THE

DORMANT, ABEYANT, FORFEITED, AND EXTINCT PEERAGES.

A

GENEALOGICAL HISTORY

OF THE

Dormant, Abeyant, Forfeited, and Extinct

PEERAGES

OF THE

BRITISH EMPIRE.

BY

SIR BERNARD BURKE, C.B., LL.D.,

ULSTER KING OF ARMS,

AUTHOR OF "THE PEERAGE AND BARONETAGE," "HISTORY OF THE LANDED GENTRY,"
"VICISSITUDES OF FAMILIES," "REMINISCENCES ANCESTRAL AND ANECDOTAL," &c.

New

Edition.

CLEARFIELD

Reprinted for
Clearfield Company by
Genealogical Publishing Co.
Baltimore, Maryland
2008

ISBN-13: 978-0-8063-0789-3
ISBN-10: 0-8063-0789-7

Made in the United States of America

This edition originally published in London in 1883.
Reprinted, in association with Burke's Peerage Ltd.,
by Genealogical Publishing Co., Inc.
Baltimore, Maryland 1985, 1996
Library of Congress Catalogue Card Number 77-88158

TO

His Grace the Duke of Leinster,

THE REPRESENTATIVE OF

The Geraldines,

AN ILLUSTRIOUS RACE, SECOND TO NONE, FOR ANTIQUITY AND RENOWN,

IN THE EXTANT OR EXTINCT PEERAGE,

THIS VOLUME IS INSCRIBED.

J. BERNARD BURKE,

Ulster.

Record Tower,
Dublin Castle.
26 *May*, 1883.

PREFACE.

THE noble families, of which this volume is the record—families unsurpassed in the whole range of European Genealogy—are so associated with our national annals, have at all times exercised so powerful an influence on the political events of their country, that their history must of necessity abound in interest. Fortunately the Nobility of the British Empire still endures in all its original grandeur, and includes on its roll the names of Howard, Nevill, Percy, Devereux, Grosvenor, Talbot, Courtenay, Hastings, Cavendish, Bruce, Stanley, FitzGerald, Butler, O'Brien, Brabazon, Nugent, Bertie, Russell, Seymour, Clifford, Ashburnham, Hamilton, Campbell, Graham, Douglas, Stuart, Murray, Gordon, Lindsay, Forbes, Montgomerie, and others of equal fame; but it must be confessed that many of the most distinguished Houses have passed away and now form part of the Dormant and Extinct Peerage.

It is a fact no less strange than remarkable that the more conspicuous a man is for his great mental powers, the more rarely does he leave a representative to perpetuate his name. Neither Shakespeare, nor Milton, nor Marlborough, nor Napoleon, nor Nelson, nor Walter Scott, nor Chatham, nor Edmund Burke, nor William Pitt, nor Fox, nor Canning, nor Macaulay, and, I may add, nor Palmerston, nor Beaconsfield, has a descendant, in the male line, living. May not the same observation be applied with equal truth to those families which stand out the most prominent in the pages of history? May not the splendour of race like the splendour of mind have too much brilliancy to last? Beauchamp, De Vere, Beaufort, De Clare, De Lacy, Dunbar, Bohun, De la Pole, Sydney, Holland, Tudor, Plantagenet, and Mortimer are "entombed in the urns and sepulchres of mortality." This ever-recurring extinction of English titles of honour formed the subject of a chapter in my work on "The Vicissitudes of Families," and I venture to reproduce from it the following passages which bear strikingly on the Dormant and Extinct Peerage:—

"After William of Normandy had won at Hastings the broad lands of England, he partitioned them among the chief commanders of his army, and conferred about twenty Earldoms: not one of these now exists, nor one of the honours conferred by William Rufus, Henry I., Stephen, Henry II., Richard I., or John.

"All the English Dukedoms, created from the institution of the Order down to the commencement of the reign of Charles II., are gone, except only Norfolk and Somerset, and Cornwall, enjoyed by the Prince of Wales. At one time, in the reign of Elizabeth, Norfolk and Somerset having been attainted, the whole order of Dukes became extinct, and remained so for about fifty years, until James 1. created George Villiers, Duke of Buckingham.

" Winchester and Worcester (the latter now merged in the Dukedom of Beaufort) are the only existing English Marquessates* older than the reign of George III. !

" The Earl's coronet was very frequently bestowed under the Henrys and the Edwards : it was the favourite distinction, besides being the oldest ; and yet of all the English Earldoms created by the Normans, the Plantagenets, and the Tudors, eleven only remain ; and of these six are merged in higher honours, the only ones giving independent designation being Shrewsbury, Derby, Huntingdon, Pembroke, and Devon.

" The present House of Lords cannot claim amongst its members a single male descendant of any one of the Barons who were chosen to enforce Magna Charta, or of any one of the Peers who are known to have fought at Agincourt ; and the noble house of Wrottesley is the solitary existing family, among the Lords, which can boast of a male descent from a Founder of the Order of the Garter. Sir William Dugdale's " History of the Baronage of England," published in 1675, contains all the English Peerages created up to that time. The index of these titles occupies fourteen closely printed columns, a single one of which would easily include the names of all the dignities that remain now out of the whole category."

There are at present six English counties which are unrepresented, if I may so express myself, among the existing nobility ; but which formerly gave titles of great historic fame now to be found in the Dormant and Extinct Peerage only, viz.,

1. DORSET, made so memorable by the Beauforts, Greys, and Sackvilles ; 2. YORK, always, and 3. GLOUCESTER, frequently, a Royal appanage ; 4. OXFORD, for twenty Earls, the inheritance of DE VERE ; 5. MONMOUTH, principally remembered in connection with the ill-fated son of Charles II.; and 6. MIDDLESEX, the title of a series of three Earls of the family of Cranfield, before it became the second dignity of the Sackvilles.

WALES has only two counties unappropriated, MERIONETH and FLINT, but IRELAND has seven, viz., KILKENNY, WEXFORD, MONAGHAN, KING'S COUNTY, QUEEN'S COUNTY, CLARE, and ROSCOMMON ; and SCOTLAND, twelve, viz., BANFF, BERWICK, FORFAR, INVERNESS, ROSS, CLACKMANAN, STIRLING, DUMBARTON, LIN-LITHGOW, KIRKCUDBRIGHT, WIGTON, and KINROSS.

Several of the most ancient and historic of our Peerage dignities are under attainder : otherwise the Earl of Stamford would be Marquess of Dorset ; the Duke of Buccleuch, Duke of Monmouth ; the Marquess of Abergavenny, Earl of West-morland ; and Mr. Marmion Ferrers, of Baddesley Clinton, might prove his right to be Earl of Derby of a creation older than that of the Stanleys.

In course of time, it may be fairly anticipated that these Attainders will be reversed ; and that some of the dormant titles may be restored to the extant Peerage. The Earldom of Wiltes has a collateral heir male in Mr. Scrope of Danby, the male representative of the house of Scrope, and the Barony of Scrope of Bolton appears to belong to Henry James Jones, Esq., the heir-general ; Mr. Lowndes, of Chesham, and Mr. Selby Lowndes, of Whaddon, are among the co-heirs to the Baronies of Montacute and Monthermer ; Sir Brooke George Bridges, Bart., of Goodneston, Kent, is, in all probability, entitled to the Barony of Fitz-Walter ; the

---

* I do not, of course, include Marquessa'es—the second titles of Dukedoms—titles which neither have nor ever can have separate existence.

Earl of Dufferin is undoubtedly the senior heir of the Earls of Clanbrassill; Mr. Anstruther-Thomson, of Charleton, co. Fife, is heir-general of the St. Clairs, Earls of Orkney, and Lords Sinclair; a Dillon is, unquestionably, in existence, *de jure* Earl of Roscommon; a Fitz-Patrick, who ought to be Lord Upper Ossory, and a Barnewall who may, some day or other, establish that he is Viscount Kingsland. Many other heirs and representatives of dormant honours will be found named in the following pages.

It is also possible that heirs to some of our old titles might be discovered in foreign countries; most certainly there are in Spain, France, Italy, and Germany descendants of several of those noble families which preferred exile to disloyalty; and very probably there are in America other scions of the British nobility besides the Fairfaxes, the Aylmers, and the Livingstones. A Lord Willoughby of Parham may yet be found on the other side of the Atlantic.

To the perfecting of this book I have devoted the most laborious revision—the most anxious and unremitting attention. Public Documents and Records, Heralds Visitations, Post Mortem Inquisitions, Patent Rolls, Lords' Entries, and Funeral Certificates have been referred to; printed authorities, especially Dugdale's "Baronage," Wood's edition of Sir Robert Douglas's "Peerage of Scotland," Archdale's "Lodge," Sir Harris Nicolas's "Synopsis" (edited under the title of "The Historic Peerage," by the late Mr. Courthope, Somerset Herald), Milles, Brooke, Collins, Jacob, Banks, and Heylin have been consulted and largely drawn on, as well as many privately printed family memoirs. In fact, no available source of information has been neglected which I thought would improve my work, and no trouble or research has been spared.

In this, as in my other literary productions, I have received most valuable aid from many friends and correspondents—a co-operation demanding my most grateful acknowledgment. Thousands and thousands of communications have been made to me in furtherance of my "History of the Landed Gentry," and my "Extant Peerage and Baronetage," as well as of this, my present work, and an amount of knowledge has been thus acquired which could not otherwise be obtained. The gentlemen of England did for "The History of the Landed Gentry" in the 19th century what their ancestors did for the Heralds Visitations of the 16th and 17th; they submitted freely and courteously their pedigrees and family documents, thus enabling me to produce a work which has, for a long series of years, been most favourably received.

With these few remarks, I submit my "History of the Dormant and Extinct Peerage" to the judgment of the public, with some confidence and much hope. My readers, I am convinced, will take into account the toilsome nature of the undertaking, the countless dates, and names and facts, that the following pages comprise, and will make allowance for mistakes and errors which may, despite of the most sedulous care and minute revision, have been overlooked. Their indulgence thus accorded to me, I feel safe as to the general correctness of the whole.

J. BERNARD BURKE,
ULSTER.

CONTENTS.

ROBINSON, BARONS ROKEBY.

Created 26 February, 1771.

Lineage.

The estate of Rokeby, in the North Riding of the co. of York, was purchased in 1610, by

WILLIAM ROBINSON, Esq., a merchant of London, from Sir Thomas Rokeby, whose progenitors had resided there from the Conquest. He m. Mary, dau. of Thomas Hall, Esq. of Thornton, co. York, by whom he had,

Thomas, of Gray's Inn, barrister-at-law, who changed his profession at the breaking out of the civil war, and was slain near Leeds, when a colonel in the service of the parliament. He m. Frances, dau. of Leonard Smelt, Esq. of Kirkby Fleetham, and left,

WILLIAM, successor to his grandfather.

Leonard (Sir), chamberlain of the city of London; d. in 1696, leaving by his wife Deborah, dau. of Sir James Collet, Knt., an only son,

Thomas, of Enfield Chase, Middlesex, who d. 1700, leaving a son,

Matthew, of Edgely, co. York, who m. 3 June, 1772, Elizabeth, dau. of Robert Drake, Esq. of Cambridge, by Sarah his wife, granddau. of Thomas Morris, Esq. of Mountmorris, and dying in 1778, left issue,

1 MATTHEW, of Edgely, 2nd Lord Rokeby.
2 Morris, m. 13 Feb. 1757. Jane, dau. of John Greenland, of Lovelace; and dying in 1777, left,

MORRIS, 3rd baron.

MATTHEW, who assumed the surname and arms of MONTAGU in 1776, and s. as 4th baron.

3 Robert, capt. E.I.C.S., d. unm. in China.
4 William, in holy orders, rector of Burfield, in Berkshire, and of Denton, co. Kent; m. Mary, dau. of Adam Richardson, Esq. of Kensington, co. Middlesex, and had issue,

Matthew (Rev.), rector of Burfield, m. Mary-Anne, dau. of Henry Parsons, Esq., and d. s. p. 10 Aug. 1827. His widow d. 2ndly, Sept. 1827, John Blagrave, Esq. of Calcot Park, Berks, and is dec.
Sarah-Elizabeth, m. to Samuel Truman, Esq.; and d. in 1834, leaving a son and a dau., viz., Matthew Truman, M.D., and Mary Truman.
Mary, m. to Sir Samuel Egerton Brydges, Bart., and had issue. She d. his widow 27 Nov. 1844.

5 John, fellow of Trinity Hall, Cambridge.
6 Charles, recorder of Canterbury, M.P.; m. Mary, 2nd dau. of John Greenland, Esq., and widow of R. Dukes, Esq., and had an only dau., Sarah, widow of William Hougham, Esq., of co. Kent.

1 Elizabeth, b. 2 Oct. 1720; m. 5 Aug. 1742, to Edward Montagu, Esq. of Allerthorpe, Yorkshire, M.P., who d. 25 Aug. 1800. This lady was the gifted and well-known Mrs. Montagu, whose correspondence was published after her death.
2 Sarah, m. to George-Lewis Scott, Esq., commissioner of excise.

Mr. Robinson (first settler at Rokeby) d. in 1643, and was s by his grandson,

WILLIAM ROBINSON, Esq. of Rokeby, who m. Mary, eldest dau. and co-heir of Francis Layton, Esq. of Rawdon, and was s. by his only son,

THOMAS ROBINSON, Esq. This gentleman m. Grace, dau. of Sir Henry Stapylton, Bart. of Myton, co. York; and dying in 1719, was s. by his only son,

WILLIAM ROBINSON, Esq., who m. Anne, dau. and heir of Robert Walters, Esq of Cundall, co. York, by whom he left at his decease, in 1719,

THOMAS, created a Baronet 10 March, 1730, with remainder to his brothers; and after those, to his kinsman, Matthew Robinson, Esq. of Edgely, co. York. Sir Thomas m. twice, but d. s. p. 1777, when the title devolved upon his next brother, William, as 2nd baronet; who d. unm. in 1785, when the title devolved upon his brother, Lord Rokeby.
Henry, major in the army; killed at Carthagena, in 1741.
RICHARD, of whom presently, as LORD ROKEBY.
Septimus (Sir), gentleman usher of the Black Rod, lieut.-gen. of the guards; d. unm. in 1765.

Anne, m 1st to Robert Knight, Esq., father of Robert, Earl of Catherlough (ext.); and 2ndly, to James Cresset, Esq.
Grace, m. to the Very Rev. William Freind, D.D., dean of Canterbury.

The 4th son,

RICHARD ROBINSON, Archbishop of Armagh, Primate of all Ireland, and prelate to the order of St. Patrick, was elevated to the peerage, 26 Feb. 1777, as BARON ROKEBY, of Armagh, with remainder to Matthew Robinson, the reversionary heir to the baronetcy. This prelate went to Ireland, in 1751, as first-chaplain to the lord-lieutenant, his Grace the Duke of Dorset, and was promoted in that year to the see of Killala. When the Duke of Bedford was viceroy, his lordship was translated to the united sees of Leighlin and Ferns, and in 1761, to that of Kildare. In 1765, during the government of the Duke of Northumberland, he was elevated to the primacy, and nominated lord-almoner. His grace s. to the baronetcy upon the decease of his brother Sir William, 2nd baronet, in 1785; and d. unm. 10 Oct. 1794 when the honours devolved, according to the limitation, upon

MATTHEW ROBINSON, Esq. of Edgely, as 2nd baron (refer to descendants of Sir Leonard Robinson, chamberlain of the city of London, 2nd son of Thomas, of Gray's Inn, son of the purchaser of Rokeby). His lordship d. unm. 30 Nov. 1800, when the family honours passed to his nephew,

MORRIS, 3rd baron. This nobleman d. unm. 19 April, 1829, when the honours devolved upon his brother,

MATTHEW MONTAGU, Esq., as 4th Lord Rokeby; b. 23 Nov. 1762; m. 9 July, 1785, Elizabeth, dau. and heir of Francis Charlton, Esq., by whom (who d. 7 March, 1817) he had issue,

EDWARD, 5th peer.
John, lieut.-col. Coldstream guards; d. 12 Dec. 1843.
HENRY, last peer.
Spencer-Dudley, b. 11 April, 1807 m. 1st, 15 Dec. 1842, Anna - Louisa, only dau. of Sir C.-W. Flint, and widow of Joseph Jekyll, Esq. of Wargrave Hill, Berks, and by her (who d. 17 Oct. 1865) had a dau., Emily-Jane, m. 3 Aug. 1865, to the Rev. John Climenson, vicar of Shiplake, Oxford. The Hon. S.-D. Montagu m. 2ndly, 1 Jan. 1868, Henrietta-Elizabette-Harriet, 2nd dau. of Christopher-Robert Pemberton, Esq. of Newton, Cambridge, and d. 31 March, 1882, leaving by her (who d. 16 May, 1871) a dau., Henrietta-Mary, b. 29 April, 1871.
Elizabeth, m.- to Charles - Oldfield Bowles, Esq. of North Aston, co. Oxford, who d. 1862; she d. 12 April, 1875.
Catherine, m. in 1831, to Mr. Serjeant Goulburn, and d. 6 April, 1865. The Serjeant d. 24 Aug. 1868.
Jane, m. 20 Dec. 1811, to the Right Hon. Henry Goulburn, M.P.; and d. his widow, 1 Feb. 1857.
Mary, m. 24 May, 1820, to Lieut.-Col. Ellison, gren.-guards, who d. in 1843; she d. 24 March, 1877.
Eleanor, m. in 1822, to John-Nicholas Fazakerly, Esq., and d. in 1847; he d. in 1852.
Caroline, m. 7 June, 1843, to Lord William-Godolphin Osborne, brother of the Duke of Leeds, and d. 10 Nov. 1867.
Emily, d. 24 Nov. 1832.

His lordship d. 1 Sept. 1831, and was s. by his eldest son,

EDWARD, 5th baron; b. 6 July, 1787; who d. unm. 7 April, 1847, and was s. by his brother,

HENRY, 5th Baron, G.C.B., a general in the army (retired list), col. Scots guards, comm. of Legion of Honour, and knight of the Medjidie; commanded a division of the British army in the Crimea; b. 2 Feb. 1798; m. 18 Dec. 1826, Magdalen, eldest dau. of Lieut.-Col. Thomas Huxley, and widow of Frederick Croft, Esq., and by her (who d. at Nice, 7 Dec. 1868) had issue,

I. Edmund, b. 4 May, 1835; d. 3 April, 1852.
I. Mary, m. 29 Nov. 1855, John, Marquess of Winchester, and d. 5 Sept. 1868.
II. Harriet-Lydia, m. 19 April, 1855, Lionel-Seymour-William Dawson-Damer, Esq., M.P. for Portarlington.
III. Magdalen, m. 16 Sept. 1856, to the Hon. and Very Rev. Gerald Wellesley, Dean of Windsor.
IV. Elizabeth.

His lordship d. 25 May, 1883, when his honours became EXTINCT.

Arms—Quarterly, 1st and 4th, arg., three lozenges conjoined in fesse gu, within a bordure sa., and, for difference, a mullet on a mullet, for MONTAGU; 2nd and 3rd, or, an eagle displayed vert, for MONTHERMER.

Abrincis.
(E. Chester.)

Albini.
(E. Arundel.)

Alexander.
(E. Starling.)

Alington.
(B. Alington.)

Amorie.
(B. D'Amorie.)

Archer.
(B. Archer.)

Argentine.
(B. Argentine.)

Arundel.
(B. Arundel.)

Audley.
(B. Audley.)

Aungier.
(E. Longford.)

Badlesmere.
(B. Badlesmere.)

Baliol.
(B. Baliol.)

R.R. Baker. sc.

PEERAGES:

EXTINCT, DORMANT, AND IN ABEYANCE.

ABERCROMBY—LORD GLASFORD.

By Letters Patent, dated 5 July, 1685.

Lineage.

ALEXANDER ABERCROMBY, of Fetterneir, younger brother of James Abercromby, of Birkenbog, in Banffshire (ancestor of the ABERCROMBYS, Baronets of Birkenbog), m. Jean, dau. of John Seton, of Newark, and had three sons, FRANCIS, John, and Patrick, a physician, author of the "Martial Achievements of the Scottish Nation," as well as of "Memoirs of the Family of Abercromby." The eldest son and heir,

FRANCIS ABERCROMBY, of Fetterneir, having married Anne, Baroness Sempill, in her own right, was created a peer of Scotland, *for life only*, 5 July, 1685, as LORD GLASFORD. He had several children (of whom Francis, 9th Lord Sempill, was the eldest, and Hugh, 11th Lord Sempill (great grandfather of the present BARONESS SEMPILL), the 4th son), but the dignity of Glasford became, of course, EXTINCT at Lord Glasford's decease. (*See* SEMPILL, BURKE's *Extant Peerage*.)

Arms—Arg., a chev. gu. between three boars' heads erased az., langued of the second.

ABERCROMBY—BARON DUNFERMLINE.

(*See* ADDENDA.)

ABRINCIS—EARLS OF CHESTER.

Created by WILLIAM THE CONQUEROR, anno 1070.

Lineage.

Upon the detention, a prisoner in Flanders, of GHERBOD, a Fleming who first held the Earldom of Chester, that dignity was conferred, A.D. 1070, by the CONQUEROR, upon (his half-sister's son) HUGH DE ABRINCIS,[*] surnamed LUPUS, and called by the Welch, *Vras*, or "the Fat." "Which Hugh," says Dugdale, "being a person of great note at that time amongst the Norman nobility, and an expert soldier, was, for that respect, chiefly placed so near those unconquered *Britains*, the better to restrain their bold incursions: for it was, 'consilio prudentium,' by the advice of his council, that King WILLIAM thus advanced him to that government; his power being, also, not ordinary; having royal jurisdiction within the precincts of his earldom—which honor he received *to hold as freely by the sword as the King himself held England by the crown*. But, though the time of his advancement was not till the year 1070, certain it is, that he came into England with the CONQUEROR, and thereupon had a grant of Whitby, in Yorkshire, which lordship he soon afterwards disposed of to William de Percy, his associate in that famous expedition." In the contest between WILLIAM RUFUS, and his brother ROBERT CURTHOSE, this powerful nobleman sided with the former, and remained faithful to him during the whole of his reign. He was subsequently in the confidence of HENRY I., and one of that monarch's chief councillors. "In his youth and flourishing age," continueth the author above quoted, "he was a great lover of worldly pleasures and secular pomp; profuse in giving, and much delighted with interludes, jesters, horses, dogs, and other like vanities; having a large attendance of such persons, of all sorts, as were disposed to those sports: but he had also in his family both clerks and soldiers, who were men of great honor, the venerable Anselme (abbot of Bec, and afterwards archbishop of Canterbury) being his confessor; nay, so devout he grew before his death, that sickness hanging long upon him, he caused himself to be shorn a monk in the abbey of St. Werburge, where, within three days after, he died, 27 July, 1101." His lordship m. Ermentrude, dau. of Hugh de Claremont, Earl of Bevois, in France, by whom he had an only son,

RICHARD, his successor.

Of his illegitimate issue were Ottiwell, tutor to those children of King HENRY I., who perished at sea; Robert, originally a monk in the abbey of St. Ebrulf, in Normandy, and afterwards abbot of St. Edmundsbury, in Suffolk; and Geva,[*] the wife of Geffery Riddell, to whom the Earl gave Drayton Basset, in Staffordshire.

That this powerful nobleman enjoyed immense wealth in England is evident, from the many lordships he held at the general survey; for, besides the whole of Cheshire, excepting the small part which at that time belonged to the bishop, he had nine lordships in Berkshire, two in Devonshire, seven in Yorkshire, six in Wiltshire, ten in Dorsetshire, four in Somersetshire, thirty-two in Suffolk, twelve in Norfolk, one in Hampshire, five in Oxfordshire, three in Buckinghamshire, four in Gloucestershire, two in Huntingdonshire, four in Nottinghamshire, one in Warwickshire, and twenty-two in Leicestershire. It appears too, by the charter of foundation to the abbey of St. Werburge, at Chester, that several eminent persons held the rank of baron under him. The charter runs thus:— "Hæc sunt itaque dona data Abbatiæ S. Werburge, quæ omnia ego Comes Hugo et Richardus filius meus et Ermentrudis Comitissa, et mei Barones, et mei homines dedimus, &c," which *Barones et Homines* mentioned therein, were the following:—

1 William Melbanc; 2 Robert, son of Hugo; 3 Hugo, son of Norman; 4 Richard de Vernun; 5 Richard de Rullos; 6 Ranulph Venator; 7 Hugo de Mara; 8 Ranulph, son of Ermiwin; 9 Robert de Fremouz; 10 Walkelinus, nephew of Walter de Vernon; 11 Seward; 12 Gislebert de Venables; 13 Gaufridus de Sartes; 14 Richard de Mesnilwarin; 15 Walter de Vernun.

The charter concludes—"Et ut hæc omnia essent rata et stabilia in perpetuum, ego Comes Hugo et mei Barones confirmavimus (&c.), ita quod singuli nostrum propriâ manu, in testimonium posteris signum in modum Crucis facerunt:"— and is signed by the earl himself,

Richard, his son; Hervey, bishop of Bangor; Ranulph de Meschines, his nephew, who eventually inherited the earldom; Roger Bigod; Alan de Perci; William Constabular; Ranulph Dapifer; William Malbanc; Robert FitzHugh; Hugh FitzNorman; Hamo de Masci; and Bigod de Loges.

---

[*] The legitimacy of this lady is maintained from the circumstance of her father having bestowed upon her the manor of Drayton, in free marriage, which the lawyers say could not be granted to a bastard; but had she been legitimate, she would surely have succeeded to the earldom before her aunt.

Those barons, be it remembered, were each and all of them men of great individual power, and large territorial possessions. Hugh Lupus, Earl of Chester, was *s.* by his only son (then but seven years of age),

RICHARD DE ABRINCIS, as 2nd earl. This nobleman, after he had attained maturity, attached himself faithfully to King HENRY I., and never subsequently swerved in his allegiance. He *m.* Maud, dau. of Stephen, Earl of Blois, by Adela, dau. of WILLIAM THE CONQUEROR, but had no issue—himself and his countess being soon afterwards amongst the victims of the memorable shipwreck (Dec., 1119), wherein the king's two sons, WILLIAM and RICHARD, with their tutor Ottiwell, the earl's bastard brother, Geffery Riddell, his sister Geva's husband, and many others of the nobility perished. Upon the demise thus of Richard de Abrincis, 2nd Earl of Chester, the male line of the family becoming EXTINCT, the earldom passed to the deceased nobleman's 1st cousin, RANULPH DE MESCHINES, son of Ralph de Meschines, by Maud de Abrincia, sister of Earl Hugh Lupus—(*see* Meschines, Earls of Chester).

Arms—Az., a wolf's head, erased, arg.

AGAR—BARON CALLAN.

By Letters Patent, dated 4 June, 1790.

Lineage.

JAMES AGAR, Esq., of Gowran Castle, co. Kilkenny, M.P., son and heir of Charles Agar, Esq., of York, left by Mary, his 2nd wife (who *d.* 1771, aged 106), eldest dau. of Sir Henry Wemyss, Knt., of Danesfort, two sons and two daus., viz.,

I. HENRY, of Gowran Castle, M.P., father of JAMES, 1st VISCOUNT CLIFDEN, and of CHARLES, 1st EARL OF NORMANTON. (*See* BURKE's *Peerage and Baronetage*.)
II. JAMES, of whom presently.
I. ELLIS, *m.* 1st, March, 1726, Theobald, 7th Viscount Mayo; and 2ndly, 7 August, 1745, Francis, Lord Athenry. Her ladyship was created COUNTESS OF BRANDON, 1 August, 1758, but *d. s. p.* in 1789, when the peerage became EXTINCT.
II. Mary, *m.* to James Smyth, Esq., of Tinny Park, co. Wicklow.

He *d.* 30 November, 1733; his 2nd son,

JAMES AGAR, Esq., of Ringwood, co. Kilkenny, M.P. for Gowran, *b.* 7 September, 1713, *m.* 6 July 1740, Rebecca, only dau. of William, Lord Castle Durrow, and by her (who *d.* 8 March, 1789,) had issue,

GEORGE, his heir.
Charles, *b.* 18 April, 1754, archdeacon of Emly, *d. s p.,* 5 May, 1789.
John, deceased.
Mary, *m.* 30 August, 1761, to Lieut. Philip Savage (of General John Campbell's dragoons), and was mother of JAMES SAVAGE, Esq., of Kilgibbon, co. Wexford, whose only dau. and heiress, MARGARET, *m.* HARRY ALCOCK, Esq., of Wilton, co. Wexford.

Mr. Agar (whose will is dated 20 October, 1761) *d.* 3 August, 1769, and was *s.* by his son,

THE RT. HON. GEORGE AGAR, of Ringwood; *b.* 4 December, 1751, M.P. for Callan in 1789; who was raised to the peerage of Ireland, as BARON CALLAN, of Callan, co. Kilkenny, 4 June, 1790. His lordship *d.* however, without issue, 29 October, 1815, when the title became EXTINCT.

Arms—Az., a lion rampant, or.

AGAR—COUNTESS OF BRANDON.
(*See* AGAR *Lord Callan.*)

AIREY—BARON.
(*See* ADDENDA.)

AIRMINE—BARONESS BELASYSE.
(*See* ARMINE.)

ALAN, FERGAUNT, EARL OF RICHMOND.
(*See* DE DREUX, *Earls of Richmond.*)

ALBINI—EARLS OF ARUNDEL.

By feudal tenure of ARUNDEL CASTLE, A.D. 1189.

Lineage.

WILLIAM DE ALBINI, surnamed *Pincerna*, son of Roger de Albini, and elder brother of Nigel de Albini, whose posterity assumed, and attained such eminence under the name of MOWBRAY, accompanied the CONQUEROR into England, and acquired extensive territorial possessions by royal grants in

Norfolk and other counties. Of these grants was the lordship of Bokenham, to be holden by the service of being BUTLER to the Kings of England on the day of their coronation, and in consequence we find this William styled in divers charters, "*Pincerna Henrici Regis Anglorum.*" William de Albini founded the abbey of Wymondham in Norfolk, and gave to the monks of Rochester the tithes of his manor of Elham; as also one carucate of land in Achestede, with a wood called Acholte. He likewise bestowed upon the abbey of St. Etienne at Caen, in Normandy, all his lands lying in Stavell, which grant he made in the presence of King HENRY and his baron's. He *m.* Maud, dau. of Roger Bigot, with whom he obtained ten knights' fees in Norfolk, and had issue,

| WILLIAM. | Nigel. | Oliver. |

Oliva, *m.* to Raphe de Haya, a feudal baron of great power.

At the obsequies of Maud, William de Albini gave to the monks of Wymondham, the manor of Hapesburg, in pure alms, and made livery thereof to the said monks by a cross of silver, in which (says Dugdale) was placed certain venerable reliques, viz., "part of the wood of the cross whereon our Lord was crucified; part of the manger wherein he was laid at his birth; and part of the sepulchre of the blessed Virgin; as also a gold ring, and a silver chalice, for retaining the holy eucharist, admirably wrought in form of a sphere; unto which pious donation his three sons were witnesses, with several other persons." The exact time of the decease of this great feudal baron is not ascertained, but it is known that he was buried before the high altar in the abbey of Wymondham, and that the monks were in the constant habit of praying for his soul, by the name of "William de Albini, the king's butler." He was *s.* by his eldest son,

WILLIAM DE ALBINI, surnamed "William with the strong hand," from the following circumstance, as related by Dugdale:—

"It happened that the Queen of France, being then a widow, and a very beautiful woman, became much in love with a knight of that country, who was a comely person, and in the flower of his youth : and because she thought that no man excelled him in valour, she caused a tournament to be proclaimed throughout her dominions, promising to reward those who should exercise themselves therein, according to their respective demerits; and concluding that if the person whom she so well affected should act his part better than others in those military exercises, she might marry him without any dishonour to herself. Hereupon divers gallant men, from forrain parts hasting to Paris, amongst others came this our William de Albini, bravely accoutred, and in the tournament excelled all others, overcoming many, and wounding one mortally with his lance, which being observed by the queen, she became exceedingly enamoured of him, and forthwith invited him to a costly banquet, and afterwards bestowing certain jewels upon him, offered him marriage; but, having plighted his troth to the Queen of England, then a widow, he refused her, whereat she grew so much discontented that she consulted with her maids how she might take away his life; and in pursuance of that designe, inticed him into a garden, where there was a secret cave, and in it a fierce lion, unto which she descended by divers steps, under colour of shewing him the beast; and when she told him of its fierceness, he answered, that it was a womanish and not a manly quality to be afraid thereof. But having him there, by the advantage of a folding door, thrust him in to the lion; being therefore in this danger, he rolled his mantle about his arm, and putting his hand into the mouth of the beast, pulled out his tongue by the root; which done, he followed the queen to her palace, and gave it to one of her maids to present her. Returning thereupon to England, with the fame of this glorious exploit, he was forthwith advanced to the EARLDOME OF ARUNDEL, and for his arms the LION given him."

He subsequently obtained the hand of the Queen ADELIZA, relict of King HENRY I., and daughter of Godfrey, Duke of Lorraine, which Adeliza had the castle of Arundel in dowry from the deceased monarch, and thus her new lord became its feudal earl. The earl was one of those who solicited the Empress Maud to come to England, and received her and her brother Robert, Earl of Gloucester, at the port of Arundel, in August 1139, and in three years afterwards (1142), in the report made of King STEPHEN's taking William de Mandevil at St. Albans, it is stated—"that before he could be laid hold on, he underwent a sharp skirmish with the king's party, wherein the Earl of Arundell, though a stout and expert souldier, was unhorsed in the midst of the water by Walkeline de Oxeai, and almost drowned." In 1150, his lordship wrote himself Earl of Chichester, but we find him styled again Earl of Arundel, upon a very memorable occasion — namely, the reconciliation of Henry Duke of Normandy (afterwards HENRY II.) and King

STEPHEN at the siege of Wallingford Castle in 1152. "It was scarce possible," says Rapin, "for the armies to part without fighting. Accordingly the two leaders were preparing for battle with equal ardour, when, by the prudent advice of the Earl of Arundel, who was on the king's side, they were prevented from coming to blows." A truce and peace followed this interference of the earl's, which led to the subsequent accession of HENRY after STEPHEN's decease, in whose favour the earl stood so high that he not only obtained for himself and his heirs the castle and honour of Arundel, but a confirmation of the Earldom of Sussex, of which county he was really earl, by a grant of the *Tertium Denarium* of the pleas of that shire. In 1164, we find the Earl of Arundel deputed with Gilbert Foliot, bishop of London, to remonstrate with LEWIS, King of France, upon affording an asylum to Thomas à Becket within his dominions, and on the failure of that mission, despatched with the archbishop of York, the bishops of Winchester, London, Chichester, and Exeter,—Wido Rufus, Richard de Invecestre, John de Oxford (priests)—Hugh de Gundevile, Bernard de St. Valery, and Henry Fitzgerald, to lay the whole affair of Becket at the foot of the pontifical throne. Upon levying the aid for the marriage of the king's daughter, 12th of HENRY II., the knights' fees of the honour of Arundel were certified to be ninety-seven, and those in Norfolk belonging to the earl, forty-two. In 1173, we find the Earl of Arundel commanding, in conjunction with William, Earl of Essex, the king's army in Normandy, and compelling the French monarch to abandon Verneuil after a long siege, and in the next year, with Richard de Lucy, justice of England, defeating Robert Earl of Leicester, then in rebellion at St. Edmundsbury. This potent nobleman, after founding and endowing several religious houses, departed this life at Waverley, in Surrey, on the 3 October, 1176, and was buried in the abbey of Wymondham. His lordship left by Adeliza, his wife, widow of King HENRY I., four sons and three daughters, the eldest of whom, Alice, m. John, Earl of Ewe. The eldest son,

WILLIAM DE ALBINI, 2nd earl, had a grant from the crown, 23rd HENRY II., of the Earldom of Sussex, and in the 1st of RICHARD I., had a confirmation from that prince, of the castle and honour of Arundel, as also of the *Tertium Denarium* of the county of Sussex. He d. 1196, and was s. by his son,

WILLIAM DE ALBINI, 3rd earl, who, in 1218, embarked in the Crusade, and was at the celebrated siege of Damietta, but died in returning, anno 1221. He m. Maud, dau. and heiress of James de St. Hillary, and widow of Roger de Clare, Earl of Hertford, by whom he left issue,

  I. WILLIAM, } successors to the earldom.
  II. HUGH, }
  I. MABEL, m. to Sir Robert de Tateshall, and was mother of Robert de Tateshall, b. in 1223; a participator in the wars of HENRY III., and subsequently in those of EDWARD I., summoned to parliament as BARON TATESHALL from 24 June, 1295, to 26 August, 1296. He m. Joan. 2nd dau. and co-heir of Ralph FitzRanulph, Lord of Middleham, co. York, with whom he acquired a considerable accession of property. His lordship d. in 1272, leaving a son and successor, ROBERT DE TATESHALL, 2nd baron, and it is supposed, on strong presumptive evidence, a younger son, JOHN DE TATESHALL, living 21st EDWARD I., ancestor of the TATTERSHALLS, of *Wanstede and Little Wultham, co. Essex, of Hilden, co. Kent, of Finchhampstead, co Berks, and of Gatton, co. Surrey.*
  II. ISABEL, m. to JOHN FITZALAN, Baron of Clun and Oswestry, ancestor, by her, of the FITZALANS, EARLS OF ARUNDEL (*which see*).
  III. NICOLA, m. to Roger de Somerie, Lord of Dudley, and had four daus., her co-heirs, viz ,
    1 Joan, m. to John Le Strange.
    2 Mabel, m. to Walter de Sulcy.
    3 Maud, m. to Henry de Erdington, and left a son, Henry, Lord Erdington, ancestor of the ERDINGTONS, *of Erdington, co. Warwick,* long since EXTINCT.
    4 Margery, m. 1st, to Ralph Cromwell, of Tatshall (*see* CROMWELL, BARONS); and 2ndly, to William de Bifield.
  IV. CECILIA, m. to Roger de Montalt, a great feudal baron, and had two sons, John and Robert (whose issue became EXTINCT), and one dau., Leucha, m. to Philip de Orreby the younger.

The earl was s. by his elder son,

WILLIAM DE ALBINI, 4th earl, who m. Mabel, second of the four sisters and co-heiresses of Ranulph, Earl of Chester, with whom he obtained great landed property. As he, however, died issueless in 1224, or, by some statements, in 1233, his honours devolved upon his only brother (then in minority),

HUGH DE ALBINI, 5th earl, who gave 2,500 marks fine to the king for the possession of all the lands and castles which descended to him from his brother, and those which he inherited from his uncle *Ranulph,* EARL OF CHESTER. At the nuptials of King HENRY III. we find the Earl of Warren serving the king with the royal cup in the place of this earl, by reason he was then but a youth, and not knighted. He m. Isabel, dau. of

William, Earl of Warren and Surrey, but *d. s. p.,* in 1243, when this branch of the great house of Albini expired, while its large possessions devolved upon the earl's sisters as co-heiresses —thus,

  Mabell Tateshall, had the castle and manor of Buckenham.
  Isabel Fitzalan, had the castle and manor of Arundel, &c., which conveyed the earldom to her husband.
  Nichola de Somery, had the manor of Barwe, co. Leicester.
  Cecilie de Montalt, had the castle of Rising, co. Norfolk.
The earl had another sister, Colet, to whom her uncle Ranulph, Earl of Chester, gave £30 towards her marriage portion, which gift was confirmed by King HENRY III.

Arms—Gu., a lion rampant, or, armed and langued, az.

ALDEBURGH—BARONS ALDEBURGH.

By Writ of Summons, dated 8 January, 1371, 44th EDWARD III.

Lineage.

WILLIAM DE ALDEBURGH was summoned to parliament as a BARON, from 8 January, 1371, to 8 August, 1386, in which latter year his lordship died, leaving by Elizabeth, his wife, dau. of Robert, Lord Lisle of Rugemont, an only son,

WILLIAM DE ALDEBURGH, 2nd baron, who dying *s. p.,* 20 August, 1391, the Barony of Aldeburgh fell into ABEYANCE at his lordship's decease, between his two sisters,

  I. Elizabeth, who m. 1st, Sir Bryan Stapleton, of Carleton, co. York; and 2ndly, to Richard or Edward Redman.
  II. Sybilla, m. to William de Myther, of Harewood.

Arms—Az., a fesse, arg., between three cross-crosslets, or.

ALEXANDER—VISCOUNT AND EARL OF STIRLING.

Viscounty, by Letters Patent, dated 4 September, 1630.
Earldom, by Letters Patent, dated 14 June, 1633.

Lineage.

This family is esteemed a branch of the Macdonalds, Lords of the Isles, one of whom,

ALEXANDER MACDONALD, obtained the lands of Menstrie, in the county of Clackmannan, in *feu,* from the family of Argyll, where he fixed his residence, and his posterity assumed the surname of ALEXANDER, from his Christian name.

THOMAS ALEXANDER, was one of the arbiters betwixt the abbot of Cambuskenneth and Sir David Bruce, of Clackmannan, in a dispute concerning the marches of their lands, which was settled 6 March, 1505. His descendant (probably his grandson),

ALEXANDER ALEXANDER, of Menstrie, living 1529, m. Elizabeth Douglas, of Lochleven, and d. 1545. He was great-grandfather of

SIR WILLIAM ALEXANDER, of Menstrie (son of Alexander Alexander, of Menstrie, and grandson of Andrew Alexander, also of Menstrie,) was a celebrated poet. He accompanied the Earl of Argyll upon his travels, was knighted by King JAMES VI., and made master of requests. Henry, Prince of Wales, honoured Sir William with particular notice, and brought him to court. He had a grant of the territory of Nova Scotia by charter, dated 10 September, 1621, and the king gave him permission to divide that territory into one hundred parcels, and to dispose of these tracts, with the title or BARONET, for the purpose of improving the colony. Sir William obtained about £200 from each purchaser; and he likewise had the privilege of coining a sort of base copper money, denominated "Turners," by which he acquired much wealth. He had charters of the lordship of Canada, in America, 2 February, 1628; and of the barony of Menstrie, 30 July following; of the barony of Largis, 11 April, 1629; and of the barony of Tullibody, 30 July, in the same year. He was sworn of the privy council, and appointed secretary of state in 1626; keeper of the signet in 1627; a commissioner of the exchequer in 1628; and one of the extraordinary lords of Session in 1631. He was created *Lord Alexander, of Tullibody,* and *Viscount Stirling,* by patent, dated 4 September, 1630, to himself and his heirs male bearing the name and arms of ALEXANDER; and was raised to the dignity of *Earl of Stirling, Viscount Canada,* and *Lord Alexander, of Tullibody,* by patent, dated 14 June, 1633, with the same remaindership. His lordship m. Janet, dau. and co-heiress of Sir William

Erskine, Knt., parson, of Campsie, commendator of the bishopric of Glasgow, and had issue,

1. WILLIAM, Viscount Canada, who m. Lady Margaret Douglas, eldest dau. of William, 1st Marquess of Douglas; and dying in the lifetime of his father, in March, 1638, left issue,
 1 WILLIAM, successor to the honours.
2 CATHERINE, m. Walter, Lord Torphichen, and left two daus.,
 Anne, m. Robert Menzies, Esq., and had a dau., Katherine, m. to John Menzies, M.D., of Culterallers, and a son, Sir Robert Menzies, Bart., of Menzies, who m. Christian, dau. of Lord Neil Campbell, and had a son, Sir Robert, who d. s. p., and a dau., Christian, who also d. s. p., wife of Mackintosh, of Mackintosh.
 Catherine, m. to David Drummond, of Cultmalindie, s. p.
3 MARGARET, m. to Sir Robert Sinclair, Bart., of Longformacus.
4 LUCY, m. to Edward Harrington, Esq, page of honour to the Prince of Orange in 1630.
II. Anthony (Sir), d. s. p. 1637.
III. HENRY, who s. as 3rd earl.
IV. JOHN. It was from this John that ALEXANDER HUMPHREYS pretended that he was maternally descended; his claim to the title of Earl of Stirling has long been disproved and set at rest.
V. Charles, left a son, Charles, who d. s. p.
VI. Ludovic, d. s. p.
VII. James, left a dau., Margaret.
 I. Jean, m. to Hugh, Viscount Montgomery, of Great Ardes, co. Down, and had a son,
 Hugh, created EARL OF MOUNT ALEXANDER.
 II. Mary, m. 3 August, 1620, to Sir William Murray, Bart., of Clermont.

The earl d. in 1640, and was s. by his grandson,

WILLIAM, 2nd earl; who d. in three months after, and was s. by his uncle,

HENRY, 3rd earl. This nobleman m. a dau. of Sir Peter Vanlore, an alderman of London; and dying in 1650, was s. by his son,

HENRY, 4th earl; who m. Judith, dau. of Robert Lee, Esq., of Binfield, Berks, and had four sons, who all d. s. p., and two daus., viz.,

Mary, m. to — Phillips, Esq., and had a son,
 William Phillips-Lee, of Binfield and York.
Judith, m. to Sir William Trumbull, of East Hampstead Park, Berks, and had a son,
 WILLIAM TRUMBULL, who m. Mary, dau. of Montagu, Lord Blundell, and left an only dau.,
 MARY, m. to the Hon. Martyn Sandys, and left an only dau. and heiress,
 MARY, who m. 1786, to Arthur, 2nd Marquess of Downshire, and was created BARONESS SANDYS in 1802, Her ladyship d. 1 August, 1836, leaving several children, of whom the eldest, Arthur-Blundell-Sandys-Trumbull, 3rd MARQUESS OF DOWNSHIRE, K.P., was father of the present MARQUESS OF DOWNSHIRE, K.P.

His lordship d. in 1690, and was s. by his eldest son,

HENRY, 5th earl. This nobleman m. Elizabeth, widow of John Hobey, Esq.; but d. s. p. in 1739, since which time the Earldom of Stirling has remained unacknowledged, although it was claimed and borne by WILLIAM ALEXANDER, commander-in-chief of the American forces, who d. 1795.

There are several families of Alexander settled in Ireland who claim descent from the noble house of Stirling; among these are the ALEXANDERS, of Foyle Park, co. Derry, of Ahilly, co. Donegal, of Milford, co. Carlow, of London, of Portglenone, co. Antrim, of Forkhill, co. Armagh, and of Somerhill, co. Kent; the ALEXANDERS, Earls of Caledon, the ALEXANDERS, Baronets, and the ALEXANDERS, of Maryville, co. Galway. Of this last-named family, the first ancestor in Ireland, JAMES ALEXANDER, is stated to have been cousin-german of the 1st Earl of Stirling, and only son of James Alexander, of Lancarse, 3rd son of Andrew Alexander, of Menstrie, co. Clackmannan, the grandfather of the 1st earl. The present representative of the Alexanders, of Maryville, is ARTHUR ALEXANDER, of Maryville, only surviving son of the late John Alexander, Esq., of Maryville.

Arms—Per pale, arg. and sa., a chev., and in base, a crescent, all counterchanged.

ALINGTON—BARON'S ALINGTON, OF WYMONDLEY.

By Letters Patent, dated 5 December, 1682.

Lineage.

SIR HILDEBRAND DE ALINGTON, Under Marshal to WILLIAM THE NORMAN at the battle of Hastings, had Alington Castle, by gift of the CONQUEROR.

An old pedigree of the Alingtons, now in the possession of

Mr. Alington, of Swinhope, narrates that after the Norman Conquest "The Kentish men, not well suffering the loss of their liberties, and the late loss of their Prince, conferred with Stigurd, archbishop of Canterbury, and others, to entrap the King, which they did at Swannercote, beside North Fleet, in Kent, and there took hostages of the King for the due performance of their liberties. After which Stigurd was sent into Normandie, and there pined in prison, and the lands of the others were confiscated; whereupon Medwaycester, one of the forfeited castles, was given to Sir Hildebrand Alington, Knt. The former proprietor, Sir John, had, however, a fair daughter named Emlyn, who as she sued earnestly for the life of her father, even so, Sir Hildebrand was as earnest a suitor to her for marriage, which taking effect, the inheritance was conferred again to the right heir."

SIR ALAN DE ALINGTON, "who," to quote the same old pedigree, "was in great favour with WILLIAM RUFUS, and a great devisor of building, and was thought to be the chief doer for the building of Westminster Hall, which then was Palatium Regium, and by KING HENRY I. converted to the use it now is and much beautified by EDWARD III." His son,

SIR SOLOMON DE ALINGTON, Knt., "was in great authority in the reign of HENRY I., and builded the Castell of Alington, where he erected one notable tower after his own name, called the 'Solomon's Tower.'" His descendant,

SIR WILLIAM ALINGTON, Knt., privy councillor to King HENRY VI., treasurer of Normandy in the time of HENRYS V. and VI., and also of Ireland, m. Joane, dau. and heir of Sir Wm. Burgh, lord chief justice of the Court of King's Bench, (2 RICHARD II.), and had a son,

WILLIAM ALINGTON, of Horseheath, in Cambridgeshire, sheriff of Cambridge and Huntingdon (16 HENRY VI.), who had issue,

I. WILLIAM, of whom presently.
II. John, m. Mary, dau. and co-heir of John Anstys, and d. s. p.
III. Robert, of Bottlesham, m. 1st, Mary, dau. of Sir Robert Bruose, of Norfolk; and 2ndly, Joan, sister and heir of John Argentine.

The eldest son,

WILLIAM ALINGTON, Esq., high sheriff of the counties of Cambridge and Huntingdon, in the reign of EDWARD IV., m. Elizabeth, only dau. and heiress of John de Argentine, and acquired by her the manor of Wymondeley, in the co. of Hertford, held in grand serjeanty, by service of presenting the first cup at the coronation of the kings of England; which service was claimed and allowed at the coronation of King JAMES II., and has ever since been performed by the lords of that manor. From this William Alington and Elizabeth, his wife, derived

SIR GILES ALINGTON, who m. Mary, only dau. and heiress of Sir Richard Gardiner, Knt., and had several children, of whom three of the younger sons, George, John, and Richard, were the founders of families; GEORGE ALINGTON, the 2nd son, being the direct ancestor of the ALINGTONS, of Swinhope, co. Lincoln, whose present representative, GEORGE MARMADUKE ALINGTON, Esq., of Swinhope, is also male representative of the family of the LORDS ALINGTON (see BURKE's Landed Gentry). Sir Giles was s. by his eldest son,

GILES ALINGTON, Esq., of Horseheath, co. Cambridge; high sheriff of that shire in the 22nd of HENRY VIII., and of Huntingdon in the 37th of the same monarch. Mr. Alington appears to have attended King HENRY VIII. as master of the ordnance at the siege of Boulogne, by the inscription of a clock which he brought from that siege, and affixed over the offices at Horseheath Hall, in which was the alarum bell of the garrison of Boulogne. He d. in 1586, and from him lineally descended

WILLIAM ALINGTON, Esq., of Horseheath Hall, co. Cambridge, who was elevated to the peerage of Ireland, as BARON ALINGTON, of Killard, on 28 July, 1642. His lordship m. Elizabeth, dau. of Sir Lionel Tollemache, Bart., of Helmingham, by whom he had, with five sons, three daus.; viz.,

Elizabeth, m. to Charles, Lord Seymour, of Troubridge.
Catherine, m. to Sir John Jacob, Bart., of Gamlinghay, co. Cambridge.
Diana, d. unm.

Lord Alington was s. by his 2nd, but eldest surviving son,

WILLIAM ALINGTON, 2nd baron, who was created a peer of England on 5 December, 1682, by the title of BARON ALINGTON, of Wymondley, in the co. of Herts. His lordship m. 1st, Catherine, 2nd dau. of Henry Lord Stanhope, son of Philip, 2nd earl of Chesterfield, by whom he had no issue. He m., 2ndly, Joanna, dau. of Baptist, Lord Campden. and had a dau., JULIANA, who m. Scroope, Lord Howe, and was grandmother of the famous RICHARD EARL HOWE, the great admiral, whose co-representatives are Earl Howe and the Marquess of Sligo.

lord Alington m. 3rdly, Diana, dau. of William Russell, 1st Duke of Bedford, by whom he had one surviving son, GILES, and two daus.; viz.,

Diana, m. Sir George Warburton, Bart., of Arley, co. Chester, and d. in 1705, leaving an only dau., DIANA, who m. Sir Richard Grosvenor, Bart., of Eaton, co. Chester, but had no issue. Sir Richard, who acquired a third part of the Alington estates with his wife, purchased the shares of Lady Howe and Sir Nathaniel Napier, and thus became possessed of the entire manor of Wymondley, which entitled him to present the first cup of silver at the coronations of GEORGE II. and GEORGE III.

Catherine, m. to Sir Nathaniel Napier, Bart., of Middlemarsh Hall, co. Dorset.

His lordship d. in 1684, and was s. by his son,

GILES ALINGTON, 3rd baron of the Irish creation, and 2nd of the English. This nobleman dying in his tenth year, anno 1691, the English peerage EXPIRED, while that of Ireland reverted to his uncle,

The HON. HILDEBRAND ALINGTON, son of the 1st lord, as 4th baron; but his lordship did not inherit the fortune. William, the 2nd lord, having devised his estates, the most extensive in the co. of Cambridge, to his widow during the minority of his children, with a power of granting leases to raise portions for his daus., that lady, in consequence of an error in the will, found herself possessed of the power of leasing ad infinitum, and she accordingly made a lease of the whole to Henry Bromley, Esq., afterwards Lord Montfort, for 999 years; to whom, subsequently, Hildebrand, Lord Alington, also disposed of the small interest then remaining to him in the estates. His lordship dying s. p. in 1722, the Irish barony of ALINGTON, OF KILLARD likewise became EXTINCT

Arms—Sa., a bend engrailed between six billets, as.

ALINGTON, IN THE PEERAGE OF IRE-LAND—BARON ALINGTON.

(See ALINGTON, Baron Alington, in the Peerage of England.)

ALLEN—VISCOUNT ALLEN.

By Letters Patent, dated 27 August, 1717.

Lineage.

JOHN ALLEN, a distinguished architect of the city of Dublin, who, with singular humility, styles himself "Bricklayer," in his Will, dated April, 1641, left by Mary, his wife, a son,

SIR JOSHUA ALLEN, Knt., an eminent and opulent merchant of Dublin, who was lord mayor of that city in 1673, and was knighted. Sir Joshua completed the house at Mullynahack (near Dublin), begun by his father, called Allen's Court. He m. Mary Wybrow, of the co. Chester, sister of Capt. Richard Wybrow, by whom he had three surviving daus., viz., 1 Elizabeth, m. to Anthony Shephard, Esq., of Newcastle, co. Longford, M.P.; 2 Elinor, m. 1700, to Henry Westenra, Esq., of Dublin; and 3 Mary, m. to Arthur Cooper, Esq. of Markree, co. Sligo; and one son, his successor,

JOHN ALLEN, M.P. for the co. Wicklow, who was elevated to the peerage of Ireland, 27 August, 1717, in the dignities of Baron Allen, of Stillorgan, and VISCOUNT ALLEN. His lordship m. in 1684, Mary, eldest dau. of Robert FitzGerald, Esq., and sister of Robert, Earl of Kildare, and had issue,

I. JOSHUA, his successor.

II. Robert, M.P. for the co. Wicklow, d. in 1741, leaving, of several children, two surviving daus.,

1 Mary, m. 1732, Robert Boswell, Esq., of Ballycurry, co. Wicklow; and d. 1799, leaving a son, John Boswell, Esq. (who m. Frances Coote, sister of Charles, Earl of Bellamont, and left two daus. only, who both d. unm.), and a dau., Frances, m. in 1766, to Charles Tottenham, Esq., grandfather, by her, of CHARLES TOTTENHAM, Esq., of Ballycurry.

2 Frances, m. 3 April, 1738, William-Paul Warren, Esq. of Grangebegg, co. Kildare; and d. 1763, leaving a son, Richard Warren, d. s. p., and a dau., FRANCES, who m. FRANCIS RYVES, Esq., of Ballyskiddane, co. Limerick.

III. Richard, M.P. for the co. Kildare, b. 16 July, 1696; m. Dorothy, dau. and co-heiress of Major Green, of Killaghy, co. Tipperary; and dying 14 April, 1745, left issue,

1 JOHN, } successively viscounts.
2 JOSHUA,

3 Richard.

1 Elizabeth, m. 1767, to Captain Browne.

His lordship d. 8 November, 1726, and was s by his eldest son,

JOSHUA, 2nd viscount, b. in 1685; m. 18 October, 1704, Margaret, dau. of Samuel Du Pass, Esq.. of Epsom, by whom he h id,

JOHN, his heir.

5

ELIZABETH, m. 1750, John, 1st Lord Carysfort, and had a dau., Elizabeth, m. to Thomas-James Storer, Esq., and a son, John-Joshua, 1st Earl of Carysfort, father of Granville-Leveson, EARL OF CARYSFORT.

FRANCES, m. the Right Hon. Sir William Mayne, Bart., afterwards created Lord Newhaven, and had one child only, a son, who d. young.

His lordship d. 5 December, 1742, and was s. by his only surviving son,

JOHN, 3rd viscount. This nobleman being insulted in the public streets by some disorderly dragoons, 26 April, 1745, received a wound in the hand, which occasioned a fever, and caused his death 25 May following. As he d. unm., his sisters became his heirs, and the peerage devolved upon his first cousin (refer to children of the Hon. Richard Allen, youngest son of the 1st viscount),

JOHN, 4th viscount, at whose decease unm., 10 November, 1753, the honours passed to his next brother,

JOSHUA, 5th viscount, b. 26 April, 1728; m. in 1781, Frances, eldest dau. of Gaynor Barry, Esq., of Dormstown, co. Meath, by whom (who d. in 1833) he had a son and two daus., viz.,

I. JOSHUA-WILLIAM, last viscount.

1. Frances-Elizabeth, d. unm., 31 January, 1826.

II. LETITIA-EMILY-DOROTHEA, m. 17 May, 1806, the Hon. and Very Rev. William Herbert, LL.D., dean of Manchester. son of Henry, 1st Earl of Carnarvon, and by him (who d. 28 May, 1847), had, with other issue,

1 HENRY-WILLIAM-HERBERT, b. 7 April, 1807; d. 2 September, 1859.

2 Frederick-Charles-Herbert.

1 Louisa-Catherine-Georgina, m. Major-General Godfrey-Charles Mundy; and d. 1860, leaving issue.

2 Cecilia-Augusta-Henrietta, m. to Col. A.-T. Ferguson.

He d. 1 February, 1816, and was s. by his only son,

JOSHUA-WILLIAM, 6th viscount, a military officer, who served under Wellington in the Peninsula. He d. 21 September, 1845, when the honours became EXTINCT.

Arms—Arg., two bars, wavy, and a chief, az., the latter charged with an estoile, between two escallops, or.

AMORIE—BARONS D'AMORIE.

By Writ of Summons, dated 20 November, 1317.

Lineage.

GILBERT DE AUMARI, in the 18th HENRY II., gave fifteen marks for livery of his lands at Winford, in the co. of Somerset: after this Gilbert came another,

GILBERT D'AMORIE, who in the 22nd EDWARD I. was in the expedition made into Gascony. This Gilbert had three sons, viz.,

I. ROGER (Sir), of whom presently.

II. NICHOLAS, who, in the 6th EDWARD II., obtained a charter of free warren, in all his demesne lands within the manors of Bokenhall and Blechesdon, co. Oxford, and Thornebergh, co. Bucks. He was s. by his son,

SIR RICHARD D'AMORIE, who was summoned to parliament as a BARON from 20th EDWARD II. to 4th EDWARD III. This nobleman was in the wars of Scotland in 1320, and in three years afterwards, being at the time steward of the king's household, had command to besiege the castle of Wallingford, then in possession of the rebellious lords. His lordship d. in 1330, leaving issue.

RICHARD, 2nd baron. His lordship, who was engaged in the Flemish and French wars from 1341 to 1347, d. without issue in 1375, when this BARONY EXPIRED, but the estates devolved upon his sisters,

ELIZABETH, m. to Sir John Chandos, K.G.

ELEANOR, m. to Roger Colyng.

MARGARET, whose only child, Isabel, m. Sir John Annesley, Knt.

III. RICHARD (Sir), continued the male line after the extinction of his elder brothers, and from him sprang, it is asserted, the family of DAMER, EARLS OF DORCHESTER, now represented by Henry-John-Reuben Dawson-Damer, Earl of Portarlington.

The eldest son,

SIR ROGER D'AMORIE, was summoned to parliament as a BARON, from 20 November, 1317, to 15 May, 1321. This nobleman obtained in the 13th EDWARD II., from the crown, confirmed by the parliament then held at York, the manors of Sandall, in Yorkshire, Halghton, in Oxfordshire, and Faukeshall, in Surrey, as likewise 100 marks per annum to be paid out of the exchequer. His lordship was engaged in the wars of Scotland, and was governor at different times of Knaresborough Castle, the castle of Gloucester, and St. Briavel's Castle. He was also warden of the forest of Dene. He joined, however, in the confederacy against the Spencers, and enrolling himself under the banner of Thomas, Earl of Lancaster, marched on Burton-upon-Trent, and thence to Tutbury Castle, co. Stafford, where falling ill, he *d.* in 1322, and was buried in the priory at Ware, in Hertfordshire. His lordship *m.* Elizabeth, 3rd sister and co-heir of Gilbert de Clare, Earl of Gloucester (who had been previously twice a widow. 1st of John de Burgh, Earl of Ulster, and 2ndly, of Theobald de Verdon, she was also niece of King EDWARD II.). By this lady he had issue, two daus., his co heirs, viz.,

> Elizabeth, *m.* to John, Lord Bardolph, by whom she had,
> WILLIAM, Lord Bardolph, whose son,
> THOMAS, Lord Bardolph, being attainted, the BARONIES OF BARDOLPH AND D'AMORIE fell) under the attainder and EXPIRED in 1404,
> Eleanor, *m.* to John de Raleigh, progenitor, it is said, of the celebrated Sir Walter Raleigh.

Upon the decease of Lord D'Amorie, orders were given to seize all his lands as an enemy and rebel, and to make livery of them to Elizabeth de Burgh, his widow. This lady *d.* in the 34th EDWARD III., leaving, Dugdale says, Elizabeth Lady Bardolph, then above thirty years of age; Nicolas calls this Elizabeth the only dau. and heir of Roger, Lord D'Amorie; as such, she of course inherited the Barony of D'Amorie, and it EXPIRED as stated above, with *that* of Bardolph; but Banks mentions the other dau., who if Sir Walter Raleigh sprang from her, left descendants, amongst some of whom the BARONY OF D'AMORIE may yet be in ABEYANCE.

One branch of this ancient house was long seated at Yatt, co. Gloucester; and another has migrated to America where, in the United States, the name and family of Amory are well known and esteemed.

Arms—Barry of six, nebulée, ar. and gu., a bend, az.

ANGUS—EARL OF MORAY.

ANGUS, EARL OF MORAY, was killed at Strickathrow, in Forfarshire, in 1130.

ANNESLEY—EARLS OF ANGLESEY.

By Letters Patent, dated 20 April, 1661.

Lineage.

The ancient family of ANNESLEY, derived their surname from the town of Annesley, co. Nottingham, which was possessed in 1079, by

RICHARD DE ANNESLEY, from whom lineally descended

SIR JOHN ANNESLEY, Knight of Hedynton, co. Oxford, M.P. for Notts, *temp.* EDWARD III and RICHARD II. He *m.* Isabel, dau., by Sir John Ireland, and heir of Margaret, 3rd sister and co-heir of Sir John Chandos, K.G., Baron of St. Saviour le Viscount, in Normandy, whereby becoming interested in that barony, he cited Thomas de Caterton, who had been governor of the castle of St. Saviour le Viscount, into the Court of Chivalry, to appear before the Lord High Constable of England and others, at Westminster, on 7 May, 1380, to answer his delivering up to the French the said castle of St. Saviour's, a third part whereof being Sir John's property, in right of his wife. And the said Thomas, endeavouring to avoid the challenge by frivolous exceptions, John, Duke of Lancaster, 3rd son of King EDWARD III., swore, that if he did not perform what he ought to do therein, according to the law of arms, he should be drawn to the gallows as a traitor. The combat took place in the March following, in the Palace Yard of Westminster, and "Caterton," says Barnes, in his History of EDWARD III., ' was a mighty man of valour, of a large stature, and far overtopped the knight, being also of great expectation in such matters. But, however, whether justice, or chance, or valour, only decided the business, the knight prevailed, and Caterton, the day after the combat (as some say) died of his wounds, though, considering the laws attending duels in such cases, I rather inclined to Fabian, who affirms he was drawn to Tyburn, and there hanged for the treason, whereof being vanquished he was proved guilty." The king taking into consideration the damage done to this Sir John Annesley, was pleased, 26 May, 1385, to grant to him, and Isabel his wife, for their lives, an annuity of £40 per annum out of the exchequer. He was *s* by his son,

THOMAS ANNESLEY, of Annesley, co. Nottingham, M.P. for that shire, *temp.* RICHARD II., from whom descended

ROBERT ANNESLEY, of Newport-Pagnel, co. Bucks, who *d.* 1st Queen MARY. And we pass to his great grandson,

SIR FRANCIS ANNESLEY, Knt., of Newport-Pagnel, who was created a BARONET OF IRELAND, upon the institution of that order by King JAMES I. And filling the offices in the Irish

government of *vice-treasurer and secretary of state*, he was elevated to the peerage of that kingdom, by letters patent, dated 8 February, 1628, as BARON MOUNT NORRIS, of Mount Norris, co. Armagh, having been created the year previously VISCOUNT VALENTIA, co. Kerry, to hold immediately after the death of Henry Power, the then Viscount Valentia, in case the said Henry died without male issue, which dignity he accordingly enjoyed upon the decease of that nobleman. In the 19th JAMES I., Sir Francis, then one of the principal secretaries of state, was in commission with the lord deputy, the lord chancellor, and the archbishop of Armagh, to enquire into the clerical affairs of Ireland. During the lieutenancy of the Earl of Strafford, his lordship was, however, committed to prison, and sentenced to lose his head, by a most extraordinary stretch of power, which proceeding afterwards constituted the 5th article of the impeachment of Lord Strafford. The charge against Lord Mountnorris, upon which he was tried and condemned by a council of war, was thus set forth by the Lord Deputy himself:—" That within three or four days, or thereabouts, after the end of the parliament, it being mentioned at the Lord Chancellor's table, that after we, the Lord Deputy, had dissolved the parliament, being sitting down in the presence-chamber, one of our servants in moving a stool, happened to hurt our foot, then indisposed through an accession of gout; that one then present at the Lord Chancellor's table, said to the Lord Mountnorris, being there likewise, that it was Annesley, his lordship's kinsman, and one of our, the Lord Deputy and general's gentlemen ushers, had done it: whereupon the Lord Mountnorris then publicly, and in a scornful, contemptuous manner, answered, ' *Perhaps it was done in revenge of that public affront which my Lord Deputy had done him formerly; but he has a brother that would not take such a revenge.*' " which public affront the lord deputy thus explains:—" That his said kinsman (being one of the horse troop commanded by us, the Lord Deputy), in the time of exercising the said troop, was out of order on horseback, to the disturbance of the rest, then in exercising; for which we, the Lord Deputy, in a mild manner, reproving, as soon as we turned aside from him, we observed him to laugh and jeer us for our just reproof of him; which we disliking, returned to him, and laying a small cane (which we then carried) on his shoulders (yet without any blow or stroke then given him therewith), told him, that, if he did serve us so any more, we would lay him over the pate." And the Lord Deputy draws this inference thus against Lord Mountnorris:—" We conceive offence to contain an incitement to revenge in these words, ' *but he has a brother that would not take such a revenge;*' which incitement might have given encouragement to that brother, being then and now in this kingdom, and lieutenant of the said Lord Mountnorris's foot company." Upon this frivolous accusation Lord Mountnorris was found guilty, and adjudged "to be imprisoned, to stand from henceforth deprived from all the places, with the entertainments due thereunto, which he holds now in the army, to be disarmed, to be banished the army, and disabled from ever bearing office therein hereafter; and, lastly, to be shot to death, or to lose his head, at the pleasure of the general. Given at his Majesty's Castle of Dublin, 12th day of December, 1635." Although the extremity of this iniquitous sentence was not put into execution, his lordship was deprived, in conformity with it, of all his offices, and confined in the castle of Dublin for nearly a year and a-half. He lived, however, to witness the disgrace and public execution of his persecutor, the Earl of Strafford. Lord Mountnorris, who became Viscount Valentia, *m.* 1st, Dorothy, dau. of Sir John Philips, of Picton Castle, co. Pembroke, by whom he had, with other issue,

> I. ARTHUR, his successor.
> II. John, of Ballysonan, co. Kildare, *m.* Charity, dau. of Henry Warren, Esq., of Grange Begg, co. Kildare, and had issue.
> I. Anne, *m.* to George Cook, Esq., of Pebmarsh, co. Essex.

His lordship *m.* 2ndly, Jane, dau. of Sir John Stanhope, Knt., sister of Philip, Earl of Chesterfield, and widow of Sir Peter Courteen, Knt., of Aldington, co. Worcester, by whom he had surviving issue,

> I. Francis, of Castle Wellan, co. Down, who *m.* Debora, dau. of Dr. Henry Jones, bishop of Meath, and widow of John Boudler, Esq., of Dublin, and was *s.* by his son,
> Francis, M.P. for Downpatrick and for Westbury, *m.* Elizabeth, dau. of Sir John Martin, of London, by whom, with several other children, he had FRANCIS, ancestor of the ANNESLEYS, OF BLETCHINGTON, co. Oxford, now VISCOUNTS VALENTIA; and WILLIAM, ancestor of the EARLS ANNESLEY.
> I. Catharine, *m.* to Sir Randal Beresford, Bart., of Coleraine.

The viscount *d.* in 1660, and was *s.* by his eldest son,

ARTHUR ANNESLEY, 2nd Viscount Valentia. This nobleman

was appointed in the lifetime of his father (anno 1645), first of the three commissioners then nominated by parliament to govern the kingdom of Ireland. And a little before the Restoration, in the year 1660, being president of the council, he evinced, according to Lord Clarendon, a strong disposition towards the exiled monarch, for which, and his subsequent adhesion to the restored government, he was sworn of the privy council, and created, 20 April, 1661, a peer of England, by the titles of *Baron Annesley*, of Newport-Pagnel, co. Bucks, and EARL OF ANGLESEY.

His lordship subsequently held the office of privy seal. He was a person of learning—a distinguished statesman, and an able political writer. The earl m. Elizabeth, one of the daus. and co-heirs of Sir James Altham, Knt., of Oxey, co. Herts, one of the barons of the exchequer, by whom he had five sons and five daus., viz.,

I. JAMES, Lord Annesley.
II. ALTHAM, who was created an Irish peer, 14 February, 1680, by the title of BARON ALTHAM, with limitation to his younger brothers. His lordship m. 1st, Alice, dau. and sole heiress of Charles Leigh, Esq., of Leighton Buzzard, co. Bedford, but had no issue. He m. 2ndly, Ursula, dau. and heir of Sir Robert Markham, Bart, and dying 1699, was s. by his only son,

JAMES-GEORGE, 2nd Lord Altham, at whose decease, in infancy, the dignity reverted to his uncle, the Hon. and Very Rev.

III. RICHARD ANNESLEY, dean of Exeter, as 3rd Lord Altham, who d. in 1761, the year in which he succeeded to the peerage, and was s. by his son,

ARTHUR, 4th Lord Altham, who m. Mary, illegitimate dau. of John Sheffield, Duke of Buckingham; but dying, as supposed, issueless, 16 November, 1727, the title devolved upon his brother,

RICHARD, 5th Lord Altham, of whom hereafter as 6th EARL OF ANGLESEY.

IV. Arthur.   V. Charles.
I. Dorothy, m. to Richard Power, Earl of Tyrone.
II. Elizabeth, m. to the Hon. Alexander Macdonnell, 2nd son of the Earl of Antrim.
III. Frances, m. 1st, to Francis Windham, Esq., of Felbrigg, and 2ndly, to Sir John Thompson, of Haversham, Bucks Bart, afterwards Lord Haversham.
IV. Philippa, m. 1st, to Charles, Lord Mohun; and 2ndly, to Thomas Coward, Esq., co. Somerset, serjeant-at-law.
V. Anne, m. to — Baker, Esq.

His lordship d. 6 April, 1686, and was s. by his eldest son,

JAMES ANNESLEY, 2nd Earl of Anglesey, who m. Lady Elizabeth Manners, dau. of John, Earl of Rutland, and had issue,

JAMES, Lord Annesley, } successively Earls of Anglesey.
JOHN,
ARTHUR,

Elizabeth, m. to Robert Gayer, Esq., of Stoke Poges, co. Bucks.

His lordship d. in 1690, and was s. by his eldest son,

JAMES ANNESLEY, 3rd Earl of Anglesey. This nobleman m. 28 October, 1699, Lady Catherine Darnley, natural dau. of King JAMES II., by Catherine, dau. of Sir Charles Sedley, Bart., by whom he had an only dau. and heiress,

Catherine, who m. William Phipps, Esq., son of Sir Constantine Phipps, Knt., lord chancellor of Ireland, and had issue,

CONSTANTINE PHIPPS, created Baron Mulgrave, in the peerage of Ireland, a dignity inherited by his descendant, the Marquess of Normanby.

His lordship d. 18 January 1701-2, and having no male issue, the honours devolved upon his brother,

JOHN ANNESLEY, 4th Earl of Anglesey, who, in the year 1710, was constituted vice-treasurer, receiver-general, and paymaster of the forces in Ireland, and sworn of the privy council. His lordship m. in 1706, Lady Henrietta Stanley, eldest dau. and co-heir of William, Earl of Derby, by whom he had an only dau., Elizabeth, who d. in infancy. The earl d. 18 September, 1710, and was s. by his only surviving brother,

ARTHUR ANNESLEY, 5th Earl of Anglesey. Upon the death of Queen ANNE, this nobleman was chosen by King GEORGE I, to be one of the lords justices, until his Majesty's arrival from Hanover; after which he was sworn of the privy council. He was afterwards joint treasurer of Ireland, and treasurer at war. His lordship was also high steward of the University of Cambridge, which seat of learning he represented in three successive parliaments while a commoner. He m. Mary, dau. of John Thompson, Lord Haversham, but dying without issue, the honours were assumed by his kinsman,

RICHARD ANNESLEY, 6th Lord Altham, as 6th Earl of Anglesey (revert to issue of Arthur, 2nd Viscount Valentia and 1st Earl of Anglesey). Soon after the assumption of the dignity by this Earl Richard, a claimant to the honours arose in Mr. James Annesley, who asserted himself to be the son of Arthur, 4th Lord Altham, by Mary, his wife, and a publication entitled "The Adventures of an Unfortunate Young Noble-

man,' sets forth his case in a very curious and interesting narrative. In that statement it is alleged that Mr. Annesley is the true and lawful son and heir of Arthur, Lord Altham, and that he had been kidnapped and transported by his uncle Richard, to make room for his own accession to the honours and estates of the family. Mr. Annesley did more, however, to establish his legitimacy. He commenced a suit at law for the recovery of his property from his uncle, and after a trial in the Court of Exchequer in Ireland, James Annesley against Richard, called Earl of Anglesey, commenced 11 November, 1743, and continued by adjournment daily to the 25th of the same month, he obtained a VERDICT. But he does not appear to have made any effort for the peerage, for Richard survived the issue of the suit eighteen years, and was always esteemed Earl of Anglesey. [For a full narrative of the marvellous incidents in the life of James Annesley, as well as of the Annesley litigation, refer to BURKE's *Vicissitudes of Families*.]

The earl m. 15 September, 1741, Juliana, dau of Rickard Donovan, Esq., and by her (who d. 1776) had issue,

ARTHUR, heir to the Irish honours.
Richarda, m. 1761, to Robert Phaire, Esq., of Temple Shannon,
Juliana, m. to Sir Frederick Flood, Bart.
Catherine, m. to John O'Toole, Esq.

His lordship d. 4 February, 1761, when the legitimacy of his son was contested by the heir-at-law, John Annesley, Esq., of Ballysax, who petitioned the Irish parliament to be admitted to the honours of the family. The matter excited great public interest, and was pending in the Irish House of Lords nearly four years, when their lordships came to a decision establishing the marriage with Miss Donovan, and confirming the rights of her son, ARTHUR, as Baron Mountnorris, Baron Altham, and Viscount Valentia, and as a Baronet of Ireland, and his lordship took his seat accordingly when he came of age, anno 1765, in the House of Lords. He then applied for his writ to the English House of Peers, as Earl of Anglesey, but there the decision as to his legitimacy and the marriage of his mother, was against him, and the writ was denied; upon the decease, therefore, of Richard, Earl of Anglesey, in 1761, the Earldom of Anglesey was deemed to have EXPIRED, and the dignity has since been conferred upon another family. Arthur, Lord Valentia, continued, however, to sit in the Irish parliament (his case being again investigated and his right confirmed), and was created, 3 December, 1793, EARL OF MOUNTNORRIS, in the peerage of Ireland. His lordship m. 1st, in 1767, Lucy, only dau. and eventual heir of George, 1st Lord Lyttleton, by whom (who d. 1783) he had

GEORGE, last earl.
Juliana-Lucy, m. John, Lord Farnham; and d. s. p. 1833.
Hester-Annabella, m. in 1801, Major-Gen. Norman Macleod and d. 14 August, 1844, leaving, with other issue, a son and heir, Arthur-Lyttelton Macleod, Esq., who changed his name for that of his maternal ancestors, and became ARTHUR-LYTTELTON ANNESLEY, Esq., of Arley Castle, co. Stafford

The earl m. 2ndly, 20 December, 1783, Sarah, 3rd dau. of the Rt. Hon. Sir Henry Cavendish and the Baroness Waterpark, by whom (who d. 1849) he left at his decease, in 1816,

Henry-Arthur, d. s. p. in 1818.
Catherine, m. Lord John Somerset, and had issue.
Frances-Caroline, m. in 1810, to Sir James-Webster Wedderburn, late of the 10th hussars; and d. 22 January, 1837.
Juliana, m. 26 October, 1837, to Robert Bayly, Esq., of Bally. duff.

The earl d. 4 July, 1816, and was s. by his son,

GEORGE, 2nd Earl of Mountnorris, F.R.S., F.S.A., b. 1769; m. 1790, Anne, 8th dau. of William, 2nd Viscount Courtenay, and by her (who d. 1835) had issue,

GEORGE-ARTHUR, Viscount Valentia, b. 20 October, 1793; m. 21 October, 1837, Frances-Cockburn, one of the late Charles-James Sims, Esq; and d. s. p. 16 March, 1841.
Lady Valentia d. 27 January, 1856.
William, in holy orders, b. 19 February, 1796; d. unm. 1 November, 1830.

The earl d. 23 July, 1844, when the Earldom of Mountnorris became EXTINCT, and the VISCOUNTY OF VALENTIA passed to his kinsman, ARTHUR ANNESLEY, Esq., of Bletchington, co. Oxford. (See BURKE's *Extant Peerage*.)

Arms—Paly of six, arg. and az., a bend, gu.

ANNESLEY—EARLS OF MOUNTNORRIS, AND ANNESLEY—BARONS ALTHAM.

See ANNESLEY, EARLS OF ANGLESEY.

7

ANSON—BARON ANSON, OF SOBERTON, CO. SOUTHAMPTON.

By Letters Patent, dated 13 June, 1747.

Lineage.

The family of Anson has resided in the co. of Stafford for several generations; first, at Dunston; but since the time of JAMES I. at Shugborough, which manor was then purchased by

WILLIAM ANSON, Esq., who had been an eminent lawyer in the previous reign. This William Anson m. Joan, dau. of Richard Mitchel, of Oldbury, in Warwickshire; and dying at an advanced age, about the year 1644, was s. by his son,

WILLIAM ANSON, Esq., of Shugborough, who m. Elizabeth, dau. of Thomas Stafford, Esq., of Botham Hall, in Derbyshire, and was s. by his son,

WILLIAM ANSON, Esq., of Shugborough. This gentleman m. Isabella, dau. and co-heir of Charles Carrier, Esq., of Wirksworth, and had issue,

  I. THOMAS, his successor.
  II. GEORGE, of whom presently.
  1. Janette, m. to Sambrooke Adams, Esq., of Sambrooke, co. Salop, and left a son, GEORGE ADAMS, who assumed the name of ANSON.
  II. Isabella.   III. Anna.   IV. Johanna.

Mr. Anson d. in 1720, and was s. by his elder son,

THOMAS ANSON, Esq., of Shugborough, M.P. for Lichfield, who, at his decease, s. p., bequeathed his property to his nephew, George Adams. Thomas Anson's younger brother,

GEORGE ANSON, so celebrated for his voyage round the world, was soon after his return appointed rear-admiral of the Blue, and one of the lords of the admiralty. In April, 1745, he was made rear-admiral of the White, and in July, 1746, vice-admiral of the Blue. In 1747 (13 June), he was elevated to the peerage by the title of LORD ANSON, *Baron of Soberton, co. Hants,* and the same year appointed vice-admiral of the Red. In 1751, his lordship was constituted first lord of the admiralty; and he continued in that high office, with a very brief interval, until his death. This gallant and enterprising seaman m. Lady Elizabeth Yorke, dau. of Philip, 1st Earl of Hardwicke; but d. s.p. 6 June, 1762, when the Barony of Anson became EXTINCT, while his fortune devolved upon his nephew, GEORGE ADAMS, Esq., who subsequently inherited the estates of his elder uncle, THOMAS, and assumed, by sign-manual, 30 April, 1773, the surname and arms of ANSON. His great-grandson is the present EARL OF LICHFIELD.

Arms—Arg., three bends engr., gu.

AP-ADAM—BARONS DE AP-ADAM.

By Writ of Summons, dated 6 February, 1299

Lineage.

SIR JOHN AP ADAM, possessor in his own right of lands in Gorste and Beteale within Tidenham, co. Gloucester, having m. in the 19th EDWARD I., Elizabeth, dau. and heiress of John de Gurnay, Baron of Beverstone, co. Gloucester, by Oliva, his wife, dau. of Henry Lovel, Baron of Castle Cary, obtained considerable landed property in that shire by the alliance, and in five years afterwards, an accession of estates in Somersetshire, upon the decease of the lady's mother, Oliva. This John had a royal charter (in the 21st of EDWARD I.,) for a weekly market and a yearly fair to be holden at Beverstone, and another charter in the 26th of the same monarch, for a weekly market and annual fair to be holden at his manor of Netherwere. In this latter year he was engaged in the Scottish wars; and again, in eight years subsequently. He was summoned to parliament from the 25th of EDWARD I. to the 2nd of EDWARD II. inclusive. His lordship d. 4 EDWARD II., leaving in minority a son and heir,

SIR THOMAS AP-ADAM, whose wardship Ralph de Monthermer obtained, in consideration of 6,000 marks. This Thomas arrived at maturity in the 18th of EDWARD II., and had livery of his lands upon doing homage. He was living in 1330, having then alienated the greater part of the estates he had inherited from the Gurnays, and sold the castle and manor of Beverstone to Thomas de Berkeley and Margaret his wife: his three sons, Robert, Hamund, and John, all appear to have d. s p: but his only dau.—heiress to her brothers—and wife of Thomlyn Huntley ap Philipot, left a son and heir, JOHN HUNTLEY AP THOMLYN, who succeeded to his uncle Robert ap Adam's lands in Tidenham: by Johanna, his wife, this John ap Thomlyn left daus., his co-heiresses, of whom MARGARET was wife of Edmund ap Gwylyn ap Hopkin; and MARGERY, of Thomas Parker, of Monmouth, ancestor of the Powells of Llanllowel. Badamscourt, with the manor of Betteslay, and a third of the manor of Gorste, the last Gloucestershire fragment of the once great estate of the Baron ap Adam was purchased in 1580 from Dr. John Symings, an eminent London physician, by William Lewis, Esq., of St. Pierre, co. Monmouth, and after passing through the families of Williams, of Tidenham and Cosby, was sold to GEORGE ORMEROD, Esq., D.C.L., of Sedbury.

There is a family of ADAMS seated at Middleton Hall, co. Carmarthen, which has assumed the surname of ABADAM, and claims to be descended from this baronial house.

Arms—Arg., on a cross, gu., five mullets, or; in the old painted glass of Tidenham church, the mullets are "pierced of the field."

ARCHDEKNE—BARONS ARCHDEKNE.

By Writ of Summons, dated 15 May, 1321.

Lineage.

THOMAS LE ARCHDEKNE, of Shepestall, co. Cornwall, petitioned the king, in parliament (35 EDWARD I.), soliciting that an investigation might he instituted, touching the seizure of his lands for neglect of service in the wars of Scotland, whereas neither himself nor his ancestors have been bound to perform such service, and praying for the restitution of the said lands. In the 6th of EDWARD II., this Thomas Le Archdekne was governor of Tintaget Castle, in the co. of Cornwall, and, in twelve years afterwards, a commissioner, with Ralph Lord Basset, of Drayton, and Arnold de Durefort, to receive all such persons, in the duchy of Aquitaine, into protection as should submit to the king's authority. He was summoned to parliament as BARON ARCHDEKNE, from the 15 May, 1321, to 13 September, 1324; and, dying, was s. by his son,

JOHN LE ARCHDEKNE, 2nd baron—summoned to parliament on 25 February, 16th EDWARD III. This nobleman distinguished himself in the expedition to Flanders, in the 13th of EDWARD III., and, two years afterwards, was in Scotland, in the train of William de Many. In the next year we find him serving under Oliver de Ingham in the wars of Gascony; and, in the 19th of EDWARD III., upon the great expedition then made into France, he had summons to fit himself with horse and arms, so that he might be in readiness against the Feast of St. Lawrence to attend the king upon that enterprise. Again, in the 29th of the same monarch, Lord Archdekne attended Henry Duke of Lancaster upon another expedition against France. His lordship m. Cecilie, dau. and heiress of Sir Jordan FitzStephen Haccombe, of Haccombe, and was s. by his son,

WARINE LE ARCHDEKNE, 3rd baron, who m. Elizabeth, one of the sisters and co-heiresses of John Talbot, of Richard's Castle, and had issue,

  I. ALIANORE (or ELIZABETH), m. to Walter de Lucie, by whom she had,
    1 William, who d. s. p.
    1 Alianore, m. to Thomas Hopton.
    2 Maud, m. to Thomas Vaux.
  II. PHILIPPA, m. to Hugh Courtenay, of Haccomb, Knt., and had a dau., Joan, m. 1st, to Sir Nicholas Carew, of Mohuns Ottery; and 2ndly, to Sir Robert Vere.
  III. MARGARET, m. to Thomas Arundel.

At the decease of Warine, Lord Archdekne, in 1400, the barony fell into ABEYANCE, and so continues amongst the representatives of his daus.

Arms—Arg., three chevronells, sa.

ARCHER—BARONS ARCHER, OF UMBERSLADE, CO. WARWICK.

Created by Letters Patent, dated 14 July, 1747.

Lineage.

The Archers of Umberslade were a family of considerable distinction, long antecedent to their elevation to the peerage. One line, deriving descent from Fulbert L'Archer, the Norman, was settled, at a very remote period, at Kilkenny, in Ireland; and its descendants may still be traced in that kingdom, one being the present GRAVES-CHAMNEY ARCHER, Esq., of Mount John, co Wicklow.

ROBERT L'ARCHER, son of Fulbert L'Archer, who came into England with the CONQUEROR, obtained considerable grants from King HENRY I., whose tutor he had been, and acquired the lands of Umberslade, co. Warwick, as a marriage portion with his wife Sebit, dau. of Henry de Villiers, sewer to William de Newburgh, Earl of Warwick, all which possessions were confirmed by HENRY II. to his son,

WILLIAM L'ARCHER, whose son,

JOHN L'ARCHER, being champion to Thomas, Earl of Warwick, obtained special charter from that nobleman, granting to himself and his heirs the privilege of hunting and hawking everywhere within the territory of Taneworth, except the park, and of exercising all other liberties belonging to the earl within Monkspath and Ombersladc, paying to the said earl and his heirs twelve broad arrow heads and a couple of capons yearly, at Whitsuntide, as an acknowledgment. This John d. in the 35th HENRY III., leaving four sons and two daus. The three younger sons appear to have been churchmen. Thomas, the 2nd, was prior of St. John's of Jerusalem, in England, temp. EDWARD II. The eldest son,

JOHN ARCHER, purchased of William de Olenhale the manor of Monkspath, adjoining Omberslade. This John m. Margery, dau. of Sir William Tracey, of Todington, co. Gloucester, and was s. by his eldest son,

JOHN ARCHER, who m. Isabel, dau. of Ralph Erscote, Esq., of Erscote, co. Warwick, by whom he had two sons and two daus.; and, dying in the 22nd of EDWARD III., was s. by the elder son,

THOMAS ARCHER. This gentleman m. Margaret, dau. and co-heiress of John Malley, Esq., of Malley, co. Salop, and had issue,

THOMAS, his successor.
Gilbert, who, writing himself of Taneworth, had license from the crown, in the 16th RICHARD II., to give to the prior and convent of Kenilworth one messuage, with divers lands at Hitchenden, in the co. of Buckingham.
Joane, m. to William Shelly, Esq.

This Thomas Archer's will is dated "Thursday next after the Feast of St. Thomas the Martyr, 1372," and he was s. in that year by his elder son,

THOMAS ARCHER, one of the gallant soldiers of the martial reign of EDWARD III. In 1373 he had a command in the army of John of Gaunt, and fell into the hands of the French and Burgundians in a rencounter at Ouchy le Château, near Soissons, on 20 October in that year, being surprised when foraging with Sir Matthew Redmayn, Sir Thomas Spencer, Sir Hugh Bradenel, Sir John Bourchier, and several other knights and esquires, In the 49th of EDWARD III. we again find him in France under Thomas Beauchamp, Earl of Warwick, from whom he received a pension for his services, dated at Worcester "20 Martii, 1 RICH. II.," in the 21st of which latter reign he received a special pardon dated 8 June, for all manner of transgressions, and for whatever he had acted contrary to his allegiance, &c. in behalf of Thomas, late Duke of Gloucester, Richard, late Earl of Arundel, and Thomas, Earl of Warwick; after which, in the same year, he was in commission for assessing and collecting a fifteenth and tenth, then granted to the king in parliament. This Thomas Archer m. Agnes, dau. of Sir Walter Cokesey, of Cokesey, co. Worcester, and grand-dau. of Hugh Cokesey and of Dionis his wife, one of the four sisters and co-heiresses of Edmund le Botcler, by whom he had three sons. He died, after being bedridden for three years, in the 84th year of his age, on the Feast of Pentecost, in 1426, and was s. by his 2nd but eldest surviving son,

RICHARD ARCHER, who was one of the persons of note in the county of Warwick summoned in the 7th of HENRY V. to serve the king in person for the defence of the realm, being, according to the writ, "one that did bear ancient arms from his ancestors." This gentleman m. 1st, Alice, dau. of William Hugford, Esq., of Hugford and Middleton, co. Salop, sister and heiress of William Hugford, and widow of Sir Thomas Lucy, Knt., of Charlecote, by whom he had one son,

JOHN, who m. in the 25th HENRY VI., Christian, widow of Henry Sewal, of London, and only dau. and heiress of Ralph Blacklow, of the same city, and of his wife, Joan, only dau. and heiress of Thomas Coke, alias Malling, of West Malling, Kent, by whom he had an only son, JOHN. King HENRY VI., by his letters patent, dated 12 May, in the 8th year of his reign, retained this John Archer, Esq., by his factors or attorneys, to convey in ships all manner of provisions for victualling the town and fortress of Calais. Mr. Archer fell in battle in 1463, on the side of the Earl of Warwick, against King EDWARD IV. His widow remarried, in the 3rd of EDWARD IV., Henry Becch, Esq.

Richard Archer m. 2ndly, Margaret, relict of Thomas Newport, Esq., of Ercall, in Shropshire, ancestor of the Earls ..radford, and 3rdly, Joane, dau. and heiress of William Ley, of Stotford, co. Stafford. In the 7th of HENRY VI. Mr. Archer had summons to attend the king in France, to be present at his coronation there; Sir Ralph Bruce, Knt., Sir Edward Dodingfell, and Nicholas Burdett, with others of the county of Warwick, being also summoned. In the 19th of the same monarch, he served the office of sheriff for the county of Salop, and the next year that of sheriff for the county of Stafford, in which shire he resided at Stotford. He d. in the 55th year of his age, anno 1471, when his large estates in the counties of Salop, Stafford and Bedford, devolved upon his grandson,

9

JOHN ARCHER, Esq., b. in 1449; m. Alice, dau. of Sir Baldwin Mountford, Knt., of Coltshill, co. Warwick, and dying at Omberslade, 4 December, 1519, was s. by his only son,

JOHN ARCHER, Esq., who m. Margaret, dau. of Humparcy Stafford, Esq., of Blatherwicke, co. Northampton, by whom he had four sons and a dau. He d. in a year after his father, and was s. by his eldest son,

RICHARD ARCHER, Esq., escheator of the co. of Warwick in the 22nd of HENRY VIII., and justice of the peace for that shire. This gentleman m. Maud, 2nd dau. of Nicholas Delamere, Esq., of Little Hereford, co. Hereford, and co-heiress with her sister Susan, wife of John Dansey, Esq., of her brother Edmund Delamere, Esq., and had issue, HUMPHREY, b. in 1527, Miles, b. in 1530, Edward, b. in 1533, d. unm., Francis, b. in 1534, Anne, b. in 1526, and Winifrede, b. in 1535.

In the 32nd of HENRY VIII. Mr. Archer was appointed steward of the manor of Knole, co. Warwick, being then, as recited in the letters patent, one of the esquires of the king's body, and in two years afterwards, he was commanded to take the muster of all able men, as well horsemen as foot, that he could furnish both of the king's tenants, inhabiting upon farms whereof he had the stewardship, as also his own servants and tenants dwelling on his own lands, &c. He d. 5 October, 1544, and was s. by his eldest son,

HUMPHREY ARCHER, Esq., who m. 4th of EDWARD VI. (6 October) Anne, dau. of Sir Robert Townshend, Knt., chief justice of the Marches of Wales and Chester, and grand-dau. of Sir Roger Townshend, of Raynham, Norfolk, one of the justices of the Court of Common Pleas, ancestor of the Lords Townshend, by whom he had surviving issue,

ANDREW, his successor.
John, m, Eleanor, dau. and heiress of Richard Frewin, Esq., of Handley, co. Worcester.
Bridget, m. to John Bancroft, Esq., of Handbury, co. Worcester.
Margery, m. to John Colles, Esq., of Hatfield, co. Hertford.
Elizabeth, m. to John Hereford, Esq., of Sufton, co. Hertford.

Mr. Archer d. at Omberslade, 24 October, 1562, and was s. by his eldest son,

ANDREW ARCHER, Esq., who extended his territorial possessions by the purchase of large estates in the reigns of Queen ELIZABETH and King JAMES I. In the 7th year of which latter reign, he was sheriff of the co. of Warwick. He m. in 1580, Margaret, dau. of Simon Raleigh, Esq., of Farnborough, co. Warwick, and had issue,

Thomas, who d. in his twenty-fourth year, before his father, unm.
SIMON, successor to the estates,
Richard, m. Mary, dau. and sole heiress of Rowland Bull, Esq., of Neithropp, co. Oxford (with whom he acquired that estate), and had a son, Rowland.

Mr. Archer d. 23 April, 1629, and was s. by his eldest surviving son,

SIR SIMON ARCHER, Knt., sheriff of Warwickshire, in the 3rd year of King CHARLES I. and member for Tamworth, in the parliament which assembled on the 30th April, 1640. This gentleman was distinguished as a man of letters and an antiquary, and Sir William Dugdale acknowledges himself greatly indebted to him in compiling his antiquities of Warwickshire. Sir Simon m. Anne, dau. of Sir John Ferrers, Knt., of Tamworth Castle, co. Warwick, by whom he had surviving issue,

THOMAS, his successor.
Anne, m. to Philip Young, Esq., of Keneton, co. Salop.
Elizabeth.
Penelope, m. to Erasmus de Ligne, Esq., of Harlaxton, co. Lincoln.

Sir Simon Archer was s. at his decease, by his son,

THOMAS ARCHER, Esq. of Umberslade, who, at the commencement of the civil wars was a colonel in the parliament army, and raised a troop of horse at his own expense; but, so soon as he discovered the designs of the parliamentarians, he threw up his commission, and, emigrating, remained abroad until the restoration of the monarchy, when he represented the city of Warwick in parliament. He m. Anne, dau. of Richard Leigh, Esq., of London, and had issue,

ANDREW, his successor.
Thomas, groom-porter to Queen ANNE and to Kings GEORGE I and II., d. s. p. in 1743.
Leigh, d. unm.
Elizabeth, m. Sir Herbert Croft, 1st bart., of Croft Castle, co. Hereford; and d. 1709, leaving three daus., Elizabeth, m. to A. Moseley, Esq.; Margaret, m. to Richard Oakeley, Esq., of Oakeley; and Frances, m. to Robert Dyer, Esq.; and two sons, Sir Archer Croft, 2nd bart., whose son, Sir Archer, d. s. p. m.; and Francis, ancestor of the present Sir Herbert-George-Denman Croft, Bart.
Frances, m. to Sir Francis Rous, Bart., of Rous-Lench, co. Worcester.

Mr Archer d. in 1685, and was s. by his eldest son,

ANDREW ARCHER, Esq., M.P. for the county of Warwick in the reigns of WILLIAM and MARY, Queen ANNE, and King GEORGE I., and one of the commissioners appointed in 1711 to inquire into the numbers and quality of the forces in her Majesty's pay in Portugal, and to examine the accounts relating to the said forces, and to the garrisons of Portmahon and Gibraltar. Mr. Archer m. Elizabeth, dau. of Sir Samuel Dashwood, lord mayor of London in 1702, and had issue,

THOMAS, his successor.
Henry, M.P. for Warwick, m. Lady Elizabeth Montagu, sister of George, Earl of Halifax; and d. in 1768.
Anne.   Elizabeth.   Sarah.
Diana, m. Thomas Chaplin, Esq. of Blankney Hall, co. Lincoln, ancestor, by her, of the CHAPLINS of Blankney, and the CHAPLINS of Tathwell Hall, Lincolnshire.

Mr. Archer d. at Umberslade, which he had rebuilt, on 31 December, 1741, and was s. by his elder son,

THOMAS ARCHER, Esq., M.P. for Warwick, and subsequently for Bramber, who was elevated to the peerage, 14 July, 1747, by the title of BARON ARCHER, OF UMBERSLADE, IN THE COUNTY OF WARWICK. His lordship m. Catharine, dau. and co-heiress of Sir Thomas Tipping, Bart., of Wheatfield, co. Oxford, and Anne, his wife, dau. and heiress of Thomas Cheke, Esq., by his wife, Letitia, dau. and eventually sole heiress of Edward Russell (brother of William, 1st Duke of Bedford) and sister and heiress of Edward Russell, Earl of Orford, by whom he had issue,

ANDREW, his successor, M.P. for Coventry.
Catharine, m. 11 August, 1750, to Other-Lewis, 4th Earl of Plymouth.
Anne, m. 15 March, 1756, to Edward-Garth Tournour, Esq., of Shilingley Park, co. Sussex, created subsequently EARL OF WINTERTON, in Ireland.

His lordship d. in 1768, and was s. by his only son,

ANDREW ARCHER, 2nd baron. This nobleman m. in 1761, Sarah, elder dau. of James West, Esq., M.P. of Alscot, co. Warwick, by whom he had three daus., his co-heirs, viz.,

I. SARAH, m. 1st, 1788, to Other-Hickman, Earl of Plymouth, by whom she had issue,

1 Other-Hickman, 6th earl, d. s. p. 1833.
1 MARIA, m. 25 October, 1811, Arthur, 2nd Marquess of Downshire, K.P.; and d. 7 April, 1855, leaving with other issue, Arthur-Wills-Blundell-Sandys-Trumbull-Windsor Hill, MARQUESS OF DOWNSHIRE, K.P., one of the co-representatives of the LORDS ARCHERS.
2 HARRIET, now BARONESS WINDSOR, m. 1819, to Hon. Robert Henry Clive, who d. 29 January, 1854.
The Countess of Plymouth m. 2ndly, William Pitt, 1st Earl Amherst, by whom she was mother of the present EARL AMHERST.
II. ELIZABETH-ANNE, m, Christopher Musgrave, Esq. (2nd son of Sir Philip Musgrave, Bart., of Edenhall), and had, with two daus., two sons, Christopher and William.
III. MARIA, m. 4 November 1788, Henry Howard, Esq., of Corby, co. Cumberland; and d. 9 November, 1789, s. p.

Lord Archer d. in 1778, when the title EXPIRED.

Arms—Az., three arrows, or.

ARDEN—BARON ALVANLEY, OF ALVANLEY, CO. CHESTER.

By Letters Patent, dated 22 May, 1801.

Lineage.

"The elder branch of the Ardernes," says Lysons, in his Cheshire, "whose chief seat was at Aldford, where they had a castle, became extinct in the principal line by the death of Walkeline Arderne, in or about the reign of RICHARD II. The present John Arden, Esq., for so the family have of late years spelt the name, is descended from Sir John Arderne, a younger brother of Walkeline before mentioned, whose posterity settled in the parish of Stockport in the 15th century; and he is also the representative of the Barons of Montalt, and of the ancient family of the Dones, of Utkington and Flaxyards. A younger branch of the Ardernes settled at Alderley about the beginning of the reign of EDWARD III., and ended, after a few descents, in a female heir, who married into the Weever family, whose heiress married the ancestor of Sir J.-T. Stanley, Bart. The Ardernes of Leicestershire were descended from a younger son of Ralph Arderne, of Harden, in the 15th century."

SIR RALPH ARDERNE, of Harden, d. about 1420, leaving, by the dau. of Stanley of Houton, two sons; the younger, Thomas, was the progenitor of the Ardernes of Leicestershire, and the elder,

JOHN ARDERNE, inherited Harden. From this gentleman descended through several generations,

SIR JOHN ARDERNE, Knt., whose grandson,

JOHN ARDEN, Esq., of Arden, co. Chester, m. Mary, dau. of Cuthbert Pepper, Esq., of Pepper Hall, co. York, and heiress of her brother, Preston Pepper, Esq., and had two sons, viz., John, of Arden, and

RICHARD-PEPPER ARDEN, Esq., b. in 1755, who was appointed solicitor-general in 1782, attorney-general in 1784, master of the rolls in 1788, and constituted lord chief justice of the court of Common Pleas in 1801, when he was elevated to the peerage, 22 May, 1801, in the dignity of BARON ALVANLEY, of Alvanley, co. Chester.* His lordship m. in 1784, Anne-Dorothea, eldest dau. of Richard Wilbraham Bootle, Esq., and sister of Edward, Lord Skelmersdale, by whom (who d. in 1825,) he left issue,

I. WILLIAM, his heir.   II. RICHARD-PEPPER, 3rd lord.
1. Sarah, d. young.
II. FRANCES-HENRIETTA, b. 1791; m. 21 June, 1831, Sir John Warrender, Bart., of Lochend, East Lothian; and d. 20 Feb. 1852, leaving an only child,
HELEN-CATHERINE, m. 17 October, 1854, to George, Lord Binning, now Earl of Haddington.
III. CATHERINE.

The baron d. 19 March, 1804, and was s. by his eldest son,

WILLIAM, as 2nd baron, b. 20 February, 1789, who d. unm. 16 November, 1849, when the title devolved on his brother,

RICHARD-PEPPER, as 3rd baron, b. 8 December, 1792; m. 30 April, 1831, Arabella, youngest dau. of William-Henry, 1st Duke of Cleveland, by whom (who survived him) he had no issue. His lordship, who had been a lieutenant-colonel in the army, d. 24 June, 1857, when the title became EXTINCT.

Arms—Gu., three cross-crosslets, fitchée, or, on a chief, of the second, a crescent, of the first.

ARGENTINE—BARONS DE ARGENTINE.

By Writ of Summons, dated 26 January, 1297.

Lineage.

REGINALD DE ARGENTINE, left a widow, Maud, who had license to marry again in the 5th year of STEPHEN, upon giving a composition to the king for her dowry. This Reginald d. before the year 1139, and was s. by

REGINALD DE ARGENTINE, sheriff of the counties of Cambridge and Huntingdon, from the 5th to the 8th years of RICHARD I., and in the next year for the counties of Hertford and Essex, for one half of the year. He d. about the year 1223, and was s. by his son,

RICHARD DE ARGENTINE, who being sheriff for the counties of Essex and Hertford, in the 8th of HENRY III., was constituted governor of the castle of Hertford. He was likewise sheriff of the counties of Cambridge and Huntingdon, and subsequently (11th HENRY III.) one of the stewards of the king's household. In the 14th of HENRY III., this Richard being (in the words of M. Paris), a noble knight and valiant in arms, went on a pilgrimage to the Holy Land, and dying there in the year 1246, was s. by his son,

GILES DE ARGENTINE, a knight also of great valour, who, in the 16th of HENRY III., being with the king in an expedition made that year into Wales, fell into the hands of the enemy in a sharp conflict near Montgomery. In ten years afterwards he had summons with other important personages to attend the king with horse and arms into Gascony, and the next year he was appointed governor of Windsor Castle; but soon after we find him joining the rebel barons, at the battle of Lewes, and elected by them one of the nine councillors to assume the government of the kingdom. The barons being, however, defeated at the subsequent battle of Evesham, his lordship's lands and those of his son Reginald were sequestered. Giles m. Margery, dau. and heir of Sir R. de Aiguillon, and d. in the 11th of EDWARD I, seised of the manor of Great Wymondeley, co. Cambridge, holden by grand serjeantie, viz., "to serve the king upon the day of his coronation with a silver cup." His son and successor (then in minority),

---

* The manor of Alvanley, in the parish of Frodsham, was held under the Fitzalans, Earls of Arundel, at an early period, by Richard de Pierpont and Robert de Alvanley, who sold it to Sir Philip de Orreby, father of Philip, whose dau. and heir, Agnes, brought it and other possessions, in the reign of HENRY III., to Walkeline de Arderne, ancestor of John Arden, the present proprietor. A farm-house, called Alvanley Hall, occupies the site of an ancient mansion belonging to the Arden family, called by Webb, in 1622, "a very fine house, belonging to Henry Arderne, Esq., Tyrone Cheshire.

REGINALD DE ARGENTINE, who doing homage, had livery of all his father's lands in the counties of Cambridge, Norfolk, Suffolk, and Hertford. This nobleman was summoned to parliament in the 25th EDWARD I., 26 January, 1297. His lordship m. Lora, dau. of Robert de Vere, Earl of Oxford, and dying in 1307, was s. by his son,

JOHN DE ARGENTINE, 2nd baron, who had livery of his father's lands, but was never summoned to parliament. This nobleman m. 1st, Joane, dau. and heir of Sir Roger Bryan, Knt., Lord of Throcking, Herts, and had issue,

Joane, co-heir of her mother, who m. Sir John le Boteler, and was mother of Sʳ Edward Boteler.
Elizabeth, m. Sir William le Botiller, brother of Sir John.
Dionysia, co-heir of her mother.

His lordship m. 2ndly, Agnes, dau. and heir of William Bereford, of Burton, co. Leicester, and dying in the 12th year of EDWARD II., was s. by his only son, then but six months old,

SIR JOHN DE ARGENTINE, 3rd baron, who was seised of the manors of Wymondeley, Herts, and Milburn, co. Cambridge: he received the honour of knighthood 4th of EDWARD III., but was never summoned to parliament. He m. Margaret, dau. and heir of Robert D'Arcy, of Stretton, and by her had issue,

Maud, m. to Sir John or Ivo FitzWarren.
Joan, m. to Sir Bartholomew Naunton.
Elizabeth, m. Sir Baldwin St. George, and was mother, by him, of SIR BALDWIN ST. GEORGE, Knt., who m. 4 RICHARD II., Johanna, a dau. and co-heir of Sir John Engaine, and was ancestor of the ST. GEORGES of Hatley St. George, co Cambridge, the ST. GEORGES of Dunmore, co. Galway, the ST. GEORGES, LORDS ST. GEORGE (whose heir-general is the DUKE OF LEINSTER), the ST. GEORGES of Tyrone, co. Galway, the ST. GEORGES, Barts., of Woodsgift, &c.

John Lord de Argentine d. 1382-3, without legitimate male issue,* when the barony fell into ABEYANCE amongst his daus. and co-heirs.

Arms—Gu., three covered cups, arg.

ARMINE—BARONESS BELASYSE, OF OSGODBY.

By Letters Patent, dated 25 March, 1674.

Lineage.

SIR WILLIAM ARMINE, Bart., of Osgodby, co. Lincoln, b. 1622, m. Anne, dau. and co-heiress of Sir Robert Crane, Bart., of Chilton, co. Suffolk, and by her (who m. 2ndly John, Lord Belasyse,) left two daus. his co-heirs,

I. SUSAN, created a peeress for life.
II. ANNE, m. 1st, SIR THOMAS WODEHOUSE, Knt., by whom she had, with a dau., a son, Sir John Wodehouse, Bart., of Kimberley, grandfather of the 1st LORD WODEHOUSE. Her ladyship m. 2ndly, Thomas, 2nd Lord Crewe, of Stene, and by him had four daus., viz.,
1 Jemima Crewe, m. to Henry de Grey, Duke of Kent, and had issue,
ANTHONY, Earl of Harold, summoned to parliament as Baron Lucas, of Crudwell, in 1719. He m. Lady Mary Tufton, but d. s. p. in 1723. His death is mentioned as having arisen from an ear of barley which his lordship had inadvertently put into his mouth, by which he was choked.
Henry, d. unm.

*Sir William de Argentine, illegitimate son of the last Lord Argentine, was given the manor of Wymondeley. He m. 1st, Isabel, dau. of Sir Wm. Kerdeston; and 2ndly, Margaret. —By the former he left an only son,
JOHN DE ARGENTINE, at whose decease the manor of Wymondeley was carried by his dau. and heiress, Elizabeth, into the family of Alington, upon her marriage with William Alington, Esq., ancestor of the Lords Alington. This manor of Wimley or Wymondeley is said to have fallen to the Argentines by marriage with the heiress of FitzTees, who derived themselves from David D'Argenton, a Norman, who came over with WILLIAM THE CONQUEROR.
Note: "Of this family," says Dugdale, "was Reginald de Argentine, who, in 21 HENRY III., being a knight-templar, was standard bearer of the Christian army in a great battle against the Turks near Antioch, in the Holy Land, and carried it till his hands and legs being broken, he was there slain. So likewise was Sir Giles Argentine, Knt., slain in Scotland at the battle of Bannoksburne, near Strivelin, in 7th EDWARD II. It is said, that the king himself, being in that fatal battle, and seeing the danger, by the advice of this Sir Giles (who being then lately come from the wars of Henry de Luzemburgh, the Emperour, and reputed a stout warrior), fled to Dunbar; and that this Sir Giles, saying that he was not wont to fly, returned to the English host, and was slain."

Amabel, m. John, Viscount Glenorchy, and hence descend the EARL COWPER, K.G., and the MARQUESS OF RIPON.
Jemima, m. to John, 3rd Lord Ashburnham, and was ancestor of the present peer.
Anne, m. to Lord Charles Cavendish
Mary, m. to Dr. Gregory, dean of Christchurch.
2 Armine Crewe, m. to Thomas Cartwright, Esq., of Aynho ancestor of the present WILLIAM CORNWALLIS CARTWRIGHT Esq., of Aynho.
3 Catherine Crewe, m. to Sir John Harpur, Bart., of Calke Abbey; and the great-grandson of this marriage SIR HENRY HARPUR, Bart., of Calke Abbey, assumed by Royal License, in 1808, the surname and arms of CREWE.
4 Elizabeth Crewe, m. to Charles Butler, Earl of Arran.
Anne, Lady Crewe, m. 3rdly, Arthur, Earl of Torrington.

The elder dau. and co-heiress of Sir William Armine,
SUSAN ARMINE, m. 1st, Hon. Sir Henry Belasyse, K.B., son and heir of John, Baron Belasyse, of Worlaby, and had a son,

HENRY BELASYSE, who s. to the title of Belasyse, of Worlaby, upon the decease of his grandfather, his father, Sir Henry, dying previously (see BELASYSE, of Worlaby).

Lady Belasyse m. 2ndly, —— Fortrey, Esq., of Chequers, but by him had no issue. Her ladyship was created a peeress for life, by King CHARLES II., by letters patent dated 25 March, 1674, as BARONESS BELASYSE OF OSGODBY. She d. 6 March, 1712-13, when the dignity EXPIRED.

Arms—Erm., a saltire engr., gu., on a chief of the last a lion passant, or, armed and langued, az.

ARUNDEL—BARONS ARUNDEL, OF TRERICE.

By Letters Patent, dated 23 March, 1664.

Lineage.

RANDEL ARUNDEL, m. Elizabeth, dau. and heiress of John Steward, and left a son,
RALPH ARUNDEL, living in the 31st of EDWARD III., who m Jane, dau. and heiress of Michael Trerice, by whom he had two sons, NICHOLAS and THOMAS, and a dau. Jane, m. to Robert Trevanion. The elder son,
NICHOLAS ARUNDEL, m. Elizabeth, dau. of John Pellocer, and sister and co-heiress of Martin Pellocer, and was s. by his son,
SIR JOHN ARUNDEL, of Trerice, co. Cornwall, who m. Joan, dau. and heiress of John Durant, and was s. by his eldest son,
NICHOLAS ARUNDEL, who m. Jane, dau. of Edward St. John, Esq., by whom he had four sons and four daus. He was s. by his eldest son,
SIR JOHN ARUNDEL, Knt., sheriff of Cornwall in 1471. "This gentleman being forewarned," says Carew in his Survey of Cornwall, "that he should be slain on the sands, forsook his house at Elford, as too maritime, and removed to Trerice, his more inland habitation in the same county; but he did not escape his fate, for being sheriff of Cornwall in that year, and the Earl of Oxford surprising Mount Michael, for the house of Lancaster, he had the king's commands, by his office, to endeavour the reducing of it, and lost his life in a skirmish on the sands thereabouts." Sir John Arundel m. 1st, Margaret, dau. of Sir Hugh Courtenay, Knt., by whom he had two sons, who d. young; and 2ndly, Anne, dau. of Sir Walter Moyle, Knt., by whom he had also two sons, and was s. by the elder,
SIR JOHN ARUNDEL, sheriff of Cornwall, anno 1524. He m. Joan, dau. of Thomas Greenvil, Esq., and was s. by his only son,
JOHN ARUNDEL, Esq., who received the honour of knighthood at the battle of Spurs. This gallant person, who was vice-admiral to Kings HENRY VII. and VIII., acquired great renown by the defeat and capture of Duncan Campbell, the Scottish pirate, in a sea fight. Sir John Arundel m. 1st, Mary, dau. and co-heiress of John Beville, of Gwarnick, Cornwall, by whom he had a son, Roger, and three daus., viz.,

Elizabeth, m. to Robert Tredenham, Esq.
Catherine, m. to Richard Prideaux, Esq., of Thuborough.
Jane, m. to William Wall, Esq.

Sir John m. 2ndly, Julian, dau. of Jacob Erisey, Esq., by whom he had issue,

JOHN, who became his heir.
Margaret, m. to Robert Beckett, Esq.
Jane, m. to Wm. Vyel, Esq., of Treworder.
Grace, m. to John Dinham, Esq.
Margery, m. to John Trengough.

He was s. by his only surviving son,
JOHN ARUNDEL, Esq., who m. 1st, Catherine, dau. and co-heiress of John Coswarth, Esq., and relict of Allan Hill, Esq., by whom he had four daus., viz.,

Mary, *m.* to Oliver Dynham, Esq.
Dorothy, *m.* to Edward Cosworth, Esq.
Julian, *m.* to Richard Carew, Esq., of Antony, Cornwall.
Alice, *m* to Henry Somaster, Esq., of Painsford.

Mr. Arundel *m.* 2ndly, Gertrude, dau. of Robert Dennis, Esq., of Holcomb, by whom he had two sons, JOHN and Thomas, and two daus., Anne, *m.* to William Cornfew, Esq., of Bucclesly, and Catherine, *m.* to John St. Aubyn, Esq. He *d.* in 1580, and was *s.* by his elder son,

JOHN ARUNDEL, Esq., of Trerice, M.P. for Cornwall, *temp.* Queen ELIZABETH and King JAMES I., and for Tregony in the reign of King CHARLES I. At the breaking out of the civil war, this eminent person, with his four sons, espoused the cause of royalty, and took up arms for the king. Of these sons, two, John and William, lost their lives in the service of their unfortunate master, while their gallant father hurled defiance to the rebels from the battlements of Pendennis, and maintained his position there, to the very end of those unhappy conflicts, although besieged both by sea and land, being as Lord Clarendon relates, then nearly fourscore years of age, and of one of the best estates and interests in the county of Cornwall. Whitlock states, that on the 31st of August, 1646, letters came to the parliament, of the surrender of Pendennis Castle, and in it were Colonel Arundel, the governor, four knights, five colonels, and divers others of quality. That they had store of arms, but little provision. Colonel Arundel *m.* Mary, dau. of George Cary, Esq., of Clovelly, co. Devon, by whom he had four sons and two daus.; viz., RICHARD, John, William, Francis, Agnes, and Mary. The latter was *m.* 1st, to John Trevanion, Esq. (son and heir of Charles Trevanion, Esq., of Caerhayes), and 2ndly, to Sir John Arundel, of Lanherne. He was *s.* at his decease by his eldest son,

RICHARD ARUNDEL, Esq., member in the two last parliaments of King CHARLES I., for Lostwithiel, and in his military capacity, attached to the personal staff of that unhappy prince. This gallant officer had a command in the battle of Kineton, in the county of Warwick, where he displayed the hereditary valour of his family, and he was subsequently actively engaged during the whole of the civil wars, in which disastrous contest he was despoiled of the entire of his landed property. On the re-establishment of the monarchy, however, that was restored to him, and in consideration of the devotedness of his father, his brothers, and himself, to the royal cause, he was elevated to the peerage by letters patent, dated 23 March, 1664, as BARON ARUNDEL OF TRERICE, co. Cornwall. His lordship *m.* Gertrude, dau. of Sir James Bagge, Knt., of Saltram, co. Devon, and widow of Sir Nicholas Slanning, Knt., of Bickley, and was *s.*, at his decease in 1688, by his only surviving child,

JOHN ARUNDEL, 2nd baron; this nobleman *m.* 1st, Margaret, dau. and sole heiress of Sir John Acland, Knt., of Colomb-John, co. Devon, by whom he had issue,

JOHN, his successor.
Gertrude, *m.* 1st, to Sir Peter Whitcomb, of Essex; and 2ndly, to Sir Bennet Hoskins.

His lordship *m.* 2ndly, Barbara, dau. of Sir Henry Slingsby, of Scriven, co. York, Baronet, and relict of Sir Richard Mauleverer, of Allerton Mauleverer, in the same shire, by whom (who *m.* 3rdly THOMAS, EARL OF PEMBROKE), he had an only son,

Richard, M.P., clerk of the pipe, *m.* 2 Sept. 1732, Frances, dau. of John, 2nd Duke of Rutland, and *d.* 1759.

Lord Arundel *d.* 7 September, 1697, and was *s.* by his elder son,

JOHN ARUNDEL, 3rd baron, who *m.* Elizabeth, dau. of the Right Rev. William Beaw, D.D., Lord Bishop of Landaff, and dying 24 September, 1706, was *s.* by his only surviving child,

JOHN ARUNDEL, 4th baron, who *m.* in 1722, Elizabeth, dau. of Sir William Wentworth, of Ashby Puerorum, co. Lincoln, and sister of Thomas, Earl of Strafford, by whom, who *d.* in 1750, he had no issue. His lordship *d.* in 1773, when the barony EXPIRED. This nobleman, upon his marriage settled all his lands, in default of issue, on his wife's nephew, William Wentworth, Esq., of Hembury, co. Dorset, with remainder to Sir Thomas Acland, Bart., and his heirs. Mr. Wentworth, who succeeded to the estates under this settlement, levied a fine, and re-settled the manor of Trerice and the other Arundel estates on his son Frederick Thomas (afterwards Earl of Strafford), with remainder, in failure of issue, to his dau., who *m.* into the family of Kaye, of Woodsome, co. York, and on failure of issue from both (which was eventually the case) to SIR THOMAS ACLAND, Bart. The manor of Trerice and the other estates so limited became ultimately the property of Sir Thomas Dyke Acland, Bart., grandson of Sir Thomas, named in the settlement.

Arms—Quarterly: first and fourth, sa., six swallows close, three, two, and one, arg.; second and third, sa., three chevronels arg.

12

ASTLEY —BARONS ASTLEY.

By Writ of Summons, dated 23 June, 1295.

Lineage.

This noble family derived its surname from the manor of Astley (or Estley, as formerly written), in the county of Warwick, which, with other estates in that shire, belonged to the Astleys so far back as the reign of HENRY I.

PHILIP DE ESTLEY, grandson of the first possessor, was certified upon the assessment of the aid towards the marriage portion of King HENRY II.'s daughter, to hold three knight's fees of William Earl of Warwick, *de veteri Feoffamento*—by the service "of laying hands on the *earl's stirrop* when he did get upon, or alight from horseback." This feudal baron was *s.* by his son,

THOMAS DE ASTLEY, who holding certain lands of the Honour of Leicester, became a kind of bailiff to Simon de Montfort, Earl of Leicester, "as may be seen," says Dugdale, "by a fine of four score marks and a palfrey, to the king, in 9th John, to be discharged of the profits required of him for that earl's lands, during the time he had to do with them." In the 12th of King JOHN, this Thomas Astley paid 100 marks to the crown, to be excused going beyond the sea: Dugdale supposes in an expedition to Ireland. In the 17th of the same reign, he was committed prisoner to Bedford Castle, and had his lands seized for his participation in the rebellion of the barons; but returning to his allegiance, he was reinstated in his territorial possessions, in the 1st year of HENRY III., and in two years afterwards he was constituted a commissioner for restoring to the crown all the demesnes of which King JOHN was possessed at the beginning of his wars with the barons, &c. This feudal lord *m.* Maud, one of the sisters and co-heirs of Roger de Camvill, of Crecke, co. Northampton, and was *s.* by his son,

WALTER DE ASTLEY. This nobleman had been concerned in the rebellion of the barons against JOHN. He was *s.* by his son,

SIR THOMAS DE ASTLEY, Knt., who was constituted in the 26th of HENRY III., one of the king's justices for the gaol delivery at Warwick, and again in the next year, when he paid to the king 15*l.* for his relief. In the 32nd of HENRY III., this Sir Thomas de Astley was sent with several other persons of rank and power into Gascoigne: but we afterwards find him (47th HENRY III.) a leader amongst the rebellious barons, who seized upon the revenues of the crown in the counties of Warwick and Leicester; and when the king submitted to the PROVISIONS OF OXFORD, the following year, he was nominated CUSTOS PACIS for Leicestershire. Sir Thomas fell, however, soon after (49th HENRY III., 1264,) with Montford, Earl of Leicester, and other insurrectionary nobles, at the battle of Evesham, when his estates, valued at 151*l.* 16*s.* 11*d.* per annum, being confiscated, were conferred upon Warine de Bassingbourne, but the king compassionating his widow and children, reserved to them out of those estates, certain lands, valued at 34*l.* 18*s.* 1*d.* per annum, subject to one mark yearly to the said Warine and his heirs. Sir Thomas de Astley *m.* 1st, Joane, dau. of Ernald de Bois, a person of great power in the county of Leicester—and had issue,

ANDREW, his successor.
Isabel, *m.* to William de Bermingham (son and heir of Robert de Bermingham, one of the companions in arms of Strongbow, Earl of Pembroke, in his expedition into Ireland, *temp.* HENRY II.), and left a son, PETER DE BERMINGHA M, who was summoned to parliament, in Ireland, as BARON ATHENRY, in the reigns of JOHN and HENRY III.

Sir Thomas *m.* 2ndly, Editha, dau. of Peter Constable, Esq., of Melton Constable, in Norfolk, and sister of Sir Ralph Constable, Knt., by whom he had three sons and a daughter,

THOMAS, settled at Hill Morton, but dying *s. p.*, his estates devolved upon his brother,
RALPH ASTLEY, from whom the extinct Barons Astley of Reading derived, and Sir John-Henry-Delaval Astley, Bart., of Hill Morton, co. Warwick, and of Melton Constable, co. Norfolk, now BARON HASTINGS, descends. (*See* BURKE's *Peerage*.)

After the decease of Sir Thomas de Astley, his eldest son,

ANDREW DE ASTLEY, by virtue of the decree called *Dictum de Kenilworth*, was put into possession of his father's estates—paying as a compensation to Warine de Bassingbourne, 320 marks sterling, to raise which sum he sold his manor of Little Copston to the monks of Combe. He was subsequently engaged in the Scottish wars of King EDWARD I., and participated in the victory of Falkirk. Andrew de Astley was summoned to parliament as BARON ASTLEY, from 23 June, 1295, to 3 November, 1306, and was *s.* at his decease by his son,

NICHOLAS DE ASTLEY, 2nd *Lord Astley*, summoned to parliament from 4 July, 1302, to 11 July, 1309. His lordship and his brother Sir Giles de Astley attending King EDWARD II. into Scotland, were taken prisoners at Bannockburn. The period of this nobleman's decease is not ascertained, but having outlived his brother above-mentioned, and dying without issue, the title and estates devolved upon his nephew (Sir Giles de Astley's son and heir by Alice, 2nd dau. and co-heiress of Sir Thomas Wolvey, Knt.),

THOMAS DE ASTLEY, 3rd *Lord Astley*, summoned to parliament from 25 February, 1342, to 10 March, 1349. This nobleman founded a chantry in the parish church of Astley, in the 11th year of EDWARD III., and afterwards obtaining permission to change his chantry priests into a dean and secular canons, he erected a fair and beautiful collegiate church in the form of a cross, with a tall spire, covered with lead, and dedicated it to the assumption of the blessed Virgin. His lordship *m.* Elizabeth, dau. of Guy de Beauchamp, Earl of Warwick, and left issue, with daus. (of whom Alice *m.* Sir Richard Champernoune of Modbury) three sons, viz.,

WILLIAM (Sir), his successor.

THOMAS (Sir), M P. for the co. of Warwick, *m.* Elizabeth, dau. of Richard, son of Sir William Harecourt, Knt., from which union the ASTLEYS of Patshull, co. Stafford, and the ASTLEYS of Everleigh, Wilts, lineally derived. Of the Patshull family was JOHN DE ASTLEY, memorable for fighting a duel on horseback, upon the 29 August, 1438, with Peter de Massel, a Frenchman, in the street St. Antoine, at Paris, before Charles VII., King of France, where having pierced his antagonist through the head, he had the helmet, by agreement of the vanquished, to present to his lady. He subsequently fought Sir Philip Boyle, an Arragonian knight, in Smithfield, in the city of London, in the presence of King HENRY VI. and his court, which combat, we are told, was gallantly performed on foot, with battle axes, spears, swords, and daggers, and at its conclusion, that John de Astley was knighted by the king, and rewarded with a pension of one hundred marks for his life. "Yes," (says Dugdale), "so famous did Sir John de Astley grow for his valour, that he was elected a knight of the garter, and bore for his arms the coats of *Astley* and *Harecourt*, quarterly, with a *label of three points ermine.*"

The present representative of the Astleys of Everleigh, is Sir FRANCIS DUGDALE ASTLEY, Bart.; and to the Everleigh line also belongs RICHARD GOUGH, Esq., of co. Warwick, who assumed the surname of Gough in lieu of that of Astley in 1818.

Giles, ancestor of the Astleys of Wolvey.

Thomas, 3rd Lord Astley, was *s.* at his decease by his eldest son,

WILLIAM DE ASTLEY, 4th *Lord Astley*, who does not appear to have been summoned to parliament. This nobleman was included in several commissions during the reigns of HENRY IV. and HENRY VI. His lordship *m.* Joan, dau. of John, Lord Willoughby de Eresby, by whom he left an only dau.,

JOANE, *m.* 1st, to Thomas Raleigh, Esq., of Farnborough, co. Warwick, by whom she had a son, William *d.* a minor, 8 HENRY V., and a dau. Joan *m.* 1st, to Gerard Braybroke, and 2ndly, to Edward Bromflete. The heiress of Astley *m.* 2ndly, to Reginald, Lord Grey de Ruthyn (being his lordship's 2nd wife), by whom she had three sons, and a dau., viz.,

EDWARD, of whom presently,

John de Grey, of Barwell. co. Leicester.

Robert de Grey, of Enville and Whittington, co. Stafford.

Eleanor, *m.* to William Lucy, Esq., of Charlecote, co. Warwick.

EDWARD DE GREY, the eldest son, marrying Elizabeth, only dau. and heiress of Henry son, and heir of William, Lord Ferrars, of Groby, by Isabel, 2nd dau. and co-heiress of Thomas Mowbray, Duke of Norfolk, was summoned to parliament in 1446, as LORD FERRARS, *of Groby*, which barony, and *that* of ASTLEY, descended regularly to Henry Grey, 3rd marquess of Dorset, K.G. (who was created DUKE OF SUFFOLK 10 October, 1551), and became forfeited upon the decapitation and attainder of his grace in 1554.

Arms—Az., a cinquefoil, ermine.

ASTLEY—BARONS ASTLEY, OF READING

By Letters Patent, dated 4 November, 1664.

Lineage.

The Hon. RALPH DE ASTLEY, a younger son of Thomas, Lord Astley, of Astley, co. Warwick, by his 2nd wife, Editha, dau. of Peter Constable, Esq., of Melton-Constable, co. Norfolk, and sister and co-heiress of Sir Robert Constable, Knt., of the same place, was lineal ancestor of

JOHN ASTLEY, Esq., of Hill-Morton and Melton-Constable,

who *m.* Frances, dau. and heiress of John Cheyney, Esq., of Sittingborne, co. Kent, and was *s.* by his only surviving son,

ISAAC ASTLEY, Esq. This gentleman *m.* Mary, dau. of Edward Waldegrave, Esq., of Borley, Essex, and had two sons, Thomas, ancestor of the Astleys (Baronets) of Hill-Morton, co. Warwick, and

SIR JACOB ASTLEY, Knt., a distinguished captain under the royal banner during the civil wars; governor of Oxford and Reading, and pre-eminently conspicuous at the battles of Edgehill, Brentford, and Newbury; who for his gallant and faithful services was raised to the peerage by letters patent, dated 4 November, 1664, as LORD ASTLEY, of Reading, co. Bucks. His lordship *m.* Agnes Imple, a German lady, and had issue,

ISAAC, his successor.

Thomas,
Henry,
Bernard,
Edward, } all *d.* without issue.

Elizabeth, *m.* to (her cousin) Sir Edward Astley, Knt., and left SIR JACOB ASTLEY, Knt., who inherited, upon the decease of his uncle, Sir Isaac Astley, Bart., *s. p.*, in 1659, the estates of Hill-Morton and Melton-Constable, and succeeded to the entailed property of Lord Astley.

Of Jacob, Lord Astley, Clarendon says, "He was an honest, brave, plain man, as fit for the military posts he held as Christendom yielded, and was generally esteemed very discerning and prompt in giving orders, as occasion required; and most cheerful and pleasant in action. An enemy to long speeches, as usually made in council, he himself using only few, but very pertinent words." His lordship *d.* in 1651, and was *s.* by his eldest son,

ISAAC ASTLEY, 2nd lord, who *m.* Anne, 4th dau. of Sir Francis Stydolfe, Knt., of Norbury, co. Surrey, and had issue,

JACOB, his successor.

Francis *d. s p.*

His lordship *d.* in 1662, and was *s.* by his elder son,

JACOB ASTLEY, 3rd lord. His lordship *m.* Frances, dau. and co-heiress of Sir Richard Stydolfe, of Norbury, son of Sir Francis, but had no issue. Lord Astley *d.* in 1688, when the barony of Astley of Reading EXPIRED.

Arms—Az., a cinquefoil erm. within a bordure, engrailed, or

ASTON—BARON ASTON, OF FORFAR.

By Letters Patent, dated 28 November, 1627.

Lineage.

Fuller, speaking of the Astons, says: "A more noble family measuring on the level of flat and inadvantaged antiquity, is not to be met with; they have ever borne a good respect to the church and learned men."

RANDAL, or RANDULPH DE ASTONA, the first on record, who lived in the reign of EDWARD I., was father of

ROGER DE ASTON, who, in 1260, obtained from Roger de Moland, Bishop of Lichfield, the manors of Heywood and Longdon, and the keeping of the game in Caukwood, all in the co. Stafford. The 5th in descent from this Roger,

SIR ROGER DE ASTON, Knt., served the office of sheriff for Staffordshire in the reign of HENRY VI., and was one of the prime gentry returned by the commissioners for that county in 1433. Sir Roger *m.* Joyce, sister and co-heir of Sir Baldwin de Frevile, and with her acquired large estates in the co. of Warwick, and by her he had, with a dau., Joan, *m.* to Sir Roger Draycot, of Paynesley, in Staffordshire, Knt., a son and heir,

SIR ROBERT DE ASTON, of Parkhall and Heywood, Knt. By his 1st wife, whose family name has not been transmitted, he had no issue; he *m.* 2ndly, Isabel, dau. of Sir William Brereton, of Brereton, in Staffordshire, Knt., by whom he had a son and two daus.,

1. JOHN, his heir.
1. Elizabeth, *m* to Richard Bagot, of Blythefield.
11. Petrinilla, wife of Richard Biddulph.

SIR JOHN DE ASTON, sheriff of Stafford, 16th EDWARD IV. *m.* Elizabeth, dau. of Sir John Delves, of Dodrington, co. Chester, Knt., and had issue,

1. JOHN, his successor.
11. Richard, of Whorcross, co. Stafford.
111. Robert.
1. Elizabeth, *m.* to John Basset, of Blore.
11. —— *m.* to Dudley, of Sedgeley.
111. Isabella, *m* to Humphrey Okeover.
1v. —— *m.* to Braddock, of Adelbaldeston.
v. Catherine, *m.* to Thomas Blount, of Burton.

vi. Margaret, m. 1st, to Thomas Kynardesley, of Loxley; 2ndly, to Ralph Wolseley, Esq.

vii. Alice, m. to John Dodd, of Chorley.

viii. —— m. Colwich, co. Stafford.

ix. Rose, m. to Thomas Child, of Ormesley, in Shropshire.

Sir John de Aston, K.B., was a military character of great eminence in the reigns of the first two sovereigns of the house of Tudor. Sir John was with Henry VIII in the French war of 1513, and was made a banneret for his conduct at the battle of Spurs. He obtained renown likewise at the siege of Terouin and Tourney. He was sheriff of the counties of Leicester and Warwick, and thrice of Staffordshire. Sir John Aston m. Joan, only child of Sir William Littleton, of Frankley, co. Worcester, by whom he acquired the manors of Wanlip, in Leicestershire, and Tixall, co. Stafford. He was s. by his eldest son,

Sir Edward Aston, of Tixall, who built a stately mansion at that place, the ruins of which are still remaining. He m 1st, Joan, dau. of Sir Thomas Bowles, of Penho, co. Carnarvon, one of the barons of the exchequer, and by her (who d. 15 September, 1562) had issue,

i Walter, of whom presently.

ii Leonard.

iii. Anthony.

i. Catherine, m. to Sir William Gresley, of Drakelow, in Derbyshire.

ii. Mary, m. to Simon Harcourt, of Stanton Harcourt, co. Oxford, ancestor of the Earl of Harcourt.

iii. Frances. m. to Robert Needham, c? Shenton, in Leicestershire, ancestor of Earl Kilmorey.

iv. Elizabeth, m. to Lawley, of Wenlock, co. Salop.

Sir Edward m. 2ndly, Mary, dau. of Sir Henry Vernon, Knt., but had no issue.

Sir Walter Aston, of Tixall, m. Elizabeth, dau. of Sir James Leveson, of Lilleshull, and left issue,

i. Edward, his heir.

ii. Robert, of Parkhall, m. Jocosa, 2nd dau. of William Dallyson, one of the judges of the King's Bench, and had three sons, William, Robert, and John, of whom the two latter d. infants, and the former left an only child, Frances, his sole heir, who, 28 April, 1647, m. John Whitehall, into whose family she carried the estate of Parkhall.

iii. Richard, who d. s. p. 1610.

iv. William, of Millwich, ancestor of the 6th Lord Aston.

v. Hastings, d. unm.

vi. Devereux, d. unm.

i. Joan, wife of William Crompton, of Stone, in Staffordshire.

ii. Mary, m. to Thomas Astley, of Pattershull.

iii. Eleanor, m. to William Portoe, of Chesterton, co. Warwick.

iv. Elizabeth, m. to Basil Fielding, of Newnham, and was mother of the 1st Earl of Denbigh.

v Catherine, m. to Stephen, son and heir of Sir Stephen Slaney, alderman of London.

Sir Edward Aston, of Tixall. This gentleman possessed estates of the value of £10,000 annually, in the cos. of Stafford, Derby, Leicester, and Warwick. He m. Anne, only dau. of Sir Thomas Lucy, of Cherlecote, and dying in 1598, left issue,

i. Walter.

ii. Edward, m. Anne, only dau. of Leigh Sadler, of Temple Dinesley, Herts, grandson of Sir Ralph Sadler, of Standon, the able ambassador to Scotland.

iii. Thomas barrister, of the Middle Temple, London, d. unm.

i. Joyce, m. to Sir Martin Colepeper, of Deane, co. Oxford, Knt.

ii. Elizabeth, m. to Sandbech, of Broadway, co. Worcester.

iii. Anne, m. to Ambrose Elton, of Hansel, in Herefordshire.

iv. Jane, m. to Thomas Elton, M.P.

Sir Walter Aston, who, at the coronation of James I., was honoured with the order of the Bath, and subsequently, in 1611, created a baronet. In 1622 he was employed to negotiate a marriage between Charles, Prince of Wales, and the Infanta of Spain; and, in requital for his service upon that occasion, was elevated to the peerage, 28 November, 1627, as Lord Aston, of Forfar. His lordship m. 1st, Gertrude, only dau. of Sir Thomas Sadleir, of Standon (son of the celebrated Sir Ralph Sadleir—See Burke's Landed Gentry), and dying in 1689, left issue,

i. Walter, d. an infant.

ii. Walter, 2nd Lord Aston.

iii. Herbert, baptized at Chelsea, 16 January, 1614, m. Catherine, sister of Sir John Thimelby, of Irnham, co. Lincoln, Knt., and was buried at Colton, in Staffordshire, 9 January, 1689, æt. 75.

iv. John, d. an infant.

v. Thomas, d. an infant.

i. Gertrude, d. an infant.

ii. Honor, baptized at Tottenham, 17 July, 1610, d. at Vittoria, in Spain, during her father's embassy, and was buried at St. Martin's-in-the-Fields, London.

iii. Frances, baptized at Chelsea, 16 April, 1612, m. to Sir William Pechall, of Canwell, in Staffordshire.

14

iv. Gertrude, wife of Henry, brother of Sir John Thimelby.

v. Constantia, m. to Walter Fowler, of St. Thomas, near Stafford.

Walter, 2nd baron, who, at the decease of his uncle, Ralph Sadleir, Esq., of Standon, s. p. in 1660, inherited, under the will of that gentleman, the lordship of Standon, with other estates in Hertfordshire. This nobleman, a stanch and gallant supporter of the royal cause during the civil wars, m. 1629, Lady Mary Weston, 2nd dau. of Richard, Earl of Portland, K.G., lord high treasurer of England; and at his decease, 23 April, 1678, left issue,

i. Walter, 3rd Lord Aston.

ii. Thomas, m. Elizabeth, dau of Thomas Ogle, of Tissington, in Northumberland, d. s. p.

iii. Charles, d. an infant.

iv. William, d. s. p.

i. Elizabeth, m. to Sir John Southcote, of Mestham, in Surrey.

ii. Frances, m. to Sir Edward Gage, of Hengrave, in Suffolk, Bart

iii. Gertrude, d. unm.

iv. Mary, d. unm.

v. Anne, m. to Henry Somerset, of Pauntley Court, co. Gloucester, grandson of Henry, 1st Marquess of Worcester.

Walter, 3rd baron, b. 1633, m. 1st, Eleanor, dau. of Sir Walter Blount, Bart., of Soddington, co. Worcester, and relict of Robert Knightley, Esq.; and dying 10 November, 1714, left issue,

i. Edward-Walter, b. 1658, d. at Clermont Cottage, Paris.

ii. Francis, d. s. p. 1694.

iii. Walter, 4th Lord Aston.

iv. Charles, b. 1664, killed at the battle of the Boyne, 1 July, 1690.

v. William, d. an infant.

i. Mary, d. unm.

ii. Catharine, d. an infant.

Walter, 3rd. Lord Aston, m. 2ndly, Catherine, youngest dau of Sir Thomas Gage, of Firle, in Sussex, Bart., but by her had no issue.

Walter 4th baron, who m. Lady Mary Howard, only sister to Thomas, Duke of Norfolk. At his decease, 4 April, 1748, he left issue,

i. Walter, b. 16 February, 1711, d. 19 June, 1717.

ii. Edward, mentioned in Collin's Baronetage as alive 1714; d. young.

iii. James, 5th Lord Aston.

iv. Charles, b. 19 March, 1719, d. 12 April, 1730

i. Mary, b. 27 October, 1703, d. 10 December, 1704.

ii. Anne, b. 4 April, 1705, d. 24 July following.

iii. Catherine, b. 7 March, 1706, m. Edward Weld, of Lulworth Castle, co. Dorset, and d. 20 October, 1739, æt. 34.

iv. Mary, b. 31 May, 1709, d. April, 1712.

v. Eleanor, b. 22 May, 1717, d. 12 April, 1727.

vi. Margery, living unm. 4 July, 1746, as appears from her father's will.

James, 5th baron. This nobleman m. 30 June, 1742, Barbara, dau. of George, 14th Earl of Shrewsbury, and had two daus., his co-heirs, viz.,

i. Mary, m. to Sir Walter Blount, Bart., of Sodington. This lady was accidentally burnt to death by her clothes catching fire, 6 February, 1805.

ii. Barbara, who inherited Tixall, m. to the Hon. Thomas Clifford, son of Hugh Clifford, of Chudleigh. She d. in 1786, leaving twelve children, of whom

1 Thomas Hugh Clifford, the eldest son, succeeded to Tixall, He subsequently assumed the surname of Constable, and was created a Baronet. (See Constable.)

2 Arthur Clifford, who edited his great ancestor Sir Ralph Sadleir's State Papers and Letters in the year 1809.

His lordship dying thus, in 1751, without male issue, the baronetcy ceased, while the barony devolved upon

Philip Aston, Esq., as 6th baron, the great-great-grandson of the late lord's great-great-great-grand uncle, William Aston, of Milwich, in remainder to whose posterity the original patent was framed. His lordship d. unm. in 1755, when his brother,

Walter, inherited as 7th baron. At the decease of this nobleman, without male issue, in 1763, the honours descended to the son of his uncle Edward,

Walter, 8th baron. His lordship, b. 10 October, 1732, m. in 1766, Anne, dau. of Peter Hutchinson, Esq., by whom he left at his decease, 29 July, 1805, an only surviving son,

Walter-Hutchinson, 9th Baron Aston, of Forfar, a clergyman of the Church of England; b. 15 September, 1769, who m. 15 June, 1802, Elizabeth. dau. of the late Rev. Nathan Haines, D.D., but by her (who d. in 1833) had no issue. His lordship d. 21 January, 1845, when the title appears to have become EXTINCT.

Arms.—Arg., a fesse, sa., in chief, three lozenges, of the last.

ATON—BARONS DE ATON.

AUDLEY—BARONS AUDLEY, OF HELEIGH.

ATON—BARONS DE ATON.

By Writ of Summons, dated 30 December, 1324.

Lineage.

The paternal surname of this family arose from the feudal barony of ATON, in the co. of York, of which its members were lords from the Conquest; for we find that

GILBERT, son of LAOI, assumed the surname of ATON so far back as the reign of King HENRY I. from those lands; but the importance of the family was founded by the marriage of this Gilbert de Aton's great grandson,

GILBERT DE ATON, with Margerie, dau. and heiress of WARINE DE VESCI, a younger son of William de Vesci, Lord of Alnwick, co. Northumberland, through which alliance the ATONS inherited, eventually, the extensive possessions of the great Barons de Vesci: thus

> EUSTACE DE VESCI, one of the twenty-five barons appointed to enforce the observance of MAGNA CHARTA, elder brother of the above WARINE, succeeded his father; m. Margaret, dau. of WILLIAM and sister of ALEXANDER, kings of Scotland; and, dying about 1216, was s. by his son,
> WILLIAM DE VESCI, to whom s. in 1253, his son,
> JOHN DE VESCI, who had summons to parliament, as a baron, in 1264, but dying s. p., was s. by his brother,
> WILLIAM DE VESCI, summoned to parliament in the reign of EDWARD I., and one of the competitors for the Scottish throne in the same era. He d. about the year 1297, without legitimate issue, when the BARONY EXPIRED; but the estates devolved upon his natural son,
> WILLIAM DE VESCI, who was summoned to parliament in 1313; but dying in two years afterwards, s. p., that BARONY also EXPIRED, while the estates reverted to the great-grandson of the above Gilbert de Aton and Margerie de Vesci, his wife.

Gilbert de Aton d. in the 19th of HENRY III., and was s. by his son,

WILLIAM DE ATON, who was s. by his son,

SIR GILBERT DE ATON, one of the knights of the Bath, created by Prince EDWARD, in the 34th of EDWARD I. Sir Gilbert dying s. p., was s. by his brother,

WILLIAM DE ATON, who m. Isabel de Vere, and had a son and heir,

GILBERT DE ATON, inherited, in the 9th of EDWARD II., the estates of the BARONS DE VESCI, as deduced above. This Gilbert had command, the year before, to fit himself with horse and arms, and to be at NEWCASTLE-UPON-TYNE on the feast-day of the Blessed Virgin, to restrain the hostilities of the Scots. In the 13th of EDWARD II. he was in the expedition to Scotland; and in the 17th of the same monarch, he confirmed (in consideration of receiving 700 marks sterling) as heir of William de Vesci, to Henry Lord Percie, the castle and lands of Alnwick, which Anthony Beke, bishop of Durham and patriarch of Jerusalem, had sold to the said Henry, although but confided to the bishop by William Lord de Vesci in trust for his bastard son, the last William de Vesci. In the following year (30 December, 1324) Gilbert de Aton was summoned to parliament as a baron of the realm, and he was so summoned during the remainder of his life. His lordship d. in 1342, and was s. by his son,

WILLIAM DE ATON, 2nd BARON ATON, who was summoned to parliament on 8 January, 1371. His lordship m. in 1340 Isabel, dau. of Henry, 3rd Lord Percy, by whom (who was dead in 1368) he had an only son, William, who died vitâ patris, and three daus., his co-heiresses, namely—

> Anastasia, m. to Sir Edward de St. John, and left a dau. and heiress, Margaret de St. John, who m. Thomas de Bromflete, king's butler, temp. RICHARD II. (See BROMFLETE.)
> Katherine, m. to Sir Ralph de Eure.
> Elizabeth, m. 1st, to Sir William Playtz, and, 2ndly, to John Conyers, Esq., of Sokebourne, co Durham, ancestor, by her, of the families of CONYERS of Sokebourne and CONYERS of Horden: the Sokebourne line ended in a dau. and heiress, Anne, wife of Francis, 11th Earl of Shrewsbury, and mother of an only dau. and heiress, Mary, m. to John Stonor, Esq., of Stonor, co. Oxford; the male line of CONYERS of Horden (raised to a baronetcy in 1628), expired with SIR THOMAS CONYERS, Bart., of Horden, who died in the deepest poverty at Chester-le-Street, 15 April, 1810. (See "BURKE's Vicissitudes of Families.")

William, Lord Aton, was engaged in the French wars of King EDWARD III. He was sheriff of Yorkshire in the 42nd of that monarch, and governor of the castle of York, and again in the 43rd and 46th of the same reign. At his lordship's decease his estates were divided amongst his daughters, and the BARONY fell into ABEYANCE, as it still continues. (S e ADDENDA.)

Arms—Or, three bars, az., on a canton, gu., a cross patonce, arg.

AUDLEY—BARONS AUDLEY, OF HELEIGH.

By Writ of Summons, dated 8 January, 1313.

Lineage.

"That this family of *Aldithdey*, vulgarly called *Audley*, says Dugdale, "came to be great and eminent, the ensuing discourse will sufficiently manifest: but that the rise thereof was no higher than King JOHN's time, and that the first who assumed this surname was a branch of that ancient and noble family of VERDON, whose chief seat was at *Alton Castle*, in the northern part of Staffordshire, I am very inclined to believe; partly by reason that Henry had the inheritance of *Aldithdey* given him by Nicholas de Verdon, who d. in the 16th HENRY III., or near that time; and partly for that he bore for his arms the same ordinary as Vernon did, viz. *frette*, but distinguished with a large *canton* in the dexter part of the shield, and thereon a *cross paté;* so that probably the ancestor of this Henry first seated himself at *Aldithdey:* for that there hath been an antient mansion there, the large moat, northwards from the parish church there (somewhat less than a furlong, and upon the chief part of a fair ascent), do sufficiently manifest."

HENRY DE ALDITHELEY, to whom Dugdale alludes above, being in great favour with Ranulph, Earl of Chester and Lincoln (the most powerful subject of England in his time), obtained from that nobleman a grant of Newhall in Cheshire, with manors in Staffordshire and other parts—and for his adhesion to King JOHN, in that monarch's struggle with the insurrectionary barons, a royal grant of the lordship of Storton, in Warwickshire, part of the possessions of Roger de Summerville. In the four first years of King HENRY III. he executed the office of sheriff for the counties of Salop and Stafford, as deputy for his patron, the great Earl Ranulph. In the 10th of HENRY III. this Henry de Aldithdey was appointed governor of the castles of Carmarthen and Cardigan, and made sheriff the next year of the counties of Salop and Stafford and constable of the castles of Salop and Bridgenorth, which sheriffalty he held for five years. Upon his retirement from office, he had a confirmation of all such lands, whereof he was then possessed, as well those granted to him by Ranulph, Earl of Chester, and Nicholas de Verdon, as those in Ireland, given him by *Hugh de Lacy*, EARL OF ULSTER, whose constable he was in that province. He subsequently obtained divers other territorial grants from the crown, but, notwithstanding, when *Richard Mareschal*, EARL OF PEMBROKE, rebelled, and made an incursion into Wales, the king, HENRY III., thought it prudent to secure the persons of this Henry, and all the other barons-marchers. He was afterwards, however, constituted governor of Shrewsbury, in place of John de Lacy, Earl of Lincoln, and on the death of John, Earl of Chester, governor of the castle of Chester, and also of that of Beeston, then called the "Castle on the Rock," and soon after made governor of Newcastle-under-Lyne. This powerful feudal baron m. Bertred, dau. of Ralph de Meisnilwarin, of Cheshire, and had a son, JAMES, and a dau., Emme, who m. Griffin ap Madoc, Lord of Bromefield, a person of great power in Wales. He d. in 1236, having founded and endowed the Abbey of Hilton, near to his castle at Heleigh, in Staffordshire, for Cistercian monks, and was s. by his son,

JAMES DE ALDITHELEY, a great favourite of Richard, Earl of Cornwall, at whose coronation as king of Almaigne he assisted. This nobleman had livery of his lands in the 31st HENRY III., and was constituted in two years afterwards constable of Newcastle-under-Lyne. Being one of the lords-marchers he was actively employed for some years against the Welsh, and was appointed governor of the castles of Salop and Bridgenorth, and sheriff for the counties of Salop and Stafford. In the 6th of HENRY III. he was made justice of Ireland; and in the same year, upon the misunderstanding between the king and the barons, regarding the *provisions of Oxford*, being referred to the arbitration of the monarch of France, he was one of the noblemen who undertook for the king therein. The next year we find him with Roger de Mortimer and the other barons-marchers, giving battle to *Lewelin*, Prince of Wales, and afterwards joining the Earl of Gloucester at Evesham in rescuing the king, who had been captive to the Earl of Leicester at the battle of Lewes. In the 52nd of HENRY III. his lordship performed a pilgrimage to the shrine of St. James in Galicia, and the following year embarked in the Crusade. His death, occasioned by breaking his neck, occurred soon afterwards (1271). He had a dau., Joan, who m. John, son of Robert de Beauchamp, to whose child, prior to its birth, the said John being then deceased, his lordship was appointed guardian. He had also five sons, the youngest of whom, Hugh, is supposed to have been the Hugh Aldithdey, who had summons to parlia-

ment 15 May, 1321, and whose son became Earl of Gloucester.
His lordship was *s.* by his eldest son,

JAMES DE ALDITHELEY, who *d. s. p.* in 1272, and was *s.* by his
brother,

HENRY DE ALDITHELEY, between whom and John D'Eivill,
who had *m.* Maud, widow of his deceased brother, a covenant
was made in the 3rd of EDWARD I., conveying on the part of
Henry a considerable landed dowry to the said Maud. He *d.*
without issue in 1275, and was *s.* by his brother,

WILLIAM DE ALDITHELEY, who, attaining majority in a year
after his accession, had livery of all his lands, save a reasonable
dowry to Dulcia, the widow of his deceased brother Henry. In
the 10th of EDWARD I., the king, by his precept to the barons of
his exchequer, acknowledging that he was indebted to James
de Alditheley, father of this William, in the sum of
£1,288 5s. 13d., upon the surplusage of his account since he
was justice of Ireland, commanded them to discharge the said
William of £230 14s. 10d., a debt due by James to the exchequer upon another account. In this year (1275) William de
Alditheley fell in an engagement with the Welsh, wherein
several other brave warriors were slain, and the king lost
fourteen banners. Dying without issue, he was *s.* by his
brother,

NICHOLAS DE ALDITHELEY, who doing homage, had livery
of his lands, and then paid £10 for his relief of the tenth part
of the Barony of Wiche-Malbanc. In the 22nd of EDWARD I.,
this feudal lord received command to attend the king at Portsmouth, upon the 1st of September, well fitted with horse and
arms, and thence to accompany the monarch into Gascoigne;
which service he performed. In three years afterwards, 26
January, 1297, he was summoned to parliament amongst the
other barons of the realm, and was likewise in the expedition
to Scotland, with the Earls of Warren and Warwick, and participated in the victory obtained at Dunbar. His lordship *m.*
Catherine, dau. and co-heiress of John Giffard, of Brimefield, by
Maud, widow of William de Longespe, and dau. of Walter de
Clifford, and dying in 1299, was *s.* by his eldest son, then in
his tenth year,

THOMAS DE ALDITHELEY, who *m.* Eve, dau. and heiress of
John, Lord Clavering, but dying *s. p.* in 1307, the inheritance
devolved upon his brother,

NICHOLAS DE ALDITHELEY, who was summoned to parliament
from 8 January, 1313 (6th EDWARD II.), to 25 August, 1318
(12th EDWARD II.). His lordship *m.* Joane, widow of Henry
Lacy, Earl of Lincoln, and sister and co-heiress of William
Martin—Baron Martin (by writ, 23 June, 1295: which
barony fell into ABEYANCE between the descendants of the said
Joane and her sister, Eleanore, the other co-heiress, wife of
Philip de Columbers), and was *s.* at his decease, in 1319, by
his son,

JAMES DE AUDLEY—LORD AUDLEY—one of the most celebrated
warriors of the martial reign of King EDWARD III. His lordship
was but three years of age at the decease of his father, when
his castle of Heleigh and divers other estates were committed
to the guardianship of Ralph de Camoys, while he was himself
confided in ward to Roger Mortimer, Earl of March. At the
early age of twenty-three, we find him governor of Berwick-
upon-Tweed, and receiving orders to attend King EDWARD III. in
his expedition into France, with twenty men-at-arms and twenty
archers. In the next year (17th EDWARD III.), his lordship did
homage for lands inherited through his aunt Eleanore de Columbers, and then served the king with twenty men-at-arms and
twenty archers, in his wars in France. In the 19th of EDWARD
III., he had command to attend the monarch in person, and to
serve him with all his retinue, for the defence of the realm
against the French, at the king's proper cost. In two years
afterwards, he was again in France, and his lordship had the
honour of being one of the Original Knights of the Garter,[*]
upon the institution of that illustrious order. From this period,
Lord Audley was pre-eminently distinguished as a soldier
upon the French soil, until the glorious conflict of Poictiers
placed his military renown upon the highest elevation. Of his
lordship's conduct in this celebrated battle, Froissard gives the
following account:—

"The Lord James Audley went not from the Prince of a
great season, but when he saw that they should needs fight, he
said to the prince, 'Sir, I have served always truly my lord
your father, and you also, and shall do as long as I live. I say
this, because I made once a vow, that the first battel that
either the king your father or any of his children should be at,
how that I would be one of the first setters on, or else to die in
the pain; thereof I require your grace, as in reward for my
service that ever I did to the king your father, or to you, that
you would give me license to depart from you, and to set
myself there, as I may accomplish my vow.' The prince
accorded to his desire, and said, ' *Sir James, God give you this
day that grace to be the best knight of all other ;*' and so took
him by the hand. Then the knight departed from the prince
and went to the foremost front of all the battel, all onely
accompanied with four esquires, who promised not to fail
him. This Lord James was a right sage and a valiant knight
and by him was much of the host ordained and governed the
day before.

"The Lord James Audley, with his four esquires, was in
the front of the battel, and there did marvels in arms; and by
great prowess, he came and fought with *Sir Arnold D.indrahe*,
under his own banner, and there they fought long together,
and Sir Arnold was there sore handled." Froissard goes on to
say, " that his lordship continuing to combat in his advanced
position, he was sore hurt in the body, and in the visage; as
long as his breath served him, he fought. At last at the end of
the battel, his four esquires took and brought him out of the
field, and laid him under a hedge to refresh him, and they unarmed him, and bound up his wounds as well as they could

"As soon as the Earl of Warwick (continues the same
authority,) and Lord Cobham were departed, the Prince demanded regarding the Lord Audley; some answered, 'He is
sore hurt, and lieth in a litter here beside.'—' *By my faith* (said
the prince,) *of his hurts I am right sorry ; go, and know if he
may be brought hither, else I will go and see him there as he is.*
Then two knights came to the Lord Audley, and said, 'Sir, the
prince desireth greatly to see you.' 'Ah, Sir,' (said Lord
Audley,) 'I thank the prince when he thought on so poor a
knight as I am.' Then he called eight of his servants, and
caused them to bear him in his litter, to the place where the
prince was.

"Then the prince took him in his arms and kissed him
and made him great cheer, and said, '*Sir James, I ought
greatly to honor you, for by your valiance, you have this
day achieved the grace and renown of us all; and ye are reputed for the most valiant of all other.*' 'Ah, Sir,' (said the
knight,) 'ye say as it pleaseth you; I would it were so : and if
I have this day anything advanced myself, to serve you and
accomplish the vow that I made, it ought not to be reputed to
my own prowess.' '*Sir James,* (said the prince,) *I, and all
ours take you in this journey for the best doer in arms ; and to
the intent to furnish you the better to pursue the wars, I retain
you for ever to be my knight, with five hundred marks of yearly
revenues, the which I shall assign you of my heritage in
England.*' 'Sir,' (said the knight,) 'God grant me to deserve
the great goodness that he shew me.' And so he took his
leave of the prince, for he was right feeble; and so his
servants brought him to his lodging.

"The Lord James Audley gave to his four esquires the five
hundred marks revenue that the prince had given him.

"When the prince heard of this gift made by Sir James
Audley to his four esquires, he thanked him for so doing, and
gave him six hundred marks per annum more."

In confirmation of Froissard, it appears by the public records
that this eminent soldier had for his singular services at the
battle of Poictiers, a grant from Edward the Black Prince, of
an annuity of £400 during his life, and for one year after, to
be received out of the coinage of the Stanneries in Cornwall,
and the king's lands in that county. After this period, he
continued to serve in the wars, with equal renown to himself
and glory to his country. His lordship *m.*, 1st, Joane,
dau. of Roger Mortimer, Earl of March, and had issue,

> NICHOLAS, his successor.
> Joane, *m.* to Sir John Touchet, grandson of which marriage,
> Sir John Touchet, was summoned to parliament as Baron
> Audley, upon the extinction of the male line of the family.
> (*See* TOUCHET, Barons Audley.)
> Margaret, *m.* to Sir Roger Hillary.

The baron *m.* 2ndly, Isabel, dau. and co-heiress of William
Malbank, Baron of Wich-Malbank, by whom he had

> Rowland, }
> Thomas, } both of whom *d. s. p.*
> Margaret, *m.* to Fouke, son of Sir Fouke Fitz-Warine,
> Knt.

His lordship made his will in the 9th of RICHARD II., at
Heleigh Castle, by which he bequeathed his body to be buried

---

* ORIGINAL KNIGHTS OF THE GARTER :—EDWARD III., KING
OF ENGLAND, EDWARD, PRINCE OF WALES, Henry, Duke of
Lancaster, Thomas, Earl of Warwick, Ralph, Earl of Stafford,
William Montacute, Earl of Salisbury, Roger Mortimer, Earl of
March, Captall de Buche, John Lord L'Isle, Bartholomew
Burghersh, John Beauchamp, John Lord Mohun, Hugh Cour-
tenay, Thomas Holand, John Lord Grey, Richard Fitz-Simon,
Miles Stapleton, Thomas Wale, Hugh Wrottesley, Nigel Loring,
John Chandos, JAMES DE AUDLEY, Otho Holland, Henry Eam,
Sanchet Dabridgecourt, and Sir Walter Paveley.

In the quire of his abbey at Hilton, before the high altar, in case he should depart this life in the marches ; but if in Devon or Somersetshire, then in the quire of the Fryers Preachers at Exeter, before the high altar there ; and appointed that there should be about his corpse, five great tapers, and five morters of wax, burning on the day of his funeral, as also £40 sterling, then distributed to poor people, to pray for his soul. To Nicholas, his son, he gave £100 in money, and one dozen of silver vessels, with all the armour for his own body. To Fouke Fitz-Warine and Philip his uncle, all his other armour of plate and mall. To Margaret Hillary, his dau., £10 in money ; and to the monks of Hilton Abbey, to pray for his soul, £10. This great soldier d. at Heleigh, 1 April, 1386, and was s. by his eldest son,

NICHOLAS AUDLEY, Lord Audley, who was summoned to parliament from 17 December, 1387, to 12 September, 1390. His lordship m. Elizabeth, dau. of Adelice de Beaumont, by whom he had no issue ; he d. in 1392, and his half-brothers having predeceased him, without issue, the male line of this branch of the family of ALDITHELEY or AUDLEY EXPIRED, while the " Barony of Audley " devolved upon the grandson of his lordship's sister, Joane Touchet, his other sister, Margaret Hillary, having also died without issue,

Arms—Gules, a fret, or.

AUDLEY, OR DE ALDITHELEY—BARONS AUDLEY, AND SUBSEQUENTLY EARL OF GLOUCESTER.

Barony, by Writ of Summons, dated 15 May, 1321.

Lineage.

HUGH DE ALDITHELEY OR AUDLEY, brother it is presumed of Nicholas, Lord Audley of Heleigh, was summoned to parliament as " Hugh de Audley, Seniori," on 15 May, 1321, 14th EDWARD II. His lordship had been engaged during the reign of EDWARD I, in the king's service, and was called " Senior," to distinguish him from his son. Being concerned in the insurrection of Thomas, Earl of Lancaster, 15th EDWARD II., the baron was committed a close prisoner to Wallingford Castle, but making his peace with the king he obtained his release, and suffered nothing further. His lordship sat in the parliament of the 11th and 14th of EDWARD II. He m. Isolda, widow of Walter Balim, and left two sons, by the elder of whom he was succeeded,

HUGH DE AUDLEY, who had been summoned to parliament in the life-time of his father as " HUGH DE AUDLEY, JUNIORI," from 20 November, 1317, to 15 May, 1321, and after that nobleman's decease as " HUGH DE AUDLIE," from 3 December, 1326, 20th EDWARD II., to 10th EDWARD III. His lordship m. Margaret, sister and co-heiress of Gilbert de Clare, Earl of Gloucester, and widow of Piers Gaveston, by whom he left an only dau. and heiress,

Margaret, who m. Ralph, Lord Stafford, and carried the Barony of Audley into that family : it EXPIRED upon the attainder of Edward, Duke of Buckingham, with that nobleman's other honours, in 1521.

Hugh Lord Audley, was created Earl of Gloucester, 23 April, 1337, and under that title a further account of his lordship will be found. He d. in 1347.

AUDLEY—BARON AUDLEY OF WALDEN.

By Letters Patent, dated 29 November, 1538.

Lineage.

The old genealogists were quite at a loss to ascertain anything about the family of Lord Chancellor Audley ; it was reserved for the late Lord Braybrooke to discover that eminent lawyer's parentage and ancestry.

" It seems extraordinary," says his lordship, " that neither Camden, who lived so much nearer those times, nor Dugdale could with all their industry satisfy themselves as to the birthplace or extraction of Thomas Audley ; for they state only in general terms that he was of a good family ; but that his arms differed entirely from those of the ancient lords of the same name, to whom, in fact he was no way related. All doubt upon the subject has, however, been removed, by the discovery of the following entry, copied from the Burgesses Oath Book at Colchester :—

" ' A.D. 1516, Thomas Audley, Gen., natus in Colne-Comitia, in Com. Essex, Burgeus.'

" One of his ancestors, indeed, Ralph Audley, appears to have been seated at Earls' Colne as far back as the 28th of HENRY

VI., and in the 35th of that king, became possessed of the Hay House, an ancient mansion previously in the tenure of the prior of Colne, in the same parish, demolished a few years ago ; and in which, we may presume, the chancellor was born ; Geoffrey Audley, his father, subsequently made a subsequent addition to his property at Earls' Colne."

THOMAS AUDLEY, to whom these remarks refer, was an eminent lawyer in the reign of HENRY VIII., who, having attracted royal favour by his zeal in the spoliation of religious houses, as speaker of the parliament which originated that measure, attained within a short period the highest honours which royalty could bestow. In the 22nd of HENRY VIII. he was nominated attorney for the duchy of Lancaster, raised to the degree of serjeant-at-law, and appointed king's serjeant. In two years afterwards Mr. Serjeant Audley succeeded Sir Thomas More in the custody of the great seal, as lord keeper, when he received the honour of knighthood, and before the close of the year he was elevated to the dignity of lord chancellor of England. In addition to those lucrative honours, Sir Thomas had a grant of the site and precinct, with all the lands and plate thereunto belonging, of the suppressed priory of *Christchurch*, " near Aldgate, in the city of London," where he erected a mansion-house for his residence. In the 30th of the same reign his lordship sat as high steward upon the trial of Henry Courtenay, Marquis of Exeter, for conspiring to raise Reginald Pole (the subsequently eminent Cardinal Pole) to the throne. And in that year he obtained a grant of the great *Abbey of Walden*, in Essex, in compensation, as he alleged, " for having in this world sustained great damage and infamy for serving the king." Having acquired this last possession he was raised to the peerage by letters patent, dated 29 November, 1538, as BARON AUDLEY, OF WALDEN, and installed a knight of the most noble order of the Garter. His lordship m. Elizabeth, dau. of Thomas Grey, Marquess of Dorset, and had two daus., viz.

> Margaret, m. 1st, to Lord Henry Dudley, son of John, Duke of Northumberland, who fell at St. Quintin in 1557, dying *s.p.*; and 2ndly, to Thomas Howard, Duke of Norfolk, who was beheaded 2 July, 1572 ; by whom, her second husband, she had issue,
>
>> THOMAS, summoned to parliament as LORD HOWARD OF WALDEN, and afterwards created EARL OF SUFFOLK, lord high treasurer, *temp.* JAMES I. and K.G. From this nobleman descend LORD HOWARD DE WALDEN and the EARL OF SUFFOLK AND BERKSHIRE.
>>
>> Henry d. young.
>> William, ancestor of the Earls of Carlisle.
>> Elizabeth d. unm.
>> Margaret, m. to Robert Sackville, 2nd Earl of Dorset, ancestor of the Dukes of Dorset.
>
> The Duchess of Norfolk inherited the entire property of her father upon the decease of her sister.
> Mary, who d. unm.

Lord Audley d. 19 April, 1544, and the title became EXTINCT. According to a desire expressed in his will, he was buried in a chapel he had erected at Saffron Walden, where a splendid monument was raised to him with the following epitaph, which there is some reason to suppose that, in imitation of his immediate predecessor, he had himself composed :

" The stroke of death's inevitable dart,
Hath now (alas !) of life bereft the hart
Of Sir Thomas Audley of the Garter Knight,
Late Chancellor of England, under our Prince of might,
Henry the Eighth, worthy of high renown,
And made him Lord Audley of this town."

His lordship appointed, by his last testament, that his executors should, upon the next new year's day after his decease, deliver a legacy of £100 to the king, " from whom he had received all his reputations and benefits." Of this nobleman Rapin says, " Chancellor Audley was a person of good sense. He served the reformers when he could without danger : but he was too much a courtier to insist upon what he judged reasonable, if the king was against it."

Arms—Quarterly : per pale, indented, or and az. : in the second and third quarters an eagle displayed of the first, on a bend of the second a fret between two martlets of gold.

NOTE.—In the feast of Abbey Lands, King HENRY VIII. carved unto him (Thomas Audley), the first cut (and that, I assure you, was a dainty morsel), viz., the Priory of the Trinity in Aldgate Ward, London, dissolved 1531, which as a van courier fore-ran other abbeys by two years and foretold their dissolution. This I may call (afterwards called Duke's Place) the Covent-Garden Within London, as the greatest empty space within the walls, though since filled, not to say pestered with houses. He had afterwards a large partage in the Abbey Lands in several counties.—FULLER's *Worthies*, I., 507 and 508.

AUNGIER—BARON AUNGIER, OF LONG-FORD, VISCOUNT LONGFORD, AND EARL OF LONGFORD.

Barony, by Letters Patent, dated 29 June, 1621.
Viscounty, by Letters Patent, dated 8 November, 1675.
Earldom, by Letters Patent, dated 18 December, 1677.

Lineage.

SIR FRANCIS AUNGIER, Knt., descended from the Aungiers, of Cambridge, having adopted the legal profession, was appointed master of the rolls 5 October, 1609, and created BARON AUNGIER, of Longford, in the peerage of Ireland, 29 June, 1621. His lordship m. 1st, Douglas, youngest sister of Gerald, Earl of Kildare, and had by her,

  I. GERALD, his heir.
  II. Ambrose, D.D., who m. Griseld, younger dau. of Lancelot Bulkeley, archbishop of Dublin, and had issue,
    1 FRANCIS, who s. as 3rd baron.
    2 Gerald, governor of Fort St. George, East Indies, d.s.p.
    3 Ambrose.
    1 Douglas (dau.). m. in 1669, to Edmund Ludlow, Esq.
    2 ALICE, m. to SIR JAMES CUFF, Knt., M.P., and had, with other issue,
      FRANCIS CUFF, grandfather of Elizabeth, Countess of Longford.
      GERALD CUFF, ancestor of LORD TYRAWLEY. (See that title.)
  I. Elizabeth, m. 1st, to Simon Caryll, Esq., of Tangley; 2ndly, to Richard Barne, Esq.; and 3rdly, to John Matchell, Esq.
  II. Lettice, m. 1st. to E. Cherry, Esq.; 2ndly, to Sir William Danvers, Knt.; and 3rdly, to Sir Henry Holcroft, Knt.

Lord Aungier m. 2ndly, Anne, dau. of Sir George Barne, Knt., and had issue,

    George.   Frances.

He m. 3rdly, Margaret, dau. of Sir Thomas Cave, Knt., of Stanford, by whom (who m. 2ndly, Sir Thomas Wenman) he had no issue. His lordship d. 8 October, 1632, was buried at St. Patrick's, Dublin, 6 November following, and was s. by his eldest son,

GERALD AUNGIER, 2nd baron, who m. Jane, 2nd dau. of Sir Edward Onslow, of West Clandon, in Surrey, and was s. at his decease, in 1655 (having no issue), by his nephew (refer to children of Dr. Ambrose Aungier).

FRANCIS AUNGIER, 3rd baron. This nobleman was made a captain of a troop of horse in 1660. In 1668 he obtained a patent for the incorporation of the town of Longford, and was advanced to the dignity of VISCOUNT LONGFORD, with remainder to his brothers and their male heirs, by letters patent, dated 8 November, 1675. His lordship was created EARL OF LONGFORD, with the limitation, on 18 December, 1677. In 1682 he was appointed a commissioner of the revenue, and in 1697 keeper of the great seal, at which time he was a member of the privy council, governor of Carrickfergus, and master of the ordnance. His lordship m. Lady Anne Chichester, younger dau. and co-heir of Arthur, 1st Earl of Donegal, and widow of John, Earl of Gowran; but d. s. p. 22 December, 1700, when his honours devolved, according to the patents, upon his only surviving brother,

AMBROSE AUNGIER, as 2nd Earl of Longford, a commissioner of the revenue; at whose decease, without issue, 23 January, 1704, all the honours of the family became EXTINCT, while the estates devolved upon his lordship's sister, Mrs. Ludlow, and after her decease passed to his nephews, Francis Cuff and James Macartney, Esqrs., by an equal division, and to their heirs for ever.

Francis Cuff had two sons; the elder, Francis, d. s. p. in 1717, and was s. by his only brother, Michael Cuff, whose only dau. and heiress, Elizabeth Cuff, m. Thomas Pakenham, Esq. of Pakenham Hall, and was created COUNTESS OF LONGFORD. Her ladyship was s. at her decease, in January, 1794, by her grandson, Thomas Pakenham, who had s. his father, in 1792, as Baron Longford, and was the late EARL OF LONGFORD.

Arms.—Erm., a griffin, segreant, az.

BACON—BARON VERULUM, VISCOUNT ST. ALBAN'S.

Barony, by Letters Patent, dated 11 July, 1618.
Viscounty, by Letters Patent, dated 27 January, 1621

Lineage.

FRANCIS BACON, 2nd son of Sir Nicholas Bacon, lord keeper in the reign of ELIZABETH, by Anne, his 2nd wife, dau. of Sir Anthony Cook, of Gidea Hall, Essex, having been brought up to the bar, was appointed queen's counsel in 1558; and soon after the accession of King JAMES I., honoured with knighthood. In 1613 he was made attorney-general, and subsequently sworn of the privy council. In 1617, Sir Francis was constituted lord keeper of the great seal, and the next year he was entitled lord high chancellor of England. Within a few months afterwards he was elevated to the peerage, 11 July, 1618, in the dignity of BARON VERULAM, and created 27 January, 1621, VISCOUNT ST. ALBAN'S. His lordship was subsequently convicted of corruption in the exercise of his judicial functions, upon his own confession, and sentenced to pay a fine of £40,000, to be imprisoned during the king's pleasure, and to be ever afterwards incapacitated from holding office under the crown. Having, in pursuance of this judgment, suffered a brief incarceration, and the fine being eventually remitted, his lordship withdrew into retirement, and devoted the remainder of his life to the most splendid literary labours. He m. Alice, dau. and co-heir of Benedict Barnham, Esq., an alderman of London, but d. without issue, 9 April, 1626, when his honours became EXTINCT. The learned Bayle calls Lord St. Alban's one of the greatest geniuses of his age, Voltaire styles him the father of experimental philosophy, and Walpole terms him the prophet of arts, which Newton was sent afterwards to reveal. The latter author adds:—"It would be impertinent to the reader to enter into any account of this amazing genius or his works: both will be universally admired as long as science exists. As long as ingratitude and adulation are despicable, so long shall we lament the depravity of this great man's heart. Alas! that he, who could command immortal fame, should have stooped to the little ambition of power." Lord St. Alban's own brother, Anthony, d. unm.; his brothers (of the half-blood) were—I. SIR NICHOLAS BACON, the first baronet ever created, ancestor of the present SIR HENRY HICKMAN BACON, Bart.; 2. Sir Nathaniel Bacon, K.B., of Stiffkey, Norfolk, who left daus. only; and 3 Edward Bacon, Esq., of Shrubland Hall, co. Suffolk, ancestor of the BARONS of Shrubland, Ipswich, and Earlham.

Arms.—Gu., on a chief, ar., two mullets, sa., a crescent for difference.

BADLESMERE—BARONS BADLESMERE.

By Writ of Summons, dated 26 October, 1309.

Lineage.

The first mention of this family occurs in the 16th year of the reign of HENRY II. (1169-70), when

BARTHOLOMEW DE BADLESMERE had a law suit with William de Cheney concerning a landed property in the county of Kent, and in the 22nd of the same king, we find this Bartholomew amerced 20 marks for trespassing in the royal forests. To Bartholomew succeeded

WILLIAM DE BADLESMERE, who, adhering to the cause of the barons, was taken prisoner with several others, in the castle of Rochester, towards the close of King JOHN's reign, and did not obtain his freedom until the 6th year of HENRY III. (1221-2). After this William, came

GILES DE BADLESMERE, who lost his life in a skirmish with the Welsh, in the 32nd year of HENRY III, and after him

GUNCELINE DE BADLESMERE, known first as a great rebel to HENRY III., for which he was excommunicated by the archbishop of Canterbury; but subsequently, returning to his allegiance, as justice of Chester, in that office he continued until the 9th of Edward I. (1280-1). In the next year he was in the expedition made into Wales, and in the 25th of the same monarch, in that into Gascony, having previously, by the writ of 26 January in that year, been summoned to the parliament at Salisbury for the following Sunday, the feast of St. Matthew, 21 September, as Gunselin de Badlesmere. He d. four years afterwards, seised of the manor of Badlesmere, which he held in capite of the crown, as of the barony of Crevequer, by the service of one knight's fee. He *m.* the heiress of Ralph Fitz-Bernard, Lord of Kingsdowne, and was *s.* by his son, then twenty-six years of age,

BARTHOLOMEW DE BADLESMERE, who in the life-time of his father (22nd EDWARD I.) received command to attend the king at Portsmouth, upon the 1st day of September, with horse and arms, to embark with him for Gascony, and in the year that he succeeded to his paternal property was in the wars of Scotland. He was afterwards in the retinue of Robert de Clifford in the Welsh wars, and in the 1st year of EDWARD I. was appointed governor of the castle of Bristol. In two years afterwards he was summoned to parliament as Badlesmere, and had a grant from the king, through the especial influence of Gilbert de Clare, Earl of Gloucester and Hertford, and Henry de Lacy, Earl of Lincoln, of the castle and manor of Chelham, in Kent, for his own and his wife's life, which castle had been possessed by Alexander de Baliol in right of his wife Isabel, and ought to have escheated to the crown upon the decease of the said Alexander, by reason of the felony of John 'de Stra-Lolgi, Earl of Athol (Isabel's son and heir), who was hanged. In the 5th of EDWARD II., Lord Badlesmere was constituted governor of the castle of Ledes, and obtained at the same time grants of divers extensive manors. In the next year but one, his lordship was deputed, with Otto de Grandison and others, ambassador to the court of Rome, and the next year, upon the death of Robert de Clifford, he obtained a grant of the custody of the castle of Skypton in Yorkshire, as of all other castles in that county and Westmorland, whereof the said Robert died possessed, to hold during the minority of Roger de Clifford, his son and heir.

His lordship was further indebted to the crown for numerous charters for fairs and marts throughout his extensive manors; and he held the high office of steward of the household for a great number of years; but notwithstanding his thus basking in the sunshine of royal favour, his allegiance was not trustworthy, for joining the banner of Thomas, Earl of Lancaster, and other discontented nobles of that period, he went into Kent without the king's permission; where, being well received, he put himself at the head of some soldiers from his castle at Ledes, and thence proceeded to Canterbury, with 19 knights, having linen jackets under their surcoats, all his esquires being in plate armour, and thus repaired to the shrine of St. Thomas, to the great amazement of the good citizens. While Lord Badlesmere remained at Canterbury, John de Crumwell and his wife sought his lordship's aid, and, pledging himself to afford it, he hasted to Oxford, where the barons of his party had been then assembled. In the meantime the king being apprised of the baron's proceedings, despatched the queen to Ledes, and upon admission being denied to her, the castle was regularly invested by Adomere de Valence, Earl of Pembroke, and John de Britannia, Earl of Richmond, to whom it eventually surrendered, when Lord Badlesmere's wife, young son, and daughters, all falling into the hands of the besiegers, were sent prisoners to the Tower of London. The baron and his accomplices afterwards were pursued by Edmund, Earl of Kent, and John de Warren, Earl of Surrey, and being defeated and taken prisoners at the battle of Borough-bridge, his lordship was hanged, drawn, and quartered at Canterbury, and his head set upon a pole at Burgate. At the time of the baron's execution upwards of ninty lords, knights, and others concerned in the same insurrection, suffered a similar fate in various parts of the kingdom. Margaret, his lordship's widow (one of the daus. and co-heiresses of Thomas, 3rd son of Thomas, 2nd son of Richard de Clare, Earl of Gloucester), continued prisoner in the Tower, until, through the influence of William Lord Roos, of Hamlake, and others, she obtained her freedom. Whereupon betaking herself to the nunnery of *Minoresses,* without Aldgate, in the suburbs of London, she had 2*s.* a-day for her maintenance, to be paid by the sheriff of Essex; she subsequently, however, obtained a large proportion of the deceased lord's manors for her dowry. By this lady, Lord Badlesmere left issue,

1. GILES, his heir.
1. Margery, *m.* to William, Lord de Roos, of Hamlake, and had a son, THOMAS, LORD DE ROOS, from whom descended the LORDS DE ROOS, whose heir general, THOMAS MANNERS, Lord de Roos, was created EARL OF RUTLAND, 18 June, 1525. His lordship's grandson, HENRY, 2nd Earl of Rutland, and 14th Lord de Roos, *m.* Margaret, dau. of Ralph Nevil, Earl of Westmorland, and had issue: I. EDWARD, who *s.* as 3rd Earl of Rutland, whose issue became EXTINCT. II. JOHN, who became 4th Earl of Rutland. His lordship *m.* Elizabeth, dau. of Francis Charlton, Esq., of Apley Castle, Salop, and had Roger, Francis, and Sir George, successively Earls of Rutland, and two daus., 1 LADY BRIDGET MANNERS, *m.* Robert Tyrwhitt, Esq., of Kettleby, Lincolnshire, and had a son and heir, WILLIAM TYRWHITT, of Kettleby, who *m.* Katherine, dau. of Anthony Browne, 2nd Viscount Montagu, and *d.* 1642, leaving ROBERT TYRWHITT, who *s.* his father at

Kettleby, *d. s. p.* in 1648, and was *s.* by his brother, FRANCIS TYRWHITT, *b.* about 1623, *m.* Elizabeth, dau. and heir of Robert Lloyd, M.D.. and *d.* 1673. His only child and heiress, KATHERINE TYRWHITT, *m.* Sir HENRY HUNLOKE, Bart., of Wingerworth, near Chesterfield. co. Derby. 2 LADY FRANCES MANNERS, *m.* William, 3rd Lord Willoughby of Parham, and had, with other issue, ELIZABETH, *m.* to Richard Jones, Earl of Ranelagh, and had four daus., of whom LADY FRANCES JONES, *m.* Thomas, Earl Coningsby, and had, with other issue, LADY FRANCES CONINGSBY, who *m.* Sir Charles Hanbury-Williams. and had two daus. co-heirs, viz., 1 FRANCES HANBURY-WILLIAMS, *m.* 1754, William-Anne, Earl of Essex, and had issue. George. Earl of Essex, *d.s.p.* 1839, and Elizabeth, who *m.* John, 3rd Lord Monson, and their issue is EXTINCT. 2 CHARLOTTE HANBURY-WILLIAMS, *m* Admiral the Hon. Robert Boyle, who assumed the name of WALSINGHAM, and their dau. was CHARLOTTE, late BARONESS DE ROS. whose son, the present Lord de Ros, is one of the co-heirs of the Barons of Badlesmere.
II. Maud, *m.* 1st, to Robert, FitzPayn, and 2ndly. to John de Vere, Earl of Oxford. (*See* VERE, *Earl of Oxford.*) Of this 2nd dau. and co-heiress of Badlesmere, the co-heirs are, THE DUKE OF ATHOLE (descended from Katherine Neville, grand-dau. of Sir John Neville, Lord Latimer, and Dorothea Vere, his wife, sister and co-heir of John 14th Earl of Oxford), WINCHCOMBE-HENRY-HOWARD HARTLEY, Esq., of Bucklebury, Berks; and SIR RAINALD KNIGHTLEY, Bart., of Fawsley, co. Northampton (descended from Dorothy Neville, Countess of Exeter, Katherine's sister), SIR ROBERT BURDETT, Bart., JOHN, LORD ROLLO, SIR CHARLES-ROBERT TEMPEST, Bart., CHARLES STANDISH, Esq , of Standish, co. LANCASTER, and JOHN WRIGHT, Esq , of Kelvedon, co. Essex (all descended from Lucy Neville, Lady Cornwallis, another of Katherine's sisters), GEORGE-WILLIAM VILLIERS and MONTAGU, EARL OF ABINGDON (descended from Elizabeth Neville, Lady Danvers, the youngest of Kathe ine's sisters), and ADRIEN, MARQUESS DE CONRONNELL, and SIR WILLIAM HENRY DILLON (descended from Elizabeth Vere, wife of Sir Anthony Wingfield. K G , and sister of Dorothea, wife of John Neville, Lord Latimer).
III. Elizabeth, *m.* 1st to Edmund Mortimer, and 2ndly, to William Bohun, Earl of Northampton. (*See* BOHUN.)
IV. Margaret, *m.* to Sir John Tiptoft, 2nd baron of that name : (*See* TIPTOFT.) HENRY-JAMES JONES, Esq , Ralph-Gordon Noel, LORD WENTWORTH, and EMMA-PHIPPS, wife of GEORGE-POULETT SCROPE, Esq., are the co-representatives of this co-heiress.

His lordship had been summoned to parliament from 26 October, 1309, to 6 August, 1320. His unhappy fate occurred in 1322,; but notwithstanding *that,* his son,

GILES DE BADLESMERE, 2nd baron, found such favour from the king, that he had a special precept to the keeper of the wardrobe, in the Tower, to deliver unto him all his father's harneys, as well coat-armours as others. This nobleman doing homage in the 7th of EDWARD III., although not then at majority, had livery of his lands, and the next year attended the king in an expedition into Scotland, in which service he was engaged the three ensuing years. His lordship was summoned to parliament from 22 January, 1336, to 18 August, 1337. He *m.* Elizabeth, dau. of William de Montacute, Earl of Salisbury; but dying without issue, in 1338, the barony of Badlesmere fell into ABEYANCE* between his sisters and co-heiresses, and it so continues amongst their descendants and representatives.

Arms —Arg , a fesse between two bars gemelles, gules.

BALFOUR—BARON BALFOUR OF GLENAWLEY.

By Letters Patent, dated 8 November, 1619.

Lineage.

The Barony of Balfour (or Bal-or, from the water of Or running near it), in Fife, gave the name of BALFOUR to a very ancient family, who were long heritable proprietors of that place.

SIR JOHN BALFOUR, Knt. of Balgarvie, got a grant of the lands of Burleigh, which were erected into a free barony, from King JAMES II., in the 9th year of his Majesty's reign, *anno* 1445-6. From him lineally descended

---

* The Barony of Badlesmere was assumed, without any legal right by the deceased lord's sister, Maud, Countess of Oxford, and the earl her husband, and was retained in that family until the demise of John de Vere, 14th earl, without male issue, in the reign of HENRY VIII., when it was certified, 5 April, 1626, to have fallen into ABEYANCE between that nobleman's four sisters.

SIR MICHAEL BALFOUR, Knt. of Burleigh, who had charters of Mochaster, Dullectur, and Portbank, 11 July, 1502, of Easter and Wester Balgarvies, and the Mill of Sheok, 16 February, 1506, and of Schanwell, 28 May, 1512. He m. Margaret Musshett, and had a son,

DAVID BALFOUR, of Burleigh, who had a charter of Schanwell, co. Fife, 11 June, 1541, m. Agnes Forrester, and had a son,

MICHAEL BALFOUR, of Burleigh, who was served heir to his father, 1542, and had a charter of Kinloch and the office of coroner of co. Fife, 18 June, 1566. He m. Christian, dau. of John Bethune, of Creich, and had an only child, his sole heir,

MARGARET BALFOUR, who m. Sir James Balfour, Knt. of Pittendreich, co. Fife (brother of Michael Balfour, of Monquhany, commendator of Melrose, ancestor of BALFOUR of Trenaby, in Orkney (see BURKE's Landed Gentry). Sir James enacted an important part during the turbulent reigns of Queen MARY and her son JAMES VI., and was President of the court of Session, 6 Dec. 1567. By Margaret, his wife (who m. 2ndly, Sir Robert Melville), he had issue,

I. MICHAEL, his heir.
II. JAMES (Sir), created in 1619, Lord Balfour of Glenawley, of whom presently; buried at St. Anne's, Blackfriars, London, 24 October, that year.
III. Alexander, of Balgarvie, from whom several families of that name are descended.
IV. Henry, general in the army of the States of Holland, served with reputation under the Prince of Orange.
V. William, m. Hamilton, heiress of Glenawley, assumed her name, and one of their descendants was created Lord Glenawley.
VI. David, captain in his brother, Sir Henry's, regiment, perished at sea going over to Holland.
I. A dau., m. to Sir Michael Arnot, of Arnot.
II. A dau., m. to Sir John Henderson.
III. A dau., m. to Barclay, of Collairnie, in Fife.

Sir James's eldest son,

SIR MICHAEL BALFOUR, of Burleigh, had a charter of the lands of Nethertoun of Auchinhuffle, co. Banff, 28 October, 1577, and another of the barony of Burleigh, 29 November, 1606; in which latter year he was ambassador to the Duke of Tuscany and Lorraine, as appears from Sibbald's Fife, where it is stated that Sir Michael was honoured, by letters patent, bearing date at Roystoun, 7 August, 1606, with the title of LORD BALFOUR, of Burleigh. In Carmichael's Tracts it is mentioned that Sir Michael Balfour, Knt., of Balgarvie, is made and created "Barone Banaret and Lord of our Soveraine's parliament, to be stiled in all time coming Lord Balfour of Burlie, at Whitehall, 16 July, 1607," without any mention of heirs in his patent of creation. His lordship was subsequently sworn of the privy council. This nobleman m. 1st, Margaret Adamson; and 2ndly, Margaret, dau. of Lundie; by the latter lady he left at his decease, 1619, a dau., his sole heiress,

MARGARET BALFOUR, who m. Robert, son of Robert Arnot, of Newton, chamberlain of Fife, which Robert assumed, on his marriage, the surname of Balfour, and enjoyed the title of Lord Balfour, of Burleigh, sitting in parliament as a baron. At the meeting of parliament in 1610, he was chosen president thereof for the session, and continued in the office to 1641. He was one of the commissioners for the treaty of peace with England, 1640 and 1641, and was one of the privy councillors constituted "ad vitam aut culpam" by the parliament of Scotland, 13 November, 1641. His lordship was much engaged in the subsequent public transactions, and was one of the peers who opposed "the engagement" to march into England for the rescue of the king. He d. at Burleigh, 10 August, 1663, having had, by Margaret, his wife (who d. at Edinburgh, in June, 1639), one son and four daus., viz.,

1 JOHN, of whom presently.
1 Jean, m. in 1628, David, 2nd Earl of Wemyss, d. 10 November, 1649, leaving a dau., Jean, Countess of Angus and Sutherland.
2 Margaret, m. to Sir James Crawford, of Kilbirnie, d. s. p.
3 Isabel, m. to Thomas, 1st Lord Ruthven, and had issue.
4 A dau., m. to her cousin Arnot, of Ferny.

The son and heir,

JOHN BALFOUR, 3rd Lord Balfour, of Burleigh, who m. in 1649, Isabel, dau. of Sir William Balfour, Knt. of Pitcullo, lieutenant of the Tower of London, and d. before 1697, having had issue,

1 ROBERT, his heir.
2 John, of Fernie, attainted for his participation in the rising of 1715; he d. 1725, leaving three sons, of whom the eldest,

Arthur, of Fernie. an officer in the army, was restored to his estate by GEORGE II.; d. 1746, leaving three sons,
Sandford, d. s. p.
John, of Fernie, d. s. p 1795.
Francis, of Fernie, d. 1818, leaving a son,
FRANCIS BALFOUR, of Fernie, who was served heir male of the body of John, Lord Balfour, 1824, and d. 1854, leaving a son,

20

FRANCIS-WALTER BALFOUR, Esq. of Fernie, who claimed unsuccessfully the title of LORD BALFOUR of Burleigh.

3 Henry, of Dunbog, major of dragoons, father of Henry Balfour, of Dunbog.
1 Margaret, m. to Andrew, 3rd Lord Rollo, and had issue.
2 Isabel, d. unm.
3 Emilia, m. to Sir John Malcolm, Knt. of Innertiel, and had issue.
4 Jean, m. 1st, to Oliphant, of Gask, co. Perth, and 2ndly, to Sir Robert Douglas, of Kirkness.
5 Susan, m. to Robert Douglas, of Strathendry, and had issue.
6 Anne, b. 11 March, 1671; m. to Captain Robert Sinclair, s. p.

The eldest son,

ROBERT BALFOUR, Lord Balfour, of Burleigh, m. Lady Margaret Melville, only dau. of George, 1st Earl of Melville, and dying in 1713, left issue,

1 ROBERT, Master of Burleigh: in the lifetime of his father, and when very young, falling in love with a girl of inferior rank, was sent abroad to travel, in the hope of removing the attachment. Before he set out, he declared that if she married in his absence, he would put her husband to death. Notwithstanding this threat, she did marry Henry Stenhouse, a schoolmaster at Inverkeithing. Balfour, on his return, being informed of the match, proceeded directly to the school, and inflicted a mortal wound upon the unfortunate schoolmaster, in the midst of his scholars, 9 April, 1707, of which Stenhouse d. in twelve days afterwards. The Master of Balfour was tried for this foul murder in the high court of justiciary, 4 August, 1709, and sentenced, 29 November, to be beheaded, 6 January, 1710, but he escaped from prison a few days preceding by exchanging clothes with his sister. He was present at a meeting at Lochmaben, 29 May, 1714, when the Pretender's health was publicly drank at the cross; and he engaged in the rebellion the following year, for which he was ATTAINTED by act of parliament. He d. without issue in 1757.

1 Margaret, d. unm. at Edinburgh, 12 March, 1769.
2 Mary, m. in 1714, to brigadier-general Alexander Bruce, of Kennet, co. Clackmannan; d. 7 November, 1758, leaving a son and heir, ROBERT BRUCE, Esq. of Kennet, father of ROBERT BRUCE, Esq. of Kennet, a lord of session, as Lord Kennet, who d. 8 April, 1785, and was s. by his son, ALEXANDER BRUCE, Esq. of Kennet, who was s. in 1808 by his eldest son, ROBERT BRUCE, Esq. of Kennet, M.P. co. Clackmannan, m. Anne, dau. of William Murray, Esq. of Touchadam, and d. 13 Augu t, 1864, leaving a son, ALEXANDER HUGH, Lord Balfour of Burleigh, who established his right to the barony, 21 July, 1868.

Having thus carried down the senior line, we revert to Sir James Balfour's second son,

SIR JAMES BALFOUR, Knt., who having risen high in favour with JAMES I., was created by His Majesty LORD BALFOUR of Glenawley, co. Fermanagh, in the peerage of Ireland, by patent, dated 8 November, 1619. He m. 1st, Grissell, dau. and heir of Patrick Balfour, of Petcolla, co. Fife, by whom he had issue,

I. JAMES, 2nd baron. II. Alexander. III. P'erce, d s. p.
1. Margaret, m. John Gordon, of Ducherys, in Scotland.
II. Anne, m. 1st, Sir John Wemyss, Knt., of Loghly, co. Fife; and 2ndly, Archibald Hamilton, Esq., of Ballygawley, co. Tyrone, eldest son of Malcolm Hamilton, D.D., Archbishop of Cashel, by whom she had no issue.
III. Elizabeth, d. unm.

Lord Balfour m. 2ndly, Lady Elizabeth Hay, dau. of George, 6th Earl of Erroll, previously wife of Sir John Leslie, Knt., 10th Baron of Balquhain; and 3rdly, Hon. Anne Blayney, dau. of Edward, 1st Lord Blayney, but had no further issue. He d. 18 October, 1634, and was buried in the church of the Blackfriars, London, when he was s. by his eldest son, JAMES, 2nd Lord Balfour, of Glenawley, who signed his father's funeral certificate in Ulster's Office, 29 July, 1635, m. Anne, dau. of Sir Francis Goldsmith, Knt., of Gravesend, co. Kent, and d. s. p. 26 February following, leaving by his will, dated the 15th of the same month, Anne, his wife, his executrix. With his lordship the title of Glenawley EXPIRED. The will of the 1st lord, dated 16 October, 1634, was proved 5 March following. In it he mentions his relative, Sir William Balfour, Knt., of Westminster, whose dau. Susan, m. Hugh Hamilton de Deserf, and whose son was ancestor of the Balfours, now TOWNLEY-BALFOURS, of Townley Hall, co. Louth.

Arms.—Arg., a chev., sa., charged with an otter's head erased, of the first; in base, a saltier, couped, of the second.

BALIOL—BARONS BALIOL.

Lineage.

In the reign of WILLIAM RUFUS,
GUY, GUIDO, or WIDO DE BALIOL had a grant from the crown

of the Barony of Biwell, in Northumberland, and thus became its feudal lord. He was s. by his son (or, by some accounts, the son of Barnard de Baliol),

Barnard de Baliol, a military commander of reputation, who participated in the victory achieved over the Scots, in 1138, at Northallerton, known in history as the "Battle of the Standard," but was afterwards taken prisoner, at Lincoln, with King Stephen. Upon the incursion of the Scots, in the 20th Henry II., Barnard de Baliol again took up arms, and joining Robert de Stutevile, proceeded to the relief of Alnwick Castle, and having surprised the besiegers, seized the king of Scots with his own hand, and sent him prisoner to the castle of Richmond. In the course of this forced march to Alnwick, when, in consequence of a dense fog, a halt was recommended, Baliol exclaimed. "Let those stay that will, I am resolved to go forward, although none follow me, rather than dishonour myself by tarrying here." This feudal chief is supposed to have been the founder of the fortress upon the banks of the Tees, called "Barnard Castle." He was a munificent benefactor to the church, having, among other grants, bestowed lands upon the abbey of St. Mary, at York, and upon the monks at Riebault, for the health of his own soul, and that of his wife, Agnes de Pincheni. He was s. by his son,

Eustace de Baliol, who gave £100 for license to marry the widow of Robert Fitzpiers. This feudal lord had issue,

I. Hugh, of whom presently.
II. Henry, m. Lora, one of the co-heiresses of Christian, wife of William de Mandeville, Earl of Essex, and heirs of Peter, lord of the barony of Valoines, and dying in the 30th of Henry III. (1245-6), his widow, the Lady Lauretta (as termed in the record), had livery of all the lands in Essex, Hertford, and Norfolk, which he held of her inheritance. They had issue,
1 Alexander, living 56th Henry III. (1271-2).
2 Guy Baliol.
III. Eustace, m. Hawise, dau. and heiress of Ralph de Boyville de Levyngton, a baron of Northumberland, and his wife, Ada, who had been the widow of William de Furnivall. In the 45th Henry III. (1260-1), this Eustace was sheriff of Cumberland and governor of the castle of Carlisle. In nine years afterwards, assuming the cross, he attended Prince Edward to the Holy Land.

Eustace de Baliol, sen., was s. by his son,

Hugh de Baliol, who was certified to hold the barony of Biwell of the crown by the service of five knights' fees, and to find thirty soldiers for the guard of Newcastle-upon-Tyne, as his progenitors had done from the time of Rufus. He held likewise the lordship of Hiche, in Essex, in capite, as an augmentation of his barony, by the gift of Henry II. From King John he obtained the lands of Richard de Unfranville, and of Robert de Meisnell, in the county of York, in consideration of his services in the baronial war. In the 18th of that monarch's reign, he was joined with Philip de Hulcotes in defence of the northern border towards Scotland; and when the King of Scots had subjugated the whole of Northumberland for Lewis of France, those generals held out stoutly all the fortresses upon the line of the Tees, particularly that of Barnard Castle, where Eustace de Vesci (who had married the Scottish monarch's sister), coming with his royal brother-in-law to the siege, was slain. Hugh de Baliol, styled by Matthew Paris, "dives et potens," was s. by his son,

John de Baliol. This feudal lord m. Devorgilda, younger dau. and eventually sole heir, of Alan, Lord of Galloway, a great baron of Scotland, by Margaret his wife, sister of John le Scot, the last Earl of Chester, and one of the heirs of David, sometime Earl of Huntingdon, from which alliance arose the claim of the Baliols to the crown of Scotland. By this illustrious lady he acquired the Scottish barony of Galloway. In the 28th of Henry III., when ways and means were required to discharge the debt incurred by the war in Gascony, John de Baliol was one of the committee of twelve chosen to report to parliament upon the subject; and the next year he paid £30 for thirty knights' fees, which he held towards the levy in aid, for marrying the king's dau. He was afterwards sheriff of Cumberland for six successive years, and governor of the castle of Carlisle. Subsequently he had a military summons to attend the king at Chester, to oppose the Welsh, and was sheriff of the counties of Nottingham and Derby for three years; at which time he had the honour of Pevcrell committed to his custody. In the baronial contest he adhered faithfully to the king, and fell into the hands of the Earl of Leicester, with his royal master, at the battle of Lewes, in 1264; but he appears to have effected his escape, and to have joined the other loyal barons in raising fresh troops for the captive monarch's redemption. This John Baliol and his wife were the founders of the college that bears the name of Baliol, at Oxford. He d. in 1268, and was s. by his son (then twenty-eight years of age),

Hugh de Baliol, who m. Anne, or Agnes, dau. of William

21

de Valence, Earl of Pembroke, but dying in 1271, without issue, was s. by his brother,

Alexander de Baliol. The barony inherited by this feudal lord consisted of more than five-and-twenty extensive lordships He d. s. p. 1279, leaving Eleanor de Genoure, his widow, and was s. by his brother,

John de Baliol, who m. Isabel, dau. of John de Warren, 7th Earl of Surrey. This feudal nobleman was one of the chief competitors for the crown of Scotland in the reign of Edward I., and was eventually declared king, by the decision of that monarch, to whose arbitration the claimants submitted their pretensions.

To elucidate Baliol's right to the Caledonian sceptre it will be necessary to digress somewhat into the genealogy of the Scottish princes.

David, King of Scotland, had an only son Prince Henry, of Scotland, who d. v. p., leaving three sons, viz.,

I. Malcolm, who ascended the throne as Malcolm IV., and was s. by his brother.
II. William the Lion, father of Alexander II., father of

    Alexander III. This prince m. Margaret, dau. of Henry III., King of England, and had three children, viz.,
    Alexander,} both died in the lifetime of their father, s. p.
    David,   }
    Margaret, m. in 1281, Eric, King of Norway, and left an only dau.,
        Margaret, who was acknowledged Queen of Scots, but died in her passage from Norway, and with her terminated the lines of David's two sons, Malcolm and William.

III. David, Earl of Huntingdon, in England, m. Maud, dau. of Hugh, and sister and co-heiress of Ranulph, Earl of Chester, by whom he left issue at his decease in 1219,

    Henry, d. s. p.
    David, d. s. p.
    John, surnamed Le Scot, s. to the earldom of Huntingdon, and became Earl of Chester, d. s. p.
    Margaret, m. to Alan, Lord of Galloway, and had two daus. and co-heirs, Christian, m. William, Earl of Albemarle, and d. s. p.: and Devorouill, or Devorgilda, who m. John de Baliol, and was mother of John Baliol, King of Scotland, ut supra.
    Isabella, m. to Robert Bruce, and had a son, Robert Bruce, the celebrated claimant for the Scottish crown.
    Ada, m. Henry de Hastings, Lord Hastings, and left a son and heir,
        Henry, Lord Hastings, father of John, Lord Hastings, a claimant for the Scottish throne.

By this table, the claim of Baliol seems indisputable, his mother, who was then alive, having abdicated her right in his favour, but Bruce contended that he was himself one step of kindred nearer to David, Earl of Huntingdon, than Baliol, being that nobleman's grandson; and he met the question of seniority, by alleging, that he had to contest that point in reality with Baliol's mother, and that being a male, he ought to be preferred to a female, according to the law and usage of nations, of which he adduced divers precedents. Edward decided, however, in favour of Baliol, and the new king swore fealty to the English monarch, on 30 November, 1292, as his superior lord. In the oath he acknowledged the sovereignty of the king of England over Scotland, in very express and submissive terms; and he caused an authentic act of allegiance to be drawn up. Baliol's installation followed, and was performed at Scone, with the usual ceremonies, all the Scottish lords swearing fealty to him, save Robert Bruce, who absented himself. Thus the English feudal barony of Baliol merged in the royal dignity of Scotland. John Baliol, king of Scotland, d. in 1314, and his two sons, King Edward Baliol, and Henry Baliol, dying s. p., the former in 1363, the latter in 1332, the right of representation of the Kings of Scotland became vested in his, John's, sisters, of whom there were four,

Margaret, who d. s. p.
Ada, wife of William de Lindsay, of Lamberton.
Cicely, wife of John de Burgh.
Mary, wife of John Comyn, Lord of Badenoch,

The dau. and heir of Ada Baliol and William Lindsay was Christian Lindsay, wife of Ingelram Sire de Coucy. Her right to represent the royal House of Scotland (which carried along with it the representation of the Anglo-Saxon kings) descended through the House of St. Pol to that of the Royal Bourbons, and is now vested in His Royal Highness Henry, Duke of Bordeaux, Count de Chambord, and failing him, it will descend to his sister's son, Robert de Bourbon, Duke of Parma.

Cicely Baliol and John de Burgh had two daus. and co-heirs, viz.,

1 Hawys, who, by her husband, Thomas de Gresley, had a dau. Joan, wife of John, 2nd Lord de la Warre, and from her descended two brothers, viz., Sir Owen West, whose only

dan. and heir, Mary, *m.* Sir Adrian Poynings, and was mother of two co-heiresses, Mary, *m.* to Sir Edward Moore, of Larden, and Ann, *m.* to Sir George Moore, of Loseley, and GEORGE WEST, ancestor of the WESTS, EARLS OF DE LA WARRE.

2 Dervorgilla, wife of Robert, 1st Lord Fitzwalter. From her dau., Christian, wife of John le Marechal, and her grand-dau,, Hawyse, wife of Robert, 2nd Lord Morley, descended a long line of Lords Morley. William, 12th Lord Morley and Lord Monteagle, had a dau., Catherine Parker, wife of John Savage, Earl Rivers, through whose two daus. the royal blood of Baliol has descended to the families of Pitt, Lord Rivers, and Lane Fox, of Bramham, and to that of Colyear, Earl of Portmore.

MARY BALIOL *m.* JOHN COMYN, Lord of Badenoch, who was heir general of King DONALD BANE, being 4th in descent from Hextilda, that monarch's grand-dau. His son, John Comyn, Lord of Badenoch, had two daus. (in whose descendants are united the co-heirship of Baliol with that of Donald Bane), viz.;

1 Joan Comyn, wife of David de Strathbolgie, Earl of Athol. Her descendant, Elizabeth Percy, of Athol, the wife of Sir Thomas Burgh, was ancestress to a line of Lords Burgh and Baronets Boothby, of whom the co-heirship general vested in the Venerable Thomas Thorpe, archdeacon of Bristol.

2 Elizabeth Comyn, wife of Richard, 2nd Lord Talbot, and ancestress to a long line of Earls of Shrewsbury, whose elder branch ended in an heiress, Lady Alithea Talbot, who, in 1612, *m.* Thomas Howard, Earl of Arundel and Surrey. From her are descended the Dukes of Norfolk; but her two heirs general are Lords Stourton and Petre.*

Arms—Gu , an orle, arg.

BALIOL—BARONS BALIOL.

By Writ of Summons, dated 26 September, 1300.

Lineage.

SIR ALEXANDER BALIOL, of Cavers, a kinsman of JOHN DE BALIOL, King of Scotland, being in the retinue of that magnificent prelate, Anthony Beke, bishop of Durham, and Patriarch of Jerusalem, in the expedition made by King EDWARD I. into Flanders, was restored to all his lands in Scotland, in the 25th of that monarch's reign, and was summoned to parliament, as a BARON, from the 26th September, 1300, to the 3rd November, 1306. His lordship *m.* Isabell, dau. and heiress of Richard de Chilham, and widow of David de Strabolgi, Earl of Athol, by whom he obtained, for life, the castle and manor of Chilham, in the county of Kent, and was father of

SIR ALEXANDER BALIOL, of Cavers, lord chamberlain of Scotland 1290, who suffered forfeiture. His son, or brother, THOMAS BALIOL, having no issue, resigned Cavers to his brother-in-law, William, Earl of Douglas, in 1368. The BARONY OF BALIOL is EXTINCT.

BARD—VISCOUNT BELLAMONT.

By Letters Patent, dated 8 July, 1646.

Lineage.

HENRY BARD, younger of two sons of the Rev. George Bard, vicar of Staines, in Middlesex, by Susan his wife, dau. of John Dudley, and the lineal descendant of the family of Bard of North Kelsey, in Lincolnshire, returning from his travels in the East about the time the civil war of CHARLES's reign broke out, entered into the royal service, obtained a colonel's commission, and having subsequently gallantly distinguished himself, particularly at the battle of Cheriton Down, was created successively a BARONET of England, in 1644, and a peer of Ireland, as Baron Bard, of Dromboy, in the co. of Meath, and Viscount Bellamont, in the co. of Dublin, 8 July, 1646. His lordship *m.* Anne, dau. of Sir William Gardyner, Knt., of Peckham, co. Surrey, and by her (who *d.* in 1668) had two daus., of whom the elder, Anne, became mistress to her father's patron, Prince Rupert, and by him was mother of Dudley Bard, slain at the siege of Buda, in 1686; and Persiana, the younger, *m.* her cousin, Nathaniel Bard, Esq. of Caversfield.

Arms—Sa., on a chev., between ten martlets, arg., five plates.

* To the researches of my learned and esteemed friend, Alexander Sinclair, Esq., the ablest, probably, of all Scottish genealogists, I am much indebted for these details of the descendants of the royal Baliols.

BARDOLF—BARONS BARDOLF.

By Writ of Summons, dated 6 February, 1299.

Lineage.

The first of this family upon record,

WILLIAM BARDOLF, was sheriff of Norfolk and Suffolk, from the 16th to 21st of HENRY II., inclusive, and after him came his son and heir,

THOMAS BARDOLF, who, upon the scutage being levied of such barons as did not attend King HENRY II. into Ireland, in the 18th of that monarch's reign, nor contribute men or money to that service, paid £25 for the scutage of those knights' fees which formerly belonged to Ralph Hanselyn, Baron of Schelford, in the county of Nottingham, whose dau. and heiress, ROSE, he had married. This Thomas obtained from William, brother of King HENRY II., the Lordship of Bradewell, to hold to himself and his heirs, by the service of one knight's fee; three parts of which he bestowed upon his three daus., viz., ——, wife of Robert de St. Remigio; ——, wife of William Bacun; and ——, wife of Baldwin de Thoni. Thomas Bardolf was *s.* by his son,

DOUN BARDOLF, who marrying Beatrix, dau. and heiress of William de Warren, acquired by her the Barony of Wirmegay, in the county of Norfolk. He *d.* in 1209, leaving his widow Beatrix surviving, who gave 3100 marks to the king, for livery of her father's lands, and a reasonable dowry from the lands belonging to her husband; as also that she might not be compelled to marry again, contrary to her inclination. Doun Bardolf was *s.* by his son,

WILLIAM BARDOLF, who, in the 26th of HENRY III., attended that monarch in person in the expedition which he then made into France. In the next year, he had livery of the honour of Wirmegay, which during his minority had been in the hands of Hubert de Burgh, Earl of Kent; and he subsequently obtained royal charters for markets and free warren throughout his different lordships and manors. In the 41st of the same monarch, he attended the king in his expedition into Wales, and was soon after constituted governor of Nottingham Castle. He was at the fatal battle of Lewes, under the royal banner, in 1264, and was there taken prisoner, along with the king. He *d.* in the 4th of EDWARD I., *anno* 1275, and was *s.* by his son,

WILLIAM BARDOLF, who, doing homage, had livery of his lands, lying in the counties of Leicester, Lincoln, Nottingham, Norfolk, and Sussex, and soon after obtained charters for fairs and markets to be holden at his different manors. He *m.* Julian, dau. of Hugh de Gurnay, and dying before 1292, was *s.* by his son,

HUGH BARDOLF, who, in the 22nd of EDWARD I., had summons, with other eminent persons, to attend the king, to advise upon the affairs of the realm, and was subsequently summoned to parliament, as BARON BARDOLF, from the 6th of February, 1299 (27th EDWARD I.), to the 2nd of June, 1302. He *m.* Isabel, dau. and heiress of Robert Aguillon,* by whom he had two sons, Thomas and William. His lordship, who was employed in the French and Scottish wars of this reign, *d.* in 1303, and was *s.* by his elder son,

SIR THOMAS BARDOLF, K.B., as 2nd Baron Bardolf. This nobleman was summoned to parliament from 26 August, 1307, to 23 October, 1330 (4 EDW. I.), about the latter of which years his lordship *d.*, and was *s.* by his son,

JOHN BARDOLF, 3rd Baron Bardolf de Wirmegay, as latterly styled, summoned to parliament from 22 January, 1336, to 1 June, 1363. His lordship *m.* Elizabeth, dau. and co-heiress of Sir Roger D'Amorie, and, as Dugdale calls her, "that great woman," his wife, Elizabeth, by whom he acquired a considerable accession of landed property. This nobleman participated in the glories of the martial reign of EDWARD III., and attained the high dignity of BANNERET. He *d.* in 1371, and was *s.* by his son,

WILLIAM BARDOLF, 4th Baron Bardolf, summoned to parliament from 20 January, 1376, to 3 September, 1385, as "William Bardolf of Wormegay." His lordship *m.* Agnes, dau. of Sir Michael Poynings, Knt. He served in the French and Irish wars; latterly under John of Gaunt, Duke of Lancaster, and dying in 1385 (8 RICHARD II.), was *s.* by his son,

THOMAS BARDOLF DE WORMEGAY, 5th Baron Bardolf, sum-

* In Gibson's Camden's Britannia, it is stated that Sir Robert Aguillon had a castle at the manor of Addington in Surrey, which was holden in fee, by the serjeantcy, to find in the king's kitchen, on the coronation day, a person to make a dainty dish, called "Mapigernoun, or Dillegrout," and serve the same up to the king's table. This service has been regularly claimed by the lords of the said manor, and allowed at the respective coronations of the kings of England.—BANKS' *Extinct Peerage*.

moned to parliament from 12 September, 1390, to 25 August, 1404. This nobleman joining Henry, Earl of Northumberland, Thomas, earl marshal and Nottingham, and Richard Scroope, archbishop of York, in their rebellion, *temp.* HENRY IV. (for which the earl marshal and archbishop were beheaded at York), he was forced, with the Earl of Northumberland, to fly to France; but those lords returning in about three years afterwards, and again raising the standard of insurrection in Yorkshire, they were attacked by the sheriff and the power of the county at Bramham Moor, where, sustaining a total defeat, the earl fell in the field, and Lord Bardolf died soon afterwards of his wounds. His lordship had married Avicia, dau. of Ralph, Lord Cromwell, and left two daus., viz.,

Anne, *m.* 1st, to Sir William Clifford, Knt., and 2ndly, to Reginald Lord Cobham.
Joane, *m.* to Sir William Phelip, K.G. (son of Sir John Phelip, Knt., of Donynton, Suffolk), a valiant soldier in the French wars of King HENRY V., to which monarch he was treasurer of the household, and at his decease had the chief direction of his funeral. Sir William is said to have been raised to the peerage by letters patent, as LORD BARDOLF, in the reign of HENRY VI., but he was never summoned to parliament. By Joane Bardolf he left an only dau. and heiress,
Elizabeth, who *m.* John, Viscount Beaumont (*see that title*).

Thomas, the 5th and unfortunate Lord Bardolf, dying thus, and being afterwards attainted, his BARONY and large possessions became forfeited. The estates were divided between Thomas Beaufort, Duke of Exeter, the king's brother, Sir George Dunbar, Knt., and the queen; but the latter proportion, upon the petition of Sir William Clifford and his wife, and Sir William Phelip and his wife, to the king, was granted in reversion, after the queen's decease, to those representatives of the attainted nobleman. Dugdale states " that Lord Bardolf's remains were quartered, and the quarters disposed of by being set upon the gates of London, York, Lenne, and Shrewsbury, while the head was placed upon one of the gates of Lincoln; his widow obtained permission, however, in a short time, to remove and bury them."

Arms—Az., three cinquefoils, or.

BARNEWALL—VISCOUNT BARNEWALL, OF KINGSLAND.

By Letters Patent, dated 29 June, 1646.

Lineage.

This great Anglo-Norman family which with the FitzGeralds, Butlers, and Plunketts was one of the most powerful of the old English pale, has been settled in Ireland from the period of the conquest of that country by Strongbow, in the reign of HENRY II. Of the three principal lines of the family of Barnewall, the BARONETS OF CRICKSTOWN are the eldest, their representative and the present chief of the family is SIR REGINALD BARNEWALL the 8th baronet. Next in order to the house of Crickstown comes the branch of the Lords Trimleston, whose peerage, created in 1461, is still extant, and the 2nd barony on the roll of the Irish peers. The present possessor is Thomas Barnewall, 16th lord. The youngest of all the branches of this family was that of the VISCOUNTS KINGSLAND, of whom we are now about to treat.

The first of the family who came to Ireland was SIR MICHAEL DE BERNEVAL, who landed at Beerhaven, in the co. of Cork, according to tradition, previous even to the landing of Strongbow in Leinster. Sir Michael was the direct descendant of ALANUS DE BERNEVAL, the companion in arms of WILLIAM THE CONQUEROR, whose name is inscribed on the roll of Battle Abbey. From this successful soldier the 12th in descent was SIR ULPHRAM DE BERNEVAL, who *m.* a dau. of the Lord Furnival, and by her left issue.

I. SIR CHRISTOPHER, who succeeded at Crickstown, and having *m.* Matilda, dau. and heiress of the last Lord of Drakestown and Drakerath, left issue two sons,
SIR NICHOLAS, who continued the elder line at Crickstown, whose descendant and representative is SIR REGINALD BARNEWALL, Bart., and
SIR ROBERT, who was created, in 1461, Baron Trimleston; his representative is Thomas Barnewall, present and 16th Lord Trimleston.
II John of Frankestown, from whom the Viscounts Kingsland derive.

Sir Ulphram dying was succeeded at Crickstown by his eldest son, Sir Christopher, while his 2nd son, JOHN DE BERNEVAL, of Frankestown, was high sheriff of the co. Meath in 1433; he *m.* Genet, dau. and heiress of —— Netterville, of Staffordston, and by her left issue.

SIR RICHARD BARNEWALL, of Fieldston, which estate he

23

acquired by his marriage with Catherine, dau. and heiress of John de la Feld (*or Delafeld*) of Fieldston : by this lady, he left, with other issue, a son,
SIR ROGER BARNEWALL, who *m.* Alison dau. of Christopher, 2nd Lord Trimleston, and dying was succeeded by his son,
SIR PATRICK BARNEWALL, of Fieldston, Gracedieu, and Turvey. On 7 October, 1534, he was made serjeant-at-law, and solicitor-general, and on 1 October, 1550, Master of the Rolls. By his marriage with Anne, eldest dau. of Richard Luttrell, of Luttrellstown, he left issue (with three daus., the eldest of whom became the wife of Sir Patrick Barnewall, of Crickstown) a son and successor,
SIR CHRISTOPHER BARNEWALL, of Turvey, who was high sheriff of the co. Dublin in 1560 : he *m.* Marian, dau. of Patrick Sherle, of Shallon, co. Meath, and sister and heiress of John Sherle. Sir Christopher built the present mansion at Turvey, and dying in 1607, left issue,

I. SIR PATRICK, his successor.
II. Lawrence, *d. unm.*
III. James, *d.* young.
IV. John, of Flemingston, whose line is EXTINCT.
I. Catherine, *m.* Thomas Finglas, of Westpalston.
II. Margaret, *m.* Nicholas, Lord Howth
III. Genet, *m.* Richard Stanihurst, of Court Duff.
IV. Alison, *m.* Sir Edward FitzGerald, of Tecroghan.
V. Elizabeth, *m.* John Finglas, Esq.
VI. Anne, *m.* Sir John Dralcot, of Mornington.
VII. Mable, *m.* Sir Richard Masterson, of Fernes
VIII. Ismay, *m.* Richard Delahyde, of Moyclare.
IX. Eleanor, *m.* James, 1st Earl of Roscommon.
X. Maud, *m.* Richard Belinge, Esq.
XI. Mary, *m.* Patrick, Lord Dunsany.

Sir Christopher dying was succeeded by his son,
SIR PATRICK BARNEWALL, of Turvey, who *m.* Mary, dau. of Sir Nicholas Bagenal, knight marshal of Ireland, by his wife Eleanor, dau. and co-heiress of Sir Edward Griffith, of Penthorn, in Wales, and by her left (with other issue,) a son and successor,
SIR NICHOLAS BARNEWALL, of Turvey, who, in reward for his services during the civil war, was created by King CHARLES I., 29 June, 1646, VISCOUNT BARNEWALL of KINGSLAND and BARON OF TURVEY. The patent conferring these titles is dated at Ragland Castle, the seat of the devoted loyalist, the Marquess of Worcester. The 1st Viscount Kingsland *m.* Bridget, eldest dau. and co-heir of Henry, the 12th Earl of Kildare, and widow of Rory O'Donel, Earl of Tyrconnel, and by her had issue : five sons and four daus.:

I. Christopher, *d. unm.*, before his father.
II. Patrick, whose services are mentioned in the preamble to his father's patent, also *d. unm.*, in England, before his father.
III. HENRY, who succeeded to the title.
IV. Francis, of Beggstown and Woodpark, co. Meath : he *m.* Jane, dau. of Philip FitzGerald, of Allgone, and dying, left issue by her
Nicholas, of Beggstown and Woodpark, who *m.* Catherine, 4th dau. of Robert, 9th Lord Trimleston, and sister of Mathias and John, 10th and 11th lords. By this marriage Nicholas Barnewall left issue,
Mathew Barnewall, of Beggstown, who *m.* Anne, dau. of Thomas McCann, Esq., and left issue
MATHEW, who became the 6th viscount.
V. Mathew, *d. unm.*
VI. James (Col.), father of
George, of Wimbledon, co. Dublin, who *m.* Miss O'Farrell, of Coyne Castle, co. Longford, and left (with two daus.) a son and successor,
Christopher, of Wimbledon, who *m.* Miss Norman, dau. of Thomas Norman, of Lanesborough, co. Longford, and had issue,
1 George, who *d. unm.*
2 Thomas, capt. Longford militia, who presented a petition to the House of Lords in 1835, claiming the titles of Viscount Kingsland and Baron of Turvey, but the case was never adjudicated on. Capt. Barnewell *m.*, and had several children.
I. Mary, *m.* Nicholas, 6th Viscount Gormanston.
II. Mable, *m.* Christopher, 2nd Earl of Fingall.
III. Eleanor, *m.* Charles Whyte, of Leixlip.
IV. Frances, *d. unm.*

The 1st Viscount Kingsland was succeeded by his 3rd but eldest surviving son,
HENRY, 2nd viscount, who *m.* 1st, Mary, dau. of John, 2nd Viscount Netterville, and by her had an only dau., Marian, who *m.* Thomas Nugent, styled Lord Riverston; he *m.* 2ndly, Lady Mary Nugent, dau. of Thomas, 3rd Earl of Westmeath, and by her left issue at his death in 1688,

I. NICHOLAS, his successor,
II. Richard, *d. unm.*
III. Joseph, *d. unm.*
IV. Christopher, *d. unm.*

Henry, 2nd viscount, dying in 1688, was succeeded by his eldest son,

NICHOLAS, 3rd viscount, who m. Mary, youngest dau. and co-heiress (with her sisters, Elizabeth, Viscountess Ross, and Frances, Viscountess Dillon) of George, Count Hamilton (uncle of James, 6th Earl af Abercorn) by his wife, Frances, eldest dau. and co-heiress (with her sister, Sarah, Duchess of Marlborough) of Richard Jennings, of Sandridge, in Hertfordshire ; after the death of Count Hamilton she became the wife of Richard Talbot, Earl and afterwards Duke of Tyrconnel : by this marriage the 3rd viscount had two sons and four daus.,

I. HENRY-BENEDICT, his successor.
II. George, who m. in 1752, Barbara Belasyse, 2nd dau. of Thomas, 2nd Earl of Falconberg, and at his death in 1771, he left issue by her an only son,

GEORGE, who succeeded as 5th viscount.

I. Mary,
II. Harriot. } d. unm.
III. Elizabeth. }
IV. Frances, m. Hon. Richard Barnewall, 3rd son of John, 11th Lord Trimleston. The great grandson of this marriage was

THOMAS, 16th LORD TRIMLESTON, thus heir of line of the Viscounts Kingsland.

The 3rd viscount was succeeded by his eldest son,

HENRY BENEDICT, 4th viscount, who m. 1735, Honora, dau. of Peter Daly, of Quansbury, co. Galway, but by her had no issue; he d. 1744, and was succeeded by his nephew,

GEORGE, 5th viscount, who having been brought up a Protestant, took the oaths and his seat in the House of Lords in Ireland, 18 January, 1787 ; he never married, and at his death, 5 April, 1800, the Turvey and other estates devolved on Lord Trimleston, and the title remained dormant till 1814, when the House of Lords admitted the claim of MATHEW BARNEWELL, who then became the 6th viscount (vide descendants of Francis, 4th son of 1st viscount) : he was three times married, but left no issue by any of his wives : he d. in 1833 (for a narrative of this lord's changeful career, see BURKE's Vicissitudes of Families), and since that period, with the exception of the petition of Captain THOMAS BARNEWELL, already mentioned, who claims ta be descended from Christopher, 4th son of the 2nd viscount, no attempt has been made to revive the honours of the family. The petition of Captain Barnewall was before the House of Lords in 1835.

Arms—Erm., a bordure, engr., gu.

BARRET—LORD BARRET OF NEWBURGH.

By Letters Patent, dated 17 October, 1627.

SIR EDWARD BARRETT, Knt., created a peer of Scotland, by the title of LORD BARRETT, OF NEWBURGH, 17 October, 1627, held the office of chancellor of the exchequer from 1635 to 1642, and d. in 1644, without issue by his wife, Anne, dau. of Sir Edward Cary, Knt. The title of course became EXTINCT. His kinsman, the Hon. Richard Lennard, of Horsford, in Norfolk, to whom he bequeathed his property in Essex, was youngest son of Richard, Lord Dacre : he took the name of Barrett, and was ancestor of Thomas Barrett-Lennard, Lord Dacre, who d. in 1786.

Arms—Per pale, arg. and gu., barry of four pieces, counterchanged.

BARRY — BARONS BARRY, OF BARRY'S COURT, VISCOUNTS BUTTEVANT, AND EARLS OF BARRYMORE.

WILLIAM DE BARRI, of Norman origin, from whom all the Barrys descend, m. Angareth, dau. of Nesta (the dau. of Rhese Gryffith, Prince of South Wales), and sister of Robert Fitz-Stephen, and Maurice Fitzgerald; by whom he had issue,

ROBERT, } of whom presently.
PHILIP, }
Walter.
GERALD, so well known as GIRALDUS CAMBRENSIS. from Cambria, the ancient name of Pembrokeshire, in which county

24

he was born in the year 1146. at Tenby, or the castle of Mainarpir. About the time of the birth of Philip the August, we find him then twenty years of age, a student at Paris. He was subsequently prebendary of Hereford, and being a person of great learning, was elected in 1176, by the chapter of St. David's, bishop of that see; but he declined the election, because unsanctioned, according to law, by the king, and passed a second time into France, to pursue his studies at Paris, where he became so celebrated that he was chosen in 1179 professor of canon law, by the university ; he rejected the honour, however, in expectation of more solid advantages at home. In four years afterwards, he was invited to court by King HENRY II., and appointed one of the royal chaplains. In 1185, he accompanied John, Earl of Moreton (afterwards King JOHN), as his private secretary, into Ireland, and employed a five years' residence there in the collection of materials for writing the Topography of Ireland, and the Vaticinal History of its Conquest; and having already written a description of England and Wales, he travelled to Jerusalem, and wrote De Mirabilibus Terræ Sanctæ. Upon his return, his uncle David, bishop of St. David's, made him archdeacon of Brecknock ; in which capacity he assisted, anno 1188, Baldwin, archbishop of Canterbury, in preaching the Christian doctrine to the Welsh, and inciting them to the Holy War. But in 1197, Jeffry Fitz-Piers, Earl of Essex, having been made justiciary of England, and having marched with a great force into Wales, was so much incensed against Giraldus, by the bishop of Bangor's insinuations of his being an enemy to the king, that he seized upon all his lands at Brecknock, and passing, on his return, through Gloucester, directed a precept to the archdeacon of Oxford to take into his hands all the revenues Giraldus had within his archdeaconry ; whereof Gerald complained by letter to the bishop of Ely, the dean of London, and the archdeacon of Bucks, setting forth that among his other sufferings, he had been dis-seized of his prebend of Hereford and his church of Chesterton, in Oxfordshire. He afterwards refused the bishopric of Leighlin and Ferns; but accepted, in 1199, that of St. David's. He could not, however, obtain a confirmation from the Holy See, being opposed by Geoffry, prior of Lanthony, nominated by Hubert, archbishop of Canterbury, which caused his resignation of the archdeaconry. He d. about the year 1215, and was buried in the cathedral of St. David's.

The eldest son,

SIR ROBERT BARRI, accompanied Robert Fitz-Stephen into Ireland, in 1169, to assist Dermod, King of Leinster, to regain his kingdom, and after a series of gallant exploits, which obtained for him the name of " Barry-More," was slain at Lismore, about the year 1185. His brother and successor,

PHILIP DE BARRY, who built the castle of Barry's Court in 1206, was ancestor of

DAVID DE BARRY, styled the 1st VISCOUNT OF BUTTEVANT, who was appointed by the king, in 1267, lord justice of Ireland, subdued the McCarties and Geraldines, and ended the feuds between them and the Burkes. In 1273, he had free warren in all his lands, as Lord of Buttevant, being designated "a rich noble baron." His descendant,

JOHN BARRY, was living at Buttevant in 1317, and was father of

DAVID DE BARRY, from whom we pass to his lineal descendant,

WILLIAM BARRY, who in 1490 sat as premier viscount in parliament, but was slain by his brother, David, archbishop of Cork and Cloyne, in 1499; which David shared himself a similar fate, being killed by Thomas Barry ; and after he had been buried twenty days, his body was taken up and publicly burned, by the command of Maurice, Earl of Desmond. William Barry, Viscount Buttevant, left issue, Juliana, m. to Edmund de Courcy, by whom she was grandmother of John, Lord Kingsale, and his successor,

JOHN BARRY, Lord Barry and Viscount Buttevant, who was s. by his son,

JAMES FITZ-JOHN BARRY, Lord Barry and Viscount Buttevant, who on 9 February, 1556, made an entail of his estate, on failure of issue of his own body, to his cousin, James Fitz-Richard Barry-Roe ; and dying s. p. in 1557, was s. by his said kinsman,

JAMES FITZ-RICHARD BARRY-ROE, Lord of Ibawne and Viscount Buttevant, who had a special livery of the inheritance granted him, 27 April, 1561, by the title of James Barry, Viscount Barrymore, alias Lord of Barrymore, and obtained, on 12 March, 1567, from Queen ELIZABETH, a lease for twenty-one years of divers abbey lands, among which were those of Buttevant. In the parliament held at Dublin, 12 January, 1559, he sat as premier viscount. His lordship m. Ellen, dau. of Cormac MacCarthy Reagh, and had issue,

I. RICHARD, VISCOUNT BUTTEVANT, deaf and dumb, d. s. p.
II. DAVID. of whom presently.
III WILLIAM. of Lislee. whose grandson,

WILLIAM BARRY, of Lislee, forfeited his estate temp. CROM-

WELL; he m. Ellen, dau. and heir of Charles McCarthy, Esq., of Castlemore, co. Cork, and had issue; of which the eldest son, DAVID, was declared by a decree in Chancery, 1706, heir to his maternal grandmother.

From JAMES BARRY, of Ballynacraheen, co. Cork, Esq., stated to have been another son of William Barry, of Lislee, and Ellen McCarthy, his wife, descended

JAMES REDMOND BARRY, Esq., who claimed the VISCOUNTY OF BUTTEVANT, in 1825.

The 2nd son,

DAVID FITZ-JAMES BARRY, Viscount Buttevant and Baron of Ibawne, was one of the lords of the parliament held by Sir John Perrot, 26 April, 1585, but afterwards joined in the rebellion of the Earl of Desmond. He made his peace, however, in the time of Lord Grey's government, by paying a fine of £500. From that period he became remarkable for his fidelity to the crown, was of council to Sir George Carew, president of Munster, and did great service against the rebels in that province. In 1601, he was made general of the Provincials, and after the defeat of the Spaniards, and raising the siege of Kinsale, anno 1602, the president placed 1,600 men under his command: when his lordship, with his brother John, and Sir George Thornton, commander of 500 English soldiers, did considerable service; and by taking a very large prey of cattle, forced several, from the extreme misery to which they were reduced, to return to their allegiance and to sue for pardon. In recompense of these services, King JAMES I. made his lordship leases for thirty-one years of a great portion of the lands of the M'Carthys. His lordship m. Ellen, younger dau. of David, Viscount Fermoy, and had issue,

DAVID FITZ-DAVID, who m. Elizabeth, dau. of Richard, Lord Poer, and dying before his father, left a son,

DAVID, who s. his grandfather.

Honora, m. 1st, to Gerald Fitz-Gerald, of the Decies, by whom she had no issue; and 2ndly, to Patrick Browne, Esq., of Mulrankin, co. Wexford, by whom she had William, Walter, and several daus.

Helena, m. 1st, to John, son and heir of Richard, Lord Poer, of Curraghmore, by whom she had an only son, heir to his grandfather. Her ladyship m. 2ndly, Thomas, Earl of Ormonde, but had no issue; and 3rdly, in 1631, Sir Thomas Somerset (3rd son of Edward, Earl of Worcester), who was created, in 1626, Viscount Cashel, by whom she had an only dau., Helena, who d. unm.

Ellen, m. to Sir John Fitzgerald, Knt., of Ballymaloe, co. Cork.

Catherine, m. to Richard Burke, Esq., of Derry Maclaghny, co. Galway.

Margaret, m. to Robert, Earl of Roscommon.

Lord Buttevant d. 10 April, 1617, and was s. by his grandson,

DAVID BARRY, Viscount Buttevant, who highly distinguished himself by his fidelity to the English interest during the civil commotions in Ireland, and was created, 28 February, 1628, EARL OF BARRYMORE. His lordship m. 29 July, 1621, Alice, eldest dau. of Richard, Earl of Cork, and by her (who m., 2ndly, John Barry, Esq., of Liscarrol) he left at his decease, 29 September, 1642, with two daus. (Ellen, m. to Sir Arthur Denny, Knt., of Tralee; and Catherine, wife of Edward Denny, Esq., of Castle Lyons), two sons, of whom the elder,

RICHARD BARRY, 2nd Earl of Barrymore, b. in 1630, m. 1st, Susan, dau. of Sir William Killegrew, Knt., by whom he had three daus., Mary, m. to the Rev. Gerald Barry, Catherine, m. to John Townsend, of Castle Townsend, co. of Cork; and Susan. He m. 2ndly, in 1656, Martha, dau. of Henry Lawrence, Esq., by whom he had a son LAWRENCE, his heir; and a dau., Theodora, wife of Charles May, Esq.; and 3rdly, Dorothy, dau. and heir of John Ferrer, Esq., of Dromore, co. Down, by whom he had four sons and four daus., Dorothy m. to Sir John Jacob, Bart.; Anne, m. to Dr. Henry Maule, Bishop of Meath; Margaret, m. to Thomas Crosbie, Esq., of Ballyheigue; and Elizabeth, who d. young. The earl d. in 1694, and was s. by his son,

LAWRENCE BARRY, 3rd Earl of Barrymore, who m. in 1682, Catharine, dau. of Richard, Lord Santry, but by her (who m. 2ndly, in 1699, Francis Gash, Esq.; and 3rdly, in 1729, Sir Henry Piers, Bart., of Tristernagh) leaving no issue at his decease, 17 April, 1699, he was s. by his half-brother,

JAMES BARRY, 4th Earl of Barrymore, b. in 1667, a lieutenant-general in the army, who m. 1st, Elizabeth, sister of Charles, Earl of Cork, and by her had a dau., Anne, m. to James Maule, Esq. His lordship m. 2ndly, Lady Elizabeth Savage, dau. and heir of Richard, Earl Rivers, by whom he had a dau. Penelope, wife of Major-General James Cholmondeley; and 3rdly, 12 July, 1716, Lady Anne Chichester, dau. of Arthur, Earl of Donegal, by whom he had issue,

I. JAMES, his heir.

II. Richard, M.P. for Wigan; m. in 1749, Jane, dau. and heir of Arthur Hyde, Esq., of Castle Hyde, M.P. for the county of Cork, but d. s. p. 23 November, 1787.

III. Arthur, d. unm. in 1770.

IV. John-Smith, of Marbury, in Cheshire, b. 28 July, 1725; m. in 1746, Dorothy, dau. and co-heir of Hugh Smith, Esq., of Weald Hall, Essex, and had issue, with a dau., two sons.

1 JAMES-HUGH, of Marbury, Cheshire, and Foaty Island, co. Cork, b. 1748, who d. without legitimate issue: his son was the late JOHN-SMITH BARRY, Esq., of Marbury and Foaty Island.

2 Richard, d. s. p.

I. Catharine, d. in 1738.

II. Anne, m. to — Taylor, Esq., and d. 21 March, 1758.

His lordship d. at Castle Lyons, 5 January, 1747, and was s. by his son,

JAMES BARRY, 5th Earl of Barrymore, b. 25 May, 1717, who m. Margaret, dau. and heir of Paul Davys, Viscount Mountcashel, and dying 19 December, 1751, was s. by his only son,

RICHARD BARRY, 6th Earl of Barrymore (captain 9th dragoons), b. October, 1745, who m. 1767, Lady Emily Stanhope, 3rd dau. of William, Earl of Harrington, and by her (who d. in France, 1782) had issue,

I. RICHARD, his heir.

II. HENRY, successor to his brother.

III. Augustus, b. 16 July, 1773, in holy orders, d. s. p. 27 November, 1818.

I. Carolina, b. 17 May, 1768, m. July, 1788, Louis Pierre Drummond, Count de Melfort, of the French service, son of Louis, Count de Melfort.

His lordship d. at Dromana, 1 August, 1773, and was interred at Castle Lyons, co. Cork. His son,

RICHARD BARRY, 7th Earl of Barrymore, b. 14 August, 1769, M.P. for Heytesbury. Of this nobleman Sir Egerton Brydges gives the following description :—" With talents to shine in a course of honourable ambition, with wit, good nature, and engaging manners, he shone a meteor of temporary wonder and regret, by freaks which would have disgraced Buckingham or Rochester, until the accidental explosion of his musket, while he was conveying some French prisoners from Folkestone to Dover, as captain in the Berkshire militia, put an end to his troubles and his follies on 6 March, 1793." He left no issue. His brother and heir,

HENRY BARRY, 8th Earl of Barrymore, lieutenant-colonel South Cork Militia, b. 16 August, 1770, m. 16 January, 1795, Anne, eldest dau. of Jeremiah Coghlan, Esq., of Ardo, co. Waterford, but d. s. p. in 1824, when all his honours became EXTINCT.

Arms.—Arg., three bars, gemelles, gu.

BARRY—BARON BARRY, OF SANTRY.

By Letters Patent, dated 18 February, 1661.

Lineage.

The Barrys of Santry derived, it is supposed, from a branch of the Barrymore family.

SIR JAMES BARRY, b. in 1603, eldest son of Alderman Richard Barry, M.P., lord mayor of Dublin in 1610, and nephew of Nicholas Barry, ancestor of the Barrys of Newtown Barry, co. Wexford, entered on the profession of the law, and attained its highest honours, becoming eventually chief justice of the King's Bench in Ireland. He received the honour of knighthood in 1634, and in 1659 was chosen chairman of the convention which met in Dublin, and proceeded to the transaction of business, in defiance of the orders issued by the council of state in England for their dissolution. They asserted their liberty and independence, proclaimed their detestation of the king's murder, and published a declaration for the re-admission of the secluded members into the parliament of England. At the Restoration, these services were not forgotten, and Sir James was advanced, shortly after that auspicious event (by privy seal, dated 18 December, 1660, and by patent dated 18 February, 1661), to the peerage of Ireland as BARON BARRY, of Santry, co. Dublin. His lordship m. Catharine, dau. of Sir William Parsons, lord justice of Ireland, and dying 9 February, 1672, left, with four daus. (Anne, m. 1st, to Stephen Butler, of Belturbet, and 2ndly, to the Hon. Raymond Fitzmaurice; Elizabeth, m. 4 December, 1683, Thomas Anderton, Esq.; Catherine, and Mary), three sons,

I. RICHARD.   II. James.   III. William, d. s. p.

The eldest son,

RICHARD BARRY, 2nd Lord Santry, m. Elizabeth, dau. of Henry Jenery, Esq., and d. 1694, leaving (with four daus., Catharine, m. 1st, Lawrence, Earl of Barrymore; 2ndly,

Francis Gash, Esq.; 3.dly, Sir Henry Piers, of Tristernagh, Part., and d. 8 June, 1737; Frances, m. 23 November, 1696, John Keating, Esq.; Elizabeth, wife of James Napper, Esq.; and Dorothea) a son and successor,

HENRY BARRY, 3rd Lord Santry, b. in 1680, who m. 9 February, 1702, Bridget, only dau. of Sir Thomas Domvile, Bart., of Templeogue, and dying 27 January, 1734, was s. by his only son,

HENRY BARRY, 4th Lord Santry, b. 3 September, 1710, who was brought to trial before his peers, in 1739, for the murder of Loughlin Murphy, a footman, and found guilty, whereby he was attainted of high treason, condemned to suffer death, and all his estates became forfeited to the crown. By the mediation, however, of the Duke of Devonshire, the lord lieutenant, and several other noblemen, Lord Santry obtained a full pardon for his life, under the great seal, 17 June, 1739, and subsequently, in 1741, a re-grant of his estates. He m. 1st, 8 May, 1737, Anne, dau. of William Thornton, Esq., of Finglas; and 2ndly, Elizabeth Shore, of Derby, but d. without issue, 18 March, 1750-1. By his will he devised his estates to his uncle (ex parte maternd) Sir Compton Domvile, Bart., of Templeogue, co. Dublin, and Santry is now, in consequence, the seat of the present SIR CHARLES-COMPTON-WILLIAM DOMVILE, Bart.

Arms.—Arg., three bars, gemelles, gu.

BASSET—BARONS BASSET, OF WELDEN.

By Writ of Summons, dated 6 February, 1299

Lineage.

Few families in the early annals of England can boast of a more eminent progenitor than the Bassets, and the descendants of few of the Anglo-Norman nobles attained a higher degree of power than those of

RALPH BASSET (son of Thurstan, the Norman), who was justice of England under King HENRY I. We find his son Ralph, in the reign of STEPHEN, "abounding in wealth, and erecting a strong castle upon some part of his inheritance in Normandy." Ralph Basset, the justice of England, required none of the artificial aids of ancestry to attain distinction; he had within himself powers sufficient at any period to reach the goal of honour, but particularly in the rude age in which he lived. To his wisdom we are said to be indebted for many salutary laws, and among others for *that* of frank pledge. Like all the great men of his day, he was a most liberal benefactor to the church. He d. in 1120, leaving issue,

  I. THURSTINE, who s. to the manor of Colston.
  II. Thomas, ancestor of the Bassets of Heddington, from whom diverged the Wycombe Bassets.
  III. RICHARD, of whom presently. This Richard is called the eldest son by Dugdale, and by others, the 2nd.
  IV. Nicholas, who sided with King STEPHEN against the Empress Maud; and his son forfeited all the estates to HENRY II.
  V. Gilbert, of Little Rissington, co. Gloucester, ancestor of the Bassets of Little Rissington.

The 3rd son,

RICHARD BASSET, succeeded his father as justice of England, which high office he filled in the latter part of King HENRY I.'s reign, and through the whole of King STEPHEN's. In the 5th year of the latter monarch, he was sheriff of Surrey, Cambridge, and Huntingdonshire, with Aleric de Vere; and he served the same office for Essex, Hertford, Buckingham, Bedford, Norfolk, Suffolk, Northampton, and Leicestershires. He m. Maud, only dau. and heiress of Geoffrey Ridel, Lord of Witheringe, by Geva, dau. of Hugh Lupus, Earl of Chester, and had issue,

  I. Geoffrey, who, from his mother, assumed the surname of "de Ridel."
  II. Ralph, of Drayton, co. Stafford (a lordship bestowed upon his mother by the Earl of Chester).
  III. William, of Sapcoate.

He was s. by his eldest son,

GEOFFREY DE RIDEL. This feudal lord married twice, and had issue by both wives; by the 1st, two sons, viz.,

  I. GEOFFREY, who obtained the principality of Blaye, in France, and is said to have been Geoffrey "The Troubadour."
  II. RICHARD, of whom presently.

By the 2nd, one son, Hugh. Geoffrey de Ridel was s. at his decease by his eldest surviving son, who re-assuming his paternal surname, and seating himself at Welden, in Northamptonshire, became

RICHARD BASSET of Weldon, and was s. by his son,

RALPH BASSET, who, in the 2nd of HENRY III., paid 30 marks for the fifteen knights' fees he then held, upon the levy of the

first scutage for the king. He d. sometime before the year 1257, and was s. by his son,

RALPH BASSET, who had livery of his lands, upon doing homage in the 42nd HENRY III. (1257-8). He was s. by his son,

RICHARD BASSET, who d. in 1275, and was s by his son,

RALPH BASSET, who d. in 1294, and was s. by his son,

RICHARD BASSET, who was summoned to parliament, 6 February, 1299, as Richardo Basset de Welden. In the 34th EDWARD I., his lordship was in the expedition made against the Scots, in the retinue of Almare de Valence, Earl of Pembroke, and being subsequently engaged in the same service, he was slain at the battle of Strevelyn in 1314. He was s. by his son (then in minority, whose wardship was granted to Richard de Grey),

RALPH BASSET, 2nd baron, who making proof of his age, had livery of his lands in the 15th EDWARD II. (1321-2). He was summoned 1st EDWARD III. to Newcastle, *cum equis et armis*, but it does not appear, by the existing enrolments, that he was summoned to parliament. He m. Joane, dau. of John de la Pole, citizen of London, and had issue,

  I. RALPH, his successor
  I. Eleanor, m. to Sir John Knyvett, lord chancellor of England.
  II. Joane, m. to Sir Thomas Aylesbury, Knt.

His lordship was s. at his decease by his son,

RALPH BASSET, 3rd baron, who, becoming a canon regular in the priory of Laund, his son and heir,

RALPH BASSET, doing his homage, had livery of all his father's lands, and dying in the 8th of RICHARD II., was s. by his son,

RICHARD BASSET, who d. s. p. in the 10th of HENRY IV. (1408-9), leaving his cousins,

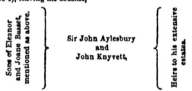

The male line of Sir John Aylesbury failed with his son, Sir Thomas, who left two daus., co-heiresses, viz.,

  I. Isabel, wife of Sir Thomas Chaworth, Knt.
  II. Eleanor, m. to Humphrey Stafford, of Grafton.

But from John Knyvett descended the KNYVETTS, of Buckenham, Norfolk (See CLIFTON, Barons), the Knyvetts, of Charlton, Wilts, the Knyvetts, of Escrick, co. York (See KNYVETT, Baron), the Knyvetts, of Plumstead, Norfolk (ancestors of Lord Berners), &c.

Arms.—Or, three piles, gu., within a bordure, sa., bezantée.

BASSET—BARONS BASSET, OF DRAYTON.

By Writ of Summons, dated 14 December, 1264.

Lineage.

"Immediately after the Norman conquest," says Collins, arose into power and importance, more especially in the midland counties, the great baronial family of Basset" (descended from Thurstan the Norman), which gave a chief justice to England, in the reign of HENRY I., in the person of Ralph Basset, from whom sprang the Lords Basset of Drayton, the Lords Basset of Heddington, &c. About the middle of the 12th century, the Bassets of Cornwall obtained the estates of Tehidy, by marriage with the heiress of the great house of De Dunstanville, and at the commencement of the 16th, the two noble seats of Umberleigh and Heanton Court came into the possession of a branch of the Bassets, elder than the Cornwall branch, by the marriage of Sir John Basset with Joan Beaumont, an heiress, descended from Sir William Beaumont and Isabel, his wife, dau. and co-heir of Sir John Willington, of Umberleigh.

In the 42nd year of King HENRY III. (1257-8),

RALPH BASSET, Lord of Drayton, co. Stafford, great-grandson of Richard Basset, justice of England, and his wife, Maud Ridel, had summons (amongst other great men) to attend the king at Chester, well furnished with horse and arms, to oppose the incursions of the Welsh. But in the 48th of the same monarch, having joined Simon Montford, Earl of Leicester, and the other rebellious barons, he was appointed the next year, after the defeat of the king's arms at Lewes, and capture of the king, governor for those lords of the castles of Salop and Bruges. He fell, however, before the close of the same year, at the battle of Evesham. It is said that when the Earl of Leicester perceived the great force and order of the royal army, calculating upon defeat, he conjured Ralph Basset and Hugh Dispenser to retire, and reserve themselves for better times; but they bravely answered, "that if he perished, they would not desire to live." Lord Basset m. Margaret, dau. of Roger de Someri, Baron of Dudley, and widow of Urian St. Pierre, and had issue,

1. RALPH, his successor.
1. Maud, m. to John, Lord Grey de Wilton.

Notwithstanding the death of Lord Basset, thus in arms against the king, his widow was so favoured by the monarch as to have the chief of his estates settled upon her for life, but soon afterwards, taking the veil, she passed her title in those lands to her son,

RALPH BASSET, 2nd baron, who had summons to parliament, 23 June, 1295, as "Radulphus Basset de Drayton." This nobleman was engaged in the French and Scottish wars of King EDWARD I. In the latter, as one of the retinue of Edmund, Earl of Lancaster, the king's brother. His lordship m. Joan,* dau. of John Grey, justice of Chester, and had issue,

1. RALPH, his successor.
1. Margaret, m. Edmund, Baron of Stafford. the great-grandson of which marriage, THOMAS, Earl of Stafford, was one of the heirs to Ralph, last Lord Basset of Drayton.
11. Maud, m. William de Heriz, and was mother of JOAN, who m. Jordan le Brett, and had a son or grandson, Sir John Brett, whose dau. Catherine, m. Sir John Caltoft, and their dau, Alice, wife of Sir William Chaworth, Knt., was one of the heirs to Ralph, last Lord Basset of Drayton. The son and heir of this Alice Chaworth was Sir Thomas Chaworth, who m. 1st, Nichola, dau. of Sir Reginald Braybroke, by whom he had a dau. Elizabeth, wife of John. 6th Lord Scrope, of Masham; and 2ndly, Isabel, dau. and co-heir of Sir Thomas Aylesbury, by whom he had two sons, Sir William and George (see p. 111).

His lordship d. in 1299, and was s. by his son,

RALPH BASSET, 3rd Lord Basset of Drayton, summoned to parliament from 29 December, 1299, to 25 February, 1342. This nobleman was one of the eminent persons made knights of the Bath with Prince Edward, in the 34th of EDWARD I., and who attended the king that year into Scotland, but returning thence without leave, orders were issued to the sheriffs of Stafford, Nottingham, and Derbyshire to seize his lands: he received, however, his pardon in the following year. His lordship was for several years afterwards in constant service in Scotland. In the 15th EDWARD II. he was joined in commission with John de Someri, to seize the castle of Kenilworth for the king, by reason of the forfeiture of Thomas, Earl of Lancaster, and in the same year was constituted steward of the Duchy of Aquitane. During his government there, Lord Basset was embroiled in a contest with the king of France, but being supported by his royal master, he bade defiance to the wrath of the French monarch. He did not remain long, however, in that government, but returning to England in the year but one afterwards, he was made constable of Dover Castle, and warden of the Cinque Ports. In the 1st and 7th of EDWARD III. he was again in the Scottish wars, and in the 8th of the same reign he was appointed justice of North Wales. His lordship m. Joane, dau. of Thomas Beauchamp, Earl of Warwick, and had issue,

RALPH, who m. Alice, dau. of Nicholas, Lord Audley, and dying before his father, anno 1323, left issue, RALPH, successor to his grandfather, and a dau. Isabel, whose illegitimacy has been almost positively established. She m. Sir Thomas Shirley, Knt.. M.P. for the county of Warwick, and was ancestor of the SHIRLEYS, EARLS FERRERS.

Ralph, Lord Basset, of Drayton, d. 25 February, 1343, and was s. by his grandson,

RALPH BASSET, 4th Lord Basset of Drayton, summoned to parliament from 25 December, 1357, to 6th December, 1389. This nobleman was distinguished in arms during the reigns of EDWARD III. and RICHARD II., and was honoured with the Garter, in consequence of which, his achievement is still to be seen in one of the stalls of the chapel at Windsor. His lordship m. Joane, sister of John, Duke of Britanny, but had no issue. He d. 10 May, 1390, directing by his will, dated 16 January, 1390 (13th RICHARD II.), that his body should be buried at Lichfield, near the altar of St. Nicholas, and devising his estates to Sir Hugh Shirley, his nephew, son of his sister Isabel (see above), upon condition

* Dugdale, under Basset of Drayton, makes this lady dau. of John, the justice of Chester, but under Grey, of Wilton, he calls her the dau. of Reginald Grey, the son of John.

27

that he should assume the surname and arms of Basset, in failure of which proviso, those estates were then to pass to his cousin, Edmund, Lord Stafford. But the matter is differently represented by other authorities; it is certain, however, that great disputes arose after the decease of Lord Basset, between Humphrey, Earl of Stafford, and Sir Thomas Chaworth, Knt., regarding the lordship of Colston-Basset, co Nottingham, but it does not appear that the Shirleys were engaged in it, nor did they take the name of Basset. Amongst other directions, Lord Basset orders in his will that the person, whomsoever it should be, that should first adopt his surname and arms, should have the use of his great velvet bed during his life; and to the same person he also bequeathed four silver basons, with two ewers, whereon his arms were graven, six silver dishes, two silver pots, and four chargers, all marked with his arms; as also a cup, with cover gilt, having one ring on the side thereof. His lordship constituted Walter Skyelaw, bishop of Durham, Richard Scrope, bishop of Chester, and Sir Richard Scrope Knt., his executors. The barony of Basset has remained in ABEYANCE since the decease of this nobleman, which can only be accounted for by the presumption that Isabel, Lady Shirley, was not the legitimate dau. of his lordship's father, and the supposition becomes almost a certainty by the inquisitions taken after the baron's decease; according to the first, Thomas, Earl of Stafford, was found to be his cousin and next heir; and by the second, the same Thomas, Earl of Stafford, and Alice, the wife of Sir John Chaworth, were found his cousins and next heirs, without any mention whatever of his next relative, were she legitimate, Isabel, Lady Shirley. Glover, the Herald, expressly calls her soror naturalis of the 1st baron, and debruises by a baton her coat of arms. (See COURTHOPE's Historic Peerage.) It is but right, however, to add that Sir Egerton Brydges, in his edition of Collins, argues strongly in favour of a contrary view of the case, and considers Isabel's legitimacy established.

Arms.—Or, three piles, gu, a canton, erm.

BASSET—BARONS BASSET OF SAPCOTE.

By Writ of Summons, dated 14 December, 1264.

Lineage.

This branch of the BASSETS was founded by

WILLIAM BASSET, one of the itinerant justices for Yorkshire, in the 21st HENRY II., who settled at Sapcote in Leicestershire, and was younger brother of Ralph Basset, Lord of Drayton: as deputy to whom he executed the office of sheriff of Warwick and Leicestershire, in the 9th of the same monarch's reign. In the 10th he was sheriff of Leicestershire himself: from the 11th to half of the 16th years, inclusive, sheriff of both shires, and from the 23rd to the 30th, sheriff of Lincolnshire. To this William Basset s. his son,

SIMON BASSET, who m. in the 6th RICHARD I. one of the daus. and co-heiresses of William Avenel, of Haddon, co. Derby, and was s. by his son,

RALPH BASSET, of Sapcote. This feudal lord held the sheriffalty of Lincolnshire from the 25th to the 29th of HENRY III., inclusive, and in four years after performed a pilgrimage to St. James in Gallicia. In the 42nd of the same monarch received command to attend the king at Chester, to repel the incursions of the Welsh, and he was constituted in that year governor of Northampton Castle. But after the battle of Lewes, being summoned to the parliament which the barons held in the king's name (49th HENRY III.) he subsequently sided with Simon Montfort, Earl of Leicester, and fell with that ambitious noble at the battle of Evesham, on 4 August, 1265. His lordship m. Milisent, one of the daus. and co-heiresses of Robert de Chaucombe, and was s. by his son,

RALPH BASSET, Lord of Sapcote, who had summons to parliament, 24 December, 1264: he m. Elizabeth, dau. of Roger Colvil, and one of the co-heirs of Robert, Lord Colvil, and left a son and successor,

SIMON BASSET, 2nd baron, who had summons in the 22nd of EDWARD I. to attend the king, wheresoever he should be, to advise touching the important affairs of the realm, and was shortly afterwards ordered to come to Portsmouth, on 1 September, well equipped with horse and arms, and to accompany the king into Gascony. His lordship was father of Ralph Basset of Sapcote, whose son, Simon Basset, was father of (COURTHOPE's Historic Peerage)

RALPH BASSET, 3rd Baron Basset, of Sapcote, who had summons to parliament from 8 January, 1371, to 6 October, 1372. His lordship was one of the gallant soldiers of the martial reign of EDWARD III., and shared in the glories of

Cressy. We find him, however, subsequently experiencing some of the vicissitudes of a soldier's fortune; for being again in France in the 46th of Edward III., under the command of the Duke of Lancaster, and sustaining great losses at Douchy and Rabymont, he was reproved by the king upon his return, which preceded that of the duke. His lordship *m.* 1st, Sybil, dau. of Sir Giles Astley, and had issue

ALICE, who *m.* SIR ROBERT MOTON, Knt., and carried into that family the estates of Sapcote and Castle Bytham (the latter came to the Bassets through the Colvilles). The grandson and heir of this marriage, SIR ROBERT MOTON, *d.* 34th HENRY VI., leaving, by Margery, his 1st wife, a son and heir, REGINALD MOTON, of Peckleton, father of two daus., his co-heirs, viz.,

    I. ANNE MOTON, who *m.* William Grimsby, and had an only dau. and heir ANNE, who *m.* RICHARD VINCENT, of Massingham, co. Lincoln, and had issue. In the heir general of this marriage vests a co-heirship to the Barony of Basset.

    II. ELIZABETH MOTON, who *m.* Ralph de la Pole, Esq., of Radborne, co. Derby, high sheriff, 1477: their grandson and heir,

        GERMAN DE LA POLE, Esq., of Radborne. *m.* Anne, dau. of Sir Robert Plompton, Knt., and *d.* 1552, having had, with other issue,

        1 FRANCIS, of Dale Abbey, in whose heir general vests a co-heirship to the BARONY OF BASSET, OF SAPCOTE; and

        2 German, of Lees, ancestor of the family of CHANDOS POLE, OF RADBORNE, co. Derby.

Lord Basset, of Sapcote, *m.* 2ndly, Alice, dau. of John Derby, and had another dau.,

ELIZABETH, who *m.* Richard, Lord Grey, of Codnor, and had two sons, whose issue became extinct, and three daus., viz.,

    I. ELIZABETH, *m.* Sir John Zouche, of Codnor: the heir general of which marriage is co-heir of the Barony of Basset, of Sapcote.

    II. ELEANOR, *m.* THOMAS NEWPORT, ancestor of THE NEWPORTS, EARLS OF BRADFORD, whose heir general is the present EARL OF BRADFORD.

    III. LUCY, *m.* SIR ROWLAND LENTHALL, and had two daus., eventual co-heirs of their mother, viz.,

        KATHERINE, *m.* to William, Lord Zouche, of Harringworth; the heirs general of this marriage is the BARONESS DE LA ZOUCHE, who is one of the CO-HEIRS of the Barony of BASSET OF SAPCOTE.

        ELIZABETH, *m.* Sir Thomas Cornewall, Baron of Burford.

His lordship *d.* in 1378, and the BARONY OF BASSET OF SAPCOTE fell into ABEYANCE between his two daus., and so continues amongst their descendants.

Arms— Arg., two bars undèe, sa.

BASSET — BARON DE DUNSTANVILLE, OF TEHIDY, AND BARON BASSET, OF STRATTON.

By Letters Patent, dated 17 June, 1796, and 30 October, 1797.

Lineage.

The Bassets of Tehidy derive descent in the direct male line from THURSTAN the Norman, and held Tehidy *temp.* RICHARD I. Their descendant,

SIR JOHN BASSET, acquired Umberleigh and Heanton, two noble seats in Devonshire, by his marriage with Joan Beaumont, an heiress (descended from Sir William Beaumont, of Shirwell, and Isabel, his wife, dau. and co-heir of Sir John de Willington, of Umberleigh), and had issue a son and heir,

SIR JOHN BASSET, of Umberleigh and White Chaple, who *m.* 1st, Elizabeth, dau. of John Denys, by whom he had an only child, Anne, *m.* to James Courtenay; and 2ndly, Honora, dau. of Sir Thomas Granville, by whom (who *m.* 2ndly, Arthur Plantagenet, Viscount Lisle) he left at his decease, in 1528,

    I. JOHN, of Umberleigh, *m.* Frances, dau. and co-heir of Arthur Plantagenet, Viscount Lisle, and was ancestor of THE BASSETS OF UMBERLEIGH and HEANTON COURT, extinct in the male line, but represented, through an heiress, by HARRIET-MARY BASSET, of Umberleigh and Watermouth, Devon, wife of Charles Henry Williams, Esq., who assumed, in 1880, the surname and arms of Basset.

    II. GEORGE, of Tehidy, of whose line we treat.

The younger son, GEORGE BASSET, Esq., had a gift from his nephew, Sir Arthur Basset, of Umberleigh, of the manor of Tehidy, in Cornwall, to him and his heirs, as appears by a conveyance dated 26 March, 1558. He *m.* Jacquetta, dau. of George Coffin, of Portledge, in Devonshire, and dying 5 November, 1589, left, with two daus., Catherine, *m.* to James Cary, of Clovelly, in Devon, and Blanch, *m.* to William Newman, an only son,

JAMES BASSET, Esq., of Tehidy, who *d.* 8 February, 1603, having *m.* Jane, dau. of Sir Francis Godolphin, of Godolphin, Knt., by whom he had, with four daus., Margery, *m.* Henry Trengrove, *alias* Nans; Joanna, *m.* to William Courtenay, of Tremara, co. Cornwall; Grace and Margaret; five sons, FRANCIS (Sir); Thomas (Sir), a major-general under King CHARLES I., commanded a division of the royal army at the battle of Stratton; Arthur (Sir), a colonel in the royal army; Nicholas; and James. The eldest son,

SIR FRANCIS BASSET, of Tehidy, *m.* Anne, dau. of Sir Jonathan Trelawny, of Trelawny, Knt., governor and owner of St. Michael's Mount, in Cornwall, and *d.* 19 September, 1645, leaving a 2nd son,

JOHN BASSET, of Tehidy, heir male of his brother Francis, who *m.* Anne, dau. and heiress of Robert Delbridge, of Barnstaple, and *d.* in November, 1656, having had issue,

    FRANCIS, his heir.
    Charles, rector of Illogan, *d. s. p.* 1709.
    John, *d. unm.*, January, 1708
    Anne, *d. unm.*, October. 1715.
    Elizabeth, *d. unm.*

The eldest son,

FRANCIS BASSET, Esq., of Tehidy, *m.* Lucy, dau. and heir of John Hele, Esq., and had issue,

FRANCIS BASSET, Esq., his only son and heir, who *m.* 1st, Elizabeth, dau. and co-heiress of Sir Thomas Spencer, Bart., of Yarnton, Oxfordshire, and widow of Sir Samuel Garrard, by whom he had no issue. He *m.* 2ndly, Mary, dau. and heiress of John Pendarves, rector of Dunsteignton, in Devonshire, and at length heiress of her uncle, Alexander Pendarves, by her he had two sons,

    JOHN-PENDARVES, his heir.
    FRANCIS, of whom presently.

Francis Basset *d.* 11 December, 1721; his elder son,

JOHN PENDARVES BASSET, Esq., of Tehidy, *d.* 25 September, 1739, and was buried at Illogan, having *m.* Anne, dau. and co-heiress of Sir Edmund Prideaux, of Netherton, Bart., by whom he had a posthumous son,

JOHN PRIDEAUX BASSET, Esq., of Tehidy, who *d.* 28 May, 1756, aged 16, and was buried at Illogan.

FRANCIS BASSET, of Torrley, in Northamptonshire, the younger son of Francis Basset, *s.* to the family estate at Tehidy on the death of his nephew. He was M.P. for Penrhyn, and *d.* November, 1769. He *m.* 19 October, 1756, Margaret, dau. of Sir John St. Aubyn, of Clowance, Bart., and by her (who *d.* 19 October, 1768) had issue,

FRANCIS (Sir), Lord de Dunstanville, his heir.
John-M., in holy orders, rector of Illogan, and of Camborne, co. Cornwall, bapt. at Illogan. 4 August, 1760; *m.* 4 October, 1790, Mary, dau. of George Wingfield, of Durham, by whom he had a son, JOHN, of whom presently.
Margaret, *m.* at St. Breock, 1776, to John Rogers, Esq., of Treassowe, and Penrose, and had issue.
Anne, *d. unm.*, 1779.   Cecilia.
Mary.   Catherine.

The elder son,

FRANCIS BASSET, Esq., of Tehidy, *b.* 9 August, 1757, was created a baronet 24 November, 1779, raised to the peerage, as BARON DE DUNSTANVILLE, 7 June, 1796, and created BARON BASSET, of Stratton, with remainder to his only dau. and her male issue, 30 November, 1797. He *m.* 1st, 16 May, 1780, Frances-Susanna, dau. of John Hippisley Coxe, Esq., of Ston Easton, co. Somerset, and by her (who *d.* 14 June, 1823) had an only child,

FRANCES, BARONESS BASSET, of Stratton, *b.* 30 April, 1781, who *d. unm.*, 22 January, 1855, when the Barony of Basset became EXTINCT.

Lord de Dunstanville *m.* 2ndly, 13 July, 1824, Harriet, dau. of Sir William Lemon, Bart., of Carclew, by whom he had no issue. His lordship *d.* 14 February, 1835, when the title of de Dunstanville became EXTINCT. The barony of Basset and the Tehidy estates passed to his dau., and the male representative of the family devolved on his nephew,

JOHN BASSET, Esq., J.P. and D.L., *b.* 1791, high sheriff of Cornwall in 1837, who *m.* June, 1830, Elizabeth-Mary, dau. of Sir Rose Price, Bart., of Trengwainton, and left at his decease three sons, viz.,

    JOHN-FRANCIS, of Tehidy, *b.* 15 July, 1831.
    Arthur, *d. unm.* 7 May, 1870.
    GUSTAVUS-LAMBERT, of Tehidy, now MALE HEIR of the great House of BASSET. (See BURKE's *Landed Gentry*) Walter-St. Aubyn,

Arms—Barry wavy of six, or and gu,

Beauchamp.
(E.Warwick.)

Belasyse.
(E.Fauconberg.)

Bermingham.
(E.Louth.)

Blount.
(E.Devon.)

Bohun.
(E.Northampton.)

Booth.
(E.Warrington.)

Bourchier.
(E.Essex.)

Browne.
(V.Montagu.)

Bruce.
(B.Bruce.)

Brydges.
(D.Chandos.)

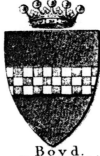
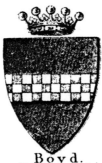

Boyd.
(E.Kilmarnock.)

Camville.
(B.Camville.)

BATEMAN—VISCOUNT BATEMAN.

By Letters Patent, dated 12 July, 1725.

Lineage.

Sir James Bateman, Knt., son of Joas Bateman, a merchant of London, and grandson of Giles Bateman, filled the civic chair of London in 1717, and was appointed sub-governor of the South Sea Company 1718. He m. Esther, youngest dau. and co-heir of John Searle, Esq., of Finchley, and had issue,

William, his heir.

Anne, who m. in 1735, William Western, Esq., of Rivenhall, Essex, and had one son and two dau.,

  1. James Western, d. in infancy.

  1. Sarah Western, m. William Hanbury, Esq., of Kelmarsh, in Northamptonshire, and d. in 1766, leaving (with a dau., Anne, wife of John Harvey-Thursby, Esq., of Abington Abbey, co. Northampton) a son,

    William Hanbury, of Kelmarsh, who inherited the estates of the Viscounts Bateman. He was father of one dau. and three sons ; of whom the eldest.

      William Hanbury, was created, in 1837, Baron Bateman, of Shobdon, co. Hereford. His lordship's eldest son is the present William Bateman, 2nd Lord Bateman. (See Burke's Peerage.)

  II. Wilhelmina-Anne Western, m. Richard Stephens, Esq.

Sir James Bateman d. in November, 1718, and was s. by his son,

William Bateman, Esq., M.P., who was raised to the peerage of Ireland as Baron Culmore and Viscount Bateman, 12 July, 1725, and, in 1731, created a knight of the Bath. He m. Lady Anne Spencer, dau. of Charles, Earl of Sunderland, and grand-dau. of the great Duke of Marlborough, and dying in 1744, left two sons, John, his heir ; and William, capt. R.N., d. 19 June, 1783, s. p. The elder son,

John Bateman, 2nd viscount, master of the buckhounds, chief steward of Leominster, and M.P. for Woodstock, m. in 1748, Elizabeth, dau. and co-heir of John Sambroke, Esq., but d. s. p. 2 March, 1802, when the peerage became extinct.

Arms—Or, on a fesse, sa., between three Muscovy ducks, ppr., a rose of the field.

BAVENT—BARONS BAVENT.

By Writ of Summons, dated 8 January, 1313.

Lineage.

In the 25th of Edward I.,

Roger Bavent was in the expedition made then into Gascony, and in the 30th of the same monarch he obtained a charter for a weekly market at Marom, co. Lincoln. From the 6th to the 15th Edward II., and from the 6th to the 9th Edward III., he was summoned to parliament as Baron Bavent.

It does not appear from the existing enrolments, that there was any subsequent summons to parliament to a member of the Bavent family, although it appears that Roger, Lord Bavent, left a son to succeed him. Vincent, the herald, in his pedigree of the Bavents, enters John Bavent, living 22 Edward III., as the grandson of Roger, Lord Bavent, and states that he d. s. p., leaving a sister and heiress, Eleanor, m. William de Braose (Courthope's Historic Peerage), and had a son, Peter de Braose, whose descendant heir-general Beatrice, m. Hugh Shirley, Esq., of Eatington, co. Warwick. Certain it is that in the 13th Edward III., Thomas de Bavent and Alice, his wife, settled Easton Bavent with Chediston, in Suffolk, on himself for life, remainder to William, his son, and Catherine, his wife, remainder to Felicia, his dau., sister of William, remainder to John, son of Thomas Ubbeston, remainder to Richard, son of John, son of Baldwin Bavent. In the 20th Edward III., William Bavent and Robert Paville were Lords of Easton Bavent.

Arms—Arg., a chief, indented, sa.

BAYNING—VISCOUNTS BAYNING, OF SUDBURY.

By Letters Patent, dated 8 March, 1627.

Lineage.

Sir Paul Bayning, Bart. (so created 24 September, 1612), of Bentley-Parva, co. Essex (son of Paul Bayning, Esq., one of the sheriffs of London, temp. Elizabeth, anno 1593), was elevated

to the peerage on 27 February, 1627, in the dignity of Baron Bayning, of Horkesley-Bentley, co. Essex, and advanced to the rank of Viscount Bayning, of Sudbury, co. Suffolk, on the 8 March, in the same year. His lordship m. Anne, dau. of Sir Henry Glemham, of Glemham, co. Suffolk, Knt., and had issue,

Paul, his successor.

Cecilia, m. Henry Viscount Newark, who s. his father, in 1643, in the earldom of Kingston, and was created Marquess of Dorchester in the following year, by whom she had two surviving daus ; viz.,

  Anne, m. to John, Lord de Ros, afterwards Earl of Rutland, a marriage dissolved by parliament in 1668.

  Grace d. unm. in 1703.

Anne, m. to Henry Murray, Esq., one of the grooms of the bedchamber to King Charles I. This lady was created Viscountess Bayning, of Foxley. (See Murray.)

Mary, m. 1st, to William Viscount Grandison, and 2ndly, to Christopher, Earl of Anglesey.

Elizabeth, m. to Francis Lennard, Lord Dacre. Her ladyship was created Countess of Shepey, for life, 6 September, 1680 : she d. 1686.

The Viscount d. "at his own house, in Mark-lane, within the city of London" on 29 July, 1629, and was s. by his son,

Paul Bayning, 2nd viscount, who m. Penelope, only dau. and heiress of Sir Robert Naunton, Knt., Master of the court of ward and liveries, by whom he left two daus. ; viz.,

Anne, m. to Aubrey de Vere, Earl of Oxford.

Penelope, m. to the Hon. John Herbert, youngest son of Philip, 4th Earl of Pembroke and 1st Earl of Montgomery.

His lordship dying thus without male issue, all his honours expired, while his estates passed to daus., as co-heiressess.

Arms—Or, two bars, sa., on each as many escallops of the first.

BEAUCHAMP—EARLS OF WARWICK.

Created by William the Conqueror or William Rufus, and conveyed to the family of Beauchamp by Isabel de Mauduit, wife of William de Beauchamp, feudal Baron of Elmley.

Lineage.

Amongst the most eminent Norman families in the train of the Conqueror, was that of Beauchamp, and amongst those that shared most liberally in the spoils of the conquest.

Hugh de Beauchamp, the companion in arms of the victorious Norman, who obtained grants to a very great extent from his triumphant chief, as he appears at the general survey, to be possessed of large estates in Hertford, Buckingham, and Bedfordshires, was the founder of this illustrious house in England This Hugh had issue,

Simon, who d. s. p.

Payne, ancestor of the Beauchamps of Bedford, that barony having been conferred upon him by William Rufus.

Walter, of whom presently, but some doubts have been thrown upon the question of his having been son of Hugh, Sir H Nicolas stating him to have been " supposed of the same family."

Milo, of Eaton, co. Bedford.

Adeline, m. to Walter Le Espec, Lord of Kirkham and Helmesley, co. of York.

The 3rd son,

Walter de Beauchamp, of Elmley Castle, co. Gloucester, having m. Emeline, dau. and heiress of Urso de Abitot constable of the castle of Worcester, and hereditary sheriff of Worcestershire (who was brother of Robert le Despenser, steward to the Conqueror), was invested with that sheriffalty by King Henry I., and obtained a grant from the same monarch (to whom he was steward) of all the lands belonging to Roger de Worcester, with a confirmation of certain lands given to him by Adelise, widow of his father-in-law, the said Urso. Walter de Beauchamp was s., as well in his estates as in the royal stewardship, by his son,

William de Beauchamp, who, for his zeal in the cause of the Empress Maud, was dispossessed of the castle of Worcester by King Stephen, to which, and all his other honours and estates, however, he was restored by King Henry II.; and in that monarch's reign, besides the sheriffalty of Worcestershire, which he enjoyed by inheritance, he was sheriff of Warwickshire (2nd Henry II.), sheriff of Gloucestershire (from 3rd to the 9th Henry II. inclusive), and sheriff of Herefordshire (from the 8th to the 16th Henry II., 1167-70 inclusive). Upon the levy of the assessment towards the marriage portion of one of King Henry's daus., this powerful feudal lord certified his knight's fees to amount to fifteen. He m. Maud, dau. of William Lord Braose, of Gower, and was s., at his decease, by his son,

William de Beauchamp, who m. Joane, dau. of Sir Thomas

Walerie; and dying before the 13th (1211-12) of King John's reign, was s. by his son (a minor, whose wardship and marriage Roger de Mortimer and Isabel, his wife, obtained for 3,000 marks),

WALTER DE BEAUCHAMP. This feudal lord was appointed governor of Hanley Castle, co. Worcester, in the 17th King John, and entrusted with the custody of the same shire in that turbulent year. Walter de Beauchamp m. Bertha, dau. of William Lord Braose, by whom he had two sons, Walcheline and James. Of this nobleman we find further. that, being one of the *barons-marchers*, he gave security to the king for his faithful services (with the other lords-marchers), until peace should be fully settled in the realm; and for the better performance there *f*, gave up James, his *younger son*, as a hostage. He d. in 1235, and was s. by his elder son,

WALCHELINE DE BEAUCHAMP, omitted in Sir H. Nicholas' account of the family, m. Joane, dau. of Roger, Lord Mortimer, and dying in the same year as his father, was s. by an only son,

WILLIAM DE BEAUCHAMP, feudal Lord of Elmley. This nobleman attended King HENRY III., in the 37th year of his reign (1252-3), into Gascoigne, and in two years afterwards marched under the banner of Robert de Clare, Earl of Gloucester, against the Scots. In the 41st of the same reign he had summons (with other illustrious persons) to meet the king at Chester on the feast day of *St. Peter de Vincula*, well fitted with horse and arms to oppose the incursions of Llewelyn, Prince of Wales. Lord Beauchamp m Isabel, dau. of William Mauduit, of Hanslape, co. Bucks, heritable chamberlain of the exchequer, and sister and heiress of WILLIAM MAUDUIT, EARL OF WARWICK (who inherited that dignity from his cousin, Margery de Newburgh, Countess of Warwick, in the year 1263). His lordship made his will in 1268, the year in which he died. Besides the daus. mentioned above, Lord Beauchamp left four sons, viz.,

WILLIAM. of whom presently.
John, of Holt, co. Worcester.
Walter, of Powyke and Alcester.
Thomas, d. s. p.

The eldest son,

WILLIAM DE BEAUCHAMP, inherited not only the feudal barony of Elmley from his father, but had previously derived from his mother the EARLDOM OF WARWICK (originally possessed by the Newburghs), and the barony of Hanslape (which had belonged to the Mauduits). This eminent nobleman was a distinguished captain in the Welsh and Scottish wars of King EDWARD I. "In the 23rd year of which reign (1294-5), being in Wales with the king," as Dugdale relates, "he performed a notable exploit; namely, hearing that a great body of the Welsh were got together in a plain, betwixt two woods, and to secure themselves, had fastened their pikes to the ground, sloping towards their assailants, he marched thither with a choice company of cross-bowmen and archers, and in the night time encompassing them about, put betwixt every two horsemen, one cross-bowman, which cross-bowman killing many of them that held the pikes, the horse charged in suddenly, and made a very great slaughter. This was done near Montgomery." His lordship m. Maud, widow of Girard de Furnival, and one of the four daus. and co-heiresses of Richard Fitz-John, son of John Fitz-Geffery, chief justice of Ireland, by whom he had surviving issue,

GUY, his successor.
Isabel, m. to Peter Chaworth.
Maud, m. to — Rithco.
Margaret, m. to John Sudley.
Anne, ⎰ nuns at Shouldham, co. Norfolk, a monastery founded
Amy, ⎱ by his lordship's maternal great grandfather.

William de Beauchamp, 1st Earl of Warwick of that family, d. in 1298, having previous to his mother's death used the style and title of Earl of Warwick, with what legality appears very doubtful, and was s. by his eldest son,

GUY DE BEAUCHAMP, 2nd earl, so called in memory of his celebrated predecessor, the Saxon, GUY, EARL OF WARWICK. This nobleman acquired high military renown in the martial reign of EDWARD I., distinguishing himself at the battle of Falkirk, for which he was rewarded with extensive grants of lands in Scotland, at the siege of Caerlaverock, and upon different occasions besides beyond the sea. In the reign of EDWARD II. he likewise played a very prominent part. In 1310 his lordship was in the commission appointed by parliament to draw up regulations for " the well governing of the kingdom and of the king's household," in consequence of the corrupt influence exercised at that period by *Piers Gaveston*, in the affairs o. the realm, through the unbounded partiality of the king: and In two years afterwards, when that unhappy favorite fell into the hands of his enemies upon the surrender of Scarborough Castle, his

lordship violently seized upon his person, and after a summary trial, caused him to be beheaded at Blacklow Hill, near Warwick. The earl's hostility to Gaveston is said to have been much increased by learning that the favourite had nicknamed him "*the Black Dog of Ardenne*." For this unwarrantable proceeding his lordship, and all others concerned therein, received within two years the royal pardon, but he is supposed to have eventually perished by poison, administered in revenge by the partizans of Gaveston. The earl m. Alice, relict of Thomas de Laybourne, dau. (by Lady Alice de Bohun) of Ralph de Toni, of Flamsted, co. Herts, and sister and heiress of Robert de Toni, by whom he had issue,

THOMAS, his successor, whose sponsors were, Thomas Plantagenet, Earl of Lancaster, and Henry, his brother, and Thomas de Warrington, prior of Kenilworth.
John, a very eminent person in the reign of EDWARD III., being captain of Calais, admiral of the fleet, STANDARD BEARER at CRESSY, and one of the original knights of the Garter. He was summoned to parliament as a BARON, but dying s. p. the dignity EXPIRED.
Maud, m. to Geoffrey, Lord Say.
Emma, m. to Rowland Odingsels.
Isabel, m. to John Clinton.
Elizabeth, m. to Sir Thomas Astley, Knt.
Lucis, m. to Robert or Roger de Napton.

This great Earl of Warwick was, like most of the nobles of his time, a munificent benefactor to the church, having bestowed lands upon several religious houses, and founded a chantry of priests at his manor of Elmley. His will bears date, "at WARWICK CASTLE,[*] on *Munday* next after the feast of St. James the Apostle, an. 1315," and by it he bequeaths to Alice his wife a proportion of his plate, with a crystal cup, and half his bedding; as also, all the vestments and books belonging to his chapel; the other moiety of his beds, rings, and jewels, he gives to his daus. To his son Thomas, his best coat of mail, helmet, and suit of harness; to his son John, his second suit of mail, &c., appointing that all the rest of his armour, bows, and other warlike provisions, should remain in Warwick Castle for his heir. Alice, widow of the earl, had very extensive estates assigned her in dowry, in the November following the death of her husband, and in the next year she paid a fine of 500 marks, for license to marry William La Zouche, of Ashby, co. Leicester, to whom she was accordingly married. The earl d. at Warwick Castle, on 12 August, 1315, and was s. by his eldest son, then but two years of age,

THOMAS DE BEAUCHAMP, 3rd earl, regarding whom we find the king (Edward II.) in two years subsequently soliciting a dispensation from the pope, to enable him to marry his cousin Catherine, dau. of Roger de Mortimer, Lord of Wigmore, under whose guardianship the young earl had been placed; an alliance eventually formed, when his lordship had completed his fifteenth year. In two years, afterwards, the earl, by special licence from the crown, was allowed to do homage, and to assume his hereditary offices of sheriff of Worcestershire, and chamberlain of the exchequer. This nobleman sustained in the brilliant reign of EDWARD III. the high military renown of his illustrious progenitor, and became distinguished in arms almost from his boyhood. So early as the third year of that monarch, he commanded the left wing of the king's army at Wyzonfosse, where Edward proposed to give the French battle, and from that period was the constant companion of the king, and his gallant son, in all their splendid campaigns. At Cressy, he had a principal command in the van of the English army, under the Prince of Wales, and at Poictiers, where Dugdale says he fought so long and so stoutly, that his hand was galled with the exercise of his sword and pole-axe; he personally took William de Melleun, archbishop of Sens, prisoner, for whose ransom he obtained 8,000 marks. After these heroic achievements in France, the earl arrayed himself under the banner of the cross, and reaped fresh laurels on the plains of Palestine, whence upon his return he brought home the son of the King of Lithuania, whom he had christened at London by the name of Thomas, answering for the new convert himself at the baptismal font; for his lordship was not more distinguished by his valour than his piety, as his numerous and liberal donations to the church while living, and bequests at his decease, testify. This nobleman rebuilt the walls of Warwick Castle, which had been demolished in the time of the Mauduits; adding strong gates, with fortified gateways, and embattled towers; he likewise founded the choir of the collegiate church of St. Mary, built a

---

[*] Warwick Castle was almost rebuilt by Thomas, 4th Earl of Warwick, and Richard, his heir and successor, in the reigns of EDWARD III. and RICHARD II. The much admired polygon, Guy's Tower, which is thirty-eight feet in diameter and one hundred and six feet in height was erected it is said by the latter.

booth hall in the market place, and made the town of Warwick toll free. His lordship had issue, by the Countess already mentioned, seven sons and nine daus.: viz.,

Guy, called by Dugdale, a "stout soldier," m. Philippa, dau. of Henry, Lord Ferrars, of Groby, and dying before his father, left three daus.; viz.,

Katherine,
Elizabeth, } nuns at Shouldham, in Norfolk.
Margaret,

Thomas, inheritor of the honours.

Reynburne, who left an only dau., Alianore, wife of John Knight, of Hanslope, in co. Bucks, by whom she left a dau., Emma, who m. William Forster, from whom the Forsters of Hanslope derived.

William (Sir), K.G., Lord of Abergavenny.

John,
Roger, } all d. unm.
Hierom,

Maud,* m. to Roger de Clifford.

Philippa, m. to Hugh, Earl of Stafford.

Alice, m. to John, Lord Beauchamp, of Hacche, co. Somerset.

Joane, m. to Ralph, Lord Basset, of Drayton.

Isab 1, m. 1st, to John, Lord Strange, of Blackmere, and 2ndly, to William Ufford, Earl Suffolk.

Margaret, m. to Guy de Montford, after whose decease she took the veil at Shouldham.

Agnes, m. 1st, — Cokesay, and afterwards — Bardolf.

Juliana, d. unm.

Catharine, took the veil at Wroxhall, in Warwickshire.

The earl was one of the original knights of the Garter. His lordship d. 13 November, 1369, of the plague at Calais, where he was then employed in his military capacity, and had just achieved a victory over the French; he was s. by his eldest son,

Thomas, 4th earl, K.G., who was appointed by parliament governor of the young king, Richard II., in the third year of that monarch's reign, but did not long enjoy the office, for we find him in arms with Thomas, Duke of Gloucester (the king's uncle), long before the majority of Richard, constraining the assembling of parliament, for which proceeding, however, in several years afterwards, he was seized at a feast given to him by the king—tried and condemned to death—a sentence commuted by the king, at the instance of the Earl of Salisbury, to banishment to the Isle of Man, while his castle and manors of Warwick, with his other estates, were granted to Thomas Holland, earl of Kent, to whom the custody of his son and heir, Richard Beauchamp, was also confided. From the Isle of Man, the earl was brought back to the Tower of London, and imprisoned there during the remainder of King Richard's reign; but upon the accession of Henry IV. he was released, and re-instated in all his honours and possessions. His lordship m. Margaret, dau. of William, Lord Ferrars, of Groby, and had issue,

Richard, his successor, for whom King Richard II. and Richard Scrope, then bishop of Coventry and Lichfield (afterwards archbishop of York), stood sponsors.

Katherine d. young.
Margaret, } nuns.
Katherine,
Elizabeth.

The earl d. in 1401, and was s. by his son,

Richard de Beauchamp, 5th earl, b. 28 January, 1381. This nobleman was made a knight of the Bath at the coronation of King Henry IV., and at the coronation of the Queen in the following year, attained high reputation for the gallantry he had displayed in the lists. In the 4th year of the same monarch (1402-3), he was pre-eminently distinguished against Owen Glendower, whose banner he captured, and put the rebel himself to flight; and about the same time he won fresh laurels in the memorable battle of Shrewsbury, against the Percys, after which, he was made a knight of the most noble order of the Garter. Of his lordship's pilgrimage to the Holy Land, Dugdale gives the following account: — "In the 9th Henry IV., obtaining license to visit the Holy Land, he fitted himself with all necessaries for that journey, and passed the sea: in which voyage, visiting his cousin, the Duke of Barr, he was nobly received and entertained by him for eight days, who thence accompanied him to Paris; where being arrived, the king of France then wearing the crown, in reverence of that holy feast, made him to sit at his table, and

* Those ladies' portraitures are curiously drawn, and placed in the windows on the south side of the quire of the collegiate church at Warwick, in the habit of their time. Seven of them were married, and have their paternal armes upon their inner garments; and on their outer mantle their husbands' armes; the picture of Isabel, who married twice, is twice drawn.—Dugdale's Baronage.

at his departure, sent an herald to conduct him safely through that realm. Out of which, entering Lumbardy, he was met by another herald from Sir Pandulph Malacet, with a challenge to perform certain feats of arms with him at Verona, upon a day assigned, for the order of the Garter; and in the presence of Sir Galiot of Mantua; whereunto he gave his assent. And as soon as he had performed his pilgrimage at Rome, returned to Verona, where he and his challenger were first to just, next to fight with axes, afterwards with arming swords, and lastly with sharp daggers. At the day and place assigned for which exercises, came great resort of people, Sir Pandulph entering the lists with nine spears borne before him: but the act of spears being ended, they fell to it with axes; in which encounter Sir Pandulph received a sore wound on the shoulder, and had been utterly slain, but that Sir Galiot cried peace.

"When he came to Jerusalem, he had much respect shewed him by the partiarch's deputy, and having performed his offerings at the sepulchre of our Saviour, he set up his arms on the north side of the temple. While at Jerusalem, a noble person, called Baltredam (the Soldan's lieutenant), hearing that he was descended from the famous Sir Guy of Warwick, whose story they had in books of their own language, invited him to his palace, and royally feasting him, 'presented him with three precious stones of great value,' besides divers cloaths of silk and gold given to his servants. Where this Baltredam told him privately, that he faithfully believed as he did, though he durst not discover himself; and rehearsed the articles of the creed. But on the morrow he feasted Sir Baltredam's servants, and gave them scarlet, with other English cloth, which being shewed to Sir Baltredam, he returned again to him, and said, he would wear his livery, and be marshal of his hall. Whereupon he gave Sir Baltredam a gown of black peak, furred; and had much discourse with him, for he was skilful in sundry languages." At the coronation of King Henry V., in whose service, when Prince of Wales, his lordship had been engaged, the earl was constituted High Steward of England for that solemnity, and in the next year, we find him actively engaged for the king against the Lollards. In the 3rd of Henry V (1415-16), he was at Calais, and there his chivalric disposition led him into an encounter with three French knights, the result of which Dugdale thus relates:—"which letters (challenges sent by the earl under fictitious names) were sent to the king's court at France, where three French knights received them, and promised their fellows to meet at a day and place assigned: whereof the first was a knight called Sir Gerard Herbaumer, who called himself Le Chevalier Rouge; the second, a famous knight, named Sir Hugh Launey, calling himself Le Chevalier Blanc; and the third a knight named Sir Collard Fines. Twelfday, in Christmas, being appointed for the time that they should meet, in a land called the Parkhedge of Gynes. On which day the earl came into the field with his face covered, a plume of ostrich feathers upon his helm, and his horse trapped with the Lord of Toney's arms (one of his ancestors), viz. argent a manch gules; where, first encountering with the Chevalier Rouge, at the third course he unhorsed him, and so returned with closed vizor, unknown to his pavilion, whence he sent to that knight a good courser. The next day he came into the field with his vizor closed, a chaplet on his helm, and a plume of ostrich feathers aloft, his horse trapped with the arms of Hanslap, viz. silver two bars gules, where he met with the Blanc knight, with whom he encountered, smote off his vizor thrice, broke his besagurs and other harneys, and returned victoriously to his pavilion, with all his own habiliments safe, and as yet not known to any; from whence he sent the Blanc knight a good courser But the morrow after, viz, the last day of the justs, he came with his face open, and his helmet as the day before, save that the chaplet was rich with pearls and precious stones; and in his coat of arms, of Guy and Beauchamp quarterly; having the arms of Toney and Hanslap on his trappers; and said, 'That as he had, in his own person, performed the service the two days before, so with God's grace he would the third.' Whereupon, encountering with Sir Collard Fines, at every stroke he bore him backward to his horse; insomuch, as the Frenchman saying, 'that he himself was bound to his saddle;' he alighted and presently got up again, but all being ended, he returned to his pavilion, sent to Sir Collard Fines a fair courser, feasted all the people, gave to those three knights great rewards, and so rode to Calais with great honour." About this time the earl attended the deputation of bishops and other learned persons from England to the Council of Constance, and during his stay there slew a great duke in justing. In the next year, he was with King Henry at the siege of Caen, and upon the surrender of that place was appointed governor of that castle. His lordship continued actively engaged in military and diplomatic services during the remainder of the reign of King Henry V., by whose will he was appointed governor to his infant son and successor, HENRY VI., which charge having fulfilled with great wisdom and fidelity, his lordship was appointed, upon the death of John Plantagenet, Duke of Bedford, Regent of France, LIEU-TENANT-GENERAL of the whole REALM OF FRANCE and DUCHY OF NORMANDY. The earl, who had been created EARL OF ALBEMARLE, for life, in 1417, *d.* in the castle of Roan, in his French government, on 30 April, 1439—having by his will ordered his body to be brought over to England, where it was afterwards deposited, under a stately monument,* appointed by the deceased lord to be erected in the collegiate church of St. Mary, at Warwick. His lordship *m.* 1st, Elizabeth, dau. and heiress of Thomas, Lord Berkeley, Viscount Lisle, by whom he had three daus., viz.,

Margaret, *m.* to John Talbot, Earl of Shrewsbury (his lordship's 2nd wife, by whom he had one son, John Talbot, Lord Viscount Lisle, of whom the Dudleys, Earls of Warwick, derived).

Alianor, *m.* 1st, to Thomas, Lord de Ros, from whom the Dukes of Rutland derive; and 2ndly, to Edmund, Duke of Somerset

Elizabeth, *m.* to George Nevil, Lord Latimer.

The earl *m.* 2ndly, Isabel, dau. and eventually heiress of Thomas le Despencer, Earl of Gloucester, and widow of his cousin, Richard Beauchamp, Earl of Worcester (for which marriage he obtained a papal dispensation), and had a son and dau.,—namely,

HENRY, his successor, whose sponsors were Cardinal Beaufort, Humphrey, Earl of Stafford, and Joane, Lady Bergavenny.

Anne, who *m.* Sir Richard Nevil, son and heir of Richard, Earl of Salisbury, and grandson of Ralph Nevil, 1st Earl of Westmoreland.

The Earl of Warwick was *s.* by his son,

HENRY DE BEAUCHAMP, 6th earl. K.G. This nobleman having, before he had completed his nineteenth year, tendered his services for the defence of the Duchy of Acquitaine, was created by charter dated 2 April, 1444, PREMIER EARL OF ENGLAND, and his lordship obtained, at the same time permission for himself and his heirs male to wear a golden coronet about his head, in the presence of the king and elsewhere. In three days after he was advanced to the dignity of DUKE OF WARWICK, with precedence immediately after the Duke of Norfolk, and before the Duke of Buckingham: which extraordinary mark of royal favour so displeased the latter nobleman, that an act of parliament was subsequently passed to appease his jealousy, declaring that from 2 December, then next ensuing, the two dukes should take place of each other alternately year about, but with precedency of the first year to the Duke of Warwick. After which, his Grace of Warwick had a grant in reversion, upon the death of the Duke of Gloucester, of the Isles of Guernsey, Jersey, Serke, Erme, and Alderney, for the annual rent of a rose; also the hundred and manor of Bristol, for £60 a-year, with all the royal castles and manors in the Forest of Dene, for £100 per annum: and he was shortly before his death crowned KING OF THE ISLE OF WIGHT, by the hand of HENRY VI. himself. His grace *m.* in the life-time of his father, when but ten years old, and then called Lord Despencer, Cicily, dau. of Richard Nevil, Earl of Salisbury, whose portion was 4,700 marks—by whom he left an only dau. and heiress,

ANNE.

His grace *d.* in the twenty-second year of his age, on 11 June, 1445, when the dukedom (and the male line of this branch of the Beauchamps) EXPIRED, but his other honours devolved upon his dau.,

ANNE DE BEAUCHAMP, *Countess of Warwick,* then but two years old, who was committed to the guardianship, 1st, of Queen MARGARET, and afterwards of William de la Pole, Duke of Suffolk Her ladyship dying however in a few years afterwards, on 3 January, 1449, the honours of the illustrious house of Beauchamp reverted to the young countess's aunt,

ANNE, wife of Richard Nevil, Earl of Salisbury, who then became Countess of Warwick, and her husband, the celebrated "King-Maker," was subsequently created Earl of Warwick.—(*See* NEVIL, EARL OF SALISBURY and WARWICK),

Arms.—Gules, a fesse between six cross crosslets, or.

* This magnificent tomb (which yet remains in uncommon splendour) is inferior to none in England, unless that of HENRY VII. in Westminster Abbey.

BEAUCHAMP—BARONS ST. AMAND.

By Writ of Summons, dated 25 March, 1313,

Lineage.

WALTER DE BEAUCHAMP, younger son of John, Lord Beauchamp, of Powyke, a military person of celebrity in the reigns of HENRY IV. and HENRY V., *m.* Elizabeth, dau., and co-heiress of Sir John Roche, Knt. of Broham, and had issue,

WILLIAM, of whom presently.

Richard, bishop of Salisbury, supposed to have been the first chancellor of the order of the Garter.

Elizabeth *m.* to Sir Richard Dudley, and had a son and a dau., the latter of whom, Joane Dudley, became heiress to her brother, and *m.* Sir John Bayntun, Knt., from which marriage, through a long line of distinguished ancestors, descended Edward Bayntun Rolt, Esq., of Spye Park, co. Wilts, who was created a baronet in 1762, an honour now EXTINCT (*see* p. 588).

The elder son,

WILLIAM DE BEAUCHAMP, *m.* Elizabeth (afterwards wife of Roger Touchet), eldest dau. and co-heiress of Gerard de Braybrooke, (grandson, and eventually heir of Almaric St. Amand, 3rd and last Baron St. Amand of that family,) and was summoned to parliament in right of his wife, "as William de Beauchamp, Baron of St. Amand," from 2 January, 1449, (the barony had been forty-six years previously in ABEYANCE,) to 26 May, 1455. His lordship was soon afterwards, being then sewer to the king, constituted chamberlain of North Wales. He made his will 18 March, 1457, and *d.* the following day, being succeeded by his only son,

RICHARD DE BEAUCHAMP, 2nd Baron St. Amand, of the family of Beauchamp, attainted in the 1st of RICHARD III., (1483-4) but fully restored upon the accession of HENRY VII. This nobleman, *b.* four years before his father's death, was in the expedition made in the 8th of HENRY VII. (1492-3), in aid of Maximilian the Emperor against the French. He *d.* in 1508, and by his testament dated 12 June, in that year, he desires to be interred in the Black Friers' Church, near Ludgate, within the city of London, and for lack of issue by Dame Anne his wife, settles divers lordships in the cos. Wilts, Bedford, Berks, Huntingdon, and Hereford, upon his natural son by Mary Wroughton, Anthony St. Amand, and the heirs of his body. The BARONY at the decease of this nobleman, Nicolas, in his Synopsis, presumes became vested in the descendants and representatives of Isabella, sister of Almaric St. Amand, 2nd Baron St. Amand of that family (Maud wife of John Babington and Alianore, the sisters of Elizabeth Braybrooke, who brought the barony into the family of Beauchamp, the other co-heiresses of Gerard de Braybrooke having died issueless), which Isabella *m.* 1st, Richard Handlo, and 2nd, Robert de Ildesle; but Sir Harris Nicolas observes further in a note, "that although no other issue is assigned to William Beauchamp, 4th Lord St. Amand (or *first* of that family), in either of the numerous pedigrees he had consulted, than his son Richard the last Baron, it is to be remarked, that in the will of the said Richard, Lord St. Amand, he bequeathes a cup to his *niece Leverseye.* This expression was probably used to describe his *wife's niece;* but it must be observed, that if he had a sister of the whole blood who left issue, the barony became vested in her and her descendants," upon the death of the last lord.

Arms.—Gules, a fesse between six martlets, or, within a bordure, arg.

BEAUCHAMP—BARON BEAUCHAMP, OF BLETSHO.

By Writ of Summons, dated 1st June, 1363.

Lineage.

ROGER DE BEAUCHAMP, one of the eminent warriors in the reign of EDWARD III., younger son of Giles, and grandson of Walter de Beauchamp, of Alcester, was summoned to parliament, as Roger de Bello Campo, BARON BEAUCHAMP, OF BLETSHO, from 1 June, 1363, to 20 October, 1379. In the 20th of EDWARD III. (1346-7), we first find this gallant person serving in France, and the next year the king confirming unto him and his wife, Sibel, the manor of Lydeard-Tregoz, in the co. Wilts, granted to them by Peter de Grandison; which Sibel was eldest of the four sisters and co-heirs of Sir William de Patshul, Knt., and grand-dau., maternally, of Mabel, eldest of the four sisters and co-heirs of Otto de Grandison. In the 28th of EDWARD III., Roger de Beauchamp was captain of Calais

In the 33rd of the same monarch he attended the king in his expedition into Gascoigne, and in the next year he obtained, in right of his wife, the manor of BLETNESHO, or BLETSHO, in the co. Bedford, which he made the chief place of his residence. In the 46th of EDWARD III., being still captain of Calais, his lordship had license to transport his household goods and other necessaries thither without the payment of any custom upon the same, and in the next year he had a special commission to take care that the peace then made between King EDWARD and the Earl of Flanders should be preserved within the marches of Calais. In the 5th of EDWARD, being then CHAMBERLAIN OF THE HOUSEHOLD, Lord Beauchamp had a pension for life of 100 marks per annum, in consideration of his eminent services, out of the farm of the castle and town of Devizes, in Wiltshire. His lordship d. in 1379, and was s. by his son,

ROGER DE BEAUCHAMP, as second BARON BEAUCHAMP, of Bletsho; but this nobleman was never summoned to parliament. His lordship proving his age in the 7th of RICHARD II., had livery of all his lands. In the 18th (1394-5) of the same reign, we find this nobleman attending the king into Ireland; but of his lordship, who m. Johanna Clopton, nothing more is known than that he was succeeded by his son,

JOHN DE BEAUCHAMP, 3rd baron, but never summoned to parliament. This nobleman doing homage in the 8th of HENRY IV. (1406-7), had livery of his lands; but he d. in six years afterwards. He m. Edith, dau. of Sir John Stourton, and left by her (who m. 2ndly Sir Robert Shottesbrook) a son and heir,

JOHN DE BEAUCHAMP, 4th baron, then only two years old, at whose decease the title and estates passed to his only sister and heiress,

MARGARET DE BEAUCHAMP, who m. 1st, Sir Oliver St. John, Knt., and conveyed the BARONY OF BEAUCHAMP, OF BLETSHO, into that family, from which it was carried by Anne St. John, of Bletsho—(see BURKE's Peerage and Baronetage, article ST. JOHN)—into the family of William, Lord Howard, son and heir of Charles, 1st Earl of Nottingham, whose dau. and heiress, Elizabeth, m. John Mordaunt, 1st Earl of Peterborough, and the barony of Beauchamp of Bletsho, with that of Mordaunt, is now vested in the co-representatives of the Dukes of Gordon (see that title); Margaret de Beauchamp m. 2ndly, John Beaufort, Earl of Somerset, and by him was mother of Margaret, Countess of Richmond, whose son ascended the British throne as King HENRY VII.

BEAUCHAMP—BARONS BEAUCHAMP, OF HACHE, IN THE CO. SOMERSET.

By Writ, dated 29 December, 1299.

Lineage.

The first of this Somersetshire family of whom mention is made by Dugdale, is

ROBERT DE BEAUCHAMP, who, in the 3rd of HENRY II. (1156-7), accounted the king £6 for a mark of gold, and, in the 9th of the same monarch, was sheriff of the cos. Somerset and Dorset. In three years afterwards, this Robert, upon the assessment of the aid for marrying the king's dau., then levied, certified his knight's fees, veteri feoffamento, to amount in number to seventeen, for which, in the 14th of HENRY II., he paid £7 1s. 8d., that is 8s. 4 l. for each knight's fee. In the 22nd of the same HENRY, he again enjoyed the sheriffalty for the same cos., and continued in office for five years, and one half of the sixth year following. This feudal lord d. in 1228, leaving in minority, and in ward to Hubert de Burgh, his son and heir,

ROBERT DE BEAUCHAMP, who d. before 1251, and was s. by his son,

ROBERT DE BEAUCHAMP. Of this feudal baron nothing is known beyond his being engaged against the Welsh with HENRY III., and his founding the priory of Frithelstoke, in the co. Devon. He was yet living in 1257, and was s. by his son,

JOHN DE BEAUCHAMP, who, in the 5th of EDWARD I. (1276-7), was made governor of the castles of Kaermerdin and Cardigan. He m. Cicely, dau. and heiress of Maud de Kyme, dau. of William Ferrers, Earl of Derby, by her second husband, William de Vivonia, which William was son of Hugh de Vivonia, by Mabel, one of the co-heirs of William Mallet, a great baron, who d. temp. HENRY III. This John de Beauchamp, who d. 1283, was s. by his son,

JOHN DE BEAUCHAMP, who was summoned to parliament as a baron by the style of "Io de Bello Campo (de Somerset)," on 29 December, 1229, 28th of EDWARD I., and in the 34th of

the same reign was one of the distinguished persons who received the honour of knighthood with Prince Edward, the king's eldest son, being in the expedition made into Scotland in that year. In the 8th of EDWARD II. his lordship was again in the Scottish wars; and in the 14th of the same king he succeeded to the very extensive landed possessions of his mother, comprising the manor of Sturminster-Marshal, in the co. Dorset, a moiety of the manor of West Kington, in the co. Wilts, of the whole manor of Wadmersh, in the co. Surrey, of the manor of Bullingham, in the co. Cambridge, also the hamlets of Watweton and Widecombe. In two years afterwards Lord Beauchamp was made governor of the castle of Bridgewater. In the 7th of EDWARD III. (1333-4), he obtained license to fortify his manor houses at Hacche, Estokes, and South Hainedon, and to embattle their walls. His lordship d. in 1336, up to which period he had regular summonses, and was s. by his son,

JOHN DE BEAUCHAMP, 2nd Lord Beauchamp, of Hacche, summoned to parliament from 24 August, 1336, to 24 February, 1343. This nobleman participated in the glories of EDWARD III.'s reign, being constantly engaged in the French wars of that monarch. His lordship d. in 1343, and was s. by his son (then twelve years of age, and under the guardianship of Robert de Ferrers, and Reginald de Cobham),

JOHN DE BEAUCHAMP, 3rd baron, summoned to parliament from 15 November, 1351, to 20 November, 1360. This nobleman was in the expedition made into Gascoigne, in the 33rd of EDWARD III., and of the retinue of Thomas de Beauchamp, Earl of Warwick, whose dau. Alice he had married. His lordship d. in 1360 without issue, when the BARONY OF BEAUCHAMP OF HACCHE fell into ABEYANCE between his three sisters and co-heiresses, and in that state it still continues amongst their descendants. Those ladies were

I. Cecily, m. 1st, to Sir Roger Seymour, by whom she had a son, William, from whom the Duke of Somerset, and Marquess of Hertford, derive; and 2ndly, to Richard Turberville, of Bere Regis, in Dorset, by whom she left a dau., Juliana Turberville.

II. Margaret, wife of Thos. Challons.

III. Eleanor, m. to —— Meriet, and left a son, John Meriet, whose dau. and heiress, Elizabeth, m. a Seymour.

Upon the division of the estates, Cecily had for her share the manors of Hacche, Shipton, Beauchamp, Murifield, and one-third of the manor of Shipton Mallet, in the co. Somerset, with certain lands in Sturminster Marshal, in the co. Dorset; the manors of Boultberry and Harberton, in Devonshire; the manor of Dourton, in Buckinghamshire; of Little Hawes, in Suffolk, and two parts of the manor of Selling, in Kent.

Arms.—Vaire as. and arg.

BEAUCHAMP—BARONS BEAUCHAMP, OF KYDDERMINSTER.

By Letters Patent (the 1st Barony so created), dated 10 October, 1387.

Lineage.

SIR JOHN DE BEAUCHAMP, Knt., of Holt, in co. Worcester, (great grandson of William de Beauchamp, Lord of Elmley, and his wife, Isabel, dau. and heiress of William Mauduit, of Hanslope,—see Beauchamp, Earls of Warwick) having participated in the high achievements of his distinguished family, during the martial reign of EDWARD III., obtained a grant, in the 11th of RICHARD II. (1387-8), of the manors and lands belonging to the priory of Deerhurst, in the co. Gloucester, being then steward of the king's household, and was elevated to the peerage by letters patent, dated 10 October, 1387, (the 1st barony* so conferred), as LORD BEAUCHAMP, OF KYDDERMINSTER. This honour, however, he did not long enjoy, for, in the same year, he was attainted of high treason along with Sir John Tresilian, chief justice of the King's Bench.

---

* That the solemn investure of this John, and all other barons who were thenceforth created by patent, was performed by the king himself, by putting on a robe of scarlet, as also a mantle (with two gards on the left shoulder) and a hood, and all furred with minever, there is no doubt; which form of creation continued until the 13th year of King JAMES, that Sir James Hay (a Scotchman) was advanced to the dignity of a baron of this realm by letters patent, date Junii, by the title of Lord Hay, of Sauley, the lawyers then declaring that the delivery of the letters-patent was sufficient without any ceremony.—DUGDALE.

and several others, by the parliament which the nobles forced the king to assemble, and beheaded upon Tower-hill, his sentence being so commuted from hanging and quartering, which latter punishment the chief justice underwent. Lord Beauchamp *m.* Joane, dau. and heiress of Robert le Fitzwith, and was *s.* by his only son (then but ten years of age, the lordship of Holt being committed, during his minority to Thomas, Earl of Warwick),

JOHN DE BEAUCHAMP, 2nd baron (the attainder being, we presume, repealed). This nobleman attended King RICHARD II. into Ireland, in the 22nd year of that monarch's reign (1398-9), and executed the office of escheator of the co. Worcester, in the 8th of HENRY IV. (1406-7). His lordship *d.* in 1420, leaving an only dau. and heiress, Margaret, who *m.* 1st, John Pauncefort, and 2ndly, John Wysham, when the BARONY OF BEAUCHAMP, OF KYDDERMINSTER, EXPIRED.

BEAUCHAMP—BARONS BEAUCHAMP, OF POWYKE.

By Letters Patent, dated 2 May, 1447.

Lineage.

WALTER DE BEAUCHAMP, a younger son of William de Beauchamp, Lord of Elmley, and his wife, Isabel, sister and heiress of William Mauduit, Earl of Warwick (*see* Beauchamp, Earls of Warwick), having purchased from Reginald Fitzherbert a moiety of the manor of Alcester, co. Warwick, made that one of his principal seats, calling it Beauchamp Court; the other being at Powyke, co. Worcester. This Walter, who was a very eminent person at the period in which he lived, having signed with the cross for a pilgrimage to the Holy Land, had a legacy of 200 marks bequeathed to him by his father, for his better performance of that voyage. He was steward of the household to King EDWARD I., and attended that monarch to Flanders, and into Scotland, where he shared in the honours of Falkirk on 22 July, 1298. In the 29th of the same reign he was one of the lords in the parliament of Lincoln, being then styled *Dominus de Alcester*, who signified to the pope, under their seals, the superiority of King EDWARD over the kingdom of Scotland. His lordship *m.* Alice de Tony, and had issue,

  I. WALTER, successor to his father,
  II. William, a military man of celebrity, who succeeded to part of the estates of his elder brother.
  III. Giles, who inherited the lordship of Alcester, by the settlement of his eldest brother.

The eldest son,
WALTER DE BEAUCHAMP, succeeded his father in 1306, and was the next year in the expedition against the Scots. In 1317, soon after the death of Guy, Earl of Warwick, his kinsman, he had custody of all the lands belonging to Warwick Castle, together with the castle itself, during the minority of the young earl. In 1327 he had a special commission to execute the office of constable of England in a particular case; and dying in the following year, *s. p.*, was *s.* by his brother,
WILLIAM DE BEAUCHAMP, a military officer of high reputation, who had attended EDWARD I. in several of his expeditions into Flanders and Scotland. In the 10th of that monarch he acted as sheriff of Worcestershire, which office was granted to him during the minority of his kinsman, Guy, Earl of Warwick. In the 14th of EDWARD II. he was appointed governor of St. Briavel Castle, co. Gloucester, and of the Forest of Dean, and was constituted, in the year following, one of the king's commissioners for the safe custody of the city of Worcester. Dying, however, without issue, his estates devolved upon his brother,
GILES DE BEAUCHAMP, who had already inherited, by the settlement of his eldest brother, the lordment of Alcester, the manor-house of which, called Beauchamp's Court, he had license to fortify in the 14th of EDWARD III. with a wall of stone and lime, and to embattle it; and he obtained similar permission regarding his house at Fresh-Water, in the Isle of Wight, in the 16th year of the same reign, 1342-3. This Giles was *s.* by his son,
JOHN DE BEAUCHAMP, of whom little is mentioned save his founding a chantry in the parish church of Alcester, *temp.* EDWARD III., for one priest to celebrate divine service daily at the altar of All Saints, and his being in the expedition against France in the 3rd of RICHARD II. This John de Beauchamp left two sons,

  I. WILLIAM (Sir), his successor.
  II. Walter (Sir), from whom the Beauchamps, Barons of St. Amand, derived (*see* that dignity),

and was *s.* by the elder,

SIR WILLIAM DE BEAUCHAMP, Knt., who, in the 16th of RICHARD II., was made constable of the castle of Gloucester. In the 3rd of HENRY IV. (1401-2), was appointed sheriff of Worcestershire, and upon the accession of HENRY V., sheriff of Gloucestershire. He *m.* Catharine, dau.. and eventually co-heir. of Sir Gerard de Ufflete, and was *s.* by his son.

SIR JOHN DE BEAUCHAMP, Knt., who purchased from Thomas de Botreaux the other moiety of the manor of Alcester, which had continued in that family for divers descents. In the 17th of HENRY VI., this Sir John de Beauchamp (2 May, 1447) was elevated to the peerage, in consequence of the many good and acceptable services performed by him to that king, and to HENRY V. his father, by the title of Lord Beauchamp, Baron of Powyke. He was also constituted justice of South Wales, with power to exercise that office personally or by deputy: and ere long (28th HENRY VI.) was raised to the office of lord treasurer of England, and honoured with the Garter. His lordship *d.* in 1475 (says Sir H. Nicholas), and by his last testament, dated 9 April, 1475, bequeathed his body to sepulture in the church of the Dominican Friars, at Worcester, in a new chapel to be made on the north side of the choir. Lord Beauchamp was *s.* by his only son, then forty years of age,

SIR RICHARD BEAUCHAMP, 2nd Lord Beauchamp, of Powyke, who *m.* Elizabeth, dau. of Sir Humphrey Stafford, Knt. and had issue,

  1. Elizabeth, *m.* to Sir Robert Willoughby, Lord Willoughby de Broke, and had an only son, Edward, who predeceased his father, leaving by his wife Elizabeth, dau. of Richard Nevil, Lord Latimer, three daus.. of whom the eldest. Elizabeth. alone left issue; which Elizabeth *m.* Sir Fulke Greville, 2nd son of Sir Fulke Greville, of Milcote, co. Warwick, and from that union descend the extant EARLS of BROOKE AND WARWICK, the BARONS WILLOUGHBY DE BROKE, the LORD GREVILLE, &c.
  II. Anne, *m.* to Richard Lygon, Esq., of Worcestershire, and from this marriage the present EARL BEAUCHAMP derives. (*See* BURKE's *Peerage and Baronetage*.)
  III. Margaret, *m.* to Richard Rede, Esq., of co. Gloucester.

His lordship *d.* in 1496, and thus leaving no male issue, the Barony of Beauchamp of Powyke EXPIRED, while the estates of the deceased lord devolved upon the above ladies as co-heiresses. Elizabeth, Lady Willoughby de Broke, having the Manor of Alcester. and her sisters Powyke and the other lands in the co. of Worcester.

BEAUCHAMP—EARL OF ALBEMARLE.

By Letters Patent, dated 1417.

(*See* Beauchamp, 5th Earl of Warwick.)

BEAUFORT—EARL OF DORSET, AND DUKE OF EXETER.

By Letters Patent, dated—18 November, 1416.

Lineage.

This was a branch of the royal house of Plantagenet, springing from the celebrated
JOHN OF GAUNT (4th son of King EDWARD III., and so denominated from the place of his birth, Gant, or, as we spell it, Ghent, *anno* 1340), Earl of Richmond, Duke of Lancaster, and Duke of Aquitaine, K.G., who *m.*, for his 3rd wife, Katherine, dau. of Sir Payn Roet, a knight of Hainault and Guienne King of Arms, and widow of Sir Hugh (or Otes) Swinford, but had the following issue by her before his marriage, who were legitimated by parliament, in the 15th RICHARD II., for all purposes, save accession to the crown, viz.,

  JOHN, EARL OF SOMERSET.
  HENRY, bishop of Lincoln, 1397, and of Winchester, 1405; CARDINAL, 1426. This was the celebrated CARDINAL BEAUFORT, Lord Chancellor of England, who crowned Henry VI. in Paris as king of France in 1431, and *d.* at Winchester in 1447.
  THOMAS, of whom presently.
  Joane, *m.* 1st, to Sir Robert Ferrers, 2nd Lord Ferrers, of Wemme; and 2ndly, to Ralph Nevill, Earl of Westmoreland.

The youngest son (surnamed Beaufort, from the castle of Beaufort in France, part of the marriage portion of Blanch of Artois, upon her marriage with Edward Crouchback, 1st Earl of Lancaster),

SIR THOMAS BEAUFORT. having attained some eminence in the reign of RICHARD II.. was appointed admiral of the whole fleet to the northwards. In the 5th of HENRY IV., and retained to serve the king in that command with 300 men at-arms, himself and one banneret being part of the number. In the 10th of the same monarch he was made captain of Calais. and in the next year had another grant of the office of admiral, both of the northern and western seas, for life. In which employments Sir Thomas deported himself with so much discretion that he was soon afterwards (2nd HENRY IV.) appointed lord chancellor of England, with a pension of 500 marks per annum, over and above the ordinary fees and wages of that high office, to enjoy from 31 January preceding, so long as he should hold the same. He obtained likewise a grant of some of the forfeited lands of Sir Robert Belknap, and in addition to the command of the northern and western seas, the admiralship of Ireland, Aquitaine. and Picardy. with six tuns of wine yearly from the port of Kingston-upon-Hull. In the 13th of HENRY IV. he was elevated to the peerage as EARL OF DORSET, and upon the accession of HENRY V.. being then lieutenant of Aquitaine, he was retained to serve the king in that capacity for one half-year, with 240 men-at-arms and 1,200 archers. In the 2nd year of the new monarch his lordship was one of the ambassadors to negotiate a marriage between his royal master and Catherine, dau. of the king of France: and in the next year he had the honour of commanding the rear-guard at the celebrated battle of Agincourt. "consisting of archers. and such as were armed with spears. halberds, and bills," and was constituted lieutenant of Normandy. In the 4th of HENRY V. (1416-17), his lordship was created DUKE OF EXETER, for life only, in the parliament then held at London. having therewith a grant of £1,000 per annum out of the exchequer, and £40 per annum more payable from the city of Exeter. During the remainder of the martial reign of the gallant HENRY V., at whose solemn funeral he assisted as a mourner, his grace continued constantly engaged upon the plains of Normandy, and reaped fresh laurels in each succeeding campaign. Upon the accession of the new monarch (HENRY VI.) the duke's services in France were retained. with three bannerets, three knights, 182 men-at-arms, and 600 archers, and he obtained in the same year the office of justice of North Wales. His grace m. Margaret, dau. and co-heiress of Sir Thomas Nevil, of Horneby, Knt., but had no issue. He d. 27 December, 1417, when the earldom of Dorset and dukedom of Exeter EXPIRED, but his great landed possessions devolved upon his nephew, John, Duke of Somerset. In the last testament of this eminent person, dated 29 December, in the 5th of HENRY VI., he ordains that as soon after his decease (viz., the first day, if possible, or the second or third at the furthest), a thousand masses should be solemnly sung for his soul, &c., that no great cost should be incurred at his funeral and that five tapers only, in so many candlesticks, should be placed round his remains. That as many poor men as he should be years of age at the time of his death should carry a torch at his funeral, each of them having a gown or hood of white cloth, and as many pence as he himself had lived years; likewise the same number of poor women to be similarly attired and remunerated. Furthermore, he bequeathed to each poor body coming to his funeral a penny; and he appoints that at every anniversary of himself, and Margaret his wife, that the abbot of St. Edmundsbury, if present, should have 6s. 8d.; the prior, if present, 3s. 4d.; and every monk there at that time 20d.; giving to the monastery for the support of these anniversaries 400 marks. To Joane, his sister, Countess of Westmorland, he gives a book, called *Tristram*, and to Thomas Swineford, a cup of silver gilt, with a cover. To the use of poor scholars in Queen's College, Oxon, he bequeaths £100, to be deposited in a chest, to the end that they might have some relief thereby, in loan, desiring that the borrowers should in charity pray for his soul, &c., and upon the like terms he bequeaths £100 more, to be similarly placed to Trinity Hall, Cambridge. The deceased duke was a knight of the Garter.

BEAUFORT — EARLS AND DUKES OF SOMERSET, MARQUESS OF DORSET.

Earldom, by Letters Patent, *anno* 1397.
Dukedom, by Letters Patent, *anno* 1442.

Lineage.

In the 20th year of RICHARD II., the Lord Chancellor having declared in parliament that the King had created
SIR JOHN BEAUFORT, Knt., eldest son of John of Gaunt, by Catharine Swineford (*see* Beaufort, Duke of Exeter), EARL OF

35

SOMERSET. His lordship was advanced in the next year (also in open parliament) to the Marquisate of Dorset, a dignity which he soon afterwards resigned: and was created on the day of his resignation MARQUESS OF SOMERSET. He bore, however, subsequently, the former title, and as Marquess of Dorset, was made constable of Wallingford Castle, and constable of Dover Castle. and warden of the Cinque Ports. In the same year his lordship had extensive grants from the crown, and was appointed admiral of the king's fleet, both to the north and west; but upon the accession of HENRY IV., having been one of the accusers of Thomas de Woodstock, Duke of Gloucester, his right to the marquisate of Dorset was declared void by parliament, and his only title then remaining was Earl of Somerset, by which, in the same year, he was constituted lord chamberlain of England. In the 4th of the new monarch, the commons in parliament, however, petitioned for his restitution to the marquisate of Dorset; but the earl seemed unwilling to re adopt the designation of marquess, that being then so new a dignity in England. His lordship did at length, though, re sume it, for we find him in a few years after appointed, as Marquess of Dorset, lord high admiral of England. The marquess m. Margaret, dau. of Thomas Holland, and sister and co-heiress of Thomas, both Earls of Kent (who m. after his decease, Thomas, Duke of Clarence), and had issue,

HENRY, who s. as 2nd Earl of Somerset.
John, successor to his brother.
Edmund, who, in the 9th of HENRY VI., was appointed, under the title of Lord Morteign, commander of the forces in France (but of him hereafter).
Jane, m. to JAMES I. King of Scotland, who has celebrated her in his poems.
Margaret, m. to Thomas Courtenay, Earl of Devon.

His lordship, who, among other honours, was a knight of the Garter, d. in 1409-1410, and was s. by his eldest son,
HENRY BEAUFORT, 2nd Earl of Somerset, god-son to King HENRY IV., who, dying in his minority, in 1418. was s. by his brother,
JOHN BEAUFORT, 3rd Earl of Somerset, K.G., a distinguished military commander in the reigns of HENRY V. and HENRY VI., by the latter of whom he was created, in 1443, Earl of Kendal and Duke of Somerset, by which title he was made lieutenant-general of Aquitaine, and of the whole realm of France, and Duchy of Normandy. His grace m. Margaret, dau. of Sir John Beauchamp, of Bletsho, Knt., and heiress of John, her brother (which lady m. after the duke's decease, Sir Leode Welles), by whom he left an only dau. and heiress,

Margaret, who m. Edmund Tudor, surnamed of Hadham, Earl of Richmond, by whom she was mother of
HENRY, EARL OF RICHMOND, who ascended the throne as HENRY VII.

Her ladyship m. 2ndly, Sir Henry Stafford, Knt., and 3rdly, Thomas, Lord Stanley, but had issue by neither. The virtues of this distinguished lady have been greatly celebrated, and Walpole mentions her in his catalogue of noble authors, as having written upon several occasions; and by her son's command and authority, "made the orders for great estates of ladies and noblewomen, for their precedence, attires, and wearing of harbes at funerals, over the chin and under the same."

John, Duke of Somerset, d. in 1444, when that dignity and the Earldom of Kendal EXPIRED; but the Earldom of Somerset de volved upon his brother,
EDMUND BEAUFORT, Marquess of Dorset, as 4th Earl of Somerset. This nobleman commanded, in the 10th of HENRY VI., one of the divisions of the Duke of Bedford's army in Normandy, and upon the death of that eminent general, was appointed joint commander, with Richard, Duke of York, of all the English forces in the duchy. He subsequently (15th HENRY VI.) laid successful siege to Harfleur; and afterwards crossing the Somme, invested, with equal fortune, the Fort of Fulleville, when he formed a junction with Lord Talbot. In a few years following, he acquired an accession of renown by his relief of Calais, then invested by the Duke of Burgundy, and for his good services upon that occasion, was created (24 August, 1441) Earl of Dorset. His lordship continuing to distinguish himself in arms, was advanced, on 24 June, 1442, to the Marquisate of Dorset, by which title he inherited the Earldom of Somerset at the decease of his brother in 1444, and the next year was constituted Regent of France. In three years afterwards (31 March, 1448) he was created Duke of Somerset. His grace was also knight of the Garter, and lord high constable. But the fortune of war veering soon after, and Caen falling into the hands of the French, the Duke had to encounter a storm of unpopularity in England, to which he was recalled, with the hostility of Richard, Duke of York, and espousing the Lancastrian cause, in the lamentable war of the Roses, which about that period broke out, he fell in the first

battle of St. Alban's in 1455. His grace had *m.* Alianore, one of the daus. and co-heiresses of Richard Beauchamp, Earl of Warwick, and had issue,

HENRY, Earl of Morteign, his successor.
Edmund, successor to his brother.
John, slain at the battle of Tewkesbury.
Alianore, *m.* 1st, to James Boteler, Earl of Wiltshire, and 2ndly, to Sir Robert Spencer, Knt.
Joane, *m.* to the Lord Howth, of Ireland, and afterwards to Sir Richard Fry, Knt.
Anne, *m.* to Sir William Paston, Knt.
Margaret, *m.* to Humphrey, Earl of Stafford, and afterwards to Sir Richard Darell, Knt.
Elizabeth, *m.* to Sir Henry Lewes, Knt.

The duke was *s.* by his eldest son,

HENRY BEAUFORT, 2nd Duke of Somerset, K.G., a very distinguished personage in the York and Lancaster contest. His lordship, like his father, being a staunch Lancastrian, was constituted, in the 36th of HENRY VI., governor of the Isle of Wight, with the castle of Carisbroke, and in the following year appointed captain of Calais. He subsequently continued high in the confidence of his royal master, until the defeat sustained by the Lancastrians at Towton, on 11 March, 1461, when flying from the field with the unfortunate HENRY, he is accused of abandoning the fallen monarch at Berwick, and of making his peace with the new king (EDWARD IV.) by the surrender of Bamburgh Castle. Certain it is that he was taken into favour by that prince, and obtained a grant from him of 1,000 marks per annum. In the next year, however, upon the appearance of Margaret of Anjou in the north, at the head of a considerable force, his grace resumed "the Red Rose," but falling into the hands of the Yorkists at Hexham, in 1463, he was beheaded the day after the battle, and attainted by parliament in the 5th of EDWARD IV. The duke had no legitimate issue, but left by Joane Hill an illegitimate son, Sir Charles Somerset, K.G., Knight Banneret, from whom the SOMERSETS, DUKES OF BEAUFORT, directly descend. His grace was *s.* by his brother,

EDMUND BEAUFORT, who after enduring a miserable exile with his brother John in France, is said to have been restored to the honours of his family (49th HENRY VI.) upon the temporary re-establishment of the Lancastrian power, and the 10th of EDWARD IV., when he is said to have been summoned to parliament as Duke of Somerset, though he is absent from the list of summonses for that year, as observes Sir H. Nicolas. His grace commanded the archers at the battle of Barnetfield, in the next year, and upon the loss of that battle fled into Wales, to the Earl of Pembroke. He was subsequently in command at Tewkesbury, where the ill-fortune of the day was attributed to his defection. His grace fled the field, but he was soon overtaken, and paid the forfeit of his head (*anno* 1471). As he died without issue, all his honours EXPIRED, leaving attainders out of the question, while his sisters or their representatives became his heirs.

Arms.—Quarterly, France and England, a border gobony, arg. and az.

BEAUMONT—EARLS OF LEICESTER.

See BELLOMONT.

BEAUMONT—VISCOUNTS BEAUMONT.

By Letters Patent, dated 12 February, 1440.

Lineage.

The original descent of this noble family does not appear to have been clearly ascertained. Some authorities deduce it from Lewis, son of Charles, Earl of Anjou, a younger son of LEWIS VIII., king of France; some from Lewis de Brienne, 2nd son of John de Brienne, the last king of Jerusalem; and some from the Viscounts Beaumont, of Normandy. Certain it is, however, that in the reign of EDWARD I., mention is made of Isabel de Beaumont, wife of John de Vesci; of Lewis, who, in 1294, was treasurer of the church of Salisbury, and afterwards Bishop of Durham; and of

HENRY DE BEAUMONT, who attending the king, 30th EDWARD I. (1301-2), in his expedition against the Scots, obtained a precept to the collectors of the fifteenth in Yorkshire for 200 marks towards his support in those wars. In the 1st year of King EDWARD II. this Henry had a grant in fee of the manors of Folkynham, Edenham, and Barton-upon-Humber, and of all the knight's fees belonging to Gilbert de Gant, which Laura de Gant, his widow, held in dower, and in three years afterwards

had a further grant of the Isle of Man, to hold for life, by the services which the lords thereof had usually performed to the kings of Scotland. In the preceding year he had been constituted governor of Roxburgh Castle, and deputed, with Humphrey de Bohun, Earl of Hereford, and Robert de Clifford, to guard the marches. About this period he espoused Alice, dau. and eventually heiress of Alexander Cumyn, Earl of Boghan, constable of Scotland, and, doing his homage, in the 6th of EDWARD II. (1312-13), had livery of her lands. In the 10th of the same monarch, Lord Beaumont (he had been previously styled "consanguineus regis," says Nicolas, and summoned to parliament as a BARON on 4 March, 1309), being then the king's lieutenant in the north, accompanying thither two cardinals who had come from Rome, partly to reconcile the king to the Earl of Lancaster, and partly to enthronize his lordship's brother, Lewis de Beaumont, in the bishopric of Durham, was attacked, near Darlington, by a band of robbers, headed by Gilbert de Middleton, and despoiled of all his treasnre, horses, and everything else of value, as were likewise his companions. His lordship and his brother were also made prisoners, the former being conveyed to the castle of Mitford, and the latter to that of Durham, there to remain until ransomed. From this period the baron continued to bask in the sunshine of royal favour, and to receive from the crown further augmentations to his territorial possessions, until the 16th of EDWARD II., when, being required to give his advice in council, regarding a truce then meditated with the Scots, he declined, contemptuously observing, "*that he would give none therein,*" which so irritated the king, that his lordship was ordered to depart the council, and he retired, saying, "*he had rather begone than stay.*" He was in consequence committed, with the consent of the lords present, to prison, but soon after released upon the bail of *Henry de Perci*, and *Ralph de Nevile.* He seems within a short time, however, again to enjoy the king's favour, for we find him in two years constituted one of the plenipotentiaries to treat of peace with France, and in two years subsequently nominated guardian to David, son and heir of David de Strabolgi, Earl of Athol, deceased, in consideration of the sum of £1,000. His lordship after this time, entirely deserting his royal master, sided with the queen consort Isabella, and was the very person to deliver up the unhappy monarch to his enemies, upon his abortive attempt to fly beyond the sea. The king thereupon was committed close prisoner to Berkeley Castle, where he was inhumanly murdered in 1327. For this act of treachery Lord Beaumont received a grant of the manor of Loughborough, part of the possessions of Hugh le Despenser, the attainted Earl of Winchester, and was summoned to parliament on 22 January, 1334, 7th EDWARD III., as EARL OF BOGHAN. His lordship, during the reign of EDWARD III., had many high and confidential employments, and took a prominent part in the affairs of Scotland being at one time sent as constable of the king's army into that country for defence of the realm. The earl *d.* in 1340, leaving by Alice Cumyn, of Buchan, his wife, four sons and six daus., VIZ., JOHN, his heir; Richard; John; Thomas, of Bolton Percy; Alice; Elizabeth, *m.* to Nicholas de Audley; Joan, *m.* to Fulk, Lord FitzWarine; Isabel, *m.* to Henry Plantagenet, Duke of Lancaster; Beatrice, *m.* to the Count de Dammartin; and Catherine, *m.* to David, Earl of Athole. His lordship inherited, upon the decease of his sister, Isabel, wife of John de Vesci, of Alnwick, in Northumberland (one of the most powerful barons of the North), a lady of great eminence in her time, without issue, large possessions in the co. Lincoln, which, added to his own acquirements, placed him amongst the most wealthy nobles in the kingdom at the period of his death. He was *s.* by his son,

JOHN DE BEAUMONT, 2nd BARON BEAUMONT, styled in the summons to parliament, 25 February, 1342, "Johannes de Bello-monte," but never entitled Earl of Boghan. His lordship *m.* Lady Alianore Plantagenet, 5th dau. of Henry, Earl of Lancaster, and great grand-dau. of King HENRY III., by whom he had an only child, Henry, born in Brabant, during her ladyship's attendance upon Phillippa, Queen Consort of EDWARD III. This nobleman, like his father, was much engaged in the Scottish wars. His lordship *d.* in 1342, leaving by the Lady Alianore Plantagenet his wife (who *m.* 2ndly Richard Earl of Arundel) an only son,

HENRY DE BEAUMONT, 3rd Baron, whose legitimacy (owing to his being born beyond the sea) was ratified by act of parliament, in the 25th of EDWARD III. In the 34th of the same monarch, being then of full age, his lordship did homage and had livery of his lands, and was summoned to parliament from 14 August, 1362, to 24 February, 1368. He *m.* Margaret, dau. of John de Vere, Earl of Oxford, and dying in 1368, left an only son, JOHN, and a dau., Eleanor, *m.* to Richard de Molines. The only son was placed, in the 47th EDWARD III., under the guardianship of William Lord Latimer.

JOHN DE BEAUMONT, 4th baron, K.G., attaining maturity in

the 6th RICHARD II. (1382-3), had livery of his lands, and in the same year with Henry de Spencer, bishop of Norwich, was in the English army sent to oppose the adherents of Pope CLEMENT VII. In four years afterwards his lordship accompanied JOHN OF GAUNT, then called *King of Castile and Leon*, into Spain, but before the close of that year, he was expelled the court, as one of the king's evil advisers, by the great lords assembled at Haringey Park. Soon afterwards, however, he made his peace, and had license to repair to Calais, in order to engage in a tournament, and he had then the honour of tilting with the Lord Chamberlain of the King of France. In the 12th RICHARD II., he was made admiral of the king's fleets to the northwards, and one of the wardens of the marches towards Scotland; "whereupon he entered that country forty miles, spoyled the Market at FOWEE, and brought many prisoners back." In the next year he had the castle of Cherburgh in France committed to his custody, and about that time was specially enjoined to abstain from exercising any feats of arms with the French, without permission from Henry de Perci, Earl of Northumberland. In the 16th of the same reign, his lordship received a pension of £100 per annum for his services, and was constituted constable of Dover Castle and Warden of the Cinque Ports; and in the 19th, he was appointed one of the commissioners to negotiate a marriage between the King of England and Isabell, dau. of the King of France. His lordship *m.* Katherine, dau. of Thomas de Everingham of Laxton, in the co. Nottingham, and had issue,

HENRY, his successor.
THOMAS, Lord of Basquerville and Captain of Galliarde, ancestor of the BEAUMONTS, of Cole Orton, co. Leicester, Barts. (of England, and Viscounts Beaumont, of Ireland), and of the BEAUMONTS of Stoughton Grange, also in Leicestershire, now represented by SIR GEORGE HOWLAND BEAUMONT, Bart.
Richard.
Elizabeth, *m.* to William, 3rd Lord Botreaux.

The baron, who had been summoned to parliament from 20 August, 1383, to 13 November, 1393, and had the honour of being a KNIGHT OF THE GARTER, *d.* in 1396, and was *s.* by his eldest son,
HENRY DE BEAUMONT, 5th baron, who received the honour of knighthood at the coronation of King HENRY IV.; and in the 11th of the same monarch's reign, was constituted one of the commissioners to treat of peace with France. His lordship *m* Elizabeth, dau. of William Lord Willoughby de Eresby, and had issue,

JOHN, his heir.
Henry, from whom the Beaumonts of Wednesbury, in the co. Stafford, descended.

Lord Beaumont, who had been summoned to parliament from 25 August, 1404, to 22 March, 1413, *d.* in the latter year, and was *s.* by his eldest son,
JOHN DE BEAUMONT, 6th baron, a very distinguished personage in the reign of HENRY VI., and high in that monarch's favour, under whom he enjoyed the most lucrative and honourable employments, and in whose service he eventually laid down his life. In the 14th of King HENRY (1435-6) his lordship obtained by letters patent, to himself and his heirs male, the Earldom of Boloine, being at that time upon his march for the relief of Calais, and in four years afterwards, 12 February, 1440, he was created VISCOUNT BEAUMONT (being the first person dignified with such a title), with precedency above all barons of the realm, and with a yearly fee of 20 marks out of the revenues of the co. Lincoln. His lordship received, subsequently, a patent of precedency (23rd HENRY VI.) above all viscounts thenceforth to be created; and in five years afterwards was constituted Lord High Chamberlain of England. The viscount finally lost his life at the battle of Northampton, fighting under the Lancastrian banner, on 10 July, 1459. His lordship was a knight of the Garter, and had been summoned to parliament, in the BARONY OF BEAUMONT, from 26 February 1432 to 26 September, 1439. He had *m.* Elizabeth, only dau. and heiress of Sir William Phelip, Lord Bardolf, by whom he left,

WILLIAM, his successor.
Joane, *m.* to John, Lord Lovel, of Tichmersh, and dying before her brother, left a son (who succeeded as Lord Lovel, but *d.* without issue,) and two daus., viz.,
    1 Joane, *m.* to Sir Brian Stapleton, of Carlton, Knt., from which marriage lineally descended
        Miles Thomas Stapleton, Esq., of Carleton, who established his co-heirship to the Barony of Beaumont, and was summoned by writ to the House of Peers 16 October, 1840. He was *b.* 4 June, 1805, and *d.* 1854, having *m.* 9 September, 1844, the Hon. Isabella Browne, dau. of Lord Kilmaine, by whom he had issue,

HENRY, now Baron Beaumont, *b.* 11 August, 1848.
Miles, *b.* 17 July, 1850. (*See* BURKE's *Peerage*.)
    2 Fridiswide, *m.* to Sir Edward Norris, of Yattenden, Knight, whose eldest son, John, *d. s. p.* and whose second, Henry, having been attainted, 1536, his portion of inheritance in the barony was confiscated to the crown. The son of Henry, Sir Henry Norris, was summoned to parliament, 14th ELIZABETH, 1572, as Baron Norris, of Rycote, a barony now merged in the Earldom of Abingdon.

John, Viscount Beaumont, was *s.* by his only son,
WILLIAM DE BEAUMONT, 2nd viscount and 7th baron, who inherited likewise large possessions from his mother, the heiress of the Bardolfs. This nobleman adhering faithfully to the Lancastrian interest, was made prisoner by the Yorkists at Towton Field, in the 1st year of Edward IV. (1461-2), when he was attainted, and his large possessions bestowed upon Lord Hastings. From this period until the accession of King HENRY VII., his lordship shared the fallen fortunes of his party, but rising with that event, he was restored to his honours and estates by act of Parliament, passed on 7 November, 1485, in the 1st year of the new monarch's reign. The viscount *m.* 1st, Elizabeth, dau. of Richard Scrope, and niece of Lord Scrope, of Bolton; and 2ndly, Joane, dau. of Humphrey Stafford, Duke of Buckingham, but *d.* without issue in 1507, when the viscountcy EXPIRED, while the Barony of Beaumont fell into ABEYANCE, and so continued, according to the decision upon the claim of Mr. Stapleton in 1798, "between the co-heirs of William, Viscount Beaumont (in whom it was vested by descent from his father, John, Lord Beaumont, who was summoned to and sat in parliament, 2nd HENRY VI. (1423-4), as a baron in fee), descended from his sister Joane, and that the petitioner Thomas Stapleton, Esq., was one of those co-heirs." The barony, however, as already stated, was revived and assigned forty-two years subsequently to Mr. Stapleton's grand-nephew, Miles-Thomas Stapleton, Esq.

Arms.—Az., semée de lis, a lion rampant, or.

BEAUMONT—VISCOUNT BEAUMONT.

By Letters Patent, dated 1622.

Lineage.

NICHOLAS BEAUMONT, Esq., M.P. for the co. Leicester, *m. p.* ELIZABETH, lineally descended from Thomas, 2nd son of John Beaumont, 4th Lord Beaumont, in the peerage of England, *m.* Anne, dau. of Wm. Saunders, Esq., of Welford, in Northamptonshire, and had, with other issue, two sons, HENRY, his heir; and Thomas, ancestor of the present SIR GEORGE-HOWLAND BEAUMONT, Bart., of Stoughton Grange, co. Leicester. The eldest son,
SIR HENRY BEAUMONT, Knt., petitioned JAMES I., ineffectually to revive in his person the Viscounty of Beaumont, forfeited by John, Viscount Beaumont, who fell at the battle of Northampton, on the side of the Lancastrians. Sir Henry *m.* Elizabeth, dau. and heir of Thomas Lewis, Esq., and was *s.* by his only son,
SIR THOMAS BEAUMONT, of Cole Orton, M.P., who was created a Baronet of England in 1619, and raised to the peerage of Ireland, as VISCOUNT BEAUMONT, of Swords, in 1622. His lordship was a staunch supporter of the royal cause and had to compound for his estates. He *m.* Elizabeth, dau. and heir of Henry Sapcote, Esq., of Elton, co. Huntingdon, and left a son and successor,
SIR SAPCOTE BEAUMONT, Bart., 2nd Viscount Beaumont, who, like his father, suffered deeply for his adherence to the royal cause, and died before the Restoration. He *m.* Elizabeth, dau. of Sir Thomas Monson, Knt., and had issue,

I. THOMAS, his heir.
II. John, governor of Dover Castle, *d. s. p.*, 3 July, 1701.
    I. Elizabeth, *m.* Sir John Hotham, Bart., and left a son and heir, Sir John Hotham, Bart., who died without male issue in 1691.

The son and heir,
SIR THOMAS BEAUMONT, 3rd Viscount Beaumont, *m.* Mary, dau. of Sir Erasmus Fountain, Knt., but *d.* without issue, 11 June, 1702, when the peerage became EXTINCT. The estates his lordship bequeathed to Sir George Beaumont, 4th bart. of Stoughton Grange, and they are now possessed by Sir George's descendant, the present Bart. of Stoughton Grange.

Arms.—Az., semée de-lis, a lion rampant, or.

BEAUMONT—EARL OF BEDFORD.

(S e BELLAMONT, Earl of Leicester.)

BEAUMONT—BARON CRAMOND.

(See RICHARDSON, Baron Cramond.)

BEC OR BEKE—BARONS BEKE OF ERESBY.

By Writ of Summons, dated 23 June, 1295.

Lineage.

WALTER BEC, Lord of Eresby, co. Lincoln, m. Agnes, dau. and heiress of Hugh, the son of Pinco, and had issue,

I. Hugh, who d. s. p. in his return from the Holy Land.
II. Henry, being a person of weak understanding, his two next brothers shared with him the inheritance.
III. Walter, } participators, with their brother Henry, in their
IV. John, } father's lands.
Nicholas, inherited the church patronage of his father.

The eldest surviving son,
HENRY BEKE, inherited Eresby and other manors. He m. Hawse or Alice de Multon, sister of Thomas de Multon, and was s. by his son,
WALTER BEKE, Lord of Eresby, who m. Eva, niece of Walter de Grey, archbishop of York, and had issue,

I. JOHN, his successor in the lordship of Eresby.
II. THOMAS, bishop of St. David's, d. 14 April, 1293.
III. Anthony, the celebrated bishop of Durham, and patriarch of Jerusalem. "This Anthony," says Dugdale, "was signed with the cross in the 54th HENRY III., in order to his going to the Holy Land with Prince Edward; and on the 3rd of EDWARD I., being then a clerk, was made constable of the Tower of London. Moreover, in anno 1283, being present at the translation of St. William, archbishop of York, and at the whole charge of that great solemnity (the king, queen, and many of the nobility being also there), he was then consecrated bishop of Durham, by William Wickwane, archbishop of York, in the church of St. Peter, within that city. After which, anno 1294 (22nd EDWARD I.), the king discerning his great losses in Gascoigne, he was sent to Rodolph, king of Almaine, to make a league with him; and the same year, upon the arrival of the cardinals to treat of peace between King EDWARD and the King of France, he readily answered their proposals in the French tongue. Furthermore, in anno 1296, King EDWARD entered Scotland with a powerful army; he brought thither to him no less than 500 horse and 1,000 foot, besides a multitude of Welsh and Irish. After which, the same year, being sent ambassador into that realm, he was solemnly met by the king and nobles; and after much dispute, brought them to such an accord that they totally submitted themselves to the pleasure of King EDWARD. Also, upon that rebellion, which again broke out there the next year following (at which time they used great cruelties to the English), he was again sent thither to inquire the truth, and to advertise the king thereof. And in the 26th of EDWARD I. was again sent into Scotland, with certain forces, at which time he assaulted the castle of Dulton, and took it. And lastly, in 33rd of EDWARD I., being with the Earl of Lincoln and some other bishops, sent to Rome, to present divers vessels of pure gold from King EDWARD to the Pope, his holiness taking especial notice of his courtly behaviour and magnanimity of spirit, advanced him to the title of 'Patriarch of Jerusalem.'"

"Amongst other works of this great prelate," continues Dugdale, "he founded the collegiate churches of Chester and Langcester, as also the collegiate chappel at Bishops-Auckland, all in the county palatine of Durham. Moreover, it is reported that no man in all the realm, except the king, did equal him for habit, behaviour, and military pomp, and that he was more versed in state affairs than in ecclesiastical duties; ever assisting the king most powerfully in his wars; having sometimes in Scotland 26 standard-bearers, and of his ordinary retinue 140 knights; so that he was thought to be rather a temporal prince than a priest or bishop; and lastly, that he d 3 March, 1310, and was buried above the high altar in his cathedral of Durham." This prelate was the first bishop that presumed to lie in the church, on account of the interment of the holy St. Cuthbert, and so superstitious were they in those days that they dared not bring in the remains at the doors, but broke a hole in the wall, to convey them in at the end of the church, which breech is said to be still visible.
I. Margaret, m. to Galfridus de Thorpe.
II. Another dau., a nun

The eldest son,

JOHN BEKE, s. his father in the feudal lordship of Eresby, and was summoned to parliament as Baron Beke of Eresby, on 23 June, 20 September, and 2 November, 1295, and 26 August, 1296, having previously (4th of EDWARD .., 1275 6) had license to make a castle of his manor-house at Eresby; his lordship m. ——, and had issue,

I. WALTER, who must have d. s. p. and vità patris, before the gift of Eresby to Robert Willoughby.
I. Alice, m. to Sir William de Willoughby, Knt., and had issue,
ROBERT WILLOUGHBY, who inherited, at the decease of his grand uncle, Anthony Beke, bishop of Durham, the great possessions of that eminent prelate, and was summoned to parliament, temp. EDWARD II., as LORD WILLOUGHBY DE ERESBY. (See that dignity in BURKE's Peerage and Baronetage.)
II. Margaret, m. to Sir Richard de Harcourt, Knt., ancestor of the Harcourts, Earls of Harcourt.
III. Mary, d unm.

Lord Beke gave Eresby to his grandson, Robert Willoughby, and d. 1303-4, when the Barony fell into ABEYANCE between his two daus. and co-heirs, the Ladies Willoughby and Harcourt, and so continues amongst their descendants.

Arms.—Gules, a cross moline, arg.

BECHE—BARONS LA BECHE.

By Writ of Summons, dated 26 February, 1342.

Lineage.

Of this family, De la Beche, of Aldworth, co. Bucks,
NICHOLAS DE LA BECHE was constituted constable of the Tower of London in the 9th of EDWARD III., and had a grant from the crown in two years afterwards of the manor of Whitchurch, with other lands. About this period, too, he obtained license to encastellate his houses at De La Beche, Beaumya, and Watlyington. He was subsequently distinguished in the wars in Brittany, and was summoned to Parliament as a baron on 25 February, 1342. In 1343 his lordship became seneschal of Gascony, and the next year was constituted one of the commissioners to treat with ALPHONSUS, king of Castile, touching a marriage between the eldest son of that monarch and Joane, dau. of the king of England.
Lord de la Beche d. in 1347, and leaving no issue, the Barony EXPIRED, but the estates passed to the sisters of John de la Beche, who d. nineteen years previously, and is supposed to have been the elder brother of the baron; consequently the co-heiresses were his lordship's sisters likewise. Of those ladies, the elder, JOAN, m. 1st, Sir Andrew Sackville, and 2ndly, Sir Thomas Langford; and the younger m. Robert Danvers.

Arms.—Vaire arg. and gules.

BELASYSE — BARONS FAUCONBERG, OF YARM, CO. YORK. VISCOUNTS FAUCONBERG, OF HENKNOWLE, CO. OF DURHAM. EARLS OF FAUCONBERG.

Barony, by Letters Patent, dated 25 May, 1627.
Viscounty, by Letters Patent, dated 31 January, 1643.
Earldom, by Letters Patent, dated 1st, 9 April, 1689; 2ndly, 15 June, 1774.

Lineage.

This eminent Norman family deduced an uninterrupted descent from
BELASIUS, one of the commanders in the army of the Conqueror, distinguished for having suppressed the adherents of Edgar Ethling, in the Isle of Ely, whence the spot where he had pitched his camp was named Belasius Hill, now known by the corrupted designation of Belsar's Hill. The son of this gallant soldier,
ROWLAND, marrying Elgiva, dau. and heiress of Ralph de Belasyse, of Belasyse, co. Durham, assumed, upon succeeding to the inheritance of his wife, the surname of "Belasyse, of Belasyse," and his descendants ever afterwards adhered to the same designation, although the spelling has frequently varied. The great-grandson of this Rowland Belasyse,
SIR ROWLAND BELASYSE attained the honour of knighthood by his gallant bearing at the battle of Lewes, in the 48th of HENRY III. Sir Rowland m. Mary, dau. and heiress of Sir

Henry Spring, Lord of Howton-le-Spring, in the bishopric of Durham, by whom he acquired a considerable accession of property, and was *s.* by his son,

SIR ROGER BELASYSE, Knt., who *m.* Joan, dau. of Sir Robert Harbottle, Knt., and had issue,

ROBERT, his successor.
John, *m.* to Mary, dau. of Roger Bertram, Esq.
Elizabeth, *m.* to Thomas Madison, Esq., of Unthank Hall.

Sir Roger was *s.* by his elder son,
SIR ROBERT BELASYSE, *m.* Anne, dau. of Sir Wm. Goulbourne, and had issue,

JOHN, his successor.
Mary, *m.* to John de Lambton.
Anne, *m.* to Robert Fowbray.
Ursula, *m.* to James de Claxton.
Frances, *m.* to Wm. de Wickliffe.

SIR JOHN BELASYSE *m.* Oswold, dau. of Sir Wm. Talbois, and by her had two sons and three daus,

I. JOHN, his heir.
II. Thomas, *m.* Mary, dau. of Thos. de Whitwell.
I. Dionysia, *m.* to Sir Gerald Salveyn, Knt.
II. Jane, *m.* to Robert de Buckton.
III. Elizabeth, *m.* to Hamon Byrd, of Newcastle-upon-Tyne.

The elder son,
JOHN BELASYSE *m.* Alice, dau. of John de la Hay, by whom he had issue,

I. WILLIAM, his heir.
II. John, *m.* Maud, dau. of John Doolard, of Aukland.
I. Mary, *m.* to William de Featherstonhaugh, of Featherston-haugh, in Northumberland.

The elder son,
WILLIAM BELASYSE, *m.* Maud, dau. and co-heiress of William Bellingham, of Bellingham, by whom he had issue,

JOHN, his heir.
Joan, wife of John Bussy, Esq.

SIR JOHN BELASYSE, Knt., *m.* Alice, dau. of Sir Robert Hansard, of Walworth, Knt., and had issue,

I. ROBERT, his heir.
I. Elizabeth, *m.* 1st, to Thomas Bingham, Esq., and 2ndly, to Sir John Cranlington, Knt.
II. Julian, *m.* 1st, to John Fishburn, of Fishburn, in the bishopric of Durham, and 2ndly, to Sir John Waddon. Knt.

ROBERT BELASYSE, *m.* Alice, dau. of Robert Lamplugh, of Lamplugh, in Cumberland, and by her had four sons, JOHN, WILLIAM, ROBERT, and GEOFFREY.

JOHN BELASYSE, *m.* Jonetta, dau. of Thomas Tipping, Esq., and *d.* 18th HENRY VII., leaving a dau. Alice. His brother,

WILLIAM BELASYSE, Esq., *of Belasyse,* who *m.* 1st, Cecily, dau. and heiress of William Hottan, Esq., and had a son,

THOMAS BELASYSE, *m.* Margery, dau. of Richard Dalton, Esq., and by her had two daus., who both *d.* young.

He *m.* 2ndly, Margaret, dau. of Sir Lancelot Thirkeld, of Malmerby, in Yorshire, Knt., and had issue,

RICHARD, his successor.
Anthony, LL.D., master in Chancery in 1545, when he was one of the four especially appointed to hear causes and pass decrees in the Court of Chancery, in the absence of the lord chancellor, Sir Thomas Wriothesley. And in the reign of EDWARD VI., being written Anthony Belasis, Esq., was one of the king's council in the north. On the dissolution of the monastries he obtained from the crown a grant of Newburgh Abbey, co. York, which he afterwards gave to his nephew, Sir William Belasyse.
Elizabeth, *m.* to William Clervaux, of Crofts, co. York.
Anne, *m.* to Anthony Smith, Esq., of Kalton.

RICHARD BELASYSE, Esq., LL.D., the son and heir, was constituted constable of Durham for life, to officiate in person, or by deputy. He *m.* Margery, eldest dau. and heiress of Richard Errington, Esq., of Cockley, in Northumberland, and dying 26 March, 1540, left issue,

William, who *d.* an infant; WILLIAM, his heir; Anthony Francis, Thomas, Anthony, Richard, who all *d. unm.*; Cecilia; Anne; Margaret, *m.* to Wm. Pulleyne, Esq., of Scotton, co. York; and Jane, *m.* John, son and heir of Sir Ralph Hedworth, of Harraton, in Durham.

The eldest surviving son,
SIR WILLIAM BELASYSE, Knt., who served the office of sheriff for Yorkshire in the 17th year of ELIZABETH, 1574-5. He *m.* Margaret, dau. of Sir Nicholas Fairfax, of Walton and Gilling, co. York, and had issue,*

HENRY (Sir), his heir.
Bryan, of Morton House, and sometime of Brandon, co. Durham; *d.* 12 July, 1608; leaving, by Margaret, his wife, dau.

*From the Westmoreland branch of the family of Belasyse, descended MR. SERJEANT BELLASIS.

and co-heir of William Lee, Esq., of Brandon, a son and heir,

SIR WILLIAM BELASYSE, Knt., of Morton House, *m.* Margaret, eldest dau. and co-heir of Sir George Selby, Knt., and has issue,

I. Richard (Sir), of Ludworth, father of General Sir Henry Belasyse, of Brancepeth Castle, co. Durham, and of other issue, all of whom are now EXTINCT.
II. WILLIAM,

The 2nd son,
WILLIAM BELASYSE, of Morton House, *b.* 30 December, 1617, *m.* Martha, dau. of Sir Henry Curwen, of Workington, co. Cumberland, and by her (who *d.* 1665) had issue,

I William, *d. s.p.,* between the years 1678 and 1682.
II. RICHARD, of whom presently.

The 2nd son,
THE REV. RICHARD BELASYSE, rector of Haughton-le-Skerne, co. Durham, *m.* Margaret, dau. of Lodowick Hall, Esq., of Great Chilton, co. Durham, and by her (who *d.* 1728), had issue,

I. THOMAS, of whom presently.
II. William, *m.* Jane, dau. of Seth Loftus, of Wickall, co. York, left a son Charles, who was living, under age, 1738.
I. A dau., *d.* in childhood.

The Rev. Richard Belasyse *d.* 1 November, 1721. His elder son, THOMAS BELASYSE, Esq., of Haughton-le-Skerne, *m.* Alice, dau. of Robert Hilton, and widow, 1st, of Christopher Blacket, Esq., of Newham; 2ndly, of Francis Smart, Esq., and by her (who *d.* November, 1761), had a sole child and heiress,

Martha-Maria Belasyse, *b.* 8 March, 1721, who *m.* January, 1740-1, at Cleasby, co. York, Richard Bowes, Esq., of Darlington, descended from Bowes, of Boythorp and Bugthorpe, co. York, and *d.* July 1767, leaving a son,

Thomas Bowes, Esq., of Darlington, *bapt.* 15 Aug. 1753, *m.* 8 February, 1776, Dorothy, dau. of — Stephenson, Esq., of Huntingdon, and *d.* April, 1806, leaving a son,

THOMAS BOWES, Esq., of Darlington, bapt. 23 February, 1777; *m.* 31 December, 1907, Elizabeth, dau. of David Crawford, Esq., of Howledge Hall, co. Durham, and *d.* 3 October, 1846, leaving issue,

I. THOMAS, of Darlington, co. Durham, *b.* 1813,
II. Richard, *m.* Hester, dau. of Mons. Le Forestier, of Havre de Grâce, France.
III. George.
I. Dorothy.
II. Catherine.
III. Elizabeth, *m.* to John Hull Fell, Esq., of Belmont, Uxbridge.

Sir William *d.* at an advanced age, 13 April, 1604, and was *s.* by his eldest son,

SIR HENRY BELASYSE, of Newborough, co. York, who, having received the honour of knighthood from King JAMES I., at York, in his majesty's journey to London, 17 April, 1603, was created a BARONET upon the institution of that dignity, 29 June, 1611. Sir Henry *m.* Ursula, dau. of Sir Thomas Fairfax, of Denton, co. York, and had issue,

THOMAS, his successor.
Dorothy, *m.* to Sir Conyers Darcy, Knt. of Hornby.
Mary, *m.* to Sir William Lister, Knt., of Thornton, co. York.

He was *s.* at his decease by his son,
SIR THOMAS BELASYSE, 2nd baronet, advanced to the peerage by the title of BARON FAUCONBERG, *of Yarm,* co. York, 25 May, 1627. His lordship, adhering faithfully to the fortunes of King CHARLES I., was created, 31 January, 1643, VISCOUNT FAUCONBERG, of Henknowle, co. palatine of Durham. His lordship was subsequently at the siege of York, and at the battle of Marston Moor, under the Duke of Newcastle, with whom he fled to the continent after that unfortunate defeat. He *m.* Barbara, dau. of Sir Henry Cholmondeley, Bart., of Roxby, co. York, and had issue,

HENRY, M.P. for co. York; of whom Clarendon writes:— "Harry Belasis, with the Lord Fairfax, the two knights who served in parliament for Yorkshire, signed articles for a neutrality for that county, being nearly allied together, and of great kindness, till their several opinions and affections had divided them in this quarrel; the Lord Fairfax adhering to the parliament, and the other, with great courage and sobriety, to the king." Mr. Belasyse *m.* Grace, dau. and heiress of Sir Thomas Barton, of Smithells, co. Lancaster, and dying in the lifetime of his father, left issue,

THOMAS, successor to his grandfather.
Henry, *d. unm.*
Rowland (Sir), K.B., *m.* Anne, eldest dau. and heiress of James-Humphrey Davenport, Esq., of Sutton, co. Chester, and dying in 1699, left

THOMAS, who *s.* as 3rd Viscount Fauconberg.

Henry, *d. unm.*
John, *d. s. p.*
Rowland, *m.* Frances, dau. of Christopher, Lord Teyn-
ham, by whom he had, with other issue,
    Anthony, who *m.* Susannah, dau. of John Clarvet,
    Esq., and had issue,
        ROWLAND, who *s.* as 6th viscount.
        Raymond, *d.* in infancy.
        Charles, D.D., of Sorbonne, who *s.* as 7th viscount.
        Thomas, *b.* 11 September, 1751, *m.* in 1788, Marie
        Louise de Maneville, and had five daus., Mary,
        Frances, Elizabeth, Anne, and Barbara.
        Mary, *d.* April, 1790.
        Frances, *b.* 1753.
        Barbara, *b.* in 1754.
William, *d.* an infant.
John, *d.* young.
Charles, *d.* young.
William, *d.* young.
Mary.
Barbara.
Grace, *m.* to George, Viscount Castleton, in Ireland.
Frances, *m.* to Sir Henry Jones, of Ashton, co. Oxford, Knt.,
of which marriage there was an only dau. and heiress,
    FRANCES, *m.* to Richard, Earl of Scarborough.
Arabella, *m.* to Sir William Frankland, Bart., of Thirkleby,
co. York.
Margaret.
Barbara, *m.* 1st, to Walter Strickland, Esq., son of Sir
Robert Strickland, of Sizergh; and 2ndly, to Sir Marma-
duke Dalton, of Huxwell, Yorkshire.
John, created LORD BELASYSE, *of Worlaby*, 27 January, 1644,
(*see that dignity*).
Margaret, *m.* to Sir Edward Osborne, of Kiveton, ancestor of
the DUKE OF LEEDS.
Mary, *m.* to John, Lord Darcy, of Aston.
Barbara, *m.* to Sir Henry Slingsby, Bart., of Scriven, co. York,
who was put to death under Cromwell's usurpation, and *d.*, as
he said on the scaffold, for being an honest man.
Ursula, *m.* to Sir Walter Vavasor, of Haslewood, Bart.
Frances, *m.* to Thomas Ingram, Esq., eldest son of Sir Arthur
Ingram, of Temple Newsom, Yorkshire.

His lordship *d.* in 1652, and was *s.* by his grandson,

THOMAS BELASYSE, 2nd viscount, who *m.* 1st, Mildred, dau.
of Nicholas, Viscount Castleton, by whom he had no issue;
and 2ndly, 18 November, 1657, at Hampton Court, Mary, dau.
of the protector Cromwell. Of this nobleman Lord Clarendon
gives the following account:—"After Cromwell was declared
protector, and in great power, he married his dau. to the Lord
Fauconberg, the owner of a very great estate in Yorkshire,
and descended of a family eminently loyal. There were many
reasons to believe that this young gentleman, being then about
three or four-and-twenty years of age, of great vigour and
ambition, had many good purposes that he thought that alliance might qualify and enable him to perform. His marriage
was celebrated at Whitehall (Wood has given the time at
Hampton Court), with all imaginable pomp and lustre. And it
was observed, that, though it was performed in public, according
to the rites and ceremonies then in use, they were presently
afterwards, in private, married by ministers ordained by bishops,
and according to the form in the book of Common Prayer,
and this with the privity of Cromwell." In 1657, his lordship
was made one of the council of state, and sent the next year,
by his father-in-law, with a complimentary message to the
court of Versailles. This was the only employment Lord
Fauconberg had under the Usurper; for, as the noble author
before-mentioned relates, "his domestic delights were lessened
every day; he plainly discovered that his son Fauconberg's
heart was set upon an interest destructive to his, and grew to
hate him perfectly." Of Lady Fauconberg, Burnet writes:—
"She was a wise and worthy woman, more likely to have
maintained the post (of protector) than either of her brothers;
according to a saying that went of her, *that those who wore
breeches deserved petticoats better ; but if those in petticoats had
been in breeches, they would have held faster.*" That his lordship forwarded the Restoration, is evident from his being
appointed, by the restored monarch, in 1660, lord-lieutenant
of the bishopric of Durham, and in the same year, lord-
lieutenant and custos-rotulorum of the North Riding of Yorkshire. He was soon afterwards accredited ambassador to the
state of Venice and the princes of Italy, and nominated captain
of the band of gentlemen pensioners. In 1679, Lord Fauconberg was sworn of the privy council; and again, in 1689, upon
the accession of King WILLIAM and Queen MARY, when his
lordship was created EARL FAUCONBERG, by letters patent,
dated 9 April, in that year. He *d.* 31 December, 1700, and
leaving no issue, the EARLDOM EXPIRED, while his other honours
reverted to his nephew (refer to Sir Rowland Belasyse, K.B.,
3rd son of the 1st lord).

THOMAS BELASYSE, Esq., as 3rd Viscount Fauconberg. He
m. Bridget, dau. and eventual heir of Sir John Gage, of Firle,

40

Bart., and co-heiress of her mother, who was dau. of Thomas
Middlemore, Esq., of Edgbaston, co Warwick, by whom he
had surviving issue,
    THOMAS, his successor.
    Henry.
    Rowland, *d. unm.*, 9 April, 1768.
    John, *d.* an infant.
    Mary, *m.* 4 April, 1721, to John Pitt, Esq., 3rd son of
    Thomas Pitt, Esq., governor of Fort St. George.
    Anne and Penelope, both of whom *d. unm.*

His lordship *d.* 26 November, 1718, and was *s.* by his elder
son,

THOMAS, 4th Viscount, who was created EARL FAUCONBERG,
of Newborough, co. York, 15 June, 1756. His lordship *m.* 5
August, 1726, Catherine, dau. and heiress of John Betham,
Esq., of Rowington, co. Warwick, and co-heiress of William
Fowler, Esq., of St. Thomas, co. Stafford, by whom (who *d.* 30
May, 1760) he had issue,
    Thomas, *d.* an infant.
    Thomas, *b.* 29 June, 1740.
    HENRY, his successor.
    Catherine, *d.* 12 January, 1788.
    Barbara, *m.* in April, 1752, to the Hon. George Barnewall,
    only brother of Henry Benedict, Viscount Kingsland, buried
    at St. Pancras Church, Middlesex.
    Mary, *m.* 23 July, 1776, to Thomas Eyre, Esq., of Hassop, co.
    Derby.
    Anne, *m.* 20 April, 1761, to the Hon. Francis Talbot, brother
    of George, 14th Earl of Shrewsbury.

His lordship, who conformed to the established church, *d.* 4
February, 1774, and was *s.* by his son,

HENRY BELASYSE, 2nd earl. His lordship *m.* 1st, 29 May,
1766, Charlotte, dau. of Sir Matthew Lamb, of Brocket Hall, co.
Hertford, Bart., and had four daus., his co-heirs, viz.,
    CHARLOTTE, *b.* 10 January, 1767, *m.* to Thomas Edward
    Wynn, Esq. (3rd son of Colonel Glynn Wynn), who assumed
    the surname and arms of BELASYSE, in addition to his
    own.
    ANNE, *b.* 27 December, 1760, *m.* Sir George Wombwell, Bart.,
    of Wombwell, co. York, and *d.* 7 July, 1808, leaving a son
    and heir, SIR GEORGE WOMBWELL, Bart., who *m.* 23 June,
    1824, Georgiana, 2nd dau. of the late Thomas Orby Hunter,
    Esq., of Crowland Abbey, and had with other issue, the
    present SIR GEORGE ORBY WOMBWELL, Bart., who now pos-
    sesses Newburgh Hall, the old seat of the Belasyses.
    ELIZABETH, *b.* 17 January, 1770, *m.* 23 April, 1789, to Bernard
    Howard, Esq. (afterwards 12th Duke of Norfolk), from whom
    she was divorced in 1794, when she re-married Richard, 2nd
    Earl of Lucan.
    HARRIOT, *b.* 21 April, 1776, *d. unm.*

The earl *m.* 2ndly, Miss Chesshyre, but had no issue. He *d.*
23 March, 1802, when the EARLDOM became EXTINCT, but the
other honours devolved upon his kinsman (*refer* to descendants of the Hon. Henry Belasyse, eldest son of Sir Thomas
Belasyse, the 1st Viscount),

ROWLAND BELASYSE, as 6th Viscount, who *d. s. p.* in 1810, and
was *s.* by his brother,

The REV. CHARLES BELASYSE, D.D., of the Roman Catholic
Church, as 7th Viscount, *b.* 7 May, 1750, at whose decease, in
1815, the Barony and Viscounty of Fauconberg became EX-
TINCT.

Arms—Quarterly, 1st and 4th, arg., a chev. gu., between
three fleurs-de-lis, az.; 2nd and 3rd, arg., a pale ingrailed between two pallets, plain, sa.

BELASYSE—BARONS BELASYSE, OF WOR-
LABY, IN THE COUNTY OF LINCOLN.

By Letters-Patent, dated 27 January, 1644.

Lineage.

THE HON. JOHN BELASYSE, 2nd son of Thomas, 1st Viscount
Fauconberg, having distinguished himself as one of the gallant
leaders of the royal army during the civil wars, was elevated
to the peerage on the 27 January, 1644, as LORD BELASYSE, *of
Worlaby, co. Lincoln*. At the commencement of the rebellion,
this eminent person arrayed six regiments of horse and foot
under the royal banner, and had a principal command at the
battles of Edge-Hill, Newbury, and Knaresby, and at the sieges
of Reading and Bristol; and being appointed, subsequently,
governor of York, and commander-in-chief of the king's forces
in Yorkshire, he fought the battle of Selby with Lord Fairfax.
His lordship being lieutenant-general of the counties of Lincoln,
Nottingham, Derby, and Rutland, and governor of Newark,
valiantly defended that garrison against the English and

Scotch armies, until His Majesty came in person, and ordered it to surrender; at which time he had also the honour of being general of the king's horse-guards. In all those arduous services, General Belasyse deported himself with distinguished courage and conduct, was frequently wounded, and thrice incarcerated in the Tower of London. At the restoration of the monarchy, his lordship was made lord lieutenant of the east riding co. York, governor of Hull, general of His Majesty's forces in Africa, governor of Tangier, and captain of the king's guards of gentlemen pensioners. In the reign of King JAMES II., Lord Belasyse was first lord of the treasury. His lordship m. 1st, Jane, dau. and sole heiress of Sir Robert Boteler, Knt., of Woodhall, co. Hertford, by whom he had issue,

HENRY (Sir), K.B., who m. 1st, Rogeresa, dau. and co-heir (with her sister Elizabeth, Duchess of Richmond and Lenox) of Richard Rogers, Esq., of Brianston, co. Dorset, by whom he had no issue; and 2ndly, Susan, dau. and co-heiress of Sir William Armine, Bart., of Osgodby, co. Lincoln (which lady, who d. in 1713, was created, 25 March, 1674, BARONESS BELASYSE, of Osgodby, for her own life, after the decease of her husband), by whom he left, at his decease, in 1668, an only son,
HENRY, of whom presently, as 2nd LORD BELASYSE.
Mary, m. to Robert, Viscount Dunbar, of Scotland.

Lord Belasyse m. 2ndly, Anne, dau. and co-heiress of Sir Robert Crane, of Chilton, co. Suffolk; and 3rdly, Anne, dau. of John, 5th Marquess of Winchester, by whom he had several children, of which the following alone survived infancy,

Honora, m. to George Lord Abergavenny, and d. s. p.
Barbara, m. Sir John Webb, Bart., of Oldstock, Wilts, and had, with other issue, a son, Sir Thomas Webb, Bart., father of two sons, Sir John Webb, 5th Bart. (whose granddau. and heiress, Lady Barbara Ashley-Cooper, m. Hon. William Francis Ponsonby who was created BARON DE MAULEY, and Sir Thomas Webb, 6th Bart., father of Sir Henry Webb, 7th Bart.
Katherine, m. to John Talbot, Esq., of Longford
Isabella, m. to Thomas Stoner, Esq., of Stoner, co. Oxford, d. s. p. 1706.

His lordship d. in 1689, and was s. by his grandson,
HENRY BELASYSE, 2nd baron, who m. Anne, dau. of Francis, son and heir of Robert Brudenel, Earl of Cardigan; but died s. p. in 1692, when the BARONY OF BELASYSE became EXTINCT, while the estates reverted to his lordship's aunts by the half blood, as co-heiresses.

Arms—Arg. a chevron gu. between three fleurs-de-lis, az. with due difference.

BELLENDEN—LORD BELLENDEN.

By Letters-Patent, dated 10 June, 1661.

SIR WILLIAM BELLENDEN, of Broughton, the only son of Sir James Bellenden, of Broughton, and grandson of Sir Lewis Bellenden, Knt., of Auchinoule, adhered to the royal cause during the civil war, and was created a peer, by the title of LORD BELLENDEN, OF BROUGHTON, 10 June, 1661. The same year he was constituted treasurer-depute, and was sworn a privy councillor. He d. unm. about 1671, having previously made a resignation of his title and estate into the hands of CHARLES II., in favour of John Kerr, 4th son of William, 2nd Earl of Roxburghe, who accordingly succeeded to them at his death, and was 2nd Lord Bellenden.

Arms—Gu., a hart's head, couped, between three cross-crosslets, fitchée, all within a double treasure, counterflowered, or.

BELLEW—BARON BELLEW, OF DULEEK.

By Letters Patent, dated 1686.

Lineage.

The first who settled in Ireland appears to have been ROGER DE BELLEW, the common ancestor of the various families of the name seated in the sister island. From him directly descended*
SIR JOHN BELLEW, Knt., of Bellewstown and the Roach, successor to his father in 1542, who m. Margaret, dau. of Sir

Oliver Plunket, of Beaulieu, and left, with other issue, a son and successor,
SIR JOHN BELLEW, Knt., of Bellewstown, who m. 1st, in 1599, Margaret, dau. of Oliver Plunket, Lord Louth; 2ndly, Janet Sarsfield, of the Lucan family; and 3rdly, Ismay Nugent. By his 1st wife, Sir John had several children. The 3rd son, JOHN, of Lisfrannan and Willystown, was progenitor of Patrick, LORD BELLEW, of Barmeath, lord lieutenant of the co. Louth : of SIR CHRISTOPHER BELLEW, Bart., of Mount Bellew, co. Galway: of HENRY CHRISTOPHER GRATTAN-BELLEW, Esq., &c. The eldest son,
SIR CHRISTOPHER BELLEW, Knt., of Bellewstown, m. 1st, Alice,* dau. of Sir Thomas Cusack, lord chancellor of Ireland; and 2ndly, Catherine, dau. of Sir William Sarsfield, of Lucan. By the former he left at his decease a son and successor,
SIR JOHN BELLEW, of Bellewstown, knighted 5 November, 1626, who m. Aminetta, dau. of John Barnewell, Esq., recorder of Drogheda, and was father of
SIR CHRISTOPHER BELLEW, Knt., of Bellewstown, who m. Frances, dau. of Matthew Plunket, Lord Louth, and had issue,

I. JOHN (Sir), his heir, created BARON BELLEW.
II. Matthew, of Rogerstown, an officer in JAMES's army, slain at the Boyne, leaving for Frances, his wife,
  1 Matthew, of Rogerstown, whose dau. and heiress m. Dominick Trant, Esq. and had issue. This line is extinct.
  2 Patrick, who m. Honor, dau. of G. Neville, Esq., and had an only son,
    ROBERT BELLEW, Esq., of Castle Martyr, co. Cork (where his father settled and was buried), who m. Bryanna, dau. and co-heir (with her sisters, Mrs. Hanning, of Kilcrone, and Mrs. Forster) of — Wright, Esq., co. Cork, and left, with two daus., a son and heir,
    PATRICK BELLEW, Esq., of Ballendiness, Castle Martyr who m. Sarah, sister of the late Gen. John Pratt, R.I.A., and cousin to Sir Charles Pratt, Col. Kenah, &c., and had issue,
      ROBERT, his heir.
      Patrick, major 54th foot; d. s. p. at Gibraltar.
      Bryanna, m. to Richard Fitton, Esq., of Gawsworth, near Cork.
    The elder son,
    ROBERT BELLEW, Esq., barrister-at-law, m. Sophia, dau. of Joseph Fowke, Esq., and had issue,
      Patrick-Edward, lieutenant of engineers, d. young, s. p.
      FRANCIS-JOHN, of whom presently.
      Christopher, H.C.S., deceased
      Henry-Walter, captain H.C.S., and dep.-assist.-quarter-master-general in Bengal, m. in 1830, Anna, 3rd dau. of Captain Jeremie, and has Henry, Patrick, and other issue.
      Frances, d. unm.
      Louisa, m. to John-Baker Graves, Esq., of Fort William, co. Limerick, now of Somerset, co. Wexford, nephew of Dean Graves, and had issue, Frances, m. to Mumford Campbell, Esq., of Sutton Place, Kent; Sydney, and other children.
      Sarah-Margaret, d. unm.
    The 2nd but eldest surviving son,
    FRANCIS-JOHN BELLEW, Esq. captain on the retired list, H.C.S., and formerly dep.-assist.-commissary-general, Bengal; b. 19 January, 1799; m. in November, 1819, Ann, dau. of the late Simon Temple, Esq., formerly of Hylton Castle, co. Durham, sister of the Rev. William-S. Temple, rector of Dinsdale, co. Durham, and had Francis, Patrick-Beckett, Sophia, and other children.
  3 Robert, of Ballydonell, co. Louth, left issue.
  4 Thomas, of Gaffney.

The eldest son,
SIR JOHN BELLEW, of Bellewstown, knighted by King JAMES II., was elevated to the peerage of Ireland, as BARON BELLEW, of Duleek, 29 October, 1686. He m. (Mar. Lic. 28 November, 1663), Mary, eldest dau. and co-heir of Walter Bermingham, Esq., of Dunfert, co. Kildare, and had two sons and a dau., Margaret, wife of Thomas, Earl of Westmeath. His lordship dying 12 January, 1692, having been mortally wounded at Aughrim, was s. by his son,
WALTER BELLEW, 2nd Lord Bellew, who commanded a troop in the Duke of Tyrconnel's regiment of horse: he m. 1686, Frances-Arabella, eldest dau. of Sir William Wentworth, of Northgatehead, Yorkshire, sister to the Earl of Strafford, and by her (who d. 1723) had two daus., his co-heirs,
MARY, m. 1702, to Denis Kelly, Esq., of Aughrim, co. Galway.
FRANCES ARABELLA, m. — Horncastle, Esq., and d. 1732.

His lordship d. in 1694, and was s. by his brother,
RICHARD BELLEW, 3rd Lord Bellew, who m. 1695, Frances,

---

* The intermediate Lords of Bellewstown and Duleek intermarried with the D'Arcys, Fitzgeralds (Earls of Kildare), St. Lawrences, Flemings, Gernons, and Prestons.

* From Alice's sister descended the late Marquess of Thomond and Lord Shannon.
† Grandmother of Clement Forster, Esq., of Ballumalos Castle, near Cloyns.

3rd dau. of Francis, Lord Brudenell, and by her, who d. in 1735, had two sons, JOHN, his heir, and Walter-Bermingham, b. 1707, d. young, and one dau., Dorothea, b. 1696, m. 1st, 1717 Gustavus Hamilton, Esq., father of Viscount Boyne; 2ndly, to William Cockburn, Esq., of Redford, King's County; and 3rdly, to Captain Dixon. Lord Bellew, who was attainted, but afterwards restored, having conformed to the Protestant religion, d. 22 March, 1714, and was s. by his son,

JOHN BELLEW, 4th Lord Bellew, b. in 1702, who m. 1st, 1731, Lady Anne Maxwell, dau. of William, Earl of Nithsdale, and had by her, who d. 3 May, 1735, a dau., Mary-Frances, b. in Italy, 1733, who d. s. p.; he m. 2ndly, Mary, only dau. of Maurice Fitzgerald, Esq., of Castle Ishen, relict of Justin, 5th Earl of Fingall, and of Valentine, Earl of Kenmare, by whom he had two daus., Emilia, m. to General Count Taafe, of Bohemia, brother to R. Viscount Taafe; and Anne, m. to — Butler, Esq. His lordship m. 3rdly, Lady Henrietta Lee, dau. of George-Henry, Earl of Lichfield, but by her had no child to survive infancy. He d. in 1770, when the Barony of Bellew became EXTINCT.

Arms—Sa., fretty, or.

BELLOMONT—EARLS OF LEICESTER.

By Charter of Creation, dated anno 1103.

Lineage.

ROBERT DE BELLOMONT, OR BEAUMONT (son of Roger, grandson of Turlof of Pont Audomere, by Wevia, sister to Gunnora, wife of RICHARD I., Duke of Normandy), came into England with the CONQUEROR, and contributed mainly to the Norman triumph at Hastings. This Robert inherited the earldom of Mellent in Normandy, from his mother Adelina, dau. of Waleran, and sister of Hugh (who took the habit of monk in the abbey of Bec), both Earls of Mellent. Of his conduct at Hastings, William Pictavensis thus speaks: "A certain Norman young soldier, son of Roger de Bellomont, nephew and heir to Hugh, Earl of Mellent, by Adelina his sister, making the first onset in that fight, did what deserveth lasting fame, boldly charging and breaking in upon the enemy, with that regiment which he commanded in the right wing of the army," for which gallant services he obtained sixty-four lordships in Warwickshire, sixteen in Leicestershire, seven in Wiltshire, three in Northamptonshire, and one in Gloucestershire, in all ninety-one. His lordship did not however arrive at the dignity of the English peerage before the reign of HENRY I., when that monarch created him EARL OF LEICESTER. The mode by which he attained this honour is thus stated by an ancient writer: "The city of Leicester had then four lords, viz., the king, the bishop of Lincoln, Earl Simon, and Yvo the son of Hugh de Grentmesnel. This Earl of Mellent, by favour of the king, cunningly entering it on that side which belonged to Yvo (then governor thereof, as also sheriff, and the king's farmer there), subjecting it wholly to himself; and by this means, being made an earl in England, exceeded all the nobles of the realm in riches and power." His lordship m. 1096, Isabel, dau. of Hugh, Earl of Vermandois, and had issue,

WALERAN, who s. to the earldom of Mellent.
ROBERT, successor to the English earldom.
Hugh, surnamed Pauper, obtained the EARLDOM OF BEDFORD from King STEPHEN, with the dau. of Milo de Beauchamp, upon the expulsion of the said Milo. Being a person (says Dugdale) remiss and negligent himself he fell from the dignity of an earl to the state of a knight; and in the end to miserable poverty.

With several daus., of whom,

Elizabeth, was concubine to HENRY I., and afterwards wife of Gilbert Strongbow, Earl of Pembroke.
Adeline, m. to Hugh de Montfort.
A dau., m. to Hugh de Novo Castello.
A dau., m. to William Lupellus, or Lovel.

This great earl is characterised as "the wisest of all men betwixt this and Jerusalem, in worldly affairs; famous for knowledge, plausible in speech, skilful in craft, discreetly provident, ingeniously subtile, excelling for prudence, profound in council, and of great wisdom." In the latter end of his days he became a monk in the abbey of Preaux, where he d. in 1118, and was s. in the earldom of Leicester by his 2nd son,

ROBERT (called Bossu), as 2nd earl. This nobleman stoutly adhering to King HENRY I. upon all occasions, was with that monarch at his decease in 1135, and he afterwards as staunchly supported the interests of his grandson, HENRY II., upon whose accession to the throne, his lordship was constituted

42

Justice of England. He m. (1119) Amicia, dau. of Ralph de Waer, Earl of Norfolk, by whom he had a son, ROBERT, and two daus.; one, the wife of Simon, Earl of Huntingdon, the other of William Earl of Gloucester. The earl, who was a munificent benefactor to the church, and founder of several religious houses, d. in 1167, after having lived for fifteen years a canon regular in the abbey of Leicester, and was s. by his son,

ROBERT (surnamed Blanchmaines, from having white hands), as 3rd earl, who adhering to Prince Henry, in the 19th of HENRY II., in his rebellion, incurred the high displeasure of that monarch. The king commanding that his town of Leicester should be laid waste, it was besieged, and the greater part burnt; the inhabitants having permission for £300 to move whither they pleased. He was received however into royal favour in four years afterwards (1177), and had restoration of all his lands and castles, save the castle of Montsorel, in the co. of Leicester, and Pacey in Normandy; but surviving King HENRY, he stood in such favour with RICHARD I., that those castles were likewise restored to him, and he was appointed to carry one of the swords of state at that monarch's coronation. His lordship m. Patronil, dau. of Hugh de Grentemesnil, with whom he had the whole honour of Hinkley, and stewardship of England, and had issue,

ROBERT FITZPARNEL, his successor.
Roger, bishop of St. Andrews, in Scotland.
William, founder of the hospital of St. Leonards, at Leicester. It is from this William that the great Scottish house of HAMILTON is said to be descended, but the statement is scarcely reconcileable with dates and circumstances. It is more probable that the ancestor of the Hamiltons, if a Bellomont, was a younger son of Robert, 2nd Earl of Leicester.
Amicia, m. to Simon de Montfort, who after the earldom of Leicester expired, with the male line of the Bellomonts, was created Earl of Leicester by King JOHN (see Montfort, Earl of Leicester).
Margaret, m. to Sayer de Quincy.

The earl d. in his return from Jerusalem, at Duras in Greece anno 1190, and was s. by his son,

ROBERT (surnamed Fitz-parnel from his mother), 4th earl, who in 1191, being at Messina, on his journey to the Holy Land, was invested into his father's earldom of Leicester, by King RICHARD, with the cincture of a sword. After which, whilst his royal master was detained in captivity by the emperor, the King of France having invaded Normandy, and taken divers places, this earl coming to Roan, excited the inhabitants to so vigorous a defence, that the French monarch was obliged to retreat. Furthermore, it is related of him, that making a pilgrimage into the Holy Land, he there unhorsed and slew the Soldan in a tournament, when returning into England, he d. in 1204, and was buried in the abbey of Leicester, before the high altar, betwixt his mother and grandfather. His lordship had m. Lauretta, dau. of William, Lord Braose, of Brember, but having no issue, the EARLDOM OF LEICESTER became EXTINCT, while his great inheritance devolved upon his two sisters as co-heirs, which was divided between them, thus—

SIMON DE MONTFORT, husband of Amicia, had one moiety of the earldom of Leicester, with the honour of Hinkley, and was created EARL OF LEICESTER; he also enjoyed the stewardship of England, as in right of the said honour of Hinkley.
SAYER DE QUINCEY, husband of Margaret, had the other moiety of the earldom of Leicester, and was shortly after created EARL OF WINCHESTER. (See that dignity.)

Arms.—Gu., a cinquefoil, erm., pierced of the field.

BELLOMONT—EARL OF BEDFORD.

(See Beaumont, Earl of Leicester.)

BENHALE—BARON BENHALE.

By Writ of Summons, dated 3 April, 1360.

Lineage,

ROBERT DE BENHALE, a soldier of distinction in the expedition made into France, in the 10th year of EDWARD III., and again in two years afterwards, in the expedition made into Flanders, was summoned to parliament as BARON BENHALE, on 3 April, 1360, but nothing further is known of his lordship, or his descendants, "who never," says Sir Harris Nicolas, "ranked among the barons of the realm." Banks states, however, that this Robert de Benhale was the 4th husband of Eva, dau. and heir of John, Lord Clavering, and that he d. s. p., and was buried in the Abbey of Langley.

BENSON—BARON BINGLEY.

By Letters Patent, dated 21 July, 1713.

Lineage.

ROBERT BENSON, Esq., M.P., for the city of York, son of Robert Benson, Esq., of Wrenthorn, co. York, by Dorothy, dau. of Tobias Jenkins, Esq., having filled the offices of commissioner, and chancellor, and under treasurer of the exchequer, was elevated to the peerage, as BARON BINGLEY, on 21 July, 1713. His lordship was subsequently ambassador to the court of Madrid. He m. Elizabeth, eldest dau. of Heneage Finch, 1st Earl of Aylesford, and had an only dau. and heiress.

HARRIOT, who m. George Fox Lane, Esq., M.P. for the city of York, who was created LORD BINGLEY, in 1772 (see that title.)

His lordship d. 9 April, 1730, and thus leaving no male issue, the Barony of BINGLEY became EXTINCT, while £100,000, and £7,000 a-year, devolved upon his dau., with the fine seat of Bramham Park, erected by the deceased lord.

Arms.—Arg., three trefoils in bend, sa., cotised, gu

BERESFORD—BARON AND VISCOUNT BERESFORD.

Barony—By Letters Patent, dated 17 May, 1814.
Viscounty—By Letters Patent, dated 22 April, 1823.

Lineage.

SIR WILLIAM CARR BERESFORD, D.C.L., G.C.B., G.C.H., K.T.S., VISCOUNT BERESFORD, of Beresford, co. Stafford, and Baron Beresford, of Albuera and of Dungarvan, co. Waterford; governor of the Royal Military Academy at Woolwich, a com missioner of the Royal Military College and Royal Military Asylum, a general officer in the army, governor of Jersey, and colonel of the 16th foot; Duke of Elvas, Marquess of Campo Major and Count Francozo, in Portugal, and a field-marshal in that kingdom; was illegitimate son of George de la Poer Beresford, 1st Marquess of Waterford, and was b. 2 October, 1768. At the age of seventeen he commenced his military career as ensign 6th foot; in 1793 was in the Mediterranean, at the capture of Toulon, and at Bastia in 1795; attained the rank of colonel, and, after service with Sir Ralph Abercromby, in the West Indies, commanded a brigade under Sir David Baird, in Egypt, 1799. He next participated in the reconquest of the Cape of Good Hope, and was thence sent as brigadier-general to Buenos Ayres That disastrous expedition suffered a fearful repulse, and Beresford was taken prisoner; but in 1807, he effected his escape, and was made governor of Madeira. In the following year, he accompanied the army of Sir John Moore to Spain, fought at Corunna, and assisted in covering the final embarkation of the British force. Subsequently he returned to Portugal with the rank of major-general, to organize and command the Portuguese forces, and, in this important employment, exhibited such unwearied exertion and such sound judgment that the Portuguese became admirably efficient and contributed mainly to the victory of Busaco in 1810. During the following campaigns in the Peninsula, Beresford was one of the ablest and most distinguished of Wellington's lieutenants, commanding-in-chief at the sanguinary but glorious battle of Albuera, and being present at Badajoz, Salamanca, Vittoria, the Pyrenees, Nivelle, Nive, and Orthes. For Albuera, Marshal Beresford received the thanks of parliament. In 1814, he was in command of the forces which occupied Bordeaux, and took a prominent part in the battle of Toulouse.

In 1811 and 1812, he was elected M.P. for the co. of Waterford; in 1814, elevated to the peerage as BARON BERESFORD; in 1822, made lieutenant-general of the ordnance; in 1823 created a viscount; and appointed in 1828 quartermaster-general of the ordnance.

In further consideration of his eminent services, parliament passed a bill in 1814, granting an annuity of £2,000 to himself and his two immediate successors in the barony. His lordship m. 29 November, 1832, Louisa, widow of Thomas Hope, Esq., of Deepdene, in Surrey, and dau. of the Most Reverend Wm. (Beresford) Lord Decies, Archbishop of Tuam, but d. 8 January, 1854, having no issue.

By his will, bearing date 21 January, 1851, Lord Beresford devised his English estates—including his seat, Bedgebury

Park, Kent (anciently the residence of the Colepepers), and Beresford Hall. co. Stafford (the original home of the Beresfords), to ALEXANDER-JAMES-BERESFORD HOPE, Esq., youngest son of the late Thomas Hope, Esq., of Deepdene, co. Surrey, by his wife, the Hon. Louisa Beresford (afterwards Viscountess Beresford), dau. of the Most Rev. William Beresford Lord Decies, archbishop of Tuam. Mr. Alexander Hope assumed, in consequence, the additional and prefix surname of Beresford. His Irish estates, Lord Beresford bequeathed to DENIS WILLIAM PACK, Esq., capt. roy. art., 2nd son of the late Major-General Sir Denis Pack, K.C.B., by his wife, Lady Elizabeth Louisa de la Poer Beresford, dau. of George de la Poer Beresford, 1st Marquess of Waterford ; and Captain Pack having, in obedience to Lord Beresford's testamentary injunction, taken the additional surname and arms of Beresford, is the present DENIS WILLIAM PACK-BERESFORD, Esq., of Fenagh Lodge, co. Carlow, M.P., for that county.

Arms—Arg., semée of cross-crosslets fitchée. three fleurs-de-lis, two and one, sa., within a bordure, wavy, pean.

BERKELEY—VISCOUNT BERKELEY, EARL OF NOTTINGHAM, AND MARQUESS OF BERKELEY.

Viscounty, by Letters Patent, dated 12 April, 1481.
Earldom, by Letters Patent, dated 28 June, 1483.
Marquessate, by Letters Patent, dated 1488.

Lineage.

The family of Berkeley,* established in England at the Norman conquest, was founded by a leading chief in the CONQUEROR's army, named

ROGER. who is styled, in the 20th of WILLIAM's reign, "Rogerus senior de Berkele," from the possession of Berkeley Castle,† co. Gloucester. This Roger bestowed several churches upon the priory of Stanley, with the tithes and lands thereunto belonging, and being shorn a monk there, in 1091, restored the lordship of Shoteshore, which he had long detained from that convent. He was s. at his decease by his nephew,

WILLIAM DE BERKELEY, 2nd feudal lord of Berkeley Castle, who was s. by his son,

ROGER DE BERKELEY. This nobleman, adhering to the Empress MAUD (an adherence, however, denied by SMITH and FOSBROKE, in the Lives of the Berkeleys, page 11), "under went," says Dugdale, "a very hard fate, through the perfidiousness and cruelty of Walter, brother to Milo, Earl of Hereford, his seeming friend (and kinsman by consanguinity), being treacherously seized on, stripped naked, exposed to scorn, put into fetters, and thrice drawn by a rope about his neck, on a gallows, at his own castle gates, with threats that if he would not deliver up his castle to the earl, he should suffer a miserable death; and when he was, by this barbarous usage, almost dead, carried to prison, there to endure further tortures." This feudal baron was s. by his son,

ROGER DE BERKELEY, living in 1165 (11th HENRY II.), the last of the original family of Berkeley, of Berkeley Castle, whose dau. and heiress, Alice, at the instigation of King HENRY II., married,

MAURICE DE BERKELEY (son of Robert FitzHardinge, upon whom had been conferred, for his attachment to the Empress MAUD, the lordship of Berkeley and Berkeley Her nesse, the confiscated possessions of the above Roger, the adherent of King STEPHEN ; but, to reconcile the parties, King HENRY, who had restored to Roger his manor and castle of Dursley, caused an agreement to be concluded between them that the heiress of the ousted lord should be

---

* There is a family of Berkeley or Barclay of high distinction in Scotland, viz., " the BARCLAYS of URIE," now represented by ARTHUR KETT BARCLAY, Esq., of Bury Hill, co. Surrey, which is of the same lineage as this noble House of Berkeley.
† "The castle," says Budder, "was began in the 17th HENRY I., by Roger de Berkeley the 2nd, and finished by Roger the 3rd, in the reign of King STEPHEN. At first it comprehended only the inmost of the three gates and what was within the same; the two outmost, and all the buildings within them, were added by Thomas, eldest son of Robert, and by Thomas the 2nd, in the 6th EDWARD III. (1332-3), and of Thomas the 3rd (8th EDWARD III.)—SMITH and FOSBROKE's History of the Berkeleys. A plan of the buildings is given in PARKER's Domestic Architecture, vol. iii. part II.

given in marriage to the heir of the new baron; and thus passed the feudal castle of Berkeley to another chief, which Maurice de Berkeley became feudal lord of Berkeley upon the decease of his brother Henry, and dying in 1189, left six sons, and was *s.* by the eldest,

ROBERT DE BERKELEY, who, in the turbulent times of King JOHN, forfeited his castle and lands by his participation in the rebellious proceedings of the barons, but upon submission, and paying a fine of £965, and one mark, had all restored save the castle and town of Berkeley, in the 1st of HENRY III. This nobleman, who had been a munificent benefactor to the church, *d. s. p.* in 1219, and was *s.* by his brother,

THOMAS DE BERKELEY, who, in the 8th of HENRY III. (1223-4), upon giving his two nephews as pledges for his fidelity, had restitution of Berkeley Castle. His lordship *m.* about the year 1217, Joane, dau. of Ralph de Somery, Lord of Campden, co. Gloucester, and niece of William Marshal, Earl of Pembroke, and dying, aged seventy-six, November 29, 1243, left issue, MAURICE, his heir; Thomas, *d. s. p.*; Robert; Henry, *d. s. p.*; William; Richard; and one dau. Margaret, wife of Sir Anselm Basset: the eldest son,

MAURICE DE BERKELEY, *m.* in 1240, Isabel, dau. of Maurice de Credonia, by his wife Isabel, sister of William de Valence, Earl of Pembroke, *d.* 4 April, 1281, and was *s.* by his 2nd son (the eldest, Maurice, having been killed in a tournament at Kenilworth),

THOMAS DE BERKELEY, *b.* at Berkeley in 1245, who was summoned to parliament by writ as a baron, from 23 June, 1295, to 15 May, 1321. This nobleman was of great eminence in the reigns of EDWARD I. and EDWARD II., being in the French, Welsh, and Scottish wars of those periods, particularly at the celebrated siege of Caerlaverock. He was involved, however, at the close of his life, in the treason of Thomas, Earl of Lancaster. His lordship *m. circa* 1267, Jane, dau. of William de Ferrars, Earl of Derby, and dying July 23, 1321 (his wife *d.* 19 March, 1309), left issue,

  I. MAURICE, 2nd baron, of whom later.
  II. Thomas, ancestor of the Berkeleys of Wymondham, co. Leicester, extinct in Sir Henry Berkeley, living 1622.
  III. John, *d. s. p.* 10th EDWARD II.
  IV. James, a bishop.
  I. Isabel, } both *d. unm.*
  II. Margaret, }

The eldest son,

MAURICE DE BERKELEY, 2nd baron, *b.* 1281, *d.* 1326, having *m.* Eve, dau. of Eudo le Zouch. He received summons to parliament from 1308 to 1321, during his father's lifetime. He had issue,

  I. THOMAS, 3rd baron, of whom later.
  II. Sir Maurice, who *d.* at Calais, 21st EDWARD III., having *m.* Margaret, dau. and heiress of Sir Maurice Berkeley, of Uley, by whom he was ancestor of the family of Stoke-Giffard.
  III. John, constable of Bristol Castle, ancestor of the Shropshire Berkeleys.
  IV. Eudo.
  V. Peter.
  I. Isabel, *m.* 1st, Robert, Lord Clifford; 2ndly, Thomas, Lord Musgrave.

The eldest son,

THOMAS, 3rd baron, *m.* 1st, Margaret, dau. of Roger Mortimer, Earl of March, and 2ndly, in 1347, Catherine, dau. of Sir John Clyvedon, widow of Sir Peter le Veel. This lord having adhered to the interests of the Queen, Mortimer, and Prince Edward, afterwards the third of that name, furnished "the only precedent," says Smith, "of a peer being tried by knights, as the peers would have been both judges and jurors." He first assumed a mitre for his crest. He was summoned to parliament from 1329 to 1360. He had issue by his 1st wife, besides his heir, three sons, who *d. s. p.*, and one dau., Joan, wife of Sir Reginald Cobham; by his 2nd wife he had, with three sons, who *d. s. p.*, a 4th, John, ancestor of the Berkeleys of Beverstone. He *d.* 1361, and was *s.* by his son,

MAURICE, 4th baron, *b.* 1330, was knighted at seven years of age, *to prevent wardship*, which was also avoided by early marriages, and accordingly he *m.* when eight years old, Elizabeth, dau. of Hugh, Lord De Spencer, whose portion was 1,000 marks, payable by half-yearly instalments of 200 marks. He was summoned to parliament from 1362 to 1368, and *d.* in August, 1368. He had issue, with daus., who *d. unm.*,

  I. THOMAS, 5th baron.
  II. Sir James, *m.* Elizabeth, dau. and heiress of Sir John Bluet, by whom he got Ragland, and by whom (who remarried William Thomas, a Welsh gentleman) he left at his decease, in 1405, a son,

JAMES, 6th Lord Berkeley, of whom later.

44

III. John *d. s. p.*
IV. Maurice, *m.* Joan, by whom he got the manors of Dodscote, &c., co. Devon, and had a son,
  Maurice, living 45th EDWARD III. (1371-2).

The eldest son,

THOMAS, 5th Lord Berkeley, *m.* Margaret (*d.* aged thirty), dau. and heiress of Gerard Warren, Lord Lisle (contracted when but seven years of age, and required to remain for four years with her father), by whom he left an only child,

  Elizabeth,[*] *m.* to Richard Beauchamp, Earl of Warwick (also contracted when under seven years of age), and had three daus., viz.,
    1 Margaret, *m.* to John Talbot, 1st Earl of Shrewsbury, (his lordship's 2nd wife).
    2 Eleanor, *m.* 1st, to Thomas, Lord de Ros, and 2ndly, to Edmund, Duke of Somerset.
    3 Elizabeth, *m.* to John Nevill, Lord Latimer.

His lordship *d.*, say some, on 13 July, 1416; Smith and Fosbroke say 1417, which appears more probable, but even this is not perfectly clear, as this lord received summons to parliament from 16 July, 1381, to 3 September, 1417: his nephew,

JAMES BERKELEY, became his heir; and inheriting, by virtue of a special entail and fine, the castle and lordship of Berkeley, with other lordships in the said fine specified, was summoned to parliament from 9 October, 1421, to 23 May, 1461. His lordship *m.* 1st, a dau. of Humphrey Stafford, of Hooke, co. Dorset, by whom he had no issue; and 2ndly, Isabel, widow of Henry, son and heir of William, Lord Ferrers, of Groby, and the dau. and co-heir of Thomas Mowbray, 1st Duke of Norfolk, earl marshal of England, by Elizabeth, his wife, eldest sister and co-heiress of Thomas FitzAlan, Earl of Arundel, by whom he had issue,

  I. WILLIAM, his successor.
  II. Maurice, successor to the barony at the decease of his brother, as 8th baron.
  III. James, killed in France.
  IV. Thomas, *d.* 1484, who *m.* Margaret, dau. of Richard Guy, Esq., of Minsterworth, and had Richard, of Dursley, husband of Margaret Dyer, and by her father of William, who *m.* Elizabeth Burgwash, and had Rowland, of Spetchley, M.P. for Worcester, who *d.* 1611, and by his wife, Catherine, dau. of Thomas Heywood, Esq., left, with others,
    1 WILLIAM, of Cotheridge, *b.* 1582, father of Sir Rowland, one of the intended knights of the royal oak, who was succeeded by the son of his eldest dau. Elizabeth, wife of Henry Green, Esq., of Wykin, Rowland Green, who assumed the name of Berkeley, and dying in 1731, had issue, Rowland Berkeley, Esq., of Cotheridge, whose issue failed, and the Rev. Lucy Berkeley, of Great Whitley, &c., father of the Rev. Rowland Berkeley, LL.D., whose 2nd surviving son, WILLIAM BERKELEY, Esq., of Cotheridge, *v.* to the property in 1850. (*See* BURKE'S *Landed Gentry*.)
    2 SIR ROBERT, of Spetchley, *b.* 1584, who *m.* Elizabeth, dau. and co-heiress of Thomas Conyers, Esq., of East Barnet, and was *s.* by his son, Thomas, husband of Anne, dau. of William Dayrell, Esq., of Scotney (founders kin to archbishop Chicheley), and father by her of Thomas, who *m.* Elizabeth, dau. and heiress of William Holyoke, Esq., of Morton Bassett, and was *s.* at his death (1719) by his son, Thomas, who *m.* Mary, dau. and heiress of Robert Davis, Esq., of Clytha, and had issue, Robert, who *d. s. p.* 1804, and John, who, by Catherine, dau. of Charles Bodenham, Esq., had Robert, of Spetchley, *m.* 1792, Apollonia, dau. of Richard Lee, Esq., of Llanfoist, co. Monmouth, and left an only surviving son, ROBERT BERKELEY, Esq., of Spetchley. (*See* BURKE'S *Landed Gentry*.)
  I. Elizabeth, *m.* to Thomas Burdett, Esq., of Arrow, co. Warwick.
  II. Isabel, *m.* to Thomas Trye, Esq., of Hardwick, co. Gloucester.

---

[*] "According to the usual descents of baronies in fee (says Nicolas, in a note to his Synopsis), the barony of Berkeley, created by writ of summons of the 23rd EDWARD I., devolved on the said Elizabeth, dau. and heir of Thomas, Lord Berkeley, instead of the heir male; but whether this anomaly arose from an idea then prevailing, that the tenure of the castle of Berkeley conferred the barony, or that the heir male had the greatest political influence, cannot now, perhaps, be ascertained; the inference which may be drawn from the relative situations of the husband of the said Elizabeth, who was one of the most powerful noblemen of the time, and that of James Berkeley, who succeeded to the barony, is, that the tenure of Berkeley Castle was then considered to confer the dignity of baron on its possessor, and consequently that the said James was allowed that dignity as his right rather than by favour of the crown. If, however, modern decisions may be applied to the subject, the barony of Berkeley created by the writ of the 23rd EDWARD I. is now in ABEYANCE between the descendants and representatives of the three daus. and co-heirs of Elizabeth, Countess of Warwick, above mentioned; and the barony merged in the present E rldom of Berkeley is the new one created by the writ of the 5th of HENRY V. to James Berkeley."

III. Alice, m. to Richard Arthur, Esq., of Clapton, co. Somerset.

His lordship m. 3rdly, Joan (by whom he had no issue, and whose portion was 100 marks), dau. of John Talbot, 1st Earl of Shrewsbury, which lady, after his decease, m. Edmund Hungerford, Esq. Lord Berkeley d. 22 October, 1463, and was s. by his eldest son,

SIR WILLIAM DE BERKELEY, Knt., 7th Baron Berkeley, who had been, when a boy, in the retinue of Henry Beaufort, cardinal bishop of Winchester. This nobleman having a dispute with Thomas Talbot, Viscount Lisle, regarding some landed property, the contest ran so high, that they encountered, with their respective followers, at Wotton-under-Edge, in 1469, when Lord Lisle was mortally wounded by an arrow shot through his mouth. In the next year, when the Duke of Clarence and the Earl of Warwick took up arms against the king, we find Lord Berkeley commanded, with Maurice Berkeley, of Beverstone, to muster and array all fitting to bear arms in the county of Gloucester; and so great a regard had King EDWARD IV. for his lordship that he created him Viscount Berkeley, on 21 April, 1481, with a grant of 100 marks per annum, payable out of the customs of the port of Bristol, for life. The viscount was advanced to the Earldom of Nottingham (a dignity enjoyed by his ancestors, the Mowbrays), by King RICHARD III., on 28 June, 1483; but his lordship afterwards espousing the cause of the Earl of Richmond, upon the accession of that nobleman to the throne, as HENRY VII., was constituted in 1485—giving for this purpose "all his part and purpart of 27 manors in Wales and the marches adjoining Shropshire"—earl marshal of England, with limitation of that great office to the heirs male of his body; and created on 28 January, 1489-90, Marquess of Berkeley. His lordship m. 1st, Elizabeth, dau. of Reginald West, Lord de la Warre, from whom he was divorced without having issue; 2ndly, Jane, widow of Sir William Willoughby, Knt., and dau. of Sir Thomas Strangwayes, Knt., by whom he had Thomas and Catherine, who both died young; and 3rdly, Anne, dau. of John Fiennes, Lord Dacre, but had no issue. The marquess d. s. p. on 14 February, 1492, when all the honours acquired by himself became EXTINCT, while the barony and castle of Berkeley, with his lordship's other estates, should have devolved upon his brother Maurice—from whom the title has descended to the present time (see BURKE's Peerage)—but for a settlement made by the deceased nobleman (who seems to have been offended with his brother for marrying lowly) of the castle of Berkeley upon King HENRY VII. and the heirs male of that monarch's body, which castle and lands were thus alienated until the decease of King EDWARD VI., the last male descendant of HENRY VII., when they returned to the house of Berkeley, and have since been enjoyed by that noble family.*

Arms—Gu., a chev. between ten crosses pattée, six in chief, and four in base, arg.

---

* The dispute between Viscount Lisle and William Lord Berkeley is thus mentioned by Dugdale:—" But it was not long after, ere this Viscount L'Isle arrived at his full age; and thirsting after the castle of Berkeley, practised with one Thomas Holt, the keeper of Whitley Park, and one Maurice King, porter of the castle, to betray it into his hands; one Robert Veel (the viscount's engineer) being likewise an active person in that design, giving bond to Maurice King in the sum of £100 that as soon as the work should be accomplished, he should be made keeper of Wotton Park, with the fee of five marks per annum during his life. But this plot being discovered by Maurice King so much perplexed the Viscount L'Isle, that he forthwith sent this Lord Berkeley a challenge, 'requiring him of knighthood and manhood, to appoint a day, and to meet him half way, to try their quarrel and title, to eschew the shedding of Christian blood'; or to bring the same day the utmost of his power.' This letter of challenge, under the hand of that viscount, was sent 19 Martii, 10th EDWARD IV., he being then not full 22 years of age, having sued out his livery on 14 July before; and his wife then with child of her first-born. Unto which the Lord Berkeley returned this answer in writing, viz., 'that he would not bring the tenth man he could make; and bid him to meet on the morrow, at Nybley Green, by eight or nine of the clock, which standeth (saith he) on the borders of the Livelode that thou keepest untruly from me.' Whereupon they accordingly met, and the Viscount L'Isle's vizor being up, he was slain by an arrow shot through his head."

BERKELEY—BARON BOTETOURT.

By Writ of Summons, dated 10 March, 1308.

Lineage.

SIR MAURICE BERKELEY, of Uley, co. Gloucester, Knt. (son of Maurice Berkeley, Baron Berkeley, of Berkeley Castle), d. at the siege of Calais, 21st EDWARD III., leaving (by Margaret his wife) a son and a dau.,

I. THOMAS, of whom presently.
I. Isabel, aunt, and for a time heir of Maurice, son of Thomas Berkeley.

The son and heir,

THOMAS DE BERKELEY, of Uley, m. Catherine, dau. of John de Bottetourt, Baron Bottetourt, sister of John, and aunt of Joyce Burnel, and d. 35th EDWARD III., having had issue,

MAURICE.   Edmund, s.p.   John, s.p.

The eldest son,

MAURICE DE BERKELEY, m. Johanna, dau. of Sir John Dinham, Knt., and d. 2nd HENRY IV. His son and heir,

MAURICE BERKELEY, of Stoke Gifford, co. Gloucester, born after the death of his father, m. Ellen, dau. of William Montfort, and d. 26 November, 4th EDWARD IV., leaving a son and heir.

WILLIAM BERKELEY, of Stoke, who was attainted 1st HENRY VII., and restored 11th HENRY VII. He m. Anne, dau. of Sir Humphrey Stafford, Knt., and was father of

RICHARD BERKELEY, Esq., of Stoke, who m. Elizabeth, dau. of Humphrey Coningsby, Knt., and d. 5th HENRY VIII., having had issue,

I. JOHN, of whom presently.
II. Maurice (Sir), of Bruton, Knt., m. 1st, Catherine, dau. of William Blount Baron Mountjoy, and was ancestor of the BERKELEY's of BRUTON, and of Pylle (see BURKE's Peerage;) of Berkeley Portman, Lord Portman, and of the BERKELEYS, VISCOUNTS FITZ-HARDING; Sir Maurice m. 2ndly, Elizabeth, dau. of Anthony Sandes, Esq., and by her was ancestor of the BERKELEYS of BOYCOT, co. Kent.
I. A dau., m. to Sir Thomas Speke, of White Lackington, Knt.
II. A dau., m. to William Francis, of Combe Flore.

The elder son,

SIR JOHN BERKELEY, of Stoke Gifford, Knt., æt. three, 5th HENRY VIII., m. Isabella, dau. of William Dennys, and d. 28 June, 37th HENRY VIII., leaving (with two daus., Mary, m. 1st, Nicholas Walsh, and 2ndly, William Herbert, of Swansey, Knt.; and Elizabeth m. Henry Lison, of Upton St. Leonard), a son and heir,

SIR RICHARD BERKELEY, of Stoke Gifford, Knt., who m. 1st, Elizabeth Ann Beade, of Melton, and 2ndly, Elizabeth, dau. of Robert Jermy, of Antingham, and by her (who had m. 1st, Robert Roe, and was mother by him of Sir Thomas Roe, Knt., and of Mary, wife of Richard Berkeley, of Stoke and Rendcombe, Esq.), had, at his decease, 26 April, 2nd JAMES I., two sons and five daus., viz.,

I. HENRY, of whom presently.
II. William.
I. Elizabeth, m. to Sir Thomas Throckmorton, of Tortworth, co. Gloucester, Knt.
II. Catharine, m. to R. Lee, of Longborow.
III. Mary, m. to Sir John Hungerford, Knt.
IV. Anne.   V. Dorothy.

The eldest son,

SIR HENRY BERKELEY, of Stoke, Knt., m. Mary, dau. of Thomas Throckmorton, of Caughton, co. Warwick, and d. 7 February, 6th JAMES I., leaving (with a dau. Margaret, m. to John Tomlinson, of Bristol,) a son and heir,

RICHARD BERKELEY, Esq., of Stoke and Rendcombe, who m. 1st, Mary, dau. of Robert Roe, by Elizabeth, his wife, dau. of Robert Jermy, of Antingham, and had issue,

I. MAURICE (Sir), of whom presently.
II. John.   III. Thomas.   IV. Giles.   V. Richard, s. p.
VI. Robert, of Eycotta, co. Gloucester, m. Rebecca, dau. of Henry Stretton, of Wilts, and had issue, Richard; Robert; John; Rebecca, Mary; Muriel; and Frances, unm., 1682.
I. Elizabeth.   II. Muriel.   III. Catherine.
IV. Mary.   V. Margaret.

Richard Berkeley, who m. 2ndly, Jane, dau. of Thomas Murcott, of Remnam, Berks, d. 12 May, 1661, æt. eighty-three, and was buried at Stoke. His eldest son and heir,

SIR MAURICE BERKELEY, Knt., of Stoke, who m. 1st, Elizabeth, dau. of Sir Edward Coke, Knt., lord chief justice of the King's Bench, and by her had a dau. Frances; and 2ndly, a dau. of Sir Geo. Tipping, of Oxfordshire, and had a son and heir.

RICHARD, of whom presently. Sir Maurice *d. v. p.*, and was buried at Stoke, 3 January, 1654. His son and heir,

RICHARD BERKELEY, Esq., of Stoke, *m.* Elizabeth, dau. and heiress of Henry Symms, Esq., of Frampton Cotterell, co. Gloucester, and *d.* January, 1670, having had two sons, George, whose will bears date, 20 June, 1684, *d. s. p.*, and

JOHN SYMMS BERKELEY, Esq., of Stoke Gifford, co. Gloucester, *b.* 1 February, 1662, *m.* Elizabeth, widow of Edward Devereux, 8th Viscount Hereford, and dau. and co-heir of Walter Narborne, Esq., of Calne, in Wilts, and by her (who *d.* 17 November, 1742, and was buried at Canterbury, co. Oxford,) had issue,

NARBORNE, of whom presently.
Elizabeth, *b.* 17 January, 1718-19, *m.* 1 May, 1740. Charles Noel Somerset, Duke of Beaufort, and *d.* 8 April, 1799, leaving issue,

  1 HENRY SOMERSET, Duke of Beaufort, ancestor of the present Duke of Beaufort.
  1 Anne, *b.* 11 March, 1740-41, *m.* 13 September, 1759, Charles Compton, Earl of Northampton.
  2 Elizabeth, *b.* 12 March, 1742; *d. unm.* 7 May, 1760.
  3 Rachel, *b.* at Badmington, and bapt. there, 21 August, 1746, buried 7 May, 1747.
  4 Henrietta, *b.* 26, and bapt. 30 April, 1748, *m.* 13 April, 1769, to Sir Watkin W. Wynne, Bart, and *d. s. p.*, 24 July, 1770.
  5 Mary Isabella, *b.* 1 and bapt. 27 August, 1756, *m.* 26 December, 1775, to Charles Manners, Duke of Rutland, and had issue.

The only son and heir,
NARBORNE BERKELEY, Esq., claimed the BARONY OF BOTETOURT, which had been in abeyance from the decease of Joyce, Lady Burnell, *s. p.* in 1406, grand-dau. of John de Botetourt (*see* Botetourt, Barons Botetourt), and his right being established, he was summoned to parliament in that ancient dignity, on the 13 April, 1764. But as he *d.* without issue in 1776, it again fell into ABEYANCE, and so remained, until once more called out in favour of Henry Somerset, 5th Duke of Beaufort, son and heir of Charles, 4th duke, by Elizabeth (who *d.* in 1799), sister and sole heiress of the above mentioned Narborne, the deceased lord. The BARONY OF BOTETOURT is now therefore merged in the DUKEDOM OF BEAUFORT.

BERKELEY—BARONS BERKELEY, OF STRATTON.

By Letters Patent, dated 19 May, 1658.

Lineage.

Descended from the BARONS BERKELEY, of BERKELEY CASTLE, was

SIR RICHARD BERKELEY, Knt., of Stoke-Gifford, co. Gloucester, who *d.* in 1514, leaving issue by his wife, Elizabeth, dau. of Sir Humphrey Coningsby, Knt., two sons, namely, Sir John Berkeley, of Stoke-Gifford, ancestor to Lord Botetourt, and

SIR MAURICE BERKELEY, K.B., of Bruton, co. Somerset, standard-bearer to King HENRY VIII., and EDWARD VI., and to Queen ELIZABETH. Of this gentleman it is mentioned, that, in the 1st year of Queen MARY, riding casually in London, he met with Sir Thomas Wyat at Temple Bar, and persuading him to yield himself to the queen, Sir Thomas took his advice, and, mounting behind Sir Maurice, rode to the court. Sir Maurice Berkeley *m.* 1st, Catherine, dau. of William Blount, Lord Mountjoy, and by her (who *d.* 25 February, 1559) had issue, two sons and four daus., viz.,

HENRY, of whom presently.
Edward
Gertrude, *m.*, to Edward Horne, Esq.
Elizabeth, *m.* to James Percival, Esq., of Weston, Gorriano, co. Somerset.
Anne, *m.* to Nicholas Poynings, Esq., of Adderley.
Frances, *d. unm.*

Sir Maurice *m.* 2ndly, Elizabeth, dau. of Anthony Sandes, Esq., by whom (who *d.* 16 June, 1585) he had two sons and a dau. He was *s.* at his decease by his eldest son,

SIR HENRY BERKELEY, Knt., of Bruton, who *m.* Margaret, dau. of William Lygon, Esq., of Madresfield, co. Worcester, and was *s.* by his eldest son,

SIR MAURICE BERKELEY, who received the honour of knighthood from the Earl of Essex, while serving under that nobleman in the expedition to Calais, *anno* 1596. Sir Maurice *m.* Elizabeth, dau. of Sir Henry Killigrew, of Hanworth, co. Middlesex, and had issue five sons and two daus.; viz.,

1. CHARLES, who received the honour of knighthood at Bewley, in 1623, and, being eminently loyal to King CHARLES I., was sworn of the privy council upon the restoration of the monarchy, and appointed first comptroller, and then treasurer, of the household. Sir Charles *m.* Penelope, dau. of Sir William Godolphin, of Godolphin, co. Cornwall, Knt., and had issue,

  1 Maurice, created a baronet 2 July, 1660, successor to the viscounty of Fitzhardinge, &c. at the decease of his father. He *m.* Anne, dau. and co-heir of Sir Henry Lee, but *d. s. p.*

  2 CHARLES, who for his fidelity to King CHARLES II. during his Majesty's exile, and other eminent services, was created a peer of Ireland, as *Baron Berkeley, of Rathdown,* and VISCOUNT FITZHARDINGE, with remainder to his father, and his issue male; and a peer of England, 17 March, 1664, by the titles of *Baron B. tetourt, of La gport, co. Somerset,* and Earl of Falmouth. His lordship *m.* Elizabeth, dau. of Colonel Hervey Bagot, 2nd son of Sir Henry Bagot. Bart., of Blithfield, co. Stafford, by whom he had an only dau.,

    Mary, *m.* to Gilbert Cosyn Gerrard, Esq., eldest son of Sir Gilbert Gerrard, Bart., of Feskerton, co. Lincoln, from whom she was divorced in 1684, and *d.* in 1693.

  Lord Falmouth fell in a naval engagement with the Dutch, 3 June, 1665, and his remains were honourably interred in Westminster Abbey. At the decease of his lordship, his English honours EXPIRED, while those of Ireland reverted, according to the patent, to his father, Sir Charles Berkeley.

  3 William (Sir), governor of Portsmouth, and vice-admiral of the White, killed at sea in 1666.
  4 John, who succeeded his eldest brother, as VISCOUNT FITZHARDINGE, was treasurer of the chamber, and one of the tellers of the exchequer, in the reign of Queen ANNE. He *m.* a dau. of Sir Edward Villiers, and sister to the Earl of Jersey, governess to his royal highness William, Duke of Gloucester, and had issue,

    Mary, *m.* to Walter Chetwynd, Esq., of Ingestre, co. Stafford, who was created, in 1717, Baron Rathdown and Viscount Chetwynd, with remainder to the heirs male of his father.
    Frances, *m.* to Sir Thomas Clarges, Bart.

  His lordship *d.* 19 December, 1712, and thus leaving no male issue, the Irish *Barony of Berkeley,* and VISCOUNTY OF FITZHARDINGE, became EXTINCT.

Sir Charles Berkeley, upon the decease of his 2nd son, Charles, Earl of Falmouth, succeeding to that nobleman's Irish honours, became *Baron Berkeley, of Pathdown,* and VISCOUNT FITZHARDINGE, of the kingdom of Ireland; and dying 12 June, 1668, those honours descended to his eldest son, Sir Maurice Berkeley, Bart.

II. Henry (Sir).
III. Maurice (Sir).
IV. William (Sir).
V. JOHN (Sir), of whom presently.
1. Margaret.   II. Jane.

The youngest son,
SIR JOHN BERKELEY, having a command in the army raised to march against the Scots, in 1638, received the honour of knighthood from the king at Berwick, in the July of that year, and at the breaking out of the rebellion, appearing in arms for his sovereign, was one of those very good officers (as Lord Clarendon calls them), who were ordered, with the Marquess of Hertford, to form an army in the west. But, before entering upon that duty (in 1642) Sir John safely conducted a supply of arms and ammunition from the queen into Holland. Soon after this, being constituted commissary-general, he marched into Cornwall at the head of about one hundred and twenty horse, and not only secured the whole of that county, but made incursions into Devonshire; and being in joint commission with Sir Ralph Hopton, obtained divers triumphs over the insurgents of those western shires in the several battles of Bradock, Saltash, Launceston, and Stratton, as also at Modbury, co. Devon; subsequently investing Exeter, he reduced that garrison, and gallantly repulsed the enemy's fleet, then at Topsham, under the command of the Earl of Warwick; when he was constituted governor of Exeter, and general of all his majesty's forces in Devon. Sir John Berkeley stood so high in the estimation of the queen, that her majesty selected the city under his protection as the place of her accouchement, and was delivered, at Exeter, of the Princess Henrietta Maria; "Farewell, my dear heart: behold the mark * which you desire to have, to know when I desire any thing in earnest. I pray begin to remember what I spoke to you concerning Jacke Berkeley, for master of the wards." Exeter subsequently surrendered to Sir Thomas Fairfax, but its governor obtained the most honourable terms for its inhabitants and garrison. Sir John Berkeley was afterwards employed with Mr. Ashburnham; in endeavouring to negotiate terms for the unfortunate CHARLES and in a statement which he has given of the affair, attributes the ruin of the king to his misplaced confidence. after his escape from Hampton Court, in Colonel Hammond, governor

cf the Isle of Wight, at the instigation of Ashburnham, by whom Rapin is of opinion that Charles was betrayed: but Clarendon considers Ashburnham faithful, but outwitted by Cromwell. During the usurpation, Sir John Berkeley remained in exile with the royal family, and after the death of Lord Byron, in 1652, was placed at the head of the Duke of York's family, having the management of all his receipts and disbursements. In a few years afterwards, he was elevated to the peerage by the exiled monarch, as BARON BERKELEY, of *Stratton, co. Somerset* (one of the scenes of his former triumphs), by letters patent, dated at Brussels in Brabant, 19 May, 1658, in the 10th year of his majesty's reign. Upon the restoration of the monarchy, his lordship was sworn of the privy council; and at the close of the year 1669, was constituted lord lieutenant of Ireland, where he landed in 1670, and continued in the government for two years, when his lordship was succeeded by the Earl of Essex. In 1675, he was accredited ambassador extraordinary to the court of Versailles, and d. 28 August, 1678. His lordship had married Christian, dau. and heiress of Sir Andrew Riccard, president of the East India Company, and widow of Henry Rich, Lord Kensington, son and heir of Henry, Earl of Holland, by whom he had three sons, all of whom eventually succeeded to the title, and one dau., Anne, married to Sir Dudley Cullum, Bart., of Hawsted, co. Suffolk. Lord Berkeley was *s.* by his eldest son,

CHARLES BERKELEY, 2nd baron, captain of the "Tiger" man-of-war, who *d.* at sea, unmarried in the twenty-fourth year of his age, 21 September, 1682, and was *s.* by his brother,

JOHN BERKELEY, 3rd baron, groom of the stole, and 1st gentleman of the bed-chamber to Prince George of Denmark, and in the reign of King WILLIAM, one of the admirals of the fleet, and colonel of the 2nd regiment of marines. His lordship *m.* Jane Martha, dau. of Sir John Temple, Knt., of East Sheen, co. Surrey (who was afterwards *m.* to William, Earl of Portland), by whom he had no surviving issue. He *d.* 27 February, 1697, and was *s.* by his brother,

WILLIAM BERKELEY, 4th baron, who was constituted chancellor of the Duchy of Lancaster, and sworn of the privy council to Queen Anne, 20 September, 1710 His lordship *m.* Frances, youngest dau. of Sir John Temple (aforesaid), and had issue,

I. JOHN, his successor,
II. William, captain of the "Tiger" man-of-war, on board of which he died, 25 March, 1733, *s. p.*
III. Charles, *b.* 21 June, 1701, *m.* in 1745, Frances, dau. of Colonel John West, and dying in 1765, left one surviving child,
SOPHIA, *m.* 1769, SIR JOHN WODEHOUSE, Bart., of Kimberley, co. Norfolk, who was created BARON WODEHOUSE in 1797.
I. Jane, *d. unm.*
II. Francis, *m.* 1st, 1720, to William, Lord Byron, ancestor, by her, of the subsequent LORDS BYRON; and 2ndly to Sir Thomas Hay, Bart., of Alderston, N.B.
III. Barbara, *m.* in 1726, to John Trevanion, Esq., of Caerhayes, co. Cornwall, by whom she had a son, William Trevanion, Esq., M.P. of Caerhayes, who *d. s. p.*, and two daus. eventual co-heirs, viz.,
1 FRANCES, who *m.* John Bettesworth, Esq., LL.D., ancestor by her of the BETTESWORTH-TREVANIONS, of Cornwall; and
2 SOPHIA, who *m.* Admiral the Hon. John Byron, grandfather, by her, of George Gordon, LORD BYRON, the POET, and of George Anson, 7th LORD BYRON.
IV. Anne, *m.* in 1737, to James Cocks, Esq., M.P. for Reigate, by whom she left at her decease in 1729, an only child,
James Cocks, Esq., who *d. unm.*, being slain at St. Cas, on the French coast, in 1758.

His lordship *d.* 24 March, 1740, and was *s.* by his eldest son,

JOHN BERKELEY, 5th baron, who was constituted, in 1743, captain of the yeomen of his majesty's guard, sworn of the privy council in 1752, and appointed captain of the band of gentlemen pensioners in 1746. His lordship was subsequently constable of the Tower of London, and lord lieutenant of the Tower Hamlets. He *m.*, but *d. s. p.* 1773, when the BARONY OF BERKELEY, OF STRATTON, became EXTINCT.

Arms.—Gu., a chev. erm., between ten crosses pattée, arg.

BERKELEY—EARL OF FALMOUTH.

By Letters Patent, dated 17 March, 1664.

Lineage.

CHARLES BERKELEY, Esq., 2nd son of Sir Charles Berkeley, Knt., and nephew of John, 1st Lord Berkeley, of Stratton,

standing high in the favour of King CHARLES II., was elevated by that monarch to the peerage of Ireland, as Baron Berkeley and Viscount Fitzhardinge, with remainder, in default of male issue, to his father, and his male descendants; and afterwards created, 17 March, 1664, a peer of England, in the dignities of *Baron Botetourt, of Langport, co. Somerset,* and EARL OF FALMOUTH. His lordship *m.* Elizabeth, dau. of Colonel Hervey Bagot, 2nd son of Sir Henry Bagot, Bart., of Blithfield, co. Stafford, by whom he had an only dau.,

Mary, who *m.* Gilbert Cosyn Gerrard, Esq., eldest son of Sir Gilbert Gerrard, Bart., of Feskerton, co. Lincoln, from whom she was divorced in 1684, and *d.* in 1693.

Lord Falmouth fell in a bloody naval engagement with the Dutch, 3 June, 1665, and his remains were honourably interred in Westminster Abbey. Dying thus without male issue, his lordship's English honours EXPIRED, while those of Ireland reverted, according to the limitation of the patent, to his father, Sir Charles Berkeley, who then became Charles, 2nd Viscount Fitzhardinge, of that realm.

Arms.—Gu., a chev. between ten crosses formée, arg., a label of three points.

BERKELEY—VISCOUNT FITZHARDINGE.

(See BERKELEY, Baron Berkeley, of Stratton, in the *Peerage of England.*)

BERKELEY—BARON SEGRAVE, AND EARL FITZHARDINGE.

Barony by Letters Patent, dated 10 September, 1831.
Earldom by Letters Patent, dated 17 August, 1841.

Lineage.

COLONEL WILLIAM FITZHARDINGE BERKELEY, who bore during the lifetime of his father, Frederick Augustus, 5th Earl Berkeley the courtesy-title of Viscount Dursley, and had a seat in the lower house of parliament, under that designation, presented a petition to the crown at the earl's death in 1810, for a writ of summons as EARL BERKELEY, but doubts having arisen touching the marriage upon which the petitioner's right to the peerage rested, the petition was referred to the House of Lords, and their lordships came to a resolution, that the petitioner had not substantiated his claim. Colonel Berkeley was, however, some years after, 10 September, 1831, raised to the peerage by patent as BARON SEGRAVE, of Berkeley Castle, co. Gloucester, and made EARL FITZHARDINGE, 17 August, 1841. His lordship, *b.* 26 September, 1786, was lord lieutenant of the co. Gloucester, and colonel of the South Gloucester Militia; he *d. unm.* 10 October, 1857, when his honours became EXTINCT. His estates devolved under the entail created by the 5th earl on Admiral Sir MAURICE F. FITZ-HARDINGE BERKELEY, G.C.B., who was created Baron Fitzhardinge 5 August, 1861.

BERMINGHAM—BARONS BERMINGHAM.

By Writ of Summons, dated in 1326.

Lineage.

This family assumed its surname from the town of BERMINGHAM, in Warwickshire, which

PETER DE BERMINGHAM, steward to Gervase Paganell, Baron of Dudley, held of that nobleman in the 12th of HENRY II. (1165-6), with no less than nine knight's fees, *de veteri feoffamento,* of which William his father, had been enfeoffed in the reign of HENRY I. This Peter had a castle at Bermingham, which stood scarcely a bow-shot from the church to the westward and by a charter from the crown held a weekly Thursday market there, by which charter he had the liberties of *Thol, Theam, Sock, Sack, Infangthef,** to him and his heirs for ever. This Peter was *s.* by his son,

WILLIAM DE BERMINGHAM, who having *m.* Isabell, dau. of

---

* *Toll, &c.*—A power of punishing offenders within his own bounds; a power of obliging all that live in his jurisdiction to plead in his courts: a cognizance of all courts; a power to punish natives for theft.

Thomas de Estley (or Astley), a great feudal lord, and joining his father-in-law in rebellion, fell at the battle of Evesham, in the 94th of HENRY III., and was s. by his son,

WILLIAM DE BERMINGHAM, who, in the 22nd of EDWARD I., was in the expedition made then into Gascony, and in three years afterwards, he accompanied the Earl of Lincoln and Sir John de St John to the relief of Belgrade, then besieged by the Earl of Arras. But the English army forming into two divisions, that under General St. John, in which William de Bermingham immediately served, had the misfortune to encounter the whole force of the enemy, led by the Earl of Arras himself, and to be totally routed, numbers falling in the field, and numbers being made prisoners, of which latter was this William Bermingham; to whom s. at his decease, his son,

WILLIAM DE BERMINGHAM, who was s. by his son,

WILLIAM DE BERMINGHAM, who having filled several eminent employments during the reign of EDWARD II., was summoned to parliament as BARON BERMINGHAM, in the 1st year of EDWARD III. But (says Dugdale) never afterwards, so that I shall not pursue the story of him nor his descendants any further, than to observe, that his grandson,

SIR THOMAS DE BERMINGHAM, left issue one sole dau. and heiress, Elizabeth, m. to Thomas de la Roche, of which marriage there were two daus., co-heiresses, viz.,

Elena, m. 1st, to Edward, Lord Ferrars, of Chartley, now represented by the Marquis Townshend; and 2ndly, to Philip Chetwynd.
Elizabeth, m. to George Longvill, Esq., ancestor of Charles Longvill, Baron Grey, of Ruthyn and Hastings, now represented by the Marquis of Hastings.

LODGE, in his *Irish Peerage*, says that "the family continued to possess the lordship of Bermingham until the reign of HENRY VIII., when Edward Bermingham, Esq., the last male heir, was wrested out of that lordship by John Dudley, afterwards Duke of Northumberland."

Arms.—Per pale, indented, or and gules.

BERMINGHAM—BARONS ATHENRY AND EARL OF LOUTH.

Barony by Writ.
Earldom, by Letters Patent, dated 3 April, 1759.

Lineage.

PIERS DE BERMINGHAM, Lord of Thetmoy in Offaley, is usually reckoned the 1st BARON of ATHENRY, and was the progenitor of this family, which was known to the Irish as MACFEORIS (MacPierce), in consequence of their descent from him. Throughout the whole of "the Annals of the Four Masters" the name of Bermingham never once occurs; notices of the family are very frequent but always under the adopted Celtic name of MacFeoris. From this ancient family of the Berminghams is descended a branch settled in Scotland which still retains this old Celtic name of MACIORIS, or, as they to began to write it in the beginning of the 18th century, MACGEORGE. From this line descended the late ANDREW MACGEORGE, of Hillside, co. Dumbarton, writer in Glasgow (see BURKE's *Landed Gentry*, ed. 1864), and the present Lieutenant-Colonel WILLIAM MACGEORGE, of Her Majesty's Indian Army. Piers de Bermingham obtained by his sword large possessions in Connaught. His younger son, JAMES, was father of Piers, feudal Baron of Thetmoy (now Monastereoris), from whom the MacFeoris or MacYeoris, of Tipperary. His eldest son MEYLER, 2nd Lord Athenry acquired a large territory in Tipperary by marriage with Basilia, sister and heir of William de Wygornia (descended from Philip de Wygornia, lord deputy of Ireland), but exchanged it with Piers, Lord Bermingham, of Thetmoy for other lands. His son,

PETER DE BERMINGHAM, Lord of Athenry, summoned to parliament, d. 1307. He had issue,

I. Meiler d. v. p., leaving by Joan his wife, two daus., Philippa, and Elizabeth.
II. RICHARD, of whom presently.
III. Peter.

The 2nd son,

RICHARD DE BERMINGHAM, sheriff of Connaught, 1299, 1310, and 1316, left by Finwola, a son and heir,

THOMAS DE BERMINGHAM, Lord of Athenry, a minor at his father's death. He m. Edina Snymecaga, and by her (who d. 1384) he had four sons,

I. Richard, slain by O'Kelly, 1371, s. p
II. John, d. s. p.
III. William, d. s. p.
IV. WALTER, of whom we treat.

The 4th son,

WALTER DE BERMINGHAM, Lord of Athenry, was summoned to parliament 1377, 1380, and 1382. He had issue,

I. John, slain by O'Kelly, 1426.
II. Thomas, Lord of Athenry, in parliament temp. HENRY VI.: d. 1473, having had a son,
1 Thomas, Lord of Athenry, summoned to parliament 1490, m. Annablyna de Burgo, and had issue, John, who d. s. p., v. p., and Meyler, Lord of Athenry, 1526, m. Honora, dau. of Richard oge Bourke, son of Rickard, Lord Clanricarde.
III. RICHARD, of whom we treat.

The 3rd son,

RICHARD DE BERMINGHAM, called "Old Richard," and "Richard of the Wine," was father of EDMUND DE BERMINGHAM, who had a son,

SIR RICHARD DE BERMINGHAM, Lord of Athenry, 1547, s. Meyler, Lord Athenry, who d. 1529. He m. before 1540, Catherine, dau. of Teige O'Kelly, of Gallagh, chief of his name, and d. 1580, having had a son,

EDMUND DE BERMINGHAM, Lord Athenry, b. 1540, m. Cicely dau. of Teige O'Kelly, of Mullaghmore, and by her (who d ir 1593), had two sons, viz.,

I. RICHARD, of whom presently.
II. Meyler Buy, was seated at Connaught, but that place being lost in the troubles of 1641. the family settled at Dalgan. He m. Sarah, dau. of Walter Boyle MacJordan, of Tolrachan, co. Mayo, and had a son, REDMOND, who m. a dau. of Sir Christopher Garvey, and was father of

MILES, of Clondargin and Dalgan, who m. Cicely, dau. of Dudley MacCostello, Esq., of Tolaghan, co. Mayo, and was father of FRANCIS (his heir), a captain in the service of King JAMES II., who m. (mar. art. dated 28 February, 1684) Bridget, dau. of Andrew O'Crean, of Knock, co. Galway, and by her had a son and heir,

JOHN BERMINGHAM, of Clondargin and Dalgan, who m. Maud, eldest dau. of John Bermingham, Esq., of Killbegg, and d. in November, 1777, æt. eighty-five, having had five sons and a dau., viz.,

Francis, d. s. p.
John, of Dalgan, J. P., m. 1st, Jennett, dau. of John Puech, of St. Christopher's, which lady d., 1768. He m. 2ndly, Dorothea Matthews, of Demerara.
Michael, d. unm.
Redmond, a general in the Neapolitan service, d. unm.
Edward, m. in 1777, Anne, dau. of James Waddell, and had issue,

John, of Dalgan, major in the army, slain at Badajos.
Edward, of Dalgan and Clondargin, who claimed, 1830, the BARONY of ATHENRY.
Francis, who by Susanna his wife had an only child, Francis, who d. unm.
Bridget, m. to Charles Croghan, Esq., of Wingfield, co. Roscommon.

III. Thomas (Duffe), of Birmingham, m. a dau. of Burke, of Cloghroake, co. Galway, and had besides three younger sons, the eldest son and heir,

EDMUND, who by his wife, the dau. of Burke, of Ballylillie, was father of Thomas, who m. a dau of Burke, of Castletogher, and had a son and heir,

JOHN BERMINGHAM of Killbegg, co. Galway, who m. Elizabeth, 2nd dau. of John Browne, Esq , of Westport, co. Mayo, and had issue, five sons and five daus., viz.,

John, m. Anne dau. of — Chambers, and left an only son, William Bermingham, Esq., of Ross, who left two daus. his co-heirs, viz., Mary, Countess of Leitrim, and Anne, Countess of Charlemont.
Thomas.
Francis, m. the dau. of O'Byrne, of Athlone.
Peter, m. Elizabeth Holyday, and had two sons and five daus.,—Francis. John; Jane, m 1750, to John Chambers, Esq., of Kilboyne, co. Mayo; Elizabeth, Margery, Mary, and Honora.
Gilbert, d. unm.
Maud, m. to John Bermingham, Esq., of Dalgan.
Bridget, d. unm.
Mary, m. to Christopher O'Fallon, Esq., of Ballinderry, co. Roscommon.
Honora, m. to Richard Kirwan, Esq., of Carrunegarry, co. Galway.
Elizabeth, m. to Bryan O'Kelly, Esq., of Gardenford, co. Roscommon.

The eldest son and successor,

RICHARD DE BERMINGHAM, Lord Athenry, m. 1st, the dau of William Lally, archbishop of Tuam, and had a son,

EDWARD, of Dunmore, co. Galway, who m. Mary, dau. of Feagh Bourke, of Dunamon, co. Galway, and d. in his father's lifetime, before 1641, having had two sons,

1 Edward, a Dominican friar, who by deed, 20 February, 1645, conveyed all his right to the title and estate to his younger brother.
2 FRANCIS, of whom presently.

Richard de Bermingham m. 2ndly, Giles, dau. of Ulick Bourke, and relict of Dermot O'Shaughnessy, and by her (who d. 20 November, 1635,) had a son,

John, of Turloghvaughan, who m. Elizabeth, dau. of Martin Darcy, of Galway, alderman, and widow of Hugh O'Flaherty, but by her left no male issue.

Richard de Bermingham d. circa 1645, and was s. by his grandson,

FRANCIS BERMINGHAM, who s. to the title of Lord Athenry by virtue of the surrender executed by his elder brother Edward in 1645. He m. Bridget, dau. of Sir Lucas Dillon, Knt., of Lough Glyn, co. Roscommon, by Jane his wife, dau. of Garrett Moore, Esq., of Ball, co. Mayo, and had numerous children, of whom two sons and two daus. only survived,

EDWARD, his heir.
Remigius, LL.D., m. Elizabeth, dau. of Leeson, of co. Huntingdon, d. s. p.
Bridget, m. 1st, to James Talbot, Esq., of Mount Talbot, co. Roscommon (son of Sir Henry Talbot); and 2ndly to Capt. Thomas Bourke, youngest son of Colonel Richard Bourke, of Partry, and d. 1699.
Jane, m. to Myles, Viscount Mayo, and d. 6 June, 1687.

The Lord Athenry d. 12 April, 1677, and was s. by his eldest son and heir,

EDWARD BERMINGHAM, 20th lord, who m. 1st, Lady Mary Burke, elder dau. of Richard, 8th Earl of Clanricarde, and widow of Sir John Burke, of Derrymaclaghtny, co. Galway, and by her (who d. 13 August, 1685,) had two daus., both of whom d. young. He m. 2ndly, Bridget, eldest dau. of Colonel John Browne, of Westport, co. Mayo, ancestor of John, Earl of Altamont, and by her (who d. 13 January, 1702,) had issue,

FRANCIS, his heir.
John, d. 1704.   Richard, d. young.
Bridget, m. to George Browne, Esq., of the Neale, co. Mayo, and d. 24 September, 1747, s. p.
Maud, d. an infant.

His lordship d. in May, 1709, and was s. by his eldest son and heir,

FRANCIS BERMINGHAM, 21st lord, b. 1692, who m. 1st, 22 September, 1706, Lady Mary Nugent, eldest dau. of Thomas, Earl of Westmeath, and by her (who d. 26 July, 1725,) had issue,

THOMAS, his successor.
John, captain in the navy, killed in action.
Edmund, lieut. in the army, d. 1743.
Bridget, m. to James Daly, Esq. of Dunsandle, and d. s. p. 1730.
Margaret, m. 1741, to Gregory, eldest son of Charles Byrne, Esq., of Byrne-Grove, co. Kilkenny, and grandson of Sir Gregory Byrne, of Tymogue, Queen's Co., Bart, d. s. p.
Mary, m. in October, 1748, to Edmund Costello, Esq., barrister-at-law, and had issue,
Charles, b. 1750; Francis d. young; and another son, b. 1762.
Mary and Alice.
Catherine, m. 1st, in July, 1750, to Patrick Wemyss, Esq., of Danescourt, M.P. for co. Kilkenny, who d. 1762; and 2ndly, to Captain John Cullen, and d. s. p. 1773.

His lordship m. 2ndly, 17 August, 1745, Ellis, eldest dau. of James Agar, Esq., of Gowran, and widow of Theobald, Viscount Mayo, but by her (who subsequently was created Countess of Brandon,) had no issue. His lordship d. 4 March, 1749, and was s. by his only surviving son,

THOMAS BERMINGHAM, 22nd Lord Athenry, b. 16 November, 1717, M.P. for co. Galway, who was created by privy seal, 3 April, 1759, and by patent, 23rd of the same month, EARL OF LOUTH. He m. 1st, in November, 1745, Jane, eldest dau. of Sir John Bingham, Bart., of Castlebar, co. Mayo (sister of the 1st Earl of Lucan), and by her (who d. 11 September, 1746,) had a dau., d. in infancy. His lordship m. 2ndly, 10 January, 1750, Margaret, youngest dau. of Peter Daly, Esq., of Quansborough, co. of Galway, and by her had (with two sons, Francis and Peter, both d. young,) three daus., co-heiresses,

I. ELIZABETH, b. 24 October, 1756, m. 1st, to Thomas-Baily-Heath Sewell, Esq., son and heir of the Right Hon. Sir Thomas Sewell, master of the Rolls, and had, with a dau., a son and heir,

THOMAS-BERMINGHAM-DALY-HENRY SEWELL, who claimed the Barony of Athenry in 1800. He m. in 1796, the Hon Harriet Beresford, dau. of William, 1st Lord Decies, arch-

---

bishop of Tuam, and had four daus, the eldest of whom, Elizabeth, m. 9 May, 1814, Rev. Solomon Richards, of Solsborough, co. Wexford, and d. 26 January, 1861, leaving SOLOMON RICHARDS, Esq., of Solsborough, lieut.-general in the army, and other issue.
Lady Elizabeth Sewell m. 2ndly, 19 June, 1779, Francis Duffield, Esq.; 3rdly, Joseph Russell, Esq.; and d. in 1838.
II. MARY, m. 1 June, 1777, William, 2nd Earl of Howth, and left four daus.,
1 HARRIET, m. to Arthur French St. George, Esq., of Tyrone, co. Galway, and was one of the claimants to the BARONY OF ATHENRY; the son and heir of this marriage, CHRISTOPHER ST. GEORGE, Esq., of Tyrone, d. 1877, leaving two daus., his co-heirs.
2 Isabella, m. 19 May, 1803, to William-Richard, Earl Annesley, and d. in 1827, leaving an only child, Lady Mary, who m. 1828, Wm.-John M'Guire, Esq., of Rostrevor, and d. 1837, leaving William-Richard-Bermingham McGuire, and other issue.
3 Mary, m. November, 1805, to Clifford Trotter, Esq., of Charleville Cottage, co. Wicklow, and d. in 1825; her grandson and heir, WILLIAM CLIFFORD BERMINGHAM RUTHVEN, Esq., of Quansborough, co. Galway, m. 12 October, 1865, Frances-Margaret, dau. of Admiral Robert-Jocelyn Otway, and has issue.
4 Matilda, m. to Major William Burke, of Keelogues, and had an only surviving dau.,
Mary-Isabella, m. 11 June, 1833, John-Joseph-Andrew Kirwan, Esq., of Hillsbrook, and had,
Martin-FitzJohn-Kirwan; d. s. p. 11 November, 1865.
William-Joseph-Kirwan, m. Katherine, dau. of Martin Kirwan; and d. 9 June, 1862, leaving an only dau., MARY-LYDIA KIRWAN.
Matilda, m. Joseph Burke, Esq., of The Abbey, Roscommon.
III. LOUISA, m. 1st, Joseph-Henry Blake, Esq., of Ardfry, co. Galway, and was mother of Anastasia Blake, who m. Luke, 2nd Lord Clonbrock, and was mother of ROBERT, LORD CLONBROCK. Lady Louisa Blake m. 2ndly, James Daly, Esq., of Great Charles Street, Dublin.
The earl d. 1799, when the Earldom of Louth became EXTINCT, and the BARONY OF ATHENRY suspended.

Arms—Per pale, indented, or and gu.

BERMINGHAM—EARL OF LOUTH.

By Charter, dated 12 May, 1319.

Lineage.

SIR JOHN BERMINGHAM, 2nd son of Peter, 3rd Lord Athenry, being appointed, in 1318, commander-in-chief of the English forces in Ireland, achieved a signal victory over Edward le Bruce and his adherents, and was in consequence created by EDWARD II., 12 May, 1319, EARL OF LOUTH. He m. Catharine, 4th dau. of Richard, Earl of Ulster, by whom he had an only son Richard, who predeceased him, and three daus., his co-heirs, viz., Matilda, m. to Sir Eustace le Poer, ancestor of the Earl Tyrone; Bartholomea, m. to John, son of Richard FitzRicher, and had a son Richard; and Catharine, m. to Edward Lacie. His lordship acted a conspicuous part in the political and military proceedings of his time, but was eventually most treacherously murdered, 10 June, 1329, when, as he had no male issue, the title became EXTINCT.

Arms—Party per pale, indented, or and gu.

BERMINGHAM—BARON CARBERY.

By Letters Patent, dated 17 June, 1541.

Lineage.

SIR WILLIAM BERMINGHAM, Knt., descended from a common ancestor with the Lords Athenry, was created, in June, 1541, Baron of Carbery. co Kildare. His lordship m. 1st, Rose, dau. of Gerald Fitzgerald, Esq., of the Blackwood, by whom he had no issue; and 2ndly, of Sir John Plunket, Knt., of Beaulieu, by whom (who m. 2ndly, Robert Plunket, Esq.) he left at his decease, 17 July, 1548, an only son,

EDWARD BERMINGHAM, 2nd Lord Carbery; at whose decease, without male issue, the peerage became EXTINCT, the manor of Dunfert, in Kildare, devolving on his lordship's next heir,

WALTER BERMINGHAM, Esq., of Meylerston, son of John, brother of the 1st Lord Carbery. He d. 27 November, 1591, and was s. by his son,

THOMAS BERMINGHAM, Esq., of Dunfert, who m. 1st, Margaret, dau. of Robert Talk, of Cookstown, co. Meath, and widow of

Robert Scurlock; and 2ndly, Cecilia, dau. of — Fitzgerald, and had issue,

WILLIAM, his heir.
Edward.
JOHN, *s.* to his brother.
Anne.   Margaret.
Catharine, *m.* to Richard Plunket, Esq., of Tullynoch, co. Meath
Mary.
Maud, *m.* to Patrick Vernon, Esq.

The eldest son and heir,
WILLIAM BERMINGHAM, *s.* his father at Dunfert and Carryck, and dying *s. p.* in 1603, left his estates to his brother,
JOHN BERMINGHAM, who *m.* Mary, dau. of Sir Christopher Barnewall, Knt., and by her (who *m.* 2ndly, Thomas Nugent, Esq., of Delvin, co. Westmeath,) had one son, WALTER. Mr. Bermingham *d.* about 1608, his son,
WALTER BERMINGHAM, a minor at his father's death, had a livery of his estate, 2 July, 1629. He *m.* Margaret, 2nd dau. of Thomas the 18th Lord of Kerry, and *d.* 12 June, 1638, having had two sons and two daus. The sons, John and Thomas, both *d. unm.*, and the two daus. became co-heirs. They were

Mary, *m.* to John, 1st Lord Bellew.
Anne, *m.* to Maximilian O'Dempsey, the last Viscount of Clanmalier.

Arms.—As Bermingham, Earl of Louth.

BERTIE — DUKES OF ANCASTER AND KESTEVEN, CO. LINCOLN, MARQUESSES OF LINDSEY.

Barony, by Writ of Summons, dated 26 July, 1313.
Marquisate, by Letters Patent, dated 29 December, 1706.
Dukedom, by Letters Patent, dated 16 July, 1715.

Lineage.

The family of BERTIE came originally into England from Bertiland, in Prussia, with the Saxons, and obtained from one of our Saxon monarchs a castle and town in the co. Kent, which was denominated from them Bertie-stad (Saxon-town), now Bersted, near Maidstone.

It appears from an old manuscript in the Cotton Library, that
LEOPOLD DE BERTIE was constable of Dover Castle, *temp.* King ETHELRED, but opposing strongly the government upon some occasion, his son and heir,
LEOPOLD DE BERTIE, upon succeeding to the inheritance, apprehensive of his safety, in consequence of his father's proceedings, fled to ROBERT, King of France, and marrying a French woman, settled in that kingdom, where his posterity continued until the year 1154, when his descendant,
PHILIP BERTIE, *de eadem familiâ,* accompanying King HENRY II. to England, was restored by that monarch to his ancient patrimony in Bersted. From this Philip lineally descended
THOMAS BERTIE, Esq., of Bersted, who having "a long tyme used himself in feates of arms" was appointed by HENRY VIII. *capitanus castri de Hurst.* He *m.* Alicia Say, and left a son and heir,
RICHARD BERTIE, Esq., *b.* 1518, who *m.* in 1553, Katherine Willoughby, Baroness Willoughby de Eresby, in her own right, and Duchess of Suffolk, in right of her 1st husband, Charles Brandon, Duke of Suffolk, and had issue,

PEREGRINE, his successor.
Susan, *m.* 1st, to Reginald Grey, Earl of Kent, and 2ndly, to Sir John Wingfield.

During the reign of Queen MARY, the Duchess of Suffolk, being a zealous supporter of the Reformation, was obliged to retire, accompanied by Mr. Bertie from England, and they subsequently encountered great privations and dangers upon the continent, until received under the protection of the King of Poland, and placed by that monarch in the earldom of *Crozan* in Sanogelia (see "*Five Generations of a Loyal House*"). Mr. Bertie and his wife returned to England at Queen MARY's death. The duchess *d.* 19 September, 1580, and Mr. Bertie 9 April, 1582; the son,
PEREGRINE BERTIE, Baron Willoughby de Eresby, being born in the duchy of Cleves, was naturalized by patent, dated 2

August, 1559, and declared by order of Queen ELIZABETH, by the Lord Treasurer Burleigh, the Lord Chamberlain Sussex, and the Earl of Leicester, in the Star Chamber, on 11 November, 1580, entitled to the ancient Barony of Willoughby—just as those high personages were about to sit down to dinner, when his lordship was placed by them in his proper situation at table; and he took his seat in parliament on the Monday following, next to Lord Zouch, of Haringworth. His lordship was deputed in 1582 to attend, with the Earl of Leicester, and other nobles, upon the Duke of Anjou, into Antwerp, and was sent in the same year to FREDERICK, King of Denmark, with the ensigns of the order of the Garter. In the 29th of ELIZABETH (1586-7), Lord Willoughby, reputed "one of the queen's first swordsmen and a great master of the art military," was employed at the siege of Zutphen, in the Netherlands, and in an encounter with the forces of the garrison, overthrew General George Cressiak, commander-in-chief of the cavalry, and took him prisoner. His lordship, in the next year, upon the retirement of the Earl of Leicester, was appointed commander-in-chief of the English auxiliary forces in the United Provinces, and most valiantly defended Bergen-op-Zoom against the Prince of Parma. He subsequently commanded an English army sent into France, in aid of the King of Navarre. Of this nobleman Sir Robert Naunton speaks with high commendation, in his *Fragmenta Regalia.* His lordship *m.* Mary, dau. of John Vere, Earl of Oxford, sister and heiress of the whole blood to Edward, 17th Earl of Oxford, and had issue five sons and one dau.,

I. ROBERT, his successor.
II. Peregrine, K.B., *m.* Margaret, dau. of Nicholas Saunderson, VISCOUNT CASTLETON, and *d.* 1640, having had issue,
    Nicholas, of St. Martin-in-the-Fields, who *d.* January, 1671. He *m.* Mary, dau. of Edward Raybone, of Chard, co. Somerset, and had a son Peregrine, *b.* 14 January, 1655, and *d.* in 1721, leaving issue,
        Peregrine, from whom the Berties of Low Layton, co. Essex, are descended.
III. Henry, *m.* Dorothy, dau. of Corbet, of Clipstow, co. Rutland, and was ancestor of the Berties of Lound, co. Lincoln,
IV. Vere.   v. Roger.
I. Catherine, who *m.* Sir Lewis Watson, of Rockingham Castle, co. Northampton, afterwards Lord Rockingham.

Lord Willoughby *d.* in 1601, and was *s.* by his eldest son,
ROBERT BERTIE, as 10th Baron Willoughby de Eresby. This nobleman claimed the earldom of Oxford, and the baronies of Bulbec, Sandford and Badlesmere, with the office of Lord High Chamberlain of England, in the right of his mother, but succeeded in establishing his right to the chamberlainship only; he was, however, created EARL OF LINDSEY, 22 November, 1626, and in four years after elected a knight of the most noble order of the Garter. In the 7th of CHARLES I. he was constituted constable of England, for the trial of Lord Rea and David Ramsey. In the 11th of the same reign, he was made Lord High Admiral; and in 1639, upon the Scots taking up arms, he was appointed governor of Berwick. His lordship was chosen general of the king's forces at the breaking out of the civil war, and fell at the battle of Edge Hill, in 1642. Lord Willoughby *m.* Elizabeth, only child of Edward, 1st Lord Montague, of Boughton, and grand-dau., maternally, of Sir John Jefferies, Lord Chief Baron of the Exchequer, and by her (who *d.* 30 November, 1654), had issue,

MONTAGU, his successor.
Roger (Sir), K.B., *m.* Ursula, dau. and heiress of Sir Edward Lawley, Knt., and *d.* 15 October, 1654, leaving a son Robert, who *d. s. p.* in August, 1699.
Robert, *d.* in 1608.
Peregrine, *m.* Anne, dau. of Daniel Hardby, Esq., of Eveden, co. Lincoln, with whom he acquired that seat and settled there. He left at his decease an only dau. and heiress, Elizabeth, who *m.* William, Lord Widrington.
Francis, captain of horse, killed in the king's service, in Ireland, *anno* 1641.
Robert, fellow of Sidney College, Cambridge. *m.* 1st, Alice, dau. of Richard Barnard, Esq., and widow of Francis Osbaston, of Beehive, in Essex, which lady *d.* 1677; 2ndly, Elizabeth, 2nd dau. of Sir Thomas Bennet, of Baberham, co. Cambridge; and 3rdly, Mary, dau. of Robert Halsey, of Great Gaddeston, co. Hertford, and relict of John Crosby, Esq.
Henry, captain of horse, killed at Newberry, fighting under the royal banner.
Vere, *b.* 1 January, 1619, *d. unm.*
Edward, *b.* 17 October, 1624; *d.* 25 December, 1686, and was buried at Richmond, in Surrey. He *m.* Jane, dau. of Francis Rogers, of Maidencroft, co. Hertford, Esq.
Catherine, *m.* to Sir William Paston, Bart., of Oxnead, co. Norfolk, and *d.* in 1636.
Elizabeth, *m.* to Sir Miles Stapleton, of Carlton, co. York, and *d.* 28 February, 1683.
Anne, *d. unm.* 1660.

Sophia, m. to Sir Richard Chaworth, Knt., and d. 20 December, 1689.

Mary, m. 1st, to the Rev. John Hewit, D.D., beheaded for his loyalty to King CHARLES I., and 2ndly, to Sir Abraham Shipman, Knt.

His lordship was s. by his eldest son,

MONTAGU BERTIE, 2nd earl, who commanded the king's royal regiment of guards, at Edge Hill, and being near his gallant father, when that nobleman fell wounded into the hands of the enemy, voluntarily surrendered himself to a commander of the horse on the rebel side, in order to be in attendance upon his afflicted parent. Being afterwards exchanged, he continued zealously to support the royal cause, and at the head of the guards fought at the three battles of Newberry, at Cropredy, at Lostwithiel, and at the fatal fight of Naseby, where he was wounded; nor did he forsake his royal master to the very last, for being one of the lords of the bedchamber, and of the privy council, he attended personally upon the unhappy monarch, until his majesty put himself into the hands of the Scots. After the death of the king, Lord Lindsey compounded for his estate, and lived in privacy until the restoration of the monarchy, when he was called to the privy council, and elected a knight of the most noble order of the Garter. His lordship had the honour and gratification too of officiating at the coronation of King CHARLES II., as LORD HIGH CHAMBERLAIN OF ENGLAND. The earl m. 1st, Martha, dau. of Sir William Cockain, of Rushton, co. Northampton, Knt., and widow of James Ramsay, Earl of Holderness, by whom (who d. in July, 1641) he had,

ROBERT, his successor.

Peregrine, m. Susan, dau. and co-heiress of Sir Edward Monins, Bart., of Waldershare, Kent, and had three daus.,

Bridget, wife of John, Earl of Poulet.

Elizabeth, d. unm.

Mary, m. 1st, to Anthony Henley, Esq., of the Grange, Hants; and 2ndly, to the Honourable Henry Bertie, 3rd son of James, Earl of Abingdon.

Richard, capt. in the army, of Creton, co. Lincoln, d. unm. in 1685, æt. fifty.

Vere, justice of the Common Pleas, temp. CHARLES II., d. unm. 13 February, 1680.

Charles, of Uffington, co. Lincoln, m. Mary, dau. of Peter Tryon, Esq., of Harringworth, co. Northampton, and widow of Sir Samuel Jones, by whom he had issue: his great-grandson, ALBEMARLE BERTIE, inherited the EARLDOM OF LINDSEY at the death of the last DUKE OF ANCASTER. (See BURKE's Peerage.)

Elizabeth, m. to Baptist Noel, Viscount Campden.

Bridget, m. to Thomas Osborne, Duke of Leeds.

Catherine, m. to Robert Dormer, Esq., of Dourton, Bucks.

The earl m. 2ndly, Bridget, dau. and sole heiress of Edward Wray, Esq. (3rd son of Sir W. Wray, of Glentworth, co. Lincoln, Bart.), by Elizabeth, his wife, dau. and heiress of Francis, Lord Norreys and Earl of Berkshire, and had issue,

JAMES, who succeeded to the Barony of Norreys, of Rycote, co. Oxford, and was created Earl of Abingdon : his lordship is ancestor to the extant Earls of Abingdon.

Edward, d. young.

Henry, m. Philadelphia, dau. of Sir Edward Norris, of Western, co. Oxford, d. in 1734.

Mary, m. to Charles Dormer, Earl of Caernarvon.

His lordship d. 25 July, 1666, and was s. by his eldest son,

ROBERT BERTIE, 3rd earl. This nobleman m. 1st, Mary, 2nd dau. and co-heir of John Massingberd, Esq., and had an only dau. Arabella, m. to Thomas Savage, Earl of Rivers. He m. 2ndly, Elizabeth, dau. of Philip, Lord Wharton, by whom he had five sons, viz.,

ROBERT, his successor, who was summoned to the house of peers as Baron Willoughby.

Peregrine, vice-chamberlain of the household to Queen ANNE, and one of the tellers of the exchequer, d. s. p. 10 July, 1711.

Philip, d. unm. 15 April, 1728.

Noreys, d. unm.

Albemarle, M.P., auditor of the duchy of Cornwall, d. unm. 23 January, 1741-2.

His lordship m. 3rdly, Elizabeth, dau. of Thomas Pope, Earl of Down, in Ireland, by whom he had a son Charles, and a dau. Elizabeth, who both d. unm. The earl d. 8 May, 1701, and was s. by his eldest son,

ROBERT BERTIE, Lord Willoughby de Eresby, as 4th earl, who was created MARQUESS OF LINDSEY, 29 December, 1706; and upon the decease of Queen ANNE, was appointed one of the lords justices until the arrival of King GEORGE I. His lordship was subsequently called to the privy council, appointed lord-lieutenant and custos-rotulorum of the county of Lincoln, and elevated, 20 July, 1715, to the DUKEDOM OF ANCASTER AND KESTEVEN. His grace m. 1st, 30 July, 1678, Mary, dau. of Sir

Richard Wynn, of Gwydyr, co. Caernarvon, Bart., by whom he had issue,

Robert, b. 6 January, 1683-4, and d. at Wolfenbuttle, on his travels.

PEREGRINE, his successor.

Elizabeth, Eleanor, and Mary, who all d. unm.

He m. 2ndly, Albinia, dau. of Major-General William Farington, of Chiselhurst, in Kent, by whom (who m. 2ndly, James Douglas, Esq., and d. 29 July, 1745,) he had issue,

Vere, M.P. for Boston, m. in 1736, to Miss Anne Casey, of Braunston, near Lincoln, and left, in 1768, two sons, who d. young, and two daus., his co-heirs; viz.,

Albinia, m. 27 May, 1757, to the Hon. George Hobart, who succeeded his brother as 3rd Earl of Buckinghamshire.

Louisa, m. 19 April, 1778, to General Sir Charles Stuart, K.B., son of John, Earl of Bute.

Montagu, capt. R.N., m. Elizabeth, dau. of William Piers, Esq., M.P. for Wells, and left, in 1753, two daus.,

Augusta, m. in 1758, to John, Lord Burghersh, afterwards Earl of Westmoreland.

Frances.

Robert, a general officer in the army. In 1756 he happened to be on board the "Ramillies" (proceeding to join his regiment in Minorca,) with Admiral Byng, in the engagement with the French fleet off that island, and gave a very clear and candid evidence in behalf of that unfortunate officer, at his trial in the January following. Lord Robert sat in parliament successively for Whitechurch, Hants, and Boston in Lincolnshire. He m. 5 April, 1762, Chetwynd, dau. and heir of Montagu, Viscount Blundell, in Ireland. He d. 10 March, 1782.

Thomas, capt. R.N. d. unm. 21 July, 1749.

Louisa, m. in 1736, to Thomas Bludworth, Esq., gentleman of the horse to the Prince of Wales, and one of the grooms of the bedchamber.

His grace d. 26 July, 1723, and was s. by his eldest son,

PEREGRINE BERTIE, 2nd duke, b. 29 April, 1686, who had been summoned to parliament, in the lifetime of his father, as LORD WILLOUGHBY DE ERESBY. His grace was called to the privy council in 1724, and appointed in the same year lord-lieutenant and custos-rotulorum of the county and city of Lincoln. In 1734 he was constituted lord warden and justice in Eyre of all his majesty's parks, chases, forests, &c. north of the Trent. The duke m. Jane, one of the four daus. and co-heirs of Sir John Brownlow, Bart., of Belton, co. Lincoln, by whom he had,

I. PEREGRINE, his successor,

II. — who d. unm. 16 May, 1765.

III. BROWNLOW, who s. as 5th duke.

1. Mary, m. 21 February, 1747, to Samuel Greatheed, Esq., of Guy's Cliffe, co. Warwick, and d. 23 May, 1774, leaving a son,

BERTIE BERTIE-GREATHEED, Esq., of Guy's Cliffe, co. Warwick, whose grand-dau. and heiress, ANNE CAROLINE GREATHEED, of Guy's Cliffe, co. Warwick, 22 March, 1822, the Hon. CHARLES PERCY, who assumed, in 1826, the surname and arms of BERTIE, in addition to and before PERCY.

II. Albinia, m. Francis Beckford, Esq., of Basing Park, Hants, and d. in 1754.

III. Jane, m. General Edward Mathew, governor of Grenada, and had issue, four daus. and one son, BROWNLOW, who took the name of BERTIE, and had issue, Bertie, d. s.o., and four daus., of whom Jane, m. Field-Marshal the Marquis de la Marmora.

IV. Carolina, m. to George Dewar, Esq., and d. in 1774.

His grace d. 1 January, 1742, and was s. by his eldest son,

PEREGRINE BERTIE, 3rd duke, who m. 1st, 22 May, 1735, Elizabeth, dau. and sole heiress of William Blundell, Esq., of Basingstoke, Hants, and relict of Sir Charles Gunter Nicholls, K.B., but had no issue. His grace m. 2ndly, 27 November, 1750, Mary, dau. of Thomas Panton, Esq., by whom he had surviving issue,

ROBERT, his successor.

PRISCILLA-BARBARA-ELIZABETH, m. 23 February, 1779, to Peter Burrell, Esq., of Beckenham, Kent, afterwards created a baronet, and elevated to the peerage, as BARON GWYDIR. (See WILLOUGHBY DE ERESBY—BURKE's Peerage and Baronetage.)

GEORGIANA-CHARLOTTE, m. 25 April, 1791, to James, 1st Marquess Cholmondeley.

In 1745, on the breaking out of the rebellion in Scotland, his grace raised a regiment of foot for his majesty's service, and attained through the different gradations, the rank of general in the army in 1772. At the coronation of King GEORGE III., the duke officiated as LORD GREAT CHAMBERLAIN OF ENGLAND. In 1766, he was appointed master of the horse; he was also recorder of Lincoln. He d. 12 April, 1778, and was s. by his son, ROBERT BERTIE, 4th duke, at whose decease, unm., 8 July, 1779, the BARONY OF WILLOUGHBY DE ERESBY fell into ABEYANCE between his grace's two sisters, but was called out by the crown, in the following year, in favour of the elder, PRISCILLA (who d. 29 December, 1828) and was s. by her son and heir, Peter Robert, 2nd Lord Gwydyr and 19th Lord Willoughby de Eresby. The LORD GREAT CHAMBERLAINSHIP devolved jointly upon the two ladies; while his grace's other honours reverted to his uncle,

LORD BROWNLOW BERTIE, as 5th duke. This nobleman m. 1st, 6 November, 1762, Harriot, dau. and sole heiress of George Morton Pitt, Esq., of Twickenham, Middlesex, but her grace d. in the following year without issue. He m. 2ndly, 2 January, 1769, Mary Anne, youngest dau. of Major Layard, by whom (who d. 13 January, 1804,) he had an only dau., MARY-ELIZABETH, m. 26 May, 1793, to Thomas, Viscount Milsington, afterwards Earl of Portmore, and left at her decease, in 1797, an only son, BROWNLOW-CHARLES, who inherited the great personal estates of his grandfather, the Duke of Ancaster, but died at Rome, in 1818, of wounds received from banditti. His grace d. in 1809, when the DUKEDOMS OF ANCASTER AND KESTEVEN, and the MARQUISATE OF LINDSEY, became EXTINCT.

Arms—Arg., three battering rams, barways, in pale, proper, armed and garnished, az.

BERTRAM—BARONS BERTRAM, OF MITFORD.

By Writ of Summons, dated 14 December, 1264.

Lineage.

At the time of the Conquest the castle of Mitford, in Northumberland, was held by Sir John de Mitford, whose only dau. and heiress, SYBILLA MITFORD, was given in marriage by the CONQUEROR to a Norman knight of the name of Richard Bertram, and from this alliance sprang the Lords Bertram, of Mitford. From Matthew, the brother of Sir John de Mitford, descend the Mitfords, now of Mitford Castle, Northumberland, the Mitfords of Pitshill, co. Sussex, the Mitfords of Exbury, Hants, the Mitfords, Lords Redesdale, &c. In the reign of King HENRY I.,

WILLIAM BERTRAM (son of Richard Bertram, by Sybella Mitford his wife,) founded, with the approbation of his wife and sons, the Augustinian Priory of BRINKBURNE, in Northumberland, m. Hawyse, dau. of Sir William Merley, of Morpeth, and left issue, ROGER, Guy, William, and Richard. The eldest son,

ROGER BERTRAM, in the 12th of HENRY II., upon the assessment in aid of the marriage portion of the king's dau., certified his knight's fees to be six and a half; and, in the 18th of the same monarch, paid £6 10s. scutage for not going in person, nor sending soldiers, upon the expedition then made into Ireland. To this feudal lord s. his son and heir, by Ada, his wife,

WILLIAM BERTRAM, who obtained a grant from the crown, in the 5th year of King JOHN, of the manor of Felton, in Northumberland, with all the woods thereunto belonging. He m. Alice, dau. of Robert de Umfravil, and d. in or before the 7th year of the same reign, for at that time we find King JOHN conferring the wardship of his lordship's son and heir, ROGER, upon Peter de Brus, with the custody of his lands during the minority, in consideration of the sum of 300 marks. To the possession of which lands succeeded, when at full age, the said

ROGER BERTRAM. This feudal lord being involved in the proceedings of the barons, in the 17th King JOHN, 1215-16, his castle and lands of Mitford were seized, and conferred upon Philip de Ulecotes; but afterwards making his peace, and Philip de Ulecotes not seeming willing to obey the king's mandate in restoring those lands, he was threatened with the immediate confiscation of his own territorial possessions in the cos. of York, Nottingham, and Durham. After this period Roger Bertram appears to have enjoyed the royal favour; and in the 13th of HENRY III., when ALEXANDER of Scotland was to meet the English monarch at York, he was one of the great northern barons who had command to attend him thither. He d. in 1241, and was s. by his son,

ROGER BERTRAM, who, in the 42nd of HENRY III., had command, with other barons of the north, to march into Scotland for the rescue of the young King of Scots, the King of England's son-in-law, out of the hands of his rebellious subjects; but, in the 48th of the same monarch, being in arms with the other rebellious barons, he was taken prisoner at Northampton, and his castle of Mitford seized upon by the escheator of the crown,* while he was himself committed to the custody of William de Valence. He must, however, have made his peace very soon afterwards, for we find him summoned to parliament as a

BARON (the first by writ,) in the next year, 14 December, 1264. His lordship had issue, by Joan, his wife (who m. 2ndly, Robert de Neville,)

ROGER, his successor.
Agnes, m. to Thomas Fitz-William, Lord of Elmeley and Sprotborough, co. York, and had issue,
   WILLIAM FITZ-WILLIAM, who was succeeded by his son,
      WILLIAM FITZWILLIAM (from whom the extant Earls Fitz-William descend), one of the co-heirs of the BARONY and estates at the decease of his cousin, AGNES BERTRAM.
Isabel, m. to Philip Darcy, and had Norman Darcy, who was s. by his son,
   PHILIP DARCY, one of the co-heirs of the BARONY and estates at the decease of his cousin, AGNES BERTRAM. He d. young and s. p.
Christian, m. to Penulbury, and had a son,
   ELIAS DE PENULBURY, one of the co-heirs to the BARONY and lands, at the decease of his cousin, AGNES BERTRAM.
Ada, m. to — de Vere, and had a dau., Isabel, whose son,
   GILBERT DE ATON, was one of the co-heirs to the BARONY and lands, at the decease of his cousin, AGNES BERTRAM.

The baron was s. at his decease by his son,
ROGER BERTRAM, 2nd baron, but never summoned to parliament. This nobleman d. in 1311, leaving, by EVA his wife, an only dau. and heiress,

AGNES BERTRAM, at whose decease, without issue, the BARONY OF BERTRAM OF MITFORD fell into ABEYANCE, between her ladyship's cousins and co-heirs, mentioned above, and so continues amongst their representatives.

Arms—Az., an escutcheon, or.

BICKERSTETH—BARON LANGDALE.

By Letters Patent, dated 1836.

Lineage.

HENRY BICKERSTETH, Esq., of Kirkby Lonsdale, surgeon, m. Elizabeth, dau. of John Batty, Esq., and d. in May, 1851, having had issue,

JAMES, who went at an early age to sea, and was not heard of after 1796.
JOHN, in holy orders, rector of Sapcote, co. Leicester.
HENRY, of whom we treat.
Edward, b. 19 March, 1786, who was brought up to the law, and settled as an attorney at Norwich, but abandoning that profession in 1815, he entered into holy orders, and became a distinguished minister of the church, and rector of Walton, co. Herts. He m. 9 May, 1812, the eldest dau. of Thomas Bignold, Esq., of Norwich, and d. 2 February, 1850, leaving an only son, Edward Henry, in holy orders, who m. his cousin Rosa, dau. of Samuel Bignold, Esq., of Norwich, and five daus., of whom the eldest m. the Rev. T. R. Birks, rector of Kelshall, Herts.
Robert, a surgeon in Liverpool.
Mary Anne.   Charlotte.

The 3rd son,
HENRY BICKERSTETH, b. 18 June, 1783, at Kirkby Lonsdale, co. Westmoreland, was brought up to his father's profession, which he followed for some time, and travelled as medical adviser with the Earl of Oxford, through whose encouragement he entered at Caius College, Cambridge, where he graduated as senior wrangler and first Smith's prizeman in 1808, and subsequently entering the Inner Temple, was called to the bar 1811. Assiduously pursuing the arduous duties of his profession, he attained the different grades of king's counsel, bencher of the Inner Temple, &c.; and in January, 1836, s. Lord Cottenham as MASTER OF THE ROLLS, and at the same time was called to the House of Peers as BARON LANGDALE. His lordship m. 17 August, 1835, Lady Jane Elizabeth Harley, eldest dau. of the Earl of Oxford, by whom (who resumed her maiden name of HARLEY, as heiress of the Earls of Oxford, and d. 1 September, 1872) he had one dau.,

JANE-FRANCES, m. 16 December, 1857, to Alexander, Count Teleki de Szèh, and d. 3 May, 1870.

This very learned and distinguished lawyer d. 18 April, 1851, and, as he had no male issue, the title became EXTINCT.

Arms—Arg., a cross, flory, sa., charged with four mullets, or, on a chief, az., three roses of the third.

---

* The precedence of the escheator was next to the judges.

BIGOD—EARLS OF NORFOLK.

By creation of King STEPHEN, and also of King HENRY II.

Lineage.

The first of this great family that settled in England, was ROGER BIGOD, who in the CONQUEROR'S time possessed six lordships in Essex, and a hundred and seventeen in Suffolk, besides divers manors in Norfolk. This Roger adhering to the party that took up arms against WILLIAM RUFUS, in the 1st year of that monarch's reign, fortified the castle at Norwich, and wasted the country around. At the accession of HENRY I. being a witness of the king's laws, and staunch in his interests, he obtained Framlingham in Suffolk, as a gift from the crown. We find further of him that he founded, in 1103, the abbey of Whetford, in Norfolk, and that he was buried there at his decease in four years after, leaving, by Adeliza his wife, dau. and co-heir of Hugh de Grentesmesnil, high steward of England, a son and heir,

WILLIAM BIGOD, steward of the household to King HENRY I., one of the unhappy persons who perished with the king's children and several of the nobility in the memorable shipwreck which occurred in the 20th of that monarch's reign. This feudal lord leaving no issue his great possessions devolved upon his brother,

HUGH BIGOD, also steward to King HENRY I., who being mainly instrumental in raising Stephen, Earl of Boloigne, to the throne, upon the decease of his royal master was rewarded by the new king with the EARLDOM OF THE EAST ANGLES, commonly called NORFOLK, and by that designation we find him styled in 1140 (6th STEPHEN). His lordship remained faithful in his allegiance to King STEPHEN through the difficulties which afterwards beset that monarch, and gallantly defended the castle of Ipswich against the Empress MAUD and her son, until obliged at length to surrender for want of timely relief. In the 12th HENRY II. this powerful noble certified his knight's fees to be one hundred and twenty-five "de veteri feoffamento," and thirty-five "de novo," upon the occasion of the assessment in aid of the marriage of the king's daughter; and he appears to have acquired at this period a considerable degree of royal favour, for we find him not only re-created EARL OF NORFOLK, by charter, dated at Northampton, but by the same instrument obtaining a grant of the office of steward, to hold in as ample a manner as his father had done in the time of HENRY I. Notwithstanding, however, these and other equally substantial marks of the king's liberality, the Earl of Norfolk sided with Robert, Earl of Leicester, in the insurrection incited by that nobleman in favour of the king's son (whom HENRY himself had crowned,) in the 19th of the monarch's reign; but his treason upon this occasion cost him the surrender of his strongest castles, and a fine of 1,000 marks. After which he went into the Holy Land with the Earl of Flanders, and died in 1177. His lordship had married twice; by his 1st wife, Julian, dau. of Alberic de Vere, he had a son, ROGER; and by his 2nd, Gundred, he had two sons, Hugh and William. He was s. by his eldest son,

ROGER BIGOD, 2nd earl, who, in the 1st year of RICHARD I., had a charter dated at Westminster, 27 November, reconstituting him EARL OF NORFOLK, and steward of the household, his lordship obtaining at the same time restitution of some manors, with grants of others, and confirmation of all his widespreading demesnes. In the same year he was made one of the ambassadors from the English monarch to PHILIP of France, for obtaining aid towards the recovery of the Holy Land. Upon the return of King RICHARD from his captivity, the Earl of Norfolk assisted at the great council held by the king at Nottingham; and at his second coronation, his lordship was one of the four earls that carried the silken canopy over the monarch's head. In the reign of King JOHN he was one of the barons that extorted the great CHARTERS OF FREEDOM from that prince, and was amongst the twenty-five lords appointed to enforce their fulfilment. His lordship m. Isabel, dau. of Hamelyn, Earl of Warrenne and Surrey, and had issue,

HUGH, his successor.
William, m. Margaret dau. of Robert de Sutton, with whom he acquired considerable property.
Thomas.
Margery, m. to William de Hastings.
Adeliza, m. to Alberic de Vere. Earl of Oxford.
Mary, m. to Ralph Fitz-Robert, Lord of Middleham.

The earl d. in 1220, and was s. by his eldest son,
HUGH BIGOD, 3rd earl, who m. Maud, eldest dau. of William Mareschal, Earl of Pembroke, and by her (who m. 2ndly, William Earl of Warrenne and Surrey,) had issue,

53

1. ROGER, his successor.
II. Hugh, an eminent lawyer, appointed CHIEF JUSTICE OF ENGLAND by the barons in 1257. He m. 1st, Joane, dau. of Robert Burnet, by whom he had issue,
  1 ROGER, successor to his uncle in the earldom.
  2 John.
He m. 2ndly, Joane, dau. of Nicholas Stuteville, and widow of — Wake, but had no issue. His lordship fell under the baronial banner at the battle of Lewes.
III. Ralph, m. Berta, dau. of the Baron Furnival, and had a dau.,
  Isabel, who m. 1st, Gilbert, son of Walter de Lacy, Lord of Meath, in Ireland; and 2ndly, John Fitz Geoffrey.

His lordship, who was also one of the twenty-five barons appointed to enforce the observance of MAGNA CHARTA, d. in 1225, and was s. by his eldest son,

ROGER BIGOD, 4th earl, whose guardianship ALEXANDER, King of Scotland, obtained for 500 marks. This nobleman attained high reputation in all martial and warlike exercises. Skilful and valiant alike in the tilting and battle field, he held a high rank amongst the chivalrous spirits of his day, and won many a trophy in court and camp. In the tournament held at Blithe, in Nottingham (21st HENRY III., 1237), which terminated in a conflict between the southern and northern lords, the Earl of Norfolk was pre-eminently distinguished, and in a few years afterwards he gained new laurels at the battle of Zantoigne. But the most remarkable event in his lordship's life was his personal dispute with King HENRY III., as thus stated by Dugdale :—" In the 39th HENRY III. the Earl of Norfolk, making a just apology for Robert de Ros (a great baron of that age), then charged with some crime, which endangered his life. he had very harsh language given him by the king, being openly called *traytor;* whereat, with a stern countenance, he told him (the king) *that he lied; and, that he never was, nor would be a traytor;* adding, '*if you do nothing but what the law warranteth, you can do me no harm.*'—'*Yes,*' quoth the king, ' *I can thrash your corn, and sell it, and so humble you.*' To which he replied, '*If you do so, I will send you the heads of your thrashers.*' But by the interposing of the lords then present this heat soon passed over, so that (shortly after) he was, together with the Earl of Leicester and some others, sent on an embassy to the King of France, to treat with him for restoring some rights which he withheld from the king." His lordship was subsequently appointed by the barons, after their victory at Lewes (48th HENRY III.), governor of the castle of Orford, in Suffolk. To this nobleman, by reason of his mother Maud being the eldest co-heiress of William Mareschal, Earl of Pembroke, the MARSHALSHIP OF ENGLAND, with the rights thereunto belonging, was assigned. His lordship m. Isabel, sister of ALEXANDER, King of Scotland, but died issueless in 1270, when all his honours and possessions devolved upon his nephew (refer to Hugh, 2nd son of the 3rd earl),

ROGER BIGOD, 5th Earl of Norfolk, and 2nd earl marshal of this family. This nobleman took a distinguished part in the wars of King EDWARD I., having previously, however, in conjunction with the Earl of Hereford, compelled even that resolute monarch to ratify the GREAT CHARTER AND CHARTER OF THE FOREST. His lordship m. 1st, Aliva, dau. and heiress of Philip, Lord Basset, and widow of Hugh Despencer, slain at Evesham, and 2ndly, Joane, dau. of John de Avenne, Earl of Bayonne, but had no issue by either. In the 29th of EDWARD I. the earl constituted that monarch his heir, and surrendered into his hands the marshal's rod, upon condition that it should be returned in the event of his having children, and that he should receive £1,000 prompt, and £1,000 a-year for life; in consequence of which surrender his lordship was re-created EARL OF NORFOLK in 1302, with remainder to his heirs male by his 1st wife, but dying without issue, as stated above, in five years afterwards, the EARLDOM became (according to the surrender) EXTINCT in the BIGOD family, although his lordship left a brother,

JOHN BIGOD, his heir-at-law, whose right seems to have been annihilated in this very unjust and extraordinary manner, and so completely destroyed that he did not even inherit any of the great estates of his ancestors.

Arms—Gules, a lion passant, or.

BLAKENEY—BARON BLAKENEY,

By Letters Patent, dated 1756.

Lineage.

The Blakeneys, originally of Norfolk, settled in Ireland, temp. ELIZABETH, the senior branch being now represented by

JOHN BLAKENEY, Esq., of Abbert, co. Galway. A younger brother of the ancestor of the Abbert family,

WILLIAM BLAKENEY, of Mount Blakeney, near Kilmallock, was father of two sons, WILLIAM and GEORGE. The younger was a colonel in the army; the elder, WILLIAM BLAKENEY, Esq., of Thomastown, co. Limerick, was father of four sons, WILLIAM, Charles, John, and Robert, of whom the eldest,

SIR WILLIAM BLAKENEY, K.B., colonel of the 27th foot, and lieutenant-general in the army, distinguished by his defence of Stirling Castle in 1746, and Fort St. Philips in 1756, was raised to the peerage of Ireland as BARON BLAKENEY in the latter year. His lordship was for some time governor of Minorca. He d. s. p., 20 September, 1761, aged ninety-one, and was interred with great funeral pomp in Westminster Abbey. With him the title became EXTINCT. His lordship's brother, ROBERT BLAKENEY, Esq., of Mount Blakeney, co. Limerick, whose will was proved in 1763, m. Deborah, dau. of Grice Smyth, Esq., of Ballynatray, co. Waterford, and had issue, 1 William Blakeney, Esq., of Mount Blakeney, who m. Gertrude, dau. of Richard Smyth, Esq., of Ballynatray, and was father of the Rev. Robert Blakeney, of Great Eaton, co. Somerset, who d. s. p. 1824; 2 Grice Blakeney, lieutenant-general in the army, d. unm.; 1 Gertrude, m. Robert Blakeney, Esq., of Abbert; and 2 Jane, m. Robert Uniacke Fitzgerald, Esq., of Corkbegg, co. Cork. and was mother of Gertrude, wife of John La Touche, Esq., of Harristown, co. Kildare.

Arms—Sa., a chev., erm., between three leopards' faces, or.

BLAYNEY—BARON BLAYNEY.

(*See* ADDENDA.)

BLOOMFIELD—BARON.

(*See* ADDENDA.)

BLOUNT—BARONS MOUNTJOY AND EARL OF DEVON.

Barony, by Charter, dated 20 June, 1465.

Earldom, by Letters Patent, dated 21 July, 1603.

Lineage.

The origin of this most ancient and distinguished family is traced from the COUNTS OF GUISNES, in Picardy, a race of nobles descended from the Scandinavian rulers of Denmark. Rodolph, 3rd Count of Guisnes, had three sons, by his wife Rosetta, dau. of the Count de St. Pol, all of whom accompanied WILLIAM THE CONQUEROR in his expedition against England, in 1066, and contributing to the triumph of their chief, shared amply in the spoils of conquest. One of the brothers returned to his native country; the other two adopted that which they had so gallantly helped to win, and abided there. Of these, Sir William le Blount, the younger, was a general of foot at Hastings, and was rewarded by grants of seven lordships in Lincolnshire; his son was seated at Saxlingham, in Norfolk, and the great-granddau. of that gentleman, sole heiress of her line, Maria le Blount, marrying, in the next century, Sir Stephen le Blount, the descendant and representative of her great-great-great-uncle, Sir Robert le Blount, united the families of the two brothers.

SIR ROBERT LE BLOUNT had the command of the CONQUEROR'S ships of war, and is styled "Dux Navium Militarium." His portion of the *spolia opima* embraced thirteen manors in Suffolk, in which county he was the 1st feudal Baron of Ixworth (the place of his residence), and Lord of Orford Castle. He m. Gundreda, youngest dau. of Henry, Earl Ferrers, and had a son and heir,

GILBERT LE BLOUNT, 2nd Baron of Ixworth, who came into England with his father. This feudal lord founded a priory of black canons at Ixworth, and marrying Alicia de Colekirke, was s. by his son,

WILLIAM LE BLOUNT, 3rd Lord of Ixworth, *temp.* HENRY II., who rebuilt the priory of Ixworth, which had been destroyed during the contest between the Empress MAUD and King STEPHEN. By his wife, Sarah, dau. of Hubert de Monchensi, he was father of

GILBERT or HUBERT LE BLOUNT, 4th baron, living 20th HENRY II. (1173), who m. Agnes de L'Isle (de Insulâ), alive 10th RICHARD I. (1198), and had two sons, viz.,

   I. WILLIAM, b. in 1153, who s. as 5th LORD OF IXWORTH, and, marrying Cecilia de Vere, had issue,

     1 WILLIAM, his successor.

     1 Agnes, m. to Sir William de Crickelot; and Roisia, m. to Robert de Valoings, Lord of Orford, in Suffolk, co-heirs to their brother.

54

This baron d. at the age of thirty-two, in 1185, and was s. by his son,

    WILLIAM LE BLOUNT, 6th Lord of Ixworth, who was standard-bearer to Simon de Montford, Earl of Leicester, and fell at Lewes on 14 May, 1264. He was afterwards attainted in parliament, when the Barony of Ixworth became FORFEITED. He had m. Alicia de Capella (who lived to the 10th EDWARD I., anno 1281), but having no issue, his sisters became his co-heirs.

   II. STEPHEN (Sir), of whose line we treat.

The chief branch of the family, the Barons of Ixworth, having, as just stated, EXPIRED with the 6th feudal lord, at the battle of Lewes, the representation devolved upon the line of the younger son of Gilbert, by Agnes de L'Isle, viz.,

SIR STEPHEN LE BLOUNT, living in the 10th RICHARD I., anno 1198. He m. his kinswoman, Maria le Blount, sole dau. and heiress of Sir William le Blount, the descendant and representative of Sir William le Blount, of Saxlingham, in Suffolk, one of the brothers who came over with the CONQUEROR, and thus the lines of the brothers merging formed the parent stock, whence have since sprang the different families of the name. Of this marriage there were two sons, Sir John Blount (the younger), who m. Constance, one of the sisters and co-heirs of Sir Richard de Wrotham, justice of the Common Pleas, and the son and heir,

SIR ROBERT LE BLOUNT, who was a witness to the charter of Wilton Abbey, in Staffordshire, in the 8th HENRY III. (anno 1223). He m. Isabel, dau. and co-heir of the feudal lord of Odinsels, and acquired the manor of Belton, co. Rutland, as a part of the lady's portion. He d. in the 17th EDWARD I. (anno 1288), leaving two sons, viz.,

   I. RALPH (Sir), Lord of Belton, who recovered lands 14th EDWARD I. (anno 1285), in Saxlingham, which had been his grandfather's. He m. Cecilia or Alicia, dau. and co-heir of Sir John Lovet, of Hampton Lo·et, co. Worcester, and was grandfather of Sir Thomas Blount, summoned to parliament as BARON BLOUNT, of Belton, in the 1st EDWARD III. (anno 1327), and of NICHOLAS LE BLOUNT, who adopted the surname of CROKE, and was ancestor of the Crokes of Studley Priory.

   II. WILLIAM (Sir).

The younger,

SIR WILLIAM LE BLOUNT, m. the Lady Isabel de Beauchamp, dau. of William, 1st Earl of Warwick, and widow of Henry Lovet, of Elmley Lovet, co. Worcester, and d. 9th or 10th of EDWARD II. (1316 or 1316), having had issue,

PETER, one of the chamberlains in 1313 to King EDWARD II., d. s. p.

WALTER, of whom we treat.

The 2nd son,

SIR WALTER LE BLOUNT, of the Rock, co. Worcester, m. JOHANNA, 3rd sister and co-heir of SIR WILLIAM DE SODINGTON, who d. 30th EDWARD I. (anno 1301), and thus became proprietor of the manor of Sodington, co. Worcester. He d. in 1322, and was s. by his son,

SIR WILLIAM LE BLOUNT, of Sodington, who had a command in Scotland in 1335. He m. Margaret, 3rd dau. and co-heir of Theobald de Verdon, Lord of Alton Castle, co. Stafford, lord justice of Ireland. The lady was b. in 1310; there was no issue of the marriage, and Sir William dying, 11th EDWARD II. (anno 1337), seized of the castle of Weobly, in Herefordshire, Batterby, and lands in Fenton, Romesore, and Biddulph, in Staffordshire, Sodington and Timberlake, in Worcestershire, was s. by his brother,

SIR JOHN LE BLOUNT, then thirty nine years of age, who was in the service of the Earl of Lancaster, and had obtained from that nobleman a grant for life of the manor of Passingham, co. Northampton. He had also lands from the earl in Holland and Duffield, co. Derby, and Tiberton, in Gloucestershire. He had two wives, 1st, ISOLDA, dau. and heir of Sir Thomas de Mountjoy, by whom he acquired a large accession of estates, and had issue,

JOHN (Sir), who m. twice, 1st, Juliana, dau. of —— Foulhurst, and 2ndly, Isabella, dau. and heir of Sir Bryan Cornwall, of Kinlet. By the 2nd he was ancestor of the BLOUNTS of Kinlet, co. Salop, whose heir-general is WILLIAM LACON CHILDE, Esq., of Kinlet. By his 1st wife, Juliana Foulhurst, Sir John had a son,

    JOHN BLOUNT, of Sodington, ancestor of the BLOUNTS, Baronets of Sodington.

Walter, d. s. p.

Sir John Blount's 2nd wife was Eleanor, 2nd dau. of John Beauchamp, of Hache, co. Somerset, and widow of John Meriet, of Meriet, in the same shire. By this lady he left at his decease, 32nd HENRY III. (1358), a son, the heroic

SIR WALTER BLOUNT, so celebrated for his martial prowess in

the warlike times of EDWARD III., RICHARD II., and HENRY IV., and immortalized by the muse of Shakespeare for his devotion, even unto death, to King HENRY. Sir Walter fell at the battle of Shrewsbury, 22 June, 1403, wherein, being standard bearer, he was arrayed in the same armour as his royal master, and was slain, according to the poet, in single combat, by the Earl of Douglas, who had supposed he was contending with the king himself.

In 1367 we find Sir Walter accompanying the BLACK PRINCE and his brother, the DUKE OF LANCASTER (John of Gaunt), upon the expedition into Spain to aid PETER THE CRUEL, King of Castile, and assisting on 3 April in that year at the battle of Najore, which restored PETER to his throne. Thenceforward for a series of years, indeed until the prince's decease, he appears to have been immediately and confidentially attached to the duke, having chosen his wife, whom he m. about the year 1372, from amongst the ladies in the suite of CONSTANTIA OF CASTILE (eldest dau. of PETER, and his successor on the throne, who became the royal consort of JOHN OF GAUNT) when the princess visited England in 1369. In 1398 the duke granted 100 marks a-year to Sir Walter for the good services which had been rendered to him by the knight and his wife, the Lady Sancia. The Lady Sancia's maiden designation was DONNA SANCHA DE AYALA; she was the dau. of DON DIEGO GOMEZ DE TOLEDO, alcalde mayor and chief justice of Toledo, and notario mayor or principal secretary of the kingdom of Castile, by his wife, Inez Alfon de Ayala, one of the most ancient and illustrious houses in Spain. JOHN OF GAUNT, at his decease, appointed Sir Walter one of his executors, and bequeathed him a legacy of 100 points, £ 6 6s. 8d.

In 1374, Sir Walter's half-brother, Sir John Blount, of Sodington, conveyed to him numerous manors, which he had inherited from his mother, Isolda, heiress of the Mountjoy family. In 1381 he became proprietor, by purchase, of the large estates of the BAKEPUIZ family, in cos. Derby, Stafford, Leicester, and Hertford. In 1385 he obtained a charter for a fair and free warren in his demesne lands at Barton, and other manors in Derbyshire. In 1399 he was ranger of Needwood Forest and knight of the shire for co. Derby. By his wife, Donna Sancha, who survived him, and lived until 1418, he left issue,

I. JOHN (SIR), his heir, one of the great warriors who have immortalized the reign and times of HENRY V.
II. THOMAS (SIR), successor to his brother.
III. James (Sir), who m. Anne, dau. of Roger Parker, Esq., of Lillinghall, and was father of Roger Blount, of Grendon, ancestor of the BLOUNTS of Grendon, Eldersfield, Orleton, &c.; the present male representative of the BLOUNTS of Orleton, co. Hereford, is WILLIAM BLOUNT, Esq., of that place.
IV. Peter, d. s. p.
I. Constantia, m. to John Sutton, Lord Dudley.
II. Anne, m. to Thomas Griffith, of Wichnor, co. Salop, living in 1415.

Sir Walter was s. by his eldest son,

SIR JOHN BLOUNT, K.G., who was governor of Calais, and defeated in Aquitaine, in 1412, a French army commanded by a marshal of France, for which achievement he was created a knight of the Garter the next year. In 1418, when Rouen was besieged by King HENRY V., Sir John Blount assisted at the siege. He d. without issue, and was s. by his brother,

SIR THOMAS BLOUNT, treasurer of Normandy, who was then seated at Elvaston, in Derbyshire, and to whom the Duke of Exeter gave 1,000 marks (£666 6s. 8d.) to found a charity at Leicester. Sir Thomas m. 1st, Margaret, dau. of Sir Thomas Greseley, Knt., of Greseley, and dying in 1456, left issue,

I. WALTER (SIR), Lord High Treasurer of England, of whose line we treat.
II. THOMAS (SIR), of Milton Ross, co. Leicester, ancestor of the BLOUNTS of Maple Durham, co. Oxford, still resident at that ancient seat. (See BURKE's Landed Gentry)
I. Elizabeth, m. to Ralph Shirley, of West Heaton, in Sussex.
II. Sanchia, m. to Edward Langford.
III. Agnes, m. to —— Wolseley.

The eldest son,

WALTER BLOUNT, was made treasurer of Calais, 39th of HENRY VI., and had the same office confirmed to him upon the accession of King EDWARD IV. In the 4th year of which latter monarch's reign, he was constituted, by letters patent, dated 24 November, LORD TREASURER OF ENGLAND, and the next year, advanced, by charter, dated 20 June, to the peerage, by the title of BARON MOUNTJOY, of Thurveston, co. Derby. This nobleman became so stanch an adherent of the House of York, that he shared largely in the confiscated estates of the leading Lancastrians—particularly in those of Sir William Carey, Sir William Vaux, and Thomas Courtenay, Earl of Devon, obtaining thereby extensive territorial possessions in the counties of Devon, Cornwall, and Worcester. He was also honoured with the Garter. His lordship m. 1st, Helena, dau.

of Sir John Byron, of Clayton, Lancashire; and by her (who was buried at Grey Friars, London) he had three sons;

I. WILLIAM, m. Margaret, dau. and heir of Sir Thomas Echingham, d before his father in 1471, leaving issue,
  1 John, d. s. p.
  2 EDWARD, 2nd Lord Mountjoy.
  1 Elizabeth, m. to Andrews, Lord Windsor.
  2 Anne, m. 1st, Sir Thomas Oxenbridge, and 2ndly, Sir David Owen.
II. JOHN, 3rd Lord Mountjoy, s. his nephew.
III. James (Sir), knighted by HENRY VII. on his landing at Milford Haven, and made knight banneret 2nd HENRY VII., after the battle of Newark.

His lordship, who m. 2ndly, Anne, dau. of Ralph Nevil, Earl of Westmoreland, and relict of Humphrey, Duke of Buckingham, d. 1 August, 1474, and was s. by his grandson,

EDWARD BLOUNT, 2nd baron, who died the following year, having attained only the eighth year of his age, when his estates devolved upon his sister, but the Barony of Mountjoy reverted to his uncle,

SIR JOHN BLOUNT, 3rd baron, who d. in 1485, leaving by his will, bearing date 6 October in that year, a chain of gold with a gold lion set with diamonds, to his son, Rowland Blount, and to his dau., Constantia, £100 for her marriage portion. His lordship, who was governor of Guisnes, m. Lora, dau. of Sir Edward Berkeley, of Beverton Castle, co. Gloucester. His issue were, WILLIAM, his heir; Rowland, d. s. p., 1509; Lora, d. 1480; and Constantia, m. to Sir Thomas Tyrrell, of Heron, Essex. The elder son,

WILLIAM BLOUNT, 4th baron, K.G., was called to the privy council upon the accession of HENRY VII., and was constituted in the 1st year of HENRY VIII. master of the Mint in the Tower of London, as also throughout the whole realm of England, and the town of Calais. His lordship subscribed, in the latter reign, to the articles against Cardinal Wolsey, and the letter to Pope CLEMENT VII., regarding the king's divorce from Queen CATHERINE. He m. 1st, Elizabeth, dau. and co-heiress of Sir William Say, by whom he had two daus., Gertrude, m. to Henry Courtenay, Marquess of Exeter; and Mary, m. to Sir Henry Bourchier, Earl of Essex. His lordship m. 2ndly, Alice Kebel, and had a son CHARLES, his heir; and a dau. Catherine, m. 1st, to John Champernon, and 2ndly, to Sir Maurice Berkeley, of Bruton. His lordship m. 3rdly, Dorothy, dau. of Thomas Grey, Marquis of Dorset, relict of Robert Willoughby, Lord Brooke, and had issue, John, d. s. p.; Dorothy, m. to Roger Blewet; and Mary, m. to Sir Robert Dennys. He d. in 1535, and was s. by his son,

CHARLES BLOUNT, 5th baron, who in the 36th HENRY VIII., served in the rear-guard of the army then sent into France. His lordship d. 14 October. 1544, leaving issue by his wife Anne, dau. and heir of Robert Willoughby, Baron Brooke, JAMES; John d. s. p.; Francis m. Catherine, dau. of John Carleton, Esq., of Brightwell, OXON, and d. s. p.; and William, d. s. p. The eldest son,

JAMES BLOUNT, s. as 6th baron. This nobleman was one of the peers who sat in judgment upon Thomas, Duke of Norfolk, temp. ELIZABETH. His lordship m. Catherine, dau. and sole heir of Sir Thomas Leigh or Lee, of St. Oswalds, co. York, and had issue, WILLIAM; Charles; Christopher (Sir), m. Letitia, eldest dau. of Sir Francis Knowlis, K.G., and was beheaded in 1601; and Anne, d. s. p. He d. in 1593, and was s. by his eldest son,

WILLIAM BLOUNT, 7th baron, who d. in 1594, s. p., and wa, s. by his brother,

CHARLES BLOUNT, 8th baron. Before he inherited the peerage, this nobleman, being a person of high military reputation, had a command in the fleet which defeated the famous Spanish Armada; and a few years afterwards succeeded the Earl of Sussex in the governorship of Portsmouth. In 1597 his lordship was constituted lord lieutenant of Ireland; and in two years after repulsed the Spaniards with great gallantry at Kinsale. Upon the accession of King JAMES, he was reinvested with the same important office, and created by letters patent, dated 21 July, 1603, EARL OF DEVONSHIRE, being made at the same time a knight of the Garter. The high public character of the earl was, however, considerably tarnished by one act of his private life, the seduction of Penelope, sister of the Earl of Essex, and wife of Robert, Lord Rich. By this lady he had several children; and upon his return from Ireland, finding her divorced from her husband, he married her at Wanstead, in Essex, on 26 December, 1605, the ceremony being performed by his chaplain, William Laud, afterwards archbishop of Canterbury. Camden says that this nobleman was so eminent for valour and learning, that in those respects "he had no superior, and but few equals," and his secretary Moryson, writes, "that he was beautiful in person, as well as valiant; and learned, as well as wise." His lordship *d.* 3 April, 1606, and leaving no *legitimate* issue, all his honours became EXTINCT.

Arms—Barry nebulée of six, or and sa.

BLOUNT—EARL OF DEVONSHIRE.

By Letters Patent, dated 21st July, 1603.

Lineage.

(*See* COURTENAY, Earls of Devon.)

BLOUNT—BARONS MOUNTJOY, OF THURVESTON, CO. DERBY, AND EARLS OF NEWPORT.

Barony, by Letters Patent, dated 1627.
Earldom, by Letters Patent, dated 3 August, 1628.

Lineage.

MOUNTJOY BLOUNT Esq., illegitimate son of Charles Blount, Earl of Devonshire, by Penelope, dau. of Walter Devereux, 1st Earl of Essex, of that family—the divorced wife of Robert, Lord Rich (whom the Earl of Devonshire subsequently married)—was elevated to the peerage of Ireland, as LORD MOUNTJOY, OF MOUNTJOY FORT, by King JAMES I., and created in the follow ingreign, *anno* 1627, BARON MOUNTJOY, *of Thurveston, co. Derby,* and EARL OF NEWPORT, on 3 August, 1628. His lordship *m.* Anne, dau. of John, LORD BUTLER, of Bramfield, Herts, and dying 12 February, 1665, left issue,

  I. GEORGE, his successor.
  II. Charles *d.* when two years old, buried in St. Martin-in-the-Fields.
  III. HENRY, 3rd earl.
  I. Isabella, *m.* to Nicholas Knollys, who bore the title of Earl of Banbury.
  II. Anne, *m.* to Thomas Porter, 4th son of Endymion Porter, groom of the bedchamber to King CHARLES I.

The eldest son was

GEORGE BLOUNT, 2nd earl, at whose decease, *unm.,* in 1676, the honours devolved upon his brother,

HENRY BLOUNT, 3rd earl. This nobleman *m.* Susanna, dau. of John Briscoe, Esq., of Grafton, co. Kent, and widow of Edmund Mortimer, Esq., but dying *s. p.,* in 1681, all his honours EXPIRED.

BLOUNT—BARON BLOUNT.

By Writ of Summons, dated 3 December, 1326.

Lineage.

SIR THOMAS LE BLOUNT, Lord of Belton (son of Sir Ralph le Blount, Lord of Belton, by Cecilia Lovet, his wife—*refer to* BLOUNT, BARONS MOUNTJOY), an accomplished soldier, *temp.* EDWARD I., was appointed governor of Drosselan Castle, in Wales, in 1311, and was summoned to parliament as a BARON, from 3 December, 1326, to 16 June, 1328. He *m.* twice, the name of the 1st, whom he *m.* in 1325, is unknown; the 2nd was Juliana de Leyborne, a great Kentish heiress, only child of Sir Thomas de Leyborne, and widow of John de Hastings, Lord Bergavenny. In the 20th of EDWARD II., Lord Blount being steward of the king's household, espoused the cause of the queen after the taking of Bristol, and the flight of the king into Wales. He *d.* in 1330, leaving no issue by his 2nd wife Juliana, who *m.* for her 3rd husband, Sir William de Clinton, Earl of Huntingdon. By his 1st wife he appears to have had two sons, WILLIAM and NICHOLAS. From the 2nd, NICHOLAS, sprang the family of Croke, *alias* Le Blount, so distinguished in our legal annals, and the CROKES, of Studley Priory, Oxfordshire, whose representative, the late SIR ALEXANDER CROKE, wrote a very able and elaborate *History of the Blounts.* The elder son, SIR WILLIAM LE BLOUNT, Lord of Belton, had, with a dau. Isabel, *m.* Alanus de Atkinson, a son Sir John Blount, custos of London, constable of the Tower, Lord of Belton. By his 1st wife, whose name is unknown, Sir John was father of Sir Thomas Blount, Lord of Belton, who was beheaded, *s. p.,* in 1400; by his 2nd wife, Elizabeth Fourneaux, he had William,

56

who *d. s. p.,* by Maud his wife; and Alice, who *m.* 1st, Richard Stafford, 2ndly, Sir Richard Stury, and *d. circa* 1415, *s. p:* when Sir John Blount, of Sodington, was found to be her heir.

Arms—Barry nebulée of six, or and sa

BLOUNT—BARON BLOUNT.

By Writ of Summons, dated 25 January, 1340.

Lineage.

WILLIAM LE BLUND or BLOUNT (eldest son of Sir Walter le Blount, of Rock, by Joanna his wife, sister and heir of Sir William de Sodington (*refer to* BLOUNT, BARONS MOUNTJOY), having *m.,* in the 2nd EDWARD III., Margaret, one of the daus. and co-heiresses of Theobald de Verdon, Lord Justice of Ireland, obtained a livery of the castle of Weobley, co. Hereford, with divers other lands and lordships, as her portion of the inheritance, and was summoned to parliament as a BARON, from 25 January, 1330, to 18 August, 1337. His lordship had a command in the Scottish wars in the 9th EDWARD III. He *d.* in 1337, and leaving no issue, the BARONY OF BLOUNT EXPIRED, while his lordship's estates devolved upon his brother and heir, John Blount, of Sodington, co. Worcester, from whom descend the PRESENT BARONETS (Blount) of Sodington.

Arms—Barry nebulée of six, or and sa.

BLOUNT—BARON MOUNTJOY, IN IRELAND.

(*See* BLOUNT, Baron Mountjoy, of Thurveston, in the *Extinct Peerage of England.*)

BLUNDELL—VISCOUNT BLUNDELL.

By Letters Patent, dated 22 November, 1720.

Lineage.

The noble family of BLUNDELL was a junior branch of the BLUNDELLS of Ince, co. Lancaster, whose direct male heir, CHARLES ROBERT BLUNDELL, Esq., *d. s. p.* 1838, having bequeathed his estates, including Ince Blundell, to Thomas Weld, Esq., their present possessor.

SIR FRANCIS BLUNDELL (brother and heir of Sir George Blundell, Knt., of Cardington, Bedfordshire, who had a grant of the manor of Blundell, King's Co.), was appointed, in 1619, secretary for the affairs of Ireland, and made a BARONET of that kingdom, 13 October, 1620. He *m.* Joyce, dau. of William Serjeant, Esq., of Waldridge, co. Bucks, and by her (who *m.* 2ndly, Nicholas Whyte, Esq.) had a son and successor,

SIR GEORGE BLUNDELL, 2nd bart., M.P. for Philipstown, who *m.* Sarah, dau. and eventual heir of Sir William Colley, Knt., of Edenderry, and had with two daus. (Elizabeth, *m.* to Sir Henry Wemys, of Danesfort, co. Kilkenny; and Sarah, *m.* to Deliverance Barrow, Esq.), three sons, viz.,

FRANCIS, his heir.
William, who *m.* Miss Anne Taillour, and by her, who *d.* in 1732, had two sons and three daus.
Winwood, who *m.* Margaret, dau. of Henry Bollard, of Dublin, and by her (who *m.* 2ndly, the Rev. William Nelson,) had two daus.,
  Frances, who *d. unm,*
  Sarah, wife of Arthur Graham, of co. Longford.

The eldest son,

SIR FRANCIS BLUNDELL, 3rd bart., *b.* 30 January, 1643, M.P. for the King's Co., left by Anne, his 2nd wife, only dau. of Sir Henry Ingoldsby, Bart., a dau. Anne, *m.* in 1696, to Col. Robert Echlin, of Monaghan, a son and successor,

SIR MONTAGUE BLUNDELL, 4th bart., *b.* in 1689, who represented Haslemere in parliament, and was raised to the peerage of Ireland, 22 November, 1720, as *Baron of Edenderry* and VISCOUNT BLUNDELL. His lordship *m.* in 1709, Mary, only dau. of John Chetwynd, Esq., of Grendon, co. Warwick, and had issue,

Montagu, who *d. unm.* 21 January, 1732.
Elizabeth.
Mary, *m.* in 1733, to William Trumbull, Esq., *of* East Hampstead Park, Berkshire, and had a dau. Mary, who *m.* the Hno.

Martyn Sandys, and was mother of MARY, BARONESS SANDYS, who *m.* 1786, Arthur, 2nd Marquess of Downshire, and was grandmother of the present Arthur-Wills-Blundell-Sandys-Trumbull Hill, MARQUESS OF DOWNSHIRE, K.P.

Chetwynd, *m.* in 1741, to Robert, Lord Raymond.

Lord Blundell *d.* in 1756, and with him the peerage EXPIRED.

Arms.—AZ., ten billets, four, three, two, one; and a canton, or, charged with a raven, ppr.

BOHUN—EARLS OF HEREFORD, EARLS OF ESSEX, EARLS OF NORTHAMPTON, AND HIGH CONSTABLES OF ENGLAND.

First earldom, by Charter of Creation, dated 28 April, 1199,
Second, by the same, of King HENRY III.
Third, by the same, dated 17 March, 1337.

Lineage.

The founder of this family in England was

HUMPHREY DE BOHUN, kinsman and companion in arms of WILLIAM THE CONQUEROR, generally known as "*Humphrey with the Beard.*" Of this Humphrey little more is ascertained than that he possessed the lordship of Taterford, in Norfolk, and was *s.* by his son,

HUMPHREY DE BOHUN, surnamed the GREAT, who by command of King WILLIAM RUFUS *m.* Maud, dau. of Edward de Saresbury (progenitor of the ancient Earls of Salisbury), by whom he acquired large estates in the co. of Wilts, and had issue, Maud, and his successor,

HUMPHREY DE BOHUN, who was steward and sewer to King HENRY I. This feudal lord *m.* Margery, dau. of Milo de Gloucester, Earl of Hereford, Lord High Constable of England, and sister and co-heiress of Mabel, last Earl of Hereford, of that family. At the instigation of which Milo, he espoused the cause of the Empress MAUD and her son, against King STEPHEN, and so faithfully maintained his allegiance that the empress, by her especial charter, granted him the office of steward and sewer, both in Normandy and England. In the 20th of HENRY II., this Humphrey accompanied Richard de Lacy (Justice of England) into Scotland, with a powerful army to waste that country; and was one of the witnesses to the accord made by WILLIAM, King of Scots and King HENRY as to the subjection of that kingdom to the crown of England. He *d.* 6 April, 1187, and was *s.* by his son,

HUMPHREY DE BOHUN, who was EARL OF HEREFORD and CONSTABLE OF ENGLAND, in right of his mother, if the Chronicles of Lanthony be correct. His lordship *m.* Margaret of Scotland, dau. of Henry, Earl of Huntingdon, sister of WILLIAM, King of Scots, and widow of Conan le Petit, Earl of Britanny and Richmond, and was *s.* by his son,

HENRY DE BOHUN, who in reality was the 1st EARL OF HEREFORD of this family, being so created by charter of King JOHN, dated 28 April, 1199; but the constableship he inherited from his father. His lordship, taking part with the barons against King JOHN, had his lands sequestered, but they were restored at the signing of MAGNA CHARTA, at Runnimede, the earl being one of the twenty-five lords, appointed there, to enforce the observance of the celebrated charters. His lordship was subsequently excommunicated by the pope, and he became a prisoner at the battle of Lincoln, in the 1st year of HENRY III. He *m.* Maud, dau. of Geoffrey Fitz-Piers, Earl of Essex, and eventually heiress of her brother, William de Mandeville, last Earl of Essex of that family (*see* MANDEVILLE, Earls of Essex), by whom he acquired the honour of Essex and other extensive lordships,—and had issue, Henry, *d.* young, HUMPHREY, and Ralph, and a dau. Margery, who *m.* Waleran, Earl of Warwick. His lordship *d.* 1 January, 1220, and was *s.* by his son,

HUMPHREY DE BOHUN, as EARL OF HEREFORD, and possessing the honour of Essex through his mother, was created EARL of that county by King HENRY III., at whose marriage his lordship performed the office of marshal in the king's house, and in three years afterwards, *anno* 1239, was one of the godfathers at the font, for Edward, eldest son of the king, there being no less than nine sponsors on the occasion, viz., five temporal and four spiritual lords. He was Lord High Constable of England. In 1250 he took up the cross and proceeded to the Holy Land. In three years afterwards, his lordship was present, with other peers, when that formal curse was denounced in Westminster Hall, with *bell, book, and candle,* against the violators of Magna Charta; in which year he founded the church

of the Fryers Augustines, in Broad-street, within the city of London. In the great contest between the king and his barons, this nobleman fought for the latter at Evesham, where he was taken prisoner, but he did not long continue in bondage, for we find him soon after again in favour, and receiving new grants from the crown. His lordship *d.* 1275, having *m.* 1st, Maud, dau. of Ralph, Count d'Eu, by Yolande his wife, dau. of Robert, Count de Dreux, Earl of Ewe, and had issue,

HUMPHREY, a very distinguished person amongst the rebellious barons, in the reign of HENRY III. In the 47th of that monarch he was excommunicated, with Simon de Montfort, Earl of Leicester, and others, for plundering divers churches and committing sacrilege. He was afterwards one of the commanders at the battle of Lewes, where the king was made prisoner, and was constituted governor of Goodrich and Winchester Castles In the year following he commanded the infantry at the battle of Evesham, where he fell into the hands of the royalists, and was sent prisoner to Beeston Castle in Cheshire, where he soon afterwards died. leaving issue, by his wife Eleanor, dau. and co heir of William de Braose, of Brecknock, and co-heir of her mother Eve, one of the five daus. and co-heirs of William Marshal, Earl of Pembroke,

HUMPHREY, who *s.* his grandfather.

Maud, *m.* to Anselm Mareschal, Earl of Pembroke.
Alice, *m.* to Roger Thony.
——, *m.* to — Quincy.

Humphrey, Earl of Hereford and Essex, *d.* 1275, and was *s.* by his grandson,

HUMPHREY DE BOHUN, Earl of Hereford, Earl of Essex, and Lord High Constable. This nobleman inheriting the high and daring spirit of his predecessors, often strenuously opposed the measures of the court, and was often therefore in disgrace, but he appears at the close of his career to have regained royal favour, for we find him attending the king into Scotland when that monarch (EDWARD I.) obtained a great victory near Roxburgh. His lordship *m.* Maud, dau. of Sir Ingelram de Fiennes, and dying in 1297, was *s.* by his son,

HUMPHREY DE BOHUN, as Earl of Hereford, Earl of Essex, and Lord High Constable. In the 30th EDWARD I., this nobleman gave and granted unto the king, by a formal conveyance, the inheritance of all his lands and lordships, as also of his earldoms of Hereford and Essex, and the constableship of England, which, upon his marriage with Elizabeth Plantagenet, widow of John, Earl of Holland, and dau. of the king, were regranted to him, and entailed upon his issue lawfully begotten by that lady; in default thereof, and from and after the death of himself and wife, then the lordship of Plassets, and certain other lordships in Essex, and elsewhere, together with the constableship, should remain wholly to the king and his heirs for ever. In the 34th of the same reign he had a grant similarly entailed of the whole territory of Annandale, in Scotland. After this his lordship was in the wars of Scotland and was taken prisoner, in the 7th EDWARD II. (1313-14), at the disastrous battle (to the English) of Stryvelin. But he was exchanged for the wife of Robert Bruce, who had long been captive in England. From this period we find him constantly engaged in the service of the crown, until the 14th year of the king's reign, when EDWARD learning that the earl was raising forces in the marches of Wales, against Hugh de Spencer the younger, sent him a peremptory command to forbear, which his lordship not only refused obeying, but forthwith joined Thomas, Earl of Lancaster, in the great insurrection then incited by that nobleman, for the redress of certain grievances, and the banishment of the Spencers. In this proceeding, however, he eventually lost his life, being run through the body by a soldier at the battle of Boroughbridge, in Yorkshire, where his party received so signal a defeat on 16 March, 1321. The earl had issue five surviving sons and two surviving daus., viz.,

JOHN; HUMPHREY; and Edward; successors primogeniturely to the honours. The eldest was made a knight of the Bath in the 20th EDWARD II., having, by special command of Prince Edward, the robes for that solemnity out of the royal wardrobe, as for an earl.
WILLIAM, a personage of great eminence in the turbulent times in which he lived, and one of the gallant heroes of Cressy. In the parliament held at London, in the 11th EDWARD III., upon the advancement of the Black Prince to the dukedom of Cornwall, he was created EARL OF NORTHAMPTON (17 March, 1337), and from that period his lordship appears the constant companion in arms of the martial EDWARD, and his illustrious son. At Cressy he was in the second battalia of the English army, and he was frequently engaged in the subsequent wars of France and England. He was entrusted at different periods with the most important offices, such as ambassador to treat of peace with hostile powers, commissioner to levy troops, &c., and he was finally honoured with the Garter. His lordship *m.* Elizabeth, dau. of Bartholomew de Badlesmere, one of the co-heirs of her brother Giles, and widow of Edmund de Mortimer, by whom he had issue,

HUMPHREY, 2nd Earl of Northampton, of whom hereafter, as successor to his uncle in the earldoms of Hereford and Essex and constableship of England.

Elizabeth, m. to Richard Fitzalan, 10th Earl of Arundel.

He d. in 1360.

Alianore, m. 1st, to James Butler, Earl of Ormonde, and 2ndly, to Sir Thomas Dagworth, Lord Dagworth.

Margaret, m. to Hugh Courtenay, son of the Earl of Devon.

The earl was s. by his eldest son,

SIR JOHN DE BOHUN, K.B., as Earl of Hereford, Earl of Essex, and Lord High Constable. This nobleman, who had served in the Scottish wars, being in an infirm state of health, was allowed in the 4th EDWARD III. to depute his brother Edward to execute the duties of constable. His lordship m. 1st, Lady Alice Fitz-alan, dau. of Edmund, Earl of Arundel, and 2ndly, Margaret, dau. of Ralph, Lord Basset, of Drayton, but had no issue. He d. in 1335, when all his honours and estates devolved upon his next brother,

HUMPHREY DE BOHUN, Earl of Hereford, Earl of Essex, and Lord High Constable, K.G. This nobleman was one of the great lords who assisted, in the 15th of EDWARD III., at the celebrated feast and justs which the king then held at London in honour of the Countess of Salisbury, and, in the 20th of the same monarch, attended the king to the relief of Aguilon, then besieged by the French. His lordship never married, and dying in 1361, his honours and estates reverted to his nephew,

HUMPHREY DE BOHUN, K.G., 2nd Earl of Northampton, then a minor, and under the guardianship of Richard, Earl of Arundel. His lordship did not, however, long enjoy this great accumulation of wealth and honour, for he d. in 1372, in the thirty-second year of his age, leaving by his wife Joane, dau. of his late guardian, the Earl of Arundel, two daus., his co-heirs, viz.,

ALIANORE, m. to Thomas, of Woodstock, Duke of Gloucester, 6th son of King EDWARD III.

MARY, m. to Henry, Earl of Derby (son of John of Gaunt, Duke of Lancaster), who afterwards ascended the throne as HENRY IV.

Upon the decease of this nobleman, the EARLDOM OF HEREFORD EXPIRED; but his son-in-law, the Earl of Derby was subsequently created (in 1397) DUKE OF HEREFORD, prior, of course, to his becoming KING OF ENGLAND, while the lordships of Essex and Northampton, and the constableship fell to his other son-in-law, the Duke of Gloucester, and the EARLDOMS OF ESSEX and NORTHAMPTON became EXTINCT.

Arms—Az., a bend, arg., between two cottises and six lions rampant, or.

BOHUN—BARONS BOHUN, OF MIDHURST.

By Writ of Summons, dated 1 June, 1363.

Lineage.

In addition to the illustrious house of Bohun, Earls of Hereford, Essex, and Northampton, there was another family of the same name, and probably descended from the same source, whose chief seat was at Midhurst, co. Sussex.

ENGHILER DE BOHUN, temp. WILLIAM THE CONQUEROR, was father of SAVARIC DE BOHUN, temp. HENRY I., who had two sons, Savaric, who d. s. p., and JELDEWIN DE BOHUN, whose son,

FRANCO DE BOHUN (1st RICHARD I.), Lord of Midhurst Ford, Clemping, and Rushington, was father of

JOHN DE BOHUN, who m. Sibel, dau. of William Ferrars, 2nd Earl of Derby, and d. 12th of EDWARD I., having had two sons and a dau.,

1. John d. s. p.
II. JAMES. of whom presently.
I. Elizabeth, m. to Sir John Lesley, and had two daus. and co-heirs,
 1 Elizabeth, m. to John Bramshott, and had issue, Thomas.
 2 Eva, m. to Sir John Barford, and was mother of a dau. and heir,
  Elinor, m. to Thomas Cooke, of Wreckham, and was mother of Richard Cooke, of Rushington, ancestor of the COOKES, of Westburton and Goring. Their descendant, Sir John Cooke had a dau. and heir,
  Elizabeth, m. to John Covert, of Sullington, in 1558.

The 2nd son,

JAMES DE BOHUN (4th EDWARD I.), m. Joan, dau., and co heir of William de Braose, Lord of Bramber, and was father of

JOHN DE BOHUN, who was summoned to parliament as Baron of Midhurst, 1364 (37th EDWARD III.) "This is he (says Dugdale) who for his great services in Flanders, and elsewhere beyond sea, in 11th EDWARD III. (when the king first laid claim

to the crown of France), as also in that famous expedition into France, 19th EDWARD III. (shortly after which, the king obtained that glorious victory at Cressy, whereof our historians make ample mention), became afterwards one of the BARONS of the realm, being summoned to sit in parliament, in 37th, 38th, and 39th of that king's reign." By his 1st wife, Isabel, he had a dau. Joan, m. to John de Lisle de Gatcombe, in the Isle of Wight, and by his 2nd wife, Cicely, dau. and heir of John Filliol, he had a son John. His lordship d. 41st EDWARD III., his son,

JOHN DE BOHUN (7th RICHARD II.) had two sons, JOHN and Humphrey (Sir), of Midhurst, who d. s. p. 1468. The eldest son,

JOHN DE BOHUN (10th HENRY VI., 1432), left two daus. and co-heirs,

MARY, m. to SIR DAVID OWEN, of Easebourn, Knt., natural son of Owen Tudor, grandfather of King HENRY VII., &c., and was mother of HENRY, Jasper, Roger, and Anne. The eldest son,
 SIR HENRY OWEN, of Easebourn, m. Dorothy West, dau. of Thomas La War, and had issue.
Ursula, m. to Sir Robert Southwell, of Norfolk, and d. s. p.

Sir David Owen, having married MARY, at length sole heir of the last John Bohun, who d. temp. HENRY VII., s. to their several manors of Midhurst, Easebourn, Ford, and Clemping; and in 1528 (19th HENRY VIII.) sold them to Sir William Fitzwilliam, K.G., treasurer of the king's household, for the sum of £2,198 6s. 8l. But after the demise of Sir David Owen, the said manors of Ford and Clemping to revert to Sir Henry Owen, his son and heir, abating of the above-mentioned sum, £1,432 6s. 8d. But by a subsequent indenture, dated 1532, it appeared that Sir Henry Owen having no right, a fine and recovery were suffered, and Sir William Fitzwilliam gained immediate possession. By an inquisition held at East Grinstead, 1545, three years after his death, it is certified that he died seized of these and other manors, holden of Sir Anthony Browne, K.G. For, in 1539, he had by indenture settled all his manors of Midhurst, Cowdray, and Rushington, to his own use, and that of Mabel his wife; and then to his brother of the half-blood, Sir Anthony Browne, K.G. Then to his bastard son, Thomas Fitzwilliam, otherwise Fisher; and lastly to John Fitzwilliam, son of Thomas Fitzwilliam, of Masborough, co. York. These manors were held in capite of the crown, by the said Sir Anthony Browne, in 1547, and descended to George Samuel, 8th Viscount Montague, who in 1793, when they passed to the Hon. Elizabeth Mary Browne, his only sister and heir, the wife of William Stephen Poyntz, Esq., M.P. for Callington, co. Cornwall.

Arms—Or, a cross, az

BOLEYNE—VISCOUNT ROCHFORD, EARL OF WILTSHIRE AND EARL OF ORMONDE.

Viscounty, by Letters Patent, dated 18 June, 1525.

Earldoms, by Letters Patent, dated 8 December, 1529.

Lineage.

The family of Bullen, or Boleyne, is said to have been of ancient date in the county of Norfolk; we shall, however, begin with

SIR GEOFFREY BOLEYNE (son of Sir Geoffrey Boleyne, of Salle. co. Norfolk, by Alice Bracton his wife), who, settling in the city of London, attained great opulence there, and filled the lord mayor's chair in the year 1458, when he was made a knight. He m. Anne, eldest dau. and co-heiress of Thomas, Lord Hoo and Hastings, by whom (who m. 2ndly, Sir T. Fynes), he had several children, of which the eldest son,

SIR WILLIAM BOLEYNE, K.B., settled at Brickling, in Norfolk, and m. Margaret, youngest dau. and co-heiress of Thomas Butler, 7th Earl of Ormonde, and niece and co-heiress of James Butler, Earl of Wiltshire, by whom, with other issue, he left, at his decease (10 October, 1505), a son and heir,

SIR THOMAS BOLEYNE. This gentleman took up arms in the 12th of HENRY VII., with his father and other persons of rank, against the Cornish rebels; and in the beginning of the next reign, being one of the knights of the king's body, was constituted governor of the castle of Norwich, jointly with Sir Henry Wyatt, Knt., master of the king's jewel-house. In the next year he was one of the ambassadors to the Emperor MAXIMILIAN, touching a war with France; and a few years afterwards was appointed sole constable of Norwich Castle. In the 11th of the same reign, being ambassador to France, he arranged the preliminaries for the famous interview between his royal master and FRANCIS I., between Guisnes and Ardres. In three years afterwards he was ambassador to the court of Spain, and was advanced to the peerage 18 June, 1525, in the dignity of VISCOUNT ROCHFORD. In 1527 his lordship was one of the commissioners to invest the King of France with the order of the Garter. In 1529 he subscribed the articles then exhibited against Cardinal Wolsey; and on 8 December, in the same year, being then a knight of the Garter, he was advanced to the EARLDOMS OF WILTSHIRE AND ORMONDE—the former to the heirs of his body, and the latter to heirs-general, to the injury, however, of Sir Piers Butler, the 8th earl rightfully of Ormonde, who instead was created Earl of Ossory. In the January following, his lordship was nominated lord privy-seal, soon after which he was again accredited to the court of Spain. The earl m. Elizabeth, dau. of Thomas Howard, Duke of Norfolk, and had issue,

    I. GEORGE, who was summoned to parliament in the lifetime of his father, viz., 5 January, 1533, as VISCOUNT ROCHFORD This nobleman was deputed by King HENRY to announce his private marriage with his lordship's sister, Anne Boleyne, to the King of France, and to solicit that monarch's advice regarding its public avowal. In two years afterwards he was made constable of Dover Castle, and lord warden of the Cinque Ports. Again the viscount was accredited to Versailles in the 27th (1535-6) of his brother-in-law's reign, touching a projected union between the king's infant dau. Elizabeth, and one of the sons of France. His lordship, who had risen with his sister, shared in the downfall of that unhappy lady—was committed to the Tower 2 May, 1536, and arraigned and beheaded on the 17th of the same month. He m. Jane, dau. of Sir Henry Parker (eldest son and heir of Henry, Lord Morley), an infamous woman, who continued a lady of the bed-chamber to the three succeeding queens, but eventually shared the fate of Katherine Howard. His lordship had no issue. He was attainted soon after his execution.

    I. ANNE, created MARCHIONESS OF PEMBROKE, 1 September, 1532, m. in the following year to King HENRY VIII., and thus became QUEEN CONSORT OF ENGLAND. Beheaded in 1536, leaving an only child,

       ELIZABETH, who ascended the English throne, as QUEEN REGNANT, at the decease of her half-sister, Mary, 17 November, 1558.

    II. Mary, m. to William Carey, Esq., whose son and heir was created, in 1559, Baron Hunsdon (see CAREY, LORD HUNSDON).

The Earl of Wiltshire and Ormonde d. in 1538, two years after his unhappy son and dau., when the VISCOUNTY OF ROCHFORD and EARLDOM OF WILTSHIRE became EXTINCT; that of ORMONDE being to heirs-general, fell into ABEYANCE between the representatives of his daus. "On the death of Queen ELIZABETH," says Nicolas, "the only issue of Anne Boleyne, the eldest co-heir, became EXTINCT, when it is presumed that the abeyance, agreeably to the limitation, terminated, and consequently that dignity reverted to the representative of the other co-heir, the heir-general of whom is the present Earl of Berkeley, and under the said limitation, must probably be considered as EARL OF ORMONDE."

    Arms—Arg., a chev., gu., between three bulls' heads, sa., armed, or.

BOLEYNE—MARCHIONESS OF PEMBROKE.

By Letters Patent, dated 1 September, 1532.

Lineage.

This dignity was conferred by King HENRY VIII. upon his unhappy Queen Anne Boleyne, prior to his marriage. For that unfortunate lady's family see BOLEYNE, EARL OF WILTSHIRE AND ORMONDE.

BONVILE—BARON BONVILE.

By Writ of Summons, dated 23 September, 1449.

Lineage.

In the 4th of RICHARD II.,

SIR WILLIAM DE BONVILE was constituted sheriff of the cos. of Somerset and Dorset, which trust he also held the next ensuing year; and in the 13th of the same reign was sheriff of Devonshire. He d. in 1408, and was s. by his grandson,

SIR WILLIAM BONVILE (son of John de Bonvile, by Elizabeth his wife, Lady of Chuton, dau. of Henry FitzRoger). This Sir William, in the 5th of HENRY V., in the expedition then made into France, was of the retinue of Thomas, Duke of Clarence, the king's brother. In the 1st of HENRY VI. Sir William was appointed sheriff of Devonshire, and being afterwards engaged in the French wars, wherein he deported himself with great valour, he was constituted seneschal of the duchy of Aquitaine, and had summons to parliament as a BARON, from 23 September, 1449, to 30 July, 1460, under the title of LORD BONVILE, of Chuton. His lordship subsequently espousing the interests of the house of York, was one of those to whom the custody of King HENRY VI. was committed after the battle of Northampton, but the tide of fortune turning, his lordship lost his head, with the Duke of Exeter and the Earl of Devon, after the second battle of St Alban's. Lord Bonvile m. Margaret Meriet, and had (with a dau. Mary, m. to Sir William Courtenay), an only son,

    WILLIAM, who d. before the baron, having m. Elizabeth de Harrington, dau. and heir of William, Lord Harrington, and leaving an only child,

       WILLIAM, commonly called Lord Harrington, who m. Lady Catherine Nevil, dau. of Richard, Earl of Salisbury, and had an only dau., Cecily. This William was slain at the battle of Wakefield, fighting under the banner of the house of York, in the 39th HENRY VI.

Lord Bonvile was s. at his decease by his great-grand-dau. the above-mentioned CECILY BONVILE, who m. 1st, Thomas Grey, Marquess of Dorset, and 2ndly, Henry Stafford, Earl of Wiltshire, but had issue by the former only. Through this union the BARONIES OF BONVILE AND HARRINGTON were conveyed to, and continued in the family of Grey, until the attainder of Henry Grey, Duke of Suffolk (grandson of the said Thomas and Cecily), in 1554, when, with his grace's other honours, those dignities EXPIRED.

    Arms—Sa., six mullets, arg., pierced, gu.

BOOTH—BARONS DELAMERE, OF DUNHAM MASSIE, CO. CHESTER, AND EARLS OF WARRINGTON.

Barony, by Letters Patent, dated 20 April, 1661.
Earldom, by Letters Patent, dated 17 April, 1690.

Lineage.

The family of BOOTH was of great repute and honourable station in the cos. of Lancaster and Chester for several centuries before it arrived to the dignity of the peerage.

ADAM DE BOOTHS, so called from his place of abode in Lancashire, was father of

WILLIAM DE BOOTHS, living in 1275, who m. Sibel, dau. of Sir Ralph de Brereton, Knt., and was s. by his son,

THOMAS DE BOOTHS, to whom s. his son,

JOHN DE BOOTHE, living temp. EDWARD II., who m. Agnes, dau. and heiress of Sir Gilbert de Barton, and was s. by his son,

SIR THOMAS BOOTH, of Barton, called "Tomalin of the Boothes," m. Ellen, dau. of Thomas de Workesley, of Workesley, now Worsley, co. Lancaster, and had issue,

    I. JOHN, his successor.
    II. Henry, left a son, John.
    III. Thomas, left a son, Robert.
    I. Alice, m. 1st, to William Leigh, Esq., of Paguley, co. Chester, and 2ndly, to Thomas Duncalf, Esq., of Foxwist.
    II. Catherine.
    III. Margaret.
    IV. Anne, m. to Sir Edward Weever.

Sir Thomas was s. by his eldest son,

JOHN BOOTH, Esq., of Barton, who lived in the reigns of RICHARD II. and HENRY IV., and m. 1st, Joan, dau. of Sir Henry Trafford, of Trafford, co. Lancaster, by whom he had issue,

    I. THOMAS, who received the honour of knighthood in the 14th HENRY VI. Sir Thomas m. a dau. of Sir George Carrington, Knt., and widow of —— Weever, and had issue,
       Sir John Booth, Knt., to whom King HENRY VII. granted an annuity of 10 marks sterling for his good services. Sir John fell at Flodden Field, in the 5th of HENRY VIII., and his male line ceased with his great-grandson JOHN, who left, at his decease, three daus., co-heiresses.
    II. ROBERT, of whom presently, as ancestor of the Lords Delamere.

III. William, archbishop of York.
IV. Richard, of Strickland, near Ipswich, co. Suffolk.
V. Roger, m. Catherine, dau. and heiress of Ralph Hatton, Esq., of Mollington, near Chester, and had issue,

1 Robert Booth, Esq., of Sawley, co. Derby.
1 Isabel, m. to Ralph Nevil, 3rd Earl of Westmoreland, and had issue,

ANNE, who m. William, Lord Coniers.

VI. John, bishop of Exeter, anno 1465; buried in the church of St. Clement Danes, London, in 1478.
VII. Ralph, archdeacon of York.
I. Margery, m. to John Byron, Esq., of Clayton, co. Lancaster.
II. Joan, m. 1st, to Thomas Sherborne, Esq., of Stonyhurst, co. Lancaster, and 2ndly, to Sir Thomas Sudworth, Knt.
III. Catherine. m. to Thom s Ratcliffe, Esq., of Wimmorley.
IV. Alice, m. to Sir Robert Clifton, Knt., of Clifton, co. Nottingham.

Mr. Booth m. 2ndly (but the lady's name is not known), and left a son,

Laurence Booth, who was chancellor of the university of Cambridge, bishop of Durham, and afterwards archbishop of York. His lordship was appointed keeper of the privy seal in the 35th of HENRY VI., and Lord Chancellor of England in the 12th of EDWARD IV. He d. in 1480

The line of Sir Thomas Booth, the eldest son, terminating, as stated above, in co-heiresses, we proceed with the 2nd son,
SIR ROBERT BOOTH, Knt., of Dunham Massie, co. Chester, which seat he acquired by his wife Douce, dau. and co-heiress of Sir William Venables, of Bollen, in the same shire; which Sir William was son of Joane, dau. and heir of Hamon Fitton, who was grandson of John Fitton, of Bollen, by Cicelie his wife, eldest dau. and co-heir of Sir Hamon de Massie, the 6th and last Baron of Dunham Massie, one of the eight feudal lordships instituted by Hugh Lupus, Earl of Chester, in the time of the CONQUEROR. By this lady Sir Robert Booth had no less than nine sons and five daus. Of the former,

I. WILLIAM, the eldest, inherited the fortune.
II. Raufe, m. Margaret, dau. and heir of Thomas Sibell, of Sandwich, co. Kent, and had three daus., Dowse, m. to —— Gomer, of London ; Margaret, m. to William Mere, son and heir of Thomas Mere, of Mere ; and Jane, m. to Robert Leycester, of Toft.
III. Geoffrey.
IV. Hamond, in holy orders
V John, bishop of Exeter, and warden of Manchester college, d. 1478.
VI. Robert.   VII. Edward.   VIII. Peter.
IX. Philip, the youngest. m. the dau. and heiress of Sir William Hampton, of Wellington, Knt.

The daus. were
I. Lucy, m. to John Chantler, Esq., of the Bache, near Chester.
II. Ellen, m. to Robert Legh. Esq., of Adlington. co. Chester.
III. Alice, m. to Robert Hesketh, Esq., of Rufford, co. Lancaster, ancestor of the Baronets Hesketh.
IV. Joan, m. to Hamond Massie, Esq., of Rixton, co. Lancaster.
V. Margery, m. to James Scaresbrich, Esq.

Sir Robert and his eldest son had a grant of the office of sheriff of Cheshire for both their lives, and to the survivor of them, by patent, dated at Chester 8 March, in the 21st of HENRY VI., with all fees appertaining to the said office, and to execute its duties, either personally or by deputy. Sir Robert d. 16 September, 1450, and was s. by his eldest son,
SIR WILLIAM BOTHE, who m. Maud, dau. of John Dutton, Esq., of Dutton, co. Chester, by whom he had issue,
GEORGE, his heir.
Lawrence.   John.   William.
Douce, m. to Thomas Leigh, Esq., of West Hall, co. Chester.
Anne, m. 1st, to John Leigh, Esq., of Booths, Cheshire, and 2ndly, to Geoffery Shakerly, of Shakerly, co. Lancaster.
Ellen, m. to Sir John Leigh, of Baguley, co. Chester.
Margery, m. to John Hyde, Esq., of Haighton, Lancashire.
Alice, m. to John Ashley, Esq., of Ashley, co. Chester.
Elizabeth, m. to Thomas Fitton, Esq., of Pownall, Cheshire.
Joane, m. to William Holt, Esq.
Isabella.   Catherine.

Sir William d. in 1476, and was s. by his eldest son,
GEORGE BOTHE, Esq. This gentleman m. Catherine, dau. and heiress of Robert Mountford, Esq., of Bescote, co. Stafford, and of Monkspath, Warwickshire (younger son of Sir William Montford, of Coleshill, co. Warwick), by whom he acquired considerable estates in the cos. of Salop, Stafford, Warwick, Leicester, Wilts, Somerset, Cornwall, and Hereford, and had issue,
WILLIAM, his successor.
Laurence.   Roger
Alice, m. to William Massie, Esq., of Denfield, co. Chester,
Ellen, m. 1st, to Thomas Vaudrey, Esq., and 2ndly, to Trafford, Esq., of Bridge Trafford.

60

Mr. Bothe d. in 1483, and was s. by his eldest son,
SIR WILLIAM BOTHE, Knt., who m. 1st, Margaret, dau. and co-heir of Sir Thomas Asheton, of Ashton-under-Lyne, co. Lancaster, and of his wife Anne, dau. of Ralph, Lord Greystock, by which alliance a great accession of property came to the family of Bothe. He had issue of this marriage,
GEORGE, his successor.
John, m. to Margery, dau. of Sir Piers Dutton, of Dutton, co. Chester, and had two sons, William and Robert.

Sir William m. 2ndly, Ellen, dau. of Sir John Montgomery, of Throwley, co. Stafford, and had

William, m. to a dau. of — Smith, Esq., of co. Leicester.
Hamnet, m. to a dau. of Humphrey Newton, Esq.
Edward, m. to Mary, dau. and co-heir of Roger Knutsford, Esq., of Twemlow, co. Chester, from whom descended the BOOTHS of TWEMLOW HALL.
Henry, m. to a dau. of — Bowdon, Esq., of co. Chester.
Andrew.
Jane, m. 1st, to Hugh, son and heir of Sir Piers Dutton, of Dutton, co. Chester, and 2ndly, to Thomas Holford, Esq., of Holford, in the same shire.
Dorothy, m. to Edward, son and heir of Laurence Warren, Esq., of Poynton, co. Chester.
Anne, m. to Sir William Brereton, of Brereton, Cheshire.

Sir William d. 9 November, in the 11th HENRY VIII. (1519), and was s. by his eldest son,
GEORGE BOTHE, Esq., who m. Elizabeth, dau. of Sir Thomas Boteler, of Beausey, near Warrington, and had issue,
GEORGE, his successor.
John, m. to Elizabeth, dau. of John Dutton, Esq., and left four sons,
William.   Robert.   Edmund.   Henry.
Robert, in holy orders, rector of Thornton-in-the-Moors, co. Chester.
Ellen, m. to John Carrington, Esq., of Carrington, co. Chester.
Anne, m. to William Massie, Esq., of Podington.
Margaret, m. to Sir William Davenport, of Bramhall.
Elizabeth, m. to Richard Sutton, Esq., of Sutton, near Macclesfield.
Dorothy, m. to Robert Tatton, Esq., of Withenshaw.
Alice, m. to Peter Daniel, Esq., of Over Tabley.
Cecilie, m. unm.

Mr. Bothe d. in the 22nd HENRY VIII. (1531), and was s. by his eldest son,
GEORGE BOTHE, Esq., of Dunham, who m. Elizabeth, dau. of Sir Edmund Trafford, of Trafford, co. Lancaster, and by her (who m. 2ndly, James, brother and heir of Sir John Done, of Utkinton, and 3rdly, Thomas Fitton, of Gawesworth,) left, at his decease in 1548 (35th HENRY VIII.), a son and three daus., viz.,
WILLIAM, his successor.
Elizabeth, m. to William Chauntrell, Esq., of the Bache, near Chester.
Mary, m. to Randle Davenport, Esq., of Henbury, co. Chester.
Anne, m. to — Wentworth, Esq., of co. York

To this George Bothe, Queen JANE SEYMOUR commanded a letter to be written, acquainting him with the birth of a son (afterwards King EDWARD VI.), bearing date, at Hampton Court, the very day of her delivery, 12 October (29th HENRY VIII.) Mr. Bothe had also the honour of a letter from King HENRY himself, dated at Westminster, 16 February, in the 34th year of his reign, concerning forces to be raised to war against the Scotch. Mr. Bothe was s. by his son,
WILLIAM BOTHE, or BOUTHE, who, being then but three years old, was in ward to the king. He received the honour of knighthood in 1578. Sir William m. Elizabeth, dau. of Sir John Warburton, of Warburton and Arley, co. Chester, and had seven sons and six daus. Of the former,
GEORGE, s. his father.
Edmund, a lawyer, d. s. p.
John, m. to a dau. of — Preistwich, of Hulme, near Manchester, and had several children. He was buried 1 August, 1644.
Robert, bant 11 December, 1570, a soldier in Holland.
Peter, b. 1576, d. an infant.
Richard, m. a dau. and heiress of — Massie, of Cogshull.

The married daus. were,
Elizabeth, m. 1st, to William Basnet, Esq., of Eaton, co. Denbigh, and 2ndly, to Edward Walsh, Esq., of Clonmaynine, co. Wicklow.
Dorothy, m. to Ralph Bunnington, Esq., of Barrowcote, co. Derby.
Alice, m. to — Panton, Esq.,
Susan. m. 1st, to Sir Edward Warren, of Pointon, co. Chester, and 2ndly, to John Fitton, Esq., of the city of Chester.

Sir William d. 28 November, 1579, and was s. by his eldest son,
SIR GEORGE BOOTH, whose extensive estates were placed by

Queen ELIZABETH, during his minority, under the guardian-ship of her favourite, Robert Dudley, Earl of Leicester. In the latter end of her majesty's reign Sir George received the honour of knighthood, and upon the institution of the order of baronet, he was amongst the first raised to that dignity, on 22 May, 1611. Sir George Booth *m*. 1st, 18 February, 1577, his 2nd cousin Jane, only dau. and heiress of John Carrington, Esq., of Carrington, co. Chester, by whom he had no issue, nor did he live long with her, yet he inherited the lands of her father; the same being strictly so settled by that gentleman before the marriage of his daughter, to descend to the family of Booth: in which settlement, among other provisions, is one particu-larly worthy of notice :—" That if she, the said Jane, should, after marriage, be detected of incontinency, the estate should remain to the family of Booth." After the decease of this lady, Sir William *m*. Catherine, dau. of Chief Justice Anderson, of the court of Common Pleas, and had several children, of whom

   I. WILLIAM, the eldest son, *m* in May, 1619, Vere, 2nd dau and co-heir of Sir Thomas Egerton, eldest son of Thomas, Viscount Brackley, Lord Chancellor of England, and pre-deceasing his father (26 April, 1636), left issue,

     1 GEORGE, of whom presently, as successor to the baro-netcy.
     2 Nathaniel, *b*. 1627, *m*. Anne, 3rd dau. of Robert Ravens-croft, Esq., of Bretton, co. Flint, whose line terminated with his great-grand-dau., Hannah Vere Booth, in 1765.
     1 Catherine, *m*. to Sir John Jackson, of Hickleton, co. York, baronet

   II. John, the youngest son, having actively espoused the cause of King CHARLES II., received the honour of knight-hood after the Restoration, *anno* 1660. Sir John *m*. 1st, Dorothy, dau. of Sir Anthony St. John, younger son of Oliver, Earl of Bolingbroke, and, 2ndly, in 1659, Anne, widow of Thomas Legh, Esq., of Adlington, and by the former left several children at his decease, in 1678.

     I. Alice, *m*. George Vernon, Esq., of Heslinton, co. Chester, afterwards Judge Vernon.
     II. Susan, *m*. Sir William Brereton, of Handforth, co. Ches-ter, Bart.
     III. Elizabeth, *m*. to Richard, Lord Byron (his lordship's 2nd wife), and *d*. *s*. *p*.

Sir George Booth, who served the office of sheriff of Cheshire twice, and as often of Lancashire, *d* 24 October, 1652, and was *s*. in his title and estates by his grandson (whose guardian-ship he had purchased from the crown for £4,000),

   SIR GEORGE BOOTH, 2nd baronet. This gentleman was com-mitted prisoner to the Tower of London during the usurpation, for his zeal in the royal cause and his efforts to restore the exiled prince. He had the pleasure eventually, however, of being chosen one of the twelve members deputed by the House of Commons, in May, 1660, to carry to that prince the recal of the house, in answer to his majesty's letters. And on Monday, 13 July, 1660, the House of Commons ordered, "that the sum of £10,000 be conferred on Sir George as a mark of respect for his eminent services and great sufferings in the public cause;" which order obtained the sanction of the House of Lords in the ensuing month. In addition to which honour-able grant, the baronet was elevated to the peerage, by letters patent, dated 20 April, 1661, as BARON DELAMERE, *of Dunham Massie, in the county of Chester*. His lordship *m*. 1st, Lady Katharine Clinton, dau. and co-heir of Theophilus, Earl of Lincoln, by whom (who *d*. 5 August, 1643) he had an only dau., Vere, who *d*. *unm* in 1717, in the 74th year of her age. He *m* 2ndly, Lady Elizabeth Grey, eldest dau. of Henry, Earl of Stamford, by whom he had seven sons and five daus., of whom,

   I. William, *d*. before his father, 1662.
   II. HENRY, succeeded to the title.
   III. Charles.
   IV George, *m*. Lucy, dau. of the Right Hon. Robert Robartes, Viscount Bodmin, son and heir of John, Earl of Radnor, by whom he had an only son, Charles-Henry, who *d*. *unm*.
   V. Robert, in holy orders, archdeacon of Durham in 1691, and dean of Bristol in 1708. This gentleman *m*. 1st, Ann, dau. of Sir Robert Booth, chief justice of the court of Common Pleas in Ireland, by whom he had a son, Henry, who died an infant. He *m*. 2ndly, Mary, dau. of Thomas Hales, Esq., of Howlets, in Kent, and had five sons and four daus., of whom,

     1 NATHANIEL, the 4th and only surviving, succeeded to the BARONY OF DELAMERE, but of him hereafter.
     1 Mary, *d*. *unm*.
     2 Elizabeth, *m*. to Charlton Thruppe, Esq., of the city of London.
     3 Vere, *m*. to George Tyndale, Esq., of Bathford, Somerset-shire, and dying 31 May, 1758, had a son,

       George Booth Tyndale, Esq., of Bathford, barrister-at-law. father of the late George Booth Tyndale, Esq., of Hayling, Hants, and of two other sons (*see* BURKE's *Landed Gentry*).

61

   I. Elizabeth, *m*. to Edward, Earl of Conway.
   II. Diana, *m*. to Sir Ralph Delaval, Bart., of Seaton-Delaval, Northumberland, and after his decease to Sir Edward Blacket, Bart., of Newby, co. York.

George, 1st Lord Delamere, *d*. 8 August, 1684, and was *s*. by his eldest surviving son,

   HENRY BOOTH, 2nd baron. This nobleman, who had been committed to the Tower prior to the death of King CHARLES II., was brought to trial, in the reign of King JAMES, for high treason, before the Lord Chancellor Jeffreys, constituted high steward on the occasion, and a select number (27) of peers, but was most honourably acquitted. After which he lived in retirement until the revolution, when espousing the cause of the Prince of Orange, he was deputed with the Marquess of Halifax, and the Earl of Shrewsbury, upon the arrival of the prince at Windsor, 17 December, 1688, to bear a message to the fallen monarch, requiring that his majesty should remove from Whitehall; an office which his lordship executed so delicately that King JAMES was afterwards heard to remark, " that the Lord Delamere, whom he had used ill, treated him with much more regard than those to whom he had been kind, and from whom he might better have expected it." His lordship was afterwards sworn of the privy council, and appointed chancellor of the exchequer, an office which he held but one year ; when, upon his retirement, he was advanced to the dignity of EARL OF WARRINGTON, by letters patent, dated 17 April, 1690. The earl *m*. Mary, dau. and sole heiress of Sir James Langham, Bart., of Cottesbrooke, co. Northampton, by whom (who *d*. 23 March, 1690,) he had four sons and two daus., viz.,

   James, died an infant.
   GEORGE, his successor.
   Langham, groom of the bedchamber to GEORGE II., and M.P for co. Chester. *b*. 1684, *d*. *unm*. 12 May, 1724.
   Henry, *b*. 17 July, 1687, *d*. 2 February, 1726.
   Elizabeth, *m*. to Thomas Delves, Esq., son and heir apparent of Sir Thomas Delves, Bart., of Doddington, co. Chester, and *d*. *s*. *p*. in 1697.
   Mary, *m*. to the Hon. Russel Robartes, and had issue,

     Henry, last Earl of Radnor of that family.

His lordship, who published a Vindication of his friend Lord Russell, and other literary productions mentioned in Walpole's Catalogue, *d*. on 2 January, 1693-4, and was *s*. by his 2nd, but eldest surviving son,

   GEORGE BOOTH, 2nd Earl of Warrington. This nobleman *m*. Mary, eldest dau. and co-heiress of John Oldbury, Esq., of London, merchant, by whom he had an only dau. and heiress,

     MARY, who *m*. in 1736, Henry Grey, 4th Earl of Stamford, and *d*. 10 December, 1772, having had issue,

      GEORGE HARRY, 5th EARL OF STAMFORD, created in 1796, EARL OF WARRINGTON (*see* BURKE's *Peerage*).
      Booth, *b*. 1740, M.P. for Leicester, *m*. 10 May, 1782, Elizabeth, dau. of Charles Mainwaring, Esq., of Brom-borough, and had issue,

       BOOTH, of Aston Haye, co. Chester, *d*. *s*. *p*., and Eliza-beth Kynaston, *m*. 1826, to Rev. Charles Mytton, who took the name of Thornycroft.
      John, *b*. 1743, *m*. 22 July, 1773, Susanna, 4th dau. of Ralph Leycester, Esq., of Toft, and *d*. 12 July, 1802, having had issue,

       HARRY, *b*. 8 July, 1783, *m*. 14 May, 1811, Frances, dau. of Hugh Ellis, Esq., of Carnarvon.
       Henrietta, wife of the Rev. Charles Mytton. M.A., rector of Eccleston.
       Mary.
       Emma, *m*. to Thomas William Tatton, Esq., of Witten-shaw.
       Anna Maria, *m*. to the Rev. I. Clarke.

His lordship *d*. 2 August, 1758, when his estates passed to his dau. Mary, Countess of Stamford; the EARLDOM OF WARRINGTON EXPIRED, while the barony reverted to his cousin (*refer* to the Very Reverend Dean Robert Booth, son of the 1st Lord Delamere),

   NATHANIEL BOOTH, Esq., as 4th Baron Delamere. His lord-ship *m*. Margaret, dau. of Richard Jones, Esq., of Ramsbury Manor, Wilts, by whom he had two sons, who both *d*. young, and a dau. Elizabeth, who *d*. *unm*., in 1765. Lord Delamere was appointed chairman of the committees of the House of Lords in 1765, and *d*. in 1770, when the BARONY OF DELAMERE became EXTINCT.

Arms—Arg., three boars' heads, couped and erect, *sa*.

BOSCAWEN, EARL OF FALMOUTH.

By Letters Patent, dated 14 July, 1821.

Lineage.

This is a very ancient family, deriving its surname from the lordship and manor of Boscawen-Rose, co. Cornwall, possessed since the reign of King JOHN.

JOHN DE BOSCAWEN, who *s.* to that inheritance in 1334, *m.* Johan, dau. and heir of John de Tregothnan, of Tregothnan, with whom he acquired that estate; and dying in 1357, was *s.* by his elder son,

JOHN DE BOSCAWEN, who *m.* Johan. dau. and heir of Otho de Abalanda, and was father of JOHN BOSCAWEN, *temp.* RICHARD II.; he *m.* Rose, dau. of William Brett, Esq., and was *s.* by his son,

HUGH BOSCAWEN, who *m.* Johan, only dau. of John Trenoth, and had a son,

RICHARD BOSCAWEN, who *m.* Maud, dau. and co-heir of Lawrence Hallop, and *d.* 4 HENRY VII., leaving a son and heir,

JOHN BOSCAWEN, who *m.* Elizabeth, dau. of Nicholas Lower, and *d.* 13 October, 1515, leaving a son,

HUGH BOSCAWEN, of Tregothnan, who paid a fine of four marks for not attending the coronation of Queen MARY, 1 October, 1553. He *m.* Philippa, dau. and co-heir of Nicholas Carminow, Esq., of Carminow, and had issue: the 3rd son,

NICHOLAS BOSCAWEN, eventually continued the line, *m.* Alice, dau. and co-heir of John Trevanion, Esq. of Trevanion; and dying 1626, was *s.* by his only son,

HUGH BOSCAWEN, Esq. of Tregothnan, M.P. for the co. Cornwall, *m.* Margaret, dau. of Robert Rolle, Esq. of Heanton-Satchville, Devon, and had eight sons and three daus., of whom the eldest son,

   I. NICHOLAS BOSCAWEN, Esq., *s.* his father. This gentleman joined the parliamentarian army with a regiment of horse raised from amongst his own tenantry. He *d. s. p.,* when the estates devolved upon his next brother,

   II. HUGH BOSCAWEN, Esq., who *m.* Margaret, dau. and co-heir of Theophilus Clinton, Earl of Lincoln, by whom he had eight sons, who all *d.* issueless, and two daus., the younger of whom,

     BRIDGET, *m.* to Hugh Fortescue, Esq. of Filleigh, in Devonshire, became eventually sole heir,

The male line of the elder sons drawing thus to a close, we proceed with the 5th son (continuator of the family),

EDWARD BOSCAWEN, Esq., member of the Restoration parliament. This gentleman *m.* Jael, dau. of Sir Francis Godolphin, K.B., and had,

   HUGH, his heir.
   Anne, *m.* to Sir John Evelyn, Bart.
   Dorothy, *m.* to Sir Philip Medows.

Mr. Boscawen dying in 1685, was *s.* by his eldest son,

The RIGHT HON. HUGH BOSCAWEN. warden of the Stannaries and comptroller of the household, who was created, 9 June, 1720, Baron Boscawen Rose and Viscount Falmouth. He *m.* 23 April, 1700, Charlotte, elder dau. and co-heir of Charles Godfrey, Esq., and niece maternally of the 1st Duke of Marlborough, and had (with junior issue) Hugh, his successor, and Edward, the famous Admiral Boscawen. The eldest son,

HUGH, 2nd Viscount, general officer, *d. s. p.* 4 Feb. 1782, and was *s.* by (the son of Adm. Hon. Edward Boscawen) his nephew,

GEORGE EVELYN, 3rd Viscount, *b.* 6 May, 1758; who *m.* in 1784, Elizabeth Anne, dau. and heiress of John Crewe, Esq., of Bolesworth Castle, co. Chester; and *d.* 8 Feb. 1808, leaving (with two daus.) two sons,

   I. EDWARD, his heir.
   II. John Evelyn (Rev.), Canon of Canterbury, who *m.* 4 May, 1814, Catherine-Elizabeth, eldest dau. of Arthur Annesley, Esq., of Bletchington Park, Oxford; and *d.* 1851, leaving (with other issue) EVELYN, present VISCOUNT FALMOUTH.

The elder son,

EDWARD BOSCAWEN, 4th Viscount Falmouth, *b.* 10 May, 1787, was created EARL OF FALMOUTH, 14 July, 1821. He *m.* 27 August, 1810, Anne-Frances, dau. of Henry Bankes, Esq., of Kingston House, co. Dorset, and dying 29 December, 1841, was *s.* by his only son,

GEORGE-HENRY, 5th viscount and 2nd Earl of Falmouth, high steward of Wallingford, *b.* 8 July, 1811, at whose decease *unm.,*

---

29 August, 1852, the earldom became EXTINCT, while the other honours devolved on his cousin, EVELYN, present VISCOUNT FALMOUTH (*see* Burke's *Peerage*).

Arms—Erm., a rose, gu., barbed and seeded, ppr.

BOTELER — BARONS BOTELER, OF BRAMFIELD, CO. HERTFORD.

By Letters Patent, dated 20 September, 1628.

Lineage.

From the BOTELERS or BUTLERS, Barons of Wemme and Oversley, descended

SIR JOHN BUTLER, Bart., of Hatfield Woodhall, Herts (so created in 17th JAMES I.), who was advanced to the peerage 20 September, 1628, as BARON BUTLER OF BRAMFIELD, in the same shire. His lordship *m.* Elizabeth, sister of George Villiers, Duke of Buckingham, and had issue, six sons, five of whom died in his lifetime *unm.,* and six daus., who became ultimately co-heiresses, viz.,

   I. Aubrey, *m.* 1st, Sir Francis Anderson, Knt., of Eyworth : and 2ndly, Francis Leigh, Earl of Chichester, by whom she had issue, two daus., co-heiresses,

     1 Elizabeth, 2nd wife of Thomas Wriothesley, 4th Earl of Southampton.
     2 Mary, *m.* George Villiers, 4th Viscount Grandison, and had, with other issue, an eldest son, Edward, brig.-gen., *m.* 1677, Catherine, dau. and heir of John FitzGerald, Esq., of Dromana, co. Waterford; and *d.* 1693, leaving (with other issue) John, 1st Earl Grandison (*see* p. 561); and Harriet, wife of Robert Pitt, and mother of the 1st Earl of Chatham.

   II. Helena, *m.* Sir John Drake, Knt., of Ashe, and had, with other issue, an eldest son and heir, Sir John Drake, Bart., of Ashe, and a dau., Elizabeth, wife of Sir Winston Churchill, and mother of the great Duke of Marlborough.

   III. Jane, *m.* 1st, James Ley, Earl of Marlborough; and 2ndly, Major-Gen. Ashburnham, and *d. s. p.*

   IV. Olive, *m.* Endymion Porter, Esq., of Wandsworth, groom of the bedchamber to CHARLES I., the celebrated courtier and one of the handsomest men of his time. Among Vandyke's finest pictures is a family piece containing portraits of Endymion himself and his wife, the co-heiress of Lord Butler, of Bramfield. The eldest son and heir of this marriage,

     George Porter, of Wandsworth, groom of the bedchamber to CHARLES II., *m.* Lady Diana Covert, dau. of George Goring, 1st Earl of Norwich, and *d.* 1683; his eldest dau. Mary, was wife of Philip Smyth, 4th Viscount Strangford, and his eldest son, George Porter, vice-chamberlain to Queen CATHERINE. He *d.* in 1111, leaving by Mary, his wife, dau. and heir of John Mawson, Esq., a son and successor, John Porter, of Allarthing, Wandsworth, Surrey, *b.* in 1696; who *m.* Catherine, eldest dau. of Lieut.-Gen. Richard Sutton, of Scofton, Notts, and had, with daus., an only son, John Porter, of Allarthing, who *d. s. p.,* and was *s.* by his nephew, Pierce Walsh, Esq., who assumed the surname and arms of Porter.

   V. Mary, *m.* Lord Howard, of Escrick, and was mother of Anne, Countess of Carlisle.

   VI. Anne, *m.* Mountjoy Blount, Earl of Newport; and 2ndly, Thomas Weston, Earl of Portland.

His lordship *d.* in 1637, and was *s.* by his only surviving son,

WILLIAM, 2nd baron, at whose decease without issue, in 1647, the BARONY OF BUTLER, of Bramfield, EXPIRED, while his lordship's estates devolved upon his sisters, or their representatives, and were purchased afterwards by George, Viscount Grandison, in Ireland, who thereby obtained possession of the manor of BRAMFIELD.

Arms—Gu., a fesse, counter compony, arg. and sa., between six crosses, pattée fitchée of the second.

BOTELER—BARONS BOTELER, OF OVERSLEY AND WEMME.

By Writ of Summons, dated 10 March, 1308.

Lineage.

In the reign of the 1st HENRY.

RALPH BOTELER, so called, from holding the office of butler to Robert, Earl of Mellent and Leicester, seated himself at

Oversley, co. Warwick, where he erected a strong castle, and at a mile distant, founded a monastery for Benedictine monks (anno 1140, and 5th STEPHEN). This Ralph was *s.* by his son,

ROBERT BOTELER, who was *s.* by his son,

RALPH BOTELER, one of the barons who took up arms against King JOHN, and whose lands were seized in consequence; but making his peace he had restitution on paying 40 marks upon the accession of HENRY III., in whose reign he was constituted a commissioner for collecting the fifteenth then levied in the counties of Warwick and Leicester. In the former of which shires he was likewise a justice of assize. He was *s.* at his decease by his son,

MAURICE BOTELER, one of the justices of assize for the co. of Warwick, in the 13th and 16th HENRY III., and a commissioner for assessing and collecting the fourteenth part of all men's moveable goods, according to the form and order then appointed. This feudal lord filled the office of justice of assize for the same shire, a second and third time, and was repeatedly justice for the gaol delivery at Warwick, in the same king's reign. He was *s.* by his son,

RALPH BOTELER, who *m.* Maud, dau. and heiress of William Pantulf, by whom he acquired the great lordship of Wemme, in the co. of Salop. This feudal baron had divers summonses to attend the king, HENRY III., in his wars with the Welsh, and adhering faithfully to that monarch, against Simon de Montfort, and the revolted barons, he was amply rewarded by grants of lands and money from the crown. He was *s.* at his decease by his son,

WILLIAM BOTELER, who, in the lifetime of his father, had *m.* Ankaret, niece of James de Aldithley. He died, however, in a very few years after inheriting his paternal property (anno 1283), leaving three sons, JOHN, GAWINE, and WILLIAM, and was *s.* by the eldest,

JOHN BOTELER, at whose decease in minority, anno 1286, the inheritance devolved upon his brother,

GAWINE BOTELER, who, dying issueless (1289), was *s.* by his brother,

WILLIAM BOTELER, who, in the 24th EDWARD I., was in ward to Walter de Langton, lord treasurer of England, and Walter de Beauchamp, of Alcester, steward of the king's household. This feudal lord obtaining renown in the Scottish wars of the period, was summoned to parliament as a BARON from 10 March, 1308, to 10 October, 1325. His lordship *m.* 1st, Ankaret, dau. of Griffin, and had an only son, WILLIAM, his successor. He *m.* 2ndly, Ela, dau. and co-heiress of Roger de Herdeburgh, by whom he had two sons, Edmund and Edward, who both died issueless, and four daus., viz.,

Ankaret, *m.* to John, Lord Strange, of Blackmere.
Ida, *m.* to Wm. Trussell.
Alice, *m.* to Nicholas Langford.
Dionyse, *m.* to Hugh de Cokesey.

He *d.* in 1334, and was *s.* by his eldest son,

WILLIAM BOTELER, 2nd Baron Boteler, of Wemme, but never summoned to parliament. This nobleman *m.* Margaret, dau. of Richard FitzAlan, Earl of Arundel, and dying in 1361, was *s.* by his son,

WILLIAM BOTELER, 3rd Baron Boteler, of Wemme, summoned to parliament from 23 February, 1368, to 6 April, 1369. His lordship *m.* Joane, elder sister and co-heir of John, Lord Sudley, and dying in 1369, left an only dau. and heiress,

Elizabeth, who *m.* 1st, Sir Robert Ferrers, a younger son of Robert, 2nd Baron Ferrers, of Chartley, and conveyed to him the lordship of Wemme, co. Salop, and the said Robert was summoned to parliament as "Robert Ferrers de Wemme, Chev." in the 49th EDWARD III. Elizabeth Boteler *m.* 2ndly, Sir John Say, and 3rdly, Sir Thomas Molinton, who styled himself "Baron of Wemme," but was never summoned to parliament. Her ladyship had no issue by her second and third husbands, but by the first she left a son,

ROBERT FERRERS, who inherited the Barony of Boteler, as well as that of Ferrers of Wemme, but was never summoned to parliament. His lordship *d.* in 1410, leaving two daus.-co-heiresses viz.,

Elizabeth, *m.* to John, son of Ralph, Lord Greystock.
Mary, *m.* to Robert Nevill, Earl of Westmoreland.

Between whose representatives those BARONIES are still in ABEYANCE.

Arms—Gu., a fesse componée, or and sa., between six crosses patée, arg.

BOTELER—BARON SUDLEY.

(See SUDLEY, Baron Sudley.)

BOTELER—BARONS BOTELER, OF WARINGTON.

By Writ of Summons, dated 23 June, 1295.

Lineage.

The first of this family who assumed the surname of BOTELER was

ROBERT LE BOTELER, from filling the office of botelor or butler to Ranulph de Gernons, Earl of Chester, and under that designation he founded an abbey for Cistercian monks in the year 1158. This Robert left a son Robert, but nothing further is known of the family until the time of King JOHN, when

WILLIAM LE BOTELER was certified to hold eight knight's fees, in capite of the king, in the co. of Lancaster. To this William *s.* another,

WILLIAM LE BOTELER, who, in the 43rd of HENRY III., was constituted sheriff of the co. of Lancaster, and governor of the castle there. But being involved with the turbulent barons of that period he appears subsequently to have lost his lands, until making his peace in the 49th of the same monarch, soon after the battle of Evesham, the sheriff of Lancashire had orders to restore them. In the early part of the next reign this William le Boteler had charters from the crown to hold markets and fairs upon some of his manors, and was summoned to parliament as a BARON, from 23 June, 1295, to 26 August, 1296. In the 34th of EDWARD I. his lordship was engaged in the Scottish war, having been previously upon military service in Gascony. He was *s.* at his decease by his son and heir,

JOHN LE BOTELER, who had summons to parliament in the 14th EDWARD II., but after this nobleman nothing further is known of the family.

Arms—Az., a bend between six garbs, or.

BOTETOURT—BARONS BOTETOURT.

By Writ of Summons, dated 10 March, 1308.

Lineage.

JOHN DE BOTETOURT, governor of St. Briavel's Castle, co. Gloucester, and admiral of the king's fleet in the reigns of EDWARD I. and EDWARD II., was summoned to parliament as a BARON by the latter monarch, from 10 March, 1308, to 13 September, 1324. His lordship *m.* Matilda, sister and heiress of Otto Fitz Thomas, and dau. of Thomas Fitz Otho, by Beatrix his wife, dau. and co heir of William de Beauchamp, Baron of Bedford, by whom he had issue,

  I. THOMAS, who *m.* Johanna, dau. of Roger de Somery, and sister and co-heiress of John de Somery, Baron of Dudley, and dying before his father left an only son,

    JOHN, who *s.* his grandfather.

  II. John, of Gestingthorp and Belchamp Otho, in Essex, who *d.* 1339, left, by Margaret his wife (who *d.* 1376), a son and heir,

    John, who *m.* Johanna, dau. and heiress of John Gernon. and left an only dau. and heiress,

      Johanna *m.* to Sir Robert Swynburne, Knt.

  III. Otho, of Mendlesham, *m.*, and had issue,

    John, who *m.* Catherine, dau. of Sir William Wayland, Knt., and had an only dau. and heiress,

      JOANE, *m.* to John, son and heir of Sir John Knyvet, Knt.

  IV. Robert.

  I. Elizabeth, *m.* 1st, to William, Lord Latimer, and 2ndly, to Robert Ufford.

  II. Johanna, contracted to Robert, son and heir of Robert Fitzwalter, Lord of Wodeham, in Essex.

Lord Botetourt, who was one of the eminent military characters of the reign of EDWARD I., took a leading part in the Scottish wars of that monarch, and was entrusted with the government of the strongest castles, the command of the fleet, and other duties of the highest importance. His lordship *d.* in 1324, and was *s.* by his grandson,

JOHN DE BOTETOURT, 2nd baron, who had livery of his lands in the 14th EDWARD III., and in two years afterwards attended the king in the expedition made then into France, in the train of Thomas de Beauchamp, Earl of Warwick. From that period his lordship appears to have been constantly engaged in the French wars of his sovereign, and was summoned to parliament from 25 Febuary, 1342, to 3 February, 1385. He *m.* 1st, Matilda, dau. of John de Grey, Baron Grey, of Rutherfield, and had two daus., Elizabeth, *m.* or contracted to be *m.* to Sir Baldwin Freville, of Tamworth, Knt., and Joyce, who *m.* 1st,

Baldwin Freville, Esq., of Tamworth; and 2ndly, to Adam Pershal, of Weston-under-Lizeard, co. Stafford, Knt., and had issue by the former,

BALDWIN FREVILLE, who dying before his mother, left by his wife, Johanna, dau. of Sir Thomas Green, Knt.,

BALDWIN, who d. young.
Elizabeth, m. Thomas, 2nd son of William, Lord Ferrers, of Groby.
Margaret, m. 1st, to Sir Hugh Willoughby, Knt., and 2ndly, to Sir Richard Bingham, Knt.
Joyce, m. to Sir Roger Aston, Knt.

His lordship m. 2ndly, Joyce, dau. of William, Lord Zouche, of Mortimer (aunt and heir of Hugh de la Zouche, of Richard's Castle), and had issue,

JOHN, who m. Maud, dau. of John, Lord Grey, of Rotherfield, and predeceasing his father, left a son, John, who died before his grandfather, and a dau., Joyce, who m. Sir Hugh Burnell, Knt., and d. s. p. in 1406.
Matilda, abbess of Polesworth.
Agnes, a nun at Elstow.
Alice, m. to John Keriell, and had an only dau. and heiress, Johanne, who m. John Wykes, and left two daus., Agnes, who d. unm., and Joyce, m. to Hugh Stanley.
Katherine. m. to Maurice de Berkeley, of Stoke Gifford, co. Gloucester, and left an only son and heir,

MAURICE DE BERKELEY, who m. Joan, dau. of Sir John Denham, Knt., and his descendant (refer to BERKELEY, Baron Botetourt),

NARBONNE, was summoned to parliament as BARON BOTE-TOURT in 1764, and d. s. p. in 1776, which caused the title to fall once more into ABEYANCE.
Elizabeth, heiress to her brother, m. to Charles, 4th Duke of Beaufort, in favour of whose son, Henry, 5th duke, the Barony of Botetourt was revived, by patent dated 4 June, 1803, to him and the heirs of his body.

John, 2nd Lord Botetourt, d. in 1385, leaving Joyce, Lady Burnell, his grand-dau., his heiress; but that lady dying in 1406, the BARONY OF BOTETOURT then fell into ABEYANCE between his three surviving married daus., and so continued amongst their descendants for more than three centuries and a-half, when it was at length called out in favour of the representative of Katherine de Berkeley (see BERKELEY, Baron Botetourt).

Arms—Or, a saltier engr., sa.

BOTHWELL—LORD HOLYROODHOUSE.

By Letters Patent, dated 20 December, 1607.

Lineage.

JOHN BOTHWELL, of Alhammer, eldest son of Adam Bothwell, bishop of Orkney, was, on his father's resignation, appointed a lord of session, 2 July, 1593, and sworn of the privy council to JAMES VI., whom he accompanied to England in 1603. He was created a peer by the title of LORD OF HOLYRUDHOUSE, by charter, dated at Whitehall, 20 December, 1607, to him and the heirs male of his body; which failing, to the heirs male of Adam, bishop of Orkney, his father; which failing, to his heirs and assigns. He d. in November, 1609, leaving (by Mary his wife, dau. of Sir John Carmichael, of Carmichael, with whom he got 12,000 marks of portion) a son,

JOHN BOTHWELL, 2nd Lord Holyroodhouse, who was served heir to his father, 17 January, 1629; and d. unm. 1635; from which period the Barony of Holyroodhouse has remained dormant, although claimed, in 1734, by Henry Bothwell, of Glencorse (great-great-grandson of William Bothwell, 3rd son of Adam, bishop of Orkney), who petitioned the crown for an acknowledgment of his title, but no decision was ever come to respecting his claim.

Arms.—Az., a chevron between three trefoils, slipped, or.

BOULDE, or BOLDE, BARON OF RATOATH.

By Letters Patent, dated 13 August, 1468.

Lineage.

SIR ROBERT BOULD, or BOLDE, Knt., was created BARON RATOATH, in the peerage of Ireland, by patent, dated at Drogheda, 13 August, 1468. His lordship m. twice. By his 2nd wife, Ismay, dau. and heir of Sir John Serjeant, of Castle Knock, near Dublin, and widow of Sir Nicholas Barnewall, of Cricks-

town, he had no child; but by his 1st wife, whom he had married in England, he had a dau. and heir, KATHARINE, who m. Edmund Barnewall, Esq., of Dunbrow, co. Dublin, and had issue, Robert Barnewall, of Dunbrow, and Elizabeth, m. to Richard Talbot, of the house of Templeogue.

BOURCHIER—BARONS FITZ-WARINE, EARLS OF BATH.

Barony, by Writ of Summons, dated 23 June, 1292.
Earldom, by Letters Patent, dated 9 July, 1536.

Lineage.

SIR WILLIAM BOURCHIER (3rd son of WILLIAM BOURCHIER, EARL OF EWE, in Normandy, and Anne his wife, dau. and heiress of Thomas, of Woodstock, Duke of Gloucester, youngest son of King EDWARD III.,) having m. Thomasine, dau. and heiress of Richard Hanckford, Esq., by Elizabeth his wife, sister and heiress of Fulke Fitz-Warine, 7th and last Baron Fitz-Warine, of that family, who d. s. p., in 1429, was summoned to parliament, *jure uxoris*, as BARON FITZ-WARINE, from 2 January, 1449, to 7 September, 1469. This nobleman, who was one of the foresters in the reign of EDWARD IV., had license from that monarch to export, duty free, a thousand woollen cloths of his own goods. His lordship appears to have married 2ndly, Catherine, widow of —— Stukeley, by whom he had a dau. Elizabeth, to whom her mother bequeaths in her last will, dated in 1466, "a girdle of red tissue." Lord Fitz-Warine d. about the year 1470, and was s. by his son,

SIR FULKE BOURCHIER, Knt., who was summoned to parliament on 19 August, 1472. This nobleman m. Elizabeth, sister and heiress of John, Lord Dynham, and had issue,

JOHN, his successor.
Joane, m. to James, Lord Audley.
Elizabeth, m. 1st, to Sir Edward Stanhope, Knt., and 2ndly, to Sir Richard Page, Knt.

His lordship d. in 1479, and was s. by his son,

JOHN BOURCHIER, 3rd Baron Fitz-Warine, who, in the 6th of HENRY VII., being of full age, had livery of his lands, and was summoned to parliament from 12 August, 1492, to 8 June, 1536. His lordship inherited, likewise, the large estates of his mother, the heiress of the Lords Dynham. This nobleman signed the celebrated letter to Pope CLEMENT VII., in the 22nd HENRY VIII., wherein the subscribing lords apprised his holiness of the frail tenure of his supremacy, should he refuse the pontifical assent to the divorce of the king from Queen KATHERINE. Lord Fitz-Warine was subsequently advanced, by letters patent, dated 9 July 1536, to the EARLDOM OF BATH. His lordship m. Cecilia, dau. of Giles, Lord D'Aubeney, and sister and heiress of Henry D'Aubeney, Earl of Bridgewater, and had, with other issue,

JOHN, his successor.
Elizabeth, m. to Edward Chichester, Esq.
Dorothy, m. to Sir John Fulford, Knt.

The earl d. 30 April, 1539, leaving amongst other directions in his will, "that an honest secular priest should sing mass for the health of his soul, for the space of twenty years after his decease." His lordship was s. by his eldest son,

JOHN BOURCHIER, 4th Baron Fitz-Warine, and 2nd EARL OF BATH. This nobleman, upon the decease of EDWARD VI., being amongst the first to declare for Queen MARY, was constituted one of the commissioners for receiving the claims of those who in respect of their tenures were to perform service upon the day of her majesty's coronation. His lordship m. 1st, Elizabeth, dau. of Sir Walter Hungerford, Knt., by whom he had one dau., Elizabeth. He m. 2ndly, Eleanor, dau. of George Manners, Lord Ros, and sister of Thomas, 1st Earl of Rutland, of that family, and had issue,

I. John, Lord Fitz-Warine, who d. in the lifetime of his father, leaving by his wife Frances, dau. of Sir Thomas Kitson, Knt., of Hengrave, co. Suffolk,

WILLIAM, who s. to the honours of his grandfather.

II. Henry.
III. George (Sir), general of the army sent to suppress the rebellion in the province of Munster, in Ireland, anno 1580; m. Martha, dau. of William, Lord Howard, of Effingham, and had issue,

Sir Henry Bourchier, Knt., who s. as 6th EARL OF BATH.

IV. Fulke.
I. Mary, m. to Hugh Wyot, of Exeter.
II Cecilia, m. to Thomas Peyton, Customer of Plymouth.

The Earl m. 3rdly, Margaret, dau. and heiress of John Donington, Esq., and widow of Sir Richard Long, Knt., and of this
marriage there were two daus., viz.,

Susanna.
Bridget, wife of Thomas Price, Esq., of Vaynor, co. Montgomery.

Ilis lordship d. in 1560, and was s. by his grandson,

WILLIAM BOURCHIER, 5th baron and 3rd earl. This nobleman was in the expedition (28th ELIZABETH) to the Netherlands, in aid of the Dutch, under Robert, Earl of Leicester.
His lordship m. Elizabeth, dau. of Francis Russell, Earl of Bedford, and had surviving issue,

EDWARD, who was made knight of the Bath at the coronation
of HENRY, Prince of Wales, anno 1610.
Frances, d. unm.

The earl d. 12 July, 1623, and was s. by his son,

EDWARD, 6th baron and 4th earl, who m. 1st, Dorothy, dau.
of Oliver, Lord St. John, of Bletso, and sister of Oliver, Earl of
Bolingbroke, by whom he had surviving issue,

ı. Elizabeth, m. to Basil, Earl of Denbigh, and d. s. p.
ıı. Dorothy, m. to Thomas, Lord Grey, of Groby, eldest son
of Henry Grey, 1st Earl of Stamford, and had issue,
1 Thomas, who s. his grandfather as Earl of Stamford, his
father dying previously, but d. s. p. viv. in 1719-20, when
his cousin s. as 3rd earl.
1 Elizabeth, m. to Henry Benson, Esq.
2 Anne, m. to James Grove, Esq., serjeant-at-law.
Her ladyship m. 2ndly, Gustavus Mackworth, Esq., by whom
she had
Mary, m. ——.
ııı. Anne, m. 1st, to James Cranfield, Earl of Middlesex, by
whom she had a dau.,
Elizabeth, m. to John, Lord Brackley, but d. s. p.
Lady Middlesex m. 2ndly, Sir Chichester Wrey, Bart., from
whom the present Sir Bourchier-Palk Wrey descends, and
who inherits the mansion of Tawstock, co. Devon, the chief
seat of the Earl of Bath

Ilis lordship m. 2ndly, Anne, dau. of Sir Robert Lovet, Knt., of
Liscombe, co. Buckingham. The earl dying thus in 1636, without male issue, the BARONY OF FITZ-WARINE fell into ABEYANCE
between his three daus., and so continues among their descendants, of whom the present Sir Bourchier-Palk Wrey, Bart.,
is one, while the EARLDOM OF BATH devolved upon (General
Sir George Bourchier's son, refer to the 3rd son of the 2nd earl)
his cousin,

HENRY BOURCHIER, 5th earl, who m. Rachael, dau. of Francis
Fane, Earl of Westmoreland, but d. s. p. 15 August, 1654, when
the EARLDOM OF BATH became EXTINCT.

Arms—Arg., a cross engrailed, gu., between four water
bougets, sa., a label of three points, az., charged with nine fleurs-
de-lis, or.

—————

BOURCHIER—BARONS BOURCHIER,
EARLS OF ESSEX.

Barony by Writ of Summons, dated 25 February, 1342.
Earldom, by Letters Patent, dated 30 June, 1461.

Lineage.

In the reign of King EDWARD II.,
SIR JOHN DE BURCER, or BOURCHIER, Knt., one of the justices
of the Court of King's Bench, marrying Helen, dau. and heiress
of Walter de Colchester, and niece maternally of Roger de
Montchensy, acquired the manor of Stansted Hall, co. Essex,
and took up his abode there. Sir John had two sons, ROBERT
and John, and was s. at his decease by the elder,

ROBERT DE BOURCHIER, who in the 4th EDWARD III. (1330-1),
obtained a royal charter for holding a court leet at Halsted,
and in the 10th of the same monarch, had permission to impark
his woods there. In four years afterwards this eminent person
was constituted Lord Chancellor of England, with £500 a-year
above the customary fees, for his suitable maintenance; and
in the next year he had license to make a castle of his mansion-
house at Halsted. Uniting the civic and military characters,
his lordship was subsequently distinguished in arms, particularly at the battle of Cressy, where he was attached to the
division of the army under the immediate command of the
Black Prince. He m. Margaret, dau. and sole heiress of Sir
Thomas Prayers, of Sible-Hedingham, co. Essex, by Anne,
dau. and heiress of Hugh de Essex, descended from a younger

son of Henry de Essex, Baron of Raleigh, standard-bearer of
England, and had issue,

JOHN, his successor.
William, m. Eleanor, dau. and heiress of Sir John de Lou-
vaine, and dying in 1365, left,
WILLIAM, who was made constable of the Tower of London,
and created EARL OF EWE, in Normandy, by HENRY V.
His lordship m. ANNE PLANTAGENET, widow of Edward,
Earl of Stafford, and dau., and eventually sole heiress of
Thomas of Woodstock, Duke of Gloucester, son of King
EDWARD III., and left at his decease four sons and a dau.,
viz.,
HENRY, EARL OF EWE, of whom hereafter, as EARL OF
ESSEX.
Thomas, bishop of Ely, and subsequently archbishop of
Canterbury.
William, Lord Fitz-Warine, see that dignity.
John, Lord Berners.
Anne, m. to John Mowbray, Duke of Norfolk.

Lord Bourchier, who had been summoned to parliament from
25 February, 1342, to 10 March, 1349, d. in the latter year, and
was s. by his elder son,

SIR JOHN BOURCHIER, Knt., as 2nd Baron Bourchier; summoned to parliament from 16 July, 1381, to 30 September,
1399. This nobleman was engaged during the greater part of
his life in the French wars of EDWARD III. and RICHARD II.,
and was installed a knight of the Garter for his gallant services
therein. In the 9th year of the latter king his lordship was
appointed chief governor of Flanders, and particularly of the
town of Gaunt, at the express desire of the Flemings. Prior
to his decease he obtained a special exemption, owing to age
and infirmity, from parliamentary duties, and from attending
councils. His lordship m. Elizabeth, dau. of Sir John Coggeshall, and dying in 1400, was s. by his only son,

BARTHOLOMEW BOURCHIER, 3rd Baron Bourchier, summoned
to parliament from 5 September, 1400, to 26 October, 1409.
This nobleman obtained, like his father, when he became old
and infirm, an exemption from parliament and council, and
from military service in Scotland and beyond the seas. His
lordship m. 1st, Margaret, widow of Sir John de Sutton, but
had no issue. He m. 2ndly, Idonea Lovey, widow, first, of
Edmund, son of Sir John de Brooksburn, and afterwards of
John Glevant, and dying in 1409, left an only dau.,

ELIZABETH BOURCHIER, Baroness Bourchier, who m. 1st, Sir
HUGH STAFFORD, Knt., who thereupon assumed the dignity of
LORD BOURCHIER, but had summons to parliament from 21 September, 1411, to 22 March, 1415, as "Hugoni Stafford" only.
His lordship d. however, s. p., and his widow remarried with
Sir Lewis Robsart, K.G., standard-bearer to King HENRY V.,
who assumed also the title of LORD BOURCHIER, but was summoned,
in like manner, in his own name only, from 24 February, 1425,
to 3 August, 1429. He likewise d. issueless in 1431, and upon
the decease of Lady Bourchier, in 1432, the barony devolved
upon her ladyship's cousin and next heir,

HENRY BOURCHIER—(revert
to William, 2nd son of Robert, 1st Baron Bourchier)—who had
summons to parliament in the 13th HENRY VI., viz., 5 July,
1435, in his Norman dignity, but never subsequently under
that title. In the 25th HENRY VI., 14 December, 1446, his
lordship was advanced to the dignity of VISCOUNT BOURCHIER,
and had summons accordingly; and in the 33rd of the same
monarch he was constituted Lord Treasurer of England. But,
notwithstanding such sterling marks of royal favour, the Lord
Treasurer forsook his royal master, and espousing the interests
of the Earls of March and Warwick, was re-invested with the
treasurership by the former (his brother-in-law) upon his
accession as EDWARD IV., and created, by letters-patent, dated
30 June, 1461, EARL OF ESSEX. His lordship m. Isabel, dau. of
Richard, Earl of Cambridge, Protector of England (grandson
of King EDWARD III.), and aunt of King EDWARD IV., by whom
he had issue,

ı. WILLIAM, who m. Anne, dau. of Richard Widvile, Earl
Rivers, and sister of Elizabeth, queen of King EDWARD IV.,
and by her (who m. 2ndly, George, Earl of Kent) he left at
his decease, v. p., a son and a dau.,
HENRY, successor to his grandfather.
Cecily, m. to John Devereux, Lord Ferrers, of Chartley,
who left a son, SIR WILLIAM DEVEREUX, Lord Ferrers, of
Chartley, from whom sprang the house of DEVEREUX,
EARLS OF ESSEX, which s. to the Barony of Bourchier on
the death of Anne, Lady Parr (see later), that title falling
into ABEYANCE on the death, in 1646, of the Earl of Essex,
and though the Barony of Ferrers, of Chartley, was revived
in favour of the heir-general of Sir Robert Shirley, viz., the
Marquess Townshend; that of Bourchier was overlooked
and continued in abeyance.
ıı. HENRY (Sir), m. Elizabeth, dau. and heiress of Thomas,
Lord Scales.
ııı. Humphrey, m. Joane, niece and co-heiress of Ralph, Lord
Cromwell.

iv. John (Sir), m. Elizabeth, niece and heiress of William Lord Ferrers, of Groby.

v. Thomas (Sir), m. Isabel, dau. and heiress of Sir John Barre, Knt., and widow of Humphrey Stafford, Earl of Devon.

vi. Edward (Sir), slain at the battle of Wakefield.

i. Fulke, } both d. young.
ii. Isabel, }

This nobleman shared largely in the confiscated estates of the Lancastrians, particularly in those of the attainted Earls of Devon (Thomas Courtenay) and Wiltshire, and the Lord Roos. His lordship d. in 1483, and was s. by his grandson,

HENRY BOURCHIER, 2nd Earl of Essex, who had special livery, 9th HENRY VII. (1493-4), of the great estates which descended to him from the Earl of Essex, his grandfather, his father, Isabel his grandmother, Anne his mother, and Sir Thomas Bourchier, Knt., his uncle, to all of whom he was heir. This nobleman, who is represented to have been a person of singular valour and worth, was of the privy council of King HENRY VII., and had a chief command at the battle of Blackheath, in the 12th of that monarch. Upon the accession of HENRY VIII. his lordship was appointed captain of the king's horse-guard, then newly constituted as a body-guard to that monarch. The corps consisted of 50 horse, "trapped with cloth of gold, or goldsmith's work; whereof every one had his archer, a demilance, and coustrill." In the 5th of the same king he attended his highness into France, as lieut.-general of all the spears; and at the famous tournament which HENRY held on 19 and 20 May, 1516, in the 8th year of his reign, in honour of his sister, MARGARET, Queen of Scotland, the Earl of Essex, with the king himself, the Duke of Suffolk, and Nicholas Carew, Esq., answered all comers. In the 12th of HENRY his lordship again attended his sovereign into France, and swelled the pageantry of the monarch in his magnificent interview with FRANCIS I. upon the *Field of the Cloth of Gold*. The earl m. Mary, eldest dau. and co-heiress of Sir William Say, Knt., by whom he had an only dau.,

ANNE, who m. Sir William Parr, Knt. (brother of Queen Katherine Parr), but that marriage was annulled by parliament in the 5th of EDWARD VI. (1551-2), and the issue thereof bastardized.

The earl died in consequence of a fall from his horse, at his manor of Basse, co. Hereford, in 1539, when the EARLDOM OF ESSEX, the VISCOUNTY OF ESSEX, and, apparently, the VISCOUNTY of BOURCHIER EXPIRED; while the BARONY OF BOURCHIER devolved upon his only dau., Anne Lady Parr; but that lady's issue being, as above stated, *illegitimated*, it passed, at her decease, to Walter Devereux, Baron Ferrers, of Chartley, son and heir of Cecily, the deceased earl's sister—(*see descendants of William, eldest son of the 1st earl*)—and became united with the Barony of Ferrers, until the decease, issueless, of Robert, 11th Baron Ferrers, of Chartley, and Earl of Essex, in 1646, when it fell into ABEYANCE between his lordship's two sisters and co-heiresses, Frances, Marchioness of Hertford, and Dorothy, wife of Sir Henry Shirley, Bart.; and it so continues between the Duke of Buckingham and Chandos, as heir-general of Frances, the elder co-heir; and Marmion Edward Ferrers, Esq., of Baddesley Clinton, co. Warwick; and Lady Elizabeth-Margaret Boultbee, the co-representatives of the junior.

Arms—Arg., a cross engrailed, gu., between four water bougets, as.

BOURCHIER—BARON CROMWELL.

(*See* CROMWELL, BARON CROMWELL, OF TATSHALL.)

BOURKE—VISCOUNT BOURKE, OF MAYO.

By Letters Patent, dated 21 June, 1628.

Lineage.

SIR EDMOND-ALBANAGH BOURKE, 4th in descent from William Fitzadelm, and great-grandson of Richard de Burgo, Lord of Connaught and Trim, who d. in 1243, was ancestor of the Mayo Bourkes, and, by the law of tanistry, became elective head of

that family, with the title of Lord Mac William Bourke, five years after the murder of his kinsman, William de Burgo, (the Brown) Earl of Ulster, by Sir John Mandeville, in 1333. Sir Edmond d. "well stricken in years," in 1375, leaving one son, by his wife Sabina, dau. of Dermott O'Malley, of the Owles (the Baronies of Murrisk and Burrishoole, co. Mayo).

SIR THOMAS BOURKE, who s. his father as Lord MacWilliam Bourke, and d. in 1402, leaving five sons by his wife, O'Connor's dau.,

i. Walter, of Kilmaine (barony), co. Mayo, s. his father as Lord MacWilliam Bourke, which title he held for twenty years, and was ancestor of the Bourkes, of the Neale, Gwesshedan, Cloneen, Elestran, Cloonegashel, Shrule, Ballinrobe, Cloghens, Daurus, and Castle Carra, co. Mayo, and of those of Newtown and Thomastown, co. Tipperary, now EXTINCT. He founded the cell of Armagh (for the abbey of Cong).

ii. EDMOND OF THE BEARD, of whom presently.

iii. Thomas, of Moyne, co. Mayo, was elected Lord Mac William Bourke on the death of his brother Edmond, in 1458, and founded the abbey of Moyne, in the said county, two years afterwards.

iv. John, ancestor of the Bourkes of Munster-Creachane, Moyla-Lebinsy, and Moinycrower, co. Mayo. The present Earl of Mayo is descended from him.

v. Richard, of Turlough, co. Mayo, s. his brother Thomas in the MacWilliamship in 1460, and d. nine years after (having previously resigned his lordship). He was ancestor of the Bourkes of Turlough. Thomas Bourke, of this family, was M.P. for co. Mayo in 1639, and Sir William was included in the royal declaration of thanks, as for services beyond sea. In 1689, Walter Bourke, of Turlough, was M.P. for co. Mayo, and colonel of a regiment in the service of King JAMES. Two of his brothers were in the same service; Theobald as colonel, and Thomas, who was M.P. for Castlebar, as captain. Colonel Walter Bourke and Captain Thomas Bourke were included in the royal commission of 10 March, 1690. After the treaty of Limerick, the former retired to France with his regiment, called the regiment of Athlone. He was greatly distinguished in subsequent campaigns, and d. a field-marshal in 1715. At the siege of Cremona, which he defended against Prince Eugene in 1703, his regiment, and that of Henry Dillon, repulsed the Austrians, who had surprised the sleeping garrison.

The 2nd son,

EDMOND BOURKE OF THE BEARD, of Newport and Burrishoole, co. Mayo, s. his brother as Lord Mac William Bourke, and d. in 1458, leaving three sons, by his wife Honoria, dau. of Ulick Roe MacWilliam, of Clanricarde,

i. Sir RICHARD-O'CORKSEY, ancestor of the BOURKES OF CASTLEBAR, represented in the female line by the Earls of Lucan), the BOURKES of Tyrawley, Ardnaree, Castlerea, Carrowkeel, Curraghleagh, &c.

ii. ULICK, ancestor of the Viscounts Mayo. Another member of this family described as of Castle Bourke, co. Mayo, was one of those included in the before-mentioned outlawries. From Ulick were descended the Bourkes of Partry, one of whom, Colonel Richard Bourke was father of David Bourke, a colonel in the service of King JAMES, and killed at Aughrim, and of Richard, who d. in holy orders.

iii. Thomas-Roe, of Newport, Burrishoole, Castle Laffy, and Moyne, co. Mayo, ancestor of the Bourkes, of Ballinglen, in that co. William Bourke, of this family, was a captain in the service of King JAMES, and d. abroad.

The 2nd son,

ULICK BOURKE, m. a dau. of Saba O'Kelly, of Callow, and had three sons, EDMOND; Walter Fitz-Ulick, ancestor to the Bourkes called Sloght-Illiac, or the Offspring of Ulick; and William, an abbot. EDMOND, who succeeded, had also three sons, David; William Corran; and Rickard, who d. in Spain, leaving a son of his own name, called *Iringus*. DAVID, the eldest son, m. 1st, the dau. of John Fitz-Oliver Bourke, of Tyrawley, by whom he had WALTER (Fadda the Long), of Partry; and 2ndly, Finola O'Flaherty, and by her he had two sons, RICHARD AND JERAN (IRON DICK), ancestor to the LORDS MAYO; and William, called by the Irish Theabb-Kiagh, or the blind abbot. The elder son of David's 2nd marriage,

SIR RICHARD BOURKE, a distinguished member of the ancient family of Bourke, marrying Grana, dau. of Owen O'Maly, of the Owles, an Irish chief, had, with other issue, a son and successor,

SIR THEOBALD BOURKE, Knt., who represented, in 1613, the co. Mayo in parliament, and being possessed of a large estate, and distinguished for his eminent attachment to the crown, was advanced by King CHARLES I. (in 1628,) to the dignity of VISCOUNT BOURKE, OF MAYO. He m. Maud, dau. of Charles O'Conor, Esq., and had issue,

i. MILES (Sir), his successor.

ii. David, d. s. p.

iii. Theobald (surnamed the Strong), of Cloghan, co. Mayo, who d. in 1654, leaving issue.

iv. Richard (surnamed *Iron Dick*), who m. Anne, dau. of Thomas MacMahon. of Ennismore, co. Clare, and had issue.
  i. Mary, m. to the O'Conor Don.
  ii. Honora, m. 1st, to Murrogh O'Flaherty, Esq., of Aghnamurra, co. Galway; and 2ndly, to Ulick Bourke, Esq., of Castle Hacket.
  iii. Margaret, m. to Theobald Bourke, Esq., of Turlough.

His lordship d. 18 June, 1629, and was s. by his eldest son,
Sir MILES BOURKE, 2nd viscount, who took his seat in parliament 4 November, 1634. His lordship m. 1st, Honora, dau. of Sir John Bourke, of Derrymaclaghtny, co. Galway, by the Lady Margaret Bourke, dau. of Ulick, 3rd Earl of Clanricarde, and had, with other issue,

  THEOBALD (Sir), his successor.

The viscount m. 2ndly, Isabella Freake, and dying before 1649, was s. by his son,
Sir THEOBALD BOURKE, 3rd viscount; who m. 1st, Elinor Talbot, and by that lady had two sons and two daus.,

  THEOBALD, his successor.
  MILES, 5th viscount.
  Margaret, m. to Sir Henry Lynch. Bart., of Galway.
  Maud, m. to John Browne, Esq., of Westport, co. Galway.

His lordship m. 2ndly, Elinor, dau. of Sir Luke Fitzgerald, Knt., of Tecroghan, co. Meath, and had by her a son, Luke, who d. young. The viscount was shot at Galway, by order of Cromwell, 16 December, 1652. He was s. by his son,
THEOBALD BOURKE, 4th viscount; who d. s. p. in 1676, and was s. by his brother,
MILES BOURKE, 5th viscount. This nobleman m. Jane, dau. of Francis Birmingham, Lord Athenry; and dying in 1681, was s. by his only son,
THEOBALD BOURKE, 6th viscount, b. 6 January, 1681, who m. 1st, 1702, his 1st cousin Mary, dau. of Colonel John Browne, of Westport, and had issue,

  i. THEOBALD, his successor.
  ii. JOHN, who s his brother.
  i. Joan, who m. Murrough O'Flaherty, Esq., of Lemonfield.
  ii. Elizabeth, abbess of Channel Row Nunnery, Dublin.
  iii. Bridget m. in 1731, to Barnaby Gunning, Esq., of Castle Coote, co. Roscommon, and had issue,
    1 John Gunning, a general officer in the army, whose only child, Jane, m. Major James Plunkett.
    1 Maria Gunning, m. to George William, 6th Earl of Coventry.
    2 Elizabeth Gunning, m. 1st, to James, Duke of Hamilton, and 2ndly, to Colonel Campbell, who became Duke of Argyll, in 1776. This lady was herself created Baroness Hamilton.
    3 Catherine Gunning, m. to Robert Travis, Esq.

His lordship m. 2ndly, in June, 1731, Margaret, eldest dau. of Bryan Gunning, and relict 1st, of John Edwards, Esq., of Dublin, 2ndly, of William Lyster, of Athleague, co. Roscommon, and 3rdly, of Captain Francis Houston, of Ashgrove, co. Roscommon. He d. in 1741, and was s. by his elder son,
THEOBALD BOURKE, 7th viscount, who m. in 1726, Alice, eldest dau. of James Agar, Esq., of Gowran, co. Kilkenny, M.P., and by her, who m. 2ndly, Francis, Lord Athenry, had two sons, who d. in infancy. His lordship d. without surviving issue, and was s. by his brother,
JOHN BOURKE, 8th viscount. This nobleman m. Catherine, dau. and heir of Whitgift Aylmer, Esq., descended from Dr. John Aylmer, bishop of London, and from Dr. John Whitgift, archbishop of Canterbury (both in the reign of ELIZABETH), and widow of Mr. Hamilton, of co. Galway, and had issue,

  AYLMER, b. 17 November, 1743; d. in the lifetime of his father, in July, 1748.
  Bridget, m. to Edmund Lambert, Esq., of Boyton, co. Wilts, and left a son,
    AYLMER-BOURKE LAMBERT.

His lordship d. 12 January, 1767, when the VISCOUNTY OF BOURKE, OF MAYO, became DORMANT, and his estates devolved upon his only dau., the Hon. Mrs. Lambert, and passed from her to her son, the late
AYLMER-BOURKE LAMBERT, Esq., of Boyton, co. Wilts, heir-general and representative of the VISCOUNTS BOURKE, OF MAYO.

Arms—Per fesse, or and erm., a cross, gu.; the 1st quarter charged with a lion rampant, and the 2nd with a dexter hand, couped at the wrist, and erect, sa.

BOURKE—BARON BOURKE, OF CASTLE-CONNELL.

By Letters Patent, dated 16 May, 1580.

Lineage.

SIR EDMOND DE BURGO, custos-rotulorum of Connaught in 1336, 3rd son of Richard the Red, Earl of Ulster, was killed in 1338, leaving by his wife, dau. of Turlogh O'Brien, Lord of Thomond, four sons, of whom the eldest,
RICHARD BOURKE, of Castle-Connell, co. Limerick, licensed to treat with the rebels in 1355, was father of
WALTER BOURKE, of Castle-Connell, styled Walter Duff, great-great-grandfather of
SIR WILLIAM BOURKE, of Castle-Connell, who received the honour of knighthood 16 September, 1535, and was created BARON BOURKE, of Castle-Connell, by patent, dated 16 May, 1580. He d. in 1584, having had by Catherine, his 1st wife, dau. of Maurice Fitzjames Fitzgerald, Earl of Desmond, five sons, viz.,

  i. THEOBALD, a principal commander against Lord Desmond, who m. Mary, dau. of Donough O'Brien, Earl of Thomond; and d. 19 August, 1578 (being slain in battle), leaving issue,
    JOHN,
    RICHARD, } successive Lords Bourke, of Castle Connell.
    THOMAS.
    THEOBALD, created LORD BURGH, BARON OF BRITTAS, in the co. of Limerick, 28 January, 1618. His lordship m. Lady Margaret Burke, dau. of Richard, 2nd Earl of Clanricarde; and dying in 1654, left two sons and one dau.; of the former, the elder,
      JOHN BOURKE, 2nd Lord Brittas, m. Margaret, dau. of Thomas Fitzmaurice. Lord Kerry, and widow of Walter Bermingham, Esq., of Dunfert, and had two daus., Margaret, wife of John Macnamara, Esq., of Corthagh, co. Clare; and Honoria, m. 1st, to Pierce Power, Esq., and 2ndly, to Charles MacCarty, Esq. Lord Brittas was s. at his decease by (the son of his brother William, lieut.-colonel in Lord Castle-Connell's regiment, who was executed at Cork, by Cromwell's orders. in 1653) his nephew.
      THEOBALD BOURKE, 3rd Lord Brittas, who, in consequence of his adherence to JAMES II., in whose army he served as lieut.-colonel, forfeited his estate, and was attainted in 1691. His lordship m. Lady Honora O'Brien, dau. of Morough. Earl of Inchiquin, and was father of a dau. Elizabeth, wife of Jas Mathew, Esq., and of a son,
        JOHN BOURKE, but for the attainder, 4th Lord Brittas, and as heir to the senior branch of the family, 9th Lord CASTLE-CONNELL. He resided at St. Germains, near Paris, and d. in France, leaving by Catherine his wife, dau. of Colonel Gordon O'Neill, two sons,
        JOHN, styled 5th Lord Brittas, captain in the French service.
        Thomas, lieut.-general in the Sardinian service.
  ii. Ullick, of Garanceky, co. Limerick.
  iii. William, slain in battle, in 1578.
  iv. David.
  v. John, of Cappagh.

Lord Castle-Connell was s. by his grandson,
JOHN BOURKE, 2nd Lord Bourke, of Castle-Connell, who sat in parliament in Dublin, 26 April 1585. He was slain at Hounslow, Middlesex, by Arnold Cosby, 14 January, 1592, and leaving no issue. was s. by his brother,
RICHARD BOURKE, 3rd Lord Bourke. of Castle-Connell, killed by Dermot O'Connor Sligo, at Ballynecargy, co. Limerick, 28 February, 1599, in the rebellion excited by Lord Tyrone. His lordship d. s. p., and was s. by his next brother,
THOMAS BOURKE, 4th Lord Bourke, of Castle-Connell, who was also slain by Dermot O'Connor Sligo, a few hours after his brother. He had m. Honora, dau. of Connor O'Mulryan, of Annagh, co. Limerick, and left a son and successor,
EDMUND BOURKE, 5th Lord Bourke, of Castle-Connell, an infant at his father's death. For some years he was deprived of his rights by his uncle Theobald, but eventually regained them, and sat in parliament in 1634. He d. in the following year, aged forty-seven, leaving by Thomasin his wife, dau. of Sir Thomas Browne, Knt., of Hospital, co. Limerick, two sons and three daus., WILLIAM, his heir; Thomas, who m. Elizabeth, dau of Sir Lawrence Parsons, of Birr, but d. s. p.; Mary, m. to Thomas Harris, of Klifinan; Elizabeth and Honoria. The elder son,
WILLIAM BOURKE, 6th Lord Bourke, of Castle-Connell, commander in the Munster army in 1641, was outlawed in 1643, but restored in 1661. His lordship m. Ellen, dau. of Maurice Roche, Viscount Fermoy, and had three sons; the two younger. Edmund and Theobald, both d. s. p. The eldest,
THOMAS BOURKE, 7th Lord Bourke, of Castle-Connell, m.

Margaret, dau of Mathew Hore, Esq., of Shandon, co. Waterford, and was father of

WILLIAM BOURKE, 8th Lord Bourke, of Castle-Connell, who followed King JAMES II. into exile; and *d. s. p.* in France, whereupon the succession to the Barony of Castle Connell vested in the LORDS BRITTAS.

Arms.—Or, a cross, gu., in the first quarter, a lion rampant, sa.

BOURKE, BARON BRITTAS.

(*See* BOURKE, LORDS CASTLE-CONNELL.)

BOWES, BARON BOWES.

By Letters Patent, dated 15 August, 1758.

Lineage.

MR. SERJEANT JOHN BOWES, an eminent lawyer, who had been called to the English bar (Inner Temple) 29 June, 1718, was appointed solicitor-general of Ireland, 1730, and attorney-general, 1739; he succeeded Marlay as chief baron of the Irish Exchequer in 1741; was constituted LORD CHANCELLOR OF IRELAND, 22 March, 1757, in succession to Lord Jocelyn, and created in the following year (15 August) BARON BOWES, of Clonlyon, co. Meath. His lordship. *d.* 22 July, 1767, and with him the title EXPIRED. He made his will in the year of his death, and mentions his brothers, Samuel Bowes and Rumsey Bowes, Esqs., of Binfield, co. Surrey.

Arms.—Erm , three bows strung, in pale, gu.

BOYD, LORDS BOYD AND EARLS OF KILMARNOCK.

Barony, by Letters Patent, dated 1459.
Earldom, by Letters Patent, dated 7 August, 1661.

Lineage.

The first recorded ancestor of this noble family, SIMON, brother of Walter, high steward of Scotland, witnessed the foundation charter of the monastery of Paisley in 1160, and is therein designated "frater Walteri filii dapferi." He was father of ROBERT, called BOTT or BOYD, from his complexion (the Celtic word *Boidh* signifying *fair*), and from him derived the various families of the name. The lands of Kilmarnock were granted by ROBERT THE BRUCE to his gallant adherent, SIR ROBERT BOYD, who had been among the first associates of the prince in his arduous attempt to restore the liberties of Scotland. Sir Robert was father of three sons, SIR THOMAS, his heir; Alan, who commanded the Scottish archers at the siege of Perth, in 1339, where he was slain; and James. The eldest son,

SIR THOMAS BOYD was taken prisoner, together with King DAVID II., at the battle of Durham, in 1346. His son and successor,

SIR THOMAS BOYD, of Kilmarnock, *m.* Alice, dau. and co-heir of Hugh Gifford, of Yester, and had a son and heir,

SIR THOMAS BOYD, of Kilmarnock, one of the hostages for the ransom of King JAMES I., in 1424. He *d.* 1432, leaving, by Joanna, dau. of Sir John Montgomery, of Ardrossan, two sons, viz.,

THOMAS (Sir), his heir.
William, abbot of Kilwinning, who received a dispensation from Rome, and had a charter from JAMES III. He also obtained lands in Lanarkshire, which descended to his representative the Rev. WILLIAM BOYD, D.D., of Mertor Hall, co. Wigton, grandfather of the present MARK BOYD, Esq., of Mertou Hall, co. Wigton.

The elder son,
SIR THOMAS BOYD, of Kilmarnock, was killed in a feud, 1439, leaving issue,

ROBERT, his heir.
Alexander (Sir), of Duncrow, executed 1469.
Janet, m. to John Maxwell, of Calderwood.
Margaret, m. to Alexander, Lord Montgomerie.

The son and heir,
ROBERT BOYD, was created in 1459, by King JAMES III., a

peer of parliament, as LORD BOYD, twice sent ambassador to England, constituted governor of the kingdom till the sovereign came of age, and appointed great chamberlain of Scotland for life, in 1467 The power of the house of Boyd was destroyed as speedily as it arose. In 1469, the mind of the king became alienated from the Boyds; and their chief, the Lord Boyd, having had recourse to arms, sentence of high treason was passed upon them. Sir Alexander Boyd was beheaded on the Castle Hill of Edinburgh, 22 November, 1469, and his brother, the Lord Boyd, escaped to England, where he died in poverty at Alnwick, in 1470. His lordship *m.* Mariota, dau. of Sir Robert Maxwell, of Calderwood, and had (with two daus., Elizabeth, *m.* to Archibald, 5th Earl of Angus; and Annabella, wife of Sir John Gordon, of Lochinvar) three sons, viz.,

THOMAS, EARL OF ARRAN. (*See that title.*)
ALEXANDER, of whom presently.
Archibald, 1st of the Boyds, of Bonshaw.

The 2nd son,
ALEXANDER BOYD, chamberlain of Kilmarnock for the crown in 1505, *m.* a dau. of Sir Robert Colvill, of Ochiltree, and had three sons,

ROBERT, his heir,
Thomas, of Pitcon, ancestor of the BOYDS OF PITCON, the last male descendant of whom in Ayrshire was THOMAS BOYD, comptroller of customs in Irvine. Pitcon was sold by the Boyds in 1770, and is now, after various changes, the property of Alexander Alison, Esq.
Adam, of Pinkill, co Ayr, *m.* Helen, dau. of John, Lord Kennedy, and was ancestor of the BOYDS of Pinkill and Trochrig, whose male descendant and representative the late SPENCER BOYD, Esq., of Pinkill, *m.* Margaret, dau. of William Losh, Esq., of Newcastle, and *d.* in 1827, leaving an only son, SPENCER BOYD, Esq., now of Pinkill.

The eldest son,
ROBERT BOYD, of Kilmarnock, a man of judgment and resolution, had a confirmation from Queen MARY of all the estates, honours, and dignities that had belonged to his grandfather, the late Robert, Lord Boyd. He *m.* Helen, dau. of Sir John Somerville, of Cambusnethan, and left (with a dau. Margaret, wife of John Montgomery, of Lainshaw,) a son and successor,

ROBERT BOYD, 4th Lord Boyd, a devoted adherent of MARY STUART, who *m.* Margaret, or Mariot, dau. and heir of Sir John Colquhoun, of Glins; and *d.* 3 January, 1589, leaving issue,

I. Robert, Master of Boyd, *d. s. p.*
II. THOMAS, 5th Lord Boyd.
III. Robert, of Badenheath, *d.* in July, 1611.
I. Egidia, *m.* Hugh, 4th Earl of Eglinton, and was mother of the 5th earl.
II. Agnes, *m.* to Sir John Colquhoun, of Luss.
III. Christian, *m.* to Sir James Hamilton, of Evendale.
IV. Elizabeth, *m.* to John Cunningham.

The 2nd son,
THOMAS BOYD, 5th Lord Boyd, fought with his father for Queen MARY at Langside. His lordship *m.* Margaret, 2nd dau. of Sir Matthew Campbell, of Loudoun; and dying in 1611, left issue,

I. ROBERT, Master of Boyd. *d.* before his father in May, 1597. He *m.* Lady Jean Ker, eldest dau. of Mark, 2nd Earl of Lothian, and by her (who *m.* 2ndly, David, 10th Earl of Crawford,) had two sons,
1 ROBERT, 6th Lord Boyd.
2 JAMES, 8th Lord Boyd.
II. Thomas (Sir), of Bedlay.
III. Adam, *m.* Marion, sister of Robert Galbraith, of Kilcroich.
IV. John.
I. Marion, *m.* to James, 1st Earl of Abercorn.
II. Isabel, *m.* to John Blair, of Blair.
III. Agnes, *m.* Sir George Elphinstone, of Blythswood.

The eldest son,
ROBERT BOYD, 6th Lord Boyd, *m.* 1st, Margaret, dau. of Robert Montgomery, of Giffin, and relict of Hugh, 5th Earl of Eglinton, but by her had no issue. His lordship *m.* 2ndly, Lady Christian Hamilton, eldest dau. of Thomas, 1st Earl of Haddington, and relict of Robert, 10th Lord Lindsay, of Byres, and by her left at his decease, in 1628, a son and six daus., viz.,

I. ROBERT, 7th Lord Boyd.
I. Helen, who *d. unm.*
II. Agnes, *m.* to Sir George Morison, of Dairsie, in Fife.
III. Jean, *m.* to Sir Alexander Morison, of Prestongrange, co. Haddington.
IV. Marion, *m.* to Sir James Dundas, of Arnistoun.
V. Isabel, *m.* 1st, to John Sinclair, of Stevenston; 2ndly, to John Grierson Fiar, of Sag.
VI. Christian, *m.* to Sir Wm. Scott, of Harden.

The eldest son,

ROBERT BOYD, 7th Lord Boyd, who m. Lady Anne Fleming, 2nd dau. of John, 2nd Earl of Wigton. but by her (who m. 2ndly, George, Earl of Dalhousie) he left no issue at his decease, which occurred 17 November, 1640, when he was s. by his uncle,

JAMES BOYD, 8th Lord Boyd, 2nd son of Robert. Master of Boyd. He m. Catharine, dau. of Robert Creyke, Esq. of Cottingham, co. York, the disinherited son of Ralph Creyke, Esq., of Marton, and had (with a dau. Eva, wife of Sir David Cunningham, of Robertland,) a son and successor,

WILLIAM BOYD, 9th Lord Boyd, s. his father in 1654, and was created EARL OF KILMARNOCK, by patent to him and his heirs male for ever, 7 August, 1661. His lordship m. 25 April, 1661, Lady Jean Cunninghame, eldest dau. of William, 9th Earl of Glencairn; and dying in 1692, left (with two daus., Mary, wife of Sir Alexander Maclean, and Catherine, m. to Alexander Porterfield, of Porterfield,) four sons,

I. WILLIAM, 2nd EARL of KILMARNOCK.
II. James (Capt.)
III. Charles (Capt.), d. in September, 1737.
IV. Robert.

The eldest son,

WILLIAM BOYD, 2nd Earl of Kilmarnock, m. Lettice, dau. of Thomas Boyd, Esq., of the city of Dublin, and had two sons, viz.,

WILLIAM, his heir.
Thomas, an advocate, m. Eleanora, dau. of Sir Thomas Nicolson, Bart., of Carnock, co. Stirling; and that lady m. 2ndly, John Craufurd Esq., of Craufurdland, and was by him, mother of Lieut.-Col. John Walkinshaw Craufurd, of Craufurdland, who attended Lord Kilmarnock to the scaffold; and held, according to tradition, a corner of the cloth which received the earl's head.

The earl d. 20 May, 1692, and was s. by his son,

WILLIAM BOYD, 3rd Earl of Kilmarnock, a steady supporter of the Union and of the Hanoverian succession; who m. Eupheme, eldest dau. of William, 11th Lord Ross, and dying in September 1717, was s. by his son,

WILLIAM BOYD, 4th Earl of Kilmarnock; who engaging in the rising of 1745, was taken prisoner at Culloden, conveyed to London, convicted of high treason, and executed on Tower Hill, 18 August, 1746, when the honours and estates of his family were forfeited. His lordship m. Lady Anne Livingstone, dau. and heir of James, 5th Earl of Linlithgow and Calender. by Lady Margaret Hay his wife, dau. of John, 12th Earl of Erroll, and by her (who d. 18 September, 1747,) left three sons,

I. JAMES, Lord Boyd, who served in the Scots Fusiliers, at Culloden, on the side opposed to his father, and recovered eventually, in 1752, the lands of Kilmarnock, which he afterwards sold to the Earl of Glencairn; in 1758 he succeeded to the EARLDOM OF ERROLL, and d. 3 June, 1778; his great-grandson, William-Henry, is the present EARL OF ERROLL, who, were it not for the attainder of 1746, would also be EARL OF KILMARNOCK.
II. Charles, who was in Charles Edward's army at Culloden. He escaped to France, where he married a French lady, but eventually returning home, he resided at Staines Castle, Aberdeenshire. He d. 1782, leaving a son and a dau.
III. William, a naval and afterwards a military officer; at the time of his father's execution he was serving on board Commodore Barnet's ship.

Arms—Az., a fess chequy, arg. and gu.

NOTE.—There are families of Boyd settled in Ireland, all claiming descent from this Scottish House of Boyd: the BOYDS of Ballycastle, co. Antrim. the BOYDS of Ballymacool, co. Donegal: the BOYDS of Rosslare, co. Wexford: and the BOYDS now of Middleton Park, co. Westmeath.

BOYD—EARL OF ARRAN.

SIR THOMAS BOYD, eldest son of Robert, Lord Boyd, on his marriage with Mary, eldest dau. of King JAMES II., obtained the Isle of Arran, and other lands, and was created EARL OF ARRAN, as appears from a charter, 26 April, 1467. But he enjoyed the dignity for a brief period only, being ATTAINTED and FORFEITED in 1469; and he died soon afterwards. His widow m. 2ndly, in 1474, James, 2nd Lord Hamilton, and her son by that nobleman, James, was created, in August, 1503, Earl of Arran. By the Earl of Arran her ladyship had a son and a dau., viz.,

JAMES, who was restored to the property of the family by two charters, dated in 1482; and d. in 1483: "in ipso adolescentia flore periit inimicorum insidiis circumventus."
Margaret, who m. 1st, Alexander Lord Forbes, and 2ndly, to David, Earl of Cassilis, but d. s. p.

BOYLE—BARONS CLIFFORD, OF LANES-BOROUGH, CO. YORK, EARLS OF BURLINGTON.

Barony, by Letters Patent, dated 4 November, 1644.
Earldom, by Letters Patent, dated 20 March, 1664.

Lineage.

RICHARD BOYLE, 2nd Earl of Cork, having m. (5 July, 1635,) Lady Elizabeth Clifford, only dau. and heiress of Henry, 5th and last Earl of Cumberland, of that family, was created a peer of England, by letters patent, dated 4 November, 1644, as BARON CLIFFORD, of Lanesborough, co. York, and advanced to the EARLDOM OF BURLINGTON on 20 March, 1664, having been constituted previously Lord High Treasurer of Ireland. His lordship was a zealous supporter of the royal cause during the civil wars, and one of the chief promoters of the Restoration. His eldest son,

CHARLES, Lord Viscount Dungarvan (who predeceased the earl in 1694), was summoned to the English parliament by writ, in 1682, as Lord Clifford. His lordship m. 1st, Lady Jane Seymour, youngest dau. of William, Duke of Somerset, by whom he had surviving issue,

CHARLES, successor to his grandfather
Henry, chancellor of the exchequer, and a principal secretary of state in the reign of Queen ANNE, created BARON CARLTON (see that dignity).
Elizabeth, m. to James, Earl of Barrymore.
Mary, m. in 1685, to James Douglas, Duke of Queensbury, afterwards created Duke of Dover.
Arabella, m. to Henry, Earl of Shelburne.

His lordship m. 2ndly, Arethusa, dau. of George, Earl Berkeley, and had,

Arethusa, m. to James Vernon, Esq.

Richard, 1st Earl of Burlington, d. 15 January, 1697, and was s. by his grandson,

CHARLES BOYLE, 2nd Earl of Burlington (3rd Earl of Cork), Lord High Treasurer of Ireland. This nobleman (who was esteemed one of the most accomplished gentlemen in England) m. Juliana, dau. and heiress of Henry Noel, Esq., of Luffenham, co. Rutland, and had issue,

RICHARD, Lord Dungarvan.
Elizabeth, m. in 1719, to Sir Henry-Arundel Bedingfeld, Bart.
Juliana, m. in 1719, to Charles, Lord Bruce, son and heir of Thomas, Earl of Aylesbury. and d. s. p. in 1739.
Henrietta, m. in 1726, to Henry Boyle, Esq., of Castle Martyr, co. Cork, created EARL OF SHANNON.

His lordship d. 9 February, 1704, and was s. by his son,

RICHARD BOYLE, 3rd Earl of Burlington (4th Earl of Cork), Lord High Treasurer of Ireland, K.G., who claimed and was allowed the barony of Clifford, created by writ of summons, 1628. His lordship m. Lady Dorothy Savile, eldest dau. and co-heir of William, Marquess of Halifax, by whom he had issue,

Dorothy, b. in 1724; m. in 1741, to George, Earl Euston, and d. s. p. in 1742.
Juliana, b. in 1727, and d. in 1730.
Charlotte-Elizabeth, b. in 1731; m. in 1748, to William, Marquess of Hartington, son and heir of the Duke of Devonshire.

His lordship, who was distinguished by his patronage of the arts, and a very splendid and refined taste in architecture, d. 4 December, 1753, when the EARLDOM OF BURLINGTON and BARONY OF CLIFFORD, in the peerage of England, created by the patent of 1644, EXPIRED, while the Irish honours and the barony devolved upon his kinsman, JOHN, 5th EARL OF ORRERY (see Earl of Cork in BURKE's Peerage). The deceased nobleman's extensive estates at Chiswick, co. Middlesex, and at Lismore, co. Waterford, with Burlington House, in London, passed, together with the Barony of Clifford, created by the writ of 1628, to his lordship's only surviving dau. and heiress, Charlotte-Elizabeth, Marchioness of Hartington, afterwards Duchess of Devonshire. Her grace's co-heirs-general are the EARLS OF CARLISLE and GRANVILLE, between whom the Barony of Clifford is now in ABEYANCE, and her heir male is the DUKE OF DEVONSHIRE.

Arms—Per bend crenellé, arg. and gu.

BOYLE—BARON CARLTON.

By Letters Patent, dated 26 October, 1714.

Lineage.

The Right Honourable HENRY BOYLE (3rd son of Charles, Lord Clifford, by his 1st wife, Lady Jane Seymour, dau. of William, Duke of Somerset), representative in parliament for the university of Cambridge, and for the city of Westminster, was elevated to the peerage of England, on 20 October, 1714, in the dignity of BARON CARLTON, and was constituted lord president of the council, 14 March, 1724. His lordship had previously filled the offices of chancellor of the exchequer (1701), and principal secretary of state (1707). He was made high treasurer of Ireland in 1704, during the minority of Richard, Earl of Cork, and he was constituted one of the commissioners for the union with Scotland in 1706. His lordship d. unm. 14 March, 1725, when the BARONY OF CARLTON became EXTINCT

BOYLE—VISCOUNTS BLESINTON.

By Letters Patent, dated 23 August, 1673.

Lineage.

The Most Rev. MICHAEL BOYLE, archbishop of Armagh, lord primate, lord almoner, and lord chancellor of Ireland (son of Richard Boyle, archbishop of Tuam, and grandson of Michael Boyle, who was youngest brother of RICHARD BOYLE, the 1st and great EARL OF CORK), d. at the advanced age of ninety-three, on 10 December, 1702, leaving, with other issue, by his 1st wife Margaret, dau. of the Right Rev. George Synge, D.D., bishop of Cloyne, an only surviving son,

MURROUGH BOYLE, who had been elevated to the peerage of Ireland, 23 August, 1673, in the dignity of VISCOUNT BLESINTON, with limitation to the heirs male of his father. His lordship m. 1st, Mary, eldest dau. of his Grace Dr. John Parker, archbishop of Dublin, by whom (who d. in 1668) he had an only child, Mary, m. in 1684, to Sir John Dillon, of Lismullen, co. Meath. He m. 2ndly, in 1672, Anne, dau. of Charles Coote, 2nd Earl of Montrath, by whom he had issue,

CHARLES, his successor.
Alicia, m. in 1697, to Pierce, Viscount Ikerrin; and d. 28 October, 1700, leaving a son James, Viscount Ikerrin, who d. young and unm. 1712.
Anne, m. 1st, in 1696, to WILLIAM STEWART, Viscount Mountjoy, and had
William, who was created, 7 December, 1745, EARL OF BLESINTON. (See STEWART.)
Her ladyship m. 2ndly, John Farquharson, Esq.; and d. in 1741.

His lordship, who was governor of Limerick and constable of Limerick Castle, a privy councillor in Ireland, one of the commissioners of the great seal in that kingdom in 1693, and lord justice in 1696, d. 26 April, 1718, and was s. by his son,

CHARLES, 2nd viscount; who m. 1st, Rose, dau. of Colonel Richard Coote, and 2ndly, Martha, eldest dau. of Samuel Matthews, Esq., of Bonnettstown, co. Kilkenny, but had no surviving issue. His lordship d. 2 June, 1732, when his estates devolved upon his only surviving sister Anne, Viscountess Mountjoy, but the VISCOUNTY OF BLESINTON became EXTINCT.

Arms—Per bend, crenellée, arg. and gu.

BOYLE—VISCOUNT SHANNON.

By Letters Patent, dated 1660

Lineage.

The Hon. FRANCIS BOYLE, of Shannon Park, 6th son of Richard, Earl of Cork, having distinguished himself in suppressing the rebellion in Ireland, was rewarded, in 1660, with the title of VISCOUNT SHANNON, co. Limerick, and admitted of the privy council. His lordship m. Elizabeth, dau. of Sir Robert Killigrew, Knt., vice chamberlain to Queen MARY, and had issue,

Richard, who predeceased his father, leaving three sons and one dau.
Charles.
Elizabeth, m. to John Jephson, Esq., of Mallow. M.P

70

Lord Shannon was s. at his decease by his grandson,

RICHARD BOYLE, 2nd Viscount Shannon, an eminent warrior who eventually attained the rank of joint field-marshal with John, Duke of Argyle, of all his majesty's forces. His lordship m. 1st, in 1695, Lady Mary Sackville, dau. of Richard, Earl of Dorset, and widow of Roger, Earl of Orrery; and 2ndly, Grace, dau. and co-heir of John Senhouse, Esq., of Netherhall, in Cumberland. By the latter, who d. in 1755, he had an only dau. Grace, who m. in 1744, Charles, Earl of Middlesex, and d. s. p. Lord Shannon d. 20 December, 1740, aged sixty-six, and as he left no male issue, the peerage became EXTINCT.

Arms—Per bend, crenellée, arg. and gu.

BOYLE—COUNTESS OF GUILDFORD.

By Letters Patent, dated 14 July, 1660.

Lineage.

LADY ELIZABETH FEILDING, dau. of William, 1st Earl of Denbigh, m. Lewis Boyle, Viscount Boyle, of Kynalmeaky, in the peerage of Ireland (2nd son of the 1st Earl of Cork), by whom she had no issue. His lordship fell at the battle of Liscarroll, in 1642, and her ladyship was advanced to the peerage of England *for life*, on 14 July, 1660, as COUNTESS OF GUILDFORD; she d. in 1673, when the dignity, of course, EXPIRED.

BRADESTON—BARONS BRADESTON.

By Writ of Summons, dated 25 February, 1322.

Lineage.

The first person of this family, of whom anything memorable occurs, is

SIR THOMAS DE BRADESTON (son of Henry de Bradeston, by Isabel his wife), seated at Bradeston, co. Gloucester, the ancient residence of his predecessors (all of whom were homagers to the castle of Berkeley, for their manors of Bradeston and Stinchcombe, which they held by knight's service). In the 10th and 13th of EDWARD II. he was engaged in the Scottish wars, but in the 15th (1321-2) of the same monarch, adhering to the Lord Berkeley against the favourite Spencer, his lands were seized by the crown: he was, however, the next year included in a general amnesty, and upon paying 100 marks and renewing his oath of allegiance, had his property restored. He was afterwards constituted keeper of Kingswood Chase, near Bristol, and governor of Berkeley Castle; and subsequently taking part with the queen consort, Isabella, he was made one of the gentlemen of the privy chamber, at the accession of the young king, EDWARD III. In the 11th of EDWARD III. (1337-8), he had a grant of a ship, called "The Christmas," taken in fight from the French by the merchants of Bristol; and, in the next year, was in the grand expeditions made into Flanders and Scotland, and for his good services was made a KNIGHT BANNERET. Continuing actively engaged in foreign warfare, and acquiring fresh reputation each succeeding campaign, Sir Thomas de Bradeston was summoned to parliament as a BARON 25 February, 1342, and from that period until 3 April, 1360, during which interval his services were remunerated by extensive territorial grants, and by high and lucrative employments. This nobleman appears to have had one son, ROBERT, who predeceased him, leaving an only son, Thomas. Of Robert, the only thing memorable is, that having been taken prisoner in the 19th of EDWARD III., by the citizens of Pisa, on his journey to the Holy Land, the English monarch caused all the merchants of Pisa, as well as those of St. Luca, then in London, with their goods, to be seized, until he was released, twelve of the principal of whom were committed to the Tower, and not discharged until bail was given that young Bradeston should be forthwith enlarged. His lordship d. in 1360, and was s. by (the son of Robert de Bradeston and Isabel his wife) his grandson,

SIR THOMAS DE BRADESTON, 2nd baron. This nobleman was in the expedition against France, in the 43rd of EDWARD III before he had attained majority. He d. however, in five years afterwards, leaving (by his wife Adela de Burgh) an infant, only dau. and heiress,

ELIZABETH, who, in the reign of Richard II., made proof of her age, and had livery of her lands, being then the wife of

Sir Walter de la Pole (1st cousin of William, Earl of Suffolk), by whom she left a dau. and heiress,

Margaret, who m. Sir Thomas Ingoldsthorpe, whose grand-dau. and heir-general, ISABEL (only child of Sir Edmund Ingoldsthorpe, by Joan Tiptoft, a co-heiress), m. 1st. JOHN NEVIL. Marquess of Montacute, brother to the celebrated Richard Nevil, Earl of Warwick; and 2ndly, Sir William Norreys. (See NEVILLE, MARQUESS OF MONTACUTE.)

Arms—Arg., on a canton, gu., a rose, or, barbed, vert.

BRANDON—DUKES OF SUFFOLK.

By Letters Patent, dated 1 February, 1514.

Lineage.

SIR WILLIAM BRANDON, KNT., living 12 HENRY VII., m. Elizabeth, dau. of Sir Richard Wingfield, of Letheringham, by Elizabeth his wife, dau. and co-heir of Sir Robert Goushill, by Elizabeth his wife, Duchess of Norfolk, and had issue,

I. WILLIAM (Sir), his heir.
II. THOMAS (Sir), K.G., who living to witness the accession of has patron to the crown, as HENRY VII., was made one of the esquires of that king's body, and bore his buckler at the battle of Stoke. In consideration of which, and other services, he obtained the wardship of Richard Fenys, son and heir of William Fenys, Lord Say, with the benefit of his marriage; and before the termination of the same reign, was installed a knight of the most noble order of the Garter. Sir Thomas d. in the 1st year of HENRY VIII., being then one of the knights of the king's body, and marshal of the court of Common Pleas. He left no issue.
III. Robert (Sir), d. s. p.
I. MARGARET, m. Sir Gregory Lovell, and had a dau. and heiress,
MARGARET LOVELL, m. to John Kersey, Esq.
II. Ann, m. to John Sydney, Esq., of Penshurst (See SYDNEY, EARL OF LEICESTER).
III ALIANORE, m. John Glenham, Esq.
IV. KATHERINE, m. Henry Gurney, Esq., and had three daus., co-heiresses, viz.,
  1 Christian Gurney, æt. fifty, 1552, m. James Darnell, Esq., and had a son,
    Adam Darnell, Esq., of Thornholme.
  2 Elizabeth Gurney, m. Walter Ayscough, and had issue.
  3 Elizabeth, m John Trye, Esq., of Hardwicke, co. Gloucester, and had a son,
    JOHN TRYE, Esq., ancestor of the TRYES of Hardwicke, and the TRYES of Leckhampton Court, co. Gloucester.
V. ELIZABETH, m. to John Cavendish, Esq.

The eldest son,
SIR WILLIAM BRANDON, standard-bearer at Bosworth, fell by the hand of King RICHARD in that celebrated field, leaving by his wife Elizabeth, dau. and co-heir of Sir Henry Bruyn, Knt., a son and heir,
CHARLES BRANDON, K.G. "Which Charles," says Dugdale, "being a person of comely stature, high of courage, and conformity of disposition to King HENRY VIII., became so acceptable to him, especially in all his youthful exercises and pastimes, as that he soon attained great advancement, both in titles of honour and otherwise." In the 1st of HENRY he was made one of the esquires of the king's body, and chamberlain of the principality of North Wales; in the 4th he distinguished himself in a naval engagement off Brest; and the next year, attending the king upon the expedition of *Therouenne and Tournay*, he was elevated to the peerage (5 March, 5th HENRY VIII.) as VISCOUNT L'ISLE, and appointed commander of the advanced guard of the army; in which campaign he behaved so valiantly, that, in reward of his distinguished services, he was created in the following February (anno 1514) DUKE OF SUFFOLK; and shortly afterwards, assisting at the coronation of the Lady Mary (King HENRY's sister), then wife of LEWIS XII. of France, at St. Denis, he acquired so much renown by overthrowing the knight with whom he tilted at a princely tournament, celebrated upon the occasion, that he won the affections of the queen, who, upon the decease of her royal husband, which occurred soon after, bestowed upon him her hand; and having reconciled the Kings of England and France to the union, he obtained from the former a grant in general tail of all the lordships, manors, &c., which had previously belonged to Edmund de la Pole, Duke of Suffolk (who was beheaded and attainted in 1513). His grace made one of the retinue of his royal master at his magnificent interview with FRANCIS I. upon "the Field of the Cloth of Gold," between Guisnes and Ardres, in Picardy; and, in the next year (15th HENRY VIII.) he led an army almost to the gates of Paris, to the great consternation of the good citizens, whose destruction was averted only by the recall of the general. In the 21st of HENRY VIII.

he was one of the peers who subscribed the articles against Cardinal Wolsey, and, in the next year, the declaration to Pope CLEMENT VII. regarding the king's divorce from Queen Katherine. His grace was afterwards constituted chief justice in Eyre of all the king's forests, and at the dissolution of the great monasteries he had a large proportion of the spoil. The duke was also a knight of the most noble order of the Garter. His grace married no less than four wives, 1st, Margaret, dau. of John Nevil, Marquess of Montagu, and widow of Sir John Mortimer, by whom he had no issue; 2ndly, Anne, dau. of Sir Anthony Browne, Knt., governor of Calais, by whom he had two daus.,

Anne, m. to Sir Edward Grey. Lord Powys.
Mary, m. to Thomas Stanley, Lord Monteagle.

His grace m. 3rdly at Greenwich, 13 May, 1515, the Lady Mary Tudor, 2nd dau. of King HENRY VII., and Queen Dowager of Louis XII., King of France, by whom he had issue,

I. HENRY, created EARL OF LINCOLN in 1525, who predeceased the duke unm., when the EARLDOM of Lincoln EXPIRED.
I. Frances, m. 1st, to Henry Grey, 3rd Marquess of Dorset, who was created DUKE OF SUFFOLK after the decease of his wife's half brother, Henry Brandon (last duke of that family), in 1551, but beheaded and attainted in three years afterwards. The issue of this marriage were
  1 LADY JANE GREY, the amiable but unfortunate aspirant to the crown at the decease of EDWARD VI. She m. Lord Guildford Dudley, but was beheaded 12 February, 1554, leaving no issue.
  2 Lady Katherine Grey, died a prisoner in the Tower, (1567), m. 1st, Henry, Lord Herbert, and 2ndly, Edward Seymour, Earl of Hertford, by the latter of whom she had a son, Edward, Lord Beauchamp, father of two sons, William, Duke of Somerset (husband of Arabella Stuart), and Francis, Lord Seymour, of Trowbridge.
  3 Lady Mary Grey, m. to Martin Keys, groom porter to Queen ELIZABETH, and d. s. p. 1578.
  Her grace m. 2ndly, Adrian Stokes.
II. Eleanor, m. to Henry Clifford, Earl of Cumberland, and left an only dau. and heiress,
MARGARET, m. to Henry Stanley, Earl of Derby.

His grace m. 4thly, Catherine, Baroness Willoughy de Eresby (only dau. and heiress of William, Lord Willoughby), who d. in 1525, by whom he had two sons,

HENRY, his successor.
Charles.

CHARLES BRANDON, DUKE OF SUFFOLK, d. in 1545, and was s. by his elder son,

HENRY BRANDON, 2nd duke, who, with his brother Charles, died in minority, on the same day, 14 July, 1551, at the residence of the bishop of Lincoln at Bugden, in Huntingdonshire, when the DUKEDOM OF SUFFOLK became EXTINCT. The patent of the VISCOUNTY OF L'ISLE was cancelled soon after its creation, owing to the refusal of Elizabeth Grey (only dau. and heiress of John Grey, Viscount L'Isle at whose decease that dignity EXPIRED in the Grey family, in 1512) to fulfil, on coming of age, her marriage contract with his grace, then Charles Brandon, Viscount L'Isle, the said patent being in reversion to his issue by that lady. Miss Grey afterwards m. Henry Courtenay, 2nd Earl of Devonshire, and died issueless.

Arms—Barry of ten, arg. and gu., over all a lion rampant, or, crowned per pale, of the first and second.

NOTE—In the 2nd of ELIZABETH, the extensive possessions of this celebrated Duke of Suffolk were shared amongst the descendants of Sir William Brandon, his grandfather, viz.,

Sir Henry Sydney, Knt., descended from John Sydney and Anna Brandon.
William Cavendish, Esq., from John Cavendish and Elizabeth Brandon.
Thomas Glenham, Esq., from Alianora Brandon.
Francis Kersey, Esq., son of John Kersey, by Margaret Lovell, dau. and heiress of Margaret Brandon, by her husband, Lovell.
Christian Darnell, widow.
Walter Ascough, Esq., and his son, Henry
John Trye, Esq., of Hardwicke.

BRANDON—EARL OF LINCOLN.

(See BRANDON, DUKE OF SUFFOLK.)

BRAOSE—BARON BRAOSE, OF GOWER.

By Writ of Summons, dated 29 December, 1299.

Lineage.

WILLIAM DE BRAOSE came into England with the CONQUEROR, and held at the general survey considerable estates in the counties of Berks, Wilts, Surrey, Dorset, and Sussex. He was *s.* by his son, PHILIP DE BRAOSE, whose son WILLIAM, *m* Berta, dau. of Milo de Gloucester, Earl of Hereford, and co-heir of her brother, William, Earl of Hereford, by whom he acquired Brecknock, with other extensive territorial possessions. He had two sons, WILLIAM and Reginald, and was *s.* by the elder,

WILLIAM DE BRAOSE, who likewise inherited the large estates of his grandmother, and besides possessed the Honour of Braose, in Normandy. This feudal lord was a personage of great power and influence during the reigns of HENRY II. and RICHARD I., from the former of whom he obtained a grant of the "whole kingdom of Limeric, in Ireland," for the service of sixty knight's fees, to be held of the king and his younger son, JOHN For several years after this period he appears to have enjoyed the favour of King JOHN, and his power and possessions were augmented by divers grants from the crown. But in the 10th of the king's reign, when the kingdom laboured under an interdiction, and JOHN deemed it expedient to demand hostages from his barons to ensure their allegiance, should the Pope proceed to the length of absolving them from obedience to the crown, his officers who came upon the mission to the Baron de Braose, were met by Maud his wife, and, peremptorily informed that she would not intrust any of her children to the king, who had so basely murdered his own nephew, Prince ARTHUR. De Braose rebuked her, however, for speaking thus, and said that if he had in any thing offended the king, he was ready to make satisfaction, according to the judgment of the court, and the barons his peers, upon an appointed day, and at any fixed place, without however giving hostages. This answer being communicated to the king, an order was immediately transmitted to seize upon the baron's person, but Braose having notice thereof fled with his family into Ireland. This quarrel between De Braose and King JOHN, is, however, differently related by other authorities. The monk of Lanthony states, that King JOHN disinherited and banished him for his cruelty to the Welsh, in his war with Gwenwynwyn, and that his wife Maud, and William, his son and heir, died prisoners in Corfe Castle. While another writer relates, "that this William de Braose, son of Philip de Braose, Lord of Buelt, held the lands of Brecknock and Went, for the whole time of King HENRY II., RICHARD I., and King JOHN, without any disturbance, until he took to wife the Lady Maud de St. Walerie, who, in revenge of Henry de Hereford, caused divers Welshmen to be murthered in the castle of Bergavenny, as they sat at meat: and that for this, and for some other pickt quarrel, King JOHN banished him and all his out of England. Likewise, that in his exile, Maud his wife, with William, called *Gam,* his son, were taken and put in prison; where she died, the 10th year after her husband fought with Wenwynwyn, and slew three thousand Welch." From these various relations, says Dugdale, it is no easy matter to discover what his demerits were; but what usage he had at last, take here from the credit of these two historians, who lived near that time. "This year, viz. anno 1210," quoth MATTHEW OF WESTMINSTER, "the noble lady Maud, wife of William de Braose, with William, their son and heir, were miserably famished at Windsore, by the command of King JOHN; and William, her husband, escaping from Scorham, put himself into the habit of a beggar, and privately getting beyond sea, died soon after at Paris, where he had burial in the abbey of St. Victor." And Matthew Paris, putting his death in anno 1212 (which differs a little in time), says, "That he fled from Ireland to France, and dying at Ebula, his body was carried to Paris, and there honourably buried in the abbey of St. Victor." "But after these great troubles in his later days," continues Dugdale, "I shall now say something of his pious works. Being by inheritance from his mother, Lord of Bergavenny, he made great grants to the monks of that priory, conditionally, that the abbot and convent of St. Vincenti, in Maine (to which this priory of Bergavenny was a cell) should daily pray for the soul of him, the said William, and the soul of Maud his wife."

This great, but unfortunate personage, had issue by his wife, Maud de St. Walerie.

    I. William, who perished by starvation with his mother, at Windsor. He *m.* Maud, dau. of the Earl of Clare, with whom he had the town of Buckingham, in frank marriage, and left a son,

        JOHN, surnamed *Tadody,* of whom hereafter.

    II. GILES, bishop of Hereford
    III. REGINALD, who *s.* his brother, the bishop, in the representation of the family.
    IV. John (Sir), who is stated to have had from his father the manor of Knylle, or Knill, in the marches of Wales, and thence to have adopted the surname of KNILL, and to have been ancestor of

        JENKIN KNILL, Esq., of Knill, who *m.* Anne, dau. and co-heiress of Sir Richard Devereux, 2nd son of William, Lord Ferrers, K.G., and *d.* in 1508. His grandson,
        FRANCIS KNILL, Esq., of Knill, a justice of the peace for Herefordshire, *temp.* ELIZABETH, *m.* Joane, dau. of Thomas Lewis, Esq., of Harpton Court, in Radnorshire, and dying in 1590, was *s.* by his only son,
        JOHN KNILL, Esq., of Knill, who *d. unm.* in 1609, when his estates devolved upon his sister and heiress,
        BARBARA KNILL, who conveyed them to her husband, John Walsham, Esq., of Presteigne, by whose lineal descendant,
        SIR JOHN WALSHAM, Bart., they are still possessed.

    I. Joane, *m.* to Richard, Lord Percy.
    II. Loretta, *m.* to Robert Fitz-Parnell, Earl of Leicester.
    III. Margaret, *m.* to Walter de Lacy.
    IV. Maud, *m.* to Griffith. Prince of South Wales, living *circa* 1188, son of Rhys ap Griffith, Prince of South Wales, called "the Lord Rhys," and dying in 1202, left, with junior issue, two sons: Rhys ap Griffith, Prince of South Wales, whose only dau. and heiress, Gwellian, *m.* Gilbert de Talbot, ancestor of the Earls of Shrewsbury, and Owen ap Griffith, Prince of South Wales, ancestor of the dynasty of South Wales.

When the contest between King JOHN and the barons broke out, GILES DE BRAOSE, bishop of Hereford, arraying himself under the baronial banner, was put in possession of the .people of Bergavenny and the other castles of the deceased lord; and eventually King JOHN, in the last year of his reign, his wrath being then assuaged, granted part of those lands to the bishop's younger brother and heir,

REGINALD DE BRAOSE, which grant was confirmed by King HENRY III., and he had livery of the castle and honour of Totness, with the honour of Barnstaple, having had previous possession of other estates. He *m.* Græcia, dau. of William de Bruere, and dying in 1221, was *s.* by his son,

WILLIAM DE BRAOSE. This feudal lord fell a victim to the jealousy of LLEWELLYN, Prince of Wales, who suspecting an intimacy between him and the princess, his wife, King HENRY's sister, invited him to an Easter feast, and treacherously cast him into prison at the conclusion of the banquet. He was soon afterwards put to death with the unfortunate princess. He had married Eve, dau. of Walter Mareschal, and sister of Richard, Earl of Pembroke, by whom he had four daus., his co-heirs, viz.,

    I. ISABEL, *m.* 1st, to Prince David, who on the demise of his father, 1240, usurped the crown of North Wales, eldest son (by Joan, his 3rd consort, natural dau. of JOHN, King of England) of LLEWELYN, the Great King of North Wales. David ap Llewelyn *d. s. p.* Isabel his widow *m.* Peter Fitzherbert.
    II. MAUD, *m.* to Roger, Lord Mortimer, of Wigmore.
    III. EVE, *m.* to William de Cantilupe, Lord of Abergavenny, *jure uxoris,* and left a son, and two daus.,

        1 George, who *d. s. p.*
        } Milicent, *m.* 1st, to John de Montalt, and 2ndly, to Eudo le Zouche, ancestor by her of the ZOUCHE, of Haryngworth.
        2 Joan, *m.* to Henry de Hastings.
    IV. Eleanor, *m.* to Humphrey de Bohun (*see* BOHUN, *Earl of Hereford*).

The line of this branch thus terminating in heiresses, we proceed with that founded by the bishop of Hereford's nephew.

    JOHN DE BRAOSE, surnamed *Tadody,* who had been privately nursed by a Welch woman, at Gower. This John had grants of lands from King HENRY III., and was also possessed of the Barony of Brembye, in Sussex, where he died in 1231, by a fall from his horse, his foot sticking in the stirrup. He married, it is stated, Margaret, dau. of LLEWELLYN, Prince of Wales, by whom (who *m.* afterwards Walter de Clifford) he had a son, his successor,

    WILLIAM DE BRAOSE, who in the 41st HENRY III., when Llewellyn ap Griffith menaced the marches of Wales with a great army, was commanded by the king to defend his own marches about Gower, and the next year he had a military summons to attend the king at Chester. In two years afterwards, he was again in arms, under Roger de Mortimer, against the Welsh; and was one of the barons who became pledged for King HENRY, abiding the award of LOUIS, King of France. He *d.* in 1290, leaving by Isabel de Clare, his first wife, a son,

    WILLIAM DE BRAOSE, who in the 22nd of EDWARD I., had summons to attend the king with other great men, to advise regarding the important affairs of the realm. And about the beginning of the ensuing September, was one of those who embarked at Portsmouth, with .horse and arms, in the king's service, for Gascony. In the 28th and 29th of the same reign, he was in the wars of Scotland, and in the latter year he had summons to parliament as a BARON. In the 32nd, he was again in the Scottish wars, and then enjoyed so much favour, that the king not only confirmed to him and his heirs, the grant of Gower Land, made by King JOHN to his ancestor, but granted that he and they should thenceforward enjoy all regal jurisdiction, liberties, and privileges there, in as ample a manner as Gilbert de Clare, son of Richard de Clare, sometime Earl of Gloucester, had in all his lands of Glamorgan. For several years afterwards his lordship appears to have been constantly engaged upon the same theatre of war, and was always eminently distinguished. In the 14th EDWARD II., being, according to Thomas of Walsingham, "a person who had a large patrimony, but a great unthrift," his lordship put up for sale his noble territory of Gower Land, and absolutely sold it under the king's license to the Earl of Hereford; but its contiguity to the lands of the younger SPENCER (who was then high in royal favour, and the king's chamberlain,) attracting the attention of that minion, he forcibly possessed himself of the estate, and thus gave rise to the insurrection headed by Thomas Plantagenet, Earl of Lancaster. Lord Braose m. Aliva, dau. of Thomas de Moulton, and had issue,

ALIVA, m. 1st, to John de Mowbray, and 2ndly, to Sir Richard de Pershall, younger brother of Adam de Pershall, Lord of Pershall, co. Stafford, and had issue by each. Elizabeth, grand-dau. and heiress of Sir Richard de Pershall, m. 1st, Henry Grendom, and 2ndly, Sir Richard Bacon, Knt JOANE, m. to John de Bohun, of Midhurst.

His lordship, who had regular summons to parliament, to 18 September, 1322, d. in that year, when the BARONY OF BRAOSE, OF GOWER, fell into ABEYANCE between his daus. and co-heirs, and it so continues with their representatives.

Arms—Az., semée of cross-crosslets, a lion rampant, or, armed and langued, gu.

BRAOSE—BARONS BRAOSE.

By Writ of Summons, dated 25 February, 1342.

Lineage.

SIR THOMAS DE BRAOSE, Knt., son of Peter, half-brother of William. Lord Braose, of Gower, was found heir to his grandmother, Mary de Ros (his grandfather, William de Braose's 3rd wife), and having distinguished himself in the wars of EDWARD III., was summoned to parliament as a BARON, from 25 February, 1342, to 15 July, 1353. His lordship m. Beatrix, dau. of Roger de Mortimer, and widow of Edward, son of Thomas, of Brotherton, Earl of Norfolk, and Earl Marshal of England, by whom he had issue,

  1 JOHN, his successor.   2 Thomas (Sir).   3 Peter, *s. p.*
  1 Joane, *d. s. p.*
  2 Beatrice, *m.* William Lord Say, and was mother of Elizabeth, Lady Heron.

He d. in 1361, and was s. by his elder son,

JOHN DE BRAOSE, 2nd Baron, who m. Elizabeth, dau. of Edward de Montague, but dying s. p., was s. by his brother,

SIR THOMAS DE BRAOSE, 3rd baron, who d. 1395, leaving by Margaret, his wife, a son, Thomas, and a dau. Joan, who both d. young, when the BARONY OF BRAOSE became EXTINCT, and the estates passed to Elizabeth, wife of Sir William Heron, Knt., the niece, through his sister Beatrice, of the last baron.

Arms—Az., semée of cross-crosslets, a lion rampant, or, armed and langued, gu.

BRAYE—BARONS BRAYE.

By Writ of Summons, dated 3 November, 1529.

Lineage.

The descent of this barony, twice in abeyance but now enjoyed by the heir-general, is still retained in this work as explanatory of the devolution of baronies in fee.

The name of the SIEUR DE BRAY occurs in the roll of Battel Abbey, and although the authenticity of that record has been questioned, in this the statement is confirmed by the fact of WILLIAM DE BRAY being one of the subscribing witnesses to the charter of the year 1080, conferred by the CONQUEROR on the abbey he had founded. The family supplied sheriffs to Northamptonshire, Bedfordshire, Bucks, and some other counties, between 1202 and 1273.

SIR RICHARD BRAY, the descendant and representative of the Norman knight, is said by some to have been of the privy

council to HENRY VI.; by others he is called the king's physician; the former is the more probable, as he was buried in Worcester Cathedral. He had two wives; by the 1st, Margaret, dau. of John Sandes, Esq., of Furnes Felles, in Lancashire, he had an only son, JOHN (Sir), whose only dau. and heir, Margaret, m. Sir William Sandys, Baron Sandys of the Vine; by the 2nd, Joan, Sir Richard had two other sons, viz., SIR REGINALD BRAY, knight-banneret, and K.G., Lord Treasurer *temp.* HENRY VII., and

JOHN BRAY, Esq., who was buried in the chancel of the church at Chelsea, had (with a dau., the wife of Sir John Norris) three sons,

  I. EDMUND (Sir), summoned to parliament as Baron Bray, 21st HENRY VIII., ancestor of the BARONS BRAYE.
  II. EDWARD (Sir), ancestor of the BRAYS OF SHERE, co. Surrey. (*See* BURKE's *Landed Gentry*.)
  III. Reginald, of Barrington, co. Gloucester, ancestor of the BRAYS OF BARRINGTON.

The eldest son,

SIR EDMUND BRAYE, Knt., of Braye, co. Bedford, was summoned to parliament as a BARON, it was alleged, 21st HENRY VIII.; but as neither the original writ issued to him, nor the enrolment thereof, could be found, the fact could not, in the investigation recently before the House of Lords, be *positively* substantiated. The reasoning in support of the allegation, however, and the cases adduced in point were deemed conclusive. Lord Braye m. Jane, dau. and heir of Sir R. Hallighwell, of Holwell, and dying 18 October, 1539, left issue,

  I. JOHN, his heir.
  I. ANNE BRAYE, m. to George Brooke, Lord Cobham. Her grandsons,
    HENRY BROOKE, Lord Cobham, who d. in 1619, *s. p.*, and GEORGE BROOKE, being both attainted of high treason (the latter was executed), and the attainder never having been reversed, the representation of this, the elder co-heir, vested in the crown.
  II. ELIZABETH BRAYE, m. to Sir Ralph Verney, Knt., of Pendley and Middle Claydon, co. Bucks, and had issue, 1 Edward Verney, d. s. p. in 1558; 2 John Verney, d. s. p.; and 3 SIR EDMUND VERNEY, m. 1st, Frances, dau. of John Hastings, Esq., of Ilford, co. Oxford, but by her had no issue. He m. 2ndly, Audrey, dau. of William Gardner, Esq., of Fulmere, Bucks, and widow of Sir Peter Carew, and by that lady had an only child, SIR FRANCIS VERNEY, of Penley, who m. Ursula, dau. and co-heir of William St. Barbe; and *d. s. p.* abroad, having sold the estate. Sir Edmund m. 3rdly Mary, dau. of John Blackney, Esq., of Sparrowham, and widow of Geffrey Turvile, of Leicestershire, and had by her, SIR EDMUND VERNEY, Knt., marshal and standard-bearer to King CHARLES I., killed at the battle of Edge Hill, 23 October, 1642, leaving by Margaret his wife, dau. of Sir Thomas Benton, Knt., a son, SIR RALPH VERNEY, who was created a baronet in 1696, and was *s* by his son, SIR JOHN VERNEY, 2nd baronet, who was created a peer of Ireland, *temp.* ANNE, as Baron Verney and VISCOUNT FERMANAGH. He m. Elizabeth Palmer, of Little Chelsea, and had issue,
    1. RALPH VERNEY, 2nd VISCOUNT FERMANAGH, who was created EARL VERNEY. His lordship's line entirely failed on the death of his grand-dau., Mary Verney, who was created BARONESS FERMANAGH, and d. s. p. in 1810.
     1 ELIZABETH VERNEY, d. unm. in 1767.
    2 MARY VERNEY, m. to Col. John Lovett, of Soulbury, Bucks, and her issue all d. unm.
    3 MARGARET VERNEY. m. Sir Thomas Cave Bart., of Stanford Hall, co. Leicester, and was great-grandmother of SARAH OTWAY-CAVE, late BARONESS BRAYE.
  III. FRIDESWIDE-BRAYE, m. Sir Percival Hart, Knt., of Lullingstone, and from her descended (her representative) SIR PERCIVAL HART-DYKE, Bart., who was one of the co-heirs to the BARONY OF BRAYE.
  IV. MARY BRAYE, m. Sir Robert Peckham. Her descendants are presumed to be EXTINCT.
  V. DOROTHY BRAYE, m. to Edmund, Lord Chandos; and her grand-dau., the HON. CATHERINE CHANDOS, having m. Francis Russell, 4th Earl of Bedford, she is now represented by William, Duke of Bedford.
  VI. FRANCES BRAYE, m. to Thomas Lifield, Esq., of Stoke d'Aubernon, co. Surrey, and had a dau. and heiress,
    JANE LIFIELD, who m. Thomas Vincent, Esq., and from that marriage descends SIR FRANCIS VINCENT, Bart., of Stoke d'Aubernon, who was stated to have been one of the co-heirs of the BARONY OF BRAYE.

Lord Braye was *s.* by his son,

JOHN BRAYE, 2nd baron, summoned to parliament from 3 November, 1545, to 21 October, 1555. This nobleman was a commanding officer in the expedition made into France under the Earl of Hertford, in the 38th of HENRY VIII.; and upon the insurrection in Norfolk, in the 2nd of EDWARD VI., his lordship marched with the Marquess of Northampton for its suppression; and in three years afterwards he was appointed to attend the same nobleman upon his embassy into France, as bearer of the order of the Garter to the French monarch. In the 4th year of MARY, he assisted at the siege of St. Quintins, in Picardy. His lordship m. Anne, dau. of Francis, Earl of Shrewsbury, but dying *s. p.* 19 November, 1557, was buried at Chelsea Church. His estates devolved upon his sisters, and the BARONY OF BRAYE fell into ABEYANCE amongst these ladies, and so continued until 2 October, 1839, when the abeyance was determined in favour of

SARAH OTWAY CAVE, by letters patent, to hold the said dignity to her and the heirs of her body, she being one of the co-heirs of John, Lord Bray, who was the only son of Sir Edmund Braye, summoned to parliament by writ, 21st HENRY VI. Her ladyship m. in 1790, Henry Otway, Esq., of Castle Otway, co. Tipperary, and by him (who *d.* 13 September, 1815,) had issue,

   I. Robert, M.P. for co. Tipperary, m. 19 October, 1838, Sophia, eldest dau. of Sir Francis Burdett, Bart., and *d. s. p.* 30 November, 1844.
   II. Thomas, major in the army, *d. unm.* 19 January, 1831.
   I. Maria, *d. unm.* 13 May, 1879.
   II. Anne, m. 1st, in 1828, to J. A. Arnold, Esq., of Lutterworth, who *d. s. p.* in 1841; and 2ndly, 2 December, 1817, the Rev. Henry Kemp Richardson, rector of Leire, co. Leicester. She *d. s. p.* 22 May, 1871.
   III. Catherine, m. 1st, in 1826, to Henry Murray, Esq., (youngest son of Lord George Murray,) who *d.* 26 November, 1830; and 2ndly, 11 February, 1850, to Earl Beauchamp, who *d.* in 1853. She *d. s. p.* 4 November, 1875.
   IV. Henrietta, m. 24 September, 1844, the Rev. Edgell Wyatt Edgell, rector of North Cray, Kent, and had issue.

Her ladyship *d.* 21 February, 1862, when her barony again fell into ABEYANCE, and so remained until 1879, when it devolved on the youngest and last surviving co-heiress, HENRIETTA, late BARONESS BRAYE (*see* BURKE'S *Extant Peerage*).

Arms—Arg., a chev., between three eagles' legs, erased à la quisé, sa.

BRERETON—BARON BRERETON.

By Letters Patent, dated 11 May, 1624.

Lineage.

RALPH DE BRERETON (son of William de Brereton, and grandson of William de Brereton,) was father (besides a 2nd son, Gilbert, and a dau., Isolda, wife of Gilbert de Stoke,) of an elder son and heir,

SIR WILLIAM BRERETON, of Brereton, Knt., living *temp.* JOHN and HENRY III., who m. Margery, dau. of Randle of Thornton, and had a son, RALPH, and a dau., wife of Thurstan de Smethwick. The former

SIR RALPH BRERETON, of Brereton, Knt., had two sons, WILLIAM (SIR), and Gilbert, father of Henry and Sibella, wife of William de Bouths. The elder son,

SIR WILLIAM BRERETON, of Brereton, Knt., m. the dau. of his guardian, Sir Richard de Sandbach, Knt., and was father of

SIR WILLIAM BRERETON, of Brereton, Knt., who m. Roesia, dau. of Ralph de Vernon, and had issue,

   I. WILLIAM, m. Margery, dau. of Richard de Coaley, and *d.* in his father's lifetime, leaving issue,
      1 WILLIAM (SIR), of whom presently.
      2 John.   3 Ralph, in holy orders.
      4 Robert.   5 Hugh.
      1 Margaret, wife of Henry, brother of Sir John Delves.
      2 Jane, wife of Adam de Bostock.
   II. John, in holy orders
   III. Peter   IV. Richard.
   V. Nicholas, who by Margaret his wife, had two sons, John and William.
   I. Margery, wife of John Davenport, of Davenport.
   II. Matilda, wife of John Dunville.

Sir William was *s.* by his grandson,

SIR WILLIAM BRERETON, of Brereton, living 49th EDWARD III., who m. 1st, Ellen, dau. of Philip, and sister and finally heiress of David Egerton, of Egerton, and by her had a son and successor,

WILLIAM.

He m. 2ndly, Margaret, dau. of — Done, of Utkinton, and widow of John Davenport, and by her had a son and two daus.,

   Randle, who m. Alicia, dau. and heir of William de Ipstones, and was ancestor of the BRERETONS OF MALPAS HALL AND SHOCKLACH, from whom the BRERETONS OF BRINTON, co. Norfolk, deduce their descent.
   Elizabeth, wife of William Cholmondeley.
   Another dau., wife of Spurstow, of Spurstow.

The eldest son,

SIR WILLIAM BRERETON, of Brereton, m. 1st, in 1386, Ang Ha dau. of Hugh Venables, and by her had issue,

   I. WILLIAM. *d.* before his father, having m. Alice, sister and heiress o Richard Corbett, of Leighton, and by her (who m. 2ndly, John Stretley, Esq.,) had issue,
      1 WILLIAM (SIR), successor to his grandfather,
      2 Ralph.
      1 Alice, wife of Peter Corbett, of Leighton.
      2 Johanna, wife of Robert Aston, of Parkhall, co. Stafford
   II. Hugh.   III. Matthew.
   I. Elizabeth, wife of Sir John Savage.
   II. Margery, wife of Richard Patten, *alias* Wanflet, of Wanflet.

Sir William m. 2ndly, Elena, dau. of Sir William Massy, of Tatton, Knt., and by her, who m. 2ndly, Sir Gilbert Halsall, Knt., had a son,

Thomas, in holy orders, rector of Brereton, 1433.

Sir William *d.* 4th HENRY VI., and was *s.* by his grandson.

SIR WILLIAM BRERETON, of Brereton, Knt., who m. Philippa, dau. of Sir Hugh, and sister of Thomas Hulse, and had issue,

   I. WILLIAM, m. Katherine, dau. of Sir John Byron. and *d. s. p.*
   II. ANDREW (SIR , of whom presently.
   III. John (Sir), m. 1st, Katherine, dau. of Maurice Berkeley, of Beverston, and relict of John, Lord Stourton, and by her had a dau. and heiress,
      Werburga, m. 1st, to Sir Francis Cheney; and 2ndly, to Sir William Compton.
   Sir John m. 2ndly, Jane, dau. and heiress of Geoffrey Massy, of Tatton, and relict of Sir William Stanley, and by her had a son,
      Philip, who *d. s. p.*
   IV. Robert.   V. Roger.
   VI. Henry.   VII. Matthew.
   VIII. Hugh, of Wimbersley. m. Anne, dau. of Robert Done.
   I. Elizabeth, wife of John Radcliffe, of Ordeshall.
   II. Jane, wife of Cotton, of Rudware.
   III. Eleanor, m. 1st, Thomas Bulkeley, of Eyton. and 2ndly, to Hugh Cholmondeley.
   IV. Matilda, wife of Thomas Needham, of Shavington.

The eldest surviving son,

SIR ANDREW BRERETON, of Brereton, Knt., m. Agnes, dau. of Robert Legh, of Adlington, and had issue,

   I. WILLIAM (SIR), his heir.
   II. John, of Leek, co. Stafford.
   III. Andrew.   IV. Matthew.
   I. Ellen, wife of John Fitton, of Gawsworth.
   II. Alice, wife of William Moreton, of Little Moreton.
   III. Elizabeth, m. 1st, to Philip Legh, of Boothes; and 2ndly, to John Carington, of Carington.
   IV. Catherine, m. to Thomas Smith, of Hagh.
   V. Matilda, m. to John Davenport, of Davenport.
   VI. Johanna. m. to Lawrence Dutton, of Marshe, brother and heir of Sir Thomas Dutton, of Dutton.

The eldest son and heir,

SIR WILLIAM BRERETON, of Brereton, Knt., chief justice and lord high marshal of Ireland, m. 1st, Alice, dau. of Sir John Savage, Knt., of Clifton, and by her had a son,

   I. WILLIAM, who m. Anne, dau. of Sir William Booth, of Dunham, and predeceasing his father, left issue,
      1 WILLIAM (SIR), successor to his grandfather.
      2 Andrew. m. Catherine, dau. of Sir Andrew FitzSimon, of Dublin, Knt., and had issue.
      3 Robert.   4 Arthur   5 John.
      6 Edward, m Edith, dau. of William Birche, of Birche, co. Lancaster, and had issue,
         HENRY BRERETON, ancestor it is believed, of the BRERETONS OF QUEEN'S Co. (*see* LANDED GENTRY).
      1 Ellen. m. 1st, to John Carenton; and 2ndly, to Lawrence Winington, of Hermitage.
      2 Jane, wife of Richard Clyve, Esq., of Huxley.
      3 Margaret.

The chief justice m. 2ndly, Eleanor, dau. of Sir Ralph Brereton, of Ipstones, co. Stafford, and widow of — Egerton, and by her had issue,

   I. John, a captain in Ireland.
   II. Ralph, m. Thomasine, dau. and heiress of George Ashley, of Ashley, and had issue.
   III. Henry.
   I. Margaret, m. 1st, to William Goodman, and 2ndly, to William Mostyn.
   II. Katherine, m. 1st, to Edward Fulleshurst, and 2ndly, to Roger Brereton.
   III. Elen, wife of Robert Dokenfeld, of Dokenfeld.
   IV. Anne. wife of David Kynaston, of Hanney.
   V. Mary, wife of Sir John Warburton, of Arley.

Sir William, who was buried at Kilkenny, in Ireland, 4 February, 1541, was *s.* by his grandson,

SIR WILLIAM BRERETON, Knt., of Brereton, who m. Jane,

eldest dau. of Sir Peter Warburton, by Elizabeth Wynynton, his wife, and by her (who *m.* 2ndly, Sir Lawrence Smith, of Hough', had issue,

  I. WILLIAM (SIR), his heir.
  I. Mary.
  II. Elizabeth, wife of Thomas Venables, Esq., of Kenderton, and *d.* June, 1591.
  III. Jane, *m.* to John Legh, Esq., of Boothes.
  IV. Anne, *m.* to Sir Thomas Smith, mayor of Chester, 1596, sheriff of the county in 1600.
  V. Susanna.

Sir William, who was buried at Brereton, 4 September, 1559, was *s.* by his son,

SIR WILLIAM BRERETON, of Brereton, Knt., *bapt.* 6 February, 1550, who built the Hall of Brereton in 1586, and was created Baron Brereton, of Leighlin, co. Carlow, 11 May, 1624. His lordship *m.* Margaret, dau. of Sir John Savage, Knt., by Elizabeth his wife, dau. of the Earl of Rutland, and by her (who *d.* 7 April, 1597,) had issue, besides other children, who *d.* young,

  I. John (Sir), of Brereton, *b.* 25 March, 1591. *m.* Anne, dau. of Sir Edward Fitton, of Gawsworth, in the lifetime of his father, left by her (who *m.* 2ndly, Sir Gilbert Gerard, Knt.,) three sons and two daus., viz.,
    1 WILLIAM, successor to his grandfather as 2nd baron.
    2 John, *b.* 1624, *d.* 22 October, 1656.
    3 Edward.
    1 Mary, wife of Sir Michael Hutchinson.
    2 JANE (eventual heiress of the family), *m.* about 1646, to Sir Robert Holte, Bart., and *d.* 1648, leaving a son,
      SIR CHARLES HOLTE, Bart., who *m.* Anne, eldest dau. and co-heiress of Sir John Cloberry, of Bradstone, co. Devon, and had with other issue, a son and successor,
      SIR CLOBERRY HOLTE, Bart., who *m.* Barbara, dau. and heir of Thomas Lister, of Whitfield, co. Northampton, and left two sons,
      SIR LISTER HOLTE, Bart., who *m.* twice, but *d. s. p.*
      Sir Charles Holte, Bart., *s.* his brother. He *m.* Anne, dau. of Pudsey Jesson, Esq., of Langley, co. Warwick, and *d.* 12 March, 1782, leaving an only dau. and heiress,
        MARY ELIZABETH, who *m.* 12 September, 1775, ABRAHAM BRACEBRIDGE, Esq., of Atherstone, co. Warwick, and was mother of
        CHARLES HOLTE BRACEBRIDGE, Esq., of Atherstone Hall, co. Warwick.
  I. Mary, *m.* 13 July, 1608, to Henry, Lord Inchiquin.

Lord Brereton *d.* in 1631, and was *s.* by his grandson,

WILLIAM BRERETON, 2nd Lord Brereton, *b.* 28 February, 1611, who *m.* Elizabeth, dau. of George, Lord Goring, Earl of Norwich, and by her (who *d.* in 1687) had, with other issue, a son, WILLIAM, his successor. His lordship *d.* in 1664, and was *s.* by his eldest son,

WILLIAM BRERETON, 3rd Lord Brereton, *b.* 4 May, 1631, who was distinguished as a man of letters, and was one of the founders of the Royal Society. He *m.* Frances, dau. of Francis, Lord Willoughby, of Parham; and dying in 1679, left a son and successor,

JOHN BRERETON, 4th Lord Brereton, who *m.* Mary, dau. of Sir Thomas Tipping; but *d. s. p.* in 1718, and was *s.* by his brother,

FRANCIS BRERETON, 5th Lord Brereton; at whose decease, *unm.*, in 1722, the title became EXTINCT.

Arms—Arg., two bars, sa.

BRIDGES—BARON FITZWALTER.

By Letters Patent, dated 17 April, 1868.

(*See* BURKE's *Extant Peerage and Baronetage*, BRIDGES, B.)

BROMFLETE—BARON OF VESCY.

By Writ of Summons, dated 24 January, 1449.

Lineage.

In the 11th year of RICHARD II.,

THOMAS DE BROMFLETE obtained a charter of free warren in all his demesne lands in the co. of York, and marrying in two years afterwards, Margaret, dau. and heiress of Sir Edward St John, Knt., by Anastasia his wife, dau. and co-heir of William de Aton, Lord of Vescy, had livery of the lands of her inheritance. In the 19th of the same reign he was constituted the king's chief butler, and received the honour of knighthood. He *d.* in the 9th of HENRY VI. (1430-1), and was *s.* by his only surviving son,

SIR HENRY DE BROMFLETE, Knt., who had then livery of his lands. In the 12th of HENRY VI., Sir Henry was sent ambassador to the great council holden at Basil, in Germany; having license to take with him, in gold, silver, jewels, and plate, to the value of £2,000 sterling, and an assignation of £300 for every half year he should be detained upon the mission, beyond the first six months. In the 27th of the same reign, he was summoned to parliament by special writ, dated 24th January (1449), as "HENRICO BROMFLETE DE VESCI, CHEVALIER," in remainder to the heirs *male* of his body, being the *first* and *only* writ with *such a limitation*. His lordship had afterwards a specific dispensation from the duty of attending parliament, in consideration of his eminent services to King HENRY V., in that monarch's wars of France and Normandy, for which he had never received any remuneration, and in consideration, likewise, of his advanced age. Lord Vesey *d.* 6 Jan., 1468, without male issue, when the BARONY EXPIRED, according to the terms of the writ. A portion of his lordship's estates were devoted, by his will, to religious purposes, while the remainder devolved upon his only dau. (by Eleanor his wife, dau. of William, Lord Fitzhugh),

MARGARET DE BROMFLETE, who *m.* 1st, John Clifford, Lord Clifford, who fell at the battle of Towton, in the 1st of Henry IV. (*See* CLIFFORD, Lords Clifford). And 2ndly, Sir Lancelot Threlkeld, Knt., by whom she had a son, Sir LANCELOT THRELKELD, father of three daus., viz.,
  GRACE, *m.* to Thomas Dudley.
  A dau., *m.* to James Pickering.
  Winifred, *m.* to William Pickering, brother of James.

Henry Bromflete, Lord Vesey, was summoned to parliament, altogether, from 24 January, 1449, to 28 February, 1466.

Arms—Sa., a bend florée counter-florée, or

BROMLEY, BARONS MONTFORT.

By Letters Patent, dated 9 May, 1741.

Lineage.

SIR WALTER BROMLEGHE, of Bromleghe, co. Stafford, living in the reign of King John, *m.* Alice, eldest sister and one of the heirs of Roger de Burwardeslegh, son of Warin de Burwardeslegh, lord of the manor of Estelegh, co. Stafford, and had issue,

GALFRIDUS DE BROMLEGHE, who was found to be the heir to John, son of John de Ipstone, in 21st EDWARD I. He *d.* 1st EDWARD I, and left two sons, RICHARD, of whom presently, and Robert, who was knighted, and had the estate of Asteley. he *d.* 1st EDWARD II., leaving a son, John, of Asteley, who dying 1332, left John, his son and heir, who *d.* 23rd EDWARD III, leaving a dau. and heir, Alice, wife of John de Frodesham, of Frodesham. The elder son of Galfridus,

RICHARD DE BROMLEGH, inherited the estate of Bromlegh, and was father of

RANULPH DE BROMLEGH, who *m.* and had issue,

  I. RICHARD DE BROMLEGH, who, by Agnes his wife, was father of John Bromley.
  II. Walter.
  III. Roger (Sir), *d. s. p.* 13th EDWARD III.
  IV. John, of Badynton, who, by his wife Joan, had issue,
    1 Walter, left a dau. and heir,
    Lettice, *m.* to John Cholmondeley, of Chorley.
    2 William, of Badinton, *m.* Annabella, sister and heir of William de Chettleton, son of Henry, son of Robert (called Shirrard), son of William de Chettleton, by which marriage he had two sons,
      JOHN, of whom presently.
      Richard, *m.* Anne, dau. and co-heir of William Praers, of Badeleighe, in Cheshire, by Letitia his wife, one of the heirs of William Wittenhall, of Cholmeston, in the said county, by whom he had John, his son and heir, who *m.* Margery, dau. of Sir Thomas Massey, of Tatton, also in Cheshire, Knt., by whom he had issue, Thomas, Edward, Ralph, who all *d. s. p.*, and William, who *m.* Margaret, dau. and heir of Ralph Manwaring, of Badeleighe, and left issue, Sir John de Bromley, Knt., who *d.* 3rd HENRY VII., leaving by Joan his wife, dau. and heir of William Hexstall, three daus., his co-heirs.

JOHN DE BROMLEY (son and heir of William, by Annabella de Chettleton), *m.* Agnes, dau. of John Trentham, and left issue by her,

WALTER DE BROMLEY, who *m.* Joan, dau. of Richard de Delves, by whom he had a son,

ROGER BROMLEY, who was of Mitley, in right of Jane, his

wife, dau and heir of Richard de Mitley, of the co. Salop; they had two sons,

> ROGER, of whom presently.
> Nicholas, whose posterity was of Hampton-Norbury, in Cheshire.

The elder son,

ROGER BROMLEY, was father, by his wife, the dau. of David Broe, of Malpas, in Cheshire, of four sons,

> WILLIAM, of whom presently.
> John, who left a dau., Anne, who d. s p.
> Roger. m. Jane. dau. of Thomas Jennings, and had issue.
> William Bromley, of Stoke, and THOMAS BROMLEY, 2nd son, who was constituted LORD CHIEF JUSTICE of England in the 1st year of Queen MARY; he left issue, Margaret, his dau. and heir, wife of Sir Richard Newport, Knt., who by her was ancestor of the Earls of Bradford.
> Humfry, living 7th HENRY VII.

The eldest son,

WILLIAM BROMLEY, Esq., of Mitley, m. Beatrice, dau. of Humphrey Hill, of Blore and Buntingdale, and by her had issue, a son, GEORGE, of whom we treat; and three daus., Elizabeth. wife of Rowland Jenens; Joan, m. to Richard Sandford; and Dorothy, m. to William Leighton. The son and heir,

GEORGE BROMLEY, seated at Hodnet, in Shropshire, m. Elizabeth, dau. of Sir Thomas Lacon, of Witley, and had issue,

> GEORGE (Sir). appointed justice of Chester, 1581, his dau. Mary was m. to GEORGE COTTON, Esq., ancestor to the Cottons of Cumbermere.
> THOMAS, of whom presently.

The 2nd son,

SIR THOMAS BROMLEY, Knt., was one of the most eminent lawyers of his day, appointed solicitor-general 11th ELIZABETH; treasurer of the Inner Temple, 16th ELIZABETH; and constituted LORD HIGH CHANCELLOR, 21st ELIZABETH. This learned person m. Elizabeth, dau. of Sir Adrian Fortescue, K.B., and dying in 1587 (was buried in Westminster Abbey), left issue,

> I. HENRY, of whom presently.
> II. Thomas.
> III. Gerard, m. Elizabeth, dau. of Thomas Darell, and left two sons, Thomas and Alexander.
> IV. Edward.
> I. Anne, m. to Richard Corbet, of Stoke, in Shropshire.
> II. Muriel, m. to John Littleton, of Frankley.
> III. Jane, m. to Edward Grevill, of Milcot, co. Warwick.
> IV. Elizabeth, m. to Sir Oliver Cromwell, of Hinchinbroke Castle, Huntingdonshire, K.B., uncle to the Lord Protector.

The eldest son,

SIR HENRY BROMLEY, who received the honour of knighthood from Queen ELIZABETH in 1592, and was returned to parliament in the same year by the co. of Worcester. He m. 1st, Elizabeth, dau. of Sir William Pelham, Knt., and had (with four daus., Elizabeth, m. 6 October, 1604, to Thomas Scriven, Esq., of Frodesley, co. Salop; Eleanor; Mary, bapt. 5 September, 1588, m. to John Prynne, Esq.; and Catherine, who d. young), a son, THOMAS. He m. 2ndly, Elizabeth, dau. of Hugh Verney, of Somersetshire, and by her (who was buried at Holt, 17 March, 1592), had a son, John. Sir Henry m. 3rdly, Anne, dau. of Mr. Alderman Beswick, alderman of London, and by her (who was m. 10 February, 1622, to Dr. John Thornborough, bishop of Worcester, and was buried at Holt, 2 January, 1628,) had three more sons, Henry, bapt. at Holt, 9 May, 1596; Philip, bapt. 4 February, 1598; and Robert, b. 20 April, 1600, buried 14 August, 1604. He d. 15 May, 1615, and was s. by his eldest son,

SIR HENRY BROMLEY, of Holt Castle, who m. Anne, dau. and co-heir of Sir Richard Welshe, Knt., of Sheldsley Welshe, in Worcestershire, and dying in 1541, left (with two daus., Muriel, m. to — Bastard, and Joyce, m. to William Cotton, of Bellaport, in Shropshire, Esq.,) two sons, HENRY, his heir; and John, of the College of Worcester, who m. Elizabeth, dau. of Sir Henry Longueville, of Wolverton, Bucks, Knt., father of Edward Longueville, created a baronet of Nova Scotia by CHARLES I. in 1638. The elder son,

HENRY BROMLEY, Esq., of Holt Castle, m. 10 January, 1627, Beatrice, dau. of Sir Richard Newport, of High Ercol, co. Salop, and dying in 1652, left issue,

> I. Thomas, } d. infants.
> II. John, }
> III. HENRY, his heir.
> IV. Francis, b. 5 January, 1643, m. Anne, dau. of Joseph Walsh, Esq., of Abberley, co. Worcester, and had issue.
>> 1 William, of Abberley, who m. 1st, Elizabeth, dau. of John Holloway, Esq., of Oxford, son of Judge Holloway, by whom he had a son, William, who d. young; and 2ndly, Sarah, dau. and co-heir of William Paunceforte, Esq., of Careswell, co. Gloucester, by whom he had Henry and

Thomas, who d. unm.; and Robert of Abberley, who d 10 March, 1803.
> 2 Henry, d. 1698, æt. five.
> 1 Margaret.
> 2 Anne.   3 Elizabeth.
> 4 Octavia, d. 1713, æt. nine.
> 5 Catherine, d. 1714, æt. fifteen.
> I. Diana, b. 16 December, 1646.

The 3rd son,

HENRY BROMLEY, Esq., of Holt Castle, M.P. for the co. of Worcester, who m. Mercy, dau. of Edward Pytts, Esq., of Keyer, in the same shire, and d. 30 September, 1670, having had two sons, Henry, buried at Holt, 6 May, 1658, and WILLIAM, his successor.

WILLIAM BROMLEY, Esq., M.P for the co of Worcester, b. 26 June, 1656. This gentleman m. Margaret, dau. of Sir Rowland Berkeley, of Cotheridge, in Worcestershire, and had two daus., his co-heirs, viz.,

> MERCY, of whom presently.
> Dorothy. m. to John Jennings, Esq., of Hayes, co. Middlesex, and d. s. p.

The eldest dau.,

MERCY BROMLEY, who, on the decease of her sister, became sole heir, m. 10 August, 1704, John Bromley, Esq., eldest son and heir of John Bromley, Esq., of Horseheath Hall, co. Cambridge, and by her (who d. 29 August, 1705,) left at his decease, in 1718, an only son,

HENRY BROMLEY. Esq., of Horseheath Hall and Holt Castle, b. 20 August, 1705, who represented the co of Cambridge in parliament from 1727, until elevated to the peerage by letters patent, dated 9 May, 1741, as LORD MONTFORT, BARON OF HORSEHEATH, in that shire. His lordship m. Frances, dau. of Thomas Wyndham, Esq., and sister and sole heir of Sir Francis Wyndham, Bart., of Trent, co. Somerset, by whom (who d. in 1733,) he had

> THOMAS, his successor.
> FRANCES, m. 28 May. 1747, to Charles Sloane, 1st Earl of Cadogan, and d in 1768.

The baron d. 1 January, 1755, and was s. by his son,

THOMAS, 2nd baron, b. in 1732. This nobleman m. 29 February, 1772, Mary-Anne, dau. of Patrick Blake, Esq., and sister of Sir Patrick Blake, Bart., of Langham, co. Suffolk, by whom he had an only son, HENRY, his heir. His lordship (who sold Horseheath,) d. 24 October, 1799, and was s. by his son,

HENRY BROMLEY, 3rd Lord Montfort, D.L., Baron of Horseheath, co. Cambridge; b. 14 May, 1773, who m. 1st, 5 September, 1793, Miss Elizabeth Watts, but by her (who d. 10 December, 1847,) had no issue; and 2ndly, 23 December, 1847, Anne, dau. of the late William Burgham, Esq., of Upton Bishop, co. Hereford, by whom he had no child. His lordship d. 30 April, 1851, when the BARONY OF MONTFORT became EXTINCT.

Arms — Quarterly: per pale dovetail, gu. and or.

BROOKE—BARONS COBHAM.

By Writ of Summons, dated 8 January, 1313.

Lineage.

This ancient barony came into the family of Brooke with Joane, only dau. and heiress of Sir Reginald Braybroke, and his wife, Joane de la Pole, grand-dau. and heiress of John Cobham, 2nd and last Lord Cobham of that family (see COBHAM, Barons Cobham), which

JOANE BRAYBROKE, m. SIR THOMAS BROKE, Knt., and had issue,

EDWARD, of whom we treat.
Reginald, of Aspall, co. Suffolk, from whom derived, 9th in descent,

> FRANCIS BROOKE, Esq., of Woodbridge, father, by Anne his wife, dau. and heiress of Samuel Thompson, Esq., of Ufford, Place, co. Suffolk, of the REV. CHARLES BROOKE, of Ufford Place, whose only child was FRANCIS CAPPER BROOKE, Esq., of Ufford Place.

The eldest son,

SIR EDWARD BROOKE, Knt., summoned to parliament as "EDWARD BROOKE DE COBHAM, CHEVALIER," from 13 January, 1445, to 30 July, 1460. (The Barony of Cobham had lain dormant from the execution of Sir John Oldcastle, Lord Cobham, until the issue of the first of these summonses.) His lordship was a zealous supporter of the house of York, under whose banner he participated in the victory of St. Albans, in the

83rd of HENRY VI., and commanded the left wing of the Yorkshiremen at Northampton, He *m.* Elizabeth, dau. of James, Lord Audley, and dying in 1464, was *s.* by his son,

JOHN BROOKE, who was summoned to parliament as LORD COBHAM, from 19 August, 1472, to 16 January, 1497. This nobleman distinguished himself in arms in the reigns of EDWARD IV. and HENRY VII. His lordship *m.* Margaret, dau. of Edward Nevil, Lord Abergavenny, and dying in 1506, was *s.* by his son,

THOMAS BROOKE, summoned to parliament from 17 October, 1509, to 12 November, 1515. His lordship attended King HENRY VIII. into France at the taking of Tournay. He *m.* thrice, but had issue only by his 1st wife, Dorothy, dau of Sir Henry Heyden, and dying in 1529, was succeeded by his eldest son,

GEORGE BROOKE, summoned to parliament, from 8 November, 1529, to 20 January, 1558. Upon the dissolution of the greater monasteries in the reign of HENRY VIII., this nobleman obtained a grant in fee of the manor of Chattingdon in Kent; as also of the college of Cobham, and in the 5th of EDWARD VI., on some apprehension of danger from the French, he was constituted lieutenant-general of those forces which were sent into the north for the purpose of fortifying some havens there. At the accession of Queen MARY he was committed to the Tower on suspicion of being implicated in the treason of Sir Thomas Wyat, but was soon afterwards liberated. His lordship *m.* Anne, dau. of Edmund, Lord Bray, and had issue, WILLIAM, his successor, with seven other sons, the 5th of whom, HENRY, was father of JOHN BROOKE, of Hekington, created BARON COBHAM, in 1645, and two daus., viz.,

Elizabeth, *m.* to William Parr, Marquess of Northampton (his lordship's 2nd wife).
Katherine, *m.* to John Jerningham, Esq.

Lord Cobham, who was a knight of the Garter, *d.* at Cobham Hall, on 29 September, 1558, and was *s.* by his eldest son,

WILLIAM BROOKE, summoned to parliament, from 1558, to 1593. This nobleman being lord warden of the Cinque Ports at the death of Quee:. MARY, was deputed to announce to the Spaniards, in the Netherlands, the accession of ELIZABETH, and to acquaint them that her majesty had added to the commission appointed to negotiate a peace at Cambray, William, Lord Howard, of Effingham. In the 14th of ELIZABETH (1571-2), his lordship being one of those committed to the Tower of London for participating in the designs of the Duke of Norfolk, regarding that nobleman's marriage with MARY, Queen of Scots, made a discovery of all he knew of the affair, in the hope of obtaining his own pardon. The baron was subsequently employed upon two occasions to treat of peace with France. He was afterwards constable of Dover Castle, and warden of the Cinque Ports, lord chamberlain of the household, and a knight of the Garter. His lordship *m.* 1st, Dorothy, dau. of George, Lord Abergavenny, by Mary, dau. of Edward, Duke of Buckingham, by whom he had an only dau.,

Frances, *m* 1st, to Thomas Coppinger, Esq., of Kent, and 2ndly, to Edmund Beecher, Esq. Francis Coppinger. Esq., the 2nd son of the marriage of Frances Brooke with Thomas Coppinger, *m.* the Hon. Frances Burgh. and their great-great-grandson, FYSH COPPINGER, Esq., of West Drayton, co. Middlesex, assumed in 1790, the surname and arms of DE BURGH.

Lord Cobham *m.* 2ndly, Frances, dau. of Sir John Newton, and by her (who *d.* 1592) had issue,

I Maximilian, who *d.* before his father, *s. p.*
II. HENRY, successor to the title.
III. George, attainted and executed as a participator in "Raleigh's Conspiracy," 5 December, 1603. He left issue, by his wife Elizabeth, dau. of Thomas, Lord Borough,

WILLIAM. K.B., restored in blood, *m.* 1st, Pembroke, dau. of Henry Lennard, Lord Dacre, by Crisagon his wife. and by her had a dau. Pembroke. *m.* to Mathew Tomlinson, and had two daus., Jane, *m.* to Philip Owen, and *d. s. p.* 1703, and Elizabeth. who *d. unm.* 1692. He *m.* 2ndly, Penelope, dau. of Sir Moyses Hill, Knt., and left three daus.,* viz.,

1 HILL, *m.* to Sir William Boothby. Knt., of Broadlow Ash. co. Derby: the heir-general of this marriage is ARCHDEACON THOMAS THORP.
2 MARGARET, 2nd wife of Sir John Denham, the poet, K.B., sometime governor of Fareham Castle, the "Majestic Denham," of Pope. They both figure in Grammont's Memoirs. She *d. s. p.* 1605.
3 Frances, *m.* 1st, to Sir Thomas Whitmore, of Bridgenorth, K.B.; and 2ndly, to Matthew Harvey of Twickenham.

IV. William (Sir), killed in 1597.
I. Elizabeth, *m.* to Robert, Earl of Salisbury.
II. Frances, *m.* 1st, to John, Lord Stourton, *s. p.*, and 2ndly, to Sir Edward Moore.
III. Margaret, *m.* to Sir Thomas Sondes, Knt., and had,

FRANCES, *m.* to Sir John Leveson, Knt., and left issue,
SIR RICHARD LEVESON, K.B., of Trentham, co. Stafford, *m.* Lady Catherine Dudley, but *d. s. p.*
SIR JOHN LEVESON, Knt., of Haling, Kent, and Lilleshul, co. Salop, who had two daus. his co-heirs, viz.,

FRANCES, *m.* to Sir Thomas Gower, Bart., of Stittenham, ancestor of the DUKES OF SUTHERLAND
CHRISTIANA, *m.* to Sir Peter Temple, of Stowe, Bucks, whose grandson, Sir Richard Temple, was created in 1714, Baron Cobham, and in 1718, Viscount and Baron Cobham. (*See* TEMPLE, Lord Cobham, under the head of BUCKINGHAM, in BURKE'S *Peerage and Baronetage*).

His lordship *d.* in 1596, and was *s.* by his eldest son,

HENRY BROOKE, summoned to parliament on 24 October, 1597. This nobleman was constituted by Queen ELIZABETH warden of the Cinque Ports ; but in the reign of King JAMES, being arraigned with his brother George for participation in the alleged treason of Sir Walter Raleigh, they were found guilty and condemned to death, but George Brooke alone suffered. His lordship was reprieved, yet nevertheless attainted and left to drag on in misery, and the most wretched poverty, the remainder of an unhappy life in imprisonment, wherein he died 24 January, 1618. His wife was Frances, dau. of Charles Howard, Earl of Nottingham, but he had no issue. Under the attainder of this unfortunate nobleman the ancient BARONY OF COBHAM EXPIRED, although his nephew and heir, William Cobham (son of the beheaded and attainted George), was restored in blood in 1610, but "not to enjoy the title of Lord Cobham without the king's especial grace," which was never conferred upon him.* Cobham Hall. Lord Cobham's fine seat near Gravesend. was granted by King JAMES I. to James Stewart, Duke of Richmond, and has descended to his grace's heir-general, the EARL OF DARNLEY.

Arms—Gu., on a chev., arg., a lion rampant, sa., crowned, or.

BROOKE—BARON COBHAM.

By Letters Patent, dated 3 January, 1645.

Lineage.

SIR JOHN BROOKE OF HEKINGTON (son of the Honourable Henry Brooke, 5th son of George, 4th Lord Cobham of that family), having eminently distinguished himself in the cause of King CHARLES I., was elevated to the peerage 3 January, 1645, as LORD COBHAM, "to enjoy that title in as ample a manner as any of his ancestors had done," save that the remaindership was limited to heirs male of his body, a new barony being thus created. His lordship *d.* in 1651, *s. p.*, when the barony EXPIRED.

Arms—Gu., a chev., arg., a lion rampant, sa., crowned, or.

---

* The plot in which Henry, Lord Cobham, and his brother the Honourable George Brooke were involved, is known as the "Raleigh Conspiracy," and amongst the principal actors were the Lord Grey, of Wilton, Sir George Carew, and other persons of eminence. Lord Cobham appears to have been not many degrees removed from a fool, but enjoying the favour of the queen, he was a fitting tool in the hands of his more wily associates. Upon his trial he was dastardly to the most abject meanness.
The mode of bringing the prisoners on the scaffold, and aggravating their sufferings, with momentary expectation of their catastrophe, before the pre-intended pardon was produced. was a piece of management and contrivance for which King JAMES was by the sycophants of the court very highly extolled, but such a course was universally esteemed the pitiful policy of a week contemptible mind.
On this occasion, however, says Sir Dudley Carleton, Cobham, who was now "to play his part," did much cozin the world, for he came to the scaffold with good assurance and contempt of death. And in the short prayers he made, so outprayed the company which helped to pray with him, that a stander-by observed, "that he had a good mouth in a cry, but was nothing single."

---

* To these ladies notwithstanding the attainder, the king granted the precedency of a baron's daus.

BROTHERTON—EARL OF NORFOLK.

(*See* PLANTAGENET, Earl of Norfolk.)

BROUNCKER—VISCOUNT BROUNCKER.

By Letters Patent, dated 12 September, 1645.

Lineage.

The family of Brouncker, or Brunker, was early seated in the co. of Wilts. In 1544, HENRY BRUNKER, Esq., of Melksham and Erlestoke, M.P. for Devizes (son of Robert Brunker de Melksham), added to his estates in that county, about which time the town of Melksham was called Melksham-Brunker, as appears by old title deeds.

This Henry Brunker (or Brounker, as sometimes spelt,) had two wives. By his 2nd wife he had two sons, Sir WILLIAM and Sir HENRY BROUNCKER, Knights. The elder SIR WILLIAM BROUNCKER, m. Maria, dau. of Sir Walter Mildmay, from which alliance descended the Erlestoke branch of the family, terminating in co-heiresses, 1707. The younger son,

SIR HENRY BROUNCKER, Knt., lord president of Munster, d. 3 June, 1607, and was buried in St. Mary's, in Cork, leaving by Anne his wife, dau. of Parker, Lord Morley, with three daus., three sons,

WILLIAM, his heir.
Edward, of Wadham College, who d. s. p.
Henry, from whom FRANCIS BROUNCKER, Esq., of Boveridge, Dorset, claimed descent.

The eldest son,

SIR WILLIAM BROUNCKER, Knt., b. in 1585, gentlemen of the privy chamber to CHARLES I., and vice chamberlain to CHARLES II., when Prince of Wales, was created a peer of Ireland, 12 September, 1645, as Baron Brouncker, of Newcastle, and Viscount Brouncker, of Lyons, co. Dublin. He m. Winifred, dau of Sir William Leigh, Bart., of Newnham, Warwickshire, and by her, who d. in London, 20 July, 1649, had issue,

WILLIAM, his heir.
HENRY, successor to his brother.
Katherine.
Elizabeth, m. to Charles Skrymsher, of Johnston, Staffordshire.

Lord Brouncker, who had grant of the monastery of Clonnis, co. Monaghan, d. at Oxford in 1645, and was buried in the cathedral of Christ-church, Oxford, where there is a handsome monument erected to his memory and that of his wife Winifred. Lord Brouncker was s. by his eldest son,

SIR WILLIAM BROUNCKER, 2nd Viscount Brouncker, famous for his proficiency in mathematical knowledge, who for fifteen years filled the president's chair of the Royal Society. He was also chancellor to Queen KATHERINE, and held other places of honour and profit. Lord Brouncker d. unm. in 1684, aged sixty-four, and was buried in the church of St. Katherine, near the Tower of London. He was s. by his brother,

HENRY BROUNCKER, 3rd and last Viscount Brouncker, cofferer to King CHARLES II., and gentleman of the bedchamber to the Duke of York. This Lord Brouncker m. Rebecca Rodway, widow of the Hon. Thomas Jermyn (brother to the Earl of St. Albans), and d. in 1687-8, aged sixty-three s. p., when the honours became EXTINCT.

Arms—Arg., six pellets, three, two, and one; a chief embattled, sa.

BROWNE—VISCOUNTS MONTACUTE, OR MONTAGU.

By Letters Patent, dated 2 September, 1554.

Lineage.

SIR ANTHONY BROWNE, who was made knight of the Bath at the coronation of King RICHARD II., left two sons, the younger, Sir Stephen Browne, lord mayor of London, in 1439, imported, during his mayoralty, large cargoes of rye from Prussia, in consequence of the scarcity of wheat, and distributed them amongst the poorer classes of the people. The elder son,

SIR ROBERT BROWNE, of Beechworth, co. Surrey, was father of SIR THOMAS BROWNE, of Beechworth Castle, co. Surrey, treasurer of the household to King HENRY VI., who m. Eleanor, dau. and co-heiress of Sir Thomas Fitz-Alan, and niece of John, Earl of Arundel, and had issue,

I. ANTHONY.
II. George (Sir), of Beechworth Castle, who, in the 1st RICHARD III., was amongst those ordered to be apprehended as adherents of the Duke of Buckingham. He m. Elizabeth, dau. of — Paston, and widow of Richard, Lord Poynings, and was beheaded, 1483: he left issue,

1 Richard, who m. the dau. of — Sands, and had two sons.
2 William, the father of Richard and Edmond.
3 Mathew (Sir), of Beechworth, m. Fridiswide, dau. of Sir Richard Guildford, K.G., of Hemsted, co. Kent, and had issue,

Henry, of Beechworth Castle, m. 1st, Mary, dau. of John Fitzherbert; 2ndly, Catherine, dau. of Sir William Shelley, of Michel Grove, co. Sussex, and had a son,

Sir Thomas Browne, of Beechworth Castle, who m. 1st, Helen, dau. and heir of William Harding, Esq., and widow of Richard Knevet, and was father of Richard Browne, who m. Margaret, dau. and heir of James Astyn, of Westerham, co. Kent, and had issue, John, of Shingleton, co. Kent, m. Elizabeth, dau. of Edward Scott, of Scott's Hall; Thomas; Robert; Cecilia, m. 1st, Francis Knollys, 2ndly, Richard Whitehead, and d. September, 1677; Margaret, m. to Walter Bourchier, of Barnesley, co. Gloucester; Elizabeth; and Anne. Sir Thomas Browne, m. 2ndly, Mabel, dau. and heir of Sir William FitzWilliams, and had (with two daus., Elizabeth, m. to Robert Honywood, and Jane, m. to Sir Oliff Leigh, of Addington, co. Surrey), a son,

Sir Mathew Browne, of Beechworth Castle, m. Jane, dau. of Sir Thomas Vincent, of Stoke Dabernon, co. Surrey, and had issue,

Sir Ambrose Browne, of Beechworth Castle, created a baronet, 7 July, 1627, lord of the manor of Shapwick Egle, co. Sussex, m. Elizabeth, dau. of William Adam, of Saffron Waldron, co. Essex, and by her (who was buried at Dorking, 17 October, 1657) left at his decease, 16 August, 1661, a son, Sir Adam Browne, Baronet, whose only son, Ambrose, d. v. p., unm., when the baronetcy and line terminated at his decease; Edward, d. abroad. 1622; Thomas, living 1623; Jane, m. Sir Robert Kempe, and Mabel, d. unm.

III. Robert (Sir), m. Mary, dau. of Sir William Mallet, Knt., and had a dau. and heiress, Eleanor, m. 1st, to Sir Thomas Fogge; and 2ndly, Sir William Kempe, of Olantye, co. Kent.
I. Katherine, m. to Humphrey Sackvile, Esq., of Buckhurst, co. Sussex.

The eldest son,

ANTHONY BROWNE, was appointed in the 1st year of HENRY VII. standard-bearer for the whole realm of England and elsewhere; and the next year, being one of the esquires of the king's body, was constituted governor of Queenborough Castle, Kent. At this period, participating in the victory achieved over the Earl of Lincoln and Lambert Simnell at Newark, he received the honour of knighthood, 1486. He m. Lucy, 4th dau. and co-heir of JOHN NEVIL, MARQUESS OF MONTAGU, and widow of Sir Thomas FitzWilliams, of Aldwarke, co. York, and had issue,

ANTHONY, his successor.
Elizabeth, m. to Henry Somerset, Earl of Worcester.
Lucy, m. 1st, to Sir Thomas Clifford, Knt., 3rd son of Henry, Earl of Cumberland; and 2ndly, John, son of Sir John Cutts, Knt.

Sir Anthony was s. by his son,

SIR ANTHONY BROWNE, who was with the Earl of Surrey, Lord High Admiral, at Southampton, in the 14th HENRY VIII. (1522-3), when he conveyed the emperor from that port to Biscay; and after landing at Morleis, in Britanny, was knighted for his gallantry in the assault and winning of that town. In two years afterwards, being then an esquire of the household, he was one of the challengers in feats of arms held at Greenwich before the king; and the next year he was appointed lieutenant of the Isle of Man during the minority of the Earl of Derby. After this he was twice deputed on important occasions ambassador to the court of France; and obtained in 30th of the same reign a grant of the office of master of the horse, with the annual fee of £40; in which year he had also a grant of the house and site of the late monastery of Battle, co. Sussex. In the next year he was elected, with the Lord Chancellor Audley, a knight of the most noble order of the Garter. In the 30th of HENRY, Sir Anthony was constituted standard-bearer to the king, and was nominated by his majesty one of the executors to his will. Sir Anthony Brown m. Alice, dau. of Sir John Gage, K.G., and by her (who was buried at Battley,) had issue,

I. ANTHONY, his heir.
.2. William, *m.* Anne. dau. and co-heiress of Sir Hugh Hastings, by whom he acquired Elsing, co. Southampton, ancestor of the BROWNES, of Elsing.
III. Henry
IV. Francis, *m.* Anne, dau. of Sir William Goring. of Burton, co. Sussex, Knt., and relict of Sir George Lyne, Knt.
V. Henry.
I. Mary, *m.* 1st, to John Grey, 2nd son of Thomas, Marquess of Dorset; and 2ndly, to Sir Henry Capel, of Hadham, co. Herts, Bart.
II. Mabel, *m.* to Gerald, Earl of Kildare.
III. Lucy, *m.* to Thomas Roper, Esq., of Eltham, in Kent.

Sir Anthony *d.* 6 May, 1548, and was *s.* by his eldest son,
SIR ANTHONY BROWNE, Knt., sheriff of Surrey and Sussex in the last year of EDWARD VI., who was elevated to the peerage by Queen MARY on 2 September, 1554, in the dignity of VISCOUNT MONTAGU, and immediately after deputed, by order of parliament, with Thomas Thurlby, bishop of Ely, to the Pope, for the purpose of reuniting the realm of England with the church of Rome. In the next year his lordship was installed a knight of the most noble order of the Garter; but upon the accession of Queen ELIZABETH his name was left out of the privy council, and he voted soon after, in his place in parliament, with the Earl of Shrewsbury against abolishing the Pope's supremacy. Yet, according to Camden, he contrived to ingratiate himself with her majesty. "Queen ELIZABETH," says that writer, "having experienced his loyalty, had great esteem for him (though he was a stiff Romanist), and paid him a visit some time before his death; for she was sensible that his regard for that religion was owing to his cradle and education, and proceeded rather from principle than faction, as some people's faith did." His lordship *m.* 1st, Jane, dau. of Robert Ratcliffe, Earl of Sussex, and had issue,

I. ANTHONY, who predeceased him on 29 June, 1592, leaving by his wife Mary, dau. of Sir William Dormer, Knt., of Ethorp, co. Bucks. and who re-married successively Sir Edward Twedale and Sir Thomas Gerard, of Bryn, Bart.,

1 ANTHONY MARY, who *s.* as 2nd viscount.
2 John, *m.* Anne, dau. of — Giffard, Esq., and had a son, STANISLAUS, of Eastbourne, co. Sussex, father of

Stanislaus, of Eastbourne. *m.* Honor, dau. of — Malbrank, merchant, of Cadiz, heir to her brother, Claudius, in the manor of Methley, and was buried in the family vault, at Midhurst, co. Sussex. His issue were,

Francis, a merchant, at Cadiz, gave up his estate to his brother Mark, *d. unm.*, and was buried at St. Lucar.
Nicholas, *d. unm.*
Stanislaus, *d. unm.*

Mark, of Eastbourne, Lord of Methley, in Fillongley, co. Warwick, *m.* 1st, Mary, dau. of —— Simpson, of Monksherborne, co. Hants, which lady was buried at St. James's, Winchester, *s. p.* He *m.* 2ndly, 7 February, 1744, Anastasia, 4th dau. of Sir Richard Moore, of Fawley, co. Berks, Bart., and by her (who was buried at Eastbourne, 26 December, 1780) he had issue, 1 Mark Anthony, of Eastbourne, co. Sussex, *b.* 2 March, 1745, *unm.* 1774. He lived at Fontainbleau, in France 2 Stanislaus, *b.* 26 February, 1752, *d.* 26 February, 1763. 1 Anastasia, *b.* 10 May, 1749. *m.* 17 April, 1780. Sir Thomas Mannock, Bart., of Gifford's Hall, co. Suffolk. 2 Mary, *b.* 3 July, 1747, *m.* 19 May, 1772, Oliver John du Moulin, merchant, of London. Mark Browne *d.* 7 February, 1755, and was buried at Midhurst.

Anna, *m.* Henry Mathew, of Heathhouse Bureton, co. Hants, and *d.* 28 April, 1750.
Mary, *m.* Roger Langley, of Higham Gobious, co. Bedford, and *d.* 29 April, 1757.
Elizabeth, *m.* — Astley, of Escott Hall, co. Warwick.
Mary, *m.* to Robert Alwyn, Esq., of Treford, co. Sussex.

3 George.
1 Dorothy, *m.* to Edward Lee, Esq., of Stanton Barry, co. Bucks.
2 Jane, *m.* to Sir Francis Englefield, Bart.
3 Catharine, *m.* to — Treganion, Esq.

I. Mary, *m.* 1st, to Henry Wriothesley, Earl of Southampton; 2ndly, to Sir Thomas Heneage, Knt.; and 3rdly, to Sir William Harvey, Bart., created Lord Ross in Ireland, and Baron Kidbrook in England.

The viscount *m.* 2ndly, Magdalen, dau. of William, Lord Dacres, of Gillesland, and had, with other issue,

I. George (Sir), of Wicham-Brews, co. Kent, *m.* Mary, dau. of Sir Robert Tyrwhitt, of Kettleby, co. Lincoln, Knt., and had (with four daus., Mary, wife of Thomas Paston, Esq., of Norfolk; Jane, Elizabeth, and Frances. One son,

George, *m.* Eleanor, dau. of Sir Richard Blount, of Mapledurham, co. Oxford, Knt., and had two sons and three daus. (all nuns).

George, K.B., had issue, two daus.
John, of Caverham, created a baronet in 1665, had

1 Anthony, *d. s. p.*
2 Sir John, *d. s. p., s.* his father as baronet
3 Sir George, who *d.* 1729-30, had issue,

1 Sir John, who succeeded.
2 Anthony, an officer of marines.
3 James, in the Austrian army.

II. Henry (Sir), of Kiddington, co. Oxford, *m.* Anne, dau. of Sir William Catesby, Knt., and had

PETER (Sir), who was slain in the service of King CHARLES I., leaving two sons,

HENRY, created a baronet in 1658, with remainder to his brother.
Francis.

III. Anthony (Sir), of Effingham, Knt., *m.* Anne Bell, of Norfolk, and *d. s. p.*
IV. Thomas. *d. unm.*
V. Philip. *d.* in the lifetime of his father.
VI. William, *d.* in the lifetime of his father.
I. Elizabeth, *m.* to Sir Robert Dormer, afterwards Lord Dormer.
II. Mabel, *m.* to Sir Henry Capel, ancestor to the Earl of Essex.
III. Jane, *m.* to Sir Francis Lacon, of Willey, co. Salop, Knt.

His lordship, who was on the trial of MARY, Queen of Scots, *d.* 19 October, 1592, and was *s.* by his grandson,
ANTHONY-MARY BROWNE, 2nd viscount, who *m.* in February, 1591, Jane, dau. of Thomas Sackville, Earl of Dorset, Lord High Treasurer of England, and had issue,

FRANCIS, his successor.
Mary, *m.* 1st, to William, Lord St John, of Basing; and 2ndly, to William, 2nd son of Thomas, Lord Arundel, of Wardour.
Catherine, *m.* to William Tyrwhitt, Esq., of Kettleby.
Anne,
Lucy, } became nuns abroad
Mary, *m.* to Robert, Lord Petre.

His lordship *d.* 23 October, 1629, and was *s.* by his son,
FRANCIS BROWNE, 3rd viscount. This nobleman suffered considerably in the royal cause during the civil wars, but lived to hail the restoration of the monarchy. His lordship *m.* Elizabeth, youngest dau. of Henry Somerset, Marquess of Worcester, and had issue, FRANCIS and HENRY, successively viscounts, and Elizabeth, *m.* to Christopher Roper, 5th Lord Teynham. His lordship *d.* 2 November, 1682, and was *s.* by his elder son,
FRANCIS BROWNE, 4th viscount. This nobleman, who was a zealous catholic, was appointed lord lieutenant of Sussex, by King JAMES II., in 1687. His lordship *m.* Mary, dau. of William Herbert, Marquess of Powis, and widow of Robert Molineux, eldest son of Carryl, Viscount Molineux, but dying *s. p.* in 1708, his honours devolved upon his brother,
HENRY BROWNE, 5th viscount, who *m.* Barbara, dau. of James Walsingam, Esq., of Chesterford, co. Essex, and had issue,

ANTHONY, his successor.
Mary, *d. unm.*
Elizabeth, a nun.
Barbara, *m.* to Ralph Sheldon, Esq., and had a dau. Catherine, who *m.* George Collingwood, Esq., and had a dau., the wife of Sir Robert Throgmorton, Bart.
Catherine, *m.* to George Colingwood, Esq., of Estlington, co. Northumberland.
Anne, *m.* to Anthony Kemp, Esq., of Slindon, in Sussex.
Henrietta, *m.* to Richard Harcourt, Esq., and had a dau., wife of — Carrington, Esq.

His lordship *d.* 25 June, 1717, and was *s.* by his son,
ANTHONY BROWNE, 6th Viscount Montagu, who *m.* in 1720, Barbara, dau. of Sir John Webb, Bart., of Hathorp, co. Gloucester, by whom (who *d.* 7 April, 1779) he left at his death, 23 April, 1767 (having also had a dau. Mary, *m.* to Sir Richard Bedingfield, Bart.), a son,
ANTHONY JOSEPH BROWNE, 7th viscount, *b.* 1730. This nobleman *m.* in 1765, Frances, sister of Sir Herbert Mackworth, Bart., and widow of Alexander, Lord Halkerton, by whom he had issue,

GEORGE-SAMUEL, his successor.
Elizabeth Mary, *b.* 5 February, 1767, *m.* in 1794, to William Stephen Poyntz, Esq., of Midgham, Berks.

His lordship *d.* 9 April, 1787, and was *s.* by his son,
GEORGE-SAMUEL BROWNE, 8th viscount, *b.* 26 June, 1769, who met an untimely fate in a rash attempt to pass the waterfalls of Schauff hausen, accompanied by his friend, Mr. Sedley Burdet, in a small flat-bottomed boat, contrary to the advice, and even restriction of the local magistrate, who, knowing the certain result of so unprecedented an enterprise, had placed guards to intercept the daring travellers. They found means, however, to elude every precaution, and having pushed off, passed the first fall in security, but in attempting to clear the second they disappeared, and were never afterwards seen or heard of. It is presumed that the boat, impelled by the

violence of the cataract, got jammed between the two rocks, and was thus destroyed. This melancholy event occurred in 1793, and about the same period his lordship's magnificent mansion at Cowdray* was accidentally burnt to the ground. His lordship (b. 26 June, 1769) dying *unm.* the viscounty was supposed to devolve upon (the great-grandson of Stanislaus Browne, Esq., son and heir of John Browne, Esq., brother of Anthony, 2nd viscount, and grandson of the 1st lord) his cousin, MARK ANTHONY BROWNE, Esq., 9th Viscount Montagu, at whose decease, in 1797, without issue, the dignity is supposed to have become EXTINCT.

Arms—Sa., three lions passant, in bend, between two double cotisses, arg.

BROWNLOW—VISCOUNT TYRCONNEL.

By Letters Patent, dated 1718.

Lineage.

RICHARD BROWNLOW, Esq., of Belton, co. Lincoln, prothonotary of the Court of Common Pleas, *temp.* ELIZABETH and JAMES I., m. Katherine, da :. of John Page, Esq., a master in chancery, and dying in 1638, left two sons, viz.,

JOHN (Sir), of Belton, created a baronet 1641, *d. s. p.*, 1680.
WILLIAM (Sir), of whose line we treat.

The 2nd son,
SIR WILLIAM BROWNLOW, of Great Humby, co. Lincoln, was created a BARONET of England, 27 July, 1641. He m. Elizabeth, dau. and co-heir of William Duncombe, Esq., and d. in 1666, being s. by his son,
SIR RICHARD BROWNLOW, 2nd Baronet of Humby, who m. Elizabeth, dau. of John Freke, Esq., of Stretton, co. Dorset, and was father of
SIR JOHN BROWNLOW, 3rd Baronet of Humby, who m. Alice, dau. of Richard Sherrard, Esq., and had issue four daus., his co-heirs, viz.,

Jane, m. to Peregrine, Duke of Ancaster.
Elizabeth, m. to John, Earl of Exeter.
Alicia, m. to Francis, Lord Guilford.
Eleanor, m. to her cousin, Sir John Brownlow, Bart., afterwards Lord Tyrconnel

Sir John d. 16 July, 1697, and was s. by his brother,
SIR WILLIAM BROWNLOW, 4th Baronet of Humby, who m. Dorothy, dau. and co-heir of Sir Richard Mason, of Sutton, and had issue. The son and heir,
SIR JOHN BROWNLOW, 5th Baronet of Humby, M P. for Lincolnshire, was elevated to the peerage of Ireland as Baron Charleville and VISCOUNT TYRCONNEL, in 1718. His lordship m. 1st, Eleanor, dau. and co-heir of his uncle, Sir John Brownlow, Bart.; and 2ndly, Elizabeth, dau. of William Cartwright, Esq., of Marnham, Notts.; but *d. s. p.* in 1754, when the peerage became EXTINCT. The estates of the family devolved on Lord Tyrconnel's sister, ANNE, who m. SIR RICHARD CUST, Bart.; and from this marriage descends the present EARL BROWNLOW.

Arms—Or, an inescutcheon, within an orle of eight martlets, sa.

BRUCE—BARON BRUCE, OF ANANDALE.

By Writ of Summons, dated 23 June, 1295.

Lineage.

ROBERT DE BRUS was a wealthy baron in Yorkshire in the reign of WILLIAM THE CONQUEROR, with whom he had come from Normandy. He had the castle and manor of Skelton, in Yorkshire, and Hert and Hertness, in the Bishoprick of Durham, and before the end of the reign of the CONQUEROR was possessed of ninety-four lordships in Yorkshire. His son (or, by by some accounts, the son of his son ADAM),
ROBERT DE BRUCE, Lord of Skelton, made a figure at the

court of King HENRY I., where he became intimate with Prince David of Scotland, that monarch's brother-in-law. When the Prince became King of Scotland, as DAVID I., in 1124, Bruce obtained from him the lordship of Annandale, and great possessions in the south of Scotland. Robert de Bruce *d.* in 1141, and was buried at Gysburn, the place of his birth. He m. Agnes, dau. of Fulk de Paganell (and 2ndly, according to Drummond, Agnes de Annan), and had issue,

ADAM DE BRUCE, of Skelton, in Yorkshire. He inherited his father's great English estates, and was ancestor to the family of Bruce of Skelton, which failed in the male line in 1271, at the decease *s. p.* of PETER DE BRUS, Lord of Skelton, whose sisters and co-heirs were

1 Agnes, m. to Walter de Fauconberg.
2 Lucy, m. to Marmaduke de Thweng.
3 Margaret, m. to Robert de Ros, and had issue. The descendant and heir-general of this marriage, ELIZABETH DE ROS. m. Sir Wm. Parr, Knt., ancestor by her of PARR, MARQUESS OF NORTHAMPTON, and of Queen Katharine Parr.
4 Laderina, m. to John de Bellew.

ROBERT.

The 2nd son,
ROBERT DE BRUCE became Lord of Annandale, as his father's gift, and was founder of the great House of Bruce in Scotland. He flourished under DAVID I., MALCOLM IV., and WILLIAM THE LION. The name of his wife was Euphemia, by whom he had issue, ROBERT and WILLIAM.

ROBERT DE BRUCE, lord of Annandale, m. in 1183, Isabel, natural dau. of King WILLIAM THE LION by whom he had no issue : he was *s.* before 1191, by his brother,
WILLIAM DE BRUCE lord of Annandale, and possessor of large estates in the north of England. He obtained from King JOHN the grant of a weekly market at Hartilpool, and he granted lands to the canons of Gysburn. He *d.* in 1215, and was *s.* by his son,
ROBERT DE BRUCE, lord of Annandale. He m. Isabel, 2nd dau. of David, Earl of Huntingdon, son of Henry, Prince of Scotland, and grandson of King DAVID I. It was in consequence of this royal alliance, that their son entered into competition for the Scottish crown, and that their descendants became co-heirs of the ancient Scoto-Pictish and Anglo-Saxon kings. Isabel was co-heir of her brother, John the Scot, Earl of Chester; she *d.* in 1251, having survived her husband six years. He *d.* in 1245, and was *s.* by his son,
ROBERT DE BRUCE, lord of Annandale. He was an able and strenuous baron, and acted a great part in the reign of ALEXANDER III. In 1255, he was appointed one of the fifteen Regents of Scotland. In 1284, he was one of the Magnates Scotiæ who consented to accept Margaret of Norway as their sovereign, on the demise of ALEXANDER III. In 1291, he entered into an unsuccessful competition with John Baliol for the crown of Scotland. He *d.* at Louhmaben Castle, in 1295, aged eighty-five. In 1240, he m. Isabella, dau. of Gilbert de Clare, 3rd Earl of Gloucester, by whom he had

ROBERT, his heir.
BERNARD, of Conington and Exton. Sir Bernard Bruce was the ancestor of the only cadet branch of the House of Bruce which can boast of royal descent. He was seated at Exton, co. Rutland, and was father of SIR JOHN BRUCE, of Exton, whose only dau. and heir, JANE BRUCE, of Exton, was wife of Sir Nicholas Green. Her dau. and heir, JOAN GREEN, of Exton, was wife of Sir Thomas Culpeper, and her dau. and heir, CATHERINE CULPEPER, of Exton, was wife of Sir John Harington. Her descendant in the fourth degree, SIR JOHN HARINGTON, of Exton, heir-general of the only cadet branch of the royal Bruces, m. Lucy Sydney, dau. of Sir William Sydney of Penshurst, by whom he had a son, JOHN HARINGTON, created Lord Harington, of Exton, by King JAMES I., whose line fail d, and a dau., ELIZABETH HARINGTON, wife of Sir Edward Montague, of Boughton. Through her three families of the House of Montague, viz., the DUKES OF MONTAGUE and MANCHESTER, and the EARL OF SANDWICH: SONDES, EARL OF FEVERSHAM, and his descendants, LORDS MONSON and SONDES; and CHOLMELEY, BARONET OF EASTON; are all descended from the royal blood of Bruce. The competitor for the Scottish crown had also a dau., CHRISTIAN BRUCE, wife of Patrick Dunbar, 7th Earl of March, ancestress to a long line of Earls of March.

Robert Bruce, the competitor, was *s.* by his eldest son,
ROBERT BRUCE, Lord of Annandale, who was Earl of Carrick, in right of his wife, Margaret, Countess of Carrick (to whom he was m. in 1271), dau. and heir of Niel, Earl of Carrick, and widow of Adam de Kilconcath, Earl of Carrick. On the death of his countess, in 1292, he resigned the Earldom of Carrick to his eldest son. In 1296, he, along with his eldest son, swore fealty to King EDWARD I., and was summoned to parliament as a BARON of England from 23 June, 1295, to 26 January, 1297. He *d.* in 1304. By the Countess of Carrick he had issue,

* Views of this fine Elizabethan structure have been published in the *Monumenta Vetusta,* though in a manner not remarkable for either faultless perspective or artistic finish.

80

I. ROBERT, eventually King of Scotland.
II. EDWARD, crowned King of Ireland in 1316, and killed at the battle of Dundalk, in 1318. He had issue, ROBERT, ALEXANDER, and THOMAS (stated to have been illegitimate), who were successively Earls of Carrick.
III. Thomas, *s. p.*   IV. Alexander. *s. p.*
V. Nigil, *s. p.*
1. ISABEL, wife, 1st, of Sir Thomas Randolph, high chamberlain of Scotland; 2nd, of the Earl of Athol; 3rd, of Alexander Bruce. By Randolph she had issue, THOMAS RANDOLPH, EARL OF MORAY, Regent of Scotland, whose dau. and eventual heir, AGNES RANDOLPH, *m.* her cousin, Patrick Dunbar, 9th Earl of March. Her son, GEORGE, 10th Earl of March, was father of the 11th earl, and of two daus., 1 ELIZABETH, betrothed in 1399 to the Duke of Rothsay; 2 JANET, wife, 1st, of Sir John Seton; and 2ndly, of Sir Adam Johnstone. She was ancestress to the Earls of Winton, and the Johnstones, baronets of Westerhall.
II. MARY, wife, 1st, of Sir Neil Campbell, of Lochowe, by whom she was ancestress to the House of Argyle; 2nd, of Sir Alexander Frazer, high chamberlain of Scotland.
III. CHRISTIAN, wife, 1st, of Gratney, Earl of Mar; 2nd, of Sir Christopher Seton; 3rd, of Sir Andrew Moray, of Bothwell.
IV. MATILDA, wife of Hugh, Earl of Ross.

The three other daus. are said to have *m.* into the families of Carlyle, Dishington, and Brechin.

ROBERT BRUCE, the eldest son, *b.* 11 July, 1274, was the glorious restorer of the Scottish monarchy. He became Earl of Carrick on his father's resignation, in 1292, and *s.* as 2nd Baron Bruce. He asserted his claim to the Scottish crown, and ascended the throne of his ancestors, being crowned at Scone, in 1306. His power and the liberties of his country were finally vindicated by the splendid victory of Bannockburn, in 1314. He *d.* in June, 1329, in the fifty-fifth year of his age. King ROBERT I. *m.* 1st, Isabella, dau. of Donald, 10th Earl of Mar, by whom he had an only dau., PRINCESS MARJORY, his eldest co-heir, who, failing her brother, was heiress of the Scottish crown. She was wife of WALTER, LORD HIGH STEWARD of Scotland, by whom she had issue, ROBERT, who afterwards ascended the throne of Scotland as King ROBERT II., and who was ancestor of the long line of STUART Kings; his heirs-general are the DUKE OF MODENA, the DUKE OF PARMA, and the KING OF NAPLES. King ROBERT I. *m.* 2ndly, Elizabeth de Burgo, dau. of Richard, 2nd Earl of Ulster, by whom he had issue a son, who *s.* him as King DAVID II.; and two daus.,

The Princess MARGARET, his junior co-heir. She was wife of William, 4th Earl of Sutherland. Her descendant and representative is GEORGE, 2nd DUKE OF SUTHERLAND, who is junior co-heir general of King ROBERT BRUCE.
The Princess MATILDA, his junior co-heir, wife of Thomas de Izac, by whom she had a dau., JOANNA LE IZAC, the wife of John de Ergadia, Lord of Lorn, by whom she had a dau., who transmitted to her descendants and representatives the junior co-heirship of King ROBERT BRUCE, viz., JANET DE ERGADIA, wife of Robert Stewart, brother of John Stewart, of Innermeath. She was ancestress of the STEWARTS OF ROSSYTHE, co. Fife, and of the STEWARTS OF CRAIGIE HALL, afterwards of NEW HALLS, co. Linlithgow.

King ROBERT had also a dau., who is believed to have been illegitimate, who was wife of Sir Walter Oliphant, of Aberdalgy, the ancestor of the Lords Oliphant. King ROBERT was *s.* in 1329 by his only son,

DAVID II., King of Scotland, who was crowned at Scone, in 1331. He had no issue by either of his wives—the Princess Joanna of England, dau. of EDWARD II., or Margaret of Logie, and he closed his inglorious reign in 1371, in the forty-seventh year of his age. With him and his cousin, Sir John Bruce, of Exton, ended the royal male line of Bruce, which continued to be represented as heirs-general by the STUART KINGS OF SCOTLAND, (the EARLS OF SUTHERLAND, the STEWARTS OF ROSSYTHE, and (of the junior branch) the HARINGTONS OF EXTON.

But the great House of Bruce continued to be perpetuated in the male line .by a most distinguished family of baronial rank, which has been prolific of high and important branches. The family of Bruce of Clackmanan, from which all the principal houses of the name in Scotland are descended, claims to be of the same stock with the ancient Lords of Annandale and of Skelton, and this claim, was distinctly admitted by the head of the family, King DAVID II., in a charter to Sir Robert Bruce, of the son of Thomas Bruce, of the castle and manor of Clackmanan, together with the lands of Wester Kennet, Garlet, &c., dated 9 December, 1359. In this charter, the King designates Sir Robert Bruce thus: "Dilecto et fideli consanguineo suo Roberto de Bruis."

The family of BRUCE of CLACKMANAN was the parent stem of the BRUCES of KENNET, co. Clackmanan, whose chief is Alexander Hugh Bruce, Esq., of Kennet, and their junior branch of Garlet, now represented by William Downing Bruce, Esq., F.S.A., of Lincoln's Inn, barrister-at-law; of the BRUCES of

Blair Hall, whose chief is the EARL OF ELGIN; the BRUCES of AIRTH, and their cadet in Ireland, BRICE or BRUCE, of KILLROOT; the BRUCES of STENHOUSE, &c., &c. Their detailed pedigrees may be seen in DRUMMOND'S "Noble British Families."

Arms—Or, a saltier and chief, gu.

BRUCE—EARL OF CARRICK.

(*See* BRUCE, Baron Bruce, of Annandale.)

ROBERT BRUCE, "THE BRUCE OF BANNOCKBURN," son of Robert de Brus (Bruce), Lord of Annandale, inherited the Earldom of Carrick, in 1292, at the decease of his mother, MARGARET, Countess of Carrick (only dau. and heir of Niel, Earl of Carrick, and grand-dau. of Duncan, the son of Gilbert, living *temp.* WILLIAM THE LION, who was created Earl of Carrick), and the dignity, upon his accession to the throne, merged in the crown of Scotland.

Arms—Or, a saltier and chief, gu.

BRUCE—EARLS OF AILESBURY, BARONS BRUCE, OF WHORLTON, CO. YORK.

Barony, by Letters Patent, dated 1 August, 1641.
Earldom, by Letters Patent, dated 18 March, 1664.

Lineage.

THOMAS BRUCE, 1st Earl of Elgin in the peerage of Scotland, was created a peer of England, 1 August, 1641, as BARON BRUCE, OF WHORLTON, *in the co. of York*, and dying in 1643, was *s.* by his only son,

ROBERT BRUCE, 2nd Earl of Elgin, who was advanced in the peerage of England, 18 March, 1664, to the dignities of Baron Bruce, of Skelton, co. York, Viscount Bruce of Ampthill, co. Bedford, and EARL OF AILESBURY. His lordship *m.* Diana, dau. of Henry, 2nd Earl of Stamford, and dying in 1685, was *s.* by his only surviving son,

THOMAS BRUCE, 3rd Earl of Elgin, and 2nd Earl of Ailesbury, who *m.* 1st, in 1676, Elizabeth Seymour, dau. of Henry, Lord Beauchamp, and heiress of her brother, William, 3rd Duke of Somerset, by whom he had issue,

I. CHARLES, his successor, who was summoned to parliament in 1711, as LORD BRUCE, OF WHORLTON.
1. Elizabeth, *m.* to George Brudenell, 3rd Earl of Cardigan, and had issue,
1 GEORGE, 4th Earl of Cardigan, *m.* Mary, dau. of John, Duke of Montagu, and, assuming the surname of Montagu, was advanced, at the decease of his father-in-law, to the Marquisate of Monthermer, and DUKEDOM OF MONTAGU. His grace *d.* in 1790, leaving one married dau.,
ELIZABETH, Duchess of Buccleuch, grandmother of the present DUKE OF BUCCLEUCH.
2 James, successor to his brother, as 5th Earl of Cardigan.
3 Robert, whose son inherited as 6th Earl of Cardigan.
4 THOMAS, who, upon succeeding his uncle, the Earl of Ailesbury, in the Barony of BRUCE, of Tottenham, assumed the surname of Bruce, and was subsequently created EARL OF AILESBURY.

His lordship, who *m.* 2ndly, Charlotte, Countess of Sannu, and had an only dau., Charlotte-Maria, wife of Prince Horne, *d.* in 1741, and was *s.* by his only surviving son,

CHARLES BRUCE, 3rd Earl of Ailesbury, and 4th Earl of Elgin. This nobleman *m.* 1st, Anne, eldest dau. and one of the co-heirs of William Savile, Marquess of Halifax, by whom he had issue,

Robert, *m.* Frances, dau. of Sir William Blackett, Bart., and *d. s. p.* before his father.
MARY, *m.* 1728, Henry Brydges, 2nd Duke of Chandos, and was mother of James Brydges, 3rd Duke of Chandos, whose only dau. and heiress, ANNE ELIZA, *m.* in 1796, Richard, Earl Temple, afterwards DUKE OF BUCKINGHAM AND CHANDOS; and was grandmother of Richard-Plantagenet-Campbell, DUKE OF BUCKINGHAM AND CHANDOS, who thus, by descent from the Bruces and Seymours, derives in a direct line from the Princess Mary, and, in her issue, sister and co-heir of King HENRY VIII.

Elizabeth, *m.* in 1732, to Hon. Benjamin Bathurst, son and heir of Allen, Lord Bathurst, and *d. s. p.*

His lordship *m.* 2ndly, Juliana, 2nd dau. of Charles Boyle, Earl of Burlington, but had no issue. He *m.* 3rdly, in 1739, Caroline, only dau. of John Campbell, 4th Duke of Argyll, by whom he had an only dau.,

Mary, *m.* in 1757, to Charles, Duke of Richmond.

After the decease of his son, the Earl of Aylesbury and Elgin obtained, by letters patent, dated 17 April, 1746, the English Barony of BRUCE OF TOTTENHAM, co. Wilts, in remainder to his nephew, the Hon. Thomas Brudenell. His lordship *d.* 10 February, 1747, when the earldom of Elgin and barony of Bruce passed to the Earl of Kincardine, the heir male, and the barony of Kinloss devolved on the Duke of Chandos, as heir general. (See ELGIN, BURKE's *Peerage and Baronetage*.) The English BARONY OF BRUCE OF TOTTENHAM as limited, and the EARLDOM OF AILESBURY, with his lordship's other English honours EXPIRED.

Arms—Or, a saltier and chief, gu., on a canton, arg., a lion rampant, az.

BRUGES—EARL OF WINCHESTER.

By Creation in open Parliament, 13 October, 1472,

Lineage.

LEWIS DE BRUGES, Lord of Gruthuse, and Prince of Steenhouse, in Burgundy, "who" (says COURTHOPE, *Historic Peerage*) "was a knight of the Golden Fleece, and is stated by Philip de Comines to have been governor in Holland for the Duke of Burgundy," having evinced the greatest sympathy for King EDWARD IV., during that monarch's exile (when forced to fly by the Lancastrians in the 10th year of his reign,) at the court of his brother-in-law, Charles de Valois, Duke of Burgundy, was received in two years afterwards by EDWARD, then re-established monarch in his English dominions, with the highest honours, and as a testimony of the gratitude felt by the nation towards so stanch a friend of its sovereign, the House of Commons, in parliament assembled, besought the king, through their speaker, William Alyngton, to bestow upon the foreign Prince some especial mark of royal favour. In compliance with which request EDWARD advanced him, 13 October, 1472, to the dignity of EARL OF WINCHESTER, in the parliament chamber, by cincture with a sword, and granted to the new peer for upholding the dignity, the sum of £200 annually. In the November following his lordship obtained a patent of arms as Earl of Winchester, viz., " Azure dix mascles d'or orné d'une canton de armes de Angleterre; c'estasavoir de gules, a une léopard passant d'or, armé d'azure," which were so depicted in colours in the roll wherein his patent for them is recorded. But in the 15th of HENRY VII (1499), which was about twenty-seven years after, both these grants were surrendered to the king, then at Calais, and upon each of their enrolments a *vacat* made, without having any reason assigned for the proceedings. His lordship *m.* Margaret, dau. of Henry de Boreslie, and had issue,

JOHN, *Lord of Gruthuse*, father of REGINALD, who *d.* without male issue.

Arms.—Az., ten mascles, four, three, two, and one, or, on a canton, gu., a lion passant guardant of the second.

BRYAN—BARON BRYAN.

By Writ of Summons, dated 25 November, 1350.

Lineage

In the 29th of HENRY III.,

GUY DE BRIAN, whose chief seat was in the marches of Wales, received command to assist the Earl of Gloucester against the Welch; and in the 42nd of the same reign, he had a second military summons for a similar service. We find him subsequently, however, arrayed under the baronial banner, and constituted after the victory of his party, at Lewes, governor of the castles of KARDIGAN and KERMERDYN, but he soon afterwards returned to his allegiance, and was one of the sureties (51st HENRY III.) for Robert de Vere, Earl of Oxford, that that nobleman should thenceforward deport himself peaceably, and abide by the *dictum of Kenilworth*, for the redemption of his lands. This Guy de Brian, *m* twice: one of his wives being Eve, only dau. and heiress of Henry de Traci, and had by her an only dau., Maud, *m.* to Nicholas

82

Martin, Baron of Kemes. By the other wife, Guy de Bryan left at his decease a son,

SIR GUY DE BRYAN, who, in the 4th Edward III., was constituted governor of the castle of Haverford, but he was found next year to be of unsound mind—when an agreement was made, that the Barony of *Chastel Walweyn* should at once come into possession of his son GUOYEN, upon his undertaking to provide for his two sisters from the revenues thereof. This

GUOYEN DE BRYAN, thus invested with the Barony of Chastel-Walweyn, served in the Scottish wars, in the 11th of EDWARD III., and in consideration of his special services, had an annuity of £40 granted him by the king, out of the exchequer, for life. In the 15th of the same reign, he was made governor of St. Briavel's Castle, and warden of the forest of Dene, co. Gloucester; and from the 16th to the 20th he was engaged in the French wars. He *d.* in 1350, and was *s.* by his son,

GUY DE BRYAN, who became a person of considerable note. About the time of his father's death he was standard-bearer to King EDWARD III., in the celebrated fight with the French at Calais, and deporting himself with great valour upon that occasion, he had a grant of 200 marks per annum, out of the exchequer, for life. He was also constituted governor of St. Briavel's Castle, and warden of the forest of Dene; and was summoned to parliament as a BARON from 25 November, 1350, to 6 December, 1389. In 1354 his lordship was one of the ambassadors to the court of Rome to procure the papal ratification of a league, then made, between the Kings of England and France; the next year, he attended King EDWARD in his expedition into France, when he was made a banneret, and he continued for several years subsequently in the French wars. In 1361 he was again accredited upon a mission of importance to the holy see, and being some years afterwards once more engaged against the French, he was made admiral of the king's fleet, a command renewed to his lordship in the next year (44th EDWARD III), and he was soon after elected a knight of the Garter. In the reign of RICHARD II., Lord Bryan also served against the French, and he was in the expedition made with him, with Edward Mortimer, Earl of March. His lordship *m.* Elizabeth, dau. of William de Montacute, Earl of Salisbury, and widow of Hugh le Despenser, by whom (with two younger sons, who *d* issueless), he had,

GUY, who *d.* in 1368, in the lifetime of his father, leaving issue,

PHILIPPA, *m.*, 1st, to John Devereux, and 2ndly, to Sir Henry le Scrope, Knt., but *d. s. p.* 8th HENRY IV.

ELIZABETH, *m.* to Sir Robert Lovell, Knt., and had an only dau. and heiress,

MAUD LOVELL, who *m.*, 1st, John Fitzalan, Earl of Arundel, and had issue,

HUMPHREY, EARL OF ARUNDEL, *d. s. p.*

Her ladyship *m.* 2ndly, Sir Richard Stafford, and had a dau.,

AVICE, *m.* to James Butler, Earl of Ormonde, and *d. s. p.* in 1456.

His lordship *d.* in 1390, leaving his two grand-daus., Philippa, then twelve, and Elizabeth, nine years of age, his co-heirs, between whom the BARONY OF BRYAN fell into ABEYANCE, and it became EXTINCT, at the decease of Avice, COUNTESS OF ORMONDE, in 1456.

Arms.—Or, three piles meeting in point, az.

BRYDGES—BARONS CHANDOS, OF SUDELEY CASTLE, CO. GLOUCESTER, EARLS OF CARNARVON, DUKES OF CHANDOS.

Barony, by Letters Patent, dated 8 April, 1554.
Earldom, by Letters Patent, dated 19 October, 1714.
Dukedom, by Letters Patent, dated 30 April, 1729.

Lineage.

SIR SIMON DE BRUGGE, of the county of Hereford, supposed to have sprung from the old Counts de Rethel, in the province of Champagné, in France, having taken part against HENRY III., lost by confiscation a great proportion of his lands, which were conferred upon Roger, Lord Clifford. Sir Simon was father of another

SIMON DE BRUGGE (commonly omitted in the printed pedigrees), who *m.* the dau. of Walwyn, a family of distinction in the co. of Hereford even to the present times, and had issue,

JOHN DE BRUGGE, M.P. for the cc. of Hereford, 16th EDWARD II., 1322, who left issue,

SIR BALDWIN DE BRUGGE (his son and heir), who was seated in the county of Hereford, in the time of EDWARD III., and who left, at his decease, by Isabel, his wife, three sons,

THOMAS, his heir

John (Sir), who was in the battle of Agincourt, 25 October, 1415, and the next year served the office of sheriff of Herefordshire, at which period he bore for his arms, arg., on a cross, sa., a leopard's face, or, as since used, and has been borne by Simon de Brugge, one of the same family, when he was sheriff of this county, in 1379. Sir John was also sheriff of Gloucestershire, in the 7th HENRY V., and was returned to parliament by that county the following year. He left at his decease, an only dau. and heiress,

Joanna, who m. Sir John Baskerville, of Erdisley, Herefordshire.

Simon, of the Leye, co. Hereford, left a numerous posterity, of whom the chief branch was still living at the Leye, when Gregory King made his visitation of that county in 1684 And hence descended Sir John Bridges, who was lord mayor of London, 12th HENRY VIII., whose dau. Winifrede. m. 1st, Sir Richard Sackville, by whom she was mother of Thomas Sackville, Lord Buckhurst, and Earl of Dorset, the celebrated poet. Her ladyship m. 2ndly, John Powlett, Marquess of Winchester.

Sir Balwin Brugge was s by his eldest son,

THOMAS BRUGGE, or BRUGES, who m. Alice, dau. and co-heir of Sir Thomas Berkeley, of Coberley, co. Gloucester, by Elizabeth, sister and co-heiress of Sir John Chandos (see that dignity), and acquired the seat of Coberley, and other large estates, which descended down to George Brydges, 6th Lord Chandos, who d. in 1654. By this great heiress, Thomas Bruges had issue,

GYLES, of whom presently.

Edward, of Lone, co. Gloucester, who d. in 1436, leaving a dau. and heiress, ISABEL, who m. John Throckmorton, Esq. (younger son of John Throckmorton, Esq., and Eleanor his wife, dau. and co-heir of Sir Guy de Spineto, Lord of Coughton, co. Warwick), and was mother of John Throckmorton, Esq., ancestor of the Throckmortons, extinct Baronets of TORTWORTH.

The elder son,

SIR GYLES BRUGES, was seated at Coberley, co. Gloucester, and in the 7th HENRY V. (1419) was amongst the persons of note of that county who had command to serve the king in person for the security of the realm, all those then required so to do being such (as the words of the writ impart,) "as did bear ancient arms by descent from their ancestors." In 1429, he was sheriff of Gloucestershire, and again in 1453. In the next year, Sir Gyles Bruges and William Whittinton were returned members of parliament for that shire. He m. Catherine, dau. of James Clifford, Esq., of Frampton, co. Gloucester, and widow of Anselm Guise, Esq., of Elmore, by whom he had,

THOMAS, his successor.

Cicily, who m. 1st, Thomas Gates, Esq.; and 2ndly, John Wellesborne, Esq.

Sir Gyles d. in 1466, and was s. by his son,

THOMAS BRUGES, Esq., of Coberley, who was returned to parliament by the co. of Gloucester in 1459, and by the co. of Hereford in 1472. He m. Florence, dau. of William Darell, Esq., of Littlecot, in Wilts, and had issue,

I. GILES, his successor.
II. Henry, of Newberry, Berks, who m. a dau. of John Hungerford, Esq., and had a dau., m. to Gifford, of Itchel House, Hants, and a son and heir,

SIR RICHARD BRIDGES, of Shefford, Berks, and of Ludgershall, Wilts, K.B., who m. Jane, dau. of Sir William Spencer, of Wormleighton, ancestor to the Duke of Marlborough, and had issue,

1 ANTHONY, of Great Shefford, whose heiress, ELEANOR, carried that estate to Sir George Browne, of the Montague family, by whom she had no issue.
2 Edmund, of Bradley, co. Somerset.

I. Elizabeth, m. to William Cassey, Esq., and subsequently to Walter Rowdon, Esq.
II. Elice, m. to Thomas Chichelev, of Wimpole, co. Cambridge.
III. Eleanor, m. to Sir Thomas Pauncefoot, Knt.

The eldest son,

SIR GILES BRUGES, of Coberley, received the honour of knighthood, for his valour at the battle of Blackheath, 22 June, 1497. He m. Isabel, dau. of Thomas Baynham, and had issue,

I. JOHN, of whom presently.
II. Thomas, of Cornbury, Oxfordshire, and Keinsham Abbey, Somersetshire. This gentleman was sheriff of Gloucestershire in the 3rd of EDWARD VI., and of Berkshire and Oxfordshire in the 3rd and 4th of PHILIP and MARY. In the reign of Queen MARY, he was an officer of the Tower, under his brother, Lord Chandos. He d. 14 November, 1559, leaving issue by Anne, dau. and co-heiress of John Sidenham, Esq., of Orchard, co. Somerset, Mary, m. to Rowland Arnold,

Esq, of Higham, co. Gloucester; Ellen, m. to John Ashfield, Esq.; and a son and heir, HENRY BRYDGES, Esq., of Keinsham, who m. Anne, dau. of John Hungerford, Esq., of Down Ampney, co. Gloucester; and was s. by his son, SIR THOMAS BRYDGES, of Keinsham, whose son, THOMAS BRYDGES, Esq. m. Philippa, dau. of Sir George Speke, K.B., and left with a dau. Philippa, who m. Major Henry Guise of Winterbourne, a son, SIR THOMAS BRYDGES, of Keinsham, an eminent loyalist, who m. Anne, dau. and co-heiress of Sir Edward Rodney, of Stoke Rodney, co. Somerset, by whom he had, with other issue,

1 HARRY BRYDGES, Esq., who inherited the estates, and m. Lady Diana Holles, dau. of John, 2nd Earl of Clare, by whom he had a dau., Arabelle, m. to John Mitchell, Esq., of Kingston Russel, Dorset. Mr. Brydges m. 2ndly, Miss Freeman, and had two more daus.; upon his decease, his estates devolved, by an entail, upon his nephew, GEORGE-RODNEY BRYDGES.

2 GEORGE-RODNEY BRYDGES, of Avington, Hants, m. Lady Anne Maria Brudenell, dau. of Robert, 2nd Earl of Cardigan, and widow of Francis Talbot, 11th Earl of Shrewsbury, and had a son,

GEORGE-RODNEY BRYDGES, of Avington, who inherited the estates upon the decease of his uncle, Harry Brydges, as stated above. He was M.P. for the city of Winchester from 1714 to 1751. This gentleman was found drowned in the canal of his garden, at Avington, in the seventy-second year of his age: leaving no issue, the greater part of his estates reverted to the Chandos branch of the family, but he devised a property at Alresford, in Hampshire, to George Brydges Rodney, afterwards the great Admiral, Lord Rodney.

Sir Giles Bruges d. 1511, and was s. by his elder son and heir,

SIR JOHN BRUGES, who was under age at his father's decease, and was in ward to King HENRY VIII. He had an early ambition of military glory, and though very young, attended the king in his expedition into France, 1513, when Terouenne and Tournay were taken. He was likewise at the battle of Spurs, and for his valiant conduct in those engagements received the honour of knighthood. In the 10th of HENRY VIII., Sir John covenanted to serve the king with 100 archers under his command; and being one of the knights of the king's body, was in his train at Bulloign, at the interview at Sadingfield with the French king, attended by three servants and one horse keeper, according to the appointment then made. In 1537 he was constituted constable of Sudeley Castle, and in the same year was, amongst those of the court, summoned with the nobility and bishops to be present, October 15, at the christening of Prince Edward. In the year 1544 he passed the seas with the king, and for his gallant behaviour at the siege of Bulloign. was, on the surrender thereof, appointed deputy-governor of the town; in which post he was continued by King EDWARD VI. He had also, in the 1st year of that king, a grant of divers manors in consideration of his services. In 1549 (3rd EDWARD VI.), Bulloign being besieged by the French, he had the command of the place as deputy-governor, and successfully defended it against the French king in person, and an army flushed with the conquest of Newhaven and other places. On the death of EDWARD VI., Sir John Bruges waited upon Queen MARY, assisted her against those who had usurped the government; and upon her majesty's entrance into London to the Tower, was one of the principal persons in her train; for which services he was then appointed governor of the Tower, and had a grant, at the same time, of the castle and manor of Sudeley, in Gloucestershire. He was subsequently, Sunday, 8 April, 1554, elevated to the peerage in the dignity of BARON CHANDOS, of Sudeley, to him and the heirs male of his body, "in consideration not only of his nobility and loyalty, but of his probity, valour, and other virtues." Four days afterwards he attended Lady Jane Grey to the scaffold, and that unhappy lady presented him (as related by some), in testimony of his civilities to her, with her prayer book; but according to others it was a table book, which with some Greek and Latin verses which she wrote in it, upon his lordship's begging her to write something that he might retain as a memorial of her. His last will bears date 2 March, in the 2nd and 3rd of PHILIP and MARY, and he d. 4 March following (1557), an adherent to the old religion. His lordship m. Elizabeth, dau. of Edmund, Lord Grey de Wilton, sister to the gallant soldier, William, Lord Grey de Wilton, and aunt to Arthur, Lord Grey de Wilton, the celebrated lord-deputy of Ireland. By this lady he had seven sons and three daus., of the latter, Catherine, m. Edward Sutton, Lord Dudley; Elizabeth, m. John Tracy, Esq., of Todington, co. Gloucester, and Mary, m. George Throckmorton, Esq., son of Sir George Throckmorton, of Coughton; of the sons

EDMUND, inherited the title.

Charles, of Wilton Castle, near Ross, in Herefordshire, became cup bearer to King PHILIP, and was deputy-lieutenant of the Tower to his father, John, Lord Chandos, when the warrant came for executing the Princess Elizabeth, which he refused to obey, until he should receive orders from the king and queen, and thereby was the means of saving her life · for the order being disowned at court, a stop was put to the execution. Mr. Brydges lived to an advanced age, and was sheriff of Herefordshire, in the 32nd of ELIZABETH. He *m.* Jane, dau. of Sir Edward Carne, of Ewenny, co. Glamorgan, Knt., and dying in 1619, was *s.* by his eldest son,

GILES BRYDGES, Esq. of Wilton Castle, who was created a baronet, 17 May, 1627. Sir Giles *m.* Mary, dau. of Sir James Scudamore, and was *s.* by his eldest son,

SIR JOHN BRYDGES, 2nd baronet, who *m.* Mary, only dau. and heir of James Pearle, Esq., of Dewsal and Anconbury, co. Hereford, and dying in 1651, was *s.* by his only son,

SIR JAMES BRYDGES, 3rd baronet, of whom hereafter, as 8th LORD CHANDOS.

Anthony, *m.* Catherine, dau. of Henry Fortescue, Esq., of Faulkbourn Hall, Essex; from this marriage the Rev. EDWARD TYMEWELL BRYDGES, who eventually claimed the Barony of Chandos at the death of the last Duke of Chandos, endeavoured, unsuccessfully, to establish a descent.

Lord Chandos was *s.* by his eldest son,

EDMUND BRUGES, 2nd baron, who adopted early the profession of arms, and served under the Earl of Hertford, in the reign of King HENRY VIII., and in 1547, behaving himself with great bravery in the famous battle of Musselburgh, he was made a knight banneret by the Duke of Somerset. In the reign of Queen ELIZABETH he was elected a knight of the Garter, and installed at Windsor, 17 June, 1572. His lordship *m.* Dorothy, 5th dau., and eventually co-heir of Edmund, Lord Braye, and dying 11 September, 1573, was *s.* by his elder son,

GILES BRUGES, 3rd baron, who, in the lifetime of his father, represented the co. of Gloucester in parliament. His lordship *m.* Lady Frances Clinton, dau. of Edward, 1st Earl of Lincoln, admiral of England, by whom he had two daus., Elizabeth, who *m.* Sir John Kennedy, of Scotland, and *d. s. p.* and Catherine, *m.* to Francis, Lord Russell, of Thornhaugh, afterwards Earl of Bedford. Those ladies were his heirs. His lordship *d.* 21 February, 1593-4, and was *s.* in the peerage by his brother,

WILLIAM BRUGES, 4th baron, who *m.* Mary, dau. of Sir Owen Hopton, lieutenant of the Tower, and dying in 1602, was *s.* by his elder son,

GREY BRUGES, 6th baron, K.B. This nobleman, from the magnificence of his style of living at his mansion, in Gloucestershire, and the splendour of his retinue when he came to court, acquired the title of KING OF COTSWOULD. He had an ample fortune, which he expended in the most generous and liberal manner. His house was open three days in the week to the gentry, and the poor were fed as constantly from the remnants of his entertainments. On 8 November, 1617, Lord Chandos was appointed to receive and introduce the Muscovite ambassadors, who had brought rich and costly presents from their master to the king. His lordship *m.* Lady Anne Stanley, dau. and co-heir of Ferdinando, 5th Earl of Derby, and great grand-dau. of the Princess Mary Tudor, by her husband, Charles Brandon, Duke of Suffolk, and dying 10 August, 1621, was *s.* by his elder son,

GEORGE BRUGES, 6th baron. This nobleman, who was but a year old at the decease of his father, became at the breaking out of the civil wars, in 1641, a stout supporter of the royal cause. At the battle of Newbury his lordship had three horses killed under him, which so far from damping his ardour, roused his valour to a higher pitch, for mounting a fourth charger he renewed the attack, and was mainly instrumental in breaking the enemy's cavalry. In consideration of his splendid conduct in this action, Lord Chandos had an offer from the king to be created *Earl of Newbury*, but he modestly declined, until it should please God to restore his majesty to the crown, an event which he did not survive to see: but, on the contrary, many severe mortifications and sufferings, and much mental adversity, as well as worldly oppression. When the parliamentarians triumphed, his lordship, besides having suffered imprisonment, paid at one time £3,973 10*s.*, and what was left him he generously bestowed in relieving the distressed clergy, and those who had suffered by the wars.

In the year, 1652, Lord Chandos had a difference with Colonel Henry Compton, grandson of Henry, Lord Compton, which unhappily ended in a duel at Putney Heath, on 13 May, when Colonel Compton fell. His lordship and his second, Lord Arundel, of Wardour, having been imprisoned more than a year, were at length arraigned in the upper bench, 17 May, 1654. and found guilty of manslaughter. He *d.* in the February of the following year of the small-pox, and was buried at Sudeley. His lordship *m.* 1st, Susan, dau. of Henry, Earl of Manchester, and had two daus., Mary, *m* to William Brownlow, Esq., of Humby, co. Lincoln, and Elizabeth, *m.* 1st, to Edward, Lord Herbert of Cherbury; and 2ndly, to William, Earl of Inchiquin; and 3rdly, to Charles, Lord Howard, of Escrick. Lord Chandos *m.* 2ndly, Jane, dau. of John Savage, Earl Rivers, by whom he

had with two other daus. that *d unm.*, Lucy, *m.* to Adam Loftus, Viscount Lisburne, in Ireland. His lordship dying thus, without male issue, the major part of his fortune passed under settlement to Jane, his last wife, who afterwards *m.* George Pitt, Esq., of Strathfieldsay, ancestor of the Pitts, Lords Rivers, and conveyed to that gentleman Sudeley Castle, and other lands of great value. The peerage devolved upon his lordship's brother,

WILLIAM BRUGES, 7th baron, who *m.* Susan, dau. and co-heir of Gerrot Keire, of London, merchant, but having no male issue (he left three daus., Mary, Frances, and Rebecca), the title devolved at his decease, in 1676, upon his kinsman (*refer* to Charles, 2nd son of John, 1st Lord Chandos),

SIR JAMES BRYDGES, Bart., of Wilton Castle, as 8th Baron Chandos. This nobleman was accredited ambassador to Constantinople in 1680, where he resided for some years in great honour and esteem. His lordship *m.* Elizabeth, eldest dau. and co-heir of Sir Henry Bernard, Knt., an eminent Turkey merchant. By this lady he had no less than twenty-two children, of which number fifteen only were christened, and seven of those dying young, the remainder were,

    I. JAMES, his successor.

    II. Henry, in holy orders, of Adlestrop, Gloucestershire, archdeacon and prebendary of Rochester, and rector of Agmondesham, Bucks. Mr. Brydges *m.* Annabella, dau. of Henry, and grand-dau. of Sir Robert Atkyns, lord chief baron of the Exchequer, by whom he had issue,

      1 Robert, a lunatic, *d. s. p.* 1779.

      2 James, of Pinner, *m.* Jane, dau. and co-heir of John, Marquess of Carnarvon, and *d. s. p.* 1789.

      1 Elizabeth Louisa, *m.* Sir Robert Walter, Bart., of Saresden, and *d. s. p.*

      2 Annabella, *m.* to Colonel Inwood.

      3 Mary, *m.* to Simon Whorwood Adeane, Esq., ancestor, by her, of the Adeanes of Babraham, co. Cambridge.

      4 Henrietta, *m* the Rev. John Kearney, D.D., and had issue.

      5 Catherine, *m* to Lindley Simpson, Esq.

    III. Francis, receiver general of the duties on malt, *m.* Sarah Western, and *d. s. p.* 1714.

    I. Mary, *m.* to Theophilus Leigh, Esq., of Adlestrop, co. Gloucester, ancestor, by her, of the Leighs of Adlestrop, Lords Leigh, of Stoneleigh.

    II. Elizabeth, *m.* 1st, to Alexander Jacob, Esq.; and 2ndly, to the Rev Dr. Thomas Dawson, vicar of Windsor.

    III. Emma, *m.* to Edmund Chamberlayne, Esq., of Maugersbury House, co. Gloucester, ancestor, by her, of the present Joseph Chamberlayne-Chamberlayne, Esq., of Maugersbury House.

    IV. Anne, *m.* Charles Walcot, Esq., of Walcot, co. Salop, ancestor, by her, of the Walcots now of Bitterley Court, co. Salop.

    V. Catherine. *m.* 1st, to Brereton Bourchier, Esq., of Barnsley Court, co. Gloucester; and 2ndly, to Henry Perrot, Esq., of North Leigh, co. Oxford.

His lordship *d.* in 1714, and was *s.* by his eldest son,

JAMES BRYDGES, 9th baron, who, upon the accession of King GEORGE I., was created, by letters patent, dated 19 October, 1714, *Viscount Wilton*, and EARL OF CARNARVON, with a collateral remainder to the issue male of his father; and in the November following, a patent passed the great seal, granting to his lordship and his two sons, John and Henry, the reversion of the office of clerk of the hanaper in chancery. In 1729, on 30 April, his lordship was advanced to the *Marquisate of Carnarvon*, and DUKEDOM OF CHANDOS, and he acquired by his magnificence the appellation of the *princely* Chandos. He *m.* 1st, 28 February, 1696-7, Mary, only surviving dau. and heir of Sir Thomas Lake, of Cannons, Middlesex, by whom he had two surviving sons,

    I. JOHN, Marquess of Carnarvon, *d. v. p.* 8 April, 1729; *m.* in 1724, Lady Catharine Tollemache, dau. of Lionel, 2nd Earl of Dysart, by whom he had issue,

      1 Catherine, *m.* 1st, to William Berkeley Lyon, Esq., of the horse-guards; and 2ndly, to Edwyn Francis Stanhope, Esq. (a descendant of the 1st Earl of Chesterfield), and was grandmother of SIR EDWYN FRANCIS SCUDAMORE-STANHOPE, Bart., of Holme Lacy, co. Hertford.

      2 Jane (a posthumous child), *m.* her cousin, James Brydges, Esq., of Pinner, and *d. s. p.*

    II. HENRY, Marquess of Carnarvon, after the decease of his brother.

His grace *m.* 2ndly, Cassandra, dau. of Francis Willoughby, Esq., and sister of Thomas Willoughby, Lord Middleton ; and 3rdly, Lydia Catharine Van Hatten, widow of Sir Thomas Davall, Knt., but had no issue by either of these ladies. He *d.* at his noble seat of Cannons, near Edgeware, 9 August, 1744, and was *s.* by his only surviving son,

HENRY BRYDGES, 2nd duke, who *m.* in 1728, Mary, eldest dau. and co-heir of Charles, Lord Bruce, only son and heir apparent of Thomas, Earl of Aylesbury, by whom he had issue,

JAMES, Marquess of Carnarvon.

Caroline. *m.* 10 March, 1755, John Leigh, Esq., of Adlestrop, co. Gloucester, and was grandmother of Chandos Leigh, Esq., created in 1839, BARON LEIGH, of Stoneleigh.

His grace *m.* 2ndly, 25 December, 1744, Anne Jeffreys, and by her he had a dau., Augusta-Anne, *m.* to Henry John Kearney, Esq. The duke *m.* 3rdly, 18 July, 1767, Elizabeth, 2nd dau. and co-heir of Sir John Major, Bart., of Worlingworth Hall, Suffolk, by whom he had no issue. He *d.* 28 November, 1771, and was *s.* by his son,

JAMES BRYDGES, 3rd duke, *b.* 27 December, 1731. This nobleman, upon the accession of his majesty King GEORGE III., was appointed one of the lords of his bed-chamber. In 1775, he was sworn of the privy council, and was afterwards constituted lord-steward of the household. His grace *m.* 22 March, 1753, Margaret, dau. and sole heiress of John Nicol, Esq., of Southgate, Middlesex, by whom he acquired Minchenden House at Southgate, together with the whole fortune of his father-in-law. By this lady, who *d.* in 1768, he had no issue. The duke *m.* 2ndly, 21 June, 1777, Anne-Eliza, dau. of Richard Gamon, Esq., and widow of Roger Hope Elletson, Esq., by whom he had one surviving dau. and heiress,

ANNE-ELIZA, who *m.* in 1796, RICHARD, *Earl Temple*, afterwards DUKE OF BUCKINGHAM AND CHANDOS, and left issue.

His grace *d.* without male issue 29 September, 1789, when all his honours became EXTINCT, but the BARONY OF CHANDOS was immediately claimed by the Rev. EDWARD TYMEWELL BRYDGES, M.A., of Wootton Court, Kent, as next heir male of the body of Sir John Brydges, LORD CHANDOS, the first grantee, who *d.* in 1557. The first hearing of this celebrated cause took place before the committee of privileges of the House of Lords, 1 June, 1790; the second, 21 December, in the same year; the 3rd, 4th, 5th, 6th, and 7th, in 1794; the 8th and 9th in 1795; the 10th, 11th, 12th, and 13th, in 1802; thirteen other hearings in 1803; and at length, after a few more investigations, it was resolved by the committee for privileges, 17 June, 1803, "that the said Rev. Edward Tymewell Brydges had not made out his claim to the said barony." Mr. Brydges, the claimant, was elder brother of the late distinguished writer, SIR SAMUEL EGERTON BRYDGES, Bart.

BULKELEY—BARONS BULKELEY, OF BEAUMARIS, IN THE ISLE OF ANGLESEY: VISCOUNTS BULKELEY IN IRELAND.

Barony, by Letters Patent, dated 14 May, 1784.
Viscounty, by Letters Patent, dated 6 January, 1643.

Lineage.

he ancient family of Bulkeley derives descent from ROBERT DE BULKELEY, lord of the manors of Bulkeley, Eaton, Tarporley, Rudhall, Heathhall, Orton Madox, Pettyhall and Prestland, in the cos. of Chester and Salop, living *temp* King JOHN, as appears by an inquisition taken in the reign of EDWARD IV., whose son and successor,

WILLIAM BULKELEY, lord of the manor of Bulkeley, co. Chester, *m.* the dau. of Thomas Butler, of Bewsey, feudal Lord of Warrington, co. Lancaster, and had issue five sons,

I. ROBERT, his successor.
II. WILCOCK, of Pettyhall, co. Chester, *m.* Mary, dau. of Hugh Venables, Baron of Kinderton, and had an only son, Willcock.
III. Roger, of Orton Madoc, co. Chester.
IV. Ralph, of Rudhall, co. Chester.
V. David, who *m.* Helen, heiress of Bickerton, co. Chester, and was father of a son, Robert Bulkeley, ancestor of the Bulkeleys of Bickerton, extinct in 1802.

The eldest son,

ROBERT BULKELEY, of Bulkeley, *m.* Jane, dau. of Sir William Butler, Knt., and had issue,

I. WILLIAM, of whom presently.
II. Peter Bulkeley, *jure uxoris* of Were, co. Salop, who by the heiress of Were, dau. and heir of Bird, of Were, had a son, John Bulkeley, of Were, who *m.* Awdry, dau. and heir of Sir John Audley, of Wirral, co. Chester, progenitor by her of the Bulkeleys of Were.
I. Agnes, *m.* Griffith Vychan, whose name occurs 1231, 3rd son (by Matilda, sister and co-heir of Ralph Le Strange, Baron of Knocklyn, Alveley and Weston) of Griffith, Lord of Sutton, son of Prince Jorwerth Gôch, *alias* Gervase Gôch, Lord of Mochnant-ys Rhaiadr. son, by his 2nd consort (Efa, dau. of Blettrws ap Ednowen Bendew) of Meredith ap

Bleddyn, Prince of Powys. Of this marriage there was issue a son, GRIFFITH, of Cae Howel and Kynaston, co. Salop, ancestor of the several families of Kynaston of Kynaston; Kynaston of Storks; Kynaston of Oteley, and Kynaston of Hardwicke, Barts. (*Refer to Cherlton of Powys.*)

Robert Bulkeley was *s.* by his eldest son,

WILLIAM BULKELEY, living at Bulkeley in 1302, who *m.* twice. By his 2nd wife, Alice, dau. of Bryan St Pierre, he had issue an only son, RICHARD, on whom he conferred the manor of Prestland, co. Chester, from which the latter assumed the surname of Prestland, and was ancestor of the family of that name. By his 1st wife Maud, dau. of Sir John Davenport, Knt., of Davenport, co. Chester, living in 1302, he had four sons, viz.,

I. William Bulkeley, of Bulkeley, whose line terminated with his grand-dau., Alice, heiress of Bulkeley, who *m.* Thomas Holford, of Holford, co. Chester, *jure uxoris* Lord of Bulkeley.
II. ROBERT, of whom presently.
III. Roger, of Norbury, co. Chester, whence his descendants derived the patronymic of "Norbury."
IV. Thomas Bulkeley, *m.* Alice, heiress of Alpraham. dau. and co-heir of Mathew Alpraham, esq., of Alpraham, co. Chester, by whom he left an only child and heir, Ellin, heiress of Alpraham, who *m.* Sir Thomas Ardern, Knt., of Elford, co. Stafford.

The 2nd son,

ROBERT BULKELEY, lord of the manor of Eaton, co. Chester, high sheriff of Cheshire, 3rd EDWARD II. (1309-10), was father, by Agnes his wife, of two sons and a dau., viz.,

I. Robert Bulkeley, high sheriff of Cheshire 15th EDWARD II. (1341-2), his father being then alive, *m.* Isabel, dau. of Philip Egerton, of Malpas, co. Chester, and was father (with a younger son, Robert Bulkeley, whose only child and heir, Ellin, *m.* William, son of Robert Whettenhall), of an elder son, JOHN BULKELEY, of Eaton, living 20th RICHARD II. (1397), father of Sir WILLIAM BULKELEY, Knt., of Eaton, chief justice of Chester, *temp.* HENRY IV., living 30th HENRY VI. (1451), who *m.* Margaret, dau. (by Elizabeth, dau. of Sir Thomas Stanley, K.G., 1st Baron Stanley, summoned to parliament 15 January, 34th HENRY VI., 1456) of Sir Richard Molineux, Knt., of Sefton, co. Lancaster, slain at Bloreheath, 23 September, 1459. Of this marriage there was issue,

1 Thomas Bulkeley, of Eaton, who by Jane his wife, dau. of Sir Geoffrey Warburton, Knt., had two sons and two daus.,

    Thomas Bulkeley, of Eaton, father, by Eleanor his wife, dau. of Sir William Brereton, Knt., of Brereton, of a son, Thomas Bulkeley, Esq., of Eaton, who *m.* Elizabeth, dau. of Thomas Venables, and *d. s p.*
    Robert Bulkeley, father of two sons, Robert and Richard, who both *d. s. p.*
    Jonet, eventual co-heir of the Bulkeleys of Eaton, *m.* Roger Puleston, Esq., of Emral, co. Flint, living 9 August, 38th HENRY VI. (1460), and 12th EDWARD IV (1484), and was mother of a son, Sir Roger Puleston, Knt., of Emral, who *d.* 18 January, 36th HENRY VIII. (1545), ancestor of the Pulestons of Emral, from whom derive maternally the Pulestons (paternally Prices) of Emral, baronets.
    Elizabeth, co-heir, *m.* John Frobisher, of Chirk, co. Denbigh.

2 Arthur Bulkeley, father of four sons, Richard, William, Thomas, and Edward.
3 Richard Bulkeley, living 18th HENRY VI. (1439).
4 Ralph Bulkeley, *m.* the dau. and heir of Vernon, of Wheatcroft, co. Chester, and of Parwich, co. Derby. From this marriage derive the Bulkeleys of Parwich; Bulkeleys of Stanton, co. Stafford; Bulkeleys of Bradnop; Bulkeleys of Huntley, and Bulkeleys of Stapenhill.
1 Maud, *m.* Thomas Holford, of Holford, co. Chester, and was mother of a son, Sir George Holford, Knt., of Holford, great-grandfather of Christopher Holford, of Holford, whose dau. and heir *m.* Sir Hugh Cholmondeley, Knt.. of Cholmondeley, co. Chester, ancestor by her of GEORGE-HORATIO CHOLMONDELEY, 2nd and present Marquess Cholmondeley.
2 Petronel, *m.* Richard Brett, Esq., of Dunham, co. Chester.
3 Catherine, *m.* Randal Brereton, Esq., of Malpas, co, Chester.
4 —, *m.* John Minshull, Esq., of Minshull, co. Chester.

II. RICHARD BULKELEY, of whose line we treat.
I. Ciceley, *m.* Thomas Weaver, Esq.

The 2nd son of Robert Bulkeley,

RICHARD BULKELEY, *jure uxoris* lord of the manor of Cheadle, co. Chester, *m.* in 1307, Agnes, heiress of Cheadle, dau. and co-heir of Roger Cheadle, Esq., of Cheadle, and was *s.* by his son and heir,

RICHARD BULKELEY, of Cheadle, who, by Alice his wife, dau. of Sir Ralph Bostock, Knt., was father of a son and successor,

WILLIAM BULKELEY, Esq., of Cheadle, constable of Beaumaris Castle, Anglesey, in the reign of HENRY VI., who prevented the Duke of York, on his return from Ireland, from effecting a landing at Beaumaris. He *m.* Ellin, dau. (by his 2nd wife,

Jonet, widow of Robert Paris, chamberlain of North Wales, and dau. of Sir William Stanley, Knt., of Hooton, co. Chester) of Gwylim ap Griffith, of Penrhyn, co. Carnarvon, and *jure primæ uxoris* of Penmynydd, co. Anglesey, who *d.* 18th HENRY IV. (1440), derived from Ednyfed Vychan, Lord of Brynfenigle. By this lady he was father of a son,

ROWLAND BULKELEY, Esq., of Beaumaris and Cheadle, who *m.* Alice, dau. and heir of William Beconsal, of Beconsal, co. Lancaster, and had two daus., and five sons, of whom,

  I. SIR RICHARD BULKELEY, *s.* his father.
  II. William Bulkeley *m.* Ellin, heiress of Porthamel, co. Anglesey, dau. and co-heir of Richard ap Meredith, of Porthamel, derived from Llywarch ap Bran, Lord of Menai, and was ancestor of the Bulkeleys of Porthamel.
  III. Robert Bulkeley, of Gronant, co. Anglesey, who by Jonet his wife, dau. of Morris, of Llanfwrog, son of Rhys, of Clygyrog, son of Howel y Rharf, Lord of Trejorwerth, derived from Hwfa ap Cynddelew, Lord of Llyslyffon, was ancestor of the Bulkeleys of Gronant.

The eldest son,

SIR RICHARD BULKELEY, Knt., of Beaumaris, chamberlain of North Wales in 1534, *m.* Catherine, dau. (by his 1st wife, Jane, dau. of Sir Thomas Stradling, Knt., of Donald's Castle,) of Sir William Griffith, Knt., of Penrhyn, co. Carnarvon, son of Sir William Griffith, Knt., of Penrhyn, surnamed "the Liberal," chamberlain of North Wales. Of this marriage there was issue three sons and three daus., viz.,

  I. SIR RICHARD BULKELEY, Knt., of whom presently.
  II. Rowland Bulkeley, Esq., of Cremlyn, whose will, dated 2 April, 1592, was proved at Bangor, 13 October following. He *m.* Elizabeth (who became subsequently the 2nd wife of Richard Bulkeley, Esq., of Porthamel), dau. of Rhys Wynn, Esq., of Bodychan, co. Anglesey, who *d.* 1559, and was by her father of an only child, JANE, heiress of Tre'rmoelgoch, co Anglesey, to whom her father devised all his lands in Lwydiarth and Tre'rmoelgoch, with remainder to the heirs of her body, with remainder to the heirs male of his nephew, Sir Richard Bulkeley, of Beaumaris. She *m.* Rowland Bulkeley, Esq., of Porthamel, son (by his 1st wife Mary, dau. of William Lewis, Esq., of Presaddfed, co. Anglesey) of Richard Bulkeley, Esq., of Porthamel, who *m.* 2ndly, the widow of Rowland Bulkeley, Esq., of Cremlyn, and mother of Jane. From this marriage derive the Bulkeleys of Porthamel.
  III. John Bulkeley, named in the will of his brother Rowland Bulkeley, Esq., of Cremlyn.
  I. Jane, who became the 1st wife of Morris Wynne, Esq., of Gwydyr, named in the will of his brother-in-law, Rowland Bulkeley, Esq., of Cremlyn, son of John Wynne ap Meredith, of Gwydyr, who *d.* in 1553, derived from Owen Gwynedd, Prince of North Wales, and was by him mother of four sons and four daus., of whom the eldest son, Sir John Wynne, of Gwydyr, Bart, so created in 1611, was ancestor of the Wynnes of Gwydyr, Baronets, EXTINCT, represented as senior co-heirs by Peter-Robert-Drummond Willoughby, Baron Willoughby d'Eresby, and George-Horatio Cholmondeley, 2nd Marquess of Cholmondeley; and as junior co-heir by Sir Watkin Williams Wynn, 6th Baronet of Wynnstay, co. Denbigh.
  II. Jonet, *m.* to Ralph Ardern, Esq.
  III. —, *m.* William Thom s Wynn, Esq., of The Vaynols, named in the will of his brother-in-law Rowland Bulkeley, Esq., of Cremlyn.

Sir Richard Bulkeley was *s.* by his eldest son,

SIR RICHARD BULKELEY, Knt., of Beaumaris and Cheadle, knighted 1576, M.P. for Anglesey in the reigns of Queen MARY and ELIZABETH, who married twice : 1st, Margaret, dau. (by Lady Elizabeth, dau. of Charles Somerset, Earl of Worcester) of Sir John Savage, Knt., of Rock Savage, co. Chester, ancestor of the Savages, Earls Rivers, extinct, by whom he had, with four other sons and two daus.,

  I. SIR RICHARD BULKELEY, his heir.
  II. Daniel Bulkeley, *m.* Ellin, dau. (by Alice, dau. of John Conway, of Bodryddan, co. Flint) of Rowland Bulkeley, Esq , of Porthamel, who *d.* in 1590.
  I. Elizabeth, *m,* Owen Holland, Esq., of Berw, co. Anglesey, ancestor by her of the Hollands of Berw, represented (1864) as heir-general by Richard Trygarn Griffith, Esq., of Carreglwyd, Trygarn and Berw.
  II. Catherine, *m.* Griffith ap John Griffith, of Cefnamlwch, co. Carnarvon, who *d.* at Oxford, and was buried there in St. Mary's Church, in 1599, ancestor by her, of the Griffiths of Cefnamlwch.
  III. Jane, *m.* Robert Pugh, Esq., of Penrhyn-yn-Creyddyn, co. Carnarvon.

Sir Richard Bulkeley *m.* 2ndly, Agnes, dau. (by Anne, dau. of Sir John Talbot, of Grafton) of Thomas Needham, Esq., of Shenton, ancestor of the Needhams, Earls Kilmorey, and by her had issue eight sons and two daus., of whom five *d.* young,

  I. Lancelot Bulkeley, consecrated archbishop of Dublin, 11 August, 1619, and sworn of the privy council, who, dying 8 September, 1650, æt. eighty-one, was buried in St. Patrick's Cathedral, Dublin. This prelate *m.* Alice, living in 1652,

dau. of Rowland Bulkeley, Esq., of Beaumaris, and had with other issue,

  Sir Richard Bulkeley, of Old Bawn, Ireland, baronet, so created 1672, who left, at his decease, in 1685, I Sir Richard Bulkeley, 2nd baronet, of Old Bawn, who *d. s. p.* in 1710, when the baronetcy became EXTINCT. II. — Bulkeley (dead in 1710 , whose only dau. and heir, Anne, heiress of her uncle, *m.* I. W. Tynte, Esq.

II. Arthur Bulkeley, vicar of Coydan, living 36th ELIZABETH, 1596, *m,* Anne, heiress of Coydan and Brynddu, co Anglesey, only child and heir of Rhys ap William of Clygyrog-Ucha, derived from Yarddur, Lord of Llehwedd, grand forester of Snowdon, by Elizabeth his wife, heiress of Coydan and Brynddu, younger dau. and co-heir of Hugh ap Llewelyn, of Bodowyr in Bodedern, derived from Llywarch Holbwrch, Lord of Monodog. By the heiress of Coydan and Brynddu, Arthur Bulkeley was father, with other issue, of an eldest son, WILLIAM BULKELEY, Esq., of Brynddu, who *m.* twice : 1st, Mary, 2nd dau. (by Barbara, widow of Humphrey Lloyd, Esq., of Denbigh "the antiquary," and sister and eventual heir of John Lumley, Baron Lumley in 1547, and dau of George Lumley, executed for high treason, 29th HENRY VIII. (1538), son of John de Lumley, 5th Baron Lumley) of William Williams, Esq., of Cochwillan, co. Carnarvon. By his 2nd wife, Anne, dau. of Rhys Wynn, of Lwydiarth, he was father of an only child, Anne, who *m.* 1st, William Lewis, Esq., of Cemlyn, and 2ndly, the Rev. Richard Hughes, brother of Hugh Hughes, Esq., of Plas Côch, Anglesey, and left issue by both these marriages. William Bulkeley was *s.* by his eldest son, WILLIAM BULKELEY, Esq., of Brynddu, who *m.* 1st, 20 May, 1624, Gaynor, dau. of Cadwalader Wynne, Esq., of Voelas, co. Denbigh, and by her was father of an only child, WILLIAM, his successor. By his 2nd wife, Margaret, dau. of Richard Parry, bishop of St. Asaph, he had four sons and two daus. His eldest son and heir, WILLIAM BULKELEY, Esq., of Brynddu, *m.* Mary, dau. of Ffacknallt, of Ffacknallt, co. Flint, and had, with other issue, an eldest son. WILLIAM BULKELEY, Esq., of Brynddu, high sheriff of Anglesey in 1715, who *m.* Lettice, youngest of the three daus. and co-heirs of Captain Henry Jones, of Llangoed, co. Anglesey, and was father of an eldest son,

  WILLIAM BULKELEY, Esq., of Brynddu, presumptive heir male of the Baronhill branch of the Bulkeleys, contingent on the decease without surviving male issue of James, 6th Viscount Bulkeley. This gentleman *m.* Jane, dau. of the Rev. Ambrose Lewis, of Cemlyn, by whom he was father of a son and dau., viz.,

    WILLIAM BULKELEY, Esq., barrister-at-law, who *d. unm.* in the lifetime of his father, 23, and was buried 27 December, 1751
    MARY, heir of her brother, *m.* Fortunatus Wright, a merchant of Liverpool, who, accepting letters of marque from the crown in the war of the Spanish succession, by his enterprise and gallantry as a naval captain in command of the "St. George" privateer, acquired an honourable place in the history of his country Of this marriage there was issue, with an eldest son, William Bulkeley Wright, who *d.* an infant, and was buried at Leghorn, in Italy, 21 December, 1756, and four daus., who *d. unm.*, an eldest dau. and heiress,

      ANNE, heiress of Brynddu, devisee of her grandfather William Bulkeley, Esq., of Brynddu. This lady, who was *bapt.* 10 February, 1738, *m.* (settlement previous to marriage dated 12 and 13 July, 1765) William Hughes Esq., of Plâs Côch, in Mendi, co. Anglesey, and of Llan goed, in the same county, high sheriff of Anglesey in 1768, and of Carnarvonshire in 1789, XVIIITH in direct male descent from Llywarch, ap Bran Lord of Menai. By Mr. Hughes, the heiress of Brynddu, who *d.* 13 March, 1807, was mother, with other issue, of an eldest son,

        SIR WILLIAM HUGHES, Knt., of Plâs Côch and Brynddu, high sheriff of Anglesey in 1803, who *m.* Elizabeth, 2nd dau., and in her issue senior co-heir of Rice Thomas, Esq., of Coedhelen and Glascoed, po. Carnarvon, lord of the manor of Kemmees, co. Anglesey, of Pentrehobyn, co. Flint, of Glanhafon. co. Montgomery, and of Trevor Hall, including Valle Crucis Abbey, co. Denbigh. By this lady Sir William Hughes, who *d.* 6 December, 1836, was father, with other children, of an eldest son and heir, the late

          WILLIAM BULKELEY HUGHES, Esq., of Plâs Côch and Brynddu, lord of the manor of Kemmees, high sheriff of Anglesey in 1861, and M.P. for the Carnarvon boroughs from 26 June, 1837, until 1859. This gentleman *m.* 19 April, 1825, Elizabeth, widow of Henry Wormald, Esq., of Woodehouse, co York, and dau. and co-heir of Jonathan Nettleship, Esq., of Mattersey Abbey, co. Nottingham. He *d.* 8 March, 1882.

III. Tristram Bulkeley, the youngest son, *m.* Mary, living 1694, dau. of Jeuan ap Llewelyn ap Griffith, of Llangristiolus.
I. Grizzel, who *d.* 17 September, 1641, and was buried with her husband, *m.* Sir Henry Power, Knt., of Bersham, co. Denbigh, constable of the castle of Maryborough, created

Viscount Valentia, 1 March, 1620, *d. s. p.* 8 September, 1641, and was buried in St. Patrick's Cathedral, Dublin.

II. Mary, *m.* James Eaton, of Pentre Madog, Duddlestone, co. Salop.

Sir Richard Bulkeley was *s.* by his eldest son,

Sir RICHARD BULKELEY, Knt., of Beaumaris, who erected the mansion at Baronhill in 1618. "Before that time the residence of the family was at Court Mawr, in Beaumaris, and afterwards in another house, called Plâs Hen, or Old Hall" (Pennant's *Tours in Wales*), more recently known as "Plâs Bulkeley," an ancient house, possessing great architectural feature, and beautifully carved ceilings and panelling, now in extreme dilapidation from neglect. Sir Robert Bulkeley *m.* twice, 1st, Mary, dau. of William Borough, Lord Borough, of Gainsborough, co. Lincoln, by whom he had two sons,

I. Sir Richard Bulkeley, Knt., who *m.* Anne, dau. of Sir John Wilford, Knt., of Ildington, co. Kent, *d.* 25 January, 1645, and was buried in the church of Penmon Priory, Anglesey, where there is a monument to him. By this lady (who *m.* 2ndly, Sir Thomas Cheadle, Knt., deputy to the Earl of Dorset, constable of Beaumaris Castle in 1642) Sir Richard Bulkeley was father of,

Richard Bulkeley, who *d. unm.*

Mary, *m.* Richard Bodychen, 2nd son and eventual heir of John Bodychen, of Bodychen, co. Anglesey.

During the marriage of Sir Richard Bulkeley and Anne Wilford his wife, the latter was mother of several sons who bore the surname of Bulkeley, but were repudiated by her as illegitimate.

II. THOMAS BULKELEY, of whom presently.

Sir Richard Bulkeley *m.* 2ndly, Catherine, dau. of Sir William Davenport, Knt., of Brome Hall, co. Chester, and had issue,

I. Richard Bulkeley, named in the will of his great uncle, Rowland Bulkeley, Esq., of Cremlyn, *m.* Anne, dau. of George Needham. Esq., of Jamaica, younger son of Thomas Needham, Esq., of Pool Park, 2nd son of Robert Needham, Esq., of Shenton, co, Salop, ancestor of the Needhams, Earls Kilmorey.
I. Elizabeth, *m.* George Shelton, of Heath Hall, co. York.
II. Catherine, named in the will of her great-uncle, Rowland Bulkeley, Esq., of Cremlyn.
III. Margaret, *m.* Sir Thomas Potter, Knt.
IV. Penelope, *m.* in 1614 Sir Edwyn Sandys, Knt., of Worsburgh, eldest son and heir of Sir Samuel Sandys, of Ombersley, co. Warwick, and from this marriage derived Samuel Sandys, Baron Sandys, of Ombersley, so created 1743, speaker of the House of Lords, whose grand-dau. and eventual heir, Mary, dau. of his 4th son, Colonel Martin Sandys, was created Baroness Sandys, of Ombersley, with remainder to her 2nd and younger sons by her husband Arthur Hill, Marquess of Downshire.

Sir Richard Bulkeley, who *d.* 28 June, 1621, *æt.* eighty-eight, was *s.* by his 2nd son,

THOMAS BULKELEY, of Baronhill, who espousing zealously the cause of King CHARLES I., was created by that monarch, by patent, under the privy seal, dated at Oxford, 6 January, 1643, VISCOUNT BULKELEY, of CASHEL, in the peerage of Ireland. His lordship *m.* twice, 1st, Blanch, dau. (by Lumley, dau. of Humphrey Lloyd, Esq., "the antiquary," by Barbara his wife, sister and heir of John, Lord Lumley) of Robert Coytmore, Esq., of Coytmore, co. Carnarvon, derived from Yarddur, Lord of Llechwedd, great forester of Snowdon. By this lady Viscount Bulkeley had issue,

I. Colonel Richard Bulkeley, who held Beaumaris Castle for the king until 1646, when it was surrendered on honourable terms to General Mytton. This gentleman, who *d. s. p.* in the lifetime of his father, was treacherously murdered at Traethlavan by Richard Chedle, for which crime that person was executed at Conway.
II. ROBERT, successor to his father.
III. Captain Thomas Bulkeley, of Dinas, co. Carnarvon, *m.* Jane, widow of William Williames, brother of Sir William Williames, Bart., of Vaynol, co. Carnarvon, and dau. and co-heir of Griffith Jones, Esq., of Castllemarch, co. Carnarvon, derived from Meirion Goch.
IV. Henry Bulkeley, master of the household to CHARLES II. and JAMES II. He *m.* Lady Sophia Stewart, maid of honour to the queen, by whom he had two daus. and co-heirs,

Anne, who in 1700 became the 2nd wife of James Fitz-James, Duke of Berwick, illegitimate son, by Arabella Churchill, sister of the celebrated Duke of Marlborough, of JAMES II. The Duke of Berwick, marshal of France, who was attainted in England in 1695, was created Duc de Fitz-James in France, with remainder to the issue of his 2nd marriage, and that dignity is enjoyed by the descendant of his marriage with Anne Bulkeley, the present DUC DE FITZ-JAMES.
—, dau. and co-heir, who *m.* John Howard.

V. Edwin Bulkeley, *d. s. p.*
I. Mary, *m.* Sir Roger Mostyn, of Mostyn, co. Flint, Baronet, so created in 1660, ancestor by her of the Mostyns of Mostyn, Barts., extinct, represented as heir-general by Edward, 2nd and present Lord Mostyn.
II. Lumley, who *d.* in 1669, *m.* Pierce Lloyd, Esq., of Lligwy,

co. Anglesey, derived from Gwerydd ap Rhys Goch, and was mother of a son, Pierce Lloyd, Esq., of Lligwy, whose grandson *d. s. p.* in 1723, when the family estates were sold to Sir William Irby, Bart., created 16 April, 1761, Lord Boston.

III. Catherine, who *d.* at Branas-in-Edeirnion, co. Merioneth, 5 September, 1706, æt. sixty-nine, and was buried in the churchyard of Llandrillo, in Edeirnion, where there is a handsome monument to her. She *m.* twice, 1st, Richard Wood, Esq., of Rhosmore, co. Anglesey, who *d. s. p.* in 1629, and 2ndly, Richard Wynne, Esq., of Branas-in-Edeirnion, and of Garthgynan, co. Denbigh, high sheriff of Merionethshire in 1667, only son of William Wynne, Esq., of Branas (which he acquired by purchase from Humphrey Branas, Esq., of Branas), son of Sir John Wynne, of Gwydyr, co. Carnarvon, Bart., so created in 1611. By this gentleman she had only issue William, Richard, and Mary, who *d.* infants.

IV. Penelope, *m.* twice, 1st, Sir Griffith Williames, 4th Baronet of Vaynol, who was fourteen years of age at his father's death, 1 November, 1658, great-grandson of Sir William Williames, of Vaynol, Bart., so created 15 June, 1622, eldest son of Thomas Williames, Esq., of Vaynol, younger brother of William Wynn, *alias* Williames, of Cochwillan, co. Carnarvon, derived from Ednyfed Vychan, Lord of Brynfenigle. Of this marriage there were two sons,

Sir Thomas Williames, 5th baronet, *d. s. p.*
Sir William Williames, 6th and last Baronet of Vaynol, who *m.* his cousin, Ellin, dau. of Robert, 2nd Viscount Bulkeley, and, dying *s. p.*, devised his estates to King WILLIAM III.

Penelope *m.* 2ndly, Colonel Hugh Wynn, of Bodscallen, co. Carnarvon, who was buried at Llanrwst, 6 December, 1674, a scion of the house of Gwydyr, by whom she had no issue.

Viscount Bulkeley *m.* 2ndly, Miss Cheadle, dau. of Mr. Cheadle, sometime his lordship's steward, and was *s.* at his decease by his eldest surviving son,

ROBERT BULKELEY, 2nd Viscount Bulkeley, M.P. for Anglesey in the parliament which restored CHARLES II. He *m.* Sarah, dau. of Daniel Harvey, Esq., of Combe, co. Sussex, alderman of London, and by her, who survived him, and *d.* at Rhiwlas, in the parish of Llanfor, co. Merioneth, 18 June, 1718, and was buried in Llanfor Church, co. Merioneth, where there is a monument to her, had issue twelve children,

I. RICHARD, of whom presently.
II. James Bulkeley, LL.D., and M.P. for Beaumaris.
III. Thomas Bulkeley, M.P., for the co. of Carnarvon.
IV. Robert Bulkeley.
I. Elizabeth, *m.* John Griffith, Esq., of Cefnamlwch, co. Carnarvon, who *d. s. p.* at Paris.
II. Catherine, who died æt. sixty-five, April, 1727, and was buried at Llanfor, co. Merioneth, where there is a monument to her; *m.* the Rev. Philip Atkinson, D.D., rector of Kingsthorpe, co. Northampton, and was mother of a son, Lewis Atkinson, who *m.* the dau. of Thomas Ffowlkes, Esq., of The Vaynols, co. Flint, father of an only son, Thomas Atkinson, who *d.* young.
III. Ellin, *m.* her cousin, Sir William Williames, 6th and last Baronet of Vaynol, co. Carnarvon.
IV. Lumley.   V. Penelope.   VI. Eleanor.   VII. ——.
VIII. Martha, who *d.* 22 February, 1742-3, and was buried at Llanfôr, where there is a monument to her, *m.* Roger Price, Esq., of Rhiwlas, co. Merioneth, high sheriff of that co. in 1710, derived from Marchweithian, a chief of Ysaled, ancestor of the Prices of Plâs Yollyn, co. Merioneth; Wynnes of Voelas, co. Denbigh; and Parrys, of Twysog, co. Flint. By this lady Mr Price, who *d.* 17 October, 1719, and was buried at Llanfôr, had with other children, none of whom had issue, an eldest son, William Price, Esq., of Rhiwlas, who *m.* 1st, the Hon. Mary-Devereux, sister and co-heir of Price Devereux, 10th Viscount Hereford, by whom he had three sons, of whom the eldest and youngest *d. unm.*, and were survived by the 2nd, RICHARD-THELWALL PRICE, Esq., of Rhiwlas, M.P. for Beaumaris, who was *b.* 26 May, 1720, and *d.* without legitimate issue. Mr. Price of Rhiwlas, *m.* 2ndly, the Hon. Elizabeth Bulkeley, dau. of Richard, 4th Viscount Bulkeley, by whom he had no issue.

Viscount Bulkeley *d.* 18 October, 1688, and was *s.* by his eldest son,

RICHARD BULKELEY, 3rd viscount, M.P. for the co. of Anglesey, *b.* 1658. This nobleman *m.* twice, 1st, Mary, eldest dau. of Sir Philip Egerton, Knt , of Egerton and Oulton, co. Chester, by whom he had an only son, RICHARD. By his 2nd wife, Elizabeth, dau. of Henry White, Esq., of Hawthlin, co. Pembroke, Lord Bulkeley, who *d.* 9 August, 1704, left no issue. He was *s.* by his only son,

RICHARD BULKELEY, 4th viscount, M.P. for Anglesey, which honour, together with the constableship of Beaumaris Castle, and chamberlainship of North Wales, had been almost uninterruptedly in his family from the reign of Queen ELIZABETH. His lordship *m.* Lady Bridget Bertie, eldest dau. of James Bertie, summoned to parliament as Baron Norreys, of Rycote, 22 October, 1675, and created Earl of Abingdon in 1682, son of Montague Bertie, Earl of Lindsey, and had issue,

i. RICHARD, } successive viscounts.
ii. JAMES, }

i. Eleanor-Mary, *m.* George Hervey, Esq., of Tiddington, co. Oxford.

ii. Anne, *m.* the Rev. William Bertie, D.D., brother of William, 3rd Earl of Abingdon.

iii. Elizabeth, *b.* 1704, *d.* 21 August, 1778, æt. seventy-four, and was buried at Llanfôr, where there is a monument to her. She became the 2nd wife of William Price, Esq., of Rhiwlas, by whom she had no issue.

Viscount Bulkeley, *d.* 4 June, 1724, and was *s.* by his eldest son,

RICHARD BULKELEY, 5th viscount, who was *b.* 1708 ; *m.* in January, 1731, Jane, dau. and heir of Lewis Owen, Esq., of Penniarth, co. Merioneth, by whom he had no issue. Lady Bulkeley, *m.* 2ndly, Edward Williams, Esq., 3rd son of John Williams, Esq., 2nd son of Sir William Williams, of Landfordd, Bart. Viscount Bulkeley, who *d.* 15 March, 1738, was *s.* by his brother,

JAMES BULKELEY, 6th viscount, constable of Beaumaris Castle, and chamberlain of North Wales, *b.* in 1717 ; *m.* 5 August, 1749, Emma Bridget, heiress of Nant, co. Carnarvon, and of Castellor, co. Anglesey, only surviving child and heir (by Ellin, heiress of Caerau and Castellor, dau. and heir of William Roberts, Esq., of Caerau and Castellor) of Thomas Rowlands, Esq., of Nant, *alias* Ystrad-Ucha. By this lady, Lord Bulkeley, who *d.* 23 April, 1753, left issue, with two daus., Bridget and Elinor, who both *d.* young, an only son and heir,

THOMAS-JAMES.

Viscountess Bulkeley *m.* 2ndly, Sir Hugh Wlliames, 8th Baronet of Penrhyn, co. Carnarvon, derived, through Sir Griffith Williames of Marl, co. Carnarvon, who *s.* to the estates of his uncle, John Williams, archbishop of York, and was created a baronet, 17 June, 1661, from Ednyfed Vychan, Lord of Brynfenigle. Sir Hugh Williames, who *d.* 19 August, 1796, was father by Viscountess Bulkeley of an eldest son, Sir Robert Williames, 9th bart , who *b.* 20 July, 1764, *m.* in 1799, Anne, sister of William-Lewis Hughes, 1st Lord Dinorben, and had with other issue an eldest son, SIR RICHARD-BULKELEY WILLIAMES, 10th bart., M.P. for the co. Anglesey, and lord-lieutenant for the co. Carnarvon, who assumed, by sign manual, 26 June, 1827, the additional surname of BULKELEY, having *s.* in 1822, by will, to Baronhill and the other estates of his father's uterine brother Thomas-James, 7th and last Viscount Bulkeley. The only son of Lord Bulkeley,

THOMAS JAMES BULKELEY, 7th viscount, born posthumous 10 December, 1752, was created a peer of Great Britian, 11 May, 1784, as Baron Bulkeley, of Beaumaris. His lordship *m.* 26 April, 1777, Elizabeth Harriett, only dau. and heir of Sir George Warren, K.B., upon which occasion he assumed the name of Warren before that of Bulkeley. He *d. s. p.* in 1822, when all his honours became EXTINCT, devising Baronhill and his other estates to the eldest son of his uterine brother, the present Sir Richard-Bulkeley Williames, 10th bart., who assumed the name of Bulkeley.

Arms—Sa., a chev.,between three bulls heads, arg., armed, or.

BULMER—BARON BULMER.

By Writ of Summons, dated 25 February, 1342

Lineage.

In the reign of King HENRY I.,

ALAN DE BULMER, son of Henry de Bulmer, Lord of Bulmer and Brancepeth, *m.* and had three sons, viz.,

i. BERTRAM, Lord of Bulmer and Brancepeth, whose only dau. and heiress, *m.* Robert, Lord Neville of Raby.

ii. ANKETELL, of whom presently.

iii. Alphonsus.

The 2nd son,

ANKETELL DE BULMER, gave twelve oxgangs of land, lying in Bramham, to the canons of Nostell, and was father of

BERTRAM DE BULMER, sheriff of Yorkshire *temp.* King STEPHEN and HENRY II., and founder of the priory of Barton, in that county. This Bertram was *s.* by

STEPHEN DE BULMER, who, upon the aid being levied in the 12th HENRY II., towards the marriage portion of that monarch's dau., certified his knights' fees to amount to the number of five *de veteri ffeoffamento*, and one-and-a-half, and fourth part, *de novo*, for which, in two years afterwards, he paid six marks and a-half. Stephen de Bulmer was *s.* by his son,

THOMAS DE BULMER, who, in the 18th HENRY II., paid a hundred shillings scutage for not joining the expedition then made into Ireland. He was *s.* by his son,

ROBERT DE BULMER, living 26th HENRY II, who was *s.* by his son,

BERTRAM DE BULMER. This feudal lord left an only dau. and heiress,

Emme, who *m.* Geffrey de Nevill, and conveyed to the Nevills the Lordship of Branspeth, co. Durham, which had previously been the family seat of the Bulmers.

The male line of the original feudal house thus failing, the next of the name met with is

JOHN DE BULMER, who in the 53rd HENRY III., *m.* Theophania, one of the three daus. and co-heiress of Hugh de Morewyke, of Morewyke, co. Northumberland, whose son and heir,

RALPH DE BULMER, obtained a special charter from the crown, in the 4th EDWARD II., enabling him to hold his park at Riceberg, and keep dogs to hunt therein, and to have free warren in all his demesne lands. In the 9th of the same monarch, we find this Ralph doing homage, and having livery of the estates which descended to him upon the decease of his mother ; and in the next year he was in the wars of Scotland, and again in two years afterwards. In the 20th EDWARD II. he was made deputy governor of the castle of York, to William de Ros, of Hamlake, and upon the accession of King EDWARD III. was summoned to parliament (viz., 25 February, 1342, and until 10 March, 1349) as a BARON. In four years afterwards he had special license to make a castle of his manor-house of Milton, co. York, being the same year constituted sheriff of Yorkshire, and governor of the castle at York. His lordship participated again (the 8th EDWARD III.) in the wars of Scotland. He *d.* in 1357, and was *s.* by his son, then in his sixteenth year,

RALPH BULMER, who was placed under the guardianship of the king's dau. Isabel, and by her assigned to Ralph de Nevill. He had livery of his lands, upon attaining maturity, in the 36th EDWARD III., after which, 40th EDWARD III., he had license, together with William, a younger son of Ralph, Lord Nevill, of Raby, to travel into foreign parts. He *d.* at the close of that year, but does not appear by the existing enrolments to have been summoned to parliament, leaving a son and heir, then but a year old,

RALPH BULMER, "whose descent," says Dugdale, "I shall not trace down farther, in regard that none of this family after the before-specified Ralph, who was summoned to parliament from the 1st till 23rd EDWARD III., were barons of the realm." The male line of this branch of Bulmers continued, however, to the time of PHILIP and MARY, when it terminated with Sir Richard Bulmer, Knt.

Arms—Gu., a lion rampant, between twelve billets, or.

BULWER BARON DALLING AND BULWER.

Created, March 23, 1871 ; extinct, 23 May, 1872.

(*See* BURKE's *Extinct Peerage*, LYTTON, E.)

BURGH—EARL OF KENT.

By Charter of Creation, dated 11 February, 1226.

Lineage.

JOHN, EARL OF COMYN, and Baron of Tonsburgh, in Normandy, being general of the king's forces, and governor of his chief towns, there obtained the surname " DE BURGH," and took his motto, " Ung roy, ung foy, ung loy," from that of Caen, a chief town in his jurisdiction. He had issue. The eldest son,

HARLOWEN DE BURGH, *m.* Arlotta, mother of WILLIAM THE CONQUEROR, and dying before his father, left issue,

ODO, bishop of Bayeux, created Earl of Kent (*see* ODO, EARL OF KENT), and

ROBERT, EARL OF MORETON, in Normandy, who, participating with his brother, the bishop of Bayeux, in the triumph of Hastings, was rewarded by his victorious kinsman, Duke William, with the EARLDOM OF CORNWALL (anno 1068), and grants of not less than seven hundred and ninety-three manors. This nobleman *m.* Maud, dau. of Roger de Montgomery, Earl of Shrewsbury, and had issue,

WILLIAM, his successor,

and three daus., one of whom *m.* Andrew de Vetrel ; another, Guy de La Nal ; and the youngest, the Earl of Thoulouse, brother of Raymond, Count of St. Giles, who behaved so valiantly in the Jerusalem expedition. The period of the decease of Robert, Earl of Moreton and Cornwall, is not ascertained, but he appears to have been s. by his son,

WILLIAM DE MORETON, Earl of Cornwall, who, rebelling against King HENRY II., died a prisoner, having had his eyes put out by order of that monarch, and his earldom of Cornwall transferred to Stephen of Blois (see DE MORETON, Earl of Cornwall). This unfortunate nobleman left two sons,

ADELME, from whom the extant house of CLANRICARDE, and the numerous families of De Burgh, Burgo, Burke, and Bourke, derive their descent,

And

JOHN DE BOURGH, whose son,

HUBERT DE BOURGH, became one of the most eminent and conspicuous nobles of his time; and as a subject was considered the greatest in Europe during the reigns of King JOHN and HENRY III. "The first mention of this Hubert, I find," says Dugdale, " is that he was servant to King RICHARD I., as also to King JOHN, being sent by the latter from Roan, in the 1st year of his reign, to treat of a marriage for him with a daughter to the king of Portugal; and had such great estimation from that king, that in the 3rd of his reign, being lord-chamberlain of the household, he was constituted warden of the marches of Wales, and had a hundred soldiers to attend him in those parts." In the next year we find him employed on an embassy to PHILIP of France, to treat for the restitution of Normandy, then seized upon by that monarch—and for some years after engaged in the important duties of sheriff for the cos. of Dorset, Somerset, Hereford, Berks, and Lincoln. At the period that the barons rose against King JOHN, this even then powerful nobleman was seneschal of Poictou, and, taking part with his royal master, he was nominated one of the commissioners to treat with the insurrectionary lords at Runnymede, in which capacity he witnessed the signing of MAGNA CHARTA, and was advanced by the king, before he left the field, to the high station of Justice of England. In ten days afterwards he was constituted sheriff of the cos. of Kent and Surrey, and governor of the castle of Canterbury, and within a month made sheriff of Herefordshire, governor of the castle of Hereford, and governor of the castles of Norwich and Oxford. In the October following he obtained a grant of the lordship and hundred of Hoa, in Kent, part of the possession of Robert Bardolph; and was again constituted, on 19 of the ensuing November, one of the commissioners upon the part of the king to treat with Richard, Earl of Clare, and others, then deputed by the barons, in the church of Erith, in Kent, touching a peace between the king and those turbulent nobles. He subsequently augmented his reputation by the gallant defence of Dover Castle against Louis of France, when King JOHN was compelled to fly to Winchester, and after the death of that monarch, by still faithfully holding the castle for the young king, HENRY III., although the highest honours and rewards were tendered him personally by the French prince for its surrender. In the 4th year of the new king he succeeded William Mareschall, Earl of Pembroke, just then deceased, in the guardianship of young Henry (at that time but fourteen years of age), and in the government of the kingdom; and he suppressed in the next year a dangerous insurrection of the Londoners, begun by one Constantine, a chief man of the city, whom he caused to be hanged. His great power soon after, however, exciting the jealousy of the barons, the Earl of Chester, and others of the discontented party, signified to the king, that unless he forbore to require their castles, and to hearken to the counsels of this Hubert, who then assumed a higher deportment than any nobleman in the kingdom, they would all rise in rebellion against him; but it does not appear that this cabal prevailed, for we find in the next year, when the king solemnized the festival of Christmas at Westminster, this Hubert, by especial royal appointment, proposing to the lords spiritual and temporal, then assembled, an aid "for vindicating the injuries done to the king and his subjects in the parts beyond sea." And soon afterwards, having executed the office of sheriff for the cos. of Norfolk and Suffolk, from the 1st to the 9th of HENRY III. inclusive, and of the co. of Kent, from the 3rd to to the 11th of the same reign, he was created (on 11 February, 1226,) EARL OF KENT, with most extensive territorial grants from the crown. Within the year, too, he was constituted, by the advice of the peers of the whole realm, Justice of England. His lordship afterwards, however, incurred the temporary displeasure of his royal master, as Dugdale thus states—"But before the end of this thirteenth year (about Michaelmas), the king having a rendezvous at Portsmouth, of the greatest army that had been seen in this realm (it consisting of English, Irish, Scotch, and Welch), designing therewith the recovery of what his father had lost in foreign parts,

and expecting all things in readiness, with ships for their transportation, but finding not half so many as would suffice for that purpose, he wholly attributed the fault to this Hubert, and publicly calling him Old Traytor, told him that he had taken 5,000 marks as a bribe from the Queen of France, and thereupon drawing out his sword would have killed him on the spot, had not the Earl of Chester, and some others, prevented it, but displaced him from his office of Justice, whereupon he withdrew until the king grew better pacified, as, it seems, he soon was; for the next ensuing year, when divers valiant knights, coming to the king out of Normandy, earnestly besought him to land forces in that country, assuring him that it might be easily recovered, this Hubert wholly dissuaded him from attempting it, and prevailed with him to make an expedition into Gascony and Poictou, where he succeeded so well, that having little opposition, he freely received the homage of the inhabitants of those countries."

His lordship subsequently so fully re-established himself in royal favour, that he obtained permission, under certain circumstances, to execute the office of Justice of England by deputy, and he soon afterwards had a grant of the office of Justice of Ireland; and was appointed governor of the Tower of London, castellan of Windsor, and warden of Windsor Forest. Here, however, he appears to have reached the summit of his greatness, for, sharing the common fate of favourites, he was soon afterwards supplanted in the affections of the king, and exposed to the hostility of his enemies, so that at one period his life was sared only by his taking sanctuary in the church of Merton. He was afterwards dragged from before the altar of the chapel at the bishop of Norwich's manor-house in Essex, and conveyed prisoner, with his legs tied under his horse, by Sir Godfrey de Crawcombe, to the Tower of London; "whereof," (says Dugdale,) "when they made relation to the king, who had sate long up to hear the news, he went merrily to bed. Howbeit," (continues the same authority,) "the next morning, Roger, bishop of London, being told how they had dragged him from the chappel, went immediately to the king, and boldly rebuked him for thus violating the peace of holy church, saying, that if he did not forthwith free him of his bonds, and send him back to that chappel, whence he had been thus barbarously taken, he would pronounce the sentence of excommunication against all who had any hand therein. Whereupon the king, being thus made sensible of his fault, sent him back to the same chappel upon the 5th calend of October, but withall directed his precept to the sheriff of Essex and Herefordshire, upon pain of death, to come himself in person, as also to bring with him the posse comitatus, and to encompass the chappel, so to the end he should not escape thence, nor receive any manner of food, which the sheriff accordingly did, making a great ditch, as well about the bishop's house as the chappel, resolving to stay there forty days." From this perilous situation the earl was relieved through the influence of his stanch friend, the archbishop of Dublin, upon condition of expatriating himself, being conveyed in the interim again to the Tower; when the king, learning that the disgraced lord had deposited great treasure in the new temple of London, peremptorily demanded the same, but the Templars as peremptorily refused surrendering the property entrusted to them, without the consent of the owner, which latter being obtained, "great store of plate, both of gold and silver, much money, and divers jewels of very great value" were seized and deposited in the royal treasury. His lordship was subsequently committed close prisoner to the castle of Devizes, where, it is said, upon hearing of the death of his great enemy, the Earl of Chester (5 November, 1233,) "he fetched a deep sigh, and exclaimed, God have mercy on his soul; and calling for his psalter, stood devoutly before the cross, ceasing not before he had sung it all over, for the health of his soul." Soon after this the earl received a full and free pardon for his flight and outlawry, with a grant that his heirs should enjoy all the lands of his own inheritance, but as to such as he had otherwise acquired, "they should stand to the king's favour and kindness, and such terms as the king should think fit." Whereupon, relinquishing his title to the office of Justice of England, and entering into obligation upon oath never again to claim it, he had restitution of numerous extensive lordships and manors. He did not, however, obtain his freedom, but was still closely confined at Devizes, from whence he eventually made his escape into Wales, and was ultimately pardoned, with the other English nobles who had joined Llewellyn, Prince of Wales, upon the conclusion of peace with that chieftain. Again, though, he incurred the displeasure of the king, in consequence of his dau. Margaret having m. Richard, Earl of Gloucester, a minor, without license, but was pardoned upon clearing himself of all cognizance of the matter, and paying a fine. He was, however, again in disgrace, and again mulct, and so on until he was stript of almost all his splendid possessions.

The Earl's marriages are differently given by different authorities. Dugdale assigns him four wives, but Milles, three only. According to Milles, he m. 1st, Margaret, dau. of Robert de Arsic, by whom he had two sons; 2ndly, Isabel, dau. and co-heiress of William, Earl of Gloucester, and widow of Geoffrey de Mandeville; and 3rdly, Margaret, dau. of WILLIAM, King of Scotland. By the last he is said, but erroneously, to have had two sons; his only issue by the Princess were two daus., who both d. s. p., Margaret, m. to Richard de Clare, Earl of Gloucester and Magota. The Earl had, however (besides these two daus., his only children by the princess), two sons previously mentioned, viz.,

    i. John (Sir), m. Hawyse. dau. and heiress of William de Lanvalay, and left issue a son, John. This Sir John de Burgh never inherited the Earldom of Kent. He fought under the banner of the barons at the battles of Lewes and Evesham, in the reign of HENRY III. The period of his decease is not ascertained. His son and heir,

      JOHN, d. in the 8th EDWARD I., leaving the extensive manors and estates which he inherited from his father and mother to three daus., as co-heirs, viz.,

        1 Hawyse, m. to Robert de Greilly.
        2 Dervorgild, m. to Robert Fitz-Walter.
        3 Margerie, a nun at Chiksand, co. Bedford.

    ii. HUBERT, ancestor of the BARONS BOROUGH, of Gainsborough.

Hubert de Bourgh, thus celebrated as Earl of Kent, d. 4 March, 1243, and his remains were honourably interred within the church of the Friars preachers (commonly called the Black-Friars), in the city of London. With his lordship the EARLDOM OF KENT, in the family of Burgh, EXPIRED, which Collins accounts for in his parliamentary precedents, by the allegation that the patent by which the earldom was conferred, was in remainder to his heirs male by the Scottish princess only, and that lady leaving no male issue, the dignity of course ceased.

Arms—Gu, seven lozenges vairé, three, three and one.

BURGH—BARONS BURGH, OR BOROUGH, OF GAINSBOROUGH CO. LINCOLN.

By Writ of Summons, dated 1 September, 1487.

Lineage.

This family sprang directly from HUBERT DE BURGH, younger son of the celebrated HUBERT DE BURGH, EARL OF KENT,[b] but it does not appear to have attained much importance until the reign of EDWARD IV., when,

SIR THOMAS DE BURGH joined Sir William Stanley in rescuing that prince from Neville, Earl of Warwick, whose prisoner he was at the castle of Middleham, but allowed the privilege of hunting for his recreation, upon one of which recreations his escape was effected. Sir Thomas fought afterwards under the banner of the same monarch, and shared with him in the fruits of the victory of Barnet Field. He m. Elizabeth, dau. and co-heiress of Sir Henry Percy, of Athol, Knt., son of Sir Thomas Percy (2nd son of Henry, 1st Earl of Northumberland), by his wife, Elizabeth, dau. and co-heiress of David Strabolgi, Earl of Athol, by which lady the Percys acquired the manor of Gainsborough, and thus it passed to the De Burghs. Sir Thomas de Burgh was s. by his son,

SIR THOMAS DE BURGH, who was created a knight of the Garter by King RICHARD III., and was summoned to parliament as BARON BOROUGH, OF GAINSBOROUGH, 1 September, 1487, and until 14 October, 1495. His lordship m. Margaret, dau. of Thomas, Lord Roos, of Hamlake, and widow of Sir Thomas Botreaux, by whom he had issue,

    EDWARD (Sir).   Thomas.
    Elizabeth, m. to Richard. Lord Fitz-Hugh.
    Anne, m. to Sir George Talbois, of Kyme.

The baron d. in 1496, and was s. by his son,

EDWARD DE BURGH, 2nd baron, but never summoned to parliament, who m. Anne, dau. and heiress of Sir Thomas Cobham, of Sterborough, and had two sons,

THOMAS, his heir.
Henry, m. Catherine, dau. of Sir Ralph Neville, and had a dau., Anne, wife of Richard Vaughan.

The elder son,

THOMAS DE BURGH, 3rd baron, summoned to parliament from 3 November, 1529, to 8 September, 1552. This nobleman m. Anne, dau. of Sir Thomas Tyrwhit, of Kettleby, co. Lincoln, and dying in 1552, was s. by his son,

THOMAS DE BURGH,[*] 4th baron, who m. 1st, Elizabeth, dau. of Sir David Owen, Knt., but the lady proving faithless, and having children by another person, his lordship obtained an act of parliament to bastardize those children. By Alice, his 2nd wife, he had issue,

Henry d. in the lifetime of his father, s p.
WILLIAM, successor to the title.
Dorothy, m. to Sir Anthony Nevill, Knt.

His lordship was s. by his son,

WILLIAM DE BURGH, 5th baron, summoned to parliament from 14 August, 1553, to 23 January, 1559, one of the peers who sat in judgment upon the Duke of Norfolk, in the reign of ELIZABETH (called 4th baron by Nicolas). His lordship m. Katherine, dau. of Edward Clinton, Earl of Lincoln, and had issue,

THOMAS, his successor.
Henry, slain by Holcroft.
John (Sir), d. in 1594, "late admiral of England, renowned for his exploits by sea and land; governor of Duisburgh. He was twice knighted, 1st, in Holland, by his excellency the Earl of Leicester, next by HENRY IV., King of France, on the victory of St. André; but, unhappily, fighting the enemy, who fought with much courage, he fell by an untimely death, to the great grief of his men, and his country's loss, in the fifty-third year of his age, March 7, 1594."
Mary, m. to — Bulkeley.
Elizabeth, m. to — Rider.
Anne, m. to Sir Henry Ashley, Knt.

The baron was s. at his decease by his eldest son,

THOMAS BURGH, 6th baron, summoned to parliament 11 January, 1563. This nobleman was sent, in the 36th ELIZABETH, upon an embassy into Scotland to incite King JAMES against the Spanish faction there, and in four years afterwards succeeded Sir William Russell in the lieutenancy of Ireland. His lordship m. and had issue,

    i. ROBERT, his successor.
    ii. Thomas, d. in minority, s. p.
    i ELIZABETH, m. to George Brooke, 4th son of Lord Cobham, and had issue,

      Sir William Brooke, K.B., who m. Penelope, dau. of Sir Moyses Hill, of Hillsborough Castle, and left two daus. and co-heirs, the eldest of whom,

        HILL BROOKE, m. 1st, the Hon. Mr. Wilmot, eldest son of Lord Wilmot; 2ndly, Sir William Boothby, Bart.; and 3rdly, Edward Russell, brother of the Earl of Bedford. Hill's heir-general, THOMAS THORP, archdeacon of Bristol, was one of the co-heirs of the Barony of Burgh.

    ii. FRANCES, m. to Francis Coppinger, Esq., her heir-general, is HUBERT DE BURGH, Esq., of West Drayton, co. Middlesex one of the co-heirs of the Barony of Burgh.
    iii. ANNE, m. to Sir Drew Drury.
    iv. CATHERINE, m. to Thomas Knevit, Esq., and d. in 1640. Her heir-general is LORD BERNERS, one of the co-heirs of the Barony of Burgh.

His lordship, who was a knight of the Garter, d. in 1594, and was s. by his elder son,

ROBERT BURGH, 7th baron, at whose decease, unm. in minority (his brother having d. previously), his estates devolved upon his sisters and co-heiresses, while the BARONY OF BOROUGH, OF GAINSBOROUGH, fell into ABEYANCE amongst those ladies, and so continues with their representatives.

Arms—Az., three fleurs-de-lis, erm.

BURGH—BARONS SOMERHILL, VISCOUNTS TUNBRIDGE, EARLS OF ST. ALBANS.

Barony and Viscounty, by Letters Patent, dated 3 April, 1624.
Earldom, by Letters Patent, dated 23 August, 1628.

Lineage.

RICHARD BURKE, OR DE BURGH, 4th Earl of Clanricarde, in the peerage of Ireland, was created a peer of England, 3 April, 1624, as BARON SOMERHILL AND VISCOUNT TUNBRIDGE, both in Kent, and advanced to the EARLDOM OF ST. ALBANS, 23 August,

---

    * SIR HUBERT DE BURGH, 2nd son of the renowned Hubert de Burgh, Earl of Kent, was the ancestor of the BARONS BOROUGH OF GAINSBOROUGH. (See BURKE'S *Peerage*, CLANRICARDE.)

    * Sir Harris Nicolas omits this Thomas de Burgh as if he considered him identical with Thomas, the 3rd baron.

1628. His lordship m. Frances, dau. and heiress of Sir Francis Walsingham, and widow of Sir Philip Sydney, and of the unfortunate Earl of Essex, by whom he had issue,

ULICK, his successor.

Margaret. m. to the Hon. Edmond Butler, son of James, Earl of Ormonde.

Honora, m. to John Paulett, Marquess of Winchester.

His lordship d. 12 November, 1635, and was s. by his son, ULIC & BURKE, OR DE BURGH, 5th Earl of Clanricarde, and 2nd Earl of St. Albans, who was created MARQUESS OF CLANRICARDE, in Ireland, 21 February, 1644. This nobleman, who was appointed lord-lieutenant of Ireland in 1650, took so distinguished a part against the rebels in the unhappy times of CHARLES I., that he was excepted from pardon for life or estate, in the act passed by Cromwell's parliament for the settlement of Ireland, 12 August, 1652. His lordship m. in December, 1622, Lady Anne Compton, then only dau. of William, Earl of Northampton, and by her had an only child,

Margaret, who m. 1st, Charles, Viscount Muskerry, and had issue,

CHARLES JAMES, who s. his grandfather, Donogh, Earl of Clancarty.

Frances, d. unm.

Her ladyship m. 2ndly, in 1676, Robert Villiers, called Viscount Purbeck, by whom she had an only son,

John Villiers, who claimed the Earldom of Buckingham.

She m. 3rdly, Robert Fielding, Esq., and d. in 1698.

His lordship d. in 1659, when the Irish marquisate, and the English EARLDOM OF ST. ALBANS, with the minor English honours, became EXTINCT; his other dignities passed to his heir at law.

Arms—Or, a cross, gu., in the dexter canton a lion rampant, sa.

BURGH—BARONS DOWNES.

By Letters-Patent, dated 10 December, 1822.

Lineage.

The family of DOWNES, from which the last Lord Downes maternally descended, and through which he inherited the peerage, appears to have been of considerable antiquity in the co. Suffolk, its progenitors having been seated there so far back as the 14th century. From this root branches subsequently spread into Norfolk and Northampton.

DIVE DOWNES, of East Haddon, d. in 1629, leaving an only son,

THE REV. LEWIS DOWNES, rector of Thornby, father of DIVES DOWNES. This gentleman, having finished his education at Trinity College, Dublin, took holy orders, was made archdeacon of Dublin in 1690, and consecrated bishop of Cork and Ross in 1699. He m. four times. By his 1st and 2nd wives he had no issue; by the 3rd, Elizabeth, dau. of Thomas Becher, Esq., of Sherkin, co. Cork, he had one dau., Elizabeth; and by the 4th (whom he m. 19 August, 1707), Catherine, sister of Robert, 19th Earl of Kildare he left a son,

ROBERT, his heir,

and a posthumous dau.,

Anne, who m. Thomas Burgh, Esq., of Bert, co. Kildare, and had, with other children,

Thomas Burgh, Esq., who m. Anne, only dau. of David Aigoin, Esq.; and d. in 1810, leaving

ULYSSES, last Lord Downes.

The bishop was s. at his decease by his only son,

ROBERT DOWNES, Esq., of Donnybrooke, M.P. for the co. Kildare; who m. 18 February, 1737, Elizabeth, dau. of Thomas Twigge, Esq., of Donnybrooke, by whom he had issue,

Dive, in holy orders, LL.D., who d. unm. in 1798,

and

WILLIAM DOWNES, Esq., who was called to the bar of Ireland in 1786, elevated to the bench there in 1792, and constituted, in 1803, upon the death of Lord Kilwarden, lord chief justice of the Court of King's Bench, and sworn of his Majesty's most honourable privy council in Ireland. His lordship retired from the judicial seat in 1822, when he was elevated to the peerage of Ireland (10 December in the same year), by the title of BARON DOWNES, with remainder, in default of male issue, to his cousin

Sir Ulysses Burgh, upon whom, at the decease of his lordship, 2 March, 1826, the dignity devolved. Lord Downes was vice-chancellor of the university of Dublin

FAMILY OF BURGH.

On the murder of WILLIAM, 3rd Earl of Ulster, his kinsmen seized such portions of his daughter's inheritance as lay in the Irish districts, and adopted Irish names and habits, as it was only thus they could hope to hold them adversely to the heir-general, who according to Norman, but not to Irish notions, had a better right to them than the cadets of the De Burgos.

Mr. Lodge derives McWilliam Eighter, represented by the Marquess of Clanricarde, and McWilliam Oughter, from whom the extinct viscounts and extant Earls of Mayo descend, alike from Sir William de Burgo, brother to the 1st Earl of Ulster; whilst he makes the Bourkes, Lords Castle Connell and Brittas, spring direct from the 1st earl himself

A barony of Clanwilliam in Tipperary, and a barony with the same name in the co. of Limerick, bear testimony to the early period at which the Bourkes were settled in that country. But the name seems also to imply that they were descended from Sir William.

The BOURKES, of Dromkeen, in Clanwilliam, however, known as "Sloght Meyler," are clearly of the MacWilliams, and were the senior branch of MacWilliam Oughter.

EDMOND, the 1st McWILLIAM OUGHTER, was s. in that Irish chieftainship by his eldest son, THOMAS. This rank henceforth went by tanistry, and hence it was enjoyed in turn by the eldest and 2nd sons of this Thomas. From the latter the EXTINCT VISCOUNTS MAYO descended. But Walter, the eldest son, left three sons. Of the 2nd, Lodge states that the male line is EXTINCT. The EARL OF MAYO descends from the 3rd, whilst the eldest, JOHN BOURKE, acquired Dromkeen, in Clanwilliam (co. Limerick), with the third part of that barony, from the Bourkes of Clanwilliam in exchange for his wife's territory of Ooshma.

He d. at Dromkeen, and his eldest son, WILLIAM DUFFE BOURKE, was father of MEYLER BOURKE, of Dromkeen, who gave a patronymic to this branch of the De Burgos.

The early pedigree of this family is recorded in Ulster's office. But the change of name, temp. CHARLES I., requires two or three descents to be noticed.

RICHARD OGE BOURKE, who d. 6 June, 1596, was then chief of this family, and was found by inquisition to be seized of Drom keen and Drumrusk, &c.

WILLIAM BOURKE, the eldest son, inherited the chief part of the property, but it eventually passed to the grandson of his brother Meyler; which MEYLER succeeded to Drumrusk on his father's death in 1596. His son, Ulick, was father of RICKARD BURKE, who adopting the established religion, and taking holy orders, anglicised, as was not uncommon, his name, and was the first to write it Burgh. He inherited the Dromkeen property under an entail, and it passed at his death to his eldest son, ULICK (anglicised to ULYSSES) BURGH, D.D., also in holy orders, rector of Grean and Kilteely (near Dromkeen), in 1672, and dean of Emly in 1685. He adhered to the Prince of Orange, and when he, as WILLIAM III., advanced to the siege of Limerick, Dr. Burgh received him at Dromkeen, and attended him throughout the siege, being of much service to the army from his personal acquaintance with that district. When that first siege proved abortive, the Irish party burned Dromkeen, but King WILLIAM rewarded the owner with the bishoprick of Ardagh in 1692, a preferment which he only held for a few months, dying soon after his consecration. He had m. Mary, dau. of William Kingsmill, Esq., of Ballyowen, colonel in the army, and M.P. for Mallow, by Dorothy, dau. of Sir Warham St. Leger, Knt., by Ursula, dau. of George, Lord Abergavenny, and grand-dau. of Edward Stafford, Duke of Buckingham. From this alliance spring the BURGHS of Dromkeen, the BURGHS of Oldtown, the BURGHS of Bert, of whom SIR ULYSSES BURGH, G.C.B., became 2nd LORD DOWNES, and, in the female line, the HUSSEY-BURGHS of Donore and Dromkeen. By Mary Kingsmill his wife, Bishop Burgh had issue,

I. RICKARD, in holy orders, who s. at Dromkeen, and was father of two sons, THOMAS, of Dromkeen, whose dau and heir, m. Philpot Wolfe, Esq.; and RICKARD, of Mount Bruis, co. Tipperary, in holy orders, whose only dau. Mary, m. in 1781, Captain William Byam, 3rd son of William Byam, Esq., of Byams, in Antigua, and left surviving issue,

1 Richard-Burgh Byam, in holy orders, vicar of Kew and Petersham.

2 Edward-Samuel Byam.

1 Martha.

2 Alicia-Juliana, wife of Major William Leeves, of Tortington House, Sussex.

II. WILLIAM, of whom presently.

III. Thomas, of Old Town, co. Kildare, engineer and surveyor-general, who m. Mary, dau. of William Smith, bishop of Kilmore, and had (with a son, THOMAS, of Old Town, grandfather of the late Very Rev. John T. Burgh, dean of Cloyne) two daus., of whom Elizabeth, m. Ignatius Hussey, Esq., and was mother of WALTER HUSSEY-BURGH, lord chief baron of the Court of Exchequer in Ireland, whose grandson was the late WALTER HUSSEY-BURGH, Esq., of Dromkeen and Donore. (See BURKE's Landed Gentry.)

I. Dorothy, m. to Thomas Smyth, D.D., Bishop of Limerick, ancestor of Viscount Gort.

II. Catherine, m. to the Rev. Alexander Alcock, of Ferns, co. Wexford.

The 2nd son,

WILLIAM BURGH, Esq., of Bert, co. Kildare, m. in 1693, Margaret, dau. of Thomas Parnell, Esq., of Congleton, in Cheshire; and dying about the year 1744, was s. by his eldest surviving son,

THOMAS BURGH, Esq., of Bert, who m. Anne, dau. of the RIGHT REV. DIVE DOWNES, bishop of Cork and Ross (as in the lineage of the family of DOWNES), and had issue,

I. WILLIAM, LL.D., his successor.

II. Thomas, comptroller-general and commissioner of the revenue in Ireland.

III. Robert, of the E. I. Co.'s service, m. Anne, dau. of Hugh Hickman, Esq., of Fenloe, co. Clare, and left two daus.,

1 Mary, m. to the Rev. John Hussey-Burgh, of Dromkeen.
2 Catherine, m. to Alexander Hamilton, Esq.

I. Margaret-Emilia, m. the Right Hon. John Foster, and was created Baroness Oriel and Viscountess Ferrard.

II. Anne, m. to the celebrated WALTER HUSSEY-BURGH, lord chief baron of the exchequer.

III. Dorothy, m. to John Rochfort, Esq., of Clogrenane, co. Carlow.

IV. Harriet-Charlotte.

Mr. Burgh, whose will bears date 15 November, 1754, was s. by his eldest son,

WILLIAM BURGH, LL.D., who m. Mary, dau. and heir of George Warburton, Esq., of Firmount, co. Kildare; but d. s.p., when the estate devolved upon his brother,

THOMAS BURGH, Esq., of Bert House, co. Kildare, who m. in 1775, Anne, only dau. of David Aigion, Esq., and by her (who d. in 1831) left issue,

ULYSSES, 2nd Lord Downes.
Anne, m. to Nathaniel Sneyd, Esq.
Mary, m. to John-Staunton Rochfort, Esq., of Clogrenane, co. Carlow.
Elizabeth.
Charlotte, m. 17 February, 1815, to the Rev. Zachariah Cornock, of Cromwell's Fort, co. Wexford; and d. in 1827.

Mr. Burgh d. in 1810: his son and heir,

SIR ULYSSES BURGH, G.C.B., K.T.S., and S.A., a general officer, colonel 29th foot, b. 15 August, 1788, s. his cousin, William, Lord Downes, as 2nd BARON DOWNES, 2 March, 1826, and became a representative peer for Ireland. His lordship m. 1st, 20 June, 1815, Maria, only dau. and heir of the late Walter Bagenal, Esq., heir male and representative of the great family of Bagenal, of Bagenalstown, and by her (who d. 20 August, 1842) had two daus.,

ANNE, m. 27 April, 1838, to John-Henry, Earl of Clonmel.
CHARLOTTE, m. 12 February, 1851, to the Hon. Lieut.-Colonel James Colborne, now Lord Seaton, and d. 26 April, 1863.

His lordship, m. 2ndly, 4 August, 1846, Christopheria, widow of John-Willis Fleming, Esq., of Stoneham, Hants, and dau. of James Buchanan, Esq. (which lady d. 18 October, 1860). In 1848, his lordship and his cousins, Thomas Burgh, Esq., of Oldtown, Rev. Walter Burgh, vicar of Naas, Major John Burgh, and Rev. William Burgh, were authorized to re-assume their ancient name of DE BURGH. Lord Downes d. without male issue 26 July, 1864, when the barony became EXTINCT.

Arms—Quarterly: first and fourth, or, a cross, gu., for BURGH; second and third, arg., three pales, wavy, gu., for DOWNES.

BURGHERSH—BARONS BURGHERSH.

By Writ of Summons, dated 12 November, 1303.

Lineage.

In the 26th year of EDWARD I.,

ROBERT DE BURGHERSH had his commission renewed, as constable of Dover Castle and lord warden of the Cinque Ports, and was summoned to parliament in six years afterwards, as BARON BURGHERSH; in which dignity he had summons from 12 November, 1303, to 13 June, 1305. His lordship d. in 1306, and was s. by his son,

STEPHEN DE BURGHERSH, 2nd baron, but never summoned to parliament; this nobleman had issue,

BARTHOLOMEW, his successor.

Henry, bishop of Lincoln, temp. EDWARD II., and in the reign of EDWARD III. Lord Treasurer and Lord Chancellor. This distinguished prelate d. at Ghent, in 1343, and his remains were brought over and interred in Lincoln Cathedral. A story subsequently circulated—that his lordship having incurred many a bitter curse, for despoiling his poorer tenantry of their grounds, to form a park at Tynghurst, appeared after his decease, to a certain person (who had been one of his esquires), in the habit of a keeper, with his bow, quiver of arrows, and a horn by his side, arrayed in a short green coat, and thus addressed him—"Thou knowest how I have offended God, and injured the poor, by my inclosure of this park: for this cause, therefore, am I enjoined penance, to be the keeper of it, till it be laid open again. Go, therefore, to the canons of Lincoln (my brethren), and intreat them from me to make a restitution to the poor of what I thus wrongfully took from them." Whereupon having delivered the message to the canons, they sent one of their company, called William Batchelor, to see the desired restitution accomplished; who caused the banks and pales to be forthwith thrown down, and the ditches to be filled up.

Stephen de Burghersh was s. by his elder son,

BARTHOLOMEW DE BURGHERSH, 3rd baron, who had summons to parliament from 25 January, 1330 (4th EDWARD III.), to 15 March, 1354, latterly with the addition of "Seniori." This nobleman was in the wars of Scotland and France, temp. EDWARD II., in the retinue of Bartholomew, Lord Badlesmere; but in the 15th of the same reign, joining Thomas, Earl of Lancaster, against the Spencers, he was taken prisoner with Lord Badlesmere, after the battle of Borough-bridge, upon the surrender of that nobleman's castle of Leeds, in Kent, and sent to the Tower of London. He was restored, however, to his freedom and rank, on the arrival of Queen Isabel and Prince Edward, and constituted governor of Dover Castle and warden of the Cinque Ports—trusts confirmed to him by King EDWARD III., in whose reign his lordship became still more highly distinguished, participating in the glories of Cressy, and filling several important offices, such as lord chamberlain of the household, constable of the Tower, &c. Lord Burghersh, m. Elizabeth, dau. and co heiress of Theobald de Verdon, a great Staffordshire baron, by whom he had issue,

Henry, who m. Isabel, one of the sisters and co-heirs of Edmund de St. John, but d. s. p.
BARTHOLOMEW, his successor.
Joane.
A dau., m. 5th Earl of Kildare.

His lordship d. in 1355, and was s. by his only surviving son,

BARTHOLOMEW DE BURGHERSH, 4th baron, summoned to parliament from 15 December 1357 (31st Edward III.), to 24 February, 1368. This nobleman was one of the most eminent warriors of the martial times of EDWARD III., having served in the immediate staff (as we should now call it) of the BLACK PRINCE in the French wars, and attaining therein so much renown, as to be deemed worthy of one of the original Garters, upon the institution of that order. In a few years afterwards, he journeyed into the Holy Land; and he was subsequently, for several years, again in attendance upon his royal master, the BLACK PRINCE, during which period he participated in the triumph of Poictiers. His lordship m. 1st, Cecily, dau. and heiress of Richard de Weyland, by whom he had an only dau., and, eventually, heiress,

ELIZABETH, who m. Sir Edward le Despencer, K.G., and carried the Barony of Burghersh into the family of her husband. The great-grand-dau. and representative of this marriage,

Elizabeth Beauchamp, m. Edward, a younger son of Ralph Nevil, Earl of Westmoreland, and her great-grand-dau.,

MARY, only dau. and heiress of Henry Nevil, last Lord Abergavenny and Despencer, m. Sir Thomas Fane, Knt., whose son, Sir Francis Fane, K.B., was created, in 1624, BARON BURGHERSH, and EARL OF

WESTMORELAND, honours now enjoyed by his lordship's descendant, Francis-William-Henry Fane, 12th EARL OF WESTMORELAND, C.B.

Lord Burghersh m. 2ndly, Margaret, sister of Bartholomew Lord Badlesmere, but had no issue. His lordship d. in 1369, in which year, his last will and testament bears date, at London, 4 April. By this instrument he directs that his body be interred in the chapel of Massingham, before the image of the blessed Virgin; that a *dirge* be there said, and in the morning a mass; and that a dole should be daily given to the poor of that place, at the discretion of his executors. To Sir Walter Pavely (whom, with Lord Badlesmere, he had constituted executors) he bequeathed a standing cup, gilt, with an L upon the cover, as also his whole suit of arms for the justs, with his coat of mail and sword. Upon the demise of this nobleman, the last male representative of this branch of the family of Burghersh, the BARONY OF BURGHERSH, passed with his dau., as stated above, into the family of Despencer, and the dignity is now vested, although not assumed, in Mary-Frances Boscawen, Baroness Le Despencer, Viscountess Falmouth.

Arms.—Gu., a lion rampant, double quevée, or.

NOTE.— Of this family was
JOHN DE BURGHERSH, who m. Maud, one of the daus. and heiresses of Edmund Bacon, of the co. Essex, and left a son,
SIR JOHN DE BURGHERSH, Knt., who was in the expedition, made in the 47th EDWARD III. into Flanders. This Sir John m. Ismania, dau. of Simon Hanap, of the co. Gloucester, and by her (who m. Sir John Raleigh of Nettlecomb, Knt.) he left two daus., his co-heirs, viz.,
    Margaret, m. 1st, to Sir John Greneville, Knt., and 2ndly, to John Arundell, Esq., of the co. of Cornwall, by whom she had a son, Sir John Arundell of Lanherne, who m, Catherine, dau. of Sir John Chidiock, and widow of Sir William Stafford, Knt., of Southwick, and by her had (with a dau. Elizabeth, Lady Daubeuy,) a son, Sir Thomas Arundell, K.B.
    Maud. m. to Thomas Chancer, son of the celebrated poet, and dying in 1436 or 1437, left au only d-u.,
        Alice Chaucer, who m. 1st Sir John Philip; and 2ndly William de la Pole. Duke of Suffolk, K.G., lord chancellor and lord high admiral

BURKE—VISCOUNT BURKE.

By Letters Patent, dated 20 April, 1629.

Lineage.

THE HON. JOHN BURKE, 5th son of Ulick, 3rd Earl of Clanricarde, was raised to the peerage of Ireland, 20 April, 1629, as VISCOUNT BURKE, of Clanmorris, with limitation of the honour to the heirs male of his father. His lordship m. Catherine, 3rd dau. of Sir Anthony Brabazon, Knt., of Ballinasloe, co. Galway, and dying 16 November, 1635, was s. by his son,
THOMAS BURKE, 2nd Viscount Burke, of Clanmorris, who m. Margaret, dau. of Christopher Fleming, Lord of Slane; but d. s. p. The peerage, however, did not become extinct, but reverted to the Earls of Clanricarde, and is now vested in their representative, the present marquess, though it is not assumed by his lordship.

Arms—Or, a cross, gu.; in the dexter canton, a lion rampant, sa.

BURKE — BARON TYAQUIN AND VISCOUNT GALWAY.

By Letters Patent, dated 2 June, 1687.

Lineage.

THE HON. ULICK BURKE, 4th son of William, 7th Earl of Clanricarde, by Lettice his wife, only dau. of Sir Henry Shirley, Bart., was created, 2 June, 1687, Baron of Tyaquin and VISCOUNT GALWAY. His lordship commanded a regiment of foot in JAMES the SECOND's army, and was slain at Aughrim, 12 July, 1691. He m. Frances, only dau. of George Lane, Viscount Lanesborough, and by her (who m. 2ndly, Henry Fox, Esq., of East Horsley, co. Surrey,) had an only dau. who d. in infancy.

Arms—Or, a cross, gu.; in the dexter canton, a lion rampant, sa.

BURKE—BARON LEITRIM.

By Letters Patent, dated 6 May, 1583.

Lineage.

JOHN BURKE, Esq., of Meelick Castle, co. Galway, was created BARON LEITRIM, in the peerage of Ireland, by patent, dated 6 May, 1583, but d. shortly after, in the same year, when the title became EXTINCT.

His lordship is stated to have had two sons, JOHN, executed for treason, and Redmond, a fugitive in Spain, in 1615.

Arms—Or, a cross, gu.; in the dexter canton, a lion rampant, sa.

BURNELL—BARONS BURNELL.

By Writ of Summons, dated 19 December, 1311.

Lineage.

"That this family," says Dugdale, "hath been of great antiquity, here in England, an old Martyrologe (sometime belonging to the abbey of Buldewas, co. Salop,) doth plainly demonstrate; for thereby appeareth that Sir Robert Burnell, Knt., d. 15 November, 1087; Sir Philip, 14 December, 1107; Sir Roger, 5 February, 1140; Sir Hugh, 7 January, 1149; Sir Richard, 20 January, 1189; Sir Hugh, 12 May, 1242; and another Sir Robert, 6 December, 1249."

The next persons of the name upon record are
WILLIAM BURNELL, who took part with the rebellious barons at the close of King HENRY III.'s reign, and his brother,
ROBERT BURNELL, who, in the 54th of the same monarch, obtained a charter for a weekly market, and two fairs yearly, to be holden at his manor of Acton Burnell, co. Salop; and before the end of the same year we find him, amongst others, signed with the cross for a voyage to the Holy Land with Prince Edward. He was, however, drowned, along with his above-mentioned brother, in 1282, when he was s. by his nephew (the son of his brother Philip),
PHILIP BURNELL, who was s. by his 1st cousin (son of his uncle, Hugh Burnell), Philip Burnell, who, in the 19th of EDWARD I., had a charter for free warren in all his demesne lands in the co. of Salop, and in two years afterwards inherited estates in the cos. of Southampton, Wilts, Berks, Stafford, Essex, and Surrey, from his uncle, Robert Burnell, bishop of Bath and Wells. This feudal lord m. Maud, dau. of Richard Fitz-Alan, Earl of Arundel, and had issue,
EDWARD, his successor.
Maud. m. 1st. to John Lovel, of Tichmarch, co. Northampton, by whom she had issue,
    John Lovel, who was deprived of his inheritance by fine.
Maud. m. 2ndly, John de Handlo, who was summoned to parliament, as BARON HANDLO, in 1342. (*See that dignity.*)

Philip Burnell d. in the 28rd of EDWARD I., and was s. by his son,
EDWARD BURNELL, who, being in the wars of Scotland, had summons to parliament, as BARON BURNELL, from 19 December, 1311, to 24 October, 1314. His lordship m. Olivia, dau. of Hugh le Despenser, but dying s. p. in 1315, the barony EXPIRED, while his estates, save those held by his widow in dower, devolved upon his only sister MAUD (mentioned above), as sole heiress,

Arms—Arg., a lion rampant, sa, crowned, or, within a bordure, az.

BURNELL—BARONS BURNELL, OF HOLGATE, CO. SALOP.

By Writ of Summons, dated 25 November, 1350.

Lineage.

MAUD BURNELL, sister and sole heiress of Edward Lord Burnell, who d. in 1315, when his barony EXPIRED, took for her 2nd husband John de Handlo, afterwards summoned to parliament as LORD HANDLO, and had issue, two sons, viz.,

Richard, who *d. v. p.*, leaving a son,

Edmund de Handlo, who *s.* to the Barony of Handlo. (*See* HANDLO.

And

NICHOLAS DE HANDLO, who inherited in the 22nd EDWARD III., the estates of his mother, and assumed, in consequence, the surname of BURNELL ; by which designation he was summoned to parliament, as a BARON, on 25 November, 1350. His lordship distinguished himself in arms, and participated in the glory acquired by his victorious sovereign upon the French soil. He *d.* 19 January, 1383, and was *s.* by his son,

SIR HUGH BURNELL, Knt., as 2nd BARON BURNELL. This nobleman was constituted governor of the castle of Bridgenorth, co. Salop, in the 10th of RICHARD II.; but being denounced, in the next year, as one of the favourites and evil counsellors of that unhappy prince, he was banished the court. He regained popular favour, however, so much within a few years, that upon the deposal of his royal master, he was one of the lords deputed to receive the unfortunate king's resignation of the crown and government, at the Tower of London. In the next reign we find Lord Burnell entrusted with the government of several strong castles on the Welch border. His lordship *m.* 1st, Lady Philippa de la Pole, dau. of Michael, 2nd Earl of Suffolk, and 2ndly, Joyce, dau. of John Botetourt, and grand-dau. and heiress of John, 2nd Lord Botetourt; by the latter he had no issue; but by the former he had an only son,

EDWARD, who, dying *v. p.*, left, by his wife Alice, dau. of Thomas, Lord Strange, three daus., viz.,

Joyce, *m.* to Thomas Erdington, Esq., and *d. s. p.*

Margery, *m.* to Edmund, son of Sir Walter Hungerford, Knt., and had issue. In the co-representatives of this marriage, one moiety of the BARONY OF BURNELL now vests.

Katherine, *m.* to Sir John Ratcliffe, whose son, Sir John Ratcliffe, K.G., *m.* Elizabeth, dau. and heiress of Walter, Lord Fitz-Walter. In the representatives of this marriage, a moiety of the BARONY OF BURNELL now vests.

Lord Burnell, who had been summoned to parliament from 20 August 1383, to 21 October, 1420, *d.* in the latter year; when his above-mentioned grand-daus. became his heirs, and the BARONY OF BURNELL fell into ABEYANCE amongst them, as it still continues with their representatives.

Arms—Arg., a lion rampant, sa., crowned, or, a bordure, az.

BURY—EARL OF CHARLEVILLE.

(*See* ADDENDA.)

BUTLER—EARL OF WILTSHIRE.

By Letters Patent, dated 8 July, 1449.

Lineage.

JAMES BUTLER, son and heir of James, 4th Earl of Ormonde, in Ireland, by Joan, dau. of William Beauchamp, Lord Abergavenny, was elevated to the peerage of England, by letters patent, dated 8 July, 1449, as EARL OF WILTSHIRE, and succeeded to the Irish honours, as 5th Earl of Ormonde, at the decease of his father, in 1452. This nobleman, who was a stanch adherent of the house of Lancaster, was made lieutenant of Ireland in the 30th HENRY VI., and in three years afterwards Lord Treasurer of England. Shortly after this his lordship was with King HENRY in the first battle of St. Albans, where the Yorkists prevailing, he fled, and cast his armour into a ditch. In the 38th of the same monarch he was reconstituted Lord Treasurer, and appointed keeper of the forest of Pederton, co. Somerset, and of Craneburn Chase, lying in the cos. of Wilts and Dorset; being at the same time honoured with the Garter. His lordship participated this year in the triumph of his party at Wakefield, where the Duke of York fell; but sharing also their defeat at Mortimer Cross, he fled the field : and pursuing a similar course after the unfortunate issue to the Lancastrians, of Towton Field, he was taken prisoner by Richard Salkeld, Esq., and beheaded at Newcastle, 1 May, 1461. His lordship *d. s. p.*, and being attainted by parliament in the November following his execution, his EARLDOM OF WILTSHIRE EXPIRED, as should the Irish honours of the family, the deceased lord's brother and heir, John Butler, being also attainted for his Lancatrian principles, and being likewise engaged at the battle of Towton, but that the said John was restored in blood by King EDWARD IV., and thus enabled to inherit as 6th Earl of Ormonde. James, Earl of Ormonde and Wiltshire, *m.* thrice; 1st, Amy, dau. of John

94

Fitz-Alan, Earl of Arundel ; 2ndly, Amicea, dau. of Sir Richard Stafford, a great heiress; and 3rdly, Eleanor, dau. of Edmund Beaufort, Duke of Somerset, but never had issue.

Arms—Or, a chief indented, az., a label of five points, arg

BUTLER — BARON BUTLER, OF WESTON, CO. HUNTINGDON.

By Letters Patent, *anno* 1673.

Lineage.

LORD RICHARD BUTLER, 2nd son of James, 1st Duke of Ormonde, was advanced to the peerage of Ireland, as EARL OF ARRAN, in 1662, and created a peer of England, by the title of BARON BUTLER, OF WESTON, in 1673. Upon his father's quitting Ireland in 1682, this nobleman was left deputy until his return, and performed great service against the mutinous garrison of Carrick-Fergus. His lordship distinguished himself also in the celebrated naval engagement with the Dutch in 1673. He *m.* 1st, Mary, dau. of James Stuart, Duke of Richmond and Lenox, but had no issue. He *m.* 2ndly, Dorothy, dau. of John Ferrers, Esq., of Tamworth Castle, co. Warwick, by whom he had an only surviving dau.,

CHARLOTTE, *m.* to CHARLES, LORD CORNWALLIS. (*See that title.*)

He *d.* in 1685. when leaving no male issue, all his HONOURS EXPIRED, but were revived in the person of his nephew, the Hon. Charles Butler (*see* BUTLER, Baron Butler, of Weston).

Arms—Or, a chief indented, az.

BUTLER—BARON BUTLER, OF WESTON, CO. HUNTINGDON.

By Letters Patent, dated 23 January, 1693.

Lineage.

The Honourable

CHARLES BUTLER. 2nd son of the celebrated Thomas, Earl of Ossory (by courtesy), and Lord Butler, of Moorpark, by writ, eldest son of James, Duke of Ormonde, was elevated to the peerage of England on 8 March, 1693, as *Baron Cloghgrenan, Viscount Tullough*, and EARL OF ARRAN, and created at the same time a peer of England, by the title of BARON BUTLER, OF WESTON, co. Huntingdon. This nobleman was one of the lords of the bedchamber, and colonel of horse, in the reign of King WILLIAM; governor of Dover Castle, and deputy-warden of the Cinque Ports, and master of the ordnance in Ireland, *temp.* Queen ANNE, and chancellor of the university of Oxford in the reign of King GEORGE I. His lordship *m.* Elizabeth, 4th dau. and co-heiress of Thomas, Lord Crew, of Stene; but dying *s. p.* in 1759, all his HONOURS EXPIRED. His lordship was also lord high steward of Westminster, and a lieut.-general in the army.

Arms—Or, a chief indented, az.

BUTLER — BARONS BUTLER, OF LANTHONY, CO. MONMOUTH, EARLS OF BRECKNOCK, IN THE PEERAGE OF ENGLAND, AND DUKE OF ORMONDE.

By Letters Patent, dated 20 July, 1660.
Marquesses and Dukes of Ormonde, and Earls of Ossory, in Ireland.

Lineage.

The Right Honourable

JAMES BUTLER, Marquess of Ormonde, and Earl of Ossory. In Ireland, for his faithful adherence to King CHARLES I., was created a peer of England at the restoration of the monarchy (20 July, 1660,) in the dignities of *Baron Butler, of Lanthony*, co. Monmouth, and EARL OF BRECKNOCK,* and the next year advanced to the Irish DUKEDOM OF ORMONDE, while he was elevated to the same rank in England by the same title on 9 November, 1682. This nobleman distinguished himself first in public life by a disposition to oppose the government of the Earl of Strafford in Ireland, and his political career commenced in the following singular manner. Lord Strafford, upon calling a parliament to meet at Dublin Castle, issued a proclamation that none of the members, lords or commons, should enter with their swords; an injunction obeyed by all but the young Marquess of Ormonde, who told the black rod at the door "that he should have no swords of his except in his guts." This so irritated the lord-deputy, that the refractory lord was called upon in the evening to account for his conduct; when he produced his majesty's writ, summoning him to parliament, "cinctus cum gladio." So resolute a reply, at once fixed his lordship's fortune, and it being deemed more prudent to conciliate than to provoke so ardent a spirit, he was immediately called to the privy council; from that period he attached himself zealously to the cause of the king, and used all his efforts to defeat the accusations against the Earl of Strafford, who thenceforward felt so much gratitude towards him that he made it his last request to his royal master to bestow the Garter upon Ormonde; a request cheerfully complied with. The marquess was afterwards lord-lieutenant of Ireland, and his valour, conduct, and loyalty were in the highest degree conspicuous throughout the whole of the Civil Wars. He was a second time chief governor of Ireland after the Restoration. Burnet says of this eminent person, "that he was every way well fitted for a court; of a graceful appearance, a lively wit, and a cheerful temper; a man of great expense, but decent even in his vices, for he always kept up the forms of religion : too faithful not to give always good advice; but when bad ones were followed, too complaisant to be any great complainer. He had got through many transactions with more fidelity than success; and in the siege of Dublin, miscarried so far, as to lessen the opinion of his military conduct : but his constant attendance on his master and his great sufferings raised him (after the Restoration) to be lord steward of the household and lord-lieutenant of Ireland."

His grace m. Elizabeth, only dau. of Richard Preston, Earl of Desmond, by whom he had issue,

I. Thomas, who d. young.
II. THOMAS, EARL OF OSSORY, who was summoned to parliament 24 September, 1666, as LORD BUTLER, of Moor Pa. k, co. Herts. This nobleman was b. at Kilkenny, on 8 July, 1634, and by the time he reached majority, gave such proofs of discretion, talent, and noble bearing, that Sir Robert Southwell thus depicts him at that period. "He was a young man with a very handsome face; a good head of hair; well set; very good natured; rides the great horse very well; is a very good tennis player, fencer, and dancer; understands music, and plays on the guitar and lute; speaks French elegantly; reads Italian fluently; is a good historian; and so well versed in romances, that if a gallery be full of pictures and hangings, he will tell the stories of all that are there described. He shuts up his door at eight in the evening, and studies till midnight; he is temperate, courteous, and excellent in all his behaviour." In 1661 his lordship was general of the horse in Ireland, and a member of the privy council. He was deputy to his father while lord-lieutenant, and attained the highest reputation in the cabinet and in the field. His lordship pre-eminently distinguished himself in the great naval engagement with the Dutch in 1673, "wherein" (saith Anthony Wood,) "he gallantly acted beyond the fiction of romance." He m. in 1659, Amelia, eldest dau. of Louis de Nassau, Lord of Auverquerque, natural son of Maurice, Prince of Orange, by whom he had two surviving sons, and three daus., viz,

1 JAMES, who s. his grandfather.
2 Charles, created Earl of Arran.
1 Elizabeth, m. to William Richard George, 9th Earl of Derby.
2 Emilia.
3 Henrietta, m. to Henry D'Auverquerque, Earl of Grantham.

His lordship d. v. p. of a fever, at Whitehall, deeply lamented by the kingdom at large, on 30 July, 1680.
III. Richard, created Earl of Arran in Ireland, and LORD BUTLER, OF WESTON, in England.
IV. John, created EARL OF GOWRAN, d. s. p. in 1677.

The duke d. the year of the revolution, 1688, and was s. by his grandson,
JAMES BUTLER, 2nd Duke of Ormonde, both in England and Ireland, and 2nd EARL OF BRECKNOCK, IN ENGLAND This nobleman being one of the first to espouse the cause of the Prince of Orange, was made a knight of the Garter, upon the elevation of his highness to the throne : and constituted Lord High Constable of England for the day, at the coronation of his Majesty and Queen MARY. In 1690 his grace attended King WILLIAM at the battle of the Boyne, and in three years after wards was at Landen, where he received several wounds, had his horse killed under him, and was taken prisoner by the French, and carried to Namur. In 1702 he was appointed by Queen ANNE commander-in-chief of the land forces sent against France and Spain, when he destroyed the French fleet and the Spanish galleons, in the harbour of Viga, for which he received the thanks of parliament. In 1712, he succeeded the Duke of Marlborough, as captain-general and commander-in chief of all his majesty's land forces in Great Britain, or employed abroad in conjunction with her allies; and on the Queen's death was one of the privy council who signed the proclamation, disclaiming GEORGE I. King of England; on whose arrival he was at first graciously received by his majesty, but in a few days after was removed from his great offices; and within a short time (1715,) impeached in parliament of high crimes and misdemeanours. Whereupon retiring into France, he was attainted, his estates confiscated, and all his honours EXTINGUISHED, on 20 August, 1715. But in 1721, an act of parliament passed, enabling his brother the Earl of Arran to purchase the escheated property, which he accordingly did. The duke m. twice, 1st, Lady Anne Hyde, dau. of Laurence, Earl of Rochester, who d. with her only infant child; and 2ndly, Lady Mary Somerset, dau. of Henry Duke of Beaufort, by whom he had an only surviving dau., Mary, m. to John, Lord Ashburnham. He d. at Madrid, at the advanced age of ninety-four, on 16 November, 1745.

Arms—Or, a chief indented, az.

NOTE.—The illustrious house of ORMONDE originally sprang from the great feudal family of Walter:
In the 3rd HENRY II., in the sheriff's account for Norfolk and Suffolk, mention is made in those shires of
HUBERT WALTER, to whom s.
HENRY WALTER, who had five sons, Hubert, THEOBALD, Walter, Roger, and Hamon, of whom,
Hubert, the eldest, a churchman, became archbishop of Canterbury;
and the 2nd,
THEOBALD WALTER, obtained from King RICHARD I. a grant in fee of the lordship of PRESTON, in Lancashire, with the whole wapentake and forest of Amundernesse, to hold by three knights' fees: which grant bears date 22 April, in the 1st year of that king's reign, being the Friday immediately after his coronation. And five years after he was appointed sheriff of the co. Lancaster, and continued to fulfil the duties of that high office from the 6th of RICHARD to the 1st of JOHN, inclusive. This feudal lord was a great benefactor to the church, and a founder of several religious houses, amongst which were the Augustinian Abbey of Cockersand, in Lancashire, and (being BUTLER of Ireland) the monastery of Arklow, and the abbeys of Motheny, co. Limerick, and Nenagh, co. Tipperary, in Ireland. In the 5th of King JOHN he gave two palfreys for license to go into that kingdom, and having m. Maud, dau. of Robert Vavasour, with whom he acquired the manors of Edlington and Newborough, and the lands of Boulton, departed this life in the 9th of the same monarch; when Robert Vavasour above-mentioned gave to the king a fine of 1,200 marks, and two palfreys, for the benefit of the widow's marriage and dowrie. The lady m. subsequently Fulke Fitz-warine. Theobald Walter left issue,

THEOBALD, who assumed from his office in Ireland the surname of BOTELER OF BUTLER, and from this great feudal lord, who m. Maude, sister of the celebrated Thomas-à-Becket, archbishop of Canterbury, immediately descended the BUTLERS OF ORMONDE.

Maud, whose tuition King JOHN committed to Gilbert Fitz-Reinfrid, Baron of Kendall.

BUTLER—EARL OF ARRAN.

(See BARON BUTLER, of Weston, in the Exti. et Peerage of England.)

---

* James Butler, Earl of Ormonde, his lordship's ancestor, m. Allanore, dau. of Humphrey de Bohun, Earl of Hereford and Essex, LORD OF BRECKNOCK. and constable of England, by Elizabeth Plantagenet, dau. of EDWARD I.—(See BOHUN, Earl of Hereford.)

BUTLER—EARL OF GOWRAN.

By Letters Patent, dated 13 April, 1676.

Lineage.

LORD JOHN BUTLER, *b.* in 1643, 3rd son of James, 1st Duke of Ormonde, was created, 13 April, 1676, Baron of Aughrim, Viscount of Clonmore, and EARL OF GOWRAN, co. Kilkenny, in the peerage of Ireland. His lordship *m.* in 1676, Lady Anne Chichester, only dau. of Arthur, Earl of Donegal; but *d. s. p.* in August, 1677, when all his honours became EXTINCT.

Arms—Or, a chief indented, az.

BUTLER—VISCOUNT BUTLER.

By Letters Patent, dated 4 August, 1603.

Lineage.

THEOBALD BUTLER, youngest son of Sir Edmond Butler, of Roscrea and Cloughrenan, who was 2nd son of James, 9th Earl of Ormonde, had, by patent, dated at Westminster, 13 July, 1603, the titles of Ormonde and Ossory, entailed and secured to him after the death of Thomas, then Earl of Ormonde, without male issue, and was elevated, 4 August following, to the peerage of Ireland, as VISCOUNT BUTLER, of Tulleophelim, co. Carlow. His lordship *m.* his cousin, Lady Elizabeth Butler, only dau. of the said Thomas, Earl of Ormonde, but *d. s. p.* In January, 1613, when the viscounty became EXTINCT. His widow *m.* 2ndly, Sir Richard Preston, Lord Dingwall.

Arms—Or, a chief indented, az.

BUTLER—BARONS CAHER, VISCOUNTS CAHER, AND EARLS OF GLENGALL.

Barony, by Letters Patent, dated 6 May, 1583.
Earldom and Viscounty, by Letters Patent, dated 22 January, 1816.

Lineage.

The feudal barony of Kiltenenen, of which Cahir Castle became the chief seat, with Knockgrafton, &c., were granted by King JOHN to Philip de Wygornia, lord-deputy of Ireland, in 1184, and very incorrectly supposed by some writers to be the same with his enemy, Philip de Brnose. The heiress of this family, Basilia, brought it in marriage to Meyler de Bermingham, Lord Athenry, who exchanged it with Piers de Bermingham, Lord of Thetmoy, for other lands (*circa* 1290); and his descendants, styled MAC FEORIS or MAC YORIS, retained this barony until Ellice, dau. and heir of MAC FEORIS MORE, brought it in marriage to PIERCE BUTLER, sprung from James le Botiller, illegitimate son of James, 3rd Earl of Ormonde, but upon whose family the Ormonde estates were entailed by the 10th earl, next after the Lords Dunboyne. His eldest son,

THOMAS BUTLER, of Cahir-dun Eske, Esq., *m.* Ellice, dau. of Thomas, 8th Earl of Desmond, and was father of EDMUND BUTLER, who, by Catharine, dau. of Sir Pierce le Poer, Knt., left issue,

 I. THOMAS, of whom presently.
 II. Pierce, who was father of
 THEOBALD, who became Baron Caher.

The eldest son,

THOMAS BUTLER, Esq., was elevated to the peerage of Ireland, 10 November, 1543, by the title of *Baron of Caher*, with remainder to his heirs-general. His lordship *m.* Eleanor, 5th dau. of Pierce, Earl of Ormonde, and by her had a surviving son EDMUND, his successor. He *m.* 2ndly, Ellen, dau. of Thomas, Earl of Desmond, and left two daus., Joan, *m.* to Thomas Prendergast, Esq., of Newcastle; and Eleanor, *m.* 1st, to Sir John Fitzgerald, Knt., brother of the Earl of Desmond; and 2ndly, to Sir John Oge, Knt. His lordship *d.* 1557, and was *s.* by his only surviving son,

EDMUND, 2nd baron, who *d. s. p.*, when the barony EXPIRED, and his two half-sisters became his heirs. The dignity was, however, revived 6 May, 1583, by a new patent granted to his lordship's 1st cousin,

SIR THEOBALD BUTLER, Knt., who thus became Baron Caher. The queen did not, however, feel authorized in conferring the Barony of Caher again, though by a new creation, and with only the new precedence to do so, without the consent of the heirs-general. But one of these heirs who had *m.* Mr. Prendergast, dying during the negotiations, the queen then

96

signed the patent, the release being executed a little later by the son of the deceased lady, though only ten years of age at the time. This nobleman received the honour of knighthood, in 1567, from the Lord-Deputy Sidney, who thus mentions him in a letter to the lords of the council, dated Limerick, 27 February, 1577 :—"There were with me that descended of English race, Sir Maurice Fitzgarrold, brother to the Vicounte Decies; Sir Thibald Butler, whose uncle and cozen-germaine were Baronnes of the Cayre, whose lands he lawfullye and justlye enjoyeth, and better deserveth that title of honor than any of theim ever did; for whome I entende more speciallye to write; for trulye, for his deserte, he is worthie any commendation." His lordship *m.* Mary, dau. of Sir Thomas Cusack, of Cussington, co. Meath, lord chancellor of Ireland, and left,

 I. THOMAS, his successor.
 II. Edmund, of Cloghcallie, co. Tipperary, *m.* Eleanor, dau. of Pierce Butler, Esq., of Callan, co. Kilkenny, and left a son,
   THOMAS, who *s.* as 3rd baron.
 III. Pierce, *d. s. p.*
 IV. Richard, of Clonbrogan, father of Thomas, who *d.* 1680 (leaving an only child, Ellen, *m.* to Theobald Stapleton, Esq.), and of Pierce, of Knockanamonagh, who *m.* a dau. and heir of Donogh O'Brien, and was father of THEOBALD, 5th Lord Caher.
 V. JAMES, of Knocklofty, *m.* 1st, Honor, dau. of Walter Walsh, Esq., of Castlehoel, co. Kilkenny ; and 2ndly, Margaret ——, and dying 17 April 1630, was buried in the abbey of Clonmel, having had issue,
   1 Theobald, of Knocklofty, who took a prominent part in the rebellion of 1641, and was deprived of his estates by Cromwell, *æt.* twenty-three, *ann.* 1630, and had issue,
    JAMES, of Glengall, in Tipperary, whose will, dated 28 May, 1732, was proved 29 January, 1737 ; he had issue,
     1 Theobald, *d. unm.*
     2 Richard, *m.* Jane, dau. of Richard Butler, of Ballynahinch, in Tipperary, and *d.* before 1750, leaving issue, JAMES, who *s.* his cousin PIERCE, as 9th Lord Baron Caher.
     1 Ellen. *m.* to — Ryan, of Banshigh.
     2 Anastatia, wife of — Murphy.
     3 Elinor, wife of — Macenery.
     4 Mary, wife of — Fitzgerald, and had issue.
   2 Thomas.   3 Richard.
   1 Mary   2 Catharine.   3 Ellinor.
 VI. John, of Cloughbridy, father of three sons, Edward, John, and Walter.
 I Ellen, *m.* to Richard Butler, Esq., of Ballyboe, co. Tipperary.
 II. Mary, *m.* to Sir Cormac M'Carthy, of Blarney.

Lord Caher *d.* in 1596, and was *s.* by his eldest son,

THOMAS BUTLER, 2nd baron. This nobleman *d.* 31 January, 1627, and leaving an only dau. and heir, Margaret, who *m.* Edmund, 3rd Lord Dunboyne, the barony devolved upon his nephew,

THOMAS BUTLER, 3rd baron (*refer to* 3rd son of 1st lord). His lordship *m.* Eleanor, dau. of Richard, Lord Power, and was *s.* by his grandson,

PIERCE BUTLER, 4th baron (only son of the Hon. Edmund Butler, by Eleanor, 2nd dau. of Edmund, Lord Dunboyne). His lordship *m.* in 1663, Elizabeth, dau. of Toby Mathew, Esq., of Thurles, by whom (who *m.* 2ndly, Daniel M'Carty, of Carrignavar) he had four daus., Elinor, *m.* to Sir John Everard, Bart., of Fethard ; Margaret, *m.* to Theobald, Lord Caher ; Anne, who *d. unm.* ; and Mary, *m.* to Robert Walsh, Esq., but dying in 1676, without male issue, the dignity devolved upon his kinsman,

THEOBALD BUTLER, Esq., of Knockanamonagh, as 5th baron (grandson of Richard, 4th son of the 1st lord). This nobleman was outlawed in 1691 for his adhesion to JAMES II., and suffered much privation in consequence, having had his estates for some time laid waste, and afterwards seized upon by the crown. The outlawry was, however, reversed in Michaelmas term, 1693, and his lordship restored to his honours and estates. He *m.* 1st, Mary, eldest dau. of Sir Redmond Everard, Bart., of Fethard, by whom he had one son and two daus., Mary, wife of James Long, Esq., of Dublin, and Joanna, *m.* to James Butler, Esq., of Caherbane ; and 2ndly, Margaret, 2nd dau. of Pierce, 4th Lord Caher, and had one son, and two daus., nuns at Ypres. His lordship *d.* in 1700, and was *s.* by his eldest son,

THOMAS BUTLER, 6th baron, who *m.* in 1709, Frances, eldest dau. of Sir Toby Butler, Knt., solicitor-general to JAMES II., and dying 22 May, 1744, left issue,

 I. JAMES, 7th lord.
 II. Theobald, *d.* young.
 III. PIERCE, 8th lord, successor to his brother.
 IV. Jordan, *d. s. p.*   V. Thomas, *d. s. p.*   VI. John. *d. s. p.*
 I. Mary.
 II. Margaret, *m.* to Andrew Kennedy, Esq.

He was *s.* by his eldest son,

JAMES BUTLER, 7th baron, at whose decease, *s. p.*, at Lyons, in France, 6 June, 1786, the title devolved upon his brother,

PIERCE BUTLER, 8th baron, who *d.* at Paris, 10 June, 1788, when this branch of the family being deemed to have become EXTINCT, the title and estates devolved upon

JAMES BUTLER, 9th Lord Caher, who *m.* Sarah Nichols; *d.* 1788, having had issue,

I. RICHARD, his heir.
II James, *d.* young.
I. Jane, *m.* to the Right Hon. Thomas Manners, high chancellor of Ireland.

He was *s.* by his son,

RICHARD BUTLER, Esq., as 10th baron. He took his seat in the Irish House of Lords, 4 February, 1796. His lordship, *b.* 13 November, 1775, *m.* 13 August, 1793, Emily, youngest dau. of James St. John Jefferys, Esq., of Blarney Castle, co. Cork, by Arabella his wife, sister of John Fitzgibbon, Earl of Clare, and by her (who *d.* in 1836) he had issue,

RICHARD, his heir.
Harriet-Anne, *m.* in 1822, to George-Hamilton, Earl of Belfast, afterwards Marquess of Donegal, and *d.* 14 September, 1860.
Charlotte, *m.* in December, 1835, to Christopher-Rice Mansel Talbot, Esq., M.P., of Margam, Glamorganshire, and *d.* 23 March, 1846.
Emily-Arabella-Georgiana, *m.* 1st, 1836, to Richard Pennefather, Esq., of Darling Hill, who *d.* 1849; and 2ndly, 1852, to Major-General H.-A. Hankey.

Lord Caher was created VISCOUNT CAHER and EARL OF GLENGALL 22 January, 1816; he *d.* 30 January, 1819, and was *s.* by his son,

RICHARD BUTLER, 2nd Earl of Glengall, a representative peer; *b.* in May, 1794, who *m.* 20 February, 1834, Margaret-Lauretta, younger dau. and co-heir of the late William Mellish, Esq., of Woodford, Essex, and by her (who *d.* 1863) had issue,

MARGARET, *m.* 2 August, 1858, to Lieut.-Colonel the Hon. RICHARD CHARTERIS, 2nd son of Francis, 8th Earl of Wemyss.
MATILDA, *d. unm.* 18 March, 1861.

His lordship *d.* 22 June, 1858, when the Earldom of Glengall and Viscounty of Caher became EXTINCT, but it is possible that the Barony of CAHER may be still successfully claimed.

Arms—Quarterly: first, arg., a cross Calvary, gu., thereon a representation of our Saviour, or (borne in memory of the family having fought against the infidels): second, or, a chief, indented, az., with a crescent for difference; third, gu., three covered cups, or, for BUTLER.

BUTLER—EARL OF KILKENNY.

By Letters Patent, dated 20 December, 1793.

Lineage.

EDMUND, 12th VISCOUNT MOUNTGARRET, *b.* 16 January, 1771, was advanced to the *Earldom of Kilkenny* by patent, 20 December, 1793. He *m.* 8 June, 1793, Mildred, eldest dau. of the Most Rev. Robert Fowler, archbishop of Dublin; but by her (who *d.* 30 December, 1838) he had no issue. The earl *d.* 16 July 1846, when the earldom became EXTINCT, but he was *s.* in the viscounty by his nephew, HENRY-EDMUND, present VISCOUNT MOUNTGARRET.

Arms—Or, a chief indented, az.

BUTLER—VISCOUNT GALMOYE.

By Letters Patent, dated 16 May, 1646.

Lineage.

THOMAS BUTLER, 10th Earl of Ormonde and Earl of Ossory, K.G., surnamed, from the darkness of his complexion, the "Black Earl," left at his decease, in 1614, a legitimate dau. and heiress, and had besides an illegitimate son,

PIERS-FITZ-THOMAS BUTLER, in whose favour the earl executed a deed of conveyance, in 1597 (when the said Piers had reached majority), of certain church-lands, considerable in amount, which had been granted by Queen ELIZABETH, in 1576, to James Butler, the earl's brother, and which reverted to his lordship at the decease of the said James' son, James, without issue. This Piers-Fitz-Thomas *m.* Katherine, eldest dau. and co-heiress of Thomas, Lord Slane, by whom he had two sons, and dying in 1601, was *s.* by the elder,

SIR EDWARD BUTLER, Knt., who was elevated to the peerage of Ireland, 16 May, 1646, as VISCOUNT OF GALMOYE, in the co.

of Kilkenny. His lordship *m.* Anne, dau. of Edmund, 2nd Viscount Mountgarret, by whom he had two sons, viz.,

I. PIERS, of Barrowmount, colonel of dragoons in the royal army, who fell at the battle of Worcester in 1650; he *m.* Margaret, dau. of Nicholas, 1st Lord Netterville (settlement dated 20 November, 1626), and had issue,

1 EDWARD, who *s.* his grandfather.
2 Nicholas, *d. s. p.* in 1653.
3 Richard, *d.* in 1678, without male issue.
4 James, *d. s. p.*
5 EDMUND, of Killoshulan, co. Kilkenny, ancestor of the present family, of whom hereafter.
1 Frances, *m.* to Hervey Morres, grandfather of the 1st Viscount Mountmorres.
2 Eleanor, *m.* to William Grace, Esq., of Ballylinch, and had a younger son, John Grace, ancestor of the DUKES OF BUCKINGHAM (*see* BURKE's *Landed Gentry*).

II. Thomas, whose only child,
Anne, *m.* William Cook, Esq., of Painstown.

The viscount *d.* in 1653, and was *s.* by his grandson,

EDWARD, 2nd viscount; who *m.* Eleanor, Lady Aston, dau. of Sir Nicholas White, Knt., of Leixlip, co. Kildare, by whom he had two sons,

I. PIERS, his successor.
II. Richard, a col. in the army, and captain in the royal guards, who *m.* Lucy Kavanagh, of the Borris family, and by her (who *d.* 1708) had with other issue who *d. unm.*, an eldest son,

1 JAMES, who assumed the title as 4th viscount, and *d. s. p.* in 1769.
1 Sophia, *m.* William Hay, Esq., of Nantes, ancestor of the Chevalier Hay, of the same place.

His lordship *d.* in 1667, and was *s.* by his elder son,

PIERS, 3rd viscount, a distinguished officer in the royal army (King JAMES's) at the battle of the Boyne, who was outlawed in consequence, 11 May, 1691; but being in the October following one of the commissioners for the surrender of Limerick, his lordship was included of course in the celebrated treaty of that city. Following, however, the fortunes of his royal master (who had created him Earl of Newcastle) into France, he was despoiled of all his estates, and attainted in 1697, by the statute of 9th William III., c. 5. His lordship, who had the rank of lieutenant-general in the French service, *m.* Elizabeth, dau. of Theobald Mathew, of Thurles, co. Tipperary, and had an only son, Edward, colonel in King JAMES's army, who *d.* in the lifetime of his father, having been slain in the battle of Malplaquet, 11 September, 1709, *s. p.* His lordship *d.* 18 June, 1740, without male issue, when the viscounty was assumed, notwithstanding the attainder, by his nephew and next male heir,

COL. JAMES BUTLER, of the Irish brigade in the French service (eldest son of the deceased lord's only brother, the Hon. Richard Butler, of his majesty King JAMES's bodyguard), as 4th viscount. His lordship *d. s. p.* 1771, when the dignity was assumed by the illegitimate son of his youngest brother, Captain Francis-Piers Butler, of the Irish brigade, by Catherine-Julie de Vallory (a lady whom Captain Butler eventually married, and acknowledging the said son, legitimated him according to the laws of France, but, indisputably, not according to the laws of England),

PIERS-LOUIS-ANTOINE, as 5th viscount. This Piers dying without issue in 1826, it is of no importance whether he assumed, *consistently* with the English law of descent, the representation of the family or not; but while he lived, the branch which should have inherited the peerage did not urge their claim, owing to ignorance of the taint in the birth of the said Piers; but upon his decease, the next claimant and male heir to the (assumed) 4th viscount, Garret Butler, Esq., of Garrendenny Castle, Queen's Co., lost no time in asserting his right, upon which the law officers of Ireland came to the favourable conclusion hereafter mentioned.

We shall now deduce the line of the said GARRET:—

EDMOND BUTLER, Esq., of Killoshulan, co. Kilkenny (youngest son of the Hon. Piers Butler, and brother of Edward, the 2nd viscount), a major in the army of King JAMES II., *m.* Catharine, dau. of Sir Nicholas Crisp, of Luddenham, co. Kent; and dying in 1691, left a son,

PIERS BUTLER, Esq., of Newtown and Urlingford, major of dragoons in King JAMES's army, comprehended within the articles of Limerick. This gentleman *m.* Domvile, eldest dau. of Sir Robert Hartpole, Knt. of Shrule, and grand-dau. of Sir William Domvile, King CHARLES the SECOND's attorney-general, by whom he had EDMOND BUTLER, Esq., capt. of dragons in the service of King GEORGE II., who conformed to the protestant faith in 1719. This gentleman served as high sheriff for the co. Kilkenny. He *m.* Miss Anne Skellerin, by whom he had several children, and was *s.* by his son,

PIERS BUTLER, Esq. (who but for the attainder would have succeeded at the decease of the 4th Viscount Galmoye, in 1769, owing to the illegitimacy of the person who assumed the dignity as 5th viscount). He m. Mary, only dau. of Theobald Mandevile. Esq., of Ballydine, and was s. by his only son,

EDMOND-THEOBALD-MANDEVILE BUTLER, Esq., of E. T. M. Ville and Garrendenny, Queen Co., who m. Elizabeth, dau. of Garret Nevile, Esq., and niece of Sir Robert-Adare Hodson, Bart., by whom he had,

    I. PIERS-THEOBALD, his heir.
    II. GARRET, heir to his brother.
    III. WILLIAM, m. Maria, 3rd dau. and coheiress of Sir Joshua-Colles Meredyth, Bart., and d. in 1848, leaving,

        PIERS MANDEVILLE, d. unm., 9 February, 1857
        MARIA-ELIZABETH, m. 20 August, 1867, John Kilkelly, Esq., LL.D., of Upper Mount Street, Dublin, and d. 24 Nov. 1871, leaving an only child,

            JOHN-PIERS BUTLER, who assumed, by royal licence, dated 1 May, 1878, the surname and arms of BUTLER.

    IV. THEOBALD, of E. T. M. Ville, co. Tipperary, m. 1840, Eliza, dau. of Robert Neville, Esq., of Marymount, co. Kilkenny, and has issue.

Mr. Butler d. in 1815, and was s. by his eldest son,

PIERS-THEOBALD BUTLER, Esq., at whose decease, unm., in 1824, the estates and representation of the family devolved upon his next brother,

GARRET BUTLER, Esq., who upon the demise of the (illegitimate) 5th Viscount Piers, Louis Antoine, in 1826, petitioned the crown for the recognition of his right to the peerage; and upon a reference to the law officers of the crown in Ireland, the following report was made:—

"Upon the whole of this case we are humbly of opinion that the said Garret Butler, the claimant of said title of Viscount of Galmoye, has well proved his right to the same, in case said attainder were out of the way; and that his majesty may, if he shall be graciously pleased so to do, recommend the proper measures to be taken to reverse the attainder created by the said act of William III., in order that the said title, honour, or dignity of Viscount of Galmoye, of the kingdom of Ireland, may be revived in the person of the petitioner, the said Garret Butler; the more so as such attainder arose from the acts of Piers, the 3rd viscount, who was not the lineal ancestor of the said claimant, he having, as before stated, shown his right to the said title through the uncle of the said Piers.

"All which is humbly submitted to your excellency as the report of your excellency's obedient and very humble servants,
      (Signed)   "H. JOY,
                  "JOHN DOHERTY.
"Dublin, 29 June, 1828."

Garret Butler (titular), Lord Galmoye, d. s. p. in 1861.

Arms—Or, a chief indented, az., within a bordure, vert.

BUTLER—BARON BUTLER, OF MOOR PARK CO. HERTS.

See BUTLER, EARLS OF BRECKNOCK.
(Thomas, Earl of Ossory, son of the 1st lord.)

CADOGAN—BARON CADOGAN, OF READING, BERKS, VISCOUNT CAVERSHAM, EARL CADOGAN.

Barony, by Letters Patent, dated 21 June, 1716.
Earldom, &c., by Letters Patent, dated 8 May, 1718.

Lineage.

WILLIAM CADOGAN (eldest son of Henry Cadogan, barrister-at-law, by Bridget his wife, dau. of Sir Hardress Waller, Knt.), a general officer of great celebrity, the companion in arms of the Duke of Marlborough, and his grace's successor in the command of the army, was elevated to the peerage 21 June, 1716, as BARON CADOGAN, of Reading, Berks, and created, 8 May, 1718, Baron Cadogan, of Oakley, co. Bucks, with remainder, in default of male issue, to his brother, Charles Cadogan, VISCOUNT CAVERSHAM, in the co. of Oxford, and EARL CADOGAN. His lordship m. Margaretta-Cecilia, dau. of William Munter, councillor of the court of Holland, by whom he had two daus., his co-heirs, viz.,

    I. SARAH, m. 4 December, 1719, to Charles, 2nd Duke of Richmond, K.G., and d. 1751, leaving issue, with five daus., two sons, viz.,

        1 Charles, 3rd Duke of Richmond, K.G., who d s. p. 1806.

        2 Lord George Henry Lennox, father of Charles, 4th Duke of Richmond, K.G.

    II. MARGARET. m. to the Hon. Charles-John, Count Bentinck, (2nd son of William, Earl of Portland) who d. 1779.

The earl d. 17 July, 1726, when the BARONY OF CADOGAN, of Reading, the VISCOUNTY OF CAVERSHAM, and the EARLDOM OF CADOGAN, became EXTINCT, while the Barony of Cadogan of Oakley devolved, according to the limitation, upon his lordship's brother, Charles Cadogan, and is now enjoyed by the present Earl Cadogan.

Arms—Quarterly; 1st and 4th. gu., a lion rampant, reghrdant, arg.; 2nd and 3rd, arg., three boars' heads, couped, sa.

CAILLI—BARON CAILLI.

By Writ of Summons, dated 4 March, 1309.

Lineage.

Many of the names which have been of note and nobility in this country, says Camden, are derived from localities situate in Normandy; as instances of which he mentions D'Arcy, Devereux, Gournay, Cayley, D'Aubigny, &c. The place, Cailly (Cailleium), from which this family takes its name, is in the arrondissement of Rouen, a few miles to the north-east of that town, and in the "Ballivium Caleti," or bailiwick of Caux. Here there was a fortress called "Castellum Cailleii," which was held by a baronial tenure, as the "Honour (or barony) de Cailly."

SIMON DE CAILLY, Lord of Massingham, Cranwich. Brodercross, Hiburgh, &c., in Norfolk (son of Humphrey de Cailly, temp. the CONQUEROR), m. Alice, and had two sons,

    ROGER, his heir.
    Jordanus (Sir), who held a knight's fee in Norfolk under Hugh Bigod, Earl of Norfolk, and another fee in Warwickshire under Robert Marmion.

The eldest son,

ROGER DE CAILLY, temp. HENRY II., was one of the most wealthy and influential barons of the time. His name appears, temp. HENRY II., as witness to a deed, along with the archbishop of Canterbury, the constable de Humez, and other distinguished nobles of the same date. His son,

    JOHN DE CAILLY, as appears by a trial, was Lord of Cranwich, temp. RICHARD I. He was also Lord of Massingham, Bradenham, Oxburgh, Denver, Hillington, Hecham, Hildeburgh, &c. His dau. Beatrix m. William de Butery. His son,
    JOHN DE CAILLY, was lord of these manors, 4th JOHN (1202). He m. Margery, who, after his death, m. Michael de Poynings. His son was,
    ADAM DE CAILLY. In the 17th JOHN there is a mandate to Hervey Belet, "that he do not receive into the king's peace Hugh de Plaiz, Michael de Poynings, William de Stuteville, William de Mortimer, Adam de Cayly, and Robert de Clere, until the king otherwise commands.—Witness the king at Stamford, 28 February." Adam de Cailly paid £5 to plead before the king, in the case of waste in Bradenham Forest, during the dower of Margerie, his mother, who was m. to Michael de Poynings, she being to have only reasonable estovers of house-bote, hedge-bote, and wood to burn, by view of the forester of Adam de Kayly. By Mabel his wife, he had, besides other sons,

    OSBERT, his heir.
    HUGO (SIR), of Owby, ancestor of the CAYLEYS, of Brompton, co. York, Baronets, and the CAYLEYS, of Wydale House, in the same co.

The eldest son,

SIR OSBERT DE CAILLI, m. Emma,[*] eldest dau. and co-heiress of Robert, Lord Tatshall, of Bokenham, and had by her Buckenham Castle and its large estates. This castle had been built by William, 1st Earl of Arundel, and was held by the service of being chief butler, or pincerna, which William Albini had been at that time (HENRY I.). It came into the Tateshall family by Mabel, eldest dau. and co-heiress of William, 3rd Earl of Arundel, which Mabel m. Robert de Tatshall, grandfather of Emma. William, 1st Earl of Arundel, m. Queen ADELICIA, the widow of HENRY I., dau. of Godfrey, Count of Brabant and Lorraine, who was lineal descendant and repre

---

[*] Many of the authorities differ as to whether Adam or Osbert de Cailly married the heiress of the Albinis.

sentative of CHARLEMAGNE. Sir Osbert, *temp.* EDWARD I., claimed assize of bread and beer, view of frankpledge, &c., in the towns of Bradenham, Oxburgh, Cranwich, and Hilburgh, as having been possessed by his father from the time of the Conquest. Sir Osbert had a dau. Margerie, *m.* to Roger de Clifton, and two sons,

ADAM (Sir). In the list of knights-bannerets, in the early part of EDWARD II.'s reign, appears " Sire Adam de Cayli. Chekere de or e de goules a une bende ermine." In the 2nd year of EDWARD III. he was ransomed from captivity in Scotland. Sir Adam appears to have been by a former wife, and not by Emma de Tatshall, as his son, Edmund de Cailly, who inherited Denver and other manors anciently belonging to the family, did not succeed to Buckenham.

THOMAS (Sir), of Buckenham Castle.

The 2nd son,

SIR THOMAS DE CAILLI, of Buckenham Castle, lord of the Barony of Buckenham, to which he succeeded through his mother, Emma, was, in 1308, summoned to perform military service against the Scots' muster at Carlisle, 22 August. In 1309 he was summoned to parliament as Baron de Cailly, of Buckenham, to attend at Westminster, 27 April; again, in the same year, at Stamford; again (8 February, 1310), he was summoned at York; and at London in 1311. Thomas, Lord Cayley, *d. s. p.*, and all his large estates went to his sister Margerie, who *m.* Roger de Clifton, esquire to her brother. Her son, Sir Adam de Clifton, was afterwards summoned to parliament as Baron Clifton, of Buckenham (*see that title*). There is an inquisition, 10th EDWARD II., apparently on the death of Thomas de Cailli, in which there is notice of his large possessions in Norfolk, and also of his having lands at Hunmanby and Fynehey, in Yorkshire. This is remarkable, as showing a very early connexion with Yorkshire.

Arms—Arg., four bendlets, gu.

CALVERT—BARON BALTIMORE, OF BALTIMORE.

By Letters Patent, dated 16 February, 1624.

Lineage.

LEONARD CALVERT, Esq., of Danbywiske, co. York, son of John Calvert, *m.* Alicia, dau. of John Crossland, Esq., of Crossland, in the same co., and left a son,

GEORGE CALVERT, Esq., *b.* 1578, who having served as secretary to Sir Robert Cecil, when secretary of state, and afterwards as clerk to the privy council, received the honour of knighthood in 1617, and was appointed, in the beginning of the ensuing year, secretary of state to the king, who employed him in the most important affairs, and settled, in 1620, a pension of £1,000 a-year upon him beyond his salary. Sir George changing his religion, however, and turning Roman catholic in 1624, voluntarily resigned his post. The king continued him, nevertheless, in the privy council, and having made him large grants of lands in Ireland, elevated him to the peerage of that kingdom 16 February, 1624, as BARON BALTIMORE, *of Baltimore*, co. Longford, Sir George being at the time representative in parliament for the university of Oxford. Whilst secretary of state his lordship obtained a grant of the province of Avalon, in Newfoundland, with the most extensive privileges, and expended £25,000 in the settlement thereof. This place he visited thrice in the reign of King JAMES I., but after contending with great spirit against the French encroachments, he was obliged to abandon it altogether; whereupon he obtained from King CHARLES I. a patent of Maryland to him and his heirs for ever, with the same title and royalties as in Avalon, to hold in common soccage as of the manor of Windsor, paying yearly, as an acknowledgment to the crown, two Indian arrows at Windsor Castle, upon Easter Tuesday, and the fifth part of the gold and silver ore. His lordship did not live, however, to see the grant pass the great seal, and his son Cecil, the succeeding Lord Baltimore, had it made out in his own name, bearing date 20 June, 1632. The province of Maryland was so named by the king in the honour of his queen, HENRIETTA MARIA. His lordship *m.* Anne, dau. of George Mynne, Esq., of Hertingfordbury, co. Hertford, by whom he had a numerous family, of which

CECIL, *s.* to the title.
Leonard, was constituted by his brother. In 1633, the 1st governor of Maryland, jointly with Jeremy Hawley and Thomas Cornwallis, Esqrs.
Anne, *m.* William Peaseley, Esq.
Grace, *m.* Sir Robert Talbot, of Carton, co. Kildare.

The baron *d.* 15 April, 1632, and was *s.* by his eldest son.

CECIL, 2nd baron; who *m.* Anne, 3rd dau. of Thomas, Lord Arundel, of Wardour, and was *s.* by his son,

JOHN, 3rd baron. This nobleman was present in King JAMES's Irish parliament, in 1689, and dying soon afterwards, was *s.* by his son,

CHARLES, 4th baron, who was outlawed for high treason in Ireland, although he had never been in that kingdom, but King WILLIAM, upon his lordship's representation, caused the outlawry to be reversed, 25 January, 1691. He inherited the estates of Woodcote Park and Horton, under the will of Elizabeth Evelyn, a dau. of the house of Mynn, a relative of his great-grandmother. His lordship *d.* 21 February, 1714, and was *s.* by his son,

BENEDICT LEONARD, 5th baron, who had conformed to the established church in 1713, and was afterwards returned to the British parliament for Harwich. His lordship *m.* 2 June, 1698, Lady Charlotte Lee, eldest dau. of Edward Henry, 1st Earl of Lichfield, by Lady Charlotte Fitzroy, natural dau. of King CHARLES II., and had issue,

CHARLES, his successor.
Benedict-Leonard, M.P. for Harwich, and governor of Maryland. Died in his passage home, 1 June, 1732.
Edward-Henry, commissary-general and president of the council of Maryland. His widow *m.* 15 October, 1741, James Fitzgerald, Esq.
Cecil, *b.* 1702.
Charlotte, *m.* to Thomas Breerwood, Esq., and *d.* December, 1744.
Jane, *m.* — Hyde, of Bucks, and *d.* July, 1778.

His lordship *d.* 16 April, 1715, and was *s.* by his eldest son,

CHARLES, *b.* 29 September 1699, 6th baron, who filled several high official employments between the years 1731 and 1745, and represented for some time the co. of Surrey in parliament. His lordship *m.* 20 July, 1730, Mary, youngest dau. of Sir Theodore Janssen, Bart., of Wimbledon, co Surrey, and had issue,

FREDERICK, his heir.
CAROLINE, *m.* Sir Robert Eden, Bart., governor of Maryland (grandfather by her of the late Sir William Eden, Bart., of Auckland and Truir).
LOUISA, *m.* to John Browning, Esq., of Lincolnsnire.

His lordship *d.* 24 April, 1751, and was *s.* by his only surviving son,

FREDERICK, 7th baron, *b.* 6 February, 1731-2, who *m.* in 1753, Lady Diana Egerton, dau. of Scrope, Duke of Bridgwater; but *d. s. p.* at Naples, 4 September, 1771, when the title became EXTINCT. (His lordship had sold his estates before going abroad to Mr. John Trotter, of Soho, London.)

Arms—Paly of six, or and sa., a bend counter-changed.

CAMPBELL—DUKE OF GREENWICH.

See p. 535.

CAMPBELL — EARL AND MARQUESS OF ARGYLL, BARON ARASE AND DUNOON, EARL OF ILAY, ETC.

(*See* DUKE OF ARGYLL in BURKE's *Extant Peerage*.)

CAMPBELL—EARL OF ATHOLL.

Upon the forfeiture of David de Strathbogie, 11th Earl of Atholl, his estates were granted to Sir Niel Campbell, and Mary his wife, sister to the king, and John, their son. This SIR JOHN CAMPBELL, of Moulin, 2nd son of Sir Niel Campbell, of Sochon, was created EARL OF ATHOLL, as appears from the charter of King DAVID II. to Robert, Lord Erskine, of the customs of Dundee, and third part of Pettarache, in Forfarshire, which sometime pertained to John Campbell, Earl of Atholl, and a charter granted by John Campbell, Earl of Atholl, to Roger de Mortimer, of the lands of Bellandre. He was killed in the battle of Halidon Hill, 19 July, 1333, without issue, whereby the title reverted to the crown.

CAMPBELL—BARON CLYDE.

(*See* ADDENDA.)

CAMPBELL—EARL OF CAITHNESS.

(*See* CAMPBELL, Earl of Breadalbane, in BURKE's *Extant Peerage*.)

CAMPBELL—MARQUESS OF BREADAL-BANE.

(*See* CAMPBELL, Earl of Breadalbane, in BURKE's *Extant Peerage*.)

CAMPBELL—EARL OF IRVINE.

By Letters Patent, dated 28 March, 1642.

JAMES CAMPBELL, only son of Archibald, 7th Earl of Argyll, by his 2nd wife, Anne, dau. of Sir William Cornwallis, was, when very young, created a peer by royal charter, dated 12 February, 1626, under the title of Baron of Kintyre, to himself and his heirs male and assigns. He had in some years afterwards (12 December, 1636) a charter of the Barony of Lundie, in Forfarshire ; and entering the military service of LOUIS XIII. of France, in that monarch's wars with the Spaniards, obtained the command of a regiment, and distinguished himself so valiantly, that on his return to his native country he was advanced by King CHARLES I. to the dignity of EARL OF IRVINE and Lord of Lundie, by patent, dated at York, 28 March, 1642, in remainder to the heirs male of his body. The district of Kintyre was settled upon him by his father; he sold it to his brother, the Marquess of Argyll; and *d. s. p.* in France before the Restoration, when the titles of Lord of Lundie and EARL OF IRVINE became EXTINCT.

Arms—Gironny of eight, or and sa.

CAMVILLE—BARONS CAMVILLE, OF CLIFTON.

By Writ of Summons, dated 23 June, 1295.

Lineage.

In the 5th of King STEPHEN,
GERALD DE CAMVILLE, of Lilburne Castle, co. Northampton, granted two parts of the tithes of Charleton-Camville, in Somersetshire, to the monks of Bermondsey, in Surrey. To this Gerald *s* his son,
RICHARD DE CAMVILLE, who was *founder*, in the time of King STEPHEN, of Combe Abbey, co. Warwick, and was one of the witnesses, in the 12th of the same reign, to the convention between that monarch and Henry, Duke of Normandy, regarding the succession of the latter to the crown of England. This feudal lord appears to be a person of great power during the whole of King HENRY's reign, and after the accession of RICHARD I. we find him one of the admirals in the expedition made by that monarch into the Holy Land. He was subsequently governor of Cyprus; whence he went without the king's permission to the siege of Acre and there died His lordship left four sons and a dau., viz.,

I. GERALD, his heir, who purchased from King RICHARD the custody of Lincoln Castle and the province adjacent. This Gerald was a very powerful feudal lord in the reign of JOHN, to which monarch he stanchly adhered. He *m.* Nichola, eldest dau. and co-heiress of Richard de Haya, and left an only son and heir,
  RICHARD, who *m.* Eustachia, dau. and heiress of Gilbert Basset, and widow of Thomas de Vernon, and left an only dau. and heiress,
    IDONEA, who *m.* William, son of William de Longespee, Earl of Salisbury.
II. Walter, left issue,
  1 Roger, who had an only dau.,
    Matilda, *m.* to Nigel de Mowbray, and *d. s p.*
  1 Patronilla, *m.* to Richard Curzon.
  2 Matilda, *m.* to Thomas de Astley.
  3 Alicia, *m.* to Robert de Esseby.

100

III. Richard, left issue,
  1 Richard, *d s p.*
  1 Isabella, heiress of her brother, *m.* in the 4th of RICHARD I., Richard Harcourt, of Bosworth, co. Leicester.
IV. WILLIAM, with whom we shall proceed.
  1. Matilda, *m.* to William de Ros.

WILLIAM DE CAMVILLE, the youngest son, *m.* Albreda, dau. and heiress of Geoffrey Marmion, and had issue,

I GEOFFREY, his successor.
II William, of Sekerton, co. Warwick, father of
  Thomas, whose grandson, Sir Gerard de Camville, of Arrow, co. Warwick, left a dau. and heiress,
    Elizabeth, *m.* to Robert Burdett, ancestor of the BURDETTS *of Arrow, co. Warwick, and Foremark, co. Derby*.
III. Thomas.

William de Camville was *s.* by his eldest son,
GEOFFREY DE CAMVILLE, who, in the 22nd EDWARD I. had summons to attend the king at Portsmouth, with horse and arms, to embark in the expedition then proceeding to Gascony ; and was subsequently summoned to parliament as BARON CAMVILLE, *of Clifton, co. Stafford*, from 23 June, 1295, to 22 February, 1307. His lordship *m.* Maud, dau. and heir of Sir Guy de Bryan, by Eve, dau. and heir of Henry de Traci, and had an only child,

WILLIAM, his successor.

He *d.* in 1309, seised of the lordships of Freymington, Bovey-Traci, Nymet-Traci, Barnstaple, the fourth part of the manor of Toriton, and of the hamlet of Nimet St. George, as also of the lordship of Clifton Camville, co. Stafford, which he held by the service of three knights' fees ; and which lordship and manors were holden by him (as tenant by the courtesy of England) in right of Maud his wife. His lordship was *s.* by his son,
WILLIAM DE CAMVILLE, 2nd baron, summoned to parliament 4 March, 1309, and 16 June, 1311, but never afterwards. Of the issue of this nobleman there are different statements. He *d.* however, without a son, when the BARONY OF CAMVILLE fell into ABEYANCE, as it probably so continues. One authority, Burton, in his "Leicestershire," gives his lordship two daus., his co-heiresses, viz.,

Maud, *m.* to Sir Richard Stafford, of Pipe, co. Stafford (2nd son of Baron Stafford), whose son,
  Richard, was summoned to parliament as Lord Stafford, of Clifton.
Margery, *m.* to Sir Richard Vernon, of Haddon, co. Derby.

Another, Erdswic, the historian of Staffordshire, says, he had but one dau.,

MAUD, who *m.* 1st, Richard Vernon, and 2ndly, Sir Richard Stafford.

While a third authority, Dr. Vernon, rector of Bloomsbury, in an interleaved copy of Erdswic, states that William de Camville, of Clifton-Camville, had issue five daus. and heirs, viz.,

Maud, *m.* to Sir William Vernon, Knt., of Haddon, co. Derby.
Isabella, *m.* 1st, to Sir Richard Stafford, and 2ndly, to Gilbert de Bermingham.
Eleanor.
Nichola, *m.* to John St. Clere.
Catherine, *m.* to Robert Griesly.

Arms—Vert, three lions passant, arg., armed and langued, gu.

CANNING — EARL CANNING, AND CANNING, VISCOUNT STRATFORD DE REDCLIFFE.

(*See* ADDENDA.)

CANTILUPE—BARONS CANTILUPE.

By Writ of Summons, dated 29 December, 1299.

Lineage.

WILLIAM DE CANTILUPE, the first of this family upon record, served the office of sheriff for the cos. of Warwick and Leicester in the 3rd, 4th, and 5th years of King JOHN. In the next year he was made governor of the castles of Hereford and Wilton, and he was subsequently sheriff of Herefordshire. In the 11th of the same reign, being then the king's steward, he gave 40 marks for the wardship of Egidia, Lady of Kilpeck, widow of William Fitz-Warine, and in three years

Carew.
(E.Totness.)

Carey.
(E.Dover.)

Carmichael.
(E.Hyndford.)

Carteret.
(B.Carteret.)

Chandos.
(B.Chandos.)

Cherlton.
(B.Cherlton.)

Clare.
(E.Pembroke.)

Colepeper.
(B.Colepeper.)

Coningsby.
(E.Coningsby.)

Conway.
(E.Conway.)

Coote.
(E.Mountrath.)

Cornwallis.
(M.Cornwallis.)

afterwards, when the king was excommunicated by Pope INNOCENT III., he remained so faithful as to become one of the monarch's chief counsellors. We find him, however, arrayed afterwards under the baronial banner, and joining in the invitation to Louis of France. But within the same year he returned to the king, when he obtained grants of all the forfeited estates of Richard de Engaine and Vitalis de Engaine, two leading barons in the insurrection; and was appointed governor of Kenilworth Castle, co. Warwick. In the reign of HENRY III. he continued attached to the cause of royalty, and acquired immense possessions in the shape of grants from the crown of forfeited lands. He d. in 1238, leaving five sons, viz.,

I. WILLIAM, his heir, also steward to the king, and a person of great power, m. Milicent, dau. of Hugh de Gournai, and widow of Almeric, Earl of Eureux, and d. 1250, having had issue,

1 WILLIAM, who m. Eve, dau. and co-heiress of William Broase, Lord of Brecknock and Abergavenny, and in her right became possessed of that honour He d. in the flower of his youth, leaving issue,

George, who d. s. p

Milicent, m. 1st, to John de Montalt, and 2ndly, to Eudo le Zouche, from which latter union descended the LORDS ZOUCHE, of Haryngworth.

Joan, m. to Henry de Hastings, and had a son, John Hastings, Lord of Abergavenny, ancestor of the Hastings, Earls of Pembroke.

2 Thomas, bishop of Hereford, and in the 34th EDWARD I. canonized.

1 Julian, m. to Robert de Tregoz.

II. Walter, a priest, employed by King HENRY as his agent to the court of Rome, afterwards bishop of Worcester.

III. John, Lord of Snitterfield, co. Warwick, m. Margaret, dau. and heiress of William Cumnin, of that place, and was s. by his son,

JOHN, who d. in the 17th EDWARD II. He m. Margaret, dau. of John, Lord Mohun, of Dunster, and had issue,

John, d. v. p., s. p.

ELEANOR CANTILUPE, who m. Sir Thomas West, Lord West, from which union lineally descend the Earls of DELAWARE and VISCOUNTS CANTILUPE.

IV. NICHOLAS, of whom presently.

V. Thomas, elected Lord Chancellor of England by the barons in the 49th HENRY III.

NICHOLAS DE CANTILUPE, of Ilkeston, co. Derby, the 4th son, m. Eustachia, sister, and eventual heiress, of Hugh FitzRalph, Lord of Greseley, co. Nottingham, and was s. by his son,

WILLIAM DE CANTILUPE, who having distinguished himself in the French and Scottish wars of King EDWARD I., was summoned to parliament as BARON CANTILUPE, from 29 December, 1299, to 5 August, 1308. His lordship d. in the following year, and was s. by his elder son,

WILLIAM DE CANTILUPE, 2nd baron, but never summoned to parliament. This nobleman dying s. p. was s. by his brother,

SIR NICHOLAS DE CANTILUPE, 3rd baron. This nobleman served in the Flemish and Scottish wars of EDWARD III. and had summons to parliament from 23 April, 1337, to 13 March, 1354. His lordship d. in 1355, seised of the manor of Eselburgh, co. Buckingham; Ilkeston, co. Derby; Greseley, co. Nottingham; and Livingston and others, co. Lincoln. He m. 1st, Typhania, and 2ndly, Joane, widow of William de Kyme: his grandson, Nicholas (son of his son William) was his heir; this last-named Nicholas d. s. p. 45th EDWARD III., and his brother Sir William d. s. p., circa 14th RICHARD II.

Arms.—Gu., three leopards' heads inverted, jessant three fleurs-de-lis, or.

CAPEL—BARON CAPEL, OF TEWKSBURY, CO, GLOUCESTER.

By Letters Patent, dated 11 April, 1692.

Lineage.

SIR HENRY CAPEL, K.B., 2nd son of Arthur, 1st Baron Capel, of Hadham, co. Hertford, and brother of Arthur, 1st Earl of Essex, having distinguished himself as a leading and eloquent member of the House of Commons, was elevated to the peerage 11 April, 1692, as BARON CAPEL, of Tewksbury. His lordship m. Dorothy, dau. of Richard Bennet, Esq., of Kew, in Surrey, and niece of Sir Richard Bennet, Bart., of Babraham, in Cambridgeshire, but had no issue. Lord Capel was one of the lords justices of Ireland, upon the recal of Lord Sydney, in 1693, and d. Lord-Lieutenant of that kingdom, at the castle of Dublin, 30 May, 1696. His lordship was buried at Hadham.

where an inscription states that he was of the privy council to King CHARLES II., one of the lords of the treasury, and of the privy council to King WILLIAM. At his lordship's decease the BARONY OF CAPEL, of Tewksbury, became EXTINCT.

Arms—Gu., a lion rampant, between three cross crosslets, fitchée, or, with due difference.

CAREW—BARON CAREW, OF CLOPTON, CO. WARWICK, EARL OF TOTNESS.

Barony, by Letters Patent, dated 4 May, 1605.
Earldom, by Letters Patent, dated 5 February, 1625.

Lineage.

Of this family, one of great antiquity in the western parts of England, and which derived its surname originally from Carew Castle, co. Pembroke, was

SIR NICHOLAS CAREW, Knt., m. Jane, dau. of Sir Hugh Courtenay, and had a son,

SIR THOMAS CAREW, who, by Joan his wife, dau. of John Carminow, was father of

SIR EDMUND CAREW, Knt., who, by Catherine his wife, dau. of Sir William Huddersfield, had a son,

GEORGE CAREW, who, being a churchman, was, first archdeacon of Totness, in Devon, next dean of Bristol and chief chanter in the cathedral of Salisbury, afterwards dean of the king's chapel and dean of Christ's Church, Oxford, lastly dean of Exeter and Windsor. This very reverend personage m. Anne, dau. of Sir Nicholas Harvey, Knt., and had with other issue,

GEORGE CAREW, who was in the expedition to Cadiz, in the 38th of ELIZABETH, and afterwards served with great reputation in Ireland. He was made president of Munster, when uniting his forces with those of the Earl of Thomond, he reduced several castles and other strong places, obtained many triumphs over the rebels, and brought the Earl of Desmond to trial. He was likewise a privy councillor in Ireland and master of the ordnance. Upon the accession of King JAMES I. he was constituted governor of the Isle of Guernsey, and having m. Joyce, only dau. and heiress of William Clopton, Esq., of Clopton, co. Warwick, he was elevated to the peerage 4 May, 1605, as BARON CAREW, of Clopton. After which he was made master of the ordnance for life, and sworn of the privy council; and, in the 1st year of King CHARLES I., created EARL OF TOTNESS. "Besides," says Dugdale, "these, his noble employments, 'tis not a little observable, that being a great lover of antiquities, he wrote an historical account of all those memorable passages which happened in Ireland during the term of those three years he continued there, intituled 'Hibernia Pacata,' printed at London in 1633, and that he made an ample collection of many chronological and choice observations, as also of divers exact maps, relating to sundry parts of that realm, some whereof are now in the public library at Oxford, but most of them in the hands of Sir Robert Shirley, Bart., of Stanton Harold, co. Leicester, bought of his executors." His lordship d. 27 March, 1629, at the Savoy in the Strand, "in the suburbs of London," leaving an only dau. and heiress,

LADY ANNE CAREW, who m. 1st, — Wilford, Esq., of Kent, and 2ndly, Sir Allen Apsley, lieutenant of the Tower of London.

The earl dying thus, without legitimate male issue, all his honours became EXTINCT.

Arms.—Or, three lions passant, sa.

CAREY—BARONS HUNSDON, VISCOUNTS ROCHFORT, EARLS OF DOVER.

Barony, by Letters Patent, dated 13 January, 1559.
Viscounty, by Letters Patent, dated 6 June, 1621.
Earldom, by Letters Patent, dated 8 May, 1628,

Lineage.

This family had their residence, anciently, at Cockington, co. Devon.

ADAM DE KARRY, Lord of Castle Karry, in Somersetshire, m. Anne, dau. of William Trevet, and was father of

JOHN KARRY, who, by Elizabeth, his wife, dau. of Sir Richard Stapleton, had a son and heir,

WILLIAM KARRY, who held the manor of West Polworth, co.

Devon, at his decease, 31st EDWARD I. He m. Alice, dau. of Sir William Beaumont, Knt., and was father of

SIR WILLIAM KARRY, who m. the dau. of Sir John Archdeacon, and had two sons, JOHN (Sir), his heir, and WILLIAM (Sir), M.P. for Devonshire, 36th and 42nd EDWARD III., living 11th RICHARD II., *d. s. p.* The elder son,

SIR JOHN CAREY, Knt., one of the barons of the exchequer, *temp.* RICHARD II., m. 1st, Agnes, dau. of Lord Stafford, and 2ndly, Margaret, dau. of William Holwell, of Holwell, in Devon, and widow of Sir Guy de Brian; by the latter he had issue, John, bishop of Exeter, *anno.* 1419, and an elder son, his heir,

SIR ROBERT CAREY, Knt., a person so valorous and so skilful in arms that few presumed to enter the lists with him. Amongst his other exploits is recorded his triumph over an Arragonian knight in Smithfield; upon which occasion he was knighted, and allowed to adopt the arms of his vanquished rival—namely, "Three roses on a bend." Sir Robert. m. twice; by Margaret his 1st wife, dau. of Sir Philip Courtenay, of Powderham, co. Devon, he left a son and heir,

PHILIP CAREY, Esq., of Cockington, who m. Christian, dau. and heir of William Orchard, Esq., and by her (who m, 2ndly, Walter Portman, Esq.) was father of

SIR WILLIAM CAREY, Knt., an eminent Lancastrian, who, upon the issue of the battle of Tewkesbury, 10th EDWARD IV., fled to a church for sanctuary, but was brought forth, under a promise of pardon, and beheaded. Sir William m. 1st, Anne, dau. of Sir William Paulet, Knt., and from that marriage descended the Carys, who continued at Cockington, and were ancestors of the CARYS *of Torr Abbey and Follaton,* co. Devon. He m. 2ndly, Alice, dau. of Sir Baldwin Fulford, Knt., and by her had a son,

THOMAS CAREY, Esq., of Chilton Follot, who m Margaret, 2nd dau. and co-heir of Sir Robert Spencer, by Eleanor his wife. dau. and coheir of Edmund Beaufort, Duke of Somerset, by whom he had two sons, viz.,

> JOHN (Sir), who m. Joice, sister of Sir Anthony Denny, Knt., and left issue,
>
> > EDWARD (Sir), of Berkhamsted, who m. Catherine. dau. of Sir Henry Knevet, and widow of Henry, Lord Paget, by whom he had,
> >
> > > HENRY, created VISCOUNT FALKLAND, in the peerage of Scotland, a dignity still EXTANT.
>
> WILLIAM, of whose line we treat.

The younger son,

WILLIAM CAREY, an esquire of the body to King HENRY VIII., and a favourite of that monarch, m. Lady Mary Boleyne, dau. of Thomas, EARL OF WILTSHIRE, and sister of the unfortunate Queen ANNE STAFFORD, Knt., and by her, who m. 2ndly, Sir William Stafford, Knt., had issue,

> HENRY, his heir
> Catherine, m. to Sir Francis Knollys, K.G.

He d. in 1528, being then of the bedchamber to the king, and was s. by his son,

HENRY CAREY, who, soon after the accession of his first cousin, Queen ELIZABETH, to the throne, received the honour of knighthood, and upon 13 January following (*anno* 1559) was elevated to the peerage, by letters patent, as BARON HUNSDON, with a grant of the mansion of Hunsdon, co. Hertford, and a pension of £4,000 a-year. In the 5th of ELIZABETH his lordship was sent with the order of the Garter to the King of France, then at Lyons; and in five years afterwards, being governor of Berwick, he drove the insurrectionary Earls of Northumberland and Westmoreland into Scotland; the former of whom he subsequently got into his hands, and had beheaded at York. In the 29th ELIZABETH, Lord Hunsdon was appointed general warden of the marches towards Scotland and lord chamberlain of the household. In 1588, the memorable year of the menaced Spanish invasion, his lordship had the protection of the queen's person, in the camp at Tilbury, with the command of the army for that purpose. He was likewise captain of the pensioners and a knight of the Garter. He m. Anne, dau. of Sir Thomas Morgan, Knt., of Arkestone, co. Hereford, by Anne his wife, dau. of Jean, Sire de Merode, and had issue,

> I. GEORGE, his successor.
> II. John.
> III. Edmund, who was knighted for his valour by the Earl of Leicester, in 1587. Sir Edmund m. 1st, Mary, dau. and heiress of Christopher Crocker, Esq., of Croft, co. Lincoln; 2ndly, Elizabeth, dau. and co-heir of John, Lord Latimer, and widow of Sir John Danvers, Knt.; and 3rdly, Judith, dau. of Lawrence Humphrey, D.D., and had three sons and two daus., and was *s.* by his son,
> > ROBERT (Sir), a captain of horse, under Horatio, Lord Vere of Tilbury, in the Netherlands, m. Alletta, dau. of Mynheer

Hogenhove, secretary to the States General, by whom he had three sons, HORATIO, Ernestus, and Ferdinand, and was *s.* by the eldest,

> > > HORATIO, captain of horse in the service of King CHARLES I., m. Petronilla, dau. of Robert Conyers, Esq., and was father of
> > > > ROBERT, of whom hereafter, as 6th LORD HUNSDON.

> IV. ROBERT, created EARL OF MONMOUTH (*See that dignity*).
> I. Catherine, m. to Charles Howard, EARL OF NOTTINGHAM.
> II. Philadelphia, m. to Thomas, Lord Scrope.
> III. Margaret, m. to Sir Edward Hoby, Knt.

The illness which occasioned his death is said to have arisen from disappointed ambition, in never having been able to attain the dignity of EARL OF WILTSHIRE. Fuller, in his "Worthies of England," relates that, "when he lay on his death-bed, the queen gave him a gracious visit, causing a patent for the said earldom to be drawn, his robes to be made, and both to be laid on his bed; but this lord (who could not dissemble, neither well nor sick,) replied, '*Madam, seeing you counted me not worthy of this honour while I was living, I count myself unworthy of it now I am dying!*'" His lordship d. at Somerset House, 23 July, 1596, æt. seventy-two, and was s. by his eldest son,

GEORGE CAREY, 2nd Baron Hunsdon, who had been educated for the public service from his earliest youth, and obtained in the lifetime of his father the honour of knighthood, for his distinguished conduct in the expedition made into Scotland, in the 13th of ELIZABETH, under the Earl of Sussex. Sir George succeeded his father as captain of the band of pensioners, and was soon afterwards made lord chamberlain and a knight of the Garter. His lordship m. Elizabeth, dau. of Sir John Spencer, of Althorp, Knt., by whom (who m. 2ndly, Sir Thomas Chamberlain, and 3rdly, Ralph, Lord Eure) he had an only dau. and heiress,

> Elizabeth, who m. Sir Thomas Berkeley, Knt., son and heir of Henry, Lord Berkeley, and d. 23 April, 1635.

He d. 9 September, 1603, and leaving no male issue, the peerage devolved upon his brother,

SIR JOHN CAREY, Knt., warden of the east marches towards Scotland, as 3rd Baron Hunsdon. His lordship m. Mary, dau. of Leonard Hyde, Esq., of Throgkyn, Herts, and widow of Richard Peyton, and had issue,

> HENRY, his successor.
> Charles.
> Anne, m. to Sir Francis Lovell, Knt., of East Harlyng, Norfolk.
> Blanch, m. to Sir Thomas Wodehouse, Knt., of Kimberley, Norfolk.

He d. in April, 1617, and was *s.* by his eldest son,

HENRY CAREY, 4th Baron Hunsdon, who was advanced, 6 June, 1621, to the *Viscounty of Rochfort,* and created 8 May, 1627, EARL OF DOVER. His lordship m. 1st, Judith, dau. of Sir Thomas Pelham, Bart., of Loughton, Sussex, by whom he had issue,

> JOHN, *Viscount Rochfort,* who was made a knight of the Bath at the coronation of King CHARLES I.
> Henry, d. January, 16:0-1.
> Pelham (Sir), m. 24 June, 1630, Mary, dau. and heir of John Jackson, and d. *s. p.*
> George, d. *s. p.*
> Mary, m. to Sir Thomas Wharton, K.B., brother of Lord Wharton.
> Judith, d. *unm.*
> Philadelphia, d. *unm.*

His lordship, who m. 2ndly, Mary, dau. of Richard Morris, d. in 1668, and was *s.* by his eldest son,

JOHN CAREY, 2nd EARL OF DOVER and 5th Baron Hunsdon. This nobleman m. 1st, Lady Dorothy St. John, dau. of Oliver, EARL OF BOLINGBROKE, by whom he had no issue. His lordship m. 2ndly, Abigail, dau. of Alderman Sir William Cokayne, Knt., of London, by whom he had an only dau.,

> Mary, m. to William Heveningham, Esq., of Heveningham, Sussex, by whom she had,
> > Sir William Heveningham, Knt.
> > Abigail, m. to John, son and heir of Sir John Newton, Bart,

He d. in 1677, and leaving thus no male issue, the *Viscounty of Rochfort* and EARLDOM OF DOVER EXPIRED, while the BARONY OF HUNSDON reverted to his lordship's kinsman,

SIR ROBERT CAREY, Knt. (*revert to the descendants of the Hon.* Sir Edmund Carey, 3rd son of the 1st lord), as 6th Baron Hunsdon. His lordship m. Margaret, dau. of Sir Gervase Clifton, Bart., and widow of Sir John South, Knt., but dying *s. p.* in 1692, the title devolved upon (the son of his uncle Ernestus,) his cousin,

ROBERT CAREY, as 7th Baron Hunsdon, who, at the time of

his succession, was said to pursue the humble avocation of a *weaver*. His lordship *d. unm.* in September, 1702, when the title devolved upon (the grandson of Colonel Ferdinand Carey, uncle of the last lord,) his cousin,

WILLIAM FERDINAND CAREY, as 8th Baron Hunsdon. This nobleman was *b.* in Holland, the son of William Carey and Gertrude Van Oustoorn, but being naturalized in 1690, he inherited the honours of his family, and took his seat in the House of Peers on 1 March, 1708. His lordship *m.* Grace, dau. of Sir Edward Waldo, Knt., and relict of Sir Nicholas Wolstenholme, Bart., but dying *s. p.* in 1765, the BARONY OF HUNSDON became EXTINCT.

Arms.—Arg., on a bend, sa. three roses of the field, barbed and seeded, ppr., a crescent for difference.

CAREY—BARONS CAREY, OF LEPPINGTON, CO. YORK, EARLS OF MONMOUTH.

By Letters Patent, dated 5 February, 1626.

Lineage.

The Honourable
ROBERT CAREY, 4th son of Henry, 1st LORD HUNSDON, was elevated to the peerage by King JAMES I., by letters patent, dated 5 February, 1626, as *Baron Carey, of Leppington, co. York*, and EARL OF MONMOUTH. This eminent person, whose Memoirs, written by himself, were published by JOHN, EARL OF CORK AND ORRERY, in 1759, was *b.* about 1560. At the age of seventeen he accompanied Sir Thomas Leighton in his embassies to the States General and to Don John of Austria; and he soon afterwards went with Secretary Walsingham into Scotland, where he appears to have insinuated himself into the good graces of JAMES, the future King of England. He was on board the fleet, in 1588, at the destruction of the Armada, and he states, "that he won a wager of £2,000 the next year by going on foot in twelve days to Berwick." "After this," goes on the memoir, "I married a gentlewoman, Elizabeth, daughter of Sir Hugh Trevanion, more for her *worth* than her *wealth*, yet for her estate was but £500 a-year jointure. She had between £500 and £600 in her purse. Neither did she marry me for any great wealth; for I had in all the world but £100 a-year out of the exchequer, as a pension, and that was but during pleasure; and I was near £1,000 in debt. Besides the queen was mightily displeased with me for marrying, and most of my best friends, only my father, was no ways offended at it, which gave me great content." The tide of fortune, which he took in the spring, was the opportunity afforded him by the familiar intercourse with which his kinswoman, Queen ELIZABETH, condescended to treat him, of being the first to announce her majesty's decease to her successor. Visiting her (he says) in her last illness, and praying that her health might amend, she took him by the hand, and wringing it hard, replied, "No, Robin, I am not well," and fetching at the same time no fewer than forty or fifty sighs, which she declares, except for the death of Mary of Scotland, he never in her whole life knew her to do before. By those sighs the wily politician judged her majesty was near her dissolution, and with great candour he proceeds, "I could not but think in what a wretched state I should be left, most of my livelihood depending on her life. And hereupon I bethought myself with what grace and favour I was ever received by the King of Scots whensoever I was sent to him." Upon the decease of the queen, Carey immediately proceeded to Scotland, and was the first person to announce to King JAMES his accession to the crown of England, producing and presenting to his majesty in proof of his veracity, a certain blue ring.* The king received

him, of course, most graciously, and observed, "I know you have lost a near kinswoman, and a mistress, but take here my hand, I will be a good master to you, and will requite this service with honour and reward." Notwithstanding this royal pledge, however, full nineteen years elapsed before he attained the peerage, and in his Memoirs he observes, "I only relied on God and the king. The one never left me, the other, shortly after his coming to London, decieved my expectations, and adhered to those who sought my ruin. By the said lady, Elizabeth his wife, dau. of Sir Hugh Trevanion, Knt., of Correheigh, his lordship had issue,

HENRY, his successor, made a knight of the Bath at the creation of Charles, Prince of Wales, *anno* 1616.
Thomas, one of the grooms of the bedchamber to King CHARLES I., and amongst that unfortunate monarch's most faithful servants; so faithful and attached, indeed, that upon the execution of his royal master, he fell sick of grief, and died about the year 1649, in the thirty-third year of his age. The Hon. Thomas Carey obtained celebrity as a poet, and his remains repose in Westminster Abbey. He *m.* Margaret, dau. and heir of Sir Thomas Smith, of Parsons Green, clerk of the council to King JAMES I., by Frances his wife, dau. of William, 4th Lord Chandos, and left an only dau.,
   Elizabeth, who *m.* John Mordaunt, who was created *Viscount Mordaunt*, of Avelon, and left a son,
      CHARLES, created EARL OF MONMOUTH.
Philadelphia, *m.* to Sir Thomas Wharton, Knt.

His lordship *d.* in 1639, and was. *s.* by his elder son,
HENRY CAREY, 2nd *Earl of Monmouth*. This nobleman, according to Anthony Wood, was noted, upon succeeding to his father's honours, as a person well skilled in the modern languages, and a generous scholar; the fruit whereof he found in the troublesome times of the rebellion, when by a forced retiredness, he was capacitated to exercise himself in studies, while others of the nobility were fain to truckle to their inferiors for company's sake." He wrote much; but as Walpole observes, "we have scarce anything of his own composition, and are as little acquainted with his character as with his genius." His lordship *m.* Lady Martha Cranfield, dau. of the lord treasurer, Lionel, Earl of Middlesex, by whom he had issue,

Lionel, who fell *ex parte regis*, at Marston-Moor, in 1644, *unm.*
Henry, *d.* of the small-pox, 1641, also *unm.*
Anne, *m.* to James Hamilton, Earl of Clanbrassil.
Philadelphia, *d. unm.*
Elizabeth-Mary, *m.* William, Earl of Desmond.
Trevaniana, *d. unm.*
Martha, *m.* to John, Earl of Middleton, in Scotland.
Theophila, } *d. unm.*
Magdalen, }

His lordship *d.* 13 June, 1661, and leaving no male issue, the BARONY OF CAREY, *of Lepington*, and the EARLDOM OF MONMOUTH, became EXTINCT.

Arms.—Az., on a bend, sa., three roses of the field, a crescent for difference.

CARLETON—BARON AND VISCOUNT CARLETON.

Barony, by Letters Patent, dated 1 November, 1789.
Viscounty, by Letters Patent, dated 7 November, 1797.

Lineage.

At Dugdale's visitation of Cumberland, in 1665, Sir William Carleton, of Carleton Hall, near Penrith, certified his descent, eighteen generations in all, from Baldwyn de Carleton, who flourished shortly after the CONQUEST, and "from that family (as Sanford says in his Cumberland MSS., deposited at the Chapter House, Carlisle) all the famous Carletons of England are descended." The representative of the above line is the present Lord Dorchester, whose ancestor Lancelot, of Brampton Foot, settled at Rossfad, in Ireland, *temp.* CHARLES I. From the same family also sprang Guy, bishop of Bristol, 1671, and of Chichester, 1678, whose line is represented by the Carletons of Gulsons Farley, Sussex. A branch appears to have settled in Lincolnshire, where we find Adam de Carleton living *temp.* EDWARD I., and also in Nottinghamshire, where Thomas de Carleton held Whitehall, 10th EDWARD II., from John de Londham. Adam de Carleton was the ancestor of the celebrated statesman and ambassador, Baron Carleton, of Imbercourt, Viscount Dorchester (1628). Some other of his descendants settled in Surrey and Middlesex, and from them derived FRANCIS CARLETON, Esq., who settled in Ireland, *temp.*

---

* *Blue Ring.*—The account of the *blue ring* which Lady Elizabeth Spelman (dau. of Martha, Countess of Middleton, who was dau. of the 2nd earl of Monmouth, and grand-dau. of the nobleman to whom the anecdote refers) gave to Lord Cork was this :—King JAMES kept a constant correspondence with several persons of the English court for many years prior to Queen ELIZABETH's decease; among others, with Lady Scroope (sister of this Robert Carey) to whom his majesty sent, by Sir James Fullerton, a sapphire ring, with positive orders to return it to him by a special messenger, as soon as the queen actually expired. Lady Scroope had no opportunity of delivering it to her brother Robert whilst he was in the palace of Richmond: but waiting at the window till she saw him at the outside of the gate, she threw it out to him, and he well knew to what purpose he received it.—Banks.

CHARLES I., and together with Thomas Hunt, Esq., had a grant of lands in Beladare, Skahanagh, and Moyclare, barony Garrycastle, and Lehensie and Kilmucklin, barony Kilcoursie, all in King's Co., and another grant in Tewistowne, barony Kells, co. Kilkenny. He was *s.* by his son,

RICHARD CARLETON, of Knocknaming, *alias* Darlinghill, near Clonmel, Tipperary. He *m. circa* 1665, Elinor, youngest dau. of Capt. Francis Drew, of Kilwinny, co. Waterford, and dying 1682, was *s.* by his son,

COL. JOHN CARLETON, of Darlinghill, high-sheriff for Tipperary, 1717. He purchased Butler's land (now Clare) in 1705, from the Hollow-Sword Blade Company, and also obtained the forfeited estate, Bardenshill, in Tipperary, He *m. ci.ta* 1695, Jane, 5th dau. of Robert Stratford, Esq., of Baltinglass, and *d.* 1730, leaving issue,

   I. ROBERT, living 1730.
   II. Richard, *b.* 1698; *d.* 1742. He *m.* Isabella, dau. of Robert Connell, Esq., registrar of the diocese of Ossory (she *m.* 2ndly, John Jephson, Esq.), and by her he had issue,
     1 JOHN, who sold Darlinghill to the Pennefathers, and *d.* 1769.
     2 Hugh.
     1 Jane, *d.* 1750.
   III. JOHN.   IV. FRANCIS.

FRANCIS CARLETON (4th son of Col. Carleton) was *b.* 1713. He *m.* 1734, Rebecca, dau. of Hugh Lawton, Esq., of Lake Marsh, co. Cork, and by her (who *d.* February, 1797) he left at his decease, 1791,

   I. Robert, *d.* young.
   II. Francis, of Rostrevor, *m.* Dorcas, dau. of Roger Hall, Esq., of Narrow Water.
   III. HUGH, of whom presently.
   IV. John, *b.* 1742; *m.* 1776, Elizabeth, dau. and heir of Thomas Hodgson, Esq., of Dublin, brother of Lorenzo Hodgson, of Coolkenno, co. Wicklow, who *m.* Elizabeth Hutchinson, of Knocklofty, great-grandmother to the 1st Earl of Donoughmore; John Carleton *d.* 1781, and left issue a son and a dau., Francis, of Clare, and Dorothea, who *m.* Edward Reeves, Esq., of Ballyglissane, co. Cork, and had issue.
   I. Mary, *d.* 1769.
   II. Isabella, *d.* 1771.
   III. Rebecca, *d.* young.
   IV. Rebecca, *m.* Hugh Millerd, Esq., and *d.* July, 1804, *s. p.*
   V. Anne.
   VI. Sarah, *d.* 1766.
   VII. Grace, *m.* Sampson Jervois, Esq., and *d. s. p.*

The 3rd son,
HUGH CARLETON, Esq., *b.* 11 September, 1739, being brought up to the bar, became solicitor-general of Ireland in 1779; in 1787 was appointed Lord Chief Justice of the Common Pleas in that kingdom; and raised to the peerage in two years after (7 November, 1789) as *Baron Carleton*, of Anner. In 1797 he was further advanced to be VISCOUNT CARLETON, *of Clare, co. Tipperary.* His lordship *m.* 1st, 2 August, 1766, Elizabeth, only dau. of Richard Mercer, Esq., which lady *d. s,* p. 27 May, 1794; and 2ndly, 15 July, 1795, Mary Buckley, 2nd dau. of Abednego Mathew, Esq., by whom, who *d.* 13 March, 1810, he had no issue. His lordship *d.* in 1825, when the title became EXTINCT, and his nephew, FRANCIS CARLETON, Esq., became his representative. (*See* BURKE's *Landed Gentry.*)

Arms—Arg., on a bend, sa., three mascles of the field.

CARLTON—BARON CARLTON, OF IMBERCOURT, CO. SURREY, VISCOUNT DORCHESTER.

Barony, by Letters Patent, dated 21 May, 1626.
Viscounty, by Letters Patent, dated 25 July, 1628.

Lineage.

SIR DUDLEY CARLTON, Knt., son of Anthony Carlton, Esq., of Baldwin Brightwell, co. Oxford, *b.* 10 March, 1573, having been employed, for a series of years, as ambassador to Venice Savoy, and the Low Countries, was elevated to the peerage 21 May, 1626, as BARON CARLTON, *of Imbercourt, ca. Surrey,* and in two years afterwards created VISCOUNT DORCHESTER; in which year he was constituted one of his majesty's principal secretaries of state. His lordship *m.* 1st, Anne, dau. and co-heiress of George Gerard, Esq., 2nd son of Sir William Gerard, Knt., of Dorney, co. Bucks, by whom he had a son, Henry, who *d.* young. He *m.* 2ndly, Anne, dau of Sir Henry Glen-

ham, Knt., and widow of Paul, Viscount Bayning, which lady survived him, and gave birth to a posthumous child, Frances, who *d.* young. Lord Dorchester, whose negotiations have been published, had the reputation of being an able diplomatist, and a polished statesman. He was master of different languages, and a good ancient and modern historian He composed some pieces, which are noticed by Walpole, and was esteemed a graceful and eloquent speaker. He *d.* 15 February, 1631, and his honours, in default of male issue, became EXTINCT. His estates, however, devolved on his nephew,

SIR JOHN CARLETON, of Brightwell, son and heir of George Carleton, Esq., of Brightwell, by Elizabeth his wife, dau: and co-heir of Sir John Brockett, of Brockett Hale, Herts; he *m.* 1627, Anne, eldest dau. of Sir R. Hoghton, Knt., of Hoghton Tower, and relict of Sir John Cotton, of Landwade, by whom he had one son and two daus., viz.,

   George (Sir), Bart., *d. unm.*
   Anne, *m.* George Garth, Esq., of Morden, Surrey.
   Catherine, *m.* to John Stone, Esq.

Sir John Carleton *d.* 1637; his estates passed eventually to his daus. as co-heirs, Brightwell becoming the property and residence of CATHERINE CHARLOTTE LOWNDES STONE. (*See* BURKE's *Landed Gentry.*)

Arms—Arg., on a bend, sa., three mascles of the first.

CARLYLE—LORD CARLYLE.

Lineage.

SIR WILLIAM CARLYLE, 1st of Torthorwald, attended Margaret of Scotland into France, in 1436, on her marriage to Louis the Dauphin. He left issue, Sir JOHN, who succeeded him; Adam, the ancestor of the family of Bridekirk; James, rector of Kirkpatrick; and Margaret, who *m.* Sir William Douglas, of Drumlanrig, 3rd Marquess of Queensberry. The eldest son,

SIR JOHN CARLYLE, Knt., of Torthorwald, was mainly instrumental in suppressing the rebellion of the Earls of Douglas, in 1455. For this service he was rewarded with the half of the lands of Pettinain, upon the Clyde; and in 1470-1, he was raised by JAMES III. to the peerage, and his residence styled the town of Cairleill. Shortly after he appeared as chief justice of Scotland south of the Firth; and in 1477 he went on an embassy to France. By Janet his wife, he had issue,

   JOHN, Master of Carlyle, *d.*, leaving a son, WILLIAM, who *s.* as 2nd Lord Carlyle.
   Robert, had a charter of the office of steward of Kirkcudbright, with the custody of the castle of Crief, 28 October, 1487.
   Catherine, *m.* Simon Carruthers, of Menswald.

John, Lord Carlyle, *m.* 2ndly, Margaret Douglas, widow of Sir Edward Maxwell, of Monreith, and had two sons,

   John.   George.

WILLIAM CARLYLE, 2nd Lord Carlyle, knighted 29 January 1487-8, *m.* Janet Maxwell, dau. of Robert Lord Maxwell, and had two sons,

   JAMES, 3rd lord.
   MICHAEL, 4th lord.

The eldest son,
JAMES CARLYLE, 3rd Lord Carlyle, having *d. s. p.* before 27 December, 1529, was *s.* by his younger brother,

MICHAEL CARLYLE, 4th Lord Carlyle, in 1529. Michael *d.* in 1579, in comparatively reduced circumstances. He had five sons, William, Michael, Edward, John, and Peter, and a dau., Estote. William, Master of Carlyle, predeceased his father in 1572, leaving an only child, Elizabeth, who although she could not carry off the title, which was a male fee, was styled Dame Elizabeth Carlel, Soon after the death of her grandfather, she *m.* Sir James Douglas, son of George Douglas, natural brother to James, Earl of Morton, regent of Scotland; and after a litigation of fourteen years with her uncle Michael, she conveyed the family estates to the house of Douglas, through her eldest son, Sir James, who was created Lord Torthorwald, in 1609.

Michael, the 2nd son of Michael, the last Lord Carlyle, after losing all but the small property of Locharthur, which he acquired through his wife Grizel, dau. of Lord John Maxwell, did not assume the title which still remained in him, but his male descendants were careful to preserve and assert their right. The last Michael *d.* in 1763. Of the other sons of Lord Michael, viz., Edward, of Limekilns, John, of Boytath, and

Peter—no males but the issue of Edward survived. On the deaths of Adam Carlyle, last of Limekilns, and his six sons, the male representation of the family devolved upon the branch to which Professor Joseph-Dacre Carlyle, chancellor of Carlyle, belonged. On 6 February, 1798, he was served heir to Michael, last Lord Carlyle; but his only son *d.* in 1798; he himself followed in 1804; and John Carlyle, Esq., then of Jamaica, afterwards of Shawhill, in Ayrshire, succeeded to the claim, as belonging to a younger branch of the Limekilns family. By his death, *s. p.,* in October, 1824, the claim to dormant peerage passed through a still younger branch, into the person of the then only surviving male representative, Thomas Carlyle, Esq., advocate, Edinburgh.

Arms.—Quarterly: 1st and 4th, arg. (the first Sir William bore the field or), a cross flory, gu., for Carlyle; 2nd and 3rd, or, a cross, gu., for Corsvie; and by way of surtout, arg., a saltier, az., to show their connexion with the family of Bruce.

CARMICHAEL—EARL OF HYNDFORD.

By Letters Patent, dated 25 June, 1701.

Lineage.

This ancient family derived its name from the lands and barony of Carmichael, co. Lanark.

Sir John Carmichael, of Carmichael, whose ancestors had possessed that barony for many generations, was one of the noble Scottish warriors sent to assist Charles VI. of France against the English. He signalized his valour at the battle of Baugé in 1422. He *d.* in 1436. By his wife Mary Douglas, a dau. of the house of Angus, he had issue,

I. William, his successor.
II. John Carmichael, of Meadowflat, captain of the castle of Crawford. This gentleman was twice married. By his 1st wife he had issue, with a dau., Margaret, wife of David, Earl of Crawford, Duke of Montrose, a son, John Carmichael, of Meadowflat, who *d.* in 1507. His son, John Carmichael, of Meadowflat, captain of Crawford Castle, *d.* in 1567, and was *s.* by his grandson, Sir John Carmichael, of Meadowflat, captain of Crawford Castle, who, by his 1st wife, Elizabeth Scott, a dau. of the house of Buccleuch, had issue a dau., Grizzel, wife of Walter Carmichael, of Hyndford. By his 2nd wife, Jane Wallace, he had issue a son, John, whose son, Sir John Carmichael, of Meadowflat, captain of Crawford Castle, *d. s. p.* 1638. The 1st John Carmichael, of Meadowflat, captain of Crawford Castle, *m.* 2ndly, Isabella Sibbald, widow of George, 4th Earl of Angus, and was mother of "Earl Bell-the-cat," by whom he had a son, James Carmichael, founder of the house of Balmedie, in Fifeshire. His descendant in the 5th degree, Sir David Carmichael, of Balmedie, knighted in 1648, *m.* 1st, the Honourable Anne, dau. of James, 1st Lord Carmichael, and 2ndly, Cecilia, dau. of Fotheringham, of Powrie, by whom he had a son, David Carmichael, of Balmedie, who *d.* in 1676. His descendant in the 4th degree was Sir James Carmichael Smythe, major-general R.E., governor of British Guiana, created a baronet in 1821. His son, Sir James Robert, the 2nd baronet, dropped the name of Smythe, and resumed his paternal name of Carmichael only, and on the extinction of the male line of Earls of Hyndford, appears to be the male head of the great house of Carmichael.

The eldest son of Sir John Carmichael, the hero of Baugé, was

William Carmichael, of Carmichael, who was alive in 1437. He had two sons, Sir John, his heir, and George, promoted to the episcopal see of Glasgow in 1482. The elder son,

Sir John Carmichael, of Carmichael, *d.* 1495. His son,

William Carmichael, of Carmichael, *d.* 1530. He had three sons,

I. Bartholomew, who *d. s. p.* in 1510.
II. William, his heir.
III. Walter, of Park and Hyndford, of whom hereafter.

William Carmichael, of Carmichael, was alive in 1532. His son,

John Carmichael, of Carmichael, *m.* Elizabeth, dau. of Hugh, 5th Lord Somerville, and *d.* 1580. His son was

Sir John Carmichael, of Carmichael. He was warden of the middle marches. In 1588 he was one of the ambassadors sent to Denmark to negotiate the marriage of King James VI. with the Princess Anne. In 1590 he was sent ambassador to Queen Elizabeth. In 1598 he was warden of the west marches, in the exercise of which office he was murdered in 1600. By Margaret Douglas, sister of David, 7th Earl of Angus, and James, Earl of Morton, Regent of Scotland, he had, with other issue, a son,

105

Sir Hugh Carmichael, of Carmichael, a privy councillor, master of the horse in 1593, and ambassador to Denmark. By Abigail, dau. of William Baillie, of Lamington, he had a son, John, and a dau. Jean, wife of James Lockhart, of Cleghorn.

Sir John Carmichael, of Carmichael, *m.* Elizabeth, dau. of Sir Patrick Home, of Polwarth. He had a charter, dated 1619. He *d. s. p.* about the year 1640. His affairs were in very great disorder, and previous to his death his estates had been transferred to Sir James Carmichael, of Hyndford. The line of the house of Carmichael was then carried on by the said Sir James Carmichael, of Hyndford, who was a descendant of Walter Carmichael, of Hyndford and Park, great-great-grand-uncle to the last Sir John.

Walter Carmichael was father of

Gavin Carmichael, of Hyndford, of which he had a charter in 1547. His son,

James Carmichael, of Hyndford, *m.* Marian Campbell, dau. of Sir Hugh Campbell, of Loudon, by Lady Elizabeth Stewart, dau. of Matthew, Earl of Lennox, and great-grand-dau. of James II., King of Scotland, and Queen Mary of Gueldres. By her he had, with other issue, a son,

Walter Carmichael, of Hyndford, who *d.* in 1616. By his wife Grizzel Carmichael, dau. of Sir John Carmichael, of Meadowflat, captain of Crawford Castle, he had a son James, and six daus., of whom the eldest, Marian, was wife of James Stewart, of Allanton, and from her are descended Stewart, of Allanton, Hamilton, of Barns, Hamilton Dundas, of Duddingston, and Gray, of Carntyne.

James Carmichael, of Hyndford, was distinguished by the favour of King James VI., to whom he stood in the degree of 3rd cousin, and to whom he was cup-bearer, carver, and chamberlain. He was created a baronet 17 July, 1627. On the death of Sir John, between 1640 and 1650, he became head of the house of Carmichael. He was lord justice clerk in 1634, and lord of session in 1639. In 1641 he was made privy councillor for life, and 27 December, 1647 he was created, by King Charles, Lord Carmichael, to him and his heirs-male whatsoever. He *m.* Agnes, sister of John Wilkie, of Foulden, by whom he had issue,

I. William, Master of Carmichael, in his youth one of the gens d'armes of Louis XIII. of France, one of the committee of parliament in 1644-5; fought in 1646, at Philiphaugh, against Montrose; *d.* 1657. By Lady Grizzel Douglas his wife, 3rd dau. of William, 1st Marquess of Douglas, he had issue,

  1 John, who *s.* his grandfather as 2nd Lord Carmichael.
  1 Mary, *m.,* in 1665 to Sir Archibald Stewart, Bart., of Castlemilk.
  2 Rachel, wife of James Weir, of Stonebyres.

II. David (Honourable Sir), *d. s. p.*
III. James (Honourable Sir), of Bonnytoun. His son, Sir John, *s.* him in 1691, and *m.* in 1684, Lady Hariet Johnstone, dau. of James, Earl of Annandale, by whom he had a son, Sir James Carmichael, Bart., of Bonnytoun, who *m.* Margaret Baillie, heiress of Lamington, by whom he had a son, Sir William, who *d. s. p.* 1738, and a dau. Henrietta, heiress of Lamington and Bonnytoun, who *m.* Robert Dundas, of Arniston, lord president of the Court of Session, and *d.* 1755. Their eldest dau. Elizabeth, *m.* Sir John Lockhart Ross, of Balnagown, and had issue.

  I. Mary, wife, 1st, of Sir William Lockhart, of Carstairs, and 2ndly, of Sir William Weir of Stonebyres.
  II. Agnes, wife of Sir John Wilkie, of Foulden.
  III. Anne, wife of Sir David Carmichael, of Balmedie. Her only child, Anne, was, in 1670, wife of John Dundas, of Duddingston, and was ancestress of John Hamilton Dundas, late of Duddingston, and of the Rev. John Hamilton Gray, of Carntyne.
  IV. Martha, wife of John Kennedy, of Kirkmichael.

James, 1st Lord Carmichael, *d.* 29 November, 1672, and was *s.* by his grandson,

John, 2nd Lord Carmichael, *b.* 28 February, 1638, commissioner of the privy seal and privy councillor in 1689. He was high commissioner to the general assembly of the church of Scotland in 1690, and from 1694 to 1699; and secretary of state in 1696. He was created Earl of Hyndford, Viscount of Inglisberry and Nemphlar, and Lord Carmichael, of Carmichael, 25 June, 1701, to him and to his heirs male and of entail. He was a promoter of the union in 1705, and *d.* in 1710, aged seventy-three. He *m.* 9 October, 1669, the Honourable Beatrix Drummond, 2nd dau. of David, 3rd Lord Maderty, by whom he had issue,

  I. James, 2nd Earl of Hyndford,
  II. William, of Skirling, who *m.* 1st, in 1709, Ellen, only child of Thomas Craig, of Riccarton, and had issue,

    1 John, 4th Earl of Hyndford.
    2 James, of Hailes, *d. s. p.* in 1781.
    3 Thomas, *d.* young.

1 Elizabeth, *d. unm.* in 1783.
2 Helen, wife of John Gibson, of Durie. Her descendant and heir is the Rev. Sir William Gibson Carmichael, Bart., of Skirling and Castlecraig.

He *m.* 2ndly, without issue, Margaret Menzies, *b.* 1710.

III. Daniel, of Mauldslie, who *d.* in 1707, leaving, by Barbara his wife, dau. of Sir George Lockhart, of Carnwath, a son,

DANIEL, of Mauldslie, who *m.* 1742, Emilia, dau. of the Rev. John Hepburn; and *d.* in 1765, leaving issue, Daniel, John, and William, who all *d. unm.*; THOMAS, who *s.* as 5th Earl of Hyndford; ANDREW, successor to his brother; and Grizel, wife of Archibald Nisbet, of Carfin, by whom she had a son, Archibald Nisbet, of Carfin and Mauldslie, and a dau. Jane, wife of Thomas Gordon, of Harperfield.

IV. David, who *d. s. p.*
V. and VI. John and Charles, lost at sea. *s. p.*
VII. Archibald, *d.* young.
I. Beatrix, *m.* in 1700, to John Cockburn, of Ormiston.
II. Mary, *m.* to John Montgomery, of Giffen.
III. Anne, *m.* to Sir John Maxwell, Bart., of Pollock.

The eldest son,

JAMES, 2nd Earl of Hyndford, was a brigadier-general in 1710. He *m.* Lady Elizabeth Maitland, only dau. of John, 5th Earl of Lauderdale, and by her (who *d.* 27 November, 1753) he had issue,

I. JOHN, 3rd Earl of Hyndford.
II. William, archdeacon of Bucks in 1742, bishop of Clonfort in 1753, and of Meath in 1758, archbishop of Dublin in 1765, in which year he *d. s. p.*
III. James, M.P. for Lanark, *d. s. p.* 1754.
IV. Archibald, *d. s. p.* 1745.
V. Charles, *d. s. p.* 1732.
I. Margaret, *m.* in January, 1717, Sir John Anstruther, Bart., of Anstruther, M.P. Her descendant, SIR WINDHAM CARMICHAL ANSTRUTHER, Bart., is the present possessor of the Carmichael estates, and is heir-general of the family.
II. Mary, *m.* to Charles O'Hara, Esq., of Annaghmore, co. Sligo.
III. Anne, *m.* to Gerard Dusign, of Bath.
IV., V., and VI. Elizabeth, Rachel, and Grace, *d.* young

James, 2nd Earl, *d.* 16 August, 1707, and was *s.* by his eldest son,
JOHN, 3rd Earl of Hyndford, *b.* 15 March, 1701, lord-lieutenant of the co. of Lanark in 1739, high commissioner to the general assembly in 1739-40, envoy extraordinary and plenipotentiary to the King of Prussia in 1741, ambassador to Russia in 1744, and to Vienna from 1752 to 1764. He was a knight of the Thistle and vice-admiral of Scotland. He *d.* 19 July, 1767, aged sixty-seven. He *m.* 1st, in 1732, Elizabeth, dau. of Admiral Sir Cloudesley Shovel, and widow of Robert, 1st Lord Romney; and 2ndly, 1756, Jean, dau. of Benjamin Vigor, of Fulham. Dying *s. p.*, he was *s.* by (the son of his uncle) his cousin,
JOHN, 4th Earl of Hyndford. He *m.* 16 January, 1749, Janet, dau. and heir of William Grant, of Preston Grange, lord of session. He *d. s. p.* 21 December, 1787, and was *s.* by (the grandson of his uncle) his cousin,
THOMAS, 5th Earl of Hyndford, who *d. unm.* 14 February, 1811, and was *s.* by his brother,
ANDREW, 6th Earl of Hyndford, who *d. unm.* in 1817. Since his death the family titles have been DORMANT or EXTINCT. He was *s.* in his paternal estate of Mauldslie by his nephew, ARCHIBALD NISBET, of Carfin, while the great family estates of Carmichael devolved on SIR JOHN ANSTRUTHER, Bart., of Anstruther, the heir-general of the house of Carmichael, and are now held by Sir Windham Carmichael Anstruther, Bart.

Arms—Arg., a fess wreathy, az. and gu.

CARPENTER — BARONS CARPENTER, VISCOUNTS CARLINGFORD, AND EARLS OF TYRCONNEL.

Barony, by Letters Patent, dated 29 May, 1719.
Viscounty and Earldom, by Letters Patent, dated 1 May, 1761.

Lineage.

WILLIAM CARPENTER, Esq., of Holme, descended from a very ancient Herefordshire family, *d.* in the year 1520, and from him lineally descended
THOMAS CARPENTER, Esq., who bequeathed his estate to his 2nd cousin,
LIEUT.-GEN. THE RIGHT HON. GEORGE LORD CARPENTER. This nobleman, who was a younger son, commenced his career as page to the Earl of Montagu in his embassy to the court of France in 1671, and on returning in the next year, rode as a private gentleman in the 3rd troop of guards, from which station (then deemed an honourable introduction to a military

life) Mr. Carpenter was appointed quartermaster to the Earl of Peterborough's regiment of horse, the lieut.-colonelcy of which he subsequently attained. In 1693, Colonel Carpenter *m.* Alice, dau. of William, 1st Viscount Charlemont, and widow of James Margetson, Esq., and purchased afterwards for 1,800 guineas, a part of his lady's dowry, the king's own regiment of dragoons, the command of which he retained until his decease; distinguished himself at its head in the battle of Almanza in 1707, the battle of Almenara in 1710, and upon other eminent services. In 1709 he had attained the rank of lieut.-general, and in 1715 he forced the rebels under Lord Derwentwater to surrender at discretion at Preston, thus securing the throne to the present reigning family. In 1716, Gen. Carpenter was appointed governor of Minorca, and subsequently commander-in-chief of all the forces in Scotland, when he was elevated to the peerage of Ireland, by patent dated 29 May, 1719, as BARON CARPENTER, *of Killaghy, co. Kilkenny.* His lordship *d.* 10 February, 1731, and was *s.* by his only son,
GEORGE, 2nd baron, lieut.-colonel of the 1st regiment of horse guards. His lordship *m.* in 1722, Elizabeth, only dau. of David Petty, Esq., of Wanstead, co. Essex, and dying 12 July, 1749, left (with a dau. Alicia-Maria, *m.* 1st, to Charles, 2nd Earl of Egremont, and 2ndly, to Count Bruhl) an only son,
GEORGE, 3rd baron, *b.* 26 August, 1723. This nobleman *m.* in March, 1747-8, Frances, only dau. and heiress of Sir Robert Clifton, Bart., of Clifton, co. Nottingham, and heiress of her mother, Lady Frances Coote, only dau. of Nanfan, 2nd Earl of Bellamont, by whom he had issue,

I. GEORGE, his successor.
II. Charles, a naval officer of rank, *b.* 3 January, 1757; *m.* 10 May, 1785, Elizabeth, only dau. of Thomas Mackenzie, Esq., and dying 5 September, 1803, left issue by her (who *d.* 23 February, 1842),
  1 GEORGE, who *s.* as 3rd earl.
  2 JOHN-DELAVAL, 4th earl.
I. Almeria, *d.* 5 October, 1809.   II. Elizabeth.
III. Caroline, *m.* to Uvedale Price, Esq., of Foxley (afterwards created a baronet), and *d.* 16 July, 1826.

Lord Carpenter was advanced to the dignities of Viscount Carlingford and EARL OF TYRCONNEL 1 May, 1761, and dying the year after was *s.* by his elder surviving son,
GEORGE, 2nd earl, *b.* in 1750; *m.* 1st, in 1772, Frances Manners, eldest dau. of the celebrated military commander, Lieut.-General John, Marquess of Granby, and grand-dau. of John, 3rd Duke of Rutland, which marriage was dissolved by act of parliament in 1777, and the lady *m.* Philip Anstruther, Esq. His lordship *m.* 2ndly, in 1780, the Hon. Sarah Hussey Delaval, youngest dau. and co-heir of John, Lord Delaval, and left an only dau.,
SUSAN-HUSSEY, who *m.* in 1805, Henry, 2nd Marquess of Waterford, and *d.* 7 June, 1827.

The earl *d.* 15 April, 1805, when the honours devolved upon his nephew,
GEORGE, 3rd earl. This nobleman, who was *b.* in 1788, impelled by the love of military enterprise, entered into the Russian army as a volunteer, and *d.* at Wilna, 20 December, 1812, in that service, from his zeal and excessive fatigue in pursuit of the French forces under Bonaparte. His lordship was *unm.* and the honours devolved at his decease upon his brother,
JOHN DELAVAL, 4th Earl of Tyrconnel, Viscount Carlingford, of Carlingford, and Baron Carpenter, of Killaghy, co. Kilkenny, G.C.H., *b.* 16 December, 1790. He *m.* 1 October, 1817, Sarah, only child of Robert Crowe, Esq., of Kiplin, co. York, by Anne his wife, dau. of Christopher Buckle, Esq., of Burgh, in Banstead, and had a dau., Elizabeth Anne, *b.* 19 February, 1847, and *d.* same day. His lordship *d.* 25 June, 1853, whereupon all his titles became EXTINCT.

Arms—Paly of six, arg. and gu., on a chev., az., three cross-crosslets, or

---

CARR—VISCOUNT ROCHESTER, EARL OF SOMERSET.

Viscounty, by Letters Patent, dated 25 March, 1611
Earldom, &c., by Letters Patent, dated 3 November, 1613.

Lineage.

SIR ROBERT CARR, K.B., of the ancient House of Ker, of Fernihurst, in Scotland, and half brother of Andrew, 1st Lord

Jedburgh, having ingratiated himself into the favour of King JAMES I., was appointed, upon the decease of George, Lord Dunbar, treasurer of Scotland, and elevated to the peerage, as VISCOUNT ROCHESTER, 25 March, 1611. In the May following his lordship was installed a knight of the Garter, and created, 3 November, 1613, BARON CARR, *of Branspeth*, in the bishopric of Durham, and EARL OF SOMERSET, being also nominated lord chamberlain of the household, and sworn of the privy council. At this time the earl was esteemed the first favourite of the court. "But having," says Dugdale, "thus seen his rise, let us now behold his fall, which I shall briefly here relate, with the occasion and chief circumstances thereof, from the report of the most Rev. Dr. Spotswood, late archbishop of St. Andrew's in Scotland."

"This earl falling in love with the Lady Frances Howard, dau. of Thomas, Earl of Suffolk (wife to Robert, Earl of Essex, from whom she had procured a divorce), having formerly received into his intimate familiarity a knight of excellent parts, called Sir Thomas Overburie, was frequently by him dissuaded from her company, which being discerned by Overburie, and that, notwithstanding what had been said, he had a purpose to marry her; he so far presumed upon the friendly freedom which he had otherwise given him, to press him more earnestly to forbear her. And one night, dealing more plainly with him, said to this effect, 'My lord, I perceive you are proceeding in this match, from which I have often dissuaded you, as your true servent and friend: I now again advise you not to marry that woman, for if you do, you shall ruine your honour and yourself,' adding, 'that, if he went on in that business, he should do well to look to his standing.' Which free speech, this earl taking impatiently, because he had touched the lady in her honour, replied in passion, 'That his legs were strong enough to bear him up, and that he should make him repent those speeches.' But Overburie, interpreting this to be only a sudden passion, thought not that their long continued friendship would break off by this occasion, and therefore continued his wonted attendance; neither did this earl wholly abandon him. Howbeit, having discovered his words to the lady, she never ceased, but by all means sought his overthrow. It happening, therefore, about this time, that Overburie being designed for ambassador into Russia, this earl (whose counsel he asked) advised him to refuse the service, but to make some fair excuse. Which advice he followed, supposing that it did proceed of kindness; but for his refusal he was committed to the Tower. The lady thus having him where she wished, and resolving to dispatch him by poison, wrought so with Sir Gervase Elways, then lieutenant of the Tower, as that he admitted one Richard Weston, upon her recommendation, to be his keeper, by whom (the very evening after he was so committed) a yellow poison was ministered to him in a broth at supper. But neither this nor the other poisons, which were continually put into his meats, serving to dispatch him, Mistress Turner (the preparer of all,) procured an apothecary's boy to give him a poisoned clyster, which soon brought him to his end. Being thus dead, he was presently buried; a general rumour, however, prevailed that he had died by poison, but the greatness of the procurers kept all hidden for a time, till at length it pleased God to bring everything to light, after a miraculous manner, It happened that the Earl of Shrewsbury, in conference with a counsellor of state, recommended the lieutenant of the Tower to his favour, as a man of good parts, and one who desired to be known to him. The counsellor answered, that he took it as a favour from the lieutenant that he should desire his friendship, but added, that there lay upon him an heavy imputation for Overburie's death, whereof he wisht that the gentleman should clear himself. Which being related to the lieutenant, he was stricken with it, and said to his knowledge some attempts were made against Overburie, but that the same took no effect. Which being told to the king, he willed the counsellor to move the lieutenant to set down in writing what he knew of that matter, as he accordingly did. Whereupon certain of the council were appointed to examine and find out the truth. From Weston somewhat being found, he was made prisoner, Turner and Franklyn, the preparers of the poison, being examined, confessed everything; whereupon all breaking forth, this earl and his lady, as also the lieutenant, were committed. But Weston at his first arraignment stood mute, yet afterwards was induced to put himself on the trial of his country, and being found guilty suffered death at Tyburn. Mistress Turner and James Franklyn were in like sort executed. The lieutenant, who had winked at their doings, being judged accessary to the crime, and condemned, suffered death also, express-ing great penitency. And in May following, this earl and his lady were both brought to their trial, though, by their friends, laboured earnestly to eschew it. But King JAMES would not be intreated for the love he had to maintain justice. Thomas,

Lord Ellesmere, at that time Lord Chancellor of England, was, by commission, constituted high steward for that occasion, having for his assistants, Sir Edward Coke, Knt., Lord Chief Justice of the Court of King's Bench, Sir Henry Hobert, Knt., Lord Chief Justice of the Common Pleas, and others. With the lady there was much ado; she, with many tears, confessing the fact, and desiring mercy. But this earl, being the next day presented, made some defence, which served no purpose; for the confessions of those who had suffered death already for the fact, and a letter which he himself had sent to the king, did so clearly convict him of being at least an accessary, that both himself and his lady had sentence of death passed upon them. Nevertheless, through his majesty's great clemency, their lives were spared." The event proved, however, miserable to both these guilty persons, ending in a total separation and hatred of each other. The abandoned countess *d.* 23 August, 1632. The earl, who was released from the Tower in 1621, but afterwards confined to the house of Viscount Wallingford, *d.* in July, 1645, leaving an only dau.,

ANNE, who *m.* William, 5th Earl of Bedford, and was mother of the illustrious patriot, William, LORD RUSSELL. The Countess of Bedford was as distinguished for purity as her unhappy mother had been for the reverse.

Upon his lordship's decease the *Viscounty of Rochester* and EARLDOM OF SOMERSET became EXTINCT.

Arms—Gu., on a chev., arg., three mullets, sa., in the dexter part of the escutcheon, a lion passant guardant, or.

CARROLL—BARON ELY O'CARROLL.

(See O'CARROLL.)

CARTERET — BARONS CARTERET, OF HAWNES, CO. BEDFORD, VISCOUNTS CARTERET, EARLS GRANVILLE.

Barony, by Letters Patent, dated 19 October, 1681.
Earldom, &c., by Letters Patent, dated 1 January, 1714.

Lineage.

All the English Carterets derive their origin and descent from the ancient and noble family of this name, of St. Ouen's manor, in the island of Jersey; the present lineal representative of which, maternally, is EDWARD CHARLES MALET DE CARTERET, Seigneur de St. Ouen.

In the charters of the cathedral of Coutances, and of the abbeys of Fontenelle and Bec, in Normandy, great and honourable mention is made of the De Carterets, of whom the chief, in 1002, took on him sovereign authority in the barony of Carteret, situated on the coast of that duchy, opposite the eastern part of the island of Jersey. The ancient Norman historians, Louis de Oouis, in his "History of the Crusades," and Du Moulin, in his "History of Normandy," speak largely of this family, which, during upwards of seven centuries, has held the seigneurie of St. Ouens, which takes precedence of every other feudal tenure in Jersey, and bears the ancient title of "*Le Grand Fief Haubert de St. Ouen*," with two knights' fees and service, in addition to that of its lord or seigneur. Anciently this honour and lordship fell into the charge and keeping of the sovereign, during the minority of its heir; and the honourable and responsible post of keeper of the fortresses of the island was, of right, confided to the Seigneurs de St. Ouen, in the absence by death or otherwise of the governor.

Our limits do not permit us to make more than a very cursory mention of a few of the members of this race of insular heroes and statesmen who have sprung up in rapid succession from this house, whose sons, in one long and *unbroken* line, are recorded, from 1066 to 1859, at the College of Arms, London; and whose history, replete with events affording ample and singular proof of their energy of purpose and chivalrous bravery, is to be found in numerous and authenticated public and private sources in England, Normandy, and Jersey.

ONFREY and MAUGER DE CARTERET fought at Hastings in 1066, and as deserving knights are made mention of in the "Roman du Rou."

REGINALD DE CARTERET accompanied Robert, Duke of Normandy, and Godfroi de Bouillon, to the first great crusade in 1096, and his arms are recorded by Du Moulin.

PHILIP DE CARTERET, in fulfilment of a pious vow, made when in great danger of shipwreck off the coast of Guernsey, built in 1129, at his own cost, the church of Torteval, in that island.

SIR REGINALD DE CARTERET, Knt., who assumed the chief command of the insular forces when Drogo de Barentin, the governor, was killed, after performing prodigies of valour, succeeded in forcing the French, who had made several destructive forays and descents on the island, to abandon it; and afterwards joining the fleet commanded by Reynold de Cobham and Geoffrey d'Harcourt, was chiefly instrumental, by the reinforcement of his troops, in recovering the island of Guernsey, of which the French had obtained possession. And his grandson, the celebrated SIR REGINALD DE CARTERET, Knt., captain of the king's castles in Jersey, had the signal honour of compelling the illustrious Du Guesclin to raise the siege of Mount-Orgeuil Castle, which he had closely invested in 1374 with an army of 10,000 men, among whom were comprised the flower of the French chivalry and the Duke de Bourbon. For this glorious achievement the honour of knighthood was conferred, the same day, on Sir Reginald and his seven sons by EDWARD III.

SIR PHILIP DE CARTERET, Knt. (grandson of Sir Reginald), who m. Margaret, dau. of Sir William Newton, Knt., of Gloucester, also displayed, in an eminent degree, those great qualities which were peculiar to his race, preserved for the second time the island of Jersey from French possession, and succeeded in expelling Pierre de Brézé, Comte de Maulevrier, grand sénéchal of Normandy, who during five years, from 1461 to 1466, had retained under subjection the six eastern parishes of Jersey.

PHILIP DE CARTERET, Sir Philip's grandson, Lord of St. Ouen, who m. Margaret, only dau. of Sir Richard Harliston, governor of Jersey, nearly fell victim to a foul plot of accusation of treachery, based on a forged letter, purporting to offer to betray basely the island to France, produced against him by his enemy, Sir Matthew Baker, the governor, whose vexatious and unjust exactions exercised on the inhabitants had been withstood and severely commented upon by De Carteret: this letter was written by one Le Boutillier, whom the Seigneur de St. Ouen had saved from capital punishment. By the connivance of the then bailli, Clement le Hardy, Sir Philip was imprisoned in Mount-Orgeuil Castle, and stinted of food in order to render unequal the trial by combat, which he was unjustly condemned to accept from this miscreant on the feast of St. Lawrens. That side of the lists from which he was to do battle was subsequently found to be studded with numerous pitfalls, artfully covered over to hasten his destruction; but his heroic wife, to obtain her husband's liberation, clandestinely left the island in an open boat with only one trusty servant, in the depth of winter, and four days only after her confinement; and obtaining an audience of the king, HENRY VII., who at that time held his court at Salisbury, returned to Jersey successful; the king having by writ under the great seal fully reinstated her injured husband. This Lady of St. Ouen was mother of twenty sons and one daughter, all presented to the king the same day. From this gallant personage we pass to his descendant,

SIR PHILIP CARTERET, who undertook, in the reign of ELIZABETH, to plant such a colony in the island of Sark as should keep out the French, and he accordingly enlarged the settlement, and thereby improved his own estate. He m. Rachel, dau. and heir of Sir George Paulet, son and heir of Lord Thomas Paulet, of Cossington, co. Somerset, 2nd son of William, Marquess of Winchester, and had, with other issue,

I. PHILIP (Sir), his successor, Lord of St. Ouen, b. 1583, a gallant and devoted royalist, who held Elizabeth Castle, as his wife did that of Mount Orgueil, for the king. He m. Anne, dau. of Sir Francis Dowse, Knt., of Wallop, Hants, and had issue; one of his sons, Francis, became attorney-general of Jersey, and through him by female descent the seigneury of St. Ouen has been held by the families of Le Maistre and MALLET; the eldest son and heir of the cavalier, Sir Philip, was s. by his eldest son,

SIR PHILIP DE CARTERET, Lord of St. Ouen and royal bailli of Jersey, knighted by CHARLES II., when Prince of Wales, 29 April, 1645. He m. Anne Dumaresq, and dying in 1662, was s. by his son,

PHILIP, created a BARONET 4 June, 1670. He m. Elizabeth, dau. of Sir Edward Carteret, and dying in 1693, was s. by his only son,

CHARLES (Sir), 2nd baronet, who was one of the gentlemen of the privy chamber to Queen ANNE, and high bailiff of the island of Jersey. Sir Charles d. in 1715 (when the baronetcy EXPIRED), and was buried in Westminster Abbey. In him the elder male line of the family EXPIRED.

II. HELIER, of whom presently.

1. Rachael, m. 1st, to de Beauvoir, Esq., of the island of Jersey, and 2ndly, to — de Vic, Esq.

II. Judith, m. to Sir Brian Johnson, of Buckinghamshire.

The 2nd son,

HELIER CARTERET, Esq., deputy-governor of Jersey, m. Elizabeth Dumaresq, and had, with other children, a son,

SIR GEORGE CARTERET, b. 1599, a naval officer of high reputation, who, through the influence of the Duke of Buckingham, was appointed in the 2nd of King CHARLES I. joint governor of Jersey, and at the breaking out of the civil war held the office of comptroller of the navy. Sir George was, however, so much esteemed by all parties, that when the parliament passed the ordinance for the Earl of Warwick to command the fleet, then fully and entirely at their disposal, they likewise resolved that Captain Carteret should be vice-admiral; but he declined the appointment at the express command of the king. Upon which Lord Clarendon observes, "his interest and reputation in the navy was so great, and his diligence and dexterity in command so eminent, that it was generally believed he would, against whatsoever the Earl of Warwick could have done, have preserved the major part of the fleet in their duty to the king."

Having thus retired from the navy, he withdrew with his family to Jersey; but subsequently returned to aid the projects of the royalists, when he was created by King CHARLES a baronet, 9 May, 1645. He again, however, went back to his government in Jersey, and there, in the ruin of the royal cause, afforded an asylum to the Prince of Wales (who appointed him his vice-chamberlain), Mr. Hyde, afterwards Lord Clarendon, and other refugees of distinction. After this he defended the island of Jersey in the most gallant manner against the parliamentarians, and ultimately only surrendered upon receiving the command of King CHARLES II. so to do. At the Restoration Sir George formed one of the immediate train of the restored monarch in his triumphant entry into London: and the next day he was sworn of the privy council and declared Vice Chamberlain. He was afterwards returned to parliament by the corporation of Portsmouth. Sir George m. Elizabeth, dau. of Sir Philip Carteret, Knt., of St. Ouen, and had issue,

I. PHILIP (Sir), m. Jemima, dau. of Edward Montagu, 1st Earl of Sandwich, vice-admiral of England, and had issue,

1 GEORGE, who s. his grandfather.

2 Philip, captain of marines; lost at sea in 1693.

3 Edward, M.P., joint-postmaster-general, m. Bridget, dau. of Sir Thomas Exton, judge of the high court of admiralty, and d. in 1739, leaving issue.

Sir Philip Carteret being with his father-in-law, Lord Sandwich, in the great naval engagement off Solebay, 28 May, 1672, was blown up with that gallant officer in the "Royal James."

II. James, captain R N , in the reign of King CHARLES II.

III. George, d. unm, in 1656.

1. Anne, m. to Sir Nicholas Slanning, Bart., K.B., of Maristow, co. Devon.

II. Caroline, m. to Sir Thomas Scot, of Scot's Hall, Kent.

III. Louisa-Margaretta, m. to Sir Robert Atkins, of Saperton, co. Gloucester.

Sir George d. 13 January, 1679, and was s. by his grandson,

SIR GEORGE CARTERET, 2nd baronet, who was elevated to the peerage 19 October, 1681, as BARON CARTERET, of Hawnes, with remainder, in default of male issue, to his brothers, and their heirs male. This nobleman, when only eight years of age, was m. to Lady Grace Granville, youngest dau. of John, Earl of Bath, and co-heiress of her nephew, William-Henry, last Earl of Bath of that family; a marriage agreed upon by his grandfather, Sir George Carteret, and the Earl of Bath, to cement the friendship which had long subsisted between them. By this lady his lordship had issue, JOHN, his successor, with another son, Philip, and a dau., Jemima, who both d. unm. His lordship, who was a zealous supporter of the revolution, d. at the early age of twenty-six, in 1695. His widow, Lady Carteret, having succeeded as co-heiress to the great Bath estates, upon the decease of her nephew, William-Henry Granville, Earl of Bath, in 1711 (when that dignity became EXTINCT), was created 1 January, 1714, Viscountess Carteret, and COUNTESS GRANVILLE, with remainder of the viscounty, in default of male issue in her son John, Lord Carteret, to the uncle of that nobleman, Edward Carteret, Esq., and his male heirs. Her ladyship d. in 1744, and was s. by her only surviving son,

JOHN CARTERET, 2nd Lord Carteret, as Earl Granville. His lordship was appointed one of the lords of the bedchamber at the accession of King GEORGE I., and constituted in 1716 lord-lieutenant and custos rotulorum of the co. of Devon. In 1719 he was accredited ambassador extraordinary to the court of Sweden. In 1721 he was declared principal secretary of state, and in 1724 constituted Lord-Lieutenant of Ireland, which high office he retained for the six following years. He was thrice one of the lords justices during the occasional absence of the king, and a knight of the Garter. His lordship *m.* 1st, 17 October, 1710, Frances, only dau. of Sir Robert Worsley, Bart., and grand-dau. maternally of Thomas Thynne, Viscount Weymouth, by whom he had surviving issue,

  I. ROBERT, his successor.
  I. Grace, *m.* 1729, Lionel, Earl of Dysart, and *d.* 23 July, 1755, leaving issue: the co-heirs of the line of this marriage are the EARL OF DYSART and JOHN TOLLEMACHE, Esq., M.P., of Helmingham Hall, co Suffolk, and Pickforton Castle, co. Chester.
  II. Louisa, *m.* to Thomas Thynne, Viscount Weymouth, and had issue,
    1 THOMAS, Viscount Weymouth, K.G., created Marquess of Bath, *d.* in 1784, and left
      THOMAS, 2nd Marquess of Bath, K.G., and other issue,
    2 HENRY-FREDERICK, having *s.* to the Carteret estates under the will of his grandfather, John, Earl of Granville, after the decease of his uncle, assumed the surname and arms of CARTERET, and was created 29 Jan 1784 BARON CARTERET, *of Hawnes*, with remainder to the younger sons of his brother, the Marquess of Bath. His lordship *d.* in 1826, and the barony passed according to the limitation to his nephew, LORD GEORGE THYNNE, 2nd LORD CARTERET. (*See* THYNNE, BARONS CARTERET.)
  III. Georgiana-Carolina, *m.* 1st, to the Hon John Spencer, and 2ndly, to William, Earl Cowper.
  IV. Frances, *m.* to John, Marquess of Tweeddale.

The earl *m.* 2ndly, Lady Sophia Fermor, dau. of Thomas, Earl of Pomfret, and had an only dau.,

Sophia, who *m.* in 1765, William Petty, 2nd Earl of Shelburne, afterwards Marquess of Lansdowne, by whom she had an only son,
  JOHN, 2nd Marquess of Lansdowne, who *d. s. p.* 15 November, 1809.

His lordship *d.* 2 January, 1763, and was *s.* by his son, ROBERT CARTERET, 3rd Lord Carteret and 2nd Earl Granville. His lordship *d. s. p.* in 1776, when the BARONY OF CARTERET, and EARLDOM OF GRANVILLE, with the VISCOUNTY OF CARTERET, became EXTINCT, but the Barony of Carteret was re-created in 1784 (*revert* to issue of Lady Louisa Carteret, 2nd dau. of John, 1st earl).

Arms.—Quarterly: 1st and 4th, gu., four fusils in fesse, arg., for CARTERET; 2nd and 3rd, gu., three horsemen's rests, or, for GRANVILLE.

NOTE.—The three principal branches of the ancient house of Carteret are now represented in the present branches of St. Ouen, by EDWARD CHARLES MALLET DE CARTERET, Esq., of the 88th regt.; that of England, founded at Hawnes, co. Bedford, by SIR GEORGE DE CARTERET, Bart., vice-chamberlain to CHARLES II., treasurer of the navy (whose grandson was raised to the peerage), by the Marquess of Bath, and the Earl of Dysart, and John Tollemache, Esq., as co-heirs; and that of Trinity manor, in Jersey, by the Count de St. George, son of Miss de Carteret, sister of the late Lady Symonds, who was eldest sister of the gallant and distinguished Sir Philip de Carteret Sylvester, captain R.N., who *d. s. p.*

CAVANAGH—BARON BALLYANE.

(*See* KAVANAGH.)

CAVENDISH — BARON OGLE AND VISCOUNTS MANSFIELD, EARLS OF NEWCASTLE-UPON-TYNE, &c., MARQUESSES OF NEWCASTLE, DUKES OF NEWCASTLE, &c.

Barony and Viscounty, by Letters Patent, dated 3 Nov., 1620.
Earldom, &c., by Letters Patent, dated 7 March, 1628.
Marquisate, by Letters Patent, dated 27 October, 1643.
Dukedom, &c., by Letters Patent, dated 16 March, 1664.

Lineage.

This noble family, and the existing ducal house of Devonshire, had a common progenitor in

The Right Honourable SIR WILLIAM CAVENDISH, who, by his 3rd wife ("Bess of Hardwick"), Elizabeth, dau. of John Hardwick, Esq., of Hardwick, co. Derby, and eventually co-heiress of her brother, James Hardwick, had issue,

Henry, of Tutbury Priory, co. Stafford, M.P. for Derbyshire, who *d. s. p.* 12 October, 1616.
WILLIAM, created EARL OF DEVONSHIRE, ancestor of the extant DUKES.

and

SIR CHARLES CAVENDISH, Knt., of Welbeck Abbey, Notts, who *m.* 1st, Margaret, eldest dau. and co-heir of Sir Thomas Kitson, of Hengrave, Suffolk, by whom he had no issue; and 2ndly, Catherine, dau. of Cuthbert, 7th Baron Ogle, who becoming eventually his lordship's sole heiress, succeeded to the Barony of Ogle, which was confirmed to her ladyship by letters patent, dated 4 December, 1628: by this lady he left an only surviving son,

SIR WILLIAM CAVENDISH, K.B., who was elevated to the peerage, 3 November, 1620, as *Baron Ogle, of Bothal*, and VISCOUNT MANSFIELD, *in the co. of Nottingham*. This nobleman, afterwards so celebrated as a royalist general, filled originally the post of governor to the Prince of Wales, eldest son of King CHARLES I., and was advanced in the peerage by that monarch, on 7 March, 1628, in the dignities of *Baron Cavendish, of Bolsover, in the co. of Notts*, and EARL OF NEWCASTLE. When the proceedings of the Long Parliament ceased to be equivocal, his lordship hastened to rear the royal standard in the north, and planting it on the battlements of the Castle of Tynemouth, manned and fortified the town of Newcastle. He then levied forces, and, though in the midst of winter, placing himself at their head, routed the rebels in all directions in the county of York, and became master of their principal strong places there. In 1642 he received the queen, upon her majesty's arrival with arms and ammunition, and conducting her in safety to the king, at Oxford, was rewarded, by letters patent, dated 27 October, 1643, with the MARQUISATE OF NEWCASTLE. Subsequently, his lordship sustained, upon every occasion, his high reputation, but particularly in his gallant defence of the city of York against three powerful armies of English and Scotch. He retired to the continent however, after the fatal battle of Marston-Moor, owing to some misunderstanding between himself and PRINCE RUPERT, a misunderstanding which the royalists had eventually most deeply to deplore. Upon the restoration of the monarchy, the marquess was created, 16 March, 1664, *Earl of Ogle* and DUKE OF NEWCASTLE, as some compensation for the immense losses he had sustained, amounting in the aggregate, to nearly three parts of a million sterling! His grace *m.* 1st, Elizabeth, dau. and heiress of William Basset, Esq., of Blore, co. Stafford, and widow of the Hon. Henry Howard, youngest son of Thomas, Earl of Suffolk, by whom he had surviving issue,

  CHARLES, who *m.* Elizabeth, dau. of Richard Rogers, Esq., of Brianston, Dorset, but *d. v. p., s. p.* His widow *m.* 2ndly, Charles, 6th Duke of Richmond and Lennox.
  HENRY, his successor.
  Jane, *m.* to Charles Cheney, Esq., of Chesham-Boys, Bucks.
  Elizabeth, *m.* to John, 2nd Earl of Bridgewater.
  Frances, *m.* to Oliver St. John, Earl of Bolingbroke.

The duke *m.* 2ndly, Margaret, sister of the Lord Lucas, but had no issue. Of his grace, Walpole, in his "Noble Authors," says, that "he was a man extremely known from the course of life into which he was forced, and who would soon have been forgotten in the walk of fame which he chose for himself: yet as an author he is familiar to those who scarce know any other, from his Book of Horsemanship. Though amorous in poetry and music, as Lord Clarendon says, he was fitter to break Pegasus for a menage, than to mount him on the steeps of Parnassus. Of all the riders of that steed, perhaps there have not been a more fantastic couple than his grace and his faithful duchess, who was never off her pillion."

His grace, who, amongst his other honours, was a knight of the Garter, *d.* in 1676, and a costly monument in Westminster Abbey records his virtues, dignities, and high public employments. He was *s.* by his only surviving son, HENRY CAVENDISH, 2nd duke, who *m.* Frances, dau. of William, 2nd son of Robert Pierpoint, Earl of Kingston, by whom he had surviving issue,

  1 HENRY, Earl of Ogle, who *m.* Lady Elizabeth Percy, only surviving child and heiress of Joceline, 11th and last Earl of Northumberland of the old Percys, upon which occasion his lordship assumed the surname of PERCY. He *d. s. p.* 1 November, 1680, and his widow *m.* in two years afterwards, *Charles Seymour*, DUKE OF SOMERSET, of which union the present DUKE OF ATHOLE is heir-general.
  I. Elizabeth, *m.* 1st, to Christopher Monk, Duke of Albemarle, and 2ndly, to Ralph Montagu, Duke of Montagu, but *d. s. p.*

109

II. Frances, m. to John, 2nd Earl of Breadalbane, but d. s. p.

III. Margaret, m. to John Holles, 4th Earl of Clare, who was created, 14 May, 1694, Marquess of Clare and DUKE OF NEW-CASTLE, by whom she had an only dau.,

Lady Henrietta-Cavendish Holles, who m. Edward, Lord Harley, son and heir of Robert, Earl of Oxford, to whom she carried a very great real and personal estate. Her only dau. and heiress, LADY MARGARET CAVENDISH HARLEY, m. 1734, William, 2nd DUKE OF PORTLAND, and her heir-general, the Duke of Portland, is one of the co-heirs of the Barony of Ogle.

His grace (John Holles, Duke of Newcastle) dying thus without male issue, the honours ceased in the Holles family, but were revived in the descendants of his sister, GRACE HOLLES, who m. Thomas Pelham, Lord Loughton, and had issue,

1 THOMAS, created Earl and Marquess of Clare, and DUKE OF NEWCASTLE, d. in 1768. s. p., when the husband of his niece inherited the dukedom.

2 Henry Pelham, m. to Catherine, dau. of John, Duke of Rutland, and left issue,

Catherine, m. to Henry Clinton, EARL OF LINCOLN, who s. his wife's uncle in the DUKEDOM OF NEWCASTLE, and from him descend the extant DUKES OF NEWCASTLE.

1 Grace, m. to George Naylor, Esq.
2 Frances. m. to Christopher Viscount Castlecomer.
3 Gertrude, m. to David Polhill, Esq.
4 Lucy, m. to Henry, 7th Earl of Lincoln.
5 Margaret, m. to Sir John Shelley, 4th bart., of Michelgrove.

IV. Catherine, m. to Thomas, 6th Earl of Thanet, and had five daus., co-heiresses, viz.,

1 Catherine, wife of Edward Viscount Sondes, and great-great-grandmother of Sophia, Baroness de Clifford, one of the co-heirs of the Barony of Ogle.
2 Anne, m. James, Earl of Salisbury, and the heir-general of this marriage, the MARQUESS OF SALISBURY, is one of the co-heirs of the Barony of Ogle.
3 Margaret, m. Thomas Coke, Earl of Leicester, and d. s. p.
4 Mary, m. 1st, to Anthony, Earl of Harold, and 2ndly, to John, Earl of Gower; the Duke of Sutherland is her heir-general, and one of the co-heirs to the Barony of Ogle.
5 Isabella, m. 1st, to Lord Nassau Paulet, and 2ndly, to Sir F. Blake Delaval, K.B.

V. Arabella, m. to Charles, Earl of Sunderland, and left an only dau.,

FRANCES, who m. in 1717, Henry, 4th Earl of Carlisle, and had surviving issue,

Arabella, m. to Jonathan Cope, Esq., of Orton Longueville, and the heir-general of this marriage is the MARQUESS OF HUNTLEY, one of the co-heirs of the Barony of Ogle.

Diana, m. to Thomas Duncombe, Esq., of Duncombe Park, co. York, and had an only dau. and heiress,

ANNE, who m. 1774, Robert Shafto, Esq., of Whitworth, co. Durham, and was mother of ROBERT EDEN DUNCOMBE SHAFTO, Esq., of Whitworth, M.P., father of ROBERT DUNCOMBE SHAFTO, Esq., M.P., one of the co-heirs of the Barony of Ogle.

His grace d. in 1691, when, as he left no male issue, the dignities created in 1620, in 1628, in 1643, and in 1644 (see commencement of this article), became EXTINCT, while the old Barony of OGLE, which came into the family with Catherine, Lady Ogle, wife of Sir Charles Cavendish, of Welbeck Abbey, fell into ABEYANCE between his grace's five daus. and co-heiresses, and so continues amongst their descendants.

Arms—Sa., three bucks' heads, cabossed, arg , attired, or, a crescent for difference.

CECIL—BARON CECIL, OF PUTNEY, CO. SURREY, VISCOUNT WIMBLEDON.

Barony, by Letters Patent, dated 9 November, 1625.
Viscounty, by Letters Patent, dated 25 July, 1626.

Lineage.

SIR WILLIAM CECIL, Baron Burghley, treasurer to Queen ELIZABETH, m. 1541, Mary, dau. of Peter Cheke, and sister of Sir John Cheke, tutor to King EDWARD VI., and was father of SIR THOMAS CECIL, 1st Earl of Exeter, who m. Dorothy, dau. and co-heir of John Nevil, Lord Latimer, and had issue,

WILLIAM, 2nd earl, who m. Eliza, sister and co-heir of Sir Robert Drury, Knt., of Halsted, Suffolk, and left only daus. and co-heirs.

RICHARD, ancestor of the Earls of Exeter.

EDWARD (Sir).

The 3rd son,

The HONOURABLE SIR EDWARD CECIL, b. 1571, having adopted

a military life, attained celebrity in the wars in the Netherlands, where he was engaged for a space of thirty-five years. He was marshal, lieutenant, and general of the forces sent by King JAMES and King CHARLES I. against the Spaniards and Imperialists, and was elevated to the peerage by King CHARLES I., 9 November, 1625, as Baron Cecil, of Putney, and created 25 July, 1626, VISCOUNT WIMBLEDON. Walpole in his "Noble Authors," mentions that in the king's library are two manuscript tracts drawn up by this nobleman on the several subjects of war and the military defence of the nation; and he likewise states, that a manuscript was found by the Earl of Huntingdon in an old chest, purporting to be a warrant of King CHARLES I., directing, at the instance of Lord Wimbledon, the revival of the old English march, so famous in all the honourable achievements and glorious wars of this kingdom in ancient times; but which, by neglect, had been nearly lost and forgotten. His lordship m. thrice; 1st Theodosia, dau. of Sir Andrew Noel, of Dalby, co. Leicester, Knt., by whom he had four daus., viz.,

Dorothy.

Albinia, m. to Sir Christopher Wray, Knt., of Barlings. co. Lincoln, and had a dau., Albinia, m. to Richard, son of Sir Richard Betenson, Bart., of Scadbury, co. Kent.

Elizabeth, m. to Frances, Lord Willoughby, of Parham.

Frances, m. to James, son and heir of William, Viscount Saye and Sele, and had a dau. Frances, m. to Andrew Ellis, of Alrey, co. Flint, and d. 1687.

The viscount m. 2ndly, Diana, dau. of Sir William Drury, of Halstede, co. Suffolk, Knt.; and 3rdly, Sophia, dau. of Sir Edward Zouche, of Woking, Surrey, by whom he had a son,

Algernon, who d. in infancy.

His lordship d. at Wimbledon, 16 November, 1638, where he was interred, and leaving no male issue, his honours became EXTINCT.

Arms—Barry of ten, arg. and az., on six escutcheons, su., three, two, one, as many lions rampant of the first.

CHANDOS—BARON CHANDOS.

By Writ of Summons, dated 20 December, 1337.

Lineage.

The first of this family upon record,

ROBERT DE CHANDOS, came from Normandy with the CONQUEROR, and obtained by arms large possessions in Wales. He was subsequently a munificent benefactor to the church. To this Robert s. another

ROBERT DE CHANDOS, who, upon the assessment in aid of marrying the king's dau., in the 12th HENRY II., certified his knights' fees to be thirteen and a sixth part, for which he paid £8 15s. 6d. He d. in 1173, and was s. by his eldest son,

ROBERT DE CHANDOS. This feudal lord paid 40 marks for livery of the lands of his inheritance, in the 8th RICHARD I. He was s. by

ROBERT DE CHANDOS, who was s. by his son and heir,

ROGER DE CHANDOS, whose wardship was granted by the crown to William de Cantilupe. This Roger along with other barons-marchers had frequent summonses in the reign of HENRY III. to march against the Welsh. He was s. by his son,

ROBERT DE CHANDOS, who, in the 50th HENRY III., doing his homage, had livery of the lands of his inheritance, and in the 10th EDWARD I. was in the expedition then made into Wales. Upon his death, which happened in the 30th EDWARD I., it was found that he held the manor of Snodhull, with its appurtenances, by barony and the service of two knights' fees. He was s. by his son,

SIR ROGER DE CHANDOS. This feudal lord was in the Scottish wars temp. EDWARD II., and received the honour of knighthood with Prince Edward, and many others, by bathing, prior to going upon one of those expeditions. In the 15th EDWARD II. he was made sheriff of Herefordshire, and again in the 1st EDWARD III., when he was made governor of the castle of Hereford. "But of his successors," says Dugdale, "I am not able to continue a direct series." We come therefore to

ROGER DE CHANDOS, brother and heir of Thomas de Chandos, deceased. This Roger performing his fealty in the 7th EDWARD III., had livery of his lands, and the next year was constituted sheriff of Herefordshire and governor of the castle of Hereford. In the 19th of the same reign, being then a banneret, he received a military summons to attend the king into France, and was summoned to parliament as a BARON from 20 December, 1337, to 22 October, 1355. He m. 1st, Catherine, dau. of Richard, Lord Talbot; and 2ndly, Maud, dau. of Sir John Acton, and d. 1355, leaving by her a son,

SIR THOMAS DE CHANDOS, Knt., who does not appear by the existing enrolments to have been summoned to parliament. He was *s.* by his son,

SIR JOHN CHANDOS, Knt., who *d.* in 1430, leaving his sister, Margaret, his heir; which

MARGARET CHANDOS, *m.* Sir Thomas Berkeley, Knt., of Coberley, and left two daus., her co-heirs, viz.,

> Margaret, *m.* to Nicholas Mattesden.
> Alice, *m.* to Thomas Bruges, whence the DUKES OF CHANDOS.

Arms—Or, a pile, gu.

NOTE—There was a family of the same stock as the Barons Chandos, which gained considerable military reputation. It was seated at Radborne, co. Derby, an estate acquired by the marriage, *temp.* HENRY III., of SIR JOHN CHANDOS, Knt., with Margery, dau. and co-heir (with her sister Ermintrude, wife of Robert de Talbot, ancestor by her of the Talbots of Bashall, co. York) of Robert de Ferrars, Lord of Egginton and Radborne. Their son and heir was

SIR HENRY CHANDOS, Knt., of Radborne, who gave lands to find two lamps in the church of Radborne, A.D. 1280. By Eleanor his wife, he left a son and successor,

SIR JOHN CHANDOS, Knt., of Radborne, living 16th and 28th EDWARD I., who *m.* Elizabeth, dau. and co-heir of Sir Henry Braylesford, and was *s.* by his son,

SIR EDWARD CHANDOS, Knt., of Radborne, who *m.* Isabel, dau. of Sir John Twyford, Knt., and had issue,

I. JOHN (Sir), his heir.
II. Robert, *d. unm.*
 I. Margaret, who *m.* Robert de Ireland, and had a dau., Isabella de Ireland, one of the co-heirs of Sir John Chandos. She *m.* Sir John de Annesley, Knt., but *d. s. p.*
 II. Elizabeth, *d. unm.*
 III. ALIANORE, who *m.* Sir John Lawton, Knt., and had an only dau. and heir,

> ELIZABETH LAWTON, who *m.* Sir Peter de la Pole, and was ancestress of the POLES of RADBORNE, co. *Derby.*

The elder son and successor,

SIR JOHN CHANDOS, of Radborne, a distinguished warrior, one of the original knights of the Garter at the foundation of that illustrious order, acted a brilliant part in the various military achievements of his time. On the memorable field of Cressy, he was entrusted by King EDWARD with the task of directing and defending the Prince of Wales; in the 30th EDWARD III., he fought at Poictiers; and in three years after, in consideration of his gallantry, obtained a grant from Prince Edward of two parts of the manor of Kirketon, in Lincolnshire, to hold for life. In the same year, being retained by King EDWARD to serve him in the office of vice-chamberlain, he received £100 per annum out of the exchequer, and shortly after, in recompense of "his great services in the wars and otherwise," had a grant to himself and his heirs for ever of the Barony of St. Saviour le Viscount, whereon he erected a castle. In 1364, the battle of Auray was fought against Charles of Blois, in which the famed Bertrand du Guesclin was made prisoner, and the victory there achieved is ascribed by all historians to the ability and prowess of Sir John Chandos, who had the chief command of the army of the Comte de Montfort. In the 41st EDWARD III., Sir John accompanied the expedition of the BLACK PRINCE into Spain on behalf of PETER, King of Castile, and held a high command at the battle of Nazar. He subsequently became constable of Aquitaine and seneschal of Poictiers. The career of this gallant soldier "the pride of English chivalry," soon after terminated, for in 1369, he was slain in the wars of Gascoigne in a skirmish at the bridge of Lussac, "to the great sorrow," adds Dugdale, "of both kingdoms, whereof the King of France himself was so apprehensive, that he passionately said, there was not any souldier living so able to make peace betwixt both crowns as he." "Sir John Chandos," says Froissart, "kept a noble and great establishment, and he had the means of doing it, for the King of England, who loved him much, wished it should be so. He was certainly worthy of it; for he was a sweet-tempered knight, courteous, benign, amiable, liberal, courageous, prudent, and loyal in all affairs, and bore himself valiantly on every occasion." He was buried at Mortemer, and his epitaph is recorded in " Les Annales d'Aquitaine par Bouchet." He left no issue.

CHAVENT—BARON CHAVENT.

By Writ of Summons, dated 29 December, 1299

Lineage.

PETER DE CHAUMPVENT, OR CHAVENT, having been engaged in the wars of Gascony *temp.* EDWARD I., was summoned to parliament as a BARON, 29 December, 1299, and *d.* in 1302, leaving a son and heir, John de Chavent (COURTHOPE's *Historic Peerage*), who did not, however, receive a summons to parliament.

Arms—Paly of six, arg. and az., a fesse, gu.

CHAWORTH—BARON CHAWORTH.

By Writ of Summons, dated 6 February, 1299.

Lineage.

About the latter end of King WILLIAM THE CONQUEROR'S reign,

PATRICK DE CADURCIS, vulgularly called Chaworth, a native of Little Brittany, made a grant of certain mills in Gloucestershire to the monks of St. Peter's Abbey. To this Patrick *s.*

PATRICK DE CHAWORTH, who in the 33rd HENRY II., upon the collection of the scutage of Galway, accounted six pounds for the knight's fees belonging to the honour of Striguil. This feudal lord was *s.* by

PAIN DE CHAWORTH, who, in the 2nd HENRY III., being at that time one of the barons marchers, became surety for Isabel de Mortimer that she should come to the king's exchequer on the octaves of St. Michael to satisfy for such debts as she owed to the late King JOHN. Pain de Chaworth *m.* Gundred, dau. and heir of William de la Ferte (heir to Margaret de la Ferte, 2nd dau. and co-heir of William de Briwere, a great feudal lord, who *d.* in 1226), and was *s.* at his decease by his son,

PATRICK DE CHAWORTH, who in the 23rd HENRY III., being then under age, compounded with the king for his own wardship and marriage, paying £500 for the same. In the 29th of the same reign he received a precept from the crown, whereby he was commanded to use all his power and diligence to annoy the Welsh then in hostility. He *m.* Hawyse, dau. and heir of Sir Thomas de Londres, Lord of Kidwilly, in Wales, and had issue,

> PAIN,   } all of whom, in 54th Henry III., joining the
> Hervey, } Crusade, attended Prince Edward to the Holy
> Patric,   } Land.

with two daus., Eve, *m.* to Robert Tibetot, and Anne. This feudal lord *d.* in 1257, and was *s.* by his eldest son,

PAIN DE CHAWORTH, who, in the 5th Edward I., was constituted general of the king's army in West Wales: whereupon Roger de Mortimer had command to aid him with all his power, and to admit him into all his castles and garrisons; at which time he was so successful that the Welsh sued for peace, and did homage to the king. This gallant soldier *d. s. p.* in 1278, and was *s.* by his only surviving brother,

PATRIC DE CHAWORTH, who *m.* the Lady Isabel de Beauchamp, dau. of William, Earl of Warwick, and *d.* in 1382, leaving by her (who *m.* 2ndly, Hugh le Despenser), an only dau. and heiress,

> MAUD DE CHAWORTH, who *m.* Henry Plantagenet, Earl of Lancaster, nephew of King EDWARD I.

Thus terminated this great feudal branch of the family, but another branch had diverged from

WILLIAM DE CHAWORTH, son of Robert, brother of Patric, the first feudal lord. This William, in the 2nd year of King JOHN, paid £5 fine that he might not go beyond sea. He was *s.* by his son and heir,

ROBERT DE CHAWORTH, who in the 6th of JOHN, paid a fine of 100 marks, and one palfrey for his relief, and that he might have the king's charter for those lands he then held by military service, whereof he had no grant. He *d. s. p.*, and was *s.* by his brother,

WILLIAM DE CHAWORTH, who *m.* Alice, dau. of Robert, and sister and co-heir (with her sister Joane, wife of Robert de Latham, of Lancashire) of Thomas de Alfreton, and was *s.* at his decease by his son,

THOMAS DE CHAWORTH, who was summoned to parliament as a BARON 6 February, 1299. But his lordship had no other summons, nor had any of his descendants, who long flourished in the cos. of Derby and Nottingham. One of these descendants, THOMAS CHAWORTH, Esq., of Wyverton, Notts, *m.* Jane, dau. of Galfrid Luttrell, and was father of THOMAS CHAWORTH, who *d. v. p.*, leaving by Joan-Margaret his wife, dau. of Sir Richard Pole, a son, WILLIAM CHAWORTH, whose wife was Alicia, dau. and heir of Sir John de Caltoft, and whose son and heir was SIR THOMAS CHAWORTH, who *m.* 1st, Nicola, dau. of Sir Reginald Braybrook, and by her had a dau. Elizabeth, *m.* to John, 5th Lord Scrope, of Masham. Sir Thomas *m.* 2ndly, Isabella, dau. and co-heir of Sir Thomas Aylesbury, and had with other issue,

> WILLIAM (Sir), his heir, *m.* Elizabeth. dau. of Sir Nicholas Bowet, Knt., of Repinghall, and left issue,
> THOMAS, *m.* Lady Margaret Talbot, and *d. s. p.* 22nd EDWARD IV.
> JOAN, *m.* John Ormond, Esq., and left three daus., co-heirs,

viz., JOAN, *m.* Thomas Dinham, Esq.; ELIZABETH, *m.* to Sir Anthony Babington, of Dethick; and ANNE, *m.* to William Mering.

George (3rd son). *m.* Alicia Annesley, and was father of Thomas, who *m.* Ankaret Serleby, and had a son, George, who *d.* 1521, leaving by Catherine Babington his wife, a son, Sir John, who *m.* Maria Paston, and had a son, Sir George Chaworth, who *m.* Anne Paston.

Arms of the feudal Barons Chaworth—Barry of ten, arg. and gu., an orle of martlets, sa.

Arms borne by Lord Chaworth—Being the arms of Alfreton, viz., az , two chevrons, or.

CHAWORTH—VISCOUNT CHAWORTH.

By Letters Patent, dated 4 March, 1627.

Lineage.

SIR GEORGE CHAWORTH, Knt., son of John Chaworth, Esq., of Crophill Butler, co. Nottingham (a descendant of the old feudal Lords Chaworth), by Jane his wife, dau. of David Vincent, Esq., of Stoke D'Abernon, in Surrey, was created a peer of Ireland, as BARON CHAWORTH, *of Trim, co. Meath,* and VISCOUNT CHAWORTH, *of Armagh,* 4 March, 1627. He *m.* Mary, dau. of Thomas Knyveton, Esq., of Myrcaston, co. Derby, and left at his decease a son and successor,

JOHN CHAWORTH, 2nd Viscount Chaworth, who *m.* Penelope, dau. of Edward Noel, Viscount Campden, and had issue,

PATRICIUS, his heir.
Elizabeth, who *m.* William, 3rd Lord Byron, and was mother of William, 4th Lord Byron, great-grandfather of GEORGE-GORDON, 6th LORD BYRON, *the Poet.*
Mary, *m.* to Sir Michael Armine, Bart.

The son and successor,
PATRICIUS CHAWORTH, 3rd Viscount Chaworth, *m.* Grace, 2nd dau. of John, 8th Earl of Rutland, and by her (who *m.* 2ndly, Sir William Langhorn, Bart.) had a dau. and heiress, viz.,

JULIANA, who *m.* Chambre, 5th Earl of Meath, and had, with other issue, a son,
EDWARD, 7th Earl of Meath, great-grandfather of WILLIAM, present EARL OF MEATH.

At his lordship's decease, 15 February, 1699, the title became EXTINCT. A considerable portion of the estates of the Chaworth family eventually centered in MARY-ANNE CHAWORTH, of Annesley, co. Nottingham, only child of WILLIAM CHAWORTH, Esq.,

"Herself the solitary scion left
Of a time-honoured race—."

That lady, celebrated in the poems of Lord Byron, *m.* in 1805, John Musters, Esq., of Colwick Hall, Notts., and *d.* at Wyverton Hall, in February, 1832, in consequence of the alarm and danger to which she had been exposed during an attack on Colwick Hall by a party of rioters from Nottingham. Her grandson is the present JOHN CHAWORTH-MUSTERS, Esq., of Annesley, Colwick, and Wyverton, Notts.

Arms—Barry of ten, arg. and gu., three martlets, sa.

CHENEY—BARON CHENEY, OF TODDINGTON, CO. BEDFORD.

By Writ of Summons, dated 6 May, 1572.

Lineage.

RICHARD CHENEY, of Shurland, *m.* one of the daus. and co-heirs of Robert Cralle, of Cralle, co. Sussex, and had two sons,
WILLIAM, of whom presently.
Symon, ancestor of the Cheneys of Higham.

The eldest son,
SIR WILLIAM CHENEY, Knt., *d.* 21st HENRY VI., and was buried in St. Benet's Church, Paul's Wharf, leaving by Eleanor, his wife, a son and heir.
SIR JOHN CHENEY, who *m.* Elinor, dau. of Sir John Shottisbroke, and *d.* 7th EDWARD IV., leaving with other issue,
JOHN (Sir). of Shurland, who had summons to parliament as Lord Cheney. 3rd HENRY VII., *d. s. p.*, and was buried in Salisbury Cathedral.
WILLIAM.

The 2nd son,
WILLIAM CHENEY, constable of Queenborough Castle, *m.*
112

twice; by his 1st wife he had a son, Sir Francis, constable of Queenborough Castle, who *d. s. p.*; by his 2nd wife he was father of
SIR THOMAS CHENEY, K G. (nephew and heir of John, Lord Cheney, a dignity that expired in 1496), *m.* 1st, Frideswide, dau. and co-heiress of Sir Thomas Frowyke, Knt., chief justice of the Court of Common Pleas, and had issue,

JOHN, *m.* Margaret, dau. of George Nevil, Lord Abergavenny, and *d. s. p.*
Catherine, *m.* Thomas Kemp, Esq., of Glendich, in Kent.
Frances, *m.* to Nicholas Cripps, Esq., son and heir of Sir Henry Cripps, Knt.

Sir Thomas *m.* 2ndly, Anne, dau. and co-heiress of Sir John Broughton, of Toddington, co. Bedford, grandson of Sir John Broughton, by Mary his wife, dau. and heir of Thomas Peyvre,* of Toddington, by whom he acquired that estate, and had with an only son, HENRY, of whom hereafter, a dau., Anne, who *m.* Sir John Perrot, Knt., and had a son, Sir Thomas Perrot. Sir Thomas Cheney appears to have been a person of great gallantry and note, in the reign of HENRY VIII. At the celebrated interview between that monarch and FRANCIS I., at Ardres, he was one of the challengers, against all gentlemen, who were to exercise feats of arms, on horseback, or on foot, for thirty days. He was a knight of the Garter, warden of the Cinque Ports, and treasurer of the king's household. Upon the death of King EDWARD VI. he espoused the interests of Queen MARY, and he was called to the privy council in the 1st year of ELIZABETH: he *d.* 8 December, 1st ELIZABETH, and was *s.* by his son,

SIR HENRY CHENEY, Knt., who was summoned to parliament as BARON CHENEY, OF TODDINGTON, co. Bedford, from 8 May, 1572, to 15 October, 1586. His lordship, who was one of the peers, on the trial of MARY Queen of Scots, *m.* Jane, dau. of Thomas Wentworth, Lord Wentworth, but *d. s. p.* in 1587, when his estates devolved upon his widow, and the Barony of CHENEY, OF TODDINGTON, became EXTINCT. His lordship erected a noble mansion at Toddington, wherein he resided.

Arms—(Originally), erm., on a bend, sa., three martlets, or.

CHENEY—BARON CHENEY.

By Writ of Summons, dated 1 September, 1487.

Lineage.

JOHN CHENEY, Esq., of Shurland, in the Isle of Sheppey (son of Sir William Cheyney, by Eleanor, his wife, dau. of John Salern, of Joen, and grandson of Richard Cheney, Esq. by his wife, a dau. and co-heiress of Robert Cralle), was descended from Ralph de Caineto, who came into England with the CONQUEROR. He *m.* Eleanor, dau. and co-heir of Sir John Shottisbrook, by Edith Stourton his wife, and had issue,

I. JOHN (Sir), his heir. III. Edward, dean of Salisbury
II. William. IV. Robert (Sir).
V. Roger (Sir). VI. Alexander (Sir).
VII. Geoffrey.
I. Edith, *m.* to Sir William Sandys, of The Vine, Hants.

The son and heir,
SIR JOHN CHENEY, K.G., an eminent soldier in the army of Henry, Earl of Richmond, at Bosworth, whom, it is said, King RICHARD personally encountering, felled to the ground, although he was a person of great bodily strength. Upon the accession of his chief to the crown, as HENRY VII., Sir John Cheney was called to the privy council, and soon after, again stoutly fought for the king against the Earl of Lincoln and his adherents, at Stoke. In the 3rd year of the new monarch, he was summoned to parliament as a BARON, and from that period to 14 October, 1495. His lordship was also a knight banneret and a knight of the most noble order of the Garter. He *d. s. p.* in 1496, when the BARONY OF CHENEY EXPIRED, while his lands devolved upon his nephew, Sir Thomas Cheney (*see* CHENEY, of Toddington).

Arms—Az., six lions rampant, arg., a canton, erm:

* Thomas Peyvre was 6th in descent from Pauline Peyvre (counsellor and favourite of King HENRY III.), whose mansion of Toddington, which he erected "with palace-like grandeur," was "the astonishment of beholders."

CHERLTON—BARONS CHERLTON OF POWYS.

By Writ of Summons, dated 26 July, 1313,

Lineage.

The Barony of Cherlton, of Powys, was created by writ of summons to John de Cherlton, who acquired the feudal Barony of Pole (Welshpool), co. Montgomery, comprised in the ancient principality of Powys, in right of his wife Hawys, heiress of the Wenwynwyn branch of the sovereigns of Powys, derived from MERVYN, King of Powys, 3rd son of Rhodri Mawr, who by inheritance and marriage re-uniting the states of North Wales, South Wales, and Powys, became King of all Wales, A.D. 843, 5th in lineal succession to his memorable progenitor, St. Cadwalader Bendigelig (the Blessed), "as well saint as monarch," crowned King of the Britains, A.D. 676, whose standard displayed the "red dragon," transmitted as the distinctive cognizance of his royal race.

Sixth in descent from Mervyn ap Rhodri Mawr, was Meredith ap Bleddyn, Prince of Powys, who adopted the "black lion of Powys" (arg., a lion rampant, sa.) in substitution of his father's arms, "or, a lion rampant, gu." By his 2nd wife Efa, dau. of Blettrws ap Ednowain Bendew, Lord of Tegeingle (Flint), he was father of

Jorwerth, *alias* Gervase Goch ap Meredith, Lord of Mochnant-is-Rhayadr, whose name occurs in deeds, 1157-1171, and who bore "the black lion of Powys." This noble, who acquired lands in the fief of Gerard de Tournay, in Shropshire, including Sutton, Brockton, and Ellardine, and received the manor of Rowton, near High Ercall, from HENRY II., *m.* Matilda, dau. of Sir Roger de Manly, of Manly, co. Chester, and had issue,

   I. Madoc ap Gervase Goch, Lord of Sutton, who, about 1167, as son and heir, granted to Wombridge Priory the advowson of his church of Sutton, and willed that his body, wherever he might chance to die, might be buried at that monastery. He *d. s. p. circa* 1194.

   II. Griffin ap Jorwerth, *alias* Gervase Goch, Lord of Sutton, who confirmed the charter which his brother had given to Wombridge Priory, and directed that he should be buried at Wombridge. In 1195 and 1196, he is named in the Salop Pipe Roll as fining for his lands; and by a return of the year 1211, it appears that he then held, among other lands, the manor of Sutton, by the gift of King HENRY II., by the service of being *latimarius* (interpreter) between England and Wales He *m.* before Michaelmas, 1196, Matilda, sister and co-heir of Ralph le Strange, Baron of Knockyn, Alveley and Weston, and appears, with the husbands of the other co-heiresses as fining 200 marks for seizin of their lands. This lady, who *d.* 4 May, 1242, surviving her husband twenty-two years, brought him and his heirs the whole villa of Dovaneston (Dovaston) and Kineverdeston (Kynaston), for which she concurred with her husband in surrendering her third part of Knokyn to her cousin, John le Strange, of Ness. Kynaston became a seat of a branch of Griffins' and Matilda's descendants, and from it was derived the patronymic of their widespread line. Griffith ap Jorwerth, *alias* Gervase Goch, who *d. circa* January, 1221, had issue,

     1 Madoc ap Griffin, Lord of Sutton, whose name occurs 1221-1262. Soon after his succession, "Madoc, son of Griffin, and Duce his wife," are found suing Imbert, prior of Wenlock; and the case was heard by the king himself, when, in August, 1226, he visited Shrewsbury. In Michaelmas Term, 1228, the prior of Wenlock was prosecuting a suit at Westminster against "Madoc, son of Griffin, and Cecilia" his wife, tenants of lands in Sutton, but the king had issued a mandate to his Justices *in banco* that the case should be postponed till Madoc should be released from prison, he having been arrested by Llewelyn, Prince of North Wales. Madoc de Sutton was returned in 1253-4, as one of eleven persons in the cos. of Salop and Stafford, who, being of less than baronial degree, were yet possessed of lands to the extent of £20 annual value. He alienated the manor of Sutton-Madoc, as well as Rowton and Ellardine, to John le Strange, 3rd Baron of Ness and Cheswardine, who *d.* early in 1269. Madoc *m.* Duce, *alias* Cecilia, whose name occurs 1226-9, and had a dau.,

      Isabel, who *d.* about January, 1302, *m.* between 1255 and 1274 to Henry de Morf, living 1274, whose name occurs also October, 1292, and 12 July, 1296. By him, who was dead in 1302, Isabel was mother of

       1 William de Morf, whose name occurs 1303.
       2 Henry de Morf, *b. circa* 1257, and living 1323.

     2 Howel ap Griffin, whose name occurs *circa* 1245.
     3 Griffin ap Griffin, whose name occurs *circa* 1231, father (by Agnes, dau. of Robert Bulkeley, Lord of Bulkeley, co. Chester) of

      Griffith, of Cae Howel and Kynaston, who, by the name of "Griffith de Kynaston," witnessed, in 1313, a grant from Hugh Fitz-Philip to Haghmond Abbey, of lands near Oswestry, ancestor of the Kynastons of Kynaston; the Kynastons of Stocks, co. Salop; the Kynastons of

Oteley, co. Salop; and the Kynastons of Hardwick, barts., of which last line John Kynaston, Esq., M.P. for Salop, claimed in 1731, and his grandson, John Kynaston, Esq., in 1800, the Barony of Cherlton of Powys.

   III Jorwerth ap Jorwerth, *alias* Gervase Goch, Baron of Main-yn-Meifod, progenitor of the Barons of Main-yn-Meifod; the Mathews of Tref; the Moris's of Bryngwallie; the Powys's, Lords Lilford; the Parrys of Main-yn-Meifod; and the Lloyds of Sharpley, in Llanarmon, Dyffryn Clwyd.

Meredith ap Bleddyn, whose demise took place in 1132, was father, by his 1st consort Hunydd, dau. of Eunydd ap Gwernwy, Lord of Dyffryn Clwyd, with other issue, of two sons,

   I. Madoc ap Meredith, Prince of Lower Powys, from him called Powys Fadoc, who *d.* at Winchester in 1160, and was buried in Meifod Church, near Mathrafal, his castle-palace on the banks of the Vwrnwy, where the carved stone lid of his coffin, with the cognizance of the dragon, is still to be seen. According to the Welch chronicle he was "one who feared God and relieved the poor." By the Princess Susanna his consort, dau. of GRIFFITH AP CYNAN, King of North Wales, this monarch had, with other issue,

   1 Griffith Maelor ap Madoc, who *s.* as Lord of Maelor or Bromfield, and Mochnant ys Rhaiadr, in Powys Fadoc, a man "wise and liberal, nor was he less brave, nor less a friend to his country. He was valiantly engaged at the head of his men of Bromfield at the battle of Crogen (Chirk Castle) where HENRY II was repulsed." Griffith, who bore paley of eight, arg. and gu., over all a lion rampant, sable, *d.* in 1191, and was buried at Meifod, leaving, by his wife the Princess Angharad, dau. of Owen Gwynedd, Prince of North Wales, an only son,

     Madoc ap Griffith, Lord of Bromfield, ancestor of Griffith Vychan, Lord of Glyndwrdwy, paternal representative of the sovereigns of Powys, who *m.* the Lady Eleanor, elder dau. and co-heir of Thomas ap Llewelyn, Lord of South Wales, representative of the princes of South Wales, by his wife Eleanor Goch, dau. and heir of Philip ap Ivor, Lord of Cardigan, by the Princess Catherine, dau. and heir of Llewelyn, Prince of North Wales. By this illustrious alliance the Lord of Glyndwrdwy was father of two sons,

      1 Owen ap Griffith Vychan, Lord of Glyndwrdwy, the chivalrous Owen Glyndwr, who, representing the royal lineage of North Wales, South Wales, and Powys, asserted his claim by arms to the sovereignty of his country.

      2 Tudyr ap Griffith Vychan, Lord of Gwyddelwern in Edeirnion, upwards of twenty-four years old, 3 September, 10th RICHARD II., when, as "Tudor de Glyndore," he appeared as a witness in the Scrope and Grosvenor controversy. Terminating a gallant career at the battle fought between the English and the Welch forces, 15 March, 1405, at Mynydd-y-Pwll-Melyn, in Brecknockshire, he left, by Mawd his wife, dau. and heir of Jeuan ap Howel, derived from Tudor Trevor, Lord of Hereford, a dau. and heir,

       LOWRY, Lady of Gwyddelwern and a Baroness of Edeirnion, representative, in her issue, of her uncle Owen Glyndwr. This lady *m.* Griffith ap Einion. of Corsygedol, co. Merioneth, living Michaelmas, 1400, and 2nd and 3rd HENRY V., ancestor by her of the Vaughans of Corsygedol, represented as heir-general by Edward Lloyd Mostyn, 2nd Lord Mostyn; Yales of Plas-yn-Yale, co. Denbigh, whose representation in the female line devolved on the Lloyds of Plymog and Gwerclas; and the Wynnes of Bryntangor, represented as heir-general by the Hughes's of Gwerclas.

   2 Owen Vychan ap Madoc, Lord of Mechain-Yscoed, living 1165, when he despoiled his uncle, Jorwerth, *alias* Gervase Goch, of Mochnant-ys-Rhayadr, and slain at Carreghwfa in 1186 by Gwenwynwyn ap Owen Cyfeiliog. By Eleanor his wife, dau. of Maelgwyn Vychan, grandson of Rhys ap Tudyr Mawr, King of South Wales, he had two sons,

     Llewelyn ap Owen Vychan, presumed to have been dead in March, or the beginning of May, 1241, father of

      Llewelyn Vychan ap Llewelyn, who, in March, or the beginning of May, 1241, with his uncle, by the description of "*Llewelinus Wagham et Audoenus Wagham avunculus suus*," had fined £50, that they might have seizin of their lands in Maghemant. King HENRY, by a letter dated Newborough, 14 July, 1241, charges David ap Llewelyn, who had usurped the throne, with having unjustly deforced Owen Vaughan and his nephews of the lands which had been adjudged to them, and among the barons who did homage to HENRY at the commencement of 1245, is "*Llewelinus filius Llewelini de Methaim*." This noble was father of two sons,

       1 Meredith ap Llewelyn Vychan, Lord of Mechain, living 1258.
       2 Llewelyn Vychan ap Llewelyn Vychan

     Owen Vychan ap Owen Vychan. whose name occurs with that of his nephew, Llewelyn Vychan, 14 July 1241, and 1245, father of a dau. and heir,

Angharad, who is stated to have *m.* Griffith ap Jor-werth Voel.

3 Ellis ap Madoc, who received from his father Crogen (Chirk Castle) and adjoining lands, but despoiled of his territory and the castle of Crogen. had assigned to him seven townships. He was living in 1202, and is supposed to have *d. s. p.*

4 Owen Brogyntyn ap Madoc, Lord of Edeirnion, Dinmael, and Abertanat, in Powys Fadoc, one of the most distin-guished warriors of his age, took a conspicuous part in the most prominent incidents of a period peculiarly eventful in the anna's of the Cymry. Accepting (it is supposed in succession to his father, who resided at Oswestry and Caereinion, which he built.) the Shropshire fee of Porking-ton (the "Burtone" of Doomsday Book), near Oswestry, he was designated by the Welch "Owen Brogyntyn," and by the English, "Owen de Porkington," a fee which he must have held immediately under King HENRY II., then pala-tine earl of Shropshire by escheat. Before 1161 the sheriff of Shropshire, by the king's order, had paid to "Oen de Porchinton" the livery of £30 10*s.* 6*d.*, equivalent to £1,500 a-year modern currency. In 1162, "Oen de Por-chinton" received £27 7*s.* 6*d.*; in 1163, £27 7*s.* 6*d.*; in 1165, £5 13*s.* 4*d.*; in 1166, £56; and in 1169, forty *sol per breve regis* (Rot. Pipe, 15th HENRY II., Salop). Notwithstanding the close alliance implied by these grants, the Lord of Edeirnion must have wavered in steady attachment to the English monarch. The Welch chronicle, in reference to the league against King HENRY and the events of the summer of 1165, states that "the sonnes of Madoc ap Meredith and the power of Powys were against the king," and local tra-dition records that, entering with his brother, Griffith Maelor, into alliance with Owen Gwynedd, Prince of North Wales. and RHYS AP TUDOR, King of South Wales, to resist the renewed attempt of HENRY on Cambrian independence. Owen Brogyntyn, as one of the leaders of the allied forces, contributed essentially to the victory over the English monarch at the battle of Crogen, fought beneath *Castell Crogen,* the present Chirk Castle, where the battle-field is still called *Adwyr Beddel,* or the pass of the graves. This abandonment of HENRY by Owen Brogyntyn is confirmed by the total or partial suspension in 1164-5 of the payments previously made to him, but the subsequent charges on the Pipe Roll indicate his renewed adhesion to HENRY. "Owen de Brogyntyn" made a grant to Basingwerk Abbey of Bala Lake, witnessed by Rainer, bishop of St. Asaph, 1186-1224 (Sebright MSS., cited by Pennant). David ap Llewelyn, Prince of North Wales, by charter, dated 1240, on the day of St. James the Apostle. confirms to the monastery of Basingwerk all the donations of his father Llewelyn and other ancestors, "*item ex dmo Hoen de Porkentona in totum Wenhewa cum omnibus maneribus ejusdem villæ et cum pertinentiis*" (Dugdale's *Monast.,* new edit., vol. ii., p. 203). Owen Brogyntyn, whose arms were "the black lion of Powys," *m.* Marredd, dau. of Einion ap Seyssyllt, Lord of the Cantref of Merioneth, subsequently wife of Thomas, Lord of Rhiwllwyd ap Rhodri, Lord of Anglesey, ancestor by her of the house of Gwydyr. By this lady he had, with junior issue, three sons,

Griffith ap Owen Brogyntyn, Lord of Half Edeirnion, living 1200, and 6 January, 29th HENRY III., proge-nitor of the early Barons of Crogen and Branas in Edeirnion, Barons of Edeirnion, represented as heirs-general by the house of Gwerclas, and the Lords of Hendwr in Edeirnion, Barons of Edeirnion.

Bleddyn ap Owen Brogyntyn, Lord of Dinmael, living 25 May, 2nd HENRY III., the date of a writ tested at Wood-stock, whereby that monarch intimates to Llewelyn, Prince of Wales, that "*B edh filius Oeni de Porkington*" and others, "*venerunt ad fidem et servicium nostrum*" (Rhymer's "Fœdera," 1816. i., 151), ancestor of the Lords of Rug in Edeirnion, Barons of Edeirnion. represented as heir-general by Spencer Bulkeley Wynn. 2nd Lord New-borough, whose 2nd son, the Honourable Charles-Henry Wynn, *s.* to Rug, pursuant to the will of Sir Robert-Williames Vaughan, 3rd and last Baronet of Nanney (*see* BURKE's *Landed Gentry,* ed. 1864, Wynn of Rug), and the Maesmores of Maesmore, in Dinmael (*see* BURKE's *Landed Gentry,* ed. 1846, Supplement, Lloyd of Maesmore).

Jorwerth ap Owen Brogyntyn, Lord of Half Edeirnion, ancestor, by the Lady Efa, dau. and heir of Prince Madoc Goch, Lord of Mowddwy, younger son of Gwen-wynwyn, Prince of Powys Cyfeiliog. of the Hughes's of Gwerclas, Lords of Kymmer-yn-Edeirnion, represented as heir-general by John Hughes Lloyd, Esq., com-mander R.N., 2nd son but eventual heir of the late Richard Hughes Lloyd, Esq., of Plymog, Gwerclas, and Bashall; and as heir-male by the Rev. William O'Farrell Hughes, grandson and heir of the late William Hughes, Esq., of Pen-y-Clawdd (*see* BURKE's *La ded Gentry,* ed. 1846, and ed. 1863, Hughes of Gwerclas).

II. GRIFFITH AP MEREDITH, of whose line we treat.

The 2nd son of King MEREDITH AP BLEDDYN, viz.,

GRIFFITH AP MEREDITH, Lord of Mowddwy, submitted with his father to HENRY I., and was it stated, summoned by that monarch to his baronial parliaments. Griffith, who bore

" or, a lion's gamb., erased, in bend, gu.," took an active part in the feuds and warfare of the period, and *d. v. p.* in 1128, leaving, by Gwertyl his wife, dau. of Gwrgenas ap Howel, of Caer-a-Chydewin, an only child,

OWEN CYFEILIOG AP GRIFFITH, Prince of Powys Cyfeiliog, or Higher Powys, to which he *s.* on the demise of his grandfather, Meredith ap Bleddyn. In 1176 he attended the summons of HENRY to a conference with him at Oxford on Welch affairs. Owen Cyfeiliog, "Lord of Mathrafal, the poet and the prince" (Southey), was a distinguished bard, and among other produc-tions of his muse, which have been transmitted to us, is his Welch ode called "Hirlas," or the "Blue Long Horn." In the year 1170 this prince founded the Cistercian abbey of Ystrad-Marchell (Strata Marcella), and *d.* in 1197, leaving, by the Princess Gwenllian, his consort, dau. of Owen Gwynedd, Prince of North Wales, an only child,

GWENWYNWYN AP OWEN CYFEILIOG, Prince of Powys Cyfeiliog, from him called Powys Wenwynwyn. This prince, so finely pourtrayed in the "Betrothed" of Sir Walter Scott, recovered his castle from archbishop Hubert, who commanded the armies of RICHARD I. against the Welch. He next assisted Maelgwyn to surprise and imprison his brother Griffith, Lord of South Wales, and Griffith's person being delivered to Gwenwynwyn, he was given up to the English. Two years after, in 1198, ambitious of achieving the independence of his country, he raised a large army, and besieged William de Braose in his castle of Payn, in Radnor, but was defeated in a battle near the castle. By a grant dated 1199, the original of which, in perfect preservation, is now in the possession of Miss Conway Griffith, of Carreglwyd, Anglesey, "*Wenwnwen filius Oveni*" sold to the monks of Ystrad Marchell certain lands near the abbey. King JOHN of England granted 15 April, in the 1st year of his reign, to "Wenonwen," the manor of *Euseford-i-Derebinr.* By the same monarch a safe conduct was granted to "Wenonwen," 3 August, 6th JOHN (1206). In 1208 he was in arms with Llewelyn, Prince of North Wales, and with other great men of Wales, and the two princes drove King JOHN from the country. Gwenwynwyn adhered but two years to Llewelyn, deserted again to JOHN, and a convention between the English king and "*Wenon filius Hoeni de Keneloc*" being concluded at Shrews-bury, 10th JOHN (1210), Gwenwynwyn was pursued by Llewelyn and driven within the walls of Chester. In the 2nd of HENRY III. (1218) Gwenwynwyn appears to have been dead, his widow Margaret living, and his heirs under age. By Margaret his consort, dau. of Robert Corbet, feudal Baron of Caus, Gwen-wynwyn, who resumed the arms of his line, subsequently borne by his descendants, viz., "or, a lion rampant, gu.," had issue two children,

I. GRIFFITH AP GWENWYNWYN, of whom presently.

II. Madoc Goch ap Gwenwynwyn, Lord of Mowddwy and Caereinion, ordered 15 July, 1223, to be sent to Bridgenorth, and certified to have arrived there on the 19th following We find him designated "*Maddoc filius Wenunnuna,*" a baron of North Wales, 6 January, 29th HENRY III. (1245) "*Madant filius Wenwynwyn*" is party (with "*Dominus Llewelinus, filius Grifini principis Walliæ*" and others) to a treaty "*inter Magnates Scotiæ et Walliæ quod non fucient pacem cum Rege Angliæ sine mutuo consensu et assensu,*" 42nd HENRY III. (1258). This prince dying without male issue, his lordships of Mowddwy and Caereinion became the apanage of his nephew William, 4th son of Prince Griffith ap Wen wynwyn. Madoc Goch *m.* and was father of a dau. and heir,

The Lady Efa, who *m.* Jorwerth, Lord of Half Edeirnion, 3rd son of Owen Brogyntyn, Lord of Edeirnion, Dinmael, and Abertanat, and was mother by him of Griffith ap Jor werth, living 20 and 22 July, 12th EDWARD I. (1284), on the former of which days he received a royal pardon (Rot. Wal. 2nd EDWARD I., memb. 5), and on the latter a gran of confirmation to hold his land "*per baroniam*" (*ibid*); ancestor of the Hughes's of Gwerclas in Edeirnion. co Merioneth, lords of Kymmer-yn-Edeirnion and barons o, Edeirnion. The Lady Efa *m.* 2ndly, Owen ap Bleddyn. of the lineage of Tudor Trevor, Lord of Hereford, father by her of Jorwerth Gam ap Owen, ancestor of the distin-guished house of Mostyn of Mostyn, whose heir-general is the present Edward Lloyd Mostyn, 2nd Lord Mostyn.

Gwnwynwyn was *s.* by his elder son,

GRIFFITH AP GWENWYNWYN, Prince of Powys-Wenwynwyn. On 15 July, 1223, Ranulph, Earl of Chester, was ordered to see that the constable of Brug (Bridgenorth), Shropshire, do send the sons of Gwnwynwyn to Gloucester; and on the 19th, the king being then at Gloucester, the earl certifies their arrival. As the penalty of disaffection to Llewelyn, Prince of North Wales, Griffith's country was taken by that monarch; but, temporising, he joined Llewelyn, and, as a test of his sincerity, took and demolished the castle of Mold, then a frontier town. He must still have changed, for it is a matter of com-plaint on the part of Llewellyn, that EDWARD I. of England had received and protected his rebel subject, Griffith ap Gwnwynwyn. In 1274 "*Dominus Griffinus filius Wenwwin Powisiæ Dominus*" proceeded to England, leaving his son Owen with Llewelyn in free custody. Griffith *m*. Hawys, dau. of John le Strange, feudal Lord of Knockyn and Cheswardine, and by her, who had a royal grant of the manor of Strettondale, and the wardship of the lands *in capite* of her grandson, Griffin de la Pole, had six sons and one dau.,

  I. OWEN AP GRIFFITH, of whom presently.

  II. Llewelyn ap Griffith, living after the Epiphany, 1257, and also 18th EDWARD I., who *s*. to Mochnant Ucha and Mechain Uwch Coed. "Llewelyn, the son of Griffin, the son of Wenwnwin," granted to his brother Owen, all his right in the lands and tenements which had been their father's in Wales, with certain exceptions to himself; and " Owen, the son of Griffith, the son of Wenonwyn." granted to his brother Llewelyn the lands of "Motnant Hatrhaiadr" (Mochnant Llanrhaiadr). By a deed of *inspeximus* of 20 July, 3rd HENRY V., Edward Cherlton, Lord of Powys, confirmed a charter "which that nobleman Llewelyn, son of Griffith, son of Wenwinwin our kinsman (*consanguineanus*). made to his burgesses of Llanfyllin in these words: ' Know that I, Llewelyn, son of Griffith, Lord of Mechain-uscheaet and Mochnant-unrhaidd, have given, granted, and by this present charter confirmed, to my trustie and well-beloved burgesses of Llanfyllin, &c., &c.' " Llewelyn *m*. Margaret, dau. of Meredith Goch, Lord of Mochnant, grandson of Jorwerth. *alias* Gervase Goch, Lord of Mochnant-ys-Rhaiadr, and was by her father of a dau.,

    Efa, who *m*. Madoc ap David, Lord of Hendwr in Edeirnion. living 15th EDWARD II. (1321-2), and was by him mother of an eldest son David ap Madoc, Lord of Hendwr, living 2 November, 8th EDWARD III., who *d*. 20th RICHARD II., and a dau. Gwerfyl, mother, by her husband Grono ap Tudyr, of a son Sir Tudyr ap Grono, grandfather of Sir Owen Tudor, Knt., progenitor of the royal house of Tudor.

  III. John ap Griffith, who had the third part of Caereinion, released at Westminster, 16 June, —— to his brother Owen his right in their father's lands; and by an agreement acknowledged in the Chancery at Westminster, 17 May, 17th EDWARD I. (1289), his brother Owen granted to him five villa in Carregmaen. He *d. s. p.*

  IV. William ap Griffith, *alias* Wilcox, surnamed " De la Pole," Lord of Mowddwy, which was granted to him by his brother Owen. to be held of himself. This noble, who was living 17th EDWARD I., and dead 9th EDWARD II. (1315). *m*. the Lady Eleanor, junior co-heir of the monarchs of South Wales and Powys, 3rd dau. of Thomas ap Llewelyn, Lord of Yscoed, twenty-eight years of age and upwards, Sunday next after the Feast of St. Michael, 2 October, 2nd EDWARD III. (1328), and sister and co-heir of Owen ap Thomas, Lord of Half Yscoed, Monday next after the Feast of the Exaltation of the Holy Cross, 18th EDWARD III. (20 September, 1334). By .his lady he had,

    1 Griffith ap William, son and heir, 12th EDWARD II., and as "Griffin, son of William de la Pole," Lord of Mowddwy, appointed high sheriff of Merionethshire, 4th EDWARD III.

    2 John ap William, Lord of Mowddwy, under age at the death of his father, 12th EDWARD II., *m*. Catherine, only dau. and heir of Sir Foulk Corbet, Knt., of Watlesborough, and had with a son, Fowlk ap John, Lord of Mowddwy, who *d. s. p* , seized of the manor of Watlesborough, a dau., ELIZABETH, who as heiress of her brother, succeeded to Mowddwy. She *m*. Sir Hugh de Burgh, Knt., and with him had seizin of the manor of Watlesborough, 9th HENRY VI. (1438), and they held the fourth part of the Barony of Caus, co. Salop, viz., a moiety of the manor of Worthen, and the manors of Over Garthor and Banghaltre. Their son, SIR JOHN DE BURGH, Knt., son and heir, 9th HENRY VI., high sheriff for Shropshire in 1442, *d*. 9th EDWARD IV. He *m*. Johanna, dau. and heir of Sir William Clopton, Knt., of Clopton, co. Warwick, and Radbrooke, co. Gloucester; the latter of whom *d*. seized of Radbrooke, 7th HENRY IV. In 14th EDWARD IV., the manor of Watlesborough, with other extensive domains, was released and confirmed for life to this lady, as relict of Sir John Burgh, by Sir John Lingen, Knt., William Newton, John Leighton, Thomas Mytton, Esqrs., and others. By her Sir John de Burgh had four daus. and co-heirs,

      1 Angharad, Lady of Watlesborough and Cardeston, who *m*. John Leighton of Stretton, co. Salop, *jure uxoris* Lord of Watlesborough and Cardeston, and by him, who was thrice high sheriff of Shropshire, was mother of Sir Thomas Leighton, knight-banneret and knight of the body to HENRY VII., M.P. for Shropshire in the reigns of HENRY VII. and HENRY VIII., ancestor of Sir Baldwin Leighton of Watlesborough, 7th baronet.

      2 Isabel, dau. and co-heir. *m*. Sir John Lingen, Knt., of Lingen and Sutton, co. Hereford, high sheriff of Herefordshire, *temp*. EDWARD IV. and HENRY VII., and was by him mother of Sir John Lingen, Knt., from whom derived, 8th in descent, Robert Lingen, Esq., of Radbrooke, co. Gloucester, who assumed in 1748, by Act of Parliament, the surname and arms of BURTON, eldest son of Thomas Lingen, Esq , of Sutton Court, co. Hereford, by Anne his wife, sister and heir of Thomas Burton, Esq., of Longnor, &c., co. Salop.

3 Elizabeth (the elder), dau. and co-heir. *m*. William Newport, Esq., ancestor of the NEWPORTS, Earls of Bradford, extinct, whose heiress, Anne, dau. of Richard Newport, 2nd Earl of Bradford, *m*. Sir Orlando Bridgeman, Bart., from which alliance derive the BRIDGEMANS, Earls of Bradford.

4 Elizabeth (the younger), dau. and co-heir, Lady of Mowddwy, *m*. Thomas Mytton, Esq., *jure uxoris*, Lord of Mowddwy, M.P. for Shrewsbury in 1472, high sheriff for Shropshire in 1483, who *d*. in 1504, by whom she was mother of William Mytton, Esq., Lord of Mowddwy, M.P. for Shrewsbury in 149!, ancestor of the Myttons of Halston, co. Salop, Lords of Mowddwy, represented by John Fox Mytton, Esq., son and heir of the late John Mytton, Esq., of Halston, co. Salop, last hereditary Lord of Mowddwy, M.P. for Shrewsbury; —— Thornycroft, Esq., of Thornycroft, son of the Rev. Charles Mytton, rector of Eccleston, co. Chester, who assumed the name of Thornycroft, derived from Charles Mytton, Esq. of Chester, 4th son of Richard Mytton, Esq., of Halston, Lord of Mowddwy, and M.P. for Shrewsbury; the Myttons of Garth and Pontyscowryd, co. Montgomery, represented by Richard Herbert Mytton, Esq., of Garth and Pontyscowrdy; of Sir Peter Mytton, of Llannerch Park, co. Denbigh, whose dau. and co-heir Anne *m*. Robert Davies, Esq , of Gwyssney, co. Flint, ancestor by her of the Davies's of Gwysaney, represented (1865) as heirs-general, by the COOKES of Owston and Gwystaney, and as heir male by Owen Davies. Esq., son of the late Thomas Davies, Esq., of Trefynant, co. Denbigh.

  V. Griffith Vychan ap Griffith, who had Ddeuddwr, Merchel, and the tower tref or the towns on the border. An agreement was made at Westminster, 17 May, 17th EDWARD I., between " Owen, son of Griffith ap Wenowin and Griffith. his brother," granting to Griffith the land of Mechain Yscoed, with the appurtenances; by commission and writ, tested at Westminster, 18 June, 3rd EDWARD II. (1310), Griffin de la Pole and John de Cheriton were requested to allow 400 soldiers to be raised " *de terra sua de Powys;*" and by a writ tested at Westminster, 16 October, 7th EDWARD II., Griffith de la Pole obtains a pardon as an adherent of the Earl of Lancaster for his participation in the death of Gaveston, and the disturbance occasioned thereby. Griffith Vychan *d. s. p*.

  VI. David ap Griffith succeeded to the fourth part of Caereinion; and by deed, dated at Westminster, 16 May, 17th EDWARD I., "David, the son of Griffin, the son of Wenonwin," released to his eldest brother, Owen, all his right to his lands, as well in England as in Wales, for which Owen gave all the land of Mawddoc. David ap Griffith *d. s. p*.

  I. Margaret, Verch Griffith ap Gwenwynwyn, *m*. Foulk Fitzwarine, summoned to parliament as a BARON 23 June, 1295, and from that period to 12 October, 1314, and by him, who with her acquired the territory of Ballesley, was mother of Foulk Fitzwarine, 2nd baron, summoned to parliament from 6 October, 1315, to 22 January, 1336.

Griffith ap Gwenwynwyn was *s*. by his eldest son,

  OWEN AP GRIFFITH, Prince of Powys-Wenwynwyn, designated "Lord de la Pole," Welchpool, Montgomeryshire, seated at Powys Castle. who succeeded to the comots of Cyfeiliog, Arwstli, Llannerchydol, and the half of Caereinion. On him David, brother of Llewelyn ap Griffith, Prince of North Wales, conferred (*concessit*) his eldest dau., "*in sponsor*." He was with his father living Sunday next " *post clausum parchæ,*" 4th EDWARD I., and his inquisition *post mortem* as "Owen de la Pole," was taken 21st EDWARD I, (1292-3). It is stated that, summoned to a parliament held at Shrewsbury, Owen acknowledged his lands to be held under the crown of England *in capite*, under the tenure of free baronage, and resigned to the English monarch and his heirs the sovereignty of Powys-Wenwynwyn. This prince *m*. Johanna, only surviving child (by Katherine, dau. of Lord Strange of Knokyn) of Sir Robert Corbet, Knt., of Moreton Corbet, co. Salop, and sister of Thomas Corbet, who *d. s. p*. before his father; the Corbet estates passing to the issue of Sir Robert, by his 2nd marriage. By this lady, to whom, with other manors, that of Cyfeiliog was assigned for her dower, Owen ap Griffith had issue a son and a dau., viz.,

  GRIFFITH AP OWEN, surnamed "De la Pole," only son and heir, who *d. unm*., 2nd EDWARD II. (1309), and was *s*. by his sister and heir,

  HAWYS GADARN (the Hardy), said to have been *b*. in 1291, æt. nineteen years 4th EDWARD II.,and living 9th EDWARD II. (1315), *m*. by the gift of King EDWARD II, JOHN DE CHERLTON, *b*., it is stated, in 1268 (younger son of Sir John de Cherlton, Knt., of Appley Castle, co. Salop), who obtained, 1st EDWARD II., a charter of free warren in all his demesne lands at Cheriton and Pontisbury, co. Salop; and the next year had a confirmation of the manor of Pontisbury, sometime belonging to Rhys ap Howel. In right of Hawys, John de Cheriton acquired the feudal Barony of Pole, held *in capite* of the Crown. The uncles of Hawys, with the exception of William ap Griffith, preferred a claim to her possessions, contending that she as a

CHE

female, could not inherit her father's lands. They besieged
Powys Castle, occupied at the time by her and her husband,
whereupon the king directed his precept to Roger de Mortimer, then Justice of Wales, to march thither for their relief and
protection. Again, however, they were disturbed by the
uncles, including Griffith Vychan, who had summons to appear
before the king to answer for his proceedings; and to render
Hawys and John de Cherlton more secure in their title, they
had a royal charter, 7th EDWARD II., confirmatory of all their
lands and castles in North Wales, South Wales, and Powys.
In the same year, 26 July. 1313, John de Cherlton was summoned to parliament as Baron Cherlton de Powys, and from
that period to 25 July, 1353. By writ, tested at York, 4 and 8
June, 12th EDWARD II. (1319) John de Cherlton was requested
to raise 500 foot soldiers "*de terris suis de Powys.*" His lordship was subsequently engaged in the wars of France. His
armorial bearing was, "or, a lion rampant, gu.," the arms of
the Prince of Powys, presumed to have been adopted consequent on his marriage. By Hawys Gadarn his wife (who *d.*
before her husband, and was buried in the house of the Grey
Friars at Shrewsbury, which she had founded), Lord Cherlton
left, at his decease in 1353,

JOHN DE CHERLTON, 2nd baron, summoned to parliament
from 15 March, 1354, to 20 November, 1360, as BARON CHERL-
TON, and from 14 August, 1362, to 4 October, 1373, as Lord
Cherlton, of Powys. This nobleman being Lord Chamberlain to the king, was in the wars of Gascony, in attendance
upon the BLACK PRINCE. His lordship *m.* Joan, dau. of Ralph,
1st Earl of Stafford, K.G., and dying in 1374, was *s.* by his son,

JOHN DE CHERLTON, 3rd baron, summoned to parliament as
"*Johanni de Cherlton de Powys,*" from 9 August, 1382, to
3 October, 1400. His lordship *m.* Maud, dau. of Roger de
Mortimer, Earl of March; but *d. s. p. anno* 1400, and was *s.* by
his brother,

EDWARD DE CHERLTON, 4th baron, summoned to parliament
from 2 December, 1401, to 26 February, 1421. In the 9th of
HENRY IV. this nobleman sustained great loss by the insurrection of the Welsh under Owen Glendower. In the next
reign he had the thanks of parliament for his activity in
apprehending the unfortunate Sir John Oldcastle, Lord Cobham,
within the territory of Powys. His lordship *m.* Alianore, dau.
of Thomas Holland, and sister and co-heir of Edmund Holland,
both Earls of Kent, and widow of Roger Mortimer, Earl of
March, by whom he had issue,

1. Joane, *m.* to Sir John Grey, K.G., Earl of Tankerville, in
Normandy, whose grandson, John Grey, was summoned to
parliament as "*Johanni Grey de Powys,*" 15 November,
1482 (*see* that dignity).
11. Joyce, *m.* to Sir John de Tiptoft, who was summoned to
parliament, from 7 January, 1426, to 3 December, 1441. Dugdale says he bore the title of Lord Tiptoft and Powys, but
he was never summoned by any other designation than
"*Johanni Tiptoft, Chl'r*") and had issue,

i JOHN, created EARL OF WORCESTER, 1449, but attainted
and beheaded in 1470, when his honours EXPIRED, but
his son,
EDWARD DE TIPTOFT, was restored in blood, as EARL OF
WORCESTER, dying, however, *s. p* in 1485, his aunts
became his co-heiresses to the BARONY OF TIPTOFT, and
to his estates, while the EARLDOM EXPIRED.
1 Philippa, *m.* to Thomas, Lord de Ros.
2 Johanna, *m.* to Sir Edmund Inglethorpe.
3 Joyce, *m.* to Edmund Sutton, son and heir of John, Lord
Dudley.

His lordship *d.* 1422, when the BARONY OF CHERLTON OF POWYS
fell into ABEYANCE, between his daughters, and his estates
devolved upon them as co-heirs. The lordship of Powys coming
to the eldest dau. Joane. that lady's grandson, John Grey,
had summons to parliament, in 1482, as LORD GREY, OF POWYS,
but Sir Harris Nicolas, in his "Synopsis," considers *that* summons a new creation, and not a revival of the original dignity,
and he is borne out in the opinion, he says, by a careful
examination of the parliamentary rolls, wherein he finds
the old lords denominated in almost all instances, LORDS
CHERLTON, and he thence argues, that if it were meant to
revive the suspended barony in the great-grandson of Edward,
4th and last Lord Cherlton, that personage would have been
summoned as BARON CHERLTON, of Powys, and not as Lord
Grey—a course which appears indisputable. The BARONY OF
CHERLTON must therefore be deemed still in ABEYANCE.

Arms.—Or, a lion rampant, gu.

NOTE.—A younger branch of this family, was
ALAN DE CHERLTON, brother of the 1st baron, who in the 11th
EDWARD II. had a charter for free warren in all his demesne
lands at Appley, and other places in the co. of Salop, and was
constituted in three years afterwards, governor of Montgomery

116

Castle; *m.* Ellen, widow of Nicholas de St. Maur, and one of
the daus. and co-heirs of Lord Zouch—from which union
descended the family of Charlton, of Apley Castle, co.
Salop.

CHEVERS—VISCOUNT MOUNT-LEINSTER.

By Patent dated 23 August, 1689.

Lineage.

The Anglo-Norman of Cheevers claimed descent from the
Lords of Chievres, a town of the Netherlands, in the county of
Hainault.

SIR WILLIAM CHEVRE, one of the knights who accompanied
Strongbow in the invasion of Ireland, received a knight's fee
of land in the co. of Wexford. He is one of the witnesses to
the foundation charter to Tinterne Abbey in that county.

PATRICK CHEVERS held one knight's fee in Ballyhaly, co.
Wexford, of the Earl of Pembroke, in 1307, and is witness to
that nobleman's charter to the town of Wexford, dated 1317.

JOHN CHEVERS, Esq., of Ballyhaly, grand seneschal of the co.
in 1416, was father of

WILLIAM CHEVERS, Esq., who held four manors, and was
appointed second justice of the Court of Common Pleas,
24 March, 13th HENRY VI. He had a son,

WALTER CHEVERS, Esq., of Ballyhaly, co. Wexford, and Mace-
town, co. Meath, a commissioner in the latter co., 3rd EDWARD
IV., *m.* Ellen, dau. of Sir William Wells, Lord Chancellor of
Ireland, and had with a dau., Margaret, wife of Bartholomew
Aylmer, of Lyons, a son and successor,

SIR NICHOLAS CHEVERS, Knt., of Ballyhaly and of Macetown,
who *m.* Alison, dau. of Robert Fitzsimons, Esq., and by her
(who *m.* 2ndly Sir Nicholas St. Lawrence, Baron of Howth), he
left with a dau., Joan, wife of William Hore, of Harperstown,
co. Wexford, a son and successor,

SIR WALTER CHEVERS, of Macetown, Knt., who *m.* Elena,
dau. of Nicholas, Lord Howth. and had with two younger sons,
John and Thomas, an eldest son,

SIR CHRISTOPHER CHEVERS, Knt., of Ballyhaly, and of Bally-
cullen, co. Wexford, who acquired also the lordship of Tartaya,
co. Meath. He was knighted in 1566, and appointed one of the
commissioners for muster, in that county, in 1579. He *m.* Maud,
dau. of Walter Kelly, alderman of Dublin, and had John, Patrick,
Nicholas, and Walter Thomas, and three daus., the eldest *m.*
to — Golding; the 2nd, Margaret, to Robert Kent; and the
3rd, Katherine, to Patrick Talbot, father of Richard Talbot,
Esq., of Malahide. He *m.* 2ndly, Anne Plunkett (her will is
dated 1583), by whom he had four daus., Elenor, Ellis, Jenet,
and Margaret. Sir Christopher Chevers, *d.* 20 March, 1581
(his will bears date 18 March, 1550, and was proved in 1581),
and was *s.* by his eldest son,

JOHN CHEVERS, Esq., of Macetown, *b.* in 1540; who *d.*
30 April, 1599, leaving by Catherine his wife, dau. and co-heiress
of Henry Travers, Esq., of Monkstown Castle, co. Dublin, issue,

I. CHRISTOPHER, his heir.
II. Henry, of Monkstown, who *m.* Catherine, dau. of Sir
Richard Fitzwilliam, Knt., of Merryon; and *d.* 7 July, 1640,
having had issue,
1 Walter Chevers, Esq., of Monkstown Castle, *d.* 20 December, 1678, leaving by Alison his wife, 3rd dau. of Nicholas,
1st Viscount Netterville,
MARY, eventual heiress, who *m.* in 1678, John Byrne, Esq.
of Cabinteely.
2 Thomas. 3 Patrick, *d. unm.*
1 Margaret, *d. unm.*
III. Richard.
I. Jennet. II. Frances.
III. Eleanor, *m.* to Thomas Luttrell, Esq., of Luttrellstoun, *d.*
1610.

The elder son,

CHRISTOPHER CHEVERS, Esq., of Macetown, *b.* 1580, had a
grant of the manor and castle of Rathmore, co. Kildare, and
of the manor, mansion-house, and castle of Grangeforth, co.
Carlow, 10 October, 9th JAMES I. He *m.* 1st, Elinor, 4th dau.
of Sir Christopher Nugent, 4th Lord Delvin, and by her (who
d. 31 August, 1636) had issue,

I. JOHN, of whom presently.
II. Christopher.
III. Garrett, *m.* Katherine, dau. of Hamon Chevers, Esq. of
Killain, co. Wexford.
IV. Richard. V. Anthony. VI Peter.
I. Mary, *m.* to Edmond Dalton, of co. Armagh, Gent
II. Bridget. III. Anne, *d.* young.

Christopher Chevers *m.* 2ndly, Jane dau. of Jerome Bath,

gent, of Edickstown, co. Meath, and *d.* 7 November, 1640, having had three sons, viz.,

   ı. William.   ıı. JEROME, of whom presently.
   ııı. Francis.

The eldest son,

JOHN CHEVERS, Esq., of Macetown, Ballyhaly, &c., transplanted to Connaught by Cromwell, who *m.* 1st, Mary, dau. of Sir Henry Bealing; and 2ndly, Joan, dau. of Edward Sutton, Esq. He *d. circa* 1688, leaving issue,

   ı. EDWARD, of whom we treat.
   ıı. Andrew, of Cregan, co. Galway.
   ııı. John, of Külyan, *m.* Ellis, dau. of Edward Geoghegan, Esq., and had issue,

      1 MICHAEL, *m.* Margaret O'Flyn, of Turlough, co. Galway and was great-grandfather of the present MICHAEL-JOSEPH CHEVERS, Esq., of Killyan House, co. Galway. (*See* BURKE's *Landed Gentry*).
      2 Edward, of Leckafin, *m.* Bridget Telberton, and had issue, William, Captain of Regiment of Hibernia. Spain, who *d. s. p.* 1778; Margaret, *m* 1759 to James O'Neill, Esq., of Crakenstown and Rathcarron; and Ellis, *m.* to John, son of Philip O'Reilly, Esq., of Balli-Kilcriest, now Anneville, co. Longford, and had several sons, and three daus.
      3 Christopher.
      4 Matthias, Knt. of St. Jago, Governor of Fuentarabia, *d. s. p.* October, 1771.
      5 Augustin, R.C. Bishop of Meath, *b.* 1666, *d.* 18 Aug , 1778.
      6 Hyacinth.
      1 Margaret, *m.* to Richard Burke, Esq., of Glynsk.
      2 A dau. *m.* to Hugh O'Connor, Esq., in Spain, and had issue.

The eldest son,

EDWARD CHEEVERS, Esq., of Macetown, *m.* Anne, sister of the gallant Patrick Sarsfield, Earl of Lucan, and was created by JAMES II., by patent, dated 23 August, 1689, VISCOUNT MOUNT LEINSTER, co. Carlow, and Baron Bannow, co. Wexford. The creations of JAMES subsequent to his abdication, were not acknowledged by his successors; but as Dr. Burke observes in his *Hibernia Dominicana*, this title was more honourably extinguished by failure of male issue. Lord Mount Leinster joined his connexions in their strenuous support of JAMES II., entered the Irish army, and acted as aide-de-camp to that unfortunate monarch at the battle of the Boyne. Although specially included in the articles of Limerick, Lord Mount Leinster relinquished the benefits of the capitulation, and accompanied his sovereign into exile. The title became EXTINCT on his decease.* His uncle, of the half blood,

JEROME CHEEVERS, *m.* and had two sons, Christopher and Francis. Like the decayed gentlemen of those days, he resided amongst his more fortunate friends, some of whom resided at Drogheda, where his situation and misfortunes attracted the attention of Chief Justice Singleton, the friend and companion of Swift. Christopher Cheevers, the eldest son, *d. unm.*, but FRANCIS CHEEVERS the younger, *m.* Jane Cosgrave, and had a son, William, who was killed in the revolutionary war of America; and five daus., the eldest of whom *m.* Colombo Brodigan, of Drogheda, and had a son, Francis Brodigan, of Drogheda, who *d.* 29 April, 1831, and was interred in the family burial place in the churchyard of Coppe. His eldest son is the present THOMAS BRODIGAN, Esq., of Piltown, near Drogheda.

Arms—AZ., three goats rampant, arg.

CHEYNE—VISCOUNT OF NEWHAVEN.

By Letters Patent, dated 17 May, 1681.

Lineage.

THOMAS CHEYNE, of Chesham Boys, Bucks (brother of Sir John Cheyne, Knt., of Cogenho, who *d.* in 1468, æt. one hundred), *m.* Eleanor, dau. and heir of Sir John Chesham, and was *s.* by his grandson (the son of his son John, by Perinda, dau. of Sir Robert Whitney),

JOHN CHEYNE, Esq., of Chesham Boys, heir also to his granduncle, Sir John, of Cogenho: he *m.* Elizabeth, dau. of Sir Edmund Brudenell, of Rains, and *d.* in 1496, leaving a son, JOHN CHEYNE, Esq., of Cogenho, who *m.* Margaret, dau. of Robert Ingylton, of Thornton, and *d.* 1 July, 1535. His son and heir, ROBERT CHEYNE, Esq., of Cogenho, was father, by Elizabeth his wife, dau. of John Webb, of JOHN CHEYNE, Esq., of

* BARBARA CHEVERS, a co-heiress, descended from the family of Cheevers, Lord Mount Leinster, *m.* Lawrence-Coyne Nugent, Esq., and had an only dau. and heir, MARIA, *m.* to Sir Joshua-Colles Meredyth, Bart.

Cogenho and Chesham Boys, who *m.* 1st, Winifred, dau. of John, Lord Mordaunt, and by her (who *d.* 1562) had a dau., Temperance; he *m.* 2ndly, Joyce, dau. of Sir Anthony Lee, and by her had JOHN and Francis (Sir), who *d. s. p.* 1619. John Cheyne *d.* 1585, his elder son (whom he disinherited), JOHN CHEYNE, Esq., *m.* Mary, dau. of Sir Thomas Skipwith, of St. Albans, and *d.* 1587, leaving a son, FRANCIS CHEYNE, Esq., who *s.* his uncle, Sir Francis, and was of Cogenho. By Ann his wife, dau. of Sir William Fleetwood, he left at his decease in 1644, a son,

CHARLES CHEYNE, of Cogenho, who purchased from William and Anne, Duke and Duchess of Hamilton, the estate of Chelsea, co. Middlesex, in 1657, and the manor thereof in 1660. He was chosen member of parliament for Amersham in that year, and created a peer of Scotland, by the titles of VISCOUNT OF NEWHAVEN, co. Edinburgh, and LORD CHEYNE, by patent, dated 17 May, 1681, to him and the heirs-male of his body. He *d.* 13 July, 1698, in the seventy-fourth year of his age, and was buried at Chelsea. He *m.* 1st, Lady Jane Cavendish, dau. and co-heir of William, Duke of Newcastle; and 2ndly, Isabella, Dowager Countess of Radnor. By the former (who *d.* 1 November, 1669, and was buried under a stately monument in Chelsea Church,) he had issue,

WILLIAM, his heir.
Elizabeth, *bapt.* at Chelsea, 18 May, 1656; *m.* to Sir Henry Monson, Bart., of South Carlton, in Lincolnshire, M.P. for the city of Lincoln. He *d. s. p.* 6 April, 1718, and his relict was buried at South Carlton, 29 April, 1725, aged sixty-nine.
Catherine, who dying *unm.*, was buried at Chelsea, 25 March, 1670.

His only son was

WILLIAM CHEYNE, 2nd Viscount of Newhaven, *bapt.* at Chelsea, 14 July, 1657, M.P. for Buckinghamshire, of which co. he was appointed lord-lieutenant in 1712; but removed from that office on the accession of GEORGE I., 1714. He *m.* at Chelsea, 16 December, 1675, the ceremony being performed by the bishop of Winchester, Elizabeth Thomas, grand-dau. of Lady Morgan; and 2ndly (his 1st wife *d.* in 1687), Gertrude, sister of Evelyn Pierrepont, Duke of Kingston; but *d. s. p.* 14 Dec., 1738, when the honours became EXTINCT. The manor of Chelsea, in which parish several localities still retain the name of Cheyne, was sold by the 2nd Lord Newhaven to Sir Hans Sloane in 1712.

Arms—Chequy, or and az., a fesse, gu., fretted, arg.

CHICHESTER—BARON CHICHESTER, OF BELFAST.

By Letters Patent, dated 23 February, 1612.

Lineage.

The celebrated
SIR ARTHUR CHICHESTER, Knt., so distinguished for his services in Ireland, of which he was lord-deputy during the reign of JAMES I., was elevated to the peerage by that monarch, 23 February, 1612, by the title of BARON CHICHESTER, *of Belfast*. He *m.* Letitia, dau. of Sir John Perrott, and widow of Vaughan Blackham, Esq.; but *d. s. p.* 19 February, 1624, when the barony EXPIRED; but the great estates which his lordship had acquired devolved upon his brother, SIR EDWARD CHICHESTER, afterwards Viscount Chichester, ancestor of the MARQUESSES OF DONEGAL. (*See* BURKE's *Peerage*.)

Arms—Chequy, or and gu., a chief., vair.

CHILD—VISCOUNTS CASTLEMAINE AND EARLS TYLNEY.

Viscounty, by Letters Patent, dated 24 April, 1718.
Earldom, by Letters Patent, dated 11 January, 1731.

Lineage.

SIR JOSIAH CHILD (2nd son of Richard Child, Esq., of London, by Elizabeth his wife, dau. of — Roycroft, Esq., of Weston's Wick, co. Salop, and descended from the ancient family of Childs, for many ages seated at Northwick, Poole-Court, Shrowley, and Pencock, co. Worcester), an eminent London merchant, and sometime governor of the East India Company, was created a BARONET, 18 July, 1678. He *m.* 1st, Anne, dau. of Edward Boat, Esq., of Portsmouth, by whom he had a dau. Elizabeth, wife of John Howland, Esq., and mother of Elizabeth, Duchess of Bedford. Sir Josiah *m.* 2ndly, Mary, dau. of William Atwood, Esq., of Hackney, and widow of Thomas Stone, of London, merchant, by whom he had, with two daus. (Rebecca, *m.* 1st, to Charles Somerset, Lord Herbert, eldest son of the Marquess of Worcester, and 2ndly, to John, Lord Granville; and Mary, *m.* 1st, to Edward Bullock, Esq., of Faulkbourn Hall, Essex, and 2ndly, to — Hutchinson, Esq.) a son and successor, JOSIAH. Sir Josiah *m.* 3rdly, Emma, youngest dau. and co-heir of Sir Henry Bernard, Knt., of Stoke, Salop, and relict of Sir Thomas Willoughby, of Wollaton, co. Notts, and had by her, two sons, Bernard, who *d. unm.* in June, 1698, and RICHARD. He *d.* 22 June, 1699, and was *s.* by his son,

SIR JOSIAH CHILD, Bart., M.P. for Wareham, who *m.* Elizabeth, eldest dau. of Sir Thomas Cooke, Knt., of the city of London; but *d. s. p.* 20 January, 1703-4, when the baronetcy passed to his half-brother,

SIR RICHARD CHILD, Bart., of Wanstead, M.P. for Essex, who was created, 24 April, 1718, Baron of Newtown, co. Donegal, and VISCOUNT CASTLEMAINE, in the co. Kerry, and 11 January, 1731, EARL TYLNEY, *of Castlemaine,* all in the peerage of Ireland. His lordship *m.* Dorothy, only surviving dau. and heir of John Glynne, Esq., of Henley Park, Surrey, by Dorothy his wife, dau. of Francis Tylney, Esq., of Rotherwick, and by her (who *d.* 23 February, 1743) had issue,

   I. Richard, *d.* 19 Feb., 1783-4.
   II. JOHN, his heir.
   III. Josiah, lieut. of dragoons.
   I. EMMA, eventual heiress; who *m.* 29 May, 1735, Sir Robert Long, Bart., M.P. of Draycot, Wilts, and conveyed Wanstead, and the other extensive estates of the Child family, to the Longs; she *d.* 8 March, 1758, leaving issue, with others, a son and heir,

     SIR JAMES LONG, Bart., of Draycot, who assumed the additional surname of TYLNEY, and was M.P. for Wilts. By Catherine his wife, dau. of Other Windsor, 4th Earl of Plymouth, he left at his decease, 28 November, 1794, one son and three daus., viz.,

      SIR JAMES TYLNEY LONG, Bart., of Draycot, *d.* 14 September, 1805, being the last known male descendant of the Longs of Wraxall and Draycot.
      CATHERINE LONG, of Draycot, *b.* 1789, *m.* 14 March, 1812, WILLIAM POLE-TYLNEY-LONG-WELLESLEY, 4th Earl of Mornington, who on his marriage assumed the additional surnames of TYLNEY and LONG. She *d.* 12 September, 1825, and had issue, William-Arthur, 5th Earl of Mornington; James-FitzRoy-Henry-William, *d.* 1851; and Victoria-Catherine-Mary. (See BURKE's *Peerage.*)
      Dorothy, *unm.*
      Emma, *unm.*

By Act of parliament, passed 24 March, 1734, his lordship's eldest son and his heirs assumed the surname of Tylney, on account of the large estates which devolved on his wife, Lady Tylney, as heiress of Anne, Lady Craven, dau. of Frederick Tylney, Esq., of Rotherwick. Lord Tylney *d.* in 1749, and was *s.* by his eldest surviving son,

JOHN CHILD, 2nd earl; at whose decease *s. p.*, 17 September, 1784, all the honours became EXTINCT.

Arms—Gu., a chev., engr., erm, between three eagles, close, arg

---

CHOLMONDELEY—VISCOUNT CHOLMONDELEY, EARL OF LEINSTER, IN THE PEERAGE OF IRELAND, BARON CHOLMONDELEY, IN THE PEERAGE OF ENGLAND.

Viscounty, by Letters Patent, dated 2 July, 1628.
Earldom, by Letters Patent, dated 5 March, 1645-6.
Barony, by Letters Patent, dated 1 September, 1645.

Lineage.

SIR HUGH CHOLMONDELEY, Knt., of Cholmondeley (eldest son of Sir Hugh Cholmondeley, and his wife Anne, dau. and co-heiress of George Dorman, Esq., of Malpas), *m.* Mary, only dau. and heiress of Christopher Holford, Esq., of Holford, and had issue,

ROBERT, of whom presently.
Hugh, *m.* Mary, dau. of Sir John Bodville, of Bodville Castle, co. Carnarvon, and dying in 1655, left
   ROBERT, who inherited the estates of his uncle, and was the founder of the present noble house of Cholmondeley.

Thomas, of Vale Royal, from whom the present Lord Delamere descends.

Sir Hugh *d.* in the 43rd of ELIZABETH, and his lady (designated by King JAMES I. "the bold lady of Cheshire," in consequence of the spirit she displayed in carrying on a law suit with George Holford, Esq., of Newborough, for more than forty years, which finally terminated by compromise,) *d.* 15 August, 1626. Sir Hugh was *s.* by his eldest son,

ROBERT CHOLMONDELEY, Esq., who was created a baronet on 29 June, 1611, and advanced to the peerage of Ireland, 2 July, 1628, as *Viscount Cholmondeley, of Kells,* co. Meath. His lordship afterwards, "in consideration of his special service in raising several companies of foot in Cheshire, in order to the quenching of those rebellious flames which began to appear *anno* 1642, and sending many other to the king (CHARLES I.) then at Shrewsbury (which stood him in high stead in that memorable battle of Kineton, happening soon after), as also raising other forces for defending the city of Chester, at the first siege thereof by his majesty's adversaries in that county, and courageous adventure in the fight of Tilton Heath, together with his great sufferings, by the plunder of his goods and firing his house," was created a peer of England, by letters patent, dated 1 September, 1645, in the dignity of BARON CHOLMONDELEY, *of Wiche Malbank,* otherwise Nantwich, co. Chester, and advanced 5 March, 1645-6, to the Irish EARLDOM OF LEINSTER. Subsequently, under the rule of the parliament, his lordship was obliged to compound for his estates, and paid the large fine of £7,742. He *m.* Catherine, dau. of John, Lord Stanhope of Harrington, but *d. s. p.* 2 October, 1659, when his large possessions devolved upon his nephew, Robert Cholmondeley (son of his brother Hugh), immediate ancestor of the existing noble house of Cholmondeley—and his lordship's honours, namely, the Irish BARONY *or* CHOLMONDELEY of Kells, and the EARLDOM OF LEINSTER, with the English BARONY OF CHOLMONDELEY *of Nantwich,* became EXTINCT.

Arms—Gu., two helmets in chief, ppr., garnished, or, in base a garb of the last.

CHURCHILL—BARON CHURCHILL.

By Letters Patent, dated 14 May, 1685.

JOHN CHURCHILL, subsequently the great Duke of Marlborough, was created a peer of Scotland 14 May, 1685, as BARON CHURCHILL, *of Eyemouth, Berwick;* but his grace *d.* without male issue, 16 June, 1722, when the title became EXTINCT. (See BURKE's *Peerage,* MARLBOROUGH.)

Arms—Sa., a lion rampant, arg., on a canton of the last, a cross, gu.

CLARE — LORDS OF CLARE, EARLS OF HERTFORD, EARLS OF GLOUCESTER.

The feudal Lordship of Clare, from the Conquest.
The Earldom of Hertford, *temp.* King STEPHEN.
The Earldom of Gloucester, by marriage with the heiress of Gloucester.

Lineage.

GEOFFREY, natural son of RICHARD I., Duke of Normandy, had a son,

GISLEBERT, surnamed Crispin, *Earl of Brion,* in Normandy, whose eldest son,

RICHARD FITZGILBERT, having accompanied the CONQUEROR into England, participated in the spoils of conquest, and obtained extensive possessions in the new and old dominions of his royal leader and kinsman. In 1073 (6th WILLIAM THE CONQUEROR,) we find him joined under the designation of *Ricardus de Benefacta,* with William de Warren, in the great office of Justiciary of England; with whom, in three years afterwards, he was in arms, against the rebellious lords, Robert de Britolio, Earl of Hereford, and Ralph Waher, or Guader, Earl of Norfolk and Suffolk, and behaved with great gallantry. But afterwards, at the time of the General Survey, which was towards the close of WILLIAM's reign, he is called *Ricardus de Tonebruge,* from his seat at Tonebruge (now Tunbridge), in Kent, which town and castle he obtained from the archbishop of Canterbury, in lieu of the castle of Brion; at which time he enjoyed thirty-eight lordships in Surrey, thirty-five in Essex, three in Cambridgeshire, with some others in Wilts and Devon, and ninety-five in Suffolk, amongst those was CLARE, whence he was occasionally styled RICHARD DE CLARE; and that place in a few years afterwards becoming the chief seat of the family, his descendants are said to have assumed thereupon the title of EARLS OF CLARE. This great feudal lord *m.* Rohese, dau. of Walter Giffard, Earl of Buckingham, and had issue,

  I. GILBERT, his successor.
  II. Roger, an eminent soldier in the reign of HENRY I., *d. s. p.,* when his estates devolved upon his elder brother's son, Gilbert.
  III. Walter, who having license from the king to enjoy all he could conquer in Wales, possessed all NETHER-WENT; he also *d. s. p.*
  IV. Richard, a monk of Bec, in Normandy, and last abbot of Ely.
  V. Robert, steward to King HENRY I., *m.* Maud, dau. of *Simon St. Liz,* EARL OF HUNTINGDON, and had Walter Fitz-Robert, whose son, Robert Fitz-Walter, was one of the most distinguished of the barons who rebelled against JOHN, and was styled, Marshal of the Army of God and Holy Church.
  I. A dau. *m.* to Ralph de Telgers.
  II. A dau. *m.* to Eudo Dapifer.

Richard de Tonebruge, or de Clare, who is said to have fallen in a skirmish with the Welsh, was *s.* by his eldest son,
  GILBERT DE TONEBRUGE, who resided at Tonebruge, and inherited all his father's lands in England. This nobleman joined in the rebellion of Robert de Moubray, Earl of Northumberland, but observing the King (William RUFUS) upon the point of falling into an ambuscade, he relented, besought pardon, and saved his royal master. We find him subsequently, however, again in rebellion, in the same reign, and fortifying and losing his castle at Tunbridge. He *m.* in 1113, Adeliza, dau. of the Earl of Cleremont, and had issue,
  RICHARD, his successor.
  Gilbert, created EARL OF PEMBROKE, *anno* 1138 (*see* that dignity.) This nobleman was father of RICHARD, surnamed Strongbow, so celebrated for his conquest of Ireland.
  Walter, founder of the abbey of Tintern, in Wales, *d. s. p.*
  Hervey, famous in the conquest of Ireland, by the name of Hervey de Monte Mariscoe, but *d.* a monk at Canterbury.
  Baldwin, who left three sons, William, Robert, and Richard, and a dau. Margaret, *m.* to Montfichet.

Gilbert de Tonebruge, who was a munificent benefactor to the church, was *s.* by his eldest son,
  RICHARD DE CLARE, who first bore the title of EARL OF HERTFORD, and being one of those, who by power of the sword entered Wales, there planted himself and became lord of vast territories, as also of divers castles in those parts, but requiring other matters of moment from the king, in which he was unsuccessful, he reared the standard of revolt, and soon after fell in an engagement with the Welsh. His lordship in 1124 removed the monks out of his castle at Clare into the church of St. Augustine, at Stoke, and bestowed upon them a little wood, called Stoke-Ho, with a doe every year out of his park at Hunedene. He *m.* Alice, sister of Ranulph, 2nd Earl of Chester, and had issue, GILBERT, his successor, with two other sons, and a dau. Alice, who *m.* Cadwalader-ap-Griffith, Prince of North Wales. His lordship *d.* 1139, and was *s.* by his eldest son,
  GILBERT DE CLARE, 2nd Earl of Hertford, who is said by Dugdale to have also borne the title of Earl of Clare; but Hornby observes, that *that* meant only *Earl at Clare;* for his earldom was certainly at *Hertford.* This nobleman, in the 8th of King STEPHEN, *anno* 1145, was a hostage for his uncle Ranulph, Earl of Chester, and subsequently, being in rebellion against the power of STEPHEN, was taken prisoner, and held in captivity, until he surrendered all his strong places. He *d.* in 1151, and having no issue, was *s.* by his brother,
  ROGER DE CLARE, 3rd Earl of Hertford, who is likewise said to have borne the title of Earl of Clare. In the 3rd HENRY II., this nobleman obtaining from the king all the lands in Wales which he could win, marched into Cardigan with a great army, and fortified divers castles thereabouts. In the 9th of the same reign, we find him summoned by the celebrated Thomas-à-Becket, archbishop of Canterbury, to Westminster, in order to do homage to the prelate for his castle of Tonebruge; which at the command of the king he refused, alleging that holding it by military service it belonged rather to the crown than to the church. His lordship *m.* Maude, dau. of James de St. Hillary, by whom (who *m.* after his decease William d'Aubigny, Earl of Arundel) he had a son,
  RICHARD, his successor.

This earl, who, from his munificence to the church, and his numerous acts of piety, was called the *Good, d.* in 1173, and was *s.* by his son,
  RICHARD DE CLARE, 4th Earl of Hertford, who, in the 7th

RICHARD I., gave £1,000 to the king for livery of the lands of his mother's inheritance, with his proportion of those sometime belonging to Giffard, Earl of Buckingham. His lordship *m.* Amicia, 2nd dau. and co-heiress (with her sisters Mabell, wife of the Earl of Evereux, in Normandy, and Isabel, the divorced wife of King JOHN) of William, EARL OF GLOUCESTER, by whom he had issue,

  GILBERT, his successor.
  Joane, *m.* to Rhys-Grig, Prince of South Wales.

This earl, who was one of the twenty-five barons appointed to enforce the observance of MAGNA CHARTA, *d.* in 1218, and was *s.* by his son,
  GILBERT DE CLARE, 5th Earl of Hertford, who, after the decease of Geoffrey de Mandeville, Earl of Essex, the 2nd husband of Isabel, the divorced wife of King JOHN (one of the co-heiresses mentioned above of William, Earl of Gloucester), and in her right EARL OF GLOUCESTER, and her own decease, *s. p.,* as also the decease of Almarick D'Evereux, son of the Earl of Evereux, by Mabell, the other co-heiress, who likewise succeeded to the Earldom of Gloucester, became EARL OF GLOUCESTER, in right of his mother Amicia, the other co-heiress. This nobleman was amongst the principal barons who took up arms against King JOHN, and was appointed one of the twenty-five chosen to enforce the observance of MAGNA CHARTA. In the ensuing reign, still opposing the arbitrary proceedings of the crown, he fought on the side of the barons at Lincoln, and was taken prisoner there by William Marshall, Earl of Pembroke; but he soon afterwards made his peace. His lordship *m.* Isabel, one of the daus., and eventually co-heiresses of William Mareschal, Earl of Pembroke, by whom (who *m.* after his decease, Richard, Earl of Cornwall, brother of King HENRY III.) he had issue,
  RICHARD, his successor.
  William.   Gilbert.
  Amicia, *m.* to Baldwin de Redvers, 4th Earl of Devon.
  Agnes.
  Isabel, *m.* to Robert de Brus.

The earl *d.* in 1229, and was *s.* by his eldest son,
  RICHARD DE CLARE, 6th Earl of Hertford, and 2nd Earl of Gloucester, then in minority. The wardship of this young nobleman was granted to the famous Hubert de Burgh, Earl of Kent, Justiciary of England, whose dau., Margaret, to the great displeasure of the king (HENRY III.) he afterwards (1243) clandestinely married, but from whom he was probably divorced for we find the king marrying him the next year to Maude, dau. of John de Lacy, Earl of Lincoln, in consideration whereof the said John paid to the crown 5,000 marks, and remitted a debt of 2,000 more. His lordship, who appears to have been a very distinguished personage in the reign of HENRY III., was one of the chief nobles present in Westminster Hall (40th HENRY III.), when Boniface, archbishop of Canterbury, with divers other prelates, pronounced that solemn curse, with candles lighted, against all those who should thenceforth violate MAGNA CHARTA. In two years afterwards an attempt was made by Walter de Scotenay, his chief counsellor, to poison the earl and his brother William, which proved effective as to the latter, while his lordship narrowly escaped with the loss of his hair and nails. In the next year the earl was commissioned with others of the nobility, by the appointment of the king, and the whole baronage of England, to the parliament of France, to convey King HENRY III.'s resignation of Normandy, and to adjust all differences between the two crowns; and upon the return of the mission, his lordship reported proceedings to the king, in parliament. About this period he had license to fortify the isle of Portland, and to embattle it as a fortress. It is reported of this nobleman, that being at Tewkesbury, in the 45th HENRY III., a Jew, who had fallen into a jakes upon the Saturday, refusing to be pulled out in reverence to the Jewish sabbath, his lordship prohibited any help to be afforded him on the next day, Sunday, the Christian sabbath, and thus suffered the unfortunate Israelite to perish. He *d.* himself in the July of the next year (1262), having been poisoned at the table of Peter de Savoy, the queen's uncle, along with Baldwin, Earl of Devon, and other persons of note. His lordship left issue,

  I. GILBERT, his successor.
  II. Thomas, governor of the city of London, 1st EDWARD I., and was killed in battle in Ireland fourteen years after, leaving by Amy, his wife, dau. of Sir Maurice FitzMaurice.
    1 Gilbert, who *d. s. p.*
    2 Richard, *d. v. p.,* leaving a son, Thomas, who *d. s. p.*
    3 Thomas, whose daus. and eventual co-heiresses were
      Margaret, wife of Bartholomew, 1st Lord Badlesmere.
      Maud, wife of Robert, Lord Clifford, of Appleby.
  I. Rose, *m.* to Roger de Mowbray.
  II. Margaret, *m.* to Edmund, Earl of Cornwall, and *d. s. p.*

The earl was *s* by his elder son,

GILBERT DE CLARE, surnamed the Red, 7th Earl of Hertford, and 3rd Earl of Gloucester, who, by the king's procurement, *m.* in 1257, Alice, dau. of Guy, Earl of Angoulesme, and niece of the king of France, which monarch bestowed upon the lady a marriage portion of 5,000 marks. This nobleman, who, like his predecessors, was zealous in the cause of the barons, proceeded to London immediately after the defeat sustained by the insurrectionary lords at Northampton (48th HENRY III.), in order to rouse the citizens, which, having effected, he received the honour of knighthood, from Montford, EARL OF LEICESTER, at the head of the army at Lewes; of which army, his lordship, with John Fitz-John and William de Montchensi, commanded the second brigade, and having mainly contributed to the victory, in which the king and prince became prisoners, while the whole power of the realm fell into the hands of the victors, the earl procured a grant under the great seal of all the lands and possessions, lying in England, of John de Warren, Earl of Surrey, one of the most faithful adherents of the king, excepting the castles of Riegate and Lewes, to hold during the pleasure of the crown, and he soon after, with some of the principal barons, extorted from the captive monarch a commission authorizing Stephen, then bishop of Chichester, Simon Montford, EARL OF LEICESTER, and himself, to nominate nine persons of "the most faithful, prudent, and most studious of the public weal," as well prelates· as others, to manage all things according to the laws and customs of the realm, until the consultations at Lewes should terminate. Becoming jealous, however, of the power of LEICESTER, the earl soon after abandoned the baronial cause, and having assisted in procuring the liberty of the king and prince, commanded the second brigade of the royal army at the battle of Evesham, which restored the kingly power to its former lustre. In reward of these eminent services he received a full pardon for himself and his brother Thomas, of all prior treasons, and the custody of the castle of Bergavenny, during the minority of Maud, wife of Humphrey de Bohun. His lordship veered again though in his allegiance, and he does not appear to have been sincerely reconciled to the royal cause, until 1270, in which year demanding from Prince Edward repayment of the expenses he had incurred at the battle of Evesham, with livery of all the castles and lands which his ancestors had possessed, and those demands having been complied with, he thenceforward became a good and loyal subject of the crown. Upon the death of King HENRY, the Earl of Hertford and Gloucester was one of the lords who met at the New Temple in London, to proclaim Prince Edward, then in the Holy Land, successor to the crown, and so soon as the new monarch returned to England, his lordship was the first to entertain him and his whole retinue, with great magnificence for several days at his castle of Tonebruge. In the 13th EDWARD I., his lordship divorced his wife Alice, the French princess, and in consideration of her illustrious birth, granted for her support during her life, six extensive manors and parks, and he *m.* in 1289, JOANE OF ACRE, dau. of King EDWARD I., upon which occasion he gave up the inheritance of all his castles and manors, as well in England as in Wales, to his royal father-in-law, to dispose of as he might think proper; which manors, &c., were entailed by the king upon the earl's issue, by the said Joane, and in default, upon her heirs and assigns, should she survive his lordship. By this lady he had issue,

I. GILBERT, his successor.
I. Alianore, *m.* 1337, 1st, to Hugh le Despencer the younger, and 2ndly, to William, Lord Zouche, of Mortimer.
II. Margaret, *m.* 1st, to Piers Gavestone Earl of Cornwall, and 2ndly, to Hugh de Audley, who was eventually created Earl of Gloucester.
III. Elizabeth, *m.* 1st, to John de Burgh, son of Richard, Earl of Ulster, by whom she had issue,

   William, EARL OF ULSTER, who *m.* Maud, sister of Henry Plantagenet, Duke of Lancaster, and left a dau. and heiress,

      ELIZABETH DE BURGH, who *m.* Lionel Plantagenet, DUKE OF CLARENCE, K.G., and had an only dau. and heiress,

         PHILIPPA PLANTAGENET, who *m.* Edward Mortimer, EARL OF MARCH.

Elizabeth, widow of John de Burgh, *m.* 2ndly, Theobald de Verdon; and 3rdly, Roger d'Amory: by the last she had two daus, Elizabeth, *m.* to John, Lord Bardolph, and Eleanor, *m.* to John de Raleigh.

His lordship *d.* in 1295, and the Countess Joane, surviving, *m.* a "plain esquire," called Ralph de Monthermer, clandestinely, without the king, her father's knowledge; but to which alliance he was reconciled through the intercession of Anthony Beke, the celebrated bishop of Durham, and became eventually much attached to his new son-in-law,

RALPH DE MONTHERMER, who, during the lifetime of the Princess Joane his wife, enjoyed the Earldoms of HERTFORD AND GLOUCESTER, and was summoned to parliament in those digni-

ties from 6 February, 1299, to 3 November, 1306, *jure uxoris*, but Joane dying in 1307, he never afterwards was so summoned but as a baron, under the designation of "Radulpho de Ma n-thermer" (*see* MONTHERMER). We now return to

GILBERT DE CLARE, who *s.* his father, and at the decease of his mother, Joane, became EARL OF HERTFORD and EARL OF GLOU-CESTER. His lordship *m.* Maud, dau. of Richard de Burgh, EARL OF ULSTER, but was slain at the battle of Bannockburn in 1313, leaving no issue, whereupon his large possessions devolved upon his three sisters as co-heiresses, and the EARL-DOMS OF GLOUCESTER AND HERTFORD became EXTINCT.

Arms—Or, three chevs., gu.

CLARE—EARLS OF PEMBROKE.

By Creation, *anno* 1138, 3rd of King STEPHEN.

Lineage.

GILBERT DE CLARE, 2nd son of Gilbert de Tonebruge, feudal Lord of Clare, and brother of Richard de Clare, 1st Earl of Hertford, having obtained from King HENRY I. a license to enjoy all the lands he should win in Wales, marched a large force into Cardiganshire, and brought the whole country under subjection: here he soon afterwards built two strong castles; and his power increasing, he was created by King STEPHEN, in 1138, EARL OF PEMBROKE. His lordship *m.* Elizabeth, sister of Waleran, Earl of Mellent, and dau. of Robert, Earl of Leicester, and had issue,

RICHARD, surnamed Strongbow, his successor.
Baldwin, who fell at the battle of Lincoln, fighting under the banner of King STEPHEN.
Basilia, *m.* to Reymond, son of William Fitz-Gerald of Ireland.

The earl *d.* in 1149, and was *s.* by his elder son,

RICHARD DE CLARE (the celebrated Strongbow), 2nd Earl of Pembroke. This nobleman was one of the witnesses to the solemn agreement, made in 1153, between King STEPHEN and Henry, Duke of Normandy, whereby the latter was to succeed to the English throne upon the decease of the former. But the leading part he subsequently had in the subjugation of Ireland procuring him a conspicuous place in history, we shall relate the particulars of that event in the words of the Monk of Jorevaulx—"The realm of Ireland," saith he, "being miserably opprest with warr by the many kings there who banded against each other, one of them sent his son into England to procure souldiers thence for his aid. Which souldiers for the hope of gain, giving him assistance, were so well recompenced, as that they rather chose to stay there than return into England. But after a short time the stoutest people of Ireland, being much offended with that king for getting aid from England, the English already fixed in Ireland sent for more from hence to strengthen their party, and because they had no chief they made choice of this EARL RICHARD (a stout and valiant man), to be their captain, who, yielding to their request, rigging a good fleet, prepared for the journey. Whereupon there were some who, in the king's behalf, endeavoured to restrain him. Howbeit, getting on shipboard, and landing safe, he assaulted Dublin, and took it; the tidings whereof so terrified those that lived afar off, that they were content to be at peace with him; and, to confirm what he had got, gave him in marriage, Eva, daughter of Dermot McMurrough, one of their kings, with whom he had in dower a great part of the realm. Whereat the King of England growing much displeased, as well for that he had not only, without his consent, but forbidden, made so great an attempt, seized upon all his patrimony here, prohibiting that he should have further aid; and threatening him otherwise very sore, compelled him so to such a compliance as that he got Dublin from him, and all the principal places he had won, requiring him to be content with the rest, and his patrimony in England; soon after raising a great army, the king sayled thither, himself." In the end the earl was constituted Justice of Ireland by King HENRY II., and having founded the priory of Kilmainham, in the province of Leinster, for knights hospitallers, "this eminent person," Dugdale concludes "died untimely upon the nones of April, *anno* 1176, and was buried in the Chapter house at Gloucester, as may be seen by this inscription on the wall there, '*Hic jacet* RICARDUS STRONG-BOW, *filius* GILBERTI, *Comitis de* PEMBROKE,'" leaving issue, as some say, one son, scarce three years old, to be his heir, but by others it is reported that, being by treachery abused and wounded, he departed this life the 5th year after his acquisition of the province of Leinster, and that he was buried at Dublin, leaving issue one only dau. and he ress,

ISABEL, who became in ward to King HENRY II. and remained under the royal guardianship for the space of fourteen years, when she was given in marriage to William Marshal, who thereupon became EARL OF PEMBROKE (see MARSHAL, Earl of Pembroke).

Arms—Or, three chevs., gu., a label of five points, az.

NOTE—Hacket, in his collection of Epitaphs, gives the following from the tomb of Strongbow, at Christ's Church, Dublin:—

"Nate ingrate, mihi pugnanti terga dedisti,
Non mihi, sed genti, regno quoque terga dedisti."

"This alludes," says Banks, "to a story that Strongbow's only son, a youth about seventeen, frighted with the numbers and ululations of the Irish in a great battle, ran away, but being afterwards informed of his father's victory, he joyfully returned to congratulate him. But the severe general having first upbraided him with his cowardice, caused him to be immediately executed by cutting him off in the middle with a sword. Such, in former times was the detestation of dastardliness!!! '

CLARE—BARON CLARE.

By Writ of Summons, dated 26 October, 1309.

Lineage.

RICHARD DE CLARE was summoned to parliament as a BARON on 26 October, 1309, but never afterwards. Of this nobleman Dugdale makes no mention at all, but COURTHOPE (*Historic Peerage*) says that "there can be little doubt but that he was brother and heir of Gilbert de Clare, and æt. twenty-two, 1st EDWARD II., and 2nd son of Thomas, son of Richard de Clare, Earl of Gloucester. He was slain in battle at Dysert, in Ireland, in 1318; he left issue, Thomas, who *d. s. p.*, and apparently a minor in the 14th EDWARD II., leaving his aunts (sisters of his father) Margaret, the wife of Bartholemew de Badlesmere, and Maud, then the wife of Robert de Welle (and 2ndly, before 1st EDWARD III., of Robert de Clifford), his heirs."

CLAVERING—BARONS CLAVERING.

By Writ of Summons, dated 2 November, 1295.

Lineage

EUSTACE DE BURGH, Baron Tonsburgh, in Normandy, younger brother of HARLOWEN DE BURGH, the ancestor of the Lords Clanricarde, and the numerous families of DE BURGH, BURKE, and BOURKE, had two sons,

SERLO, of whom presently.
JOHN, surnamed *Monoculus*, from having but one eye.

The elder son,

SERLO DE BURGH, erected the castle of Knaresborough, which passed at his decease, *s. p.*, to his brother,

JOHN *Monoculus*, who had three sons,

PAGANUS, } These brothers were witnesses to the foundation
EUSTACE, } of the abbey of Cirencester, co. Gloucester,
William, } 1133.

The elder son, PAGANUS, dying *s. p.*, was *s.* by his brother,

EUSTACE FITZ-JOHN (nephew and heir of SERLO DE BURGH, founder of Knaresborough Castle), one of the most powerful of the northern barons, and a great favourite with King HENRY I., who m. 1st, Agnes, eldest dau. of William Fitz Nigel, Baron of Halton, constable of Chester. By this lady he acquired the Barony of Halton, and had an only son,

RICHARD FITZ-EUSTACE, of whom presently.

EUSTACE FITZ-JOHN m. 2ndly, Beatrice, only dau. and heiress of Yvo de Vesci, Lord of Alnwick, in Northumberland, and of Malton, in Yorkshire, by whom he had issue,

WILLIAM, progenitor of the great baronial house of De Vesci.

The eldest son,

RICHARD FITZ-EUSTACE, Baron of Halton, and constable of Chester, m. Albreda, dau. and heir of Robert de Lizures, and half sister of Robert de Lacy, and had issue,

JOHN, who assumed the surname of Lacy, and *s.* his father as constable of Chester. He d. 25th HENRY II., leaving one son,

Henry de Lacy, whose only dau. m. the Earl of Lancaster.

Robert, the hospitaller, that is of the Hospital of St. John of Jerusalem in England.
ROGER.

The youngest son,

ROGER FITZ-RICHARD, who was feudal Baron of Warkworth, co. Northumberland, a lordship granted to him by King HENRY II., m. Alianor, dau. and co-heir of Henry of Essex, Baron of Raleigh, and was *s.* by his only son,

ROBERT FITZ-ROGER, who m. Margaret, only child and heiress of William de Cheney, by whom he acquired the Barony of HORSFORD, co. Norfolk, and had an only son, JOHN. This Robert obtained a confirmation, upon the accession of King JOHN, of the castle and manor of Warkworth, of the manor of Clavering, in Essex, and of the manor of Eure, in Buckinghamshire, to hold by the service of one knight's fee each. And in that monarch's reign he served the office of sheriff for Northumberland, Norfolk, and Suffolk; for each county thrice. In the conflict between JOHN and the barons, this powerful person, although indebted to the crown for immense territorial possessions, took part in the first instance with the latter, but under the apprehension of confiscation, and the other visitations of royal vengeance, he was very soon induced to return to his allegiance. He was *s.* by his son,

JOHN FITZ-ROBERT, to whom King JOHN, in the 14th year of his reign, ratified the grant of the castle and manor of Warkworth, made by King HENRY II. to his grandfather, Roger Fitz-Richard, as also of the manor of Clavering. In three years afterwards he was appointed joint governor with John Marshall, of the castles of Norwich and Oxford; but joining in the insurrection of the barons, and being chosen one of the twenty-five appointed to exercise the regal authority, his lands were seized by the king, and a part confiscated. Returning, however, to his allegiance in the next reign, his castles and estates were restored to him. In the 9th of HENRY III. he was constituted sheriff of Northumberland, and governor of the town of Newcastle-upon-Tyne; and in the 13th of the same monarch, he was one the great northern barons appointed by special command of the king to wait upon ALEXANDER, King of Scotland, at Berwick-upon-Tweed, and to conduct that prince to York, there to meet the king of England, "to treat upon certain affairs of great importance." His lordship m. Ada, dau. and heir of Hugh de Baliol, and grand-aunt of BALIOL, King of Scotland, and had issue,

ROGER, his successor.
Hugh, surnamed "De Eure," from whom the Lords Eure descended.
Robert, ancestor of the Eures of Axholm, in Lincolnshire.

He d. in 1240, and was *s.* by his eldest son,

ROGER FITZ-JOHN, feudal Baron of Warkworth and Clavering, who d. in 1249, and was *s.* by his son,

ROBERT FITZ-ROGER, then in infancy, whose tuition was committed to William de Valence, the king's half-brother, although Ada de Baliol, the grandmother of the child, offered 2,200 marks for the wardship. This feudal lord became eventually so eminent in the Scottish wars of King EDWARD I., particularly in the battle of Falkirk, and other memorable conflicts, that he was summoned as "Robert Fitz-Roger" to parliament as a BARON, from 2 November, 1295, to 16 June (4th EDWARD II.), 1311, and subsequently assisted with his son JOHN, who assumed, by the king's appointment, the surname of Clavering, at the celebrated siege of Kaerlaverok. His lordship m. Margaret de la Zouche, and had issue, seven sons, viz.,

JOHN, his successor.
Edmund,
Alexander,
Robert, } all *d. s. p.*
Henry,
Roger,
ALAN (SIR), m. Isabella, eldest dau. and co-heir of William Riddell; and from this union descended t. e CLAVERINGS OF CALLALY, in Northumberland, the Baronets CLAVERING of Axwell, co. Durham, the Claverings of Learchild, the Claverings of Tilmouth, co. Durham, &c.

He d. about the year 1311, and was *s.* by his eldest son,

JOHN DE CLAVERING, 2nd baron, who had summons to parliament from 10 April, 1299, to 20 November, 1331. This nobleman had distinguished himself, in his father's lifetime, in the French and Scotch wars, and was taken prisoner at the battle of Strivelyn. His lordship m. Hawyse, dau. of Robert de Tibetot, and had an only dau.,

Eve, who m. 1st, Ralph de Ufford 2ndly, Thomas de Audley, and 3rdly, Robert Benhale.

Lord Clavering, long before his death, being doubtful of having male issue, made a feoffment to Stephen de Trafford whereby he vested the inheritance of his castle and manor of Wark-worth in the said Stephen, with other manors, for the intent that he should reconvey them to his lordship for life, with remainder to the king and his heirs. In consideration whereof the king granted unto the baron and his heirs divers lands and hereditaments, then valued at £400 pe. annum. His lordship d. at his manor of Aynho, in Northamptonshire, in 1332, when those great estates falling to th crown, were divided thus—

Warkworth, and the manors in Northumberland, granted to Henry de Perci, are still part of the possessions of the ducal family of Northumberland.

Aynho and Horsford, in Northamptonshire and Norfolk, to Ralph de Neville, and his heirs.

Clavering, in Essex, to the deceased lord's brother Edmund, for life, and in remainder to the above Ralph Neville and his heirs.

In this very unjustifiable manner were the descendants of his lordship's youngest brother deprived of their fair inheritance.

Arms—Quarterly: or and gu., over all a bend, sa.

CLAYTON—BARON SUNDON.

By Letters Patent, dated 2 June, 1735.

Lineage.

RALPH CLAYTON, Esq., descended, it is said, from the Clay-tons of Fullwood, co. Lancaster, m. Mary Frances, and had by her three sons and three daus., viz.,

I. JOHN, who m. Mrs. Mary Norgate, a widow, and had, with two daus. (Frances, Mrs. Comling; and Ann, m. to Thomas Stuteville,) a son,
  ROBERT, who m. Miss Ann Tabram, and had issue,
    1 ROBERT, who d. s. p.
    2 William, whose only dau. d. unm.
    3 John, d. unm.
    1 Ann. m. to Tomkinson Cooper, Esq.
    2 Elizabeth, m. to William Cole, Esq.
    3 Frances, m. to William Hale, Esq., of Dunstable, Beds.
    4 Margaret, m. to James Smyth, Esq.
II. WILLIAM, of whom presently.
III. Richard, d. unm.
I. Jane, m. to Richard Searle, Esq., and had a son. Richard, whose dau., Catharine Searle, m. George Elkins, Esq.
II. Elizabeth, m. to Walter Fyson, Esq., and had two sons, William and Joseph.
III. Frances, Mrs. Westrop.

The 2nd son,
WILLIAM CLAYTON, m. Ann, dau. of John Huske, of New-market, and was father of
WILLIAM CLAYTON, Esq., a clerk in the treasury, who was deputy auditor of the exchequer, 1716, and held also the im-portant trust of being one of the managers of the Duke of Marlborough's estates during his grace's absence. Mr. Clayton represented at one time Westminster in parliament, and was elevated to the peerage of Ireland, as BARON SUNDON, of Ardagh, co. Longford, 2 June, 1735, being then described as "William Clayton, Esq., one of the commissioners of His Majesty's Treasury." His lordship m. Charlotte Dyves, sister of Lewis Dyves, Esq., an officer of the 2nd horse guards, a lady who became the favourite of Sarah, Duchess of Marlborough, and obtained great influence at court, becoming eventually mistress of the robes to CAROLINE, Queen of GEORGE II. Through that influence her husband acquired the Irish peerage, and several members of her own family were promoted; her nieces, Frances, Dorothy, and Charlotte Dyves, became attendants on the princesses, one in the capacity of maid of honour. He d. s. p. 29 April, 1752, aged about eighty, being at the time M.P. for St. Maws (his wife having predeceased him, 1 January, 1742), and with him the title EXPIRED.

Arms—Arg., a cross, sa., between four pellets.

CLIFFORD — EARLS OF CUMBERLAND AND BARONS CLIFFORD.

Earldom, by Letters Patent, dated 18 June, 1525.
Barony, by Writ, dated 17 February, 1628.

Lineage.

The first of this ancient family of whom Dugdale takes notice, was called Ponce, who is represented as leaving three sons, Walter and Dru, considerable landed proprietors in the CONQUEROR's survey, and

RICHARD FITZPONCE, a personage of rank in the time of RICHARD I., and a liberal benefactor to the church; this Richard left also three sons, of whom the 2nd, Walter, having obtained Clifford Castle, in Herefordshire, with his wife Mar-

garet, dau. of Ralph de Toney, a descendant from William Fitzosborn, Earl of Hereford, by whom the castle was erected, assumed thence his surname, and became

WALTER DE CLIFFORD. This feudal lord, who was in in-fluence in the reign of HENRY II., left at his decease, two sons and two daus., viz.,

WALTER, his heir.
Richard, from whom the CLIFFORDS of Frampton, in Glouces-t .rshire, descended.
ROSAMOND, so well known as "Fair Rosamond," the celebrated mistress of HENRY II., by whom she was mother of William Longespee, Earl of Salisbury.
Lucia, m. 1st, to Hugh de Say, of Richard's Castle, and 2ndly, to Bartholomew de Mortimer.

Walter de Clifford was s. by his elder son,
WALTER DE CLIFFORD, who m. Agnes, only dau. and heiress of Roger de Cundi, lord of the manors of Covenby and Glen-tham, co. Lincoln, by Alice his wife, Lady of Horncastle, dau. and heiress of William de Cheney, lord of those manors in the CONQUEROR's time, by whom he had issue, WALTER, Roger, Giles, and Richard. He was sheriff of Herefordshire in the 1st, 8th, 9th, and 17th JOHN, and dying in the 7th of HENRY III., was s. by his eldest son,

WALTER DE CLIFFORD. This feudal lord held a very high place in the estimation of King HENRY III. until the rebellion of Richard Mareschal, Earl of Pembroke, when, taking part with that nobleman, his lands were confiscated, and himself outlawed. The royal displeasure did not, however, endure any length of time, for we find him soon afterwards restored to his castle of Clifford, and during the many subsequent years of the same reign, enjoying the full confidence of the crown At the coronation of Queen Eleanor, consort of King HENRY, he claimed with the other barons-marchers, as jus marchæ, to carry the canopy which belonged to the barons of the Cinque Ports. This Walter de Clifford m. Margaret, dau. of Llewellyn, Prince of Wales, and widow of John de Braose, by whom he had an only dau. and heiress,

Maud, who m. 1st, William de Longespee, Earl of Salisbury, and 2ndly, Sir John Gifford of Brimsfield.

Walter de Clifford d. in the 48th HENRY III., when the con-tinuation of the male line of the family devolved upon his nephew,

ROGER DE CLIFFORD (son of Roger de Clifford, by Sibill, dau. and co-heiress of Robert de Ewyas, a great baron of Hereford-shire, and widow of Robert, Lord de Tregoz), who, for his stanch adherence to HENRY III., was appointed, after the victory of Evesham, justice of all the king's forests south of Trent, and obtained a grant at the same time of the lordship of Kings-bury, co. Warwick, forfeited by Sir Ralph de Bracebrigge, Knt. He was afterwards frequently employed against the Welsh, and lost his eldest son, Roger, who had m. Isabel, dau. and co-heiress of Robert de Vipount, lord and hereditary sheriff of Westmoreland, in one of those conflicts. Roger de Clifford d. in 14th of EDWARD I., and was s. by (the son of his deceased son above-mentioned) his grandson,

ROBERT DE CLIFFORD, who was summoned to parliament as a BARON, from 29 December, 1299 (28th EDWARD I), to 26 Novem-ber, 1313 (7th EDWARD II.) This nobleman participated in the Scottish wars of King EDWARD I., and had a principal com-mand in the English army. He fell in the following reign at the battle of Bannockburn. His lordship m. Maud, dau. and co-heiress of Thomas, 2nd son of Richard de Clare, 7th Earl of Gloucester, and had issue, besides an elder son, Roger, Lord of Westmoreland, who d. s. p. 1327. A 2nd son,

ROBERT DE CLIFFORD, b. 1305, who d. 20 May, 1344. He m. 1328, Isabel, dau. of Maurice, Lord Berkeley, and had issue four sons,

I. Robert, who m. Eufamia, dau. of Radolphus, Lord Nevill, of Meddleham, and d. s. p.
II. ROGER, who s. his father.
III. John.
IV. Thomas, from whom descended Richard, Bishop of Wor-cester, afterwards a Cardinal.

The 2nd but eldest surviving son,
ROGER DE CLIFFORD, Lord of Westmoreland, m. Maud, dau. of Thomas Beauchamp, 3rd Earl of Warwick, and d. 13 July, 1390, having had, with four daus., three sons,

THOMAS, his heir.
William, m. Anne, eldest dau. and co-heir of Thomas, Lord Bardolph. and d. s. p. 6th HENRY V.
Lewis (Sir) K.G., ancestor of the Cliffords of Chudleigh.

The eldest son and heir,
THOMAS DE CLIFFORD, d. abroad, 15th RICHARD II., leaving by Elizabeth his wife, dau. of Thomas, Lord Ros of Hamlake, an only son and heir,
JOHN DE CLIFFORD, Lord Clifford and Westmoreland

Elizabeth, dau. of Henry, Lord Percy (surnamed HOTSPUR), son and heir of Henry, Earl of Northumberland, and by her, who m. 2ndly, Radulphus Nevill, 2nd Earl of Westmoreland, left at his decease, in 1422, a son and heir,

THOMAS, Lord Clifford and Westmoreland, b. 1415, who m. Johanna, dau. of Thomas, Lord Dacre, of Gillesland, and was s. at his decease, 22 May, 1455, by his son,

JOHN, Lord Clifford and Westmoreland, b. 1435, who m. Margaret, only dau. and heir of Henry Bromflete, Baron de Vesci, and d. 1st EDWARD IV., having had issue,

HENRY, his heir.
Richard, slain in the Netherlands.
Thomas (Sir), m. Ellen, dau. and co-heir of John Swarby, of Brakenburgh, co. Lincoln.
Elizabeth, m. to Robert Aske, Esq.

The eldest son and heir,

HENRY, Lord Clifford and Westmoreland, b. 1453, m. 1st, Anne, dau. of John St. John, of Bletnesho, and had besides five daus., all married, two sons, HENRY his heir, and Thomas, who m. Lucia, dau. of Anthony Brown. He m. 2ndly, Florence, dau. of Henry Pudsey, of Barfoot, co. York, by whom he had three sons who d. young, and one dau. He d. 23 April, 15th HENRY VIII., and was s. by his eldest son,

HENRY DE CLIFFORD, the 11th baron, b. 1493, who was created, by letters patent, dated 18 June, 1525, EARL OF CUMBERLAND, and dignified with the Garter in 1532. This nobleman obtained large grants out of the monastic spoliations, and was entrusted with a principal command in the army which invaded Scotland in the 34th of HENRY VIII. His lordship m. 1st, Margaret, dau. of George Talbot, Earl of Shrewsbury, by whom he had no issue; and 2ndly, Margaret, dau. of Henry Percy, 5th Earl of Northumberland, by whom he had

I. HENRY, Lord Clifford, his successor.
II. Ingeram (Sir), who m. Anne, dau. and sole heiress of Sir Henry Ratcliff, but dying s. p., left his property to his nephew, George, Earl of Cumberland.
I. Catherine, m. 1st. to John, Lord Scroope, of Bolton; and 2ndly, to Sir Richard Cholmondeley, by the latter of whom she had

     SIR HENRY CHOLMONDELEY, of Grandmount and Roxby, who had

         RICHARD (Sir), sheriff of Yorkshire in the last year of King JAMES I., whose son,

            HUGH, was created a baronet, 10 August, 1641, and was s. by his son,

                SIR WILLIAM, 2nd baronet, who left daus. only, his co-heirs, the eldest of whom,

                    Elizabeth, m. Sir Edward Dering, of Surenden.

II. Maud, m. to John, Lord Conyers, of Hornby, co. York.
III. Elizabeth, m. to Sir Christopher Metcalf, of Nappa, co. York.
IV. Jane, m. to Sir John Huddlestone, of Millum Castle, co. Cumberland.

By the last will and testament of this nobleman, he devised, amongst other bequests, 300 marks to be expended upon his funeral; to his dau. Elizabeth, £1,000 if she should marry an earl or an earl's son; if a baron, 1,000 marks; if a knight, 800 marks. His lordship, d. 22 April, 33rd HENRY VIII., and was s. by his elder son,

HENRY CLIFFORD, 2nd earl, b. 1517, who had been made a knight of the Bath at the coronation of Queen Anne Boleyne. This nobleman m. 1st, in 1537, Eleanor, dau. and co-heiress of Charles Brandon, Duke of Suffolk, and niece of King HENRY VIII., by whom he had an only surviving child,

Margaret, b. 1540, m. to Henry Stanley, then Lord Strange, and afterwards Earl of Derby.

His lordship m. 2ndly, Anne, dau. of William, Lord Dacre, of Gillesland, by whom he had surviving issue,

GEORGE, Lord Clifford.
FRANCIS, 4th earl.
Frances, m. to Philip, Lord Wharton,

The earl d. 8 January, 1569, and was s. by his elder son,

GEORGE CLIFFORD, 3rd earl, then in his eleventh year, who was placed by Queen ELIZABETH under the guardianship of Francis Russell, 2nd Earl of Bedford, whose 3rd dau., Lady Margaret Russell, he m. in 1577, and had an only surviving dau.,

ANNE, b. 30 January, 1578, who m. 1st, Richard Sackville, 2nd Earl of Dorset, by whom she had three sons, who d. young, and two daus., viz.,

MARGARET, m. to John Tufton, 2nd Earl of Thanet.
Isabel, m. to James, Earl of Northampton.

The Countess of Dorset, m. 2ndly, Philip Herbert, Earl of Pembroke and Montgomery, K G., and lord-chamberlain of the household: but had no issue. This lady claimed the Barony of Clifford in 1628, and the hearing of her petition was appointed for the next session: but no further proceed-

ings ensued. Her ladyship d. in 1675. Her descendant, however, Thomas, 6th Earl of Thanet, preferred his claim to the barony, and had it acknowledged by the House of Lords in 1691; but the dignity fell into ABEYANCE at his decease. In 1729, between his daus and co heirs, and so remained until terminated by the crown, in 1734, in favour of the 3rd dau., Margaret, Countess of Leicester, at whose decease, in 1775, it again became suspended, until again revived in favour of EDWARD SOUTHWELL, Esq. who became Lord de Clifford (see BURKE'S Extant Peerage).

Earl George was educated at the university of Cambridge, and attaching himself to the study of mathematics, imbibed so decided a passion for navigation, that he became soon afterwards eminent as a naval commander, having undertaken at his own expense several voyages for the public service; but that, and a passion for tournaments, horse-racing, and similar pursuits, made such inroads upon his fortune, that he was said to have wasted more of his estate than any one of his ancestors. His lordship was elected a knight of the Garter in 1592. His character is thus depicted in the MS. Memoirs of his celebrated dau., Anne, Countess of Dorset and Pembroke:—"He was endowed with many perfections of nature befitting so noble a personage, as an excellent quickness of wit and apprehension, an active and strong body, and an affable disposition and behaviour. But as good natures, through human frailty, are oftentimes misled, so he fell to love a lady of quality, which did, by degrees, draw and aliene his love and affections from his so virtuous and well-deserving wife; it being the cause of many discontents between them for many years together, so that at length, for two or three years before his death, they parted houses, to her extreme grief and sorrow, and also to his extreme sorrow at the time of his death; for he died a very penitent man. He d. in the duchy-house, called the Savoy, 30 October, 1605, aged forty-seven years, two months, and twenty-two days, being born at Brougham Castle, 8 August, 1558."

His lordship leaving no male issue, the barony remained for some years in abeyance, but eventually devolved upon the descendants of his daus., by one of whom it is at present inherited, while the earldom passed to his only brother,

FRANCIS CLIFFORD, 4th earl, who m. Grissel, dau. of Thomas Hughes, of Uxbridge, and widow of Edward Nevill, Lord Abergavenny, by whom he had surviving issue,

HENRY, Lord Clifford.
Margaret m. to Sir Thomas Wentworth, of Wentworth-Woodhouse, co. York, afterwards Earl of Strafford.
Frances, m. to Sir Gervase Clifton, Bart., of Clifton, co. Nottingham (his 2nd wife).

Of this nobleman, the Countess of Dorset says, "He was an honourable gentleman, and of a good, noble, sweet, and courteous nature." His lordship d. in 1641, and was s. by his son,

HENRY CLIFFORD, 5th earl, who m. Frances, only dau. of Robert Cecil, Earl of Salisbury, and had an only surviving dau. and heiress,

ELIZABETH, m. to Richard, 2nd Earl of Cork and 1st Earl of Burlington, who was created BARON CLIFFORD, of Lanesborough, co. York, in 1644.

The earl d. 1643, when the Earldom of Cumberland became EXTINCT, but the BARONY OF CLIFFORD (which originated in the writ, addressed, 17 February, 1628, to this Henry Clifford, when son and heir-apparent of Francis, 4th Earl of Cumberland, under the erroneous supposition that the ancient Barony of Clifford was vested in his father) devolved on his dau., Elizabeth, Countess of Cork and Burlington, and is now in ABEYANCE between the EARLS OF CARLISLE and GRANVILLE, as co-heirs of William Spencer, late Duke of Devonshire, Baron Clifford, &c., grandson of the said Elizabeth, Countess of Cork and Burlington.

Arms—Chequy, or and az., a fesse, gu.

NOTE.— " Beneath the altar in Skipton Church," says Whittaker, in his "History of the Deanery of Craven, in the county of York," "is the vault of the Cliffords, the place of their interment from the dissolution of Bolton Priory to the death of the last Earl of Cumberland, which, after having been closed many years. I obtained permission to examine, 29 March, 1803. The original vault, intended only for the 1st earl and his 2nd lady, had undergone two enlargements; and the bodies having been deposited in chronological order, first, and immediately under his tomb, lay Henry, the 1st earl, whose lead coffin was much corroded, and exhibited the skeleton of a short and very stout man, with a long head of flaxen hair, gathered in a knot behind the skull. The coffin had been closely fitted to the body, and proved him to have been very corpulent as well as muscular. Next lay the remains of Margaret Percy his 2nd wife, whose coffin was still entire. She must have been a slender and diminutive woman. The third was 'the lady Ellinor's grave,' whose coffin was much decayed, and exhibited the skeleton (as might be expected in a dau. of Charles Brandon, and the sister of HENRY VIII.) of a tall and large-limbed female. At her right hand was Henry, the 2nd earl, a very tall and rather slender man, whose then envelope of lead really resembled a winding-sheet, and folded like a coarse drapery round the limbs. The head was beaten to the left side: something of the shape of the face might have been distinguished, and a long prominent nose was very conspicuous. Next lay Francis, Lord Clifford, a boy. At his right hand was his father, George, the 3rd earl, whose lead coffin precisely resembled the outer case of an Egyptian mummy, with a rude face, and something like a female mammæ cast upon it, as were also the figures and letters 'G. C. 1605.' The body was closely wrapped in ten folds of coarse cere cloth, which, being removed, exhibited the face so entire (only turned to a copper colour,) as plainly to resemble his portraits. All his painters, however, had the complaisance to omit three large warts upon the left cheek. The coffin of Earl Francis, who lay next to his brother, was of the modern shape, and alone had an outer shell of wood, which was covered with leather. The soldering had decayed, and nothing appeared but the ordinary skeleton of a tall man. This earl had never been embalmed. Over him lay another coffin, much decayed, which I suspect had contained the Lady Anne Dacre, his mother. Last lay Henry, the 5th earl, in a coffin of the same form with that of his father. Lead not allowing of absorption, nor a narrow vault of much evaporation, a good deal of moisture remained in the coffin and some hair about the skull. Both these coffins had been cut open). Room might have been found for another slender body; but the Countess of Pembroke chose to be buried at Appleby, partly, perhaps, because her beloved mother was interred there, and partly that she might not mingle her ashes with rivals and enemies."

CLIFTON—BARONS CLIFTON.

By Writ of Summons, dated 1 December, 1376

Lineage.

ROGER DE CLIFTON, esquire to Thomas, LORD CAILLI, m. Margerie, the sister of that nobleman, and left issue,

ADAM DE CLIFTON, who, in his ninth year, inherited the great estates of his uncle, Lord Cailli, which included those of the family of Tatshall, derived by that nobleman from his mother, Emme, one of the co-heirs of Robert de Tatshall. This Adam m. Eleanor, dau. of Robert Mortimer, of Attilbergh, and had a son, CONSTANTINE, who predeceased him, and having m. Catherine, dau. of Sir William de la Pole, left a son, the said Adam's successor,

JOHN DE CLIFTON, who was summoned to parliament as a BARON from 1 December, 1376, to 28 July, 1388. His lordship d. in the latter year at Rhodes, possessed, amongst other lands, of the castle of Bokenham, and manor of Babingle, co. Norfolk; which castle he held by performing the office of butler at the king's coronation. He m. Elizabeth, dau. and heir of Sir Ralph Cromwell, and was s. by his son,

CONSTANTINE DE CLIFTON, 2nd baron, summoned to parliament from 13 November, 1393, to 20 of the same month in the next year. This nobleman m. Margaret, dau. of Sir John Howard, only surviving son of Sir Robert Howard, by Margery his wife, dau. of Robert, Lord Scales, and d. in 1395, leaving issue,

JOHN (Sir), his heir.
Elizabeth, m. to Sir John Knyvett, Knt. and had issue,

    JOHN KNYVETT, who m. Alice, dau. and heir of William Lynnes, and was father of SIR WILLIAM KNYVETT, attainted 1st RICHARD III., but afterwards restored; he m. Alice, dau. of John Grey, brother of Reginald, Lord Grey de Ruthyn, and had a son and heir, SIR EDMUND KNYVETT, of Buckenham, drowned in a sea-fight, temp. HENRY VIII., leaving by Eleanor his wife, dau. of Sir William Tyrrell, Knt., with other issue, two sons, viz.,

    1 THOMAS (Sir), of Buckenham, K.B., standard-bearer to King HENRY VIII., ancestor of KNYVETT of Buckenham, and KNYVETT, LORD KNYVETT, of Escrick (which see).
    2 EDMUND, of Ashwellthorpe, co. Norfolk, ancestor of LORD BERNERS (see BURKE's Peerage).

His lordship's son and heir,
SIR JOHN DE CLIFTON, 3rd baron, but who does not appear by the existing enrolments to have been summoned to parliament, m. Joane, dau. and co-heir of Sir Edward Thorpe, by whom he had a dau. and heiress,

Margaret, who m. Sir Andrew Ogard, but d. s. p.

At his lordship's death, and the death s. p. of his only child, Lady Ogard, the BARONY OF CLIFTON became vested in JOHN KNYVETT, amongst whose descendants and representatives it is now in ABEYANCE.

Arms—Chequy, or and gu., a bend. erm

CLINTON—BARON CLINTON, EARL OF HUNTINGDON.

Barony, by Writ of Summons, dated 6 September, 1330.
Earldom, by Letters Patent, dated 16 March, 1337.

Lineage.

SIR WILLIAM DE CLINTON, Knt., younger son of John de Clinton, Baron Clinton, m. 1330, Julian, dau. and heiress of Sir Thomas de Leyburne, Knt., and widow of John, Lord Hastings, of Bergavenny, by which alliance it is presumed that his subsequent advancement in life was considerably promoted; he was, however, himself a very eminent person, and fully entitled by his own deeds to the high honours he attained. In the year ensuing his marriage, Sir William was made justice of Chester, and within less than two months afterwards constable of Dover Castle and warden of the Cinque Ports. Shortly after this being one of those who surprised the great Mortimer, at Nottingham Castle, he had summons to parliament as BARON CLINTON, 6 September, 1330, and from that period to 14 January, 1337. In three years subsequently his lordship was constituted Lord Admiral of the Seas, from the Thames westwards, and in that year he was engaged in the Scottish wars, as he was in the 9th and 10th of the same reign. In the 11th EDWARD III., then enjoying the highest favour of the king, his lordship was created, by letters patent, dated 16 March, 1337, EARL OF HUNTINGDON, having, at the same time, not only £20 per annum given him out of the issues of the county to be paid by the sheriff, but 1,000 marks per annum in land, to hold to himself and his male heirs for ever. He subsequently participated in his gallant sovereign's wars, both in Scotland and France, and was frequently employed in foreign embassies of the first importance. He was a second time constituted Lord admiral, and a second time appointed constable of Dover Castle, and lord warden of the Cinque Ports. His lordship d. in 1354, leaving, according to Banks, an only dau.,

Elizabeth, who m. Sir John Fitzwilliam, of Sprotborough, ancestor of the present EARL FITZWILLIAM.

The earl having no male issue the dignity of EARL OF HUNTINGDON became EXTINCT, but the BARONY OF CLINTON, created by writ, should have devolved upon his dau., if legitimate, and if so, is still extant in her descendants, the Earls Fitzwilliam. Of this, however, there must be strong doubt. Dugdale mentions no dau., but says that he left all his extensive possessions to his nephew, Sir John de Clinton, Knt. Nicolas, in his Synopsis, confirms Dugdale, by stating that the Earl of Huntingdon d. s. p., "when his honours became EXTINCT;" while Banks gives the particulars of the dau. as above. Collins and Jacob call the lady "Elizabeth, dau. of William, Lord Clinton." Had she been legitimate, she would, doubtless, have been his lordship's heiress, and BARONESS CLINTON.

Arms—Arg., six cross crosslets fitchée, sa., on a chief, az., two mullets, or, pierced, gu.

COBHAM—BARONS COBHAM OF KENT.

By Writ of Summons, dated 8 January, 1313.

Lineage.

In the 12th of King JOHN, HENRY DE COBBEHAM gave to that monarch 1,000 marks for his royal favour. This Henry had three sons, viz.,

JOHN, of whom presently.
Reginald, justice itinerant in Essex, in the 32nd HENRY III., and the ensuing year in Middlesex and Wilts, when he was constituted sheriff of Kent, and he continued to execute the duties of that office for the nine following years. In the 39th of the same monarch he was made constable of Dover Castle and warden of the Cinque Ports, when he had command to attend the ambassadors from the King of Castile, who then landed at Dover, to afford them hospitable entertainment, and to conduct them to the new temple at London, where they were to be lodged. He d. in three years afterwards.
William, one of the justices itinerant in the cos. of Sussex, Southampton, and Wilts in the 39th HENRY III., and for Norfolk and Suffolk in the 41st of the same reign.

JOHN DE COBBEHAM, the eldest son, executed in the 26th HENRY III. the office of sheriff of Kent, on behalf of Peter de Savoy, brother of Queen Eleanor, for one-half of the year, and on behalf of Bertram de Criol, for the other half. He was also one of the justices of the Court of Common Pleas from the 28th to the 35th of the same reign. This eminent person m. 1st, ——, dau. of Warine Fitz-Benedict, by whom he had issue,

JOHN, his successor.

Henry (Sir), of Rundell, governor of the Islands of Guernsey and Jersey, and constable of the castle of Dover and warden of the Cinque Ports, *temp.* EDWARD I. Sir Henry *m.* Joane, elder dau. and co-heiress of Stephen de Pencestre, and had issue,

STEPHEN (*see* COBHAM, BARON COBHAM OF RUNDELL).
RALPH (*see* COBHAM OF NORFOLK).

He, *m.* 2ndly, Joane, dau. of Hugh de Nevill, and had a son,

REGINALD, from whom the COBHAMS *of Sterborough* sprang.

JOHN DE COBHAM, the eldest son, *s.* his father, and was one of the justices of the courts of King's Bench and Common Pleas, and a baron of the exchequer, in the reigns of HENRY III. and EDWARD I. This learned person *m.* Joane de Septvaus, one of the co-heirs of Roese, the widow of Stephen de Pencestre, and had issue,

HENRY, his successor.

Reginald, *m.* Joane, dau. of William de Evere, and obtained a charter in the 32nd EDWARD I. for free warren in all his demesne lands at Pipard's Clive, co. Wilts.

The elder son,

HENRY DE COBHAM, *s.* his father, and doing homage in the 28th EDWARD I. had livery of his lands. In the 4th EDWARD II., being then styled Henry de Cobham, jun. (his uncle Henry, of Rundell, then living), he was in an expedition into Scotland; and, in four years afterwards, he was constituted constable of Dover Castle and warden of the Cinque Ports. In the 10th of the same reign he was again in the wars of Scotland, and in the 15th he was made governor of the castle of Tonebrugge. He had been summoned to parliament as a BARON on 8 January, 1313, and in continuation for the remainder of his life. His lordship *m.* Maud de Columbers; *d.* in 1339, and was *s.* by his eldest son,

JOHN DE COBHAM, 2nd Baron Cobham, summoned to parliament from 12 September, 1342, to 20 November, 1360. This nobleman, who had been made admiral of the king's fleet from the mouth of the Thames westward in the 9th EDWARD III., had the next year in remuneration of his services, whilst he was a justice of Oyer and Terminer, in Kent, a grant of 100 marks out of the 200 which the commons of that county gave to the king in furtherance of the Scottish war. In the 28th of the same monarch he was made a banneret. His son and heir (by Joan his wife, dau. of John Beauchamp),

JOHN DE COBHAM. was summoned to parliament from 24 February, 1368, to 9 February, 1406. In the beginning of RICHARD II.'s reign his lordship was appointed ambassador upon two occasions to negotiate a peace with the French, and joined in commission by the same monarch with John, Duke of Lancaster, and others, to treat with the Earl of Flanders and others of that country, for the appeasing of certain discords between them and the English. In the 10th RICHARD he was one of the thirteen lords then appointed to govern the kingdom, but being impeached in the 21st of the same king, he had judgment pronounced against him; his lordship received, however, a pardon, but was sent prisoner to the Isle of Jersey. Lord Cobham *m.* Margaret, dau. of Hugh Courtenay, Earl of Devon, and had issue,

Joane, who *m.* Sir John de la Pole, Knt., and dying *v.p*, left an only dau.,

   JOANE, who *m.* 1st, Sir Robert Hemengdale, but had no surviving issue. Her ladyship *m.* 2ndly, Sir Reginald Braybroke, by whom she had one surviving dau.,

      JOANE, *m.* to Sir Thomas Brooke, Knt. (*see* BROOKE, LORD COBHAM).

   She *m.* 3rdly, Sir Nicholas Hawberke, but had no surviving issue; 4thly, SIR JOHN OLDCASTLE, Knt.; and 5thly, Sir John Harpenden.

His lordship *d.* 1409, leaving his above-mentioned grand-dau. Joane, then Lady Hawberke, his sole heiress, who marrying subsequently

SIR JOHN OLDCASTLE, Knt., that gentleman was summoned to parliament, *jure uxoris*, as BARON COBHAM, from 26 October 1409, to 22 March, 1413. Sir John Oldcastle is celebrated in history as leader of the Lollards, the first sect of reformers that arose in England, and eventually by laying down his life in maintenance of his principles. Of this celebrated person Dugdale gives the following account:—
" In the 1st of HENRY V., being tainted in his religion by those pretended holy zealots, then called Lollards, he became one of the chief of that sect, which at that time gave no little disturbance to the peace of the church; for which he was cited to appear before the archbishop of Canterbury. Whereupon, betaking himself to his castle of Couling, he was shortly after apprehended, and brought before the archbishop and others,

in the cathedral of St. Paul, and there, by reason of his obstinacy in those dangerous tenets. received the sentence of an heretick. Under the cloak of this sanctity it was that he and his party designed to murder the king upon Twelfth Night, then keeping his Christmas at Eltham, and to destroy the monasteries of Westminster and St. Albans, as also the cathedral of St. Paul in London, with all the houses of friers in that city : to which end about four score of his party were found, in arms, in the night-time, expecting no less than 25,000 the next day to appear with them in St. Giles Fields. Which pernicious purpose being seasonably prevented, divers of them suffered death at that time. But this Oldcastle escaping, lurked privily for a time in sundry places, and endeavoured to raise new commotions. Wherein failing of that success he expected, in *anno* 1417, 5th HENRY V. (the king being then in his wars of France), he incited the Scots to an invasion of this realm, which, through the vigilancy of John, Duke of Bedford (the king's brother, and his lieutenant here in his absence), was happily prevented, and, at length being taken in Wales, within the territory of the Lord Powys, was brought to his trial, where having judgment of death pronounced against him, viz., to be drawn, hanged, and burnt on the gallows; and accordingly brought to the place of execution, he desired Sir Thomas Erpingham, that in case he saw him rise again the third day after, that then he would be a means to procure favour for the rest of his sect " Walpole, in his "Catalogue of Royal and Noble Authors," gives, however, a more flattering and just character of this unfortunate, though highly gifted nobleman—" The first author, as well as the first martyr, among our nobility, was Sir John Oldcastle, called 'the good Lord Cobham,' a man whose virtues made him a reformer, whose valour made him a martyr, whose martyrdom made him an enthusiast. His ready wit and brave spirit appeared to great advantage on his trial." He wrote "Twelve Conclusions, addressed to the Parliament of England," and several other tracts. His lordship had an only dau., Joane, the heiress of Cobham, who *d.* young, and the BARONY OF COBHAM appears to have remained DORMANT from the period of his execution, until revived in the person of JOHN BROOKE. great-grandson of the above-mentioned Joane de la Pole, in 1445.

Arms—Gu., on a chev., or, three lions rampant, sa.

COBHAM—BARON COBHAM, OF RUNDELL.

By Writ of Summons, dated 3 December, 1326.

Lineage.

STEPHEN DE COBHAM, of Rundell and Alington, co. Kent, son of Henry de Cobham, by Joan his wife, dau. and co-heir of Stephen de Pencestre, was summoned to parliament from 20th EDWARD II. to 6th EDWARD III.; he *d.* in 1334, leaving JOHN, his son and heir, and Avice his wife, him surviving.

COBHAM, OF NORFOLK.

RALPH DE COBHAM, brother of Stephen, of Rundell, had summons to parliament, 30 December, 1324, and 20 February, 1325, *m.* Mary, widow of Thomas of Brotherton, Earl of Norfolk and Earl Marshal, and dau. of William, Lord Roos, and *d.* 1325, having had a son, JOHN DE COBHAM, who was in the wars of France; but neither he nor his descendants were ever summoned to parliament.

COBHAM—BARONS COBHAM, OF STER-BOROUGH, CO. KENT.

By Writ of Summons, dated 25 February, 1342.

Lineage.

REGINALD DE COBHAM, of Sterborough, sprung from the 2nd marriage of John de Cobham, of Cobham, with Joane, dau. of Hugh de Nevill, had a chief command in the English army at Cressy and Poictiers, and was summoned to parliament from the 16th to the 34th EDWARD III. ; he d. 1361, leaving, by Joan his wife, dau. of Maurice de Berkeley, a son and successor,

REGINALD DE COBHAM, summoned to parliament 44th and 46th EDWARD III. He m. 1st, Elizabeth, widow of Fulke le Strange, of Blackmore ; and 2ndly, Alianore, dau. and co-heir of John, Lord Maltravers, widow of Sir John Fitzalan, *alias* Sir John Arundel ; d. 4th HENRY IV., and was s. by his son and heir,

REGINALD DE COBHAM, who m. 1st, Eleanora, dau. of Thomas Culpepper, and 2ndly, Anne, dau. and co-heir of Thomas, Lord Bardolf, and widow of Sir William Clifford. His issue were,

I. Reginald, who d. v. p., leaving an only dau. Margaret, who was 2nd wife of Ralph Nevill, 2nd Earl of Westmoreland of that name.
II. Thomas (Sir), m. Anne, dau. of Humphrey Stafford, Duke of Buckingham, and had an only dau. Anne, who m. Edward Borough, or Burgh, whose son, Thomas, was afterwards created Baron Borough or Burgh, by HENRY VIII.
I. Elizabeth, m. to Richard, Lord Strange, of Knocking.
II. Margaret, m. to Reginald Curteys.
III. Alianore, m. to Humphrey, Duke of Gloucester.
IV. Anne, a nun at Berking.

COKAYNE—VISCOUNT CULLEN.

By Letters Patent, dated 11 August, 1642.

Lineage.

The family of Cokeyn or Cokayne was of importance in the co. of Derby soon after the Conquest, and some magnificent monuments still remain at Ashbourne, in that shire, to their memory.

ROGER COKEYN, of Ashborne, living 1284 (son of William Cokeyn, by Alice his wife, dau. of Hugh de Dalbury, which William was son of another William, son of Andreas, son of John Cokeyn, of Ashbourne, 16 STEPHEN, 1150), had, by Elizabeth his wife, two sons and three daus. The elder son,

WILLIAM COKEYN, of Ashburne, in 1299, by Sarah, his wife, had issue, 1 JOHN, living at Ashbourne, 1305, father of JOHN COKAYNE, who, by Letitia his wife, was father of SIR JOHN COKAYNE, a person of great distinction *temp.* EDWARD III. This last-named John, who represented the co. of Derby in several parliaments, m. Cecilia Ireton, of the co. of Derby, and had two sons, viz.,

EDMUND, of whom presently.
John (Sir), of Bury Hatley, co. Bedford, ancestor of the family of COCKAYNE, OF COCKAYNE-HATLEY.

The elder son,

EDMUND COKAINE, of Ashburne, slain at the battle of Shrewsbury, 1403, m. Elizabeth, dau. of Sir Richard de Herthull, of Pooley, co. Warwick, and heiress of that family. Their son and heir,

SIR JOHN COKAINE, a commissioner of assay, M.P., &c., m. Isabel, dau. of Sir Hugh Shirley, ancestor of the Earl of Ferrers, and d. 1438, having had,

I. John, who m. Anne, dau. of Sir Richard Vernon, and was ancestor of the Cokaines, of Ashburne, co. Derby, extinct in the male line, 1684.
II. WILLIAM, of whom presently.
III. Roger.
IV. Reginald.
I. Ellen (or Alice), m. to Sir Ralph Shirley, Knt.

The 2nd son,

WILLIAM COKAINE, was father of Thomas Cokaine, the father of Roger Cokaine, of Baddesley, co. Warwick, who was the father of WILLIAM COKAINE, of London, merchant-adventurer in Muscovy, Spanish Portugal, and Eastland Companies, of which last he was a governor. This William m. Elizabeth, dau. of Roger Medcalfe, of Wensleydale, and d. 18 November, 1599, leaving a son and heir,

SIR WILLIAM COKAYNE, Knt., sheriff of London in 1609, and soon after an alderman of the same city. JAMES I. having granted in the province of Ulster, *anno* 1612, a considerable tract of land to the city of London, he was appointed governor, and under his direction the city of Londonderry was founded, receiving a considerable grant in the vicinity. He was knighted 8 June, 1616. In 1619, he served the office of lord mayor, and that year purchased the manors of Elmsthorpe, co. Leicester, and of Rushton, co. Northampton. He m. Mary, dau. of Richard Morris, of London (by Maud, dau. of John Daborne, of Guildford), by whom he had,

I. CHARLES, his successor.
II. William, d. s. p.
I. Mary, m. 22 April, 1620, to Charles Howard, 2nd Earl of Nottingham.
II. Anne, m. Sir Hatton Fermor, of Easton Neston, Northamptonshire, and was grandmother of William, created Lord Lempster, ancestor of George, Earl of Pomfret.
III. Martha, m. 1st, to John Ramsay, Earl of Holdernesse; and 2ndly, in February, 1625, to Montagu Bertie, Lord Willoughby of Eresby, afterwards 2nd Earl of Lindsey.
IV. Elizabeth, m. to Thomas, Viscount Fanshawe.
V. Abigail, m. to John Carey, Earl of Dover.
VI. Jane, m. Hon. James Sheffield.

Sir William Cokayne d. 20 October, 1626. His widow (who m. 1630, Henry Carey, 1st Earl of Dover) d. January, 1648-9. Their elder son,

CHARLES COKAYNE, of Rushton, co. Northampton, was elevated to the peerage of Ireland, 11 August, 1642, in the dignity of VISCOUNT AND BARON CULLEN. His lordship m. in 1647, Lady Mary O'Brien, dau. and co-heir of Henry, 5th Earl of Thomond, by whom he had a dau. Elizabeth, and a son his successor (in 1661),

BRYAN, 2nd Viscount Cullen. This nobleman m. Elizabeth, dau. and heiress of Francis Trentham, of Rocester Priory, co. Stafford, by whom he acquired the valuable lordship of Castle Hedingham, in Essex (derived from the de Veres, Earls of Oxford). By her (who was famous for her beauty and wit, and who d. 30 November, 1713,) he had issue,

I. CHARLES, his successor.
II. Trentham, d. unm.
III. George, d. s. p.
I. Elizabeth, m. Thomas Crathorne.
II. Mary, d. unm.

His lordship d. 1687, aged fifty-six, and was s. by the elder son,

CHARLES, 3rd viscount, who m. Catharine, youngest dau. of William, 6th Lord Willoughby, of Parham (son of William, Lord Willoughby, of Parham, by his wife Lady Frances Manners, dau. of John, 4th Earl of Rutland), and was s. by his son (in 1688),

CHARLES, 4th viscount. This nobleman m. Anne, dau. of Arthur Warren, of Stapleford, Notts, by Anne, sister and heiress of Sir John Borlase, Bart. He d. 6 April, 1716, and was s. by his son,

CHARLES, 5th viscount, b. 2 September, 1710; who m. 1st, 1732, his 1st-cousin, Anne, dau. of Borlase Warren, by whom (who d. 1754), he had a son, BORLASE, his heir. His lordship m. 2ndly, Sophia, dau. and co-heir of John Baxter, by Sophia, sister and co-heir of Geo. Woodward, of Stoke Lyne, Oxon, and by her (who d. 13 July, 1802,) had a son,

Hon. William Cockayne, of Rushton Hall, co. Northampton, who m. Barbara, dau. and heir of George Hill, of Rothwell Manor House, co. Northampton, serjeant-at-law, and dying 8 October, 1809, left issue ten daus., viz.,

1 MATILDA-SOPHIA*, m. 31 December, 1804, to Rev. Robert Austen, LL.D., prebendary of Cloyne, and d. 23 February, 1860, having had, with several daus., two sons, who both d. unm. in her lifetime.
2 BARBARA-MARIA, d. 23 September, 1825.
3 MARY-ANNE*, m. 6 April, 1811, to William Adams, of Thorpe, Surrey, and of Dummer Grange, Hants, LL D. (who d. 11 June, 1851), and d. 16 June, 1873, leaving, among other issue, a son,
GEORGE - EDWARD, M.A., Norroy King of Arms, who assumed, by royal licence, 15 August, 1873, the surname and arms of Cokayne, and is of Rothwell Manor House, above-named.
4 GEORGIANA*, m. 11 October, 1824, to John-E. Maunsell, R.H.A., and d. s. p. 19 December, 1864.
5 SOPHIA, d. unm. 20 January, 1828.
6 CAROLINE-ELIZA*, m. 6 April, 1811, to Thomas-Philip Maunsell, of Thorpe Malsor, M.P. for north Northamptonshire; and d. 12 March, 1860, leaving issue.
7 CATHERINE, d. unm. 10 March, 1824.
8 SARAH-MARGARETTA, d. unm. 1 September, 1814.
9 FRANCES-ANNABELLA, m. 9 August, 1816, to William Assheton, of Downham Hall, Lancashire; and d. 25 July, 1835, leaving issue.
10 ELIZABETH-CHARLOTTE, m. 14 February, 1825, to the Hon. Edmond-Sexten Pery, youngest son of the Earl of Limerick, and has issue.

Lord Cullen d. 7 June, 1802, and was s. by his son,

BORLASE, 6th viscount, who d. unm., 11 August, 1810. The Viscounty of Cullen was supposed to have become EXTINCT, being used as one of the extinctions for the creation of the Barony of Howden in 1819. The Patent is lost, but a record in the Heralds' College (given in the ADDENDA) indicates that it contained an extended limitation.

Arms—Arg.; three cocks, gu., crested, sa.

---

* These ladies, by royal warrant, were raised to the precedence of the daughters of a Viscount.

COKE—BARON LOVEL, OF MINSTER LOVEL, CO. OXFORD, VISCOUNT COKE, OF HOLKHAM, CO. NORFOLK, EARL OF LEICESTER.

Barony, by Letters Patent, dated 28 May, 1728.
Earldom, &c., by Letters Patent, dated 9 May, 1744.

Lineage.

The learned Camden, who set forth the pedigree of this ancient family, deduced its origin from

WILLIAM COKE, of Dodington, in Norfolk, mentioned in a deed *anno* 1206, who by his wife Felice, had issue,

GEFFREY COKE, of the same place, from whom descended

SIR EDWARD COKE, the celebrated lawyer. This eminent person, the son of Robert Coke, Esq., of Mileham, in Norfolk, and Winifred his wife, dau. and one of the heirs of William Knightley, of Morgrave-Knightley, in the same shire, was born at the seat of his father, and at ten years of age sent to the grammar-school at Norwich, whence he removed to Trinity College, Cambridge, where he studied for four years, and was in some years afterwards chosen high-steward of that university. From Cambridge he removed to Clifford's Inn, and the year after he was entered a student in the Inner Temple, whence he was called to the bar, and being chosen reader in Lyon's Inn, acquired so much celebrity that he very soon obtained considerable practice. About this period he *m.* Bridget, dau. and co-heir of John Paston, Esq., of Huntingfield Hall, in Suffolk, 3rd son of Sir William Paston, of Paston, with whom he acquired a fortune of £30,000. An alliance, too, that brought him honours and preferments as well as wealth. The cities of Coventry and Norwich soon after elected him their recorder. The county of Norfolk returned him to parliament, and the House of Commons placed him in the speaker's chair. In the 35th of ELIZABETH (1592), Mr. Coke was appointed solicitor, and the next year attorney-general. In 1603 he received the honour of knighthood from King JAMES I. at Greenwich, and in three years afterwards was elevated to the bench as chief of the Court of Common Pleas, from which he was advanced, in 1613, to the dignity of chief justice of England (being the last person who bore that title) and sworn of the privy council. His lordship incurred subsequently, however, the displeasure of the court; and while in disgrace, hearing that a noble lord had solicited from the crown a portion of the lands belonging to the church at Norwich, which he had recovered and settled thereon, he cautioned the peer to desist, or that he would resume his gown and cap, and come into Westminster Hall once again to plead the cause of the church. Between his paternal property, the great marriage portion he had with his wife, and his valuable offices and lucrative practice at the bar, Sir Edward Coke realized an estate so ample, that each of his sons possessed a fortune equal to *that* of an elder brother. Camden, in his " Britannia," says, "that he was a person of admirable parts, than whom, as none ever applied himself closer to the study of the law, so never did any one understand it better. Of which he fully convinced England by his excellent administration for many years together, whilst attorney-general, and by executing the office of lord chief justice of the Common Pleas with the greatest wisdom and prudence; nor did he give less proof of his abilities in his excellent ' Reports,' and Commentaries upon our Laws, whereby he has highly obliged both his own age and posterity." His lordship *d.* 3 September, 1633, at the advanced age of eighty-three. A noble monument was erected to his memory at Tittleshall Church, Norfolk, with his effigies habited in judge's robes lying at full length, under a canopy supported by two marble pillars, on the top of which are four large figures, and between the two pillars two marble tables, bearing Latin inscriptions. Sir Edward Coke's daus., by his 2nd wife Lady Elizabeth Cecil, dau. of Thomas, Earl of Exeter, were

Elizabeth, who *d. unm.*
Frances, *m.* to John Villiers, Viscount Purbeck, son and heir of Sir George Villiers, by Mary, Duchess of Buckingham, and eldest brother of George, Duke of Buckingham, *d. s. p.*

His surviving children, by his 1st wife Bridget, dau. and co-heir of John Paston, Esq., of Huntingfield Hall, Suffolk, were

I. Robert (Sir), *m.* Theophila, only dau. of Thomas, Lord Berkeley, and *d. s. p.* 19 July, 1653.
II. Arthur, *m.* Elizabeth, dau. and heiress of Sir George Walgrave, Knt., of Hitcham, in Norfolk, and left at his decease, h December, 1629, four daus., his co-heirs.
III. John, of Holkham, in Norfolk, *m.* Meriel, dau. and heiress of Anthony Wheatley, Esq. (son of William Wheatley, pro-

thonotary of the Court of Common Pleas), by whom he had seven sons and seven daus., whereof EDWARD, his heir apparent, *d. v. p.* leaving no issue by Elizabeth his wife, dau. of George, Lord Berkeley, whereby the inheritance devolved, eventually, upon his youngest son,
    JOHN, who dying *unm.*, the estate of Holkham came to the heirs of HENRY COKE, of Thurrington, 5th son of Sir Edward Coke (next mentioned).
IV. Henry, of Thurrington, in Suffolk, *m.* Margaret, dau. and heiress of Richard Lovelace, Esq., of Kingsdown, co. Kent, and was *s.* by his eldest son,
    RICHARD, who *m.* Mary, dau. of Sir John Rous, Bart., of Henham Hall, in Suffolk, and left an only son,
        ROBERT, of whom hereafter, as inheritor of the principal part of Sir Edward Coke's fortune, and grandfather of the 1st peer.
V. Clement, *m.* Sarah, dau. and co-heiress of Alexander Redich, Esq., of Redich, co. Lancaster (by a dau. and co-heiress of Sir Robert Langley, of Agecroft, in the same shire), by whom he acquired the estate of Longford, in Derbyshire, and was *s.*, in May 1619, by his elder son,
    SIR EDWARD COKE, who was created a baronet 30 December, 1641. He *m.* Catherine, dau. and co-heiress of Sir William Dyer, Knt., of Great Stoughton, co. Huntingdon, and had issue,
        ROBERT, } successive baronets.
        EDWARD, }
        Catharine, *m.* to Cornelius Clarke, Esq., of Norton.
        Anne, *d. unm.*
        Theophila, *m.* to — Bullock, Esq.
    Sir Edward was *s.* by his eldest son,
    SIR ROBERT COKE, of Longford, 2nd baronet, M.P. for the co. of Derby, 1st JAMES II., who *m.* Sarah, 3rd dau and co-heiress of — Barker, Esq., of Abrightlee, co. Salop, but dying *s. p.*, 1617, the title and estates devolved upon his brother,
    SIR EDWARD COKE, of Longford, 3rd baronet, at whose decease, *u. m.*, 25 August, 1727, the baronetcy EXPIRED, while the estates passed by the baronet's will to Edward Coke, Esq., brother of Thomas, 1st Lord Lovel.
I. Anne, *m.* to Ralph Sadler, Esq., son and heir of Sir Ralph Sadler, Knt.
II. Bridget, *m.* to William Skinner, Esq., son and heir of Sir Vincent Skinner.

So much for the lord chief justice's children, we now return to the grandson of his son HENRY.

ROBERT COKE, Esq., of Thurrington, who upon the decease of his cousin (the son of his great-uncle JOHN), John Coke, Esq., of Holkham, in Norfolk, *unm.*, inherited that estate, and thus became possessed of the chief part of (Sir Edward Coke) his great-grandfather's property. Mr. Coke *m.* Lady Anne Osborne, dau. of Thomas, 1st Duke of Leeds, Lord Treasurer of England, by whom he had an only surviving son, his successor at his decease, 16 January, 1679,

EDWARD COKE, Esq., who *m.* Carey, dau. of Sir John Newtown, Bart., of Barrows Court, co. Gloucester, and had issue,

I. THOMAS, his successor.
II. Edward of Longford, co. Derby, who bequeathed at his decease, *unm.* in 1733, that estate to his younger brother.
III. Robert, vice-chamberlain to Queen ANNE, who *m.* June, 1733, Lady Jane Holt, widow of John Holt, Esq., of Redgrave, in Suffolk, and sister and co-heiress of Philip, Duke of Wharton, but *d. s. p.*
    I. Carey, *m.* Sir Marmaduke Wyvil, 6th baronet, of Constable Burton, co. York, and *d. s. p.*
    II. Anne, *m.* to Philip Roberts, a major in the 2nd troop of horse guards, and left a son,
        WENMAN ROBERTS, of whom hereafter, as heir to the entire of the estates of his uncle, the EARL OF LEICESTER.

Mr. Coke *d.* 13 April, 1707, and was *s.* by his eldest son,

THOMAS COKE, Esq., who was elected a knight of the Bath, 27 May, 1725, and elevated to the peerage, 28 May, 1728, as BARON LOVEL, *of Minster Lovel, Oxford.* In 1733, his lordship was constituted joint postmaster-general, and created 9 May, 1744, *Viscount Coke, of Holkham,* and EARL OF LEICESTER; his lordship *m.* 2 July, 1718, Lady Mary Tufton, 4th dau. and co-heiress of Thomas, 6th Earl of Thanet (in which lady's favour the abeyance of the BARONY DE CLIFFORD was terminated by the crown in 1734), by whom he had an only son,

EDWARD, *Viscount Coke,* who *m.* in 1747, Lady Mary Campbell, dau. and co-heiress of John, Duke of Argyll and Greenwich, but *d. s. p.* in the lifetime of his father, *anno* 1753.

The earl *d.* 20 April, 1759, and thus leaving no issue, the *Barony of Lovel* and *Earldom of Leicester,* with the *viscounty,* became EXTINCT.

His lordship commenced the stately pile of building called Holkham Hall, in Norfolk, which was completed by the countess, who survived him many years: her ladyship *d.* in 1775. The whole of the extensive estates of the Earl of Leiceeter devolved upon his nephew (*refer* to Anne, youngest dau. of Edward Coke, Esq., and Carey. dau. of Sir John Newton Bart.), WENMAN ROBERTS, Esq., who thereupon assumed the surname of COKE only, and marrying Miss Elizabeth Chamberlayne, left, with two daus., and a younger son, EDWARD, an elder son, THOMAS WILLIAM COKE, of Holkham, M.P. for the co. of Norfolk, who was created (12 August, 1837) EARL OF LEICESTER, of Holkham.

Arms—Party per pale, *gu.* and *az.*, three eagles displayed, *arg.*

COLBORNE—BARON COLBORNE.

By Letters Patent, dated 15 May, 1839.

Lineage.

NICHOLAS-WILLIAM RIDLEY-COLBORNE, Esq., M.P., 2nd son of Sir Matthew-White Ridley, 2nd Baronet of Blagdon (*see* WHITE-RIDLEY, *o.' Blag'lon*), by Sarah his wife, dau. and heir of Benjamin Colborne, Esq., of Bath, inherited the property of his maternal uncle, William Colborne, Esq., and assumed. in consequence, the additional surname and arms of COLBORNE, by sign-manual, 21 June, 1803. He was *b.* 14 April, 1779; *m.* 14 June, 1808, Charlotte, eldest dau. of the Right Hon. Thomas Steele, and by her (who *d.* 17 February, 1855) he had issue,

I. William-Nicholas. *b.* 24 July, 1814, M.P.; *d. unm.* 1846.
I. HENRIETTA-SUSANNA, *m.* 12 August, 1828, Brampton Gurdon, Esq., M.P., of Letton, in Norfolk, and has issue. Robert-Thornhagh Gurdon; William Brampton Gurdon; Charlotte, wife of Horace Broke, Esq.; and Amy-Louisa.
II. MARIA-CHARLOTTE, *m.* 13 July, 1830, to Sir George-Edmund Nugent, Bart., and has Edmund-Charles Nugent and other issue.
III. Emily-Frances, *m.* 11 April, 1833, to John-Moyer Heathcote, Esq., M.P., of Connington Castle, co. Huntingdon, and *d.* 13 October, 1849, leaving John-Moyer Heathcote and other issue.
IV. LOUISA-HARRIET, *m.* 25 September, 1819, to Harvie-Morton Farquhar, Esq., 2nd son of Sir Thomas Harvie Farquhar, Bart., and has Alfred Farquhar and other issue.

Mr. Ridley-Colborne was raised to the peerage as BARON COLBORNE, OF WEST HARDING, co. Norfolk, 15 May, 1839; but *d.* 3 May, 1854, when the title became EXTINCT.

Arms—Quarterly: 1st and 4th. arg., on a chev., gu., between three bugle horns, sa., stringed of the 2nd, as many mullets pierced, or, for COLBORNE; 2nd and 3rd. gu., on a chev., between three doves, arg., as many pellets for RIDLEY.

COLE—BARON RANELAGH.

By Letters Patent, dated 18 April, 1715.

Lineage.

SIR WILLIAM COLE, Knt., the first of the Cole family who settled in Ireland, fixed his abode, early in the reign of JAMES I., in the co. of Fermanagh, and becoming an undertaker in the northern plantation, had an assignment, in 1611, of 1,000 acres of escheated lands in the co. wherein he resided ; to which, in 1612, were added 320 in the same county, whereof 80 were assigned for the town of Enniskillen. Sir William raised a regiment and fought with great success against the rebels in 1643. He *d.* in Oct. 1653, leaving by Catherine his 2nd wife, dau. of Sir Lawrence Parsons, of Birr, 2nd baron of the Irish exchequer, two sons,

MICHAEL (Sir), Knt., M.P. for Enniskillen, ancestor of William Willoughby Cole, EARL OF ENNISKILLEN. (*See* BURKE'S *Peerage.*)
JOHN.

The 2nd son,
SIR JOHN COLE, of Newland, co. Dublin, M.P. for the co. of Fermanagh, having distinguished himself during the rebellion, particularly in the relief of Enniskillen, of which he was governor, and being instrumental in promoting the restoration of CHARLES II., was created a Baronet of Ireland 23 January, 1660. He *m.* Elizabeth, dau. of John Chichester, Esq., of Dungannon, and had issue,

I. ARTHUR, his heir.
II. Michael, born, of Derry, co. Tipperary, *m.* in September, 1701,

128

Catherine, eldest dau. of John Cusack, Esq., of Kilklaseen, co. Clare, and by her (who *d.* in 1718) had an only son, John, *b.* 1703, *d. unm.* in March 1724 : he *d.* in 1726.
III. Richard, of Archer's Grove, co. Kilkenny, M.P. for Enniskillen, *b.* 1671 ; who *m.* 1st, in 1698, Penelope, dau. and heir of Sir William Evans, Bart., of Kilcreene; and 2ndly, Mary Keating ; but *d. s. p.* in 1730, Toby Purcell, Esq., who resided at Archer's Grove.
IV. Edward, *b.* in May, 1674, buried in the chancel of St. Michan's Church, 9 January following.
I. Catharine, *m.* to Thomas Brooke, Esq., of Donegal, and had

HENRY BROOKE, Esq , M.P. for the co. of Fermanagh, who *m.* in 1711. Lettice, dau. of Mr. Alderman Benjamin Burton, of the city of Dublin, and left at his decease, in 1761, besides daus., two sons, viz.,

ARTHUR, M.P. for Fermanagh, and privy councillor, created a baronet of Ireland in 1764, which honour ceased at his demise in 1785, when he left. by his wife Margaret, only dau. of Thomas Fortescue, Esq., of Reynold's Town, co. Louth, and sister of the 1st Lord Clermont, two daus., his co-heirs,
Selina. *m.* to Thomas, 1st Viscount de Vesci.
Letitia-Charlotte, *m.* to Sir John Parnell.
Francis, who *m.* in 1765, Hannah, dau. of Henry Prittie, Esq., of Dunally, and was great-grandfather of the present SIR VICTOR ALEXANDER BROOKE, of Colbrooke.
II. Letitia, *m.* to William Fitzgerald, dean of Cloyne, afterwards bishop of Clonfert.
III. Mary, *m.* to Henry, Earl of Drogheda, ancestor by her of the Marquesses of Drogheda.
IV. Frances, *m.* Sir Thomas Domvile, Bart., but *d. s. p.*
v. Margaret, *m.* 1st, the Very Rev. John Burdett, dean of Clonfert, and 2ndly, to Thomas Lloyd, Esq., of Croghan. co. Roscommon, who *d. s. p.* : Margaret Cole left by her 1st husband, a son, Arthur Burdett, Esq., of Lismalin, ancestor of the BURDETTS of Ballymany, co. Kildare, and of Hunstanton, King's Co.
VI. Elizabeth, *m.* to Sir Michael Cole, Knt., and by him was ancestor of William Willoughby Cole, EARL OF ENNISKILLEN.
VII. Alicia, *bapt* 25 July, 1679, buried 28 December, 1680, with her brother Edward.

Sir John Cole, whose will bears date 1 August, 1688, and was proved 5 October, 1691, was *s.* by his eldest son,
SIR ARTHUR COLE, Bart., M.P., who was created by King GEORGE I., 18 April, 1715, BARON RANELAGH, *of Ranelagh*, with limitation of the title, in default of his male issue, to the heirs male of his father. His lordship *m.* 1st, Catharine, dau. of William, 3rd Lord Byron ; and 2ndly in 1748, Selina, dau. of Peter Bathurst, Esq., of Clarendon Park, Wilts; but *d. s. p.* 12 October, 1754, aged ninety, when the dignity became EXTINCT.

Arms—Arg., a bull passant, sa., armed and unguled, or, within a border of the second, charged with eight bezants ; on a canton, az., a harp, or, stringed of the field.

COLEPEPER — BARONS COLEPEPER, OF THORESWAY, CO. LINCOLN.

By Letters Patent, dated 21 October, 1644.

Lineage.

SIR THOMAS COLEPEPER, Knt., of Bay Hall, in the parish of Pepenbury, near Tunbridge, co. Kent, son and heir of Sir John Colepeper of the same place, Knt., had a son,
JOHN COLEPEPER, of Bay Hall aforesaid, Esq., who *m.* Eliza, dau. and co-heir of Sir John Hardreshall, of Hardreshall, co. Warwick, Knt., and had issue,

I. THOMAS (Sir), *m.* Jane, dau. and co-heir of Nicholas Green, by Joan his wife, dau. and heir of John Bruse, of Exton, and had a son,
SIR THOMAS, of Exton, who *m.* the dau. of Cromwell, and had an only dau. and heir, Catherine, *m.* 1st, to Robert Harington, and 2ndly, to B yan Talbot.
II. WALTER, of whom presently.
III. Thomas, *d. s. p.*
IV. Nicholas, who had a dau., Susanna Joyce.

The 2nd son,
WALTER COLEPEPER, Esq., *m.* Agnes, dau. of Edmund Roper, Esq., of St. Dunstan's, in the city of Canterbury, and had issue,

I. Richard, *m.* the dau. and co-heir of Richard Wakehurst, and *d. s. p.*
II. JOHN, of whom presently.
III. Nicholas, *m.* Elizabeth. dau. and co-heir of Richard Wakehurst, of Wakehurst, and *d.* 2nd HENRY VIII., 1510, leaving issue,

1 Richard, of Wakehurst, who *m.* Joan, dau. of Richard Naylor, of London, and had issue,

John, of Wakehurst, *m.* Emma, dau. and co-heir of Sir John Erneley, Knt., and had with other issue, a son, Thomas Wakehurst, who *m.* Phillipa. dau. of John Teacher, of Presthouse, co. Suffolk, who was father of Sir Edward Colepeper, Knt., of Wakehurst, who *m.* Elizabeth, dau. of William Farnefoulde, co. Sussex.

Gerard.   Edmund.   John, of Norfolk.
Thomas.   William.
Jasper, *m.* Anne Stafford, widow of Richard Clifford.
Elizabeth, *m.* to John Fynes, of co. Sussex.
Anne, *m.* to John Hayward.
Alice, *m.* to William Bird, of co. Sussex.
Mary, *d. s. p.*

2 Thomas.   3 George.
4 Edward, LL.D.   5 Richard.
1 Margaret.

i. Margaret.   ii. Elizabeth.

The 2nd son,

Sir John Colepeper, Knt., *m.* Agnes, dau. and heir of John Bedgebery, Esq., of Bedgebery, and *d.* 1480, having had issue,

i. Alexander (Sir), of Bedgebery, *m.* 1st, Agnes, dau. of Roger Davy, Esq., of Northfleet, co. Kent, and by her had an only dau., Alice, *m.* to Sir Adam Newington, of Withernden Ticehurst, co. Sussex, Knt.; and 2ndly, Constantia, dau. of Sir Robert Chamberlaine, of co. Sussex, Knt., by whom he had issue,

1 Thomas, of Bedgebery, *m.* 1st, Eliza, dau. and co-heir of Sir William Hawte, Knt., of Borne, and 2ndly, Helen, dau. and co-heir of Sir Walter Hendley; by his first wife he had a son,

Alexander (Sir), of Bedgebery, who *m.* Mary, dau. of William, Lord Dacre, of the North, and had a son, Sir Anthony Colepeper, of Bedgebery, Knt., who *m.* Anne. dau. and co-heir of Sir Roger Martin, of London, Knt., and had issue,

Alexander (Sir), of Bedgebery, who *m.* 1st, Elizabeth, dau. of Sir Thomas Roberts, of Glassonbery, Knt., and had an only dau., Anne, *b.* 1603; *m.* 1624, Thomas, son and heir apparent of Sir Henry Shelgrave, Knt.; and 2ndly, Jane, dau. of Ninian Burrell, of Cuckfield, co. Sussex.

William, *m.* Eleanor, dau. of Robert Say, of Ickenham, co. Middlesex.
Henry.   Roger.
Thomas.   James.
Mary, *m.* to Henry Crispe, of Quex.
Elizabeth, *m.* to John Thorpe, of Cudworth, co. Surrey.
Anne-Catherine.

2 Thomas.

3 John, *m.* Mary, dau. and co-heir of Sir Christopher Hales, Knt., custos rotulorum, and had an only dau. and heir, Anne.

1 Jane, *m.* to Richard Molins, of Perks.
2 Margaret, *m.* to Philip Choute.
3 Catherine, *m.* to Thomas Barrett.
4 Joan, *m.* to John Fitz-James, of co. Devon.
5 Elizabeth, *m.* to John Saint-Cleere, *s. p.*

ii. Walter, of whom presently.
i. Jocosa, *m.* 1st, Geratio Hume, and 2ndly, Reginald Peckham.

The 2nd son,

Walter Colepeper, *m.* Anne, only dau. and heir of John Aucher, of Losnam, in the parish of Newenden, and had (with a dau. Elizabeth, *m.* to Thomas Wilsford, Esq.), a son and heir,

William Colepeper, of Losenham and Wigsell, who *m.* Cecilia, dau. of Edward Barrett, and had issue,

i. John, of whom presently.

ii. Francis, of Greenway Court, *m.* Joane, dau. of John Pordage, of Rodmersham, and *d.* 1591, aged fifty-three, leaving a son,

Sir Thomas Colepeper, of Hollingbourne, who *m.* Elizabeth dau. of John Cheney, of Guestling, co. Sussex and by her (who *d.* 27 October, 1638, aged fifty-six) he had issue,

Cheney.
Thomas (Sir), who was father of Margaret, the wife of William Hamilton, of Chilston or Boctonplue, co. Kent.
Judith, 2nd wife of John, 1st Lord Colepeper.

The elder son,

Sir John Colepeper, of Wigsell, Knt., *m.* Elizabeth, dau. of William Sedley, of Southfleet, and had a son,

Sir John Colepeper, of Bedgebery, knight of the shire, co. Kent, in the parliament which met in 1641. He was chancellor of the exchequer, and afterwards master of the Rolls, and one of the privy-council of King Charles I., and was elevated to the peerage by that monarch, 21 October, 1644, as Lord Colepeper, *Baron of Thoresway, co. Lincoln.* His lordship adhered zealously to the royal cause during the whole of the civil

---

wars, and withdrew with King Charles II., in whose exile he shared for twelve years, but had the high gratification of witnessing the restoration of his royal master. Lord Colepeper *m.* 1st, Philippa, dau. of Sir — Snelling, Knt. and had issue,

Alexander, who *m.* Catherine, dau. and heiress of Sir Edward Ford, Knt., of Harting, co. Sussex, but *d. v. p., s. p.*
Philippa, *m.* to Thomas Harlakenden, Esq., of Wood Church, in Kent.

His lordship *m.* 2ndly, Judith, dau. of Sir Thomas Colepeper, of Hollingbourne, Knt., by whom he had four sons and three daus., viz.,

i. Thomas, his successor.
ii. John   iii. Cheney.   iv. Francis.
i. Elizabeth, *m.* James Hamilton, Esq., and was mother of
James, 6th Earl of Abercorn.
ii. Judith, *m.* to — Colepeper, Esq.
iii. Philippa.

Lord Colepeper *d.* in July, 1660, and was *s.* by his eldest surviving son,

Thomas Colepeper, 2nd baron, who *m.* Margaret, dau. and co-heir of Seigneur Jean de Hesse, of the noble family of Hesse, in Germany, by whom he had an only dau. and heiress,

Catherine, who *m.* Thomas, Lord Fairfax, and conveyed to her husband Leeds Castle, in Kent. At the decease of Robert, 7th Lord Fairfax, his nephew, the Rev. Denny Martin *s.* to Leeds Castle, which is now the seat of Charles Wykeham Martin, Esq.

His lordship *d.* in 1688, and, leaving no male issue, the title devolved upon his brother,

John Colepeper, 3rd baron. This nobleman *m.* Frances, dau. of Sir Thomas Colepeper, of Hollingbourne, co. Kent, but dying *s. p.* in 1719, was *s.* by his brother,

Cheney Colepeper, 4th baron, at whose decease, issueless (his younger brother, Francis, having previously *d. unm.*), in 1725, the Barony of Colepeper became extinct.

Bedgebery, the old residence of the Colepepers, is now the seat and property of A. B. Beresford Hope, Esq.

Arms—Arg., a bend engrailed, gu.

COLLINGWOOD—BARON COLLINGWOOD, OF COLDBURNE AND HETHPOOL, CO. NORTHUMBERLAND.

By Letters Patent, dated 20 November, 1805.

Lineage.

Cuthbert Collingwood, *b.* 1750, son of Cuthbert Collingwood, Esq., of Ditchburne, co. Northumberland, having adopted the naval profession, obtained the rank of lieutenant in 1775, was made post-captain in 1780, advanced to the rank of rear-admiral of the White in 1795, rear-admiral of the Red in 1801, vice-admiral of the Blue in 1804, in which commission he had the glory of being second in command at the memorable battle off Cape Trafalgar, 21 October, 1805, under the immortal Nelson; and for the services rendered upon that triumphant occasion, the vice-admiral obtained the professional promotion of vice-admiral of the Blue, and was advanced to the peerage 20 November, 1805, as Baron Collingwood, *of Coldburne and Hethpool, co. Northumberland.* His lordship *m.* Patience, dau. and co-heiress of Erasmus Blackett, Esq., alderman of Newcastle-upon-Tyne, by whom he had issue,

Sarah, *m.* 30 May, 1816, George Lewis Newnham Collingwood, Esq., F.R.S., and *d.* 25 November, 1851, leaving issue.
Mary-Patience, *m.* Anthony Denny, Esq., of Barhamwood Herts, and *d.* 18 September, 1823, leaving issue.

His lordship *d.* in 1810, when, leaving no male issue, the Barony of Collingwood became extinct.

COLVILE—BARONS COLVILE.

By Writ of Summons, dated 14 December, 1264.

Lineage.

In the time of King Stephen, Philip de Colvile, being opposed to that monarch, built a castle in Yorkshire, and fortified it against him, but which Stephen invested, reduced, and demolished. In the ensuing reign we find this feudal lord one of the witnesses to the agreement between the King of England and the King of Scots, by which the latter obliging himself to be faithful to King HENRY, did homage to him at York. To this Philip *s.*

WILLIAM DE COLVILE, one of the barons who took up arms against JOHN, and was excommunicated by the Pope. This William, being taken prisoner at the battle of Lincoln, in the 1st HENRY III., his wife Maude had safe conduct to the king, to treat for his liberation, and having accomplished her object, obtained a royal precept to William, Earl of Albemarle, for the restoration of her husband's castle at Birham, co. Lincoln. William de Colvile was *s.* by his son,

ROBERT DE COLVILE, who had also taken up arms against JOHN, and in the 17th of that monarch's reign had letters of safe conduct, with Roger de Jarpevill, to the royal presence, to treat of peace on behalf of the barons. Continuing, however, in rebellion, he was taken prisoner by Falcase de Breant, in the 1st HENRY III. To this Robert *s.*

WALTER DE COLVILE, a person of no less turbulent disposition than his predecessors. Joining with Montfort, Earl of Leicester, he was taken prisoner by Prince Edward, at Kenilworth, in the 49th HENRY III , but under the decree, called the "Dictum of Kenilworth," was admitted to a composition for his lands which had been seized, and he appears to have been summoned to parliament as a BARON in the same year, 24 December, 1264. His lordship *d.* in 1276, and was *s.* by his son,

ROGER DE COLVILE, 2nd baron, who was sheriff of Norfolk and Suffolk, in the 51st HENRY III., and paid £100 .line in the 14th EDWARD I. for permission to marry Ermentrude, widow of Stephen de Cressy, by whom he had issue,

1. EDMUND, his successor.
2. Elizabeth, *m.* to — Basset, of Sapcote, co. Lincoln, and had
    SIMON, whose son and heir,
    RALPH BASSET, of Sapcote, became eventually co-heir to the Colviles.
II. Alice, *m.* Sir John Gernun, and had
    John Gernun, who became eventually co-heir to the Colviles.

His lordship *d.* in 1287, and was *s.* by his son,

EDMUND DE COLVILE, 3rd baron, but who does not appear by the existing enrolments to have been summoned to parliament. This nobleman *m.* Margaret, dau. of Robert de Ufford, and dying in 1315, was *s.* by his son,

ROBERT DE COLVILE, 4th baron, summoned to parliament from 25 February, 1342, to 20 January, 1366. His lordship *d.* in 1368, and was *s.* by his son,

WALTER DE COLVILE, 5th baron, but who does not appear by the existing enrolments to have been summoned to parliament. His lordship *m.* Margaret, dau. and heiress of Giles de Bassingburne, and was *s.* by his grandson,

ROBERT DE COLVILE, son of Walter de Colvile, who *d. v. p.* Robert *d.* in early youth, leaving Ralph Basset, of Sapcote, and Sir John Gernun (above-mentioned) his heirs, between whose descendants and representatives it is presumed the BARONY OF COLVILE is now in ABEYANCE.

Arms—Or, a fesse, gu.

COLVILL—LORD COLVILL, OF OCHILTRIE.

By Letters Patent, dated 4 January, 1651.

Lineage.

ROBERT COLVILL, of Cleish, who had a charter of the Barony of Cleish, 17 November, 1574, wherein he is designated son and heir of Robert Colvill, of Cleish, *d.* in January 1634. By his wife Beatrix, dau. of John Haldane, of Gleneagles, he left issue,

ROBERT, of whom presently.
II. David, *d.* before 6 March, 1649. He *m.* (contract dated 6 July, 1630) Agnes, youngest dau. of David Beaton, of Balfour, in Fife, and had issue,
  1 ROBERT, 2nd Lord Colvill.
  2 David, *m.* (contract, dated 30 June, 1664) Margaret, dau. of Michael Barclay, advocate, and *d.* before 3 November, 1665
  3 Andrew, *d. s. p.*
  1 Jean, *m.* 2 September, 1658, to Thomas Alexander, of Sheddoway.
2. Margaret, *m.* to David Wemyss, of Fingask.

The elder son,

SIR ROBERT COLVILL, of Cleish, knighted by CHARLES I., who
130

was raised to the peerage as LORD COLVILL, *of Ochiltrie*, 4 January, 1651, by patent to him and his heirs male; he *m.* Janet, 2nd dau. of Sir John Wemyss, but by her, who *d.* April, 1655, had no issue. He *d.* at Crombie, 25 August, 1662, and was *s.* by (the son of his brother David) his nephew,

ROBERT COLVILL, as 2nd Lord Colvill, of Ochiltrie. He *m.* Margaret, dau. of David Wemyss, of Fingask, by whom he had, with two daus. (the elder, Margaret, wife of Sir John Ayton, of Ayton; and the younger, *m.* to the Rev. Mr. Logan, minister of Torry), a son,

ROBERT COLVILL, 3rd Lord Colvill, of Ochiltrie; who *d. s. p.*, leaving Robert Ayton, his grand nephew, his heir of line, who took the name of COLVILL, and was designed Robert-Ayton Colvill, of Craigflower. The title was assumed by David Colvill, son of William Colvill, tenant at Balcormie Mill, in Fife, but he never was voted as such. He held the rank of major, and *d. unm.* in London, 8 February, 1782, and his pretensions to the peerage descended to his cousin, Robert Colvill, whose vote, registered at the election of 1788, was subsequently disallowed by the House of Lords.

Arms—Arg., a cross moline, sa.

COLYEAR—EARL OF PORTMORE.

Barony, by Letters Patent, dated 1 June, 1699.
Earldom, by Letters Patent, dated 13 April, 1703.

Lineage.

ALEXANDER ROBERTSON. Esq. (who claimed descent from the ancient family of Robertson of Strowan), was created a Baronet of England 20 February, 1677. He subsequently settled in Holland, acquired a considerable fortune there, and assumed the name of Colyear. Sir Alexander had two sons, viz.,

DAVID, of whom we treat.
Walter Philip, *d.* at Maestricht, November, 1747, æt. ninety, leaving a dau. Elizabeth, maid of honour to Queen ANNE, and lady of the bedchamber to Queen CAROLINE; who *m.* in January, 1709, Lionel, Duke of Dorset; and *d.* in June, 1768, leaving issue.

The elder son,

DAVID COLYEAR, Esq., a military officer of renown, distinguished himself in 1674 as commander of the Scots regiment in the pay of the United States of Holland, and afterwards under the banner of the Prince of Orange, in the years 1689 and 1690, in Ireland. Sir David was elevated to the peerage of Scotland, 1 June, 1699, by the title of LORD PORTMORE AND BLACKNESS; and created, 13 April, 1703, EARL OF PORTMORE, Viscount Milsington, and Baron Colyear. The earl *m.* Catharine, only child of Sir Charles Sedly, Bart., of Southfleet, co. Kent, who had been created, 20 January, 1685, Baroness of Darlington and Countess of Dorchester for life. His lordship *d.* 2 January, 1730, having had two sons,

DAVID, Viscount Milsington, who *m.* 20 November, 1724, Bridget, dau. of the Hon. John Noel, of Walcot, co. Northampton, 3rd son of Baptist, Viscount Campden. All his children *d.* in infancy, and he *d.* at Piperno, 10 March, 1729.
CHARLES, 2nd earl.

The second son,

CHARLES COLYEAR, 2nd Earl of Portmore, who *m.* 7 October, 1732, Juliana, dau. and co-heir of Roger Hale, Esq., and relict of Peregrine, 3rd Duke of Leeds; and dying 5 July, 1785, left issue,

1. DAVID, Viscount Milsington, *d. unm.* 16 January, 1756, æt. eighteen.
II. WILLIAM-CHARLES, 3rd earl.
1. Caroline, *b.* December, 1733; *m.* 27 October, 1751, Sir Nathaniel Curzon, of Kedleston, co. Derby, created Lord Scarsdale, 1761; and *d.* 7 February, 1812. (*See* BURKE'S *Peerage.*)
II. Juliana, *b.* 1735; *m.* 23 November, 1759, Henry Dawkins, Esq., of Standlynch, co. Wilts. and Over Norton, co. Oxford. M.P., and had, with four daus., eight sons, viz.,
  1 JAMES DAWKINS, M.P., who assumed the surname of COLYEAR, on succeeding to the estates of his uncle, the Earl of Portmore; his issue is EXTINCT
  2 George Hay Dawkins-Pennant, of Penrhyn Castle, co. Carnarvon, whose daus. and co-heiresses were Juliana, wife of the Hon. Edward Douglas, and Emma-Elizabeth-Alicia, wife of the late Lord Sudeley.
  3 Henry Dawkins, M.P., *m.* Augusta, dau. of General Sir Henry Clinton, G.C.B., and had Colonel HENRY DAWKINS, of Over Norton, co. Oxford, and other issue.

4 William, d. an infant.   5 Richard.
6 Edward, in holy orders.
7 Charles, of the grenadier guards, d. 1799.
8 John, fellow of All Souls, d. 1844.

The 2nd son,

WILLIAM-CHARLES COLYEAR, 3rd Earl of Portmore, m. 5 November 1770, Mary, 2nd dau. of John, 8th Earl of Rothes, by whom he left issue,

I. THOMAS-CHARLES, Viscount Milsington.
II. William, an officer of rank in the army, d. s. p.
III. Francis, b. January, 1781, d 25 May, 1787.
IV. John David, lieutenant 64th foot, d. 19 March, 1801.
I. Mary, b. in 1773, } d. at Bath, 11 August, 1800.
II. Julia, b. in 1774, }
III. Catherine-Caroline, m. 1810, to James Brecknell, Esq.

His lordship d. in 1823, and was s. by his son,

THOMAS-CHARLES COLYEAR, 4th Earl of Portmore; who m. 1st, 22 May, 1793, Mary-Elizabeth, only child of Brownlow, Duke of Ancaster, by whom he had an only son, BROWNLOW-CHARLES, who s. to the great personal property of his grandfather, the Duke of Ancaster, at the decease of that nobleman in 1809, but d. at Rome, in 1819, of wounds received from banditti. The earl m. 2ndly, 6 September, 1828, Frances, youngest dau. of William Murrells, Esq. His lordship d. 18 January, 1835, and with him all the honours EXPIRED.

Arms—Gu., on a chev., between three wolves' heads, truncated and erased, arg., as many oak trees, eradicated, ppr., fructed, or.

COMPTON—BARON WILMINGTON, OF WILMINGTON, CO. SUSSEX, VISCOUNT PEVENSEY, AND EARL OF WILMINGTON.

Barony, by Letters Patent, dated 11 January, 1728.
Earldom, &c., by Letters Patent, dated 14 May, 1730.

Lineage.

The Right Honourable SIR SPENCER COMPTON, K.B., 3rd son of James, 3rd Earl of Northampton, having filled the Speaker's chair of the House of Commons in the parliaments of 1714 and 1722, and subsequently the offices of paymaster-general of his majesty's land forces, and treasurer of Chelsea Hospital, was elevated to the peerage 11 January, 1728, as Baron Wilmington. In 1730, his lordship was constituted lord privy seal, and advanced 14 May in that year to the dignities of Viscount Pevensey, and EARL OF WILMINGTON. In the December following he was declared lord president of the council, and installed, 22 August, 1733, a knight of the Garter. He was also one of the lords justices during the king's absence in Hanover, and one of the governors of the Charter House. This nobleman, who was esteemed a personage of great worth, abilities, and integrity, d. unm. in July, 1743, when all his honours became EXTINCT; while his estates passed by his lordship's bequest to his brother George, 4th Earl of Northampton, and have since been carried by that nobleman's great-grand-dau. Lady Elizabeth Compton, only dau. and heiress of Charles, 7th Earl of Northampton, into the Cavendish family, upon her ladyship's marriage in 1782, with Lord George Cavendish (afterwards Earl of Burlington), grandfather of the present Duke of Devonshire. The Barony of Wilmington was revived on 7 September, 1812, in the advancement of Charles, 9th and late earl, to the Marquisate of Northampton.

Arms—Sa., a lion passant guardant, or, between three helmets, arg.

COMYN—EARL OF NORTHUMBERLAND.

Conferred by WILLIAM THE CONQUEROR, anno 1068.

Lineage.

In the 3rd year of King WILLIAM THE CONQUEROR, that monarch conferred the Earldom of Northumberland, vacant by the death of Earl Copsi, upon

ROBERT COMYN, but the nomination accorded so little with the wishes of the inhabitants of the county that they at first resolved to abandon entirely their dwellings; being prevented doing so, however, by the inclemency of the season, it was then determined, at all hazards, to put the new earl to death. Of this evil design his lordship had intimation, through Egelivine, bishop of Durham, but, disregarding the intelligence, he repaired to Durham with 700 soldiers and commenced a course of plunder and bloodshed, which rousing the inhabitants of the neighbourhood, the town was assaulted and carried by a multitude of country people, and the earl and all his troops, to a man, put to death. This occurrence took place in 1069, in a few months after his lordship's appointment to the earldom.

Arms—Gu., three garbs, or.

CONINGSBY—BARON CONINGSBY, OF CONINGSBY, CO. LINCOLN, EARL OF CONINGSBY. BARONESS AND VISCOUNTESS CONINGSBY, OF HAMPTON COURT, CO. HEREFORD.

Barony, by Letters Patent, dated 18 June, 1715.

Earldom, by Letters Patent, dated 30 April, 1719.

Baroness and Viscountess, by Letters Patent, dated 26 January, 1716.

Lineage.

The surname of this family was originally assumed from the town of Coningsby, co. Salop, and the Coningsbys are said to have been of ancient descent, but they do not appear to have attained much importance until the period of the revolution. A THOMAS DE CONINGSBIE certainly distinguished himself in the martial reign of EDWARD III., and participated in the glory of Poictiers, and the family of which we are about to treat may have sprung from him, but of that there is no evidence.

SIR HUMPHREY CONINGSBY, Knt., was father of THOMAS, temp. HENRY VIII., who m. Cicely Salwey, dau. and co-heir of John Salwey, Esq., of Stanford, Worcestershire. Their son, HUMPHREY CONINGSBY, m. Ann, dau. of Sir Thomas Inglefield, and had a son,

SIR THOMAS CONINGSBY, who d. 1625, having m. Philippa Fitzwilliam, of Milton, Northamptonshire, by whom he had a son,

FITZWILLIAM CONINGSBY, of Hampton Court, co. Hereford, who m. Cicely, dau. of Henry, 7th Lord Abergavenny. Their son,

HUMPHREY CONINGSBY, of Hampton Court, m. Lettice, dau. of Arthur Loftus, Esq., of Rathfarnham, and had a son and heir,

THOMAS CONINGSBY, Esq., who, having zealously promoted the revolution, attended King WILLIAM into Ireland, and was present at the battle of the Boyne, where, being close to his majesty when the king received a slight wound in the shoulder, he was the first to apply a handkerchief to the hurt. He was subsequently, upon WILLIAM's departure from Ireland, constituted lord justice with Lord Sydney, and elevated to the peerage of that kingdom as Baron CONINGSBY, of Clanbrassil, co. Armagh, on 17 April, 1693; in which year his lordship was sworn of the privy council in England, and again in the reign of Queen ANNE, when he was made vice-treasurer and paymaster of the forces in Ireland. Upon the accession of King GEORGE I. he was made a peer of Great Britain (18 June, 1715), in the dignity of BARON CONINGSBY, of Coningsby, co. Lincoln, and created EARL OF CONINGSBY, also in the peerage of Great Britain, on 30 April, 1719, both honours being in remainder to MARGARET, Viscountess Coningsby, his eldest dau. by his 2nd wife, and her heirs male. His lordship m. 1st, Miss Gorges, dau. of Ferdinando Gorges, Esq., of Eye, co. Hereford, by whom he had issue,

I. THOMAS, who m. —, dau. of John Carr, Esq., of Northumberland, and dying v.p., left issue,
Thomas, who d. unm.
RICHARD, who s. his grandfather in the Irish BARONY OF CONINGSBY, of Clanbrassil. His lordship m. Judith, dau. of Sir Thomas Lawley, Bart., but d. s. p. 18 December, 1729, when the dignity EXPIRED.

I. MELIOR, m. to Thomas, 1st Lord Southwell, ancestor, by her, of the VISCOUNTS SOUTHWELL.

II. BARBARA, m. to George Eyre, Esq., of Eyre Court, Galway, and had a dau. Frances, m. to William Jackson, Esq., of Coleraine, and had issue a son and heir,

The Right Honourable RICHARD JACKSON, of Coleraine, who m. Anne. dau. and (in her issue,) heiress of Charles O'Neill, Esq., of Shanes Castle, co. Antrim, and left issue George (Sir), Bart., of Coleraine, d.s.p.; Richard, an officer in the army, d.s.p.; Anne, m. to Nathaniel Alexander, Lord Bishop of Meath, and had issue; Mary, m. to John Hamilton O'Hara, Esq., of Crebilly, and d. s. p.; and Harriet, d. unm.

III. LETTICE, m. to Henry Denny, Esq., of Tralee, co. Kerry.

IV. Mary, m. to Rev. Mr. Hathway.

Lord Coningsby m. 2ndly, Frances, dau. and co-heir of Richard, Earl of Ranelagh, by Elizabeth his wife, dau. of William, 3rd Lord Willoughby, of Parham, and by her had two surviving daus., viz.,

MARGARET, who, in the lifetime of her father (26 January, 1716) was created BARONESS AND VISCOUNTESS CONINGSBY, of Hampton Court, co. Hereford, with remainder to her heirs male.

FRANCES, m. 1732, to Sir Charles Hanbury-Williams, K.B., of Coldbrook Park, co. Monmouth, M.P., and left two daus.,

I. FRANCES, m. 1754, William, 4th Earl of Essex, and d. 19 July, 1759, leaving a son and a dau., viz.,

1 George, 5th Earl of Essex, who assumed the surname of Coningsby on succeeding to the Coningsby estates; he d. s. p. 23 April, 1839.

2 Elizabeth, m., 1777, to John, 3rd Lord Monson; their issue is EXTINCT

II. CHARLOTTE, m. 1759, Admiral the Hon. Robert Boyle Walsingham, and was mother of CHARLOTTE, late BARONESS DE ROS.

The earl d. 1 May, 1729, when the BARONY OF CONINGSBY, of Clanbrassil, devolved upon his grandson RICHARD, as stated above, and EXPIRED with that nobleman in the same year, while his dignities of Great Britain passed according to the limitation to his eldest dau. (by his 2nd wife),

MARGARET, Viscountess Coningsby, of Hampton Court, who then became COUNTESS OF CONINGSBY. Her ladyship m. Sir Michael Newton, K.B., by whom she had an only son,

John, who d. in infancy.

Lady Coningsby d. s. p. in 1761, when all her own honours and those inherited from her father became EXTINCT.

Arms—Gu., three conies sejeant, arg.

CONSTABLE—VISCOUNT OF DUNBAR.

By Letters Patent, dated 14 November, 1620.

Lineage.

SIR HENRY CONSTABLE, Knt., of Burton and Halsham, co. York, the representative of a very ancient and eminent family, s. his father in 1608; and being a man of parts and learning, highly esteemed by JAMES VI., was created a peer of Scotland, by the title of VISCOUNT OF DUNBAR, and Lord Constable, by patent, dated at Newmarket, 14 November, 1620, to him and his heirs male, bearing the name and arms of CONSTABLE. He d. in 1645, leaving by Mary his wife, 2nd dau. of Sir John Tufton, Bart., of Hothfield, in Kent, and sister of Nicholas, 1st Earl of Thanet,

I. JOHN, 2nd Viscount of Dunbar.

II. Matthew, d. s. p.   III. Henry, d.s.p.

I. Mary, m. to Robert, 2nd Earl of Cardigan, and had an only child, Lady Mary Brudenel, m. to William, 3rd Earl of Kinnoul.

II. Catherine, m. William Middleton, Esq., of Stockeld.

The eldest son,

JOHN CONSTABLE, 2nd Viscount of Dunbar, s. his father in 1645, and d. in 1666. He m. Lady Mary Brudenel, only dau. of Thomas, 1st Earl of Cardigan, and had issue,

I. John, d. v. p. unm.

II. ROBERT, 3rd Viscount of Dunbar.

III. WILLIAM, 4th Viscount of Dunbar.

I. Cecily, m. to Francis Tunstall, of Skirgill Castle, and had several children, who all d. unm., except her eldest son, CUTHBERT TUNSTALL, who succeeding to the estates of his uncle William, 4th Viscount of Dunbar, took the name of Constable, and d. in 1747. He m. the Hon. Amy Clifford, 5th dau. of Hugh, 2nd Lord Clifford, of Chudleigh, sister of

Elizabeth, Viscountess of Dunbar, and by her (who d 25 July, 1731) had three children. WILLIAM, who was in his thirteenth year, Cecily in her ninth year, and Winifred in her third year, anno 1733. William Constable, of Burton Constable, the only son, s. his father in 1747.

II. Catherine, m. to John Moore, of Kirklington, co. Nottingham.

III. Mary, a nun.

The eldest surviving son,

ROBERT CONSTABLE, 3rd Viscount of Dunbar, dying 25 November, 1714, in the sixty-fourth year of his age, was buried in the north aisle of Westminster Abbey. He m. 1st, Mary, dau. of John, Lord Belasyse, of Worlaby, co. Lincoln, by whom he had one dau.,

MARY, m. to Simon Scrope, Esq., of Danby, co. York, but d. s. p.

He m. 2ndly, Lady Dorothy Brudenel, 3rd dau. of Robert, 2nd Earl of Cardigan, and relict of Charles, Earl of Westmoreland, s. p.; she d. 26 January, 1739, in her ninety-first year, and was buried in Westminster Abbey. His lordship's brother,

WILLIAM CONSTABLE, 4th Viscount of Dunbar, s. in 1714, and died not long afterwards. He m. Elizabeth, eldest dau. of Hugh, 2nd Lord Clifford, of Chudleigh, but as he had no issue by her (who m. 2ndly, 17 November, 1720, Charles Fairfax, of Gilling, only son of Thomas, Lord Fairfax, and died 25 April, 1721), his estates, in virtue of a special entail, devolved on his nephew, Cuthbert Tunstall, Esq., and the title has ever since been DORMANT, no heir male general having appeared to claim it. The Burton Constable estate is now in the possession of SIR THOMAS-ASTON CLIFFORD-CONSTABLE, Bart., of Tixall, co. Stafford, whose father, the late Sir Thomas Clifford, Bart., took the name and arms of Constable in 1821; his grand-aunts, the Hon. Elizabeth Clifford and the Hon. Amy Clifford, both married into the Constable family, the former with William, Viscount Dunbar, the latter with Cuthbert Tunstall, Esq.

Arms—Or, three bars, az.

CONWAY—BARONS CONWAY, OF RAGLEY, CO. WARWICK, VISCOUNTS CONWAY, OF CONWAY CASTLE, CO. CARNARVON, AND EARL OF CONWAY.

Barony, by Letters Patent, dated 22 March, 1624.
Viscounty, by Letters Patent, dated 6 June, 1626.
Earldom, by Letters Patent, dated 3 December, 1679.

Lineage.

SIR HUGH CONWAY (whose ancestors had been seated at Prestatyn and Bodrhyddan, co. Flint, from the time of King EDWARD I.) received the honour of knighthood at the coronation of ELIZABETH, consort of King HENRY VII., having been previously a zealous supporter of the interests of that monarch, and master of his wardrobe. From this Sir Hugh sprang JOHN CONWAY, Esq., of Bodrhyddan, co. Flint, who m. 1st, Ellen, dau. of Edmund Minshull, Esq., by whom he had a son, HUGH (Sir), treasurer of Calais; and 2ndly, Janet, dau. of Edward Stanley, Esq. (son of Sir William Stanley, of Hooton), by whom he had, inter alios,

I. JOHN, of Bodrhyddan, whose descendant, Sir HUGH CONWAY, of Bodrhyddan, was created a Baronet 25 July, 1660; he m. Mary, dau. and heir of Richard Lloyd, Esq., and was father of SIR JOHN CONWAY, 2nd Baronet of Bodrhyddan, M.P., who m. 1st, Margaretta Maria, dau. of John Digby, Esq., of Goathurst, and had by her a dau., Maria Margaretta, wife of Sir Thomas Longueville, Bart., and a son. Harry, whose only child, HONORA, m. SIR JOHN GLYNNE, Bart., of Hawarden Castle, co. Flint. Sir John Conway, m. 2ndly, Penelope, dau. of Richard Grenville, Esq., of Wotton, by whom he had two daus., the elder of whom only married, viz., PENELOPE, who became the wife of JAMES RUSSELL STAPLETON, Esq.; their descendant is the present WILLIAM SHIPLEY CONWY, Esq., of Bodrhyddan.

II. EDWARD, of whom we treat.

III. James, of Soughton and Ruthyn. The eventual heiress of the CONWAYS of Soughton, CATHERINE CONWAY, m. the Rev. John Potter, rector of Badgeworth, co. Somerset. and d. 1775, leaving a son. JOHN CONWAY CONWAY, Esq., LL.B., of Lower Soughton, co. Flint.

IV. Henry.

The 2nd son,

EDWARD CONWAY, Esq., one of the gentlemen ushers of the

chamber to King HENRY VIII., who m. Anne, dau. and heiress of Richard Burdett, Esq., of Arrow, co. Warwick, and was s. by his son,

SIR JOHN CONWAY, Knt., who being in the great expedition made into Scotland in the 1st year of EDWARD VI., distinguished himself so highly as to be made a Banneret. Sir John M. Catherine, dau. of Sir Ralph Verney, Knt., and was s. at his decease, some time in the reign of EDWARD VI., by his son,

SIR JOHN CONWAY, who was made governor of Ostend, by Robert, Earl of Leicester, in the year 1586. He m. Elene, dau. of Sir Fulke Greville, of Beauchamps Court, co. Warwick, and dying in the 1st King JAMES I., was s. by his son,

SIR EDWARD CONWAY. This gallant person received the honour of knighthood from Robert, Earl of Essex, at the sacking of Cadiz, where he commanded a regiment in 1596. After which he served in the Netherlands, and was governor of the Brill. In the 20th JAMES I. he was constituted one of the principal secretaries of state, and elevated to the peerage on 22 March, 1624, as BARON CONWAY, of Ragley, co. Warwick, a manor acquired by purchase towards the close of Queen ELIZABETH'S reign. His lordship was appointed captain of the Isle of Wight in the December following, and being again secretary of state in the 1st King CHARLES I., was advanced to the IRISH VISCOUNTY OF KILLULTAGH, co. Antrim, 15 March, 1626, in which year, on 6 June, he was created VISCOUNT CONWAY, of Conway Castle, co. Carnarvon. His lordship filled afterwards the high office of president of the council, and was accredited upon some occasion ambassador extraordinary to the court of Vienna. His lordship m. Dorothy, dau. of Sir John Tracy, Knt., of Todington, co. Gloucester, and widow of Edward Bray, Esq ,by whom he had issue, EDWARD, his successor; Thomas (Sir), a lieut.colonel in the army in the wars in Germany; and Ralph, together with four daus., viz.,

Frances, m. to Sir William Pelham, Knt., of Brocklesby, co. Lincoln.
Brilliana, m. to Sir Robert Harley, Knt., of Brampton Bryan, co. Hereford.
Heligawrth, m. to Sir William Smith, Knt., of Essex.
Mary.

The viscount m. 2ndly, Catharine, dau. of Giles Hambler, of Ghent, and relict of Richard Fust, but by her had no issue. His lordship d. in 1630 (his widow in 1639), and was s. by his eldest son,

EDWARD CONWAY, 2nd viscount, who had been summoned to parliament in the 4th of CHARLES I., in his father's barony of Conway. His lordship m. Frances, dau. of Sir Francis Popham, Knt., of Littlecot, co. Somerset, by whom he had two surviving sons, EDWARD and Francis, and two daus., Dorothy, m. to Sir George Rawdon, Bart., of Moira, co. Down (ancestor of the Lords Moira, of Ireland), and Anne. His lordship d. in 1655, and was s. by his eldest surviving son,

EDWARD CONWAY, 3rd viscount, who was created EARL OF CONWAY, 3 December, 1679, and was for some time secretary of state. His lordship m. 1st, Elizabeth, dau. of Sir Heneage Finch, serjeant-at-law and recorder of London, and sister of the Lord Chancellor Heneage (Finch), 1st Earl of Nottingham, by whom he had an only son, Heneage, who d. in infancy. He m. 2ndly, Elizabeth, dau. of Henry Booth, Earl of Warrington; and 3rdly, Ursula, dau. of Colonel Stawel, but had no surviving issue. He d. in 1683, when all his honours became EXTINCT; but the principal part of his extensive estates passed, by his lordship's will, to the sons of Sir Edward Seymour, Bart., of Bury Pomeroy, by his 2nd wife Letitia, dau. of Alexander Popham, Esq., of Littlecote, M.P., with the injunction that the inheritor should assume the surname and arms of CONWAY. This fortune was first inherited by POPHAM SEYMOUR, Esq., who assumed, of course, the name of Conway, but that gentleman falling in a duel with Colonel Kirk, 4 June, 1699, and dying unm , it passed to his brother, FRANCIS SEYMOUR, Esq., who assumed likewise the surname of Conway, and was afterwards created BARON CONWAY, of Ragley, which barony now merges in the MARQUISATE OF HERTFORD.

Arms—Sa., on a bend cotised, arg., a rose between two annulets, gu.

CONYNGHAM—EARL CONYNGHAM.

By Letters Patent, dated 19 December, 1780.

Lineage.

The Right Honourable
HENRY CONYNGHAM, of Slane, M.P., representative of the ancient and influential family of Conyngham, was elevated to the peerage of Ireland, by the title of BARON CONYNGHAM, of

Mount Charles, co. Donegal, 3 October, 1753, and further created Viscount Conyngham, 20 July, 1756, and EARL and BARON CONYNGHAM, 19 December, 1780, the barony to descend, in case of failure of male issue, to his nephew, Francis Pierpont Burton, Esq., M.P., of Buncraggy, co. Clare. His lordship m. in 1774, Ellen, only dau. and heir of Solomon Merret, Esq.; but d. s. p. 3 April, 1781, when all his honours became EXTINCT, except the Barony of Conyngham, which devolved, according to the limitation, upon the before-mentioned Francis Pierpont Burton, Esq., whose grandson is the present MARQUESS CONYNGHAM.

Arms—Arg., a shakefork between three mullets, sa.

COOTE—EARLS OF MOUNTRATH, BARON CASTLECOOTE.

Earldom, by Letters Patent, dated 6 September, 1660.
Barony, by Letters Patent, dated 20 July, 1800.

Lineage.

This noble family, of which the senior branch still exists in Sir Charles Coote, Bart., of the Queen's Co., derived its origin from

SIR JOHN COOTE, a native of France, who m. the dau. and heiress of the Lord Boys of that kingdom, and had issue

SIR JOHN COOTE, who settled in Devonshire, and marrying a dau. of Sir John Fortescue, of that co., left a son,

SIR WILLIAM COOTE, who m. a dau. of Thomas Mansel, and was father of Sir William Coote, who m. the dau. and heir of — Worthy, Esq., of Worthy, and had a son and heir,

SIR JOHN COOTE, who m. the dau. of — Sacheveral, and was father of

ROBERT COOTE, the father, by — Grantham his wife, of

THOMAS COOTE, Esq., who m. the dau. of — Darnell and left

SIR JOHN COOTE, who had two sons, JOHN his heir, and Robert, abbot of St. Albans, and rector of St. Edmundsbury, in Suffolk. The elder,

JOHN COOTE, had three sons, viz., Richard, who m. Margaret, dau. of Sir William Calthrope, of Norfolk, and had Christopher, who m. the dau. and co-heir of the family of Whitsingham, by whom he was father of Richard, who, by Elizabeth, dau. and co-heir of — Felton, was ancestor of the Cootes, of the co. of Norfolk; JOHN, of whom presently; Robert, who m. the dau. of — Blaxton, of Blaxton, and had issue, John, who d. unm., and a dau. Anne, who became his heir: she m. Robert Waldgrave, Esq., and took with her into that family the lands in Devonshire.

The 2nd son,

JOHN COOTE, to whom his uncle Robert, the abbot, gave great possessions in Norfolk and Suffolk, m. Margaret, dau. of — Drury, Esq., and had a son,

FRANCIS COOTE, Esq., of Eaton, in Norfolk, a servant to Queen ELIZABETH, who, by Anne his wife, left a son,

SIR NICHOLAS COOTE, living in 1636. He had issue, CHARLES, his heir, and William, dean of Down. The elder son,

SIR CHARLES COOTE, removing to Ireland, served in the wars there against O'Neill, Earl of Tyrone, as captain of 100 foot. He was subsequently provost-marshal of the province of Connaught, collector and receiver of the king's composition money there, and finally vice-president. In 1620, he was sworn of the privy council, and created a baronet of Ireland, by patent, dated 2 April, 1621.

Upon the breaking out of the rebellion in 1641, Sir Charles Coote had a commission to raise 1,000 men to resist and suppress the rebels, and he was subsequently highly distinguished upon several occasions at the head of his regiment, but particularly by his gallant relief of Birr, in 1642, in which affair, heading 30 dismounted dragoons, he beat off the enemy with the loss of their captain and 40 men, relieved the castles of Birr, Borris, and Knocknemease; and having continued forty-eight hours in the saddle, returned to the camp without the loss of a single soldier. This is the surprising passage through Montrath Woods which was perpetuated in the title of honour afterwards conferred upon his posterity. Sir Charles lost his life the ensuing year in a sally from the town of Trim; and parliament, in consideration of his services and sufferings, declared their intention, 16 May, 1642, of bestowing upon his children the estate in the Queen's Co., of Florence Fitzpatrick, a rebel, but which not having been effected, the Protector ordered, 27 July, 1654, that the deceased baronet's family should be put into possession thereof, until the intention of the legislature be fulfilled.

Sir Charles Coote m. prior to the year 1617, Dorothea

younger dau. and co-heir of Hugh Cuffe, Esq., of Cuffe's Wood, co. Cork, and had issue,

ɪ. CHARLES, his successor.
ɪɪ. Chidley, of Killeater, co. Dublin, a military man like his father, who for his services and arrears under Cromwell had lands assigned him, after the Restoration, in co. Kerry. Colonel Coote represented the Queen's Co., and afterwards the co of Galway, in parliament. He m. Alice, or Anne, only dau. of Sir Thomas Philips, of Newtown-Limavady, co. Derry, and had issue,

1 CHIDLEY, of Kilmallock, co. Limerick, attainted by King JAMES's parliament in 1689, by the name of Chidley-Coote Fitz-Chidley, Esq. He was a lieut.-col. in the army, and lieutenant of the ordnance in the reigns of WILLIAM and MARY and Queen ANNE. He m. Catharine, dau. of Colonel Robert Sandys, son of Sir Edwin Sandys, of Northbourne, Kent, and had issue, Anne (m. to Bartholomew Purdon, Esq., of Ballyclogh; and Catherine, m. to Henry Boyle, Earl of Shannon), and an only son, his successor,

CHIDLEY COOTE, D.D., of Ash Hill, who m. 31 January, 1702, Jane Evans, sister of the 1st Lord Carbery, and had issue,

ROBERT, of Ash Hill, m. in 1730, Anne, dau. and heir of Bartholomew Purdon, Esq.; and d. in 1745, leaving issue,

CHIDLEY, of Ash Hill, co. Limerick, m. 31 August, 1790, Elizabeth, dau. of the Rev. Ralph Carr, of Bath; and d. 6 August, 1799, leaving issue,

CHARLES-HENRY (Sir), who s. to the Coote Baronetcy on the death of Lord Mountrath.
Robert-Carr, m. Miss Margaret Grier; and d. 5 November, 1834, leaving issue four sons and three daus.
John-Chidley, of Huntingdon, Queen's Co., J.P., b. 10 January, 1793; m. 8 May, 1827. Jane-Deborah, 2nd dau. of the Rev. Samuel Close, of Elm Park, and has,

Chidley-Samuel, b. 21 December, 1829.
Maxwell-Henry, b. 4 May, 1832.
Jane-Elizabeth-Anna, m. 2 January, 1855, to the Rev. Charles-Lyndhurst Vaughan, son of the late Baron Vaughan and the Dowager Lady St. John.
Harriet-Mary.
Ralph, in holy orders, m. 1825, Miss Harriet Close.
Mary, m. to Charles-L. Sandys, Esq., of Indiaville, Queen's Co.; and d. 6 February, 1852.
Bartholomew, whose son, Robert-Eyre-Purdon Coote, was of Ballyclough.
Charles, in holy orders.
Jane, m. to William Purdon, Esq.
Catherine, m. to the Rev. William Dobbin, D.D.

George d. unm.
Charles, dean of Kilfenora; m. 1st, in 1753, Grace, dau. of Thomas Tilson, Esq., and widow of Thomas Cuffe, Esq.; and 2ndly, in 1770, Catherine, dau. of Benjamin Bathurst, Esq., of Lydney, co. Gloucester; by the former of whom he had issue,

CHARLES HENRY, LORD CASTLECOOTE.
Eyre (Sir), lieut.-general in the army.
John.
Thomas, whose eldest son, Brigade-Major Thomas Coote, left one surviving son, Charles-Eyre Coote, of Farway House, Clifton.
EYRE (Sir), K B., of West Park, Hants, at one time commander-in-chief in India.

2 Philips (Sir), m. 1st, Jane, dau. of Dr. Henry Jones, bishop of Meath, by whom he had an only dau.,

Alice, who d. in 1680.

Sir Philips m. 2ndly, Elizabeth, dau. and co-heir of William, Earl of Meath, by whom he had two daus. and a son,

Charles, who m. Katherine, dau. of Sir Robert Newcomen, Bart., and d. in 1761, leaving an only son,

CHIDLEY, of Mount Coote, co. Limerick, who unsuccessfully claimed the BARONY OF ARDEE, as heir-general of William, Earl of Meath. He m. Jane, dau. of Sir Ralph Gore, Bart., and left at his decease, 24 February, 1764, a dau., Elizabeth, m. to James King, Esq., of Gola, and a son, CHARLES COOTE, Esq., of Mount Coote, who m. Elizabeth, dau. and co-heir of Philip Oliver, Esq., M.P., and was father of CHIDLEY COOTE, Esq., of Mount Coote, who m. Anne, dau. and co-heir of the Hon. W. W. Hewett, and d. 1843, leaving a son CHARLES CHIDLEY COOTE, Esq., of Mount Coote, and other issue. (See BURKE's Landed Gentry.)

ɪɪɪ. RICHARD, ancestor of the Earl of Bellamont.
ɪᴠ. Thomas, of Coote Hill, in Cavan; lieut.-col. of the Earl of Ossory's regiment of foot, m. Frances, dau. of Moyses Hill, Esq., and d. s. p. 27 November, 1671.
ɪ. Letitia, m. to Sir Francis Hamilton, of Killeshandra.

Sir Charles Coote was s. by his eldest son,

SIR CHARLES COOTE, 2nd bart., who was also actively employed against the rebels. He succeeded his father as provost marshal of Connaught, of which province he was made lord president by patent in 1645, and he afterwards zealously

134

defended it for the parliament. In November 1651, he joined Ireton, and took Clare; he next blockaded Galway, which surrendered in 1652, in which year he repossessed himself of Ballyshannon, with the castles of Donegal, Sligo, and Ballymote; and was appointed, 17 December, the first of the Commonwealth's commissioners for the affairs of Ireland in the province of Connaught. In January, 1659, he was made one of the commissioners of government. About this period Sir Charles entered into measures with Lord Broghill for the restoration of the king, and, according to Lord Clarendon, being president of Connaught, and having a good command and interest in the army, and being a man of courage and impatience to serve his majesty, he sent over, in February, Sir Arthur Forbes (a Scottish gentleman, of good affection to the king and good interest in the province of Ulster, where he was an officer of horse, and was afterwards created Earl of Granard) to Brussels, to the Marquess of Ormonde, "that he might assure his majesty of his affection and duty; and that, if his majesty would vouchsafe himself to come into Ireland, he was confident the whole kingdom would declare for him." This loyal declaration the king received with great satisfaction, offering, in return, to make Sir Charles an earl, to confer upon him such command as he pleased, and to take his whole family under his especial protection; and after the Restoration his majesty, in accordance with this pledge, confirmed Sir Charles in his post of president of Connaught, appointing him at the same time keeper of the castle of Athlone, and granted to him various other important immunities, while he was elevated to the peerage, by letters patent, dated 6 September, 1660, as EARL OF MOUNTRATH. His lordship m. 1st, Mary, 2nd dau. and co-heiress of Sir Francis Ruish, of Ruish Hall, in the Queen's Co., M.P. for the King's Co., and of the privy council in the reign of King JAMES I., by whom he had an only son, CHARLES, his successor. The earl m. 2ndly, Jane, dau. of Sir Robert Hannay, Bart., of Scotland, by whom he had,

ɪ. RICHARD, who having lands assigned him, by the acts of settlement, in the cos. of Kilkenny, Kerry, Roscommon, and Limerick, became seated at Tullaghmine, in the first mentioned shire. He m. Penelope, dau. of Arthur, and sister of William Hill, Esq., of Hillsborough, co. Down, by whom he had surviving issue,

1 Rose, m. to Charles Boyle, Viscount Blesinton.
2 Jane, m. to Sir William Evans, Bart., of Kilcreene, co. Kilkenny, by whom she had four daus., of whom
Catherine became eventually survivor, and then sole heiress of her father. She m. Francis Morres, Esq., of Castle Morres, co. Kilkenny, and her eldest son was advanced to the peerage as VISCOUNT MOUNTMORRES.

ɪɪ. Chidley, of Sherwood Park, co. Carlow.
ɪ. Dorothy, m. to Rev. Moses Viredett, and d. 8 February, 1677.

His lordship d. 18 December, 1661, and was s. by his eldest son,

CHARLES COOTE, 2nd earl; who m. in 1653, Alice, dau. of Sir Robert Meredyth, Knt., of Greenhills, co. Kildare, chancellor of the Exchequer, and had surviving issue,

CHARLES, his successor.
Anne, m. to Murrough Boyle, Viscount Blesinton; and d. in 1725.

His lordship d. in 1672, and was s. by his son,

CHARLES COOTE, 3rd earl. This nobleman m. Arabella Dormer, 2nd dau. and co-heir of Charles, Earl of Carnarvon, by whom he had surviving issue, three sons. His lordship, who carried the banner of Ireland at the funeral of Queen MARY, 5 March, 1694, and was one of the lords justices in 1696, d. in May, 1709, and was s. by his eldest son,

CHARLES COOTE, 4th earl, member in the English parliament for Knaresborough, and of the privy council of King GEORGE I. His lordship dying unm. in the thirtieth year of his age, 14 September, 1715, the honours devolved upon his brother,

HENRY COOTE, 5th earl; who was s. at his decease, unm., 27 March, 1720, by his brother,

ALGERNON COOTE, 6th earl, member for Castle Rising in the British parliament, anno 1723. His lordship m. in 1721, Lady Diana Newport, youngest dau. of Richard, Earl of Bradford; and dying in August, 1744, was s. by his only son,

CHARLES-HENRY COOTE, 7th earl. This nobleman having no heir to his hereditary honours, obtained a new peerage by letters patent, dated 20 July, 1800, creating him BARON CASTLECOOTE, with remainder to the Right Hon. Charles-Henry Coote, eldest son of the Very Rev. Charles Coote, dean of Kilfenora;—a creation which led to the great legal argument in the Fermoy case before the Lords Committee for Privileges in 1856. The earl d. 1 March, 1802, when the EARLDOM OF MOUNTRATH EXPIRED, while the ancient baronetcy and estates devolved upon Charles Coote, Esq., of Ballyfin, in the Queen's

Co. (*revert* to descendants of Col. Chidley Coote, of Killester, 2nd son of the 1st settler, Sir Charles Coote), and the Barony of Castlecoote passed, under the limitation, to

THE RIGHT HON. CHARLES-HENRY COOTE, as 2nd lord. He *m.* Elizabeth-Anne, eldest dau. and co-heir of the Rev. Dr. Tilson; and *d.* 22 January, 1823, leaving an only son and successor,

EYRE COOTE, 3rd Lord Castlecoote; who *m.* in July, 1822, Barbara, 2nd dau. of Sir Joshua-Colles Meredyth, Bart.; but *d. s. p.* in 1827, when the peerage became EXTINCT. His lordship's widow *m.* 2ndly, in 1828, Joseph, present Earl of Milltown.

Arms—Arg., a chev., sa., between three coots, close, ppr.

COOTE—BARONS COOTE, OF COLOONY, EARLS OF BELLAMONT.

Barony by Letters Patent, dated 6 September, 1660.
Earldom by Letters Patent, dated 2 November, 1689.

Lineage.

RICHARD COOTE, Esq., brother of Sir Charles Coote, 1st Earl of Mountrath (*see* that dignity), having cordially aided his lordship in promoting the Restoration was elevated to the peerage of Ireland, by letters patent, dated 6 September, 1660, as BARON COOTE, *of Coloony, co. Sligo.* His lordship *m.* Mary, 2nd dau. of Sir George St. George, Bart., of Carrickdrumruske, co. Leitrim, and by her (who *d.* 5 November, 1701) had issue,

I. Charles, *d.* an infant.
II. RICHARD, his successor.
III. Chidley, of Cootehall, co. Roscommon, col. of horse; *m.* 1st, April, 1698, Elinor, dau. and heiress of Isaac Walkden, Esq., of Ardmayle, co. Tipperary, by whom he had

  1 John, *d. unm.*
  1 Mary, *m.* 1st, in 1717, Guy Moore, Esq., of Abbey, in the same county, and by him (who *d.* 21 June, 1735), was mother of Guy Moore, Esq., and two daus., Mary and Elizabeth; and 2ndly, to Rev. William Gore, bishop of Limerick.
  2 Elinor, *m.* to Robert Moore, Esq. of Ardmayle, and Mooremount, co. Tipperary, and had, with other issue, a son and heir, Thomas-Bob.

Colonel Coote *m.* 2ndly, Mary, eldest dau. of Sir Robert King, Bart., of Rockingham, co. Roscommon, and by her (who *m.* 2ndly, Henry Dering, Esq., of Dublin, and *d.* in July, 1750) had issue,

  1 Chidley, buried at St. Michan's, 26 September, 1702.
  1 Olivia, *m.* 1722, to Walter Jones, Esq., of Headford, co. Leitrim, and had issue.
  2 Catharine, *m.* to Marcus-Anthony Morgan. Esq., M.P., of Cottelstown, co. Sligo, and *d.* 7 October, 1738.

IV. Thomas, of Coote Hill, co. Cavan, barrister-at-law, chosen recorder of Dublin soon after the revolution, and constituted one of the justices of the King's Bench in 1693. In 1696 he was one of the commissioners entrusted with the great seal, and was appointed the same year, with the other judges, to hear and determine all causes of persons pretending to be comprehended within the articles of Limerick and Galway. He *m.* 1st, Frances, dau. and co-heir of Colonel Christopher Copley, by his wife Mary, dau. of Roger Jones, the 1st Viscount Ranelagh, by whom he had a son, Chidley, lieut.-col. in Schomberg's regiment, who *d. unm.* 6 April, 1719. Mr. Justice Coote *m.* 2ndly, Elinor, dau. and co-heiress of Sir Thomas St. George, Knt., of Woodford, co. Essex, by whom he had a son, Thomas, who *d. s. p.*, and Mary. He *m.* 3rdly, in 1679, Anne, widow of William Tighe, Esq., of Rutland, co. Carlow, and dau. of Mr. Alderman Christopher Lovett, of Dublin, and dying 24 April, 1741, had issue by her,

  1 CHARLES, of Coote-Hill, *bapt.* 15 September, 1695, M.P. for the co. of Cavan, for which shire he served the office of sheriff in 1719; *m.* in July, 1722, Prudence, 2nd dau. of Richard Geering. Esq., one of the six clerks of the Court of Chancery; and dying 19 October, 1750, left issue,

    CHARLES, his heir, who *s.* to the BARONY OF COOTE, *of Coloony,* at the decease of Richard, 3rd Earl of Bellamont, in 1766.
    Anne, *m.* 11 March, 1748, to William Anketel, Esq., of Anketel Grove, co. Monaghan.
    Frances, *b.* 1731; *m.* 2 June, 1755, to John Boswell, Esq., of Ballycurry, co. Wicklow.
    Catharine, *b.* 1732; *m.* in 1762, to John Corry, Esq., of Sport Hall, co. Monaghan.
    Caroline, *b.* 1733; *m.* in September, 1761, to James Uniacke, Esq., of Mount Uniacke, co. Cork.
    Elizabeth, *b.* 1734; *m.* 23 October, 1752, to Chidley Coote, Esq., of Ash Hill, co. Limerick, and *d.* 1780.
    Mary, } *d. unm.*
    Prudentia, }

135

2 Francis, *m.* 17 September, 1748, Henrietta, dau. of the Right Hon. Luke Gardiner.
1 Frances, *bapt.* 4 May, 1682.
2 Elizabeth, *b. pt.* 3 September, 1687, *m.* in 1704, to Mervyn Pratt, Esq., of Cabra Castle, co. Cavan, and had issue, Joseph, in holy orders, and other children.
3 Catharine, *m.* to James Macartney, Esq., M.P. for Granard, and *d.* 29 July, 1731.
4 Anne, *bapt.* 16 February, 1692; *m.* 9 November, 1716, to Samuel Bindon, Esq., of Rockmount, M.P. for Ennis.
I. Mary, *m.* to William, 1st Viscount Mountjoy.
II. Catherine, *m.* to Ferdinando Hastings.
III. Letitia, *m.* to Robert, 1st Viscount Molesworth.
IV. Olivia, *m.* to Audley Mervyn, of Trelick, co. Tyrone.
V. Elizabeth, *m.* to Richard St. George, lieutenant-general.

Richard, 1st Lord Coote, of Coloony, *d.* 10 July, 1683, and was buried in Christ Church. His eldest surviving son,

RICHARD COOTE, 2nd baron, was member in the British parliament for Droitwich. This nobleman being one of the first to espouse the cause of the Prince of Orange, was attainted by King JAMES's parliament in 1689. His lordship was rewarded, however, immediately after the Revolution, by being appointed treasurer and receiver-general to Queen MARY, and being created, by patent, dated 2 November, 1689, EARL OF BELLAMONT, in Ireland. He filled, until his decease, 5 March, 1700, the office of governor of New York. He *m.* Catharine, dau. and heiress of Bridges Nanfon, Esq., of Bridgemorton, co. Worcester, by whom he had two sons, NANFAN and RICHARD, and was *s.* by the elder,

NANFAN COOTE, 3rd baron and 2nd earl; who *m.* in 1704, Frances, youngest dau. of Henry de Nassau, Lord of Auverquerque, sister of Henry, Earl of Grantham, by whom he had an only dau. Frances, who *m.* in 1723, Sir Robert Clifton, Bart., of Clifton, co. Notts. His lordship *d.* 12 July, 1708, when the honours devolved upon his brother,

RICHARD COOTE, 4th baron and 3rd earl. This nobleman *m.* 1st, Judith, dau. and heiress of Francis Wilkinson, Esq., of Southwark, by whom he had issue,

Richard, Lord Coloony, capt. of the foot-guards; *d.* 23 October, 1740.
Thomas, Lord Coloony, *m.* Elizabeth, eldest dau. of Thomas Bond, of Dublin, merchant; and *d. s. p.* 24 March, 1765.
Mary, } *d. unm.*
Judith, }

His lordship *m.* 2ndly, in 1721, Anne, dau. of John Holloway, Esq., of Oxford, and widow of Sir Harry Oxenden, Bart., of Dene Court, co. Kent, but had no surviving issue. His lordship sold Coloony, and divers other lands, in March, 1729, to Joshua Cooper, Esq., of Markree, co. Sligo, for £16,945 5s. 6d.; and dying without male issue, 10 February, 1766, the EARLDOM OF BELLAMONT became EXTINCT, while the Barony of Coote, of Coloony, devolved upon his kinsman,

CHARLES COOTE, Esq., of Coote Hill (*revert* to descendants of the Honourable Thomas Coote, youngest son of Richard, 1st lord), as 5th BARON COOTE, *of Coloony,* who was created, 4 September, 1767, EARL OF BELLAMONT. His lordship *m.* 20 August, 1774, Lady Emily-Maria-Margaret Fitzgerald, 2nd dau. of James, 1st Duke of Leinster, and had issue, Charles, Lord Coloony, who *d.* young in 1786; and four daus., his co-heirs, viz., MARY; PRUDENTIA, who *d.* 18 January, 1837; EMILY; and LOUISA. Lord Bellamont *d.* 20 October, 1800, when all his honours became EXTINCT.

Arms—Arg., a chev., sa., between three coots, ppr.

COPLEY—BARON LYNDHURST.

By Letters Patent, dated 27 April, 1827.

Lineage.

RICHARD COPLEY, of the co. Limerick, who emigrated to America, and became of Boston, in the United States, *m.* Sarah, younger dau. of John Singleton, Esq., and had a son,

JOHN-SINGLETON COPLEY, who settled in England, and obtaining eminence as a painter, was elected member of the Royal Academy. He *m.* Miss Clarke, and by her who *d.* 1836, left, at his decease, 1815, a son,

SIR JOHN-SINGLETON COPLEY, P.C., F.R.S., and D.C.L., of Lyndhurst, co. Southampton, *b.* 21 May, 1772; *m.* in 1819, Sarah-Garay, dau. of Charles Brunsden, Esq., and widow of Lieutenant-Colonel Charles Thomas, 1st foot-guards, who fell at Waterloo. By this lady (who *d.* 15 January, 1834) he had issue,

Sarah-Elizabeth, *m.* 8 January, 1850, to Henry John Selwyn,

Esq., now Sir H. J. Selwyn-Ibbetson, Bart. She *d.* 25 June, 1865.

Susan-Penelope, *d.* 9 May, 1847.

Sophia-Clarence, *m.* 14 December, 1854, Hamilton Beckett, Esq.

His lordship *m.* 2ndly, 5 August, 1837, Georgiana, dau. of Lewis Goldsmith, Esq., and had by her a dau.,

Georgiana-Susan, *m.* 25 June, 1863, to Sir Charles DuCane, K.C.M.G., of Braxted Park, Essex.

Sir John Copley, whose career was so eminent as an advocate, judge, orator, and statesman, attained, at the bar, a high reputation as a lawyer, and filled the law offices of solicitor and attorney-general, and the judicial one of master of the Rolls,* and was constituted lord chancellor on the retirement of the Earl of Eldon in 1827, when he obtained his peerage by patent, dated 25 April, 1827. His lordship resigned the great seal in 1830, and was appointed in 1831 lord chief baron of the Exchequer, which he resigned in 1834, to resume the chancellorship, which he then held, however, but for a brief period (from December, 1834, to April, 1835). He was subsequently, for the third time, appointed lord-chancellor in September, 1841, and finally retired in July, 1846. His lordship *d.* 12 October, 1863.

Arms—Arg., a cross patonce, sa., within a bordure, az., charged with eight escallops of the field.

COPSI—EARL OF NORTHUMBERLAND.

Conferred by WILLIAM THE CONQUEROR, *anno* 1068.

Lineage.

The earldom of the county of Northumberland was held at the time of the Conquest by

MORKAR, younger son of Algar, Earl of the co. of Chester, and he was left undisturbed in the dignity until he rose in rebellion against the new monarch, when he forfeited the earldom, which was then conferred upon

Copsi (uncle of Tofti, a very distinguished Earl of Northumberland under the Saxon rule,) in consideration of the high character he had attained in council. The new earl immediately expelled from his territory Osulph, whom Morkar had placed there as his deputy, but that chief collecting a force, compelled Earl Copsi to seek shelter in the church of Newburne, which being fired, the Earl of Northumberland was seized by his opponent in an attempt to escape, and was decapitated at the door of the church, on the fourth Ides of March, in the fifth week after he had the administration of those parts committed to him; but in the very next autumn Osulph himself was slain by a robber, with whom he came casually into conflict.

CORBET—BARONS CORBET.

By Writ of Summons, dated 23 June, 1295.

Lineage.

In the time of WILLIAM THE CONQUEROR the brothers ROGER and ROBERT, mentioned in Doomsday Book as sons of CORBET, held of Roger de Montgomery divers lordships in the co. of Salop, and were munificent benefactors to the church.

WILLIAM CORBET, the eldest son of Roger, was seated at Wattlesborough. His 2nd son,

SIR ROBERT CORBET, Knt., had for his inheritance the castle and estates of Caus, with a large portion of his father's domains. He was father of

ROBERT CORBET, also of Caus Castle, who accompanied RICHARD I. to the siege of Acre, and then bore for arms the two ravens, as now borne by all his descendants.

THOMAS CORBET, son of the last-named Robert, was sheriff of Shropshire in 1249; in 1270 he was a donor to the abbey of Shrewsbury, and in 1272 he founded the chapel of St. Margaret, in Caus. He *m.* Isabel, sister and co-heir of Reginald de Valletort, Baron of Trematon Castle, in Cornwall, and widow of Alan de Dunstanville, by whom he had issue,

PETER, his successor.

Alice, *m.* to Robert de Stafford, and had issue,

Nicholas de Stafford, whose son,

Edmund de Stafford, was father of

RALPH, LORD STAFFORD.

Emma, *m.* to Sir Bryan de Brampton, and had

Walter de Brampton, father of

Sir Bryan de Brampton, who left two daus., co-heiresses,

Margaret. *m.* to Robert Harley, Esq., ancestor of the Earls of Oxford.

Elizabeth, *m.* to Edmund de Cornwall.

His lordship *d.* in 1273, and was *s.* by his son,

PETER CORBET, who, it appears, was "a mighty hunter," for, in the 9th King EDWARD I, he obtained letters-patent from the sovereign authorizing him to take wolves in all the royal forests in various counties, a proof of the falsehood of the common belief that our island is indebted to the exertions of King EDGAR for the extirpation of that savage beast of prey. This Peter Corbet, of Caus, had summons to parliament as one of the barons of the realm, from the 22nd of EDWARD I., to his death in 1300. By Alice his wife, he had three sons, THOMAS, PETER, and JOHN. THOMAS CORBET, the eldest son, *m.* Joan, dau. of Alan Plukenet, and *d. v. p., s. p.* The 2nd son,

PETER CORBET, 2nd baron, succeeding his father in the estates of his family, joined with Harry de la Pomeroy in petitioning parliament for the domains of the Valletort family, to which estates they were now become the heirs; but, as King EDWARD II. had himself been found, by inquisition, to be heir to the Earl of Cornwall, the grantee of "Roger de Vauter," the last of the Valletorts who possessed the estates, the petitioners did not find favour in their suit. This Peter Corbet had also summons to parliament, as Baron Corbet, of Caus, until his death on 26 May, 1322. He *d. s. p.*, and the line of the family was continued by the youngest of the three brothers,

JOHN CORBET, 3rd baron, at whose decease, *s. p.*, the BARONY OF CORBET became EXTINCT, while (the descendants of the deceased lord's aunts) Ralph, Lord Stafford, and Sir Robert Harley became his heirs.

Arms—Or, a raven, ppr.

CORBET—VISCOUNTESS CORBET, OF LINCHDALE, CO. SALOP.

By Letters Patent, dated *anno* 1679. The dignity for life only.

Lineage.

DAME SARAH CORBET, widow of Sir Vincent Corbet, Bart., of Moreton Corbet, co. Salop (a descendant of the old Lords Corbet, of Caus Castle), and dau. and co-heir of Sir Robert Monson, of Carlton, co. Lincoln, was elevated to the peerage, by letters patent, dated in 1679, *for life only*, as VISCOUNTESS CORBET, *of Linchdale*. Her ladyship, who *m.* 2ndly, Sir Charles Lee, Knt., of Edmonton, was mother of Sir Vincent Corbet, 2nd baronet, who left a son, Sir Vincent Corbet, 3rd baronet, at whose decease, *s. p.*, in 1688, the baronetcy became EXTINCT. The peerage EXPIRED, of course, with the viscountess, who *d.* in 1682.

NOTE.—Upon the demise of Sir Vincent Corbet, in 1688, the estates of the family reverted to that gentleman's great uncle, Richard Corbet, Esq., of Shrewsbury, whose lineal descendant, Andrew Corbet, Esq., was created a Baronet in 1808, and was grandfather of the present SIR VINCENT ROWLAND CORBET, Bart., *of Moreton Corbet.*

CORNWALL—BARON FANHOPE, IN THE CO. HEREFORD. BARON MILBROKE, IN THE CO. BEDFORD.

Barony of Fanhope, 17 July, 1433.
Barony of Milbroke, 30 January, 1442.

Lineage.

RICHARD, King of the Romans, and Earl of Cornwall and Poictou, 2nd son of JOHN, King of England, by his 3rd wife Isabel, sister and heir of Aymer, Earl of Angoulesme, *m.* Sanchia, 3rd dau. of Raymond, Earl of Provence, sister of Queen

---

* Sir John Copley was called to the bar in 1804, and made serjeant-at-law in 1813, and became chief-justice of Chester in 1819; he was solicitor-general from 1819 to 1823; attorney-general from 1823 to 1826; and master of the Rolls from 1826 to 1827.

ELEANOR, wife of HENRY III., and by her had two sons, EDMUND, Earl of Cornwall, who *m.* Margaret, dau. of Richard de Clare, Earl of Gloucester, and *d. s. p.* in 1300, and RICHARD DE CORNWALL, who was slain at the siege of Berwick in 1296. Richard, Earl of Cornwall and Poictou, *d.* at Berkhampstead, in 1279. He had three natural children, viz., a dau., Isabella, *m.* to Maurice, Lord Berkeley, of Berkeley Castle; and two sons, RICHARD, ancestor of the family of which we treat; and Walter, to whom Edmund, Earl of Cornwall gave lands on his manor of Branell, 18th EDWARD I. The former,

RICHARD DE CORNWALL, had the manor of Thunnock, in Lincolnshire, from Edmund, Earl of Cornwall, 8th EDWARD I., *anno* 1280. He *m.* Joan, dau. of John, Lord St. Owen, and by her had issue,

   I. GEOFFREY (Sir), of whom we treat.
   II. E:moud (Sir), of Kinlet, who *m.* Elizabeth, dau. and co-heir of Sir Brien de Brampton, of Brampton Brian, co. Hereford, and had issue,

     1 EDMOND (Sir), of Kentwell, co. Suffolk, who by Isabel his wife, had a son, John, who *d. s. p.*
     2 BRIAN DE CORNWALL, who was seized of Outragorther Baughallor, Worthen, &c., *m.* Maude, dau. of the Lord Strange, of Blackmere, and had, with other issue, a son, John, of Kinlet, who *m.* Elizabeth, dau. of Sir John Wastneys, of Tixhall, co. Stafford, and *d.* 2nd HENRY V., having had three daus., viz., ELIZABETH, who *m.* Roger Corbett, of Morton Corbett, co. Salop; MATILDA, who *m.* John Wode; and ELIZABETH, *m.* Sir William Lichfield, Knt.
     3 Peter de Cornwall, *m.* a dau. of Roger Hanley, and *d.* 13 July, 10th RICHARD II., having had a son or grandson, Edmond, who left a son and heir, Thomas Cornewall.

The elder son,

SIR GEOFFREY DE CORNWALL had the manor of Ever in Bucks, from Edmund, Earl of Cornwall. He *m.* Margaret, dau. and co-heir of Hugh de Mortimer, BARON OF BURFORD, co. Salop, son of Mortimer, Lord of Wigmore; and *d.* 9th EDWARD III., having had issue,

   I. GEOFFREY, who gave to his nephew, Sir Geoffrey de Cornwall, the manor of Kingsnewton, co. Devon, and lands in Northamptonshire.
   II. RICHARD, from whom descended the CORNEWALLS, BARONS OF BURFORD, whose eventual heiress, ANNA MARIA CORNEWALL, only child of Francis Cornewall, Baron of Burford, *m.* GEORGE LEGH, Esq., of High Legh, co. Chester, ancestor by her of the present GEORGE-CORNEWALL LEGH, Esq., of High Legh, M.P.: and also the CORNEWALLS of Delbury, Berrington, and Moccas (*see* BURKE's *Landed Gentry*).
   III. JOHN (Sir), of whom we treat.

The 3rd son,

SIR JOHN DE CORNEWALL, *m.* the niece of the Duke of Britaine, and was father of

SIR JOHN CORNWALL, K.G., who occurs in the 20th RICHARD II., when, being retained to serve the king during his life, he obtained a grant of 100 marks per annum. In the 2nd of HENRY IV., Sir John, having deported himself with great gallantry in justing against a Frenchman at York, in the presence of the king, won the heart of that monarch's sister, Elizabeth, widow of John Holland, Earl of Huntingdon, whose hand he soon afterwards obtained, and with her considerable grants from the crown to enjoy during the lady's life, with a rent-charge of 400 marks per annum for his own. In five years afterwards he was again distinguished at a tournament held in London, where he triumphed over a Scottish knight; and he was subsequently one of the companions in arms of the gallant HENRY V., at the battle of Agincourt. In the 5th of the same reign he was constituted one of the commissioners to treat with the captain of the castle of Caen for the surrender of that fortress, and upon the departure of his royal master from France he was left behind for the defence of those parts, for all which important services, and in consideration of his connection with the house of Plantagenet, Sir John Cornwall was advanced by King HENRY VI., in open parliament, to the dignity of a Baron of the realm, under the title of BARON FANHOPE, *of Fanhope, co. of Hereford*, on 17 July, 1433, and created 30 January, 1442, BARON MILBROKE, to bear that title as a free denizen of this realm, &c.; but he was always summoned to parliament as "*Johanni Cornewayll, Chevalier.*" In the 12th of HENRY VI. his lordship was made governor of the town of St. Selerine, then won by assault; shortly after which he had a grant of the custody of Charles, Duke of Orleans, during the time of the restraint of that prince in England.

This gallant nobleman outlived his wife, the Princess Eliza-

137

beth, by whom he had no issue,* and *d.* in 1443, when the BARONIES OF FANHOPE AND MILBROKE became EXTINCT. His lordship left two illegitimate sons, JOHN and THOMAS, for whom he provided in his will.

Arms—Erm., a lion rampant, gu., crowned, or, within a bordure, sa., bezantée.

CORNWALLIS — BARONS, EARLS, AND MARQUESSES CORNWALLIS.

Barony, by Letters Patent, dated 20 April, 1661.
Earldom, by Letters Patent, dated 30 June, 1753.
Marquessate, by Letters Patent, dated 15 August, 1792.

Lineage.

Harvey, Clarencieux king-of-arms, in his visitation of the co. of Suffolk, made in 1561, states that

THOMAS CORNWALLEYS, of London, merchant, the first of the family mentioned in the Visitation, was a younger brother, and born in Ireland, and that he bore the same arms which the house at the time of the Visitation used. This Thomas was sheriff of London in 1378, he *d.* in 1384, and was *s.* by his son,

JOHN CORNWALLIS, who added to his patrimony the lordships of Broome and Oakley, with other lands in Suffolk, by intermarrying with Philippe, dau. and one of the heirs of Robert Bucton. This John represented the co. of Suffolk in parliament in the reign of RICHARD II., he *d.* in 1446, and was *s.* by his son,

THOMAS CORNWALLIS, who *m.* Philippe, dau. and heir of Edward Tyrrel, Esq., of Downham in Essex, and dying in 1447, was *s.* by his son,

THOMAS CORNWALLIS, Esq., M.P. for the co. of Suffolk, in the 28th of HENRY VI. The three elder sons of this Thomas having successively inherited the estate of Broome, and all dying *s. p.*, his youngest son eventually succeeded as

SIR WILLIAM CORNWALLIS, K.B., of Broome. This gentleman *m.* Elizabeth, dau. and co-heir of John Stanford, Esq., and dying in November, 1519, was *s.* by his eldest son,

SIR JOHN CORNWALLIS, steward of the household to Prince Edward, son of HENRY VIII. He *d.* in 1544, and was *s.* by his eldest son,

SIR THOMAS CORNWALLIS. This gentleman displayed great personal courage against the Norfolk rebels under Ket, the Tanner, in 1549, and he subsequently held the office of sheriff for Norfolk and Suffolk. He was also instrumental in the suppression of Wyat's insurrection, and was commissioned with the Earl of Sussex and Sir Edward Hastings for the trial of Sir Thomas Wyat, in 1554; at this time he was sworn of the privy council and constituted treasurer of Calais. In the 4th and 5th of PHILIP and MARY, Sir Thomas represented the co. of Suffolk in parliament. Upon the accession of Queen ELIZABETH, being a Roman Catholic, he was left out of the privy council, and removed from the comptrollership of the household, which he held under MARY. He then retired into the country and built Broome Hall. Sir Thomas Cornwallis *m.* Anne, dau. of Sir John Jerningham, and had issue,

   I. WILLIAM, his successor.
   II. Charles (Sir), ambassador to Spain, *temp.* JAMES I., and a person of great eminence; he *m.* 1st, Elizabeth, dau. of Thomas Farnham, Esq., of Fincham, and founded (through his eldest son, Sir William Cornwallis, a celebrated writer and essayist, whose works were published after his death) a branch of the family whose last representative was CAROLINE FRANCES CORNWALLIS, the distinguished author of a popular series

---

* "The case of Sir John Cornwall" (says COURTHOPE, "*Historic Peerage*," p. 184), "is remarkable in several respects. Both of his creations were in parliament and enrolled in parliament, but the former only was exemplified by patent; in the latter, creating him Baron of Milbroke, he is styled Sir John Cornwall only, without reference to his former creation as Baron of Fanhope, in neither case are there any words of inheritance, and although the absence of such words under ordinary circumstances would give only a life estate to the grantee, Lord Lyndhurst, in his argument on the Wensleydale Peerage, considered that his being created in parliament as a baron, 'with all and singular rights, privileges and immunities in every place within the realm of England as fully, entirely, and in the same manner and form as other barons of the same realm before this time have used and enjoyed,' gave to him amongst those rights the privilege enjoyed by other barons of transmitting his title to his posterity."

entitled "Small Books on Great Subjects," who *d. unm.* 8 January, 1859.

  I. Elizabeth, *m.* to Sir Thomas Kitson, of Hengrave, Suffolk.
  II. Anne, *m.* to William Halse, Esq., of Devonshire.
  III. Alice, *m.* to Richard Southwell, Esq.

Sir Thomas *d.* 24 December, 1604, and was *s.* by his elder son,

  SIR WILLIAM CORNWALLIS, who *m.* 1st, Lucy, eldest dau. and co-heir of John Nevill, Lord Latimer, by whom he had an only surviving son, THOMAS, and four daus. He *m.* 2ndly, Jane, dau. of Hercules Mewtas, Esq., and by that lady had an only son, FREDERICK. Sir Wiilam was *s.* by his elder son,

  THOMAS CORNWALLIS. Esq., M.P. for the co. of Suffolk, *temp.* CHARLES I.; who dying *unm.* was *s.* by his brother,

  FREDERICK CORNWALLIS, Esq., who was created a baronet 4 May, 1627, and for the active part he had taken in the civil wars, and his faithful adherence to CHARLES II. through all fortunes, was elevated to the peerage, by the title of BARON CORNWALLIS, *of Eye, co. Suffolk*, 20 April, 1661. His lordship *m.* 1st, Elizabeth, dau. of Sir John Ashburnham, by whom he had CHARLES, his successor, with two other sons and one dau. who all *d. s. p. m.* He *m.* 2ndly, Elizabeth, dau. of Sir Henry Crofts, and had a dau., Jane, who *m.* William Duncomb, Esq. Lord Cornwallis, who is characterized by Lloyd as "a man of so cheerful a spirit that no sorrow came next his heart, and of so resolved a mind that no fear came into his thoughts; a well-spoken man, competently seen in modern languages, and of a comely and goodly personage," *d.* in 1662, and was *s.* by his eldest son,

  CHARLES, 2nd baron, who *m.* Margaret, dau. of Thomas Playsted, Esq., and dying in 1673, was *s.* by his son,

  CHARLES, 3rd baron, who *m.* 1st, Elizabeth, eldest dau. of Sir Stephen Fox, Knt., by whom he had CHARLES, his successor, and other sons. He *m.* 2ndly, Anne Scot, Duchess of Monmouth and Buccleuch, relict of the unhappy James, Duke of Monmouth, and by her grace had one son, Lord George, who *d.* in youth, and two daus. His lordship filled the office of first commissioner of the admiralty during the reign of WILLIAM III., and was lord-lieutenant of the co. of Suffolk. He *d.* 29 April, 1698, and was *s.* by his only surviving son,

  CHARLES, 4th baron. His lordship was a military officer, and served in several campaigns under King WILLIAM III. He *m.* Charlotte, dau. and sole heir of Richard Butler, Earl of Arran, 2nd son of James, Duke of Ormonde, and had issue,

  I. CHARLES, his successor.
  II. Stephen, major-general in the army, *b.* in 1703; *m.* Mrs. Pearson, and *d. s. p.* in May, 1743.
  III. John, *b.* in 1706; *m.* Sarah, dau. of the Rev. Hugh Dale, and by her (who *d.* in 1768), left an only surviving dau. and heiress,
    Sarah, *m.* to the Rev. Walter Earle.
  IV. Richard, *b.* in 1708, *d. unm.* in 1741.
  V. Edward, *b.* in February, 1713, a general in the army, and governor of Gibraltar; *m.* in 1763, Mary, dau. of Charles, 2nd Viscount Townshend, but *d. s p.* 14 January, 1776.
  VI. Frederick, archbishop of Canterbury, *m.* Caroline, dau. of William Townshend, Esq., and *d. s. p.* in 1783.
  VII. William,
  VIII. Henry,
  I. Charlotte, } all *d. unm.*
  II. Elizabeth,
  III. Mary.

His lordship was appointed in 1715, joint postmaster-general with James Craggs, Esq. He *d.* 19 January, 1721-2, and was *s.* by his eldest son,

  CHARLES, 5th baron, who was created 30 June, 1753, Viscount Brome and Earl Cornwallis; his lordship *m.* Elizabeth, eldest dau. of Charles, Viscount Townshend, by whom he had issue,

  I. CHARLES, his successor.
  II. James, *b.* 10 September, 1740, *d.* April, 1761.
  III. James, in holy orders, bishop of Lichfield and Coventry, who *s.* as 4th earl.
  IV. William (Sir), G.C.B., admiral of the Red, *b.* in 1743-4; *d.* in 1819.
  I. Elizabeth, *m.* in July, 1753, to Bowen Southwell, Esq., nephew to Thomas, 1st Lord Southwell, and *d.* 20 March, 1796.
  II. Charlotte, *m.* to Spencer Madan, D.D., bishop of Peterborough, and *d.* 11 March, 1794.
  III. Mary, *m.* to Samuel Whitbread, Esq., of Cardington, Bedfordshire, and *d.* in December, 1770.

The earl was appointed constable of the Tower in 1740. He *d.* 23 June, 1762, and was *s.* by his eldest son,

  CHARLES CORNWALLIS, 2nd Earl Cornwallis, *b.* 31 December, 1738, who having distinguished himself as a great military commander in America and India, was created MARQUESS CORNWALLIS, 15 August, 1792. In 1799 his lordship was appointed lord-lieutenant of Ireland and commander of the forces there; in which high situation he acquired

the reputation of having restored public tranquillity at that unhappy period by the firmness, moderation, and humanity which governed his councils. In 1801, he signed the peace of Amiens; in 1804 had the honour of being placed a second time at the head of the government of India, as governor-general, and died there on 5 October, in the following year. His lordship *m.* in July, 1768, Jemima, dau. of Col. James Jones, of the 3rd guards, and sister of Arnoldus Jones, Esq., of Brenthwaite, Cumberland, who took the name of Skelton; and by her (who *d.* 14 February, 1779), his lordship had issue,

  CHARLES, his successor.
  Mary, *m.* 1785, to Mark Singleton, Esq., M.P., principal store-keeper to the ordnance, who *d.* 17 July, 1840.

The marquess, who was a knight of the Garter, was *s.* by his eldest son,

  CHARLES CORNWALLIS, 3rd earl and 2nd marquess, *b.* 19 October, 1774; *m.* 17 April, 1797, Louisa, 4th dau. and eventually co-heiress of Alexander, 4th Duke of Gordon, K.T., and by her (who *d.* 5 December, 1850) had issue,

  JANE, *m.* 13 May, 1819, Richard, 3rd Lord Braybroke, and *d.* 23 September, 1856, leaving issue.
  LOUISA.
  JEMIMA, *m.* 2 September, 1824, Edward-Granville, Earl of St. Germans, and *d.* 1 July, 1856, leaving issue.
  MARY, *m.* 7 April, 1825, to Charles Ross, Esq., M.P., who *d.* 22 March, 1860.
  ELIZABETH.

His lordship *d.* in 1823, when the MARQUESSATE OF CORNWALLIS EXPIRED; but the earldom and other honours reverted to his uncle,

  JAMES CORNWALLIS, D.C.L., lord bishop of Lichfield and Coventry, as 4th earl. He *m.* Catherine, dau. of Galfridus Mann, Esq., of Egerton, and sister of Sir Horace Mann, Bart., by whom he left at his decease in 1824, an only son,

  JAMES, 5th earl, *b.* 20 September, 1778; who *m.* 1st, 1804, Maria-Isabella, dau. of Francis Dickens, Esq., and by her (who *d.* 1823) had issue,

  CHARLES-JAMES, *Viscount Brome, d. unm.*, aged twenty-two, 27 December, 1835.
  JEMIMA-ISABELLA, *m.* 12 April, 1828, Charles Wykeham-Martin, Esq., of Leeds Castle, Kent, and *d.* 17 December, 1836, leaving issue.

The earl *m.* 2ndly, 1829, Laura, dau. of William Hayes, Esq., which lady *d.* 1840; and 3rdly, in 1842, Julia, dau. of Thomas Bacon, Esq., of Redlands, by whom (who *d.* 1847) he had an only surviving child,

  JULIA, *m.* 27 August, 1862, to William-Archer, Viscount Holmesdale, eldest son of Earl Amherst.

The earl *d.* 21 May, 1852, when all his honours became EXTINCT

Arms—Sa., guttée d'eau, on a fesse, arg., three Cornish choughs, ppr.

COSBY—BARON SYDNEY.

By Letters Patent, dated 14 July, 1768.

Lineage.

ALEXANDER COSBY, Esq., of Stradbally Hall, in the Queen's Co. (representative of the family of Cosby, which was established in Ireland by the celebrated Francis Cosbie, *temp.* EDWARD VI., for full details *see* BURKE's *Landed Gentry*), *d.* in 1694, leaving by Elizabeth his wife, dau. of Henry L'Estrange, Esq., of Moystown, King's Co., several sons and daus., of whom

  DUDLEY, was his heir, and
  Alexander, lieut.-col. in the army, and lieut.-governor of Nova Scotia, where he *d.* in 1743, leaving issue.

The eldest son,

  LIEUT.-COL. DUDLEY COSBY, of Stradbally, M.P. for the Queen's Co., *m.* Sarah, dau. of Periam Pole, Esq., of Ballyfin; and *d.* 24 May, 1729, leaving, with a dau. Sarah, wife of Sir Robert Meredyth, Bart., of Shrewland, a son and successor,

  POLE COSBY, Esq., of Stradbally, who *m.* Mary, dau. and co-heir of Henry Dodwell, Esq., of Manor Dodwell, co. Roscommon, and left at his decease, 20 May, 1766, with a dau. Sarah, *b.* in 1730 (*m.* 1st, to tne Right Hon. Arthur Upton, of Castle Upton; and 2ndly, to Robert, Earl of Farnham) a son and successor,

DUDLEY-ALEXANDER-SYDNEY COSBY, Esq., of Stradbally Hall, minister plenipotentiary to the Court of Denmark, who was created, by patent dated 14 July, 1768, a peer of Ireland, as Lord Sydney, of Leix, Baron Stradbally, Queen's Co. He m. December, 1773, Lady Isabella St. Lawrence, dau. of Thomas, Earl of Howth; but d. in the ensuing month (17 January, 1774) s. p., when the peerage became EXTINCT, while the inheritance reverted to (the only surviving son of Lieut.-Col. Alexander Cosby, governor of Nova Scotia) Admiral PHILLIPS COSBY, who left no issue at his decease, when the family estates passed to his kinsman, THOMAS COSBY, Esq., of Vicarstown, by whose great grand-son, ROBERT-ASHWORTH GODOLPHIN COSBY, Esq., of Stradbally Hall, they are still enjoyed.

Arms—Arg., a chev., between three leopards' faces, sa ; on a canton, or, a saltier, vert, between a cross crosslet, in chief, gu., a lizard erect in the dexter, and a salmon in the sinister, fesse point of the fourth, and a dexter hand, couped, in base, of the fifth.

COSPATRICK—EARL OF NORTHUMBERLAND.

Conferred by WILLIAM THE CONQUEROR, anno 1069.

Lineage.

Upon the death of Robert Comyn, Earl of Northumberland, COSPATRICK, son of Maldred, son of Crinan (which Maldred was progenitor to the second dynasty of the great family of Neville, still represented by the Earls of Abergavenny), obtained the earldom of the co. of Northumberland from the CONQUEROR for a large sum of money; but soon afterwards becoming dissatisfied with the sway of the new ruler, Cospatrick, with other northern chiefs, fled into Scotland, and was well received by King MALCOLM CANMORE.

From Scotland the earl made several hostile incursions into England, and was deprived of the earldom for those repeated treasons. He subsequently obtained Dunbar, with the adjacent lands in London, from the Scottish monarch for his subsistence, but d. soon afterwards, leaving issue, 1 DOLPHIN; 2 COSPATRIC, 2nd Earl of Dunbar; and 3 Waldene, of Cockermouth Castle. The 2nd son, COSPATRIC, 2nd Earl of Dunbar, who witnessed the foundation charter of the abbey of Scone, 1115, and that of Holyrood, 1128, d. 16 August, 1139, leaving a son and heir, COSPATRIC, 3rd Earl of Dunbar, styled in some charters "Cospatricius Comes, filius Cospatricii," he d. 1147. (*See* ADDENDA, under DUNBAR.)

Arms—Gu., a saltier, arg

COTTINGTON—BARON COTTINGTON, OF HANWORTH, CO. MIDDLESEX.

By Letters Patent, dated 10 July, 1631.

Lineage.

FRANCIS COTTINGTON, Esq., 4th son of Philip Cottington, Esq., of Godmanston, co. Somerset, having held the office of clerk of the council in the reign of King JAMES I., and being secretary to Charles, Prince of Wales, was created a Baronet by that monarch, 16 February, 1623. After the accession of King CHARLES I., Sir Francis Cottington was constituted chancellor and under treasurer of the Exchequer ; and being accredited ambassador to the court of Madrid for the purpose of negotiating a peace, he was elevated to the peerage, 10 July, 1631, as LORD COTTINGTON, Baron of Hanworth, co. Middlesex. His lordship was next commissioned to exercise the important office of lord treasurer during the king's absence in Scotland, in the 9th CHARLES I., and was constituted master of the wards upon his Majesty's return. During the civil wars, Lord Cottington remained faithfully attached to his royal master, and eventually went into exile with King CHARLES II., from which he never returned. His lordship m. Anne, dau. of Sir William Meredith, Knt., and widow of Sir Robert Brett, by whom he had a son and four daus., all of whom predeceased him unm. He d. at Valladolid, in 1653, when the BARONY OF COTTINGTON became EXTINCT, and his estates passed to his nephew,

139

CHARLES COTTINGTON, Esq., who had his lordship's remains brought over to England. and interred in Westminster Abbey, where he erected a stately monument.

Arms—Az., a fesse between three roses, or.

COUCI—EARL OF BEDFORD.

By Charter, dated in 1366.

Lineage.

INGELRAM, SIRE DE COUCY, Seigneur de Gynes, who d. in 1321, m. Christian, dau. and sole heir of William de Lindsay, of Lamberton, by Ada, his wife, sister and co-heir of JOHN BALIOL, King of Scotland, and dau. of John Baliol, Lord of Barnard Castle, by Dervorgil, his wife, one of the two daus. and co-heirs of Alan, Lord of Galloway (*see* p. 21). By this great alliance Ingelram left a son,

WILLIAM, SIRE DE COUCY, b. 1286, who m. Isabel de Chatillon St. Paul, and dying in 1335, left two sons, INGELRAM, his heir; and Raoul, Seigneur de Montmirail et de Bailleul. The elder son,

INGELRAM, SIRE DE COUCY, m. Catherine, dau. of the Duke of Austria, and d. 1344, leaving a son,

INGELRAM DE COUCI, who was so highly esteemed by King EDWARD III. that that monarch bestowed upon him his dau., Isabel, in marriage, and created him EARL OF BEDFORD, conferring upon him also the ribbon of the Garter. His lordship d. in 1397, leaving issue by the princess,

Mary. m. to Henry de Barr, Seigneur d'Oisy, and had a son, Robert, Count de Marle et de Soissons, who m. Jeanne de Bethune, Viscountess de Meaux, and d. 1415, leaving a dau., JEANNE, Countess de Marle et de Soissons, wife of Louis, Count de St. Paul, Constable of France, and mother of PETER, Count de St. Paul, Marle and Soissons, Chevalier de la Toison d'Or, whose dau., by his wife, Margaret, of Savoy, was MARIE DE LUXEMBURGH, Countess de St. Paul and Conversan, m. in 1487, to FRANCIS DE BOURBON, Count de Vendôme, great-grandfather by her of HENRY IV., King of France and Navarre, whose descendant and representative HENRY, DUKE DE BOURDEAUX, is heir of the De Coucys, and senior co-heir of the Baliols.

Philippa, m. to Robert de Vere, Earl of Oxford and Duke of Ireland, one of the unhappy favourites of RICHARD II.

After the death of King EDWARD III., his lordship resigned the Earldom of Bedford, as well as the insignia of the order of the Garter, and d. at Bursa, in Natolia, 18 February, 1397, when the EARLDOM OF BEDFORD became EXTINCT.

Arms—Barry of six, vairée and gu.

COURCY—EARL OF ULSTER.

(*See* ADDENDA.)

COURTENAY—BARONS COURTENAY, EARLS OF DEVON.

Barony by Writ of Summons, dated 6 February, 1299.
Earldom, by Letters Patent, dated 22 February, 1335.

Lineage.

The Courtenays, of whom a distinguished line still exists, were one of the most illustrious races amongst the British nobility, and deduced their pedigree paternally from ATHON, who himself descended from PHARAMOND, founder, in 420, of the French monarchy, and common patriarch of all the Kings of France. This ATHON, having fortified, during the reign of ROBERT THE WISE, the town of COURTENAY, in the Isle of France, thence adopted his surname. But as the power of the Courtenays in England principally arose from the great alliances formed by the first members of the family who settled here, we shall pass at once to their maternal pedigree.

GODFRY, Earl of Ewe and Brion, natural son of RICHARD I., Duke of Normandy, was father of

GILBERT, Earl of Brion, who had two sons, Richard, ancestor of the house of Clare, and

BALDWYN DE BRIONIS, who for the distinguished part he had

in the Conquest, obtained from King WILLIAM the Barony of Okehampton, the custody of the co. of Devon, and the government of the castle of Exeter in fee. He m. Albreda, dau. of Richard, surnamed Goz, Count of Avranche, and had, with other issue,

I. RICHARD, surnamed DE REDVERS.
II. Robert, governor of Brione.
I. Emma, m. 1st, to William Avenal, and 2ndly, to William de Abrincis, by the latter of whom she had issue,

ROBERT DE ABRINCIS, who upon the resignation of his uncle, Richard de Redvers, obtained a grant of the Barony of Okehampton, the office of hereditary sheriff of Devon, and the government of Exeter Castle. He m. a dau. of Godwyn Dole, and left an only dau. and heiress,

MAUD DE ABRINCIS, who m. 1st, — Deincourt, by whom she had a dau.,

HAWISE, m. to SIR REGINALD DE COURTENAY, of whom hereafter.

Maud m. 2ndly, Robert Fitz-Edith, natural son of King HENRY I., and had another dau.,

MATILDA, m. to William de Courtenay, brother of Sir Reginald.

RICHARD DE ABRINCIS, surnamed DE REDVERS, having s. to the honours and possessions of his father, resigned the Barony of Okehampton, the sheriffalty of Devon, and the custody of the castle of Exeter, in favour of his nephew, Robert de Abrincis, mentioned above, and was created by King HENRY I. EARL OF DEVON, with a grant of the Isle of Wight in fee. This nobleman (who from residing chiefly at Exeter, was generally called Earl of Exeter) m. Adeliza, dau. and co-heiress of William Fitz-Osborne, Earl of Hereford, and had issue,

I BALDWYN DE REDVERS, his successor.
II. William de Redvers, surnamed DE VERNON.
III. Robert de Redvers.
I Hadewise, m. to William de Romare, Earl of Lincoln.

Richard de Redvers, 1st Earl of Devon, d. in 1137, and was s. by his eldest son,

BALDWYN DE REDVERS, as 2nd Earl of Devon. This nobleman, upon the demise of King HENRY I., espousing the cause of the Empress MAUD, took up arms, and immediately fortified his castle of Exeter and the Isle of Wight; but being besieged by King STEPHEN, he was obliged to surrender the castle and all his other possessions, and to withdraw with his family from the kingdom. We find him, however, soon again returning, and in the enjoyment of the Earldom of Devon; but, like his father, generally styled Earl of Exeter, from residing in that city. His lordship m. Lucia, dau. of Dru de Balun, and had issue,

I. RICHARD, his successor.
II. WILLIAM, surnamed DE VERNON, of whom hereafter, as 6th Earl of Devon.
I. Maud, m. to Ralph Avenill.

He d. in June, 1155, and was s. by his son,

RICHARD DE REDVERS, 3rd Earl of Devon, who m. Dionysia, dau. of Reginald de Dunstanville (natural son of King HENRY I.), Earl of Cornwall, and had two sons, successive earls. His lordship d. in 1162, and was s. by the elder,

BALDWIN DE REDVERS, 4th Earl of Devon, at whose decease, s. p., the honours devolved upon his brother,

RICHARD DE REDVERS, 5th Earl of Devon, who also d. s. p., when the honours reverted to his uncle,

WILLIAM DE REDVERS, surnamed VERNON, as 6th Earl of Devon. This nobleman, upon the second coronation of King RICHARD I., was one of the four earls that carried the silken canopy, being then styled, "Earl of the Isle of Wight." His lordship appears to have adhered steadily to King JOHN, for we find that monarch, in the 18th of his reign, providing for the security of the earl's property against LOUIS of France, which, from his advanced age, he was unable to defend himself. He m. Mabel, dau. of Robert, Earl of Mellent, by whom he acquired a considerable accession to his landed possessions, and had issue,

I. Baldwin, who m. Margaret, dau. and heiress of Warine Fitz-gerald, and d. v. p. 1 September, 1216, leaving an only son,

BALDWIN, of whom presently, as 7th EARL OF DEVON.

Margaret, the widow, was forced, according to Matthew Paris, by King JOHN, to marry "that impious, ignoble, and base conditioned man, Falk de Breant."

I. Joane, m. 1st, to William Brewere, and 2ndly, to Hubert de Burgh, chamberlain to the king, but had no issue.
II. Mary, m. ROBERT DE COURTENAY, feudal Baron of Okehampton, son and successor of Sir Reginald de Courtenay and Maude de Abrincis (refer to Emma, dau. of Baldwin de Abrincis, 1st Baron of Okehampton), and conveyed to her husband the head of the Barony of Devonshire, with the castle of Plimton. Of this marriage, were

SIR HUGH DE COURTENAY, successor to his father.

Sir William de Courtenay, surnamed de Musberrie, who m. Joane, dau. of Thomas Basset, but d. s. p.
Hauise, m. to John de Nevil.

Robert de Courtenay, Baron of Okehampton, was s. by his elder son,

SIR HUGH DE COURTENAY, as 3rd Baron of Okehampton. His lordship m. Alianora, dau. of Hugh le Despencer (father of Hugh, Earl of Winchester) by whom (who d. 11 October, 1328) he had issue,

HUGH (Sir), his successor, of whom hereafter, as successor to the estates of the Redvers, and the person in whom the EARLDOM OF DEVON was revived.
Philip (Sir), who fell at the battle of Shivelin, 24 June, 1314, and d. unm.
Isabel, m. to John St. John, Baron St. John, of Basing.
Aveline, m. to Sir John Gifford, Knt.
Egeline, m. to Robert Scales.
Margaret, m. to John de Moels.

His lordship d. 28 February, 1291.

William, 6th Earl of Devon, d. 14 September, 1216, and was s. by his grandson,

BALDWIN DE REDVERS, 7th Earl of Devon. In the 11th HENRY III., Gilbert de Clare, EARL OF GLOUCESTER AND HERTFORD, paid a fine of 2,000 marks to the king for permission to marry his eldest daughter to this young nobleman; whereupon all his demesne lands, which were then valued at £200 per annum, were placed under the guardianship of the Earl of Gloucester, until he should attain maturity. In the 24th of the same reign, the king keeping his Christmas at Winchester, at the instance of Richard, Earl of Cornwall, under whose tuition Baldwin then was, girded his lordship with the sword of knighthood; and investing him with the EARLDOM OF THE ISLE OF WIGHT, bestowed upon him Amicia, the dau. of the said Earl of Gloucester, in marriage. The Earl of Devon d. in five years afterwards, in the flower of his youth, anno 1245, leaving issue,

BALDWIN, his successor.
Margaret, a nun at Lacock.
ISABEL, successor to her brother.

His lordship was s. by his son,

BALDWIN DE REDVERS, 8th Earl of Devon, who was committed to the tuition of Peter de Savoy, uncle of Queen ELEANOR, and a person of great note at that period. His lordship did homage, and had livery of his lands in the 41st HENRY III., in which year he espoused Avis, dau. of Thos. Comte de Savoy, by whom he had an only son, John, who d. in infancy. The earl d. in 1262, having been poisoned, with the Earl of Gloucester, and others, at the table of Peter de Savoy. With his lordship the male line of the ancient and eminent house of REDVERS EXPIRED, but its honours devolved upon his sister,

ISABEL DE FORTIBUS, widow of William de Fortibus, Earl of Albemarle and Holderness, as COUNTESS OF DEVON. Her ladyship had three sons, all of whom d. in infancy, and two daus., viz.,

Anne, d. unm.
Aveline, m. 1st, to Ingram de Percy, and 2ndly, to Edmund Plantagenet, Earl of Lancaster, but d. s. p. in the lifetime of her mother, A.D. 1273.

The countess d. in 1293, and as she left no issue, the EARLDOM OF DEVON and the other honours of the house of REDVERS EXPIRED, but so much of its extensive possessions as did not pass to the crown, devolved upon the heir-at-law,

SIR HUGH COURTENAY, feudal Baron of Okehampton (the descendant of Lady Mary Redvers, dau. of William, 6th Earl of Devon, refer to that nobleman), who was summoned to parliament as BARON COURTENAY from 6 February, 1299, to 24 July, 1334, and created 22 February, 1335, EARL OF DEVON. The latter dignity was conferred upon his lordship in consequence of a representation made by him to the King (EDWARD III.), with whom he was in high estimation, to the purpose "that he was seised of a certain annuity of £18 6s. 7d. for the tertium denarium of the county of Devon, with divers lands by right of inheritance, from Isabel de Fortibus, Countess of Albemarle and Devon, which she in her lifetime did possess; and having accordingly received the same annuity at the hands of the sheriffs of that county, for which they had allowance upon their accounts in the exchequer, until Walter, bishop of Exeter, lord treasurer to King EDWARD II., upon the investigation of some persons who were inclined to disturb the business, did refuse to admit thereof, alleging, that this annuity was granted to the ancestors of the said Isabel, by the king's progenitors, under the name and title of EARLS; and therefore, that he, the said Hugh, being NO EARL, ought not to receive the same: and, that upon the like pretence, the then sheriffs of Devon did decline to pay it any longer to him." The king immediately instituted an inquiry into the affair, and finding it as stated, removed the difficulty by creating his lordship an earl, as stated above, and despatching his royal precept to the then sheriff of Devon, commanded him to proclaim that all persons should forthwith style his lordship EARL OF DEVON. The earl m. when but seventeen years of age, Agnes, dau. of Sir John St. John, Knt., and sister of Lord St. John, of Basing, by whom he had issue,

I. JOHN, abbot of Tavistock.
II. HUGH, his heir.
III. Robert, of Moreton, who d. in youth.
IV. Thomas, of Southcombe, m. Muriel, dau. and heiress of Sir John de Moels, Knt., by whom he had,
    1 Hugh, who d. s. p.
    1 Margaret, m. to Thomas Peverell.
    2 Muriel, m. to John Dynham.
I. Eleanor, m. to Henry, Lord Grey, of Codnor.
II. Elizabeth, m. to Lord Lisle.

His lordship d. in 1377, and was s. by his son,

HUGH COURTENAY, 2nd Earl of Devon. This nobleman distinguished himself in arms during the reign of EDWARD III., and was one of the first dignified with the Garter upon the institution of that noble order. His lordship m. Margaret, dau. of Humphrey de Bohun, Earl of Hereford and Essex, and grand-dau. of King EDWARD I., by whom he had, with other issue,

I. HUGH (Sir). who was summoned to parliament as BARON COURTENAY, 8 January, 1371, and was one of the original knights of the Garter. His lordship being in the expedition made into France twenty-four years before (EDWARD III.), participated in the glory of Cressy, and being the next year in the tournament at Eltham, he had a hood of white cloth, embroidered with dancing men, and buttoned with large pearls, presented to him by the king. He m. Elizabeth, dau. of Guy Brian, Lord of Tor-Brian, in Devonshire, and sister of the famous Guy, Lord Brian, standard-bearer to the king at Cressy, and a knight of the Garter, by whom he left at his decease, in the lifetime of his father, an only son,
    Hugh, who m. Matilda, dau. of Thomas Holland, Earl of Kent, and of Joane his wife, commonly called the "Fair Maid of Kent," dau. of Edmund, of Woodstock, son of King EDWARD I., which Joane was subsequently m. to EDWARD THE BLACK PRINCE, and by him was mother of King RICHARD II. Hugh Courtenay d. in 1377, a few years after his father, and before his grandfather, leaving no issue. His widow m. 2ndly, Waleran, Earl of St. Paul.

II. Edward, of Godlington (who also d. v. p.). m. Emeline, dau. and heiress of Sir John D'Auney, Knt., and had issue,
    1 EDWARD, of whom presently, as inheritor of the honours of the family.
    2 Hugh (Sir), of Haccomb, m. 1st, Elizabeth, dau. of Sir William Cogan, and widow of Sir Fulk Fitzwarine, who d. s. p. He m. 2ndly, Philippa, dau. and co-heiress of Sir Warren Arcedekene (by Elizabeth, dau. and heiress of John Talbot, of Ricard's Castle), by whom he had an only dau.,
       Joane, m. 1st, to Nicholas, Lord Carew, of Mohuns Ottery, and 2ndly, to Sir Robert Vere.
    Sir Hugh Courtenay m. 3rdly, Maud, dau. of Sir John Beaumont, of Sherwell, Dorset, by whom he had a dau.,
       Margaret, who m. Sir Theobald Grenvill, Knt.
    and a son and heir,
       HUGH (Sir), of Boconnock, in Cornwall, who fell at the battle of Tewkesbury, leaving issue, by his wife Margaret, dau. and co-heir of Thomas Carmino, Esq., of Devonshire,
          EDWARD, who was created Baron Okehampton, and EARL OF DEVON, in 1485 (see those dignities).|
          Elizabeth, m. to John Trethrif, Esq.
          Maud, m. to John Arundel, Esq., of Talverne.
          Isabel, m. to William Mohun, Esq.
          Florence, m. to John Trelawny, Esq.

III. William, chancellor of the university of Oxford, anno 1367; bishop of Hereford, 1369; bishop of London, 1375, and archbishop of Canterbury, 1381. His grace d. in 1396.
IV. PHILIP (Sir), of Powderham Castle, lieutenant of Ireland in the reign of RICHARD II., ancestor of the existing noble house of COURTENAY, EARL OF DEVON.
V. Piers (Sir), standard-bearer to King EDWARD III., constable of Windsor Castle, governor of Calais, chamberlain to King RICHARD II., and knight of the Garter. This eminent and gallant person, who was celebrated for deeds of arms, d. unm. in 1409.
I. Margaret, m. to John, Lord Cobham.
II. Elizabeth, m. 1st, to Sir John Vere, and 2ndly, to Sir Andrew Luttrell.
III. Catherine, m. 1st, to John, Lord Harington, and 2ndly, to Sir Thomas Engaine.
IV. Joane, m. to Sir John Cheverston.

Hugh, 2nd Earl of Devon, d. in 1377, and was s. by (the elder son of his son Edward) his grandson,

EDWARD COURTENAY, 3rd earl. This nobleman served in the

beginning of the reign of RICHARD II. as a naval officer, under John of Gaunt and Thomas of Woodstock respectively, and was appointed in the 7th of the same monarch, admiral of all the king's fleet, from the mouth of the Thames westward. In the next year, being then Earl Marshal, his lordship was retained to serve the king in his Scottish wars; in two years afterwards he had the command of the fleet at sea to prevent invasion, and in the 13th of RICHARD was engaged in the French wars. His lordship m. Maud, dau. of Thomas, Baron Camois, and had issue,

Edward (Sir), K.B., and admiral of the king's fleet, who m. Eleanor, dau. of Roger Mortimer, Earl of March, but d. s. p. in the lifetime of his father.
HUGH, his successor.
James.

The earl d. 5 December, 1419, and was s. by his 2nd but eldest surviving son,

HUGH COURTENAY, 4th earl, K.B., who, in the 6th HENRY V. (his father then living), was appointed commander-in-chief of the king's fleet. His lordship m. Anne, dau. of Richard, Lord Talbot, and sister of the renowned John, Earl of Shrewsbury, by whom he had issue,

THOMAS, his successor.
John, d. unm.

His lordship d. 16 June, 1422, and was s. by his elder son,

THOMAS COURTENAY, 5th earl. This nobleman commenced his military career at the age of sixteen, and was engaged for several years in the French wars of King HENRY VI., with which monarch he sided upon the breaking out of the unhappy conflict between the houses of York and Lancaster; and the Courtenays continued to adhere to the red rose with unshaken fidelity from that period until the termination of the contest. In 1448 a dispute regarding precedency arose between the Earls of Devon and Arundel, but it was decided by parliament in favour of the latter, in consequence of the feudal possession of Arundel Castle. The earl m. Margaret Beaufort, 2nd dau. of John, Marquess of Somerset (one of the legitimated children of John of Gaunt), and had issue,

THOMAS, his successor.
Henry, beheaded as a Lancastrian.
John, slain at Tewkesbury.
Joane, m. 1st, to Sir Roger Clifford, Knt., who was beheaded in 1485, and 2ndly, to Sir William Knyvett, Knt.
Elizabeth, m. to Sir Hugh Conway, Knt.
Anne,   }
Matilda, } d. young.
Eleanor, }

His lordship d. 3 February, 1458, in the abbey of Abingdon, upon his journey to London, with other lords, to mediate between the king and the Duke of York, and was s. by his eldest son,

THOMAS COURTENAY, 6th earl, then twenty-six years of age. This nobleman inheriting the political principles, as well as honours of his deceased father, was a strenuous upholder of the cause of Lancaster, and falling into the hands of the enemy at Towton Field, he was beheaded at York, by order of King EDWARD IV. in April, 1462. Under the attainder of this earl, the honours and possessions of the house of Courtenay fell; but his next brother,

HENRY COURTENAY, Esq. (as he was styled, but who should have been 7th earl), finding favour with the new king, had restoration of some part of the lands. Engaging, however, in the Lancastrian quarrel with the zeal of his predecessors, he was attainted of treason, 4 March, 1466, before the king and justices at Sarum, and beheaded with the Lord Hungerford on the same day. The greater part of the Courtenay estates having been conferred upon Humphrey Stafford, Baron Stafford, of Southwicke, his lordship was created EARL OF DEVON, 7 May, 1469, but being beheaded and attainted in the August following, that earldom became forfeited. Upon the demise of Henry Courtenay, his only surviving brother,

JOHN COURTENAY, assumed to be 8th Earl of Devon, and the Lancastrian interest prevailing in 1470, when King EDWARD was driven into Holland by the Earl of Warwick, his lordship was restored, by parliament, with King HENRY VI., to the HONOURS and ESTATES of his family The defeat of the Earl of Warwick, however, after the return of King EDWARD by that prince, at the decisive battle of Barnet, 14 April, 1471, again placed the Earl of Devon in jeopardy; and attaching himself to Margaret of Anjou, his lordship fell, gallantly fighting at the head of the rear-guard of Margaret's army, at Tewkesbury, on 4 May following. Thus the three brothers sealed with their blood their bond of fidelity to the house of Lancaster, and with these brave soldiers expired the senior branch of the ancient and illustrious house of Courtenay. The last earl was buried at Tewkesbury, and being attainted, the HONOURS and ESTATES of DEVON became again FORFEITED.

Arms—Or, three torteaux, with a label of three points, az., in chief.

COURTENAY—MARQUESSES OF EXETER.

Earldom by Letters Patent, dated 26 October, 1485.
Marquisate, by Letters Patent, dated 18 June, 1525.

Lineage.

SIR HUGH COURTENAY, Knt., of Boconock, co. Cornwall, only son of Sir Hugh Courtenay, of Haccomb, brother of EDWARD, 3rd EARL OF DEVON, of the Courtenay family (*see* descendants of Hugh, 2nd Earl of Devon—article COURTENAY, EARLS OF DEVON), m. Margaret, dau and co-heiress of Thomas Carmino, Esq. (the last male heir of that ancient family), by whom he had issue,

1. EDWARD (Sir), his successor.
II. Walter (Sir), *d. unm.*
1. Elizabeth, *m.* to John Trethrif, Esq., and had a son,
   THOMAS TRETHRIF, who *m.* — dau. of — Travisa, and left two daus., viz.,
     Elizabeth, *m.* to John Vivian, Esq.
     Margaret, *m.* to Edward Courtenay, Esq., of Larrock.
II. Maud, *m.* to John Arundel, Esq., of Talkern.
III. Isabel, *m.* to William Mohun, Esq.
IV. Florence, *m.* to John Trelawny, Esq.

Heiresses, eventually, of their grand-nephew, Edward, 2nd Marquess of Exeter.

Sir Hugh, faithful to the Lancastrian interest, fell with his noble kinsman, the Earl of Devon, at the battle of Tewkesbury, and his elder son,

SIR EDWARD COURTENAY, being implicated with his brother, in Henry Stafford, Duke of Buckingham's conspiracy, in favour of Henry, Earl of Richmond, was forced to fly into Britanny upon the failure of that plot and the decapitation of the duke; and was attainted with the Earl of Richmond and others, by parliament, in the beginning of 1484, but returning with the earl, and assisting at the battle of Bosworth, he was elevated to the peerage by King HENRY VII., 26 October, 1485, in the ancient dignity of the family, *that* of EARL OF DEVON, the new monarch making him grants at the same time of the greater part of the castles, manors, &c., which belonged to the late Thomas Courtenay, Earl of Devon. In the March following, the king made his lordship governor of Kesterwell, in Cornwall, and a knight of the Garter. The earl was in all the parliaments of HENRY VII. He was in the expedition to France in 1491, and in six years afterwards he defended the city of Exeter against Perkin Warbeck and his adherents. He *m.* Elizabeth, dau. of Sir Philip Courtenay, of Molland, by whom he had an only son,

WILLIAM, K.B., who *m.* Katherine, 7th and youngest dau. of King EDWARD IV. In the year 1502, this gentleman, with Lord William de la Pole, Sir James Tyrrel, and Sir John Windham, were arrested on the charge of holding a traiterous correspondence with Edmund de la Pole, Earl of Suffolk (son of John, Duke of Suffolk and Lady Elizabeth, elder sister of EDWARD IV.), who had fled to his aunt, Margaret, Duchess of Burgundy, and he (Sir William Courtenay) was attainted in consequence, in 1504 ; Tyrrel and Windham were beheaded on Tower Hill, while Sir William Courtenay was doomed to incarceration during the king's reign.

The earl *d.* 24 May, 1509, and King HENRY VIII. ascending the throne in the same year, his highness immediately liberated SIR WILLIAM COURTENAY, and took him into his gracious favour ; but Sir William *d.* in the 3rd year of that monarch's reign, before he had either letters patent or a formal restoration of the earldom ; he was, however, buried "with the honours of an earl," at the *especial* command of the king. By the Lady Katherine Plantagenet, he left an only son,

HENRY COURTENAY, who being restored in blood and honours, became 2nd Earl of Devon. In 1522 his lordship obtained a grant of Caliland, in Cornwall, and of " a fair mansion," situate in the parish of St. Lawrence Poultry, in the city of London, forfeited by the attainder of Edward Stafford, Duke of Buckingham, on whose trial he was one of the twenty-six peers that sat in judgment ; and he was advanced, by letters patent, dated 18 June, 1525, to the dignity of MARQUESS OF EXETER. In the year 1530, at the interview between King HENRY VIII. and the King of France, in the vale of Arden, when the two monarchs challenged all men at justs, the Marquess of Exeter ran a course with the French prince, when

both their spears broke, and they maintained their seats. His lordship evinced his skill and valour in many other tournaments, and in the year 1532, on HENRY'S going to Calais, he was nominated by the king, prior to his highness's departure, heir apparent to the throne. His lordship subscribed the articles against Cardinal Wolsey, and the letter sent to Pope CLEMENT VII., entreating his holiness to ratify the divorce between the king and Queen CATHERINE. In 1536, he sat in judgment upon ANNE BOLEYNE, and in the same year, he suppressed, in conjunction with the Duke of Norfolk and the Earls of Shrewsbury, Huntingdon, and Rutland, a rebellion in Yorkshire ; but that very year he was committed to the Tower, with Henry Pole, LORD MONTACUTE, and Sir Edward Nevill, brother of Lord Abergavenny, accused by Sir Geoffrey Pole, brother of Lord Montacute, of high treason, and indicted for devising to maintain, promote, and advance one Reginald Pole, late dean of Exeter, enemy to the king beyond sea, and to deprive the king, &c. The Marquess of Exeter and Lord Montacute were tried on 1 and 2 December, 1539, at Westminster, and being found guilty were beheaded, with Sir Edward Nevill, on 9 January ensuing, on Tower Hill. Upon the attainder of the marquess, all his honours of course EXPIRED, and King HENRY annexed to the Duchy of Cornwall all his lands in that co., which came to the crown. The marquess had *m.* 1st, Elizabeth Grey, dau. and heiress of John, Viscount Lisle, by whom he had no issue, and 2ndly, Gertrude, dau. of William Blount, Lord Mountjoy, by whom he left an only son (the Marchioness of Exeter was attainted with the Countess of Salisbury, the year after her husband, but the latter only suffered),

EDWARD COURTENAY, who, although but twelve years of age when his father was beheaded, was committed prisoner to the Tower, and detained there during the remainder of King HENRY'S reign and that of King EDWARD VI., but upon the accession of Queen MARY he was released, and restored to his father's honours, as MARQUESS OF EXETER, &c., and to the estates which remained in the possession of the crown, by a private bill, passed in the 1st year of her majesty's reign, while another private bill reversed the attainder of his mother. His lordship had some command in suppressing Wyat's rebellion, and yet with the Princess Elizabeth was afterwards accused of being accessory thereto, and sent with her highness to the Tower. He was subsequently confined in Fotheringhay Castle, but released through the interposition of PHILIP of Spain, upon his marriage with the queen, as was also the Lady Elizabeth. His lordship after this obtained the queen's permission to go abroad, and *d.* at Padua, not without suspicion of poison, 4 October, 1556. This unfortunate nobleman seemed to be born to be a prisoner, for, from twelve years of age to the time of his death, he had scarcely enjoyed two entire years liberty. He *d. unm.*, and was the last of the family who bore the titles of MARQUESS OF EXETER and BARON OF OAKHAMPTON, those dignities expiring with his lordship, while his estates were divided amongst the four sisters of EDWARD, the 1st earl, his lordship's grand-aunts (*refer* to children of Sir Hugh Courtenay). The marquess's remains were interred in St. Anthony's Church, in Padua, where a noble monument was erected to his memory. The EARLDOM OF DEVON was DORMANT from the time of the Marquess's death to the year 1831, when a resolution of the House of Lords declared that William, Viscount Courtenay, was entitled to it. That nobleman *d unm.*, 1835, and his kinsman and heir male is now EARL OF DEVON.

Arms—Or, three torteaux, with a label of three points, az., in chief.

COVENTRY—BARONS COVENTRY, OF AYLESBOROUGH, CO. WORCESTER.

By Letters Patent, dated 10 April, 1628.

Lineage.

This family rose first into importance through

JOHN COVENTRY, an opulent mercer of the city of London, who filled the civic chair in 1425, and was one of the executors of the celebrated Sir Richard Whittington. From this worthy citizen descended

THOMAS COVENTRY, Esq., an eminent lawyer, *temp.* ELIZABETH and King JAMES I. In the 38th of the former reign he was chosen autumnal reader by the society of the Inner Temple, but was obliged to postpone the fulfilment of his task to the ensuing Lent, owing to the plague then raging in London. He was soon afterwards advanced to the dignity of the coif, and, in the 3rd of King JAMES, was appointed king's sergeant ; before the close of which year, being constituted one of the judges of the Court of Common Pleas, he took his seat upon the bench, but survived his promotion a few months only. He *m.* Margaret, dau. and heiress of — Jeffreys, Esq., of Croome-d'Abitot and had issue,

THOMAS, his successor.
William, of Ridmarley, co. Worcester.
WALTER, from whom the present Earl of Coventry derives.
Joan, *m.* to — Rogers, Esq., of Surrey.
Catherine, *m.* to William Child, Esq.
Anne, *m.* to George Frampton, Esq.

He was *s.* by his eldest son,

THOMAS COVENTRY, Esq., who, having adopted the learned profession of his father, attained the very highest honours of the bar. His advancement commenced with the recordership of London; he was then appointed solicitor-general and honoured with knighthood, and in the 18th of JAMES I. succeeded to the attorney-generalship. In the 1st of King CHARLES I. Sir Thomas was constituted lord keeper of the Great Seal, and elevated to the peerage on 10 April, 1628, as BARON COVENTRY, *of Aylesborough, co. Worcester.* His lordship *m.* 1st, SARAH, dau. of Edward Sebright, Esq., of Besford, co. Worcester, and had issue,

I. THOMAS, his successor.
1. Elizabeth, *m.* to Sir John Hare, of Stow Bardolph, in Norfolk

He *m.* 2ndly, Elizabeth, dau. of John Aldersey, Esq., of Spurstow, and widow of William Pitchford, Esq., by whom he had issue,

1. John, *m.* to Elizabeth, dau. and co-heir of John Coles, Esq., of Barton, co. Somerset, and widow of Herbert Doddington, Esq., and had

John (Sir, K. B.), member of the long parliament for Weymouth. The outrage upon this gentleman, and its provocation, which gave rise to the well-known Coventry Act, arose thus:—" Upon the occasion of a money grant being carried in the House of Commons, it was proposed by opposition that the supplies for it should be raised by a tax upon playhouses, which being resisted by the court party, upon the plea 'that players were the king's servants, and a part of his pleasure,' Sir John Coventry asked whether did the king's pleasure lie among the men or the women that acted?—an observation that excited so much indignation in the royal circle that it was determined to inflict summary punishment upon the utterer. The Duke of York told Burnet 'that he said everything to divert the king from the resolution he had taken, which was to send some guards to watch in the street where Sir John Coventry lodged, and to set a mark upon him.' The outrage, by bills of indictment, was found to have been committed by Sir Thomas Sandys, Knt., Charles O'Brien, Esq., Simon Parry, and Miles Reeves, who fled from justice, not daring to abide a legal trial. 'As Coventry was going home,' says Burnet, 'they drew about him: he stood up to the wall and held the flambeau out of his servant's hands, and with that in one hand, and his sword in the other, he defended himself so well that he got great credit by it. He wounded some of them; but was soon disarmed, and then they cut his nose to the bone, to teach him to remember what respect he owed to the king; and so they left him and went to the Duke of Monmouth's, where O'Brien's arm was dressed. The matter was executed by orders from the duke, for which he was severely censured, because he lived then upon terms of friendship with Coventry. Coventry had his nose so well needled up that the scar was scarcely to be discerned. This put the House of Commons in a furious uproar; they passed a bill of banishment against the actors of it, and put a clause in it, that it should not be in the king's power to pardon them, and that it should be death to maim any person." This Sir John Coventry, *d. unm.,* and endowed an hospital at Wiveliscomb, co. Somerset.

II. Francis, *m.* thrice, but had issue only by his 3rd wife, Elizabeth, dau. and co-heiress of John Manning, Esq., of London, and widow of Robert Cæsar, Esq., viz.,

1 Francis, who *d. unm.* in 1686.
1 Elizabeth, *m.* to Sir William Keyt, Bart., of Ebrington, co. Gloucester.
2 Ultra-Trajectina, *m.* to Sir Lacon-William Child, Knt.

III. Henry, one of the privy council of King CHARLES II., a diplomatist in the beginning of that monarch's reign, and subsequently one of his majesty's principal secretaries of state. He *d. unm.* 7 December, 1686.
IV. William (Sir), a privy councillor, secretary of the admiralty, *temp.* CHARLES II. "A man," says Burnet, "of great notions and eminent virtues; the best speaker in the House of Commons, and capable of bearing the chief ministry, as it was once thought he was very near it, and deserved it more than all the rest did." Sir William was, however, forbid the court for sending a challenge to the Duke of Buckingham; after which he resided in private until his decease in 1686, at Minster Lovel, near Whitney, in Oxfordshire. Sir William Coventry *d. unm.*
1. Anne, *m.* 1st, to Sir William Savile, Bart., of Thornhill, co. York, by whom she was mother of George, Marquess of

Halifax; and 2ndly, to Thomas Chichele, Esq., of Wimpole, co. Cambridge.
II. Mary, *m.* to Henry-Frederick Thynne, Esq., of Longlete, co. Wilts.
III. Margaret, *m.* to Anthony, 1st Earl of Shaftesbury.
IV. Dorothy, *m.* to Sir John Pakington, Bart., of Westwood, co. Worcester, M.P., the gallant Cavalier. This lady, who was distinguished by her intelligence and piety, was esteemed the author of "The Whole Duty of Man."

Thomas, Lord Coventry. *d.* at Durham House, in the Strand, London, 14 January, 1640, and Lord Clarendon says that " he discharged all the offices he went through with great abilities and singular reputation of integrity; that he enjoyed his place of lord keeper with universal reputation (and, sure, justice was never better administered) for the space of about sixteen years, even to his death, some months before he was sixty years of age." His lordship was *s.* by his eldest son,
THOMAS COVENTRY, 2nd baron, who *m.* Mary, dau. of Sir William Craven, Knt., and sister of William, Earl Craven, by whom he had two sons GEORGE, 3rd baron, and THOMAS, 5th baron. His lordship *d.* 27 October, 1661, and was *s.* by the elder,
GEORGE COVENTRY, 3rd baron. This nobleman *m.* 18 July, 1653, Margaret, dau. of John, Earl of Thanet, by whom he had surviving issue,

JOHN, his successor.
Margaret, *m.* to Charles, Earl of Wiltshire, afterwards Duke of Bolton, and *d. s. p.* in 1683.

His lordship *d.* 15 December, 1680, and was *s.* by his son,
JOHN COVENTRY, 4th baron, at whose decease *unm.,* 25 July, 1687, the title and estates reverted to his uncle.
THE HON. THOMAS COVENTRY, of Snitfield, co. Warwick, as 5th Baron Coventry His lordship was advanced by letters patent, dated 26 April, 1697, to the dignities of *Viscount Deerhurst* and EARL OF COVENTRY, the limitation extending to William, Thomas, and Henry Coventry, grandsons of Walter Coventry, brother of the Lord Keeper Coventry. He *m.* 1st, Winifrede, dau. of Pierce Edgcombe, Esq., of Mount Edgcombe, in Devon, and had two surviving sons, viz., THOMAS his successor, and GILBERT, 4th earl. His lordship *m.* 2ndly, Elizabeth, dau. of Richard Graham, Esq. (who *m.* after the earl's decease, Thomas Savage, Esq., of Elmley Castle, co. Worcester), by whom he had no issue. He *d.* on 15 July, 1699, and was *s.* by his elder son,
THOMAS COVENTRY, 2nd earl, who *m.* Anne, dau. of Henry, Duke of Beaufort, and dying in 1710, was *s.* by his only surviving son,
THOMAS COVENTRY, 3rd earl, at whose decease at Eton College, 28 January, 1712, the honours and estates reverted to his uncle,
GILBERT COVENTRY, 4th earl, who *m.* 1st, Dorothy, dau. of Sir William Keyt, Bart., of Ebrington, co. Gloucester, and had an only dau.,

Anne, *m.* Sir William Carew, Bart., of Antony, in Cornwall, and had an only child, Sir Coventry Carew, Bart., who *d. s p.* 24 March, 1748.

His lordship *m.* 2ndly, Anne, dau. of Sir Streynsham Master, but had no issue. He *d.* 27 October, 1719, when the EARLDOM and VISCOUNTY, with the bulk of his estates, passed to his relative, William Coventry, Esq., of the city of London, one of the clerks of the green cloth, according to the limitation of the patent of 1697 (from whom the extant Earl of Coventry inherits), while the BARONY OF COVENTRY OF AYLESBOROUGH became EXTINCT.

Arms—Sa., a fesse, erm., between three crescents, or.

CRANFIELD — BARONS CRANFIELD, EARLS OF MIDDLESEX.

Barony, by Letters Patent, dated 9 June, 1621.
Earldom, by Letters Patent, dated 16 September, 1622.

Lineage.

LIONEL CRANFIELD, a merchant of London, and married to a kinswoman of Villiers, Duke of Buckingham, was introduced to the court of King JAMES I. by that celebrated favourite, when he received the honour of knighthood, and soon after attracting the attention of the king, by his habits of business, he was appointed master of the requests, next master of the king's great wardrobe, then master of the wards, after which he was sworn of the privy council, and elevated to the peerage, as BARON CRANFIELD, *of Cranfield, co. Bedford,* 9 July, 1621. In the October following, his lordship was constituted Lord Treasurer of England, and created, 16 September, 1622, EARL OF MIDDLESEX (the first person, says Dugdale, to whom that county gave the title of earl). Within two short years however he was impeached by parliament, through the influence of the very nobleman who was the founder of his fortune, the favourite Buckingham, for bribery, extortion, oppression, and other misdemeanours, for which he received judgment. His lordship m. 1st, Elizabeth, dau. of Richard Shepherd, a merchant in London, by whom he had three daus., viz.,

I. Martha, m. to Henry Carey, Earl of Monmouth.
II. Elizabeth, m. to Edmund Lord Sheffield, grandson and heir of Edmund, Earl of Mulgrave.
III. Mary, d. unm.

The earl m. 2ndly, Anne, dau. of James Brett, Esq., of Hoby, co. Leicester, by Anne Beaumont his wife (sister of Mary, Countess of Buckingham), and had issue,

I. JAMES } successive earls.
II. LIONEL }
III. Edward, d. unm.
IV. William, d. young.
I. Frances, m. 1st, to Richard Earl of Dorset, and 2ndly, to Henry Poole, Esq.

His lordship d. in 1645, and notwithstanding his disgrace, was buried in Westminster Abbey, where a monument was erected to his memory. He was s. by his eldest son,

JAMES CRANFIELD, 2nd earl, who m. Anne, 3rd dau. and coheiress of Edward, Earl of Bath, by whom he had an only dau.,

Elizabeth, m. to John, Lord Brackley, eldest son of the Earl of Bridgewater.

His lordship d. in 1651, when his honours devolved upon his brother,

LIONEL CRANFIELD, 3rd earl, who m. Rachel, widow of Henry, Earl of Bath, and dau. of Francis, Earl of Westmoreland, but dying s. p. in 1674, the BARONY OF CRANFIELD and EARLDOM OF MIDDLESEX became EXTINCT, while his lordship's estates devolved upon his sister, the Countess of Dorset, whose eldest son, CHARLES, was created, BARON CRANFIELD and EARL OF MIDDLESEX in 1675, honours which have descended with the Dukedom of Dorset.

Arms—Or, on a pale, az., three fleurs-de-lis, of the first.

CRANSTOUN—BARONS CRANSTOUN.

Patent dated 14 November, 1609.

Lineage.

THOMAS DE CRANSTON had a charter of the barony of Stobbs, co. Roxburgh, from the Earl of Marr, in the reign of DAVID II. From this Thomas we pass to

SIR WILLIAM CRANSTOUN, Knt., who had a charter of the lands of New Cranstoun in 1553. He m. Elizabeth, dau. of Andrew Johnston, of Elphinston, and had a son, JOHN, who died, and seven daus., the eldest of whom,

SARAH CRANSTOUN, m. William Cranstoun, son of John Cranstoun, of Moriestoun, which William was capt. of the guards, temp. JAMES VI., and having received the honour of knighthood, became

SIR WILLIAM CRANSTOUN. He was subsequently elevated to the peerage of Scotland, 14 November, 1609, as BARON CRANSTOUN, of Creeling, with remainder to his heirs male bearing the name and arms of Cranstoun. His lordship d. in 1627, and was s. by his eldest son,

JOHN, 2nd baron; at whose decease s. p. the title devolved upon his nephew,

WILLIAM, 3rd baron (the son of the deceased lord's younger brother, James, by Lady Elizabeth Stewart, his wife, dau. of Francis, Earl of Bothwell); who m. Mary, dau. of Alexander, Earl of Leven, by whom he had one son, JAMES, 4th baron. His lordship attending CHARLES II. at the battle of Worcester, was there taken prisoner, and sent to the Tower of London, where he remained several years, his estates being sequestered, and himself excepted out of Cromwell's indemnity. He was s. by his son,

JAMES, 4th baron, m. Anne, dau. of Sir Alexander Don, Bart., and was s. by his son,

WILLIAM, 5th baron; who m. Jane, dau. of William, 2nd Marquess of Lothian, and had issue,

I. JAMES, 6th baron.
II. William-Henry, a captain in the army, b. in 1707; m. 1745, Anne, sister of Sir David Murray, Bart. of Stanhope, and being implicated in the parricide committed by Miss Blandy (who was executed in March, 1752), went abroad, and d. a religious penitent, at Furnes, in Flanders, 20 November, 1752.

III. Charles, d. unm.
IV. George, m. Maria, dau. of Thomas Brisbane, Esq.; and d. in 1788, leaving issue by her (who d. in 1807),

1 Henry-Kerr, m. 1st, Christiana Smart; and 2ndly, in 1803, Mary-Anne, dau. and co-heir of Sir John Whiteford, Bart., and had issue by the former, a dau., Christiana-Brisbane, m. to Thomas Metcalfe, Esq. He d. in 1843.
2 George, a lord of session, as Lord Corehouse; d. in 1850.
1 Margaret, m. in 1780, to William-Cunninghame, of Lainshaw, co. Argyll; and d. in 1841.
2 Jane-Anne, m. in 1797, to Godfrey-Winceslaus, Count Purgstall, a Styrian noble; and d. in 1835.
3 Helen-D'Arcy, m. in July, 1790, to Dugald Stewart, of Catrine; and d. in 1838.
I. Anne, m. to G. Selby, Esq. of Paston, co. Northumberland.
II. Mary, m. to Archibald Mellet, Esq.

Lord Cranstoun d. in 1768, and was s. by his eldest son,
JAMES, 6th baron; m. Sophia, dau. of Jeremiah Brown, Esq. of Abscourt, co. Surrey, by whom (who m. 2ndly, Michael Lade, Esq., and d. 26 October, 1779) he had,

WILLIAM, 7th baron. JAMES, 8th baron.
Charles, m. Miss Elizabeth Turner, and by her (who d. 2 Feb. 1781) had JAMES-EDWARD, 9th baron.
George, col. in the army; d. unm. at Surinam, 8 March, 1806.
Elizabeth. Charlotte.

Lord Cranstoun d. in 1773, and was s. by his eldest son,
WILLIAM, 7th baron; who d. unm. in 1788, when the honours devolved upon his brother,
JAMES, 8th baron; a naval officer, who distinguished himself as commander of the "Belliqueux," in the celebrated actions between Admiral Hood and Comte de Grasse, 25 and 26 January, 1782. He d. s. p. in 1790, and was s. by his nephew,
JAMES-EDMUND, 9th baron; who m. in 1807, Anne-Linnington, eldest dau. of John Macnamara, Esq. of the island of St. Christopher, and by her (who d. 22 November, 1858) had,

JAMES-EDMUND, 10th baron.
CHARLES-FREDERICK, 11th and last baron.
Eliza-Linnington, m. 24 February, 1838 (she was his second wife), to Richard Ford, Esq. of Heavitree, Devon; and d. 23 January, 1849; Mr. Ford, an eminent critic writer and patron of the fine arts, d. 1 September, 1858.
Anna-Caroline, d. in 1847.

Lord Cranstoun d. 5 September, 1818, and was s. by his elder son,
JAMES-EDMUND, 10th baron; b. 12 August, 1809; who m. Elizabeth, elder dau. of Sir John-Henry Seale, Bart., and had a dau., Pauline-Emily. He d. 18 June, 1869, when he was s. by his only brother,
CHARLES-FREDERICK, 11th baron, b. 1813; who d. unm. 28 September, 1869, when the barony became dormant or extinct.

Arms—Gu., three cranes, arg.

CRAVEN—BARON CRAVEN, OF HAMPSTEDMARSHALL, CO. BERKS, EARL CRAVEN, AND BARON CRAVEN OF RYTON.

(See BURKE's Extant Peerage.)

CRETING—BARON CRETING.

By Writ of Summons, dated 27 January, 1332.

Lineage.

SIR ADAM DE CRETING, Knt., having summons to attend King EDWARD I. at Portsmouth, and passing with the monarch into Gascony, was there slain by the treachery of one Walter Gifford. He was succeeded in his manor of Great Stockton, co. Huntingdon, and other lands, by his son and companion in arms,

JOHN DE CRETING, who in the 4th of EDWARD III., obtained a charter for free-warren in all his demesne lands at Great Stockton, and being a military man of reputation, was summoned to parliament, as a BARON, 27 January, 1332, but never afterwards; and nothing further is known of the family.

Arms—Arg., a chev., between three mullets, gu., pierced of the field.

CREW—BARONS CREW, OF STEINE, CO. NORTHAMPTON.

By Letters Patent, dated 20 April, 1661.

Lineage.

JOHN CREWE, Esq., of Nantwich, co. Chester, m. Alice, dau. of Humphrey Mainwaring, of Nantwich, and d. in 1598, æt. seventy-four, leaving two sons,

Ranulph (Sir), of Crewe, M.P. for Brackley, and lord chief justice of the King's Bench, m. Juliana, dau and co-heiress of John Clippesby, Esq., of Clippesby, co. Norfolk, and was ancestor of Baron Crewe, of Crewe.
THOMAS (Sir).

The 2nd son,
SIR THOMAS CREWE, serjeant-at-law, M.P. for Northampton, and speaker of the House of Commons, of Stene and Hinton, *jure uxoris*, m. Temperance, 4th dau. and co-heiress of Reginald Bray, Esq., of Stene and Hinton; and d. 1 February, 1633-4, having had issue,

John, his heir.
Thomas, of Crawley, co. Hants.
Nathaniel, of Gray's Inn, London.
Salathiel, of Hinton, d. 1686, æt. seventy-three.
Anne.   Patience.
Temperance, m. to John Browne, Esq., of Eydon, and d. s. p., 1634.
Silence.   Prudence.

The eldest son and heir,
JOHN CREWE, of Stene, co Northampton, was elevated to the peerage on 20 April, 1661, as BARON CREW, *of Stene*, in consideration for his zealous services in the restoration of the monarchy. His lordship m. October, 1648, Jemima, dau. and co-heiress of Edward Waldegrave, Esq., of Lawford, co. Essex, and by her (who d. 14 October, 1675), he had issue,

THOMAS (Sir), his successor.
John, of Newbald Vernon, co. Leicester; d. *unm.* in France, 1681.
Edward, d. *unm.* 1680.
Samuel (Rev.), d. *unm.* 1660.
NATHANIEL, bishop of Durham, s. his brother, as 3rd baron.
Walgrave, of Hinton, m. 1670, Susanna, dau of Robert Mellor, Esq., of Derby, and d. in 1673, æt. thirty-six, leaving (by this lady, who m. 2ndly, Thomas Bard, Esq.), an only son,
    Walgrave, of Gray's Inn, London, who d. s. p. 1694.
Jemima, m. to Edward, 1st Earl of Sandwich.
Anne, m. to Sir Henry Wright, Bart., of Dagenham, co. Essex.

Lord Crew d. in 1679, and was s. by his eldest son,
THOMAS CREW, 2nd baron, who m. 1st, Mary, eldest dau. of Sir George Townshend, Bart., of Rainham, co. Norfolk, by whom he had surviving issue,

Anne, m. to John Jolliff, Esq., of Coston, co Stafford, and d. s. p. before 1696.
Temperance, m. 1st, to Rowland, son and heir of Sir Thomas Alston, Bart., of Odell, co. Bedford; and 2ndly, to Sir John Wolstenholme, of Enfield, co Middlesex, 3rd baronet; and d. 18 October, 1728.

His lordship m. 2ndly, 1674, Anne, dau. and co-heiress of Sir William Airmine, Bart., of Osgodby, co. Lincoln, and relict of Sir Thomas Wodehouse, Knt., of Kimberly, co. Norfolk, and by her had four daus., viz.,

Jemima, m to Henry de Grey, Duke of Kent; and d. 2 July, 1728.
Airmine, m. to Thomas Cartwright, Esq., of Aynho, co. Northampton, and d. 1728.
Catherine, m. to Sir John Harper, 4th Baronet of Caulk, co. Derby, the great-grandson of which marriage, Sir Henry Harper, 7th baronet, assumed, by royal permission, the surname of CREWE only, and was s. at his decease by his son, SIR GEORGE CREWE, 8th Baronet of Caulk Abbey.
Elizabeth, m. 18 September, 1721, Charles Butler, Earl of Arran, and Lord Butler, of Weston, and d. s. p., 21 May, 1756.

His lordship d. 30 November, 1697, æt. seventy-three, and thus leaving no male issue, his fortune devolved upon his daus. as co-heiresses, while the title passed to his brother, the Right Reverend
NATHANIEL CREW, lord bishop of Durham, as 3rd Baron Crew, of Stene. His lordship, b. in January, 1633, m. 1st, 21 December, 1691, Penelope, dan. of Sir Philip Frowde, Knt., and 2ndly, 23 July, 1700, Dorothy, dau. of Sir William Forster, of Bamborough Castle, co. Northumberland; but not having had any issue, the BARONY OF CREW, *of Stene*, became, at his lordship's decease, 18 September, 1721, EXTINCT.

Arms—Az., a lion rampant, arg , a crescent for difference.

CRICHTON—EARL OF CAITHNESS.

By Charter, dated 1452.

Lineage.

SIR GEORGE DE CRICHTON, high-admiral of Scotland, designed son and heir of Stephen Crichton, of Cairns, was, in the year 1452, created Earl of Caithness, the honours being limited to the heirs male of his body by his 2nd wife Janet Borthwick. He d. in 1455, without legitimate issue of his 2nd marriage, and the title became EXTINCT. The large estates of the Earl of Caithness, with the exception of Barntoun and Cairns, appear to have reverted to the crown.

CRICHTON—VISCOUNT OF FRENDRAUGHT.

By Letters Patent, dated 29 August, 1642.

Lineage.

WILLIAM CRICHTON, high chancellor of Scotland (son of John Crichton, of Crichton, and grandson of William de Crichton, whose 2rd son, Stephen, of Cairns, was father of the Earl of Caithness), made a conspicuous figure in Scottish history in the reigns of King JAMES I. and II. His first public appearance was in 1423, when he went to England to wait upon King JAMES I., and conduct him home. According to Fordun, he was created Lord Crichton, 1445, and re-appointed high chancellor, 1447. The next year he passed on a solemn embassy to France to renew the alliance with that kingdom, and conclude the marriage of King JAMES II. with Mary, dau. of Arnold, Duke of Guelder, which he happily settled. On the chancellor's return home he founded the collegiate church of Crichton, 26 December, 1449, and continued prime minister of Scotland till his death in 1454. By Agnes his wife, he had issue,

JAMES, of whom presently.
Elizabeth, m. Alexander, 1st Earl of Huntly.
Agnes, m. 1st, Alexander, 4th Lord Glamis; 2ndly, Walter Ker, of Cessford.

The only son,
JAMES CRICHTON, 2nd Lord Crichton. knighted by King JAMES I., at the baptism of his eldest son, 1430, m. Lady Janet Dunbar, eldest dau. and co-heir of James, Earl of Moray, with whom he got the Barony of Frendraught. He was, under the designation of Sir James Crichton, of Frendraught, appointed great chamberlain of Scotland, 1440, and held that office till 1453. He d. about 1469, leaving issue,

WILLIAM, 3rd lord
Gavin, obtained a charter of the lands of Molyne, Rahillis, Monigep, and Cronzeantoun, in the Barony of Kirkmichael, co. Dumfries, 24 January, 1477, from his brother, and was forfeited for treason by the parliament of Scotland, 24 February, 1483-4, for engaging in Albany's rebellion.
George, also forfeited 24 February, 1483-4, for the same offence.

The eldest son,
WILLIAM CRICHTON, 3rd Lord Crichton, who having joined the Duke of Albany in his rebellion against King JAMES III., garrisoned his castle of Crichton on behalf of the duke, for which he was forfeited by the parliament of Scotland, 24 February, 1483-4. He m. Margaret, 2nd dau. of King JAMES II., by whom he had (with a dau. Margaret, m. to George, 4th Earl of Rothes), a son,
SIR JAMES CRICHTON, who m. Catherine, eldest dau. of William, Lord Borthwick, by whom he had a son,
WILLIAM CRICHTON, of Frendraught, who, by Agnes Abernethy his wife, was father of
SIR JAMES CRICHTON, of Frendraught, who by Lady Johanna Keith his wife, 6th dau. of William, 4th Earl Marischal, left issue,

JAMES, of whom presently.
George, who had a charter of the Barony of Frendraught, Conveth, &c., in Banffshire, 29 April, 1599.
Agnes, who in a charter, 1572, is designed "dau. of Sir James Crichton, future spouse of William Leslie, of Tulliferry."

The eldest son,
JAMES CRICHTON, of Frendraught, by Janet his wife, dau. of Alexander Gordon, of Lesmoir, had issue,

JAMES, his heir.
Anne, m. to William Seaton, of Meldrum.
Mary, m. to Patrick, Lord Oliphant.

The only son,
JAMES CRICHTON, of Frendraught, had the family estates made over to him by his father. He m. 25 February, 1619, Lady Elizabeth Gordon, eldest dau. of John, 12th Earl of Sutherland, by whom he had issue,

1. JAMES, of whom presently.
II. William   III. George.   IV. Francis.
I. Elizabeth.   II. Isabel.   III. Margaret.

The eldest son,
JAMES CRICHTON, of Frendraught, who was, in the lifetime of his father, advanced to the peerage, in consideration of his father being heir male of Lord Chancellor Crichton, and created VISCOUNT OF FRENDRAUGHT and Lord Crichton, to him and his heirs male and successors, by patent, dated at Nottingham, 29 August, 1642. His lordship accompanied the Marquess of Montrose in his last expedition, and was with him at Invercharron, when he was defeated by Strachan, in 1650. Montrose's horse being shot under him, he was generously remounted by the viscount, and thus escaped for a few days. "The Viscount of Frendraught," says Douglas, " being made prisoner, to prevent public vengeance, preferred a Roman death." His lordship m. 1st, Lady Margaret Lesly, 2nd dau. of Alexander, 1st Earl of Leven, by whom he had a dau.,

Janet, m. 24 August 1665, to Sir JAMES MAKGILL, of Ran-keilour, and had issue. (See BURKE's Landed Gentry.)

The viscount m. 2ndly, 8 November, 1642, Marion, dau. of Sir Alexander Irvine, of Drum, and by her had two sons,

JAMES, 2nd viscount.
LEWIS, 4th viscount.

The elder son,
JAMES CRICHTON, 2nd Viscount of Frendraught, m. Christian, dau. of Sir Alexander Urquhart, of Cromarty, and relict of Lord Rutherford, by whom (who m. 3rdly, George Morison, of Bognie) he had a son,
WILLIAM CRICHTON, 3rd Viscount of Frendraught; who d. unm. in his minority, and was s. by his uncle,
LEWIS CRICHTON, 4th Viscount of Frendraught, who accompanied JAMES II. to France, and was attainted by parliament in July, 1690. He attended the king to Ireland; and d. s. p. 26 November, 1698

Arms—Quarterly: 1st and 4th, arg., a lion rampant, az., armed and langued, gu.; 2nd and 3rd, arg., a saltire and chief, az.; over all, on an escutcheon, az., three stars, arg., within a double treasure, counterflowered, or.

CROFTS—BARON CROFTS, OF SAXHAM, CO. SUFFOLK.

By Letters Patent, dated 18 May, 1658.

Lineage.

WILLIAM CROFTS, Esq., lineal male heir of the family of Crofts, which had flourished for several ages at Saxham, co. Suffolk, and descended by females from the 1st Lord Wentworth, of Nettlested, as also from the Montacutes, Earls of Salisbury, and Nevils, Earls of Westmoreland, was elevated to the peerage on 18 May, 1658, as BARON CROFTS, of Saxham, co. Suffolk. His lordship having been brought up at court from his youth, became first, master of the horse to James, Duke of York, next captain of the guards to the queen-mother, and afterwards one of the gentlemen of the bed-chamber to King CHARLES II. He was subsequently employed as ambassador to Poland, and for his services on that occasion obtained the peerage. His lordship m. 1st, Dorothy, widow of Sir John Hele, Knt., dau. of Sir John Hobart, of Intwood, co. Norfolk, Bart. (son and heir of Lord Chief Justice Hobart, of the Common Pleas); and 2ndly, Elizabeth, dau. of William Lord Spencer, of Wormleighton; but having no issue, the BARONY OF CROFTS became, at his lordship's decease in 1677, EXTINCT.

Arms—Or, three bulls' heads, couped, sa.

CROMWELL — BARON CROMWELL, OF OKEHAM, CO. RUTLAND, EARL OF ESSEX.

Barony by Letters Patent, dated 9 July, 1536
Earldom, by Letters Patent, dated 10 April, 1539

Lineage.

THOMAS CROMWELL (son of Walter Cromwell, a blacksmith at Putney), upon his return from foreign service under the Duke of Bourbon, obtained a situation in the suite of Cardinal Wolsey, and, after the fall of that celebrated prelate, was taken into the service of the king (at HENRY's special command, from his fidelity to his old master), in which he evinced so much zeal and ability, that the road to the highest honours of the state presented very soon an unimpeded course for his ambition. In a short time he filled successively the important situations of master of the jewel-office, clerk of the hanaper, principal secretary, justice of the forests, master of the Rolls, and lord privy-seal, and was elevated to the peerage, in the dignity of BARON CROMWELL, of Okeham, 9 July, 1536. He was afterwards constituted the king's vice-regent in spirituals, honoured with the Garter, and finally (10 April, 1539) created EARL OF ESSEX, when he was invested with the Lord High Chamberlainship of England. In the dissolution of the monastic institutions, and the establishment of the spiritual supremacy of his royal master, Cromwell, considering the powerful interests with which he had to contend, exhibited a boldness of character paralleled only by the profound political dexterity that accomplished those great and daring innovations. As a recompense, he shared largely in the spoil of the fallen church, and, amongst other grants, the sacerdotal revenues of St. Osyths, in Essex, and of the Gray Friars, at Yarmouth, flowed into his coffers. But his elevation was not more rapid than his decline, and his fall was hailed by all parties with satisfaction. So long as Essex ministered to the pleasures of HENRY, the royal shield protected him from the indignation of the people; but the moment that was removed, his fate was sealed. His instrumentality in allying the king with Anne of Cleves was the rock upon which his fortunes foundered. Unprepared for such a proceeding, the earl was arrested, under the king's especial order, by the Duke of Norfolk, at the Council Table, 10 June, 1540, hurried off to the Tower, attainted unheard, and beheaded 24 July, notwithstanding archbishop Cranmer's powerful exertions in his behalf; and all the honours of the ex-minister were of course forfeited under the attainder: but his son, Gregory, who, in his lifetime, had been summoned to parliament as Lord Cromwell, had that dignity confirmed to him, by letters patent, in the December following the earl's execution. (See BARON CROMWELL.)

SIR RICHARD WILLIAMS, in someway a connection of Thomas Cromwell, Earl of Essex, assumed, at the desire of King HENRY VIII., the surname of CROMWELL. He was appointed a gentleman of the privy-chamber to King HENRY VIII., and constable of Berkeley Castle. Upon the dissolution of the monasteries, he obtained all the lands, in Huntingdonshire, belonging to any religious house in that county, and was s. by his son,

SIR HENRY CROMWELL, Knt., of Hinchinbroke, M.P. for Huntingdonshire, father, by Joan his wife, dau. of Sir Ralph Warren, of six sons and five daus. Of the latter, the 2nd, Elizabeth, m. to William Hampden, Esq., was mother of JOHN HAMPDEN, the patriot; and of the former, the eldest, SIR ROBERT CROMWELL, K.B., inherited Hinchinbroke, while the 2nd, ROBERT CROMWELL, of Huntingdon, who m. Elizabeth, dau. of William Stewart, Esq., was father of

OLIVER CROMWELL, the LORD PROTECTOR.

Arms—Az., on a fesse, between three lions rampant, or, a rose, gu. between two cornish choughs, ppr.

CROMWELL—BARONS CROMWELL AND EARLS OF ARDGLASS.

By Writ of Summons, dated 28 April, 1539.
By Letters Patent, dated 18 December, 1540.
Earldom, by Letters Patent, dated 15 April, 1645.

Lineage.

The Honourable
GREGORY CROMWELL, summoned to parliament 28 April, 1539, as LORD CROMWELL (son of Thomas Cromwell, Earl of

Essex, attainted and beheaded in July, 1540), a servant of King HENRY VIII., was created BARON CROMWELL, by letters patent, dated 18 December, 1540. His lordship *m*. Elizabeth, dau. of Sir John Seymour, sister of Edward, Duke of Somerset, and widow of Sir Anthony Oughtred, by whom he had three sons, HENRY, Edward, and Thomas, and two daus., Frances, *m*. to Edward Strode, Esq., of Devonshire; Catherine, *m*. to John Strode, Esq., co. Dorset. Lord Cromwell who had summons to parliament to the year 1548, *d*. in 1551, and was *s*. by his eldest son,

HENRY CROMWELL, 2nd baron, summoned to parliament from the 5th to the 31st ELIZABETH. His lordship *m*. Mary, dau. of John, Marquess of Winchester, and had issue, EDWARD, his successor, Sir Gregory Cromwell, Knt., and Catherine, *m*. to Sir Lionel Tollemache, Bart., of Helmingham, co. Suffolk, ancestor by her of the EARLS OF DYSART. He *d*. in 1592, and was *s*. by his elder son,

EDWARD CROMWELL, 3rd baron, summoned to parliament in the 36th ELIZABETH. This nobleman was with the Earl of Essex in his expedition at sea against the Spaniards in the 40th ELIZABETH, and joined in the insurrection three years afterwards, which cost the earl his head. Lord Cromwell received, however, an especial pardon on 9 July, 1601. His lordship *m*. 1st, —, dau. of — Umpton, Esq., and had an only dau. Elizabeth, *m*. 1st, to Sir John Shelton, of Shelton, in Norfolk, and afterwards to Thomas Fitzhughes, Esq., of Oxfordshire. The baron *m*. 2ndly, Frances, dau. of William Rugge, Esq., of Norfolk, by whom he had THOMAS, his successor, with two daus., viz., Frances, *m*. to Sir John Wingfield, of Tickencote, co. Rutland, and Anne, *m*. to Sir William Wingfield, of Poores Court, in Ireland. Lord Cromwell having alienated his estates in England by sale, purchased the Barony of Lecale, in Ireland, from Mountjoy Blount, Earl of Devon, or, according to Noble, in his "History of Cromwell," made an exchange thereof. His lordship *d*. in Ireland in 1607, and was *s*. by his son,

THOMAS CROMWELL, 4th baron, who was created 22 November, 1624, *Viscount Lecale*, and 15 April, 1645, EARL ARDGLASS, in the peerage of Ireland. His lordship remained firmly attached to the interests of the king during the civil wars, notwithstanding his friendship with the Earl of Essex. He *m*. Elizabeth, dau. and heiress of Robert Meverell, Esq., of Throwleigh, co. Stafford, by whom he had surviving issue, WINGFIELD, his successor; VERE-ESSEX, who inherited after his nephew; Oliver; and Mary, who *m*. William Fitz-Herbert, Esq., of Tissington, co. Derby. He *d*. in 1653, and was *s*. by his eldest son,

WINGFIELD CROMWELL, 5th Baron Cromwell and 2nd Earl of Ardglass. This nobleman *m*. Mary, dau. of Sir William Russell, of Strensham, co. Worcester, and was *s*. in 1668, by his only son,

THOMAS CROMWELL, 6th baron and 3rd earl, who *m*. Honora, dau. of Michael Boyle, archbishop of Armagh, and lord chancellor of Ireland, but *d*. *s*. *p*. 11 April, 1682, when his honours reverted to his uncle,

VERE-ESSEX CROMWELL, 7th baron and 4th earl. This nobleman *m*. Catherine, dau. of James Hamilton, Esq., M.P. for Bangor, co. Down, nephew of James, Viscount Claneboye; and by her (who *m*. 2ndly, Nicholas Price, Esq., of Hollymount, co. Down) had an only dau., ELIZABETH. His lordship *d*. at Booncastle, co. Down, 26 November, 1687, when the Irish VISCOUNTY OF LECALE and EARLDOM OF ARDGLASS, and the English Barony of Cromwell, created by patent, EXPIRED, but the BARONY OF CROMWELL, originating in the writ of 29 April, 1539, devolved upon his dau.,

ELIZABETH CROMWELL, as Baroness Cromwell, in which rank her ladyship assisted at the funeral of Queen MARY and coronation of Queen ANNE. She *m*. Edward Southwell, Esq., principal secretary of state for Ireland, and had issue, two sons and a dau., who all *d*. *s*. *p*., and another, a son, EDWARD SOUTHWELL, who marrying Catherine, dau. of Edward Watson, Viscount Sondes, and sole heiress of her brother, Lewis and Thomas, Earls of Rockingham, left a son.

EDWARD SOUTHWELL, who, in right of his mother, *s*. to the Barony of Clifford.

Her ladyship *d*. in 1709, and the BARONY OF CROMWELL is now supposed to be vested in the sisters and co-heirs of EDWARD, LORD DE CLIFFORD, son and successor of Edward, Lord de Clifford, mentioned above.

Arms—Quarterly: per fesse, indented, or and az., four lions passant, counterchanged.

CROMWELL — BARONS CROMWELL, OF TATSHALL, CO. LINCOLN.

By Writ of Summons, dated 10 March, 1308.

Lineage.

The family of Cromwell was of importance so far back as the time of King JOHN, for we find in the 17th of that reign,

RALPH DE CROMWELL, paying a fine of 60 marks and a palfry to make his peace for participating in the rebellion of the barons, and upon delivering up his eldest dau. in hostage, obtaining restitution of his lands. After which, in the 3rd HENRY III., he was constituted justice itinerant in the cos. of Lincoln, Nottingham, and Derby. To this Ralph *s*. another

RALPH DE CROMWELL, who *m*. Margaret, one of the sisters and co-heirs of Roger de Someri, Baron of Dudley, and was afterwards engaged in the French, Welsh, and Scottish wars of King EDWARD I. He was *s*. by his son,

SIR JOHN DE CROMWELL, who *m*. Idonea de Leyburne, younger dau. and co-heir of Robert de Vipont, hereditary sheriff of Westmoreland, and widow of Sir Roger de Leyburne, but by her had no issue. In the 33rd EDWARD I., Sir John Cromwell accused Sir Nicholas de Segrave of treason, and was answered by a defiance to battle, but the combat was not permitted. In the 1st EDWARD II. he had a grant for life from the crown of the castle of Hope, in Flintshire, and the same year was made governor of Stritguil Castle, and constable of the Tower of London. He was likewise summoned to parliament as a BARON. His lordship was subsequently engaged in the French and Scotch wars of King EDWARD II., and having had summons to parliament until the 9th EDWARD III., *d*. in the latter year (*anno* 1335), and was *s*. by his son (by a 2nd wife), or by his nephew (the son of his brother, Sir Ralph),

SIR RALPH DE CROMWELL, 2nd baron, summoned to parliament from 28 December, 1375, to 19 August, 1399, inclusive. This nobleman *m*. Maud, dau. of John Bernack, and heiress of her brother William, in whose right he became lord of the manor of Tatshall, co. Lincoln, by lineal succession from the heirs female of Robert de Tatshall, sometime owner thereof, whereupon he fixed his chief residence there. In the 10th RICHARD II., Lord Cromwell being then a banneret, was retained to serve the king in defence of the realm against an invasion apprehended at that period. His lordship *d*. 27 August, 1398, and was *s*. by his son,

RALPH DE CROMWELL, 3rd baron, summoned to parliament from 9 September, 1400, to 3 September, 1417. His lordship *d*. in 1419, and was *s*. by his son,

SIR RALPH DE CROMWELL, 4th baron, who *m*. Margaret, dau. of John, Lord Deincourt, and Joane his wife, dau. and heiress of Robert, Lord Grey, of Rotherfield, and co-heiress of her brother, William, Lord Deincourt. In the 11th HENRY VI., this nobleman was constituted treasurer of the king's exchequer, and in three years afterwards had a grant of the office of master of the king's mews and falcons. In the 23rd of the same reign his lordship was appointed hereditary constable of Nottingham Castle, and warden of the forest of Sherwood. He *d*. *s*. *p*. in 1455, and his sister became his heir, viz.,

MAUD CROMWELL, who *m*. Sir Richard Stanhope (ancestor of the existing noble houses of Chesterfield, Harrington, and Stanhope), and had issue, two daus., co-heiresses, viz.,

I. MAUD STANHOPE, *m*. 1st, Robert, Lord Willoughby de Eresby, and had a dau.,

Joane, wife of Sir Richard Wells, Knt., afterwards Lord Wells, by whom she had issue,

Robert, Lord Willoughby and Wells, who *d*. *s*. *p*.
Jane, heir to her brother; *m*. Sir Richard Hastings, Lord Wells and Willoughby (in right of his wife), and had issue,

Anthony Hastings, who *d*. *s*. *p*., thus terminating the line.

Maud, Lady Willoughby, *m*. 2ndly, Sir Thomas Nevil, Knt., a younger son of Richard, Earl of Salisbury; and 3rdly, Sir Gervaise Clifton, Knt., but had issue by neither.

II. JANE STANHOPE, *m*. SIR HUMPHREY BOURCHIER, 3rd son of Henry, Earl of Essex, which

SIR HUMPHREY BOURCHIER was summoned to parliament in right of his said wife, as BARON CROMWELL, from 25 July, 1461, to 15 October, 1470. This nobleman fell gallantly fighting at the battle of Barnet Field, on the part of EDWARD IV., in 1471, and *d*. *s*. *p*. The BARONY OF CROMWELL, upon the decease of his lordship's widow, fell into ABEYANCE amongst the descendants of Ralph, the 4th baron's three aunts,

Rawise, wife of Thomas, Lord Bardolph.

Maude, wife of Sir William Fitz-William, Knt., of Sprotboro'.

Elizabeth, wife, 1st of Sir John Clifton, Knt., and afterwards of Sir Edward Bensted, Knt.

and it still so continues, save as to the line of Bardolph, which was attainted.

Arms—Or, a chief, gu., over all a bend, az.

CROSBIE—EARL OF GLANDORE VISCOUNT CROSBIE, OF ARDFERT, BARON BRANDON.

Barony, by Letters Patent, dated 6 September, 1758.
Viscounty, by Letters Patent, dated 30 November, 1771.
Earldom, by Letters Patent, dated 22 July, 1776.

Lineage.

The ancestor of the noble family of Crosbie, which has been long settled in Ireland, left two sons,

I. PATRICK, his heir, who had a grant of the estates of the O'Moores, in the Queen's Co., in which he was *s.* by his son,

PIERCE CROSBIE (Sir), a military man of distinction, who having incurred the resentment of the Earl of Strafford, was compelled to retire from Ireland until the overthrow of that nobleman, upon whose trial Sir Pierce appeared as a witness. He was a gentleman of the privy council. He *m.* Elizabeth, dau. of Sir Andrew Noel, of Brooke, co. Rutland, and widow of George, 1st Earl of Castlehaven; but dying *s. p.* in 1646, bequeathed all his property to his cousins, Walter and David Crosbie.

II. JOHN, of whom we treat.

JOHN CROSBIE, being bred to the church, was made bishop of Ardfert, 2 October, 1600. His lordship *m.* Winefred, dau. of O'Lalor, of the Queen's Co., and *d.* September, 1621, leaving (with four daus.) two sons, viz.,

WALTER, created a Baronet of Nova Scotia; and

DAVID CROSBIE, Esq., who with his brother Walter inherited the estates of his cousin, Sir Pierce Crosbie. This gentleman was a colonel in the army, and governor of the co. of Kerry in 1641, where he stood a siege in the castle of Ballingarry for more than twelve months with great resolution. He was afterwards governor of Kinsale for the king, which he surrendered upon articles of capitulation for the garrison and his estate, to Lord Broghill, who besieged it for the parliament of England. Colonel Crosbie *m.* a dau. of the Right Rev. John Steere, D.D., lord bishop of Ardfert, by whom he had issue,

I. THOMAS, his successor.

II. Patrick, of Tubrid, *m.* Agnes Freke, aunt of Sir Ralph Freke, Bart., by whom he had a large family.
  I. The eldest dau. *m.* Richard Shovel, Esq., a captain in Lord Inchiquin's regiment of horse.
  II. The 2nd dau. *m.* Richard Chute, Esq., of Tulligaron.
  III. The 3rd dau. *m.* Garrett Reeves, Esq.
  IV. The 4th dau. *m.* Captain William Reeves.

Col. Crosbie was *s.* at his decease by his elder son,

SIR THOMAS CROSBIE, who received the honour of knighthood from James, Duke of Ormonde, in consideration of the loyalty of his family during the civil wars. Sir Thomas was seated at Ardfert, and was member for the co. of Kerry in King JAMES's parliament, held at Dublin in 1688. He remained steady in his allegiance to that unfortunate prince, and refused to take the oaths to King WILLIAM. He *m.* 1st, Bridget, dau. of Robert Tynte, Esq., of the co. of Cork, and had, with two daus. (Sarah, *m.* to Henry Stoughton, Esq., of Rattoo, co. Kerry, nephew of Murrough, 1st Earl of Inchiquin, and had two sons; and Bridget, *m.* to Philip Morgel, Esq.), four sons,

I. DAVID, his heir.
II. William, a major in the army, *d. s p.*
III. Patrick, in holy orders, *d. s. p.*
IV. Walter, of Trinity College, Dublin, *d. s. p.*

Sir Thomas *m.* 2ndly, Ellen, widow of Sir Ralph Wilson, and dau. of Garret Fitzgerald, of Ballynard, co. Limerick; and 3rdly, Elizabeth, eldest dau. and co-heir of William Hamilton, Esq., by which latter lady he had issue,

I. Thomas, of Ballyheige, co. Kerry, M.P. for that shire in 1709; *m.* in 1711, Lady Margaret Barry, dau. of Richard, 2nd Earl of Barrymore, and left issue, Anne-Dorothy, *m.* to William Carrique, Esq., of Glandyne, co. Clare, and had an only son, and Harriet-Jane, *m.* to Col. Lancelot Crosbie, of Tubrid, co. Kerry, and a son and heir, James, of Ballyheige, who *m.* Mary, dau. of his uncle, Pierse Crosbie, of Rusheen, and dying in March, 1761, left issue: *see* BURKE's *Landed Gentry*, CROSBIE, of Ballyheigue.

148

II. John, a major in the army, living in the co. of Wicklow in 1752, after being engaged for several years in active service upon the continent, where he lost an arm, and subsequently in Scotland. Amongst the most celebrated battles in which Major Crosbie participated were those of Dettingen and Culloden. He left at his decease a numerous family.

III. Pierce, barrister-at-law, of Rusheen, co. Kerry; *m.* Margaret, dau. of Sir Lancelot Sandes, of Carigfoyle; and dying in April, 1761, left an only son, Francis, and two daus.,
  1 Mary, *m.* to James Crosbie, Esq., of Ballyheige.
  2 Elizabeth.

IV. Charles, a colonel in the army, served in Flanders, in Queen ANNE's wars under the Duke of Marlborough. Colonel Crosbie *m.* 1st, the dau. of Mr. Warburton, of Chester, and sister of Jane, Duchess of Argyle, by whom he had two sons and two daus.; and *m.* 2ndly, a Cheshire heiress.
  1. Anne, *m.* 1st, to Richard Malone, Esq., of Ballynahowne. King's Co., by whom she had a numerous family; 2ndly, to William L'Estrange. Esq., by whom she had one son; and 3rdly, to Peter Holmes, Esq., of Johnstown, by whom she had another son.

Sir Thomas Crosbie *d.* in 1694, and was *s.* by his eldest son,

DAVID CROSBIE, Esq., of Ardfert, who, like his father, refused to swear allegiance to King WILLIAM. Mr. Crosbie *m.* Jane, younger dau. and co-heir of William Hamilton, Esq. (sister of his father's 3rd wife), by whom he had issue,

MAURICE, his heir.

Anne, *m.* to Henry Rose, Esq., of Mount Pleasant, co. Limerick, one of the justices of the Court of King's Bench, and *d.* 5 May, 1740, leaving three children.

Elizabeth, *m.* to Maurice Fitzgerald, Knight of Kerry, by whom she had a large family.

Margaret, *m.* 1st, to Lancelot Sandes, Esq.; and 2ndly, to John Green, Esq.; of Abbey, co. Limerick.

Mary-Anne, *m.* to John Copinger, Esq., *d.* 15 March, 1747, and had two sons, John and Maurice

He *d.* in 1717, and was *s.* by his son,

SIR MAURICE CROSBIE, Knt., who was returned to parliament by the co. of Kerry in 1713, and continued to represent that co until his elevation to the peerage of Ireland, on 6 September, 1758, in the dignity of BARON BRANDON, *of Brandon, co Kerry.* Sir Maurice *m.* in December, 1712, Anne, eldest dau. of Thomas, Earl of Kerry, and by her (who *d.* 17 December, 1757), had issue,

I. WILLIAM, his successor.

II. John, *b.* 1724; *m.* Elizabeth, dau. of Mr. Fisher; and *d. s p.* in May, 1755.

III. Maurice, in holy orders, dean of Limerick; *m.* 1st, 22 March, 1762, Elizabeth, dau. and co-heiress of William Gun, Esq., of Kilmary, co. Kerry, barrister-at-law, by whom (who *d.* 14 April, 1767), he had an only dau.,

Elizabeth, *m.* to Edward Moore, Esq., of Mooresfort, co. Tipperary.

Dean Crosbie *m.* 2ndly, Pyne, dau. of Sir Henry Cavendish, Bart., and had,

WILLIAM, in holy orders, D.D.; who inherited the BARONY OF BRANDON on the death of his cousin, John, 2nd Earl of Glandore; *m.* 3 May, 1815, Elizabeth, eldest dau. of Col. David La Touche, of Marlay, co. Dublin, and had an only child, Elizabeth-Cecilia, *m.* 1837, Henry-Galgacus-Redhead Yorke, Esq., who *d.* 1848. Lord Brandon *d.* 3 May, 1832, when the barony became EXTINCT.

Anne, *m.* 1st, 1790, to Charles-B. Woodcock, Esq., of Brentford Butts, Middlesex; and 2ndly, to Hon. Christopher Hely-Hutchinson, M.P. for Cork.

Pyne, *m.* 1st, to Sir John Gordon, Bart.; and 2ndly, to Major-General the Hon. Henry Brand-Trevor, eventually Lord Dacre.

Dorothy, *m.* William-Edward Harvey, Esq., of Kyle, son of the Rev. Christopher Harvey, D.D.

I. Jane, *m.* 1 February, 1735, to Thomas Mahon, Esq., of Strokestown, co. Roscommon, by whom she was mother of Maurice, Lord Hartland.

II. Anne, *m.* to Bartholomew Mahon, Esq., of Clonfree, co. Roscommon.

III. Elizabeth, *m.* to Lancelot Crosbie, Esq., of Tubrid, co. Kerry.

IV. Dorothy, *m.* to the Rev. Richard Pigott, of the co. of Cork.

His lordship *d.* 20 January, 1762, and was *s.* by his eldest son,

WILLIAM CROSBIE, 2nd baron; who was advanced 30 November, 1771, to the dignity of VISCOUNT CROSBIE, *of Ardfert, co. Kerry,* and created EARL OF GLANDORE on 22 July, 1776. His lordship *m.* 1st, in November, 1745, Lady Theodosia Bligh, dau. of John, 1st Earl of Darnley, by whom (who *d.* 20 May, 1777), he had issue,

I. Maurice, *b.* 17 February, 1749, *d.* 10 November, same year.

II. JOHN, *Viscount Crosbie.*

I. Anne, *b.* 1 December, 1754; *m.* in May, 1775, to John-William Talbot, Esq., of Mount Talbot, co. Roscommon, and

Cuff.
(B.Tynwley.)

Cunynghame.
(E.Glencairn.)

Dacre.
(B.Dacre.)

Darcy.
(B.D'Arcy.)

Douglas.
(D.Douglas.)

Egerton.
(E.Bridgewater.)

Eustace.
(V.Ballinglass.)

Fanshawe.
(V.Fanshawe.)

Fitz Gerald.
(E.Desmond.)

Fitz Hugh.
(B.Fitz Hugh.)

Grandison.
(B.Grandison.)

Granville.
(E.Bath.)

by him was mother of Rev. John Talbot-Crosbie, of Mount Talbot who m. 1811, Jane, dau. of T. Lloyd, Esq., and d. 1818, leaving an eldest son and heir, WILLIAM-TALBOT TALBOT-CROSBIE, Esq., of Ardfert Abbey, co. Kerry, HEIR-GENERAL of the Earls of Glandore.

II. Theodosia, b. 12 March, 1756, d. unm. 3 June, 1782.

III. Arabella, b. 21 October, 1757, m. 27 February, 1783, to the Hon. Edward Ward, 2nd son of Bernard, 1st Viscount Bangor, by whom she was mother of Edward Southwell, 3rd Viscount Bangor.

His lordship m. 2ndly, 1 November, 1777, Jane, dau. of Edward Vesey, Esq., and relict of John Ward, Esq., but by her (who d. in September, 1787), he had no issue. He d. 11 April, 1781, and was s. by his son,

JOHN CROSBIE, 3rd baron and 2nd earl, b. 25 May, 1753, who had been a member of the House of Commons for several years. His lordship m. 26 November, 1777, Diana Sackville, dau. of George, 1st Viscount Sackville; but d. s. p., 20 April, 1815, when the VISCOUNTY OF CROSBIE and EARLDOM OF GLANDORE became EXTINCT.

Arms—Az., a lion rampant, sa.; in chief, two dexter hands, gu

---

CUFF—BARON TYRAWLEY.

By Letters Patent, dated 7 November, 1797.

Lineage.

THOMAS CUFF, 2nd son of Robert Cuff, Esq., of Crych, in Somersetshire, by Catharine Cutter his wife, and grandson of John Cuff, of Crych, by Joan his wife, dau. of Sir William Denny, who was son of John Cuff, of Ilchester, co. Somerset, subscribed, upon the first breaking out of the rebellion in 1641, a large sum of money, and went over to Ireland with two of his sons, JAMES and Thomas. The younger had a considerable command in the parliamentary army, and d. in 1650.* The elder,

SIR JAMES CUFF, of Ballinrobe, devotedly attached to the royal cause, continued strenuously to promote the restoration of CHARLES II., by whom he was knighted, appointed master of the ordnance, and made a privy councillor. In 1661 he was elected M.P. for the co. of Mayo, and had a grant of the town and lands of Ballinrobe, and other extensive estates in the cos. of Mayo and Galway. He m. 14 January, 1655, Alice, dau. of Ambrose Aungier, D.D., and sister of Francis, Earl of Longford, and had issue,

  I. FRANCIS, M.P. for the co. of Mayo, who m. Honora, dau. of Primate Boyle, and relict of Thomas Cromwell, Earl of Ardglass, and d. 26 December, 1694, leaving issue,

    FRANCIS, who inherited a moiety of the estates of Ambrose Aungier, the last Earl of Longford; but dying unm., 12 November, 1715, was s. by his brother,

    MICHAEL, M.P., of Ballinrobe, b. 1694; m. 1 August, 1718, Frances, dau. of Henry Sandford, of Castlerea, Esq., by Elizabeth his wife, sister of Robert Fitzgerald, 19th Earl of Kildare, and by her (who d. 1757) had an only dau. and heiress,

      ELIZABETH CUFF, m. 5 March, 1739-40, to Thomas Pakenham, Esq., of Pakenham Hall, co. Westmeath, created Baron Longford, and had issue. Her ladyship was created in her widowhood, 5 July, 1785, COUNTESS OF LONGFORD; and dying 27 January, 1794, was s. by her grandson,

      THOMAS, Earl of Longford, father of the present peer.

  Mary, m. to Whitfield Doyne, Esq., and d. s. p.

  II. James.   III. Thomas.

  IV. Ambrose.   V. Charles.

  VI. GERALD, ancestor of LORD TYRAWLEY.

  I. A dau. m. to Mr. Lamb, a West India merchant.

  II. Jane, m. 4 September, 1677, to Sir Henry Bingham, of Castlebar, bart.

  III. Grisild, m. to the Rev. Ralph Rule, D.D.

  IV. Alice, m. James Macartney, Esq., justice of the Common Pleas, and d. 7 October, 1725.

  V. Lettice, m. to Francis Ffolliott, Esq., of Ballyshannon.

  VI. Mary, d. s. p.   VII. Doglis, d. s. p.

The youngest son,

GERALD CUFF, Esq., of Elm Hall, co. Mayo, b. 24 July, 1669, m. Dorothy, sister of Lieut.-Gen. Owen Wynne, of Hazlewood, co. Sligo, and had, with three daus. (Alice, m. to John Cuff,

Esq.; Douglas, m. to the Rev. James Miller; and Catherine, m. to George Jones, Esq.), a son and successor,

JAMES CUFF, Esq., of Elm Hall, co. Mayo, M.P. for that shire; who m. 30 April, 1731, Elizabeth, sister of Arthur, Earl of Arran; and d. 1766, having had issue,

  I. JAMES, his heir.

  II. Michael, major in the army, d. unm.

  I. Elizabeth, m. Dodwell Browne, Esq., of Raheens, co. Mayo, and was grandmother of HUGH JOHN HENRY BROWNE, Esq., of RAHEENS.

  II. Anne, d. unm.

  III. Jane, m. to George Jackson, Esq., of Enniscoe, co. Mayo, and had, with three daus., four sons, who all married, namely,

    1. GEORGE, of Enniscoe, col. of the North Mayo Militia, and M.P. for the co. of Mayo; who m. in 1783, Maria, dau. and heir of William Rutledge, Esq., of Foxford, and had with several daus., six sons, of whom the two eldest were

      WILLIAM, of Enniscoe, whose only dau. and heir (by Jane-Louisa his wife, dau. of Col. Blair, M.P. for Blair),

      MADELINE-EGLANTINE, m. in 1834, Mervyn Pratt, Esq., of Cabra Castle, co. Cavan.

      GEORGE, col. of the North Mayo Militia; who m. in 1804, Sidney, only child and heir of Arthur Vaughan, Esq., of Carramore; and d. in 1836, leaving, with younger children, a son and successor, the late

      GEORGE VAUGHAN-JACKSON, Esq., of Carramore, co. Mayo.

    2 Francis.   3 James.   4 Oliver.

  IV. Bridget, d. unm.

  V. Sarah, m. to John Blake, Esq., of Belmont House, co. Galway, J.P., and had issue: their dau. Jane, m. Edmond John Concanon, Esq., of Waterloo, co. Galway.

The elder son,

THE RIGHT HON. JAMES CUFF, of Ballinrobe, M.P. for the co. of Mayo, and one of its governors, was created 7 November, 1797, a peer of Ireland, as BARON TYRAWLEY, of Ballinrobe. His lordship m. 28 April, 1770, Mary, only dau. and heir of Richard Levinge, Esq., of Calverstown, co. Kildare (only son of Sir Richard Levinge, Bart., by his 2nd wife), which lady d. s. p. in 1808. Lord Tyrawley, d. himself in 1821, and as he left no legitimate issue, the peerage became EXTINCT at his decease.

Arms—Arg., on a bend, indented, sa, between two cotises, az., each charged with three bezants, as many fleurs-de-lis, or.

CUMYN—EARL OF BUCHAN.

Lineage.

WILLIAM CUMYN, son of Richard Cumyn, justiciary of Scotland, and ancestor, by his 1st wife, of the Cumyns, Lords of Badenoch, became Earl of Buchan in the right of his 2nd wife, Marjory, Countess of Buchan, only child of FERGUS, Earl of Buchan, temp. WILLIAM THE LION, and by her had (with a dau., Elizabeth, wife of William, Earl of Marr) three sons; of whom the eldest,

ALEXANDER CUMYN, 2nd Earl of Buchan, s. his mother, and became justiciary of Scotland. He m. Elizabeth, 2nd of the three daus. and co-heirs of Roger de Quinci, Earl of Winchester, by Helen, eldest dau. and co-heir of Alan, Lord of Galloway, constable of Scotland, and had a son and heir,

JOHN CUMYN, 3rd Earl of Buchan, constable of Scotland, who was infeoffed in the manor of Wightwicke, in Leicestershire, and doing his homage, had livery of his lands. A firm adherent of EDWARD I., his lordship raised a large force against King ROBERT BRUCE, but was defeated at Inverary, in 1308, when he retired to England. He m. Isabel, dau. of Duncan, Earl of Fife, a lady celebrated for having, in the absence of her brother, the Earl of Fife, placed the crown on ROBERT BRUCE at Scone, and for the consequent sufferings she underwent during her imprisonment in the castle of Berwick-upon-Tweed, where EDWARD I. caused her to be confined for many years in an iron cage.

ALEXANDER CUMYN, 4th Earl of Buchan, is stated to have s. his brother, on the authority of Robertson's "Index," where Margaret Cumyn, wife of John Ross, is called dau. to the Earl of Buchan; and Burton's "Leicestershire," p. 37, where Alice, wife of Henry de Beaumont, is styled dau. and heir of Alexander Comin, Earl of Buchan in Scotland. Still, however, there is room for doubt that Alexander predeceased his brother John, and of course was never Earl of Buchan, as John infeoffed his youngest brother William, in his manors in 1312-13, who gave them up to his nieces as the heirs. Alexander Cumyn de Boghan gave his oath to serve King EDWARD I.

---

* Ancestor of the Cuffs of Ballymoe, whose co-heiress, Catherine, dau. of Michael Cuff, Esq., m. to John Bagot, Esq. (see BURKE's Landed Gentry—BAGOT of Ard and Ballymoe).

against the French, along with his brother John, Earl of Buchan, 7 June, 1297. He had two daus.,

ALICE, m. about 1319-20, to Henry de Beaumont.

MARGARET, m. m. to Sir John the Ross, son to the Earl of Ross, who got with her in tocher, from King ROBERT BRUCE, the half of the Earl of Buchan's whole lands in Scotland.

The husband of the elder,

HENRY DE BEAUMONT, assumed the title of the Earl of Buchan in right of his wife, and is so designed in Rymer's "Fœdera." With her he got the manor of Whitwicke, in Leicestershire, and divers other lands and possessions, of which he had livery, 6th EDWARD II. By the treaty of Northampton, 1328, it was agreed that he should be restored to his lands and estates; but this not being performed, he was one of the disinherites who accompanied Edward Baliol into Scotland, 1332, and had a share in the decisive victory over the Scots at Duplin, 12 August, 1332. He d. 14th EDWARD III., leaving a son John, Lord Beaumont, ancestor of the BEAUMONTS, Baronets, of Cole Orton, co. Leicester.

CUNYNGHAME—LORD KILMAURS, AND EARL OF GLENCAIRN.

By Charter, dated 28 May, 1488.

Lineage.

VERNEBALD, the 1st of this family whose name appears in authentic record, was settled in the west of Scotland about the commencement of the 12th century. His son,

ROBERT, designed "Robertus, filius Vernebaldi," made a donation of the patronage of the kirk of Kilmaurs, &c., to the abbey of Kelso about 1153. He m. Richenda, dau. and heiress of Sir Humphrey de Barclay, of Gairntully.

ROBERTUS, filius Roberti filii Vernebaldi, previous to 1189, confirmed the grants made by his father.

HERVEY DE CUNYNGHAME, great grandson of the last Robert, represented the family about 1264, in which year he had a charter from ALEXANDER III. He founded a collegiate church at Kilmaurs, and is renowned in tradition for his gallant conduct at the battle of Largs against the Danes, 1263. He m. the heiress of Riddell, of Glengarnock, and was s. by his son,

SIR WILLIAM DE CUNYNGHAME, of Kilmaurs, who d. in 1285, and was s. by his eldest son,

EDWARD DE CUNYNGHAME, of Kilmaurs, who was s. by his eldest son,

GILBERT DE CUNYNGHAME, of Kilmaurs, who was s. in 1292, by his son,

SIR ROBERT DE CUNYNGHAME, of Kilmaurs, who swore fealty to EDWARD I.; but declaring afterwards for ROBERT BRUCE, had a charter from that monarch of the superiority of the lands of Lambrachtoun and Grugere, in Cunninghame, to be holden of the king, as Alan la Suche and William de Fereres held the same. He d. in 1330, and was s. by his elder son,

SIR WILLIAM DE CUNYNGHAME, of Kilmaurs, on whom DAVID II. conferred the Earldom of Carrick, 1361, as husband of Eleanor Bruce, dau. of Alexander Bruce, Earl of Carrick, son of Edward Bruce, brother of ROBERT I. As appears from a charter of the lands of Kindeven, Sir William was m. 2ndly, to a lady named Margaret, but of what family is not known. Though generally stated otherwise it would seem by Eleanor Bruce, Sir William had five sons. Robert, the eldest d. young, the 2nd,

SIR WILLIAM CUNYNGHAME, s. his father. In 1400 he resigned his estates for new infeftment, and obtained a charter from ROBERT III. to Sir William and his heirs male, failing whom to his brothers, Thomas, Alexander, and John in succession, and their heirs male, failing whom to other near relatives of the name of Cunynghame, &c., of the lands and baronies, Kilmaurs, Lambrachton, Kilbryde, Skelmorlie, and Polquharne, co. Ayr; lands and barony of Redhall, co. Edinburgh; lands of Nevy, in Forfarshire; the barony of Hassingden, in Roxburghshire; and the lands of Ranfurley, in the barony of Renfrew. Sir William m. Margaret, elder dau. and co-heiress of Sir Robert de Danyelston, and with her obtained a large addition to the family property: the division between the co-heiresses, took place in 1404, and in Sir William's share were included the Baronies of Glencairn and Fynlayston.

SIR ROBERT CUNYNGHAME, son of the preceding, succeeded. He was one of the jury who tried and condemned Murdock, Duke of Albany, in the reign of JAMES I.; by his wife Anne, only dau. of Sir John de Montgomery, of Ardrossan, he had a successor,

ALEXANDER CUNYNGHAME, who about 1450 was created Lord Kilmaurs, and for the strenuous support given to his sovereign against the rebel nobles, headed by the prince, he was raised to the dignity of an earl, with the title of GLENCAIRN, 28 May, 1488. A few days after, a battle took place between the hostile parties near Stirling, where the royal army was defeated, and where the king and newly-created earl were both slain. The rebel party having thus come into power, the parliament was convoked, and an act passed, annulling all grants of peerages or lands conferred by JAMES III., during the late struggle: amongst these was included the title of Glencairn. His lordship m. Margaret, dau. of Adam Hepburn, Lord of Hales, and had four sons,

ROBERT, his heir.

William, ancestor of CUNINGHAME OF CRAIGENDS, and of the Cunninghams of Robertland, Cairncuran, Baidland, Auchinharvie, and Ashinyards.[*]

Alexander, } both mentioned in a charter, 1483.
Edward,

The eldest son,

ROBERT CUNYNGHAME, 2nd Earl of Glencairn, was reduced to the rank of Lord Kilmaurs in October, 1488. He m. Christian, eldest dau. of John, 1st Lord Lindsay, of Byres, relict of John, Master of Seton, by whom he had a son,

CUTHBERT CUNYNGHAME, 3rd Earl of Glencairn, who m. Lady Marjory Douglas, eldest dau. of Archibald, 5th Earl of Angus, by whom he had a son,

WILLIAM CUNNINGHAM, 4th Earl of Glencairn; who d. in 1547, leaving by Margaret, or Elizabeth, his 2nd wife, dau. and heiress of John Campbell, of West Loudon, five sons and one dau., viz.,

I. ALEXANDER, his heir.
II. Andrew, ancestor of the CUNNINGHAMS OF CORSHILL, Barts.
III. Hugh, ancestor of the CUNNINGHAMS OF CARLUNG, whose heir of line is Hunter, of Kirkland.
IV. Robert, minister of the priory of Fell, in Ayrshire, ancestor of the CUNNINGHAMS OF MOUNTGRENAN.
V. William, bishop of Argyll.
I. Elizabeth, m. to Sir John Cunningham, of Caprington.

The eldest son,

ALEXANDER CUNNINGHAM, 5th Earl of Glencairn, for distinction called "the Good Earl," was among the first of the peers of Scotland who concurred in the Reformation, and the most zealous in its promotion. He m. 1st, Lady Johanna Hamilton, youngest dau. of James, Earl of Arran, and had issue,

WILLIAM, his heir.
Andrew, prior of Lesmahago.
Margaret, m. to John Wallace of Craigie.

His lordship m. 2ndly, Janet, dau. of Sir John Cunningham, of Caprington, and had by her,

Alexander, commendator of Kilwinning.
Janet, m. 1st, to Archibald, 5th Earl of Argyll; and 2ndly, to Humphry Colquhoun, of Luss.

The earl d. in 1574, and was s. by his son,

WILLIAM CUNNINGHAM, 6th Earl of Glencairn; by Janet Gordon his wife, he had issue,

I. JAMES, his heir.
II. John.
I. Jean, m. 1st, George Haldane, of Gleneagles; 2ndly, to Kirkpatrick, of Closeburn; and 3rdly, to Ferguson, of Craigdarroch.
II. Margaret, m. to Sir Hector Maclean, of Dowart, Bart.
III. Elizabeth, m. 1st, to James Crawford, of Auchinames; and 2ndly, to Alexander Cunningham, of Craigends.
IV. Susannah, m. to John Napier, of Kilmahew, co. Dumbarton.

The elder son,

JAMES CUNNINGHAM, 7th Earl of Glencairn, m. 1st, Marriot, or Margaret, 2nd dau. of Sir Colin Campbell, of Glenurchy, and by her (who d. in January, 1610) had issue,

I. WILLIAM, his heir.
II. John.
I. Jean, d. unm.
II. Catherine, m. to Sir James Cunningham, of Glengarnock, co. Ayr.
III. Margaret, m. 1st, to Sir James Hamilton, of Evandale; and 2ndly, to Sir James Mexwell, of Calderwood.
IV. Anne, m. to James, 2nd Marquess of Hamilton.
V. Mary, m. to John Crawford, of Kilbirny.
VI. Susanna, m. to Sir Alexander Lauder, of Hatton.

His lordship m. 2ndly, Agnes, dau. of Sir James Hay, of Kingask, sister of James, Earl of Carlisle. His elder son,

---

* Ashinyards was purchased from the co-heiresses of the family by a near relative, John Bowman, Esq., lord provost of Glasgow, descended from Elizabeth, dau. of William Cuninghame, of Ashinyards.

WILLIAM CUNNINGHAM, 8th Earl of Glencairn, *d.* in October, 1631. He *m.* Lady Janet Ker, 2nd dau. of Mark, 1st Earl of Lothian, and had issue,

    I. WILLIAM, his successor.
    II. Robert, usher to CHARLES II.: *m.* Anne, dau. of Sir John Scot, of Scotstarvit, and had one dau.
    III. Alexander, *b.* 8 April, 1613.
    I. Elizabeth, *b.* 7 November, 1611, *m.* to Sir Ludovick Stewart, of Minto.
    II. Jean, *m.* to John Blair, of Blair.
    III. Margaret, *m.* 1st, to David Betoun, of Creich ; and 2ndly, Chisholm of Crombie.
    IV. Marion, *m.* 1st, to James, 1st Earl of Findlater ; and 2ndly, to Alexander, Master of Salton, and *d. s. p.* 1661.
    V. Anne, *d. unm.*

The eldest son,
WILLIAM CUNNINGHAM, 9th Earl of Glencairn, *b.* about 1610; who, on the Earl of Loudon surrendering the high office of chancellor, was appointed his lordship's successor, 19 January, 1661. He *m.* 1st, Lady Anne Ogilvy, 2nd dau. of James, 1st Earl of Findlater, and had issue,

    I. William, Lord Kilmaurs, *d.* young.
    II. James, Lord Kilmaurs, *m.* Lady Elizabeth Hamilton, 2nd dau. of William, 2nd Duke of Hamilton; *d. v. p.*
    III. ALEXANDER, 10th earl.
    IV. JOHN, 11th earl.
    I. Jean, *m.* 25 April, 1661, to William, 1st Earl of Kilmarnock.
    II. Margaret, *m.* to John, 2nd Lord Bargeny.
    III. Anne, *d. unm.*
    IV. Elizabeth, *m.* to William Hamilton, of Orbistoun.

His lordship *m.* 2ndly, Lady Margaret Montgomery, eldest dau. of Alexander, 6th Earl of Eglinton, relict of John, 1st Earl of Tweeddale, but had no issue.
The 3rd son,
ALEXANDER CUNNINGHAM, 10th Earl of Glencairn, *s.* his father in 1664. He *m.* Nichola, eldest sister and co-heiress of Sir William Stewart, of Kirkhill and Strathbrock, co. Linlithgow, and had one dau.,

    MARGARET, *m.* to John, 5th Earl of Lauderdale, and *d.* 1740. Her eldest son, James, Lord Maitland, had an only child, Jean, *m.* to Sir James Fergusson, Bart., of Kilkerran, co. Ayr; and her son, Sir Adam Fergusson, unsuccessfully claimed, in her right, the title of Glencairn. Sir Adam's great-grandnephew SIR JAMES FERGUSSON, Bart., is now the heir-general of the noble house of Glencairn.

The earl *d.* 26 May, 1670, and was *s.* by his brother,
JOHN CUNNINGHAM, 11th Earl of Glencairn, who strenuously supported the Revolution, and raised a regiment of 600 foot, of which he was appointed colonel, for the service of the nation, in 1689. His lordship *m.* 1st, 5 August, 1673, Lady Jean Erskine, 2nd dau. of John, 9th Earl of Marr, and by her had one son, WILLIAM, 12th Earl of Glencairn; and 2ndly, Margaret, dau. and heiress of John Napier, of Kilmahew, relict of Patrick Maxwell, of Newark, but by her had no issue. He *d.* 14 December, 1703, and was *s.* by his only son,
WILLIAM CUNNINGHAM, 12th Earl of Glencairn, who supported the treaty of Union, was sworn a privy councillor, and appointed governor of Dumbarton Castle. His lordship *m.* 20 February, 1704, Lady Henrietta Stewart, 2nd dau. of Alexander, 3rd Earl of Galloway, and by her (who *d.* at Glasgow, 21 October, 1763, in her eighty-first year) had issue,

    I. John, Lord Kilmaurs, *d.* young.
    II. WILLIAM, 13th Earl of Glencairn.
    III. John, *d. unm.*   IV. James *d.* an infant.
    V. Malcolm Fleming, *d. unm.*
    VI. Alexander, an officer in the army, *d.* at Portobello, 1739,
    VII. Charles *d. unm.*   VIII. James, *d. unm.*
    I. Margaret, *m.* 2 April, 1732, Nicol Graham, Esq., of Gartmore, co. Perth, who *d.* at Gartmore, 16 November, 1775, in his eightieth year, and was *s.* by his only son,
        ROBERT GRAHAM, Esq., of Gartmore, who inherited, at the decease of John, last Earl of Glencairn, the estate of Finlaystone, &c., and assumed the additional surname and arms of CUNNINGHAME; his eldest son and heir,
        WILLIAM CUNNINGHAM CUNNINGHAME-GRAHAM, Esq., of Gartmore and Finlaystone, was father of ROBERT-CUNNINGHAME CUNNINGHAME-GRAHAM, Esq., of Gartmore, co. Perth and Finlaystone, co. Renfrew; *m.* 1824, Frances Laura, dau. of Archibald Speirs, Esq , of Elderslie, and had WILLIAM CUNNINGHAM and other issue.
    II. HENRIET, *m.* 20 April, 1735, to John Campbell, of Shawfield, co. Lanark; and *d.* at Edinburgh, 5 May, 1774. Her son, WALTER CAMPBELL, Esq., of Shawfield, was progenitor of the CAMPBELLS *of Islay and Shawfield*, and the CAMPBELLS *of Skipness.*

The son and heir,
WILLIAM CUNNINGHAME, 13th Earl of Glencairn, *s.* his father, 1734, and had the government of Dumbarton Castle conferred

on him in the same year. He *m.* in August, 1744, the elder dau. and heiress of Hugh Macguire, of Drumdow, in Ayrshire, and by her (who *d.* at Coats, near Edinburgh, 24 June, 1801, in her seventy-seventh year) had issue,

William, Lord Kilmaurs, *d. unm.* in 1768.
JAMES, 14th Earl of Glencairn.
JOHN, 15th Earl of Glencairn.
Alexander, *b.* in June, 1754; *d.* young.
Henriet, *m.* to Sir Alexander Don, Bart., of Newton-Don, co. Roxburgh, and had two daus., who were unfortunately drowned in the river Eden, near Newton-Don. 7 June, 1795; and one son, SIR ALEXANDER DON, Bart., who *s.* to the Barony of Ochiltree, in Ayrshire, on the death of his grandmother, the Countess of Glencairn, in 1801.
Elizabeth, *d. unm.* at Coats, 6 August, 1804.

The earl, who attained the rank of major-gen. in the army, *d.* 9 September, 1775, and was *s.* by his son,
JAMES CUNNINGHAM, 14th Earl of Glencairn, *b.* in June, 1749, who disposed of his ancient family estate of Kilmaurs to the Marchioness of Titchfield, in 1786. His lordship was a nobleman of great generosity of disposition, and *d.* deeply lamented, 30 January, 1791, in the forty-second year of his age. His kindness to Robert Burns, and the beautiful lament of the poet on his lordship's decease, have added new lustre to the name of Glencairn. Burns put on mourning for his death, and called after the earl his next-born son, James-Glencairn Burns (afterwards major of the East India Company's service). Lord Glencairn never married, and was *s.* at his decease by his brother,
JOHN CUNNINGHAME, 15th Earl of Glencairn, *b.* in May, 1750; who was an officer in the 14th regt. of dragoons, but afterwards took orders in the church of England. He *m.* in 1785, Lady Isabella Erskine, 2nd dau. of Henry-David, 10th Earl of Buchan, and relict of William Leslie Hamilton, Esq. ; but *d. s. p.,* 24 September, 1796, in the forty-seventh year of his age, when the honours became DORMANT,

Arms—Arg., a shakefork, sa.

CUNYNGHAME—EARL OF CARRICK.

Lineage.

SIR WILLIAM DE CUNYNGHAME, Knt., of Kilmaurs, who *m.* for his 2nd wife, Lady Eleanor Bruce, only dau. of Alexander Bruce, 8th Earl of Carrick, obtained in consequence a charter from DAVID II. of that earldom, which soon however reverted to the crown. The heirs-male of Edward Bruce having failed the Earldom of Carrick ought to have reverted to the crown, in terms of the charter; but exception seems to have been made in favour of his grand-dau., his only existing descendant; and according to the custom of the time, her husband became Earl of Carrick. The charter in his favour is on record, and singularly incomplete, as if there had been a doubt as to the propriety of the grant :—" *David, D. G. Rex Scottorum, sciatis nos dedisse concessisse et hac presenti-carta confirmasse dilecto consanguineo nostro Willielmo de Cuninghame militi totum comitatum de Carryk.*" Without date; the charters immediately preceding and following on the record are dated at Aberdeen, 12 September, 1361. No mention being made of heirs, it was clearly intended the earldom should revert to the elder branch of the Bruce family. Indeed, after Lady Eleanor's death, it was re-assumed by ROBERT II., and soon after conferred on his eldest son, JOHN, during Sir William's lifetime.

CUTTS—BARON CUTTS, OF GOWRAN.

By Letters Patent, dated 12 December, 1690.

Lineage.

PETER CUTT, Esq., who held the manors of Woodhall, Coggeshall-Peverals, Essex, and *d.* 22 October, 1547, left a son,
RICHARD CUTT, Esq., who *m.* Mary, dau. of Edward Elrington, of Theydon Bois, and *d.* 16 August, 1592, having had issue,

RICHARD, his heir.
WILLIAM (Sir), *s.* his brother.
Francis, *m.* Catharine, dau. of John Bondvile, of Spanton, co. York.
John.
Barbara, *m.* to Roger Godsall, Esq., of Buckenham Ferry, Norfolk.
Dorothy, *m.* to Thomas Bendishe, of Steeple Bumsted .

The eldest son,

RICHARD CUTT, Esq., s. to the second moiety of the family estates on the death s. p. of his cousin, Sir Henry Cutt, and he dying also s. p., 4 April, 1607, was s. by his brother,

SIR WILLIAM CUTTS, Knt., of Woodhall, Peveral, Rockling, &c., who m. Anne, dau. of Daniel Bettenham, Esq., of Pluckley, in Kent, and was s. at his decease, 16 December, 1609, by his son,

RICHARD CUTTS, Esq., then eleven years old, who d. 16 July, 1626, leaving a son and heir,

JOHN CUTTS, Esq., who was in wardship to King CHARLES I. He m. a dau. of Sir Richard Everard, Bart., of Much Waltham, and left a son and heir,

RICHARD CUTTS, Esq., who removed to Childerley, co. Cambridge, having had the estate of Cutts, in that co., given to him by a distant relative. He left two sons and three daus., Richard, who d. unm.; JOHN; Anne, m. to John Withers, Esq., of the Middle Temple; the 2nd dau. was m. to John Acton, Esq., of Basingstoke; and the youngest, Joanna, d. unm. The 2nd son and eventual heir to the family,

JOHN CUTTS, Esq., of Childerley, in Cambridgeshire, a gallant military officer under the Duke of Marlborough was created, 12 December, 1690, BARON CUTTS, of Gowran, co. Kilkenny. He m. 1st, the sister of Sir George Treby; and 2ndly, a dau. of Sir Henry Pickering, of Whaddon; but d. s. p. 26 January, 1706, in Ireland, whither he had gone as one of the lords justices, and with him the BARONY OF CUTTS. EXPIRED. The estate of Childerley his lordship sold, in 1686, to Felix Calvert, Esq., and the Woodhall estate, which had been long in his family, to Thomas Maynard, Esq., of Bury St. Edmunds, and it was subsequently purchased by Richard Cheeke, Esq., treasurer of Christ's Hospital, London, who d. 26 December, 1740.

Arms—Arg., on a bend, engrailed, sa., three plates.

DACRE—BARONS DACRE, OF GILLESLAND, OR THE NORTH.

By Writ of Summons, dated 15 November, 1482.

Lineage,

In the 20th year of King HENRY III.

WILLIAM DACRE, of Dacre, in Cumberland, served the office of sheriff for that shire, with John de Moore, and in the 32nd of the same reign, he was constituted sheriff of Yorkshire, and governor of the castles of Scarborough and Pickering. He d. in ten years afterwards, when again sheriff of Cumberland, and governor of the castle of Carlisle, and was s. by his son,

RANULPH DE DACRE, who had been in the lifetime of his father a stanch adherent of King HENRY III., in the conflicts between that monarch and the barons, and upon succeeding to his inheritance was appointed sheriff of Cumberland. In the 7th EDWARD I., he was constituted sheriff of Yorkshire, and continued in that trust, until the end of the 3rd quarter of the 8th succeeding year. This Ranulph m. Joane de Luci, and dying in the 14th EDWARD I., was s. by his son,

WILLIAM DE DACRE, b. 1265, who, in the 32nd EDWARD I., was in the expedition made that year into Scotland, and about the same period obtained a charter for free warren in all his demesne lands at Dacre, co. Cumberland, and at Halton, in Lancashire. In the 1st year of the next reign, he had license to encastellate his mansion at Dunwalloght, in Cumberland, on the marches of Scotland, and in three years afterwards was again engaged in the Scottish wars. His lordship m. Joane, dau. and heiress of Benedict Garnet, or according to some authorities, dau. of Sir William Bluet, and having been summoned to parliament as a Baron, from the 28th EDWARD I., to the 12th EDWARD II., departed this life in the latter year, and was s. by his son,

RANULPH DE DACRE, who had summons to parliament as BARON DACRE, from 15 May, 1321, to 15th November, 1338. His lordship was made sheriff of Cumberland and governor of Carlisle, in the 4th EDWARD III., and in the 8th of the same monarch, he obtained livery of all those castles and manors in Anandale, within the realm of Scotland, part of the possessions of Roger de Kirkpatric and Humphrey de Bois, which had been given to him by EDWARD, King of Scotland. He was also, in the same year, joined in commission with Robert de Clifford, for the defence of the town and marches of Carlisle, and for arraying so many "men at arms, hoblers, and foot soldiers," as should be needful for the service. In the next year he had license to make a castle of his house at Naworth, co. Cumberland. His lordship m. Margaret, only dau. and heiress of Thomas de Multon, BARON MULTON, of Gillesland,

152

(by writ of EDWARD II., dated 26 August, 1307), by whom he acquired considerable estates, and left at his decease, in 1339, three sons, viz.,

WILLIAM, who s. to the Barony of Dacre through his father, and to the Barony of MULTON, through his mother, but d. s. p. in 1361.

THOMAS.

RALPH, successor to his brother in the baronies, d. also s. p. in 1375.

And

HUGH DE DACRE, who s. his brother Ralph as Lord Dacre and Lord Multon, and had summons to parliament from 1 December, 1376, to 20 August, 1383. His lordship m. Ela, dau. of Alexander, Lord Maxwell, and dying in 1383, was s. by his son,

WILLIAM DE DACRE, b. 1357, summoned to parliament from 3 March, 1384, to 23 November, 1403. His lordship m. Joan, illegitimate dau. of James, Earl of Douglas, and dying about the year 1403, was s. by his son,

THOMAS DE DACRE, summoned to parliament from 1 December, 1412, to 26 May, 1455. This nobleman was constituted chief forester of Inglewood Forest, co. Cumberland, in the 8th HENRY V., and was appointed in the 2nd HENRY VI. one of the commissioners to treat for peace with JAMES I. of Scotland. His lordship m. Philippa, dau. of Ralph Nevil, Earl of Westmoreland, and d. 1458, having had issue,

Thomas, who m. Elizabeth, dau. of Richard Bowes, Esq., and dying in the lifetime of his father, left an only dau. and heiress,

   Joane, m. Sir Richard Fienes, Knt., who was declared *Baron* DACRE by King EDWARD IV., and from whom the BARONY has descended in regular succession to the present LORD DACRE.

Ranulph, a stout adherent of the house of Lancaster, had summons to parliament as a Baron in the 38th HENRY VI., but fell at Towtonfield, and was subsequently attainted, when his title and estates became forfeited.

HUMPHREY, of whom presently.
John.   Richard.   George.
Joan, m. to Thomas, 8th Lord de Clifford.
Isabel, m. to Lord Scrope, of Upsal.

SIR HUMPHREY DACRE (the 3rd son), having deported himself obsequiously to the then triumphant house of York, attended King EDWARD IV. at the sieges and surrender of the different Lancastrian castles in the north; for which good services, as well as his fidelity to the king's sister, Margaret, whom he escorted as chamberlain upon her journey into Flanders, on the occasion of her marriage with Charles, Duke of Burgundy, he was constituted master forester of Inglewood Forest for life, and continuing to enjoy the confidence of the king, he was summoned to parliament as a Baron on the 15 November, 1482, under the designation of "HUMFRIDO DACRES OF GILLESLAND, *Chevalier*." Sir Humphrey Dacre, who enjoyed Gillesland and other capital manors, by virtue of a fine levied by his father, had previously disputed the original BARONY OF DACRE, with his niece Joane, Lady Fienes, when the affair was referred to the arbitration of King EDWARD IV., who confirmed Sir Richard Fienes and his lady in the barony, with the precedency enjoyed by Lady Fienes's grandfather, and decreed to them divers castles and manors, but GILLESLAND, the ancient seat of the Vaux's, with several considerable estates, was adjudged to Sir Humphrey, who, at the same time, was created a Baron, with place next below Sir Richard Fienes, and for distinction was styled Lord Dacre, of Gillesland, or of the North; Sir Richard being entitled Lord Dacre, of the South. His lordship m. Maud, dau. of Sir Thomas Parr, Knt., of Kendal, and dying in 1509, was s. by his son,

SIR THOMAS DACRE, 2nd Lord Dacre, of Gillesland, summoned to parliament from 17 October, 1509, to 12 November, 1515. This nobleman, in the 9th HENRY VII., served under Thomas, Earl of Surrey, at the siege of Norham Castle, and his lordship obtained great celebrity in the command of a body of horse reserve, at the famous fight of Flodden, in the 4th HENRY VIII., under the same gallant leader. He was, subsequently, at different times, engaged in Scotland, and he filled the important office of warden of the West Marches from the 1st year of King HENRY VIII. He m. Elizabeth, grand-dau. and sole heiress of Ralph de Greystock, Baron Greystock, K.G., and had issue,

WILLIAM, his successor.
Humphrey.
Mary, m. to Francis, Earl of Shrewsbury.
Margaret, m. to Henry, Lord Scrope, of Bolton.
Jane.

His lordship d. in 1525, and was s. by his elder son,

SIR WILLIAM DACRE, as 3rd Lord Dacre, of Gillesland, summoned to parliament from 3 November, 1529, to 21 October,

1555, in the 1st writ as "Willielmo Dacre de Dacre and Greystok, Chl'r," afterwards as "de Gillesland," or of Greystok, or "de North." In the 26th HENRY VIII., this nobleman being accused of high treason by Sir Ralph Fenwyke, was brought to trial before his peers at Westminster in the July of that year, and acquitted, owing to the description of evidence by which the charge was sustained, namely, persons of mean degree from the Scottish border, who were either suborned, or brought forward by a vindictive feeling towards Lord Dacre, arising from the severity with which he had executed the duty of warden of the marches. In the reigns of EDWARD VI., MARY and ELIZABETH, his lordship was captain of the castle, and governor of Carlisle, and in the 2nd year of the last queen, he was joined in commission with the Earl of Northumberland to negotiate a peace with Scotland. His lordship *m.* Elizabeth, 5th dau. of George, 4th Earl of Shrewsbury, and had issue,

THOMAS, his successor.

Leonard, who being dissatisfied with the distribution of the family estates amongst his nieces, at the decease of his nephew, George, Lord Dacre, joined in the conspiracy of the Earls of Northumberland and Westmoreland, *temp.* ELIZABETH, for the rescue of MARY, Queen of Scots, and took possession of the Dacre castles of GREYSTOCK and NAWORTH, in the north, but was eventually obliged to fly into Scotland, when he was attainted with the lords abovementioned; he *d.* abroad in great poverty, at Louvaine, in 1581, *s. p.*

Edward, attainted with his brother Leonard for the same treason, *d. s. p.* in 1579.

Francis, attainted with his brothers, and for the same treason. He lived, however, several years after, dying about the 8th CHARLES I. He left a son and dau.,

    Randal (the last male heir of Humphrey, Lord Dacre, of Gillesland), who *d.* two years after his father, without issue. The parish register of Greystock for 1634, contains the following entry (Buried), "Randal Dacre, Esq., sonne and hyre to Francis Dacre, Esquire, deceased, being the youngest son of the last Lord William Dacre, deceased, being the last hyre male of that lyne; which said Randal dyed at London, and was brought downe at the charges of the Right Hon. Thomas, Earle of Arundell and Surreye, and earle marshall of England."

    Mary, who lived to a very great age, and *d. s. p.*

Margaret, *m.* to Anthony Browne, Viscount Montacute.

Anne, *m.* to Henry Clifford, Earl of Cumberland.

Eleanor, *m.* to Henry Jerningham, Esq., of Costessy Hall, Norfolk, by whom she had, with other issue,

    HENRY JERNINGHAM, who was created a Baronet, 16 October, 1621.

Mary, *m.* to Alexander Culpepper, Esq.

Dorothy, *m.* to Sir Thomas Windsore, Knt., son and heir of William, Lord Windsore.

Lord Dacre *d.* in 1563, and was *s.* by his eldest son,

THOMAS DACRE, 4th Baron Dacre, of Gillesland, but never summoned to parliament. This nobleman *m.* Elizabeth, dau. of Sir James Leiburne, Knt. of Cunswick, in Westmoreland, and by her (who *m.* 2ndly, Thomas Howard, Duke of Norfolk), had issue,

GEORGE, his successor.

ANNE, *m.* Philip Howard, Earl of Arundel, and had issue: the heir male of this marriage is the DUKE OF NORFOLK; and the heirs-general the LORDS PETRE and STOURTON.

MARY, *m.* to Thomas, Lord Howard, of Walden, and *d. s. p.*

ELIZABETH, *m.* to Lord William Howard, and her greatgrandson, Charles Howard, Esq., was elevated to the peerage, 20 April, 1661, by the titles of *Baron Dacre, of Gilesland, Viscount Howard, of Morpeth,* AND EARL OF CARLISLE. (*See* BURKE's *Extant Peerage.*)

His lordship *d.* in 1566, and was *s.* by his only son,

GEORGE DACRE, 5th Lord Dacre, of Gillesland, who *d.* in minority, *anno* 1569, of a fall from a wooden horse, upon which he practised to leap. At the decease of his lordship the "BARONY OF DACRE, OF GILLESLAND," fell into ABEYANCE between his sisters as co-heirs, and it so continues with their descendants. Of his estates, Greystock fell to the Earl of Arundel, and is now in the possession of the Duke of Norfolk; while Naworth Castle devolved upon Lord William Howard, where he settled, and it now belongs to the Earl of Carlisle.

Arms—Gu., three escallops, arg.

DAGWORTH—BARONS DAGWORTH.

By Writ of Summons, dated 13 November, 1347.

Lineage.

In the 19th of King EDWARD II., upon the death of Lora, widow of William Peyforer, which Lora died, seised of the

third part of the office of *Huisher* (Usher), in the Exchequer Court, and crier in the King's Bench, her grandson,

JOHN DAGWORTH, being found her next heir, upon doing his homage, had livery of the lands of his inheritance. To this John, succeeded his son,

THOMAS DE DAGWORTH, a very eminent soldier in the reigns of EDWARD II., and EDWARD III. In the 20th of the latter, being then a knight and commander of the king's forces in Britanny, he is recorded as having defeated twice in one day Charles de Blois, who had usurped in right of his wife, the title of Duke of Britanny, notwithstanding the great inequality of forces, the duke having 1,500 horse, 8,000 ballistars, and 30,000 foot, being treble the army of the English commander. In the next year following up his fortune, he marched to the relief of Rochedirlan, invested by the same foe, and giving battle to the duke, obtained a decisive victory, making prisoners of 36 knights, slaying more than 500 men-at-arms, and conveying CHARLES himself a captive to the Tower of London; for which good services he was appointed lieutenant and captain-general to the king, in the dukedom of Britanny; and the next year reaping fresh laurels on the French soil, he was summoned to parliament, as BARON DAGWORTH, on the 13 November, 1347, as an additional reward for his gallantry. His lordship resided from that period in Britanny until 1359, when he is said to have been slain by the treachery of the French. He *m.* Lady Eleanor Bohun, widow of James, Earl of Ormonde, and was *s.* by his son,

SIR NICHOLAS DAGWORTH, 2nd Baron Dagworth, who does not appear from the existing enrolments to have been summoned to parliament. Like his father, this gallant person acquired the highest military renown. In the year 1366, Sir Nicholas obtained a great victory over the French in Anjou, when amongst his prisoners, were the Dukes of Orleans and Anjou. It is further reported of him, that with thirteen English horse, he encountered sixty French near Flaveny, and by the means of chariots, which he employed for his defence, utterly vanquished them. In the reign of RICHARD II., he was imprisoned by the great lords then opposed to the court, but having obtained his freedom, he was employed with Walter Skirlaw, bishop of Durham, to negotiate a peace with France —"from which period," says Dugdale, "I have not seen any more of him." Thomasine, dau. of this 2nd Lord Dagworth, *m.* William, 4th Lord Furnival.

Arms—Erm., on a bend gu., three bezants.

DAMER—BARONS MILTON, VISCOUNTS MILTON, EARLS OF DORCHESTER.

Barony, by Letters Patent, dated 10 May, 1762.
Earldom, &c., by Letters Patent, dated 18 May, 1792.

Lineage.

This family was long seated in the counties of Somerset and Dorset, and claimed descent from William D'Amory, who came into England with the Conqueror.

JOSEPH DAMER, of Chapel, co. Devon, who *m.* Jane, dau. of William St. Lo, Esq., of co. Dorset, had two sons, Robert and Ambrose, *b.* 1572. The former,

ROBERT DAMER, of Chapel, *b.* 1571, *m.* in 1600, Mary, dau. of Edward Colmer, Esq., and with a dau., Elizabeth, had a son,

JOHN DAMER, of Godmanston, *b.* 1602, who *m.* in 1628, Elizabeth, dau. of the Rev. William Maber, and had issue,

JOSEPH, of whom presently.

Edward, in holy orders, rector of Wyke Regis.

Jonathan, *b.* 1635, *d. s. p.*

Benjamin and Nathaniel, both *d. s. p.*

George, *b.* 1644, *m.* Sarah, dau. of Richard Fowler, Esq., and *d.* 1730, having had issue,

    JOHN, to whom his uncle bequeathed his estates, and of whom hereafter.

    JOSEPH, who *s.* his brother, and of whom presently.

    Elizabeth, *m.* 1717, to Edward Clavell, Esq, of Smedmore.

Elizabeth, *m.* to John Trevelian, Esq., of Mildenay, co. Somerset.

JOSEPH DAMER, eldest son of John Damer, of Godmanston, embarked early in the service of the parliament, and was advanced by Cromwell to the command of a troop of horse; being in high confidence with Oliver, he was twice deputed by him upon secret negotiations to Cardinal Mazarin. After the Restoration, Mr. Damer not deeming it safe to continue in

England, disposed of his lands in Somerset and Dorsetshire, and purchased other estates in Ireland, whither he removed. He d. 6 July, 1720, at the advanced age of ninety-one, never having experienced indisposition until three days before his decease. He d. a bachelor, and bequeathed his estates to his nephew,

JOHN DAMER, Esq., of Shronehill, co. Tipperary, who m. in 1724, Margaret, eldest dau. of Andrew Roe, Esq., of Roesborough, in the same shire, but d. without issue in 1768, when the estates devolved upon his brother,

JOSEPH DAMER, Esq., of Came, co. Dorset, b. in 1676, m. 6 December, 1714, Mary, dau. of John Churchill, Esq., of Henbury, in the same shire, and had issue,

JOSEPH. his heir.

John, of Came, Dorset, b. 27 October, 1720, M.P. for Dorchester, and LL.D., m. Martha, dau. of Samuel Rush, Esq., of Benhall, Suffolk, and d. 26 December, 1783.

George, M.P. for Dorsetshire, in 1750-1, d. in 1752, unm.

Mary, m. to William-Henry Dawson, Esq., M.P., of Dawson's Grove, Queen's Co. This gentleman was advanced to the peerage of Ireland, as Viscount Carlow, and created EARL of PORTARLINGTON. (See BURKE's Extant Peerage.)

Martha, m. 1st, in 1741, to Sir Edward Crofton, Bart., of the Moat, co. of Roscommon, and 2ndly, to Ezekiel Nesbitt, M.D.

Mr. Damer, who represented the co. of Dorset in parliament in 1722, d. 1 March, 1736-7, and was s. by his eldest son,

JOSEPH DAMER, Esq., who, having successively represented the borough of Weymouth (1741), Bramber (1747), and Dorchester (1754), in parliament, was elevated to the peerage of Ireland. 3 July, 1753, as BARON MILTON, of Shronehill, co. Tipperary, and created a peer of Great Britain, 10 May, 1762, in the dignity of BARON MILTON, of Milton Abbey, co. Dorset. His lordship m. 27 July, 1742, Lady Caroline Sackville, only surviving dau. of Lionel, 1st Duke of Dorset, by whom (who d. 24 March, 1775), he had issue,

John, b. 25 June, 1744, m. 14 June, 1767, Anne, only child of the Right Honourable Henry Seymour Conway, brother of Francis, 1st Marquess of Hertford, and d. s. p. 15 August, 1776.

GEORGE, who succeeded his father.

Lionel, b. 16 September, 1748, m. 16 April, 1778, Williamsa, dau. of William Janssen, son of Sir Stephen Janssen, and niece of Sir Stephen Theodore Janssen, Bart., and d. s. p. 28 May, 1807.

Caroline, b. 4 May, 1752, d. unm. in 1829. At the decease of this lady, the distinguished sculptor, Lady Caroline Damer, the Damer estates passed to the noble family of DAWSON.

His lordship was advanced to the dignities of Viscount Milton and EARL OF DORCHESTER, in the peerage of Great Britain, 15 May, 1792. He d. 12 February, 1798, and was s. by his eldest surviving son,

GEORGE DAMER, 2nd Earl of Dorchester, at whose decease in 1808, without issue (his brother Lionel having died previously), the Irish Barony of MILTON, with the British EARLDOM OF DORCHESTER, and inferior dignities, became EXTINCT.

Arms—Barry nebulé of six, arg. and gu., a bend engrailed, az.

DAMER—BARON MILTON, OF SHRONE-HILL, CO. TIPPERARY.

(See DAMER, Earl of Dorchester, in the Extinct Peerage of England.)

DANIEL—BARON RATHWIER.

Lineage.

The Barony of Rathwier, co. Meath, was conferred by Letters Patent, 1475, on THOMAS DANIEL, but of its descent or extinction we have not been able to ascertain any particulars. We find, however, in Morant's "History of Essex," the following reference to the family:—

Grace, only dau. and sole heir of Richard Baynard, m. before her father's decease, Thomas Langley, but took to her second husband, Edward Daniel, Esq., son of SIR THOMAS DANIEL, Baron of Rathwre, in Ireland, and lord-deputy there under King EDWARD IV., by Margaret his wife, dau. of Sir Robert Howard, Knt., and sister of John Howard, Duke of Norfolk, K.G., and had three sons and four daus., Edward; John; and Thomas; Jane, m. to Sir John Jermyn, of Melesfield, co.

Suffolk; Margaret, m. to — Green, of Witham, Essex; Elizabeth, abbess of Mullym; and Catharine. She (Grace) d. 2 January, 1508, her 2nd son John Daniel, is said to be her heir, the eldest being either dead or settled at Bulmer or Acton Hall, Suffolk. He d. 5 September, 1556. His son and successor, Edmund Daniel, d. 16 December, 1570, leaving a son,

JOHN DANIEL, aged seventeen years; his successors were Edmund and John Daniel, of Messing, Esqs.; the latter m. Hawisea, dau. of — Tyrrell, and had two daus., of whom Ursula, m. 1st, William Wiseman, Esq., of Great Badow, son of George Wiseman, Esq., of Axminster; and 2ndly, George Aylett, of Great Coggeshall

---

DANVERS—BARON DANVERS, OF DANTSEY, WILTS. EARL OF DANBY, CO. YORK.

Barony, by Letters Patent, dated 27 July, 1603.
Earldom, by Letters Patent, dated 5 February, 1626.

Lineage.

JOHN NEVIL, last Lord Latimer, of that surname, m. Lucy, dau. of Henry, Earl of Worcester, and left at his decease, in 1577, four daus., his co-heiresses, viz.,

KATHERINE, m. to Henry Percy, Earl of Northumberland, by whom she had eight sons and three daus. This earl was committed to the Tower, for a supposed plot in favour of MARY, QUEEN OF SCOTS, and there found dead in his bed, wounded by three pistol bullets, anno 1585.

DOROTHY, m. Thomas Cecil, 1st Earl of Exeter, by whom (who d. 1622), she was mother of

WILLIAM, 2nd Earl of Exeter, left at his decease, in 1640, three daus. and co-heirs, viz.,

Elizabeth, m. to Thomas, Earl of Berkshire, and their heir-general is Winchcombe H. H. Hartley, Esq.

Diana, m. 1st, to Thomas, Earl of Elgin, and 2ndly, to the Earl of Oxford, d. s. p.

Anne, m. to Henry Grey, Earl of Stamford, and their heir-general is Sir Rainald Knightley, Bart.

LUCY, m. to Sir William Cornwallis, Knt., of Brome, and dying 1608, left four daus., viz.,

FRANCES, m. to Sir Edmund Withipool, and their heir-general is Sir Robert Burdett, Bart.

ELIZABETH, m. 1st, to Sir William Sandys, and 2ndly, Richard, Viscount Lumley, and d. s. p. 1659.

CORNELIA, m. to Sir Richard Fermor, of Somerton, and their co-heir-general is Sir Charles R. Tempest, Bart. : see p. 398.

ANNE, m. to Archibald, Earl of Argyll, and their heir-general is Lord Rollo.

ELIZABETH, m. 1st, to Sir John Danvers, Knt., of Dauntsey, Wilts, and 2ndly, to Sir Edmund Carey, Knt. She d. 1636.

SIR JOHN DANVERS acquired with the Honourable Elizabeth Nevil the ancient Castle of Danby, in the North Riding of Yorkshire, and had issue,

I. CHARLES (Sir), who lost his life s. p. 1602. and was attainted for participating in the insurrection of Robert, Earl of Essex.

II. HENRY, of whom presently.

III. John (Sir), of Chelsea, one of the judges of King CHARLES I., m. 1st, Magdalen Newport; 2ndly, Elizabeth Dauntsey; and 3rdly, Grace Hawes. By his 2nd wife, who d. 1636, he had two daus., eventually co-heirs, viz.,

Elizabeth, m. to Robert Villiers, Esq : their heir-general is George-William Villiers, Esq.

Anne, m. to Sir Henry Lee, of Ditchley: their heir-general is the Earl of Abingdon.

I. Elizabeth, m. Thomas Walmesley, Esq., of Dunkenhalgh, co. Lancaster, and dying September, 1601, left issue,

1 SIR THOMAS WALMESLEY, of Dunkenhalgh, ancestor of the WALMESLEYs of Dunkenhalgh, represented by LORD PETRE, as heir-general.

1 Elizabeth, wife of Richard Sherborne, Esq., d. s. p.

2 Anne Walmesley, who m. 1st, William Middleton, Esq., of Stockeld, in the county of York; and 2ndly, Sir Edward Osborne, Bart.; by the latter she had issue,

Sir Thomas Osborne, Bart., who was created Viscount Latimer, Earl of Danby, Marquess of Carmarthen, and DUKE of LEEDS.

II. Dorothy, m. to Sir Peter Osborne, Knt., from which union the Baronets OSBORNE, of Chicksand Priory, Beds., derive.

The 2nd son,

SIR HENRY DANVERS, Knt., was elevated to the peerage, by letters patent, 27 July, 1603, as Baron Danvers, of Dantsey, co. Wilts, and in two years afterwards his lordship was restored in blood, by special act of parliament, as heir to his father, notwithstanding the attainder of Sir Charles Danvers, his elder brother. Upon the accession of King CHARLES I., Lord Danvers was created by letters patent, dated 5 February, 1626, EARL OF DANBY, and his lordship was soon afterwards chosen a knight of the Garter. This nobleman, who had adopted from his youth the profession of arms, distinguished himself both by sea and land, and was esteemed an able and gallant soldier.

His lordship was the founder of the famous Physic Garden at Oxford, which cost him little short of £5,000. He d. 20 January, 1643, when as he never married, the *Barony of Danvers* and EARLDOM OF DANBY, became EXTINCT. His remains were interred in the chancel of the parish church at Dantsey, under a noble monument of white marble, with the following inscription :—

" HENRY, EARL OF DANBY, second son to Sir John Danvers, Knt., and *Dame* ELIZABETH, dau. and co-heir of John Nevil, Lord Latimer; born at Dauntesey, co. Wilts, 28 June, ann. Dom. 1573, and baptised in this church, the 1st of July following, being Sunday. He departed this life on the 20th of January, ann. Dom. 1643, and lyeth here interred.

" He was partly bred up in the low country wars, under MAURICE, Earl of Nassau (afterwards Prince of Orange), and in many other military actions of those times, both by sea and land. He was made a CAPTAIN in the wars of France, and there knighted for his good service, under HENRY IV., then French King. He was employed as lieutenant-general of the horse, and serjeant-major of the whole army, in Ireland, under ROBERT, Earl of Essex, and Charles, Baron of Mountjoy, in the reign of Queen ELIZABETH.

" He was made Baron of DAUNTSEY, and peer of the realm, by King JAMES I.; and by him made Lord President of MUNSTER, and Governor of GARNESEY.

" By King CHARLES I., he was created Earl of Danby; made of his privy council, and knight of the most noble order of the Garter; but declining more active employments in his later time (by reason of his imperfect health), full of honour, wounds and days, he died at his house at CORNBURY PARK, in the county of Oxford, in the 71st year of his age."

Arms—Gu., a chevron between three mullets of six points, or.

D'ARCY—BARONS D'ARCY.

By Writ of Summons, dated 29 December, 1299.

Lineage.

At the time of the General Survey,

NORMAN DE ARECI enjoyed no less than thirty-three lordships in the county of Lincoln, by the immediate gift of the CONQUEROR, of which Nocton was one, where he and his posterity had their chief seat for divers after ages. This Norman, in the 6th year of WILLIAM RUFUS, being with the king in his great council held at Gloucester (together with several bishops, abbots and others), was a witness to that confirmation there made to the monks of St. Mary's Abbey, in York, of numerous possessions which had formerly been bestowed upon them. To Norman de Areci *s.* his son and heir,

ROBERT D'ARCY, who founded a priory of Augustines at his lordship at Nocton, and otherwise contributed liberally to the church. This Robert was *s.* by his son and heir,

THOMAS D'ARCY, who, upon the assessment of the aid for marrying the king's daughter in the 12th HENRY II., certified that he then held twenty knights' fees *de veteri feoffamento*, with half a knight's fee, and a fourth part *de novo*, for which he paid £13 6s. 8d. This feudal lord *m.* Alice, dau. of Ralph D'Eincurt, by whom he had three sons and four daus. He *d.* on St. Swithin's Day, *anno* 1180, leaving Thomas his son and heir, then eighteen years of age. Upon the decease of his lordship, William Bassett, sheriff of Lincolnshire seized on his whole barony for the king, and committed it to the custody of Michael D'Arcy, but the baron's widow subsequently obtained the possession with the guardianship of her children, for which she paid £200. To Thomas D'Arcy *s.* his aforesaid son and heir,

THOMAS D'ARCY, who was with King RICHARD I. in the expedition which that monarch made into Normandy in the 6th year of his reign, and in the 5th JOHN was retained to serve that king with three knights for one whole year, in consideration of which King JOHN remitted to him a debt of 225 marks, which he then owed the Jews; but besides this retainer he was to perform the like service for his barony that other barons did. His lordship was *s.* at his decease by his son.

NORMAN D'ARCY, who in the 7th of King JOHN giving 500 marks, six palfreys, with one horse for the great saddle, and doing his homage, had livery of all the lands of his inheritance : but taking part with the barons, those lands were seized upon by the crown a few years afterwards, and held until the pacification in the beginning of HENRY III's reign, when they were restored. The baron *d.* soon after, and was *s.* by his son,

PHILIP D'ARCY, who had previously, for his adhesion to the king, in the turbulent times of JOHN, a grant of all the lands of Robert de Camberling. In the 34th HENRY III., this feudal lord is said to have been the accuser of *Sir Henry de Bathe*, an eminent judge of the period, for corruption in his judicial capacity. His lordship was afterwards engaged in the French wars, and involved himself so deeply in debt in the king's service, that he was obliged to obtain in the 39th HENRY III., certain letters hortatory, to all his tenants by military service, and other, earnestly moving them to yield unto him such reasonable aid as might extricate him from his pecuniary difficulties, and for which they should receive the especial thanks of the crown. He *m.* Isabel, sister and co-heir of Roger Bertram, of Mitford, and dying in 1263, was *s.* by his son,

NORMAN D'ARCY, then twenty-eight years of age, who doing his homage, and giving security for the payment of his relief as a baron, had livery of his lands, but the very next year, being one of the barons defeated at Evesham, those lands were all seized by the crown. His brother Roger, and his uncle Thomas, were likewise involved in the defeat, but all made their peace, under the memorable decree, denominated "*Dictum de Kenilworth*," John de Burgh, of Kent, Adam de Newmarch, of York, and Robert de Ufford, all barons, undertaking for their future loyalty and quiet demeanour. He was subsequently engaged in the Welsh wars, and in the 22nd EDWARD I. had summons to attend the king forthwith, and to give him his advice in those great and difficult affairs which then concerned his crown and kingdom. This feudal lord had issue,

PHILIP, his successor.
John, summoned to parliament as a baron 28th EDWARD I. (*see* another Lord D'Arcy).
Robert, of Stailinburgh, co. Lincoln, who left by Joan his wife, an only dau. and heiress,
    Margaret, who *m.* John Argentine.

Norman D'Arcy *d.* 1296, and was *s.* by his eldest son,

PHILIP D'ARCY, who was summoned to parliament as BARON D'ARCY from 29 December, 1299, to 20 October, 1332. This nobleman was involved in the insurrection of Thomas, Earl of Lancaster, in the 15th EDWARD II., but made his peace, and had restitution of his lands. His lordship had issue,

NORMAN, his successor.
Robert, } *d. s. p.*
John, }
Julian, *m.* to Sir Peter de Limberry.
Agnes, *m.* to Sir Roger de Pedwardine.

Lord D'Arcy was *s.* at his decease by his only surviving son,

NORMAN D'ARCY, 2nd Baron D'Arcy, who was likewise implicated in Lancaster's rebellion, but had pardon for his treason and restitution of his lands. He *d.* in 1340, and was *s.* by his only child,

PHILIP D'ARCY, 3rd Baron D'Arcy, at whose decease without issue,

SIR PHILIP DE LIMBURY, KNT., son of Julian, the elder dau. of Philip, 1st Lord D'Arcy; and
AGNES, wife of SIR ROGER DE PEDWARDINE, younger dau. of Philip, 1st Lord D'Arcy.

were found to be his next heirs, and between those the BARONY OF D'ARCY fell into ABEYANCE, as it is still supposed to continue amongst their representatives.

Arms—Az., semée of cross-crosslets, and three cinquefoils, arg.

D'ARCY—BARONS D'ARCY.

By Writ of Summons, dated 27 January, 1332.

Lineage.

JOHN D'ARCY (next brother of Philip D'Arcy, who was summoned to parliament, as Baron D'Arcy, 29 December, 1299), being an active and distinguished person in the reigns of the 1st, 2nd, and 3rd EDWARDS, obtained some of the highest offices in the state, and attained eventually the peerage. In the latter years of EDWARD I., and the beginning of EDWARD II.'s reign, he was engaged in the wars in Scotland; and during the time of the last-mentioned monarch, he was governor of Norham Castle, sheriff of the counties of Nottingham, Derby, and Lancaster, and JUSTICE OF IRELAND. Upon the accession of EDWARD III., he was appointed sheriff of Yorkshire, and governor of the castle at York, and re-constituted JUSTICE OF IRELAND; to which latter post, with the government of the country, he was re-appointed the next year; and in the following year he had a grant from the king, for his good services, of the manor of Werk, in Tindale. In the 6th of EDWARD III., he was summoned to parliament, as BARON D'ARCY; and the next year, being then in his government of Ireland, his lordship marched with a great army into the province of Ulster, to avenge the death of William de Burgh, EARL OF ULSTER; but before he got thither, the people of the country having vindicated the murder, he transported himself and his army into Scotland, leaving Thomas Burke, his lieutenant, in Ireland, and joined the king, who was then pursuing the victorious course which placed EDWARD BALIOL upon the Scottish throne. In two years afterwards, Lord D'Arcy, at the head of the Irish nobles, made a second inroad upon Scotland with fifty-six ships, and wasted the Isles of Arran and Bute, for which good service the king granted to him and his heirs the manors of Rathwere and Kildalk, in Ireland. His lordship was subsequently constable of the Tower of London, and steward of the king's household; and he was accredited ambassador to the courts of France and Scotland in the 11th EDWARD III.; after which we find him acquiring fresh laurels on the French soil, until he finally shared in the glory of Cressy. His lordship obtained further great immunities from EDWARD III., and was appointed JUSTICE OF IRELAND and CONSTABLE OF THE TOWER for life. This eminent nobleman m. 1st, Emeline, dau. and co-heir of Walter Heron, of Hedleston, co. Northumberland, by whom he had issue,

JOHN, his successor.
Roger, from whom the D'Arcys of Essex derive.
Adomar.

His lordship m. 2ndly, 3 July, 1329, Joane, dau. of Richard de Burgh, Earl of Ulster, and widow of Thomas, Earl of Kildare, and had issue of this marriage,

William, of Plattyn, co. Meath, from whom the Darcys of Ireland derive; viz., the D'ARCYS of KILTULLAGH, and NEW FORREST, co. GALWAY, of Gorteen, co. Mayo, the D'ARCYS of PLATTEN and DUNMOW, co. MEATH, the D'ARCYS of HYDE PARK, co. WESTMEATH, &c., &c.
Elizabeth, m. to James, Earl of Ormonde.

Lord D'Arcy, who had summon to parliament from 1332 to 1342, d. 30 May, 1347, and was s. by his eldest son,
SIR JOHN D'ARCY, 2nd Baron D'Arcy, b. in 1317, summoned to parliament from 20 November, 1348, to 15 March, 1354. This nobleman had acquired high military fame in the life-time of his father, and was also amongst the heroes of Cressy. His lordship had custody of the king's liberty of HOLDERNESS, co. York, and was constable of the Tower of London. He m. Elizabeth, dau. and heiress of Nicholas Meinell, Lord Meinell, of Wherlton, and had issue,

JOHN, his successor.
PHILIP, successor to his brother.
Isabel.

His lordship d. in 1356, and was s. by his eldest son,
JOHN D'ARCY, 3rd Baron D'Arcy, at whose decease in minority (s. p.), 26 August, 1362, the barony devolved upon his brother,
PHILIP D'ARCY, 4th Baron D'Arcy, summoned to parliament from 4 August, 1377, to 5 November, 1397. This nobleman, in the 4th RICHARD II., was in the expedition made into France with Thomas of Woodstock, Earl of Buckingham; and arriving at Calais three days before Maudlin-tide, in July, rode with his banner displayed. He became subsequently so eminent in the French wars, that, in the 6th of RICHARD II., he was especially excused, in consequence, from repairing into Ireland, as all persons having lands there were compelled to by Act of Parliament passed three years before, for the defence of the realm against the insurgents then in arms; and in the next year he was again excused, by reason of the great charge he was at in supporting himself in those wars, and likewise "that he was then marching towards Scotland against the king's enemies there." In the 9th of RICHARD II., his lordship was constituted ADMIRAL of the king's fleet from the River Thames northward. Lord Darcy m. Elizabeth, dau. of Sir Thomas Grey, of Heton, and had issue,

JOHN, his successor.
Thomas, of Seamer.   Philip.
Elizabeth.

His lordship d 25 April, 1398, and was s. by his eldest son,
JOHN D'ARCY, 5th Baron D'Arcy, b. in 1377, summoned to

156

parliament from 19 August, 1399, to 21 September, 1411 This nobleman m. Margaret, dau. of Henry, Lord Grey de Wilton, and had issue,

PHILIP, his successor.
John, m. Joan, dau. of John, Lord Greystock; and his great-grandson, Thomas D'Arcy, was summoned to parliament as Lord D'Arcy of D'Arcy. (See that dignity.)
Elizabeth.   Maud.

His lordship d. in 1399 (leaving his widow, who m. 2ndly, Sir Thomas Swinford), and was s. by his elder son,
PHILIP D'ARCY, 6th Baron D'Arcy. This nobleman m. Eleanor, dau. of Henry, 3rd Lord Fitz-Hugh, and d. in 1418, before he had attained majority, leaving two daus., viz.,

I. ELIZABETH, m. to Sir James Strangeways, and had issue,
  1 Richard Strangeways, who m. Lady Elizabeth Nevil, one of the daus. and co-heirs of William Nevil, Lord Fauconberg, and Earl of Kent, and had issue.
  2 James, ancestor of the STRANGEWAYS of Ormsby, Little Holtby, Well and Alne, co. York.
  3 Henry.   4 John.   5 Robert.
  1 Eleanor, m. to Edmund Mauleverer, Esq.
II. MARGERY, m. to SIR JOHN CONYERS, Knt., and the heir-general of this marriage, Francis-Godolphin-D'Arcy, 7th DUKE of LEEDS, assumed the additional surname of D'Arcy. His grace d. s. p. 4 May, 1859, leaving his nephew, SACKVILLE-GEORGE LANE-FOX, now LORD CONYERS, his heir-general.

Upon the decease of his lordship, the BARONY OF D'ARCY fell into ABEYANCE between those ladies, and it so continues with their representatives.

Arms—Az., semée of cross-crosslets, and three cinquefoils, arg.

DARCY—BARONS DARCY, OF CHICHE, ESSEX.

By Letters Patent, dated 5 April, 1551.

Lineage.

This is presumed to have been a branch of the great baronial house of D'Arcy, which flourished in the counties of Lincoln and York, but the exact line could never be traced. The first of the family of note,
ROBERT DARCIE, was originally a lawyer's clerk, who laid the foundation of his fortune, by marrying Alice, the widow of John Ingoe, a rich merchant of Malden, in Essex, and dau. and co-heiress of Henry Fitz-Langley. She d. in the 26th HENRY VI., and was buried in the chapel of the Holy Trinity, within the church of All Hallows, in Malden, with this Robert Darcie, her husband, leaving issue by him,

I. SIR ROBERT DARCY, of Danbury.
II. John Darcy, of Tolleshunt, co. Essex.*

---

* D'ARCY OF TOLLESHUNT AND TIPTREE, ESSEX.

JOHN DARCY (by some called Thomas), brother of Sir Robert, of Danbury, was seated at Tolleshunt, which he acquired by his 2nd marriage with a dau. and co-heir of Bois, or Boys, of that place. His 1st wife was Anne, dau. of Sir Thomas Tyrell, of Heron, and by her, was father of
ANTHONY DARCY, who was sheriff of Essex in 1512. He m. Elizabeth, dau. of Christopher Wilson, Esq., and d. 18 October, 1540, having had issue,

Robert, who m. Joanes, dau. of John Bassel, Esq., and d. s. p. before his father, in 1535
THOMAS, of whom presently.
Anthony, settled at Norwich.

The eldest surviving son,
THOMAS DARCY, b. 1511, purchased the estate of Tiptree Priory. He m. thrice. By his 2nd wife, Anne, dau. of Sir John Mundy, Lord Mayor of London in 1522, he had issue,

I. Thomas, sheriff of Essex, 1580; m. Margaret, dau. of Eustace Sulyard, Esq., of Runnell, and d. 2 September, 1586, having had three sons and six daus.,
  1 Thomas, m. Camilla, dau. of Vincent Guiciardini, of Florence, and had by her, who m. 2ndly, Francis Harvey, Esq., of Ickworth, a son, Thomas, who d. s. p., and five daus.,
    Mary, m. to Christopher Nevill, 3rd son of Edward, Lord Abergavenny.
    Elizabeth, m. to Sir Henry Mildmay, Knt., of Woodham Walter, younger brother of Sir Thomas Mildmay, Bart.
    Bridget, m. to Sir George Fenner, Knt.

i. Eleanor, m. to Sir William Tyrell, of Heron.
ii. Anne, m. to — Montgomery.
iii. Margaret, m. to William Tyrell, of Gupping.
iv. Alice, m. to John Clopton.
v. Elizabeth, m. to Henry Bruyn.
vi. Catharine, m. to Robert Crane.

The elder son,

SIR ROBERT DARCY, of Maldon and Danbury, sheriff of Essex and Herts, 1420, m. Elizabeth, dau. of Sir Thomas Tyrell, of Heron, and had two sons and one dau., THOMAS, his heir; Robert; and Elizabeth, m. to William Barty or Berkley. He d. in the 9th EDWARD IV., and was s. by his elder son,

THOMAS DARCY, Esquire of the body to King HENRY VI. and King EDWARD IV., who m. Margaret, dau. and co-heir of John Harleston, of Suffolk, and d. in the 1st year of King HENRY VII., and was s. by his son,

ROGER DARCY, Esquire of the body to King HENRY VII., who m. Elizabeth, dau. of Sir Henry Wentworth, Knt., and widow of John Bourchier, Earl of Bath, and of Thomas Wyndham, and had a son, THOMAS, and three daus., Eleanor; Thomasine, wife of Sir Richard Southwell: and Elizabeth, wife of John Legh. He d. September, 1508, and was s. by his son,

SIR THOMAS DARCY, Knt., b. 1506, who in the 36th HENRY VIII., was constituted master of the king's artillery within the Tower of London, and in the next year made a gentleman of the privy chamber. In the 5th EDWARD VI., Sir Thomas, being then vice-chamberlain of the king's household, captain of the guard, and one of the principal knights of the privy chamber, was advanced to the peerage, as BARON DARCY, of Chiche, co. Essex, by letters patent, dated 5 April, 1551, and thereupon had summons to the parliament then sitting. He was also made a knight of the Garter. His lordship m. Lady Elizabeth de Vere, dau. of John, Earl of Oxford, and had surviving issue,

JOHN, his successor.
Thomasine, m. to Richard Southwell, Esq., of Wood Rising, Norfolk.
Constance, m. to Edmund Pyrton, Esq., of Bentley, Essex.

Lord Darcy d. in 1558, and was s. by his son,
JOHN DARCY, 2nd Lord Darcy, of Chiche. This nobleman accompanied William, Earl of Essex, into Ireland, in the 16th ELIZABETH. His lordship m. Frances, dau. of Richard, Lord Rich, lord chancellor of England, and had issue,

Frances, m. to Sir Henry Vane, Knt., secretary of state to CHARLES I.
Margaret m. to John Browne.

2 John, d. s. p.   3 EUSTACE.
1 Bridget.   2 Dorothy.
3 Margaret.   4 Anne.
5 Mary, m. to Richard Southwell, Esq., of Woodrising, co. Norfolk.
6 Elizabeth, m. to Henry Maynard, Esq., of Great Waltham.
ii. Anthony, who left an only dau.

By his 3rd wife, Elizabeth, dau. of John Heydon, of Baconsthorpe, and relict of — Bedingfeld, Esq., Mr. Thomas Darcy had further issue,

Brian, seated at Tiptree, where he erected a fine house out of the ruins of the Priory. He was sheriff of Essex, 1585. He m. Bridget, dau. of John Corbet, of Sprouston, co. Norfolk, Esq., and had besides two daus. and two sons, both d. young, an eldest son and heir,

John Darcy, created serjeant-at-law, 26 June, 1623, who m. Dorothy, dau. of Thomas Audeley, Esq., of Berechurch, and d. 1638, leaving a son,

Thomas Darcy, who m. 1621, Mary, dau. of Sir Andrew Astley, of Writtle, and by her had a dau., Mary, and a posthumous son,

Sir Thomas Darcy, b. 1632, who was of Tiptree and St. Clere Hall, in Oseth. He was created a Baronet, 20 June, 1660. He m. 1st, Cecily, dau. of Sir Symonds Dewes, Knt. and Bart., and by her had a dau., Anne, who d. young. Sir Thomas m. 2ndly, Jane, dau. and heir of Robert Cole, Esq., and by her had issue,

Robert, d. an infant.
THOMAS (Sir), s. his father in the baronetcy, and was father of Sir Thomas, the 3rd baronet, who left a son and three daus., viz.,

SIR GEORGE, the 4th bart., who d. a minor, and the estates went to his three sisters and co-heirs, viz.,
Frances, wife of Sir William Dawes, Bart., archbishop of York.
Mary, m. to Thomas Boteler, Esq.
Elizabeth, m. to William Pierpont, Esq., of Ollingham.

Brian.   William.   John.
Elizabeth.

THOMAS, his successor.
John, d. unm.
Mary, m. to Robert, Lord Lumley.

He d. in 1580, and was s. by his elder son,
THOMAS DARCY, 3rd Lord Darcy, of Chiche, who was advanced, 5 July, 1621, to the dignity of VISCOUNT COLCHESTER, with remainder to his son-in-law, Sir Thomas Savage, of Rocksavage, co. Chester, Bart., and created 4 November, 1626, EARL OF RIVERS, with a similar reversionary clause in the patent. His lordship m. Mary, dau. and heiress of Sir Thomas Kytson, Knt., of Hengrave, co. Suffolk, and had issue,

Thomas. who m. a dau. of Sir John Fitz, of Tavistock, and widow of Sir Alan Perci, but d. v. p., s. p.
Elizabeth, m. to Sir Thomas Savage, of Rocksavage, co. Chester, to whom, and his male issue, by the said Elizabeth, the viscounty and earldom of her father, were granted in reversion; but previously to inheriting those honours, Sir Thomas was himself created VISCOUNT SAVAGE, of Rocksavage, co. Chester, by letters patent, dated 6 November, 1626. He d. in 1635. His eldest son, then Sir John Savage, Bart., s. to the title of EARL OF RIVERS, in 1639.
Mary, m. to Roger Manwood, Esq., son of Sir Peter Manwood, K.B., of St. Stephen's, Canterbury.
Penelope, m. 1st, to Sir George Trenchard, Knt., of Wolverton, co. Dorset, s. p.; 2ndly, to Sir John Gage, Bart., of Firle, Suffolk (from which union the family of Gage, Viscounts Gage, and that of Gage, Baronets of Hengrave, derive); and 3rdly, to Sir William Hervey, of Ickworth, co. Suffolk.
Susan, d. unm.

His lordship d. in 1639, and his only son having d. s. p. previously, the BARONY OF DARCY, of Chiche, became EXTINCT, while the viscounty and earldom devolved, according to the limitation, and his estates passed to his four daus. as co-heiresses.

Arms—Arg., three cinquefoils, gu.

D'ARCY — BARONS D'ARCY, OF D'ARCY, BARONS D'ARCY, OF ASTON.

By Writ of Summons, dated 17 October, 1509.
Restored as Baron D'Arcy, of Aston, to *heirs male only*, by Act of Parliament, 1548.

Lineage.

The Honourable
JOHN D'ARCY, 2nd son of John, Lord D'Arcy, and Margery, dau. of Henry, Lord Grey de Wilton, became male representative of the family upon the decease of his brother Philip, Lord D'Arcy, 1418 (the barony fell, however, into ABEYANCE between the said Philip's two daus. as co-heirs, as it still continues with their descendants). Mr. D'Arcy, while a minor, living in ward to the king, m. without license, Joane, dau. of John, Lord Greystock, for which offence he paid a fine of 200 marks. Of this marriage were issue,

Richard, who d. v. p., leaving by his wife Eleanor, dau. of John, Lord Scrope, of Upsal, an only son,
WILLIAM, who s. his grandfather.
John.   George.   Thomas.   Philip.
Jane, m. 1st, to John Beaumont, and 2ndly, to Giles Daubeney.

John D'Arcy d. in the 32nd HENRY VI., and was s. by his grandson,
SIR WILLIAM D'ARCY, then but four years of age. This gentleman m. Euphemia, dau. of Sir Thomas Langton, of Farnly, co. York, and dying in the 3rd HENRY VII., was s. by his son,
SIR THOMAS D'ARCY, a person who obtained high honours and distinction in the reign of HENRY VII., and was called to the peerage by the succeeding monarch. In the 12th HENRY VII., Thomas D'Arcy was one of the northern lords that marched with Thomas, Earl of Surrey, to the relief of Norham Castle, then besieged by the King of Scotland, and the next year being a knight of the king's body, he was made constable of Bamburgh Castle, in Northumberland; in two years, subsequently, he was constituted captain of the town and castle of Berwick, as also warden of the east and middle marches towards Scotland, and he had a special commission soon afterwards to exercise the office of constable and marshal of England against certain rebels, being appointed about the same time constable of Sheriff Hoton, co. York, and steward of that lordship. In the 17th of the same reign he was one of

the commissioners appointed to receive the oath of JAMES, the 4th King of Scotland, upon a treaty of peace, and in four years afterwards being then of the privy council, he was made general warden of the marches towards Scotland. An office confirmed to him jointly with Sir Thomas D'Arcy, Knt., upon the accession of King HENRY VIII., when he was summoned to parliament, from 17 October, 1509, to 3 November, 1529, as BARON D'ARCY, OF D'ARCY, installed a knight of the Garter, and sworn of the privy council. From this period he enjoyed the confidence for several years of his sovereign, being amongst those who exhibited articles against Wolsey, and subscribed the celebrated letter to CLEMENT VII., until, at length, absenting himself from parliament sooner than sanction the dissolution of the religious houses, and finally joining in Ask's rebellion, called " The Pilgrimage of Grace," he was convicted of high treason, on the charge of delivering up Pontefract Castle to the rebels, and beheaded on Tower Hill, 20 June, 1538, when the BARONY OF D'ARCY fell under the attainder. His lordship had m. 1st, Dowsabel, dau. and heiress of Sir Richard Tempest, Knt., of Ridlesdale, co. Northumberland, by whom he had issue,

I. GEORGE, of whom presently, as the restored Lord D'Arcy.
II. Arthur, who m. Mary, dau. and co-heir of Sir Nicholas Carew, of Beddington, Surrey, K.G., and dying in 1561, left issue,

  1 Henry, m. Catherine, dau. of Sir John Fermor, and widow of M. Pulteney, Esq., and left an only dau. and heiress,

    Catherine, who m. Gervase, Lord Clifton, and had a dau.,

      Catherine, who laid claim to the Barony of Clifton in 1674, and had the same allowed in parliament.

  2 Thomas; m. Elizabeth, co-heir of John, Lord Coniers, and had issue,

    Sir Coniers D'Arcy (see D'ARCY, LORDS HOLDERNESS).

  3 Edward, from whom the D'Arcys of Kent derive.
  4 Arthur, ancestor of the D'Arcys of Aldington, co. Northampton.
  5 Francis, m. to Catherine, dau. of Ed. Leigh, Esq., of Rushall, co Stafford.
  1 Elizabeth, m. to Lewis, Lord Mordaunt.

Lord D'Arcy m. 2ndly, Elizabeth, sister of William Sandys, 1st Lord Sandys, by whom he had an only dau.,

Elizabeth, m. to Sir Marmaduke Constable, of Spaldingmoor, co. York.

GEORGE D'ARCY, the eldest son, received the honour of knighthood from King HENRY VIII., at the siege of Tournay, and was restored in blood, with the dignity of BARON D'ARCY to himself, and his heirs male, by an act of parliament passed in the 2nd EDWARD VI., anno 1548. This nobleman m. Dorothy, dau. and heiress of Sir John Melton, of Aston, co. York, by whom he had issue,

JOHN, his successor.
Agnes, m. to Sir Thomas Fairfax.
Mary, m. 1st, to Henry Babington, Esq., and 2ndly, to Henry Foljamb, Esq.
Edith, m. to Sir Thomas Dauney, Knt.
Dorothy, m. to Sir Thomas Metham, Knt.
Elizabeth, m. to Bryan Stapleton, Esq., of Carleton.

His lordship, who from the restoration of his honours bore the title of LORD D'ARCY, of Aston, d. 23 September, 1558, and was s. by his son,

JOHN D'ARCY, as 2nd BARON D'ARCY, of Aston. This nobleman was with the Earl of Essex in the expedition made into Ireland in the 16th ELIZABETH. His lordship m. Agnes, dau. of Thomas Babington, Esq., of Dethick, co. Derby, by whom he had an only son,

MICHAEL, who m. Margaret, dau. of Thomas Wentworth, Esq., and dying v. p., left issue,

JOHN, who s. to the title at the decease of his grandfather.
Margaret, d. unm.
ANNE, m. Thomas Savile, Esq., of Copley, co. York, and the great granddau. of this marriage, MARY-ELIZABETH, only child of Sir John Savile, Bart., and wife of LORD THOMAS HOWARD, is now represented by the LORDS STOURTON and PETRE.

Lord D'Arcy d. 1587, and was s. by his grandson,

JOHN D'ARCY, 3rd Lord D'Arcy, of Aston, who was summoned to parliament as "Johanni D'Arcie and Meinill." His lordship m. four times, 1st, Rosamond, dau. of Sir Peter Freschevile, of Stavely, co. Derby, and by her had issue,

JOHN, who d. v. p., unm.
Rosamond, } both d. unm.
Elizabeth, }

He m. 2ndly, a dau. of Sir Christopher Wray, and widow, 1st, of Godfrey Foljambe, Esq., and 2ndly, of Sir William Bowes. This lady dying in 1622, his lordship m. 3rdly, Mary Bellasis,

158

dau. of Lord Fauconberg, and sister of Lady Osborne, of Kiveton; and 4thly, Elizabeth West, a co-heiress of the Wests of Firbeck, which lady m. 2ndly, Sir Francis Fane. Lord D'Arcy, d. 1635, when the BARONY OF D'ARCY, of Aston, for want of a male heir, became EXTINCT.

Arms—Az., semée of cross-crosslets, and three cinquefoils, arg

---

D'ARCY—BARONS D'ARCY, EARLS OF HOLDERNESS.

Barony of D'Arcy, by Letters Patent, dated 10 August, 1641.
Earldom, by Letters Patent, dated 5 December, 1682.

Lineage.

The Honourable
SIR ARTHUR D'ARCY, 3rd son of the beheaded and attainted Lord D'Arcy, temp. HENRY VIII. m. Mary, dau., and co-heir of Sir Nicholas Carew, of Beddington, Surrey, and dying 1561, left, with several other children,

THOMAS D'ARCY, who, upon the decease of his elder brother Sir Henry D'Arcy, without male issue, became chief of the family. This gentleman m. Elizabeth, dau. and co-heir of John, Baron Conyers, and dying in 1605, was s. by his only child,

SIR CONYERS D'ARCY, who being the principal male branch then remaining of this ancient and noble family, set forth in a petition to King CHARLES I., in that parliament, begun at Westminster 3 November, 1640, that after the attainder of Thomas, Lord D'Arcy, his great-grandfather, in the 29th HENRY VIII., Sir George D'Arcy, Knt., eldest son of the said Thomas, being restored in blood by King EDWARD VI., obtained a grant of the title and dignity of LORD D'ARCY to himself and the heirs male of his body; and that by the death of John, Lord D'Arcy, lord of Aston, in Yorkshire, without issue male, in the 11th of his majesty's reign, the title and dignity of Lord D'Arcy was utterly extinct, did humbly desire, that being grandchild and heir male of Sir Arthur D'Arcy, Knt., and likewise son and heir of Elizabeth, dau. and co-heir of John, Lord Conyers, lineal heir to Margery, dau. and co-heir to Philip, Lord D'Arcy, son of John, Lord D'Arcy, one of the barons of this realm in the time of King HENRY IV., his majesty would be pleased to declare, restore and confirm to him, the said Sir Conyers D'Arcy, and to the heirs male of his body, the dignity of LORD D'ARCY with such precedency as the said John, Lord D'Arcy had, and by right from his ancestors then enjoyed. Whereupon his majesty graciously condescending, he did by letters patent, dated at Westminster, 10 August, 1641, restore and confirm to the said Sir Conyers D'Arcy, and the heirs male of his body, the dignity of BARON D'ARCY, as enjoyed by his aforesaid ancestor John, Lord D'Arcy, and he had summons to parliament accordingly.

His lordship was seated at Hornby Castle, and having m. Dorothy, dau. of Sir Henry Bellasyse, Bart., had issue,

CONYERS, his successor.
William (Sir) m. Dorothy, dau. of Sir George Selby, Knt.
Henry, of Newpark, co. York. m. Mary, dau. of William Scrope, Esq., of Highley, co. Durham.
Thomas, of Winkborne.
Marmaduke, gentleman usher of the privy council to King CHARLES II., d. unm.
James, of Sedbury Park, co York, M.P. for Richmond, anno 1660; m. Isabel, dau. of Sir Marmaduke Wyvill, Bart., and had issue,

  James, created BARON D'ARCY, of Navan.

Barbara, m. to Matthew Hutton, Esq., of Marske, co. York.
Ursula, m. to John Stillington, Esq., of Kelfield, co. York.
Dorothy, m. to John Dalton, Esq., of Hawkeswell, co. York, ancestor by her of the NORCLIFFES, OF LANGTON, and the DALTONS OF SLENINGFORD, CO. YORK.
Anne, m. to Thomas Metcalf, Esq., of Routh Park, co. Lincoln.
Grace, m. 1st, to Geo. Best, Esq., of Middleton, and 2ndly, to Sir Francis Molineux, of Mansfield, co. Nottingham.
Margaret, m. to Acton Burnell, Esq., of Winkburn Hall, co. Notts, whose descendant, D'Arcy Burnell, Esq., of Winkburn Hall, devised his estates to his cousin, Peter Pegge-Burnell, Esq.

Lord D'Arcy d. 3 March, 1653, and was s. by his eldest son,

CONYERS D'ARCY, 2nd Baron D'Arcy, summoned to parliament from 8 May, 1661, to 1 March, 1680, as " Conyers D'Arcie de D'Arcie," and in the two last writs with the addition of " Meynill." This nobleman was advanced to the dignity of

EARL or HOLDERNESS by letters patent, dated 5 December, 1682. His lordship *m.* Grace, dau. and heiress of Thomas Rokeby, Esq., of Skyers, co. York, and had issue,

> CONYERS, his successor, who had been summoned to the House of Lords, in November, 1680, as Baron Conyers.
> URSULA, *m.* to Sir Christopher Wyvill, Bart., of Constable Burton, co. York.
> Elizabeth, *m.* to Sir Henry Stapleton, Bart., of Myton, co. York.
> Grace, *m.* to Sir John Legard, Bart., of Ganton, co. York.
> Margaret, *m.* to Sir Henry Marwood, Bart., of Little Busby, co. York.

The earl *d.* 14 June, 1689, and was *s.* by his son,

> CONYERS D'ARCY, Lord Conyers, as 2nd Earl of Holderness. This nobleman *m.* no less than four times; 1st, Lady Catherine Fane, dau. of Francis, Earl of Westmoreland, by whom he had no issue; 2ndly, Lady Frances Howard, dau. of Thomas, Earl of Berkshire, by whom he had,

1. John, M.P. for the co. of York, *m.* Bridget, dau. of Robert Sutton, Lord Lexington, and predeceasing his father and grandfather, on 7 June, 1688, left issue,
   1 ROBERT, successor to his grandfather.
   2 Conyers (Sir) M.P. for the co. of York in 1707, and in several succeeding parliaments; master of the horse to Queen ANNE and King GEORGE I., and subsequently comptroller of the household, and a member of the privy council; *m.* twice, 1st, Mary, dau. of William, Earl of Portland, and widow of Algernon, Earl of Essex; and 2ndly, Elizabeth, dau. of John Rotheram, Esq., and widow of Sir Theophilus Napier, and of Thomas, Lord Howard of Effingham, but *d. s. p.* 1 December, 1758.
   1 Elizabeth, *m.* to Sir Ralph Milbanke, Bart., of Halnaby, co York.
   2 Charlotte, *m.* to Wardel George Westley, Esq., a commissioner of the customs.
II. Philip. } both *d. unm.*
III. Charles, }

The earl *m.* 3rdly, Lady Frances Seymour, dau. of William, 2nd Duke of Somerset, and widow of Richard, 1st Viscount Molineux, and of Thomas Wriothesly, Earl of Southampton. His lordship *m.* 4thly, Elizabeth, dau. and co-heir of John, Lord Frescheville, and widow of Philip Warwick, Esq., but had no issue by those ladies. He *d.* in 1692, and was *s.* by his grandson,

> ROBERT D'ARCY, 3rd Earl of Holderness, first commissioner of trade, in 1718, and sworn of the privy council. His lordship *m.* Frederica, eldest surviving dau. and co-heir of Meinhardt Schomberg, Duke of Schomberg, and had issue,

> Meinhardt-Frederic, who *d.* young.
> ROBERT, successor to the honours.
> Louisa-Carolina, *m.* to William-Henry, Earl of Ancram, afterwards (4th) Marquess of Lothian.

The earl *d.* 20 January, 1721-2, and was *s.* by his only surviving son,

> ROBERT D'ARCY, 4th Earl of Holderness. His lordship was appointed, in 1740, lord-lieutenant of the North Riding of Yorkshire, and in the following year was admitted gentleman of his majesty's bed-chamber. In June, 1744, he was accredited ambassador to the republic of Venice; in 1749, ministerplenipotentiary to the States-General of the United Provinces—and in 1751, his lordship was constituted one of the principal secretaries of state, and sworn of the privy council. In 1752, he was appointed one of the lords justices during the king's absence at Hanover. He resigned the secretaryship of state, but was reappointed in 1754. He was subsequently admiral and warden of the Cinque Ports. In 1771 he sold the estate of Aston to Mr. Verelst, governor of Bengal. His lordship *m.* at the Hague, in November, 1742, Mary, dau. of Francis Doublet, member of the States of Holland, by whom he had issue,

I. George, } both *d.* young before the earl.
II. Thomas, }
I. AMELIA, *b.* 12 October, 1754, *m.* 1st, in 1773, Francis-Godolphin then Marquess of Carmarthen, afterwards 5th Duke of Leeds, by whom she had issue,
   1 GEORGE-WILLIAM-FREDERIC, 6th Duke of Leeds.
   2 Francis-Godolphin Osborne (Lord), created BARON GODOLPHIN in 1832, father of GEORGE-GODOLPHIN, 8th DUKE OF LEEDS.
   1 Mary-Henrietta-Juliana, *m.* to Thomas, 2nd Earl of Chichester.

Her ladyship being divorced from the Marquess, by Act of Parliament in May, 1779, *m.* 2ndly, John Byron, Esq., and had an only dau.,

> Augusta-Mary Byron, *b.* 26 January, 1783, *m.* in 1807, to John Leigh, Esq.

Lady Conyers (having succeeded her father as BARONESS CONYERS), *d.* in 1784.

159

The Earl of Holderness *d.* in 1778, when the *Earldom,* for want of male issue, became EXTINCT, as did the Barony of D'Arcy, created by the patent of 1641, but the Barony of "CONYERS" devolved upon his only surviving dau., Amelia, then Marchioness of Carmarthen, and at her ladyship's decease, passed to her eldest son,

> George-William-Frederick, 6th Duke of Leeds, K.G., and is now enjoyed by his grace's grandson, SACKVILLE-GEORGE-LANE FOX, present LORD CONYERS.

Arms—Az., semée of cross-crosslets, and three cinquefoils, arg.

D'ARCY—BARON D'ARCY, OF NAVAN.

By Letters Patent, dated 13 September, 1721.

Lineage.

JAMES D'ARCY, Esq., of Sedbury Park, co. York, son of the Hon. James D'Arcy, 6th son of Sir Conyers D'Arcy, Lord D'Arcy, in the peerage of England, was created an Irish peer in 1721, as BARON D'ARCY, *of Navan, co. Meath,* with remainder to his grandson, James D'Arcy, Esq., son of William Jessop, Esq. and Mary his wife, eldest dau. of the said James Lord D'Arcy, and the heirs male of his body. His lordship *m.* 1st a dau. of — Payler, Esq., of Nunmonkton; 2ndly, Anne, eldest dau. of Ralph, Lord Stawel; and 3rdly, Mary, eldest dau. of Sir William Hicks, Bart. He had no son, but several daus. of whom,

1. MARY, *m.* William Jessop, Esq., of Broom Hall, near Sheffield, M.P. for Aldborough, and one of the justices of Chester, and *d.* 17 June, 1737, having had issue,
   1 JAMES JESSOP, who assumed the surname and arms of D'ARCY, and *s.* his grandfather as 2nd LORD D'ARCY.
   2 Barbara Jessop, *m.* to Andrew Wilkinson, Esq., M.P., of Boroughbridge, and had issue,
      Charles Wilkinson, M.P., *d. unm.* in 1782.
      William Wilkinson, col. in the army; *d. unm.* in 1761.
      Andrew Wilkinson, capt. R.N., M.P.; *m.* Dorothy, dau. of Richard Lawson, Esq., but *d. s. p.* in 1785.
      James Wilkinson, M.A., vicar of Sheffield; *d. unm.* 1805.
      Thomas Wilkinson, capt. engineers; *d. unm.* in 1773.
      George Wilkinson, East India Company's service; *d. unm.* in 1761.
      John Wilkinson, whose only dau., BARBARA-ISABELLA, *m.* the Rev. Marmaduke Lawson, M.A., and had four sons and three daus.; of the former the eldest, Marmaduke Lawson, Esq., M.P., *d. unm.* in 1823; and the 2nd, ANDREW LAWSON, Esq., was of Aldborough Lodge and Boroughbridge Hall, Yorkshire. (*See* BURKE's *Landed Gentry*)
   3 Isabella Jessop, *m.* to John Eyre, Esq., of Hopton, co. Derby, who took the name of GELL.
   4 Mary, } *d. unm.*
   5 Bethia }
II. Elizabeth, *m.* 1726, to John Hutton, Esq., of Marske, co. York.

Lord D'Arcy *d.* in 1731, and was *s.* by his grandson,

> JAMES JESSOP, 2nd Lord D'Arcy, who *d. unm.* in 1733, aged eighty-three (having devised his estate of Sedbury to his cousin, HENRY D'ARCY,* of Colborne on the Swale), and with him the Barony of D'ARCY, of Navan, EXPIRED.

Arms—Az., semée of cross-crosslets, and three cinquefoils, arg.

DAUBENEY—BARONS DAUBENEY, EARL OF BRIDGEWATER.

Barony, by Writ of Summons, dated 2 November, 1295.
Barony, by Letters Patent, dated 13 March, 1486.
Earldom, by Letters Patent, dated 19 July, 1538.

Lineage.

Amongst the most distinguished companions in arms of the CONQUEROR, was

---

* This Henry D'Arcy left an only dau., Maria-Catharine, who *m.* in 1738, Sir Robert Hildyard, Bart., of Winestead, and was mother of SIR ROBERT D'ARCY HILDYARD, Bart., who *d. s. p.* 1814. Henry D'Arcy by his will, 18 December, 1750, devised Sedbury to Sir Conyers D'Arcy, Sir Robert Hildyard, and John Hutton, Esq., of Marske (which last had married Elizabeth, dau. of James Lord D'Arcy), and two others in trust, for her grandson, Sir Robert D'Arcy Hildyard, Bart., who *d.* 6 November, 1814, and his male heirs; failing which, to Matthew, 2nd son of John and Elizabeth Hutton, and his male heirs; failing which to James, 3rd son of John and Elizabeth Hutton. Matthew *d. unm.* 1782, and James D'Arcy Hutton *s.* to Sedbury at the decease of his father

ROBERT DE TODENI, a nobleman of Normandy, upon whom the victorious monarch conferred, with numerous other grants, an estate in the county of Lincoln, upon the borders of Leicestershire. Here De Todeni erected a stately castle, and from the *fair view* it commanded, gave it the designation of Belvoir Castle, and here he established his chief abode. At the time of the General Survey, this powerful personage possessed no less than eighty extensive lordships, viz., two in Yorkshire, one in Essex, four in Suffolk, one in Cambridge, two in Hertfordshire, three in Bucks, four in Gloucestershire, three in Bedfordshire, nine in Northamptonshire, two in Rutland, thirty-two in Lincolnshire, and seventeen in Leicestershire. "Of this Robert," saith Dugdale, "I have not seen any other memorial, than that the Coucher-Book of Belvoir recordeth: which is, that bearing a venerable esteem to our sometime much celebrated protomartyr, St. Alban, he founded, near to his castle, a priory for monks, and annexed it as a cell to that great abbey in Hertfordshire, formerly erected by the devout King OFFA, in honour of that most holy man." Robert de Todeni, Lord of Belvoir, d. in 1088, leaving issue by his wife Adela, viz.,

WILLIAM, who assumed, from what reason is unascertained, the surname of ALBINI, and was known as "William de Albini, Brito," in contradistinction to another great baron, "William de Albini, Pincerna," from whom the Earls of Arundel descended.

Beringer, who had divers lordships in the co. of York, as well as others in Lincoln, Oxford, and Nottinghamshires.

Geoffery, who had three sons, Oliver, Iwan, and Geoffrey de Chauveni.

Robert.

Agnes, *m.* to Hubert de Rye, a person of note in Lincolnshire.

He was *s.* by his eldest son,

WILLIAM DE ALBINI, *Brito*, Lord of Belvoir, who, in the Chapter House of St. Albans, confirmed all the grants of his father and mother to the church of our lady at Belvoir, desiring that he might be admitted in the fraternity as those his parents had been. This feudal lord acquired great renown at the celebrated battle of Tinchebray, in Normandy, where, commanding the horse, he charged the enemy with so much spirit, that he determined at once the fate of the day. Of the exploit, Matthew Paris says, "In this encounter chiefly deserveth honour the most heroic William de Albini, the Briton, who, with his sword, broke through the enemy, and terminated the battle." He subsequently adhered to the Empress MAUD, and had his castle of Belvoir, with all his other lands, seized by King STEPHEN, and transferred to Ranulph, Earl of Chester. He *m.* Maud, dau. of Simon de St. Liz, 1st Earl of Huntingdon, widow of Robert, son of Richard de Tunbridge, and dying about the year 1155, left two sons, viz.,

I. WILLIAM, surnamed MESCHINES, and likewise BRITO, who had Belvoir Castle, and a considerable portion of his lands restored by King HENRY II. In the 14th of which monarch's reign he *d.* and was *s.* by his son, by his 1st wife, Adelisa,

WILLIAM DE ALBINI, feudal Lord of Belvoir, who, in the 6th of RICHARD I., was with that monarch in the army in Normandy. And the next year was sheriff of the counties of Warwick and Leicester, as he was subsequently of Rutlandshire. In the 2nd of King JOHN he had special license to make a park at Stoke, in Northampton, and liberty to hunt the fox and hare (it lying within the royal forest of Rockingham). Afterwards, however, he took up arms with the other barons, and leaving Belvoir well fortified, he assumed the governorship of Rochester Castle, which he held out for three months against the Royalists, and ultimately only surrendered when reduced to the last state of famine. Upon the surrender of Rochester William Albini was sent prisoner to Corfe Castle, and there detained until his freedom became one of the conditions upon which Belvoir capitulated, and until he paid a ransom of 6,000 marks. In the reign of HENRY III. we find him upon the other side, and a principal commander at the battle of Lincoln. *anno* 1217, where his former associates sustained so signal a defeat. This stout baron, who had been one of the celebrated Twenty-five, appointed to enforce the observance of MAGNA CHARTA—*m.* 1st, Margery, dau. of Odonel de Umframville, by whom he had issue,

WILLIAM.

Odinel (Sir).   Robert.

Nicholas, rector of Bottesford.

He *m.* 2ndly, Agatha, dau. and co-heir of William Trusbut, and dying in 1236, was *s.* by his eldest son,

WILLIAM DE ALBINI, feudal Lord of Belvoir, who, like his father, adhered firmly to King HENRY III. He *m.* 1st, Albreda, dau. of Henry Lord Biseth, and 2ndly, Isabel ———, and left issue by the former, an only dau. and heiress,

ISABEL DE ALBINI, who *m.* Robert de Ros, Lord Ros of Hamlake (*see* that dignity), and conveyed to him

the feudal barony and castle of Belvoir, which eventually passed from the family of Ros to that of Manners, by which they are now enjoyed in the person of the DUKE OF RUTLAND.

II. Ralph.

The 2nd son of William de Albini, Brito,

RALPH DE ALBINI, obtained fifteen knights' fees from his brother William, in the 12th of HENRY II., and in the 28th of the same reign, he gave 200 marks for license to marry Sibella de Valoines, widow of Robert, Baron Ross, of Hamlake and Werke, and had two sons,

PHILIP, his heir.

Ralph, who, by Isabel his wife, had three sons,

PHILIP *s.* his uncles.

ELIAS *s.* his brother.

Owen.

Ralph de Albini, who founded some religious houses, *d.* at Acre, in the Holy Land, in 1190, and was *s.* by

PHILIP DE ALBINI, who, in the 8th of King JOHN, was governor of Ludlow Castle, in Shropshire, and in six years afterwards of the Isle of Jersey. He was subsequently governor of the castle of Bridgnorth, and he obtained some territorial grants from the crown; but notwithstanding those favours, he enrolled himself under the baronial banner, and participated in the triumph of Runnimede. Again, however, he changed his colours, and adhered to King JOHN during the remainder of his reign. Upon the accession of HENRY III. he assisted at that monarch's coronation, and was one of his principal generals at the battle of Lincoln. Independently, however, of his military renown, he appears to have acquired the reputation of a man of learning, and Matthew Paris designates him "a most faithful teacher and instructor of the king." In this reign he was governor of Guernsey and Jersey, and governor of the castle of Devizes. Ultimately being signed with the cross, he repaired to the Holy Land, and dying there in 1235, was *s.* by his nephew,

PHILIP DE ALBINI, who had acted as lieutenant to his uncle in the government of Guernsey and Jersey, and in the 8th of HENRY III. had the hundred of Wichton granted to him for his better support in the king's service. He was *s.* at his decease in 1294 *s. p.*, by his brother,

ELIAS DAUBENEY, who was summoned to parliament as a Baron, from 2 November, 1295, to 22 January, 1305. His lordship was *s.* at his decease, in 1305, by his son (by Hawise, his wife),

SIR RALPH DAUBENEY, 2nd baron, summoned to parliament 25 February, 1342. This nobleman was one of the knights of the Bath, solemnly created in the 20th EDWARD II., and had his robes as a banneret. In the 8th of EDWARD III. he was in the expedition then made into Scotland, and again in a similar expedition made in four years afterwards. His lordship *m.* 1st, Katherine, dau. of William de Thweng, Lord Thweng, and sister and co-heir of Thomas de Thweng, Lord Thweng, a priest, by whom he had an only dau.,

ELIZABETH, *m.* to Sir William Botreaux, Knt.

The baron *m.* 2ndly, Alice Montacute, dau. of Lord Montacute, and had a son,

SIR GILES DAUBENEY, Knt., 3rd baron, but never summoned to parliament. This nobleman *m.* Alianor, dau. of Henry de Wylington, and dying in 1386, had three sons,

I. GILES, of whom presently.

II. Thomas.   III. William.

The eldest son,

SIR GILES DAUBENEY, then aged fifteen, 4th baron, but never summoned to parliament. This Giles was sheriff of Bedfordshire and Bucks, in the 10th HENRY VI. He *d.* about the year 1402, leaving a son,

JOHN DAUBENEY, aged nine, who dying in his minority in 1410, was *s.* by his brother,

GILES DAUBENEY, sheriff of Beds and Bucks, who *m.* 1st, Joan, dau. of Philip, Lord Darcy, and had a son,

WILLIAM, of whom presently.

He *m.* 2ndly, Mary, one of the daus. and co-heirs of Simon Leake, of Cotham. The son and heir,

WILLIAM DAUBENEY, 5th baron, but never summoned to parliament, who, doing homage in the 24th HENRY VI., had livery of his lands: and in the following year obtained a royal charter for a fair at his lordship of South Petherton. He *m.* Alice, dau. and co-heir of John Stornton, of Preston, and was *s.* by his son,

GILES DAUBENEY, 6th baron, who in the 17th EDWARD IV., being one of the esquires of the body to the king, had, in consideration of his many services, a grant for life of the custody of the king's park at Petherton, near Bridgewater

Upon the accession of RICHARD III., he appears to have been one of the first consulted by the friends of the Earl of Richmond, and to have cordially joined in the conspiracy to place that nobleman upon the throne. Which, being accomplished by the victory of Bosworth, he was made one of the new monarch, HENRY VII.'s, chief counsellors—appointed constable of the castle of Bristol, master of the Mint, and created by letters patent, dated 12 March, 1486,* LORD DAUBENEY. In the 2nd of HENRY VII., his lordship was retained by indenture to serve the king in his fleet at sea; and in the next year he was constituted one of the chamberlains of the exchequer. He was afterwards joined with Richard Fox, bishop of Exeter, in an embassy to France, and subsequently made justice itinerant with Sir Reginald Bray, of all the king's forests on the south of Trent. Upon the fall of Sir William Stanley, in the 10th of HENRY VII., Lord Daubeney succeeded to the lord chamberlainship of the king's household. In the 12th of the same reign his lordship was about to march at the head of a large army into Scotland, but his course was diverted by the insurrection of Lord Audley and the Cornishmen; and he participated in the victory obtained over those rebels at Blackheath—as he did in that of Taunton, the next year, achieved over Perkin Warbeck and his partisans. In the 19th of HENRY VII. he was made constable of the castle Bridgewater, and had previously been honoured with the Garter. His lordship m. Elizabeth, dau. of Sir John Arundel, of Lanhern, in Cornwall, by whom he had issue,

HENRY, his successor.
Cecily, m. to John Bourchier, Lord Fitz-Warine, afterwards Earl of Bath.

He d. 28 May, 1507, and was s. by his son,

HENRY DAUBENEY, 2nd baron under the new creation, but 7th of the old, who was created EARL OF BRIDGEWATER, 19 July, 1538. His lordship m. Lady Catherine Howard, dau. of Thomas, Duke of Norfolk, but had no issue. He d. in 1548, when the BARONY OF DAUBENEY, created in 1486, and the EARLDOM OF BRIDGEWATER, became EXTINCT—but the Barony created by the writ of EDWARD I., anno 1295, which have passed to his sister Cecily, Countess of Bath, and it is probably now vested in the descendants of that lady, if such exist; if not, it is in the heirs-general of Elias, the 1st BARON DAUBENEY.

Arms—Gu., four lozenges in fesse, arg.

D'AUNEY—BARON D'AUNEY.

By Writ of Summons, 1st EDWARD III.

Lineage.

NICHOLAS D'AUNEY, lord of the manor of Shunock, in Cornwall, was summoned to parliament as a Baron, in the 1st of EDWARD III., but never afterwards, nor any of his posterity. His lordship made a journey to the Holy Land, whence he brought home a rich and curious medal, said to be yet in the possession of the family of Burton-Dawnay, Viscounts Downe, in Ireland, which claims descent from Nicholas.

Arms—Arg., a bend, sa., between two cotises, az.

DAVYS, VISCOUNT MOUNTCASHEL.

By Letters Patent, dated 21 Jan. 1705-6.

Lineage.

SIR PAUL DAVYS, of St. Catherine's, co. Dublin, and of Kill, co. Kildare (son of JOHN DAVYS, of Kill), general and principal clerk of the council, one of the commissioners appointed 1660, to settle the affairs of Ireland, a privy councillor, prime secretary of state for Ireland 1661, and M.P. for Enniskillen 1634, and for the co. Kildare, 1661. This gentleman, who had large grants of lands in the co. Donegal, m. 1st, Margaret, eldest dau. of Arthur Ussher, Esq., and by her (who d. 20 July, 1633) had a son, JAMES, who was buried at St. Audeon's, Dublin, 22 July, 1638. Sir Paul m. 2ndly, Anne, 6th dau. of Sir William Parsons, Bart., of Garradyce, co. Leitrim, surveyor-general of Ireland, M.P., and sister of Catherine, Lady Santry, and of Elizabeth, wife of Sir William Ussher. By this lady he had issue,

George, buried 11 March, 1660.
William (Sir), knighted 3 August, 1662. He was recorder of Dublin, 1660, attorney-general for Munster, 1660, prime secretary of state and clerk of the council, and lord chief justice of the King's Bench. He m. 1st, 27 July, 1664, Martha, 3rd dau. of Michael Boyle, archbishop of Armagh, and lord chancellor of Ireland, and by her (who d. 14 May,

1680) left a dau., Mary, who was buried at St. Audeon's, 20 August, 1683. He m. 2ndly, Elizabeth, 2nd dau. of George, 16th Earl of Kildare, and widow of Callaghan McCarthy, Earl of Clancarty, but by her had no issue.
JOHN, of whom presently.
Elizabeth, m. 1st, to Sir John Bramhall, Bart., of Rathmullen, M.P., and 2ndly, to Sir John Topham, Knt.

Sir Paul m. 3rdly, Mary, dau. of William Crofton, Esq., of Temple House, co. Sligo, by Mary his wife, eldest dau. of Sir William Ussher, Knt., and had a dau., Ursula, who m. Sir Francis Blundel, Bart., M.P. for the King's Co., and was buried at St. Audeon's, 23 May, 1673. Sir Paul d. 7 September, 1672, and was s. by his son,

SIR JOHN DAVYS, of Thomastown, co. Dublin, Knt., b. 1646. This gentleman was prime secretary of state and clerk of the privy council. Sir John, whose will bears date 1684, left by Anne his wife, two sons, Paul and Robert, and one dau. The elder son,

SIR PAUL DAVYS, Knt., of St. Catherine's, near Dublin, high sheriff in 1700, was raised to the peerage of Ireland, as BARON and VISCOUNT MOUNTCASHEL, in the co. Tipperary, 21 January, 1705-6. His lordship m. Lady Catherine M'Carty, dau. of Callaghan, Earl of Clancarty, and had two sons, JAMES and EDWARD, and two daus.: Elizabeth, wife of her 1st cousin, the Hon. Justin M Carty, 2nd son of Donogh, Earl of Clancarty, and Margaret, m. 8 June, 1738, James Barry, 5th Earl of Barrymore. He d. 5 August, 1716, and was s. by his son,

JAMES, 2nd Viscount Mountcashel, at whose decease, 10 March, 1718-19, aged nine years, the title devolved on his brother,

EDWARD, 3rd viscount, who d. unm. 30 July, 1736, whereupon the title became EXTINCT.

Arms—Sa., on a chev., arg., three trefoils slipped, vert.

DAWNAY—BARON DAWNAY, OF COWICK.

(See BURKE's Extant Peerage.)

DAWSON—VISCOUNT CREMORNE.

(See DAWSON, EARL OF DARTRY, in BURKE's Extant Peerage.)

DE BURGH—EARL OF ULSTER.

Lineage.

RICHARD DE BURGH, surnamed the Great, Lord of Connaught, son of William FitzAdelm de Burgh, Lord Deputy of Ireland temp. HENRY II., was also Viceroy of that kingdom from 1227 to 1229. This Richard built the Castle of Galway, 1232; he d. on his passage to France, January, 1243, whither he was proceeding, attended "by his barons and knights," to meet the King of England at Bordeaux. He m. Una of Agnes, dau. of Hugh O'Conor (King of Connaught), son or Cathal Crobhdearg, or the red hand, and had two sons,

I. WALTER, his successor.
II. William, known by the surname of Athankip, from being put to death at that place by the King of Connaught. He was s. by his son,
    Sir William, who, having m. a dau. of the family of Mac-Jordan, left, with other issue, at his decease, in 1324,
        Ulick, ancestor of the EARLS and MARQUESSES of CLANRICARDE.
        Edmond (Sir), from whom the (extinct) VISCOUNTS BOURKE of MAYO, and the extant EARLS OF MAYO.
        Richard.
        Redmond, from whom several eminent families of BURKE, in the county of Galway, have descended.
        Thomas (Sir), appointed lord-treasurer of Ireland in 1331.
        John.
        Henry.

The eldest son,
WALTER DE BURGH, Lord of Connaught, m. Maud, dau. and heir of Hugh de Laci, Earl of Ulster (by Emmeline, his wife, dau. and heir of Walter de Ridlesford, Lord of Bray), and became in consequence EARL OF ULSTER, in her right at her father's decease in 1243, and in his own right in 1264. The issue of this marriage consisted of four sons, viz.,

I. RICHARD, his successor.
II. Theobald, who d. at Carrickfergus on Christmas night, 1303, on his return from assisting the King in Scotland.
III. William (Sir), who performed many signal services in conjunction with his brother, the Earl.
IV. Thomas, who d. 1315.

The eldest son,
RICHARD DE BURGH, 2nd Earl of Ulster, usually called the Red Earl, the most powerful subject in Ireland, and general of all the Irish forces in Ireland, Scotland, Wales, and Gascoigne, was a great soldier and statesman. He founded the Carmelite monastery at Loughrea, built the Castles of Ballymote, Corran, and Sligo, and eventually retired to the monas-

* The original barony does not appear to have been assumed from the period of the demise of Sir Ralph Daubeney, who had summons in 1342. This patent was probably but a confirmation of the dignity already in the family.

tery of Athassil, where he *d.* 28 June, 1326; he *m.* Margaret, dau. of John de Burgo, Baron of Lanville (son of John, grandson of John, the great-grandson of Hubert, Earl of Kent), and had issue,

   I. WALTER, *d.* without male issue, 1304.
   II. JOHN, *d. v. p.*
   III. Thomas, *d. s. p.* 1316.
   IV. Edmond na Feisoge, murdered by his kinsman, Edward Bourke McWilliam; he *m.* Slany, dau of Turlogh O'Brien, Lord of Thomond, and was ancestor of the BURKES, LORDS of CASTLE CONNELL and BRITTAS.
   V. William, *d.* after the year 1337.
   I. Ellen, *m.* in 1302, Robert Bruce, Earl of Carrycke, crowned King of Scotland in 1306.
   II. Maud, *m.* in 1308, to Gilbert, Earl of Gloucester.
   III. Joan, *m.* 1st, 16 August, 1312, to Thomas the 2nd Earl of Kildare; and 2ndly, in July, 1329, to Sir John Darcy, lord justice, and *d.* 12 March, 1359.
   IV. Catherine, *m.* to John Bermingham, Earl of Louth.
   V. Margaret, *m.* 16 August, 1312, Maurice, Earl of Desmond.
   VI. Eleanor, *m.* to John, Lord Multon of Egremont.

The 2nd son,

JOHN DE BURGH, *m.* Elizabeth, 3rd dau. of Gilbert, Earl of Gloucester, by his 2nd wife, the PRINCESS JOAN, of Acres, and *d.* 1313, having had one son,

WILLIAM DE BURGH, 3rd Earl of Ulster, *b.* 1312, who *s.* his grandfather in 1326, was knighted at London, 1328, and sat in the parliament held in Dublin the following year. He was murdered 6 June, 1333, by Robert Fitz-Richard Mandeville and others. He *m.* Maud, 3rd dau. of Henry Plantagenet, Earl of Lancaster, and by her (who *m.* 2ndly, Sir Ralph de Ufford, lord justice of Ireland), had an only child,

LADY ELIZABETH DE BURGH, *b.* 1332, *m.* 1352, Prince Lionel, of Antwerp, K.G., 3rd son of EDWARD III., who became, in consequence, 4th Earl of Ulster, and Lord of Connaught, and was made chief governor of Ireland in 1361; and created DUKE OF CLARENCE, 13 November, 1362. By the great heiress of De Burgh, he had an only child, PHILIPPA, wife of EDMOND MORTIMER, 3rd *Earl of March*, viceroy of Ireland in 1380, *jure uxoris* 5th *Earl of Ulster* and *Lord of Connaught*, ancestor, through his grand-dau., the LADY ANNE MORTIMER, wife of Richard Plantagenet, Earl of Cambridge, of EDWARD IV., King of England, and of the subsequent SOVEREIGNS of Great Britain. Connaught, as an earldom, was conferred, in 1764, on Prince WILLIAM HENRY, brother of GEORGE III., and as a Dukedom on Prince ARTHUR, 3rd son of Queen VICTORIA.

Arms—Or, a cross, gu.

DE COURCY—EARL OF ULSTER.
(See ADDENDA.)

DE DREUX—EARLS OF RICHMOND.
Creation of WILLIAM THE CONQUEROR.
By Letters Patent, dated 6 July, 1268.

Lineage.

The 1st Earl of Richmond was

ALAN, surnamed Rufus or Fergaunt (from his red hair), son of Hoel or Eudo, Earl of Britanny, in France; which Alan coming over into England with the CONQUEROR, commanded the rear of his army in the memorable battle of Hastings, and for his services upon that occasion, and at the siege of York, obtained the Earldom of Richmond, with all the northern part of co. York, vulgarly denominated Richmondshire, previously the honour and co. of Edwyne, the Saxon, Earl of Mercia. This nobleman was esteemed a personage of great courage and ability—and his benefactions to the church were munificent. He *m.* Constance, dau. of King WILLIAM THE CONQUEROR, but by her (who *d.* 13 August, 1090) had no issue. He *m.* 2ndly, in 1093, Ermengarde, the divorced wife of WILLIAM IXth, Duke of Aquitaine, and dying in 1119, was *s.* by his son,

CONAN LE GROS, who *m.* Matilda, natural dau. of HENRY I., King of England, and *d.* 17 September, 1148, leaving by her a son, Hoel, who *d. s. p.* 1158, whom he refused to acknowledge, and a dau. and heir,

BERTHA, who *m.* about 1137, ALAN NIGER (Earl of Richmond in her right), son of Stephen, Count of Penthievre, by an heiress of Guingamp.

ALAN NIGER, was an active partisan of King STEPHEN in his contest with the Empress MAUD. In 1142, he took the castle of Lincoln, with considerable treasure, from Ranulph, Earl of Chester, by scaling the walls at night. He also garrisoned the castle of Hotun, in Yorkshire, then part of the bishop of Durham's possessions, and made great spoil at Ripon, upon the demesnes and tenants of the archbishop of York. This Alan Niger, who is described as a most deceitful, wicked person, wrote himself Earl of Britanny, Cornwall, and Richmond: but notwithstanding that character, he appears, like

his progenitors, to have been a munificent benefactor to the church. His lordship *m.* Bertha, dau. and heir of Conan le Gros, the 3rd Duke of Bretagne (and by this marriage acquired the title of Duke of Britanny) and had issue,

CONAN LE PETIT, his successor.
Brian, father of Alan, Lord of Bedale.
Guy, ancestor of the Barons Strange.
Reginald.

He *d.* in 1165, and was *s.* by his eldest son,

CONAN LE PETIT, Earl of Richmond, who bore also the title of Duke of Britanny. Little more is recorded of this nobleman, than his numerous grants to the church. He *m.* Margaret, dau. of Henry, Earl of Huntingdon, and sister of WILLIAM, King of Scotland, by whom he had an only dau.,

CONSTANCE, who *m.* 1st, Geoffrey Plantagenet, 4th son of King HENRY II., and had issue,
   ARTHUR. said to be put to death by his uncle, John, afterwards King JOHN.
   Eleanor, *m.*
Geoffrey Plantagenet was accidentally slain in a tournament, at Paris, in the twenty-eighth year of his age. His widow, Constance, of Britanny, *m.* 2ndly, RALPH DE BLONDVILLE, Earl of Chester, but from him she was soon afterwards divorced, and she *m.* 3rdly, GUY, VISCOUNT OF THOUARS, by whom she had two daus., viz.,
   ALICE, *m.* in 1212, to PETER DE DREUX, son of Robert, Count of Dreux, of the blood royal of France.
   Katherine, *m.* to Andrew de Vitre, in Britanny.
The three husbands of Constance are said to have been in her right, EARLS OF RICHMOND, but it is very questionable how far they were entitled to the dignity.

Conan, Earl of Richmond, *d.* 20 February, 1171. The husband of his grand-dau. Alice,

PETER DE DREUX (called *Mauclerc*), obtained a grant of the dignities of Earl of Richmond and Duke of Britanny, but he does not appear to have enjoyed the whole honour of Richmond, for in 1241, we find a grant from King HENRY III., to Peter de Savoy, of divers towns, castles, manors, lands, &c., belonging to the honour of Richmond. This nobleman had issue, by Alice, co-heir of Constance of Britanny,

JOHN, his successor.
Joland, *m.* to Hugh le Brun, Earl of Picardy.

His lordship *d.* about the year 1250, but previously his son,

JOHN DE DREUX, became Earl of Richmond and Duke of Britanny on the death of his mother, 21 October, 1221, and was acknowledged as duke on attaining his twenty-sixth year in 1237. He had livery in the 50th of HENRY III., of the honour of Richmond, from Guischard de Charrun, a servant to Peter of Savoy, who had authority for granting the same. Having thus acquired Peter de Savoy's title, the king, by letters patent, dated 6 July, 1268, conferred upon him and his heirs, under the designation of JOHN, DUKE OF BRITANNY, the *Earldom of Richmond*, with the castle and honour of Richmond, &c., in fee. Soon after this he obtained a grant from the king of the honour and rape of Hastings; and the next year, he attended Prince Edward to the Holy Land. His lordship *m.* Blanch, dau. of Theobald, King of Navarre, and dying in 1286, was *s.* by his son,

JOHN DE DREUX, Earl of Richmond, and Duke of Britanny. This nobleman was an eminent military leader in the reigns of EDWARD I. and EDWARD II. In 1293, he had the command of the forces then sent into Gascony, and the ensuing year, being the king's lieutenant in Britanny, he was joined in commission with the seneschal of Aquitaine, and others, to conclude a league of amity with the King of Castile. In 1300, he was with King EDWARD in the wars of Scotland; and in 1305, he was constituted the king's lieutenant in that kingdom, as he was again upon the accession of King EDWARD II. In the 18th of which latter monarch's reign, the Earl of Richmond was one of the ambassadors deputed to the King of France for securing the Duchy of Aquitaine from further spoil from the French. His lordship *m.* the Lady Beatrix Plantagenet, dau. of King HENRY III., and had surviving issue,

ARTHUR, who inherited the Dukedom of Britanny, who *m.* 1st, Maria de Limoges, and by her had two sons,
   JOHN, *s.* his uncle in the Earldom of Richmond; and Guido, who left a dau., Joan.
He *m.* 2ndly, Jolanta de Monteforte, and by her had a son, John, Earl of Montfort and Richmond, who *d.* 1345, leaving a son, JOHN, Earl of Richmond, who *m.* 1st, Mary, dau. of King EDWARD III.; 2ndly, Joan, dau. of Thomas Holland, Earl of Kent; and 3rdly, Joan of Navarre.
JOHN, of whom presently, as inheritor of the Earldom of Richmond.
Blanch, *m.* to Philip, son of Robert, Earl of Artois.
Mary, *m.* to Guy de Chatilion, Count of St. Pol.
Alice, abbess of Fontevraud.

He *d.* in 1303, and was *s.* by his younger son,

JOHN DE DREUX, as Earl of Richmond, who was summoned to parliament as "*Johanni de Britannia Juniori*," in the 33rd EDWARD I., and the next year as Earl of Richmond. He *d. s. p.*, however, in 1334, and was *s.* by his nephew,

JOHN DE DREUX, Duke of Britany, who did his homage for the EARLDOM OF RICHMOND, and was summored to parliament as "*Johanni Duci Britanniæ, and Comiti Richmund*," on 1 April, 1335, and 22 January, 1336. This nobleman *m.* 1st, Isabel, dau. of Charles, Earl of Valois; 2ndly, Blanch, dau. of the King of Castille; and 3rdly, Margaret, dau. of Edward, Earl of Savoy, but had no issue. He *d.* in 1341, when his niece, Joane,* dau. of his brother Guy, was constituted h's heir, but the EARLDOM OF RICHMOND reverted to the crown— when King EDWARD III. created, on 20 September, 1342,

JOHN PLANTAGENET, surnamed of "Gaunt," his younger son, Earl of Richmond, but this prince resigned the dignity in 1372, when it was conferred upon

JOHN DE DREUX, surnamed *De Brenon*, Earl of Montfort, half brother of the last John, Duke of Britany and Richmond. This nobleman being deprived by the King of France of his Earldom of Montfort, for siding with King EDWARD III., had the Earldom of Richmond from the English monarch in its stead, with the castle, town, and honour of Richmond. His lordship was constantly engaged with King EDWARD in the wars of France, but ultimately falling into the hands of his great foe, Charles of Blois, he was sent to Paris, and there died in prison, about the year 1345, leaving issue, by Joane his wife, dau. of Lewis, Comte de Nevers, a dau., Joane, who *m.* Ralph, Lord Basset, of Drayton, and a son, his successor,

JOHN DE DREUX, (surnamed the *Valiant*,) in the Earldom of Richmond. This nobleman in the 1st RICHARD II., was retained by indenture to serve the king, in his French wars, for one quarter of a year, with 200 men at arms (himself accounted), 12 knights, and 187 archers. And the next year, in consideration of the castle of Brest in Britany, which he delivered up to King RICHARD, obtained a grant to himself, and Joane his wife (sister of the king), of the castle and manor of Rising, co. Norfolk. In the 3rd of the same reign, bearing the titles of Duke of Britany, Earl of Montfort, and Earl of Richmond, he was in the wars of France, but shortly after this deserting the banner of England for that of France, all his lands in the former kingdom were seized, and he was deprived of the Earldom of Richmond by special act of parliament, 7th RICHARD II., November, 1383. He is said to have been afterwards restored to the dignity, but with the proviso, that if he *d. s. p.*, the earldom and honour should revert to the king; in the 14th RICHARD II., it was however again adjudged to be forfeited, and thus terminated the family of DE DREUX, EARLS OF RICHMOND. The last earl *m.* 1st, the Lady Mary Plantagenet, dau. of King EDWARD III.; 2ndly, Joane, dau. of Thomas Holland, Earl of Kent ; and 3rdly, Joane, dau. of CHARLES THE BAD, King of Navarre, and by the last named lady (who *m.* after the duke's death HENRY IV., King of England), his lordship had issue,

I. JOHN, his successor.
II. ARTHUR, *s.* his nephew Peter.
III. Richard, Earl of Estampes, *m.* Margaret, of Orleans, and was father of

FRANCIS, Duke of Britany, in 1458, of whom presently.

The eldest son and successor,

JOHN, Duke of Britany in 1399, *m.* Jane of Flanders, and had two sons, FRANCIS, his heir, and PETER, who *s.* his brother ; the former,

FRANCIS, Duke of Britany, *m.* in 1442, Isabel of Scotland, and had two daus., Mary, wife of John, Viscount Rohan, and Margaret, *m.* to her kinsman, Francis, Duke of Britany. At Francis's death the dukedom passed to his brother,

PETER, Duke of Britany in 1450, who *m.* Frances d'Amboise and *d. s. p.* He was *s.* by his uncle,

ARTHUR, styled Earl of Richmond and Duke of Britany in 1457; he *d. s. p.*, and was *s.* by his nephew,

FRANCIS, Duke of Britany in 1458, who *m.* twice—by one wife, Margaret, his kinswoman, dau. of Francis, Duke of

Britany he had no issue, by the other wife, Margaret de Foix, he had one dau.,

ANNE, heiress of Britany, who *m.* LEWIS XII., King of France and thus annexed the Duchy of Britany to the crown of France.

Arms—Of Alan Fergaunt, and his immediate descendants— Chequy, or and az., a canton, erm. Of De Dreux—The same.

D'EIVILL—BARON D'EIVILL.

By Writ of Summons, dated 14 December, 1264.

Lineage.

In the reign of HENRY I., NIGEL DE ALBINI, being enfeoffed of the manor of Egmanton, co. Nottingham, by the crown, conferred it upon

ROBERT D'EIVILL, from whom descended another

ROBERT D'EIVILL, who, in the 15th King JOHN, attended that monarch in his expedition into Poictou, and in the 26th HENRY III., had summons to fit himself with horse and arms, and to accompany the king into Gascony. To this Robert *s.*

JOHN D'EIVILL, who, in the 38th HENRY III., was forced to fly the country under an excommunication, but soon afterwards having made his peace, had permission to return, for in the third year following, we find him constituted justice of all the forests beyond Trent, and the next year the King of Scots, King HENRY's son-in-law, being in restraint by his own subjects, he, with other of the northern barons, received summons to fit himself with horse and arms, and to be ready on command, to march into Scotland for the captive monarch's rescue. In the 44th HENRY III., he was again constituted warden of all the forests north of Trent. So, likewise, in three years afterwards, when he was appointed governor of the castle at York, and the next year he obtained license to erect a castle at a place called Hode, in Yorkshire, in which year he was constituted governor of Scarborough Castle. After this we find him arrayed with the other discontented barons against the crown, and so actively engaged in the north, that the sheriff of Yorkshire could not exercise his office for the king's service, from Michaelmas in the 48th, till the battle of Evesham in the 49th of that reign, during which period HENRY was in the hands of the barons a prisoner, and this feudal lord was summoned to parliament, by the companions then ruling, as Baron D'Eivill. The subsequent triumph of the royal cause at Evesham terminated for that time, however, the baronial sway, but it did not bring back Lord D'Eivill to his allegiance, for joining Robert, Lord Ferrers, his lordship made head again at Chesterfield, co. Derby, where, after the capture of Ferrers, he was unhorsed by Sir. Gilbert Haunsard, but effected his escape to the Isle of Arholme, co. Lincoln. Under the decree, called the "Dictum of Kenilworth," he eventually, however, made his peace, and redeemed his lands by a pecuniary fine. His lordship *m.* Maude, widow of Sir James de Aldithley, without license, for which transgression he paid a fine of £200 to the king. Of this nobleman nothing further is known, and his posterity do not appear from the existing enrolments to have been ever after summoned to parliament.

Arms—Arg., a chev., sa., a fleur-de-lis, or.

DE LA POER—EARL OF TYRONE.

(*See* POER.)

DE LACY—EARL OF ULSTER.

(*See* DE LACY, Earls of Lincoln, in the EXTANT PEERAGE OF ENGLAND.)

DELAVAL—BARON DELAVAL.

(*See* DELAVAL, Baron Delaval, of Seaton Delaval.)

---

* This lady *m.* Charles, 2nd son of Guy, Earl of Blois, who laid claim in her right to the Duchy of Britany, which caused a procrastinated war, wherein England and France became involved—one espousing the claim of John de Brenon, half-brother of the deceased Duke John ; the other that of Charles, of Blois, which latter was certainly the more legitimate, the Lady Joan being the dau. of Guy, brother to the whole blood to the duke.

DELAVAL—BARON DELAVAL, OF SEATON DELAVAL, CO. NORTHUMBERLAND.
By Letters Patent, dated 21 August, 1786.
Lineage.

SIR ROBERT DELAVAL, of Seaton, co. Northumberland, descended from the old feudal barons De la Val, who flourished in the 11th and 12th centuries, was eldest son of SIR JOHN DELAVAL, of Seaton, by Anne his wife, dau. of Ralph, Lord Ogle. He m. Dorothy, dau. of Sir Ralph Grey, of Chillingham (ancestor of the GREYS of Werk) and had issue,

I. Ralph (Sir), ancestor of the family of DELAVAL, EXTINCT BARONETS.
II. JOHN, of whom presently.
III. Robert, m. Alice, dau. of William Riddell, Esq., and had issue,
    Mary and Margaret.
IV. Edward, m. Dorothy, dau. of Mr. Whitfield.
V. Claudius, }
VI. Francis, } d. unm.
VII. Arthur. }
I. Jane, m. to Michael Milford, Esq., of Scighill.

The 2nd son,

SIR JOHN DELAVAL, of Dishington, in Northumberland, m. 1st, Anne, dau. of Sir George Bowes, Knt., by whom he had a son, Sir Robert Delaval, of Dishington, living in 1666; and 2ndly, Elizabeth, dau. of Sir James Selby, Knt., and by her had four sons, viz.: John, who d. unm.; William, who m. Mary, dau. of Sir Henry Widdrington, Knt., of Black Hedden, co. Northumberland; Ralph, d. unm.; and GEORGE, of whom we treat. The 4th son,

GEORGE DELAVAL, Esq., m. Margaret, dau. of Edward Grey, Esq., of Morpeth, and had a son,

EDWARD DELAVAL, Esq., who m. Mary, dau. and heir of Sir Francis Blake, of Coggs, co. Oxford, and by her had issue,

I. FRANCIS-BLAKE, of whom presently.
II. Robert, d. s. p.
I. Margaret, m. to R. Robinson.
II. Anne, m. to Sir Ralph Milbank, Bart.

The elder son,

FRANCIS-BLAKE DELAVAL, Esq., who m. Rhoda, dau. of Robert Apreece, Esq., of Washingly, co. Huntingdon, by Sarah his wife, dau. and eventually sole heiress of Sir Thomas Hussey, Bart., and by her (who d. in August, 1759), had issue,

FRANCIS-BLAKE, K.B., m. Isabella, dau. of Thomas, 6th Earl of Thanet, and widow of Lord Nassau Paulett, but d. s. p. in 1771.
JOHN-HUSSEY, of whom presently.
Edward-Thomas, d. unm. in 1787.
Rhoda, m. to Sir Edward Astley, Bart., of Melton Constable, Norfolk.
Anne, m. to the Hon. Sir William Stanhope, K.B., 2nd son of Philip, 3rd Earl of Chesterfield, and after his decease to Captain Morris.
Sarah, m. to John Savile, 1st Earl of Mexborough.

Mr. Blake-Delaval d. in December, 1752, and was s. by his eldest son, Sir Francis Blake-Delaval, K.B., but we pass to the 2nd,

JOHN-HUSSEY DELAVAL, who was created a Baronet in 1761, and upon the decease of his brother, Sir Francis, became the representative of the family. He was created a peer of Ireland, as BARON DELAVAL, of Redford, co. Wicklow, 17 October, 1783, and enrolled amongst the peers of Great Britain on 21 August, 1786, in the dignity of BARON DELAVAL, of Seaton Delaval, co. Northumberland. His lordship m. 1st, Susannah, dau. of R. Robinson, Esq., and widow of John Potter, Esq., by whom (who d. 1 Oct. 1783,) he had issue,

John, b. in 1755; d. in 1775, unm.
Sophia-Anne, m. to John Maximilian Jadis, Esq., and d. 24 July, 1793.
Elizabeth, m. 19 May, 1781, to George, Lord Audley, and d. in 1785, leaving issue.
Frances, m. to John-Fenton Cawthorne, Esq.
Sarah, m. to George, Earl of Tyrconnell, by whom she left an only dau. (heiress of the earl),
    Lady Susannah Carpenter, who m. Henry, 2nd Marquess of Waterford.

Lord Delaval m. 2ndly, Miss Knight, but had no issue. He d. May, 1808, when his honours became EXTINCT, and his estates devolved upon his daus. as co-heiresses, or their representatives.

Arms—Quarterly: 1st and 4th, erm., two bars, vert, for DELAVAL; 2nd and 3rd, arg., a chev. between three garbs, sa., for BLAKE.

DEMPSEY, VISCOUNT CLANMALIER.
(See O'DEMPSEY).

DENISON—VISCOUNT OSSINGTON.
By Letters Patent, dated 13 February, 1872.
Lineage.

JOHN WILKINSON, Esq. of Potterton, Barwick-in-Elmet, co. York. m. the sister of William Denison, an eminent merchant of Leeds (who purchased the manor of Ossington, co. Nottingham, 1753), and had issue,

I. EDWARD, of Potterton Hall, m. 1787, Anne, dau. of Nicholas Pearse, Esq. of Woodford, and d. 1836, leaving a son,
    JOHN-EDWARD of Potterton Hall, m. 1813, Katherine, dau. of Robert Bathurst, Esq., and d. 1850, leaving a son,
    BATHURST-EDWARD WILKINSON, Esq., of Potterton Hall (see BURKE's Landed Gentry).
II. JOHN, of whom hereafter.

Mr. Wilkinson d. May, 1789. His 2nd son s to the estates of his maternal uncles (WILLIAM DENISON, Esq. of Ossington, high sheriff of Notts, 1779; and ROBERT DENISON, of Ossington, who d. 1785) and assumed in consequence the surname and arms of DENISON. This,

JOHN DENISON, Esq. of Ossington, M.P. for Colchester, and afterwards for Minehead, m. 1st, a dau. of J. Horlock, Esq., of Ashwick, and had by her two sons, who d. young, and a dau.,

Charlotte, m. Right Hon. Charles Manners Sutton, speaker of the House of Commons, 1st VISCOUNT CANTERBURY.

He m. 2ndly, Charlotte, dau. of Samuel Estwick, Esq., M.P., and had issue,

I. JOHN-EVELYN, created VISCOUNT OSSINGTON.
II. Edward (Right Rev.), D.D., Bishop of Salisbury, b. 13 May, 1801; consecrated in 1837; m. 1st, 27 June, 1839, Louisa-Maria, 2nd dau. of Henry Ker Seymer, Esq. of Hanford House, co. Dorset, and by her (who d. 22 September, 1841), had issue,
    Edward, b. 1840.   Louisa.
He m. 2ndly, 10 July, 1845, Hon. Clementina Baillie-Hamilton, maid of honor to the Queen, dau. of the Ven. Charles Baillie-Hamilton, archdeacon of Cleveland, but by her had no issue. The Bishop d. 6 March, 1854.
III. William-Thomas (Sir), Knt., col. R.E., b. 1804; successively governor of Van Diemen's Land, of Australia, and of Madras; m. 29 November, 1838, Caroline-Lucy, 2nd dau. of Admiral Sir Phipps Hornby, K.C.B., and d. 1871, leaving,
    WILLIAM-EVELYN, capt. Royal artillery, D.L. and M.P. co. Nottingham, b. 1843; m. 23 November, 1877, Lady Elinor-Amherst, dau. of William Pitt, 2nd Earl Amherst.
IV. George-Anthony, M.A., Fellow of Oriel College, archdeacon of Taunton, b. 11 December, 1805; m. 4 September, 1838, Georgiana, eldest dau. of the Right Hon. J.-W. Henley, M.P. of Waterperry, Oxon.
V. Henry, M.A., fellow of All Souls, barrister-at-law, b. 2 June, 1810; d. 1858.
VI. Stephen-Charles, M.A., barrister-at-law, deputy judge advocate, b. 2 July, 1811; m. 1845, Susan, dau. of the Rev. F. Fellowes; d. 1871.
VII. Frank, lieut. R.N., b. 1813; d. 1843.
VIII. Robert-Alfred, settled in New South Wales, b. August, 1816.
IX. Charles-Albert, formerly lieut.-col. 52nd regt., b. 1819.
I. Julia-Grace, m. to the Rev. C. Des Vœux.
II. Henrietta-Sophia, m. 1840, to J.-H. Jacob, Esq.
III. Charlotte, m. to Rt. Hon. Sir Robert-J. Phillimore, Bart.

Mr. Denison d. 6 May, 1820, and was s. by his eldest son,

RIGHT HON. JOHN-EVELYN DENISON, of Ossington, b. 27 Jan. 1800; educated at Eton and Oxford; m. 14 July, 1827, Lady Charlotte Cavendish Bentinck, 3rd dau. of William, 4th Duke of Portland, but had no issue. Successively M.P. for Newcastle-under-Lyme, Hastings, Liverpool, Notts, Malton, and again for the northern division co. Nottingham. He was a lord of the Admiralty in Mr. Canning's administration, was chosen, by a unanimous vote, Speaker of the House of Commons in 1857, and in three subsequent Parliaments. After fifteen years' service he was raised to the peerage of the United Kingdom as VISCOUNT OSSINGTON, of Ossington, co. Nottingham, 13 Feb. 1872. His lordship d. 7 March, 1873, when the viscountcy became extinct.

Arms—Arg., on a bend, between an unicorn's head erased in chief, and a cross crosslet fitchée, in base sa. three bezants.

DENMARK, PRINCE OF—DUKE OF CUMBERLAND.
By Act of Parliament, dated 9 April, 1689.
Lineage.

GEORGE, PRINCE OF DENMARK, having espoused Her Royal Highness the Princess Anne, youngest dau. of King JAMES II., was created Baron Workingham, Earl of Kendal, and DUKE OF CUMBERLAND, with precedency of all other dukes by act of parliament, dated 9 April, 1689. He was also constituted lord high admiral of Great Britain and Ireland, and installed a knight of the Garter. By the princess, who subsequently to her marriage ascended the throne as Queen ANNE, the duke had two sons and four daus., all of whom d. before the age of maturity, and in his lifetime. His own death occurred in 1708, when his British honours became EXTINCT.

Arms—Or, three lions passant guardant, az., crowned, ppr., and semée of hearts, gu.

DENNIS—BARON TRACTON.

By Letters Patent, dated 13 December, 1780.

Lineage.

The Right Honourable JAMES DENNIS, lord chief baron of the Exchequer in Ireland (son of John Dennis, Esq., of the co. Cork, by Anne Bullen his wife), was raised to the peerage of that kingdom as BARON TRACTON *of Tracton Abbey, co. Cork,* 13 December, 1780. His lordship d. suddenly in 1782, *s. p.*, when the title expired. His estates in the co. of Kerry he bequeathed to his eldest nephew and heir-at-law, the Rev. Meade Swift, and those in the counties of Cork and Dublin to his other nephew, John Swift, subject to a jointure of £1,800 per annum to Lady Tracton, and on condition that they and their heirs should take the name and arms of DENNIS.

His lordship's only sister FRANCES, m. THOMAS SWIFT, Esq., of Lynn, co. Westmeath, and had two sons. (*See* BURKE's *Landed Gentry.*)

Arms—Gu., on a chev., betw. three fleurs-de-lis, or, as many annulets, of the first; a canton, chequy, of the second, and az.

DENNY—BARONS DENNY, EARL OF NORWICH.

Barony, by Writ of Summons, dated 27 October, 1604.
Earldom, by Letters Patent, dated 24 October, 1626.

Lineage.

SIR ANTHONY DENNY, 2nd son of Thos. Denny, Esq., was one of the gentlemen of the privy chamber to King HENRY VIII. and M.P. for co. Her s in the 1st parliament of EDWARD VI. He m. Joane, dau. of Sir Philip Champernon, of Modbury, and had issue,

  i. HENRY, his heir.   II. Arthur.
  III. Edward, ancestor of DENNY, BARONET OF TRALEE (*see* BURKE's *Peerage and Baronetage*).
  I. Douglas, m. to John Dive, Esq.
  II. Mary, m. to Thomas Astley, Esq.
  III. Honora, m. to Thomas Wingfield, Esq.

The eldest son and successor,

HENRY DENNY, Dean of Chester, b. 1540, m. 1st, Honora, dau. of William Lord Grey, of Wilton, and by her had issue,

  I. ROBERT, his successor.
  II. EDWARD, of whom presently.
  I. Katherine, m. to Sir George Fleetwood.
  II. Anne, m. to George Goring, Esq., of Hurstpierpoint, Suffolk, and had issue,
    George Goring, who was created Baron Goring, and Earl of Norwich (*see* Goring Earl of Norwich),—from Edward Goring, Esq., uncle of this nobleman, the Gorings, Baronets, of Highden, in Sussex, derive.
  III. Margaret, m. to William Purvey.

The Dean m. 2ndly, Elizabeth, dau. of John, Lord Grey, of Pirgo, and by her had a son, Henry, who d. s. p., and two daus. d. young. He was s. by his elder son,

ROBERT DENNY, then only a minor nine years old, who d. in 1576, and was s. by his brother,

SIR EDWARD DENNY, b. 14 August, 1569, who was knighted in 1589 by King JAMES I. on that monarch passing from Scotland to London on his accession to the throne, when Sir Edward being then high sheriff of co. Herts, met him with a noble retinue of 140 men well mounted and suitably apparelled, and presented his Majesty with a fine horse richly accoutred. He was summoned to parliament in the 3rd JAMES I., as BARON DENNY, *of Waltham, co. Essex,* and created by letters patent, dated 24 October, 1626, EARL OF NORWICH. His lordship m. Lady Mary Cecil, dau. of Thomas, Earl of Exeter, by Dorothy, dau. and co-heir of John Nevil, Lord Latimer, and had an only dau. and heir,

Honora, who m. Sir James Hay (of Pitcorthie, co. Fife, the celebrated favourite of King JAMES I.), Viscount Doncaster, and Earl of Carlisle, by whom she had an only son,

  JAMES, 2nd Earl of Carlisle, at whose decease, s. p., in 1660, the Viscounty of Doncaster, and Earldom of Carlisle, with the BARONY of DENNY, EXPIRED.

His lordship d. 20 December, 1630, when the EARLDOM of NORWICH became EXTINCT, but the BARONY of DENNY devolved upon his dau.,

HONORA, as Baroness Denny, who m. 6 January, 1606, Sir James Hay, Knt., subsequently created Earl of Carlisle. At her decease the title passed to her son,

THE RT. HON. JAMES HAY, 2nd Earl of Carlisle, at whose decease, in 1660, it EXPIRED, with his lordship's other honours.

Arms—Gu., a saltier, arg., between twelve crosses patée, or

DE RUVIGNY—EARL OF GALWAY.

(*See* MASSUE, EARL OF GALWAY.)

DESPENCER—EARL OF WINCHESTER.

Creation of EDWARD II. 10 May, 1322.

Lineage.

In the 18th year of WILLIAM THE CONQUEROR,

ROBERT LE DESPENCER, so called from being steward to the king, was a witness to the royal charter for removing the secular canons out of the cathedral of Durham, and placing monks in their stead. This Robert was brother of Urso de Abitot, then sheriff of Worcestershire, and he appears, as well by his high official situation, as by the numerous lordships he possessed, to have been a person of great eminence; but it has not been ascertained whether he first came into England with his royal master, or whether he was of Saxon or Norman extraction; nor is it clearly known, whether he had ever been married or had issue. In the reign of HENRY I. there was a

WILLIAM LE DESPENCER, but whether he had the name from being son of Robert, or from succeeding to the post of steward, cannot be determined.

The next person we find holding this office, and in the same reign, was

THURSTAN DISPENCER. Of this steward, Camden, in his Remains, relates the following story. " In the time of HENRY I. it was the custom of the court, that books, bills, and letters, should be drawn and signed by servitors in court, concerning their own matters, without fee. But at this time Thurstan, the king's steward, or Le Despencer, as they then called him (from whom the family of the Lord Spencer came), exhibited to the king a complaint against Adam of Yarmouth, clerk of the signet, for, that he refused to sign, without a fee a bill passed for him. The king first heard Thurstan commending the old custom at large, and charging the clerk for exacting somewhat contrary thereunto, for passing his book. Then the clerk was heard, who briefly said, ' I received the book, and sent unto your steward, desiring only of him to bestow upon me two spice cakes made for your own mouth; who returned for answer, he would not, and thereupon I desired to seal his book.' "

The king greatly disliked the steward for returning this negative, and forthwith made Adam sit down upon the bench, with the seals and Thurstan's book before him, but compelled the steward to put off his cloak, to fetch two of his best spiced cakes for the king's own mouth, to bring them in a fair white napkin, and with low curtsie to present them to Adam, the clerk. Which being accordingly done, the king commanded Adam to seal and deliver him his book, and made them friends, adding this speech—" Officers of the court must gratifie and show east of their office, not only one to another, but also to strangers, whensoever need shall require."

This Thurstan was s. by his son,

ALMARIC DE SPENCER, who served the office of sheriff of Rutland in the 34th HENRY II., and again in the 1st RICHARD I. From the latter monarch, to whom he was also steward, he obtained a confirmation in fee of the lordships of Wurdle and Stanley, in the vale of Gloucester. The former of which King HENRY II. had given to Walter, the usher of his chamber, son of Thurstan, and uncle of this Almaric, for his homage and service, reserving a pair of gilt spurs, or twelve pence, to be yearly paid for the same into the exchequer. In the 6th of King JOHN this Almaric paid a fine of 120 marks and one palfry to be exempted from attending upon the king in an expedition then proposed to be made beyond the sea. Almaric de Spencer m. Amabil, dau. of Walter de Chesnel, by whom he had two sons, Thurstan and Almaric, and was s. by the elder,

THURSTAN DE SPENCER, who appears, with his brother, to have taken arms with the other barons against King JOHN, for, in the latter part of that reign, the king committed the custody of Thurstan de Spencer to Rowland Bloet, and gave away the lands of Almaric de Spencer to Osbert Giffard, his own natural son. Thurstan seems however to have regained his rank in the next reign, and to have twice served the office of sheriff for Gloucestershire. He d. in 1248.

Contemporary with this Thurstan, and doubtless of the same family, was

HUGH DE SPENCER, whom King HENRY III., in the 9th year of his reign, constituted sheriff of the counties of Salop and

Stafford, and governor of the castles of Salop and Bruges (Bridgnorth). He was subsequently sheriff of Berkshire, and governor of Wallingford Castle. To this Hugh HENRY III. gave the manor of Rithal, co. Rutland, and in the 21st of that monarch's reign, upon the death of John Scot, Earl of Chester, he was deputed with Stephen de Segrave and Henry de Aldithley to take charge of the castles of Chester and Beeston. After this Hugh came his grandson, another

HUGH DESPENCER, who, taking part with the barons, was nominated under the baronial power in the 44th of HENRY III., justiciary of England. After the battle of Lewes he was one of those to whom the custody of the captive monarch was committed, and he was then entrusted with the castles of Orford, in Suffolk, of Devises, in Wilts, and Barnard Castle, in the bishopric of Durham. He was summoned to parliament on 14 December, 1264, as "*Hugh le Despencer, Justic' Angliæ,*" and lost his life under the baronial banner at the battle of Evesham. His lordship *m.* Aliva, dau. of Philip Bassett of Wycombe, co Bucks, and afterwards 1st wife of Roger Bigod, Earl of Norfolk, by whom he left at his decease, August, 1265, HUGH, of whom presently, and Alianore *m.* to Hugh de Courteney, father of Hugh, 1st Earl of Devonshire. After the forfeiture and decease of Lord Despencer his widow Aliva, for her father's sake, found such favour from the king, that she was enabled to retain a considerable proportion of the property, and at her death, in the 9th of EDWARD I., it devolved, on the payment of a fine of 500 marks, upon her son,

HUGH DESPENCER, senior, so called to distinguish him from his son, who bore the designation of HUGH DESPENCER, junior, both so well known in history, as the favourites of the unfortunate EDWARD II. Of HUGH, senior, we shall first treat, although as father and son ran almost the same course, at the same time, and shared a similar fate, it is not easy to sever their deeds.

HUGH DISPENSER paid a fine of 2,000 marks to the king, in the 15th of EDWARD I., for marrying, without license, Isabel, dau. of William de Beauchamp, Earl of Warwick, and widow of Patrick Cheworth; by this lady he had an only son, the too celebrated

HUGH DISPENSER, jun.

In the 22nd of the same reign, he was made governor of Odiham Castle, co. Southampton, and the same year had summons to attend the king at Portsmouth, prepared with horse and arms for an expedition into Gascony. In two years afterwards he was at the battle of Dunbar, in Scotland, where the English arms triumphed; and the next year he was one of the commissioners accredited to treat of peace between the English monarch and the kings of the Romans and of France. In the 26th and 28th years of EDWARD I. he was again engaged in the wars of Scotland, and was sent by his sovereign, with the Earl of Lincoln, to the papal court, to complain of the Scots, and to entreat that his holiness would no longer favour them, as they had abused his confidence by falsehoods. To the very close of King EDWARD I.'s reign his lordship seems to have enjoyed the favour of that great prince, and had summons to parliament from him from 23 June, 1295 to 14 March, 1322; but it was after the accession of EDWARD's unhappy son, the second of that name, that the Spencers attained that extraordinary eminence, from which, with their feeble-minded master, they were eventually hurled into the gulph of irretrievable ruin. In the first years of EDWARD II.'s reign, we find the father and son still engaged in the Scottish wars. In the 14th year the king, hearing of great animosities between the younger Spencer and Humphrey de Bohun, Earl of Hereford and Essex, and learning that they were collecting their followers in order to come to open combat, interfered, and strictly commanded Lord Hereford to forbear. About the same time, a dispute arising between the Earl of Hereford and John de Moubray regarding some lands in Wales, young Spencer seized possession of the estate, and kept it from both the litigants. This conduct, and similar proceedings on the part of the elder Spencer, exciting the indignation of the barons, they formed a league against the favourites, and placing the king's cousin, Thomas Plantagenet, Earl of Lancaster, at their head, marched, with banners flying, from Sherbourne to St. Alban's, whence they despatched the bishops of Salisbury, Hereford, and Chichester, to the king with a demand that the Spencers should be banished; to which mission the king, however, giving an imperious reply in the negative, the irritated nobles continued their route to London: when EDWARD, at the instance of the queen, acquiesced; whereupon the barons summoned a parliament, in which the Spencers were banished from England; and the sentence was proclaimed in Westminster Hall. To this decision, HUGH the elder submitted and retired; but Hugh the younger lurked in divers places; sometimes on land, an ! sometimes at sea, and was fortunate enough

to capture, during his exile, two vessels near Sandwich, laden with merchandize to the value of £40,000; after which, being recalled by the king, an army was raised, which encountered and defeated the baronial forces at Boroughbridge, in York shire. In this action, wherein numbers were slain, the Earl of Lancaster being taken prisoner, was carried to his own castle at Pontefract, and there, after a summary trial (the elder Spencer being one of his judges), beheaded. The Spencers now became more powerful than ever, and the elder was immediately created EARL OF WINCHESTER, the king loading him with grants of forfeited estates. He was about the same time constituted warden of the king's forests on the south of Trent. Young Spencer obtained, like his father, immense grants from the lands forfeited after the battle of Boroughbridge; but not satisfied with those, and they were incredibly numerous, he extorted by force whatsoever else he pleased. Amongst other acts of lawless oppression, it is related that he seized upon the person of Elizabeth Comyn, a great heiress, the wife of Richard Talbot, in her house at Kennington, in Surrey, and detained her for twelve months in prison, until he compelled her to assign to him the manor of Painswike, in Gloucestershire, and the castle and manor of Goderich, in the marches of Wales; but this ill-obtained and ill-exercised power was not formed for permanent endurance, and a brief space only was necessary to bring it to a termination. The queen and the young prince, who had fled to France, and had been proclaimed traitors through the influence of the Spencers, ascertaining the feelings of the people, ventured to return; and landed at Harwich, with the noblemen and persons of eminence who had been exiled after the defeat at Boroughbridge, raised the royal standard, and soon found themselves at the head of a considerable force; when, marching upon Bristol, where the king and his favourites then were, they received in that city with acclamation, and the elder Spencer being seized (although in his ninetieth year), was brought in chains before the prince and the barons, and received judgment of death, which was accordingly executed, by hanging the culprit upon a gallows in the sight of the king and of his son, upon St. Dennis's day, in October, 1326. It is said by some writers that the body was hung up with two strong cords for four days, and then cut to pieces, and given to the dogs. Young Spencer, with the king, effected his escape; but they were both, soon afterwards, taken and delivered to the queen, when the unfortunate monarch was consigned to Berkeley Castle, where he was basely murdered in 1327. Hugh Spencer the younger, it appears, was impeached before parliament, and received sentence "to be drawn upon a hurdle, with trumps and trumpets, throughout all the city of Hereford," and there to be hanged and quartered, which sentence was executed on a gallows 50 feet high, upon St. Andrew's eve, *anno* 1326 (20 EDWARD II.) Thus terminate l the career of two of the most celebrated royal favourites in the annals of England. The younger Hugh was a peer of the realm, as well as his father, having been summoned to parliament as a baron, from 29 July, 1314, to 10 October, 1325; but the two BARONIES OF SPENCER, and the EARLDOM OF WINCHESTER, expired under the attainders of the father and son. For the family of the younger Spencer, *see* Despencer, Earl of Gloucester.

Arms—Quarterly: arg. and gu.; in the 2nd and 3rd, a fret, or. Over all a bend, sa.

DESPENCER—BARONS DESPENCER, EARL OF GLOUCESTER.

Barony, by Writ of Summons, dated 15th June, 1338.
Earldom, *anno* 1337,

Lineage.

HUGH DESPENCER, Jun. (one of the hapless favourites of King EDWARD I.), *m.* Eleanor, dau. and co-heir of Gilbert de Clare, Earl of Gloucester, and had issue,

I. HUGH, of whom presently.
II. Edward, *m.* Anne, sister of Henry, Lord Ferrers, of Groby, and dying in 1342, left an only son,
    EDWARD, who *s.* his uncle, HUGH.
III. Gilbert, of Melton Mowbray.
IV. Philip, *m.* Margaret Gousell, and *d.* 1313.
I. Elizabeth, *m.* to Maurice, Lord Berkeley.
II. Isabel, *m.* to Richard, Earl of Arundel.

After the execution of Hugh Despencer, in November, 1326, Eleanor his widow, with her children and family, was confined in the Tower of London until the ensuing February, when she obtained her liberty, and *m.* subsequently William la Zouch, of Mortimer. She *d.* in July, 1337, possessed of several estates, in which she was *s.* by her elder son,

HUGH DESPENCER, who had already distinguished himself as a soldier in France and Scotland; and continuing actively and gallantly engaged in the same fields, he was summoned to parliament as a Baron by King EDWARD III., from 15 June, 1338, to 1 January, 1349. His lordship *m.* Elizabeth, widow of Giles de Baddlesmere, but *d. s. p.* in 1349, when the barony EXPIRED, but his lands devolved upon his nephew,

EDWARD DESPENCER, who, in the 30th EDWARD III., being then a knight, attended Edward the Black Prince into France, and shared in the glory of Poictiers. For several years afterwards Sir Edward continued in the French wars, and for his gallant conduct was summoned to parliament as BARON DE SPENCER, from 15 December, 1357, to 6 October, 1372, being also honoured with the Garter. His lordship *m.* Elizabeth, dau. and heiress of Bartholomew de Burghersh, Baron Burghersh, and had issue,

  I. THOMAS, his successor.
  II. Hugh, *d.* 1424.
  I. Cicely, who *d.* young.
  II. Elizabeth, *m.* 1st, to John Arundel, and 2ndly, to Hugh, Lord Zouch.
  III. Anne, *m.* to Hugh Hastings, and afterwards to Thomas, Lord Morley.
  IV. Margaret, *m.* to Robert, Lord Ferrers of Chartley.

Lord Despencer *d.* 1375, and was *s.* by his son,

THOMAS DESPENCER, 2nd Baron De Spencer, summoned to parliament 30 November, 1396, and 18 July, 1397. This nobleman, who was known as Lord Despencer of Glamorgan, was in the expedition to Ireland, made in the 18th RICHARD II., and in the 21st of the same reign, having the sentence of banishment reversed, which had been passed by parliament in 16th EDWARD III., against his great grandfather, HUGH DESPENCER THE YOUNGER, was created EARL OF GLOUCESTER, 21st RICHARD II., *anno* 1337, by reason of his descent through Eleanor, wife of the said Hugh, from the De Clares, Earls of Gloucester. In the petition which his lordship presented for the reversal of Hugh his ancestor's banishment, it was set forth, that the said Hugh, at the time possessed no less than fifty-nine lordships in different counties; 28,000 sheep; 1,000 oxen and steers; 1,200 kine, with their calves; 40 mares, with their colts of two years; 160 draught horses; 2,000 hogs; 3,000 bullocks; 40 tuns of wine; 600 bacons; four score carcasses of martinmas beef; 600 muttons in his larder; 10 tuns of cider; armour, plate, jewels, and ready money, better than £10,000; 36 sacks of wool, and a library of books. His lordship *m.* Constance, dau of Edmund Plantagenet, surnamed De Langley, Duke of York, 5th son of King EDWARD III., and had issue,

  I. RICHARD, who *m.* Elizabeth, dau. of Ralph, Earl of Westmoreland, and *d.* issueless, in 1414.
  I. Isabel, *m.* to Richard Beauchamp, Lord Abergavenny and Earl of Worcester, by whom she had an only dau. and heiress,
    ELIZABETH BEAUCHAMP, who *m.* Edward Nevil, a younger son of Ralph, Earl of Westmoreland, and brought into that family the Baronies of Burghersh and Despencer and Abergavenny.
  II. Elizabeth, *d.* young.

Upon the marriage of the Earl of Gloucester, he obtained from King RICHARD II. a grant of divers manors; but adhering to that unfortunate monarch, he was degraded from his earldom, and dispossessed of most of his lands by the first parliament of HENRY IV.; and before the same year elapsed, being taken prisoner, in an attempt to fly the kingdom, at Bristol, and being condemned by a vote of the House of Commons to die, he was carried into the market-place and there beheaded by the rabble, on the 3rd day after St. Hillary, in the year 1400; when the EARLDOM OF GLOUCESTER and BARONY OF DE SPENCER fell under the attainder. Richard, his eldest son, dying in fourteen years afterwards, still a minor, without issue, Isabel, his only dau., then became his heir. This lady, as stated above, *m.* Richard Beauchamp, Baron Abergavenny, and Earl of Worcester, by whom she had an only dau. and heiress, Lady Elizabeth Beauchamp. The attainder of Thomas, Lord Despencer and Earl of Gloucester, her grandfather, being reversed in the 1st year of EDWARD IV., the said Lady Elizabeth carried the Barony of Despencer (the Earldom of Gloucester could not of course be revived, having failed for want of a male heir), with the Baronies of Abergavenny and Burghersh, to her husband, the Hon. Edward Nevil, who was summoned to parliament as Lord Abergavenny, in 1450; and the dignity of Despencer continued in his descendants, the Lords Abergavenny, until the decease of Henry, 4th baron, in 1687, when his lordship's only dau. and heiress, Elizabeth,

then the wife of Sir Thomas Fane, Knt., claimed the baronies; but, after a long investigation, the House of Lords decided, that the Barony of Abergavenny belonged to the heir male at law; when the crown, by letters patent, confirmed the Barony of Le Despencer to her ladyship and her heirs. From that period it was enjoyed by Lady Fane's immediate descendants, the first seven Earls of Westmoreland; at the decease of John, the 7th earl, in 1762, the Barony of Despencer fell into abeyance between the heirs of his lordship's sisters, and was terminated the next year in favour of his nephew, Sir Francis Dashwood, at whose decease, *s. p.* in 1781, it again fell into abeyance; and so continued, until again terminated in 1788 in favour of Sir Thomas Stapleton, Baronet, late Lord Le Despencer, the descendant of Lady Catherine Paul, John, 7th Earl of Westmoreland's younger sister.

Arms—Same as those of Despencer, Earl of Winchester.

D'EVEREUX—EARLS OF SALISBURY.

Creation of the Empress MAUD.

Lineage.

Amongst the principal Normans who accompanied the CONQUEROR in his expedition against England, and participated in the triumph and spoil of Hastings, was

WALTER DE EVEREUX, of Rosmar, in Normandy, who obtained, with other considerable grants, the lordships of Salisbury and Ambresbury, which, having devised his Norman possessions and earldom to Walter, his eldest son, he bequeathed to his younger son,

EDWARD DE EVEREUX, who was thenceforward designated " of Salisbury." This Edward was subsequently sheriff of Wiltshire, and, at the time of the general survey, possessed lordships in the counties of Dorset, Somerset, Surrey, Hants, Middlesex, Hereford, Buckingham, and Wilts. When sheriff of the latter county, we are told that he received in rent, as belonging to his office, 130 hogs, 32 bacons, 2 bushels and 16 gallons of wheat, the same of barley, several bushels of oats, 32 gallons of honey or 16 shillings, 448 hens, 1,060 eggs, 100 cheeses, 52 lambs, 200 fleeces of wool; having likewise 162 acres of arable land, and, amongst the reves-land, to the value of £40 per annum. This Edward was standard-bearer at the battle of Brennevill, in Normandy, fought 20th HENRY I., King HENRY being present, and distinguished himself by his singular skill and valour. He left at his decease, a dau.,

Maude, wife of Humphrey de Bohun, and a son and heir,

WALTER DE EVEREUX, who *m.* Sibilla de Chaworth. This feudal lord founded the monastery of Bradenstoke, wherein, in his old age, he became a canon. He was *s.* by his son,

PATRICK DE EVEREUX, who, being steward of the household to the Empress MAUD, was advanced by that princess to the dignity of EARL OF SALISBURY, and was one of the subscribing witnesses, as such, to the agreement made between King STEPHEN and Henry, Duke of Normandy, in the 18th year of that monarch's reign. In the 10th HENRY II., his lordship was a witness to the recognition of the ancient laws and liberties of England, and in two years afterwards, upon the aid then assessed for marrying the king's dau., he certified his knights' fees at seventy-eight and two-fifths. The earl being the king's lieutenant in Aquitaine, and captain general of his forces there, was slain in 1167, by Guy de Lusignan, upon his return from a pilgrimage to St. James of Compostella, and was *s.* by his son,

WILLIAM DE EVEREUX, 2nd Earl of Salisbury, who, at the coronation of King RICHARD I., bore the golden sceptre with the dove on the head of it; but the next year, when the king became a prisoner in Almaine, his lordship was one of those who adhered to John, Earl of Moreton. In the 6th RICHARD I., the earl was with the king in the expedition then made into Normandy, and, upon his return to England, was one of his great council assembled at Nottingham. At the second coronation of RICHARD, in the same year, the Earl of Salisbury was one of the four earls who supported the canopy of state. His lordship *m.* Alianore de Vitrei, dau. of Tirrel de Mainers, and left, at his decease, an only dau. and heiress,

ELA, " of whom (writes Dugdale) it is thus reported: that being so great an inheretrix, one William Talbot, an Englishman, and an eminent soldier, took upon him the habit of a pilgrim, and went into Normandy, where, wandering up and down for the space of two months, at length he found her out. Likewise, that he then changed his habit, and having entered the court where she resided in the garb of a harper (being practised in mirth and jesting), he became well accepted. Moreover, that, growing acquainted with her, after some time he conducted her into England, and presented her to King RICHARD, who, receiving her very courteously, gave her in marriage to WILLIAM, surnamed *Longespee* (from the long sword which he usually wore), his brother, that is, a natural son of King HENRY II., by Fair Rosamond; and that thereupon King RICHARD rendered unto him the earldom of Rosmar, as her inheritance." Be this story true or false, it is certain, however, that the great heiress of the D'Evereux, Ela, espoused the above-named

WILLIAM LONGESPEE, who thereupon became in her right, EARL OF SALISBURY. In the beginning of King JOHN's reign this nobleman was sheriff of Wiltshire, he was afterwards warden of the marches of Wales, and then sheriff of the counties of Cambridge and Huntingdon. About this period (14th JOHN), the baronial contest commencing, William Longespee at once espoused the royal cause, and maintained it so stoutly, that he was included, by the barons, amongst the evil councillors of the crown. The next year he was again constituted sheriff of Wilts, and he held the office from that time during the remainder of his life. He had also a grant of the honour of Eye, in Suffolk, and was the same year a witness to the agreement made between King JOHN and the barons, as guarantee for the former. He was likewise a witness to the charter whereby JOHN resigned his kingdom to the Pope. After this we find him a principal leader in the royal army, until the very close of JOHN's reign, when he swerved in his loyalty, and joined for a short period the ranks of LEWIS of France. Upon the accession, however, of HENRY III., he did homage to that monarch, particularly for the county of Somerset, which the king then gave him; and joining with William Marshall (governor of the king and kingdom), raised the siege of Lincoln: when he was constituted sheriff of Lincolnshire and governor of Lincoln Castle, being invested at the same time with sheriffalty of the co. of Somerset, and governorship of the castle of Shirburne. His lordship soon afterwards accompanied the Earl of Chester to the Holy Land, and was at the battle of Damieta, in which the crescent triumphed. He served subsequently in the Gascon wars, whence returning to England, Dugdale relates "there arose so great a tempest at sea, that, despairing of life, he threw his money and rich apparel overboard. But when all hopes were passed, they discerned a mighty taper of wax, burning bright at the prow of the ship, and a beautiful woman standing by it, who preserved it from wind and rain, so that it gave a clear and bright lustre. Upon sight of which heavenly vision both himself and the mariners concluded of their future security; but everyone there being ignorant what this vision might portend except the earl; he, however, attributed it to the benignity of the blessed virgin, by reason that upon the day when he was honoured with the girdle of knighthood he brought a taper to her altar, to be lighted every day at mass, when the canonical hours used to be sung, and to the intent, that for this terrestrial light, he might enjoy that which is eternal." A rumour, however, reached England of the earls having been lost, and Hubert de Burgh, with the concurrence of the king, provided a suitor for his supposed widow, but the lady, in the interim, having received letters from her husband, rejected the suit with indignation. The earl soon after came to the king at Marlborough, and being received with great joy, he preferred a strong complaint against Hubert de Burgh, adding, that unless the king would do him right therein, he should vindicate himself otherwise, to the disturbance of the public peace. Hubert, however, appeased his wrath with rich presents, and invited him to his table, where it is asserted that he was poisoned, for he retired to his castle of Salisbury in extreme illness, and died almost immediately after, *anno* 1226. His lordship left issue, four sons and five daus., viz.,

WILLIAM, his successor.

Richard, a canon of Salisbury.

Stephen, Justiciary of Ireland. m. Emmeline, widow of Hugh de Lacy, Earl of Ulster, and dau. and heir of Sir Walter de Ridelsford, Baron of Bray, and had two daus., Ela and Emmeline. The latter m. to Maurice Fitzgerald, Baron of Offaly.

Nicholas, bishop of Salisbury, d. in 1297.

Isabel, m. to William de Vesui, Lord Vescy.

Ela, m. 1st, to Thomas, Earl of Warwick, and 2ndly, to Philip Basset, of Hedendon.

Idonea, m. to William de Beauchamp, Baron of Bedford.

Lora, a nun at Lacock.

Ela, jun., m. to William de Odingsells.

His lordship's eldest son,

WILLIAM DE LONGESPEE, "commonly called," says Sir William Dugdale, "by Matthew Paris, and most of our other historians, EARL OF SALISBURY, but erroneously; for all records wherein

mention is made of him, do not give him that title, but call him barely William Longespee. Nay, there is an old chronicle who saith expressly, that, in *anno* 1233 (17th HENRY III.), he was girt with the sword of knighthood, but not made Earl of Salisbury." This William made a pilgrimage to the Holy Land in 1240, and again in 1247, having assumed the cross for a second pilgrimage, proceeded to Rome, and thus preferred a suit to the sovereign pontiff. "Sir, you see that I am signed with the cross, and am on my journey with the King of France to fight in this pilgrimage. My name is great, and of note, viz., WILLIAM LONGESPEE; but my estate is slender; for the king of England, my kinsman and liege lord, hath bereft me of the title of earl, and of that estate; but this he did judiciously, and not in displeasure, and by the impulse of his will; therefore I do not blame him for it. Howbeit, I am necessitated to have recourse to your holiness for favour, desiring your assistance in this distress. We see here (quoth he,) that Earl Richard (of Cornwall,) who, though he is not signed with the cross, yet, through the especial grace of your holiness, he hath got very much money from those who are signed, and therefore I, who am signed, and in want, do intreat the like favour." The pope taking into consideration the elegance of his manner, the efficacy of his reasoning, and the comeliness of his person, conceded in part what he desired : whereupon he received above 1,000 marks from those who had been so signed. In about two years after this, *anno* 1249, having received the blessing of his noble mother, Ela, then abbess of Lacock, he commenced his journey at the head of a company of 200 English horse, and being received with great respect by the king of France, joined that monarch's army. In Palestine he became subsequently pre-eminently distinguished, and fell, in 1250, in a great conflict with the Saracens, near Damieta, having previously killed above 100 of the enemy with his own hand. It was reported that, the night before the battle, his mother Ela, the abbess, saw in a vision the heavens open, and her son armed at all parts (whose shield she well knew), received with joy by the angels. Remembering the occurrence, when the news of his death reached her in six months after, she held up her hands, and with a cheerful countenance said, "I, thy handmaid, give thanks to thee, O Lord, that out of my sinful flesh thou hast caused such a champion against thine enemies to be born " It was also said, that in 1252, when messengers were sent to the Soldan of Babylon, for redemption of those who had been taken prisoners, he thus addressed them—" I marvel at you, Christians, who reverence the bones of the dead, why you inquire not for those of the renowned and right noble William Longespee, because there be many things reported of them (whether fabulous or not I cannot say), viz., that, in the dark of the night, there have been appearances at his tomb, and that to some, who called upon his God, many things were bestowed from Heaven. For which cause, and in regard of his great worth and nobility of birth, we have caused his body to be here intombed." Whereupon the messenger desiring it, the remains were delivered to them by the Soldan, and thence conveyed to Acre, where they were buried in the church of St. Cross. This eminent and heroic personage m. Idonea, dau and heir of Richard de Camville, and had issue,

WILLIAM DE LONGESPEE, his son and heir, who m. Maud, dau. of Walter Clifford, and d. in the 41st HENRY III., in the flower of his age, leaving an only dau. and heiress,

MARGARET, commonly called Countess of Salisbury, who m Henry de Lacy, Earl of Lincoln, and had issue, an only dau and heiress,

ALICE, m. to Thomas, Earl of Lancaster, who being outlawed. King EDWARD II. seized upon the lands which she had made over to her husband; some of which, viz., Tenbrigge, Winterbourn, and Ambresbury, with other manors, King EDWARD III. gave to William de Montacute, to hold in as full and ample a manner, as ever the same had been holden by Margaret, Countess of Salisbury, or her predecessors.

Thus terminated the very eminent families of D'Evereux and De Longespee, EARLS OF SALISBURY.

Arms—D'Evereux, paly of six, gu. and vairé, on a chief, or, a lion passant, sa. De Longespee, az., six lions (or lioncels) rampant, or, three, two, and one.

DEVEREUX—BARONS DEVEREUX.

By Writ of Summons, dated 28 September, 1384.

Lineage.

Of this family, which derived its surname from the town of Eureux, in Normandy, and which came into England with the CONQUEROR, there were several generations, prior to that which attained the peerage. In the 7th King HENRY III.,

STEPHEN DEVEREUX, being in the king's army against the Welsh, had scutage of all his tenants in the counties of Gloucester and Hereford, who held of him by military service. To this Stephen *s.* his son,

WILLIAM DEVEREUX, who in the 42nd of HENRY III., had summons to attend the king at Chester, with horse and arms to restrain the incursions of the Welsh, and in two years afterwards, being then one of the barons marchers, received command, with the others, to repair to the marches without delay, for a similar purpose. He subsequently attended the king at the battles of Lewes, but there he forsook the royal standard, and afterwards fell fighting on the side of the barons at Evesham, in the 49th HENRY III., whereupon Maud, his widow, sister of Walter Giffard, bishop of Bath and Wells, applied to the king, for "certain jewels and harness," which had been deposited in the church of Hereford by the deceased baron, and obtained a precept to the treasurer of the cathedral, for their deliverance to her. But his lands being seized, continued with the crown, until the 51st HENRY III., when his son and heir,

WILLIAM DEVEREUX, making his composition at three years value, according to the decree called "Dictum de Kenilworth," had livery of those estates. In the 22nd of EDWARD I., we find this William Devereux employed in the great expedition made by the king himself into Gascony. To this feudal lord succeeded,

SIR JOHN DEVEREUX, Knt., who in the 42nd EDWARD III., attended Edward the BLACK PRINCE, into Gascony, and the next year was seneschal and governor of Lymosin. Upon the accession of King RICHARD II., Sir John served in the fleet at sea, and was constituted governor of Leeds Castle, in Kent. In the 3rd of RICHARD, he was made captain of Calais, and in the 8th of the same monarch, being then a banneret, was summoned to parliament as a Baron. The following year his lordship was installed a knight of the Garter, and in the second year afterwards constituted constable of Dover Castle, and warden of the Cinque Ports, but this last appointment was through the influence of the great lords then predominant. Upon the attainder of Sir Simon Burley, Knt., the castle and manor of Leonhales, co. Hereford, devolving to the crown, Lord Devereux obtained a special grant thereof, and being possessed of the lordship of Penshurst, he had a license in the 16th of RICHARD, to make a castle of his mansion house there. His lordship *m.* Margaret, dau. of Sir John Barre, Knt., and had issue,

JOHN, his successor.
Joane, *m.* to Walter Fitz-Walter, Lord Fitz-Walter.

He *d.* in 1394, and was *s.* by his son,

SIR JOHN DEVEREUX, Knt., 2nd Baron Devereux, who *m.* Philippa, one of the daus. of Guy de Brien, then deceased, and granddau. and co-heiress of Sir Guy de Brien, but *d.* in 1397, still in minority, and without issue; when his lordship's barony and estates devolved upon his sister Joane, Lady Fitz-Walter, and thenceforward became united with the Barony of Fitz-Walter.

A distinguished branch of the family of Devereux became seated in the co. Wexford, at Carrigmenan, Bulmagir and Ballyrankin.

Arms—Arg., a fesse, gu., in chief three torteaux.

DEVEREUX—EARLS OF ESSEX.

By Letters Patent, dated 4 May, 1572.

Lineage.

WALTER DEVEREUX, 2nd Viscount Hereford. was created the 4 May, 1572, EARL OF ESSEX, in consideration of his descent from the family of BOURCHIER, which had previously held that earldom. His lordship being a military man of high reputa-

169

tion. was appointed in the 12th ELIZABETH, field-marshal of the forces sent to suppress the rebellion of the Earls of Northumberland and Westmoreland; and he was afterwards employed in the wars of Ireland, with the title of earl marshal of that kingdom; he was also a knight of the Garter. His lordship *m.* Lettice, dau. of Sir Francis Knolles, K.G., and had issue,

ROBERT, his successor.
Walter, killed before Roan.
Penelope, *m.* 1st, to Robert, Lord Rich, and 2ndly, to Charles Blount, Earl of Devon.
Dorothy, *m.* 1st, to Sir Thomas Perrot, Knt., and 2ndly, to Henry, Earl of Northumberland.

The earl *d.* at Dublin, 22 September, 1576, but not without suspicion of having been poisoned, through the instigation of the infamous Robert Dudley, Earl of Leicester, who soon after repudiated his wife, Lady Douglas Howard, and *m.* the widow of his lordship. Lord Essex was *s.* by his elder son,

ROBERT DEVEREUX, 2nd Earl of Essex, the celebrated but unfortunate favourite of Queen ELIZABETH. His lordship was first brought to court, in 1585, by his step-father, the Earl of Leicester, and he subsequently attained the highest honours his sovereign could bestow. He was a privy councillor, a knight of the Garter, master of the horse, earl marshal of England, and lord deputy of Ireland: he was likewise chancellor of the University of Cambridge. His ultimate fate is so conspicuous an event in history, that it would be impertinent to dwell at any length upon it here. His lordship having conspired against his royal mistress, and made a fruitless effort at insurrection, was taken prisoner, committed to the Tower, and thence, after being convicted by his peers of high treason, led to the scaffold, 25 February, 1600. The earl left issue by his wife Frances, dau. and heir of Sir Francis Walsingham, and widow of Sir Philip Sidney, one son and two daus., viz.,

ROBERT.
Frances, *m.* to William Seymour, Duke of Somerset.
Dorothy *m.* 1st, to Sir Henry Shirley, Bart., of Stanton-Harold, and 2ndly, to William Stafford, Esq., of Blatherwick, in the co. of Northampton.

His lordship's honours expired under the attainder, but his children being restored in blood, in 1603, his son,

ROBERT DEVEREUX, succeeded to the earldom of Essex, and his late father's other dignities. This nobleman who was installed a knight of the Garter in 1638, attached himself to the royal cause until 1642, when he accepted a commission in the parliament army, and afterwards distinguished himself as a parliamentary general. He *d.* 14 September, 1646, and was interred with national obsequies in Westminster Abbey, the two houses of parliament attending the funeral. His lordship *m.* 1st, Lady Frances Howard, dau. of Thomas, Earl of Suffolk, from whom he was divorced, and that infamous woman *m.* afterwards, Sir Robert Carr, K.G., Earl of Somerset. The earl *m.* 2ndly, Elizabeth, dau. of Sir William Paulet, of Eddington, co. Wilts, one the natural son of William, 3rd Marquess of Winchester, and had a son, Robert, who *d.* in infancy. His lordship leaving no issue, the EARLDOM OF ESSEX, at his decease, became EXTINCT, while his other honours passed according to their respective limitations. (*See* Viscount Hereford, BURKE's *Peerage and Baronetage.*)

Arms—Arg., a fesse, gu., in chief three torteaux.

D'EYNCOURT—BARONS D'EYNCOURT.

By Writ of Summons, dated 6 February, 1299.
By Writ of Summons, dated 27 January, 1332.

Lineage.

Camden, in his "Britannia" (vol. i. p. 559), after referring to this family, as having flourished in a continued succession from the coming in of the Normans to the time of HENRY VI., and then to have failed for want of an heir male of William, 13th Lord d'Eyncourt, adds, "I was the more willing to take notice of this family, that I might in some measure answer the desire of Edmund, Baron d'Eyncourt, who was so very earnest to preserve the memory of his name, that, having no issue male, he petitioned King EDWARD II. for liberty to make over his manors and arms to whomsoever he pleased; for he imagined that both his name and arms would go to the grave with him, and was very solicitous to have them survive and be remembered. Accordingly the king gave him a patent for that end. Yet this surname, for aught I can find, is now quite extinct, and would have been forgotten for ever, if the memory of it had not been preserved in books."

Camden does not quite correctly state the license. It is extant, and may be found, printed at length, in Ryley's "Plac. Parl." (p. 547.) It is dated 23 February, 7th EDWARD II., and enabled Edmund, Baron d'Eyncourt, as will be seen hereafter, to settle his lands upon his grandson William, 2nd son of his eldest son, John d'Eyncourt, in exclusion of Isabel, the female heir, she being the only child of Edmund, eldest son (then deceased) of the said John d'Eyncourt, which Isabel afterwards d. s. p.; and this leads us to trace the family of d'Eyncourt, who were formerly barons by tenure, until summoned to parliament by writ, 22nd EDWARD I.

WALTER DE AYNCOURT, de Eyncourt, or d'Eyncourt, a noble Norman, one of the distinguished companions in arms of the CONQUEROR, was cousin to Remigius, bishop of Lincoln, who built the cathedral there, and obtained as his share of the spoil, sixty-seven lordships in several counties, of which many were in Lincolnshire, where Blankney was his chief seat, and the head of his feudal barony. By his wife Matilda, he had two sons, William and Ralph. WILLIAM, probably the eldest, while receiving his education in the Court of King WILLIAM RUFUS, d. there, as appears by an inscription on a plate of lead, found in the churchyard, near the west door of Lincoln Cathedral, before Dugdale published his baronage, which contains an engraving of the plate, still preserved in the library of that church. From this inscription it seems he was descended from the royal family, probably through his mother. The inscription runs as follows:—"Hic jacet Wilhelmus filius Walteri Aiencuriensis, consanguinei Remigii Episcopi Lincolniensis, qui hanc ecclesiam fecit—Præfatus Wilhelmus, regid stirp: pro-enitus, dum in curid Wilhelmi filii magni Regis Wilhelmi qui Angliam conquisivit aleretur III. Kalend. Novemb obiit."

RALPH D'EYNCOURT, 2nd baron, son of Walter, s. him. He founded Thurgarton Priory, co. Notts, and was s. by his son,

WALTER D'EYNCOURT, 3rd baron, who, with his son Oliver, fought on the side of King STEPHEN in the battle of Lincoln, 1141, and he appears, upon his son's death, subsequently, to have given lands to Walter, a priest, who had saved his son from captivity and death in that battle, to pray for his soul Walter was s. by his other son,

JOHN DEINCOURT, 4th baron, who, in the 22nd HENRY II., paid 20 marks in Nottinghamshire, for trespassing in the king's forests, and 10 marks in Northamptonshire, for a similar transgression. This John m. Ann, dau. of Ralph Murdac, and was s. by his son,

OLIVER, 5th baron, who, by his wife Annabella, had a son,

OLIVER, 6th baron, who m. Nicola, grand-dau. of Nicola de la Haye, a lady of large possessions in Lincolnshire, by her husband, William Fitzernest, and was s. by their son,

JOHN, 7th baron, who m. Agnes de Neville (whose 1st husband was Richard de Percy), and was s. by their son,

EDMUND, 8th baron, who obtained that remarkable license, above mentioned, from EDWARD II. He signed, 12 February, 1301, 29th EDWARD I., the celebrated letter sent by the barons, assembled in parliament at Lincoln, to Pope BONIFACE VIII., denying his jurisdiction in temporal affairs, and denying that Scotland was a fief of the Roman see. The duplicate of this letter exists amongst the public archives, and the seal of "Edmundus de Eyncourt" thereto appended, is in good preservation, and was engraved in 1729, in the 1st vol. of the "Vetusta Monumenta." Baron Edmund was also present, 31rd EDWARD I., when the king refused permission to the bishop of Durham to present a foreign bishop, on the Pope's recommendation. to the priory of Coldingham. He had two sons, John and William, who were with the feudal army at Carlisle, 29th EDWARD I., in the place of their father, and figure in the roll of Carlaverock, where John, it is said, "mult bien fist son devoir." He d. v. p., and subsequently, William, a commander of distinguished valour, was killed 23 June, 1314, 7th EDWARD II., before the Castle of Stirling, on the eve of the battle of Bannockburn, an event referred to by Sir Walter Scott, in his "Lord of the Isles:"

> "Back to the host the Douglas rode,
> And soon glad tidings are abroad,
> That D'Eyncourt by stout Randolph slain,
> His followers fled with loosen'd rein."

Baron Edmund's eldest son, John, left three sons, Edmund, who also d. in the baron's lifetime; William (afterwards 9th baron), and John. Edmund, the grandson, left a dau., Isabel, and the object of the above-mentioned license was, to vest the estates in her uncle, William, next brother of her father, Edmund, in order to prevent the barony descending to her, and thus passing, in case of her marriage, to another name and family. The youngest brother, John, represented Lincolnshire in parliament, 11th EDWARD III., and Nottinghamshire,

14th EDWARD III. Baron Edmund d. 20th EDWARD II., at a very advanced age. He had immense possessions, with great weight and authority: he was prominent in the chief events of his time, and attended his sovereigns on all important occasions of war or council. On his decease, his son John, and his grandson Edmund, being dead, and his great-granddau. Isabel, being also dead, without issue,

WILLIAM. 9th Lord d'Eyncourt, s. his grandfather, when twenty-six years of age, as heir by descent, as well as by virtue of the licensed entail. He was an eminent warrior and active servant of King EDWARD III., through the glorious period of his reign, participating in the immortal achievements of that era in France and Scotland, and on 17 October, 1346, he was one of the commanders in the famous battle of Neville's Cross, near Durham. He is particularly mentioned as an object of the king's gratitude, in his letter of thanks, dated 20 October, written on the occasion of that celebrated victory, when DAVID, King of Scotland, was taken prisoner. King EDWARD being then before Calais, his queen, PHILIPPA, is stated by some writers to have been present at the battle. At any rate it is clear she was in the field prior to its commencement, when she rode in front of the army on a white courser, and, in the words of the historian, "sweetly exhorted them." She was attended by Lord d'Eyncourt at the head of her guard, a post of honour and responsibility, which shows that he was deemed one of the first gentlemen of his day. This is further evidenced by the circumstance, that JOHN, King of France, taken prisoner at the battle of Poictiers—who, during his captivity in England, was treated with that respectful and generous courtesy which shed a lustre over those times—was consigned to Lord d'Eyncourt's custody, and so remained until the period when he passed out of Lincolnshire, under Lord d'Eyncourt's charge, to the metropolis, and thence to France, King EDWARD himself conducting him to the sea-side, and the BLACK PRINCE attending him to Calais, having felt his durance so little personally irksome, that he afterwards returned on a visit to King EDWARD, and died in England before it was completed. On 14 May, 1347, Lord d'Eyncourt was commanded to attend the king before Calais, and was present at all the interesting scenes there enacted, and at the final surrender of the place, followed by the heroic self-devotion of six of the inhabitants, who, with Eustace St. Pierre at their head, were saved by the gentle, but urgent intercession of Queen PHILIPPA, who, after the battle of Durham. had joined her husband at Calais. Lord d'Eyncourt d. 2 June, 1364, aged sixty-four. He m. Millicent, dau. of William, Lord Rees, of Hamlake. William, his eldest son, m. Margaret, dau. of Adam de Welle, and d. v. p., leaving an only son, who s. his grandfather as

WILLIAM, 10th Lord d'Eyncourt. He m. Alice, dau. of John, Lord Neville, of Raby and Brancepeth, co. Durham, by Maud, dau. of Henry, 2nd Lord Percy, which Alice was sister of Ralph Neville, 1st Earl of Westmoreland, who, having m. Joan, half-sister of King HENRY IV., and being, through their dau., Cecily, Duchess of York, grandfather of EDWARD IV. and RICHARD III., the d'Eyncourt family became intimately allied with both the lines of York and Lancaster, and the blood of those royal houses was afterwards brought to their posterity, as hereafter explained, by the marriage of Mr. Tennyson's ancestors, Catherine, co-heiress of Morley and Monteagle, with John Savage, Earl Rivers, and Francis, Lord d'Eyncourt, Earl of Scarsdale, with Anne Cary, of which marriage Mr. Tennyson was eldest co-heir. William, 10th baron, d. 5th RICHARD II., 1381, and was s. by his son,

RALPH, 11th Lord d'Eyncourt, who, dying an infant, s. p., was s. by his brother,

JOHN, 12th Lord d'Eyncourt, who m. Johanna, dau. and sole heiress of Robert de Grey, 5th Baron Grey, of Rotherfield, and d. 7th HENRY IV., leaving issue,

WILLIAM, 13th Lord d'Eyncourt, his son and heir, and two daus., ALICE and MARGARET. This nobleman, who was also in right of his mother, Baron Grey of Rotherfield, m. Elizabeth, sister of Viscount Beaumont, but d. s. p. in 1422, 1st HENRY VI., leaving Alice (Mr. Tennyson's ancestor), aged eighteen, and Margaret, aged seventeen, his sisters and co-heirs. Margaret m. Ralph, 4th Lord Cromwell, of Tattershall, co. Lincoln, and d. s. p. 15 September, 1455, 33rd HENRY VI., leaving her sister,

ALICE, Baroness d'Eyncourt and Grey, of Rotherfield, sole heiress of her father, mother, brother, and sister. She m. William, Baron Lovel (of Tichmarsh) and Holland, chief of the male line of the illustrious house of Yvery in Normandy, named Lupellus, afterwards Lovel. In the 24th HENRY VI., in consideration of his eminent services abroad to HENRY V. and HENRY VI., and his infirmity of body, he had exemption for life from attendance in parliament, and d. 13 June, 33rd

HENRY VI., leaving, by the said Alice D'Eyncourt, who survived him, JOHN, his successor, and WILLIAM, who ultimately became heir-male of his said father and mother, William, Lord Lovel, and Alice, Lady D'Eyncourt, and was the ancestor of the present family of Tennyson-D'Eyncourt, of Bayons Manor, co. Lincoln. Alice, Lady D'Eyncourt, afterwards *m.* Ralph, Lord Boteler of Sudeley, who *d.* 13th EDWARD IV., and by him had one son, who *d.* an infant, and she *d.* 15th EDWARD IV. Her eldest son, JOHN, became Lord Lovel and Holland, but *d.* before his mother, 4th EDWARD IV. By his wife Joane, only dau. and heiress of John, Lord Beaumont, he had a son FRANCIS, and two daus., Joane and Frideswide. The 1st *m.* Sir Bryan Stapleton, and her descendant has recently been summoned to parliament as Baron Beaumont, by descent from her; Frideswide *m.* Sir Edward Norris, and their unfortunate son was attainted and executed, with Queen ANNE BOLEYN, 28th HENRY VIII. On the death of John, Lord Lovel, he was *s.* by his only son,

FRANCIS, Lord Lovel and Holland, who, on the death of his grandmother, Alice, became also Lord d'Eyncourt (15th from the Conquest), and *Lord Grey of Rotherfield*. (*See* LOVELL.)

The late RIGHT HON. CHARLES TENNYSON, of Bayons Manor, co. Lincoln, superadded the name and arms of d'Eyncourt to those of Tennyson, by royal license, dated 27 July, 1835, in compliance with a condition attached to the enjoyment of certain manors and estates, by a codicil to the will of his father, George Tennyson, Esq., of Bayons Manor, " in order to commemorate his descent from the ancient and noble family of D'Eyncourt, Barons D'Eyncourt of Blankney, and his representation in blood, as co-heir of the Earls of Scarsdale, Barons D'Eyncourt of Sutton."

Arms—Az., a fesse indented, between ten billets, or, four in chief, six in base.

DIGBY—BARONS DIGBY OF SHERBORNE, CO. DORSET, EARLS OF BRISTOL.

Barony, by Letters Patent, 25 November, 1618.
Earldom, by Letters Patent, 15 September, 1622.

Lineage.

SIR JOHN DIGBY, Knt., younger brother of Sir Robert Digby, ancestor of the LORDS DIGBY, and 2nd son of Sir George Digby of Coleshill, by Abigail his wife, dau. of Sir Arthur Henningham, Knt., of Ketteringham, having filled some high situations in the court of JAMES I. and being twice accredited ambassador to the court of Spain, was elevated to the peerage, 25 November, 1618, as BARON DIGBY, *of Sherborne, co. Dorset.* His lordship was subsequently employed upon different embassies, but particularly to the court of Spain, in 1622, touching a marriage between Prince Charles and the Lady Maria, when he was created EARL OF BRISTOL. In 1624, his lordship had a difference with the Duke of Buckingham, and they mutually impeached each other. From that period he lived in retirement, until the breaking out of the civil war, in which he first sided with the parliament, but afterwards went over to the king, and eventually withdrew into France. The earl *m.* Beatrix, dau. of Charles Walcot, Esq., of Walcot, co. Salop, and had issue,

GEORGE, his successor.
John, who was a general of horse in Lord Hopton's army, and afterwards a secular priest, at Pontoise, in France, *d.* after the restoration.
Abigail, *m.* to George Freke, Esq., of Shroton, co. Dorset, and *d. s. p.*
Mary, *m.* to Arthur, Earl of Donegal, had no surviving issue.

His lordship *d.* in 1652, and was *s.* by his elder son,
GEORGE DIGBY, 2nd Earl of Bristol, K.G. This nobleman suffered considerably during the civil wars, having had his estates confiscated and himself banished. He lived however to be restored with the monarchy, to his country and fortune; but having become a Roman Catholic while abroad, he was thereby incapacitated from holding any place in the government. His lordship is noticed by Walpole as an author, and a person of singularity, whose life was one contradiction. "He wrote against popery, and embraced it. He was a zealous opposer of the court, and a sacrifice for it; was conscientiously converted in the midst of his prosecution of Lord Strafford, and was most unconscientiously a prosecutor of Lord Clarendon. With great parts, he always hurt himself and his friends. With romantic bravery, he was always an unsuccessful commander. He spoke

for the Test Act, though a Roman Catholic; and addicted himself to astrology, on the birthday of true philosophy." His lordship *m.* Anne, dau. of Francis, 4th Earl of Bedford, by whom he had issue,

JOHN his successor.
Francis, slain in the sea-fight with the Dutch, 28 May, 1672, and *d. s. p.*
Diana, *m.* to the Baron Moll, in Flanders.
Anne, *m.* to Robert, Earl of Sunderland, from whom descend the Dukes of Marlborough, and the Earls of Spencer.

His lordship *d.* in 1676, and was *s.* by his only surviving son,
JOHN DIGBY, 3rd Earl of Bristol, who *m.* 1st, Alice, dau. and heiress of Robert Bourne, Esq., of Blackhall, co. Essex; and 2ndly, Rachael, dau. of Sir Hugh Windham, Knt., but having no issue, the BARONY OF DIGBY, and the EARLDOM OF BRISTOL, became, at his lordship's decease, in 1698, EXTINCT, while his large estates devolved upon his only surviving sister, Anne, Countess of Sunderland, whose son George, 3rd Earl of Sunderland, *m.* for his 2nd wife, Anne, 2nd dau. of John, 1st and celebrated DUKE OF MARLBOROUGH.

Arms—Az., a fleur-de-lis, arg., with a mullet for difference.

DIGBY—BARONESS OFFALEY.

Lineage.

THE HON. LETTICE FITZGERALD, dau. and sole heir of Gerald, Lord Offaley, and grand-dau. of Gerald, 11th Earl of Kildare, *m.* SIR ROBERT DIGBY, Knt., of Coleshill, in Warwickshire, and had several sons, from whom descended the Earl Digby, the Digbys of Landenstown, the Rev. John Digby, of Osberstown, &c. Sir Robert Digby *d.* 24 May, 1618, and in two years after (1620) his widow was created BARONESS OFFALEY for life. Her ladyship *d.* in 1658, and of course the peerage EXPIRED with her.

Arms—Az., a fleur-de-lis, arg.

DIGBY—EARL DIGBY AND VISCOUNT COLESHILL.

(*See* BURKE's *Extant Peerage*.)

DILLON—EARL OF ROSCOMMON.

Lineage.

SIR HENRY LE DILLON, who, accompanying the Earl of Moreton (afterwards King John), into Ireland, in 1185, obtained those extensive territorial grants in the cos. of Longford and Westmeath then denominated *Dillon's Country*, but altered by statute, 34th HENRY VIII., to the Barony of Kilkenny West. Sir Henry *m.* a dau. of John de Courcy, Earl of Ulster, and was afterwards styled "Premier Dillon, Lord Baron Dromrany." From this feudal lord lineally sprang

GERALD DILLON, Lord of Dromrany, who *m.* Lady Emily FitzGerald, dau. of the Earl of Desmond, and had issue,
I. SIR MAURICE, of Dromrany, ancestor of the DILLONS of Dromrany, the DILLONS of Kilcornan (now represented by COMTE AUGUSTE HENRI DILLON, resident at Mons, in Belgium), the DILLONS, VISCOUNTS DILLON, &c.
II. John   III. JAMES (Sir).

The 3rd son,
SIR JAMES DILLON, of Proudstown, was ancestor of
SIR ROBERT DILLON, of Newton, attorney general for Ireland to HENRY VIII. in 1545, appointed, in 1553, by Queen MARY, 2nd Justice of the Court of Queen's Bench, whence he was advanced, in the following reign, to the chief justiceship of the Common Pleas; and was subsequently for sometime speaker of the House of Commons. He *m.* Jenet, youngest dau. of Edward Barnewall, Esq., of Crickstown, by Elizabeth his wife, dau. of Sir Thomas Plunket, of Dunsoghly, Knt., lord chief justice of the Common Pleas, and had issue,
I. LUCAS (Sir) of whom presently.
II. Roger, of Ballydromny, co Cavan, *m.* Margaret, dau. and heir of Richard Dillon, Esq., of Ballydromny, and had a son,
James, of Ballydromny, Ballynecor, who *m.* 1st, Margaret, dau. of Edward Nugent, of Trim, Esq., and had four children, who all *d. unm.*; 2ndly, Mary, dau. of Richard Linham, Esq., of Adamstown, co. Meath, and had a son and heir, Lucas, of Ballydromny; 3rdly, Catherine, dau. of Edmund Dalton, of Mullinvichan, co. Meath, Esq., and *d.* 23 October, 1633, leaving by her a son, Bartholomew.

III. Thomas, of Kilmackeron, co. Westmeath, m. 1st, a dau. of Walter Pepper, and by her had two sons, Talbot, of Kilmackeron, who d. 9 July, 1599, leaving a son and heir, Thomas; and Luke. He m. 2ndly, Margaret Cashel, and had a son, Robert, of Cannerstown, Ballymulvey, and Ballymahon, co. Longford, who was aged seventeen, in 1592, and who m. Margaret, dau. of Theobald, 1st Viscount Dillon.

IV. John, of Davidstown and Walterston.

I. Elizabeth, m. to Thomas Plunket, Alderman of Dublin.

II. Alson, m. to Lord Slane.

The eldest son,

SIR LUCAS DILLON, of Newtown and Moymet, co. Meath, attorney-general for Ireland in 1567, speaker of the House of Commons; constituted in 1572, chief-baron of the Exchequer, and sworn of the privy council. Sir Lucas m. Jane, dau. of James Bathe, Esq., chief-baron of the Exchequer, and by her (who d. 1581) he had issue,

I. JAMES, of whom presently.

II. Thomas, of Kentstown, and Prephans, co. Meath. m. Elizabeth Colepeper, and d. 18 April, 1609, leaving issue,

    1 Henry, of Kentstown, m. Jane, dau. of Sarsfield of Sarsfieldstown, co. Meath, Esq., and had issue,

        Robert, who m. the dau. of O'Connor Roe, and was father of Charles, and of Magdalen the wife of Edmund O'Kelly, Esq., and of Clare, wife of Michael O'Connor, Esq.

        Henry, settled in the co. Tipperary.

    2 Theobald, of Waterstown.

    3 Lucas, settled in Munster.

    4 James.

III. Christopher, d. s. p.

IV. Alexander, d. s. p.

V. John, d. s. p.

VI. Robert, settled in the King's co., and left issue.

I. Genet, wife of Christopher, Lord Killeen.

II. Elinor, wife of Robert Rochfort, Esq., of Kilbride.

III. Elizabeth, m. to John Sarsfield, Esq., of Shurnings, co. Kildare.

IV. Anne, m. to Richard Plunket, Esq., of Rathmore.

V. A dau., wife of Christopher Plunket, of Courtstown, Esq.

VI. A dau., wife of Bartholomew Dillon, Esq.

The eldest son was

SIR JAMES DILLON, who was elevated to the peerage of Ireland, 24 January, 1619, as *Lord Dillon, Baron of Kilkenny West*, and advanced to the dignity of EARL OF ROSCOMMON, 5 August, 1622. His lordship m. Elinor, dau. of Sir Christopher Barnewall, Knt. of Turvey, and had, (with six daus.),

I. ROBERT, Lord Dillon, his successor.

II. Lucas, of Trinity Island, co. Cavan, m. Mary, dau. of Sir John Thorpe, and was s. by his son,

    James, of Rathwire, who m. Jane, dau. of Sir Anthony Mulledy of Robertstown, co. Meath, Knt., and had issue,

        1 Lucas, d. s. p.

        2 Patrick, of Twomore, m. Dymphna, dau. of Col Arthur Talbot and grand niece of Richard, Earl of Tyrconnell, and had issue,

           James, d. s. p.

           Robert, 9th Earl of Roscommon, but did not assume the title, d. unm. in France, 1770.

           John, 10th Earl of Roscommon, he assumed the title, but did not sit in Parliament, being a Roman Catholic, Arthur, d. unm.   John, d. unm.

           1 Mary.   2 Jane.   3 Ellinor.

III. Thomas, d. s. p.

IV. Christopher, d. s. p.

V. George, d. s. p.

VI. John, d. s. p.

VII. Patrick, of Rath, King's Co., m. Jane, dau. of Edmund Malone, of Ballynahoune and Clanmullen, chief of his name, and had,

    James, of Rath, m. 1st, Elizabeth, dau. of John Veale, of Lancaster, and had issue,

        Edward, of Dublin, m. Penelope Sharpless, an English lady, and d. 1734, leaving (by her who m. 2ndly, Colonel John Dillon, of the 7th Dragoon Guards), a son, Robert, who claimed to be 11th Earl of Roscommon, but failed, as Patrick the 11th earl proved his legitimacy.

        Veale, who m. Margaret, dau. of Walsh, and had an only child, Jane, who m. Anthony Fox, of Clotanny, King's Co., Esq., and had an only son, Anthony.

    Mr. Dillon, of Rath, m. 2ndly, Penelope, sister of James Horan, Gent., and had issue,

        Michael, m. Mary, dau. and heir of John Jennet, of Recluse and Skeden, co. Dublin, Esq., and had issue,

           John, d. young.

           James, of Dublin, surgeon, m. 1st, the dau. of Butler, of Waterford, but by her had no issue; 2ndly, Elizabeth dau. of Joseph Plunket, Esq., and had,

               Michael, capt. in the Dublin Militia, killed before the battle of Ross, 1798, he m. Mary, dau. of the Rev. Richard Griffith, of Kilbritain, co. Cork, and had a son, Michael-James-Robert Dillon, 12th Earl of Roscommon, and a dau. Elizabeth, who d. young.

Anthony, d. unm.

James, m. 3rdly, Anne, dau. of Mark Burne of Johnstown, co. Wicklow, and had,

    James, who d. young.

    Henry, d. young.

    Mary.

James. m. 4thly, Mary, dau. of Capt. Patrick Quinlan, Esq., of Limerick, and by her had issue,

    Patrick.   John.

    Thomas, d. unm.

    Peter Quinlan Dillon, of Alharuin, near Malaga, in Spain, who m. Margaret, dau. of John Power of London; d. s. p.

    Elizabeth.   Margaret.

    Catharine, wife of Bernard Colyer, of Dublin, Esq. Maria, d. young.

Francis, father of Francis, who m. Elizabeth Sherving ton, and who was father of Veale, who d. young, Robert, m. Catherine, dau. of Luke Shervingham.

James, 1st Earl of Roscommon, was s. by his eldest son,

ROBERT, 2nd earl; a privy-councillor in Ireland, and twice included in the commission of lords-justices for that kingdom. His lordship m. 1st, Margaret, dau. of David, Earl of Barrymore, by whom he had JAMES, Lord Dillon, Lucas, who d. s. p., and Daniel, d. s. p. The earl m. 2ndly, Lady Dorothy Hastings, youngest dau. of George, 4th Earl of Huntingdon, and widow of Sir James Stewart, by whom he had Henry, who d. unm. 21 April, 1640; and 3rdly, Anne, dau. of Sir William Stroud, and widow of Lord Folliott, by whom he had a son, CARY, who s. as 5th earl. His lordship d. 7 September, 1642, and was s. by his eldest son,

JAMES, 3rd earl. "This nobleman," says Anthony à Wood, "was reclaimed, when young, from the superstitions of the Romish church by primate Usher, and sent by him into England, as a jewel of price, to be committed to the care and trust of Doctor George Hakewell, who finding him to be a young man of pregnant parts, placed him in Exeter College in 1628, under the tuition of Lawrence Bodley, B.D., in which college continuing some years, he became an accomplished person." His lordship m. Elizabeth, youngest dau. of Sir William Wentworth, Bart., and sister of Thomas, Earl of Strafford, lord-lieutenant of Ireland, and was s. in 1649, by his son,

WENTWORTH, 4th earl, the celebrated poet, thus characterized by Dryden and Pope:—

"Roscommon, whom both court and camps commend,
True to his prince, and faithful to his friend;
Roscommon first in fields of honour known,
First in the peaceful triumphs of the gown."—*Dryden*.

"Roscommon, not more learned than good,
With manners gen'rous as his noble blood;
To him the wit of Greece and Rome was known,
And every author's merit but his own."—*Pope*.

His lordship m. 1st, Lady Frances Boyle, dau. of Richard, Earl of Burlington and Cork, and 2ndly, Isabella, dau. of Matthew Boynton, Esq., 2nd son of Sir Mathew Boynton, Bart., of Barnston, in Yorkshire, but dying s. p. 20 January, 1684, the honours reverted to his uncle, (see Robert, 2nd earl),

CARY, 5th earl, bapt. July, 1627; master of the Mint, commissary-general of the horse, colonel of foot, and a privy-councillor. His lordship m. Katherine, dau. of John Werden, Esq., of Chester; and dying 24 November, 1689, left (with two daus. Catharine m. Hugh, Earl of Mount Alexander, and d. s. p. 26 June, 1674, buried in St. Michans Church, Dublin, and Anne, m. to Sir Thomas Nugent) a son,

ROBERT, 6th earl; who m. Margaret, dau. of Sir Thomas Putt, Bart., of Combe Gillisham, Devonshire; and dying in 1715, was s. by his eldest son,

ROBERT, 7th earl, m. Anne, dau. of Sir Charles Ingoldsby, of Clondiralaw, co. Clare, and dying s. p., 9 January, 1721, the honours devolved upon his brother,

JAMES, 8th earl who d. unm. in 1746, when the honours devolved upon his kinsman,

ROBERT DILLON, Esq., as 9th earl, (refer to descendants of the Hon. Lucas Dillon, 2nd son of 1st earl). This nobleman entered early into the military service of France, and attained the rank of marshal with the command of the corps called "The Roscommon Regiment," previously "De Rothe's." His lordship d. unm. in 1770, and was s. by his brother,

JOHN, 10th earl, who m. Eleanor, dau. of Edward O'Fallon, Esq., of Kye, co. Roscommon, by whom he had,

    Margaret, m. to Lawrence Manning, Esq.

    Dymphna, m. to Edward Hanly, Esq.

    Helen, m. to Mathew Manning, Esq.

His lordship m. 2ndly, Bridget Mullaly, and dying in 1782, left an only son,

PATRICK, 11th earl, b. 15 March, 1769, who m. Barbara, dau

of Ignatius Beg, Esq., of Belrea, co. Roscommon, by whom he had an only dau., Maria. His lordship d. 17 November, 1816, and the honours became dormant, and so remained until restored, 19 June, 1828, after a procrastinated investigation by the House of Lords, to MICHAEL-JAMES-ROBERT DILLON, Esq., who s. as 12th Earl of Roscommon. He was b. 2 October, 1798; m. 19 August, 1830, Charlotte, 2nd dau. of the late John-Joseph Talbot, Esq., and sister of John, 16th Earl of Shrewsbury, which lady d. s. p. 21 November, 1843. His lordship d. s. p. 15 May, 1850, since which time the honours have remained DORMANT.

Arms—Arg., a lion rampant, between three crescents, each beneath an estoile of six points, gu.; over all a bar, az.

DINAN—BARON DINAN.

By Writ of Summons, dated 23 January, 1295.

Lineage.

The surname of DINAN appears to have been first adopted by Fouke, one of the knights of Roger de Montgomery, Earl of Shrewsbury, upon whom that nobleman conferred the castle which he had erected at Dinan (now called Ludlow), and he was thence designated Sir Fouke de Dinan.

GEFFERY DINAN had summons, with other persons of note, in 41st HENRY III., to repair to the king at Bristol, well fitted with horse and arms, in order to march against the Welsh. He d. in two years afterwards, seised of the manor of Hertland, co. Devon, which he held by service of two knights' fees, and was s. by his son,

OLIVER DINAN, who, upon doing homage in 48th HENRY III., had livery of his lands. This Oliver, having m. Isabel, dau. of Hugh, Earl of Oxford, and widow of John de Courtenay, without license, had to pay a fine of £100 to the crown in consequence. In the 14th EDWARD I. he procured the royal charter for free warren in all his demesne lands in the counties of Devon, Somerset, and Cornwall; and was summoned to parliament as a Baron, from 23 June, 1295, to 29 December, 1299, and dying in the following year, was s. by his son,

JOSCE DINAN, 2nd Baron Dinan, who does not appear from the existing rolls to have been summoned to parliament; he d. soon after his father (29th EDWARD I.), leaving two sons, viz.,

JOHN, his successor.
Oliver, who d. in 20th EDWARD III. and left a son,
  Oliver, who left, by his 1st wife, a son Oliver, who d. s. p.; and by his 2nd, Margaret, dau. of Richard de Hydon, three daus., viz.,
    Margaret, m. to William de Asthorpe.
    Elene, } nuns.
    Isabel, }

The elder son,

JOHN DINAN, s. his father, and was s. himself by his son,

JOHN DINAN (Dynant, or Dynham, as the name was differently written), of Hertland, 4th baron. He was b. 1320; m. 1369, Joane, dau. of Sir Thomas Courtenay and Muriell his wife, dau. and co-heir of John, Lord Moells; which Joane was heiress of her brother, Sir Hugh Courtenay, Knt. To this nobleman, who d. 1382, s. his son,

JOHN DYNHAM, 5th baron. He m. Philippa, dau. of John, Lord Lovell; d. 1428, and was s. by his son,

SIR JOHN DYNHAM, 6th baron, who served in the wars of King HENRY VI., and d. in the 36th of that monarch, leaving by his wife Joane, dau. and heiress of Richard de Arches, the following issue,

JOHN, his successor.
Elizabeth, m. 1st, Fouke, Lord Fitz-Warren; and 2ndly, to Sir John Sapcoate, Knt.
Joane, m. to John, Lord Zouche, of Harringworth.
Margaret, m. to Sir John Carewe, Knt.
Catherine, m. to Sir Thomas Arundel, Knt.

Sir John Dynham was s. by his son,

SIR JOHN DYNHAM, Knt., who being in high favour with King EDWARD IV., was summoned to parliament as a Baron,* by that monarch, 28 February, 1466, and continuing one of the most zealous and gallant supporters of the House of York, his lordship obtained, in two years afterwards, the custody of the forest of Dartmore, with extensive territorial grants, amongst

---

* No writ of summons appears to have issued for several generations (from the reign of EDWARD I.), Sir John Dynham, although unquestionably a Baron by descent, is presumed to have been only raised to the dignity by this writ; and this has been deemed erroneously a new creation.

173

which were several manors, part of the possessions of Humphrey Stafford, Earl of Devon, then in the crown, by reason of the death of that earl, without issue, and the forfeiture of Thomas Courtenay, Earl of Devon. In the 15th EDWARD IV., Lord Dynham was sworn of the privy council, and had a grant of an annuity of 100 marks for his attendance on that service, to be received out of the petty customs in the port of London; in which office of privy councillor he was continued by King HENRY VII., and constituted by that monarch treasurer of the Exchequer. His lordship was also a knight of the Garter. He m. Elizabeth, dau. and heiress of Walter, Lord Fitz-Walter, and widow of Sir John Ratcliffe; but dying s.p. 30 January, 1500, his barony, supposing it a new creation, EXPIRED; but that created by the writ of EDWARD I. fell into ABEYANCE between his heirs at law, and so continues amongst their representatives. Those heirs were

Elizabeth, his lordship's sister, m. 1st, Fouke, Lord Fitz-Warren, who d. 1478; and 2ndly, Sir John Sapcoate, Knt., and by him had a son,
  Richard Sapcoate, who m. Alice Vaux, and was father of William Sapcoate, who m. Anne St. Mark, of Thornhaugh, and had a son, Sir Guy Sapcoate, who m. Margaret, dau. and heir of Guy Wolston, and had a dau. and heir,
    Ann, m. 1st, to Sir John Broughton, of Tuddington, and 2ndly, John, 1st Earl of Bedford.
Joane, his lordship's sister, widow of John, Lord Zouche, of Haryngworth.
Sir Edmund Carewe, of Mohun's Ottery, his lordship's nephew, son of his sister Margaret, Lady Carewe.
Sir John Arundel, K.B., of Lanherne, co. Cornwall, his lordship's nephew, son of his sister Catherine, Lady Arundel. This Sir John Arundel m. 1st, Eleanor, dau. of Thomas Grey, Marquess of Dorset, from which union the noble family of ARUNDEL OF WARDOUR derives.

Arms—Gu., a fesse dancettee, erm.

DISRAELI, EARL OF BEACONSFIELD AND VISCOUNT HUGHENDEN OF HUGHENDEN MANOR.

VISCOUNTESS BEACONSFIELD OF BEACONSFIELD.

Earldom, by Letters Patent, dated 21 August, 1876.
Viscounty of Hughenden, by Letters Patent, same date.
Viscounty of Beaconsfield, by Letters Patent, dated 30 November, 1868.

Lineage.

The family of Disraeli settled first in Spain, and then in Venice.

BENJAMIN DISRAELI, b. 22 September, 1730, came to England in the year 1748. He m. in 1765, Sarah Villareal de Seproot, a branch of the Villareals of Portugal, and d. 28 November, 1816, leaving an only child,

ISAAC DISRAELI, Esq. of Bradenham Manor, co. Buckingham, D.C.L., b. May, 1766 (author of the well-known work, "The Curiosities of Literature"), who m. 10 February, 1802, Maria, sister of George Basevi, Esq., of Brighton, D.L., originally of a Venetian family, by whom (who d. 21 April, 1847) he had four children,

BENJAMIN, created Earl of Beaconsfield.
Ralph, deputy clerk of the Parliaments, m. 15 August, 1861, Katherine, dau. of Charles Trevor, Esq., and has issue,
  CONINGSBY-RALPH, who s. to Hughenden Manor, b. 25 February, 1867.
  Doro.hy.   Sybil-Isabel.
  Margaret-Katherine.
James, commissioner of Her Majesty's Inland Revenue, m. 24 September, 1856, Isabella-Anne, dau. of William Cave, Esq., of Brentry, co. Somerset, and d. s. p. 22 December, 1868.
Sarah, d. unm. 19 December, 1859.

Mr. Disraeli d. 19 January, 1848. His eldest son,

THE RIGHT HON. BENJAMIN DISRAELI, EARL OF BEACONSFIELD, Viscount Hughenden, of Hughenden, in the county of Buckingham, K.G., P.C., LL.D., D.C.L., First Lord of the treasury, and lord privy seal, 1874 to 1880, a commissioner of education for Scotland, one of the committee of council on education, an elected trustee of the British Museum, and an elder brother of the Trinity House; was b. 21 December, 1804; m. 28 August, 1839, Mary-Anne, widow of Wyndham Lewis,

Esq., M.P., of Greenmeadow, co. Glamorgan, only dau. of Capt. John-Viney Evans, R.N., of Bampford Speke, Devon, and niece and eventual heiress of General Sir James Viney, K.C.H., of Taignton Manor, co. Gloucester. This lady was created, 30 November, 1868, Viscountess Beaconsfield of Beaconsfield, co. Bucks, in the peerage of the United Kingdom, but *d.* without issue, 15 December, 1872, when that title became extinct.

Author, orator. and statesman, the Earl of Beaconsfield is pre-eminently distinguished in literature and politics. He was M.P. for Maidstone, 1837-41, for Shrewsbury, 1841-7, and for co. Buckingham from 1847 to 1876. From March to December, 1852, from February, 1858, to June, 1859, and from June, 1866, to February, 1868, he held office as Chancellor of the Exchequer; and from February, 1868, till December of the same year, and from February, 1874, to April, 1880, was first lord of the treasury. He was elevated to the peerage of the United Kingdom, by Letters Patent, dated 21 August, 1876, and was appointed (with the Marquess of Salisbury) Her Majesty's plenipotentiary to the Congress of European Powers assembled at Berlin, 1878. Upon his return he was invested with the Garter, 22 July same year, and *d.s.p.* 19 April, 1881, when all his honours became extinct.

Arms—Per saltire gu. and arg., a castle triple towered in chief, of the last, two lions rampant in fesse sa, and an eagle displayed in base or.

DOCKWRA—BARON DOCKWRA, OF CULMORE.

By Letters Patent, dated 15 May, 1621.

Lineage.

Sir Henry Dockwra, Knt., a distinguished soldier in the Irish wars of the reign of Elizabeth, was created Baron Dockwra, of Culmore, co. Derry, by patent, dated at Westminster, 15 May, 1621. Lord Dockwra, who was treasurer at war, one of the privy council, and governor of Loughfoyle, received a grant of lands in the co. Wicklow, 4 August, 1623. He *m.* Anne, dau. of Frances Vaughan, of Sutton-upon-Derent, and by her (whose will bears date 20 July, 1648), he had issue,

I. Theodore, 2nd baron.
II. Henry, *d.* 25 December, 1627, and was buried in Christ Church, Dublin.
I. Frances, *d. unm.* 26 June, 1624, and was buried in Christ Church, Dublin.
II. Anne, *m.* Capt. William Shore, and *d.* 22 December, 1657.
III. Elizabeth. *m.* Sir Henry Brooke, governor of Donegall, was buried in Christ Church, Dublin, leaving two sons, George and Henry.

Lord Dockwra (whose will bears date 10 March, 1630), *d.* 18 April, 1631, and was *s.* by his elder son,

Sir Theodore Dockwra, Knt., 2nd baron, aged twenty-one, in 1631. He *d. unm.*, whereupon the title became extinct.

Arms—Quarterly : 1st sa., a chev. engrailed, arg., between three plates, each charged with a palet for Dockwra; 2nd arg., on a bend, gu., three martlets, or, for Danvers; 3rd erm., a bend, gu., charged with two chevrons, or; 4th az., a fesse wavy, or, between three swans, arg., for Swan.

DODINGTON—BARON MELCOMBE, OF MELCOMBE REGIS, CO. DORSET.

By Letters Patent, dated 6 April, 1761.

Lineage.

George Bubb, Esq., *b.* in 1692, assumed by Act of Parliament, in pursuance of the testamentary injunction of his maternal uncle, George Dodington, Esq., of Eastbury, co. Dorset, the surname of Dodington; and under that designation was a very versatile and busy politician in the reigns of George I. and George II.; during which period, he was member of parliament for Winchelsea, Bridgewater, Weymouth, and Melcombe Regis, and held many posts of importance, being at one time envoy extraordinary at the Court of Spain; but his own curious and well-known "Diary," published after his decease, best shows the place he held in public life. He was elevated to the peerage 6 April, 1761, by the title of Lord Melcombe, *of Melcombe Regis, co. Dorset* ; but *d.* 28 July in the following year, *unm.*, at his villa of La Trappe, Ham-

mersmith, when the dignity became extinct. This nobleman, the patron of Thomson and Young, the poets, is so generally known, that it would be a work of supererogation to enter more into detail regarding him upon the present occasion. His mansion at Eastbury, when finished by his lordship, was esteemed a most superb and costly structure; it passed, at his decease to the Duke of Buckingham, and was pulled down and sold piece-meal; but the bulk of his fortune he left to Thomas Wyndham, Esq.

Arms—Arg. a chev., between three bugle horns, sa.

DORMER—EARLS OF CARNARVON.

By Letters Patent, dated 2 August, 1628.

Lineage.

Robert Dormer (son of the Hon. William Dormer, and Alice, dau. of Sir Richard Molineux, of Sefton), *s.* as 2nd Baron Dormer, *of Wenge*, at the decease of his grandfather, Robert, 1st lord, in 1616, and was advanced 2 August, 1628, to the Viscounty of Ascot and Earldom of Carnarvon. His lordship, who took up arms in the royal cause during the civil wars, was eminently distinguished as a military leader in those unhappy times. In the year 1643 he had the command of a regiment of horse, and went with Prince Rupert, the Marquess of Hertford, Prince Maurice, and Colonel Howard, into Dorsetshire, and charged as a volunteer in Sir John Byron's regiment, at the battle of Roundway-down, co. Wilts; after which he joined the king before Gloucester, being then a general of horse, but was slain at Newbury on 20 September following. His lordship *m.* Anna-Sophia, dau. of Philip Herbert, Earl of Pembroke and Montgomery, and was *s.* by his only son,

Charles Dormer, 3rd Baron Dormer, and 2nd Earl of Carnarvon. This nobleman *m.* Elizabeth, dau. of Arthur, Lord Capel, by whom he had surviving issue,

Elizabeth, *m.* to Philip Stanhope, Earl of Chesterfield.
Isabella, *m.* to Charles Coote, Earl of Mountrath.
Anna-Sophia, *d.* of the small-pox, *unm.*, in the twenty-second year of her age, *anno* 1695.

His lordship *m.* 2ndly, Mary, dau. of Montagu Bertie, Earl of Lindsey, but had no issue. He *d.* 29 November, 1709, when the Earldom of Carnarvon became extinct, while the Barony of Dormer devolved upon his kinsman, Rowland Dormer, Esq., of Grove Park, co. Warwick, great-grandson of Robert, 1st lord, through his 2nd son, the Hon. Anthony Dormer ; and is still extant.

Arms—Az., ten billets, four, three, two, and one, or, on a chief of the 2nd a demi lion issuant, sa., armed and langued, gu.

DOUGLAS—EARL OF DOUGLAS.

Creation, 4 February, 1356-7.

Lineage.

William Douglas, created Earl of Douglas, 4 February, 1356-7, was son of Archibald Douglas, regent of Scotland, and nephew of the good Sir James Douglas who commanded the centre of the Scottish army at Bannockburn ; and is still more celebrated in history by the journey he undertook for the purpose of depositing Bruce's heart in the sepulchre of our Lord of Jerusalem. The 1st Earl Douglas *m.* 1st, Lady Margaret Marr, dau. of Donald, 12th Earl of Mar, sister and heiress of Thomas, 13th of the old Earls of Mar and thereupon assumed the designation of Earl of Douglas and Mar in 1377. Of this marriage there were two children,

James, who *s.* to the honours.
Isabel, who became eventually Countess of Marr.

The countess survived him, and as his widow *m.* 2ndly, Sir John Swinton, of Swinton. Lord Douglas* *d.* 1384, and was *s.* by his son,

James Douglas, Earl of Douglas and Mar. This distinguished chieftain fell at the battle of Otterburn (Chevy Chase) just as he had achieved a victory over Hotspur, 19 August, 1388. He *m.* Margaret, eldest dau. of King Robert II., but left no legitimate issue, whereupon his only sister, Isabel, succeeded as

---

* The earl had also a son whom he never acknowledged, George Douglas, born of Margaret, Countess of Angus and Mar, his sister-in-law, whom he could not marry. He became Earl of Angus, by King Richard II.'s sanction to his mother, with a view to prepare him to be his son-in-law.

Countess of Mar, while the Earldom of Douglas passed, apparently, in consequence of a special entail executed before the birth of George, Earl of Angus, to an illegitimate* son of the good Sir James Douglas,

ARCHIBALD DOUGLAS, Lord of Galloway, as 3rd Earl of Douglas, called "the Grim," the most powerful subject of his time, who m. Jean, or Johanna, dau. and heir of Thomas Moray, Lord of Bothwell, and had (with two daus., Marjory, m. to David, Duke of Rothsay, and Eleanor, wife of Sir Alexander Fraser, of Philorth) two sons,

ARCHIBALD, his heir.
JAMES, who s. as 7th earl.

The elder,

ARCHIBALD DOUGLAS, 4th Earl of Douglas, inheriting, with the brilliant coronet of his house, its martial and chivalrous spirit,—

"And Douglases were heroes every age,"—

commanded the Scots at the battle of Homildon, 14 September, 1402, where he was wounded in five places, lost an eye, and was taken prisoner by Henry Percy. In 1416, his lordship engaged himself, with 200 horse, and a like number of infantry, in the service of HENRY V.; but that monarch dying the next year, and CHARLES VII. of France being anxious to secure the personal aid of so renowned a warrior, Douglas arrived in France in the spring of 1424, and on 19 April following, had a gift of the Duchy of Touraine. He received, likewise, the appointment of lieutenant-general of the French forces; but held that high dignity for a brief period only, falling at the saguinary battle of Verneuil, 17 August, 1424. His lordship m. Margaret, eldest dau. of ROBERT III., and left (with one dau., Elizabeth, m. 1st, to John, Earl of Buchan, Constable of France; 2ndly, to Thomas Stewart, styled Earl of Garioch, natural son of Alexander, Earl of Mar; and 3rdly, to William, 3rd Earl of Orkney) a son and successor,

ARCHIBALD DOUGLAS, 5th Earl of Douglas, and 2nd Duke of Touraine, who distinguished himself at the battle of Baugé. His lordship m. 1st, Lady Matilda Lindsay, eldest dau. of David, 1st Earl of Crawford; and 2ndly, Lady Euphemia Graham, eldest dau. of Sir Patrick Graham, by Euphemia his wife, Countess of Strathern. By the latter (who m. 2ndly, in 1440, James, 1st Lord Hamilton) the earl had issue,

WILLIAM, his heir.
David, executed with his brother, in 1440.
Margaret, "the Fair Maid of Galloway," m. 1st, to William, 8th Earl of Douglas; 2ndly, to James, 9th Earl of Douglas; and 3rdly, to John, Earl of Atholl. She had issue by the latter, two daus., who carried her estates into the families of Gordon and Gray.

Lord Douglas d. 26 June, 1438, and was s. by his son,

WILLIAM DOUGLAS, 6th Earl of Douglas, 3rd Duke of Touraine, and 2nd Count of Longueville, in France, a young nobleman of an impetuous spirit and princely magnificence, whose power had risen to so formidable a height, that the Chancellor Crichton determined on its abasement. By plausible invitations and flatteries, the Earl of Douglas, his brother David, and Malcolm Fleming, of Cumbernauld, a faithful adherent of the family, were inveigled into the castle of Edinburgh, and after an insidious entertainment, and a brief and desultory trial, were beheaded, 24 November, 1440. Upon this event, the Duchy of Touraine reverted to the King of France, while the Scottish earldom devolved on his granduncle,

JAMES DOUGLAS, 7th Earl of Douglas: who had been created, in 1437, EARL OF AVONDALE. Of this nobleman, called "James the Gross," the Chronicle of JAMES II. records that "he had in him four stane of talch and mair." His lordship d. 24 March, 1443, leaving by Lady Beatrix Sinclair his wife (dau. of Henry, Earl of Orkney), six sons and four daus., viz.,

I. WILLIAM, his heir.
II. JAMES, 9th earl.
III. Archibald, Earl of Moray, } attainted 1445.
IV. Hugh, Earl of Ormond, }
V. John (Sir, Knt.), Lord of Balveny, forfeited in 1455.
VI. Henry, in holy orders.
I. Margaret, m. to James, 3rd Lord Dalkeith.
II. Beatrix, m. to William, 1st Earl of Erroll, Constable of Scotland.
III. Janet, m..to Robert, Lord Fleming.
IV. Elizabeth, m. to William Wallace, of Craigie.

The eldest son,

WILLIAM DOUGLAS, 8th Earl of Douglas, lieut.-general of the kingdom, restored the splendour and power of the house of Douglas, by his marriage with his cousin "the Fair Maid of

Galloway." The fate of the earl whom JAMES II. stabbed in Stirling Castle with his own hand and while under the royal safeguard, is familiar to all who read Scottish history. He d in 1451, leaving no issue, and was s. by his brother,

JAMES DOUGLAS, 9th Earl of Douglas, who got a dispensation to marry his cousin, the Fair Maid of Galloway, on the ground that the marriage with his brother had not been completed. He m, however, 4th EDWARD IV., Lady Anne Holland, dau. of John, 2nd Duke of Exeter, K.G., widow, 1st, of John, Lord Neville; and 2ndly, of Sir John Neville. His lordship, in revenge for the late earl's death, took up arms against King JAMES, and it cost him little more than the waving of his banner to collect an army of full 40,000 men, with which he encamped on the south side of the Carron, to await the attack of the royal army. Owing, however, to the desertion of Hamilton and other chieftains, the troops of Douglas dissolved like a snow-wreath on a sudden thaw; and on the fearful morning succeeding that on which the Earl Douglas led out his mighty host, his empty camp scarce contained 100 soldiers, save his own household troops. Douglas himself, in the spring of 1455, fled into England, with very few attendants. His three brothers, Moray, Ormond, and Balveny, remaining in Ewesdale, maintained their followers by military license, and harassed the adjacent country, until completely routed at Arkinholm. Moray fell in the action; Ormond was made prisoner, condemned, and executed; and of the brethren of Douglas, Balveny alone effected his escape. In the June following, a parliament met in Edinburgh, and decreed the forfeiture of Douglas and his brothers. The title of Douglas accordingly ceased; and thus fell, and for ever, the formidable power of the house of Douglas, which had so lately measured itself against that of monarchy. "It can only," to quote a beautiful simile of Sir Walter Scott, "be compared to the gourd of the prophet, which, spreading in such miraculous luxuriance, was withered in a single night." The earl was received with favour by the ruling party in England. EDWARD IV. granted him a pension, admitted him to the privileges of an English subject, and invested him with the order of the Garter. In 1483, having raised 500 horse and a small body of infantry, the exiled lord advanced to Lochmaben; but the west-border men rose to repel the incursion, and the invaders were defeated. Struck from his horse, and surrounded by enemies, the aged Douglas surrendered himself to a son of Kirkpatrick, of Closeburn, and was conveyed to the royal presence; but, either from shame or scorn turned his back on the son of JAMES II., the destroyer of his house. A ray of pity illuminated the despotic mind of the king; he merely sentenced Douglas to the religious retirement of Lindores Abbey; while the earl's indifference muttered—"He who may no better be must be a monk." In this retreat he d. after four years' penance and peace, 15 April, 1488.

Arms—As Douglas, Duke of Douglas.

DOUGLAS—DUKE OF DOUGLAS.

By Letters Patent, dated 18 April, 1703.

Lineage.

GEORGE DOUGLAS, only son of William, 1st Earl of Douglas, by Margaret his 3rd wife, Countess of Angus, obtained, on his mother's resignation in parliament, 1389, a grant of the Earldom of Angus, to himself and the heirs of his body. He m. in 1397, Mary, 2nd dau. of King ROBERT III., and by her (who m. 2ndly, Sir James Kennedy, of Dunure; 3rdly, Sir William Graham, of Kincardine; and 4thly, Sir William Edmonstone, of Duntreath) had issue,

I. WILLIAM, 2nd Earl of Angus.
II. GEORGE, 4th Earl of Angus.
I. Mary, m. Alexander, 1st Lord Forbes.

The elder son,

WILLIAM DOUGLAS, 2nd Earl of Angus, warden of the Middle Marches, who routed Sir Robert Ogle at Piperdean, in 1435. He m. in 1425, Margaret, only dau. of Sir William Hay, of Yester; and dying in 1437, was s. by his son,

JAMES DOUGLAS, 3rd Earl of Angus; who m. Lady Johanna Stewart, 3rd dau. of King JAMES I., but by her (who m. 2ndly, James, Earl of Morton) he had no issue. He was alive in 1445. His uncle and successor,

GEORGE DOUGLAS, 4th Earl of Angus, a gallant warrior, m. Isabel, dau. of Sir Andrew Sibbald, of Balgony, in Fifeshire, and by her, who m. 2ndly, Robert Douglas, of Lochleven, left at his decease, 14 November, 1462,

1. ARCHIBALD, 5th earl.
  II. Anne, *m.* to William, Lord Graham.
  III. John de Douglas, who appears to have *d. s. p.*
  IV. Isabel, *m.* to Sir Alexander Ramsay, of Dalhousie.
  V. Elizabeth, *m.* (contract dated 1476) to Sir Robert Graham, of Fintry.
  VI. Margaret, *m.* to Sir Duncan Campbell.
  VII. Elizabeth.   **VIII.** Jonet, *m.* George, Earl of Rothes.
  IX. Giles, or Egidia   **X.** Alison.

The only son,
  ARCHIBALD DOUGLAS, 5th Earl of Angus, is known in history as "Archibald, Bell-the-Cat." His lordship accompanied JAMES IV. in his fatal expedition to England, and shortly before the conflict of Flodden, which laid low the flower of the Scottish chivalry, strongly remonstrated against the king's imprudence in accepting Surrey's challenge. "If you be afraid, Angus," said his majesty, coldly, in reply to the earl's arguments, "you may go home." Angus would not remain in the camp after the affront; he departed with tears of anger and sorrow, leaving his two sons and his followers, with a command to stand by their royal master to the last; in defence of whom they gallantly fought, and at length fell, with 200 gentlemen of their name. Angus retired to the priory of Whithorn, in Galloway, and there passed the brief residue of his life in acts of devotion and charity, until his death in 1514. He *m.* 1st, 4 March, 1468, Elizabeth, only dau. of Robert, Lord Boyd, and had issue,

  I. GEORGE, master of Angus, who fell at Flodden, leaving, by Elizabeth his wife, 2nd dau. of John, 1st Lord Drummond,
    1 ARCHIBALD, successor to his grandfather.
    2 George (Sir), of Pittendriech, who fell at Pinkie in 1547, leaving, by Elizabeth his wife, dau. and heir of David Douglas, two sons, DAVID, who *s.* as 7th Earl of Angus; and JAMES, created Earl of Morton; and two daus., Margaret, wife of Sir John Carmichael; and Mary, *m.* to Sir George Auchinleck, of Balmanno.
    3 William, prior of Coldingham.
    1 Elizabeth, *m.* about 1509, to John, 3rd Lord Yester.
    2 Jean, *m.* 1st, John, 8th Lord Glammis; 2ndly, Archibald Campbell, of Skipnish
    3 Margaret, *m.* 1513, to Sir James Douglas, of Drumlanrig.
    4 Alison, *m.* 1st, 1510, to Robert Blackader, of Blackader, in Berwickshire; and 2ndly, to David Home, of Wedderburn.
    6 Isabel, *m.* to Robert Crawford, of Auchinames.
  II. William (Sir, Knt.), of Glenbervie, also fell at Flodden, father of Sir Archibald Douglas, of Glenbervie, whose son *s.* as 9th Earl of Angus.
  III. Gawen, bishop of Dunkeld, translator of Virgil's "Æneid."
  I. Mariot, *m.* to Cuthbert, Earl of Glencairn.
  II. Elizabeth, *m.* to Robert, 2nd Lord Lyle.
  III. Janet, *m.* to Andrew, son and heir of Herbert, Lord Herries, of Terregles.

He *m.* 2ndly, Catherine, dau. of Sir William Stirling, of Keir, by whom he had a dau., Mary, wife of James, 1st Lord Ogilvy, of Airly; and a son, Archibald (Sir), of Kilspindie, high treasurer of Scotland, the king's "Grey steil," who *d.* in France, broken-hearted—a victim to royal ingratitude. The earl's grandson and successor,
  ARCHIBALD DOUGLAS, 6th Earl of Angus, one of the council of regency, and afterwards high chancellor of Scotland, acted a conspicuous part in Scottish history. He held, for a considerable period, uncontrolled sway in the affairs of state, and, soldier as well as statesman, frequently distinguished himself in the military transactions of his time. At Ancrum Muir he behaved with great courage, and at Pinkie commanded the van of the Scottish army. He *m.* 1st, Lady Mary Hepburn, 2nd dau. of Patrick, 1st Earl of Bothwell, who *d. s. p.*; and 2ndly, 6 August, 1514, MARGARET, of England, queen dowager of JAMES IV., by whom (who *m.* 3rdly, Henry Stewart, Lord Methven) he had an only dau.,

  MARGARET, *b.* 18 October, 1515, *m.* to Matthew, 4th Earl of Lennox; and *d.* in 1577. Her eldest son,
    HENRY, Lord Darnley, was husband of Queen MARY, and father of King JAMES VI.

His lordship *m.* 3rdly, 9 August, 1543, Margaret, only dau. of Robert, 5th Lord Maxwell, and by her (who *m.* 2ndly, Sir William Baillie, of Lamington) had a son, James, who *d. v. p.* The earl *d.* in 1556, and was *s.* by his cousin,
  DAVID DOUGLAS, 7th Earl of Angus, who *m.* Margaret, dau. of Sir John Hamilton, of Clydesdale, and *d.* 1558, leaving (with two daus., Margaret, *m.* 1st, to Sir Walter Scott, of Buccleuch; and 2ndly, to Francis, Earl of Bothwell; and Elizabeth, *m.* 1st, to John, 7th Lord Maxwell, and 2ndly, to Sir Alexander Stuart, of Garlies) a son and successor,
  ARCHIBALD DOUGLAS, 8th Earl of Angus, called "the Good Earl," who *m.* 1st, Lady Mary Erskine, only dau. of John, 6th Earl of Marr, regent of Scotland (divorced); 2ndly, Lady Margaret Lesley, 4th dau. of Andrew, 4th Earl of Rothes; and

3rdly, in 1586, Jean, eldest dau. of John, 10th Lord Glammis, and relict of Robert, Master of Morton. By the two first he had no issue, but by the last (who *m.* 3rdly, Alexander, Lord Spynie) had a son, who had separate guardians appointed for the Earldoms of Angus and Morton in 1588 9; a dau., Elizabeth, who *d.* young. His lordship *d.* in 1588. His kinsman and eventual male heir (the grandson of Sir William Douglas, 2nd son of Archibald, 5th Earl of Angus)
  SIR WILLIAM DOUGLAS, Knt., of Glenbervie, succeeded as 9th Earl of Angus. His lordship obtained a charter from King JAMES V., in 1591, confirming all the ancient privileges of the family of Douglas—namely, *The first vote in council or parliament; to be the king's hereditary lieutenant; to have the leading of the van of the army in the day of battle; and to carry the crown at coronations;* to himself and his heirs male. All these were again confirmed by a charter under the great seal, in 1602. The earl *m.* Egidia, dau. of Sir Robert Graham, of Morphie, and dying in 1591, left issue,

  I. WILLIAM, 10th earl.
  II. Robert, of Glenbervie, whose eldest son, SIR WILLIAM, created a Bart. of Novia Scotia, 30 May, 1625, was grandfather of the gallant SIR ROBERT DOUGLAS, of Glenbervie. He *m.* 1st, Mary, dau. of Sir William Ruthven, of Douglass, he had a son, Sir William Douglas, who *d. s. p.* 27 July, 1764, æt. seventy-five; and 2ndly, Janet, dau. of — Paterson, of Dunmure, in Fife, which lady *d* 9 February, 1750.
  III. Gavin, of Bridgeford.
  IV. John, of Barras.
  V. Archibald.
  VI. Duncan.
  I. Margaret, *m.* to William Forbes, of Monymusk.
  II. Elizabeth, *m.* to Sir Alexander Gordon, of Cluny.
  III. Jean, *m* to James Wishart, of Pittarrow.
  IV Sarah, *m.* 1st, to Sir Alexander Strachan, of Thornton, Bart. ; 2ndly, to Sir George Auchinleck, of Balmanno.

The eldest son,
  WILLIAM DOUGLAS, 10th Earl of Angus, who *m.* Elizabeth, eldest dau. of Lawrence, 4th Lord Oliphant, and had issue,

  WILLIAM, his heir.
  James, created LORD MORDINGTON.
  Francis (Sir), of Sandilands, *m.* a sister of the Earl of Wigton, and *d. s. p.*
  Mary, *m.* to Alexander, 2nd Earl of Linlithgow.
  Margaret, *m.* to Sir John Campbell, of Calder.

The earl *d.* 3 March, 1611, was buried at St. Germain de Prez, and was *s.* by his son,
  WILLIAM DOUGLAS, 11th Earl of Angus, a devoted partisan of CHARLES I., by whom he was created MARQUESS OF DOUGLAS, 17 June, 1633. He *m.* 1st, the Hon. Margaret Hamilton, only dau. of Claude, Lord Paisley, and had by her (with three daus., Margaret, wife of William, Lord Alexander; Jean, *m.* to John, 1st Lord Bargeny; and Grisel, *m.* to William, Master of Carmichael) two sons,

  ARCHIBALD, who was created, in the lifetime of his father, Earl of Ormond, Lord Bothwell and Hartside, with remainder to the heirs male of his 2nd marriage, 3 April, 1651. He *m.* 1st, Lady Anne Stuart, 2nd dau. of Esme, Duke of Lennox, by whom he had a son, JAMES, 2nd Marquess of Douglas. His lordship *m.* 2ndly, 22 April, 1649, Lady Jean Wemyss, by whom he had, with a dau., a son, ARCHIBALD, afterwards Earl of Forfar. He *d.* 15 January, 1665.
  James, a distinguished general in the service of LOUIS XIV., slain at Douay in 1655.

He *m.* 2ndly, 15 September, 1632, Lady Mary Gordon, dau. of George, Marquess of Huntly, and had issue,

  I. WILLIAM, Earl of Selkirk, afterwards DUKE OF HAMILTON.
  II. George, created EARL OF DUMBARTON.
  III. James, colonel in the army, *d. s. p.*
  I. Henriet, *m.* to James, Earl of Annandale.
  II. Catherine, *m.* to Sir William Ruthven, of Dunglas.
  III. Isabel, *m.* in 1657, to William, 1st Duke of Queensberry.
  IV. Jean, *m.* 18 January, 1670, James, Earl of Perth, High Chancellor of Scotland.
  V. Lucy, *m.* Robert, 4th Earl of Nithsdale.
  VI. Mary, *d. unm.*

The marquess *d.* 19 February, 1660, and was *s.* by his grandson,
  JAMES DOUGLAS, 2nd Marquess of Douglas, *b.* 1646, who *m.* 1st, 7 September, 1670, Lady Barbara Erskine, eldest dau. of John, 9th Earl of Marr, by whom he had a son, JAMES, killed at the battle of Steinkirk, *unm.* 3 August, 1692; and 2ndly, 13 December, 1692, Lady Mary Ker, 3rd dau. of Robert, 1st Marquess of Lothian, by whom he had (with a dau., JANE, *m.* to Sir John Stewart, Bart., of Grandtully, co. Perth, and *d.* 24 November, 1753, aged fifty-six) two sons,

  William, Earl of Angus, *b.* 15 October, 1693, *d.* 20 May, 1694, buried at Douglas.
  ARCHIBALD, 3rd marquess.

The 2nd son,

ARCHIBALD DOUGLAS, 3rd Marquess of Douglas, *s.* his father in 1700. His lordship was created DUKE OF DOUGLAS, Marquess of Angus and Abernethy, Viscount of Jedburgh Forest, and Lord Douglas, of Bonkill, by patent, dated 18 April, 1703. He *m.* in 1758, Margaret, eldest dau. of James Douglas, of Mains; but *d. s. p.* in 1761, when the ducal honours became EXTINCT. The Marquessate of Douglas devolved on the Duke of Hamilton; and the Duke of Douglas's nephew, ARCHIBALD STEWART, was returned heir of line and provision to that nobleman; but the Duke of Hamilton, disputing the return, on the ground of Mr. Stewart's birth being surreptitious, and the Scotch courts determining in favour of Hamilton, an appeal was made to the House of Lords, which reversed the Scottish judgment, in February, 1769. This suit (known so well by the name of the "Douglas cause") made a noise all over Europe, and is one of the most extraordinary ever litigated. (*See* "*Vicissitudes of Families,*" *3rd Series.*) Mr. Stewart, becoming thus entitled to the estates, assumed the surname and arms of "DOUGLAS," and was elevated to the peerage, as BARON DOUGLAS, *of Douglas Castle,* 9th July, 1790.

Arms—Arg., a heart, gu., imperially crowned, or, on a chief, az., three mullets of the field.

NOTE.—At an armed conclave of nobles held in Lauder Church, in 1483, to adopt means of resisting the power and influence of the king's favourite, the base-born Cochrane, Earl of Marr, Lord Gray reminded the assembly of the fable in which the mice are said to have laid a project for preventing the future ravages of the cat by tying a bell around her neck. "An excellent proposal," said the orator, "which fell unexpectedly to the ground, because none of the mice had the courage to fasten the bell." "*I will bell the cat,*" exclaimed Angus, and thus obtained the appellation by which he is so well known. Cochrane was seized immediately after, and, with the king's other favourites, hanged over the bridge of Lauder.

DOUGLAS—EARL OF ATHOLL.

SIR WILLIAM DOUGLAS, Lord of Liddisdale, designated "the flower of chivalrie," eldest son of Sir James Douglas de Loudonia, ancestor of the Earls of Morton, had the earldom conferred upon him not long after the death of John Campbell, Earl of Atholl, who fell at Halidon Hill, in 1333, but the precise date does not appear. William Douglas, Earl of Atholl, resigned his title, and gave a charter of the Earldom of Atholl to Robert Stewart, great steward of Scotland, at Aberdeen, 16 February, 1341. This dignity thereby became vested in the royal family on the Steward's accession to the throne of England.

DOUGLAS—EARL OF DUMBARTON.

By Letters Patent, dated 9 March, 1675.

Lineage.

LORD GEORGE DOUGLAS, 3rd son of William, 1st Marquess of Douglas, was, in his younger years, page to LOUIS XIV., King of France, and afterwards entering the French army, and participating in most of the battles and sieges between the French and the Confederates, attained the rank of major-gen. After the treaty of Nimeguen, in 1673, he was called over to Britain by King CHARLES II., who created him EARL OF DUMBARTON, by patent, dated 9 March, 1675; and upon the accession of King JAMES II., he was constituted commander-in-chief of the forces in Scotland, in which capacity he defeated the Earl of Argyll's invasion. He *m.* a sister of the Duchess of Northumberland, and had a son,

GEORGE DOUGLAS, 2nd Earl of Dumbarton, who had the commission of lieut.-col. of Dubourgay's regt. of foot in the British service, 1715, and the appointment of ambassador to Russia, 1716. He *d. s. p.*, and with him the title became EXTINCT.

DOUGLAS—EARL OF FORFAR.

By Patent, dated 3 April, 1351.

Lineage.

ARCHIBALD DOUGLAS, Earl of Angus (eldest son and heir apparent of William, 1st Marquess of Douglas), was, by patent, dated 3 April, 1651, created Earl of Ormond, Lord Bothwell and Hartside, with remainder to the heirs male of his 2nd marriage. He *d.* 15 January, 1655, and, in terms of the patent, was *s.* by the only son of his 2nd marriage with Lady Jean Wemyss, afterwards Countess of Sutherland,

ARCHIBALD DOUGLAS, 2nd Earl of Ormond, *b.* 1653, who obtained a new patent, dated 20 October, 1661, creating him EARL OF FORFAR, Lord Wandale and Hartside, with remainder to his heirs-male. He early espoused the Revolution, was sworn a privy councillor to King WILLIAM, and appointed one of the commissioners for executing the office of keeper of the privy seal. He was also of the privy council to Queen ANNE, and one of the commissioners of the Treasury, which he held till the dissolution of that court, in consequence of the treaty of Union. He *m.* Rabina, dau. of Sir William Lockhart, Knt., of Lee, in the co. of Lanark, ambassador extraordinary to the court of France, grandniece of Oliver Cromwell and by her (who *d.* at Bothwell Castle, 20 March, 1749, aged seventy-nine) left at his decease, 12 December, 1712, a son and successor,

ARCHIBALD DOUGLAS, 2nd Earl of Forfar, an officer in the army, who was appointed col. of the 3rd regt. of foot, or buffs, 13 April, 1713, and nominated envoy extraordinary to Prussia, in 1714. He served as a brigadier-gen. at the battle of Sheriffmuir, 13 November, 1715, when he received a shot on the knee, was made prisoner, and *d.* of his wounds, at Stirling, on 8 December following, *unm.*, when his titles and estates devolved on the Duke of Douglas.

DOUGLAS—EARL OF MORAY.

(*See* RANDOLPH, Earl of Moray.)

DOUGLAS—EARL OF MORTON.

(*See* that title in BURKE'S *Extant Peerage.*)

DOUGLAS—EARL OF ORMOND.

Lineage.

HUGH DOUGLAS, 4th son of James, 7th Earl of Douglas, was created EARL OF ORMOND in 1445; but engaging in the rebellion of the Douglases, was attainted and executed in 1455. His son Hugh, dean of Brechin, *d. s. p.*

DOUGLAS—VISCOUNT OF BELHAVEN.

By Letters Patent, dated 24 June, 1633.

Lineage.

SIR ROBERT DOUGLAS, of Spott, co. Haddington (son of Malcolm Douglas, of Mains, in Dumbartonshire, descended from Nicol Douglas, of the family of Morton,) was page of honour to Henry, Prince of Wales, and afterwards his master of the horse. Upon the death of that prince, he was appointed one of the gentlemen of the bedchamber to King JAMES I., and continued in that office to King CHARLES I., by whom he was also constituted master of the household, and sworn a privy councillor. He was created a peer of Scotland, by the title of VISCOUNT OF BELHAVEN, co. Haddington, to himself and the heirs-male of his body, by patent, dated 24 June, 1633. His lordship *m.* Nicolas, eldest dau. of Robert Moray, of Abercairny but had no issue. He *d.* at Edinburgh, 14 January, 1639, in the sixty-sixth year of his age, and was buried in the abbey church of Holyrood House, where is a fine monument erected to his memory by Sir Archibald and Sir Robert Douglas, the sons of his elder brother, his heirs.

Arms—*See* DOUGLAS, Duke of Douglas.

DOUGLAS—LORD MORDINGTOUN.

By Letters Patent, dated 14 November, 1641.

Lineage.

Sir James Douglas, 2nd son of William, 10th Earl of Angus, m. Anne, only child of Laurence, 5th Lord Oliphant. A controversy arose between her and the male heir for the title of Lord Oliphant, which was determined in presence of Charles I., in the court of Session, 1633, when it was adjudged that Anne Oliphant had no right to the honours; but the king was pleased to create her husband a peer, by the title of Lord Mordingtoun, 14 November, 1641, with the precedency of Oliphant (1458). He d. 11 February, 1656, leaving a son and a dau., viz.,

William, 2nd Lord Mordingtoun.
Anne, m. to Robert, 7th Lord Sempill.

The son and heir,
William Douglas, 2nd Lord Mordingtoun, m. Elizabeth, eldest dau. of Hugh, 5th Lord Sempill, and had two sons, James, 3rd lord; Lewis, d. 1682. The elder,
James Douglas, 3rd Lord Mordingtoun, m. the Hon. Jean Seton, eldest dau. of Alexander, 1st Viscount of Kingston, and was father of
George Douglas, 4th Lord Mordingtoun, who d. in Covent Garden, 10 June, 1741. He m. Catherine, dau. of Dr. Robert Lauder, rector of Shenty, in Hertfordshire, and by her had a son,
Charles Douglas, 5th Lord Mordingtoun, who adopted the naval profession early in life, and did not return home till after his father's death, when, having no landed property, he did not assume the title. In 1745, he joined the young Pretender, was taken prisoner, and arraigned at Carlisle, 11 September, 1746, under the designation of Charles Douglas, Esq.; he pleaded, however, his peerage as Lord Mordingtoun, and proving his descent, his trial was put off, and he was remanded back prisoner to the castle of Carlisle. Dying s. p., his lordship was s. by his sister,
Mary Douglas, Baroness Mordingtoun, who assumed that title. Her ladyship m. William Weaver, Esq., an officer of the royal regiment of horse-guards, who was at the battle of Dettingen and Fontenoy, but by him (who d. 28 April, 1796) had no issue. She d. 22 July, 1791.

Arms—Quarterly: 1st and 4th, arg., a man's heart, gu., ensigned with an imperial crown, ppr.; on a chief, az., three stars, of the 1st, for Douglas; 2nd and 3rd, gu., three crescents, arg., for Oliphant.

DOUGLAS—BARON CARLYLE.

By Letters Patent, dated 1609.

Lineage.

Sir James Douglas, eldest son of Sir James Douglas, of Parkhead, by Elizabeth his wife, only child of William Carlyle, master of Carlyle, had the title of Carlyle conferred on him in 1609. His lordship m. 1st, Grizel, youngest dau. of Sir John Gordon, of Lochinvar; and 2ndly, Anne Saltonstall. By the latter he had a son, James, b. at Edinburgh, 2 January, 1621; and by the former, it is said, a son, William, who sold his estate, and d. abroad s. p. According to Crawford, James, Lord Carlyle, resigned his title, in 1638, to William, Earl of Queensbury.

Arms—As Douglas, Duke of Douglas.

DOUGLAS—DUKES OF DOVER.

By Letters Patent, dated 26 May, 1708.

Lineage.

James Douglas, who s. his father in 1695, as 2nd Duke of Queensbury, in the Scottish peerage, having taken a prominent part in the Revolution, was appointed in 1693 one of the lords of the treasury in Scotland, and the following year had a patent to sit and vote in the parliament of that kingdom as Lord High Treasurer. After his accession to the Dukedom

of Queensbury, his grace was made by King William, lord privy seal of Scotland, and one of the extraordinary lords of Session; and in 1700 appointed lord high commissioner to represent the king in the parliament of Scotland, where he held two sessions under two distinct patents. Upon his return to court, his grace was elected a knight of the most noble order of the Garter: and at Queen Anne's accession to the crown, he was made secretary of state for Scotland In 1703 he, for the fourth time, filled the office of lord high commissioner, and again in 1706, being the last session of the parliament of Scotland, in which, with the utmost efforts, his grace carried the measure of union between the two kingdoms, For all these eminent services the duke was rewarded with a pension of 3,000l. a-year out of the post-office, and the first peerage of Great Britain, under the titles of Baron Ripon, Marquess of Beverley, and Duke of Dover, with remainder to his 2nd son, Charles, Earl of Solway. His grace m. 4 December, 1685, Mary, 2nd dau. of Charles, Lord Clifford, and granddau. of Richard Boyle, Earl of Burlington and Cork, and by her (who d. 2 October, 1709) had, with other issue,

James, an imbecile.
Charles, b. 24 November, 1698, created 17 June, 1706, Viscount Tibbers, and Earl of Solway.
George, b 20 February, 1701; d. unm. at Paris, 1725.
Jane, m 5 April, 1720, to Francis, Earl of Dalkeith, afterwards Duke of Buccleuch, and d. 31 August, 1729.
Anne, m. 25 January, 1733, to the Hon. William Finch, brother of Daniel, Earl of Winchelsea and Nottingham, d. s. p. 26 October, 1741.

The duke d. in 1711, and was s. by his eldest surviving son,
Charles Douglas, Earl of Solway, as 2nd Duke of Dover. His grace m. 10 March, 1720, Lady Catherine Hyde, 2nd dau. of Henry, Earl of Clarendon and Rochester, and had two sons,

Henry, Earl of Drumlanrig, b. 30 October, 1722; m. 24 July, 1754, Lady Elizabeth Hope, eldest dau. of John, 2nd Earl of Hopetown, and was killed 19 October, 1754, by the accidental discharge of his own pistol. The countess d. s. p. 7 April, 1756.
Charles, Earl of Drumlanrig, b. 17 July, 1726, d. unm. 24 October, 1756.

The duke d. at the age of eighty, on 22 October, 1778, and leaving no issue, the Dukedom of Dover, and his other British honours became extinct. The Scottish dignities devolved on different heirs, and are now enjoyed in part by the Duke of Buccleuch as heir of line, and in part by the Marquess of Queensbury, as heir male.

Arms—Quarterly, 1st and 4th, arg., a heart, gu., crowned with an imperial crown, or, on a chief, az., three mullets of the field, for Douglas; 2nd and 3rd, a bend between six cross-crosslets, fitché, or, (for the Earldom of Mark,) the whole within a bordure, or, charged with a double treasure, fleury and counterfleury of the 2nd, being an augmentation; as was also the heart in the 1st quarter, used in memory of the pilgrimage made by Sir James Douglas, ancestor of his grace, to the Holy Land, in the year 1330, with the heart of King Robert Bruce, which was there interred according to that monarch's own desire. The double treasure was added by King Charles II., when he honoured the family with the Marquessate of Queensbury, the bordure previously being plain.

Note.—The officers of state in Scotland, prior to the Union, had seats in parliament ex officio and when an office was placed in commission the crown had the privilege to appoint any one person to represent the said office in parliament.

DOUGLAS—BARON DOUGLAS, OF AMBRESBURY.

By Letters Patent, dated 8 August, 1786.

Lineage.

William Douglas, 3rd Earl of March, who s. in 1778, as 4th Duke of Queensbury, in Scotland, was created a peer of Great Britain, 8 August, 1786, as Baron Douglas, of Ambresbury, co. Wilts, but dying unm., 23 December, 1810, the barony became extinct.

Arms—Four grand quarterings, viz., 1st and 4th, quarterly: 1st and 4th, arg., a human heart, gu., imperially crowned ppr. on a chief, az., three mullets of the field, for Douglas: 2nd and 3rd, az., a bend between six cross-crosslets, fitché, or, for Mark, all within a bordure of the last, charged with the double tressure of Scotland, which tressure was added by King Charles II., when he honoured the family with the Marquessate of Queensbury; 2nd and 3rd grand quarters. gu., a lion rampant, arg., within a bordure of the last, charged with eight roses of the 1st, for March.

DOUGLAS—BARON DOUGLAS, OF DOUGLAS CASTLE.

By Letters Patent, dated 9 July, 1790.

Lineage.

SIR JOHN STEWART, Bart. of Grandtully (brother and successor of Sir George Stewart, of Balcaskie, who inherited the estate of Grandtully, and 2nd son of Sir Thomas Stewart of Balcaskie, created a *Baronet of Nova Scotia*, 2 January, 1683), *m.* for his 2nd wife,

THE LADY JANE DOUGLAS, only dau. of James, 2nd Marquess of Douglas, by whom he had two sons (twins), Sholto, the younger, who *d.* in infancy; and

ARCHIBALD STEWART, *b.* 10 July, 1748. This gentleman, upon the demise of his uncle, Archibald, Duke of Douglas, without issue, 21 July, 1761 (when the dukedom expired), was returned heir of line and provision to that nobleman; but the Duke of Hamilton, who had inherited his grace's Marquessate of Douglas, disputing his return, on the ground of Mr. Stewart's birth being surreptitious, and the Scotch court determining in favour of Hamilton, an appeal was made to the House of Lords, which reversed the Scottish judgment, 27 February, 1769.* Mr. Stewart becoming thus entitled to the estates, assumed the surname and arms of DOUGLAS, and was elevated to the peerage as BARON DOUGLAS, *of Douglas Castle,* 9 July, 1790. His lordship *m.* 1st, in June, 1771, Lucy, only dau. of William, 2nd Duke of Montrose, by whom (who *d.* 13 February, 1780), he had issue,

ARCHIBALD, 2nd baron.
CHARLES, late peer.
Jane-Margaret. *m.* 1804, to Henry-James, Lord Montagu, of Boughton, who *d.* in 1845.

Lord Douglas *m.* 2ndly, 13 May, 1783, Frances, posthumous dau. of Francis, Earl of Dalkeith, and sister of Henry, 3rd Duke of Buccleuch, by whom he had,

Sholto-Scott. *b.* in 1785; *d.* in 1821.
JAMES. in holy orders, 4th lord
George. capt. R.N., *b.* 2 August, 1788; *d. unm.* in 1838.
Caroline-Lucy, *m.* 27 October, 1810, to Admiral Sir George Scott, K.C.B., who *d.* in 1841. She *d.* 20 April, 1857.
Frances-Elizabeth, *m.* 1826, William-Moray Stirling, Esq., of Abercairny and Ardoch, N.B., who *d.* 9 November, 1850. She *d.* 14 September, 1854.
Mary-Sidney, *m.* in 1821, to Robert Douglas, Esq., of Strathany, who *d.* in 1844.

His lordship *d.* 26 December, 1827, and was *s.* by his elder son,

ARCHIBALD, 2nd baron, *b* 25 March, 1773, who *d. unm.* in January, 1844, and was *s.* by his brother,

CHARLES, 3rd baron, who *d.* 10 September, 1848, and was *s.* by his brother,

JAMES DOUGLAS, 4th Baron of Douglas Castle, co. Lanark, in holy orders, hereditary sheriff of the co. Forfar, *b.* 9 July, 1787; *m.* 18 May, 1813, Wilhelmina, 2nd dau. of the late Gen. Hon. James Murray; *d. s. p.* 6 April, 1857, when the title became EXTINCT, and the estates devolved on his lordship's half-sister, Lady Montagu.

Arms—Quarterly : 1st. az., a lion rampant, arg., crowned with an imperial crown, or, for the EARLDOM OF GALLOWAY; 2nd, or, a lion rampant, gu., surmounted of a bend, sa., for LORD ABERNETHY; 3rd, arg., three piles, gu.. for WISHART *of Brechin;* 4th, or, a fesse, chequy, az. and arg., surmounted of a bend, gu., charged with three buckles of the 1st, for STEWART *of Bonkle;* over all, upon an escutcheon, arg., a man's heart, gu., ensigned with an imperial crown, ppr.; on a chief, az., three stars, of the 1st, the paternal coat of DOUGLAS.

---

* Sir John Stewart asserted that he had twin sons by the Lady Jane Douglas, born at the house of a Madame le Brun, 10 July, 1748, in the Faubourg St. Germain, at Paris, her ladyship being then in her 51st year. One of these children, Sholto, *d.* an infant, and against the other, ARCHIBALD STEWART, inheriting the estates of his maternal uncle, Archibald, Duke of Douglas, on that nobleman's decease, 21 July, 1761, to whom he was returned heir of line and provision, the guardians of James-George (the minor), Duke of Hamilton, instituted a suit-at-law, and the Scottish courts determined in favour of his grace. From the decision an appeal was made to the House of Lords, which eventually reversed it, and confirmed Sir Archibald in the possession of the Douglas estates. One of the guardians of the duke and institutors of the suit, Sir Andrew Stuart, subsequently published, in January 1773, some very strong letters, addressed to Lord Mansfield, arraigning the conduct of his lordship during the progress of this celebrated litigation, and maintaining the rectitude of the Scottish decision (*See* "*Vicissitudes of Families.*")

DOUGLAS—BARON GLENBERVIE.

By Letters Patent, dated 29 December, 1800.

Lineage.

JOHN DOUGLAS, Esq. (3rd son of Sylvester Douglas, by Margaret his wife, dau. and heir of George Keith, Esq., of Whiteriggs, in Kincardineshire, and grandson of Robert Douglas, bishop of Dumblane, who was lineally descended from Archbold Douglas, the great Earl of Angus), *m.* Margaret, dau. and co-heir of James Gordon, of Fectrel, and had, with a dau. (*m.* to Major Mercer, the poet), one son,

SYLVESTER DOUGLAS, Esq., *b.* 24 May, 1743, barrister-at-law, and editor of the "Reports" which pass under his name. This gentleman, who attained considerable forensic eminence, represented Fowey in parliament, and having filled successively the appointments of chief secretary to the lord-lieutenant of Ireland, lord of the treasury, commissioner for Indian affairs. and governor of the Cape of Good Hope, was raised to the peerage of Ireland, in 1800, as BARON GLENBERVIE. His lordship was subsequently joint paymaster-general of the forces, and surveyor-general of the woods and forests. He *m.* in 1789, Catherine, eldest dau. of Frederick, 2nd Earl of Guilford (the celebrated Lord North), and had an only son,

FREDERICK - SYLVESTER - NORTH, M.P. for Bambury, *b.* 3 February, 1791; who *m.* Harriet, eldest dau. of William Wrighston, Esq., of Cusworth, in Yorkshire, but *d. v. p., s. p.,* His widow *m.* 26 April, 1825, the Hon. Lieut.-Col. Hely-Henry Hutchinson, brother of the Earl of Donoughmore.

Lord Glenbervie *d.* in 1823, when the peerage became EXTINCT.

Arms—Arg., a heart, gu., imperially crowned, or; on a chief, az., three mullets of the field.

DRUMMOND—BARON PERTH.

By Letters Patent, dated 14 October, 1797.

Lineage.

JAMES DRUMMOND, 11th Earl of Perth, who became possessed of the Drummond estates in 1785, was created a British peer, as LORD PERTH, Baron Drummond, of Stobhall, to him and the heirs-male of his body, 14 October, 1797. His lordship *m.* in 1785, the Hon. Clementina Elphinstone, 4th dau. of Charles, 10th Lord Elphinstone; and dying 2 July, 1900 (when his title EXPIRED,) left an only dau. and heir,

CLEMENTINA-SARAH, *m.* 20 October, 1807, the Hon. Peter-Robert Burrell, who assumed the additional surname and arms of DRUMMOND. He inherited the Barony of Gwydyr in 1820, and that of WILLOUGHBY DE ERESBY in 1828.

His heir-male was James-Lewis Drummond, Duke of Melfort, who *d.* in 1800. His nephew is the present GEORGE DRUMMOND, EARL OF PERTH (*See* BURKE's *Peerage*).

Arms—Or, three bars, wavy, gu.

DRUMMOND—DUKE OF MELFORT.

By Letters Patent, dated 12 August, 1686.

Lineage.

The HON. JOHN DRUMMOND, 2nd son of James, 3rd Earl of Perth, was appointed general of the ordnance, and deputy-governor of the castle of Edinburgh, 1680; treasurer-depute in 1682; and one of the principal secretaries of state in September, 1684. On the accession of King JAMES VII., 1685, he was continued in that office, and created VISCOUNT OF MELFORT, in Argyllshire (part of the forfeited estate of Argyll), and LORD DRUMMOND, of Gilestoun, 14 April, 1685; and for the better support of that honour. got a grant of the barony of Melfort, and estate of Duchal, which was dissolved from the crown by act of parliament. He was created EARL OF MELFORT, Viscount of Forth, Lord Drummond, of Riccartoun, Castlemains, and Gilston, 12 August, 1686, the patents of his honours being taken to him and the heirs-male of his body of his 2nd marriage; which failing, to the heirs-male whatever of his body, as he was disappointed by the family of Lundin, who were zealous Protestants, in his attempt to educate his two sons of the 1st marriage in the Catholic faith. When the Order of the Thistle was revived, in 1687, the Earl of Melfort was constituted one of the knights companions thereof, continued in the office of secretary till the Revolution, when he repaired to King JAMES in France; attended him to Ireland, in the year 1690, and was by him created DUKE OF MELFORT and Marquess of Forth, and invested with the Order of the Garter. Not returning to Scotland within the time limited by law, he was outlawed by the court of justiciary, 23 July, 1694, and attainted. 2 July, 1694, by act of parliament. By a clause it was provided that his forfeiture should no ways affect or taint the blood of the children procreated betwixt him and Sophia Lundin his 1st wife. He had the chief administration at St. Germains for several years, and d. there in January, 1714. He m. 1st, 30 April, 1670, Sophia, dau. and heiress of Margaret Lundin, of Lundin, in Fife, by the Hon. Robert Maitland, brother of John, Duke of Lauderdale, and by her had issue (see DRUMMOND, Earl of Perth, BURKE'S *Extant Peerage*); he m. 2ndly, Euphemia, dau. of Sir Thomas Wallace, of Craigie, a lord of Session, and by her (who lived to be above ninety years of age, and was supported by keeping one of the two faro tables authorized by LOUIS XIV.,) had issue,

I. John, b. 1679; d. s p.
II. James, d. s. p. 1698.
III. Robert, s. his brother in 1698 to the estate of Lundin, near Largo, in Fife, on which he assumed her surname; m. 1704, Anne, dau. of Sir James Inglis, of Cramond.
IV. John. styled Duke of Melfort.
V. Thomas, an officer in the service of CHARLES VI., Emperor of Germany; who d. unm. 1715.
VI. William, abbé-prirol of Liege; who d. in Spain, 1742.
VII. Andrew, a general of horse in the French service; m. Magdalene Silvia de St. Hermione, and had a son, Louis, designed Count de Melfort, a major-gen. in the same service, who m. Jean-Elizabeth de la Porte, dau. of Peter-John-Francis de la Porte, intendant of Dauphiny, by whom he had a son, Lewis-Peter-Francis-Malcolm Drummond, of Melfort, who m. 1st, Lady Caroline Barry, dau. of the Earl of Barrymore; and 2ndly, Caroline, dau. of the Earl of Seaforth, and d. in 1838, leaving issue, Louis and Edward.
VIII Bernard, d. young, at Douay.
IX. Phillip, an officer in the French service; d. of wounds received in the wars of LOUIS XIV.
1 Henrietta, d. unm. 1752.
II. Mary, m. to Don Jose de Rozas, Count Castel Blanco, a Spanish nobleman; but d. s. p. 1713.
III. Frances, m. by dispensation from the pope, to her brother-in-law, Count Castel Blanco; and d. 1726, leaving a son, who m. an heiress in Spain, and two daus., the eldest m. 1st, to M. de Campillo, prime minister to PHILIP V., King of Spain; 2ndly, to Peter, 2nd son of the Duke of Liria, a grandee of Spain, and grandson of the Marshal Duke of Berwick; the youngest, Lady Margaret, m. also a Spanish grandee.
IV. Louisa, d. at Paris, unm.
V. Teresa-Margareta, d. unm.

JOHN DRUMMOND, the eldest surviving son, b. 1682, assumed the title of DUKE OF MELFORT, and d. 1754. He m. 1707, Mary Gabrielle d'Audebert, Countess de Lusanne, widow of Henry Fitzjames, Duke of Albemarle, natural son of King JAMES II., and had four sons,

I. John, d. unm. 1735.
II. JAMES, his successor.
III. Lewis, major-gen. in the French service, col. of the regt. of royal Scots; who, on the reduction of that corps, got a considerable pension from the court of France, d. s. p. 1792.
IV. John, lieut. of the guards of the King of Poland, Elector of Saxony, with the rank of major-gen., d. s. p.

JAMES DRUMMOND, the eldest surviving son, assumed the title of the DUKE OF MELFORT, and had a considerable estate in Lower Languedoc. He m. Mary de Berenger, by whom he had issue, four sons and two daus., viz., James-Lewis, general in the French service, commander of the Order of St. Louis, d. s. p. 1788 ; Charles-Edward, prelate in the household of the Pope, d. at Rome, 1840 ; Henry-Benedict, in the French navy, chevalier of the Order of St. Louis, killed 1778; Leon-Maurice ; Mary-Cecilia-Henrietta, and Emilia-Felicitas. Leon-Maurice Drummond, m. 1794, Mary Longuemare, and had two daus., Leontina, who d. 1809, aged sixteen, and Lady Lucy-Clementina, m. to Francis-Henry Davies, Esq., registrar of the Court of Chancery, and a son, GEORGE, EARL OF PERTH AND MELFORT. (See BURKE'S *Extant Peerage*.)

Arms—Or, three bars, wavy, gu.

DUDLEY—VISCOUNTS L'ISLE, EARLS OF WARWICK, DUKE OF NORTHUMBERLAND.

Viscounty, by Letters Patent, dated 12 March, 1542.
Earldom, by Letters Patent, dated 17 February, 1547.
Dukedom, by Letters Patent, dated 11 October, 1551.

Lineage.

SIR JOHN SUTTON, K.G., 4th Baron Dudley, of that family, m. Elizabeth, dau. and co-heir of Sir John Berkeley, Knt., of Beveston, and widow of Sir Edward Charlton, Lord Powis, and had, with other issue, John, his 2nd son, who assuming the name of Dudley, became

JOHN DUDLEY; this gentleman m. Elizabeth, one of the daus. and co-heirs of John Bramshot, Esq., of Bramshot, and was father of

EDMUND DUDLEY, so well known, with his colleague, Richard Empson, as the rapacious minister of King HENRY VII. Dudley was brought up to the bar, having studied at Gray's Inn, and before he entered the service of the king, he had attained considerable eminence in his profession. Upon the accession of HENRY, he was sworn of the privy council, and he subsequently filled the speaker's chair of the House of Commons; whilst in the latter office, they were about making him a serjeant-at-law, when he petitioned the king, for what reason does not appear, that he might be discharged from assuming that dignity. This occurred in the 19th of HENRY VII., and in three years afterwards he obtained the stewardship of the rape of Hastings, in the county of Suffolk. "Whether (writes Dugdale), Dudley, with Richard Empson, another lawyer, son to a sieve-maker, discerning King HENRY to be of a frugal disposition, did first project the taking advantage against such as had transgressed the penal laws, by exacting from them the forfeitures according to those statutes, or whether the king perceiving so fair a gap open, to rake vast sums of money from his subjects, finding those persons to be fit instruments for his purpose, did put them upon such courses for filling his coffers, 'tis hard to say. But certain it is, that these were they, whom he constituted his *judices fiscales* (Dudley being an eminent man, and one that could put hateful business into good language, as Lord Verulam saith)." The extortions of those men exciting universal clamour, HENRY VIII. commenced his reign by the popular acts of submitting their oppressive conduct to judicial investigation before a criminal court; Dudley was tried at Guildhall, in the city of London, and Empson at Northampton, and both being found guilty, were beheaded together on Tower Hill, on 28 August, in the 2nd year of HENRY VIII. Dudley, in the day of his power, having obtained the wardship of Elizabeth Grey, dau. of Edward, 1st Viscount L'Isle, and Elizabeth Talbot, dau. of John Talbot, Viscount L'Isle, and sister and co-heir of Thomas Talbot, 2nd and last Viscount L'Isle, of the Shrewsbury family, m. the said Elizabeth Grey, and left issue by her,

JOHN, of whom presently.
Andrew (Sir), involved in the conspiracy to elevate Lady Jane Grey to the throne, and received sentence of death in the 1st year of MARY.
Jerome.
Elizabeth, m. to William, 6th Lord Stourton.

Of these, JOHN, the eldest son, had scarcely attained his eighth year at the period of his father's execution, and being in ward to Edward Guildeford, Esq., of the body of the king, that gentleman petitioned that the attainder of Edmund Dudley might be repealed, and obtained a special act of parliament (3rd HENRY VIII.), which restored the said

JOHN DUDLEY, in name, blood and degree, so that he might inherit all his deceased father's lands. From this period twelve years elapsed before John Dudley appeared in public, and the first we afterwards hear of him is his receiving the honour of knighthood from Charles Brandon, Duke of Suffolk, general of the army sent into France against the Duke of Bourbon. In the 19th of HENRY VIII., Sir John Dudley was in the train of Cardinal Wolsey upon an embassy into France; and in eight years afterwards, "being the king's servant," he was made master of the armoury in the Tower of London for life, with the wages of twelve-pence per day for himself, and three-pence per day for his groom in the office. In the 31st of the same reign he was appointed master of the horse to Anne of Cleves; and the next year, in the jousts held at Westminster, Sir John was one of the principal challengers, his horse being accoutred with white velvet. In about two years after this he was elevated to the peerage, in the ancient dignity enjoyed by his mother's family, that of VISCOUNT L'ISLE, and made, the same year, lord admiral of England for life. In this capacity his lordship displayed great gallantry, and did good service against France and Scotland. "To say truth," remarks Sir John Howard, " he was the minion of that time; so as few things he attempted, but he achieved with honour, which made him the more proud and ambitious. Generally he always increased both in estimation with the king and authority amongst the nobility ; but doubtful, whether by fatal destiny to the state. or whether by his virtues or appearance of virtues." His lordship was one of the executors to the will of his royal master; and upon the accession of EDWARD VI., he was created EARL OF WARWICK, with a grant of Warwick Castle. At this period he was made lieut.-gen. of the army, and acquired an accession of military fame under the Earl of Hertford, in Picardy and Scotland, as well as by his successful defence of Boulogne, of which he was governor. In the 3rd of EDWARD VI. he was again made admiral of England, Ireland, and Wales, and the next year constituted lord steward of the household. Henceforward his lordship's ambition appears to have known no bounds, and to have hurried him into acts of great baseness and atrocity. Through his intrigues the quarrel arose between the Protector Somerset and his brother, Thomas, Lord Seymour, which terminated in the public execution of the latter; and he is at this period accused of acquiring considerable wealth by plunder of the church. In the 6th of the same reign he was advanced to the dignity of DUKE OF NORTHUMBERLAND, a peerage which, by the death of the last Earl of Northumberland, s. p., and the attainder and execution of his brother, Sir Thomas Percy, with the Percy estate, became vested in the crown. His grace had previously been constituted earl-marshal of England. Having now attained the highest honour in the peerage, and power the most unlimited, the duke proceeded, with scarcely the semblance of restraint, in his ambitious projects; and the Protector Somerset, one of his earliest and steadiest patrons, soon fell a victim to their advancement. That distinguished personage was arraigned, through the intrigue of Northumberland, before his peers, and though acquitted of high treason, was condemned for felony, and sentenced to be hanged. The eventual fate of this unhappy nobleman is well known, and, considering his own conduct to his brother, not deplored. He was executed by decapitation on Tower Hill. From the death of Somerset, the Duke of Northumberland became so unremitting in his attentions upon the king, and had so much influence over him, that he prevailed upon his majesty to sign and seal a patent conferring the succession upon Lady Jane Grey, the wife of his son, Lord Guilford Dudley. His subsequent efforts, after the decease of EDWARD VI., to establish this patent by force of arms, proving abortive, he was arrested, upon a charge of high treason, at Cambridge, and being condemned thereof, he was beheaded, on Tower Hill, upon the 22nd of August, 1553, when all his honours became forfeited under the attainder. His grace m. Jane, dau. of Sir Edward Guildeford, Knt., and had issue,

Henry, d. at the siege of Boulogne.
John, Earl of Warwick, d. v. p., s. p.
Ambrose, created EARL OF WARWICK. (See Dudley, Earl of Warwick.)
GUILFORD, who m. LADY JANE GREY, eldest dau. of Henry, Duke of Suffolk, by MARY, Queen Dowager of France, and sister of King HENRY VIII. Lady Jane Grey was therefore grand-niece to King HENRY VIII. Lord Guilford Dudley was attainted and beheaded with his father.
Robert, K.G., created baron of Denbigh and Earl of Leicester. (See those dignities.)
Henry, slain at St. Quintin.
Charles, d. young.
Mary, m. Sir Henry Sidney, K G,
Catherine, m. Henry Hastings, Earl of Huntingdon.

Arms—Or, a lion rampant, az., double queued, vert.

NOTE.—John Sutton, the 7th Lord Dudley of the Sutton family, disposed of Dudley Castle to the Duke of Northumberland, and having alienated other property, was ever afterwards known as *Lord Quondam.*

DUDLEY—DUCHESS OF DUDLEY.

By Letters Patent, dated 23 May, 1644

Lineage.

ROBERT DUDLEY, Earl of Leicester, the notorious favourite of Queen ELIZABETH, m. for his 2nd wife, Douglas Howard, dau. of William, Lord Effingham, and widow of John, Lord Sheffield, by whom he had an only son,

ROBERT.

The earl apprehending a diminution of his influence with his royal mistress, made an attempt to get rid of this wife, as he did of his 1st, the unhappy Amy Robsart, by poison, but ineffectually. He repudiated her, however, and denied his marriage—but he bequeathed, at his decease, the greater part of his property to their issue, calling him nevertheless his base son,

SIR ROBERT DUDLEY, who having in vain endeavoured to establish his legitimacy, retired in umbrage to Italy : whence, through the influence of his enemies, being summoned to return, and disobeying the mandate, his lands were seized under the statute of fugitives. Sir Robert m. Alice Leigh, dau of Sir Thomas Leigh, Bart., and his wife, Catherine, dau. of Sir John Spencer, of Wormleighton, co. Warwick, and aunt of Thomas, 1st Lord Leigh, of Stoneleigh, by whom he had issue,

Alice, } *d. unm.*
Douglas, }
Catherine, m. to Sir Richard Leveson, K.B.
Frances, m. to Sir Gilbert Kniveton, of Bradley, co. Derby.
Anne, m. to Sir Richard Holbourne, solicitor-general to King CHARLES I.

Sir Robert Dudley took up his abode in the territories of the Grand Duke of Tuscany, with which prince he became a favourite, owing to his extraordinary accomplishments, being not only well skilled in all kinds of mathematical learning, in navigation, and architecture, but being a great chymist and skilful physician; and his fame reaching the imperial courts, the emperor FERDINAND II., by letters patent, dated 9 March, 1620, conferred upon him the dignity of DUKE, when he assumed the title of Duke of Northumberland. Sir Robert, like his father, deserted his lady, and took with him to the continent Miss Southwell, dau. of Sir Robert Southwell, of Wood Rising, co. Norfolk, and there married her, under the pretence that his marriage with Alice Leigh was, by the canon law, illegal, inasmuch as he had carnal knowledge of her during the lifetime of his 1st wife, Miss Cavendish, sister of Thomas Cavendish, the navigator. By Miss Southwell, Sir Robert Dudley had several children, of which Charles, the eldest son, bore, after his decease, the title of Duke of Northumberland. Notwithstanding the conduct of Sir Robert, his lady, who remained in England,

ALICE DUDLEY, was elevated to the peerage for life, by King CHARLES I., by letters patent, dated 23 May, 1644, as DUCHESS OF DUDLEY, and her surviving daus. were allowed the precedency of a duke's children.

The following is a copy of the grant, viz. :

" CHARLES, by the grace of God, &c.

" Whereas, in the reign of King JAMES, a suit was commenced in the Star Chamber Court against Sir Robert Dudley, for pretending himself lawful heir to the honours and lands of the earldoms of Warwick and Leicester, as son and heir of Robert, Earl of Leicester, by Douglas, wife to the said earl, and all proceedings stayed in the ecclesiastical courts, in which the said suit depended for proof of his legitimation ; yet, nevertheless, did the said court vouchsafe liberty to the said Sir Robert to examine witnesses in the Star Chamber Court, to make good his legitimacy. Whereupon, by full testimony of the Lady Douglas herself, and other witnesses it was made appear. But a special order being made, that the depositions should be sealed up, and no copies taken, did cause the said Sir Robert, to leave the kingdom; whereof his adversaries taking advantage, occasioned his lands to be seized on, to the king, our father's use. And not long after, Prince Henry made overture to the said Sir Robert, to obtain his title by purchase of Kenilworth Castle, &c., valued at £50,000, but bought by the prince in consideration of £14,500, and promise of his princely favour to restore Sir Robert in honours and fortunes; but before payment thereof was made (if any at all), to the said Sir Robert's hands, the prince was dead. And it appearing that Alice, Lady Dudley, wife of Sir Robert had an estate of inheritance in the same, descendible unto her posterity, in the 19th of JAMES I., an act was passed to enable her to alien her estate from her children as a feme sole; which she accordingly did, in consideration of £4,000, and further payments yearly to be made out of the exchequer, &c.; which having not been accordingly paid for many years, are to the damage of the said Lady Alice and her children, to a very great value. And the said Sir Robert settling himself in Tuscany, within the territories of the great duke, (from whom he had extraordinary esteem,) had from the emperor, FERDINAND II., the title of a duke given him, to be used by himself and his heirs throughout the sacred empire.

" And whereas, our father not knowing the truth of the lawful birth of the said Sir Robert, (as we piously believe), granted away the titles of the said earldom to others, which we now hold not fit to call in question. And yet having a very deep sense of the injuries done to Sir Robert Dudley, and the Lady Alice, and their children, &c., and holding ourselves in honour and conscience obliged to make reparation; and also taking into consideration the said great estate which the Lady Alice had in Kenilworth, and sold at our desire to us at a very great undervalue, and yet not performed or satisfied to many thousand pounds damage. And we also, casting our princely eye upon the faithful services done by Sir Richard Leveson, who married the Lady Catherine, one of the daughters of the said duke, and also the great services which Robert Holbourne, Esq., hath done us by his learned pen, and otherwise, who married Anne, another of the daughters; we have conceived ourselves bound in honour and conscience to give the said Lady Alice and her children such honours and precedencies as is, or are due to them in marriage or blood. And therefore we do not only give and grant unto the said Lady Alice Dudley the title of Duchess of Dudley for life, in England, and other our realms, &c., with such precedencies as she might have had, if she had lived in the dominions of the sacred empire, &c.; but we do also further grant unto the said Lady Catherine and Lady Anne, her daughters, the places, titles, and precedencies of the said duke's daughters, as from the time of their father's creation during their respective lives, &c. Conceiving ourselves obliged to do much more for them, if it were in our power, in these unhappy times of distraction, &c., witness ourself, at Oxford, 23rd May, in the 20th year of our reign."

This honour was also confirmed to her grace by King CHARLES II.

The Duchess of Dudley d. 22 January, 1669-70, and was buried at Stoneleigh, co. Warwick, under a noble monument erected by herself, when her peerage, being for life only, EXPIRED.

DUDLEY—EARL OF WARWICK.

By Letters Patent, dated 26 September, 1561.

Lineage.

Through the especial favour of the Queen, in the 3rd and 4th of PHILIP and MARY,

LORD AMBROSE DUDLEY, then eldest surviving son of the attainted John Dudley, Duke of Northumberland, was restored in blood; and in the 1st year of ELIZABETH, he obtained a grant of the manor of Ribworth Beauchamp, co. Leicester, to be held by the service of pantler to the kings and queens of England at their coronations, which manor and office his father and other of his ancestors, Earls of Warwick, formerly enjoyed. In the next year he was made master of the ordnance for life, and two years afterwards, 25 December, 1561, advanced to the peerage as BARON L'ISLE, preparatory to his being created next day Earl of WARWICK, when he obtained a grant of Warwick Castle, and divers other lordships in the same co., which had come to the crown upon the attainder of his father. His lordship was afterwards elected a knight of the Garter. In the 12th ELIZABETH, upon the insurrection in the North of the Earls of Northumberland and Westmoreland the Earl of Sussex being first despatched against the rebels with 700 men, the Earl of Warwick, with the Lord Admiral Clinton, followed with 13,000 more, the earl being nominated lieut-gen. of the army. The next year his lordship was constituted chief butler of England, and soon afterwards sworn of her majesty's privy council; in which latter year, 15th ELIZABETH, he was one of the peers who sat in Westminster Hall on the trial and judgment of Thomas, Duke of Norfolk, as he did in fourteen years after at Fotheringay, on the trial of Mary of Scotland.

His lordship m. 1st, Anne, dau. and co-heir of William Whorwood, Esq., attorney-general to King HENRY VIII.; 2ndly, Elizabeth, dau. and heir of Gilbert Talboys, and sister and heir of George, Lord Talboys; and 3rdly, Anne, dau. of Francis, Earl of Bedford; but d. s. p. in 1589, when all his honours became EXTINCT, and the lordships and lands, which he had obtained by grant (part of the inheritance of the old Earls of Warwick), reverted to the crown. Of these the ancient park of Wedgenock was granted in 1601 by Queen ELIZABETH to Sir Fulke Greville, to whom, in four years afterwards, King JAMES likewise granted the castle of Warwick, with the gardens and dependencies. This Sir Fulke Greville

was descended through his grandmother, Elizabeth, one of the daus. and co-heirs of Lord Beauchamp, of Powyk, from the old Beauchamps, Earls of Warwick; and from him have sprung the existing Earls of Brooke and Warwick.

Arms.—Or, a lion rampant, az., double queued, vert.

DUDLEY—BARON DENBIGH, EARL OF LEICESTER.

Barony, by Letters Patent, dated 28 September, 1563.
Earldom, by Letters Patent, dated 29 September, 1563.

Lineage.

SIR ROBERT DUDLEY, a younger son of John, Duke of Northumberland, and brother of Lord Guilford Dudley, the unhappy husband of Lady Jane Grey, was appointed according to his biographist, Sir John Hayward, in the 5th of EDWARD VI., one of the six gentlemen in ordinary of the privy-chamber to that king; and Hayward adds, "that he was the true heir, both of his father's hate against persons of nobility, and cunning to dissemble the same; and afterwards for lust and cruelty, a monster of the court. And, as apt to hate, so a true executioner of his hate; yet rather by practice than by open dealing, as wanting rather courage than wit: and that, after his entertainment into a place of so near service the king enjoyed his health not long." Upon the accession of MARY, Dudley was sent to the Tower with his father, and attainted; but, escaping the fate of that ambitious nobleman, he was soon afterwards restored, and made master of the ordnance. By Queen ELIZABETH he was at once taken into favour, raised to high rank, and invested with wealth and power. In the 1st year of her majesty's reign, he was made master of the horse, with a fee of 100 marks per annum, and elected a knight of the most noble order of the Garter. He was soon afterwards constituted constable of Windsor Castle for life, and the queen subsequently proposed that he should become the husband of the beautiful but unfortunate MARY STUART, promising, in the event of the princess's assent, that she would, by authority of parliament, declare her heir to the crown of England, in case she died herself without issue. The alliance was marred, however, through the influence of France, although the favourite had been advanced the same year, that he might be deemed the more worthy of his royal bride, to the dignities of *Baron Denbigh* and EARL OF LEICESTER. But this proceeding of ELIZABETH has been considered as a mere experiment to enable herself to espouse Dudley with less dishonour, if he had been accepted by the Queen of Scots. In 1572 his lordship was one of the peers who sat upon the trial of the Duke of Norfolk, and he was appointed some years afterwards captain-general of an expedition sent into the Low Countries for the service of the United Provinces against the Spaniards; but in this enterprise, incurring, by his insolence, incapacity, and caprice, the displeasure of the Dutch, he was recalled, and constrained upon his return to humble himself to the queen, and with tears to beg of her majesty, "that, having sent him thither with honour, she would not receive him back with disgrace; and that whom she had raised from the dust, she would not bury alive!" He intended afterwards to retire to his castle of Kenilworth, and commenced his journey thither, but died on the way at Cornbury Park, in Oxfordshire, 4 September, 1588. His lordship was a knight of the Garter, and a knight of St. Michael, a privy-councillor, master of the horse, steward of the queen's household, constable of Windsor Castle, chancellor of the university of Oxford, justice in eyre of all the forests south of Trent, and lieutenant and captain-general of the English forces in the Netherlands. "His death," says Rapin, "drew tears from the queen, who, nevertheless, ordered his goods to be sold at public sale for payment of the sums she had lent him. This infamous nobleman m. 1st, the beautiful AMY ROBSART, dau. of Sir John Robsart, Knt.; and that unhappy lady he is accused but too justly of having murdered in the house of Forster, one of his tenants, at Cumnor, near Oxford. To this lone habitation she was removed, and there, after poison had proved inefficacious, she was strangled, and her corpse flung from a high staircase, that her death might appear to have been occasioned by the fall. He m. 2ndly, Douglas, dau. of William, Lord Howard, of Effingham, and widow of John, Lord Sheffield, by whom he had a son,

ROBERT (Sir).

Fearing that this latter alliance would cause a diminution of his influence with the queen, he tried by every means to repu-

.liate her ladyship, and he subsequently attempted her life by poison, but unsuccessfully. His child by her, Sir Robert Dudley, he terms, in his will, his base son, but leaves him the principal part of his fortune. His 3rd wife was Lettice, dau of Sir Francis Knolles, and widow of Walter, Earl of Essex: but by her he had no surviving issue. In the year 1575, Queen ELIZABETH paid the earl a visit at Kenilworth, and was there magnificently entertained by his lordship for seventeen days, at the enormous expense of £60,000. About this period appeared a pamphlet, written with much force, entitled a Dialogue between a Scholar, a Gentleman. and a Lawyer, wherein the whole of Leicester's conduct was canvassed with great truth. The queen herself caused letters to be written from the privy-council, denying the charges, and vindicating the character of the favourite; but the book was not the less read nor credited.

Upon the decease of the earl, his honours became EXTINCT. His son, Sir Robert Dudley, failing to establish his legitimacy, retired to Italy in disgust, and lived there the remainder of his life. (See Dudley, Duchess of Dudley.) Of Dudley, Walpole, in his Royal and Noble Authors, thus speaks: " Robert Dudley, called the natural son, probably the legitimate son of the great Earl of Leicester, having been deprived of his birthright, and never acknowledged as a peer of England, could not with propriety be classed among that order; yet he was too great an honour to his country to be omitted; and it is the duty of the meanest historian, and his felicity to have it in his power, to do justice to the memory of the deserving, which falls not within the compass of particulars to procure to the living. The author of those curious Lives of the Dudleys in the Biographia has already retrieved the fame of this extraordinary person from oblivion; and therefore I shall touch very few particulars of his story. He was educated under Sir Thomas Chaloner, the accomplished governor of Prince HENRY, and distinguished his youth by martial achievements, and by useful discoveries in the West Indies : but it was the house of Medici, those patrons of learning and talent, who fostered this enterprising spirit, and who were amply rewarded for their munificence by his projecting the free port of Leghorn. He flourished in their court, and in that of the emperor, who declared him Duke of Northumberland, a dukedom remarkably confirmed to his widow, whom CHARLES I. created Duchess of Dudley. Anthony Wood says, ' the duke was a complete gentleman in all suitable employments, an exact seaman, an excellent architect, mathematician, physician, chymist, and what not. He was a handsome, personable man, tall of stature, red-haired, and of admirable comport, and, above all, noted for riding the great horse, for tilting, and for his being the first of all that taught a dog to sit in order to catch partridges.' "

Arms—Or, a lion rampant, double queued, vert.

DUFF—BARON FIFE.

By Letters Patent, dated 5 July, 1790.
By Letters Patent, dated 28 April, 1827.

Lineage.

JAMES DUFF, 2nd Earl Fife, in the peerage of Ireland, was created a peer of Great Britain, in the dignity of BARON FIFE, 5 July, 1790. His lordship m. in 1766, Lady Dorothea Sinclair, sole heir of Alexander, 9th Earl of Caithness; but dying without male issue, 24 January, 1809, the British BARONY OF FIFE became EXTINCT, while his lordship's Irish honours devolved upon his brother, the HON. ALEXANDER DUFF, as 3rd Earl Fife, whose eldest son, JAMES, 4th Earl Fife, was created a Baron of the United Kingdom, as BARON FIFE, 28 April, 1827, but d. s. p. 9 March, 1857, when that title became EXTINCT.

Arms—Quarterly : 1st and 4th, or, a lion rampant, gu. for MAC DUFF; 2nd and 3rd, vert, a fesse, dancettée, erm. between a hart's head, caboosed, in chief, and two escallops in base, or, for DUFF.

DUNBAR—EARLS OF DUNBAR AND MARCH.
(See ADDENDA.)

DUNBAR—BARON DUFFUS.
(See ADDENDA.)

DUNBAR—EARL OF MORAY.
(See RANDOLPH, Earl of Moray.)

DUNCOMBE—LORD FEVERSHAM, BARON OF DOWNTON, CO. WILTS.

By Letters Patent, dated 23 June, 1747.

Lineage.

The Duncombes, originally of Barley-End, co. Buckingham, spread in different branches into other counties during the reigns of King HENRY VIII. and his son EDWARD VI.

WILLIAM DUNCOMBE, of Ivingho (at the time of the Visitation in 1634), m. Mary, dau. of John Theed, gentleman, and had four sons, of whom the 2nd,

ANTHONY DUNCOMBE, Esq., of Drayton, Bucks, m. — dau. of Paulye, lord of the manor of Whitchurch, and had issue,

Charles (Sir), a banker in London. who served the office of sheriff for that city, anno 1700, and filled, in nine years afterwards, the civic chair. Sir Charles d. unm., possessed of immense wealth, acquired by himself, which he devised to his nephews, Anthony Duncombe, the son of his brother, and Thomas Brown, the son of his sister.

ANTHONY, of whom presently.

Mary, m. to Thomas Brown, Esq., of the city of London; by whom she had an only son,

Thomas, whose grandson, Charles Duncombe, Esq., of Duncombe Park, co. York, was created Baron Feversham in 1826. (See BURKE's *Extant Peerage*).

ANTHONY DUNCOMBE, Esq. (the 2nd son) m. Jane, eldest dau. and co-heiress of the Hon. Frederick Cornwallis, 2nd son of Frederick, 1st Lord Cornwallis, and had an only son,

ANTHONY DUNCOMBE, Esq., who inherited, as stated above, a moiety of his uncle, Sir Charles Duncombe's large fortune, and was elevated to the peerage by letters patent, dated 23 June, 1747, as LORD FEVERSHAM, *Baron of Downton, co. Wilts.* His lordship m. 1st, the Hon. Margery Verney, dau. of George, Lord Willoughby de Broke; by whom he had three sons, Charles and Anthony, who both d. young, and George, who attained his nineteenth year, but d. in 1741; he had likewise a dau. that d. in infancy. Lord Feversham m. 2ndly, Frances, dau. of Peter Bathurst, Esq., of Clarendon Park, Wilts; this lady d. in childbed, 21 November, 1757; and he m. 3rdly, Anne, dau. of Sir Thomas Hales, Bart., by whom he had a dau.,

Anne, who m. Jacob, 2nd Earl of Radnor, by whom she was mother of William, 3rd Earl of Radnor, and other issue.

His lordship d. in 1763, and leaving no male issue, the BARONY OF FEVERSHAM, OF DOWNTON, became EXTINCT. His widow m. 22 July, 1765, William, 1st Earl of Radnor.

Arms—Per chev., engrailed, gu. and arg., three talbots' heads erased, counterchanged.

NOTE.—Sir Saunders Duncombe (probably a member of this family), a gentleman pensioner to King JAMES I. and his son King CHARLES, was the introducer of *sedans* or close chairs into this country in 1634, when he obtained a patent, vesting in himself and his heirs the sole right of carrying persons "up and down in them " for a certain sum. It is somewhat singular that the *same year* introduced hackney coaches into London; they were first brought into use by Captain Bayley.

DUNDAS—BARON AMESBURY.

By Letters Patent, dated 10 May, 1832.

Lineage.

ALEXANDER DUNDAS, of Fingask, son of James Dundas, of Dundas, by Christian his wife, dau. of John, Lord Innermeath and Lorn, was returned heir to his father in divers lands, anno 1431. He m. Eupham, dau. of Sir Alexander Livingston, of Callendar, and d. in 1451, during his confinement in Dumbarton Castle, wherein he had been imprisoned through the hostility of William, Earl of Douglas : he was s. by his son,

ALEXANDER DUNDAS, of Fingask, who m. Isabel, dau. of Lawrence, Lord Oliphant, and had several sons, and one dau., the wife of Law, of Lawbridge. He fell at Flodden, in 1513, together with four of his sons. and was s. by his eldest son,

ALEXANDER DUNDAS, of Fingask, who m. Elizabeth, dau. of Sir David Bruce, of Clackmannan, and had issue. He was slain at Pinkie, and s. by his eldest son,

ARCHIBALD DUNDAS, of Fingask, a man of much influence in the time of JAMES VI., who was s. at his decease by his son,

WILLIAM DUNDAS, of Fingask, who m. in 1582, Margaret, eldest dau. and heir of Sir David Carnegie, of Clouthie, but having no issue, was s. by his brother,

ARCHIBALD DUNDAS, of Fingask, who m. 1st, Jane, dau. of Sir David Carnegie, by Eupham, his 2nd wife, dau. of Sir David Wemyss, of Wemyss, and had a son, JOHN, his heir; and a dau. Nicholas, m. to Fairlie, of Braid. Archibald m. 2ndly, Giles, dau. of Lawrence Mercer, of Aldie, and had a son, Lawrence, professor of humanity at Edinburgh. The eldest son,

SIR JOHN DUNDAS, of Fingask, received the honour of knighthood from CHARLES I. at Dunfermline, in 1633. Enthusiastically attached to the unfortunate monarch, and nearly related by his mother to the great and gallant Marquess of Montrose, he devoted his energies and fortune to the royal cause, and ruined his estate—the transmitted inheritance of so long a line of ancestry. He m. 1st, Anne, dau. of Sir William Moncrief, of that ilk, but had no issue; and 2ndly, Margaret, dau. of George Dundas, of Dundas, by whom he had an only son, his successor in 1670,

JOHN DUNDAS, of Fingask, who m. Magdalen, dau. of Thomas Allardice, son of Allardice, of that ilk, and was s. in 1724, by his son,

THOMAS DUNDAS, of Fingask, who acquired a considerable estate in the co. of Stirling, and got a charter under the great seal, anno 1739, for erecting his lands into a barony, under the designation of the barony of Fingask. He m. Berthea, dau. of John Baillie, of Castlecarry, and had two sons, namely, THOMAS, his heir; and LAURENCE, of Kerse, ancestor of the EARL OF ZETLAND. The elder son,

THOMAS DUNDAS, Esq., of Fingask, M.P. for the stewartry of Orkney and Shetland, m. 1st, Anne, dau. of James Graham, of Airth, judge of the High Court of Admiralty for Scotland, but had no issue; and 2ndly, 1744, Lady Janet Maitland, dau. of Charles, 6th Earl of Lauderdale, and had issue,

I. THOMAS, his heir, of Fingask and Carron Hall, co. Stirling, M.P., a general officer of distinction, m. 9 January, 1794, Lady Elizabeth-Eleanora Home, dau. of Alexander, 9th Earl of Home, and by her (who survived until 10 April, 1837) he had THOMAS and other issue. He d. in the public service at Guadaloupe, 3 June, 1794, and in the following year a monument was ordered by the House of Commons to be erected to his memory in St. Paul's Cathedral. His son and heir,

LIEUT.-COL. THOMAS DUNDAS, of Carron Hall, who m. Charlotte-Anne, dau. of Lieut.-Col. Joseph Moore Boultbee, and left at his decease, 24 May, 1860, one surviving son and heir, JOSEPH DUNDAS, Esq., of Carron Hall; and two daus., viz., Charlotte-Anna, m. 1st, to Col. Armine Mountain, who d. 1854; and 2ndly, 1860, to Col. Henry Lefroy, R.A.; and Clementina m. 1856, to Vincent Bartolucci.

II. CHARLES, of whom presently.
I. Margaret, m. to A. Gibson, Esq.
II. Berthia, m. to George Haldane, Esq.
III. Mary, m. to James Bruce, Esq., of Kinnaird.
IV. Janet, m. to JAMES DEANS, Esq., M.D.

Mr. Dundas d. in 1786. His 2nd son,

CHARLES DUNDAS, Esq., of Barton Court, co. Berks, for many years representative in Parliament for that shire, was elevated to the peerage 10 May, 1832, as BARON AMESBURY, of Kentbury Amesbury, but enjoyed the honour for two months only. He m. 1st, Anne, dau. and sole heiress of Ralph Whitley, Esq., of Aston Hall, in Flintshire (lineally descended from Richard Whitley and Margaret his wife, dau. and heir of William de Messam, of Aston, which William de Messam was great-grandson of Henry de Messam by his wife, the dau. and heir of Richard Aston, of Aston), and had by her an only dau.,

JANET, who m. 28 April, 1808, her cousin, the late VICE-ADMIRAL SIR JAMES WHITLEY DEANS-DUNDAS, G.C.B., of Barton Court, co. Berks, J.P., and D.L., and by him (who m. 2ndly, 3 August, 1847, Lady Emily Moreton, sister of the 1st Earl of Ducie, and d. 30 October, 1862), had issue,

1 Charles-James, of the coldstream-guards, b. 15 January, 1811, M.P. for the Flint district, 1838; m. 20 March, 1837, his cousin Janet-Lindsay, dau. of John Jardine, and grand-dau. of Bruce, the traveller, and had issue, Charles Amesbury, b. 30 November, 1845. He d. 11 April, 1856.
2 James, in holy orders, M.A., of Magdalen Coll., Cambridge, vicar of Kintbury.
1 Ann, m. to John-Archer Houblon, Esq., of Great Hallingbury.
2 Janet, m. to Henry Robarts, Esq.
3 Sophia, m. to James-Coutts Crawford, Esq., and d. 1850.

Lord Amesbury, m. 2ndly, his cousin Margaret, 3rd dau. of the late Charles Barclay, and widow 1st of Charles Ogilvy, Esq.; and 2ndly, of Major Archibald Erskine. His lordship d. 30 June, 1832, when the title became EXTINCT.

Arms—Arg., a lion rampant, within a bordure, flory-counter flory, gu.

DUNGAN—EARL OF LIMERICK.

(See ADDENDA.)

184

DUNNING—BARON ASHBURTON, OF ASHBURTON, CO. DEVON.

By Letters Patent, dated 8 April, 1782.

Lineage.

JOHN DUNNING, 2nd son of John Dunning, of Gnatham, co. Devon, m. Agnes, dau. of Henry Judsham, of Old Port, in the same shire, and left at his decease, 1 December, 1780, an only surviving son,

JOHN DUNNING, b. at Ashburton, 18 October, 1731, who having applied himself to the study of the law, was called to the bar, and soon attained the first rank in his learned profession. In 1767, Mr. Dunning was appointed solicitor-general, an office which he resigned in 1770. He was elected to parliament by the borough of Calne, in 1768, and continued a member of the lower house until elevated to the peerage upon the accession of Lord Shelburne, his great patron, to power, by patent, dated 8 April, 1782, as BARON ASHBURTON, of Ashburton, co. Devon. On the 13th of the same month his lordship was appointed chancellor of the Duchy of Lancaster. He was also recorder of Bristol, and a member of the privy council. He m. 31 March, 1780, Elizabeth, dau. of John Baring, Esq., of Larkbear, co. Devon. and sister of Sir Francis Baring, Bart., by whom he had two sons, John, who d. at about seventeen months old in April, 1783, and RICHARD-BARRE, his successor. Of this eminent lawyer, Sir Egerton Brydges says, "He was a man whose talents were so peculiar, and had such a singular kind of brilliance, that they are not yet forgotten at the bar. They were more remarkable for acuteness and for wit, than for elegance and chasteness. The combination of his words were so singular, and the tones of his discordant voice so served in him to rivet the attention, that, as they always conveyed powers of thinking eminently sharp and forcible, he was constantly listened to with eagerness and admiration. His temper was generous, his spirits lively, and his passions violent. The popular side which he took in politics increased his fame; and he died generally lamented, just as he had attained the fond object of his ambition, aged fifty-two." His lordship d. 18 August, 1783, and was s. by his son,

RICHARD-BARRE DUNNING, 2nd baron, b. 16 September, 1782. His lordship m. 17 September, 1805, Anne, dau. of the late William Cuninghame, Esq., of Lainshaw, but had no issue. He d. in 1823, when the BARONY OF ASHBURTON became EXTINCT.

Arms—Bendy sinister of eight, or and vert, a lion rampant, sa.

DUNSTANVILL—EARL OF CORNWALL.

By creation, 1140.

Lineage.

REGINALD DE DUNSTANVILL 3rd of the fourteen illegitimate sons of King HENRY I., by the dau. of Robert Corbet, was made EARL OF CORNWALL, by King STEPHEN, anno 1140. Notwithstanding which, he subsequently espoused the cause of the Empress MAUD, and was in rebellion, and the fall of STEPHEN's power at the battle of Lincoln. From which period we find nothing remarkable of him until the 10th HENRY II., when he appears to have been an unsuccessful mediator between that monarch and the haughty prelate, Thomas à Becket. His lordship was afterwards in arms on the side of the king, against Robert, Earl of Leicester (who had reared the standard of revolt in favour of Prince Henry, the king's son), and joined Richard de Luci, justice of England, in the siege of Leicester; the town of which they carried, but not the castle. His lordship m. Beatrice, dau. of William Fitz-Richard, a potent man of Cornwall, and d. in 1175, when leaving no legitimate male issue, the EARLDOM OF CORNWALL reverted to the crown, and was retained by King HENRY II. for the use of JOHN, his younger son, excepting a small proportion which devolved upon the deceased lord's daus., viz.,

Hawyse, m. to Richard de Redvers.
Maud, m. to Robert, Earl of Mellent.
Ursula, m. to Walter de Dunstanvill.
Sarah, m. to the Viscount of Limoges.
Reginald de Dunstanvill d. 1175.

Arms—Gu., two lions passant guardant, or, a baton sinister, az.

NOTE.—Besides his legitimate daus. above-mentioned, the

earl left by Beatrice de Vaus, lady of Torre and Karswell, two bastard sons, HENRY and William, whereof the elder,

HENRY, surnamed FITZ-COUNT, became a person of great celebrity. In the 4th King JOHN he had an assignation of £20 current money of Anjou, for his support in the king's service in Roan; and about that time gave 1,200 marks for the lands of William de Traci; which lands Hugh de Courtenay and Henry de Tracy afterwards enjoyed. In the 17th JOHN he had a grant from the king of the whole county of Cornwall, with the demesnes, and all other appurtenances, to farm, until the realm should be in peace, and the king clearly satisfied, whether he ought to hold it in right of inheritance, or as a part of the demesne of the crown; and being then made constable of the castle of Launceston, rendered up the government of the castle of Porcestre, which he had previously held. In the 4th of King HENRY III., it appears that he stood indebted to the king in £597 and one mark, which sum was due by him to King JOHN, and that the same year disobeying the king's commands, and departing the court without permission, the king discharged all his subjects, and in particular those of Cornwall, from having anything to do with him. He made his peace, however, soon after, through the mediation of the bishops of Norwich, Winchester, and Exeter, and the friendship of Hubert de Burgh, then justice of England, upon surrendering to the crown the castle of Launceston, and the county of Cornwall, with all the homage and services thereto belonging as fully as King JOHN enjoyed them at the beginning of the war with the barons; saving the right which he, Henry Fitz-Count, preferred to the county, and in which the king promised to do him justice when he attained maturity. The claimant d. 6th HENRY III., and the matter was consequently never determined. By some it has been thought that this HENRY FITZ-COUNT s. his father in the Earldom of Cornwall, because he obtained a grant of the county from the crown. "But considering," says Dugdale, "that the title of earl was never attributed to him, I cannot conceive anything more passed by that grant, than the barony or revenue of the county."

DURAS—BARON DURAS, OF HOLDENBY, CO. NORTHAMPTON, EARL OF FEVERSHAM.

Barony, by Letters Patent, dated 19 January, 1673.
Earldom, by Letters Patent, dated 8 April, 1676.

Lineage.

LEWIS DE DURAS, Marquis de Blanquefort, and brother of the Duc de Duras, in France, was naturalized by act of parliament, 17th King CHARLES II., being at that period captain of the guard to the Duke of York, whom he afterwards attended in the celebrated sea-fight with the Dutch, in June, 1665, and behaved very gallantly therein. He was subsequently elevated to the peerage by letters patent dated 19 January, 1673 (in consideration of this and other services), in the dignity of Baron Duras, of Holdenby. His lordship m. Mary, elder dau. and co-heiress of Sir George Sondes, of Lees Court, co. Kent, K.B., which Sir George was elevated to the peerage (See Sondes), as Baron Throwley, Viscount Sondes, and EARL OF FEVERSHAM, with remainder, in default of male issue, to his son-in-law, Lord Duras, by letters patent, dated 8 April, 1676. In the following year, the Earl died, and Lord Duras, became Earl of Feversham. His lordship had a command at the battle of Sedgemoor, and was commander of the army of King JAMES (by whom he was made a knight of the Garter), when the Prince of Orange came to Whitehall. He survived the Revolution, and d. s. p. in 1709, when all his honours became EXTINCT.

Arms—Gu., a lion rampant, arg. (a label of three points)

EARDLEY—BARON EARDLEY.

By Patent, dated October, 1789.

Lineage.

SAMPSON GIDEON, Esq., of Spalding, co. Lincoln, a gentleman of large estate, paternal and personal, m. Jane, dau. of Charles Ermell, Esq., and by her he left at his decease, 17 October, 1762, a son and two daus.,

I. SAMPSON, his successor.
I. Susanna, d. unm.
II. Elizabeth, m. in 1757, to William Hall, 2nd Viscount Gage, and had an only son, who d. an infant.

The only son and heir,

SIR SAMPSON GIDEON, Bart., of Spalding, in Lincolnshire, and of Belvidere, in Kent, assumed, by sign manual, in July, 1789, the additional surname of EARDLEY, and was created, in the October following, BARON EARDLEY, of Spalding, in the peerage of Ireland. He m. 6 December, 1766, Maria-Marow, dau. of the Right Hon. Sir John-Eardley Wilmot, chief justice of the Common Pleas, and by that lady (who d. 1 March, 1794) had issue two sons, both in the army, who predeceased their father, s. p., and three daus., co-heirs,

MARIA-MAROW, m. 8 September, 1794, George-William, Lord Saye and Sele, and d. 5 September, 1834, leaving a son, WILLIAM-THOMAS, late Lord SAYE and SELE, and a dau., Maria-Elizabeth, who m. 1825, George-Ernest, Count de Gersdoff, of Prussia, and d. 1826.
CHARLOTTE-ELIZABETH, m. 22 September, 1792, to Culling Smith, Esq., afterwards Sir Culling Smith, Bart., and had issue; her grandson and representative was the late SIR EARDLEY-GIDEON-CULLING EARDLEY, Bart., of Hadley.
SELINA, m. March, 1797, to John-Walbanke Childers, Esq., of Cantley, in Yorkshire, and had John Walbanke-Childers, Esq., of Cantley, and other issue.

Lord Eardley, a nobleman of great generosity and benevolence, d. at the age of eighty, 25 December, 1824, when the peerage became EXTINCT, his extensive property devolving on his daughters.

Arms—Arg., on a chev., az., three garbs, or; a canton, gu., charged with a fret of the 3rd.

EDEN—EARL OF AUCKLAND.

By Letters Patent, dated 11 December, 1839.

Lineage.

GEORGE EDEN, 2nd Lord Auckland, b. 25 August, 1784, having filled the important office of governor-general of India was made a knight Grand Cross of the Bath, and created Baron Eden, of Norwood, in Surrey, and EARL OF AUCKLAND, in 1839. His lordship became subsequently first Lord of the Admiralty. He d. unm., 1 January, 1849, when the Earldom of Auckland and Barony of Eden became EXTINCT, but his other honours devolved on his brother, ROBERT-JOHN EDEN, D.D., now BARON AUCKLAND.

Arms—Gu., on a chev., arg., between three garbs, or, as many escallops, az.

EDRINGTON—BARON EDRINGTON.

By Writ of Summons, dated 22 January, 1336.

Lineage.

The surname of this family was assumed from the lordship of Edrington, co. Warwick, bestowed by Gervase Paganell, Baron of Dudley, upon

HENRY DE EDRINGTON, whose grandson,

THOMAS DE EDRINGTON, was appointed, with Richard de Altacvipa, in the 6th King JOHN, bailiff or substitute to Geoffrey Fitzpiers, then sheriff of the counties of Salop and Stafford. He was afterwards chamberlain to the king, and obtained some territorial grants from the crown. In the 15th of JOHN, when the baronial influence predominated, this Thomas de Edrington, and Ralph Fitz-Nicholas, are said to have been despatched secretly by the king to Admiralius Murmelius, king of Africa and Spain, to offer to the infidel the whole realm of England, as a tributary state; and that he, JOHN, would renounce the cross, and assume the crescent, if the Mahomedan monarch would afford him assistance against his powerful and rebellious subjects. Thomas de Edrington m. Roese de Cockfield, and dying in the latter end of JOHN's reign, was s. by his son,

GILES DE EDRINGTON, who, in the 35th HENRY III., was one of the justices itinerant for the city of London, and the next was constituted one of the justices of the court of Common Pleas: he was likewise one of the justices of assize for the co. Warwick, from the 34th to the 53rd of the same reign inclusive. This learned person was a munificent benefactor to the church. He was s. at his decease by his son,

HENRY DE EDRINGTON, who m. Maud, one of the daus., and eventually co-heiresses of Roger de Someri, Baron of Dudley; and also one of the co-heirs of Nichola, dau. and co-heir of

Hugh Albini, Earl of Arundel, and dying in the 10th EDWARD I., was *s.* by his son,

HENRY DE EDRINGTON, who, in the 30th EDWARD I., upon the decease of his mother, had livery of her lands. In four years afterwards he was made a knight of the Bath, and he then attended Prince Edward in the expedition made into Scotland: wherein he attained so much celebrity that he was summoned to parliament as a BARON 22 January, 1336. His lordship *m.* Joane, dau. and co-heir of Sir Thomas de Wolvey, of Wolvey, co. Warwick, by whom he had an only son,

GILES, who, not appearing in the 19th EDWARD III., to receive the honour of knighthood, obtained pardon for that omission.

Lord Edrington had but one summons, and his descendants none. He was *s.* by his son,

GILES DE EDRINGTON, whose great grandson,

THOMAS EDRINGTON, who lived in the reign of HENRY VI., was the last of the family that enjoyed the lordship of Edrington, co. Warwick.

Arms—Or, two lions passant, in pale, as.

EGERTON—BARON GREY DE WILTON.

By Letters Patent, dated 15 May, 1784.

Lineage.

This, and the noble house of BRIDGEWATER, originated with a common ancestor; but the branch of Grey de Wilton was the senior.

DAVID DE MALPAS, *alias* DE EGERTON, son and heir of Philip Goch, 2nd son of DAVID DE MALPAS, surnamed Le Clerk, *m.* Cecilia, dau. of Randle le Roter, and was father of

PHILIP DE EGERTON, sheriff of Cheshire 23rd and 24th EDWARD I., who *m.* Margaret, dau. of Richard de Wrenbury, and was father, with other issue, of

DAVID, his heir.
Urian, lord of Caldecote *jure uxoris*, ancestor of the Egertons of Betley, &c.

The eldest son and heir,

DAVID DE EGERTON, sheriff of Cheshire 7th EDWARD III., *m.* Isabella, dau. of Ric de Fulleshurst, Lord of Crewe, and had issue,

Philip, who *m.* twice, and whose only son, David, *d. s. p.,* leaving his two sisters his co-heiresses. The elder of whom, Elena, became eventually sole heiress. She *m.* Sir William Brereton, Knt., of Brereton, and had issue.
David, *d. s. p.*
URIAN, of whose line we treat.

The youngest son,

URIAN DE EGERTON, living 29th EDWARD III., *m.* Amelia. dau. of John Warburton, and was *s.* by his eldest son,

PHILIP DE EGERTON, who *m.* Matilda, dau. of David de Malpas, and co-heir of her niece, Ellen, wife of Urian de Brereton, and by her was father of

SIR JOHN EGERTON, Knt., who was slain at the battle of Blore Heath, leaving, by Margaret his wife, dau. of Sir John Fitton, Knt., an eldest son and heir,

PHILIP EGERTON, Esq., of Egerton, who *m.* Margery, dau. of William Mainwaring, Esq., of Ightfield, and had issue. His eldest son,

WILLIAM EGERTON, Esq., *m.* Margaret, dau. of Sir Ralph Egerton, of Wrinehill, but dying *s. p., v. p* was *s* by his next surviving brother,

JOHN EGERTON, Esq., who *m.* Elizabeth, dau. and heir of Hugh Done, Esq., of Oulton, and was father of

PHILIP EGERTON, of Egerton and Oulton. who *m.* Joana, dau. and co-heir of Gilbert Smith, of Cuerdley, and widow of Richard Winnington, and left a son and heir,

SIR PHILIP EGERTON, of Egerton and Oulton, Knt., who *m.* Eleanor, dau. of Sir Randle Brereton, Knt., of Malpas, and was father of

JOHN EGERTON, of Egerton and Oulton, who *m.* Jane, dau. of Piers Mostyn, Esq., of Talacre, and dying in 1590, was *s.* by his eldest son,

SIR JOHN EGERTON, of Egerton and Oulton, knighted by Queen ELIZABETH, who *m.* Margaret, dau. of Sir Rowland Stanley, of Hooton, Knt., and was father of

SIR ROWLAND EGERTON, Knt., of Egerton and Oulton, co.

Chester (the latter estate inherited through an heiress of the Dones, from the family of Kingsley), who was created a baronet 15 April, 1617. This gentleman resided at his manor of Ferminghoe, co. Northampton, and *m.* Bridget, dau. of Sir Arthur Grey, 14th Lord Grey de Wilton, lord-lieutenant of Ireland in 1580, and heir of her brother, Thomas Grey, 15th and last baron of that family (*see* GREY, BARONS GREY DE WILTON), by whom he had, with other issue,

Thomas, who *m.* Barbara, dau. of Sir John St. John, Bart., and *d. s. p., v. p.*
JOHN. his successor.
Philip (Sir), of Oulton, whose descendant is the present Baronet of Egerton and Oulton.

Sir Rowland *d.* in 1646, and was *s.* by his eldest surviving son,

SIR JOHN EGERTON, 2nd baronet, who *m.* Anne, dau. of George Wintour, Esq., of Derham, co. Gloucester, and dying in 1674, left three daus., Bridget, *m.* 1st, to Ralph Thickness, of Barterly; and 2ndly, to Timothy Hildyard, Esq., of co. Lincoln; Margaret, *m.* to Windsor Finch, Esq., of Rushout, co. Worcester; and Anne, *m.* to John Gardener, Esq., and an only surviving son,

SIR JOHN EGERTON, 3rd baronet. This gentleman *m.* 1st Elizabeth, dau. of William, and sister and sole heir of Edward Holland, Esq., of Heaton and Denton, in Lancashire, by whom he had six sons and two daus.

HOLLAND, his heir.
Thomas, in holy orders, rector of Sefton, co. Lancaster, and of Cheadle, co. Chester, *m.* Frances, dau. of John Beresford, Esq., and *d. s. p.* 1762.
William, in holy orders, *m.* the widow of — Bateman, Esq., and had a dau., Frances.
John, *d. unm.*
Edward, of Hurleston, co. Stafford.
Ralph.
Anne.   Elizabeth.

He *m.* 2ndly, Anne, sole dau. and heir of Francis Wolferstan, Esq., of Statfold, in Staffordshire. Sir John *d.* 4 November, 1729, and was *s.* by his eldest son,

SIR HOLLAND EGERTON, 4th baronet, who *m.* in 1712, Eleanor, youngest dau. of Sir Roger Cave, of Stanford, in Northamptonshire, Bart., and had besides other sons, who *d. unm.,*

EDWARD (Sir), his heir.
THOMAS-GREY (Sir), successor to his brother.
Mary, *m.* Sir Ralph Assheton, Bart., whose 2nd wife was Eleanor, dau. and co-heir of the Rev. John Copley.
Charlotte-Elizabeth, *m.* to the Rev. Ashburnham Legh, rector of Davenham.

Sir Holland *d.* 25 April, 1730, and was *s.* by his elder surviving son,

SIR EDWARD EGERTON, 5th baronet, at whose decease *unm.,* in 1743, the title devolved upon his brother,

SIR THOMAS-GREY EGERTON, 6th baronet, who *m.* Catherine, dau. and co-heir of the Rev. John Copley, rector of Thornhill, co. York, *d.* 17 August, 1756, æt. thirty-five, and was *s.* by his only son,

SIR THOMAS-GREY EGERTON, 7th baronet, who represented the county of Lancaster in three parliaments, and was elevated to the peerage, by letters patent, dated 15 May, 1784, in the dignity of BARON GREY DE WILTON, in the co. Hertford. His lordship *m.* 12 December, 1769, Eleanor, dau. and co-heir of Sir Ralph Assheton, Bart., of Middleton, co. Lancaster, by whom he had two sons and three daus., of which one dau. alone lived to maturity, namely,

ELEANOR, who *m.* 28 April, 1794, Robert, Viscount Belgrave (late MARQUESS OF WESTMINSTER).

The baron was advanced, 26 June, 1801, to the dignities of *Viscount Grey de Wilton* and EARL OF WILTON, with special remainder to Thomas Grosvenor, the 2nd, and to the younger sons, successively, of his dau. Eleanor, by her then husband, Robert, Viscount Belgrave, or to her male issue by any future husband. His lordship *d.* 23 September, 1814, when the baronetcy reverted to John-Grey Egerton, Esq., of Oulton Park. The viscounty and earldom devolved, according to the limitation, upon his grandson, the Hon. Thomas Grosvenor now EARL OF WILTON, and the BARONY of GREY DE WILTON became EXTINCT.

Arms—Arg., a lion rampant, gu., between three pheons' heads, sa.

EGERTON — BARONS OF ELLESMERE, VISCOUNTS MARQUESSES OF BRACKLEY, EARLS OF BRIDGEWATER, DUKES OF BRIDGEWATER.

Barony, by Letters Patent, dated 17 July, 1603.
Viscounty, by Letters Patent, dated 7 November, 1616.
Earldom, by Letters Patent, dated 27 May, 1617.
Marquessate and Dukedom, by Letters Patent, dated 18 June, 1720.

Lineage.

Sir Thomas Egerton, b. in 1540, the illegitimate son of Sir Ralph Egerton, of Ridley, by Alice Spark, having been brought up to the bar, attained the highest honours of his profession, and filled during the reign of Elizabeth, successively the offices of solicitor and attorney-general, master of the Rolls, and lord keeper of the great seal. Upon the accession of James I., Sir Thomas was appointed Lord High Chancellor of England, and elevated to the peerage, 21 July, 1603, as Baron of Ellesmere, in co. Salop, and further advanced, 7 November, 1616, to the dignity of Viscount Brackley. His lordship m. three times, 1st, Elizabeth, dau. of Thomas Ravenscroft, Esq., of Bretton, co. Flint, by whom he had two sons and a dau., viz.,

Sir Thomas Egerton, Knt., who d. v. p.
John, his successor; and Mary, m. to Sir Francis Leigh, of Newnham Regis, co. Warwick, K.B., father of Francis, Earl of Chichester.

Sir Thomas m. 2ndly, Elizabeth, sister of Sir George More, of Losely Farm, co. Surrey, and widow of Sir John Wolley, of Pitford, chancellor of the Garter; and 3rdly, Alice, dau. of Sir John Spencer, of Althorp, co. Northampton. He d. 15 March, 1616-17, in the seventy-seventh year of his age having received an intimation, immediately before his decease, that it was his majesty's intention to confer upon him the dignity of an earl and an accompanying pension. This learned and distinguished nobleman was s. by his only surviving son,

John Egerton, 2nd viscount, K.B., who was created, 27 May, 1617, Earl of Bridgewater. His lordship was appointed lord president of Wales and the marches thereof, 12 May, 1633, and to this appointment the world is indebted for Milton's celebrated mask of Comus. Warton gives the following account of the circumstance which afforded the subject to the poet; "I have been informed from a manuscript of Oldys's that Lord Bridgewater, being appointed lord president of Wales, entered upon his official residence at Ludlow Castle with great solemnity. On this occasion he was attended by a large concourse of neighbouring nobility and gentry. Among the rest, came his children; in particular Lord Brackley, Mr. Thomas Egerton and Lady Alice,

——— to attend their father's state
And new intrusted sceptre.

They had been on a visit at a house of the Egerton family, in Herefordshire; and, in passing through Staywood forest, were benighted, and the Lady Alice even lost for sometime. This accident which in the end was attended with no bad consequences, furnished the subject for a mask, for a Michaelmas festivity, and produced Comus." The earl m. Frances, 2nd dau. and one of the co-heiresses of Ferdinando Stanley, Earl of Derby, and dying in 1649, was s. by his only surviving son,

John Egerton, 2nd earl, who m. Elizabeth, 2nd dau. of William Cavendish (then earl, but subsequently), Duke of Newcastle, and dying 26 December, 1686, had issue,

I. John, 3rd earl.
II. William, b. 15 August, 1649, m. Honora, sister of Thomas, Lord Leigh, of Stoneleigh, by whom he had issue, an only son, John who d. young, and four daus., Jane, Mary, Elizabeth, who d. unm.; and Honora, b. 11 August, 1685, m. Thomas-Arden Bagot, of Pipe Hall, co. Stafford.
III. Thomas, of Tatton Park, co. Chester, ancestor of the Egertons of Tatton, co. Chester, whose eventual heiress,

Hester Egerton, m. May, 1747, William Tatton, Esq., of Withenshaw, and upon inheriting her brother's possessions, resumed, by sign-manual, 8 May, 1780, her maiden name. She d. the 9th of the following July, leaving a dau., Elizabeth Tatton, the wife of Sir Christopher Sykes, Bart., of Sledmere, M.P., and a son and successor,

William Tatton Egerton, Esq., of Tatton and Withenshaw, M.P., b. 9 May, 1749. He m. thrice and dying in 1806, was s. in the Withenshaw estates by his 2nd son, Thomas-William, who took the name of Tatton, and in the Egerton estates by his eldest son, Wilbraham Egerton, Esq., of Tatton, father of Lord Egerton, of Tatton.

The eldest son,
John Egerton, 3rd earl, K.B., was b. 9 November, 1646. This nobleman m. 1st, Elizabeth, dau. and heir of James Cranfield, Earl of Middlesex, by Anne, dau. and co-heir of Edward Bourchier, Earl of Bath, and by her (who d. 3 March, 1669), had a son John, b. 11 January, 1668, who d. 31 March, 1670, and a dau. who d. in infancy; and 2ndly, Jane, eldest dau. of Charles, Duke of Bolton, and by her (who d. 22 March, 1714,) had issue,

I. Charles, Viscount Brackley, b. 7 May, 1675, burnt to death, April, 1687.
II. Thomas, b. 15 August, 1679, burnt to death, April, 1687.
III. Scroope, 4th earl.
IV. William, b. 5 November, 1684, m. Anna-Maria, dau. of Sir George Saunders, one of the commissioners of the navy, and left issue, three daus., Jane, m. to Thomas Revel, of Fetcham, Surrey, M.P. for Dover, whose heiress m. Sir George Warren, K.B.; Henrietta; and Anne, m. to Thomas Russell, D.D., of Hereford.
V. Henry, one of the canons of Christchurch, consecrated bishop of Hereford. He m. 18 December, 1720, Lady Elizabeth Ariana Bentinck, dau. of William, Earl of Portland, and d. 1 April, 1746, having had issue,

1 John, b. 30 November, 1721, bishop of Durham, m. 1st, 21 November, 1748, Lady Anne-Sophia de Grey, dau. and co-heir of Henry, Duke of Kent, and by her (who d. 24 March, 1780), he had issue,

John-William, 7th earl.
Francis-Henry, in holy orders, rector of Whitchurch, in Shropshire, afterwards 8th Earl of Bridgewater.
Amelia, m. Sir Abraham Hume, of Wormleybury, co. Hertford, Bart., and had two daus., her co-heirs, Amelia, m. Charles Long, Lord Farnborough, G.C.B., but d. s. p., and Amelia-Sophia, m. 1810, John, Lord (afterwards Earl) Brownlow, by whom she had issue.

The bishop of Durham m. 2ndly, 31 March, 1782, Mary, sister of Sir Edward Boughton, but by her who survived him had no issue. He d. 18 June, 1787.
2 William, lieut.-col. in the army, M.P., m. Mary, dau. of Robert Kirke, Esq., and d. 26 March 1783, having had three daus., viz.,

Ariana-Margaret.
Elizabeth, m. 19 February, 1783, to Charles-Benjamin Saladin of Crans, near Geneva, and had issue, a son, Charles-William Saladin, of Crans; and a dau. Charlotte-Ariana, m. 1st, to the Baron A. de Courval, and 2ndly, to Lieut.-Col. John Huber.
Isabella-Frances, m. to Richard Master, Esq., M.P., governor of Tobago, where he d. leaving, issue.

3 Henry, D.D., prebendary of Durham, d. s p.
4 Charles, lieut.-col. in the army, d. 13 May, 1793.
5 Francis, d.s.p.
1 Anne, d. unm.

VI. John, page to the Duke of Gloucester, d. unm.
VII. Charles, b. 7 November, 1725, m. Catharine, sister of William, Lord Brooke, and by her (who d. July, 1735,) had two sons,

1 Scroop, who m. Miss Sarah Pope, and d. 23 April, 1767, leaving two sons and a dau., viz., Scroop, d. young; Dodington, lieut. in the 2nd troop of horse guards, d. 12 September, 1713, s.p.; and Elizabeth, who m. Hayter, of Salisbury, and was mother of Francis Hayter, Esq., of Roche Court, Salisbury, who took the name of Egerton.
2 Dodington, one of the gentlemen of the Privy Chamber to His Majesty, d. s. p.
1 Mary, m. in 1703, to William, Lord Byron, d. 1703.
2 Elizabeth, m. 1718, Thomas Catesby, Lord Paget.

The eldest surviving son,
Scroope Egerton, 4th earl, b. 11 August, 1681, created Marquess of Brackley and Duke of Bridgewater, 18 June, 1720. His grace m. twice, 1st, Elizabeth, 3rd dau. and co-heiress of John, 2nd Duke of Marlborough, by whom he had one surviving dau. Anne, who m. 1st, Wriothesley, 3rd Duke of Bedford; and 2ndly, William, Earl of Jersey, and d. 15 April, 1763. The Duke of Bridgewater m. 2ndly, 4 August, 1722, Rachel, sister to his son-in-law, the Duke of Bedford, and by her (who m. 2ndly, Sir Richard Lyttleton, K.B.,) had issue,

I. Charles, Marquess of Brackley, b. 27 July, 1725, d. 2 May, 1731.
II. John, Marquess of Brackley, 2nd duke.
III. William, b. 15 January, 1728-9, d. 10 February following.
IV. Thomas, b. 18 April, 1730, d. 1 May following.
V. Francis, 3rd duke.
I. Louisa, b. 30 April, 1723, m. 28 March, 1748, Granville, Viscount Trentham afterwards Earl Gower, and Marquess of Stafford, and d. 14 March, 1761. From this marriage descended the ducal house of Sutherland and the Earl of Ellesmere.
II. Caroline, b. 21 May, 1724, d. unm.
III. Diana, b. 3 March, 1731-2 m. 9 March, 1753, Frederick, Lord Baltimore.

His grace who was lord-lieutenant and custos rotulorum of the co. Bucks, d. 11 January, 1745. His eldest surviving son,

JOHN EGERTON, 2nd duke, d. unm. 26 February, 1748, when the honours devolved upon his brother,

FRANCIS EGERTON, 3rd duke, b. 21 May, 1736. This nobleman justly acquired the reputation of being the great founder of inland navigation in this country by his enterprising speculation in the celebrated canal which bears his name, and which has realized a princely revenue for his successors. His grace d. unm. 9 March, 1803, when the dukedom and marquessate EXPIRED, and the greater portion of his immense wealth devolved on his nephew, George, Marquess of Stafford, afterwards Duke of Sutherland, and is now enjoyed by his grandson, the EARL OF ELLESMERE. The earldom of Bridgewater and minor titles, together with the family estates, reverted to the Duke's cousin,

GENERAL JOHN-WILLIAM EGERTON, 7th earl, son of the Right Reverend John, Lord Bishop of Durham, grandson of Doctor, Henry Egerton, Lord Bishop of Hereford, and grand nephew of the 1st duke. Lord Bridgewater was b. 17 April, 1753, and entering into the army attained the rank of lieutenant-general, 1 January, 1801. He m. 14 January, 1783, Charlotte-Catherine-Anne, only dau. and heiress of Samuel Haynes, Esq., but d. s. p. 21 October, 1823, (having bequeathed £8,000 for the production of "the Bridgewater Treatises") when the family honours devolved upon his only brother,

FRANCIS-HENRY EGERTON, 8th Earl of Bridgewater, co. Somerset, a clergyman of the established church, and prebendary of Durham, at whose decease s. p., 11 February, 1829, his honours became EXTINCT, and the great Bridgewater estates have devolved, after much litigation, on the Earl of Brownlow. (See "Vicissitudes of Families," 1st Series, p. 310.)

Arms—Arg., a lion rampant, gu., between three pheons, sa.

ELIOTT—BARONS HEATHFIELD, OF GIBRALTAR.

By Letters Patent, dated 6 July, 1787.

Lineage.

SIR GILBERT ELIOTT, of Stobbs, co. Roxburgh, a baronet of Nova Scotia, m. Eleanor, dau. of William Eliot, of Weld, or Wells, in the same shire, and had, with other issue,

JOHN, his successor in the baronetcy.

And

GEORGE-AUGUSTUS ELIOTT, 8th son, who was born at Stobbs, the paternal seat, 25 December, 1717, and received the rudiments of his education under a private tutor. At an early age was sent to the university of Leyden, where he made rapid progress in classical learning, and spoke with elegance and fluency the German and French languages. Being designed for a military life he was sent from thence to La Fere, in Picardy. This school was rendered the most celebrated in Europe, by means of the great Vauban, under whom it was conducted. It was afterwards placed under the management and care of the Count de Hourorille; here it was that the foundation was laid of that knowledge of military science in all its branches, and particularly in the arts of engineering and fortification, which afterwards so greatly distinguished this renowned officer. He completed his course, by a tour upon the continent, for the purpose of witnessing the practical effect of what he had been studying theoretically. Mr. Eliott returned in his seventeenth year, to his native country of Scotland, and was introduced by his father, Sir Gilbert, in 1735, to Lieut.-Col. Peers, of the 23rd regiment, then lying in Edinburgh. Sir Gilbert presented him as a youth anxious to bear arms for his king and country; he was accordingly entered as a volunteer in that regiment, and continued as such for more than a year. From the 23rd he went into the engineer corps at Woolwich, and made great progress in that study, until his uncle, Col. Eliott, brought him in as adjutant of the 2nd troop of horse guards, with which he went on service to Germany, and was wounded at the battle of Dettingen. Of this regiment he eventually became lieut.-col., and was soon afterwards appointed aide-de-camp to King GEORGE II. In the year 1759, he quitted the 2nd troop of horse grenadier guards, being selected to raise, form, and discipline the 15th regiment of light horse, called after him, "Eliott's light horse." As soon as this corps was fit for service, he was appointed to the command of the cavalry in the expedition on the coasts of France, with the rank of brigadier-general, thence he passed into Germany, and from that was appointed second in command in the memorable expedition against the Havannah. In 1775, General Eliott succeeded General A'Court, as commander-in-chief of the forces in Ireland. But he did not continue long on that station; not even long enough to unpack his trunks. He solicited his recal,

188

which being complied with, he was appointed to the command of Gibraltar. The system of his life, as well as his education, peculiarly qualified him for this trust. He was perhaps the most abstemious man of the age. His food was vegetables, his drink water. He never slept more than four hours at a time, so that he was up later and earlier than most other men. He had so inured himself to habits of severity, that the things which to others are painful, were to him of daily practice, and rendered agreeable by use. It could not be easy to starve such a man into a surrender. It would be quite as difficult to surprise him. The example of the commander-in-chief in a besieged garrison, has a most persuasive efficacy in forming the manners of the soldiery. Like him, his gallant followers came to regulate their lives by the most strict rules of discipline, before there arose a necessity for so doing; and severe exercise, with short diet, became habitual to them by their own choice. Thus General Eliott maintained his station upon the rock for three years of uninterrupted investment (1779 to 1783) in which the whole resources of Spain and France were employed. All the eyes of Europe were on his garrison, and his conduct justly raised him to a most elevated place in the military annals of his country.

On his return to England General Eliot received the thanks of both Houses of Parliament, was made a knight of the Bath, and raised to the peerage by the title of LORD HEATHFIELD, BARON GIBRALTAR, by letters patent, dated 6 July, 1787, a permission being granted at the same time to his lordship to take the arms of the fortress he had so bravely defended, to perpetuate to posterity his heroic conduct. His lordship m. 10 June, 1748, Anne-Pollexfen Drake, dau. of Sir Francis Drake, Bart., of Buckland, co. Devon, and had surviving issue,

FRANCIS-AUGUSTUS, his successor.

Anne, m. 1777, John-Trayton Fuller, Esq., of Erightling, co. Sussex, by whom she had six sons and five daus.,

1 Augustus-Eliott Fuller, of Rosehill, and Ashdown House, co. Sussex, b. 7 May, 1777; m. in 1801, Clara, eldest dau. and co-heir of O.-P. Meyrick, Esq., of Bodorgan, Anglesey, and dying 1857, left issue,

    Owen-John-Augustus, of Bodorgan, who has assumed the additional surname of MEYRICK. (See BURKE's Landed Gentry).

    Clara, m. to George-W. Tapps, Esq., M.P., subsequently a baronet; and d. leaving issue.

    Lucy-Ann.   Catharine-Sarah.
    Augusta-Maria.

2 Francis-John Fuller, capt. 20th dragoons, d. unm.

3 THOMAS-TRAYTON FULLER, who assumed the additional surnames of ELIOTT and DRAKE and was created a Bart. (see BURKE's Peerage and Baronetage).

4 William-Stephen Fuller, captain R.N.; d. s. p. 10 September, 1815.

5 Rose-Henry Fuller, captain R. N.; m. Margaretta, dau. of the late Sir Robert Sheffield, Bart., and has surviving issue, a son, Francis-George-Augustus, b. 24 December, 1837, lieut. royal horse-guards, and two daus., Jane-Eliza-Anne-Pollexfen; and Eleanor-Halford, m. 7 August, 1856, to C. Eales, Esq., and d. 21 October, 1858.

6 Robert-Fitzherbert Fuller, in holy orders; rector of Chalvington, Sussex; m. Ursula, dau. of Sir Robert Sheffield, Bart., and has issue.

1 Eliza-Fuller, m. John Hamilton, Esq., and has issue.

2 Sarah-Maria Fuller.

3 Cordelia-Eleonora Fuller.

4 Louisa Fuller.   5 Charlotte Fuller.

Lord Heathfield died in the seventy-third year of his age, at his château, at Aix-la-Chapelle, 6 July, 1790, and was s. by his son,

FRANCIS-AUGUSTUS ELIOTT, 2nd baron, b. 31 December, 1750. This nobleman was also a military man, and attained the rank of lieutenant-general. He d. s. p. in 1813, when the BARONY OF HEATHFIELD EXPIRED.

Arms—Gu., on a bend arg., a baton, az.: on a chief, az., the fortress of Gibraltar, under it, PLUS ULTRA, as an augmentation.

ELPHINSTON—LORD BALMERINOCH.

By Charter, dated 20 February, 1603-4.

Lineage.

THE HON. SIR JAMES ELPHINSTON (3rd son* of Robert, 3rd Lord Elphinston), designed of Innernochtie, was under that designation appointed a lord of session, 4 March, 1586. In

---

* From John Elphinstone, of Baberton, 2nd son of Robert, 3rd Lord Elphinstone, and next brother of James, 1st Lord Balmerinoch, descended

JOHN ELPHINSTONE, captain in the British, and admiral in the Russian navy, who commanded the fleet of the czar at the

1595 he was constituted one of the eight commissioners of the Treasury; in 1598, secretary of state; and as he continued to rise in the king's favour, the lands belonging to the Cistertian Abbey of Balmerinoch, in Fife, were erected into a temporal lordship in favour of him, his heirs male, and heirs of tailzie and provision, by charter, under the great seal, dated 20 February, 1603-4; and he accordingly took his seat as a peer in parliament, by the title of Lord Balmerinoch. In 1605, he became president of the court of Session. His lordship m. 1st, Sarah, dau. of Sir John Monteith, of Carse, by whom he had one son,

JOHN, 2nd Lord Balmerinoch.

He m. 2ndly, Marjory, dau. of Hugh Maxwell, of Te-ling, by whom he had another son and two daus.,

James, Lord Coupar.
Anne, m. to Andrew, 1st Lord Frazer.
Mary, m. to John Hamilton, of Blair.

Lord Balmerinoch was found guilty of the fabrication of a letter purporting to be from JAMES VI. to Pope CLEMENT VIII., and sentenced to death, but obtained a pardon. He d. in 1612, and was s. by his son,

JOHN ELPHINSTONE, 2nd Lord Balmerinoch, a stanch covenanter, whose trial and conviction proved ruinous in its consequences to King CHARLES's interest in Scotland. He m. Anne, dau. of Sir Thomas Ker, of Fernyhirst, and had a son,

JOHN ELPHINSTONE, 3rd Lord Balmerinoch, b. 18 February, 1623; who d. 10 June, 1704, aged eighty-two, having m. at the abbey of Holyrood-house, 30 October, 1649, Lady Margaret Campbell, only dau. of John, Earl of Loudoun, lord high chancellor of Scotland, and by her (who d. in January, 1666, and was buried at Restalrig) had

JOHN ELPHINSTONE, 4th Lord Balmerinoch, b. 28 December, 1652; who m. 1st, 16 February, 1672, Lady Christian Montgomery, 3rd dau. of Hugh, 7th Earl of Eglintoun, by whom he had (with two daus., Margaret, wife of Sir John Preston, of Preston Hall; and Jean, m. to Francis, 8th Earl of Moray) two sons, Hugh, slain at the siege of Lisle in 1708, s. p.; and JOHN, who s. his father. His lordship m. 2ndly, 7 June, 1687, Anne, dau. of Arthur Ross, the last archbishop of St. Andrew's, and by her (who d. 10 November, 1712,) had two sons, ARTHUR, 6th Lord Balmerinoch; Alexander, who d. unm. 1733; and Anne, who d. unm. The eldest son,

JOHN ELPHINSTONE, 5th Lord Balmerinoch, b. 24 November, 1675; d. at Leith, 5 January, 1746, aged seventy-one; and leaving no issue by his wife, Lady Elizabeth Carnegie, dau. of David, 4th Earl of Northesk (who survived till 21 September, 1767), was s. by his half-brother, the ill-fated adherent of the exiled family of Stuart,

ARTHUR ELPHINSTONE, 6th Lord Balmerinoch, b. in 1688; who suffered decapitation, 18 August, 1746, for his participation in the rising of the previous year. His lordship m. Margaret, dau. of Capt. Chalmers, but d. s. p. The title became forfeited by his lordship's attainder.

Arms—ARG., on a chevron, sa., between three boars' heads, erased, gu., as many buckles of the field.

ELPHINSTONE—LORD COUPAR.

By Charter, dated 20 December, 1607.

Lineage.

By royal charter, bearing date 20 December, 1607, King JAMES VI. united the lands and baronies which belonged to the dissolved Cistertian Abbey of Coupar in Angus into a temporal lordship, with a title of a lord of parliament, by the style of BARON COUPAR, in favour of

THE HON. JAMES ELPHINSTONE (only son of James, 1st Lord Balmerinoch, by his 2nd wife, Marjory, dau. of Hugh Maxwell, of Tealing) and the heirs male of his body; which failing, to his father and his heirs male and of entail. Lord Coupar was appointed one of the extraordinary lords of session, 7 June, 1649, in place of his brother, Lord Balmerinoch, deceased. His lordship m. 1st, Margaret, dau. of Sir James

battle of Tchesme, and succeeded in destroying his infidel opponents. He m. Amelia, dau. of John Warburton, Esq., Somerset Herald; and d. in 1785, leaving, with other issue,

SAMUEL-WILLIAM, capt. Russian navy, whose son,
CAPT. ALEXANDER ELPHINSTONE, R.N., a noble in Livonia, claimed to be heir to the title of Balmerinoch.

HOWARD, who was created a Baronet in 1815. (*See* BURKE's *Peerage and Baronetage*.)

189

Halyburton, of Pitcur; and 2ndly, Lady Marion Ogilvy, eldest dau. of James, 2nd Earl of Airly, who afterwards became wife of John, 3rd Lord Lindores, but had no issue by either. He d. in 1669, and his title and estates devolved, in terms of the patent and entail, upon his nephew, JOHN, 3rd Lord Balmerinoch.

Arms—Arg., a chev., sa., charged with three hearts of the field, between three boars' heads, erased, gu.

ENGAINE—BARONS ENGAINE.

By Writ of Summons, dated 6 February, 1299, which became extinct; but revived by Writ, dated 25 February, 1342.

Lineage.

The first of this family taken notice of by our public records, is,

RICHARD INGAINE, chief engineer to King WILLIAM THE CONQUEROR, from which office he derived his surname; to whom succeeded,

VITALIS ENGAINE; and after him came,

RICHARD ENGAINE, Lord of Blatherwick, co. Northampton, *temp.* HENRY II., who m. Sara, dau. of the Earl of Oxford, and d. 10th King JOHN, having had two sons,

RICHARD, his successor.
Vitalis.

He was s. by the elder,

RICHARD ENGAINE, one of the insurrectionary barons, in the reign of King JOHN, whose lands were in consequence seized by the crown. He d. in 1216, and was s. by his brother,

VITALIS ENGAINE, who had likewise espoused the baronial cause, and had not, therefore, possession of the estates of the family until the accession of King HENRY III. In the 26th of this reign, this feudal lord made partition with William de Cantelupe, of Bergavenny, of the manor of Badmundsfields, in Suffolk, as heirs to William de Courtenai. He m. 1st, Clemence, dau. of Aubrey, Earl of Oxford, widow of Sir Jordan de Sackville; and 2ndly, Roese, one of the three sisters and co-heirs of the honour of Montgomery, in Wales, and was s. at his decease in 1248, by his son,

HENRY ENGAINE, who in the 42nd HENRY III. had a military summons to march against the Welsh: but afterwards taking part with the barons, he was involved in the defeat at Evesham, and had his lands sequestered. They were soon restored, however, under the *Dictum of Kenilworth*. This feudal lord never married, and dying in 1271, was s. by his brother,

JOHN ENGAINE, who m. Joane, dau. and heir of Henry Gray, and dying in 1296, was s. by his son,

JOHN DE ENGAINE. This feudal lord having distinguished himself in the wars of Scotland, *temp.* EDWARD I., was summoned to parliament as a BARON by that monarch, from 6 February, 1299, to 15 May, 1321. His lordship d. however, the next year, when the BARONY became EXTINCT, but his landed property devolved upon his nephew as heir at law, namely—

JOHN DE ENGAINE (son of Nicholas de Engaine, by Amicia, dau. of Walter Fauconberg), who making proof of his age had livery of his estates. This John, in the 19th EDWARD III., then residing in Huntingdonshire, had a military summons to attend the king into France, and was summoned to parliament as a BARON, from 25 February, 1342, to 20 November, 1360. His lordship had previously the high military rank of knight banneret. He m. Joane, dau. of Sir Robert Peverell, and had issue,

THOMAS, his successor.
Joyce, m. to John de Goldington.
Elizabeth, m. to Sir Lawrence Pabenham.
Mary, m. to Sir William Bernak.

His lordship d. at his seat at Dillington, co. Huntingdon, seised of the manors of Haighton, co. Leicester; Noteley, in Essex: Handsdon, in Herts; Saundey, in Bedfordshire; Gideling and Dillington, in Huntingdonshire; and Laxton, co. Northampton, in which he was s. by his son,

THOMAS DE ENGAINE, 2nd baron, but never summoned to parliament. His lordship m. the Lady Katherine Courtenay, dau. of Hugh, Earl of Devonshire, and widow of Lord Harington, but dying s. p. in 1367, his great landed possessions devolved upon his sisters as co-heirs, while the BARONY of ENGAINE fell into ABEYANCE amongst them, as it still continues with their representatives.

Arms—Gu., a fesse indented between seven cross-crosslets, four in chief, three in base, or.

ESMONDE—BARON ESMONDE.

By Patent, dated 20 May, 1622.

Lineage.

This family is of very ancient establishment in the co. of Wexford, where we find John Esmond was consecrated bishop of Ferns, about the middle of the 14th century.

The immediate ancestor of the present house,

JOHN ESMONDE, Esq., of Johnstown, co. Wexford, m. Isabel, dau. of Thomas Rosseter, Esq., of Rathmacknee Castle, and left a son,

LAURENCE ESMONDE, Esq., of Johnstown. This gentleman m. Eleanor, dau. of Walter Walsh, of The Mountains, by whom he had two sons, and was s. by the elder,

WILLIAM ESMONDE, Esq., who m. Margaret, dau. of Michael Furlong, Esq., of Horetown, and had, with seven daus., four sons, viz.,

ROBERT, living in 1618, who continued the line of Johnstown, which became EXTINCT a few years since in the male line.
LAURENCE, of whom presently.
James.   Patrick.

The 2nd son,

SIR LAURENCE ESMONDE, abandoning the religious creed of his ancestors, declared himself a partisan of ELIZABETH, and a convert to Protestantism In 1601-2, he commanded a troop of 150 foot and horse in her Majesty's service, was knighted by Sir Henry Sydney the viceroy, and served in Connaught in the same corps d'armée, on the expeditions of the Irish chieftains, Morough-ni-doe O'Flaherty, Dynast of West Connaught, and Sir Theobald Bourke, 1st Viscount Mayo, who, to preserve their estates, had made their submission a short time previously to the lord-deputy, and accepted commands in the queen's service. Sir Laurence Esmonde's zeal and activity in his military operations procured for him, in an especial degree, the favour of the court; and his ambition increasing with his fortune, he was raised to the peerage 20 May, 1622 (being at the time major-general of all the king's forces in Ireland, and governor of Duncannon Fort), as LORD ESMONDE, Baron of Limerick, co. Wexford. During one of his campaigns in Connaught, having fallen in love with the beautiful sister of O'Flaherty, he m. her, and had one son, THOMAS It happened, however, that Lady Esmonde, a devout Roman Catholic, fearing that her child might be brought up a Protestant, formed the resolution of carrying off the infant by stealth, and returning to her family in Connaught. This act of maternal devotion appears to have been not at all disagreeable to Sir Laurence, as affording him a pretext for casting suspicion on the legality of his union, that of a Protestant with a Catholic; yet, without resorting to legal measures to annul the marriage in due form, he sometime after m. Elizabeth, 2nd dau. of the Hon. Walter Butler, 4th son of James, 9th Earl of Ormonde, but by her had no issue. His lordship d. 26 March, 1646, bequeathing all his extensive estates to his only son, SIR THOMAS ESMONDE, 1st baronet. The severity and singularity of his case created considerable interest; and there is scarce a doubt that, but for the melancholy state of civil war, usurpation, and destruction of property, at that period, upon legal investigation into the matter and the accompanying circumstances, the conduct of Lord Esmonde towards his lady, and the legality of his second marriage (his first undivorced wife still living), Sir Thomas Esmonde's right of succession to his father's peerage could not fail to have been acknowledged. Before, however, that could have taken place, Sir Thomas died; and his successor had to occupy himself with entering into possession of his grandfather's property. Sir Thomas Esmonde, as already noticed, was reared and educated with his maternal relations; and upon his uncle being raised in the peerage to the dignity of Viscount Bourke, of Mayo, by privy-seal, dated at Westminster, 8 February, 1626, and by patent, 21 June, 1627, Sir Thomas, who was subsequently knighted for his eminent services in the cause of royalty, as general of horse in the armies of CHARLES I. was created, through Lord Mayo's influence, a few months later (28 January, 1628), a BARONET OF IRELAND. Sir Thomas m. Ellis, widow of Thomas Butler, 4th Lord Cahir, and dau. of Sir John Fitzgerald, of Dromana, co. Waterford of the line of Desmonde, and was ancestor of the ESMONDES, now of Ballynastra, co. Wexford, BARONETS of Ireland.

Arms—Erm., on a chief, gu., three mullets, arg.

EURE, OR EVRE — BARONS EURE, OR EVRE, OF WILTON, CO. DURHAM.

By Letters Patent, dated 24 February, 1544.

Lineage.

The surname of this family was derived from the lordship of EVRE, co. Buckingham, where HUGH, a younger son of the Bacons of Werkworth, in Northumberland (which Bacons were afterwards known under the name of Clavering), took up his abode, in the reign of HENRY III., and thus became,

HUGH DE EVRE. He was s. by his son and heir,

SIR JOHN EVRE, who in the 35th Edward I., obtained a charter for free-warren, in all his desmesne lands, at Esby, in Cleveland, co. York: and in the 8th EDWARD II., was in the expedition then made into Scotland. In two years afterwards, Sir John Evre, was constituted one of the commissioners to negotiate a truce with the Scots; and in the 12th of the same reign, we find him again in the Scottish wars. From Sir John Evre descended,

SIR RALPH EURE, who m. Katharine, one of the daus. and co-heirs of Sir William Aton, 2nd Lord Aton, and in the 13th RICHARD II., made partition with the other co-heirs, of those lands which were of their inheritance; Sir Ralph being at that time sheriff of Northumberland, and governor of Newcastle-upon-Tyne. He was afterwards sheriff of Yorkshire, and constable of the Castle of York, and again sheriff of Northumberland. Sir Ralph Eure was s. by his son,

RALPH EURE, whose son and successor,

SIR WILLIAM EURE, m. Maud, dau. of Henry, Lord Fitz-Hugh, and had issue,

SIR RALPH EURE, who fell at Towton-field, in the 1st EDWARD IV., and from him descended,

SIR WILLIAM EURE, who, in the 30th HENRY VIII., was made captain of the Town and Castle of Berwick-upon-Tweed, and afterwards, being warden of the west marches towards Scotland, was elevated to the peerage, by letters patent, dated 24 February, 1544, as BARON EURE, of Wilton, co. Durham; his lordship m. Elizabeth, sister of William, Lord Willoughby de Eresby, and had issue,

RALPH (Sir), who being constable of Scarborough Castle, in the 28th HENRY VIII., held that fortress so gallantly against the insurgents, calling themselves the "Pilgrimage of Grace," that he was made commander-in-chief of all the king's forces appointed for guarding the marches towards Scotland. A post which he defended for several years with great reputation. Sir Ralph Eure after distinguishing himself by many valiant inroads upon Scotland, fell at last, in 1544, at the battle of Halydon Hill He m. Margaret, dau. of Ralph Bowes, Esq., of Streatlam Castle, co. Durham, and left issue,
WILLIAM, who s. his grandfather.
Ralph.   Thomas.
Frances, m. to Robert Lambton, Esq., of Lambton, co. Durham, from which marriage the present EARL OF DURHAM descends.
Anne, m. to Lancelot Merfeild, Esq.
Henry.
Anne, m. to Anthony Thorp, Esq., of Conyl Thorp, co. York.
Muriel, m. 1st. to George Bowes, Esq., and 2ndly, to William Wicliff, Esq., of Wicliff.
Margaret, m. to William Buckton, Esq.

Lord Eure, who was one of the commissioners appointed in 5th EDWARD VI., to convey the Garter to the King of France, d. 1548, and was s. by his grandson,

WILLIAM EURE, 2nd baron. This nobleman was constituted one of the commissioners in the 29th of ELIZABETH, to negotiate a league with Scotland. His lordship m. Margaret, dau. of Sir Edward Dymoke, of Scrivelsby, co. Lincoln, and had issue,

RALPH, his successor.
Francis (Sir), m. 1st, Elizabeth, dau. of John Leonard, Esq., and had issue,
HORACE, who m. Debora, dau. and co-heir of John Bret, Esq., and had, with other issue,
GEORGE, }
RALPH, } who inherited as 7th and 8th lords.
Elizabeth, m. to William Kay. Esq.
Deborah, m. to John Pickering, Esq.
Sir Francis Eure m. 2ndly, Ellin, heiress of Clenenney, co Carnarvon, widow of John Owen, Esq., secretary to Lord Walsingham, 4th son of Owen ap Robert, of Bodsilin, co Anglesey, and elder dau. and co-heir of William Morris, Esq., of Clenenney, son (by Margaret, dau. and heir of John Lacon, Esq., of Sir William Morris, Knt., of Clenenney, living 1598, great-grandson of Morris ap John, of Rhiwaedog Park, co. Merioneth, and· Clenenney, derived, with the

Wynnes, of Gwyder, from Owen Gwynedd, Prince of North Wales. Of this marriage there was an only son,

COMPTON EURE, in whom, if he survived his nephew, Ralph Eure, 8th baron, and in his male issue, if any, vested the barony.

William.   Charles.

Anne, m. to John Malory, Esq.

Meriol, m. to Richard Goodricke, Esq., of Ribstone, and her grandson,

SIR JOHN GOODRICKE, Knt., of Ribstone Hall, co. York, was created a BARONET 14 August, 1641.

Martha, m. to William Ayrmin, Esq.

William, Lord Eure, d. in 1594, and was s. by his eldest son,

RALPH EURE, 3rd baron, who was constituted, in the 5th of JAMES I., the king's lieutenant within the principality of Wales. His lordship m. 1st, Mary, only dau. of Sir John Dauney, of Cessay, co. York, and had an only son,

WILLIAM, his successor.

He m. 2ndly, Lady Hunsdon, widow of George, 2nd Lord Hunsdon, but had no issue. He was s. at his decease, in 1618-9, by his son,

WILLIAM EURE, 4th baron. This nobleman m. Lucia, dau. of Sir Andrew Noel, Knt., of Dalby, co. Leicester, and had issue,

RALPH, who d. in the lifetime of his father, leaving by his wife, Catherine, dau. of Thomas, Lord Arundel, of Wardour, an only child,

WILLIAM, who inherited as 5th lord.

WILLIAM, who s. as 6th lord.

Mary, m. to Sir William Howard, Knt., of Naworth Castle, co. Cumberland, and had, with other issue,

CHARLES HOWARD, who was elevated to the peerage, 20 April, 1661, as Baron Dacre, of Gillesland, Viscount Howard, of Morpeth, and EARL OF CARLISLE (see BURKE'S Extant Peerage).

His lordship was s. by his grandson,

WILLIAM EURE, 5th baron. This nobleman dying unm., the BARONY reverted to his uncle,

WILLIAM EURE, 6th baron. This nobleman, who was a colonel in the army of King CHARLES I., fell at Marston Moor in 1645. His lordship m. the dau. of Sir Thomas Denton, Knt., of Helsden, co. Bucks, and left two daus., viz.,

Margaret, m. to Thomas Danby, Esq., of Thorpe, co York, 1st mayor of Leeds.

Mary, m. to William Palmes, Esq., of Lindley, co. York.

Lord Eure dying thus without male issue, the Barony of Eure passed to his kinsman (revert to issue of Sir Francis Eure, 2nd son of William, 2nd lord),

GEORGE EURE, as 7th baron. This nobleman dying unm. in 1672, was s. by his brother,

RALPH EURE, 8th baron, at whose decease, in 1698, s. p., the BARONY OF EURE is presumed to have become EXTINCT.

Arms—Quarterly: or, and gu., on a bend, sa., three escallops, arg.

EUSTACE—VISCOUNT BALTINGLASS.

By Letters Patent, dated 29 June, 1541.

Lineage.

JOHN FITZ-EUSTACE, a Norman lord, accompanied STRONGBOW to Ireland, and founded in that country the historic family of FITZ-EUSTACE or EUSTACE, a great but unfortunate race, whose history, replete with spirit-stirring incident, romance, and vicissitude, records at one time vast power and influence, and at another, unmerited suffering and ruin. The 3rd Viscount of Baltinglass, the ally and friend of the Earl of Desmond, forfeited all but life for what he conceived to be his duty; and died an exile in Spain. The Eustaces were attainted almost by hundreds, their broad lands seized on and their Chiefs destroyed. The descendant, however, of one of the branches of the family, more fortunate than the rest, was the famous Lord Chancellor SIR MAURICE EUSTACE, whose classical and poetical quotations in his address to Strafford on the opening of parliament are highly significant of the literary taste of the day. King CHARLES II. thought he could never do enough for this stanch supporter of his father and himself; he lavished on him the confiscated estates of his attainted kinsmen, and made a parliamentary borough of his pleasure grounds at Harristown, which continued to return two members to the Irish House of Commons up to the time of the Union.

The Viscounty of Baltinglass is one of the few peerages supposed to be under attainder, which has not been restored: so far back as 1839, the late male heir of the 3rd lord, the REV.

191

CHARLES EUSTACE, presented a petition to the crown that his right to the title might be acknowledged: the petition was referred by the Queen to the Attorney-General for Ireland, who having investigated the case, made an elaborate report thereon, concluding in these words—

"I am of opinion that the petitioner has shown sufficient evidence of his right to the dignity of Viscount of Baltinglass, in case the attainder of James, the 3rd viscount, created by the Act of Queen ELIZABETH, were reversed.—MAZIERE BRADY."

Subsequent reference was made by the crown to the Attorney-General for England, who gave in a report fully confirming that of the Attorney-General of Ireland.

Despite, however, of the recommendations of the law officers, this historic title has been allowed to remain obscured by the forfeiture of Queen ELIZABETH's time, and still remains affected by that attainder—a harsh measure it would seem when we consider that Her Majesty's Attorney-General acknowledged and confirmed the claimant's descent in 1839, and that the descent comes from a brother of the attainted lord who was not included in the forfeiture.

The Act passed in the time of Queen ELIZABETH, was presumed to have attainted the title; but recent researches seem to show that the legality of the attainder cannot be sustained, and that consequently the dignity is at this moment unobscured by any penal enactment. The claimant rests his case on the following grounds:

I. The previous sanction of the English privy council had not been obtained before the introduction of the act into the Irish parliament. This initiatory proceeding, under Poyning's Law, then in full force, was indispensable.

II. James, 3rd Viscount Baltinglass, against whom the act was specially directed, had died three years previously.

III. There is no record of the attainder to be found in the archives of the privy council, London

IV. The pardon and promise of indemnity granted by the parliament of JAMES I., to all who had opposed the government of ELIZABETH destroyed the attainder, even if such attainder were effectual.

V. The title was borne and recognized by two viscounts long subsequent to the passing of the statute

SIR ROWLAND FITZ-EUSTACE, Knt., lord of Kilcullen, lord deputy to the Duke of Clarence, and lord high treasurer of Ireland, which latter high post he held for thirty-eight years, was created by patent, 5 March, 1462, for his many services, LORD BARON PORTLESTER This Sir Rowland who was son and heir of Edward Fitz-Eustace (Rot. Pat. 1 EDWARD IV., Can. Dub.), m. Margaret, dau. and heir of Jenico Dartas (Mem. Rot. 22nd HENRY VII., m 12 Ch. R. Off), and widow of John, son of Sir John Dowdall, and had, with other issue, a dau. and co-heir,

ALISON, who m. Gerald, the 8th EARL OF KILDARE, surnamed "the Great," and by him was mother of Gerald, 9th Earl of Kildare, ancestor of the ducal house of LEINSTER. Alison Eustace, Countess of Kildare, d. in 1480, and was buried in the new chapel of Kilcullen.

Sir Rowland, Lord Portlester, d. 14 December, 1496, and was buried in the convent of Minors Friars, at Kilcullen (New abbey), which he and his wife Margaret, had founded and built. In the churchyard of Ballycultane (now Cotlandstown), co. Kildare, there is a curious stone about a foot square and four feet long, apparently the shaft of some ancient cross: on one side is "Eustace, Lord of Portlester, 1496," and on the other the "saltire" and baron's coronet. At Lord Portlester's decease, the male heir of the great house of Eustace was

SIR THOMAS EUSTACE, Knt., created Baron of Kilcullen, co. Kildare, in 1541, and Viscount of Baltinglass, co. Wicklow, in 1542. His lordship made a settlement of all his estates upon the marriage of his son, SIR ROWLAND EUSTACE, 2nd viscount, with Joan, dau. of James, Lord Dunboyne. The 1st Viscount Baltinglass m. Margaret, dau. of Sir Peter Talbot, of Malahide Castle, co. Dublin, by Lady Catherine his wife, dau. of Gerald, Earl of Kildare, and had issue,

   I. ROWLAND, of whom presently.
   II. Richard.
   I. Anne, m. O'Toole, of Magnelle.
   II. Janet, m. to Bryan McCahir Cavanagh.
   III. Margaret, m. to George Burnell.

The eldest son,

SIR ROWLAND EUSTACE, Knt., 2nd Viscount Baltinglass, Baron Kilcullen, aged thirty-five in 1540, had livery of his estates 16 November, 1549. He m. Joan, dau. of James Butler, Lord Dunboyne, by the Lady Joan Butler, his wife, dau. of Peter, 8th Earl of Ormonde, and had issue,

EUS EUS

I. JAMES, of whom presently.
II. Edmund, of Tubber, who fled from Ireland, being attainted in 1585. He m. Frances, dau. of Rober. Pipho.
III. WILLIAM, of Naas, of whom hereafter, as ancestor of the present representative of the family.
ıv. Thomas.
v. Walter, executed in Dublin, 1583.
VI. Richard fled from Ireland.

The eldest son,

JAMES EUSTACE, 3rd Viscount Baltinglass, acted a conspicuous part in the political drama of his time; having, with other Lords of the Pale complained in 1576 to Queen ELIZABETH that their liberties and privileges had been annulled by the cess, and that no tax ought to be levied upon them but by Act of Parliament, he was, with the Lords Delvin, Howth, and Trimlestown, by order of her Majesty, committed prisoner to the castle of Dublin. "And in like manner their lawyers, whom they had sent with their complaints to her Majesty, were committed prisoners to the Tower of London. In consequence of which, and for the sake of his religion, he being a Catholic, and the Protestant religion having been (as Spenser says) forced upon the Irish people with great terrors and sharp penalties, he did join the Earl of Desmond in arms, in the hope of placing Queen MARY of Scotland upon the throne of those kingdoms." But, despite of all his exertions and gallantry, the attempt proved abortive, and Baltinglass had to escape to Spain in 1583, where he soon after died of grief. The Viscount Baltinglass (says Holinshed, Chronicles), "being advertised of the death of the Earl of Desmond, which was no small grief unto aim, and he also very wearie of his trolling and wandering on foot amongst bogs, woods, and desert places (being altogether distressed and in great misery, and now destitute of all his friends and acquaintances, and not able to hold head any longer against her Majesties force), did imbarke himself for Spain in hope to have some relief and succour and to procure some aid from the king of Spain, and by that meanes to be of some abilitie to renew his force and rebellion. But he found in the end very small comfort. And therefore of a very melancholy grief and sorrow of mind as it is thought, he died, being in very extreme poverty and need." In two years after the death of Lord Baltinglass, in 1585, an act of parliament was passed against the family, called the Statute of Baltinglass, which not only made estates tail forfeitable for treason, but did also (as Spenser says) cut off and frustrate all such family settlements, as had been made for the twelve years prior to the rebellion, but the difficulty with which that Act had been obtained was so great that was it to have been passed again, he was very sure it never could. By these post facto laws the family of Eustace was deprived of their estates and titles.
The 3rd viscount m. Mary, dau. and co-heir of Sir Henry Travers of Monkstown Castle, co. Dublin, by Genet Preston his wife, but d. s. p. His brother and eventual heir,
THE HON. WILLIAM EUSTACE (who had not been engaged in the rebellion), on the departure of Lord Baltinglass for Spain, retired with his family to England, and, in consequence of the edict of pardon and oblivion, published by King JAMES on his accession, together with the confirmatory acts of parliament of that and the subsequent reign, is recorded in the Heralds' College, London, as living as Viscount Baltinglass, in 1610. He m. Margaret, dau. of Ashe, of Great Forenass, co. Kildare, and had (with a dau., Jane, wife of Captain Archbold) an only son,
ROWLAND EUSTACE, m. Elizabeth Bigland, a Yorkshire lady, dau. of Mary Strickland, of Sizergh, one of the "Maries" residing with Mary Stuart at the time of her execution. In memory, a drinking cup has been handed down in the Eustace family, and is still in the possession of Mrs. Eustace of Robertstown, widow of Capt. Charles Stannard Eustace: it bears this inscription:—"This was MARY Queen of Scott's drinking cup: ye day she was beheaded, she gave it to her goddaughter, Mary Strickland, to be kept for her sake. Jon. Eustace, great great-grandson to the said Mary Strickland had it mounted in this silver in the year 1754." By her he had two sons, of whom the elder, James, an officer in the army, died in early youth, of the plague. The younger,
RICHARD EUSTACE, became representative of the family. He served as sovereign of Naas, and inherited the property of Ashe's Castle there, derived from his grandmother, Margaret Ashe. By Mary his wife, dau. of Sir William Forster, he had issue,

I. John, d. unm. at a very advanced age.
II. CHARLES, of whom presently.
III. William d. very old and unm.
I. Elizabeth.
II. Avis, m. 1688, to Alexander Graydon, Esq.
III. Mary.

Richard Eustace's will was dated 21 August, 1702, and proved 10 September in the same year. His 2nd son,
192

CHARLES EUSTACE, Esq., m. Elizabeth, dau. of Captain Borrowes, of Ardenode, co. Kildare, and had issue,
I. RICHARD, of Naas, whose line is EXTINCT. II. JOHN.
III. William, d. s. p. IV. Borrowes, d. young.
v. Alexander, in holy orders, d. unm., will proved in 1779, probate to his nephew Charles, son of his brother John.
VI. Thomas, d. young.
I. Mary and Elizabeth, both d. young.
The will of Charles Eustace was dated 28 April, 1732, and proved 2 February, same year. His 2nd son, whose descendants became eventually representatives of the family,
JOHN EUSTACE, Esq., of Naas, m. Elizabeth, dau. of Robert Graydon, of Russellstown (marriage licence dated 7 December, 1736); and dying 16 November, 1769, was s. by his only son,
CHARLES EUSTACE, Esq., of Robertstown, co. Kildare, and of Corbally, Queen's Co., a lieut.-general in the army, and member in the Irish parliament. He m. (licence dated 23 December, 1762) Alice, dau. of Oliver McCausland, Esq., of Stranorlar, M.P. for Strabane, and had,
I. CHARLES, his heir.
II. Oliver, cornet of horse, d. unm.
III. Henry, of Corbally, Queen's Co., lieut.-gen. in the army; m. 1819, Henrietta, dau. of Peter, Count D'Alton, and d. 5 October, 1844, leaving issue,
1 HENRY, of Corbally, Queen's Co., and Grennanstown, co. Tipperary, HEIR MALE OF THE FAMILY; m. 9 October, 1861, Albertina, widow of the late Count Foschi, and youngest dau. of the late Lieut.-Gen. Marquis Paulucci, Gov.-gen. of Genoa, Knt. of the Annunciata, &c., and has issue.
2 Charles-Edward, late lieut. 46th regiment.
3 John-Rowland. 1 Henrietta, d. young.
2 Rosalie, m. 15 August, 1853, to the Marquis Ricci Paracciani, of Rome.
IV. William-Cornwallis (Sir), lieut.-gen. in the army, K.C.H., C.B., of Sandford Hall, Essex, m. 1st, in 1809, Catherine-Frances, dau. of Lord Talbot of Malahide, by whom he had,
1 Alexander-Talbot-Eustace-Malpas, m. 1845, Georgia ı:, dau. of John Drummond, Esq., and d. 1870, leaving issue.
1 Frances-Catherine-Elizabeth, m. 1st, in 1841, to Robert King, Esq.; and 2ndly, to the Rev. Samuel Lloyd.
2 Alicia-Margaret-Maria, who d. unm. in 1840.
Sir William m. 2ndly, Caroline-Margaret, dau. of John King, Esq., under secretary of state, and by her had two sons,
1 John-Thomas. 2 Robert-Henry.
He m. 3rdly, Emma, 2nd dau. and co-heir of Admiral Sir Eliah Harvey, of Chigwell, and by her had one dau.,
Emma-Louisa, m. 1854 to Miles-L. Fornby, Esq., late of the carbineers.
Sir William d. 9 February, 1855.
v. Alexander, capt. of dragoons, killed at Vimiero.
VI. John Rowland (Sir), K.H., of Baltrasney, co. Kildare, lieut.-general, high sheriff, co. Kildare, 1848, d. unm. 1864.
I. Elizabeth, m. to the Rev. Henry Johnson.
II. Alicia, m. to Nicholas Barnewall, 14th Lord Trimlestown, but had no issue. She afterwards m. Lieut.-Gen. Sir Evan Lloyd, by whom she left a son and two daus.
III. Mary-Anne, m. to Robert Shearman, Esq. of Grange.

Lieut.-Gen. Eustace d. in 1800, and was s. by his eldest son,
THE REV. CHARLES EUSTACE, of Robertstown, who claimed in 1839 the Viscounty of Baltinglass, and had his right confirmed by the law officers of the Crown, subject to the Act of Attainder. He m. in 1800, Cassandra, dau. and co-heir of John Stannard, of Ballyduyle, son of Eaton Stannard, Esq., recorder of Dublin, and prime serjeant, M.P., and had issue,
I. CHARLES STANNARD, his heir.
I. Alicia, m. to Robert Robertson, Esq., sheriff substitute for Stirlingshire, and has one surviving son, Col. R. J. EUSTACE ROBERTSON EUSTACE, late 60th rifles (m. Lady Kath.rine Legge), and one dau., Alicia-Trimleston, wife of James Jameson, Esq., of Airfield, co. Dublin.
II. Elizabeth, m. to Henry Leader, Esq. of Mount Leader, co. Cork, and has issue.
III. Catherine, m. to Sir Alexander-D.-Y. Arbuthnot, vice-admiral, R.N., and has issue.
IV. Jane, m. to William-H. Connor, Esq., Capt. R.N., brother of Daniel Connor, Esq. of Ballybricken, co. Cork, and has issue.
The Rev. Charles Eustace was s. by his only son,
CHARLES-STANNARD EUSTACE, Esq., of Upper Grosvenor Street, London, Robertstown, co. Kildare, and Bally Doyle, co. Cork, late a capt. in the army, HEIR MALE AND REPRESENTATIVE of the Viscounty of Baltinglass, m. 1st, Laura, dau. of C. T. Tower, Esq., of Weald Hall, Essex, and 2ndly, 1864, Rosetta-Philippa, youngest dau. of the late Lieut.-Col. Cameron, of Dan-y-graig, and granddau. of Lieut.-Gen. Sir Alan Cameron, K.C.B., of Erracht, Inverness-shire, who raised and commanded the 79th or Queen's Own Cameron Highlanders. Sir Alan's wife was dau. of Nathaniel Phillips, Esq., of Slebech Hall, Pembrokeshire. Capt. Eustace d. 1875, when he was s. in his estates by his widow, Mrs. Eustace, now of Robertstown and Bally Doyle. The present HEIR MALE of the family is HENRY EUSTACE, of Corbally and Grennanstown.

Arms—Or. a saltier gu.

EVERINGHAM—BARONS EVERINGHAM.

By Writ of Summons, dated 4 March, 1309.

Lineage.

In the 14th HENRY III.,

ROBERT DE EVERINGHAM m. Isabel, dau. of John de Birkin, and sister and sole heiress of Thomas de Birkin, (feudal lords who flourished to nearly the middle of the 13th century,) and paid a fine of 200 marks to the crown for livery of her lands, and likewise for livery of the Bailiwick of the forest of Sherwood, that being also part of her inheritance. This Robert held then five knights' fees and a half in the county of Nottingham, and one in Lexinton. He had issue,

ADAM, his successor.
John, to whom his mother gave the manor of Birkin.
Robert, a clergyman, rector of the church of Birkin.

He d. in the 30th HENRY III., and was s. by his eldest son,

ADAM DE EVERINGHAM, who in six years after, at the decease of his mother, had livery of her lands, upon doing homage, and giving security for the payment of £50 for his relief. In the 42nd HENRY III. this feudal lord was in the expedition made then into Wales, but he afterwards took up arms with Montfort, Earl of Leicester, and the other discontented barons of that period, and was at the battle of Evesham. He d. 9th EDWARD I., being at the time seised of a moiety of the barony of Schelford, in Nottinghamshire, into which moiety twelve knights' fees and a half in several counties appertained, whereof ten were for the Bailiwick of Sherwood. He likewise possessed the manors of Everingham and Farburne, co. York, and Westbury, co. Lincoln. He was s. by his son,

ROBERT DE EVERINGHAM, who m. Lucia, dau. and heiress of Robert de Thwenge, a great feudal lord, temp. EDWARD I., (the lady been previously the wife of Sir William Latimer, and divorced,) and dying in the 15th EDWARD I., was s. by his son,

ADAM DE EVERINGHAM, who, in the 31st of EDWARD I., was in the wars of Scotland, and in three years afterwards was created a knight of the Bath with Prince Edward, and other persons of rank, when he attended the prince upon the expedition then made into Scotland. After which, in the 2nd of EDWARD II., he was summoned to parliament as a BARON; and from that period to the 9th inclusive; during those years he was constantly engaged in the wars of Scotland; but afterwards taking up arms with Thomas, Earl of Lancaster, he was made prisoner at the battle of Boroughbridge, and forced to pay a fine of 400 marks to the king to save his life. In the 11th EDWARD III., his lordship entailed his manor of Lexinton, in Notts, where he principally resided, upon ADAM, his eldest son, and so successively in default of male issue upon Robert, Edmund, Alexander, and Nicholas, his younger sons. This manor was holden of the archbishop of York, by the service of performing the office of butler in the prelate's house, upon the day of his inthronization. Lord Everingham d. in 1341, and was s. by his eldest son,

ADAM DE EVERINGHAM, 2nd baron, summoned to parliament, as "Adam de Everingham de Laxton," 8 January, 1371. This nobleman, who was several years actively engaged in the French wars, shared in the glory of Cressy. His lordship m. Joan, dau. of John Deyville and d. 9 February, 2nd RICHARD II., having had issue,

WILLIAM, who m. Alice, dau. of John, Lord Grey, of Codnor, and dying v. p. 43rd EDWARD III., left issue,

ROBERT, who s. his grandfather.
Joan, m. to Sir William Elys, Knt.
Catherine, m. to John Elton, Esq.

Reginald, who inherited the manor of Westburgh, co. York, m. 1st, Agnes, dau. of John Longvillers, and 2ndly, Joan, dau. of ———, and d. 1st HENRY VI., leaving a son,

Edmund, who d. s. p.; and several daus.

The baron d. in 1371, and was s. by his grandson,

ROBERT DE EVERINGHAM, 3rd baron. This nobleman d. in minority a few months after he inherited the title, leaving his two sisters his heirs, and the BARONY OF EVERINGHAM fell into ABEYANCE, between those ladies, as it has continued since with their representatives.

Arms—Gu., a lion rampant, vairée, arg. and az.

———

EYRE—BARON EYRE.

By Letters Patent, dated 16 July, 1768.

Lineage.

THOMAS EYRE, Esq., of New Sarum (eldest son of Robert Eyre, Esq., M.P. for New Sarum in 1557, and a lineal descendant of Humphrey Le Heyr, of Bromham, Wilts), held lands in Wimborne, Dorset, 21st ELIZABETH: he m. Elizabeth, dau. of John Rogers, Esq., of Poole, and d. 1628, having had issue, with four daus. who married, six sons, viz.,

1. Robert Eyre, Esq., of Chillhampton and Sarum, barrister-at-law, b. 1569, who m. Anne, b. at Hadleigh, co. Suffolk, 1581, sister of the Rev. John Still, of Westbower, near Bridgnorth, prebendary of Sarum, ancestor of the Stills of the Bury, lords of the manor of Doynton, co. Gloucester, represented by the de Pearsalls of Willsbridge House, co. Gloucester, and dau. of John Still, bishop of Bath and Wells, who d. 1607. By his 1st wife Anne (who d. 15 February, 1593 and was buried at Hadleigh, where there is a monument to her), dau. of Thomas Arblaster, Esq., of Hadleigh, Mr. Eyre had issue, besides an eldest dau. Anne, and a youngest dau. Elizabeth,

   1 Robert Eyre, Esq., of Chillhampton and New Sarum, whose male representative is the present HENRY-SAMUEL EYRE, Esq., of St. John's Wood, Middlesex.
   1 Blanche, m. Thomas Pelham, of Compton Valence, Herts, grandson of Anthony Pelham, of Buxted, younger brother of Sir William Pelham, Knt., ancestor of the DUKES OF NEWCASTLE and EARLS OF CHICHESTER. The heir general of this marriage is the present THOMAS THISTLETHWAYTE, Esq., of Southwick Park, Hants.
   2 Catherine, m. 1630, Charles Chauncey, Esq., President of Hayward College, New England, bapt. 1592; d. 19 February, 1671-2, in New England. From this marriage derived CHARLES SNELL CHAUNCEY, Esq., of Dane End, Herts, lord of the manor of Minden.

II. GILES, of whom presently.
III. Christopher Eyre, Esq., b. 1578, founder of Eyre's Hospital in Sarum, d. s. p. 5 January, 1624.
IV. Thomas Eyre, b. 1580, mayor of Sarum in 1610, ancestor of the EYRES of Box, who merged in the EYRES of Botley Grange.
v. William Eyre, Esq., barrister-at-law, bequeathed his estate of Bonham to his great-nephew, Sir Samuel Eyre, grandson of his eldest brother Robert, and d. November, 1646.
VI. John Eyre.

The 2nd son,

GILES EYRE, Esq., of Brickworth, Wilts, high sheriff of that co. in 1640, was bapt. in 1572, he m. Jane, dau. of Ambrose Snelgrove, Esq., of Redlynch and had issue,

GILES, of Brickworth, M.P., ancestor of the Eyres of Brickworth, whose heiress, Frances-Elizabeth Eyre, m. in 1821, Thomas Bolton, Esq., afterwards Earl Nelson.
Ambrose, of Newhouse.
John, ancestor of Lord Eyre.
Henry, recorder and M.P. for New Sarum.
William, rector of St Edmond's, Sarum.
Edward, from whom descends the family of HEDGES EYRE, of Macroom Castle, co. Cork.
Thomas, M.P. for Wilts.

The 3rd son,

The RIGHT HON. JOHN EYRE, colonel in the army, accompanied General Ludlow to Ireland, and having made several large purchases of land in the cos. of Galway, Tipperary, and King's Co., established himself at Eyre Court Castle, in the first named shire of which he was M.P. He m. Mary, dau. and co-heir of Philip Bygoe, Esq., high sheriff of the King's Co., in 1662, and d. in 1685, leaving two sons and two daus.,

JOHN, his heir.
Samuel, colonel in the army at Limerick in 1690, and M.P. for the town of Galway in 1715. He m. 1st, Jane, dau. of Edward Eyre, Esq., by whom he had a son,
   JOHN, who m. Mary, dau. of Thomas Willington, Esq., and was progenitor of
      THOMAS STRATFORD EYRE, Esq., of Eyreville, co. Galway. Colonel Samuel Eyre m. 2ndly, Anne, 6th dau. of Robert Stratford, Esq., M.P., of Baltinglass, co. Wicklow, and had issue,
   Stratford, governor of Galway, and vice-admiral of Munster, d. s. p.
   Thomas, colonel in the army, M.P., and master of the ordnance in Ireland; d. s. p. in 1772.
   Anne, m. in 1717, to Robert, only son of Richard Powell, Esq., of New Garden, co. Limerick, and was great-great-grandmother of Eyre-Burton Powell, Esq.
Mary, m. to Thomas Crosadaile, Esq.
Mary, m. 1679, to Right Hon. George Evans.
Anne, m. 1686, to Richard St. George, Esq., of Dunmore.

The elder son,

JOHN EYRE, Esq., of Eyrecourt Castle, m. 7 February, 1677, Margery, dau. of Sir George Preston, of Craigmillar, in Mid-

..lian, niece of the Duchess of Ormonde, and had three sons, GEORGE, JOHN, and GILES, of whom hereafter, and five daus., Mary; Elizabeth. m. to Frederick Trench, Esq., M.P.; Emilia, m. 1st, to William Wilson, Esq., and 2ndly, to John Rochfort, Esq.; of Clogrenane; Margery, m. to Shuckburgh Whitney, Esq.; and Jane. The eldest son,

GEORGE EYRE, Esq., of Eyrecourt Castle, succeeded his father in 1709. He m. Barbara, dau. of Richard, Lord Coningsby, and had an only dau. Frances, who m. in 1729, William Jackson, Esq., of Coleraine (see p. 132). Mr. Eyre d. 7 March, 1710, and was s. by his brother,

JOHN EYRE, Esq., of Eyrecourt Castle, who m. 1st, Rose, dau. of Mathew, Lord Louth; and 2ndly, Jane Waller, but d. s. p. in 1745, when he was s. by his brother,

THE VERY REV GILES EYRE, dean of Killaloe, whose Will was dated 3 January, 1747: he m. Mary, dau. of Richard Cox, Esq., eldest son of Sir Richard Cox, Lord Chancellor of Ireland; and left issue,

JOHN, his heir.
Richard, who m. 1st, Emilia, dau. of Frederick Trench, Esq., of Garbally, by whom he had a dau., Elizabeth; and 2ndly, Anchoretta, dau. of Samuel Eyre, Esq., of Eyreville, by whom he left at his decease, 1780, four sons, GILES, John, Richard and Samuel.
Robert.
Mary, m. to Edward D'Alton, Esq., of Deer Park, co. Clare.

The eldest son,
JOHN EYRE, Esq., of Eyrecourt Castle, was elevated to the peerage of Ireland, by patent dated 16 July, 1768, as BARON EYRE, of Eyrecourt, co. Galway. His lordship m. 1746, Eleanor, dau. of James Staunton, Esq., of Galway, and had an only dau.,

MARY, m. to the Hon. Francis Caulfeild, and had a son, James Eyre Caulfeild, and a dau., Eleanor, m. the Hon. William Howard, afterwards EARL OF WICKLOW.

Lord Eyre d. 30 September, 1781, when the title became EXTINCT. His estates devolved on his nephew, GILES EYRE, Esq., colonel of the Galway militia, who d. in 1829, leaving, with other issue, a son and successor, JOHN EYRE, Esq., of Eyrecourt, who m. 21 August, 1818, and d. in 1856, leaving with other issue a son, JOHN EYRE, Esq., of Eyrecourt Castle.

Arms—Arg., on a chev., sa., three quatrefoils, or.

FAIRFAX—VISCOUNT FAIRFAX.

By Letters Patent, dated 10 February, 1628.

Lineage.

WILLIAM FAIRFAX, Esq., of Walton, co. York, m. Catherine, dau. of Sir Humphrey Nevil, of Thornton Bridge, and d. 31st HENRY VI., having had a son,

SIR THOMAS FAIRFAX, K.B., who m. Elizabeth, dau. of Sir Robert Sherburne, of Stoneyhurst, co. Lancaster, and d. 1505, leaving with other issue an eldest son,

SIR THOMAS FAIRFAX, who m. Anne, dau. of Sir Wm. Gascoigne, of Gawthorpe, co. York, by Lady Margaret Percy his wife, 3rd and youngest dau. of Henry, 3rd Earl of Northumberland, and d. 1520, leaving with other issue an eldest son,

SIR NICHOLAS FAIRFAX, of Walton and Gilling, sheriff of the co. York, who m. 1st, Alice, dau. of Sir John Harrington, by whom he had no issue; and 2ndly, Jane, dau. of Guy Palmes, Esq., of Lindley, second sergeant-at-law to HENRY VII., and by her left at his decease in 1570, an eldest son and successor,

SIR WILLIAM FAIRFAX, sheriff of York, 31st HENRY VIII. He m. Agnes, eldest dau. of George Lord D'Arcie, of Menel, but by her had no issue; 2ndly, Jane, dau. and heir of Bryan Stapleton, Esq., of Nottingham and Burton, grandson of Geo. Stapleton, of Ribston, descended from Alleyne Lord Stapleton, and by her had an only son,

SIR THOMAS FAIRFAX, Knt., of Gilling Castle, co. York, sheriff for the co. York, who was elevated to the peerage of Ireland, 10 February, 1628, as VISCOUNT FAIRFAX, of Elmley, co. Tipperary. He m. 1st, Mary, dau. of Robert Ford, Esq., of Bultey Abbey, and relict of Sir William Bamburgh, of Howton, co. York, Knt. and Bart., but by her had no issue; and 2ndly, Catherine, sister of Henry Viscount Dunbar, and dau. of Sir Henry Constable, of Burton Constable, in Holderness, and by her he left issue,

I. THOMAS, his successor.
II. Henry, m. Frances, dau. of Henry Baker, Esq., of Hurst, by whom he had
Henry, of Hurst, Berks, who left an only child, Frances, who m. 1697, David Erskine, Earl of Buchan.
John.
Frances.

194

Henry d. 4 April, 1650, and was buried in the church of Hurst.
III. WILLIAM, m. Mary, dau. of Marmaduke Cholmeley, Esq., of Brandsby, co. York, and had two sons, viz.,
1 Charles, who m. 1st, the widow of Charles Walmesley, Esq., of Selby, co. York, by whom he had an only child, Charles, who d. young; 2ndly, the widow of — Middleton, Esq.; and 3rdly, the widow of — Mullins, Esq., but by neither of the last named ladies had he issue.
2 WILLIAM, 9th viscount.
IV. Nicholas, m. Isabel, eldest dau. and co-heir of Thomas Beckwith, Esq., of Acton.
V. Jordan. VI. John.
I. Jane m. to Cuthbert Morley, Esq.
II. Margaret, m. 1st, to Watkinson Payler, Esq.; and 2ndly, to Sir John Hotham, son of Sir John Hotham, Bart., who was beheaded by the parliament just before his father.
III. Catherine, m. 1st, Robert Stapleton, of Wigill, Esq.; and 2ndly, Sir Matthew Boynton, of Barmston, Knt. and Bart.
IV. Mary, m. to Sir Thomas Layton, of Eslayton, Knt.
V. Dorothy, m. to John Ingram, Gent.; and 2ndly, to Sir Thomas Nordliffe, of Langton, co. York.

The eldest son,
THOMAS FAIRFAX, 2nd Viscount Fairfax, m. Alathea, youngest dau. of Sir Philip Howard, grandson of Thomas, 2nd Duke of Norfolk, and by her (who d. 3 September, 1677,) he left at his decease, 24 September, 1641, five sons and two daus., viz.,
I. WILLIAM, 3rd viscount.
II. CHARLES, 5th viscount.
III. John, m. Mary, dau. of Col. Thomas Hungate, son of Sir Philip Hungate, of Saxton, Bart.
IV. Nicholas, m. Elizabeth, 4th dau. of Sir Thomas Davison, of Blackiston, in the bishopric of Durham, and widow of John Chaytor, Esq., of Croft, and had issue,
1 NICHOLAS, 6th viscount.
2 CHARLES, 8th viscount.
1 Alathea, m. to John Forcer, Esq.
V. Philip.
I. Mary.
II. Catherine, m. 1st to George Meham, Esq., of Meham; and 2ndly, to Sir Arthur Ingram, of Temple Newsham, co. York, Knt.

The eldest son,
WILLIAM FAIRFAX, 3rd Viscount Fairfax, b. at Naworth Castle, 6 June, 1630; m. Elizabeth, dau. of Alexander Smith, Esq., of Norfolk, and by her (who m. 2ndly, Sir John Goodricke, Bart.,) his lordship left at his decease, in 1648, two sons and a dau., viz.:
I. THOMAS, 4th viscount.
II William, d. in infancy.
I. Catherine, m. to Benjamin Mildmay Lord Fitzwalter, and d. 20 March, 1724, leaving a son, Charles, Lord Fitzwalter, who d. s. p.

The elder son,
THOMAS FAIRFAX, 4th Viscount Fairfax; d. in infancy, and was s. by his uncle,
CHARLES FAIRFAX, 5th viscount, 2nd son of the 2nd viscount; who m. Abigail, dau. of Sir John Yates, Knt., and had an only child, Alathea, m. to William, Lord Widdrington, of which marriage Charles Standish, Esq., M.P., of Standish, became heir-general. Lord Fairfax d. 6 July, 1711, and was s. by (the son of his brother Nicholas) his nephew,
NICHOLAS FAIRFAX, 6th Viscount Fairfax; who m. Mary, dau. of William Weld, Esq., of Lulworth Castle, co. Dorset, and by her (who m. 2ndly, Sir Francis Hungate, Bart.), had a dau. Mary, m. to Charles Gregory, 10th Viscount Fairfax, and a son,
CHARLES FAIRFAX, 7th Viscount Fairfax; who d. young, and was s. by his uncle,
CHARLES FAIRFAX, 8th Viscount Fairfax; at whose decease unm., the honours devolved on his kinsman,
WILLIAM FAIRFAX, 9th Viscount Fairfax. His lordship was son of the Hon. William Fairfax, 3rd son of Thomas, 1st viscount. He m. Elizabeth, dau. of Capt. Gerard; and dying in November, 1738, left, with a dau., ALATHEA, m. to Ralph Pigott, Esq., of Whitton, Middlesex, a son and successor,
CHARLES GREGORY FAIRFAX, 10th Viscount Fairfax; who m. 1st, 17 September, 1720, Elizabeth, dau. of Hugh, Lord Clifford, of Chudleigh, and relict of Viscount Dunbar, by whom (who d. 25 April, 1721,) he had no issue; and 2ndly, Mary, dau. of Nicholas, 6th Viscount Fairfax, by whom (who d. 1 July, 1741,) he left an only surviving dau. and heir,
ANNE, who d. unm. in 1793, when the estates passed to her cousin, Charles Gregory Pigott, Esq., who assumed the surname of Fairfax, and became of Gilling Castle, co. York (See BURKE's *Landed Gentry*).

Lord Fairfax d. in 1741, when the title expired.

Arms—Arg., three bars, gemelles, gu., surmounted by a lion rampant, sa.

FALVESLEY—BARON FALVESLEY.

By Writ of Summons, dated 20 August, 1383.

Lineage.

SIMON FITZROBERT, son of ROBERT FITZWALTER, of Daventry, purchased the manor of Falewesle, from Thomas de Capes, of Fawsley and Preston Capes, in 1301, and adopted the local appellation of Simon de Falwesle. He d. 1331, and was s. by his son (by Petronilla his wife, dau. of William Stanford, and widow of John Crawford of Ashby Ledgers).

THOMAS DE FALWESLE, of Fawsley, who d. 1353, leaving a son and heir,

SIR JOHN FALVESLEY, lord of Falvesley, co. Northampton, one of the great military characters of the reign of EDWARD III., who having m. 1383, Elizabeth Say, dau. of William Lord Say, and sister and heiress of John, Lord Say, had livery of all her lands lying in the counties of Kent, Sussex, and Hertford, and the same year attended John, Duke of Lancaster, in the expedition then made into Spain. Sir John was summoned to parliament, as "Johanni de Falvesley, Chevalier," from 20 August, 1383, to 8 September, 1392. His lordship's last martial occupation was in the fleet, under the command of the Lord Admiral, Richard, Earl of Arundel, in the 11th RICHARD II. He d. about the year 1392, when, as he left no issue, the BARONY OF FALVESLEY became EXTINCT. His widow m. 2ndly, Sir William Heron, who was summoned to parliament as Baron Say, jure uxoris, from 17th RICHARD to 5th HENRY IV., and d. s. p. 1404.

Arms—Gu., two chevs., or.

FANE—BARON CATHERLOUGH.

By Letters Patent, dated 4 October, 1733.

Lineage.

JOHN FANE, 7th Earl of Westmoreland, having distinguished himself during the lifetime of his brother, the 6th earl, in the Duke of Marlborough's wars, was elevated to the peerage of Ireland, 4 October, 1733, by the title of BARON CATHERLOUGH. His lordship subsequently attained the rank of lieut.-general in the army. He m. Mary, only dau. and heir of Lord Henry Cavendish, 2nd son of William Duke of Devonshire, but d. s. p., 26 August, 1762, when the Irish peerage EXPIRED, while the Barony of Despencer, which he enjoyed, was confirmed to Sir Francis Dashwood, Bart., and the Earldom of Westmoreland reverted to the next male heir, Thomas Fane, Esq., M.P. for Lyme Regis, ancestor of the present earl.

Arms—Az., three dexter gauntlets, backs affronté, or.

FANE—VISCOUNT FANE.

By Letters Patent, dated 22 April, 1718.

Lineage.

SIR HENRY FANE, K.B., of Bassilden (son of Sir Francis Fane, K.B., of Fulbeck, co. Lincoln, 3rd son of Francis, 1st Earl of Westmoreland), m. Elizabeth, dau. and heir of Thomas Sapcott, Esq., of Exeter, and by her (whose will bears date 28 October, 1724), he had a son, CHARLES, his successor. Sir Henry's will, dated 10 July, 1701, was proved in 1706. The son, CHARLES FANE, Esq., of Bassilden, co. Berks, was raised to the peerage of Ireland, 22 April, 1718, by the titles of VISCOUNT FANE, and Baron of Loughguyre, co. Limerick. His lordship m. Mary, youngest dau. of Alexander Stanhope, Esq., and sister of James, Earl Stanhope, by whom he had issue,

CHARLES, his heir.
Mary, m. in 1735, Jerome, Count de Salis, and was grandmother of the late
  JEROME, COUNT DE SALIS, who assumed, by sign-manual, in 1835, the additional surname and arms of FANE.
Elizabeth.
Dorothy, m. in 1740, to John, Earl of Sandwich.
Charlotte.

Lord Fane d. 7 July, 1744, and was s. by his son,

CHARLES FANE, 2nd Viscount Fane, M.P. for Tavistock, a diplomatist of the first grade, who was successively resident at Florence, and ambassador at Turin and Constantinople. He m. Lady Juxon, and d. s. p. in 1766, when the peerage became EXTINCT. The estates devolved on the De Salis family, by whom they are still enjoyed.

Arms—Az., three dexter gauntlets, backs affronté, or.

FANSHAWE—VISCOUNT FANSHAWE.

By Letters Patent, dated 5 September, 1661.

Lineage.

ROBERT FANSHAWE, Esq., of Fanshawe Gate, in the parish of Dronfield, co. Derby, had two sons, I. JOHN, of whom presently; and II. Henry, of Jenkins, in Essex, remembrancer of the Exchequer, temp. Queen ELIZABETH, d. in London, 28 October, 1568, leaving, by Dorothy his wife, dau. of Sir George Stonherd, two daus., his co-heirs, Anne, wife of William Fuller, Esq., and Susanna, m. to Timothy Lucy, Esq., of Valence, Essex, uncle of Sir Thomas Lucy, of Charlecote. The elder son,

JOHN FANSHAWE, Esq., of Fanshawe Gate, b. 1504, d. 1578, leaving by Margaret his wife, dau. of Rowland Eyre, Esq., of Hassop, four sons and three daus.,

  I. THOMAS, his heir.
  II. Henry, d. young.
  III. Robert, who d. 24 June, 1613, and was ancestor of the FANSHAWES of Dronfield, co. Derby, and Hartlip, Kent.
  IV. Godfrey, d. unm. 1587.
  I. Margaret, m. to Richard Castle, Esq., of Dronfield.
  II. Alice, m. to Edward Eliott.
  III. Elizabeth, d. young.

The eldest son,

THOMAS FANSHAWE, Esq., s. his uncle as Queen's Remembrancer of the Exchequer, and purchased Ware Park, Herts, and Dengey, and Westbury, Essex. He m. 1st, Mary, dau. of Anthony Bouchier, and had by her a son, HENRY (Sir), K.B. Thomas Fanshawe m. 2ndly, Joan Smyth, sister of Thomas, Viscount Strangford, and had by her two sons and six daus.,

  I. THOMAS (Sir), of Jenkins, co. Essex, K.B., surveyor-general and clerk of the Crown, who d. in 1631, leaving by Anne his wife, dau. of Urian Bebington, of London, a son, Thomas Fanshawe, Esq., of Jenkins, clerk of the Crown, m. Susan, dau. and co-heir of Matthias Otten, Esq., of Putney, and had a dau., Alice, wife of John Fanshawe, Esq., of Paralces, a son, Sir Thomas Fanshawe, of Jenkins, knighted in 1660, who m. 2ndly, Elizabeth, 4th dau. of Thomas, 1st Viscount Fanshawe, and left an only dau. and heiress, Susan, m. to Baptist Noel, 4th son of Baptist, Viscount Campden.
  II. WILLIAM, ancestor of the Fanshawes, of Fanshawe Gate, co. Derby, who eventually succeeded to the estates of Simon, last Viscount Fanshawe, and are now represented by the REV. CHARLES SIMON FAITHFUL FANSHAWE, of Dengey Hall, co. Essex. From this line descend also the Fanshawes of Paralces, co. Essex. (See BURKE'S Landed Gentry.)
  I. Alice, m. to Sir Christopher Hatton, K.B.
  II. Margaret, m. to Sir Benjamin Ayloff, Bart., of Braxsted and Brittons.
  III. Catherine, m. to John Bullock, Esq., of Darley and Norton, co. Derby.
  IV. Mary, m. to Thomas Hardwick, of Leeds, Esq.

The eldest son,

SIR HENRY FANSHAWE, Knt., of Ware Park, remembrancer of the Exchequer, M.P. for Westbury and Boroughbridge, m. Elizabeth, dau. of Thomas Smythe, Esq., of Ostenhanger, and by her, who d. in 1631, had several sons and daus. Of the former, the 4th, Richard, was created a BARONET of England 2 September, 1650, and the eldest,

SIR THOMAS FANSHAWE, K.B., was raised to the peerage of Ireland, as VISCOUNT FANSHAWE, of Dromore, 5 September, 1661. His lordship m. 1st, Anne, dau. of Sir Giles Alington, of Horseheath, in Cambridgeshire; and 2ndly, Elizabeth, dau. of Sir William Cockaine, Knt., which lady m. 2ndly, Sir Thomas Rich, Bart. By his 1st wife Lord Fanshawe left, with four daus. (of whom the youngest, Elizabeth, m. Sir Thomas Fanshawe, of Jenkins), three sons, THOMAS, 2nd viscount; CHARLES, 4th viscount; and SIMON, 5th viscount. Lord Fanshawe d. in 1665, and s. by his eldest son,

THOMAS FANSHAWE, K.B., 2nd viscount; who m. 1st, Catharine, dau. and heir of Knighton Ferrers, Esq., of Beyford, Herts; and 2ndly, Sarah, dau. of Sir John Evelyn, Knt., of West Dene, and widow of Sir John Wray. By this lady his lordship left at his decease, in 1674, a dau., Katharine, and a son,

EVELYN FANSHAWE, 3rd Viscount Fanshawe, who *d.* at Aleppo, in Turkey, 10 October, 1687, aged nineteen, and was *s.* by his uncle,

CHARLES FANSHAWE, 4th Viscount Fanshawe who *d. s. p.* in 1710, and was *s.* by his brother,

SIMON FANSHAWE, 5th Viscount Fanshawe ; at whose decease *s. p.*, 23 October, 1716, the peerage became EXTINCT.

Arms—Or, a chev., between three fleurs-de-lis, sa.

FELTON—BARONS FELTON.

By Writ of Summons, dated 8 January, 1313.

Lineage.

In the 25th EDWARD I.

ROBERT DE FELTON obtained a charter from the crown for a weekly market at his manor of Luchin, co. Norfolk, and likewise for free-warren there. In the 34th of the same reign he was in the expedition then made into Scotland, and in 4th EDWARD II., he had a military summons for a similar service. The next year he was constituted governor of Scarborough Castle, and was summoned to parliament as a BARON, 8 January, 22 May, 26 July, and 26 November, 1313. His lordship *d.* in 1314, and was *s.* by his son,

JOHN DE FELTON, 2nd baron, who (according to Dugdale) had summons* to parliament in the 16th EDWARD III., but not afterwards. This nobleman was governor of Alnwick Castle in the 8th EDWARD II., and for some years afterwards, he was engaged in the Scottish wars. In the 18th of the same reign he was in the expedition then made into Gascony, being at that time one of the admirals of the fleet sent out to annoy the French and their commercial adventurers. Of his lordship nothing further appears known, except that he was an ancestor of the Feltons of Playford, co. Suffolk, one of whom was created BARONET in 1620, an honour now extinct. Contemporary with this John, Baron Felton, was

WILLIAM DE FELTON, governor of Bamburgh Castle, co. Northumberland. *temp.* EDWARD II., and governor of Roxburgh Castle, in Scotland, in the 11th EDWARD III. This personage, who appears to have taken a distinguished part in the wars of Scotland and France, was summoned to parliament as a BARON, 25 February, 1342, but not afterwards. In the 39th EDWARD III. he attended Prince Edward into Gascony, and being then seneschal of Limosin, he vanquished a considerable party of the Britains there ; but in two years subsequently, being in Spain with the Duke of Lancaster, and wishing to prove his charger, he made a descent upon a body of the enemy, with his spear in his rest, and piercing it through a knight, he was immediately surrounded and slain, 19 March, 1367, leaving a son and heir,

SIR JOHN DE FELTON, who *d.* 31 March, 1396, having m. twice ; by his 1st wife, Joan, dau. of Sir John Fitz-William, he had two daus., Elizabeth, aged fifteen at her father's death, who *m.* Sir Edward Hastinge, and Joan, aged thirteen at her father's death, who *m.* Walter Falconberg, and was mother of John Falconberg. By his 2nd wife, he had a son,

SIR JOHN FELTON, who *d. s. p.* in 1402, when John, the son of Walter Falconberg, by Joan his wife, was found sole heir of the whole blood ; and Elizabeth, his half-sister, wife of Sir Edward Hastings, was found to be heir of the half blood. She left issue, Sir John Hastings, father of Sir Edmund, father of Sir Roger, æt. twenty-six in 1489, amongst whose descendants this barony is in ABEYANCE.

Arms—Gu., two lions passant, erm., crowned, or.

FERMOR—EARL OF POMFRET.

(*See* ADDENDA.)

FERRERS—EARLS OF DERBY.

Creation of King STEPHEN, *anno* 1138.

Lineage.

The first of this eminent family that settled in England was HENRY DE FERIERS (son of Walcheline de Feriers, a Norman), who obtained from WILLIAM THE CONQUEROR, a grant of

* His name does not appear in the list of summonses for that year.—NICHOLAS.

196

Tutbury Castle, co. Stafford, with extensive possessions in other shires, of which 114 manors were in Derbyshire. This person must have been of considerable rank, not only from these enormous grants, but from the circumstance of his being one of the commissioners appointed by the CONQUEROR to make the great survey of the kingdom. He was the founder of the priory of Tutbury, which he liberally endowed. By Berta his wife, he had issue, Egenulph, *d. v. p.* ; William, *d. v. p* ; ROBERT, his successor ; Gundred ; and Emmeline. His only surviving son and heir,

ROBERT DE FERRERS, having contributed, at the head of the Derbyshire men, to King STEPHEN'S victory over King DAVID, of Scotland, at Northallerton (commonly called the battle of the Standard), was created by that monarch EARL OF DERBY. By Hawise his wife, he had William, who *d. s. p.* ; ROBERT, his successor ; Walcheline, of Okeham ; Isolda, *m.* to Stephen de Beauchamp ; and Maud, *m.* to Bertram de Verdon. The earl *d.* in 1139, and was *s.* by his son,

ROBERT DE FERRERS, as 2nd Earl of Derby, living 1141. This nobleman was distinguished by his munificence to the church. His lordship was buried at the abbey of Meervale, co. Warwick, one of the religious houses which he had founded, wrapped in an ox's hide, according to his own desire. He had (with a dau., Petronilla, *m.* to Henry de Stafford) a son,

WILLIAM DE FERRERS, 3rd Earl of Derby, who, in the 12th HENRY II., upon levying the aid for marrying the king's daughter, certified the knights' fees then in his possession to be in number seventy-nine, for which he paid the sum of 68 marks. This nobleman was also a liberal benefactor to the church. His lordship *m.* Margaret, dau. and heiress of William Peverel, of Nottingham, by whom he had issue,

ROBERT. of whom presently.
Walcheline de Ferrers, Lord of Eggington, co. Derby, father, by Goda his wife, dau. of Robert de Toni, of
Robert de Ferrers, Lord of Eggington and of Radbourne, who left at his decease, 9th HENRY III., two daus. and co-heirs,
    1 Ermentrude, who *m.* Robert de Talbot, Lord of Gainsburg, in Lincolnshire, living 18th King JOHN, and was grandmother of
        THOMAS TALBOT DE BASHALL, co. York, ancestor of the knightly house of Bashall, represented by the late Richard Hughes Lloyd, Esq., of Plymog, Gwerclas, and Bashall, father of the present
        JOHN-HUGHES LLOYD, Esq., commander R.N. (*See* BURKE'S *Landed Gentry.*)
    2 Margery, who *m.* Sir John Chandos, Knt., and from this marriage lineally derives the family of CHANDOS POLE, *of Radbourne Hall, co. Derby.* (*See that name* BURKE'S *Landed Gentry.*)

The earl was *s.* by his elder son,
ROBERT DE FERRERS, 4th Earl of Derby. This nobleman rebelled against HENRY II., and marching at the head of the Leicestershire men (19th HENRY II.), upon Nottingham, then kept for the king by Reginald de Luci, got possession of the town, which he sacked, putting the greater part of the inhabitants to the sword, and taking the rest prisoners. He was soon afterwards, however, reduced to submission, and obliged to surrender to the crown his castles of Tutbury and Duffield, which were demolished by order of the king. His lordship *m.* Sibilla, dau. of William de Braose, Lord of Abergavenny and Brecknock, by whom he had issue,

WILLIAM, his successor.
Milicent, *m.* to Roger, Lord Mortimer, of Wigmore.
Agatha. This lady being a concubine to King JOHN, had by that prince a dau.,
    Joane, 3rd consort of Llewelyn the Great, Prince of North Wales ap Iorwerth Drwyndwn, by her, who *d.* 1237, and was buried at Llanfaes, Anglesey, where, over her tomb Prince Llewelyn erected the Friary of Llanfaes, had issue,
        DAVID AP LLEWELYN, Prince of North Wales by usurpation, living 5 May, 4th HENRY III., 1229 ; *d. s. p.* 30th HENRY III., 1246, having *m.* Isabella, dau. and co-heir of William de Braose, of Brecknock.
        HELEN, *m. circa* 6th HENRY III., 1220, John Le Scott, 8th Earl Palatine of Chester and Earl of Huntingdon, brother of WILLIAM THE LION, king of Scotland, who *d. s. p.* 7 June, 1244. She *m.* 2ndly, Robert de Quiney, who *d.* 41st HENRY III., 1277, son of Sahir de Quiney, created Earl of Winchester, *circa* 1210.
        MARGARET, *m. circa* 2nd HENRY III., 1217, John de Braose, surnamed *Tadody*, who *d.* 16th HENRY III., 1231-2. She *m.* 2ndly, Walter de Clifford, who *d.* 48th HENRY III., 1263.
        Gwladys Ddû, *m. circa* 1215, Reginald de Braose, who dying 1221, left no issue by her. She *m.* 2ndly, Ralph de Mortimer, of Wigmore, who living November, 1227, *d.* 30th HENRY III., 1245-6. His widow *d.* at Windsor,

1253. From the marriage of Gwladys Ddû and Ralph de Mortimer, derived by direct representation, EDWARD IV., KING OF ENGLAND.

Angharad, m. Llewelyn Vychan ap Maelgwyn, grandson of the Lord Rhys, Prince of South Wales.

This earl, who was also a benefactor to the church, having founded the priory of Woodham, commonly called Woodham-Ferrers, in Essex, was s. at his decease by his son, WILLIAM DE FERRERS, 5th Earl of Derby. This nobleman was ousted of his dignities of Derby and Nottingham by King RICHARD I., but they were soon afterwards restored to him, and we find him accompanying the lion-hearted monarch to the Holy Land, where he lost his life at the siege of Acon, anno 1191. His lordship, amongst other gifts to the church, gave, in the 1st RICHARD I., for the health of his soul, and the soul of Sibel his wife, to the monks of St. Denis, in France, one wax taper yearly, price thirteen pence; as also a stag and boar in their proper seasons, to be sent annually thither at the feast of St. Denis, by himself and his heirs. He was s. by his son, WILLIAM DE FERRERS, 6th Earl of Derby. This nobleman, upon the return of King RICHARD from captivity, took arms in his behalf, and joining the Earl of Chester, besieged Nottingham Castle, which, after a brief resistance, surrendered. For this and other acts of fidelity, he was chosen by the king to sit with the rest of the peers in the great council held at the said castle of Nottingham in the ensuing March. Moreover, at RICHARD's second coronation he was one of the four that carried the canopy over the king's head. Upon the accession of King JOHN, his lordship, with the Earls of Clare and Chester, and other great men, swore fealty to the new monarch, but upon the condition that each person should have his right. His lordship was present at the coronation of King JOHN, and 7 June following, being solemnly created EARL OF DERBY by special charter, dated at Northampton, he was girt with a sword by the king's own hands (being the first of whom in any charter that expression was used). He had also a grant of the third penny of all the pleas before the sheriff throughout the whole county, whereof he was earl, to hold to him and his heirs as amply as any of his ancestors had enjoyed the same. Moreover, in consideration of 4,000 marks, he obtained another charter from the king of the manor of Higham-Ferrers, co. Northampton, with the hundred and park; as also of the manors of Bliseworth and Newbottle, in the same shire; which were part of the lands of his great grandfather, William Peverel, of Nottingham. King JOHN also conferred upon him a mansion-house, situated in the parish of St. Margaret, within the city of London, which had belonged to Isaac, a Jew, at Norwich, to hold by the service of waiting upon the king (the earl and his heirs), at all festivals yearly, without any cap, but with a garland of the breadth of his little finger upon his head. These liberal marks of royal favour were felt so gratefully by the earl, that in all the subsequent struggles between the king and the refractory barons, his lordship never once swerved from his allegiance, but remained true to the monarch; and after King JOHN's decease, he adhered with the same unshaken loyalty to the interests of his son, King HENRY III. His lordship assisted at the coronation of the new monarch; and immediately after the ensuing Easter he took part with the famous William Marshall (governor of the king and kingdom), the Earls of Chester and Albemarle, and many other great men in the siege of Mountsorell Castle, in Leicestershire, then held by Henry de Braybroke, and ten other stout knights. And the same year, was likewise with those noble persons at raising the siege of Lincoln, which place the rebellious barons with LEWIS, King of France, had invested. His lordship m. Agnes, sister, and one of the co-heirs of Ranulph, Earl of Chester, by whom he had two sons, William and Thomas. He d. of the gout in 1246, and his countess d. in the same year, after a union, according to some authorities, of seventy-five, and by others, of fifty-five years. His lordship was s. by his elder son,

WILLIAM DE FERRERS, 7th Earl of Derby, who, upon doing homage in the 32nd HENRY III., had livery of Chartley Castle, and the other lands of his mother's inheritance; and the same year he sat in the parliament held in London; wherein the king made so stout an answer to the demands of his impetuous barons. His lordship m. 1st, Sibel, one of the daus. and co-heirs of William Mareschal, Earl of Pembroke, by whom he had seven daus., viz.,

Agnes, m. to William de Vesci.
Isabel, m. 1st, to Gilbert Basset, of Wycombe, and 2ndly, to Reginald de Mohun.
Maud, m. 1st, to William de Kymes; 2ndly, to William de Vyvon, and 3rdly, to Emerick de Rupel Carnardi.
Sibil, m. 1st, to John de Vipont; 2ndly, to Franco de Mohun.
Joane, m. to William Aguillon; and 2ndly, to John de Mohun.
Agatha, m. to Hugh Mortimer, of Chechmarsh.

Eleanor, m. 1st, to William de Vallibus; 2ndly, to Roger de Quincy, Earl of Winton; and 3rdly, to Roger de Leybourne, but had no issue.

The earl m. 2ndly, Margaret, one of the daus. and co-heirs of Roger de Quinci, Earl of Winchester, and had issue,

ROBERT, his successor.
William, upon whom his mother conferred the lordship of Groby, co. Leicester. (See FERRERS, BARONS FERRERS, of Groby, ancestor of the families of FERRERS, of Groby, and of FERRERS, of Baddesley, Clinton.)
Joan, m. to Thomas, Lord Berkeley.
Agnes, m. to Robert de Muscegros, Lord of Deerhurst.

His lordship, who from his youth had been a martyr to the gout, and in consequence, obliged to be drawn from place to place in a chariot, lost his life by being thrown, through the heedlessness of his driver, over the bridge of St. Neots, co. Huntingdon, in 1254. (38th HENRY III.) He was s. by his elder son,

ROBERT DE FERRERS, 8th Earl of Derby. This nobleman being a minor at the time of his father's decease, the queen and Peter de Savoy gave 6,000 marks for the custody of his lands, during his minority. His lordship, when arrived at manhood, became one of the most active of the discontented nobles arrayed against HENRY III., and commencing his career by the plunder and destruction of Worcester, the king, to retaliate, sent a force under Prince Edward, into the cos. of Stafford and Derby, which wasted the earl's lands with fire and sword, and demolished his castle at Tutworth. His lordship joining, afterwards, with Montford, Earl of Leicester, and Clare, Earl of Gloucester, participated in the victory achieved at Lewes, in Sussex, wherein the king and the prince were made prisoners; but continuing to adhere to Leicester, he was defeated, with that nobleman, by his former companion in arms, the Earl of Gloucester, at Evesham, and obliged to throw himself upon the mercy of the king, which, in consideration of a cup of gold, adorned with precious stones (obtained from Michal de Tony, upon a mortgage on one of his manors in Northamptonshire), and 1,500 marks, was extended to him, and he received a full pardon for all his misdemeanours, the king undertaking to protect him against Prince Edward, and all others, towards whom, at any time during the troubles, he had done wrong: upon condition, that if he should transgress again, he was without hope of favour, to be wholly disinherited. For the strict observance of which provision, the earl not only obliged himself by special charter, then freely sealed to the king, but by his oath of allegiance at the time renewed. The charter and oath, however, were but feeble restraints upon his lordship, for in the very next spring, we find him again at the head of a powerful army in the northern part of Derbyshire, and soon after defeated in a pitched battle, at Chesterfield, by Prince Henry, eldest son of the King of Almaine. Here, his lordship was amongst those who made their escape from the field, but hiding himself under some sacks of wool in a church, he was there discovered, through the treachery of a woman, and thence conveyed a prisoner to London; whereupon he was totally disinherited, by the parliament then sitting at Westminster, as well of the EARLDOM OF DERBY, as of his territorial possessions, the greater part of which were conferred by the king upon his 2nd son, Edmund (surnamed Crouchback), Earl of Leicester and Lancaster; to whom many writers of authority attribute also the dignity of Earl of Derby; but Dugdale expressly says, "although he (the prince) had possession of the greater part of this Robert's land, and exercised (perhaps) the power of earl in that county, I am not satisfied that he really was Earl of Derby; in regard, I cannot find that the same Edmund had any patent of creation to that honour, as he had to those of Leicester and Lancaster." It seems that this unfortunate nobleman continued in confinement about three years, but in the 53rd HENRY III., there was so much interest made for him, that the king accepted of security, whereby he might receive satisfaction for his lordship's misdemeanours, and issued his precept to Prince Edmund, to make restitution of his lands; when an agreement was entered into between the disinherited earl and the prince, by which the latter, for the sum of £50,000, to be paid at once upon a certain day, was to relinquish all interest in the lands; but that payment not being made good, the securities to the covenant passed over the lands to Prince Edmund and his heirs for ever. Subsequently, however, the ousted lord instituted a suit in the Court of King's Bench, against the prince, for the restitution of his property, upon the allegation that the agreement he had sealed was extorted from him when a prisoner, and under apprehension of his life; but after divers pleadings, a decision of the court in the beginning of EDWARD I.'s reign, confirmed the lands to Prince Edmund.

This Robert de Ferrers, last Earl of Derby, of the family, m. 1st, Mary, dau. of Hugh le Brun, Earl of Angoulosme, and niece of King HENRY III., by whom he had no issue; and 2ndly, Eleanore, dau. of Ralph, Lord Basset, by whom he had an only son,

JOHN, who inherited Chartley Castle. (*See* FERRERS, BARONS FERRERS, *of Chartley*.)

The earl *d.* 7th EDWARD I., the last EARL OF DERBY of the house of FERRERS. The descendant, and existing male representative of this once powerful family is MARMION-EDWARD FERRERS, Esq., of Baddesley Clinton, co. Warwick.

Arms—Arg., six horse-shoes, sa., pierced, or, three, two, and one.

FERRERS—BARONS FERRERS, OF WEMME, CO. SALOP.

By Writ of Summons, dated 28 December, 1375.

Lineage.

SIR ROBERT FERRERS, Knt., younger son of Robert, 2nd Lord Ferrers, of Chartley, having *m.* Elizabeth, only dau. and heiress of Robert, Lord Boteler, of Wemme, was summoned to parliament as BARON FERRERS, *of Wemme*, from 28 December, 1375, to 16 February, 1379. His lordship acquired, by this alliance, the lordship of Wemme, in Shropshire, and that of Oversley, co. Warwick, with other extensive estates, and by her (who *d.* 1410) had an only son,

ROBERT, his successor.

This nobleman, prior to his marriage, was engaged in the Flemish wars of EDWARD III. His lordship *d.* in 1380, and his widow *m.* two husbands afterwards, viz., Sir John Say and Sir Thomas Molinton, but had issue by neither. Lord Ferrers was *s.* by his son,

SIR ROBERT FERRERS, 2nd Baron Ferrers, of Wemme, but never summoned to parliament. His lordship, *b.* 1370, *m.* Joane, dau. of John of Gaunt, by Catherine Swinford, and had issue, two daus.,

Elizabeth, *b.* 1392, *m.* to John, 6th Lord Greystock, son of Ralph, Lord Greystock (who *s.* to the barony in 1417), and had issue,

Ralph, Lord Greystock, who *m.* Elizabeth, dau. of William, Lord Fitzhugh, and was *s.* in 1487 by his grand-dau.,

Elizabeth, who *m.* Thomas, Lord Dacre, of Gillesland.

Elizabeth, *m.* to Roger Thornton, Esq., whose only dau. and heiress,

Elizabeth, *m.* Sir George Lumley, whose descendant, and eventual representative,

Barbara Lumley, *m.* Humphrey Lloyd, Esq., of Denbigh; the great-great-grandson of this marriage, Rev. Dr. Robert Lloyd claimed, unsuccessfully, the Barony of Lumley in 1723.

Mary, *m.* to Ralph, a younger son of Ralph Nevil, Earl of Westmoreland, and had issue.

JOHN NEVIL, who *m.* Elizabeth, dau. and heiress of Robert Newmarch, and left an only dau. and heiress.

JOANE NEVIL, *m.* to Sir William Gascoign, whose dau. and heiress,

MARGARET GASCOIGN, *m.* 1st, Thomas Wentworth, ancestor of the Wentworths, Earls of Strafford; and 2ndly, Sir James Harington.

Robert, Lord Ferrers, *d.* in 1410, when the BARONY OF FERRERS, *of Wemme*, fell into ABEYANCE between his daus., Elizabeth Greystock and Mary Nevil. His widow Joane, *m.* 2ndly, the above-mentioned Ralph Nevil, Earl of Westmoreland (his 2nd wife). Elizabeth, Lord Ferrers' mother, outlived his lordship, and at her decease, the BARONY OF BOTELER, *of Wemme*, fell also into ABEYANCE between her ladyship's grand-daus., the said Elizabeth and Mary, and both baronies continue in the same state with their representatives.

Arms—Vairée, or, and gu., a lion passant guardant of the 1st, in a canton.

FERRERS—BARONS FERRERS, OF GROBY, CO. LEICESTER.

By Writ of Summons, dated 26 January, 1297.

Lineage.

The Honourable

WILLIAM FERRERS, 2nd son of William, 7th Earl of Derby, obtained, by gift of Margaret, his mother, one of the daus. and co-heirs of Roger de Quinci, Earl of Winchester, the manor of Groby, co. Leicester, whereupon he assumed the arms of the family of De Quinci. He *m.* 1st, Joane, dau. of Hugh le Despencer; and 2ndly, Eleanor, dau. of Matthew Lovaine, and by the former had issue,

WILLIAM, his successor.
Anne, *m.* to John, Lord Grey, of Wilton.

He *d.* in 1288, and was *s.* by his son,

WILLIAM FERRERS, who doing homage, had livery of his lands in England, in the 21st EDWARD I., and in the 24th, of the lands which he inherited in Scotland. In the following year he was summoned to parliament as BARON FERRERS, *of Groby*. His lordship was engaged in the wars of Scotland in the reigns of EDWARD I. and EDWARD II. He *m.* Margaret, dau. of John, 2nd Lord Segreve, and dying in 1325, left two sons and a dau., Henry and Thomas, and Anne, *m.* to Edward le Despencer, who *d.* in 1342. The former,

HENRY FERRERS, 2nd Baron Ferrers, of Groby, summoned to parliament, from 5 June, 1331, to 20 November, 1342. This nobleman, being actively engaged in the wars of King EDWARD III., both in Scotland and France, acquired very large territorial possessions, by grants from the crown, for his services. His lordship *m.* Isabel, 4th dau. and co-heir of Theobald, 2nd Lord Verdon, and in the 5th EDWARD III., upon doing homage, had livery of the lands of her inheritance lying in Ireland. Of this marriage there were issue,

WILLIAM, his successor.
Ralph, *m.* Joan, dau. of Richard, Baron Grey, of Codnor, and widow of Sir William Harcourt, of Bosworth, co. Leicester.
Philippa, *m.* to Guy de Beauchamp, son and heir of Thomas, Earl of Warwick.
Elizabeth, *m.* David, Earl of Athol.

His lordship *d.* in 1343, and was *s.* by his son,

WILLIAM FERRERS, 3rd Baron Ferrers, of Groby, summoned to parliament, from 15 March, 1354, to 6 April, 1369. In the 29th EDWARD III., his lordship was in the expedition then made into France in the retinue of his father-in-law, Robert de Ufford, Earl of Suffolk; and again, in the 33rd and 34th, in the latter of which years, his lands in Ireland being seized for the defence of that realm, the king directed his precept to the justice, chancellor and treasurer there, to discharge them, in consequence of his lordship being then in the wars in France, with divers men at arms and archers, at a very considerable expense. His lordship *m.* 1st, Margaret, dau. and co-heir of Robert de Ufford, Earl of Suffolk, by whom he had issue,

HENRY, his successor.
Elizabeth, a nun, in the convent of Minoresses-without, Aldgate, in the suburbs of London.
Margaret, *m.* to Thomas Beauchamp, Earl of Warwick.

He *m.* 2ndly, Margaret, dau. of Henry, 2nd Lord Percy, and widow of Robert, son and heir of Gilbert de Umfravil, Earl of Angus, and dying in 1372, was *s.* by his son,

HENRY FERRERS, 4th Baron Ferrers, of Groby, summoned to parliament from 4 August, 1377, to 17 December, 1387. This nobleman was uninterruptedly engaged in the French wars from the 1st to the 7th RICHARD II. inclusive; and the next year, being then a banneret, he was retained to serve the king in the wars of Scotland. Upon the death of William de Ufford, Earl of Suffolk, his mother's brother, without issue, Lord Ferrers was found to be one of the deceased earl's next heirs. His lordship *m.* Joane, dau. of Lucas Poynings, Lord St. John, and dying in 1388, was *s.* by his son,

WILLIAM FERRERS, 5th Baron Ferrers, of Groby, summoned to parliament from 30 November, 1396, to 3 December, 1441. This nobleman was also in the French wars. His lordship *m.* 1st, Philippa, dau. of Roger, Baron Clifford, by Matilda his wife, dau. of Thomas Beauchamp, Earl of Warwick; and 2ndly, Margaret, dau. of John Montacute, 3rd Earl of Salisbury, and by the former had issue,

1. HENRY, who *d. v. p.* 1394, leaving (by Isabel his wife, eldest dau. of Thomas Mowbray, Duke of Norfolk, by Elizabeth his wife, sister and co-heir of Thomas FitzAlan, Earl of Arundel and Surrey, which lady *m.* 2ndly, James, Baron Berkeley), an only dau. and heiress,

ELIZABETH, heiress to the Barony of Ferrers, of Groby, at the decease of her grandfather, *m.* 1st, Sir Edward Grey,

Knt. (eldest son of Baron Grey de Ruthin), who was summoned to parliament as Baron Ferrers of Groby. (*See* GREY, *Baron Ferrers.*) She m. 2ndly, Sir John Bourchier, 4th son of Henry, Earl of Essex.

II. Thomas (Sir), of Tamworth, *jure uxoris*, who m. Elizabeth, sister and co-heir of Sir Baldwin Frevile, Knt., of Tamworth Castle, co. Warwick, and had issue,

1 THOMAS (Sir), 2nd Lord of Tamworth Castle, ancestor of the family of FERRERS of Tamworth Castle, the eventual heiress of which, ANNE FERRERS, m. the Hon. Robert Shirley, eldest son of Robert, 1st Earl Ferrers, and 13th Lord Ferrers of Chartley, and had an only dau. and heiress, ELIZABETH SHIRLEY, BARONESS FERRERS, who m. James Compton, Earl of Northampton. Their only dau. and heiress, LADY CHARLOTTE COMPTON, Baroness Ferrers and Compton, m. George, 1st MARQUESS TOWNSHEND, and had a son and successor, GEORGE, EARL OF LEICESTER, who became 16th Baron Ferrers of Chartley. His lordship was created Earl of Leicester in 1784, and inherited the MARQUESSATE OF TOWNSHEND at the decease of his father, as 2nd marquess. He m. Charlotte, dau. of Eaton-Mainwaring Ellerker, Esq. of Risby Park, and had George, 2nd Marquess Townshend, 17th Baron Ferrers of Chartley, who *d. s. p.* 1855; Lord Charles V. F. Townshend, who also *d. s. p.*, and three daus., co-heirs, viz., Lady Charlotte-Barbara, wife of Lieut.-Col. Bishop, who *d. s p.* and Lady Harriet-Anne Townshend m. EDWARD FERRERS, Esq., of BADDESLEY CLINTON, and Lady Elizabeth-Margaret, m. J. M. BOULT- BEE, Esq.

2 HENRY (Sir), ancestor of the family of FERRERS, *of Baddesley Clinton, co. Warwick*, now represented by MARMION EDWARD FERRERS, Esq., of Baddesley Clinton, who is senior co-heir of the Barony of FERRERS, of Chartley ; and HEIR MALE, also, of the House of Ferrers, Earls of Derby.

III. John.
IV. Edmund, of St. Albans.

William, 5th Baron Ferrers, of Groby, *d.* in 1445, when the BARONY OF FERRERS, *of Groby*, devolved upon his grand-dau., Elizabeth, in which dignity, her husband, Sir Edward Grey, was summoned to parliament (*see* GREY, BARON FERRERS, *of Groby*).

Arms—Gu., seven mascles voided, or (the arms of Quinci).

FERRERS—BARONS FERRERS OF CHART-
LEY.

By Writ of Summons, dated 6 February, 1299.

Lineage.

JOHN DE FERRERS (only son of Robert de Ferrers, 8th and last Earl of Derby of that family), after the forfeiture of his father was summoned to parliament as BARON FERRERS *of Chartley*, co. *Stafford*, 6 February, 1299. (A seat which came into the family of Ferrers, by the marriage of William, 5th Earl of Derby, with Agnes, sister and co-heir of Ranulph, Earl of Chester.) This John, inheriting the turbulent spirit of his father, joined the Earl of Hertford and others, in the 25th EDWARD I., in opposing the collection of the subsidies granted by the parliament then held at St. Edmundsbury, to the crown, but the ferment was allayed by the king's confirming Magna Charta, and the charter of the Forests ; and by declaring that in future no tax should be imposed upon the subject without the consent of parliament, at the same time granting a pardon to the discontented lords and their adherents, in which pardon John de Ferrers is especially named. Soon after this he petitioned Pope NICHOLAS III., that his holiness should interfere to procure him the lands of his late father which had been conferred upon Edmund, Earl of Lancaster, but his suit was ineffectual. He was subsequently in the Scottish wars, and was then raised to the peerage as stated above. His lordship m. Hawyse, dau. and heiress of Sir Robert de Muscegros, of Charlton, co. Somerset, by whom he acquired a great increase to his fortune. In the 34th EDWARD I., he was again in the wars of Scotland, and, subsequently, in the 4th EDWARD II., the year following which he was constituted seneschal of Aquitaine. He *d.* in 1324, and was *s.* by his son,

ROBERT DE FERRERS, 2nd Baron Ferrers, of Chartley, summoned to parliament 25 February, 1342. This nobleman, who was of a martial character, served frequently in the Scotch and French wars of HENRY III., and finally, the year before his decease, participated in the glorious victory of Cressy, (23rd EDWARD III.) His lordship m. Agnes, dau. of Humphrey de Bohun, Earl of Hereford, by whom he had issue,

JOHN, his successor.
Robert, summoned to parliament as Baron Ferrers, of Wemme (*see* that dignity).
199

He *d.* in 1350, and was *s.* by his elder son,

JOHN DE FERRERS, 3rd Baron Ferrers, of Chartley, but never summoned to parliament. This nobleman was in the wars of Gascony in the 33rd EDWARD III. His lordship m. Elizabeth, dau. of Ralph, 1st Earl of Stafford, and widow of Fulke, Lord Strange of Blackmere, and dying beyond the seas, 2 April, 1367, was *s.* by his son,

ROBERT DE FERRERS, 4th Baron Ferrers, of Chartley, but never summoned to parliament. His lordship m. Margaret, dau. of Edward, Lord Le Despencer, and dying 13 March, 1412-13, had (with a dau. Philippa, m. to Sir Thomas Green, of Boughton), three sons, EDMUND, his heir ; Thomas and Edward. The eldest son,

EDMUND DE FERRERS, 5th Baron Ferrers, of Chartley, but never summoned to parliament, was *b.* 1389. This nobleman participated in most of the great victories of King HENRY V. His lordship m. Eleanor, dau. and co-heir of Thomas de la Roche, by Elizabeth Bermingham his wife, by whom he acquired large landed possessions, amongst which was that of Castle Bromwich, co. Derby, and by her (who m. 2ndly, Philip Chetwynd of Ingestre, and *d.* 1439-40), he had issue,

WILLIAM, his successor.
Edmund, upon whom the estates were entailed.
John.

He *d.* 1435-6, and was *s.* by his eldest son,

WILLIAM DE FERRERS, 6th Baron Ferrers, of Chartley, who m. Elizabeth, dau. of Sir Hamon Belknap, Knt., and by her (who *d.* 28 May, 1470), left an only dau.,

ANNE, wife of Walter Devereux, Esq., upon whom the Barony of FERRERS, *of Chartley*, devolved, and among whose descendants, M. E. FERRERS, Esq., of Baddesley Clinton, and HENRY TOWNSHEND BOULTBEE, Esq., it is now in ABEYANCE.

His lordship's great landed possessions passed in conformity with the entail upon his only brother, the Hon. Edmund Ferrers. William, the 6th Baron, *d.* 9 June, 1450.

Arms—Vairée, or and gu.

FIENES—VISCOUNTS SAYE AND SELE.

By Letters Patent, dated 7 July, 1624.

(*See* Lords Saye and Sele in BURKE'S *Extant Peerage.*)

FINCH—BARON FINCH, OF FORDWICH,
CO. KENT.

By Letters Patent, dated 7 April, 1640.

Lineage.

SIR THOMAS FINCH, Knt. (son of Sir William Finch, of Mote, by Elizabeth his wife, dau. of Sir James Crowner, Knt., and widow of Sir Richard Lovet, Knt.) was a gallant soldier in the reigns of MARY and ELIZABETH. He m. Catherine, elder dau. and co-heiress of Sir Thomas Moyle, of Eastwell, co. Kent, and had issue,

MOYLE (Sir), from whom the extant EARLS of WINCHILSEA and NOTTINGHAM descend.
HENRY, of whom presently.
Thomas, m. ——, dau. of —— Wilkins, Esq., of Tonge, and *d. s. p.*

The 2nd son,

SIR HENRY FINCH, serjeant-at-law, m. Ursula, dau. and heiress of John Thwaites, Esq., and had an only son,

SIR JOHN FINCH, an eminent lawyer, who filled the chair of the House of Commons in 1627, became attorney-general to the queen in 1635, justice of the Common Pleas the following year, and chief justice afterwards. In 1639, Sir John was appointed lord keeper of the great seal, and in the beginning of the next year (7 April, 1640), he was advanced to the peerage, in the dignity of BARON FINCH, *of Fordwich, co. Kent.* His lordship m. 1st, Eleanor, a dau. of Sir George Wyat, of Bexley, and 2ndly, Mabel, dau. of the Very Rev. Charles Fortherby, dean of Canterbury, but as he had one child only—a dau., who m. the Right Hon. Sir George Radcliffe, of Ireland, the BARONY OF FINCH, at his lordship's decease, 20 November, 1660, became EXTINCT.

Arms—Az., a chev., between three garbs, or.

FITTON—BARON FITTON.

By Patent, dated 1 April, 1689.

Lineage.

Sir Edward Fitton, Knt., representative of the Gawsworth branch of the ancient Cheshire family of Fitton, *temp.* Henry VIII., served as sheriff for the palatinate 35th of that reign. He m. Mary, dau. and co-heir of Guicciard Harbottle, of Northumberland, and had issue,

Edward (Sir), his heir.
Thomas, of Liddington, d. 20 April, 1699, m. Anne, dau. of Peter Warburton, and had two daus.,
  Frances, m. to John Wills, of Staffordshire.
  Margaret, m. to Robert Hyde, of Norbury.
Francis, m. 1588, Catherine, Countess Dowager of Northumberland, and d. s. p.
Anthony, d. in Ireland.
George.   John.
Jane, m, to — Kynaston, of Oteley.
——, m. to Sir Francis Inglefield.
——, m. to Sir Richard Leveson, of Trentham.
Katherine, m. to John Mere, Esq., of Mere.

Sir Edward d. 17 February, 2 Edward VI., and was s. by his son,
  Sir Edward Fitton, Knt., of Gawsworth, lord president of Connaught and Thomond, and treasurer of Ireland, who m. in 1539, Anne, dau. of Sir Peter Warburton, Knt., of Arley, in Cheshire, and had issue,

Edward (Sir), his heir, who was ancestor of the Fittons, Barts. (*See* Burke's *Extinct Baronetcies*).
Alexander, of whom we treat.
John, d. s. p.   Richard, d. s. p.
Margaret, m. to Sir Randle Mainwaring, Knt., of Peover.

The 2nd son,
  Alexander Fitton, settled in Ireland, and m. Jane, dau. of Mac Bryen O'Connogh, and had a 2nd son,
  William Fitton, Esq., of Awne, in Ireland, on whom Sir Edward settled the estate as heir male. He m. Eve, dau. of Sir Edward Trevor, Knt., of Brynkynalt, and had two sons,

Alexander, of whom presently.
Edward, supposed to have d. s. p.

The 2nd son,
  Sir Alexander Fitton, Knt., was constituted lord chancellor of Ireland, 12 February, 1687, and created Baron Fitton, *of Gawsworth, co. Limerick,* in the peerage of that kingdom, by King James II., 1 April, 1689, but the title, like the other creations of the unfortunate James subsequent to his abdication of the English throne, has not been acknowledged. His lordship m. Anne, dau. of Thomas Joliffe, Esq., of Cofton, co. Worcester, and by her (who d. 7 October, 1687, and was buried in St. Patrick's Cathedral) had an only dau., Anne.

Arms—Arg., on a bend, az., three garbs, or.

FITZ-ALAN—EARLS OF ARUNDEL, BARONS MALTRAVERS.

Earldom by feudal possession of Arundel Castle.
Barony by Writ of Summons, dated 5 June, 1330.

Lineage.

In the time of William the Conqueror,
  Alan, the son of Flathald (or Flaald) obtained, by the gift of that King, the castle of Oswaldestre, with the territory adjoining, which belonged to Meredith, Prince of Powys ap Bleddyn, King of Powys. This Alan, having m. the dau. and heir of Warine, sheriff of Shropshire, had, in her right, the Barony of Warine, and was s. by his son,
  William Fitz-Alan, who, in the contest between King Stephen and the Empress Maud, being then governor of Shrewsbury and sheriff of the county of Salop, held the castle of Shrewsbury for the latter, until it was taken by assault. He was also with the empress at the siege of Winchester Castle, in the 6th Stephen, when she and her whole army were put to flight; and afterwards, continuing to adhere stoutly to the same cause, he was reconstituted sheriff of Salop, so soon as King Henry attained the crown. This William m. Isabel, dau. and heir of Helias de Say, Lady of Clun, niece of

Robert, Earl of Gloucester, and dying some time before 1160, was s. by his son,
  William Fitz-Alan, who, in the 12th Henry II., upon the assessment, in aid of marrying the king's daughter, certified his knights' fees to be in number thirty-five and a half. He d. about 1172, and was s. by his son,
  William Fitz-Alan. This feudal lord served the office of sheriff for Shropshire, from 2nd Richard I., until the 3rd of John, inclusive. He m. Mary, dau. of Thomas de Erington. and d. 1214, having had a son,

William, who d. s. p.

He was s. by his brother,
  John Fitz-Alan, who took up arms with the other barons, *temp.* John; but, upon the accession of King Henry, having had letters of safe conduct to come in and make his peace, he had livery of the lands of his inheritance, upon paying, however, a fine of 10,000 marks. This feudal lord m. 1st, Isabel, 2nd dau. of William de Albini, Earl of Arundel, and sister and co-heir of Hugh, last earl of that family, by whom he had a son,

John, his successor.

He m. 2ndly, Haws de Blancminster, and dying in 1239, was s. by his son,
  John Fitz-Alan, who, in the 28th Henry III., upon the division made of the property of Hugh Albini, Earl of Arundel, then made, had the castle of Arundel assigned to him for his principal seat, thus becoming 5th Earl of Arundel; and soon after that, in consideration of £1,000 fine, had livery of his own castles of Clun, Blancminster and Schrawurthen. In the 42nd Henry III., his lordship was made captain-general of all the forces designed for guarding the Welsh marches, and in the baronial war, he appears first to have sided with the barons, and afterwards with the king. He d. 1267, having m. Maud, dau. of Roesia de Verdun (which lady m. 2ndly, Richard de Amundevill), by whom he had a son and successor,
  John Fitz-Alan, 6th Earl of Arundel, who m. Isabel, dau. of Sir Roger Mortimer (which lady m. 2ndly, Ralph de Arderne, and 3rdly, Robert de Hastings), and dying 1269, was s. by his son,
  Richard Fitz-Alan, 7th Earl of Arundel, who m. Alice, dau. of the Marquess of Saluce in Italy, and had issue,

Edmund, his successor.
John (Sir), in holy orders, mentioned in his nephew, Earl Richard's will.
Maud, m. to Philip, Lord Burnel.
Margaret, m. to William, Baron Boteler, of Wemme.

His lordship d. in 1302, and was s. by his son,
  Edmund Fitz-Alan, 8th Earl of Arundel. We find this nobleman, from the 34th Edward I., when he was made a knight of the Bath with Prince Edward, to the 4th of the ensuing reign, constantly engaged in the wars of Scotland; but he was afterwards involved in the treason of Thomas, Earl of Lancaster, yet not greatly to his prejudice, for, in the 10th Edward II., his lordship was constituted lieutenant and captain-general to the king, from the Trent northwards, as far as Roxborough in Scotland, and for several years subsequently, he continued one of the commanders of the English army in Scotland, in which service he so distinguished himself, that he obtained a grant from the crown of the confiscated property of Lord Baddlesmere, in the city of London and county of Salop, as well as the escheated lands of John, Lord Moubray, in the Isle of Axholme, and several manors and castles, part of the possessions (also forfeited) of Roger, Lord Mortimer, of Wigmore. But those royal grants led, eventually to the earl's ruin; for, after the fall of the unhappy Edward into the hands of his enemies, Lord Arundel, who was implacably hated by the queen and Mortimer, suffered death by decapitation at Hereford, in 1326. His lordship m. 1305, the Lady Alice Plantagenet, sister and sole heir of John, last Earl of Warren and Surrey of that family, by whom he had issue,

Richard, his successor.
Edmund (Sir), m. Sibil, dau of William Montacute, Earl of Salisbury, and had one dau., Alice, m. to Leonard, Lord Carew.
Alice, m. to John de Bohun, Earl of Hereford.
Jane, m. to Warine Gerrard, Lord L'Isle.
Alaive, m. to Sir Roger le Strange.

His lordship was s. by his eldest son,
  Richard Fitz-Alan, b. 1306, who being restored by parliament, 4th Edward III., had the castle of Arundel (which had been given to Edmund, Earl of Kent, the king's uncle,) rendered to him, and thus became 9th earl. In the 7th Edward III., this nobleman was constituted governor of Chirke Castle, co.

Denbigh, and the ensuing year had a grant of the inheritance of that castle, with all the territories thereunto belonging, being part of the possessions of Roger Mortimer, the attainted Earl of March; he was soon afterwards made governo. of Porchester Castle, and the same year had a command in the w..s of Scotland, where he continued engaged for some years. After this he was constituted admiral of the western seas, and governor of Caernarvon Castle. In the 14th EDWARD III., his lordship embarked in the French wars, and participated in the glories of the subsequent campaigns. He was at the siege of Vannes, the relief of Thouars, and the immortal battle of Cressy. Besides his great military services, the earl was frequently employed in diplomatic missions of the first importance, and was esteemed one of the most eminent generals and statesmen of the era in which he lived. His lordship, who with his other honours, had the Garter, contracted in minority and under constraint, marriage with Isabel, dau. of Hugh le Despencer, and had issue by her, an only dau.,

Philippa, m. to Sir Richard Sergeaux, Knt., of Cornwall.

In 1345, he was divorced from this lady, and m. Lady Eleanor Plantagenet, dau. of Henry, Earl of Lancaster, and widow of John, Baron Beaumont, by whom he had issue,

I. RICHARD, his successor.
II. John, marshal of England in 1377, summoned to parliament 1st to 3rd RICHARD II. He d. 1379, having m. Eleanor, grand-dau. and co-heir of John, Lord Maltravers, in whose right he bore that title, and by her (who m. 2ndly, Reginald, Lord Cobham,) had issue,

1 JOHN, b. 1365: who m. Elizabeth, dau. of Hugh le Despencer, and d. 1391, having had issue,
JOHN, Lord Maltravers, who s. as 12th Earl of Arundel.
Edmund.
Thomas (Sir), of Beechwood, whose dau. and heir, Eleanor, m. Sir Thomas Browne, Knt., treasurer of the household to HENRY VI.
Margaret, m. to William, Lord Ros.
2 William, K.G.
3 Thomas (also called Edward).
4 Henry.   1 Joan.

III. Thomas, called Arundel, successively bishop of Ely, archbishop of York, and archbishop of Canterbury, Lord Chancellor of England. This prelate was impeached and banished the kingdom in the reign of RICHARD II., but returned with HENRY IV., and was restored to the see of Canterbury. He was a person of great eminence in his time, but is accused of being a religious persecutor, particularly of the Wickliffites, and of Sir John Oldcastle, Lord Cobham. He d. 19 February, 1413, and was buried in the cathedral church of Canterbury.
I. Joane, m. to Humphrey de Bohun, Earl of Hereford.
II. Alice, m. to Thomas Holland, Earl of Kent.
III. Mary, m. to John, Lord Strange, of Blackmere.
IV. Eleanor, m. to Robert, son of William de Ufford, Earl of Suffolk.

His lordship d. 1376, and was s. by his eldest son,
RICHARD FITZ-ALAN, 10th Earl of Arundel, K.G. In the 1st RICHARD II., this nobleman being constituted admiral of the king's fleet in the westwards, and soon after that to the southwards, was retained by indenture to serve the king at sea for one quarter of a year, in the company of John, Duke of Lancaster, King of Castile. He was afterwards engaged for some years in Scotland; and was in the commission (9th EDWARD II.), for the trial of Michael de la Pole, and some other of the king's favourites, whom the Commons had then impeached. His lordship was appointed the next year admiral of the whole fleet, and putting to sea, encountered and vanquished the united fleets of France and Spain, taking no less than 100 ships, great and small, all laden with wines, comprising 19,000 tuns. This gallant exploit he followed up by entering the port of Brest, and reducing one of its castles and burning the other. He now returned to England in great triumph, but had to encounter the jealousy and hatred of the king's favourites, particularly of the Duke of Ireland, whose influence over the king he strenuously resisted. His lordship afterwards entered into the confederation of the Earls of Derby and Warwick, which assembled in arms at Haringhay Park (now Hornsey), in Middlesex, and compelled the king to acquiesce in their views. He was then, by the general consent of parliament (11th RICHARD II.), made governor of the castle and town of Brest, and shortly after captain-general of the king's fleet at sea, with commission to treat of peace with John de Montfort, then Duke of Britanny; whereupon hoisting his flag, soon after met with the enemy, of whose ships he sunk and took fourscore; entered the Isle of Rhò, which he burnt and spoiled, and several other ports which he likewise plundered, putting to flight all the French and Britons that made any resistance. From this memorable period in the life of Lord Arundel, little is known of him, until the 15th RICHARD,

when the king regaining his power, summoned a parliament at Westminster, and dismissed several of the great officers of state, amongst whom his lordship was removed from his command as admiral; and in two years afterwards, the parliament then sitting, he was accused of treason by the Duke of Lancaster, but escaped for the moment, and sought to retire from public life. The king entertaining, however, the strongest feeling of personal enmity to all those who had previously opposed his minions, contrived to get the Earl of Arundel into his hands by stratagem, and having sent him prisoner to the Isle of Wight, brought him to immediate trial, when he was condemned to be hanged, drawn, and quartered as a traitor. The sentence was however somewhat mitigated, and the gallant nobleman was simply beheaded at Cheapside, in the city of London, 21st RICHARD II., the king himself being a spectator, and Thomas de Mowbray, Earl Marshal (who had m. his dau.), the executioner, who bound up his eyes, and according to some, the person who actually struck off his head. It is stated that when the earl saw his son-in-law, Mowbray, and the Earl of Kent, his nephew, guarding him to the place of execution, he told them, it had been much more fit that they should have absented themselves: "For the time will come," said he, "when as many shall wonder at your misfortune as they now do at mine." His lordship m. 1st, 1359, Lady Elizabeth de Bohun, dau. of William, Earl of Northampton, and had surviving issue,

THOMAS, his successor.
Elizabeth, m. 1st, to William de Montacute, eldest son of William, Earl of Salisbury, which William was unhappily slain by his father in a tilting at Windsor, 6th RICHARD II. Her ladyship m. 2ndly, Thomas, Lord Mowbray, Earl Marshal, and through the dau. of this marriage, the
LADY MARGARET MOWBRAY, eventual heiress of the Mowbrays, who m. Sir Robert Howard, Knt., the Dukedom of Norfolk, the Earl Marshalship, and other honours, came into the family of Howard, which they have since enjoyed.
Lady Elizabeth m, 3rdly, Sir Gerard Uffiete, Knt., and 4thly, Sir Robert Goushill, Knt.
Joan, m. William Beauchamp, Lord Abergavenny, K.G.
Margaret, m. to Sir Rowland Lenthall, of Hampton Court, co. Hereford.
Alice, m. to John Cherleton, Lord Powis.

The earl was s. by his son,
THOMAS FITZ-ALAN, who being restored in blood in the parliament 1st HENRY IV., when the judgment against his father was reversed, became 11th Earl of Arundel. This nobleman was made a knight of the Bath at the coronation of King HENRY IV. He was afterwards made a knight of the Garter, and upon the accession of King HENRY V. he was constituted constable of Dover Castle, and lord warden of the Cinque Ports, as also Lord Treasurer of England. His lordship m. Beatrix, an illegitimate dau. of JOHN, King of Portugal, and the nuptials were celebrated with great pomp in London, the king and queen assisting. He d. however without issue, in 1415, leaving his four sisters his heirs, as to certain parts of his great possessions; but the castle of Arundel, and with it the earldom, devolved upon his cousin,
JOHN FITZ-ALAN, Lord Maltravers, as 12th Earl of Arundel* (refer to issue of Richard, 9th earl). This nobleman was in the king's fleet at sea under his kinsman, Richard, Earl of Arundel, and he was subsequently in the wars of Scotland and France. His lordship m. Eleanor, dau. of Sir John Berkeley, Knt., of Beverston, co. Gloucester, by whom (who m. 2ndly, Sir Richard Poynings, and 3rdly, Sir Walter Hungerford) he had issue,

---

* Nicolas has the following note in his Synopsis:—"Until the 11th HENRY VI., when it was decided that the tenure of the castle of Arundel alone, without any creation, patent, or investiture, constituted its possessor Earl of Arundel, neither this John, nor John his son and heir, were regularly considered to have possessed that dignity, although they were both seized of the said castle; in proof of which John Fitz-Alan, 12th earl, was never summoned to parliament, and John, his son and heir,¡was summoned in the 7th HENRY VI., as a baron only; nor was it until 3 December, 1441, that the inheritor of the castle of Arundel sat in parliament by that title, which probably arose from this circumstance, that at the time of the decision alluded to, in the 11th HENRY VI,, 1432, John, Earl of Arundel, was engaged in the wars of France, and continued to be so until his death, which happened within two years afterwards; and Humphrey, his son and heir, d. in 1437, then only ten years of age, and was s. by William, his uncle and heir, who was accordingly summoned to parliament as Earl of Arundel. Notwithstanding what has been observed, that John Fitz-Alan, who s. in 1415, was not admitted to this earldom, it is manifest he was generally styled Earl of Arundel, for Alice, his widow, in her will, describes herself as Countess of Arundel, and speaks of her late husband as John, Earl of Arundel."

JOHN, his successor.
William, who *s.* as 15th earl.

Lord Arundel *d.* in 1421, and was *s.* by his elder son,

JOHN FITZ-ALAN, 13th Earl of Arundel, who, in the 7th HENRY VI., was summoned to parliament as Lord Maltravers, and the next year, according to Dugdale, as Earl of Arundel. In the 11th HENRY VI., this nobleman petitioned parliament for the confirmation of his title, as annexed to the castle, honour, and seigniory of Arundel, which was adjudged to him by virtue of the tenure only, after much opposition from John Mowbray, Duke of Norfolk, who was heir to Elizabeth, one of the sisters and co-heirs of Thomas, 11th earl. His lordship was in the wars of France, under the celebrated general, John Talbot, 1st Earl of Shrewsbury, and for his achievements was created by HENRY VI., Duke of Touraine, in France, and invested with the Garter. But eventually having his leg shattered by a cannon ball, in an engagement with the enemy, he was taken prisoner, and conveyed to Beauvois, where he departed this life in 1435. The earl *m.* 1st, Constance, dau. of John Cornwall, Lord Fanhope, but by her had no issue; and 2ndly, Maud, dau. of Sir Robert Lovel, by Elizabeth, dau. of Sir Guy Bryen, the younger, Knt., and by her (who *m.* 2ndly, Sir Richard Stafford) had issue,

HUMPHREY, his successor.
Amicia, *m.* to James Butler, Earl of Ormonde and Wiltshire, and *d. s. p., temp.* EDWARD IV.

His lordship was *s.* by his son,

HUMPHREY FITZ-ALAN, as Duke of Touraine, and 14th Earl of Arundel, then but six years old. This nobleman *d.* 1438, when the dukedom of Touraine EXPIRED, but the castle of Arundel reverted to his uncle,

WILLIAM FITZ-ALAN, who thus became 15th Earl of Arundel. Between this nobleman and Thomas Courtenay, Earl of Devon, there arose, in the 23rd HENRY VI., a great dispute in parliament regarding precedency, which being renewed in the parliament held four years afterwards, was then referred to the judges, who refused, however, to give any opinion upon the subject, declaring, "that it was a matter of parliament belonging to the king's highness, and to his lords spiritual and temporal in parliament, by them to be decided." The question at issue was whether this earl should have precedency of the Earl of Devon or not? The Act of 11th HENRY VI., expressing *only* that John, *then* Earl of Arundel, should have the place, precedency, &c., as Earl of Arundel, without mentioning his heirs. Upon which the lords ultimately resolved, "that he should have his place in parliament, and the king's council, as earl, by reason of the castle, lordship, and honour of Arundel, for himself and his heirs for evermore, above the said Earl of Devon, and his heirs, as worshipfully as any of his ancestors Earls of Arundel before that time ever had." The Earl of Arundel, in the 10th EDWARD IV., was made constable of Dover Castle, and warden of the Cinque Ports, being then also justice of all the king's forests south of Trent, a post renewed to him upon the accession of HENRY V. He was also a knight of the Garter. His lordship *m.* the Lady Joane Nevil, dau. of Richard, Earl of Salisbury, by whom he had issue, THOMAS, Lord Maltravers, his successor, William, George, and John, with a dau., Mary. He *d.* in 1488, and was *s.* by his eldest son,

THOMAS FITZ-ALAN, 16th Earl of Arundel, who had been summoned to parliament, in 22nd EDWARD IV., and 1st HENRY, as "Thomas Arundel, of Maltravers, Knt." his father being then alive. His lordship, who was a knight of the Garter, was one of the English nobles sent over to Flanders, 5th HENRY VII., to assist the Emperor MAXIMILIAN against the French. He *m.* Margaret, dau. of Richard Widvile, Earl Rivers, and had issue,

WILLIAM, Lord Maltravers, his successor.
Edward.
Margaret, *m.* to John de la Pole, Earl of Lincoln.
Joane, *m.* to George Nevill, Lord Bergavenny.

The earl *d.* in 1524, and was *s.* by his elder son,

WILLIAM FITZ-ALAN, 17th Earl of Arundel, K. G. This nobleman's signature appears to the letter of remonstrance transmitted to Pope CLEMENT II., in the 22nd HENRY VIII., regarding the king's divorce from Queen Katherine. His lordship *m.* 1st, Anne, sister of Henry, Earl of Northumberland, upon which occasion he had grants from the crown of three manors, co. Somerset, and that of Hunton, in Southamptonshire, to hold by the service of a red rose yearly. By this lady he had issue, HENRY, Lord Maltravers, his successor, and two daus., who both *d. unm.* He *m.* 2ndly, Elizabeth, dau. of Robert Willoughby, Lord Broke, by whom he had two daus., Margaret and Elizabeth, who likewise *d.unm.* In conformity with the policy recommended by CROMWELL to the king upon the confiscation of the church lands, the Earl of

Arundel was obliged to exchange several of his manors for those which had belonged to the religious houses. His lordship *d.* in 1544, and was *s.* by his son,

HENRY FITZ-ALAN, 18th Earl of Arundel, K.G. This nobleman, in the 36th HENRY VIII., was field-marshal of the king's army at the siege of Boulogne, and in two years afterwards was constituted one of the assistants to that monarch's executors. After the fall of the Protector Somerset, *temp.* EDWARD VI., the Earl of Arundel having declined to enter into the views of Dudley, Earl of Warwick, was removed from the council by the intrigues of that nobleman, and fined £12,000 upon the frivolous charge of having removed bolts and locks from Westminster, and given away the king's stuff, in his capacity of lord chamberlain: and the ensuing year he was committed prisoner to the tower. Upon the death of King EDWARD, his lordship zealously espoused the cause of Queen MARY, and was mainly instrumental in her ascending the throne without any effusion of blood; for which and other eminent services, he was made constable of the day at her majesty's coronation, as he was also the day immediately preceding the coronation of Queen ELIZABETH, at which he officiated as lord high steward. His lordship at this period aspired to the hand of the virgin queen, but being disappointed in his hopes he obtained permission to travel, and while abroad served in the wars against the Turks. After his return to England he was upon the commission instituted to inquire into the murder of Henry, Lord Darnley, husband of MARY, Queen of Scots, and subsequently favouring the pretensions of the Duke of Norfolk, to the hand of that beautiful but unfortunate princess, he suffered imprisonment (14th ELIZABETH). His lordship *m.* 1st, Lady Catherine Grey, dau. of Thomas, Marquess of Dorset, by whom he had,

HENRY, Lord Maltravers, who *d.* in the lifetime of his father, *s. p.*
Joanna, *m.* to John, Lord Lumley, by whom she had no surviving issue.
Mary, *m.* to Thomas Howard, Duke of Norfolk, and had issue,

   Philip Howard, who having inherited Arundel Castle, was summoned to parliament, 16 January, 1580, as EARL OF ARUNDEL, and the castle and dignity have since remained in the family of Howard.

The earl *m.* 2ndly, Mary, dau. of Sir John Arundel, of Lanherne, co. Cornwall, and widow of Robert Ratcliffe, Earl of Sussex, but had no issue. His lordship, who with the other high offices already enumerated, was president of the council of Queens MARY and ELIZABETH, *d.* in 1580, when the EARLDOM OF ARUNDEL and the castle passed with his dau., and eventually sole heiress, Lady Mary Fitz-Alan, to her husband, Thomas Howard, Duke of Norfolk, with the BARONY OF MALTRAVERS, which descended to her son, Philip Howard, who was attainted in the 32nd ELIZABETH, when the barony became FORFEITED; it was, however, restored to his son, Thomas Howard, 20th Earl of Arundel, and by act of parliament, 3rd CHARLES I., the Barony of Maltravers, with the Baronies of Fitz-Alan, Clun, and Oswaldestre, were annexed to the title, dignity, and honour of Earl of Arundel, and settled upon Thomas Howard, then Earl of Arundel and Surrey, and his heirs male, &c. Until the passing of this act, FITZ-ALAN was not a parliamentary barony, it was merely feudal. Thus terminated the noble and ancient family of Fitz-Alan, EARLS OF ARUNDEL.

Arms—Az., a lion rampant within a bordure, or.

FITZ-CHARLES—EARL OF PLYMOUTH.

By Letters Patent, dated 29 July, 1675.

Lineage.

CHARLES FITZ-CHARLES, illegitimate son of King CHARLES II., by Catherine, dau. of Thomas Pegg, Esq., of Yeldersley, co. Derby, was elevated to the peerage, 29 July, 1675, as *Baron Dartmouth, Viscount Totness,* and EARL OF PLYMOUTH. His lordship *m.* Lady Bridget Osborne, dau. of Thomas, 1st Duke of Leeds, but *d. s. p.* at Tangier, during the siege of that city by the Moors, in 1680, when all his honours became EXTINCT.

Arms—England, with a baton sinister, vairé, arg and az.

FITZGERALD—BARON FITZGERALD AND VESEY.

By Letters Patent, dated 27 June, 1826.

Lineage.

WILLIAM VESEY, Esq., settled in Ireland, *temp.* ELIZABETH. He *m.* a dau. of — Ker, of Cessford, co. Roxburgh, and had a son,

The REV. THOMAS VESEY, archdeacon of Armagh, who was father of

THE MOST REV. JOHN VESEY, archbishop of Tuam, privy councillor, and LORD JUSTICE OF IRELAND, who *m.* 1st (licence dated 1662) Rebecca Wilson, and by her had (with a dau., Mary, wife of Sir Thomas Staples) a son,

SIR THOMAS VESEY, Bart., bishop of Killaloe, who *m.* Mary, only surviving child and heir of Denny Muschamp, Esq., of Horsley, co. Surrey, and was ancestor of VISCOUNT DE VESCI (*See* BURKE's *Peerage.*)

He *m.* 2ndly, Anne, dau. of Agmondisham Muschamp, and by her had issue,

I. Agmondisham, of Lucan, co. Dublin, *m.* 1st, Charlotte, dau. and heir of William Sarsfield, Earl of Lucan, and by her (whose will bears date 18 March, 1732) had two daus., Anne, wife of Sir John Bingham, Bart., and Henrietta, wife of Cæsar Colclough, Esq., of Duffrey Hall. He *m.* 2ndly, Jane, dau. of Capt. Edward Pottinger, and relict, 1st of John Reynolds, of Killabride, and 2ndly, of Sir Thomas Butler, Bart., and by her (whose will bears date 19 February, 1745), he had issue,

  1 Agmondisham, of Lucan, M.P., accountant-general of Ireland, *m.* Elizabeth, dau. of Sir Thomas Vesey, Bart., and relict of William Handcock, Esq., M.P., of Twyford, co. Westmeath, but by this lady (who was the accomplished Mrs. Vesey, the friend of Dr. Johnson) he had no issue. Mr. Vesey's will bears date 1772, and was proved in 1785.
  2 Edward.   3 Charles, R.N.
  4 George, *m.* 1754, Letitia, dau. of his uncle, the Rev. George Vesey, and had issue,

    George, of Lucan, who *m.* Emily, dau. of the Right Hon. David La Touche, and had an only dau. and heir, Elizabeth, who *m.* in 1818, Sir Nicholas-Conway Colthurst, Bart., and whose 2nd son is the present CHARLES-COLTHURST VESEY, Esq., of Lucan, (*See* BURKE's *Landed Gentry*).

  1 Jane.
  2 Letitia, *m.* to — Meredyth.
  3 Catherine, *m.* to Anthony Jephson, Esq., of Mallow.
  4 Semira.

II. JOHN, of whom presently.
III. William, *m.* Mary Dixon, widow of — Ormsby, Esq. His will bears date 13 March, 1735, and was proved 19 July following.
IV. George, of Hollymount, co. Mayo, *m.* Frances, dau. of Archibald Stewart, Esq., of Ballintoy, co. Antrim, and was great grandfather of SAMUEL VESEY, Esq., of Derrabard House, co. Tyrone, J.P. and D.L. (*See* BURKE's *Landed Gentry*).
V. Muschamp, in holy orders, archdeacon of Leighlin, *m.* Elizabeth, dau. of Matthew Forde, Esq., of Seaforde. His will bears date 9 August, 1761, and was proved 4 February, 1762.
  I. Elizabeth, *m.* 25 February, 1723-4, Richard Dawson, Esq., M.P. for the co. of Monaghan, and was mother of Thomas, Viscount Cremorne.
  II. Leonora, *m.* (licence dated 19 July, 1714), the Rev. Archibald Stewart, of Ballintoy.
  III. Elizabeth, *m.* to — Walker, Esq.
  IV. Catherine, *m.* to the Ven. James Smyth, archdeacon of Meath.
V. Anne, *m.* the Right Hon. Henry Bingham, M.P., and had issue,

  1 John, *m.* 1 June, 1738, Frances, eldest dau. and co-heir of Sir Arthur Shaen, Bart., of Kilmore, co. Roscommon, and had a son,

    Henry, who *m.* Letitia, 2nd dau. of Denis Daly, Esq., of Raford, by Anne de Burgh, his wife, sister of John, 11th Earl of Clanricarde, and was father of John Bingham, 1st Lord Clanmorris (*See* BURKE's *Extant Peerage*).

  2 Henry.
  1 Mary, *m.* (articles dated 5 May, 1729) Joshua Cooper, Esq., of Markree, and was great grandmother of EDWARD-JOSHUA COOPER, Esq., of Markree Castle, co. Sligo (*See* BURKE's *Landed Gentry*).
  2 Anne, *m.* Alderman Francis Leigh, of Drogheda, M.P., and had a dau., Letitia, who *m.* 20 February, 1768, Blayney Balfour, of Townley Hall, co. Louth, from whom descends Blayney Townley Balfour, Esq., of Townley Hall (*See* BURKE's *Landed Gentry*).
  3 Susan, *m.* to Rev. Dr. Forster.
  4 Catherine, *m.* to the Rev. Chamberlain Walker, rector of Rosconnell, Queen's Co., and was mother of Sarah, who

m. Rev. William Hamilton, D.D., J.P., and had issue: William, M.D.; Bingham-Walker, M.A., *d. unm.*; Balfour-Rowley, R.N., *d. unm.*; John-Vesey, rector of Little Chart, Kent; Catherine, *m.* to Capt. Silas Hood, R.N.; Elizabeth, *m.* to Rev. William Johnson, prebendary of Clenore; Sarah, *m.* to Rev. John Southcomb, rector of Rose Ash, Devon, and Vescina, *m.* to John Litton, Esq., of Ardavilling, co. Cork, J.P., M.A.

The 2nd son,
  THE REV. JOHN VESEY, archdeacon of Kilfenora, *m.* Anne, dau. of the Rev. Fielding Shaw, Warden of Galway, and had issue,

    I. Agmondisham, of Newport Pratt, whose will, dated 30 January, 1789, was proved 20 August following.
    II. HENRY, of whom presently.
    III. John, in holy orders, whose will, dated 13 July, 1762, was proved 8 February, 1763.
    I. Elizabeth, *m.* to Richard Martin, Esq., of Dangan, from whom she was divorced.
    II. Lady Fielding Ould.
    III. Mrs. Henry Ellis.

The 2nd son,
  THE REV. HENRY VESEY, Warden of Galway, *m.* Mary, dau. and co-heir of George Gerry, of Galway, alderman, by whom he had one son and two daus, viz.,

    JOHN, his heir.
    Rebecca, *m.* to James Irwin, Esq., and had issue, James-John-Vesey Irwin, who *d. unm.*, and Mary Irwin, wife of Col. Poole-Hickman Vesey.
    CATHERINE, late BARONESS FITZGERALD AND VESCI.

Mr. Vesey's will, dated 21 April, 1767, was proved 24 October, 1774. His only son,
  JOHN VESEY, Esq., of Oranmore, co. Galway, *s.* to the estates of his uncles, John and Agmondisham Vesey; and dying *unm.* in 1779, bequeathed those estates to his two sisters, with an injunction that their heirs male should bear the surname and arms of VESEY. The younger of these ladies,
  CATHERINE VESEY, was elevated to the peerage of Ireland as BARONESS FITZGERALD AND VESEY, 27 June, 1826. She *m.* the Right Hon. James Fitzgerald, one of his majesty's privy council in Ireland, and formerly prime serjeant-at-law there (son of William Fitzgerald, Esq., of Inchicronan, by Eliza his wife, dau. and co-heir of Pierce Lynch, Esq., of Grange), and left issue at her decease, in January, 1832 (Mr. Fitzgerald *d.* 20 January, 1835, aged ninety-three),

  I. WILLIAM, successor to his mother.
  II. HENRY, late peer.
  I. Mary-Geraldine, *m.* 1809. Sir Ross Manon, Bart., who *d.* 1835; she *d.* March, 1859, leaving issue.
  II. Letitia, *m.* in 1814, John-Leslie Foster, Esq., M.P. for the University of Dublin, and afterwards one of the barons of the Exchequer in Ireland, and had issue, William-Vesey-Leslie Foster, Esq., John-Fitzgerald-Leslie Foster, Esq., James-Leslie Foster, Esq., and Letitia-Leslie Foster. The Hon. Mrs. Leslie Foster, assumed, by royal license, 7 May, 1860, the surnames and arms of VESEY and FITZGERALD, for herself and her issue.
  III. Catherine-Geraldine.

Her ladyship was *s.* by her eldest son,
  WILLIAM, 1st baron, who assumed, 13 February, 1815, the additional surname of VESEY. His lordship, who was a privy councillor, and successively chancellor of the Irish Exchequer, paymaster-general of the forces, president of the Board of Trade, and president of the Board of Control, was made a peer of the United Kingdom, by patent, in 1835, as *Baron Fitzgerald, of Desmond and Clan Gibbon, co. Cork.* He was lord-lieut. of the co. Clare, and *d. unm.*, 11 May, 1843, when the British peerage expired, and the Irish barony devolved on his next brother,
  HENRY VESEY-FITZGERALD, LL.D., Baron Fitzgerald and Vesey, dean of Kilmore, vicar of Ballintemple, and rector of Castleraghan; *m.* 7 September, 1825, Elizabeth, dau. of the late Standish O'Grady, Esq., of Elton, and by her (who *d.* 1834) had five daus. and co-heiresses,

    I. Mabella-Geraldine, *m.* 23 April, 1857, to the Rev. Beauchamp-W. Stannus, incumbent of Woodbury-Salterton, Devon, 2nd son of the Very Rev. the Dean of Ross.
    II. Letitia.
    III. Elizabeth, *d.* 3 November, 1856.
    IV. Catherine-Geraldine, *m.* 16 October, 1856, to Walter-Trevor Stannus, Esq., 4th son of the Very Rev. the Dean of Ross.
    V. Georgiana.

Lord Fitzgerald and Vesey *d.* 30 March, 1860, and, as he left no male issue, the title became EXTINCT.

Arms—Quarterly: 1st and 4th, arg., a saltier, gu., for FITZGERALD; 2nd and 3rd, or, on a cross, sa., a patriarchal cross of the field, for VESEY.

FITZGERALD—BARON LECALE.

By Patent, dated 1800.

Lineage.

LORD CHARLES-JAMES FITZGERALD, 2nd son of James, 1st Duke of Leinster, was created BARON LECALE in the peerage of Ireland, in 1800. His lordship *m.* Julia, widow of Thomas Carton, Esq., and *d. s. p.* in 1810, when the title became EXTINCT.

Arms—Arg., a saltier, gu.

FITZGERALD—EARLS OF DESMOND.

By Patent, dated 22 August, 1329.

Lineage.

WALTER FITZOTHO, constable of Windsor and keeper of the forests of Berkshire, *m.* Gladys, dau. of Rhiwallon ap Cynvyn, Prince of North Wales, and had issue,

  I. GERALD FITZWALTER, of whom presently.
  II. William de Windsor, Baron of Estaines.
  III. Robert de Windsor, ancestor of the EARLS OF PLYMOUTH.

The eldest son,

GERALD FITZWALTER, constable of Pembroke, lieutenant to Arnolph de Montgomery, *m.* Nesta, dau. of Rhys ap Tudor Mawr, Prince of South Wales, and had issue,

  I. MAURICE FITZGERALD, of whom presently.
  II. David FitzGerald, archdeacon of Cardigan, and bishop of St. David's from 1147 to 1176.
  III. William FitzGerald, ancestor of FitzMaurice, Marquess of Lansdowne, the Lord Gerald of Ince, and the great houses of Carew and Grace,
    I. Anghared, *m.* to Wm. de Barry, ancestor of the Earls of Barrymore, &c.

The eldest son,

MAURICE FITZGERALD, who was Baron of Naas and Wicklow by the gift of Strongbow, accompanied his half brother Robert FitzStephen to Ireland. He had half a cantred in Offaly, and dying at Waterford about the calends of December, was buried in the Grey Friars at Waterford. By his wife Alice, dau. of Arnolph de Montgomery (by his wife Lafracoth, dau. of Murrough O'Brien, King of Munster) he had issue,

  I. William FitzMaurice, Baron of Naas, ancestor of the Barons of Naas.
  II. Gerald FitzMaurice, Lord of Offaly, ancestor of the EARLS of KILDARE, and DUKES of LEINSTER.
  III. THOMAS FITZMAURICE, of whom presently.
  IV. Alexander FitzMaurice, held the lands of Compton in England, from William de Windsor, and with his brother Gerald, the castle and lands of Wicklow, of which they were deprived by William FitzAdelm, lord deputy, who gave them in recompense the castle of Ferns, co. Wexford.
  V. Walter FitzMaurice.
  VI. Redmond FitzMaurice.
  VII. Hugh FitzMaurice.
  I. Nesta, *m.* Hervey de Monte Marisco, constable of Ireland, who *d. s. p.*

The 3rd son,

THOMAS FITZMAURICE, Lord of O'Connelloe, co. Limerick, *m.* Elinor, dau. of Jordan de Marisco, and sister of Hervey, and Geoffrey de Marisco, lord justice of Ireland, and *d.* 1213, leaving a son,

JOHN FITZTHOMAS, called "John of Callan," Lord of O'Connelloe and of Decies, Desmond, and Dungarvan, granted to him by Edward, Prince of Wales, by charter dated at Bermundescye, 7 November, 44th HENRY III., (1259). He was killed at the battle of Callan, and was buried in the north part of the monastery of Tralee, of which he was the founder. He *m.* Margery, dau. and co-heir of Thomas FitzAnthony, Lord of Decies and Desmond, seneschal of Leinster, and BAILIFF of the co. of Kerry, by whom he had issue,

  I. MAURICE FITZJOHN.
  II. John.
  I. Olyvia, *m.* Elias Ketyng.

he elder son,

MAURICE FITZJOHN was killed at Callan with his father and buried with him. By his wife Matilda, dau. of the Lord Barry of Olethan, he left issue,

204

  I. THOMAS FITZMAURICE, of whom presently.
  II. Sir Richard FitzMaurice, ancestor of the Seneschal of Imokilly.

The elder,

THOMAS FITZMAURICE, called "Thomas a Nappagh," or "Thomas Simiacus," who was lord justice, was summoned to parliament, 1295, and *d.* 1296, leaving by his wife Margaret, dau. of John, Lord Barry (who *re-m.* in 1300, Reginald de Rosel), three sons and a dau.,

  I. Thomas Fitz-Thomas, *b.* 1290, *d.* in or before 1309.
  II. MAURICE FITZTHOMAS, of whom presently.
  III. Sir John FitzThomas, called "Sir John of Athassell," who was buried there 1319, or, according to Clyn, 1324; and through his son Thomas FitzJohn was ancestor of "MacThomas Geraldyn."
  I. Joan, *m.* John (Kittogh) Lord Barry.

The 2nd son,

MAURICE FITZTHOMAS, called Maurice the Great, lord justice of Ireland, who had livery of Decies and Desmond in 1312, and of Kerry in 1315, was created EARL OF DESMOND, 22 August, 1329, *d.* in Dublin, 25 January, 1355, and was buried at Tralee. He *m.* 1st, at Grenecastel, 16 August, 1312, Margaret, 5th dau. of Richard, "the Red Earl of Ulster," and by her (who *d.* at Dublin, 1331,) had issue,

MAURICE FITZMAURICE, 2nd earl.

He *m.* 2ndly, Margaret, dau. of Conor O'Brien, of Thomond, by whom he had a dau. *m.* to James Barry Roe, Lord of Ibawne; and 3rdly Aveline, dau. of Nicholas FitzMaurice, Lord of Lixnaw, by whom he had issue,

NICHOLAS FITZMAURICE, 3rd earl.
GERALD FITZMAURICE, 4th earl.

The eldest son,

MAURICE FITZMAURICE, 2nd Earl of Desmond, *m.* Beatrix, dau. of Ralph, 1st Earl of Stafford, by whom (who *m.* 2ndly, in 1368, Thomas, Lord Ros, of Hamlake) he had issue, a dau. and sole heir, Joan, who *m.* Donal Oge MacCarthy More, who *d.* in 1358, and was buried in Tralee Abbey. He was *s.* by his half brother,

NICHOLAS FITZMAURICE, 3rd Earl of Desmond, who was an idiot, and dying *s. p.* about 1367, was *s.* by his brother,

GERALD FITZMAURICE, 4th Earl of Desmond, called "Gerald the poet," who disappeared in 1398. He *m.* in 1359, Eleanor, dau. of James, 2nd Earl of Ormonde, and by her (to whom her father gave the barony of Inchiquin in Imokilly) had issue three sons and two daus., viz.,

  I. JOHN FITZGERALD, of whom presently.
  II. Maurice FitzGerald, *d. s. p.* 1410.
  III. JAMES FITZGERALD, who *s.* as 7th earl.
  I. Joan, *m.* Maurice FitzJohn, Lord of Kerry.
  II. Catherine, *m.* John FitzThomas, ancestor of MacThomas of Knocknione.

The eldest son,

JOHN FITZGERALD, 5th Earl of Desmond, *m.* Joan, dau. of Roche, Lord Fermoy, was drowned in 1399, at Ardfinnan, on the Suir, and was buried at Youghal. His only son was,

THOMAS FITZJOHN, 6th Earl of Desmond. This unfortunate nobleman was deprived of his earldom, in 1418, and *d.* in exile, at Rouen, 10 August, 1420. His misfortunes arose from his imprudent marriage with Catherine, dau. of William MacCormac of Abbeyfeale, one of his own dependents. This alliance was looked upon by his clan as so great a degradation that he was at once deprived of his earldom, and forced to fly. It is said that, by his wife, he left two sons, Maurice, ancestor of the FitzGeralds of Adare and Broghill, and John Claragh, who *d.* 1452. He was *s.* by his uncle.

JAMES FITZGERALD, 7th Earl of Desmond, called "James the Usurper," who, however, was not acknowledged as earl till 1422, but in 1420, was, by James, Earl of Ormonde, made Seneschal of Imokilly, Inchiquin, and the town of Youghal. He *m.* Mary, dau. of Ulick or William FitzRickard Burke (Mac William Eighter), and had issue,

  I. THOMAS FITZJAMES, 8th earl.
  II. Sir Gerald More FitzGerald, ancestor of the FITZGERALDS of Dromana, co. Waterford, Lords of Decies. (See under VILLIERS.)
  I. Honor, *m.* Thomas FitzPatrick, Lord of Kerry, called "Thomas the Stammerer."
  II. Joan, *m.* Thomas FitzJohn, 7th Earl of Kildare, founder of the monastery of Adare.

He *d.* in 1462, and was buried at Youghal. His elder son,

THOMAS FITZJAMES, 8th Earl of Desmond, lord justice, called "Thomas of Drogheda," was beheaded there 15 February, 1467, and buried at St. Peter's. He *m.* Elizabeth, dau. of John or William Barry, Viscount Buttevant, by whom he had issue,

  I. JAMES FITZTHOMAS, 9th earl.
  II. MAURICE FITZTHOMAS, 10th earl.
  III. SIR THOMAS FITZTHOMAS, 12th earl

IV. Sir JOHN FITZTHOMAS, father of the 14th earl.

V. Sir Gerald FitzThomas, of Macollop in Coshbride, and the Sheane, who by his wife, grand-dau. of Owen MacTeige MacCarthy Muskery, had issue four sons,

James Fitzgerald, of Macollop, who had issue, 1 Maurice FitzJames, of Macollop, (who had issue Maurice, living in 1615; James, whose son, Gerald, d. in France, 1655; and John, living 1615); 2 Gerald, had issue, James d. s. p. 1663, and Garret Oge ; 3 Thomas.

Maurice FitzGerald of the Shaen, had issue two sons and a dau., Thomas FitzMaurice, who was attainted and had a son, John Grany, who was "drowned in rebellion ;" Gerald FitzMaurice who was also attainted; and Ellis, m. to James, Lord Barry.

Thomas FitzGerald, of Kilmacow, m. Lady Honora O'Brien, dau. of the Earl of Thomond, by whom he had issue,

Thomas Oge, attainted.

John FitzGerald, of Kilmacow, m. Margaret, dau. of Garret Nugent, of Cloncoskeran, co. Waterford, by Hannah, dau. of O'Brien Conagh, and had issue,

Thomas FitzGerald, who m. Eleanor, dau. of Edmond Supple, of Aghadoe, and had a son, Gerald, who by his wife, Ellen, dau. of Richard Condon, Lord of Condon, had two sons, James, living 1687, who m. Miss Brien, of Comeragh (he was the last of the male line of Desmond, and commonly called Earl of Desmond, and d. in a state of great poverty, leaving two daus.;) and Gerald.

John FitzGerald, of Strancally, who had a son, James FitzJohn, attainted with his sons James, Gerald, John, Thomas, and Maurice.

I. Catherine, m. 1450, Finin MacCarthy Reagh.

II. Ellen, m. 1st, Thomas Butler of Caher, and 2ndly, Turlogh Mac I.-Brien Ara, of Duharra, bishop of Killaloe

The eldest son,

JAMES FITZTHOMAS, 9th Earl of Desmond, m. Margaret, dau. of Teige O'Brien, of Thomond, by whom he had a dau. and heir, Joan, who m. Maurice, "the mad" Lord Fermoy. The Earl was "feloniously slain" by John Murtagh, one of his servants, at Rathkeale, by "the stroke of a bullet," 7 December, 1487, and was buried at Youghal. He was s. by his brother,

MAURICE FITZTHOMAS, 10th Earl of Desmond, called "Maurice Baccagt," "Maurice of the Chariot," or "Maurice Bellicosus." He m. 1st, Ellen, dau. of Maurice Roche, Lord Fermoy, by whom he had issue,

I. Thomas FitzMaurice, who d. v. p., leaving a dau. and heir, m. to H. Butler of Polestown.

II. JAMES FITEMAURICE, 11th earl.

I. Joan, m. to Cormac Oge MacCarthy.

II. Ellis, m. to Conor O'Brien, of Thomond.

He m. 2ndly, Honor, dau. of the White Knight, and dying 1520, was buried at Tralee. He was s. by his only surviving son, JAMES FITZMAURICE, 11th Earl of Desmond, who m. Amy, dau. of Turlogh Mac I.-Brien Ara, bishop of Killaloe, and had issue a dau. and heiress, Joan, who m. 1st, James-FitzPiers, 9th Earl of Ormonde, and 2ndly, Sir Francis Bryan, lord justice, who d. s. p. 2 February, 1549; and 3rdly, Gerald FitzJames, 16th Earl of Desmond, and d. 1564, and was buried at Askeaton. The earl d. at Dingle 18 June, 1529, and was buried at Tralee. He was s. by his uncle,

SIR THOMAS FITZTHOMAS, 12th Earl of Desmond, b. 1454, called "Sir Thomas the Bald," and "Thomas the Victorious," m. 1st, Celia, dau. of Cormac Oge Laider MacCarthy Muskery, of Blarney, by whom he had a son,

MAURICE FITZTHOMAS, who d. v. p. 1529 within six months after the earldom fell to his father, and was buried at Youghal, leaving by his wife Joan, dau. of John-FitzGarret FitzGibbon, the White Knight, with a dau. Ellen, 2nd wife of Thomas, 1st Lord Cahir, an only son,

JAMES FITZMAURICE, 13th earl.

He m. 2ndly, Catherine, dau. of John, Lord of Decies, who survived him by seventy years, dying in 1604, at the age of one hundred and forty. This was the famous "Old Countess of Desmond," whose only dau. Catherine, m. Philip Barry Oge. Sir Thomas d. in Rathkeale, 1534, and was buried at Youghal. He was s. by his grandson,

JAMES FITZMAURICE, 13th Earl of Desmond, called "the Court Page," having been hostage for his grandfather at the court of Windsor. He m. Mary, dau. of his grand uncle, Cormac Oge MacCarthy which laig d. 1548, having m. 2ndly, Donal O'Sullivan More. The unfortunate court page did not long enjoy his honours, for he was murdered at Leacan Sgail in Kerry, by his cousin Maurice A. Totan, 19 March, 1540. As he d. s. p. the title reverted to the line of his grand uncle,

SIR JOHN FITZTHOMAS, (styled Earl of Desmond, by his partizans, who denied the right of the 13th Earl to inherit). He was accused of having instigated the murder of his brother James, the 9th earl in 1487. He m. More, dau. of Donogh Dubh O'Brien, of Carrigogonnell, Lord of Poble O'Brien, by whom he had issue,

I. Thomas FitzJohn, who was slain v. p. s. p. m. at Kilmallock by "the stroke of a bullet." By his 1st wife, Ellisdau. of Richard, Lord Poer, he had two daus. one m. FitzGerald of Caherass, the other to Walter Butler, of Polestown. By his 2nd wife, Slany ny Brien, he left a dau. Catherine, m. to Garret MacMorris of Thomastown.

II. SIR JAMES FITZJOHN, 14th earl.

III. Maurice FitzJohn, Lord of Kerricurrihy called "Maurice A Totan," or, "Maurice Duff Macan Early." He m. Sile, dau of Diarmid O'Mulrian, of Sulloghode, co. Tipperary, and widow of Mac I. Bryen Ara, and was killed in 1565, at the age of eighty, by the horsemen of his son-in-law, Sir Diarmid MacTeige MacCarthy Muskery, leaving issue,

1 James FitzMaurice, called "James Geraldine," the Pope's generalissimo, and by English writers, "the arch traitor." He m. Catherine, dau. of William Bourke, chief of his sept, by whom he had issue,—Fitz James, a fugitive in Spain, in 1615, said to have d. s. p., and Honor, who m. 1st, John FitzEdmund Fitz Garret, seneschal of Imokilly; and 2ndly, Sir Edmund FitzJohn. This James FitzMaurice killed his cousin Tibbot Bourk, in 1579, and in the same year was "killed in [rebellion," by the sons of Sir William Bourk, Lord of Castleconnell, and was hung in chains in the market place of Kilmallock

1 Eleanor, m. to Maurice, Lord Roche, of Fermoy, or to Maurice, Viscount Buttevant.

2 Ellen, m. to Sir Diarmid MacTeige MacCarthy Muskery

3 Ellis, m. O'Mahen Carbery, of Kilnalmeaky.

4 Joan, m. to Sir Donogh MacCarthy Reagh.

IV. Gerald FitzJohn, d. s. p.

V. John FitzJohn, of Ballyteige called "John Oge, of Desmond," m Ellen, dau. of Lord Roche, and had with many other children,

Maurice, a fugitive in Spain in 1600, at that time married and having issue.

James, killed in rebellion in 1580.

John Oge, m. Eleanor, dau. of
Thomas, Lord Cahir, d. s. p. } killed in rebellion.
Gerald,
Thomas,

Ellis, m. 1st. to the White Knight; 2ndly, to Cormac Oge MacDiarmid of Muskery, 3rdly, to MacDonogh, Lord of Duhallow ; 4thly, to O'Sullivan More, of Irrigh ; and 5thly to O'Callaghan. Lord of Pobble O'Callaghan.

I. Eleanor, m. 1st, Thomas Tobin, of Cumshinagh and Killaghy; 2ndly, John Oge FitzJohn FitzGibbon, the White Knight, who was attainted in 1571.

II. A dau. m. Sir William Bourke, 1st Lord Castleconnell.

III. Anne, m MacCarthy Reagh.

He d. about Christmas in 1536, and was s. by his 2nd but elder and surviving son,

SIR JAMES FITZJOHN, 14th Earl of Desmond, Lord High Treasurer of Ireland, by English writers called "the Traitor Earl." He m. 1st, his cousin Joan, dau. of "Maurice the Mad," Lord Fermoy, and by her (whom he repudiated on account of consanguinity) he had a son,

SIR THOMAS FITZJAMES, Lord of Killnataloon and Castle more, by his father's will, called "Sir Thomas Ruagh." He d. 18 January, 1595, leaving by his wife, dau. of David Lord Roche,

JAMES FITZTHOMAS, 17th earl.

John FitzThomas, called Count of Desmond, in Spain, 1615, who d. at Barcelona, leaving by his wife, a dau. of Richard Comerford, of Dunganmow, co. Kilkenny, one son, Gerald FitzJohn, Count of Desmond, who d. s. p. in Germany, in 1632.

Gerald FitzThomas, a count in Spain, d. s. p.

Margaret, m. Donal MacCarthy Reagh.

A dau., m. Donogh, son of Sir Owen MacCarthy Reagh.

The earl m. 2ndly, More, dau. of Sir Molrony MacShane O'Carroll, Lord of Ely O'Carroll, called "Molrony the Bearded," and by her (who d. 1548) he had issue,

I. GERALD FITZJAMES, 15th earl.

II. Sir John Fitz-James, called Sir John Desmond, of Moygeely, co. Cork, knighted 1567, killed in rebellion, August, 1581, in the woods near Castlelyon, by Captains Zouche and Dowdall, and had his head cut off and sent to Dublin, and his body hung by the heels at the north gate of Cork. By his wife Ellen, dau. of Teige MacCormac MacDiarmid MacCarthy Muskery he had issue a dau. Ellen, m. to Donald MacCarthy.

III. Maurice FitzJames, d. s. p.

I. Honor, m. Donal MacCarthy More, Earl of Clancare.

II. Margaret, m. to Thomas FitzEdmond FitzMaurice, Lord of Kerry.

III. Ellis, m. to John More, Lord Poer of Curraghmore.

IV. Joan, m. 1st, John, Lord Barry ; 2ndly, Sir Donal O'Brien, 2nd, son of Donogh, Earl of Thomond, and 3rdly, Sir Piers Butler, of Caher.

V. Ellis, m. James, Viscount Buttevant.

The earl m. 3rdly, Catherine, dau. of Piers, 8th Earl of Ormonde, and widow of Richard, Lord Poer, and by her (who d. 17 March, 1552-3, at Askeaton) had no issue. He m. 4thly, Eleanor, dau. of Donal MacCarthy More, and sister of Donal Earl of Clancare, by whom (who d. his widow in 1560), he had issue,

1. Sir James FitzJames, called "Sir James Sussex," who was christened, 26 June, 1558, was taken prisoner in rebellion, August, 1580, by Sir Cormac MacTeige MacCarthy Muskery, and beheaded, quartered, and hung in chains, at Cork in the same year. He had no issue by his wife Honor, dau. of Sir Owen MacCarthy Reagh.

   i. Eleanor, m. 1st, Sir Edmund Butler, of Clogrennane, and 2ndly, Brian O'Rorke.

The earl d. at Askeaton, 14 October, 1558, and was buried 1 November following. He was s. by his eldest son, by his 2nd marriage,

GERALD FITZ-JAMES, 15th Earl of Desmond, called by English writers, "The Rebel Earl," and "ingens rebellibus exemplar." He was attainted 15 November, 1582, and killed at Glanaginty, under Slieve Loghra, 11 November, 1583, by Daniel Kelly, who got a grant in 1585, " in consideration of his having slain the traitor Desmond and his very good service done therein." He was buried in the chapel of Killanamannagh, having had by his 1st wife Joan, dau. and sole heir of James Fitz-Maurice, 11th earl, no issue; but by his 2nd wife, Eleanor, dau. of Edmond, Lord Dunboyne (who re-m. Sir Donogh O'Conor, Sligo, and d. 1656), he had issue,

   I. JAMES FITZ-GERALD, 16th earl.
   II. Eleanor.
     1. Margaret, m. to Diarmid O'Conor, of Connaught.
     II. Joan, m. Diarmid O'Sullivan Bere, who d. s. p. 25 November, 1619.
   III. Catherine, m. 1st, Maurice, Lord Roch, who d. s. p.; and 2ndly, Sir Donal O'Brien, of Carrigichouly, brother of Donogh, Earl of Thomond, and ancestor to the Viscount Clare. He was living 1615.
   IV. Ellen, m. 1st, Sir Donogh O'Conor, Sligo; and 2ndly, Sir Robert Cressy; and 3rdly, Edmond, Lord Dunboyne. She d. 1660, and was buried in Cong Abbey.
   V. Ellis, m. Valentine Browne, of Ross, in Kerry.

The eldest son,
JAMES FITZ-GERALD, 16th Earl of Desmond, called " The Queen's Earl," was restored 1 October, 1600, and d. unm a prisoner in the Tower of London, 1601. He was s. by his 1st cousin,

JAMES FITZ-THOMAS, 17th Earl of Desmond, called "The Sugan Earl," or "Earl of Straw," who was attainted 10 March, 1600-1, and taken prisoner by the White Knight and Diarmid O'Conor, 29 May, 1601. He d. s. p., in the Tower of London, 1608, having had two or three wives : 1st, a dau. of Theobald, Lord Caher; 2ndly, a dau. of John Lord Poer; and 3rdly, Ellen, dau. of Maurice Fitz-Gibbon, the White Knight. With him disappeared from Ireland the great house of Desmond. Their vast estates had been parcelled out among "undertakers" from England, and those estates now form the possessions of a great portion of the existing landed proprietors of the counties of Cork and Kerry. The Geraldine Earls of Desmond suffered perhaps more than any other great race in Ireland the severest reverses of fortune. (See BURKE's Vicissitudes of Families.)

Arms—Erm., a saltier, gu.

FITZGIBBON — BARON FITZGIBBON, OF LOWER CONNELLO, CO. LIMERICK, LORD FITZGIBBON, OF SIDBURY, CO. DEVON, AND EARL OF CLARE

Irish Barony, by Letters Patent, dated 16 June, 1789.
Earldom, by Letters Patent, dated 12 June, 1795.
British Barony, by Letters Patent, dated 24 September, 1799.

Lineage.

JOHN FITZGIBBON, Esq., of Mount Shannon, co. Limerick, barrister-at-law, M.P., m. Isabella, dau. of John Grove, Esq., of Ballyhimmock, co. Cork, and had issue,

   JOHN, his successor.
   Isabella, m. to James-St.-John Jefferyes, Esq., of Blarney Castle.
   Elizabeth, m. in 1763, to the Hon. and Most Rev. William Beresford, archbishop of Tuam.
   Eleanor, m. to Dominick Trant, Esq., of Dunkettle, co Cork.

Mr. Fitzgibbon d. 11 April, 1780, and was s. by his son,
   The RIGHT HON. JOHN FITZGIBBON, barrister-at-law, b. 1748, who was appointed attorney-general of Ireland in 1784, and constituted LORD CHANCELLOR of that kingdom in 1789, when he was raised to the peerage 16 June, 1789, as *Baron Fitzgibbon of Lower Connello*. His lordship was created, 6 Decem-

ber, 1793, *Viscount Fitzgibbon, of Limerick*, and 12 June, 1795, EARL OF CLARE. He was enrolled amongst the British peers, in September, 1799, as *Lord Fitzgibbon of Sidbury, co. Devon*. He m. 1 July, 1786, Anne, eldest dau. of Richard Chapel Whaley, Esq., of Whaley Abbey, and had issue, I. JOHN, his successor; II. RICHARD-HOBART, last earl; I. Isabella-Mary-Anne, b. 20 January, 1795. His lordship d. 28 January, 1802; the countess, in January, 1844. His elder son,

JOHN, 2nd earl, K.P. and G.C.H., b. 10 June, 1792, lord-lieutenant and custos rotulorum of the co. Limerick; m. 14 April, 1826, Elizabeth Julia Georgiana, dau. of Peter, 1st Lord Gwydyr ; but d. s. p. 18 August, 1851, when he was s. by his brother,

RICHARD HOBART FITZGIBBON, 3rd Earl of Clare, lord-lieut. of the co. and city of Limerick; b. 2 October, 1793; m. in 1325, Diana, eldest dau. of the late Charles Bridges Woodcock, Esq., of Brentford Butts, co. Middlesex (the lady's marriage with Maurice-Crosbie Moore. Esq., had been previously dissolved by parliament), and had issue,

   I. JOHN CHARLES-HENRY, *Viscount Fitzgibbon*, an officer 8th hussars, b. 2 May, 1829; killed at Balaklava.
   I. FLORENCE, m. 16 August, 1847, to JOHN LORD WODEHOUSE, now Lord Lieutenant of Ireland (see BURKE's *Extant Peerage*).
   II. Louisa Isabella Georgina, m. 22 May, 1817, to the Hon. Gerald-Normanby Dillon.
   III. Eleanor Sophia Diana, m. 24 April, 1856, to Francis, 2nd son of Gen. the Hon. Henry Cavendish.

His lordship d. 10 January, 1864, when the title became EXTINCT.

Arms—Erm., a saltier, gu.; on a chief, arg., three annulets, of the 2nd.

FITZ-HERBERT—BARON ST. HELENS.
(See ADDENDA.)

FITZ-HERBERT — BARON FITZ-HERBERT,
By Writ of Summons, dated 8 June, 1294.

Lineage.

In the 5th year of King STEPHEN,
HERBERT FITZ-HERBERT, then lord chamberlain to that monarch, gave £333 in silver, for livery of his father's lands. This Herbert m. 1st, — the dau. and co-heiress of Robert Corbet, Lord of Alcester, co. Warwick, who had been some time concubine to King HENRY I. He m. 2ndly, Lucy, 3rd dau. and co-heir of Milo, Earl of Hereford, and by her had three sons, Reginald, who d. s. p.; PETER, his successor; and Matthew, sheriff of Sussex, 12th JOHN. The 2nd son,

PETER FITZ-HERBERT, who, being very obsequious to King JOHN, was reputed one of that prince's evil counsellors. In 1214, he was constituted governor of Pykering Castle, co. York, and sheriff of the shire : but afterwards falling off in his allegiance, his lands at Alcester were seized by the crown, and given to William de Camvill. Returning, however, to his duty upon the accession of HENRY III., those lands were restored to him. He m. 1st, Alice, dau. of Robert Fitz-Roger, a great baron in Northumberland, but by her had no issue; and 2ndly, the 3rd dau. and co-heir of William de Braose, Baron of Brecknock, and d. 1235, leaving a son,

HERBERT FITZ-PETER, who, in the 26th HENRY III., had a military summons to attend the king into France. He d. soon after, however (anno 1247), and, leaving no issue, was s. by his brother,

REGINALD FITZ-HERBERT. This feudal lord had summons to march against the Welsh in the 42nd HENRY III., and in two years afterwards received orders, as one of the barons marchers, to reside in those parts. In the 45th of the same reign, he was made sheriff of Hampshire, and governor of the Castle of Winchester; and in the 48th, he was one of those barons who undertook for the king's performance of what the king of France should determine regarding the ordinances of Oxford. He m. Joane, dau. of William de Fortibus, Lord of Chewton, co. Somerset, and dying in 1285, was s. by his son,

JOHN FITZ-REGINALD, who had summons to parliament, as a baron, 8 June, 1294, and from that period to 26 January, 1297. He was afterwards summoned from 29 December, 1299, to 26 August, 1307; but his descendants, who all bore the surname of FITZ-HERBERT, were never esteemed barons, nor had any of them summons to parliament as such. From PETER, a brother of this John, Lord Fitz-Reginald, the Fitz-Herberts, EARLS OF PEMBROKE, are said to descend.

Arms—Arg., a chief vair, or, and gu. Over all a bend, az.

FITZ-HUGH—BARONS FITZ-HUGH.

By Writ of Summons, 2nd EDWARD I.

Lineage.

Although the surname of FITZ-HUGH was not appropriated to this family before the time of EDWARD III., it had enjoyed consideration from the period of the Conquest, when its ancestor,

BARDOLPH, was Lord of Ravenswath, with divers other manors, in Richmondshire. This Bardolph assumed in his old age the habit of a monk, in the Abbey of St. Mary, at York, to which he gave the churches of Patrick Brompton and Ravenswath, in pure alms. He was *s.* by his son and heir,

AKARIS FITZ-BARDOLPH, who in the 5th of STEPHEN, founded the Abbey of Fors, co. York, then called the Abbey of Charity; and dying in 1161, was *s.* by his elder son,

HERVEY FITZ-AKARIS, who being a noble and good knight, and much esteemed in his country, gave consent that Conan, then Earl of Richmond and Brittany, should translate the Abbey of Charity into the fields at East Wilton, and there place it on the verge of the river Jore, from which it was thenceforward called JOREVAULX. This Hervey *d. circa* 1182, and was *s.* by his son,

HENRY FITZ-HERVEY, who *m.* Alice, dau of Randolph Fitz-Walter (ancestor of the Barons of Greystoke), by whom he acquired considerable estates in the north. He *d.* in 1201, and was *s.* by his son,

RANDOLPH FITZ-HENRY. This feudal lord *m.* Alice, dau. and heiress of Adam de Staveley, Lord of Staveley, by Alice, dau. of William de Percy, of Riddel, and dying in 1262, was *s.* by his elder son,

HENRY FITZ-RANDOLPH, who *d.* 1262, and was *s.* by his son,

RANDOLPH FITZ-HENRY. This feudal baron dying *s. p.*, was *s.* by his brother,

HUGH FITZ-HENRY, summoned to parliament 2nd EDWARD I.; also 29th EDWARD I., who *d.* in 1304, and was *s.* by his son,

HENRY FITZ-HUGH, from whom his descendants ever afterwards adopted the surname of Fitz-Hugh. This Henry was engaged in the Scottish wars from the 3rd to the 8th of EDWARD II., the next year he was constituted, owing to the minority of the Earl of Warwick (whose inheritance it was), governor of Barnard Castle, in the bishopric of Durham; and being again employed in Scotland, he was summoned to parliament as a baron from 15 May, 1321, to 15 November, 1351. In 1327, his lordship acquitted Sir Henry Vavasor, Knt., of a debt of 500 marks, by special instrument under his seal, upon condition that Henry Vavasor, Sir Henry's son, should take to wife Annabil Fitz-Hugh, his dau. In the 7th, 8th, and 9th EDWARD III., Lord Fitz-Hugh was again in arms upon the Scottish soil. His lordship *m.* Eve, dau. of Sir John Bulmer, Knt., and had, besides the dau. already mentioned, a son,

HENRY, who *d. v. p.*, leaving issue by his wife, Joane, dau. of Sir Richard Fourneys, and sister and heiress of William Fourneys,

    Hugh, *m.* Isabel, dau. of Ralph, Lord Nevill, and *d. s. p.*
    HENRY, who *s.* his grandfather.

Lord Fitz-Hugh *d.* in 1356, and was *s.* by his grandson,

HENRY FITZ-HUGH, 3rd baron, summoned to parliament from 4 August, 1377, to 8 August, 1385. This lordship was engaged in the French wars of King EDWARD III., almost uninterruptedly from the 33rd to the 43rd of that gallant monarch's reign. He *m.* Joane, dau. of Henry, Lord Scrope, of Masham, and had issue,

    John, slain in the battle of Otterbourne.
    HENRY, successor to his father.

His lordship *d.* in 1386, and was *s.* by his only surviving son,

HENRY FITZ-HUGH, 4th baron, summoned to parliament from 17 December, 1387, to 1 September, 1423. This nobleman attained great eminence in the reigns of HENRY IV. and HENRY V. In the beginning of the former we find his lordship included in a commission to negotiate a truce with Scotland, and afterwards to accomplish a league of amity between the two crowns (of England and Scotland). In the 8th HENRY IV., he was accredited upon an important mission to Denmark, and in five years afterwards he was again a commissioner upon the affairs of Scotland. On the coronation of King HENRY V. Lord Fitz-Hugh was appointed constable of England for that solemnity, and the next year he obtained a grant from the crown of £100 per annum. He was afterwards lord chamberlain of the king's household, and assisted at the council of Constance. For which, and his other eminent services, he had a grant of

all the lands which had belonged to the attainted Henry, Lord Scrope, of Masham, lying in Richmondshire, to hold during the term that those lands should continue in the king's hands and upon the surrender of that grant in the same year, he had another grant for life of the manors of Masham, Clifton, Burton-Constable, and ten others, likewise part of the possessions of the aforesaid Lord Scrope. From the 5th to the 9th HENRY V. his lordship was uninterruptedly engaged in the French wars, during which period he was at the siege of Roan with the Duke of Exeter.

It is further reported of Lord Fitz-Hugh, that he travelled more than once to Jerusalem, and beyond that celebrated city, to Grand Cairo, where the souldan had his residence, and that on his return he fought with the Saracens and Turks. It is also stated by that the help of the knights of Rhodes, he built a castle there, called St. Peter's Castle. His lordship *m.* Elizabeth, dau. and heir of Sir Robert Grey, Knt., son of John, Lord Grey, of Rotherfield, by Avice, sister and co-heir of Robert, Lord Marmion, by whom he had, with other issue,

    I. Henry, drowned.   II. John, *d.* young
    III. WILLIAM, his successor.
    IV. Geffery.
    V. Robert, in holy orders, bishop of London.
    VI. Ralph, *d.* in France.   VII. Herbert.
    VIII. Richard. *d. young.*
    I. Joane, *m.* to Sir Robert Willoughby, Lord Willoughby de Eresby.
    II. Eleanor, *m.* 1st, to Philip D'Arcy, and 2ndly, to Thomas Tunstal.
    III. Maud, *m.* to Sir William Eure, ancestor of the Lords Eure.
    IV. Laura, *m.* to Sir Maurice Berkeley, Knt., of Beverstone.
    V. Lucy.
    VI. Elizabeth, *m.* to Sir Ralph Grey, Knt., of Northumberland.

Henry, Lord Fitz-Hugh, K.G., *d.* 11 January, 1424, and was *s.* by his eldest surviving son,

SIR WILLIAM FITZ-HUGH, 4th baron, *b.* 1398, summoned to parliament from 12 July, 1429, to 5 September, 1450. This nobleman attained distinction in the life-time of his father in the French wars, and after his accession to the title, he was in commission (11th HENRY VI.), to treat with the commissioners of King JAMES I., of Scotland, regarding compensation for injuries inflicted by the Scots upon the English. In two years afterwards his lordship was joined with the Earls of Northumberland and Westmoreland, and the great northern Lords Dacre, Clifford, Greystoke, and Latimer, to repel an irruption of the Scots. Lord Fitz-Hugh *m.* Margery, dau. of William, Lord Willoughby de Eresby, and had issue,

    HENRY, his successor.
    Margery, *m.* to Sir John Melton, Knt., of Aston.
    Joane, *m.* to John, Lord Scrope, of Bolton.
    Eleanor, *m.* to Thomas, Lord Dacre.
    Maud, *m.* to William Bowes.
    Lora, *m.* 1st, to John Musgrave, and 2ndly, to John Constable, of Halsham.
    Lucy, a nun at Deptford.
    Elizabeth, *m.* Ralph, Lord Greystock.

His lordship *d.* in 1452, and was *s.* by his son,

HENRY FITZ-HUGH, 5th baron, *b.* 1430, summoned to parliament from 26 May, 1455, to 15 October, 1470. His lordship obtained, in 38th HENRY VI., a grant of the stewardship of the honour of Richmond, and also of the office of chief forester of the new forest of Arkilgarth-Dale, and Le Hoppe, then escheated to the king by the forfeiture of Richard, Earl of Salisbury, to hold for life. During the reign of King HENRY VI. Lord Fitz-Hugh remained firmly attached to the Lancastrian interest, but he seems nevertheless to have successfully cultivated the good opinion of King EDWARD IV., the champion of York, for we find his lordship, soon after the accession of that monarch, employed in his military capacity, and as a diplomatist. In 1468 he made a pilgrimage to the Holy Sepulchre, and upon his return founded a chantry for two priests in his castle at Ravenswath, there to celebrate divine service for himself and Alice during their lives, and for the health of their souls after their decease. His lordship *m.* Lady Alice Neville, dau. of Richard, Earl of Salisbury, and had issue,

    I. RICHARD, his successor.
    II. Thomas,
    III. John,
    IV. George,   } *d. s. p.*
    V. Edward,
    I. Alice, *m.* to Sir John Fienes, Knt., and was mother of THOMAS, LORD DACRE.
    II. Elizabeth, *m.* 1st, to Sir William Parr, Knt., and had (with William, created Lord Parr, of Horton),
      SIR THOMAS PARR, who *m.* Maud, dau. and co-heir of Sir Thomas Green, Knt., of Horton, and had one son and two daus, viz.,

1 William Parr, Marquess of Northampton, *d. v. p.*

1 Anne Parr, *m.* to William Herbert, Earl of Pembroke, and her male descendant continues to the present time to inherit that dignity, but Philip, 7th Earl of Pembroke, leaving at his decease an only dau.,

LADY CHARLOTTE HERBERT, who *m.* 1st, John, Lord Jeffreys and 2ndly, Thomas, Viscount Windsor, the co-heirship to the Barony of Fitz-Hugh was thus severed from the Earldom of Pembroke. The representatives of her ladyship are Sir Thomas George Fermor Hesketh and Lady Henrietta-Louisa Ogilvy, co-heirs of the last Earl of Pomfret; and the Marquess of Bute.

2 CATHERINE PARR, *m.* 1st, to Edward Borough; 2ndly, to John Neville, Lord Latimer; 3rdly, to King HEN Y VIII., and 4thly, to Thomas, Lord Seymor, of Sudley, but *d. s. p.*

Elizabeth Fitz-Hugh, *m.* 2ndly, Nicholas, Lord Vaux.

I. Anne, *m.* to Francis, Lord Lovell, but had no issue.
II. Margery, *m.* to Marmaduke Constable, *d. s. p.*
III. Joane, a nun at Deptford.

Henry, 5th Baron Fitz-Hugh, *d.* in 1472, and was *s.* by his only son,

RICHARD FITZ-HUGH, 6th baron, summoned to parliament from 15 November, 1482, to 1 September, 1487. This nobleman was constituted. in the 1st HENRY VII., governor of the castles of Richmond and Middleham, and of Barnard Castle. His lordship *m.* Elizabeth, dau. of Sir Thomas Borough, Knt., and was *s.* at his decease, about the year 1508, by his only child,

GEORGE FITZ-HUGH, 7th baron, summoned to parliament from 17 October, 1509, to 28 November, 1511, but dying *s. p.* in 1512, his aunt Alice, Lady Fienes, and his cousin, Sir Thomas Parr, Knt. (*refer* to issue of Henry, 5th baron,) were found to be his next heirs, and between those the BARONY OF FITZ-HUGH fell into ABEYANCE, as it still continues amongst their representatives. Which representatives are at present, we believe,

Thomas-Crosbie-William-BrandTrevor, Lord Dacre, descended from Alice, Lady Fienes, whose husband, Sir John Fiennes, was father of Thomas, Lord Dacre. His lordship, if we be correct, is co-heir therefore to the barony of Fitz-Hugh.

Sir Thomas-George Fermor Hesketh, nephew, and Lady Henrietta-Louisa Ogilvy, sister, co-heirs of the 5th Earl of Pomfret, descended from Hon. Henrietta-Louisa Jefferys, only child of Lady Charlotte Herbert, by her 1st husband.

John-Patrick-Crichton Stuart, Marquess of Bute, the representative of Lady Charlotte Herbert, by her 2nd husband, Thomas, Viscount Windsor.

} Co-heir to the barony of Fitz-Hugh.

Arms—Az., three chevronels in base, or, and a chief of the 2nd.

FITZJAMES—DUKE OF BERWICK.

By Letters Patent, dated 19 March, 1687.

Lineage.

JAMES FITZ-JAMES, illegitimate son of King JAMES II., by Arabella Churchill, sister of the celebrated John Churchill, Duke of Marlborough, was *b.* in 1671, and elevated to the peerage, 19 March, 1687, in the dignities of *Baron Bosworth, in the county of Leicester, Earl of Tinmouth, in the county of Northumberland,* and DUKE OF BERWICK UPON TWEED. His grace withdrew into France with his father, and entering into the French service, became one of the most distinguished commanders of the reign of LOUIS XIV. In 1690, he was at the siege of Londonderry, and the battle of the Boyne, and returning soon after the last engagement to France, he acquired high reputation at the sieges of Mons, Charleroi, and Ath, and at the battles of Lenze, Steinkirk, and Nerwinde. In the last-named he was taken prisoner, and detained until exchanged for the Duke of Ormonde. In 1693, the French king made him lieutenant-general of his armies, and in ten years afterwards he commanded the expedition sent to aid the King of Spain. By the latter monarch he was created in 1704, a Spanish grandee of the 1st class. After a very successful campaign, the duke returning into France, was nominated (*anno* 1715,) to the command of the troops destined to act against the fanatics in Languedoc, and upon the favourable issue of that campaign, he was presented with a marshal's baton. Subsequently sent a second time into Spain, he achieved over the combined forces of England and Portugal, the great victory of Almanza, for which eminent service PHILIP V., granted to him, with the dignity of Duke, the towns of Liria, and Xerica, in Valentia. Upon his return, the duke was placed at the head of the army on the Rhine, destined to oppose Prince

208

Eugene, of Savoy, in which service, after a long series of brilliant achievements, he fell at the siege of Philipsburg, *anno* 1734. His grace *m.* 1st in 1695, Honora de Burgh, widow of Patrick Sarsfield, Earl of Lucan, and dau. of the Earl of Clanricarde, by whom (who *d.* in 1698), he had issue,

JAMES-FRANCIS, Duke of Liria and Xerica, Grandee of Spain, an officer of eminence, *m.* Katherine, dau. of Pierre, Duke of Veragues; and had several children. His posterity, still existing in Spain, perpetuates the senior line of the descendants of the Marshal DUKE OF BERWICK, LIRIA, and XERICA.

The Duke of Berwick *m.* 2ndly, in 1700, Anne, dau. of Henry Bulkeley, Esq., by Sophia Stuart, maid of honour to the queen, and had issue,

JAMES, Duc de Fitz-James, *b.* in 1702, *m.*[Victoire Felicité, dau. of John de Durfort, Duke of Duras, but *d. s. p.* in the lifetime of his father, *anno* 1721.

Francis, bishop of Soissons, who having entered into holy orders, never assumed the French title. He *d.* 1764.

Henry, the "Abbé de Berwick." *d.* 1731.

CHARLES, *b.* in 1714, heir eventually to the French Dukedom of Fitz-James, and the estates in that kingdom, and eventually a marshal of France. He *m.* in 1741, Sophie-Goyon de Matignon, dau. of the Marquess de Matignon, and had with other issue a son and heir,

JOHN-CHARLES, 3rd Duke Fitz-James, *b.* in 1743, *m.* Marie, dau. of Charles, Count de Thiard, and was father of EDWARD, Duc de Fitz-James, Chevalier of St. Louis, and officer of the Legion of Honour, peer of France. *b.* 10 January, 1776; *m.* 1st, Mademoiselle de La Touche, and 2ndly, Mademoiselle de Torcy, and left by the former two sons, of whom the younger, Charles, Comte de Fitz-James, was *b.* in 1801, and the elder, JAMES, Duc de Fitz-James, in 1799; he *m.* 1825, Marguerite de Marmier, and *d.* 1846, leaving with other issue, a son, EDWARD-ANTHONY-SIDOINE, DUC DE FITZJAMES, who *m.* 1851, Marguerite-Augusta, dau. of Gustavus-Charles-Frederick, Comte de Loevenhielm, Swedish Minister at Paris, and has issue.

Edward, lieutenant-general, *d.* 1748.
Henrietta, *m.* to the Marquess Clermont d'Amboise.
Laura, *m.* to the Marquess de Montaigu.
Emilia, *m.* to the Marquess d'Escars.
Sophia, a nun.

Marshal Berwick was attainted in 1695, when the Dukedom of Berwick, and the minor English honours became FORFEITED. His grace was besides Duke of Liria and Xerica, in Valentia, a dignity which he transferred in his life-time to his eldest son, JAMES, who then became Duke of Liria, and having *m.* as already stated, Katherine, dau. of Pierre, Duke of Veraguez, was *s.* in 1738, by his eldest son, JAMES, *b.* in 1718, surnamed STUART, who was himself *s.* by his brother, PETER, *b.* in 1720, created MARQUESS OF ST. LEONARD, in 1764. The Duke of Berwick was created DUC DE FITZ-JAMES in France, with remainder to the issue of his 2nd marriage, and that dignity is enjoyed by his descendant, the present DUC DE FITZ-JAMES.

Arms—Quarterly of four; 1st, England and France; 2nd, Scotland; 3rd, Ireland; 4th as the 1st, within a border componé. gu. and az, the gu. charged with lions of England, the az, with fleurs-de-lis of France.

FITZ-JOHN—BARONS FITZ-JOHN.

By Writ of Summons, dated 14 December, 1264.
By Writ of Summons, dated 23 June, 1295.

Lineage.

JOHN FITZ-GEOFFREY, son of Geoffrey Fitz-Piers, Earl of Essex, by Aveline his 2nd wife, being next male heir of that family on the death of William Fitz-Piers, Earl of Essex, in 1227, paid a fine to the king of 300 marks for those lands which were his father's and did by hereditary right belong to him, whereof this last Earl William died seised. In the 18th of HENRY III., this John was constituted sheriff of Yorkshire; and in the 21st of the same reign, upon the treaty then made between the king and the barons, whereby, in consideration of the great charter and charters of the forest being confirmed, a thirtieth part of all men's moveables were given to the king, this feudal lord was admitted one of the privy council; and the same year, there being a grand council held at London, he was one of those at the time sent to the Pope's legate, to prohibit hisattempting anything therein prejudicial to the interests of the king and kingdom. In eight years afterwards, John Fitz-Geoffrey was one of the commissioners sent from King HENRY (with Roger Bigod, Earl of Norfolk, and others) to the council at Lyons, in order to complain of the great exactions made upon the realm by the holy see; and the next year he was constituted Justice of Ireland, where, for his services, he received a grant from the crown of the Isles of Thomond. He *m.* Isabel, dau. of Sir Ralph Bigod, 3rd son of Hugh, Earl of Norfolk, sister of John Bigod, and widow of Gilbert de Laci, and dying in 1256, was *s.* by his son,

JOHN FITZ-JOHN, who had a military summons to march against the Welsh in the 42nd HENRY III. To this feudal lord, who *d.* 1258, *s.* his son,

JOHN FITZ-JOHN, who *m.* Margery, dau. of Philip Basset, Justice of England. Joining Montford, Earl of Leicester, and the other turbulent barons, this John Fitz-John had a chief command at the battle of Lewes; after which, marching towards Wales, he reduced Richard's Castle (the chief seat of Hugh de Mortimer), and the Castle of Ludlow. He was subsequently constituted, by a grant from the barons, sheriff of Westmoreland, and keeper of the castles in those parts; & likewise governor of Windsor Castle; but sharing the fate of his party at the battle of Evesham, he became a prisoner in the hands of the royalists, when the inheritance of his lands appears to have been given, by the king, to Clare, Earl of Gloucester: but he had permission afterwards to compound for them under the "dictum of Kenilworth." He was summoned to parliament as a baron, 14 December, 1264, but *d. s. p.* 1276, when that dignity expired. His lordship was *s.* in his estates by his brother,

RICHARD FITZ-JOHN, who, upon doing homage, and paying his relief, had livery of all his lands in the counties of Norfolk, Bucks, Devon, Surrey, Wilts, Southampton, Essex, and Northampton. In the 10th EDWARD I., this feudal lord was in the Welsh wars, and he was summoned to parliament as a baron, 23 June, 1295, but *d. s. p.* 1297, in the wars of France, when the Barony of Fitz-John became EXTINCT, while his lands devolved upon his heirs, viz.,

MAUD, *Countess of Warwick*, his eldest sister, who *d.* 1300.
ROBERT CLIFFORD, son of Isabel de Clifford, dau. of ... ... Isabell de Vipount, his
IDONEA DE LEYBURNE, another dau. of ... 2nd sister.
RICHARD DE BURGH, *Earl of Ulster*, son of Aveline, his 3rd sister.
JOANE, wife of Theobald le Boteler, his 4th sister.

FITZ-PATRICK—BARONS AND EARLS OF UPPER OSSORY, IN IRELAND, AND BARONS UPPER OSSORY, OF AMPT-HILL, CO. BEDFORD.

Irish Baronies, by Patent, dated 11 June, 1541, and 27 April, 1715.
Irish Earldom, by patent, dated 5 October, 1751.
British Barony, by Patent, dated 12 August, 1794.

Lineage.

The noble house of Fitz-Patrick claimed descent from HEREMON, son of Milesius, King of Spain, the first Irish monarch of the Milesian race. The first peer of the family was BARNARD, BRYAN, or BARNABY MACGILL PATRICK, who, 8 October, 1537, made his submission to the king's commissioners for the settlement of the kingdom, after the rebellion of the Fitzgeralds was suppressed, and was, as "Bernard McGyllepatricke, Esq.," created BARON OF UPPER OSSORY, by patent, dated 11 June, 1541, entailing the honour on his issue male. He was knighted 1 July, 1543, but afterwards taken prisoner and confined in the city of Waterford, until he made restitution of some preys he had seized in Leix. He *m.* 1st, Margaret, eldest dau. of Pierce, Earl of Ormonde, and widow of Thomas Fitzgerald, 2nd son of the Earl of Desmond, by whom he had four sons and one dau., viz.:

BARNABY, his heir.
FYNIN, or FLORENCE, who *s.* his brother.
Teige, or Thady, who in 1546, was sent prisoner to Dublin by his father, and there executed for his crimes.
Geoffry, and
Grany or Grizell, *m.* to Edmund, 2nd Viscount Mountgarret.

He *m.* 2ndly, Elizabeth, 3rd dau. of Bryan O'Conor, of Offaley, by his wife, Mary, dau. of Gerald, Earl of Kildare, but by her (who survived him) he is said to have left no issue. His eldest son,

SIR BARNABY FITZ-PATRICK, 2nd baron, enjoyed a large share of the esteem of King EDWARD VI., and was the constant companion of that prince. At an early age, he served as a volunteer in France, under King HENRY II., against the Emperor, and after his return from that kingdom, behaved with great bravery against Sir Thomas Wyatt, who had raised

disturbances in England. In 1558, he was knighted by the Duke of Norfolk, at the siege of Leith, in Scotland; and was present in Queen ELIZABETH's parliament, held at Dublin, 12 January, 1559. He *m.* in 1560, Joan, dau. of Sir Rowland Eustace, Viscount Baltinglass, by his wife Je_A, dau. of James, Lord Dunboyne, by whom he had an only dau., Margaret, *m.* to James, Lord Dunboyne (grandson of the aforesaid James), who *d.* 18 February, 1624. Sir Barnaby had the honour of receiving several autograph letters from King EDWARD VI., which are now in the possession of the Right Hon. J. W. FitzPatrick, who has had them printed for private circulation. His lordship, whose will bears date 9 September, 1581, was *s.* by his brother,

FYNIN or FLORENCE FITZ-PATRICK, 3rd baron, who sat in Sir John Perrott's parliament, in 1585. His lordship having repaired to the court of Queen ELIZABETH, her Majesty was pleased, at his solicitation, to direct, by letter, dated at Greenwich, 21 July, 1600, that the territory and country of Upper Ossory should be "made and reduced into shire ground, annexed and made parcel of our countie called the Queen's county." She likewise granted by letters patent, dated 10 April, 1601, to the said Florence Fitz-Patrick, Lord Baron of Upper Ossory, the late monastery of Aghmacart, the friary of Aghavoe, and sundry other rectories in the same district. He had likewise a grant, by letters patent, 16 August, 42nd of ELIZABETH, of numerous castles and manors in the country of Upper Ossory, with tithes oblations, &c., to hold to him, Florence, lord Baron of Upper Ossory, and John, his son, remainder to his sons, Geoffry, Barnaby, and Edmond, remainder to his heirs male, and to the heirs of his father, Barnaby, late Baron, and of his grandfather, Barnaby.—*Chancery Rolls of Ireland.* This baron *m.* Catherine, dau. of Patrick (or Rory) O'More, of Leix, in the Queen's co., and *d.* in the reign of JAMES I., having had five sons and two daus.,

I. THADY, his successor.
II. JOHN, of Castletown, ancestor of the BARONS OF GOWRAN and EARLS OF UPPER OSSORY, of whom hereafter.
III. Geoffry, of Ballyraghin, or Ballyharagh. He *m.* Mary, dau. of Fergus Ferrall, of Tenelick, co. Longford, and widow of Sir John O'Reilly, and *d.* 13 August, 1638, having had issue two daus., 1 Ellice, *m.* 1st, Thomas Butler, Esq., of Pollardstown, co. Limerick, 5th son of James, 2nd Lord Dunboyne, and had issue. James, Margaret, Mary, Ellen, and Ellice; and 2ndly, William Burke, also of Pollardstown, younger son of Theobald, 1st Lord Brittas, and had by her, Theobald, 3rd Lord Brittas, Richard and Honora; 2 Catherine, who *d. unm.*
IV. Barnaby, of Water Castle.
V. Edmond, of Castle Fleming, living 1641, father of Andrew, who was engaged in the rebellion.
I. Catherine, *m.* in May, 1592, James Eustace, Esq., of Newland, co. Kildare.
II. Joan, *m.* to John Butler, son and heir of James, 2nd Lord Dunboyne.

The eldest son,

THADY FITZ-PATRICK, 4th baron, *m.* Joan, dau. of Sir Edmund Butler, of Tullow, co. Carlow, 2nd son of James, Earl of Ormonde, and by her (who *d.* 1631, and was interred in the cathedral of St. Canice, Kilkenny) had issue,

I. BRYAN, his successor.
II. Dermoid, or Darby, *m.* 1st, Elan, dau. of Nicholas Shortall, Esq., of Clara, co. Kilkenny, and 2ndly, Ellinor, dau. of Richard Comerford, Esq., of Ballybirr, and widow of John Kennedy, Esq., of Ballynegarry, co. Tipperary.
III. Tirlagh, executor to his mother's will, dated 16 September, 1631, *m.* Onera, dau. of Oliver Grace, Esq., of Courtstown.
IV. John.
I. Margaret, *m.* to Thomas Hovenden, Esq., of Tankerston, Queen's co.
II. Onora.
III. Joan, *m.* to William Butler, Esq., of Lynon, co. Tipperary.
IV. Catherine, *m.* 6 February, 1637, to Callaghan Fitzgerald, gent., of Cloquhoyle, Queen's co.

The 4th baron *d.* in December, 1627, and was *s.* by his eldest son,

BRYAN FITZ-PATRICK, 5th baron, took his seat in parliament, 14 July, 1634, *m.* Margaret, eldest dau. of Walter, Earl of Ormonde, and dying 1641, left issue,

I. BRYAN, his heir.
II. Edmond.   III. Derby.

The eldest son,

BRYAN or BARNABY FITZ PATRICK, 6th baron, took his seat in the House of Peers, 16 March, 1639. He *m.* Catherine, dau. of Sir Edward Everard, Knt., of Fethard, co. Tipperary, and had three sons and two daus.,

I. BRYAN, his successor.
II. John, who *m.* Elizabeth, dau. of Bryan Kavanagh, of Borris, co. Carlow, and had issue,

BRYAN, or BARNABY, who assumed the title on the death of his uncle.

Catherine.   Mary.

III. James, who d. in England.

I. Ellen, d. young.   II. Mary, d. young.

The eldest son,

BRYAN or BARNABY FITZ-PATRICK, 7th baron, captain in the army of JAMES II., was outlawed 11 May, 1691, but in the Act to hinder the reversal of several outlawries and attainders, passed 6th King WILLIAM, it was provided the outlawries of Barnaby, late Baron of Upper Ossory, should not be confirmed, but that the same might be capable of being reversed in such manner as if that Act had never been made. He m. 1st, Margaret, dau. of Pierce, 1st Viscount Ikerrin, by whom he had Bryan, who d. unm., 1687; Keran; John, who d. an infant; and Catherine, d. an infant; and 2ndly, Margaret, dau. and heir of James, Lord Dunboyne; and 3rdly, Dorothy Wagstaffe, and dying before the year 1696, was s. by his nephew (son of his brother John),

BARNABY FITZ-PATRICK, Esq., who assumed the title, which was disallowed 2 December, 1697, by the House of Lords, who found from the report of the committee appointed to inspect the journals, that the said Barnaby, or Bryan was outlawed 11 May preceding. The barony was again claimed by Lieut. James Fitz-Patrick, who had a son Henry, who m. in January, 1749-50, Jane, dau. of Mr. Richard Farren, but the Earl of Cavan reported from the committee appointed to consider the return of the Lords, that the title of Baron of Upper Ossory was extinct, and Ulster King of Arms was ordered to leave it out of the list of peers.

We now return to JOHN FITZPATRICK, of Castletown (2nd son of Florence or Fynin, 3rd baron). He m. temp. JAMES I., Mabel St. John, of the Queen's co., and had three sons,

     I. FLORENCE, his heir.
     II. John, of Bardwell.
     III. James, of Grantstown, Queen's co., from whom the Rev. JOSEPH FITZ-PATRICK, of Dromondragh, derived his descent.

The eldest son,

FLORENCE FITZ-PATRICK, Esq., who, with his two brothers, were engaged in the rebellion of 1641, m. Bridget, dau. of — D'Arcy, Esq., of Platen, co. Meath, and had a son,

JOHN FITZ-PATRICK, Esq., of Castletown, doctor of laws, who m. Elizabeth, 4th dau. of Thomas, Viscount Thurles, sister of James, 1st Duke of Ormonde, and widow of James Purcell, Baron of Loughmoe, by whom (who d. 6 December, 1675) he had issue,

EDWARD, his successor.

RICHARD, successor to his brother.

Mr. Fitz-Patrick, who suffered during the usurpation of Cromwell for his fidelity to the house of Stuart, was involved in King JAMES's general act of attainder in 1089, and d. in 1093. His elder son,

EDWARD FITZ-PATRICK, Esq., had the command of a regiment given him at the Revolution, 31 December, 1688; was made colonel of the royal fusiliers, 1 August, 1692, and promoted to the rank of brigadier-general in 1694. General Fitz-Patrick was drowned in his passage from England to Ireland, 10 November, 1696, and d. unm. His brother,

RICHARD FITZ-PATRICK, Esq., being bred to the sea-service, had the command of a ship of war, in which station he signalized himself by his valour and conduct; and to him and his brother, in consideration of their faithful services, King WILLIAM III., granted, in 1696, the estate of Edmond Morris (one of the adherents of King JAMES, killed at the battle of Aughrim), situated in the Queen's co. Mr. FitzPatrick was elevated to the peerage of Ireland, 27 April, 1715, as BARON GOWRAN, of Gowran, co. Kilkenny, and took his seat in parliament 12 November following. His lordship m. in July, 1718, Anne, younger dau. and co-heir of Sir John Robinson, Bart., of Farming-Woods, co. Northampton, and had two sons,

JOHN, his heir, and

Richard, who m. Anne, dau. of Mr. Usher, of London, and by her (who d. 28 March, 1759) he had a son and three daus., of whom the last survivor, ANNE, m. 9 March, 1789, John Henry, BARON DE ROBECK.

He d. 9 June, 1727, and was s. by his elder son,

JOHN FITZ-PATRICK, 2nd baron, who was advanced to the EARLDOM OF UPPER-OSSORY, in the peerage of Ireland, 5 October, 1751, with limitation to his issue male. His lordship, who was M.P. for Bedford, in 1754, m. in July, 1744, Lady Evelyn Leveson-Gower, eldest dau. of John, Earl Gower, and by her (who re-m. in February, 1759, Richard Vernon, Esq., M.P. of Hilton, co. Stafford, secretary to John, Duke of Bedford, Lord-Lieutenant of Ireland) had issue,

JOHN, Lord Gowran.

Richard, b. 21 January, 1748, a general officer in the army, a privy councillor, and M.P. for the county of Bedford. In 1783, General Fitz-Patrick was appointed secretary-at-war, which office he resigned in the course of the year. Under the whig administration of 1806 he again filled the same department, and for hardly a longer period. He d. s. p.

Mary, m. 20 April, 1766, to Stephen Fox, 2nd Lord Holland.

Louisa, b. 1755, m. in 1779, to William, 2nd Earl of Shelburne, and 1st Marquess of Lansdowne (his lordship's 2nd wife).

The earl d. 23 September, 1758, and was s. by his elder son,

JOHN FITZ-PATRICK, 2nd earl, b. in May, 1745, who was created a peer of Great Britain on 12 August, 1794, as BARON OF UPPER OSSORY, of Ampthill, co. Bedford. His lordship m. 26 March, 1769, Anne, dau. of Henry Liddell, Lord Ravensworth, by whom (who had been divorced from the Duke of Grafton, and d. in 1804) he had two children only, viz., Anne, b. 10 February, 1774, and Gertrude, both of whom d. unm.

The earl d. 1 February, 1818, when all his honours became EXTINCT. The earl had likewise a dau., Emma-Mary, m. to Robert Vernon Smith, now Lord Lyveden, and two sons, JOHN-WILSON and Richard, the younger, d. unm., the elder, the Right Hon. JOHN-WILSON FITZPATRICK, of Lisduff and Grantstown Manor, Queen's co., was created Baron Castletown in 1869; and d. 1883 (see BURKE'S Extant Peerage).

Arms—Sa., a saltier, arg., on a chief, az., three fleurs-de-lis, or.

FITZ-PAYNE—BARONS FITZ-PAYNE.

By Writ of Summons, dated 6 February, 1299.

Lineage.

The first that assumed this surname was ROBERT, son of Pain Fitz-John, whose nephew, taking the name of VESCI, was founder of that eminent family. This

ROBERT FITZ-PAIN served the office of sheriff for the counties of Dorset and Somerset, from the 31st to the 34th HENRY II. inclusive; and in the 13th of JOHN, upon the collection of the scutage of Wales, he paid 30 marks for 15 knights' fees. He was s. by

ROGER FITZ-PAIN, who m. Margery, eldest of the three sisters and co-heirs of Alured de Lincolne, and thereby acquired considerable property in the counties of Somerset, Dorset, Wilts, and Devon, whereof Ockford Fitz-pain, in Dorsetshire, constituted a part. He d. about the year 1237, and was s. by his son,

ROBERT FITZ-PAIN, who, during his homage in the 30th HENRY III., had livery of his lands in the counties of Wilts, Somerset and Dorset, and Netherwent, in Wales. In the 41st of the same reign, he had two military summonses to march against the Welsh; but after this he appears to have joined the barons, and to have taken a prominent part in the battle of Lewes, where the baronial banner waved in triumph. He d in 1280, and was s. by his son,

ROBERT FITZ-PAYNE. This feudal lord was in the expedition made against the Welsh, in the 10th EDWARD I., and the same year, during his homage, had livery of the lands of his inheritance. He was summoned to parliament as a baron on 6 February, 1299, and from that time to 23 October, 1314. In 1303 he was in the Scottish wars, and again in 1306, in the immediate train of Prince Edward, having been created a knight of the Bath in the same year. In the 1st EDWARD II., his lordship was constituted governor of the castle of Winchester, and the next year, being then steward of the king's household, he was deputed, with Otto de Grandison, upon an important mission to the sovereign pontiff. In the 8th of the same reign he had a military summons to march against the Scots, but d. the ensuing year, 1315, seized of manors in the counties of Devon, Wilts, Dorset, Gloucester, and Somerset; and, jointly with his wife Isabel, of the manor of Stourton, in Wiltshire. His lordship was s. by his son,

ROBERT FITZ-PAYNE, 2nd baron, summoned to parliament, from 7 August, 1327, to 15 November, 1351. This nobleman was in the wars of Scotland in the 10th and 12th EDWARD II., and in the 16th EDWARD III. (residing then at his seat of Mershwode, co. Dorset) he had command to provide ten men at arms, and ten archers, for the king's service in France, and in three years afterwards, being then a banneret, he had a military summons to attend the king into that realm. His lordship *m.* Ela, dau. and co-heir of Guy de Bryan, and dying in 1354, left an only dau. and heir,

ISABEL FITZ-PAYNE, then thirty years of age, and the wife of John Chideock, by whom (who *d.* 1387) she had a son and heir,

SIR JOHN CHIDEOCKE, Knt., whose son and heir was

SIR JOHN CHIDEOCKE, Knt., aged fifteen, in 1416, who left two daus., his co-heirs, viz.,

1 KATHERINE CHIDEOCKE, *m.* 1st, to Sir William Stafford, of Frome, and had an only child,

HUMPHREY STAFFORD, EARL OF DEVON, who *d.s.p.*

She *m.* 2ndly, Sir John Arundell, Knt., and from this union descend the LORDS ARUNDELL, OF WARDOUR.

2 Margaret Chideocke, *m.* to William, 2nd Lord Stourton, and from this marriage the Lord Stourton descends.

The Barony of Fitz-Payne, upon the decease of ROBERT, the 2nd baron, appears to have been suspended, and it is now in ABEYANCE between the representatives of Sir John Chideocke's co-heirs, namely, the above-mentioned Katherine and Margaret Chideocke; which representatives are,

JOHN-FRANCIS, LORD ARUNDELL, OF WARDOUR, grandson of Mary Christiana, elder dau. and co-heir of Henry, 8th Lord Arundel, of Wardour.	Co-heirs to a moiety of the Barony of Fitz-Payne.
CHARLES-HUGH, LORD CLIFFORD, OF CHUDLEIGH, grandson of ELEANOR-MARY, younger dau. of Henry, 8th Lord Arundell, of Wardour.	

CHARLES, LORD STOURTON, heir to a moiety of the BARONY OF FITZ-PAYNE.

Arms—Gu., three lions passant, guardant, in pale, over all a bend, az.

Certain manors in the county of Dorset, part of the property of Robert, last Lord Fitz-Payne, and Ela, his wife, being so entailed, devolved, at the decease of the said Ela (then his lordship's widow) upon her presumed brother-in-law,

The HON. ROBERT GREY, of Charlton Grey, co. Somerset, younger son of Richard, Lord Grey, of Codnor, who thereupon assumed the surname of FITZ-PAYNE, and Dugdale says, was summoned to parliament as BARON FITZ-PAYNE; but the name of such a baron does not appear upon the roll. He *m.* Elizabeth, dau. and co-heir of Guy de Bryan (sister of Ela, Lady Fitz-Payne), and left an only dau. and heiress,

ISABEL FITZ-PAYNE, who *m.* Richard, Lord Poynings, and was mother of

ROBERT, LORD POYNINGS, whose grand-dau. and heiress,

ALIANORE POYNINGS, *m.* Sir Henry Percy, son and heir of the Earl of Northumberland, and conveyed her great inheritance to the noble HOUSE OF PERCY. Through this alliance, the Percys claimed the ancient BARONY OF FITZ-PAYNE, but they had no pretensions whatever to it.

FITZ-PIERS—EARL OF ESSEX.

(*See* Mandeville, Earl of Essex.)

FITZ-ROY—DUKES OF CLEVELAND, DUKES OF SOUTHAMPTON.

Dukedom of Cleveland, by Letters Patent, dated 3 August, 1670.
Dukedom of Southampton, by Letters Patent, dated 10 September, 1674.

Lineage.

BARBARA VILLIERS, dau. and heiress of William Villiers, Viscount Grandison, in Ireland, grand-niece of George, Duke of Buckingham, the celebrated favourite of King JAMES I., and wife of Roger Palmer, Earl of Castlemaine, in Ireland, becoming the mistress of King CHARLES II., was elevated to the peerage by letters patent, dated 3 August, 1670, as *Baroness Nonsuch, in the county of Surrey, Countess of Southampton,* and DUCHESS OF CLEVELAND, with remainder to

Charles and George Fitzroy, two of her sons by the king. Her grace had issue by his majesty,

CHARLES, of whom presently.
Henry, created Duke of Grafton, from whom the present Duke of Grafton descends.
George, created Duke of Northumberland, *d.s.p* in 1716, when that dignity expired. (*See below.*)
Charlotte, *m.* to Edward Lee, Earl of Lichfield.

The duchess *m.* 2ndly, 25 November, 1705, Robert Fielding, Esq., from whom she was divorced 24 May, 1707, his 2nd wife, Mary Wadsworth, being then alive. She *d.* 9 October, 1709, and was *s.* by her eldest son,

CHARLES FITZROY, *b.* in June, 1662, who had been elevated to the peerage himself by letters patent, dated 10 September, 1674, as *Baron Newbury, in the county of Berks, Earl of Chichester, in the county of Sussex,* and DUKE OF SOUTHAMPTON, with remainder, in default of male issue, to his brother George. He was installed a knight of the Garter the year preceding. His grace *m.* 1st, Mary, dau. and sole heiress of Sir Henry Wood, one of the clerks of the Green Cloth, *temp.* CHARLES II., which lady *d.s.p.* 1680; but in Michaelmas term, 1685, the duke had a decree in Chancery against his uncle, Doctor Thomas Wood, bishop of Lichfield and Coventry, for £30,000, as a portion for his fortune. His grace *m.* 2ndly, Anne, dau. of Sir William Pulteney, of Misterton, co. Leicester, Knt., by whom he had,

WILLIAM, his successor.
Charles. *b.* in 1699, *d.* in 1723.
Henry, *b.* in 1701, *d.* in 1708.
Barbara, *d. unm.*
Grace, *m.* in 1725, to Henry Vane, 3rd Baron Barnard, of Barnard Castle (who was created V.scount Barnard and Earl of Darlington) From this marriage descend the DUKES OF CLEVELAND of later creation. (*See Extant Peerage.*)
Anne, *m.* to Francis Paddy, Esq.

The duke *d.* 9 September, 1730, and was *s.* by his eldest son,

WILLIAM FITZROY, 2nd Duke of Cleveland and Southampton. His grace *m.* Lady Henrietta Finch, dau. of Daniel, Earl of Winchelsea, but *d. s. p.* in 1774, when all his honours became EXTINCT.

Arms—Quarterly: 1st and 4th, grand quarters, France and England; 2nd, Scotland, and 3rd, Ireland (being the arms of King CHARLES II.), over all a baton, sinister, counter-componé, erm. and az.

FITZ-ROY—EARL AND DUKE OF NORTH-UMBERLAND.

Earldom, by Letters Patent, dated 1 October, 1674.
Dukedom, by Letters Patent, dated 6 April, 1683.

Lineage.

GEORGE FITZ-ROY, natural son of King CHARLES II., by Barbara, Duchess of Cleveland (*see preceding article*), was created on 1 October, 1674, *Baron of Pontefract, Viscount Falmouth,* and *Earl of Northumberland;* and he was advanced, 6 April, 1683, to the DUKEDOM OF NORTHUMBERLAND. He was also invested with the Garter. His grace *m.* Katherine, dau. of Thomas Wheatley, Esq., of Brecknock, co. Berks, and widow of Thomas Lucy, Esq., of Charlecote, but *d. s. p.* in 1716, when all his honours became EXTINCT.

Arms—England, with a border componée, erm., and az.

FITZ-ROY—DUKE OF RICHMOND AND SOMERSET.

By Letters Patent, dated 18 June, 1525.

Lineage.

HENRY FITZ-ROY, natural son of King HENRY VIII., by Elizabeth, widow of Gilbert, Lord Talboys of Kyme, and dau. (by Catherine, heiress of Wyrley, co. Stafford, who *d.* 32nd HENRY VIII., dau. and co-heir of Sir Hugh Pershall, Knt., of Knightley, co. Stafford, lord of the manor of Wyrley, who *d.* 4th

HENRY VII., 1488), of Sir John Blount, Knt., of Kinlet, co. Salop; was first made a knight of the Garter, and then created by letters patent, dated 18 June, 1525, *Earl of Nottingham*, and DUKE OF RICHMOND AND SOMERSET; the ceremony being performed at the royal palace, called Bridewell, in the city of London, at which time he was little more than six years of age. Upon the same day he was appointed lieutenant-general of all the king's forces north of Trent, and warden of the marches of Scotland. In five years afterwards, his grace was constituted lieutenant of Ireland, and Sir William Skeffington appointed his deputy there. The duke was educated with Henry, Earl of Surrey, at Windsor Castle, and went with that nobleman to Paris in 1532, when he formed an attachment to the earl's sister, Lady Mary Howard, and married her, but the marriage was never consummated. His grace was a youth of great promise, and much beloved by his royal father He d. aged about seventeen, in 1536, when all his honours became EXTINCT.

FITZWALTER—BARONS FITZWALTER.

By Wr.. Summons, dated 23 June, 1295.

Lineage.

ROBERT, 5th son of Richard FitzGilbert, Earl of Clare (ancestor of the Earls of Hertford), being steward to King HENRY I., obtained from that monarch the Barony of Dunmow in Essex, as also the honour of Baynard's Castle, in the city of London, both of which came into the possession of the crown by the forfeiture of William Baynard. This Robert m. in 1112, Maud de St. Liz, Lady of Bradham, dau. of Simon de St. Liz, 1st Earl of Huntingdon, and by her (who d. 1140, m. 2ndly, Saer de Quincy, *see that name*,) had two sons,

WALTER, his successor.
Simon, to whom he gave Daventre, in Northamptonshire.

He d. in 1134, and was s. by his elder son,
WALTER FITZ-ROBERT, who in the 12th of HENRY II., upon the assessment in aid of marrying the king's dau., certified his knights' fees to be in number sixty-three and a half, *de Veteri feoffamento;* and three and a fourth part, *de Novo*, for all of which he paid £44 10s. In the great controversy between John, Earl of Moreton, (brother of King RICHARD,) and William de Longcamp, bishop of Ely, whom the king left governor of the realm during his absence in the Holy Land, this Walter adhered to the bishop, and had at that time the custody of the castle of Eye, in Suffolk. He m. 1st, Margaret de Bohun, who d. in 1146; and 2ndly in 1148, Maud de Lucy, with whom he had the lordship of Dia, in Norfolk, and by whom he left at his decease, 1198, a son,

ROBERT FITZ-WALTER. This feudal lord, upon the assessment of the scutage of Scotland, in the 13th of JOHN, had the king's especial writ of acquittal for sixty-three knights' fees and a half, which were of his own proper inheritance; and for thirty knights' fees, and a third part which he had acquired by marriage. But the next year he was forced to fly with his family into France in order to avoid being arrested, upon the first disposition of the barons to revolt; and was soon afterwards charged with treason and rebellion, when his house, called Baynard's Castle, in the city of London, was demolished by order of the king.

"The primary occasion of these discontents," says Dugdale, "is by some thus reported: viz.—that this Robert Fitz-Walter having a very beautiful dau. called Maude, residing at Dunmow, the king frequently solicited her chastity, but never prevailing, grew so enraged, that he caused her to be privately poisoned, and that she was buried at the south side of the quire at Dunmow, between two pillars there."

FitzWalter, however, is said, subsequently, to have made his peace with King JOHN, by the great prowess and valour he displayed at a tournament, held in Normandy before the kings of France and England; where, running a tilt with his great lance, he overthrew his rival at the first course, which act of gallantry caused the English monarch to exclaim, "*By God's Tooth, he deserves to be a king who hath such a soldier of his train;*" and afterwards, ascertaining the name of the victorious knight, he immediately sent for him, and having restored his barony, gave him liberty to repair his castle of Baynard. In the 17th of King JOHN, FitzWalter had so far regained the confidence of the crown, that he was appointed governor of the castle at Hertford; but soon after, arraying himself under the baronial banner, his lands were all seized, and those in

Cornwall committed to Prince Henry, the king's son; a course of proceeding that had the immediate effect of riveting the haughty baron to the cause which he had espoused, while his high rank, tried courage, and acknowledged abilities, soon gave him a lead amongst his compeers. We find him, therefore, amongst the first commissioners nominated to treat with the king, when it was agreed, that the city of London should be delivered up to the barons, and twenty-five of those powerful feudal chiefs chosen to govern the realm. The insurrectionary lords subsequently assembled at St. Edmundsbury, and there pledged themselves, by solemn oath at the high altar, that if the king refused to confirm the laws and liberties granted by EDWARD THE CONFESSOR, they would withdraw their allegiance from him and seize upon his fortresses. After which, forming themselves into a regular army, they appointed this Robert FitzWalter their general, with the title of Marshal of the army of God and the Church, and under his command, they eventually extorted the Great Charters of Freedom from JOHN on the plains of Runnymede, when Fitz-Walter was elected one of the celebrated twenty-five, appointed to see the faithful observance of those laws. He continued, during the remainder of JOHN's reign, equally firm to his purpose; and after the accession of HENRY III., until the battle of Lincoln, where the baronial army sustained a signal defeat under his command, and he became a prisoner himself, after displaying a more than ordinary degree of valour. He does not appear, however, to have remained long under restraint, for we find him, the very next year, in the Holy Land, and assisting at the great siege of Damietta. This eminent feudal baron m. 1st, Gunnora, dau. and heiress of Robert de Valonies, and had issue,

WALTER, his successor.
Matilda.
Christian, m. 1st, to William Mandevil, Earl of Essex, and 2ndly, to Raymond de Burgh.

He m. 2ndly, Rose ——, and dying at the siege of Damietta in 1234, was s. by his son,
WALTER FITZ-WALTER, who, in the 24th HENRY III., paid into the exchequer a fine of 300 marks for livery of his lands, and in the 42nd of the same king had a military summons to march against the Welsh, and d. 1259, leaving by Maud his 1st wife, a son and heir,
SIR ROBERT FITZ-WALTER, who had a license, in 1275, to pass away the inheritance of Baynard's Castle to Robert Kilwardby, then archbishop of Canterbury, which prelate translated thereto the Dominican or Black Friars, from Holborn, near Lincoln's-inn. In alienating this part of his property, Sir Robert took especial care, however, to preserve the immunities of his barony, which, as appertaining to Baynard's Castle, were thus specified: "That the said Robert, as constable of the Castle of London, (so Baynard's Castle was designated), and his heirs ought to be banner-bearers of that city, by inheritance as belonging to that castle; and in time of war, to serve the city in the manner following, viz., to [ride upon a light horse, with twenty men-at-arms on horseback, their horses covered with cloth or harness, unto the great door of St. Paul's church, with the banner of his arms carried before him."

This Robert Fitz-Walter was in the wars of Gascony, in the 22nd EDWARD I., in the retinue of Edmund, Earl of Lancaster, and continued there the next year; at which period he was summoned to parliament, as a baron, and from that time to the 19th EDWARD II. His lordship was afterwards continually engaged in the Scottish wars. He m. 1st, Devorgil, one of the daus. and co-heirs of John de Burgh, and grand-dau. of Hubert de Burgh, Earl of Kent, and by her (who d. 1284), had an only dau.,

1. Robert, b. 1291, m. 1305, — Boutetourt.
1. Christian, m. to John le Marshal, and left a son,
  William Marshal, who left two children, viz ,
    John Marshal, who d s. p.
    Hawyse, who m. to Robert Morley.

His lordship m. 2ndly, Alianore, dau., of William Ferrers, Earl of Derby, and had an only son,
ROBERT, his successor.
Ida, m. to John de la Ward.

The baron d. in 1325, and was s. by his son,
ROBERT FITZ-WALTER, 2nd baron, but never summoned to parliament, b. 1300. This nobleman m. Joane, dau. and co-heir of John de Multon, of Egremond, and dying in 1328, was s. by his son,
JOHN FITZ WALTER, 3rd baron, b. 1316, summoned to parliament from 3 March, 1341, to 20 November, 1360. In the latter year, being then in the wars of France with the king, his lordship was one of those appointed to assist Sir Walter Manny

in an attack upon the barriers of Paris, the Duke of Normandy being at the time within the city; and he was knighted for his good services therein. Lord Fitz-Walter *m.* Eleanor, dau. of Henry, Lord Percy, and was *s.* at his decease in 1361, by his son,

WALTER FITZ-WALTER, 4th baron, summoned to parliament from 6 April, 1369, to 3 September, 1385. This nobleman, in the 44th EDWARD III., was in the expedition made into Gascony, being esteemed at that time one of the most expert soldiers in the realm; but being taken prisoner, he was constrained to mortgage his castle and lordship of Egremond for the sum of £1,000 to accomplish his release by ransom. In three years afterwards, he was again in France under John, Duke of Lancaster; and in the 1st of RICHARD II., he served with Thomas of Woodstock against the Spaniards. In the 5th of the same reign, he did great service in Essex against Jack Straw, and the next year he was constituted one of the wardens of the west marches towards Scotland. In the 9th, being with John, Duke of Lancaster, in his expedition into Spain, when he went to receive possession of the kingdom of Castile, his lordship displayed great valour in storming the forts raised against the castle of Brest, in Britanny, and relieving that fortress, then closely besieged. He *m.* 1st, Eleanor — —, but had no issue; and 2ndly, Philippa, dau. and co-heir of John de Mohun, Lord of Dunster, and afterwards wife of Edward, Duke of York, and dying in 1386, was *s.* by his son,

WALTER FITZ-WALTER, 5th baron, summoned to parliament from 12 September, 1390, to 25 August, 1404. This nobleman *m.* Joane, dau. of Sir John Devereux, and sister and heiress of John, 2nd Baron Devereux, (by which alliance the baronies of Fitz-Walter and Devereux became united,) and had issue,

HUMPHREY,
WALTER,   } successive barons.
Eleanor.

His lordship *d.* in 1407, and was *s.* by his elder son,

HUMPHREY FITZ-WALTER, 6th baron, *b.* 1398, who *d.* a minor, *s. p.,* about 1419, and was *s.* by his brother,

WALTER FITZ-WALTER, 7th baron, *b.* 1400, summoned to parliament from 12 July, 1429, to 27 November, 1430. This nobleman became so distinguished in the French wars of King HENRY V., that he obtained from that monarch, in consideration of his services, a grant to himself and his heirs male of all the lands and lordships which Sir John Cheney held within the duchy of Normandy, and which had reverted to the crown upon the decease *s. p.* of the said Sir John. At this time Lord Fitz-Walter had not attained his full age; he was, however, equally eminent in after years His lordship had an only dau. and heiress,

ELIZABETH, who *m.* Sir John Ratcliffe, K.G., and conveyed the baronies of Fitz-Walter and Devereux into that family.

He *d.* in 1432, when the male line of the FITZ-WALTERS became EXTINCT; but the honours of the family passed, as stated above, to the Ratcliffes. (*See* RATCLIFFE, *Barons Fitz-Walter.*)

Arms—Or, a fesse, between two chevronels, gu

FITZ-WARINE—BARONS FITZ-WARINE.

By Writ of Summons, dated 23 June, 1295,

Lineage.

Amongst the first persons of note, to whom WILLIAM THE CONQUEROR committed the defence of the Marches towards Wales, was

GUARINE DE MEER (a member of the house of Lorraine), to whose custody he confided Adderbury, co. Salop, and Alestoun, co. Gloucester, of which former county Guarine was sheriff, in the year 1083; and he was at the same time one of the chief councillors to Roger de Montgomerie, Earl of Shrewsbury. Of this Guarine, it is stated, that having heard that William, a valiant knight, sister's son to Pain Peverell, Lord of Whittington, in Shropshire, had two daus., one of whom, Mallet, had resolved to marry none but a knight of great prowess; and that her father had appointed a meeting of noble young men, at Peverel's Place, on the Peke, from which she was to select the most gallant, he came thither; when entering the lists with a son of the King of Scotland, and with a Baron of Burgundy, he vanquished them both, and won the fair prize, with the lordship and castle of Whittington. At this place he subsequently took

up his abode, and founded the Abbey of Adderbury He was *s.* at his decease, by his son,

SIR FULKE FITZ-WARINE, who being under the tutelage of Sir Josce de Dinant, fell in love with his dau., Hawise, and marrying her, proceeded with her father to Ireland, and assisted him in his wars against Walter de Lacie. This Fulke was constituted by King HENRY I., about the year 1122, lieutenant of the Marches of Wales, and afterwards steward of the household, and lord and governor of those Marches. Of Sir Fulke it is stated, that at one time falling out with Prince John, King HENRY's son, at a game of chess, and having had his head broken by a blow of the chess-board from the prince, he returned the assault so violently, as nearly to deprive his opponent of life. He *d.* some time before the year 1195, leaving a dau. Eve, and was *s.* by his eldest son,

FULKE FITZ-WARINE, who had a castle at Adderbury, the ruins of which were remaining at the time Dugdale wrote. This Fulke was left by King RICHARD I., to defend the Marches of Wales, when that monarch set out himself for the Holy Land; and in the 7th of the same reign, he paid 40 marks to the crown for livery of Whittington Castle, in conformity with the judgment then given in his favour, by the Court of King's Bench. After the accession of JOHN, however, this castle was forcibly seized by the crown, and conferred upon another person, which act of injustice drove Fitzwarine and his brothers into rebellion, and they were in consequence outlawed; but through the mediation of the Earl of Salisbury (the king's brother), and the bishop of Norwich, the outlawry was reversed, and Fitz-Warine, upon paying 200 marks, and two courses, had livery of the castle as his hereditary right; command being given to the sheriff of Shropshire to yield him possession thereof accordingly. About this time he paid to the crown, 1,200 marks and two palfreys, for permission to marry Maud, dau. of Robert Vavasour, and widow of Theobald Walter. In the 12th JOHN, he attended that prince into Ireland, and in the 17th he had livery of his wife's inheritance, lying in Amundernesse, in Lancashire. After this we find him active in the baronial cause, and amongst those excommunicated by the Pope; nor did he make his peace until the 4th of HENRY III., when he compromised by paying £262, and two great coursers, for the re-possession of Whittington Castle, which, in the baronial conflict, had again been alienated. Whereupon undertaking that it should not be prejudicial to the king, he had licence the next year, to fortify the same; and he thenceforward evinced his loyalty, by the good services he rendered against the Welsh, under William Marshal, Earl of Pembroke, and by his personal attendance upon the king himself, in his army at Montgomery. He had subsequently military summonses upon several occasions, and fought at the battle of Lewes, *anno* 1263, under the royal banner; in which action he lost his life, by being drowned in the adjacent river. This celebrated feudal lord. *m.* 1st, as already stated, Maud, dau. of Robert Vavasour; and 2ndly, Clarice ——. He left at his decease a dau. Eve, who became 2nd consort of Llewelyn the great Prince of North Wales ap Iorwerth Drwyndun, and a son, his successor,

FULKE FITZ-WARINE, who having distinguished himself in the Welsh wars, was summoned to parliament as a baron, by King EDWARD I., 23 June, 1295, and he had summons from that period, to 24 October, 1314. His lordship was afterwards equally eminent in the wars of Scotland and Flanders, and was made a knight of the Bath, prior to attending Prince Edward into the former kingdom, in the expedition made against Robert Bruce. Lord Fitz-Warine *m.* the Princess Margaret, dau. (by Hawys, dau. of John Le Strange, feudal Lord of Knockyn and Cheswardine, co. Salop) of Griffith ap Wenwynwyn, Prince of Powys-Wenwynwyn, 1274. By the Princess Margaret, Lord Fitz-Warine acquired the territory of Ballesley, and dying *circa* 1314, was *s.* by his son,

FULKE FITZ-WARINE, 2nd baron, summoned to parliament from 6 October, 1315, to 22 January, 1336. This nobleman being at the time of his father's death, in the wars of France, Alianore, his wife by the king's especial favour, had livery of the manor of Whittington until his return. During the remainder of King EDWARD II.'s reign, he was engaged either in Scotland or Gascony, and he was constable of the royal army which advanced against the barons in insurrection under the Earl of Lancaster. In the 7th of EDWARD III., he was again in Scotland; and in the 20th, he was in the expedition then made into France. His lordship, who *m.* 2ndly, Joan, dau. of Henry, Lord Beaumont, styled Earl of Buchan, in right of his wife Alice Cumyn, *d.* in 1349, and was *s.* by his son,

FULKE FITZ-WARINE, 3rd baron, *b.* 1342. This nobleman and his successors do not appear from the existing enrolments to have been summoned to parliament. In the 41st EDWARD III., he attended Edward, the Black Prince, into

Gascony, and was subsequently engaged in the wars in Flanders. His lordship m. Margaret, dau. of James, Lord Audley, and 3rd sister and co-heir of Nicholas, Lord Audley, of Heleigh, co. Stafford, and dying circa 1374, was s. by his son,

FULKE FITZ-WARINE, 4th baron, d. in 1377, and was s. by his son,

FULKE FITZ-WARINE, 5th baron, b. 1363. His lordship making proof of his age, in 7th RICHARD II., had livery of his lands. He m. Elizabeth, sister and heir of Sir William Cogan, Knt. of Baunton, by Elizabeth, afterwards m. to Sir Hugh Courtenay, Knt., of Haccomb, and was s. at his decease, in 1391, by his son,

FULKE FITZ-WARINE, 6th baron. His lordship m. Alice, dau. of William, Lord Botreaux, afterwards m to William, Lord Clinton, and dying in minority, anno 1407, was s. by his son,

FULKE FITZ-WARINE, 7th baron. This nobleman d. also in minority, anno 1429, and left his only sister,

ELIZABETH FITZ-WARINE, his heir, b. 1403. This lady m. afterwards, Richard Hankford, Esq., and left an only dau. and heiress,

THOMASINE HANKFORD, who m. SIR WILLIAM BOURCHIER, Knt., who was summoned to parliament, in her right, as LORD FITZ-WARINE. (See BOURCHIER, Barons Fitz-Warine.)

Arms—Quarterly : arg. and gu., per fesse, indented.

FITZ-WARINE—BARONS FITZ-WARINE.

By Writ of Summons, dated 25 February, 1342.

Lineage.

Besides the barony of Fitz-Warine, conferred by the writ of EDWARD I., upon Fulke Fitz-Warine, in 1295, and which barony was eventually conveyed by an heiress to a branch of the great house of Bourchier, another member of the same family,

WILLIAM FITZ-WARINE, called Le Frere, was elevated to the peerage, as a baron, by writ of summons, dated 25 February, 1342. This William had been constituted governor of the castle of Montgomery, in the beginning of King EDWARD III.'s reign, and was afterwards engaged in the French and Scottish wars. The year he attained the peerage he was in France, being then of the rank of banneret, with one knight, eight esquires, and ten archers, on horseback, in his immediate train—and again in four years afterwards. His lordship m. Amicia, dau. and heir of Henry Haddon, of Candel Haddon, co. Dorset, and dying in 1361, possessed of estates in the counties of Berks, Somerset, and Dorset, was s. by his son,

IVO or JOHN FITZ-WARINE, 2nd baron, but never summoned to parliament. This nobleman was at the siege of Nantes in the beginning of the reign of RICHARD II., under Thomas of Woodstock. He d. in 1414, leaving an only dau. and heiress,

ELEANOR FITZ-WARINE, who m. Sir John Chediock, and left a son,

SIR JOHN CHEDIOCK, Knt., who m. Katherine, dau. of Ralph Lumley, and left, at his decease, two daus. his co-heirs, viz.,

Margaret, m. to William, 2nd Lord Stourton, ancestor of the present lord.
Katherine, m. 1st, to Sir William Stafford, and 2ndly, to Sir John Arundel, from whom the Lords Arundel, of Wardour, descend.

Arms—Quarterly : gu., and erm., per fesse, indented. In the first quarter a fret, gules.

FITZWILLIAM — VISCOUNT FITZWILLIAM, AND EARL OF TYRCONNEL.

Viscounty, by Patent, dated 5 August, 1629.
Earldom, by Patent, dated 20 April, 1663.

Lineage.

This family, presumed to have been a branch of the ancient house of Fitzwilliam in England, has been settled in Ireland since the reign of JOHN.

RICHARD FITZWILLIAM, of Ballymon, living in the reign of EDWARD II., left issue by Ellena his wife, two sons, WILLIAM and Robert, living 1342. The elder son,

WILLIAM FITZWILLIAM, built the castle of Wicklow, of which he was made constable, and in 1375 he was appointed chief commander and governor of all that part of the country. He left (with a dau. Elizabeth, m. to Sir Thomas de Musgrave) a son,

WILLIAM FITZWILLIAM, who was sheriff of the co. Meath, 1381, and in 1382, constable of the castle of Wicklow. He d. in 1397, leaving a son,

JOHN FITZWILLIAM, who had a pardon from the king for all his transgressions. He left, by Christiana his wife, a son, HENRY FITZWILLIAM, who was s. by

THOMAS FITZWILLIAM, constable of the town of Swords, who had,

I. RICHARD, of whom presently.
1. Felicia, m. to Walter, 3rd son of Sir Robert Cruise, of Graltagh and Tirrelstown.

RICHARD FITZWILLIAM, of Donnybrook, near Dublin, presumed to be the father of

PHILIP FITZWILLIAM, Esq., to whom King HENRY VI. granted a certain sum of money out of the crown rents, which he had to pay for his manor of Thorn Castle, in order to enable him to build a fort there. To this Philip s.

STEPHEN FITZWILLIAM, who, in 1463, held the manor of Thorn Castle. He was s. by

WILLIAM FITZWILLIAM, who m. Anne, only dau. of Robert Cruise, Esq., of the Maull, co. Dublin, and left a son and heir,

RICHARD FITZWILLIAM, who m. Genet Hollywood, and

THOMAS FITZWILLIAM, Esq., of Merrion, Bray, and Baggotrath, co. Dublin, of which county he was sheriff, in 1511. He m. Eleanor, dau. of John Dowdall, Esq., 3rd son of Sir John Dowdall, of Newtown, and d. 1529, having had three sons and two daus., viz. :

I. RICHARD, of whom presently.
II. William (Sir), clerk of the Hanaper, and M.P. for Carlow, who by Jane his wife, had four daus., Mabel, Elizabeth, Catharine, who m. Christopher, Viscount Gormanston, and d. in 1595, and Elizabeth.
III. Nicholas, (Sir). a priest, prebendary of Ballymore, and treasurer of the Cathedral of St. Patrick's.
I. Margaret, m. to William Walsh, Esq., of Carrigmaine, co. Dublin.
II. Alison, m. 1st, Christopher Usher, bailiff of Dublin and twice mayor thereof.

The eldest son,

RICHARD FITZWILLIAM, Esq., of Baggotrath, gentleman of the king's bed-chamber in 1527. This Richard m. Catherine, dau. of Robert Bathe, Esq., of Kepoke, co. Dublin, and had three sons,

I. THOMAS, his successor.
II. Michael, of Donamore, co. Meath, surveyor-general of crown lands. He m. Mary, dau. of Jenico, 3rd Viscount Gormanston, and had issue,
1 William, of Donamore, had a dau. Elizabeth, who m. 1st, Edward Plunket, of Loghgor, and 2ndly, Peter Taaffe, Esq.
2 Patrick.
1 Eleanor, m. to Howell Walsh, Esq.
2 Catherine, the 2nd wife of George King, Esq., of Clontarf.
3 Jane.
4 Elizabeth, m. to Gerald Fitz-Gerald, who was executed for murder in the time of the rebellion.
III. John.

He d. 20 Dec. 1541, and was s. by his eldest son,

SIR THOMAS FITZWILLIAM, Knt., of Meryon and Baggotrath, M.P., and sheriff for the co. Dublin, who m. Genet, dau. of Patrick Finglas, Esq., of Westpalston, chief baron of the Exchequer, and d. 9 Nov., 1592, having had issue,

I. RICHARD, his successor.
II. Nicholas, of Molmpatrick and Balldungan, co. Dublin, who m. Mabel, dau. of Walter Nangle, Esq., of Kildalky, co. Meath, and d. 5 Dec. 1635, having had issue two sons and five daus.,
1 Thomas.   2 Nicholas.
1 Mary, m. to Bartholomew Russell, Esq., of Seaton, co. Dublin.
2 Jane.
3 Elizabeth, m. to John, son of Sir Richard Bolton, chief baron of the Exchequer.
4 Eleanor, m. to James Bermingham, Esq., of Ballogh.
5 Margaret, m. to William Underwood, of Dublin, merchant.
III. Thomas, of Moylagh, who m. Mary, dau. of Christopher Segrave, Esq., of Dublin, and had a son, Thomas, who d. s. p.

2. Catharine, *m.* 1st, to James Plunket, Esq., of Dunsoghly, son and heir of Sir John Plunket, chief justice of the King's Bench; and 2ndly, to Christopher, 4th Viscount Gormanston. She was buried 10 Feb, 1602.

The eldest son,

SIR RICHARD FITZWILLIAM, of Merrion, constable of the castle of Wicklow and lord warden of the marches of Leinster. He *m.* Jane, dau. of — Preston, and had issue,

I. THOMAS, his successor.
II. William, of Dundrum, *m.* in 1614, Mary, dau. of Mr. Smyth, and widow of Dr. Henry Ussher, archbishop of Armagh, but *d. s. p.* 16 July, 1616.
III. Christopher, *d. s. p.* in 1649.
IV. Patrick, killed by Sir Robert Newcomen, *unm.*
V. Richard, of the Rock, *m.* the dau. of Sir Thady Duffe, of Dublin, Knt., and sister of Richard Duffe, Esq.
1. Catharine, *m.* to Henry Chevers, Esq., of Monktown, co. Dublin, 2nd son of John Chevers, Esq., of Macetown.
II. Mary, *m.* 1st, to Matthew Plunket, 5th Lord Louth, and 2ndly, to Gerald Aylmer, Esq.

The eldest son,

SIR THOMAS FITZWILLIAM, Knt. of Merrion, co. Dublin, sheriff of that county, 1609, was created, 5 August, 1629, *Baron Fitzwilliam, of Thorncastle*, and VISCOUNT FITZWILLIAM, of Merrion, co. Dublin, in the peerage of Ireland. This nobleman repaired, the day after the breaking out of the rebellion, in 1641, to Dublin, and waiting upon the lords justices, made a tender of his best services to the crown; but, being a Roman catholic, he was rejected, and compelled to go into England, where, with his two sons, he faithfully and zealously served King CHARLES I., who, in recompense, granted h.s lordship a privy-seal for a British earldom, dated at Oxford, 1 May, 1645, but the great seal not being then in the power of that unhappy monarch, the patent could not be legally perfected, and it eventually never was. His lordship *m.* 23 Aug. 1605, Margaret, eldest dau. of Oliver, 4th Lord Louth, by his 1st wife Frances, dau. of Sir Nicholas Bagenall, Knt., Marshal of Ireland, and had issue,

I. Richard, *m.* Ellinor Stanihurst, widow of Sir Henry Pierce, of Shercock, co. Cavan, and *d. v. p. s. p.*
II. OLIVER, 2nd viscount.
III. Christopher, *m.* Jane, dau. of Brereton, Esq., of Malpas, in Cheshire, and left a dau. Alicia.
IV. WILLIAM, 3rd viscount.

The 2nd son,

OLIVER FITZWILLIAM, 2nd Viscount Fitzwilliam, was a military officer, and being a lieutenant-general under the Marquess of Ormonde, achieved a victory at Roscommon, by which he gained the whole province of Connaught to the king's service. His lordship was created *Earl of Tyrconnel* by CHARLES II., by patent dated 20 April, 1663. He *m.* 1st, Dorothy, sister of his brother Christopher's wife; and 2ndly, Lady Eleanor Holles, eldest dau. of John, 1st Earl of Clare, but *d. s. p.* 11 April, 1667, when that dignity expired, while the other honours devolved upon his brother,

WILLIAM FITZWILLIAM, 3rd Viscount Fitzwilliam, governor of Whitchurch, in Cheshire, during the civil wars, and lieutenant-general of that co. He *m.* a dau. of Thomas Luttrell, Esq., of Luttrellstown, and sister of Thomas Luttrell, Esq., of Ranaghan, in Westmeath, and dying before 1681, had issue,

I. THOMAS, his successor.
1. Mary, *m.* in May, 1685, to John Browne, Esq., of Clongoosewood, co. Kildare, son and heir of Thomas Browne, Esq., counsellor-at-law, and by him, who *d.* in 1693, had issue,
  1 Stephen-Fitzwilliam: 2 Christopher, of Castle Browne; 3 Bruno, counsellor-at-law; 1 Alice, *m.* to Mr. John Taylor; and 2 Anne, who *d. unm.* in 1737.
II. Rose, *m.* to Christopher Malpas, Esq., of Winston, and *d.* 1 March, 1744, leaving a son, John Malpas, Esq., of Rochestown, co. Dublin.
III. Margaret, *m.* to James Crawley, Esq.
IV. Catharine, *m.* to Nicholas, son of Robert Netterville, Esq., of Crucerath, co. Meath.
V. Dorothy, *m.* to Thomas Magher, Esq., of the Queen's co.

The son and heir,

THOMAS FITZWILLIAM, 4th Viscount Fitzwilliam, for his attachment to King JAMES II. was outlawed, but the outlawry was subsequently reversed. His lordship *m.* 1st, Mary, dau. of Sir Philip Stapleton, of Wighill, co. York, Bart., by whom he had RICHARD, his heir, and a dau. *m.* to her 1st cousin, Stephen-Fitzwilliam Browne, of Castle Browne, co. Kildare; and 2ndly, the sister of George Pitt, Esq., of Strathfieldsea, co. Southampton, and by her had a dau. Mary, *m.* 11 March, 1718, to George, Earl of Shrewsbury. His lordship *d.* 20 Feb. 1704, and was *s.* by his only son,

RICHARD FITZWILLIAM, 5th Viscount Fitzwilliam, who conformed to the established church, and took his seat in the Irish house of peers, 25 May, 1710. His lordship *m.* Frances, only

215

dau. of Sir John Shelley, Bart., of Michael Grove, in Sussex, and by her (who *d.* 11 Dec. 1771) had three sons and two daus. viz.,

I. RICHARD, his successor.
II. William, bapt. 11 Sept. 1712, Usher of the Black Rod in Ireland, *m.* the only dau. of Thomas Bourchier, Esq., and had an only child, Julia, who *d.* in 1770.
III. John, bapt. 28 March, 1714, page of honour to H.R.H the Prince of Wales, a lieut.-general and M.P. He *m.* in October, 1751, Barbara, dau. of Dr. Chandler, bishop of Durham.
1. Mary, maid of honour to Caroline, Princess of Wales, *m.* 1st, 28 August, 1733, to Henry, Earl of Pembroke, and by him, who *d.* 9 January, 1749, she had an only son,
  Henry, Earl of Pembroke.

She *m.* 2ndly, in September, 1751, North-Ludlow Bernard, Esq., major of dragoons, and *d.* 13 February, 1769.
II. Frances, *m.* 18 May, 1732, to George, Lord Carbery.

His lordship *d.* 6 June, 1743, and was *s.* by his eldest son,

RICHARD FITZWILLIAM, 6th Viscount Fitzwilliam, K.B., a privy-councillor of Ireland, and vice-admiral of Leinster, bapt. 24 July, 1711. His lordship *m.* 3 May, 1744, Catharine, dau. of Sir Matthew Decker, Bart., of Richmond, co. Surrey, by whom he had four sons,

I. RICHARD, 7th viscount.
II. William, *m.* 25 August, 1782, the only dau. and heir of John Eames, Esq., master of the court of Chancery in England.
III. John.
IV. Thomas, *m.* in July, 1780, Agnes, dau. of — Macclesfield, Esq.

His lordship *d.* 25 May, 1776, and was buried in Donnybrook Chapel, near Dublin. He was *s.* by his eldest son,

RICHARD FITZWILLIAM, 7th Viscount Fitzwilliam, *b.* in August, 1745, who *d. unm.* in 1816, when the principal part of his estates passed to the Earl of Pembroke, and are now enjoyed by GEORGE-ROBERT-CHARLES, EARL OF PEMBROKE, son and heir of the late Right Hon. Sydney Herbert, Lord Herbert, of Lea: the honours devolved upon the 7th lord's brother,

JOHN FITZWILLIAM, 8th Viscount Fitzwilliam; at whose decease *s. p.* in 1833, the honours of the family became EXTINCT.

Arms—Lozengy, arg. and gu.

FITZ-WILLIAM—BARON FITZ-WILLIAM.

By Writ of Summons, dated 5 April, 1327.

Lineage.

In the reign of HENRY II., William, the son of William Fitz-Godrick, was the first, according to Dugdale, who assumed this surname, and called himself

WILLIAM FITZ-WILLIAM, in which opinion Seager, Garter-king-of-arms, *temp.* CHARLES I., coincides. William Fitz-Godrick is stated to have been cousin in blood to King EDWARD THE CONFESSOR, and to have been deputed upon an embassy by that monarch to William Duke of Normandy, at whose court he remained until he returned with the expedition in 1066, as marshal of the invading army, and it is added that the CONQUEROR bestowed upon him a scarf from his own arm, for the gallantry he had displayed at Hastings. Sir William Fitz-William (Fitz-Godrick's son), *m.* Eleanor, dau. and heir of Sir John de Elmley, Lord of Elmley and Sprotborough, in Yorkshire, and was *s.* by his son,

SIR WILLIAM FITZ-WILLIAM, who was living in 1117, Lord of Elmley and Sprotborough. This feudal lord *m.* Ella, dau. and co-heir of William, Earl of Warren and Surrey, and had Roger, to whom the Earl of Warren gave the lordship of Gretewell; and an elder son, his successor,

SIR WILLIAM FITZ-WILLIAM, lord of Elmley and Sprotborough, who *m.* Albreda, dau. and heir of Robert de Lizures, widow of Richard Fitz-Eustace, constable of Chester, and sister of the half blood to Robert de Laci, Baron of Pontefract, and had issue, a dau. Donatia, to whom her mother gave lands in Crowle—with a son, his successor,

SIR WILLIAM FITZ-WILLIAM. This feudal lord took up arms in the baronial cause, *temp.* King JOHN, but returned to his allegiance in the 5th HENRY III. He *m.* Ella, dau. of Hamlyn, Earl Warren and Surrey, and was *s.* by his son,

SIR THOMAS FITZ-WILLIAM, who *m.* Agnes, one of the daus. and co-heirs of Roger Bertram, feudal lord of Mitford, by whom he had three sons,

WILLIAM, his successor.
Roger (Sir), who had the lands of Woodhall from his father.
Peter, who was settled at Denby.

He had besides five daus., Margaret, Agnes, Bertha, Rometa, and Alberda, *m.* Sir Richard Walleis, Knt., of Burgh Walleis. Sir Thomas Fitz-William was *s.* by his eldest son,

SIR WILLIAM FITZ-WILLIAM, of Sprotborough, who, in the 29th EDWARD I., was in the Scottish wars; but the next reign, joining in the great insurrection of Thomas, Earl of Lancaster, he was made prisoner with that nobleman at Boroughbridge, and hanged immediately after at York. He *m.* Agnes, dau. of Richard, Lord Grey, of Codnor, and left an only son,

SIR WILLIAM FITZ-WILLIAM, who was summoned [*] to parliament in the 1st EDWARD III., as a baron, but never afterwards. This nobleman *m.* Maud, dau. of Edmund, Lord Deincourt, and had several children, but as none were subsequently esteemed barons, we presume, with Nicolas, that the summons was not a parliamentary, but a military one. From this Sir William the present noble house of Fitz-William, Earls Fitz-William, lineally derive.

Arms—Lozengy, arg. and gu.

FITZ-WILLIAM—EARL OF SOUTHAMPTON.

By Letters Patent, dated 18 October, 1537.

Lineage.

From Sir William Fitz-William, son of William Fitz-Godrick, marshal of the victorious army at Hastings, descended,

SIR WILLIAM FITZ-WILLIAM, who *m.* Agnes, dau. of Richard Lord Grey, of Codnor, and had issue a son,

SIR WILLIAM FITZ-WILLIAM, summoned to parliament as a baron, 5 April, 1327. (*See* FITZ-WILLIAM, BARON FITZ-WILLIAM). He *m.* Maud, dau. of Edmond, Lord Deincourt, and had, with other issue, a son,

SIR JOHN FITZ-WILLIAM, who *m.* Joan, dau. of Sir Adam Reresby, Knt., and had a son,

SIR JOHN FITZ-WILLIAM, who *m.* Elizabeth, dau. and heiress of William Clinton, Earl of Huntingdon, and had several children, of whom,

EDMOND FITZWILLIAM, was grandfather of

SIR THOMAS FITZWILLIAM, Knt., of Aldwarke, co. York, who *m.* Lucy, dau. and co-heir of John Nevill, Marquess of Montacute, and had issue, THOMAS, slain at Flodden Field, in the 4th HENRY VIII., and another son,

WILLIAM FITZ-WILLIAM, who was made by King HENRY VIII one of the esquires of his body, and knighted soon after for his good services at the siege of Tournay. Upon the attainder of Edward Stafford, Duke of Buckingham, Sir William Fitz-William, being then vice-admiral of England, obtained a grant of the manor of Navesby, in the county of Northampton, part of that nobleman's possessions. In the 15th HENRY VIII. Sir William, as admiral of the English fleet, went to sea for the purpose of intercepting the Duke of Albany, who was about returning to Scotland with a large body of French. The next year he was captain of Guisnes, in Picardy, and he was soon after, being at the time treasurer of the household, deputed with John Taylor, doctor of law, to take the oath of the Lady Regent, then at Lyons, (King FRANCIS I. being a prisoner in Spain,) for ratifying the articles of a treaty just concluded between the crowns of England and France. In the 24th of the same reign he was joined in another embassy to France with the Duke of Norfolk and Dr. COX, regarding the marriage of the French King's third son, with the English monarch's daughter, the Lady Elizabeth; after which (28th HENRY VIII.), being a knight of the Garter, treasurer of the household, and chancellor of the Duchy of Lancaster, he was constituted Admiral of England, Wales, Ireland, Normandy, Gascony, and Aquitaine, and elevated to the peerage, by letters patent, dated 18 October, 1537, as EARL OF SOUTHAMPTON. He was subsequently appointed lord privy seal. His lordship *d.* at Newcastle in 1543, upon his march into Scotland, leading the van of the English army, but so highly was he esteemed, that to do honour to his memory, his standard was borne in the forward, throughout the whole of the ensuing campaign. The earl *m.* Mabel, dau. of Henry, Lord Clifford, and sister of Henry, 1st

---

Earl of Cumberland, but had no issue, in consequence of which the Earldom of Southampton at his decease, became EXTINCT. while his estates devolved upon (his brother's daus.) his nieces,

Margaret Fitz-William, wife of Godfrey Fuljambe, Esq.
Alice Fitz-William, wife of Sir James Fuljambe, Knt.

Arms—Lozengy, arg. and gu., a mullet for difference.

FLEMING — VISCOUNT LONGFORD AND BARON SLANE.

Lineage.

ARCHEMBALD, a nobleman of Flanders, accompanied WILLIAM THE CONQUEROR to England, and acquired the manor and lordship of Bratton, in Devonshire, with other manors in that county and Cornwall, which ne held in 1087. His son,

STEPHEN FITZ-ARCHEMBALD, Lord of Bratton, paid a fine of ten silver marcs to the king for trespass, in 1139; and in 1145 he witnessed the charter of Henry de Tracy to the abbey of Barnstaple by the name of Stephen of Flanders. His son,

ARCHEMBALD, of Flanders, was, in 1165, returned as possessor of the family estates which he held "*de veteri feoffamento.*" He attended HENRY [ ] in his invasion of Ireland, and obtained the lordships of Ast...ayn and Eskertenen, in Tipperary, and Newcastle and Slane, on the river Boyne, from the latter of which he and his male descendants took their title of honour. He was a great baron of Ireland, and that dignity, subsequently known as that of a lord of parliament, continued to be enjoyed by his descendants until they were excluded from their seat in parliament by the penal laws. He was *s.* by his son,

STEPHEN, of Flanders, who, in 1185, by the express command of the king, with a retinue of nine knights and fifty horsemen, attended Prince John, then appointed lord of Ireland, to take possession of his government. He *d.* in the 14th year of the reign of JOHN. His son,

BALDWIN LE FLEMING, 3rd Baron of Slane, was, in 1242, with twenty-one Irish kings and princes, and nine other great barons, summoned to accompany HENRY III. in his Scotch wars, and when the king made peace, specially thanked by him. In 1260 he was, as a magnate of England, ordered to attend the king in London, to perform the services due to him, and to hear his commands. He was *s.* by his son,

RICHARD LE FLEMING, 4th Baron of Slane, who as a tenant in capite of the crown, for his manors in Devon and Cornwall, accompanied the king, in 1293, in his wars in Wales, and in 1295 and 1300, in those of Scotland, in which he lost his life. He *m.* Maria, dau. of Nicholas Lord Martyn, by whom he had issue,

BALDWIN LE FLEMING, 5th Baron of Slane, who received various writs of military and parliamentary summons during the reign of EDWARD II. In 1318 he was specially thanked by the king for his services against Edward Bruce, who had been crowned king of Ireland. He *d.* 1332, having *m.* Matilda, dau. and co-heir of Sir Symon de Geynville, 2nd son of Geffry, next brother of Jean, Sire de Joinville, the celebrated historian and friend of St. Louis, by whom he had issue,

SYMON FLEMING, 6th Baron of Slane, who was, by letters patent, 20th EDWARD III., appointed conservator of the peace for the county of Meath. He *d.* in 1371, leaving issue by Cecilia his wife, dau. of Sir Thomas Champernon, of Modberrie, in Devonshire, a son and successor,

THOMAS FLEMING, 7th Baron of Slane, who was, with the Lords Gormanston and Delvin, guardian of the marches of Meath during the reigns of HENRY IV. and HENRY V. He *m.* 1st, Elizabeth, dau. of Robert Preston, Lord Gormanston, by whom he had issue,

CHRISTOPHER, his successor.

He *m.* 2ndly, Catherine, dau. of James, Earl of Ormonde, by whom he had issue,

   William, of Newcastle, who left issue by Jenetta Rochford, his wife, three sons, viz.,

     1 James, who *s.* as 12th Lord Slane.
     2 John, whose male issue failed before 1515.
     3 Robert, ancestor of the FLEMINGS of Drogheda, and of several branches of the family.

Thomas, Lord Slane, *d.* in 1436, after having enjoyed his peerage for more than half a century, and was *s.* by his son,

CHRISTOPHER FLEMING, 8th Baron of Slane, whose services in the wars were gratefully acknowledged by HENRY VI., in 1436 He *m.* 1st, Levita, dau. and co-heir of Martin Ferrers, of Beere Ferrers, in Devonshire, by whom he had issue,

---

[*] So says Dugdale, "but it appears from his list of summonses in that year, that Sir William Fitz-William was not included in either of the summonses *to parliament,* but only in the summons dated at Ramsay, 5 April, 1324, to attend at Newcastle-upon-Tyne, with horse and arms.   "NICOLAS."

216

John Fleming, who *d. v. p.*, leaving issue,

Christopher, heir to his grandfather.
Anne, *m.* to Walter Dillon, Esq. }
Amia, *m.* to John Bellew, Esq. }

Lord Christopher *m.* 2ndly, Elizabeth, dau. and co-heir of John, son and heir apparent of Sir David Wogan, by whom he had issue,

David Fleming, who *s.* as 10th Lord Slane.

Christopher, Lord Slane, *d.* in 1447, and was *s,* by his grandson, CHRISTOPHER FLEMING, 9th Baron of Slane, who sat in parliament in 1450; and *d.* in 1457, *s. p.*, leaving his two sisters his co-heirs. He was *s.* by his uncle,

DAVID FLEMING, 10th Baron of Slane, who *m.* Alicia, dau. of Sir Robert Dillon, by whom he had issue,

THOMAS, his successor.
Elizabeth.
Anne. }
Margaret, *m.* to John D'Arcy, Esq. of Platten. } †

David, Lord Slane, *d.* in 1462, and was *s.* by his son,

THOMAS FLEMING, 11th Baron of Slane, who was seven years old on his father's death. His wardship was confirmed to the Earl of Kildare, by act of parliament, in 1463. In 1470 he had livery of all his lands by statute, although he was then under age. He *d.* in the following year *s. p.*, leaving his sisters, his co-heirs, and was *s.* by his cousin,

JAMES FLEMING, 12th Baron of Slane (*refer* to the issue of Thomas, 7th Lord Slane, by his 2nd wife), who, in 1480, was made member of the order of St. George, then established in Ireland. In 1487, he, with the other peers of Ireland, signed the letter to HENRY VII. in favour of the Earl of Kildare, the lord deputy of Ireland, and in the following year attended that monarch at Greenwich. He *m.* Elizabeth, widow of Christopher, Lord Killeen, and dau. and co-heir of Sir William Welles, lord chancellor of Ireland, only brother of Lionel, Lord Welles, lord lieutenant of that kingdom, in the reign of HENRY VI., by whom he had issue,

I. Christopher, his successor.
II. George (Sir), of Stephenston, who *m.* Margaret, sister of Piers, Earl of Ormonde, by whom he had,
George, who *d. s. p.*
James, who *m.* Ismay, dau. of Sir Bartholomew Dillon, by whom he had an only son,
THOMAS, who *s.* as 15th Lord Slane.
III. Thomas, of Derpatrick, who *m.* Alison, dau. of Walter Cruice, of Navan, by whom he had,
WILLIAM, of Derpatrick, who *m.* Alice, dau. of Oliver Eustace, of Liscarton, by whom he had an only son,
George, of Derpatrick, who *m.* Mary, only child of Walter Cusack, of Kilkarn, by whom he had,
WILLIAM, who *s.* as 16th Lord Slane.
Edward, of Sydon.
IV. John.
V. William.

James, Lord Slane, *d.* in 1491, and was *s.* by his son,

CHRISTOPHER FLEMING, 13th Baron of Slane, who, in 1513, was. by letters patent, appointed lord high treasurer of Ireland, which high office he retained to the period of his death. He *m.* Ellys, dau. of Gerald, Earl of Kildare, but his marriage with her was set aside, and he afterwards *m.* Elizabeth, dau. of Nicholas Stukeley, of Affeton, co. Devon, Esq., by whom he had issue,

JAMES, his successor.
Ellinor, *d. s. p.*
Catherine, who became sole heir of her brother. She *m.* Sir Christopher Barnewall, Knt., of Crickstown, and had issue. Their descendant and heir-male is the present SIR REGINALD BARNEWALL, Bart.

Christopher, Lord Slane, *d.* in 1518, and was *s.* by his son,

JAMES FLEMING, 14th Baron of Slane, who sat in the parliament of 1541, which made HENRY VIII. King of Ireland. He constantly served with the Earl of Essex, who in a letter to the queen, dated 1573, stated that he was the only nobleman who would consent to accompany him in his wars against O'Neal. He *d. s. p.* in 1576, leaving his sister his heir, and was *s.* by his kinsman,

THOMAS FLEMING, 15th Baron of Slane (*refer* to the issue of James, 12th Lord Slane), who highly distinguished himself in the service of Queen ELIZABETH. He *m.* Katherine, dau. of Jenico, Lord Viscount Gormanston, by whom he had issue,

Catherine, *m.* to Piers Butler, Esq. of the Old Abbey.
Ellinor, who *m.* her cousin, William Fleming, who *s.* as Lord Slane.

Thomas, Lord Slane, *d.* in 1597, and was *s.* by his kinsman,

WILLIAM FLEMING, 16th Baron of Slane (*refer* to the issue of Thomas, 3rd son of James, 12th Lord Slane), who had livery of all his estates in 1605. He *m.* as before mentioned, his cousin Ellinor, by whom he had,

CHRISTOPHER, his successor.
George.
Thomas.   James.

William, Lord Slane, *d.* in 1612, and was *s.* by his son,

CHRISTOPHER FLEMING, 17th Baron of Slane; who *m.* Ellinor, dau. of Sir Patrick Barnewall, of Turvey, by whom he had issue,

THOMAS, his successor.
WILLIAM, afterwards Baron of Slane.
John.   Patrick.
James.   Laurence

Christopher, Lord Slane, *d.* in 1625, and was *s.* by his son,

THOMAS FLEMING, 18th Baron of Slane, who being a friar of the order of St. Francis, petitioned the king, in 1629, that his brother might enjoy the dignity of Baron of Slane; which petition his Majesty was pleased to grant, and to confirm the dignity to William, and the heirs male of his body, during the lifetime of Thomas. Thomas resided in his convent in the Netherlands, until he was made Roman Catholic Archbishop of Dublin, when he returned to Ireland. For a long period, with the aid of the retainers and friends of his family, he carried on a destructive war against the parliamentary forces.

WILLIAM FLEMING, who became, as before mentioned, 19th Baron of Slane, *m.* Anne, dau. of Randal, Earl of Antrim, and widow of Christopher, Lord Delvin, by whom he had issue,

I. CHARLES, his successor.
II. RANDAL, who *s.* his brother.
III. Michael, who *d. s. p.*
IV. William, of Gillenstown, who *d.* before his brother Randal, leaving issue,
William, who became *de jure* Baron of Slane, on the death of Christopher, Viscount Longford, and assumed that title. He had a pension of £300 a year, and *d.* in 1747, leaving an only son, Christopher, who also assumed the title of Lord Slane, who *d.* without issue male in 1772, and on his death the male issue of William, the 19th Lord Slane became extinct.

William, Lord Slane, was outlawed, after his death, in 1641; but afterwards declared, both by the king and the commissioners appointed under the act of settlement, innocent. After the Revolution, his outlawry was brought forward to deprive the family of the peerage. Lord William was *s.* by his eldest son,

CHARLES FLEMING, 20th Baron of Slane, who was excepted from pardon for life and estate by Cromwell's act for the settlement of Ireland, passed in 1652. He with his half-brother, Lord Westmeath, long maintained the royal cause in Ireland, and they were the last royalists in arms in that kingdom. He afterwards, with 10,000 troops, entered into the service of LOUIS XIV., in which he lost his life, in Italy, in 1661. He was *s.* by his brother,

RANDALL FLEMING, 21st Baron of Slane, who was restored to all his estates on the Restoration. He *m.* 1st, Ellinor, dau. of Sir Richard Barnewall, Bart., of Crickstown, by whom he had,

Mary, who *m.* 1st, Richard Fleming, Esq., of Staholmock, and afterwards Colonel Oliver O'Gara. By her 2nd husband she had a son Charles, who *d. unm.* 1785. By her 1st husband, she was mother of an only son, James, who *d. unm.*, and an only dau BRIDGET, *m.* to RANDALL PLUNKETT, 11th LORD DUNSANY.

Lord Randall *m.* 2ndly, Penelope, dau. of Henry, Earl of Drogheda, by whom he had,

CHRISTOPHER, his successor.
Henry, } who both *d. s. p.* in the lifetime of their
Randall, } brother.
Alice, *m.* Sir Gregory Byrne, Bart., and their grand-dau and eventual heiress, Catherine Xaveria Byrne, *m.* George Bryan, Esq., and was mother of GEORGE BRYAN, Esq., of Jenkinstown, co. Kilkenny.

Randall, Lord Slane, *d.* in 1676, and was *s.* by his son,

CHRISTOPHER FLEMING, 22nd Baron of Slane, who was seven years old on the death of his father. In 1691 he was attainted for his adherence to JAMES II., whom he followed to France. In 1708 he was restored in blood and to his peerage, by an English act of parliament; and, in 1713, created by Queen ANNE, VISCOUNT LONGFORD. He *d.* in 1726, without male issue, and although on his death the dignity was assumed by his cousin William, and on the death of William by his son Christopher, the attainder of 1641 was alleged as a bar to the descent of the dignity, notwithstanding that it had been admitted from the time of the Restoration until the succession of Viscount Longford, who was actually outlawed as Christopher Lord Slane, in

* These ladies became co-heirs of their brother, and succeeded to estates in Devonshire and Cornwall, as well as to some property in Ireland.
† These ladies became co-heirs of their brother.
217

1691. Both William and his son Christopher adhered to the Roman Catholic religion, and therefore could not sit in parliament. The dignity was recently claimed by the late George Bryan, of Jenkinstown, co. Kilkenny, Esq., as sole heir of the Hon. Alice Fleming, youngest dau. of Randall, Lord Slane; but this claim was opposed by James Fleming, Esq., now one of Her Majesty's Counsel, who claimed to be the heir male of the family, and alleged that the barony was descendable solely in the male line. On 1 September, 1835, the House of Lords, after an investigation which lasted more than five years, resolved that Mr. Bryan had not made out his claim to the Barony of Slane.

Arms—Vair, a chief, chequy, or and gu.

*** The motto of this family is in Flemish, the only instance of an English or Irish family continuing to bear a motto in that language.

FLEMING—EARL OF WIGTON.

By Patent, 19 March, 1606.

Lineage.

This family has common origin with the Flemings of Slane, and, after the Union of the crowns of England and Scotland, the Lords Slane, in all the settlements of their estates, made remainders, on failure of the prior branches, in favour of the Earls of Wigton.

SIR MALCOLM FLEMING was sheriff of Dumbarton in the reign of King ALEXANDER III. He was great grandson of a distinguished Flemish leader, Baldwin Flandrensis, who had a grant of the lands of Biggar from King DAVID I., and was sheriff of Lanark in the reigns of MALCOLM IV. and WILLIAM THE LION. Baldwin was a younger son of Stephen Flandrensis, or Stephen of Flanders, of Bratton, which Stephen first assumed the surname from Flanders.

ROBERT FLEMING of Biggar, the son of Sir Malcolm, was a faithful adherent of King ROBERT BRUCE, and obtained from that monarch the lands of Cumbernauld on the forfeiture of the great house of Comyn. He d. before 1314. He left two sons; I. SIR MALCOLM, whose son, SIR MALCOLM, was created EARL OF WIGTON, in 1341, but his line failed in the person of his grandson, the 2nd earl, soon after 1332; II. SIR PATRICK FLEMING, of Biggar.

There was a long succession of Lords of Biggar and Cumbernauld in this family, and in the reign of JAMES II., SIR ROBERT FLEMING was created a peer of parliament as BARON FLEMING. In 1606, the ancient title of EARL OF WIGTON was revived in the person of John, 6th Lord Fleming. In 1747, the earldom of Wigton became EXTINCT, and the estates of Biggar and Cumbernauld devolved on Lady Clementina Fleming, only surviving child of John, 6th earl.

The matrimonial alliances of the successive generations of the Flemings were illustrious, Robert, Duke of Albany, Regent of Scotland; Douglas, Earl of Douglas; Livingston, Lord Livingston; Drummond, Lord Drummond; JAMES IV., King of Scotland, natural dau.: Ross, Lord Ross; Graham, Earl of Montrose; Livingston, Earl of Linlithgow; Drummond, Earl of Perth; Seton, Earl of Dunfermline; and last and not least, Keith, Earl Marischal.

JOHN, 6th Lord Fleming (only son of John, 5th lord, by Elizabeth, his wife, only child of Robert, Master of Ross, and grandson of Malcolm, 3rd Lord Fleming, by Johanna Stewart, his wife), was created EARL OF WIGTON, LORD FLEMING AND CUMBERNAULD, by patent, dated at Whitehall, 19 March, 1606. His lordship m. 1st, Lady Lillias Graham, only dau. of John, 3rd Earl of Montrose, and had issue,

  I. JOHN, 2nd Earl of Wigton
  II. James, of Boghall, who m. in 1612, Janet Brisbane, dau. of the Laird of Bishoptoun, and d. in 1622. His son, John, came of age, 1643.
  III. Malcolm.   IV. Alexander.
  I. Jean, m. in 1603, to George, Master of Loudoun, and was mother of Margaret, Countess of Loudoun.
  II. Anne, m. to Sir William Livingston, of Darnchester, eldest son of Sir William Livingston, of Kilsyth.
  III. Margaret, m. in 1613, to Sir John Charteris, of Amisfield, and had issue.
  IV. Lillias, m. in 1627, to Sir David Murray, of Stanhope, and had issue.
  V. Mary, m. 1634, to Archibald Stewart, the younger, of Castlemilk, and had issue.
  VI. Rachel, m. in 1624, to George Lindsay, of Covington.

The earl m. 2ndly, Sarah Maxwell, eldest dau. of John, Lord Herries, relict of Sir James Johnston, of Johnston, and by her (who m. 3rdly, Hugh Montgomery, Viscount of Airds, in Ireland, and was buried at Edinburgh, 27 March, 1636) had two daus., Sarah and Jean. The earl d. 1619: his eldest son, JOHN FLEMING, 2nd Earl of Wigton, m. Lady Margaret Liv-

ingston, 2nd dau. of Alexander, 1st Earl of Linlithgow, and had issue,

  I. JOHN, 3rd Earl of Wigton.
  II. William, chamberlain of the household of CHARLES d. s. p.
  I. Eleanor, m. at Cumbernauld, 23 April, 1650, to David, 2nd Earl of Wemyss, and d. s. p. 20 April, 1652.
  II. Anne, m. 1st, to Robert, 7th Lord Boyd; 2ndly, to George, 2nd Earl of Dalhousie, and d. 20 April, 1661, having had issue
  III. Jean, m. in 1641, to Sir John Grierson, of Lag, co. Dumfries, and had issue.

The Earl of Wigton d. 7 May, 1650, and was s. by his son,
  JOHN FLEMING, 3rd Earl of Wigton, who joined Montrose, was at the battle of Philiphaugh, 1645, and escaped with the marquess to the highlands, where he lay concealed for some time. His lordship was served heir to his father, 20 August, 1652. He m. Lady Jane Drummond, eldest dau. of John, 2nd Earl of Perth, and had issue,

  I. JOHN, 4th Earl of Wigton.
  II. Robert (Sir), d. unm.
  III. James, d. unm.   IV. Harry, d. unm.
  V. WILLIAM, 5th Earl of Wigton.
  VI. Charles, d. unm.
  I. Margaret, d. unm.
  II. Lillias, m. to Richard Storry, Esq.   III. Jean.

The eldest son,
  JOHN FLEMING, 4th Earl of Wigton, who had a charter to John, Lord Fleming, and Anne Ker, his wife, of the Earldom of Wigton, 10 May, 1662, and s. his father, 1665. He m. Anne, 2nd dau. of Harry, Lord Ker, son and heir apparent of Robert, 1st Earl of Roxburghe, and by her had one dau.,

  Jean, m. to George, 3rd Earl of Panmure; and d. in April, 1683. William, 5th Earl of Wigton, was served tutor-at-law as nearest heir of her, 21 September, 1669.

The earl d. in April, 1668, and was s. by his brother,
  WILLIAM FLEMING, 5th Earl of Wigton, who m. at Dalgety in September 1670, Lady Henriet Seton, dau. of Charles, 2nd Earl of Dunfermline, and by her (who m. 2ndly, William, 18th Earl of Crawford) had issue,

  JOHN, 6th Earl of Wigton.
  CHARLES, 7th Earl of Wigton
  Mary, m. 30 March, 1695, to the Hon. Harry Maule, of Kelly, and was mother of William, Earl of Panmure.

The eldest son,
  JOHN FLEMING, 6th Earl of Wigton, s. his father in 1681; attended JAMES II. to St Germains; opposed the treaty of Union in the parliament, 1706, voting against every article; and was committed prisoner to the castle of Edinburgh, at the breaking out of the rebellion, by warrant of Major-General Williams, 20 August, 1715. His lordship required the governor of the castle, under form of instrument, 19 June, 1716, to set him at liberty. The governor answered, that his lordship being committed in time of war, could not be released without a special warrant from the king, or those having power from him. The court of Justiciary, however, ordained the governor to set the prisoner at liberty, 24 June, 1716. He had the appointment of king's chamberlain of Fife, 1736; and dying at Edinburgh, 10 February, 1744, in the seventy-first year of his age, was buried at Biggar. (WOODS' DOUGLAS.) He m. 1st, 14 March, 1698, Lady Margaret Lindsay, 2nd dau. of Colin, 3rd Earl of Balcarres, by whom he had a dau.,

  Margaret, m. to Sir Archibald Primrose, Bart., of Dunipace, co. Stirling; but d. s. p.

The earl m. 2ndly (contract dated 8 February, 1711), Lady Mary Keith, eldest dau. of William, 9th Earl Marischal, and by her (who d. 1721) had one dau.,

  CLEMENTINA, m. in 1735, to CHARLES, 10th LORD ELPHINSTONE; and d. 1 January, 1799, aged eighty. Her grandson,
  THE HON. CHARLES ELPHINSTONE FLEMING, admiral in the royal navy, M.P. for the county of Stirling, succeeded in her right to the estates of Cumbernauld and Biggar, the ancient inheritance of the Earls of Wigton. He m. in 1816, Donna Catalina-Paulina-Alessandro, a Spanish lady, and by her (who m. 2ndly, Captain Katon, R.N.) had,
    1 JOHN-ELPHINSTONE-FLEMING, 14th Lord Elphinstone, d. unm., 13 January, 1861.
    1 Clementina, m. 24 March, 1845, Cornwallis, Viscount Hawarden, and d. in January, 1865, leaving issue.
    2 Mary-Keith, m. 1st, 20 April, 1843, to Alexander Macalister, Esq., of Torridale (which marriage was dissolved in 1847); and 2ndly, to Morgan Lloyd, Esq.; and d. 11 March, 1859.
    3 Anne-Elizabeth, m. 12 June, 1851, to William Cunninghame Bontine, Esq., of Ardoch, eldest son of R.-C. Cunninghame-Graham, Esq., of Gartmore and Finlayston.

His lordship m. 3rdly, Eupheme, dau. of George Lockhart, of Carnwath, co. Lanark, author of the *Memoirs of Scotland*, but had no issue by her, who m. 2ndly, Peter Mac Elligot, major-general in the service of MARIA-THERESA. The earl was *s.* by his brother,

CHARLES FLEMING, 7th Earl of Wigton; who *d. unm.* at Elphinstone, 26 May, 1747, when the family estates devolved on his niece, Lady Clementina Elphinstone, whose senior co-representative is the HON. CORNWALLIS MAUDE.

The title of Earl of Wigton was assumed at his lordship's decease by CHARLES-ROSS FLEMYNG, M.D., of Dublin, son of James Flemyng, rector of Castlane, Kilderry, &c., chaplain to the lord-lieutenant of Ireland, and grandson of James Flemyng, rector of Ramochy, co. Donegal, whose father was stated to have been Alexander, son of John, 6th Lord Fleming, and 1st Earl of Wigton. Dr. Flemyng bore the title for a time, but was debarred by the Lords' Committee for Privileges from such assumption until he should establish his claim. He *m.* 26 December, 1743, Anne, sister of William Hamilton, Esq., of Queen Anne's Street, London, and had a son and heir, Hamilton Flemyng, Esq., an officer in the army, who *m.* 14 December, 1769, Mary-Charlotte, dau. and heir of William Child, Esq., and *d.* 13 June, 1809, leaving an only dau. and heiress, Harriot-Jane-Laura, *m.* 13 October, 1794, to WILLIAM GYLL, Esq., of Wyrardisbury, Bucks, capt. 2nd life guards. He *d.* 18 October, 1769.

Arms—Quarterly 1st and 4th, arg., a chev., within a double treasure, flowered and counter-flowered with fleurs-de-lis, gu. for FLEMING; 2nd and 3rd, az., three cinquefoils, arg., for FRASER.

FOLIOT—BARON FOLIOT.

By Writ of Summons, dated 23 June, 1295.

Lineage.

In the 12th of King HENRY II.
ROBERT FOLIOT, upon the assessment of the aid for marrying the king's dau., certified that he had fifteen knights' fees, which his ancestors had held from the Conquest. This feudal lord *m.* Margery, dau. and heiress of Richard de Reincurt. Lord of Sutton, co. Bedford, whereupon King HENRY II. confirmed to him the manor of Burton, in the co. of Northampton, and all the other lands and honour of Guy de Reincurt, ancestor of the said Richard. He was *s.* by his son,
RICHARD FOLIOT, living 1199, who left an only dau. and heiress,
Margery, who *m.* Whyschard Ledet, son of Christian Ledet, Lady of Langtone, co. Leicester. The inheritance of this lady (Margery Foliot) was litigated in the 8th RICHARD I., by Thomas Foliot, Richard de Hidon, Emme de Boterel, and Geffrey de Barinton, grand-children of Robert Foliot, and the suit was pending in the reign of King JOHN.

With this heiress this branch of the family appears to have terminated, but many of the same race were distinguished for several years afterwards, until the reign of EDWARD I., when
JORDAN FOLIOT was summoned to parliament as a Baron from 23 June, 1295, to 26 January, 1299, leaving a son,
RICHARD FOLIOT, æt. fifteen, of whom nothing is known, but that he left, besides a son, RICHARD, two daus.,
Margery, *m.* before 1330, Hugh de Hastings, a younger son, (by his 2nd marriage) of John, Lord Bergavenny.
Margaret, *m.* to John de Camoys.
The son,
RICHARD FOLIOT *d. s. p.* in 1326, and the barony remains in ABEYANCE between the descendants of his two sisters.

Arms—Gu., a bend, arg.

NOTE.—Gilbert Foliot, bishop of Hereford, *anno* 1149, and of London, in 1161, is another eminent person of this name.

FOLLIOTT—BARON FOLLIOTT, OF BAL-LYSHANNON.

By Letters Patent, dated 22 January, 1619.

Lineage.

THE RT. HON. SIR HENRY FOLLIOTT, governor of Ballyshannon, co. Sligo (son of Thomas Folliott, Esq. of Pyrton, co. Worcester, by Katherine, his 2nd wife, dau. of William Lygon, Esq., and the lineal descendant of a younger branch of the old baronial family of Folliott, which was established in England at the Conquest,) was knighted by Robert, Earl of Essex, lord-

219

lieutenant of Ireland, 6 September, 1599, and commanded a regiment at the victory of Kinsale. Subsequently he was raised to the peerage of Ireland, as *Baron Folliott of Bally-shannon, co. Donegal,* 22 January, 1619. His lordship *m.* Anne, dau of Sir William Strode, of Stoke-under-Hampden, in Somersetshire, and by her (who *m.* 2ndly, Robert, Earl of Roscommon,) had issue,

I. THOMAS, his heir.
II. Michael, *d.* 17 November, 1638, and was buried in St. Werburgh's Church. Dublin.
III. Arthur, *d.* an infant.
IV. Henry, *d. s. p.*
V. Charles, living 1622.
I. Frances, *m.* to Sir Robert King, of Kingsborough (son of the Right Hon. Sir John King, of Abbey Boyle, co. Roscommon, Muster-Master of Ireland, P.C.); and *d.* 13 March, 1637, having had issue,
  1 John (Sir), created BARON KINGSTON, 4 September 1660.
  2 Henry.
  3 Robert, created a Baronet, 27 September, 1682, ancestor of the EARL OF KINGSTON and of VISCOUNT LORTON.
  4 William, *d.* 11 June, 1662.
  1 Catherine.   2 Anne.   3 Mary.
  4 Elizabeth.   5 Anne.   6 Frances.
II. Elizabeth, *m.* 1st, in 1640, to Richard Wingfield, Esq., of Powerscourt; 2ndly, in 1646, to Edward Trevor, Esq.; and 3rdly, to Col. Sir John Ponsonby, of Bessborough, and by him had issue,
  1 Henry (Sir), *d. s. p.*
  2 William, 1st Baron Bessborough, and Viscount Duncannon, ancestor of the EARL OF BESSBOROUGH.
  1 Elizabeth, *m.* 1673, to Richard, Viscount Shannon.

His lordship *d.* 10 November, 1622, and was *s.* by his son,
THOMAS FOLLIOTT, 2nd Lord Folliott, governor of Londonderry; *b.* in 1613; who *m.* Rebecca French, relict of Mr. Waterhouse, or Waters, of Dublin, and had issue,

I. HENRY, his heir.
I. Anne, *m.* to John Soley, Esq. of Lickhill, co. Worcester.
II. Rebecca, *m.* to Job Walker, Esq., of Wotton, Salop, and was mother of
  Rebecca Walker, who *m.* in 1717, Humphrey Sandford, Esq., of the Isle of Rossall, co. Salop, and was grandmother of
    FOLLIOTT SANDFORD, Esq., of the Isle of Rossall, who *m.* Isabella, dau. of William Deuchars, and was grandfather of HUMPHREY SANDFORD, Esq., of the Isle of Rossall, co. Salop (see *Landed Gentry*).
III. Elizabeth, *m.* 1st, to Samuel Powell, Esq., of Stanedge, co. Radnor: and 2ndly, to the Rev. Thomas Jones, of Combe, co. Flint; by the former she had, with other issue,
  Samuel Powell (2nd son) who *m.* Elizabeth, dau. of the Rev. Richard Richmond and was ancestor of
    HENRY FOLLIOTT POWELL, Esq., of Bradlesome Hall, co. Lancaster.
IV. Frances, *m.* to Mr. Mason.
V. Mary, *m.* to Rowland Baugh, Esq., of Stone House, co. Salop.
The son and heir,
HENRY FOLLIOTT, 3rd Lord Folliott, *m.* Elizabeth, dau. and co-heir of Henry Dudley, Esq., of Langley Hall, co. Warwick, or (as otherwise stated) dau. and co-heir of George Pudsey, Esq., but *d. s. p.* in 1716, when the title became EXTINCT.

Arms—Arg., a lion rampant, double queued, purpure, ducally crowned, or, a crescent for difference on the neck of the lion.

⁂ The FFOLLIOTTS now of HOLLYBROOK HOUSE, co. Sligo, descend from a common ancestor with the Lords Folliott, of Ballyshannon.

FORBES—LORD FORBES OF PITSLIGO.

By Letters Patent, dated 24 June, 1633.

Lineage.

SIR WILLIAM FORBES, 2nd son of Sir John de Forbes, *m.* Agnes, dau. of William Fraser, of Philorth, and had a son,
SIR ALEXANDER FORBES, of Pitsligo, who *m.* the dau. of the Erroll family, and had, with four daus., three sons,
I. ALEXANDER (Sir), his successor.
II. George, ancestor of the Forbeses of Lethinty.
III. Arthur (Sir), progenitor of the Forbeses of Rires.
The eldest son,
SIR ALEXANDER FORBES, who obtained a charter of the

barony of Pitsligo and Kynaldy, 10 October, 1476, m. Christian, dau. of Sir John Ogilvy, of Lintrethan, and left two sons,

JOHN (Sir), his heir.
William, of Dauch and New, ancestor of the families of Forbes of New, whose last male heir, Major Forbes, of New, d. in 1792; and of Forbes of Bellabeg, now represented by Sir Charles Forbes, Bart., of Newe, &c.

The elder son,
SIR JOHN FORBES, Knt., m. Margaret, dau. and heiress of Sir Patrick Wemys, of Rires, and had a son,
JOHN FORBES, of Pitsligo, who m. Jean, dau. of Sir William Keith, of Innerugy, and had issue,

I. ALEXANDER.
II. Arthur, killed at the battle of Pinkie. 1547, s. p.
III. William.
IV. John.

The eldect son,
ALEXANDER FORBES, of Pitsligo, m. Beatrix, dau. of Alexander, 4th Lord Abernethy, of Saltoun, and by her had issue,

I. WILLIAM (Sir).
II. ALEXANDER, of whom presently.
III. John, of Boyndlie, m. Agnes Gray, dau. of the Laird of Shives, and had issue.
IV. Arthur, m. Margaret Lesly, a dau. of the Laird of Pitcaple.
V. George.   VI. Hector.
I. Anne, m. to Alexander Gordon, of Lesmoir.

The 2nd son,
ALEXANDER FORBES, of Pitsligo, m. 1st, Elizabeth Anderson, relict of Forbes, of Tolquhoun, by whom he had a dau., Violet, m. to Gilbert Menzies. He m. 2ndly, Barbara, 2nd dau. of William, Lord Keith, son and heir-apparent of William, 4th Earl Marshal, and had, with a dau. Margery, m. to John Forbes, of Brux, a son,
SIR JOHN FORBES, of Pitsligo, who m. Christian, eldest dau. of Walter, 1st Lord Ogilvy, of Deskford, and d. in September, 1625, having had issue,

I. Alexander, his successor.
I. Anne, m. to Alexander, 10th Lord Forbes.
II. Jean, m. to Forbes, of Tolquhoun.
III. Mary, m. to Ogilvy, of Boyne.
IV. Christian, m. to Fraser, of Strichen.

SIR ALEXANDER FORBES, Knt., of Pitsligo, who was raised to the peerage of Scotland, 24 June, 1633, as BARON FORBES, of Pitsligo, with limitations to his heirs male whatsoever. His lordship m. Jean Keith, dau. of William, 6th Earl Marischal, and left at his decease, 1635 (with a dau., Mary, m. to Sir John Gordon, of Haddo), a son and successor,
ALEXANDER FORBES, 2nd Lord Forbes; who m. Lady Mary Erskine, eldest dau. of James, Earl of Buchan, and was father of
ALEXANDER FORBES, 3rd Lord Forbes; who m. Sophia, dau. of John, 9th Earl of Marr; and dying in 1691, left, with a dau. (Mary, m. 1st, to John Forbes, Esq., of Monymusk, and 2ndly, to James, 15th Lord Forbes,) a son,
ALEXANDER FORBES, 4th Lord Forbes; who m. 1st, Rebecca, dau. of John Norton, merchant of London, and had a son, John, who d. s. p.; and 2ndly, Elizabeth Allan, an English lady, but by her had no issue. His lordship was attainted for his participation in the rebellion of 1745, and the title has since remained under attainder. The male heir is the present SIR CHARLES JOHN FORBES, Bart., of Newe and Bellabeg.

Arms—Az., three boars' heads, couped, arg., muzzled, gu.

FORTESCUE—EARL OF CLINTON.

By Letters Patent, dated 5 July, 1746.

Lineage.

LADY MARGARET CLINTON, one of the daus. and co-heirs of Theophilus, 4th Earl of Lincoln, and 10th Baron Clinton, m. Hugh Boscawen, Esq., of Tregotham, co. Cornwall, and left an only dau. and heiress,
BRIDGET BOSCAWEN, who m. Hugh Fortescue, Esq., of Filley, co. Devon, and had (with two other sons and two daus., all of whom d. s. p.) a son and heir,
HUGH FORTESCUE, Esq., in whose favour the abeyance of the ancient barony of Clinton was terminated by the crown, and he was summoned to parliament, as LORD CLINTON, 16 March, 1721. His lordship was made a knight of the Bath in 1725, and created, by letters patent, dated 5 July, 1746, *Baron Fortescue, of Castle Hill*, and EARL OF CLINTON, with special remainder of the barony to his half brother, Matthew Fortescue,

Esq. The earl d. in 1751, s. p., when the barony of Clinton fell again into ABEYANCE between his sister and heir, Margaret Fortescue, and Margaret, Countess of Orford, dau. of Lady Arabella Clinton, by her husband, Robert Rolle, Esq., of Heanton, co. Devon, and so remained until called out in favour of R. G. W. Trefusis, Esq., the descendant of Lady Arabella, in 1794. The barony of Fortescue passed according to the limitation, and is enjoyed by the present Earl Fortescue, while the earldom of Clinton became EXTINCT.

Arms—Az., a bend, engrailed, arg., cotised, or.

FORTESCUE-ALAND—BARON FORTESCUE.

By Letters Patent dated 15 August, 1746.

Lineage.

SIR JOHN FORTESCUE-ALAND, Knt., b. 7 March, 1670 (son of Edmond Fortescue, Esq. of London, by Sarah, his wife, eldest dau. of Henry Aland, Esq., of Waterford, and nephew of Arthur Fortescue, Esq., of Filleigh, ancestor of Earl Fortescue), having adopted the legal profession, became a Baron of the Exchequer in 1717, and continued to sit as a judge in the superior courts of Westminster for thirty years. On his retirement he was, in testimony of his services, created by patent dated at Dublin, 15 August, 1746, BARON FORTESCUE, *of Credan, co. Waterford*, in the kingdom of Ireland. His lordship survived the elevation but a brief period, and d. 19 December following, when he was s. by his son,
DORMER FORTESCUE-ALAND, 2nd Lord Fortescue, at whose death, s. p., in 1781, the title became EXTINCT.

Arms—Az., a bend, engr., arg., cotised, or.

FORTESCUE, EARL OF CLERMONT.

By Letters Patent, dated 10 February, 1777.

Lineage.

This family of Fortescue derives its origin from Sir Richard le Fort, a person of extraordinary strength and courage, and a distinguished soldier, who accompanied William, Duke of Normandy, in his expedition to England, and bearing a strong shield before the Duke, at the decisive battle of Hastings, in Sussex, against King HAROLD, wherein he was exposed to imminent danger, having three horses killed under him, contribute d greatly to his preservation; and from that signal event were assumed the name and motto of the family, the word *scutum* in Latin, or *escu* in French (a shield) being added to *Fort* composes the name, and the motto is "Forte Scutum, Salus Ducum."
SIR JOHN FORTESCUE, of Winston, co. Devon (son of Adam Fortescue, Esq.), principal commander in the army raised under William, Lord Brewer, in aid of King JOHN against the rebellious barons, was father of RICHARD FORTESCUE, the father of WILLIAM FORTESCUE, who had a son,
WILLIAM FORTESCUE, of Winston, who m. Elizabeth, or Isabella, dau. of Richard Beauchamp, Earl of Warwick and Albemarle, sister and co-heir of Thomas Beauchamp, Lord of Kyme, and widow of Richard Branscomb, and had two sons,

I. William of Winston, ancestor of the Fortescues of Winston, Preston, and Fallapit: he m. Mabella, dau. of John Fowell, Esq., and had a son, John, who, by Joan, dau. of John Preston, of Preston, had issue three sons,
   1 John, of Winston, who m. Isabella, dau. of Thomas Gibbons, Esq., by whom he had Thomas, whose son Thomas, marrying Cicely, dau. of Thomas Strode, Esq., had an only dau., Jane, m. to Edmond Babington, of Wyke, co. Worcester.
   2 William, of Preston, who m. Elizabeth, dau. of Richard Champernon, Esq., and had an only son, Henry, who, by the d au. and heir of William St. Maur, of North Melton, had John, of Preston, who m. Elizabeth, dau. of Robert Wood, Esq.
   3 John, of Spirelston, co. Devon, ancestor of the FORTESCUES *of Fallapit, co. Devon*, &c.
II. JOHN, of whom we treat.

The 2nd son,
SIR JOHN FORTESCUE, signalized himself at the battle of Agincourt, 1415, and was appointed, 1424, for his valour and conduct at the reduction of Meaux, governor and captain thereof. He m.

Eleanor or Joan dau. and heir of Henry or of William Norreis, Esq., of Norreis, Devon, by whom he had three sons,

i. Henry (Sir), Chief Justice of the Common Pleas in Ireland, m. 1st, Joan, dau. of Wood. in Devon, by whom he had John, of Wood, father of William, the father of Robert, whose son William, m. Elizabeth, dau. of William Hynstone, Esq , of Bonwell, left a son, Anthony, of Wood, whose only dau. Elizabeth was m. to Lewis Fortescue, Esq., of Preteston, and in her right of Wood, whose descendant, Peter Fortescue, was created a baronet, 29 January, 1666. Sir Henry m. 2ndly, the heiress of the family of Fallapit, of Fallapit, in East Allington, co. Devon, and had a son and successor, Richard Fortescue, Esq., the father of John, whose dau. and heir Elizabeth, m. Lewis Fortescue, a Baron of the Exchequer, 3rd son of John Fortescue, Esq., of Spirelstone, and had issue.

ii. John, of whom presently.

iii. Richard, m. Alice, dau. and heir of Richard Hallacomb, Esq., of Hallacomb, and had two sons,

1 Richard, whose only dau., Amelia, m. John Rolle, Esq., of Stevenstone.
2 John (Sir), of Punsburn, otherwise Pombery, Herts, m. Alice, youngest dau. of Sir Jeffrey Bullein, Lord Mayor of London (by Anne, his wife, dau. and co-heir of Thomas, Lord Hoo and Hastings, K.G.), aunt of Thomas Bullein, Earl of Wiltshire and Ormonde, the father of Queen ANNE, the mother of Queen ELIZABETH, and by her had two sons,

John (Sir), sheriff of Hertford and Essex, in 1481, and 1486. He m. the dau. of Sir Peter Speccott, of Thornbury, co. Devon, and had Anthony, his heir, who m. Eleanor, dau. of Humphrey Walrond, Esq., of Bradfield, Wilts; and John, of Punsburn, who had a son, Henry, sheriff of Hertfordshire, in 1563.
Adrian (Sir), K.B., m. 1st, Anne, dau. of William Stonor, of Stonor, co. Oxford, by whom he had two daus, Margaret, m. to Thomas, Lord Wentworth, and Frances, m. to Thomas, Lord Kildare. He m. 2ndly, Anne, dau. of Sir William Rede, of Rockingham Castle, co. Northampton, and by her had three sons and two daus., viz.,

John (Sir), M.P., chancellor and under treasurer of the Exchequer. He acquired a good estate near Newport, in Bucks, where he built Salden House. He m. 1st, Alice, dau. and heir of Edward Ashfield, Esq , and 2ndly, Eleanor, dau. of Edward Hubbard, Esq., and by her (who is buried in the chancel of St. Sepulchre's Church, London) he had two sons and one dau., Francis (Sir), K.B., and M.P., and sheriff for the co. Bucks; John (Sir), who d. 29 September, 1656, whose descendants remained possessed of the estate and fine seat at Salden, until they became extinct by the death, without issue, 11 November, 1729, of Sir Francis Fortescue; and Margery, m. to Sir John Pulteney, of Misterton, co. Leicester, and d. 19 March, 1613.
Thomas.
Anthony (Sir), comptroller of the household to Pole, archbishop of Canterbury. He m. his niece, Catherine, eldest dau. of Sir Jeffrey Pole, of Lordington, in Sussex, and had a son, John.
Mary, m. to William, son and heir of John Norris, Esq., of Fyfield, Berks.
Elizabeth, m. to Sir William Bromley, Lord Chancellor of England, and by him was ancestor of Henry, Lord Montfort, Baron Horseheath, co. Cambridge.

The 2nd son,

SIR JOHN FORTESCUE, governor of Lincoln's Inn, constituted chief justice of England 1442, and made Lord Chancellor by HENRY VI., was author of "De Laudibus Legum Angliæ." He d. at Ebrington, near Cambden, co. Gloucester, aged ninety, in the chancel of which church a monument was erected. He m. Elizabeth, dau. of Sir Miles Stapleton, and left a son and heir,

MARTIN FORTESCUE, Esq., of Filleigh, and of Ware, Giffard who m. Elizabeth, dau. and heir of Richard Deynsell, Esq., of Filleigh, and had two sons,

i. John, of Filleigh, who m. Jacquetta, eldest dau. of Randal St. Leger, Esq., and had a son, Bartholomew Fortescue, Esq., of Filleigh, and Ware Giffard, who had issue two sons, and a dau.,

1 Richard, of Filleigh and Ware, father of several children, of whom the eldest, Hugh, m. Elizabeth, eldest dau. of Sir John Chichester, of Raleigh, and had a son, John, who, by Elizabeth, dau. of Sir John Specot, Knt., was father of Hugh Fortescue, who m. Mary Rolle, and dying 1661, left five sons,

Robert (colonel), m. 1st, Grace, dau. of Sir Bevill Granville, of Stow, sister of John, Earl of Bath, and 2ndly, the dau. of Sir John Northcotta, but left no issue.
Arthur, by the dau. of — Elford, Esq., had four sons, viz., 1 Hugh, of Filleigh, who m. 1st, Bridget, dau. and heir of Hugh Boscawen, Esq., of Tregothan, co. Cornwall, by his wife Margaret, 5th dau. and co-heir of Theophilus Earl of Lincoln, and Baron Clinton, by whom he had (with a dau., Margaret, eventually co-heiress of the Barony of Clinton)

221

two sons, HUGH, who was created, 5 July, 1746, Lord Fortescue, Baron of Castlehill, co. Devon (with limitation to his half-brother, Matthew Fortescue, Esq.), and EARL OF CLINTON (See BURKE'S Extant Peerage); and Theophilus, M.P. for the co. Devon, who d. unm. 13 March, 1745; Hugh, of Filleigh, m. 2ndly, Lucy, dau. of Matthew, Lord Aylmer, and by her he had 1 Matthew, successor to the brother as Lord Fortescue; 2 John, of Penwarn, co. Cornwall; 3 Arthur, of St. Endar, and of Penwarn, who d. in October, 1735, leaving a son. John; 4 Joseph; and 1 Lucy, m. 1742 to George, Lord Lyttleton.
Edmond, of London, m. Sarah, eldest dau. of Henry Aland, Esq., of Waterford, and had with other issue, a son. SIR JOHN FORTESCUE-ALAND, Baron Fortescue (See that dignity).
Joseph.
Samuel, of Ware, left a son, John, father of Samuel, of Ware.

2 Levi, m. Mary, dau. of William Giffard, Esq., of Hattsbury, and had three sons, James, Nicholas, and Martin.
1 Mary, m. to Robert Yeo, Esq., of Heanton-Sackville, co. Cornwall.

ii. WILLIAM, of whom we treat.

The 2nd son,

WILLIAM FORTESCUE, Esq., of Buckland Filleigh, co. Devon, m. Maud, dau. and heir of John Atkyns, Esq., of Milton Abbot, co. Devon, and had issue,

i. John, of whom presently.
ii. Edward.   iii. James.
i. Jacquetta, m. to William Dennis, Esq., of Southcombe.

The eldest son,

JOHN FORTESCUE, Esq., Buckland Filleigh, m. Christian, dau. of John Arscott, Esq., of Hollesworthy, Devon, and had issue,

i. WILLIAM, of whom presently.
ii. John.
i. Alice, m. to John Farry, Esq.

The elder son,

WILLIAM FORTESCUE, Esq., of Buckland Filleigh, m. Anne, dau. of Sir Roger Giffard, Knt., of Brightleigh, and had (with eight daus., the eldest of whom, Elizabeth, m. John Yeo, Esq., of Hewish) four sons,

i. JOHN, of whom presently.
ii. Faithful (Sir), a distinguished soldier temp. Queen ELIZABETH; d. circa 1608, aged ninety-six, having issue, three sons and several daus.,

1 John, of Northam, who left a son, John, of Parkham, who d. in the reign of GEORGE I., having had two sons, John and William.
2 Faithful (Capt.), who was sent into Flanders to learn the art of war; he went over to Ireland to visit his cousin, Sir Faithful.

iii. Martin.   iv. Bartholomew.

The eldest son,

JOHN FORTESCUE, Esq., of Buckland Filleigh, m. 1st, Anne, dau. of Walter Porter, Esq., of Thetford, co. Norfolk, and widow of D. Thorne, Esq., and had a son,

i. Roger, father of John who m. the dau. of Humphrey Prideaux, Esq., of Soldon, and had three sons, 1 William; 2 James (who had three sons, John, who d. s. p., James, who left a son, George, and George, who had issue, George, James, John, and William); and 3 John, of Shebbear. William, the eldest son, was ancestor of the FORTESCUES of Buckland Filleigh.

He m. 2ndly, Susanna, dau. of Sir John Chichester, of Raleigh and sister of Sir Arthur Chichester, lord deputy of Ireland, and had two sons,

i. John. d. unm.
ii. FAITHFUL (Sir), of whom we treat.

The 2nd son,

SIR FAITHFUL FORTESCUE, Knt., of Dromisken, co. Louth, went over to Ireland in the beginning of the reign of JAMES I., and commanded a regiment of foot there under his uncle, the Lord Deputy Sir Arthur Chichester. Sir Faithful is the subject of a privately-printed memoir by the present Lord Clermont. He m. 1st, Anne, dau. of Gerald Moore, 1st Viscount Drogheda, and by her (who d. 5 September, 1634), had issue,

i. Chichester, M.P., d. v. p., leaving an only child, Elizabeth, m. to Sir Richard Graham, Bart., of Norton-Conyers, co. York.
ii. John, d. unm. 1668.
iii. THOMAS (Sir), who s. to the estate.
iv. Roger.   v. Garret.   vi. William.
i. Lettice, m. to Sir Thomas Meredyth, of Dollardstown, co. Meath, Knt., who d. 1677, having had issue.
ii. Eleanor, m. 1st, to Thomas Burnet, Esq., of Ballyleck, co. Monaghan; and 2ndly, to Brent Moore, Esq
iii. Mary.   iv. Elizabeth.
v. Alice, living unm. in 1656.

Sir Faithful Fortescue *m.* 2ndly, 1639, Eleanor Symonds, a widow. The eldest surviving son of this eminent personage was

SIR THOMAS FORTESCUE, Knt., of Dromisken, lieutenant-colonel of Prince Charles's horse guards, governor and constable of Carrickfergus. He *m.* twice, and *d.* in 1710, aged nearly ninety, leaving by Sidney, his 2nd wife, dau. of Colonel Kingsmill, two sons namely,

I. CHICHESTER, of Dromisken, ancestor of the FORTESCUES of Dromisken Castle, co. Louth, now represented by THOMAS FORTESCUE, LORD CLERMONT.
II. WILLIAM, of whose line we have to treat.

The younger son,

WILLIAM FORTESCUE, Esq., of Newragh, co. Louth, a distinguished military officer, *m.* in 1681, Margaret, only dau. of Nicholas Gernon, Esq., of Miltown ; and *d.* in 1733, leaving issue,

I. THOMAS, his heir.
II. Chichester.
III. Matthew, lieutenant of a ship of war.
IV. Faithful, of Corderry, co. Louth, counsellor-at-law, M.P., co. Louth, and recorder of Derry, *m.* Elizabeth, dau. of Thomas Tipping, Esq., of Castletown, and *d.* 22 March, 1740, having had two sons, Thomas, *b.* 30 June, 1731, *d.* 6 November, 1733; and Faithful, *d.* 1785.
V John, in holy orders, of Whiterath, rector of Haynestowne, in the diocese of Armagh, *m.* Elizabeth, eldest dau. of Henry Bellingham, Esq., of Castle Bellingham, and had James, his heir, and other children.
I. Alice, *m.* to George Vaughan, Esq., of Buncranagh, co. Donegal, and had no issue.
II. Mary, *m.* to John Foster, Esq., of Dunleer, co. Louth, *d.* 29 October, 1762.

The eldest son,

THOMAS FORTESCUE, Esq., of Randalston, M.P. for Dundalk, *m.* Elizabeth, sister of James, Earl of Clanbrassil, and by her who *d.* 12 August, 1756), had issue,

I. WILLIAM-HENRY, of whom presently.
II. James (Rt. Hon.), of Ravensdale Park, co. Louth, M.P., and P.C., *b.* 15 May, 1725, *m.* Henrietta, eldest dau. of Thomas-Orby Hunter, Esq., of Crowland Abbey, in Lincolnshire; and dying in 1782, left issue,
  Thomas, M.P., who *d.* in 1795.
  WILLIAM-CHARLES, who *s.* as 2nd Viscount Clermont.
  Maria, *m.* 1st, in 1781, Captain Sloper, and had issue; the Hon. Mrs. Sloper *m.* 2ndly, Col. George-Francis Barlow, of the Manor House, Hampton-on-Thames, by whom she had an only dau., who *d. unm.* She *d.* a widow about 1853.
  Charlotte, *m.* in 1796, to Sir Harry Goodricke, Bart.
  Emily, *m.* in 1811, to Captain Charles Grantham, R.N., of Ketton, who *d. s. p.* 21 Dec·mber, 1859.
III. Matthew, *b.* 7 November, 1726.
IV. John, *b.* 28 February, 1730.

He *d.* in February, 1769, aged eighty-six, and was *s.* by his eldest son,

WILLIAM-HENRY FORTESCUE, Esq., of Clermont, co. Louth, M.P. for that shire, and postmaster-general, was created a peer of Ireland, as *Baron Clermont,* of Clermont, co. Louth, 26 May, 1770; made, 23 July, 1776, VISCOUNT and BARON CLERMONT, with remainder to his brother, the Right Hon. James Fortescue, and his male issue ; and further advanced 10 February, 1778, to be EARL OF CLERMONT, co. Louth. His lordship *m.* 29 February, 1752, Frances, eldest dau. of Colonel John Murray, M.P. for co. Monaghan, but *d.* without issue male,* in 1806, when the earldom and the 1st barony expired, while the viscounty and barony created in 1776 devolved on his nephew,

WILLIAM-CHARLES FORTESCUE, as 2nd viscount; at whose decease, *s. p.,* 24 June, 1829, the honours became EXTINCT, while the estates passed, under his lordship's will, to his nephew, Sir Harry Goodricke, Bart., and are now possessed by Thomas Fortescue, of Clermont, the present LORD CLERMONT, in whose favour the title was revived in 1852.

*Arms—*Az., a bend, engr., arg., cotised, or

FORTIBUS—EARLS OF ALBEMARLE.

Creation of the CONQUEROR.

Lineage.

ODO, Earl of Champaigne, having married Adeliza, sister of the CONQUEROR, obtained from that monarch the Isle (as he calls it) of Holderness. and he had from the archbishop of Roan, the city of Albemarle, upon the condition, that in all expedi-

tions where that prelate went in person, he should be his standard-bearer with twelve knights. Holderness, at this period being a barren country, producing nought but oats, so soon as his wife brought him a son, Odo entreated the king to give him some land which would bear wheat, " whereby he might better nourish his nephew," the king granted him therefore the lordship of Bytham, in Lincolnshire. Others mentioning this gift to Odo, call it *Comitatum Holderness,* the county or earldom of Holderness, which included a large portion of Yorkshire, upon the north-eastern side. Of this Earl Odo nothing further is known, than his joining Robert de Mowbray, Earl of Northumberland, and others, *anno* 1096, in a conspiracy to depose WILLIAM RUFUS, and to place STEPHEN (afterwards king) upon the throne ; for which conduct he suffered imprisonment. He *d.* in 1096, leaving a dau. Judith, *m.* to Waltheof, Earl of Northumberland and Huntingdon, and a son, his successor,

STEPHEN, Earl of Albemarle, who, in the contest between WILLIAM RUFUS, and his brother, Robert Curthose, remained faithful to the former ; but that difference being adjusted, he embarked with Curthose for the Holy Land, and in the great victory achieved over the infidel near Antioch, had a principal command in the Christian army. He subsequently joined Hugh de Gornay in an unsuccessful attempt to depose HENRY I. in favour of Robert Curthose, and he made a similar effort afterwards for Curthose's son, Prince William. In the last attempt some lost their lives, others were disinherited or imprisoned, but of the fate of the Earl of Albemarle nothing certain is known. He *m.* Hawise, dau. of Ralph de Mortimer, and had, with other issue, a son and successor,

WILLIAM, Le Grosse, 3rd Earl of Albemarle. In 1138 he was chief of those great nobles that gave battle to, and defeated, the Scots at North Allerton, when DAVID, King of Scotland, had invaded the north with a mighty army, claiming Northumberland for his son Henry, in right of Maud, dau. and heir of Earl Waltheof. Upon this memorable occasion Thurston, archbishop of York, caused a famous standard to be erected in the English camp, displaying the banners of St. Peter, St. John of Beverley, and St. Wilfrid, of Rippin, with the sacred host From which circumstance the ground whereon the battle was fought has ever since been termed Standard Hill. The Earl of Albemarle was rewarded for his gallantry with the Earldom of Yorkshire, and Robert de Ferrers with that of the county of Derby. His lordship, under the title of Earl of York, was subsequently under King STEPHEN at the battle of Lincoln, where that monarch sustained so signal a defeat. He *m.* Cicily, dau. of William Fitz-Duncan, (nephew of MALCOLM, King of Scotland,) by Alice, dau. of Robert de Romeley, Lord of the Honour of Skipton, in Craven, &c., by which marriage he enjoyed, as her inheritance, all that part of Yorkshire called Craven. By this lady he had two daus.,

  Hawyse, who *m.* 1st, William de Mandeville, Earl of Essex, and 2ndly, William de Fortibus.
  Amicia, *m.* to — Eston, by whom she had a son,
    Ranulph, whose son,
      John, was father of
        John de Eston, or Aston, who, as right heir after Aveline de Fortibus, claimed, in the 6th of EDWARD I., the Earldom of Albemarle, and had certain lands in Thornton to the value of £100 per annum, assigned to him to release his right therein.

William, Le Grosse, *d.* in 1179, and was *s.* in the Earldom of Albemarle by his son-in-law,

WILLIAM DE MANDEVILLE Earl of Essex, who *d. s. p.* in 1190; and Hawyse, his widow, marrying

WILLIAM DE FORTIBUS, he became, in her right, EARL OF ALBEMARLE, and *Lord of Holderness.* This William was constituted, by RICHARD I., one of the admirals of the fleet, in which that monarch soon afterwards sailed towards Jerusalem. His lordship *d.* in 1194, leaving a son and heir, WILLIAM DE FORTIBUS, but in regard that Hawyse, the deceased lord's widow, was heir to the earldom, and that she married

BALDWINE DE BERTUNE, Earl of the Isle of Wight, that William was postponed to Baldwine in the enjoyment of the Earldom of Albemarle, but Baldwine dying *s. p.* in 1212, the dignity then devolved upon the said

WILLIAM DE FORTIBUS, to whom King JOHN, in the sixteenth year of his reign, confirmed all the lands which accrued to him by inheritance from his mother. The next year the earl, arraying himself on the side of the barons, was one of the celebrated twenty-five chosen to enforce the observance of Magna Charta ; but he subsequently deserted his party, and was with King JOHN in his expedition into the north, so marked by spoil and rapine. He was then constituted governor of the castles of Rockingham, in Northamptonshire, Saubey, in Leicestershire, and Bitham, co. Lincoln, with strict command to destroy all

---

* His only dau., Lady Louisa Fortescue, *m.* 21 September 1778, the Rev. Mr. Harrington.

the houses, parks, and possessions of those barons who were in arms against the king. In the reign of HENRY III. his lordship fought at the battle of Lincoln under the royal banner, and shared largely in the spoils of victory. He was subsequently for and against the king by turns, and eventually *d.* at sea, in his progress to the Holy Land. He *m.* Aveline. dau. and co-heir of Richard de Munfichet, a great baron in Essex, and was *s.* by his son,

WILLIAM DE FORTIBUS, Earl of Albemarle. This nobleman enjoyed the sheriffalty of Cumberland from the 41st HENRY III. until the time of his decease. His lordship *m.* 1st, Christian, dau. and co-heir of Alan, of Galoway, but that lady *d. s. p.* He *m.* 2ndly, Isabel, dau. of Baldwine, Earl of Devon, by whom he had three sons, John, Thomas and William, and one surviving daughter, Aveline. The earl, journeying into France, *d.* at Amiens in 1259, when the tuition of his two surviving sons, Thomas and William, was committed to their mother, Isabel, but these children appear to have lived only a short time, when the whole inheritance passed to the earl's dau.,

AVELINE DE FORTIBUS, whose wardship was granted by the king to Richard de Clare, Earl of Gloucester, for the whole term of fifteen years of her minority. This grant was, however, shortly after surrendered, and the king conferred the guardianship of the heiress to his eldest son, Prince Edward, who assigned the castle and barony of Skipton, in Craven, to ALEXANDER, King of Scotland, during her minority, in consideration of the sum of £1500. This lady, independently of the great inheritance of the Fortibus family, became also heiress to her mother. Isabel, (who, upon the death of her brother Baldwine, 5th Earl of Devon, styled herself Countess of Albemarle and Devon) and thus with both inheritances, she was heir to the Earldoms of Albemarle and Devon, to the Barony of Skipton and the Sovereignty of the Isle of Wight. Her ladyship *m.* EDMUND PLANTAGENET, surnamed *Crouchback,* afterwards Duke of Lancaster: the king and queen and almost all the nobility of England attending at the wedding. She *d.* however, within a short time *s. p.* and her honours passed into other families.

Arms—Arg., a chief, gules.

FOX—BARONS HOLLAND.

By Letters Patent, dated 6 May, 1762.
By Letters-Patent, dated 16 April, 1763.

Lineage.

This family and that of Fox, Earls of Ilchester, had a common progenitor in

SIR STEPHEN FOX, a distinguished senator during the reigns of CHARLES II., JAMES II., WILLIAM III., and Queen ANNE. By his marriage, in 1703, with Christian, dau. of the Rev. Charles Hope, of Naseby, co. Lincoln, he had two sons, Stephen, created EARL OF ILCHESTER, and

HENRY FOX, *b.* 1705, who filled several high official situations in the reign of GEORGE II. (amongst others those of secretary at war, and secretary of state), from 1735, when he was first returned to parliament for Hendon, until the accession of his Majesty GEORGE III., at which period he was a member of the privy council, and enjoyed the office of paymaster-general to the forces, which he soon afterwards resigned. The right hon. gentleman *m.* in 1744, Georgiana-Carolina, eldest dau. of Charles, 2nd Duke of Richmond, and had issue,

I. STEPHEN, his successor.
II. CHARLES-JAMES (*b.* 13 Jan. O. S. 1748-9), one of the most eminent statesmen of modern times. Mr. Fox first came into parliament for Midhurst, in 1768, before he was of age. In 1770, he was appointed a lord of the Admiralty, which post he retained till May, 1772. In 1773, he was made lord of the Treasury, an office he resigned the following year, to oppose Lord North and the American war. Upon the fall of the North administration, March, 1782, Mr. Fox was constituted secretary of state, but held the seals only till the death of Lord Rockingham, in the following July. When the brief-lived Shelburne cabinet ceased, Mr Fox formed the celebrated coalition with Lord North, and became again secretary of state, 2 April, 1783. His power was as fleeting, however, as before, and he retired on 19 December following, to make room for Mr. Pitt, who at once became premier. After the death of Mr. Pitt, Mr. Fox came again into office, and he *d.* 15 September, 1806, when nominally secretary of state for foreign affairs, but virtually prime minister of England. He had *m.* Elizabeth-Bridget Armstead, but had no issue. His widow survived until 8 July, 1842.
III. Henry-Edward, a general officer in the army, and col. of the 16th foot; *m.* Marianne, dau of William Clayton, Esq; and *d.* in 1811, leaving

---

1 Henry-Stephen, *b.* 22 September, 1791; *d.* in October, 1846.
1 Louisa-Amelia, *m.* to Sir H.-E. Bunbury, Bart.; and *d.* in 1828.
2 Caroline. *m.* to the late Lieut.-Gen Sir William-F.-P. Napier, K.C.B.; and *d.* 26 March, 1860.

Lady Georgiana Fox was elevated to the peerage, as *Baroness Holland, of Holland, co. Lincoln,* 6 May, 1762; and Mr. Fox himself was created BARON HOLLAND, *of Foxley, co. Wilts,* 16 April, 1763. His lordship *d.* 1 July, 1774, and was *s.* by his eldest son,

STEPHEN, 2nd baron; who inherited likewise the Barony of Holland of Holland, at the demise of his mother, the 24th of the same month, in the same year. His lordship *m.* 20 April, 1766, Mary, eldest dau. of John Fitzpatrick, 1st Earl of Upper Ossory, by whom (who *d.* in 1778) he had issue,

HENRY-RICHARD, his heir.
Caroline, *d.* 12 March, 1845.

He *d.* 16 December, 1774, and was *s.* by his only son,

HENRY-RICHARD, F.R.S., F.S.A., 3rd baron, recorder of Nottingham; *b.* 21 November, 1773; who *m.* 9 July, 1797, Elizabeth, dau. and heir of Richard Vassall, Esq., (who had been previously *m.* to Sir Godfrey Webster, Bart.), by whom (who *d.* in Nov. 1845) he had issue,

HENRY-EDWARD, his heir.
Mary-Elizabeth (heiress of her brother), *m.* 22 May, 1830, Thomas, 3rd Lord Lilford, and had a son, Thomas Littleton, 4th Lord Lilford, and other issue,

His lordship, in consequence of his marriage, assumed the surname of VASSALL. Lord Holland, who was a cabinet minister, and chancellor of the Duchy of Lancaster, *d.* deeply lamented, 22 October, 1840, and was *s.* by his son,

HENRY-EDWARD, 4th lord, *b.* 7 March, 1802. He was M.P. for Horsham 1826-7, and from 1839 to 1842 minister-plenipotentiary at the court of Tuscany. He *m.* 9 May, 1833, Augusta-Mary, dau. of George-William, Earl of Coventry, but had no surviving issue. His lordship *d.* at Naples, 18 December, 1859, when the title became EXTINCT.

Arms—Erm. on a chevron, az., three foxes' heads erased, or, on a canton of the 2nd, a fleur-de-lis of the 3rd.

FRASER—BARON FRASER.

By Letters Patent, dated 29 June, 1633.

Lineage.

ANDREW FRASER, son and heir of Andrew Fraser, of Kinmundie, by Lady Elizabeth Douglas, his wife, 2nd dau. of Robert, Earl of Buchan, was created a peer of Scotland, 29 June, 1633, as BARON FRASER, with limitation of the title to his heirs male for ever. He *m.* Anne, eldest dau. of James, 1st Lord Balmerinoch, and *d.* 10 December, 1636, and was *s.* by his son,

ANDREW FRASER, 2nd Lord Fraser; who *m.* Anne, dau. of Haldane, of Gleneagles; and dying 24 May, 1674, left a son and successor,

ANDREW FRASER, 3rd Lord Fraser; who *m.* Ca'herine, 3rd dau. of Hugh, 8th Lord Lovat, relict of Sir John Sinclair, of Dunbeath, and of Robert, 1st Viscount Arbuthnott, by whom he had a son,

CHARLES FRASER, 4th Lord Fraser; who *m.* Lady Margaret Erskine, eldest dau. of James, Earl of Buchan, and relict of Fraser, of Innerlachy, but had no issue. His lordship engaged in the rising of 1715; and after its suppression, remained concealed until his death, which occurred 12 October, 1720; since which period the title has remained DORMANT.

Arms—Az., three fraizes, arg.

FRENCH—BARON DE FREYNE.

Created 16 May, 1839.
Extinct 29 September, 1856.

(*See* BURKE's *Extant Peerage*)

FRESCHEVILLE—BARON FRESCHEVILLE, OF STAVELEY, CO. DERBY.

By Letters Patent, dated 16 March, 1664.

Lineage.

In the 9th HENRY III., upon the death of Hubert Fitz-Ralph, Lord of Cryche. in Derbyshire,

RALPH DE FRESCHEVILLE, being his heir, and paying 100 marks for his relief, had livery of his lands. This Ralph, in the 26th of the same reign, paid a fine of 30 marks to be excused from attending the king into Gascony. He d. in 19 years afterwards, and was s. by his son,

ANKERE DE FRESCHEVILLE, who, having joined the baronial standard, was made prisoner at the battle of Northampton, when his lands were seized by the crown, and conferred upon Brian de Brompton, according to the tenor of the Dictum de Kenilworth, until the heir of the said Ankere should accomplish his full age. Ankere d. in the 54th HENRY III., when it was found that he held the manor of Boney, co. Nottingham, by barony, of the king in capite, so likewise the manor of Cryche, in Derbyshire. He m. Amice, eldest dau. and co-heir of Sir Nicholas Musard, Lord of Staveley, co Derby, and sister and co-heir of Nicholas Musard, and was s. by his son,

RALPH DE FRESCHEVILLE, who, in the 15th EDWARD I., doing his homage, had livery of all his father's lands, save the manor of Boney, which Richard de Grey still retained until the fine imposed by the Dictum of Kenilworth should be liquidated. In ten years afterwards this Ralph distinguished himself in the wars of Scotland, and was summoned to parliament as a baron, in the 25th EDWARD I., but never afterwards. His lordship was s. by his son,

RALPH DE FRESCHEVILLE, who was never summoned to parliament, nor esteemed a baron; nor were any of his descendants. Of whom his direct male heir,

SIR PETER DE FRESCHEVILLE, had the honour of knighthood conferred upon him by King EDWARD VI., for his valour at the battle of Musselborough, in Scotland. Sir Peter was great grandfather of

JOHN FRESCHEVILLE, Esq., of Staveley, co. Derby, who, having adhered firmly to the royal cause during the civil wars, was elevated to the peerage by King CHARLES II., 16 March, 1664, as BARON FRESCHEVILLE, of Staveley. In 1677, his lordship claimed to be allowed to sit in the House of Peers under the writ of summons to his ancestor, Ralph, in the reign of EDWARD I., but it being contended, that to give the party summoned to parliament an estate of inheritance, a sitting under the writ was necessary, as the onus of proving such sitting rested with the party claiming the dignity, and no such proof being extant in the case of Ralph Frescheville, the claim was not admitted. Lord Frescheville m. 1st, Sarah, dau. of Sir John Harington, Knt., and had three daus., viz.,

Christian, m. to Charles Paulet, then Lord St. John, afterwards Duke of Bolton.
Elizabeth, m. 1st, to Philip, son and heir of Sir Philip Warwick, Knt., and 2ndly (his lordship's 4th wife), to Conyers Darcy, 2nd Earl of Holdernesse.
Frances, m. to Col. Thomas Colepeper. This lady became eventually sole heiress of her father.

His lordship m. 2ndly, Anna-Charlotta, dau. and heir of Sir Henry Vick, Knt., but had no issue. He d. s. p. m. in 1682, when the Barony of Frescheville, of Staveley became EXTINCT.

Arms—Az., a bend, between six escallop shells, arg.

———

FREVILLE—BARON FREVILLE.

By Writ of Summons, dated 5 April, 1327.

Lineage.

This family was anciently seated in the county of Cambridge, and of considerable note. In the 15th HENRY III.,

BALDWIN DE FREVILLE, having obtained the wardship of Lucia, dau. and heir of Richard de Scalers, for which he gave 200 marks, made her very soon after his wife ; and in the 36th of the same reign, paid towards the marriage-portion of the king's dau., £15 for fifteen knights' fees which he had of her inheritance. To this Baldwin s. his son and heir,

RICHARD DE FREVILLE, who was engaged in the Welsh wars. He was s., at his decease, by his son,

224

BALDWIN DE FREVILLE, who d. s. p., and was s. by his brother,

ALEXANDER DE FREVILLE who m. Joane, dau. of Mazera, 2nd dau. and co-heir of Sir Philip Marmion, and wife of Ralph de Cromwell. This Alexander was in the Scottish wars of EDWARD I., and had a military summons for that service in the 8th EDWARD II.; in the 3rd of which latter monarch's reign, upon partition of the lands of Isabel, wife of William Walraund, he had, in right of his wife, heir to the said Isabel, the manors of Winterborne and Asserton, co. Wilts. He was afterwards summoned to parliament as a baron, in the 1st EDWARD III., but never again, nor any of his descendants. On referring to Dugdale's List of Summonses, it appears that this Alexander is not included in either summons to parliament issued in that year, but only in a summons dated at Ramsey, 5 April, 1st EDWARD III., 1327, to be at Newcastle-upon-Tyne, with horse and arms, to serve against Robert Bruce.—NICOLAS. Alexander de Freville d. in 1328, leaving a son,

BALDWIN DE FREVILLE, who d. in the 17th EDWARD III., and was s. by his son,

BALDWIN DE FREVILLE, then twenty-six years of age, who, doing homage, the next ensuing year had livery of the lands of his inheritance lying in the cos. of Warwick, Hereford, Salop, Stafford, Wilts, Norfolk and Suffolk. In the 38th EDWARD III., this Baldwin was made seneschal of Fantoigne for life, by EDWARD the renowned Black Prince, and he was afterwards in the wars of Gascony, with that illustrious personage. He m. 1st, Elizabeth, sister and co-heir of Sir John Montfort, of Beldesert, co. Warwick : 2ndly, Ida, dau. of — Clinton, a lady of honour to Queen Philippa, and 3rdly, Joane, dau. of Lord Strange, and dying in the 49th EDWARD III., was s. by his son,

SIR BALDWIN DE FREVILLE, who, in the 1st RICHARD II., claimed, as feudal lord of Tamworth Castle, co. Warwick, to be the king's champion on the day of his coronation; but the same was determined against him, in favour of Sir John Dymoke, Knt. (*see* Marmion), in right of the tenure of the manor of Scrivelsby, co. Lincoln, and the Dymokes have ever since enjoyed that honour. Sir Baldwin Freville m. two wives, both co-heirs of Sir John de Botetourt, 2nd Baron Botetourt, summoned to parliament from 25 February, 1342, to 3 February, 1385. Elizabeth, his 1st wife, d. very young. By his 2nd wife, Joyce (widow of Sir Adam de Pershall, Knt., of Weston-under-Lizard, who d. 7th HENRY V., 1419, leaving issue by her), Sir Baldwin Freville had issue,

SIR BALDWIN DE FREVILLE, who m. Joane, dau. of Sir John Green, Knt., and had issue,

BALDWIN, his successor.
Elizabeth, m. to Sir Thomas Ferrers, 2nd son of William, Lord Ferrers, of Groby, from whom lineally descended

Anne Ferrers, granddau. and heiress of Sir John Ferrers, of Tamworth Castle, who d. in 1680. This great heiress m. the Hon Robert Shirley, 1st Earl of Ferrers of that family, and had issue,

Robert, who d. s p. in 1714.
Elizabeth, heir to her brother, m. to James, 5th Earl of Northampton, and carried the baronies of Ferrers, of Chartley, &c., &c., into that family.

Margaret, m. to Sir Hugh Willoughby, Knt., and afterwards to Sir Richard Bingham, Knt., one of the justices of the King's Bench.
Joice, m. to Roger Aston, Esq., ancestor of the Lord Astons, of Forfar, in Scotland.

Sir Baldwin d. in the 2nd HENRY IV., and was s. by his son,

BALDWIN DE FREVILLE, at whose decease in minority, and issueless, 6th HENRY V., his sisters became his heirs, and the great possessions of the Frevilles were thus divided :—

Sir Thomas Ferrers had the castle and manor of Tamworth, with other estates in the co. Warwick, and lands in Hereford and Stafford shires.
Roger Aston had the manor of Newdigate, in Surrey, with other lands in Wiltshire and Warwickshire.
Sir Richard Bingham obtained the manors of Middleton and Whitnash, in Warwickshire, and other lordships in the cos. of Nottingham and Hereford.

Arms—Or, a cross patonce, gu.

———

FURNIVAL—BARONS FURNIVAL.

By Writ of Summons, dated 23 June, 1295.

Lineage.

In the time of RICHARD I.

GIRARD DE FURNIVAL came into England from Normandy, and, accompanying the King to the Holy Land, assisted at the celebrated siege of Acon. To this gallant soldier succeeded his son, another

GIRARD DE FURNIVAL, who m. Maud, dau. and heiress of William de Luvetot, a powerful Nottinghamshire baron, and had livery of her lands in the 5th year of King JOHN. This feudal lord, being one of the barons who adhered to JOHN, was included in the commission to treat, on part of the monarch, with Robert de Ros and the other insurrectionary lords, and was appointed by the king to reside at Bolsover Castle, co. Derby, for the better preservation of the peace in those parts. He d. at Jerusalem, in the 3rd HENRY III., leaving three sons. viz.,

  I. THOMAS, of whom presently.
  II. Gerard, who m. Christian Ledet, dau. and heiress of Guischard Ledet, and widow of Henry de Braybroc, in whose right he held the barony of Wardon. He left at his decease, a son, Sir GERARD DE FURNIVAL. who m Joan, dau. and co-heir of Hugh de Morvill, and left at his decease, two daus. and co-heiresses, LORETTA, m. to John Uffiet, and Christian, who m. Sir John Eynsford, and was mother of Elizabeth, wife of Sir John Milborne.
  III. William, m. Ada ——, but had no issue.

The eldest son,

THOMAS DE FURNIVAL, s. to the feudal barony, and HENRY III. committed to his wardship William de Moubray, son of Roger de Moubray, a great Yorkshire baron. Of this Thomas nothing more is known, than his being slain by the Saracens in the Holy Land, whither he had journeyed upon a pilgrimage, and that his body was brought from thence by his brother Girard, and buried at Worksop. By Bertha, his wife, he had a son and successor,

THOMAS DE FURNIVAL, who had licence, in the 54th HENRY III., to make a castle of his manor-house of Sheffield, co. York. To this Thomas s. his son and heir,

GERARD DE FURNIVAL, who m. Maud, eldest of the four sisters and co-heirs of Richard Fitz-John, and by her (who m. 2ndly, William 11th Earl of Warwick), had a son,

THOMAS DE FURNIVAL, who, in the 22nd EDWARD I., had summons, amongst other great men, to attend the king, in order to advise of the affairs of the realm; and having so done, received command to repair to Portsmouth, upon the first day of the ensuing September, well fitted with horse and arms, for the expedition then intended against France. In the next year, 23 June, 1295, he was first summoned to parliament as a baron, and from that period his lordship appears, for several years, to have taken a distinguished part in the Scottish wars. In the 27th EDWARD I., he was constituted captain-general and lieutenant to the king for the cos. of Nottingham and Derby, and had summons to parliament, uninterruptedly, until 27 January, 1332 (6th EDWARD III.), but he did not hold his lands by barony. Lord Furnival m. Elizabeth, dau. of Peter de Montfort, of Beldesert Castle, co. Warwick, and was s. at his decease, in 1332, by his eldest son,

THOMAS DE FURNIVAL, who was himself a baron, having been summoned to parliament as "Thomæ de Furnival, Junior," from 25 August, 1318, to 27 January, 1332, and without "junior," until 15 November, 1338 (12th EDWARD III). This nobleman, who, like his father, was engaged in the Scottish wars, m. Joan, eldest dau. and co-heiress of Theobald de Verdon, but without the king's licence, for which he had to pay a fine of £200. By this lady he acquired extensive estates in co. Stafford, and had two sons, THOMAS and William. His lordship d. in 1339, and was s. by the elder,

THOMAS DE FURNIVAL, 3rd baron, b. 1322. In the 19th EDWARD III. this nobleman embarked in the expedition made into France, and the next year participated in the glories of Cressy. His lordship continued in the French wars some years subsequently, and he was afterwards in Scotland under Henry, Lord Percy. He d. about the year 1366, having been summoned to parliament, from 20 November, 1348, to 4 October, 1364, and leaving no issue, was s. by his brother,

WILLIAM DE FURNIVAL, 4th baron, summoned to parliament, from 20 January, 1366, to 7 January, 1383. This nobleman permitted the park of his park at Worksop to be so defective, that

divers of the king's deer, out of the forest of Sherwood, came freely into it, and were destroyed. In consequence of which, William de Latimer, warden of the forests beyond Trent, seized the said park for the king; but it was soon afterwards released, and Lord Furnival pardoned, upon the payment of a fine of £20. His lordship m. Thomasin, dau. and heiress of —- Dagworth (in whose right he acquired the manor of Dagworth, Suffolk), by whom he had an only dau.,

Joane, who m. Thomas Nevill, brother of Ralph, 1st Earl of Westmoreland.

With this nobleman, in the year 1383, expired the male line of the Furnivals, and the barony was conveyed by his heiress, Joane Nevill, to her husband,

THOMAS NEVILL, who was summoned to parliament 20 August, 1383 (7th RICHARD II.) as "Thomæ Nevyll de Halumshire," and thenceforward styled "Lord Furnival." In which year, making proof of his wife's age, he had livery of her great inheritance. By this lady he had,

Maud, m. 1408, Sir John Talbot, 1st Earl of Shrewsbury.
Joane, who d. unm.

His lordship m. 2ndly, Ankaret Strange, of Blackmere, widow of Richard, Lord Talbot, and by her had a dau. Joan, who m. 1st, Sir Hugh Cokesey; and 2ndly, Hams de Belknap. This nobleman, who was a personage of distinction, in the reigns of RICHARD II. and HENRY IV., d. in 1406, leaving his two daus. his co-heiresses. The elder of whom, Maud, as stated above, m. the celebrated

GENERAL SIR JOHN TALBOT, 2nd son of Richard, Lord Talbot, of Blackmere, who was summoned to parliament as "Lord Furnival," from 26 October, 1409, to 26 February, 1421; and subsequently, 20 May, 1442, for his many heroic achievements, was created EARL OF SHREWSBURY, in the peerage of England, and EARL OF WATERFORD AND WEXFORD, in that of Ireland. In these higher honours the Barony of Furnival merged for two centuries, until the demise of Gilbert, 7th Earl of Shrewsbury, in 1616, without male issue, when the earldom passed to that nobleman's brother; but the baronies of Talbot, Furnival, Strange, and Blackmere, &c., fell into ABEYANCE between his three daus., viz.,

  Mary, m. to William, Earl of Pembroke.
  Elizabeth, m. to Henry, Earl of Kent.
  Alethea, m. to Thomas Howard Earl of Arundel; by which marriage the manor of Worksop came into the Howard family; and by virtue of possessing which, the Dukes of Norfolk claim to support the king's left arm on the day of coronation, so long as his majesty holds the royal sceptre; George, 4th Earl of Shrewsbury, having exchanged with tho crown, his manor of Farnham Royal (holden by that tenure), for the inheritance of the site of the priory of Worksop, with divers other lands.

The baronies finally, however, devolved upon Alethea, Countess of Arundel, and thenceforward became merged in the Earldom of Arundel and the Dukedom of Norfolk, until the decease of Edward Howard, 9th duke, 20 September, 1777, without issue, when the higher honours passed to the male heir; and the baronies in fee, amongst which was that of Furnival, fell into ABEYANCE between the daus. of his grace's deceased brother, Philip Howard, of Buckingham, co. Norfolk: the said

PHILIP HOWARD, m. 1st, Winefrede, dau. of Thomas Stonor, Esq., of Watlington Park, co. Oxford, and had issue,

  Thomas, who d. in 1763, s. p.
  Winifred, m. WILLIAM, 15th Lord Stourton, and had issue,
    CHARLES-PHILIP, 16th Lord Stourton, grandfather of the present Lord Stourton.

Mr. Howard m. 2ndly, Harriet, dau. and co-heir of Edward Blount, Esq., by whom he had,

  Edward, who d. unm. in 1767.
  Anne, m. Robert-Edward, 9th Lord Petre, by whom she had, ROBERT-EDWARD, 10th Lord Petre, grandfather of the present Lord Petre.

The baronies still continue in ABEYANCE between the Lords Stourton and Petre.

Arms—Arg., a bend, between six mascles, gu.

GAGE—BARON GAGE, OF FIRLE, CO. SOMERSET.

By Letters Patent, dated 7 October, 1780.

Lineage.

WILLIAM HALL GAGE, 2nd Viscount Gage, in the peerage of Ireland (*see* the extant Viscounts Gage, BURKE's *Peerage and Baronetage*), was created a peer of Great Britain 7 October, 1780, as BARON GAGE, *of Firle, co. Somerset*. His lordship *m.* 1757, Elizabeth, sister of Sampson, Lord Eardley, by whom he had an only son, who *d.* in infancy. His lordship obtained, subsequently, 1 November, 1790, another British peerage, as Lord Gage, of High Meadow, co. Gloucester, with remainder to his nephew and presumptive heir, Major-General Henry Gage, who inherited that dignity and the Irish viscounty at his decease, 11 October, 1791, when the Barony of Gage, of Firle, became EXTINCT.

Arms—Per saltier, az. and arg., a saltier, gu.

GALLOWAY—LORD DUNKELD.

By Letters Patent, dated 15 May, 1645.

Lineage.

SIR JAMES GALLOWAY. of Carnbie, in Fife, son of Patrick Galloway, minister of Perth, by Mary, his wife, dau. of Mr. James Lawson, a minister of Edinburgh, was master of requests to JAMES VI. and CHARLES I., became a privy councillor, was conjunct secretary of state with William, Earl of Stirling, 1640, and was created a peer, by the title of LORD DUNKELD, 15 May, 1645. He *m.* a dau. of Sir Robert Norter, Knt., and dying in 1662, left a son and heir,

THOMAS GALLOWAY, 2nd Lord Dunkeld; who *m.* Margaret, dau. of Sir Thomas Thomson, Bart., of Duddingstone, and had issue,

JAMES, 3rd Lord Dunkeld.
John.   Andrew.
Catherine, *m.* to Thomas Forbes, of Waterstoun, in Aberdeenshire.
Margaret, *m.* to Thomas Rattray, of Craighall, in Perthshire.
Mary, *m.* to John Falconer, D.D.
Grizel, *m.* to Patrick Crichton, of Ruthven.
Jean, *b.* 4 April, 1667.

The eldest son,

JAMES GALLOWAY, 3rd Lord Dunkeld, an officer in the army, joined Lord Dundee in 1689, and was at the battle of Killicrankie, for which he was outlawed. He retired to the court of St. Germains, was afterwards a colonel in the French service, and fell in battle, leaving a son, JAMES, and a dau., Mary, who entered into the nunnery of Val de Grâce. The only son, JAMES GALLOWAY, took the title of Lord Dunkeld, and was an officer in the French service, in which he served with distinction, and rose to the rank of lieutenant-general.

Arms—Arg., a lion, rampant, az.

GAMBIER—BARON GAMBIER.

By Letters Patent, dated 3 November, 1807.

Lineage.

NICHOLAS GAMBIER, of the parish of St. Mary-le-bow, London, came from Caen, in Normandy, and settled in England, about 1690. He *d. circa* February, 1724, leaving by Hesther, his wife, four sons and two daus,

I. JAMES, of whom presently.
II. John. living 1741.
III. David, *d. unm.*, buried 18 November, 1726.
IV. Henry, *b.* 1694, who by Catherine-Judith, his wife, had issue,
    1 Samuel-Henry, *bapt.* 13 October, 1725.
    2 William-James, *b.* 24 August, 1718, *d.* 16 March, 1797; *m.* 31 March, 1744, Mary, dau. of the Rev. Richard Venn,

rector of St. Antholins, London; and by her (who *d.* 17 March, 1791), had three sons and four daus.,

James-Edward, in holy orders, A.M., rector of Langley, co. Kent, *bapt.* 15 August, 1759, *m.* 7 November, 1782, Eleanor, dau. of — Bardwell, of Beccles, co. Suffolk, by whom he had issue, William-Edward, *b.* 8 July, 1785, *d.* 24 March, 1786; William-Henry, *b.* 2 November, 1790; Edward-Morton, *b.* 6 April, 1793, *d.* 2 November, 1795; Philip-Venn, *b.* 8 January, 1795; Eleanora-Catherina; Anna-Maria *b.* 21 January, 1787; a dau., *d.* 1800; and Charlotte-Sophia, *b.* 3 August, 1797.
Richard-Henry, *d.* an infant.
James-Henry, *d.* an infant.
Charlotte-Mary, *bapt.* 3 October, 1760, *m.* 7 December, 1779, to Edward Venn, son of Edward Venn, M.D., of Ipswich.
Mary-Charlotte, *d.* an infant.
Catherine-Mary, *b.* 19 January, 1752; *m.* 30 December, 1775, to James Walker, Esq., marshal of the King's Bench.
Elizabeth-Mary, *b.* 12 January, 1756; *d.* 6 March, 1750.
Maria-Henrietta-Judith, *b.* 23 January, 1745; *m.* 3 July, 1770, to John Wright, of St. Martin Pomeroy, London, and *d.* 30 August, 1803, having had issue.
    1 Hesther-Judith, *bapt.* 20 September, 1724.

The eldest son,

JAMES GAMBIER, Esq., *b.* 1692, warden of the Fleet, and formerly of St. Andrew's, Holborn, *m.* Mary Mead, and had issue,

I. JOHN, of whom presently.
II. James, *b.* 19 August, 1725, admiral of the red squadron, *d.* 28 January, 1789. He *m.* 1st, Mary Ruck, of Betshanger, co. Kent, but by her (who was buried at Ripple,) he had no issue. He *m.* 2ndly, Jane, dau. of Colonel Monpesson, of London, and had (with two daus., Jane, *m.* to Sir William Wake, Bart., and Katherine, *m.* to John Allen Cooper, Esq.,) two sons,
    1 Samuel-John, a lieut. in the navy, *d. unm.* 1789.
    2 James (Sir), Knt., *b.* 15 February, 1772, of the life guards, consul-general in the Netherlands, *m.* 21 April, 1797, Jemima, 2nd dau. of William Snell, Esq., of Salisbury Hall, co. Hertford, by whom he had issue,
        William, *b.* 14 September, 1802.
        Robert-Fitzgerald, rear-admiral, *b.* 21 March, 1803.
        James Mark, *b.* 9 December, 1807.
        Maria Jane, *m.* George Jenyns, Esq.
        Wilhelmina-Frederica, *m.* 1820, to Richard Norris, Esq., of Basing Park, Hants.
        Frederica-Elizabeth-Sophia.
III. Samuel, a lawyer, *d. s. p.* in the Bahama Islands.
IV. Robert, *d. s. p.* June, 1787.
I. Susan, *m.* Sir Samuel Cornish, Bart., and *d.* before him.
II. Elizabeth, *d. unm.*
III. Margaret, *m.* to Sir Charles Middleton, Bart., Lord Barham, and *d.* about 1792.

James Gambier's eldest son,

JOHN GAMBIER, Esq., *b.* 15 June, 1723, lieutenant-governor of the Bahama Islands, *m.* Deborah Stiles, of Bermuda, and *d.* 5 April, 1782, having had issue,

I. Samuel, *b.* in September, 1752, 1st commissioner of the navy, *m.* Jane, dau. of Daniel Matthew, Esq., of Felix Hall, co. Essex, by whom he had issue,
    1 Charles-Samuel, *b.* 1790, *d.* 1848.
    2 Robert, of Sharnbrook, co. Bedford, *b.* 1791, admiral R.N., *m.* 1815, Caroline, dau. of General Gore Browne, and has issue.
    3 Edward-John (Sir), late chief justice at Madras, *b.* 1794, *m.* Emilia, dau. of C. Morgell, Esq., M.P.
    4 George Cornish, *b.* 1795.
    5 Frederick, *b.* 1796.
    6 Francis-Shee, *b.* 22 May, 1802, *d.* July, 1813.
    7 Samuel-James, in holy orders, *m.* 1830, Maria Rowlanda, dau. of Rear-Admiral Money, C.B.
    1 Mary, *m.* to Richard Parry, Esq.
    2 Henrietta-Maria.
    3 Emily-Jane, *m.* 1816, to Edward Morant Gale, Esq.
    4 Louisa.
    5 Caroline-Penelope, *m.* 1819, to James Gordon Murdock, Esq.
    6 Sophia-Rose.   7 Frances.
II. JAMES, of whom presently.
III. John, a midshipman in H. M. S. "Rippon," *d. s. p.*
IV. Cornish, in the East India Company's service, *d.* 1800.
I. Mary, *m.* to Samuel Pitchford, who took the name of CORNISH, admiral of the red squadron.
II. Susannah, *m.* to Richard Sumner, Esq.
III. Harriet, *m.* to the Rev. Lascelles Iremonger.
IV. Margaret, *m.* to William Morton Pitt, Esq., M.P. for the co. Dorset, by whom she had Sophia, *m.* September, 1806, to Charles, Viscount Marsham, Earl of Romney.

The 2nd son,

SIR JAMES GAMBIER, of Iver, co. Buckingham, admiral of the fleet, and K.C.B.; *b.* in 1756, being brought up to the naval profession, attained the rank of post captain in 1778, and continuing to distinguish himself, particularly under Lord Howe on the memorable 1st June, 1794, when he commanded the

"Defence," was appointed colonel of marines. In March, 1795, he was nominated a lord of the Admiralty, which office he retained until February, 1801, when he hoisted his flag on board the "Neptune," as third in command of the channel fleet. In April, 1802, he was appointed commander-in-chief of the fleet, and governor of Newfoundland. Thence he returned to the Admiralty in 1804, was removed in 1806, and re-appointed in 1807, in which latter year he was nominated naval commander-in-chief of the expedition against Copenhagen, and upon its successful termination, was elevated to the peerage by the title of Baron Gambier, *of Iver*, 9 November, 1807. His lordship *m.* in 1798, Louisa, 2nd dau. of Daniel Matthew, Esq., of Felix Hall, co. Essex, by whom he had no issue, and the title became extinct at his decease 19 April, 1833.

Arms—Erminois, a fess wavy, az., between three starlings, sa., beaked, and legged, gu.

GANT—EARLS OF LINCOLN.

Inherited by marriage from the family of Romare,
(*see* Romare, Earl of Lincoln.)

Lineage.

GILBERT DE GANT, son of Baldwin, Earl of Flanders, by Maud, sister of WILLIAM THE CONQUEROR, accompanied his uncle into England, and participating in the triumph of Hastings, obtained a grant of the lands of a Danish proprietor, named Tour, with numerous other lordships. This Gilbert happened to be at York, *anno* 1069, and had a narrow escape, when the Danes, in great force on behalf of Edgar Etheling, entered the mouth of the Humber, and marching upon that city, committed lamentable destruction by fire and sword, there being more than 3,000 Normans slain. Like most of the great lords of his time, Gilbert de Gant disgorged a part of the spoil which he had seized to the church, and amongst other acts of piety restored Bardney Abbey, co. Lincoln, which had been utterly destroyed many years before by the Pagan Danes, Inquar and Hubba. He *m.* Alice, dau. of Hugh de Montfort, and had issue,

    I. HUGH, assumed the name of Montfort.
    II. WALTER, his successor.
    III. Robert, lord chancellor of England, *anno* 1153.
    I. Emma, *m.* to Alan, Lord Percy.

This great feudal chief *d.* in the reign of WILLIAM RUFUS; his son,

WALTER DE GANT, a person of great valour and piety; at an advanced age commanded a brave regiment of Flemings and Normans, in the celebrated conflict with the Scots, at Northallerton, in Yorkshire, known in history as the Battle of the Standard, "where," says Dugdale, "by his eloquent speech and prudent conduct, the whole army received such encouragement, as that the Scots were utterly vanquished." He *m.* Maud, of Brittany, and had issue,

    I. GILBERT, his heir.
    II. ROBERT, of whom presently.
    III. Geffery.

He *d.* in 1138, and was *s.* by his eldest son,

GILBERT DE GANT, who, in his youth, being taken prisoner with King STEPHEN, at the battle of Lincoln (1142), was compelled by Ranulph, Earl of Chester, to marry his niece the Lady Hawyse Romare, dau. and heir of William de Romare, Earl of Lincoln, whereby he became eventually in her right Earl of Lincoln. He *d.* in 1160, leaving two daus., his co-heirs, viz.,

    Alice, *m.* to Simon de St. Liz (the last of that name,) Earl of Huntingdon and Northampton.
    Gunnora, *d. s. p.*

At the decease of these ladies *s. p.*, the great inheritance reverted to their uncle,

ROBERT DE GANT, who does not, however, appear to have *s.* to the Earldom of Lincoln. This Robert *m.* 1st, Alice, dau. and heir of William Paganel, and of Avice de Romelli (dau. and co-heir of William Meschines, Lord of Copeland,) by whom he had an only dau.,

    ALICE, *m.* to Robert Fitzhardinge, *of* the family of Fitzhardinge, from which the Earls of Berkeley derive.

Robert de Gant *m.* 2ndly, Gunnora, niece of Hugh de Gournay, and had two sons, GILBERT and Stephen. He *d.* about the 4th RICHARD I., and was *s.* by his elder son,

GILBERT DE GANT, then under age, and in ward to William de Stutevill. In the last year of King JOHN's reign, this Gilbert adhering to the barons, was constituted EARL OF LINCOLN, by LEWIS, of France, at that time in London, and at the head of the baronial party, and was despatched into Nottinghamshire, to oppose the royalists. Shortly after which, assisted by Robert de Ropesle, he reduced the city of Lincoln, but at the subsequent battle, the baronial force being totally broken, he was taken prisoner, and never after assumed the title of Earl of Lincoln, which dignity was then conferred upon Randall de Meschines, surnamed Blundaville, Earl of Chester. This ex-earl *d.* in 1241, leaving issue,

    GILBERT, who inherited a considerable property, for in the 29th HENRY III., he paid £68 for as many knights' fees, upon collection of the aid for marrying the king's dau. In the 42nd of the same reign he was made governor of Scarborough Castle, but afterwards adhering to the barons, he was taken prisoner at Kenilworth, and was obliged to pay no less than 3,000 marks for the redemption of his lands; whereupon the king received him again into favour; but he *d.* soon afterwards, *anno* 1274, leaving issue,

        GILBERT, summoned to parliament as a baron (*see* Barons Gant).
        Margaret, *m.* to William de Kerdeston.
        Nichola. *m.* to Peter de Mauley.
        Julian, *d. unm.*

Julian, *m.* to Geffrey, son of Henry de Armentiers.

Arms—Barry of six, or and az., a bend, gu.

GANT—BARON GANT.

By Writ of Summons, dated 23 June, 1295.

Lineage.

GILBERT DE GANT, grandson of Gilbert, last Earl of Lincoln of that family (*see* Gant, Earls of Lincoln,) *s.* to his father's possession in 1274, and having served in the Welsh wars of King EDWARD I., was summoned to parliament as a baron from 23 June, 1295, to 26 August, 1296. His lordship *m.* Lora, sister of Alexander de Baliol, but having no issue, he constituted King EDWARD I. his heir in the lands of his barony; viz., Falkingham, Barton, Heckyngton, and Edenham, retaining only Swaledale, and his portion of Skendelley. He *d. s. p.* in 1297, when the barony of Gant became extinct, and his property passed to Roger, son of William de Kerdeston, by Margaret, his eldest sister; Peter, son of Peter de Mauley, by Nicola, his 2nd sister; and Julian de Gant, his 3rd sister, who *d. unm.*

Arms—Barry of six, or and az., a bend, gu

GARDINER — EARL OF BLESSINGTON, BARON MOUNTJOY, VISCOUNT MOUNT-JOY.

Barony, by Letters Patent, dated 19 September, 1789.
Viscounty, by Letters Patent, dated 30 September, 1795.
Earldom, by Letters Patent, dated 1816.

Lineage.

THE RIGHT HON. LUKE GARDINER, a member of the Irish parliament and privy council, and vice-treasurer of Ireland, *m.* in 1711, Anne, only dau. and sole heiress of the Hon. Alexander Stewart, 2nd son of William, 1st Viscount Mountjoy, and was *s.* by his son,

THE RIGHT HON. CHARLES GARDINER, of the city of Dublin, M.P and P.C., who inherited the fortune of his maternal great grandfather, in 1769, upon the demise of William, 3rd Viscount Mountjoy and 1st Earl of Blessington, when the male line of that Stewart family ceased. He was *b.* 21 February, 1720; *m.* 20 March, 1741, Florinda, only dau. of Robert Norman, Esq., of Lagore, co. Meath, and by her (who was *b.* 17 October, 1722) left at his decease, 15 November, 1769, three sons and two daus, viz.,

    I. LUKE, of whom presently.
    II. William, *b.* 23 October, 1748, a major-general in His Majesty's service, *m.* Harriet, dau. of the Rev. Sir Richard Wrottesley, Bart., of Staffordshire.
    III. Robert, *b.* 3 March, 1749, surveyor of His Majesty's stores in Dublin.
    I. Anne, *b.* 13 May, 1746, *m.* 30 October, 1762, to William-Power Keating Trench, Esq., of Garbally, co. Galway, M.P.

II. Florinda, b. 12 January, 1760, m. Thomas Burgh, Esq., of Oldtown. co. Kildare. M.P. for the borough of Harristown

The eldest son,

THE RIGHT HON. LUKE GARDINER, who was b. 7 February, 1745, represented the co. Dublin in parliament, was a privy councillor in Ireland, and colonel of the Dublin militia. He m. 1st, 3 July, 1773, Elizabeth, eldest dau. of Sir William Montgomery, Bart., of Magbie Hill, in Scotland, and by her (who was b. 4 May, 1751, and d. 7 November, 1783) he had issue.

  I. Luke, b. 1780, d. 15 September, 1781.
  II. CHARLES-JOHN, his successor.
  I. Florinda, b. 1774, d. 8 March, 1786.
  II. Louisa, b. 27 June, 1775, m. 30 January, 1796, to the Right Rev. Robert Fowler, D.D., bishop of Ossory.
  III. Harriet, b. 18 August, 1776.
  IV. Emily, b. 20 October, 1777, d. 12 September, 1788.
  V. Caroline. b. 5 December, 1778, d. 6 November, 1782.
  VI. Elizabeth, b. 26 October, 1783, d. 31 January, 1790.

On 19 September, 1789, Mr. Gardiner was created BARON MOUNTJOY, of Mountjoy, co. Tyrone, and 30 September, 1795, advanced to the dignity of VISCOUNT MOUNTJOY, both in the Peerage of Ireland. He m. 2ndly, 20 October, 1793, Margaret, eldest dau. of Hector Wallis, Esq., by whom he had,

Luke, d. unm. 24 April, 1810.
Margaret, who m., 1822, John Hely-Hutchinson, Esq., M.P. for the co. Tipperary. (afterwards Earl of Donoughmore) and d. 13 October, 1825, leaving issue.

Lord Mountjoy fell at the head of his regiment at the battle of Ross, in Ireland, in 1798, and was s. by his son,

CHARLES-JOHN GARDINER, 2nd Viscount Mountjoy, who was created EARL OF BLESSINGTON, in the peerage of Ireland, in 1816. His lordship, b. 19 July, 1782, m. 1st, in 1812, Mary Campbell, widow of Major William Brown, and had by her a dau. and heiress,

HARRIETT-ANNE-FRANCES, m. 1st, in 1827, to Count Alfred D'Orsay, who d. 4 August, 1852, and 2ndly, 1 September, 1852, to Hon. Charles Spencer Cowper. She d. 17 December, 1869, without surviving issue.

Lord Blessington m. 2ndly, in 1818, Mrs. Farmer, widow of M. St. Leger Farmer, Esq., and dau. of Edmund Power, Esq., by whom (who d. 4 June, 1849) he had no issue. He d. 25 May, 1829, and at his decease all the honours became EXTINCT.

Arms—Or., a griffin passant, az., on a chief, sa., three pheons heads, arg.

GAVESTON—EARL OF CORNWALL.

Lineage.

WILLIAM THE CONQUEROR gave the EARLDOM OF CORNWALL to his relation, ROBERT, EARL OF MORTEYNE, commonly called MORETON, who m. Maud, dau. of Roger de Montgomery, and had a son, WILLIAM, who forfeited the title, temp. HENRY I. The natural son of that monarch, Reginald Fitz-Henry, who was invested with the title by King STEPHEN, left no legitimate male issue. HENRY II. gave the earldom to his son, John. After this, Henry, Fitz-Count, natural son of Reginald above-mentioned, enjoyed it for a few years by sufferance. In 1219, he resigned it into the hands of King HENRY III., and in 1224, the king's son, Richard, afterwards King of the Romans, was created EARL OF CORNWALL. This Richard, Earl of Cornwall, left an only son, Edmund, who dying without legitimate male issue, in 1300, the title again lapsed to the crown. EDWARD II. gave it to his favourite,

PIERS DE GAVESTON, who was elevated to the peerage by that monarch, as Baron Wallingford and EARL OF CORNWALL.

Gaveston, the son of a private gentleman in Gascony, who had been distinguished in the wars, was brought to court by King EDWARD I., as a companion for his son, Prince Edward, but that monarch before his death was so sensible of the danger incurred by the prince in having so evil an adviser, compelled Gaveston to abjure the realm, and forbad his son recalling him, under the penalty of his curse. Upon the accession of the young monarch, however, he not only invited Gaveston back, but elevated him to the peerage, and loaded him so profusely with favours, that the rest of the nobility found it imperatively necessary to interfere, and to beseech the king to remove him. EDWARD for the moment acquiesced—but only for the moment—Gaveston was recalled, and new honours awaited him. This at length so exasperated the haughty nobles, that they flew to arms, under Thomas Plantagenet, Earl of Lancaster, and determined to compel the king to comply with their wishes. EDWARD being apprised of these

proceedings, conducted the favourite to Scarborough Castle and there left him with sufficient forces for its defence, whilst he himself marched into Warwickshire. The lords thereupon invested Scarborough, and the unhappy Gaveston soon after surrendered upon conditions of personal safety. He was, however, conveyed by the Earl of Warwick to Warwick Castle, and beheaded by his orders at Blacklow Hill, about a mile from the town of Warwick, without any form of trial whatsoever.

Gaveston m. Margaret, dau. of Gilbert de Clare, Earl of Gloucester, by Joan of Acres, the king's sister, and co-heir of her brother, Gilbert de Clare, Earl of Gloucester, by whom (who m. after his decease, Hugh de Audley) he had an only dau., Joane, who d. young. The execution of his lordship took place in 1314, when the Earldom of Cornwall became EXTINCT. After this the title was not revived till 1328, when EDWARD III. bestowed it on his 2nd brother, John, of Eltham. The following year the king created his eldest son (afterwards known as the Black Prince) Duke of Cornwall, and some years afterwards procured an Act of Parliament for settling the title on the 1st begotten son of the King of England.

Arms—Vert, six eagles displayed, or, membered and beaked, gu.

———

GENEVILL—BARON GENEVILL.

By Writ of Summons, dated 6 February, 1299.

Lineage.

In the 28th HENRY III.,
PETER DE GENEVILL, a Provencal, stated by Matthew of Paris, to have been a man of humble birth, and by others to have been Lord of Vancouleur, and brother of John de Geneville. or Joinville, the historian of the crusade of St. Louis, was governor of Windsor Castle, and dying in 1249, was s. his son and heir,

Sir GEOFFREY DE GENEVILL, who, in the 38th HENRY III., had livery of the castle of Trim, in Ireland. In four years afterwards he received a military summons to march against the Welsh, and in the 44th of the same king, being then one of the barons marchers, he had command to repair to the castle of Wales, and to reside there. In the 10th EDWARD I. he was in the expedition made against the Welsh, and in fifteen years subsequently he was in the wars of Gascony. For all which services he was summoned to parliament as a baron, 6 February, 1299, and from that period to 3 November, 1306. He m. Maud, dau. and heir of Gilbert de Lacey, son of Walter de Lacey, Lord of Meath, and had issue,

  I. Geoffrey, who d. s. p. in the life-time of his father.
  II. PETER, his successor.
  III. Simon (Sir), Lord of Culmullin, m. Joan Fitz-Leon, Lady of Culmullin, and had issue daus. only, viz., Matilda, m. to Baldwyn, Lord Slane; Elizabeth, m. Sir William de Loundres, Baron of the Naas; and Joan, m. to John Cusack. (See ADDENDA.)

His lordship d. 1307, and was s. by his son,
PETER DE GENEVILL, 2nd baron, but never summoned to parliament, who m. Joane, dau. of Hugh le Brune, Earl of Angolesme, and had three daus., viz.,

JOANE, who m. Roger Mortimer, Earl of March, and conveyed eventually the whole inheritance of the Genevills, and half the lands of the Lacies, into that family.
Isabel, }
Beatrice, } nuns at Aconbury.

Upon the decease of this Peter, the Barony of Genevill, if Peter were ever esteemed a baron, fell into ABEYANCE between his daus.

Arms—Az., three horses' bits, or, on a chief, ermine, a demi-lion, issuant, gu.

———

GEORBODUS—EARL OF CHESTER.

Creation of the CONQUEROR.

Lineage.

The Earldom of Chester, after the Norman conquest, was first conferred upon
GEORBODUS, a Fleming, who, having encountered many difficulties, as well from the English as his troublesome neighbours the Welsh, and being at length sent for into Flanders by

some of his friends, to whom he had entrusted his affairs there, obtained licence from King WILLIAM to attend the summons, but he had no sooner reached his native soil, than, falling into the power of his enemies, he was cast into prison, where he remained a considerable time. He does not appear to have ever returned to England, and the Earldom of Chester was subsequently bestowed upon HUGH DE ABRINCES (*See* Abrinces, Earl of Chester).

GERARD—BARONS GERARD, OF GERARD'S BROMLEY, CO. STAFFORD.

By Letters Patent, dated 21 July, 1603

Lineage.

In the 1st year of Queen MARY, GILBERT GERARD, a branch of the ancient Gerards, of Bryn, in Lancashire, derived from the great Geraldine stock, in Ireland, having attained eminence in the profession of the law, was chosen autumn reader by the benchers of Grey's Inn, and the next year appointed, with Nicholas Bacon (afterwards lord-keeper), joint treasurer of the society. In some time after, when the Princess Elizabeth was brought before the council, Mr. Gerard advocated her cause so ably, that he was committed to the Tower, where he remained during the rest of Queen MARY'S reign. Upon the accession of ELIZABETH, he was released, and constituted attorney-general. He afterwards received the honour of knighthood, and was appointed master of the Rolls, when he had held the attorney-generalship no less than 23 years. This Sir Gilbert erected a stately mansion in the county of Stafford, where he resided, called Gerard's Bromley. He *m.* Anne, dau. of Thomas Ratcliffe, Esq., of Wimersley, co. Lancaster, only sister and heir of the half-blood of William Radcliffe, Esq., and had issue,

I. THOMAS, his successor.
II. Ratcliffe, barrister-at-law, from whom the Gerards, Barons Gerard, of Brandon, and Earls of Macclesfield derived. (*See* Gerard, Barons Gerard, of Brandon.)
III. Gilbert, *m.* Ellen, dau. of William Pearson, of Chester.
I. Frances. *m.* to Sir Richard Molineux, Bart., ancestor of the extant Earls of Sefton.
II. Margaret. *m.* to Peter Leigh, Esq., of Lyme.
III. Catherine, *m.* to Sir Richard Hoghton, Bart., of Hoghton Tower, co. Lancaster, ancestor of the Baronets Hoghton.
IV Ratcliffe, *m.* to Thomas Wingfield, Esq.

Sir Gilbert Gerard *d.* in 1592, and was *s.* by his eldest son, SIR THOMAS GERARD, who was advanced to the peerage 21 July, 1603, as BARON GERARD, *of Gerard's Bromley, co. Stafford;* and in the 14th of King JAMES I., was constituted lord president of Wales. His lordship *m.* 1st, Alice, dau. and heiress of Sir Thomas Rivet, Knt., and had besides other issue, who *d. s. p.,* two sons,

I. GILBERT, his heir.
II. John, who *d.* 1673, having had a son and heir, Richard, who *d.* the same year, leaving issue,
CHARLES. heir to Digby, 5th Lord Gerard, by settlement, *m.* Mary, dau. of Sir John Webb, of Oldstock, co. Wilts, and *d. s. p.* 21 April, 1707.
William, *d. s. p.*
Philip, 1st Lord Gerard, of Bromley, disinherited.
Joseph, *d. s. p.* 23 April, 1705.
Frances, *m.* to Thomas Fleetwood, Esq., and had issue.

He *m.* 2ndly, Elizabeth, dau. of — Woodford, Esq.; but had no issue. He *d.* in 1617, and was *s.* by his eldest son, GILBERT GERARD, 2nd Baron Gerard, of Gerard's Bromley, who *m.* in 1609, Eleanor, dau. and heiress of Thomas Dutton, Esq., of Dutton, co. Chester, by whom, who *m.* 2ndly, Robert Nedham, Esq., of Shaventon, co. Salop, he had surviving issue,

I. DUTTON, his successor.
I. Alice, *m.* to Roger Owen, Esq., son and heir of Sir William Owen, of Cundover, co. Salop, Knt.
II. Frances, *m.* to the Hon. Robert Needham, son and heir of Robert, Viscount Kilmorey.
III. Elizabeth, *m.* to Sir Peter Leicester, Bart., of Nether Tabley, the celebrated antiquary and historian of Cheshire, maternal ancestor of the present Lords de Tabley.

His lordship *d.* in 1622, and was *s.* by his son, DUTTON GERARD, 3rd Baron Gerard, *b.* 4 March, 1613. This nobleman *m.* 1st, Lady Mary Fane, dau. of Francis, Earl of Westmoreland, by whom he had issue,

CHARLES, his successor.
Mary, *m.* to Sir Anthony Cope, Bart., of Hanwell, co. Oxford.

His lordship *m.* 2ndly, Lady Elizabeth O'Bryen, dau. and co-heir of Henry, Earl of Thomond, in Ireland, and had an only dau.,

Elizabeth, *m.* to William Spencer, of Ashton, co Lancaster, 3rd son of William, Lord Spencer, and had a dau.,
Elizabeth Spencer, who *m.* Robert Hesketh, Esq., of Rufford, co Lancaster, and left a dau. and heiress,
ELIZABETH HESKETH, who *m.* Sir Edward Stanley, Bart., afterwards 11th Earl of Derby, and had, with other issue,
JAMES, Lord Stanley, father of Edward, 12th Earl of Derby.

Lord Gerard *d.* in 1640, and was *s.* by his son, CHARLES GERARD, 4th Baron Gerard, who *m.* in 1660, Jane, only surviving dau. and heiress of George Digby, Esq., of Sandon, co. Stafford; and by her (who *m.* 2ndly, Sir Edward Hungerford, Bart.), had an only son DIGBY. He *d.* in 1667, and was *s.* by his only child, DIGBY GERARD, 5th Baron Gerard. This nobleman *m.* his distant relation, Elizabeth, dau. of Charles Gerard, 1st Earl of Macclesfield, and had an only dau. and heiress, ELIZABETH, who *m.* James, Duke of Hamilton, in Scotland, and 1st Duke of Brandon, in England.

Lord Gerard *d.* 8 November, 1684, when the title devolved on CHARLES GERARD, 6th baron, who *d.* without male issue, 12 April, 1707, when the title became EXTINCT.

Arms—Quarterly: 1st and 4th, arg., a saltier, gu., 2nd and 3rd, az., a lion rampant, crowned, or.

GERARD—BARONS GERARD, OF BRANDON, CO. SUFFOLK, EARLS OF MACCLESFIELD.

Barony, by Letters Patent, dated 8 October, 1645.
Earldom, by Letters Patent, dated 21 July, 1679.

Lineage.

RATCLIFFE GERARD, Esq., of Halsall, co. Lancaster, 2nd son of Sir Gilbert Gerard, attorney-general and master of the Rolls, in the reign of ELIZABETH, *m.* Elizabeth, dau. and heiress of Sir Charles Somerset, K.B., and grand-dau. of Edward, Earl of Worcester, and had issue,

I. CHARLES (Sir), his heir.
II. Thomas, *d. s. p.*
III. Radclyffe, twin with Gilbert, lieut.-colonel in the army, *m.* Jennet, dau. of Edward Barret, Esq., of co. Pembroke, and had issue.
IV. Gilbert (Sir), governor of Worcester for CHARLES I., *m.* Anne, dau. and heir of Sir John Fitton, and relict of Sir John Brereton, son and heir of William, Lord Brereton, and *d. v. p.*

The eldest son, SIR CHARLES GERARD, Knt., of Halsall, co. Lancaster, who *m.* Penelope, sister and co-heir of Sir Edward Fitton, of Gosworth, co. Chester, Knt., and had three sons and a dau.,

I. CHARLES, his heir.
II. Edward.
III. Gilbert (Sir).
I. Charlotte, *m.* to Roger Whitley, Esq., of Ashton and Hawarden Castle, co. Flint.

Sir Charles was *s.* by his eldest son, CHARLES GERARD, who, being brought up from his youth to the profession of arms, upon the usual theatre of European warfare, the Netherlands, joined his majesty. King CHARLES I., at Shrewsbury, soon after he had reared the royal standard, and became eminently distinguished amongst the cavaliers. First, at Kineton, where he received some dangerous wounds. And soon afterwards at the taking of Lichfield, the first battle of Newberry, and the relief of Newark. General Gerard then accompanied Prince Rupert into South Wales, and acquired high reputation by his victories at Cardiffe, Kidwelly, and Caermarthen—and his success in taking the castle of Cardigan, and other fortresses, and reducing the strong garrison of Haverford-West, with the castles of Picton and Carew. In consideration of which gallant services he was made, by the king, lieutenant-general of his horse, and elevated to the peerage, as BARON GERARD,* *of Brandon*, 8 October, 1645. His lordship, after the Restoration, was created, 21 July, 1679, *Viscount Brandon*, and EARL OF MACCLESFIELD—but in the time of JAMES II., he was committed, with the Earl of Stamford and the Lord Delamere, to the Tower, and condemned to death, but pardoned. He lived to see the Revolution, and, " in fact, to witness," says Banks, "three singular occurrences in the annals of British history;" (he might have characterized them as the three *most* singular,) " first, the deposition and decapitation of King CHARLES I. ; 2ndly, the restoration of his son; and 3rdly, the Revolution and total expulsion of the royal family so recently restored." His lordship married a French lady, and had issue,

> CHARLES, }
> FITTON, } successively earls.
>
> Charlotte, *m*. 1st, Thomas Mainwaring, Esq., of Cheshire, and had a dau.,
>> CHARLOTTE, who *m*. Charles, Lord Mohun To this nobleman, Charles, 2nd Earl of Macclesfield, left the chief of his estates, which causing a law-suit between him and James, Duke of Hamilton, an unhappy personal quarrel arose, which terminated in a duel, wherein both lost their lives, 15 November, 1712.
>
> Lady Charlotte Mainwaring *m*. 2ndly, Sir Thomas Orby, of Lincolnshire.
> Anne, *m*. to Captain Ebrington.
> Elizabeth, *m*. to Digby, Lord Gerard, of Bromley, and had a dau., Elizabeth, *m*. to James, Duke of Hamilton, who fell in the duel with Lord Mohun.

The earl† *d*. in 1693, and was *s*. by his elder son,

CHARLES GERARD, 2nd Earl of Macclesfield, a colonel in the army. This nobleman was ambassador to Hanover, upon the subject of the succession to the throne of England. His lordship *m*. 1st, the dau. of Sir Richard Mason, Knt., of Shropshire, from whom he separated; and 2ndly, Miss Harbourd, but had no issue. His lordship *d*. in 1701, leaving the greater part of his estates to Charles, Lord Mohun (who had *m*. his niece, Miss Mainwaring), owing to some dispute with his brother and successor,

FITTON GERARD, 3rd Earl of Macclesfield, who *d. unm.* in 1702, when the Barony of Gerard, of Brandon, with the Viscounty of Brandon, and Earldom of Macclesfield, became EXTINCT.

Arms—Arg., sa., saltier, gu., a crescent for difference.

GHISNES—BARON GHISNES.

By Writ of Summons, dated 23 June, 1295.

Lineage.

The Barons Ghisnes derived descent from the Counts de Ghisnes in Flanders, who were also great feudal Lords in England so far back as the reigns of JOHN and HENRY III.

INGELRAM DE GHISNES (brother of Baldwin de Ghisnes, and grandson of ARNOLD, Comte de Ghisnes, who sold the county of Ghisnes to the King of France), *m*. Christian, dau. and heir of William de Lindsay, by Ada, his wife, sister and co-heir of JOHN BALIOL, King of Scotland, descended from Alice, one of the sisters and co-heirs of William de Lancaster, and doing his fealty in the 11th EDWARD I., had livery of the lands of her inheritance, amongst which was the manor of Wyresdale, in Lancashire. This feudal lord having distinguished himself in the wars of Scotland, was summoned to parliament, as a baron, from 23 June, 1295, to 14 March, 1322. His lordship, who took the name of DE COUCI, *d*. in the 17th EDWARD II., seised of the manor of Middleton, near Richmond, and was *s*. by his son,

---

* Besides his lordship, there were of his family the following persons actively engaged upon the royal side, in those unhappy conflicts—

His brothers, { Edward Gerard, a colonel of foot, wounded in the first battle of Newbury.
Sir Gilbert Gerard, slain near Ludlow.

His uncles, { Sir Gilbert Gerard, governor of Worcester.
Ratcliffe Gerard, lieut.-colonel to his brother. This gentleman had three sons,

Radcliffe.
John, put to death by Cromwell.   } All in the battle of Kineton.
Gilbert, created a baronet.

† His lordship was first created Earl of Newberry, but the title was changed to MACCLESFIELD.

---

of the manor of Middleton, near Richmond, and was *s*. by his son,

WILLIAM DE GHISNES, Sire de Coucy, 2nd baron, but never summoned to parliament. He *d*. in 1335, leaving a son and heir,

INGELRAM DE GHISNES, who *d*. in 1347, without being summoned to parliament. His son and heir,

INGELRAM DE COUCY, *m*. the Lady Isabella Plantagenet, one of the daus. of King EDWARD III., and was created Earl of Bedford (*see* DE COUCY, Earl of Bedford). The barony of Ghisnes is now vested in the descendant and representative of INGELRAM, who was summoned to parliament in the reign of EDWARD I.

Arms—Barry of six, vairée and gu.

GIFFARD—EARLS OF BUCKINGHAM.

Creation of WILLIAM THE CONQUEROR, *circa* 1070.

Lineage.

OSBORNE DE BOLEBEC, a noble Norman, living *temp.* RICHARD *sans peur* Duke of Normandy, *m*. Avelina, sister of Gunnora, Duchess of Normandy, and had two sons, WALTER, of whom we treat; and OSBORNE, ancestor of the GIFFARDS, Lords Giffard, of Brimsfield, and of the Giffards of Chillington, co. Stafford. The elder son.

WALTER GIFFARD, Earl of Longueville, in Normandy, was granted for his gallant services at the battle of Hastings, the title of EARL OF BUCKINGHAM. At the time of the General Survey, this nobleman was sent with Remigius, bishop of Lincoln, and others, into Worcestershire, and some other counties, to value the lands belonging to the crown, as well as to private individuals in those parts. He himself possessed at that time two lordships in Berkshire ; one in Wilts ; one in Somersetshire ; one in Huntingdon ; five in Cambridgeshire ; nine in Oxfordshire ; nine in the co. of Bedford ; three in Suffolk ; twenty-eight in Norfolk ; and forty-eight in Buckinghamshire ; in all one hundred and seven. In 1089, his lordship adhering to WILLIAM RUFUS, fortified his mansions in Normandy, for that king, and became chief general of his army there ; yet in some years afterwards (1102), he sided with ROBERT COURTHOSE, against King HENRY I. The earl *m*. Agnes, dau. of Gerard Flaitell, and sister of William, bishop of Eureux, and had, with other issue,

WALTER, his successor.
Rohais, *m*. to Richard Fitz-Gilbert, feudal lord of Clare, co. Suffolk (*see* Clare), and had, besides other children,
> GILBERT, who *m*. Adeliza, dau. of the Earl of Claremont, and was father of
>> Richard de Clare, Earl of Hertford.
>> GILBERT DE CLARE, created Earl of Pembroke, whose son,
>>> RICHARD, surnamed STRONGBOW, became so distinguished in the conquest of Ireland.
Isabel, *m*. to Richard Granville, or Grenville, progenitor of the noble house of Grenville, now Dukes of Buckingham.

His lordship *d*. in 1102, and was *s*. by his son,

WALTER GIFFARD, 2nd Earl of Buckingham. This nobleman adhered faithfully to King HENRY I., and distinguished himself in that monarch's cause at the battle of Breneville in 1119, against the French, commanded by their king in person, where HENRY obtained a victory. His lordship, during this reign, founded the Abbey of Nutley, co. Bucks. He *d*. in 1164, without issue, when the lands of his barony came, according to Dugdale, to be shared amongst his relatives; " for it seems," (says that writer), " in the 1st RICHARD I., that Richard de Clare, Earl of Hertford (in respect of his descent from Rohaise, sister of the earl, and wife of Richard Fitz-Gilbert, his lineal ancestor), and William Mareschall, Earl of Pembroke (in right of Isabel de Clare, his wife), obtained a confirmation from that king, of all the lands of this Walter, Earl of Buckingham, both in England and Normandy ; of which lands, Richard, Earl of Hertford, was to have the chief seat in England, and William, Earl of Pembroke, the chief seat in Normandy ; the residue in both countries to be equally divided between them." Thus terminated the house of Giffard, Earls of Buckingham. The title is said by Camden to have been subsequently borne by Richard de Clare, surnamed Strongbow, Earl of Pembroke.

Arms—Gu., three lions passant, arg.

GIFFARD—BARONS GIFFARD, OF BRIMS-FIELD, CO. GLOUCESTER.

By Writ of Summons, dated 24 June, 1295.

Lineage.

This family was descended from Count Giffard, a great Norman nobleman and a general in the CONQUEROR's army. In the CONQUEROR's time,

OSBORNE GIFFARD, held one lordship in Berkshire; one in Oxfordshire; three in Cornwall; one in Dorsetshire; and four in Gloucestershire, whereof Brimsfield was one, and his chief seat. To this feudal lord, who *d.* before the year 1086, *s.* his son,

HELIAS GIFFARD, who, in conjunction with Ala his wife, granted in about 1100, part of his woods, with three borderers, to the Abbey of St. Peter, at Gloucester. He left two sons, HELIAS, his heir, and GILBERT, ancestor of GIFFARD of CHIL-LINGTON. The elder son,

HELIAS GIFFARD, was, like his father, a liberal benefactor to the church, having made grants to divers religious houses, amongst which was the above mentioned Abbey of St. Peter, upon which he conferred his lordship of Cronham. His grandson was,

HELIAS GIFFARD. This feudal lord, upon the assessment for the marriage portion of King HENRY II.'s dau., Maud, certified that he possessed nine knights fees, and the same year (12th HENRY II.) gave 100 marks fine, for livery of his inheritance. He *d.* in 1190, and was *s.* by

THOMAS GIFFARD, who in the 6th RICHARD I., paid £9 upon levying the scutage for the king's redemption. He was *s.* by his son,

HELIAS GIFFARD, who took up arms with the other barons against King JOHN, and in the 18th of that monarch's reign, all his lands in the cos. of Wilts, Northampton, Gloucester, Somerset, Dorset, Oxford, and Berks, were given by order of the king, to Bartholomew Peche, but restored by HENRY III., at the general pacification. By the inquisition taken after the death of this feudal baron, 33rd HENRY III., he appears to have been possessed of the manor of Winterborne, co. Wilts, and that that lordship was then the head of his barony He *d.* 33rd HENRY III., and was *s.* by his son,

JOHN GIFFARD, then in his seventeenth year, during whose minority the queen had a grant of his lands, towards the maintenance of Prince Edward. In the 41st HENRY III., this John Giffard was commanded to be at Bristol with horse and arms, thence to march into South Wales, against Lewelin ap Griffin. In six years subsequently, he was constituted governor of St. Briavel's Castle, and warden of the Forest of Dean, in Gloucestershire; but soon after, taking part with the rebellious barons, was amongst those whom the archbishop of Canterbury ordered to he excommunicated. He was at the battle of Lewes, under the baronial banner, but adopting a different course at the battle of Evesham, he obtained pardon for his former treasons, in consideration of the services which he then rendered to the royal cause.

In the 55th HENRY III., Maud de Longespée, widow of William Longespée, son of William, Earl of Salisbury, and dau. and heiress of Walter de Clifford, having by letter complained to the king, that this John Giffard, had taken her by force from her manor house, and carried her to his Castle of Brimsfield, where he kept her in restraint; he was summoned before the king, when denying the charge, but confessing his marriage with the lady without the royal licence, he made his peace by paying a fine of 300 marks.

In the 10th EDWARD I. John Giffard was in the expedition made by Gilbert, Earl of Gloucester, against Lewelyn ap Griffith, Prince of North Wales; and observing that Lewelyn, had separated, with a small party, from the body of his army, he joined with Edward Mortimer, and slaying the prince, despatched his head to the king, who caused it to be set upon the Tower of London, crowned with ivy. In the 18th of the same reign he was constituted governor of Dynevor Castle, in Wales, and having had summons to parliament as a baron, from 24 June, 1295, to 10 April, 1299, *d.* in the latter year, and was buried at Malmesbury. His lordship *m.* 1st (as already stated), Maud, widow of William Longespée, by whom he had issue,

Katherine, *m.* to Nicholas Aldithley, 1st Baron Aldithley, or Audley, of Helegh.

Alianore, *m.* to Fulk le Strange, Baron Strange, of Blackmere.

He *m.* 2ndly, Alicia Maltravers, by whom he had no child; and 3rdly, Margaret de Nevile, by whom he had an only son, JOHN. He *d.* 27th EDWARD I. (1299), and was *s.* by his son,

SIR JOHN GIFFARD, K.B., 2nd baron, summoned to parliament, from 8 October, 1311, to 15 May, 1321, as "Johanni Giffard de Brymesfield." This nobleman was constituted, in the 9th EDWARD II., constable of the castles of Glamorgan and Morgannoc. Adhering subsequently, however, to Thomas, Earl of Lancaster, in his opposition to the Spencers, he sat in the parliament by which those favourites were condemned to banishment, and afterwards, when the king marched into Wales, plundered the royal carriages, which so incensed EDWARD, that, in passing from Cirencester towards Worcester, he sent a party of soldiers to demolish Lord Giffard's castle at Brimsfield. His lordship eventually, sharing the fortune of his leader, the Earl of Lancaster, was taken prisoner with that nobleman, after the defeat at Boroughbridge, and being condemned for high treason, was hanged at Gloucester in 1322, when the barony of Giffard fell under the attainder; but the proceedings against Thomas, Earl of Lancaster, and his adherents, being reversed in the 1st EDWARD III., *anno* 1327, the dignity was revived, and may now probably be considered to be vested in the descendants and representatives of his half-sisters, the above-mentioned

Katherine. Lady Aldithley, and
Alianore, Lady Strange, of Blackmere.

Arms—Gu., three lions passant, in pale, arg., and langued, az.

GINKEL—EARL OF ATHLONE.

By Letters Patent, dated 4 March, 1692.

Lineage.

GODART DE GINKEL, commander-in-chief of King WILLIAM's army in the Irish campaign of 1691, having achieved an important victory at Aughrim, near Athlone, 12 July in that year, was elevated to the peerage of Ireland, 4 March, 1692, as *Baron of Aughrim*, and EARL OF ATHLONE, obtaining at the same time a grant of 26,000 acres of land, the confiscated estate of William Dongan, Earl of Limerick. This grant was, however, subsequently reversed by parliament, and the earl returned to his native country, there to reap fresh laurels as a military commander. His lordship *d.* 11 February, 1720, and was *s.* by his son,

FREDERICK-CHRISTIAN, 2nd earl, *b.* 1668, who, continuing to reside in Holland, was a member of the nobles for the province of Utrecht, and lieutenant-general of the Dutch army. His lordship *m.* Henrietta, Countess of Nassau Zulenstein, youngest dau. of William, Earl of Rochfort, by whom he left at his decease, 15 August, 1719, two sons and a *s.* by the elder,

GODARD-ADRIAN, 3rd earl, at whose decease *unm.* 8 October, 1736, the honours devolved upon his brother,

FREDERICK-WILLIAM, 4th earl, *b.* 1717, and educated with his brother in the university of Marbourg. His lordship *m.* Louisa, Baroness de Wassenaar, and dying 1748, left two sons and a dau., viz.,

FREDERICK-CHRISTIAN, his heir.
Arent William, *b.* 1747, *m.* Heijlwig Adrianna-Amarante, Baronne de Lynden, and left issue, William-Frederick, Baron de Reede Lynden.
Maria Frederika, *m.* to Sigismund Pieter Alexander, Count Heyden.

He was *s.* by his elder son,

FREDERICK-CHRISTIAN-RYNHART, 5th Earl of Athlone, *b.* 31 January, 1743, who *m.* in 1765, Anna-Elizabeth-Christina, Baroness de Tuijll de Serooskerkin, and *d.* in 1808, leaving issue,

  I. FREDERICK-WILLIAM, his heir.
  II. Charles-William-Lewis, royal horse artillery, *d.* young in 1793.
  III. REINAUD-DIEDRICK-JACOB, 7th earl.
  IV. John-Gerard-Reinaud, *d.* 13 March, 1818.
  V. WILLIAM-GUSTAUF-FREDERICK, 9th and last earl.
    I. Jemima-Helena, *m.* in 1785, Count John-Charles Bentinck, and *d.* in 1829, leaving William-Christian-Frederick, Count Bentinck, and more issue. (See DUKEDOM OF PORTLAND, BURKE's *Extant Peerage*.)
    II. Maria-Wilhelmina, *d. unm* in 1852.
    III. Christiana-Maria-Isabella-Henrietta, *m.* in 1793, her cousin, William-Frederick, Baron Van Reede Lynden; and *d.* 16 January, 1800.
    IV. Christiana-Renira, *d. unm.* in 1847.

The eldest son,

FREDERICK-WILLIAM, 6th earl, *b.* in 1766; *m.* 1st, in 1789, Miss Munter; and 2ndly, in 1800, Maria, dau. of the late Sir John Eden, Bart., but *d. s. p.* in 1810; his widow *m.* 2ndly,

Si: William Johnstone Hope, G.C.B. and *d.* in 1851. The peerage honours devolved on his lordship's brother,

REINAUD-DIEDRICH-JACOB, 7th earl, *b.* in 1773; who *m.* in 1818, Henrietta-Dorothea-Maria, dau. of John Williams Hope, Esq., of Amsterdam, and by her (who *m.* 2ndly, in 1825, William Gambier, Esq , and *d.* in 1830) left at his decease, 31 October, 1823, a son and a dau.,

GEORGE-GODART-HENRY, 8th earl.

Elizabeth, *b.* 18 December, 1821, *m.* 12 July, 1842, Hon. Frederic-William Child-Villiers, 3rd son of George Child, 5th Earl of Jersey.

The only son,

GEORGE-GODART-HENRY, 8th earl, *b.* 20 November, 1820; *d. unm.,* 2 March, 1843, when the title reverted to his uncle,

WILLIAM-GUSTAUF-FREDERICK, 9th earl, *b.* 21 July, 1780, who *m.* 7 September, 1814, Wendela-Eleanor, dau. of M Burcel, but *d. s. p.* 21 May, 1844, when the peerage became EXTINCT.

Arms—Arg., two bars, dancettée, *sa.*

GODOLPHIN—BARONS GODOLPHIN, OF RIALTON, CO. CORNWALL, EARLS OF GODOLPHIN, BARONS GODOLPHIN, OF HELSTON, CO. CORNWALL.

Barony, by Letters Patent, dated 8 September, 1684.
Earldom, by Letters Patent, dated 29 December, 1706.
Barony, by Letters Patent, dated 23 January, 1735.

Lineage.

This family derived its surname from Godolphin* (anciently written Godolghan), co. Cornwall,

JOHN DE GODOLPHIN was living about the time of the Norman Conquest, and amongst his other feudal possessions was lord of the manor of Godolphin, and resided there. He *m.* Margaret, dau. of Roger de Trewargen, of Trewargen, and was *s.* by his son,

RICHARD DE GODOLPHIN, father of

JAMES DE GODOLPHIN, whose son and heir,

JOHN DE GODOLPHIN, was father of

THOMAS DE GODOLPHIN, his son and successor,

EDWARD DE GODOLPHIN, *m.* Maud, dau. of William Boteler, Esq., of Camerton, and was father of

WILLIAM DE GODOLPHIN, whose son,

THOMAS DE GODOLPHIN, was *s.* by his son,

EDWARD DE GODOLPHIN, Esq., of Godolphin, who *m.* Christian, dau. of Thomas Prideaux, Esq., and was father of

ALEXANDER GODOLPHIN, who *m.* Mary, dau. of Sir John de Tregour, and had a son,

WILLIAM GODOLPHIN, who was father of

DAVID GODOLPHIN, Esq., who *m.* Meliora, dau. of John Cowling, Esq., of Trewerveneth, and left an only dau. and heiress,

ELEANOR GODOLPHIN, who *m.* John Rinsey, Esq., and being a great heiress, covenanted, that her issue should bear her own family name. The heir of this marriage was,

THOMAS GODOLPHIN, Esq., of Godolphin, who *m.* Isabel, dau. of — Benne, Esq., of Boskenne, co. Cornwall, and was father of

JOHN GODOLPHIN, Esq., who *m.* Elizabeth, dau. of John Beauchamp, Esq., of Bennerton, and had a son,

JOHN GODOLPHIN, Esq., who by Elizabeth, his wife, dau. of John Killegrew, Esq., was father of

JOHN GODOLPHIN, Esq., of Godolphin, who was sheriff of Cornwall in the 19th and 28rd HENRY VII.; he was also joint steward with Sir Robert Willoughby, Lord Brooke, of the mines in Cornwall and Devonshire. He *m.* Margaret, dau. of John Trenouth, Esq., and had issue,

I. WILLIAM (Sir), his successor.
II. John, whose descendants were seated at Morewall and Trewerveneth, co. Cornwall.
I. Elizabeth, *m.* to William Canell, Esq.

He was *s.* by his son,

WILLIAM GODOLPHIN, Esq., who *m.* Margaret, dau. and co-heir of John Glinne, Esq., of Moreval and Lowewater, by whom he had two sons, viz.,

I. WILLIAM (Sir), his successor.
II. Thomas, who *m.* the dau. of Edmund Bonithon, Esq., and left issue,

FRANCIS, who *s.* his uncle, Sir William Godolphin, and carried on the line of the family.
William, M.P. for Helston, in the 28th ELIZABETH, *m.* a dau. and co-heir of — Gaurigan.

Mr. Godolphin was *s.* by his elder son,

SIR WILLIAM GODOLPHIN, a very distinguished person in the reign of HENRY VIII., who, for his services, had the honour of knighthood, and was constituted warden and chief steward of the Stanneries. Sir William lived to an advanced age, and was chosen several times one of the knights of the shire for Cornwall, in the parliament of King HENRY VIII. and King EDWARD VI. He was thrice sheriff of Cornwall, in the reign of HENRY VIII., and once in the reign of EDWARD VI., and again in that of ELIZABETH. He likewise, attained a high military reputation, particularly for his gallant conduct at the siege of Boulogne. Mr. Carew, in his Survey of Cornwall, ranks Sir William Godolphin amongst the principal worthies of that shire; thus speaking of him : " He demeaned himself very valiantly beyond the seas, as appeared by the scars he brought home, no less to the beautifying of his fame, than the disfiguring of his face." Sir William *m.* Blanch, dau. of Robert Langden, Esq., and had issue,

Margaret, *m.* to Sir Robert Verney.
Grace, *m.* to Sir John Sydenham, of Brimpton, co. S merset.
Anne, *m.* to Sir John Arundel, of Talvern, co. Cornwall.

Having thus no male issue, the estates passed at Sir William's decease to his nephew,

SIR FRANCIS GODOLPHIN, M.P. for the co. Cornwall, in the 31st ELIZABETH, and colonel of a regiment of twelve companies armed with 470 pikes, 490 muskets, and 240 calivers. He was also governor of Scilly, " which," Carew says, " by her majesty's order, was reduced to a more defensible plight by him, who with his invention and purse, bettered his plot and allowance, and therein so tempered strength and delight, and both with use, as it serveth for a sure hold, and a commodious dwelling." Of Sir Francis, this same author gives the following character :—" Sir Francis Godolphin, Knt., whose zeal in religion, uprightness in Justice, providence in government, and plentiful housekeeping, have won him a very great and reverent reputation in his country ; and these virtues, together with his services to her majesty, are so sufficiently known to those of highest place, as my testimony can add but little light thereunto. But by his labours and inventions in tin matters, not only the whole county hath felt a general benefit, so as the several owners have thereby gotten very great profit out of such refuse works, as they before had given over for unprofitable; but her majesty hath also received increase of her customs by the same, at least to the value of £10,000. Moreover, in those works, which are of his own particular inheritance, he continually keepeth at work three hundred persons or thereabouts; and the yearly benefit, that out of those his works accrueth to her majesty, amounteth *communibus annis* to £1,000 at the least, and sometimes so much more. A matter very remarkable, and, per chance, not to be matched again, by any of his sort and condition in the whole realm." Sir Francis undertook the coinage of silver out of the mines in Wales and Cornwall ; and King CHARLES I. granted him the power of coining at Aberrusky, in Cornwall. The pence, groats, shillings, half-crowns, &c., there afterwards coined, were distinguished by a plume of ostrich feathers, the badge of the English Princes of Wales. Sir Francis Godolphin *m.* Margaret, dau. of John Killigrew, Esq., of Arnwick, in Cornwall, and had three sons and six daus., of whom,

WILLIAM, was his successor.
Blanch, *m.* George Kekewich, Esq., of Catch-French.
Ursula, *m.* — Creyde, Esq.
Thomasin, *m.* Sir George Carew, afterwards Earl of Totness.

Sir Francis was *s.* by his eldest son,

SIR WILLIAM GODOLPHIN, who accompanied Robert, Earl of Essex, in his expedition to Ireland against the rebels in 1599, and received the honour of knighthood for his gallantry at Arklow. In the following year he was so highly esteemed by the lord deputy, Mountjoy, that he entrusted him with the command of his own brigade of horse, in the decisive battle between the queen's forces, and the Spaniards and Irish, fought 24 December, in the immediate vicinity of Kinsale : which victory was chiefly owing to his courageous conduct, having broken through the Spanish line, and made prisoner of their commander, when the whole was put to the rout. Sir William was slightly wounded in the thigh with a halbert; but in six days afterwards was so far recovered, that when Don John D'Aquila, commander of the Spaniards in the town of

---

Godolphin, in Cornish, signifies a *White Eagle,* which was always borne in arms of this family.

Kinsale, offered a parley, desiring the lord deputy that some gentlemen of special trust and sufficiency might be sent into the town to confer with him. he was employed in the negotiation. Sir William Godolphin represented the co. Cornwall in the first parliament of King JAMES, and dying in 1613, left issue by Thomasin, dau. and heir of Thomas Sidney, Esq., of Wrighton, co. Norfolk,

FRANCIS, his successor.

Sidney, a very accomplished personage, and a poet of some celebrity, of whom Lord Clarendon thus speaks :—" A young gentleman of incomparable parts, who being of a constitution and education more delicate and unacquainted with contentions, upon his observation of the wickednes of those men in the House of Commons, of which he was a member, out of pure indignation of his soul against them, and conscience to his country, had, with the first, engaged himself with that party in the west ; and though he thought not fit to take command in a profession he had not willingly chosen, yet as his advice was of great authority with all the commanders, being always one in the council of war, and whose notable abilities they had still use of in their civil transactions, so he exposed his person to all action, travel, and hazard ; and by too forward engaging himself, (in this action at Chagford,) received a mortal shot by a musket, a little above the knee, of which he died in the instant " He was buried at Oke-hampton, 10 February, 1642, leaving an only dau. Mary, m. to her cousin, Dr. Henry Godolphin.

William, was colonel of a regiment, and performed many signal services for King CHARLES I., in several remarkable actions in the west.

Penelope, m. to Sir Charles Berkeley, Viscount Fitz-hardinge.

Sir William was s. by his eldest son,

FRANCIS GODOLPHIN, Esq., M.P. for St. Ives, prior to the breaking out of the rebellion. After which unhappy proceeding he retired to his seat in Cornwall, secured the Island of Scilly for the king, and raised a regiment of foot, the command of which was given to his brother, Colonel William Godolphin. He subsequently waited upon his majesty at Oxford, and was amongst those members who met there by royal appointment in January, 1643. The Island of Scilly was under Mr. Godolphin's command, until the incarceration of the king, when finding it hopeless any longer to resist, he capitulated upon honorable terms : the Commons having voted, 4 January, 1646-7, "that Mr. Godolphin, governor of Scilly, upon his surrender of that island, with all forts, &c., should enjoy his estate, and be free from arrest from any acts of war." For these services, and his known loyalty, he was created a knight of the Bath at the coronation of King CHARLES II. He m. Dorothy, 2nd dau. of Sir Henry Berkeley, Knt., of Yarlington, co. Somerset, and had no less than sixteen children, of whom,

I. WILLIAM, (the eldest son.) was created a baronet 29 April, 1661, Sir William lived in retirement, and dying u.m. 17 August, 1710, bequeathed his estates to his nephew, the Earl of Godolphin.
II. Francis, d. unm. 1675.
III. SIDNEY, of whom presently.
IV. Henry, D.D., provost of Eton College, and dean of St. Paul's. Dr. Godolphin, who was greatly esteemed for his learning, piety, and benevolence, d. at the advanced age of eighty-four, 29 January, 1732-3, leaving, by Mary, his wife, dau. of Sidney Godolphin, governor of Scilly, a son and dau., viz.,

FRANCIS, who s. to the Barony of Godolphin, of Helston, upon the decease of Francis, 2nd Earl of Godolphin.
Mary, m. to William Owen, Esq., of Porkington, and their descendant and representative is JOHN RALPH ORMSBY-GORE, Esq.

The 3rd son,

SIDNEY GODOLPHIN, was, from his youth, in the service of King CHARLES II., who, when Prince of Wales, coming into Cornwall, there took particular notice of him, and after the Restoration made him one of the grooms of the bed-chamber. In 1678 he was accredited to the States General upon a special mission, and the next year, upon the dismission of the Earl of Danby from the office of lord high treasurer of England, he was constituted one of the commissioners of the Treasury, and sworn of the privy council. Soon after which he acquired, by his prudent management, a great ascendant in the council, and Sir William Temple informs us, "that the Earl of Sunderland, Mr. Hyde, and Mr. Godolphin were esteemed to be alone in the secret and management of the king's affairs, and looked upon as the ministry." On the resignation in 1684 of Sir Leoline Jenkins, one of his majesty's principal secretaries of state, Mr. Godolphin was sworn into that office, but he returned to the Treasury in a few months after as first commissioner, and was elevated to the peerage 8 September in that year, as BARON GODOLPHIN, of Rialton, co. Cornwall. Upon the accession of King JAMES II. his lordship was appointed lord chamberlain to

the Queen, and upon the removal of the Earl of Rochester from the lord treasurership in January, 1686-7, he was again consti tuted one of the commissioners of the Treasury. After the landing of the Prince of Orange, his lordship was one of those deputed by the reigning sovereign to wait upon the prince, and to demand the object he had in view; and when King JAMES retired, in the debates regarding the vacancy of the throne that followed, his lordship voted for a regency : nevertheless, when their majesties, King WILLIAM and Queen MARY were proclaimed king and queen of England, knowing his great abilities and integrity, they constituted him one of the lords commissioners of the Treasury, and he was sworn of the privy council. In the year 1695 his lordship was declared one of the seven lords justices, for the administration of the government during the king's absence beyond the seas, as he was again in the following year, as also in the year 1701.

Upon the accession of Queen ANNE, Lord Godolphin was constituted lord high treasurer of England. Under his lordship's administration in this high office, public credit, which had previously been declining, revived. The war was carried on with success, and the nation was entirely satisfied with his prudent management. He neglected nothing that could engage the subject to bear the burthen of war with cheerfulness ; and it was owing to his lordship's advice that her majesty contributed £100,000 out of the civil list towards that object. In 1704, he was installed a knight of the Garter ; the next year he was constituted lord-lieutenant of the county of Cornwall ; and his lordship so managed affairs before the end of that year, that her majesty was empowered by the parliaments, both of Scotland and England, to appoint commissioners to treat about a union. This important affair was set on foot by King JAMES I but no prince before Queen ANNE, nor any council but here could effect it : for by the assiduity and dexterity of Lord Godolphin, all obstacles were removed, and the long-desired union of the two kingdoms accomplished. For those eminent services her majesty created his lordship, 29 December, 1706, Viscount Rialton and EARL OF GODOLPHIN, and constituted him lord high treasurer of Great Britain : from which office he was removed by the spirit of political animosity in 1710, the celebrated trial of Dr. Sacheverel having previously taken place. His lordship. who had laboured for some years under an indisposition of the stone and gravel, d. 15 September, 1712, and was buried the 8th of the next month, in the south aisle of Westminster Abbey, where a monument was erected to his memory by his daughter-in-law, the Duchess of Marlborough.

His lordship m. Margaret, 4th dau. and one of the co-heirs of Thomas Blague. Esq., groom of the bed-chamber to Kings CHARLES I. and II., by whom he left, at his decease, 15 September, 1712, an only child,

FRANCIS GODOLPHIN, 2nd earl, b. 3 September, 1678. This nobleman represented the county of Oxford, in the life-time of his father, in parliament ; and in the reign of Queen ANNE, was lord warden of the Stannaries, and cofferer to her majesty. In 1723, his lordship was appointed groom of the stole, and first gentleman of the bed-chamber, and the same year was constituted one of the lords justices during the temporary absence of the king. In 1733, the earl was appointed governor of the Islands of Scilly, and he was created, 23 January, 1735, BARON GODOLPHIN, of Helston, with special remainder, (in default of his own male issue,) to the heirs male of his deceased uncle, the Very Reverend Henry Godolphin, D.D., dean of St. Paul's (revert to issue of Henry Godolphin, Esq., father of the 1st earl). He was subsequently sworn lord privy-seal. His lordship m. Lady Henrietta Churchill, eldest dau. and co-heir of John Churchill, the great Duke of Marlborough, which lady upon her illustrious father's decease, became Duchess of Marlborough, by virtue of the act of parliament which entailed her grace's honours upon his daus. By this lady the earl had issue,

WILLIAM, Marquis of Blandford, M.P. for Woodstock. His lordship m., in 1729, Maria-Catherine, dau. of Peter D'Jong, of the province of Utrecht, but d. s. p. 24 August, 1731.
Henry, d. young.
Henrietta, m. to Thomas Pelham Holles, Duke of Newcastle, and d. s. p.
Margaret, d. young.
Mary (eventually sole heiress), m. 1740, Thomas Osborne, 4th Duke of Leeds, K.G. (See BURKE's Extant Peerage.)

Her grace d. 24 October, 1733, and his lordship, 17 January, 1766, when the Earldom of Godolphin, Viscounty of Rialton, and Barony of Godolphin, of Rialton, became EXTINCT ; but the Barony of Godolphin, of Helston, devolved, according to the limitation, upon his 1st cousin,

FRANCIS GODOLPHIN, Esq., of Baylis, co. Bucks, as 2nd baron, who had previously represented Helston in parliament. His lordship m. 1st, in 1734, Lady Barbara Bentinck, dau. of

William, Earl of Portland. He *m.* 2ndly, Lady Anne Fitz-William, dau. of John, Earl Fitz-William: but dying *s. p.* in 1785, the Barony of Godolphin, of Helston, also EXPIRED.

Arms—Gu., an eagle with two heads displayed, between three fleurs-de-lis, arg.

GORDON—DUKE OF GORDON.

By Letters Patent, dated 1 November, 1684.

Lineage.

GEORGE GORDON, 4th Marquis of Huntly, *b.* about 1650, was elevated to the DUKEDOM OF GORDON, in the Peerage of Scotland, 1 November, 1684. His grace *m.* in October, 1676, Lady Elizabeth Howard, 2nd dau. of Henry, Duke of Norfolk, and left at his decease, 7 December, 1716, (with a dau. Jane, *m.*—contract dated 5 October, 1706—James Drummond, son of James, 4th Earl of Perth,) a son and successor,

ALEXANDER GORDON, 2nd Duke of Gordon, a zealous adherent of the Chevalier St. George, in 1715. He *m.* in 1706, Lady Henrietta Mordaunt, dau. of the celebrated general, Charles, Earl of Peterborough and Monmouth, by whom he had issue,

    I. COSMO-GEORGE, his heir.
    II. Charles, *d. unm.* 26 April, 1780.
    III. Lewis, lieut. in the navy, *d. unm* 15 June, 1754.
    IV. Adam, a general in the army, and commander-in-chief of the forces in Scotland; *m.* 2 September, 1767, Jane, dau. of John Drummond, of Megginch, co. Perth, dowager of James, 2nd Duke of Athole; *d.* 13 August, 1801. *s. p.*
    I. Henrietta, *d. unm.* 17 February, 1789, æt. eighty-one.
    II. Mary, *d. unm.* 26 July, 1782.
    III. Anne, *m.* to William, Earl of Aberdeen; and *d.* 22 June, 1791.
    IV. Betty, *m.* to the Rev. John Skelly.
    V. Jean, *d. unm.* 17 January, 1792.
    VI. Catherine, *m.* to Francis, 5th Earl of Wemyss.

The duke *d.* 28 November, 1728, and was *s.* by his son,
COSMO-GEORGE GORDON, 3rd Duke of Gordon; who *m.* 3 September, 1741, Catherine, dau. of William, Earl of Aberdeen, and by her (who *m.* 2ndly, Staats-Long Morris, a general in the army, M.P., and *d.* 10 December, 1779,) had issue,

    I. ALEXANDER, his heir.
    II. William, deputy ranger of St. James's park; *m.* 13 February, 1781, Frances, dau. of Charles, 9th Viscount Irvine; and *d.* in 1823, leaving a dau., Frances, who *d. unm.* 2 September, 1831.
    III. George, so well known as leader of the rioters, in 1780; *d. unm.* 1793.
    I. Susan, *m.* 1st, 28 May, 1767, to John, 9th Earl of Westmoreland; and 2ndly, 28 December, 1778, to Lieutenant-Colonel Woodford.
    II. Anne, *m.* 1782, to Rev. Alexander Chalmers.
    III. Catherine, *m.* to Thomas Booker, Esq.

His grace *d.* in France, in 1752, and was *s.* by his eldest son,
ALEXANDER GORDON, 4th Duke of Gordon, K.T., *b.* 18 June, 1743, who was created a peer of England, as *Baron Gordon, of Huntly,* and EARL OF NORWICH, 12 February, 1784. His grace inherited the Baronies of Beauchamp, of Bletsoe, and Mordaunt, of Turvey, at the decease of Mary-Anastasia, Baroness Mordaunt, issueless, in 1819. The duke *m.* 1st, 28 October, 1767, Jane, dau. of Sir William Maxwell, Bart., and by her, who *d.* in 1812, had issue,

    I. GEORGE, his heir.
    II. Alexander, *d. unm.* 8 January, 1808.
    I. Charlotte, *m.* 9 September, 1789, Charles, 4th Duke of Richmond, and their eldest son, Charles, 5th Duke of Richmond, K.G., assumed the additional surname of GORDON, and *s.* to Gordon Castle.
    II. Madelina, *m.* 1st, 2 April, 1789, to Sir Robert Sinclair, Bart.; and 2ndly, 25 November, 1805, to Charles-Fyshe Palmer, Esq., of Luckley Park. She *d.* 1847.
    III. Susan, *m.* 7 October, 1793, William, 5th Duke of Manchester, and *d.* 1828.
    IV. Louisa, *m.* 17 April, 1797, Charles, 2nd Marquess of Cornwallis, and *d.* 1850, leaving issue, Jane, Lady Braybrooke, Louisa, Jemima, Countess of St. Germans, Mary, wife of Charles Ross, Esq., M.P., and Elizabeth.
    V. Georgiana, *m.* 23 June, 1803, to John, 6th Duke of Bedford.

His grace *m.* 2ndly, in 1820, Mrs. Christie, by whom, (who *d.* in 1824) he had no issue. He *d.* 17 June, 1827, and was *s.* by his son,
GEORGE GORDON, 5th Duke of Gordon, G.C.B., a general officer, colonel of the Scots fusiliers, and governor of the castle of Edinburgh, *b.* in 1770; *m.* 11 December, 1813, Elizabeth,

234

dau. of the late Alexander Brodie, Esq., of Arnhall, N.B.; but *d. s. p.* 28 May, 1836, when the Dukedom of Gordon, with the English peerages of Norwich and Gordon, became EXTINCT. The Baronies (by writ) of Mordaunt and Beauchamp fell into abeyance; and the Marquisate of Huntly devolved on George, Earl of Aboyne.

Arms—Az., a chev., between three boars' heads, couped, within a double tressure, flory within, and adorned with crescents without, or.

GORDON—EARL OF NORWICH.

By Letters Patent, dated 12 February, 1784.

See GORDON, DUKE OF GORDON.

GORDON—VISCOUNT OF ABOYNE.

By Letters Patent, dated 20 April, 1632.

Lineage.

GEORGE, LORD GORDON, eldest son of George, 1st Marquess of Huntly, was, by patent, dated at Whitehall, 20 April, 1632, created VISCOUNT ABOYNE in the Peerage of Scotland during the life of his father, with remainder, after his death or succession to the marquessate, to his son, James, and his heirs male bearing the name and arms of Gordon. He became 2nd Marquess of Huntly on the death of his father, 1636, whereupon the title of Viscount of Aboyne went, in terms of the patent, to his 3rd son,
LORD JAMES GORDON, 2nd Viscount of Aboyne; who taking the field for King CHARLES I. against the Covenanters, was defeated by the Earl Montrose at the bridge of Dee, 19 June, 1639, but effected his escape by sea to England. Being summoned before the council, 1643, to answer for his negotiations with the Earl of Antrim, and not appearing, he was forfeited, and declared a traitor. When Montrose sided with the king, the Viscount of Aboyne attended him to Scotland, took Dumfries; but being obliged to retreat to Carlisle, obtained the command of the garrison of that place. He was excommunicated by the general assembly at Edinburgh, 24 April, 1644, joined Montrose in Menteith, in April, 1645, and continued with him until September following, when he proceeded to the north with his troop of horse just before the battle of Philiphaugh. He was excepted from pardon, 1648, made his escape to France, and was at Paris when the intelligence of the execution of CHARLES I. arrived there, which had such an effect on his mind that he *d.* a few days after (in 1649).

GORDON—VISCOUNT MELGUM.

By Letters Patent, dated in 1627.

Lineage.

LORD JOHN GORDON, 2nd son of George, 1st Marquess of Huntly, was created a peer of Scotland, as VISCOUNT MELGUM, and BARON ABOYNE, in 1627; but did not long enjoy the honours, as he was burnt to death in the house of Frendraught, in October, 1630. He *m.* Lady Sophia Hay, 5th dau. of Francis, 9th Earl of Errol, and had an only dau.

GORDON—VISCOUNT KENMURE.

By Letters Patent, dated 8 May, 1633.

Lineage.

SIR ADAM DE GORDOUN, a knight of great renown, was the representative of the family in one of the most momentous periods of Scottish history. Although his possessions were almost on the borders of England, he long held out against the power of EDWARD I., and for a long time resisted the bond of fealty and submission prescribed by EDWARD in 1292; but that bond having become generally subscribed by the successively conquered Scotch nobility, and Sir Adam's own son, William de Gordoun, having been obliged to do so, the valiant knight was compelled to succumb, 28 July, 1296. Baliol's subsequent resignation of the crown to EDWARD gave Sir Adam a pretence to fly to arms, and thereafter, like Wallace and others, he leagued his fortunes with those of ROBERT BRUCE, from whom he obtained for his services a grant of the lands of Strathbogie in the north, forfeited by the desertion of the Earl of Atholl. These Sir Adam never however possessed, for the donation became ineffective by the return of the earl to his allegiance. Sir Adam had another son, who shone conspicuously at Halidon Hill, in 1333, but it has not yet been ascertained whether William or Alexander was the elder son. But it appears from the records, that Sir Adam, in 1306, took a charter of his barony of Stitchill in life-rent to himself, and in fee to his son,

SIR WILLIAM DE GORDOUN, who subscribed the bond of fealty, 12 July, 1296, and was designed in a writ, in 1331, as Signor de Stitchill. He was s. by his son,

ROGER DE GORDOUN, who was s. by his son,

SIR ALEXANDER DE GORDOUN, who d. in 1432, leaving a son and successor,

WILLIAM DE GORDOUN, who fixed his residence in Galloway, and was the first who designated himself of Lochinvar. He d. in 1450, and was s. by his son,

SIR JOHN GORDON, of Lochinvar, who had three sons,

Alexander, a valiant knight, who d. v. p., falling with his sovereign, JAMES IV., at Flodden, in 1513.
ROBERT (Sir), successor to his father.
William, of Craichlaw and Culvennan. (See BURKE's Landed Gentry.)

Sir John d. in 1517, and was s. by his son,

SIR ROBERT GORDON, who m. Marion, dau. and sole heir of John Accarson, of Glenshireburne; and dying in 1520, was s. by his eldest son,

SIR JAMES GORDON, of Lochinvar, who m. Margaret. dau. and sole heir of Robert Crighton, of Kilpatrick, and had, with other issue,

JOHN, his successor.
William, of Pennygame. who m. Helen, dau. of Alexander Stewart, of Garlies, and was s. by his son,
    JOHN, of Pennygame, who was s. by his son,
        ALEXANDER, of Pennygame, who d. about the year 1645, and was s. by his son,
            WILLIAM, of Pennygame, who left two sons,
                John, d. s. p. in 1662.
                ALEXANDER, of whom hereafter, as 5th VISCOUNT KENMURE.

Sir James fell at the battle of Pinkie, 10 September, 1547, and was s. by his elder son,

SIR JOHN GORDON, of Lochinvar. This gentleman m. 1st, in 1563, Juliana, dau. of Home, of Wedderburne, and had an only dau., Margaret, m. to Hugh, 1st Lord Loudoun. Sir John espoused 2ndly, Elizabeth, dau. of John, Lord Herries; and dying in 1604, was s. by his eldest son,

SIR ROBERT GORDON, of Lochinvar, remarkable for his great bodily strength and activity, who, at a tournament proclaimed by JAMES VI., obtained, as one of the three successful champions, a prize from the hands of the Princess Elizabeth. He m. Lady Isabel Ruthven, dau. of William, 1st Earl of Gowrie, and dying in 1628, was s. by his eldest son,

SIR JOHN GORDON, of Lochinvar. This gentleman disposed of Stitchill, the ancient inheritance of the family, and is said to have given the produce in a purse to the Duke of Buckingham, to insure his grace's interest in forwarding his claim to the Earldom of Gowrie. But the duke falling the very next day by the hand of the assassin Felton, the expectation proved abortive. Sir John was, however, elevated to the peerage, as Lord Lochinvar and VISCOUNT KENMURE, in the Peerage of Scotland, by patent, dated 8 May, 1633, with remainder to his heirs male whatsoever bearing the surname and arms of Gordon. His lordship m. Jane, dau. of Archibald. 7th Earl of Argyll, and dying in 1634, was s. by his only son,

JOHN, 2nd viscount; who d. s. p., in 1509, when the peerage reverted to (the eldest son of James Gordon, of Barncrosh, by Margaret, dau. of Sir John Vans, and relict of John Glendonwyn, of Drumrash) his lordship's cousin and next male heir,

JOHN, 3rd viscount. This nobleman d. unm. in October, 1643, when the honours devolved upon his brother,

ROBERT, 4th viscount, b. in November, 1622, was a devoted adherent to the house of Stuart, and suffered in consequence. He d. s. p. in 1663, when the peerage descended to his cousin,

ALEXANDER GORDON, Esq., of Pennygame, as 5th viscount.

235

His lordship m. thrice, and was s. in 1698 by his eldest son (by his 2nd wife, Marian, dau. of Maculloch, of Ardwell),

WILLIAM, 6th viscount. This unfortunate nobleman inheriting the attachment of his family to the Stuarts, took up arms, in 1715, against GEORGE I. He was made prisoner at Prestonpans the following year, and thence conveyed to London, where he was tried, condemned, and executed on Tower Hill, 24 February ensuing, when the honours of his house fell under an attainder. He m. Mary Dalzell, only sister of Robert, 6th Earl of Carnwath, by whom he left three sons (the eldest and youngest d. unm.) and a dau., Harriet, m. to John Dalzell, Esq. When his lordship's estate was brought to the hammer, his dowager purchased it; and when her son Robert, came of age, delivered it up to him free of debt; which son,

ROBERT GORDON, was styled 7th viscount. He d. unm. 1 August, 1741, when the estates devolved on his brother,

JOHN GORDON, by courtesy 8th viscount; who m. Frances, only dau. of William, 5th Earl of Seaforth, and had issue,

WILLIAM, his successor.
JOHN, 10th viscount.
Adam, who d. in 1806, leaving issue by Miss Davies,
    ADAM, of the R.N., 11th viscount.
    LOUISA (Hon.), m. 19 August, 1815, Charles Bellamy, Esq., and, in her widowhood, resumed her maiden name of GORDON.

John, 8th viscount, d. in June, 1769, and was s. by his eldest son,

WILLIAM GORDON, by courtesy 9th viscount; a capt. in the army; who d. 7 February, 1772, unm., and was s. by his brother,

JOHN GORDON, 10th viscount and Lord Lochinvar, who was restored by act of parliament, 17 June, 1824, to the honours forfeited by the 6th viscount; he was b. in 1750; m. in 1791, Miss Morgan, by whom (who d. in 1815) he had no issue. The viscount who was vice-lieutenant of the stewartry of Kirkcudbright, d 21 September, 1840, and was s. by his nephew,

ADAM, 11th viscount; b. 9 January, 1792, who m. November, 1843, Mary-Anne, dau. of the late James Wildey, Esq., and d. s. p. 1 September, 1847. Since that time the Viscounty of Kenmure has remained DORMANT.

Arms—Az., three boars' heads, erased, or, armed and langued, gu.

GORE—BARON GORE, VISCOUNT BEL-LEISLE AND EARL OF ROSS.

Barony. by Letters Patent, dated 30 June, 1764.
Viscounty, by Letters Patent, dated 25 August, 1768.
Earldom, by Letters Patent, dated 4 January, 1772.

Lineage.

GERARD GORE (son of John Gore, Esq., of London), alderman of the city of London, m. Helen, dau. of John Davenant, Esq., of Davenant Land, in Essex, and by her (who d. 13 February, 1607) had eight sons, of whom,

RICHARD, the eldest, M.P. for London, d. leaving seven daus.
JOHN (Sir), the 4th son, was Lord Mayor of London, 1624; from this gentleman descend the families of GORE-LANGTON, of Newton Park, and GORE, of BARROW COURT, co. Somerset (See BURKE's Landed Gentry).
PAUL (Sir), of whom we treat.

Gerard Gore d. 11 December, 1607. His youngest son, PAUL GORE, Esq., captain of a troop of horse, went over to Ireland with his regiment in the reign of ELIZABETH, and obtaining large grants of land, which he condensed into a manor, designated "Manore Gor," settled there. He m. Isabella, dau. of Francis Wickliffe, and niece of Thomas, Earl of Strafford, by whom he had issue,

I. RALPH, his heir.
II. Arthur, created a BARONET OF IRELAND, 10 April, 1662. He was ancestor of the Gores, Earls of Arran (see BURKE's Peerage).
III. Henry, lieut.-col., m. Mary, elder dau. and co-heir of Robert Blaney, of Tregonar, co. Montgomery, also of Castle Blayney, co. Monaghan, and nephew of Edward, 1st Lord Blayney. He d. 2 November, 1751, leaving a dau., Frances, who m. 1st, Sir Robert King, grandfather of Edward, Earl of Kingston, and 2ndly, Robert Choppyne, Esq., of Newcastle, co. Longford.
IV. Francis (Sir), of Artaman, co. Sligo, m. Anne, dau. and heir of Robert Parke, Esq., of Newtown, co. Leitrim, and

was ancestor of the present SIR ROBERT-GORE BOOTH, Bart. (*see* BURKE's *Peerage and Baronetage*).

v. Robert.   vi. Charles.

1. Lettice, *m.* Sir Archibald Erskine, of Clogh, K.B., and *d. s. p.*

11. Angel, *m.* Edward Archdall, Esq., of Castle Archdall, co. Fermanagh.

111. Elizabeth, *m.* to Henry Wray, Esq., of Castle Wray, co. Donegal.

IV. Isabella, *m.* to the Rev. Humphry Galbraith.

v. Anne, *m.* to — Stewart, Esq., of Dunduffe.

VI. Sidney, *m.* to Lewis, 3rd son of Sir Edward Wingfield, Knt.   VII. Rebecca.

Sir Paul *d.* in September, 1629, and was *s.* by his eldest son,

SIR RALPH GORE, 2nd bart , of Manor Gore, who *m.* Anne, 2nd dau. of William, 2nd Lord Caulfeild, of Charlemont, and had a son,

SIR WILLIAM GORE, 3rd bart., of Manor Gore, P. C., and custos rotulorum, co. Leitrim. He *m.* Hannah, elder dau. and co-heir of James Hamilton, Esq., son and heir of Sir Frederick Hamilton, of Manor Hamilton, co. Leitrim, and niece of Gustavus Hamilton, created Viscount Boyne, and by her (who *d.* 16 May, 1733) he had issue,

I. RALPH, his heir.

11. William, in holy orders, dean of Down, *d.* 6 January, 1731. He *m.* Honora Prittie, of the co. Tipperary, and had issue,

   1 Ralph, *d.* young.

   2 William, bishop of Limerick, *m.* 1st, Mary, eldest dau. of Col. Chidley Coote, of Coote Hall, co. Roscommon, and relict of Guy Moore, Esq., of Abbey, co. Tipperary, but by her had no issue; he *m.* 2ndly, Mary, dau. of William French, of Oak Port, co. Roscommon, dean of Ardagh, and dying 25 February, 1784, left issue, William, 14th dragoons, who *m.* in July, 1788, Maria, dau. of Michael Head, Esq , of Derry, co. Tipperary.

   3 Hamilton, capt. R.N., lost on the coast of Newfoundland, about the year 1775.

   4 Henry, lieut.-col., *m.* 14 May, 1749. Mrs. Nesbitt, sister of Lady Cairnes, and *d.* 1787, having had a son, who *d.* young

   5 Frederick, M.P. for the borough of Tulske, *m.* 1st, Mary, only child of John, 2nd Viscount Molesworth ; and 2ndly, 27 October, 176?, Mary, youngest dau. of his uncle, Sir Ralph Gore, and *d. s. p.* 1764.

   6 Francis.

   1 Catherine, *m.* to the Right Hon. Nathaniel Clements, whose son, Robert, was created Lord Leitrim.

   2 Elizabeth, *m.* to Robert Brereton, vicar of Aghmacart, Queen's co.

111. Frederick, capt. of foot, and provost-marshal-general of Ireland, *d.* in December, 1761, leaving issue.

The eldest son,

SIR RALPH GORE, 4th bart., of Manor Gore, became in right of his mother possessed of the estates of Manor Hamilton. This gentleman was chancellor of the Exchequer, and Speaker of the House of Commons, and on 22 April, 1730, he was sworn one of the lord justices of the kingdom. He *m.* 1st, a dau. of Sir Robert Colvill, Knt., of Newtown, co. Down, and by her he had two daus., Hannah, who *m.* 28 June, 1727, John Donnellan, Esq.; and Rose, who *m.* in July, 1733, the Right Hon. Anthony Malone, uncle of Richard, Lord Sunderlin; and 2ndly, Elizabeth, only dau. of Dr. St. George Ashe, bishop of Clogher, and by her (who *d.* 7 December, 1741) he left issue,

I. ST. GEORGE, 5th bart.

11. RALPH, 6th bart.

111. Richard, *b.* 16 October, 1728, settled at Sandymount.

1. Jane, *b.* 25 January, 1719, *m.* 1744, to Charles Coote. Esq.

11. Elizabeth, *b.* 17 March, 1720, *m.* 6 April, 1713, to Frederick-Cary Hamilton, Esq., 2nd son of Henry Cary, Esq., of Dungiven, co. Derry.

111. Catherine, *b.* 7 November, 1723, *m.* 14 June, 1744, to James Daly, Esq., of Carrownekelly, co. Galway, and had issue.

IV. Mary, *m.* 27 October, 1762, Frederick Gore, Esq., 5th son of her uncle William.

The eldest son,

SIR ST. GEORGE GORE, 5th bart., *b.* 25 June, 1722, assumed the surname of St. George, as heir to his mother. He *m.* Anne, only dau. of the Right Hon. Francis Burton, of Buncraggy, and sister of Francis Pierpoint, Lord Conyngham, which lady *d.* 23 April, 1745. He *d. s. p.* 25 September, 1746, and was *s.* by his next brother,

SIR RALPH GORE, 6th bart., of Manor Gore, co. Donegal, *b.* 23 November, 1725. This gentleman was a distinguished military officer, having obtained the command of a battalion at the battle of Laffeldt, 2 July, 1747, when only a captain, owing to the fall of his senior officers, distinguished himself so highly that he received the thanks of the Duke of Cumberland, on the following day, at the head of his regiment. He subse-

quently represented the co. Donegal in parliament, and was elevated to the peerage of Ireland, 30 June, 1764, by the title of *Baron Gore, of Manor Gore, co. Donegal.* On 25 August, 1768, he was advanced to the *Viscounty of Bellelsle,* and created EARL OF ROSS, 4 January, 1772. In 1788, the earl, who had attained the rank of lieut.-general, was appointed commander-in-chief in Ireland, in the absence of Lieut.-General Pitt. His lordship *m.* 1st, 23 February, 1754, Catherine, dau. of the Right Hon. Thomas Connolly, by whom he had no issue; and 2ndly, Alice, dau. of the Right Hon. Nathaniel Clements, and sister of Robert, Lord Leitrim, by whom he had an only son, Ralph, Viscount Belleisle, who *d. s. p.,* in 1789. His lordship *d.* in 1802, when the peerage EXPIRED ; but the baronetcy devolved upon his nephew, RALPH GORE, who then became SIR RALPH GORE, 7th Baronet (*See* BURKE's *Peerage*).)

Arms—Gu., a fesse, arg., between three crosses-crosslet, fitchée, or

---

GORE—BARON ANNALY.

By Letters Patent, dated 17 January, 1766; and 23 September, 1789.

Lineage.

GEORGE GORE, Esq., 4th son of Sir Arthur Gore, Bart., of Newtown Gore, co. Mayo, filled the office of attorney-general in Ireland, and was subsequently one of the judges of the Court of Common Pleas there. He *m.* 4 February, 1702, Bridget, dau. and eventual heir of John Sankey, Esq., of Tenelick, co. Longford, and *d.* 1753, having had, with a dau. (Bridget, wife of Cutts Harman, A.M., dean of Waterford), three sons. The 2nd, but at length eldest surviving,

JOHN GORE, Esq., barrister-at-law, *b.* 2 March, 1718, became chief justice of the court of King's Bench, in Ireland, and was advanced to the peerage of that kingdom, 17 January, 1766, as BARON ANNALY, *of Tenelick, co. Longford.* His lordship was chosen Speaker of the House of Lords, in 1767, on the demise of Lord Chancellor Powis. He *m.* 1747, Frances, 2nd dau. of Richard, Viscount Powerscourt; but *d. s. p.* 3 April, 1784, when the peerage became EXTINCT ; his estate descended to his only surviving brother,

HENRY GORE, Esq., lieutenant-colonel in the army, and M.P. for the co. Longford, *b.* 8 March, 1728, who was created, 23 September, 1789, BARON ANNALY, of Tenelick. His lordship *m.* Mary, dau..of Skeffington Smyth, Esq., but *d. s. p.* 5 June, 1793, when the Barony of Annaly, of the 2nd creation, also became EXTINCT.

Arms—Gu., a fesse, between three crosses-crosslet, fitchée, or.

GORGES—BARON GORGES.

By Writ of Summons, dated 4 March, 1309.

Lineage.

In the 41st HENRY III.,

RALPH DE GORGES, (son of Ivo de Gorges of Tamworth,) had a military summons to march against the Welsh, and in a few years afterwards, in 1273, was made governor of Sherburne and Exeter Castles. He was likewise sheriff of the co. Devon. He *m.* Elena, dau. and heir of John de Moreville, who was descended from Endo de Moreville, by his wife, the dau. and heiress of Richard de Wrokeshale. In the 54th of the same reign, he attended Prince Edward to the Holy Land, and dying within the two next years, was *s.* by his son,

RALPH DE GORGES, who, in the 21st EDWARD I., was marshal of the king's army in Gascony, and the next year, continuing in those parts, was made prisoner and carried to Paris. He was not detained long, however, in captivity, for we find him soon after again in active service upon the same field, and subsequently engaged in the wars of Scotland; in consideration of which services he was summoned to parliament, as a baron, by King EDWARD II., 4 March, 1309, and from that period to 18 September, 1322; but his descendants enjoyed no similar honours. He *m.* and had one son, and three daus.,

RALPH, his heir.

Elizabeth, *m.* to — Ashton, whose issue failed in its next generation.

ELEANOR, *m.* to Theobald Russell, and of whom presently.

Joan, *m.* to Sir William Chency.

His lordship d. in 1323, and was s. by his son,

RALPH DE GORGES, who was never summoned to parliament and dying s. p., was s. by his sister,

ELEANOR DE GORGES, who m. Sir Theobald Russel, son of Sir William Russel, of Kingston-Russel, co. Dorset, and had issue,

THEOBALD, of whom presently.

Ralph (Sir), of Kingston-Russel and Derham, m. ——, and left issue,

Theobald,}
John,   } d. without issue.

Maurice (Sir), of Kingston-Russel, who had issue,

Thomas-Fitzmaurice, whose dau.,

Mary, d. s. p.

Isabel, m. to Sir Stephen Heytfield.

Margaret, m. 1st to Gilbert Denys, Esq., and 2ndly to John Kemys, Esq.

Sir Theobald, by a 2nd marriage, with the dau. and heir of John de la Tour, was direct ancestor of the Earls of Bedford. The elder son,

SIR THEOBALD RUSSEL, assuming his maternal surname, became Sir Theobald Gorges. He also adopted the armorial bearings of the family which occasioned a dispute in the 21st EDWARD III., between him and Warburton of Cheshire, for bearing also those arms; but the latter established his right thereto in the court of the Earl Marshal, Henry, Earl of Lancaster, and Gorges had then assigned him, a *chevron gules on the lozenge, or and az.*, for difference; which his posterity bore for some time, until they again resumed their ancient and hereditary coat, namely, "*Arg., a gurges (or whirlpool) az.*" Sir Theobald d. in the 4th RICHARD II., leaving by Agnes, his wife, four sons,

Ralph,
Bartholomew, } all of whom d. without issue.
William   }

And

THOMAS GORGES, who s. his brothers, and carried on the line of the family. He m. Agnes, widow of Thomas Norton, Esq., and dying in the 5th HENRY IV., was s. by his son,

JOHN GORGES, who d. in minority, 1st HENRY VI., and was s. by his brother,

SIR THEOBALD GORGES, m. twice, by his 2nd wife, Agnes, dau. of John de Wyke, to whom he was m. 15 October, 1333, he left at his decease 10th EDWARD IV., two sons,

I. WALTER, of Wraxhall, his heir, who m. Mary, dau. and heir of William Ouldhall, and d. v. p. leaving a son,

Edmund, created a knight of the Bath, at the creation of Arthur, Prince of Wales, son of HENRY VII. He m. Anne, dau. of John Howard, Duke of Norfolk, and had issue, five sons and three daus. The eldest son and successor,

Sir Edward Gorges, of Wraxhall, m. 1st, Mary, dau. of Sir John Newton, by whom he had besides a dau. Anne, a son and successor,

Edward Gorges, of Wraxhall, b. 1526; m. a dau. of Sir John Walsh, and was father of

Sir Edward Gorges, of Wraxhall, b. in 1564; who m. Dorothy, dau. of Sir George Speke, of White Lackington, K. B. and by her had besides several daus., of whom Elizabeth, m. Francis Trenchard, Esq., of Lutteridge, and Anne, m. Edward Tynte, Esq., of Chelvy; two sons, viz.:

Sir Robert Gorges, who d. s. p. in 1638, and Samuel Gorges, Esq. of Wraxhall, who m. Jane, dau. of — Cotterell, of Winford, and was s. at his decease, in 1671, by his son and heir,

Edward Gorges, Esq., of Wraxhall, who m. Grace, dau. of William Winter, Esq., of Clapton, and d. in 1708, leaving a son and heir,

Samuel Gorges, Esq., the last male heir of the Wraxhall branch of the family. He d. in 1699, leaving an only dau. and heiress,

Elizabeth Gorges, who m. in 1709, John Codrington, Esq., of Codrington, co. Gloucester, who in her right became possessed of Wraxhall, which with the other estates descended to his only surviving dau. and heir,

Jane Codrington, who m. in 1742, Sir Richard-Warwick Bamfylde, Bart.

Sir Edward Gorges m. 2ndly, Mary, dau. of Sir Anthony Poyntz, of Iron Acton, co. Gloucester, and by her had further issue,

William.   Arthur.
Ferdinand.
Thomas (Sir), of Langford, co. Wilts, m. Helena

Snakenberg, relict of William Parr, Marquis of Northampton, and d. 1610, having had issue,

Sir Edward Gorges, created a peer of Ireland by the title of *Baron of Dundalk*, 13 July, 18th JAMES I., and was father of Richard Gorges, 2nd Baron Dundalk, who d s. p.

Sir Theobald Gorges, who m. Anne, dau. of Sir Henry Poole. Knt. of Sapperton, co. Gloucester, by Anne, his wife, dau. of Sir William Wroughton, of Broad Hinton, Wilts.

Elizabeth, m. to Sir Hugh Smith, of Long Aston, co. Somerset.

II. Richard Gorges, of Stourminster Marshall, co. Dorset, who d. 20th EDWARD IV., leaving a son, Marmaduke Gorges.

NOTE.—There were other branches of this family in the cos. of Hereford, Somerset, and Wilts, particularly at Langford, in the latter shire; one of which was created a baronet in the reign of JAMES I., and an Irish peer, by the title of Lord Dundalk.

GORGES—BARON GORGES OF DUNDALK.

By Letters Patent, dated 13 July, 1620.

Lineage.

SIR EDWARD GORGES, Knt., eldest son and heir of Sir Thomas Gorges, of Langford, co. Wilts, was created a Baronet of England by JAMES I., 25 November, 1612, and advanced to the peerage of Ireland, 13 July, 1620, as BARON GORGES, *of Dundalk*, co. Louth. He m. 1st, Katherine, dau. of Sir Robert Osborne, Knt., of Kelmarsh, co. Northampton, and relict of Edward Haselwood, Esq., of Maidwell, by whom he had a son, Thomas, who predeceased him. His lordship m. 2ndly, Jane, dau. of — Throxton, and widow of Sir John Levingstone, and by her left a son and successor,

SIR RICHARD GORGES, Bart., 2nd Lord Gorges, of Dundalk, who m. Bridget, dau. of Richard Kingsmill, Esq., of Sidmanton, Hants; but d. without surviving issue, in 1712, when all his honours became EXTINCT.

Arms—Arg., a whirlpool, az.

*** For the early ancestry of the Gorges family in England, refer to BURKE's *Extinct and Dormant Baronetage*. In Ireland a branch of the ancient stock still remains, deriving from

ROBERT GORGES, LL.D., of Kilbrew, co. Meath, who m. Jane, dau. of Sir Arthur Loftus, Knt., and sister of Adam, Viscount Lisburn. By this lady, who d. in 1728, Dr. Gorges had, with other issue, (of which Elizabeth m. William Jackson, Esq., of Coleraine,) a son and heir,

LIEUT.-GEN. RICHARD GORGES, of Kilbrew, bapt. in 1662; who m. 1st, in 1704, Nichola-Sophia, dau. of Hugh Hamilton, Lord Glenawley, and relict of Sir Tristram Beresford; and 2ndly, Dorothy, Countess Dowager of Meath; by the former, who d. in 1713, he left at his decease, 12 April, 1728, two sons and two daus., namely,

I. RICHARD, of Kilbrew, M. P. for Aughter and Enniskillen, who m. Elizabeth, dau. of John Fielding, governor of Jamaica, and had issue,

1 Richard, of Kilbrew, lieutenant-colonel of Lord Drogheda's regiment of dragoons; m. Catharine, dau. of Thomas Christmas, Esq., of Whitfield, co. Waterford; and d. without surviving issue, in 1765.

2 John, d. s. p.

3 HAMILTON, of Kilbrew, captain of foot, b. in 1739; who d. M.P. for Meath, 14 June, 1802, leaving by Catherine, his 1st wife, dau. and co-heir of Edmund-Gorges Howard, Esq.,

HAMILTON, of Kilbrew, who m. 1st, in 1797, Alicia, dau. of Arthur French, Esq., of French Park, M.P. for Roscommon; and 2ndly, Miss Cunningham; by the former he had a son Hamilton, and other issue.

John, who m. Frances, dau. of Solomon Richards, Esq., of Solsborough, co. Wexford; and d. leaving issue.

Isabella, m. 1st, to Edward Cooke, Esq.; and 2ndly, to Sir Henry Fane.

Eliza, Mrs. Vicars.

Susannah, m. to the Hon. and Rev. George-D. Beresford, son of Lord Decies, archbishop of Tuam.

4 Robert, dean of Kilmacduagh, whose dau. m. J. Blennerhasset, Esq., of Mount-st., Dublin.

II. Hamilton, of Castlegrove, M.P. for Swords, who m. Catherine, dau. of John Keating, Esq., and had a son,

Richard, who m. the dau. and heir of Arthur-Francis Meredyth, Esq., of Dollardstown, co. Meath, assumed the surname of Meredyth, and was created a Baronet in 1787. His only dau. and heir,

　　Mary-Anne, who m. Sir Marcus Somerville, Bart., and was mother of the present Sir William Somerville, Baron Athlumney.

III. Lucy, m. 1st, to Lord Howth; and 2ndly, to Nicholas Weldon, Esq.

IV. Dorothy, m. to John Cuffe, created Earl of Desart.

GORING — BARONS GORING, OF HURST-PIERPOINT, CO. SUSSEX, EARLS OF NORWICH.

Barony by Letters Patent, dated 14 April, 1628.
Earldom, by Letters Patent, dated 8 November, 1646.

Lineage.

Robert de Goring, living *temp.* Edward III., son of John de Goring, and grandson of John de Goring, Lord of Goring, had besides two sons, Thomas and Simon, who both *d. s. p.*, another son,

John de Goring, of Lancing, co. Sussex, who was father of

John Goring, of Lancing, who was *s.* by his son, another

John Goring, of Lancing, who, by Agnes, his wife, was father of

John Goring, who m. Margaret, dau. of Ralph, and sister and heir of Sir William Radimill, and his son,

John Goring, of Burton, whose will is dated 11th Henry VII., left by Joan, his wife, relict of Humphrey Hewster, (besides a a dau. Elizabeth, who m. Thomas Dyke, and other issue, who *d. s. p.*) a son and heir,

John Goring, of Burton, who m. Constance, dau. and co-heir of Henry or Roger Dyke, by Elizabeth, his wife, dau. and heir of Sir Edward St. John and Eva, his wife, dau. and heir of Sir William Dawtrey, and *d.* 1521, having had with several daus. of whom Constance m. Sir John Kingsmill, of Sidmanton, Hants, and a younger son George, an elder son and heir,

Sir William Goring, of Burton. Knt., one of the gentlemen of the privy chamber to Edward VI., who m. Elizabeth, dau. and heir of John Covert, of Slaugham, and *d.* 1553, having had issue,

I. Henry (Sir), his heir of Burton, ancestor of the Gorings, Baronets of Burton, extinct since 1723, when Sir William, the 3rd and last baronet *d. s. p.*, (*see* Burke's *Extinct Baronetage*) and ancestor of the Gorings of Highden, Barts. (*see* Burke's *Peerage and Baronetage*.)

II. George, of whom presently.

III. Robert, m. Mary, dau. of Francis Onley, Esq., and had a dau. Elizabeth.

I. Anne, m. 1st, to Sir George de Lalind, and 2ndly, to Thomas Browne, brother of Viscount Montague.

II. Elinor, m. to John Fenner, of Crawley, and was mother of Sir Edward Fenner, Justice of the King's Bench, who *d.* in 1611.

The 2nd son,

George Goring, Esq., of Ovingdean and Lewes, m. Mary, dau. and co-heir of William Everard, and widow of — Rolling-ham, and was father of

George Goring, Esq., of Hurstpierpoint and Ovingdean, co. Suffolk, who m. Anne, dau. of Henry Denny, Esq., of Waltham Abbey, co. Essex, eldest sister of Sir Edward Denny, Baron Denny, and Earl of Norwich, (an earldom that expired in 1630,) and was *s.* by his son,

Sir George Goring, Knt., vice chamberlain to the queen, who was elevated to the peerage, 14 April, 1628, as Baron Goring, *of Hurstpierpoint, co. Sussex,* and in two years afterwards obtained a grant of the offices of secretary, clerk of the signet, and clerk of the council within the principality of Wales. His lordship subsequently rendering the highest services to King Charles I., after the breaking out of the civil wars, was advanced to the dignity of Earl of Norwich, by letters patent, dated 8 November, 1646. He m. Mary, dau. of Edward, Lord Abergavenny, by whom he had issue,

I. George, so gallantly distinguished in the civil wars as General Goring. This heroic personage fought to the last in the cause of his royal and unfortunate master, and after the surrender of Oxford, retiring to the Netherlands, he acquired fresh laurels as lieutenant-general of the King of Spain's army: he m. Lettice, dau. of Richard, Earl of Cork, and *d. s. p.* in 1662, in the life-time of his father.

II. Charles, 2nd earl.

I. Elizabeth, m. to Lord Brereton, of Ireland.

II. Lucy, m. to Sir Dru Dene, of Maptested, co. Essex, Knt.

238

III. Diana, m. 1st, to Thomas Covert, Esq., of Slaugham, Sussex; and 2ndly, to George, eldest son of Endymion Porter, Esq.

IV. Catherine, m. to William Scott, Esq., of Scott's Hall, Kent.

His lordship *d.* in 1662, and was *s.* by his only surviving son,

Charles Goring, 2nd Earl of Norwich. His lordship m. Alice, dau. of Robert Leman, Esq., and widow of Sir Richard Baker, Knt., but *d. s. p.* in 1670-1, when the Barony of Goring and Earldom of Norwich, became extinct.

Arms—Arg., a chevron between three annulets, gu.

Note.—From Edward Goring, Esq., uncle of George, 1st Earl of Norwich, the extant baronets Goring, of Highden, in Sussex, derive descent.

GRAHAM—VISCOUNT PRESTON.

By Letters Patent, dated 12 May, 1681.

Lineage.

Sir Richard Graham, of Eske and Netherby, created a Baronet of England, 29 March, 1639. m. Catherine, dau. and co-heiress of Thomas Musgrave, of Cumcatch, by whom he had issue,

I. George, of whom presently.

II. Richard, (Sir) of Norton Conyers, co. York, created a Baronet of England, 17 November, 1662, ancestor of the Grahams of Norton Conyers.

I. Catherine, *d. unm.*

II. Mary, m. to Sir Edward Musgrave, Bart., of Hayton, in Cumberland.

III. Elizabeth, m. to Sir Cuthbert Heron, of Chipchase, in Northumberland.

IV. Susan, m. to Reginald Carnaby, of Halton.

The elder son,

Sir George Graham, 2nd Baronet of Esk, co. Cumberland, *d.* 1657, leaving by Lady Mary Johnstone, his wife, dau. of James, 1st Earl of Hartfell,

I. Richard (Sir), of whom presently.

II. James, col. of Levens, in Westmoreland, M.P., m. Dorothy, eldest dau. of the Hon. William Howard, 4th son of Thomas, 1st Earl of Berkshire, by whom he had an only child, Catherine, m. 5 March, 1709, to her cousin-german, Henry-Bowes, 11th Earl of Suffolk and Berkshire, and *d.* 14 February, 1762, leaving issue.

III. Fergus. *d. s. p.*

IV. Reginald, who left a son Metcalfe Graham, Esq.

V. William, dean of Carlisle, D.D., ancestor of the present Sir Edward Graham, Bart., of Esk.

I. Margaret.

The eldest son,

Sir Richard Graham, 3rd baronet, was advanced, 12 May, 1681, to the peerage of Scotland, as *Baron Graham, of Esk,* and Viscount Preston. His lordship was British ambassador to the Court of France for many years, and subsequently secretary of state to James II. At the Revolution, the viscount was committed to the Tower, but soon released from imprisonment. Being afterwards, however, apprehended in an attempt to escape to his old master in France, he was arraigned for high treason, and condemned, but pardoned through the intercession of his friends, under the sign manual, in June, 1691. He m. Anne, 2nd dau. of Charles Howard, 1st Earl of Carlisle, by whom he had (with two daus.) a son, his successor in 1695,

Edward Graham, 2nd Viscount Preston; who m. Mary, dau. and co-heir of Sir Marmaduke Dalton, of Hawkswell, Yorkshire, and dying in 1709, was *s.* by his only son,

Charles Graham, 3rd Viscount Preston, who m. Anne, dau. of Thomas Cox, Esq., of London; but *d. s. p.* 22 February, 1739, when the peerage expired. His lordship's extensive estates passed to his aunts, Lady Widdrington and the Hon. Mary-Susan Graham, daus. of the 1st viscount; and devolved, by the will of the former of those ladies, in 1757, upon the Rev. Robert Graham, D.D., father of Sir James Graham, Bart. of Netherby; while the ancient baronetcy of the family reverted to the deceased lord's cousin, the Rev. William Graham.

Arms—Or, on a chev., sa., three escallops of the field.

GRAHAM—VISCOUNT OF DUNDEE.

By Letters Patent, dated 12 November, 1688.

Lineage.

SIR WILLIAM GRAHAM, Lord of Kincardine, chief of the name, and ancestor of the Duke of Montrose, *m.* in 1406 for his 2nd wife, the Lady Mary Stuart, dau. of ROBERT III., King of Scotland, and widow of George, Earl of Angus, and of Sir James Kennedy, of Dunure. Of this marriage the sons were,

ROBERT, who became of Fintry.
Patrick, archbishop of St. Andrews.
William, of Garvock, co. Perth, ancestor of the Græmes of that place, now represented by Robert Græme, Esq., of Garvock, and of the Grahams of Balgowan. (*See* LYNEDOCH.)
Harry.
Walter, from whom descended the Grahams of Knockdolian and Wallacetown.

The eldest son,
SIR ROBERT GRAHAM, Knt. of Fintry, *m.* Janet, dau. and heir of Sir Richard Lovel, of Balumbie, by Elizabeth, his wife, dau. of Sir Henry Douglas, of Lochleven, and left, with two daus., two sons,

ROBERT, ancestor of the GRAHAMS of Fintry, now represented by Robert Graham, Esq. (*See* BURKE's *Landed Gentry*.)
JOHN, ancestor of GRAHAM of Claverhouse.

The 2nd son,
JOHN GRAHAM, of Balargus, co. Forfar, *m.* Matilda, dau. of Sir James Scrimgeour, constable of Dundee, and was *s.* by his son,
JOHN GRAHAM, of Balargus and Claverhouse, who *m.* Margaret, dau. of John Bethune, of Balfour, and was father of
JOHN GRAHAM, of Claverhouse, living in 1541; who *m.* Anne, dau. of Robert Lundin, of Balgony, and had two sons, WILLIAM, his heir, and John. The elder,
SIR WILLIAM GRAHAM, of Claverhouse, who *d.* in October, 1642, leaving by Maria, his wife, dau. of Thomas Fotheringhame, of Powrie, two sons; the younger, Walter, was ancestor of the GRAHAMS of Duntrune, co. Forfar (*see Landed Gentry*) : the elder,
GEORGE GRAHAM, of Claverhouse, *d.* April, 1645, and was *s.* by his son,
SIR WILLIAM GRAHAM, of Claverhouse, who *m.* Lady Jean Carnegy, 4th dau. of John, 1st Earl of Northesk, and had two sons, JOHN, and DAVID, 3rd Viscount Dundee; and two daus., Margaret, *m.* to Sir Robert Graham, of Morphy, and Anne, *m.* to Robert Young, of Auldbar. His eldest son,
JOHN GRAHAM, the gallant Graham of Claverhouse, who zealously supported episcopacy and royalty under CHARLES and JAMES, asserted, with distinguished military skill, the rights of the latter after the Revolution, and at length sealed his devotion to that ill-fated prince by his heroic death in the arms of victory at Killiecrankie, 26 May, 1689, was created a peer of Scotland, by the title of VISCOUNT OF DUNDEE, and *Lord Graham, of Claverhouse*, by patent dated 12 November, 1688, to him and the heirs male of his body; which, failing to his other heirs male. He *m.* the Hon. Jean Cochrane, youngest dau. of William, Lord Cochrane, and by her (who *m.* 2ndly, William, 3rd Viscount of Kilsyth) had a son,
JAMES GRAHAM, 2nd Viscount of Dundee; who *d.* an infant, in December, 1689, and was *s.* by his uncle,
DAVID GRAHAM, 3rd Viscount of Dundee, who was with his brother at Killiecrankie. After the act of outlawry passed against him, in 1690, he retired to the court of St. Germains in 1692, and was, by King JAMES II., invested with the order of the Thistle. He *d. s. p.* in 1700, when the representation of the family devolved on David Graham, of Duntroon, who *d.* in January, 1706. His son, William Graham, of Duntroon, assumed the title of Viscount of Dundee, engaged in the rebellion of 1715, and was attainted by act of parliament. James Graham, of Duntroon, styling himself Viscount of Dundee, was forfeited for his adherence to the insurgents in 1746, had a company in Lord Ogilvy's regiment in the French service, and *d.* at Dunkirk in 1759.

Arms—Or, three piles, (for Lovel, of Balumby,) waved, sa., within a double tressure, counterflowered, gules; and on a chief of the 2nd, three escallops of the 1st.

GRAHAM—BARON LYNEDOCH.

By Letters Patent, dated 3 May, 1814.

Lineage.

JOHN GRAHAM, 2nd son of John Graham, or Græme, of Garvock, purchased, in 1584, the estate of Balgowan, co. Perth, from James, Lord Innermeith. He *m.* Marjory, eldest dau. of Andrew Rollo, of Durcurb, and widow of George Græme, of Inchbrakie, and was father of JOHN GRAHAM of Balgowan, who *m.* 1st, 1605, Isabel, dau. of Ninian Bonar, of Keltie, by whom he had an only son, JOHN. He *m.* 2ndly, Helen, dau. of Thomas Blair, of Balthayoch, by whom he had four sons and five daus., and was *s.* by his eldest son,
JOHN GRAHAM, Esq., of Balgowan, dying *unm.*, was *s.* by his half-brother,
THOMAS GRAHAM, Esq., of Balgowan, who *m.* 1st, 1671, Anne, dau. of Sir James Drummond, of Machany, by Anne, his wife, dau. of Sir George Hay; and 2ndly, 1716, Christian, 3rd dau. of David, 2nd Lord Newark; by the former of whom he had five sons and four daus., of whom,

JOHN, his heir.
David, *d. s. p.*
Robert, *m.* Elizabeth, dau. of Sir D. Threipland, of Fingask, and had an only son, JOHN, of Eskbank, who *m.* Mary Scott, of Usan, and was father of ROBERT, who *s.* Lord Lynedoch in the Balgowan estate.

He *d.* 1735, and was *s.* by his son,
JOHN GRÆME, or Graham, Esq., of Balgowan, who *m.* 1702, Elizabeth, dau. of James Carnegie, of Balnamoon, and *d.* 1749, having had, with four daus., five sons, all of whom *d. s. p.*, except the eldest,
THOMAS GRAHAM, Esq., of Balgowan, *m.* 8 April, 1749, Lady Christian Hope, 4th dau. of Charles, Earl of Hopetoun, and *d.* 6 December, 1766, leaving a son,
THOMAS GRAHAM, Esq., of Balgowan, M.P., the celebrated commander in the Peninsular war, who achieved the memorable victory of Barossa, 5 March, 1811, and was created 3 May, 1814, BARON LYNEDOCH. He *m.* 26 December, 1774, the Hon. Mary Cathcart, dau. of Charles, 9th Lord Cathcart, but by her (who *d.* 26 June, 1792) had no issue. Lord Lynedoch *d. s. p.* 1843, when the title became EXTINCT. His estate of Balgowan devolved on his kinsman, ROBERT GRAHAM, Esq., J.P. and D.L., who sold it in 1844, and *d. s. p.* 1859, when JOHN MURRAY, Esq., of Murrayshall, co. Perth. *s.* under Lord Lynedoch's settlement, to a portion of the unentailed estate, and to the additional name and arms of GRAHAM.

Arms—Or, three piles, gu., issuing from a chief, sa., charged with as many escallops of the 1st, within a double tressure, flory counterflory, to mark the royal descent.

GRAHAM—EARL OF STRATHERN, AND EARL OF MONTEITH AND AIRTH.

Lineage.

SIR PATRICK GRAHAM, *m.* Euphemia, Countess of Strathern in her own right, only dau. and sole heiress of Prince David, Earl-Palatine of Strathern, eldest son of the second marriage of King ROBERT II. of Scotland, in right of which their descendants quarter the royal arms of Stuart. (*See* some account of them in *The Vicissitudes of Families*, 3rd series.) Their only son,
MALISE GRAHAM, inherited the title of Earl of Strathern; but King JAMES I. divested him of that earldom, under pretence that it was a male fee, and conferred it on his uncle Walter, Earl of Atholl and Caithness, for life, by charter, dated 22 July, 1427. To Malise, the king gave the lands of Craynis, &c., which he erected, 6 September, 1427, into the EARLDOM OF MENTETH (more usually spelled "Monteith,") to be held in a free earldom by Malise and the heirs male of his body; which failing, to return to the crown. Under the designation of Earl of Menteth, his lordship went to England, 9 December, 1427, as a supplementary hostage in place of Robert Erskine, and was not released till 17 June, 1453, when he was ordered to be liberated out of the castle of Pontefract; Alexander, his son and heir, surrendering himself as a hostage in his stead, and the Earl of Douglas and Lord Hamilton becoming sureties for his return in the event of Alexander dying or escaping. Malise, Earl of

Menteth, was dead before 17 May, 1491, when Marioun, Countess of Menteth, John of Drummond, her spouse, and John, Lord Drummond, appeared as pursuers in a civil cause, and the deceased Malise, Earl of Menteth, is mentioned; also Alexander, then Earl of Menteth. Malise, Earl of Menteth, *m.* 1st, Lady Anne Vere, dau. of Henry, Earl of Oxford, and had three sons,

    Alexander, who *d. v. p.* 17 June, 1453, being at the time a prisoner, at Pontefract as hostage for his father, leaving a son, ALEXANDER, heir to his grandfather.
    John, of Kilbride, called Sir John with the Bright Sword, ancestor of the Grahams, Viscounts of Preston, extinct 1739; Grahams, of Gartmore; Grahams, of Netherby; Grahams, of Norton Conyers, Barts.; and other families of that name.
    Walter, 1st of the Grahams, of Buckquhaple.

The earl was *s.* by his grandson,

ALEXANDER GRAHAM, 2nd Earl of Menteth; who was served heir of his grandfather, 6 May, 1493. He *m.* Margaret, dau. of Walter Buchanan, of Buchanan, and had two sons,

    WILLIAM, 3rd Earl of Menteth.
    Walter, who had a charter of the lands of Gartur, from the Abbot of Inchmahoomo, 1553, ancestor of the Grahams of Gartur, who appear to be heirs male of this family.

The elder son,

WILLIAM GRAHAM, 3rd Earl of Menteth, *d.* in 1537, leaving by Margaret, his wife, dau. of Mowbray, of Barnbougle, three sons and a dau., viz.,

    JOHN, 4th Earl of Menteth.
    Robert, of Gartmore, who *d. s. p.*
    Gilbert, of Gartmore, whose male line is EXTINCT.
    Margaret, *m.* to Archibald, 4th Earl of Argyll, and had issue.

The eldest son,

JOHN GRAHAM, 4th Earl of Menteth, was one of the prisoners taken at the rout of Solway, 1542, and ransomed for 200 marks, 1 July, 1543, being designed in Rymer, Lord Monkereth. He was killed in a scuffle with the tutor of Appin, in October, 1547, leaving by Marian, eldest dau. of George, 5th Lord Seton (which lady *m.* 2ndly, John, 10th Earl of Sutherland,) two sons and two daus.,

    WILLIAM, 5th Earl of Menteth.
    George, whose son, James, son and heir-apparent of George Graham, in Reidnoche, brother-german of the deceased William, Earl of Menteth, had a charter of the king's lands of Easter Rednoche, in Perthshire. 12 June, 1598 Marion, grand-dau and heiress of George, brought that estate to her husband, John Graham, of Duchray.
    Mary, *m.* to John Buchanan, of Buchanan.
    Christian, *m.* to Sir William Livingston, of Kilsyth.

The elder son,

WILLIAM GRAHAM, 5th Earl of Menteth, *m.* Margaret, eldest dau. of Sir James Douglas, of Drumlanrig, relict of Edward, Lord Crichton, of Sanquhar, and by her (who *m.* 3rdly, Wauchope, of Niddery) he had a son,

JOHN GRAHAM, 6th Earl of Menteth; who was served heir to his father, 29 October, 1587; and *d.* in December, 1598. He *m.* Mary, 3rd dau. of Sir Colin Campbell, of Glenurchy, by whom he had issue,

    WILLIAM, 7th Earl of Menteth.
    James, who *m.* Lady Margaret Erskine, 2nd dau. of James, Earl of Buchan; but *d.* without male issue. They had a dau.,
        MARION, *m.* to Walter Graham, of Gartur.
    Christian, *m.* to Sir John Blackader, of Tulliallan.

The elder son,

WILLIAM GRAHAM, 7th Earl of Monteith, *b.* 1589, *s.* his father in December, 1598, and was served heir to him 7 August, 1610. He *m.* in 1611, (contract dated at Dundee, 30 January, 1610), Agnes, dau. of Patrick, Lord Gray, a curious account of whom will be found in a letter of her husband printed in Chambers's "Edinburgh Journal," 2 July, 1836. The earl was served heir of David Stewart, Earl of Strathern, of Patrick Graham, Earl of Strathern, and of Malise, Earl of Menteith, 25 May, 1630. In August, 1628, his lordship was constituted justice-general of Scotland; in the November following, made an extraordinary lord of session; and appointed, in 1629, president of the privy council. He had besides, being high in royal favour, charters of various lands and baronies from 1626 to 1632, amongst which was a charter of the lands and barony of Airth, wherein he had the title of Strathern allowed him, being styled Earl of Strathern and Menteith, &c. Subsequently, however, King CHARLES I. and his ministers for Scotland began to view with jealousy his lordship's pedigree, which reached to David, eldest son of King ROBERT II., by Euphemia Ross, and the incautious although true, acknowledgement in his retours and patent of his being lineally descended from the said David was deemed an ad-

240

mission of his having the preferable title to the throne of Scotland. Popular rumour became busy on the occasion ; the earl was accused to King CHARLES I. of having renounced his claim to the crown, with the reservation of the rights of his blood, and of having used the expression—" That he had the reddest blood in Scotland." Drummond of Hawthornden addressed a special memorial to his majesty on the subject, dated December, 1632, wherein he says—" The restoring the Earl of Menteith in blood, and allowing his descent and title to the Earldom of Strathern, is thought to be disadvantageous to the king's majesty, and that a more dangerous blow could not have been given to the nobleman himself." Eventually, the earl's retours and patent were set aside by the court of session, 22 March, 1633, upon the erroneous plea that David, Earl of Strathern, *d. s. p.*, and he being thus deprived of his rightful honours, and his titles, the king was pleased to confer upon him, by patent, dated at Whitehall, 21 January following, (in 1633, sealed 28 March, 1633), the title of EARL OF AIRTHE, annexing the same to the Earldom of Montethe, with precedence from the date of the original patent of the Earldom of Montethe, namely 6 September, 1428, to him and his heirs. He was thenceforward styled Earl of Airth and Monteith. His lordship was afterwards deprived of his public offices and retired to his castle of Monteith where he died. He had with other issue, (including James; and his 2nd dau. Margaret, *m.* Lord Garlies, but left no surviving issue)

JOHN GRAHAM, Lord Kinpont, who joined Montrose with 400 royalists in August, 1644, just before the battle of Tippermuir, but was murdered with two "Irish rebels at the kirke of Collace," three or four days afterwards in September of that year by his friend and companion James Stewart of Ardvorlick. The melancholy fate of this gallant young nobleman, and the singular circumstances attending the birth and history of his murderer (who was pardoned by parliament in 1645,) are the facts on which Sir Walter Scott, has founded his beautiful "Legend of Montrose." Lord Kinpont, who thus *d. v. p.*, *m.* in April, 1632, Lady Mary Keith, eldest dau. of William, 6th Earl Marischal and had issue,

    WILLIAM, who *s.* his grandfather as 2nd (and last) Earl of Airth and Monteith.
    MARY,   ⎧ of whose lines we shall presently proceed to treat
            ⎨ more fully as co-heirs of their brother in the
    ELIZABETH, ⎩ earldom.

The only son,

WILLIAM GRAHAM, 2nd Earl of Airth and Monteith, *b.* before January, 1644; *m.* 1st, Anne Hews, and 2ndly, Catherine, 2nd dau. of Thomas Bruce, of Blairhall, who *d.* in 1693. This nobleman had charters of certain lands 4 February, 1670 and 1680, and sat in parliament down to 1693. Not having issue by either of his wives, he disposed of the reversion of all his property to his kinsman, the Marquess of Montrose, and his nephews, Sir George Allardice and Sir John Graham, of Gartmore, the latter of whom he charged to inter him and his wife in the family burial place, and to provide a suitable mausoleum, of which, however, in 1784, no trace was to be found. This nobleman dying *s. p.* 12 September, 1694, the titles went into ABEYANCE between his sisters, and has since remained DORMANT.

The following are the particulars of the descendants of the Ladies Elizabeth and Mary Graham, co-heirs of the Earldoms :

LINE OF LADY MARY GRAHAM.

LADY MARY GRAHAM, so styled, supposed to be the elder, *m.* at Arbuthnot, 8 October, 1662 (contract dated 26 September),

SIR JOHN ALLARDICE, of Allardice, chief of an ancient family, who possessed the Barony of Alrethes, co. Kincardine, *temp.* WILLIAM THE LION, and assumed its name therefrom. Dying before 14 November, 1690 (will dated 27 January, 1676), he left by her, who survived to 1720, and was buried at Arbuthnot, 2 December of that year (with four daus., Mary, wife of Sir Alexander Ogilvy, Bart., of Forglen; Helen, who *d. unm.* in 1743, aged seventy-nine; Anna, *m.* to John Gordon, of Breakley; and Margaret, *b.* in 1673), two sons JOHN and GEORGE. The elder,

JOHN ALLARDICE, of Allardice, bapt. at Arbuthnot, 6 August, 1667, *m.* 23 or 28 October, 1690, at the same place (contract dated 17 October), Elizabeth, dau. of William Barclay, Laird of Balmackewan, who afterwards *m.*— Wood, of Drumlagair, and had three daus. He and his father had a charter of the Barony of Allardice, 26 May, 1671. Dying within ten weeks after his marriage in the December following it, and having had no issue, he was *s.* by his only brother,

SIR GEORGE ALLARDICE, of Allardice, *b.* 17 August, and bapt. at Arbuthnot, 27 August, 1672, M.P., and master of the mint, was served heir to his father and brother, 14 October, 1697. He m. Lady Anne Ogilvy, eldest dau. of James, Earl of Findlater and Seafield, and was buried at Arbuthnot, 17 October, 1709, leaving issue,

JAMES, his heir.   Anna, b. 1695.
Helen, b. 1697.
Katherine. b. 15 October, 1699
William, b. 17 December, 1700.
John, bapt. 11 December, 1701. He was 2nd son in 1719.
Elizabeth, b. 5 October, 1703; buried 8 May, 1705.
Mary, m. Andrew Hay, of Mount Blairy (now represented by Andrew Hay, of London, barrister-at-law, eldest son of the late General Hay, who was killed at Bayonne, in 1814).

The eldest son,

JAMES ALLARDICE, of Allardice, b. and bapt. at Arbuthnot, 25 July, 1693. He had a charter of resignation, 27 July, 1719. He m. in 1720 (contract dated 31 May), Mary, dau. of Robert Mill or Milne, of Balwhyllie, and d. in 1728 (buried 21 May), leaving with a dau., Mary, wife of James Macdonald, sheriff-substitute of Kincardineshire (she d. in 1802 or 3), an only son and successor,

JAMES ALLARDICE, of Allardice, b. 29 January, 1727, at Arbuthnot. He had a charter of the Barony of Allardice, as only son, 26 July, 1748. He m. in 1756 (contract dated 7 April), Anne, only dau. of James Barclay, of London, banker, and dying 14 July, 1765, was buried in Arbuthnot church. His wife d. in giving birth to her only child,

SARAH-ANN ALLARDICE, of Allardice, b. 13 July, 1757. She m. 1st, in December, 1776, Robert Barclay, Esq., of Urie, in Kincardineshire, M.P. for that county, whose 2nd wife she was (see BARCLAY, in BURKE's Landed Gentry). She had a charter, as sole issue of her father, 3 July, 1777, and was, 26 February, 1785, served nearest and lawful eldest heir portioner in general of William, Earl of Airth and Menteith, &c. Her husband assumed the additional surname of ALLARDICE on his marriage; and by him, who was b. 1731-2, and d. 8 April, 1797, she had issue, eight children,

Robert (1st), d. 8 April, 1797.
ROBERT (2nd), of whom presently.
James, 2nd son, in 1800, b. 3 July, 1784; d. unm. at Madras, 3 March, 1804.
David-Stuart, 3rd and youngest son in 1800, b. 3 March, 1787; d. unm. after 1793.
Anne, b. 13 September, 1777; d. 1781.
Une-Cameron, b. 13 September, 1778; m 25 July, 1802, John Innes, Esq., of Cowie, Kincardineshire, and by him, who d. in April, 1832, had issue (see INNES, of Raemoir House, in BURKE's Landed Gentry).
MARGARET, b. 14 October, 1780; m. in 1809, HUDSON GURNEY, Esq., of Keswick, co. Norfolk, M.P. (see Landed Gentry), and d. 16 December, 1855, her husband surviving to November, 1864.
Mary, twin with Margaret, d. in June, 1799.
Rodney, a dau., b. 29 April, 1782, living 1793.

Mrs. Barclay-Allardice was in September, 1793, divorced from her husband, and m. 5 August, 1795, at Christ Church, Surrey, John Nudd, of that parish. She d. in June, 1833, and was buried at Sprowston, in Norfolk. The eventual eldest son of the former marriage,

ROBERT BARCLAY-ALLARDICE, Esq., of Allardice and Urie, b. 25 August, 1779; was served heir-male to his father, 17 December, 1799, and to his mother, 9 November, 1833, and had a charter of the Barony of Allardice, &c., 2 June, 1800. He m. in 1819, Mary Dalgarno. Mr. Barclay-Allardice claimed in 1839 the Earldom of Airth, and his claim was investigated by the House of Lords. For full particulars refer to the minutes of evidence. He styled himself sole heir of the body of Prince David, son of ROBERT II., King of Scotland. His only child,

MARGARET BARCLAY-ALLARDICE, m. 2 April, 1840, Samuel Ritchie, and has issue.

LINE OF LADY ELIZABETH GRAHAM.

LADY ELIZABETH GRAHAM (see above), m. in 1663 (contract dated 19 December), her relative, Sir William Graham, of Gartmore, co. Perth, who was created a Baronet, 28 June, 1665. She d. 1672, having had issue by him, who d. in December, 1684, an only son, Sir John Graham, of Gartmore, 2nd and last baronet, who was executor of his uncle the last earl, he was cognosced insane in 1696, and d. unm. 12 July, 1708 (see GRAHAM, of Gartmore, in BURKE's Landed Gentry); and a dau., and eventual sole heiress,

MARY GRAHAM, who m. James Hodge, Esq., of Gladsmuir, advocate, and was served heir to her uncle, Sir John Graham, 4 November, 1708. This lady had an only child and heir, whose birth she did not survive more than a year. This dau.,

MARY HODGE, heiress of Gartmore, was b. 1687. She m. at the age of fourteen, 28 February, 1701, her mother's cousin, William Graham, of Dumbarton, writer, younger son of Walter Graham, of Gallingad, brother of Sir William, the 1st baronet. She sold Gartmore to her cousin, Robert Graham, in 1708, for 10,000 marks Scots. She d. before 1740, and her husband between that and 1742. They had issue,

I. James, living in 1708, d. s. p. before 1740.
II. WILLIAM, b. 1720. He was described as "only heir-male now existing" in 1740, and of full age in 1741, and was in 1744 a student of medicine, at Edinburgh. He assumed the title of Earl of Menteith, and voted as such at the general election of Scottish peers of parliament, from 12 October, 1744, to 5 May, 1761, after which he was ordered by the House of Lords, on a report from the committee of privileges (before which he neglected to appear), not to take upon himself the title until he should substantiate his claim in due course of law. He d. unm. 30 June, 1783, while passing through the parish of Bonhill, by the road side, and was buried there. Sir William Scott, of Ancrum, Bart., was in 1830, served heir to this William Graham, in right of his mother, Harriet, dau. of William Graham, Esq., of Gartmore, and in a 1839, he claimed this peerage before the House of Lords
I. Grizel, eldest dau., living 1742-8, d. unm. 12 June, 1774.
II. Mary, 2nd dau., of whom presently.
III. Margaret, youngest dau., unm. in 1726; m. John Colquhoun, of the family of Luss, and d. s. p. a widow, 18 or 19 February, 1782.

The eventual heir,

MARY GRAHAM, m. before 1741, 1st, John Bogle, of Glasgow, an officer of excise, at Edinburgh, head of a respectable old family, Lairds of Hutchiston, near Glasgow, whose pedigree is given in the minutes of evidence. His father was seated at Bogles Hole, near Glasgow. Mrs. Bogle d. 20 January, 1779, and was buried at Dumfries. Her husband, who was living at Kirkcudbright, from 1778 till 1 May, 1787, d. an aged man in the latter year; intestate, having had issue,

JOHN, only son, only brother of Mary, of whom presently.
Mary, living 1776, d unm 12 November, 1821. She lived at Edinburgh, and always insisted on being called "Lady Mary Bogle," or "Lady Grahame Bogle." She was in 1805 served heir of line of her great-grandfather Sir William Graham, of Gartmore, as only surviving child, and so considered herself his only existing descendant in 1819. Calls herself her brother's heir-at-law, and says no one else can have any claim but herself, being the last of her family.
Grizell, living 1776, lately deceased, unm. 1802. She was the only sister of Mary.

The only son,

JOHN BOGLE was a miniature portrait painter of Edinburgh, and afterwards (from 1772), of Panton-square, London. He had a large collection of evidences on this peerage claim, which passed into the hands of Deuchar, the genealogist. He m. 7 August, 1769, May, only dau. of John Wilson, of Spango, Nithsdale, and d. at Edinburgh, about 1803, leaving no issue. His will, dated 9 December, 1786, was proved 28 July, 1803, in London, by his widow and sole executrix, who survived him till about 1823.

From the foregoing pedigree, founded on the evidence submitted to the House of Lords by Mr. Barclay-Allardice, it would appear that the line of Lady Elizabeth Graham is EXTINCT But the House of Lords, not being satisfied on that point made no decision. The Lord Advocate argued that the Earldom of Airth being attached to the Earldom of Menteith, which was granted to heirs male, could not descend to heirs female, but this question was not decided. We accordingly subjoin, as fully as the information obtained will admit of, the pedigree of another claimant, viz.:

LINE OF JAMES-BOGLE-DENTON-GRAHAM MATTHEWS, ESQ.

JOHN BOGLE, one of the family of Bogles Hole (originally "Hold"), near Glasgow, m. MARY GRAHAM, stated to have been a sister or dau. of the last Earl of Menteith, and during the Rebellion of 1715, having been obliged to leave Scotland on account of his religious opinions, settled, according to tradition, in or near Strabane, Ireland. He acquired a small property called Ballycommon, or Balwaggie, half a mile from Strabane, and d. there. The tombstone of himself and his wife is in the churchyard of Strabane. They had issue, besides Joseph, James (whose son James had an only dau., m. a Mr. Delap, and had a son, James-Bogle Delap), and another, an eldest son,

SAMUEL BOGLE, who m. Elizabeth Graham (she had a brother, James, whom she survived), and had issue,

ANDREW, his heir.
Samuel, who lived near Strabane, took possession of the land,

and disposed of it by lottery, when, it is said, his nephew, Mr. Bogle-French won it. Samuel Bogle m., but d. s. p. Mark, d. young.

James, a posthumous child, of Jamaica and of London, m. Miss French, an heiress, and took her name in addition to his own. They had Nathaniel, who m. and had issue; and Mary, Mrs. Smith, mother of Horace Smith (joint author of "Rejected Addresses").

A dau., m. Mr. Baird, and had a dau., Mrs. Moffat, living near Strabane in 1809, and during sixty years previously.

Agnes, m. Thomas, eldest son of William Buchanan, Esq., of Hordoch, and had issue.

Samuel Bogle d. suddenly, intestate, and his widow, who m. a Mr. Somerville, continued to reside near Strabane, and she built a house on the estate. The eldest son,

ANDREW BOGLE, M.D., went out to Jamaica, with Mr. Bogle-French, and settled at Black River. He m. Eleanor, dau. of — Richardson, of Killeleagh, co. Down, and d. in Jamaica leaving (with a dau., m. to Mr. McConnell, of Donegall-place, Belfast, and had issue,) an only son,

JAMES-ANDREW BOGLE, b. in Edinburgh, m. at St. Andrew's, Newcastle-upon-Tyne, about 1769, Mary Skiddaw, and d. at Lambeth, in April, 1809, aged sixty-three, having had issue, (besides an only son, William, who d. æt. nine or twelve) an only dau.,

MARY-ELEANOR BOGLE, b. at Whitehaven, Cumberland, who m. at Isleworth, Middlesex, January, 1796, Nicholas Donnithorne Bishop, Esq., attorney-at-law, of Crossdeep Lodge, Twickenham, co. Middlesex, and d. at Richmond, Surrey, on Christmas-day, 1846, aged seventy-four, leaving by him, who d. 26 December, 1840 (besides an only son, who d. young), an only dau.,

MARY-ELEANOR BISHOP, b in Essex-street, London, 1 January, 1797; m. in 1824, Richard-Hunt Matthews, Esq., H.E.I.C.S., of Buxar, East Indies, and afterwards of Crossdeep Lodge, Twickenham, and by him (who d. in 1840) she had issue, an only dau., Mary-Eleanor-Graham and an only son, of whom presently. Mrs. Matthews is possessed of the ancient steel seal of the Earl of Monteith, with the coat of arms, quartering the royal arms of Scotland. She has likewise a large collection of papers on this peerage claim. Her only son,

JAMES-BOGLE-DENTON-GRAHAM MATTHEWS, Esq., b. 1 July, 1830; m. at Hanworth, Middlesex, 11 April, 1855, Rosa-Robinson, dau. of W. Reed, Esq., and has a son, ALFRED-GRAHAM, b. 1856, and other issue. This gentleman's grandfather and grandmother petitioned the House of Lords, in 1839, on their own and his behalf, as entitled to the Airth peerage, in opposition to the claim of Mr. Barclay-Allardice, whereupon the House made no decision, and the title has since remained DORMANT.

GRANDISON—BARON GRANDISON.

By Writ of Summons, dated 21 September, 1299.

Lineage.

In the 55th HENRY III.,

OTHO DE GRANDISON attended Prince Edward into the Holy Land; and after that prince ascended the throne as EDWARD I., he was constituted governor of the islands of Guernsey and Jersey. In this reign he appears to have been a person of great note, and to have held some high political employment. amongst others that of secretary to the king. He was knighted, and deputed ambassador to Rome (17th EDWARD I.), when he had the king's letters to the merchants of Luca, to supply him with money there, by bills of exchange He had previously obtained grants from the crown of the town of Tipperary, and other extensive possessions in Ireland, all which he transferred, with the sanction of the king, to his brother, William de Grandison. In the 24th of the same reign Sir Otho was joined in commission with the bishop of Ely and others, to treat of peace with the French; and he was summoned to parliament, as a baron, 21 September, 1299. The period of his lordship's death is not ascertained, but in the 12th EDWARD II., all those castles, manors, and lands, which he held in Ireland for life, were given, by the king, to Prince Edward, his eldest son, and to his heirs, Kings of England. He d. s. p., when the barony of Grandison became EXTINCT.

Arms—Paly of six, arg. and vert, on a bend, gu., three eagles displayed, or.

GRANDISON--BARONS GRANDISON.

By Writ of Summons, dated 6 February, 1299.

Lineage.

WILLIAM DE GRANDISON (younger brother of Sir Otho de Grandison, secretary to King EDWARD I., and afterwards Lord Grandison), being originally a menial servant to Edmund, Earl of Lancaster, obtained from that prince, in consideration of his own faithful services, and the services of his ancestors, a grant of the manors of Radley and Menstreworth, co. Gloucester. In the 20th EDWARD I., he procured license to make a castle of his house at Asperton, co. Hereford, and in two years afterwards he was in the expedition into Gascony, where he continued for some time, and while so engaged was summoned to parliament as a baron. He was afterwards engaged in the Scottish wars His lordship m. Sibilla, youngest dau. and co-heiress of Sir John de Tregoz, and upon partition of the lands of that inheritance, acquired the manors of Burnham, co. Somerset, and Eton, in Herefordshire. He had issue by this lady, three sons and a dau., viz.,

I. PETER, his successor.
II. John, bishop of Exeter
III. Otho, a distinguished soldier in the reigns of EDWARD II. and EDWARD III., m. Beatrix. dau. and co-heir of Nicholas Malmains, and dying in 1364, had issue,
THOMAS, who s. his uncle, the bishop of Exeter, in the barony of Grandison.
Elizabeth, d. unm.
I. Mabella, m. Sir John Patteshul.
II. Katherine, m. to William de Montacute, Earl of Salisbury.
III. Agnes, m. to Sir John de Northwode, and had a son and heir, Roger de Northwode, who was father of John Northwode, aged thirty in 1375.

His lordship d. before 1335, and was s. by his eldest son,

PETER DE GRANDISON, 2nd baron, summoned to parliament from 23 April, 1337, to 28 March, 1349. This nobleman being implicated in the insurrection of Thomas, Earl of Lancaster, 15th EDWARD II., was obliged to pay 300 marks fine for his pardon. He was afterwards in the wars of France, and attained the rank of banneret. His lordship m. Blanch, one of the daus. of Roger de Mortimer, Earl of March, but had no issue. He d. in 1358, and was s. by his brother,

JOHN DE GRANDISON, bishop of Exeter, 3rd baron, but never summoned to parliament as Lord Grandison, having already a seat in his episcopal dignity. Of this prelate it is related, that he got the wealth of all the clergy in his diocese into his own hands, by inducing them to leave him everything they possessed at their death, for the purpose of laying the same out in charitable uses, in endowing churches, and building hospitals and colleges; trusts which he is said, however, very piously to have performed. He d. in 1369, and was s. by his nephew,

SIR THOMAS GRANDISON, as 4th Baron Grandison, who d. s. p. in the 49th EDWARD III., and the barony is now vested in the representatives of his lordship's aunts and co-heirs.

The late Sir Henry Paston Bedingfeld, having claimed to be one of the co-heirs of the Barony of Grandison, the case was referred to Her Majesty by the House of Lords, and after several hearings, the Committee for Privileges reported, "that it is the opinion of this Committee, that the Barony of Grandison was created in the person of Sir William Grandison, by writ of summons to and sitting in parliament in the reign of King EDWARD the First, and fell into abeyance on the death of Thomas, Lord Grandison, grandson of the said William, Lord Grandison, in the 46th year of the reign of King Edward the Third, between Mabella, who married Sir John Patteshul, Katherine, who married the Earl of Salisbury, and Agnes, who married Sir John Northwode, the three daughters and co-heirs of the said William Lord Grandison, and the heirs of their respective bodies; and that the petitioner, Sir Henry Paston Bedingfeld, has proved his descent as sole heir of the body of Katherine Tuddenham, the second of the four daughters and co-heirs of the said Mabella; and that the Duke of Richmond Sir John Gordon Sinclair, Baronet, the Duke of Manchester, such of the following five daughters of the late Louisa, Marchioness Cornwallis, namely, Jane Lady Braybrooke, Jemima Countess of St. Germans, the Lady Mary, wife of Charles Ross, Esquire, the Lady Louisa Cornwallis, and the Lady Elizabeth Cornwallis, as are now living, and the heirs of the bodies (if any) of such of them as are deceased, and Lord Wriothesley Russell, are the co-heirs of the body of Sibella, the eldest daughter and co-heir of the said Mabella; and that the heirs of the body of Elizabeth Neville, who married Sir Richard Strangways, and the heirs of the body of Alice Neville, who married Sir John Conyers, became the co-heirs of the body of Matilda, the third daughter and co-heir of the said Mabella; and the descendants of the said Elizabeth have not been traced beyond the seventeenth century; and that the Duke of Leeds is the heir of the body of the said Dame Alice Conyers; and that descendants from Alice, the fourth daughter and co-heir of the said Mabella, who married Sir Thomas Wake, have been traced into the sixteenth century, and no further; and that the Most Honorable Henry Marquess of Hastings, William Lowndes of Chesham, Esquire, and William Selby Lowndes of Whaddon, Esquire, are the co-heirs of the body of the said Katherine Countess of Salisbury; and that Sir Anchitel Ashburnham, Baronet, is the heir of the body of Agnes, who married Sir John Northwode."

Arms—Paly of six, arg. and vert, on a bend, gu. three eagles displayed, or.

GRANT—BARON GLENELG.

By Letters Patent, dated 11 May, 1835.

Lineage.

Patrick Grant (3rd son of Robert Grant, of Shewglie, co. Inverness), *m.* a dau. of Hugh Fraser, of Erebet, and had a son and successor,

Robert Grant, Esq., who, by his wife, the niece of Chisholm, chief of that name, left

Alexander Grant, Esq., who *m.* Margaret, dau. of Donald Macbean, Esq., a descendant of the Macbeans of Kinchyle, and by her had,

Charles Grant, Esq., *b.* in 1746, who for many years represented the co. of Inverness in parliament, and was one of the most distinguished directors of the East India Company. He *m.* in 1770, Jane, dau. of Thomas Fraser, Esq., a younger son of Fraser of Balnain, co. Inverness, by whom (who *d.* 23 January, 1827) he had (with daus., of whom one, Charamelle, was *m.* to the Right Hon. Samuel March-Phillipps, Esq., under-secretary of state for the Home Department, and another to Patrick Grant, Esq., of Redcastle) three sons,

Charles, Lord Glenelg.
Robert (the Right Hon. Sir), G.C.H., governor of Bombay; who *m.* 11 August, 1829, Margaret, only dau. of Sir David Davidson, of Cantray, co. Nairn, and *d.* in 1838, leaving issue by her (who *m.* 2ndly, 8 August, 1848, Hon. Josceline Percy),

  1 Charles, *b.* 22 February, 1836.
  2 Robert, *b.* 10 August, 1837.
  1 Constance-Charemile, *d.* July, 1843.
  2 Sibylla-Sophia. *m.* 19 March, 1844, to Richard Ryder, Esq., of the Inner Temple.

Thomas-William, *d.* 15 May, 1848.

The eldest son,
The Right Hon. Charles Grant, P.C., *b.* 26 October, 1778, was some time principal secretary of state for the Colonial Department. He was raised to the peerage of the United Kingdom by letters-patent, bearing date 11 May, 1835, by the title of Baron Glenelg, of Glenelg, co. Inverness. He had previously represented the co. of Inverness in parliament. He *d. unm.* 23 April, 1866, at Cannes, in France, when the title became extinct.

Arms—Gu., on a fesse, between three antique crowns, or, a lion, passant-guardant, of the field, imperially crowned, ppr., between two cinquefoils, also of the first.

GRANVILLE—EARLS OF BATH.

By Letters Patent, dated 20 April, 1661.

Lineage.

The celebrated,
Sir Bevil Granville, Knt., of Stow and Bideford, one of the boldest and most successful of the cavalier leaders, the "Bayard" of England, was *b.* 23 March, 1595 (*see* Burke's *Landed Gentry*). He was educated at Exeter College, Oxford, and made so rapid a progress in learning, that the degree of B.A. was conferred on him at the age of 17. He represented the co. of Cornwall in parliament, 18th James I., 1620 to 1623; again, in the reign of Charles I., was member for Launceston, 1625, and for several succeeding parliaments. In 1638, he raised, at his own expense, a troop of horse, with which he accompanied the king in his first expedition against the Scottish rebels, and on that occasion received the honour of knighthood. In 1642, on the first outbreaking of the civil wars, he joined the royal standard, and marching into Cornwall, rescued that whole county from the parliament, attacking the partizans of the Commons who had risen in great numbers in the west, and routed them at Bodmin, Launceston, and Stratton. His last and most brilliant action was at Lansdowne Hill, near Bath, where he fell in the arms of victory, on 5 July,

1643. "On the king's part," says Clarendon, in detailing this engagement, "there were more officers and gentlemen of quality slain than common men, and more hurt than slain. That which would have clouded any victory, and made the loss of others less spoken of, was the death of Sir Bevil Granville. He was, indeed, an excellent person, whose activity, interest, and reputation, was the foundation of what had been done in Cornwall; and his temper and affection so public, that no accident which happened could make any impression on him, and his example kept others from taking anything ill, or at least seeming to do so. In a word, a brighter courage and a gentler disposition were never married together to make the most cheerful and innocent conversation." Sir Bevil *m.* Grace, dau. of Sir George Smythe, of Matford, in Heavitree, near Exeter, Knt., and had issue, seven sons and six daus., of whom survived and married,

  I. John, *b.* 1628, of whom presently.
  II. Bernard, *b.* 1630, father of George Granville, Lord Lansdowne.
  III. Dennis. *b.* 1637, dean of Durham, rector of Easington and Elwycke, and chaplain in ordinary to Charles II. He *m.* Ann, 4th dau. of John Cosyn, lord bishop of Durham, but *d.* without issue.
  I. Elizabeth, *b.* 1621; *m.* to Sir Peter Prideaux, of Netherton, co. Devon.
  II. Grace, *b.* 1624; *m.* to Colonel Robert Fortescue, of Fileigh.
  III. Bridget, *b.* 1629; *m.* 1st, to Sir Simon Leach; and 2ndly, to Sir Thomas Higgons.
  IV. Joane, *b.* 1635; *m.* to Colonel Richard Thornhill.

The eldest surviving son of Sir Bevil,
John Granville, Esq., who attended Charles II., in all his wanderings abroad, was only sixteen years old when he took the command of his father's regiment, and was in all the considerable battles of the west of England, as well as the battle of Newbury, where he was severely wounded. Sir John was chosen negotiator and messenger from the king, to deliver to both Houses of Parliament the king's letters from Breda, and received their acknowledgments for his services in that transaction. Thus pointed out to his country as a principal instrument of the Restoration, he was further rewarded with such honours as his services and those of his family might justly claim. He was, therefore, on the restoration of Charles II., created Earl of Bath, *Viscount Lansdowne and Baron Granville, of Bideford and Kilkhampton;* also permitting him to use the titles of Earl of Corboile, Thorigny, and Granville (as his ancestors had done), to him and his posterity. He *m.* Jane, dau. of Sir Peter Wyche, and dying in 1701, left issue,

  I. Charles, 2nd Earl of Bath.
  II. John, created, by Queen Anne, 9 March, 1702, Baron Granville, *of Potheridge, co. Devon,* *m.* Rebecca, dau. of Sir John Child, of Wanstead, in Essex, and widow of Charles, Marquess of Worcester, but had no issue. His lordship was lord warden of the Stanneries. He *d.* in 1707, when the barony became extinct.
  I. Jane, *m.* to Sir William-Leveson Gower, ancestor of the Duke of Sutherland.
  II. Catherine, *m.* to Craven Peyton, warden of the Mint.
  III. Grace, *m.* to Sir Geo. Carteret, afterwards Lord Carteret, and had issue. Lady Carteret surviving her husband, was herself elevated to the peerage as Countess Granville. Her ladyship's grand-daughter, the Lady Louisa Carteret, *m.* Thomas Thynne, Viscount Weymouth, and was grandmother of Thomas, Marquess of Bath, and of George, Lord Carteret.

His lordship *d.* in August, 1701, and was *s.* by his eldest son,
Charles Granville, 2nd Earl of Bath, who had been summoned to parliament in the lifetime of his father, *anno* 1689, and had been created a count of the Roman empire by the Emperor Leopold, for his eminent services in the war of Hungary, where he was a volunteer in the army that defeated the Turks before Vienna, in 1683, and was the same year at the taking of Gran. His lordship *m.* 1st, Lady Martha Osborne, dau. of Thomas, 1st Duke of Leeds, by whom he had no surviving issue. He *m.* 2ndly, Isabella, dau. of Henry de Nassau, Velt Marshal Auverquerque, commander of the Dutch forces under the Duke of Maalborough, and had an only child,

William-Henry, his successor.

The earl *d.* in twelve days after his father, being killed by the accidental discharge of his own pistol, at the time he was preparing for the interment of that nobleman. He was *s.* by his son,
William-Henry Granville, 3rd Earl of Bath, *b.* 30 January, 1691-2, but *d. unm.*, of the smallpox, in May, 1711; when the Earldom of Bath and inferior dignities became extinct, while his estates passed to his lordship's aunts (revert to issue of John, 1st earl) as co-heiresses.

Arms—Gu., three suffines or organ rests, or

GRANVILLE—BARON LANSDOWNE, OF BIDDEFORD, CO. DEVON.

By Letters Patent, dated 1 June, 1712.

Lineage.

BERNARD GRANVILLE, 2nd surviving son of the famous Sir Bevil Granville, of Stow, by Grace Smythe, his wife, was very young at his father's decease, and made his escape from school to join his brother John in defence of the Scilly islands, besieged by Admiral Blake, to which place he conveyed large reinforcements. He was ever after very active in the service of CHARLES II. during his exile : " When all was concluded for his Majesty's restoration, and his brother Sir John Granville had received the thanks of both houses of parliament for the letters he brought, General Monk thought it proper to send his last despatches by one he could trust, which was Bernard Granville, his first cousin,* who was to inform his Majesty that every-thing was ready for his reception." He was gentleman of the bedchamber to the Duke of Gloucester during his exile, and after the Restoration, gentleman of the horse and groom of the bedchamber to CHARLES II. He was M.P. for Lostwithiel the 1st of CHARLES II., and served for Launceston, Saltash, and Bodmin, in all the parliaments in that reign ; also for Plymouth 1st JAMES II.; also for Saltash again in the reign of WILLIAM till the day of his death. He m. Anne, only dau. and heir of Cuthbert Morley, Esq., of Haunby, co. York, and dying in 1701, was buried at Lambeth, leaving issue,

1. BEVIL (Sir), knighted by JAMES II., a major-general, M.P. for Fowey, 1st JAMES II., Governor of Barbadoes, d. 1706, s. p.
11. GEORGE, of whom we treat.
VII. Bernard, of Buckland, co. Gloucester, colonel by com-mission from Queen ANNE, lieutenant-governor of Hull, M.P. for the boroughs of Camelford and Fowey. He m. Mary, dau. of Sir Martin Westcombe, Bart., consul at Cadiz, who, dying in 1747, was buried at Gloucester Cathedral. He d. in 1723, leaving issue two sons and two daus., viz.,

  1 Bernard, his heir, who purchased from the Fleetwoods, the estate of Calwich Abbey, in Staffordshire. He d. unm. 1775, being the last male heir of this ancient family, bequeathing his name and estates to his sister Anne's son, JOHN D'EWES, of whom presently.
  2 Bevil, in holy orders, m. Mary-Anne, dau· of Richard Rose, Esq., d. s. p.
  1 Mary, b. 1700, m. 1st, Alexander Pendarves, Esq., of Roscrow, in Cornwall; and 2ndly, to the Very Rev. Patrick Delany, D.D., dean of Down, but d. s. p. 1788. This lady,† so justly celebrated for her great literary acquirements, was much esteemed by King GEORGE III., and Queen CHARLOTTE, and resided constantly with their Majesties both at Kew and Windsor.
  2 Anne, b. 1707; m. at Gloucester, 1740, John D'Ewes, Esq., of Wellesbourne, co. of Warwick, and had issue: the only dau., Mary, m. John Port, Esq., of Ilam, and was grand-mother of Lady Llanover; the 3rd son, the Rev. John D'Ewes, took the name and arms of GRANVILLE, on suc-ceeding to his uncle Bernard Granville's estates, but d. without surviving issue in 1826, when the property devolved upon his nephew (the son of his elder brother, Bernard D'Ewes), COURT GRANVILLE, Esq., grandfather of the present BEVIL GRANVILLE, Esq., of Wellesbourne Hall, co. Warwick. (See Landed Gentry.)
z. Anne, m. Sir John Stanley, Bart. of Grangegormam
11. Elizabeth, d. unm.; maid of honour.

The 2nd son,
GEORGE GRANVILLE, Esq., was elevated to the peerage, on 1 January, 1712, as BARON LANSDOWNE, of Biddeford, co. Devon. His lordship m. Lady Mary Villiers, dau. of Edward, Earl of Jersey, and had issue,

Anne, d. unm.
Mary, m. to William Graham, Esq., of Platten, near Drogheda.
Grace, m. to Thomas Foley, Esq., of Stoke, co. Hereford, who was created Baron Foley, of Kidderminster, in 1776.
Elizabeth, d. unm

Lord Lansdowne was secretary-at-war, and comptroller and treasurer of the household, in the reign of Queen ANNE. He d. 1734, when the Barony of Lansdowne became EXTINCT, and his estates devolved on his daus. as co-heirs.

Arms—Same as those of Granville, Earls of Bath.

---

* Bernard Granville's mother, and George Monk's mother, were sisters, daus. of Sir George Smythe.
† See Mrs. Delany's Autobiography, edited by Lady Llanover.

GRANVILLE—BARON GRANVILLE.

Refer to GRANVILLE, *Earl of Bath.*

GRENDON—BARON GRENDON.

By Writ of Summons, dated 29 December, 1299.

Lineage.

ROGER DE GRENDON, living *temp.* King STEPHEN, was the first who adopted this surname. He had with other issue,
RICHARD, his heir.
Walchelinus, of Bromcote, whose son, William de Bromcote, was father of William de Grendon, lord of Bromcote, whose son and heir Robert de Grendon, living 22nd EDWARD I., had a son, Thomas de Grendon, 18th EDWARD II., who was father of Thomas de Grendon, who left an only dau and heir, Mar-garet, who m. 1st,—Charnels, and 2ndly, Thomas Malory.

The eldest son,
RICHARD DE GRENDON, had by Margaret his wife, a son and heir,
SIR ROBERT DE GRENDON, Knt., who m. Avicia, dau. (and in her issue heir) of William de Brae, and had two sons,
ROBERT and Roger. The former,
SIR ROBERT DE GRENDON, Knt., as heir to his maternal grand father, became possessed of Shenston, a fair lordship in Staf-fordshire. He was a justice of assize, and in the 34th HENRY III. was constituted sheriff of the cos. Stafford and Salop, and also governor of the castles of Salop, Bruges, and Ellesmere He contracted matrimony with one Joane le Botiller, but does not seem to have received her as his wife, as appears by a sentence of the spiritual court of Lichfield; he was quit of her and m. Emma, dau. of William Bassett, of Sapcote, and by her had issue,

John, living 55th HENRY II., who had issue, Henry ; Thomas ; Nicolas; Robert; and Ranulph
RALPH, of whom we treat.
Alicia, m. to John de Clinton.

The 2nd son was
SIR RALPH DE GRENDON, Knt., who in the 26th EDWARD I., had a summons to be at Carlisle on Whitsun eve (with other sundry great men of the time) well furnished with horse and arms to march against the Scots. Three years after he received another command to attend the king at Berwick to march into Scotland. By Johanna, his 1st wife, he had a son and succes-sor, RALPH (Sir), and by his 2nd, A. de Clinton, had three daus., Johanna, m. to Sir Roger Chetwind: Alicia, m. to Sir Philip Chetwind, and was mother of Sir William Chetwind, of Inges-tre ; and Margaret, m. to John de Freford. The son and heir,
SIR RALPH DE GRENDON, d. 5th EDWARD III., leaving a son ROBERT, his heir ; and a dau., Joane, m. to John Rochford, Esq., and was mother of Sir Ralph Rochford, who had a dau. and heir Margery. The son,
ROBERT GRENDON, 2nd baron. This being a person of weak intellect, Sir Roger de Chetwind, and Sir Philip de Chetwind, Knts., with John de Freford, who had m. his aunts, Joane, Alice, and Margaret Grendon, alleging that A. de Clinton, 2nd wife of old Sir Ralph de Grendon, father of the late baron, had a joint estate with her husband in all their lands, challenged the whole inheritance, and accordingly entered upon the land; whereupon ROBERT sought the protection of Henry Duke of Lancaster, yielding unto his grace the entire manor of Shen-ston, near Lichfield, co. Stafford, conditionally, that he would protect him in the possession of Grendon, and cer-tain other lands in other places. In consequence of which arrangements, his uncles and aunts relinquished their pre-tended claim. He d. about the 22nd EDWARD III., when those lands descended to his nephew, Sir Ralph Rochfort, Knt., whereupon Sir Ralph entailed them upon the issue of his own body, by Joane, his wife, dau. of Sir Hugh Meynil, with remainder to his three sisters successively, and then to Sir Richard Stafford, Knt., and his heirs. According to which settlement the possession continued for divers years, until Sir Ralph Rochfort's death, when Joane, his widow, marrying 2ndly, Hugh de Ashby, made an agreement with Sir William Chetwynd, Knt. (son and heir of Sir Philip), by which Grendon at length came into the possession of the Chetwynds, and is now held by Sir George Chetwynd, Bart. The barony of Grendon, which fell into ABEYANCE amongst the Rochforts, so continues with their representatives, if such exist.

Arms—Arg., two chevrons, gu.

GRENVILLE—BARON GRENVILLE.

By Letters Patent, dated 25 November, 1790.

Lineage.

WILLIAM-WYNDHAM GRENVILLE, D.C.L., F.S.A., and F.R.S. of Wotton-under-Bernwood, co. Bucks, 2nd son of the Right Hon. George Grenville, by Elizabeth, his wife, dau. of Sir William Wyndham, Bart., b. 25 October, 1759, having attained very high reputation as an orator and statesman, and having filled some of the most important ministerial offices during the reign of GEORGE III., was elevated to the peerage 25 November, 1790, by the title of BARON GRENVILLE. Lord Grenville was auditor of the Exchequer, chancellor of the university of Oxford, an elder brother of the Trinity House, one of the governors of the Charter House, and high steward of Bristol. His lordship m. 18 July, 1792, the Hon. Anne Pitt, only dau. of Thomas, 1st Lord Camelford, and sister and sole heiress of Thomas, 2nd and last lord; but d. s. p. 12 January, 1834, when his title became EXTINCT. His widow survived until 13 June, 1864. At her Ladyship's decease, her large estates, in accordance with the wish of her husband, devolved by her will on the Hon. George Fortescue.

Arms—Vert, on a cross, arg., five torteaux.

GRENVILLE—BARON GLASTONBURY.

By Letters Patent, dated 20 October, 1797.

Lineage.

JAMES GRENVILLE, Esq., (son of the Right Hon. James Grenville, uncle to George, 1st Marquess of Buckingham, by Mary, dau. and heiress of James Smyth, Esq., of Harden, co. Herts,) having been sworn of his majesty's most honourable privy council, and constituted one of the lords of the Treasury in 1782, was elevated to the peerage 20 October, 1797, as Baron Glastonbury, of Butley, co. Somerset, with remainder to his brother, General Grenville, who predeceased him in 1823, unm. His lordship d. s. p. in 1826, when the barony of Glastonbury became EXTINCT.

Arms—Vert, on a cross, arg., five torteaux.

GRESLEY—BARON GRESLEY.

By Writ of Summons, dated 10 March, 1308.

Lineage.

In the year 1184,

ROBERT DE GRESLEI, of Manchester, co. Lancaster, having a large proportion of marsh land, at Swineshed, in Lincolnshire, founded an abbey of Cistertian monks there. To this Robert s. his son,

ALBERT DE GRESLEI, who m. 1st, Agnes, dau. of Nigel, Baron of Halton, and 2ndly, a dau. of Thomas Basset. He d. about the year 1185, and was s. by his son,

ROBERT DE GRESLEI, who in the 6th RICHARD I., being then of full age, attended that monarch in the expedition made into Normandy; but taking part with the barons towards the close of King JOHN's reign, his lands were all seized by the crown. Making his peace, however, in the 2nd HENRY III., he had restitution of those lands, which lay in the cos. Oxford, Rutland, Lincolnshire, Lancashire, Norfolk, and Suffolk. He m. a dau. of Henry de Longchamp (brother of William de Longchamp, chancellor to King RICHARD I.), and dying in 1230, was s. by his son,

THOMAS DE GRESLEI, who, in the 26th HENRY III., had a military summons to march into France, but paid 100 marks, besides his ordinary scutage, to be freed from the journey. In the 42nd of the same reign, he had another military summons to march against the Welsh, and the next year he was constituted warden of the king's forest, south of Trent. He d. about the year 1261, and was s. by his son,

THOMAS DE GRESLEI, who, in the 8th EDWARD I., having m. Hawyse, one of the daus. and co-heirs of John de Burgh, son of Hubert, Earl of Kent, had livery of her share of her father's

lands: namely, Waukerley, Ringeston, and Porteslade. He d. in 1283, and was s. by his son,

THOMAS DE GRESLEY, who, in the 34th EDWARD I., was made a knight of the Bath, and was summoned to parliament as a baron, from the 1st to the 4th EDWARD II., inclusive. His lordship d. s. p. 1347, when the barony of Gresley became EXTINCT, but his great estates devolved upon his only sister and heiress,

JOANE DE GRESLEY, who m. John, son of Roger de la Warre, and brought her noble inheritance into that family.

Arms—Vairée, ermines and gu.

GREY—BARONS GREY OF WILTON, CO. HEREFORD.

By Writ of Summons, dated 23 June, 1295.

Lineage.

SIR JOHN DE GREY, 2nd son of Henry de Grey, of Thurrock, co. Essex (see GREY, of Codnor), served the office of sheriff for the cos. Buckingham and Bedford, in the 23rd HENRY III., and had summons to attend the king, in the 26th of the same reign, with horse and arms, upon the expedition then made into Flanders. "In the 35th HENRY III.," says Dugdale, "the Lady Joane Peyvre, widow of Pauline Pevere (a great man in that age), being possessed of all her husband's estate, sold to this John, the marriage of her son, for 500 marks, he undertaking to discharge her of any fine to the king; whereupon he married him to his own daughter; and when this Joane heard that the king had given her in marriage (as she was a widow) to one Stephen de Salines, an alien, she, by the advice of her friends (being then in London), matched herself to this John de Grey, which being told to the king, he grew much offended, but at length accepted of a fine of 500 marks from him for that transgression." In the 37th HENRY III., Sir John de Grey was made governor of Northampton Castle, and the next year constituted steward of all Gascony, but in three years afterwards, "being an aged knight, much esteemed for his civility and valour, as also chief of the king's council," yet weary of the vanities of the court, he withdrew from public life. In the very next year, however, we find him nominated to the governorship of Shrewsbury Castle, and soon after appointed constable of that of Dover. In the 47th HENRY III., he was sheriff of Herefordshire, and governor of Hereford Castle. The next year he had the custody of all the lands of Anker de Frescheville, in the cos. of Nottingham and Derby; and was one of those barons who undertook that the king should abide the arbitration of LEWIS, King of France, touching the misunderstanding with the barons. Remaining subsequently loyal to the king, he was appointed after the victory of Evesham, sheriff for the cos. of Nottingham and Derby. Sir John de Grey d. in 1265, and was s. by his son,

REGINALD DE GREY, b. 1287, who, in consideration of his faithful services to the king, obtained special livery of all his father's lands, although he had not then done his homage. In the 9th EDWARD I., he was made justice of Chester, and merited so well, that for his manifold services, he had part of the honour of Monmouth conferred upon him by the king; and in further recompense of his services obtained the castle of Ruthyn and other lands. In 22nd EDWARD I., he received command to be at Portsmouth, to attend the king in Gascony, then menaced by the French, and the next year was summoned to parliament as a baron. In two years afterwards, King EDWARD going into Flanders, committed the government of England in his absence to Prince Edward, and appointed Lord Grey the prince's assistant, and the same year his lordship was one of the sureties on the part of the king, for the observance of the charters; after this we find him in the wars of Scotland. His lordship m. Maud, dau. and heiress of William, Lord Fitz-Hugh, by Hawys, dau. and heiress of Hugh de Longchamp, of Wilton Castle, co. Hereford, which came into the family of Grey by this marriage—by whom he had issue,

JOHN, his successor.
Joane, m. to Ralph, Lord Basset.

The baron, who had been summoned to parliament, from 23 June, 1295, to 26 August, 1307, d. in 1308, and was s. by his son,

JOHN DE GREY, 2nd baron, summoned to parliament, from 9 June, 1309, to 18 September, 1322. In the 10th EDWARD II., he was constituted justice of North Wales, and governor of the castle of Caernarvon. His lordship m. 1st, Anne, dau. of William, Lord Ferrers, of Groby, and had issue,

HENRY, his successor.

He m. 2ndly, Maud, dau. of Ralph, Lord Basset, and had,

Roger, who was summoned to Parliament, as Lord Grey de Ruthyn, in the 18th EDWARD II., a dignity, which eventually devolved on the 4th Marquess of Hastings, and at his death *s. p.*, 1868, fell into abeyance between his sisters (*see* YEL-VERTON, Earl of Sussex and Baron Grey de Ruthyn).

His lordship d. in 1323, seized, among other possessions, of the manor of Eston Grey, in Wilts, and the castle of Ruthyn, in North Wales, and was *s.* by his elder son,

HENRY DE GREY, 3rd baron, summoned to parliament from 30 December, 1324, to 12 September, 1342. This nobleman being abroad in the French wars at the time of his father's death, and therefore not able to come to claim his inheritance so soon as he should, according to custom, have done, King EDWARD III., in the 1st year of his reign, in consideration of his eminent services remitted him a debt he owed to the exchequer. His lordship m. Anne, dau. and heiress of Ralph Rockley, by Elizabeth, his wife, dau. of William Clare (a younger son of Robert, Earl of Clare), and dying 1342, was *s.* by his only son,

REGINALD DE GREY, 4th baron, summoned to parliament from 24 February, 1343, to 20 November, 1360. His lordship m. Maud, dau. and co-heir of John Botetourt, of Weoly, and dying in 1370, was *s.* by his son,

SIR HENRY DE GREY, 5th baron, summoned to parliament as "Henry Grey, of Shirland," 1 December, 1376, and as "Henry Grey, of Wilton," from 4 August, 1377, to 20 November, 1394. This nobleman, during the lifetime of his father, was in the immediate retinue of John of Gaunt, in the expedition made by that prince into Gascony, in 40th EDWARD III. His lordship m. Elizabeth, dau. of Thomas, Lord Talbot, and had issue,

RICHARD, his successor.
Margaret, m. to John, Lord Darcy.

Lord Grey d. in 1395, and was *s.* by his son,

RICHARD DE GREY, 6th baron, but never summoned to parliament. This nobleman, at the decease of his father, was but three years of age, so that nothing occurs regarding him, until the 3rd HENRY V., when he appears to have been in the retinue of Thomas, Earl of Dorset, uncle of the king, and governor of Normandy, in an expedition made thither. His lordship m. 1st, Blanche, dau. and co-heiress of Sir Philip de la Vacche, K.G., by whom he had a son,

REGINALD, his successor.

He m. 2ndly, Margaret, dau. of William, Lord Ferrers, of Groby, and had another son,

William, aged nineteen, 20th HENRY VI.

His lordship d. in 1442, and was *s.* by his elder son,

SIR REGINALD DE GREY, 7th baron, summoned to parliament from 13 January, 1445, to 14 October, 1495, as "Reginaldo Grey de Wilton, chevalier." His lordship m. Tacina, sister of Owen Tudor, and dying in 1495, was *s.* by his son,

JOHN DE GREY, 8th baron, summoned to parliament as "Johanni Grey de Wilton," 16 January, 1497. In the 1st RICHARD III., this nobleman obtained a grant from the crown of the manor of Wilsamsteda, co. Bedford; and in the 11th HENRY VII., he fought stoutly at Blackheath, against the Cornishmen, then in rebellion, under James, Lord Audley. In the next year he was in the wars of Scotland, under Giles, Lord D'Aubeny. His lordship m. Anne Grey, dau. of Edmund, Earl of Kent, lord-treasurer, and dying before 1506, was *s.* by his son,

SIR EDMUND DE GREY, 9th baron, summoned to parliament, as "Edmundo Grey de Wilton, Chl'r," 17 October, 1509. His lordship m. Florence, dau. and co-heir of Sir Ralph Hastings, 3rd brother of William, 1st Lord Hastings, by whom he had issue,

GEORGE,
THOMAS,
RICHARD,
WILLIAM,
} all successively Lords Grey, of Wilton.
Elizabeth, m. to John Brydges, 1st Lord Chandos.

His lordship d. in 1511, and was *s.* by his eldest son,

GEORGE DE GREY, 10th baron, who d. in minority, and was *s.* by his brother,

THOMAS DE GREY, 11th baron, at whose decease, also in minority, the title devolved upon his brother,

RICHARD GREY, 12th baron, likewise a minor at his decease, when the title devolved upon his brother,

SIR WILLIAM GREY, 13th baron, summoned to parliament from 3 November, 1529, to 5 November, 1558, as "Willielmo Grey de Wilton, Chl'r." This nobleman was one of the commanders in the expedition made into France in the 36th HENRY VIII., under John, Lord Russell; and in the 1st year of EDWARD VI., being then a field-marshal and captain-general of horse in the army sent into Scotland, he placed himself at its head, and in that position made the first charge against the enemy. In the next year his lordship fortified Haddington, fired Dalkeith, and won the castle, spoiling much of the country around Edinburgh; after which, upon the commotions raised in England against the reformation, he marched, at the head of 1500 horse and foot, into Oxfordshire, and immediately restored tranquillity. His lordship was afterwards committed to the Tower as one of the partizans of the Protector Somerset, but was restored to his liberty after the decapitation of that unfortunate nobleman, and the next year made deputy of Calais, and governor of the castle of Guisnes, in Picardy. Lord Grey joined the Duke of Northumberland in his abortive effort to place Lady Jane Grey upon the throne; and it was to him the duke observed, in reference to the multitude of people that stood gazing at them when about to march from London, "Do you see, my Lord, what a conflux of people here is drawn together to see us march?—and yet, of all this multitude, you hear not so much as one that wisheth us success."

As governor of the castle of Guisnes, his lordship, after a gallant defence of that fortress against the French, was obliged to surrender it, and became, with all his officers, prisoner to the Duke of Guise, then commander-in-chief of the French army, by whom he was transferred to Marshal Stozzy, and finally passing to Count Rouchefoucault, he continued in captivity until ransomed for 20,000 crowns, which considerably impaired his fortune. "How he came to be attainted," says Dugdale, "I have not seen; but in the 1st ELIZABETH he was restored in blood;" and the next year being then a knight of the Garter, he was constituted governor of Berwick-upon-Tweed, and warden of the east and middle marches towards Scotland. His lordship m. Mary Somerset, dau. of Charles, Earl of Worcester, and had issue,

ARTHUR, his successor.
William.
Honora, m. to Henry Denny, Esq

Lord Grey d. in 1562, at Cheston, in Hertfordshire, at the house of his son-in-law, Denny; and it was remarked, "that on the same day died the greatest scholar and the greatest soldier of the nobility," namely Henry Manners, Earl of Rutland, and William Grey, Lord Grey, of Wilton. His lordship was *s.* by his elder son,

SIR ARTHUR GREY, 14th baron, summoned to parliament as "Arthuro Grey de Wilton, Chl'r," from 30 September, 1566, to 19 February, 1593. This nobleman was lord lieutenant of Ireland in 1580, and acquired great fame by suppressing the rebellion of Desmond. He was subsequently one of the commissioners who sat in judgment on the unfortunate MARY, Queen of Scots, at Fotheringay. and he afterwards defended Secretary Davison from the accusation of delivering the warrant of execution without the knowledge of ELIZABETH, and, in a long speech, justified the foul murder of the Scottish princess. In the 31st ELIZABETH, he was one of the council of war, for the defence of the ports and havens against the celebrated Armada. His lordship m. 1st, Dorothy, natural dau. of Richard, Lord Zouch, of Harringworth, by whom he had an only dau.,

Elizabeth, m. to Sir Francis Goodwin, by whom she had a son,
Arthur Goodwin, who m. Jane, dau. of Sir Richard Wenman, of Thame, and had an only dau. and heiress,
Jane, who m. Philip, Lord Wharton.

Lord Grey m. 2ndly, Jane-Sibylla, dau. of Sir Richard Morison, Knt., and Countess Dowager of Bedford, and had issue,

THOMAS, his successor.
William, d. s. p. in 1605.
Bridget, m. to Sir Rowland Egerton, Bart.

His lordship, who was a knight of the Garter, d. in 1593, and was *s.* by his elder son,

SIR THOMAS GREY, 15th baron, summoned to parliament from 24 October, 1597, to 27 October, 1601. This nobleman being involved in what has been termed "Raleigh's Conspiracy," was arrested 12 July, 1603, and tried with Lord Cobham, at Winchester, 25 and 26 November following. Sir Dudley Carleton says, that after the abject defence of Cobham, "Grey, quite in another key, began with great assurance and alacrity, telling the lords, the judges, and the king's council, their duties in a long speech, and kept them the whole day to subtle traverses and subterfuges; but the evidence that he was acquainted with the surprise of the king, was too conspicuous, by Broke's and Markham's confessions." "The lords," continues Sir Dudley, "were long ere they could agree, and loth to come out with so hard a censure against him; most of them strove with themselves, and would fain, as it seems, have dispensed with their consciences, to have shewn him favour. After sentence, when he was asked what he would say against its being denounced? he replied, 'I have nothing to say, yet a word of Tacitus comes in my mouth:

'Non eadem omnibus decora.'

The house of Wilton have spent many lives in their prince's service, and Grey cannot ask his.'" His lordship was removed to the Tower, where he d. 6 July. 1614, having received a pardon so far as the remission of the capital part of the sentence: but the barony of Grey of Wilton expired under his lordship's attainder, and his estates became forfeited. Those at Whaddon, in Buckinghamshire, were, after his attainder, leased out to his widow, and after his death granted in fee to the favourite George Villiers, Duke of Buckingham. Wilton Castle, on the banks of the Wye, in Herefordshire, had been sold in the reign of ELIZABETH, to the Hon. Charles Brydges, ancestor to the Dukes of Chandos, and upon the decease of the 1st duke it was, together with other large estates in the neighbourhood, sold to Guy's Hospital. Lord Grey having d. s. p., and his only brother, William, previously, also without issue, his sister of the whole blood, Bridget, wife of Sir Rowland Egerton, of Egerton, in Cheshire, became his heir. Her ladyship's interest in the estates, according to Carte, was purchased by Villiers for £11,000, and the procuring a baronetcy for Sir Rowland. Villiers was subsequently himself created Baron Whaddon, the mansion of the Greys.

From Sir Rowland Egerton, and Bridget Grey, his lady, descended lineally,

Sir Thomas Egerton, the 7th baronet, who was elevated to the peerage, 15 May, 1784, as Baron Grey, of Wilton Castle, co. Hereford, and advanced, 26 June, 1801, to the dignities of *Viscount Grey de Wilton* and EARL OF WILTON, with remainder to the 2nd and younger sons of his dau. Eleanor, who had *m.* in 1794, Robert, Viscount Belgrave, afterwards Marquess of Westminster, and the said honours, at the Earl's decease in 1814, were inherited by his grandson (according to the limitation),

The Hon. Thomas Grosvenor, who assumed the name of Egerton, and became EARL OF WILTON.

Arms—Barry of six, arg. and az., in chief, three torteaux, a label of as many points, arg.

GREY—BARONS GREY, OF ROTHERFIELD, CO. OXFORD.

By Writ of Summons, dated 26 January, 1297.

Lineage.

ROBERT DE GREY, 4th son of Henry de Grey, of Thurroc (*see* BARONS GREY, *of Codnor*), obtained from his brother, Walter de Grey, archbishop of York, a gift of the major part of the lordship of Rotherfield, co. Oxford, and was *s.* by his son,

WALTER DE GREY, to whom the same prelate extended his bounty by a grant of all his lands in Gilesford, in Kent, Brighthelmstone, in Sussex, with Herdewyke and Coges, co. Oxford which he had by assignment from Joan and Alice, the daus. and co-heirs of Robert de Arsic, Baron of Coges, and likewise the residue of the manor of Rotherfield, together with divers other lordships. This Walter d. in 52nd HENRY III., and was *s.* by his son,

ROBERT DE GREY, who *m.* Avice, dau. of William de St. Lis, and dying in 1295, was *s.* by his son,

JOHN DE GREY, then twenty-four years of age, who, soon after doing his homage, had livery of his inheritance; and in the 25th EDWARD I., had summons to the parliament then held at Westminster, as a baron. This nobleman appears to have taken part in the Scottish wars of EDWARD I. His lordship *m.* Margaret, dau. and co-heiress of William de Odingsells, of Maxtock, co. Warwick, and dying 5th EDWARD II., was *s.* by his son,

JOHN DE GREY, 2nd baron, one of the founders of the order of the Garter, *b.* 1300, who in the 15th EDWARD II., making proof of his age, had livery of his lands; and in the 1st EDWARD III., was in the wars of Scotland. In the 6th of

the same reign, upon some difference between his lordship and William le Zouch, of Haryngworth, another great baron, which was heard before the king, Lord Grey, under the irritation of the moment, drew his knife upon Lord Zouch in the royal presence, whereupon both lords were committed to prison; but the Lord Zouch was soon afterwards released, while Lord Grey was remanded, and his lands seized upon by the crown. He was, however, within a short time, upon making submission, restored to favour: and in three years afterwards we find his lordship in Scotland upon the king's service, being of the retinue with Henry, Earl of Lancaster. From this period, for several years, he was engaged in the French wars, and in the 20th of EDWARD's reign, he obtained license to fortify his houses at Rotherfield Grey, co. Oxford, and Sculcotes, co. York, with embattled walls of lime and stone. The next year there being a tournament held at Eltham, in Kent, amongst other accoutrements prepared for that military exercise, his lordship had a hood of white cloth, embroidered with dancing men, in blue habits, buttoned before with large pearls, presented to him by the king. In the 28th EDWARD III., he was one of the commissioners in the cos. Oxford and Berks, for arraying and arming all men of ability within those shires, and leading them against the king's enemies, invasion being at that time threatened by the French. In the next year he was steward of the king's household, and had summons to parliament from the 1st to the 29th EDWARD III. inclusive. His lordship *m.* 1st, Katherine, dau. and co-heiress of Bryan Fitz-Alan, of Bedall, co. York, and had issue,

JOHN, his successor.
Maud, *m.* 1st, to John de Botetourt, of Weoley, and 2ndly, to Thomas de Harcourt.

He *m.* 2ndly, Avice, dau. and co-heir of John, Lord Marmion, and had two sons, John and Robert, who both assumed their mother's name of Marmion (*see* Barons Marmion). Lord Grey d. in 1359, and was *s.* by his eldest son,

JOHN DE GREY, 3rd baron, summoned to parliament as "Johanni de Grey de Rotherfeld," from 20 November, 1360, to 4 October, 1373. His lordship had issue,

JOHN, who *m.* Elizabeth, dau. of Sir Richard de Poynings, Knt., and dying before his father, left issue,
BARTHOLOMEW, who *s.* his grandfather.
ROBERT, who *s.* his brother.
Richard, *d. s. p.*

Robert, who *d.* without male issue, in the 41st EDWARD III

Lord Grey d. in 1375, and was *s.* by his grandson,

BARTHOLOMEW DE GREY, 4th baron, but never summoned to parliament. This nobleman, dying in 1376, *unm.*, the title and estates devolved upon his brother,

ROBERT DE GREY, 5th baron, summoned to parliament in the 1st RICHARD II., but not afterwards. His lordship *m.* Elizabeth, dau. and co-heir of William de la Plaunche, of Haversham, co. Bucks, and by her (who afterwards became the 2nd wife of John, 3rd Lord Clinton) he left at his decease in 1387, an only dau. and heiress,

JOANE, who *m.* in 1401, John, Baron d'Eyncourt, and by him left, at her decease, two daus., viz.,

Alice, *m.* 1st, Ralph Boteler, of Sudeley, who *d. s. p.*, and 2ndly, William, Lord Lovel.
Margaret, *m.* Ralph, Lord Cromwell, of Tatshall, and *d. s. p.*

The barony of Grey, of Rotherfield, vested, eventually, in John, Lord Lovel, son and heir of the above-mentioned Alice d'Eyncourt, by William, Lord Lovel, and passed, at his decease, to his son Francis, Viscount Lovel, K.G., under whose attainder, in 1487, it EXPIRED.

Arms—Same as Grey, of Codnor.

GREY—BARON GREY, OF CODNOR, CO. DERBY.

By Writ of Summons, dated 6 February, 1299.

Lineage.

In the 6th year of King RICHARD I., that monarch conferred the manor of Thurrock, co. Essex (afterwards called Thurrock Grey), upon

HENRY DE GREY, which grant was confirmed by King JOHN, who vouchsafed, by special charter, to permit the said Henry de Grey to hunt the hare and fox in any land belonging to the crown, save the king's own demesne-parks. In the 1st HENRY III. he had also a grant of the manor of Grimston, co. Nottingham, and having afterwards *m.* Isolda, niece and heiress of Robert Bardolf, shared in the inheritance of his lands. By this lady Henry de Grey had issue,

  RICHARD, of whom presently.
  John, some time justice of Chester, progenitor of the Greys of Wilton, and Greys of Ruthyn.
  William, of Landford, co. Notts, and Sandiacre, co. Derby.
  Robert, of Rotherfield.
  Walter, archbishop of York. This prelate lies buried in the cathedral church of York, under a tomb of curious Gothic workmanship, having the bishop's effigy at full length, with his crosier lying at the bottom part.
  Henry.

  RICHARD DE GREY, of Codnor, co. Derby, the eldest son, having adhered to King JOHN, had the lands of John de Humez, in Leicestershire, and Simon de Canci, in Lincolnshire, two of the rebellious barons, conferred upon him; and in the 10th HENRY III he was made governor of the Isles of Guernsey, Jersey, Alderney, and Sarke; of which, in the 36th of the same king, he had a grant, in fee farm, for 400 marks, to be paid yearly into the king's exchequer. In which year the king, intending a pilgrimage to the Holy Land, and causing the bishops of Worcester and Chichester to preach a similar course to the people, this Richard and John, his brother, came forward, although, generally speaking, the discourses of the prelates had but little effect, which so pleased the king, that he embraced them in his arms, kissed them, and called them brothers In a few years afterwards (42nd HENRY III.), we find Richard de Grey constable of Dover Castle and warden of the Cinque Ports, and being both diligent and trusty in those offices, discovered much treasure, which the Poictovins (then in high favour with the king), had ready to convey into France. "But about this time," says Dugdale, "there being no little contest, touching Athelmure, the king's brother, by the mother, then elect bishop of Winchester; divers of the great barons opposing him, in regard he was of that party, against whom they took high exception, for misleading the king, and consuming the wealth of the land. Whereupon he fled to Rome, and by false suggestions, procured the pope's letters for his institution, which were sent by Walescho, a grey friar, who landed at Dover. The barons grew so incensed, that they forthwith sent Hugh Bigot, then justice of England, thither, to inquire, by what authority he was suffered to come on shore; who went to this Richard (then constable of the castle), and said, 'Have you been trusted by the people of England, as a faithful warden of the ports, and suffered this person to land, without our knowledge, to the manifest violation of your oath? We thus tell you, not only unworthy of this place any longer, but to be farther questioned, for so great a transgression, tending to the public damage of the whole realm.' And thereupon took the custody of the castle, and of all the ports into his own hands." Subsequently to this period Richard de Grey arrayed himself under the baronial standard, and being, with his son John, in the army of young Simon de Montfort, at Kenilworth, was surprised in the night-time by a party from Prince Edward's army, and taken prisoner, with several other barons. For this treason his lands were seized upon by the crown; but were afterwards restored, upon the payment of a fine under the decree, denominated "Dictum de Kenilworth." Richard de Grey *m.* Lucia, dau. and heiress of the John de Humes mentioned above, and (with two daus., Agnes, *m.* to Sir William Fitz-William; and Isabel *m.* William, son of Henry de Fauconberg), had a son,

  JOHN DE GREY, who *m.* Lucy, dau. of Reginald, Lord Mohun, *d.* in 1271, and was *s.* by his son,

  HENRY DE GREY, who being in the king's army in Wales, in the 10th EDWARD I., had scutage from all his tenants, in the cos. Norfolk, Suffolk, Kent, Nottingham and Derby, that held of him by military service, and had summons, in the 22nd of the same monarch, amongst other great men, to repair forthwith to the king, to consult about the urgent affairs of the realm, as also to be at Portsmouth, upon the first of the ensuing September, with horse and arms, to attend the king in his expedition into Gascony. After which he had summons to parliament as a baron, from 6 February, 1299, to 6 August, 1308. His lordship was, for several years, actively engaged in the French and Scottish wars in the latter of which he formed one of the immediate retinue of Prince Edward. He *m.* Lady Eleanor, dau. of Courtenay, Earl of Devon, and *d.* 1308, having had two sons, RICHARD, his heir, and Nicholas, of Rydale, co. York. The elder son,

  RICHARD DE GREY, 2nd baron, summoned to parliament from 4 March, 1309, to 3 February, 1335. This nobleman was seneschal of Gascony in the 6th EDWARD II. In the 12th of the same reign he was in the wars of Scotland, and again the next year, when he was in the retinue of Thomas de Brotherton, Earl of Norfolk. In four years after, he was constituted

steward of the duchy of Aquitaine, and within two years appointed constable of Nottingham Castle. In the 7th EDWARD III., he had summons to attend the king at Newcastle, with horse and arms, to march against the Scots, but had a special dispensation from the service in consequence of his bodily infirmities. By Johanna, his wife, his lordship had issue,

  JOHN, his successor,
  Robert, of Cheriton-Grey, co. Somerset, which, with other lands, he inherited from Robert Fitz-Payn, and in consequence assumed the surname of Fitz-Paine. He *m.* Elizabeth, dau. and co-heir of Sir Guy de Bryan, and left an only dau. and heiress, ISABEL, who *m.* Richard, Lord Poynings.

  Richard, Lord Grey, *d.* in 1335, and was *s.* by his elder son,

  JOHN DE GREY, 3rd baron, *b.* 1305, summoned to parliament from 1st April, 1335, to 8 September, 1392, as "Johanni Grey de Codenore." This nobleman, during the lifetime of his father, attained distinction in the Scottish wars, and, after his accession to the title, was engaged in those of Flanders; and so eminent were his services esteemed by the king, that his lordship received, about the 20th year of EDWARD's reign, from the hands of the monarch himself, a hood of white cloth, embroidered with blue men, buttoned before with great pearls; and being to perform divers military exercises in a tournament at Canterbury, had certain accoutrements of Indian silk, whereon the arms of Sir Stephen Cosyngton, Knt., were painted, bestowed upon him by the king. In two years afterwards, he again went into France, continuing in the retinue of Henry, Earl of Lancaster; and in four years subsequently, we find him joined in commission with Lord D'Eincourt, to array all the knights, esquires, and other able persons residing in the counties of Nottingham and Derby, and to conduct them to such places as should be needful for the defence of the realm, there being an invasion threatened at that time by the French. In the 29th EDWARD III., his lordship was once more in France, as he was again in the 33rd. But after all these military services, he obtained license, in the 39th EDWARD III., to go on a pilgrimage; and in the 45th of the same reign, being then very aged, and not able to endure the fatigues of travelling, he had a special dispensation from the king (wherein his great and manifold services were gratefully acknowledged), to exempt him from coming to parliament and councils, and likewise from being charged with setting forth any soldiers whatsoever in the wars of that king, his heirs, or successors. His lordship *m.* Alice de Insula, and had issue,

  HENRY, *m.* Johanna, dau. of Reginald, Lord Cobham, of Sterborough, and dying in the lifetime of his father, left his son,
    RICHARD, who inherited the title.
  John.
  Alice, *m.* to William de Everingham, of Laxton, Notts.

  John, Lord Grey, of Codnor, knight of the Garter, *d.* about the year 1392, and was *s.* by his grandson,

  RICHARD DE GREY, 4th baron. This nobleman, who was in the French wars in the 17th and 21st RICHARD II., was made admiral of the king's fleet from the mouth of the Thames to the northward, in the 2nd HENRY IV., and soon afterwards constituted joint-governor of the castle of Roxborough, in Scotland, with Sir Stephen le Scrope. In the next year he was again in France upon the king's service; and in the 8th of the same monarch, his lordship was constituted constable of the castle of Nottingham, and chief ranger of Shirewood Forest, for life. After this we find him constantly employed upon confidential missions to the courts of France and Scotland, and he had summons to parliament, as "Richardo Grey de Codenore," from 13 November, 1393, to 3 September, 1417, being also a knight of the Garter. His lordship *m.* Elizabeth, dau. and co-heir of Ralph, Lord Basset, of Sapcoate, and had issue,

  JOHN, his successor.
  Henry, successor to his brother.
  William, bishop of Ely, *d.* 1478.
  Elizabeth, *m.* to Sir John Zouche.
  Eleanor, *m.* to Thomas Newport, of Bradford.
  Lucy, *m.* to Sir Rowland Lenthall.

  His lordship *d.* in 1418, and was *s.* by his elder son,

  JOHN DE GREY, 5th baron, summoned to parliament from 26 February, 1420, to 3 August, 1428, as John Grey, of Codnor. This nobleman *d. s. p.* 9th HENRY VI., and was *s.* by his brother,

  HENRY DE GREY, 6th baron, summoned to parliament, as Henry Grey, of Codnor, from 27 November, 1430, to 3 December, 1441. His lordship *m.* Margaret, dau. and co-heir of Sir Henry Percy, of Athol, by whom (who *m.* after his decease, Sir Richard Vere, Knt.), he had an only son, his successor, at his decease in 1443,

Grey.
(B. Grey.)

Hamilton.
(E. Cambridge.)

Hamilton.
(E. Clanbrassill.)

Harcourt.
(E. Harcourt.)

Harington.
(B. Harington.)

Harley.
(E. Oxford.)

Hastings.
(E. Pembroke.)

Hepburn.
(E. Bothwell.)

Herbert.
(E. Powis.)

Holland.
(E. Kent.)

Hungerford.
(B. Hungerford.)

Hyde.
(E. Clarendon.)

HENRY DE GREY, 7th baron, summoned to parliament, from 9 October, 1459, to 14 October, 1495, as "Henrico Grey, Militi," but never with the addition of Codnor. This nobleman much affecting the study of chemistry, obtained, in the 3rd EDWARD IV., a license from the crown to practise the transmutation of metals. His lordship *d.* in 1495, and, leaving no legitimate issue, his estates reverted to his aunts,

Elizabeth, wife of Sir John Zouche, of Codnor;
Eleanor, wife of Thomas Newport;
Lucy, wife of Sir Rowland Lenthall;

amongst whom, the barony of Grey, of Codnor, fell into ABEYANCE, as it continues with their descendants.

Lord Grey left two illegitimate sons,

Richard Grey, to whom he devised the manor of Radcliffe-upon-Trent, co. Notts.
Henry Grey, from whom the Greys of Langley, co. Leicester, descended.

Arms—Barry of six, arg. and az., in chief three torteaux.

NOTE.—"The last Lord Grey, of Codnor," says Leland, "left three daughters, whereof one was married to Sir Rowland Lentalle, of Nottynghamshire; another to Newport, in Shropshire; and the third to one Zouche, a younger brother of the house of the Lord Zouches. These three had the Lord Greyes landes in copartion, whereof the lordship of Ailesford, in Kent, and How Hundred, was parte. There were some of the Lord Greyes, of Codnor, byried at Ailesford Freres."
"Lentalle, dying without issue male, left two daughters, whereof one, called Catherine, was married to one of the Lord Zouches; the other to Cornwale, baron of Burford; and so cam they to be co-partiners in the Lord Grey of Codnor's lands."

GREY—BARONS GREY, OF GROBY, MARQUESSES OF DORSET, DUKE OF SUFFOLK.

Barony, by Writ of Summons, dated 26 September 1449.
Marquessate, created 18 April, 1475.
Dukedom, created 11 October, 1551.

Lineage.

SIR EDWARD GREY, Knt. (eldest son of Reginald, Lord Grey, of Ruthyn, by Joan, his 2nd wife, dau. and he.r of Sir William de Astley, son and heir of Thomas, 7th Lord Astley), *m.* Elizabeth Ferrers, grand-dau. and heir of William Ferrers, Lord Ferrers, of Groby, and was summoned to parli.ment in her right, as *Baron Ferrers, of Groby*, from 14 December, 1446, to 2 January, 1449, and as LORD GREY, OF GROBY, from 23 September, 1449, to 26 May, 1455. That his lordship bore, in 1446, the former title is evident, from a special dispensation, which he obtained 8 November in that year, from John Stafford, then archbishop of Canterbury, whereby, in consequence of the distance of the manor house of Groby from the parish church, and "foulness of the ways thereto," he had license to christen the child, of which his lady was then pregnant, by the vicar of his chapel. The dispensation being addressed thus—"Nobili viro Edmundo Domino de Ferrers de Groby." His lordship had issue,

JOHN (Sir), his successor.
Edward, who *m.* Elizabeth Talbot, eldest dau. of Thomas, Lord L'Isle, and was created Viscount L'Isle. *d.* 1492.
Reginald, slain at the battle of Wakefield, 31 December, 1460.
Anne, *m.* to Sir Edward Hungerford.

He *d.* 18 December, 1457, and was *s.* by his eldest son,

SIR JOHN GREY, 2nd baron, but never summoned to parliament, who *m.* Elizabeth Widville, dau. of Richard Widville, K.G., 1st Earl Rivers, and by her (who *d.* 1492) had issue,

THOMAS (Sir), his successor.
Richard (Sir), beheaded, 1483.

Sir John Grey, who was *b.* 1435, fell 17 February, 1460, at the battle of St. Albans, fighting under the colours of Lancaster. His widow becoming subsequently a suitor to King EDWARD IV., for some lands which had been given to her in jointure, the king was so enamoured of her beauty and gracefulness, that he, upon his part, became a suitor to the lady. But she, it is said, wisely answered him when he became importunate, "that as she did account herself too base to be his wife, so she did think herself too good to be his harlot." The result is well known. The king married her, and thereby incurred the wrath of the Earl of Warwick, which had nearly lost him his crown. In consequence of this great alliance her eldest son,

SIR THOMAS GREY, was created, 4 August, 1471, *Earl of*

Huntingdon,* and advanced, 18 April, 1475, to the MARQUESSATE OF DORSET, *only* "per Cincturam Gladii et Capœ Honoris impositionem." On which day he sat in his habit at the upper end of the table, among the knights, in St. Edward's chamber; and in the 22nd EDWARD IV., had livery of his lands without making proof of his age. But on the death of King EDWARD he was attainted of high treason, 1st RICHARD III., owing to his near relationship to the young King EDWARD V.; he was, however, fortunate enough to make his escape into Britanny, and joined the Earl of Richmond, who, after the battle of Bosworthfield, having ascended the throne, as HENRY VII., sent for the Marquess of Dorset, and restored him to all his honours. His lordship subsequently enjoyed the favour of the king. although at one time he was committed to the Tower. In the 7th HENRY VII. he was with the army sent to assist the Emperor MAXIMILIAN against the French; and in four years afterwards we find him one of the commanders who vanquished Lord Audley and the rebels at Blackheath. His lordship *m.* 1st, Anne, dau. and heir of Henry Holland, Duke of Exeter, and 2ndly, Cecilia, dau. and heir of William, Lord Bonvile and Harrington, and had issue,

I. Edward. *d. s. p.*　　　　II. Anthony.
III. THOMAS, his successor.
IV. Richard, *m.* Florence Pudsey, who had a son Henry, who *d. s. p.*
V. John, *m.* Anne, dau. of William Barlow, and *d. s. p.*
VI. Leonard, created Viscount Graney of the kingdom of Ireland, executed 31st HENRY VIII.
VII. George, in holy orders.
I. Cecily, *m.* to John Sutton, Lord Dudley.
II. Bridget.　　　　　　III. Anne.
IV. Dorothy, *m.* 1st, to Robert, Lord Willoughby de Broke, and 2ndly, to William, Lord Mountjoy.
V. Elizabeth, *m.* to Gerald Fitz-Gerald, 9th Earl of Kildare.
VI. Margaret, *m.* to Richard Wake, of Blisworth.
VII. Eleanor, *m.* to Sir John Arundel, of Lanhern, co. Cornwall.
VIII. Mary, *m.* to Walter, Viscount Hereford.

The Marquess, who was a knight of the Garter, *d.* in 1501, and was *s.* by his eldest son,

THOMAS GREY, who was summoned to parliament 17 October, 1509, as *Lord Ferrers, of Groby*, but in the second parliament, in 1511, as MARQUESS OF DORSET. This nobleman, in the 3rd HENRY VIII., was commander-in-chief of the army sent about the beginning of May into Spain, consisting of ten thousand men, whereof a moiety were archers, who, along with their bows and arrows, carried halberts, which they pitched in the ground until their arrows were shot, and then resumed them to charge the enemy. In this expedition were also his lordship's brothers, Lord Thomas Howard, son and heir of the Earl of Surrey, and the Lords Brooke, Willoughby, and Ferrers. This armament returned, however, to England, without performing any service. It was designed as an augmentation of the forces of the Emperor FERDINAND in the invasion of Guyenne, but that monarch proposing another designation, not warranted by the commission which the general had received, he thought it his duty to re-embark, not, however, before he had lost some of his soldiers by sickness, and suffered indisposition himself. In two years afterwards the marquess and his brothers were with the Duke of Suffolk in France, at a just at St. Denis, where he acquired singular honour, as also in those celebrated tournaments, the 12th HENRY VIII., at the interview, in Picardy, between the English and French monarchs. In the 14th of the same reign his lordship was sent to Calais, to attend the Emperor, CHARLES V., into England, who was at that period so sumptuously entertained by King HENRY, being himself lodged in Black Friers, and his train in the king's (then newly beautified,) palace at Bridewell. "This Thomas, Marquess of Dorset, was esteemed the best general of those times for embattling an army, always observing the number, strength, and experience of his camp, and the nature and extent of the place, as well as the time, ground, persons, and quality of his enemies. And he was ever careful of good pay, lest his soldiers mutinied; of good diet and quarters, lest they failed; and of order, discipline, and temperance, lest they should be confused by sudden attacks, or enfeebled by sickness and distemper. His speech was soldier-like, plain, short, smart, and material; and notwithstanding the times could not endure his virtues, nor he their vices; he died full of honour at court, and applause in the country, with this monument from the king, (HENRY VIII.,) 'That honest and good man.' The collegiate church of Astley, co. Warwick, (founded by Thomas, Lord Astley, whose heiress general *m.* the ancestor of this marquess,) a most rare and beautiful piece of workmanship, having fallen down, a new chancel was erected by the parishioners. When, on opening

---

* This dignity he relinquished upon being created Marquess of Dorset.

the vault where the body of the marquess was laid, a large and long coffin of wood was found, which, at the curious desire of some, being burst open, the body, which had lain there seventy-eight years, appeared perfect in every respect, neither perished nor hardened, but the flesh, in colour, proportion, and softness, alike to any ordinary corpse newly interred. The body was about five feet eight inches in length. the face broad, and the hair yellow. All which seemed so well preserved from the strong embalming thereof." The marquess was one of those lords who, in the 22nd HENRY VIII., signed the celebrated letter to Pope Clement, touching the king's divorce: and was also one who subscribed the forty-four articles of impeachment against Cardinal Wolsey. His lordship *m.* 1st, Eleanor, dau. of Oliver, Lord St. John, but had no issue. He *m.* 2ndly, Margaret, dau. of Sir Robert Wotton, Knt., of Bocton, in Kent, by whom he had (with other issue),

I. HENRY, his successor.
II. Edward, *d. s. p.*
III. Thomas, beheaded, 23 April, 1554.
IV. John, of Pirgo, co. Essex, from whom the present Earl of Stamford derives.
I. Mary, *s. p.*
II. Catherine, *m.* Henry, Earl of Arundel.
III. Elizabeth, *m.* 1st, Thomas, Lord Audley, of Walden; and 2ndly, George Norton.
IV. Anne, *m.* to Sir Henry Willoughby, of Wollaton, Notts.

This eminent personage *d.* in 1530, and was *s.* by his eldest son, HENRY GREY, 3rd Marquess of Dorset, who in the 1st EDWARD VI., was constituted lord high constable of England, for three days only, by reason of the solemnity of the king's coronation. In the fourth of the same reign, he was made justice in eyre of all the king's forests, and the next year warden of the east, west, and middle Marches, towards Scotland. His lordship was created DUKE OF SUFFOLK, 11 October, 1551, and installed a knight of the most noble order of the Garter. He *m.* 1st, Katherine, dau. of William, Earl of Arundel, but by her had no issue. His grace *m.* 2ndly, Frances Brandon, eldest dau. and co-heir of Charles, Duke of Suffolk, by Mary, dowager Queen of France, and sister of King HENRY VIII., by whom he had

JANE, who *m.* Lord Guildford Dudley, and having aspired to the crown, at the decease of EDWARD VI., suffered decapitation for high treason. with her husband, Lord Guildford Dudley. In Walpole's Catalogue of Noble Authors, he terms the Lady Jane Grey, "this admirable young heroine," and the fairest ornament of her sex. "The works of this lovely scholar's writing," he says "are four Latin epistles; three to Bullinger, and one to her sister, the Lady Katherine, which was written the night before her death, in a Greek Testament, in which she had been reading, and sent to her sister. Her conference with Feckenham, Abbot of Westminster, who was deputed to convert her to the Catholic religion. A letter to Dr. Harding, her father's chaplain, who had apostatised a prayer for her own use, under imprisonment. Four Latin verses written in prison, with a pin." Her speech on the scaffold; and various others, of which mention is made by Faker and Hollingshed.
Katherine, *m.* 1st, Henry, Lord Herbert, eldest son of William, Earl of Pembroke, from whom she was divorced. Her ladyship *m.* 2ndly, Edward Seymour, Earl of Hertford, but not having the permission of Queen ELIZABETH, she was committed, as well as her husband, to the Tower, where she *d.* 26 January, 1567; having had, by her first husband, three sons: Edward, the eldest, who *d.* young; Thomas, the youngest, who *m.* Isabel, dau. of Edward Onley, Esq., of Catesby, co. Northampton, and died without issue—and
EDWARD, Lord Beauchamp, who *m.* Honora, dau. of Sir Richard Rogers, Knt., and left two sons, William, Marquess of Hertford, and Francis, Lord Seymour, of Trowbridge; the elder son, WILLIAM, MARQUESS OF HERTFORD, *m.* 1st, Lady Arabella Stuart; and 2ndly, Lady Frances Devereux, by the latter of whom he had a son HENRY, LORD BEAUCHAMP, whose dau. and eventual heiress, Elizabeth, having *m.* Thomas Bruce, 1st Earl of Ailesbury, had issue,
CHARLES, Earl of Ailesbury, whose eldest dau. and co-heir, Mary, *m.* Henry Brydges, Marquess of Carnarvon; afterwards 2nd Duke of Chandos, and her grand-dau. ANNA-ELIZA, who *m.* 16 April, 1796, Richard, 2nd Marquess of Buckingham and Chandos, was sole representative of this branch of the Grey family; and of Frances, eldest dau. of Charles Brandon, Duke of Suffolk, and his wife Mary, Queen Dowager of France, sister of King HENRY VIII.

Mary, *m.* to Martin Keyes, Groom Porter to Queen ELIZABETH, and *d. s. p.* 1578.

Upon the demise of King EDWARD VI., the Duke of Suffolk, at the instigation of Dudley, Duke of Northumberland, (father of Lord Guildford Dudley,) proclaimed his dau. the LADY JANE GREY, QUEEN OF ENGLAND, upon the allegation that the deceased monarch had so designated her ladyship in his will. This attempt proving abortive, the unhappy lady and her youthful husband, with her father-in-law, the ambitious Northumberland, were brought to the block, while Suffolk himself

250

was reserved for a subsequent fate, for joining in Wyat's rebellion, he made an effort to raise the people in the cos. of Warwick and Leicester, but being pursued by the Earl of Huntingdon, at the head of some forces, he was obliged to conceal himself within a hollow tree, in his park, at Astley, when being betrayed by Underwood, one of the keepers in whom he had confided, he was delivered up to his enemies, and beheaded on Tower Hill, 23 February, 1554; being also attainted, his honours, viz., the Dukedom of Suffolk, the Barony of Grey, of Groby, the Marquessate of Dorset, and the Baronies of Astley, Bonvile and Harrington, became EXTINCT.

Arms—Barry of six, arg. and az., three torteaux in chief, and a label of three points, ermine.

GREY — EARL OF TANKERVILLE, AND BARONS GREY, OF POWIS.

Earldom by Letters Patent, dated 31 January, 1418.
Barony by Writ of Summons, dated 15 November, 1482.

Lineage.

EDWARD DE CHERLTON, Lord Powys, whose ancestor had been summoned to parliament in that dignity, in the 7th EDWARD II., *d.* in 1422, leaving two daus., his co-heirs, (between whom the barony fell into abeyance,) namely,

JOAN, *m.* to Sir John de Grey, of whom we are about to treat.
JOYCE, *m.* to John, Lord Tiptoft, and had issue,
JOHN, created Earl of Worcester, who was attainted of treason, 10th EDWARD IV., 1478.

The husband of the elder dau.,
SIR JOHN DE GREY, Knt., who was son of Sir Thomas Grey, of Berwyke, co. Northumberland, by Jane, dau. of John, Lord Moubray, was a very eminent military character in the time of HENRY V. In the 2nd of that monarch's reign, he was with the king at the siege of Caen, and behaved himself so valiantly, that he had a grant of the castle and lordship of Tilye, in Normandy, then forfeited by Sir William Harcourt, an adherent of the king's enemies. He was subsequently sent with a guard into Powisland, where Sir John Oldcastle, the chief of the Lollards, had been taken, to bring that unfortunate personage before parliament. The next year, (6th HENRY V.,) being again in the French wars, we find him Captain of Maunt, and obtaining, in further consideration of his services, a grant of the EARLDOM OF TANKERVILLE, in Normandy, to hold by homage, and delivery of a bassinet, or helmet, at the castle of Roan, on the feast of St. George, yearly. Continuing in those wars, his lordship had several further grants, and was made governor of the castle of Tournay. But he was soon after slain, (at the battle of Baugy Bridge,) in fording a river, near the castle of Beaufort, with the Duke of Clarence, and divers others of the English nobility. His lordship was *s.* by his son,
SIR HENRY GREY, Knt., as Earl of Tankerville. This nobleman being young at the time of his father's decease, (9th HENRY V.) had not livery of his lands until the 20th HENRY V., yet the 4th year of that reign, he was knighted, by John, Duke of Bedford: at which time, the king himself received the same honour, at Leicester. He *m.* Antigone, natural dau. of Humphrey Plantagenet, Duke of Gloucester, and dying in the 28th HENRY VI., (1449,) left issue,
RICHARD, his successor.
Humphrey, who *d.* without issue.
Elizabeth, *m.* to Sir Roger Kynaston, Knt., from whom lineally descended,
John Kynaston, Esq., who claimed the Barony of Grey de Powis, in 1731. He *d.* in 1733, and was *s.* by his elder surviving son,
Edward Kynaston, Esq., who *d. s. p.* in 1772, and was *s.* by his brother,
Roger Kynaston, Esq., who *m.* Mary, only child of Henry Powell, Esq., of Worthen, co. Salop, and dying in 1788, was *s.* by his eldest son,
John Kynaston, who assumed, by sign manual, the additional surname of POWELL. This gentleman claimed unsuccessfully, in 1800, the Barony of Powis. He was subsequently created a baronet in 1818. (See KYNASTON, BURKE's *Peerage and Baronetage.*)

The elder son,
RICHARD GREY, Earl of Tankerville, adhering to the house of York, was attainted, with divers others, in the 38th HENRY VI. He was with the Earl of Warwick at the siege of

Alnwick Castle, in the 2nd EDWARD IV. "It does not appear," says Nicolas, "that this nobleman was ever summoned to parliament, but strong evidence exists that he sat in that assembly as a baron of the realm, in 1455." His lordship *m.* Margaret, dau. of James, Lord Audley, and dying 6th EDWARD VI., left issue,

JOHN, of whom hereafter.

And a (presumed) dau.,

Elizabeth, who *m.* Sir John Ludlow, of Hodnet, co. Salop, and had issue,

ANNE, *m.* to Thomas Vernon, Esq., of Stokesley, from whom descended through his dau., Eleanor Vernon, who *m.* Francis Curzon, Esq., of Kedleston, Sir Nathaniel Curzon, Bart., who opposed the claim of Mr. Kynaston, to the Barony of Powis, and from whom the Lords Scarsdale derive.

Alice, *m.* to Humphrey Vernon, Esq., (brother of the above Thomas), from whom descended,

Sir Henry Vernon, Bart., (so created in 1660,) who left a dau. Elizabeth (who *m.* Robert Cholmondeley, Esq., and was ancestor of the HEBERS of HODNET), and a son,

Sir Thomas Vernon, 2nd baronet, who *d.* in 1684, leaving two daus., Diana and Harriot, who both *d. unm.*, and a son, his successor,

Sir Richard Vernon, 3rd baronet, at whose decease *unm.*, his title and line became EXTINCT.

The Earldom of Tankerville, fell not only by the attainder of the earl, but France being lost to the English crown, it shared a similar fate. His lordship's son,

JOHN GREY, who obtained livery of his lands, in the 20th EDWARD IV., without making proof of his age, was summoned to parliament as a baron, under the designation of "Johanni Grey de Powes," from 15 November, 1482, 22 EDWARD IV., to 16 January, 1497, 12th HENRY VII. His lordship *m.* Anne Herbert, dau. of William, Earl of Pembroke, and dying in 1497, was *s.* by his son,

JOHN GREY, 2nd Baron Grey, of Powis, who *m.* Margaret, dau. of Edward, Lord Dudley, and dying in 1504. was *s.* by his son,

SIR EDWARD GREY, 3rd Baron Grey, of Powis, summoned to parliament, from 3 November, 1529, to 23 January, 1552. This nobleman accompanied the Duke of Suffolk, 15th HENRY VIII., in the expedition then made into France, and was at the taking of Bray and other places, won, at that time, from the French. His lordship *m.* Anne Brandon, dau. and co-heir of Charles, Duke of Suffolk, by whom he had no issue. He had illegitimate children by one Jane Orwell, namely, Edward, Anne, Jane, and — Grey, upon whom he entailed the greater part of his estates, composing the Barony of Powis. His lordship *d.* in 1552, when the Barony of Grey de Powis fell, it is supposed, into ABEYANCE, but between whom, has not been determined. Sir Harris Nicolas, in his *Synopsis of the Peerage* (an admirable and much improved edition of which has been produced by Mr. Courthope, *Somerset Herald*, under the title of "the Historic Peerage"), deems the BARONY OF GREY DE POWIS created by the summons of EDWARD IV., not a continuation of that of CHERLETON OF POWIS, but a new and distinct peerage, and if he be right, the former is EXTINCT.

Arms—Gu., a lion rampant, within a border, engrailed, arg.

GREY—BARONS L'ISLE, VISCOUNTS L'ISLE.

Barony, by Letters Patent, dated in 1475.
Viscounty, by Letters Patent, dated 28 June, 1483.

Lineage.

SIR EDWARD GREY, Knt., 2nd son of Edward Grey, Lord Ferrers, of Groby, having *m.* Elizabeth Talbot, eldest dau. of John Talbot, Viscount L'Isle, and sister and co-heir of Thomas Talbot, last Viscount L'Isle of that family, was created in the 15th EDWARD IV., BARON L'Isle, the patent reciting to the effect of the preamble in that granted to John Talbot (see Talbot, Viscount L'Isle), and further stating, "that the said John Talbot had issue, Thomas, late Viscount L'Isle, and Elizabeth, then the wife of Edward Grey, Lord L'Isle, and Margaret, late the wife of George Vere; that the manor of Kingston L'Isle, descended to Thomas, late Viscount L'Isle, and that he dying *s. p.*, the manor descended to Elizabeth and Margaret, as his heirs, and Margaret, dying without issue, Edward Grey, Lord L'Isle, and Elizabeth, his wife, were seised

251

in fee of the manor, in right of Elizabeth, and had issue, John and others; the king, therefore, considering the premises, and that Warine L'Isle before mentioned, by reason of the lordship and manor of Kingston L'Isle, aforesaid, had the dignity of Baron and Lord de L'Isle, &c., recognized the right to the dignity of Edward Grey, and the heirs of his body, by the aforesaid Elizabeth, and granted the said barony to him, and the heirs of his body by the said Elizabeth." His lordship was subsequently created VISCOUNT L'ISLE, also by patent, dated 28 June, 1483. This nobleman in the 14th EDWARD IV., was retained by indenture to serve the king, in his "Duchy of Normandy and realm of France," for one whole year, with seven spears and fifty archers. In the 4th HENRY VII., he was one of the commissioners for choosing archers in the co. Warwick, for the relief of the Duchy of Britanny. By the heiress of Talbot (who *d.* 8 September, 1487), his lordship had issue,

JOHN, his successor.
Anne, *m.* to John Willoughby.
Elizabeth, *m.* 1st, to Edmund Dudley, so notorious in the reign of HENRY VII., and had, with other issue,

JOHN DUDLEY, created VISCOUNT L'ISLE (see Dudley, Viscount L'Isle).

Muriel, *m.* to Henry Stafford, Earl of Wiltshire, and *d. s. p.*

The viscount had a 2nd wife, Jane, who survived him, but he had no issue by her. He *d.* in 1492, and was *s.* by his son,

JOHN GREY, 2nd Viscount L'Isle, who *m.* Muriel Howard, dau. of Thomas, Duke of Norfolk, and dying in 1512, left an only dau. and heiress,

ELIZABETH GREY,

Upon the decease of Lord L'Isle, the Viscounty of L'Isle expired, but the barony must have devolved upon his dau., as his sole heiress, and likewise tenant of the manor of Kingston L'Isle. This lady was contracted to Charles Brandon (afterwards Duke of Suffolk), who was therefore created Viscount L'Isle, but refusing when at majority to fulfil the contract, the patent was cancelled. She afterwards *m.* Henry Courtenay, 2nd Earl of Devon, but *d. s. p.* before 1526, leaving her aunt Elizabeth, her father's only surviving sister, her heir, and who being seised of the manor of Kingston L'Isle, and heir general of John Talbot, Viscount L'Isle, is presumed to be legally entitled to the Barony of L'Isle, both under that patent, of 26 June. 1443, and under that to Edward Grey, her father; at her decease both these qualifications devolved upon her son (by her 1st husband), John Dudley,* but who never enjoyed the dignity; he was, however, created Viscount L'Isle (see Dudley, Lord L'Isle).

Arms—Barrule of six, arg. and az., in chief three torteaux, a label, arg.

GREY — EARLS OF KENT, VISCOUNT GOODERICH, OF GOODERICH CASTLE, CO. HEREFORD, EARL OF HAROLD, CO. BEDFORD, MARQUESS OF KENT, DUKE OF KENT, MARQUESS DE GREY.

Earldom of Kent, 3 May, 1465.
Marquessate of Kent, and minor honours, 14 December, 1706.
Dukedom, 28 April, 1710.
Marquisate, 9 May, 1740.

Lineage.

EDMUND GREY. 4th Lord Grey, of Ruthyn, having espoused the cause of the Yorkists, after the battle of Northampton, obtained from King EDWARD IV., the estate of Ampthill, co. Bedford, and other lands, which had belonged to the Lord Fanhope, and was subsequently made lord treasurer of England. Leland gives the following account of this nobleman's conduct upon that occasion. "In the time of the civil war betwixt King HENRY VI. and King EDWARD IV, there was a

---

* Sir John Dudley, sold the manor of Kingston L'Isle, to Mr. Hyde, from whom it passed in lineal succession to John Hyde, Esq., who *d.* seised thereof, in May, 1745, and his widow sold the same in the following year to Abraham Atkins, Esq., of Clapham, in Surrey, whose case, as claimant to the Barony of L'Isle, as possessor of the manor of Kingston L'Isle, and consequently assignee of John Talbot, 1st Viscount L'Isle, was drawn up by the Hon. Hume Campbell, in 1790, under the title of "Case of the Barony of L'Isle."

battle fought without the south suburbs of Northampton. The Lord Fanhope took totally King HENRY's part. The Lord Grey, of Ruthyn, did the same in countenance; but a little afore the field, he practised with King EDWARD. Others saying that he had a title to the Lord Fanhope's lands at Antehille, and thereabout, or depraving him with false accusations, so wrought with King EDWARD, that he, with all his strong band of Walshemen, fell to King EDWARD's part, upon promise, that if EDWARD wan the field, he should have Antehille, and such lands as Fanhope had there. EDWARD wan the field, and Grey obtained Antehille, *cum pertinentiis*, &c.[*] His lordship appears to have attained in a very great degree the favour of King EDWARD, who besides conferring the treasurership upon him, created him (he then bearing the titles of Lord Hastings, Weaford, and Ruthyn), EARL OF KENT, with limitation to his heirs male. Which dignity was confirmed by King RICHARD III., and afterwards by HENRY VII., so that his lordship seems to have played the part of the vicar of Bray, long before that celebrated divine is supposed to have existed; and to have reposed in equal security upon a bed of *white* or *red roses*. The earl *m.* Katherine Percy, dau. of Henry, Earl of Northumberland, and had surviving issue,

Anthony, *d. unm. v. p.*
GEORGE, his successor.   John.
Elizabeth, *m.* to Sir Robert Greystock, Knt., son and heir of Ralph, Lord Greystock.
Anne, *m.* to John, Lord Grey, of Wilton.

His lordship *d.* in 1489, and was *s.* by his eldest surviving son,

GEORGE GREY, 5th Baron Grey de Ruthyn, and 2nd Earl of Kent, who, being a military commander of high reputation, was one of the principal persons in the army, sent the 7th HENRY VII. into France, under Jasper Tudor, Duke of Bedford, to the assistance of the Emperor MAXIMILIAN, but which army returned in a short time, without achieving any memorable action, by reason that MAXIMILIAN, for want of money, was unable to make his appearance. The earl was afterwards the chief commander against the Cornish men, who had risen under Lord Audley, and defeated those insurgents at Blackheath. His lordship *m.* 1st, Anne, dau. of Richard Wldville, Earl Rivers, and widow of William, Viscount Bouchier, by whom he had an only son, RICHARD, his successor. He *m.* 2ndly, Katherine Herbert, dau. of William, Earl of Pembroke, and had issue,

HENRY (Sir), of Wrest, who inherited as 4th earl.
George, *d. unm.*
Anthony, of Branspeth, whose grandson, the REV. ANTHONY GREY, rector of Burbache, inherited as 9th earl.
Anne, *m.* to John, Lord Hussey.

The earl *d.* in 1504, and was *s.* by his eldest son,
RICHARD GREY, 6th Baron Grey de Ruthyn, and 3rd Earl of Kent, K.G. This nobleman attended King HENRY VIII., at the siege of Therouenne; but becoming an inveterate gamester, he wasted the whole of his estate, and *d.* in poverty at the sign of the George, in Lombard-street, within the city of London, *anno* 1523. He *m.* Elizabeth, dau. of Sir William Hussey, Knt., chief justice of the King's Bench, and sister of John, Lord Hussey, but having no issue, the honours devolved upon his half brother,
SIR HENRY GREY, of Wrest, co. Bedford, who should have been 7th Baron Grey de Ruthyn, and 4th Earl of Kent, but from the narrowness of his estate he declined assuming the peerage. He *m.* Anne, dau. of John Blanerhasset, Esq., by whom he had an only son,

HENRY, who *d.* in the lifetime of his father, *anno* 1545. This gentleman *m.* Margaret, dau. of John St. John Esq., of Bletsho, by whom he had issue,

REGINALD,
HENRY,   } successively Earls of Kent.
CHARLES,

Katherine. *m.* 1st, — Spencer, Esq.; and 2ndly, — Slayton, Esq., but *d. s. p.*

Sir Henry Grey *d.* in 1562, and was *s.* by his grandson,
REGINALD GREY, 8th Baron Grey de Ruthyn, and 5th Earl of Kent, which honours, having by frugality much improved his fortune, he assumed in 1571, and sat as one of the peers on the trial of the Duke of Norfolk in two years afterwards. His lordship *m.* Susan, dau. of Richard Bertie, Esq., and Katherine, Duchess of Suffolk, but dying *s. p.* in 1572-3 was *s.* by his brother,

SIR HENRY GREY, as 9th Baron Grey de Ruthyn, and 6th Earl of Kent. This nobleman was one of the peers on the trial of the unhappy Mary of Scotland (29th ELIZABETH), and "evinced," says Dugdale, "much more zeal for her destruction than befitted a person of honour." His lordship *m.* Mary, dau. of Sir John Cotton, and widow of Edward, Earl of Derby, by whom he had no issue, and dying in 1615, was *s.* by his brother,

CHARLES GREY, 10th Baron Grey de Ruthyn, and 7th Earl of Kent. His lordship *m.* Susan, dau. of Sir Richard Cotton, of Bedhampton, co. Hants, and had issue,

HENRY, his successor.
Susan, heir to her brother, *m.* Sir Michael Longueville, and her son,
CHARLES LONGUEVILLE, was confirmed in the barony of Grey de Ruthyn, in 1640. His lordship *d.* in 1643, leaving an only dau. and heiress,
SUSAN LONGUEVILLE, Baroness Grey de Ruthyn, who *m.* Sir Henry Yelverton, Bart., and from this marriage descended,
BARBARA YELVERTON, Baroness Grey de Ruthyn, who *d.* 18 November, 1858, when the barony of Grey de Ruthyn devolved on her son the MARQUESS OF HASTINGS, and at his death *s. p.* 1868, fell into abeyance between his sisters.

The earl *d.* in 1625, and was *s.* by his son,
HENRY GREY, 11th Baron Grey de Ruthyn, and 8th Earl of Kent, who *m.* Elizabeth, dau. and co-heir of Gilbert Talbot, Earl of Shrewsbury, but *d.* in 1639 *s. p.*; when the Barony of Grey de Ruthyn, devolved upon his sister, Susan, Lady Longueville, and has since been enjoyed by her descendants; while the Earldom of Kent passed according to the limitation to his distant relation (revert to children of George, 2nd earl),
THE REV. ANTHONY GREY, rector of Burbache, co. Leicester, as 9th Earl of Kent. This nobleman resisted strenuously the claim of Charles Longueville, to the Barony of Grey de Ruthyn, upon the plea, "that when a barony by writ was once involved in an earldom, it should wait upon such earldom, and might not be subsequently transferred to another family, by a dau. and heiress, so long as the earldom continued in the male." But the decision was against his lordship, and it established the point, that an earldom, or other superior dignity, does not attract a barony in fee. The earl *m.* Magdelene, dau. of William Purefoy, Esq., of Caldecote, co. Warwick, by whom he had, with other issue,

HENRY, his successor.
John.   Bob.   Theophilus.
Nathaniel.
Grace, *m.* to James Ward, Esq.
Magdelen, *m.* to John Brown, Esq.
Christian, *m.* to — Burdet, Esq.
Patience, *m.* to — Wood, Esq.
Priscilla.

His lordship *d.* in 1643, and was *s.* by his eldest son,
HENRY GREY, 10th Earl of Kent, who *m.* 1st, Mary, dau. of Sir William Courteen, Knt., by whom he had a son,

Henry, who *d.* young, in the earl's lifetime.

His lordship *m.* 2ndly, Amabel, dau. of Sir Anthony Benn, recorder of London, and widow of the Hon. Anthony Fane, a younger son of Francis, Earl of Westmoreland, by whom he had issue,

ANTHONY, his successor.
Elizabeth, *m.* to Banastre Maynard, 3rd Lord Maynard.

The earl *d.* in 1651, and his lady, who, from her numerous acts of benevolence, was called the "Good Countess," lived to the advanced age of ninety-two, surviving her husband forty-seven years. The earl was *s.* by his only son,
ANTHONY GREY, 11th Earl of Kent. His lordship *m.* Mary, dau. and heiress of John, 1st Baron Lucas, of Shenfield, co. Essex, which lady was created, 7 May, 1663, BARONESS LUCAS, *of Crudwell, co. Wilts*, with remainder to her heirs male by the said earl; failing which, "the title not to be suspended, but to be enjoyed by such of the daus. and co-heirs, if any shall be, as other indivisible inheritances, by the common law of this realm, are usually possessed." The earl had issue by her ladyship,

HENRY, his successor.
Amabel, who *d. unm.*

His lordship *d.* in 1702, and was *s.* by his only son,
HENRY GREY, Lord Lucas (a dignity which he had inherited at the decease of his mother in 1700), as 12th Earl of Kent. His lordship was created, 14 December, 1706, *Viscount Goodrich, of Goodrich Castle, co. Hereford; Earl of Harold, co. Bedford*, and MARQUESS OF KENT. On 22 April, 1710, his lordship obtained a dukedom, as DUKE OF KENT, and in three years

---

[*] This account seems however quite erroneous, for Lysons, in his "Magna Britannia," relates, that the Lord Fanhope *d.* in peace at Ampthill, 17 years before the battle.

252

afterwards was installed a knight of the Garter. At the demise of Queen ANNE, he was one of the lords entrusted with the administration of the kingdom, until the arrival of his majesty, King GEORGE I., by whom he was received with so much favour as to have several of the most honourable and important places and offices· at court conferred upon him. Nor was he less esteemed by King GEORGE II., at whose coronation he carried St. Edward's staff, and was afterwards constituted lord-lieutenant and custos-rotulorum of the county of Bedford. His grace m. 1st, Jemima, eldest dau. of Thomas, Lord Crewe, of Steane, by whom he had, with two other sons who both d. young,

1. ANTHONY, Earl of Harold, who was summoned to parliament as Lord Lucas, of Crudwell, in 1719, and the next year appointed one of the lords of the bedchamber. His lordship m Lady Mary Tufton, dau. of Thomas, Earl of Thanet; but d. s. p. in 1723. His death is mentioned as having arisen from an ear of barley which his lordship had inadvertently put into his mouth, by which he was choked.

II Henry, d. in the twenty-first year of his age, in 1717.

1. Amabel, m. John, 3rd Earl of Breadalbane; and dying in 1727, left an only dau.,

  Lady Jemima Campbell, who m. Philip, 2nd Earl of Hard-wicke, and had two daus.,

    Amabel, who s. as Baroness Lucas, and was created Countess de Grey.

    Mary-Jemima, m. to Thomas Robinson, 2nd Lord Gran-tham, and had issue,

      Thomas-Philip, EARL DE GREY, who d. 1859, leaving two daus.,

        Anne-Florence, Baroness Lucas, m. George-Augus-tus, 6th Earl Cowper; and d. 23 July, 1880, when she was s. by her eldest son,

          FRANCIS THOMAS DE GREY, 7th Earl Cowper, as 7th Baron Lucas, K.G.

        Mary-Gertrude, m. to Capt. Henry Vyner.

      Frederick-John, Earl of Ripon, father of the Marquess of Ripon, K.G.

II. Jemima, m. to John, 1st Earl of Ashburnham.

III. Anne, m. to Lord Charles Cavendish, brother of William, Duke of Devonshire.

IV. Mary, m. to Dr. Gregory, dean of Christ Church.

His grace m. 2ndly, Sophia, dau. of William, Duke of Devon-shire, by whom he had a son, who d. in infancy, and a dau.,

  Anne-Sophia, m. John Egerton, D.D., Bishop of Durham.

The duke was created MARQUIS DE GREY 9 May, 1740, with limitation to himself and his issue male ; and in default thereof to his grand-dau., Lady Jemima Campbell, and her issue male. His grace d. 5 June, 1741, when all his honours became EXTINCT, save the MARQUISATE DE GREY and the BARONY OF LUCAS, which devolved upon his aforesaid grand-dau., then Lady Jemima York, at whose decease, in 1770, without male issue, the MARQUISATE also became EXTINCT; but her ladyship's eldest dau., Lady Amabel York, who m. in 1772, Alexander, Lord Polwarth (created a British peer, as Lord Hume, of Berwick), s. to the BARONY OF LUCAS (now inherited by Earl Cowper), and was created, 5 October, 1816, COUNTESS DE GREY, with remainder in default of male issue, to her sister, Jemima, Lady Grantham, and her male issue, a dignity now inherited by the Marquess of Ripon.

Arms—Barry of six, arg. and az. ; in chief three torteaux.

GREY, EARL OF WARRINGTON—BARON DELAMER.

(*See* ADDENDA.)

GREY—VISCOUNT GRANEY.

By Letters Patent, dated 2 January, 1535.

Lineage.

LORD LEONARD GREY (2nd son of Thomas, 1st Marquess of Dorset), marshal and lieutenant of the army in Ireland, was created VISCOUNT GRANEY, in the peerage of Ireland, 2 January, 1535; but in five years afterwards, 28 July, 1541, he was beheaded and attainted, and the title fell under the forfeiture.

Arms—Barry of six, arg., and az., three torteaux, in chief, and a label of three points, erm.

GREY—BARONS GREY, OF WERKE, EARL OF TANKERVILLE.

Barony, by Letters Patent, dated 11 February, 1624.
Earldom, &c., by Letters Patent, dated 11 June, 1695.

Lineage.

SIR THOMAS GREY, of Berwyke, co. Northumberland, m. Jane (or Anne), dau. of John, Lord Mowbray, and had issue,

JOHN, from whom descended the Barons Grey de Powis (see that dignity).
THOMAS (Sir), of whom presently.
Henry (Sir), of Ketteringham, in Suffolk.
William, bishop of London.
Maud, m. to Sir Henry Ogle, Knt.

From the 2nd son,

SIR THOMAS GREY, of Heton, descended,
RALPH GREY, who m. Isabel, dau. and heir of Sir Thomas Grey, of Horton, and had issue,
WILLIAM GREY, Esq., of Chillingham, who was created a baronet, 15 June, 1619, and elevated to the peerage, 11 February, 1624, as BARON GREY, of Werke, co. Northumberland. His lordship m. Anne, dau. and co-heir of Sir John Wentworth, of Gosfield, co. Essex, and had surviving issue,

RALPH, his successor.
Elizabeth, d. in 1668.
Katherine, m. 1st, to Sir Edward Moseley, Bart., of Hough, co. Lancaster; and 2ndly, to Charles, eldest son of Dudley, Lord North.
Lord Grey* d. in 1674, and was s. by his son,
RALPH GREY, 2nd Lord Grey, of Werke, who m. Catherine, dau. of Sir Edward Forde, Knt., of Hartling, co. Sussex, and widow of Alexander, eldest son of John, Lord Colepeper, by whom he had issue,

FORDE, his successor.
RALPH, who s. his brother.   Charles.
Catherine, m. to Richard Neville, Esq., and had issue,
  GREY, m. Elizabeth, dau. of Sir John Boteler, and d. s. p. in 1723.
  HENRY, who assumed the surname of Grey, and d. s.p in 1740, leaving a widow, Elizabeth, who re-m. John Wallop, Earl of Portsmouth.
  Catherine, m. to Richard Aldworth, Esq , of Stanlake, co. Oxford. and dying in 1740, left a son,
    RICHARD, who assumed the surname and arms of Neville, and was father of
      RICHARD-ALDWORTH NEVILLE, who s. as 2nd LORD BRAYBROOKE.

His lordship d. in 1675, and was s. by his eldest son,
FORDE GREY, 3rd Lord Grey, of Werke. This nobleman joining in the rebellion of the Duke of Monmouth, commanded the horse at Sedgemoor, where he is accused of having treacherously deserted his post, and of flying at the first charge; certain it is, that he subsequently made terms for himself, and preserved his life by giving evidence against his associates. After the Revolution, his lordship obtained the favour of King WILLIAM, and was created by letters patent, dated 11 June, 1695, Viscount Grey, of Glendale, and EARL OF TANKERVILLE. He was afterwards a lord of the Treasury, sworn of the privy council, and in 1700, lord privy-seal. He m. Mary, dau. of George, Lord Berkeley, and had an only dau.,

Mary, m. to Charles Bennet, 2nd Lord Ossulston, who was created, after the extinction of the male line of the Greys, EARL OF TANKERVILLE. His lordship was great-great-great-grandfather of the Earl of Tankerville.

His lordship d. in 1701, when the Earldom of Tankerville and Viscounty of Glendale, became EXTINCT, while the Barony of Grey, of Werke, devolved upon his brother,
RALPH GREY, as 4th baron. This nobleman attended King WILLIAM in most of his campaigns, and was made governor of Barbadoes, in 1698. He d. s. p. in 1706, when the Barony of Grey, of Werke, EXPIRED. His lordship devised a considerable estate to his cousin, William, Lord North and Grey, son of Charles, Lord Grey, of Rolleston.

Arms—Gu., a lion rampant, within a border engrailed, arg.

---

* When the Lord Keeper Lyttleton deserted the House of Lords, in 1643, and carried the great seal to King CHARLES. at Oxford, this William, Lord Grey, of Werke, was elected speaker for the House at Westminster.

GREYSTOCK—BARONS GREYSTOCK.

By Writ of Summons, dated 23 June, 1295.

Lineage.

This barony the Earl of Ranulph de Meschines gave to one Lyolf, or Lyulphe, and King Henry I. confirmed the same unto Phorne, son of the said Lyulphe, whose posterity took their surname from the place, and were called de Graystock. Phorne was *s.* by his son Ivo, who was father of Walter; his son, Ranulph *d.* 12th King John, and was *s.* by his son William, whose son and successor,

Thomas de Greystoke obtained a royal charter, 29th Henry III., to hold a weekly market and yearly fair. This Thomas *m.* Christian, dau. of Roger de Viteripont, the first of that name of Appleby Castle, and was *s.* by his son,

Robert de Greystock, who dying in the 38th Henry III., was *s.* by his brother,

William de Greystock, who paying £100 for his relief, and doing his fealty, had livery of the lands of his inheritance. This William had a military summons to attend the king at Chester, 42nd Henry III., in order to restrain the hostilities of the Welsh. He *m.* Mary, the eldest dau. and co-heir of Roger de Merlay, an eminent baron of the north, by whom he acquired the manor of Morpeth, in Northumberland, and had issue, two sons, John, and William, and a dau., Margaret, *m.* to Sir Robert de la Val, Knt. This feudal lord *d.* in 1288, and was *s.* by his elder son,

John de Greystock, who in the 22nd Edward I., had summons with other great men, to attend the crown to advise upon certain important affairs of the nation, and in pursuance of that advice, went with the king into Gascony, the French monarch having then invaded those territories; where distinguishing himself in arms, he was the next year summoned to parliament as a baron, and subsequently to all the parliaments of his time. In two years afterwards, we find his lordship again in the wars of Gascony, and then in the retinue of Anthony Bec, bishop of Durham, and patriarch of Jerusalem. In the 28th and 29th Edward I., he was in the wars of Scotland. His lordship *d.* without issue in 1305, when he settled his manor and barony of Greystock upon his cousin, Ralph, son of William Fitz-Ralph, Lord of Grimthorpe, in Yorkshire, son of the baron's aunt, Joane; his brothers and uncles being then all dead, without issue male, which

Ralph Fitz-William, in the 10th Edward I., paid a fine to the king of 100 marks for license to marry Margery, widow of Nicholas Corbet, and dau. and heir of Hugh de Bolebec; and in the 24th of the same reign, as brother and heir of Geffery Fitz-William, of Yorkshire, had livery of the said Geffery's lands upon doing his homage. This nobleman was much engaged in the wars of Scotland; and in the 7th Edward II., we find him governor of Berwick, and joined in commission with John, Lord Moubray, and others, in the wardenship of the marches. He was the next year governor of Carlisle, and founded a chantry at Tinemouth, for the soul of John, Lord Greystock, his kinsman, and all his ancestors. His lordship *d.* in 1316, having had summons to parliament as a baron, under the designation of "Ralp Fitz-William," from 23 June, 1295, to 6 October, 1315. He was *s.* by his 2nd but eldest surviving son,

Robert Fitz-Ralph, 2nd baron, but never summoned to parliament, who *m.* Elizabeth, dau. of — Nevill, of Stainton, co. Lincoln, and dying the year after his father, was *s.* by his son,

Ralph de Greystock, *b.* 1298, which surname he assumed, and was summoned to parliament by that designation, from 15 May, 1321, to 17 September, 1322. His lordship, by virtue of a special dispensation from the Pope, *m.* Alice,* dau. of Hugh, Lord Audley, they being within the 3rd and 4th degrees of consanguinity; and had an only son, William. Lord Greystock having been a principal in seizing Sir Gilbert de Middleton, in the castle of Mitford, for treason, was soon afterwards poisoned, while at breakfast, through the contrivance of that person. He was *s.* by his son,

William de Greystock, 4th baron, *b.* 1321, summoned to parliament from 20 November, 1348, to 15 December, 1357.

---

* Dugdale, in one place, calls this lady, "Alice de Audeley," dau. of Hugh, Lord Audeley, and in another, "Alice," dau. of Ralph, Lord Nevill.

This nobleman served in France under the Black Prince. He obtained permission to make a castle of his manor house, at Greystock, and was constituted governor of Berwick; but during his governorship, being commanded to attend, personally, King Edward into France, Berwick fell into the possession of the Scots, whereupon the king was much offended; it being clearly proved, however, that Lord Greystock was absent on no other occasion, he obtained his pardon at the request of Queen Philippa. His lordship *m.* 1st, Lucy de Lucie, dau. of Lord Lucie, from whom he was divorced, without issue. He *m.* 2ndly, Joane, dau. of Lord Fitz-Hugh, by whom (who *m.* after his decease, Anthony de Lucie, and Sir Matthew Redman, Knt.), he had issue, Ralph, his successor, William and Robert, and a dau., Alice, *m.* Sir Robert de Harrington, and *d. s. p.* He *d.* 10 July, 1359, and was *s.* by his eldest son,

Ralph de Greystock, 5th baron, summoned to parliament from 28 November, 1375, to 5 October, 1417, as "Radulfo Baroni de Greystok." This nobleman was constituted in the 50th Edward III., governor of Loughmaban Castle, in Scotland, and one of the commissioners for guarding the west marches. Moreover, in the 1st Richard II., he was joined in commission with Henry, Duke of Northumberland, and others, for guarding the east and west marches, and the next year he assisted the earl in taking the castle of Warwick, of which the Scots had possessed themselves, by surprise. In the 4th Richard II. his lordship had the direction of the military expedition against the Scots; but was made prisoner by George, Earl of Dunbar, at Horseridge, in Glendall. His ransom cost 3,000 marks. His brother William went as a hostage for him to Dunbar, and *d.* there of the pestilence. After his enlargement he was again constituted one of the commissioners for guarding the west marches. His lordship *m.* Catherine, dau. of Roger, Lord Clifford, and dying in 1417, had, with a dau., Maud, *m.* to Eudo, son and heir of John, 4th Lord Welles, a son,

Sir John de Greystock, 6th baron, *b.* 1389, summoned to parliament from 24 August, 1419, to 5 July, 1435. This nobleman was constituted, 9th Henry V., governor of Roxborough Castle, in Scotland, for four years, with an allowance of £1,000 per annum in time of peace, and £2,000 in war. In the 1st Henry VI. he was joined in commission, with the bishop of London, and others, to treat of peace with James, King of Scotland; and was twice subsequently in a similar commission. In the 13th of the same reign his lordship was one of the chief commanders sent with the forces to the relief of Berwick, then besieged by the Scots. He *m.* Elizabeth, eldest dau. and co-heir of Robert Ferrers, of Wemme, by Elizabeth his wife, sole dau. and heir of William Boteler, Lord of Wemme, and had issue, Ralph, his successor, with three other sons, William, Richard, and Thomas, and a dau., Elizabeth, *m.* to Roger Thornton, whose only child and heiress, Elizabeth Thornton, *m.* Sir George Lumley, Lord Lumley, from whom the present Earl of Scarborough collaterally descends. Lord Greystock *d.* in 1436, and was *s.* by his eldest son,

Sir Ralph de Greystock, 7th baron, summoned to parliament from 29 October, 1436, to 15 September, 1485. This nobleman, who was frequently in commissions to treat with the Scots, *m.* Elizabeth, dau. of William Fitzhugh, Lord Ravenswath, and had (with a dau. Elizabeth, who *m.* 1st, Thomas, 5th Lord Scroop, of Masham, and 2ndly, Sir Gilbert Talbot of Grafton) an only son,

Robert (Sir), who *m.* Elizabeth, dau. of Edmund Grey, Earl of Kent, and dying in the lifetime of his father, 1st Richard III., left an infant dau. and heiress,

Elizabeth, who *m.* Thomas, Lord Dacre, of Gillesland, K.G., and conveyed the Barony of Greystock to her husband, when it became united with that of Gillesland.

Lord Greystock *d.* in 1487, and was *s.* by his grand-dau., Elizabeth, who *m.* as stated above, Lord Dacre, of Gillesland—by this marriage, as also stated above, the baronies of Dacre and Greystock became united, and so continued until the decease of George, 5th Baron Dacre, of Gillesland, and Baron Greystock, in 1569, when it fell into abeyance between his lordship's three sisters and co-heirs, viz.,

Anne, *m.* to Philip Howard, Earl of Arundel, ancestor of the Dukes of Norfolk.

Mary, *m.* to Thomas, Lord Howard, of Walden, and *d. s. p.*

Elizabeth, *m.* to Lord William Howard, ancestor of the Earls of Carlisle.

And between the representatives of these co-heirs the Barony of Greystock is presumed still to be in abeyance. Those representatives are,

William-Bernard, Lord Petre, Charles, Lord Stourton, { Representatives of Anne Dacre, through Winifred Howard, who m. William, 15th Lord Stourton, and Anne Howard, who m Robert-Edward, 9th Lord Petre, sisters and co-heirs of Philip Howard, brother of Edward, 9th Duke of Norfolk.

William-George, Earl of Carlisle, representative of Elizabeth Dacre.

Arms—Barry of six, arg. and az., over all three chaplets gu.

GRIFFIN — BARONS GRIFFIN, OF BRAY-BROKE CASTLE, CO. NORTHAMPTON.

By Letters Patent, dated 3 December, 1688.

Lineage.

By a pedigree attested by Sir Richard St. George, and William Camden, it appears, that in the reign of Edward II., Sir John Griffin, of Gumley Ewing, 20th Edward III., m. Elizabeth, dau. and co-heir of John Favell, of Weston-Favell, co. Northampton, and left a son and heir,

Sir Thomas Griffin, Knt., who m. Elizabeth, sister of Edward le Latimer, and heir to her brothers, and dying 33rd Edward IV., had issue,

Richard, his heir.
Thomas, m. Maude, dau. of Henry Mulshoe, of Geddington.
Hugh.
Elizabeth, wife of — Teakin; and
Anne, wife of — Hardwicke.

The eldest son,

Richard Griffin, m. Anne, dau. of Sir Richard Chamberlaine, of Coates, co. Northampton, and had, besides a dau. Margaret, wife of Richard Cheshull, two sons, John, cousin and heir to Edward, Lord Latimer, d. s. p. 22nd Henry VI., and

Sir Nicholas Griffin, of Braybrook, who. m. Catharine, dau. of Sir Thomas Pilkington, Knt., and d. 15th Henry VI., having had issue,

John, d s. p.
Nicholas, of whom presently.
Henry.   Richard.   Thomas

The eldest surviving son,

Nicholas Griffin, m. 1st, Katharine, dau. of Richard Curson, and by her had,

John, of whom hereafter.
Richard, d. at Windsor.
Edward, m. a dau. of — Leigh, of Burton, and had two sons, Henry and Thomas.
Isabel, wife of Thomas Nevil, of Rolleston.
Katharine, wife of Sir John Digby, Knt., of Eye Kettleby.

He m. 2ndly, Marina, dau. and co-heir of John Beler, Esq., of Eye Kettleby, and relict of Thomas Green. of Green's Norton, and by her had three daus., Elizabeth, wife of — Sandford; Anne, wife of — Villiers; and Joan, wife of — Pinchbeck. Nicholas Griffin d. 22nd Edward IV., and was s. by his eldest son,

John Griffin, who m. Emmote, dau.. of Richard Wheathill, of Calais, and by her, (who d. 13th Henry VIII.) had issue,

Nicholas (Sir), his heir.
George.   David.
Mary, m. to John Touchet, Lord Audley.

He d. 1st Henry VII., and was s. by his eldest son,

Sir Nicholas Griffin, who was made one of the knights of the Bath at the marriage of Prince Arthur, eldest son of King Henry VII., 17 November, 1501, and was sheriff of Northamptonshire in 1504. Sir Nicholas m. Alice, dau. of John Thornborough, Esq., and had, besides other issue, two sons,

I. Thomas (Sir), who s. his father, and was sheriff of the co. Northampton in the 26th and 36th Henry VIII. Sir Thomas m. Jane, eldest dau. and co-heir of Richard Newton, Esq., of Weeke, and dying 1569, was s. by his son,

Rice (Sir), who m. Elizabeth, dau. of Sir Thomas Brudenel, Knt., of Dean, co. Northampton, and left an only dau. and heiress,

Mary Griffin, who m. Thomas Markham, Esq., of Allerton. Thus terminated this branch of the family.

II. Edward.

255

Sir Nicholas d. in 1509, his younger son,

Sir Edward Griffin, having pursued the study of the law, was constituted solicitor-general in the 37th Henry VIII., and retained in that office till 6th Edward VI., when he was advanced to the attorney-generalship, which he continued to hold during the reign of Mary. Sir Edward m. 1st, Elizabeth, dau. of Robert Palmer, Esq., of Bowden, co. Northampton, by whom he had (with three daus., Frances, m. to Sir Gregory Cromwell, Knt., 2nd son of Henry, Lord Cromwell; Elizabeth, m. to Cecil, son of Arthur Hall, Esq., of Grantham; and Anne, m. to Sir William Villiers, Bart , of Brokesby),

Edward, his successor.

He m. 2ndly, Anne, dau. of Mr. Baron (John) Smith, of the Exchequer, but had no issue; and he m. 3rdly, Elizabeth, dau. and heiress of Geffrey Chambers, Esq., of Stonmore, in the co. Middlesex, relict, first of Sir Walter Stonor, Knt., and then of Reginald Conyers, Esq., by whom he had a son,

Rice (Sir), of Bickmarsh, who left a son,
Edward, who d. in 1659, leaving,
Nicholas.
Lucy.

The attorney-general was s. by his elder son,

Sir Edward Griffin, of Dingley, K.B., Lord of Gumley 1612, who m. Lucy, dau. of Reginald Conyers, Esq., of Wakerly, by his step-mother, (the attorney general's last wife) and had issue,

Thomas (Sir) of Dingley and Braybrook, m. 1st, Catharine, dau. of Sir John Morison, of Carleton. co. Lincoln, and 2ndly, Elizabeth, dau. of George Touchet, Lord Audley, and relict of Sir John Stowell, and d. v. p. in 1615, leaving issue by his 2nd wife, an only dau.,

Lucy, m. to Sir Richard Wiseman, Knt., of Torrel's Hall, Essex.

Edward (Sir), of whom presently.
Frances.   Elizabeth.   Anne.

Sir Edward d. in 1620. His eldest surviving son,

Sir Edward Griffin, Knt., Lord of Gumley, m. Frances, dau. of Sir William Uvedale, Knt., of Wickham, and dying 5 May, 1681, was s. by his son,

Sir Edward Griffin, lieut.-col. of the Duke of York's regiment of foot guards, (now called the Coldstream,) in the reign of King Charles II., who was advanced to the peerage, by letters patent. dated at Salisbury, 3 December, 1688, in the dignity of Baron Griffin, *of Braybroke*. His lordship m. the Lady Essex Howard, only dau. and heiress of James, 3rd Earl of Suffolk, and Baron Howard, of Walden. Lord Griffin adhering to the fortunes of King James II., attended that monarch on his abdication into France, and was outlawed. He remained abroad until 1708, when upon an intended invasion of Scotland, he embarked on the Salisbury man-of-war at Dunkirk, and was taken prisoner, with several others, by Sir John Byng, off the coast of North Britain. His lordship was then committed to the Tower of London, where he d. 10 November, 1710, and was s. by his only son,

James Griffin, 2nd Baron Griffin, of Braybroke, who m. Anne, dau. and sole heiress of Richard Rainsford, Esq., eldest son of Sir Richard Rainsford, of Dallington, co. Northampton, lord chief justice of England, by whom he had issue,

Edward, his successor.
James, d. unm.
Richard, d. young.
Elizabeth, m. 1st, to Henry Grey, Esq., of Billingbear. co. Berks, and 2ndly, to John Wallop, Earl of Portsmouth, but d. without issue in 1762.
Anne, m. to William Whitwell, Esq., of Oundle, co. Northampton. This lady s. eventually as sole heiress of her brother, Edward, Lord Griffin. Her eldest son,

John Griffin-Whitwell, having obtained from his aunt, the Countess of Portsmouth, her share of the estate of Saffron Walden, in Essex, assumed the surname and arms of Griffin, and having his claim to the ancient Barony of Howard, of Walden, admitted, (as great grandson of Lady Essex Howard. only child of James, Earl of Suffolk and Lord Howard, of Walden,) was summoned to parliament in that dignity He was afterwards created Baron Braybroke, with a special remainder, and that barony is now *extant* under the limitation.

His lordship d. 31 October, 1715, and was s. by his son,

Edward Griffin, 3rd Baron Griffin, who, 1 February, 1726-7, took the oaths and his seat in parliament, having conformed to the established church. His lordship m. Mary, dau. of Anthony Welden, Esq., of Well, co. Lincoln, some time governor of Bengal, by whom he had an only dau , Essex, who d. unm. 20

September, 1738. His lordship *d.* in 1742, when the Barony of Griffin, of Braybroke, became EXTINCT, and his estates devolved upon his sisters, as co-heirs (refer to the daus. of James, 2nd baron).

Arms.—Sa., a griffin segreant. arg., his beak and forelegs, or.

GUELPH—DUKE OF CAMBRIDGE.

By Letters Patent, dated 9 November, 1706.

Lineage.

GEORGE-AUGUSTUS, Prince Electoral of Hanover, only son of GEORGE I., was created a peer of Great Britain, 9 November, 1706, in the dignities of *Baron Tewkesbury, of Twkesbury, co. Gloucester, Viscount Northallerton, co. York, Earl of Milford Haven,* and MARQUESS AND DUKE OF CAMBRIDGE (created Prince of Wales, 22 September, 1714). The prince *s.* to the throne as GEORGE II., 11 June, 1727.

GUELPH—DUKE OF YORK AND ALBANY.

By Letters Patent, dated 29 June, 1716.

Lineage.

His Majesty GEORGE I. created his brother,

PRINCE ERNEST-AUGUSTUS, K.G., Bishop of Osnaburgh, DUKE OF YORK AND ALBANY, in the peerage of Great Britain, and Earl of Ulster in that of Ireland. He *d. unm.* in 1728, when his honours became EXTINCT.

GUELPH—DUKE OF EDINBURGH.

By Letters Patent, dated 26 July, 1726.

Lineage.

PRINCE FREDERICK-LEWIS, K.G., eldest son of George, Prince of Wales, and grandson of GEORGE I., was created a peer of Great Britain, 26 July, 1726, as *Baron of Snowdon, co. Carnarvon, Viscount of Launceston, co. Cornwall, Earl of Eltham, co. Kent, Marquess of the Isle of Ely. co. Cambridge,* and DUKE OF EDINBURGH, and was created Prince of Wales, 8 January, 1729. H.R.H. *m.* 8 May, 1736, Augusta, dau. of Frederick II., Duke of Saxe Gotha, and *d.* during the lifetime of his father, GEORGE II., 31 March, 1751, when he was *s.* by his eldest son,

GEORGE - WILLIAM - FREDERICK, 2nd Duke of Edinburgh, created Prince of Wales, 20 April, 1751, who ascended the throne at the death of his grandfather, GEORGE II., 25 October, 1760, as GEORGE III., when the dukedom and minor titles merged in the crown.

N.B.—In the London Gazette of 11 January, 1717-18, it was announced, under date of the 10th inst., that the king had directed Letters Patent to be passed creating Prince Frederick, eldest son of the Prince of Wales, *Duke of Gloucester,* and he was so styled till 1726, when he was created DUKE OF EDINBURGH. No warrant, however, ever passed the signet, nor did such a patent ever pass the great seal.

GUELPH—DUKE OF CUMBERLAND.

By Letters Patent, dated 27 July, 1726.

Lineage.

PRINCE WILLIAM-AUGUSTUS, K.G., 2nd son of GEORGE II., was created a peer of Great Britain by his grandfather, GEORGE I., 27 July, 1726, as *Baron of the Isle of Alderney, Viscount Trematon, in Cornwall, Earl of Kennington, Marquess of Berkhampsted,* and DUKE OF CUMBERLAND. His royal highness, who adopted early in life the profession of arms, attained a very high military reputation for courage, conduct, and ability. He was with his father at the battle of Dettingen, and there displaying great gallantry, receiving a wound in the brunt of the engagement. In this conflict the British arms were victorious; but, subsequently, sustained a defeat under his royal highness at Fontenoy, owing, in a great measure, to the valour of the Irish Brigade, which formed the rear-guard of Marechal Saxe's army. It was upon that memorable occasion that the English monarch is said to have exclaimed in the bitterness of his fortune, "curst be those laws that array my own subjects against me." The duke, in 1746, commanded the English troops against the CHEVALIER, and terminated that very formidable rebellion by his decisive victory of Culloden.

The duke *d. unm.* in 1765, when all his honours became EXTINCT.

GUELPH—DUKE OF YORK AND ALBANY.

By Letters Patent, dated 1 April, 1760.

Lineage.

PRINCE EDWARD-AUGUSTUS, 2nd son of Frederick, Prince of Wales, and brother of GEORGE III., was created DUKE OF YORK AND ALBANY, in the peerage of Great Britain, and Earl of Ulster, in Ireland, 1 April, 1760, but at his decease, in 1767, those honours became again EXTINCT.

GUELPH—DUKE OF GLOUCESTER AND EDINBURGH.

By Letters Patent, dated 17 November, 1764.

Lineage.

PRINCE WILLIAM-HENRY, 3rd son of Frederick, Prince of Wales, and brother of GEORGE III., *b.* 14 November, 1743, K.G., was created DUKE OF GLOUCESTER AND EDINBURGH, in the peerage of Great Britain, and Earl of Connaught, in that of Ireland, 17 November, 1764. His royal highness *m.* 6 September, 1766, Maria, Countess-Dowager Waldegrave, and illegitimate dau. of the Hon. Sir Edward Walpole, K.B., by whom he left, at his decease in 1805,

WILLIAM-FREDERICK, his heir.

Sophia-Matilda, ranger of Greenwich Park, *b.* 20 May, 1773; *d.* 29 November, 1844.

The only son,

WILLIAM-FREDERICK, 2nd Duke of Gloucester and Edinburgh, *b.* at Rome, 15 January, 1776; K.G., G.C.B., field-marshal in the army, &c.; who *m.* in 1816, his first cousin, the Princess Mary, sister of his Majesty King WILLIAM IV., and *d. s. p.* 30 November, 1834, when all his honours became EXTINCT.

GUELPH—DUKE OF CUMBERLAND AND STRATHERN.

By Letters Patent, dated 18 October, 1766.

Lineage.

PRINCE HENRY - FREDERICK, K.G., 3rd son of his royal highness, Frederick, Prince of Wales, and brother of GEORGE III., was created a peer of Great Britain, as DUKE OF CUMBERLAND AND STRATHERN, and of Ireland, as Earl of Dublin, 18 October, 1766. His highness *m.* in 1771, the Lady Anne Horton, widow of Christopher Horton, Esq., of Catton Hall, co. Derby, and dau. of Simon Luttrell, 1st Earl of Carhampton. This marriage was received very unfavourably at court, and gave rise to the law soon after passed, known as the Royal Marriage Act, by which the subsequent marriages of the royal family were confined within specific limitations. His royal highness *d.* in 1790, *s. p.,* when all his honours became EXTINCT.

GUELPH—DUKE OF KENT AND STRA-THERN.

By Letters Patent, dated 23 April, 1799.

Lineage.

PRINCE EDWARD, 4th son of his Majesty King GEORGE III., *b.* 2 November, 1767, was created a peer of Great Britain, as DUKE OF KENT AND STRATHERN, and of Ireland, as Earl of Dublin, 23 April, 1799. His royal highness was a knight of the Garter, and of St. Patrick, a knight grand cross of the Bath, a field-marshal in the army, and colonel of the 1st regiment of foot. The duke *m.* in 1818, her Serene Highness Victoria-Mary-Louisa, widow of Emich-Charles, Prince of Leiningen, and dau. of Francis, Duke of Saxe-Coburg-Saalfield, by whom (who *d.* 16 March, 1861), he had an only child,

ALEXANDRINA-VICTORIA, who ascended the throne at the decease of her uncle King WILLIAM IV., and is her present Most Gracious Majesty QUEEN VICTORIA.

His royal highness *d.* deeply lamented, 23 January, 1820, when all his honours became EXTINCT.

GUELPH—DUKE OF YORK AND ALBANY.

By Letters Patent, dated 27 November, 1784.

Lineage.

PRINCE FREDERICK, 2nd son of his Majesty King GEORGE III., *b* 16 August, 1763, was elected the following year bishop of Osnaburgh, and chosen a knight of the Bath in 1767. In June,

1771, he was elected a knight of the most noble order of the Garter, and installed at Windsor, 25th of the same month His royal highness was created a peer of Great Britain, as DUKE OF YORK AND ALBANY, and of Ireland, as Earl of Ulster, 27 November, 1784. The prince adopting the profession of arms, attained the rank of field-marshal and held for several years the high and important office of commander-in-chief of all the king's land forces in the United Kingdom. The Duke ... ... 20 September, 1791, Princess Frederica-Charlotte, eldest dau. of Frederick, King of Prussia, by whom (who *d.* 6 August, 1820), he had no issue. His royal highness *d.* 5 January, 1827, when all his honours became EXTINCT.

GUELPH—DUKE OF CLARENCE.

By Letters Patent, dated 20 May, 1789.

Lineage.

PRINCE WILLIAM HENRY, 3rd son of King GEORGE III., *b.* 21 August, 1765, was created 20 May, 1789, DUKE OF CLARENCE AND ST. ANDREWS in the peerage of Great Britain, and Earl of Munster in the peerage of Ireland. He *m.* 11 June, 1818, the Princess Adelaide, eldest dau. of George, Duke of Saxe Meiningen, and had two daus., who *d.* in infancy. His royal highness, who was at one time lord high admiral of England, ascended the throne as King WILLIAM IV., 26 June, 1830, when his peerage honours merged in the crown. His Majesty *d.* 20 June, 1837. Queen Adelaide survived until 2 December, 1849.

GUELPH—DUKE OF SUSSEX.

By Letters Patent, dated 7 May, 1801.

Lineage.

PRINCE AUGUSTUS-FREDERICK, *b.* 27 January, 1773 (6th son of King GEORGE III., brother of King WILLIAM IV., and uncle of her present Majesty) was created a peer as DUKE OF SUSSEX, *Earl of Inverness and Baron of Arklow*, all in the peerage of the United Kingdom, 7 November, 1801, and installed a knight of the most noble order of the Garter; *m.* at Rome by a protestant minister, 4 April, 1793, and at St. George's, Hanover Square, London, 5 December in the same year, Lady Augusta de Ameland, dau. of John (Murray) 4th Earl of Dunmore, by whom (who *d.* 5 March, 1830) he had issue,

SIR AUGUSTUS-FREDERICK D'ESTE, K.G.H., a colonel in the army, *b.* 13 January, 1794; *d. unm.* 28 December, 1848.
AUGUSTA, Mademoiselle D'Este, *b.* 11 August, 1801; *m.* 13 August, 1845, to Thomas, 1st Lord Truro, lord chancellor, 1850 to 1852; she *d.s.p.* 21 May, 1866.

The nuptials having been deemed a violation of the Royal Marriage Act (12th GEORGE III. c. ii.), were declared by the Prerogative Court null and void, and dissolved accordingly in August, 1794. His royal highness *m.* 2ndly, Cecilia, Duchess of Inverness (*see* that title). He *d.* 21 April, 1843, when all his honours became EXTINCT.

HACCHE—BARON HACCHE.

By Writ of Summons, dated 6 February, 1299.

Lineage.

EUSTACE DE HACCHE, originally a menial servant to King EDWARD I., obtained from that monarch a charter of freewarren in all his demesnes lands at Hacche, co. Wilts, as also at Norton-Merhull and Cestreton, in Warwickshire. He was afterwards, 22nd EDWARD I., made governor of Portsmouth, in which year he accompanied Edmund, Earl of Lancaster, in the expedition then made into Gascony. In the 26th EDWARD I., he was at the battle of Falkirk. He was summoned to parliament, as a baron, from 6 February, 1299, to 22 January, 1305. He *d.* in the following year, leaving an only dau. and heiress,

JULIAN, *m.* to John Hansard, in whose representatives, if such there be, the Barony of Hacche is vested.

Arms—Or, a cross, engrailed, gu.

HALL—BARON LLANOVER.

By Letters Patent, dated 27 June, 1859.

Lineage.

This family formerly resided for many generations in the county of Pembroke, and afterwards removed to that of Glamorgan.

BENJAMIN HALL, D.D., chancellor of the diocese of Llandaff; *b.* in July, 1742; *m.* Elizabeth, sister of Henry Grant, Esq. of Gnoll Castle, co. Glamorgan, and had issue,

I. BENJAMIN, his heir.   II. Henry, *d. s. p.*

Dr. Hall *d.* 20 February, 1825, and was *s.* by his son,

BENJAMIN HALL, Esq. of Abercarn, co. Monmouth, and Hensol Castle, co. Glamorgan, *b.* 29 September, 1778; M.P. in several parliaments for Totnes and Westbury, and for some years previous to his death, for the co. of Glamorgan. At his decease, a splendid marble monument was erected to his memory in Llandaff Cathedral, with the following inscription:—

"In a vault near this place are deposited the remains of Benjamin Hall, of Hensol Castle, Esq., Member of Parliament for this county, who died XXXI July, MDCCCXVII, aged XXXIX. To record the high sense they entertained of his industry, talent, and integrity, and as a tribute due to the man whose life was sacrificed to the zealous discharge of his public duties, this monument was erected by a considerable body of the nobility, clergy, gentry, and freeholders of the county of Glamorgan."

Mr. Hall *m.* 16 December, 1801, Charlotte, dau. of William Crawshay, of Cyfarthfa, Esq., co. Glamorgan, by whom (who *m.* 2ndly, S. Hawkins, Esq. of Court Herbert, co. Glamorgan) he had issue,

BENJAMIN, created LORD LLANOVER.
Richard-Crawshay, *m.* and had issue.
Henry, *d.* young.
Henry-Grant, *d.* young.
Charles-Ranken (Rev.), rector of Shire Newton, Chepstow, co. Monmouth; *m.* Harriette, dau. of John Baker, Esq., and had issue.
William-Thomas, capt. in the army, *b.* 23 March, 1818; *m.* 23 September, 1840, Louisa-Astley, youngest dau. of John Alliston, Esq., and had issue.
Charlotte, *m.* to Jenkin-Davies Berrington, Esq. of Woodland Castle, co. Glamorgan, and has issue.

Mr. Hall *d.* 31 July, 1817, and was *s.* by his eldest son,

SIR BENJAMIN HALL, P.C., of Llanover and Abercarn, in the co. of Monmouth, lord-lieut. co. Monmouth, *b.* 8 November, 1802; *m.* 4 December, 1823, Augusta, dau. and co-heir of Benjamin Waddington, of Llanover, Esq. (by Georgina-Mary-Ann his wife, dau. of John Port, Esq. of Ilam, co. Derby, by Mary his wife, only dau. of John D'Ewes, of Wellesbourn, Esq., and Ann Granville his wife, dau. of Col. Bernard Granville, grandson of the illustrious Sir Bevil Granville, and younger brother of George, Lord Lansdowne, Lady Llanover, derived, in a direct line, from the royal house of PLANTAGENET, as well as from the ancient royal and noble families of Wales (*see* BURKE's *History of the Royal Families*), and had issue,

I. Benjamin-Hanbury-Stuart, *b.* 9 January, 1826; *d.* at Llanover, 11 February, 1845.
II. Benjamin-Caradoc-Trevor-Francis-Zacchia, *b.* in Rome, 23 May, 1830; *d.* in London, 8 June, 1835.
I. AUGUSTA-CHARLOTTE-ELIZABETH, *m.* 12 November, 1846, to John-Arthur Herbert, Esq. of Llanarth, co. Monmouth, and has issue,
   1 IVOR-JOHN-CARADOC. J.P. and D.L., capt. grenadier guards, *b.* 16 July, 1851; *m.* July, 1873, Hon. Albertina Denison, dau. of Lord Londesborough.
   2 Arthur-James. *b.* 24 August, 1855.
   3 Edward-Bleithian, *b.* 23 January, 1858.
   4 Stephen-Charles, *b.* 18 December, 1864.
   1 Henrietta-Mary-Arianwen.
   2 Florence Catherine-Mary, *m.* 13 October, 1874, Joseph Monteith, Esq., only son of Robert Monteith, Esq. of Carstairs, N.B.

Sir Benjamin was for several years M.P. for the borough of Monmouth, and afterwards, during many years, for Marylebone, and was, in 1854-5, president of the board of health, and subsequently, from 1855 to 1858, first commissioner of public works, was created a BARONET, July, 1838, was made a privy councillor in 1854, and was raised to the peerage of the United Kingdom, 27 June, 1859, as BARON LLANOVER of Llanover and Abercarn, co. Monmouth. He was in October, 1861, appointed lord lieut. co. Monmouth. He *d.* 27 April, 1867, when his peerage and baronetcy became extinct.

Arms—Per pale, arg. and or, on a chevron, between three talbots' heads, erased, sa., their necks encircled with mural crowns, gold, three hawks' lures, of the first, as many of the second.

HALYBURTON—LORD HALYBURTON, OF DIRLETON.

By Letters Patent, dated 1440 or 1441.

Lineage.

SIR WALTER HALYBURTON, of Dirleton, high treasurer of Scotland, son and heir of Sir John Halyburton, of Dirleton, by Margaret, his wife, dau. and co-heir of Sir John Cameron, Knt., of Ballegarno, was created a peer in the year 1440 or 1441, and sat as such in parliament. He *m.* Lady Isabel Stewart, eldest dau. of Robert, Duke of Albany, Regent of Scotland, and relict of Alexander, Earl of Ross, by whom he had issue,

JOHN, his heir.

Walter, who m. Catherine, dau. and co-heir of Alexander de Chisholm, with whom he got the Barony of Pitcur, in Forfarshire, and had a charter of these lands, 1432. That barony was eventually inherited by Agatha Halyburton (dau. and heir of James Halyburton, Esq.), who m. James Douglas, Earl of Morton, and became eventually the property of her grandson, Lord Douglas Gordon Halyburton, M.P. of Pitcur. Lord Douglas d. 1841.

Robert.   William.

Christian, m. to George, 1st Earl of Rothes.

The eldest son,

JOHN, 2nd Lord Halyburton, m. Janet, dau. of Sir William Seton, of Seton, and by her (who m. 2ndly, Edward Congalton, 2nd son of John Congalton, of Congalton, and was alive in 1493) had two sons. The elder,

PATRICK, 3rd Lord Halyburton, m. Margaret, eldest dau. of Patrick, 1st Lord Hales, but d. s. p. He was s. by his brother,

GEORGE, 4th Lord Halyburton, who had three sons,

Archibald, living in 1586; who m. Helen, dau. of Shaw, of Sauchie; and dying v. p. left a son,

JAMES, successor to his grandfather.

PATRICK, who s. as 6th Lord.

Andrew.

His lordship was s. by his grandson,

JAMES, 5th Lord Halyburton, d. s. p. His uncle,

PATRICK, 6th Lord Halyburton of Dirleton, m. 1st, Margaret, dau. of James Douglas, of Pompherstoun, and had,

JANET, his heiress, m. to William, 2nd Lord Ruthven.

Mariota, m. to George, 4th Lord Home.

Margaret, m. to George Ker, of Faudonside.

He m. 2ndly, Christian Wawane, of Segy, Kinross-shire, dau. of Thomas Wawane, of Stevenstoun, co. Haddington, but by her (who m. 2ndly, William, 1st Earl of Montrose) had no issue. His lordship d. 1506, and was s. by his eldest dau.,

JANET, Lady Ruthven, who inherited both the estate and title of Dirleton. The title of Lord Dirleton remained in Patrick her son; her grandson William, bearing the title of Lord Ruthven and Dirleton, was created Earl of Gowrie, 1581. Her great-grandson, John, Earl of Gowrie, forfeited it in 1600, and thus the title of Lord Halyburton, or Dirleton, returned to the crown.

Arms—Quarterly: 1st and 4th, or, on a bend, az., three mascles of the 1st, for Halyburton; 2nd, or, three bars, gu., for Cameron; 3rd, arg., a bend, gu., for Vaux, or de Vallibus, Lord of Dirleton.

HAMILTON—EARLS OF CAMBRIDGE.

(See BURKE's Peerage, HAMILTON, DUKE OF.)

HAMILTON—LORD BARGENY.

By Letters Patent, dated 14 November, 1641.

Lineage.

SIR JOHN HAMILTON, of Carriden (only son of Sir John Hamilton, of Letrick, who was natural son of John, 1st Marquess of Hamilton), was created a peer of Scotland, by the title of LORD BARGENY, 14 November, 1641, with limitation to the heirs male of his body. He accompanied the Duke of Hamilton in his unfortunate expedition into England, 1648; and his attachment to the royal cause was so conspicuous, that Cromwell excepted him out of his act of grace and pardon, 12 April, 1654. His lordship m. Lady Jean Douglas, 2nd dau. of William, 1st Marquess of Douglas; and d. in 1658, having had issue,

I. JOHN, 2nd Lord Bargeny.

II. William, m. 3 April, 1662, Mary, dau. of Sir Patrick Hay, of Pitfour, relict of George Butler, of Clasbeny.

  I. Margaret, m. 1st, to John Kennedy, of Culzean, who d. 1665; and 2ndly, to Sir David Ogilvy, of Clova.

  II. Anne, m. to Sir Patrick Houston, Bart., of Houstoun, co. Renfrew, and d. 1678.

  III. Grizel, d. 1678.

  IV. Margery, m. to William Baillie, of Lamington.

  V. Catherine, m. 1676, William Cunningham, of Enterkine, in Ayrshire, and d. 1740.

The elder son,

JOHN HAMILTON, 2nd Lord Bargeny, m. 1st, Lady Margaret Cunningham, 2nd dau. of William, 9th Earl of Glencairn, lord high chancellor of Scotland, and had by her,

JOHN, master of Bargeny, who m. in 1639, Jean, dau. of Sir Robert Sinclair, Bart.; and dying before his father, left a only dau. and heir,

  JOHANNA, m. in 1707, to Sir Robert Dalrymple, Knt., of Castleton.

WILLIAM, who s. his father.

Nicolas, m. 24 April, 1690, to Sir Alexander Hope, Bart., of Kerse.

His lordship m. 2ndly, in 1676, Alice, Dowager Countess of Clanbrassil, eldest dau. of Henry, 1st Earl of Drogheda, but by her had no issue. He d. 25 May, 1693, and was s. by his only surviving son,

WILLIAM HAMILTON, 3rd Lord Bargeny; who m. 1st, Mary, eldest dau. of Sir William Primrose, of Carrington, sister of the 1st Viscount of Primrose, by whom he had a dau.,

  Grizel, m. 15 February, 1713, to Thomas Buchan, of Cairnbulg, advocate, and had three daus.,

    Mary, } both d. unm.
    Anne, }

    Nicola, m. to Thomas Buchan, of Auchmacoy, co. Aberdeen, and had issue,

      Thomas Buchan, who m. Euphame, dau. of Robert Turner, of Menie, and d. 1819, leaving a son and heir,

        JAMES BUCHAN, Esq., of Auchmacoy.

      Charles, d. in infancy.

      James, m. to Elizabeth Brebner.

      John Buchan, W.S., d. in Jamaica, 1796.

      Mary, m. to Robert Fullarton, Esq., of Jamaica.

      Grace.

      Jane, m. to Thomas Arbuthnot, of Nether Kinmundy.

      Nicolas, m. to James Watson, Esq., W.S., and left a dau., Nicolas.

Lord Bargeny m. 2ndly, Margaret, eldest dau. of Robert Dundas, of Arniston, a lord of session, sister of the 1st President Dundas, by whom he left at his decease, about 1712, a son and successor,

JAMES HAMILTON, 4th Lord Bargeny, b. 29 November, 1710; who completed his education by visiting foreign countries, as appears from Hamilton of Bangour's epitaph on the companion of his travels, who

  "With kind Bargeny, faithful to his word,
  Whom Heaven made good and social, though a lord,
  The cities view'd of many languaged men."

His lordship d. unm. at Edinburgh, 28 March, 1736, in the 26th year of his age, and was buried, 5 April, in the abbey church of Holyroodhouse; since which period the dignity has remained DORMANT. A competition arose for the estate between—

  The children of Johanna, Lady Dalrymple, only dau. of John, master of Bargeny;
  The children of the Hon. Mrs. Buchan, of Cairnbulg, dau. of the 3rd lord; and
  Sir Alexander Hope, Bart., of Kerse, son of the Hon. Nicolas Hope, dau. of the 2nd lord:

And was ultimately decided in favour of the first: the heir-general of the Dalrymple-Hamiltons, of Bargeny, Henrietta-Dundas, m. in 1822, Augustin-Louis-Joseph-Casimer Gustave, DUC DE COIGNY, and the heir male is the present SIR HEW-HAMILTON DALRYMPLE, BART.

Arms—Quarterly; 1st and 4th, gu., three cinquefoils, ermine, for Hamilton; 2nd and 3rd, arg., a ship with her sails furled up, sable, for Arran; all within a bordure, gobonated, arg. and az., the 1st charged with hearts, gules, and the 2nd with mullets of the 1st.

HAMILTON—EARL OF RUGLEN.

By Letters Patent, dated 14 April, 1697

Lineage.

LORD JOHN HAMILTON, 4th son of William and Anne, Duke and Duchess of Hamilton, bapt. at Hamilton 26 January, 1665, was created a peer of Scotland, by the titles of EARL OF RUGLEN, Viscount of Riccartoun, and Lord Hillhouse, by patent, dated 14 April, 1697, to him and the heirs male of his body; which failing, to the heirs whatsoever of his body; and he took the oaths and his seat in parliament, 19 July, 1698. On the death of his brother, Charles, Earl of Selkirk, in 1739, that title and the Barony of Crawford-John, in Lanarkshire, devolved on him; but the Barony of Riccartoun then went, in terms of the entail, to Lord Archibald Hamilton, his youngest brother, the Earl of Ruglen, who was thenceforward styled the Earl of Selkirk and Ruglen; d. at Edinburgh, 3 December, 1741, in the eightieth year of his age, and was buried at Cramond. He was *s.* in the title of Selkirk and Barony of Crawford-John by his grandnephew, Dunbar Hamilton, of Baldoon, and in the title of Ruglen and his other extensive property by his eldest dau. His lordship *m.* 1st (contract dated 21 June, 1694), his cousin-german, Lady Anne Kennedy, only dau. of John, 7th Earl of Cassilis, by his 1st wife, Lady Susan Hamilton, and by her had issue,

William, at first designed Lord Riccartoun, and after his father became Earl of Selkirk, Lord Daer. *b.* 1695; *d. unm.* at Edinburgh, 20 February, 1742, in the forty-sixth year of his age.
Anne, Countess of Ruglen.
Susan, *b.* 1 November, 1699; *m.* 26 October, 1738, to her cousin John, 8th Earl of Cassilis; and dying *s. p.* at Barnton, 8 February, 1763, in her sixty-fourth year, was buried in the abbey church of Holyrood-house, being succeeded in her large personal property by her nephew, the Earl of March.

The Earl of Selkirk and Ruglen *m.* 2ndly, at Edinburgh, 22 March, 1701, Elizabeth Hutchinson, relict of John, Lord Kennedy, and mother of John, 8th Earl of Cassilis; he had no issue by her, who had a jointure of £500 per annum out of the Cassilis estate, and *d.* at Barnton, 10 March, 1734. His lordship's elder dau.,

Anne Hamilton, Countess of Ruglen, *b.* 5 April, 1698; *m.* 1st, William, 2nd Earl of March, and by him (who *d.* at Barnton, 7 March, 1731, aged thirty-five,) had an only child, William, Duke of Queensberry, Earl of March and Ruglen; and 2ndly, in January, 1747, Anthony Sawyer, Esq., paymaster of the forces in Scotland, by whom she had no issue. On the death of her father, in 1744, she *s.* as Countess of Ruglen; and *d.* at York, on her way to London, 21 April, 1748, in her fifty-first year, when the title of Ruglen devolved on her son, William Douglas, Earl of March and Ruglen, afterwards 4th Duke of Queensberry; who *d.* in December, 1810, *s. p.*, when the Earldom of Ruglen became extinct.

Arms—Gu., three cinquefoils, erm.

HAMILTON—BARON HAMILTON, OF GLENAWLY.

By Letters Patent, dated 2 March, 1660.

Lineage.

Malcolm Hamilton, archbishop of Cashel, consecrated in 1623, *d.* in 1629. He had issue by his 1st wife, Mary, dau. of Robert Wilkie, of Sachtonhill,

i. Archibald, of Ballygally and Moyner, co. Tyrone, who by his wife, the Hon. Anne Balfour, dau. of James, Lord Glenawley, had no issue.
ii. Hugh, of whom presently.
iii. John, a captain in the army, was seated at Ballygally. By his wife Jean, dau. of James Somerville, descended from the house of Camnethan, he had issue two sons,

　1 Malcolm, ancestor to the Barons Hamilton.
　2 Hugh, ancestor to the Counts Hamilton.

The elder son,
Malcolm, entered the Swedish service in 1654: and rose to the rank of general. In 1664, he was naturalised among the Swedish nobles, and in 1689 he was created Baron Hamilton de Hagbey. He *d.* in 1699. His descendant in the 5th degree is Hugh-Adolphe, the present Baron Hamilton de Hagbey, *b.* in 1802. The younger son of Capt. John Hamilton,
Hugh, like his elder brother, entered the Swedish service, where he attained to great distinction. He was general and master-general of the Swedish artillery; he was created, along with his brother, Baron Hamilton de Hagbey, in 1689; he *d.* in 1724. Besides several sons whose lines are now extinct, he had a son, Gustavus-David, Baron Hamilton, *b.* 1699, who was one of the most distinguished generals in the Swedish service. In 1751, he was created Count Hamilton de Barsebeck; in 1765, he was field-marshal; he was knight of the Seraphim; he *d.* 1788. He had, with other issue, three sons, ancestors of the Counts Hamilton.

　1 Hugh-William, 2nd Count Hamilton de Barsebeck, whose line failed in his son, Gustavus, 3rd Count Hamilton de Barsebeck, in 1854.

　2 Adolphe-Louis, Count Hamilton, had issue,

　　Count Gustavus-Walter, who *d.* in 1835. His grandson, Count Adolphe-Louis-Wathier, *b.* 1839, became in 1854, 4th Count Hamilton de Barsebeck, and head of the family. His 2nd son, Count Hening-Hugh-Louis, *b.* 1814, has had the distinguished honour of being thrice appointed Chief of the Nobles, or President of the

Swedish Diet. He is knight of the Seraphim, and Senator.
Count Adolphe-Louis, *d.* 1844, and left issue.
Count Hugh-David, *b.* 1789, has issue, among other sons, Count Adolphe-Louis, *b.* 1820; in 1862 appointed Governor of Upsala.

　3 Axel, Count Hamilton, who had numerous issue, viz.,
　　Count Axel-Hugh-Raoul Hamilton, who has issue.
　　Count Adolphe-James-Charles Hamilton, *d.* in 1822, and left issue.
　　Count Axel-Louis-Adolphe-Malcolm Hamilton, who has issue.
　　Count Malcolm-Casimir Hamilton.
　　Count Hugh-Dieterich Hamilton, who has, with other issue, a son.
　　Count Gustavus-Malcolm Hamilton, *b.* 1826, who has issue.
　　Count John-David Hamilton, *d.* 1843.
　　Count James-Essen Hamilton, governor of Stockholm, knight of the Seraphim. He has issue.
iv. Malcolm, a clergyman.

The archbishop *m.* 2ndly, Jean, dau. of John Crawford, of Crawfordland, by whom he had,

v. Louis, who entered the Swedish service, and in 1654 was created Baron Hamilton de Deserf, in Sweden. He had a son, Gustavus, governor of Enniskillen.

The 2nd son,
Hugh Hamilton, created Baron Hamilton de Deserf, in Sweden, returned to Ireland, seated himself at Ballygally, co. Tyrone, and was advanced to the Irish peerage, 2 March, 1660, as *Lord Hamilton, Baron of Glenawly, co. Fermanagh.* By his 2nd wife, Susanna, youngest dau. of Sir William Balfour, of Pitcullo (who *m.* 2ndly, Henry Mervyn, Esq., of Trelick) he had issue,

William, his heir.
Henrietta-Amelia, *d.* in 1669.
Arabella-Susanna, *m.* 1st, 3 July, 1683, to Sir John Magill, Bart., of Gill Hall, co. Down; and 2ndly, to Marcus, Viscount Dungannon.
Nichola-Sophia, *m.* 1st, in 1687, to Sir Tristram Beresford, Bart., of Coleraine, by whom she was mother of four daus. and of one son, Marcus, Earl of Tyrone. She *m.* 2ndly, in 1704, Lieut.-Gen. Richard Gorges, by whom she had also issue. (*See title* Gorges.)

Lord Hamilton *d.* in April, 1679, and was *s.* by his son,
William Hamilton, 2nd Lord Hamilton, of Glenawly; at whose decease *s. p.*, in February, 1680, the title became extinct.

Arms—Gu., a crescent between three cinquefoils, arg.

HAMILTON—VISCOUNT CLANEBOYE, EARL OF CLANBRASSILL.

Viscounty, by Letters Patent, dated 4 May, 1622.
Earldom, by Letters Patent, dated 7 June, 1647.

Lineage.

The Hamiltons, Earls of Clanbrassill, were a powerful family in the north of Ireland: their senior heir-general is Lord Dufferin and Claneboye.
The Rev. Hans Hamilton,[*] vicar of Dunlop, Ayrshire, *b.* 1536; *m.* Margaret Denham, dau. of the Laird of Weshiels; and dying 30 May, 1608, left,

i. James (Sir) of whom hereafter.
ii. Archibald, of Haleraig, or Harrage, co. Lanark, *m.* 1st, Rachel Carmichael, and had issue,

　1 John, whose dau. Rachel *m.* John Stevenson, Esq.
　2 James, of Neilsbrook, co. Antrim, who inherited one-fifth of the Earl of Clanbrassil's estates. He *m.* Agnes Kennedy, and had three daus.,

---

[*] In the churchyard of Dunlop there is a tomb erected to his memory, and on a flag-stone in the floor is the following inscription :—" Here lies Hans Hamilton, vicar of Dunlop, who deceased the 30th of May, 1608, at the age of 72 years; and Janet Denham, his spouse." Under a marble arch, within two pillars of the composite order; in front are two statues kneeling on a marble monument, in the attitude of devotion, and habited according to the fashion of the times. There is also a long inscription on a marble slab in the wall, stating that he was the son of Archibald Hamilton, of Raploch, and that his wife was Janet, 2nd dau. of Denholme, of Westshiels; that they lived together forty-five years, during which time he had served the cure of the church.

Rose, who m. William Fairlie, but d. s. p.
Rachel, d. unm.
Anne, m. to Hans Stevenson, Esq., of Ballygrot, and left an only son, James Stevenson, whose eldest dau. and co-heir, Dorcas Stevenson, m. Sir John Blackwood, Bart., and was created Baroness Dufferin and Clanboye, in 1810. Her descendant, Frederick-Temple Hamilton-Blackwood, Lord Dufferin and Claneboye, K.P., K.C.B., is now heir-general and representative of the Hamiltons, Earls of Clanbrassill.
3 Gawen, ancestor of the Hamiltons of Killyleagh Castle, co. Down, now represented by Gawen-William-Rowan Hamilton, Esq., of Killyleagh Castle.
4 William, d. s. p.
5 Robert.
iii. Gawen, of Ballygally.
iv. John, of Coronary, co. Cavan, and Monella, co. Armagh, ancestor of the Hamiltons, of Mount Hamilton, co. Armagh and of the Hamiltons of Abbotstown, co. Dublin.
v. William, of Bangor, co. Down. m. Jane, dau. of Sir John Melville, and dying 1627, left issue,
1 James, of Newcastle, M.P. for Bangor, æt. ten years, 1627, killed at Blackwater fight, 5 Ju. 1646, m. Margaret, dau. of Francis Kynaston, Esq., of Laule, co. Down, and had issue,
James of Bangor (will dated 20 July, 1701, proved 26 February, 1706), m. Hon Sophia Mordaunt, dau. of John, 1st Viscount Avalon, and sister to Charles, Earl of Peterborough and Monmouth, and had issue,
James, M.P for Bangor, 1692, d. s. p.
Anne-Catherine, m. in 1709, Michael Ward, Esq., M.P. for the co. Down, 1715, judge of the Queen's Bench in 1727, father of Bernard Ward, Viscount Bangor.
Margaret, m. Thomas, Viscount Ikerrin.
Catherine, m. 1st, Vere Essex Cromwell, 4th Earl of Ardglass, Viscount Lecale, and 7th Baron Cromwell. He d. 1687, when the earldom and viscounty expired, and the Barony of Cromwell, originating in the writ of 28 April, 1539, devolved upon his dau.,
Elizabeth, Baroness Cromwell, m. Edward Southwell, secretary of state for Ireland.
Catherine m. 2ndly, Nicholas Price, of Hollymount, co. Down.
2 John (capt), of the co. Cavan, m. Jane Echlin, d. s. p.
3 Hans. M.P. of Carnisure, co. Down (will dated 2 December, 1655, proved 20 July, 1656), d. 28 December, 1655, and was buried at Hollywood. He m. Margaret, sister of David Kennedy, Esq., and had issue,
James, b. 1654 (will dated 2 June, 1690, proved 10 August, 1691), m. Christian, dau. of William Hamilton, of Erinagh, and had issue, Margaret, m. John Cuffe, Lord Desart, and d. s. p.; Christian, d. s. p.; Anne, d. s. p.
4 William, of Erinagh, co. Down, d. 26 January, 1680; m. 1st, Ellen, dau. of Phelim Magennis, Esq., and had issue,
James, of Tollymore, co. Down, will dated 28 December, 1693, proved 1700, m. Hon. Anne Mordaunt, grand-dau. of John, 1st Earl of Peterborough, and sister to Mrs. Hamilton, of Bangor, and had issue,
James, Earl of Clanbrassil (of the second creation), created in 1756; m. Lady Harriet Bentinck, dau. of William, Earl of Portland, and had,
James, Earl of Clanbrassil, knt. of St. Patrick, d. s. p. in 1798, when the honours became extinct, and his lordship's sister, the Countess of Roden, inherited the estates.
Anne, m. Robert, Earl of Roden, grandfather of Robert, Earl of Roden.
Caroline, d. unm.
William, d. young.
John, d. young.
Sophia, m. Frederick Hamilton, eldest son of Viscount Boyne.
Elizabeth, m. Thomas Fortescue, Esq., father of William-Henry, Earl of Clermont.
Cary.
Elinor, m. — Matthews, Esq.
He m. 2ndly, Christian, dau. of Joselin Ussher, son of Mark, son of the Right Rev. Henry Ussher, archbishop of Armagh, and had issue,
Joselin, d. s. p., will dated 17 November, 1689, proved 1690.
Christian, will dated 4 February, 1691, proved 19 January, 1692, m. James Hamilton, of Carneyshten.
1 Ursula, m.
vi. Patrick, m. Elizabeth Glen, and had issue, three sons and one dau.
The eldest son,
Sir James Hamilton, Knt., of Killyleagh and Bangor, serjeant-at-law, and privy councillor to James I., was elevated to the peerage of Ireland, 4 May, 1622, as Viscount Claneboye. He m. thrice: by Jane, his 3rd wife, dau. of Sir John Phillips, Bart., of Picton, he left, at his decease 1643, a son and heir,

James Hamilton; 2nd Viscount Claneboye; who was advanced to the Earldom of Clanbrassill, co. Armagh, 7 June, 1647. His lordship m. Lady Anne Carey, eldest dau. of Henry, Earl of Monmouth, and by her (who m. 2ndly Sir Robert Maxwell, Bart.), he had issue,
i. James, b. 7 September, 1642, d. unm. 8 May, 1658.
ii. Henry, 2nd earl.
iii. Hans, buried with his father at Bangor.
His lordship d. 20 June, 1659, and was buried at Bangor. His only surviving son,
Henry Hamilton, 2nd Earl of Clanbrassill, d. s. p., 12 January, 1675, when all the honours expired. His lordship left a widow, Alice, dau. of Henry Moore, 1st Earl of Drogheda; which lady m. 2ndly, John, Lord Bargany. The senior representation of the Earls of Clanbrassill has devolved (through Anne Hamilton, dau. and co-heiress of James Hamilton, of Neilsbrook, cousin-german of James, 1st Earl of Clanbrassill) on Lord Dufferin.
Arms—Gu., three cinquefoils, pierced, erm., and on a chief, or, a lion passant, gu.

HAMILTON—EARL OF CLANBRASSILL.

By Letters Patent, dated 24 November, 1756.

Lineage.

James Hamilton, Esq., M.P., son and heir of James Hamilton, Esq., of Tollymore (of a younger branch of the preceding family), by Anne, his wife, sister of Charles, Earl of Peterborough, was created in 1719, Baron Claneboye, and Viscount Limerick; and 24 November, 1756, advanced to the Earldom of Clanbrassill. His lordship m. 15 October, 1728, Lady Henrietta Bentinck, 3rd dau. of William, 1st Earl of Portland, and had issue,
James, his heir
Anne, m. 11 December, 1752, to Robert, Earl of Roden.
Caroline, d. unm. 13 October, 1762.
The earl was s by his only son,
James Hamilton, 2nd Earl of Clanbrassill, b. in 1729, who m. in 1774, Grace, dau. of Thomas Foley, Esq., afterwards Lord Foley, but d. s. p. in 1798, when all the honours became extinct, his lordship's sister, the Countess of Roden, inheriting the estates.
Arms—Gu., three cinquefoils, pierced, erm., on a chief, or, a lion passant.

HAMPDEN—VISCOUNTS HAMPDEN.

See Trevor, Viscounts Hampden.

HANDLO—BARON HANDLO.

By Writ of Summons, dated 25 February, 1342.

Lineage.

John de Handlo was summoned to parliament as a baron, 25 February, 1342, but never afterwards. His lordship m. twice, by his 1st wife he had a son, Richard, who predeceased him, leaving a son, Edmund, heir to his grandfather, and two daus., co-heirs to their brother, Margaret, m. 1st, to Gilbert Chastelyn, and 2ndly, to John de Apulby, and by the latter only had issue, viz., an only dau., Joan, m. to John Conghull; Elizabeth, m. to Edmund de la Pole, and had issue. He m. 2ndly, Maud, sister and heir of Edward Burnell, Baron Burnell, and widow of John Lovell, and by her had a son,
Nicholas, who assumed his mother's surname, and was summoned to parliament from 1350 to 1380. He d. 1420, having had a son,
Edward, who predeceased him, leaving three daus., viz , Joyce, wife of Thomas Elrington, Jun., s. p.
Margery, wife of Edward Hungerford.
Katherine, m. to Sir John Radcliffe.
His lordship d. in 1346. His grandson and heir,
Edmund de Handlo d. under age in 1355, leaving his two sisters above named. his co-heirs, between the descendants of whom whatever dignity was vested in John de Handlo is in abeyance.

HANGER—BARON COLERAINE.

By Letters Patent, dated 26 February, 1762.

Lineage.

GABRIEL HANGER, Esq., 3rd son of Sir George Hanger, Knt., of Dryffield, co. Gloucester, represented successively Maidstone and Bridgwater in parliament, and was raised to the peerage of Ireland, as BARON COLERAINE, *of Coleraine, co. Londonderry,* 26 February, 1762. His lordship *m.* Elizabeth. dau. and heir of Richard Bond, Esq., of Clowbury, Herts, and had three sons and one dau., Anne, *m.* in 1773, to Col. Arthur Vansittart, M.P., of Shottesbrooke House, Berks. Lord Coleraine *d.* 27 January, 1773, and was *s.* by his son,

JOHN HANGER, 2nd Lord Coleraine; who *d.* in 1794, and was *s.* by his brother,

WILLIAM HANGER, 3rd Lord Coleraine; who *d.* in 1814, and was *s.* by his brother,

GEORGE HANGER, 4th Lord Coleraine; at whose decease *unm.* in 1824, the barony became EXTINCT.

Arms—Erm., a griffin, segreant, per fess, or and az.

HANMER—BARON HANMER.

(*See* BURKE's *Extant Peerage*, HANMER, Bart.)

HARCLA—BARON HARCLA, EARL OF CARLISLE.

Barony, by Writ of Summons, dated 15 May, 1321.
Earldom, by Charter, dated 25 March, 1322.

Lineage.

ANDREW DE HARCLA (son of Michael de Harcla, sheriff of Cumberland, from the 13th to the 16th EDWARD I. inclusive), having distinguished himself in the Scottish wars, was constituted by King EDWARD II., governor of the castle of Carlisle, warden of the marches, and elevated to the peerage, by writ of summons, dated 15 May, 1321, as BARON HARCLA; in which year his lordship had the good fortune to completely rout the insurgents under Thomas Plantagenet, Earl of Lancaster, at Boroughbridge, and to seize the earl himself, whom he conveyed a prisoner to the king at York, and had soon afterwards executed at Pontefract. In consideration of this eminent service, his lordship was created an earl, under the title of EARL OF CARLISLE, by the girding of a sword, accompanied by a charter in which it was covenanted, that for the better support of the dignity, he should have to himself, and the heirs male of his body, lands and rents in the cos. of Cumberland and Westmoreland, of 1,000 marks per annum value, and 500 marks per annum more in the marches of Wales, and until such provision should be made, that he should receive 1,000 marks per annum out of the exchequer. Besides these substantial records of royal favour, this charter, for the first time in such a grant, set forth in the preamble, a detail of the merits of the dignified person: it was dated at Pontefract, 25 March, 15th EDWARD II., *anno* 1332. "Thus elevated," says Dugdale, "from a mean condition, he grew so lofty, that he began to manifest the hatred publicly, which he had long privately borne, towards Hugh le Despencer (the greatest and most powerful favourite of his time), whom the king had recently advanced to the Earldom of Winchester." This feeling towards Despencer led the earl to make private overtures to the Scots, which being communicated to the king, he was seized (by Anthony de Luci) at Carlisle, and brought to trial there, by virtue of a commission, dated at Knaresborough, 27 February, 16th EDWARD II., and directed to Edmund, Earl of Kent, John, Lord Hastings, Sir Ralph Basset, Sir John Peche, Sir John Wisham, and Geffrey le Scrope, Esq. Before this court, his lordship was accused of having conspired with James Douglas, a Scot, whereby the king, for lack of his assistance, was defeated in a battle, near the abbey of Biland, in Yorkshire; so that he was necessitated for the security of his person, to fly to York; and the earl being found guilty, sentence was then and there pronounced against him: viz.—"That his sword should be taken from him, and his gilt spurs hacked from his heels. That he should then be drawn and hanged by the neck; his heart and bowels taken out of his body, burnt to ashes and winnowed; his body cut into quarters; one to be set on the principal tower of Carlisle Castle; another upon the tower at Newcastle-upon-Tyne; a third upon the bridge at York; and the fourth at Shrewsbury; while his head was to be placed upon London Bridge;" which judgment was executed upon the unhappy nobleman accordingly, on the morrow after St. Chad's day (3 March) 1322, and all his honours became, of course, FORFEITED.

His lordship had a brother, John de Harcla, who *d.* the same year, seized of the manor of Whitehall, co. Cumberland, leaving a son and heir, ANDREW, then three years of age.

Arms—Arg., a cross, gu., in the 1st quarter, a martlet, sa.

HARCOURT — BARONS HARCOURT, OF STANTON HARCOURT, CO. OXFORD, VISCOUNTS HARCOURT, EARLS HARCOURT.

Barony, by Letters Patent, dated 3 September, 1711.
Viscounty, by Letters Patent, dated 24 July, 1721.
Earldom, by Letters Patent, dated 1 December, 1749.

Lineage.

This ancient and eminent family traced its pedigree to BERNARD, a nobleman of the royal blood of Saxony, who acquired, in 876, when ROLLO, the Dane, made himself master of Normandy, the lordships of Harcourt, Caileville, and Beaufidel, in that principality. Bernard's son,

TORF, called "the Rich," had three sons. The eldest, Tourade, is said to be the ancestor of Beaumont or Bellemont, Counts of Mellent, in France, and Earls of Leicester. The 2nd son,

TURCHETIL, Seigneur de Turqueville and Turquerange, was governor to WILLIAM II., Duke of Normandy. His eldest son,

ANCHETIL, Sire de Harcourt, being lord of that place was the first to assume the surname. Of his seven sons, the eldest, Anguerrand or Errand de Harcourt, attended William, Duke of Normandy at the Conquest, and returned to Normandy in 1078. The 2nd son,

ROBERT DE HARCOURT, built the castle of Harcourt in Normandy, A.D. 1100. He had besides three younger sons,

WILLIAM, his heir.
Richard (Sir), a Knight Templar.
Philip, dean of Lincoln, who assisted at the coronation of HENRY II., *d.* 1162.

The eldest son,

WILLIAM DE HARCOURT was Lord of Harcourt, Caileville, Beaufice, and lord of the manor of Stanton-under-Bardon, co. Leicester: he had issue,

Robert, Seigneur and Baron de Harcourt, &c., ancestor of the Dukes de Harcourt, peers of France and of the Counts d'Aumale, Counts de Tankerville, Viscounts de St. Sauveur and other branches of that illustrious house.
Ivo, of whom we treat.
Simon, *m.* Adeliza dau. and co-heir of Osbert de Arden, of Kingsbury, co. Warwick, and *d. s. p.*
Beatrix, *m.* to Robert de Basset.

Of the above sons,

IVO DE HARCOURT had, with a younger, Sir John, an elder son and heir,

SIR ROBERT DE HARCOURT, Knt., sheriff of the cos. of Warwick and Leicester in 1199-1201 and 1202, in which last year he died. He *m.* Isabel, only child and heir of Richard de Camville, by Milicent his wife, cousin to Adeliza, King HENRY I.'s 2nd consort. By this lady Sir Robert had issue,

WILLIAM (Sir), his heir.
Oliver, who joined Lewis, Prince of France, and his party, against King JOHN, but was made prisoner at the battle of Lincoln, 1217.
John, seated at Rodeley, co. Leicester, *m.* Hawis, dau. of Sir William Burdet.
Robert (Sir), *m.* Dionysia, dau. and co-heir of Henry Pipard, of Lapworth, co. Warwick.
Alice, *m.* 1st, to John de Limesi; and 2ndly, Walleran de Newburgh, Earl of Warwick.

The eldest son,

SIR WILLIAM DE HARCOURT, Knt., of Stanton-Harcourt, lord of the manor of Ellenhall, co. Stafford, *jure uxoris*, was called "The Englishman," to distinguish him from others of the same name. He *m.* Alice, eldest dau. and co-heir of Sir Thomas Noel, of Ronton, and Ellenhall, by Margaret his wife, eldest dau. and co-heir of Guy le Strange. By this lady Sir William had two sons and one dau.,

RICHARD (Sir), his heir.
Henry (Sir), knighted in 1278, *m.* Emma, dau. and heir William Mansel, of Erdington, and had an only dau. and heir, Margaret, who *m.* 1st, to John Pipe, and 2ndly, to John Saundershed.
Helen, *m.* to Hugh Bigot, justiciary of England.

The eldest son and heir,

SIR RICHARD DE HARCOURT, Knt. of Stanton-Harcourt, Ellenhall, &c., m. Arabella, dau. of Sayer de Quinci, Earl of Winchester, by Margaret his wife, dau. of Robert de Bellemont, and sister and co-heir of Robert, Earl of Leicester. By this lady, with whom he acquired the manor of Bosworth, &c., he had issue, WILLIAM (Sir), his heir; Sayer; and Maud, m. to Sir Giles Peneston, Knt. Sir Richard d. in 1258, and was s. by his elder son and heir,

SIR WILLIAM DE HARCOURT, Knt., of Stanton-Harcourt, Ellenhall and Bosworth, who m. 1st, Alice, dau. of Roger, and sister of Alan la Zouche, Lord of Ashby; and 2ndly, Margaret, m. to Sir John Cantilupe, s. p.; and Arabella, m. to Sir Fulke Pembrugge. Sir William m. 2ndly, Hillaria (or Eleanor), dau. of Henry, Lord Hastings, by Ada his wife, dau. of David, Earl of Huntingdon, and by her had an only son and successor, SIR RICHARD DE HARCOURT, Knt., of Stanton-Harcourt, &c., who m. Margaret, dau. of Sir John Beke, and sister and co-heir of Walter Beke, Lord of Eresby, and dying 21st EDWARD I. (1293), was s. by his elder son and heir,

SIR JOHN DE HARCOURT, knighted 1306, who m. 1st, Eleanor, dau. of Eudo la Zouche, by Milicent de Montalt his wife, dau. of William, and sister and co-heir of George, Lord Cantilupe; and 2ndly, Alice, dau. of Peter Corbett, of Causcastle, co. Salop, and by the former had a son and heir, WILLIAM (Sir). Sir John d. in 1330, and was s. by his son,

SIR WILLIAM DE HARCOURT, who m. Jane, dau. of Richard, Lord Grey, of Codnor, and by her (who m. 2ndly, Ralph de Ferrers) had two sons,

Richard (Sir), who predeceased his father, leaving, by Joan his wife, dau. and heir of Sir William Skareshull, Knt., of Skareshull, co. Stafford, an only dau. and heir, Elizabeth, m. to Thomas Astley, Esq., of Nelston, co. Leicester (2nd son of Thomas, Lord Astley), from whom the Astleys of Patishull descend.

THOMAS (Sir), successor to his father.

Sir William d. 6 June, 1349, and was s. by his surviving son, SIR THOMAS HARCOURT, knighted in 1366, and M.P. for co. Oxford, 1376, who m. Maud (or Alice, according to the Monasticon, or Eleanor, according to the Visitation of co. Stafford), dau. of Robert, Lord Grey, of Rotherfield, and widow of Sir John Bottetort, of Woody, Lord Bottetort, and by her had issue. He d. 12 April, 1417, and was s. by his eldest son.

SIR THOMAS HARCOURT, Knt, who m. Joan, dau. of Sir Robert Frauncels, of Foremark, co. Derby, and by her had, with other issue,

ROBERT (Sir), his heir and successor, K.G He m. Margaret, dau. of Sir John Byron, Knt., of Clayton, co. Lancaster, and, by her, had besides three younger sons, all of whom d. s. p., an eldest son and heir,

John (Sir), who m. Anne, dau. of Sir John Norris, Knt., of Bray, co. Berks, and d. 26 June, 1485, leaving an only surviving son,

Robert (Sir), standard bearer to King HENRY VII., at Bosworth, and K.B. He m. Agnes, dau. of Thomas Limericke, Esq., and by her had one son, John, who predeceased him, s. p., and five daus., who became his co heirs, viz., Elizabeth, m. to Robert Gainsford, Esq., of Hampton Park, co. Oxford; Letitia, m. 1st, to Humphrey Peshall, Esq., and 2ndly, to Thomas Nevil, Esq.; Catherine, m. to Thomas Stonor, Esq.; Ellen, m. to Richard Beckenham, Esq., of Pudlicot, co. Oxon; and another dau. m. to William Cope, Esq., of Hanwell, co. Oxon.

RICHARD (Sir), of whose line we treat.

The 2nd son,
SIR RICHARD HARCOURT, Knt., of Wytham, co. Berks, m. 1st, Edith, dau. and co-heir of Thomas St. Clere, of Burstow, co. Surrey, and by her had issue,

CHRISTOPHER HARCOURT, of whom presently.
William d. 31 August, 8th HENRY VIII., leaving two sons,
1 Francis, of Witham, who d. 27th HENRY VIII., having had issue, Robert; Simon; and three daus., Elizabeth; Anne; and Margaret.
2 Richard, of Cornbury Park.
Anne, m. 1st, to Henry Fiennes, Lord Saye and Sele; and 2ndly, to John, son of Simon Montfort.
Alice, m. to William Besilles.

Sir Richard m. 2ndly, Eleanor, dau. of Sir Roger Lewkenor, Knt., of Raunton, co. Stafford, and by her had, besides several daus.,

John, of Raunton, who m. Margaret, dau. of William Bracy, of Pembridge, co. Suffolk.
Thomas, of Raunton, who m. Isabel, dau. of Hugh Egerton, of Wrynhill, and d. 8 February, 1510, having had, besides a dau., Katherine, m. to John Pershall, two sons.
John, of Raunton, who m. Anne, dau. of Sir Randall Brereton, Knt., of Malpas, co. Chester, and by her, who m. 2ndly, John Pershall, of Horsley, had besides three daus., five sons,

Robert, of Raunton, m., but d. s. p.
Simon, m. Roisa, dau. of Richard Cave, of Peckwell, and had one dau., Elizabeth, m. 1st, to Michael Ludford, of Witherly, co. Leicester, and 2ndly, to Clement Throckmorton.
Richard, m. —— dau. of —— Clive.
Anthony.
William, m. —— dau. and heir of —— Leftwicke

Richard, of Church Eaton, m. and had two sons, Thomas, d. s. p.; and Walter, of Tamworth, m. Mary, dau. of Humphrey Comberford, of Comberford, co. Stafford, and had two sons, Edward and Thomas.

Sir Richard m. 3rdly, Katherine, dau. and heir of Sir Thomas de la Pole, Knt. (son of Michael, Earl of Suffolk), and relict of Sir Miles Stapleton, of Bedale, and Ingham, co. York. The eldest son,

CHRISTOPHER HARCOURT, predeceased his father, having had by Jane his wife, dau. and co-heir of Sir Miles Stapleton, Knt., three sons, Miles, d. unm.; Richard, of Abingdon, Berks, who m. twice, but d. s. p., and

SIR SIMON HARCOURT, of Stanton Court, who received the honour of knighthood for his distinguished bravery at the sieges of Terouenne and Tournay, &c. He m. 1st, Agnes, dau. of Thomas Dayrell, of Scotney, and 2ndly, Elizabeth, dau. of Lord Darcy and Meynell, and relict of Sir Richard York, Knt., and by the former only had issue, JOHN (Sir), his successor; Edmund; and Florence, m. to Sir William Cottesmere, of Baldwin Brightwell, Oxon. Sir Simon d. in 1547, and was s. by his elder son,

SIR JOHN HARCOURT, Knt., who m. Margaret, dau., and at length co-heir of Sir William Barentyne, Knt., of Hasely, co. Oxford, and by her had six sons and several daus. He d. 19 February, 1565, and was s. by his eldest son,

SIMON HARCOURT, who m. 1st, Mary, dau. of Sir Edward Aston, of Tixhall, co. Stafford, Knt.; 2ndly, Grace, dau. of Humphrey Fitzherbert, of Upsall, co. Hereford, and widow of William Robinson, Esq., of Drayton Bassett, co. Stafford; and 3rdly, Jane, dau. of Sir William Spencer, of Wormleighton, co. Warwick, Knt. (ancestor of the Duke of Marlborough), and relict of Sir Richard Bruges, Knt., of Shefford, co. Berks. By the 1st wife, he had, with other issue, WALTER (Sir), his heir; John, who m. Mary, dau. of Walter Jones, of Witney, and had an only son, Essex; Elizabeth, m. to Richard Chamberlayne, of Astley, co. Warwick; Jane, m. to John Gray, of Envill, co. Stafford. The eldest son and heir,

SIR WALTER HARCOURT, was knighted by the Earl of Essex, at Rome, and was possessed of Stanton-Harcourt and Ellenhall. He m. Dorothy, dau. of William Robinson, of Drayton Basset, co. Stafford, and had issue, ROBERT, his heir; Michael, captain of a ship under Sir Walter Raleigh; Jane, m. to Sir William Essex, Bart., of Lamborne; Elizabeth, maid of honour to Queen Anne, consort of JAMES I. The elder son and heir,

ROBERT HARCOURT, Esq., joined Sir Walter Raleigh on a voyage of discovery to Guiana. He m. twice, 1st, Frances, dau. of Jeffrey de Vere (4th son of John, 5th Earl of Oxford; and 2ndly, Elizabeth, dau. of John Fitzherbert, of Norbury, co. Derby, but had issue only by the first, viz.,

SIMON (Sir), his heir.
Francis, d. s. p.
Vere, D.D., archdeacon of Notts, m. Lucy, dau. of Sir William Thornton, Knt., of Snailswell, co. Cambridge, by Mary his wife, dau. of Sir Thomas Eden, Knt., of Bollington Hall, Essex, and d, in 1683, having had issue.

Vere, m., and had a son, Vere, living in 1707.
Simon, clerk of the Crown, who m. 1st, Elizabeth, only dau and heir of Sir Richard Anderson, of Pendley, Bart., by Elizabeth his wife, one of the sisters of George, Viscount Hewet, of Ireland; and 2ndly, Elizabeth, dau. of George Morse, of Henbury, co. Gloucester, and relict of Sir Samuel Astry, Knt. By his 1st wife, with whom he acquired the estate of Pendley, Mr. Harcourt had with other daus., and a younger son, Simon, who d. unm., two other sons,

Henry, who m. Sarah-Frances, dau. and heir of Nathaniel Bard, by Persiana his wife, dau. of Henry Bard, Viscount Bellamont, and d. in 1743, having had with younger issue, an elder son, Richard-Bard Harcourt, who m. Rachel, dau. of Albert Nesbit, Esq., and had an only son, Henry, and a dau., Elizabeth-Sophia, m. to Charles-Amadis Harcourt, a colonel in the French army.
Richard of the Middle Temple, barrister-at-law, who m. 1st, Elizabeth, dau. of Sir Philip Harcourt, Knt., of Stanton-Harcourt, and by her had, besides two daus., a son,

Richard, of Wigsell, who m. Phœbe, dau. of Charles, and sister of Sir Charles Palmer, Bart., of Dorney, co. Bucks, and by her had two daus. and co-heirs, Phœbe, who m. Anthony Sawyer, of Heywood Lodge, and Elizabeth, who m. William Boys, of Hawkhurst, co. Kent, Esq., and had a son, William-Hooper Boys,

Esq., of Hawkhurst, who m. Sarah, 3rd dau. of Sir Harry Colles Meredyth, Bart., and left issue, a son William; and two daus., Corinna, m. 1st to Ambrose Crawley, Esq., and 2ndly, to the Cavaliére Vigliani, Prefect of Naples; and Lydia m. 1st, to the Chevalier de Letterstedt; and 2ndly, to M. Paul de Juvencel.

Mr. Robert Harcourt, whose will is dated 3 March, 1608, was s. by his eldest son,

Sir Simon Harcourt, who was knighted at Whitehall, 26 June, 1627. He was a military officer of high renown, and was appointed governor of Dublin Castle in 1643, and immediately raised the blockade of that city, then invested by the rebels, but fell soon afterwards mortally wounded before the castle of Carrickfellain, co. Wicklow. He m. Anne, dau. of William, Lord Paget, and by her, who m. 2ndly, Sir William Walter, of Osterly Park, left a son and successor,

Sir Philip Harcourt, knighted 5 June, 1660, and M.P. for co. Oxford, 1680-1, who m. 1st, Anne, dau. of Sir William Waller, of Osterly Park, by Lady Anne his wife, dau. of Thomas Finch, Earl of Winchelsea, and by her had a son and heir Simon (Sir), of whom presently. Sir Philip m. 2ndly, Elizabeth, dau. and heir of John Lee, Esq., of London and Ankerwyke, co. Bucks, and had issue,

Philip, of Wigsell, who m. Elizabeth, dau. and heir of T. Woodruffe, M.D., of Lawton Hope, co. Hereford, and d. in 1708, having had issue,

Philip, of Ankerwycke, and of the Middle Temple, who m. Sarah, dau. of Henry Hall, of Hutton Hall, Essex, and had two daus., Elizabeth and Philippa.
Lee, of Bombay, d. about 1726, s. p.
John, of Ankerwycke, heir to his brother, Philip. He m. 1st, Anne Parker; and 2ndly, Margaret Irene, dau. of John Sarney, Esq., of Somerset house, London, and by the latter, who m. 2ndly, Molyneux, Lord Shuldham, and 3rdly, John Meade, Earl of Clanwilliam, had, with two younger sons, Philip-Francis, d. young, and George-William-Richard, major-gen. in the army, who d. unm., an eldest son and heir,

John-Simon, of Ankerwycke, and of Yardley-place, co. Herts, b. 1772, who m. Elizabeth-Dale, dau. of Major Henniker, and niece of Lord Henniker, and left with a dau., who d. in 1813, an only son,

George Simon, of Ankerwycke, high sheriff of Bucks in 1834, and formerly M.P., who m. 1st, 24 June, 1833, Jessy, 2nd dau. of John Rolls, Esq., of Bryanstone-square, London, and of The Hendre, co. Monmouth, and by her, who d. at Paris, in 1842, had surviving issue,

John-Simon-Chandos, of Ankerwycke, b. 28 September, 1835. (See Burke's Landed Gentry.)
Anna-Phillipa-Mary, m. to F. S. Mansfield, Esq.

Mr. Harcourt m. 2ndly, Gertrude-Charlotte, dau. of George Lucas, Esq., by whom also he had issue.

Sir Philip Harcourt d. 20 March, 1688, and was s. by the only son of his 1st marriage,

Sir Simon Harcourt, Knt., 1st Baron Harcourt, a lawyer of eminence, who filled the offices of solicitor and attorney-general, with little interruption, from 1702 until 1710, when he was nominated lord-keeper of the great seal, and sworn a member of the privy council. In the following year, 3 September, 1711, he was elevated to the peerage, by the title of Baron Harcourt, of Stanton-Harcourt, co. Oxford; and 7 April, 1712, declared lord high chancellor of Great Britain, which great office he continued to fill until the accession of George I., in 1714. On 24 July, 1721, his lordship was created Viscount Harcourt, and, in the following month, again called to the council board. The viscount was appointed one of the lords-justices in 1723, 1725, and 1727. His lordship m. 1st, Rebecca, dau. of the Rev. Thomas Clark, M.A., 2ndly, Elizabeth, dau. of Richard Spencer, of London, and relict of Richard Anderson; and 3rdly, Elizabeth, dau. of Sir Thomas Vernon, Knt., and relict of Sir John Waller, Bart., but had issue by his 1st wife only, viz.,

1. Simon, M.P. for Aylesbury and Abingdon, who m. Elizabeth, sister of Sir John Evelyn, Bart., and d. v. p. 1720, leaving,

Simon, successor to his grandfather.
Martha, m. George, 1st Lord Vernon.

1. Anne, m. to John Barlow, of Alebeak, co. Pembroke.
11. Ar bella, m. to Herbert Aubrey, of Clayhanger.

He d. 29 July, 1727, and was s. by his grandson,

Simon Harcourt, 2nd Viscount, who was created, 21 December, 1749, Viscount Nuneham, of Nuneham-Courtney, and Earl of Harcourt, of Stanton-Harcourt. His lordship was the 27th in paternal descent from Bernard, Lord of Harcourt, in Normandy. He m. in 1735, Rebecca, only dau. and heiress of

Charles Le Baas, Esq., of Pipwell Abbey, co. Northampton, by Mary his wife, dau., and at length sole heir of, Sir Samuel Moyer, Bart., by whom he had issue,

George-Simon, his successor.
William, successor to his brother.
Elizabeth, who was one of the ten young ladies, daus. of dukes and earls, who supported the train of Queen Charlotte, at her majesty's nuptials, 8 September, 1761. Her ladyship m. in 1763, Sir W. Lee, Bart., and d. in 1811, leaving issue,

The earl, who had filled some high diplomatic stations during the reign of King George II., was constituted, in 1751, governor to his late Majesty, King George III., then Prince of Wales; and in 1761, his lordship was nominated ambassador extraordinary to demand the Princess Charlotte, of Mecklenburgh Strelitz, in marriage for that monarch. In 1772 he was appointed viceroy of Ireland. His lordship lost his life, 16 September, 1777, by unfortunately falling into a well in his own park, at Nuneham, and was s. by his eldest son,

George-Simon Harcourt, 2nd earl, who m. 26 September, 1765, Elizabeth, dau. of George Venables Vernon, Lord Vernon, and d. s. p. 20 April, 1809, when the honours devolved upon his brother,

William Harcourt, 3rd earl. This nobleman was b. 20 March, 1743, and, adopting the profession of arms, attained the rank of field-marshal. He was colonel of the 16th regiment of dragoons, and a knight grand cross of the Bath. His lordship m. in 1778, Mary, relict of Thomas Lockhart, Esq., and dau. of the Rev. William Danby, D.D., of Marhamshire, co. York; but dying s. p. 18 June, 1830, all his honours became extinct, and his estates devolved on his first cousin, Hon. and Most Rev. Edward Vernon, Archbishop of York, who thereupon assumed the surname and arms of Harcourt, and was grandfather of Edward William Harcourt, Esq., M.P., of Stanton-Harcourt and Nuneham Courtenay, co. Oxford. (See Burke's Landed Gentry.)

Arms—Gu., two bars, or.

HARE—BARON COLERAINE.

By Letters Patent, dated 31 August, 1625.

Lineage.

John Hare, Esq., of an ancient Suffolk family, having eventually inherited the estates of his brother, Sir Nicholas, became of Stow Bardolph. He had a numerous family, seven sons and three daus. Of the former,

Richard, the eldest, was ancestor of the Hares, of Stow Bardolph, raised to the degree of Baronet in 1641. (See Burke's Extinct Baronetage.)

John Hare, Esq., the youngest, a bencher of the Middle Temple, m. Margaret, dau. of John Crouch, Esq., of Cornbury, Herts, and by her (who m. 2ndly, Henry, 1st Earl of Manchester) had a son,

Hugh Hare, Esq., of Langford, co. Wilts, a faithful adherent of Charles I., by whom he was created Baron Coleraine, co. Londonderry, 31 August, 1625. His lordship m. Lucy, dau. of Henry, 1st Earl of Manchester, and had Henry, his heir, and Hugh, from whom sprang the Hares, of Docking, in Norfolk, &c. The eldest son,

Henry Hare, 2nd Lord Coleraine, a celebrated antiquary, m. Constantia, dau. of Sir Richard Lucy, Bart., of Broxbourne, and had two sons and one dau., viz.,

Hugh, who d. v. p., leaving by Lydia his wife, dau. of Matthew Carlton, Esq., of Edmonton, two sons and three daus.,

Henry, who s. his grandfather as 3rd lord.
Hugh, d. unm.
Lucia,
Constantia, } d. unm.
Lydia, m. to the Rev. Dr. John Rogers, rector of Wrigton, in Somersetshire.

Lucius, d. unm.
Constantia, m. to Hugh Smithson, Esq., of Tottenham, who d. s. p.

Lord Coleraine was s. at his decease by his grandson,

Henry Hare, 3rd Lord Coleraine; who m. Anne, dau. of John Hanger, Esq., governor of the bank of England; but d. s. p. when the peerage became extinct.

Arms—Gu., two bars, and a chief, indented, or.

HARINGTON—BARONS HARINGTON.

By Writ of Summons, dated 30 December, 1324.

Lineage.

The family of Harington derived their surname from Haverington, co. Cumberland, a lordship which they very anciently possessed; but from the time of EDWARD I. their chief seat and residence was at Aldingham, in Lancashire, which manor was acquired by

ROBERT DE HARINGTON, with his wife Agnes, sister and heir of William de Cancefield, or Cavefeld, son and heir of Richard de Cancefield, by Alice his wife, sister and heir of Michael Flameng, Lord of Aldingham. He had with a younger son, Robert, an elder son,

JOHN DE HARINGTON, who, in the 34th EDWARD I., amongst the rest of those stout young soldiers which were then to attend the king into Scotland, received the honour of knighthood, with Prince Edward, by bathing and other sacred ceremonies. Sir John had a military summons, in the 4th EDWARD II., for the Scottish wars. In the 12th of the same reign he had a charter of free-warren in all his demesne-lands in the cos. York and Lancaster, and in the 14th EDWARD III., a license to impark 600 acres of wood, moor, and marsh, within the precincts of his lordship of Aldingham. He was summoned to parliament as a baron, from 30 December, 1324, to 13 November, 1345. His lordship m. Margaret, dau. of Sir Richard Barlingham, Knt., and had an only son,

ROBERT, who d. v. p., leaving issue, by his wife Elizabeth, one of the daus. and co-heirs of John de Multon, of Egremond,

JOHN, successor to his grandfather.

Robert, from whom descended the Lords Harington, of Exton.

Simon, ancestor of the Haringtons, of Bishton.

Lord Harington d. in 1348, and was s. by his grandson,

JOHN DE HARINGTON, 2nd baron, summoned to parliament from 14 February, 1348, to 10 March, 1349. This nobleman d. in 1363, seized of the third part of the manor of Multon, co. Lincoln, of the manors of Aldingham, Thirnum, and a moiety of the manor of Ulveston, in Lancashire, of the manor of Austwyke, co. York, and of those of Millum, Mosearghe, Haverington, with its members, and a third part of the manor of Egremond, in Cumberland. He d. 1363, and was s. by his son, then in minority,

ROBERT DE HARINGTON, 3rd baron, summoned to parliament from 4 August, 1377, during the remainder of his life. This nobleman received the honour of knighthood at the coronation of RICHARD II., and was the same year employed in that monarch's service at Calais. His lordship m. Isabel, dau. and co-heir of Sir Nigel Loryng, K.G., and had issue,

JOHN (Sir), his successor.

WILLIAM, successor to his brother.

He d. in 1405, and was s. by his elder son,

SIR JOHN DE HARINGTON, 4th baron, summoned to parliament under the misnomer of ROBERT,* from his accession to the peerage until 3 September, 1417. This nobleman was in the expedition made into France in the 3rd HENRY V.; and the next year, being retained by indenture to serve the king in those wars, he received £295 in hand, towards his wages, upon that account. But soon after, purposing to travel into foreign parts, he declared his testament, 8 June, 1417, bequeathing his body to be buried wheresoever he should happen to die, and leaving to Elizabeth his wife, one-half of all his silver vessels; after which he survived not a year, for the probate of that will bears date 27 April, next ensuing year. Leaving no issue, his lordship was s. by his brother,

SIR WILLIAM DE HARINGTON, 5th baron, K.G., summoned to parliament from 26 February, 1421, to 6 September, 1439. This nobleman served the office of sheriff for Yorkshire, and was governor of the castle at York, in the 10th HENRY V., he was afterwards several years engaged in the wars of France in the reigns of HENRY V. and HENRY VI. His lordship m. Elizabeth,

---

* The name of *Robert* de Harington occurs regularly in the summonses to parliament, from 1st RICHARD II. to 4th HENRY V.; but as Robert, the last baron d. in 1405 (twelve years before the latter period), and as *John*, Baron Harington, is stated in the rolls of parliament to have been present 22 December, 8th HENRY IV., 1406, it may be inferred that all the writs after the 7th HENRY IV. were directed to this baron, and that the christian name of *Robert* on the rolls, after that year, was an error.—NICOLAS

s'ster of Hugh Courtenay, Earl of Devon, and had an only child,

ELIZABETH (who d. v. p.), m. to William, Lord Bonville, and had a son,

WILLIAM BONVILLE, who, in her right, became Lord Harington, d. v. p., leaving a dau.,

CECILY BONVILLE, who m. 1st, Thomas Grey, Marquess of Dorset, and 2ndly, Henry Stafford, Earl of Wiltshire.

Lord Harington d. in 1457, leaving his grandson, WILLIAM BONVILLE, above-mentioned, his heir. CECILY BONVILLE, the dau. and heiress of the said William, having m. Thomas Grey, 1st Marquess of Dorset, for her 1st husband, she conveyed the Baronies of Bonville and Harington to the noble house of Grey, where they continued until the attainder in 1554 of Henry Grey, Duke of Suffolk, grandson of the said Cecily Bonville, and the said Thomas, Marquess of Dorset, when those dignities, along with his grace's other high honours, became FORFEITED. By her 2nd husband, Henry Stafford, Earl of Wiltshire, Cecily Bonville had no issue.

Arms—Sa., a fret, arg.

HARINGTON—BARONS HARINGTON, OF EXTON, CO. RUTLAND.

By Letters Patent, dated 21 July, 1603.

Lineage.

This is a branch of the ancient family of Harington, barons by writ, springing from

SIR ROBERT DE HARINGTON, grandson of Sir John de Harington, who had been summoned to parliament in the reign of EDWARD II., and 2nd son of Robert de Harington, and his wife Elizabeth, dau. and co-heir of John de Multon, of Egremond. This Sir Robert left a son,

JOHN DE HARINGTON, who m. Agnes, dau. of Lawrence Flete, Esq., of Flete, co. Lincoln, and dying in 1421, was s. by his son,

ROBERT DE HARINGTON, who m. one of the daus. and co-heirs of John de la Laund, and was s. by his son,

JOHN DE HARINGTON, who having m. Catherine, dau. and heir of Sir Thomas Colepeper, acquired thereby the manor of Exton, in Rutlandshire, and fixed his residence there. He was s. by his son,

ROBERT HARINGTON, Esq., of Exton, who served the office of sheriff for the co. Rutland in 1492 and 1498. This nobleman m. Maud, dau. of Sir John Prisett, Knt., chief justice of the court of Common Pleas, and dying in 1501, was s. by his son,

SIR JOHN HARINGTON, Knt., of Exton, sheriff of Rutland, who m. Alice, dau. of Henry Southill, and was s by his eldest son,

SIR JOHN HARINGTON, Knt., of Exton, high sheriff of the co. Rutland, and treasurer of the army to HENRY VIII., at Boulogne, who m. Elizabeth, dau. and heir of Robert Moton, of Peckleton, co. Leicester, and was s. at his decease by his son,

SIR JAMES HARINGTON, Knt., of Exton, who m. Lucy, dau. of Sir William Sidney, of Penshurst, and sister of Sir Henry Sidney, K.G., by whom he had three sons, viz.,

JOHN, his successor.

Henry (Sir).

James, of Ridlington, co. Rutland, who was created a baronet 29 June, 1611; a dignity now enjoyed by his descendant, Sir Richard Harington, Bart., of Ridlington.

Mabel, m. to Sir A. Noel.

Sir James d. in 1592, and was s. by his eldest son,

SIR JOHN HARINGTON, Knt., who was elevated to the peerage by letters patent, dated 21 July, 1603, as BARON HARINGTON, *of Exton*. His lordship was tutor to the Princess Elizabeth, dau. of King JAMES I., until her marriage with the Electoral-Palatine, when he attended her royal highness into Germany. He m. Anne, only dau. and heiress of Robert Kelway, Esq., surveyor of the court of wards and liveries, and had issue,

JOHN, his successor.

Lucy, m. to Edward Russell, 3rd Earl of Bedford, and d. s. p.

Frances, m. to Sir Robert Chichester, K.B., and had an only dau.,

Anne, m. to Robert, Lord Kinloss, 1st Earl of Elgin, by whom she was mother of

Robert, 2nd earl created, now represented by the Duke of Buckingham and Chandos, who inherits the Barony of Kinloss.

His lordship d. in 1613, and was s. by his son,

JOHN HARINGTON, 2nd baron, at whose decease in the following year (1614), the Barony of Harington, of Exton, became EXTINCT, and his lordship's estates devolved upon his sisters. The Countess of Bedford, Dugdale says, notwithstanding her large fortune, wasted by her profuseness, not only her own estate, but some portion of her husband's. Pennant, in describing the pictures at Woburne Abbey, notices "a full length of that fantastic lady, Lucy, Countess of Bedford, dressed in as fantastic a habit, with an immense veil distended behind her. Her ladyship was a patroness of literature, and there are several Epistles of Daniel, the poet, and the celebrated Doctor John Donne, dedicated to her."

Nicholas Stone, statuary to King JAMES I., made a tomb for her father, mother, brother, and sister, and for which the countess paid him £1020, and had it erected at Exton.

Arms—Sa., a fret, arg.

HARLEY—EARL OF OXFORD.

By Letters Patent, dated 24 May, 1711.

Lineage,

The family of Harley can be traced to a period antecedent to the Conquest, and its station was then so eminent, that the great house of Harlai, in France, deduces its origin from the Harleys of England.

SIR ROBERT DE HARLEY (eldest son of Sir Richard de Harley, Knt., who d. about the 13th EDWARD II.) m. Margaret, eldest dau. and co-heir (with her sister, Elizabeth, wife of Sir Richard de Cornwall, son of Richard, Earl of Cornwall, King of the Romans, brother of King HENRY III.) of Sir Bryan de Brampton; by which marriage he acquired a great estate and the seat of Brampton Castle, which continued for centuries the chief residence of his descendants. His great-grandson,

SIR JOHN HARLEY, of Brampton Castle, received the honour of knighthood from EDWARD IV., on the field of battle, at Gaston, near Tewkesbury, 9 May, 1471, and was sheriff of Shropshire in the 21st year of the same monarch. From him lineally descended

THOMAS HARLEY, Esq.,* of Brampton Castle, who was born about the year 1543, and obtained a grant from King JAMES I. of the honour and castle of Wigmore, co. Hereford. He m. Margaret, dau. of Sir Andrew Corbet, Knt., of Morton Corbet; and 2ndly, Anne, dau. of Walter Griffith, Esq., of Burton Agnes, and dying in 1631, was s. by his only surviving son,

SIR ROBERT HARLEY, K.B., M.P. for the co. Hereford. This gentleman had a grant, 12 September, 1626, of the office of master and worker of moneys to be coined in the tower of London during his life, with a salary of £4,000 a-year; but, after the murder of the king, refusing to coin with any other than the die of the deceased monarch, he was removed by parliament. Sir Robert m. 1st, Anne, dau. of Charles Barrett, Esq., of Belhouse, Essex; 2ndly, Mary, dau. of Sir Francis Newport; by neither of whom, however, had he any issue to survive; and 3rdly, Brilliana (so christened from *Brill*, of which her father was governor at the time of her ladyship's birth), dau. of Edward, Viscount Conway, by Dorothy, dau. of Sir John Tracy, of Todington, co. Gloucester, and sister to Mary, wife of the celebrated General Sir Horace Vere, Lord Vere, of Tilbury (by which alliance the Harleys became connected with the Veres, Earls of Oxford, Holles's, Earls of Clare, and other ancient families). Lady Brilliana Harley was celebrated for her gallant defence of Brampton Castle, during the civil wars, when invested, in 1643, by the rebels, whom she forced to raise the siege after seven weeks of unavailing hostility. Her ladyship dying, however, in the October following, the besiegers returned to the castle, which, after a second gallant resistance, being forced to surrender, was burnt to the ground. Sir Robert Harley d. 6 November, 1656, and was s. by his eldest son,

COLONEL SIR EDWARD HARLEY, member for the co. Hereford in the parliament which restored CHARLES II., by whom he was appointed governor of Dunkirk. Sir Edward m. 1st, in 1654, Mary, dau. of Sir William Button, of Parkgate, by whom he had two daus., Brilliana, wife of Alexander Popham, Esq., and Martha, wife of Samuel Hutchins, Esq.; and 2ndly, Abigail, dau. of Nathaniel Stephens, Esq., of Essington, co. Gloucester, by whom he had (with other issue),

ROBERT, of who.n presently, as Earl of Oxford.
Edward. of Eyewood, co. Hereford, M.P., recorder of Leominster, and one of the auditors of the Imprest, m. Sarah, 3rd dau. of Thomas Foley, Esq., of Whitley, co. Worcester, and had,

    EDWARD, who s. to the Earldom of Oxford.
    Robert, M.P., recorder of Leominster, d. unm. in 1774.
    Abigail, m. to the Hon. John Verney, master of the Rolls.

Colonel Sir Edward Harley d. 8 December, 1700, and was s. by his eldest son,

ROBERT HARLEY, Esq., b. 5 December, 1661. This gentleman was first returned to parliament for Tregony, in Cornwall; and afterwards, in 1690, for the town of Radnor, which he continued to represent so long as he remained a commoner. On 11 February, 1700-1, Mr. Harley was elected speaker of the House of Commons. In 1704, he was sworn of the privy council, and constituted one of the principal secretaries of state, filling the speaker's chair at the same time. In 1710, he was appointed chancellor of the Exchequer. About this period Mr. Harley had a miraculous escape from assassination, having been stabbed with a pen-knife by the Marquess of Guiscard, then under examination before a committee of the privy council at Whitehall. On 24 May, 1711, the right hon. gentleman was elevated to the peerage, by the titles of *Baron Harley, of Wigmore, co. Hereford*, EARL OF OXFORD, and EARL OF MORTIMER, with remainder, in default of male issue, to the heirs male of his grandfather, Sir Robert Harley, knight of the Bath; and 29 May, in the same year, his lordship was constituted lord high treasurer of England. The earl m. 1st, Elizabeth, dau. of Thomas Foley, Esq., of Whitley Court, co. Worcester, by whom he had,

EDWARD, his successor.
Abigail, m. to George, Earl of Kinnoul; and d. in 1750.
Elizabeth, m. to Peregrine Hyde, Duke of Leeds.

His lordship m. 2ndly, Sarah, dau. of Thomas Middleton, Esq., but had no other issue. On 10 June, 1715, Lord Oxford was impeached by the Commons of high treason, and was committed to the Tower by the House of Lords, where he suffered imprisonment until 1 July, 1717, when he was acquitted, after a public trial by his peers. His memory is celebrated by Pope in the following lines:—

    "A soul supreme, in each hard instance tried,
    Above all pain, all anger, and all pride,
    The rage of power, the blast of public breath,
    The lust of lucre, and the dread of death."

The earl d. 21 May, 1724, and was s. by his only son,

EDWARD, 2nd earl. This nobleman devoted himself much to literature; and the country is much indebted to him for the celebrated collection so well known as the *Harleian Miscellany*, purchased by parliament from the countess in 1754, after the earl's decease, and deposited in the British Museum. His lordship m. 31 October, 1713, Lady Henrietta Cavendish Holles, only dau. and heir of John Holles, last Duke of Newcastle of that family (the dignity expired in 1713), by whom he had an only dau. and heir, Margaret-Cavendish, who m. in 1734, William, 2nd Duke of Portland. The earl dying without male issue, 16 June, 1741, the honours devolved, according to the reversionary clause in the patent, upon his first cousin,

EDWARD HARLEY, Esq., M.P. for the co. Hereford, as 3rd earl (refer to children of Col. Sir Edward Harley). His lordship m. in 1725, Martha, eldest dau. of John Morgan, Esq. of Tredegar, co. Monmouth, by whom (who d. in 1774) he left,

  I. EDWARD, his successor.
  II. John, D.D., bishop of Hereford, and dean of Windsor; b. 29 September, 1728; m. 23 February, 1770, Roach, dau. of Gwynne Vaughan. Esq. of Trebarry, co. Radnor; and dying 7 January, 1788, left,

    1 EDWARD, who inherited as 5th earl.
    2 John, in holy orders; b. 31 December, 1774; d. unm 20 October, 1815.
    1 Frances, d. 25 November, 1848, aged seventy six.
    2 Martha, d. 25 January, 1824.

  III. Thomas, b. 24 August, 1730; an alderman of London, M.P. for that city, and lord mayor in 1768; m. 15 March, 1752, Anne, dau. of Edward Bangham, and had five daus., co-heirs to his fortune, viz.,

    1 Martha, m. 30 December, 1779, to George Drummond, Esq. of Stanmore; and d. in 1788.
    2 Anne, m. to George, 2nd Lord Rodney; and d. in 1840..
    3 Sarah, m. to Robert, 9th Earl of Kinnoull; d. in 1837.
    4 Elizabeth, m. 8 October, 1793, to David Murray, Esq.; and d. 9 July, 1824.
    5 Margaret, m. to Sir John Boyd, Bart.; and d. 20 November, 1830.

    Alderman Harley d. 1 December, 1804; his wife d. 15 January, 1798.

  IV. William, in holy orders, prebendary of Worcester; d. 8 July, 1769.

---

* Jane, sister of this Thomas Harley, of Brampton, m. Roger Mynors, Esq., of Treago, ancestor of Peter Rickards-Mynors, Esq., of Treago.

i. Sarah, *d. unm.*, 1737.

ii. Martha, *m.* 20 April, 1764, Charles Milborne, Esq., of Wonaston, The Priory, Abergavenny, co. Monmouth, and had an only dau. and heir, Mary, wife of Thomas Swinnerton, Esq., of Butterton, co. Stafford.

His lordship *d.* 11 April, 1755, and was *s.* by his eldest son,

EDWARD, 4th earl, *b.* 2 September, 1726. His lordship *m.* 11 July, 1751, Susannah, eldest dau. of William Archer, Esq. of Welford, co. Berks; but *d.* without issue in 1790, when the family honours devolved upon his nephew (revert to the Hon. and Right Rev. Dr. John Harley, bishop of Hereford).

EDWARD, 5th earl, *b.* 20 February, 1773; *m.* 3 March, 1794, Jane-Elizabeth, dau. of the Rev. James Scott, A.M., rector of Stokin, co. Southampton, by whom (who *d.* 20 November, 1824) he had issue,

EDWARD, *Lord Harley*, *b.* 20 January, 1800; *d. s. p.* 1 January, 1828.

ALFRED, last earl.

JANE, *m.* 17 August, 1835, Henry Bickersteth, Esq., afterwards Lord Langdale, and had a dau.. Jane-Frances, *m.* 16 December, 1857, to Alexander, Count Teleki de Szék, Lady Langdale resumed her maiden name of Harley, after the death of her brother, the last Earl of Oxford.

Charlotte-Mary, *m.* to General Bacon.

Anne, *m.* in 1835, to the Cavaliére San Giorgio, deceased.

Frances, *m.* in 1835, to Henry-Vernon Harcourt, Esq., who *d.* 25 February, 1853.

Louisa, *d.* young.

His lordship *d.* in January, 1849, and was *s.* by his son,

ALFRED, 6th earl, *b.* 10 January, 1809; who *m.* 17 February, 1831, Miss Eliza Nugent, but *d. s. p.* 19 January, 1853, when the honours became EXTINCT.

Arms—Or, a bend, cotised, sa.

HASTANG—BARON HASTANG.

By Writ of Summons, dated 19 December, 1311

Lineage.

Of this family whose chief seat was at Lemington, co. Warwick, and thence called Lemington Hastang, was

ATROP HASTANG, who gave to the canons of Nostell, co. York, the churches of Lemington and Newbold; and bestowed on the canons of Kenilworth, the church of Whitnash. To this Atrop *s.* his son,

ATROP HASTANG, who was *s.* by his son,

HUMPHREY HASTANG, who, joining the rebellious barons against King John, had his lands seized, but returning to his allegiance, they were restored in the 1st HENRY III. This Humphrey was *s.* by his son,

ROBERT HASTANG, who *m.* Joane, dau. and co-heir of William de Curli. This Robert gave a mark in gold, in 41st HENRY III., for respiting his knighthood. But afterwards taking part with Montford, Earl of Leicester, he was one of those who held out the castle of Kenilworth, for which his lands were seized, and given to Sir James de Aldithley and Sir Hugh de Turbervill. He had restitution of them, however, upon paying a fine under the "Dictum de Kenilworth." Robert de Hastang was *s.* by his son,

ROBERT DE HASTANG, who in the 10th EDWARD II., was constituted one of the commissioners to treat with Robert de Brus. and his party in Scotland, upon a truce betwixt both realms; and was summoned to parliament as a baron in 5th EDWARD II.; his son,

JOHN DE HASTANG, 2nd baron, does not appear from the existing rolls, to have been summoned to parliament; his son, (it is presumed)

THOMAS DE HASTANG, 3rd baron, had summons 25 February, and 20 November, 1342, but his name does not afterwards occur in the list of summonses. His lordship *m.* Maud, widow of John Strange of Knockyn, and had a son,

SIR JOHN DE HASTANG, who *m.* 1st.. Blanch ——— but had no issue, and 2ndly, Maud, dau. of Sir William Trussel, Knt., by whom he left at his decease, 1360, two daus., his co-heirs,

Maud, *m.* to Ralph de Stafford, of Grafton.

Joane, *m.* to Sir Johne Salisbury, Knt.

In the representatives of those ladies, the Barony of Hastang is now vested.

Arms—Az., and a chief gu., over all a lion rampant, or.

HASTINGS—BARONS HASTINGS, EARLS OF PEMBROKE.

Barony, by Writ of Summons, dated 14 October, 1264.
Earldom, by Letters Patent, dated 13 October, 1339.

Lineage.

This noble family derived its surname from Hastings, (one of the Cinque Ports,) in Sussex, the lastage of which they farmed for a considerable period from the crown.

ROBERT, Portreve of Hastings, was *s.* by

WALTER DE HASTINGS, who held the office of steward to King HENRY I., by Sergeantie, in respect of his tenure of the manor of Ashele, in the county of Norfolk, viz., by the service of taking charge of the naperie, (table linen,) at the solemn coronation of the kings of this realm. This Walter, by Hadewise, his wife, had a son,

HUGH DE HASTINGS, Lord of Fillongley, co. Warwick, who *m.* Erneburga, dau. of Hugh de Flamville, and niece and heir of Robert de Flamville, of Aston-Flamville, co. Leicester, by whom he acquired that manor, as well as Gressing, in Norfolk, and the stewardship of the abbey of St. Edmundsbury, and had two sons and a dau., viz.,

WILLIAM, his successor.

Richard, a priest, rector of Barewell, in Leicestershire.

Mahant, to whom he gave the manor of Arke, in Devonshire, on her marriage with Robert de Wyford; from this lady descended,

Sir Geffery de Anke, or Hanke, who, *temp.* HENRY III., conveyed that estate, in marriage with his dau., to Michael Davyll.

Hugh de Hastings was *s.* by his elder son,

WILLIAM DE HASTINGS, steward to HENRY II., who *m.* 1st, Maude, dau. of Thurstan Banaster, and had two sons,

i. Henry, who *d. s. p.*
ii. WILLIAM, of whom we treat.

William de Hastings *m.* 2ndly, Ida, dau. of Henry, Earl of Ewe, and had a son,

THOMAS, ancestor of the Earls of Huntingdon.

The 2nd son,

WILLIAM DE HASTINGS, *m.* 1st, Margery, dau., of Roger Bigot, Earl of Norfolk, and had, (with a dau. Ida, *m.* to Stephen de Segrave) a son,

HENRY DE HASTINGS, who, upon paying a fine of 50 marks, and doing his homage, had livery of his lands in the cos. Warwick, Leicester, Salop, Bedford, Norfolk, and Suffolk. This Henry *m.* Ada, 4th dau. of David, Earl of Huntingdon, and of Maud, his wife, dau. of Hugh, and one of the sisters and coheirs of Ranulph, Earl of Chester; and through her he eventually shared in the great estates of the Earls of Chester. By this lady he had issue, HENRY, his successor, and two daus., Margery and Hillaria, who, at the time of his decease, were in the nunnery of Alneston, and their tuition was then committed to William de Cantelupe. This Henry de Hastings attending King HENRY into France, in the 26th of that monarch's reign, was taken prisoner at the great defeat which the English army then sustained at Zante, but was soon afterwards released. In a few years subsequently he accompanied Richard, Earl of Cornwall, with divers other of the principal nobility, into France, whither the said earl proceeded at that period with a splendid retinue, but for what purpose does not appear. About the close of the same year (1250) Henry de Hastings *d.* and was *s.* by his son,

HENRY DE HASTINGS, then in minority, whose wardship was granted to Guy de Lusignan, King HENRY III.'s half brother. This Henry, in the 44th HENRY III., had a military summons to be at Shrewsbury, with horse and arms, to march against the Welsh; and the next year had a similar summons to be at London. But very soon afterwards we find him in arms with Simon de Mon fort, Earl of Leicester, and other turbulent spirits, against the king, and with those excommunicated by the archbishop of Canterbury. After which he became one of the most zealous of the baronial leaders, and distinguished himself at the battle of Lewes, wherein the king was made prisoner, received the honour of knighthood at the hands of Montfort; and was constituted governor of Scarborough and Winchester castles. This stout baron was *s.* at his decease in 1249, by his son,

HENRY DE HASTINGS, who *m.* Eve, sister, and at length coheir, of George de Cantilupe, Baron of Bergavenny, and had issue,

JOHN, his successor.

Edmund, who had summons to parliament, as a baron, from 29 December, 1299, 28th EDWARD I., to 26 July, 1313, 7th EDWARD II., but nothing is known of his descendants.

And three daus. Audra, Lora, and Joane. This feudal lord was summoned to parliament, as BARON HASTINGS, 14 December, 1264. He d. in 1268, and was s. by his son,

JOHN HASTINGS, 2nd baron, summoned to parliament as LORD HASTINGS, from 23 June, 1295, to 22 May, 1313, although in right of his mother, and the tenure of the castle of Bergavenny, he was unquestionably BARON OF BERGAVENNY. This nobleman was in the expedition to Scotland in the 12th EDWARD I., and in three years afterwards attended Edmund, Earl of Cornwall, regent of the kingdom during the king's sojourn in Gascony, into Wales. He was subsequently in an expedition to Ireland, and again in Scotland, 28th EDWARD I., where he performed military service for five knights' fees. The next year he continued in the Scottish wars, under Edward, Prince of Wales, and in the 31st EDWARD I. he assisted at the celebrated siege of Kaerlaverock. His lordship had afterwards, 34th EDWARD I., a grant from the king of the whole co. Menteth, with the isles, as also of all the manors and lands of Alan, late Earl of Menteth, then declared an enemy and rebel to the king. He was likewise seneschal of Aquitaine, and one of the competitors, in 1290, for the crown of Scotland, in right of his descent from Ada, dau. of David, Earl of Huntingdon, brother of MALCOLM and WILLIAM, Kings of Scotland. His lordship m. 1st, Isabel, dau. of William de Valence, Earl of Pembroke, half brother of King HENRY III., and sister and co-heir of Aymer de Valence, Earl of Pembroke, by whom (who d. 3 October, 1305) he had, with other issue,

JOHN, his successor.
Elizabeth, m. to Roger, Lord Grey, of Ruthyn.

Lord Hastings m. 2ndly, Isabel, dau. of Hugh Despencer, Earl of Winchester, and had two other sons, viz., HUGH, (Sir) of Gressing Hall, co. Norfolk, who m. Margery, dau. of Sir Jordan de Foliot, and sister and co-heir of Sir Richard Foliot, and Thomas. From the elder son lineally descended EDWARD HASTINGS, of whom in the sequel, as competitor with Lord Grey de Ruthyn, for the arms of Hastings. His lordship d. in 1313, and was s. by his eldest son,

JOHN HASTINGS, 3rd baron, summoned to parliament as LORD HASTINGS, from 26 November, 1313, to 22 February, 1325. This nobleman was actively engaged in the wars of Scotland from the 4th to the 12th EDWARD II., and the next year, upon the insurrection of the lords, when they banished the two Spencers, his lordship being one of their adherents, deserted the barons, and joined the king at Cirencester. Moreover, he was the same year again in the Scottish wars; and in the 16th EDWARD II., he was made governor of Kenilworth Castle. Lord Hastings married Julian, grand-dau. and heir of Thomas de Leybourne, Baron Leybourne, which lady m. 2ndly, Thomas le Blount, and 3rdly, William de Clinton, Earl of Huntingdon. His lordship d. in 1325, and was s. by his son,

LAURENCE HASTINGS, 4th baron, then but five years of age, who, upon attaining majority, was, by royal favour, by letters patent dated 13 October, 1339, declared EARL OF PEMBROKE: and about the same time, was in the expedition made into Flanders. The next year he attended King EDWARD III., in the notable adventure at sea against the French, where he participated in the glory of the victory achieved near Slugs. He was afterwards constantly in the French wars, wherein he displayed great valour. The earl m. Agnes, dau. of Roger Mortimer, Earl of March, and dying in 1348, was s. by his only son,

JOHN HASTINGS, 2nd Earl of Pembroke, K.G., who, in the 46th EDWARD III., being selected for his experience and valour, was sent lieutenant into Aquitaine, and arrived at the port of Rochel, then besieged by the French, on the eve of St. John the Baptist. But no sooner had he got his ships within the harbour, than being suddenly attacked by the Spanish fleet, before he had been able to form his line of battle, he suffered so signal a defeat that few of his men escaped. His squadron was entirely consumed, himself and his principal officers made prisoners, and treasure to the amount of 20,000 marks, which King EDWARD had sent over to maintain the war, became a prize to the enemy. He subsequently endured four years' harsh captivity in Spain, from which he was eventually released through the interference of Bertrand Clekyn, Constable of France, but died on his journey from Paris (whither he had removed from Spain) to Calais, being considered to have been poisoned by the Spaniards, 16 April, 1375. His lordship m. 1st, the Lady Margaret Plantagenet, 4th dau. of King EDWARD III., by whom he had no issue. He m. 2ndly, Anne, dau. and at length sole heir of Sir Walter Manny, K.G., by Margaret, Duchess of Norfolk, by whom he had an only son,

JOHN, his successor.

This John, Earl of Pembroke, according to Dugdale, in the 43rd EDWARD III., having obtained the king's license for so doing, made a feoffment of all his castles, lordships, manors, &c., in

267

England and Wales, to certain uses. Which feoffment upon his decease, was, by the feoffees, delivered to the king's council at Westminster to be opened; when it was found, that in case he died without issue of his body, the town and castle of Pembroke should come to the king, his heirs and successors; and the castle and lordship of Bergavenny, with other lands in England and Wales, to his cousin, William de Beauchamp (his mother's sister's son), in fee, provided he should bear the arms of Hastings, and endeavour to obtain the title of Earl of Pembroke—in default thereof, then to his kinsman, William de Clinton, upon similar conditions. This Earl of Pembroke was the first English subject who followed the example of King EDWARD III., in quartering of arms; as may be seen in his escutcheon on the north side of that monarch's tomb, in Westminster Abbey, wherein he beareth quarterly, Or, a maunch, gules, for HASTINGS, and Barry, arg., and az., an orle of martlets, gules, for VALENCE. His lordship d. in 1375, and was s. by his son,

JOHN HASTINGS, 3rd Earl of Pembroke, then but two years and a half old. At the coronation of RICHARD II., this nobleman (not having attained his fifth year) claimed to carry the great golden spurs; and proving his right to that honourable service, it was adjudged that by reason of his minority, another should be appointed in his behalf; viz., Edmund Mortimer, Earl of March, whose dau. Philippa, he m. although very young. The 13th RICHARD II., that monarch keeping his Christmas at Woodstock, his lordship, only then seventeen years of age, adventuring to tilt with Sir John St. John, was so severely wounded, by an unlucky slip of Sir John's lance, in the abdomen, that he died almost immediately, 30 December, 1391, when leaving no issue, the Earldom of Pembroke became EXTINCT. At his lordship's thus premature decease, REGINALD, LORD GREY DE RUTHYN, (grandson of Roger, Lord Grey, and his wife, Elizabeth Hastings, dau. of John, 2nd Baron Hastings,) was found to be his heir of the WHOLE BLOOD. And Hugh, Baron Hastings, eldest son of Hugh Hastings, of Gressing Hall, co. Norfolk, (eldest son of the said John, 2nd Baron Hastings, by his 2nd wife, Isabel, dau. of Hugh de Spenser, Earl of Winchester) his heir of the HALF BLOOD; between the son of this Lord Hastings of Gressing Hall, Edward Hastings, and Reginald Lord Grey, there was a memorable competition in the court military, before the constable and marshals of England, for the right of bearing the arms of Hastings, which lasted the full period of twenty years, and was eventually decided against Hastings, who, besides being condemned in the heavy costs of £970 17s. 1d. was imprisoned sixteen years for disobeying the judgment.

"Unless the BARONY OF HASTINGS," says Nicolas, "be considered the same as Bergavenny," (and he proves that it was totally unconnected with the feudal tenure of the castle of Bergavenny,) "it must be vested in the descendants and representatives of the said Edward Hastings."

NOTE.—The superstition of the period attributed the untimely fate of the last and youthful Earl of Pembroke to a divine judgment upon the family, in regard that Aymer de Valence, Earl of Pembroke, his ancestor, was one of those who passed sentence of death upon Thomas Plantagenet, Earl of Lancaster, at Pontefract: for it was observed, that subsequently to that judgment, none of the Earls of Pembroke saw his father, nor any father of them took delight in seeing his children.

Arms—Or, a maunch, gu.

HASTINGS — BARON HASTINGS, OF GRESSING HALL, CO. NORFOLK.

By Writ of Summons, dated 25 February, 1342.

Lineage.

JOHN HASTINGS, 2nd Lord Hastings, (grandfather by his 1st wife of Laurence Hastings, Earl of Pembroke,) m. for his 2nd wife, Isabel, dau. of Hugh Despencer, Earl of Winchester, and had, with a younger son,

HUGH HASTINGS, of Gressing Hall, co. Norfolk, whose grandson,

HUGH HASTINGS, of Gressing Hall, having distinguished himself in arms in Flanders, was summoned to parliament as a baron by King EDWARD III., 25 February, 1342. In the 20th of the same reign, being designated the king's cousin, his lordship was constituted lieutenant of Flanders, and commander of all the king's forces there, against the French. At this period, he took 300 prisoners, and brought them all to England. In 1359, Lord Hastings was in the wars of Gascony, and in some years afterwards, he attended John Duke of Lan caster, into Spain; but further nothing is mentioned of this nobleman, because neither himself nor any descendants were subsequently summoned to parliament. His son and eventual heir,

EDWARD HASTINGS, who assumed the title of LORD HASTINGS AND STOTVILLE, but by what authority remains to be established, is the person mentioned in the account of the Hastings, Earls of Pembroke, as having twenty years' litigation with the Lord Grey de Ruthyn, regarding the right to bear the arms of Hastings (viz.: or, a maunch, gu). This celebrated cause was heard and decided in the court military, by the constable and marshal of England, and it went finally against Hastings, who was also condemned in heavy costs, and imprisoned sixteen years for disobeying the judgment of the court. Edward Hastings, having likewise questioned the entail of John Hastings, 2nd Earl of Pembroke, by which the Bergavenny and other estates passed to William de Beauchamp. "Beauchamp invited," says Dugdale, "his learned counsel to his house in Pater-Noster-Row, in the city of London; amongst whom were Robert Charlton (then a judge), William Pinchebek, William Brenchesley, and John Catesby (all learned lawyers;) and after dinner, coming out of his chappel, in an angry mood, threw to each of them a piece of gold, and said, ' *Sirs, I desire you, forthwith to tell me, whether I have any right* and title to HASTINGS' lordships and lands?' whereupon Pinchebek stood up (the rest being silent, fearing that he suspected them), and said, '*No man here, nor in England, dare say that you have any right in them, except* HASTINGS *do quit his claim therein; an I should be do it, being now under age, it would be of no validitie.*' "Perhaps," (continues the same authority), "there had been some former entail, to settle them upon the heir male, of the family; but whatever it was, HASTINGS apprehended the injury thereby done to him, to be so great, that with extreme anguish of mind, at his latter end, he left God's curse and his own, upon his descendants, if they did not attempt the vindication thereof."

Nicolas considers the Barony of Hastings, which had belonged to the Earls of Pembroke, to be vested in the representatives of this Edward Hastings.

HASTINGS—BARON HASTINGS, OF LOUGHBOROUGH, CO. LEICESTER.

By Letters Patent, dated 19 January, 1558.

Lineage.

GEORGE HASTINGS, 1st Earl of Huntingdon, *m.* Lady Anne Herbert, widow of Sir Walter Herbert, Knt., and dau. of Henry Stafford, Duke of Buckingham, by whom he had, with several other children, FRANCIS, his successor in the Earldom of Huntingdon, and

SIR EDWARD HASTINGS, a very eminent person in the time of Queen MARY. In the 4th EDWARD VI., he served the office of sheriff for the cos. Warwick and Leicester; and the same year, he was sent with his brother, the Earl of Huntingdon, to dislodge the French from a position which they had taken up between Bologne and Calais. Upon the accession of MARY, he was constituted receiver of the honour of Leicester, parcel of the Duchy of Lancaster, cos. Leicester, Warwick, Northampton, and Nottinghamshire; and being the same year made a privy councillor to the queen, and master of her horse, was appointed collector-general to all her revenues within the city of London, and the cos. of Middlesex, Essex, and Hertfordshire. He obtained a grant at this time of the manor of Bosworth, co. Leicester; and was subsequently made a knight of the Garter. In the 4th and 5th of PHILIP and MARY, Sir Edward was constituted lord-chamberlain of the household, and was elevated to the peerage, by letters patent, dated 19 January, 1558, as BARON HASTINGS, *of Loughborough, co. Leicester.* His lordship *d.* at Stoke Pogis, co. Bucks (where he had built a chapel, and founded and endowed an hospital), in 1558, when, as he left no male issue, the barony became EXTINCT.

Arms—Arg., a maunch, sa.

HASTINGS—BARON HASTINGS OF LOUGHBOROUGH.

By Letters Patent, dated 22 October, 1643.

Lineage.

HENRY HASTINGS, 5th Earl of Huntingdon. *m.* Elizabeth, 3rd dau. and co-heir of Ferdinand Stanley, 5th Earl of Derby, and had, besides two daus., Ferdinando, who *s.* as 6th Earl of Huntingdon, and

HENRY HASTINGS, who having espoused, zealously, the cause of King CHARLES I., at the breaking out of the rebellion, and become one of the most distinguished in arms, amongst the gallant cavaliers, was elevated to the peerage by the ill-fated monarch, 22 October, 1643, as BARON HASTINGS, *of Loughborough, co. Leicester*, a dignity which had been borne by, and expired with his gallant ancestor, Sir Edward Hastings, K.G., in the reign of Queen MARY. His lordship had the gratification of living to witness the restoration of the monarchy, but dying *unm.* in January, 1665-6, the Barony of Hastings, of Loughborough, for the second time, EXPIRED.

Arms—Arg., a maunch, sa.

HASTINGS—MARQUESS OF HASTINGS.

(*See* RAWDON-HASTINGS, Earl of Moira and Marquess of Hastings in ADDENDA.)

HATTON—BARONS HATTON OF KIRBY, CO. NORTHAMPTON, VISCOUNTS HATTON, OF GRETTON.

Barony, by Letters Patent, dated 29 July, 1643.
Viscounty, by Letters Patent, dated 17 January, 1682.

Lineage.

This family which derived its surname from the lordship of Halton, in Cheshire, deduced its pedigree from Nigel, Baron of Halton, in that co., and constable to the old Earls of Chester.

The principal branch of the Hattons, in the days of Queen ELIZABETH, was,

CHRISTOPHER HATTON, Esq., son of William Hatton, Esq., of Holdenby, and grandson of John Hatton, who *s.* to Holdenby on the death of his mother, Elizabeth, sister and heir of William Holdenby, of Holdenby, and relict of Henry Hatton, Esq., a cadet of an ancient Cheshire family. He was then of Holdenby, co. Northampton, "who," says Dugdale, "being a private gentleman of the Inns of Court. was for his activity and comeliness, taken into favour." "Besides those accomplishments," continues the same author, "and the grace of dancing, he had likewise the addition of a strong and subtle capacity, so that, soon learning the discipline and garb of the times and court, he first became one of the queen's gentlemen pensioners; afterwards gentleman of the privy chamber, captain of the guard, vice chamberlain, and one of the privy council, lastly, Lord Chancellor of England, and a knight of the most noble order of the Garter."

Of this eminent person, the following character is given. "He had a large portion of gifts and endowments; his features, his gait, his carriage, and his prudence, strove to set him off. Everything he did, was so exactly just and discreet, and what he spoke so weighty, that he was chosen to keep the queen's conscience, as her chancellor, and to express her sense as her speaker. The courtiers that envied him, were forced by his superior power to own themselves in error; and the serjeants, who at first refused to plead before him, could not at length but confess his abilities. His place was above his law, but not above his parts, which were infinitely pregnant and comprehensive. His station was great, but his humility was greater; giving an easy access to all addresses. He was so just, that his sentence was a law to the subject, and so wise, that his opinion was an oracle with the queen." Sir Christopher Hatton *d.* a bachelor, 20 November, 1591, of a broken heart, it is stated, in consequence of his royal mistress having demanded rigorously, an old debt, which he owed her. He adopted (his sister Dorothy's son, by her husband, John Newport, Esq.), his nephew,

SIR WILLIAM NEWPORT, Knt., who thereupon assumed the name of HATTON. This gentleman m. Elizabeth, dau. and heiress of Sir Francis Gawdy, chief justice of the court of Common Pleas, and left at his decease 12 March, 1596, an only dau., FRANCES, who m. Robert Rich, Earl of Warwick. Upon his decease, the greater part of the estates of the Lord Chancellor Hatton, devolved by virtue of an entail upon the the great-great nephew of that eminent individual,

SIR CHRISTOPHER HATTON, K.B., who m. Alice, dau. of Thomas Fanshaw, Esq., of Ware Park, and dying, 11 September, 1619, was s. by his son,

SIR CHRISTOPHER HATTON, who was made a knight of the oath at the coronation of King CHARLES I., and afterwards distinguishing himself by his ardent zeal in the royal cause, he was elevated to the peerage 29 July, 1643, as BARON HATTON, of Kirby, co. Northampton. Upon the restoration of King CHARLES II., his lordship was sworn of the privy council, and constituted governor of Guernsey. Lord Hatton m. Elizabeth, eldest dau. and co-heir of Sir Charles Montague, and niece of Henry, Earl of Manchester, by whom he had issue,

CHRISTOPHER, his successor.
Charles.
Mary.   Jane.   Alice.

He d. in 1670, and was s. by his eldest son,

CHRISTOPHER HATTON, 2nd baron. This nobleman like his father, was governor of Guernsey, and while in that government had one of the most singular escapes from death probably upon record. During his residence at Cornet Castle, the magazine of powder caught fire at midnight by lightning; and his lordship while sleeping in his bed, was blown out of the window, and remained for some time struggling on the ramparts, without sustaining any injury. His lady, and several of her female attendants perished : but one of his children, an infant, was found the next day alive, sleeping in its cradle, under a beam. His lordship was advanced in 1682, to the dignity of VISCOUNT HATTON, of Gretton, co. Northampton. He m 1st, Lady Cecilia Tufton, dau. of John, Earl of Thanet, and had one surviving dau.,

ANNE, who m. Daniel Finch, 2nd Earl of Nottingham, and 6th Earl of Winchelsea, and had, with three elder sons,

The Hon. EDWARD FINCH, who assumed the additional surname of HATTON, and his grandson,

GEORGE FINCH-HATTON, Esq., inherited in 1826, the Earldoms of Winchilsea and Nottingham (see BURKE'S Peerage).

The viscount m. 2ndly, Frances, only dau. of Sir Henry Yelverton, of Gaston Mauduit, co. Northampton, Bart., by whom he had no surviving issue. He m. 3rdly, Elizabeth, dau. and co-heir of Sir William Haslewood, of Maidwell, co. Northampton, and had three sons, William, Charles, and John, and three daus., Elizabeth, Penelope, and Anne. His lordship d. in 1706, and was s. by his eldest son,

WILLIAM HATTON, 2nd viscount, who dying s. p. in 1760, was s. by his brother,

HENRY-CHARLES HATTON, 3rd viscount, at whose decease, the Barony and Viscounty of Hatton became EXTINCT. The estates eventually devolved upon the Hon. Edward Finch Hatton mentioned above.

Arms—Az., a chevron, between three garbs, gu.

HAUSTED—BARON HAUSTED.

By Writ of Summons, dated 20 July, 1332.

Lineage.

JOHN DE HAUSTED, in the 1st year of EDWARD II., obtained a grant to himself and the heirs of his body, of the manor of Deusangre, and divers other lands in the co. Northumberland; he was subsequently engaged in the wars of Scotland, and was invested with the power of receiving into protection all those who in the co. Northumberland, and parts adjacent, submitted to the authority of the king. In the 15th of the same monarch he had the castle and honour of Clare, co. Suffolk, committed to his charge; and after the accession of EDWARD III. he was made seneschal of Gascony. For all these services he obtained a grant of 200 marks sterling, to be received yearly during his life out of the customs of Bordeaux, until such time as provision should be made for the payment thereof within this realm : and he was summoned to parlia-

ment as a baron from 20 July, 1332, to 22 January, 1336. He d. in 1337 leaving a son and heir,

SIR WILLIAM DE HAUSTED, aged thirty, who d. before 1346, without ever having been summoned to parliament. His sister Elizabeth was found to be his heir but nothing further is known of her.

Arms—Gu., a chief, componée, or. and az.

HAWLEY—BARON HAWLEY.

By Letters Patent, dated 8 July, 1646.

Lineage.

SIR FRANCIS HAWLEY, Bart. of Buckland House, Somersetshire, descended from Francis Hawley, Esq., M.P. for Corfe castle, temp. ELIZABETH, was raised to the peerage of Ireland, as LORD HAWLEY, Baron of Donamore, co. Meath, 8 July, 1646. His lordship d. 22 December, 1684, and was s. by (the son of his son Francis) his grandson,

FRANCIS HAWLEY, 2nd Lord Hawley, M.P. for Bramber in 1713 and 1715; who m. Lady Elizabeth Ramsay, only dau. of William, Earl of Dalhousie; and dying in 1743 was s. by his son,

FRANCIS HAWLEY, 3rd Lord Hawley, lieutenant-governor of Antigua; who m. Margaret, dau. of Thomas Tyrrel, Esq. of London; but d. s. p. 24 August, 1772, when the honours became EXTINCT,

Arms—Vert, a saltire, engr., arg.

HAY—BARONS HAY, OF SAWLEY, VISCOUNTS DONCASTER, EARLS OF CARLISLE.

Barony, by Letters Patent, dated 29 June, 1615.
Viscounty, by Letters Patent, dated 5 July, 1618.
Earldom, by Letters Patent, dated 13 September, 1622.

Lineage.

Amongst the natives of Scotland who accompanied King JAMES I. into England was a gentleman of the name of Hay, whom Sir Anthony Weldon thus describes: "The king no sooner came to London, but notice was taken of a rising favourite, the first meteor of that nature appearing in our climate; as the king cast his eye upon him for affection; so did all the courtiers, to adore him, his name was

MR. JAMES HAY, a gentleman that long lived in France, an l some say of the Scottish guard to the French king; this gentleman coming over to meet King JAMES, and share with him in his new conquest (according to the Scottish phrase), it should seem had some further acquaintance with the then leiger embassadour in Scotland for the French monarch, who coming with his majesty into England, presented this gentleman as a well accomplished person to the king, in such high commendation as engendered such a liking as produced a favourite; in thankful acknowledgement whereof, he did him many fair offices for the present, and coming afterwards an extraordinary embassador to our king, made him the most sumptuous feast at Essex House, that ever was seen before, never equalled since, in which was such plenty, and fish of that immensity, brought out of Muscovia, that dishes were made to contain them (no dishes in all England before could ne'er hold them), and after that a costly voydee, and after that a mask, of choyse noble-men and gentlemen, and after that a most costly banquet, the king, lords, and all the prime gentlemen then about London being invited thither. Truly, he was a most compleat, and well accomplished gentleman, modest and court-like, and of so fair a demeanour, as made him be generally beloved; and for his wisdom, I shall give you but one character for all : he was ever great with all the favourites of his time, and although the king did often change, yet he was (temper idem), with the king and favourites, and got by both; for although favourites had that exorbitant power over the king, to make him grace and disgrace whom they pleased, he was out of that power, and the only exception to that general rule; and for his gettings, it was more than almost the favourites of his time, which appeared

In those vast expenses of all sorts, and had not the bounty of his mind exceeded his gettings, he might have left the greatest estate that ever our age or climate had heard of; he was, indeed, made for a courtier, who wholly studied his master, and understood him better than any other."

"He was employed in very many of the most weighty affairs, and sent with the most stately embassies of our times, which he performed with that wisdom and magnificency, that he seemed an honour to his king and country, for his carriage in state affairs." This celebrated favourite having, by the influence of his royal master, obtained Honora, sole dau. and heir of Edward, Lord Denny, in marriage, had a grant of the name and title of LORD HAY, with precedence next to the barons of England, but no place or voice in parliament. On 29 June, 1615, he was, however, advanced to the dignity of a baron of the realm, under the title of LORD HAY, of Sauley, co. York, without any solemn investiture, his lordship being the first ever so created, the lawyers then declaring that the delivery of the letters patent was sufficient without any ceremony. He was the next year sent ambassador to the court of France. In March, 1617, his lordship was sworn of the privy council, and created Viscount Doncaster, 5 July, 1618, preparatory to his proceeding upon an embassy into Germany. In 1622 he was again employed as ambassador in France, and was advanced 13 September in that year to the EARLDOM OF CARLISLE. Besides all these high honours and trusts he was master of the great wardrobe, gentleman of the robes to King JAMES I., and knight of the most noble order of the Garter. He was also first gentleman of the bed-chamber to King CHARLES I. His lordship *m.* as already stated, Honora, only dau. and heiress of Edward, Lord Denny, and after her decease he *m.* the Lady Lucy Percy, youngest dau. of Henry, Earl of Northumberland. He *d.* 25 April, 1636, and was *s.* by his only surviving son,

JAMES HAY, 2nd Earl of Carlisle, who *m.* Lady Margaret Russell, dau. of Francis, Earl of Bedford, but *d. s. p.* in 1660, when all his honours became EXTINCT.

Arms—Arg., three escutcheons, gu.

HENLEY—BARONS HENLEY, OF GRAINGE, EARLS OF NORTHINGTON.

Barony, by Letters Patent, dated 27 March, 1760.
Earldom, &c., by Letters Patent, dated 19 May, 1764.

Lineage.

ANTHONY HENLEY, Esq., *m.* Mary, dau. and co-heir of the Hon. Peregrine Bertie, a younger son of Montagu, Earl of Lindsey, and was father of

SIR ROBERT HENLEY, Knt., a lawyer of great eminence, who was appointed, in 1756, attorney-general, when he received the customary honour of knighthood, and the next year he was constituted keeper of the great seal. In 1760, Sir Robert was elevated to the peerage as BARON HENLEY, of Grainge, co. Southampton, and appointed lord chancellor of England in 1761. In three years afterwards he was advanced to the dignities of Viscount Henley, and EARL OF NORTHINGTON. His lordship officiated as lord high steward at the trial of Earl Ferrers. He *m.* Jane, dau. of Sir John Huband, of co. Warwick, and had surviving issue,

ROBERT, his successor.
Bridget, *m.* 1st, to Robert. only son of Lord Bingley; and 2ndly, to the Hon. John Talmash, but had no issue.
Jane, *m.* to Sir Willoughby Aston, Bart.
Mary, *m.* to Earl of Legonier, and *d. s. p.*
Catherine, *m.* to George, Viscount Deerhurst.
Elizabeth, *m.* to Frederick Morton Eden, Esq., a diplomatist of the 1st grade, who was created a peer of Ireland, as BARON HENLEY of Chardstock, and had with other issue.

ROBERT-HENLEY, father of the present ANTHONY HENLEY-HENLEY, BARON HENLEY.

The earl *d* in 1772, and was *s.* by his son,

ROBERT HENLEY, 2nd Earl of Northington, who was constituted lord-lieutenant of Ireland in 1783, but filled the vice-regal office until the next year only. His lordship who was a knight of the Thistle, *d. unm.* in 1786, when the Barony and Viscounty of Henley, with Earldom of Northington, became EXTINCT, while his estates devolved upon his sisters as co-heirs.

Arms—Quarterly, 1st and 4th, az., a lion rampant. arg., ducally crowned, or, within a border, arg, charged with eight torteaux, for HENLEY: 2nd and 3rd, arg., three battering rams bar-ways ppr. (Brown) armed and garnished, az., for BERTIE.

HEPBURN—EARL OF BOTHWELL.

By Letters Patent, dated 17 October, 1488.

Lineage.

SIR PATRICK HEPBURN, of Hales, eldest son of Sir Adam Hepburn, of Hales, was created a peer of Scotland, by the title of LORD HALES, under which designation he sat among the nobility in the parliament, 16 October, 1467. He left issue,

I. ADAM, 2nd Lord Hales.
II. George, dean of Dunkeld, and treasurer of the diocese of Moray.
I. Margaret, *m.* to Patrick, 3rd Lord Haliburton, of Dirleton.
II. Eupheme, *m.* to Andrew Macdowall.

The elder son,

ADAM HEPBURN, 2nd Lord Hales, is mentioned as a paramour of Mary of Guelders, dowager of King JAMES II., in 1462. He *m.* Helen, eldest dau. of Alexander, 1st Lord Home, and by her (who *m.* 2ndly, Alexander, 10th Lord Erskine) had,

I. PATRICK, 3rd Lord Hales.
II. Adam (Sir), of Craigs, master of the king's stables, *m.* Elizabeth, dau. and co-heir of Walter Ogistoun, of Ogistoun.
III. George, provost of Bothwell and Lincluden, fell at the battle of Flodden, 9 September, 1513.
IV. John, prior of St. Andrews, founder of St. Leonard's College. 1512.
V. James, rector of Dalry, bishop of Moray, 1516, buried in the cathedral of Elgin.
I. Margaret, *m.* to Alexander, 1st Earl of Glencairn.
II. Agnes, *m.* to William, 1st Lord Livingstone.
III. Elizabeth, *m.* to Alexander, master of Home.
IV. Helen, *m.* to John, 3rd Lord Somerville.

The eldest son,

PATRICK HEPBURN, 3rd Lord Hales, led the Hepburns in the vanguard against the unfortunate monarch, JAMES III., at the battle fought near Bannockburn, 11 June, 1488, where his majesty fell. For his services on that occasion, the new king created his lordship EARL OF BOTHWELL, 17 October, 1488, and conferred upon him the office of high admiral of Scotland for life. The earl *m.* Lady Janet Douglas, only dau. of James, 1st Earl of Morton; and *d.* about the year 1507, having had issue,

I. ADAM, 2nd Earl of Bothwell.
II. John, bishop of Brechin. III. Patrick, bishop of Moray.
I. Janet, *m.* to George, 4th Lord Seton.
II. Mary, *m.* to Archibald, Earl of Angus.
III. Margaret, *m.* to Henry, Lord Sinclair

The eldest son,

ADAM HEPBURN, 2nd Earl of Bothwell, high admiral of Scotland, who commanded the reserve at the battle of Flodden, and advanced to support the king's attack with such gallantry, that the standard of the Earl of Surrey was endangered; but the fortune of the day changing, Bothwell fell, with his royal master and the flower of Scottish chivalry, on that disastrous day. His lordship *m.* Agnes Stewart, natural dau. of James, Earl of Buchan, and by her (who *m.* 2ndly, Robert, 5th Lord Maxwell) left at his decease, in 1513, a son and successor,

PATRICK HEPBURN, 3rd Earl of Bothwell, who *d.* in 1556, leaving by Margaret Home, his wife, one son and one dau namely,

JAMES, his heir.
Jean, *m.* 1st, to John Stewart, prior of Coldinghame, natural son of JAMES V. ; and 2ndly, John, master of Caithness, by both who had issue.

The son and successor, the too famous

JAMES HEPBURN, 4th Earl of Bothwell, *b.* in 1536, who played so conspicuous a part in Scottish history, during the reign of the ill-fated MARY STUART, was created by her majesty, 12 May, 1567, a few days after the affair of Cramond Bridge, and two days prior to their marriage, MARQUESS OF FIFE, and DUKE OF ORKNEY. He had previously been married to Lady Jean Gordon, 2nd dau. of George, 4th Earl of Huntley, from whom he was divorced; and who *m.* 2ndly, Alexander, 11th Earl of Sutherland ; and 3rdly, Alexander Ogilvy, of Boyne. Immediately after his grace's marriage to the queen, an association of the principal nobility was formed against him, and her majesty compelled to dismiss her favourite. Bothwell retreated to the Orkneys, and, driven thence, committed some outrages on the trade of Denmark. He was finally taken, and immured in the castle of Malmoe, in Norway, where he *d* insane, after ten years' confinement, about the end of 1575, before he had attained the 40th year of his age—a melancholy example of "vaulting ambition, which o'erleaps itself." He was forfeited by the parliament of Scotland, 29 December, 1567, and his titles and vast possessions fell under the attainder.

Arms—Gu., on a chev., arg., two lions pulling at a rose, of the 1st

HERBERT — BARONS HERBERT, OF HERBERT, AND OF CHEPSTOW, EARLS OF PEMBROKE, EARL OF HUNTINGDON.

Barony, by Writ of Summons, dated 26 July, 1461.
Earldom of Pembroke, by Letters Patent, dated 8 September, 1468.
Earldom of Huntingdon, by Charter, dated 4 July, 1472.

Lineage.

The house of HERBERT deduces descent from PETER FITZREGINALD, brother of John Fitzreginald, summoned to parliament as a baron, 1294-1307, (refer to Fitzherbert, Baron Fitzherbert) derived from Herbert Fitzherbert, son of Herbert, chamberlain to WILLIAM RUFUS, and grandson of Peter, stated to have been brother of Herbert, Count of Vermandois, and son of Otho, Count of Vermandois, 7th in descent, through the Counts of Vermandois and Kings of Italy and Lombardy, from PEPIN, King of Italy and Lombardy, who d. A. D. 810, youngest son of CHARLEMAGNE, Emperor of the West.

PETER FITZREGINALD, b. in 1275, had a grant from his mother, Joan, dau. and co-heir of William de Vivonia, (de Fortibus) of the manor of Chewyton, or Chuton, co. Somerset, of which he d. seized in 1323, æt. forty-eight years. He m. Alice, dau. and heir of Blethin Broadspear, Lord of Llanllowel, near Uske, in Monmouthshire, and had issue,

 I. Roger Fitzpeter, who d. in his father's lifetime, leaving a son and heir, Sir Henry Fitzroger, whose grand-dau. and heir m. John Bonville.
 II. HERBERT FITZPETER.

The younger son,

HERBERT FITZPETER, was father, by Margaret, his wife, dau of Sir John Walsh, Knt., of a son and heir,

ADAM FITZHERBERT, Lord, by inheritance from his grandmother, of Llanllowel, and of Bettesley or Beachley. He m. Christian, dau. and heir of Gwarin Ddu, the "Black Lord" of Llandilo, a mansion of great magnificence near Abergavenny, afterwards designated Gwarinddû, now Wernddû, and by her had two sons,

 I. Sir John ap Adam, Knt., Lord of Llanllowel, whose grand-dau. and heir, Margaret, m. Thomas Huntley, of Llanarth, co. Monmouth and of Treowen, in the same county, son and heir of Thomas Huntley, of Treowen, by Alice, dau. and heir of William Wallis, of Llanarth, and was mother of two daus. and co-heirs,
  1 Mary, Lady of Llanllowell, whose husband was Thomas Parker, of Monmouthshire.
  2 Margaret, who m. David ap Jenkin, jure uxoris of Treowen, derived from Adam Fitzherbert, Lord of Llanllowel, and was mother cf Thomas ap David, of Treowen, progenitor of the house of Llanarth.
 II. JOHN, alias JENKIN HERBERT.

The younger son,

JENKIN HERBERT AP ADAM, Lord of Gwarinddû, by Gwenilian, his wife, dau. of Sir Aaron ap Bleddyn, Knt., had a son and heir,

WILLIAM AP JENKIN alias HERBERT, Lord of Gwarinddû, living at Perthir, near Monmouth, from 20th to 50th EDWARD III., who m. Gwenllian, dau. of Howel Ichon, and had four sons, viz.,

 I. John ap Jenkin ap Gwyllim, of Gwarinddû, ancestor of the family of Prodgerse of Gwarinddû.
 II. David ap Gwyllim, of Chapell, ancestor of the Morgans of Arxton.
 III. Howel ap Gwyllim, grandfather of David ap Jenkin, jure uxoris, of Treowen, co. Monmouth whose descendant, William Jones, son of Sir Philip Jones, Knt.. temp. CHARLES I., removed to Llanarth Court, co. Monmouth, and was ancestor of Jones, of Llanarth Court, whose representative, John Jones, Esq., of that place, had, with other issue,
  1 John Jones, Esq., of Llanarth Court, father of JOHN-ARTHUR-EDWARD JONES, Esq., who by royal sign manual has assumed the name of HERBERT, and is now of Llanarth Court.
  2 Philip Jones, Esq., of the Hill House, Abergavenny, and of Perthir, co. Monmouth.
  3 William Jones, Esq., of Clytha House, father, with other issue, of an eldest son,
   WILLIAM-REGINALD-JOSEPH-FITZHERBERT.
 IV. SIR THOMAS AP GWYLLIM, Knt.

The 4th son,

SIR THOMAS AP GWYLLYM, Knt., who m. Maud, dau. and co-heir of Sir John Morley, Knt., of Raglan Castle, and acquired thereby Llansaintffraid, where he afterwards resided, was buried 8 July, 1438, having had issue,

I. Philip ap Thomas, of Llansaintffraid, who d. 9 November, 1460; he m. Johanne, dau. and heir of Thomas Blethin, Esq., of Pentre, and was father by her, who d. 7 June, 1453, of a son and heir, David, of Llansaintffraid, who d. 19 December, 1510, having m. Katharine, who d. 26 March, 1520, dau. of Sir Roger Vaughan, Knt. Their son, Thomas, of Llansaintffraid, m. Jane, dau. of John ap Thomas, of Treowen, Esq., who d. 13 August, 1533, mother by him, who d. 3 April, 1537, of a son John, of Llansaintffraid, who d. 30 May, 1554. He m. Gwen, who d. 23 September, 1597, dau. of Edward Jones, Gent., of Abergavenny, and had issue, a son and heir, Walter Jones, Esq., of Llansaintffraid, who d. 17 April, 1606, having m. Lettice, who d. 19 June, 1623, dau. of John Williams, Gent., of Newport. The representative of this marriage, HENRY JONES, Esq., of Llansaintffraid, left an only surviving dau. and heir, Susan, who m. George Richards, Esq , of Bredon's Norton, co. Worcester, mother of a son JOHN RICHARDS, Esq., living 1800, who subsequently sold Llansaintffraid to John Jones, Esq., of Llanarth Court.
 II. Even ap Thomas, ancestor of the GWYNS and RAGLANS OF Glamorganshire.
 III. David ap Thomas, progenitor of the HUGHES's of Caelwch or Killough.
 IV. Howel ap Thomas, of Perthir, near Monmouth, ancestor of the POWELLS of Perthir.
 V. SIR WILLIAM AP THOMAS, Knt.

The 5th son,

SIR WILLIAM AP THOMAS, alias HERBERT, Knt., who resided at Raglan Castle, in the reign of HENRY V., and was knighted in the French wars of that monarch, m. 1st, Gwladys, widow of Sir Roger Vaughan, Knt. who fell at Agincourt, by the side of HENRY V., and dau. of Sir David Gam, knighted by HENRY V. at Agincourt; and 2ndly, Margaret, dau. of Thomas ap Griffith, by whom he had issue, Margaret, wife of Sir Henry Woogan, Knt., of Wiston, co. Pembroke. Sir William ap Thomas was buried with his 1st wife, Gwladys, in the centre of the chapel of Abergavenny, under a richly carved alabaster monument, and had issue by her, three sons, viz.,

 I. WILLIAM HERBERT, 1st EARL OF PEMBROKE, his heir.
 II. Thomas Herbert, of Troy House, near Monmouth.
 III. Richard Herbert (Sir), of Colebrooke, co. Monmouth, ancestor of the LORDS HERBERT, of Chirbury, the HERBERTS of Muckross, eo. Kerry, &c.

The eldest son,

SIR WILLIAM DE HERBERT, Knt., was Lord of Raglan, co. Monmouth, an estate which he derived from Maud, his grandmother, dau. and heiress of Sir John Morley, Knt. He was a stanch supporter of the house of York, and for his fidelity and services King EDWARD IV., soon after his accession, constituted him chief justice and chamberlain of South Wales, and made him likewise steward of the castle and lordship of Brecknock, and of all the other castles of Humphrey, Duke of Buckingham, in the same part of the principality. Sir William was summoned to parliament, as BARON HERBERT, of Herbert, 26 July, 1461, and by letters patent, bearing date 3 February following, wherein his manifold services and eminent deserts are recorded, (such as hazarding his life in numerous conflicts against King HENRY VI. and the Lancastrians, particularly against Henry Holland, Duke of Exeter, Jasper Tudor, Earl of Pembroke, James Butler, Earl of Wiltshire, &c., reducing castles, fortresses, &c.,) obtained a grant in general tail of the castle, town, and lordship of Pembroke, with all its appurtenances. His lordship had subsequently other extensive grants; was constituted chief justice of North Wales for life, and created EARL OF PEMBROKE, 8 September, 1468. He was afterwards appointed chief forester of Snowdon, and constable of Conway Castle. In the August ensuing the earl won the cast e of Harlow, one of the strongest forts in Wales, by assault, and he was shortly after elected a knight of the Garter.

Upon the breaking out of the insurrection anno 1469, 9th EDWARD IV., in the north, on behalf of the Lancastrians, headed by Sir John Coniers, Knt., and Robert Hillyard, who called himself Robin of Riddesdale, the Earl of Pembroke was despatched by the king, with his brother, Sir Richard Herbert, of Colebrooke, in command of 18,000 Welshmen, to meet the rebels, but being deserted by Humphrey Stafford, Earl of Devonshire, who had joined him with 6,000 archers at Banbury, he was compelled to give the insurgents battle with an inferior force, and experienced a signal defeat at Danesmoore, Northamptonshire, when himself and his brother fell into the hands of their enemies, and were immediately executed at Northampton, in 1469, with Richard Widvile, Lord Rivers, and his son, by order of the Duke of Clarence, and the Earl of Warwick, who had recently revolted from the banner of York. His lordship m. 1st, Anne, dau. of Sir Walter Devereux, and sister of Walter, Lord Ferrers, of Chartley. The lady's father covenanted, (10 August, 27th HENRY VI.) to give her 500 marks as a fortune; to find meat and drink for Sir W. Herbert and 40 of his men and horses; and to supply the bride with "apparel competent perta ning to her degree." By her he had issue,

WILLIAM, his successor.   Walter (Sir).

George (Sir), of St. Julians, otherwise St. Gillians, upon Uske, co. Monmouth, who *s.* eventually to a portion of the estates of the Earl of Pembroke; and his descendant, the inheritor of those estates, Mary Herbert, *m.* the celebrated Edward, Lord Herbert, of Chirbury. From the Herberts of St. Julians and Magor descended, as heir general, Mrs. JANE HAWKINS, of Tredunnock.

Philip, of Lanyhangel.

Cecilie, *m.* to Lord Greystock.

Maud, *m.* to Henry Percy, Earl of Northumberland.

Katherine, *m.* to George Grey, Earl of Kent.

Anne, *m.* to John Grey, Lord Powys.

Isabel, *m.* to Sir Thomas Cokesev, Knt.

Margaret, *m.* 1st, to Thomas Talbot, Viscount L'Isle, and 2ndly, to Sir Henry Bodringham, Knt.

William, 1st Earl of Pembroke had, besides his issue by Anne, his wife, two sons who have been generally considered illegiti: mate, viz.,

I. SIR RICHARD HERBERT, Knt., of Ewyas and of Grove Radnor, co. Hereford, father, with other issue, of an eldest son, SIR WILLIAM HERBERT, K.G., EARL OF PEMBROKE, so created 12 October, 1551, who had two sons,

     1 Sir Henry Herbert, K.G., 2nd Earl of Pembroke, ancestor of Thomas, 8th Earl of Pembroke, and 5th Earl of Montgomery, who was father, with younger issue, of

         Henry, 9th Earl of Pembroke and 6th Earl of Montgomery, progenitor of George, 13th and present Earl of Pembroke, and 10th Earl of Montgomery.

         William, Earl of Carnarvon, so created 3 July, 1793, ancestor of Henry, 4th and present Earl of Carnarvon.

     2 Sir Edward Herbert, Knt., of Powys Castle, co. Montgomery, the inheritance of the Greys and Cherletons, Barons of Powys, through the marriage of John de Cherleton with Hewys, heir general of the sovereigns of Powys Wenwynwyn. (refer to Cherleton of Powys) purchased by him 29th ELIZABETH, from Edward Grey, natural son of Edward, 3rd Baron Grey, of Powys. The eldest son of Sir Edward Herbert, viz., Sir William Powis, Knt., was created BARON POWIS, *of Powis Castle,* 2 April, 1629, and the grandson and heir of the latter, viz., William, 3rd Lord Powis, was created 4 April, 1674, EARL OF POWIS, and 24 March, 1686, MARQUESS OF POWIS; his son William, 2nd Marquess of Powis, had issue,

         1 WILLIAM, 3rd and last Marquess of Powis, who *d. unm.,* when his honours became extinct.

         2 Edward Herbert, who *d.* before his brother, father of a dau. and heir, Barbara, heiress of her uncle, who *m.* Henry Arthur Herbert, Esq., created *Baron Powis, of Powis Castle, Viscount Ludlow,* and EARL OF POWIS, 27 May, 1748; his son George, 2nd Earl of Powis, *d. s. p.,* when the estates vested in his sister and heir, Lady Henrietta-Antonia, who *m.* Edward, Lord Clive, created 13 August, 1794, EARL OF POWIS, and was mother, by him, of Edward, 2nd Earl of Powis, father of Edward-James Herbert, 3rd and present Earl of Powis.

II. Sir George Herbert, Knt., of Swansea, ancestor of the Herberts of Swansea.

William, 1st Earl of Pembroke was *s.* by his eldest son,

WILLIAM HERBERT, 2nd Earl of Pembroke. King EDWARD IV. wishing to confer the Earldom of Pembroke upon his son, Prince Edward, this nobleman made a resignation* thereof to the crown, and was created in stead EARL OF HUNTINGDON, by charter, bearing date, at York, 4 July, 1479 (Thomas Grey, Earl of Huntingdon, having previously resigned that title on obtaining the Marquessate of Dorset). In the 1st RICHARD III., his lordship was constituted justice of South Wales, and in the February ensuing, he entered into covenants with that king, to take Dame Katherine Plantagenet, his dau., to wife, before the feast of St. Michael following; as also to make her a certain jointure, and the king to settle lands and lordships of a large annual value upon them, and the heirs male of their bodies. The king further undertaking to be at the expense of the wedding. But this lady dying in her early years, the marriage did not take effect. His lordship afterwards *m.* Lady Mary Widvile, dau. of Richard, and sister and co-heir of Richard, Earl Rivers, by whom he had an only dau. and heiress,

ELIZABETH HERBERT, who *m.* Sir Charles Somerset, Knt., illegitimate son of Henry Beaufort, 3rd Duke of Somerset of that family, which Charles was created in 1514, EARL OF WORCESTER, and from this union the present Ducal family of BEAUFORT derives.

In the 3rd year of HENRY VII., his lordship obtained from the crown a confirmation of the Earldom of Huntingdon. He *d.* 1491, when the Barony of Herbert, created by the writ of

* Resolutions of the House of Lords in 1640 and 1678, declare that no surrender of a patent can be a bar to a claim of the dignity so surrendered; but previously such surrenders were not uncommon.

272

EDWARD IV., devolved upon his dau., and the Earldom of Huntingdon is considered to have become EXTINCT, although the charter of EDWARD IV would appear to create a dignity descending to heirs general.

Arms—Per pale, az., and gu., three lions rampant, arg., a border, componée, or, and of the 2nd bezantée.

HERBERT—BARONS HERBERT, OF CHIRBURY.

By Letters Patent, dated 7 May, 1629.

Lineage.

SIR RICHARD HERBERT, Knt., of Colebrooke, co. Monmouth, 3rd son of Sir William ap Thomas, *alias* Herbert, Knt., of Raglan Castle, and youngest brother of William, 1st Earl of Pembroke, resided at Montgomery Castle, was commissioned, with his brother, the Earl of Pembroke, 9th EDWARD IV., 1469, to command a Welsh army, to resist the Lancastrian insurrection, headed by Sir John Conyiers, but, defeated at Danes Moore, in Northamptonshire, he was executed with the earl, at Northampton, 27 July, 1469, and was buried at Abergavenny, where, between the chapel and the choir, there is a sumptuous monument to him. This gallant knight *m.* Margaret, dau. of Sir Thomas Griffith Nicholas, Knt., of Carmarthen and had issue, four sons,

I. SIR RICHARD HERBERT, Knt., of whom presently.

II. Sir William Herbert, Knt., of Colebrooke, *m.* Jane, widow of Thomas Mostyn, of Mostyn, co. Flint, and dau. (by Jane, dau. of Sir Thomas Stradling, Knt., of St. Donat's Castle, co. Glamorgan) of Sir William Griffith, Knt., of Penrhyn, co. Carnarvon, chamberlain of North Wales, and had issue, a son and five daus.,

     1 Rhys Herbert, Esq., of Colebrooke, who, by Elizabeth his wife, dau. and heir of Sir Weston Browne, Knt., was father of William Herbert, Esq., of Colebrooke, high sheriff of Monmouthshire in 1584. This gentleman *m.* twice. By his 1st wife, Dennis, dau. of Sir Edmund Armondsham, Knt., of Buckinghamshire, he had a son, WILLIAM, of whom presently. By his 2nd wife, Jane, dau. of John ap Thomas ap John, of Treowen, he was father of a son,

         Charles Herbert, Esq., of Hadnock House, near Monmouth, whose son,

         GILES HERBERT, Esq., of Hadnock House, *m.* Eleanor, dau. (by Lady Lucy Somerset) of Henry Herbert, Esq., of Wynastow, near Monmouth, a seat of the Herberts, erected *temp.* HENRY VI.

     The eldest son,

         WILLIAM HERBERT, Esq., of Colebrooke, *m.* Katherine, dau. of Thomas Morgan, Esq., of Tredegar, co. Monmouth, and was *s.* by his son, WILLIAM HERBERT, Esq., of Colebrooke, who, by Priscilla, his wife, dau. of Edmund Pigot, Esq., of Buckinghamshire, was father of HENRY HERBERT, Esq., of Colebrooke, who *m.* Mary, dau. of John Rudiard, of London, and had issue a son, SIR JAMES HERBERT, Knt., of Colebrooke, who *d.* 6 June, 1709, æt. sixty-four, having had, by Judith, his wife, who *d.* 12 November in the same year, dau. of Edward Moyle, Esq., an only dau. and heir, JUDITH, who *m.* Sir Thomas Powell, of Broadway, co. Carmarthen, Bart., Judge of the King's Bench, son of the intrepid judge, Sir John Powell, who defended the seven bishops, *temp.* JAMES II. Of this marriage there were three daus. and co-heirs, of whom,

         MARY, *m.* Lord Anne Hamilton, godson of Queen ANNE, 3rd son of James, 4th Duke of Hamilton and 1st Duke of Brandon, K.G., and had issue. (*Refer to* BURKE'S *Peerage*, DUKES OF HAMILTON.)

         ANNE, *m.* Sir Thomas Pryce, of Newtown, Bart.

     1 Maud, *m.* Howel Madoc, of Powys, and 2ndly, Parry, of Carnarvonshire.

     2 Margaret, 2nd wife of Sir George Mathews, Knt., of Adyr, co. Glamorgan, living *temp.* HENRY VIII., ancestor by his 1st wife, Barbara, dau. of Sir John Brent, Knt., of Somers, of a son, Sir William Mathew, whose dau. and co-heir, Mary, *m.* Rheinborn Mathew, living 1615, ancestor by her of Francis Mathew, of Thomastown, co. Tipperary, created November, 1797, Earl of Llandaff.

     3 A dau., *m.* Thomas ap Rhys, of North Wales.

     4 A dau., *m.* Philip-Thomas Watkin, of Pont-yr-illos.

     5 Jane, *m.* twice; 1st, Sir William Thomas, knight-banneret, of Aberglassney, parish of Llangathen, co. Carmarthen, derived from Cadwgan ap Elystan Glodrydd, Lord of Fferlys, living 19th HENRY VIII.; and 2ndly, Rhys Llwyd, son of Thomas Llwyd, Esq., of Builth, co. Radnor. By her 1st husband she was mother of

         RHYS THOMAS, Esq., Lord of Aber, co. Carnarvon, high

sheriff for Anglesey in 1553 and 1564, and for Carnarvonshire in 1574; a commissioner appointed 23 October, 9th ELIZABETH, to hold the celebrated Eisteddfod,
at Caerwys, co. Flint, in 1569, ancestor of RHYS
THOMAS, Esq., of Coedhelen, co. Carnarvon, who had
with other children, a dau., ELIZABETH, sister, and
in her issue, senior co-heir of Rhys Thomas, Esq.,
of Coedhelen, Lord of Kemmees, co. Anglesey, of
Glascoed, co. Carnarvon, of Pentrehobyn. co. Flint,
of Glanhafon. co. Montgomery, and of Trevor Hall,
including Valle Crucis Abbey, co. Denbigh, high
sheriff of Anglesey in 1817, and of Carnarvonshire in
1931. This lady m. 2 August, 1792, Sir William Hughes,
Knt., of Plâs Côch, in Menai, co. Anglesey, and was
mother, with other issue, of an eldest son,

WILLIAM-BULKELEY HUGHES, Esq., of Plâs Côch, and
of Brynddû, co. Anglesey, Lord of Kemmees, M.P. for
the Carnarvon boroughs, which he represented from
1837 to 1859, and high sheriff for Anglesey in 1861:
18th inheritor of his family property, and 19th
descendant paternally, from Llywarch ap Brân, Lord
of Menai, in the 12th century.

III. John Herbert, of Llacherne, co. Carmarthen, m. Janet,
dau. of Jenkin Llwyd Vychan. of Pwhldyfaich, co. Pembroke, and had daus. and co-heirs.
IV. Thomas Herbert, Esq., of Abergavenny. b. 1462, and
buried at Abergavenny, 1529. father of Richard Herbert,
Esq., b. 1488, and d. 1557, ancestor, it is stated, of SIR THOMAS
HERBERT, Bart., author of Herbert's Travels.

The eldest son,
SIR RICHARD HERBERT, Knt., of Colebrook and Tefaldwyn, the
Welsh name of the town of Montgomery, who resided at Montgomery Castle, was steward of the lordships and marches of North
Wales, East Wales, and Cardiganshire, te mp. HENRY VIII., and
was buried in St. Nicholas Church, Montgomery, formerly a
chapel of Chirbury, the upper monument in the chancel, being
erected to him. By his 1st wife, Margaret, dau. and heir of
Griffith ap Rhys ap Philip ap David, of Llwynhowel, he had
issue, a son and dau.,

EDWARD HERBERT, of whom presently.
Anne, m. Humphrey ap Howel, of Ynysymaengwyn. co.
Merioneth, deputy sheriff to John Sandown, high sheriff for
Merionethshire in 1525, derived from Einion ap Griffith,
of Corsygedol, and was by him mother of

1 John Wynne ap Humphrey, of Ynysymaengwyn, whose
heir-general is William-Thomas-Rowland Powell, Esq., of
Nanteos. co Cardigan.
2 Lewis Gwyn, m. Anne, 2nd dau. of Hugh Gwyn, of
Llwyngriffri.
1 Jane, m. Griffith Nanney. Esq., of Nanney. co. Merioneth,
represented by the Vaughans of Nanney, Baronets,
extinct.
2 Elizabeth, m. Morgan Lloyd, Esq., of Crogen, in Edeirnion, co. Merioneth, and was mother of an eldest surviving
son, David ap Morgan Lloyd, living 17 January, 1594,
when he signed his visitation pedigree by Lewis Dwn.
By Gwenwhyfar his wife, dau. of Jeuan ap Griffith, of
Bodweni, co. Merioneth, derived from Owen Gwynâd,
Prince of North Wales, he was father of an only son,
MORGAN LLOYD, Esq., of Crogen, who m. Margaret, dau. of
Peter Meyricke, Esq., of Ucheldre, co. Merioneth, and had
numerous issue. This gentleman sold Crogen to Maurice
Wynne, Esq., son of Sir John Wynne, of Gwydyr, co.
Carnarvon, Baronet.

The only son,
EDWARD HERBERT, Esq., resided at Montgomery Castle, and
subsequently at Blackhall, Montgomery, which he built in his
old age on the north-east side of the town of Montgomery,
a mansion of great extent, which was destroyed by fire, and
the site is now only indicated by the foss. This gentleman, a
courtier, a gallant soldier, and repressor of turbulence in his
neighbourhood, d. at the age of about eighty, and was buried
in Montgomery Church. He left besides several daus., four
sons,

I. RICHARD HERBERT, his successor.
II. Mathew Herbert, of Dolgeog. a seat bestowed on him by
his father, on his return from the Low Countries.
III. Charles Herbert, who, after his return from the Low
Countries, m. an heiress, and was father, with other children, of an eldest son, Sir Edward Herbert, attorney-
general.
IV. George Herbert, of New College, Oxford, a person of great
piety, who d. in middle age.

The eldest son,
RICHARD HERBERT, Esq., of Llyssyn, aliter Llysmâwr, Montgomery, m. Magdalen, dau. of Sir Richard Newport, Knt., of
High Ercall, co. Salop, by Margaret his wife, dau. and heir of
Sir Thomas Bromley, Knt. By this lady, who d. 1627, (having
m. 2ndly, Sir John Danvers, Knt., brother of Henry. Earl of
Danby), Richard Herbert, who d. 1597, and was buried in the
south transept of the Llysmâwr chancel. in Montgomery
church, where there is a monument to him, had issue,

I. SIR EDWARD HERBERT, of whom presently.
II. Richard Herbert, who served with reputation as an officer
in the Low Countries, where he d., and was buried at Bergen-
op-Zoom.
III. William Herbert, an officer who d. in the Low Countries
IV. Charles Herbert, Fellow of New College, Oxford, d
young.
V. Rev. George Herbert, an accomplished scholar and public
orator of the university of Cambridge, rector of Bamerton,
near Salisbury, he d. between 1630 and 1640. His poems wen'
printed at London in 1635, under the title of The Temple,
and his Priest to th' Temple, in 1652. Lord Bacon dedicated
to him a translation of some psalms into English verse.
VI. Henry Herbert, gentleman of the king's privy chamber,
and master of the revels, whose only son,
HENRY HERBERT, Lord Herbert, of Chirbury, so created,
26 April, 1694, d. in 1709, leaving a son, Henry, 2nd Lord
Herbert, of Chirbury, who d. s. p., when his honours
expired.
VII. Thomas Herbert, a naval officer, buried in St. Martin's
Church, Charing Cross, London.
I. Elizabeth, m. Sir Henry Jones, of Albemarle.
II. Margaret, m. John Vaughan, son and heir of Owen
Vaughan, of Llwydiart.
III. Frances, m. Sir John Browne. Knt., of Lincolnshire, and
had issue.

The eldest son was the celebrated
EDWARD HERBERT, 1st Lord Herbert, of Chirbury, of whom
we shall speak in the words of that chivalrous and eminent
person himself. "My father was Richard Herbert, Esq., son
of Edward Herbert, Esq., and grandchild of Sir Edward
Herbert, Knt., of Colebrook, in Monmouthshire, of all whom I
shall say a little. And first, of my father, whom I remember to
have been black-haired, and bearded, as all my ancestors of his
side are said to have been, of a manly or somewhat stern look,
but withal very handsome, and well compact in his limbs, and
of a great courage, whereof he gave proof, when he was so
barbarously assaulted by many men, in the churchyard at
Lanervil, at what time he would have apprehended a man who
denied to appear to justice; for defending himself against
them all, by the help only of one John ap Howell Corbet, he
chased his adversaries, until a villian coming behind him, did
over the shoulders of the others, wound him on the head
behind, with a forest bill, until he fell down, though recovering
himself again, notwithstanding his skull was cut through to the
pia mater of the brain, he saw his adversaries fly away, and
after, walked home to his house at Llyssyn, where after he was
cured, he offered a single combat to the chief of the family, by
whose procurement it was thought the mischief was committed;
but he disclaiming wholly the action as not done by his consent,
my father desisted from prosecuting the business further. My
grandfather was of a various life; beginning first at court,
when, after he had spent most part of his means, he became a
soldier, and made his fortune with his sword, at the siege of
St. Quintens in France, and other wars, both in the north, and
in the rebellions happening in the times of King EDWARD VI.,
and Queen MARY, with so good success, that he not only came
off still with the better, but got so much money and wealth, as
enabled him to buy the greatest part of that livelihood which
is descended to me. My grandfather was noted to be a great
enemy to the outlawys and thieves of his time, who robbed in
great numbers in the mountains of Montgomeryshire, for the
suppressing of whom he went often, both day and night, to
the places where they were; concerning which, though many
particulars have been told, I shall mention one only. Some
outlaws being lodged in an alehouse, upon the hills of Llandi-
nam, my grandfather and a few servants coming to apprehend
them, the principal outlaw shot an arrow against my grandfather, which stuck in the pommel of his saddle; whereupon
my grandfather coming up to him with his sword in his hand,
and taking him prisoner, he shewed him the said arrow, bidding
him look what he had done; whereof the outlaw was no
farther sensible, than to say, he was sorry that he left his
better bow at home, which he conceived would have carried
his shot to his body; but the outlaw being brought to justice,
suffered for it. My grandfather's power was so great in the
country that divers ancestors of the better families now in
Montgomeryshire were his servants, and raised by him. He
delighted also much in hospitality; as having a very long
table twice covered every meal, with the best meats that could
be gotten, and a very great family. It was an ordinary saying
in the country at that time, when they saw any fowl rise, fly
where thou wilt, thou wilt light at Blackhall; which was a low
building, but of great capacity, my grandfather erected in his
age; his father and himself, in former times, having lived in
Montgomery Castle. Notwithstanding, yet these expenses
at home, he brought up his children well, marrying his daughters to the better sort of persons near him, and bringing up
his younger sons at the university; from whence his son

Matthew went to the Low Country wars; and, after some time spent there, came home and lived in the country, at Dolegeog, upon a house and fair living, which my grandfather bestowed upon him. His son also, Charles Herbert, after he had passed some time in the Low Countries, likewise returned home, and was after married to an inheretrix, whose eldest son, called Sir Edward Herbert, Knt., is the king's attorney-general. His son, George, who was of New College, in Oxford, was very learned, and of a pious life, died in a middle age of a dropsy. My grandfather died at the age of fourscore, or therebouts and was buried in Montgomery church, without having any monument made for him, which yet for my father is there set up in a fair manner. My great grandfather, Sir Richard Herbert, was steward, in the time of King HENRY VIII., of the lordships and marches of North Wales, East Wales, and Cardiganshire and had power, in a marshal law to execute offenders; in the using thereof he was so just, that he acquired to himself a singular reputation; as may appear upon the records of that time, kept in the paper chamber at Whitehall, some touch whereof I have made in my history of HENRY, of him I can say little more, than that he likewise was a great suppressor of rebels, thieves, and outlaws, and that he was just and conscionable. He lieth buried likewise in Montgomery; the upper monument of the two placed in the chancel being erected for him. My great-great-grandfather, Sir Richard Herbert, of Colebrook, was that incomparable hero, who (in the history of Hall and Grafton, as it appears), twice passed through a great army of northern men alone, with his battle-axe in his hand, and returned without any mortal hurt. This Sir Richard Herbert lieth buried in Abergaveny, in a sumptuous monument for those times: whereas his brother, the Earl of Pembroke,* being buried in Tintirne Abbey, his monument together with the church, lie now wholly defaced and ruined. This Earl of Pembroke had a younger son, who had a daughter, which married the eldest son of the Earl of Worcester, who carried away the fair castle of Ragland, with many thousand pounds yearly, from the heir male of that house, which was the second son of the said Earl of Pembroke, and ancestor of the family of St. Gillians, whose daughter and heir I after married, as shall be told in its place. My mother was Magdalen Newport, daughter of Sir Richard Newport, and Margaret, his wife, daughter and heir of Sir Thomas Bromley, one of the privy council, and executors of King HENRY VIII. By these ancestors I am descended of Talbot, Devereux, Grey, Corbet, and many other noble families, as may be seen in their matches, extant in the many fair coats the Newports bear. The names of my brothers and sisters were, Richard, William, Charles, George, Henry, Thomas, Elizabeth, Margaret, and Frances (I was myself the eldest). My brother Richard, after he had been brought up in learning, went to the Low Countries, where he continued many years with much reputation, both in the wars, and for fighting single duels, which were many; insomuch, that between both, he carried as I have been told, the scars of four-and-twenty wounds upon him to his grave, and lieth buried in Bergen-op-zoom. My brother William, also a person of great bravery, died a military man in the Low Countries. My brother Charles was fellow of New College, Oxford, where he died young. My brother George,† was so excellent a scholar, that he was made the public orator of the university of Cambridge. Henry came to court, and was made gentleman of the king's privy chamber, and master of the revels; by which means, as also by a good marriage, he attained to great fortunes for himself and posterity to enjoy. Thomas was a naval officer, who won a very high reputation, but finding himself, after many eminent services, as he thought undervalued, he retired to a private and melancholy life, being much discontented to find others preferred to him; in which sullen humour having lived many years, he died, and was buried in London in St. Martin's, near Charing Cross. Elizabeth, my eldest sister, was married to Sir Henry Jones, of Albemarle. Margaret was married to

* In the 9th EDWARD IV. an insurrection, headed by Sir John Coniers and Robert Riddesdale, in favour of HENRY VI., having broken out, this earl and his brother, Sir Richard Herbert, being sent to suppress it, were joined by the Earl of Devonshire, but a dispute arising between the two earls, the Earl of Devon separated from Pembroke who, engaging the enemy at Danesmoore, near Edgcote, in Northamptonshire, was defeated and taken prisoner, with his brother, and both were put to death, with Richard Widville, Earl Rivers, father of the queen, by command of the Duke of Clarence and the Earl of Warwick, who had revolted from Edward.

† George took orders, and was rector of Bemerton, near Salisbury. He died between 1630 and 1640. His poems were printed at London in 1635, under the title of *The Temple* and his *Priest to the Temple*, in 1652. Lord Bacon dedicated to him a translation of some psalms into English verse.

John Vaughan, son and heir of Owen Vaughan, of Llwydiart. Frances, my youngest sister, was married to Sir John Brown, Knt., of the county of Lincoln, who had by her divers children; the eldest son of whom, although young, fought divers duels, in one of which it was his fortune to kill one Lee, of a great family in Lancashire. I shall now come to myself. I was born at Eyton, in Shropshire, in 1581;" but as our limits prevent our proceeding farther. so much in detail—we shall state at once that Mr. Herbert married about the time that he had attained his fifteenth year, his kinswoman, Mary, dau. and heir of Sir William Herbert of St. Gillians, co. Monmouth, (the lady had been enjoined by the will of her father to marry a Herbert), then twenty-one years of age, and had issue, RICHARD, Edward, Beatrix, and Florence. About the year 1608 he resolved to travel, and for that purpose came to court and obtained license to go beyond sea. In his sojourn upon the continent he became a proficient in military exercises, and a most accomplished cavalier. He was made a knight of the Bath at the coronation of King JAMES I., and was afterwards of that monarch's council for military affairs, and his Majesty's ambassador to LEWIS XIII. of France, to mediate for the relief of the Protestants of that kingdom, in which service he continued more than five years; managing the high trust with so much fidelity and discretion, that he was advanced to the dignity of a baron of Ireland, (where had a fair estate), by the title of Lord Herbert, of Castle Island: and afterwards proving himself a faithful servant of King CHARLES I., in the council and the field, his lordship was created a peer of England by letters patent, dated 7 May, 1629, as BARON HERBERT *of Chirbury, co. Salop.* "This noble lord," (says Dugdale), "was author of that learned Philosophical Tract (in Latin), *de Veritate*, printed in 1658, and since, as I have heard, translated into sundry languages." As also of these others—

De Causis Errorum, et de Religione Laici, Edit. Lon. 1658.
De Expeditione in Ream Insulam, Edit. Lon. 1649.
The Life and Reign of King Henry VIII., Edit. Lon. 1619.
De Religione Gentilitium, &c., Ed. Amstelodami, 1663.

The history of HENRY VIII.'s reign was undertaken by command of King JAMES I., and is much esteemed. His lordship's historical collections are preserved in the library of Jesus College, Oxford. This, the celebrated Lord Herbert, of Chirbury, d. in 1648, and was s. by his eldest son,

RICHARD HERBERT, 2nd Lord Herbert, of Chirbury, who, during his father's life-time, being a person of great courage and valour, served King CHARLES I. as captain of a troop of horse, in the first engagement against the Scotch; and afterwards in England against the parliamentarians. His lordship m. Mary, dau. of John, Earl of Bridgewater, and had issue,

EDWARD, his successor.
John, who d. young.
Henry, captain in the service of King CHARLES I.
Thomas, d. unm.
Frances, m. to William Brown, Esq.
Florence. m. to her kinsman, Richard Herbert, Esq., of Oakley Park, and her son,
    HENRY-ARTHUR HERBERT, had the dignity of HERBERT, *of Chirbury,* revived in his favour in 1743; *see* Herbert, Earl Powis.
Arabell, d. unm.
Alicia, m. John Buzzard, Esq., of Barby Manor, M.P., elder brother of Paul Buzzard, Esq., of Walhampton, ancestor of the Buzzards, Baronets.

His lordship d. 13 May, 1655, and was s. by his eldest son,

EDWARD HERBERT, 3rd Lord Herbert, of Chirbury. This nobleman, like his predecessors, was zealously attached to the fortunes of King CHARLES I., and had the gratification to witness the restoration of the monarchy. His lordship m. 1st, Anne, dau. of Sir Thomas Middleton, Knt., of Chirk Castle, co. Denbigh, and 2ndly, Elizabeth, dau. and co-heir of George Brydges, 6th Lord Chandos. but by her (who m. 2ndly, William, Earl of Inchiquin and 3rdly, Charles, Lord Howard of Escrick), he had no issue, and the honours, at his lordship's decease, 9 December, 1678, devolved upon his brother,

HENRY HERBERT, 4th Lord Herbert, of Chirbury, who m. Lady Catherine Newport, dau. of Francis, Earl of Bradford, but having no issue, the Irish barony, and that of Herbert, of Chirbury, at his lordship's decease, 21 April, 1691, became EXTINCT.

The HERBERTS of Muckruss, co. Kerry, descended from Sir Richard Herbert, of Colebrook, brother of the 1st Earl of Pembroke of the 1st creation, are now the male representatives of the noble house of Herbert.

Arms—Per pale, az., and gu., three lions rampant, arg., armed and langued, or.

HERBERT—BARONS POWIS, OF POWIS CASTLE, CO. MONTGOMERY, EARLS OF POWIS, MARQUESSES OF POWIS.

Barony, by Letters Patent, dated 2 April, 1629.
Earldom, by Letters Patent, dated 4 April, 1674.
Marquessate, by Letters Patent, dated 24 March, 1687.

Lineage.

The Hon. Sir Edward Herbert, Knt., of Red Castle, anciently called Poole Castle, but now Powis Castle,* 2nd son of William Herbert, 1st Earl of Pembroke, of the existing peerage, m. Mary, only dau. and heiress of Thomas Stanley, Esq., of Standen, co. Hertford, master of the Mint in 1570, by whom he had issue,

William, his successor.
George, d. unm.
John (Sir), d. s. p.　　　　　Edward, d. unm.
Anne, m. to William, son and heir of Sir William Stanley, of Horton, co. Chester.
Catherine, m. to Sir William Massey, of Puddington, in Cheshire.

The eldest son,

William Herbert, was made a knight of the Bath, at the coronation of King James I., and elevated to the peerage, as Baron Powis, of Powis Castle, 2 April, 1629. His lordship m. Eleanor, dau. of Henry Percy, Earl of Northumberland, and had issue,

Percy, who was created a baronet in the lifetime of his father, 16 November, 1622.
Katherine, m. 1st, to Sir Robert Vaughan, Knt., of Lydiard, co. Montgomery; and 2ndly, to Sir James Palmer, Knt., of Dorney Court, Bucks, father of Roger, Earl of Castlemain.
Lucy, m. to William Abington, Esq., of Hinlop, co. Worcester.

His lordship d. at the advanced age of eighty-three, 7 March, 1655, and was s. by his son,

Sir Percy Herbert, Bart., 2nd Lord Powis. This nobleman m. Elizabeth, dau. of Sir William Craven, an alderman of London, and sister of William, Earl Craven, by whom he had,

William, his successor.
Mary, m. to George, Lord Talbot, eldest son of John, Earl of Shrewsbury.

His lordship d. in 1667, and was s. by his son,

William Herbert, 3rd Lord Powis, who was created 4 April, 1674, Earl of Powis, 24 March, 1687, Viscount Montgomery, and Marquess of Powis. This nobleman attaching himself to the fortunes of his royal master, withdrew with his Majesty into France, at the revolution, and was subsequently created by the fallen monarch Marquess of Montgomery, and Duke of Powis, but those dignities were never recognized in England. His lordship was outlawed for not returning within a certain period, and submitting to the new government. He m. Lady Elizabeth Somerset, dau. of Edward, Marquess of Worcester, and had issue,

William, his successor.
Mary, m. 1st, to Richard, son of Carril, Viscount Molineaux, in Ireland; and 2ndly, to Francis, 4th Viscount Montague.
Frances, m. to Kenneth Mackenzie, 4th Earl of Seaforth.
Anne, m. to Francis Smith, 2nd Lord Carrington.
Winifred, m. to William Maxwell, 5th Earl of Nithisdale.
Lucy, a nun at Bruges.

The marquess d. at St. Germains, 2 June, 1696, and his son,

William Herbert, was restored to the dignities of Viscount Montgomery, and Earl and Marquess of Powis, and took his seat in the House of Lords, 8 October, 1722. His lordship m. Mary, dau. and co-heir of Sir Thomas Preston, Bart., of Furness, co. Lancaster, by whom she had issue,†

* This castle, anciently the seat of inheritance of the Cherletons and Greys, Barons Powis, was purchased by the Herberts, in the reign of Elizabeth.
† Of this marriage (that of William Herbert, 2nd Marquess, and Mary, dau. of Sir Thomas Preston) there was issue also several daus., the eldest, Lady Mary, who is represented in her portrait, at Powys Castle, as "Minerva," was conspicuous in her time. She was engaged deeply in the Mississippi scheme, and dreamt of millions; aimed at being royal consort to the late Pretender: failed in her plans, and with another noble adventurer, retired to Spain, in search of the gold in the mines of Asturias. She fell under the satire of Pope—

　"The crown of Poland, venal twice an age,
　To just three millions stinted modest Gage,
　But nobler scenes Maria's dreams unfold;
　Hereditary realms, and worlds of gold.
　Congenial souls! whose life one av'rice joins,
　And one fate buries in the Asturian mines "

275

William, his successor.
Edward, who m. 7 July, 1734, Henrietta, dau. of the Earl of Waldegrave, and dying in November of that year, left his lady enceinte, who was delivered of a dau., Barbara Herbert, who m. Henry-Arthur Herbert, Esq., created Lord Herbert, of Chirbury, in 1743, and Earl of Powis, in 1748 (see that dignity). Lady Henrietta Herbert m. 2ndly, Mr. Beard, the comedian.
Mary, m. Joseph, Count Gage, brother of the 1st Viscount Gage.
Anne, m. Henry, 6th Lord Arundel, of Wardour.
Charlotte, m. 1st, Edward Morris, Esq.; and 2ndly, Edward Williams, of Yeslyn, Esq.
Theresa, m. Sir R. Throckmorton, Bart.

The marquess d. in 1745, and was s. by his elder son,

William Herbert, 3rd Marquess of Powis. This nobleman dying unm. in 1748, the Marquessate and Earldom of Powis, with his other honours, became extinct; but he devised the whole of his estates to the husband of his niece, Henry-Arthur, Lord Herbert of Chirbury.

Arms—Per pale, az. and gu., three lions rampant, arg., a crescent for difference.

HERBERT—BARONS HERBERT, OF CHIRBURY.

By Letters Patent, dated 28 April, 1694.

Lineage.

Henry Herbert, only son and heir of Sir Henry Herbert, gentleman of the king's chamber, and master of the revels, and nephew of the celebrated Edward, Lord Herbert of Chirbury, was elevated to the peerage by King William III., 28 April, 1694, as Baron Herbert, of Chirbury. His lordship m. Anne, dau. and co-heir of Mr. Alderman Ranney, of the city of London; and dying in 1709, was s. by his only son,

Henry Herbert, 2nd baron. This nobleman m. Mary, dau. of John Wallop, Esq., of Farley, co. Southampton; but dying in 1738 s. p., this Barony of Herbert of Chirbury became extinct.

Arms—Per pale, az. and gu., three lions rampant, arg., armed and langued, or.

HERBERT—EARL OF TORRINGTON.

By Letters Patent, dated 29 May, 1689.

Lineage.

Edward Herbert, grand-nephew of the celebrated William Herbert, Earl of Pembroke and Huntingdon, had three sons; Richard, ancestor of the Lords Herbert of Chirbury; Matthew, of the Earls of Powis; and Charles, father of Sir Edward Herbert, an eminent lawyer, and attorney-general to Charles I., who d. 1657, leaving issue,

Arthur Herbert, Esq., who was elevated to the peerage by King William III., 29 May, 1689, as Baron Torbay, and Earl of Torrington, co. Devon, with remainder, failing his issue male, to his brother Charles. His lordship, who was brought up to the naval service, had the command of a fleet, temp. Charles II., before Tangier, and afterwards against Algiers; but being removed from his commission by King James II., he retired into Holland, and was graciously received by the Prince of Orange. "He was a man of good understanding, but profusely luxurious, and on every occasion so sullen and peevish, that it was plain he valued himself much, and expected the same from others; and it was thought, his private quarrel with Lord Dartmouth, for having more of the king's confidence than himself, was the root of his resentment against his Majesty. The reputation he had gained with the people in England, and his skill in sea affairs, made it necessary to endeavour to keep him in good temper, so far as homage and observance could do it." His lordship was admiral of the Dutch fleet, on the coming over of the Prince of Orange, and was subsequently first commissioner of the Admiralty, and commander-in-chief of the British fleet. In 1690, he engaged the French fleet, near Beechy Head, but although he fought most gallantly against a superior force, yet not achieving a victory, subjected him to considerable reprehension, deprivation of his command, and committal to the Tower. He was eventually tried by court-martial and acquitted, but never again employed. His lordship m. 1st, Miss Anne Hadley ; and 2ndly, Anne, dau. of Sir William Airmine, and widow of Sir Thomas Woodhouse, but having no issue, the Earldom of Torrington and minor dignity, at his lordship's decease, 14 April, 1716, became EXTINCT, his brother Charles having predeceased him *s. p.*

Arms—Per pale, az. and gu., three lions rampant, arg., a mullet for difference.

HERBERT—BARONS HERBERT, OF CHIRBURY, EARLS OF POWIS, &c., BARONS HERBERT, OF CHIRBURY AND LUDLOW.

Barony, by Letters Patent, dated 21 December, 1743.
Earldom, &c., by Letters Patent, dated 27 May, 1748.
Barony, with special remainder, by Letters Patent, dated 7 October, 1749.

Lineage.

SIR WILLIAM AP THOMAS of Raglan Castle, left issue, with an elder son, William, Earl of Pembroke and Huntingdon (*see* those titles), a younger son, Sir Richard, of Colebrooke and Montgomery, from whose eldest son descend the HERBERTS of MUCRUSS in IRELAND, whilst Sir Richard, the 2nd son, steward of the Welsh marches, was father of Edward Herbert, Esq., who had three sons, Richard, ancestor of the Lords Herbert of Chirbury of the 1st and 2nd creation ; MATTHEW and Charles, grandfather of the Earl of Torrington (*see* that title).

MATTHEW HERBERT, Esq., M.P. for Monmouth, 5th ELIZABETH, was father of Sir Matthew, created a baronet in 1660, but *d. s. p.*, and of Francis, of Oakley Park, whose eldest son, Richard, marrying Florence, sister and co-heir of Edward and Henry, 3rd and 4th Lords Herbert of Cherbury, was father of HENRY-ARTHUR HERBERT, Esq., who, (becoming heir male to the Chirbury family on the death of Henry, 2nd baron of the 2nd creation, in 1738), was created Baron Herbert of Chirbury, 21 December, 1743, and was advanced, 27 May, 1748, to the *Barony of Powis, of Powis Castle*, the *Viscounty of Ludlow*, and the EARLDOM OF POWIS. He m. Barbara, only dau. of Lord Edward Herbert, and niece of William, 3rd and last Marquess of Powis, and *s.*, under the will of that nobleman, to his large estates. The earl obtained another peerage, 16 October, 1749, as BARON HERBERT OF CHIRBURY AND LUDLOW, with remainder, failing the heirs male of his own body, to his brother Richard, and the heirs male of his body, in default of which, to Francis Herbert, Esq., of Ludlow, and the heirs male of his body. His lordship *d.* in 1772, and was *s.* by his son,

GEORGE-EDWARD-HENRY-ARTHUR HERBERT, 2nd Earl of Powis, who *d. s. p.* in 1801, when the Barony of Herbert of Chirbury, the Earldom of Powis and its minor dignities, with the Barony of Herbert of Chirbury and Ludlow (his lordship's uncle having predeceased him *unm.*, to whom the last barony was in reversion), became EXTINCT, while the earl's estates passed to his sister, Lady Henrietta-Antonia Herbert, who m. in 1784, Edward, Lord Clive, of the kingdom of Ireland, which nobleman was advanced subsequently to the EARLDOM OF POWIS, *Barony of Herbert, of Chirbury, &c.*, and from him they have descended to the present earl.

Arms—Per pale, az. and gu., three lions rampant, arg., armed and langued, or.

HERBERT—BARON HERBERT, OF CASTLE ISLAND.

See HERBERT, Baron Herbert of Chirbury.

HERON—BARON HERON.

By Writ of Summons, dated 13 November, 1393.

Lineage.

SIR WILLIAM HERON, of Applynden, grandson of Odonel Heron (3rd son of William, the last baron by tenure) and grand nephew of the Lord Heron of Ford, having m. Elizabeth, widow of John de Falvesley, dau. and heiress of William, Baron Say, and cousin and heiress of Thomas de Brewose, had summons to parliament, from 13 November, 1393, to 25 August, 1404, as "Willielmo Heron, Chl'r," although it is certain that he was generally considered as Lord Say, *jure uxoris ;* for in a charter of 1st HENRY IV., to which he was a witness, he is styled "Willielmo Heron, Dominus de Say, Seneschallus Hospitii Regis." This nobleman was a gallant soldier and an eminent diplomatist. He *d.* 30 October, 1404, *s. p.*, when, if his barony be deemed a distinct dignity from that of Say, it became EXTINCT.

Arms—Gu , a chevron between three herons, arg.

HERON—BARON HERON.

By Writ of Summons, dated 8 January, 1371.

Lineage.

About the beginning of King JOHN's reign, JORDAN HAIRUN, possessed a barony in Northumberland, which he held by the service of one knight's fee, as his ancestors had done from the time of King HENRY I., who enfeoffed them thereof. His grandson, WILLIAM HERON, in the 32nd HENRY III., was made governor of Bamburgh Castle, co. Northumberland, and in the 39th of the same reign was governor of the castle of Pickering, in Yorkshire, and warden of the forests north of Trent. The next year he filled the office of sheriff of Northumberland, and was constituted governor of Scarborough Castle. He m. Mary, dau. and heir of Odonel de Ford, *d.* 1256, and was *s.* by his son, WILLIAM HERON. This feudal lord was one of the barons on the part of the king at the battle of Lewes; and was summoned by EDWARD I., with the other northern barons to meet him at Norham, with horse and arms, when he went to give judgment between the competitors for the crown of Scotland. William Heron m. Christian, dau. and heir of Roger de Notton, and had issue,

> WALTER, who m. Alicia de Hastings, and dying before his father, left an only dau. and heir, EMMELINE, m. to John, Lord D'Arcy, steward of the household to EDWARD III., and who, on the decease of her grandfather, was his heir, whereby the Darcy family became possessed of the ancient Barony of Heron, and of the manors of Silkeston and Notton, co. York.
>
> ROGER, of whom presently.
> Odonel.

At the decease of his father, his elder brother having *d.* previously, as stated above, the representation of the family devolved upon ROGER HERON, who inherited the manors of Ford and Bokenfield, co. Northumberland; and with his brother Odonel, attended EDWARD I., as one of his knights, to the siege of Stirling Castle. In the 10th EDWARD II. he was governor of Bamburgh Castle, and was *s.* at his decease by his son, WILLIAM HERON. This feudal lord obtained license in the 12th EDWARD III., to make a castle of his house at Ford—and was summoned to parliament, as a baron, 8 January, 1371, but never afterwards. The Barony of Heron became, therefore, at his decease, EXTINCT.

Arms—Gu., a chevron between three herons, arg.

HERVEY—BARON HERVEY, OF KIDBROKE, CO. KENT.

By Letters Patent, dated 7 February, 1628.

Lineage.

WILLIAM HERVEY, Esq., of Ickworth, co. Suffolk (said to have descended from Robert Fitz-Hervey, a younger son of Hervey, Duke of Orleans, who came over with the CONQUEROR), *d.* in 1538, leaving, with other issue,

JOHN HERVEY, ancestor of the Marquesses of Bristol, and
SIR NICHOLAS HERVEY, of the privy-chamber to King
HENRY VIII., and ambassador from that monarch to the
emperor's court at Ghent. This eminent person *m.* 1st, Eliza-
beth, dau. of Sir Thomas Fitz-Williams, and widow of Sir
Thomas Mauleverer, by whom he had an only son,

THOMAS (Sir), knight-marshal to Queen MARY.

Sir Nicholas *m.* 2ndly, Bridget, dau. and heiress of Sir John
Wiltshire, of Stone Castle, co. Kent, and relict of Sir Richard
Wingfield, of Kimbolton Castle, co. Huntingdon, by whom he
had two sons, viz.,

HENRY, his successor.
George, ancestor of the Herveys, of Marshal, in Essex.

Sir Nicholas was *s.* by his elder son,

HENRY HERVEY, who *m.* Jane, dau. of James Thomas, Esq.,
and had a son and heir,

WILLIAM HERVEY, Esq., of Kidbroke, co. Kent, who obtained
great eminence as a military character in the reigns of Queen
ELIZABETH, King JAMES I., and King CHARLES I, Mr. Hervey
first signalized himself in the memorable conflict with the
Armada, having boarded one of the galleons, and killed the
captain, Hugh Moncade, with his own hand. He was subsequently knighted; and being employed successfully in Ireland,
was created a baronet, 31 May, 1619, and in the following year
elevated to the peerage of that kingdom, in the dignity of
Baron Hervey, of Ross, co. Wexford. His lordship, continuing
his eminent public services, was created a peer of England,
7 February, 1628, as BARON HERVEY, of *Kilbroke, co. Kent.*
He *m.* 1st, Mary, relict of Henry, Earl of Southampton, and
dau. of Anthony, Viscount Montacute, by whom he had no
issue. His lordship *m.* 2ndly, Cordelia, dau. and co-heir of
Brian Ansley, Esq., of Lewisham, in Kent, and had issue,

William, killed in Germany.
John, who *d.* in Ireland.
Henry, *d.* young.
ELIZABETH, *m.* to John Hervey, Esq., of Ickworth, who *d.* in
1679, *s. p.* when his estate devolved upon his brother, Sir
Thomas Hervey, whose eldest surviving son, John Hervey,
was created Baron Hervey, of Ickworth, and Earl of Bristol,
dignities enjoyed by the present Marquess of Bristol.

Lord Hervey *d.* in June, 1642, and his sons having pre-deceased
him, the Irish Barony of Hervey, of Ross, with the baronetcy
and English Barony of Hervey, of Kidbroke, became EXTINCT,
while his estates devolved upon his only surviving child, ELIZA-
BETH HERVEY

Arms—Gu., on a bend, arg., three trefoils slipped, vert.

HERVEY—BARON HERVEY, OF ROSS.

By Patent, dated 5 August, 1620,

(*See* HERVEY, Baron Hervey, of Kidbroke.

HEWETT—VISCOUNT HEWETT.

By Patent, dated 9 April, 1689.

Lineage.

SIR GEORGE HEWETT, 2nd Baronet of Pishobury, Herts (for
preceding lineage, *see* BURKE's *Extinct Baronetage*), was raised
to the peerage of Ireland, 9 April, 1689, as *Baron of James-
town, co. Longford,* and VISCOUNT HEWETT, *of Gowran, co.
Kilkenny;* but *d. unm.* 2 December following, when all his
honours EXPIRED, the manor of Pishobury passing to his
sister, Lady Reade, of Bardwell, by whom it was sold.

Arms—Gu., a chev., engr., between three owls, close, arg.

HILL—BARON HILL, OF ALMAREZ AND HAWKESTONE.

By Letters Patent, dated 17 May, 1814.

Lineage.

SIR ROWLAND HILL (2nd son of Sir John Hill, 3rd baronet, of
Hawkestone. co. Salop, by Mary Chambré, his wife), *b.* 11
August, 1772, having adopted the profession of arms, attained
the rank of general, and having eminently distinguished himself during the Peninsular war, was rewarded with the Grand
Cross of the Bath, and subsequently elevated to the peerage,
17 May, 1814, as *Baron Hill, of Almarez, and of Hawkestone, co.
Salop.* His lordship obtained a second patent, dated 16 January,
1816, conferring a similar dignity, with the additional designation *of Hardwicke,* and in remainder to the male issue of his
deceased brother, John Hill, Esq., of Hawkestone. Lord
Hill was commander-in-chief from 1828 until 1842, when he
resigned; upon which occasion he was raised to a *Viscounty,*
with remainder similar to that of his last barony. Viscount Hill
d. unm. 10 December, 1842, when the Barony of Hill of
Almarez became EXTINCT, but his other honours devolved on
his nephew, SIR ROWLAND HILL, Bart., the 2nd VISCOUNT
HILL. (*See Extant Peerage.*)

Arms—Erm., on a fesse, sa., a castle triple towered, arg.

HILTON—BARON HILTON, OF HILTON, CO. DURHAM.

By Writ of Summons, dated 23 June, 1295.

Lineage.

ROBERT DE HILTON, of Hilton Castle, co. Durham, was summoned to parliament, as a baron, in the 23rd, 24th, and 25th
EDWARD I. His lordship *m.* Margaret, one of the three co-
heirs of Marmaduke de Thwenge, by whom he acquired large
estates. and left two daus.,

Isabel, *m.* to Walter de Pedwardyn.
Maud, *m.* to Sir John Hotham, Knt.

At his lordship's decease the Barony of Hilton fell into ABEY-
ANCE between those ladies, as it continues amongst their
representatives, should any exist.

** The castle of Hilton stands low and sequestered in the
Vale of Wear, three miles to the west of Wearmouth Bridge, co
Durham, on the old road to Newcastle. Here for twenty-three
descents, extending over six centuries, dwelt in high renown
the famous Barons of Hilton, a race of gentlemen of the first
consideration. Of the title of "Baron," so constantly bestowed
on each successive Lord of Hilton, a few words may not be
inappropriate. The designation does not appear to have had
any reference to a peerage honour, but was given by the
general courtesy of the country, either from respect to the immemorial existence of the family in a *gentle* state, long before
the creation of barons by writ, or else with reference to the
rank which the Hiltons undoubtedly held, of "Barons of the
Bishopric," sitting with a sort of provincial peerage, in the
great council of their ecclesiastical Palatine. Certain it is,
that the name of Hilton always stands first in every episcopal
commission, and that popular respect never failed to concede to
its chief the precedence of nobility. In 1669, Mr. Arden, complaining to Miles Stapleton, Esq., of the unseemly pride of
Dean Carleton and his daus., adduces, as a superlative instance
of it, that "the Dean himself had taken a place above Baron
Hilton at the quarter sessions, to the great disgust and reluc-
tancy of the county gentry; and that, moreover, the young
Carletons had crowded themselves into a pew in the cathedral
before Baron Hilton's daughters."

The origin of the Hiltons is lost in the obscurity of distant
ages. Every ancient house has its fabulous age, and the
Hiltons are not without their ill contrived Williams and Adams,
who flourished under Saxon Athelstans, and Edwys; their
Lancelots, who died at Hastings, or Feversham, in 1066, and
their Henry, whom the CONQUEROR gifted with broad lands on
the Wear.

ROMANUS, Knight of Hilton, the genuine "homo propositus"
of the family, held three knights' fees in 1166, and was probably, by no means the first settler, as his lands were held of
"ancient feoffment." His successor, Alexander, appears in a
deed of compact, with the prior and convent of Durham, relative to the chapel of Hilton in 1172.

JOHN HILTON, the last Baron of Hilton, was a man of mild
and generous disposition, though of reserved habits, and is
remembered, with personal respect, as the final representa-

tive of a great and ancient house. He sat in parliament for the borough of Carlisle, but took little part in public affairs. His death occurred in 1746. His sisters and co-heiresses were,

I. Dorothy.
II. Anne, m. to Sir Richard Musgrave, Bart., of Hayton Castle. and d. in 1766. Her heir general is,
HEDWORTH HYLTON-JOLLIFFE, LORD HYLTON, co-heir of the blood of Hylton.
III. Elizabeth, who m. Thomas Younghusband, Esq., and d. in 1751, leaving an only dau., who m. twice, but had no issue.
IV. Catherine, m. John Brisco, D.D., of Crofton, co. Cumberland, and was mother of Sir John Brisco, Bart., of Crofton Hall.

Arms—Arg., two bars, az., and fleur-de-lis, or.

HILTON—BARON HILTON.

By Writ of Summons, dated 27 January, 1332.

Lineage.

ALEXANDER DE HILTON, who served in the Scottish wars under Ralph, Lord Neville, had summons to parliament as a baron, from 27 January, 1332, to 22 January, 1336. He left an only dau. and heiress, Elizabeth, who m. Roger Widdrington, and his descendant William, the last Lord Widdrington, was his heir male and heir general. Lord Widdrington was attainted in 1716, when his honours became forfeited. Lord Widdrington d. s. p., leaving his nephew, Thomas Eyre, Esq., of Hassop (son of his sister Mary) his heir; but he also dying issueless, the representation of Elizabeth Hilton, dau. and heir of Alexander Baron Hilton, became vested in Charles Towneley. Esq., in right of his grandmother, Mary Widdrington, aunt of the last Lord Widdrington. By the death of Mr Towneley s. p., his only sister, Cecilia, or the heir general of her body, became heir of the Barony of Hilton. She m. 1st, Charles Strickland, Esq., of Sizergh, and 2ndly, Gerard Strickland, Esq , and had issue by both husbands.

Arms—Arg., two bars, az., and fleur-de-lis, or.

HOBHOUSE – BARON BROUGHTON.

(*S e* ADDENDA.)

HOESE OR HUSEE--BARON HOESE OF BEECHWORTH, CO. SURREY.

By Writ of Summons, dated 20 November, 1349.

Lineage.

ROGER HOESE, or HUSE, son of John Husee, presumed to be of the same family as the Lords Hoese of Herting, in Sussex, having distinguished himself in the wars of Scotland, was summoned to parliament as a baron, from 20 November, 1348, to 10 March, 1349. His lordship d. in 1361, seised, amongst other lands, of the manor of West Beechesworth, and Heggercourt, co. Surrey; Ringstede, in Dorsetshire; a moiety of Burton Sacy, co. Southampton; and Northinkton, and Kingston Deverell, in Wilts. Roger d. 1361, leaving JOHN, his brother and heir, then æt. forty, whereupon the barony became EXTINCT. The said brother,

SIR JOHN HUSEE, of Beechworth castle, had livery of his inheritance. The only dau. of this Sir John, Alice, is said, by Collins, to have m. Richard de Wallop, ancestor of the Earls of Portsmouth, and the lady is called heir of Robert Husee, her brother; but Vincent mentions her as sister of Sir John, and dau. of course, of Roger, Lord Huse. It would appear by both authorities, however, that the Earls of Portsmouth represent this branch of the old baronial house of HOESE or HUSEE.

Arms—Barry of six, ermine and gules.

HOESE—BARON HOESE.

By Writ of Summons, dated 23 June, 1295.

Lineage.

GEOFFREY DE HOESE, son of Henry Hosatus, or de Hoesé, a justice itinerant and sheriff co. Oxon, d, 1199, and was s. by his son and heir,
HENRY HOESE, who d. 1213; his son and heir,
HENRY HOESE, had livery of his lands 1213, and was living 1253.
HENRY DE HOESE, Lord of Harting, co. Sussex, 1165, elder brother of Geoffrey, above-named, was father of
GEOFFREY DE HOESE, whose son and heir,
HENRY DE HOESE, d. 1234, leaving a son and heir,
MATTHEW DE HOESE, who d. 1262, and was s. by his son,
HENRY DE HOESE, who d. 1289; his son and heir was,
HENRY HOESE. This feudal lord had summons 22nd EDWARD I., 8 June in that year, to attend the king, with divers other persons of note, to advise concerning the important affairs of the realm; and the next year he was summoned to parliament as a Baron, under the designation of "Henrico Husee," and from that period to 10 October, 1325 (19th EDWARD II.). His lordship, who was engaged in the wars of Scotland, d. in 1332, and was s. by his son,
HENRY HOESE, 2nd baron, summoned to parliament, from 18 August, 1337, to 10 March, 1349. This nobleman, 21st EDWARD III., on the marriage of Henry, his son and heir, with Elizabeth, the dau. of John de Bohun, settled certain estates upon him and her, and their issue (in default), to Richard, another son, with remainder to the issue of himself, by Catherine, his then wife, and in default of such issue, on Elizabeth, his dau. His lordship d. 1349, leaving Henry, his grandson and heir (son of Mark, his eldest son, who pre-deceased him). But neither this Henry nor any one of his descendants was ever summoned to parliament.

Arms—Barry of six, ermine and gu.

HOLAND—BARONS HOLAND.

By Writ of Summons, dated 29 July, 1314.

Lineage.

That this family was of great antiquity in the county of Lancaster is evident from the register of Cokersand Abbey, to which religious house some of its members were benefactors in King JOHN's time. The first person of the name of any note was
ROBERT DE HOLAND, who was in the wars of Scotland, 31st EDWARD I., and who owed his advancement to his becoming secretary to Thomas, Earl of Lancaster, for previously he had been but a *"poor knight."* In the 1st EDWARD II. he obtained large territorial grants from the crown, viz., the manors of Melburne, Newton, Osmundeston, Swarkeston, Chelardeston, Normanton, and Wybeleston, in the county of Derby, and the same year had a military summons to march against the Scots. In the 8th EDWARD II. he was first summoned to parliament as a baron; and in the 10th and 12th, he was again in the wars of Scotland, in which latter year he had license to make a castle of his manor house of Bagworth, co. Leicester. Upon the insurrection of his old master, Thomas, Earl of Lancaster (15th EDWARD II.) his lordship promised that nobleman, to whom he owed his first rise in the world, all the aid in his power; but failing to fulfil his engagement, Lancaster was forced to fly northwards, and was finally taken prisoner at Boroughbridge, when Lord Holand rendered himself to the king at Derby, and was sent prisoner to Dover Castle. For which duplicity he became so odious to the people, that being afterwards made prisoner a second time, anno 1328, in a wood, near Henley Park, towards Windsor, he was beheaded on the nones of October, and his head sent to Henry, Earl of Lancaster, then at Waltham Cross, co. Essex, by Sir Thomas Wyther, and some other private friends. His lordship m. Maud, one of the daus. and co-heirs of Alan le Zouch, of Ashby, and had issue,

I. ROBERT, his successor.
II. Thomas, who became Earl of Kent (*see* HOLAND, EARL OF KENT.)
III. Alan, who had the manors of Dalbury and Weeksworth, co. Derby.
IV. Otho, a person of great valour in the reign of EDWARD III., and one of the original knights of the Garter. He fell into disgrace, however, by suffering the Earl of Ewe (a prisoner at war), who had been committed to his custody, to go at large armed, and was committed to the Marshalsea, after

being examined in the presence of the lord chancellor and other noblemen. He *d.* soon after in Britanny (33rd EDWARD III.), where he was engaged in his military capacity, and having no issue, his elder brother, Sir Robert Holand, by his last will, became his heir.

I. Jane, *m.* 1st, Sir Edmund Talbot of Bashall, who was constituted steward of Blackburnshire, 28th EDWARD I., by Henry de Lacy, Earl of Lincoln, and was, 32nd EDWARD I., 1303, in the great expedition against Scotland. In the preceding year he received the honour of knighthood by bathing and other ceremonies along with Prince Edward, afterwards EDWARD II. From this marriage derived the Talbots of Bashall, co. York, represented by John Hughes Lloyd, Esq., commander R.N., son of the late Richard Hughes Lloyd, Esq., of Plymog, Gwerclas, and Bashall. Jane Holand, Lady Talbot *m.* 2ndly, Sir Hugh Dutton, Knt., of Dutton, co. Chester.

II. Mary, *m.* Sir John Tempest, Knt., of Bracewell, co. York.

Robert, Lord Holand, was *s.* by his eldest son,

SIR ROBERT HOLAND, 2nd baron, summoned to parliament from 25 February, 1342, to 6 October, 1372. This nobleman was engaged for several years in the French wars of King EDWARD III., part of the time under Thomas de Beauchamp, Earl of Warwick, and the remainder in the retinue of his brother, Thomas Holland. His lordship *d.* in 1373, leaving his grand-dau. (dau. and heir of his eldest son Robert, who had pre-deceased him),

MAUD HOLLAND, then seventeen years of age, his sole heir: who *m.* John Lovel, 5th Lord Lovel, of Tichmersh, and carried the Barony of Holland into that family (*see* Lovel, Barons Lovel, of Tichmersh).

Arms—Az., a lion rampant guardant, between six fleurs-de-lis, arg.

HOLLAND—BARONS HOLLAND, EARLS OF KENT, AND BARONS WOODSTOCK AND WAKE, DUKE OF SURREY.

Barony, by Writ of Summons, dated 15 July, 1353.
Earldom, &c., by marriage with Joane Plantagenet, the Fair Maid of Kent.
Dukedom, 29 September, 1397.

Lineage.

SIR THOMAS DE HOLLAND, 2nd son of Robert de Holand, Lord Holland, having been engaged from the 14th to the 20th EDWARD III., in the wars of France, and in the last year commanded the van of Prince Edward's army at the famous battle of Cressy, was made a knight of the Garter, and summoned to parliament as a baron. At the siege of Caen, Sir Thomas had the good fortune to make prisoner of the Earl of Ewe, then constable of France, whom he delivered up to King EDWARD, for the sum of 4000 florens: and he (Sir Thomas) subsequently assisted at the siege of Calais. His lordship *m.* Joane Plantagenet, celebrated for her beauty, under the name of "the Fair Maid of Kent," only dau. of Edmund Plantagenet, surnamed "of Woodstock," Earl of Kent, 2nd son of King EDWARD III. This distinguished woman inherited, upon the decease of her brother, John, 3rd Earl of Kent, *that* dignity, with the Barony of Woodstock, honours of her father, and the Barony of Wake, a dignity of her mother's; from which latter peerage she styled herself "LADY OF WAKE."

In the 28th EDWARD III., his lordship was made lieutenant, and captain-general of the Dukedom of Britanny, and he was constituted, in two years afterwards, governor of the islands of Jersey and Guernsey. He had summons to parliament as LORD HOLLAND, from the 27th to the 31st EDWARD III., but in the 34th (*anno* 1360), he assumed the title of EARL OF KENT, and was so summoned, 20 November, in that year, in right of his wife, for it does not appear that he had any other sort of creation. In this year his lordship was appointed the king's lieutenant and captain-general in France and Normandy. He did not long, however, enjoy that high office, for he *d.* 28 December, in the same year, leaving issue by the great heiress of Kent (who *m.* after his lordship's decease, Edward the Black

* It is said by some that this Thomas, being steward of the household to William de Montacute, Earl of Salisbury, married his mistress, viz., Joane, daughter of Edmund, and sister and heir of John, Earl of Kent. But herein there is a mistake : for by his petition to Pope Clement VI., representing that the said Earl of Salisbury had a purpose to have wedded her, had not a precontract with her by him been formerly made, and carnal knowledge ensued : also that nevertheless the same earl, taking advantage of his absence in foreign parts, made a second contract with her, and unjustly withheld her. His holiness, upon a full hearing of the cause, gave sentence for him ; in which the Earl of Salisbury acquiesced. DUGDALE.

279

Prince, and was mother of King RICHARD II.), three sons and a dau., viz.,

THOMAS, his successor.   Edmund.
John, created EARL OF HUNTINGDON, AND DUKE OF EXETER (*see* Holland, Duke of Exeter).
Maud, *m.* 1st, Hugh, 3rd son of Hugh, Earl of Devon, and 2ndly, Waleran, Earl of St. Paul.

Thomas Holland, Earl of Kent, was *s.* by his eldest son.

THOMAS HOLLAND, 2nd Earl of Kent, Baron Woodstock, Baron Wake, and Baron Holland. This nobleman was engaged in the French wars in the immediate retinue of his gallant step-father, Edward, the Black Prince, and attained distinction at the battle of Castile. Upon the accession of his half-brother, King RICHARD II., his lordship obtained a grant of £200 per annum out of the exchequer, and was constituted general warden of all the forests south of Trent. In the 9th of the same reign, at the decease of his mother Joane, Princess of Wales, he had special livery of all the lands of her inheritance ; having had previously his grant out of the exchequer extended to £1000 a year. He was also constituted marshal of England, but he was afterwards discharged of that office, which was conferred upon Thomas Mowbray, Earl of Nottingham : and appointed governor of Carisbroke Castle for life. His lordship *m.* Alice Fitz-Alan, dau. of Richard, Earl of Arundel, by whom he had, with other issue,

THOMAS, } successively EARLS OF KENT.
EDMUND, }

Alianore, *m.* 1st, to Roger Mortimer, Earl of March, and 2ndly, to Edward Cherleton, Lord Powis. The senior co-representative of Alianore, Countess of March, is the ex-Duke of Modena. Among the other co-representatives are the Duke of Buckingham, the Earl of Jersey, the Duke of Sutherland, &c.
Margaret, *m.* 1st, to John Beaufort, Earl of Somerset and Marquess of Dorset, and 2ndly, to Thomas Plantagenet, Duke of Clarence, son of King HENRY IV.
Joane, *m.* 1st, to Edward, Duke of York, 2ndly, to William, Lord Willoughby, 3rdly, to Henry, Lord Scrope, of Masham, and 4thly, to Sir Henry Bromflete, afterwards Lord Vesci, and *d. s. p.* 1431.
Eleanor, *m.* to Thomas Montacute, Earl of Salisbury. The co-representatives of this marriage were WILLIAM LOWNDES, Esq., of Chesham, Bucks, WILLIAM SELBY-LOWNDES, Esq., of Whaddon, Bucks, and the MARQUESS OF HASTINGS.
Elizabeth, *m.* to Sir John Nevill, Knt., son and heir apparent of Ralph, 1st Earl of Westmoreland. Of Elizabeth, Lady Nevill, one of the co-representatives was the late SIR ROW-LAND ERRINGTON, Bart.
Bridget, a nun at Barking.

The earl *d.* 25 April, 1397, and was *s.* by his eldest son,

THOMAS HOLLAND, 3rd Earl of Kent. This nobleman, upon the attainder of Thomas de Beauchamp, Earl of Warwick, 22nd RICHARD II., had a grant in special tail of the castle, manor, and lordship of Warwick, with sundry other manors : having been created DUKE OF SURREY, the preceding year, by his uncle, King RICHARD, sitting in Parliament, with the crown upon his head. He was also constituted marshal of England, and about the same time appointed lieutenant of Ireland. The Earl was likewise a knight of the Garter. But all his honours terminated with the power of his unhappy and royal kinsman ; for being engaged in a conspiracy to subvert the government, after the accession of the Duke of Lancaster, as HENRY IV., he was taken prisoner and beheaded, with the Earl of Salisbury, by the populace, at Cirencester, in 1400, when his head was sent to London, and placed upon the bridge there, and parliament passed an act of attainder, by which his honours and lands became FORFEITED. His lordship *m.* Joane Stafford, dau. of Hugh, Earl of Stafford, but had no issue. Notwithstanding the attainder (although no reversal is upon record), the earl's brother and heir,

EDMUND HOLLAND, appears to have succeeded to the Earldom of Kent, and, of course, to the Baronies of Woodstock, Wake, and Holland. He had, subsequently, a special livery of certain castles, manors, and lands, which had devolved upon him by virtue of an old entail made of them by his ancestors. In the 9th HENRY IV. his lordship was appointed one of the commissioners to treat of peace between the king and the Duke of Britanny, and was constituted lord admiral of England. But soon after that besieging the castle and isle of Briak, in Britanny, he received a mortal wound in his head by an arrow from a cross-bow, 15 September, 1407. His lordship *m.* in 1406, Lucy, dau. of the Duke of Milan, but having no legitimate issue, his sisters, or their representatives, became his heirs (*revert* to the children of Thomas, 2nd earl), and, amongst those, the Baronies of Woodstock, Wake, and Holland, are in ABEYANCE, supposing them unaffected by the attainder of Thomas, Duke of Surrey. With Edmund, Earl of Kent, who was a knight of the Garter, that earldom expired in the Holland family.

Arms— Az., semée de lis, a lion rampant guardant, or.

HOLLAND—EARL OF HUNTINGDON, DUKE OF EXETER.

Earldom, 2 June, 1387.
Dukedom, 29 September, 1397.

Lineage.

JOHN DE HOLLAND, 3rd son of Thomas de Holland, Earl of Kent, by the celebrated heiress, Joane Plantagenet, "the Fair Maid of Kent" (see Holland, Earls of Kent), was in the expedition made into Scotland in the 29th EDWARD III., and after the accession of his half-brother, KING RICHARD II., was constituted justice of Chester. From which period we seldom find him out of some great public employment. In the 7th RICHARD he attended the king in the expedition then made into Scotland, when having some dispute with Ralph de Stafford, elder son of the Earl of Stafford, he slew the said Ralph with his dagger, and fled to sanctuary at Beverley. But the king becoming highly incensed at this foul murder, caused the assassin to be indicted and outlawed for the crime, and seized upon all his lands and offices.

It is said that the Princess Joane, his mother, hearing that the king had vowed that Holland should suffer according to law, sent earnestly to him, imploring his favour (she being their common parent), and that upon return of the messenger to Wallingford, where she then was, finding that her request availed not, she became so absorbed in grief that she died within five days. De Holland, however, eventually made his peace through the mediation of the Duke of Lancaster, and other noblemen, and was pardoned by the Earl of Stafford. The year after this unfortunate affair he was retained to serve the king in his Scottish wars for 40 days, and the next year being in Castile with the Duke of Lancaster, he tilted at Besances with Sir Reginald de Roy, in the presence of the King of Portugal, being then constable of the duke's host. About this time, being also in the wars of France, he obtained a grant of 500 marks per annum during his life. And, at length, in expiation of the murder he had the misfortune to commit, he came to an agreement with the Earl of Stafford to find three priests to celebrate divine service every day, to the world's end, for the soul of Ralph Stafford, in such places as the king should appoint. In the 11th of the same reign he was again in the wars of France, and also in Spain, with John of Gaunt, Duke of Lancaster, and upon his return was created EARL OF HUNTINGDON, at the especial desire of the commons in parliament assembled, having therewith a grant of £20 per annum out of the profits of the county: as also lands of 2000 marks per annum, to himself and Elizabeth, his wife, and to the heirs male of their bodies. Shortly after which he was made admiral of the king's fleet westwards, and constituted governor of the castle, town, and bastile of Brest, in Britanny, for three years, where he accordingly went to reside. He subsequently obtained large grants from the crown, and was constituted great chamberlain of England for life. His lordship was one of those nobles who impeached the Duke of Gloucester, in the parliament held at Nottingham, and he is accused of having assisted at the execution of his grandfather, Richard, Earl of Arundel. He was advanced in 1397 to the DUKEDOM OF EXETER, by King RICHARD, in open parliament, being at the time captain of Calais: and he accompanied that monarch soon afterwards into Ireland. Upon the accession, however, of the Duke of Lancaster, as HENRY IV., his grace was doomed to a reverse of fortune, and parliament adjudged that he should lose his honours and lands. He retained, however, the Earldom of Huntingdon, which, with his whole estate, he might probably have continued to enjoy, had he not joined with his brother, the Earl of Kent, in a conspiracy to overturn the new government. The plot having, however, failed, he endeavoured to escape beyond sea, but was driven back by contrary winds to the coast of Essex, where he landed, and was made prisoner by the populace while at supper at the house of a friend. He was immediately conveyed to Chelmsford, and thence to Plessy, where he was beheaded by the common people on the very spot where the Duke of Gloucester had suffered in the reign of his brother, King RICHARD. His grace d. in 1400, and was subsequently attainted. He had m. the Lady Elizabeth Plantagenet, dau. of John of Gaunt, and had issue,

Richard, d. unm.
John, his heir, created DUKE OF EXETER (see Holland, Duke of Exeter).
Edward (Sir).
Constance, m. 1st, to Thomas Mowbray. Duke of Norfolk; and 2ndly, to John Grey, son of Reginald, 3rd Lord Grey, of Ruthyn.

280

By this alliance, John, Earl of Huntingdon, and Duke of Exeter, was brother-in-law to King HENRY IV., the monarch, for conspiring against whom he lost his life. The earldom and dukedom fell under the attainder of his grace.

Arms—Of England, and a bordure of France.

HOLLAND—DUKES OF EXETER.

By Letters Patent, dated 6 January, 1443.

Lineage.

JOHN HOLLAND, 2nd but eldest surviving son of John Holland, Earl of Huntingdon and Duke of Exeter (attainted and beheaded in 1400), was restored in blood, as heir to his father and brother, in the 4th HENRY V., and the next year made general of all the men at arms and archers at that time employed in the king's fleet at sea, in which capacity he assisted at the siege of Caen. He did not, however, make proof of his age until the ensuing year, when it was stated by the witnesses then examined, that the abbot of Tavestoke, co. Devon, being one of his godfathers, gave him, immediately after the baptism, a cup of gold, with a circle about it, framed after the fashion of a lily, and with ten pounds in gold therein, and to the nurse twenty shillings. That the prior of Plimpton, being the other godfather, gave him twenty pounds in gold; and that Joane, the wife of Sir John Pomeraie, Knt., carried him to the church to be christened: her husband, and Sir John Dynham, Knt. conducting her by the arms. Likewise, that twenty-four men did precede them, bearing twenty-four torches, which torches, as soon as the name was given, were kindled.

This John Holland was engaged, during the whole reign of HENRY V., in active warfare upon the French soil, and displayed extraordinary skill and valour. He was at the siege of Roan; and the next year, upon the taking of Pontoise by the Captain de la Bouche, he intercepted those of the garrison who endeavoured to get to Paris; and he was in that great fight against the French who came to raise the siege of Freney, wherein 5000 were slain and 600 made prisoners. He was subsequently commissioned to reduce all the castles and strong places in Normandy that continued to hold out against the king; and he was soon after, in consideration of his eminent services, constituted constable of the Tower of London. In the reign of HENRY VI., he continued his gallant career in France, and assisted, in 1431, at the coronation of that monarch, then solemnized at Paris. In the 11th of the same reign, he had a grant of the office of marshal of England, to hold during the minority of John, son and heir of John, late Duke of Norfolk; and two years afterwards, being sent ambassador to the city of ARRAS, to treat of peace with the French, he had license to carry with him gold, silver, plate, jewels, robes, twenty-four pieces of woollen cloth, and other things, to the value of £6000 sterling. In the 14th he was joined in commission with the Earl of Northumberland for guarding the east and west marches towards Scotland, and at the same time constituted admiral of England and Aquitaine. He was afterwards in a commission to try all manner of treasons and sorceries which might be hurtful to the king's person; and was created, by letters patent, dated at Windsor, 6 January, 1442-3, DUKE OF EXETER, with this special privilege, "that he and his heirs male should have place and seat in all parliaments and councils, next to the Duke of York and his heirs male."

His grace was constituted lord high admiral of England, Ireland, and Aquitaine, for life, in the 24th HENRY VI., his son Henry being joined in the grant, and, the next year, made constable of the Tower of London, his son, Henry, being, in like manner, joined with him. His lordship m. 1st, Anne, widow of Edward Mortimer, Earl of March, and dau. of Edmund, Earl of Stafford, by whom he had an only son,

HENRY, his successor.

He m. 2ndly, Lady Anne Montacute, dau. of John, Earl of Salisbury, and had a dau.,

Anne, m. to John, Lord Nevil, son and heir of Ralph, Earl of Westmoreland, which Lord Nevil fell at Towton-Field, and d. s. p. Her ladyship m. 2ndly, Sir John Nevil, Knt., uncle of her first husband, and by him was mother of Ralph Nevil, 3rd Earl of Westmoreland.

His grace, who was a knight of the Garter, d. in 1446, and was s. by his only son,*

---

* A family of this name was established in Wales, which branched into several houses of repute and territorial pos-

HENRY HOLLAND, 2nd Duke of Exeter, who, in the 28th HENRY VI., in consideration of his father's services, had livery of all his castles, manors, and lands, both in England and Wales, although at that time he had not accomplished his full age; after which, (33rd HENRY VI.) the Yorkists then prevailing, his grace having fled to sanctuary at Westminster, he was forced thence, and sent prisoner to Pontefract Castle. We find him, however, at the battle of Wakefield, sharing the triumph of the Lancastrians: when King HENRY VI., being re-established in power, his grace's fidelity was rewarded by a grant of the office of constable of Fotheringay Castle. But the tide again turning, the duke fled from Towton-Field, with the Duke of Somerset and some others, to York, where the king and queen then were, and thence proceeded with the royal fugitives into Scotland. In the parliament assembled upon the accession of King EDWARD IV., his grace, with the other leading Lancastrians, was attainted; but nothing further is recorded of him until he appeared again in arms under the red banner of Lancaster, at Barnet-Field, where his party sustained so signal a defeat. In this conflict the Duke of Exeter fought with extraordinary courage and resolution, and being severely wounded, was left for dead, from seven o'clock in the morning until four in the afternoon, when, being conveyed to the house of one of his servants, called Ruthall, he had the assistance of a surgeon, and was then carried for sanctuary to Westminster: but in the 13th EDWARD IV., 1473, he was found dead in the sea between Calais and Dover; by what accident, however, was never ascertained. *Comines* reports that he saw this unhappy nobleman in such deep distress, (after the defeat at Barnet, it is presumed,) that he ran on foot, bare-legged, after the Duke of Burgundy's train, begging his bread for God's sake, but that he uttered not his name; and that when he was known, the duke conferred upon him a small pension. His grace m. Anne, dau. of Richard, Duke of York, and sister of King EDWARD IV., by whom, according to Sandford, he had an an only dau., ANNE, m. to Thomas Grey, Marquess of Dorset. From his lady the Duke of Exeter was divorced, *at her suit*, and his dukedom fell under the attainder, in 1461, twelve years before his melancholy death. Thus terminated the career of one of the stanchest partizans of the house of Lancaster, although brother-in-law to King EDWARD, the successful monarch of the house of York. Such was the heart-rending dissension which that terrible quarrel had sown amongst the nearest and dearest connections, and such the misery and wretchedness it entailed upon a great majority of the most illustrious houses in England.

Arms—Of England, and a bordure of France.

HOLLES—BARONS HOUGHTON, EARLS OF CLARE, DUKES OF NEWCASTLE.

Barony, by Letters Patent, dated 9 July, 1616.
Earldom, by Letters Patent, dated 2 November, 1624.
Dukedom, by Letters Patent, dated 14 May, 1694.

Lineage.

The first of this family who became of note was SIR WILLIAM HOLLES, an alderman of London, and lord mayor in 1540. This opulent citizen left three sons, viz.,

---

session. Its descent is traditionally deduced from Sir Thomas Holland, Knt., who is supposed to have settled, with a brother, in the northern principality during a period of civil convulsion. "I have reason," says Pennant, "to suppose them to have been William and Thomas, the two youngest sons of John Holland, Duke of Exeter, who d. in 1446, and left to each of them an annuity of forty pounds." (DUGDALE's *Baronage*, II. 81.)— "Pierce Holland, 11th in descent from Sir Thomas, made a settlement at Kynmel by his marriage with Katharine, dau. to Richard ap Evan ap Dafydd Fychan, and Alice, his wife, heiress of the place, dau. of Gryfydd Lloyd. In the last century (the 17th), one of his descendants had two daus. Colonel Carter, an officer in the service of the parlement, made choice of Catherine, the youngest, and took the estate with her. A wag said that he had chosen the best piece of *Holland* in the country. He left the eldest sister, Mary, to Colonel Price, of Rhiwlas, a royalist." From Sir Thomas Holland, also derived the Hollands of Bern, in Anglesey, acquired by the marriage of John Holland, 6th in descent from Sir Thomas, with Ellen (living 1525), heiress of Bern, dau. and co-heir of Ithel ap Howel, of Bern, derived from Llywarch ap Bran, Lord of Menai. The heir general of this marriage is the present Richard-Trygarn Griffith, Esq., of Carreglwyd, Trygarn, and Bern, father of an only child and heiress presumptive, MARIA GRIFFITH, who, by royal sign manual has assumed the name of Conway.

281

Thomas (Sir), who succeeded to a considerable estate, but squandered the whole, and d. in prison.
WILLIAM, of whom presently.
Francis, d. s. p.

The 2nd son,

WILLIAM HOLLES, inherited the manor of Houghton, co. Nottingham, and took up his abode there. He m. Anne, dau. and co-heir of John Denzell, Esq., of Denzell, in Cornwall, and had, with other issue, DENZELL, who m. Anne, sister of John Sheffield, Lord Sheffield, and dying before his father, left a son (who eventually s. to the estates),

JOHN HOLLES, of Houghton, who was elevated to the peerage by King JAMES I., 9 July, 1616, (through the influence of the Duke of Buckingham, to whom he paid £10,000,) in the dignity of BARON HOUGHTON, *of Houghton*, and was created, under the same powerful patronage, for the additional sum of £5,000, EARL OF CLARE,* 2 November, 1624. His lordship m. Anne, dau. of Sir Thomas Stanhope, of Shelford, co. Nottingham, and had surviving issue,

JOHN, his successor.
DENZELL, created BARON HOLLES, *of Ifeild.* (see that dignity.)
Eleanore, m. to Oliver Fitz-William, Earl of Tyrconnel, in Ireland
Arabella, m. to Thomas Wentworth, 1st Lord Strafford.

His lordship d. 4 October, 1637, and was s. by his eldest son,

JOHN HOLLES, 2nd earl, who m. Elizabeth, eldest dau., and one of the co-heirs of the celebrated General Sir Horatio Vere, Lord Vere, of Tilbury, and had issue,

GILBERT, his successor.
Anne, m. to Edward Clinton, Lord Clinton, eldest son of Theophilus, 4th Earl of Lincoln, and was mother of Edward, 5th Earl of Lincoln.
Elizabeth, m. to Wentworth, Earl of Kildare.
Arabella, m. to Sir Edward Rossiter, Knt., of Somerley, co. Lincoln.
Susan, m. to Sir John Lort, Bart., of Stackpole Court, co. Pembroke.
Diana, m. to Henry Bridges, son and heir of Sir Thomas Bridges, of Keynsham, co Somerset.
Penelope, m. to Sir James Langham, Bart., of Cottesbroke, co. Northampton.

Of this nobleman, Lord Clarendon says, "he was a man of honour and of courage, and would have been an excellent person, if his heart had not been too much set upon keeping and improving his estate." His lordship appears to have lived in retirement at his country houses during the usurpation. He survived to witness the restoration of the monarchy, and dying 2 January, 1665, was s. by his son,

GILBERT HOLLES, 3rd Earl of Clare. This nobleman opposed strongly the measures of the Stewarts, and was a strenuous supporter of the revolution. He m. Grace, dau. of William Pierpont, of Thoresby, co Nottingham, 2nd son of Robert, Earl of Kingston, and had issue,

JOHN, who s. to the honours.
William, who fell at Luxemburgh, in the twenty-first year of his age.
Denzell, d. unm.
Elizabeth, m. to Sir Christopher Vane, Knt., who was created Baron Barnard, of Barnard Castle, co. Durham. From this marriage HARRY-GEORGE, present DUKE OF CLEVELAND, is 5th in lineal descent.
Mary, m. to Hugh Boscawen, Esq.   Ann,
Grace, m. to Sir Thomas Pelham, Bart., created afterwards Baron Pelham, of Loughton, co. Sussex, and had, with other issue, a son THOMAS, who inherited the greatest part of the Holles estates, and had the honours of the family partly revived in his person, (see Pelham-Holles, Earls of Cl re).

His lordship d. 16 January, 1689, and was s. by his eldest son, JOHN HOLLES, 4th Earl of Clare. This nobleman having m. Margaret Cavendish, 3rd dau. and co-heir of Henry, 2nd Duke of Newcastle, inherited the greater part of his grace's estates upon his decease in 1691, and was created 14 May, 1694, *Marquess of Clare* and DUKE OF NEWCASTLE. He likewise s. to the fortune of his kinsman, Denzell, Lord Holles of Ifeild, and thus became one of the richest subjects in the kingdom. His grace enjoyed several high offices at court, and was a knight of the Garter. He d. from the effects of a fall while stag-hunting, 15 July, 1711, leaving an only dau.,

LADY HENRIETTA CAVENDISH HOLLES, who m. in 1713, Edward, Lord Harley, son and heir of Robert, Earl of Oxford, to whom she conveyed a very considerable estate, and by whom she had an only surviving dau.,
LADY MARGARET CAVENDISH HARLEY, who m. William Bentinck, 2nd Duke of Portland, K.G.

---

* This dignity had been just before refused to Robert Rich, Earl of Warwick, on a solemn declaration by the crown lawyers, that it was a title peculiar to the royal blood, and not to be conferred upon a subject.

At the decease of the Duke of Newcastle all his honours became EXTINCT. He had adopted his nephew, THOMAS PELHAM, eldest son of Thomas, Lord Pelham, who s. to a portion of his great estates, and assumed the surname and arms of HOLLES (see Pelham Holles, Earl of Clare).

Arms—Erm., two piles in point, sa.

HOLLES - PELHAM — BARONS PELHAM, EARLS OF CLARE, DUKE OF NEW-CASTLE.

Barony, by Letters Patent, dated 29 December, 1706.
Earldom, by Letters Patent, dated 26 October, 1714.
Dukedom, by Letters Patent, dated 11 August, 1715.

Lineage.

SIR THOMAS PELHAM, Bart., was elevated to the peerage, 29 December, 1706, as BARON PELHAM, of Loughton, co. Sussex. He had m. previously, Lady Grace Holles, youngest dau. of Gilbert, 3rd Earl of Clare, and dying in 1712, was s. by his eldest son,

THOMAS PELHAM-HOLLES, as 2nd Baron Pelham. This nobleman having been adopted by his uncle, John Holles, 4th Earl of Clare, and 1st Duke of Newcastle, assumed the additional surname and arms of HOLLES, upon the decease of his grace, and was created 26 October, 1714, Viscount Pelham, of Houghton, and EARL OF CLARE. His lordship was advanced the next year to the dignities of Marquess of Clare and DUKE OF NEWCASTLE, with remainder, default of male issue, to his brother, the Right Honourable Henry Pelham. His grace, under the three first sovereigns of the house of Brunswick, fulfilled the several posts of lord chamberlain of the household, secretary of state, first lord of the Treasury, and one of the lords justices, during the temporary absences of Kings GEORGE I. and II. The duke was likewise chancellor of the university of Cambridge, a privy councillor, and a knight of the Garter. His grace m. Harriet Godolphin, dau. of Francis, Earl of Godolphin, by Henrietta, his wife, dau. of the celebrated John Churchill, Duke of Marlborough, but had no issue.

The duke was created, in 1756, DUKE OF NEWCASTLE UNDER LYNE, with special remainder to his nephew, Henry Fiennes-Clinton, 9th Earl of Lincoln, K.G., son of his grace's sister, the Honourable Lucy Pelham, by Henry, 7th Earl of Lincoln; and he was also created, 4 May, 1762, BARON PELHAM, of Stanmere, in Sussex, with remainder to his kinsman, Thomas Pelham, Esq., of Stanmere (grandson of Henry Pelham, younger brother of the 1st Lord Pelham), which honours devolved, at his grace's decease, in 1768, according to the said limitations, and are now enjoyed by the DUKE OF NEWCASTLE and the EARL OF CHICHESTER (see those dignities in BURKE'S Extant Peerage and Baronetage,) while all his own honours, including the Dukedom of Newcastle, in remainder to his brother, the Right Honourable Henry Pelham (that gentleman having predeceased his grace, leaving daus. only) became EXTINCT.

Arms—Quarterly, 1st and 4th, az., three pelicans. arg., vulning themselves in the breast, gu.; 2nd and 3rd, erm., two piles in point, sa.

HOLLES—BARONS HOLLES OF IFIELD, CO. SUSSEX.

By Letters Patent, dated 20 April, 1661.

Lineage.

THE HON. DENZILL HOLLES, 2nd son of John, 1st Earl of Clare, by Anne, eldest dau. and co-heir of John Denzill, of Danzill, in Cornwall, serjeant-at-law, was elevated to the peerage, at the Restoration, by letters patent, dated 20 April, 1661, as BARON HOLLES, of Ifield, co. Sussex. This nobleman, in the beginning, opposed the assumed prerogative of CHARLES I. and his ministers; carrying up the impeachment against Laud; suffering a severe imprisonment, and being marked by the king in that wild attempt of accusing the five members. When brought before the privy council, with Sir Henry Hammond and others, in those times of arbitrary power, Mr. Holles deported himself with a more than ordinary degree of firmness, and as characteristic of the epoch, we give the following passage from his examination. "Why did you sit above some of the privy council, so near the speaker's chair ?"

"I seated myself there, some other times before, and took it as my due, there and in any place whatsoever, on account of my noble birth, as son of the Earl of Clare !" continuing to state, "that he came into the house, with as much zeal as any other person to serve his majesty: yet, finding his majesty was offended, he humbly desired to be the subject, rather of his mercy than of his power." To which the treasurer Weston answered, "You mean rather of his majesty's mercy than of his justice." Mr. Holles replied emphatically, "I say of his majesty's power." Subsequently discovering the designs of the republican party, and disgusted with them, he exerted himself zealously, at the decease of Cromwell, in furtherance of the restoration; and for some time after the accomplishment of that great event, accepted employments and embassies from the court. In 1663, his lordship was ambassador extraordinary to France, and afterwards plenipotentiary to the treaty of Breda; but he again joined the ranks of opposition, and maintained the consistency of his patriotic character.

Burnet thus describes this patriotic personage :—"He was a man of courage,* and as great pride. The head of the presbyterian party for many years, and who, during the whole course of his life, never once changed side. He had indeed the soul of an old stubborn Roman in him; was a faithful, but a rough friend; and a severe, but open enemy. His sense of religion was just; his course of life regular; and his judgment, where passion did not bias him, sound enough. He was well versed in the records of parliament, and argued well but too vehemently; for he could not bear any contradiction."

His lordship m. 1st, Dorothy, only dau. and heiress of Sir Francis Ashley, of Dorchester, by whom he had one surviving son, FRANCIS, who was created a baronet. He m. 2ndly, Jane, eldest dau. and co-heir of Sir John Shirley, of Isville, in Sussex; and 3rdly, Esther, 2nd dau. and co-heir of Gideon de Lou, lord of the manor of Columbiers, in Normandy, but had no other issue. He d. 17 February, 1679-80, and was s. by his son,

SIR FRANCIS HOLLES, Bart., of Winterbourne St. Martin, co. Dorset, as 2nd Lord Holles. His lordship m. 1st, Lucy, youngest dau. of Sir Robert Carr, of Sleford, co. Lincoln, Bart., by whom he had two daus., who both d. young. He m. 2ndly, Anne, eldest dau. and co-heir of Sir Francis Pile, Bart., of Compton Beauchamp, co. Berks, and had a son, DENZILL, his successor, and a dau. Jane, who d. in infancy. His lordship d. 1 March, 1689-90, and was s. by his son,

DENZILL HOLLES, 3rd baron. This nobleman d. unm. in his nineteenth year, anno 1694, when the Barony of Holles, of Ifield, with the baronetcy became EXTINCT, while his lordship's estates devolved upon his heir-at-law, John Holles, Duke of Newcastle.

Arms—Erm., two piles, sa., a crescent for difference.

HOLMES—BARON HOLMES, OF KILMALLOCK.

By Letters Patent, dated 11 September, 1760.

Lineage.

HENRY HOLMES, Esq., of Yarmouth, in the Isle of Wight, lieutenant-governor of that island, m. Mary, dau. of Sir Robert Holmes, Bart., and d. 23 June, 1738, having had (with other children, who d. young), issue,

I. THOMAS, his heir.
II. Robert, bapt. 16 November, 1701, d. s. p., buried 13 May, 1711.
III. Henry, a lieutenant-general in the army, bapt. 28 February, 1703, d. s. p., buried 15 August, 1762.
IV. William, bapt. 21 August, 1705, d. an infant.
V. Charles, rear-admiral of the white, bapt. 19 September, 1711, d. unm.
I. Anne, d. unm. 23 December, 1766.
II. Mary, m. David Wray, and d. s. p.
III. Elizabeth, b. in 1696; who m. Thomas Troughear, D.D.; and d. in 1788, leaving, inter alios, a son,

The REV. LEONARD TROUGHEAR, who assumed the surname of HOLMES, and was created BARON HOLMES, in the peerage of Ireland, in 1797. His lordship m. Elizabeth Tyrrell, and d. in January, 1804, having had two daus.,

* A remarkable instance of his spirit was his challenging General Ireton, who pleading, "That his conscience would not permit him to fight a duel;" Holles pulled him by the nose; telling him, "That if his conscience would not let him give redress, it ought to prevent his offering injuries."

I ELIZABETH, *m.* 1st, to Edward-Meux Worsley. Esq., and 2ndly, to Sir Henry Worsley-Holmes, Bart. By the former she had a dau. Jane, wife of Colonel Alexander Campbell, of Gatcombe, and by the latter a son and successor,

    SIR LEONARD-THOMAS WORSLEY-HOLMES, Bart., who *d.* in 1825, leaving two daus., Elizabeth, *m.* to William-Henry, Lord Heytesbury, who assumed the surname of HOLMES; and Anne-Emily.

2 Catherine, *m.* to Edward Rushworth, Esq.

Leonard, Lord Holmes, *d.* in January, 1804, when the peerage became EXTINCT.

    IV. Margaret, *d. unm.*

    V. Lucretia, *m.* Marmaduke Sowle, and *d.* 10 January, 1775, leaving issue.

    VI. Jane, *m.* to Robert Worsley, Esq , of Pidford, and had issue.

    VII. Valentine, *m.* William Atkinson, and *d. s. p.*

The eldest son,

THOMAS HOLMES. Esq., of Newport in the Isle of Wight, bapt. 2 November, 1699, was created 11 September, 1760, BARON HOLMES, *of Kilmallock, co. Limerick,* in the peerage of Ireland. He *m.* Ann Apsley (who *d.* in 1743) but *d. s. p.* in 1764, when the title became EXTINCT.

Arms—Barry. wavy of six, or and az ; on a canton, gu., a lion, passant guardant, of the 1st.

HOLMES—BARON HOLMES.

See preceding article.

HOME—EARL OF DUNBAR, AND HOME—EARL OF MARCHMONT.

See HUME.

HOO — BARON OF HOO, CO. BEDFORD, AND OF HASTINGS, CO. SUSSEX.

By Letters Patent, dated 2 June, 1447.

Lineage.

Of this family, whose chief seat was at Hoo, in Bedfordshire, were divers persons of note, prior to its elevation to the peerage.

ROBERT DE HOO, obtained the king's charter, 20th EDWARD I., for a weekly market, and an annual fair, at his manor of Knebbeworth, co. Hertford. As also free-warren in all his desmesne lands, within his respective lordships of the above-mentioned Knebbeworth, and Harpenden, in the same shire; of Hoo and other estates in the co. of Bedford; of Clopton, in Cambridgeshire, and Sivethorpe, co. Oxford. The next of the family we meet with,

SIR THOMAS HOO, Knt., had similar grants for fairs and markets, upon his different estates, in the 11th EDWARD III. He was *s.* by his son,

SIR WILLIAM HOO, Knt., who, in the 10th RICHARD II., assisted Michael de la Pole, Earl of Suffolk, in effecting his escape to Calais, in which garrison Sir William afterwards served (8th HENRY IV.) under John, Earl of Somerset, then captain thereof. Sir William Hoo *m.* Alice, dau. and heir of Sir Thomas St. Maur (by Jane, his wife, dau. and heir of Nicholas Malmains), and was *s.* by his son,

SIR THOMAS HOO, who, having been employed in the suppression of a rebellion in Normandy, obtained a grant, 20th HENRY VI., in consideration of his special services, and great expenses in the wars, of £11 a year during his life, out of the revenues in the co. York. In the 24th of the same reign, having again distinguished himself in the French wars he was elevated to the peerage, by letters patent, dated 2 June, 1447, by the titles of LORD HOO, *of Hoo, co. Bedford,* and of HASTINGS, *co. Sussex,* with remainder to the heirs male of his body. Moreover, he was made a knight of the most noble order of the Garter. His lordship *m.* 1st, Elizabeth, dau. and heir of Sir Thomas Felton, Knt., by whom he had an only son, Thomas, who *d.* in his father's life-time without issue. He *m.* 2ndly, Elizabeth, dau. and heir of Sir Nicholas Wichingham, Knt., by whom he had an only dau., Anne, who *m.* Sir Geffery Bullen, Knt., sometime Lord Mayor of London. His lordship *m.* 3rdly,

Alianore, dau. of Leo, Lord Welles. and sister and co-heir of Richard, Lord Welles, by whom he had issue,

    Alianore, *m.* to Sir James Carew, Knt., of Beddington, co Surrey.

    Jane, *m.* to Sir Roger Copley, Knt., from which marriage Sir Joseph-William Copley, Bart., of Sprotborough, co. York, maternally descends.

    Elizabeth, *m.* to Sir John Devenish, Knt., of Hellingleigh. in Sussex, and their descendant, and eventually co-heir general, ELIZABETH, dau. of WILLIAM DEVENISH, Esq., *m.* Henry Walrond, Esq., of Sea, co. Somerset, and is represented by HENRY WALROND, Esq., of Dulford, co. Devon.

Lord Hoo *d.* about the year 1453, and thus leaving no male issue, the Barony of Hoo became EXTINCT.

Arms—Quarterly, sa., and arg.

HOOD—BARON BRIDPORT, VISCOUNT BRIDPORT.

Barony, by Letters Patent, dated 13 June, 1796.
Viscounty, by Letters Patent, dated 16 June, 1800.

Lineage.

ALEXANDER HOOD, a very eminent naval officer, having served as rear-admiral, under Lord Howe, at the relief of Gibraltar, in 1782, was invested with the military order of the Bath; and having, as second in command, contributed to the ever-memorable victory of the 1st June, 1794, was rewarded with a peerage of Ireland, in the dignity of Baron Bridport, of Cricket St. Thomas. In 1795, his lordship achieved a splendid victory over the French fleet, and was made, in consequence, a peer of Great Britian, 13 June, 1796, as BARON BRIDPORT, *of Cricket St. Thomas, co. Somerset.* On 16 June, 1800, he was advanced to the dignity of VISCOUNT BRIDPORT, being then vice-admiral of Great Britain, and general of marines. His lordship *m.* 1st, Maria, dau. of the Rev. Dr. West, prebendary of Durham; and 2ndly, Maria-Sophia, dau. and heiress of Thomas Bray, Esq., of Edmonton, but dying *s. p.*, 3 May, 1814, his English honours, namely, the Barony and Viscounty of Bridport, became EXTINCT, while the barony in the Irish peerage devolved according to a special limitation in the patent on his great nephew, SAMUEL HOOD, who became 2nd BARON BRIDPORT. (*See* BURKE'S *Extant Peerage.*)

Arms—Az., a fret, arg., on a chief, or, three crescents, sa.

HOPTON—BARON HOPTON OF STRATTON, CO. CORNWALL.

By Letters Patent, dated 4 September, 1643.

Lineage.

ROBERT HOPTON, Esq., of Wytham. co. Somerset, *m.* Jane, dau. and heir of Rowland Keymish, Esq., of Wardry, co. Monmouth, and left a son,

SIR RALPH HOPTON, who was made a knight of the Bath, at the coronation of King CHARLES I., and became afterwards one of the most zealous supporters of that unfortunate monarch. Sir Ralph represented Welles, in parliament in 1642, when, perceiving the course of public affairs, he took up arms in the royal cause, and obtained distinction at Sherbourne Castle, Lanceston, Saltash, and Bradock, but particularly at Stratton, in Cornwall, when, in consideration of the gallant part he had in that victory, he was elevated to the peerage, 4 September, 1643, as BARON HOPTON, *of Stratton ;* with limitation, in default of male issue, to his uncle, Sir Arthur Hopton, Knt., and the heirs male of his body. His lordship was subsequently constituted general of the ordnance, in his Majesty's armies throughout the whole realm of England, and dominion of Wales. Lord Hopton *m.* Elizabeth, dau. of Arthur Capel, of Hadham, co. Hertford, Esq. and widow of Sir Justinian Leven, Knt., but had no issue. During the usurpation, his lordship retired to Bruges, where he *d.* in 1652, when (his uncle having predeceased him also without issue) the Barony of Hopton of Stratton became EXTINCT.

Sir Arthur Hopton, upon whom the title was entailed, *d.* about the year 1650, *s. p.*, when his four sisters, or their representatives became his heirs. Those sisters were,

Rachel, *m.* to — Morgan, Esq.

Mary, *m.* 1st, to — Hartop, Esq., and 2ndly, to Sir Henry Mackworth, Bart.

Catherine, *m.* to John Windham, Esq.

Margaret, *m.* to Sir Baynam Throgmorton, Bart.

Arms—Erm., on two bars, sa., six mullets, or.

HOWARD—BARONS HOWARD.

By Writ of Summons, dated 15 October, 1470.

Lineage.

The first of this very eminent family, mentioned by Dugdale, after a fruitless inquiry to discover a more ancient founder,

Sir William Howard, was chief justice of the court of Common Pleas from 1297 to 1308. This learned person had large possessions in Wigenhale, in the north-west parts of the county of Norfolk; and he had summons in the 23rd Edward I. amongst the rest of the judges, and the king's learned council, to the parliament then held at Westminster, as also to those parliaments of 25th, 28th, and 32nd of Edward I., and 1st Edward II. Sir William *m.* 1st, Alice, dau., and eventually heir of Sir Edward Fitton, Knt., by whom he had two sons, John and William. He *m.* 2ndly, Alice, dau. of Sir Robert Ufford, but had no issue. He was *s.* by his elder son,

Sir John Howard, of Wiggenhall, who, in the 34th Edward I., being one of the gentlemen of the king's bedchamber, obtained the wardship of the lands and heir of John de Crokedale, a person of note in Norfolk: and on the accession of King Edward II., had orders to attend his coronation at Westminster, the Sunday next after the feast of Saint Valentine. He subsequently distinguished himself in the wars of Gascony and Scotland; and was sheriff of the cos. Norfolk and Suffolk, from the 11th to the 16th Edward II. inclusive. Sir John *m.* Joan, sister of Richard de Cornwall, and dying in 1331, was *s.* by his son,

Sir John Howard, who, in the 9th Edward III., was constituted admiral and captain of the king's navy from the mouth of the Thames northward, and the next year had an assignation of £153 *1s.* 6*d.* for the wages of himself, with his men-at-arms and archers in that service. This gallant person *m.* Alice, dau. of Sir Robert de Boys, ancestor and heir of Sir Robert de Boys, of Fersfield, in Norfolk, by which marriage the whole inheritance of the Boyses came into the Howard family. He had issue,

Robert (Sir), of Fersfield. This gentleman was committed in the 2nd Richard II., to the Tower, for detaining Margery de Narford, from Alice, Lady Nevil, her grandmother, with whom, on her petition to the king and council, she had been appointed to remain till the cause of divorce between her and John de Brewer should be determined in the court of Rome. This Sir Robert Howard *m.* Margaret, dau. of Robert, Lord Scales, of Newcells, and, at length, one of the heirs of that family, by whom he left at his decease (1388), prior to the death of his father.

John, successor to his grandfather.

Margaret, *m.* to William de Lisle.

Sir John Howard was *s.* by his grandson,

Sir John Howard, who was sheriff of the cos. Essex and Hertford, 2nd Henry IV., and again in the 3rd and 7th Henry V., and in the 9th of the latter reign he was one of the knights of the shire for the co. Cambridge. He *m.* 1st, Margaret, dau. and heir of Sir John Plaiz, of Tofte, in Norfolk, and of Slansted Mountfitchet, in Essex, by whom he had issue,

John (Sir), who *m.* Joan, dau. of Sir Richard Walton, and sister and heir of John Walton, Esq. of Wivenhoe, in Essex, by whom, dying in the life-time of his father, he left an only dau. and heir.

Elizabeth, who *m.* John de Vere, Earl of Oxford, whereby the Barony of Scales centered in the Veres.

Margaret, *m.* 1st, to Sir Constantine Clifton, of Buckenham Castle, co. Norfolk, and 2ndly, to Sir Gilbert Talbot.

Sir John Howard *m.* 2ndly, Alice, dau. and heir of Sir William Tendring, of Stoke Neyland, co. Suffolk, and had two sons, viz.,

Robert (Sir), who *m.* Margaret, eldest dau. and eventually co-heir of Thomas de Mowbray, Duke of Norfolk, by Elizabeth, his wife, dau. and co-heir of Richard Fitz-Alan, Earl of Arundel, and cousin and co-heir of John Mowbray, Duke of Norfolk. By this marriage the inheritance of those great families became eventually vested in this of the Howards, and by Isabel, the other co-heir in that of Berkeley. Sir Robert dying before his father, left issue by this great heiress,

John, successor to his grandfather.

Margaret, *m.* to Sir William Daniel, Baron of Rathwire, in Ireland.

Catherine, the 2nd wife of Edward Nevil, Lord Abergavenny.

Henry, who, by the gift of his father, had Wigenhall, and other manors, in the co. Norfolk, *m.* Mary, dau. of Sir Henry Hussey, and left an only dau. and heiress,

Elizabeth Howard, who *m.* Henry Wentworth, Esq., of Codham, in Essex.

Sir John Howard was *s.* by his grandson,

Sir John Howard, an eminent Yorkist, distinguished not only by his birth and possessions, but by the various places of high trust which he filled during the reigns of Edward IV. and Richard III. He was first summoned to parliament as a baron 15 October, 1470, and had summons from that period as Lord Howard until 15 November, 1482. In the next year he was created Duke of Norfolk, and made earl marshal of England. The ultimate fall of this nobleman, at Bosworth-field, under the banner of Richard III., is so well known that it is hardly necessary to mention it here. From the creation of the Dukedom of Norfolk, in the Howard family, the Barony of Howard continued merged therein, and was included in the numerous forfeitures and restorations which attended that dignity until the demise of Edward Howard, 11th Duke of Norfolk, in 1777, when, with several other baronies, it fell into abeyance be ween the two daus. and co-heirs of his grace's brother, Philip Howard, Esq., of Buckenham, co. Norfolk, namely, Winifrede, Lady Stourton, and Anne, Lady Petre, thus :—

Henry Howard, created Baron of Castle Rising, and Earl of Norwich, *m.* Anne, dau. of Edward, Marquess of Worcester, and left issue,

Henry, who *s.* his uncle as Duke of Norfolk.

Thomas, who *m.* Elizabeth-Maria, only dau. and heir of Sir Henry Savile, Bart., of Copley, co. York, and had issue,

Thomas, who *s.* his uncle as Duke of Norfolk.

Edward, who *s.* his brother as Duke of Norfolk, and *d. s. p.* in 1777.

Philip, *m.* 1st, Winifrede, dau. of Thomas Stonor, Esq., and had an only surviving dau.,

Winifrede, *m.* to William, Lord Stourton, by whom she was mother of

Charles-Philip, Lord Stourton. (*See* Burke's *Peerage*.)

Mr. Philip Howard *m.* 2ndly, Harriet, dau. and co-heir of Edward Blount, Esq., and had an only surviving dau.,

Anne, who *m.* Robert-Edward, Lord Petre, and was mother of

Robert-Edward, Lord Petre. (*See* Burke's *Peerage*.)

Upon the decease of Edward Howard, 11th Duke of Norfolk, in 1777, without issue, as stated above, the Barony of Howard separated from the dukedom and fell into abeyance between his grace's nieces, as it still continues between their descendants, the Lords Petre and Stourton.

Arms—Gu., on a bend, between six cross-crosslets, fitchée. arg., an escutcheon or, charged with a demi-lion rampant, pierced through the mouth by an arrow, within a double tressure flory, counterflory of the first.

HOWARD—VISCOUNTS HOWARD, OF BINDON, CO. DORSET.

By Letters Patent, dated 13 January, 1559.

Lineage.

Thomas Howard, 3rd Duke of Norfolk, *m.* 1st, the Lady Anne Plantagenet, one of the daus. of King Edward IV., by whom he had an only son, Thomas, and another son, who both *d.* young. His grace *m.* 2ndly, Lady Elizabeth Stafford, dau. of Edward, Duke of Buckingham, by whom he had issue,

Henry, the celebrated Earl of Surrey, who suffered decapitation in 1547, leaving a son, Thomas, who inherited the honours of the house of Norfolk.

Thomas, of whom presently.

Mary, *m.* to Henry Fitz-Roy, Duke of Richmond, natural son of King Henry VIII.

The 2nd son,

Lord Thomas Howard, was restored in blood (his father having been attainted, and only saved from execution by the death of King Henry VIII.), in the 1st year of Queen Mary, and was elevated to the peerage 13 January, 1559, as Viscount

HOWARD. *of Bindon,*[*] co. Dorset. His lordship m. 1st, Elizabeth, younger dau. and co-heir of John, Lord Marney, by Christian, dau., and eventually sole heiress of Sir Roger Newburgh, of East Lullworth, co. Dorset. By this lady Lord Bindon acquired very considerable estates in Dorsetshire, amongst which was the manor of Bindon, and had issue,

 HENRY, his heir.
 THOMAS, who *s.* his brother.
 Francis, ⎫
 Giles, ⎬ *d. young.*
 Elizabeth, *d. uam.*
 Grace, *m.* John, son and heir of Sir John Horsey, of Clifton, co. Dorset, but *d. s. p.*

His lordship m. 2ndly, Gertrude. dau. of Sir William Lyte, of Billesdon, in Somersetshire, and had a son,

 Charles Lyte Howard, who left two daus., viz.,
  Catherine, *m.* to Thomas Thynne, Esq., and had issue,
  Sir Henry Thynne, Bart., ancestor of the Marquess of Bath.
  Anne, *m.* to Sir William Thornyhurst, Knt., of Agencourt, in Kent.

Lord Bindon m. 3rdly, Mabel, dau. of Nicholas Burton, Esq., of Carshalton, in Surrey, by whom he had a dau., Frances, *m.* 1st, to Henry Pranel, Esq., of Barkway, co. Hertford; 2ndly, to Edward Seymour, Earl of Hertford; and 3rdly, to Lodowick Stuart, Duke of Richmond, but had no issue. His lordship m. 4thly, Margaret, dau. of Henry Manning, Esq. of Greenwich. He *d.* 5 April, 1582, and was *s.* by his eldest son, HENRY HOWARD, 2nd viscount, who espoused Frances, dau. of Sir Peter Mewtas, Knt., of Essex, by whom he had an only dau., Douglass, who *m.* Sir Arthur Gorges, Knt. His lordship *d.* in 1590, and was *s.* by his brother, THOMAS HOWARD, 3rd viscount, who was installed a knight of the Garter in May, 1606. His lordship *m.* Grace, dau. of Bernard Duffield, Esq., but *d. s. p.* in 1610, when the Viscounty of Bindon became EXTINCT. His lordship devised his estate to his kinsman, Thomas, Earl of Suffolk, and entailed it on Henry, Viscount Howard, Giles Howard, Henry, Earl of Northampton, William, Lord Howard, and their heirs.

Arms—Same as the other noble house of Howard.

HOWARD—EARL OF NORTHAMPTON.

By Letters Patent, dated 13 March, 1604.

Lineage.

HENRY HOWARD, the celebrated EARL OF SURREY, beheaded on Tower Hill, 19 January, 1547, left by Frances his wife, dau. of John de Vere, Earl of Oxford,

 THOMAS, who was restored to the Dukedom of Norfolk HENRY, of whom presently.
 Jane, *m.* to Charles Neville, Earl of Westmoreland.
 Margaret, *m.* to Henry, Lord Scrope, of Bolton
 Catherine, *m.* to Henry, Lord Berkeley.

The 2nd son,

HENRY HOWARD, who, with his three sisters, was restored in blood, in the first parliament of Queen ELIZABETH, during the remainder of that reign, having but a limited fortune, lived in retirement, and made little figure ; but upon the accession of King JAMES he rose rapidly into honour, wealth, and power. He was first sworn of the privy council, soon afterwards constituted warden of the Cinque Ports, and constable of Dover Castle, and elevated to the peerage, 13 March 1604, in the dignities of *Baron Howard, of Marnhill,* and EARL OF NORTHAMPTON. The next year he was made one of the commissioners for exercising the office of earl marshal, and installed a knight of the Garter, and in 1608 he was appointed lord privy seal.

"The character of this nobleman," says Banks, " is unnoticed by the Baronagians in general, though other authors represent him as the most contemptible and despicable of mankind ; a wretch, that it causes astonishment to reflect, that he was the son of the generous, the noble, and accomplished Earl of Surrey ! He was a learned man, but a pedant, dark and mysterious, and consequently far from possessing masterly abilities. He was the grossest of flatterers; as his letters to his friend and patron, the Earl of Essex, demonstrate. But while he professed the most unbounded regard for Essex, he yet paid his suit to the treasurer Burghley; and on the fall of

Essex, insinuated himself so far into the confidence of his mortal enemy, Cecil, as to become the instrument of the secretary's correspondence with the King of Scots, which passed through his hands. Wherefore, this circumstance, his intriguing spirit, and the sufferings of his family, for MARY, Queen of Scots, may, in some measure, account for the very great favour he experienced on the accession of King JAMES I."

His lordship *d. unm.*, 15 June, 1614, at the palace he had erected at Charing Cross, (the present Northumberland House,) when the Barony of Howard, of Marnhill, and the Earldom of Northampton, became EXTINCT.

Arms—Gu., on a bend between six crosslets, fitchée, arg., an escutcheon, or, charged with a demi-lion, vulnerated in the mouth with an arrow, all within a double tressure counterflory gu., a crescent for difference.

HOWARD—VISCOUNT STAFFORD, EARLS OF STAFFORD.

By Letters Patent, dated 12 September, 1640.

Lineage.

The Barony of Stafford having been surrendered by Roger Stafford, the last male heir of that illustrious family, to King CHARLES I., (see Stafford, Barons Stafford, Earls Stafford, &c.) that monarch created by letters patent, dated 12 September, 1640,

SIR WILLIAM HOWARD, K.B., (younger son of Thomas, Earl of Arundel,) and his wife, Mary Stafford, only sister and heiress of Henry Stafford, Lord Stafford, who *d.* in 1637, BARON and BARONESS STAFFORD, with remainder to the heirs *male*, of their bodies, failing of which, to the *heirs female* ; and in two months after, 11 November, his lordship was advanced to the VISCOUNTY OF STAFFORD. The unjust fate of this nobleman is so well known, that it were a waste of time and space to particularise it here, further than his having been tried at Westminster Hall, for high treason, as a participator in the mock popish plot, and his becoming the last victim of Titus Oates and his perjured associates. His lordship suffered death by decapitation, on Tower Hill, 29 December, 1680, and having been attainted, his honours became FORFEITED, while the barony of his lady was placed pretty much in a similar situation, owing to the bar raised by that penal act, to the inheritance of her children. The viscount left issue,

 HENRY, of whom presently.
 John, *m.* 1st, Mary, dau. of Sir John Southcote, Knt., of Merstham, co. Surrey, and had issue,
  WILLIAM, who *s.* his uncle.
  JOHN-PAUL, who *s.* his nephew.
  Mary, *m.* to Francis Plowden, Esq., 2nd son of Edmund Plowden, Esq., of Plowden, co. Salop, and had issue, an only dau. and heiress,
   MARY PLOWDEN, who *m.* Sir George Jerningham, Bart., and was mother of Sir William Jerningham, whose son and heir Sir George-William Jerningham, Bart., was restored in 1824, to the BARONY OF STAFFORD created in 1640, by the reversal of the iniquitous attainder of Viscount Stafford, in 1678. (*See* BURKE's *Extant Peerage*).
 John Howard *m* 2ndly, Theresa, dau. of Robert Strickland, Esq., and had a son and dau., Edward and Harriott.
 Francis, *m.* Eleanor, dau. of Henry Stanford, Esq., and had a son,
  Henry, who *d. s. p.*
 Isabella, *m.* to John Paulet, Marquess of Winchester.
 Anastasia, *m.* to George Holman, Esq., of Warkworth, co. Northampton.

After the decease of the viscount, the viscountess was created, 5 October, 1688, Countess of Stafford, for life (a dignity that expired at her decease in 1693). Upon the same day that her ladyship had this new honour, her eldest son,

HENRY STAFFORD HOWARD, was created Earl of Stafford, with remainder, in default of male issue, to his brothers. Upon the abdication of King JAMES II., his lordship, following the fortunes of the fallen monarch, retired into France, and there *m.* 3 April, 1694, Claude-Charlotte, eldest dau. of Philibert, Count de Gramont, and Elizabeth, dau. of Sir George Hamilton, Knt., but dying in 1719. *s. p.* was *s.* by his nephew,

WILLIAM-STAFFORD HOWARD, 2nd Earl of Stafford, who *m.* his first cousin, Anne, dau. of George Holman, Esq., and had issue,

 WILLIAM-MATHIAS, his successor.
 Mary, *m.* to Count Chabot, of the house of Rohan, in France
 Anastasia, ⎫
 Anne,   ⎬ nuns.

His lordship *d.* in France, in January, 1733-4, and was *s.* by his son,

WILLIAM-MATTHIAS STAFFORD-HOWARD, 3rd Earl of Stafford. This nobleman *m.* in 1743, Henrietta, dau. of Richard Cantillon, Esq., banker, of Paris, but by her (who *m.* 2ndly, 1759, Robert, 1st Earl of Farnham), had no issue. He *d. s. p.* in February, 1750-1, and was *s.* by his uncle,

JOHN-PAUL STAFFORD-HOWARD, 4th Earl of Stafford, who *m.* Elizabeth, dau. of — Ewen, Esq., of co. Somerset, but as he had no issue, the Earldom of Stafford, at his lordship's decease, in 1762, became EXTINCT.

The Barony of Stafford, created in 1640, has since been restored, in the person of Sir George-William Jerningham, Bart., (*see* issue of the 1st Viscount) by the reversal of the unjust attainder of Sir William Howard, 1st Baron Stafford.

Arms—Gu., a bend between six crosslets, fitchée, arg., a crescent for difference.

HOWARD—BARONS HOWARD, OF CASTLE RISING, CO. NORFOLK, EARLS OF NORWICH.

Barony by Letters Patent, dated 27 March, 1669.
Earldom, by Letters Patent, dated 19 October, 1672.

Lineage.

HENRY HOWARD, 2nd son of Henry-Frederick Howard, Earl of Arundel, Surrey, and Norfolk, who *d.* in 1652, was created, 27 March, 1669, *Baron Howard, of Castle Rising*, and advanced, 19 October, 1672, to the EARLDOM OF NORWICH. His lordship *s.* his brother THOMAS, (who had been restored to the dukedom) as DUKE OF NORFOLK, in 1677. His grace was likewise created Earl Marshal of England. He *m.* 1st, Anne, eldest dau. of Edward, Marquess of Worcester, and had issue,

HENRY, his successor.

Thomas, of Worksop, co. Nottingham. who *m.* Mary-Elizabeth. dau. and sole heiress of Sir John Saville, Bart., of Copley. co. York, and had, with other issue,

THOMAS,⎫ who succeeded in turn to the honours.
EDWARD,⎭

Philip, of Buckenham, co. Norfolk, who left two daus. and co-heirs, namely,

WINIFRED, *m.* to WILLIAM, LORD STOURTON.
ANNE, *m.* to ROBERT-EDWARD, LORD PETRE.

His grace *m.* 2ndly, Jane, dau. of Robert Bickerton, Esq., and had four sons, all of whom *d. s. p.* and three daus. He *d.* in 1684, and was *s.* by his elder son,

HENRY HOWARD, 7th Duke of Norfolk, and 2nd Earl of Norwich, K.G. His grace *m.* Mary, dau. and heiress of Henry Mordaunt, Earl of Peterborough, from whom he was divorced. in 1700. He *d.* in the following year, and leaving no issue, the honours devolved upon his nephew,

THOMAS HOWARD, 8th Duke of Norfolk, and 3rd Earl of Norwich. His grace *m.* Mary, dau. and sole heiress of Sir Nicholas Shireburne, of Stoneyhurst, co. Lancaster, but dying *s. p.* in 1732, was *s.* by his brother,

EDWARD HOWARD, 9th Duke of Norfolk, and 4th Earl of Norwich, and Baron Howard, of Castle Rising. This nobleman *m.* Mary, 2nd dau. and co-heiress of Edward Blount, Esq., of Blagdon, co. Devon, but dying *s. p.* 20 September, 1777, the Baronies of Mowbray, Howard, &c., fell into abeyance, between his two nieces, the daus. and co-heirs of Philip Howard, of Buckenham, as they still continue with their representatives. The Dukedom of Norfolk, &c., passed to the heir-at-law, while the Barony of Howard, of Castle Rising, and Earldom of Norwich, became EXTINCT.

HOWARD—EARLS OF BINDON.

By Letters Patent, dated 30 December, 1706.

Lineage.

THOMAS HOWARD, VISCOUNT BINDON, at whose decease, *s. p.* in 1619, that dignity expired, devised his estate to his kinsman, Thomas Howard, Earl of Suffolk, from whom lineally descended

HENRY HOWARD, 5th Earl of Suffolk, who *m.* Mary Stewart, only dau. and heiress of Andrew, Lord Castle Stewart, of Ireland, and had, with other issue,

HENRY HOWARD (the eldest son), who was elevated to the peerage in the life-time of his father, by letters patent dated 30 December, 1706, as *Baron Chesterford, co. Essex*, and EARL OF BINDON. His lordship was likewise constituted deputy earl marshal, and in that capacity he held a court of chivalry, 26 September, 1707. The Earl Suffolk dying in 1709, Lord

Bindon *s.* as 6th Earl of Suffolk. His lordship *m.* 1st, Penelope, dau. of Henry, Earl of Thomond, and had issue,

CHARLES WILLIAM, his successor.

James, ⎫
Thomas, ⎬ all *d. unm.*
Arthur, ⎭

Sarah, *m.* in 1721, to Thomas Chester, Esq., of Knole Park, co. Gloucester, and *d.* in the following year.

The earl *m.* 2ndly, Henrietta, dau. of Henry, Duke of Beaufort, but had no issue. He *d.* 2 October, 1718, and was *s.* by his eldest son,

CHARLES-WILLIAM HOWARD, 7th Earl of Suffolk, as 2nd Earl of Bindon. This nobleman *m.* Arabella, dau. and co-heir of Sir Samuel Astry, Knt., but had no issue. His lordship, who was lord-lieutenant and custos rotulorum of the co. Essex, *d.* in February, 1722, when the Earldom of Suffolk devolved upon his uncle, and the Barony of Chesterford and Earldom of Bindon became EXTINCT.

HOWARD—DUKES OF NORFOLK.

The DUKEDOM OF NORFOLK came into the Howard family by the creation of JOHN HOWARD, Earl Marshal and Duke of Norfolk, 28 June, 1483. The said John Howard was son and heir of Sir Robert Howard, by Margaret, his wife, dau. of Thomas Mowbray, 1st Duke of Norfolk of that family, and cousin, and ultimately co-heir of John Mowbray, 4th and last Duke of Norfolk, of the Mowbrays. The Dukedom of Norfolk has since been frequently forfeited by the Howards; but as it has now been continued for four centuries in the family, it is deemed more correct to place it amongst *extant* honours than in his work; the reader is therefore referred to BURKE's *Extant Peerage* for a full detail of the family of Howard, Dukes of Norfolk.

A few words, however, as to the parentage of Sir William Howard, the judge, and the origin of the name of Howard may not be irrelevant here:—The name is certainly identical with the Saxon name Herward or Hereward, and Robert, the grandfather of the judge, was called Robert, *filius* Hawardi, in a fine of the 12th HENRY III.; and in an undated charter made by him, he described himself as Robert Herward. Herward was a well known name amongst the Saxons, and besides Earl Hereward, many chiefs of note bore that appellation.

In no less than five charters, all relating to property in Norfolk formerly possessed by the Howard family, Sir William, the judge, is described as the son of John Howard, and, in one, his mother is named as Lucia Germund, and as the widow of John. Copies of all these charters, from the originals at Norfolk House, are still preserved at Corby Castle, the seat of Philip Henry Howard, Esq. In a charter made by Richard Fitz-William de Wigenhall to a convent in Norfolk, a copy of which is also now at Corby Castle, two of the witnesses are John Howard and William his son. In the first writs addressed to William as a judge, the name is written either Heyward or Haward, and the word Howard does not appear in the enrolments until after the accession of EDWARD II.

John Howard, the father of the judge, was the son of Robert Howard or Herward. There are several charters preserved in which Robert was either a grantor or a witness; and in a fine of the 12th of HENRY III. he is judicially described as Robertus, *filius* Hawardi. In his own charters, he is sometimes named Robert Herward, Robert Haward, and Robert Howard.

Howard or Herward, the father of Robert, who describes himself solely by his name of Harward or Herward, in a grant which he made to the church of St. Mary at Lynn, in the time of HENRY II., a charter made with the consent of Wiburg his wife, directed that prayers should be said for the repose of the soul of his father Haward, and of the soul of his grandfather Haward. In this charter, the original of which was, in the 17th century, in the possession of the de Veres, Earls of Oxford, and a copy of which is at Corby, after the last-named Haward, there is inserted the word "exul," meaning either *the banished man*, or *the exile*. The pedigree is thus carried up to Haward or Herward, the exile, who must have lived in the time of, or shortly after, the Norman Conquest.

HOWARD — EARLS OF NOTTINGHAM, EARLS OF EFFINGHAM, CO. SURREY.

Earldom of Nottingham, by Letters Patent, dated 22 Oct., 1596.
Earldom of Effingham, by Letters Patent, dated 8 Dec., 1731.

Lineage.

LORD WILLIAM HOWARD, eldest son of Thomas, Duke of Norfolk, by Agnes, his 2nd duchess, sister and heiress of Sir Philip Tilney, of Boston, co. Lincoln, having been accredited by King HENRY VIII. and EDWARD VI., upon numerous confidential missions to foreign courts, amongst others, in 1553, to the Czar of Muscovy (being the first ambassador from England to Russia), was elevated to the peerage in the first year of Queen Mary, 11 March, 1554, as Baron Howard, of Effingham, and constituted in the same month lord high admiral of her majesty's dominions. His lordship was soon afterwards installed a knight of the Garter, and in the ensuing reign he was made lord chamberlain of the household, and then lord privy seal. His lordship m. 1st, Katherine, one of the sisters and heirs of John Broughton, Esq., by whom he had an only dau., Agnes, who m. William Paulet, 3rd Marquess of Winchester, and d. in 1601. Lord Howard m. 2ndly, Margaret, 2nd dau. of Sir Thomas Gamage, Knt., of Coity, co. Glamorgan, and had issue,

Charles, his successor.
William (Sir), of Lingfield. co. Surrey, who m. Frances, dau. of William Gouldwell, Esq., of Gouldwell Hall, Kent, and had issue,

Edward, }
Francis, } all knights.
Charles, }
Sir William d. in 1600, and was s. by his eldest son,
Sir Edward Howard, who d. s. p. in 1620, and was s. by his brother,
Sir Francis Howard, of Great Bookham, who m. Jane, dau. of Sir William Monson, of Kinnersley, in Surrey, and was s. by his eldest son,

Sir Charles Howard   This gentleman m. Frances, dau. of Sir George Courthope, of Wyleigh, co Sussex, and dying in 1685, had issue,

Francis, who s. as 5th Lord Howard, of Effingham.
George, who m. Anne Kidder, and was father of Lieutenant-General Thomas Howard, who d. 1753, leaving by Mary Morton, his wife, besides two daus., two sons, 1 Sir George Howard, K.B., field marshal, who d. 1796, leaving by Lady Lucy Wentworth, his 1st wife, an only child Ann, m. to General Richard Vyse, and 2 Henry Howard, Esq., of Arundel, father of

Kenneth-Alexander Howard, Esq., who s. to the barony upon the decease of the last Earl of Effingham, in 1816, and was created Earl of Effingham, 1838.

Douglas, m. 1st, to John, Lord Sheffield; 2ndly, to Robert, Earl of Leicester; and 3rdly, to Sir Edward Stafford, of Grafton, Knt.
Mary, m. 1st to Edward, Lord Dudley, and 2ndly, to Richard Mompesson, Esq.
Frances, m. to Edward, Earl of Hertford, and d. s. p. in 1598.
Martha, m. to Sir George Bourchier, Knt., 3rd son of John, Earl of Bath.

His lordship d. in 1573, and was s. by his eldest son,
Sir Charles Howard, 2nd Baron Howard, of Effingham, so celebrated for his glorious defeat of the formidable armada. This eminent person was initiated, in the life-time of his father, in the affairs of state, having been deputed by Queen Elizabeth on a special embassy to Charles IX. of France. On his return he was elected to parliament for the county of Surrey, and was made general of horse, in which capacity he distinguished himself in suppressing the rebellion raised by the Earls of Northumberland and Westmoreland. The following year he was sent with a fleet of men of war to convey the Lady Anne of Austria, dau. of the Emperor Maximilian, going into Spain, over the British seas. In 1574, he was installed a knight of the Garter, and appointed lord chamberlain of the household, and in 1586, his lordship was one of the commissioners for the trial of Mary, Queen of Scotland. Having succeeded the Earl of Lincoln, as lord high admiral of England, Lord Howard of Effingham, achieved his historic fame by the defeat and dispersion of the Spanish Armada in 1588. For this great service his royal mistress not only rewarded him with a pension, but ever after considered him as a person born for the especial preservation of her realm. His next achievement was the conquest of Cadiz, for which he was created, 22 October, 1596, Earl of Nottingham. Upon the accession of King James I., his lordship was continued in the post of lord admiral, and constituted for the occasion of that monarch's coronation lord high steward of England. We afterwards find the earl taking a prominent part at the nuptials of the Princess Elizabeth with the Elector Palatine, which is thus recorded by Arthur Wilson:—"In February (1612) following the death of Prince Henry, the prince palatine, and that lovely princess, the Lady Elizabeth, were married on Bishop Valentine's day, in all the pomp and glory that so much grandeur could express. Her vestments were white, the emblem of innocency; her hair dishevelled, hanging down her back at length, an ornament of virginity; a crown of pure gold upon her head, the cognizance of majesty, being all over beset with precious gems, shining like a constellation; her train supported by twelve young ladies in white garments, so adorned with jewels, that her path looked like a milky way

287

She was led to church by her brother, Prince Charles, and the Earl of Northampton. And while the archbishop of Canterbury was solemnizing the marriage some coruscations and lightnings of joy appeared in her countenance, that expressed more than an ordinary smile, being almost elated to a laughter, which could not clear the air of her fate, but was rather a fore-runner of more sad and dire events; which shews how slippery nature is to toll us along to those things that bring danger, yea sometimes destruction with them.

"She returned from the chapel between the Duke of Lenox, and the Earl of Nottingham, lord high admiral, two married men. The city of London (that with high magnificence feasted the prince palatine and his noble retinue,) presented to the fair bri e a chain of oriental pearl, by the hand of the lord mayor and aldermen, (in their scarlet and gold chain accoutrements,) of such a value as was fit for them to give, and her to receive. And the people of the kingdom in general being summoned to a contribution for the marriage of the king's daughter, did shew their affections by their bounty. And though it be the custom of our kings to pay their daughter's portions with their subjects' purses, yet an hundred years being almost passed since such a precedent, it might have made them unwilling (if their obedience had not been full ripe,) to recal such obsolete things, as are only in practice now by the meanest of the people."

In 1619, the earl resigned the office of lord admiral. He was now eighty-three years of age, and desirous of repose; but not caring to lose the precedence which that dignity gave him, he obtained from the king, according to Collins, by special patent, the privilege of taking place, as his ancestor (John, Lord Mowbray, Earl of Nottingham) had done in the time of Richard II. His lordship m. 1st, Katharine Carey, dau. of Henry, Lord Hunsdon, and had issue,

William, who was summoned to parliament in his father's life-time. He m. Anne, dau. and sole heir of John, Lord St. John, of Bletsoe, but d. before his father, leaving an only dau. and heiress,
Elizabeth, who m. John, Lord Mordaunt, afterwards Earl of Peterborough.
Charles, who s. his father as 2nd earl.
Elizabeth, m. 1st, to Sir Robert Southwell, of Woodrising, in Norfolk, and 2ndly, to John Stewart, Earl of Carrick, in Scotland.
Frances, m. 1st, to Henry, Earl of Kildare, and 2ndly, to Henry Broke, Lord Cobham.
Margaret, m. to Sir Richard Leveson, of Trentham, in Staffordshire.

The earl m. 2ndly, Lady Margaret Stewart, dau. of James, Earl of Moray, and had an only surviving son,

Sir Charles Howard who s. his half-brother in the dignities.

This great person d. at Haling House, in Surrey, 14 December, 1624, and was s. by his eldest surviving son,
Charles Howard, 2nd Earl of Nottingham, who m. 1st, in 1597, Charity, dau. of Robert White, of Christ Church, Hants, and widow of William Leche, of Sheffield, in Fletching, in Sussex. He m. 2ndly, Mary, eldest dau. of Sir William Cockayne, Knt, alderman, and sometime lord mayor of London; but had issue by neither. He d. 3 October, 1642, and was s. by his half-brother,
Sir Charles Howard, 3rd Earl of Nottingham. This nobleman m. Arabella, dau. of Edward Smith. Esq., of the Middle Temple, and sister of Sir Edward Smith, lord-chief justice of the court of Common Pleas in Ireland; but d. s. p. 26 April, 1681, when the Earldom of Nottingham became extinct, and the Barony of Howard, of Effingham, devolved upon his kinsman, (refer to descendants of Sir William Howard, of Langfield, 2nd son of 1st baron,)

Francis Howard, Esq., of Great Bookham, in Surrey, as 5th Baron Howard, of Effingham. This nobleman was governor of Virginia in the reign of Charles II. His lordship m. 1st, Philadelphia, dau. of Sir Thomas Pelham, Bart., great-grandfather of Thomas, Duke of Newcastle, and had surviving issue,

Thomas, }
Francis. } successive peers.
Elizabeth, m. 1st, to William Roberts, Esq., of Wellesden, co. Middlesex; and 2ndly, to William Hutcheson, Esq.

Lord Howard m. 2ndly, Susan, dau. of Sir Henry Felton, of Playford, co. Suffolk, and widow of Thomas Herbert, Esq. ; but had no issue. He d. 30 March, 1694, and was s. by his elder son,
Thomas Howard, 6th Baron Howard, of Effingham. This nobleman, who was one of the gentlemen of the bed-chamber to George, Prince of Denmark, m. 1st, Mary, dau. and heir of Ruishe Wentworth, Esq., son and heir of Sir George Wentworth, a younger brother of Thomas, Earl of Strafford, by whom he had two daus.,

Anne, m. to Sir William Yonge, K.B., and Baronet of Escote, Devon.

Mary, m. to George Venables Vernon, Esq., of Sudbury, in Derbyshire, afterwards created LORD VERNON.

His lordship m. 2ndly, Elizabeth, dau. of John Rotheram, Esq., of Much-Waltham, co. Essex, and widow of Sir Theophilus Napier, Bart., of Luton-Hoo, co. Bedford ; but had no issue. He d. 10 July, 1725, and was s. by his brother,

FRANCIS HOWARD, as 7th Lord Howard, of Effingham. This nobleman, who was a military officer of high rank, was advanced to the EARLDOM OF EFFINGHAM, 8 December, 1731, in consideration of his gallant professional services. In the same year he was constituted deputy-earl marshal of England. His lordship m. 1st, Diana, dau. of Major-General O'Farrel, by whom he had an only son,

THOMAS, his successor.

He m. 2ndly, Anne, sister of Robert Bristow, Esq., one of the commissioners of his majesty's board of green cloth, by whom he had a son,

George, who d. young.

The earl d. 12 February, 1742-3, and was s. by his only surviving son,

THOMAS HOWARD, 2nd Earl of Effingham, who, on the decease of his father, was appointed deputy earl-marshal of England. This nobleman was also a military character, and attained the rank of lieutenant-general in the army. His lordship m. in 1745, Elizabeth, dau. of Peter Beckford, Esq., of the Island of Jamaica, by whom (who m. after the earl's decease, Sir George Howard, K.B.) he had issue,

THOMAS,
RICHARD, } successive earls.

Elizabeth, m. 26 January, 1774, Henry Reginald Courtenay, bishop of Exeter, and by her, who d. 31 October, 1815, left at his decease, 9 June, 1803,

  William Courtenay, who s. as 11th Earl of Devon, 29 May, 1835.

  Thomas-Peregrine Courtenay, a privy councillor. who m. 5 April, 1805, Anne, dau. of Philip-Wynell Mayow, Esq

Anne, m. to Lieut.-Col. Thomas Carleton, of the 29th regiment of foot, who d. in Canada, 1787.

Maria, m. to Guy Carleton, Lord Dorchester, who d. in 1808.

Frances-Herring, d. unm. in 1796.

His lordship d. 19 November, 1763, and was s. by his elder son,

THOMAS HOWARD, 3rd Earl of Effingham, who m. in 1765, Catherine, dau. of Metcalfe Proctor, Esq., of Thorpe, near Leeds, in Yorkshire, by whom he had no issue. His lordship was deputy marshal of England. In 1782 he was appointed treasurer of the household, and, in 1784, master of the Mint. He was afterwards constituted governor of Jamaica, in which government he d. 15 November, 1791, when his honours devolved upon his brother,

RICHARD HOWARD, 4th Earl of Effingham. This nobleman m. in 1785, Miss March, dau. of John March, Esq., of Waresley Park, co. Huntingdon, but had no issue. His lordship d. 11 December, 1816, when the Barony of Howard, of Effingham, devolved upon his kinsman, Kenneth-Alexander Howard, Esq. (refer to descendants of Sir William Howard, 2nd son of the 1st lord,) while the Earldom of Effingham became EXTINCT.

Arms—Gu., a bend, between six cross-crosslets, fitchée, arg., on a bend; an escocheon, or, charged with a demi-lion rampant, pierced through the mouth with an arrow, within a double tressure, flory, counterflory, gu.

HOWARD—BARONS HOWARD, OF ESCRICK, CO. YORK.

By Letters Patent, dated 12 April, 1628.

Lineage.

SIR EDWARD HOWARD, K.B. (7th son of Lord Thomas Howard, who had been created EARL OF SUFFOLK, in 1603), having derived the lordship of Escrick, from his mother, Catherine, eldest dau. and co-heiress of Sir Henry Knevit, and heir of her uncle, Thomas, Lord Knevit, of Escrick, was elevated to the peerage 12 April, 1628, as BARON HOWARD, of Escrick. This nobleman acquired an infamous immortality by his betrayal of the celebrated patriots, Lord Russel and Algernon Sidney. His lordship, who was involved in the conspiracy for which these illustrious persons suffered in the reign of CHARLES II., was the chief evidence against Russel, and the only one against

Sidney, and thus made his own peace with the court. Lord Howard m. Mary, dau. and co-heir of John, Lord Butler, of Bramfield, and had issue,

THOMAS,
WILLIAM. } successors to the barony.

Cecil, (Sir), had an only dau. who d. in infancy.

Edward, killed before Dunkirk, d. s. p.

Anne, m. to Sir Charles Howard, Earl of Carlisle.

His lordship d. in 1675, and was s. by his eldest son,

THOMAS HOWARD, 2nd baron. This nobleman m. 1st, Elizabeth, dau of John, Earl of Peterborough, by whom he had no surviving issue. He m. 2ndly, Joane, dau. of — Drake, Esq., but had no issue. His lordship d. in 1678, and was s. by his brother,

WILLIAM HOWARD, 3rd baron, who m. Frances, dau. of Sir James Bridgman, of Castle Bromwich, co. Warwick, and niece of the lord keeper, Sir Orlando Bridgman, by whom he had Charles, with three other sons, and two daus. who all d. s. p. His lordship d. in 1694, and was s. by his eldest son,

CHARLES HOWARD, 4th baron. This nobleman m. Elizabeth, dau. and co-heir of George Brydges. Lord Chandos, widow of the Earl of Inchiquin, and of Lord Herbert of Chirbury, but dying s. p. in 1715, the Barony of Howard, of Escrick, became EXTINCT.

Arms—Gu., on a bend, between six cross-crosslets, fitchée, arg., an escocheon, or, thereon a demi-lion rampant, pierced through the mouth with an arrow, within a double tressure, counterflory, gu., with a fleur-de-lis for difference.

HOWARD—BARON LANERTON.

(See BURKE's Extant Peerage, CARLISLE, E.)

HOWARD—BARONS FURNIVAL.

(See FURNIVAL.)

HOWE—BARONS CHEDWORTH.

By Letters Patent, dated 12 May, 1741.

Lineage.

This is a branch of the family of HOWE, Earls Howe, in the existing peerage.

JOHN HOWE, Esq., of Stowell, s. to the estates of Sir Richard Howe, Bart., of Compton, co. Gloucester, and Wishford, Wilts, at the decease, s. p. of that gentleman, in 1730, and was elevated to the peerage, 12 May, 1741, as BARON CHEDWORTH, of Chedworth, co. Gloucester. His lordship m. Dorothy, dau. of Henry-Frederick Thynne, Esq., grandfather of Thomas, Viscount Weymouth, by whom he had surviving issue,

JOHN-THYNNE, his successor.

HENRY-FREDERICK, successor to his brother.

Thomas, m. Frances, dau. of Thomas White, Esq., and left JOHN, who inherited as 4th baron.

Charles, d. unm. in 1640.

James, m. Susanna, dau. of Sir Humphrey Howarth, and d. s. p.

William, d. in 1782.

Mary, m. to Alexander Wright, Esq

Anne, m. to Roderick Gwynne, Esq.

His lordship d. in 1742, and was s. by his eldest son,

JOHN-THYNNE HOWE, 2nd Baron Chedworth. This nobleman m. Martha, dau. and co-heir of Sir Philip Parker-a-Morley Long, Bart., of Arwarton, Suffolk, but dying s. p. in 1762, the title devolved upon his brother,

HENRY-FREDERICK HOWE, 3rd Baron Chedworth, who d. unm. in 1781, and was s. by his nephew,

JOHN HOWE, 4th Baron Chedworth, at whose decease, unm 29 October, 1804, the barony became EXTINCT.

Arms—Or, a fesse between three wolves' heads, couped, sa., a crescent for difference.

HOWE—VISCOUNT HOWE, EARL HOWE.

Viscounty, by Letters Patent, dated 20 April, 1782.
Earldom, by Letters Patent, dated 19 August, 1788.

Lineage.

RICHARD HOWE, so celebrated as Admiral Howe, succeeded his brother General George Augustus Howe, Viscount Howe, of Ireland, in that dignity in 1758, and was created for his own gallant achievements a peer of Great Britain, 20 April, 1782, as VISCOUNT HOWE, of Langar, co. Nottingham, and 19 August, 1788, he was advanced to the EARLDOM OF HOWE, being at the same time created Baron Howe, of Langar, with remainder of the latter dignity in failure of male issue, to his daus. and their male descendants respectively. His lordship was elected a knight of the Garter in 1797. He m. in 1758, Mary, dau. of Chiverton Hartopp, Esq., of Welby, in Nottinghamshire, by whom he had three daus., viz.,

SOPHIA-CHARLOTTE, who inherited the barony at his lordship's decease. Her ladyship m. 1st, 31 July, 1787, the Hon. Penn-Assheton Curzon, eldest son of Assheton, 1st Viscount Curzon, by whom (who d. 1797) she had, with other issue, a son,

RICHARD - WILLIAM - PENN CURZON - HOWE, 1st EARL HOWE.

She m. 2ndly, in 1812, Sir Jonathan Wathan Waller, Bart., by whom she had no child. She d. in 1836.

Maria-Juliana, d. unm.

Louisa-Catherine, m. 1st, to John-Dennis, Marquess of Sligo; and 2ndly, to Sir William Scott, Knt., Lord Stowell.

His lordship d. 5 August, 1799, when the Viscounty and Earldom of Howe EXPIRED. The Barony of Howe passed according to the limitation, to his eldest dau., and his Irish honours devolved upon the General, Sir William Howe, with whom they also EXPIRED.

Arms—Or, on a fesse between three wolves' heads erased, sa

HOWE—VISCOUNT HOWE.

For ample details of this dignity, which was conferred, in 1701, on SIR SCROPE HOWE, Knt., member for the co. Notting-ham in the Convention Parliament, and which expired with his descendant, WILLIAM, LORD HOWE, the well-known general during the American war in 1814, refer to HOWE, EARL HOWE, in BURKE's Extant Peerage.

Arms—Or, a fesse between three wolves' heads, erased, sa.

HUGHES—BARON DINORBEN.

By Letters Patent, dated 10 September, 1831.

Lineage.

REV. EDWARD HUGHES, A.M., of Kinmel Park, co. Denbigh, and of Dinorben, in the same county, son of Hugh Hughes, Esq., of Lliniog, in Anglesey, m. MARY LEWIS, dau. and co-heir (with her sister Sidney, of Madryn, wife of Love Parry, Esq.) and also co-heir to her uncle, William Lewis, from whom she inherited Llysdulas, co. Anglesey, and had issue,

I. WILLIAM-LEWIS, his heir, 1st Lord Dinorben.
II. HUGH-ROBERT, seated at Bache Hall, co. Chester, who m. 1st, Barbara, dau. of John-Bodychan Sparrow, Esq., of Red Hill, co. Anglesey, by Anne, his wife, only child and heiress of Ambrose Lewis, Esq., of Trwysclwn, co. Anglesey, and by her had four daus., viz.,

  1 Mary-Anne, m. 7 January, 1834, to Richard Massie, Esq., eldest son of the Rev. Richard Massie, of Coddington, co. Chester, and d. 20 February, 1841, s. p.
  2 Margaret-Grace, d. unm, 14 January, 1838.
  3 Elizabeth-Henrietta, m. 29 October, 1840, to Philip Stapleton Humberston, Esq., of Chester, M.P. for that city, 1859.
  4 Anne-Barbara, d. unm. 18 March, 1847.

Mr. Hughes m. 2ndly, 12 June, 1826, Anne, dau. of Thomas Lance, Esq., of Wavertree, co. Lancaster, and by her had,

  1 HUGH-ROBERT HUGHES, Esq., now of Kinmel Park and Dinorben (see BURKE's Landed Gentry).
  2 Edward-Owen, b. 29 June, 1829; d. 25 September in the following year.
  1 Adelaide-Elinor, m. 10 November, 1856, to the Hon. Walter Bouldler Devereux, captain R.N., 3rd son of Henry, 14th Viscount Hereford, and has issue, two daus.
III. James, col. in the army. C.B.: b. 12 November, 1778; m 16 March, 1841, Fanny, eldest dau. of the Hon. Sir Francis

---

Charles Stanhope, K.C.H., 6th son of Charles, 3rd Earl of Harrington, and d. s. p. 29 November, 1845.
I. Margaret, m. in July, 1792, to Owen Williams, Esq., of Temple House, Berks, and Craigydon, co. Anglesey, M.P. for Great Marlow. and d. in 1821, leaving issue: her eldest son, Thomas-Peers Williams, Esq., of Temple House and Craigydon, M.P.; d. 1875, leaving issue.
II. Anne, m. 11 June, 1799, to Sir Robert Williams, Bart., of Penrhyn, co. Carnarvon, and d. in September, 1837, leaving by him (who d. 1 December, 1830) issue, of whom the eldest son is the present Sir Richard Williams-Bulkeley, Bart., of Penrhyn, M.P.
III. Martha, m. 1st, in 1809, to Cynric Lloyd, Esq., 3rd brother of Edward Price Lloyd, Baron Mostyn. He d. s. p. 1822. She m. 2ndly, in 1829, Sir Henry Wyatt, lieut.-col. in the 2nd guards, and d. 9 April, 1839.

The eldest son,

I. WILLIAM-LEWIS HUGHES, of Kinmel Park, Dinorben, and Llysdulas, Esq., M.P., b. 10 November, 1767, created BARON DINORBEN, of Kinmel Park, co. Denbigh, 10 September, 1831 · m. 1st, 8 March, 1804, Charlotte-Margaret, 3rd dau. of Ralph-William Grey, Esq., of Backworth, co. Northumberland, and by her (who d. 21 January, 1835), had issue,

EDWARD, b. 5 November, 1806; d. 3 March, 1814.
WILLIAM-LEWIS HUGHES, 2nd Baron Dinorben.
Charlotte-Mary, m. 27 May, 1828, to Sir Richard Williams-Bulkeley, Bart., of Penrhyn, co. Carnarvon, and d. s. p. 17 May, 1829.
Frances-Margaret, m. in 1835, to Alan Legge, 3rd Baron Gardner, and d. s. p. 8 December, 1847.
Maria-Mary.
Eliza-Anne, d. young, 1815.
Laura, also d. young, 1816.
Caroline-Anne, d. unm. 19 April, 1832.
Emily.
Augusta, d. young, 1852.

Lord Dinorben m. 2ndly, in 1840, Gertrude, youngest dau. of Grice Smyth. Esq., of Ballynatray, co. Waterford, and sister of Penelope, consort of H.R.H. the Prince of Capua, son of the King of Naples, and by her had two daus.,

Gertrude-Cecilia, d. an infant, 1843.
Gwen-Gertrude.

Lord Dinorben d. 10 February, 1852, and was s. by his only surviving son,

II. WILLIAM-LEWIS, 2nd baron, b. 5 November, 1821, who d. unm. 6 October, 1852, when the title became EXTINCT. The entailed estates devolved on his first cousin and heir male, the present

HUGH-ROBERT HUGHES, Esq., of Kinmel and Dinorben, co. Denbigh, J.P. and D.L., b. 11 June, 1827; m. 18 April, 1853, Florentia, 2nd dau. of Henry-Thomas, Lord Ravensworth, and has issue.

Arms—Gu., two lions passant, and a rose in chief, arg.

HUME OR HOME—BARON HUME, OF BERWICK, AND EARL OF DUNBAR.

Barony, by Letters Patent, dated 7 July, 1604.
Earldom, by Letters Patent, dated 3 July, 1605.

Lineage.

SIR GEORGE HOME, Knt., 3rd son of Alexander Home, of Manderston, and great-grandson of Sir David Home, of Wedderburn, having accompanied King JAMES I. into England, was elevated to the English peerage, 7 July, 1604, as BARON HUME, of Berwick. He had previously succeeded Lord Elphinston in the treasurership of Scotland, and was created a peer of that kingdom, 3 July, 1605, in the dignity of EARL OF DUNBAR. His lordship, who was in great favour with his royal master, was a knight of the Garter, chancellor of the Exchequer, and master of the wardrobe. He is characterized by the Archbishop of St. Andrews "as a person of deep wit, few words; and in his majesty's service, no less faithful than fortunate. The most difficile affairs he compassed without any noise, never returning when he was employed, without the work performed that he was sent to do." He m. Catherine, dau. of Sir Alexander Gordon, of Gight, and had two daus., his co-heirs, viz.,

I. ANNE, m. Sir James Home, of Coldingknows.
II. ELIZABETH, m. to Theophilus Howard, 2nd Earl of Suffolk, K.G.

The earl d. at Whitehall, 29 January, 1611, and was buried at Dunbar. At his decease, all his honours became EXTINCT.

Arms—Vert, a lion rampant, arg.

HUME-CAMPBELL—BARON HUME, OF BERWICK.

By Letters Patent, dated 20 May, 1776.

Lineage.

HUGH HUME, 3rd Earl of Marchmont, in the peerage of Scotland, lord keeper of the great seal in that kingdom, from January, 1764, to May, 1766; m. 1st, in 1731, Anne, dau. of — Western, Esq., by whom he had three daus, viz.,

Anne, m. to John Paterson, Esq., eldest son and successor of Sir John Paterson, Bart., of Eccles.
Margaret, m. to Colonel James Stuart.
Diana, m. to Walter Scot, Esq., of Arden.

His lordship m. 2ndly, Elizabeth, dau. of Mr. Windmill Crompton, of London, by whom he had an only son,
ALEXANDER HUME (by courtesy Viscount Polwarth), who m. in 1772, Amabel, elder dau. and co-heir of Lady Jemima Campbell, Marchioness Grey, by her husband, Philip, Earl of Hardwicke, and was created a peer of England 20 May, 1776, as BARON HUME, of Berwick. His lordship assumed the additional surname of CAMPBELL. He d. s. p. in 1781, when the Barony of Hume became EXTINCT. (See Countess de Grey, BURKE's Peerage and Baronetage).

Arms—Quarterly: 1st grand quarter, counter quartered; 1st and 4th, vert, a lion rampant, arg., for HUME; 2nd and 3rd, arg., three popinjays of the 1st, for PEPDIE; 2nd, arg., three piles engrailed, gu., for POLWARTH; 3rd, arg., a cross engrailed, sa., for SINCLAIR; the 4th grand quarter as the 1st; and over all, as a surtout, an escutcheon, arg., charged with an orange, ensigned with an imperial crown, all ppr., as a coat of augmentation, given by King WILLIAM III., when he created his lordship's ancestor, Sir Patrick Hume, Lord Polwarth.

HUME OR HOME—EARL OF MARCHMONT.

By Letters Patent, dated 23 April, 1697.

Lineage.

SIR PATRICK HUME OR HOME, of Polwarth, b. 13 January, 1641, the eldest son of Sir Patrick Home, Bart., of Polwarth, and the descendant of Sir David Home, 2nd son of Sir Thomas Home, of Home, s. his father 1648, and became one of the most conspicuous characters of the age. After enduring imprisonment and long-continued persecution for his opposition to the measures of the court, he at length effected his escape to Holland, and thence accompanied the Prince of Orange to Britain in 1688, when he took his seat in the convention as member for the county of Berwick. The forfeiture passed against him in 1685 was rescinded by parliament, he was sworn a privy councillor, nominated a commissioner for the then projected union, and created a peer of Scotland, by the title of Lord Polwarth, "to him and the heirs male of his body, and to their heirs," by patent, dated at Kensington, 26 December, 1690, when the king assigned to him an orange, proper, ensigned with an imperial crown, to be placed as a surtout in his coat of arms. He was appointed sheriff of Berwickshire, 2 October, 1692; one of the extraordinary lords of session, 28 November, 1693; constituted high chancellor of Scotland 2 May, 1696, and created EARL OF MARCHMONT, Viscount of Blasonberrie, Lord Polwarth, of Polwarth, Redbraes and Greenlaw, by patent, dated at Kensington, 23 April, 1697, to him and his heirs male whatsoever; and the same year he was appointed one of the commissioners of the Treasury and Admiralty. His lordship m. Grizel, dau. of Sir Thomas Ker, of Cavers, and by her (who d. at Edinburgh, 11 October, 1703, and was buried in the Canongate churchyard) had issue,

Patrick, Lord Polwarth, who d. s. p.
Robert, who d. s. p. 27 October, 1692.
ALEXANDER, 2nd Earl of Marchmont.
Andrew, of Kimmerghame, co. Berwick, who was appointed a lord of session, on the resignation of his brother, 25 November, 1714, and d. in 1730. He m. Elizabeth, dau. of John Douglas, Esq., by whom he had a son, John, an officer in the army, murdered at Roscrea, in Ireland, 28 September, 1738, without issue, by his wife, a dau. of Drummond, of Blair; and two daus., Elizabeth, m. to Charles St. Clair, of Herdmanston, and d. 12 March, 1784, leaving a son, Andrew St. Clair, to whose son, Charles, the title of Lord Sinclair was adjudged by the House of Lords, 1782; and Helen, m. in June, 1735, to Andrew Wauchope, of Niddrie Marischal, chief of one of the oldest families in the shire of Edinburgh, and had three sons (see Landed Gentry).

290

Grizel, b. at Redbraes Castle, 25 December, 1665; m. 17 September, 1692, to George Baillie, M.P. of Jerviswood, one of the lords of the Treasury, who d. at Oxford, 6 August, 1738, aged seventy-five. She d. 6 December, 1746, in the eighty-first year of her age, and was buried at Mellerstain.
Christian, d. in 1688, aged about twenty-one, in Holland
Anne, m. to Sir John Hall, Bart., of Dunglass, co. Berwick, and had issue. She d. in January, 1699.
Juliana, m. to Charles Billingham, Esq., warden of the Mint, and had a dau., Jean, b. 5 July, 1703.
Jean, b. 26 March, 1683; m. to James, 7th Lord Torphichen, and had a numerous issue.

The eldest surviving son,
ALEXANDER HOME, 2nd Earl of Marchmont, lord clerk register, and a diplomatist of the first grade, m. 29 July, 1697, Margaret, dau. and heiress of Sir George Campbell, of Cessnock, in Ayrshire, and had issue by her,

George, Lord Polwarth, b. 17 January, 1704, who d. unm. at Montpelier, 13 October, 1724, in the twenty-first year of his age.
Patrick, d. 1724.
HUGH, 3rd Earl of Marchmont.
Alexander-Hume-Campbell, M.P. for Berwickshire, an eminent barrister, and lord clerk register of Scotland He d. s. p., 1760, in his fifty-third year
Anne, b. 3 August, 1698; m. to Sir William Purves, Bart., of Purveshall, co. Berwick, who d. 18 June, 1762.
Grizel, b. 9 March, 1701; d. unm.
Jean, b. 1 July, 1709; m. in January, 1743, to James Nimmo. Esq., receiver-general of Excise, and d. at Edinburgh, 10 October, 1770, aged sixty-two, s. p.
Margaret, who d unm.

Lord Marchmont d. in 1740, and was s. by his son,
HUGH HOME, 3rd Earl of Marchmont, b. at Edinburgh, 15 February, 1708, who soon gained distinction by his learning and the brilliancy of his genius. His lordship was a leading parliamentary debater, and held in high estimation by his contemporaries, among whom were Chatham, Walpole, Lyttelton, and Wyndham. Lord Cobham gave his bust a place in the Temple of Worthies, at Stow; and Pope thus mentions his lordship, in the well-known inscription in the grotto at Twickenham:

"There the bright flame was shot through Marchmont's soul!"

In 1747, the earl was appointed first lord of police, and in 1764, keeper of the great seal of Scotland. He m. 1st, in May, 1731, Miss Anne Western, of London, and by her (who d. at Redbraes, 9 May, 1747), had one son and three daus.,

Patrick, Lord Polwarth, who d. young.
Anne, m. at Redbraes 2 October, 1755, to Sir John Paterson, Bart., of Eccles co. Berwick; and d. at Newcastle, 27 July, 1790, leaving an only dau., who m. at Eccles, 17 February, 1778, Sir Philip Anstruther, Bart., but d. s. p.
Margaret, m. 20 September, 1763, to Major-General James Stuart, 3rd son of Archibald Stuart, of Torrance; and d. s. p. at Edinburgh, 7 January, 1765.
DIANA, m. at Redbraes, 18 April, 1754, to Walter Scott, M.P. of Harden, co. Berwick (who d. at Tunbridge, 25 January, 1793), and had one son, HUGH SCOTT, of Harden, who claimed and was allowed the BARONY OF POLWARTH, in 1835.

The Earl of Marchmont m. 2ndly, at London, 30 January, 1748, Miss Elizabeth Crompton, of Hatton Garden, and by her (who d. at Hemel Hempstead, 12 February, 1797), had one son,

Alexander, Lord Polwarth, b. 1750; created a peer of Great Britain, by the title of BARON HUME, of Berwick, 14 May, 1776. He m. 16 July, 1772, Lady Annabella Yorke, eldest dau. of Philip, 2nd Earl of Hardwicke, but d. s. p. at Wrest, 9 March, 1781, when the title became extinct.

Lord Marchmont d. 10 January, 1794, since which period the title, although claimed by Alexander Home, Esq., R.N., as heir male general of the last earl, has remained DORMANT; but the Barony of Polwarth has been allowed to Hugh Scott, Esq., of Harden.

Arms—Quarterly: 1st grand quarter, counter quartered; 1st and 4th, vert, a lion rampant, arg., armed and langued, gu., for HOME; 2nd and 3rd, arg, three popinjays, vert, beaked and membered, gu., for PEPDIE; 2nd, arg., three piles. engr., gu., issuing from the chief, for POLWARTH; 3rd, arg., a cross, engr., az., for ST. CLAIR, of Herdsmanstoun; 4th, as the 1st. Over all, in the centre, an escutcheon, arg., charged with an orange, ppr., stalked and slipped, vert, ensigned with an imperial crown, ppr., as a coat of augmentation.

HUNGERFORD—BARONS HUNGERFORD.

By Writ of Summons, dated 7 January, 1426.

Lineage.

WALTER DE HUNGERFORD, who m. Maud de Heytesbury, was father of

WALTER DE HUNGERFORD, living A.D., 1308, who had two sons,

ROBERT, and Walter.

The elder son,

SIR ROBERT DE HUNGERFORD, who, in the 1st year of EDWARD III., was constituted one of the commissioners to inquire and certify the state of the Exchequer what lands and tenements, &c., Hugh le Despencer, Earl of Winchester, and Hugh, his son (with others who suffered death in the last year of King EDWARD II.'s reign), were possessed of. This Sir Robert, who was distinguished by his piety, gave to the warden of the hospital of St. John, at Calne, lands of considerable value, to maintain a priest to pray for the soul of Joane, his wife, for the health of his own soul, and those of his parents, benefactors, and all the faithful deceased. But in the event of the said warden failing to fulfil the trust thus reposed in him, the said lands were to devolve upon his brother WALTER. Sir Robert m. Geva, widow of Adam de Stokke, d. s. p. 1364, and was s. by his said brother,

SIR WALTER DE HUNGERFORD, who m. Elizabeth, dau. of Sir Adam Fitz-John, of Cherill, Wilts, and was s. by his son,

SIR THOMAS DE HUNGERFORD, of Farley, who, in the 30th EDWARD III., was escheator for the co. Wilts; and in the 51st of the same reign, filled the chair of the House of Commons as Speaker, being the first person elected to that high office; the Commons not having had previously such an officer. In the 3rd RICHARD II., Sir Thomas obtained a confirmation of the office of forester of Selwood, which he had formerly acquired from Roger de Sturton. In the 6th of the same monarch he purchased from Elizabeth, the widow of Edward, Lord Spenser, the manor of Heytesbury, called the West Court, together with the hundred of Haytesbury. The next year having fortified his house at Farle Montford, co. Somerset, without license, he obtained a pardon for the same, and soon after procured a charter for free warren in all his demesne lands. Sir Thomas m. Joane, dau. and co-heir of Sir Edmund Hussey, Knt., of Holbrook, and d. 3 December, 1398, having had issue,

   I. Rhodolph,
   II. Thomas, } d. s. p., v. p.
   III. John,
   IV. WALTER, of whom we treat.

The 4th son,

SIR WALTER HUNGERFORD, Knt., in consideration of his eminent services obtained, upon the accession of King HENRY IV., a grant of £100 per annum, to be received out of the lands of Margaret, Duchess of Norfolk. In three years afterwards Sir Walter was engaged in the wars of France, and, subsequently, for his expenses in those wars, and especially at Calais, where he acquired great honour by encountering a knight of France, he had a further grant of 100 marks per annum, payable out of the town and castle of Marlborough, in Wilts, and the same year was constituted sheriff of that co. In the 13th HENRY IV., upon the death of Joane, his mother, he' had livery of the manors of Heytesbury and Tesfount-Ewyas, co. Wilts, and of Farle-Mountfort, and others in Somersetshire, his homage being respited. In the 4th HENRY V. Sir Walter was constituted admiral of the whole fleet under John, Duke of Bedford, and during that and the next two years he appears to have been entirely engaged in the wars of France. In the latter year, being at the time steward of the king's household, and in his service at the siege of Roan, he obtained a grant in special tail, of the Barony of Homet, in Normandy, which had formerly been enjoyed by Sir William de Montney, Knt.; rendering to the king and his heirs one lance, with a fox-tail hanging thereat yearly, upon the feast day of the exaltation of the Holy Cross; and finding ten men at arms and twenty archers, to serve him, or his lieutenant during his wars with France. About this time Sir Walter was chosen a knight of the Garter. Continuing to acquire fresh laurels on the French soil, this gallant soldier obtained a further grant for his services in the 9th of the same reign, of the castle of Neville, and territory of Breant, in Normandy, with divers other lands, which had been the possession of Sir Robert de Breant, Knt. Sir Walter was one of the executors to the will of HENRY V., and in the 2nd of the ensuing reign he was con-

stituted, by advice of the lords then sitting in parliament, steward of the household to the young king; and in two years afterwards he was appointed treasurer of the Exchequer. In the 6th HENRY VI., bearing then the title of "Sir Walter Hungerford, Knt., Lord of Heightresbury and Homet, and treasurer of England," he gave to the dean and canons of the Free-Royal-Chapel of St. Stephen, within the king's palace at Westminster, divers houses and shops in the parish of St. Anthony, within the city of London, in consideration whereof, they covenanted to make him partaker of all their masses and suffrages, during his life, and after his death to celebrate his obit annually, with Placebo and Dirige, and mass of Requiem, and to make distribution thereat, of twenty pence to the dean, to every canon twelve pence, to every vicar six pence, to every clerk four pence, and to the verger six pence. In three years afterwards, being still lord treasurer of England, his lordship had license to transport 3,000 marks for the ransom of Sir Walter Hungerford, his son, then a prisoner in France. His lordship m. 1st, Catherine, one of the daus. and co-heirs of Thomas Peverell, by his wife, Margaret, dau. of Sir Thomas Courtenay, Knt., by whom he had issue,

   I. Walter (Sir), who d. in Provence, before his father.
   II. ROBERT (Sir), of whom presently.
   III. Edmund (Sir), m. Margaret, dau. and co-heir of Edward Burnell, and grand-dau. and co-heir of Hugh, Lord Burnell, between whom and her sisters, the Barony of Burnell fell into ABEYANCE in 1420, and so remains with their representatives. He d. in 1484, having had issue, two sons,

      1 THOMAS (Sir); ancestor of the HUNGERFORDS of DOWN AMPNEY, co Gloucester, whose eventual heiress, Bridget (dau. of Sir Anthony Hungerford, of Down Ampney), m. Edmund Dunch, Esq., the HUNGERFORDS of WINDRUSH,* co. Oxford; the HUNGERFORDS of BLACK BOURTON, also in Oxfordshire, and afterwards of FARLEY CASTLE, Berks.

      2 EDWARD (Sir), m. Anne, dau. of Edward Grey, Lord Ferrers, of Groby, and was ancestor of the HUNGERFORDS, of Cadenham, co. Wilts, whose descendant, Sir George Hungerford, m. Frances, dau. of Lord Seymour, of Trowbridge, and d. in 1714, leaving two sons, whose issue became extinct, and four daus., 1 Ann, who m. Edward Luttrell, and was mother of Southcott Hungerford Luttrell, Esq.; 2 Frances, who m. John Keate, Esq., and had a son. John Hungerford Keate, Esq., who m. Penelope, dau. and heir of Henry Fleming, D.D., and had a dau. and eventual heiress who m. George Walker, Esq., of Calne, who assumed the surname of Hungerford, and had a dau., HENRIETTA-MARIA-ANNA HUNGERFORD. wife of the Hon. JOHN CREWE. 3 Catharine, who m. Henry Blaake, Esq., and had with other issue a dau., Frances, m. to Robert Duke, Esq., of Lake; and 4 Mary.

   IV. Walter, m. Margaret, dau. of Sir John St. Legor.
   1 Philippa, m. to Sir Thomas Seymour.
   2 Margaret, m. to John Ferrers, of Plowden, Wilts.
   3 Lettice.
   4 Anne, m. to Henry Barker.
   5 Jane, m. to James Ryall.
   6 Christiana

     I. Elizabeth, m. to Sir Philip Courtenay, of Powderham.
     II. Margaret, m. to Sir Walter Rodney, Knt.

Lord Hungerford m. 2ndly, Eleanor, Countess of Arundel, dau. of Sir John Berkeley, Knt., but had no issue. He was summoned to parliament as a Baron, from the 4th to the 26th of King HENRY VI 's reign inclusive. By his testament bearing date 1 July, 1449, wherein he styleth himself Lord Hungerford, Heytesbury, and Homet, he directs his body to be buried in a certain chapel in the cathedral church at Salisbury, in which he had founded a perpetual chantry for two chaplains, and wherein Catherine, his 1st wife, lay buried; and after some pious bequests, he leaves to Alianore, Countess of Arundel, his then wife, all his plate, both of silver and gold, and likewise all those other goods and chattels, which were hers while she was unmarried. To Sir Robert Hungerford, his son, his best Dorser of Arras. To the Lady Margaret, wife of his said son, his best legend of the lives of saints, written in French, and covered with red cloth. To Robert Hungerford, Lord Molines, his grandson, his best pair of cuirasses, with all belonging thereto; to be made choice of by him, out of the armory at Farley-Hungerford. To his son, Sir Edmund Hungerford, Knt., a cup of gold, with a cover, and a sapphire on the head thereof. To Elizabeth, his dau., a cup of gold. To Margaret, his other dau., a bed of silk, of black and green colour. And because his much honoured lord, the Viscount Beaumont, was lineally

---

*The last male heir of the Windrush branch was the late John Peach Hungerford, Esq., M.P., of Dingley Park, co. Northampton, who d. 4 June, 1809, aged ninety, having devised his estates to Henry Hungerford Holdich, Esq., who has assumed the additional surname of Hungerford (see BURKE's Landed Gentry—HUNGERFORD, of Dingley Park).

descended from the Dukes of Lancaster, he bequeathed unto him a cup of silver, with a cover bordered with gold, with which cup the most noble Prince John, Duke of Lancaster, his often served; and in which he did use to drink so long as he lived. And lastly, for the better advancement of Arnulph and William Hungerford (sons of the said Sir Robert Hungerford, Knt., his son), in their marriages, and Mary, dau. of the said Sir Robert, he bequeaths to them 700 marks sterling. His lordship d. in 1449, and was s. by his eldest surviving son,

SIR ROBERT HUNGERFORD, Knt., as 2nd Baron Hungerford, summoned to parliament from 5 September, 1450, to 26 May, 1455. Of this nobleman very honourable mention is made regarding his services in France, during the life-time of his father, under the Regent Bedford. In the 17th HENRY VI. he inherited the estates of his aunt, Alianore Talbot, the only sister of his mother, and the co-heir of Thomas Peverell. His lordship m. Margaret Botreaux, only dau. and heir of William, Lord Botreaux, (who d. in 1477), and had issue,

> ROBERT, his successor, who inherited the Barony of Botreaux, in right of his mother.
> Arnulph.　　　　William.
> Catharine, m. to Richard Lord Delaware.
> Mary.

Lord Hungerford d. in 1458, and was s. by his eldest son,

ROBERT HUNGERFORD, 3rd Baron Hungerford, who had been summoned to parliament (having m. the heiress of Molines), in the life-time of his father, as LORD MOLINES, from 13 January, 1445 to 20 January, 1453, but never summoned as Baron Hungerford. This nobleman served in the French wars, under the great captain, Sir John Talbot, the gallant and renowned Earl of Shrewsbury, and was with him at the unfortunate battle of Chastillon, where that illustrious soldier lost his life, and Lord Molines became a prisoner. Whereupon Alianore, Countess of Arundel, some time wife of his grandfather, Walter, Lord Hungerford, bestowed upon him all the wool then in her manor of Heytesbury, valued at 100 marks, towards the payment of his ransom, provided that he came alive out of prison. By which, and considerable supplies from Margaret, Lady Hungerford and Botreaux, his mother, he obtained his freedom, after an incarceration of seven years and four months. In the 38th HENRY VI., his lordship, in consideration of his services and his sufferings, obtained license to transport 1,500 sacks of wool into any foreign parts, without payment of custom for the same: as also to travel beyond sea, and to take as many with him in his company, with gold, silver, and other necessaries, as should be suitable to his degree. Upon this occasion, his lordship travelled into Italy. But returning before long, he espoused the Lancastrian interests, and fought under the red banner at Towton-field, from which conflict, after the defeat of his party, he fled to York, where he joined King HENRY, and thence accompanied the monarch into Scotland. His lordship was, in consequence, attainted by the parliament assembled in the 1st EDWARD IV. Notwithstanding which, King EDWARD regarded his wife, Alianore, and his younger children, with such feelings of compassion, that he committed them to the care of Lord Wenlok, to whom he had granted the attainted lord's estates, for a fitting support. In three years afterwards, the Lancastrians again making head, Lord Hungerford was in their ranks at the battle of Hexham, and being made prisoner, he was conveyed to Newcastle, and there beheaded, anno 1463. He was buried in the cathedral church of Salisbury. His lordship m. Eleanor, dau. and heir of William, Lord Molines, and had issue,

> THOMAS (Sir), of whom presently.
> Walter, ancestor of the LORDS HUNGERFORD, OF HEYTESBURY, see that dignity.
> Leonard.
> Fridiswide, who became a nun at Sion.

Upon the attainder of Robert, Lord Hungerford and Molines, these honours became EXTINCT. His lordship's widow m. Sir Oliver Manningham. His eldest son,

SIR THOMAS HUNGERFORD, sided for a while with Richard Nevil, Earl of Warwick, who then espoused the cause of EDWARD IV., but afterwards falling off, and exerting his influence for the restoration of King HENRY VI., he was seized, and tried for his life at Salisbury, in the 8th EDWARD IV., and having had judgment of death as a traitor, was executed the next day. Sir Thomas m. Anne, dau. of Henry, Earl of Northumberland, by whom (who m. 2ndly, Sir Laurence Raynesford, Knt., and 3rdly, Sir Hugh Vaughan, Knt.), he had an only dau. and heiress,

> MARY HUNGERFORD, who m. EDWARD HASTINGS, son and heir apparent of William, 1st Lord Hastings, of Ashby-de-la-Zouche. This Mary, the attainders of her father and grandfather having been reversed in the first parliament of King HENRY VII., had restitution of the honours and estates of

her family, and in consequence bore the title of Lady Hungerford, Botreaux, and Molines. Her ladyship's son and successor, George Hastings, was created EARL OF HUNTINGDON, in which earldom, those baronies became merged until the death of Francis, 10th earl, in 1789, without issue, when they became vested in Elizabeth, his sister and heir, wife of John, Earl of Moira, of the kingdom of Ireland, and they are now enjoyed by her descendant, CHARLES EDWARD HASTINGS, Earl of Loudoun, Baron Hungerford Botreaux, &c.

Arms—Sa., two bars, arg., in chief, three plates.

HUNGERFORD — BARON HUNGERFORD, OF HEYTESBURY, CO. WILTS.

By Writ of Summons, dated 8 June, 1536.

Lineage.

THE HON. SIR WALTER HUNGERFORD, 2nd son of Robert, 3rd Baron Hungerford, who was attainted and beheaded in 1463, having joined the banner of the Earl of Richmond, shared in the triumph of Bosworth, and participated in the spoils of conquest. We find him subsequently again in arms for his royal master, against Perkin Warbeck, and the Cornish men, who had risen in his behalf, and he was eventually of the privy council, to King HENRY VIII. He m. Jane Bulstrode, and had issue,

> EDWARD, (Sir), his successor.
> Elizabeth, m. to Sir John Bourchier.

He d. 1516, and was s. by his son,

SIR EDWARD HUNGERFORD, Knt., of Heytesbury, co. Wilts, who m. Jane, dau. of John Lord Zouche of Harringworth, and was s. by his only son,

SIR WALTER HUNGERFORD, of Heytesbury, who was summoned to parliament as BARON HUNGERFORD, *of Heytesbury*, 8 June, 1536. His lordship m. 1st, Susanna, dau. of Sir John Danvers, Knt., and had issue,

> I. WALTER (Sir), of whom presently.

Lord Hungerford m. 2ndly, Alicia, dau. of William, Lord Sandys, by whom he had,

> Edward (Sir), gentleman pensioner to Queen ELIZABETH, m. 1st, Jane, relict of William Foster, and 2ndly, Cicely, dau. of Sir John Tufton, and d. s. p. in 1608. His widow m. Thomas, Earl of Rutland.
> Mary, m. 1st, to Thomas Baker, Esq., and 2ndly, Thomas Shaa.
> Anne.

This nobleman in the 31st HENRY VIII., being attainted in parliament, was beheaded on Tower Hill, with Cromwell, Earl of Essex, 28 July, 1541, when the Barony of Hungerford of Heytesbury, EXPIRED. The crimes laid to his lordship's charge, were "retaining a chaplain, called William Bird, who had called the king a heretic.—Procuring certain persons to ascertain, by conjuration, how long the king should live;—and having been guilty of unnatural offences." The attainder of Lord Hungerford was reversed by Queen MARY in favour of his children, to all intents and purposes, save the enjoyment of the peerage. The eldest son,

SIR WALTER HUNGERFORD, Knt., of Farley Castle, m. 1st, Ann Basset, and 2ndly, Anne, dau. of Sir William Dormer, Knt., and had issue,

> Edmund, d. s. p.
> Susan, m. 1st, to Michael Ernley, Esq., of Cannings, co. Wilts; 2ndly, to John Moring; and 3rdly, to Sir Crew Reynolds.
> Lucy, m. 1st, to Sir John St. John, of Lydiard; and 2ndly, to Sir Anthony Hungerford.
> Jane, m. to Sir John Carne, Knt., of Ewenny, co. Glamorgan.

On the branch of the family settled at Black Bourton, co. Oxford, Farley Castle eventually devolved and was one of the great possessions of Sir EDWARD HUNGERFORD, knight of the Bath, surnamed "the Spendthrift," by whose boundless extravagence the family property, immense though it was, was utterly destroyed (*See Vicissitudes of Families*, 1st series). He d. in 1711, having had a son, Edward, who d. before him without surviving issue, and a dau. RACHEL, m. to Clotworthy, VISCOUNT MASSEREENE. "Thus terminated," says Sir Richard Hoare, "the glory and good fortune of the Hungerford family. Even the name has become extinct in England though I have reason to think it survives in Ireland." Sir Richard Hoare, was correct in his surmise; a very flourishing offshoot of the family still remains in Ireland, one branch being seated at the Island, near Clonakilty, co. Cork, and the other at Cahirmore, near Roscarbery, in the same co. Colonel Richard Hungerford of the Island, is called "cousin" in the will dated 24 May, 1729, of one of his English kinsmen, and Capt. Thomas Hungerford, who d. 1680, is described on his monument in Roscarbery Cathedral, as "descended of Sir Edward Hungerford of Down Ampney, in the co. Gloucester."

Arms—Sa., two bars arg., in chief, three plates.

HUNTERCOMBE—BARON HUNTERCOMBE.

By Writ of Summons, dated 23 June, 1295.

Lineage.

In the 25th HENRY III., WILLIAM DE HUNTERCOMBE, having m. Isabel, one of the daus. and co-he'rs of Robert de Muscamp, had livery of the lands of her inheritance, and in some years after had summons to be at Chester, well fitted with horse and arms, to oppose the hostilities of the Welsh. And in the 54th of the same reign he was signed with the cross, in order to accompany Prince Edward in a voyage to the Holy Land. He d. the next year, seised of the manor of Huntercombe, co. Oxford, and other estates, and was s. by his son,

SIR WALTER DE HUNTERCOMBE, Knt., who, in the 5th EDWARD I., answered £50 for his relief of the moiety of the Barony of Muschamp, which he then possessed. In the 10th year of the same reign we find him in an expedition made into Wales. In the 22nd he had summons to attend the king at Portsmouth, with horse and arms, thence to sail into Gascony, and the next year (23 June, 1295), he was summoned to parliament as a Baron. In the 25th his lordship was in the expedition made into Scotland, and the 26th he was made governor of Edinburgh Castle. In the 27th he was constituted lieutenant of Northumberland, and for several years subsequently he continued with the army in Scotland. In the 35th he petitioned parliament, setting forth his being in all the Scottish wars, first at Berwick, with twenty light horse; afterwards at Strivelin, with thirty-two in the retinue of the Earl Warren; next at La Vaire Chapelle, with thirty in the retinue of the bishop of Durham; lastly, at Galloway, with sixteen. And since that, in the last battle, that he sent eighteen, though absent himself, being then warden of the marches towards Northumberland. And his lordship prayed that his scutage for all these expeditions might be remitted, which request was accordingly conceded. Lord Huntercombe m. Alice, one of the daus. and co-heirs of Hugh de Bolebec, of Bolebec, co. Northumberland, and also co-heir of Richard de Montfichet, by reason that Margery, the mother of the said Hugh, was one of the sisters and co-heirs of the said Richard. His lordship d. in 1312, s. p., when his nephew, Nicholas, son of Richard de Newbaud, and Gunnora, his sister, succeeded to his lands, and the Barony of Huntercombe became EXTINCT.

Arms—Erm., two bars gemells, gu.

HUNTINGFEILD—BARONS HUNTINGFEILD.

By Writ of Summons, dated 8 June, 1201.

Lineage.

In the time of King STEPHEN, WILLIAM DE HUNTINGFEILD, with the consent of Roger, his son and heir, gave the whole Isle of Mendham, co. Suffolk, and divers other lands, to the monks of Castle Acre, co. Norfolk. He d. in 1155, and was s. by his said son and heir,

ROGER DE HUNTINGFEILD, who was s. by his son,

WILLIAM DE HUNTINGFEILD, who being made constable of Dover Castle in the 5th King JOHN, obliged himself, by oath in the king's presence, faithfully to preserve the safe custody of that fortress, so that it should not be surrendered to any person, save the king himself, or the lord chamberlain, Hubert de Burgh, and as hostages for his loyalty, delivered up his son and dau., the former to remain in the hands of the Earl of Arundel, the latter in those of the Earl Ferrers. In the 8th of JOHN this William de Huntingfeild, paid a fine of two marks

and two palfreys, for the wardship of the heir and lands of Osbert Fitz-Hervie, and the next year obtained a grant of all the possessions of Roger de Huntingfeild, his brother, which had been seized by the crown by reason of the interdict. In the following year we find him justice-itinerant for Lincoln, and afterwards sheriff for the counties of Norfolk and Suffolk; for four successive years subsequently, however, he became eminent amongst the barons who extorted the Great Charters from JOHN, and was one of the twenty-five chosen to enforce their observance, for which conduct he came under the excommunication of the Pope, and had his lands in Lincolnshire seized by the crown, and transferred to Nichola de Haya during the king's pleasure. In the reign of HENRY III., he seems to have made his peace, for he then journeyed to the Holy Land with a license from the crown. This feudal lord m. Alice de St. Liz, and had issue,

ROGER, his successor.
Alice, m. to Richard de Solers, whom she survived, and her father, in the 15th JOHN, she being then a widow, gave to the king six fair Norway goshawkers for license to have the disposal of her in marriage, and for an assignation of her dowry out of the lands of her deceased husband.

His lordship was s. at his decease, in 1240, by his son,

ROGER DE HUNTINGFEILD, who, in the 26th HENRY III., paid a fine of 200 marks, to be exempted from the expedition then making into Gascony. He m. Joane, one of the daus. and co-heirs of William de Hobrugg, and dying in 1252, was s. by his son,

WILLIAM DE HUNTINGFEILD, who, at the battle of Evesham, 49th HENRY III. was one of the principal barons in hostility to the crown. He d. in 1282, and was s. by his son,

ROGER DE HUNTINGFEILD, who, in the 22nd EDWARD I., had summons, with other eminent persons, to attend the king with all despatch to advise about the important affairs of the realm; and soon after received command to be at Portsmouth well fitted with horse and arms, to sail into Gascony. He was summoned to parliament as a baron, 8 June, 1294 and 26 January, 1297, but never afterwards. His lordship m. Joyce, dau. of John de Engaine, and dying in 1301, was s. by his son,

WILLIAM DE HUNTINGFEILD, 2nd baron, who does not appear from the existing enrolments to have been summoned to parliament. This nobleman was engaged in the Scottish wars, temp. EDWARD I. and EDWARD II., and d. in 1313, being then possessed of the manor of Bekesworth, co. Cambridge, and the manors of Mendham and Huntingfeild, co. Suffolk, as also divers lordships and lands in other shires. His wife Sibell survived him, and m. William, Lord Latimer. His lordship was s. by his son,

ROGER DE HUNTINGFEILD, 3rd baron. This nobleman m. Cecilia, dau. of Sir Walter de Norwich, Knt., and dying in 1337, was s. by his son,

SIR WILLIAM DE HUNTINGFEILD, 4th baron, summoned to parliament from 15 November, 1351, to 20 January, 1376. His lordship served in the French wars in the 33rd and 34th EDWARD III., being latterly of the retinue of Henry, Duke of Lancaster. He d. in 1377, s. p. "leaving his aunt Alice, dau. of William, his grandfather, and widow of Sir John Norwich, Knt., his heir; but according to another inquisition, the said Alice, and Sir John Copledick, grandson, of Johanna, dau. of the said William, his grandfather, by Sybilla, his 2nd wife, were his heirs."[*] Amongst whose descendants, if the writ of EDWARD I. be that which created the dignity, the Barony of Huntingfeild is now in ABEYANCE.

Arms—Or, on a fesse, gu., three plates.

HUNTINGFEILD—BARON HUNTINGFEILD.

By Writ of Summons, dated 14 August, 1362.

Lineage.

JOHN DE HUNTINGFEILD, was summoned to parliament as a baron, from 14 August, 1362, to 6 April, 1369, but nothing further is known of his lordship or his descendants.

Arms—Or, on a fesse, gu., three plates.

---

[*] COURTHOPE's *Historic P.erage.*

HUSSEY — BARON HUSSEY, OF SLEFORD, CO. LINCOLN.

By Writ of Summons, dated 5 January, 1534.

Lineage.

SIR WILLIAM HUSSEY, Knt., an eminent lawyer in the time of EDWARD IV., after filling the office of attorney-general, and having been called by writ to the degree of serjeant at law, was constituted lord chief justice of the court of King's Bench, in the 17th of that monarch's reign, when he received an allowance of 140 marks, for greater state. He was living *temp.* HENRY VII., as is evident by this inscription over his arms, in the semicircular or bow window, of Grey's Inn Hall, viz.,

" W. House miles capitalis justiciarius in banco regis, temp. R. HENRY VII."

In one of the windows of the chapel, belonging to the same Inn, are his arms impaling those of his wife, with the following inscription,

" Will. Hussee miles capitalis Justic. ad placita coram rege, et Elizabetha uxor ejus filia Thomæ Berkeley arm."

The lady mentioned above, was of the Berkeleys of Wymondham, and Sir William had issue by her,

JOHN, his successor.
Robert (Sir), whose grandson, Sir Edward Hussey, Bart., of Honington, co. Lincoln, (so created by King JAMES I.,) was grandfather of Sir Thomas Hussey, with whom the baronetcy expired. Sir Thomas left two surviving daus. his co-heirs, viz.,
> Elizabeth, *m.* to Richard Ellis, Esq., and *d. s. p.*
> Sarah, *m.* to Robert Apreece, Esq., of Washingley, co. Huntingdon, and had issue,
>> THOMAS APREECE, whose son and heir,
>> THOMAS-HUSSEY APREECE, Esq., of Washingley, was created a baronet, 4 June, 1782.
William, from whom descended the Husseys of Yorkshire.
Elizabeth, *m.* to Richard Grey, Earl of Kent.
Mary, *m.* to William, Lord Willoughby.

The eldest son,
SIR JOHN HUSSEY, Knt., in the 2nd HENRY VII., was in arms for the king at the battle of Stoke, against John, Earl of Lincoln, and his adherents; and in the 13th HENRY VIII., was made chief butler of England. In the 21st of the same reign, he was one of the knights of the king's body; and being summoned as BARON HUSSEY, *of Sleford, co. Lincoln* (where he had erected a noble mansion), to the parliament begun at Westminster, 3 November, in that year, was admitted into the house 1 December following; but his lordship's name does not occur in the list of summonses for that year, nor before 5 January, 1534, yet it is clear that he was summoned; for the year after (22nd HENRY,) he had, under the title of Lord Hussey, a grant of the custody of the manor of Harewoole, co. York; and he was one of the lords, who at that time signed the declaration to the Pope, regarding the king's divorce. In 1533, being then a lord of the council, he had a grant of the wardship and marriage of Thomas, the son and heir of Christopher Wymbushe, deceased; but in a few years afterwards, engaging in the common insurrection, (anno 1537,) when the feuds and differences about religion broke out, he was attainted of high treason; his manor of Sleford, with lands adjacent, worth £5,000 a year, confiscated, and he himself beheaded at Lincoln, when the Barony of Hussey, of Sleford, EXPIRED. His lordship *m.* 1st, Anne Grey, dau. of George, Earl of Kent, and had issue,

Giles, } who both *d. s. p.*
Thomas, }
Bridget, *m.* 1st, to Sir Richard Morrison, Knt., by whom she had issue,
> Charles, whose son, Sir Charles Morrison, Bart., of Cashiobury, co. Herts, left an only dau., and heiress, ELIZABETH, who *m.* Arthur, LORD CAPELL, OF HADHAM, from whom the present EARL OF ESSEX descends, and inherits Cashiobury Park.
> Elizabeth, *m.* 1st, to Henry Norris, Esq., and 2ndly, to Henry Clinton, Earl of Lincoln.
> Mary, *m.* to Barth Hales, Esq.
> Jane-Sibilla, *m.* 1st, to Edward, Lord Russell, and 2ndly, to Arthur, Lord Grey, of Wilton.
> Bridget, Lady Morrison, *m.* 2ndly, Henry, Earl of Rutland; and 3rdly, Francis, Earl of Bedford, but had issue by neither.
Elizabeth, *m.* to — Hungerford, Esq.
Anne, *m.* 1st, to Sir Humphrey Browne, Knt., one of the justices of the Court of Common Pleas; and 2ndly, to — Dimock, Esq.
Dorothy, *m.* to — Dockwray, Esq.

Lord Hussey *m.* 2ndly, Margaret, dau. and heir of Sir Simon Blount, of Mangotsbury, co. Gloucester, and had issue,

294

William (Sir), of whom presently
Giles (Sir), of Caythorpe, co. Lincoln.
Gilbert (Sir).   Reginald.
Elizabeth.

The attainder of his lordship was reversed in parliament, the 5th ELIZABETH, and his children restored in blood, but neither the estate nor honour granted to the heir, which heir, SIR WILLIAM HUSSEY, was sheriff of the co. Lincoln, in the 22nd HENRY VIII. He *m.* Ursula, dau. and co-heir of Sir Robert Lovell, Knt., and left two daus., viz.,

Margaret, *m.* to Richard D'Isney, Esq , of Norton D'Isney, co. Lincoln, ancestor by her of the D'Isneys of Swinderby, co. Lincoln, and of the Hyde, co. Essex.
Anne, *m.* to William Gell, Esq., of Darley, co. Derby.

Sir William *d.* in the 3rd and 4th PHILIP and MARY.

Arms—Or, a cross, vert.

HUSSEY—BARON AND EARL OF BEAULIEU.

Barony, by Letters Patent, dated 11 May 1762.
Earldom, by Letters Patent, dated 6 July, 1784.

Lineage.

SIR HUGH HUSSEY, who went to Ireland, 17th HENRY II., *m.* the sister of Theobald Fitz-Walter, the first Butler of that kingdom, and *d.* seized of large possessions in the co. Meath, from the grant of Hugh de Lacie. His son Walter Hussey, was father, by Agnes his wife, dau. and heir of Hugh de Lacie, Sen., Earl of Ulster, of HUGH HUSSEY, who *m.* a dau. of Adam de Hereford, and had a son, William Hussey, who, by Catherine Fitzgerald his wife, a dau. of the house of Kildare, was father of Sir John Hussey, Knt., 1st Baron of Galtrim, summoned to parliament 25 March and 22 November, 1374, and 22 January, 1377. From him descended the great house of HUSSEY, *Barons of Galtrim.*

PETER HUSSEY, Esq., 2nd son of James Hussey, Baron of Galtrim, by Mary, his wife, dau. of Richard Aylmer, Esq., of Lyons, *m.* Mary, only dau. and heir of Bartholomew Bellew, Esq. of Westown, co. Dublin, and had a son,

LUKE HUSSEY, Esq., of Westown, whose will bears date 17 April, 1671. He *m.* Elizabeth Barnewall, and was father of a dau., Katharine, *m.* 1st, to Christopher D'Arcy, Esq., of Stidall, and 2ndly, to Thomas D'Arcy ; and of a son,

COL. EDWARD HUSSEY, of Westown, whose will was proved 25 November, 1742; he *m.* Mabel Barnewall and had issue,

I. JAMES, his heir.
II. George, *d. unm.*   III. Luke, *d. unm.*
IV. Nicholas, who *d. unm.*
1. Mabel, *m.* to Matthias Barnewall, Esq , of Castletown, co. Meath.
II. CATHERINE, who *m.* SIR ANDREW AYLMER, Bart., of Balrath, co Meath, and by him who *d.* 5 November, 1740, left at her decease in 1746, with other issue, a dau.,
> MABEL AYLMER, who *m.* JOHN STRONG, of Mullafin, co. Meath, and had five sons and seven daus. ; ANDREW; Simon, a priest; John, a priest; GERALD, of whom presently, as the inheritor of the Westown estates; and Robert; Bridget, a nun; Mary, *m.* to James Dromgoole, of Drogheda; Margaret, *m.* to Bartholomew Ennis; Frances, *m.* 1785, to Richard Dowdall, Esq., son of Lawrence Dowdall, Esq. of Lisnawilly ; Alice, *m.* to William Cruise, Esq.; Catherine, *m.* to John Segrave, Esq.; and Arabella, *m.* to Thomas-A. Knight, Esq.

The eldest son,
JAMES HUSSEY, Esq., of Westown, co. Dublin, and of Courtown, co. Kildare, *m.* 1705 (M. L. dated 6 July) Catherine, dau. of Richard Parsons, Viscount Rosse, and by her who *d.* in March, 1766, had issue (with four daus., Frances, Elizabeth, Mabel, and Mary, wife of James Hussey, Esq., of Galtrim), three sons, EDWARD, his heir; Richard, *d. s. p.*; James, *d. s. p.* Mr. Hussey *d.* in 1759, and was *s.* by his eldest son,

EDWARD HUSSEY, Esq., of Westown, who *m.* in 1743, Isabella, eldest dau. and co-heir of John, Duke of Montague, and relict of William Montague, Duke of Manchester, and assumed at the decease of his father-in-law, the name and arms of MONTAGUE. In 1753, he was installed a knight of the Bath; in 1762, created a peer of Great Britain as BARON BEAULIEU, *of Beaulieu;* and in 1784, advanced to be EARL BEAULIEU. By the co-heiress of Montague, his lordship had an only son, JOHN, who *d. unm.*, and one dau., Isabella, who also *d. unm.* in 1772. He *d.* in 1802 (when the peerage expired), and was *s.* in the Irish estates by his brother, RICHARD HUSSEY, Esq. of Westown, who *d. unm.*, having devised his property to his cousin (the grandson of Catherine Hussey, by her husband, Sir Andrew Aylmer, Bart.),

Gerald Strong, Esq., who assumed, in consequence, the name and arms of Hussey. Owing, however, to the will of Lord Beaulieu, who had bequeathed the estates to Lord Sidney Osborne, youngest son of the Duke of Leeds, litigation ensued, and was at length terminated by a compromise and division of the property under an act of parliament, 51st George III. Mr. Strong-Hussey m. in 1781, Mary, dau. of Anthony Lynch, Esq., of La Vally, co. Galway, and had issue,

Anthony, his heir.

Margaret, m. in 1812, to Francis Magan, Esq., of Emoe, co. Westmeath, and had three daus., co-heiresses, viz.,

1 Mary, m. to John Lentaigne, Esq., J.P. and D.L., of Tallaght, co. Dublin.

2 Margaret, m. to Michael Cahill, Esq., J.P., of Ballyconra, co. Kilkenny.

3 Anna-Maria, m. to Michael Corcoran, Esq., barrister-at-law.

Isabella, m. in 1814, to Col. William Meall, E. I. Co.'s service, and d. leaving one surviving dau., Mary Meall.

Mr. Strong-Hussey d. 30 November, 1811, and was s. by his son,

Anthony Strong-Hussey, Esq., of Westown, b. 24 August, 1782; who m. 19 August, 1811, Mable, eldest dau. of Malachi Donelan, Esq., of Ballydonelan, co. Galway, and dying 12 July, 1859, left, with other issue, a son and heir, the late Malachi Strong-Hussey, Esq., of Westown.

Arms—Barry of six, erm. and gu., on a canton of the last, a cross, or.

HUTCHINSON—BARON HUTCHINSON.

By Letters Patent, dated 5 December, 1801.

Lineage.

The Hon. John Hutchinson, a gen. officer in the army, col. of the 18th regiment of foot, governor of Stirling Castle, and a knight grand-cross of the Bath; b. 15 May, 1757, succeeded Sir Ralph Abercromby in the command of the army in Egypt, and was raised to the peerage for his military services, as *Baron Hutchinson of Alexandria and Knocklofty*, 5 December, 1801, a pension of £2,000 per annum being attached to the barony. His lordship as 2nd Earl of Donoughmore, 22 August, 1825, and d. unm. 29 June, 1832, when his own immediate barony expired, while the family honours he had inherited passed to his nephew, John-Helt-Hutchinson, 3rd Earl of Donoughmore.

Arms—1st and 4th, per pale gu., and az., a lion rampant, between eight cross-crosslets, arg., for Hutchinson; 2nd, az., a fesse between three stags' heads, erased in chief, and a demi-lion rampant, in base, arg., for Hely; 3rd, az., a garb between three wolves' heads, erased, arg, for Nixon.

HYDE—BARONS HYDE OF HINDON, EARLS OF CLARENDON, BARONS HYDE OF WOTTON BASSETT, VISCOUNTS HYDE, OF KENILWORTH, EARLS OF ROCHESTER.

Barony of Hyde, of Hindon, by Letters Patent, dated 3 November, 1660.
Earldom of Clarendon, by Letters Patent, dated 20 April, 1661.
Barony of Hyde, of Wotton Bassett, and Viscounty of Hyde, of Kenilworth, by Letters Patent, dated 23 April, 1681.
Earldom of Rochester, by Letters Patent, dated 29 November, 1682.

Lineage.

Sir Edward Hyde, Knt., a person eminently learned in the law, and as eminent for his attachment to the Charleses, was made chancellor of the Exchequer and a privy councillor, by the first monarch of that name; and having shared the fortunes of the second was declared by his Majesty, while in exile at Bruges, in Flanders, lord high chancellor of England, in the year 1657, which office he held until 1667, when he was succeeded by Sir Orlando Bridgman. Sir Edward was elevated to the peerage by letters patent, dated 3 November, 1660, as *Baron Hyde, of Hindon, co. Wilts*, and created 20 April, 1661, *Viscount Cornbury*,

and Earl of Clarendon.* His lordship obtained celebrity, not only as a lawyer and a statesman, but as a man of letters. By command of King Charles II., he wrote his popular *History of the Rebellion*, and he produced several other works, which are enumerated in Walpole's Catalogue of Royal and Noble Authors. "One may pronounce," says Walpole, "on my Lord Clarendon, in his double capacity of statesman and historian, that he acted for liberty, but wrote for prerogative;" and Burnet characterizes him, "as a good minister, indefatigable in business, but little too magisterial, and not well enough acquainted with foreign affairs." "He was a good chancellor," continues the same authority, "and impartial in the administration of justice; but a little too rough. He had a levity in his wit, and a loftiness in his carriage, that did not well become the station he was in; for those that addressed him, and those that thought themselves neglected he was apt to reject with contumely, and some disparagement of their services, which created him many enemies, and at last procured his fall." Upon his disgrace the earl retired into France, and d. at Roan, in Normandy, 19 December, 1674. His lordship m. Frances, dau. and eventually sole heir, of Sir Thomas Aylesbury, Bart., and had four sons, and two daus., viz.,

I. Henry, Viscount Cornbury, his successor.

II. Laurence, master of the robes to King Charles II., who was advanced to the peerage, 23 April, 1681, as *Baron Hyde, of Wotton Bassett, co. Wilts*, and *Viscount Hyde, of Kenilworth, co. Warwick*, and was created Earl of Rochester, 29 November, 1682. This nobleman concurred in the revolution of 1688, and was constituted lord-lieutenant of Ireland, in 1700. He was a person of great natural parts, and esteemed as a statesman, incorruptible: indeed his disposition was deemed too warm to be insincere. He m. Henrietta Boyle, dau. of Richard, Earl of Burlington, and had issue,

Henry, his successor.
Anne, m. to James, Duke of Ormonde.
Henrietta, m. to James, Earl of Dalkeith, eldest son of James, Duke of Monmouth, and from this marriage the Dukes of Buccleuch descend.
Mary, m. to Francis Seymour, Lord Conway, ancestor of the extant Marquesses of Hertford.
Catherine, d. unm.

His lordship d. in 1711, and was buried in Westminster Abbey. He was s. by his son,

Henry, 2nd Earl of Rochester, of whom hereafter, as 4th Earl of Clarendon.

III. Edward, student at law, d. unm.

IV. James, drowned on board the "Gloucester" frigate, in his passage to Scotland, with several other persons of distinction, in the train of the Duke of York.

I. Anne, m. to James, Duke of York, afterwards King James II. This lady was maid of honour to the princess royal, and her marriage with the duke was concealed until her pregnancy compelled an avowal. The prince is accused of using both promises and menaces, to deter her from claiming him as a husband, and even so far as to employ the spirit to declare, that it should be known she was his wife, the consequences what they might.

II. Frances, m. to Sir Thomas Knightley, K.B., of Hartingfordbury, co. Herts.

Edward, Earl of Clarendon, was s. at his decease in 1709, by his eldest son,

Henry Hyde, 2nd Earl of Clarendon, who in the 1st year of King James II., was lord privy seal, but retired from office the next year. At the Revolution, he refused to act with the new government, and lived subsequently, in retirement. His lordship m. 1st, Theodosia Capel, dau. of Arthur, 1st Lord Capel, by whom he had an only son, Edward, Viscount Cornbury, his successor. He m. 2ndly, Flower, dau. and sole heir of William Backhouse, Esq., of Sallowfield, but had no issue. His lordship d. 31 October, 1709, and was s. by his son,

Edward Hyde, 3rd Earl of Clarendon. This nobleman, in the lifetime of his father, was master of the horse to Prince George of Denmark, and in the reign of Queen Anne, his lordship was governor of New York. He m. Catherine, dau. of Henry, Lord O'Brien, eldest son of Henry, Earl of Thomond, which Catherine, at the decease of her mother, became Baroness Clifton. By this lady he had issue,

Edward, Viscount Cornbury, who d. unm., aged twenty-two, 12 February, 1712-13.

* Clarendon. This title, first enjoyed by Sir Edward Hyde was derived from a spacious park, near Salisbury, formerly the site of a royal palace, but more remarkable, as the place where King Henry II. summoned the great council of peers and prelates, in 1164, from which emanated the celebrated regulations, so well known as "The Constitutions of Clarendon," by which the clergy were made amenable to the jurisdiction of the civil power. From those regulations arose the subsequent hostility between Henry II. and Thomas à Becket.

Catherine, d. unm.

Theodosia, m. 24 August, 1713, John Bligh, Esq., M.P. (afterwards Earl of Darnley), and from this marriage the extant Earl of Darnley derives, who enjoys the Barony of Clifton, through this lady.

His lordship d. 31 March, 1723, and his only son having d. previously, the honours devolved upon his kinsman (revert to Laurence, 2nd son of Edward, 1st earl),

HENRY HYDE, 2nd Earl of Rochester, as 4th Earl of Clarendon. This nobleman was joint treasurer of Ireland with Arthur, Earl of Anglesey. His lordship m. Jane, youngest dau. of Sir William Leveson-Gower, and sister of John, Lord Gower, by whom he had surviving issue,

HENRY, Viscount Cornbury, who was summoned in his father's lifetime, 22 January, 1750, and placed in his father's Barony of Hyde, of Hindon. He d. in 1753, before his father.

Jane, m. to William Capel, 3rd Earl of Essex, and had four daus. of whom two lived to maturity, viz.,

CHARLOTTE, who became heir to her grandfather, Henry, Earl of Clarendon and Rochester. Her ladyship m. the Hon. Thomas Villiers, 2nd son of William, 2nd Earl of Jersey, which Thomas was elevated to the peerage 31 May, 1756, as Baron Hyde, of Hindon, and created EARL OF CLARENDON, 8 June. 1776. From this marriage descends VILLIERS, EARL OF CLARENDON (see BURKE's Peerage).

Mary, m. in 1758, to Admiral the Hon. John Forbes, 2nd son of George, 3rd Earl of Granard.

Catherine, m. to Charles, Duke of Queensberry and Dover. This lady was the celebrated Duchess of Queensberry, the patroness of Gay, the poet.

The earl d. 1753, and his only son deceasing in the same year before him, the Barony of Hyde, of Hindon, the Viscounty of Cornbury, the Earldom of Clarendon, the Barony of Hyde, of Wotton Bassett, the Viscounty of Hyde, of Kenilworth, and the Earldom of Rochester, all became EXTINCT.

Arms—Az., a chev., between three lozenges, or.

HYDE—EARLS OF ROCHESTER.

See Hyde, Earls of Clarendon.

INGHAM—BARON INGHAM.

By Writ of Summons, dated 15 June, 1328.

Lineage.

In the 2nd year of King JOHN,

JOHN DE INGHAM, of Ingham, co. Norfolk, having m. Albreda, one of the daus. and co-heirs of Walter Waleran, paid a fine of 60 marks, and one palfrey to the king, for livery of the third part of his barony, and for the relief due thereupon, excepting the serjeanty of the forest, which William de Nevill then had. He d. in the 5th of the same reign, and was s. by his son,

OLIVER DE INGHAM, who d. in the 10th EDWARD I., possessed of estates in the cos. Norfolk, Southampton, Dorset, and Wilts, and was s. by his son,

JOHN DE INGHAM, of Ingham, who was s. by his son,

OLIVER DE INGHAM, of Ingham, who was summoned to parliament as a Baron, in the 2nd EDWARD III., and from that period to the 16th of the same reign. This nobleman was a very eminent person during the martial times in which he lived. In the beginning of EDWARD II.'s reign he was in the wars of Scotland, and we find him for several years afterwards actively engaged in that kingdom. In the 14th EDWARD II., he was constituted governor of the castle of Ellesmere, in Shropshire, and upon the breaking out of the insurrection under Thomas, Earl of Lancaster, he marched with the king to Cirencester, Gloucester, Shrewsbury, and other places. The next year he was made governor of the castle at Devizes, in Wilts, and sheriff of Cheshire; and in two years afterwards seneschal of Aquitaine, when he proceeded thither at the head of 7,000 men. Upon the deposition of EDWARD II., his lordship was appointed one of the twelve guardians of the young King EDWARD III., and soon after constituted justice of Chester for life. In this reign (EDWARD III.), his patent for the seneschalsy was renewed, and he obtained a grant of 500

marks sterling for his support in that service. His lordship had issue,

Elizabeth, m. to John Curson, and d. before her father, leaving a dau.,

MARY CURSON, m. to Stephen de Tumbye, and d. s. p.

Joane, m. 1st, to Roger le Strange, Lord Strange of Knokyn, by whom she had no issue; she m. 2ndly, Sir Miles Stapleton, K.G., of Bedale, co. York, by whom she had issue: their line terminated after several generations in two daus. Elizabeth, m. 1st, Sir Philip Calthorp; 2ndly, Sir John Fortescue, chief justice of England; and 3rdly, Sir Edward Howard, lord high admiral of England; and Joan, m. 1st, Christopher Harcourt, Esq., of Stanton Harcourt, 2ndly, Sir John Hudleston.

Lord Ingham d. 1344, when the Barony of Ingham fell into ABEYANCE between his grand-dau., Mary Curson, and his dau., Joane, Lady Strange, his co-heirs.

Arms—Per pale, or and vert, a cross recercele, or, moline, gu.

INGRAM—VISCOUNT IRVINE.

By Letters Patent, dated 23 May, 1661.

Lineage.

The founder of this family,

HUGH INGRAM, a wealthy citizen and merchant of London, d. in 1612, leaving a large fortune to his two sons by his wife, Anne Galthorpe. The elder, SIR WILLIAM INGRAM, LL D., secretary to the council of the North, d. 24 July, 1623, leaving issue. The younger,

ARTHUR INGRAM, made extensive purchases in the co. York, including the manor of Temple Newsom, on the river Aire, two miles below Leeds, from the Duke of Lennox.[*] He served the office of sheriff for Yorkshire in the 18th JAMES I., and represented the city of York in parliament. He m. 1st, Susan, dau. of Richard Brown, of London, and had by her (with a younger son, John, who m. 1st, Anne, dau. and heir of William Calverley, of Eccleshill; and 2ndly, Dorothy, dau. of Thomas, Viscount Fairfax, but d. s. p.; and one dau., the wife of Sir Simon Bennet, Bart.), ARTHUR (Sir), his heir. He m. 2ndly, Alice Ferrers, dau. of a citizen of London, and by that lady had Sir Thomas Ingram, of Sheriff-Hutton, chancellor of the Duchy of Lancaster, privy councillor to King CHARLES I., who m. the Hon. Frances Belasyse, dau. of Viscount Fauconberg, and had a dau., Mary. Arthur Ingram m. 3rdly, Mary, dau. of Sir Edward Grevile. of Milcote, in Warwickshire, and had another son, who d. young. He was s. at his decease by his eldest son,

SIR ARTHUR INGRAM, of Temple Newsom, high sheriff of co. York, 6th CHARLES I., who m. 1st, Elizabeth, dau. of Sir Henry Slingsby, Bart., of Red House, and had issue,

I. Thomas, who m. Elizabeth, dau. of Watkinson Payler, and d. s. p.

II. HENRY, his successor.

III. Arthur, of Barrowby, living 1712. He m. Jane, dau. of Sir John Mallory, of Studley, and had a son, Thomas, who d. 1703, leaving, by Frances, his wife, dau. of John Nicholson, Esq., of York, M.D., two sons and a dau , Arthur, d. 1708; Thomas, and Frances.

I. Elizabeth, m. to Robert, Lord Rich, afterwards Earl of Warwick.

II. Anne, m. to Henry, 3rd son of Robert Stapylton, Esq., of Wighill.

Sir Arthur m. 2ndly, Catherine, dau. of Thomas, Viscount Fairfax, of Emely, and relict of Robert Stapylton, Esq., of Wighill, and of Sir Matthew Boynton, Bart., and by her, who afterwards m. William Wickham, Esq., had a dau., Catherine, m. to Sir Charles Nevile, of Amber, Knt. He d. 4 July, 1655, and was s. by his eldest surviving son,

HENRY INGRAM, of Temple Newsom, bapt. at Stratford-le-Bow, 20 June, 1616. This gentleman was created a peer of Scotland, with remainder to the heirs male of his body, as Lord Ingram, VISCOUNT OF IRVINE, by letters patent, dated 23 May, 1661. He m. Lady Essex Montagu, dau. of Edward, Earl of Manchester, and had two sons, EDWARD and ARTHUR. His lordship d. in 1666, and was s. by his elder son,

EDWARD INGRAM, 2nd Viscount Irvine, who d. 16 September, 1688, and was s. by his brother,

---

[*] The manor of Temple Newsom was granted by HENRY VIII., in 1544, to Matthew Stewart, 4th Earl of Lennox.

Ingram.
(V. Irvine.)

Johnstone.
(M. Annandale.)

Keith.
(E. Marischal.)

Knyvett.
(B. Knyvett.)

Lacy.
(E. Lincoln.)

Lamb.
(V. Melbourne.)

Langdale.
(B. Langdale.)

Latimer.
(B. Latimer.)

Lee.
(E. Lichfield.)

Lindsay.
(D. Montrose.)

Lovelace.
(B. Lovelace.)

Lovel.
(B. Lovel.)

ARTHUR INGRAM, 3rd Viscount Irvine, who *m.* Isabel, eldest dau. of John Machel, Esq., of Hills, in Sussex, M.P. for Horsham, and had nine sons, of whom five, EDWARD, RICHARD,* ARTHUR, HENRY, and GEORGE, became 4th, 5th, 6th, 7th, and 8th Viscounts Irvine. George, the 8th viscount, who was in holy orders, a canon of Windsor, and prebendary of Westminster, *s.* in 1761; and *d. s. p.* in 1763, when he was *s.* by his nephew, son of his next brother,

CHARLES INGRAM, 9th Viscount Irvine, *b.* in 1696; who *d.* 28 November, 1748, leaving a son,

CHARLES INGRAM, 10th Viscount Irvine, who *m.* in 1756, Miss Shepherd, a lady of large fortune, and had five daus., his co-heirs (who all bore the additional name of Shepherd), viz.,

   I. ISABELLA - ANNE INGRAM - SHEPHERD, who *m.* in 1776, Francis, 2nd Marquess of Hertford, and had an only son, FRANCIS - CHARLES, 3rd MARQUESS OF HERTFORD.

   II. FRANCES INGRAM-SHEPHERD, *m.* 6 March, 1781, to Lord William Gordon, 2nd son of Cosmo-George, 3rd Duke of Gordon, and *d. s. p.*

   III. ELIZABETH INGRAM-SHEPHERD, *m.* 2 August, 1782, to Hugo Meynell, Esq., of Hoar Cross, co. Stafford, and *d.* 17 May, 1800, leaving issue. Her eldest son adopted the surname of INGRAM. and became HUGO-CHARLES MEYNELL-INGRAM, Esq., of Temple Newsom, co. York, and Hoar Cross, co. Stafford. (*See* BURKE'S *Landed Gentry.*)

   IV. HARRIET INGRAM-SHEPHERD, *m.* 16 September, 1789, to Colonel Henry Hervey Aston, and left a dau., Harriet-Elizabeth, who *m.* Lieut.-Col. Bridgeman, and *d.* in 1853; and two sons, 1 Henry-Charles Hervey-Aston, Esq., of Aston Hall, Cheshire, who *m.* Margaret, dau. of William Barron, Esq., and *d.* 1820, leaving (with a dau., Harriet, *m.* in 1832, to the Hon. and Rev. Arthur Talbot), a son, Arthur-Wellington, lieut. 1st life-guards, *d.* 1839; 2 Sir Arthur Ingram-Aston, G.C.B., late of Aston Hall, Cheshire, *b.* in 1798, who was attached to the embassy at Vienna, April, 1819, became secretary of legation at Rio de Janeiro, April, 1826, was secretary of embassy at Paris, January, 1833, and was envoy-extraordinary and plenipotentiary at Madrid from June, 1839, to November, 1843, and *d.* 5 May, 1859.

   V. LOUISA-SUSAN INGRAM-SHEPHERD, *m.* 5 June, 1787, to Sir John Ramsden, Bart., of Byrom. co. York, and had issue. Her eldest grandson is the present SIR JOHN-WILLIAM RAMSDEN, Bart., of Byrom.

His lordship, who was chosen one of the representative peers of Scotland, in 1768, *d.* at Temple Newsom, 27 June, 1778, when having no male issue, the peerage became EXTINCT.

Arms—Erm., on a fesse, gu., three escallops, or.

IPRE—EARL OF KENT.

Creation of King STEPHEN, *anno* 1141.

Lineage.

WILLIAM DE IPRE, said to be an illegitimate son of Philip, Earl of Ipre, in Flanders, having distinguished himself previously in arms, joined in 1137, the banner of King STEPHEN, then reared in Normandy against the Empress Maud, and continuing actively engaged in that prince's cause, was created by him in 1141, EARL OF KENT; in which year he commanded one of the divisions of King STEPHEN's army at the battle of Lincoln, where the king's forces experienced a signal defeat, and the monarch himself became a prisoner. The earl, however, effected his retreat, and recruiting his army, encountered, subsequently, the empress at Winchester, where he retrieved the fortunes of his royal master, and restored him to

* Richard, 5th Viscount Irvine, *m.* Lady Anne Howard, 3rd dau. of Charles, 3rd Earl of Carlisle, but by her (who *m.* 2ndly, in 1737, Col. James Douglas) had no issue. Of this lady there is a portrait in Parke's Walpole. She was a poetess, and printed the following works:—In 1759, *A Character of the Princess Elizabeth ; An Ode to George III.,* in 1761; *An Answer to some Verses of Lady Mary Wortley Montague,* printed in a *Supplement to Pope's Works; A Poetical Essay on Mr. Pope's Characters of Women.* For this last her ladyship was thus noticed in Duncombe's *Feminead*—

    " By generous views, one peeress more demands
    A grateful tribute from all female hands;
    One, who to shield them from the worst of foes,
    In their just cause dar'd Pope himself oppose.
    Their own dark forms, deceit and envy wear,
    By Irwin touch'd with truth's celestial spear."

---

freedom and a crown. In the heat of these feuds his lordship is accused of burning the Abbey of Wherwell, co. Southampton, because the nuns had harboured some of the partisans of the empress, but after peace was restored, he made restitution by founding the Cistertian Abbey, at Borley, in Kent, *anno* 1144. Upon the death of King STEPHEN, the Earl of Kent, then a widower, departed from England, and assuming the cowl in the Abbey of Laon, in Flanders, *d.* there about the year 1162. The earl had a son, who is said to have been cruelly murdered by the ministers of Theodoric, Earl of Flanders; in consequence of which, upon the decease of his lordship, the Earldom of Kent became EXTINCT; while his estates passed, acccording to "Hasted's History of Kent," to his only sister, Matilda, wife of Norman Fitz-Dering, ancestor of the Baronets Dering, of Surrenden Dering, co. Kent.

Arms—Girony of ten, or and az., an escutcheon, gu., a baton sinister, humettée, arg.

JEFFREYS—BARONS JEFFREYS, OF WEM, CO. SALOP.

By Letters Patent. dated 15 May, 1685.

Lineage.

The family of Jeffreys of Acton, near Wrexham, Denbighshire, a "race," observes Pennant, "which, after running uncontaminated from an ancient stock, had the disgrace of producing George Jeffreys, Chancellor of England," is a junior branch of the honourable stem of Jones, of Lwynon, in the same county and vicinity, still flourishing, after a succession of twenty generations, at that seat. Their progenitor was TUDOR TREVOR, Lord of Hereford, a powerful chieftain at the close of the 10th and beginning of the 11th centuries, who *m.* A.D. 907, Angharad, dau. of Howel Ddâ, King of South Wales, and had issue,

   I. GRONWY AP TUDOR TREVOR, Lord of Hereford, who *d.* without male issue,

   II. Lluddoka, ap Tudor Trevor. Lord of both Maelors and Oswestry, progenitor of 1 Mostyns, of Mostyn, co Flint, baronets, whose heir-general is Edward-Price-Lloyd Mostyn, 2nd Lord Mostyn ; 2 Mostyns of Lluesog and Segroyt, represented by the present THOMAS-ARTHUR-BERTIE MOSTYN, Esq., of those places ; 3 Mostyns, of Talacre, baronets, and Mostyns, Lords Vaux ; 4 Trevors, of Brynkynallt, from whom derives maternally LORD ARTHUR-EDWIN HILL, of Bryntrynallt, who has assumed the name and arms of TREVOR ; 5 Trevors of Allington, ancestors of Trevors, of Trevallyn. from whom descends with other co-heirs Boscowen Trevor Griffith, Esq., of Trevallyn Hall ; 6 Lloyd of Leighton Knowles ; 7 Lloyd, of Penley ; 8 Wynn, of Eyarth ; 9 Pennant, of Downing ; 10 Pennant, Lord Penrhyn ; 11 Dymoke, of Penley Hall ; 12 Eyton, of Eyton ; 13 Eyton, of Rhuabon ; 14 Edwards, of Kilhendre ; 15 Edwardes, of Shrewsbury, baronets ; 16 Vaughan, of Burlton.

   III. DINGAD AP TUDOR TREVOR, of whose line we have to treat.

The 3rd son,

DINGAD AP TUDOR TREVOR, was grandfather of CYNRIC AP RHIWALLON AP DINGAD, Lord of Whittington, slain A.D. 1073, who by Judith his wife, dau. of Ivor Hên, Lord of Rhôs, had issue,

   I. Ednyfed ap Cynric, progenitor of 1 the Denbighshire house of Bersham ; 2 Broughton, of Broughton, from whom derived as co-heirs, 1 the present Whitehall Dodd, Esq., of Llannech and Cloverley Hall ; 2 Davises, of Gwysaney, represented as heir-general by Philip Davies Cooke, Esq., of Owston, Gwysanney and Havod-y-wern ; 3 Broughton, of Marchwiel ; 4 Powel, of Alrhey.

   II. Hwfa ap Cynric, father of a dau. and heir, Angharad, who *m.* Cynric ap Jorwerth, Lord of Brynfenigle, and was by him, mother of a son,

      Ednyfed Vychan, Lord of Brynfenigle, ancestor of the Morgans, of Goulden Grove ; Williams-Bulkeleys, baronets; Lloyd, of Plymog, Gwerclas and Bashall, and THE ROYAL HOUSE OF TUDOR.

   III. NINIAU AP CYNRIC.

   IV. Llewelyn ap Cynric, *d. s. p., m.*

The 3rd son,

NINIAU AP CYNRIC, was grandfather of IORWERTH VYCHAM, of Llwynon, co. Denbigh, ap Ieuaf ap Niniau, who had issue,

1. Griffith ap Jorwerth Vychan, of Llwynon, who *m.* Margaret, dau. of Rhys Vychan, and had with other issue, an eldest and 4th son,

    Jorwerth ap Griffith, from whom derived 12th in descent, John Jones, Esq., of Llwynon, æt. fifteen, A.D. 1657, father of two sons, JOHN, Thomas, seated at Plâs Hên, co. Montgomery, whose son, John Jones, of Plâs Hên, had a dau. and eventual heir, Mary, mother by her husband, John Hughes, Esq., of Pen-y-Clawdd, co. Denbigh, of the late William Hughes, Esq., of that place (*see* BURKE's *Landed Gentry*). From the elder son, John Jones, Esq., of Llwynon, derive 1 Thomas-Love-Duncombe Jones Parry, Esq., of Madryn Castle, paternal representative of Jones, of Llwynon; 2 Robert-Lloyd-Jones Parry, Esq., of Aberdinant; 3 Thomas-Parry-Jones Parry, Esq., of Llwynon; 4 Lieut.-Colonel William-Parry Yale, of Plas-yn Yale, co. Denbigh, who assumed the name of Yale, in substitution of that of Parry.

    The 4th son of Griffith ap Jorwerth, viz.,

    David Goch ap Griffith, was ancestor of Roberts, of Havod-y-bwch, co. Denbigh, whose eventual heiress, Mary, dau. of Hugh Roberts. Esq., of Havod-y-bwch, *m.* David Lloyd, Esq., of Hendwr and Tyfôs, in Edeirnion, co. Merioneth, son of Thomas Lloyd, of Typôs, by Susan, dau. and heir of Nathaniel Jones, Esq., of Hendwr, Of this marriage, there was issue a son and two daus.,

      1 Gwyn Lloyd, Esq., of Hendwr and of Gwersyllt Park, co. Denbigh, who *m.* 12 March, 1746, Sarah, sister of Sir Rowland Hill, Bart., of Hawkestone, and *d. s. p. leg.* 19 March, 1774.

      I. Catherine, co-heir of Hendwr, Tyfôs and Gwersyllt, *d. unm.*, æt. ninety, March, 1787.

      II Mary, co-heir and eventually sole heir of Hendwr, Tyfôs and Gwersyllt, *d. unm.*, æt. ninety-five, and buried 5 April, 1789.

  II. Hwfa ap Jorwerth Vychan, of Havod-y-wern, ancestor of the house of Havod-y-wern, whose heir-general is the present Philip Davies Cooke, of Owston, Gwysaney and Havod-y-wern, Esq.

  III. IORWERTH VYCHAN AP IORWERTH VYCHAN.

The 3rd son,

IORWERTH VYCHAN AP IORWERTH was ancestor of HUGH AP ROBERT, of Acton, co. Denbigh, who *m.* Jonet, eldest dau. and co-heiress of Madoc Lloyd ap Llewelyn, of the line of Tudor Trevor, and was father of JEFFREY AP HUGH, of Acton, whose son,

JOHN JEFFREYS, Esq., one of the judges of the North Wales circuit, *m.* Margaret, dau. of William Lloyd, Esq., of Halghton, co. Flint, and was father of

JOHN JEFFREYS, Esq., of Acton, and Ryeton, living in 1654. Of this gentleman there was preserved at Acton a good portrait, painted in 1690, the eighty-second year of his age. He survived all his children. By Margaret, his wife, dau. of Sir Thomas Ireland, Knt., of Beausay, near Warrington, co. Lancaster, he had issue, besides George, his 5th son, of whom presently, an eldest son, John Jeffreys, Esq., of Ryeton, who *m.* Dorothy, dau. of Sir Griffith Williams, of Penrhyn and of Marle, co. Caernarvon, Baronet, so created, 17 June, 1661, and dying in 1670, æt. thirty-four, was by her father of a son Griffith Jeffreys. A brother of George Jeffreys, was dean of Rochester, and *d.* on his road to visit the chancellor, when confined in the Tower. Another brother, Sir Thomas Jeffreys, was a knight of Alcantara, of whom there was a fine full-length portrait at Acton, in the costume and cross of the order, in reference to whom, it is observed by Pennant, that for the honour of the descendants of Tudor Trevor, the proofs of Sir Thomas's descent were admired even by the proud Spaniards, among whom he had long resided at Alicant and Madrid, rendering himself so acceptable to the Spanish ministry as to be recommended to our Court to succeed Lord Lansdowne, a promotion which was stopped by the revolution. Another son, the youngest, was canon of Canterbury, and grandfather of Dr. Jeffreys, residentiary of St. Paul's, in 1799. The 5th son of John Jeffreys,

SIR GEORGE JEFFREYS, Baronet, elevated to the peerage, 15 May, 1685, as BARON JEFFREYS, *of Wem, co. Salop*, was the infamous "JUDGE JEFFREYS." The rudiments of education he acquired at a school in the country, whence he removed to Westminster, and thence became student of the Middle Temple. He was subsequently a practising barrister, in good business, although it is asserted that he was never regularly called to the bar. His first official employment was that of a Welsh judge, from which he was promoted in 1680 to the chief justiceship of Chester. In 1681, he was created a baronet, and in two years afterwards sworn of the privy council, and constituted lord chief justice of the court of King's Bench. The conduct of this iniquitous Judge has rendered his memory odious, and made his name the most opprobrious epithet by which the bench can be assailed. His deeds in the west, after the suppression of Monmouth's rebellion, have been so indelibly im-

printed in blood, that the tide of time washes over them without removing a single stain; and so long as the English language finds a tongue JEFFREYS will be a synonyme for everything unjust, cruel, and tyrannical. In 1685 he was constituted lord high chancellor, and in the same year he presided as lord steward of England, at the trial of Lord Delamere, who was acquitted. Upon the landing of the Prince of Orange, Jeffreys attempted to withdraw in disguise from the kingdom, and for that purpose had got on board a Newcastle collier, which was to convey him to Hamburgh, but he was discovered, seized, brought before the lords of the council, and by them committed to the Tower, where he remained until his decease in 1689. By his wife, he had one surviving son, JOHN, his successor, and two daus., viz.,

  Margaret, *m.* to Sir Thomas Stringer, of Durance, Middlesex.
  Sarah, *m.* to George Harnage, colonel of marines, 3rd son of Edward Harnage, Esq., of Belswardyne.

His lordship *m.* 2ndly, Lady Jones, widow of Sir John Jones, of Fonmon, in Glamorganshire, and dau. of Sir Thomas Bloodworth. Lord Jefferys was *s.* by his son,

JOHN JEFFERYS, 2nd baron, who *m.* Lady Charlotte Herbert, dau. and heir of Philip, Earl of Pembroke, by whom he had an only surviving dau.,

  Henrietta-Louisa, who *m.* Thomas, 1st Earl of Pomfret, and was mother of
    GEORGE, 2nd Earl of Pomfret. (*See* BURKE's *Peerage*.)

His lordship *d.* in 1703, when the Barony of Jeffreys of Wem became EXTINCT. His widow *m.* Viscount Windsor.

Arms—Erm., a lion rampant and a canton, *sa.*, with a mullet for difference.

JENKINSON—EARL OF LIVERPOOL.

By Letters Patent, dated 28 May, 1796.

Lineage.

SIR ROBERT JENKINSON, of Walcot (son and heir of Sir Robert Jenkinson, of Walcot, co. Oxford, and the heir of the celebrated Anthony Jenkinson, employed by Queen ELIZABETH on many delicate missions, and twice as her ambassador in Russia), represented the co. of Oxford in the first and other parliaments of CHARLES I., and was created a baronet 16 May, 1661. Sir Robert was the friend of Sir Mathew Hale and the philosopher Robert Boyle. He *m.* Mary, dau. of Sir John Bankes, of Kingston Hall, co. Dorset, lord chief-justice of the court of Common Pleas; and he *d.* in 1677, leaving issue, together with one dau., an only son,

SIR ROBERT JENKINSON, also M.P. for the co. of Oxford; who *m.* Sarah, dau. of Thomas Tomlins, Esq., of Bromley, co. Middlesex, and sole heiress of her brother, by whom he had, surviving him, a dau. Mary, *m.* to Sir John-Jonathan Cope, Bart., of Brewerne, co. Oxford, and three sons,

  I. ROBERT, his successor, 3rd baronet.
  II. ROBERT-BANKES, 4th baronet.
  III. Charles, a col. in the army; *m.* Amarantha, dau. of Wolfran Cornewall, Esq., capt. R.N.; and *d.* 1750, leaving one dau., Elizabeth, *m.* to the Right Hon. Charles Wolfran Cornewall, Speaker of the House of Commons; and three sons,
    1 CHARLES, of whom presently, as 1st Lord Hawkesbury, 1st Earl of Liverpool, and 7th baronet.
    2 John, col. in the army, joint secretary for Ireland; *m.* Frances, dau. of Admiral Parker, and had issue,
      CHARLES, 10th baronet.
      John-Bankes, D.D., Lord Bishop of St. David's; *d.* 1840, leaving issue, with two daus. (one Augusta, *m.* to Arthur Tower, Esq., comm. R.N.), two sons,
      GEORGE-SAMUEL, 11th baronet.
        John-Henry, *b.* 1823; *m.* 17 November, 1852, Alice-Henrietta, dau. of Sir William Gordon Cumming, Bart., which lady was killed accidentally by an overdose of chloroform, 9 December, 1859.
      George, lieut.-col. of artillery; *d. unm.* in 1823.
      Robert-Henry, governor of Dover Castle.
      Fanny, *m.* to Sir W. Boothby, Bart.; *d.* in 1838.
    3 Robert, in the Guards; *d. unm.*

The elder son,
  SIR ROBERT JENKINSON, also M.P. for the co. of Oxford, *d. unm.* in 1717, and was *s.* by his brother,
  SIR ROBERT-BANKES JENKINSON, also M.P. for the co of Ox-

ford; *m.* Catherine, 3rd dau. of Sir Thomas Dashwood, Bart., and left at his decease two surviving sons, ROBERT and BANKES, successively 4th and 5th baronets; and on his decease in 1738, was *s.* by his eldest son,

SIR ROBERT JENKINSON, also M.P. for the co. of Oxford; he *d. unm.* in 1766, and was *s.* by his brother,

SIR BANKES JENKINSON, who also *d. unm.* in 1789, and was *s.* by his cou-in,

S R CHARLES JENKINSON, 1st Lord Hawkesbury, and 1st Earl of Liverpool, the eldest son of Charles, 3rd son of the 2nd baronet. This eminent person (*b.* 16 May, 1727) was educated at the Charter House, and was under-secretary of state in 1761, secretary to the Treasury in 1763, lord of the Admiralty in 1766, lord of the Treasury from 1767 to 1773, and chancellor of the duchy of Lancaster, he was elevated to the peerage as *Baron Hawkesbury, co. Gloucester,* in 1786, and advanced, 28 May, 1796, to the EARLDOM OF LIVERPOOL; *m.* 1st, Amelia, dau. of William Watts, Esq., governor of Fort William, in Bengal, by whom (who *d.* in 1770) he had an only son,

ROBERT-BANKES, 2nd Earl of Liverpool.

He *m.* 2ndly, in 1782, Catherine, dau. of Sir Cecil Bisshopp, Bart., relict of Sir Charles Cope, Bart., of Brewerne, and mother of the Duchess of Dorset, and Countess of Aboyne, by whom he had

CHARLES-CECIL COPE, 3rd Earl of Liverpool.
Charlotte, *m.* in 1807, to James-Walter, Earl of Verulam.

His lordship *d.* 17 December, 1808, and was *s.* by his eldest son,

SIR ROBERT-BANKES JENKINSON, Baron Hawkesbury, as 2nd Earl of Liverpool, *b.* 7 June, 1770; his lordship was FIRST LORD OF THE TREASURY from 1812 to 1827, and a K.G. He *d. s. p,* 4 December, 1828, having *m.* 1st, Lady Louisa-Theodora Hervey, 3rd dau. of the Bishop of Derry, 4th Earl of Bristol (*d.* in 1821); and 2ndly, Mary, dau. of Charles Chester, Esq., formerly Bagot, brother of the 1st Lord Bagot (*d.* in 1846). He was *s.* by his half brother,

SIR CHARLES-CECIL-COPE JENKINSON, G.C.B., *b.* in 1784; *m.* Julia-Evelyn Medley, only child of Sir George-Shuckburgh Evelyn, and by her (who *d.* 8 April, 1814), had issue, Catherina, *m.* to Lieut.-Colonel Vernon Harcourt; Selina, *m.* 1st, Viscount Milton, son of Earl Fitzwilliam; and 2ndly, George-Savile Foljambe, Esq., of Osberton Hall, co. Derby; Louisa, *m.* to John Cotes, Esq., of Woodcote Hall, Shropshire. The earl *d.* 3 September, 1851, without issue male, whereupon his peerage honours became EXTINCT, and the baronetcy passed to his cousin, SIR CHARLES JENKINSON, *b.* 23 February, 1779, for many years M.P. for Dover; *m.* Catherine, 5th dau. of Walter Campbell, Esq., of Shawfield, co. Lanark, and of Islay, co. Argyle, and had

Georgiana-Elizabeth, *m.* in 1833, to Walter Nugent, Esq., who *d.* 1864: their dau., Ismay, is wife of Lord Southampton.
Katherine-Frances, *m.* in 1833, to the late R.-S. Guinness, Esq., M.P.
Eleanora-Mary, *m.* in 1830, to Napoleon Lannes, Duc de Montebello, and *d.* 14 October, 1863.

Sir Charles *d.* 6 March, 1855, and was *s.* by his nephew, the present baronet, SIR GEORGE-SAMUEL JENKINSON, Bart., of Hawkesbury, co. Gloucester.

Arms—Az., a fess wavy, arg., charged with a cross patée, gu., in chief two estoiles, or.

JERMYN — BARONS JERMYN, OF ST, EDMUNDSBURY, CO. SUFFOLK, EARL OF ST. ALBANS.

Barony by Letters Patent, dated 8 September, 1643.
Earldom, by Letters Patent, dated 27 April, 1660.

Lineage.

SIR THOMAS DE JERMYN, *m.* Agnes, sister and co-heir of Thomas de Rushbroke, with whom he acquired the manor of Rushbroke, co. Suffolk. From this Sir Thomas descended

SIR THOMAS JERMYN, of Rushbroke, treasurer of the household to King CHARLES I., who had two sons,

I. Thomas, father of Thomas, 2nd baron.
II. HENRY, of whom we treat.

The 2nd son,

HENRY JERMYN, master of the horse to the queen, having devoted himself with a more than ordinary degree of zeal to the fortunes of his royal master, during the civil wars, was elevated to the peerage, 8 September, 1643, as BARON JERMYN, *of St. Edmundsbury, co. Suffolk,* with remainder, in default of male issue, to his elder brother, Thomas Jermyn. His lordship subsequently attended the queen into France, and presided over her majesty's small establishment for a great many years. While abroad he was employed in several embassies by King CHARLES II., and in consideration of all his faithful services, his lordship, immediately upon the Restoration, was created, by letters patent, dated at Breda, 27 April, 1660, EARL OF ST. ALBANS. He was soon after made a knight of the Garter, and constituted lord chamberlain of the household. His lordship *d. unm.* in 1683, when the Earldom of St. Albans became EXTINCT, and the Barony of Jermyn devolved upon (his deceased brother Thomas's son,) his nephew,

THOMAS JERMYN, 2nd Baron Jermyn. This nobleman was governor of Jersey. By Mary, his wife, he had issue,

A dau. ——, *m.* to Thomas Bond, Esq., and *d.* in the life-time of her father.
Mary, *m.* to Sir Robert Davers, Bart.
Merelina, *m.* 1st, to Sir William Spring, and 2ndly, to Sir William Gage, Bart., of Hengrave, but had no issue.
Penelope, *m.* to Grey-James Grove, Esq.
Delarivierre, *m.* to Sir Symonds D'Ewes, Bart.

He *d.* in 1703, when the Barony of Jermyn, of St. Edmundsbury, became EXTINCT.

Arms—Sa., a chevron, between two mullets, in pale, arg.

JERMYN—BARON JERMYN, OF DOVER.

By Letters Patent, dated 13 May, 1685.

Lineage.

HENRY JERMYN, next brother of Thomas, 2nd Lord Jermyn, of St. Edmundsbury, was himself elevated to the peerage, 13 May, 1685, as BARON JERMYN, *of Dover.* His lordship *d. s. p.* in 1708, when the barony became EXTINCT—and his estates devolved upon his nieces, the daus. of the above mentioned brother.

Arms—Same as JERMYN, Earl of St. Albans, with the requisite difference.

JERVIS—EARL OF ST. VINCENT.

By Letters Patent, dated 23 June, 1797.

Lineage.

JOHN JERVIS, Esq., 2nd son of Swynfen Jervis, Esq., a lawyer of eminence (descended from James Jervis, of Chatkyll, co. Stafford, living *temp.* HENRY VIII.), by Elizabeth, dau. of George Parker, Esq., of Park Hall, was *b.* at Meaford, 19 January, 1734, and having entered the royal navy at a very early period of life (in his tenth year), attained the highest honours of that gallant profession, and was elevated to the peerage, 23 June, 1797, by the titles of *Baron Jervis, of Meaford, co. Stafford,* and EARL OF ST. VINCENT, as a reward for the splendid victory he had achieved, in that year, over the Spanish fleet off Cape St. Vincent. His lordship was nominated first lord of the Admiralty in 1801; and created, 27 April, in the same year, VISCOUNT ST. VINCENT, with remainder, in default of male issue, to his nephews, William-Henry Ricketts, and Edward-Jervis Ricketts successively, and afterwards to these gentlemen's sister, Mary, Countess of Northesk, and her male descendants. The earl *m.* in 1783, Martha, dau. of Lord Chief Baron Parker, which lady *d. s. p.* in 1816. His lordship *d.* 13 March, 1823, when the earldom and barony EXPIRED, but the viscounty devolved upon his younger nephew (the elder, Captain William-Henry Ricketts, of the royal navy, having been unfortunately drowned 26 January, 1805, leaving only daus.), EDWARD-JERVIS, 2nd viscount, who was 2nd son of William-Henry Ricketts, Esq., of Canaan, in the island of Jamaica, by the deceased earl's sister, Mary, who *d.* in 1828. His grandson is CARNEGIE-ROBERT-JOHN JERVIS, present and 3rd Viscount.

Arms—Sa., a chev., erm., between three martlets, arg.

JOHNSTONE—MARQUESS OF ANNANDALE.

By Letters Patent, dated 4 June, 1701.

Lineage.

This family can be traced, through ancestors of baronial and knightly rank, to the reign of ALEXANDER II., King of Scotland, when

HUGO DE JOHNSTONE flourished, and was proprietor of large estates in East Lothian. He was father of

SIR JOHN DE JOHNSTONE, of the co. Dumfries, who made a donation of a portion of his lands in East Lothian to the monastery of Soltra in 1285. His son

JOHN DE JOHNSTONE, was witness to a charter of lands in Annandale, granted by Thomas Randolph, Earl of Moray, before the year 1332. His son

GILBERT DE JOHNSTONE, d. about 1360, and was s. by his son,

SIR JOHN DE JOHNSTONE, a man of great note in the reign of King ROBERT II. He was Warden of the west marches in 1371, and fought valiantly against the English Borderers in 1378. He d. in 1383, and was s. by his son,

SIR JOHN DE JOHNSTONE, of Johnstone. He was nominated by the Earl of Douglas the chief Warden of the marches, one of the sureties for keeping a truce with the English in 1398. He d. in 1420, and was s. by his son,

SIR ADAM JOHNSTONE, of Johnstone. He assisted at the victory gained over the English at Sark in 1448. He was instrumental in suppressing the rebellion of the Douglases against the king in 1455, for which service the king granted him the lands of Pedinaine in Lanarkshire. By his 1st wife he had a son JOHN, his heir. His 2nd wife was Lady Janet Dunbar, only dau. of George Dunbar, 11th Earl of March, and maternally descended from the royal family of Scotland, and from the Anglo Saxon kings through Robert Bruce, the competitor for the crown, by whom he had a son MATTHEW, of Pedinaine, ancestor to the Johnstones, Baronets of Westerhall, the Johnstones of Alva, and the Johnstones, Baronets of Hackness. The Johnstones of Elphinstone claim a descent from Sir Adam through their ancestor, Sir Gilbert Johnstone, who m. the heiress of Elphinstone before 1472. But his filiation is not proved. Sir Adam d. in 1455, and was s. by his eldest son,

SIR JOHN JOHNSTONE, of Johnstone, who was one of the Wardens of the marches in 1459. He d. before 1484. He m. Mary, eldest dau. of John, 4th Lord Maxwell, by whom he had issue,

I. JAMES, his heir.
II. John, of Wamphrey, whose line became EXTINCT, when the estate reverted to the family of Johnstone.

His son,

JAMES JOHNSTONE, of Johnstone, was father of

ADAM JOHNSTONE, of Johnstone, who was father of

JAMES JOHNSTONE, of Johnstone, who had a charter of the lands of Whiteriggs and Meiklehouse, in 1516. He d. in 1529, and left with other issue, a son,

JOHN JOHNSTONE, of Johnstone. He had various charters of lands in 1542, 1545, and 1550. He fought at the battle of Pinkie in 1547. He was appointed commissioner to settle disputes in the borders in 1552, and d. in 1558. He m. 1st, Elizabeth Jardine by whom he had issue,

JAMES, his heir.
Robert.
Dorothea, wife of John Maitland, of Auchincastle.
Margaret, wife of C. Irving, of Bonshaw.

He m. 2ndly, Nicola Douglas, dau. of Douglas of Drumlanrig, by whom he had James and John. His eldest son, James Johnstone, d. v. p., in 1559, leaving by his wife, Margaret Hamilton, a son, JOHN, successor to his grandfather, and two daus., Margaret, wife of Sir Robert Douglas, of Cashogle; and Jean, wife of Sir William Levingstone, of Jerviswood.

JOHN JOHNSTONE, of Johnstone, s. his grandfather in 1568. He was appointed by King JAMES VI., Warden of the west marches, and Justice-general in 1570. He d. in 1586. By his wife, Margaret, dau. of Sir Walter Scott, of Buccleugh, he had issue a son, JAMES, and three daus. Margaret, wife of James Johnstone of Westerhall, and d. s. p.; Elizabeth, wife of Alexander Jardine, of Applegirth; and Grizzel, wife of Sir Robert Maxwell, of Orchardton. His son,

SIR JAMES JOHNSTONE, of Johnstone, was knighted at the coronation of Queen ANNE of Denmark, and was appointed Warden of the west marches in 1596. He was murdered by John, Lord Maxwell, in 1608. He m. Sarah, sister of John,

Lord Herries (who afterwards m. John Fleming, Earl of Wigton and Hugh Montgomery, Viscount Airds), by whom he had an only son,

JAMES JOHNSTONE, of Johnstone, who in 1633, was created by King CHARLES I., Lord Johnstone, of Lochwood, to him and his heirs male. The same monarch created him, in 1643, Earl of Hartfell to him and his heirs male. He d. in 1653. He m. 1st, Lady Margaret Douglas, eldest dau. of William, 1st Earl of Queensberry, by whom he had issue,

I. JAMES, 2nd Earl of Hartfell.
II. William, } both of whom d. s. p.
III. Thomas, }
I. Mary, wife 1st, of Sir George Graham, of Netherby; and 2ndly, of Sir George Fletcher, of Huttonhall.
II. Janet, wife of Sir William Murray, of Stanhope, Bart.
III. Margaret, wife of Sir Robert Dalzell, of Glenae.

He m. 2ndly, Elizabeth, dau. of Sir Samuel Johnstone, of Elphinstone; and 3rdly, 1647, Lady Margaret Hamilton, 3rd dau. of Thomas, 1st Earl of Haddington, widow of David, Lord Carnegie. He was s. by his only son,

JAMES JOHNSTONE, 2nd Earl of Hartfell. The Earldom of Annandale became EXTINCT in 1658, on the death of James Murray, 2nd earl. And in 1661, the Earl of Hartfell made a surrender of his title to King CHARLES II., who also in 1661, granted a new patent to "James, Earl of Annandale and Hartfell, Viscount Annand, Lord Johnstone of Lochwood, Lochmaben, Moffatdale, and Evandale, and to the heirs male, whom failing to the eldest heirs female of his body, and the eldest heirs male of the body of such heirs female, with the original precedency of the Earldom of Hartfell." He m. Lady Henrietta Douglas, 4th dau. of William, 1st Marquis of Douglas, by whom he had issue,

I. WILLIAM, his successor.
II. John, who d. s. p.
I. Mary, wife in 1670, of William, 18th Earl of Crawford, and 2nd Earl of Lindsay.
II. Margaret, wife of Sir James Montgomery, of Skelmorley.
III. Harriet, wife in 1684, of Sir John Carmichael, of Bonnytown.
IV. Anne.

The earl d. in 1672, and was s. by his son,

WILLIAM JOHNSTONE, 3rd Earl of Annandale and Hartfell. He was a minor. In 1679 Sir James Johnstone, of Westerhall, was cited as his nearest of kin. He was lord of the Treasury, and president of the parliament of Scotland in 1695. He was high commissioner to the general assembly of the church of Scotland in 1701. He was created 4 June, 1701, MARQUESS OF ANNANDALE, Earl of Hartfell, Viscount Annand, Lord Johnstone of Lochwood, Lochmaben, Moffatdale, and Evandale, to him and his heirs male, whatever. In 1703, he was president of the privy council. In 1704, he was made a knight of the Thistle. In 1705 one of the principal secretaries of state. In 1714, keeper of the privy seal. In 1715 he was lord lieutenant of the cos. of Dumfries, Kirkcudbright and Peebles. He d. 1721. He m. 1st, in 1682, Sophia, dau. and heir of John Fairholm, of Craigiehall, by Sophia, dau. of Joseph Johnston, of Hilton, by whom he had issue,

I. JAMES, 2nd marquess.
II. John, d. young.
III. William, d. unm., 1721.
I. Henrietta, wife of Charles, 4th Earl of Hopetoun, of whom hereafter.

He m. 2ndly in 1718, Charlotte, only dau. and heir of John Vanden Bempde, and by her (who m. 2ndly, Colonel John Johnstone, 2nd son of Sir William Johnstone, Baronet, of Westerhall, by whom he had issue, Sir Richard Vanden Bempde Johnstone, Baronet of Hackness-hall, and Charles), he had issue,

I. GEORGE, 3rd marquess.
II. John, d. unm., 1742.

The marquess was s. by his eldest son,

JAMES JOHNSTONE, 2nd Marquess of Annandale, who dying unm. in 1730, was s. by his half brother,

GEORGE JOHNSTONE, 3rd Marquess of Annandale, who d. unm. in 1792, in the seventy-second year of his age. On the death of the Marquess his large property was divided. The great landed estates of the Annandale family devolved on his grand-nephew, James Hope, 3rd Earl of Hopetoun. The large accumulation of personal property was divided amongst his next of kin, while the Vanden Bempde fortune, which he had inherited from his mother the Marchioness, devolved on her son by her 2nd marriage, Sir Richard Vanden Bempde Johnstone, Bart. With the 3rd Marquess of Annandale, EXPIRED the male line of Sir John Johnstone, of Johnstone, the eldest son of Sir Adam Johnstone, of Johnstone, who d. in 1755; and consequently the representative of Matthew Johnstone, of

Pedinaine, Sir Adam's 2nd son, became head of the house of Johnstone. This was Sir James Johnstone, 4th Baronet, of Westerhall, who became claimant of the dignity of Marquess of Annandale ; as that title had been granted to the 1st Marquess and his heirs male whatsoever. We therefore proceed to trace the descent of the knightly family of Johnstone, of Westerhall, as heir male of the house of Johnstone, and claimant of its highest honours. But before doing so, we must trace the descent of the heir general of the Johnstone family through Lady Henrietta Johnstone, dau. of the 1st, and half sister of the 3rd marquess, and wife of Charles, 1st Earl of Hopetoun, by whom she had issue,

I. JOHN, 2nd Earl of Hopetoun.
II. Charles, who inherited through his mother the estate of Craigiehall. He m. 1st in 1733, Catherine, only dau. and heir of Sir William Weir or Vere, Baronet, of Blackwood, by whom he had with other issue,

  1 William, b. 1736, grandfather of the present William Edward Hope Vere, of Craigiehall and Blackwood.
  2 John, b 1739, who had issue, Charles, b. 1763, lord president of the court of session in Scotland ; John, a general officer; William, of whom hereafter as husband of Lady Anne Hope Johnstone, and father of J J. Hope Johnstone, the heir general of the Annandale family.

Charles-Hope Vere m. 2ndly, Lady Anne Vane, d. of Henry, 1st Earl of Darlington, by whom he had issue. He m. 3rdly, Helen Dunbar, by whom he had issue.

I. Sophia, m. James, Earl of Findlater.
II. Henrietta, m. Francis, Lord Napier.
III. Margaret, m. John Dundas, of Duddingston.
IV. Helen, m. James Watson, of Saughton.
V. Christian, m. Thomas Graham, of Balgowan.
VI. Charlotte, m. Thomas, Lord Erskine.

Henrietta, Countess of Hopetoun, d. in 1750, and the earl, her husband, d. in 1742. Their eldest son,
JOHN, 2nd Earl of Hopetoun, was b. 1704. He m. 1st, 1733, Lady Anne Ogilvie, dau. of James, 5th Earl of Findlater, by whom he had issue,

I. Charles, Lord Hope, who. d. v. p.
II. JAMES, 3rd Earl of Hopetoun.
I. Elizabeth, wife of Henry, Earl of Drumlanrig, eldest son of Charles, 3rd Duke of Queensberry.
II. Henrietta.
III. Sophia, wife of Charles, 8th Earl of Haddington.

The earl m. 2ndly, in 1762, Jean, dau. of Robert Oliphant, of Rossie, by whom he had a son,

I. JOHN, a distinguished general, created, for his great military services, Lord Niddrie, in 1814. On his brother's death, in 1817, he became 4th Earl of Hopetoun. By his 2nd wife, Dorothea, dau. of Sir John Wedderburn, Bart of Ballindean, he had numerous issue. His great-grandson is JOHN-ADRIAN-LOUIS, 7th and present EARL OF HOPETOUN.
I. Lady Jean, wife, 1st, of Henry, 1st Viscount Melville, and 2ndly, of Lord Wallace.

The earl m. 3rdly, in 1767, Lady Elizabeth Leslie, 2nd dau. of Alexander, 5th Earl of Leven and Melville, by whom he had issue,

I. Charles, a general officer, m. Louisa-Anne, dau. of George-Finch Hatton.
II. Alexander, of Luffness, a general officer, G.C.B., m. Georgiana Brown, by whom he had numerous issue.
I. Elizabeth, wife of Rev. John Kemp.
II. Charlotte, wife of the Right Hon. Charles Hope, lord president of the court of Session.
III. Margaret, wife of Alexander Maclean, of Ardgour.
IV. Mary, wife of Sir Patrick-Murray Baronet, of Auchtertyre.

The earl d. in 1781, and was s. by his eldest surviving son,
JAMES, 3rd Earl of Hopetoun. On the death of his grand-uncle, George, 3rd Marquess of Annandale, he became heir general of the Annandale family, and inherited the great Annandale estates, together with a claim to the Earldoms of Annandale and Hartfell. He was, in 1809, created a British peer, as Lord Hopetoun. He m. in 1766, Elizabeth, eldest dau. of George, 6th Earl of Northesk, by whom he had issue,

I. Lady ANNE, of whom hereafter.
II. Georgiana, wife in 1793, of the Hon. Andrew Cochrane, son of the 8th Earl of Dundonald.
III. Jemima, wife in 1803, of Admiral Sir George Hope, of Carriden, G.C.B.

On the death of the 3rd Earl of Hopetoun, in 1817, his eldest dau. Anne, became the heir general of the Johnstone family, as LADY ANNE-HOPE JOHNSTONE, of Annandale. She m. in 1792, Admiral Sir William Hope, G.C.B., grandson of the Hon. Charles-Hope Vere, of Craigie Hall, and by him (who m. 2ndly, Maria, Countess Dowager of Athlone, and d. in 1831), she had issue,

I. JOHN-JAMES, her heir.
II. William-James, vice-admiral, b. 1798, m. Ellen, dau. of Sir Thomas Kirkpatrick, Bart., and had issue.

301

III. Charles-James, captain R. N., b. 1801; m. Eliza Wood, and had issue. He d. 1835.
IV. George-James. captain R. N., b. 1803, m. Maria Rankine, and d. in 1842; having had issue.
I. Mary, wife of Hon. and Right Rev. Hugh Percy, bishop of Carlisle.
II. Eliza.

Lady Anne-Hope Johnstone, of Annandale, d. in 1818, and was s. by her eldest son,
JOHN-JAMES-HOPE JOHNSTONE, of Annandale, b. 1796; m. in 1816, Alicia-Anne, dau. of George Gordon, of Hallhead, by whom he had issue,

I. William-James, b. 1819, m. the Hon. Octavia-Sophia-Bosville Macdonald, youngest dau. of the 3rd Lord Macdonald. He d. in 1850, leaving, with other issue, an eldest son, JOHN-JAMES.
II. George-Gordon, m. 1845, Adelaide. dau. of Sir George Sinclair, Bart., of Ulbster, by whom he had issue.
III. John Charles.
IV. Robert-Gordon, m. in 1855, Agnes, dau. of Col. Swanston.
V. Charles, d. 1855.
VI. David-Baird, m. 1860, Margaret-Elizabeth, dau. of Col. Grierson.
I. Anne-Jemima. II. Lucy-Wilhelmina.
III. Alice, wife in 1845, of Sir Graham Montgomery, Bart., of Stanhope.

John-James-Hope Johnstone is M.P. for the co. of Dumfries. He is heir general of the family of Johnstone, and claimant of the Earldom of Annandale and Hartfell.
On the death of the 3rd Marquess of Annandale, the headship of the house of Johnstone, and the claim to the marquessate of Annandale devolved on
SIR JAMES JOHNSTONE, 4th Baronet of Westerhall, descended from
MATTHEW JOHNSTONE, son of Sir John Johnstone, of Johnstone, by his 2nd wife, Janet Dunbar, dau. of George, 11th Earl of March, and widow of John, 1st Lord Seton. In consequence of this maternal descent, the Johnstones of Westerhall claim the blood of the ancient kings of Scotland, and the Saxon kings of England, WILLIAM THE CONQUEROR, and the Capetian kings of France. Lady Agnes Randolph, the wife of the 10th Earl of March, having been grand-daughter of Isabel, sister of King ROBERT BRUCE, and Christian Bruce. the wife of the 7th Earl of March, having been dau. of Robert Bruce, the competitor for the Scottish crown. Matthew Johnstone, of Pedinaine, d. in 1491. By his wife, Elizabeth Graham, a dau. of the house of Montrose, he had a son,
JOHN JOHNSTONE, of Westerhall, who d. 1508. His son,
HERBERT JOHNSTONE, of Westerhall, d. 1555 He had a son, HERBERT JOHNSTONE, who d. v. p., in 1545. By a dau. of the family of Douglas, Earl of Angus, he had a son,
JAMES JOHNSTONE, of Westerhall, who s. his grandfather, and d. in 1570. By his wife, Flora, dau. of John Somerville, of Camnethan, grandson of the 3rd Lord Somerville, he had a son,
SIR JAMES JOHNSTONE, of Westerhall, who m. 1st, Margaret Johnstone, dau. of his relation, Sir John Johnstone, of Johnstone, by whom he had no issue ; 2ndly, the Hon. Euphemia Oliphant, dau. of Laurence, 4th Lord Oliphant, by Lady Margaret Hay, dau. of George, 6th Earl of Errol. He d. in 1639, and was s. by his son,
JAMES JOHNSTONE, of Westerhall. He m. Isabella, dau. of Sir William Scott, of Harden, and d. in 1643. His son,
SIR JAMES JOHNSTONE, of Westerhall, was cited in 1679, as nearest of kin to WILLIAM JOHNSTONE, 3rd Earl of Annandale and Hartfell, afterwards 1st Marquess of Annandale. He m. Margaret, dau. of James Bannatyne, of Corehouse, by Grizzel, dau. of Sir James Lockhart, of Lee and Carnwath, by whom he had issue,

I. JOHN, his heir.
II. WILLIAM, of whom presently.

He d. in 1699, and was s. by his son,
JOHN JOHNSTONE, of Westerhall, created a baronet in 1700. He m. Rachel, eldest dau. of James Johnstone, of Schiennes, brother of Sir Archibald Johnstone, Lord Wariston, by Anna Hamilton, dau. of Sir John Hamilton, lord register of Scotland, brother of Thomas, 1st Earl of Haddington. By her he had issue, a dau. Philadelphia, wife of Douglas, of Dornock. Sir John Johnstone d. in 1711, without male issue, and was s. by his brother,
SIR WILLIAM JOHNSTONE, 2nd baronet, of Westerhall. He m. Henrietta, 2nd dau. of James Johnstone, of Schiennes, brother of Lord Wariston, by Anna Hamilton, dau. of Sir John Hamilton, brother to Thomas, 1st Earl of Haddington, by whom he had,

I JAMES, his heir.
II. John, a colonel in the army, m. Charlotte Vanden Bempde,

Dowager Marchioness of Annandale, mother of George, 3rd Marquess, and *d.* in 1743, leaving issue,

1 Richard, who was created a baronet in 1795, and who *d.* in 1792, *s.* to the great maternal property of his half-brother, the 3rd Marquess, and became Sir Richard-Vanden-Bempde Johnstone, Baronet of Hackness Hall, co. York. By his wife. Margaret Scott, he left issue, JOHN, and Charles, in holy orders, who had issue. Sir Richard was *s.* by his son, Sir John-Vanden-Bempde Johnstone, 2nd baronet, who, by his wife, Louisa-Augusta Vernon, dau. of the Archbishop of York, had HARCOURT, created *Lord Derwent*, 1881.

2 Charles, who left numerous issue.

Sir William Johnstone, 2nd baronet, of Westerhall, was *s.* by his eldest son,

SIR JAMES JOHNSTONE, 3rd baronet, of Westerhall. He *m.* the Hon. Barbara Murray, dau. of Alexander, 4th Lord Elibank, by whom he had, with other children, who *d. unm.*, four sons and four daus., viz.,

I. JAMES, his heir.
II. William, who *s.* his brother.
III. George, who carried on the line of the family.
IV. John, of Alva, *b.* 1734, acquired great distinction and a large fortune in India, and greatly contributed to the victory of Plassey, where he commanded the artillery. He *m.* Elizabeth-Caroline Keene, dau. of Colonel Keene, brother of Edmund Keene, bishop of Ely, and Sir Benjamin Keene, minister at the court of Spain. He purchased Alva, Hangingshaw, and other estates in Scotland. He was for sometime a member of parliament, and *d.* in 1795, in his sixty-second year. He had issue, with a dau. Elizabeth, the wife of James Gonlon, of Craig, an only son,

James-Raymond Johnstone, of Alva, who *m.* Mary-Elizabeth, dau. of Montague Cholmeley, of Easton Hall, and sister of Sir Montague Cholmeley, Bart., by whom he had issue,

1 JAMES, his heir.
2 John, *b.* 1802, a colonel in the service of the East India Company, *m.* 1844, Caroline, dau. of the Rev. — Pannel. by whom he left issue, a dau. Mary-Elizabeth. Colonel Johnstone perished with half of his regiment in the Indian seas, in May, 1854.
3 Montague-Cholmeley, *b.* 1804. major-general in the army and commander of the forces in the Mauritius. He *m.* Louisa Somerset, dau. of Gen. Sir Henry Somerset, and grand-daughter of Lord Charles Somerset, son of the 5th Duke of Beaufort, by whom he has issue four sons and four daus.
4 George-Dempster, in holy orders, rector of Creed, in Cornwall. He *m.* Mary Anne, dau. of — Hawkins, of Bignor, in Sussex, brother of Sir Christopher Hawkins, Bart., of Trewithan, in Cornwall, by whom he has a son Haywood, and a dau.
5 Charles-Kinnaird, captain in the East Indian naval service, knight of the Lion and Sun. He *m.* Elizabeth, dau. and heir of Francis Gordon, of Craig. He has taken her name, on her succession to the family estates, and has issue four daus., of whom the eldest, Elizabeth-Isabella; *m.* Hugh Scott, of Gala.
6 Henry-Wedderburn, *b.* 1810, commander R.N., is *m.* and has issue.
7 Robert-Abercrombie, *b.* 1813, in holy orders, *m.* Anne Walker, and has no issue.
8 Francis-William, *b.* 1818, a captain in the army; *m.* Maria, dau. of Pierce Mahony, by whom he has issue.
1 Elizabeth-Caroline, *m.* 1829, the Rev. John-Hamilton Gray, of Carntyne, in the county of Lanark, by whom she has issue, a dau. Caroline-Maria-Agnes-Robina, wife of John-Anstruther Thomson, of Charleton, co. Fife. Mrs. Hamilton Gray has acquired great distinction in the literary world by her works on Etruscan and Roman history, and on Etruscan antiquities.
2 Emily-Sarah.
3 Mary-Anne, *m.* 1839, James Dewar, by whom she has issue.
4 Catherine-Lucy.
5 Sophia-Matilda, *m.* 1832, Sir John-Muir Mackenzie, Bart., of Delvine, co. Perth, by whom she has issue. Her eldest son is Sir Alexander-Muir Mackenzie, 3rd Baronet of Delvine.
6 Jemima-Eleanora, *m.* 1848, Lord Frederick Beauclerk, of Little Grimsby Hall, co. Lincoln, 2nd son of William, 8th Duke of St. Albans, by whom she has issue, Neilthorpe and Frederick.
7 Mary-Cecilia, *m.* 1837, the Hon. Lawrence-Harman-King Harman, of Newcastle, co. Longford, son of General Viscount Lorton, and heir to his grandfather's (the Earl of Rosse) estates in Longford, by whom she has issue, Edward and Wentworth, and several other sons, and a dau. Frances.
8 Charlotte-Octavia, wife of Major James-Harrison Cholmeley, 2nd son of Sir Montague Cholmeley, Bart., who *d.*1853, without issue.

James-Raymond Johnstone, *d.* at Alva House, in 1830, and was *s.* by his eldest son, James Johnstone, of Alva, *b.* 1801, formerly M.P. for the cos. Kinross and Clackmannan. He *m.* 1st, 1845, the Hon. Augusta Norton, youngest sister of Lord Grantley, by whom he has issue, Augustus, *b.*

302

1847, and Caroline. He *m.* 2ndly, 1862, Sarah L'Estrange, dau. of Colonel L'Estrange, of Moystown

I. Barbara, *m.* Charles, 6th Lord Kinnaird, and mother of the 7th Lord Kinnaird, and *d.* in 1765.
II. Margaret, *m.* David, Lord Ogilvie, eldest son of John, 4th Earl of Airlie, and was mother of David Ogilvie, titular Earl of Airlie, and of Lady Margaret, wife of Sir John Wedderburn, Bart. She *d.* 1757.
III. Elizabeth.
IV. Charlotte, wife of James Balmain. Her dau. Caroline, Elizabeth, *m.* the Hon. Fletcher Norton, Baron of Exchequer-and was mother of Lord Grantley.

Sir James Johnstone *d.* 1772, and was *s.* by his eldest son,
SIR JAMES JOHNSTONE, 4th baronet, of Westerhall, *b.* 1725. On the death of the 3rd Marquess of Annandale, in 1792, he became head of the family of Johnstone, and claimant of the Marquessate of Annandale. He was for many years M.P. for co. Dumfries. He *d. unm.* in 1794, and was *s.* by his next surviving brother,
SIR WILLIAM JOHNSTONE, 5th baronet, of Westerhall, *b.* 1729, and *d.* one of the richest subjects in Great Britain, in 1805. He *m.* 1st, in 1760, Frances, dau. and heir of Daniel Pulteney, cousin and heir of William, Earl of Bath, and on succeeding to the immense fortune of that family he took the name of PULTENEY. By her he had an only dau., Henrietta-Laura Johnstone Pulteney, created Baroness of Bath, in 1792, and Countess of Bath, in 1803. She *m.* in 1794, Sir James Murray, Bart., and *d. s. p.* in 1808, when her Earldom and Barony became EXTINCT. Sir William *m.* 2ndly, in 1804, Margaret, dau. of Sir William Stirling, Bart., of Ardoch, widow of Andrew Stewart, of Torrance and Castlemilk, by whom he had no issue. Sir William, who was for many years a distinguished member of parliament, was *s.* in 1805, by his nephew, JOHN, son of his next brother,
GEORGE JOHNSTONE, *b.* 1750. He was a member of parliament, governor of Florida, and commissioner to treat for peace with America. He *m.* Charlotte Dee, (who *m.* 2ndly, Admiral Nugent,) and dying in 1787, he left one son,
SIR JOHN-LOWTHER JOHNSTONE, who *s.* his uncle as 6th baronet, of Westerhall. He *m.* Charlotte Gordon, dau. of Charles Gordon, of Clunie, by whom he had issue a son, GEORGE FREDERICK, his heir, and two daus., Charlotte-Margaret, *m.* to Rev. Henry W. Buckley, and has issue, and Anne, *m.* to the Rev. Edmund-Bucknall Estcourt, and has issue. Sir John Lowther Johnstone *d.* in 1811, and was *s.* by his son,
SIR GEORGE-FREDERICK JOHNSTONE, 7th baronet, of Westerhall, *b.* in 1810. He *m.* in 1840, Lady Louisa Craven, only dau. of the 1st Earl of Craven, who *m.* 2ndly, Alexander Oswald, of Auchencruive Sir Frederick *d.* in 1841, and left two posthumous sons,
I. FREDERICK-JOHN-WILLIAM.
II. George Charles-Keppel.

SIR FREDERICK-JOHN-WILLIAM JOHNSTONE was, at his birth, 9th baronet, of Westerhall. He is heir male and head of the house of Johnstone, and claimant of the Marquessate of Annandale. The claim to the Marquessate was prosecuted by Sir John, and by his son Sir Frederick, but it has never yet been brought to a decision by the House of Lords.

Arms.—Arg., a saltire, sa., on a chief, gu., three cushions, or.

JONES—EARL OF RANELAGH.

(See BURKE's *Extant Peerage*.)

KAVANAGH—BARON BALLYANE.

By Letters Patent, dated 8 February, 1554.

Lineage.

In ancient times the ancestors of the great house of Kavanagh were Monarchs of Ireland, and at the period of the Anglo-Norman invasion, were Kings of Leinster.

CAHIR MAC ART KAVANAGH, chief of his name, was created BARON OF BALLYANE, co. Wexford, for life, by patent dated 8 February, 1554, wherein he is recognized as "chief of his sept, and captain over all others the inhabitants of the countries of the Macomores, the Duffrey, &c.," and was directed to keep yearly on those territories, eighty kernes for himself, and twelve for Maurice, *alias* Morghe Kavanagh, "Qui proximus post cum in gradum Baronis de Cowelelyene futurus sit." His lordship *m.* Lady Alice Fitzgerald, dau. of Gerald, Earl of Kildare, by Elizabeth Grey, his wife, dau. of the Marquess of Dorset, and *d.* before 1555, having had issue,

MURROUGH, or Maurice, Baron of Cowelelyene, co. Wexford, d s. p.

Dermot, d. s. p.

BRYAN, a celebrated warrior, who d. before 1572, leaving by Eleanor, his wife. dau. of George Byrne, of Roscrea, a son,

MORGAN KAVANAGH, Esq., of Borris, co. Carlow, who d. in 1636, leaving by Eleanor, his wife, dau. of Edmund, 2nd Viscount Mountgarret, sixteen children, of whom the eldest son was,

BRYAN KAVANAGH, Esq., of Borris, who d. in 1662, leaving a son and successor,

MORGAN KAVANAGH, Esq., of Borris, who m. Mary, dau. of John Walsh, Esq., of Piltown, by Lady Helena Power, his wife, dau. of Richard, Earl of Tyrone, and was father of

MORGAN KAVANAGH, of Borris, who m. Frances, dau. of Sir Lawrence Esmonde, Bart., and had issue, BRYAN, his heir; Henry, d. in 1741; Charles, a general in the Austrian service, governor of Prague; and Mary. The eldest son,

BRYAN KAVANAGH, Esq., of Borris, m. Mary, dau. of Thomas Butler, Esq., of Kilcash, and dying in 1741, left, with six daus., of whom the eldest, Margaret, m. Richard Galwey, Esq., a son and heir,

THOMAS KAVANAGH, Esq. of Borris, who m. Lady Susan Butler, sister of John, Earl of Ormonde and Ossory, and d. in 1790, having had issue,

Walter, d. s. p. 1818.   Bryan. d. s. p.

Morgan, m. in 1792, Alicia, only child of Michael Grace, Esq., of Gracefield, Queen's co., and d. s. p. 1804.

THOMAS, eventual inheritor.

Helena, m. to James Archbold, Esq., of Davidstown.

Mary, m. to George Butler, Esq., of Ballyraggct.

Honora, a nun.

The youngest son and eventual inheritor, was THOMAS KAVANAGH, Esq., of Borris, M.P. for the co. Carlow; b. 10 March, 1767; m. 1st, 24 March, 1799, Lady Elizabeth Butler, sister of the Marquess of Ormonde, and had by her a son, WALTER, b. 20 March, 1814, and d 1836, and nine daus., of whom six d. unm. The other three were, Anne, m. in 1820, to Colonel Henry Bruen, of Oak Park, co. Carlow, and d. 1830; Susanna, m. to Major Doyne; and Grace, m. to John-St. George Deane, Esq., of Berkeley Forest, co. Wexford, and d. s. p. Mr. Kavanagh m. 2ndly, 28 February, 1825, Lady Harriet Le Poer Trench, dau. of Richard, Earl of Clancarty, and left at his decease, in 1837, by her, three sons and a dau., viz., Thomas, his successor, who d. unm. in 1852; Charles, d. unm. the following year; ARTHUR McMURROUGH KAVANAGH, now of Borris, and Harriett-Margaret. m. to Col. W. A. Middleton, royal artillery.

Arms—Arg., a lion passant, gu., in base two erescents of the 2nd.

KEITH—EARL MARISCHAL.

Lineage.

This great and illustrious family has held from the earliest ages the dignified post of Great Marischals of Scotland. Without attempting to trace the line of hereditary Great Marischals of Scotland from the year 1010, when Robert, the direct ancestor of this family, was invested with that dignity by King MALCOLM II., we will commence with SIR WILLIAM KEITH, Great Marischal of Scotland, the 11th in direct descent from the founder of the family, and who d. prior to 1476. He was created Earl Marischal of Scotland prior to 1458. By Mary, dau. of Sir James Hamilton, of Cadzow, he had, with other issue, a son,

WILLIAM KEITH, 2nd Earl Marischal. He m. Muriella, dau. of Thomas, 1st Lord Erskine, by whom he had issue,

I. WILLIAM, 3rd earl.
II. Robert.
III. Alexander, of Auquhorsk, ancestor of the late Rev. Dr. George Skene Keith.
IV. John, of Craig, ancestor of the late Sir Robert Murray Keith, K.B., a distinguished ambassador.

The eldest son,

WILLIAM KEITH, 3rd Earl Marischal, d. 1530. He m. 1482, Lady Elizabeth Gordon, dau. of George, 2nd Earl of Huntley, and grand-dau. of JAMES, 1st King of Scotland and Queen Jane Beaufort, by whom he had issue,

I. ROBERT, Lord Keith.
II. William, slain at Flodden, 1513, s. p.
III. Alexander, ancestor of Keith, of Urras, and Bishop Robert Keith, the ecclesiastical historian of Scotland.
I. Janet, wife of William, 2nd Earl of Montrose.
II. Elizabeth, wife, 1st, of Colin, master of Oliphant, 2ndly, of William, 2nd Lord Sinclair.
III. Agnes, wife of Sir Archibald Douglas, of Glenbervie.
IV. Beatrix, wife of Alexander Frazer, of Philorth.

The eldest son,

ROBERT, LORD KEITH, fell at Flodden, 1513, leaving by his wife, Lady Elizabeth Douglas, dau. of John, 2nd Earl of Morton, and great grand-dau. of JAMES I., King of Scotland and Queen Jane Beaufort,

I. WILLIAM, 4th Earl Marischal.
II. Robert Keith, Commendator of the abbey of Deer, father of Andrew Keith, created Lord Dingwall in 1587, who d. s. p. (see that title).
I. Elizabeth, wife of George, 4th Earl of Huntley.
II. Janet, wife of John, 7th Lord Glamis.
III. Christian, wife of Sir Robert Arbuthnott, of that ilk.

The eldest son,

WILLIAM KEITH, 4th Earl Marischal, was a man of immense property, which lay in so many counties that he could travel from Berwick to the northern extremity of Scotland, eating every meal, and sleeping each night on his own estates. He m. Margaret, dau. and co-heir of Sir William Keith, of Innerugie, by whom he had issue,

I. WILLIAM, Lord Keith.
II. Robert, created LORD ALTRIE (see that title).
I. Anne, m. 1st in 1561, James, Earl of Moray, regent Scotland; and 2ndly, Colin, 6th Earl of Argyle.
II. Elizabeth, m. to Sir Alexander Irvine, of Drum.
III. Alison, m. to Alexander, Lord Saltoun.
IV. Mary, m. to John Campbell, of Calder.
V. Beatrix, m. to John Allardice, of Allardice.
VI. Janet, m. to James Crichton, of Frendraught.
VII. Margaret, m. to Sir John Kennedy, of Blairquhan. All these ladies had issue.

William, 4th earl, d. in 1581. His eldest son,

WILLIAM, Lord Keith, m. Lady Elizabeth Hay, dau. of George, 6th Earl of Errol, by whom he had issue,

I. GEORGE, 5th Earl Marischal.
II. William, }
III. Robert, } d. s. p.
IV. John, }
I. Christian, m. to Robert Arbuthnott, of Arbuthnott.
II. Barbara, m. to Alexander Forbes, of Pitsligo.
III. Margaret, m. to Sir William Keith, of Ludquhaim.
IV. Jean, m. to James Gordon, of Haddo. All these ladies had issue.

The eldest son,

GEORGE, 5th Earl Marischal, was one of the most important and powerful men of his day in Scotland. He was sent ambassador to Denmark, to negotiate the marriage of King JAMES VI., in 1589. He founded the Marischal college in Aberdeen in 1593. He was royal commissioner to the parliament of Scotland in 1609. He d. in 1623. He m. 1st, Margaret, dau. of Alexander, 5th Lord Home, by whom he had issue,

I. WILLIAM, 6th Earl Marischal.
I. Anne, m. to William, 7th Earl of Morton.
II. Margaret, m. to Sir Robert Arbuthnott, of that ilk.

He m. 2ndly, Margaret, dau. of James, 6th Lord Ogilvie, by whom he had,

I. James, of Benholm, who had no male issue.
II. John, who had no issue.

The eldest son,

WILLIAM, 6th Earl Marischal, m. Lady Margaret Erskine, dau. of John, Earl of Marr, by whom he had issue,

I. WILLIAM, 7th earl.
II. GEORGE, 8th earl.   III. Robert, d. unm.
IV. John, who was in 1677, created Earl of Kintore and Lord Keith, of Inverury. He d. in 1714. By Lady Margaret Hamilton, dau. of Thomas, 2nd Earl of Haddington, he had issue,

William, 2nd Earl of Kintore, father of the 3rd and 4th Earls of Kintore, who had no issue, and of Lady Catherine-Margaret Keith, wife of David, 5th Lord Falconner, of Halkerton, ancestress of the present Earl of Kintore.

I. Mary, m. to John, Lord Kinpont, son of William, Earl of Monteith.
II. Jean, m. to Alexander, Lord Pitaligo.

The 6th Earl Marischal d. 1635. His son,

WILLIAM, 7th Earl Marischal, was a faithful friend to King CHARLES I., and suffered severely for his loyalty. He was made lord privy seal by King CHARLES II. He d. 1661. He m. 1st.

in 1637, Lady Elizabeth, dau. of George, 2nd Earl of Winton, by whom he had issue,

  i. William, Lord Keith, *d.* young.
  i. Mary, *m.* 1st, in 1657, to Sir James Hope, of Hopetoun, and 2ndly, to Sir Archibald Murray, of Blackbarony.
  ii. Elizabeth, *m.* to Robert, 2nd Viscount Arbuthnott.
  iii. Jean, *m.* to George, 3rd Lord Banff.
  iv. Isabel, *m.* to Sir Edward Turner, Bart., speaker of the House of Commons, and chief baron of Exchequer

The earl *m.* 2ndly, 1654, Lady Anne Douglas, dau. of Robert, 8th Earl of Morton, and dying without male issue, he was *s.* by his brother in 1661,

  GEORGE, 8th Earl Marischal, *m.* Lady Mary Hay. dau. of George, 2nd Earl of Kinnoul, by whom he had an only son, his successor, in 1694,

  WILLIAM, 9th Earl Marischal. He vehemently opposed the measures of King WILLIAM III.'s Government and the Union, in the reign of Queen ANNE. He *d.* 1712. He *m.* Lady Mary Drummond, eldest dau. of James, 4th Earl of Perth, lord chancellor of Scotland (Duke of Perth), by Lady Jane, dau. of William, 1st Marquis of Douglas, by whom he had issue,

  i. GEORGE, 10th Earl Marischal.
  ii. James, *b.* 1696; engaging in the rebellion in 1715, he was attainted of high treason. He retired to the continent, and entered the Spanish service, and then the Russian, where he became a general. In 1740 he entered the service of FREDERICK II., King of Prussia, where he became field-marshal. He fell at the battle of Hochkirchen, in 1758, aged sixty-three, and *unm.*
  i. Mary, *m.* in 1711, to John, 6th Earl of Wigton.
  ii. Anne, *m.* to Alexander, 6th Earl of Galloway.

The eldest son,

GEORGE, 10th Earl Marischal, entered into the rebellion in 1715, and in consequence an act of attainder was passed against him. His titles, estates, and office of Great Marischal were forfeited. He retired to the continent, first of all to Spain, and then to Prussia, where he acquired the special favour of King FREDERICK II. He was knight of the Black Eagle, and ambassador from Prussia to the court of France in 1750, and to that of Spain in 1759. He was governor of Neufchatel. He was received favourably by GEORGE III., in 1760, and by act of parliament, he was enabled to hold real property in England, and thus he inherited the entailed estates of the Earls of Kintore, on the death of the 4th earl, in 1761. He *d.* aged eighty-six, at Potsdam, in 1778, in the enjoyment of the intimate friendship of FREDERICK II., of Prussia. As his lordship *d. unm.*, the representation of the house of Keith, Earls Marischal, as heir general devolved on the descendant and representative of his eldest sister,

LADY MARY KEITH, *m.* in 1711, to John Fleming, 6th Earl of Wigton. She *d.* in 1721, leaving an only dau.,

LADY CLEMENTINA FLEMING, who was *m.* in 1735, to Charles, 10th Lord Elphinstone. This lady, on the death of her uncle, the Earl Marischal, became heir general of the Keiths, Earls Marischal, and Drummond Earls of Perth, as she was heir general of her father, the Earl of Wigton. The Sixteen Quarters of this lady were remarkable for their high nobility, not one of them being under the rank of Earl. She *d.* in 1799, aged eighty. By Lord Elphinstone, she had, with other issue,

  i. JOHN, 11th Lord Elphinstone.
  ii. William Fullerton Elphinstone, of Carberry, *m.* 1774, Elizabeth Fullerton. He was grandfather of William Buller Fullerton Elphinstone. present and 15th Lord Elphinstone.
  iii. George Keith, admiral of the Blue in 1814, created Viscount Keith, *m.* 1st, in 1787, Jane, dau. of William Mercer, of Aldie, by whom he had issue, Margaret, now Baroness Keith and Nairne, wife of Count de Flahault; and 2ndly, in 1808, Hester-Maria, dau. of Henry Thrale, by whom he had issue, Georgiana, wife of Hon. Augustus Villiers, son of the 5th Earl of Jersey. He *d.* in 1823.
  i. Eleanor, *m.* in 1777, to the Right Hon. William Adam, baron of Exchequer, lord chief commissioner of the Jury Court, by whom she had issue : 1 Admiral Sir Charles Adam, K.C.B., M.P., father of William Adam, of Blairadam, M.P.; 2 The Right Hon. General Sir Frederick Adam, G.C.B., governor of Madras, and lord high commissioner of the Ionian Islands ; and a dau., Clementina, wife of John Anstruther Thomson, of Charleton, and mother of John Anstruther Thomson, now of Charleton.
  ii. Clementina, *m.* to James Drummond, Lord Perth, and mother of Clementina-Sarah, heir general of the Earls of Melfort, wife of Peter Robert, Lord Willoughby d'Eresby.

Lady Elphinstone's eldest son,

JOHN, 11th Lord Elphinstone, *m.* Anne, dau. of James, 3rd Lord Ruthven, by whom he had issue,

  i. JOHN, 12th Lord Elphinstone.
  ii. Charles, admiral in the navy, who, on inheriting the

estates of the Wigton family, took the name of Fleming. He had with other issue, a son, John, 14th Lord Elphinstone, and a dau., Clementina, who *m* in 1845, Cornwallis, Viscount Hawarden.
  iii. James Ruthven.
  iv. Mountstuart, governor of Bombay.
  And three daus., of whom Keith was wife of David Erskine, of Cardross.

The eldest son,

JOHN, 12th Lord Elphinstone, a lieut.-general in the army, on the death of his grandmother, Clementina, Lady Elphinstone, became heir general of the Earls of Wigton, the Earls Marischal, and the Earls of Perth. He *m.* Janet Elliot, Lady Carmichael ; *d.* in 1813, and was *s.* by his only son,

JOHN, 13th Lord Elphinstone, G.C.H. and G.C.B., governor of Madras, and governor of Bombay; dying *unm.* in 1860, he was *s.* by his cousin,

JOHN, 14th Lord Elphinstone, who dying *unm.* in January, 1861, was *s.* as heir general of the Earls of Wigton, Earls Marischal, and Earls of Perth, by his eldest sister,

CLEMENTINA, VISCOUNTESS HAWARDEN, who has issue a son and six daus.,

Arms—Arg., on a chief, gu., three pallets, or.

KEITH—LORD DINGWALL.

By Charter, dated 3 August, 1587.

Lineage.

ROBERT KEITH (2nd son of William, Lord Keith, killed at the battle of Flodden, 9 September, 1513, eldest son and heir of William, 3rd Earl Marischal) was abbot of the Cistertian Monastery of Deer, in Aberdeenshire, in the reign of King JAMES V., and dying at Paris, 12 June, 1551, was buried before the altar of St. Ninian, in the Carmelite church there. According to Dempster, he was "eruditione et vitæ continentia clarus, et multa egisse dicitur, quo collapsos ecclesiastici ordinis mores restitueret; nonnulla scripsit." The compliment paid to his continence, however, appears unfounded, as he was father of

ANDREW KEITH, who was, by JAMES VI., created a peer, by the title of LORD DINGWALL, to him and his heirs male and assigns, by charter, dated at Falkland, 3 August, 1587. He *d. s. p.*, having previously resigned his estate and honours in favour of William Keith, of Delney, who thereupon had a charter of the lands of Dingwall, to him and his heirs male whatsoever bearing the name and arms of Keith, with a seat in parliament, by the title of Lord Dingwall, dated at Holyrood House, 22 January, 1592-3. This title, however, was extinct before 1606, as it does not appear in the decreet of ranking of the peers of that year, and Sir Richard Preston was created Lord Dingwall, 1607.

Arms—See KEITH, Earl Marischal.

KEITH—LORD ALTRIE.

By Letters Patent, dated 29 July, 1587.

Lineage.

ROBERT KEITH (2nd son of William, 4th Earl Marischal) was commendator of the Cistertian Abbey of Deer, in Aberdeenshire, and had the whole lands and baronies belonging to that monastery erected into a temporal lordship, to himself in life-rent, and George, Earl Marischal, his nephew, in fee, with the title of LORD ALTRIE, by charter, dated 22 July, 1587. His lordship *m.* Elizabeth, dau. and heir of Robert Lundie, of Benholm, and had two daus.,

Elizabeth, *m.* to Alexander Hay, of Dalgety.
Margaret, *m.* to John Erskine, of Dun.

Lord Altrie *d. s. p.* 1593.

KEPPEL—VISCOUNT KEPPEL, OF ELVE-DEN, CO. SUFFOLK.

By Letters Patent, dated 22 April, 1732.

Lineage.

The Hon. Augustus Keppel (2nd son of William-Anne, 2nd Earl of Albemarle), a naval officer of eminence, was constituted first lord of the Admiralty, and created a peer of the realm, as Viscount Keppel, *of Elveden, co. Suffolk,* by letters patent, dated 22 April, 1782.

This celebrated officer was with Commodore Anson in the South Seas, where at the taking of Paita, he had a narrow escape from a cannon ball, which shaved off the peak of a jockey cap, then on his head, close to his temple. In 1751, he was commodore of a squadron in the Mediterranean, and took the island of Goree from the French in 1759. The same year he was with Admiral Hawke, in that memorable battle with Conflans, when at a second broadside he sunk a seventy-four gun ship with all her crew. In 1762 he accompanied his brother, the Earl of Albemarle, and was present at the siege of Havannah, where, under Admiral Pococke, he was greatly instrumental in taking that important place and its dependencies. In 1778, he attained the rank of admiral of the blue but, while in command of the British fleet, his conduct in the engagement with the French, under Compte D'Orvilliers, was deemed so unsatisfactory, that he was brought before a court-martial, by which, however, he was honourably acquitted.

His lordship *d. unm.* in 1786, when the Viscounty of Keppel, of Elveden, became extinct.

Arms—Gu., three eschallop shells, arg., a crescent for difference.

KER—EARLS KER, OF WAKEFIELD.

By Letters Patent, dated 24 May, 1722.

Lineage.

Robert Ker, who *s.* his father in the Dukedom of Roxburghe, in the peerage of Scotland, *anno* 1741, had been previously created a peer of Great Britain, by letters patent, dated 24 May, 1722, as *Baron Ker* and *Earl Ker, of Wakefield, co. York.* His grace *m.* in 1739, Essex, dau. (by Lady Essex Finch, dau. of the Earl of Nottingham) of Sir Roger Mostyn, 3rd Bart., of Mostyn, co. Flint, and had issue,

John, his successor.
Robert, lieut.-col., who *d. unm.* in 1781.
Essex (dau.)   Mary.

The duke *d.* in 1755, and was *s.* by his eldest son,

John Ker, 3rd Duke of Roxburghe, and 2nd Earl Ker. This nobleman, who was a knight of the Garter, and a knight of the Thistle, and groom of the stole to King George III., *d. unm.,* 19 March, 1804, when his Scottish honours passed to his kinsman, William, Lord Bellenden, and the British Earldom of Ker, with the inferior dignity, expired.

Arms—Quarterly: 1st and 4th, vert, on a chevron, between three unicorns' heads, erased, arg., as many mullets, sa.; 2nd and 3rd, gu., three muscles, or.

KERDESTON—BARONS KERDESTON.

By Writ of Summons, dated 27 January, 1332.

Lineage.

In the 1st year of King John's reign,

Roger de Kerdeston paid a fine to the crown of 30 marks, to have a confirmation of those lands which formerly belonged to Hubert de Rie. To this Roger *s.*

William de Kerdeston, who was sheriff of Norfolk, and Suffolk, in the 25th and 26th Edward I. He *m.* Margaret dau. of Gilbert de Gant, Baron of Folkingham, in Lincolnshire, and was *s.* by his son,

Roger de Kerdeston, who, in right of his mother, was one of the co-heirs of his uncle, Gilbert de Gant, Lord Gant, who *d. s. p.* in 1297; and doing homage, had livery of the lands which so descended to him. In the 34th Edward I. this Roger received the honour of knighthood with Prince Edward, by bathing, &c., having his livery of robes, and all accoutrements relating to that solemnity out of the king's wardrobe. In the 5th Edward III. he was made sheriff of Norfolk and Suffolk, and governor of the castle at Norwich. In the next year (1332), he was summoned to parliament as a Baron, and from that period to 21 June, 1337. His lordship *d.* in the latter year, and was *s.* by his son,

William de Kerdeston, 2nd baron, summoned to parliament from 20 December, 1337, to 3 April 1360. This nobleman distinguished himself in the French wars, and had the honour of participating in the glories of Cressy. He *d.* in 1361, leaving according to some inquisitions, William, his son and heir, then thirty-six years of age: which

Sir William de Kerdeston, Knight, claimed part of his father's lands as his heir, and not being opposed, was admitted to them. He was, however, never summoned to parliament, and probably some doubt hung over his legitimacy. In Morant's History of Essex, which is partly corroborated by a pedigree in the College of Arms, it appears that William de Kerdeston, the last baron, left issue by William de Kerdeston, his 2nd wife, a son, William; but by his 1st wife, two daus., who are called in the MS. pedigree above cited, his co-heirs, viz.,

Margaret, who *m.* Sir William de Tendring; and her son and heir,

Sir William Tendring, left issue,

Alice, *m. to* Sir John Howard, ancestor of the Lords Stourton and Petre, as heirs general of the Howards and of the Dukes of Norfolk, as heirs male.

Maud, *m.* to John de Burghersh, and left two daus., his co-heirs,

Margaret, *m.* 1st, to Sir John Granville, and 2ndly, to Sir John Arundel.
Maud, *m.* to Thomas Chaucer, son of the poet. Geoffrey Chaucer, and left at her decease, 1436, an only child,

Alice Chaucer, who was thrice *m.,* her last husband being William De la Pole, Duke of Suffolk.

Upon the failure of issue of Sir William de Kerdeston, the reputed son of the last baron, the barony of Kerdeston fell into abeyance, as it still continues with the descendants of Margaret, Lady Tendring and Maud de Burghersh.

Arms—Gu., a saltier, engrailed, arg.

KING—BARON KINGSTON.

By Letters Patent, dated 4 September, 1660.

Lineage.

Sir John King, Knt., eldest son of Sir Robert King, muster-master-general of Ireland, and brother of Sir Robert King, of Rockingham, ancestor of the present Earl of Kingston, was elevated to the peerage of Ireland, 4 September, 1660, as Baron Kingston. His lordship *m.* Catherine, dau. of Sir William Fenton, of Mitchelston, co. Cork, by Margaret, his wife, sister and heir of Maurice Oge Fitz-Maurice Fitz-Edmund Fitz-Gibbon, and cousin and heir of Edmund Fitz-Gibbon, the White Knight; dying in 1676, Lord Kingston was *s.* by his son,

Robert King, 2nd Lord Kingston; who *d. s. p.* in 1693, having settled and limited his estates in remainder to his uncle, Sir Robert King, in consequence of his brother and the inheritor of his honours,

John King, 3rd Lord Kingston, having conformed to the church of Rome; but this nobleman appears afterwards to have enjoyed the estates. He was made a gentleman of the privy chamber to James II., and following the fortunes of his master into France, was outlawed; but after his brother's death, returning to Ireland, he had a pardon from the crown. His lordship *m.* Florence O'Cahan, and *d.* in 1727, leaving (with two daus., Catherine, *m.* to George Butler, Esq., of Ballyragget, co. Kilkenny, and Sophia, *m.* to Brettridge Badham, Esq.,) an only surviving son,

James King, 4th Lord Kingston, *m.* 1st, Elizabeth, dau. of Sir John Meade, of Ballintobber, and widow of Sir Ralph Freke, of Rathbarry, co. Cork, Bart.; and 2udly, Lady Ogle,

widow of Sir Chaloner Ogle, Knt., admiral of his Majesty's
fleet, but had issue only by the former, who *d.* 6 October, 1759,
viz., one son, WILLIAM, who *m.* the only dau. of Samuel
Burroughs, Esq., of Dewsbury, co. York, master in chancery,
but *d. s. p. v. p.*, and one dau., Margaret. He *d.* without male
issue in 1761, when the barony EXPIRED; while an estate of
£6,000 a year, and a large personal fortune, devolved upon his
only surviving dau.,

MARGARET, who *m.* RICHARD FITZGERALD, Esq., of Mount
Ophaley, co. Kildare, and had an only child and heiress,

CAROLINE, *m.* 1769, Robert, 2nd EARL OF KINGSTON. (*See*
BURKE's *Extant Peerage*).

Arms—Gu., two lions rampant, combattant, supporting a
dexter hand couped at the wrist, and arg.

KINNAIRD—BARON ROSSIE.

(*See* BURKE's *Extant Peerage*).

KIRKETON—BARON KIRKETON.

By Writ of Summons, dated 25 February, 1342.

Lineage.

THOMAS DE KIRKETON was summoned to parliament as a
baron, 25 February, 1342, but never afterwards, and Dugdale
makes no further mention of him or his descendants.

Arms—Barry of six, gu. and arg.

KIRKETON—BARON KIRKETON.

By Writ of Summons, dated 14 August, 1362.

Lineage.

JOHN DE KIRKETON, of Kirketon, in that part of the co.
Lincoln, called Holland, received the honour of knighthood, in
the 19th EDWARD II., by bathing, &c., having had allowance
of his robes for that solemnity out of the king's wardrobe; and
being possessed of the castle and manor of Tatahall and manor
of Tumby, in the same shire, with the knight's fees and advow-
sons of churches thereunto belonging, made a feoffment in
the 16th EDWARD III., of that castle and lordship, to Adam de
Welles and others, to stand feoffed thereof, to the use of himself, and Isabel, his wife; and to the heirs of their two bodies
lawfully begotten, with divers remainders; his lands at Kirketon
being at the time valued at £10 per annum.

In the 26th EDWARD III., upon the danger of an invasion by
the French, Sir John de Kirketon was constituted one of the
commissioners of Array, in the co. of Lincoln, for arming all
knights, esquires, and others for defending the sea coasts in
that shire. And in the 33rd of the same reign, King JOHN of
France being then prisoner in England, he was one of the
persons appointed to remove that prince from the castle of
Hertford to Somerton Castle, co. Somerset, and there to secure
him. Sir John de Kirketon was summoned to parliament as
a Baron, 14 August, 1362, and 1 June, 1363. He *d.* in 1367,
s. p., when the barony became EXTINCT. His lordship *d.* seized
of the manor of Tatshall, by the grant of Sir Ralph de Cromwell, Knt., and Maud, his wife, as also of the manors of Tumby,
Kirkeby, &c., leaving Sir John de Tudenham, Knt., Richard de
Lina, John de Tilney, and William de Sutton, rector of the
church of Whitwell, his next heirs.

Arms—Barry of six, gu. and arg.

KIRKHOVEN—BARON WOTTON, OF WOT-
TON, CO. KENT, AND EARL OF BELLO-
MONT, IN IRELAND.

Barony, by Letters Patent, dated 31 August, 1650.
Earldom of Ireland, by Letters Patent, dated 11 February,
1680.

Lineage.

EDWARD WOTTON, *b.* 1548, was created Baron Wotton, of
Marley, co. Kent, 13 May, 1603, and dying about the year
afterwards, was *s.* by his son,

THOMAS WOTTON, 2nd Baron Wotton, of Marley, in Kent,
who *d.* in 1630, without male issue, when that title became

EXTINCT; his lordship left, however, by his wife, Mary, dau.
and co-heir of Sir Arthur Throckmorton, of Paulers-Perry, in
Northamptonshire, four daus., his co-heirs, viz.,

KATHERINE, who *m.* 1st, to Henry, Lord Stanhope, son and
heir of Philip, Earl of Chesterfield, by whom, who predeceased his father, she had,

Phil p, who *s.* to the Earldom of Chesterfield, and from
whom the present earl directly descends

Mary, who *d. unm.*

Katherine, *m.* to William, Lord Alington.

Her ladyship *m.* 2ndly, John Polliander de Kirkhoven, Lord
of Heenfleet, in Holland, and had a son,

CHARLES HENRY DE KIRKHOVEN, of whom presently.

She *m.* 3rdly, Colonel Daniel O'Neile, one of the grooms of
the bedchamber to CHARLES II., but had no issue by him.
This lady was governess to the Princess of Orange, dau. of
CHARLES I., and attending her highness in Holland, sent
over money, arms, and ammunition, to his Majesty's aid,
for which service she was created, at the Restoration,
COUNTESS OF CHESTERFIELD for life (*see* Wotton, Countess of
Chesterfield).

Hesther, *m.* to Baptist, 3rd Viscount Campden, and was
mother of the 1st Earl of Gainsborough.

Margaret, *m.* to Sir John Tufton, Knt.

Anne, *m.* to Sir Edward Hales, Knt., of Tunstal, Kent.

The eldest of these co-heiresses, Katherine, had, by her 2nd
husband, as stated above, an only son,

CHARLES HENRY DE KIRKHOVEN, who, by reason of his
descent, was created BARON WOTTON, of *Wotton, in Kent,* by
letters patent, dated 31 August, 1650; and was naturalized by
act of parliament, in September, 1660. His lordship was
advanced to the EARLDOM OF BELLOMONT in Ireland, 11 February, 1680. but *d. s. p.* in 1683, when all his honours became
EXTINCT, and his estates devolved, by his lordship's bequest,
upon his nephew by the half-blood, CHARLES STANHOPE, a
younger son of his half-brother, Philip, Earl of Chesterfield,
who, upon inheriting, assumed the surname of WOTTON, and
d. s. p.

Arms—Arg., a saltier, sa.

KNIGHT—EARL OF CATHERLOUGH.

By Letters Patent, dated 14 May, 1762.

Lineage.

ROBERT KNIGHT, Esq., of Barrells, co. Warwick, descended
from Robert Knight, Esq., who purchased that estate in 1554,
having represented Great Grimsby and Castle Rising in four
parliaments, was created a peer of Ireland, in 1746, as BARON
LUXBOROUGH; and further advanced, 14 May, 1762, to be
Viscount Barrells, and EARL OF CATHERLOUGH. His lordship
m. 1st, 10 June, 1727, Henrietta, only dau. of Henry, Viscount
St. John, and sister of Viscount Bolingbroke, secretary of state
to Queen ANNE, and had issue,

HENRY, Viscount Barrells, who *m.* 21 June, 1750, the dau. of
Thomas Heath, Esq., of Stanstead, in Essex; but *d. s. p.* in
his father's lifetime.

Henrietta, *m.* to the Hon. Josiah Child, brother of the Earl
of Tylney.

The earl *m.* 2ndly, in 1756, Lady Le Quesne, but had no issue
by her. He *d.* 30 March, 1772, and with him the peerage
EXPIRED. His lordship left two natural sons,

ROBERT KNIGHT, to whom he devised all his estates in the cos.
of Warwick, Worcester, and Flint. This gentleman, the late
ROBERT KNIGHT, Esq. of Barrels, co. Warwick, M.P., *m.*
1791, Frances, dau. of Charles Lord Dormer, and left two
daus., his co-heirs, viz., FRANCES-ELIZABETH, and GEORGINA,
m. to Edward-Bolton King, Esq.

HENRY-RALEIGH KNIGHT, lieut.-gen. in the army, *m.* Miss
Boulton, and *d.* in 1836, having had issue a son, Raleigh,
capt. in the army, and two daus.

Arms—Arg., three bendlets, gu.; on a canton, az., a spur,
with the rowel downwards, buckled and strapped, all gold.

KNIVET.

See Knyvett.

KNOLLYS—BARON KNOLLYS, VISCOUNT WALLINGFORD, EARL OF BANBURY.

Barony, by Letters Patent, dated 13 May, 1603.
Viscounty, by Letters Patent, dated 14 November, 1616.
Earldom, by Letters Patent, dated 18 August, 1772.

Lineage.

In the 41st EDWARD III.,

SIR ROBERT KNOLLYS, K.G., having from humble fortune attained great wealth and high reputation, in the Norman wars, was chosen by the Black Prince to accompany him into Spain, in aid of DON PEDRO, then King of Castile and Leon, against Henry, the bastard son of (his father) King ALFONSUS. And in three years afterwards was made gen ral of all the forces then sent by King EDWARD into France. In the 1st RICHARD II., Sir Robert was governor of the castle of Brest, and in the 3rd, he went with Thomas Plantagenet (of Woo!-stock), Earl of Buckingham, and other gallant persons, to assist the Duke of Britanny against the French, when, landing at Calais, they marched quite through France, without resistance. The next year, upon the breaking out of Jack Straw's insurrection, Sir Robert led the citizens of London against the rebels. Besides his military achievements which rendered him famous in those days, Sir Robert Knollys left o'her memorials behind him. He erected a stately bridge over the River Medway, near Rochester, in Kent, called Rochester Bridge, and he enlarged the house of Friers-Carmelites, commonly called White Friers, in the city of London. He likewise founded a collegiate church of secular priests, at Pontefract, in Yorkshire. He d. at his seat of Scene Thorpe, co. Norfolk, anno 1407, and was buried with the Lady Constance his wife, in the body of the church at the White Friers. From th s gallant personage descended,

ROBERT KNOLLYS, who, in the 9th HENRY VIII., being then one of the gentlemen ushers of the privy chamber, had a lease for a certain number of years, from the king, of the manor of Rotherfield Grey, commonly called Greys, co. Oxford. He was s. by his son,

SIR FRANCIS KNOLLYS, who obta'ned from King HENRY VIII., a grant of the lordship in fee of Rotherfield Grey, or Greys, and was one of that monarch's gentlemen pensioners. In the reign of EDWARD VI., he was so stanch an upholder of the reformation, that he deemed it prudent, upon the accession of MARY, to retire into Germany. But when ELIZABETH ascended the throne, he returned and enjoyed in a high degree, the favour and confidence of the crown. He was immediately sworn of the privy council, made vice-chamberlain of the household; next, captain of the guard; afterwards treasurer; and lastly, installed a knight of the most noble order of the Garter. In the 11th ELIZABETH, Sir Francis Knollys had the custody of MARY, Queen of Scots, then confined at Bolton Castle, in Yorkshire, and in eighteen years afterwards, he was one of those who sat in judgment upon her life. Sir Francis m. Catherine, dau. of William Carey, Esq. (by Mary his wife, dau. of Thomas Boleyn, Earl of Wiltshire, and sister of Queen Anne Boleyn), and a dau., Lettice, m. to Walter Devereux, Earl of Essex, a son,

WILLIAM KNOLLYS, treasurer of the household in the reign of ELIZABETH, who was advanced to the peerage by King JAMES I., by letters patent, d ted 13 May, 1603, in the dignity of LORD KNOLLYS, of Grey. co. Oxford (his chief seat). In 1614, his lordship was appointed master of the wards, and within a short time installed a knight of the Garter. In 1616, he was created VISCOUNT WALLINGFORD, and advanced by King CHARLES I., 18 August, 1626, to the EARLDOM of BANBURY, with precedency of all earls who were created before him. His lordship m. 1st, Dorothy, dau. of Edward, Lord Bray, sister and co-heir of John, Lord Bray, and widow of Edmund, Lord Chandos, by whom he had no issue. He m. 2ndly, Elizabeth Howard, dau. of Thomas, Earl of Suffolk, and dying 25 May, 1632, at the advanced age of eighty-eight, was buried in .he church of Greys. The subsequent history of this peerage is one of the most curious in the whole record of peerage claims. Upon the decease of the EARL OF BANBURY, the inquisition found that he d. s. p., but leaving a widow, Elizabeth, his last wife. His honours were then deemed EXTINCT, and his estates passed to his collateral heirs, excepting such as he had devised to his widow, who re-married Lord Vaux. In a few years this lady produced two sons, born during her marriage with Lord Banbury, then Earl, They had at fir-t been called VAUX, but now she set them up as the sons of the Earl of Banbury, and gave to the eldest the title of that earldom. They were not of age before the civil wars had broken up the House of Lords. The elder died. Nicholas, the survivor, availing of the con-

vention parliament in 1660, took his seat therein, and during the continuation of its sittings, voted upon several occasions. It seems, however, that on 13 July, 1660, it was moved, "That there being a person that now sits in this house as a peer of the realm, viz., the Earl of B nbury, it is ordered that this business shall be heard at the bar by counsel, on Monday come sennight." Whether, in fact, any such hearing did take place or not, the journals are silent, yet they furnish abundant proof, that the doubt had been removed by some means: for they show, that the said earl was present in the house every day preceding the day appointed for the hearing. That he was also present on that very day : and that the day following he was named of the committee on the excise bill. That he was present on 13 September, when the king was in the house; and, in short, was only absent seven days, between 13 July, when the said motion was made, and 21 November, when it was ordered, "That the Earl of Banbury hath leave to be absent for some time." Shortly after this, however, the parliament was dissolved, viz., 29 December, 1660; and in the new parliament, which met 8 May, 1661, the name of the Earl of Banbury was omitted; his lordship presented, therefore, a petition to the king for his writ of summons, which petition was referred to the lords, for their opinion, and by them transferred to a committee for privileges. Here a regular examination of witnesses took place, and the attorney-general, who attended on behalf of the crown, confessed the law to be clear ; when the committee reported to the house, 1 July, 1661, "That Nicholas, Earl of Banbury, was a legitimate person." Upon receiving the report, the house ordered that the cause should be heard at the bar; where having been accordingly heard, it was again referred to the committee for privileges, with an additional direction, to consider the matter of the right of precedency between the said earl and several other peers; which committee once more having taken the matter into consideration, on 19 July, 1661, reported, "That the Earl of Banbury, in the eye of the law, was son of the late William, Earl of Banbury ; and the House of Peers should therefore advise the king to send him a writ to come to parliament, and that he ought to have a place in the House of Peers, according to the date of his patent, and not according to that part thereof, which ranked him before the other earls created before William, Earl of Banbury." This report was made on Friday, and the house resolved to take it into consideration on the Monday following; but nothing appears to have been done on that day: from which period it was postponed day after day, to 9 December; when it appears from the journals, that a bill was brought in, and read a first time, entitled, " An Act for declaring Nicholas, called Earl of Banbury, to be illegitimate." But such a measure was found too unjust to become a law, and the bill therefore dropped. Nicholas, the petitioner, d. 14 March, 1673-4, without bringing the matter to a conclusion, leaving a son, CHARLES, then twelve years of age. When Charles, in the first parliament after he came of age, anno 1685, presented a petition to the House of Peers, who referred it to a committee for privileges, and he was treated with the same procrastination as his father had experienced. He had, however, the misfortune to kill his brother-in-law, Philip Lawson, Esq., in a duel, in 1692, and that event placed his right to the peerage in a different point of view, and raised a new question upon it. He was indicted at the quarter sessions of Middlesex, and the indictment being removed by certiorari, into the Court of King's Bench, the assumed Earl of Banbury petitioned the lords to be tried by his peers. The house having again entered into the investigation of his father's legitimacy, resolved, that he had no right to the Earldom of Banbury, and the petition was ordered to be dismissed. Meantime, the proceedings went on in the King's Bench, and he being indicted in the name of Charles Knollys, pleaded in abatement that he was Earl of Banbury. To this the attorney-general rejoined, that he was not Earl of Banbury, because the lords adjudged that he had no right to that honour. To this he demurred as a bad replication, contending that the lords had no jurisdiction over that question. And the point which the Court of King's Bench had now to determine, was "whether the plea or replication was good."

Lord Holt and his brother judges finally adjudged " the replication ba-l, and the resolution of the lords invalid."

The claimant now again petitioned for his writ of summons, and the crown again, anno 1693, referred it to the lords, who got rid of the affair, by sending a message to his Majesty "that they had already determined the question, of which they supposed the King was not aware." In the reign of Queen ANNE the claimant once more petitioned, and it was referred to the privy council, but what became eventually of the petition is not known.

On the accession of GEORGE II., 1727, the claimant again

petitioned. Sir Philip Yorke, afterwards Lord Hardwicke, was then attorney-general, and this petition being referred to him, he reported, that whether the crown would refer it to the lords, was a matter of discretion, not of law: the crown therefore declined to interfere. Thus the claim continued to be hung up from reign to reign. Lord Hardwicke was undoubtedly right: it was a matter of pure option on the part of the crown, whether it would take the opinion of the lords; and prudence counselled the negative, after the flame which had been kindled between the House of Peers and the courts of law. At length, in 1776, the heirship devolved upon William Knollys, an officer in the army, who had attained the rank of general, who from that time enjoyed, as his ancestors had, since the Restoration, the *titular* honour, and had been so named in all the king's commissions. The awkwardness of his situation, however, impelled him to make an effort in his own person to have the question of his right to a writ of summons finally decided. He accordingly petitioned the crown; and the case was referred to the attorney-general, Sir Vicary Gibbs, in 1808. That able lawyer reported that he was bound by the high authority of the judgment of Lord Chief Justice Holt, in 1693, to give it as his opinion, that the resolution of the lords on that occasion was not conclusive, because, if that judgment had been erroneous it might have been reversed by a writ of error.

The case thus again came before a lords' committee, Sir Samuel Romilly being counsel for the claimant, and a decision was come to by their lordships, in 1813, that the claimant was not entitled to the Earldom of Banbury.

DESCENT OF THE BANBURY PEERAGE THROUGH THE ASSUMED EARLS OF BANBURY.

Nicholas Knollys (or Vaux, the person whose birth was concealed by his mother, during the lifetime of her first husband, William, Earl of Banbury), assumed the dignity of Earl of Banbury, and as such voted in the convention parliament. He *m.* 1st, Isabella, dau. of Mountjoy Blount, Earl of Newport, and had a dau.,

Anne, *m.* to Sir John Briscal, Knt.

His lordship *m.* 2ndly, Anne, dau. of William Sherard, Lord Leitrim, in Ireland, and had, with other issue, his successor, in 1673-4,

Charles Knollys, who also assumed the title of Earl of Banbury. He *m.* 1st, Margaret, dau. of Edward Lister, Esq., of Burwell, co. Leicester, and had issue,

Charles, Viscount Wallingford, who *d. s. p.*, in the lifetime of his father.

His lordship *m.* 2ndly, Mary, dau. of Thomas Woods, Esq., and dying in 1740, was *s.* by the son of this marriage,

Charles Knollys, assumed Earl of Banbury, *m.* Miss Martha Hughes, and had with other issue,

William, his successor.
Thomas-Woods, successor to his brother.

He *d.* 13 March, 1771, and was *s.* by his elder son,
William Knollys, assumed Earl of Banbury, who *d. unm.*, 29 August, 1776, and was *s.* by his brother,
Thomas-Woods Knollys, assumed Earl of Banbury, *m.* Mary, dau. of William Porter, Esq., of Winchester, and left, with other issue,
William Knollys, a general officer in the army, who, unsuccessfully, preferred his claim to the Earldom, 1808-13, and was father of
Right Hon. Sir William-Thomas Knollys, K.C.B., general in the army, colonel 62nd regt., gentleman usher of the Black Rod, receiver-general of the Duchy of Cornwall, hon. groom of the stole to the Prince of Wales, *b.* 1797; *m.* 1830, Elizabeth, dau. of Sir John St. Aubyn, Bart., and has issue.

Arms—Quarterly: 1st and 4th, semée of cross-crosslets, a cross moline, couped, or, voided throughout of the field: 2nd and 3rd, gu., on a chev., arg., three roses of the field.

KNOVILL—BARON KNOVILL.

By Writ of Summons, dated 23 June, 1295.

Lineage.

Bogo de Knovill, in the 16th King John, had livery of those lands at Horsed, in Cambridgeshire, which Stephen of Oxford some time held. But in the 18th Henry III., being involved in the insurrection of Richard, Earl Marshal, all his possessions were seized by the crown. Upon making submission, however, he obtained precepts to the sheriffs of Northamptonshire, Buckinghamshire, Sussex, Herefordshire, and Cambridgeshire, to make restitution to him of what lay in their respective counties. To this Bogo *s.* (his son and heir it is presumed)

Bogo de Knovill, who, in the 3rd Edward I., was constituted sheriff of the cos. Salop and Stafford, and governor of the castle of Blaneminster (subsequently called Oswestre), in the former shire. In which office he continued for three years, and was then made governor of Dolvoron Castle, in the marches of Wales. This feudal lord was summoned to parliament as a baron, from 23 June, 1295, to 26 August, 1307, in which latter year he *d.*, leaving a son and heir, then thirty years of age,

Bogo de Knovill, who doing homage, had livery of his lands, but, according to Dugdale, was never summoned to parliament. His name appears, however, in the rolls of the first year of King Edward II., amongst others therein mentioned, as having been summoned to the parliament held at that period. In the 4th Edward II., this Bogo was in the wars of Scotland, and in four years after he had a military summons for the same field. He was subsequently involved in the rebellion of Thomas, Earl of Lancaster, and paid the very large fine of £1,000 to preserve his life. He then resided in Gloucestershire. Of this nobleman, or his descendants, Dugdale gives no further account.

Kimber, in his Baronetage states, that Eleanor, dau. and co-heir of Sir John Knovill, *m.* about the 13th Edward III., Grey de St. Aubyn, ancestor of Sir John St. Aubyn, Baronet, of Clowance, co. Cornwall.

Arms—Arg., three estoiles, gu.

KNYVETT — BARON KNYVETT, OF ESCRICK, CO. YORK.

By Writ of Summons, dated 4 July, 1607.

Lineage.

The very ancient family of Knyvett came at length to possess Buckenham Castle, in Norfolk, through the Cliftons.

Sir John Knyvett, Knt. (son of Richard Knyvett, by Joan his wife, and great-grandson of Sir John Knyvett, Lord of Southwick), was constituted chief justice of the King's Bench, 39th Edward III., and became subsequently lord chancellor of England. He *m.* Eleanor, eldest dau. of Ralph, 2nd Lord Basset, of Welden, and his eldest son and heir,

John Knyvett, was one of the knights of the shire for Huntingdon, 21st Richard II. He left with two daus., an only son,

Sir John Knyvett, who *m.* Elizabeth, dau. of Sir Constantine de Clifton, 2nd Baron Clifton, and eventually co-heir of her noble family. By her he acquired Castle Buckenham, in Norfolk, and other estates. His only son and heir,

Sir John Knyvett, in whom, or his representative, the Barony of Clifton became vested, on the death of his uncle, Sir John Clifton, *m.* 1st, Alice, dau. of Reginald, Lord Grey, of Ruthyn, and by her had a son and heir, Edmund. He *m.* 2ndly, Joan, dau. of Humphrey Stafford, Duke of Buckingham, and relict of William, Viscount Beaumont, and by her had a son, Edward (Sir), high sheriff of Norfolk and Suffolk, 31st Henry VIII. Sir John *d.* 7th Henry VII., and was *s.* by his elder son,

Sir Edmund Knyvett, Knt., of Buckenham, who *m.* Eleanor, sister of Sir James Tyrell, Knt., and had with a dau., Anne (*m.* to Sir George St. Leger), five sons, viz.,

Thomas (Sir), of whose line we here treat.
Edmund, serjeant porter to Henry VIII., who *m.* Jane, only surviving dau. of Sir John Bourchier, 2nd Baron Berners, and by this great heiress had three sons and three daus., viz.,
  1 John, who left a son and heir, Sir Thomas Knyvet, whose descendant, Elizabeth Knyvet, *m.* Henry Wilson, Esq., and their grandson Robert Wilson, was summoned to parliament in 1832, as Lord Berners.
  2 William, ancestor of the Knyvetts of Fundenhall, in Norfolk.
  3 Edmund.
  1 Rose, *m.* to Oliver Reymes.
  2 Alice, *m.* to Oliver Spiers.
  3 Christian, *m.* to Thomas Foster.

The eldest son,
Sir Thomas Knyvett, of Buckenham, was made knight of the Bath at the coronation of Henry VIII., and became subse-

quently master of the horse. He *m.* Muriel, dau. of Thomas, Duke of Norfolk, and relict of John Grey, Viscount Lisle, and had issue,

    i. EDMUND (Sir), his heir, whose great grandson, PHILIP KNYVETT, was created a Baronet at the institution of the order, 22 May, 1611, which dignity became extinct on the death of his son, SIR ROBERT, the 2nd bart., about 1699 (*see* BURKE's *Extinct Baronetage*). Sir Robert's sisters and co-heirs were

      1 Dorothy, *m.* to James, 6th Earl of Buchan.
      2 Katherine, *d. unm.*
      3 Eleanor, *m.* 1st, to Sir Henry Hastings, of Braunston, co. Leicester, and 2ndly, to Thomas Waldron, Esq., of Charley, co. Leicester.

    ii. Ferdinando.   iii. HENRY (Sir), of whom we treat.

The 3rd son,

SIR HENRY KNYVETT, knighted by Queen ELIZABETH, in 1574, *m.* Anne, dau. and heir of Sir Christopher Pickering, and thence descended the brother,

    HENRY (Sir), Knt., of Charlton, co. Wilts, who left two daus., his co-heirs, viz.,

      Katherine, who *m.* 1st, the Hon. Richard Rich, but had no issue. She *m.* 2ndly, Thomas Howard, 1st Earl of Suffolk, and the estate of Charlton passed to her 2nd son, the Hon. Thomas Howard, who was created Earl of Berkshire.
      Elizabeth, *m.* to Thomas, 3rd Lord Lincoln, ancestor of the Dukes of Newcastle.

THOMAS (Sir).

The 2nd son was,

SIR THOMAS KNYVETT, Knt., one of the gentlemen of the privy chamber to King JAMES I., who, in 1605, upon the mysterious intimation conveyed by letter to the Lord Monteagle, was sent, being a justice of the peace in Westminster, to make search, with others, in the vaults and cellars under the House of Lords, where Guydo Faux, was discovered, and the Gunpowder Plot detected and prevented. After which, he was summoned to the parliament then sitting, 4 July, 1607, as BARON KNYVETT, *of Escrick, co. York.* His lordship *m.* Elizabeth, widow of Richard Warren, Esq., and dau. of Sir Rowland Hayward, an alderman of London, but had no issue. He *d.* 27 April, 1622, when the Barony of Escrick became EXTINCT. His lordship's estates devolved upon his niece, Elizabeth, dau. and co-heir of Sir Henry Knyvett, of Charlton, co. Wilts; which Elizabeth, *m.* Thomas Howard, Earl of Suffolk, and her 7th son, Sir Edward Howard, K.B., was created BARON HOWARD *of* ESCRICK, 29 April, 1628 (*see that dignity*).

Arms—Arg., a bend, sa., and a border, engrailed, of the last.

KYME—BARONS KYME.

By Writ of Summons, dated 23 June, 1295.

Lineage.

Of this ancient family, which assumed the surname of *Kyme*, from a fair lordship, the principal place of their residence in Kesteven, co. Lincoln, the first mentioned is

SIMON DE KYME (the son of William), who founded, *temp.* STEPHEN, the priory of Bolington, in Lincolnshire. This Simon *m.* Roese, dau. of Robert *Dapifer* (that is steward to Gilbert de Gant, Earl of Lincoln), which lady was commonly called Roese de Bolinton. He was *s.* by his son,

PHILIP DE KYME, who was constituted sheriff of Lincolnshire, in the 14th HENRY II., and was one of the barons in the great council held at London in the year 1177, where he was a subscribing witness to the instrument of arbitration there made by King HENRY II., for according the difference betwixt ALFONSO, King of Castile, and SANCTIUS, King of Navarre. This feudal lord was the founder of the priory of Kyme, and he granted twenty acres of land to the canons and nuns at Bolinton, for supporting the charge of their garments. He was steward to Gilbert de Gant, Earl of Lincoln, and was *s.* at his decease (before 1194) by his son,

SIMON DE KYME, who, in the 21st HENRY II., was indebted to the crown in the sum of forty marks, as a fine for not disclaiming his right to certain lands after he had lost them upon a trial by battle. In the 6th EDWARD I. he paid 100 marks to be excused serving in Normandy, and in the 8th of the same reign he was sheriff of Lincolnshire. In the reign of JOHN he took up arms with the barons, and was excommunicated by the pope, when his lands were all seized and transferred to Geoffrey Nevill. He subsequently negotiated for their restoration, but *d.* before anything effectual in the matter could be accomplished. He *d.* in 1219, and was *s.* by his son,

PHILIP DE KYME, who, upon paying £100 for his relief, had the lands of his father restored to him. He *m.* Agnes de Wales, and dying in 1242, was *s.* by his eldest son,

SIMON DE KYME, who *d. s. p.* 1247, and was *s.* by his brother, WILLIAM DE KYME, who also *d. s. p.* in 1258, and was *s.* by

309

PHILIP DE KYME. This feudal lord had a military summons in the 22nd EDWARD I., for the French wars, and in three years afterwards he was engaged in Gascony. This eminent person was summoned to parliament as a Baron, from 23 June, 1295, to 26 November, 1313. His lordship *m.* a dau. of Hugh Bigot (to which Hugh he had been a ward in his minority), and dying in 1322, was *s.* by his son,

WILLIAM DE KYME, 2nd baron, summoned to parliament, from 26 December, 1323, to 22 January, 1336. His lordship *d. s. p.* in 1338, leaving Joane, his widow, who *re-m.* Nicholas de Cantilupe. Whereupon Robert de Umframvill, Earl of Angus, who had *m.* LUCIE DE KYME, his lordship's sister, came by virtue of a fine levied in the 8th EDWARD III., to possess the inheritance; and amongst the descendants of the said Robert and Lucie the Barony of Kyme must now be considered to be in ABEYANCE.

Arms—Gu. a chevron, between ten crosslets, or.

LABOUCHERE—BARON TAUNTON.

By Letters Patent, dated 18 August, 1859.

Lineage.

The family of Labouchere left France at the period of the revocation of the edict of Nantes, and became established in Holland. The first who settled in England was

PETER-CÆSAR LABOUCHERE, Esq., a partner in the great mercantile house of Hope, who purchased the estates of Hylands, in Essex, and Over Stowey, co. Somerset. He *m.* 26 November, 1796, Dorothy-Elizabeth, 4th dau. of Sir Francis Baring, 1st Bart. of Larkbeer, and had issue,

    i. HENRY, created LORD TAUNTON.
    ii. John, J.P., of Broome Hall, Dorking, Surrey, *b.* 1799; *m.* 1830, Mary-Louisa, 2nd dau. of James Du Pré, Esq. of Wilton Park, co. Bucks; and *d.* 29 July, 1863, having had, with other issue,

      Henry, M.P. for Northampton, *b.* 1831.
      Arthur, *b.* 1842.
      Louisa, *m.* 1861, Rev. G.-W. Hillyar, of Coldharbour, Dorking.
      Fanny-Adelaide, *m.* 28 August, 1860, to Stuart-Herbert-Crichton Stuart, younger son of Lord James-Chrichton Stuart, and nephew of John, 2nd Marquis of Bute.

Mr. Labouchere *d.* 16 January, 1839, and was *s.* by his eldest son,

THE RIGHT HON. HENRY LABOUCHERE, P.C., M.A., *b.* 15 August, 1798; *m.* 1st, 10 April, 1840, Frances, youngest dau. of Sir Thomas Baring, 2nd Bart. of Larkbeer, and by her (who *d.* 25 May, 1850) had,

    i. Mary-Dorothy, *b.* 22 May, 1842; *m.* 19 September, 1872, Edward-James Stanley, Esq. of Cross Hall, co. Lancaster (*see Extant Peerage,* DERBY, E.).
    ii. Mina-Frances, *b.* 23 June, 1843; *m.* 2 May, 1864, to Capt. Arthur-E.-A. Ellis, grenadier guards (*see Extant Peerage,* HOWARD-DE-WALDEN, B.).
    iii. Emily-Harriet, *b.* 24 June, 1844; *m.* 18 October, 1881, Henry-Cornwallis, 5th Earl of St. Germans.

He *m.* 2ndly, 13 July, 1852, Lady Mary-Matilda-Georgiana Howard, dau. of George, 6th Earl of Carlisle. He was a lord of the admiralty from 1832 to 1834, vice-president of the board of trade and master of the mint from 1835 to 1839, chief secretary for Ireland from 1846 to 1847, and again president of the board of trade from 1847 to 1852, and secretary of state for the colonies from 1855 to 1858. He was raised to the peerage of the United Kingdom by letters patent, dated 18 August, 1859, as BARON TAUNTON *of Taunton, co.* Somerset, and *d.* without male issue, 13 July, 1869, when his title became EXTINCT.

Arms—Quarterly: erm. and az., in the 2nd and 3rd quarters a cross patonce, or.

LACY—EARLS OF LINCOLN.

By Charter of Creation, dated 23 November, 1232.

Lineage.

WALTER DE LACI, and ILBERT DE LACI, came into England with the CONQUEROR, but in what degree allied, if at all, has not been ascertained. From ILBERT, the noble house of which we are about to treat, derived, and to him and his descendants, after disposing of the line of Walter, we shall direct our attention. First then, as to the

LINE OF WALTER DE LACI.

WALTER DE LACI was one of the commanders whom WILLIAM THE CONQUEROR sent into Wales to subjugate the principality, and being victorious acquired large possessions there, in addition to those already obtained as his portion of the spoil of Hastings. He was killed in April, 1084. Walter de Laci left three sons, Roger, Hugh, and Walter, a monk in the abbey of St. Peter's, at Gloucester. The eldest son,

Roger de Laci, had large possessions in the cos. of Berks, Salop, Gloucester, Worcester, and Hereford, where the castle of Ewyas was the head of his barony. But joining in the rebellion against William Rufus, in favour of Robert Curthose, he was banished England, and all his lands were conferred upon his brother,

Hugh de Laci, who, with many other Norman soldiers of fortune, had been permitted by Rufus to invade the principality of Wales, and to acquire by their good swords, lands thereabouts—which lands Sir John Doddridge, Knt., one of the justices of the Court of King's Bench, a learned antiquary as well as lawyer, describes as becoming, when conquered, *Baronies Marchers* held in *capite* of the crown—wherein the barons enjoyed a kind of palatine jurisdiction, with power to administer justice to the tenants in each of their territories, holding courts, invested with divers privileges, franchises, and immunities, so that the king's writs were not current, unless the whole barony had been in question. Such was the state of the government of the marches of Wales down to the reign of Henry VIII. This Hugh, who upon all occasions liberally supported the church, was the founder of the priory of Lanthony, in Wales. He *d. s. p.*, bequeathing his great inheritance to his two sisters, Ermeline, who had no children, and Emme, whose son,

Gilbert, assumed the surname of Laci. This feudal lord, in the conflict between Stephen and the Empress, espoused the cause of the latter. He eventually became a knight Templar, and was *s.* by (whether son or brother not known),

Hugh de Laci, who was employed in the conquest of Ireland, and for his services there obtained from King Henry II., the whole county of Meath. He was subsequently constituted governor of Dublin, and justice of Ireland. But incurring the displeasure of his royal master by marrying without license the king of Connaught's dau., he was divested in 1181, of the custody of the metropolis. In four years afterwards he was murdered by one Malvo Miadaich, a mean person, in revenge for the severity with which he had treated the workmen employed by him in erecting the castle of Lurhedy. He left issue,

Walter, his successor.
Hugh, constable of Ireland, who, according to Matthew Paris, a most famous soldier, obtained the earldom of Ulster from King John, by betraying and delivering into that monarch's power the celebrated John de Courcy, Earl of Ulster. He subsequently, however, incurred the displeasure of the king, and was himself driven out of Ireland. His wife was Emeline, dau. and heir of Walter de Riddlesford, by whom (who *m.* 2ndly, Stephen de Longespee) he left at his decease, 26th Henry III., an only dau and heir,

Maud de Lacy, who *m.* Walter de Burgh, Lord of Connaught and Earl of Ulster.

Elayne, *m.* to Richard de Beaufo.

The elder son,
Walter de Laci, obtained, 9 King John, a confirmation of his dominion of Meath, to be held by him and his heirs for the service of fifty knights' fees; as also of all his fees in Fingall, in the valley of Dublin, to be held by the service of seven knights' fees. But in three years afterwards, King John passing into Ireland with his army, Laci was forced to deliver himself up and all his possessions in that kingdom, and to abjure the realm. He was subsequently banished from England, but in the 16th of the same reign, he seems to have made his peace, for he was then allowed to repossess Ludlow, with the castle; and the next year he recovered all his lands in Ireland, except the castle and lands of Drogheda, by paying a fine of 4,000 marks to the crown. After this we find him sheriff of Herefordshire, in the 18th of John, and 2nd of Henry III., and in the 14th of the latter king, joined with Geffrey de Marisco, then Justice of Ireland, and Richard de Burgh, in subduing the King of Connaught, who had taken up arms to expel the English from his territories. So much for the secular acts of this powerful feudal baron. In Ireland he founded the abbey of Beaubec, which was first a cell to the great abbey of Bec, in Normandy, and afterwards to Furneise, in Lancashire. Walter Laci *m.* Margaret, dau. of William de Braose, of Brecknock, and in the year 1241, being then infirm and blind, departed this life, " *Vir, inter omnes nobiles Hiberniæ, eminentissimus,*" leaving his great inheritance to be divided amongst females, viz., the daus. of Gilbert de Lacy, his son (who *d.* in his life time), and Isabel his wife, sister of John Bigod. Which daus. were,

Maud, wife of Peter de Geneva, who had livery of Ludlow Castle in her right, and after this in the 38th Henry III., of Geffrey de Genevill, who had livery of the castle of Trim, in the co. of Meath, as part of her inheritance.

Margery, *m.* to John de Verdon, and had for her share of the property, the castle of Webbeley. The honour of Ewyas-Lacy having been assigned for the dower of Isabel, her mother.

310

Having thus brought the line of Walter de Lacy, the companion of the Conqueror, to a close, we return to his fellow-soldier, if not kinsman, and proceed to deduce the

Line of Ilbert de Laci.

Ilbert de Laci, to whom King William gave the castle and town of Brokenbridge, co. York, which he afterwards denominated, in the Norman dialect, " Pontfract," had besides other territorial graots of vast extent; and at the time of the General Survey possessed nearly one hundred and fifty lordships in Yorkshire, ten in Nottingham, and four in Lincolnshire. This Ilbert left two sons, Robert and Hugh. The elder,

Robert de Laci, otherwise Robert de Pontfract, had a confirmation from King William Rufus, of all those lands whereof Ilbert, his father, died possessed. Attaching himself, however, to the interest of Robert Curthose, after the death of Rufus, himself and his son, Ilbert, were expelled the realm by King Henry I., and the honour of Pontfract bestowed upon Henry Travers; which Henry, having shortly after been mortally wounded by one Pain, a servant of his own, caused himself to be shorn a monk, and so *d.* within three days. After that the king gave this honour to Guy de la Val, who held it until King Stephen's time, when, it is stated by an old historian, that Robert de Laci's son,

Ilbert de Lacy (the personage mentioned above as exiled with his father), by the special favour of Stephen, re-obtained his Barony of Pontefract, and was ever afterwards one of the stanchest adherents of that monarch. In the 3rd year of that reign he was a principal commander at the celebrated battle of the Standard, fought at Northallerton, where the Scots sustained so signal a defeat from the northern barons. He subsequently obtained a pardon on behalf of his servants, for all forfeitures whatsoever; and especially for the death of William Maltravers. This feudal lord *m.* Alice, dau. of Gilbert de Gant, but dying *s p.*, he was *s.* by his brother,

Henry de Lacy, who was received into favour by the empress, and her son, King Henry II., and obtained from them a remission of the displeasure which King Henry I. bore towards Robert, his father; as also of the forfeiture, which he himself had made before he did his homage; with full restitution of his whole honour of Pontfract, and all other his lands in England and Normandy. He was *s.* by his son,

Robert de Lacy, who attended as one of the barons at the coronation of King Richard I. This feudal lord *d. s. p.* in 1193, when (the dau. of his mother, Albrida, by her 2nd husband, Eudo de Lisours,) his half sister,

Albreda Lisours, then the wife of Richard Fitz-Eustace, feudal baron of Halton, and constable of Chester, possessed herself of the Barony of Pontfract, and all the other lands of her deceased brother, under pretence of a grant from Henry de Lacy, her 1st husband. By Fitz-Eustace, she had a son, John, who becoming heir to his half uncle, Robert de Lacy, assumed that surname, and inherited, as

John de Lacy, the Baronies of Halton and Pontfract, with the constableship of Chester. This feudal lord *m.* Alice de Vere, and dying in the Holy Land, *anno* 1179, was *s.* by his eldest son,

Roger de Lacy, constable of Chester. This nobleman assisted at the siege of Acon, in 1192, under the banner of the lion-hearted Richard, and shared in the subsequent triumphs of the chivalrous monarch. At the accession of John, he was a person of great eminence, for we find him shortly after the coronation of that prince, deputed with the sheriff of Northumberland, and other great men, to conduct William, King of Scotland, to Lincoln, where the English king had fixed to give him an interview; and the next year he was one of the barons present at Lincoln, when David, of Scotland, did homage and fealty to King John.

In the time of this Roger, Ranulph, Earl of Chester, having entered Wales at the head of some forces, was compelled, by superior numbers, to shut himself up in the castle of Rothelan, where, being closely besieged by the Welsh, he sent for aid to the constable of Chester. Hugh Lupus, the 1st Earl of Chester, in his charter of foundation of the abbey of St. Werberg, at Chester, had given a privilege to the frequenters of Chester fair, " That they should not be apprehended for theft, or any other offence during the time of the fair, unless the crime was committed therein." This privilege made the fair, of course, the resort of thieves and vagabonds from all parts of the kingdom. Accordingly, the constable, Roger de Laci, forthwith marched to his relief, at the head of a concourse of people, then collected at the fair of Chester, consisting of minstrels, and loose characters of all descriptions, forming altogether so numerous a body, that the besiegers, at their approach, mistaking them for soldiers, immediately raised the siege. For this timely service, the Earl of Chester conferred upon De Lacy and his heirs, the patronage of all the minstrels in those parts, which patronage the constable transferred to his steward, Dutton, and his heirs; and it is enjoyed to this day by the family of Dutton. It is doubtful, however, whether the privilege was transferred to the Duttons by this constable, or his successor. The privilege was, "That, at the midsummer fair held at Chester, all the minstrels of that country, resorting to Chester, do attend the heir of Dutton, from his lodging to St. John's Church (he being then accompanied by many gentlemen of the country, one of them walking before him in a surcoat of his arms, depicted on taffata; the rest of his fellows proceeding two and two, and playing on their several sorts of musical instruments.") When divine service terminates, the like attendance upon Dutton to his lodging, where a court being kept by his steward, and all the minstrels formally called, certain orders and laws are made for the government of the society of minstrels.

Roger de Lacy's son and successor,

JOHN DE LACY, constable of Chester, who, in the 15th year of King JOHN, undertook the payment of 7,000 marks to the crown, in the space of four years, for livery of the lands of his inheritance, and to be discharged of all his father's debts due to the exchequer; further obliging himself by oath, that in case he should ever swerve from his allegiance, and adhere to the king's enemies, all his possessions should devolve upon the crown; promising also, that he would not marry without the king's license. By this agreement it was arranged that the king should retain the castles of Pontefract and Dunnington, still in his own hands; and that he, the said John, should allow £40 per annum, for the custody of those fortresses. But the next year he had Dunnington restored to him, upon hostages. About this period he joined the baronial standard, and was one of the celebrated twenty-five barons, appointed to enforce the observance of Magna Charta. But the next year, he obtained letters of safe conduct to come to the king to make his peace, and he had similar letters, upon the accession of HENRY III, in the 2nd year of which monarch's reign, he went with divers other noblemen into the Holy Land. He m. MARGARET, dau. and heir of Robert de Quincy, Earl of Winchester (see that title), by Hawyse, 4th sister and co-heir of Ranulph de Mechines, Earl of Chester and Lincoln, which Ranulph, by a formal charter under his seal, granted the EARLDOM OF LINCOLN, that is, so much as he could grant thereof, to the said Hawyse, "to the end that she might be countess, and that her heirs might also enjoy the earldom;" which grant was confirmed by the king, and at the especial request of the countess, this John de Lacy, constable of Chester, was created by charter, dated at Northampton, 23 November, 1232, EARL OF LINCOLN, with remainder to the heirs of his body, by his wife, the above-mentioned Margaret. In the contest which occurred during the same year, between the king and Richard Marshal, Earl of Pembroke, Earl Marshal, Matthew Paris states that the Earl of Lincoln was brought over to the king's party, with John le Scot, Earl of Chester, by Peter de Rupibus, bishop of Winchester, for a bribe of 1,000 marks. In 1237, his lordship was one of those appointed to prohibit Oto, the pope's legate, from establishing anything derogatory to the king's crown and dignity, in the council of prelates then assembled: and the same year he had a grant of the sheriffalty of Cheshire, being likewise constituted governor of the castle of Chester. The earl d. in 1240, leaving Margaret, his wife, surviving, who re-m. William Marshal, Earl of Pembroke. His lordship left issue,

EDMUND, his successor.

and two daus., which ladies in the 27th HENRY III., were removed to Windsor, there to be educated with the king's own daus.; of these, Maud, m. Richard de Clare, Earl of Gloucester. The earl was s. by his son,

EDMUND DE LACI (presumed 2nd Earl of Lincoln). This young nobleman m. in 1247, "an outlandish lady," says Dugdale, "from the parts of Savoy, brought over purposely for him, by Peter de Savoy, uncle to the queen, which occasioned much discontent amongst the nobles of England." The lady thus designated was Alice, dau. of the Marquess of Saluces, in Italy, and cousin of the queen. By her his lordship had issue,

HENRY, his successor.
John.
Margaret, m. to George de Cantilupe, Baron of Bergavenny.

As to the title of EARL OF LINCOLN, this nobleman never used it, nor was it ever attributed to him in any charter, by reason that he died before his mother, through whom the dignity came; but as he enjoyed the Tertium Denarium of that county, he must nevertheless be esteemed the 2nd earl, and

Sir Harris Nicolas so places him. His lordship d. in 1257, and was s. by his elder son,

HENRY DE LACY, 3rd Earl of Lincoln, who having m. Margaret, dau. and co-heir of William de Longespee, son of William de Longespee, Earl of Salisbury, became jure uxoris, EARL OF SALISBURY. This nobleman was one of the most eminent of the period in which he lived, and enjoyed the highest favour of King EDWARD I., in whose Welsh wars he had early a distinguished part, and obtained from the king the land of Denbigh, upon which he began the town of that name, walling it in and protecting it by a castle, upon the front whereof was his statue in long robes. In 1290 (18th EDWARD I.), his lordship was appointed the chief commissioner for rectifying and discovering abuses and briberies amongst the judges, complained of in parliament; when Thomas Weyland, Chief Justice of the Common Pleas, was banished, and all his estates forfeited; Sir John Lovetot, compounded for 500 marks; Roger Leicester (clerk), for 1,000; Sir William Brompton for 6,000, with several others, who were also fined; a proof that the judgment-seat is not always as immaculate as it is represented to be. In the 21st year of EDWARD I., his lordship was sent ambassador to the King of France, to treat concerning the restraint of pirates; and the next year he attended the king into Wales, where he experienced a great repulse, not far from the castle of Denbigh. He was subsequently, for some years, engaged in the French wars: first under Edmund, Earl of Lancaster, but after the decease of that prince, he had the sole command of the army himself. In the 27th and 28th of the same reign, his lordship was in the wars of Scotland; in the 29th he was constituted governor of Corff Castle, and two years afterwards, joined in commission with the bishop of Winchester and others, to treat of peace with the court of France. In 1305, the earl was deputed, with the bishops of Lichfield and Worcester, to the solemn inauguration of the Pope at Lions, and presented his holiness with divers vessels of pure gold, from his royal master. After this, we again find him in the wars of Gascony and Scotland; and in the 3rd EDWARD II., upon that monarch's march into Scotland, the Earl of Lincoln was constituted governor of England, during the king's absence. His lordship d. in 1312, "at his mansion house, called Lincoln's Inn, in the suburbs of London, which he himself had erected, in that place, where the Black-friars habitation anciently stood." Immediately before his decease, he called his son-in-law, the Earl of Lancaster, to his bedside, and addressed him in words to the following effect: "Seest thou the church of England, heretofore honourable and free, enslaved by Romish oppressions, and the king's unjust exactions? Seest thou the common people impoverished by tributes and taxes, and from the condition of freemen, reduced to servitude? Seest thou the nobility, formerly venerable through Christendom, vilified by aliens, in their own native country? I therefore charge thee, in the name of Christ, to stand up like a man; for the honour of God, and his church, and redemption of thy country; associating thyself to that valiant, noble, and prudent person, Guy, Earl of Warwick, when it shall be most proper to discourse of the public affairs of the kingdom; who is so judicious in counsel, and mature in judgment. Fear not thy opposers, who shall contest against thee in the truth. And if thou pursuest this, my advice, thou shalt gain eternal Heaven!" This great earl left an only dau. and heiress,

ALICE DE LACY, who m. 1st, Thomas Plantagenet, Earl of Lancaster, who is said to have been Earl of Lincoln, in her right; she m. 2ndly, Eubold le Strange; and 3rdly, Hugh le Frenes. Her ladyship assumed the title of COUNTESS OF LINCOLN AND SALISBURY, but d. s. p. in 1348, when those honours became EXTINCT, in the family of Lacy.

Arms—Or, a lion rampant, purpure.

LACY—EARL OF ULSTER.
(See preceding Memoir.)

LAKE—BARONS AND VISCOUNTS LAKE.

Barony, by Letters Patent, dated 13 September, 1804.
Viscounty, by Letters Patent, dated 4 November, 1807.

Lineage.

SIR THOMAS LAKE, of Canons, co. Middlesex (eldest son of Almaric Lake, of Southampton, and brother of Arthur Lake, bishop of Bath and Wells), was born at Southampton, bred a scholar, and afterwards taken into the service of Sir Francis Walsingham, secretary of state, as his amanuensis. By this minister he was recommended to Queen ELIZABETH, to whom he read French and Latin. A little before her Majesty's death, she made him clerk of her signet, and after her decease, he was deputed by the state in that capacity, to attend JAMES I. from Berwick. That monarch soon after employed him in French affairs, and knighted him. After Sir Robert Cecil (Salisbury) attained the administration of affairs, the secretaryship of state was divided, and Sir Thomas Lake was appointed one of the secretaries, "and so continued," says A. Wood, "with honourable esteem of all men, till malice and revenge, two violent p·ssions, overruling the weaker sex,* concerning his wife and dau., involved him in their quarrel, the chief and only cause of his ruin." Sir Thomas *m.* Mary, dau. and heir of Sir William Ryther, lord mayor of London, and had issue,

THOMAS (Sir).   LANCELOT (Sir).
Elizabeth, *m.* to Lord Roos.
Anne, *m.* to William Stonor, Esq., of Stonor.
Mary, *m.* to John Ingleby, Esq.
Bridget, *m.* to Sir William Domville.

Sir Thomas *d.* at his seat of Canons, co. Middlesex (which he had bought in 1604), 17 September, 1630, and was *s.* by his eldest son,

SIR THOMAS LAKE, of Canons, who *d.* in 1653, and was *s.* by his brother,

SIR LANCELOT LAKE, of Canons, who *m.* Frances, dau. of Sir Thomas Cheeke, of Pirgo, by Elizabeth, his wife, dau. of Robert Rich, Earl of Warwick, and *d.* in 1680, leaving, with other issue,

THOMAS (Sir), who inherited Canons, and marrying Rebecca, dau. of Sir James Langham. Bart., had several children, of whom,

MARY became eventually sole heir, and marrying John Brydges, Duke of Chandos, conveyed to that nobleman the seat of Canons.

And
WARWICK LAKE, Esq., who *m.* Elizabeth, only dau. and sole heir of Sir Charles Gerard,† Bart., of Flamberds, and granddaughter, maternally, of Charles Seymour, Lord Seymour, of Trowbridge, and dying in 1712, left an only son.

LAUNCELOT-CHARLES LAKE, Esq. This gentleman *m.* Letitia, dau. and co-heir‡ of John Gumley, Esq., of Isleworth, and had two sons, Gerard and Warwick, of whom,

GERARD LAKE, Esq., having adopted the profession of arms attained the rank of general in the army, with the colonelcy of the 60th regiment of foot: and was elevated to the peerage, 1 September, 1804, as BARON LAKE, *of Delhi, Laswaree, and of Aston Clinton, co. Bucks,* in consideration of the high military talents and personal valour he had displayed in the command of the army during the Mahratta war, receiving, at the same time, the thanks of both houses of parliament. His lordship

* From a statement made by Saunderson, who was secretary to Lord Roos, during that nobleman's embassy in Spain, (1611,) we extract the cause and issue of the great feud between Frances, 2nd wife of Thomas, 1st Earl of Exeter, and the Lake family, alluded to above. We must previously premise that Thomas, 1st Earl of Exeter, espoused, for his 2nd countess. Frances Brydges, dau. of William, Lord Chandos, and widow of Sir Thomas Smith, master of requests to JAMES I.. and that the lady was thirty-eight years younger than her noble husband. It is necessary also to observe, that Lord Roos, who *m.* Elizabeth, dau. of Sir Thomas Lake, was only son of William, 2nd Earl of Exeter (son and successor of the 1st earl), by Elizabeth, only dau. and heir of Edward Manners, Earl of Rutland. He was thus *step-grandson* to Frances, Countess of Exeter.

Upon Lord Roos's return from Spain, falling into some neglect of his wife and her kindred, and soon after withdrawing into Italy, where he became a Roman catholic, Lady Lake and her daughter, Lady Roos, asserted that an improper intimacy had subsisted between his lordship and the countess, his step-grandmother; and that the discovery of the intrigue had caused his lordship's flight into Italy. The matter at length assumed so serious a character that it was finally investigated before JAMES I., in person, when the whole story was found to have originated in the malice of Lady Lake and her dau., and the latter (Lady Roos) made an ample confession of the plot, in the middle of the trial, for which she was exempted from penal sentence. Sir Thomas Lake and his wife were condemned to pay £10,000 to the crown, and £5,000 to the countess, while Sarah Wharton, one of the perjured witnesses, was sentenced to be whipped through the streets at the cart's tail, and to do penance in St. Martin's Church.

† The Gerards of Flamberds were a younger branch of the family of Gerard, of Ince, in Lancashire. The 3rd baronet, SIR CHARLES GERARD, left at his decease, in 1701, an only child, ELIZABETH, *m.* 1st, to Warwick Lake, Esq., and 2ndly, to Miles Stapleton, Esq. (*see* BURKE's *Extinct Baronetage.*)

‡ The other co-heirs of Mr. Gumley were,
Anna-Maria, *m.* to William Pulteney, Earl of Bath.
Mary, *m.* to Francis Colman, Esq., and was mother of George Colman, the dramatist.

was advanced to a viscounty, by s·milar titles, 31 October, 1807. He *m.* 1770, Elizabeth, only dau. of Edward Barker, Esq., of St. Julians, co. Herts, and had issue,

FRANCIS-GERARD. his successor.
George-Augustus-Frederick, lieutenant-colonel 29th foot, a distinguished officer, slain at Vimiera, 1808.
WARWICK, present peer.
Anna-Maria, *m.* in 1799, to Sir Richard Borough. Bart.
Amabel, *m.* 1803, to Joseph Brooks, Esq., of Everton, near Liverpool, and *d.* 1831.
Elizabeth, *m.* in 1806, to Lieut.-Gen. Sir John Harvey, K.C.B., one of his late Majesty's aides-de-camp, and *d.* 1851, leaving issue.
Frances, *d.* 4 June, 1853.
Anne, *m.* 1812, to Lieut.-Gen. John Wardlaw, and *d.* 1815.

His lordship *d.* 20 February, 1808, and was *s.* by his son,
FRANCIS-GERARD, 2nd viscount, a lieutenant-general in the army; *b.* in 1772; *m.* 1st, 1 January, 1800, Priscilla, eldest dau. of Sir Charles Whitworth, Knt., widow of Sir Bellingham Graham, Bart.; and 2ndly, 12 August, 1833, Anne, second dau. of the late Admiral Sir Richard Onslow, Bart., but by her ladyship (who *m.* 2ndly, 14 September, 1837, Henry Gritton, Esq., of Woolwich, and *d.* 4 April, 1853.) had no issue. His lordship *d.* 12 May, 1836, and was *s.* by his brother,
WARWICK, 3rd viscount, *m.* 28 November, 1815, Elizabeth, dau. of James-Beveridge Duncan, Esq., of Damside, and left two daus, viz.,

ISABELLA-ELIZABETH-AUGUSTA.
ELIZABETH-GEORGIANA.

His lordship *d.* 24 June, 1848, when all his honours became EXTINCT.

Arms—Sa., a bend, between six cross-crosslets, fitchée, arg.; on a chief of augmentation of the last, a representation of the fish of Mogul, barways, per pale, or and vert, banded, vert and gu., pierced by shafts, one erect, supporting a crescent, and others in saltier, headed variously with golden balls, an an nulet, &c.

LAMB—BARONS AND VISCOUNTS MELBOURNE, BARON BEAUVALE.

Barony of Ireland, by Letters Patent, dated 8 June, 1770.
Viscounty, by Letters Patent, dated 11 January, 1781.
Baronies of the United Kingdom, by Letters Patent, dated 11 August, 1815 and 1839.

Lineage.

PENISTON LAMB, Esq., of Lincoln's-Inn, *d.* 31 January, 1734, without issue, bequeathing his property between his nephews, Robert Lamb, D.D., bishop of Peterborough, who *d.* in 1769, Sir Matthew Lamb, Bart., and his niece, Elizabeth, wife of the Rev. Henry Middleditch. The second of these, his nephew,

MATTHEW LAMB, Esq., of Brocket Hall, co. Herts, was created a baronet, 17 January, 1755. He *m.* Charlotte, dau. of the Right Hon. Thomas Coke, of Melbourne, co. Derby (teller of the Exchequer, and vice chamberlain to Queen ANNE), and eventually heir of her brother, George-Lewis Coke, Esq. (*see* BURKE's *Commoners,* vol. iv.), by whom he had issue,

I. PENISTON, his successor, Viscount Melbourne.
II. Charlotte, who *m.* Henry, 2nd and last Earl of Fauconberg, and *d.* in 1790, leaving four daus, viz.,
   1 Lady Charlotte Belasyse, *m.* to Thomas-Edward Wynn, Esq., who assumed the name of Belasyse.
   2 Lady Anne Belasyse, *m.* 19 July, 1791, to Sir George Wombwell, 2nd baronet, and *d.* 7 July, 1808, leaving issue, (*see* BURKE's *Peerage and Baronetage*).
   3 Lady Elizabeth Belasyse, *m.* 1st, to Bernard-Edward Howard, Esq. (afterwards Duke of Norfolk), and 2ndly, 26 May, 1794 (having been divorced from Mr. Howard, by act of parliament, in 1794), to Richard, 2nd Earl of Lucan. Her ladyship *d.* 24 March, 1819, leaving issue. (*See Extant Peerage.*)
   4 Lady Harriet Belasyse.
III. Anne.

Sir Matthew, who had represented Peterborough in three parliaments, was one of his Majesty's council for the board of trade and plantations, and custos-rotulorum of the liberty of Peterborough: he *d.* 6 November, 1768, and was *s.* by his son,
SIR PENISTON LAMB, as 2nd baronet; *b.* 29 January, 1748. He was elevated to the peerage of Ireland, 8 June, 1770, as LORD MELBOURNE, *Baron of Kilmore, co. Cavan.* He *m.* 13 April, 1769, Elizabeth, only dau. of Sir Ralph Milbanke, 5th baronet

of Halnaby, co. York, and by her, (who d. 6 Apr'l, 1818) had issue,

   ɪ. Peniston, b. 3 May, 1770, M.P. for the co. Herts; d. unm. 24 January, 1805.

   ɪɪ. WILLIAM, of whom presently, as 2nd Viscount.

   ɪɪɪ. FREDERICK-JAMES (Sir). G.C.B., P.C., Lord Beauvale, heir to his brother and 3rd Viscount.

   ɪᴠ. George, M.P., late under-secretary of state for the Home Department; b. 11 July, 1784; m. in 1809, Mademoiselle Caroline-Rosalie St. Jules, and d. s. p. 2 January, 1834.

   ɪ. EMILY-MARY, m. 1st. 20 July, 1805. Peter-Leopold, 5th Earl Cowper (who d. 27 June. 1847, leaving issue); and 2ndly, 16 December, 1839, Henry-John, 3rd VISCOUNT PALMERSTON, K.G., who d. 18 October, 1865.

   ɪɪ. Harriet-Anne, d. 9 June, 1803.

His lordship was created VISCOUNT MELBOURNE, in the peerage of Ireland, 11 January, 1781, and was enrolled amongst the peers of the United Kingdom, 11 August, 1815, as BARON MELBOURNE. of Melbourne, co. Derby. He d. 22 July, 1828, and was s. by his son,

SɪR WILLIAM LAMB, 2nd viscount, b. 15 March, 1779; m. 3 June, 1805, Lady Caroline Ponsonby, only dau. of Frederick, 3rd Earl of Bessborough, and by her ladyship (who d. 25 January, 1828) had an only child,

   GEORGE-AUGUSTUS FREDERICK, b. 11 August, 1807; d. unm. 27 November, 1836.

Lord Melbourne was secretary of state for the home department in the Grey administration, from 1830, until he became FIRST LORD OF THE TREASURY (prime minister) 18 July, 1834, on the resignation of Earl Grey, in which high station (except for the brief tenure of office by Sir Robert Peel, from 26 December, 1834, to 18 April following,) he continued until 1841, at the head of the Government, which derived its name from him. His lordship d. 24 November, 1848, and was s. by his brother,

FREDERICK-JAMES, Lord Beauvale, G.C.B., as 3rd Viscount Melbourne. His lordship, who was b. 17 April, 1782, attained considerable distinction as a diplomatist and was envoy extraordinary and minister plenipotentiary at the court of Vienna, in 1831. In 1839 he was created a peer of the United Kingdom, as BARON BEAUVALE, of Beauvale, co. Nottingham. He m. 25 February, 1841, the Countess Alexandrina-Julia-Theresa-Wilhelmina-Sophia, dau. of the late Joachim-Charles-Louis-Mortimer, Count of Maltzan, but by her (who m. 2ndly, 10 June, 1856, John-George Weld, Lord Forester,) had no issue. His lordship d. 29 January, 1853, when all his honours became EXTINCT.

Arms—Sa., on a fesse. erminois, between three cinquefoils, arg., two mullets of the field.

LANCASTER—BARON LANCASTER.

By Writ of Summons, dated 29 December, 1299.

Lineage.

The LANCASTERS, feudal Lords of Kendal, deduced their descent from Ivo TAILBOYS, brother of Fulk, Earl of Anjou, through his great grandson, WILLIAM, who assumed, Dugdale presumes, from being governor of Lancaster Castle, the surname of Lancaster. This

WILLIAM DE LANCASTER. Baron of Kendal, m. Gundred. dau. of William, 2nd Earl of Warren, and widow of Roger. Earl of Warwick; by whom he had issue, William, his successor, and a dau., Avicia, m. to Richard de Morevill. He was s. at his decease by his son, called

WILLIAM DE LANCASTER the 2nd, who was steward to King HENRY II. This William m. Helewise de Stuteville, and left an only dau. and heiress,

   HELEWISE DE LANCASTER, whom RICHARD I., shortly after his coronation gave in marriage to (the son and heir of Roger Fitz-Reinfride, one of the justices of the King's Bench)

GILBERT FITZ-REINFRIDE, and in consideration of a fine of 60 marks of silver, relieved him and his heirs from a certain tribute, called NUTEGELD, which used to be paid by his lands in Westmoreland and Kendall. This Gilbert obtained a grant of the honour of Lancaster for life from King JOHN, and filled the office of sheriff of Lancashire from the 7th to the 17th year of the same reign. But we find him, notwithstanding, taking up arms with the other barons, and only reduced to allegiance by the capture of his son and heir, William, by the royalists, upon the fall of Rochester Castle. This event compelled the

haughty baron to sue for pardon, which the king granted with the freedom of the captive, in consideration of the sum of 12,000 marks, the custody of some of his castles, and hostages for future good conduct. This Gilbert d. in 1219, leaving issue,

WILLIAM, his heir, of whom presently.

Helewise, m. to Peter de Brus, of Skelton, and left a son, Peter, who d. s. p., and four daus.,

   1 Margaret, m. to Robert de Ros (see Ros`, whose descendant, in the 5th degree, and representative of the family,

      Elizabeth de Ros, m. Sir William de Parre. Knt., the great-great-great grand-children of which marriage were

         WILLIAM PARR (see PARR), Baron of Kendall, and Marquess of Northampton.

         KATHERINE PARR, last Queen of King HENRY VIII.

         Anne Parr, 1st wife of William Herbert, 1st Earl of Pembroke.

   2 Agnes m. to Walter de Fauconberg (see NEVILL, LORD FAUCONBERG).

   3 Lucy, m. to Robert de Tweng.

   4 Laderine, m. to John de Bella-Aqua.

Alice, m. to William de Lindesey, whose descendant,

   Christian de Lindesey, m. Ingleram de Ghisnes. Lord of Coucy, in France.

Serota, m. to Allan de Multon, and d. s. p.

Gilbert Fitz-Reinfride, was s. by his son.

WILLIAM, who assumed his maternal surname of LANCASTER, of whose history some particulars have been given above. This feudal lord was sheriff of Lancashire from the 18th to the 30th HENRY III. inclusive, and had likewise the custody of the honour of Lancaster. He d. about the year 1246 s. p., when his estates devolved upon the representatives of his two elder sisters, the youngest sister having d. s. p., and were thus divided. The Brus's had what was called the Marquess and Lumley fee; the Lindesays the Richmond fee. Thus terminated the legitimate line of the Lancasters, Barons of Kendall. The last baron, however, had a bastard brother, called

ROGER DE LANCASTER. who held the manor of Barton, co Westmoreland, by gift of his brother, as also that of Patterdale, in the same shire, and was sheriff of Lancashire, in 49th HENRY III. He m. Philippa, eldest dau., and one of the co-heirs of Hugh de Bolebec, of the co. Northumberland, and dying in 1290, was s. by his son,

JOHN DE LANCASTER. This feudal lord having distinguished himself in the wars of Scotland, temp. EDWARD I., was summoned to parliament as a Baron from 29 December, 1299, to 12 December. 1309. His lordship d. in 1334, s. p. when the BARONY OF LANCASTER became EXTINCT, whilst his estates, which included the feudal Barony of Rydale, in Westmoreland, with divers other lordships, in the cos. of Northumberland and Essex, devolved upon his heir-at-law, Richard, the son of Richard de Plaiz, then twelve years old.

Arms—Arg., two bars gules, on a canton of the 2nd, a lion passant guardant, or.

LANE—VISCOUNT LANESBOROUGH.

By Letters Patent, dated 31 July, 1676.

Lineage.

RICHARD LANE, Esq., of Tulske, co. Roscommon, who was created a Baronet of England, in 1660-1, m 1st, Mabell, dau. and heir of Gerald Fitzgerald, Esq., of Clonbolg and Rathaman, and 2ndly, Mary, dau. of Thomas Leicester, Esq. By the former, he left at his decease, 5 October, 1668, a son and successor,

SɪR GEORGE LANE, 2nd baronet, an eminent politician, who filled the office of secretary of state for Ireland, and was raised to the peerage of that kingdom, as VISCOUNT LANESBOROUGH, co. Longford. 31 July, 1676. His lordship m. 1st, Dorcas, dau. of Sir Anthony Brabazon, Knt., of the noble family of MEATH; and 2ndly, Lady Frances Sackville, dau. of Richard, 5th Earl of Dorset. His son and successor,

SɪR JAMES LANE, 2nd Viscount Lanesborough, m. Mary, dau. of Sir Charles Compton, Knt.; but d. s. p. 2 February, 1724, when all his honours became EXTINCT, and the estates devolved on his sister and heiress,

THE HON. FRANCES LANE, who became in 1691, the 2nd wife of HENRY FOX, Esq. (see Landed Gentry), and had issue,

I. GEORGE FOX, M.P. for York, who assumed the additional surname of LANE, and was created BARON BINGLEY (*see next article*).

II. JAMES FOX, who inherited the Surrey estates of his grandmother, Lady Lanesborough, and *d. s. p.* in 1753.

III. Sackville Fox, *m.* Anne Holloway. From him descend GEORGE LANE-FOX, Esq., of Bramham Park, Yorkshire, and Sackville George-Lane Fox, LORD CONYERS.

I. Denny-Henrietta, *d.* young.

II. Jane.　　III. Frances.　　IV. Anne.

Arms—Arg., a lion rampant, gules, within a border, sable; on a canton of the 1st, a harp and crown, or.

. The title of Lanesborough, in the peerage of Ireland, has since been revived in the Butler family. (*See Extant Peerage.*)

LANE-FOX—BARON BINGLEY.

By Letters Patent, dated 13 May, 1762.

Lineage.

GEORGE FOX, Esq., M.P. for the city of York, eldest son of Henry Fox, Esq. (for whose descent refer to BURKE's *Landed Gentry*). by his wife, the Hon. Frances Lane, sister and heiress of James. 2nd and last Viscount Lanesborough *s.* by will to the extensive property of Lord Lanesborough, and assumed. by act of parliament, 22 March, 1750-1, in accordance with the testator's injunction, the additional surname and arms of LANE: he *m.* in 1731, Harriet, dau. and sole heiress of Robert Benson, Lord Bingley (*see* that name); and was, on the extinction of his father-in-law's title, advanced to the peerage in the same dignity, being created, 13 May, 1762, BARON BINGLEY, *of Bingley, in the co. of York*. By his wife, with whom he is stated to have acquired £100,000, and £7,000 a-year, he had an only son,

ROBERT, *b.* 5 August, 1732, who *m.* 1st, Mildred, dau. and heir of John Bourchier, Esq., of Benningborough; and 2ndly, in 1761, Lady Bridget Henley, eldest dau. of Robert, 1st Earl of Northington, lord chancellor of England, but *d.* in his father's lifetime, *s. p.* His widow *m.* 2ndly, in 1773, the Hon. John Tollemache, capt. R.N., 3rd son of Lionel, 3rd Earl of Dysart, and *d.* 13 March, 1796.

Lord Bingley having devised his great estates in England and Ireland to his nephew, JAMES FOX-LANE, M.P. (son of his brother, Sackville), grandfather of GEORGE LANE-FOX Esq , of Bramham Park, co. York (*see Landed Gentry*), *d.* in 1772, when his barony became EXTINCT.

Arms—Quarterly: 1st and 4th, arg.. a lion rampant, gu., within a border, sa.; on a canton of the 1st, a harp and crown, or, for LANE. 2nd and 3rd : arg.. a chev., between three foxes' heads, erased, gu., for Fox.

LANGDALE—BARONS LANGDALE, OF HOLME.

By Letters Patent, dated 4 February, 1658.

Lineage.

The family derived its surname from the town of LANGDALE, in the hundred of Pickering, in Yorkshire, of which they were lords prior to the time of King JOHN.

In the reign of EDWARD II.

PATRICK DE LANGDALE *m.* Amanda, dau. and heiress of Lawrence de Elton, and was *s.* by his son,

PATRICK DE LANGDALE, who *m.* Helen. dau. and heir of Sir Thomas Houghton, of Houghton, co. York, and with her acquired that estate; from this Patrick descended

ANTHONY LANGDALE, of Houghton, who *d.* in the 19th of ELIZABETH (1577), leaving with other issue, RICHARD, his successor, at Houghton, and

PETER LANGDALE, who was seated at Pighill, near Beverley, and having *m.* Anne, dau. of Michael Wharton, Esq., of Beverley Park, was *s.* by his son,

SIR MARMADUKE LANGDALE, of Holme, in Spaldingmore, Yorkshire. This gentleman received the honour of knight-

hood from King CHARLES I., at Whitehall. in 1627, "and was esteemed," says Banks, "a serious and wise man, of most scholarlike accomplishments, and of good husbandry." During the civil wars, Sir Marmaduke became one of the most distinguished amongst the cavalier generals. At the head of a corps raised by himself, consisting of three companies of foot, and a troop of seventy horse, he encountered and defeated the Scots at Corbridge, in Northumberland; and next, being commander-in-chief of the troops sent by the king into Lincolnshire, he there encountered the rebels under Colonel Rosseter. Thence marching against the Lord Fairfax, and putting that officer to rout, he relieved Pontefract Castle, then beleaguered by a numerous body of the northern insurgents. He subsequently besieged and reduced Berwick-upon-Tweed, and the strong castle of Carlisle. But afterwards, involved in the defeat of the Duke of Hamilton and the Scotch army at Preston, Sir Marmaduke was made prisoner. He was fortunate enough, however, to effect his escape, and retiring abroad, became one of the attendants of King CHARLES II., in his exile, by whom he was elevated to the peerage, on 4 February, 1658. as BARON LANGDALE, *of Holme, in Spaldingmore, co. York*. His lordship is thus mentioned by Lloyd: "He was a very lean and much mortified man, so that the enemy called him ghost (and deservedly, they were so haunted by him); and carried that gravity in his converse, that integrity and generosity in his dealings, that strictness in his devotion, that experience, moderation, and wariness in his counsel, and that weight in his discourse. as very much endeared strangers to his royal master's cause, and to his own person. in all the countries he travelled, as he did in many; and to all the armies he engaged in, as he did in most them afoot in Europe. till he was restored with his Majesty in 1660; when, after appearing in parliament as Baron Langdale, of Holme, he returned to his considerable estates in Yorkshire; having lost £160,000 in his Majesty's service, without any other recompense, than the conscience of having suffered in a good cause, acquitted himself bravely, and played the man." His lordship *m.* Lenox, dau of Sir John Rodes, of Barlborough, in Derbyshire, by whom he had surviving issue,

MARMADUKE, his successor.
Philip.
Lenox, *m.* to Cuthbert Harrison, Esq., of Alaster Selby, co. York.
Mary.　　　　　Anne.

Lord Langdale returned to England at the Restoration, and *d.* at his seat, Holme, on 5 August, 1661. He was *s.* by his elder son,

MARMADUKE LANGDALE, 2nd baron, who *m.* Elizabeth, dau. of the Hon. Thomas Savage, of Beeston Castle, co. Chester, and niece of John Savage, Earl Rivers (*see that name*), by whom he had issue,

MARMADUKE, his successor.
Philip, } both *d. s. p.*
Peter, }
Jane. *m.* to Michael Anne, Esq., of Frickley. Yorkshire.
Elizabeth, *m.* to Sir Hugh Smithson, 3rd Bart., and was grandmother of SIR HUGH SMITHSON, 1st EARL OF NORTHUMBERLAND, of that family. (*Refer to* BURKE's *Extant Peerage.*)
Bridget, *d. unm.*

This nobleman was governor of Hull in the reign of JAMES II., where, upon the landing of the Prince of Orange, he was surprised and made prisoner by Col. Copeley. His lordship *d.* in 1703, and was *s.* by his eldest son,

MARMADUKE LANGDALE, 3rd baron, who *m.* Frances, dau. of Richard Draycott, Esq., of Painesley, co. York, and had issue,

MARMADUKE, his successor.
Elizabeth, *m.* to Peter Middleton, Esq., of Stockeld, in Yorkshire.
Frances, *m.* to Nicholas Blundell, Esq., of Crosby, co. Lancaster (*see Landed Gentry*).

His lordship *d.* 12 December, 1718, and was *s.* by his son,

MARMADUKE LANGDALE, 4th baron, who *m.* Elizabeth, youngest dau. of William, Lord Widrington, and had issue,

I. MARMADUKE, who *s.* to the title.
I. Alathea, *d. unm.*
II. Dorothy, *m.* to Sir Walter Vavasor, Bart., of Hazlewood, co. York, and by him (who *d.* 13 April, 1766), had two surviving sons, Walter Vavasor and Thomas Vavasor, successive baronets, with the latter of whom the baronetcy expired, and Sir Thomas bequeathed his estates to his cousin, the Hon. EDWARD-MARMADUKE STOURTON (*see below.*)
III. Elizabeth.

His lordship *d.* in 1771, and was *s.* by his only son,

MARMADUKE LANGDALE, 5th baron. This nobleman *m.*

Constantia, dau. of Sir John Smythe, 3rd bart., of Acton-Burnel, co. Salop, by whom he had,

    I. MARMADUKE, who *d.* young, and before his father.
    I. Constantia, *d.* young.
    II. ELIZABETH, *m.* to Robert Butler, Esq., of Ballyragget, in Ireland.
    III MARY, *m.* 15 June, 1775, to Charles-Philip, 16th LORD STOURTON, and *d.* 12 April, 1811, leaving, with other issue,
        WILLIAM, 17th Lord Stourton.
        Edward-Marmaduke Stourton, who assumed the surname of VAVASOUR, on succeeding to the estates of his cousin as above mentioned, and was created a baronet in 1828. (*Refer to* BURKE's *Peerage and Baronetage.*)
        CHARLES STOURTON, who assumed in 1815 the surname of LANGDALE, only, in compliance with the testamentary injunction of Philip Langdale, Esq., of Houghton, co. York, a senior branch of the family of Lord Langdale. The Hon. Mr. Langdale *m.* and had issue.
    IV APOLONIA, *m.* in 1780, the 5th Lord Clifford, of Chudleigh, who *d. s p.* 15 January, 1795.

Lord Langdale *d.* in 1777, when his Barony of Langdale, of Holme, became EXTINCT.

⁎⁎⁎ The Langdales of Garston, co. Surrey (*see Landed Gentry*), claim descent from the same stock as this noble house.

Arms—Sa., a chevron between three estoiles, arg.

LASCELS—BARON LASCELS.

By Writ of Summons, dated 23 June, 1295.

Lineage.

"Of this ancient family, seated in the county of York, were divers persons," says Dugdale, "of great note many ages since." The chief of whom was

ROGER DE LASCELS, who, in the 22nd EDWARD I., had summons, with several of the peers of the realm, and other eminent persons, to attend the king, and to advise touching the most important affairs of the kingdom. Sir H. Nicolas doubts whether this writ could be deemed a baronial summons to parliament, as he observes, that none of the higher temporal nobility, nor any of the spiritual peers, were included in it, and that no regular day was fixed for the meeting. The same learned authority further remarks, "that the writ in question is the earliest on record, excepting that of the 49th HENRY III. (1265), that the majority of the persons summoned by it were never again summoned save in the 23rd EDWARD I. (A. D. 1295); that several of those persons were not considered as barons by tenure; and that of those who were barons by tenure, and summoned on those occasions, many were never included in any subsequent summons to parliament. The writ has however (continues Nicolas), on one occasion (in the case of the Barony of Roos), admitted as a writ of summons to parliament at the bar of the House of Lords; but the last 'General Report of the Lords' Committee,' appointed to search for matters touching the dignity of a peer of the realm, appears to confirm the objections thus raised." Roger de Lascels was, however, summoned in the following year, 23 June, 30 September, 2 November, and 26 August, 1296. His lordship *d.* about the year 1297, leaving four daus., his co-heirs, amongst whom the Barony of Lascels fell into ABEYANCE, and it still continues in that state with the representatives of those ladies.

⁎⁎⁎ The noble house of Lascelles, Earls of Harewood, claim descent from this ancient baronial family.

Arms—Arg., three chaplets, gu.

LASCELLES—BARON HAREWOOD.

By Letters Patent, dated 9 July, 1790.

Lineage.

EDWIN LASCELLES, Esq., of Harewood, &c., in Yorkshire, was elevated to the peerage 9 July, 1790, as BARON HAREWOOD, of Harewood Castle, co. York. His lordship *m.* twice, but dying

s. p. 25 January, 1795, the Barony of Harewood became EXTINCT, while his lordship's estates passed to his heir-at-law, EDWARD LASCELLES, Esq., who was in the following year elevated to the peerage by the same title, having been created Baron Harewood, and who was subsequently advanced to the Earldom of Harewood. (*See Extant Peerage.*)

Arms—Sa., a cross flory, within a bordure, or.

LATIMER—BARONS LATIMER, OF DANBY.

By Writ of Summons, dated 29 December, 1299.

Lineage.

The surname of LATIMER is remarked from an old inquisition to have been attributed to Wrenoc, the son of Meirric, who held certain lands by the service of being *latimer*, that is *interpreter* between the Welsh and English. Of this name, English history has a nee boasted of several distinguished personages.

WILLIAM LE LATIMER, in the 2nd RICHARD I., 1190–1, paid 100 shillings to have a trial at law with Geffry de Valoins, who had possessed himself of part of his park at Billenges, co. York. To this William *s.* another,

WILLIAM LE LATIMER, who, in the 38th HENRY III, A.D. 1254, was made sheriff of Yorkshire, and governor of the castle at York, and the next year governor of Pickering Castle. In this sheriffalty he continued for nearly five years, during which period he had a military summons to march into Scotland in aid of (the minor) King ALEXANDER (HENRY III.'s son-in-law), against his rebellious subjects: and he was constituted escheator-general throughout all the cos. of England In the 47th HENRY III., 1263, he obtained the king's precept to the conservators of the peace, in the cos. of York, Cumberland, Northumberland, Lincoln, and Northampton, to make restitution to him of all his lands which had been seized in the baronial war. He appears, however, in those contests to have sided with the crown, for we find him upon the full re-establishment of the power of the king again filling the office of sheriff of Yorkshire, and again governor of the castles at York and Scarborough. He also received a compensation of 100 marks for the expenses he had incurred. In the 54th HENRY III., 1270, he was, amongst others, signed with the cross, to accompany Prince Edward to the Holy Land. In the 10th EDWARD I., 1282, he was in an expedition against the Welsh, and in several years after he accompanied the famous soldier, John St. John, in an expedition into Gascony. From this period he seems to have been almost uninterruptedly employed in the wars of Scotland and Gascony, and for his services he was summoned to parliament as a Baron, from 29 December, 1299, to 22 January, 1305. He obtained about the same time, a grant from the crown, of the manor of Danby, co. York. His lordship *m.* Alice, eldest dau. and co-heir of Walter Ledet, *alias* Braybrook, by whom he acquired a moiety of the barony of Warden, in the county of Northampton, and a moiety of the town and whole hundred of Corby, in the same shire. He had, with other issue,

  WILLIAM, his successor.
  John (Sir), who *m.* Joane, dau. and at length heir of Sir William de Gouis, Knt., by whom he acquired, amongst other estates, the manor of Duntish, co. Dorset, where he and his posterity continued to flourish, eminent for several generations, until the attainder of
    SIR NICHOLAS LATIMER, in the reign of EDWARD IV., but that attainder was subsequently reversed. Sir Nicholas *d.* in 1505, leaving an only dau. and heiress, EDITH LATIMER, who *m.* Sir John Mordaunt, Knt., ancestor of the Earls of Peterborough, by which alliance those (now extinct) noblemen acquired Duntish, and other considerable lordships in Dorsetshire It is however stated (in a MS. collection of pedigrees by William Parsons, Lancaster, now in the British Museum) that Sir Nicholas left, by another wife, another dau., Elizabeth, who *m.* William Aprecce, Esq., of Washingley, co. Huntingdon, lineal ancestor of Sir Thomas Hussey Aprecce, Bart.

Lord Latimer *d.* in 1305, and was *s.* by his eldest son,

WILLIAM LE LATIMER, who had himself been summoned to parliament as a Baron, under the designation of "Willielmo de Latimer, juniori," from 6 February, 1299, to 22 January, 1305, and enjoyed precedency of his father. After the decease of that nobleman, he was summoned without the addition of "junior," until 20 December, 1327. His lordship was an experienced soldier, and highly distinguished in the Scottish wars of Edward I. and Edward II. In the latter reign he fought at Bannockburn, and was made prisoner there. He was subsequently involved in the treason of Thomas, Earl of Lancaster, but obtained a pardon; and in three years afterwards (15th Edward II., 1321-2), upon the breaking out of the grand insurrection of that prince, Lord Latimer was one of the principal commanders by whom he was defeated at Boroughbridge: for which service his lordship was the next year made governor of the city of York. He m. 1st, Lucie, dau. and heir of Robert de Thweng, and grand-dau. of Marmaduke, Baron Thweng. (See that title.) This lady seems to have proved unfaithful, for during one of his lordship's campaigns in Scotland, she was taken away from his manor house of Brunne, in Yorkshire, and the king's precept to the sheriff of the shire immediately issued, directing a strict search to be instituted after her. His lordship was, however, eventually divorced from her by sentence from the court of Rome, pronounced in the ecclesiastical consistory at York, and her ladyship m. Nicholas de Meinill, and then Robert de Everingham; and after him she m. Bartholomew de Fancourt. Lord Latimer m. 2ndly, Sibill, widow of William de Huntingfield, and dying in 1327, was s. by his son (by his 2nd wife),

WILLIAM LE LATIMER, 3rd baron, b. 1301, summoned to parliament from 6 August, 1327, to 1 April, 1335. This nobleman having, without license, purchased the office of coinage in the Tower of London, and city of Canterbury, from Maud, the widow of John de Botetourt (who held it by inheritance of the king in capite), obtained pardon for that offence in the 3rd Edward III., A.D. 1329. His lordship m. Elizabeth, dau. of Lord Botetourt, and d. in 1335, leaving by her (who afterwards m. Robert, Lord D'Ufford) a son,

WILLIAM LATIMER, 4th baron, b. 1330, summoned to parliament from 24 February, 1368, to 20 October, 1379. This nobleman was one of the eminent warriors of the martial times of Edward III. At the period he succeeded to the representation of his family he was in minority, and did not make proof of his age until the year 1351, when his homage was respited in consequence of his being then engaged in the king's service at Calais. His lordship continued for several succeeding years in France, performing numerous gallant exploits:—amongst others he is celebrated for a victory achieved over Charles de Blois at the siege of Doveroy; where, with only 1,600 men (English and Britons), he encountered that prince, who had come to the relief of the place at the head of 3,600 men, and defeated and slew him, with nearly 1,000 knights and esquires; taking prisoners, 2 earls, 27 lords, and 1,500 men-at-arms. In the 43rd Edward III., 1369, his lordship was again in the wars of France, being at that time steward of the king's household; and in the next year he was constituted lieutenant, captain, and governor of the castle, town, and viscounty of St. Saviour's, in Normandy. Nevertheless, in a few years afterwards, we find him, with the Duke of Lancaster, falling under the displeasure of the Commons, and impeached by the parliament (then 50th Edward III.) assembled at Westminster, of peculation, and of squandering, whilst belonging to the king's council, the royal treasure. Being convicted of these offences he was deprived of all his public offices, and sentenced to pay a fine of 20,000 marks, and to be imprisoned during the king's pleasure; but the fine and imprisonment were both remitted by the king. The parliament roll of that year states, that the loss of the town of St. Saviour's, in Normandy, and Becherell, in Britanny, were laid to his charge: but afterwards that the lords and commons, representing to the king, that he had been deprived of his offices, and erased from the privy council by untrue suggestions, he was reinstated in those offices again. Upon the death of King Edward III., Lord Latimer was one of those whom King Richard II. deputed to acquaint the citizens of London with the event; and for the remainder of his life he enjoyed the full confidence of the new monarch, was of his privy council, a knight of the Garter, &c., &c. In this reign his lordship's last service was at the siege of Nantes, with Thomas of Woodstock, being then constable of the Host. He m. the Lady Elizabeth Fitz-Alan, dau. of Richard, Earl of Arundel, and dying in 1380, left an only dau. and heiress,

ELIZABETH LATIMER, who m. John de Nevill, Lord Nevill, of Raby, (his lordship's 2nd wife), and had issue,

JOHN NEVILL, of whom presently.
ELIZABETH NEVILLE.
Margaret, d. s. p.

She m. 2ndly. as 3rd wife, Robert, 4th Lord Willoughby de Eresby, and d. in the 7th Richard II., A D. 1383-4.

The son of the above Elizabeth Latimer,
JOHN NEVILL, was summoned to parliament in right of his mother, as BARON LATIMER, from 25 August, 1404, to 27 November, 1430. His lordship m. Maud, dau. of Thomas, Lord

Clifford, and widow of Richard Plantagenet, Earl of Cambridge, but d. s. p., 1430, when the Barony of Latimer devolved upon his only surviving sister of the whole blood,

ELIZABETH NEVILL, who m. SIR THOMAS WILLOUGHBY, Knt., Lady Willoughby's great-grandson (refer to Extant Peerage),

ROBERT, LORD WILLOUGHBY DE BROKE, claimed the BARONY OF LATIMER, in the reign of HENRY VIII. against RICHARD NEVILL, 2nd LORD LATIMER, under a new writ 10th HENRY VI., A.D. 1432. "To end this contest," says Banks, "the Lord Broke was informed by a herald, that Sir George Nevill, grandfather to Richard, had been created Lord Latimer, by a new title, which therefore lineally descended to Richard, by Henry, son and heir of the said George; and that the Lord Broke had made a wrong claim, who should have claimed his style from William Latimer, first created Lord Latimer, of Danby (the head of the barony), temp. EDWARD I. On this, Lord Broke perceiving his error, and having a title of his own, was contented to conclude a match between their children; and Richard suffered a recovery on certain manors and lordships, demanded by the Lord Broke; with which adjustment, both parties were well satisfied." Notwithstanding, however, that his lordship did not prosecute his claim, the original BARONY OF LATIMER must still be considered as vested in his descendant, the present Lord Willoughby de Broke.

Arms—Gu., a cross patonce, or.

LATIMER—BARON LATIMER, OF BRAY-BROOKE.

By Writ of Summons, dated 29 December, 1299.

Lineage.

JOHN LE LATIMER, brother of William, 1st Lord Latimer, of Danby (see preceding article), m. Christian, 2nd dau. and co-heir of Walter Ledit, alias Braybrook, great grandchild and co-heir of Henry de Braybroke (Lord Latimer, of Danby, m the other dau.), and dying in the 11th EDWARD I., A.D. 1283, was s. by his son (then twelve years of age),

THOMAS LATIMER, who took up his abode at Braybroke, co. Northampton (part of his mother's inheritance), and in the 32nd Edward I., 1304, obtained license to make a castle of his manor house there. In the 18th EDWARD II., 1324-5, being then called Thomas le Latimer Bochard, he was in the expedition, made at that time, into Scotland; and he was summoned to parliament as a Baron from 29 December, 1299, to 16 June, 1311. He d. in 1334, seized, amongst other manors, of those of Warden and Braybroke, co Northampton, and was s. by his son,

WARINE LATIMER, who, being subsequently a banneret, was in the expedition made into France, in the 19th EDWARD III., and d. in four years afterwards, never having been summoned to parliament. He m. Catherine, sister of John, Lord de la Warre, and was s. by his eldest son,

JOHN LATIMER, who d. s. p., and was s. by his brother,

SIR THOMAS LATIMER, who, in the 39th EDWARD III., 1365, was of the retinue of Prince Edward in Gascony. This Sir Thomas is deemed the same person whom historians mention as a leader in the religious sect so well known, as "Lollards," in the reign of RICHARD II. He d. s. p., and was s. by his brother,

EDWARD LATIMER, who d. s. p. in 1411, then seized of the manor of Warden, and castle of Braybrooke, with divers other estates in Northampton and other shires, which devolved upon his nephew (son of his sister, Elizabeth, by her husband, Sir Thomas Griffin), JOHN GRIFFIN, whose descendant,

EDWARD-GRIFFIN, was created in 1688, BARON GRIFFIN, of Braybroke Castle, a dignity that expired with his grandson, EDWARD GRIFFIN, 3rd baron, who d. s. p. in 1742.

ANNE GRIFFIN, his lordship's younger sister, and eventually sole heiress, m. William Whitwell, Esq., of Oundle, co. Northampton, and her son,

JOHN GRIFFIN WHITWELL, Esq., having assumed, by Act of Parliament, 1748-9 (22 GEORGE II.), the surname and arms of GRIFFIN, and established his claim to the barony of HOWARD DE WALDEN, was summoned to parliament in that dignity, 3 October, 1784. He was created 6 September, 1788, BARON OF BRAYBROKE, with special remainder. (Refer to Extant Peerage.)

Arms—Gu., a cross patonce, or.

LAW—EARL OF ELLENBOROUGH.
(See BURKE's Extant Peerage.)

LEE

LEE

LAWLEY—BARON WENLOCK.

(*See* BURKE's *Extant Peerage.*)

LEA—BARON DUDLEY.

(*See* SUTTON, Barons Dudley.)

LECHMERE—BARON LECHMERE.

By Letters Patent, dated 4 September, 1721.

Lineage.

This is a younger branch of the ancient Worcestershire family of Lechmere, of Hanley, full details of the pedigree of which will be found in the *Extant Peerage and Baronetage,* LECHMERE, Baronet; and in the *Landed Gentry.*

NICHOLAS LECHMERE, Esq., an eminent lawyer, 2nd son of Edmund Lechmere, Esq., of Hanley Castle, by Lucy, his wife, dau. of Sir Anthony Hungerford, of Farley Castle, co. Somerset, and younger brother of Anthony Lechmere, Esq., of Hanley Castle, M.P., whose grandson, Anthony, was created a baronet in 1818, and was grandfather of the present Sir Edmund Anthony Harley Lechmere, Bart., of the Rhyd, co. Worcester, having filled the office of solicitor and attorney-general, was elevated to the peerage by King GEORGE I., in the dignity of BARON LECHMERE, *of Evesham, co. Worcester,* by letters patent, dated 4 September, 1721. His lordship was likewise chancellor of the duchy of Lancaster. He m. Lady Elizabeth Howard, dau. of Charles, 3rd Earl of Carlisle, but dying without issue in 1727, the barony of Lechmere became EXTINCT.

Arms—Quarterly: 1st and 4th gules, a fesse and in chief two, pelicans, or, vulning themselves, of the first; 2nd : vert, frettée, or; 3rd : arg., a chevron engrailed between three chess rooks, sa.

LEE—EARLS OF LICHFIELD.

By Letters Patent, dated 5 June, 1674.

Lineage.

The pedigree is given in Lipscombe's *History of Bucks.* The family derived its surname from the lordship of Lee, in Cheshire, where resided in the time of EDWARD III.,

SIR WALTER LEE, Knt., who was father of

SIR JOHN LEE, of Lee Hall, who by Isabelle Dutton, his wife, was father of

JOHN LEE, who m. Isabella, dau. of Thomas Folhurst, and had a son,

THOMAS LEE, who m. Alice, dau. and heir of Sir John Aston, Knt., and was father of

JOHN or THOMAS LEE, of Lee Hall, m. Margaret, dau. of Sir Ralph Hocknel, and had issue, Thomas, his successor at Lee; John, of Aston; William and Robert, of Aston; and

BENEDICT LEE, who, in the reign of EDWARD IV., became seated at Quarendon, co. Bucks. This gentleman m. Elizabeth, dau. and heir of John Wood, Esq., of Warwick, and with other issue had a son,

RICHARD LEE, of Quarendon, who altered his arms to "*Argent ; a fesse between three crescents, sa,*" and marrying Elizabeth, dau. and co-heir of William Sanders, Esq., of co. Oxford, had issue,

I. ROBERT (Sir), of Burston, co. Bucks, who was father of Sir Anthony, of Quarendon, who was father of Sir Henry Lee, K.G., *temp.* ELIZABETH.

II. BENEDICT, of whose line we treat.

III. Roger, of Pickthorn.

IV. John, from whom the Lees of Binfield, co. Berks, derived

The 2nd son,

BENEDICT LEE, Esq., of Hulcote, m. for his 2nd wife, Elizabeth, dau. of Robert Cheney, Esq., of Chesham-Boyce, co. Bucks, and was father of

317

SIR ROBERT LEE, Knt., of Hulcot, who m. Lucia, dau. of Thomas Pigot, Esq., of Beauchampton, and was father of

SIR HENRY LEE, of Quarendon, co. Bucks, who was cousin and heir of the above-named Sir Henry Lee, K.G., and was knighted. In the 9th JAMES I., A.D. 1611, this gentleman was created a Baronet. He m. Eleanor, dau. of Sir Richard Wortley, Knt., of Wortley, co. York, and was s. by his son,

SIR FRANCIS-HENRY LEE, of Ditchley, co. Oxford, and of Quarendon, Bucks, as 2nd baronet. This gentleman m. Anne, eldest dau. of Sir John St. John, of Lidiard-Tregoz, co. Wilts, Bart., and had two sons, HENRY and FRANCIS, successive baronets. The elder,

SIR HENRY LEE, of Ditchley, co. Oxon, 3rd bart., m. Anne, dau. of Sir John Danvers, Knt. of Cornbury. co. Oxon, and by her who was heiress of the Danvers, of Daunsey, in Wilts, had two daus., co-heiresses.

I. ELEANOR, m. James Bertie. created EARL OF ABINGDON.

II. ANNE, m. Thomas, MARQUESS OF WHARTON. (*See* that title).

Sir Henry having no male issue was s. by his brother,

SIR FRANCIS-HENRY LEE, Knt., of the Temple, London, and of Ditchley, co. Oxford. 4th baronet, m. Elizabeth Pope, dau. and co-heir of Thomas, Earl of Downe, in Ireland, and her (who m. 2ndly, Robert, 3rd Earl of Lindsay,) had a son and successor,

SIR EDWARD-HENRY LEE, 5th baronet, colonel of the 1st foot guards, was elevated to the peerage by letters patent, dated 5 June, 1674, as *Baron of Spellesbury, co. Oxford, Viscount Quarendon, Bucks,* and EARL OF LICHFIELD. His lordship m. Lady Charlotte Fitz-Roy, natural dau. of King CHARLES II., by Barbara Villiers, Duchess of Cleveland, and had surviving issue,

I. Edward-Henry, col. of royal regiment of guards, who d. unm., 1713.

II. James, capt. R.N., m. Sarah, dau. of John Bagshaw, and d. in 1711, s. p.

III. Charles, d. unm., 1708.

IV. GEORGE-HENRY, who s. his father.

V. Fitzroy-Henry, vice-admiral, R N., d. s. p. in 1720.

VI. ROBERT, who inherited as 4th earl

I. Charlotte, m. to Benedict Calvert, Lord Baltimore.

II. Anne, d. young

III. Elizabeth, m 1st, to Col. Lee, and 2ndly, to Rev. Dr. Edward Young.

IV. Barbara, m. to Sir Charles Browne, Bart., of Kiddington.

The Earl of Lichfield, who refused to swear allegiance to the new government of the Revolution, d. in 1716, and was s. by his eldest surviving son,

GEORGE-HENRY LEE, 2nd Earl of Lichfield, who took his seat in the House of Lords soon after his accession to the peerage. His lordship m. Frances, dau. of Sir John Hales, Bart., of St. Stephens, Tunstall, and Woodchurch, in Kent, and had issue,

I. GEORGE-HENRY, his successor.

II. Edward-Henry, d. in 1742.

III. Charles-Henry, d. in 1740.

I. CHARLOTTE, m. 26 October, 1745, Henry, 11th Viscount Dillon. Lady Charlotte became eventually heiress of her father; and her fortune was inherited by her descendants, the VISCOUNTS DILLON. (*See Extant Peerage*).

II. Mary, m. to Cosmas-Henry-Joseph Nevill, Esq., of Nevill Holt, co. Leicester.

III. Frances, m. to Viscount Cornbury.

IV. Harriet, m. to John, Lord Bellew.

V. Anne, m. in 1749, to Hugh, 4th Baron Clifford, of Chudleigh.

The earl d. 13 February, 1742, and was s. by his eldest son,

GEORGE-HENRY LEE, 3rd earl. This nobleman was chancellor of the university of Oxford, captain of the band of gentlemen pensioners, and custos-brevium in the Common Pleas. His lordship m. Dinah, dau. and co-heiress of Sir Thomas Frankland, 3rd baronet, of Thirkelby. co. York; but as he d. s. p. in 1772, the honours reverted to his uncle,

ROBERT LEE, as 4th earl, who had previously represented the city of Oxford for some time in parliament. He m. Katherine, dau. of Sir John Stonhouse, Bart., of Radley, Berks, but had no issue. His lordship d. 4 November, 1776, when the Earldom of Lichfield and minor honours became EXTINCT.

Arms —Arg., a fesse between three crescents, sa.

LEGGE—BARONS OF STAWEL.

By Letters Patent, dated 20 May, 1760.

Lineage.

For the line of the STAWELS, refer to STAWEL, BARONS STAWEL, of Somerton.

EDWARD STAWEL, 4th LORD STAWEL, of Somerton, left at his decease, in 1755, when his peerage became EXTINCT, an only dau. and heiress,

THE HON. MARY LEGGE, then the wife of the RIGHT HON. HENRY-BILSON LEGGE, b. 29 May, 1708, (whom she had m. 3 September, 1750,) 4th son of William, 1st Earl of Dartmouth. (See Extant Peerage.) Mr. Legge, who was one of the most prominent statesmen of his time, sat in the eighth parliament of Great Britain for one of the Cornish boroughs, at which period he was a commissioner of the navy, and soon afterwards joint secretary to the Treasury. He subsequently represented the county of Hants, was appointed a lord of the Admiralty in 1746, and the next year a lord of the Treasury. In 1748 he was accredited envoy extraordinary to the court of Berlin, and upon his return, in 1749, was constituted treasurer of the navy. In 1754 he was appointed chancellor of the Exchequer, and sworn of the privy council, and was, subsequently, twice removed from, and twice reappointed to the same important office, from which, however, he was finally dismissed, or, to use his own expression, turned out, upon the change of administration in 1762. He had previously obtained, by letters patent, dated 20 May, 1760, the dignity of BARONESS STAWEL, of Somerton, co. Somerset, for his wife, with remainder to the heirs male of her body by himself, and dying 21 August, 1764, left an only son,

HENRY-STAWEL, 2nd Lord Stawel.

The Baroness became, in 1768, the 2nd wife of the Right Hon. Wills Hill, Earl of Hillsborough, afterwards Marquess of Downshire, but had, by him, no issue. Her ladyship d. in 1780, when the Barony of Stawel devolved upon her only child,

HENRY-STAWEL LEGGE, as Baron Stawel. This nobleman m. in 1779, the Hon. Mary Curzon, youngest dau. of Asheton, 1st Viscount Curzon (see Extant Peerage: Howe), by whom (who d. in 1804) he left an only dau. and heiress,

MARY, who m. 11 August, 1803, John, 2nd Baron Sherborne, and d. 21 October, 1864, leaving issue. (See Extant Peerage.)

Lord Stawel d. in 1820, when this Barony of Stawel became EXTINCT.

Arms—Gu., a cross of lozenges, arg., for STAWEL; a buck's head, cabossed, arg., for LEGGE.

———

LEIGH—BARON LEIGH OF STONELEIGH.

By Letters Patent, dated 1 July, 1643.

Lineage.

This is a junior branch of the family of which the present Lord Leigh, of Stoneleigh, of the later creation, is the representative, and full details of the earlier pedigree of both lines will be found in BURKE's Extant Peerage. The history of many other branches of the family are given in the Landed Gentry.

SIR THOMAS LEIGH, of Stoneleigh, in the co. of Warwick (2nd son of Sir Thomas Leigh, lord mayor of London,) was knighted by Queen ELIZABETH, and created a baronet, upon the institution of that order, 29 June, 1611. Sir Thomas m. Catherine, 4th dau. of Sir John Spencer, Knt., of Wormleighton, co. Warwick, and had issue,

JOHN (Sir), m. 1st, Ursula, dau. of Sir Christopher Hoddesdon, Knt., lord of the manor of Leighton, in Bedfordshire, by whom he had a son,

THOMAS, successor to his grandfather.

Sir John m. 2ndly, Anne, eldest dau. of Sir Anthony Cope, of Hanwell, in Oxfordshire, who was created a baronet, but by her had no issue. He d. before his father.

Thomas (Sir), } both d. without issue.
Ferdinando, }

Alice, m. to Sir Robert Dudley, Knt., and was created Duchess of Dudley fur life. (See that name.)

318

Sir Thomas d. in February 1625, and was s. by his grandson,

SIR THOMAS LEIGH, 2nd baronet, a stanch cavalier, and M.P. for the co. Warwick, temp. CHARLES I., who, for his zeal in the royal cause, was elevated to the peerage by letters patent, dated at Oxford, 1 July, 1643, as BARON LEIGH, of Stoneleigh, co. Warwick. He had pleased the king particularly in one matter, which was this: before the king set up his standard at Nottingham his Majesty marched to Coventry, but finding the gates shut against him, and that no summons could prevail with the mayor and magistrates to open them, he went the same night to Stoneleigh, the house of Sir Thomas Leigh, where, as Clarendon observes, his Majesty met with a warm and loyal welcome, and right plenteous and hospitable entertainment from his devoted subject, Sir Thomas. After having become Lord Leigh, he persevered in his ardent attachment to royalty, and at one time paid no less than £4,895. as a compensation for his estate. He had the gratification, however, of seeing the monarchy restored. His lordship m. Mary, one of the daus. and co-heirs of Sir Thomas Egerton, eldest son of Sir Thomas Egerton, 1st Lord Ellesmere, lord chancellor of England, by whom he had, with other issue,

  I. THOMAS (Sir), who m. 1st, Anne, dau. and sole heir of Richard Bingham, Esq., of Lambeth, in Surrey, by whom he had an only dau. Anne, who d. young, Sir Thomas m. 2ndly, Jane, dau. of Patrick Fitz-Maurice, Lord Kerry, in Ireland, and dying before his father, left

    THOMAS, who s. his grandfather.
    Honora, m. 1st, to Sir W. Egerton, and 2ndly, to Hugh Lord Willoughby, of Parham.
    Mary, m. to Arden Bagot, Esq., of Pipe Hall, co Warwick.
    Jane, m. to William, 4th Viscount Tracey.

  II. Charles, of Leighton, who m. twice, but surviving his children, left his estates to his grand nephew, the Hon. Charles Leigh.
  I. Elizabeth, m. to John, 3rd Viscount Tracey, and d. in 1688, leaving issue. (See Extant Peerage: SUDLEY.)
  II. Vere, m. to Sir Justinian Isham, of Lamport, Notts, 2nd baronet.
  III. Ursula, m. to Sir William Bromley, K.B., of Bagington, co. Warwick.

Lord Leigh, d. 22 February, 1671, and was s. by his grandson,

THOMAS LEIGH, 2nd baron. This nobleman m. 1st, Elizabeth, dau. and heir of Richard Brown, Esq., of Shingleton, but had no issue. He m. 2ndly, Eleanor, eldest dau. of Edward, Lord Rockingham, by whom he had surviving issue,

EDWARD, his successor.
Charles, who s. to the estates of his uncle, the Hon. Charles Leigh, of Leighton, and m. Lady Barbara Lumley, dau. of the Earl of Scarborough, but d. s. p. in 1749.
Anne, d. unm. in 1734.
Eleanor, m. to Thomas Verney, Esq., and d. in 1756.

His lordship d. in 1710, and was s. by his elder son,

EDWARD LEIGH, 3rd baron, who m. Mary, only dau. and heiress of Thomas Holbech Esq., of Fillongley, co. of Warwick, by Elizabeth his wife, heiress of Bernard Paulet, Esq., and had issue,

Edward, who d. v. p. anno 1737.
THOMAS, his successor.
Mary.
Eleanor, } d. unm,
Anne, }

His lordship d. 9 March, 1737-8, and was s. by his only surviving son,

THOMAS LEIGH, 4th baron. This nobleman m. 1st, Maria-Rebecca, dau. of the Hon. John Craven, and sister of William, 5th Lord Craven, by whom he had surviving issue,

EDWARD, his successor.
Mary, d. unm.

His lordship m. 2ndly, Catherine, dau. of Rowland Berkeley, Esq., of Cotheridge, co. Worcester, and had a dau. Anne, who m. Andrew Hacket, Esq. Lord Leigh d. 30 November, 1749, and was s. by his son,

EDWARD LEIGH, 5th baron. This nobleman d. unm. 26 March, 1786, when the estates devolved on his sister, the HON. MARY LEIGH, at whose decease s. p., 2 July, 1806, the property passed to the Adlestrop branch of the family. The Barony of Leigh, of Stoneleigh, EXPIRED at the death of the last-mentioned baron. It was, however, revived by a new creation, in 1839: see Extant Peerage.

Arms—Gu., a cross engrailed, arg., a lozenge in the dexter chief of the 2nd.

———

LEIGH—BARON DUNSMORE AND EARL OF CHICHESTER.

Barony, by Letters Patent, dated 31 July, 1628.
Earldom, by Letters Patent, dated 3 June, 1644.

Lineage.

This is a junior branch from the stock of the present noble family of Leigh, of Stoneleigh.

Sir William Leigh, Knt., of Newnham-Regis, in Warwickshire (3rd son of Sir Thomas Leigh, lord mayor of London), m. Frances, dau. of Sir James Harington, of Exton, co. Rutland, and was s. by his son,

Sir Francis Leigh, K.B., who m. the Hon. Mary Egerton, dau. of Thomas Egerton, lord chancellor of England, created Lord Ellesmere, and by her left a son and heir,

(Sir) Francis Leigh, of Newnham, who was created a baronet, 24 December, 1618, and was ten years later elevated to the peerage as Baron Dunsmore, of Dunsmore, co. Warwick, by letters patent, dated 31 July, 1628. His lordship m. 1st, Susan, dau. and heir of Richard Northan, Esq., but by her had no issue. He m. 2ndly, Audrey, dau. and co-heir of Sir John Butler, Baron Butler, of Bramfield (by Elizabeth, sister of George Villiers, Duke of Buckingham), and widow of Sir Francis Anderson, Knt., by whom he had issue, two daus.,

Elizabeth, m. to Thomas Wriothesley, Earl of Southampton (his lordship's 2nd wife).

Mary, m. to George Villiers, 4th Viscount Grandison, in the peerage of Ireland.

Lord Dunsmore having distinguished himself by his zeal in the royal cause during the civil wars, was advanced 3 July, 1644, to the Earldom of Chichester, with the remainder to the before-named Earl of Southampton, and his issue male by his lordship's above-mentioned dau., Elizabeth. The earl d. 21 December, 1653, when the Barony of Dunsmore with the Baronetcy became extinct, and the Earldom of Chichester devolved according to the special limitation upon his son-in-law,

Thomas Wriothesley, 4th Earl of Southampton (refer to that name) who d. s. p.; m. û 1667, when the Earldom of Chichester, of this creation, expired.

Arms—Gu., a cross engrailed, and in the 1st quarter a lozenge, arg.

LEIGH—BARON KINGSDOWN.

(See Pemberton-Leigh in Addenda.)

LEIGH—DUCHESS DUDLEY.

By Letters Patent (for life only), dated 23 May, 1644.

(See Dudley, Duchess Dudley.)

LEKE—BARONS DEINCOURT, AND EARLS OF SCARSDALE.

Barony, by Letters Patent, dated 26 October, 1624.
Earldom, by Letters Patent, dated 11 November, 1645.

Lineage.

Upon the institution of the order of baronet,

Sir Francis Leke, Knt., of Sutton, co. Derby, being a person of very ancient family in those parts, and of ample fortune, was advanced to that dignity by patent, dated 22 May, 1611, and elevated to the peerage 26 October, 1624, as Baron Deincourt, of Sutton, co. Derby. This manor of Sutton "was acquired," says Banks, "by the marriage of Richard de Grey (son of William de Grey, of Landford, Notts, and Sandiacre, in Derbyshire, a younger son of Henry de Grey, of Thurrock), with Lucy, dau. and heir of Robert de Hareston, Lord of Sutton, in the Dale; which, with divers other lordships, by issue male failing, came by a female branch to the Hilarys; who took the name of Grey; by a female heir of which line, m. to Sir John Leke, in the reign of Henry IV., the same came to this family." Lord Deincourt, taking an active part during the civil war in the cause of King Charles I., under whose banner two of his sons laid down their lives, was created by that monarch, by letters patent, dated 11 Novem-

ber, 1645, Earl of Scarsdale. He m. Anne, dau. of Sir Edward Carey, Knt., of Berkhampstede, co. Hertford, and sister of Henry, Viscount Falkland, by whom he had issue, viz.,

i Francis, slain in France.
ii Nicholas, his successor.
iii Edward, } fell fighting under the royal banner.
iv Charles, }
v Henry, d. unm.
i. Anne, m. Henry Hildyard, Esq., of Winestead, in Holderness, co. York, whose grandson and heir, Christopher Hildyard, Esq., of Kelstern, co. Lincoln, left four daus. and co-heirs, of whom Dorothy, m. George Clayton, Esq., of Grimsby, co. Lincoln (her first husband). Their eventual sole surviving dau. and heiress, Elizabeth Clayton, m. Michael Tennyson, Esq., of Preston, and was grandmother of the Right Hon Charles Tennyson, M.P., of Bayons Manor, co. Lincoln, who superadded the name and arms of D'Eyncourt to those of Tennyson, by royal license, dated 27 July, 1835 (see Burke's Landed Gentry).
ii. Catherine, m. Cuthbert Morley, Esq.
iii. Elizabeth, } d. unm.
iv. Muriel, }
v. Frances, m. Viscount Gormanston, and d. s. p.
vi. Penelope, m. Charles, Lord Lucas, and was ancestress of Lord Methuen.

His lordship became so much mortified, it is said, by the murder of King Charles I., that he clothed himself in sackcloth, and causing his grave to be dug some years before his death, laid himself therein every Friday, exercising himself frequently in divine meditation and prayer. He d. in 1655, and was s. by his eldest surviving son,

Nicholas Leke, as 2nd Earl of Scarsdale, who m. Lady Frances Rich, dau. of Robert, Earl of Warwick (see that name), and had issue,

i. Robert, Lord Deincourt, his successor.
ii. Richard, who m. Mary, dau. of Sir John Molineux, Bart., and had issue,

1 Nicholas, who s. as 4th earl.
2 Robert, d. young.
1 Frances.   2 Lucy.
i. Mary.

His lordship d. in 1680, and was s. by his eldest son,

Robert Leke, 3rd Earl of Scarsdale. This nobleman, in the reign of James II., was lord-lieutenant of the co. of Derby, colonel of horse, and groom of the stole to Prince George of Denmark. His lordship m. Mary, dau. and co-heir of Sir John Lewis, Bart., of Ledstone, co. York, by whom he had no surviving issue. He d. in 1707, and was s. by his nephew,

Nicholas Leke, 4th Earl of Scarsdale. This nobleman dying unm. in 1736, the Barony of D'Eyncourt and Earldom of Scarsdale, as well as the baronetcy became extinct.

Arms—Arg., on a saltier engrailed, sa., nine annulets, or.

LENNARD—EARL OF SUSSEX.

By Letters Patent, dated 5 October, 1674.

Lineage.

Thomas Lennard, 15th Baron Dacre (see Extant Peerage), was created Earl of Sussex, 5 October, 1674. His lordship m. Lady Anne Palmer, dau. of Barbara, Duchess of Cleveland, prior to her formal separation from her husband, Roger Palmer, Earl of Castlemain, which Anne was acknowledged by King Charles II. as his natural dau., and his Majesty assigned her the royal arms, with the baton sinister. By this lady the Earl of Sussex had two sons, who both d. in infancy, and two daus., viz.,

i. Barbara, who m. Lieutenant-General Charles Skelton, of the French service (eldest son of Bevil Skelton, son and heir of Sir John Skelton, lieutenant-governor of Plymouth, which Bevil was envoy extraordinary to the States General, temp. James II., and followed the fortunes of his fallen master into France). Lady Barbara Skelton d. s. p. in 1741.
ii. Anne, who eventually became Baroness Dacre m. 1st, her cousin, Richard Barret Lennard, grandson of Richard Barret, 2nd son of Richard, 13th Baron Dacre, and by him had an only son,

Thomas Barret-Lennard, who s. as 17th Lord Dacre.

Lady Anne Lennard m. 2ndly, Henry, 8th Lord Teynham, by whom she had, with other children,

Charles Roper, whose son,

Trevor-Charles Roper, s. as 18th Baron Dacre, but

dying *s. p.* in 1794, was *s.* by his sister, GERTRUDE, as Baroness Dacre From her descends the present Baron Dacre. (*See Extant Peerage.*)

Her ladyship *m.* 3rdly, the Hon. Robert Moore, 6th son of Henry, 3rd Earl of Drogheda, by whom she had one son, Henry.

The Earl of Sussex, who was one of the lords of the bed-chamber, entering deeply into the dissipations of the court, considerably impaired his estate; a great part of which he was obliged at different times to dispose of, particularly the fine seat at Hurstmonceaux, in Sussex. He *d.* in 1715, when as he left no male issue, the Earldom of Sussex became EXTINCT, and the Barony of Dacre fell into ABEYANCE between his daus., but the elder, Lady Barbara Skelton, dying *s. p.* in 1741, the younger, Lady Anne Lennard, became then sole heiress, and BARONESS DACRE.

*Arms—*Or, on a fesse, gu., three fleurs-de-lis of the 1st.

LESLIE—BARON LINDORES.

By Charter, dated 31 March, 1600.

Lineage.

THE HON. SIR PATRICK LESLIE, of Pitcairly, commendator of Lindores, 2nd son of Andrew, 4th Earl of Rothes (*refer to Extant Peera e*), was in high favour with King JAMES VI., who conferred on him the honour of knighthood, and appointed him one of his gentlemen of the bedchamber. He *m.* Lady Jean Stewart, 2nd dau. of Robert, Earl of Orkney, and by her (who *m.* 2ndly, Robert, Lord Melville, of Monymail) left at his decease, with other issue,

  I. PATRICK, 1st Lord Lindore, his heir.
  II. JAMES, successor to his brother, as 2nd lord.
  III. DAVID, created LORD NEWARK. (*See that title.*)
  IV. Robert. *m.* and had issue, but his male line is extinct.
  V. Ludovick, who served under GUSTAVUS ADOLPHUS, and was governor of Berwick, and *d. s. p.*
  I. Helen, *m.* (contract dated 30 April, 1622) to John, 2nd Lord Maderty.
  II. Elizabeth, *m.* to Sir James Sinclair, of Mey.
  III. Jean. *m.* George Leslie, of Leslie.
  IV. Janet, *m.* Sir John Cunningham, of Broomhill.
  V. Mary, *m.* to Sir David Barclay, of Cullairnie.

The eldest son,

PATRICK LESLIE, was created, by charter, dated 31 March, 1600, BARON LINDORES, which charter was ratified to him and his heirs male and assignees whatsoever, by act of parliament, 1606. He *d. s. p.* in August, 1649, and was *s.* by his brother,

JAMES LESLIE, 2nd Lord Lindores, who *m.* 1st, Mary, 3rd dau. of Patrick, 7th Lord Grey, by whom he had a son,

  JOHN, his heir.

His lordship *m.* 2ndly, Miss Clepburn, of Yorkshire, by whom he had a dau., Jean, *m.* 1st, to John Stewart, of Innernytie; and 2ndly, to John Bruce, of Blairhall. Lord Lindores *d.* before 20 July, 1667, and was *s.* by his son,

JOHN LESLIE, 3rd Lord Lindores, who *m.* 1st, Lady Marion Ogilvy, eldest dau. of James, 2nd Earl of Airly, and relict of James, Lord Coupar, by whom he had a son, DAVID, his heir; and 2ndly, 6 September, 1695, Jean Gibson, relict of Sir Hugh Macculloch, of Piltoun, by whom he had no issue. His lordship *d.* in 1706, and was *s.* by his son,

DAVID LESLIE, 4th Lord Lindores, who *m.* Margaret, dau. of Sir Archibald Stewart, of Dunearn, and relict of Sir Archibald Stewart, of Burray; but *d. s. p.* in July, 1719, when the title devolved on his kinsman,

ALEXANDER LESLIE, of Quarter, as 5th Lord Lindores. His lordship was son of John Leslie, of Quarter, son of Major Andrew Leslie, who was 2nd son of the Hon. Sir John Leslie, of Newton, a lord of session, son of Andrew, 4th Earl of Rothes, and uncle of the 1st Lord Lindores. He entered the army early in life, and attained the rank of major-general. He *m.* Jean, dau. of Colin Campbell, Esq.; and dying in 1765, was *s.* by his son,

FRANCIS-JOHN LESLIE, 6th Lord Lindores, who *d. s. p.* 30 June, 1775.

The title was thereupon assumed by (the descendant of James Leslie, of Lumquhat, 3rd son of the Hon. Sir John Leslie, of Newton),

JOHN LESLIE, of Lumquhat, who voted as Lord Lindores, at several elections without challenge; but in 1790 was objected to, and the House of Lords, in 1793, resolved that "the votes given by the Lord Lindores at the said election were not good."

*Arms—*Arg., on a bend, az., three buckles, or.

LESLIE—LORD NEWARK.

By Letters Patent, dated 31 August, 1661.

Lineage.

DAVID LESLIE (5th son of Patrick, commendator of Lindores, *refer to preceding article*), went into the service of GUSTAVUS ADOLPHUS, King of Sweden, and having eminently distinguished himself in Germany, rose to the rank of colonel of horse. Returning home when the civil war broke out in Scotland, he was appointed major-general to the army under the command of the Earl of Leven, which marched into England in 1644, and greatly contributed to the defeat of the royalists at Marston Moor, in July of that year, the cavalry under his command breaking and dispersing the right wing of the enemy. He routed Musgrave and Fletcher in Cumberland, was recalled into Scotland to oppose Montrose in 1645, and defeated that gallant chieftain at Philiphaugh, 13 September in that year. For this acceptable service the parliament voted him 50,000 marks out of the fine imposed on the Marquess of Douglas, 18 March, 1646. In 1647 he completely suppressed the civil war in Scotland, was declared lieutenant-general of the forces, and had a pension of £1000 a month settled on him over and above his pay as colonel of the Perthshire horse. In 1648 he refused to serve in the engagement for the rescue of King CHARLES I., of which he was appointed general of horse, and threw up the commission. In 1650 he again advanced against Montrose, whom he made prisoner. In the same year, when Cromwell invaded Scotland, Leslie had the chief conduct of the Scottish army, and his cool and vigilant sagacity baffled the impetuosity of Oliver, and hemmed him up at Dunbar in such a manner that the ruin of the English seemed inevitable But the operations of the Scottish commander were controlled by a committee of church and state, by whom he was compelled to descend from his commanding situation, and he was attacked and defeated by Cromwell, 3 September, 1650. Leslie, with the dispirited remains of a numerous army, retired to Stirling to secure the passes to the north; but justice was done to his abilities: he was acquitted of misconduct, and restored to the command. He marched with CHARLES II. to Worcester, and after that disastrous battle, was, on his retreat, intercepted in Yorkshire, and committed to the Tower of London, where he remained till 1660. After the Restoration, he was, in consideration of his eminent services and sufferings in the royal cause, gratified with a pension of £500 per annum, and created LORD NEWARK, by patent, dated 31 August, 1661, to him and the heirs male of his body. His lordship *m.* Jean, dau. of Sir John Yorke, Knt., by whom he had surviving issue,

  I. DAVID. his heir.
  I. Elizabeth, *m.* to Sir Archibald Kennedy, Bart., of Cullean
  II. Mary, *m.* 1st, to Sir Francis Kinloch, of Gilmerton; and 2ndly, to the Hon. Sir Alexander Ogilvy, Bart., of Forglen
  III. Margaret, *m.* to the Hon. Colonel James Campbell, 4th son of Archibald, 9th Earl of Argyll.

His lordship *d.* in 1682, when his only son,

DAVID LESLIE, 2nd Lord Newark, *m.* 20 May, 1760, Elizabeth, 7th dau. of Sir Thomas Stewart, of Grandtully, and had five daus., namely,

  I. JEAN, of whom presently.
  II. Mary. *d. unm.*
  III. Elizabeth, *d. unm.*
  IV. Christian, *m.* to Thomas Graham, of Balgowan; and *d.* 1752.
  V. Grizel, *m.* to Thomas Drummond, of Logiealmond.

Lord Newark *d.* 15 May, 1694, and with him the title appears to have become EXTINCT.

However, his lordship's eldest dau.,

JEAN LESLIE, it appears, *s.* her father as BARONESS NEWARK; but unless some other patent were granted save that of the 31 August, 1661, which limited the title to the heirs male of the body of the grantee, she was unentitled to the dignity.

Her ladyship m. Sir Alexander Anstruther, Knt., and had several children; of whom the last surviving son, Alexander, unsuccessfully claimed the Barony of Newark in 1793.

Arms—Arg., on a bend, az., three buckles, or.

LEY—BARONS LEY, OF LEY, CO. DEVON, AND EARLS OF MARLBOROUGH.

Barony, by Letters Patent, dated 31 December, 1625.
Earldom, by Letters Patent, dated 5 February, 1626.

Lineage.

JAMES LEY (6th son of Henry Ley, Esq., of Teffont Ewias, co. Wilts,) having been bred to the bar, and having attained great eminence in his learned profession, was raised to the coif, in the 1st JAMES I., A.D. 1603-4, and the next year constituted Chief Justice of the Court of King's Bench, in Ireland. In the 17th of the same reign, his lordship, then residing at Westbury, in Wilts, was created a baronet, having previously had the honour of knighthood; and the next year was appointed Chief Justice of the Court of King's Bench, in England. In three years afterwards he was constituted Lord Treasurer of England, and upon the last day of the same year, elevated to the peerage as BARON LEY, *of Ley, co. Devon.* In 1626, his lordship was advanced to the EARLDOM OF MARLBOROUGH, and was soon after appointed president of the council. He m. 1st, Mary, dau. of John Pettey, Esq., of Stoke-Talmage, co. Oxford, and had issue,

  I. HENRY, Lord Ley, his successor.
  II. James, who d. unm. in 1618.
  III. William, who s. his nephew, as 4th earl.
  I. Elizabeth, m. to Morice Carant, Esq., of Somersetshire.
  II. Anne, m. to Sir Walter Long, of Draycot, Wilts.
  III. Mary, m. to Richard Erisey, Esq., of Erisey, in Cornwall.
  IV. Dionysia, m. to John Harington, Esq., of Kelneyton, in Somersetshire.
  V. Margaret, m. to — Hobson, Esq., of Hertfordshire.
  VI. Esther, m. to Arthur Fuller, Esq., of Bradfield, Hertfordshire.
  VII. Martha, d. unm.
  VIII. Phœbe, m. to — Biggs, Esq., of Hurst, co. Berks.

His lordship m. 2ndly, Mary, widow of Sir William Bower, Knt.; and 3rdly, Jane, dau. of John, Lord Butler, of Bramfield, but had no issue by either of these ladies.
The Earl of Marlborough, who was esteemed a person of talents and integrity, and who left behind him several learned works, both in law and history, d. 14 March, 1628, and was s. by his eldest son,

HENRY LEY, 2nd Earl of Marlborough, who had previously been summoned to parliament in his father's barony of Ley. He m. Mary, dau. of Sir Arthur Capel, of Hadham, in Hertfordshire, by whom he had a son JAMES, his successor, and a dau. Elizabeth, who d. unm. His lordship was s. at his decease, 1 April, 1638, by his son,

JAMES LEY, 3rd Earl of Marlborough. This nobleman, who was an eminent mathematician and navigator, was appointed, being a naval officer, lord admiral of all his Majesty's ships at Dartmouth, and parts adjacent. In 1662, he was employed in the American plantations. But in 1665, commanding "that huge ship called the *Old James*, in that great fight at sea, with the Dutch off Lowestoffe, upon the 3rd June, was there slain by a cannon bullet." His lordship *d. s. p.*, when his honours reverted to his uncle,

WILLIAM LEY, who thereupon became 4th earl. This nobleman m. Miss Hewet, dau. of Sir William Hewet, Knt., but d. without issue, in 1679, when the Barony of Ley, and Earldom of Marlborough, became EXTINCT.

Arms—Arg., a chevron between three seals, heads couped, sa.

₊ The Dukedom of Marlborough, conferred in 1702, upon the great warrior, John Churchill, was in no way connected with this earldom.

LEYBURN—BARON LEYBURN.

By Writ of Summons, dated 6 February, 1299.

Lineage.

In the 10th RICHARD I., A.D. 1198-9, ROBERT OF ROGER DE LEYBURN being dead, Stephen de Turnham paid 300 marks to the king, for the wardship and marriage of his son and heir, SIR ROGER DE LEYBURN. This feudal lord espousing the cause of the barons, at the commencement of the contest, in the reign of King JOHN, was made prisoner, with several of his associates, at Rochester Castle, and committed to the custody of John Mareschall. In the time of HENRY III., we find him first mentioned, in the 36th year of that king's reign (1251-2) as slaying, presumed accidentally, but shrewdly suspected, designedly and through revenge, Sir Ernauld de Mountney, in a tournament, held at Walden, in Essex. The next year, after this unhappy affair, he attended the king in an expedition into Gascony. In the 44th of the same reign, he was constituted constable of the castle at Bristol, but before two years elapsed, again siding with the barons, he was one of those prohibited by royal precept, to meet at any tournament, without especial license, and soon after included in the excommunication of the archbishop of Canterbury. Within a very short period, however, he forsook the baronial banner (drawn off it was said, by promised rewards,) and was made warden of the Cinque Ports. He was subsequently one of the most zealous commanders in the royal army—at the taking of the town and castle of Northampton—in defending Rochester, when assaulted by the insurrectionary lords, where he was severely wounded, and at the battle of Lewes. For these services, after the king's restoration to power, by the victory of Evesham, he was made warden of all the forests beyond the Trent, sheriff of Cumberland and Kent, and warden of the Cinque Ports. He obtained likewise a grant of the wardship of Idonea, younger of the two daus. and co-heirs of Robert de Vipount, a great baron in the north, and in the 50th HENRY III., joining with Robert de Clifford, the guardian of Isabel, the elder coheir, he procured the king's pardon for those ladies, for the rebellious proceedings of their father, in the time of the grand insurrection of Montfort, Earl of Leicester, and his adherents. He was afterwards re-appointed sheriff of Cumberland and Kent, and governor of the castle of Carlisle. This great feudal lord m. 1st, Idonea, dau. of Sir Robert de Vipont, Lord of Westmoreland (Dugdale calls her "Eleanor de Turnham"); and 2ndly, Eleanore widow of Roger de Quinci, Earl of Winchester (*see* QUINCY). The baron d. in the 56th HENRY III., and was *s.* by his son,

WILLIAM DE LEYBURN, of Leyburn, who, in the 10th EDWARD I., 1281-2, was in the expedition then made into Wales. In the 22nd of the same reign, he was made constable of the castle of Pevensey; and about this period, the king having concluded a league with RODULPH, King of the Romans, and sending in conformity with its provisions, an army into Gascony, this William de Leyburn was appointed admiral of the fleet, lying at Portsmouth, upon which one-third of the expedition was to embark. In three years afterwards he attended the king into Flanders; and he was summoned to parliament as a Baron, 6 February, 1299. His lordship was subsequently engaged in the Scottish wars. He d. in 1309, leaving his grand-dau. JULIANA (dau. of his son, Thomas de Leyburn, by Alice de Tony, his wife,) his heir. This lady, b. in 1303, m. 1st, John de Hastings, Lord Bergavenny, father of Laurence, 1st Earl of Pembroke of that family; 2ndly, Sir Thomas le Blount; and 3rdly, Sir William de Clinton, Earl of Huntingdon, but d. s. p. in 1369. Her two uncles Sir Simon de Leyburn and Sir Henry de Leyburn were both knighted at Carlaveroch, and her aunt, Idonea de Leyburn, m. Geoffrey de Saye.

Arms—Az., six lioncels rampant, arg.

LEYBURN—BARON LEYBURN.

By Writ of Summons, dated 21 June, 1337.

Lineage.

SIR JOHN DE LEYBURN, of the co. Salop, having been involved in the insurrection of Thomas, Earl of Lancaster, in the 15th EDWARD II., A.D. 1321-2, had all his lands in the co. Northumberland seized by the crown; but paying a fine in two years afterwards, he had full restitution of those estates. The next year he accompanied John de Felton in the expedition then made into Gascony; and in the 4th EDWARD III., 1330-1 upon the death of John le Strange, of Cheswardyne, co. Salop, he was found to be his next heir; that is, son of Lucia, sister of the said John. In three years afterwards, he had summons to attend the king in his Scottish wars; but being prevented by some unforeseen circumstances, he obtained pardon for his absence, upon his humble petition setting forth the cause in the 9th EDWARD III. The next year he was, however, in those wars. In the 19th of the same reign, being then a banneret, and residing in Shropshire, he had a military summons to attend the king into France, and the next year distinguished himself in the celebrated battle of Durham, wherein DAVID, King of Scotland, was vanquished and made prisoner. Sir John was summoned to parliament as a Baron, from 21 June, 1337, to 14 February, 1348, in the latter of which years he *d. s. p.*, when this Barony of Leyburn became EXTINCT.

LIDDELL—BARON RAVENSWORTH.

By Letters Patent, dated 29 June, 1747.

Lineage.

THOMAS DE LIDDEL, or LYDDALE, *m.* Margaret, dau. of John de Layburne, and was *s.* by his eldest son,

THOMAS LIDDELL, Esq., an alderman of Newcastle-upon-Tyne, who *m.* Barbara, dau. and heiress of Richard Strangeways, Esq., and by her had four sons and two daus. This gentleman acquired by purchase, in 1607, Ravensworth Castle, and other estates, in the co. Durham, in which he was *s.* by his eldest son,

THOMAS LIDDELL, Esq., of Ravensworth Castle, who *d.* in 1619, and was *s.* by his eldest son,

THOMAS LIDDELL, Esq., of Ravensworth Castle, who, being a zealous supporter of King CHARLES I., was created a Baronet, 2 November, 1642, in consideration of his gallant defence of Newcastle against the Scots, during the civil wars. Sir Thomas *m.* Isabel, dau. of Henry Anderson, Esq., by whom he had two daus. and six sons, of whom the eldest son was,

SIR THOMAS LIDDELL, Knt., who *m.* Bridget, dau. of Edward Woodward, Esq., of Lee, maid of honour to the Queen of Bohemia, and *d. v. p.*, leaving an only son, THOMAS, 2nd bart.

Sir Thomas *d.* in 1650, and was *s.* by his grandson,

SIR THOMAS LIDDELL, 2nd bart. This gentleman *m.* Anne, dau. of Sir Henry Vane, the elder, of Raby Castle, co. Durham, by whom he had five sons and three daus., and dying in 1697, was *s.* by his eldest son,

SIR HENRY LIDDELL, 3rd baronet, who *m.* Catherine, dau. and heiress of Sir John Bright, Bart., of Badsworth, co. York, and of Carbrook, co. Derby, by whom he had a dau., and five sons, of whom were,

  I. Thomas, the eldest son, who *m.* in 1707, Jane, eldest dau. of James Clavering, Esq., of Greencroft, co. Durham, and *d. v. p* 1715, leaving

    1 HENRY, successor to his grandfather, created Lord Ravensworth.

    2 Thomas, *m.* Margaret, dau. of Sir William Bowes, of Gibside, and had a son, HENRY-GEORGE, who *s.* as 5th baronet, and was father of Sir Thomas-Henry. In whose favour the Barony of Ravensworth was again created.

  II. John, who having been adopted by his grandfather, Sir John Bright, assumed the surname of Bright, and was seated at Badsworth. This gentleman's son, Thomas Bright, left an only dau. and heiress, Margaret, who *m.* Charles Watson Wentworth, Marquess of Rockingham.

  III. Henry, of Carbrook.

  1. Elizabeth, *m.* Robert Ellison, Esq., of Hepburn, co. Durham.

Sir Henry *d.* 1 September, 1723, and was *s.* by his grandson,

SIR HENRY LIDDELL, 4th baronet, M.P., who was elevated to the peerage, 29 June, 1747, as BARON RAVENSWORTH, *of Ravensworth Castle.* His lordship *m.* in 1735, Anne, only dau. of Sir Peter Delme, Knt., alderman and lord mayor of London, by whom he had an only dau.,

  Anne, who *m.* Augustus-Henry, Duke of Grafton, from whom she was divorced, and afterwards *m.* the Earl of Upper-Ossory (*see* FITZPATRICK).

His lordship *d.* 1749, without male issue, when the Barony of Ravensworth of this creation, became EXTINCT, while the baronetcy devolved upon his nephew, HENRY-GEORGE LIDDELL, Esq., as 5th baronet. He was father of the 6th baronet, Sir Thomas-Henry Liddell, of Ravensworth Castle, in whose favour the BARONY OF RAVENSWORTH was again created in 1821. (*See Extant Peerage*).

Arms—Arg. a fret, gu., on a chief of the 2nd, three leopards' faces, or.

LIGONIER—BARON AND EARL LIGONIER, AND VISCOUNT LIGONIER.

Irish Viscounty, by Letters Patent, dated 21 December, 1757: and 20 May, 1762.
English Barony, by Letters Patent, dated 27 April, 1763.
English Earldom, by Letters Patent, dated 10 September, 1766.

Lineage.

JOHN LIGONIER, of an ancient French family, having distinguished himself under the Duke of Marlborough, in Flanders, and attained high reputation, *temp.* GEORGE II., in Germany, was made a knight banneret, under the royal standard, at the battle of Dettingen, in 1742. Sir John, being then a Field Marshal, was raised to the peerage of Ireland, by letters patent, dated 21 December, 1757, as VISCOUNT LIGONIER, *of Enniskillen, co. Fermanagh;* and in 1762, he obtained a new patent, conferring upon his lordship the VISCOUNTY OF LIGONIER, *of Clonmell,* in the same kingdom, with remainder to Lieut.-Col. Edward Ligonier. In the next year he was made a peer of Great Britain, as BARON LIGONIER, *of Ripley, co. Surrey,* and three years later he was created EARL OF LIGONIER, by patent, dated 10 September, 1766. His lordship, after filling the first military offices, and establishing the highest military reputation, died in 1770 at the advanced age of ninety-one, and was buried in Westminster Abbey. As he left no issue, the British Barony and Earldom of Ligonier became EXTINCT, while the Irish Viscounty of Ligonier, of Clonmell, passed according to the patent to the aforesaid

EDWARD LIGONIER, Esq., who became 2nd Viscount Ligonier, and was created Earl Ligonier of Clonmell, co. Tipperary, in the peerage of Ireland, July, 1776. He *m.* 1st, Penelope, eldest dau. of George Pitt, created Lord Rivers. She was divorced from him, and *re-m.* in 1784, Captain Smith. Lord Ligonier *m.* 2ndly, Mary, dau. of Robert, Earl of Northington, but *d. s. p.* in 1782, when the Irish Viscounty of Ligonier of Clonmell likewise EXPIRED.

Arms—Gu., a lion rampant, arg.; on a chief of the 2nd, a crescent between two mullets, az.

LINDSAY—DUKE OF MONTROSE.

Dukedom, by Charter, dated 1488; and, for life by Charter, dated, 19 September, 1489.

Lineage.

The illustrious house of Lindsay has found a historian not less learned than eloquent in the heir of its ancient honours. Lord Lindsay (the late Earl of Crawford), in his *Lives of the Lindsays,* contributed an important addition to the historical literature of Scotland, in which his ancestors have during seven centuries acted such a distinguished part.

Sir William Dugdale mentions several considerable families of Lindsay in England in the 11th and 12th centuries, observing that the surname was first assumed by the proprietors of the lands and manor of Lindsai, co. Essex. It is the opinion of Scotch antiquaries, that one of these Lindsays, coming with King MALCOLM CANMORE into Scotland, and settling there, obtained the lands of Wachopdale, and other possessions from the crown, and founded the family of Lindsay beyond the Tweed. Certain it is that the Lindsays began to be of note in Scotland *temp.* ALEXANDER I. (the son of MALCOLM), who *s.* to the throne in 1107.

Descended from a great Norman family, which traced its pedigree from Randolph, Sire de Toeny, living in 1018, was

WILLIAM DE LINDSAY, Lord of Ercildown and Crawford. He was one of the MAGNATES SCOTIÆ, *temp.* MALCOLM IV., and WILLIAM THE LION. Between 1189 and 1199 he held the office of high justiciary of the Lothians. He *m.* the Princess Marjory, sister of MALCOLM IV. and WILLIAM THE LION, and dau. of David, Prince of Scotland, son and heir of King DAVID I., by Adele de Warren, who was thus descended from the kings of Scotland, the Saxon kings of England, WILLIAM THE CONQUEROR, and the Capetian kings of France. By the Princess his wife, he had three sons, ɪ David (Sir), of Crawford, whose male line became extinct. His heir-general, Sir Robert de Pinkney, was in 1292, one of the claimants of the Scottish crown, through his ancestress, Princess Marjory.

ɪɪ. Walter (Sir), of Lamberton. His great grandson, Sir William Lindsay. m. another lady of royal blood, Ada Baliol, sister of John Baliol, King of Scotland, and their dau. and heir, Christina Lindsay, carried the right of representation of the ancient Scottish kings and the Saxon kings of England, through the great French family of De Coucey, into the house of Bourbon, and their heir is H.R.H. the Duke of Bordeaux.

ɪɪɪ. William, of whose line we treat.

The 3rd son,

William Lindsay, of Luffness, d. about 1236, and was s. by his son,

Sir David Lindsay, of Luffness, who m. a dau. of Sir John Crawford, of Crawford. He was high justiciary of Lothian, from 1243 to 1249., His son,

Sir David Lindsay, of Luffness, was one of the regents of Scotland during the intestine troubles of 1255, high chamberlain in 1256, and he d. whilst accompanying St. Louis on his last crusade in 1268. His son,

Sir Alexander Lindsay, of Luffness, was one of the Magnates Scotiæ, who, at the great council of Brigham, in 1289, consented to the marriage of Margaret of Norway with Edward, Prince of Wales. On the forfeiture of Sir Henry de Pinkney, he obtained the Barony of Crawford. He d. in 1307. His son,

Sir David Lindsay, of Crawford, in 1325, m. Mary, dau. and co-heir of Hugh, Lord Abernethy. He was one of the Magnates Scotiæ, who, in 1320, signed the famous letter to the Pope. He fought at the battle of Halidonhill in 1333, and was keeper of the castle of Edinburgh in 1346. He d. in 1355, leaving three sons,

ɪ. James (Sir), of Crawford, who, by his wife, Egidia Stewart, sister of Robert II. of Scotland, had a son, Sir James, whose line failed.

ɪɪ. Alexander (Sir), of whose line we treat.

ɪɪɪ. William, ancestor of the Lords Lindsay, of the Byres, Earls of Lindsay (and Crawford eventually) and Viscounts Garnock. See those titles.

The 2nd son,

Sir Alexander Lindsay, m. Catherine, dau. and heir of Sir John Stirling, of Glenesk, by whom he had a son,

Sir David Lindsay, of Glenesk, who became on his cousin's death, 7th feudal Lord of Crawford. He m. the Princess Elizabeth of Scotland, dau. of King Robert II. "This Sir David Lindsay acted the principal part in the celebrated tournament at London Bridge, in May, 1390. John, Lord Welles, ambassador from Richard II. to Scotland, at a solemn banquet, where the Scots and English were discoursing of deeds of arms, said, ʻ Let words have no place: if you know not the chivalry and valiant deeds of Englishmen, appoint me a day and place, where you list, and you shall have experience.ʼ Whereupon Sir David Lindsay assenting, Lord Welles selected London Bridge as the place for a trial of skill. Lindsay repaired to London with a gallant train of thirty persons; and on the day appointed, appeared in the lists against Lord Welles. At the sound of trumpet they encountered each other, upon their barbed horses, with square grounden spears. In this adventure, Lindsay sat so strong that, notwithstanding Lord Welles' spear was broken upon his helmet and visage, he stirred not, insomuch that the spectators cried out that, contrary to the laws of arms, he was bound to his saddle. Whereupon he dismounted, got on his horse again without assistance, and in the third course, threw Lord Welles out of his saddle to the ground. Then dismounting, he supported his adversary, and with great humanity, visited him every day, till he recovered the effects of the fall." Sir David was created by his brother-in-law, King Robert III., a peer of Scotland, by the title of Earl of Crawford, 21 April, 1398, being, says Fordun, "valens miles et in omni probabitate bellicâ quamplurimum commendatus." His lordship had issue,

ɪ. Alexander, his successor.
ɪɪ. David, of Newdosk.
ɪɪɪ. Gerald.
ɪᴠ. Ingelram, bishop of Aberdeen.
ɪ. Matilda, m. Archibald, 5th Earl of Douglas, Duke of Touraine.
ɪɪ. Marjory, m. Sir William, Douglas of Lochleven.
ɪɪɪ. Elizabeth m. Sir Robert Keith, Marischal of Scotland.

The earl d. in 1412, and was s. by his eldest son,

Alexander Lindsay, 2nd Earl of Crawford; who m Mariota, dau. and heiress of David Dunbar of Cockburn, and grand-dau. of George, Earl of March, and dying in 1438, left a son,

David Lindsay, 3rd Earl of Crawford, who m. Marjory, dau. of Alexander Ogilvie, of Auchter House, and had issue,

323

ɪ. Alexander, of whose line we treat.
ɪɪ. Walter, of Edzell, ancestor of the Earls of Balcarres. (See below, and refer to Extant Peerage.)
ɪɪɪ. William, ancestor of the Lindsays of Evelick.
ɪᴠ. John, of Pitcairly, killed at the battle of Brechin.
ᴠ. James, keeper of the privy seal in 1453; who m. a lady of rank in Germany, and acquired with her a considerable estate near Augsburg.

The Earl of Crawford was slain at the battle of Arbroath, 13 January, 1445-6, and s. by his son,

Alexander Lindsay, 4th Earl of Crawford, who entering into a treasonable convention with the Earl of Douglas and other discontented nobles, took up arms against the royal authority, but was defeated at Brechin, by the Earl of Huntly, 18 May, 1452. An act of forfeiture passed against him; but subsequently submitting in the most humble manner to the king's mercy, his lordship was received with some degree of favour. The king rode to visit him at Finhaven, where he was magnificently entertained; and James is said to have thrown a flagstone from the battlements of the castle down into the ditch, that he might, without injury to the earl or his mansion, fulfil a vow which he had made in his anger, that he would " make the highest stone of that house the lowest." The Earl of Crawford m. Marjory Dunbar, of the house of March, and dying in 1454, left (with a dau. Elizabeth, wife of Sir John, Lord Drummond,) two sons, David, 5th earl, and Alexander, 7th earl.

The elder son

David Lindsay, 5th Earl of Crawford, was constituted, in 1475, admiral of the fleet, appointed master of the household in 1482; great chamberlain of Scotland in 1484; and justiciary of the north in 1487. In the following year, James III., King of Scotland created the Earl of Crawford, Duke of Montrose, by a patent granted to him and his heirs 18 May, 1488; and it is alleged that in the September after, King James IV., who had dethroned and murdered his father, rescinded the creations of peerages during the last year of the deceased monarch's reign; but an act of grace previously passed, preserved the Duke of Montrose from the damaging effects of this recissory Act, and he was recognised as Duke of Montrose, subsequently to the passing of it. In September, 1489, a deed was granted by King James IV., to the Duke, of which no copy exists, and which is only known by an imperfect abridgement, interpolated in the Register of the Great Seal, which, in so far as it goes, re-echoes and enforces the original patent, repeating the intention of the crown to exalt the title borne by the ancient Earls of Crawford into a Dukedom. In this deed the words " pro toto tempore vite sue " occur, but they are accompanied by words which seem to include the limitation to heirs in the original patent of 1488. The Duke m. 1st, Elizabeth, eldest dau. of James, 1st Lord Hamilton, by whom he had two sons, Alexander, who d. v. p., s. p.; and John, who s. as 6th earl. The Duke m. 2ndly, Margaret, dau. of Carmichael, of Meadowflat, by whom he had two daus., Margaret, wife of John Blair, and Elizabeth, m. to David Lyon. The Duke d. in 1495, and was s. by his only surviving son (the subsequent holders of the Crawford honours did not assume the ducal title),

John Lindsay, as 6th Earl of Crawford, who was slain at Flodden, where he had a chief command, 9 September, 1513. He had m. Mariota, sister of Alexander 2nd Lord Home, but d. s. p., whereupon the title passed to his uncle,

Alexander Lindsay, 7th Earl of Crawford, who m. Margaret, dau. of Campbell of Ardkinglass; and dying in 1517, left, (with a dau. m. to Sir Archibald Douglas, of Kilspindie) two sons; of whom the elder,

David Lindsay, 8th Earl of Crawford, m. 1st, Lady Mariana Hay, dau. of William, 3rd Earl of Errol, by whom he had a son,

Alexander, master of Crawford, who was killed in Dundee, towards the end of 1541, leaving by Jean, his 1st wife, dau. of Henry, Lord Sinclair, a son,

David, who s. as 10th earl.

His lordship m. 2ndly Isabel, dau. of Lundin, of Lundin, and had by her three sons and a dau., namely,

John, d. s. p.
Isabel, m. to John, 5th Lord Borthwick.
Margaret, m. to James, 3rd Lord Ogilvy, of Airly.
Elizabeth, m. to John Erskine, of Dun.

Alexander, Master of Crawford, and his brother, John Lindsay, having seized, fettered, and imprisoned their father, the Earl of Crawford, were disinherited in consequence by his lordship, who assigned by deed, dated 20 December, 1541, with the approbation of the crown, his honours and estates to his cousin, and next male heir after those sons,

David Lindsay, Esq., of Edzell, the grandson of Walter, the brother of Alexander, 4th Earl of Crawford, (one of the lineal progenitors of Earl Balcarres,) and the said David inherited at the earl's decease, in 1542, (the Master and his brother having previously died, the latter *s. p.*) but being of a generous disposition, he re-conveyed the titles and estates to David Lindsay, son of the said Mas·er of Crawford, but with the express provision, that future heirs male of this David's body (which eventually happened) the estate and honours of Crawford should descend to the heirs male of Edzell. He likewise reserved to himself the title for life, with sufficient property to maintain his rank. He *d.* in 1558, and was *s.* in accordance with the terms of the charter of 1546, by the said

DAVID LINDSAY, as 10th Earl of Crawford. This nobleman joined the association for Queen MARY in 1568, and adhered with fidelity to her cause. He *m.* in April, 1546, Margaret, dau. of the Cardinal David Betoun, archbishop of St. Andrew's and had issue,

    I. DAVID, his heir.
    II. HENRY, who *s.* as 13th earl.
    III. John (Sir), of Ballinscho and Woodhead, whose only son, Col. Henry Lindsay, *d. s. p.* at Hamburg in 1639.
    IV. ALEXANDER, created LORD SPYNIE. (*See that title.*)
    I. Helen, *m.* to Sir David Lindsay, of Edzell.

The earl was *s.* at his decease by his son,

DAVID LINDSAY, 11th Earl of Crawford, who *m.* 1st, Lilias, dau. of Lord Drummond; and 2ndly, Lady Grizel Stewart, eldest dau. of John, 4th Earl of Atholl; and dying 22 November, 1607, was *s.* by his son,

DAVID LINDSAY, 12th Earl of Crawford, who *m.* Lady Jean Ker, eldest dau. of Mark, Earl of Lothian, and relict of Robert, Master of Boyd, and had an only child, Jean. He *d.* in 1621, when the title devolved on his uncle,

HENRY LINDSAY, 13th Earl of Crawford, who *m.* 1st, Beatrix, dau. and heir of George Charteris, of Kinfauns, and had two sons,

    JOHN (Sir), of Kinfauns, K.B., *d. s. p. m.* and *v. p.*
    GEORGE, successor to his father.

Lord Crawford *m.* 2ndly, Elizabeth, dau. of Sir James Shaw, of Sauchie, and had by her two sons, ALEXANDER, 15th earl, who *d. s. p.*, and LUDOVICK, 16th earl. His lordship *d.* in 1623, and was *s.* by his son,

GEORGE LINDSAY, 14th Earl of Crawford, who *m.* Lady Anne Sinclair, only dau. of George, 5th Earl of Caithness, and had a dau. Margaret, who appears to have *d.* young. Lord Crawford was *s.* by his brother,

ALEXANDER LINDSAY, 15th earl, who *d. s. p.* 1639, and was *s.* by his brother,

LUDOVICK LINDSAY, 16th Earl of Crawford, who, early in life, entered the Spanish service and attained high military rank. At the outbreak of the civil war in England, his lordship sided with the king's party, and gained considerable distinction as a cavalier commander. He participated with his regiment of horse in the victory of Lansdowne; joined Montrose in the first unsuccessful attempt for King CHARLES; fought at Marston Moor and at Philiphaugh, and finally effected his escape to Spain, where he *d.* about the year 1648. After the battle of Marston Moor, Lord Crawford was taken prisoner at the siege of Newcastle, and sent to Edinburgh, where he remained in confinement until after Montrose's victory at Kilsyth. His lordship *m.* Lady Margaret Graham, dau. of William, Earl of Strathern (*see that name*), and relict of Alexander, Lord Garlies, but had no issue.

At the earl's decease, the male representation of the family devolved on George Lindsay, 3rd Lord Spynie; and upon his demise *s. p.* in 1672, on John Lindsay, of Edzell, lineally descended from David, 8th earl, and entitled, in terms of the charters of 1546 and 1565, and of the act of parliament of 1567, to the earldom of Crawford, to which he unsuccessfully preferred his claim in the second parliament of JAMES II.

The title was taken up by the Earl of Lindsay, who on sentence of forfeiture having been passed against Ludovick, the 16th earl, in 1644, had obtained a ratification from the parliament of Scotland of his lordship's right and patent as Earl of Crawford; this ratification was confirmed by act of parliament after the Restoration. As to the final devolution of this title on the EARL OF BALCARRES, *see* BURKE's *Extant Peerage.*

In 1853, James, 24th Earl of Crawford, and 7th Earl of Balcarres, the undoubted heir male of the Duke of Montrose claimed the dukedom, which claim being referred to a Committee for Privileges of the House of Lords, was unsuccessful. His son,

The late Earl of Crawford and Balcarres wrote to the author an interesting letter on the subject of this claim to the Dukedom of Montrose. Some extracts are here appended :—

Dunecht, September, 1865.

My dear Sir Bernard,

    I venture to believe that the following narrative of my father's claim to the (original) Dukedom of Montrose, as urged before the House of Lords in 1853 (on grounds still maintained by him to be sound and valid), will not be unacceptable to you for insertion in the appendix to the new edition of your *Dormant and Extinct Peerage* of Great Britain. The claim is one of great interest and curiosity, not only from its connection with history and the important precedents which are involved in its discussion, but for the extraordinary divergences of opinion between the claimant and the noble and learned lords who moved the Resolution as to matters of simple fact, patent before the eyes of the Committee of Privileges, and from the novel interpretations of peerage law, and law generally, started and applied for the first time by the noble and learned lords in question, and which, if hereafter sustained and acted upon, must revolutionize from this time forward the whole system of peerage law.

    In 1488, on the occasion of the rebellion against JAMES III. of Scotland (headed by the king's eldest son, afterwards JAMES IV., and which ended in the defeat and death of the king, on the 11th June that year, at the battle of Stirling), David, 5th Earl of Crawford, having joined the royal standard with a large force of his vassals and friends, was in reward of his loyalty created by the king DUKE OF MONTROSE by charter or patent, dated the 18th of May in that year, "changing" his earldom into a dukedom, with limitation to him " et heredibus suis." This patent and the rights conveyed by it could only, by peerage law, be annulled in one of three modes, that is to say, by attainder of the family, by special annulment, or by resignation to the crown, none of which, it is admitted, took place. After the duke's death the dignity was not assumed by his heirs, and it has been dormant (in the claimant's view) ever since. But dormancy is no bar in peerage claims.

    In 1850, my father, James, 24th Earl of Crawford, heir and representative of Duke David in terms of the patent, petitioned the Queen to recognize his right to the dukedom ; and his petition was referred to the House of Lords for their opinion and advice. The case was heard and reported upon in July and August, 1853. It was admitted (as I have said) that there had been no attainder, that no resignation of the dukedom had taken place, and that there had been no special annulment of the patent. But it was objected that the dukedom had been annulled by a statute—styled, for convenience in the discussion, the Act Rescissory—passed on the 17th October, 1488, by the victorious party assembled in parliament, and purporting to annul, in general terms and without specification, "all alienations of lands, heritage, land tacks, few-ferms, offices, tailzies, blench-ferm, creation of new dignities," conferred "sene (since) the second day of Februar last by-past be umquhile our Sovereign Lord's fader, whom God assoilzie ! quhilk might be prejudicial to our Sovereign Lord and to the crown that now is," with the inductive clause, "because that sic alienation, gifts, and privileges were grantit sene (since) the said time, for the assistance to the perverst counsale that were contrar the common good of the realm, and cause of the slaughter of our Sovereign Lord's fader." In reply to this objection the claimant, after pointing out certain legal considerations which governed the interpretation of the statute, adduced evidence to prove that the Act Rescissory took no effect whatever on any of the grants struck at by it, and least of all on the Dukedom of Montrose ; and further that by peerage law, as established by a leading case and precedent (that of the Dukedom of Norfolk) in the same century, such a general and penal act could not *per se* and without specification affect a dignity. But the Committee of Privileges disallowed the argument from law and overruled the evidence on the matter of fact ; and the House reported to the Crown " that the charter bearing date the 18th day of May, 1488, by which JAMES THE THIRD of Scotland granted the Dukedom of Montrose to David, Earl of Crawford 'et heredibus suis,' was annulled and made void by the Act of the first year of the reign of JAMES THE FOURTH of Scotland, called the Act Rescissory,—that the grant of the dukedom made by King JAMES THE FOURTH to the said David, Earl of Crawford in 1489 " (a matter quite, as the claimant holds, of a secondary nature in regard to the present claim, but to which the Committee attached great importance) "was a grant for the term of his life only,—and that the petitioner James, Earl of Crawford and Balcarres, has not established any title to the Dukedom of Montrose, created in 1488."

    Such is a brief summary or historical outline of the Montrose claim up to the present moment. It cannot, however, be appreciated without some more special details, which I will give you as succinctly as possible.

The facts adduced in evidence before the Committee of Privileges and the arguments based upon them for and against the claim may be divided into, I. Primary—those which determine the history and govern the law of the case; and, II. Secondary—those which are in themselves immaterial and superfluous in the presence of the dominant and ruling facts previously established.

I. *Primary Facts and Arguments.*

The main fact in dispute between the claimant and the crown before the Committee of Privileges was (it must be repeated) this,—'Did the Act Rescissory, 17th October, 1488, or did it not, take effect upon the dukedom?' Every other consideration (it was admitted) was immaterial. The claimant contended that the Act neither could nor did affect the patent, on grounds which I shall proceed to specify. To go into these grounds minutely would occupy too much of the space which your courtesy allows me. The controversy may be said to turn upon the question whether the Act Rescissory did or did not cut down a dignity granted within the same period and under identical circumstances with the dukedom, viz., the Earldom of Glencairn. I shall, therefore, lay special stress upon that point; and I will merely indicate in the first instance, with as much conciseness as possible, the other points of the argument, simply premising that the claimant conceives that the evidence produced on these points would have been of itself sufficient, by peerage law and precedent, to establish his claim, even if there had been no such identical case as that of Glencairn.

*   *   *   *   *

II. *Secondary Facts and Arguments.*

These embrace the matter of the second grant of the dukedom in September, 1489, and the report to the Crown, or rather the speech of Lord Chancellor Loughborough, the report being in general terms—on the claim to the Earldom of Glencairn in 1797. Both the re-grant and the Glencairn report, in 1797, are admittedly immaterial to the question, if only the Act Rescissory did not cut down the original patent. They were considered by the Committee of Privileges as affording proof that such had been the case.

*   *   *   *   *

The general result amounts to this,—that the whole of the claimant's pleas against the Act Rescissory were disregarded or overruled by the Committee of Privileges; and, while it was admitted that there had been no attainder, no resignation, and no special annulment of the Montrose patent, it was held that the general Act Rescissory—in spite of the qualification, in spite of the inductive clause being inapplicable, in spite of its being necessary to alter its words in order to make it apply, and in spite of the *rationes* laid down in the Norfolk judgment to the effect that no general Act could affect a dignity—had nevertheless the effect of cutting down the patent, simply because it was the intention of the parliament to make it do so, "parliament" (according to the Lord Chancellor) being "omnipotent," and competent (all consideration of justice and equity being set aside) to "destroy a peerage, or take a person's property, or do anything else,"—the ruling decision in favour of the Glencairn patent (*in pari casu* with the Montrose) in 1648, being altogether ignored and set aside.

It may be for others to determine whether the adverse Report of the House of Lords in 1853 proceeded, or the contrary, on misapprehension of the facts proved in evidence, and on misdirection as to the law governing the question at issue. The claimant holds the affirmative in this respect. He maintains, as before, in the face of this Report:

That, if any of the grants of JAMES III. survived the Act Rescissory, all survived:—

That, if the Earldom of Glencairn, in particular, survived the Act Rescissory, the Dukedom of Montrose also survived:—And,

That, as it is admitted that no resignation of the Dukedom took place, and as nothing therefore could deprive the duke or his heirs of their legal right to the dignity if only the Act Rescissory did not, *per se*, without trial or inquiry, and without specification, cut the patent down—every other consideration and objection, misnomer, re-grant, dormancy, &c., being quite secondary and unimportant in law—THEN, on these grounds—the

325

rationes in the Norfolk judgment pronounced in 1425, and the principle of strict interpretation of penal statutes (particular in honours), falling ever to be kept in foremost view in this matter—and, above all, the standing Glencairn decision in 1648, by the only competent tribunal, acting as well by inherent right as under reference from the Crown, having settled the whole question beyond reversal in favour of the Glencairn patent, and necessarily of that of Montrose—the Committee, he submits, OUGHT to have reported in favour of the Montrose patent of 1488 and against the Act Rescissory.

The claimant cannot tax either himself or his counsel with having contributed through any failure on their part to the misadventure of 1853. They did their utmost from the first to facilitate the inquiries of the Committee of Privileges—to put everything before them that could lighten their labours. And the Committee had one peculiar and unprecedented advantage. After disallowing the right of the Duke of Montrose (of the later creation) to oppose the claim (to which he was in every respect a stranger, his title being derived from a distinct source, the barony of Old Montrose), the Committee admitted the duke's cases as those of the Crown, and thus secured to themselves the full advantage of the ability and industry of his Grace's counsel in addition to the services of the Attorney-General of England, and the Lord Advocate of Scotland. The Committee had thus every opportunity of forming a just and impartial judgment. And if they made mistakes as to matters of fact as proved by evidence, and treated the ancient and accepted maxims of peerage law as obsolete, I can only account for the former misfortune by the decision having been given before the 'Minutes of Evidence' had been printed, and for the latter by the inexperience of the noble and learned lords who advised the Committee in peerage and Scottish law, as evinced by their observations throughout the pleadings and their speeches in moving the resolution; while an impatience as to time, a continually betrayed contempt of the claim, and a predisposition to accept the views of the opposition, completed the combination of influences to which the claim thus far fell a sacrifice.

I have only further to remark that the resolution of the House of Lords on a peerage claim is not a legal judgment, final and conclusive, but a mere report to the sovereign of their opinion and advice in the matter; and it is open to the claimant to demand a reconsideration of his claim, grounded on a more careful examination of the evidence adduced, and a more just application of the law governing the case.

I pause here. That my complaint of injustice—which is not the less firm and decided because I urge it by proof and remonstrance, rather than by invective—is not unwarranted, may appear from a letter, addressed to the representative of the Lindsays of Virginia by the learned Chief Judge of the United States' Court of Claims, the Hon. J. J. Gilchrist, to whom that gentleman had sent a copy of my 'Report' of the claim:—

*   *   *   *   *

An opinion like this, so noble and just in its general sentiments, and pronounced from a point of view apart from the prejudice and passion which influence us on this side of the Atlantic, reads, I humbly submit, like the judgment of posterity.

I remain, dear Sir Bernard,
Your obliged and faithful servant,
LINDSAY.

Arms of David Lindsay, Duke of Montrose — Gu., a fess, chequy, arg. and az.: an inescutcheon of the 2nd charged with a rose of the field.

———

LINDSAY—LORD SPYNIE.

By Charter, dated 17 April, 1589,

Lineage.

SIR ALEXANDER LINDSAY, 4th son of David, 10th Earl of Crawford (for earlier ancestry refer to that title), accompanied King JAMES VI. on his matrimonial expedition to Denmark, 1589. He had a charter granted, 17 April, 1592, erecting the lordship of Spynie, Kinneder, Baffart, and other lands, in the counties of Elgin, Banff, and Inverness, into a temporal lordship, with the dignity of a peer of parliament, by the title of LORD SPYNIE, to him and Dame Jean Lyon, Countess of Angus, his wife, and the longest liver of them, in conjunct fee, and to the heirs lawfully procreated, or to be procreated betwixt them; which failing, to the nearest lawful heirs male of the said Alexander, Lord Spynie, whomsoever, and his assignees heritably.

The Earl of Crawford having assassinated his kinsman, Sir Walter Lindsay, Sir David Lindsay, of Edzell, nephew of Sir Walter, collected an armed force to revenge the murder; the parties met on the street of Edinburgh, in July, 1607, when Lord Spynie interposing between them, was inadvertently slain by Edzell. His lordship's death was much regretted for the many good qualities he possessed, and the hopes that his friends conceived of his raising again the ancient and noble house of Crawford to its former splendour and dignity. He m. Jean, eldest dau. of John, 10th Lord Glamis, relict of Robert, Master of Morton, and of Archibald, 8th Earl of Angus, and by her had issue,

 I. ALEXANDER, 2nd Lord Spynie.
 II. John, who d. young.
 I. Anne, m. to Sir Robert Graham, of Innermay.
 II. Margaret, m. to John Erskine, of Dun.

The elder son,

ALEXANDER LINDSAY, 2nd Lord Spynie, succeeded his father, 1657. He fought in Germany under the banners of GUSTAVUS, and acquired high military reputation. He m. 1st, Johanna Douglas; and 2ndly, Lady Margaret Hay, only dau. of George, 1st Earl of Kinnoul, high chancellor of Scotland; by the latter he had issue,

 I. Alexander, Master of Spynie, who m. Magdalene Carnegie, 2nd dau. of John, 1st Earl of Northesk, but had no issue by her, who took to her 2nd husband, John Lindsay, of Edzell.
 II. GEORGE, 3rd Lord Spynie.
 I. Margaret, m. about 1650, William Fullarton, Esq., of Fullarton, and was great-great-grandmother of Lieut.-Colonel William Fullarton, of Glenquich (of whom, hereafter as claimant of this title. (See Landed Gentry, for particulars of the descent.)
 II. Anne, d unm.

The 2nd son,

GEORGE LINDSAY, 3rd and last Lord Spynie, was served heir male of Alexander, Lord Spynie, his father, and Alexander, Master of Spynie, his brother, 12 June, 1646. He was a steady loyalist, opposed the surrender of King CHARLES I. to the parliament of England, January, 1647, and was colonel of the Stirlingshire and Clackmannan horse in the engagement for the rescue of the king, 1648. After the death of the ill-fated monarch, Lord Spynie ruined his patrimonial estate by raising forces for the service of his son. He accompanied CHARLES II. to the battle of Worcester, was taken prisoner, and sent to the Tower of London, being excepted out of Cromwell's act of grace and pardon, 1654.

On the death of Ludovick, 16th Earl of Crawford, the male representation of that ancient family devolved on Lord Spynie, who was served heir male of David, Earl of Crawford, "filii patris avi," 8 November, 1666. Lord Spynie d. s. p. in 1672.

On the title of Spynie, the lords of session, in their return to the House of Peers, 1740, observed, "that the patent of creation has not been found in the records, nor has any person sat in parliament under that title since 1669, neither has any person claimed a vote in virtue thereof at any election since the Union, but whether the peerage is extinct they cannot say."

This title was unsuccessfully claimed, in 1764, by Lieut.-Col. William Fullarton (above mentioned), under the supposition that the original grant had been made only to the 1st Lord Spynie's issue male. This has been clearly proved to be wrong by Mr. Riddell, the eminent writer on Scotch peerage law. Lieut.-Col. Fullarton's representative bears the name of "Lindsay-Carnegie," and styles himself "of Spynie," and is patron of that parish. (See Landed Gentry.)

L'ISLE—BARONS DE L'ISLE, OF ROUGEMONT.

By Writ of Summons, dated 19 December, 1311.

Lineage.

Of this surname were several families, springing originally from two, which had derived the designation, one from the Isle of Ely, the other from the Isle of Wight.

326

ROBERT DE L'ISLE, of Rougemont, co. Bedford, having m. Rohese de Tatshall, widow of Robert de Tatshall, and dau. and co-heir of John de Wahull, feudal lord of Wahull (now Wodhull), co. Bedford, had livery of the lands of her inheritance upon paying his relief in the 1st HENRY III., A.D. 1217, at which period he had restitution of his own estates, in the cos. of Lincoln, Kent, York, Norfolk, and Suffolk, which had been seized by the crown in the preceding reign during the baronial contest. After this feudal lord came another,

ROBERT DE L'ISLE, who, in the 48th HENRY III., was constituted governor of the castles of Marlborough and Lutgareshull, and the next year taking part with the barons, was made by them governor of Newcastle-upon-Tyne. "From this Robert," says Dugdale, "I must make a large leap to another,"

ROBERT DE L'ISLE, who was summoned to parliament as a Baron, from 19 December, 1311, to 25 February, 1342. This nobleman was in the expedition made in 1339 into Flanders, but he subsequently took holy orders, having, before doing so, settled the manors of Rampton, Cotenham, West Wike, with the advowson of the church of Wimpole. co. Cambridge, upon Alice, dau. of Robert de L'Isle, Elizabeth Peverell, and Richard Bayeaux, for life, with remainder to John, son of Robert de L'Isle, and his heirs. He was also then seized of the manors of Hayford Warin, in Oxfordshire, and Pishiobury, in Hertfordshire. His lordship d. in 1342, and was s. by his son,

JOHN DE L'ISLE, 2nd baron, summoned to parliament, by writ addressed "Johanni de Insulâ de Rubeo Monte," from 25 November, 1350, to 15 March, 1354. This nobleman, in the 10th EDWARD III., had obtained a grant from his father of the manor of Harwood, co. York, valued at 400 marks per annum, to enable him the better to serve the king in his wars. In three years subsequently he was in the English army, then drawn up to encounter the French at Vironfosse—and we find him soon after engaged in an expedition made into Gascony. In the 16th of the same reign he was one of the commanders at the siege of Nantes. In the 18th he was again in Gascony, and in the 20th he had a pension from the king of £200 per annum, to be paid out of the exchequer, to enable him to sustain his rank of banneret. It is said by some, that in the 20th EDWARD III., A.D. 1346, Sir Thomas Dagworth, Knt., with 80 men at arms, and 100 archers, worsting Charles de Bloys, and the great men of Britany, who had 1,000 horse, the king thereupon made two barons, viz., Alan Zouche, and John L'Isle, as also 50 knights; but others affirm that this was at the battle of Cressy, which happened the same year. John L'Isle was, however, so highly esteemed by King EDWARD III. for his courage and martial prowess, that he was made one of the knights companions of the Garter, at the institution of that order. He subsequently obtained from the crown a grant for life of the sheriffalty of the counties of Cambridge and Huntingdon, with the governorship of the castle of Cambridge, and the year before he d. (29th EDWARD III.), he was again with Prince Edward in the wars of France. His lordship d. 14 October, 1356, leaving issue, ROBERT, his heir; John, d. s. p.; William, d. s. p.; and Elizabeth, m. to William, Lord Aldeburgh. The eldest son,

ROBERT L'ISLE, 3rd baron, was summoned to parliament as by writ addressed "Roberto de Insulâ de Rubeo Monte," 15 December, 1357, and 20 November, 1360. He is stated to have d. in 1399, and the Somersetshire Visitation of 1623 says that he left a son, Sir William Lisle, of Waterperry, co. Oxford, but this is very doubtful.

Arms—Or, a fesse between two chevronels, sa.

L'ISLE—BARONS DE L'ISLE.

By Writ of Summons, dated 15 December, 1347.

Lineage.

BRYAN DE L'ISLE, who, in the beginning of King JOHN's reign paid 120 marks, and a palfrey, for the wardship and marriage of the heir of William Briston, m. in a few years afterwards, Maud, dau. and heiress of Thomas, son of William de Seleby, by whom he had issue three daus. This Bryan was governor of Bolsover Castle, co. Derby, and a principal commander of the royal army raised in Yorkshire. At that time King JOHN conferred upon him the lands of the Barons, Robert de Percy, and Peter de Plumpton. In the reign of HENRY III., remaining stedfast to the cause he had espoused, he had a command at the siege of Montsorel, and the subsequent battle of Lincoln. In the 5th HENRY, he was made warden of all the forests throughout England, and he was afterwards sheriff of Yorkshire. He d. about the 18th HENRY III., A.D. 1234, possessed of the manor of Brainston, otherwise Blandford Brian, in the co. Dorset—"which," says Hutchins, in his History of that shire, "is called Brientius-town, by Camden, and very properly derived its additional denomination of Brian, from Brian de Insula, or L'Isle, its ancient lord."

"I now come (says Dugdale) to

WARINE DE L'ISLE, son of Robert, son of Alice, dau. of Henry, a younger son of Warine Fitzgerald, as the descent sheweth." Which Warine in the Scottish wars, temp. EDWARD I., and in the beginning of EDWARD II.'s reign, was constituted governor of Windsor Castle, and warden of the forest. For years subsequently, he was engaged in Scotland, but joining Thomas, Earl of Lancaster, against the Spencers, 1320-1, and sharing in the discomfiture of his chief, he was taken prisoner, and hanged at York, with the Lord Mowbray, and several others. After which, it was found in A.D. 1327, that he d. seised of the manors of Bouden, Kingston, and Fanflore, in Berks; Mundiford, in Norfolk; and Kistingbury, in Northamptonshire; leaving Gerard, his son, twenty-three years of age, and Alice, his wife, sister and heir of Henry, Baron Teyes surviving, which

GERARD DE L'ISLE, having become eminent in the Scotch and French wars of EDWARD III., was summoned to parliament as a Baron, by the designation of "Gerardo de Insula," 15 December, 1347, but never afterwards. His lordship d. in 1360, and was s. by his son,

WARINE DE L'ISLE, 2nd baron, summoned to parliament from 6 April, 1369, to 24 May, 1382. This nobleman, like his father, participated in the great martial achievements of EDWARD III. In the 1st of RICHARD II., A.D. 1377-8, he was also in the wars of France—and in two years afterwards he went to Ireland. From King EDWARD he obtained license to make a castle of his house at Shirbourne, co. Oxford. His lordship m. Margaret, dau. of William Pipard, by whom he left, at his decease in 1381, an only dau.,

MARGARET DE L'ISLE, who m. Thomas, Lord Berkeley, and had an only dau. and heiress,

ELIZABETH BERKELEY, who m, Richard Beauchamp, 12th Earl of Warwick, by whom she had three daus., viz.,

I. Margaret, 2nd wife of John Talbot, 1st Earl of Shrews-bury, and d. 1467. Her eldest son, John Talbot, was created Baron L'Isle, 26 July, 1444, and VISCOUNT L'ISLE, in 1451. From him descends Lord de Lisle and Dudley.

II. Eleanor, m. 1st, to Thomas, Lord de Ros (see p. 19); and 2ndly, to Edmund, Duke of Somerset, by both of whom she had issue; and 3rdly, Walter Rodesley.

III. Elizabeth, m. to George Nevill, Lord Latimer (see p. 398).

Amongst the representatives of these descendants of Margaret de L'Isle, this Barony of L'Isle is presumed to be now in ABEYANCE. Mr. Courthope adds in a note (Historic Peerage, p. 290), the following remarks:—"In 1825, these co-heirs were stated, in the case presented to the House of Lords on the part of Sir John Shelley Sidney, Bart. (who claimed the Barony of L'Isle, but without success), to have been—Sir John Shelley Sydney, Bart., as sole heir of the body of MARGARET, COUNTESS OF SHREWSBURY; George, Earl of Essex, Sir Henry Hunloke, Bart., and Charlotte, Baroness de Ros, as co-heirs of the body of ELEANOR, wife of THOMAS, LORD DE ROS: and Hugh, Duke of Northumberland, Winchcombe Henry Howard Hart-ley, Esq., James Knightley, Esq.; Grey Jermyn Grove, Esq.; George William Villiers, Esq.; Montagu, Earl of Abingdon; Sir Francis Burdett, Bart.; William Fermor, Esq., and John, Lord Rollo, as co-heirs of the body of ELIZABETH, LADY LATI-MER. These were also, it is presumed, co-heirs of the body of the Barony of Berkeley under the writ of summons to Thomas de Berkeley, 23 June, 1295, being co-heirs of the body of the said Thomas de Berkeley" (see LATIMER).

Arms—Gu., a lion passant, arg., crowned, or.

LIVINGSTON—EARL OF LINLITHGOW.

Earldom, by Letters Patent, dated 1600.

Lineage.

It is said by some antiquaries that the head of this noble family was a Hungarian gentleman who came to Scotland with MARGARET, Queen of MALCOLM CANMORE, about 1070. Their immediate ancestor,

LIVINGUS flourished in the reigns of ALEXANDER I., and his brother DAVID I. He possessed a considerable estate in West Lothian, called Livingstone. His son,

THURSTANUS, "filius Livingi," witnessed the foundation charter of Holyrood House, 1128, and was father of

ALEXANDER LIVINGSTON, who first assumed the surname. He left a son,

SIR WILLIAM LIVINGSTON, who had three sons,

I. William, from whom descended the Livingstons of Living-ston, the last of whom, Sir Bartholomew Livingston fell at Flodden in 1513, leaving three daus. and co-heirs.

II. ARCHIBALD (Sir), of whom we treat.

III. Adam.

The 2nd son,

SIR ARCHIBALD LIVINGSTON, was father of

SIR WILLIAM LIVINGSTON, who m. a dau. of Sir John Erskine, of Erskine, and left a son and heir,

SIR WILLIAM LIVINGSTON, who accompanied King DAVID II. in his expedition to England in 1346, was knighted under the royal banner, and taken prisoner at the battle of Durham, 17 October, 1346. He had a grant of the barony of Calendar, then in the crown, by the forfeiture of Patric Calendar, whose only dau. and heir, Christian, he married. His only surviving son and successor,

SIR WILLIAM LIVINGSTON, of Calendar, d temp. King ROBERT II., leaving a son,

SIR JOHN LIVINGSTON, of Calendar, who m. 1st, a dau. of Menteth, of Carse, and had issue,

I. ALEXANDER (Sir), his heir

II. Robert, ancestor of the Livingstons of Westquarter and the Livingstons of Kynnaird, Earls of Newburgh.

III. John, ancestor of the Livingstons of Bonton.

He m. 2ndly, Agnes, dau. of Sir James Douglas, of Dalkeith, and by her had a son,

IV. William, ancestor of the Viscounts Kilsyth (see that title.)

The eldest son,

SIR ALEXANDER LIVINGSTON, of Calendar, having passed through numerous political troubles and suffering imprison-ment was eventually restored to royal favour and appointed justiciary of Scotland, and sent as ambassador to England in 1449. He m. a dau. of Dundas, of Dundas, and was s. by his eldest son,

SIR JAMES LIVINGSTON, of Calendar, co. Stirling, who had the appointment of captain of the castle of Stirling, with the tuition of the young King JAMES II., committed to him by his father, and was afterwards (previously to 30 August, 1450) created a peer of Scotland as LORD LIVINGSTON. He d. about 1467. Marion, widow of James, Lord Livingston, occurs in the records of parliament, 4 July, 1478. He had issue,

I. JAMES, 2nd Lord Livingston.

II. Alexander, father of JOHN, 3rd Lord Livingston.

I. Elizabeth, m. to John, Earl of Ross, Lord of the Isles.

II. Eupheme, m. 1st, to Malcolm, son and heir of Robert Lord Fleming; and 2ndly, to William Fleming, of the Bord.

The elder son,

JAMES LIVINGSTON, 2nd Lord Livingston, m. 1st, a dau. of Sir John Erskine, of Kinnoul; 2ndly, a dau. of Sir Robert Crichton; and 3rdly, Agnes Houstoun; but dying s. p., was s. by his nephew,

JOHN LIVINGSTON, 3rd Lord Livingston; who m. 1st, Eliza-beth, dau. of Robert, Lord Fleming, by whom he had a son, WILLIAM, 4th Lord Livingston. He m. 2ndly, a dau. of Sir John Houstoun, of Houstoun, by whom he had another son, Alexander, ancestor of the Livingstons of Glentirran, whose male line is extinct. Lord Livingston d. before 1510, and was s. by his son,

WILLIAM LIVINGSTON, 4th Lord Livingston, who m. Agnes, 2nd dau. of Adam Hepburn, the younger, of Hales, by whom he had a son and two daus.,

ALEXANDER, 5th Lord Livingston.

Margaret, m. to John, 4th Lord Hay, of Yester.

Isabel, m. to Nicol Ramsay, of Dalhousie.

The son and heir,

ALEXANDER LIVINGSTON, 5th Lord Livingston, was appointed an extraordinary lord of Session in 1542, and accompanying Queen MARY to France, in 1548, d. there in 1553. He m. 1st, Janet Stewart, who d. s. p.; and 2ndly, Lady Agnes Douglas, dau. of John, 2nd Earl of Morton, by whom he had seven children,

I. JOHN, master of Livingston, slain at Pinkie. He d. s. p.

II. WILLIAM, 6th Lord Livingston.

III. Thomas, ancestor of the Livingstons of Haining.

I. Elizabeth, m. to John Buchanan, of Buchanan.

II. Janet, m. to Sir Alexander Bruce, of Airth.

iii. **Magdalen**, *m.* 1st, to Sir Alexander Erskine, of Gogar; 2ndly to John Scrymgeour, of Glaster.

iv. **Mary**, maid of honour to Queen MARY, and "one of the four Maries" *m.* in 1567, to John Sempill, of Beltrees.

The elder surviving son,

WILLIAM LIVINGSTON, 6th Lord Livingston, fought for Queen MARY at Langside. He *m.* Agnes Fleming, 2nd dau. of Malcolm, 3rd Lord Fleming, and had issue,

  i. ALEXANDER, his heir.
  ii. John, *d.* young.
  iii. Henry, *d.* young.
  iv. George, of Ogleface, co. Linlithgow, created, in 1625, a BARONET of Nova Scotia (now extinct). (*See Vicissitudes of Families* 2nd Series, "The Lairds of Westquarter.") This family *s.* to the representation of the Earls of Linlithgow and Calendar.
  v. William, of Westquarter.
  i.Jea , *m.* to Alexander, 4th Lord Elphinston.
  ii. Margaret, *m.* 1st, to Sir Lewis Bellenden, of Auchinoule, justice-clerk; and 2ndly, to Patrick, Earl of Orkney.

Lord Livingston *d.* in 1592, and was *s.* by his son,

ALEXANDER LIVINGSTON, 7th Lord Livingston, who was created EARL OF LINLITHGOW, *Lord Livingston and Calendar*, 1600. He *m.* Lady Eleanor Hay, only dau. of Andrew, 7th Earl of Erroll, and had issue,

  i. John, Master of Livingston, *d. unm.*
  ii. ALEXANDER, who *s.* his father as Earl of Linlithgow.
  iii. JAMES, who was created EARL OF CALENDAR.
    i. Anne, *m.* to Alexander, 6th Earl of Eglington.
    ii. Margaret, *m.* to John, 2nd Earl of Wigton.

The Earl *d.* 2 April, 1622, and was *s.* by his son,

ALEXANDER LIVINGSTON, 2nd Earl of Linlithgow, who was appointed an extraordinary lord of Session, 13 January, 1610. He *m.* 1st, Lady Elizabeth Gordon, 2nd dau. of George, 1st Marquess of Huntly, and by her, who *d.* in childbed of her son, at Edinburgh, July, 1616, had issue,

GEORGE, his heir, 3rd Earl of Linlithgow.

He *m.* 2ndly, Lady Mary Douglas, eldest dau. of William, 10th Earl of Angus, by whom also he had issue,

ALEXANDER, who *s.* his uncle as 2nd Earl of Calendar under the special remainder of his patent.
Margaret, *m.* 1st, to Sir Thomas Nicholson, of Carnock; 2ndly, to Sir George Stirling, of Kier; and 3rdly, to Sir John Stirling, of Kier.
Eleanor, *d. unm.*

The elder son,

GEORGE LIVINGSTON, 3rd Earl of Linlithgow, *b.* July, 1616, was implicated in Sir James Montgomery's plot for the restoration of the abdicated royal family. He *m.* 30 July, 1650, Lady Elizabeth Maule, 2nd dau. of Patrick, 1st Earl of Panmure, dowager of John, 2nd Earl of Kinghorn, and by her (who *d.* at Castle-Huntly, in October, 1659) had issue,

GEORGE, 4th Earl of Linlithgow.
ALEXANDER, successor to his uncle as 3rd Earl of Calendar, which uncle had also inherited from an uncle, the title of Calendar being thus borne by the 2nd son of this family for three generations in succession.
Henriet, *m.* in July, 1666, to Robert, 2nd Viscount of Oxford.

The Earl *d.* 1 February, 1690, aged seventy-four, and was *s.* by his son,

GEORGE LIVINGSTON, 4th Earl of Linlithgow, who was sworn a privy councillor in 1692, and appointed one of the commissioners of the Treasury. He *m.* Henriet Sutherland, eldest dau. of Alexander, 1st Lord Duffus, but had no issue. He *d.* 7 August, 1695, when his title devolved on his nephew,

JAMES LIVINGSTON, 4th Earl of Calendar, son of Alexander Livingston, 3rd Earl of Calendar. Engaging in the rebellion of 1715, the Earl of Linlithgow and Calendar was attainted of high treason, and his estate and honours forfeited to the crown. He *m.* Lady Margaret Hay, 2nd dau. of John, 12th Earl of Erroll, and by her had a son, James, Lord Livingston, who *d.* 13 April, 1716; and a dau., Anne, who *m.* William, 4th Earl of Kilmarnock, and their eldest dau., JAMES, *s.* in her right to the Earldom of Erroll. The great Calendar property (first sold to the York Buildings Company, a London Corporation) was purchased eventually, about 1780, by WILLIAM FORBES, Esq. (*See* BURKE's *Vicissitudes of Families, 2nd Series.*)

Though "the strongholds of the Livingstones are in ruins in Scotland," a flourishing branch of the family still remains, in high honour and distinction, in the United States of America. (*See* ADDENDA.)

Arms—Arg., three cinquefoils, gu., within a double treasure of fleurs-de-lis, vert.

LIVINGSTON—EARL OF CALENDAR.

Barony, by Letters Patent, dated 19 June, 1633.
Earldom, by Letters Patent, dated 1641 and 1660.

Lineage.

THE HON. SIR JAMES LIVINGSTON (3rd son of Alexander, 1st Earl of Linlithgow), acquired a high military reputation in the wars in Bohemia, Germany, Holland, and Sweden. Returning to his native country, he was constituted one of the gentlemen of the bedchamber to King CHARLES I., and created LORD LIVINGSTON, *of Almond*, 19 June, 1633, to him and his heirs male for ever. He obtained subsequently a patent of the EARLDOM OF CALENDAR to the heirs male of his body in 1641, and a second in 1660, with specific limitations. His lordship acted a distinguished part in the civil wars. He *m.* (contract dated 1633) Margaret, only dau. of James, 7th Lord Yester, sister of John, 1st Earl of Tweeddale. dowager of Alexander, 1st Earl of Dunfermline, high chancellor of Scotland, but by her, who was buried with her first husband, at Dalgety, 20 January, 1660, had no issue; and dying in 1672, was *s.*, in terms of the patent, by his nephew,

ALEXANDER LIVINGSTON, 2nd Earl of Calendar (2nd son of Alexander, 2nd Earl of Linlithgow). He *m.* (contract dated 1663) Lady Mary Hamilton, 3rd dau. of William, 2nd Duke of Hamilton, but by her (who *m.* 2ndly, Sir James Livingstone, of Westquarter; and 3rdly, James, 3rd Earl of Findlater) had no issue. He *d.* in August, 1685, and his estate and honours devolved on his nephew,

ALEXANDER LIVINGSTON, 3rd Earl of Calendar (2nd son of George, 3rd Earl of Linlithgow), who was served heir of entail and provision of his uncle, in the baronies of Calendar, Haining, and other lands, 16 May, 1688. He *d.* in December, 1692, leaving by his wife, Lady Anne Graham, eldest dau. of James, 2nd Marquess of Montrose,

  i. JAMES, his successor, 4th earl.
  i. Henriet, *d. unm.* 25 May, 1738.
  ii. Mary, *m.* to James Graham, of Airth, co. Stirling, an advocate of great celebrity, judge of the Court of Admiralty in Scotland.

The son,

JAMES LIVINGSTON, 4th Earl of Calendar, *s.* on the death of his uncle, George, 4th Earl of Linlithgow, to the Earldom of Linlithgow, to which *refer*. His estates and honours were FORFEITED by his engaging in the rebellion of 1715.

Arms—Quarterly: 1st and 4th, sa., a bend, between six billets, or; for CALENDAR; 2nd and 3rd, arg., three cinquefoils, gu., within a double treasure, flowered and counterflowered, with fleurs-de-lis, vert; for LIVINGSTON; with a crescent in the centre for difference.

LIVINGSTON—VISCOUNT KILSYTH.

By Letters Patent, dated 17 August, 1661.

Lineage.

This is a junior branch of the same stock, from which descends the Linlithgow family, to which *refer*.

SIR WILLIAM LIVINGSTON (only son of Sir James Livingston, of Calendar, by his 2nd wife) got from his father the lands of Wester Kilsyth; had a charter from his grandfather, James Douglas, of Dalkeith, the king's brother, of some lands near Dalkeith, 29 September, 1421; and *d.* in 1459. He *m.* Elizabeth, dau. and co-heir of William de Caldcotis, with whom he got the lands of Greden, in Berwickshire, and had two sons,

  i. EDWARD, his heir.
  ii. Henry (Sir), preceptor of Torphichen.

The elder son,

EDWARD LIVINGSTON, of Kilsyth, was served heir male of his father, 22 April, 1460. His son,

WILLIAM LIVINGSTON, of Kilsyth, *m.* Mary, dau. of Thomas, Lord Erskine, and had three sons,

  i. WILLIAM, his heir.
  ii. James, of Inches, ancestor of the Viscount Teviot. (*See that title.*)
  iii. Robert, of Baldoran.

The eldest son,

WILLIAM LIVINGSTON, of Kilsyth, m. Margaret Graham, and had two sons,

I. WILLIAM.   II. Alexander.

The elder,

WILLIAM LIVINGSTON, killed at the battle of Flodden, 9 September, 1513, leaving by his wife, Janet Bruce, dau. of the Laird of Airth, a son,

WILLIAM LIVINGSTON, of Kilsyth, who m. Mary, dau of Sir Duncan Forrester, of Garden, comptroller of the household, and had (with three daus., Elizabeth, m. to Gabriel Cunningham, of Craigends; Isabel, m. to Colin Campbell, of Auchinhove; and Margaret, m. 1st, to Ninian Bruce, and 2ndly, to Alexander Baillie, of Jerviswood,) a son,

SIR WILLIAM LIVINGSTON, of Kilsyth, who was knighted in 1565, when Darnley was made Duke of Albany. He m. Lady Christian Graham, 2nd dau. of John, 4th Earl of Menteith (see that title), and had (with a dau., Christian, m. to John Lawson, of Boghall,) an only son,

SIR WILLIAM LIVINGSTON, of Kilsyth, a man of talents and learning, who attended the Duke of Lennox in his embassy to France, in July, 1601; was appointed one of the lords of the session, 6 June, 1609; sworn a privy councillor, 13 May, 1613, and the same day constituted vice chamberlain of Scotland. He m. 1st, Antonia de Bourd, a French lady of quality, by whom he had,

William (SIR), knighted at the baptism of Prince Henry, 1595: he d. v. p., having m. Lady Annie Fleming, 2nd dau. of John, 1st Earl of Wigton, by whom he had a son, William Livingston, of Kilsyth, who d. in his minority, unm., 1647.

He m. 2ndly, Margaret, dau. of Sir John Houston, of Houston, and by her had,

JAMES (SIR), of whom we treat.

Margaret, m. to Robert Montgomery, of Haslehead, in Ayrshire.

He d. in 1627, and was s. by his only son,

SIR JAMES LIVINGSTON, of Barncloich, b. 25 June, 1616. This gentleman, an eminent royalist, offered to hold out his castle of Kilsyth against Cromwell, and received a letter of thanks from King CHARLES II., dated 7 October, 1650. He was fined by Cromwell £1,500; but on the Restoration, raised to the peerage, as Lord of Campsie, and VISCOUNT KILSYTH, by patent, dated 17 August, 1661. He enjoyed his honours, however, but a few days, dying at London, 7 September, 1661. His lordship m. Eupheme, dau. of Sir David Cunningham, of Robertland, and had issue,

I. JAMES, 2nd Viscount.
II. WILLIAM, 3rd Viscount.
I. Elizabeth, m. to the Hon. Major-Gen. Robert Montgomery, 5th son of Alexander, 6th Earl of Eglinton.
II. Anne, b. 12 January, 1648, d. unm.

The elder son,

JAMES, 2nd Viscount Kilsyth, d. unm. in 1706, and was s. by his brother,

WILLIAM, 3rd Viscount Kilsyth, b. 29 March, 1650. His lordship m. 1st, Jean, relict of John, Viscount Dundee, and 3rd dau. of William, Lord Cochrane, eldest son of William, Earl of Dundonald; by whom he had a son, William, who d. an infant. He m. 2ndly, Barbara, dau. of Macdougal, of Makerstoun, co. Roxburgh, and by her had a dau., Barbara, who d. young. This nobleman, who was one of the representative peers of Scotland, engaging in the rebellion of 1715, was attainted of high treason, and his estate and honours forfeited. He d. at Rome, 12 January, 1733. In 1795, a leaden coffin in the church of Kilsyth was opened, containing the bodies of a lady, supposed to be the 1st wife of Lord Kilsyth, and her son, in perfect preservation. The lady bore evident marks of a violent death, and it is said was killed by the fall of a house in Holland.

Arms—Arg., three gillyflowers, slipped, gu., within a double tressure, flowered and counter-flowered with fleurs-de-lis, vert.

LIVINGSTON—VISCOUNT OF TEVIOT.

By Letters Patent, dated 4 December, 1696.

Lineage.

JAMES LIVINGSTON, of Inches, 2nd son of William Livingston, of Kilsyth (see Livingston, Viscount Kilsyth), acquired the lands of Brownlee and Jerviswood, of which he had a charter, 1512. He m. 1st, a dau. of Sir James Lockhart, of Lee; and

2ndly, a dau. of James Hamilton, of Silvertonhill, and had a son,

JAMES LIVINGSTON, who d. v. p., leaving by Agnes, his wife, dau. of William Cunninghame, of Bonnytoun, a son,

WILLIAM LIVINGSTON, of Jerviswood, who had a charter of that estate, 6 March, 1548. He m. Jean, dau. of John Johnston, and had two sons, John, who d. s. p., and

WILLIAM LIVINGSTON, of Jerviswood, who had a charter of those lands in 1611. He m. Janet Douglas, sister of the 1st Earl of Queensberry, and was father of two sons, William Livingston, who sold the estate of Jerviswood to George Baillie, merchant in Edinburgh, and d. without succession, in the reign of King CHARLES I., and

MUNGO LIVINGSTON, of Newbigging, who by his wife Jean, dau. of John Lindsay, of Covington, was father of

SIR THOMAS LIVINGSTON, colonel in the service of the states of Holland, commanding a regiment of foot, who was created a Baronet, by CHARLES I., 29 June, 1627. He m. a dau. of Colonel Edmond, a native of Stirling, by whom he had two sons,

THOMAS, his heir.
Alexander (Sir), who s. his brother in his baronetcy, had the command of a regiment of foot in the service of the states of Holland, and left no male issue.

The elder son,

SIR THOMAS LIVINGSTON, was an officer in the service of the states of Holland, commanded a regiment of foot under WILLIAM III. in his expedition to Britain, 1688, and signalized himself eminently in the campaigns of that monarch. He was appointed commander-in-chief of the forces in Scotland; had the rank of major-general, 1 January, 1696; and was created VISCOUNT of Teviot, by patent, dated 4 December, 1696, to himself and the heirs male of his body. He d. at London, 14 January, 1711, and was buried in Westminster Abbey, where his brother, Sir Alexander, erected a noble monument to his memory. His title of Viscount of Teviot became EXTINCT, as he left no male issue.

Arms—As LIVINGSTON, Earl of Linlithgow.

LOFTUS—VISCOUNT LOFTUS, OF ELYE.

By Letters Patent, dated 10 May, 1622.

Lineage.

ADAM LOFTUS, of Monasterevan, now called Moore Abbey, co. Kildare, son of Robert Loftus, eldest son of Edward Loftus, of Swinesbead, in the parish of Caversham, co. York, ancestor of the present noble house of Ely, having attained considerable eminence as a lawyer, was appointed Lord Chancellor of Ireland, in 1619, and created, 10 May, 1622, VISCOUNT LOFTUS, of Elye, a title which, according to the privy seal was to continue in the family "as long as there shall remain an heir male of his house," but which the patent confines to the "heirs male of his body." His lordship m. Sarah, widow of Richard Meredyth, bishop of Leighlin, and had, with two daus., four sons, of whom the eldest, Sir Robert Loftus, Knt., d. v. p. leaving an only dau. Anne, wife of Richard Lennard Barrett, Esq., of Bellhouse, Essex, and the 2nd,

EDWARD LOFTUS, 2nd Viscount Loftus, of Elye, m. Jane, dau. and co-heir of Arthur Lindley, Esq., of Midlam Castle, Yorkshire, and dying 11 April, 1680, was s. by his son,

ARTHUR LOFTUS, 3rd Viscount Loftus, of Elye, who m. 1st Douglas, dau. and co-heir of William Savage, Esq., of Castle Rheban, co. Kildare, and 2ndly, in 1676, Anne, dau. of William Hawkins, Esq., and widow of Sir Andrew Owens, Knt., by whom he had an only dau.,

JANE, m. to Charles, Lord Moore, ancestor of the noble family of Drogheda.

His lordship m. 3rdly, in 1702, Letitia, sister of Hercules Rowley, Esq., of Somerhill, co. Meath, but by her (who m. 2ndly, Nicholas, Lord Loftus) had no issue. He d. 6 November, 1725, aged eighty-two, when the title became EXTINCT; the Monasterevan estate passing to his grandson, Henry, 4th Earl of Drogheda, son of his only daughter.

Arms—Sa., a chevron, engr., erm., between three trefoils slipped, arg.

N. B.—This title was again created as stated in the next article.

LOFTUS, BARON LOFTUS, VISCOUNT LOFTUS, OF ELYE, AND EARL OF ELY.

Barony, (Irish) by Letters Patent, dated 5 October. 1751.
Viscounty, (Irish) by Letters Patent, dated 19 July, 1756.
Earldom, (Irish) by Letters Patent, dated 23 October, 1766,
and again 5 December, 1771.

Lineage.

Refer for further details to "ELY," in *Extant Peerage*, and to the *Landed Gentry*. The second of the above titles was revived in favour of

THE RIGHT HON NICHOLAS LOFTUS, M.P. for the county of Wexford, who had been previously created BARON LOFTUS, *of Loftus Hall*, and these honours were inherited by his elder son,

NICHOLAS LOFTUS, 2nd viscount, who was advanced to the dignity of EARL OF ELY, 23 October, 1766. His only son,

NICHOLAS LOFTUS, 2nd earl, and 3rd viscount. and baron, *d. unm.* 12 November, 1769, when the earldom EXPIRED, but the viscounty and barony reverted to his uncle,

HENRY LOFTUS, 4th viscount, *b.* 11 November, 1709. The Earldom of Ely was revived in his favour, 5 December, 1771, but as he *d. s. p.* 8 May, 1783, the honours all EXPIRED, the estates devolving on his lordship's nephew,

THE RIGHT HON. CHARLES TOTTENHAM, in whose favour all these titles were again created, and he was further advanced to a marquessate, as stated in *Extant Peerage, which see*

LOFTUS—VISCOUNT LISBURNE.

By Letters Patent, dated 29 January, 1685.

Lineage.

SIR ADAM LOFTUS, Knt. (eldest brother of Nicholas Loftus, of Fethard, ancestor of the present Marquess of Ely,) was constituted, in 1636, vice-treasurer, receiver-general of the revenues, and treasurer-at-war in Ireland. He *m.* Jane, dau. of Walter Vaughan, Esq., of Golden Grove, Kings co., and had, with other issue, a son and successor,

SIR ARTHUR LOFTUS, Knt., of Rathfarnham, M.P. for the co. Wexford; appointed in 1639 provost-mareschal of the province of Ulster. He *m.* in 1624, Lady Dorothy Boyle, dau. of Richard, Earl of Cork, and by her (who *m.* 2ndly, Mr. Talbot,) had, with three daus. (Letitia, *m.* to Thomas Coningsby, Esq., of Hampton Court, Herefordshire ; Eleanor, wife of Theobald, Viscount Mayo, and Jane, *m.* to Robert Gorges, Esq., of Kilbrew, co. Meath,) a son and successor,

ADAM LOFTUS, of Rathfarnham, who was created, 29 January, 1685, *Baron of Rathfarnham*, in the county of Dublin, and VISCOUNT LISBURNE. His lordship *m.* Lucia, dau. and co-heir of George Brydges, 6th Lord Chandos, by whom he had an only dau. and heir, Lucia, who became the 2nd wife of Thomas, Lord Wharton, and carried to the Whartons, the Loftus estates, which her son Philip, Duke of Wharton, sold to William Conolly, Esq., Speaker of the Irish House of Commons, for £62,000.

The viscount commanded a regiment for King WILLIAM, at the siege of Limerick, and fell there, when his honours EXPIRED.

Arms—Sa., a chev., engr., erm., between three trefoils slipped, arg.

LONG—BARON FARNBOROUGH.

By Letters Patent, dated 8 July, 1826.

Lineage.

This family derives its origin from Wiltshire, where various branches of that name have been established for several centuries.

JOHN LONGE, of Netheravon, in that co., *d.* in 1630, leaving, by Catherine, his wife, a 2nd son,

TIMOTHY LONGE, *b.* in 1610, who *m.* Jane, only dau. of the Rev. Oliver Brunsell, vicar of Wroughton, co. Wilts (by Eliza-

beth, his wife, dau. of Henry Martyn, Esq., of Upham, and Jane, his wife, dau. of Thomas Walrond, Esq., of Albourne, forester in fee of that chase), and, dying in 1691, had issue,

I. Timothy. in holy orders, *b.* in 1636, rector of St. Alphage, London. and prebendary of Southwell, Notts, *d. unm.* 14 September, 1665, during the great plague, as stated in Peck's *Desiderata*.

II. SAMUEL, of whose line we treat. This

SAMUEL LONG, the 2nd son, *b.* 1638. accompanied the expedition under Penn and Venables, which conquered Jamaica, in 1655, as a lieutenant in Colonel D'Oyley's regiment. with whom he was connected, and was further appointed secretary to Cromwell's commissioners. He received large grants of land in that island, where he became a colonel of horse, chief justice, speaker of the assembly, and one of the council. He *d.* in 1683, and had, by his wife, Elizabeth (who remarried the Rev. John Towers, rector of Swaffham Bulbec, in the co. Cambridge, grandson of John Towers, bishop of Peterborough, and *d.* in 1710) with three daus., of whom the eldest, Elizabeth, *b.* in 1670, *m.* 1st, Henry Lowe, Esq., of Goadby Marwood, co. Leicester ; and 2ndly, Henry Smallwood, Esq. ; three sons, one of whom alone survived, namely,

CHARLES LONG, of Longville, Jamaica, and of Hurts Hall, Saxmundham, co Suffolk, *b.* in 1679, M.P. for Dunwich. in 1716, who *d.* in 1723. He *m.* 1st, in 1699, Amy, eldest dau. of Sir Nicholas Lawes, Knt. governor of Jamaica, and had issue by her (who *d.* in 1702), I. SAMUEL, his heir, ancestor of the Longs of Hampton Lodge, co. Surrey *(see* BURKE's *Landed Gentry)*, and II. Elizabeth, *b.* in 1701, *m.* John Hamerton, Esq., secretary to South Carolina, and *d. s. p.* in 1772. He *m.* 2ndly, in 1703, Jane, dau. and heir of Sir William Beeston, Knt., governor of Jamaica, and relict of Sir Thomas Modyford, Bart., by whom (who *d.* in 1724) he had issue,

I. Charles, *b.* in 1705, of Hurts Hall ; *m.* Mary, dau. and heir of Dudley North. Esq.. of Glenham Hall, co. Suffolk, nephew of Francis, 1st Lord Guildford, lord keeper, &c. He *d.* in 1778, leaving by this lady (who *d* 20 August. 1834). two sons,

  1 CHARLES, *b.* in 1749, of Hurts Hall, *m.* his cousin Jane, dau. of Beeston Long. Esq.. and *d.* in 1813, having had issue. two sons, Charles and Dudley, both of whom *d.* young.

  2 Dudley, *b.* in 1749, of Glemham Hall and Hurts Hall, member in several parliaments, assumed the name of NORTH; *m.* 1802, the Hon. Sophia-Anderson Pelham, dau. of the 1st Lord Yarborough, and *d. s. p.* in 1829.

II. William, a lieutenant in the Earl of Pembroke's dragoons, *b.* in 1706 ; *d. unm.*

III. BEESTON, of whom presently.

I. Jane, *b.* in 1709 ; *m.* 1st, to Roger Drake, Esq., of Shirley, Surrey, and 2ndly, to the Marquess D'Aragona, of Modena.

II Anne, *b.* 1713; *m.* to the Rev. Philip Carter, vicar of Turnstall, Suffolk.

III. Susannah, *d. unm.* in 1820, aged one hundred and three.

The 3rd son,

BEESTON LONG, Esq., of Carshalton Park, Surrey, *b.* in 1710, *m.* in 1745, Susannah, dau. and heir of Abraham Cropp, Esq., of Richmond, in Surrey, and *d.* 1785, having had issue,

I. Samuel, of Carshalton, M.P. for Ilchester, high sheriff for Surrey, in 1790 ; *m.* Lady Jane Maitland, 4th dau. of James, 7th Earl of Lauderdale, K.T., and by her (who *m.* 2ndly, Lieut.-Gen. Sir William Houston, G.C.B.) he left, at his decease, in 1807, two sons and a dau., viz ,

  1 Samuel, formerly lieutenant-colonel Grenadier Guards, of Bromley Hill, Kent, J.P. and D.L., *b.* 1799, who *m.* 1st, 18 April, 1827, Lady Louisa-Emily, 2nd dau. of Edward, 13th Earl of Derby, K.G. (she *d.* 11 December following); 2ndly, 1827, Sydney, dau. of Arthur Atherley, Esq., M.P. for Southampton ; and 3rdly, 1854, Emily, 2nd dau. of Charles-John Herbert, Esq., of Muckruss, Killarney. (*See Landed Gentry*.)

  2 Charles-Maitland, rector of Settrington, co. York, and archdeacon of the East Riding, rector of Whitchurch, co. Salop, *m.* and had issue.

  1 Mary.

II. Richard, *d. unm.* at Oxford.

III. Beeston, of Combe House, Surrey. a bank director, who *m.* in 1786, Frances-Louisa. eldest dau. of Sir Richard Neave, Bart., and dying in 1820, left issue,

  1 William, of Hurts Hall, near Saxmundham, Suffolk, J.P. and D.L., high sheriff, 1843 ; *b.* 1802 ; *m.* 20 October, 1830, Eleanora-Charlotte Montague, sister of Sir Edward Poore, Bart., of Rushall, co. Wilts, and has, with other issue, a son,

    William Beeston, *b.* 1833, *m.* 11 May, 1859, Arethusa-Mariamme, 4th dau. of Sir Charles-Robert Rowley, Bart.

  1 Caroline-Jane, *d.* 1824.

  2 Amelia-Ann, *d s.p.*

  3 Maria, *m.* to Henry-Seymour Montague, Esq , and *d* in 1832, leaving issue.

1ᵛ. CHARLES (Sir), of whom presently.
v. George, 1st lieutenant of "the Superb," killed at the storming of Trincomalee, in 1782, *unm.*
vi. William, in holy orders, canon of Windsor, rector of Fulham, in Norfolk, and of Sternfield, in Suffolk, *d. s. p.*1835.
vii. Richard, *d. unm.*
i. Sarah, *m.* 28 April, 1774, to Sir George-William Prescott, Bart., and left issue.
ii. Jane, *m.* to her cousin, Charles Long, Esq., of Hurts Hall, *d. s. p.*
iii. Susannah, *m.* to the Rev. George Chamberlayne.

The 4th son,
THE RIGHT HON. SIR CHARLES LONG, G.C.B., P.C., F.R.S., and F.S.A., of Bromley Hill Place, co. Kent, *b.* in 1760, having filled successively the appointments of joint secretary of the Treasury in 1800, one of the lords of the Treasury in 1804, and subsequently paymaster-general of the forces, was created 8 July, 1826, BARON FARNBOROUGH in the Peerage of the United Kingdom. His lordship *m.* 28 May, 1793, Amelia, eldest dau. of Sir Abraham Hume, Bart., but left no issue at his decease, 17 January, 1838, when the title became EXTINCT.

Arms—Sa., a lion passant, arg., holding in the dexter paw a cross-crosslet, fitchée, or: on a chief of the second, three cross-crosslets of the field.

LONGFIELD—BARON AND VISCOUNT LONGUEVILLE.

Barony, by Letters Patent, dated 1795.
Viscounty, by Letters Patent, dated 1800.

Lineage.

The earlier lineage and full details as to this family will be found in the *Landed Gentry.*
RICHARD LONGFIELD, Esq., of Longueville, co. Cork, *b.* in 1734, J.P., high sheriff for that county in 1758, sat for several years in the parliament of his native country, and was M.P. for Charleville, in 1761, and afterwards for the co. Cork. He was elevated to the peerage of Ireland as *Baron Longueville,* of Longueville, in the co. Cork, by letters patent, dated 1795, and was advanced to a viscounty, being created VISCOUNT LONGUEVILLE, by letters patent, dated 1800. His lordship, who was governor of the co. Cork, and sat in the imperial parliament as a representative peer for Ireland, *m.* in 1756, Margaret, dau. of Richard White, Esq., and aunt to Richard, 1st Earl of Bantry, but *d. s. p.* 23 May, 1811, when the title became EXTINCT, while the greater portion of his lordship's estates devolved on his cousins, JOHN LONGFIELD, Esq., of Longueville, M.P. for Mallow; and MOUNTIFORD LONGFIELD, M.P. for Enniscorthy, who inherited the estates of Castle Mary, co. Cork. (*See Landed Gentry.*)

Arms—Gu., a chevron, erm., between seven cross-crosslets, fitchée.

LONGVILLIERS—BARON LONGVILLIERS.

By Writ of Summons, dated 25 February, 1342.

Lineage.

In the 25th EDWARD I (A.D. 1297)
JOHN DE LONGVILLIERS *d.* seized of the manors of Cokesford, co. Notts, and Gloseborne, in Yorkshire, and was *s.* by his brother,
THOMAS DE LONGVILLIERS, who had summons to parliament as a Baron, 25 February, 1342, but never afterwards. His lordship *d.* in 1374, when the Barony of Longvilliers became EXTINCT.
According to Dugdale, his lordship left an only sister, AGNES, wife of Robert, son of Ralph Cromwell, his next heir. Under the head of Everingham, however, the same authority states, that Agnes, dau. of John Longvilliers, *m.* Reginald de Everingham. And Collins says, that Agnes, the wife of Everingham, was dau. and co-heir of Sir John Longvilliers, whose sister, Elizabeth, was mother of Stephen Manlovel, of Rampton, whose dau. and heir, Elizabeth, *m.* Sir John de Stanhope, ancestor of the Earls of Chesterfield.

Arms—Sa., a bend between six cross-crosslets, arg.

L'ORTI—BARON L'ORTI.

By Writ of Summons, dated 6 February, 1299.

Lineage.

In the 6th of HENRY III. (A.D. 1221-2)
HENRY D'ORTAI (which is the same with *L'Orti* or *De Urtino*), having *m.* Sabina, dau. and heir of Richard Revel (a person of great note in the West, viz., sheriff of the cos. of Devon and Cornwall, from the 7th to the end of King RICHARD I's reign), and of Mabel, his wife, sister and heir of Walter de Esselegh, of Esselegh, co. Wilts, had livery of the lands of the inheritance of the said Sabina, and in some years afterwards obtained license to impark his woods in the co. Somerset, so that he might be free of any regard of the king's forests. He *d.* in 1241, and was *s.* by his son,
HENRY L'ORTI, who having been engaged in the Welsh and French wars, was summoned to parliament as a Baron, 6 February, 1299. His lordship was *s.* at his decease, 1321, by his son,
HENRY L'ORTI, summoned to parliament by writ addressed "Henrico de L'Orty," 10 October, 1325, and *d.* 1341-2. His son and heir,
JOHN L'ORTI, was never summoned to parliament. This nobleman left, at his decease, two daus., viz.,
SYBIL, wife of Sir Lawrence de St. Martin,
MARGARET, wife of Henry de Esturmie,

Amongst whose descendants and representatives the Barony of L'Orti is now in ABEYANCE.

Arms—Vert, a pale, or.

LOVEL—BARON LOVEL OF KARY.

By Writ of Summons, dated 20 November, 1348.

Lineage.

The first of this family that came into England was
ROBERT, Lord of Breherval, &c., in Normandy (where he likewise held the castle of Yvery, by the service of three knights' fees), a younger son, as it is said, of Eudes, sovereign Duke of Brittany. This nobleman accompanied WILLIAM THE CONQUEROR in 1066, and was rewarded with the lordships of Kary and Harpetre, co. Somerset; but returning into Normandy, and being there attacked by a severe illness, he became a monk in the abbey of Bec, and *d.* soon after, about the year 1083, leaving three sons, of whom the eldest,
ASCELIN GOUEL DE PERCEVAL, *s.* his father. This feudal lord like his predecessor, held a distinguished place in the Norman army of the conquest, and for his services had a grant of divers manors, particularly of Weston and Stawell, co. Somerset. He was a man of violent temper, and hence acquired the surname of LUPUS, or the Wolf. Odericus Vitalis gives the particulars of a long and extraordinary dispute which this Ascelin had with the Earl of Bretevil, in Normandy, and which terminated by his obtaining his own terms, after sustaining a siege of two months in his castle of Breherval, against a powerful army, commanded by the ablest captains of the age—which terms included the retention of the fortress, and the hand of Isabella, the Earl of Bretevil's only dau., in marriage. This lady, although illegitimate, upon the failure of the earl's legitimate issue, became, through the favour of HENRY I., heir in part to her father, and her husband, ASCELIN, was established in the Earldom of Yvery, in *Normandy,* in 1119. The issue of the marriage were seven sons and a dau., *m.* to Radulfus Rufus, a noble Norman. Of the sons, the names of three alone have been handed down to us, namely, ROBERT, WILLIAM, and John, of whom the youngest, John, acquired from his father the manor of Harpetre, and assumed that as a surname, but it was afterwards changed by his descendants to GOURNAY. Ascelin *d.* soon after his accession to the Earldom of Yvery, and was *s.* by his eldest son,
ROBERT, Earl of Yvery, who *d. s. p.* in 1121, and was *s.* in his Norman and English estates by his brother,
WILLIAM, Earl of Yvery. This nobleman was nicknamed *Lupellus,* or the little wolf, which designation was softened into *Lupel,* and thence into LUVEL, and became the surname of most of his descendants. He defended his castle of Kary in 1153, against King STEPHEN, but *d.* in two years afterwards

He *m.* Auberic, s'ster of Waleran de Bellemonte, Earl of Mellent, in Normandy, and *d.* about 1155, having had five sons, namely,

    I. WALERAN, who *s.* to the Norman dominions, and was Baron of Yvery, but the title of earl never, subsequently, occurs. His line continued until the 15th century.

    II. RALPH, of whom presently.

    III. HENRY, successor to his brother Ralph.

    IV. WILLIAM, ancestor of the BARONS LOVEL, of Tichmersh, &c., and VISCOUNT LOVEL (*see next article*).

    V. Richard, who retained the original surname of PERCEVAL, and from him descend the Percevals, Earls of Egmont.

The 2nd son having adopted the surname of LOVEL, and inherited the estate of Castle Kary, co. Somerset, became

RALPH LOVEL, Lord of Castle Kary. He *m.* Maud, dau. of Henry de Newmarch, but dying *s. p.* before 1159, was *s.* by his brother,

HENRY LOVEL. This feudal lord, upon the collection of the scutazom in 1159, paid 5 marks; and in seven years after, upon the assessment in aid of marrying the King's dau., certified his knight's fees, *de veteri feoffamento*, to be 18, and *de novo* 1. In 1176, he was amerced for trespassing in the king's forests at 100 marks. He *d.* before the year 1199, and was *s.* by his son and heir,

RALPH LOVEL, who in the 1st year of King JOHN, A.D. 1199-1200, paid £60 for livery of his Barony of Kary, and afterwards bestowed the lands of Ethelberge on the monks of Montacute. He *d.* in 1207 *s. p.*, and was *s.* by his brother,

HENRY LOVEL. This feudal lord, in the 13th King JOHN, gave 800 marks, and seven good palfries, for permission to go into Ireland. He *d.* in 1218, and was *s.* by his son,

RICHARD LOVEL, who, in the 2nd HENRY III., A.D. 1218, giving £100 as a security for payment of his relief, had livery of his Barony of Kary, and all his other lands in Somersetshire. In the 26th of the same king he paid a fine of 15 marks to be exempted from going into Gascony, and in 12 years afterwards, upon the collection of the aid for making the king's eldest son a knight, he answered for 11 knights' fees and a-half for the honor of Moreton. He *d.* in this latter year (1253), and was *s.* by his son,

HENRY LOVEL, who, in the ensuing year, paid £100 for his relief, and had livery of his lands; but enjoyed the estates only a short period. He *d.* in 1262, then seized of the manor of Castle Kary (held in *capite* from the crown, by barony, and the service of finding two soldiers in the king's army at his own charge for forty days), and was *s.* by his elder son,

RICHARD LOVEL. This feudal lord *d. s. p.* the year after his father, and was *s.* by his brother,

HENRY LOVEL, who *d.* about the year 1280, leaving a dau., Oliva, *m.* to John de Gournay, and his successor,

HUGH LOVEL, against whom his brother-in-law, John de Gournay, instituted a suit at law in the time of EDWARD I. for the fortune of his wife, Oliva: which fortune, in the 8th of that reign, 1280, the said Hugh entered into a stipulation to pay. He *d.* in 1291, and was *s.* by his son,

SIR RICHARD LOVEL, who in the 9th EDWARD III., A.D. 1335, in conjunction with Muriel, his wife, had the custody of the castles of Corf and Purbeck, co. Dorset, and was summoned to parliament as a Baron from 20 November, 1348, to 25 November, 1350. His lordship *m.* Muriel, dau. of John Soulis, of Roxburghshire, in Scotland, and had issue,

    JAMES, who *m.* Isabella, dau. of Lord Zouche, and predeceased the baron, *anno* 1342, leaving issue,

        Richard, *b.* 1335, *d. s. p.* 1342.

        MURIEL, *b.* 1332, *m.* to Sir Nicholas de St. Maur, Lord St. Maur.

    Joan, *m.* to John de Moels.

    Alianore, *m.* to Sir Roger Ruhaut.

Lord Lovel *d.* in 1351, seized of the manor of Winfred Egle, co. Dorset, and of Castle Kary and Mersh, co. Somerset. Upon the decease of his lordship the Barony of Lovel, of Castle Kary, and his estates, devolved upon his grand-dau., MURIEL LOVEL, who conveyed them to the family of her husband, Nicholas, Lord St. Maur (*see* ST. MAUR.)

Arms—Or, semé of cross-crosslets, a lion rampant, az.

LOVEL—BARONS LOVEL, OF TICHMERSH, CO. NORTHAMPTON; VISCOUNT LOVEL.

Barony, by Writ of Summons, as stated below.
Viscounty, by Letters Patent, dated 4 June, 1483.

Lineage.

This branch of the family of Lovel descends from

WILLIAM LOVEL, 4th son of William, Earl of Yvery, in Normandy, and brother of Ralph and Henry Lovel, feudal lords of Castle Kary—(*refer to preceding article*). This William, who was lord of Minster Lovel, co. Oxford, *d.* previously to the year 1196, and was *s.* by his son,

WILLIAM LOVEL, who, in the 13th JOHN, A.D. 1211, held Dockinges by barony. He was *s.* by his son,

JOHN LOVEL, Lord of Dockinges, and of Minster Lovel. This feudal baron was a minor at the period of his father's decease, and under the guardianship of Alan Basset, of Mursdewall and Wycombe, in Surrey, whose dau. Aliva, by Aliva, dau. of Stephen Gay, he eventually *m.* (as was frequently the case in those times), and settled upon her the manor of Minster Lovel. On his marriage he relinquished the ancient coat of arms of his own family, and assumed that of the Bassets, the colours only changed from az. and sa. to or. and gu. He had issue,

    I. JOHN, his successor.

    II. Philip, who, in the 25th HENRY III., 1241, being then guardian to the Jews, was charged with great bribery, in taking plate of much value to exempt some of them from the tallage then imposed, and he incurred thereby the high displeasure of the king. He made his peace, however, and through powerful interest at court got off with a fine of 1,000 marks. He was, subsequently, so well established in royal favour that he was constituted treasurer of England. But in the 43rd of the same reign, the barons caused him to be brought to trial for the offence above-mentioned, and had him removed from the treasurership; he was likewise subjected to a heavy penalty, and his estates were seized by the crown, until that penalty should be discharged. This persecution so affected him that he is supposed to have *d.* in the following year, 1258, of grief and vexation, at his rectory (having taken orders), at Hamestable. He is stated to have *m.*, of course before he became a priest, the widow of Alexander de Arsic, and had two sons,

        1 John (Sir), who left an only dau. and heiress,

          Margaret, who *m.* Thomas de Botetourt.

        2 Henry, a priest.

    III. Fulco, archdeacon of Colchester.

    I. Agnes, *m.* to Adam de Chetwynd, ancestor of the Viscounts Chetwynd.

John Lovel was *s.* at his decease by his eldest son,

JOHN LOVEL, who in the 41st HENRY III., 1220, had a military summons to march against the Welsh, and in four years afterwards was constituted sheriff of the cos. Cambridge and Huntingdon. In the 48th of the same reign he was made governor of the castle of Northampton, and subsequently governor of Marlborough Castle. He *m.* Maud Sydenham, a great heiress, by whom he acquired the lordship of Tichmersh, and had issue,

    I. JOHN (Sir), his successor.

    II. Thomas (Sir), of Tickwell.

He *d.* in 1286, and was *s.* by his elder son,

SIR JOHN LOVEL, *b.* 1255, who performing his fealty had livery of his lands in the year of his father's decease. In 1294, Sir John attended the king in his wars in Gascony, and was summoned to parliament as BARON LOVEL from 6 February, 1299, to 26 July, 1311. He had also been summoned 26 January, 1297, but it is doubtful whether that writ was a regular summons to parliament. His lordship was subsequently engaged in the Scottish wars, and deserved so well for his services there, that he was rewarded with a license from the king, 31st EDWARD I., 1303, permitting him to make a castle of his house at Tichmersh, also for a market to be held weekly, and a fair annually. He *m.* 1st, Isabel, dau. of Ernald de Bois, of Thorpe Ernald, and sister and heir of William de Bois, by whom he had an only dau.,

    Maud, *m.* to William, Lord Zouch, of Haryngworth, and, as heir to her mother, carried with her the manor of Dockinges, which had been settled on that lady.

His lordship *m.* 2ndly, Joan, dau. of Robert, Lord Ros, of Hamlake (*see* Roos), and had two sons, viz.,

    JOHN, his successor.

    James, who left a son,

        Sir Ralph Lovel, Knt.

Lord Lovel *d.* 1311, and was *s.* by his elder son,

JOHN LOVEL, 2nd baron, *b.* 1313, summoned to parliament as LORD LOVEL, *of Tichmersh*, from 8 January, 1313, to 29 July, 1314. His lordship *m.* Maud, dau. of Sir Philip Burnell, Knt., and sister and heir of Edward, Lord Burnell, by whom (who *m.* 2ndly, John Handlo), he had an only son, his successor at his decease, in 1314,

JOHN LOVEL, 3rd baron, but who never was summoned to parliament. This nobleman was engaged for several years in the wars of Scotland and France, *temp.* EDWARD III. His lordship *m.* Isabella, sister of William, Lord Zouche, of Harringworth, and had issue,

JOHN (1st), his successor.
JOHN (2nd), successor to his brother.
Isabella, *m.* to Thomas Greene.

His lordship *d.* in 1347, and was *s.* by his elder son,

JOHN LOVEL, 4th baron, *b.* 1341, who dying in minority, without issue, *anno* 1361, was *s.* by his brother,

JOHN LOVEL, 5th baron, summoned to parliament as LORD LOVEL, *of Tichmersh*, from 28 December, 1375, to 26 August, 1407. This nobleman, in 1368, being then a knight, was in the wars of France, and one of the retinue of Lionel, Duke of C'arence; he continued in this service for some years, and was constituted governor of the Castle of Banelyngham, in France. In the reign of RICHARD III., when the influence exercised by Robert de Vere, Duke of Ireland, caused so much discontent amongst the nobility, he at first espoused the popular side, but afterwards going over to the king, he was one of those expelled the court by the confederate lords. His lordship, who was a knight of the Garter, *m.* 1373, Maud, dau. and heir of Robert de Holand, Lord Holand. This lady, in the printed pedigrees produced before the House of Lords, in a committee of privileges, on the (successful) claim of the late Sir Cecil Bisshopp, to the Barony of Zouch, is called the grand-dau. and heir of Robert, Lord Holand. Lord Lovel dying in 1408 (in his testament, he styles himself, "Lord Lovel and Holand"), was *s.* by his only son,

SIR JOHN LOVEL, Baron Holand, in right of his mother, and summoned to parliament as LORD LOVEL, *of Tichmersh*, from 20 October, 1409, to 26 September, 1414. This nobleman *m.* Alianore, dau. of William, Lord Zouch, of Haryngworth, and had issue,

WILLIAM, his successor.
Wil m, *m.* Elizabeth, dau. and co-heir of Thomas St. Clere, of Barton St. John, co. Oxford.

His lordship *d.* in 1414, and was *s.* by his elder son,

SIR WILLIAM LOVEL, Baron Lovel and Holand, summoned to parliament, from 24 February, 1425, to 20 January, 1453. This nobleman was engaged in the French wars of King HENRY V. His lordship *m.* Alice, widow of Ralph Butler, of Sudley, and dau. and eventual heir, as Baroness D'Eincourt, of John Leke, Lord Deincourt (*see* LEKE), (by Johanna, dau. and sole heir of Robert, Lord Grey, of Rotherfield,) by which alliance the Baronies of Deincourt and Grey, of Rotherfield, became united with those of Lovel and Holand. Of this marriage there were issue,

I. JOHN, his successor.
II. William, *m.* Alianore, dau. and heir of Robert, Lord Morley, and was summoned to parliament as LORD MORLEY. (*See* LOVEL, Baron Morley.)
III. Robert, *d. s. p.*
IV. William (2nd).

His lordship *d.* 13 June, 1455, and was *s.* by his eldest son,

SIR JOHN LOVEL, Baron Lovel and Holand, summoned to parliament, from 9 October, 1459, to 28 February, 1463. This nobleman, in consideration of his good services, obtained a patent from the king, 38th HENRY VI. (1460), appointing him chief forester of the forest of Whichwoode, co. Northampton; but before the end of that year, the face of public affairs suddenly changed: for upon the landing of the Duke of York, this John, Lord Lovel, proceeding to London, with the Lords Scales and Hungerford, for the purpose of raising the good citizens in favour of King HENRY, was forced to take refuge in the Tower, as a place of security. Soon after which, the Yorkists prevailed in all parts of the kingdom, to the total ruin of the unfortunate HENRY, and his faithful adherents. Of this nobleman, nothing further is related, than his death, which happened in the 4th EDWARD IV., 1464. He was then seized among divers other considerable lordships, of the manors of Minster Lovel, co. Oxford: Bainton, otherwise Deincourts Manor, in Yorkshire; Tichmersh, Northamptonshire; Holgate Burnell, and Acton Burnell, in Shropshire; and likewise of the moiety of the manor of Askham-Bryan, co. ot the city of York. His lordship had *m.* Joane, only sister and heir of William,

2nd VISCOUNT BEAUMONT (*see Extant Peerage*), and by her, who *d. v. p.*, he had issue,

I. FRANCIS, his successor.
I. Joane, *m.* Sir Brian Stapleton, of Carlton. Knt. Amongst her descendants the *Barony of Beaumont* fell into ABEYANCE until called out in 1840, as stated in *Ext nt Peerage*.
II. Fridiswide, *m.* to Sir Edward Norris, Knt., of Yattenden, co. Berks, and had issue,

1 John Norris, Esquire of the body to King HENRY VIII., *m.* Elizabeth, sister of Edward, Lord Bray, but *d.* without legitimate issue.
2 HENRY NORRIS, who fell a sacrifice to the suspicious temper of HENRY VIII., and under the charge of a criminal intercourse with Queen Anna Boleyn, was tried, condemned, and executed, 14 May, 28th HENRY VIII. Henry Norris attainted, it is presumed, that the moiety of the Barony of Beaumont, to which he was heir, became vested in the crown. From him descends the present EARL OF ABINGDON.

His lordship was *s.* at his decease, in 1463, by his only son,

SIR FRANCIS LOVEL, 9th baron, summoned to parliament as such, 15 November, 1482, and created, 4 January, 1483, VISCOUNT LOVEL. He *m.* Anna, dau. of Henry Fitz-Hugh, Baron Fitz-Hugh. This nobleman being in high favour with King RICHARD III., was made, by that monarch, chamberlain of the household, constable of the Castle of Wallingford, and chief butler of England. He subsequently fought under the banner of his royal master, at Bosworth, and was fortunate enough to escape with life, from the field; whence flying to St. John's, at Colchester, he there, for some time, took sanctuary, but deeming that no place of permanent security, he removed privately, to Sir John Broughton's house, in Lancashire, and thence effected his escape into Flanders, where he was graciously received by Margaret, Duchess of Burgundy, the late king's sister; by whom, with 2,000 soldiers, under the conduct of the eminent German general, Martin Swartz, he was sent into Ireland, to uphold the pretensions of Lambert Simnell, and thence invading England, his lordship is said to have fallen at the battle of Stoke, in 1487. That circumstance, however, admits of doubt, for after the battle, he was certainly seen endeavouring, on horseback, to swim the River Trent; yet from this period, no further mention is made of him, by any of our historians. A rumour prevailed, that he had, for the time, preserved his life, by retiring into some secret place, and that he was eventually starved to death, by the treachery or negligence of thos in whom he had confided. Which report (says Banks), in later days seems to be confirmed by a very particular circumstance, related in a letter from William Cowper, Esq., clerk of the parliament, concerning the supposed finding of the body of Francis, Lord Lovel, viz.:

"Hertingfordbury Park, 9th August, 1737.

"Sir,

"I met t'other day with a me norandum I had made some years ago, perhaps not unworthy of notice. You may remember that Lord Bacon, in his history of HENRY VII., giving an account of the battle of Stoke, says of the Lord Lovell, who was among the rebels, that he fled and swame over the Trent on horseback, but could not recover the further side, by reason of the steepnesse of the bank, and so was drowned in the river. But another report leaves him not there, but that he lived long after, in a cave or vault.

"Apropos to this; on the 6th May, 1728, the present Duke of Rutland related in my hearing, that about twenty years then before, viz., in 1708, upon occasion of new laying a chimney at Minster Luvel, then was discovered a large vault underground, in which was the entire skeleton of a man, as having been sitting at a table, which was before him, with a book, paper, pen, &c.; in another part of the room lay a cap, all much mouldered and decayed. Which the family and others judged to be this Lord Lovel, whose exit has h therto been so uncertain."

From hence (continu s Banks), it may be concluded, that it was the fate of this unhappy lord, to have re ired to his own house after the battle, and there to have entrusted himself to some servant, by whom he was immured, and afterwards neglected, either through treachery, fear, or some accident which befel that person; a melancholy period to the life and fortunes of one of the greatest and most active noblemen of the era wherein he had lived. Some additional particulars relating to this matter may be gleaned from "Notes and Queries."

To complete the tragedy, King HENRY VII , aspiring to the vast inheritance of this family, confiscated, by an act of ATTAINDER, in the 1st year of his reign, the whole estate, then inferior to few or none in the kingdom; and which, by grants at different times from HENRY VIII. down to JAMES I., has p ssed to the families of Compton, Earls of Northampton;

Cecil, Earls of Salisbury, and other great houses now existing. Under this attainder, the Baronies of Lovel, of Holand, of Deincourt, and o. Grey, of Rotherfield, fell, and could not be inherited by his lordship's sisters and co-heirs; but those ladies became heirs to their maternal uncle, William, Viscount Beaumont, in the ancient BARONY OF BEAUMONT, as already stated.

Arms—Barry nebule of six, or and gu.

NOTE.—The title of BARON LOVELL, o *Minster Lovell*, co. Oxford, was revived in the person o. Sir Thomas Coke, K.B., of Holkham, co Norfolk, 28 May, 1728, but on the death of his lordship, who was subsequently created Earl of Leicester, &c., his titles became EXTINCT. (*Refer to Extant Peerage.*)

The Barony of LOVELL AND HOLAND was conferred, 7 May, 1762, upon John Perceval, 2nd Earl of Egmont, the representative of RICHARD PERCEVAL, youngest son of William, Earl of Yvery, and brother of the founders of the houses of LOVEL OF CASTLE KARY, and LOVEL OF TICHMERSH (*see* Lovel of Castle Kary).

LOVEL—BARONS MORLEY.

By Writ of Summons, dated 29 December, 1299.

See MORLEY, BARONS MORLEY.

LOVELACE — BARONS LOVELACE, OF HURLEY, CO. BERKS.

By Letters Patent, dated 30 May, 1627.

Lineage.

SIR RICHARD LOVELACE, Knt., (son of Richard Lovelace, Esq., of Hurley, Berks, and grandson of John Lovelace, who d. 1558, possessed of Hurley), was elevated to the peerage, 30 May, 1627, as BARON LOVELACE, *of Hurley, co. Berks*. His lordship m. 1st, Katherine, dau. of George Gyll, Esq., of Wydial, Herts, and widow of William Hide, Esq., of Denchworth and Kingston L'Isle, Berks, but had no issue. He m. 2ndly, Margaret, only dau. and heir of William Dodsworth, citizen of London, and had issue,

  I. JOHN, his successor.
  II. Francis, whose son,
    William, m. Mary, dau. of William King, Esq., of Iver, Bucks, and left a son, JOHN, who inherited as 4th baron.
  I. Elizabeth, m. to Henry, son and heir of Sir Henry Martin, Knt.
  II. Martha, m. to Sir George Stonhouse, 3rd baronet.

His lordship d. in 1634, and was s. by his son,

JOHN LOVELACE, 2nd baron, who m. Lady Anne Wentworth, dau. of Thomas, Earl of Cleveland, which lady, upon the decease of her niece, Henrietta-Maria Wentworth, Baroness Wentworth, in 1686, s. to that barony. They had issue,

  I. JOHN, his successor.
  I. Anne, d. unm.
  II. Margaret, m. to Sir William Noel, Bart., of Kirby-Malory, co. Leicester, and her great-grandson,
    SIR EDWARD NOEL, Bart., eventually s. in her right to the BARONY OF WENTWORTH, and was created VISCOUNT WENTWORTH, in 1762. (*See Extant Peerage.*)
  III. Dorothy, m. to Henry, son of Sir Henry Drax, Knt.

His lordship d. in 1670, and was s. by his son,

JOHN LOVELACE, 3rd baron. This nobleman, "distinguished," says Macaulay, " by his taste, by his magnificence, and by the audacious and intemperate violence of his Whiggism," was in the habit of assembling the leading friends of the Revolution, in a vault beneath the hall of his splendid mansion at Lady Place, in Berkshire; a council chamber into which he had afterwards the pleasure of introducing King WILLIAM, when that monarch honoured him with a visit. Lord Lovelace was one of the very first to rise in arms for WILLIAM, and one of the most energetic of his partizans. His lordship who was captain of the band of pensioners, lived in so much splendour and profuseness, that a great portion of his estates came to the hammer, under a decree of the Court of Chancery. He m. Margery, one of the daus. and co-heirs of Sir Edmund Pye, Bart., of Bradenham, co. Bucks, by whom he had several children, one of whom only survived himself, viz.,

  MARTHA, who upon the decease of her grandmother, ANNE, Lady Wentworth, and Dowager Lady Lovelace, (who sur-

334

vived her son, Lord Lovelace), s. to the Barony of Wentworth, to which she was declared entitled by a resolution of the House of Lords made 2 April, 1702, and confirmed by Queen ANNE. Her ladyship m. Sir Henry Johnson, an opulent ship-builder, but d. s. p. in 1745, when the Barony of Wentworth passed to her kinsman, Sir Edward Noel, Bart. (*Refer* to Margaret, dau. of the 2nd Lord Lovelace.)

His lordship d. before his mother, Lady Wentworth, in 1693, when the Barony of Lovelace passed to his cousin (*refer* to the 2nd son of 1st lord),

JOHN LOVELACE, 4th baron, who m. Charlotte, dau. of Sir John Clayton, Knt., by whom he left two surviving sons, JOHN and NEVIL, successive barons. His lordship was governor of New York, and d. in his government, 6 May, 1709, when he was s. by his elder son,

JOHN LOVELACE, 5th baron, who survived his father but a fortnight, when the barony devolved upon his only brother,

NEVIL LOVELACE, 6th baron. This nobleman d. in 1736, when the Barony of Lovelace of Hurley became EXTINCT. His sister and heiress (or, according to one account his dau.) Martha, m. Lord Henry Beauclerk.

N.B. The title of LOVELACE was again created 30 June, 1838, in favour of William, 8th Lord King, who m. 8 July, 1835, Ada, only child o. George Gordon, Lord Byron (the poet). This lady's mother, Anna-Isabella, Lady Byron, only child of the Hon. Judith Noel, (by her husband, Sir Ralph Milbanke, Bart.), s. as Baroness Wentworth in 1856, and was representative of the extinct Barons Lovelace.

Arms—Gu., on a chief indented, sa., three martlets, arg

LOWTHER — VISCOUNTS AND EARL OF LONSDALE.

Viscounty, by Letters Patent, dated 28 May, 1696.
Earldom, by Letters Patent, dated 24 May, 1784.

Lineage.

For earlier pedigree *refer* to BURKE's *Extant Peerage:*—LONSDALE.

SIR JOHN LOWTHER, 2nd baronet, was returned to parliament by the co. of Westmoreland in 1675, and he continued to represent that shire so long as he remained a commoner. At the accession of King WILLIAM, Sir John was sworn of the privy council. In 1689 he was constituted lord lieutenant of Westmoreland and Cumberland ; in 1690 appointed first commissioner of the Treasury, and elevated to the peerage 28 May, 1696, in the dignities of *Baron Lowther, of Lowther, co. Westmoreland*, and VISCOUNT LONSDALE. In 1699 he was made lord privy seal; and was twice one of the lords justices for the government of the kingdom during his majesty's absence. His lordship m. Catherine, dau. of Sir Frederick Thynne, and sister of Thomas, Viscount Weymouth, by whom he had issue,

  I. RICHARD, } successors in turn to the viscounty.
  II. HENRY, }
  III. Anthony, a commissioner of the revenue in Ireland, d. unm. in 1741.
  I. Mary, m. Sir John Wentworth, Bart., of North Elmsal and Broadsworth, Yorkshire, and had an only child,
    CATHERINE, wife of HUGH CHOLMELEY, Esq., of Whitby Abbey, co. York.
  II. Jane, d. unm.
  III. Margaret, m. to Sir Joseph Pennington, Bart, of Muncaster, in Cumberland, M.P., and had (besides an elder son, John, his successor, whose grandson was created Lord Muncaster), a dau. Catherine who m. in 1731, Robert Lowther, Esq., governor of Barbadoes, whose eldest son by her was Sir James Lowther, of whom hereafter as EARL OF LONSDALE.
  IV. Barbara, m. to Thomas, son and heir of William Howard, Esq., of Corby, in Cumberland, and had three daus., who all d. s. p.

The viscount d. 6 July, 1700, and was s. by his eldest son,

RICHARD LOWTHER, 2nd Viscount Lonsdale, who d. of the small-pox, the same year that he had attained his majority, (1713), and being unm. was s. by his brother,

HENRY LOWTHER, 3rd Viscount Lonsdale. Of this nobleman Banks thus speaks : " If considered in his attachment to the protestant succession, his love to the king, and his readiness to co-operate with his ministers whenever he thought them right, he was *a perfect courtier*. But if we regard his constant adherence to the interest of his country, his contempt of honours, and advantage to himself, and h.s steady opposition to every measure which he considered detrimental to the

Lucy.
(B. Lucy.)

Luttrell.
(E. Carhampton.)

Macaulay.
(B. Macaulay.)

M°Carty.
(E. Clancarty.)

Mackenzie.
(E. Seaforth.)

Magennis.
(V. Magennis.)

Maguire.
(B. Maguire.)

Marshal.
(E. Pembroke.)

Maule.
(E. Panmure.)

Montacute.
(E. Salisbury.)

Mordaunt.
(E. Peterborough.)

Mortimer.
(E. March.)

public, then *he was, indeed, a patriot.* Beloved by his friends, respected even by his enemies, he was in the senate honoured with attention from both: courted by all parties, he enlisted with none, but preserved through life a remarkable independency. These public virtues arose from the excellence of his private disposition, from the benevolence of his heart, from the uprightness of his intentions, from his great parts, and uncommon penetration."

His lordship *d. unm.* 12 March, 1750-1, when the Barony of Lowther (of this creation) and Viscounty of Lonsdale became EXTINCT: while the estates and baronetcy devolved upon his heir-at-law and kinsman (who was maternally his grand-nephew, as above stated),

SIR JAMES LOWTHER, 5th baronet. Sir James, who represented the cos. of Cumberland and Westmoreland for several years in parliament, was elevated to the peerage 24 May, 1784, as *Baron Lowther, of Lowther, co. Cumberland*, Baron of the Barony of Kendal, in the same co., Baron of the Barony of Bury, co. Westmoreland, Viscount Lonsdale, in co. Westmoreland, and co. Palatine of Lancaster, *Viscount Lowther and EARL OF LONSDALE*. His lordship *m.* 7 September, 1761, Lady Margaret Stuart, dau. of John, Earl of Bute. but having no issue, he obtained a new patent, dated 10 October, 1797, conferring upon him the dignities of *Baron and Viscount Lowther, of Whitehaven, co. Cumberland*, with remainder to the heirs male of his cousin, the Rev. Sir William Lowther, Bart., of Swillington. His lordship *d.* 24 May, 1802, when the Earldom of Lonsdale, and minor honours, created in 1784, became EXTINCT, while the peerage created in 1797, devolved (according to the limitation of the new patent), with the Earl's estates in Westmoreland and Cumberland upon

SIR WILLIAM LOWTHER, Bart., in whose favour the title LONSDALE was revived, he being created, 7 April, 1807, EARL OF LONSDALE. *Refer to Extant Peerage.*

Arms—Or, six annulets, sa.: three, two, and one.

LUCAS—BARON LUCAS, OF SHENFIELD, CO. ESSEX.

By Letters Patent, dated 3 January, 1644.

Lineage.

The family of LUCAS, flourished for many ages in the cos. Suffolk and Essex.

JOHN LUCAS, town-clerk of Colchester, and master of the requests to EDWARD VI., had by his 1st wife, Mary Abell, two sons,

THOMAS (Sir), and Robert *d. s. p.*
The former,

SIR THOMAS LUCAS, Knt. of St. John's, Colchester, was sheriff of Essex in 1568, and recorder of Colchester about 1575. He *m.* Mary, 3rd dau. of Sir John Fermor, of Easton Neston, co. Northampton, Knt., and *d.* 29 August, 1611, leaving with other issue, a dau. Anne, *m.* to Sir Arthur Throckmorton, of Pauler's Perry, and an eldest son and heir,

SIR THOMAS LUCAS, Knt., sheriff of Essex in 1637, who *m.* Elizabeth, dau. and co-heir of John Leighton, of London, and had issue,

I. JOHN (Sir), his heir.
II. Charles (Sir). This gallant person having become pre-eminently distinguished in the ranks of the cavaliers, was shot in cold blood, with Sir George Lisle, by order of Cromwell, upon the surrender of Colchester to the parliamentarians in 1648.

There was also another son, SIR THOMAS LUCAS, who was illegitimate, having been born prior to the marriage of his parents; the other brothers, Sir John and Sir Charles, were born subsequently.

Sir Thomas Lucas *d.* 26 September, 1625, and was *s.* by his son and heir,

SIR JOHN LUCAS, Knt., one of the most faithful and zealous supporters of the royal cause, during the civil wars, who was elevated to the peerage by King CHARLES I., 3 January, 1644, in the dignity of BARON LUCAS, *of Shenfield, co. Essex*, with remainder, in default of his male issue, to his brothers, Sir Charles Lucas, and Sir Thomas Lucas, (his lordship's gallant companions in arms in those unhappy times), and to the heirs male of their bodies. Lord Lucas *m.* Anne, dau. of Sir

335

Christopher Nevill, K.B., of Newton St. Lo, co. Somerset, by whom he had an only child,

MARY LUCAS, who *m.* Anthony Grey, 11th Earl of Kent, and was created 7 May, 1663, BARONESS LUCAS, *of Crudwell, co. Wilts*, with remainder of the dignity of Baron Lucas, of Crudwell. to her heirs male, by the Earl of Kent, failing which, "the title not to be suspended, but to be enjoyed by such of the daus. and co-heirs, if any shall be, as other indivisible inheritances by the common law of this realm are usually possessed." Her ladyship *d.* 1 November, 1700, and her title devolved as stated in BURKE's *Extant Peerage*, and is now enjoyed by EARL COWPER, K.G.

Lord Lucas *d.* in 1670, and his celebrated brother, Sir Charles Lucas, having predeceased him, as well as his elder brother. Sir Thomas Lucas, he was *s.* by the son of the latter, his nephew,

CHARLES LUCAS, 2nd baron. This nobleman *m.* Penelope, dau. of Francis Leke, Earl of Scarsdale (*see* LEKE), and had two daus., his co-heirs: the elder *m.* the Hon. Mr. Carey, and the younger, PENELOPE, *m.* Isaac Selfe, Esq., of Benacre, and was mother of Anne, wife of Thomas Methuen, Esq., ancestor by her of the present LORD METHUEN. Lord Lucas dying without male issue in 1688, the title devolved upon his brother,

THOMAS LUCAS, 3rd baron, who *d. unm.* in 1705, when the Barony of Lucas of Shenfield became EXTINCT.

Arms—Arg., a fesse between six annulets, gu.

LUCY—BARONS LUCY.

By Writ of Summons, dated 15 May, 1321.

Lineage.

The first mention of this family is in a render made by King HENRY I., of the lordship of Dice, in Norfolk (whether in requital of services, or as an inheritance, the record saith not) to

RICHARD DE LUCIE, who was governor of Falais. In Normandy, *temp.* King STEPHEN, and defended that place with great valour, when besieged by Geoffrey, Earl of Anjou; for which heroic conduct he had a grant of lands, in the county of Essex, with the services of divers persons, to hold by ten knights' fees. In the subsequent contest between STEPHEN and the Empress Maud, he remained steady in his allegiance to the former, and obtained a victory of some importance near Wallingford Castle. Upon the adjustment of the dispute, the Tower of London, and the castle of Winchester, were by the advice of the whole clergy, placed in the hands of this feudal lord, he binding himself by solemn oath, and the hostage of his son, to deliver them up on the death of King STEPHEN, to King HENRY. Which being eventually fulfilled, Richard de Lucy was constituted sheriff of Essex and Hertfordshire, in the 2nd of HENRY II., A.D. 1156, and in three years afterwards, being with the king in Normandy, he was despatched to England to procure the election of Thomas à Becket, then lord chancellor, to the archiepiscopal see of Canterbury, vacant by the death of Theobald, Abbot of Becco. Soon after that he was appointed to the high office of Justice of England. In the 12th of this reign, upon the aid then assessed for marrying the king's dau., he certified his knights' fees (lying in the cos. of Kent, Suffolk, and Norfolk) *de veteri feoffamento*, to be in number seven, and that his ancestors performed the service of Castle Guard at Dover, for the same, as also that he held one knight's fee more, *de novo feoffamento*, in the co. Devon. About this time Becket having fled into Normandy from the power of King HENRY, came to Wiceliac to celebrate the feast of the ascension, and observing several persons of distinction present, amongst whom was this Richard de Lucie, he ascended the pulpit, and there with lighted candles, pronounced the sentence of excommunication against them all, as public incendiaries betwixt the king and himself, but being neither convicted nor called to answer, they appealed and entered the church. Soon after this (13th HENRY II.), during a temporary absence of the king beyond sea, de Lucie was constituted Lieutenant of England, and again in 1173, when the Earl of Leicester and others having reared the standard of rebellion in behalf of Prince Henry, he besieged, in conjunction with Reginald, Earl of Cornwall, the town of Leicester, and having reduced it, demolished its walls, and laid it in ashes. In 1178, he founded the priory of Westwode, in the diocese of Rochester, in honour of St. Thomas, of Canterbury, the martyr: and began, about the same time the foundation of the priory of Lesnes, in Kent, which he munificently endowed. In this priory he subsequently assumed the habit of a canon regular, and departing this life soon after (about 22nd HENRY II.), was buried in the chapter-house there. He *m.* Rohais ——, and had issue,

  I. Geffrey, who *d.* in his father's life-time, leaving,

    RICHARD, his son and heir, who departing this life, *s. p.,* before 1196, the inheritance devolved upon his aunt, ROHAIS.

  II. Hubert, who had the lordship of Stanford, in Essex, and hundred of Angre, for his livelihood, but *d. s. p.*

  I. Maude, *m.* 1st, to Walter Fitz-Robert, to whom she brought the lordship of Disce; and 2ndly, to Richard de Ripariis, and *d.* 27th HENRY III., 1243, leaving issue.

  II. Rohais, *m.* 1st, to Fulbert de Dovor, Lord of Chilham, in Kent; and 2ndly, Richard de Chilham. This Rohais, upon the decease of her nephew, succeeded to the estates of her elder brother, and upon the death of her younger brother, Hubert, she had livery of the whole barony, on paying a fine to the crown, in the 9th King JOHN.

Having thus disposed of the celebrated RICHARD DE LUCIE, and his family, we come to

REGINALD DE LUCIE, whose parentage Dugdale declares his inability to discover, but who, upon the rebellion of the Earl of Leicester, in the reign of HENRY II., was governor of Nottingham for the king; and attended at the coronation of RICHARD I., with the rest of the barons. This feudal lord *m.* Annabell, 2nd of the three daus. and co-heirs of William Fitz-Duncan, Earl of Murray, in Scotland (by Alice, dau. and heir of Robert de Rumeli, Lord of Skypton), with whom he acquired the honour of Egremont, co. Cumberland, and by whom he had issue, his successor,

RICHARD DE LUCIE, who, in the 1st JOHN, (1199) paid a fine to the crown of 300 marks for livery of his lands, and licence to marry with whom he should think proper. In four years afterwards, he paid five marks and one palfrey to the king, that he might have jurors to inquire what customs and services his tenants had used to perform, and to do, him and his ancestors for their lands in Coupland. And the same year he obtained a grant from the king to himself and Ada, his wife, dau. and co-heir of Hugh de Morvill, of the forestership of Cumberland. The next year he paid 900 marks, and five palfreys, to have livery of the property of the said Ada, and to enjoy the forester-ship of Cumberland as amply as Hugh de Morvill had it, without any partition whatsoever. By an ample charter about this period, he granted to the burgesses of Egremont, divers immunities and privileges; namely, "that they should not go beyond the gates of the castle there, upon any summons, either with the lord, or his stewart, to take distresses in Coupland. That in time of war they should not be obliged to find any more than twelve armed men for forty days, for the defence of the castle, at their own proper costs. That they should not give aid, unless for making his eldest son knight, marrying one of his daughters, or towards his own ransom, in case he were taken prisoner, and at such other times as his tenants, by military service, gave aid. Moreover, that they should be quit of pawnage for their hogs in certain of his woods." But by this charter he obliged them to grind at his mills, and to give the thirteenth part for toll of their own corn, and of that which they should buy, the sixteenth part. Upon the purchase of any burgage, the buyer to give him four-pence at the taking possession. He *d.* on or before the 15th King JOHN, for then Ada, his widow, gave a fine of 500 marks for livery of her inheritance; as also for dowry of his lands, and that she might not be compelled to marry again. She espoused without compulsion, however, and without the king's licence, Thomas de Multon, in consequence of which the castle of Egremont, and her other lands, were seized by the crown. But upon paying a compensation they were restored, and she had livery of them again. Her first husband, Richard de Lucie, left two daus., his co-heirs, who became wards to her 2nd husband, and were *m.* to his sons, thus,

  Annabell de Lucie. *m.* the eldest son, Lambert de Multon, and conveyed to him the lordship of Egremont. (*See* Multon of Egremont.)

  Alice de Lucie, *m.* the younger son, Alan de Multon, and had a son,

    Thomas de Multon.

The son of the younger co-heir, Alice, Thomas de Multon, having assumed the surname of his maternal family, became THOMAS DE LUCIE, and in the 16th EDWARD I. (1288) had livery of all the lands which were of the inheritance of Alice, his mother. He *m.* Isabell, one of the daus. and co-heirs of Adam de Bolteby, by whom he acquired the manor of Langley, co. Northumberland, and dying in 1304, was *s.* by his son,

THOMAS DE LUCY, who, in the 34th EDWARD I., was in the wars of Scotland; and dying in 1308, *s. p.* was *s.* by his brother,

ANTHONY DE LUCY, who had been companion in arms of his deceased brother in the wars of Scotland. In the 10th EDWARD

II. (1316-17) this Anthony was joined in commission with William, Lord Dacre, for defending the counties of Cumberland and Westmoreland against the incursions of the Scots. The next year he was made sheriff of Cumberland, and constituted sole guardian of that county, and of Westmoreland, and again sheriff of Cumberland the ensuing year, when he was appointed governor of the castles of Carlisle and Cockermouth. He was summoned to parliament soon after, as a baron, and from that period to the 17th EDWARD III. In the 16th EDWARD II. he obtained a grant from the crown of the honour of Cockermouth, with the manor of Hapcastre, pertaining thereto, to hold by the service of one knight's fee. Amongst the other actions of this nobleman was the surprisal and capture of Andrew de Harcla, Earl of Carlisle, who had gone over to the Scots; whom he sent up to London a prisoner, where he was degraded and sentenced to death. Lord Lucy was subsequently appointed justice of Ireland, and governor of Berwick-upon-Tweed. He *m.* Elizabeth, dau. of Robert Tillioff, Lord of Scaleby, and had issue,

THOMAS, his successor.

Joane, *m.* to William de Melton, and had issue, Sir William Melton, Knt., whose descendant and representative, Dorothy Melton, *m.* George, Lord Darcy.

Lord Lucy *d.* in 1343, and was *s.* by his son,

THOMAS DE LUCY, 2nd baron, summoned to parliament 25 February, 1342, in the lifetime of his father, and afterwards from 2 April, 1344, to 4 December, 1364. This nobleman, prior to the decease of his father, had attained high eminence in arms, particularly in Flanders, and at the siege of Loughmaban Castle, 17th EDWARD III. (1343). He was afterwards constantly employed to defend the northern marches towards Scotland, and had a part in the victory of Durham, wherein DAVID, king of Scotland, was made prisoner. His lordship *m.* Mary, sister and co-heir of John de Multon, of Egremont (*see above*), by whom he acquired considerable estates in the county of Cumberland, and had issue,

ANTHONY, his successor.

Maud, *m.* 1st, to Gilbert de Umfraville, Earl of Angus, who *d. s. p.*, and 2ndly, to Henry, 1st Earl of Northumberland. Upon the marriage of this lady, then sole heiress of the Barons Lucy, with the Earl of Northumberland, it was stipulated that the castle and honour of Cockermouth, part of her inheritance, should be settled upon the Earl and herself, and the heirs male of their bodies, failing which, upon the heirs of her body; and in case she should die without issue, then upon Henry, Lord Percy, the renowned *Hotspur*, the Earl's son and heir by his first wife, and the heirs male of his body, upon condition that the said Henry and his heirs male should bear the arms of Percy quarterly with the arms of Lucy, viz., "gules, three lucies ar.," in all shields, banners, &c.; and notwithstanding the said Maud *d. s. p.* the descendants of the said Earl of Northumberland were often styled *Barons Lucy*, their pretensions to that dignity being manifestly without a shadow of foundation. In 1557, however, Thomas Percy, brother and heir of Henry, the 6th earl, was created Baron Percy, of Cockermouth and Petworth, Baron Poynings, Lucy, Bryan, and Fitzpayne—all which honours descended, as stated in BURKE's *Extant Peerage*, until, in 1670, upon the decease of Joceline, 11th Earl of Northumberland, without issue, they EXPIRED.

Lord Lucy *d.* in 1365, and was *s.* by his son,

ANTHONY DE LUCY, 3rd baron, but never summoned to parliament. This nobleman was joined with Roger de Clifford in the guardianship of the marches towards Cumberland and Westmoreland. In the 41st EDWARD III., his lordship, with divers other noble persons, procured license to travel beyond sea, and *d.* the ensuing year, 1368, leaving an infant dau., Joane, by his wife, Joane, widow of William, Lord Greystoke, which infant dau. *d.* the next year, when her aunt,

MAUD, COUNTESS OF ANGUS, *s.* to the Barony of Lucy and the honour of Cockermouth, with the other estates. (*Refer* to issue of Thomas, 2nd baron.) This lady *m.* subsequently the Earl of Northumberland, and made the settlement already stated; but she *d. s. p.*, when the BARONY OF LUCY reverted certainly to the descendant of her aunt, Joane (*refer* to issue of Anthony, 1st baron), Sir William Melton, Knt., and it is now vested in his representatives, should any such exist.

Arms—Gu., three lucies hauriant, arg.

⁂ Sir William Dugdale surmises that SIR WILLIAM DE LUCY, the 1st ancestor of the LUCYS, of CHARLECOTE, co. Warwick, who bore the surname of Lucy, did so because his mother might have been the heir of some branch of this baronial family of Lucy.

——————

LUDLOW—EARL AND BARON LUDLOW.

Earldom, by Letters Patent, dated 3 October, 1760.
Barony of the United Kingdom, by Letters Patent, dated 7 September, 1831.

Lineage.

The family of Ludlow (which derives its surname from the ancient town so denominated in the co. Salop) settled at Hill Deverell, in Wiltshire, about the middle of the 14th century, at which time lived,

WILLIAM LUDLOW, Esq., of Hill Deverell; from whom lineally descended,

SIR HENRY LUDLOW, Knt., of Maiden Bradley, co Wilts, M.P. for that shire: *b*. in 1587: who *m*. Letitia, dau. of Thomas West, Lord Delawar. by whom he had issue, (with three daus.),

EDMUND LUDLOW, the celebrated republican general during the civil wars; who *d*. in exile, at Vevay, in Switzerland, in 1693, where a monument is erected to his memory.

Henry, who was father of

STEPHEN LUDLOW, Esq., one of the clerks in the high court of Chancery, in Ireland. This gentleman *d*. in 1721, leaving issue,

PETER, his heir.

William, who *m*. Catharine, sister of James, 1st Earl of Courtoun, and had issue.

Alice, *m*. to Francis Bernard, Esq., of Castle Bernard, co Cork.

Arabella, *m*. to David Nixon, Esq., of Havensdale, co. Kildare.

Elizabeth, *m*. to Chief-Justice (John) Rogerson.

Frances, *m*. to Robert Leslie, Esq.

Stephen Ludlow was *s*. by his eldest son,

PETER LUDLOW, Esq., M.P. for the co. of Meath, in 1719 and 1727; who *m*. Mary, dau. and heir of John Preston, Esq., of Ardsalla, in that co., and had issue,

PETER, his heir.

Alice, *m*. to John Preston, Esq., of Bellinter, who was ancestor of JOHN PRESTON, Esq., of Bellinter, co. Meath.

Mary, *m*. to Sir Robert Rich, Bart., of Waverley.

He was *s*. at his decease, in 1750, by his only surviving son,

PETER LUDLOW, Esq., *b*. 21 April, 1730, M.P. for the co. Huntingdon, who was elevated to the peerage of Ireland, 19 December, 1755, as *Baron Ludlow, of Ardsalla, co. Meath*. His lordship was created, 3 October, 1760, *Viscount Preston*, and EARL OF LUDLOW, was sworn of the privy council in England, and nominated comptroller of his Majesty's household. He *m*. 20 January, 1753, Frances, eldest dau. of Thomas, Earl of Scarborough, by whom he had issue,

AUGUSTUS, 2nd earl.

GEORGE-JAMES, 3rd earl.

Frances-Mary, *d*. in 1804.

Anne-Barbara, *d*. in 1823.

Harriot, *d*. in 1833.

Charlotte, *d*. 4 April, 1831.

The earl *d*. in 1803, and was *s*. by his eldest son,

AUGUSTUS, 2nd earl, *b*. 1 January, 1755, at whose decease, *unm*. 7 November, 1811, the honours devolved upon his brother,

GEORGE-JAMES, 3rd earl, *b*. 12 December, 1758; who obtained a barony of the United Kingdom, as Baron Ludlow, by letters patent, dated 7 September, 1831. His lordship, who had lost an arm in the service of his country, was a general officer in the army, colonel of the 38th regiment of foot. lieutenant governor of Berwick, and a knight grand-cross of the Bath. He *d*. *unm*. 16 April, 1842, when his honours became EXTINCT.

Arms—Quarterly: 1st and 4th, arg., a chev., between three foxes' heads, erased. sa., for LUDLOW; 2nd and 3rd, or, on a chief, sa., three crescents of the 1st, for PRESTON.

LUMLEY—BARON LUMLEY.

By Writ of Summons dated 28 September, 1384; and By Act of Parliament, *anno* 1547.

Lineage.

The surname of this family was assumed from Lumley on the Wear, in the bishoprick of Durham, and the family deduced its lineage from

LIULPH, son of Osbert de Lumley, *m*. Ælgitha (dau. by

Elgyve, dau. of King ÆTHELRED Ii.) of Uchtred the Bold, Earl of Northumberland. Liulph, who was a nobleman of great popularity in the time of EDWARD THE CONFESSOR, was murdered by means of Leoferin, chaplain of Walcher, bishop of Durham, a crime soon after avenged by the populace of Durham sacrificing both the chaplain and the prelate to their just resentment. By Ælgitha, his wife, Liulph had issue,

I. UCHTRED.

II. Osbert de Stafford, whose dau. and heiress, Ormonda, *m* Robert de Persall. who for his attachment to Robert de Stafford and the king's service, as also "ratione consanguinitatis," held the manor of Farsall. in the parish of Eccleshall. co. Stafford, A.D. 1068, from which his descendants adopted their name.

The eldest son,

UCHTRED, assumed the name of LUMLEY, and from him lineally descended

ROGER DE LUMLEY, who *m*. Sybil, one of the daus. and co-heirs of the great Northumberland feudal Baron, Hugh de Morewic, at whose decease in 1261, his estates devolved upon his three daus., as co-heirs, namely,

Sybil, who *m*. 1st, as stated above, Roger de Lumley, and 2ndly, Roger de St. Martin.

Theophania, *m*. to John de Bulmer.

Beatrice, *m*. to John de Roseles.

Roger de Lumley was *s*. by his son,

SIR ROBERT DE LUMLEY, who *m*. Lucia, one of the three sisters and co-heirs of William, Robert, and Thomas de Thweng, Barons Thweng, of Kilton Castle, co. York (*see* THWENG), and was *s*. by his son,

SIR MARMADUKE DE LUMLEY. Knt., who first assumed the arms of his mother's family, those of the ancient house of Thweng, which his descendants have ever since borne. Sir Marmaduke was *s*. by his elder son,

ROBERT DE LUMLEY. This feudal lord *d*. *unm*. and a minor, in the 48th EDWARD III., and was *s*. by his brother,

SIR RALPH DE LUMLEY, who in the 9th of RICHARD II.; was in the expedition then made into Scotland, in the retinue of Hugh de Percy, Earl of Northumberland. In the 10th of EDWARD II., he was made governor of Berwick-upon-Tweed, and continued therein until the 12th, when he was taken prisoner by the Scots. In three years after (15th RICHARD II.), he was deputy-governor of the same place under Henry de Percy, Earl of Northumberland, and the next year had license to make a castle of his manor house at Lumley. Sir Ralph was summoned to parliament as a Baron, from the 8th RICHARD II. to the 1st HENRY IV., 1384 to 1399, inclusive. In the latter year, joining in the insurrection of Thomas de Holand, Earl of Kent, for the restoration of the former monarch. he was slain in a skirmish at Cirencester, and being ATTAINTED in 1400, his lands were seized by the crown, and the BARONY OF LUMLEY fell under the attainder. His lordship left issue by his wife, Eleanor, dau. of John, Lord Nevill, of Raby, and sister of Ralph, Earl of Westmoreland, four sons and three daus., of whom the youngest, Marmaduke de Lumley, was successively master of Trinity Hall, Cambridge, and chancellor of the University; bishop of Carlisle (1430), treasurer of England (1446), and bishop of Lincoln (1451). Lord Lumley was *s*. by his eldest son,

THOMAS DE LUMLEY, who had been attainted with his father, and *d*. *s*. *p*. in 1404, when *s*. by his brother,

SIR JOHN DE LUMLEY, *b*. 1384, who, doing his homage in the 6th HENRY IV., had livery of all the castles, manors, and lands, whereof his father, Ralph, Lord Lumley, was seized at the time of his attainder; and was restored in blood by act of parliament, in the 13th of the same reign. He was subsequently, *temp*. HENRY IV., and V., distinguished in the wars of France, and fell at the battle of Beaugé, in Anjou, 13 April, 1421. Sir John *m*. Felicia, dau. of Sir Matthew Redman, governor of Berwick, and was *s*. by his only son,

SIR THOMAS DE LUMLEY, *b*. 1408, who, in the 33rd HENRY VI., 1455, was governor of Scarborough Castle, and upon the accession of King EDWARD IV., having petitioned the parliament for the reversal of the attainder of his grandfather, Ralph, Lord Lumley, and that prayer being granted by the repeal of the said attainder, was summoned to parliament as BARON LUMLEY, 26 July, 1461, and from that period to 16 January, 1497, in which year he is supposed to have died. His lordship *m*. Margaret, dau. of Sir James Harrington, Knt., brother of Sir Wm. Harrington, K.G., and was *s*. at his decease, by his only son,

SIR GEORGE LUMLEY, 3rd baron, who does not appear to have been summoned to parliament. He was sheriff of Northumberland, 2nd EDWARD IV., 1462. This nobleman *m*. Elizabeth, dau. and co-heir of Roger Thornton, Esq., an opulent merchant of Newcastle-upon-Tyne (by his wife, Elizabeth, dau. of John, Lord Greystoke), and had issue,

I. THOMAS, who m. Elizabeth Plantagenet, natural dau. of King EDWARD IV., by Lady Elizabeth Lucy, and d. v. p. (anno 1487) leaving a son and heir, and three daus., viz.,

  1 RICHARD, who s. his grandfather, as 4th baron.
  1 Anne, m. to Ralph, Lord Ogle. (See OGLE.)
  2 Sybil, m. to William, Baron Hilton.
  3 Elizabeth, m. to William Croswell.

II. Roger, who had three daus. to survive: Agnes, wife of John Lambton, Esq. of Lambton; Isabel, wife of Richard Conyers, Esq., of Horden; Margaret, wife of Thomas Trollope, Esq., of Thornley.
III. Ralph.

Lord Lumley acquired by his marriage the lordships of Wilton, in Northumberland, and Lulworth, and Isle, in the bishoprick, but had a protracted litigation regarding those lands with Giles Thornton, the bastard son of his father-in-law, which quarrel terminated by his lordship's killing his antagonist in the ditch of Windsor Castle. The baron, who, in the 7th HENRY VII. (1492), was in the expedition then made into Scotland under the command of Thomas, Earl of Surrey, when Norham Castle was besieged, d. in 1508, and was s. by his grandson,

RICHARD DE LUMLEY, 4th baron, summoned to parliament from 17 October, 1509, to 28 November, 1511. To the last writ the following addition is made on the roll, "Mortuus est, ut dicitur." His lordship m. Anne, dau. of Sir John Conyers, K.G., of Hornby Castle, co. York, and sister of William, 1st Lord Conyers, by whom he had two sons,

I. JOHN, his successor.
II. Anthony, who m. a dau. of Richard Grey, Esq., of co. Northumberland, and left a son,

  Richard Lumley, who m. Anne Kurtwich, and had, with other issue, a son,

    SIR RICHARD LUMLEY, who s. to the estates of his kinsman, Lord Lumley, as hereafter stated, and was elevated to the peerage of Ireland, as VISCOUNT LUMLEY, and from whom the EARL OF SCARBOROUGH is lineally descended.

His lordship d. in 1510 or 1511, and was s. by his elder son,

JOHN DE LUMLEY, 5th baron, b. 1493, summoned to parliament 23 November, 1514. This nobleman was one of the barons who, in the 22nd HENRY VIII. (1530) signed the memorable letter to Pope Clement VII., but in the 28th of that reign he was one of the chiefs of those northern lords who appeared in the insurrection called the "Pilgrimage of Grace;" when a pardon being offered by the Duke of Norfolk, who commanded the army sent against the rebels, his lordship was deputed to treat with the duke, and succeeded so well, that all concerned in the affair were allowed to return home without being further molested. Lord Lumley, was at the celebrated battle of Flodden Field under the Earl of Surrey. His lordship m. Joane, dau. of Henry, Lord Scrope, of Bolton, and had an only son,

GEORGE, who, being implicated in the treason of Lord Darcy and others, was apprehended, committed to the Tower, and being convicted of high treason, was executed and attainted in the 29th HENRY VIII., 1537 (his father then living). He m. Jane, 3rd dau. and co-heir of Sir Richard Knightley, of Fawsley, co. Northampton, and left issue, an only son, and two daus., viz.,

  John, who was restored in blood, and created Baron Lumley, (see that dignity,) but by neither of his two wives had surviving issue.
  Jane, m. Geoffry Markham, Esq., and d. s. p.
  BARBARA, m. twice; 1st, Humphrey Lloyd, Esq., M.P. for Denbigh, in 1563, the celebrated antiquary and historian, and by him, who d. August, 1568, æt. forty-one, and was buried in Denbigh Church, (Whitchurch), where there is a monument to him, had issue,

  I. Splendinan Lloyd, living in 1568. who d. s. p.
  II. HARRY, or HENRY LLOYD, of Cheam, living 1568, who m. Mary, dau. of Robert Brome, Esq., of Bromfield, co. Essex, and was s. by his son, HENRY LLOYD, who m. Isabella, sister of Sir Thomas Parkyns, of Bunny, co. Nottingham, baronet, so created, 15 July, 1684, and dau. of Isham Parkyns, Esq., of Bunny, and was s. by his son, HENRY LLOYD. who m. Elizabeth, dau. of Benjamin Goodwin, Esq., of Stretham, and had with three daus., a son,
    The Rev. Dr. Robert Lloyd, who claimed the barony of Lumley, in 1723.
  III. John Lloyd, living in 1563.
  IV. Humphrey Lloyd, dead in 1568.
  I. Jane. dead in 1568.
  II. Lumley, living in 1568, who subsequently m. Robert Coytmore, Esq., of Coytmore, co. Carnarvon, and was mother, by him, of George Coytmore, Esq., of Coytmore, whose eventual heir, Mary, heiress of Coytmore, dau. and heir of Robert Coytmore, Esq., of Coytmore. m. Edward-Philip Pugh, Esq., of Penrhyn, in Creuddyn, co. Car-

narvon, and had an elder dau. and co-heir, Bridget, who m. 11 January, 1766, Lieut.-Col. Glynn-Wynn, M.P., brother of Thomas Wynn, 1st Baron Newborough, and had issue,
  1 John Glynn-Wynn, b. 6 October, 1766.
  2 Glynn-Wynn, b. 1766; who m. Elizabeth, 6th dau. of the Rev. Frederick Hamilton.
  3 William Wynn, D.D., b. 1767, who, in accordance with the will of his grandmother, assumed the name of Coytmore. He m. Eliza, dau. and heir of Thomas Tennison, chief justice of the Common Pleas in Ireland, and widow of Henry Bellingham, of Castle Bellingham, co. Louth.
  4 Thomas-Edward Wynn, of Newburgh Hall, co. York. who m. Charlotte, eldest dau. and co-heir of Henry, 2nd Earl of Fauconberg, and assumed the name and arms of Belasyse, in addition to that of Wynn.
  1 Bridget. m. John, 4th Earl of Egmont, and d. 24 January, 1826.
  2 Frances, m. Henry Soame, Esq.
  3 Dorothea.

Barbara Lumley, m. 2ndly, William Williames, Esq., of Cochwillan, co. Carnarvon, and was mother of

I. Henry Williames, Esq., of Cochwillan, who m. Jane, dau. and heir of Thomas Salesbury. Esq., of Denbigh Castle, 3rd son of Sir John Salesbury, and was father of two sons, 1 Lumley; 2 William Williames, who m. and had issue, an only son, Griffith Williames, who d. unm. 2 April, 1658, and was buried at St. Alkmonds, Shrewsbury. The elder son LUMLEY WILLIAMES, jure ux. of Ystymcollwyn, co. Montgomery. m. Dorothy, dau. and heir of Rhys Thomas, Esq., of Ystymcollwyn, and was father of an only son, Lumley Williames, Esq., of Ystymcollwyn, whose grand-daughter and heiress, Muriel, heiress of Ystymcollwyn, dau. and heir of Lumley Williames, living 1703, m. her kinsman. Arthur Williames. Esq., of Meyllionydd, living 1723, derived from Arthur Williames, of Meyllionedd, younger brother of William Williames, Esq., of Cochwillan, who m. Barbara. the heiress of Lumley. The grand-daughter and heiress of this marriage, Anne, heiress of Ystymcollwyn and Meyllionydd, m Sir Robert-Howell Vaughan, of Nanney, co. Merioneth, created a baronet, 21 June, 1791. The grandson and heir of this marriage, Sir Robert Williames Vaughan, 3rd and last Baronet of Nanney, d. s. p.

  I. Blanch, m. Richard Price, Esq., of Eglwyseg, co. Denbigh.
  II Mary, m. William Bulkeley, Esq., of Brynddû, co. Anglesey. father of an elder son, William Bulkeley. Esq., of Brynddû, living 20 May, 1624, whose heir general was the late William Bulkeley Hughes, Esq., of Plâs Coch, Brynddû, lord of the manor of Kemmus, co. Anglesey, late M.P. for the Carnarvon Boroughs.
  III. Barbara, m. Richard Herbert, of Pwke.

Upon the death of Lord Lumley (his only son, George, having been, as above stated, previously attainted) this Barony of Lumley became EXTINCT.

His lordship's grandson and heir, however,

JOHN LUMLEY, having petitioned parliament, in the 1st EDWARD VI., praying that the attainder might be reversed, it was enacted by act of parliament, in 1547, " that the said John Lumley, and the heirs male of his body, should have, hold, enjoy, and bear, the name, dignity, state, and pre-eminence of a Baron of the realm." By this law, a new barony of Lumley was created. The old one having merged in the crown under the act of attainder, nothing but a positive repeal of that statute could have restored it, and the new act did not effect that object.

Lord Lumley was one of the noblemen who sat in judgment upon MARY, Queen of Scots, and Robert Devereux, Earl of Essex His lordship m. 1st, Jane, eldest dau. and co-heir of Henry Fitz-Alan, Earl of Arundel, by whom he had a son and two daus., who all d. in infancy. He m. 2ndly, Elizabeth, dau. of John, Lord Darcy, of Chiche, but had no issue. Of Lord Lumley, Camden says, "that he was of entire virtue, integrity, and innocence; and in his old age, a complete pattern of true nobility. Having so great a veneration for the memory of his ancestors, that he caused monuments to be erected for them, in the collegiate church of Chester-le-Street (opposite Lumley Castle), in the order as they succeeded one another, from Liulphus down to his own time: which he had either picked out of the demolished monasteries, or made new. He also took care that his estates should descend to one of his own name and blood, by his last will and testament; in which he bequeaths to his kinsman and heir male, Richard, eldest son and heir apparent of Roger, the son of Anthony Lumley, brother to John, Lord Lumley, his grandfather (see above), his Castle of Lumley, together with divers manors, lands, tenements, &c."

His lordship d. 11 April, 1609, and was interred in the Church of Cheam, having a noble monument of white marble erected to his memory. With his lordship the new barony of Lumley, created by act of parliament, EXPIRED.

The aforesaid RICHARD LUMLEY, who s. to the estates of John, last Baron Lumley, was, in 1628, elevated to the peerage of

Ireland as Viscount Lumley: and his grandson was created, in 1690, Earl of Scarborough, under which title the subsequent history of this family will be found in the *Extant Peerage.*

The Barony of Lumley was claimed, in 1723, by the above mentioned Rev. Robert Lloyd, as lineal descendant of Barbara Lumley, sister of the attainted George, when the House of Lords came to the resolution, "That the petitioner had no right to a writ of summons in parliament, as prayed by his petition,"—which resolution was founded upon the previous report—

"That by the act of parliament of 1st Edward VI. (which conferred the barony upon John Lumley, son and heir of the attainted George), "a new barony of Lumley was created, and limited by express words to John, Lord Lumley, in tail male; and that upon his death, without issue male, the said barony became extinct.

"That the attainder of George Lumley is not reversed by the said act, but remains yet in force; and that the restitution of John, Lord Lumley, in blood only, while the attainder remains unreversed, could not possibly revive the ancient barony, which was before merged in the crown, in consequence of that attainder."

Note.—In consequence of the marriage of Sir Robert Lumley with Lucia de Thweng, one of the co-heirs of the Lords Thweng, a third of the Barony of Thweng devolved upon the Lumleys, which third, it is presumed, merged in the crown under the attainder of George Lumley, in the reign of Henry VIII.

Arms—Originally: Gu., six martlets arg.
After the alliance with de Thweng: Or. a fesse. gu., between three parrots, ppr. collared of the second.

LUTEREL—BARON LUTEREL.

By Writ of Summons, dated 24 June, 1295.

Lineage.

This noble family claimed descent from one of the Norman chiefs who accompanied the Conqueror to England.

In the time of Richard I., the lands of Sir Geoffrey de Luterel, in the co. Nottingham and Derby, were seized by the crown, for his adherence to the Earl of Moreton, but he was compensated, upon the accession of the earl to the throne, as King John, by extensive territorial and other grants. He m. Trethesenta, 2nd dau. and co-heir (with her sister Alicia, wife of Robert de Gant) of William Paganal, Lord of Irnham, and by her (who m. 2ndly, Henry de Newmarch), had a son and heir, Andrew. Sir Geoffrey d. in the 2nd year of Henry III., 1218, and was s. by his son,

Sir Andrew de Luterel, of Irnham, co. Lincoln, who, 14th Henry III., upon the collection of the scutage, for the first journey of that king into Britanny, accounted £30 for fifteen knights' fees. In this year, he laid claim to lands in the county of Somerset, as well as the manor of Irnham, co. Lincoln, which formerly belonged to Maurice de Gant, and had descended to him, by right of inheritance; and the next year he had livery of the same, upon paying 100 marks to the crown. He subsequently served the office of sheriff of Lincolnshire. He m. the dau. of Philip de la Mare, a rich and powerful baron; and dying in 1264, was s. by his elder son,

Geoffrey de Luterel, feudal Baron of Irnham, co. Lincoln. This Geoffrey being insane, his brother, Alexander Luterel, had the custody of his person, and William de Gray, whose dau. he had married, the education of his children. To these succeeded

Sir Robert de Luterel (whom Courthope's *Historic Peerage* calls brother of Geoffrey de Luterel). In the 5th Edward I., A.D. 1277, he was in the expedition then made into Wales, and had summons amongst other great men, in the 22nd of the same reign, to attend the king, touching the important affairs of the realm. He was summoned to parliament as a Baron, 24 June, 30 September, and 2 November, 1295, and dying in 1297, possessed of Irnham, co. Lincoln, and Hoton Paganal, co. York, left by Joan, his wife, a son and heir,

Sir Geoffrey de Luterel, feudal Lord of Irnham, who does not appear, from the existing enrolments to have been ever summoned to parliament. He m. Agnes, dau. of Sir Richard Sutton, Knt., and left three sons,

I. Andrew, his heir.
II. Geoffrey (Sir), was one of the chief knights in the army of Edward III, in Scotland, in 1365. He m. Constance, dau. of Lord Scrope, but left no issue.
III. John (Sir).

The eldest son,

Sir Andrew Luttrell, 5th Baron of Irnham and Lord of Hoton Paganal, m. Beatrice, dau of Sir Geoffrey Scrope, Lord Scrope, of Masham, and was father of

Sir Andrew Luttrell, Knt., 6th Baron of Irnham, who m. Hawisia, dau. of John le Despenser, and dying in 1397, was s. by his son,

Sir Andrew Luttrell, 7th Baron of Irnham, who d. 1st Henry IV., A.D. 1400, leaving his estates to his son,

Sir Geoffrey Luttrell, Knt., 8th Baron of Irnham, at whose decease s. p. in 1417, the Barony of Irnham and Lordship of Hoton Paganal devolved on his only sister and heiress,

Hawisia de Belesby, relict of Thomas de Belesby, and afterwards wife of Sir Godfrey de Hilton, Knt.

From the Hiltons, Irnham was conveyed by marriage to the Thimlebys, and by them, by a female, to the Conquests, an heiress of which family brought the manor to Henry, 8th Lord Arundell de Wardour, through whose daughter it passed to the Cliffords.

Arms—Or, a bend, between six martlets, sa.

LUTTRELL—EARL AND VISCOUNT CARHAMPTON AND BARON IRNHAM.

Irish Barony, by Letters Patent, dated 13 October, 1768.
Irish Viscounty, by Letters Patent, dated 9 January, 1781.
Irish Earldom, &c., by Letters Patent, dated 23 June, 1785.

Lineage.

A branch of this ancient family appears to have settled in Ireland so early as the reign of King John, when

Sir Geoffry Luttrell obtained from that Prince a grant of the lands of Luttrellstown, co. Dublin. Perhaps this was the same person who is mentioned in the preceding article. Be this as it may, certain it is that the Luttrells, of Dunster Castle, and the Luttrells, Earls of Carhampton were of the old baronial stock of Irnham.

Sir Andrew Luttrell, of Chilton, co. Devon, a scion of the family of Luttrell of Irnham, m. the Lady Elizabeth, 2nd dau. of Hugh Courtenay, Earl of Devon (by Margaret, his wife, dau. of Humphrey de Bohun, Earl of Hereford), and was father of

Sir Hugh Luttrell, who resided at Dunster, co. Somerset, an honour and castle which his mother had purchased from the Mohuns, once Lords of Dunster, Sir Hugh was M.P. for Somersetshire in the reign of Richard II., and subsequently for Devonshire. In the 8th Henry IV. (1407), he gained a suit-at-law against Edward Plantagenet, Duke of York, and the other heirs of John, last Lord Mohun, of Dunster, by which he obtained possession of the honours and castle of Dunster, the lordship of Carhampton, &c. He was afterwards ranger of Blackmore forest in Dorsetshire, a privy councillor to Henry V., and one of the commanders under that martial monarch at the reduction of Harfleur in Normandy in 1415, and at the memorable siege of Rouen. Sir Hugh m. Catherine, dau. of Sir John Beaumont, Knt., of Sherwell, and had three sons,

I. Sir John, from whom descend the Luttrells of Dunster Castle, co. Somerset, for whose lineage *refer to* Burke's *Landed Gentry*.
II. Robert, of whose line we treat.
III. Andrew.

The 2nd son,

Robert Luttrell, acquired considerable possessions in the co. Dublin, by his marriage with the dau. of Sir Elias de Ashbourne, Knt., of Devon. He d. in the 15th Henry VI. (1436-7), seized of the castle and lands of Luttrellstown, co. Dublin. He left at his decease besides a dau. Anne, m. to Simon Fleming, Lord Slane, and a son Hugh, another son,

Christopher Luttrell, who s. at Luttrellstown, and was father of,

Thomas Luttrell, who m. Catharine, dau. of Thomas Rochfort of Kilbride, ancestor of the Earl of Belvedere, and widow of Thomas Delafield, Esq., of Culduffe, and d. in April, 1455, leaving issue,

1. THOMAS, his heir.
II. RICHARD, heir to his brother.
III. Robert (Sir).
  1. Ellen, m. to Nicholas Travers, Esq., of Cortilagh, co. Meath.

The eldest son,

THOMAS LUTTRELL, m. Ellen, dau. of Philip Bellew, Esq., but dying s. p., was s. by his brother,

RICHARD LUTTRELL, of Luttrellstown, living 1540, who m. Margaret, dau. of Patrick Fitz-Leons, Esq., of co. Dublin, and had issue,

I. THOMAS (Sir), his heir.
II. Simon, alderman of Dublin, who m. Margaret, dau. of — Bath, Esq., of Landenstown, co. Kildare, and had three daus. : 1 Mary, m. to Robert Sherlock, Esq. ; 2 Catherine, m. to Patrick White, Esq., of Flemingstown; and 3 Elizabeth, m. to Christopher Cruise, Esq., of the Naule.
  I. Anne, m. to Sir Patrick Barnewell, Knt., master of the Rolls.
  II. Catharine, m. 1st to Nicholas Barnewall, Esq., of Drumnagh, and 2ndly, to Sir John Plunkett, Knt., of Dunsoghly, co. Dublin.
  III. Elizabeth, m. 1st to John Fitz-Christopher Cusack, of Turvey, and 2ndly, to Thomas Barbe, of Dublin.

The eldest son,

SIR THOMAS LUTTRELL, Knt., s. to Luttrellstown. In November, 1553, he was appointed chief justice of the court of Common Pleas in Ireland, and subsequently a privy councillor He m 1st, Anne, dau. of Bartholomew Aylmer, Esq., of Lyons, co. Kildare, and by her had two sons and two daus.,

I. RICHARD, his heir.
II. Robert, m. Elizabeth, 2nd dau. of Robert Rochfort, Esq., of Kilbride, and was father of Richard Luttrell of Tankardstown, co. Meath, who m. Anne, dau. of Robert Cusack, Esq., of Cussington, co. Meath, and d. in October, 1633, leaving two sons and two daus., viz., 1 Oliver, of Tankardstown; 2 James; 1 Jane, m. to Rowland Plunket of Cocklestown ; and 2 Mary, m. to George Bathe, of Edickston, co. Meath.
  I. Margaret, m. to Lucas Netterville, justice of the King's Bench.
  II. Anne, m. to Thomas Dillon, Esq., of Riverston, co. Meath.

Sir Thomas, m. 2ndly, Elizabeth, dau. and co-heir of Sir William Bathe, Knt., of Rathfeigh, co. Meath, and had further issue,

I. John, who m. Mary, dau. of Walter Nugent, Esq., of Moyrath, co. Meath.
II. James, m. Dame Janet Sarsfield.

Sir Thomas was s. by his eldest son,

RICHARD LUTTRELL, Esq., who m. Mary, dau. of Lord Dunsany, and widow of Thomas Plunket, Esq., of Rathmore, and by her had (besides two daus., I. Anne, d. unm.; and II. Elizabeth, m. in 1601, to Sir Christopher Nugent), one son and successor,

THOMAS LUTTRELL, Esq., M.P. for co. Dublin, in the reigns of king JAMES and King CHARLES, and a Privy Councillor. He m. 1st, in 1605, Eleanor Preston, dau. of Christopher, 4th Viscount Gormanston, and by her had,

I. SIMON, his heir.
II. Stephen.
  I. Catharine, m. to Robert Hartpole, Esq., of Shrule, Queen's County.

Mr. Thomas Luttrell m. 2ndly, in 1616, Alison, youngest dau. of Nicholas, 21st Baron of Howth, and by her had issue,

I. John.
II. Thomas, of Ranaghan, co. Westmeath, d. s. p. in 1673, and by will settled his estates on his nephew Thomas, Viscount Fitz-William.
  I. Susan, m. to Edmund Butler, Esq., of Tullahinch, co. Carlow.
  II Mary, m. to William, 3rd Viscount Fitz-William.
  III. Margaret.   IV. Alison.

Mr Luttrell d. 12 November, 1634, and was s. by his eldest son, SIMON LUTTRELL, Esq., of Luttrellstown, in whose time the castle of Luttrellstown was taken by Colonel Hewson, commander of the parliament forces, in and about Dublin, and held possession of by him till the Restoration, when Mr. Luttrell was reinstated. He m. Mary, eldest dau. of Jenico, 5th Viscount Gormanstown, and widow of Sir Thomas Alen, Bart., of St. Wolstans, and d. in 1650, leaving a son and heir,

THOMAS LUTTRELL, Esq., who was restored to his estates in fee, by the acts of settlement. He m. a dau. of William Segrave, Esq., of co. Dublin, and d. in August, 1674, having had issue,

I. SIMON, his heir.
II. HENRY, successor to his brother.
III. Thomas, who was attainted of high treason in 1688, and d s. p.

IV. Robert, m. Anne, 3rd dau. of Nicholas, 6th Viscount Gormanston.

The eldest son,

SIMON LUTTRELL, Esq., of Luttrellstown, M.P. for the co. Dublin, was governor of the town and garrison of Dublin, during the residence of JAMES II. in Ireland, a privy councillor, and colonel of a regiment of dragoons. This gentleman adhered with unshaken fidelity to his royal master's fortunes, and was killed at the battle of Landen in 1693, commanding an Irish regiment in foreign service, when, having had no issue by his wife, Catherine, dau. of Sir Thomas Newcomen, Bart., of Sutton, he was s. by his brother,

HENRY LUTTRELL, an officer of rank in King JAMES's army, whose treachery to and desertion of the cause he had espoused excited "the abhorrence of the Roman Catholic population" of Ireland. In 1702, Colonel Luttrell was appointed a majorgeneral in the Dutch army, with a regiment, and nominated to command on a military enterprise of importance; but at the death of King WILLIAM he retired to his seat at Luttrellstown, where he chiefly resided, until assassinated in his sedan-chair, by a band of ruffians, in the city of Dublin, 22 October, 1717.* He m. in 1704, Elizabeth, dau. of Charles Jones, Esq., of Halkin, co. Flint, and by her (who m. 2ndly, Nicholas Netterville, Esq., of Hollymount, co. Meath), left two sons,

ROBERT LUTTRELL, Esq., the elder, who s. his father, and d. abroad upon his travels, and

SIMON LUTTRELL, Esq., b. 1713, who s. his brother at Luttrellstown. This gentleman was advanced to the peerage of Ireland, 13 October, 1768, by the title of Baron Irnham (a title anciently borne by his ancestors in England, as stated in the preceding article), of Luttrellstown, co. Dublin; created Viscount Carhampton, of Castlehaven, co. Cork, 9 January, 1781: and EARL OF CARHAMPTON, 23 June, 1785. His lordship m. in 1737, Maria, dau. and eventually heiress of Sir Nicholas Lawes, Knt., governor of Jamaica, by whom he had issue. five sons and three daus. The earl's youngest dau., Lucy, m. Capt. Moriarty; and the eldest, Anne, after the demise of Christopher Horton, Esq., of Catton, her 1st husband, m. H. R. H. the Duke of Cumberland, brother to King GEORGE III. The earl d. 14 January, 1787, and was s. by his eldest son,

HENRY-LAWES LUTTRELL, 2nd Earl of Carhampton, b. 7 August, 1743; a general officer in the army, and colonel of the 6th dragoon guards. His lordship m. Jane, dau. of George Boyd, Esq.; but d. s. p. in 1821, when the honours devolved upon his only surviving brother,

JOHN LUTTRELL, 3rd Earl of Carhampton, who m. 1st, 1 July, 1766, the Hon. Elizabeth Olmius, only dau. of John, Lord Waltham, and eventually heiress of her brother, the last Lord Waltham. (See that title.) The earl thereupon assumed by sign-manual in 1787, the additional surname and arms of OLMIUS. They had issue,

I. John, d. young, 1769.
II. James, d. young, 1773.
  I. LADY FRANCES-MARIA LUTTRELL-OLMIUS, m. in 1789, Sir Simeon Stuart, 4th Bart., whom she survived to 4 January, 1848.

The earl m. 2ndly, in 1798, Maria, eldest dau. of John Morgan, Esq., recorder of Maidstone, and by her, who d. 18 January, 1857, had another dau.,

II. LADY MARIA-ANNE LUTTRELL-OLMIUS, m. in 1821, Lieut.-Colonel Hardress-Roberts Saunderson, grenadier guards, of Northbrook House, Hants. son of Francis Saunderson, Esq., of Castle Saunderson, co. Cavan. She d. 14 November, 1861, leaving issue. (See Landed Gentry.)

Lord Carhampton d. 17 March, 1829, when all his honours EXPIRED: the heirs-general of his lordship's family are SIR SIMEON HENRY STUART, Bart., and HARDRESS-LUTTRELL SAUNDERSON, Esq.

Arms—Arg., a fesse, between three otters passant, sa.

* Eighty years after his death, his grave, near Luttrellstown was violated by the descendants of those whom he had betrayed, and his skull was broken to pieces with a pickaxe.—MACAULAY.

LYLE—LORD LYLE.

Creation not accurately ascertained.

Lineage.

SIR ROBERT LYLE (son of Sir John Lyle, by his wife, one of the daus. and co-heirs of the family of Marr), was created a peer by King JAMES II. of Scotland, about 1446; and *d.* about 1470. He *m.* 1st, Margaret, eldest dau. of Andrew, Lord Gray, and by her he had a dau.,

Margaret, *m.*. to Alexander, son and heir of Alan Lyle, of Craigbate.

He *m.* 2ndly, Margaret Wallace, by whom he had a son and a dau.,

ROBERT, 2nd Lord Lyle.
Elizabeth, *m.* to John Stewart, of Blackhall.

The only son,

ROBERT LYLE, 2nd Lord Lyle, was a privy councillor to JAMES III., and an ambassador to England in March, 1472, when he concluded a truce with that nation. He *m.* 1st, a dau. of John, Master of Seton, who *d. s. p.*; and 2ndly, Lady Elizabeth Douglas, 2nd dau. of Archibald, 5th Earl of Angus, by whom he had a son,

ROBERT LYLE, 3rd Lord Lyle; who *d.* 1511, leaving by Mariot Lindsay, his wife, a dau. of the house of Dunrod, a son and two daus., viz.,

JOHN, 4th Lord Lyle.
Helen, *m.* to Alan, Master of Cathcart.
Catherine, *m.* to Archibald Maclachlan, of Maclachlan.

The only son,

JOHN LYLE 4th Lord Lyle, being under age at his father's death, the king assigned his wardship and marriage to James Betoun, archbishop of Glasgow, and he *m.* a niece of the archbishop's, Grissel, dau. of David Betoun, of Creich, by whom he had an only dau.,

JEAN LYLE, *m.*.to SIR NIEL MONTGOMERY, of Lainshaw, 2nd son of Sir Niel Montgomery, of Lainshaw, 3rd son of Hugh, 1st Earl of Eglinton. (*See* BURKE's *Extant Peerage*.) Her descendant, James Montgomery, of Lainshaw, tendered his vote as Lord Lyle at the election of representative peers for Scotland in 1721 and 1722, as did Sir Walter Montgomery at the general election, 1784. The heiress of the Lainshaw line, ELIZABETH, eldest dau. and heiress of David Montgomery, of Lainshaw, *m.* Captain Alexander Montgomery Cuninghame, and from this marriage descends SIR THOMAS MONTGOMERY CUNINGHAME, Bart., of Corshill.

Arms—Gu., a fret, or.

LYTTLETON—BARONS LYTTLETON OF FRANKLEY, CO. WORCESTER.

By Letters Patent, dated 18 November, 1756.

Lineage.

The Harleian MS. 5814, f. 40-65, contains valuable collections relating to this family. Selden was possessed of two grants of Lands to the monastery of Evesham, co. Worcester, in 7th HENRY II. (1161), to both of which JOHN DE LYTTLETON was a witness. This is the most ancient mention of the name of Lyttleton which has been met with ; and as the land conveyed was at Lench, near South Lyttleton, it is probable that this John was ancestor of the Lyttletons, of Frankley, in Worcestershire.

The family of LUTTLETON or LYTTLETON has been of long standing in Worcestershire, and from an ancient pedigree it appears that it was seated at Frankley about 1235, when it is recorded that,

THOMAS DE LYTTLETON *m.* his 1st wife, Emma de Frankley, an heiress, lady of the manor of Frankley, dau. of Sir Simon de Frankley, Knt., but whether he was a stranger in the country or resided in the town of South Lyttleton in the vale of Evesham, as there is reason to think he did, is a matter of doubt. They had an only dau.,

EMMA, who *m.* 1st, Angerus de Tatlington of Tredington, in Worcestershire; and 2ndly, Nicholas Whetanstede. She was a benefactress to the abbey of Hasleowen, in Shropshire, and *d.* in 1298.

Thomas Lyttleton *m.* 2ndly, Asseline, dau. and heiress of William Fitz-Waryn of Upton, in Worcestershire, one of the justices-itinerant and judge of the Common Pleas, 12th HENRY III. (1228), and sheriff of Worcestershire in the following year, and by her he had three sons,

THOMAS.
Edmund, a priest.
John, *d. unm.*

Thomas de Lyttleton was *s.* by his eldest son (or, as some say, by his son Edmund, who *d. s. p.*, and was *s.* by his youngest and only surviving brother)

THOMAS DE LYTTLETON, who resided at his manor of Coulesdon, and had lands at Newenton (*vulgo* Walton Beauchamp), co. Worcester. He was elected M.P. for that shire 9th EDWARD II. (1315-6; and 34th EDWARD III. (1360). He *m.* Lucia, dau. of John du Bois, or Attwood, of a considerable family at Wolverly, in that co. and was *s.* by his son,

THOMAS DE LYTTLETON, who *m* Julian, dau. of Robert de Somery, and had,

I. THOMAS, his successor.
II. John, who was appointed a commissioner of array, with other the chief gentlemen of the co. Worcester, 1st HENRY IV. (1400) on a rumour of foreign invasion, *m.* Beatrice Freshevel, of a noble family in the co. Warwick, by whom he had an only dau., *m.* to Jeffery Frere, Esq.

The elder son,

THOMAS DE LUTTELTON (who thus spelled the name and sealed with the chevron between three escallops, as used by his posterity), recovered the manor of Frankley, by writ of right, on failure of the issue of his cousin, Thomas de Tatlington. He was esquire of the body to (RICHARD II. ?) HENRY IV., and HENRY V., and had annual pensions to him by both kings out of the fee farm rents of Worcester *pro bono et gratuito servicio*, as expressed in the grants. He *m.* Maud, dau. of Richard Quartermain (and heir of a large estate at Ricote and North Weston in Oxfordshire), by Joan, his wife, dau. and heir of Grey of Rotherfield, by whom he had an only dau. and heiress, ELIZABETH. He *d.* about 1421, and his wife surviving, and holding Frankley in dower or jointure, *m.* 2ndly, John Massey, Esq. The only child,

ELIZABETH DE LUTTLETON *m.* THOMAS WESTCOTE, Esq., the king's servant in court, a gentleman of Devonshire, anciently descended; but she being fair and of noble spirit (to use the phraseology of *Lord Coke*) and having large possessions and inheritances from her ancestors, De Luttleton, and from her mother and other ancestors, resolved to retain her name, and therefore provided by Westcote's assent before marriage, that her issue inheritable should be called by the name of LUTTLETON. Upon this marriage her husband settled at Frankley, and served the office of escheator of Worcester, 29th HENRY VI., 1451, and *d.* soon after. By Mr. Westcote, his wife (who *m.* 2ndly, Thomas Hewster, Esq. of Lichfield,) had issue, with four daus., of whom Anne *m.* Thomas Porter, Esq., of Barston, in Warwickshire, four sons, viz.,

I. THOMAS, their heir.
II. Nicholas *m.* Agnes, dau. and heir of Edmund Vernon of Staffordshire, and was ancestor of the Westcotes of that co.
III. Guy, *m.* Greenevile of Gloucestershire, and from him descend the Westcotes of Devon and Somerset.

Nicholas and Guy retained their paternal surname of WESTCOTE, though often solicited by their mother to call themselves LYTTLETON. She once expostulating with them at their so refusing, as if they thought better of themselves than their elder brother, they answered that he had a fair estate for a reason to change his name, and if they might share with him they would do the same.

IV. Edmund, *d. unm.*

The eldest son and heir,

SIR THOMAS LUTTLETON, or (as he begun to write it) LYTTLETON, or (as with him more invariably spelled), LITTLETON, became one of the great law luminaries of his country. Having been bred to the bar, he was called to the degree of serjeant-at-law, in 1454, and appointed steward of the marshalsea of the king's household. In the next year he was constituted king's serjeant, and 13 May, 1455, rode justice of the assize on the northern circuit. Having shown some inclining to the Lancastrian party during the war of the Roses, Littleton, on the accession of EDWARD IV., sued a general pardon which was granted to him, and in the 4th of that reign, 1464, he was appointed one of the Judges of the Court of Common Pleas, when he had a grant of 110 marks out of the customs of London, Bristol, and Hull; and moreover, 106s. 11½d. for a robe and furs, and 6s. 6d. for a summer robe. In the 14th of EDWARD IV. (1473), he was made a knight of the Bath, with the Prince of Wales and several persons of the highest distinction.

Sir Thomas wrote his celebrated *Treatise on Tenures*, after he had become a judge; a book which Lord Coke has described "as the ornament of the common law, and the most perfect and absolute work that ever was wrote in any human science."

To this work, says Dr. Holand, in his additions to Camden, "the students of the common law are no less beholden, than the civilians are to Justinian's Institutes."

The celebrity and usefulness of the *Tenures* have endured to our own time; and notwithstanding the prodigious accession of statutes and reports, the changes in the law, and the accumulation of publications, Littleton, with Coke's Commentary, will ever continue a guide to student, advocate, and judge.

Sir Thomas *m.* Joan, dau. and co-heir of William Burley, Esq., of Broomscroft Castle, Shropshire, M.P., and Speaker of the House of Commons, 1436-1443, and relict of Sir Philip Chetwynd of Ingestre, in Staffordshire. By her, with whom he acquired large possessions, he had three sons,

  I. WILLIAM, his heir, of whom presently.
  II. Richard, from whom descends LORD HATHERTON. *See* BURKE'S *Extant Peerage,* for full details of intermediate pedigree.
  III. Thomas, from whom descended the Lord-keeper Littleton, created BARON LITTLETON of Mounslow. (*See next article.*)

Judge Littleton made his will 22 August, 1481, and *d.* the next day at Frankley, in a great and good old age. His widow survived him twenty-four years, and *d.* 22 March, 1505, aged nearly fourscore years, leaving a great estate which came by her father and mother (the dau. and heir of Grendon of Grendon), to her eldest son, Sir William. This son,

SIR WILLIAM LYTTLETON, of Frankley, was knighted by HENRY VII., for his conduct at the battle of Stoke. He *m.* 1st, Ellyn, widow of Thomas Fielding, Esq , and dau. and co-heir of William Walsh, Esq., of Wanslip, co. Leicester, by whom he had an only dau., Joan, who *m.* Sir John Aston, of Heywood, in Staffordshire, and carried the manor of Tixhale, in that co., and Wanlip, into the Aston family. Sir William *m.* 2ndly, Mary, dau. of William Whittington, of Pauntley, co. Gloucester, and had issue,

  JOHN, his successor.
  Elizabeth, *m.* to Thomas Rouse, Esq., of Rouse-Lench, in Worcestershire, from the issue of which marriage descend the ROUSE-BOUGHTONS, Barts.

Sir William *d.* at Frankley, in 1507, and was *s.* by his son,

JOHN LYTTLETON, Esq., of Frankley, who endowed his family (saith Habington, in his MS. Antiquities of Worcestershire), with abundance of noble blood, by having in marriage, Elizabeth, the dau. and co-heir of Sir Gilbert Talbot, of Grafton, by Anne, his wife, dau. and co-heir of Sir William Paston, by Anne, 3rd sister and co-heir of Edmund Beaufort, Duke of Somerset. She was great-great-grand-dau. (maternally) of John of Gaunt, Duke of Lancaster, son of EDWARD III., and in her right the family of Lyttelton quarters the arms of France and England within a bordure gobony. By this marriage, Mr. Lyttleton had seven sons and two daus. Dying 17 May, 1532, he was *s.* by his eldest son,

JOHN LYTTLETON, Esq., then a minor, whose wardship was granted by the king to Sir John Pakington, Knt., of Hampton Lovell. Mr. Lyttleton *m.* Bridget, dau. and heir of his guardian, and acquired a considerable increase of fortune by the alliance. He was thus enabled to rebuild, in a magnificent manner, his seat at Frankley, and to purchase other estates. In 1553, Queen MARY granted him for life the office of Constable of Dudley Castle, co. Stafford, together with the rangership of the old and new parks there. The same year he was chosen one of the knights for Worcestershire, and served the office of sheriff once in the reign of MARY, and twice in that of ELIZABETH; in which latter reign, although adhering to the Roman Catholic religion, he enjoyed places of honour and trust, and the confidence of his sovereign, being during Her Majesty's reign, one of the council of the Marches of Wales, deputy-lieutenant and custos-rotulorum of Worcestershire, and a magistrate for that co. and Staffordshire. He was also knighted by the queen, with other gentlemen of great distinction, at Kenilworth Castle, when her Majesty honoured the Earl of Leicester with a visit there. Sir John had, with other issue,

  I. GILBERT, his successor.
  II. Edward, whose picture, dated 1568, with an atchievement of arms, is preserved at Hagley Park.
  III. John (Sir).
  IV. William, *m.* to Margaret, only dau. and heir of William Smyth, Esq., of Sherford, co. Warwick, but *d.* before the age of consummation, by a fall from his horse in hunting.
  V. George, settled at Holbeach, co. Stafford, and *m.* Margaret, his brother's widow.
  I. Elizabeth, *m.* to Francis Willoughby, Esq , of Wollaton, co. Nottingham.

  II. Margaret, *m.* to Samuel Marrow, Esq., of Berkeswell, co. Warwick.
  III. Amphilis, *m.* to William Barneby, Esq., of Bockleton, in Worcestershire.

Sir John *d.* 15 February, 1591, and was *s.* by his eldest son,

GILBERT LYTTLETON, Esq., M.P. for Worcestershire, 13th and 14th ELIZABETH, 1571-2, and high sheriff in the 25th of the same reign. This gentleman resided chiefly at Prestwood, in Worcestershire, where his father had erected a large mansion. It was purchased by him from Sutton, Lord Dudley; but there was great contention between the two families, before the Lyttletons could obtain quiet possession of the estate. In the month of October, 1592, Lord Dudley armed 140 persons, and coming by night to Prestwood, forcibly carried off 341 sheep, 14 kine, 1 bull, and 8 fat oxen, which they drove to Dudley, and there kept. Replevins were immediately taken, but not delivered by the bailiffs, for fear of being cut to pieces. After Lord Dudley had killed and eaten part of those cattle, the remainder were sent towards Coventry, accompanied by sixty armed men, in order to be sold; but his lordship changing his mind, he raised the inhabitants of several villages to the number of six or seven hundred, who brought them back to Dudley Castle, where they roasted them all. Upon this violent proceeding, a bill was filed in the Star Chamber against Lord Dudley and his adherents; where, on full proof of these illegal outrages, a reference was proposed, and accepted, and articles were signed 24 May, 1595, whereby Lord Dudley agreed to pay 1000 marks to Mr. Lyttleton, and all further suit to cease. This Gilbert *m.* Elizabeth, dau. of Humphrey Coningsby, Esq , of Nyend-Solers, in Shropshire, and of Hampton Court, co. Hereford, and dying 1 June, 1599, was *s.* by his eldest son,

JOHN LYTTLETON, Esq., M.P. for Worcestershire, *temp.* ELIZABETH. This gentleman (to use the words of Sir Francis Bacon), being much respected for his wit and valour, and a Roman Catholic, was courted by Lord Essex and his friends, and in some measure drawn in by Sir Charles Danvers to that conspiracy which cost Essex his head, and Lyttleton his estate; for he was tried and convicted of high treason at the Queen's Bench bar on 20 February, 1600-1, and *d.* in prison the July following, his execution having been averted through the interest of Sir Walter Raleigh. Mr. Lyttleton *m.* Muriel, dau. of Sir Thomas Bromley, Knt., Lord Chancellor of England, which lady obtained upon the accession of JAMES I., a reversal of the attainder of her late husband, and a grant by letters patent of the whole of his estate. She was a person of so much prudence that she was enabled not only to discharge debts of her husband and his father to the amount of £9,000, but also to acquire a high reputation for benevolence and hospitality. She survived Mr. Lyttleton twenty-eight years, and brought up her children, of whom there were three sons and five daus., in the Protestant religion. The eldest son,

SIR THOMAS LYTTLETON, Knt., M.P. for Worcestershire, and sheriff of that county in 1618, was created a Baronet, 25 July, 1618.

From Sir Thomas lineally descended (*refer to* BURKE'S *Extant Peerage* for intermediate lineage)

SIR GEORGE LYTTLETON, 5th baronet, *b.* 17 January, 1709, who was M.P. for the borough of Okehampton, and in 1737, was appointed secretary to the Prince of Wales, in 1744, one of the commissioners of the Treasury; cofferer of the household in 1754, when he was sworn of the privy council; and in 1755 Chancellor and under-treasurer of the Exchequer. Sir George was elevated to the peerage 18 November, 1756, as BARON LYTTLETON, *of Frankley, co. Worcester.* This nobleman acquired the reputation of an excellent scholar, and a great patron of literature. He was also justly esteemed as an author, and his works are still highly valued, especially his *Persian Letters, Dialogues of the Dead, History of the Age and Reign of Henry II.,* &c., &c. His lordship *m.* 1st, Lucy, dau. of Hugh Fortescue, Esq., of Filleigh, co. Devon (*see Landed Gentry*), by whom, who *d.* 19 January, 1747, he had issue,

  THOMAS, his successor.
  Lucy, *m.* in 1767, Arthur Annesley, Viscount Valentia, created Earl of Mountnorris. She *d.* in 1783, having eventually become heir to her father.

Lord Lyttleton *m.* 2ndly, Elizabeth, dau of Sir Robert Rich, Bart., but had no child by that lady. His lordship *d.* 22 August, 1773, and was *s.* by his son,

THOMAS LYTTLETON, 2nd baron. This nobleman was a person of great eccentricity, and the vision which is said immediately to have preceded his dissolution, has ever been a subject of interest and marvel, to those who place implicit reliance upon narratives of that description. His lordship *m.* in 1772, Apphia, 2nd dau. of Broome Witts, Esq., of Chipping Norton, and widow of Joseph Peach, Esq., governor of Calcutta, Her ladyship survived her husband to 9 April, 1840, but Lord Lyttleton having *d. s. p.* 27 November. 1779, the Barony of Lyttleton, of Frankley, of this creation, became EXTINCT.

Arms—Arg., a chevron, between three escallops, sa.

LYTTLETON—BARON LYTTLETON, OF MOUNSLOW, CO. SALOP.

By Letters Patent, dated 18 February, 164C-1.

Lineage.

For earlier descent *refer* to LYTTLETON, Barons Lyttleton, of Frankley. The youngest son of the celebrated Judge, Sir Thomas Lyttleton, mentioned in the genealogy of that family. From an elder son descended

SIR EDMUND LYTTLETON, OR LITTLETON, of Mounslow, co. Salop. This gentleman, like his great ancestor, attained fame, honours, and fortune, by the profession of the law. In the 10th year of King CHARLES I., 1634, Mr. Lyttelton was appointed solicitor-general, when he received the honour of knighthood. In five years afterwards he was made Lord Chief Justice of the court of Common Pleas, and the next year constituted Lord Keeper of the Great Seal, when he was elevated to the peerage, 18 February, 1640, as BARON LYTTLETON, *of Mounslow, co. Salop.* The patent for this peerage, which contains portraits of the grantor, King CHARLES, and of the grantee, Lord Littleton, is still extant, and in the possession of the present Lord Littleton (*see the Herald and Genealogist*, vol. i., p. 435). Lord Lyttleton held the Great Seal from 1640 to 1645. At the commencement of the civil wars, when CHARLES retired to the city of York, the lord keeper immediately followed his Majesty with the great seal, and continued afterwards in attendance upon him. Of this eminent person, Banks says: "his learning was various and useful; his skill in the maxims of government, and of the fundamental statutes and customs of the kingdom was particular; as was his experience, long and observing. His eloquence was powerful and majestic: in fact, such a man was worthy of that honour to which he was advanced; namely, of a peer of the realm." His lordship *m.* Anne, dau. of John Lyttleton, Esq., of Frankley, M.P. for Worcestershire, by whom he had an only dau. and heiress,

ANNE, who *m.* her 2nd cousin, Sir Thomas Lyttleton, Bart.

Lord Lyttleton *d.* in 1645, when the Barony of Lyttleton, of Mounslow, became EXTINCT.

Arms—Arg., a chevron, between three escallops, sa., a mullet, or, for difference.

MACARTNEY—BARON, VISCOUNT, EARL MACARTNEY IN IRELAND, BARON MACARTNEY IN GREAT BRITAIN.

Barony of Ireland, by Letters Patent, dated 19 July, 1767.
Earldom of Ireland, by Letters Patent, dated 1794.
Barony of Great Britain, by Letters Patent, dated 8 June, 1796.

Lineage.

GEORGE MACARTNEY, Esq., of Lissanoure (younger son of George Macartney, Esq., of Auchinleck, near Kirkcudbright, in Scotland, who settled in Ireland in 1649), was called to the bar in 1700, served subsequently the office of high sheriff for the co. Antrim, was colonel of a regiment of militia dragoons there, and represented the town of Belfast for many years in parliament. He *m.* 1st, Letitia, dau. and co-heir of Sir Charles Porter, lord chancellor of Ireland; and 2ndly, Elizabeth, dau. and co-heir of William Dobbyn, Esq., of Carrickfergus, and widow of Robert South, of Ballyeaston. By his 2nd wife he had no issue, but by the 1st he was father of three sons, the eldest and youngest of whom *d. s. p.*; the 2nd,

GEORGE MACARTNEY, Esq., of Lissanoure, co. Antrim, who *s.* his father in 1757, *m.* in 1732, Elizabeth, youngest dau. of the Rev. John Winder, prebendary of Kilroot, and rector of Carmony, and by her (who *d.* July, 1755) had issue,

GEORGE, his heir.

Letitia, *m.* in 1756, to Godfrey Echlin, Esq. of Echlinville, co. Down, but *d. s. p.* in 1767.

Elizabeth, *m.* in 1759, to John Balaquier, Esq., major 13th dragoons; and *d.* in 1782, leaving an only dau., ELIZABETH, *m.* in 1787, to the REV. TRAVERS HUME.

Mr. Macartney *d.* in 1778, and was *s.* by his only son,

THE RIGHT HON. SIR GEORGE MACARTNEY, K.B., *b.* in 1737; who was sent, in 1754, as envoy extraordinary to the Empress of Russia, and knighted on his return. In 1769, having previously been elected M.P. for Armagh, he received the appointment of chief secretary to Lord Townshend, the lord-lieutenant of Ireland; in 1772, was installed a knight of the Bath; in 1775, became governor of the Caribbee Islands; and 19 July, 1776, was raised to the Irish peerage as LORD MACARTNEY, *Baron of Lissanoure, co. Antrim.* In 1792, his lordship was appointed ambassador extraordinary and plenipotentiary to the Emperor of China, and was advanced, 19 July, in the same year, to be VISCOUNT MACARTNEY, *of Dervock, co. Antrim.* He remained in the East until 1794, when he returned to England, and was created EARL MACARTNEY. In 1795, he proceeded on an important mission to Italy, and on its completion in the following year (8 June, 1796), was made a British peer, as BARON MACARTNEY, *of Parkhurst,* in Surrey, and of Auchinleck, in the stewartry of Kirkcudbright. The last public appointment the earl held was that of governor of the Cape of Good Hope, to which colony he sailed in January, 1797, and from which he came back in 1799. He *m.* 1 February, 1768, Lady Jane Stuart, 2nd dau. of John, Earl of Bute, but *d.* without issue, 31 March, 1806, when all his honours became EXTINCT. The whole of his property his lordship bequeathed, after the death of his widow, to his niece, ELIZABETH HUME, for life, with remainder to her children (beginning with the eldest son), who were to assume the surname and arms of MACARTNEY (*see Landed Gentry,* HUME MACARTNEY, *of Lissanoure*).

Arms—Or, a buck, trippant, within a bordure, gu.

MACAULAY—BARON MACAULAY.

By Letters Patent, dated 10 September, 1857.

Lineage.

THE REV. JOHN MACAULAY, A.M., Presbyterian minister successively of Barra, South Uist, Inverary, and Cardross, *b.* in 1720 (son of Rev. Aulay Macaulay, minister of Tiree and Coll); *m.* in 1757, his 2nd wife, Margaret, dau. of Colin Campbell, of Inverseger, and had twelve children. Of the sons, Aulay, the eldest, became a clergyman of the Church of England; Alexander, succeeded his father as minister of Cardross; Colin attained the rank of general; and Zachary gained distinction by the elevation of his character and his unwearied advocacy of Negro emancipation. One of the daus. of Rev. John Macaulay, Jean, *m.* in 1787, Thomas Babington, Esq., of Rothley Temple, Leicestershire, M.P.

ZACHARY MACAULAY, the son to whom we have just referred, *b.* 1768; *m.* 26 Aug. 1799, Selina Mills, a Quaker lady of Bristol, and *d.* 1838, leaving issue,

  I. THOMAS-BABINGTON, LORD MACAULAY.

  II. John (Rev.), rural dean and rector of Aldingham, Lancashire, *m.* Miss Large, and left issue. The eldest son is MAJOR CHARLES EDWARD MACAULAY, B.S.C.

  III. Henry-William, H.M. commissioner of arbitration and commissary judge at Sierra Leone, *m.* 23 November, 1841, Hon. Margaret Denman, dau. of Thomas, 1st Lord Denman, and *d.* at Bona Vista, 24 September, 1846, leaving issue,

    1 Henry - Denman, lieut. R.N., *b.* 10 August, 1843; *m.* 18 February, 1868, Selina, dau. of Sir Joseph Needham, and has issue.

    2 Zachary-William, *b.* 15 February, 1845; *d.* young.

    3 Joseph-Babington, *b.* 17 October, 1846; *m.* 8 July, 1869, Eleanor, dau. of Henry Studdy, Esq., of Waddeton Court, Devon, and has issue.

  IV. Charles, many years in the Audit Office, Somerset House, *m.* Miss Potter, and has issue.

  I. Fanny.

  II. Hannah-More, *m.* 23 December, 1834, Sir Charles Edward Trevelyan, K.C.B.; and *d.* 5 August, 1873, leaving issue,

    Right Hon. George Otto Trevelyan, Chief Secretary for Ireland and M.P. (*See* TREVELYAN, Bt., of Wallington, BURKE's *Peerage and Baronetage.*)

    Margaret - Jean, *m.* 25 November, 1858, Sir Henry T. Holland, Bart.

    Alice-Frances, *m.* 14 December, 1871, William Stratford Dugdale, Esq., of Merevale, who *d.* 9 May, 1882.

  III. Margaret, *m.* Edward Cropper, Esq., of Swaylands, Kent, and *d.* 1834.

The eldest son,

THE RT. HON. THOMAS BABINGTON MACAULAY, was b. 25 October, 1800, at Rothley Temple, co. Leicester, the seat of Thomas Babington, Esq., the husband of his father's sister, Jean. This distinguished statesman, orator, historian, essayist and poet, graduated at, and was for several years a Fellow of, Trinity College, Cambridge. In 1826, he was called to the bar by the society of Lincoln's Inn; in 1832, became secretary of the Board of Control; and subsequently went to India as 5th member of, and legal adviser to, the supreme council of India. From 1839 to 1841, he held office as secretary at war, and from 1846 to 1848, as paymaster-general of the forces. In the latter year he was elected lord rector of the University of Glasgow, and in 1850, professor of ancient history in the Royal Academy. He sat in the House of Commons as member for Calne in 1830, for Leeds in 1832, and for Edinburgh from 1840 to 1847 and from 1852 to 1856. On 10 September, 1857, he was elevated to the peerage of the United Kingdom as BARON MACAULAY, *of Rothley, co. Leicester.* He d. *unm.* 28 December, 1859, at Holly Lodge, his residence at Kensington, when his title became EXTINCT. He was buried 9 January following, in Poet's Corner, Westminster Abbey. "His body is buried in peace, but his name liveth for evermore."

A very interesting "Life of Lord Macaulay," has been written by his nephew, the Right Hon. George Otto Trevelyan, M.P.

Arms—Gu., two arrows, saltire-wise points downwards, arg., surmounted by as many barrulets compony, or and az., between two buckles in pale of the third, all within a bordure engrailed, also of the third.

M'CARTY—EARL OF CLANCARE.

By Letters Patent, dated 22 June, 1556.

Lineage.

The M'Cartys, the most illustrious, as Dr. O'Brien observes, of all those families whose names begin with Mac, trace their origin to Heber, the eldest son of MILESIUS, King of Spain, through Oiloll Olium, King of Munster, in the third century; but the first who bore the appellation of M'Carty, or "son of Cartagh," was the grandfather of Diarmod M'Carty More, whom the English found in possession of Cork, and who subjected his kingdom to HENRY II. Diarmod was slain by Theobald Butler, founder of the house of Ormonde, in 1186. His successors were, DONALD, CORMAC FIONN, DONALD ROE, DONALD OGE, and CORMAC, all of whom were distinguished as M'CARTY *More* (or Great), an adjunct continued in this senior branch until 1556, when

DONOGH M'CARTY MORE, the 7th in descent from the eldest son* of the last mentioned Cormac, was created 22 June, 1556, *Baron of Valentia*, and EARL OF CLANCARE, co. Kerry, on resigning his estates to Queen ELIZABETH, from whom he again received the investiture of them, "to hold of the crown of England, in the English manner." The earl sat in the parliament held at Dublin, 26 April, 1584, but he soon (1597) resigned his title, which he considered a badge of slavery, and resumed the native distinction of M'CARTY MORE. He *m.* Lady Honora Fitz-Gerald, dau. of James, Earl of Desmond, and had issue a son Tiego Mac Carthy More, who *d. s. p.*, and a dau. Helena, wife of Florence Mac Carthy. The Earl having *d.* without male issue, he was *s.* by his son-in-law, Florence Mac Carthy, who thereupon assumed the native title of Mac Carthy More, and whose male descendant, Charles Mac Carthy, Esq., *d. s. p.* in 1776, having devised his estates to his cousin, Mr. Herbert, of Mucruss. The Earl of Kenmare, and O'Donoghue, of the Glyns, are the presumed representatives of this ancient sept in the female line.

Arms—Arg., a stag, trippant, gu., attired and unguled, or.

MAC CARTHY—EARL OF CLANCARTY.

By Letters Patent, dated 27 November, 1658.

Lineage.

DERMOT MAC CARTHY, 2nd son of Cormac More Mac Carthy, and 1st feudal lord and founder of the house of Muskerry, killed by the O'Mahonys in 1367, was great-grandfather of

---

* The 2nd son of Cormac More, DERMOT MAC CARTY, 1st feudal Lord of Muskerry, was ancestor of the Earls of Clancarty.

344

CORMAC MAC CARTHY, surnamed "Laidhir or the Stout," Lord of Muskerry forty years. He built the castle of Blarney. He *m.* Sarah, dau. of Mulroony Ballogh O'Carrick, and being slain in 1494, left issue an only son,

CORMAC OGE LAIDHIR MAC CARTHY, Lord of Muskerry. He defeated the Earl of Desmond in the battle of Cluhar and Morne Abbey, in 1521. He *m.* the Hon. Catherine, dau. of the Right Hon. John Viscount Buttevant, and sister of Elizabeth, Countess of Desmond, dying in 1536, left with other issue an eldest son,

TIEGE MAC CARTHY, Lord of Muskerry, twenty-five years styled also of Blarney, who *m.* Julia, dau. of Donall Mac Carthy Reagh, and had with other issue an eldest son,

SIR DERMOT MAC CARTHY, Lord of Muskerry of Blarney, knighted by Sir Henry Sidney, lord deputy, 20 March, 1567, who *m.* the Lady Fitz-Gerald, dau. of Maurice Fitz-John, of Desmond, and had with other issue, a son and successor,

SIR CORMAC MAC CARTHY, of Blarney, called Cooch or Blind, Lord of Muskerry, who *m.* 1st, Mary, dau. of Sir Theobald Butler, Knt., Lord of Cahir, and by her left at his decease, 23 February, 1616, two sons,

  I. CORMAC, of whom presently.
  II. Daniel, who built the castle of Carrignavar, co. Cork, and founded the family of Carrignavar, now represented by Robert MacCarthy, Esq., eldest son of the late Justin Mac Carthy, Esq., of Carrignavar. (*See* BURKE's *Landed Gentry*).

The eldest son,

CORMAC OGE, Lord of Muskerry, was created, 15 November, 1628, VISCOUNT MUSKERRY and BARON OF BLARNEY. He *m.* 1st, the Lady Margaret O'Brien, dau. of Donogh, 4th Earl of Thomond; and 2ndly, the Hon. Ellen Roche, dau. of David, Viscount Fermoy. He *d.* in London, 20 February, 1640, having had issue, by his 1st wife, viz.,

  I. Cormac, *d.* young.
  II. DONOGH, of whom presently.
  I. Mary, *m.* 1st, Sir Valentine Browne; and 2ndly, Edward FitzGerald, of Ballymallon.
  II. Eleanor, *m.* to Charles-Mac Carthy Reagh, whose only dau Ellen, became wife of John DeCourcy, 21st Baron Kingsale.
  III. Eleanor, *m.* to John Power, and was ancestress of Frances Power, who *m.* Richard Trench, Esq., of Garbally, father of the 1st Earl of Clancarty, of the Trench family.

The 2nd son,

DONOGH M'CARTY, was created Earl of Clancarty, 27 November, 1658. His lordship, who commanded the king's forces in Munster, against Cromwell. *m.* Lady Eleanor Butler-sister of James, 1st Duke of Ormonde, and had issue,

CHARLES, who lost his life in a sea-fight against the Dutch, 3 June, 1665. He *m.* Lady Margaret Burke, dau. of Ulick, Earl of Clanricarde, and left a son,

  Charles, 2nd earl, who *d.* a child, in 1668, and was *s.* by his uncle, CALLAGHAN, 3rd earl.

CALLAGHAN, *s.* to his nephew.

Justin, created VISCOUNT MOUNTCASHEL, by JAMES II., 23 May, 1689; *m.* Lady Arabella Wentworth, 2nd dau. of Thomas, the ill-fated Earl of Stafford; but *d. s. p.*

Helena, *m.* William, 7th Earl of Clanricarde.

Margaret, *m.* Luke, Earl of Fingall.

The 2nd son,

CALLAGHAN M'CARTY, 3rd Earl of Clancarty, *m.* Lady Elizabeth Fitzgerald, 6th and youngest dau. of George, Earl of Kildare, and *d.* 16 November, 1676, having had issue,

  I. DONOGH, of whom presently.
  I. Catherine, *m.* to the Right Hon. Paul Davys, Viscount Mountcashel.
  II. Margaret, *d. s. p.*
  III. Elizabeth, *d. s. p.*

The son and heir,

DONOGH M'CARTY, 4th Earl of Clancarty, forfeited on account of his adhesion to JAMES II., the immense estates of the family, equivalent at this day to £200,000 per annum. His lordship *m.* 30 October, 1684, Elizabeth, 2nd dau. of Robert Spencer, Earl of Sunderland, and had, with a dau. (Charlotte, *m.* to John West, 7th Lord Delawarr,) two sons, Robert and Justin. The younger was an officer in the Neapolitan army, and the elder, Robert MacCarthy, called Earl of Clancarty, captain R.N., commanded the "Adventure," man-of-war, but on Sir Robert Walpole's refusal to restore him to his earldom, he deserted to France, and resided for many years at Boulogne-sur-Mer, on a pension of £1,000 per annum. He *m.* the dau. of — Pleyer, of Gosport, Hants, and dying, 1770, aged eighty-four, left two sons in the French service, who *d. s. p.*

Arms—Arg., a stag, trippant, gu., attired and unguled, or.

MACDONELL—LORD MACDONELL AND ARRASS.

By Letters Patent, dated 20 December, 1660.

Lineage.

ALEXANDER MACDONNELL, of Glengarry, descended from John, Lord of the Isles, *m.* Margaret, the eldest of the three sisters and co-heiresses of Sir Donald Macdonald, of the Isles and Lochalsh, and dau. of Celestine, brother of John, Earl of Ross. She was served heir of her brother, 1515; and by her Glengarry had a son,

ÆNEAS MACDONNELL, of Glengarry; who *m.* Janet, only dau. of Sir Hector Maclean, of Dowart, by whom he had a son,

DONALD MACDONNELL, of Glengarry; who *d.* in 1630, leaving by Margaret, his wife, dau. of Alexander Macdonald, captain of Clanronald, two sons,

ALEXANDER, his heir.

Donald Macdonell, of Scothouse, whose son, Reginald. of Scothouse, was father of Alastair, who became male heir of the family at the decease of Lord Macdonell.

The elder son,

ALASTAIR MACDONELL, of Glengarry, *d.* soon after his father, leaving by Jean, dau. of Alan Cameron, of Locheil, a son,

ÆNEAS MACDONNELL, of Glengarry, who manifested his loyalty in an eminent manner to King CHARLES I. and CHARLES II., for which he was forfeited by Cromwell, in 1651; but surviving to the Restoration, he was, in reward of his faithful services, created a peer, by the title of LORD MACDONELL AND ARRASS, by patent, dated at Whitehall, 20 December, 1660. His lordship *m.* Margaret, eldest dau. of Sir Donald Macdonald, of Slate, by whom he had an only dau., *m.* to the Hon. James Montgomery, of Coylsfield, 4th son of Alexander. 6th Earl of Eglinton, and had issue. His lordship *d.* in 1680, when his title became EXTINCT. His estate devolved on the heir male,

ALASTAIR MACDONELL, of Glengarry, grandson of his uncle, Donald Macdonell, of Scothouse. This Alastair Macdonell, of Glengarry, *d.* 1724, leaving, by Lady Mary Mackenzie, his wife, 4th dau. of Kenneth, 3rd Earl of Seaforth, a son,

JOHN MACDONELL, of Glengarry, who *m.* 1st, a dau. of McKenzie, of Hilton, and had, by her, two sons,

ALASTAIR, his heir.

Æneas, colonel in the army, who *m.* Mary Macdonald, only dau. of Alexander Robertson, of Strowan, and by her had (with a dau. Angusia, *m.* to Mackay, of Achmony) an only son,

DUNCAN, of whom presently, as heir to his uncle.

He *m.* 2ndly, a dau. of John Gordon, of Glenbucket, and had, by her, James, whose dau. Amelia, *m.* Major Simon Macdonald, of Morer; Charles, a major in the army; and a dau. Helen, *m.* to Ranald Macdonell, of Scothouse. He was *s.* by his eldest son,

ALASTAIR MACDONELL, of Glengarry, who was selected by the Highland chiefs to carry an address to Prince Charles, signed with their blood. He *d. unm.* in 1761, and was *s.* by his nephew,

DUNCAN MACDONELL, of Glengarry, who *m.* Majory, dau. of Sir Ludovic Grant, Bart., of Dalvey, and by her had (with two daus., Elizabeth, *m.* 1st, to William Chisholm, of that ilk; and 2ndly, to Sir Alexander Ramsay, Bart., of Balmain; and Margaret, *m.* to Major James Downing) five sons, ALASTER, his heir; Lewis, captain in the army, *d. unm.*; JAMES (Sir), K.C.B., lieutenant-general in the army, and principal equerry to the Queen Dowager Adelaide. distinguished at the battle of Maida, in Egypt, and at Waterloo; Angus, *d.* an infant; and Somerled, lieutenant R.N., *d.* at Curaçoa, West Indies. Duncan was *s.* by his eldest son,

ALEXANDER-RANALDSON MACDONELL, of Glengarry, who *m.* 20 Jan*s*ry, 1802, Rebecca, 2nd dau. of of Sir William Forbes, of Pitsligo, Bart., and by her, (who *d.* in 1841) had (with several sons, all of whom *d.* young),

ÆNEAS RANALDSON MACDONELL, of Glengarry, *b.* 29 July, 1808; who *m.* 18 December, 1833, Josephine, eldest dau. of William Bennet, Esq., and niece of the late Right Rev. William Bennet, D.D., bishop of Cloyne, and had issue,

I. ÆNEAS.
I. Elizabeth, *m.* to Roderick-C. Macdonald, of Castle Tioram.
II. Marcelly, *m.* 22 October. 1833, to Andrew, 4th son of the late Andrew Bonar, Esq., of Kinmerghame, co. Berwick.
III. Jemima-Rebecca, *m.* 5 July. 1833, to Charles, 2nd son of the last Sir William Forbes, of Pitsligo and Fettercairn, Bart.
IV. Louisa-Christian.   V. Caroline-Hester.
VI. Gulielmina-Forbes.
VII. Euphemia-Margaret, *d. unm.*

Glengarry *d.* in January, 1828, and was *s.* by his only surviving son, Æneas-Ranaldson Macdonell, of Glengarry.

Arms—Or, an eagle, displayed, gu., surmounted of a galley, sa., the sails furled up. and rigging ppr.; in the dexter chief point, a dexter hand. couped in fess. of the 2nd, and in the sinister, a cross-crosslet, fitchée, of the 3rd.

MACDONNELL—MARQUESS OF ANTRIM.

(*See* BURKE's *Extant Peerage*, article, "EARL OF ANTRIM.")

MACGILL—VISCOUNT OF OXFURD.

By Letters Patent, dated 19 April, 1651.

Lineage.

SIR JAMES MACGILL, Provost of Edinburgh, *temp.* JAMES V, *m.* a dau of Wardlaw, of Torrie and had two sons,

I. JAMES (Sir), of Rankeilour, co. Fife, clerk-register, ancestor of James MacGill, of Rankeilour, who, in 1734, claimed the title of Viscount Oxfurd, and *d. s. p.*: his sister, and eventual heiress, Isabella, *m.* the Rev. William Dick, minister of Cupar, and was ancestor of the family of. MAITLAND-MAC-GILL-CRICHTON, now of Rankeilour.
II. DAVID.

The 2nd son,

DAVID MACGILL, of Nisbet, and Cranstoun-Riddel, a lord of session, *m.* Elizabeth, dau. of James Forrester, of Corstorphine, and was *s.* by his son,

DAVID MACGILL, of Cranstoun-Riddel, a lord of session, who *m.* Mary, dau. of Sir William Sinclair, of Hermanstoun, and *d.* 10 May, 1607, leaving a son and heir to his brother, viz.,

SIR JAMES MACGILL, Bart., of Cranstoun-Riddel, appointed a lord of session in 1629, and created a peer, by the title of VISCOUNT OF OXFURD, and Lord Macgill, of Cousland, by patent, dated 19 April, 1651 to him and his heirs male of entail and provision whatsoever. His lordship *m.* 1st, Catherine, dau. of Sir John Cockburn, of Ormistoun, and had issue,

Andrew, *b.* 26 July, 1630; *d.* young.
Patrick, *d. unm.* in 1651.
Elizabeth, *m.* to Patrick Hamilton, of Preston. She had a dau. Jean, *b.* 2 February, 1666; and a son, Colonel Thomas Hamilton, of Preston and Fala, who *m.* Elizabeth Stewart, of the house of Grandtully, by whom he had a dau. Elizabeth, *m.* to Malcolm Gibson, Esq., a son of the family of Durie; and a son, Thomas-Hamilton Macgill, of Fala and Oxfurd, who *s.* as heir of entail to the Oxfurd property in 1759, and *d.* 18 October, 1779. He *m.* Elizabeth, dau. of Sir John Dalrymple, Bart., of Cousland, one of the principal clerks of session, and by her had one dau., Elizabeth, *m* 7 October, 1760, to her cousin, Sir John Dalrymple, Bart., who was designed Sir John-Dalrymple-Hamilton-Macgill, of Cousland, Cranstoun, and Oxfurd, and *d.* in 1810. Their eldest surviving son was the late Sir John Hamilton-Dalrymple, Bart.
Anne, *m.* to Sir James Richardson, of Smeaton.

His lordship *m.* 2ndly, C*a*ristian, dau. of Sir William Livingston, of Kilsyth, by whom he had issue,

ROBERT, 2nd Viscount of Oxfurd.
David, *b.* 16 July, 1649.
George, *b.* 11 March, 1655.
Christian, *b.* 19 February, 1654: *m.* 1st, to Alexander Crawford, of Carse; 2ndly, to George Ross, of Galstoun.

Lord Oxfurd *d.* in 1663, and was *s.* by his son,

ROBERT MACGILL, 2nd Viscount of Oxfurd, who *m.* 1st, in July, 1666, Lady Henriet Livingston, only dau. of George, 3rd Earl of Linlithgow, and by her had issue,

Thomas, *b.* 21 January, 1676; *d. s. p.* in September 1701, in the lifetime of his father.
Christian, *b* 16 March, 1677; *m.* the Hon. William Maitland, a younger son of Charles, 3rd Earl of Lauderdale, and *d.* 1707, in her thirtieth year. leaving a son Robert, who assumed the title of Viscount of Oxfurd, and voted as such at an election of a representative peer, 21 September, 1733, but *d. s. p.* 1755.
Elizabeth, *b.* 20 May, 1678; *d. unm.*
Henriet, *m.* to James Hamilton, younger, of Orbistoun, *s. p.* She assumed the title of Viscountess of Oxfurd, on her nephew's death, in 1755, when she *s. to* the estates.

His lordship m. 2ndly, Lady Jean Ramsay, eldest dau. of George, 2nd Earl of Dalhousie, relict of George, 10th Lord Ross, but had by her no issue. The viscount d. 8 December, 1706, since which period the title has remained DORMANT.

Arms—Gu., three martlets, or.

MACKENZIE — EARL OF SEAFORTH, IN SCOTLAND, VISCOUNT FORTROSE AND EARL OF SEAFORTH, IN IRELAND, AND BARON SEAFORTH, OF GREAT BRITAIN.

Scottish Earldom, by Letters Patent, dated 3 December, 1623.

Lineage.

There is a tradition, not borne out, however, by any tangible evidence or confirmation, that this very ancient family deduced its descent from a member of the house of Geraldine, in Ireland (whence sprang the noble families of Leinster, Desmond, &c.), who, with a considerable number of his followers, is stated to have settled in Scotland about the year 1261, and to have so powerfully aided ALEXANDER III., a few years afterwards, in repelling the invasion of HACO, King of Norway, that he was rewarded by a grant of the lands of Kintail, in the co. Ross, which were .erected into a free barony by charter, dated 9 January, 1266.

COLIN, 1st feudal baron of Kintail, is said to have m. a dau. of Walter, lord high steward of Scotland; and dying in 1278, was s. by his son,

KENNETH, 2nd Baron of Kintail; who was s. in 1304, by his son,

KENNETH, 3rd Baron of Kintail, who in the Gaelic was called Kenneth Mac Kenneth, which became corrupted in English into Mackenny, or Mackenzie. and hence arose all the families of Mackenzie in Scotland. From this Kenneth, 3rd baron, we pass to his great great-grandson,

ALEXANDER, 7th Baron of Kintail; who m. 1st, Lady Agnes Campbell, and 2ndly, Margaret, dau. of Sir John Macdougal, Lord of Lorn. By the latter he had two sons; of whom the elder, HECTOR, was ancestor of the present SIR KENNETH-SMITH MACKENZIE, Bart., of Gairloch; and by the former a son and heir, SIR KENNETH MACKENZIE, of Kintail, who m. for his 2nd wife Agnes, dau. of Hugh, Lord Lovat, and had four sons and two daus., namely,

JOHN, his heir.
Alexander, of Davochmaluach, ancestor of several families of Mackenzie.
Roderick, from whom derived the Mackenzies of Achilty, Fairburn, &c.
Kenneth, progenitor of the Mackenzies of Suddy, Ord, Corrovalzie, Highfield, Inverlal, Little Findon, Scatwell, &c.
Agnes, m. to Roderick Macleod, of Lewis.
Catherine, m. to Hector Monro, of Foulis.

The Chief of Kintail d. about 1506, and was s. by his son,
JOHN MACKENZIE, of Kintail, father of Kenneth, father of
COLIN MACKENZIE, of Kintail, who fought for Queen MARY at Langside. He m. 1st, Barbara, eldest dau. of John Grant, of Grant, and by her had, with two daus., four sons, viz.,

KENNETH, his heir.
Roderick, of Tarbat, from whom the Earls of Cromarty derived.
Colin, ancestor of the Mackenzies of Kennock and Pitlundie.
Alexander, ancestor of the Mackenzies of Kilcoy.

He m. 2ndly, Mary, dau. of Roderick Mackenzie, of Davochmaluach, and had by her another son. Alexander, progenitor of the Mackenzies of Applecross, Coul, Delvin, Assint, &c. The eldest son,

KENNETH MACKENZIE, of Kintail, was raised to the peerage of Scotland, 19 November, 1609, as BARON MACKENZIE, *of Kintail*. He m. 1st, Anne, dau. of George Ross, of Balnagowan, and had by her two sons and two daus., COLIN, his heir; John, of Lochslyne, whose dau. m. Sir Norman Macleod, of Bernera; Barbara, wife of Donald, 1st Lord Reay; and Janet, m. to Sir Donald Macdonald, of Slate. His lordship m. 2ndly, Isabel, dau. of Sir Alexander Ogilvy, of Powrie, and had by her four sons and one dau.,

Alexander, who d. unm. in 1614.
GEORGE, 2nd Earl of Seaforth.
Thomas, of Pluscardine.
Simon, of Lochslyne, father of the learned and accomplished Sir George Mackenzie, of Rosehaugh, lord advocate to CHARLES II. and JAMES II., whose extensive estates eventu-

ally centered in his great-great-grandson, the Hon. James-Archibald Stuart, who assumed the surname of Mackenzie, and was father of James-Archibald. LORD WHARNCLIFFE.
Sibylla, m. to John Macleod, of Macleod.

Lord Kintail d. in 1611, and was s. by his son,
COLIN MACKENZIE, 2nd Lord Kintail, who was created, 3 December, 1623, EARL OF SEAFORTH, to him and his heirs male. Very shortly after he built the stately mansion of Brahan Castle. He m. Lady Margaret Seton, 3rd dau. of Alexander, 1st Earl of Dunfermline, and had two daus.,

ANNE, m. 1st, to Alexander, 2nd Earl of Balcarres; and 2ndly, to Archibald, 9th Earl of Argyll.
JANE, m. 1st, to John, Master of Berriedale; and 2ndly, to Alexander, 1st Lord Duffus.

The earl d. 15 April, 1633, and was s. by his half-brother,
GEORGE MACKENZIE, 2nd Earl of Seaforth, a stanch royalist and adherent of the gallant Montrose. His lordship m. Barbara, eldest dau. of Arthur, 9th Lord Forbes, and had issue,

KENNETH, his heir.
Colin, who m. Miss Jean Laurie, and had (with a dau., Barbara, wife of Patrick Oliphant, of Bachilton) a son, GEORGE MACKENZIE, M.D., author of a work of authority and research, entitled *The Lives and Characters of the Most Eminent Writers of the Scottish Nation.*
Mary, m. to John, 9th Earl of Marr.
Margaret, m. to Sir William Sinclair, Bart.

His lordship d. in 1651, and was s. by his eldest son,
KENNETH MACKENZIE, 3rd Earl of Seaforth, who suffered a long imprisonment under the Commonwealth. He m. Isabella, dau. of Sir John Mackenzie, Bart., of Tarbat; and dying in 1678, left (with four daus , Margaret, Lady Duffus; Anne, who d. unm.; Isabel, m. 1st, to Roderick Macleod, of Macleod; and 2ndly, to Sir Duncan Campbell, of Lochnell; and Mary, wife of Alexander Macdonell, of Glengarry) two sons, KENNETH, his heir; and John, of Assint. The elder,
KENNETH MACKENZIE, 4th Earl of Seaforth, K.T., accompanied King JAMES to France at the Revolution, went with the expedition to Ireland, and was created, by the exiled monarch, MARQUESS OF SEAFORTH. He m. Lady Frances Her ert, 2nd dau. of William, Marquess of Powis, and had by her, who d. in 1732,

WILLIAM, his heir.
Alexander, who m. Elizabeth, dau. of John Paterson, bishop of Ross, and had (with four daus., of whom the eldest, Isabella, m. Basil Hamilton, of Baldoon; the 2nd. Jane, Dr. Alexander Mackenzie; the 3rd, Mary, Captain Dougal Stewart; and the 4th, Maria, Nicholas Price, Esq., of Saintfield, co. Down) a son,
WILLIAM, major in the army; who m. Mary, only dau. of Matthew Humberston, Esq., of Humberston, in Lincolnshire, and d. 12 March, 1770, having had issue,
THOMAS-FREDERICK, of whom presently.
FRANCIS-HUMBERSTON, heir to his brother.
Frances-Cerjat, m. to Sir Vicary Gibbs, M.P.
Maria-Rebecca, m. to Alexander Mackenzie, of Breda, in Aberdeenshire.
Elizabeth.
Helen, m. to Major-Gen. Alexander Mackenzie Fraser.
Mary, m. to John Caryl, Esq.

Lord Seaforth d. at Paris in 1701, and was s. by his son,
WILLIAM MACKENZIE, 5th Earl of Seaforth, who joined in the rising of 1715, and was attainted. He m. 22 April, 1715, Mary, only dau. and her heir of Nicholas Kennet, Esq., of Coxhow, in Northumberland; and dying in 1740, left (with a dau., Frances, wife of the Hon. John Gordon, of Kenmure) a son,
KENNETH, Lord Fortrose, M.P., for Rosshire in 1747 and 1754; who m. 11 September, 1741, Lady Mary Stewart, dau. of Alexander, Earl of Galloway; and d. in 1761, leaving (with six daus., Margaret, m. to William Webb, of London; Mary, m. to Henry Howard, Esq., father by her of Kenneth Alexander, Earl of Effingham; Agnes, m. to J Douglas, Esq.; Catherine, m. to Thomas Griffin Tarpley, Esq.; Frances, m. to Joseph Wall, Esq.; and Euphemia, m. to William Stewart, Esq., of Castle Stewart, M.P. for Wigtonshire) a son,
KENNETH MACKENZIE, who was raised to the peerage of Ireland, 18 November, 1766, as Viscount Fortrose, co. Wicklow, and further advanced, 3 December, 1771, to be EARL OF SEAFORTH, in that kingdom. His lordship m. Lady Caroline Stanhope, and had an only child, CAROLINE, m. to Comte Melfort. Lord Seaforth d. in 1781, when his honours became EXTINCT. At the decease of the Irish Earl of Seaforth, the family estates were purchased by his lordship's cousin and heir male,
COL. THOMAS-FREDERICK MACKENZIE-HUMBERSTON, a gallant and highly distinguished military officer, who was killed in the East Indies in 1783, in the twenty-eighth year of his age. His brother and heir,
FRANCIS HUMBERSTON-MACKENZIE, Esq., b. 9 June, 1754, inherited the Seaforth and Humberston estates, and was

created a peer of Great Britain, as LORD SEAFORTH, *Baron Mackenzie, of Kintail, co. Ross*, 26 October, 1797. His lordship attained the rank of lieutenant-general in the army. He *m.* 22 April, 1782, Mary, dau. of Baptist Proby, D.D., dean of Lichfield: and *d.* in 1815, having had (with four sons, who *d.* before him *unm.*), six daus., viz.,

MARY-ELIZABETH-FREDERICA,* *m.* 1st, 6 November, 1804. to Vice-Admiral Sir Samuel Hood, Bart., who *d. s. p.* 24 December, 1814; and 2ndly, to the Right Hon, James-Alexander Stewart, who assumed the additional surname of MACKENZIE, and *d.* 24 September, 1843. The Hon. Mrs. Stewart Mackenzie *d.* 28 November, 1862.
Frances-Catherine, *d.* 24 February, 1840.
Caroline, *d.* in 1823.
Charlotte-Elizabeth, *d.* 1 September, 1857.
Augusta-Anne, *d.* 16 March, 1856.
Helen-Anne, *m.* 2 January, 1821, Joshua-Henry Mackenzie, Esq., Lord of Session in Scotland, by the title of Lord Mackenzie, and *d.* 17 November, 1852.

His lordship *d.* 11 January, 1815, when his honours became EXTINCT.

Arms—Az., a stag's head, cabossed, or.

MACKENZIE—EARL OF CROMARTY.

By Letters Patent, dated 1 January, 1703.

Lineage.

This was a branch of the ancient family of Mackenzie of Kintail, founded by
SIR RODERICK MACKENZIE, Knt. of Tarbat (2nd son of Colin Mackenzie, of Kintail, and brother of Kenneth, 1st Lord Mackenzie, of Kintail), who *m.* Margaret, dau. and heir of Torquil Macleod, of Lewes, and thereupon added to his armorial bearing the achievement of Macleod; namely, "or, a rock in flames, ppr." Sir Roderick *d.* in September, 1626, having had issue,

JOHN, his successor.
Kenneth, of Scatwell, ancestor of the present SIR JAMES JOHN-RANDALL MACKENZIE, Bart.
Colin.
Alexander, of Bellone.
Margaret, *m.* to Sir John Mac Donald, Bart., of Slate

He was *s.* by his eldest son,
JOHN MACKENZIE, Esq. of Tarbat, who was created a baronet of Nova Scotia, 21 May, 1628. Sir John *m.* Margaret, dau. and co-heir of Sir George Erskine, of Innerteil, by whom he had, with other issue,

GEORGE, his successor.
Roderick, of Preston Hall, M.P. for Cromarty in 1700, and for Fortrose in 1703, in which year he was constituted one of the senators of the college of Justice, as Lord Prestonhall, which office he resigned in favour of his nephew, Sir James Mackenzie, of Roystoun, in 1710.

Sir John was *s.* by his elder son,
SIR GEORGE MACKENZIE, 2nd baronet, who, for the good services he had rendered to CHARLES II., during his Majesty's exile and the Restoration, was made by that monarch one of the judges of Session, clerk register, sworn of the privy council, and constituted justice general. His lordship was elevated to the peerage by JAMES II., 15 April, 1685, in the dignities of Lord Macleod and Castlehaven, and Viscount of Tarbat. At the Revolution he went up to court and was well received by WILLIAM; but his arbitrary proceedings in the former reigns had rendered him so unpopular in Scotland, that his name was not included in the new commission of lords of Session, 1 November, 1689. He was, however, restored to his office of lord clerk register in 1692, from which he retired in four years afterwards upon a pension of £400 per annum. On the accession of Queen ANNE, Lord Tarbat was sent for to court, and created by letters patent, dated 1 January, 1703, Lord Macleod and Castlehaven, Viscount of Tarbat, and EARL OF CROMARTY, with remainder to his heirs male and of entail.

---

* To this lady Sir Walter Scott addressed the last verse of his *Farewell to Mackenzie*—
  "And thou, gentle dame, who must bear, to thy grief,
  For thy clan and thy country, the cares of a chief,
  Whom brief rolling moons in six changes have left,
  Of thy husband, and father, and brethren bereft;
  Thine ear of affection how sad is the hail
  That salute, thee, the Heir of the line of Kintail."

317

He was at the same time appointed one of the principal secretaries of state, which office he soon after, on account of his great age, exchanged for that of lord justice general, and finally retired in 1710, after zealously promoting the Union by his parliamentary influence, as well as his writings. His lordship *m.* 1st, Anne, dau. of Sir James Sinclair, Bart., of Mey, by whom he had, with four daus. (Margaret, *m.* to Sir David Bruce; Elizabeth, *m.* to Sir George Broun, Bart., of Colstoun; Jean, *m.* to Sir James Stewart, Bart. of Balcaskie; and Anne, *m.* to the Hon. John Sinclair, of Murkle), three sons,

JOHN, who *s.* as 2nd Earl of Cromarty.
Kenneth, of Cromarty, created a baronet in 1704.
James, created a baronet in 1704 Upon the resignation of his uncle, Lord Prestonhall, he was appointed one of the senators of the college of Justice, and a lord of Justiciary, under the title of Lord Royston.

The eldest son,
JOHN MACKENZIE, 2nd Earl of Cromarty, was father (by Mary, his 2nd wife, eldest dau. of Patrick, 3rd Lord Elibank) of GEORGE MACKENZIE, 3rd Earl of Cromarty, who *m.* in 1724, Isabel, dau. of Sir William Gordon, Bart., of Invergordon, and had issue,

I. JOHN, Lord M'Leod, *m.* Margery, eldest dau. of James, 16th Lord Forbes. and *d. s. p.* 2 April, 1789. His widow *m.* John, 4th Duke of Atholl.
II. William, *d.* aged seven years, in 1736.
III. George, lieut.-col. of the 71st regiment of foot; *d. unm.* 4 June, 1787.
I. Isabella, *m.* in January, 1760, to George, 6th Lord Elibank. Her ladyship inherited the estates of the Cromarty family in 1796; and *d.* 28 December, 1801, leaving two daus., her co-heirs, viz.,
  1 Maria, *m.* to Edward Hay, Esq. of Newhall (brother of the 7th Marquess of Tweeddale), who thereupon assumed the additional surname of McKENZIE. Mr. Hay-Mackenzie left at his decease a son,
  John Hay-Mackenzie, Esq., of Newhall, Cromarty, who *m.* Anne, 3rd dau. of Sir James Gibson-Craig, Bart., and dying in 1849, left an only child and heiress, Anne, present Duchess of Sutherland, created Countess of Cromartie 21 October, 1861 (*see* BURKE's *Extant Peerage*).
  2 Isabella.
II. Mary, *m.* 1st, to Capt. Clarke; 2ndly, to Thomas Drayton, Esq.; and 3rdly, to John Ainslie, Esq.
III. Anne, *m.* 1st, to the Hon. Edmond Atkins; and 2ndly, to John Murray, Esq., M.D.
IV. Caroline, *m.* 1st, to Mr. Drane; and 2ndly, to Walter Hunter, Esq. of Polmood.
V. Jean.
VI. Margaret, *m.* to John Glassford.
VII. Augusta, *m.* to Sir William Murray, Bart.

Lord Cromarty and his eldest son, Lord Macleod, having taken an active part in the rising of 1745, and being both made prisoners in the field, were tried, convicted, and attainted of high treason, but their lives were spared. The honours, however, became forfeited; the earl was permitted to reside in England, and his son obtained leave in 1750, to accept a commission in the Swedish service, of which kingdom he was created Count Cromarty, &c. He returned in 1777, raised two battalions of highlanders, and became colonel of the 71st foot, with which he served in India, with the local rank of major-general. His lordship came home in 1784, when his forfeited estates were restored to him, and he *d.* in 1789 without issue. For more ample details of the Earls of Cromarty, *see* BURKE's *Extant Peerage*.

MACLELLAN—LORD KIRKCUDBRIGHT.

By Letters Patent, dated 25 May, 1633.

Lineage.

The Maclellans were anciently sheriffs of Galloway and Barons of Bomble; but
SIR PATRICK MACLELLAN, nephew, maternally, of the Lord Gray, happening to side with his kinsman, Lord Herries, against the Earl of Douglas, was besieged by that nobleman in his castle of Raeberry, and put to death; whereupon the Maclellans, without warrant or authority, making reprisal on the lands of Douglas, in Galloway, the office of sheriff and barony of Bomble became forfeited to the crown; but the latter was recovered, and tradition assigns the following circumstance as the cause :—In the reign of JAMES II., of Scotland, a troop of gipsies, coming from Ireland, so infested the county of Galloway, that a royal proclamation issued, offering the barony o Bomble to any person who should bring the captain,

dead or alive, before the king, an exploit which was accomplished by the Laird of Bombie's son, who carried the marauder's head upon the point of his sword to his Majesty; whence, to perpetuate the affair, he assumed that figure for his crest, with the motto of "Think on."

THOMAS MACLELLAN, of Bondby, the direct ancestor of the Lords Kirkcudbright, m. Agnes, dau. of Sir James Dunbar, of Mochrum, and d. about 1504, having had three sons,

    I. WILLIAM, of whom presently.
    II. GILBERT, of whom hereafter.
    III.ᵈ John of Auchlean, whose male line becoming EXTINCT his estate returned to the family.

The eldest son,

SIR WILLIAM MACLELLAN, of Bombie, fell at the battle of Flodden, 9 September, 1513, leaving by Elizabeth Mure, his wife, a son and successor,

THOMAS MACLELLAN, of Bombie, who was killed in the high street of Edinburgh, 11 July. 1526, by the Barons of Drumlanrig, and Lochinvar, leaving a son,

SIR THOMAS MACLELLAN, of Bombie, who m. Helen, dau. of Sir James Gordon, of Lochinvar, by whom he had a son,

SIR THOMAS MACLELLAN, of Bombie, who d. in July, 1597, and was buried in the church of Kirkcudbright. He m. Grisel Maxwell, dau. of John Lord Herries, and had three sons,

    I. ROBERT (Sir), his heir.
    II. William, of Glenshannock. father of THOMAS. 2nd baron.
    III. John, of Bourg, father of JOHN; 3rd baron, and of William of Auchlean.

The eldest son,

SIR ROBERT MACLELLAN; knight, gentleman of the bedchamber to the two first English sovereigns of the house of Stuart, was created, 25 May, 1633, BARON KIRKCUDBRIGHT, with remainder to his heirs male bearing his name and arms. His lordship m. Margaret, dau. of Sir Matthew Campbell, of Loudoun, by whom he had an only dau. Anne, m. to Sir Robert Maxwell, of Orchardtoun. The baron m. 2ndly, Mary, dau. of Hugh, Viscount Airds; but d. in 1641, without male issue when the barony devolved according to the limitation of the patent, upon his nephew,

THOMAS MACLELLAN, 2nd baron; who m. Janet, dau. of William, 1st Earl of Queensberry : but dying s. p. in 1647, was s. by his 1st cousin,

JOHN MACLELLAN, 3rd baron. This nobleman raised a regiment of foot, at his own charge, for the service of King CHARLES II.; whose train he helped to support at his Majesty's coronation, at Scone, in 1651. His lordship m. Anne, dau. of Sir Robert Maxwell; and dying in 1664, was s. by his son,

WILLIAM MACLELLAN; 4th baron; who d. in minority, in 1669, when the whole estate was carried off by his father's creditors, so that when the succession opened to the deceased lord's cousin, John Maclellan, there being nothing left to support the dignity, the sa d John never assumed it, nor did his brother James who succeeded him, whereby the Lords Kirkcudbright do not appear as sitting in parliament from the time of John, the 3rd lord. But the right of the collateral male heir was so indisputably known and acknowledged, that at the Union, this peerage was considered as a subsisting one, and as such preserv d in the roll.

JAMES MACLELLAN, son of William Maclellan, of Auchlean, and nephew of John, 3rd lord, b. in 1661, did not assume the title of Baron Kirkcudbright until the great struggle for a representative of the Scottish peerage between the Earls of Eglinton and Aberdeen, in 1721, and then his right of voting was protested against; but he voted at all elections subsequently, until 1729, when he was served nearest and lawful male heir to his uncle, Lord Kirkcudbright. His lordship d. in 1730, leaving three daus. only (viz., 1 Margaret, m. to Samuel Brown of Mollance, 2 Mary, d. unm., and 3 Janet, m. to William Maxwell, of Milton), whereupon the barony passed to the next male heir.

WILLIAM MACLELLAN, of Bourness, who experienced great difficulty in establishing his right; and at the general election, of 1741, himself and his competitor, James, eldest son of the deceased Sir Samuel Maclellan, provost of Edinburgh, voted as Lords Kirkcudbright; nor was it confirmed during his lifetime; his lordship left by Margaret Murray, his wife, a son,

JOHN MACLELLAN, Esq., a colonel in the army, who, following up his deceased father's proceedings, had his right as 7th Baron Kirkcudbright. confirmed by the House of Lords, 3 May, 1773. His lordship m. Miss Banister, of the Isle of Wight, by whom he had issue,

    SHOLTO-HENRY, his heir.
    CAMDEN-GRAY, 9.h baron.
    Elizabeth, m. in 1795, to Finlay Ferguson, Esq.

His lordship d. 24 December, 1801, in his seventy-third year, and was s. by his eldest son,

SHOLTO-HENRY MACLELLAN, 8th baron, b. 1771, who m. in 1820, Miss Cantes; but d. s. p., 16 April, 1827, when the title devolved upon his brother.

CAMDEN-GRAY MACLELLAN, 9th Lord Kirkcudbright, b. 20 April, 1774; who m. Sarah, dau. of the late Colonel Thomas Gorges, and had an only dau. and heir,

    CAMDEN-ELIZABETH, m. in 1832. to James-Staunton Lambert, Esq., of Creg Clare, co. Galway, M.P. for that shire, and has issue,

        Walter Maclellan, captain 41st regiment, b. 31 August, 1833.
        Charles-James, b. 11 October. 1837 ; d 6 February, 1855.
        Thomas Camden, b. 5 October, 1841, an officer 29th regiment.
        Robert. b. 4 February, 1844.
        James-Henry, b. 6 September. 1851.
        Sarah-Elizabeth, m. 2 October, 1858, to Charles-Edward Lewis, Esq., of St. Pierre, Monmouthshire.
        Harriette, m. 2 October, 1856, Somerset-Molyneux Clarke, Esq., captain 93rd highlanders
        Katherine-Isabella, b. 21 Sept. 1839; d. 4 Dec. 1854.

Lord Kircudbright d. at Bruges, 19 April, 1832, and since his decease the title has remained DORMANT.

Arms—Arg., two chevrons, sa.

MACNEILL—BARON COLONSAY.

(*See* ADDENDA.)

MAGENNIS—VISCOUNT MAGENNIS OF IVEAGH.

Created by Letters Patent, dated 18 July, 1623.

Lineage.

"The Magennises," says Mr. D'Alton (King JAMES's *Army List*) "were from very ancient time, territorial Lords of Iveagh, in Dalaradia (co. Down), claiming their descent from the famous warrior, Connall Cearnach, and ranking as the head of the Clanna Rory. In 1314, when EDWARD II. sought the aid of the magnates of Ireland, he directed an especial letter missive to Admilis 'Mac Anegus, Duci Hibernicorum de Onenagh,' he being then the Magennis. In 1380, when Edmund Mortimer, who had m. the grand-dau. of EDWARD III., came over to Ireland, various native chiefs waited upon him, and amongst them, Art Magennis, the Lord of Iveagh, 'who,' says the Four Masters, 'was treacherously taken prisoner at Mortimer's residence, in consequence of which the Irish, and many of the English themselves, became afraid to place any confidence in him, or trust themselves to his power."

SIR ARTHUR MAGENNIS, Knt , of Rathfrilan, co. Down, was raised to the peerage of Ireland, as Viscount Magennis, of Iveagh, in the same co., 18 July, 1623. He m. Sarah, dau. of Hugh O'Neile, Earl of Tyrone, and had issue

    I. HUGH, his heir.
    II. Con (Sir), Knt., m. Evelyn, dau. of Ever Magennis, Esq , of Castle-Wellan, co. Down.
    III. Arthur.
    IV. Daniel.
    V. Rory.
    I. Rose, m. 1st, to Moelmurry Oge O'Reilly ; and 2ndly, to Melaghlin O'Kelly, of Aughrim, co. Galway.
    II. Evelyn. m. to Sir Alexander MacDonnell, of Moyane, Bart.
    III. Elizabeth.

The 1st Lord Magennis, of Iveagh, d. 7 May, 1629, and was buried at Drumbalong, 15 June following. His eldest son and heir,

HUGH MAGENNIS, 2nd Viscount, b. 1599, m. Mary, dau. of Sir John Bellew of Castleton, and d. April, 1630, leaving issue, a dau., the wife of Lieut.-Gen. Lee, and three sons, successively viscounts. The eldest,

ART MAGENNIS, 3rd Viscount, was buried 1 May, 1683, in St. Catherine's Church, Dublin; his next brother,

HUGH MAGENNIS, 4th Viscount, was buried 5 December, 1684, in the same church, and was s. by his brother,

BRYAN MAGENNIS, 5th Viscount Magennis, of Iveagh, who m. in 1689, Lady Margaret Burke, dau. of William, 7th Earl of Clanricarde; but d. s. p. in 1693. His lordship's widow m. 2ndly, Thomas Butler, Esq., of Kilcash.

"At the close of the war of the Revolution in Ireland (we again quote from Mr. D'Alton's *Army List of* JAMES II.), Lord Iveagh did not accompany the Irish army to France, but entered the Imperial or Austrian service, with a choice battalion of 500, part of 2,000 Irish troops of King JAMES's old army, who were landed from Cork at Hamburgh, in June, 1692.

Another portion of this sept did, however, go to France, and was there embodied with followers of M'Mahon, Maguire, and other Ulster regiments."

Arms—Vert, a lion rampant. or, armed and langued, gu. on a chief, arg., a dexter hand, gu.

MAGUIRE—BARON MAGUIRE

By Letters Patent, dated 3 March, 1627.

Lineage.

THOMAS MOR MAGUIRE, Lord or Prince of Fermanagh, and chief of the name of Maguire, living 1400. *m.* Margaret, dau. of Con O'Neil, prince of Tyrone, and *d.* 1430, having had two s ms (as to whose relative seniority the authorities differ), viz.,

I. PHILIP, who *m.* and had two sons,

John, chief of his name, *d. s. p.* 1503.
Bryan, of Tempo, co. Fermanagh, father of
Cuconnaught, of Tempo, father of
John, who *d.* 1566, and of
Cuconnaught, chief of his name, *d.* 1589. He *m.* the dau. of O'Neill, Earl of Tyrone, and had issue,
Hugh, chief of his name, the famous HUGH MAGUIRE of the reign of ELIZABETH, killed by Sir Warham St. Leger, at Kinsale in 1602.
Cuconnaught, of Tempo, chief of his name, *d. s. p.* at Genoa, in Italy, 12 August, 1608, leaving a son (or by another account a brother),
Bryan of Tempo, chief of his name, who *d.* 24 April, 1655, having had a son,
Hugh, who *d.v.p.*, having *m.* the dau. of Philip McHugh O'Reilly, chief of the district of Breffney, and was father of
Constantine or Cuconnaught, of Tempo, slain at the battle of Aughrim, in the service of King JAMES, 23 July, 1691. He *m.* Mary, dau. of Ever Magennis, of Castlewellan, co. Down, Esq., and had a son,
Bryan of Tempo, Esq., who *m.* Bridget, dau. of James Nugent, Esq., of Coolamber, and *d.* 13 October, 1712, leaving *inter alios* a son,
Philip of Tempo (heir of his brother, Colonel Hugh Maguire, who *m.* the Dowager Lady Cathcart), who *d.* 1789, having *m.* Frances, dau. of Nicholas Morres, Esq., of Lateragh, co. Tipperary, and had *inter alios* a son,
Hugh, *d.* 1 October, 1800, having *m.* Phœbe, dau. of Geo. Macnamara, of Cong, co. Mayo, Esq., and by her (who *d.* 19 August, 1829,) had issue,
1 Constantine Maguire, of Tempo, chief of his name, murdered in 1834.
2 Brian, a very remarkable character, of whom a memoir may be found in "*The Vicissitudes of Families.*"
3 Stephen, who enlisted in the British service, and *d.* soon after broken hearted.
1 Frances.
2 Stephania.
3 Mary Creagh, *m.* to the Noble Marco de Zigno of Padua.
4 Eliza.
5 Catherine.

II. THOMAS.

The 2nd, or, according to some, the elder son,
THOMAS OGE MAGUIRE, Prince of Fermanagh, circa 1450, *d.* 1480. His direct descendant,
SIR BRYAN MAGUIRE, Knt., was created a peer of Ireland by King CHARLES I., by the title of LORD MAGUIRE, BARON OF ENNISKILLEN, co. Fermanagh, 3 March, 1627, with limitation of the dignity to the heirs male of his body lawfully begotten. He *m.* Rose, dau. of Art MacAvernan O'Neill, of Carrickestikin, co. Armagh, and had issue,

I. CONNOR, his heir, of whom presently.
II. Rory (Colonel), *m.* Deborah Hassett, relict of Audley Mervyn, and had a son,
RORY OGE MAGUIRE, a colonel in the army, *m.* the widow of his cousin, Mary. dau. of Philip McHugh O'Reilly, of Ballynacargy, co. Cavan.

III. Bryan.   IV. Thomas.
I. Rose.   II. Eleanor
III. Sarah.   IV Anne.

349

The 1st Lord Maguire of Enniskillen *d.* 15 December, 1633, and was buried in Aughive, co. Fermanagh. His elder son,
CONNOR MAGUIRE, 2nd Lord Maguire and Baron of Enniskillen, was one of the chief leaders in the rebellion of 1641, and one of its chief victims. He was tried for high treason in London, 10 February, 1644, and being found guilty was hung at Tyburn. With him, the title became ATTAINTED. He *m.* Mary, dau. of Thomas Fleming, of Castle Fleming, and had a son. Several of the Maguire family, many of whom served in foreign service, assumed, and were styled Lords Maguire. O'Callaghan (*History of the Irish Brigades*), and D'Alton (*Army List of King James II.*) give particulars of these later Maguires.

Arms—Vert, a horse. thereon a man in complete armour, holding in his dexter hand a sword, all ppr.

MAHON—BARON HARTLAND.

By Letters Patent, dated 30 July, 1800.

Lineage.

NICHOLAS MAHON, Esq., a distinguished person in the civil wars, *m.* Magdalene, dau. of Arthur French, Esq., of Movilla Castle, co. Galway, and had surviving issue,

I. JOHN, his successor.
II. Peter, dean of Elphin; *m.* Catherine, grand-dau. of Sir Arthur Gore, Bart.
III. Nicholas, *m.* 14 February, 1709, Eleanor, dau. of Henry, 5th Lord Blayney, and left
1 Nicholas, *m.* Mary, only dau. of Cadwallader, 7th Lord Blayney
2 Elizabeth, *m:* to Charles, 9th Lord Blayney.

Mr. Mahon *d.* 10 October, 1680, and was *s.* by his eldest son,
JOHN MAHON, Esq., who *m.* 11 February, 1697, Eleanor, dau. of Sir Thomas Butler, Bart., and was *s.* by his eldest surviving son,
THOMAS MAHON, Esq., M.P., *b.* in 1701. This gentleman *m.* 16 January, 1735, Jane, eldest dau. of Maurice. Lord Brandon, and sister of William, Earl of Glandore, and had issue,
MAURICE, his successor.
Thomas, in holy orders, *b.* 3 June, 1740: *m.* Honoria, 2nd dau. of Denis Kelly, Esq., of Castle Kelly, and *d.* 19 March, 1811, leaving issue,
Thomas, *b.* in 1785; *m.* Catherine, 3rd dau. of the Hon. Robert Annesley, and *d. s. p.* in March, 1825.
Denis, *b.* 12 March, 1787; late major in the army; *m.* 17 September, 1822, Henrietta, dau. of the Right Rev. Charles Bathurst, late bishop of Norwich, and had issue,
Thomas, *b.* 30 October, 1831; *d. unm.*
Grace-Catherine, *m.* Henry-Sandford Pakenham, Esq., who assumed, by royal license, 26 March, 1847, the additional name and arms of Mahon.
Major Mahon, who *s.* as heir-at-law to the last Lord Hartland, was barbarously murdered in 1847.
John, *b.* in 1793; *m.* in April, 1831. his first cousin, Leonora, dau. of the Rev. Armstrong Kelly, of Castle Kelly, and had issue,
Thomas-Kelly, *b.* in April, 1832.
John, *b.* in April, 1833.
Denis, *b.* in December, 1835.
Leonora.
Anne, *m.* to William Richardson, Esq., of Prospect House, co. Louth.

Anne, *m.* to David Ross, Esq. of Beaufort.
Jane, *m.* to George Knox, Esq.
Theodosia, *m.* to Conolly M'Causland, Esq.

Mr. Mahon *d.* 13 January, 1782, and was *s.* by his eldest son,
MAURICE MAHON, Esq., *b.* in 1738, M.P.; who was created a peer of Ireland, as BARON HARTLAND, 30 July, 1800. He *m.* 1 June, 1765, Catherine, youngest dau. of Stephen, 1st Viscount Mountcashell, by whom (who *d.* in March, 1834, aged ninety-five) he had issue,

THOMAS, his successor.
Stephen, lieutenant-general in the army; *b* 6 February, 1768; and *d.* 27 May, 1828.
MAURICE, last peer.

His lordship *d.* 4 January, 1819, and was *s.* by his eldest son,
THOMAS, 2nd baron, *b.* 2 August, 1766; a lieutenant-general

in the army; *m.* 16 August, 1811, Catharine. eldest dau. of James Topping, Esq., of Whatcroft Hall, co. Chester, but had no issue. He *d.* 8 December, 1835, and was *s.* by his brother, MAURICE MAHON, 3rd Baron Hartland, in holy orders, of Strokestown, co. Roscommon, *b.* 6 October, 1772, who *m.* 24 November, 1813, Jane-Isabella, dau. of William Hume, Esq., of Humewood, M.P. for the co. of Wicklow, but by her (who *d.* 12 December, 1838) had no issue. He *d.* 11 November, 1845, when the title became EXTINCT.

Arms—Or, a lion rampant, az., armed and langued. gu.

MAITLAND — DUKE OF LAUDERDALE, EARL OF GUILDFORD.

Dukedom, by Letters Patent, dated 2 May, 1672.
Earldom, by Letters Patent, dated 25 June, 1674.

Lineage.

JOHN MAITLAND, 2nd Earl of Lauderdale, in the peerage of Scotland, having distinguished himself by his zealous support of the royal cause during the civil wars, was advanced to the Scottish titles of *Marquess of March* and DUKE OF LAUDER-DALE, 1672, and created a peer of England, 25 June, 1674, as *Baron Petersham*, and EARL OF GUILDFORD. This nobleman was a conspicuous public character in the reign of CHARLES II., and under the title of Lauderdale, supplied the letter L to the CABAL administration. His grace was knight of the Garter, and high commissioner of the church of Scotland. The duke *m.* 1st, Anne, 2nd dau. and co-heir of Alexander, Earl of Home, and had an only dau. and heiress,

ANNE, who *m.* John Hay, 2nd Marquess of Tweeddale.

He *m.* 2ndly, Elizabeth, Countess of Dysart, dau. and heir of William Murray, Earl of Dysart, and widow of Sir Lionel Tolle-mache, Bart., but by her had no issue. His grace *d.* 24 August, 1682, when the English Barony of Petersham and Earldom of Guildford, with the Scottish Dukedom of Lauderdale and Mar-quessate of March, became EXTINCT, and his other honours devolved upon his brother, the Hon. Charles Maitland, as 3rd Earl of Lauderdale.

Arms—Or, a lion rampant dechaussée, within a double tres-sure, flory, counter-flory, gu.

MALISE—EARL OF STRATHERN.

Lineage.

MALISE, or MALLUS, Earl of Strathern, is named among those who witnessed the foundation of the priory of Scone, by ALEXANDER I., in 1115. He signalized himself eminently at the battle of the Standard, 22 August, 1138, when he said to King DAVID I., "I wear no armour, but they who do, will not advance beyond me this day," (*Wood's Douglas*). He was father of

FERQUHARD, FERCHARD, or FERETH, 2nd Earl of Strathern, who is mentioned by Fordun as having leagued with five other earls, against MALCOLM IV. He witnessed a charter of that monarch to the monastery of Scone, 1160. He *d.* leaving two sons,

GILBERT, 3rd Earl of Strathern.
Malise, designed brother of Gilbert, Earl of Strathern, in the foundation charter of Inchaffray.

GILBERT, 3rd Earl of Strathern, the elder son, founded the monastery of Inchaffray, Insula Missarum, the Isle of Masses, in Strathern, and largely endowed it for canons regular. He had a son and successor,

ROBERT, 4th Earl of Strathern, who witnessed a charter of ALEXANDER II., of the Earldom of Fife, in the eleventh year of his reign, 1224-5. When the differences between that monarch and HENRY II. were accommodated by the cardinal legate, at York, in 1287, the Earl of Strathern was one of the witnesses

350

to the treaty. He *d.* before 1244, leaving two daus. (Annabella, *m.* to Sir David Graham, ancestor of the Duke of Montrose. who got with her the Barony of Kincardine; and Lucia, *m.* to Sir William Sinclair), and a son,

MALISE, 5th Earl of Strathern, who was one of the guarantees of a treaty between ALEXANDER II. and HENRY III., 1244. He *m.* a dau. of Eugene, of Ergadia, relict of the King of Man, and had a son,

MALISE, 6th Earl of Strathern, who was one of the guaran-tees of the marriage treaty of Margaret of Scotland with ERIC, king of Norway, 1281. He sat in the parliament at Scone, 5 February, 1283-4, when the Scottish nobles became bound to acknowledge Margaret of Norway as their sovereign in the event of the demise of ALEXANDER III. He was one of the nobles summoned to attend EDWARD I. into Gascony, 1 Septem-ber, 1294; and was in the Scottish army that invaded England in March, 1296, for which it appears that his estates were sequestered. He, however, again swore fealty to EDWARD, 13 July, 1296, when the English monarch issued an order to the sheriff of Perth to repone Maria (quæ uxor Malisii comitis de Strathern) in her lands. Malise, Earl of Strathern, is said to have *m.* Lady Egidia Cumyn, dau. of Alexander, 2nd Earl of Buchan, by whom he had issue,

MALISE, 7th Earl of Strathern.
Mary, *m.* to Sir John Moray, of Drumsargard.

MALISE, 7th Earl of Strathern, the only son, was one of the adherents of ROBERT I. Malisius, comes de Stratheryne, signed the letter to the Pope, asserting the independence of Scotland, 1320. According to Knighton, he fell at the battle of Halidon-hill, 19 July, 1333; and his name occurs in the list of those slain in that engagement, in Dalrymple's Annals. This, however, appears to be a mistake. EDWARD BALIOL granted the Earldom of Strathern to John de Warren, Earl of Warren and Surrey; and 2 March, 1334, addressed a letter to Henry de Bellomonte, Earl of Boghan (Buchan), indicating that Malise, Earl of Stra-thern, was then alive. Considerable difficulties occur re-specting the marriage and issue of Malise, Earl of Strathern. Marjory de Muscocampo (Muschamp), Countess of Strathern, was probably the 1st wife of Malise, Earl of Strathern; per-haps his stepmother, which is most consistent with chronology. Johanna, dau. of Sir John Menteth appears to have been his 2nd wife, and mother of Johanna, Countess of Surrey and Stra-thern, who, according to Crawford, was the Countess of Stra-thern engaged in the conspiracy against ROBERT I., in 1320. Isabella, dau. of Magnus, Earl of Caithness and Orkney, ap-pears to have been his third wife, and it would seem that he had by her four daus., one *m.* to William, 7th Earl of Ross; Isabel, *m.* to Sir William Sinclair, of Roslin; Matilda de Stra-thern, mother of Alexander de L'Arde; and the 4th, *m.* to Reginald Chene, mother of Mariot Chene; and that these four daus. inherited the Earldom of Caithness and Orkney, in right of their mother, untouched by their father's forfeiture. *Wood's Douglas.*

The Earldom of Strathern was, by DAVID II., granted to SIR MAURICE MORAY, of Drumsargard, Lord of Clydesdale, nephew of Malise, 7th Earl of Strathern. He joined the Steward of Scotland at the siege of Perth, 1339, and fell at the battle of Durham, 17 October, 1346, *s. p.*, when the Earldom of Strathern reverted to the crown.

MALONE.

(See O'MALONE.*)*

MALONE—BARON SUNDERLIN.

By Letters Patent, dated 30 June, 1785.

Lineage.

EDMOND MALONE, Esq., of Ballynahown, son of Edmond Malone, Esq., grandson of Edmond Malone, Esq., by his 1st wife, a dau. of Coghlan, and great-grandson, by Margaret, his wife, dau. of Richard Dalton, Esq., of Miltown, of Edmond Malone, Esq., of Ballynahown, living *temp.* ELIZABETH, was of an ancient Irish family, deriving their descent from the O'CONORS, Kings of Connaught, which name they originally bore : he *m.* in 1644, Mary, dau. of Brassel Fox, of Kilcoursy, and had two sons,

I. EDMOND, of Ballynahown, who *m.* in 1674, Anne, dau. of Thomas L'Estrange, Esq., of Moystown, in the King's co.,

MAL

and had, with a dau., Mary (wife of Anthony Daly, Esq.), three sons, viz.,

1 RICHARD, of Ballynahown, ancestor of the MALONES, of Ballynahown. •

2 HENRY, of Litter, in the King's co., d. in 1739, leaving by Margaret L'Estrange, his wife, two daus., his co-heirs, viz., ANNE, m. to Richard Malone, Esq., M.P., and ELIZABETH m. to Henry L'Estrange, Esq., of Moystown, M.P. for Banagher.

3 Anthony, who m. Bridget, dau. of Henry Talbot, Esq., and had two sons,

Richard, who m. Mary, dau. and co-heir, of Acheson Moore, Esq., of Ravella, co. Tyrone, and relict of Roger Palmer, Esq., and d. s. p.

Edmond, major, 47th regiment, who m. Mary, eldest dau. of Richard Malone, Esq., and widow of John O'Conor, Esq., and had a son and two daus.,

Anthony, who d. in 1787.

Elizabeth, m. to Henry, 6th son of Ralph Sneyd, Esq., of Keele, co. Stafford.

Maria.

II. ANTHONY, of whose line we have to treat.

The 2nd son,

ANTHONY MALONE, Esq., m. in 1673, Mary, eldest dau. of John Reily, Esq., of Lismore, in Cavan, by Mary, his wife, dau. of Hon. Lucas Dillon, 2nd son of James, 1st Earl of Roscommon, and was father of

RICHARD MALONE, Esq., of Baronston, co. Westmeath, b. 1674, who enjoyed for a long series of years the highest reputation as a lawyer and orator. He m. 20 April, 1698, Marcella. dau. of Redmond Moledy, Esq., and had issue,

ANTHONY (Right Hon.), b. 5 December, 1700, M.P., co. Westmeath, and like his father, one of the brightest ornaments of the Irish bar. In 1740 he was appointed prime serjeant, in 1754 dismissed, and in 1757 appointed chancellor of the Exchequer, from which latter office he was removed in 1760. He m. in 1733, Rose, dau. of Sir Ralph Gore, Bart., speaker of the House of Commons; but d. s. p., 8 May, 1776.

EDMOND, of whom presently.

Richard, 2nd serjeant-at-law, and M.P for Fore, who d. in July, 1759, leaving, by Anne, his wife, dau. and co-heir of Henry Malone, Esq., of Litter, four sons and four daus., viz.,

Henry, who m. in 1765, Catherine, dau. of Richard Plunket, Esq., and had with two daus. (Alice and Catherine), a son, Richard.

Richard.   Anthony.

John, who d. soon after his father.

Mary, m. 21 September, 1752, to John O'Connor, Esq., of Mount Pleasant, in the King's co.; and d. 1787, leaving four sons and four daus.: the eldest son, Maurice-Nugent O'Connor, Esq., of Mount Pleasant, d. 1818, leaving four daus., his co-heirs, Catherine, Dowager Countess of Desart; Mary, m. to Hugh M. Tuite, Esq., of Sonna; Julia, d. unm.; and Elizabeth, m. to Rev. Benjamin Morris.

Anne.   Jane.   Frances.

John, d. in 1753, unm.

Mary, m. to Theobald Dillon, Esq., and was mother of Mary, wife of Laurence Cruise, Esq., of Cruisetown, co. Meath.

Margaret, m. to John Hussey, Esq.

Marcella, m. to John Reily, Esq.

Jane, d. unm., in 1756.

The 2nd son,

EDMOND MALONE, b. 16 April, 1704, was constituted, 13 January, 1766, one of the Judges of the Court of Common Pleas in Ireland. He m. 26 May, 1736, Catherine, dau. and heir of Benjamin Collier, Esq., of Buckholts, co. Essex (by Catherine his wife, dau. of Robert Knight, Esq., whose grandson, Robert, was created Baron Luxborough, in 1746, and Earl of Catherlogh, in 1762), and had issue,

RICHARD, his heir.

Edmond, the commentator on Shakspeare, d. 25 May, 1812.

Anthony, } who d. in their infancy.
Benjamin, }

Henrietta.   Catherine.

Mr. Justice Malone, d. 22 April, 1774, and was s. by his son,

RICHARD MALONE, M.P., who was raised to the peerage of Ireland, in 1785, as BARON SUNDERLIN, of Lake Sunderlin, co. Westmeath. His lordship m. in 1778, Dorothea-Philippa, eldest dau. of Godolphin Roper, Esq., of Great Berkhampstead, co. Herts; but d. s. p. in 1816, when the title became EXTINCT.

Arms—Quarterly: 1st and 4th, vert, a lion rampant, or between three mullets, arg.; 2nd and 3rd, arg., on a chev., az., between three demi-unicorns, gu., as many acorns, or.

• Ballynahown, co. Westmeath, is now, by purchase, the property and seat of John Ennis, Esq., M.P.

351

MAL

MALTRAVERS—BARON MALTRAVERS.

By Writ of Summons, dated 6 June, 1330.

Lineage.

Although none of this family were barons by tenure, or had summons to parliament before the time of the 3rd EDWARD, yet were they anciently persons of note. Referring to NICHOLS' Collectanea for a great deal of curious and authentic information regarding this family of Maltravers, we will commence with

SIR JOHN DE MAUTRAVERS, of Wellcombe, co. Dorset, a joint witness with Sir Walter de Mautravers to a charter between 1160 and 1184; he was father by Alice, his wife, of

JOHN MALTRAVERS, of Sumerford, Cotes, &c., co. Wilts, A.D 1221, who left a son and heir,

SIR JOHN MALTRAVERS, seneschal of the king's household, 1274. He d. 1296, seized, amongst others, of the manors of Lychet and Wychampton, co. Dorset, leaving his son and heir,

SIR JOHN MALTRAVERS, b. 1266, who m. 1st, Alianore ——, by whom he had a son, JOHN, his heir; and 2ndly, Joan, dau. and heir of Sir Walter Folliott, by whom he had three daus. He was made a knight, with Prince Edward and others, by bathing, &c., in 1306, whereupon he attended that prince into Scotland, being of the retinue with Maurice de Berkeley; and the same year he obtained a charter for free warren in all his demesne lands at Lychet-Maltravers, co. Dorset. In the 7th EDWARD II., he was again in the wars of Scotland, and the next year had a military summons to attend the king with horse and arms at Newcastle-upon-Tyne, to restrain the incursions of the Scots: in which year he had a grant for a market weekly on the Tuesday in Limerick, in Ireland, but wherefore does not appear; for although large possessions of his are enumerated in the counties of Dorset, Somerset, Wilts, Gloucester, and Berks, none are mentioned as lying out of England. Sir John d. before 5 July, 1344; his son and heir,

SIR JOHN MALTRAVERS, Knt., was at the battle of Bannockburn, 24 June, 1314, and was there made prisoner. In 1330 being in high estimation with those who were then in power, he was summoned to the parliament held in the 4th EDWARD III., as "John Maltravers, sen." The part which this nobleman is said to have taken in the murder of King EDWARD II., is too well known to need recitation here—enough, that the wretched monarch was removed from the custody of Lord Berkeley, who had treated him with some degree of humanity, and placed under Lord Maltravers and Sir Thomas Gournay, and that while in their charge the king was killed in a most cruel manner at Berkeley Castle. According to the judgment of the House of Peers, Mortimer commanded Gournay and Ogle to perpetrate the deed, and, as Maltravers was condemned by the same parliament which condemned the king's murderers, it was for a different crime, it forms a presumption that he was innocent of this (Lingard) Maltravers fled immediately after into Germany, where he remained for several years, having had judgment of death passed upon him in England for the murder of the Earl of Kent, but in the 19th of the same reign, King EDWARD III. being in Flanders, Lord Maltravers came and made a voluntary surrender of himself to the king, who, in consideration of his services abroad, granted him a safe convoy into England to abide the decision of parliament; in which he had afterwards a full and free pardon (25th EDWARD III.) That was not, however, sufficient—King EDWARD constituted him, soon after, governor of the Isles of Guernsey, Jersey, Alderney, and Sarke. His lordship m. 1st, Ela, dau. of Maurice, Lord Berkeley, and had issue,

JOHN, who was knighted, and in the reign of EDWARD III., had summons to parliament as a Baron, but d. v. p., 13 October, 1360, leaving, by Wenaliana, his wife, a son and two daus.,

HENRY, d. s. p.

Joan, m. 1st, to Sir John de Kaynes, and 2ndly, to Sir Robert Rouse, but d. s. p.

Eleanor, m. 1st, to John Fitz-Alan, 2nd son of Richard, 9th Farl of Arundel, and had issue,

JOHN FITZ-ALAN, who s. to the Barony of Maltravers, and eventually as 11th Earl of Arundel (see Fitz-Alan, Earls of Arundel).

She m. 2ndly, Reginald, Lord Cobham.

Lord Maltravers m. 2ndly, Agnes, dau. of William Bereford, and 1st relict of Sir John Argentine, Knt., and 2ndly, of Sir John Nerford, by whom he had no issue. He d. 16 February 1365.

After the decease of John, Lord Maltravers, the barony passed to his grand dau. (the eventual sole heiress of his deceased son, Sir John Maltravers), Eleanor, wife of the Hon. John Fitz-Alan, whose son, JOHN, was summoned to parliament as Lord Maltravers, and s. as 11th Earl of Arundel—and the Barony of Maltravers has since merged in the superior dignity of Arundel. Lady Mary Fitz-Alan, the dau., and ultimately the sole heiress of Henry, 18th Earl of Arundel, m. Thomas Howard, Duke of Norfolk, and brought the barony and earldom into the Howard family. Those dignities descended to her son Philip, who was attainted in the 32nd ELIZABETH, when the barony fell under the attainder, but it was restored to his son, Thomas Howard, 20th Earl of Arundel, and by act of parliament, 3rd CHARLES I., the Barony of Maltravers, together with those of Fitz-Alan, Clun, and Oswaldestre. was annexed to the title, dignity, and honour of Arundel, and settled upon Thomas Howard, then Earl of Arundel (see FITZ-ALAN, Earls of Arundel).

SR JOHN MALTRAVERS, who m. Elizabeth, dau. and heir of Robert Sifrewast, of Hooke, co. Dorset, and Crowel, co. Oxford, and became ancestor of the Maltravers, of Hooke and Crowel, grandson of Robert Maltravers, who is supposed to have been brother of Sir John Maltravers knighted in 1306. He was father of

JOHN (Sir), of Hooke and Crowel, who m. Elizabeth. dau. and co-heir of Sir William d'Aumerle, and left two daus., viz.,

Matilda. m. 1st, to Peter de la Mare, and 2ndly, to Sir John Dynham. Knt., and d. s. p., 11th HENRY IV.
Elizabeth, m. to Sir Humphrey Stafford, Knt., whose grandson and heir,
SIR HUMPHREY STAFFORD, of Hooke, was slain by Jack Cade's mob, leaving a son,
HUMPHREY STAFFORD, who d. s. p., and was s. his cousin,
HUMPHREY STAFFORD, of Suthwike (see Staffords, of Suthwike).

Arms—Sa , a fret, or, with a file of three points, erm.

MANDEVILLE—EARLS OF ESSEX.

By Special Charter of King STEPHEN.

Lineage.

On the first arrival in England of William, Duke of Normandy, there was amongst his companions a famous soldier, called

GEOFFREY DE MAGNAVIL, so designated from the town of Magnavil, in the duchy, which he then possessed, who obtained as his share in the spoil of conquest, divers fair and widespreading domains, in the cos. Berks, Suffolk, Middlesex, Surrey, Oxford, Cambridge, Herts, Northampton, Warwick, and Essex; whereof Waldene was one, which afterwards became the chief seat of his descendants. He was subsequently made constable of the Tower of London, and continued to execute the duties of that important office for the remainder of his life. This Geoffrey, among other benefactions to the church, founded a Benedictine monastery at Hurley, in Berkshire, conferring upon it the whole lordship of that place, and the woods adjoining thereto. He was s. at his decease by his son,

WILLIAM DE MAGNAVIL, corrupted into MANDEVILLE, who was keeper of the Tower of London. He m. Margaret, only dau. and heiress of Eudo de Rie Dapifer,* and had issue,

GEOFFREY, who inherited from his mother the stewardship of Normandy.
Beatrix, m. 1st, Hugh Talbot, from whom she was divorced, and 2ndly, William de Say.

He was s. at his decease by his son,

GEOFFREY DE MANDEVILLE, who in the 5th year of King STEPHEN, had livery of his inheritance, upon paying the sum of £866 13s. 4d. to the crown; and was advanced by that monarch, from the degree of baron (by special charter, dated at Westminster), to the dignity of EARL of the county of Essex, unto which charter were witnesses: "William de Ipre, Henry de Essex, John, the son of Robert Fitz-Walter, Robert de Newburgh, William de St. Clair, William de Dammartin, Richard Fitz-Urse, and William de Owe;" but notwithstanding this high honour conferred upon him by King STEPHEN, the Empress MAUD, by a more ample charter, made at Oxford, allured him to her party; for she not only conferred whatso-

---

* Dapifer, id est, Steward, to King WILLIAM for Normandy.

ever Geoffrey, his grandfather, or William, his father, ever enjoyed, either in lands, forts, or castles, particularly the Tower of London, with the castle under it, to strengthen and fortify at his pleasure; but bestowed upon him the hereditary sheriffalty of London and Middlesex, as also that of Hertfordshire, with the sole power of trying causes in those counties: for which offices and privileges he paid the sum of £360. Moreover she granted him all the lands of Eudo Dapifer, in Normandy, with his office of steward, as his rightful inheritance, and numerous other valuable immunities, in a covenant witnessed by Robert, Earl of Gloucester, and several other powerful nobles—which covenant contained the singular clause, "that neither the Earl of Anjou. her husband, nor herself, nor her children, would ever make peace with the burgesses of London, but with the consent of him, the said Geoffrey, because they were his mortal enemies." Besides this, he had a second charter, dated at Westminster, re-creating him EARL OF ESSEX, to hold to himself and his heirs, and to have the third penny of the pleas of the sheriffalty, as an earl ought to enjoy in his earldom. Of which proceedings King STEPHEN having information, seized upon the earl in the court, then at St. Alban's, some say after a bloody affray, in which the Earl of Arundel, being thrown into the water with his horse, very narrowly escaped drowning; certain it is, that to regain his liberty, the Earl of Essex was constrained, not only to give up the Tower of London, but his own castles of Walden and Blessey. Wherefore, being transported with wrath, he fell to spoil and rapine, invading the king's demesne lands and others, plundering the abbeys of St. Alban's and Ramsay; which last having surprised at an early hour in the morning, he expelled the monks therefrom, made a fort of the church, and sold their religious ornaments to reward his soldiers; in which depredations he was assisted by his brother-in-law, William de Say, a stout and warlike man, and one Daniel, a counterfeit monk. At last, being publicly excommunicated for his many outrages, he besieged the castle of Burwell, in Kent, and going unhelmed, in consequence of the heat of the weather, he was shot in the head with an arrow, of which wound he soon afterwards died, 14 September, 1144. This noble outlaw had m. Rohesia, dau. of Alberic de Vere, Earl of Oxford, chief justice of England, and had issue, Ernulph, Geoffrey, William, and Robert; and by a former wife, whose name is not mentioned, a dau., Alice, who m. John de Lacy, constable of Chester. Of his death, Dugdale thus speaks:—

"Also that for these outrages, having incurred the penalty of excommunication, he happened to be mortally wounded, at a little town, called Burwell; whereupon, with great contrition for his sins, and making what satisfaction he could, there came at last some of the Knights Templars to him, and putting on him the habit of their order, with a red cross, carried his dead corpse into their orchard, at the old Temple, in London, and coffining it in lead, hanged it on a crooked tree. Likewise, that after some time, by the industry and expenses of William, whom he had constituted prior of Walden, his absolution was obtained from Pope Alexander III., so that his body was received among christians, and divers offices celebrated for him; but that when the prior endeavoured to take down the coffin and carry it to Walden, the Templars being aware of the design, buried it privately in the church-yard of the New Temple, viz., in the porch before the west door."

After the decease of this Earl Geoffrey, his son, ERNULPH, within the same year, was taken prisoner in the castle of Ramsey, which he had fortified, banished, and d. s p.; when

GEOFFREY, surnamed the younger (the 2nd son), was restored by King HENRY II. to all the lands of his ancestors, and confirmed in the EARLDOM OF ESSEX. This nobleman being an eloquent and accomplished person, was associated with Richard de Lacy, to march against the Welsh, then near Chester, at which city falling sick, it happened that his servants being all gone to dinner, and nobody left with him, he died. Whereupon divers ancient knights then assembled there, who had served his father, and enjoyed large possessions through his bounty, consulting together, resolved to carry his corpse to Walden, there to be interred as patron of that house: and for that purpose having taken out his brain and bowels, and committed them to holy sepulture, with honour and alms, they seasoned the rest of his body with salt, then wrapt it in a good hide, and coffined it: and thus proceeded, accompanied by the earl's servants, towards Walden; but upon the way, one of the deceased lord's chaplains, named Hasculf, took out his best saddle horse, in the night, and rode to Chicksand, where the Countess Rohese then resided with her nuns, and having acquainted her with the death of her son, advised her to send speedily, whatever force she could, to intercept the corpse, and to bring it thither, to the end that the kindred and friends of the deceased. might become benefactors to the convent of Chicksand; of which design the conductors of the corpse having, however, been apprised, they immediately drew their swords, and thus brought the noble remains in safety to Walden, where they were most magnificently interred. His lordship m. Eustachia, a kinswoman of King HENRY II., but did not live long with her, and, the lady, thereupon, making a complaint to her royal relative, the king is said to have caused, in great wrath, a divorce betwixt them. The earl d. 12 November, 1165, and leaving no issue, was s. by his brother,

WILLIAM DE MANDEVILLE, as 3rd EARL OF ESSEX. This nobleman attended King HENRY II. into France, in the 19th of that monarch's reign, as one of the generals of his army. In two years afterwards (1175), his lordship was one of the witnesses of the agreement made at Windsor, between the English monarch and Roderic, King of Connaught. In 1177, the earl made a pilgrimage to the Holy Land, and upon his return, repairing to Walden, was received by the whole convent in solemn procession, "all of them singing with one heart and voice, *Benedictus qui venit in nomine Domini*." After which, ascending to the high altar, and there receiving formal benediction from the prior, he offered divers precious relics, some of which he had acquired in the Holy Land, and others from the Emperor of Constantinople, and the Earl of Flanders. Then standing before the altar, the prior began the hymn of *Te Deum Laudamus*, which being ended, he went into the chapter house, and saluted all the monks, and thence into the abbey, where he was feasted honourably. His lordship m. 1st, Hawise, dau. and heiress of William le Gros, Earl of Albemarle, in whose right he bore that additional title; and 2ndly, Christian, dau. of Robert, Lord Fitz-Walter (who m. after the earl's decease, Reymond de Burgh), but had issue by neither of those ladies. The earl being a person chiefly engaged in military affairs, spent the greater part of his life in Normandy, where he was entrusted with divers forts and castles, by King HENRY. He d. in 1190, when the Earldom must have EXPIRED, but the feudal lordship and estates devolved upon his aunt, BEATRIX, wife of William de Say, whose eldest son, William de Say, dying v. p., left two daus., viz.,

Beatrix, m. to Geoffrey Fitz-Piers.
Maud, m. to William de Boeland.

Upon the decease of William de Mandeville, Earl of Essex, as mentioned above, much dispute arose regarding the inheritance; Beatrix, his aunt and heir, in the first place, preferring her claim, sent Geoffrey de Say, her younger son, to transact the business for the livery thereof; but Geoffrey Fitz-Piers insisted upon the right of Beatrix, his wife; nevertheless, Geoffrey de Say, in consideration of 7,000 marks, promised to be paid on a certain day, obtained an instrument in right of his mother, under the king's seal, for the whole of the barony, but the said Geoffrey de Say, making default of payment, this GEOFFREY FITZPIERS, being a man of great wealth and reputation, made representation that the barony was the right of his wife; and promising to pay the money, obtained livery thereof, and procured the king's confirmation of his title. One of the earliest acts of this feudal lord, was to dispossess the monks of Walden, of certain lands which they had derived from his predecessors, a proceeding followed by a long controversy, which, after being referred to the Pope and the King, was finally compromised. Upon the removal of Hubert, archbishop of Canterbury, from the office of Justice of England, by RICHARD I., this Geoffrey was appointed to succeed him; and at the coronation of King JOHN, 26 June, 1199, he was girt with the sword, as EARL OF ESSEX, and then served at the king's table. Being nominated patron of the monastery of Walden, he appears soon after to have been received with great ceremony by the monks, and perfectly reconciled to those holy fathers. In the 7th King JOHN, he had a grant of the castle and honour of Berkhamstead, with the knights' fees thereunto belonging, to hold to him and the heirs of his body, by Aveline, his 2nd wife. His lordship m. 1st, as already stated, Beatrix de Say, by whom he had issue,

GEOFFREY, his successor.
WILLIAM, successor to his brother,
Henry, dean of Wolverhampton.　} These all assumed the name of MANDEVILLE.
Maud. m. to Robert de Bohun, Earl of Hereford, whose son and heir became eventually EARL OF ESSEX, as well as Earl of Hereford.

He m. 2ndly, Aveline ——, and had an only son, John Fitzpiers, Lord of Berkhamstead. His lordship, whom Matthew Paris characterizes as "ruling the reins of government so that after his death the realm was like a ship in a tempest without a pilot," d. 2 October, 1213, and was s. by his eldest son, GEOFFREY DE MANDEVILLE (which surname he assumed), who, in the 15th King JOHN, had livery of the lands of his inheritance, and the same year, bearing the title of EARL OF ESSEX, the king gave him to wife, Isabel, Countess of Glouces-

353

ter, 3rd dau. and co-heir of William, Earl of Gloucester, and was in her right, Earl of Gloucester, and was so styled in the convention with King JOHN, 1215 (which Isabel had first been m. to King JOHN himself, but repudiated on account of consanguinity). This nobleman afterwards distinguished himself amongst the barons, who rebelled against the tyrannical power of JOHN, and was one of the twenty-five lords chosen to enforce the observance of Magna Charta : about which period, attending a tournament at London, he received a wound from a lance, which proved mortal. His lordship d. in 1216, and leaving no children, was s. by his brother,

WILLIAM MANDEVILLE, as EARL OF ESSEX. This nobleman, like his deceased kinsman, espoused the cause of the barons, and stoutly maintained it even after the decease of King JOHN; being one of those who then assisted LEWIS of France, in the siege of Berkhamstead Castle, occupied by the king's forces. A sally having been made, however, from the garrison, much of the baggage of the besiegers was captured, and amongst other things the banner of this Earl William. His lordship seems to have made his peace soon after, for we find him engaged in the Welsh wars. He d. in the flower of his age, 25 December, 1227, and, as he left no issue, the Earldom of Essex devolved upon his sister, Mary, Countess of Hereford (see BOHUN, Earl of Hereford), while the lands which he inherited passed to his half-brother,

JOHN FITZ-PIERS, who was sheriff of Yorkshire, in the 18th HENRY III. He m. Isabel, sister of John Bigod, and was s. by his son,

John Fitz-John Fitz-Geoffrey, whose son and heir,

JOHN FITZ-JOHN, was summoned to parliament as a Baron, temp. HENRY III. (see Fitz-John).

Arms—Quarterly : or and gules.

MANNY—BARON MANNY.

By Writ of Summons, dated 13 November, 1347.

Lineage.

WALTER DE MANNY (an alien, born in the diocese of Cambray), being a person of high military repute, was made a knight of the Bath, in the 5th EDWARD III.; after which we find him one of the most gallant and enterprising characters of the martial period in which he lived. In the 8th, 9th, and 10th of the same reign, Sir Walter was engaged in the Scottish wars, and in the 11th, was constituted admiral of the king's fleet, northwards, being the same year sworn of the privy council. "Shortly after this," says Dugdale, "he was in the battel of Cagant, against the French; and seeing Henry, Earl of Derby, son to Henry, Earl of Lancaster, felled to the ground, he brought him out of danger, and cryed, *Lancaster for the Earl of Derby*." In the week also, that defiance was made to the French king, he rode through Brabant night and day, with forty spears, until he reached Hainault; having pledged himself to divers "ladies fair," previously to leaving England, that he should be the first to invade France, and to win some town or castle there; in redemption of which chivalrous promise, he entered Mortaigne, with his penon borne before him, through the high-street; but coming to the great tower, found the gate closed against him. Upon which, causing the watch of the castle to sound his horn, and cry, *Treason, treason*, he retraced his steps, and fired the adjoining street. Thence he proceeded to Condé, and on to Valenciennes, from which place he marched to Chine, and took by assault, the strong castle there; whereof, making it a garrison, he appointed his brother, Giles Manny, governor. He thence joined the King at Machline. In about two years after this, Sir Walter Manny was in an expedition made into the north of France, and there his usual fortune attended him—he spoiled the country, slew more than 1000 soldiers, and burnt 300 villages. In the same year (14th EDWARD III.) he was in the great sea fight, between the French and English before Sluce, in Flanders; and for his disbursements in that and other services, had an assignation of £2000 payable by the receiver of the subsidy then levied in Essex. In the 16th EDWARD III., he attended the king to the siege of Nantes; and in consideration of £4000, which he remitted of the sum of £8000, then due to him from the crown, he obtained a grant for life, of the sheriffalty of Merionethshire; and an assignation of sixty-eight sacks, and one quartern of the king's wools in Sussex, for the support of himself, and fifty men at arms, with fifty archers on horseback, in the expedition then made into France. His own wages as a banneret, being 4s. per day ; the knights (twelve in number), 2s. each, per day ; the esquires, 1s., and the archers, 6d. In two years afterwards, being one of the marshals of the host to the Earl of Derby, when he went to assault Bergerath, he said to his lordship, as he sate at dinner, "Sir, if we were good men at arms, we should drink this evening with the French lords at BERGERATH." Whereupon all that heard him, cried, "to arms," and the town being immediately assaulted, surrendered to its gallant assailants.

"Amongst other towns," saith Dugdale, "then won by the Earl of Derby, RYOL being one; this Wa'ter found the tombe of his father, who had been buried there, and of whose death *Froisart* makes this relation; viz. "That at a certain tournement before Cambray (there being on both parts 500 knights), he tourneyed with a knight of Gascoine, as kinsman to the bishop of Cambray, and wounded him so sore, as that he died soon after. Which so incensed the kindred of that knight, that upon a pacification made, he was, for expiation of the knight's death, to go on a pilgrimage to St. James; and that upon his return thence, finding RYOL besieged by COUNT CHARLES, OF VALOIS, brother to King PHILIP (it being then in the hands of the English), coming back at night towards his lodging from a visit, which he had made to that count, he was murthered by some of the knight's kindred, who lay purposely in wait for him. And that upon tidings brought to the count, he caused his body to be buried in a little chappel without the town; which when the town came to be enlarged, was encompassed by the walls."

Sir Walter Manny was one of the most conspicuous heroes of Cressay, having a principal command in the van of the English army. From this celebrated field he repaired to the siege of Calais, where King EDWARD and his victorious son, the Black Prince, condescended to array themselves under Sir Walter's banner, and fighting beneath it, reduced that strong and important place. About this period, in reward of all these heroic achievements, Sir Walter Manny was summoned to parliament as a Baron, 13 November, 1347, and thenceforward during the remainder of his life. He had likewise large grants from the crown, and was made a knight of the Garter. His lordship continued actively engaged in the French war, until the peace concluded with France in the 42nd EDWARD III., when he was one of those who swore to observe the articles of the treaty. His lordship m. the Lady Margaret Plantagenet, styled Duchess of Norfolk, eldest dau., and eventually co-heiress of Thomas of Brotherton, Duke of Norfolk, and widow of John, Lord Segrave, by whom he left an only dau. and heiress,

ANNE MANNY, who m. John de Hastings, Earl of Pembroke.

This great and gallant nobleman d. in 1372. His will bears date at London, upon St. Andrew's Day, in the preceding year. By that testament he bequeathed his body to be buried in the midst of the quire of the Carthusians (commonly called the Charter House), near West Smithfield, in the suburbs of London, of his own foundation, but without any great pomp; appointing that his executors should cause twenty masses to be sung for his soul; and that every poor body coming to his funeral, should have a penny to pray for him, and for the remission of his sins. To Mary, his sister (at that time a nun), he bequeathed £10. To his two bastard daus., nuns also (namely, Mailosel and Malpleasant), the one 200 franks, the other 100. To Margaret, his wife, all his silver vessels; likewise his girdle of gold, with all his girdles and knives. Also his beds, and drossers in his wardrobe; excepting his folding bed, pale of blue and red, which he gave to his dau. of Pembroke. Moreover, he ordained, that a tomb of alabaster, with his image as a knight, and his arms thereon, should be made for him, like unto that of Sir John Beauchamp, in the cathedral of St. Paul, at London, as a remembrance of him, and that men might pray for his soul. And whereas the king did owe him an old debt of £1000, by bills of his wardrobe; he appointed, that if it could be had, it should be given to the prior and monks of the Charter House, whereof he was founder. And whereas, there was due to him from the prince, from the time he had been Prince of Wales, the sum of 100 marks per annum for his salary as governor of Hardelagh Castle, he bequeathed a moiety thereof to the said prior and monks of the Charter House before-mentioned, and the other moiety to his executors (of which he constituted Sir Guyde de Bryene one), for the performance of his testament.

Upon the decease of Lord Manny, the Barony of Manny devolved upon his dau. ANNE, COUNTESS OF PEMBROKE, and at the decease of her son, John Hastings, 3rd Earl of Pembroke, without issue, in 1391, it became EXTINCT.

Arms—Sa., a cross voided, arg.

MANSEL—BARONS MANSEL, OF MARGAM, CO. GLAMORGAN.

By Letters Patent, dated 1 January, 1712.

Lineage.

The family of MANSEL, according to genealogists, sprang from an ancient stock; whereof

PHILIP MANSEL is said to have come over with the CONQUEROR: and from his eldest son,

HENRY MANSEL descended

JOHN MANSEL, who, in the reign of HENRY III., being chancellor of the church of St. Paul's, was appointed keeper of the king's seal, and was a very eminent person at that period. This John m. Joane, dau. of Simon Beauchamp, of Bedford, and was father of

SIR HENRY MANSEL, whose son,

HENRY MANSEL, settled in Glamorganshire, *temp.* EDWARD I., and from him descended

THOMAS MANSEL, Esq., who was created a Baronet, at the institution of the order, in 1611. From Sir Thomas we pass to his lineal descendant (*see* BURKE'S *Extant Baronetage*),

SIR THOMAS MANSEL, 4th baronet, who was elevated to the peerage, 1 January, 1712, as BARON MANSEL, *of Margam, co. Glamorgan.* His lordship m. Martha, dau. and heiress of Francis Millington, Esq., of the city of London, merchant, by whom he had (with three daus.),

ROBERT, who m. Anne, dau. and co-heir of the celebrated Admiral Sir Cloudesley Shovel, Knt., and dying *v. p.* (29 April, 1723), left, with one dau., one son,

THOMAS, successor to his grandfather.

CHRISTOPHER, } who both *s.* eventually to the title.
BUSSY.   }

Martha.   Elizabeth.

MARY, m. JOHN IVORY TALBOT, Esq., M.P., of Lacock Abbey, co. Wilts, and from this marriage descend the families of MANSEL TALBOT of Margam, co. Glamorgan, and TALBOT of Lacock Abbey, Wilts.

His lordship d. in 1723, and was *s.* by his grandson,

THOMAS MANSEL, 2nd baron. This nobleman d. *unm.* in 1743, when the honours reverted to his uncle,

CHRISTOPHER MANSEL, 3rd baron, who d. in the ensuing year *unm.*, and was *s.* by his brother,

BUSSY MANSEL, 4th baron. This nobleman m. 1st, Lady Betty Hervey, dau. of John, Earl of Bristol, by whom he had no issue. He m. 2ndly, Barbara, widow of Sir Walter Blacket, Bart., and dau. of William, Earl of Jersey, and had an only dau. and heiress,

LOUISA-BARBARA MANSEL, who m. George, 2nd Baron Vernon, by whom she had two daus., who both d. in infancy, a 3rd, LOUISA, who d. *unm.* in 1786. Her ladyship d. in the same year.

His lordship d. in 1750, when the Barony of Mansel became EXTINCT.

Arms—Arg., a chevron between three maunches, sa.

MARE—BARON LA MARE.

By Writ of Summons, dated 6 February, 1299.

Lineage.

Families of the surname of DE LA MARE flourished simultaneously in the cos. of Wilts, Somerset, Hereford, and Oxford, whereof

HENRY DE LA MARE (of the Oxfordshire House), upon the demise of his father, in the 5th year of King STEPHEN, paid a fine of £28 6s. 8d., that he might enjoy his office of huntsman to the king; for so he was, holding the post by petty serjeanty. To this Henry *s.*

ROBERT DE LA MARE, who was sheriff of Oxfordshire in the 34th HENRY II., and of Oxford and Berks, in the 1st and 2nd RICHARD I. He was *s.* by

GEFFERY DE LA MARE, who gave a fine of 100 marks and one palfrey, for warranty of his lands at Dudercote, in the co. Berks. From this Geffery descended

JOHN DE LA MARE, of Gersyndon, afterwards Garsyngton, co. Oxford, who, having been engaged in the French and Scottish wars of King EDWARD I., was summoned to parliament as a Baron from 6 February, 1299, to 26 July, 1313. He *d.* 9th EDWARD II.. 1315-6. But of his lordship nothing further is known, and Dugdale says that his descendants had never afterwards summons to parliament.

Arms—Gu., two lions passant, in pale, arg.

MARMYON, OF MARMION—BARONS MARMYON.

FEUDAL.

(Although it is not intended that this work shall embrace personages who were *merely* feudal lords, the present family, as that from which the CHAMPIONSHIP OF ENGLAND is inherited, demands to be noticed.)

Lineage.

At the period of the Norman conquest,

ROBERT DE MARMYON, Lord of Fontney, in Normandy, having by grant of King WILLIAM, the castle of Tamworth, in the co. Warwick, with the adjacent lands, expelled the nuns from the abbey of Polesworth, to a place called Oldbury, about four miles distant. " After which " (writes Sir William Dugdale), " within the compass of a twelvemonth, as it is said, making a costly entertainment at Tamworth Castle, for some of his friends, amongst whom was Sir Walter de Somerville, Lord of Whichover, in the co. Stafford, his sworn brother, it happened, that as he lay in his bed, St. Edith appeared to him in the habit of a veiled nun, with a crosier in her hand, and advertised him, that if he did not restore the abbey of Polesworth, which lay within the territories belonging to his castle of Tamworth, unto her successors, he should have an evil death, and go to hell. And, that he might be the more sensible of this her admonition, she smote him on the side with the crosier, and so vanished away. Moreover, that by this stroke being much wounded, he cried out so loud, that his friends in the house arose, and finding him extremely tormented with the pain of his wound, advised him to confess himself to a priest, and vow to restore the nuns to their former possessions. Furthermore, that having so done, his pain ceased; and that in accomplishment of this vow, accompanied by Sir Walter de Somervile, and the rest, he forthwith rode to Oldbury, and craving pardon of the nuns for the injury done, brought them back to Polesworth, desiring that himself, and his friend Sir Walter de Somervile, might be reputed their patrons, and have burial for themselves and their heirs in the abbey—the Marmions in the chapter house—the Somerviles in the cloyster. However (continues Dugdale), some circumstances in this story may seem fabulous, the substance of it is certainly true; for it expressly appeareth by the very words of his charter, that he gave to Osanna, the prioress, *for the establishing of the religion of those nuns there, the church of St. Edith, of Polesworth, with its appurtenances, so that the convent of Oldbury should remain in that place* And likewise bestowed upon them the whole lordship of Polesworth: which grant King STEPHEN afterwards confirmed." The castle and manor of Tamworth, in Warwickshire, and the manor of Scrivelsby, co. Lincoln, were granted by the CONQUEROR to this Robert de Marmion, to be held by grand serjeanty, "to perform the office of champion at the king's coronation" (the Marmions, it is said, were hereditary champions to the Dukes of Normandy, prior to the conquest of England). Robert Marmion was *s.* at his decease, by his son and heir,

ROBERT DE MARMYON, Lord of Fontney, in Normandy, where he possessed a fortified castle, which was besieged by Geoffrey, of Anjou, in the 4th King STEPHEN, and demolished. This Robert having a great enmity to the Earl of Chester, who had a noble seat at Coventry, entered the priory there in the 8th STEPHEN, and expelling the monks, turned it into a fortification, digging at the same time divers deep ditches in the adjacent fields, which he caused to be covered over with earth, in order to secure the approaches thereto; but the Earl of Chester's forces drawing near, as he rode out to reconnoitre, he fell into one of those very ditches, and broke his thigh, so that a common soldier, presently seizing him, cut off his head. He was *s.* by his son,

ROBERT DE MARMYON, who, in the 31st HENRY II., being constituted sheriff of Worcestershire, continued in that office until the end of the 34th year. He was also justice itinerant in Warwickshire, and some other counties—and again sheriff of Worcester in the 1st RICHARD I. In five years afterwards he attended that monarch into Normandy, and in

355

the 15th King JOHN he was in the expedition then made into Poictou. This feudal lord *d.* about the year 1217, leaving issue, by different mothers,

ROBERT, his successor.

Robert, junior, who had the estates of Witringham and Coningsby, co. Lincoln (*see* Marmion, Barons Marmion, of Witrington).

William, of Torington (*see* Marmion, Barons Marmion).

He was *s.* by his eldest son,

ROBERT DE MARMION, who appears to have sided with the French, when they se'zed upon Normandy in the beginning of King JOHN's reign, for the murder of Arthur, Duke of Britanny; but afterwards made his peace, for in the 5th HENRY III. he had livery of Tamworth Castle, and his father's other lands. He is supposed to have returned to Normandy in twelve years afterwards, and to have *d.* there in 1241, when he was *s.* by his son,

PHILIP DE MARMION, who was sheriff for the co. Warwick and Leicester, from the 33rd to the 36th HENRY III. In the latter of which years he was questioned for sitting with Richard de Mundevill, and the rest of the justices, for gaol-delivery at Warwick, having 'no commission so to do. The next year he attended the king into Gascony; upon his return whence he was taken prisoner by the French at Pontes, in Poictou, with John de Plessets, then Earl of Warwick, notwithstanding they had letters of safe conduct from the king of France. In the 45th of the same reign this feudal lord had summons to be at London with divers of the nobility, upon the morrow after *Simon and Jude's day* ; in which year the defection of many of the barons began further to manifest itself, by their assuming the royal prerogative, in placing sheriffs throughout different shires. In this period of difficulty Philip de Marmion, being of unimpeachable loyalty, had, by special patent from the king, the co. Suffolk and Norfolk committed to his custody, with the castles of Norwich and Oxford: a well-judged confidence, for through all the subsequent fortunes of HENRY III. he never once swerved from his allegiance. He was present at the battle of Lewes—and his fidelity was rewarded after the royal victory of Evesham, by some valuable grants for life, and the governorship of Kenilworth Castle. He *m.* Joane, youngest dau., and eventually sole heiress of Hugh de Kilpec, by whom he had three daus., his co-heirs, viz.,

Joane, *m.* to William Morteyn. and *d. s. p.* in 1294.

Mazera, *m.* to Ralph Cromwell, and had an only dau. and heiress,

Joane, *m.* to Alexander, Baron Freville, whose grandson,

Sir Baldwin de Freville, Lord Freville, claimed the championship in the 1st RICHARD II., by the tenure of Tamworth Castle, but the matter was determined against him in favour of Sir John Dymoke.

Maud, *m.* to Ralph Botiller, and *d. s. p.*

By a 2nd marriage Philip de Marmion had another dau. and co-heir, viz.,

Joane, *m.* 1st, to Sir Thomas de Ludlow, Knt., and 2ndly, Henry Hillary. By the former she had,

Thomas, who, by Catherine, his wife, left an only dau. and heir,

Margaret de Ludlow, who *m.* Sir John Dymoke, Knt., and brought into the family of her husband the manor of SCRIVELSBY, in Lincolnshire, by which the Dymokes have from the accession of RICHARD II. exercised the chivalrous office of Champion at the coronations of the kings of England. Our space compels us to pass over the various Champions to SIR EDWARD DYMOKE, Champion at the coronation of King CHARLES II. This gentleman *m.* 21 June, 1624, June, dau. of Nicholas Cressy, Esq., of Fulnetby, and had, with other issue,

1 CHARLES, his successor.

2 Edward, of Grebby Hall, who *d.* 1 April, 1694, leaving, by Abigail Snowden, his wife,

ROBERT, whose great-grandson,

DYMOKE WELLS, Esq., of Grebby Hall, co. Lincoln, *m.* in 1793, Anne, dau. and co-heir of Thomas Waterhouse, Esq., of Beckingham Hall, high sheriff of Notts, in 1787 ; and *d.* in 1832 (his widow *d.* 25 December, 1848), leaving issue,

THOMAS-WATERHOUSE WELLS, of Grebby Hall, *d.* in 1833.

DYMOKE WELLS, of Grebby Hall, *d.* 1852, *s. p.*

EDMUND-LIONEL WELLES, barrister-at-law, who has assumed the additional surname of DYMOKE (*see* BURKE's *Landed Gentry*).

Georgiana, *m.* to Capt. Rowland Pennington, of Whitehaven.

John, whose grandson, John Dymoke, Esq., of Tetford, co. Lincoln, who *d.* 21 August, 1782, was the next male heir to the Scrivelsby baronial estates, on the death of the hon. Champion, Lewis Dymoke, in 1760.

8 John, who m. Elizabeth, dau. of Thomas Welborne, Esq., and left a son, Charles, father of EDWARD, who s. to the estates and Championship under the will of his cousin, the hon. Champion, Lewis Dymoke.

Sir Edward was sheriff of Lincolnshire in 1662. He d. soon afterwards, and was buried at Scrivelsby, 8 January, 1663-4. He was s. by his eldest son,

SIR CHARLES DYMOKE, who officiated as Champion at the coronation of King JAMES II. He m. Eleanor, dau. of Lewis Watson, Lord Rockingham, and had issue,

　CHARLES, his heir.
　LEWIS, successor to his brother.
　ELEANOR, wife of Matthew Lister, Esq., of Burwell Park, co. Lincoln, and great-great-grandmother of the late MATTHEW-BANCROFT LISTER, Esq., of Burwell Park.

He d. about the year 1688, and was s. by his eldest surviving son,

CHARLES DYMOKE, Esq. This gentleman fulfilled the duties of Champion at the coronation of WILLIAM and MARY, and likewise at the coronation of Queen ANNE. He m. Jane, dau. of Robert Snoden, Esq., but dying s. p. 17 January, 1702-3, was s. by his brother,

LEWIS DYMOKE, Esq., who officiated as Champion at the coronation of the first two monarchs of the line of Brunswick. He was M.P. for Lincolnshire from 1702 to 1705, inclusive, and from 1710 to 1713. He d. unm. in 1760, having completed his ninety-first year, and was s. by his cousin,

EDWARD DYMOKE, Esq., of Scrivelsby, who m. Elizabeth Segrave, relict of James Coward, and dying 12 September, 1760, was s. by his son,

JOHN DYMOKE, Esq., of Scrivelsby, Champion at the coronation of GEORGE III., who m. Martha, dau. and heir of Josiah Holmes, Esq., and dying 6 March, 1784, was s. by his elder son,

LEWIS DYMOKE, Esq., of Scrivelsby, who claimed before the House of Lords the old barony of Marmyon, but unsuccessfully. He d. unm. 12 May, 1820, and was s. by his brother,

THE REV. JOHN DYMOKE, rector of Scrivelsby, prebendary of Lincoln. This gentleman being called upon to officiate as Champion at the coronation of GEORGE IV., was obliged, owing to his clerical character, to act by deputy, and he therefore appointed his eldest son, HENRY DYMOKE, who fulfilled the duties of the office accordingly. Mr. Dymoke m. 19 July, 1799, Amelia-Jane-Alice, dau. of Captain Elphinstone, of the British navy, and Admiral of the Russian fleet, by whom (who d. 26 April, 1856), he had issue. He d. 3 December, 1828, and was s. by his elder son, the said Henry, who was created a Baronet, and was the late SIR HENRY DYMOKE, Bart., of Scrivelsby, the hon. the Queen's Champion.

Upon the decease of Philip de Marmion, about 1292, his estates passed to his co-heiresses, barony and manor of Tamworth to Freville, and Scrivelsby to Dymoke.

At the coronation of King RICHARD II., Sir Baldwin Freville, then Lord of Tamworth, exhibited his claim to be king's Champion that day, and to do the service appertaining to that office, by reason of his tenure of Tamworth Castle, viz., "To ride completely armed upon a barbed horse into Westminster Hall, and there to challenge the combat with whomsoever should dare to oppose the king's title to the crown." Which service the Barons de Marmion, his ancestors, lords of that castle, had theretofore performed. But Sir John Dymoke counterclaimed the same office as Lord of Scrivelsby. Whereupon the Constable and Marshal of England, appointed the said Sir John Dymoke to perform the office at that time.

The chief part of Scrivelsby Court, the ancient baronial seat, was destroyed by fire during the last century. In the part consumed was a very large hall, on the panels of the wainscoting of which were depicted the various arms and alliances of the family through all its numerous and far-traced descents. The loss has been, in some degree, compensated by the addition which the late proprietors made to those parts which escaped the ravages of the flames. Against the south wall of the chancel in the parish church of Scrivelsby, is a very handsome marble monument, ornamented with a bust of the Hon. Lewis Dymoke, Champion at the coronation of the two first sovereigns of the House of Brunswick. On the north side of the chancel is a marble tablet to the memory of the Hon. John Dymoke, who performed the duties of Champion at the coronation of King GEORGE III. On the floor of the south side of the communion table is a plate of copper, on which is an inscription to the memory of Sir Charles Dymoke, Knt., who was Champion at the coronation of King JAMES II. At the eastern end of the aisle are two tombs, on one of which is the figure of a knight in chain armour, cross-legged, on the other that of a lady with a lion at her feet. By the side of these is the tomb of Sir Robert Dymoke, who was Champion at the coronations of RICHARD III., HENRY VII., and HENRY VIII.

On the floor of the aisle is also a stone which once contained a brass figure, with corner shields, and an inscription, all of which are now gone.

In July, 1814, Lewis Dymoke, Esq., the descendant of Sir John Dymoke above-mentioned, uncle of the late Champion, Sir Henry Dymoke, Bart., of Scrivelsby Court, co. Lincoln, presented a petition to the crown, praying to be declared entitled to the Barony of Marmion, of Scrivelsby, in virtue of the seizure of the manor of Scrivelsby; which petition was referred to the attorney-general, who having reported thereon, the same was referred to the House of Lords, where evidence was received at the bar, and the claimant's counsel summoned up, when the attorney-general was heard in reply, and tendered some documents on the part of the crown; but the claimant died before the judgment of the House was given.

" With respect to this claim," says Sir Harris Nicolas, " it is to be observed, that though the manor of Scrivelsby was held by the service of performing the office of king's Champion by Robert de Marmyon, in the reign of WILLIAM THE CONQUEROR, he was not by seizure thereof a baron, but by seizure of the barony and castle of Tamworth, which he held of the king in capite by knight's service ; so that, if at this period baronies by tenure were admitted, the possessor of the manor and lordship of Tamworth (which in the division of his property fell to the share of Joane, his eldest dau., wife of William Morteyn, and on her death s. p. to Alexander Freville, husband of Joan, dau. and heir of Ralph Cromwell, by Mazera, the next sister of the said Joan de Morteyn), would possess the claim to the barony enjoyed by Robert de Marmyon, he having derived his dignity from that barony instead of from the seizure of the manor of Scrivelsby. Moreover, if Philip Marmyon, the last baron, had died seized of a barony in fee, Lewis Dymoke was not even a co-heir of the said Philip, though he was the descendant of one of his daus. and co-heirs."

Arms—Vairée, a fesse, gules.

MARMYON, OR MARMION—BARONS MARMION OF WETRINGTON, CO. LINCOLN.

By Writ of Summons, dated 8 June, 1294, 26 January, 1297, and 26 July, 1313.

Lineage.

ROBERT DE MARMYON, eldest son by his 2nd wife of Robert de Marmyon, 3rd feudal Lord of Tamworth, had the lordships of Witringham, and Coningsby, co. Lincoln; Dueinton, co. Gloucester ; and Berwick, co. Suffolk, by especial grant of his father ; and in the 16th King John, he gave to the king 350 marks, and five palfreys, for license to marry Amice, the dau. of Jerneygan Fitz-Hugh. After which, being in arms with the rebellious barons, he obtained letters of safe conduct for coming in to the king, to make his peace. He again, however, took up arms in the baronial cause, in the ensuing reign, along with his brother William, and appears to have held out to the last. This Robert acquired a large accession of landed property with his wife, Alice Fitz-Hugh, and was s. at his decease, by his son,

WILLIAM DE MARMION, who m. Lora, dau. of Roese de Dovor, by whom he acquired the town of Ludington, in Northamptonshire, and was s. by his son,

JOHN DE MARMION, who, in the 22nd EDWARD I., had summons, with other great men, to attend the king to advise upon the affairs of the realm, and was summoned to parliament as a Baron, 8 June, 1294, 26 January, 1297, and from 26 July, 1313, to 14 March, 1322. In the 4th EDWARD II., his lordship had license to make a castle of his house, called the Hermitage, in the co. York. He d. in 1322, and was s. by his son,

JOHN DE MARMION, 2nd baron, summoned to parliament from 3 December, 1326, to 1 April, 1335. This nobleman was engaged in the Scottish wars. His lordship m. Maud, dau. of Lord Furnival, and had issue,

　ROBERT, his successor.
　Joane, m. to Sir John Bernack, Knt.
　Avice, 2nd wife of Sir John de Grey, Lord Grey, of Rotherfield, and had issue,
　　John de Grey, who assumed the surname of Marmion, d. s. p. in 1385.
　　Robert de Grey assumed the name of Marmion, m. Lora, dau. and co-heir of Herbert de St. Quintin, and had an only dau. and heiress,
　　　Elizabeth Marmion, who m. Henry, Lord Fitz-Hugh, K.G.

The baron *d.* in 1335, and was *s.* by his son,

ROBERT DE MARMION, 3rd baron, but never summoned to parliament. This nobleman being of infirm constitution, and having no issue, married his younger sister, Avice, by the advice of his friends, to Sir John Grey, Lord Grey of Rotherfield, upon condition that the issue of the said Sir John Grey and Avice should bear the surname of Marmion. At the decease of his lordship, the Barony of Marmion, of Witrington, fell into ABEYANCE between his sisters (*refer to* children of 2nd baron), the elder of whom, Joane, Lady Bernack, *d. s. p.* The younger, Avice, as stated above, m. Lord Grey, and her grand-dau., Elizabeth, m. Henry, Lord Fitz-Hugh, amongst whose representatives this barony continues in abeyance.

Arms—Vairé arg. and az., a fesse, gules.

MARMYON, OR MARMION — BARON MARMION.

By Writ of Summons, dated 24 December, 1264,

Lineage.

WILLIAM DE MARMYON, youngest son of Robert de Marmyon, 3rd feudal lord of Tamworth, having taken a leading part in the baronial wars against King HENRY III., was summoned as a Baron to the parliament called in the king's name, by those turbulent lords, after their triumph at Lewes, 24 December, 1264, but never subsequently. His lordship appears to have *d. s. p.* when the barony became, of course, EXTINCT.

Arms—Vairé, arg. and az., a fesse, gules.

MARNEY — BARONS MARNEY, OF LAYR-MARNEY, CO. ESSEX.

By Letters Patent, dated 9 April, 1523.

Lineage.

In 1254, Ralph de Mareny, uncle of William, son of Roger de Mareny, held lands in Layr-Marney, and in 1262, William de Marney purchased lands here of Robert le Carpenter and Mary, his wife.

ROBERT DE MARNEY, son of William de Marney, living *temp.* EDWARD III., m. a dau. of — Gernon, and was father of William de Marney, who m. the dau, and co-heir of — Venables, and left a son and successor,

SIR ROBERT DE MARNEY, Knt., who m. Alice, dau. and heir of Richard Layer, of Suffolk, and relict of Sir William Bruyn, of South Okendon, and was father of

SIR WILLIAM MARNEY, high sheriff of Essex and Herts in 1402. He m. Elizabeth, dau. and co-heir of Richard Sergeants, and had three sons and one dau., Thomas (Sir), *d.* in 1417, leaving an only dau., who *d. unm.*; William, *d. unm.*; and JOHN (SIR), of whom presently; and Anne, *m.* to Sir Thomas Tyrell, of East Horndon. Sir William *d.* in 1414. His youngest son,

SIR JOHN MARNEY, was *s.* by his son,

SIR HENRY MARNEY, Knt., who being "a person of great wisdom, gravity, and of singular fidelity to that prudent prince King HENRY VII.," was made choice of for one of his privy council, in the first year of his reign, and the next year he commanded against the Earl of Lincoln, at the battle of Stoke. He was subsequently engaged against Lord Audley and the Cornish rebels, at Blackheath. Upon the accession of HENRY VIII., he was re-sworn of the privy council, and soon afterwards installed a knight of the Garter. Sir Henry was subsequently appointed captain of the guard to the king, and upon the attainder of Edward Stafford, Duke of Buckingham, he had grants of a large portion of that nobleman's estates. He was appointed keeper of the privy seal in February, 1522, and elevated to the peerage in the April following, as BARON MARNEY, *of Leyr-Marney, co. Essex*

His lordship m. 1st, Thomasine, dau. of Sir John Arundel, of Lanherne, in Cornwall, by whom he had two sons, JOHN, his successor, and Thomas, who *d.* young, and a dau. Catharine, who m. Thomas Bonham, Esq. He m. 2ndly, Elizabeth, dau. of Alderman Nicholas Wifield, lord mayor of London, and had a

dau., who m. Sir Henry Bedingfield. His lordship *d.* 24 May. 1523, and was *s.* by his son,

JOHN MARNEY, 2nd baron. This nobleman, in the time of his father, was one of the esquires of the body to King HENRY VIII., and governor of Rochester Castle. His lordship m. 1st, Christian, dau. and heir of Sir Roger Newburgh, by whom he had two daus., viz.,

Katherine, m. 1st, to George Ratcliffe, Esq. (of the Sussex family), and 2ndly, to Thomas, Lord Poynings.
Elizabeth, m. to Lord Thomas Howard, afterwards created Viscount Bindon.

Lord Marney, m. 2ndly, Bridget, dau. of Sir William Waldegrave, Knt., and widow of William Finderne, Esq., but had no issue. He *d.* 27 April, 1525, when the Barony of Marney became EXTINCT, and his estates devolved upon his daus., as co-heirs.

Arms—Gu., a lion rampant guardant, arg.

MARSHAL—BARONS MARSHAL.

By Writ of Summons, dated 9 January, 1309.

Lineage.

The earliest notice of this family occurs in the time of HENRY I., when GILBERT MARESCHALL, and JOHN, his son, were impleaded by Robert de Venoiz, and William de Hastings, for the office of MARESCHAL to the king, but without success. The son (bearing the same surname, derived from his office),

JOHN MARESCHALL, attaching himself to the fortunes of MAUD, against King STEPHEN, was with Robert, the consul, Earl of Gloucester, at the siege of Winchester Castle, when the party of the empress sustained so signal a defeat. Upon the accession of HENRY II., however, his fidelity was amply rewarded by considerable grants in the so. Wilts; and in the 10th of that monarch's reign, being then marshal, he laid claim, for the crown, to one of the manors of the see of Canterbury, from the celebrated prelate, Thomas à Becket, who about that period had commenced his contest with the king. To this John *s.* his son and heir,

JOHN MARESCHALL, to whom King HENRY II. confirmed the office of marshal, and the lands which he held of the crown of England, and elsewhere. At the coronation of RICHARD I., this John Mareschall bore the great gilt spurs, and the same year obtained a grant from the crown of the manor of Boseham, in Sussex, in fee farm, paying £43 yearly, to the exchequer; with other extensive lordships. He *d.* soon after, and it appears without issue, for his brother, William Maresuhall, Earl of Pembroke, *s.* as his heir. We now come to the nephew of the said William, Earl of Pembroke,

SIR JOHN MARSHAL, who m. Aliva, elder dau. and co-heir of Hubert de Rie, feudal lord of Hingham, oo. Norfolk, by whom he acquired that lordship. Espousing the cause of King JOHN against the barons, Sir John Marshal acquired from the crown, all the forfeited lands of the Earl of Evreux, in England, as also the lands of Hugh de Gornal, lying in the cos. of Norfolk and Suffolk, whereof the said Hugh was possessed when he deserted the royal banner; and he likewise obtained a grant in fee, of the office of marshal of Ireland. He was, subsequently, in the same reign, constituted guardian of the marches of Wales, and sheriff of Lincolnshire, and afterwards joined with John Fitz-Robert, in the sheriffalty of the cos. of Norfolk and Suffolk, and the custody of the castles of Norwich and Orford. He was likewise made governor of Dorchester Castle ; moreover, he had the same year, livery of the office of marshal of Ireland, and whatsoever did appertain thereto ; so that he should appoint a knight to execute its duties effectually. Continuing steadfast in his allegiance to King JOHN, he was made sheriff of Worcestershire, and governor of the Castle of Worcester : and he was one of those who marched with the king into the north, to waste the lands of the insurrectionary barons there. Upon the accession of HENRY III., Sir John Marshal was constituted sheriff of Hampshire, and governor of the castle of Devizes, in Wilts, and retained, during the remainder of his life, the favour of that monarch. He *d.* in 1234, and was *s.* by his son,

JOHN MARSHAL, who, dying in 1242, was *s.* by his son and heir,

WILLIAM MARSHAL, who, adopting a different line of politics, joined the baronial standard, in the 49th HENRY III., and *d.* about the same period, (1264) leaving two sons, John and William, then under age, who, the next year, through the intercession of William de Saye, obtained the king's pardon for their father's transgression, and had permission to enjoy his lands, with whatever possessions they had, by gift of Aliva, their grandmother. The elder of these sons,

JOHN MARSHAL, d. in the 12th EDWARD I., and was *s.* by his son,

WILLIAM MARSHAL, who, in the 34th EDWARD I., was in the wars of Scotland, and was summoned to parliament as a Baron, from 9 January, 1309, to 26 November, 1312. His lordship d, in the next year, and was *s.* by his son,

JOHN MARSHAL, 2nd baron. In the 7th EDWARD II., this John attended the Queen into Scotland, and the ensuing year doing his homage, had livery of his lands, lying in the cos. of Norfolk and Lincoln. He *d.* soon after, about the year 1316, leaving his sister, Hawyse, wife of ROBERT, Lord Morley, his heir, who carried the Barony of Marshal into the Morley family, from which it passed into that of Lovel, and thence to the Parkers, when it finally fell into ABEYANCE, at the decease of Thomas Parker, Lord Morley, in 1686, between the issue of that nobleman's aunts,

Katherine, wife of John Savage, 2nd Earl Rivers.
Elizabeth, wife of Edward Cranfield, Esq., and amongst whose descendants it so continues.

Arms—Gu., a bend lozengé, or.

MARSHAL—EARLS OF PEMBROKE.

Earldom, conferred upon the family of CLARE in 1138.
Conveyed to the MARSHALS by an heiress.

Lineage.

ISABEL DE CLARE, only child and heiress of RICHARD DE CLARE (surnamed STRONGBOW), EARL OF PEMBROKE, and justice of Ireland, who had been under the guardianship of HENRY II., was given in marriage by King RICHARD I , to

WILLIAM MARSHAL, of the great baronial family of Mariechal (*see* MARSHAL, Barons Marshal), marshal to the king. This William is first noticed as receiving from Prince Henry, the rebellious son of HENRY II., upon the prince's deathbed, his cross, as his most confidential friend, to convey to Jerusalem. He *m.* the great heiress of the Clares, in 1189, and with her acquired the Earldom of Pembroke—in which rank he bore the royal sceptre of gold, surmounted by the cross, at the coronation of King RICHARD I.; and he was soon afterwards, on the king's purposing a journey to the Holy Land, appointed one of the assistants to Hugh, bishop of Durham, and William, Earl of Albemarle, Chief Justice of England, in the government of the realm. Upon the decease of his brother,[*] John Mareschal, marshal of the king's house, in 1199, he became lord marshal ; and on the day of the coronation of King JOHN, he was invested with the sword of the Earldom of Pembroke, being then confirmed in the possession of the said inheritance. In the first year of this monarch's reign, his lordship was appointed sheriff of Gloucestershire, and likewise of Sussex, wherein he was continued for several years. In the 5th he had a grant of Goderich Castle, in the co. Hereford, to hold by the service of two knights' fees; and in four years afterwards, he obtained, by grant from the crown, the whole province of Leinster, in I eland, to hold by the service of one hundred knights' fees. Upon the breaking out of the baronial insurrection, the Earl of Pembroke was deputed, with the archbishop of Canterbury, by the king, to ascertain the grievances and demands of those turbulent lords; and at the demise of King JOHN, he was so powerful as to prevail upon the barons to appoint a day for the coronation of HENRY III., to whom he was constituted guardian, by the rest of the nobility, who had remained firm in their allegiance. He subsequently took up arms in the royal cause, and after achieving a victory over the barons at Lincoln, proceeded directly to London, and investing that great city, both by land and water, reduced it to extremity, for want of provisions. Peace, how-

ever, being soon after concluded, it was relieved. His lordship, at this period, executed the office of sheriff for the cos. of Essex and Hertford. This eminent nobleman was no less distinguished by his wisdom in the council and valour in the field, than by his piety and his attachment to the church, of which his numerous munificent endowments bear ample testimony. His lordship had, by the heiress of Clare, five sons, who *s.* each other in his lands and honours, and five daus., viz.,

Maud, *m.* 1st, to Hugh Bigod, Earl of Norfolk; 2ndly, to William de Warren, Earl of Surrey; and 3rdly, to Walter de Dunstanville. This lady, upon the decease of her youngest brother, Anselm, Earl of Pembroke, *s. p.*, in 1245, and the division of the estates, obtained, as her share, the manor of Hempsted-Marshall, in Berks, with the office of marshal of England, which was inherited by her son ROGER BIGOD, 4th EARL OF NORFOLK, and surrendered to the crown by her grandson, Roger Bigod, 5th Earl of Norfolk. Maud, Countess of Norfolk, had likewise the manors of Chepstow and Carlogh,

Joane, *m.* to Warine de Montchensy.

Isabel, *m.* 1st, to Gilbert de Clare, Earl of Gloucester ; and 2ndly, to Richard, Earl of Cornwall. This lady had, as her portion, Kilkenny.

Sybil, *m.* to William de Ferrers, Earl of Derby, to whom she brought Kildare,

Eve, *m.* to William de Broase, of Brecknock.

The earl *d.* in 1219, and was *s.* by his eldest son,

WILLIAM MARSHAL, Earl of Pembroke, who, in the time of his father, was as strenuous a supporter of the baronial cause as that nobleman was of the royal interests, and was constituted one of the twenty-five barons appointed to enforce the observance of Magna Charta, being then styled "Comes Mareschal, Jun." After the decease of King JOHN, however, he made his peace, and, becoming loyally attached to the new monarch, obtained grants of the forfeited lands of his former companions. Saier de Quincy, Earl of Winchester, and David, Earl of Huntingdon. His lordship was subsequently engaged against the Welsh, and defeated their Prince, Llewelyn, with great slaughter; and in the 14th HENRY III., he was captain-general of the king's forces in Britanny. He *m.* 1st, Alice, dau. of Baldwin de Betun, Earl of Albemarle; and 2ndly, the Lady Alianore Plantagenet, dau. of King JOHN, and sister of HENRY III., but had issue by neither. He *d.* in 1231, and was *s.* by his next brother,

RICHARD MARSHAL, Earl of Pembroke. This nobleman returned to England upon the decease of his brother, and repairing to the king, then in Wales, offered to do homage for his inheritance, but Henry, at the suggestion of Hubert de Burgh, justiciary of England, declined receiving it, under the plea that the late earl's widow had been left in a state of pregnancy, and the king, at the same time, commanded Marshal forthwith to depart the realm within fifteen days; upon which he repaired to Ireland, where his brothers then were, who, with the army, received him cordially, and, delivering up the castles to him, did their homage. He immediately afterwards took possession of the castle of Pembroke, and prepared to enforce his rights by arms; but the king, fearing to disturb the public tranquillity, accepted his fealty, and acknowledged him EARL OF PEMBROKE. This reconciliation was not, however, of long endurance, for we find him soon afterwards in open hostility to the king, defending his own castles, storming and taking others, fighting and winning pitched battles, until his gallant career was finally arrested by the treachery of his own followers in Ireland, where, being inveigled, under the pretext of entering into a league of amity, he was assailed by superior numbers, and mortally wounded. His lordship, who is termed by Matt. Paris "the flower of chivalry," *d.* in 1234, and was buried in the oratory of the Friers Minors, at Kilkenny. As he *d. unm.*, his estates and honours devolved upon his brother,

GILBERT MARSHAL, 4th Earl of Pembroke, who was restored to the whole of the late earl's lands by the king, although he had taken part in the proceedings of that nobleman. But notwithstanding this act of grace, his lordship never appears to have been cordially reconciled to the crown. His death occurred in 1241, and was occasioned by a fall from his horse at a tournament. He had *m.* 1st, Margaret, dau. of WILLIAM, King of Scotland, and 2ndly, Maud de Lanvaley; but having no issue, he was *s.* by his brother,

WALTER MARSHAL, 5th Earl of Pembroke. This nobleman had no little difficulty in obtaining livery of his inheritance, for when he came to do his homage, the king upbraided him with the injuries he had sustained from his predecessors. First, that Earl William, his father, had traitorously suffered LEWIS of France to escape out of England. Next, that Earl Richard, his brother, was a public enemy, and slain in fight as his enemy. That Gilbert, his brother, to whom at the instance of

---

[*] He was brother and heir male, of John Marshal, otherwise Mareschall (for whose descent, *see* Marshal, Barons Marshal). This family enjoyed the office of marshal of the King's House, and from that post assumed its surname; which gave occasion, says Banks, to their being often styled Earls Marshal, as well as Earls of Strigul and Pembroke; but such denomination was matter of *curiality* more than of *reality*. The manor of Hempsted-Marshal, in Berkshire, belonging to the Marshals, was held of old by grand serjeanty of the Kings of England, to be the knights marshals, as the offices of steward, constable, &c., were in those times granted.

Edmund, archbishop of Canterbury, he had more through grace than favour, vouchsafed livery of his lands, had against his express prohibition, met at the tournament, wherein he was killed. "And thou," continued the king, "in contempt of me, wast also there. With what face, therefore, canst thou lay claim to that inheritance?" Whereupon Walter replied: "Though I could give a reasonable answer to what you have said, nevertheless I refer myself solely to your highness. You have hitherto been gracious to me, and reputed me as one of your family, and not amongst the meanest of your servants. I never demerited your favour, but now, in being at this tournament with my brother, whom I could not deny; and if all who were there should be thus disinherited, you would raise no small disturbance in your realm. Far be it from a good king, that I should suffer for the faults of all, and that amongst so great a number be the first punished." The king soon after, through the intercession of the bishop of Durham, vouchsafed him livery of the earldom and marshal's office. His lordship m. Margaret, dau and heir of Robert de Quincy, but dying s. p. in 1245, was s. by his only remaining brother,

ANSELME MARSHAL, 5th Earl of Pembroke, who enjoyed the honours but eighteen days. He d. 5 December, 1245, leaving no issue by his wife, Maud, dau. of Humphrey de Bohun, Earl of Hereford, whereupon all his honours became EXTINCT, and his great inheritance devolved on his sisters, as co-heirs (*refer to issue of the 1st earl.*)

Arms—Per pale, or and vert, a lion rampant, gu., armed and langued, az.

These arms were not borne until the family came to be Marshals of England, prior to which period the coat was, "Gu., a bend lozengé, or."

MARTIN—BARONS MARTIN.

By Writ of Summons, dated 23 June, 1295.

Lineage.

The first of this family upon record, is

MARTIN DE TOURS, a Norman, who, making a conquest of Kemys, in Pembrokeshire, founded a monastery for benedictine monks, at St. Dogmaels, which his son and successor,

ROBERT MARTIN, endowed with lands in the time of HENRY I. This Robert m. Maud Peverell, and was s. by his son,

WILLIAM MARTIN. This feudal lord m. the dau. of Rhese ap Griffin, Prince of South Wales, and dying in 1209, was s. by his son,

WILLIAM MARTIN, who, upon the decease of his father, paid 300 marks for livery of his lands, and dying in 1215, was s. by his son,

NICHOLAS MARTIN. This feudal lord m. Maud, dau. of Guy de Brien, and Eve, his wife, dau. and heir of Henry de Tracy, Lord of Barnstaple, in the co. of Devon, by which alliance he acquired that lordship. In the 29th HENRY III. this Nicholas received command to assist the Earl of Gloucester, and other barons marchers, against the Welsh. He d. in 1282, and was s. by his grandson,

WILLIAM MARTIN (son and heir of his eldest son, Nicholas who predeceased him) who, being in the Scottish wars, was summoned to parliament as a Baron, from 23 June, 1295, to 10 October, 1325. His lordship m. Eleanor, dau. of William de Mohun, and had issue,

WILLIAM, his successor.
Eleanor, m. 1st, to William Hastings; and 2ndly, to Philip, Baron Columbers, but d. s. p.
Joan, m. 1st, to Henry de Lacy, Earl of Lincoln; and 2ndly, to Nicholas de Audley, by whom she had a son,
James de Audley, Baron Audley.

He d. in 1325, and was s. by his son,

WILLIAM MARTIN, 2nd baron, summoned to parliament 10 October, 1325. His lordship d. the year after he inherited, seized of the whole territory of Kemeys, which he held of the king, *in capite*, by the fourth part of one knight's fee. Upon the baron's decease the Barony of Martin fell into ABEYANCE between his heirs, Eleanor Columbers, his sister, and James de Audley, his nephew. The present SIR MARTEINE-OWEN-MOWBRAY LLOYD, Bart., of Bronwydd, co. Cardigan, is, by right of tenure, Lord of the Barony of Keymes. (*See* ADDENDA.)

Arms—Arg., two bars, gu.

NOTE.-Of this family the MARTINS, *of Long Melford*, are said to have been a branch.

MASHAM—BARONS MASHAM, OF OTES, CO. ESSEX.

By Letters Patent, dated 1 January, 1712.

Lineage.

The family of Masham, or Massam, was anciently seated in the north part of England, and undoubtedly took their name from Masham, a village near Richmond, in Yorkshire. From John Masham, Esq. (son and heir of Sir John Masham, who, *temp.* HENRY VI., settled in Suffolk, and d. there in 1450) descended THOMAS MASHAM, Esq., seated at Bardwell-Ash, co. Suffolk, who was ancestor of the Mashams of Suffolk. He was father of

JOHN MASHAM, Esq., who had two sons, John and WILLIAM MASHAM, Esq., alderman and sheriff of London, in 1583, He was father of

WILLIAM MASHAM, Esq., who became seated at Otes, and by his wife, a dau. of — Calton, left a son,

SIR WILLIAM MASHAM, of High-Laver, co. Essex, M.P. for Maldon and Colchester, and one of the knights of the shire, in the long parliament (created a Baronet, 20 December, 1621) He m. Winifred, dau. of Sir Francis Barrington, of Barrington Hall, son of Sir Thomas Barrington, by Winifred, his wife, widow of Sir Thomas Hastings, and 2nd dau. and co-heir of Henry Pole, Lord Montagu (attainted and beheaded in 1539), son and heir of Sir Richard Pole, K.G., by his wife, Margaret, Countess of Salisbury, dau. and eventually co-heir of George Plantagenet, Duke of Clarence, younger brother of King EDWARD IV. By this marriage, the family of Masham allied itself with the noblest blood in the realm. His eldest son,

WILLIAM MASHAM, Esq., m. Elizabeth, dau. of Sir John Trevor, Knt,, who pre-deceased her father, leaving, with other issue, William (Sir), who d. unm., and

SIR FRANCIS MASHAM, 3rd baronet, M.P., who m. 1st, Mary, dau. of Sir William Scott, of Rouen, in Normandy, Bart., and by her had eight sons, all of whom pre-deceased him except the youngest, SAMUEL, of whom presently. The 4th son, Francis, left a son FRANCIS, who s. to the baronetcy on the death of his grandfather, and d. unm. Sir Francis m. 2ndly, Damaris, dau. of Dr. Cudworth, master of Christ's College, Cambridge, and by her had a son, Francis-Cudworth, accountant-general to the court of Chancery. Sir Francis d. 2 March, 1722-3, and was s. in the baronetcy, as above stated, by his grandson. His youngest and only surviving son,

SIR SAMUEL MASHAM, 4th baronet, who m. Abigail, dau. of Francis Hill, Esq., a Turkey merchant, and sister of General John Hill. This lady was nearly related to Sarah, Duchess of Marlborough, and was introduced by her grace, whom she eventually supplanted, to the notice of Queen ANNE. Sir Samuel, who was an eighth son, was originally a page to the Queen, whilst Princess of Denmark, and also one of the equerries and gentlemen of the bed-chamber to Prince George. On the discomfiture of the Marlborough party, and the establishment of his wife as the reigning favourite, he was elevated to the peerage, 1 January, 1712, as BARON MASHAM, *of Otes, co. Essex*. and having had a grant in reversion of the office of remembrancer of the Exchequer, succeeded to that post on the death of Lord Fanshaw, in 1716. His lordship had issue,

George, who d. s. p., v. p.
SAMUEL, successor to the title.
Francis, d. s. p., v. p.
Anne, m. to Henry Hoare, Esq., and had issue,
Susannah, m. 1st, to Charles, Viscount Dungarvan, and 2ndly, to Thomas, 1st Earl of Aylesbury.
Anne, m. to Sir Richard Hoare, Bart.
Elizabeth, d. unm. in 1724.

Lord Masham d. 16 October, 1758, and was s. by his only surviving son,

SAMUEL MASHAM, 2nd baron. This nobleman m. 1st, Herriot, dau. of Thomas Winnyngton, Esq., of Stanford Court, co. Worcester, by whom (who d. in 1761,) he had no issue. He m. 2ndly, Miss Dives, one of the maids of honour to the Dowager Princess of Wales, but had no issue. His lordship, who filled several public employments, d. in 1776, when the Barony of Masham became EXTINCT.

Arms—Or, a fesse humetté, gu., between two lions passant, sa.

MASSUE—EARL OF GALWAY.

Lineage.

NICHOLAS DE MASSUE, m. Helen, dau. of Anthony D'Ally, and was grandfather of

HENRY DE MASSUE, Marquis de Renneval and de Ruvigny, deputy-general of the protestant churches of France, and envoy extraordinary from the French king to the court of St. James's, m. Marie Tallemand, and was father of

HENRY DE MASSUE DE RUVIGNY, who gained distinction in the wars of Turenne, and subsequently (having been forced by religious persecution to settle in England) in the service of WILLIAM III., especially at the battle of Aughrim. He was created a peer of Ireland, as *Baron Portarlington and Viscount Galway*, 25 November, 1692, and advanced to be EARL OF GALWAY, 12 May, 1697, whereupon, a grant of supporters passed to his lordship, viz., " two savages, crowned and girt with laurel, each holding in his hand a club, and on the same arm a shield with the arms of Ireland, all ppr." De Ruvigny was sent, upon the death of Duke Schomberg, in 1691, as lieutenant-general of the forces and envoy extraordinary to Savoy, and d. 2 September, 1720, when the honours he enjoyed became EXTINCT.

Arms—Quarterly : 1st, arg., a fesse gu., in chief, three martlets, sa., on a canton, or, a battle-axe of the 3rd ; 2nd, gu., a chaplet of laurel, or, a chief chequé, arg. and az.; 3rd, arg., three mallets, gu.

MATHEW—EARL OF LLANDAFF.

By Letters Patent, dated November, 1797.

Lineage.

Captain GEORGE MATHEW, the eldest son of Edmund Mathew, m. Elizabeth, widow of Thomas Butler, Viscount Thurles, son of Walter, 11th Earl of Ormonde, who was lost at sea on the Skerries, on the 15th December, 1619. By her, George Mathew had two daus. and two daus., Toby and George ; Frances, a nun ; and Elizabeth, m. to Edward Butler, of Ballyragget. Captain George Mathew d. in 1636, at Tenby. Of TOBY MATHEW, the eldest son, more hereafter.

GEORGE MATHEW, of Reaghill, 2nd son of Captain George and Lady Thurles, settled on the demesne of Thomastown, co. Tipperary. He m. Eleanor, widow of Edmund Butler, Lord Cahir, which is thus recorded in LODGE's *Peerage*, 1757. "Eleanor, 2nd dau. of Edmund Butler, Lord Dunboyne, m. in 1641, Edmund Butler, son and heir of Thomas, Lord Cahir, who d. before his father, when she re-married with George Mathew, of Thomastown, a gentleman of great fortune, honour, ability, and integrity," and had one son, Theobald Mathew, more familiarly called Toby   This

THEOBALD MATHEW, of Thomastown, m. the dau. and heiress of Bartholomew Faulkes, and had three sons and four daus.,

I. GEORGE, of Thomastown, styled Grand George, of whom hereafter.
II. Toby, *d. unm.* in 1726.
III. Theobald, *d. unm.* in 1712.
I. Elizabeth, m. Christopher O'Brien, heir of Donogh O'Brien, of Duagh.
II. Frances, the wife of Captain John Butler, of Kilvoleghan, co. Tipperary.
III. Eleanor, wife of Kane O'Hara, of Nymphsfield.
IV. Anne, m. Pierce, 3rd Lord Galmoy.

Theobald Mathew d. 6 January, 1699, and was s. by his son,

GEORGE MATHEW, of Thomastown, (styled Grand George, for his great acquirements and style of living). He m. 1st, Elizabeth Butler, of Ballyragget, and had four sons,

I. George, *d. unm* , v. p,
II. Edmund.
III. Theobald, m. Mary-Anne, dau. of George Mathew, the younger, in 1731. He d. and she re-married Charles O'Hare They had two children, a son George, who d. an infant, an. a dau who d. a minor, in 1750, when thus failed the line of George Mathew. of Thomastown, 2nd son of Captain George and Lady Thurles.

" Grand George " m. 2ndly, Anne, widow of James de la Poer, Earl of Tyrone, and d. in 1740, leaving no issue male, when the estate came to George Mathew, the youngest, of Thurles, brother of the Mary-Anne Mathew who had m. Toby, son of Grand George. We must now revert to the Thurles branch, commencing with

TOBY MATHEW, of Thurles and Annefield, the eldest son of Captain George and Lady Thurles. Toby Mathew, who obtained of his half-brother, the Duke of Ormonde, the manor, castle, and town of Thurles, with a vast estate surrounding, m. three times; 1st, Margaret, dau. of Sir Valentine Browne, of Hospital; 2ndly, Anne Saull; and 3rdly, Catharine Neville. By his 1st wife he had, with one dau., Elizabeth, (who m. Pierce Butler, Lord Cahir), two sons, George and James, who m. a dau. of Theobald Bourke, Lord Brittas. The elder son,

GEORGE MATHEW, Esq.' (called Major George, and also George Mathew, the elder, of Thurles), m. 1st Cecilia, dau. of Francis Arundel, of Dykes, and brother of Sir John Arundel, and had one son, GEORGE, the younger, of Thurles, of whom hereafter. He m. 2ndly, the widow of Sir Simon Eaton, Bart., dau. of Sir Richard Aldworth, of Newcastle, co. Cork; by her he had one son, Justyn, who d. unm. in 1725, and two daus. The son and heir,

GEORGE MATHEW, the younger, m. 1st, Mary, Lady Shelley, widow of Sir John Shelley, of Michell Grove, and dau. of Sir John Gage, of Firle, and by her had one son, GEORGE, the youngest, of Thurles, afterwards of Thomastown, and one dau. Mary-Anne, who, as before related, m. Theobald, 3rd son of Grand George, and afterwards, Charles O'Hara. He m. 2ndly, Martha Eaton, dau. of his step-mother, but by her had no issue. The only son,

GEORGE MATHEW, Esq., the youngest, of Thurles, who s. to Thomastown, on the decease of Grand George, m. 1st, Margaret, dau. of Thomas Butler, of Kilcash, by his wife, Lady Margaret Burke, eldest dau. of the Earl of Clanricarde, and widow of Bryan, Lord Viscount Iveagh; by her, who d. in July, 1743, he had one son, who d. an infant, and a dau. Margaret, wife of Michael Aylmer, of Lyons, co. Kildare. She disputed her father's will against Thomas Mathew, of Annefield, and failed. She was ancestress of the present Earl of Kenmare. He m. 2ndly, Isabella, dau. of W. Brownlow, Esq., of Shankhill, M.P. for the co. Armagh, but had no issue. He d. 30 March, 1760, when both the Thurles and Thomastown families became extinct. He bequeathed the estates of Thurles and Thomastown, &c., to his nearest kinsman, Thomas Mathew, of Annefield, who then represented the family, entailing the whole in the strictest possible manner, first to the sons of Thomas, and then to his brothers, John, George, and Charles, of Annefield, and their issue male only, by right of priority and seniority, then to Edmund and James, and their issue male, and then to sundry female members, on failing male heirs, but all confined to the Irish descent, recognizing no others whatever, then to his own right heirs, who must take and use the name of Mathew. We now come to the ANNEFIELD family, descendants of the first Toby Mathew, (son of Captain George), by his 2nd marriage with Anne Saull, as before related.

TOBY MATHEW, eldest son of Captain George and Lady Thurles, m. three times. By his 2nd wife, Anne Saul, he had two sons and one dau.,

I. THOMAS, on whom Annefield was settled by his father. He signed an address to King CHARLES II., in 1683, and d. in 1714.
II. James, d. v. p., having m. Elizabeth, dau. of Theobald, Bourke, Lord Brittas.
I. Mary, d. unm. about 1695.

The elder son,

THOMAS MATHEW, of Annefield, m. Honora, dau. of Thomas Ryan, of Clonmell, and relict of — Furley, and by her, who d. in 1735, he had seven sons,

I. THEOBALD, his heir, of Annefield.
II. Thomas, d. young.
III. George, d. unm.
IV. Charles, of Anabeg, co. Galway.
V. James, of Borris, m. Anne, dau. of James Morris.
VI. John, d. unm.
VII. Edmund, of Annefield, who d. unm. in 1772, leaving his property to his nephews, John, George. and Charles (of whom hereafter), and appointing his well-beloved friend and kinsman, Walter Butler, of Garryricken, his executor, who was, of right, 16th Earl of Ormonde.

Thomas Mathew d. in 1714, and was s. at Annefield by his eldest son,

THEOBALD MATHEW, of Annefield, who, besides, possessed estates in the counties of Limerick and Galway. He m. Catharine, dau. of Sir John and Mary, Lady Shelley, which latter had re-married George Mathew, the younger, as before related. She left her dau. Catharine, wife of Toby Mathew, of Annefield, £2,000 in her will, dated 1722. Theobald Mathew, of Annefield, and Catharine Shelley, his wife, left four sons and one dau.,

I. THOMAS, of Annefield, who, at the demise of George Mathew, of Thurles and Thomastown, became chief of the

family, and who *s.* to all the estates of the family by George
Mathew's will and entail.

   II. John, believed to have *d. unm.*

   III. GEORGE, an officer much on foreign service, of whom hereafter.

   IV. Charles, also an officer in the army; *m.* Honora, dau. of James Mathew, of Borris, and had a dau. *m.* to Sir Hugh O'Reilly, afterwards Nugent, of Westmeath.

   I. Mary, *d. unm.* in Dublin, in 1777.

Toby Mathew *d.* at Crumlin, 24 September, 1745, and was *s.* by his son,

   THOMAS MATHEW, Esq. of Annefield, who *m.* very young Miss Mathews, dau. of Richard Mathews, of Dublin, and by her had one dau., (Catharine-Anne-Marie, *m.* 1st, to Philip Roe, Esq., and 2ndly, to John Scott, Earl of Clonmell,) and a son,

   FRANCIS MATHEW, Esq., M.P. for co. Tipperary, who *s.* his father, Thomas, and 2nd earl. He was created a peer of Ireland as Baron Llandaff, 12 October, 1783, advanced to be Viscount Llandaff, 20 December, 1793, and made EARL OF LLANDAFF, November, 1797: he *m.* in 1764, Ellis, dau. of James Smyth, Esq., of Tinny Park, co. Wicklow, and by her, who *d.* in 1781, had issue three sons and one dau.,

   I. FRANCIS-JAMES, 2nd earl.

   II. Montague, a general in the army, colonel of the 99th regiment of foot (which his father raised), and M.P. for co. Tipperary, *d. unm.* in 1819.

   II. George-Toby-Skeffington, in the army, *d. unm.* in 1832.

   I. LADY ELIZABETH, who survived all her brothers, and *d. unm.* in 1842.

The Earl of Llandaff *m.* 2ndly, 1784, Elizabeth, dau. of Clotworthy Skeffington, Earl of Massereene, and 3rdly, a dau. of Jeremiah Coghlan, Esq., but had no issue by these marriages. The earl *d.* at Swansea, in Wales, in September, 1806, and was *s.* by his son and heir,

   FRANCIS-JAMES MATHEW, 2nd Earl of Llandaff, K.P., who, *m.,* 10 July, 1797, Gertrude, dau. of John La Touche, Esq., of Harristown, co. Kildare, and *d.* 12 March, 1833, leaving no issue, when all his honours became EXTINCT. At his death, intestate, his sister, Lady Elizabeth Mathew, was put into possession of the estates, and she dying in 1842 bequeathed the property to her cousin, the Vicomte de Châbot, whose mother was Elizabeth Smyth, sister of Ellis, Countess of Llandaff.

Arms—Or, a lion rampant, sa.

MAUDUIT—EARL OF WARWICK.

(*See* NEWBURGH, Earls of Warwick.)

MAUDUIT—BARON MAUDUIT.

By Writ of Summons, dated 12 September, 1342.

Lineage.

Of the same family as William Mauduit, Earl of Warwick, was (according to Dugdale),

   JOHN MAUDUIT, who in the 8th EDWARD II., had a military summons, amongst other great men, to march against the Scots, and was engaged for some years afterwards in the wars of Scotland. In the 3rd EDWARD III., he was constituted sheriff of Wiltshire, and governor of the castle of Old Sarum; and was summoned to parliament as a Baron, 12 September, 1342. In the 19th of the same reign, his lordship obtained a charter for free warren in all his demesne lands at Farnhull, Somerford, Muuduit, Funtel and Uptele, co. Wilts, as also at Stanlake and Broughton, in Oxfordshire. His lordship *d.* in 1347, leaving a son and heir,

   JOHN MAUDUIT, but neither this John nor any of his posterity were ever summoned to parliament, or deemed barons of the realm.

The Barony of Mauduit is therefore presumed to have become EXTINCT upon the demise of the said John, Lord Mauduit.

Arms— Arg., two bars, gules.

MAULE—EARL OF PANMURE.

By Letters Patent, dated 2 August, 1646.

Lineage.

The family of Maule, of Panmure, was one of great antiquity and eminence.

   PATRICK MAULE, of Panmure (son of Patrick Maule, of Panmure, by Margaret, his wife, dau. of John Erskine, of Dun, and nephew of Robert Maule, commissary of St. Andrews, author of "De Antiquitate Gentis Scotorum,") accompanied King JAMES VI. into England in 1603, and was appointed one of the gentlemen of the bedchamber to that monarch, an office which he afterwards held under CHARLES I., who constituted him keeper of the palace and park of Eltham, and sheriff of the co. Forfar. He subsequently adhered with great fidelity to the king in his troubles, for which services he was elevated to the peerage of Scotland, 2 August, 1646, as *Baron Maule, of Brechin and Navar,* and EARL OF PANMURE. His lordship *m.* thrice; but had issue only by his 1st wife, Frances, dau. of Sir Edward Stanhope, of Grimston, co. York. He *d.* 22 December, 1661, and was *s.* by his eldest son,

   GEORGE MAULE, 2nd Earl of Panmure, who *m.* Lady Jean Campbell, eldest dau. of John, Earl of Loudoun, high chancellor of Scotland, by whom he had issue,

   GEORGE, his successor.

   JAMES, who *s.* his brother.

   Harry, of Kelly. This gentleman was a member of the convention of estates in 1689, but retired from the assembly when he discovered the determination to dethrone JAMES II. He subsequently joined the banner of the Chevalier St. George, in 1715, and *d.* at Edinburgh in 1731. He *m.* 1st in 1695, Lady Mary Fleming, only dau. of William, 1st Earl of Wigton, and had surviving issue,

     WILLIAM; his successor.

     JEAN, *m.* 1st to George, Lord Ramsay, eldest son of William, 6th Earl of Dalhousie, and was mother of CHARLES RAMSAY, 7th earl, and of GEORGE RAMSAY, 8th Earl of Dalhousie, whose 2nd son,

       WILLIAM RAMSAY, assumed the surname and arms of Maule, and was created Lord Panmure: his son, FOX MAULE, 2nd Lord Panmure, is now also EARL OF DALHOUSIE.

   Mr. Maule, of Kelly, *m.* 2ndly, Anne dau. of the Hon. Patrick Lindsay-Crawford, of Kilbirnie, and had a son,

     John, of Inverkeilor, one of the barons of the Court of Exchequer in Scotland; who *d. unm.* in 1781.

   Mr. Harry Maule, of Kelly, was much given to the study of the history and antiquities of Scotland : his eldest son,

     WILLIAM MAULE, of Kelly, who was created a peer of Ireland in 1743, as Viscount Maule, of Whitechurch, and EARL OF PANMURE, of Forth. He *d. unm.* in 1782, when his honours became EXTINCT, and his estate devolved, by a decree of the Court of Session, upon his nephew, GEORGE, EARL OF DALHOUSIE.

George, 2nd Earl of Panmure *d.* 24 March, 1671, and was *s.* by his eldest son,

   GEORGE MAULE, 3rd Earl of Panmure, who *d. s. p.* in 1686, when the honours and estates passed to his brother,

   JAMES MAULE, 4th Earl of Panmure. This nobleman joining the rising of 1715, was taken prisoner at the battle of Sheriffmuir, but rescued by his brother Harry, when he effected his escape into France. An attainder, by act of parliament, followed, and his honours and estates became forfeited to the crown. They were, however, at two different times, offered to be restored to him, provided he returned to his native land and subscribed the oath of allegiance to the house of Hanover, but he preferred sharing the fortunes of the exiled prince, and *d.* at Paris, 11 April, 1723. This Earl of Panmure made a fine collection of family charters and documents which were arranged by Mr. Crawford, and are known as the "Registrum de Panmure." His lordship *m.* Lady Margaret Hamilton, 3rd dau. of William and Anne, Duke and Duchess of Hamilton. In 1717, an act was passed to enable his Majesty to make such provision for, and settlement upon, the wife of James, late Earl of Panmure, as she should have been entitled to had her husband been naturally dead. Her ladyship *d.* in 1731. The Scottish Earldom of Panmure and Barony of Maule remain yet under the attainder; but the attainted lord's great grand-nephew, the HON. WILLIAM MAULE was created a peer of the United Kingdom, in the dignity of BARON PANMURE, *of Brechin and Navar;* his son, FOX MAULE, 2nd LORD PANMURE, *s.* 1860, as 11th EARL OF DALHOUSIE, and *d. s. p.* 6 July, 1874, when the barony of Panmure, of Brechin and Navar became EXTINCT.

MAULE—EARL OF PANMURE.

By Letters Patent, dated 2 May, 1743.

Lineage.

THE HON. HARRY MAULE, of Kelly, 2nd son of George, 2nd Scottish Earl of Panmure, was a member of the convention of estates in 1689, but retired from the assembly when he discovered the determination to dethrone JAMES II. He subsequently joined the banner of the Chevalier St. George, in 1715; and d. at Edinburgh, in 1734. He m. 1st, in 1695, Lady Mary Fleming, only dau. of William, 1st Earl of Wigton, and had issue,

WILLIAM, his heir.

Jean, m. to George, Lord Ramsay, eldest son of William, 6th Earl of Dalhousie.

Mr. Maule, of Kelly, m. 2ndly, Anne, dau. of the Hon. Patrick Lindsay Crawford, of Kilbirnie, and had a son, John, d. unm. His son and heir, by his first wife,

WILLIAM MAULE, Esq., of Kelly, was created a peer of Ireland in 1743, as *Viscount Maule, of Whitechurch,* and EARL OF PANMURE, *of Forth,* with remainder to his brother John. His lordship purchased the forfeited Panmure estates from the York Buildings Company, in 1764, for £49,157 18s. 4d. He was a military officer of high reputation, and attained the rank of general in 1770. He d. unm. in 1782, when his honours became EXTINCT, and his estates devolved, by a decree of the Court of Session, upon his nephew, George, Earl of Dalhousie, whose 2nd son, WILLIAM, assumed the surname and arms of MAULE, and was created in 1831, BARON PANMURE, *of Brechin and Navar,* and dying in 1852, was s. by his eldest son, Fox, who subsequently s. his cousin as Earl of Dalhousie, in 1860, and d. s. p. 6 July, 1874, when his barony became EXTINCT. (See BURKE'S *Extant Peerage.*)

Arms—Per pale, arg, and gu.; on a bordure eight escallops, all counterchanged.

MAULE—BARON PANMURE.

(*See* preceding Memoirs.)

MAULEY—BARONS MAULEY.

By Writ of Summons, dated 23 June, 1295.

Lineage.

The first mention of this name and family occurs when JOHN, Earl of Moreton, to clear his own way to the throne, employed Peter de Mauley, a Poictovin, his esquire, to murder his nephew, Prince Arthur, and in reward of the deed, gave to the said

PETER DE MAULEY, in marriage, Isabel, dau. of Robert de Turnham, and heiress of the Barony of Mulgrave. This Peter, throughout the whole reign of King John, adhering to his royal master, obtained considerable grants from the crown, and was esteemed amongst the evil advisers of the king. In the height of the baronial war, most of the prisoners of rank were committed to his custody, and he was constituted (18th JOHN), sheriff of the cos. of Dorset and Somerset. In the 4th HENRY III., upon the coronation of that monarch, Peter de Mauley had summons to assist thereat, and to bring with him the *regalia,* then in his custody at Corfe Castle, which had been entrusted to him by King JOHN; and the next year, being again sheriff of the cos. Somerset and Dorset, he delivered up the castle of Corfe to the king, with Alianore, the king's kinswoman, and Isabel, sister to the King of Scots, as well as all the jewels, military engines, and ammunition there, which the late monarch had formerly committed to his custody. Soon after this, he was made governor of Sherburne Castle, co. Dorset, and dying in 1221, was s. by his son,

PETER DE MAULEY, who giving 100 marks for his relief, had livery of his lands. Amongst the causes of discontent avowed by Richard Mareschall in his contest with HENRY III. was, that the king by the advice of foreigners, had dispossessed Gilbert Basset, a great baron of the time, of the manor of Nether-Haven, co. Wilts, and conferred it upon this Peter de Mauley. The king, nevertheless, continuing his favour to Peter, constituted him governor of the castle of Devizes, and the next year (20th HENRY III.,) made him sheriff of Northamptonshire. Moreover, in 1239, he was one of the godfathers, at the baptismal font to Prince Edward (the king's eldest son), and in 1241 he accompanied William de Fortibus, Earl of Albemarle, and divers other noble persons, to the Holy Land. This feudal lord m. Joane, dau. of Peter de Brus, of Skelton, and d. in 1242. Upon his decease Gerard le Grue paid 500 marks for the *ferme* of his

362

lands, and had the custody of the castle of Mulgrave; maintaining his widow with necessaries, keeping the buildings in repair, and not committing waste in the woods. Peter de Mauley was s. by his son,

PETER DE MAULEY (commonly called the 3rd), who doing his homage in the 31st HENRY III., had livery of his lands. In the 42nd of the same reign, the Scots having made a prisoner of their King ALEXANDER III. (son-in-law of the English monarch), Peter de Mauley received summons with the other northern barons to fit himself with horse and arms for the relief of the Scottish prince. He m. Nichola, dau. of Gilbert de Gant, son of Gilbert, Earl of Lincoln, and had issue,

PETER, his successor.

Edmund, a very eminent person in the reigns of EDWARD I. and II., and greatly distinguished in the Scottish wars. He had a grant of the manor of Seton, co. York. He was successively governor of the castle of Bridgenorth, of the town and castle of Bristol, and the castle of Cockermouth. He fell at the battle of Bannockburn, and dying s. p., his estates passed to his nephew,

Peter de Mauley.

He was s. at his decease by his elder son,

PETER DE MAULEY (called the 4th), who, in the 7th EDWARD I., doing his homage, and paying £100 for his relief, had livery of all his lands, which he held of the king in *capite* by barony of the inheritance of William Fossard (whose granddau. and heir, Isabel de Turnham, was wife of the first Peter de Mauley). This feudal lord having been engaged in the Welsh and Scottish wars, was summoned to parliament as a Baron by King EDWARD I., 23 June, 1295, and he had regular summons from that period to 12 December, 1309. In the 25th EDWARD I. his lordship was in the expedition then made into Gascony, and in consideration of his good services there, obtained f om the king a grant of the marriage of Thomas, the son and heir of Thomas de Multon, of Gillesland, deceased. For several years after this he was actively employed in the warfare of Scotland. His lordship m. Eleanor, dau. of Thomas, Lord Furnival, and dying in 1310, was s. by his son,

SIR PETER DE MAULEY, 2nd baron, summoned to parliament from 19 December, 1311, to 15 March, 1354. This nobleman was for several years actively engaged in the wars of Scotland, and was a commander at the battle of Durham (20th EDWARD III.), wherein the Scots, under their king, DAVID BRUS, sustained so signal a defeat, the monarch himself being made prisoner. His lordship m. Margaret, dau. of Robert, Lord Clifford, and dying in 1355, was s. by his son,

PETER DE MAULEY, 3rd baron, summoned to parliament from 20 September, 1355, to 7 January, 1383. This nobleman, in the 30th EDWARD III., shared in the glorious victory of Poictiers, and in three years afterwards he was in the expedition then made in Gascony. In the 41st of the same reign he was joined in commission with the bishop of Durham, Henry, Lord Percy, and others, for guarding the marches of Scotland; and again, in the 3rd RICHARD II., with the Earl of Northumberland. His lordship m. 1st, in the 31st EDWARD III., Elizabeth, widow of John, Lord Darcy, and dau. and heir of Nicholas, Lord Meinill, without license, for which office he paid a fine of £100, and obtained pardon. He m. 2ndly, Margery, one of the daus. and co-heirs of Thomas de Sutton, of Sutton in Holderness, and had issue (by which wife not known),

Peter, who m. Margery, one of the daus. and co-heirs of Sir Thomas de Sutton, Knt., and dying in the life-time of his father, left issue,

PETER, successor to his grandfather.

Constance, m. 1st, William Fairfax, s. p., and 2ndly, Sir John Bigot, ancestor by her of the Bigots of Moulgrave.

Elizabeth, m. to George Salvaine, Esq. "The present heir-general of the said Elizabeth Salvaine (we quote COURTHOPE'S *Historic Peerage*), "and consequently one of the co-heirs of the barony is Charles-Frederick-Ashley-Cooper Ponsonby, Lord de Mauley, son of William-Francis Spencer Ponsonby, Lord de Mauley, by Lady Barbara, dau. and sole heir of Anthony, 5th Earl of Shaftesbury, by Barbara, his wife, dau. and heir of Sir John Webb. Bart , by Mary, sister and eventually sole heir of Thomas Salvaine, Esq., the heir male and heir general of the above-mentioned George Salvaine and Elizabeth Mauley, his wife."

His lordship d. in 1383, seized of the manor and castle of Mulgrave, the manor of Doncaster with its members, and a moiety of the manor of Helagh, all in the co. York. He was s. by his grandson,

PETER DE MAULEY, 4th baron, who making proof of his age in the 22nd RICHARD II., had livery of the lands of his inheritance, as well as those derived from his grandfather, as from Thomas, his uncle. This nobleman was made a knight of the Bath at the coronation of King HENRY IV., and was summoned to parliament from 18 August, 1399, to 12 August, 1415. His lordship m. the Lady Maud Nevil, dau. of Ralph, Earl of Westmoreland, but d. in 1415, s. p., when his sisters (refer to issue of 3rd baron) became his heirs, and between those the Barony of Mauley fell into ABEYANCE, as it still continues amongst their representatives. In the distribution of the Mauley estates, Leland says, "Bigot had the castle of Maugreve, (Mulgrave), with eight tounelettes therabout tho se cost longging to it, whereof Seton thereby was one. Saulwayne had, for his part, the Barony of Eggeston on Eske, not far from Whitby; also Lokington-Barugh, not far from Watton-on-Hull ryver. Nesseark, and the lordship of Doncaster."

Arms—Or, a bend, sa.

MAXWELL—EARL OF FARNHAM.

(*See* BURKE's *Extant Peerage*, article BARON FARNHAM.)

MAXWELL—EARL OF DIRLETOUN.

By Letters Patent, dated 1646.

Lineage.

SIR JAMES MAXWELL, son of John Maxwell, by Jean Murray, sister of John, 1st Earl of Annandale, was appointed one of the gentlemen of the bedchamber to King JAMES VI., and continued in that office under CHARLES I. He was created a peer by the title of EARL OF DIRLETOUN *and* LORD ELBOTTLE, 1646, but *d.* without male issue, when the title became EXTINCT. By his wife, Elizabeth de Boussoyne, he had two daus.,

Elizabeth, *m.* 1st, to William, 2nd Duke of Hamilton, and had six children; 2ndly, to Thomas Dalmahoy, Esq., without issue.

Diana, *m.* to Charles, Viscount Cranburne, eldest son of William, 2nd Earl of Salisbury, and was mother of the 3rd Earl of Salisbury.

MAXWELL—EARLS OF NITHSDALE.

Lineage.

For ample details of the great house of MAXWELL, from which sprang the EARLS OF NITHSDALE, the MAXWELLS of Pollok, the Maxwells of Calderwood, the Maxwells, Lords Farnham, &c., reference should be made to "The Memoirs of the Maxwells of Pollok," by William Fraser, Esq., and Anderson's "Scottish Nation."

SIR HERBERT MAXWELL, of Carlaverock, knighted 21 May, 1424, and created LORD MAXWELL *circa* 1440, *m.* 1st, a dau. of Sir Herbert Herries, of Terregles, and had two sons,

ROBERT, his successor.

Edward (Sir), of Monreith, ancestor of the Maxwells, baronets, of that place.

His lordship *m.* 2ndly, Katherine, dau. of Sir William Seton, of Seton, and had, with other children, George, from whom sprang the Maxwells of Carnsalloch; and Adam, from whom the Maxwells of Southbar. Lord Maxwell's eldest son,

ROBERT MAXWELL, 2nd Lord Maxwell, was served heir to his father 4 February, 1453, and he sat as a peer in parliament, *anno* 1467. His lordship *m.* Janet Forrester, of Corstorphine, and was *s.* by his son,

JOHN MAXWELL, 3rd Lord Maxwell; who *m.* Janet, dau. of George Crichton, Earl of Caithness, and, falling at one of the battle of Kirtle, 22 July, 1484, was *s.* by his son,

JOHN MAXWELL, 4th Lord Maxwell, who *m.* Agnes, dau. of Sir Alexander Stewart, of Garlics, and was slain at Flodden, 9 September, 1513. His eldest son,

ROBERT MAXWELL, 5th Lord Maxwell, hereditary sheriff of Kirkcudbright, and guardian of the west marches. This nobleman *m.* 1st, Janet, dau. of William, 6th Lord Douglas, of Drumlanrig (ancestor of the Dukes of Queensberry), and had issue,

ROBERT, his successor.

John (Sir), who *m.* Agnes, eldest dau. and heiress of William Herries, 4th Lord Herries, of Terregles, co. Dumfries, and became, *jure uxoris*, LORD HERRIES, *of Terregles.* His lordship *d.* 1582, and was *s.* by his son,

SIR WILLIAM MAXWELL, 5th Lord Herries, of Terregles; who *m.* Katharine Kerr, sister of Mark, 1st Earl of Lothian, and dying in 1603, was *s.* by his son,

JOHN MAXWELL, 7th Lord Herries, of Terregles; who *m.* Elizabeth, dau. of John, 7th Lord Maxwell, and dying in 1631, left, *inter alios,*

JOHN MAXWELL, 8th Lord Herries, of whom hereafter, as 3rd Earl of Nithsdale.

363

James Maxwell, ancestor of the MAXWELLS of Carruchan.

The 5th Lord Maxwell *m.* 2ndly, Agnes, natural dau. of James, Earl of Buchan, relict of Adam, 2nd Earl of Bothwell. He *d.* 9 July, 1546, and was *s.* by his elder son,

ROBERT MAXWELL, 6th Lord Maxwell, of Carlaverock, warden of the west marches; who *m.* Lady Beatrix Douglas, 2nd dau. of James, Earl of Morton; and dying 14 September, 1552, was *s.* by his son,

JOHN MAXWELL, 7th Lord Maxwell, who was guardian of the west marches. Upon the execution and attainder of the Regent Morton, Lord Maxwell obtained, as representative of his mother, a new charter of the Earldom of Morton, ratified by parliament; but the attainder being rescinded, he was deprived of the dignity, which passed, in 1585, to the heir of entail. His lordship *m.* Elizabeth Douglas, dau. of David, 13th Earl of Douglas, and 7th Earl of Angus, and had issue,

JOHN, Lord Maxwell.

ROBERT, who inherited after his brother.

Elizabeth, who *m.* John Maxwell, 7th Lord Herries, of Terregles, and had a son,

JOHN, 8th Lord Herries, who *s.* his cousin as 3rd Earl of Nithsdale.

Margaret, Lady Craigie.

Agnes, Lady Penzerie.

He was killed by the Johnstones at Lockerbie in 1593, and was *s.* by his eldest son,

JOHN MAXWELL, 8th Lord Maxwell. A feud subsisting between the houses of Maxwell and Johnstone, this nobleman slew Sir James Johnstone, of Annandale, in a rencounter, and fleeing from Scotland in consequence, he was betrayed by the Earl of Caithness, and subsequently tried, beheaded, and attainted in 1613. His lordship had *m.* the Lady Margaret Hamilton, dau. of John, 1st Marquess Hamilton, Duke of Chatelherault, but had no issue. His brother,

ROBERT MAXWELL, 9th Lord Maxwell, was created, in 1620, *Lord Maxwell, of Eskdale and Carlyle,* and EARL OF NITHSDALE, in remainder to his heirs male, and with precedency of his father's Earldom of Morton (in 1581). This nobleman was celebrated, like his gallant ancestor, Sir Eustace Maxwell, in the time of EDWARD I., by a brave defence of Carlaverock, against the parliamentarians of 1640. His lordship *m.* Elizabeth, dau. of Sir Francis Beaumont, and dying in 1646, was *s.* by his son,

ROBERT MAXWELL, 2nd Earl of Nithsdale, hereditary sheriff of Kirkcudbright. His lordship dying *unm.* 5 October, 1667, was *s.* by his cousin,

JOHN MAXWELL, 8th Lord Herries, of Terregles, as 3rd Earl of Nithsdale. His lordship *m.* Elizabeth, sister of John Gordon, 1st Viscount Kenmure, and was *s.* at his decease by his son,

ROBERT MAXWELL, 4th Earl of Nithsdale: who *m.* the Lady Lucy Douglas, dau. of William, 1st Marquess Douglas. His lordship *d.* in 1685, and was *s.* by his son,

WILLIAM MAXWELL, 5th Earl of Nithsdale. This nobleman, so celebrated for effecting his escape from the Tower of London, 23 February, 1716, the night before his intended execution, through the agency of his devoted and heroic countess, was attainted, and the Earldom of the senior branch of the house of Maxwell, "the Maxwells of Carlaverock," has ever since been obscured by that penal proceeding. His lordship *m.* the Lady Winifred Herbert, youngest dau. of William, 1st Marquess of Powis; and dying at Rome, in 1744, was *s.* by his only surviving son,

WILLIAM MAXWELL, styled Earl of Nithsdale; who *m.* his 1st cousin, Lady Catharine Stewart, dau. of Charles, 4th Earl of Traquair (by Lady Mary Maxwell, dau. of Robert, 4th Earl of Nithsdale), and had an only dau., his successor at his decease in 1776,

LADY WINIFRED MAXWELL, who, but for the attainder of her grandfather, would have inherited the Barony of Herries, of Terregles. Her ladyship had *m.* in 1758, William Haggerston-Constable, Esq. (2nd son of Sir Carnaby Haggerston, Bart., of Haggerston Castle, in the county of Northumberland), and had three sons and two daus. The eldest son,

MARMADUKE-WILLIAM CONSTABLE-MAXWELL, Esq., of Everingham, *d.* in 1819, and was *s.* by his eldest son,

WILLIAM CONSTABLE-MAXWELL, of Carlaverock and Everingham, LORD HERRIES, whose right to the Barony of Herries was confirmed by the House of Lords, 23 June, 1858.

Arms—Arg., an eagle, displayed, sa., beaked and membered, gu., surmounted by an escutcheon of the 1st, charged with a saltier of the 2nd, and surcharged in the centre with a hedgehog, or.

MAYNARD—BARON MAYNARD, OF WICKLOW, AND MAYNARD—VISCOUNT MAYNARD.

(*See* ADDENDA.)

MAYNE—BARON NEWHAVEN.

By Letters Patent, dated 1776.

Lineage.

WILLIAM MAYNE, Esq. (great-grandson of William Mayne, Esq. of Pile, near Stirling, living *temp.* Queen MARY and JAMES VI.), was put in possession by his brother, Edward, of the lands of Powis and Logie, in the cos. of Perth and Clackmannan. He *m.* 1st, Euphemia, dau. of John Christie, Esq., of Lecroft, and had three sons and two daus., viz.,

I. JOHN, of London merchant, whose issue is EXTINCT.

II. JAMES, of St. Ninians, whose only dau., Euphemia Mayne, *m.* 1st, James Henderson, Esq., of Westerton, and had two sons, John and William. She *m.* 2ndly, James Alexander, Esq., provost of Stirling, by whom she was grandmother of SIR JAMES EDWARD ALEXANDER, Knt., C.B., of Powis, co. of Clackmannan.

III. Edward, of Powis, who *m.* Janet, dau. of James Henderson, Esq., and had, with several daus.,

 1 James, major in the army, who *m.* Mary, dau. of Henry Crawford, Esq., and had with two sons (Edward and Henry, who *d. unm.*) one dau.,

  Helen-Elphinstone Mayne.

 2 William, who *d.* young.

 3 Edward, who *d. unm.*

I. Catherine, *m.* to James Burn, Esq.

II. Margaret, *m.* to Sir Alexander Cunningham.

Mr. Mayne *m.* 2ndly, Helen, dau. of William Galbraith, Esq. of the Balgaer family, and by her had issue,

IV. WILLIAM, of whom presently.

V. Robert, *b.* in 1724, of Gatton Park, co. Surrey, M.P., *m.* Sarah, dau. and co-heir of Francis Otway, Esq., and *d.* 1783, leaving,

 1 William, *b.* 1776, col. life-guards; *m.* 1805, Elizabeth, dau. and co heiress of Sir John Taylor, Bart., and *d.* 11 December, 1843, leaving issue,

  Simon-William, capt. H.M.'s 40th regt., *m.* in 1829, Charlotte, relict of R. Balland, Esq., and *d.* 25 December, 1843, leaving issue, WILLIAM-SIMON, *b.* 1831.

  John, major H M.'s 1st royals, *m.* 1st, 25 March, 1829, Mary, dau. of Sir R. Armstrong, K.C.B., who *d.* in 1830. *s. p.* He *m.* 2ndly, 19 October, 1841, Lucy, dau. of N. Ives, Esq., who *d.* in 1851, *s. p.*; and 3rdly, 22 January, 1866, Amelia, dau. of Thomas Fielder, Esq., by whom he had a dau., Lalage-Elizabeth. H. *d.* 14 January, 1872, and his widow *m.* 22 September, 1874, Samuel-Robinson Carnell, Esq., of Selands House, Isle of Wight.

  Charles-Frederic, capt. in H.M.'s 61st regt., *m.* in 1839, Eliza, dau. of the Rev. Mr. Lookwood, and *d. s. p.*

  Taylor-Lambard, 3rd dragoon guards, lieut.-col. half pay, *m.* 1858, Mary-Margaret-Charlotte, only dau. of Lieut. - Gen. Foster, and has, Clyde - Frederick, and other sons.

  Eliza, *m.* 6 October, 1830, M.-E. Impey, Esq.

  Sarah-Otway, *m.* 26 September, Rev. Richard Hollings.

 2 Robert (Rev.), M.A., rector of Limpsfield, co. Surrey, D.L., *b.* 26 February, 1778; *m.* 8 June, 1803, Charlotte Cunningham, dau. of Col. Graham, of St. Laurence House, Canterbury, and by her (who *d.* 1827) he left at his decease, 7 March, 1841,

  Charles-Otway, *b.* 6 September, 1807, M.A., prebendary of Wells, and vicar of Midsomer-Norton; *m.* in 1833, Emily, dau. of G.-R. Smith, Esq., of Selsdon, Surrey, M.P., and has Ashton-George, *b.* 1834, and other issue.

  George, *b.* 1808; *d.* 1830, at Meerut, a lieutenant Bengal artillery.

  Henry-Blair, *b.* 23 August, 1813, barrister-at-law, and one of the officers of the House of Commons.

  William, *b.* 28 October, 1818, colonel Bengal army, brigadier commanding the Hyderabad Contingent. A.D.C. to the Queen; and Hon. A.D.C. to the Governor-General of India; *m.* 1844, Helen-Cunliffe, eldest dau. of T.-R. Davidson, Esq., B.C.S., resident Nagpore, and had issue, Charles-Hardinge, *b.* August, 1848, *d.* 23 November, 1855.

  Robert-Graham, *b.* 18 February, 1820, major Bengal staff corps, *m.* 1849, Eliza Landal, and has,

   Robert, *d.* 18 Sept. 1865,

   Anne, *d.* 28 August, 1865,

   Frances, *d.* 25 April, 1855.

   Charlotte-Mary.

   Frederica-Eliza-Graham.

 3 Frederic, *b.* in 1779, lost at sea, *circa* 1799.

 4 Charles-Otway, *b.* 1780, of the Manor House, Great Stan

more, capt. H.E.I.C.'s maritime service; *m.* 1815, Emma, d u. of Harry Taylor, Esq., M.C.S., and *d.* March, 1857, leaving issue,

 Henry-Otway, *b.* 11 March, 1819, H.E.I.C.'s Madras cavalry; *m.* 12 January, 1850, Mary-Ewer, youngest dau. of T.-J. Turner, Esq., B.C.S., and *d.* November, 1861, leaving issue.

 Frederic-Otway, *b.* 5 August, 1823, M.A., a chaplain on the H.E.I.C.'s Bengal establishment; *m.* 13 February, 1849, Elizabeth-Louisa, dau. of Col. James Blair, and has issue.

 Francis-Otway, *b.* 1827, H.E I C.'s Bengal civil service, married, C.B., for services during the Indian Mutiny.

 Augustus-Otway, *b.* 1829, H.E.I.C.'s Bengal horse art., killed in action before Lucknow, 14 November, 1857.

 Jasper-Otway, *b.* 1830, in H.E.I.C.'s Madras engineers; *m.* Adriana, dau. of Col. H. Blair, and has issue.

 Charles-Thomas-Otway, *b.* 6 February, 1835; *m.* 1857, Augusta, dau. of George Parry, Esq. She *d.* 1860, leaving issue.

 Emma-Otway, *m.* December, 1855, Arthur Noverre, Esq. Marianne-Otway.

 Helen Otway, *m.* 1858, Rev. Henry Barnard.

I. Helen, *m.* to John Graham, Esq., of Kernock.

II. Barbara, *m.* to James Duncanson, Esq., of Glasgow.

III. Isabel, *m.* to James Duncanson, Esq., of Inverary.

William Mayne *m.* 3rdly, Helen, dau. of the Rev. Mr. Stark, and had by her,

 THOMAS, of Lisbon, who *m.* 1st, Miss Clever; and 2ndly, Charlotte, dau. of Alexander Pringle, of Whytbank, and had a dau., Susan-Allan.

 Elizabeth, *m.* to the Rev. Archibald Smith, of Fintry.

 Jean, *m.* to John Brown, of Glasgow, merchant.

Mr. Mayne had by his three wives twenty-one children, and the cradle is said to have rocked in his house fifty years. His eldest son by his 2nd wife,

SIR WILLIAM MAYNE, *b.* 1722, M.P., a privy councillor and a distinguished Member of the House of Commons, was created a baronet, and subsequently a peer of Ireland in 1776, as BARON NEWHAVEN, of Carrick Mayne, co. Dublin: he *m.* Frances, dau. and co-heir of Joshua, Viscount Allen, and had an only son, who *d.* young. His lordship *d.* in 1794, when his title became EXTINCT.

Arms.—Arg., a chev. gu., voided of the field, between two pheons in chief, sa , and a fleur-de-lis in base, az., all within a bordure wavy of the last.

MEINILL—BARON MEINILL.

By Writ of Summons, dated 23 June, 1295.

Lineage.

About the close of King HENRY I.'s reign,

ROBERT DE MEINEL, bestowed certain lands upon the monks of St. Mary's Abbey, at York, which his son and successor,

STEPHEN DE MEINEL ratified. In the 25th HENRY II., this Stephen was fined £100 for trespassing in the forests of Yorkshire. He *d.* about the 2nd RICHARD I., and was *s.* by his elder son,

ROBERT DE MEINEL, who *m.* Emme, dau. of Richard de Malbisse, and had a son, STEPHEN, who predeceased him, leaving a son,

NICHOLAS DE MEINEL, who *s.* his grandfather in the 8th King JOHN. This Nicholas was in the Welsh wars, and in consideration of his services had a debt of 100 marks remitted by King EDWARD I., besides obtaining grants of free warren throughout all his lands and lordships in the co. York. In the year 1290 he brought a charge against Christian, his wife, of an intent to poison him, and although she clearly established her innocence, he refused ever afterwards to be reconciled to her. In the 22nd EDWARD I. he had summons, amongst many other persons of note, to attend the king, to advise about the affairs of the realm; and he was summoned to parliament as a Baron from the 23 June, 1295, to 6 February, 1299, during which interval he took a prominent part in the wars of Scotland. His lordship *d.* in 1299, and was *s.* by

NICHOLAS DE MEINILL, who was summoned to parliament from 22 May, 1313, to 14 March, 1322, and *d.* in the last year without issue, when the barony appears to have become EXTINCT.

Arms.—Az., three bars gemels, and a chief, or.

MEINILL—BARON MEINILL.

By Writ of Summons, dated 22 January, 1336.

Lineage.

NICHOLAS DE MEINILL (natural son of Nicholas, Lord de Meinill), was summoned to parliament as a Baron from 22 January, 1336, to 25 February, 1342. His lordship *m.* Alice, dau. of William, Lord Ros, of Hainlake, and left an only dau. and heiress,

ELIZABETH, who m. 1st, John, 2nd Baron D'Arcy, and conveyed the Barony of Meinill to the D'Arcy family, in which it remained till the decease of Philip, 11th Baron D'Arcy, in 1418, when, with the Barony of D'Arcy, it fell into ABEYANCE between his lordship's daus., and co-heirs, Elizabeth, m. to Sir James Strangwayes, Knt., of Harlesey Castle, co. York, and Margery, m. to Sir John Conyers, of Hornby, also in Yorkshire. Elizabeth Meinill m. 2ndly, Peter, 6th Baron Mauley. Her ladyship d. in the 42nd EDWARD III.

His lordship d. in 1342, when the Barony of Meinill devolved as stated above upon his dau. Elizabeth, who m. Lord D'Arcy.

"Although," says Nicolas, "the abeyance of the Baronies of Meinill and D'arcy has never been terminated, yet Conyers D'arcy, 2nd Baron D'arcy, under the patent of 10 August, 1641, and Baron Conyers, in right of his grandmother, probably, under the presumption that the said patent not only restored the ancient Barony of D'arcy, but also that of Meinill, was styled, in the writs of summons to parliament of 7 October (31st CHARLES II.), 1679, 1 March, and 31 March, 1680, 'Conyers D'arcie de D'arcie and Meinill, Chl'r.' He was created Earl of Holderness in 1682, which title, as well as the Barony of D'arcy, created by the patent of 1641, became EXTINCT in 1778; but it is manifest that the assumption of the title of the Barony of Meinill was without any legal foundation."

MENTETH—EARL OF MENTETH.

Lineage.

The name of Menteth is local, a considerable district in Scotland, through which the river Teith runs, being called the stewartry of Menteth.

WALTER (3rd son of Walter, 3rd High-Steward of Scotland), m. in 1258, the Countess of Menteth, and thus acquired that earldom. His name occurs frequently in the transactions of the 13th century, and we find him gallantly distinguished at the battle of Larga, in 1263, when his brother, the High-Steward, had the chief command. The earl left two sons (who both assumed the surname of Menteth), viz.,

ALEXANDER.
John (Sir), governor of Dumbarton Castle, who took an active part in the political convulsions of his time. To him tradition ascribes. whether truly or not is still a matter of historical dispute, the surrender of Sir William Wallace. Sir John's representative is the present Earl of Marr.

The elder son,
ALEXANDER MENTETH, 6th Earl of Menteth, one of the boldest defenders of Scottish independence against EDWARD I., had two sons,

ALAN.
JOHN, of Ruskey, from whom Sir Charles-Granville-Stuart-Menteth, Bart., of Closeburn, co. Dumfries, deduces his descent.

The elder son,
ALAN MENTETH, 7th Earl of Menteth, was living in 1296; his dau. and heir,

MARY, Countess of Menteth, m. Sir John Graham (executed in 1346), and had a dau.,
MARGARET, who m. Robert Stewart, Duke of Albany, and was mother of
MURDOCK, Duke of Albany, who was attainted in 1405.

MESCHINES—EARLS OF CHESTER.

Grant, temp. HENRY I.

Lineage.

RANULPH or RANDLE DE MESCHINES, surnamed de Bricasard, Viscount Bayeux, in Normandy (son of Ralph de Meschines, by Maud, his wife, co-heir of her brother, Hugh Lupus, the celebrated Earl of Chester), was given by King HENRY I., the EARLDOM OF CHESTER, at the decease of his 1st cousin, Richard de Abrincis, 2nd Earl of Chester, of that family (see Abrincis), without issue. By some of our historians this nobleman is styled Earl of Carlisle, from residing in that city; and they further state, that he came over in the train of the CONQUEROR, assisted in the subjugation of England, and shared, of course, in the spoil of conquest. He

was lord of Cumberland and Carlisle, by descent from his father, but having enfeoffed his two brothers, William, of Coupland, and Geffery, of Gillesland, in a large portion thereof, he exchanged the Earldom of Cumberland for that of Chester, on condition that those whom he had settled there, should hold their lands of the king, in capite. His lordship m. Lucia, widow of Roger de Romara, Earl of Lincoln, and dau. of Algar, the Saxon, Earl of Mercia, and had issue,

RANULPH, his successor.
William, styled Earl of Cambridge, but of his issue nothing is known.
Adeliza, m. to Richard Fitz-Gilbert, ancestor of the old Earls of Clare.
Agnes, m. to Robert de Grentemaisnil.

The earl d. in 1128, and was s. by his elder son,
RANULPH DE MESCHINES (surnamed de Gernons, from being born in Gernon Castle, in Normandy), as EARL OF CHESTER. This nobleman, who was a leading military character, took an active part with the Empress MAUD, and the young Prince Henry, against King STEPHEN, in the early part of the contest, and having defeated the king, and made him prisoner at the battle of Lincoln, committed him to the castle of Bristol. He subsequently, however, sided with the king, and finally, distrusted by all. died, under excommunication, in 1155, supposed to have been poisoned by William Peverell, Lord of Nottingham, who being suspected of the crime, is said to have turned monk, to avoid its punishment. The earl m. Maud, dau. of Robert. surnamed the Consul, Earl of Gloucester, natural son of King HENRY I., and had issue,

HUGH, his successor, surnamed Kerveliok; from the place of his birth, in Merionethshire.
Richard.
Beatrix, m. to Ralph de Malpas.

His lordship was s. by his elder son,
HUGH (Keveliok), 3rd Earl of Chester. This nobleman joined in the rebellion of the Earl of Leicester and the King of Scots, against King HENRY II., and in support of that monarch's son, Prince Henry's pretensions to the crown. In which proceeding he was taken prisoner, with the Earl of Leicester, at Alnwick, but obtained his freedom soon afterwards, upon the king's reconciliation with the young prince. Again, however, hoisting the standard of revolt, both in England and in Normandy, with as little success, he was again seized, and then detained a prisoner for some years. He eventually, however, obtained his liberty and restoration of his lands, when public tranquillity became completely re-established some time about the 23rd year of the king's reign. His lordship m. Bertred, dau. of Simon, Earl of Evereux, in Normandy, and had issue,

RANULPH, his successor.
Maud. m. to David, Earl of Huntingdon, brother of WILLIAM, King of Scotland, and had one son and four daus, viz.,
1 JOHN, surnamed Le Scot, who s. to the Earldom of Chester. d. s. p. 7 June, 1237.
1 Margaret, m. to Alan de Galloway, and had a dau.,
Devorguill, m. to John de Baliol, and was mother of JOHN DE BALIOL, declared King of Scotland in the reign of EDWARD I.
2 Isabel, m. to Robert de Brus, and was mother of ROBERT DE BRUS, who contended for the crown of Scotland, temp. EDWARD I.
3 Maud, d. unm.
4 Ada, m. to Henry de Hastings, and had issue,
HENRY DE HASTINGS. one of the competitors for the Scottish crown, temp. EDWARD I.
Mabill, m. to William de Albini, Earl of Arundel.
Agnes, m. to William de Ferrers, Earl of Derby.
Hawise, m. to Robert, son of Sayer de Quincy, Earl of Winchester.

The earl had another dau., whose legitimacy is questionable, namely,
Amicia,* m. to Ralph de Mesnilwarin, justice of Chester, "a person," says Dugdale, "of very ancient family." from which union the Mainwarings, of Over Peover, in the co. Chester, derive. Dugdale considers Amicia to be a dau. of the earl by a former wife. But Sir Peter Leicester, in his Antiquities of Cheshire, totally denies her legitimacy. "I cannot but mislike," says he, "the boldness and ignorance of that herald who gave to Mainwaring (late of Peover), the elder, the quartering of the Earl of Chester's arms: for if he ought of

---

* Upon the question of this lady's legitimacy there was a long paper war between Sir Peter Leicester and Sir Thomas Mainwaring—and eventually the matter was referred to the Judges, of whose decision Wood says, "at an assize held at Chester, 1675, the controversy was decided by the justices itinerant, who, as I have heard, adjudged the right of the matter to Mainwaring."

right to quarter that coat, then must he be descended from a co-heir to the Earl of Chester; but he was not; for the co-heirs of Earl Hugh married four of the greatest peers in the kingdom."

The earl d. at Leeke, in Staffordshire, in 1181, and was s. by his only son,

RANULPH or RANDLE, surnamed *Blundevil* (or rather Blandevil, from the place of his birth, the town of *Album Monasterium,* modern Oswestry, in Powys), as 4th EARL OF CHESTER. This noble-man was made a knight, in 1188, by King HENRY II., and the same monarch bestowed upon him in marriage, Constance, Countess of Britanny, dau. and heiress of Conan, Earl of Britanny, and widow of King HENRY's son Geffrey, with the whole of Britanny, and the Earldom of Richmond, wherefore he is designated in most charters, "Duke of Britanny and Earl of Richmond." In the 4th RICHARD I. we find his lordship aiding David, Earl of Huntingdon, and the Earl Ferrers, in the siege of Marlbo-rough, then held for John, Earl of Moreton, the king's brother; and in two years afterwards with the same parties, besieging the castle of Nottingham. In which latter year he was also with the army of King RICHARD in Normandy, and so highly was he esteemed by the lion-hearted monarch, that he was se-lected to bear one of the three swords at his second coronation. In the commencement of King JOHN's reign his lordship divorced his wife Constance, "by reason," saith Dugdale, "that the king haunted her company," and m. Clementia, sister of Geffrey de Filgiers, widow of Alan de Dinnan, and niece of William de Humet, constable of Normandy, with whom he acquired not only a large accession of landed property in France, but some extensive manors in England. In the 6th JOHN, his lordship had a grant from the crown of all the lands belonging to the honour of Richmond, in Richmondshire, ex-cepting a small proportion, which the king retained in his own hands; and he gave in the same year to the king a palfrey for a lamprey, which shews the value of that description of fish in those days.

This was the earl, who, marching into Wales too slenderly attended, was compelled to take refuge in Rothelan Castle, in Flintshire; and being there closely invested by the Welsh, was delivered from his precarious situation by the rabble, which then happened to have been assembled at the fair of Chester. For sending to Roger de Lacy, Baron of Halton, his constable of Cheshire, to come with all speed to his succour, Roger (sur-named Hell, from his fiery spirit), gathered a tumultuous rout of fiddlers, players, cobblers, debauched persons, both men and women, and marched immediately towards the earl; when the Welsh, descrying so numerous a multitude advancing, at once raised the siege, and sought safety in flight. Wherefore the earl conferred upon the constable patronage over all the fiddlers and shoemakers in Chester, in reward and memory of this service. Of which patronage De Lacy retained to himself and his heirs that of the shoemakers, and granted the fiddlers and players to his steward, DUTTON, *of Dutton,* whose heirs still enjoy the privilege. For upon Midsummer-day, annually, the fair of Chester, a Dutton, or his deputy, rides attended through the city of Chester, by all the minstrelsy of the county playing upon their several instruments, to the church of St. John's where a court is held for the renewal of their licenses.

In the conflicts between JOHN and the barons the Earl of Chester remained stoutly attached to the former, and it was through his exertions chiefly that HENRY III. ascended the throne. Of which an old monk of Peterborough gives the following narrative:—

"Upon the death of King JOHN, the great men of England fearing that the son would follow his father's steps in tyranny over the people, resolved to extirpate him, and all of his blood, not considering that saying of the prophet, viz., ' That the son shall not suffer for the iniquity of the father.' And to that end determined to set up Lewes, son to the King of France (a youth then but fourteen years old), in his stead; whom, at the instance of the rebellious barons, that king, for the purpose alleged, sent over into England, in the last year of King JOHN, under the tuition of the Earl of Perch, and other great men of that realm. Who having landed himself in England accor-dingly, and received homage of the Londoners, expecting the like from the southern nobility, advanced to Lincolne. Which being made known to the Earl of Chester, who did abominate any conjunction with them in that their conspiracy, he convened the rest of the northern peers; and being the chief and most potent of them, taking with him young Henry, son of King JOHN, and right heir to the crown, raised a puissant army, and marched towards Lincolne. To which place, at the end of four days after Lewes got thither, expecting him, he came. To whom the Earl of Perch, observing his stature to be small, said, ' Have we staid all this while for such a little man, such a dwarf.' To which disdainful expression he answered, ' *I vow*

to God and our lady, whose church this is, that before to-morrow evening I will seem to thee to be stronger, and greater, and taller than that steeple.' Thus parting with each other, he betook himself to the castle.

"And on the next morning, the Earl of Perch, armed at all parts, except his head, having entered the cathedral with his forces, and left Lewes there, challenged out our earl to battle : who no sooner heard thereof, but causing the castle gates to be opened, he came out with his soldiers, and made so fierce a charge upon the adverse party, that he slew the Earl of Perch, and many of his followers; and immediately seizing upon Lewes in the church, caused him to swear upon the gospel and relics of those saints then placed on the high altar, that he would never lay any claim to the kingdom of England, but speedily hasten out of the realm, with all his followers; and that when he should be king of France, he would restore Normandy to the crown of England. Which being done, he sent for young Henry, who during that time lay privately in a cow-house, belonging to Bardney Abbey, (near Lincolne, towards the west,) and setting him upon the altar, delivered him seisin of this kingdom, as his inheritance by a white wand, instead of a sceptre; doing his homage to him, as did all the rest of the nobility then present.

" For which signal service, the king gave him the body of Gilbert de Gant, his enemy, with all his possessions: which Gilbert was a great baron, and founder of Vaudey Abbey, in Kesteven." Thus far for the monk of Peterborough. Further, it appears that after the coronation of the king, the Earl of Cheshire brought all his resources to bear upon the rebellious barons; first in the siege of Mountsorrell, in Leicestershire, and afterwards at Lincoln, " The castle whereof," says Dugdale, " was then beleagured by a great strength of barons; which in that notable battle there, were utterly vanquished." In the course of the same year his lordship had the Earldom of Lincoln, forfeited by Gilbert de Gant, conferred upon him, to which dignity he had a claim, in right of his great grandmother, who bore the title of Countess of Lincoln. His lordship subsequently assumed the cross, for the second time, and embarked for the Holy Land, having previously granted to his Cheshire barons a very ample charter of liberties. As a soldier, the stout Earl of Chester was not less distinguished abroad than at home, and the laurels which he had so gallantly won upon his native soil, were not tarnished in the plains of Palestine. His lordship had a command at the celebrated siege of Damieta, " where," saith Henry, archdeacon of Huntingdon, " being general of the Christian army, he did glorious things." *Ubi Dux Christianæ cohortis præstitit gloriosa.* Immediately upon his return to England, *anno* 1220, the earl begun the structure of Chartley Castle, in Staffordshire, and of Breston Castle, in Cheshire, as also the abbey of Deulacres, for white monks near Leek in the former shire; which monastery he had been incited, it was said, to found by the ghost of Earl Ranulph, his grandfather, which appeared to him one night while he was in bed, as the story went, and " bade him repair to a place called Cholpesdale within the territory of Leek, and there found and endow an abbey of white monks," adding, "there shall be joy to thee, and many others, who shall be saved thereby : for there, quoth he, shall be a ladder erected, by which the prayers of angels shall ascend and descend, and vows of men shall be offered to God, and they shall give thanks, and the name of our Lord shall be called upon in that place, by daily prayers; and the sign of this shall be when the Pope doth interdict England. But do thou in the mean time, go to the monks of Pulton, where Robert Butler hath in my name built an abbey, and thou shalt there be partaker of the sacrament of the Lord; for such privileges belong to the servants of the foundation. And in the seventh year of that interdict, thou shalt translate those monks to the place I have foretold." The earl having communicated this dream, or ghost-mandate to his wife, the Lady Clementia, she exclaimed in French, *Dieu encres,* which exclamation his lordship deeming propitious, declared should give name to the projected monastery : hence the designation of Deulacres.

After this period we find the earl coinciding with the barons rather than the king, in some misunderstanding regarding the charters, which was, however, peaceably settled in the 11th of HENRY's reign. The most remarkable subsequent event of his lordship's life was his resistance to one Stephen, a commissary from the Pope, who was deputed to collect the tenths from the bishops and all religious orders; and did so throughout England, Ireland, and Wales, except within the jurisdiction of the Earl of Chester, where his lordship's proclamation interposed. This potent nobleman d. at Wallingford, 26 October, 1232, after governing the county palatine of Chester for more than half a century; and as a proof of the simplicity of the age, so far as faith in supernatural events may be so characterized, we give the following story, which, according to Henry Huntendon, met with general credence. "It is reported," saith our author, "of this earl, that when he died, a great company in the likeness of men, with a certain potent person, hastily passed by a hermite's cell, near Wallingford; and that the hermite asking one of them, what they were, and whither they went so fast? he answered, 'We are devils, and are making speed to the death of Earl Randulph, to the end we may accuse him of his sins.' Likewise that the hermites thereupon adjuring the devil, that he should return the same way, within thirty days, and relate what was become of this earl, he came accordingly, and told him, ' That he was, for his iniquities, condemned to the torments of hell; but that the great dogs of Deulacres, and with them many other, did bark so incessantly, and fill their habitations with such a noise, that their prince, being troubled with it, commanded he should be expelled his dominions; who is now, saith he, become a great enemy to us; because their suffrages, together with others, hath released many souls from purgatory.'" So much for the ingenuity of the good monks of Deulacres.

His lordship never having had issue, his great possessions devolved, at his decease, upon his nephews and sisters, viz.,

JOHN SCOT (son of Maud, Countess of Huntingdon, the earl's eldest sister, then dead), who *s.* to the Earldom of Chester (*see* Scot, Earl of Chester), with the whole county palatine, and the advowson of the priory of Coventry.

Hugh de Albany, EARL OF ARUNDEL (son of Mabel, the earl's second sister, then dead), who *s.* to Coventry, as his chief seat, with the manors of Campden, in Gloucestershire; Diney, in Buckinghamshire; and Ledes, in Yorkshire.

Agnes, COUNTESS OF DERBY, who, with her husband, William de Ferrers, Earl of Derby, had the castle and manor of Chartley, in Staffordshire, with all the lands belonging to her late brother, which lay between the rivers Ribble and Merse, together with a manor in Northamptonshire, and another in Lincolnshire.

Hawise, wife of Robert de Quincy, who had the castle and manor of Bolingbroke, co. Lincoln, and other large estates in that shire. It appears that her brother, in his lifetime, had granted to this lady, the Earldom of Lincoln, in order that she might become countess thereof, and that her heirs might also enjoy it. Which grant seems to have been confirmed by the crown so far, that at her ladyship's desire, the king conferred the dignity of Earl of Lincoln upon John Lacy, constable of Chester, and the heirs of his body, by Margaret de Quincy, the Lady Hawise's dau.

Arms, borne by RANULPH, surnamed *De Bricasard.*—Or, a lion rampant, his tail erected, gu.

Arms, borne by HUGH, surnamed *Kereliok.*—Az., six garbs, or, three, two, and one.

Arms, borne by RANULPH, surnamed *Blundevil.*—As., three garbs or, two and one.

MICKLETHWAIT—BARON AND VISCOUNT MICKLETHWAIT.

Viscounty, by Letters Patent, dated 6 June, 1727.
Barony, by Letters Patent, dated 14 August, 1724.

Lineage.

The descent of this family from the Micklethwaites of Ingburchworth, in the parish of Peniston, co. York, is given in the Visitation of Yorkshire, 1666. The Visitation pedigree was entered at York, 11 August, 1666, and begins with JOHN MICKLETHWAIT, father of another JOHN, of Ingburchworth, who had three sons, JOHN, of Ingburchworth; Francis, of York; and ELIAS. The last-named, ELIAS MICKLETHWAIT, settled as a merchant at York, became alderman, was twice lord mayor, and sat in parliament, *temp.* JAMES I. He m. 1st, Dorothy Jaques, by whom he had no issue; and 2ndly, a widow named Ardington. He *d. circa* 1630. His issue were,

I. ELIAS, of the Middle Temple, of whom no issue remained in 1666.
II. JOSEPH, of whom presently.
III. Mark, rector of Marston.
I. Susan, wife of Christopher Topham, Esq.
II. Tabitha, wife of Alderman John Geldart.

The 2nd son,

JOSEPH MICKLETHWAIT, Esq., of Swine, in Holderness, J.P., *m.* in 1621, Anne, dau. of Perceval Levett, Esq., and *d.* 1658, having had two sons, JOHN and Joseph; and two daus., Ann, *m.* to Thomas Dickenson, Esq., and Dorothy, *m.* to Thomas Stillington, Esq. The elder son,

JOHN MICKLETHWAIT, Esq., J.P., barrister-at-law, *m.* in 1653, Barbara, dau. of Timothy Middleton, Esq., of Stansted Montfitchet, co. Essex, and was *s.* by his son,

JOSEPH MICKLETHWAIT, Esq. of Swine, who *m.* in 1677, Constance, dau. of Sir Thomas Middleton, of Stansted Montfitchet, and had two sons, namely,

THOMAS, M.P. for Arundel, who inherited a considerable property from Sir John Cropley, Bart. In 1717, he was appointed one of the lords of the Treasury, and in the following year made lieutenant-general of the Ordnance; but *d.* a few days after, March, 1718.
JOSEPH, of whom we have to treat.

The 2nd son,

JOSEPH MICKLETHWAIT, Esq., of Swine and Cosham, co Durham, *b.* In 1708, secretary to the Earl of Stanhope in Spain, was created a peer of Ireland, as BARON MICKLETHWAIT, *of Portarlington, Queen's co.,* 14 August, 1724, and in three years after (6 June, 1727,) advanced to be VISCOUNT MICKLETHWAIT, *of Longford,* in the kingdom of Ireland. His lordship, who represented Arundel and Hull in parliament, *d. unm* 16 January, 1733, and with him all the honours became EXTINCT.

Arms—Cucquy, arg. and gu.; a chief, indented, az.

MIDDLETON—EARL OF MIDDLETON.

By Letters Patent, dated 1 October, 1660.

Lineage.

JOHN MIDDLETON, the eldest son of John Middleton, of Caldhame, joined at an early period the service of the parliament in the great civil war and was lieutenant-general under Sir William Waller. Returning into Scotland, he had a command in General Leslie's army, and contributed so much to the defeat of Montrose at Philliphaugh, 13 September, 1645, that the parliament voted him a gift of 25,000 marks. Subsequently siding with the royal party, he fought with great gallantry at the battle of Worcester, where, being severely wounded, he was taken prisoner, and sent to the Tower of London, whence he effected his escape, and waited on King CHARLES at Paris. In 1653, he was sent to command the royalists in Scotland. His forces suffered a defeat at Lochgeary in 1654, and Middleton himself escaped, a second time, to the Continent, where he continued to reside until the Restoration, at which propitious event he was created EARL OF MIDDLETON, *Lord Clermont and Fettercairn,* by patent dated 1 October, 1660, to him and his heirs male bearing the name and arms of Middleton. He received also the appointments of commander-in chief of the forces in Scotland, governor of Edinburgh Castle, and commissioner to the Scottish parliament. His lordship *m.* 1st, Grizel, only dau of Sir James Durham, of Pitkerrow and Luffness, and by her, who *d.* at Cranston in September, 1666, had issue,

CHARLES, 2nd Earl of Middleton.
Grisel, *m.* at Holyrood House. 12 June, 1662, to William, 4th Earl of Morton; and *d.* in March, 1666.
Helen, *m.* at Holyrood House, 23 August, 1662, to Patrick, Earl of Strathmore, and had issue.

The earl *m.* 2ndly, at St. Andrew's, Holborn, in December, 1667, Lady Martha Cary, dau. of Henry, E rl of Monmouth, but by her had no issue. He *d.* at Tangier, of which he was governor, in 1673, and was *s.* by his son,

CHARLES MIDDLETON, 2nd Earl of Middleton, member for Winchilsea in the Long Parliament. He was bred up at the court of King CHARLES II., by whom he was appointed envoy extraordinary to the court of Vienna; and on his return constituted one of the principal secretaries of state for Scotland, 26 September, 1682, and one of the extraordinary lords of session, 15 July, 1684; he was sworn a privy councillor in England, 11 July, 1684, and appointed one of the principal secretaries of state there, 25 August, following, which office be enjoyed till the Revolution, 1688, when he joined King JAMES II. in France, for which he was outlawed by the court of justiciary, 23 July, 1694, and forfeited by act of parliament, 1695. His lordship *m.* Lady Catherine Brudenell, dau. of Robert, Earl of Cardigan, and by her, who *d.* at St. Germains, 11 March, 1743, in her ninety-fifth year, had issue,

JOHN, Lord Clermont.   Charles.
Elizabeth, *m.* to Edward Drummond, son of James, Earl of Perth, high chancellor of Scotland. She had the style of

Duchess of Perth, and d. at Paris, in an advanced age, after 1773.

Mary, m. to Sir John Giffard, Knt.

Catherine, m. to Michael, Comte de Rothe, lieutenant-general in the French service; and d. at Paris, 10 July, 1763, aged seventy-eight.

Arms—Per fess, or and gu., a lion rampant within a double tressure, flowered and counter-flowered with fleurs-de-lis, all counterchanged.

MILDMAY—BARONS FITZ-WALTER, EARL FITZ-WALTER.

Barony, originally by Writ of Summons, dated 23 June, 1295, to the Mildmays; by Writ of Summons, dated 10 February, 1669.
Earldom, by Letters Patent, dated 14 May, 1730.

Lineage.

LADY FRANCES RATCLIFFE, only dau. by his 2nd wife, of Henry, 3rd Lord Fitz-Walter, and 2nd Earl of Sussex (*see* Ratcliffe, Barons Fitz-Walter), m. Sir Thomas Mildmay, Knt., of Moulsham, co. Essex, eldest son of Sir Thomas Mildmay, Knt. (who d. 21 September, 1566), by Avicia, his wife, dau. of William Gernson, Esq., of London, and grandson of Thomas Mildmay, Esq., who purchased the manor of Moulsham, from King HENRY VIII.: Lady Francis had issue,

THOMAS (Sir) created a baronet in 1611, and d. s. p. 18 February, 1625-6.
HENRY, of whom presently.

Sir Thomas d. 21 July, 1608. His 2nd son,

SIR HENRY MILDMAY, Knt., becoming at the decease of his brother representative of the family, and his mother, at the death of her nephew, by the half blood, Robert Ratcliffe, 6th Lord Fitz-Walter, and 5th Earl of Sussex, having become sole heiress of that ancient barony, preferred his claim in her right, by petition to the Long Parliament, in 1640; but the civil war breaking out immediately after, he was unable to accomplish anything in the affair. Sir Henry m. Elizabeth, dau. of John D'Arcy, Esq., of Toleshunt D'Arcy, co. Essex, and dying in 1654, left issue,

ROBERT, who m. Mary, dau. and co-heir of Sir Thomas Edmonds, Knt., and had two sons and a dau. viz.,
  1 HENRY, who petitioned for the barony, but d. s. p. before there was any decision.
  2 BENJAMIN, of whom presently, as LORD FITZ WALTER.
  3 Mary, m. to Henry Mildmay, Esq., of Graces, and had five daus., viz.,
    Mary, m. to Charles Goodwin, Esq., of Bovant, co. Sussex, and d. s. p.
    Lucy, m. to Thomas Gardiner, Esq., of Tollesbury, Essex, and had, with other issue, who d. s. p., two daus., LUCY, who m. in 1728, Sir Richard Bacon, Bart., but their issue is extinct; and Jemima, who is stated to have m. John Joseph, surgeon, and to have had an only dau., Jemima, wife of Robert Duke, woollen-draper, of Colchester, who, it is asserted, settled in America.
    Elizabeth, m. to Edmund Waterson, Esq., and d. s. p.
    Frances, m. to Christopher Fowler, Esq., and d. in 1705, leaving a son, EDMUND FOWLER, of Graces, who m. Elizabeth Pateshall, and d. in 1751, leaving a dau. and heir, FANNY, wife of Sir Brook Bridges, Bart., of Goodnestone and grandmother of Sir Brook-W.Bridges, Bart., who was declared one of the co-heirs, if not sole heir, of the old barony of FitzWalter, and was created Lord Fitz-Walter, of Woodham Walter, by patent, 17 April, 1868.
    Katherine, m. to Col. Thomas Townshend, and had issue, but since extinct.
  Henry, d. s. p.
  Charles, m. to Martha, dau. and heiress of Sir Cranmer Harris, Knt., and left an only dau.,
  Mary, m. to Sir Charles Tyrrell, Bart., of Thornton.

Sir Henry Mildmay's grandson,
BENJAMIN MILDMAY, Esq., having inherited the estates of the family, upon the decease of his brother Henry, without issue, pursued the claim to the BARONY OF FITZ-WALTER, already preferred by his grandfather and brother; but he met a strenuous opponent in Robert Cheeke, Esq., son of Henry Cheeke, Esq., by Francis Ratcliffe, dau. of Sir Humphrey Ratcliffe, of Elneston, and sister of Sir Edward Ratcliffe, who s. as 6th Earl of Sussex, and d. s. p. in 1641. when that earldom expired. (*See* Ratcliffes, Barons Fitz Walter, issue of Robert, 2nd Lord, and Earl of Sussex.) Mr. Cheeke's claim chiefly rested on the question, whether there could be a *possessio*

fratris in dignity; and after several hearings at the bar of the House of Lords, the parliament was prorogued, and nothing further was done in that session; but on 29 December following, Mr. Mildmay again petitioned the king, and his Majesty was then pleased to order, that the cause should be heard by the privy council 19 January, 1669, on which day the two chief justices and the chief baron, were directed to attend.

"The counsel for the said Robert Cheeke affirmed, that the same was a barony by tenure, and ought to go along with the land;[*] which the counsel of the petitioner denied, and offered to argue on the same; upon which both parties being ordered to withdraw, the nature of a barony by tenure being discussed, it was found to have been discontinued for many ages, and not in being, and so not fit to be revived, or to admit any pretence of right of succession thereto: and the other points urged by Mr. Cheeke[†] being overruled, it was ordered by his majesty in council, that the petitioner is admitted, humbly to address himself to his majesty, for his writ, to sit in the House of Peers, as Baron Fitz-Walter, and he was so summoned accordingly, 10 February, 1670."[‡] There being, after this, some doubts as to the place and precedency of the Lord Fitz-Walter, it was ultimately settled, that his lordship should be placed the last baron of the reign of King EDWARD I. This Benjamin, 1st Lord Fitz-Walter, of the Mildmay family, m. Catherine, dau. and co-heiress of John, Viscount Fairfax, of the kingdom of Ireland, and had surviving issue, two sons, CHARLES and BENJAMIN, who inherited, successively, the barony. His lordship d. 1 June, 1679, and was s. by the elder,

CHARLES MILDMAY, 2nd Baron Fitz-Walter. His lordship m. Elizabeth, dau. of the Hon. Charles Bertie, of Uffington, youngest son of Montagu, Earl of Lindsey, but d. 1728, s. p, and was s. by his brother,

BENJAMIN MILDMAY, 3rd Baron Fitz-Walter, who was created by letters patent, dated 14 May, 1730, *Viscount Harwich*, and EARL FITZ-WALTER. In 1735, his lordship was sworn of the privy council, appointed first lord commissioner of trade and plantations, and constituted in 1737, treasurer of the household. He m. Frederica, eldest dau. and co-heir of Meinhardt, Duke of Scombergh, and widow of Robert, Earl of Holderness, by whom he had an only son, Robert-Scombergh, who d. in infancy. His lordship d. 29 February, 1756, when the Viscounty of Harwich and Earldom of Fitz-Walter became EXTINCT, but the ancient Barony of Fitz-Walter fell into ABEYANCE between the daus. of his aunt.

In 1841, Sir Brook claimed the title and there were six hearings of his case before the Committee for Privileges of the House of Lords. After the summing up of Mr. Loftus Wigram 18 July, 1844 (the 6th hearing of the case), the committee came to the unanimous resolution that, "the barony is now in abeyance between the petitioner, Sir Brook-William Bridges, as grandson and heir of Dame Fanny Bridges, and the descendants (if any) of Jemima Duke," which, being first passed in the affirmative, was directed by the committee to be reported by the chairman to the House. The words inserted ("if any") were part of the resolution, thus intimating considerable doubt whether any descendants remain. The counsel for the petitioner were Mr. Loftus Wigram and Sir Harris Nicolas.

Arms—Arg., three lions rampant, az.

---

[*] It does not appear on what grounds Mr. Cheeke's counsel claimed the Barony of Fitz-Walter by tenure, for that barony was originally attached to the possession of the Manor of Little Dunmow, in Essex, granted to Robert Fitz-Walter, in the reign of HENRY I., and at the period when this claim was discussed, it was not the property of either of the claimants.—Nicolas.

[†] First, half blood in Mildmay; and 2ndly, that the barony or title of Lord Fitz-Walter, was merged in the Earldom of Sussex, and became extinct with that dignity. Upon which it was decided, that the half blood could not be any impediment in the case of a dignity; and that, although a baron in fee simple be created an earl, the barony shall descend to the heir general, whether or not, the earldom continue, or be extinct.

[‡] Collins's Precedents.

MOELS—BARONS MOELS.

By Writ of Summons, dated 6 February, 1299.

Lineage.

In the time of HENRY III.,

NICHOLAS DE MOELS, possessed in right of Hawyse, his wife, dau. and co-heir of James de Newmarch, the lordships of Cadebury, and Saperton, co. Somerset, part of the feudal barony of the said James. In the same reign, this Nicholas was made sheriff of Hampshire, and governor of the castle of Winchester, and continued in office for four years. He had subsequently the islands of Guernsey, Jersey, Serke, and Aureney (Alderney), committed to his care, and was again constituted sheriff of Hampshire, after which he was sheriff of Yorkshire, and held that office until the 25th of HENRY III. The next year he was deputed with Ralph Fitz-Nicholas, ambassador to France, for the purpose of denouncing war against the king of that realm; and he was soon after appointed seneschal of Gascony; being at the time a person so highly regarded by the king, that James, his son and heir, was by special command, admitted to have his education with Prince Edward; the prince's tutors, Hugh de Giffard and Berard de Savoy, having directions to receive him, with one servant, and to provide him with necessaries. In the 28th of the same reign, Nicholas de Moels obtained a signal victory over the King of Navarre, and returning to England the ensuing year, he was employed in the Welsh wars, and constituted governor of the castles of Caermarthen and Cardigan. He was subsequently appointed constable of Dover Castle, and warden of the Cinque Ports; and the March following, made sheriff of Kent, and governor of the castles of Rochester and Canterbury. This celebrated and gallant person was s. by his son,

ROGER DE MOELS, who served in the Welsh wars, and in the beginning of EDWARD I.'s reign had the honour and castle of Lampadervaur, in Cardiganshire, committed to his custody. He m. Alice, dau. and heir of William de Preux, and dying in 1294, was s. by his son,

JOHN DE MOELS, who, doing his homage in the same year, had livery of his lands. This feudal lord having distinguished himself in the Scottish wars of EDWARD I., was summoned to parliament as a Baron, from 6 February, 1299, to 16 June, 1311. His lordship m. a dau. of the noble family of Grey, and dying in 1311, was s. by his son,

NICHOLAS DE MOELS, 2nd baron, summoned to parliament from 19 October, 1311, to 6 October, 1315. This nobleman, like his predecessors, distinguished himself in arms, and was engaged in the Scotch wars. His lordship m. Margaret, dau. of Sir Hugh Courtenay, Knt., and sister of Hugh, Earl of Devon. His lordship d. in 1316, and was s. by his brother,

ROGER DE MOELS, 3rd baron, who, paying 100 marks fine, and doing homage, had livery of his lands the same year, through the king's especial favour, being at the time not of full age. His lordship d. in the 19th EDWARD II. s. p., and was s. by his brother,

JOHN DE MOELS, 4th baron. This nobleman was created a knight of the Bath, 20th EDWARD II, an l 'in the 7th EDWARD III., he was in the expedition then made into Scotland. His lordship m. Joane, one of the daus. of Sir Richard Luvel, Knt., of Castle Cary, and had issue,

MURIEL, m. to Sir Thomas Courtenay. Knt. (who d 36th Edward III.), a younger son of the Earl of Devon, and had issue,

  HUGH COURTENAY, who d. s. p.

Margaret Courtenay, m. to Sir Thomas Peverel, and had issue,

  Katherine Peverel, m. to Sir Walter Hungerford.

  Alianore Peverel, d. s. p.

Muriel Courtenay, m. to John Dinham.

ISABEL, m. to William de Botreaux, Lord Botreaux, and her great great grand-dau.,

MARGARET BOTREAUX, m. to Sir Robert Hungerford, Knt., and carried the Barony of Botreaux, with the moiety of that of Moels, to Robert, 2nd Lord Hungerford, whose mother, Katherine, Lady Hungerford, dau., and eventually sole heir of Sir Thomas Peverel, and Margaret, dau. and co-heir of Sir Thomas Courtenay, by Muriel de Moels, his wife, above mentioned, was also the co-heir of the other moiety of the Barony of Moels; which representation, viz., of one moiety, and half of the other moiety, is now vested in the present Marquess of Hastings. Baron Hungerford, Molines, and Botreaux, the heir general of the body of the said Robert, Lord Hungerford, and of Margaret, dau. and heiress of Lord Botreaux, his wife. The other half moiety of the Barony of Moels, is vested in the representatives of the Lords Dinham.

369

His lordship d. in 1337, when the Barony of Moela fell into ABEYANCE, between his daus., as it still continues, as stated above, with their representatives. His lordship's estates passed likewise to his daus., and were divided thus:

MURIEL, Lady Courtenay. had the manor of King's Creswell, with the hundred of Haytore, in the co. of Devon; the manor of Stoke-Moels, in the co. of Oxford, with 100 shillings rent, out of the manor of Langford, also in Devonshire.

ISABEL, Lady Botreaux, had the manor of North-Cadbury, in the co. of Somerset, and Duppleford, Langeford, and the hundred of Stanburgh, in the co. of Devon.

Arms—Arg., two bars gu., in chief three torteaux.

MOHUN—BARONS MOHUN.

By Writ of Summons, dated 6 February, 1299.

Lineage.

The first of this family upon record is

SIR WILLIAM DE MOHUN, one of the companions in arms of the CONQUEROR, who is stated to have had no less than 47 stout knights of name and note in his retinue, at the battle of Hastings; and for the good services rendered to his royal master in that celebrated conflict, to have obtained the Castle Dunster, with 55 manors, in the co. of Somerset, besides several other lordships in Wilts, Devonshire, and Warwickshire. Sir William was s. by his son,

WILLIAM DE MOHUN, Lord of Dunster, who, with Agnes, his wife, granted the church of Whichford to the canons of Bridlington, King HENRY I. confirming the grant. This William was s. by his son,

WILLIAM DE MOHUN, who, espousing the fortunes of the Empress MAUD, fortified his castle of Dunster on her behalf, and breaking out into open rebellion against King STEPHEN, laid the country waste around him. He subsequently, in conjunction with DAVID, King of Scotland, Robert, Earl of Gloucester, and the other partisans of MAUD, besieged Henry de Blois (STEPHEN'S brother), bishop of Winchester, in the castle at that place; and in consideration of these eminent services, is said to have been created EARL OF DORSET by the Empress. He founded the priory of Bruton, in the co. Somerset, and endowed it largely with lands in England and Normandy. He d. before the year 1165, and was s. by his son,

WILLIAM DE MOHUN, surnamed Meschyn. In the 12th HENRY II., this feudal lord, upon levying the aid for marrying the king's dau., certified his knights' fees, *de veteri feoffamento*, to be in number forty, and those *de novo*, four. He confirmed his father's grants to the priory of Bruton, and like him was buried there. He d. before the year 1202, and was s. by his son,

REGINALD DE MOHUN, who, in the 6th of JOHN, m. Alice, one of the sisters and co-heirs of William de Briwere, and by her, with whom he acquired considerable estates in the cos. of Cornwall, Devon, and Somerset, had two sons, REGINALD, his heir, and John, ancestor of the Mohuns of Ham-Mohun, co. Dorset. He d. in 1213, and was s. by his son,

REGINALD DE MOHUN, then in minority whose wardship was committed to Henry Fitz-Count, son of the Earl of Cornwall. In the 26th HENRY III., this Reginald was constituted chief justice of all the forests south of Trent; and, in some years afterwards, governor of Saubeye Castle, in Leicestershire. In the 41st of the same reign, he had a military summons to march against the Welsh. He m. 1st, Hawise, sister of Humphrey de Bohun, Earl of Hereford, and had a son, JOHN, his successor. He m. 2ndly, Isabel, dau. of William de Ferrers, Earl of Derby (and co-heir of Sibilla, her mother, sister and co-heir of Anslem Marshal, last Earl of Pembroke, of that family), by whom he had a son,

WILLIAM, who, by the gift of his father, had the manors of Ottery, Stoke-Fleming, Monkton, and Galmeton, with the manor of Mildenhall, in the co. of Wilts, and Greylkell, in the co. of Southampton. He m. Beatrix, dau. of Reginald Fitz-Piers, and left two daus., his co-heirs, viz.,

Elinor, m. to John de Carru.

Mary, m. to John de Meryet.

Reginald Mohun d. in 1256, and was s. by his elder son,

JOHN DE MOHUN, who m. Joane, dau. of William de Ferrers, Earl of Derby, and dying 1278, left a dau., Margaret, m. to Sir John Cantilupe, and a son,

JOHN DE MOHUN (called John de Mohun the 2nd). This feudal lord, at the decease of his father, was but ten years of age. He was afterwards distinguished in the wars of Gascony and Scotland, and was summoned to parliament as a Baron, from 6 February, 1299, to 23 October, 1330. In the 27th EDWARD I., he exchanged with the crown, all his lands in Ireland, for the manor of Long Compton, in Warwickshire. His lordship *m.* Auda, dau. of Sir Robert de Tibetot, and dying in 1330, was *s.* by his grandson (son of his eldest son, John de Mohun, who predeceased him),

JOHN DE MOHUN, 2nd baron, summoned to parliament from 25 February, 1342, to 4 October, 1373 (the latter part of the time as BARON MOHUN, *of Dunster*). This nobleman, one of the Founders of the order of the Garter, was one of the martial heroes of the reign of EDWARD III., and was of the retinue of the Black Prince, and subsequently of that of John of Gaunt. His lordship *m.* Joane, dau. of his guardian, Bartholomew de Burghersh, and dying about 49th EDWARD III., left at his decease, three daus., his co-heirs, viz.,

Philippa, *m.* 1st, to Sir Walter Fitz-Walter, Knt.; 2ndly, to
' Sir John Golofre; and 3rdly, to Edward, Duke of York.
Elizabeth, *m.* to William de Montacute, Earl of Salisbury.
Maud, *m.* to John, Lord Strange, of Knocking, and had a son,
     Richard le Strange.

The two elder daus. *d.* without issue, and the barony passed to Richard, Lord Strange (son of Lord Mohun's youngest dau.), his son and heir, John, Lord Strange, left an only dau. and heir, Johanna, who *m.* George Stanley, Earl of Derby, when the barony became merged in the Earldom of Derby, until the death of Ferdinand Stanley, Earl of Derby, without male issue, when it fell into abeyance between the earl's three daus. and co-heirs, viz., Anne, wife 1st, of Grey, Lord Chandos, and 2ndly, of Mervyn, Earl of Castlehaven; Frances, wife of John, Earl of Bridgewater, and Elizabeth, wife of Henry, Earl of Huntingdon, and between whose descendants and representatives it continues in ABEYANCE.

Arms—Or, a cross engr., sa.

MOHUN—BARONS MOHUN OF OKEHAMP-TON, CO. DEVON.

By Letters Patent, dated 15 April, 1628.

Lineage.

REGINALD MOHUN, Esq., of Boconnoc, in Cornwall, lineally descended from Reginald de Mohun, youngest son of John, 1st Baron Mohun, of Dunster (a dignity that fell into ABEYANCE in the time of EDWARD III.), was created a baronet by King JAMES I. He *m.* Philippa, dau. of John Hele, Esq., and was *s.* by his son,

SIR JOHN MOHUN, 2nd baronet, who was elevated to the peerage 15th April, 1628, in the dignity of BARON MOHUN, *of Okehampton, co. Devon*. His lordship, during the civil wars, was one of the chief cavalier commanders in Cornwall and the west of England, and did essential service to the royal cause. He *m.* Cordelia, dau. of Sir John Stanhope, of Shelford, Notts, and widow of Sir Roger Aston, by whom he had issue,

John, his successor.
Warwick, heir to his brother.
Charles, slain at Dartmouth, fighting under the royal banner.
Cordelia, *m.* to John Harris, Esq., of Hayne, co. Devon.
Theophila, *m.* to James Campbell, Esq., son of Mr. Alderman
     Campbell, of London.
Philadelphia.

His lordship *d.* in 1644, and was *s.* by his eldest son,
JOHN MOHUN, 2nd baron, who *d. unm.*, and was *s.* by his brother,

WARWICK MOHUN, 3rd baron. This nobleman *m.* Catherine, dau. of — Welles, Esq., of Brember, Hants, and dying in 1665, was *s.* by his son,

CHARLES MOHUN, 4th baron, who *m.* Lady Philippa Annesley. dau. of Arthur, 1st Earl of Anglesey, and by her (who *m.* 2ndly, William Coward, Esq., and *d.* 1714) had issue,

CHARLES, his successor.
Elizabeth, who *d. unm.* in 1709.

His lordship *d.* before the year 1682, and was *s.* by his son,
CHARLES MOHUN, 5th baron. This nobleman was of a vehement and passionate temper, which led him into many excesses in his youth, and subjected him to be twice arraigned for murder, but he was, upon both occasions, honourably acquitted Having had a dispute with James, Duke of Hamilton, regarding an estate left him by the Earl of Macclesfield, he

challenged that nobleman, and a duel ensued in Hyde Park, 15 November, 1712, wherein both the combatants were slain. His lordship *m.* 1st, Charlotte, dau. of Thomas Mainwaring, Esq., by Lady Charlotte Gerard, sister of Charles, Earl of Macclesfield, and 2ndly, Elizabeth, dau. of Dr. Thomas Laurence, state physician to Queen ANNE, and widow of Col. Edward Griffith, but had no issue, in consequence of which the Barony of Mohun, of Okehampton, at his decease, became EXTINCT.

Arms—Or, a cross engrailed, sa.

MOLINES—BARONS MOLINES.

By Writ of Summons, dated 18 February, 1347.

Lineage.

This family, which was of French extraction, assumed its surname from a town so called, in the Bourbonnois; but no member of the house became of note in England before the reign of EDWARD III., when

JOHN DE MOLINES attained high rank and great importance, as well from enjoying the favour of the king, as by his large possessions in several counties, but particularly in Buckinghamshire. In the beginning of King EDWARD's reign, he was one of those who surprised the castle of Nottingham, and seized the person of Mortimer, Earl of March, for which act, he shortly afterwards received a pardon. In the 14th of the same reign he had several grants from the crown, and was summoned to parliament as a Baron, 18th February, 1347. His lordship had been treasurer of the chamber to King EDWARD, and acquired a very large estate by the favour and grants of that monarch. He was engaged in the wars of France, and received the honour of knighthood for his services. He *m.* 1st, Egidia, heir of John Mauduit, of Somerford, in Wilts, and 2ndly, Margaret, dau. and co-heir of Roger Pogeys, of Stoke Pogeys, co. Buckingham, and was *s.* at his decease in 1371, by his son,

WILLIAM MOLINES, 2nd baron, who *m.* Margery, dau. and heir of Edmund Bacoun, and dying in the reign of RICHARD II., was *s.* by his son,

RICHARD MOLINES, 3rd baron, who *m.* Eleanor Beaumont, and dying in 1384, was *s.* by his son,

WILLIAM MOLINES, 4th baron, who, dying 3rd HENRY VI., left an only dau. and heiress,

ALIANORE MOLINES, who *m.* ROBERT HUNGERFORD, 2nd Lord Hungerford, who had summons to parliament as Lord Molines, in 1445. The barony is now vested in the Marquess of Hastings.

Arms—Paly of six, wavy, or and gules.

MONK—DUKES OF ALBEMARLE.

By Letters Patent, dated 7 July, 1670.

Lineage.

The family of LE MOYNE or MONK, was of great antiquity in the co. Devon, and in that shire they had, from a remote period, possessed the Manor of Potheridge, which lineally descended to

GEORGE MONK, son of Sir Thomas Monk, Knt., and Elizabeth, his wife, dau. of Sir George Smith. This distinguished person, the celebrated general under Cromwell, was, for his exertions in restoring the monarchy, created by King CHARLES II., 7 July, 1670, *Baron Monk, of Potheridge, Baron Beauchamp, of Beauchamp, Baron of Teys, Earl of Torrington*, all in the co. Devon, *and* DUKE OF ALBEMARLE; and shortly after was installed a knight of the Garter. To explain his grace's titles, it is necessary to state that Elizabeth Grey, the wife of his ancestor, Arthur Plantaganet, was sister and heir of John Grey, Viscount L'Isle, and dau. of Edward Grey, by Elizabeth, dau. and heir of John Talbot, eldest son of John, Earl of Shrewsbury, by his 2nd wife, Margaret, eldest dau. and co-heir of Richard Beauchamp, Earl of Warwick and Albemarle, by Elizabeth, his wife, dau. and heiress of Thomas, Lord Berkeley, by Margaret, his wife, dau. and heiress of Gerard Warine, Lord L'Isle, by Alice, dau. and heiress of Henry, Lord Teyes.

The military and naval achievements of Monk occupy an honourable space in the history of the period in which he lived He crowned his reputation by the course he adopted after the death of Cromwell, in restoring the monarchy, and thus healing the wounds of his distracted country. To the gloomy and jealous mind of Cromwell, General Monk was at times a cause of uneasiness and distrust; and to a letter addressed to the general himself, Oliver once added the following singular postscript: "There be that tell me there is a certain cunning fellow in Scotland, called George Monk, who is said to lie in wait there to introduce Charles Stuart: I pray you use your diligence to apprehend him, and send him up to me." From the time of the Restoration to that of his death, the Duke of Albemarle preserved the confidence and esteem of the restored monarch, and his brother, the Duke of York, the former always calling him his "political father." With the people, Monk always enjoyed the highest degree of popularity, and his death was lamented as a national misfortune. His obsequies were public, and his ashes were deposited in HENRY VII's chapel, at Westminster, with the remains of royalty. The Duke *m.* Anne, dau. of John Clarges, and sister to Sir Thomas Clarges, Bart., by whom he had an only son,

CHRISTOPHER, his successor.

His grace *d.* in 1670, and was *s.* by his son,

CHRISTOPHER MONK, 2nd Duke of Albemarle. This nobleman was made a knight of the Garter, in 1671, and sworn of the privy council. He *m.* Lady Elizabeth Cavendish, dau. and co-heir of Henry, Duke of Newcastle, by whom he had an only son, that *d.* immediately after his birth. The duke went out governor-general to Jamaica, in 1687, accompanied by Sir Hans Sloane, and *d.* there in the next year, when all his honours became EXTINCT.

Arms—Gu., a chevron between three lions' heads erased, arg.

NOTE.—The following singular circumstance occurred during the trial of an action of trespass, between William Sherwin, plaintiff, and Sir Walter Clarges, Bart., and others, defendants, at the bar of the King's Bench at Westminster, 15 November, 1700:—
"The plaintiff as heir and representative of Thomas Monk, Esq., elder brother of George, Duke of Albemarle, claimed the manor of Sutton, in the county of York, and other lands, as heir-at-law to the said duke, against the defendant devisee, under the will of Duke Christopher, his only child, who *d* in 1689, *s. p.* Upon this trial it appeared that Anne, the wife of George, Duke of Albemarle, was dau. of John Clarges, a farrier in Savoy, and farrier to Colonel Monk. In 1632, she was married at the church of St. Lawrence Pountney, to Thomas Ratford, son of Thomas Ratford, late a farrier's servant to Prince Charles, and resident in the mews. She had a dau., *b.* in 1634, who *d.* in 1638; her husband and she lived at the Three Spanish Gipseys, in the New Exchange, and sold wash-balls, powder, gloves, and such things, and she taught girls plain work. About 1647, she being sempstress to Monk, used to carry him linen. In 1648, her father and mother died; in 1649, she and her husband fell out and parted; but no certificate from any parish register appears reciting his burial. In 1652, she was married in the church of St. George, Southwark, to General George Monk, and in the following year, was delivered of a son, CHRISTOPHER, *who was suckled by Honour Mills, who sold apples, h rbs, oysters, &c.,"* which son, CHRISTOPHER, *s.* his father, as stated in the text.

MONSON—VISCOUNT MONSON.

By Letters Patent, dated 23 August, 1628.

Lineage.

SIR WILLIAM MONSON, Knt., 2nd son of Sir Thomas Monson, Bart., of Carlton, co. Lincoln, was raised to the peerage of Ireland, as VISCOUNT MONSON, *of Castlemaine, co. Kerry,* by letters patent, dated 23 August, 1628; but being subsequently instrumental in the death of CHARLES I., he was degraded, 12 July, 1661, of all his honours, and sentenced, with Sir Henry Mildmay and Mr. Robert Wallop, to be drawn in sledges, with ropes about their necks, from the Tower to Tyburn, and back again, and to remain prisoners in the Tower during their lives. His lordship *m.* three wives (but left no male issue), 1st, Margaret, dau. of James Stewart, Earl of Murray, and widow of Charles Howard, Earl of Nottingham; 2ndly, Frances, dau. of Thomas Alston, Esq., of Polstead, in Suffolk; and 3rdly, Elizabeth, dau. of Sir George Reresby, Knt., of Thrybergh, in Yorkshire, widow of Sir Francis Foljambe, and of Edward Horner, Esq.; by the last wife (who *m.* 4thly, Sir Adam Felton, Bart.),

he had an only dau., Elizabeth, *m.* 1st, to Sir Philip Hungate, Bart., of Saxton; and 2ndly, to Lewis Smith, Esq., of Wotton, in Warwickshire.

Arms—Or, two chevronels, gu.

MONTACUTE—BARONS MONTACUTE, EARLS OF SALISBURY.

Barony, by Writ of Summons, dated 26 September, 1300.
Earldom, by Charter, dated 16 March, 1337.

Lineage.

The ancestor of this celebrated family,
DROGO, surnamed DE MONTE-ACUTO, MONTACUTE, or MONTAGUE, came into England with Robert, Earl of Moreton, at the Conquest, and appears, by Doomsday Book to have held of him divers manors in Somersetshire, whereof Sceptone, or Shipton-Montacute, was one, and Sutone, otherwise Sutton-Montacute, was another. The 1st baron by writ was SIMON DE MONTACUTE, one of the most eminent persons of the period in which he lived. In the 10th EDWARD I., he was in the expedition made into Wales, and within a few years after, received considerable grants from the crown. In the 22nd, he was in the wars of France, where he appears to have been engaged for the two or three following years, and then we find him fighting in Scotland. In the 27th he was constituted governor of Corfe Castle, and summoned to parliament as a Baron from 28th EDWARD I. to 9th EDWARD II. In the 4th EDWARD II., his lordship was appointed admiral of the king's fleet, then employed against the Scots; and he obtained, in three years afterwards, license to make a castle of his mansion house, at Perlynton, in Somersetshire. He *m.* Aufrick, dau. of Fergus, and sister and heir of Orry, King of the Isle of Man, and had issue,

WILLIAM, his successor.
Simon, *m.* to Hawise, dau. of Almeric, Lord St. Amand.

His lordship *d.* about the year 1316, and was *s.* by his elder son,

SIR WILLIAM DE MONTACUTE, 2nd baron, summoned to parliament, from 20 November, 1317, to 25 August, 1318. This nobleman had distinguished himself in the Scottish wars, in the life-time of his father, and was made a knight of the Bath. In the 11th EDWARD II., being then steward of the king's household, his lordship was constituted seneschal of the Duchy of Aquitaine, and had license to make a castle of his house at Kersynton, in Oxfordshire. He subsequently obtained other extensive grants from the crown. He *m.* Elizabeth, dau. of Sir Peter de Montfort, of Beaudesert, by whom (who *m.* 2ndly, Thomas, Lord Furnival), he had surviving issue,

WILLIAM, his successor.
Simon, in holy orders, bishop of Worcester, translated to the see of Ely, in 1336.
Edward (Sir), summoned to parliament as a Baron, *temp.* EDWARD III. (*see* MONTACUTE. Baron Montacute).
Katherine, *m.* to Sir William Carrington, Knt.
Alice, *m.* to — Auberie
Mary, *m.* to Sir — Cogan.
Elizabeth, prioress of Haliwell.
Hawise, *m.* to Sir — Bavent,
Maud, abbess of Berking.
Isabel, a nun at Berking

His lordship *d.* in Gascony, 1319, but was buried at St. Frideswide, now Christ Church, Oxford. He was *s.* by his eldest surviving son,

WILLIAM DE MONTACUTE, 3rd baron, who, the next ensuing year, although in minority, obtained a grant from the king of the wardship of all his own lands, and in the 16th EDWARD II., making proof of his age and doing his homage, had livery thereof. In three years afterwards he was made a knight of the Bath, and had an allowance of robes for that solemnity as a banneret. In the 4th EDWARD III., his lordship was deputed ambassador to the Pope, with Bartholomew de Burghersh, to return thanks to his holiness, for confirming a bull of Pope HONORIUS IV., touching certain favours, by him granted, to the monks at Westminster; moreover, before the end of the year, a parliament being then held at Nottingham, he was the principal person who apprehended Roger de Mortimer, Earl of March, in the night-time, within the Queen's lodgings there, and sent him prisoner to London, where he was soon afterwards executed for high treason. For this service, Lord Montacute had a grant in tail, to himself, and Katherine, his wife, of the castle of Sherburne, co. Dorset, and of several other manors in Hants, Berkshire, Bucks, and Cambridgeshire : part of the possessions of the attainted Earl of March. He was summoned to parliament from 5 June, 1331, to 29 November, 1336. In the 8th EDWARD III. his lordship was constituted governor of the Isles of Guernsey, Jersey, &c., and the next year made constable of the Tower of London.

About this time Lord Montacute acquired great distinction in the Scottish wars, but at the expense of one of his eyes, which he lost in the campaign. In the 10th EDWARD III., he was appointed admiral of the king's fleet, westward, and 16 March, 11th EDWARD III., in consideration of his numerous gallant achievements, he was advanced by charter. in full parliament held at London, to the title and dignity of EARL OF SALISBURY, to hold to him and his heirs, with a grant of £20 out of the profits of that county. Shortly after this he was joined in command of the army in Scotland, with Richard, Earl of Arundel; and pursued his victorious career as well in Scotland as in France, for the two ensuing years, when in storming the town of L'Isle, he had the misfortune to be made prisoner with Robert de Ufford, Earl of Suffolk, and conveyed in fetters, amidst the acclamations of the places through which he passed, to Paris, where the French king would have put him to death, but for the interference of the King of Bohemia. His lordship and his fellow-captive, the Earl of Suffolk, were soon after, however, exchanged. With his liberty, he re-commenced his martial career, and won fresh laurels on the French soil. In the 16th EDWARD III., having conquered the Isle of Man, he was crowned King thereof by his royal master. His lordship m. Catherine, dau. of William, Lord Grandison, and had issue,

WILLIAM, his successor.
JOHN (SIR), a distinguished warrior, and one of the heroes of Cressy, who m. Margaret, dau. and heir of Thomas, Lord Monthermer, and was summoned to parliament as a Baron. from 15 February, 1357, to 6 December, 1389. His lordship had issue,
    JOHN, 2nd baron. who s. his uncle, as 3rd Earl of Salisbury.
    Thomas, dean of Salisbury, d. 1404.
    Robert, of Sutton-Montague, in Somersetshire. The issue of this gentleman, according to Banks, flourished there until William Montague, the last of the family, left three daus. and co-heirs, of which, EMME m. James Dupote, who, in her right, possessed one moiety of Sutton-Montague, whose son, THOMAS, was father of Henry Duport, Esq., of Leicestershire, and John Duport, D.D., Master of Jesus College, Cambridge.
    Simon (Sir), from whom the extinct Dukes of Montague, and the extant Dukes of Manchester, and the Earls of Sandwich, deduce their descent.
    Eleanor.   Sibyl, a nun.
    Katherine.   Margaret, a nun.

Robert.
Sibyl, m. to Edmund, son of Edmund, Earl of Arundel.
Phillippa, m. to Roger Mortimer, Earl of March.
Elizabeth, m. 1st, to Giles, Lord Badlesmere; and 2ndly, to Hugh le Despencer.
Anne, m. to John, son of Roger, Lord Grey.

This great earl d. in 1343, of bruises received in a tilting at Windsor, and was s. by his eldest son,

WILLIAM DE MONTACUTE, 2nd Earl of Salisbury. This nobleman, in 1346, attended King EDWARD III. into France, and was at the siege of Caen, and the battle of Cressy. From this period he was seldom absent from the theatre of war, so that his whole life may be denominated one continued campaign. At the battle of Poictiers he commanded the rear-guard of the English army, and is said to have contended with the Earl of Warwick, in the heat of action, as to which should shed most French blood. His lordship was one of the original knights of the Garter, the foundation of which noble order, tradition attributes to the love which King EDWARD bore to his lordship's countess. The earl m. 1st, Joane, dau. of Edmund Plantagenet, Earl of Kent, from whom he was divorced, on account of the lady's precontract with Sir Thomas Holland (this was the celebrated Fair Maid of Kent, who eventually became the wife of Edward, the Black Prince). His lordship m. 2ndly, Elizabeth, dau. and co-heir of John, Lord Mohun, of Dunster, and had an only son,

WILLIAM, who m. Elizabeth, dau. of Richard, Earl of Arundel, and d. v. p., s. p., 6 August, 1382.

The earl d. s. p. in 1397 (his widow was received into the Sisterhood of the Convent of St. Albans, 10 October, 1408), and was s. by his nephew,

SIR JOHN DE MONTACUTE, Baron Montacute and Monthermer, as 3rd Earl of Salisbury. This nobleman was not less distinguished than his martial predecessors. In the 21st RICHARD II. he did his homage, and had livery of the lands

372

which he inherited from his uncle, "and being," says Dugdale, "a great favourite of the king, he was one of those whom that monarch suborned to impeach Thomas, of Woodstock, Duke of Gloucester, as also the Earls of Warwick and Arundel, in the ensuing parliament." The next year his lordship was constituted marshal of England, in the absence of Thomas Holand, Duke of Surrey, then employed in Ireland : and he remained faithful to the fortunes of King RICHARD, when almost everybody else deserted him, upon the invasion of Henry, Duke of Lancaster, who eventually drove that weak monarch from the throne. "It is reported of this earl," says Dugdale, "that though, upon the disposal of King RICHARD II. (to whom he had been most obsequious) he had such fair respect from King HENRY IV., that his life was not brought in question; nevertheless, he confederated with the Earls of Huntingdon and Kent, in designing his destruction; and accordingly came with them to Windsor Castle, under the disguise of Christmas players, with purpose to murder him and his sons, and to restore King RICHARD. But finding that their plot was discovered, they fled by night to Cirencester, co. Gloucester. Whereupon the townsmen, being much affrighted at their coming thither with such numbers, at that unseasonable time, stopping up all the avenues, to prevent their passage out, there grew a sharp fight betwixt them, which held from midnight, until three of the clock next morning; so that being tired out, they yielded themselves, desiring that they might not suffer death till they could speak with the king. which was granted: but that a priest of their party setting fire to the town, to give them an opportunity for escape, so irritated the inhabitants, that (neglecting to quench the fire) they brought them out of the great fury, and beheaded them about break of the day." His lordship had m. Maud, dau. of Sir Adam Francis, Knt., of London (widow of John Aubrey, son of Andrew Aubrey, citizen of London, and of Sir Alan Buxhull, Knt.), by whom he had issue,

THOMAS, who was restored to the Earldom of Salisbury, and the other honours.
Richard, d. s. p.
Anne, m. 1st, to Sir Richard Hankford. Knt., by whom she had a dau. and heir, m. to James, 7th Earl of Ormonde ; 2ndly, to John Fitz-Lewis, by whom she was mother of Elizabeth, m. to Sir John Wingfield; and 3rdly, to John Holland, Duke of Exeter.
Elizabeth, m. to Robert, Lord Willoughby, of Eresby.
Margaret, m. to William, Lord Ferrers, of Groby.

This John, Earl of Salisbury, was one of the most zealous of the sect called Lollards. His death, as stated above, occurred 5 January, 1400, whereupon King HENRY taking compassion upon his widow and children, restored some of the late earl's manors in Devonshire for their support; and to the elder son,

THOMAS DE MONTACUTE, he also granted a large proportion of his father's estates: and in 1409 restored him to the EARLDOM OF SALISBURY, and the other honours. "This nobleman," in the words of Banks, "was concerned in so many military exploits, that to give an account of them all, would be to write the history of the reign of HENRY V. Suffice it then to say, that as he lived, so he died in the service of his country, being mortally wounded when commanding the English army at the siege of Orleans in 1421." His lordship m. 1st, the Lady Eleanor, dau. of Thomas, and sister and co-heir of Edmund, Earl of Kent, and had a dau.,

ALICE, Countess of Salisbury, who m. Sir Richard Nevill, K.G., 2nd son of Ralph, 1st Earl of Westmoreland (see Nevill, Earls of Salisbury).

The earl m. 2ndly, Alice, dau. of Thomas Chaucer, Esq., of Ewelme, and widow of Sir John Philipps, Knt., but by her (who m. lastly, William, Duke of Suffolk), had no issue. Upon the decease of his lordship, who, with his other honours, was a knight of the Garter, the earldom of Salisbury became EXTINCT, but the baronies of Montacute, created by writ in 1300, of Montacute, created by writ in 1357, and Monthermer, devolved upon his dau. and heiress,

LADY ALICE MONTACUTE, wife of SIR RICHARD NEVILL, K.G., jure uxoris, Earl of Salisbury; their great-grand-dau. and representative Margaret Plantagenet, Countess of Salisbury. m. Sir Richard Pole, K.G., and had a son,

HENRY POLE, summoned to parliament in the Barony of MONTACUTE: his co-representatives were HENRY, MARQUESS OF HASTINGS; WILLIAM LOWNDES, Esq., of Chesham, Bucks, and WILLIAM SELBY LOWNDES, Esq., of Whaddon, Bucks, all co-heirs of the BARONIES of MONTACUTE and MONTHERMER.

Arms—Arg., three lozenges conjoined in fesse, gu.

MONTACUTE—BARONS MONTACUTE.

By Writ of Summons, dated 15 February, 1357.

(*See* Montacute, Earls of Salisbury, Sir John Montacute, 2nd son of William, 1st Earl of Salisbury.)

———

MONTACUTE—BARON MONTACUTE.

By Writ of Summons, dated 25 February, 1342.

Lineage.

Sir Edward de Montacute, youngest brother of William, 1st Earl of Salisbury, in the 4th Edward III., had a grant from the crown for his good services, and to support his rank as a knight, of £100 per annum: and was summoned to parliament as a Baron, from 25 February, 1342, to 20 November, 1360. His lordship was an eminent soldier, and served with high reputation in the wars of Scotland and France, having at one time in his train nine knights, fifteen esquires, and twenty archers on horseback, when his banner bore the following arms, viz., "Arg., three lozenges in fesse, on each an eagle displayed with a lable of three points." He *m.* Lady Alice Plantagenet, dau. and co-heir of Thomas, of Brotherton, Duke of Norfolk, by whom he had an only child,

Joane, who *m.* William Ufford, Earl of Suffolk, and *d. s. p.*

His lordship *d.* in 1361, when the Barony of Montacute devolved upon his dau. Joane, and at her decease it became EXTINCT.

Arms—Arg., three lozenges in fesse, on each an eagle displayed with a lable of three points.

———

MONTAGU—BARONS HALIFAX, EARL OF HALIFAX, EARLS OF HALIFAX.

Barony, by Letters Patent, dated 13 December, 1700.
First Earldom, by Letters Patent, dated 19 October, 1714.
Second Earldom, by Letters Patent, dated 14 June, 1715.

Lineage.

The Hon George Montagu, son of Henry, 1st Earl of Manchester, by his 3rd wife, Margaret, dau. of John Crouch, Esq., *m.* Elizabeth, dau. of Sir Anthony Irby, Knt., and was father of

Charles Montagu (a younger son), who became one of the most eminent statesmen of the important period of King William III. Mr. Montagu was returned to parliament by the city of Durham, and afterwards by the city of Westminster. In 1692 he was appointed one of the commissioners of the Treasury, and in two years afterwards chancellor of the Exchequer, in which office he projected, and caused to be executed, the great recoinage of silver in 1695. In 1698 he adjusted the affairs of the East India Company to universal satisfaction; and was elevated to the peerage, in compliance with the recommendation of the House of Commons, 13 December, 1700, in the dignity of Baron Halifax, *of Halifax, co. York*, with remainder, failing his issue male, to his nephew, George Montagu, son and heir of his elder brother, Edward Montagu. In the reign of Queen Anne, his lordship was constituted a commissioner for the Union between England and Scotland; and was created, 19 October, 1714, *Viscount Sunbury*, co. *Middlesex*, and Earl of Halifax. His lordship was not more distinguished as a politician than as a wit and man of letters. "Addison," says Banks, "has celebrated this nobleman in his account of the greatest English poets. Sir Richard Steele has drawn his character in the dedication of the second volume of the Spectator, and of the fourth of the Tatler; but Pope in the portrait of Buffo, in the Epistle to Arbuthnot, has returned the ridicule which his lordship in conjunction with Prior had heaped on Dryden's Hind and Panther; besides which admirable travestie, Lord Halifax wrote divers other works, most of which have been published together in an octavo volume, with memoirs of his lordship's life (1716); and are noticed by Walpole in his Catalogue of Noble Authors."

The earl *m.* Anne, Countess Dowager of Manchester, dau. of Sir Christopher Yelverton, Bart., of Easton Mauduit, Notts,

but had no issue. His lordship, who was a knight of the Garter, *d.* in 1715, when the earldom expired but the barony devolved, according to the limitation, upon his nephew,

George Montagu, 2nd Baron Halifax, who was created, 1st June, 1715, *Viscount Sunbury* and Earl of Halifax. This nobleman was made a knight of the Bath upon the revival of that order in 1725. His lordship *m.* 1st, Richarda-Posthuma, dau. of Richard Saltenstale, Esq., of Chippen-Warden, co. Northampton, by whom he had an only dau.,

Lucy, *m.* to Francis, 3rd Lord Guilford.

The earl *m.* 2ndly, Lady Mary Lumley, dau. of Richard, Earl of Scarborough, and had issue,

George, his successor.
Frances, *m.* to Sir Roger Burgoyne.
Anne, *m.* to Joseph Jekyll, Esq.
Mary, *m.* to Sir Danvers Osborn, Bart.
Elizabeth, *m.* to Henry Archer, brother of Lord Archer.
Barbara, *d. unm.*
Charlotte, *m.* to Col. Johnstone.

His lordship *d.* in 1739, and was *s.* by his son,

George Montagu, 2nd Earl of Halifax. This nobleman *m.* Anne, dau. of William Richards, Esq., and that lady having *s.* to the estates of Sir Thomas Dunk, of Tonges, in Kent, his lordship assumed the surname of Dunk. He had issue,

Anne, *d. unm.* in 1761.
Frances, *d. unm.* in 1764.
Elizabeth, *m.* to John, 5th Earl of Sandwich.

His lordship filled the offices of first lord of the Admiralty, lord lieutenant of Ireland, in 1749, and secretary of state. He *d.* in 1772, when all his honours became EXTINCT.

Arms—Az., three lozenges in fesse gu., within a border, sa., a mullet for difference.

———

MONTAGU — BARONS MONTAGU, OF BOUGHTON, EARLS OF MONTAGU, DUKES OF MONTAGU.

Barony, by Letters Patent, dated 29 June, 1621.
Earldom, by Letters Patent, dated 9 April, 1689.
Dukedom, by Letters Patent, dated 12 April, 1705.

Lineage.

Sir Edward Montagu, 2nd son of Thomas Montagu, Esq., of Hemington, co. Northampton, by Agnes, his wife, dau. of William Dudley, Esq., of Clopton, was *b.* at Brigstock, co. Northampton, and became one of the most celebrated lawyers of the period in which he lived. He was Speaker of the House of Commons, and was knighted and appointed chief justice of the Court of King's Bench, 30th Henry VIII. He became subsequently Chief Justice of the Common Pleas, 6 November, 1546, and was of the privy council, and in such favour with King Henry VIII., that he was appointed by that monarch one of the executors of his will. He purchased the estate of Boughton, in Northamptonshire, which at an earlier period had been possessed by his family through the marriage with the heiress of the name. Sir Edward Montagu, who *d.* 10 February, 1556, and was buried in the church of Hemington, *m.* thrice; 1st, a dau. of William Lane, Esq., of Orlingbury, co. Northampton, and had issue, with three sons, Ralph, Thomas, and Robert, who *d.* young, three daus.,

i. Dorothy, *m.* Edward Watson, Esq., of Rockingham Castle, co Northampton, ancestor by her of Thomas Watson-Wentworth, created 28 May, 1728, Baron of Malton, and 19 November, 1734, Baron of Wath and Harrowden, Viscount Higham, and Earl of Malton, and after succeeding on the death of his cousin in 1746, as 5th Baron Rockingham, was, 19 April of the same year, created Marquess of Rockingham, and dying in 1750, was *s.* by his son,

Charles Watson-Wentworth, Earl of Malton, and 2nd and last Marquess of Rockingham.

ii. Anne, *m.* John Rouse, Esq., of Rouse Lench, co. Worcester.
iii. Amelia, *m.* to George Lynne, or Lyne, of Southwick.

Sir Edward Montagu *m.* 2ndly, a dau. of George Kirkham, Esq., of Warmington, co Northampton, who *d. s. p.* He *m.* 3rdly, Ellen, sister of William Roper, Esq. (who *m.* Margaret, dau. of Sir Thomas More), and dau. (by Jane, dau. of Sir John Finieux, Knt., chief justice of the Court of King's Bench), of John Roper, Esq., of Eltham and St. Dunstan's, co. Kent, prothonotary of the King's Bench, and attorney-general *temp.* Henry VIII., ancestor of the Lords Teynham. By this lady who d in 1563, he was father, with an eldest son who d. young, of five sons and six daus., viz.,

I. EDWARD (Sir), eldest surviving son, of whom presently.
II. Roger, executor of the will of his niece's husband, Hugh Hughes, Esq., of Plâs Côch, 20 and 22 June, 1st JAMES I., 1603–4.
III. Simon, m. Christian, dau. of Robert Rastlyn, and was father by her of two daus.,

  1 Elizabeth, co-heir, m. twice : 1st, Hugh Hughes, Esq., of Porthamel Issa, in Menai, formerly called Llys Llywarch, and subsequently, from the red colour of the stone, Plâs Côch, co. Anglesey, high-sheriff for that county in 1581, 1592, and 1600 ; M.P. for Anglesey in the parliament which met at Westminster, 39th ELIZABETH (1597), a bencher of Lincoln's-Inn, attorney-general to Queen ELIZABETH ; she m. 2ndly, the Rev. Robert White, LL.D., prebendary of Worcester, and of Penmynnydd, co. Anglesey, rector of Llangeinwen. and Clynnog, co. Carnarvon, and of Newborough, co. Anglesey, and archdeacon of Merioneth, from all of which preferments he was ejected at the great rebellion.
  2 Margaret, co-heir, m. Sir Stephen Board, Knt., of Board Hill, parish of Cuckfield, co. Sussex, and was mother of two daus. and co-heirs.

    Elizabeth, m. to Sir William Slingsby, Knt., brother of Sir Henry Slingsby, Knt. of Scriven Park, and younger son (by Lady Mary Percy, only sister of Thomas Percy and Henry Percy, successively Earls of Northumberland), of Francis Slingsby, Esq., of Scriven Park, who d. 1600. By this gentleman she was mother of
      Henry Slingsby, æt. seven in 1627, master of the Mint to King CHARLES II., and author of the motto on our coin "DECUS ET TUTAMEN," father of an only son, Henry, who d. s. p. in 1695.
      William Slingsby, christened 9 December, 1618, at Knaresborough Church; d. 1622.
      Elizabeth, æt. eight years in 1627.
    Thomazine, co-heir.

IV Thomas.   V William.
I. Elizabeth. m. 1st, William Markham. Esq., of Okeham, co. Northampton. She m. 2ndly, Richard Cave, Esq., of Stanford, co. Northampton, son and heir of Sir Thomas Cave, Knt., of the same place, ancestor, by a previous marriage, of the Caves of Stanford, Baronets.
II. Ellen, m. George Tirrell, of Thornton, Bucks.
III. Isabel, m. Bryan Lascelles, Esq., of the co. Northampton.
IV. Mary, m. — Walter, Esq., of Blakesley, co. Northampton.
V. Margaret, m. Robert Woode, of Colwiche, co. Nottingham.
VI. Agnes, m. John Lane, Esq., of Walgram, co. Northampton.

Sir Edward Montagu was s. by his son,

SIR EDWARD MONTAGU, Knt., of Boughton Castle, high sheriff for Northamptonshire in 1567, who m. Elizabeth, sister of John, Baron Harrington, of Exton, so created 21 July, 1603, and dau. (by Lucy, sister of Sir Philip Sidney, K.G., and dau. of Sir William Sidney, Knt., of Penshurst), of Sir James Harrington, Knt., of Exton, co. Rutland, and had issue,

I. EDWARD (Sir), his successor.
II. Sir Walter, Knt., m. Anne, dau. and heir of Henry Morgan, Esq., of Yston, niece and heir of her father's elder brother, Sir William Morgan, Knt., of Pencoed Castle, co. Monmouth. Sir Walter Montagu d. s. p. in 1615, and his widow became the 3rd wife of her kinsman, Sir John Morgan, Knt., of Chilworth, Surrey, who was knighted at Cadiz, 1596, and d. 3 April, 1621. whose eventual heir-general, Mary, dau. and heir of Morgan Randyll, Esq., of Chilworth, m. Gilbert Vane, 2nd Baron Barnard, progenitor of the Dukes of Cleveland, and the Morgan Vanes, of Bilby Hall, co. Nottingham.
III. Henry, d. an infant.
IV. Sir Henry, Knt., M.P. for the city of London, 19 March, 1st JAMES I., 1604, Recorder of London, and Chief Justice of the Court of King's Bench, 1616 : Lord Treasurer of England, 1620; Baron Montague, of Kimbolton, and Viscount Mandeville, so created 19 December, 1620, and Earl of Manchester, 5 February, 1626. From this nobleman derives 1, the Duke of Manchester ; and 2, the Montagus, Earls of Halifax, EXTINCT.
V. Sir Charles. Knt.
VI. James, bishop of Bath and Wells (1608), translated to Winchester, 1616; d. 1618, and was buried at Bath.
VII. Sir Sidney, Knt., Master of the Court of Requests to CHARLES I.; M.P. for Huntingdonshire in 1640; but expelled and committed to the Tower in 1642, for declining to subscribe an oath framed by the house; ancestor of the Earl of Sandwich.
VIII. Thomas, d. an infant.
I. Lucy, m. Sir William Wray, Knt., of Glentworth, co. Lincoln.
II. Susanna, m. Sir Richard Sondes, Knt., of Throwley, Kent.
III. Theodosia. m. Sir Henry Capel, Knt., of Raineshall, Essex, and was mother of an only son, Arthur Capel, Baron Capel of Hadham, so created 6 August, 1641, beheaded 9 March, 1648–9, father of two sons, Arthur, created Earl of Essex 20 April, 1661 (ancestor of the present (1865) Arthur-Algernon Capel, 6th Earl of Essex); and Sir Henry Capel, Baron Capel, of Tewkesbury, so created, 1692, who d. s. p., when that dignity EXPIRED.

The eldest son,

SIR EDWARD MONTAGU, K.B., who was elevated to the peerage, 29 June, 1621, as Baron Montagu, of Boughton, co. Northampton. His lordship m 1st, 1621, Elizabeth, dau. and heir of Sir John Jeffries, Knt., of Chitting Leigh, co. Sussex, chief baron of the Exchequer, by whom he had an only dau.,

  ELIZABETH, who m. Robert, Lord Willoughby, of Eresby, afterwards EARL OF LINDSEY.

His lordship m. 2ndly, Frances, dau. of Thomas Cotton, Esq., of Conington, in Huntingdonshire, and sister of Sir Robert Cotton, Bart., by whom he had,

  Christopher, who predeceased his father, dying in the twenty-fourth year of his age, anno 1641.
  EDWARD, successor to the title.
  William, lord chief baron of the Exchequer in 1687, from which he was removed by King JAMES II. He lived, subsequently, in retirement. By Mary, his wife, dau. of Sir John Aubrey, Bart., he had a son and dau.
    William, who m. Anne, dau. and heir of Richard Evelyn, Esq., of Woodcot, in Surrey.
    Elizabeth, m. 1st, to William Drake, Esq., and 2ndly, to Samuel Trotman, Esq., of Syston Court, co. Gloucester.
  Frances, m. to John, Earl of Rutland.

This nobleman is characterised "as a person of a plain, downright English spirit; of a steady courage, a devout heart; and though no puritan, severe and regular in his life and manners. That he lived amongst his neighbours with great hospitality; and was very knowing in country affairs, and exceedingly beloved in the town and county of Northampton. That he was no friend to changes either in church or state; that when the civil wars began, he was brought prisoner to town by the parliament party, and confined in the Savoy; where he d. in the eighty-second year of his age, anno 1644." His lordship was s. by his eldest surviving son,

EDWARD MONTAGU. 2nd baron, who m. Anne, dau., and eventually heir of Sir Ralph Winwood, of Ditton Park, principal secretary of state to King JAMES I., by whom he had issue,

  Edward, who was appointed by King CHARLES II. master of the house to the queen. Afterwards going to sea with his gallant kinsman, the Earl of Sandwich, he was slain in an attack upon the Dutch East India fleet, in the port of Bergen, in August, 1665.
  RALPH, successor to the title.
  Elizabeth, m. to Sir Daniel Harvey, Knt., ambassador at Constantinople in 1668.

His lordship d. 10 January, 1683, and was s. by his only surviving son,

RALPH MONTAGU, 3rd baron, who, in the lifetime of his father, represented the co. of Huntingdon in parliament, and was a very distinguished member of the house. He was an active and zealous promoter of the Revolution, and in consequence, upon the accession of King WILLIAM and Queen MARY, he was created 9 April, 1689, Viscount Monthermer, and EARL OF MONTAGU. In 1669 his lordship was ambassador to the court of France, and then formed that taste in building and landscape gardening, which he afterwards acted upon, in erecting his mansion at Boughton, as much after the model of Versailles, as the extent would permit. His town house was in Bloomsbury, and is now the site of the British Museum. In 1705, he was advanced by Queen ANNE to the Marquessate of Monthermer, and DUKEDOM OF MONTAGU. His grace m. 1st, Lady Elizabeth Wriothesley, dau. of Thomas, Earl of Southampton, and widow of Joceline, Earl of Northumberland, by whom he had issue,

  Ralph,   } who both d. in the life-time of the duke.
  Winwood, }
  JOHN, his successor.
  Anne, m. 1st, to Alexander Popham, Esq., of Littlecote, Wilts; and 2ndly, to Lieut.-General Hervey. By the former she left an only child, ELIZABETH, m. 1st, to Edward-Richard, Viscount Hinchinbroke; and 2ndly, to Francis Seymour, Esq.

The duke m. 2ndly, Lady Elizabeth Cavendish, dau. and co-heir of Henry, Duke of Newcastle, widow of Christopher Monk, Duke of Albemarle, but by her had no issue. His grace d. in 1709, and was s. by his son,

JOHN MONTAGU, 2nd duke. This nobleman officiated as lord high constable of England at the coronation of King GEORGE I. His grace m. Mary, dau. and co-heir of the celebrated General, John, Duke of Marlborough, and had three sons, John, George, and Edward-Churchill, who all d. young, in his life-time, and three daus., viz.,

  Isabella, m. 1st, to William, Duke of Manchester, by whom she had no issue; and 2ndly, to Edward Hussey, Earl of Beaulieu.
  Eleanor, d. young.

Mary, *m.* to George Brudenell, 4th Earl of Cardigan, who, after the decease of his father-in-law, was created *Marquess of Monthermer*, and DUKE OF MONTAGU.

In the reign of GEORGE I., the Duke of Montagu filled several public situations of the highest honour. He was a knight of the Garter and a knight of the Bath. At the accession of King GEORGE II. he was continued in favour, and at the coronation of that monarch, he carried the sceptre with the cross. His grace *d.* 5 July, 1749, when all his honours became EXTINCT.

Arms—Quarterly : 1st and 4th, arg., three lozenges conjoined in fesse gu., within a border, sa., for MONTAGU; 2nd and 3rd, or, an eagle displayed vert, beaked and membered gu., for MONTHERMER.

MONTAGU—DUKE OF MONTAGU, AND BARON MONTAGU, OF BOUGHTON.

Dukedom, by Letters Patent, dated 5 November, 1766.
Barony, by Letters Patent, dated 21 August, 1781.

Lineage.

GEORGE BRUDENELL, 4th Earl of Cardigan, having *m.* Lady Mary Montagu, one of the daus. and co-heirs of John, 2nd Duke of Montagu (who *d.* 1749, when his honours expired), assumed the surname and arms of MONTAGU, and was created 5 November, 1766, *Marquess of Monthermer*, and DUKE OF MONTAGU. His grace was governor of Windsor Castle, a member of the privy council, and a knight of the Garter. He had issue,

JOHN, created BARON MONTAGU, *of Boughton*, but *d. unm.* in 1770, in the life-time of his father.
Elizabeth, *m.* in 1767, to Henry, 3rd Duke of Buccleuch, by whom she had, with four daus., two sons, viz.,
  CHARLES-WILLIAM-HENRY, 4th Duke of Buccleuch.
  HENRY-JAMES, who *s.* his grandfather as Baron Montagu, of Boughton.
  Mary, Henrietta, } both *d. unm.*

The duke was created 21 August, 1786, BARON MONTAGU, *of Boughton*, with remainder to Henry, 2nd son of his dau., Elizabeth, Duchess of Buccleuch. His grace, who was governor to the Prince of Wales (GEORGE IV.), and Prince Frederick (Duke of York), sons of King GEORGE III., *d.* 23 May, 1790, when the Earldom of Cardigan devolved upon his brother, the Hon. James Brudenell; the Marquessate of Monthermer and Dukedom of Montagu became EXTINCT ; but the Barony of Montagu. of Boughton, passed, according to the limitation, to the duke's grandson,

LORD HENRY-JAMES SCOTT, *b.* 16 December, 1776, who took the name of Montagu. and was 2nd Baron Montagu. His lordship *m.* 1804, Jane-Margaret, dau. of Archibald, Lord Douglas, and *d.* without male issue, 30 October, 1845, when the title became EXTINCT. His daus. and co heiresses were,

I. Lucy-Elizabeth, *m.* 1832, to Cospatrick-Alexander, Earl of Home.
II. Mary-Margaret, *m.* to Lieut.-Col. Frederick Clinton.
III. Jane-Caroline, *d. unm.* 16 June, 1846.
IV. Caroline-Georgiana, *m.* 1836. to George-William Hope, Esq., M.P.

Arms—Same as the previous Duke of Montagu.

MONTAGU—BARON MONTAGU, OF BOUGHTON.

By Letters Patent, dated 8 May, 1762.

Lineage.

THE HON. JOHN MONTAGU, only son of George, 4th Earl of Cardigan, by Lady Mary Montagu, dau. and co-heir of John, 2nd Duke of Montagu (who *d.* in 1749), was created by letters patent, dated 8 May, 1762, BARON MONTAGU, *of Boughton, co. Northampton*, but *d. unm.* in 1770, in the life-time of his father, when the title became EXTINCT.

Arms—Same as the Dukes of Montagu.

MONTALT—BARONS MONTALT.

By Writ of Summons, dated 23 June, 1295.
By Writ of Summons, dated 6 February, 1299.

Lineage.

Upon the foundation of the abbey of St. Werberg, in the city of Chester, temp. W LLIAM RUFUS,

HUGH, the son of Norman, being at that time one of the barons to Hugh, Earl of Chester, granted certain lands to the monks of that house, Ralph and Roger, his brothers, being witnesses. To Ralph *s.* his son and heir,

ROBERT, who assumed the surname of Montalt, from the chief place of his residence, an elevation in the co. of Flint, where he erected a castle. This Robert, being steward to the Earl of Chester, was also one of his barons. After the death of Ranulph de Gernons, Earl of Chester, the lands of that great earldom were, it appears, for some time in the king's hands, for in the 6th HENRY II., this Robert de Montalt was one of those, who accounted in the king's exchequer for the farm of them; and likewise for what was then expended, in building the Castle of Chester. This Robert was *s.* by his son and heir,

ROBERT DE MONTALT, Lord of Montalt, co. Flint, who was *s.* by his son,

ROGER DE MONTALT, who was deemed one of the greatest feudal barons in the realm, temp. HENRY II., and accompanied Prince Edward to the Holy Land. This feudal lo d was constantly employed against the Welsh, and in the 44th HENRY III., he had command to repair to the borders, with the other Barons-Marchers, and there to reside for the defence of the country. He *m.* Cecilia, 2nd sister, and one of the co-heirs of Hugh de Albini, Earl of Arundel, and had issue,

JOHN.   Robert.
Leucha, *m.* to Philip de Orreby, the younger.

He *d.* in 1260, and was *s.* by his elder son,
JOHN DE MONTALT, who *m.* 1st, Elene, widow of Robert de Stockport; and 2ndly, Milisent, dau. of William de Cantilupe, but *d. s. p.*, and was *s.* by his brother,
ROBERT DE MONTALT, who had two sons, Roger and Robert, and was *s.* at his decease, in 1278, by the elder,
ROGER DE MONTALT, who was one of the barons in rebellion against HENRY III., but returning to his allegiance, he subsequently defended Cambridge for the king. In the reign of EDWARD I., he was in the wars of Gascony, and was summoned to parliament as a Baron, 23 June, 1295. His lordship *m.* Julian, dau. of Roger de Clifford, but dying *s. p.* in 1297, the barony expired while his lands devolved, upon his brother,
ROBERT DE MONTALT. This gallant person having distinguished himself in the wars of Scotland and Gascony, temp. EDWARD I. and EDWARD II., was summoned to parliament by the former monarch, 6 February, 1299, and he had summons from that period to 13 June, 1329, in which year he *d. s. p.*, when the Barony of Montalt became EXTINCT, and his extensive estates, according to a settlement made by the deceased lord, passed to Isabel, Queen Consort of England, mother of EDWARD III., for life, and afterwards to John, of Eltham, brother to the King, and his heirs for ever.

Arms—Az., a lion rampant, arg.

⁎ From this ancient house, the MAUDES, VISCOUNTS HAWARDEN and Barons de Montalt claim descent.

MONTFORT—EARLS OF LEICESTER.

Creation of King JOHN, *anno* 1206.

Lineage.

The first of this family that settled in England was
SIMON DE MONTFORT, surnamed the Bald, great grandson of Almaric. an illegitimate son of Robert,* King of France. Which Simon having *m.* Amicia, one of the two sisters and co-heirs of ROBERT DE BELLEMONT, or BEAUMONT, surnamed

---
* Thus,
ROBERT, King of France.
  Almaric, who had the town of Montfort by gift of his royal father, and thence assumed that surname.
    Simon de Montfort.
      Almaric, Earl of Montfort, father of Simon, above-mentioned.

Fitz-Parnel, 4th and last Earl of Leicester of that family, obtained a grant of the EARLDOM OF LEICESTER from King JOHN, with a confirmation of the Stewardship of England, which he acquired by the possession of the honour of Hinkley, a portion of the immense fortune of his wife. But notwithstanding these marks of royal favour, the earl, within a brief period, revolted from the King of England to the King of France, for which act of treason the Earldom of Leicester was transferred to Ranulph, Earl of Chester, the honours of Hinkley seized upon by the crown, and De Montfort himself banished the realm. Soon after this (1209) we find him, under the title of Earl of Montfort, General of the crusade against the Albigenses, and in nine years subsequently a leader in the besieging army of LEWIS, King of France, before the walls of Toulouse, where he was slain by a slinger from the battlements. His lordship had two sons by the co-heiress of Beaumont, namely, Almaric and Simon, the younger of whom,

SIMON DE MONTFORT, is said to have first sought an asylum in England from the hostility of Blanche, Queen of France, and to have obtained a restitution of the EARLDOM OF LEICESTER, and stewardship of England, from King HENRY III., through the petition of his brother Almaric, then Earl of Montfort, and constable of France. Certain it is, however, that in 1232 (16th HENRY III.), he bore the title of Earl of Leicester, and had obtained a grant of all his mother's inheritance in England from his brother. In 1236, his lordship officiated as steward at the nuptials of HENRY III., and held the ewer in which the king washed. And in two years afterwards he obtained the hand of the king's sister, Eleanor, widow of William Marshal, Earl of Pembroke; the marriage ceremony being performed by Walter, one of the royal chaplains at Westminster, "within a little chappel at the corner of the king's chamber." This marriage was, however, opposed by the princess's other brother, Richard, Earl of Cornwall (afterwards King of the Romans), and the kingdom at large, because the lady had made in her widowhood a vow of chastity, in the presence of Edmund, archbishop of Canterbury, and several of the nobility. And so strongly did public discontent manifest itself, that the earl was obliged to repair in person to Rome for the purpose of obtaining a dispensation, which with considerable difficulty he at length accomplished; and returning to England was most graciously received at court by the king, who appointed him his chief counsellor. Notwithstanding this, however, William de Abindon, a Dominican friar, and many other of the clergy, continued to exclaim against the marriage. The birth of Prince Edward, the king's eldest son, occurring soon after, the earl was chosen one of the sponsors of the royal infant, and as such officiated at the baptismal font. But before the close of the same year, he experienced the caprice of royal favour. The king observing him and his countess amongst the nobility who attended the queen at her purification, called him an excommunicated person, and prohibited his entering the church. "Which sudden unkindness," says Dugdale, " much dismaying him, he went away by water to Winchester House, which (the bishop being dead), the king had lent him. But there he could not be permitted to stay, the king in great wrath causing him to be put out of doors. Whereupon he returned sorrowing and weeping, yet could not appease his anger, the king plainly telling him, that he had abused his sister before marriage; and that, though he afterwards gave her to him for a wife, it was unwillingly, and to avoid scandal. Upbraiding him, that to ratify this his unlawful marriage, he went to Rome, and there corrupted that court with large bribes and promises: adding that, having failed in payment of the money, he ought justly to be excommunicated." This storm ultimately drove his lordship from the kingdom, but only for a short period, as we find him returning in 1240, and having then an honourable reception from the king and all his court. Soon after this he made a journey to Jerusalem, having previously disposed of one of his woods to the knights hospitallers and canons of Leicester for somewhat less than a £1000 to defray part of the necessary expenses of the undertaking. Henceforward he appears for a series of years to have enjoyed the high favour of the king, and to have fully merited it by his eminent services. In the 32nd HENRY III., his lordship was appointed commander-in-chief of the forces in Gascony, and in the end of that year he sat in the great convention of parliament held at London; about which time he obtained from the king a grant of the custody of Kenilworth Castle, for Eleanor, his wife. to hold during her life; and returning into Gascony, he forced Guaston de Bearne, who had raised the standard of rebellion, to an honourable truce. The earl came back to England the next year, and was received at court with great honour. Soon after which, in fulfilment of a vow

he had made as penance for his marriage, he began a journey to the Holy Land, and in the 34th of the same reign returned safely, with his brother-in-law, Richard, Earl of Cornwall, and others. For the two following years he was actively and victoriously employed in Gascony, until the king hearkening to complaints against him for cruelty and oppression, which appear to have been unsustainable, removed him from the seneschalship of that country. Upon the subsequent insurrection of the barons against the king, the Earl of Leicester siding with the former, was appointed their general-in-chief, in which character he fought the great battle of Lewes, where the royal army sustained so signal a defeat, the king himself being made prisoner with Prince Edward, his son, his brother, Richard, King of the Romans, and many other personages of eminence, attached to his cause. This victory placing the government in the hands of the earl and his adherents; himself, the bishop of Chichester, the Earl of Gloucester, and a few others of less note, were nominated to discharge the executive functions. One of the earliest acts of the usurpation was to summon a parliament in the king's name, by writs dated 24 December, 49th HENRY III., directed to the bishops and abbots, and to such lay lords as could be relied upon; by which, signifying " the realm to be then in peace and quiet, and the desire of the king to establish the same to the honour of God, and benefit of his people;" they were summoned to meet at London, on the octaves of St. Hilary, there to sit in parliament, "to treat and give their advice" At the same time precepts were issued to the sheriffs, ordering them to return two knights for each county; to the cities and boroughs the like number of citizens and burgesses; and to the barons of the Cinque Ports, a certain number of their discreetest men for the same purpose. This is deemed the first precedent of a parliament, such as ever since has been established, and Sir William Dugdale thus speculates upon the causes of the revolution:— " If I may be so bold as to give my opinion, what reasons these potent rebels then had, thus to alter the former ancient usage, I shall take leave to conjecture, that it was, because they discerning what large retinues the nobility and other great men in those elder times had; as also the great number of the king's tenants in capite, then called barones minores, it might have proved dangerous to themselves to permit such a multitude to come together." The new government did not, however, endure long for a breach taking place between the two chiefs, Leicester and Gloucester, the arms of those powerful persons were directed against each other, and Prince Edward effecting his escape about the same time, the Earl of Gloucester reared the royal standard, and formed a junction with the forces of the prince. With this army, marching towards Kenilworth, they surprised young Simon Montfort, the earl's son, and made prisoners of no less than thirteen of his chief adherents, almost without resistance. Elated with this triumph they proceeded to Evesham, where the Earl of Leicester and his great force lay, expecting the arrival of his son, whose banners the royal army as a stratagem of war alone displayed, and thereby completely deceived this able commander. His lordship undismayed, however, drew out his army in order of battle, and fighting gallantly to the last, fell in the midst of his enemies, when victory declared for the royal cause. It is said, that when the earl discerned the superiority and disposition of the royalist forces he swore " by the arm of St. James (his usual exclamation), they have done discreetly; but this they learned from me: let us therefore commend our souls to God, because our bodies are theirs." Nevertheless, encouraging his men, he told them, " it was for the laws of the land, yea, the cause of God and justice, that they were to fight." The principal persons slain in the memorable engagement were, the Earl himself, Henry de Montfort, his eldest son, Hugh Le Despenser, then justice of England, Ralph Basset, of Drayton, and about one hundred and sixty knights, and many other gentlemen of his party. Amongst the prisoners, were Guy de Montfort, a younger son of the earl; John Fitz-John, Humphrey de Bohun, the younger; John de Vesci, Peter de Montfort, junr., and Nicholas de Segrave. The body of the Earl was removed from the field of battle by some of his friends upon an old ladder covered with a poor torn cloth, and thus conveyed to the abbey of Evesham, where, folded in a sheet, it was committed to the grave. But within a short time, some of the monks alleging that, the earl being an excommunicated person, and attainted of treason, his remains were unworthy christian burial, the body was taken up, and interred in a remote place, known but to few. Thus fell, in 1264, Simon de Montfort, Earl of Leicester: one of the most eminent soldiers and statesmen of the period in which he lived, and, under his attainder, the earldom became EXTINCT. Of his widow, Eleanor, the king's sister, it is stated, that after the fatal battle of Evesham, she fled into France, and took up her abode in the nunnery of the order of preachers, at Montargea, which had been founded by her husband's sister. Of his issue,

Henry, fell at Evesham, leading the van of the baronial army.

Simon, who for some time gallantly defended the castle of Kenilworth, was eventually made prisoner in the Isle of Ely, by Prince Edward; afterwards effecting his escape he fled into France, and in 1270, being at Viterbuirm, in Italy, he joined with his brother, Guy, in the murder of their cousin, Henry, eldest son of Richard, King of the Romans, in the church of St. Silvester, as the prince assisted at mass.

Guy, fought in the van of the baronial army at Evesham, and being made prisoner, was confined in Dover Castle, from which escaping, he fled into Tuscany, and there acquiring high reputation as a soldier, he obtained the dau. and heiress of the Earl Rufus for his wife. Meeting with Prince Henry, son of the King of the Romans, Guy, and his brother Simon, slew him in revenge, in the church of St. Silvester, at Viterbuirm. For which barbarous act, being first excommunicated by Pope Gregory X., he was thrown into prison; but released in 1283 by Pope Martin II., and placed at the head of an army, in which situation he displayed his characteristic prowess. He subsequently at the decease of his wife's father, returned to Tuscany, and inherited a very considerable fortune. Charles I., King of Naples, made him Count de Nola. He d. 1288, leaving by Margaret, his wife, dau. of Rodolph, Count de Languillara, an only dau, Anastasia de Monfort, Countess de Nola, m. to Raymond des Ursins.

Almaric, who, when conveying his sister from France to be m. to Llewelyn, Prince of Wales, was taken prisoner, with her at sea, and suffered a long imprisonment. He was at last, however, restored to liberty, and his posterity are said to have flourished in England under the name of Wellsburne.

Eleanor, b. about Michaelmas, 1252, at Kenilworth, who m. by proxy, early in 1275, and in person at Worcester, 13 October, 1278, Llewelyn ap Griffith, Prince of North Wales. In the household book of her mother for 1265, Eleanor is styled " Demoiselle," and in a letter to Edward I., dated 6 October, 1279, she designates herself as " Al principissa Walliæ domina Snowdon." By Llewelyn ap Griffith, who was slain 10 December, 8th Edward I., 1282, she had issue two daus., and co-heirs, the younger of whom, the Princess Gwenllian, b. 19 June, 1281, a nun of Sempringham, 10th Edward II., d. there 7 June, 11th Edward III., 1337. The elder dau., the Princess Catherine, heiress of the monarchs of North Wales, was mother, by her husband, Philip ap Ivor, Lord of Cardigan, of the Lady Eleanor Goch, who m. Thomas, representative of the sovereigns of South Wales, ap Llewelyn ap Owen ap Meredith. This prince, who with his brother, Owen ap Llewelyn, lord of the half of the comot of Yscoed Ughirwen, and of one quarter of the comot of Gwynnionydd, was twenty-eight years old and upwards, 2 December, 1328, was probably dead 20 September, 1334, the date of a quo warranto against his brother Owen ap Llewelyn and his own son, Owen ap Thomas, apparently joint co-heirs of the lordship of Yscoed Ughirwen, and of half of the comot of Gwynnionydd. By Thomas ap Llewelyn, the Lady Eleanor Goch had, with an only son, Owen ap Thomas, already named, who d. s. p., an only dau., heiress of her brother, viz., the Lady Eleanor. She m. Griffith Vychan ap Griffith, Lord of Glyndwrdwy, representative of the sovereigns of South Wales, father by her of two sons: 1 Owen ap Griffith Vychan, Lord of Glyndwrdwy, the renowned " Owen Glyndwr," in whom united the representation of the three dynasties of North Wales, South Wales, and Powys. 2 Tudyr ap Griffith Vychan, Lord of Gwyddelwern in Edeirnion, æt. twenty-three. 3 September, 10th Richard II., and killed 11 March, 1405, whose senior co-heir is Lord Lostyn.

Arms—Gu., a lion rampant, queue fourché, arg.

MONTFORT—BARONS MONTFORT.

By Writ of Summons, dated 23 June, 1295.

Lineage.

Hugh de Montfort, commonly called Hugh with a Beard, son of Thurstan de Bastenburgh, accompanied William the Conqueror into England, and aided that prince's triumph at Hastings, for which eminent service he obtained divers fair lordships, and at the time of the General Survey was possessor of twenty-eight in Kent, with a large portion of Romney Marsh; sixteen in Essex; fifty-one in Suffolk; and nineteen in Norfolk. This gallant soldier eventually lost his life in a duel, with Walcheline de Ferrers, and was s. by his son,

Hugh de Montfort, who had issue by his 1st wife, two sons, viz.,

Robert, general of the army to King William Rufus, but favouring the title of Robert Curthose, in opposition to Henry I., he was impeached for his disloyalty, whereupon, being conscious of guilt, he got permission to go to Jerusalem, and left all his possessions to the king; he d. s. p.

Hugh, d. in a pilgrimage, also s. p.

Hugh de Montfort had, besides these sons, a dau. by his 2nd wife, who m. Gilbert de Gant, and had issue, Hugh, living 1124, who, on account of his mother being so great an heiress, assumed the name of Montfort; and Ada, m. to Simon, Earl of Huntingdon; which

Hugh de Montfort (otherwise Gant), inherited all the possessions of his grandfather, and was called Hugh the fourth. This Hugh, having m. Adeline, dau. of Robert, Earl of Mellent, joined with Waleran, her brother, and all those who endeavoured to advance William, son of Robert Curthose, against King Henry I., in 1124, and entering Normandy for that purpose, he was made prisoner, with the said Waleran, and confined for the fourteen years ensuing. The time of his death is not ascertained, but he left issue,

Robert. Thurstan.

Adeline, m. to William de Britolio.

Ada, m. to Richard, son of the Earl of Gloucester.

He was s. by his elder son,

Robert de Montfort. This feudal lord having in 1163, charged Henry de Essex, the King's Standard Bearer, with cowardice, in fleeing from his colours, vanquished him in a subsequent trial by battle. He does not appear to have had any issue, for he was s. at his decease by his brother,

Thurstan de Montfort, who, being enfeoffed of divers fair lordships, by Henry de Newburgh, the 1st Earl of Warwick, erected a stony castle, called Beldesert, at the chief seat of his family in Warwickshire, which it continued for several subsequent ages. To this Thurstan, who d. before 1190, s. his son,

Henry de Montfort, who in the 2nd Richard I., regained the manor of Wellesbourne, co. Warwick, commonly called Wellesbourne-Montfort, whereof he had been dispossessed by King Henry II. He was s. by

Thurstan de Montfort, who had great law suits in King John's time, with Eustace de Stutevill, and Nicholas de Stutevill, regarding a portion of the lordship of Cotingham, co. York. He d. in 1216, and was s. by his son,

Peter de Montfort. This feudal lord for several years in the reign of King Henry III., took an active part in the wars of that monarch, but at length on the breaking out of the barons' insurrection, he became one of the most zealous amongst those turbulent lords, and after the battle of Lewes, was of the nine nominated to rule the kingdom, in which station he enjoyed and exercised more than regal power, but of short duration, for he fell at the subsequent conflict of Evesham, so disastrous to the baronial cause. Peter de Montfort m. Alice, dau. of Henry de Aldithley, a great Staffordshire baron, and had issue,

Peter, his successor.

William, who by gift of his father had the manor of Uppingham, co. Rutland.

Robert, who had lands also in the co. Rutland.

The eldest son,

Peter de Montfort, participated in his father's treasons, and was taken prisoner at the battle of Evesham, but being allowed the benefit of the dictum of Kenilworth, he was restored to his paternal inheritance—and afterwards enjoyed the favour of King Edward I., in whose Welsh wars he took a very active part. He d. in 1287, leaving a dau. Elizabeth (who m. 1st, William, son and heir of Simon de Monticute, and 2ndly, Sir Thomas de Furnivall), and a son and heir,

John de Montfort, who in the 22nd Edward I., being in the wars of Gascony, was the next year summoned to parliament as a baron. His lordship m. Alice, dau. of William de Plaunch, and had issue,

John, } successively barons.
Peter,}

Elizabeth, m. to Sir Baldwin de Freville, Knt.

Maud, m. to Bartholomew de Sudeley.

He d. in 1296, and was s. by his elder son,

John de Montfort, 2nd baron, summoned to parliament 26 July, 1313, in which year he received pardon for his participation in the murder of Piers de Gaveston—and afterwards marching with the English army into Scotland, was killed at the battle of Stryvelin, when, leaving no issue, he was s. by his brother,

Peter de Montfort, 3rd baron, summoned to parliament from 22 January, 1336, to 10 March, 1349. This nobleman, prior to the decease of his brother, was in priest's orders, but upon his inheriting the honours of his family the sacred function was dispensed with. In the 15th Edward II. he was joined in commission with William de Beauchamp, and Roger de Ailesbury, in the custody of the city of Worcester, and five years afterwards was constituted governor of Warwick Castle, then vested in the crown, by reason of the minority of the Earl of Warwick. His lordship m. Margaret, dau. of the Lord Furnivzl, and had a son,

Guy, who m. Margaret, one of the daus. of Thomas de Beauchamp, Earl of Warwick, but d. v. p., s. p.

Peter, Lord Montfort, d. in 1367, when the barony fell into ABEYANCE between his sisters (refer to children of John, 1st lord), as it still continues amongst their representatives.

Arms—Bendy of ten, or and az.

NOTE.—Peter, last Lord Montfort, had by a concubine, called Lora de Ullenhale, dau. of one Richard Astley, of Ullenhale, co. Warwick, a son,

SIR JOHN MONTFORT, Knt., whose posterity flourished in the male line for several subsequent ages, at Coleshill, co. Warwick, until the attainder of Sir Simon Montfort, Knt., temp. HENRY VII., whose descendants continued at Bescote, co. Stafford.

MONTGOMERY—BARON MONTGOMERY.

By Writ of Summons, dated 25 February, 1342.

Lineage.

In the 20th EDWARD III.,

JOHN DE MONTGOMERY was in the great expedition then made into France, and the next year was made captain of Calais, as also admiral of the king's whole fleet, from the mouth of the Thames, westwards. He had summons to parliament as a Baron, 25 February, 1342, but never afterwards, and the dignity is presumed to have become EXTINCT, at his lordship's decease.

Arms—Or, an eagle displayed, az.

MONTGOMERY—EARL OF MOUNT ALEXANDER.

Viscounty, by Letters Patent, dated 3 May, 1622.
Earldom, by Letters Patent, dated 18 July, 1661.

Lineage.

ADAM MONTGOMERY, 4th Laird of Braidstane (great-grandson of Robert Montgomery, brother of Alexander, 2nd Lord Montgomerie, father of the 1st Earl of Eglinton), m. the eldest dau. of Colquhoun of Luss; and d. about 1550, leaving two sons, namely,

ADAM, his heir.
Robert, ancestor of the Montgomerys of Grey Abbey, co. Down, now represented by Hugh Montgomery, Esq. of that place. (*See* BURKE's *Landed Gentry.*)

The elder son,

ADAM MONTGOMERY, Esq., 5th Laird of Braidstane, m. the dau. of John Montgomery, of Hasclheads, and had four sons: the 2nd, George, was bishop of Meath, and left an only dau. and heir, Jane, wife of Nicholas St. Lawrence, Earl of Howth. The eldest,

SIR HUGH MONTGOMERY, Knt., 6th Laird of Braidstane, settled in Ireland, and was raised to the peerage of that kingdom, 3 May, 1622, as VISCOUNT MONTGOMERY, *of the Great Ards, co. Down.* His lordship m. 1st, in 1587, Elizabeth, 2nd dau. of John Shaw, Laird of Greenock, and 2ndly, Sarah, dau. of William, Lord Herries, and widow of John, 1st Earl of Wigtoun; by the latter he had no issue; but by the former he was father of three sons, and two daus., viz.,

HUGH, his heir.
James, (Sir, Knt.) of Rosemount, will dated 6 June, 1651; proved 16 July, 1661; who left by Katharine, his wife, dau. of Sir William Stewart, Knt., a son William Montgomery, Esq., of Rosemount, father of James Montgomery, Esq., of Rosemount, who m. Elizabeth, dau. of Archibald Edmonstone, of Duntreath, and was father of
WILLIAM MONTGOMERY, Esq., of Rosemount, who m. Isabella, 3rd dau. of John Campbell, of Mamore, 2nd son of Archibald, Duke of Argyll, and d 1743, leaving issue.
George, of Ballylissan, whose grandson, HERCULES MONT-

GOMERY, Esq., of Ballylissan, m. Jane, dau. of Rev. Archibald Macneil, and had issue.
Mary, m. to Sir Robert Maclellan, Lord Kirkcudbright.
Jean, m. to Patrick Savage, Esq., of Portaferry, co. Down.

The 1st Viscount Montgomery's will is dated 20 May, 1636; his son and heir,

HUGH MONTGOMERY, 2nd Viscount Montgomery, colonel of a regiment during the rebellion of 1641, m. in 1623, Lady Jean Alexander, eldest dau. of William, Earl of Stirling, secretary of state for Scotland, and by her (who m. 2ndly, Major-General Monroe), he left at his decease, in 1642, a son and successor,

HUGH MONTGOMERY, 3rd Viscount Montgomery, a gallant royalist during the period of the civil war, and consequently a severe sufferer in those times of confiscation and oppression. His lordship survived, however, to witness the Restoration, and was created, 1661, EARL OF MOUNT ALEXANDER. He m. 1st, in 1648, Mary, eldest sister of Henry, 1st Earl of Drogheda, and 2ndly, Catherine, dau. of Arthur Jones, Lord Ranelagh, and widow of Sir William Parsons, Bart., by the latter he had two daus., Catharine, wife of Sir Francis Hamilton, Bart., and Elizabeth, wife of Raphael Hunt, Esq., of Dollardstown, and by the former he left at his decease a son and successor,

HUGH MONTGOMERY, 2nd Earl of Mount Alexander, b. in 1650; master of the Ordnance and brigadier-general; who m. 1st, in 1672, Catharine, eldest dau. of Carey, Earl of Roscommon; and 2ndly, Eleanor, dau. of Maurice Berkeley, Viscount Fitzhardinge; but d. without surviving issue, 12 February, 1716, and was s. by his brother,

HENRY MONTGOMERY, 3rd Earl of Mount Alexander; who m. Mary, eldest dau. of William, Lord Howth; and was s. by his son,

HUGH MONTGOMERY, 4th Earl of Mount Alexander; who m. in 1703, Elinor, dau. of Sir Patrick Barnewall, Bart., of Crickstown; but dying s. p., 27 February, 1744, was s. by his brother,

THOMAS MONTGOMERY, 5th Earl of Mount Alexander; who m. Manoah, dau. of Mr. Delacherois, of Lisburn; but d. s. p., April, 1757, when the honours became EXTINCT.

Arms—1st and 4th, az., three fleurs-de-lis. or; 2nd and 3rd, gu., three annulets, or, gemmed az., all within a bordure, or, charged with a double tressure, flory, counterflory, gu.; on a surcoat, a sword and sceptre, saltier-wise, ppr.

MONTHERMER — BARON MONTHERMER, EARL OF GLOUCESTER AND HERTFORD.

Earldom, *jure uxoris*, by Writ of Summons, dated 6 Feb., 1299.
Barony, by Writ of Summons, dated 4 March, 1309.

Lineage.

RALPH DE MONTHERMER, "a plain Esquire," having m. the Lady JOANE PLANTAGENET (commonly called Joane of Acres), dau. of King EDWARD I., and widow of Gilbert, Earl of Clare, Gloucester, and Hertford, had the title of EARL OF GLOUCESTER AND HERTFORD, in her right, and was summoned to parliament as "Comiti Gloucester' et Hertf." from 6 February, 1299, to 3 November, 1306. In the 26th EDWARD I., his lordship was in the expedition then made into Scotland, and behaved so valiantly, that the king rendered to him and his wife, the said Joane, the castle and honour of Tonebrugge with other lands in Kent, Surrey, and Sussex; as also the Isle of Portland, and divers other estates belonging to the said Joane, which had being seized by the crown in consequence of her marriage without license with the said Ralph; and the king became eventually much attached to his son-in-law, to whom he had been reconciled through the intercession of Anthony Beke, the celebrated bishop of Durham. In the 31st, 32nd, and 34th of his father-in-law, the earl was again in Scotland, and in the contest with BRUCE, King EDWARD conferred upon him the whole of Anandale, with the title of Earl of Atholl, the Scottish nobleman who held that dignity, having espoused the fortunes of BRUCE. But it was not long after this that Joane of Acres departed this life (viz., 1st EDWARD II.) and he never, subsequently, obtained the title of Earl of Gloucester and Hertford although he lived for several years; in a grant of considerable landed property made to him and his sons in two years afterwards, he is styled Ralph de Monthermer only. Nor is he otherwise denominated, in the 5th EDWARD II., at which time, for recompence of his service in Scotland the king gave him 300 marks, part of the 600 marks which he was to have paid for the wardship of John ap Adam, a great man of that

age. Nor in two years afterwards, when again in the wars of Scotland, he was made prisoner at Bannockburn, but he then found favour from his former familiarity with the King of Scotland, at the court of England, and obtained his freedom without paying ransom. He was, however, summoned to parliament as a Baron from 4 March, 1309, to 30 October, 1321. His lordship m. 2ndly, Isabel, widow of John de Hastings, and sister and co-heir of Aymer de Valence, Earl of Pembroke, by whom he had no issue. But by his 1st wife, the Princess Joane, he had two sons, viz.,

THOMAS, his heir.

EDWARD, who was summoned to parliament as a Baron, 23 April, 1337, 11th EDWARD III., but never afterwards, and nothing further is known of him or his descendants.

Ralph, Lord Monthermer, d. 19th EDWARD II., and was s. by his son,

THOMAS, LORD MONTHERMER, who was constantly employed in the military service of the crown, his name does not therefore occur in the enrolment of the summonses to parliament. He was killed in a sea fight with the French in 1340, leaving by Margaret, his wife, an only dau. and heiress,

MARGARET DE MONTHERMER, who m. Sir John de Montacute, 2nd son of William, 1st Earl of Salisbury, and conveyed the Barony of Monthermer to the family of Montacute. Her eldest son,

JOHN, Baron Montacute and Monthermer, s. as 3rd Earl of Salisbury (see MONTACUTE, Earl of Salisbury).

The Barony of Monthermer was in ABEYANCE between the late MARQUESS OF HASTINGS (as representing Katherine, Countess of Huntingdon, elder dau. and co-heir of Henry, Baron Montacute), and WILLIAM LOWNDES, Esq., of Chesham, Bucks, and WILLIAM-SELBY LOWNDES, Esq., of Whaddon, in the same co., as representing, Winifred, Lady Barrington, the other dau. and co-heir of the said Henry, Baron Montacute.

Arms—Or, an eagle displayed, vert, membered and beaked, gu.

MONYPENNY—LORD MONYPENNY.

Lineage.

The family of MONYPENNY is of great antiquity in North Britain, and has at various periods produced many eminent persons. Its present representative is David Monypenny of Pitmilly, one of the lords of Session; and from the Pitmilly line also descend the MONYPENNYS of Kent.

SIR WILLIAM MONYPENNY, son of Sir William Monypenny, Knt., by Margaret, his wife, dau. of Philip Arbuthnott, of Arbuthnott, acquired the lands of Conquersall, in France, and a considerable portion of the Earl of Ormond's forfeited estates in Scotland. This distinguished personage, who was next in remainder to his kin-man, William Monypenny, of Pitmilly, came as ambassador from France to England in 1471, and acting a conspicuous part in the public transactions of his time, was created a peer of Scotland by JAMES II. His son,

ALEXANDER MONYPENNY, 2nd Lord Monypenny, exchanged, in 1495, the Barony of Earlshall, in Fifeshire, with Sir Edward Bruce, for his lands called Escariot, in France. His lordship d. s. p. m., and with him the peerage EXPIRED.

Arms—Or, a dolphin, az., finned, gu.

MOORE—EARL OF CHARLEVILLE.

Barony, by Letters Patent, dated 22 October, 1715.
Earldom, by Letters Patent, dated 16 September, 1758.

Lineage.

The Right Hon. JOHN MOORE, of Croghan, M.P. for the King's co., (sprung from Sir Thomas Moore, younger son of John Moore, Esq., ancestor of the noble house of Drogheda,) was elevated to the peerage of Ireland, 22 October, 1715, as *Baron Moore, of Tullamore*, and obtained a reversionary grant of the office of muster-master-general of Ireland. His lordship m. 1st, in 1697, Mary, dau. of Eln. than Lunn, Esq., banker, of Dublin, by whom he had an only surviving son, CHARLES, and one surviving dau.,

Jane, who m. January, 1794, William Bury, Esq., of Shannon Grove, co. Limerick, and had, with other children, JOHN BURY, Esq.

Lord Tullamore m. 2ndly, Elizabeth, widow of Sir John King, Bart. He d. 8 September, 1725, and was s. by his son,

CHARLES MOORE, 2nd baron, governor of the King's co., and muster-master-general of Ireland, who was created EARL OF CHARLEVILLE, 16 September, 1758. His lordship m. in 1737, Hester, only surviving child of James Coghill, Esq., LL.D.; but d. s. p. 17 February, 1764, when his lordship's honours EXPIRED, while his estates passed to his nephew,

JOHN BURY, Esq. of Shannon Grove, father of CHARLES WILLIAM, 1st EARL OF CHARLEVILLE, of the new creation.

Arms—Az., on a chief, indented, arg., three mullets, gu.; a crescent for difference.

MORAY—EARL OF STRATHERN.

(*See* MALISE, Earl of Strathern.)

MORDAUNT—EARLS OF PETERBOROUGH, VISCOUNTS MORDAUNT OF AVALON, EARLS OF MONMOUTH.

Earldom of Peterborough, by Letters Patent, dated 9 March, 1628.
Viscounty, by Letters Patent, dated 10 July, 1659.
Earldom of Monmouth, by Letters Patent, dated 9 April, 1689.

Lineage.

It appears from the records of this family, collected in the reign of King CHARLES II., and printed at the charge of Henry, Earl of Peterborough, that

SIR OSBERT LE MORDAUNT, a Norman knight, was possessed of Radwell, in Bedfordshire, by the gift of his brother, who derived it from the CONQUEROR, in recompense of his own and his father's good services. Sir Osbert's grandson,

EUSTACH LE MORDAUNT, m. Alice, eldest dau. and co-heir of Sir William de Alneto, modernly called Dauney, and acquired by her the lordship of Turvey, in Bedfordshire. He was s. by his son,

WILLIAM MORDAUNT, who became Lord of Turvey, Radwell, Asthull, and other manors. He was s. by his son,

WILLIAM MORDAUNT. This feudal lord had license (1297) to inclose a park at Turvey. He m. Rose, dau. of Sir Ralph Wake, and was s. by his eldest son,

ROBERT MORDAUNT, who was knight of the shire for the co. Bedford, in the parliament held at Westminster in the 15th EDWARD III. From this gentleman we pass to his descendant,

WILLIAM MORDAUNT, Esq., of Turvey, temp. EDWARD IV., who m. Margaret, dau. of John Peeke, Esq., of Cople, and had, with other issue,

JOHN, his heir.
William, ancestor of the Mordaunts of Warwickshire, now represented by Sir Charles Mordaunt, Bart.
Joan, m. to Giles Strangwayes, Esq., of Melbury.
Elizabeth, m. to Sir Whiston Browne, Knt.

The elder son,

SIR JOHN MORDAUNT, Knt., of Turvey, co. Bedford, was one of the royal commanders at the battle of Stoke, 16 June, 1484. Being likewise learned in the law, he was constituted king's serjeant in the 11th HENRY VII., justice of Chester in four years after, and subsequently chancellor of the duchy of Lancaster, and was made one of the knights of the sword at the creation of Henry, Prince of Wales, 18 February, 1502-3. Sir John d. in the 21st year of HENRY VII., and was s. by his eldest son,

WILLIAM MORDAUNT, Esq., who d. s. p., when the estates devolved upon his brother,

SIR JOHN MORDAUNT, who was sheriff of Bedford and Bucks in the 1st year of HENRY VIII., and in the 5th of the same reign was one of the commissioners, appointed by act of parliament, for assessing and collecting the poll-tax. He was knighted before, 4 June 1520, when he was one of those appointed to attend the queen at the interview with FRANCIS I. of France, and in May, 1522, he waited upon the king at Canterbury, at his second meeting in England with the Emperor

CHARLES V. In 1530 he was appointed, with others, to inquire into the landed possessions of Cardinal Wolsey, and he was summoned to parliament, as a Baron, from 4 May, 1532, to 5 November, 1558. In the year 1551, a great dearth of provisions being in the nation, his lordship was the first in commission, with other persons of rank, in the county of Bedford, to prevent the enhancing of the prices of corn, &c., and to punish offenders therein, as also to supply the said county. He *m.* Elizabeth, dau. and co-heir of Sir Henry Vere, K., of Drayton and Adington, co. Northampton, and had issue,

JOHN, his successor.
William, *m.* Agnes, dau. and heir of Charles Booth, Esq.
George, of Oakley, co. Bedford, *m.* Cecilia, dau. and co-heir of John Harding, Esq., of Harding, in Bedfordshire, and was father of
 Edmund Mordaunt, Esq., of Thundersley, in Essex.
Anne, *m.* 1st, to James Rodney, Esq., and 2ndly, to John, son and heir of Sir Michael Fisher.
Elizabeth, *m.* to Silvester Danvers, Esq., of Dauntsey, Wilts.
Margaret, *m.* to Edward Fettiplace, Esq., of Bessels Leigh, co. Berks.
Winifrid, *m. to* John Cheyney, of Chesham-Boys.
Editha, *m.* to John Elmes, Esq., of Huntingdonshire.
Dorothy, *m.* to Thomas More, Esq., of Haddon, Oxfordshire.

His lordship *d.* in 1562, and was *s.* by his eldest son,
JOHN MORDAUNT, 2nd baron, summoned to parliament from 11 January, 1563, to 8 May, 1572. This nobleman, in the lifetime of his father, was made one of the knights of the Bath at the coronation of Queen ANNE BOLEYN, 1st June, 1553, and was sheriff for Essex and Hertfordshire, in 1540. At the demise of EDWARD VI., he was one of the first in arms on behalf of Queen MARY: whereupon he was sworn of the privy council; and in her Majesty's reign served in four parliaments for Bedfordshire. His lordship *m.* 1st, Ellen, cousin and heir of Sir Richard Fitz-Lewes, of West-Thorndon, in Essex, by whom he had issue,

LEWIS, his successor.
Elizabeth, *m.* to George Monnoux, Esq., of Walthamstow.
Anne, *m.* to Clement Tanfield, Esq., of Eberton.
Margaret, *m.* to William Acklam, Esq., of Moreby, in Yorkshire.
Ursula, *m.* to Edward, son of Sir Nicholas Fairfax, of Gilling Castle, co. York.

Lord Mordaunt *m.* 2ndly, Joan, dau. of Robert Wilford, Esq., of Kent, but had no issue by that lady. He *d.* in 1572, and was *s.* by his son,
LEWIS MORDAUNT, 3rd baron, summoned to parliament from 8 February, 1576, to 24 October, 1597. This nobleman received the honour of knighthood from Queen ELIZABETH in 1567, and was one of the peers who sat in judgment upon Thomas Duke of Norfolk, and upon Queen MARY, of Scotland. His lordship *m.* Elizabeth, dau. of Sir Arthur Darcy, Knt., 2nd son of Thomas, Lord Darcy, and had issue,

HENRY, his successor.
Mary, *m.* to Thomas Mansel, Esq., eldest son of Sir Edward Mansel, Knt.
Katherine, *m.* to John Heveningham, Esq., eldest son of Sir Arthur Heveningham, Knt.
Elizabeth.

He *d.* 16 June, 1601, and was *s.* by his son,
HENRY MORDAUNT, 4th baron, summoned to parliament from 27 October, 1601, to 5 November, 1615. This nobleman, under suspicion of being concerned in the gunpowder-plot, was committed to the Tower, and fined by the star-chamber before he obtained his liberty. He *m.* Margaret, dau. of Henry, Lord Compton, by whom he had issue,

JOHN, his successor.   Henry.
Francis, *m.* Frances, dau. of Sir Edward Go+dwick, Bart.
Lewis.   Frances.
Elizabeth, *m.* to Sir Thomas Nevil, K.B.

His lordship *d.* in 1608, and was *s.* by his son,
JOHN MORDAUNT, 5th baron, summoned to parliament from 30 January, 1620, to 17 May, 1625. This nobleman, was advanced to the dignity of EARL OF PETERBOROUGH, by letters patent, dated 9 March, 1628. He *m.* Elizabeth, only dau. and heir of William Howard, Lord Effingham, son and heir of Charles, Earl of Nottingham, by whom he had (with Elizabeth, who *m.* Thomas, son and heir of Edward, Lord Howard, of Escrick), two sons, viz.,

HENRY, his successor.
JOHN; this gentleman obtained great fame by his zeal in the cause of King CHARLES II., and stood a trial during the usurpation for his exertions in behalf of the exiled monarch, but upon which he was acquitted, by the connivance chiefly, as stated by Lord Clarendon, of the celebrated John Lisle, the presiding judge. The other judges were equally divided as to the guilt or innocence of Mr. Mordaunt, and the presi-

dent gave the casting vote in his favour. He subsequently made several daring but fruitless attempts to restore the king, and for all those faithful services was, eventually, elevated to the peerage, 10 July, 1659, as BARON MORDAUNT, *of Ryg·te, co. Surrey,* and VISCOUNT MORDAUNT, *of Avalon, in Somersetshire.* His lordship and Sir John Grenville, were the bearers of the letters which the king, prior to his restoration, addressed to Monk, to parliament, and to the corporation of London. His lordship, after the Restoration, was constituted constable of Windsor Castle, and appointed lord lieutenant, and custos rotulorum of co. Surrey. He *m.* Elizabeth, dau. and sole heiress of Thomas Carey, 2nd son of Robert, Earl of Monmouth, by whom he had five sons and three daus.,

1 CHARLES, his successor.
2 Harry, M.P., lieutenant-general in the army, and treasurer of the ordnance, to which last office he was appointed in 1699. General Mordaunt *m.* 1st, Margaret, dau. of Sir Thomas Spencer, of Yarnton, co. Oxford, Bart, by whom he had, with other children,
 John (Sir), K.B., a general officer in the army.
 Eliza-Lucy, *m.* to Sir Wilfrid Lawson, Bart., of Isell, in Cumberland.
 General Mordaunt *m.* 2ndly, Penelope, dau. and heir of William Tipping, Esq., by whom he had,
 Penelope, *m.* to Sir Monnoux Cope, Bart, of Hanwell.
3 Lewis, a brigadier-general in the army, who *d.* 2 February, 1712-13, leaving issue by two wives. One of his daus. Anne-Maria, *m.* the Right Hon. Stephen Poyntz, of Midgham, co. Berks, and another, Sophia, *m.* Sir Roger Martin, Bart.
4 Osmond, slain at the battle of the Boyne.
5 George, in holy orders. This gentleman *m.* thrice, and left by his 2nd wife, Elizabeth, dau. of Sir John D'Oyly, Bart., a dau.,
 Anna-Maria (co-heiress), *m.* to Jonathan Shipley, D.D., bishop of St. Asaph, ancestor by her of the Shipley-Conwys, of Bodrhyddan, co. Flint, and of the Shipleys of Twyford House, Hants.
and by his 3rd wife, Elizabeth, dau. of Colonel Collyer, he was father of two daus.,
 Mary, *m.* to Valentine Morris, Esq., of Piercefield, Monmouthshire.
 Elizabeth, *m.* to Sir William Milner, Bart.
1 Charlotte, *m.* to Benjamin Albin, Esq.
2 Sophia, *m.* to James Hamilton, Esq., of Bangor, in Ireland.
3 Anne, *m.* to James Hamilton, Esq., of Tollymore, in Ireland.

His lordship *d.* 5 June, 1675, and was *s.* by his eldest son,
CHARLES MORDAUNT, 2nd viscount, who was created EARL OF MONMOUTH, 9 April, 1689, and *s.* to the EARLDOM OF PETERBOROUGH, at the decease of his uncle, in 1697.

The Earl of Peterborough was general of ordnance, and colonel of a regiment of foot, in the army raised in 1642, by order of parliament, under the command of Robert, Earl of Essex. His lordship *d.* in the same year, and was *s.* by his elder son,
HENRY MORDAUNT, 2nd Earl of Peterborough. This nobleman was distinguished during the civil wars by his zeal in the royal cause. He raised a regiment at his own expense, was wounded at the battle of Newbury, and often imprisoned for his loyal exertions. In 1648, he was in the rising with the Earl of Holland to release the king from his confinement; and on their defeat, though Holland was taken and beheaded, Peterborough, with his brother, escaped, but they were voted traitors to the commonwealth and their estates sequestered. His lordship was, after the Restoration, of the privy council to King CHARLES II., and entrusted with several honourable embassies. At the coronation of King JAMES II., he carried the sceptre with the cross, and was elected in the same year a knight of the Garter. After the accession of WILLIAM and MARY, the commons resolved (26 October, 1689,) that the Earl of Peterborough, and the Earl of Salisbury, should be impeached for high treason, for departing from their allegiance, and being reconciled to the church of Rome; but the impeachment was dropped. His lordship *m.* Penelope, dau. of Barnabas, Earl of Thomond, in Ireland, by whom he had issue,

Elizabeth, *d. unm.*
MARY, who became sole heiress, *m.* 1st, Henry, Duke of Norfolk, from whom she was divorced in 1700, and then *m.* Sir John Germain, Bart., but had issue by neither. Her ladyship inherited the Barony of Mordaunt, of Turvey, at the decease of her father, but the dignity again attached to the Earldom of Peterborough, at her own decease, in 1705. Her ladyship bequeathed her whole estate to her 2nd husband.

The earl *d.* in 1697, when the Barony of Mordaunt, of Turvey, devolved upon his only surviving dau., as stated above, and the Earldom of Peterborough passed to his nephew (*revert to* issue of the 1st earl),

CHARLES MORDAUNT, 1st Earl of Monmouth, as 3rd Earl of Peterborough. This nobleman, who had distinguished himself is a military character prior to the Revolution, was, upon the accession of WILLIAM and MARY, sworn of the privy council, and made one of the lords of the bedchamber, and in order to attend at their coronation as an earl, was raised to the Earldom of Monmouth, having, the day before, been constituted first lord commissioner of the Treasury. In 1692, his lordship made the campaign of Flanders, under King WILLIAM; and soon after the accession of Queen ANNE he was declared general and commander-in-chief of the forces sent to Spain; in which command he acquired great military fame, by the capture of Montjov:—by driving the Duke of Anjou, and the French army, consisting of 25,000 men, out of Spain, with a force not exceeding 10,000, and by acquiring possession of Catalonia, of the kingdoms of Valencia, Arragon, Majorca, &c. His lordship was, however, recalled from the scene of those gallant achievements, and his conduct subsequently examined by parliament; when a vote passed the House of Lords, 12 January, 1710-11, that during the time he had the command in Spain " he performed many great and eminent services ; " and his lordship received the thanks of the house, through the lord chancellor. In 1710, and 1711, he was employed in embassy to the court of Turin, and other Italian states, on special missions; and in 1713, he was installed knight of the Garter. In the reign of King GEORGE I., his lordship was constituted general of all the marine forces in Great Britain. The earl m. 1st, Carey, dau. of Sir Alexander Fraser, of Dotes, N.B., and had issue,

John, Lord Mord unt, a military officer, colonel of the grenadier guards, at the celebrated battle of Blenheim, 13 August, 1704, wherein he lost one of his arms. His lordship m. Lady Frances Powlett, dau. of Charles, Duke of Bolton, and dying of the small-pox, 6 April, 1710, left two sons,

CHARLES, who s. his grandfather in the honours of the family.
John, a lieutenant-colonel in the army, M.P., m. 1st, in 1735, Mary, sister of Scroop, Viscount How. and widow of Thomas, Earl of Pembroke. He m. 2ndly, Elizabeth, dau. of Samuel Hamilton, Esq., but d. s. p. in 1767.
Henry, a naval officer of high character, and a M.P., d. unm. (of the small-pox) 27 February, 1709-10.
Henrietta, m. to Alexander Gordon, 2nd Duke of Gordon, from whom lineally descended,

ALEXANDER, 4th Duke of Gordon, who, upon the decease of Lady Mary-Anastasia-Grace Mordaunt, dau. of Charles, 4th Earl of Peterborough, in 1819, inherited the Barony of Mordaunt, of Turvey.

His lordship m. 2ndly, in 1735, Anastasia Robinson, the celebrated public singer, of whom Dr. Burney gives an interesting account in his *History of Music*. The earl d. on his passage to Lisbon, 25 October, in the same year. At the decease of his lordship's cousin, Mary, Baroness Mordaunt, of Turvey (*revert* to issue of 2nd Earl of Peterborough,) he inherited that ancient dignity of the family. He was s. in all his honours by his grandson,

CHARLES MORDAUNT, 4th Earl of Peterborough, and 2nd Earl of Monmouth. His lordship m. 1st, Mary, dau. of John Cox, Esq., of London, and had issue,

Frances, who m. the Rev. Samuel Bulkeley, D.D., of Hatfield, in Hertfordshire, and d. s. p. 1798.
MARY-ANASTASIA-GRACE, who s. eventually to the Barony of Mordaunt, of Turvey.

The earl m. 2ndly, Robiniana, dau. of Colonel Brown, and dying in 1779, was s. by his only surviving son, by that lady,

CHARLES-HENRY MORDAUNT, 5th Earl of Peterborough, and 3rd Earl of Monmouth, b. in 1758, who d. unm. in 1814, when the Earldom of Peterborough, and the Earldom of Monmouth, with the Viscounty of Mordaunt, and Barony of Mordaunt, of Ryegate, became EXTINCT, while the Barony of Mordaunt, of Turvey, devolved upon his lordship's half-sister, Lady MARY-ANASTASIA-GRACE MORDAUNT, as Baroness Mordaunt, and at her ladyship's decease, unm., in 1819, it passed to ALEXANDER GORDON, 4th DUKE OF GORDON, as heir-general of Charles, 3rd Earl of Peterborough. He d. 17 June, 1827, and was s. by his son, GEORGE GORDON, 5th Duke of Gordon, and 13th Lord Mordaunt, who d. s. p. 28 May, 1836, when the Barony of Mordaunt fell into abeyance amongst his sisters or their representatives. Those ladies, the last Duke of Gordon's sisters, were,

I. Charlotte, m. in September, 1789, Charles, 4th Duke of Richmond, and d. 5 May, 1842. Her grandson, Charles Gordon-Lennox. Duke of Richmond, is senior co-heir of the Barony of Mordaunt, of Turvey.
II. Madelina, m. 1st, to Sir Robert Sinclair, Bart., and 2ndly, to Charles-Fyshe Palmer, Esq., of Luckley Park, Berks, who d. in January, 1843. Lady Madelina d. in June, 1847. Her grandson, Sir Robert-Charles Sinclair, Bart., became co heir of the Barony of Mordaunt.
III. Susan, m. to William, Duke of Manchester, and d. 20 August, 1828. Her grandson, William-Drogo, Duke of Manchester, is a co-heir of the Barony of Mordaunt.

IV. Louisa, m. to Charles, 2nd Marquess Cornwallis, and d. 8 December, 1850. The co-heirs of Louisa, Marchioness Cornwallis, co-heirs also of the Barony of Mordaunt, are, 1 the two daus. of Richard Cornwallis, late Lord Braybrooke; 2 Henry, Earl of St. Germans; the son and heir of the late Lady Mary Ross.
V. Georgiana, m. to John, 6th Duke of Bedford, and d. 23 February, 1853; her eldest son, Lord Wriothesley Russell, is one of the co-heirs of the Barony of Mordaunt.

Arms—Arg , a chevron between three estoiles of six points, sa.

MORDAUNT—VISCOUNTS MORDAUNT, OF AVALON, EARLS OF MONMOUTH.

(*See* MORDAUNT, *Earls of Peterborough.*)

MORETON, or (more correctly,) DE BURGO, EARLS OF CORNWALL.

Creation of WILLIAM THE CONQUEROR, in 1068.

Lineage.

HARLOWEN DE BURGO, founder of the abbey of Grestelm, in Normandy, m. Arlotta, the mother of the CONQUEROR, and dying before his father, John, Earl of Comyn, left two sons,

ROBERT, Earl of Moreton, in Normandy.
Odo, bishop of Bayeux.

who both accompanied their illustrious brother in his expedition against England, and were aggrandized after his triumph. ODO, being created Earl of Kent, and ROBERT DE MORETON, Earl of Cornwall, with a grant of 793 manors. In the time of WILLIAM RUFUS, this nobleman joining his brother, the Earl of Kent, raised the standard of rebellion in favour of Robert Curthose, and held the castle of Pevensey for that prince. He delivered it up, however, upon its being invested by the king, and made his peace. His lordship m. Maud, dau. of Roger de Montgomery, Earl of Shrewsbury, and had issue, WILLIAM, his successor, and three daus., whose christian names are unknown; the eldest m. Andrew de Vitrel ; the 2nd m. Guy de Val, and the youngest m. the Earl of Thoulouse. The time of the Earl of Cornwall's death has not been ascertained, " but if he lived," says Dugdale, "after King WILLIAM RUFUS so fatally lost his life by the glance of an arrow in New Forest, from the bow of Walter Tirell, then was it unto him, that this strange apparition happened, which I shall here speak of; otherwise, it must be to his son and successor, Earl William, the story whereof is as followeth. In the very hour that the king received the fatal stroke, the Earl of Cornwall being hunting in a wood, at a distance from the place, and left alone by his attendants, was accidentally met by a very great black goat, bearing the king all black and naked, and wounded through the midst of his breast. And adjuring the goat by the Holy Trinity to tell what that was he so carried ; he answered, I am carrying your king to judgment, yea, that tyrant, WILLIAM RUFUS, for I am an evil spirit, and the revenger of his malice which he bore to the church of God; and it was I that did cause this his slaughter; the protomartyr of England, St. Alban, commanding me so to do; who complained to God of him for his grievous oppressions in the Isle of Britain, which he first hallowed. All which the earl soon after related to his followers." His lordship was s. by his son, WILLIAM DE MORETON, 2nd Earl of Cornwall, in England, and Earl of Moreton, in Normandy. This nobleman being from childhood of an arrogant and malevolent disposition, envied the glory of King HENRY I.; and not contented with the great honours he had derived from his father, demanded the Earldom of Kent, which had been borne by his uncle ODO; giving out secretly, that he would not put on his robe, unless the inheritance, which he challenged by descent from his uncle, might be restored to him. In this demand the king refusing to acquiesce, the earl fled to Normandy, and with Robert de Belesme reared the standard of revolt in the Duchy, which caused HENRY to seize upon his possessions in England, to raze his castles to the ground, and to banish him the kingdom. He subsequently led the van at the battle of Tenerchebray, and, after displaying great personal valour, fell into th hands of his opponents, and was sent prisoner to England.

where he was treated with great cruelty, the king causing his eyes to be put out, and detaining him in captivity for life. His honours became, of course, FORFEITED. The period of his decease has not been recorded; nor does Dugdale mention either his wife or issue—but in Archdale's edition of Lodge's Peerage of Ireland (vol. I., in the article regarding the house of Clanricarde), it is stated that the unfortunate earl left two sons, viz.,

ADELM, from whom the noble house of Clanricarde derives.
JOHN, who was father of the celebrated Hubert de Burgo, Earl of Kent, justiciary of England, temp. HENRY III.

Arms—Erm., a chief indented, gu.

MORLEY—BARONS MORLEY.

By Writ of Summons, dated 29 December, 1299.

Lineage.

In the 25th EDWARD I., WILLIAM DE MORLEY was in the expeditions made in that and the next year into Scotland, and had summons to parliament as a Baron, from 29 December, 1299, to 3 November, 1306. His lordship was s. by his son,

ROBERT DE MORLEY, 2nd baron, summoned to parliament, from 20 November, 1317, to 15 February, 1357. This nobleman was one of the eminent warriors, of the martial times of King EDWARD III. In the 13th of that monarch's reign, after previously distinguishing himself in the wars of Scotland, he was constituted admiral of the king's whole fleet, from the mouth of the Thames northwards, and the next year achieved the greatest naval victory, up to that period, ever won over the French, near Sluce, in Flanders; subsequently sailing to Normandy, he burnt fourscore ships of the Normans, with three of their sea-port towns, and two villages. The next year (16th EDWARD III.), being still admiral, he was in the great expedition then made into France, and in four years afterwards, his banner waved amongst the victorious upon the plains of Cressy. His lordship continued admiral several years afterwards, and in each successive year reaped fresh laurels. In the 29th EDWARD III., he was made constable of the Tower of London. In the 33rd, he was again in arms on the French soil, and d. there the next year, while in immediate attendance upon the king. His lordship m. Hawyse, dau. and heir of Sir William Mareschall, Knt., and had issue,

WILLIAM (Sir), his successor.

He m. 2ndly, Joane, dau. of Sir Peter de Tyes, and had, with other issue,

ROBERT (S r), who, in the 41st EDWARD III, attended Prince Edward into Aquitaine; and in the reign of RICHARD II. was in the wars of France. Sir Robert had issue,
  SIR ROBERT MORLEY, father of
    SIR THOMAS MORLEY, whose dau. and heiress,
    MARGARET MORLEY, m. Sir Jeffery Ratcliffe, Knt.

His lordship d. 1360, and was s. by his eldest son,

SIR WILLIAM MORLEY, 3rd baron, summoned to parliament from 4 December, 1364, to 3 December, 1378. This nobleman, in the time of his father, was in the wars of France, with Robert de Ufford, Earl of Suffolk; and in the 38th EDWARD III., he had license to travel beyond sea; as also to grant the office of marshal of Ireland (which he had inherited from his mother) to Henry de Ferrers, to hold during good conduct. His lordship m. Cicily, dau. of Thomas, Lord Bardolph, and had an only son, THOMAS, his successor. Lord Morley d. 30 April, 1379, and by his last testament, bequeathed his body to be buried in the church of the Friers-Augustines, at Norwich. Appointing that two of his best horses should be disposed of for mortuaries, viz., his best black horse to those friers, on the day of his funeral; and, his palfrey, called Don, to the rector of the church of Hallingbury. He likewise left large sums for masses for his soul, as all the great personages of that period were in the habit of bequeathing. He was s. by his son,

SIR THOMAS MORLEY, 4th baron, summoned to parliament from 16 July, 1381, to 3 September, 1417. This nobleman in the 4th RICHARD II., arriving at Calais, with divers other English lords, rode with his banner displayed. And in the 15th of the same reign (being marshal of Ireland) was in the expedition then made into France, as he was again in the 3rd HENRY V.; and the next year he was appointed lieutenant and captain-general of all the forces assembled at London

from the different ports, in order to proceed to France. His lordship m. twice: by his 2nd wife, Anne, dau. of Edward, Lord Despencer (by Elizabeth de Burghersh, his wife), and widow of Sir Hugh de Hastings, Knt., he had no issue, but by his 1st wife he had a son,

THOMAS, or ROBERT, who d. v. p., 3rd HENRY V., leaving by Isabel, his wife, dau. of John, Lord Molines, a son,
  THOMAS, successor to his grandfather.

He d. in 1417, and was s. by his grandson,

THOMAS MORLEY, 5th baron, who was summoned to parliament from 15 July, 1427, to 5 July, 1435, in the 6th HENRY V., being then marshal of Ireland, he was in the expedition made into France, and so likewise, in the 9th of the same reign. His lordship being in the service of King HENRY V., when that gallant prince d. in France, bore one of the banners of saints, which were carried at the monarch's solemn obsequies. His lordship m. Lady Isabel de la Pole,[*] dau. of Michael, 2nd Earl of Suffolk, and dying in 1435, left issue, two daus., Elizabeth, m. to Sir John Arundel, and Anne, m. to Sir John Hastings, and a son,

ROBERT MORLEY. 6th baron, summoned to parliament, 3 December, 1441. This nobleman m. Elizabeth, dau. of William Lord Roos, and dying in 1442, left an only dau. and heir,

ALIANORE MORLEY, æt. twenty-three, 6th EDWARD IV., who m. WILLIAM LOVEL, 2nd son of William, Baron Lovel, of Tichmersh, and he was summoned to parliament, jure uxoris, as LORD MORLEY. Of this marriage there were issue,
  HENRY LOVEL, Lord Morley, who d. s. p.
  ALICE LOVEL, m. to Sir William Parker, Knt., standard bearer to RICHARD III. Upon the death of her brother, this lady inherited the barony, and her son,
    HENRY PARKER, was summoned as LORD MORLEY. from 15 April, 1523, to 28 October, 1555 (see Parker, Lords Morley).

Upon the decease of this Robert, last Lord Morley, the male line of that family EXPIRED; while his dau., ALIANORE MORLEY, carried the Barony of Morley into the family of LOVEL, whence it passed, as stated above, to that of PARKER (see Parker, Lords Morley).

Arms—Arg., a lion rampant, sa., crowned, or.

MORTIMER — BARONS MORTIMER, OF WIGMORE, EARLS OF MARCH.

Barony, by Writ of Summons, dated 8 June, 1294.
Earldom, by Charter, dated anno 1328.

Lineage.

The first of this name upon record,

ROGER DE MORTIMER, is deemed by some to have been son of William de Warren, and by others, of Walter de St. Martin, brother of that William. Which Roger was founder of the abbey of St. Victor, in Normandy. "It is reported," says Dugdale, "that in the year 1054 (which was twelve years before the Norman Conquest), when ODO, brother of Duke William, King of France, invaded the territory of Evreux, Duke William sent this Roger, then his general (with Robert, Earl of Ewe, and other stout soldiers), to resist his attempts; who meeting with Odo near to the castle of Mortimer, gave him battle, and obtained a glorious victory. It is further observable of this Roger, that he was by consanguinity allied to the Norman duke (afterwards king, by the name of WILLIAM THE CONQUEROR), his mother being niece to Gunnora, wife of Richard, Duke of Normandy, great grandmother to the CONQUEROR." The presumed son of this Roger,

RALPH DE MORTIMER, accompanying the Duke of Normandy in his expedition against England, was one of his principal commanders at the decisive battle of Hastings; and shortly after, as the most puissant of the victor's captains, was sent into the marches of Wales to encounter Edric, Earl of Shrewsbury, who still resisted the Norman yoke. This nobleman, after much difficulty, and a long siege in his castle of Wig-

---

[*] Lady Isabel, widow of Lord Morley, in her will dated 1464, and proved 1466, mentions her nephew, John, Duke of Suffolk, her sister Dame Katherine, abbess of Berkyng, her son-in-law John Hastings, and her dau. Anne, his wife, her granddau., Isabel Boswell, &c.

more, Mortimer subdued, and delivered into the king's hands. When, as a reward for his good service, he obtained a grant of all Edric's estates, and seated himself thenceforward at Wigmore. Independently of these great Welsh territorial possessions, Ralph Mortimer enjoyed by the bounty of his royal master sundry lordships and manors in other parts of the realm, which he held at the time of the general survey. In the beginning of Rufus's reign, Mortimer took part with Curthose, but he subsequently changed sides, and being constituted general of the forces sent to oppose that prince in Normandy, by King Henry I., he totally routed the enemy, and brought Curthose prisoner to the king. This gallant person m. Millicent, dau. of ——, by whom he had issue,

Hugh, his successor.
William, Lord of Chelmersh, and afterwards of Netherby.
Robert, ancestor of the Mortimers, of Richard's Castle (see Mortimer, Baron Mortimer, of Richard's Castle).
Hawise, m. to Stephen, Earl of Albemarle.

He was s. by his son,

Hugh de Mortimer, who being a person of a proud and turbulent spirit, opposed strenuously the accession of King Henry II. upon the demise of Stephen, and induced Roger, Earl of Hereford, to fortify his castles of Gloucester and Hereford against the new monarch; himself doing the same with his castles of Cleobury, Wigmore, and Brugges (commonly called Bridgenorth). Whereupon Gilbert Foliot, at that time Bishop of Hereford, addressing himself to the Earl of Hereford (his kinsman), by fair persuasions soon brought him to peaceable submission. But Mortimer continuing obstinate, the king was forced to raise an army, and at the point of the sword to bring him to obedience. Between this rude baron, and Joceas de Dynant, at that time Lord of Ludlow, existed a feud, carried to so fierce a pitch, that Dynant could not pass safely out of his castle for fear of being taken by Mortimer's men. But it so happened, that setting his spies to take all advantages of Dynant, he was surprised himself, and carried prisoner to Ludlow, where he was detained until he paid a ransom ot 3,000 marks of silver. He was oftentimes engaged against the Welsh, and he erected some strong castles in Wales. He likewise finished the foundation of the abbey of Wigmore, begun by his father, and in his old age became a canon of that house. He m. and had issue,

Roger, his successor.
Hugh. who m. Felicia de Sancto Sydonio, and had, by gift of his father, the manors of Sudbury and Chelmers.
Ralph.   William.

He d. in 1188, and was s. by his eldest son,

Roger de Mortimer, Lord of Wigmore. This feudal lord, like his predecessors, was in constant strife with the Welsh. At one time he sustained a great defeat in conjunction with Hugh de Say, but in the end he was victorious, and took twelve of their principal leaders in one battle. He also enlarged considerably his territories, and drove thieves and robbers from those parts. Being at one time present at the solemn anniversary of his father, he confirmed all his grants to the c.nons of Wigmore; adding, of his own gift, a spacious and fruitful pasture, lying adjacent to the abbey, called the *Treasure of Mortimer.* Upon which occasion his steward remonstrating with him for parting with so valuable a treasure, he replied, "I have laid up my treasure in that field, where thieves cannot steal or dig, or moth corrupt." This Roger m. 1st, Millicent, dau. of — Ferrers, Earl of Derby, and had issue, Hugh, his successor, and two daus.; the elder, m. to Stephen le Gross; the younger, to Walkeline de Beauchamp. He m. 2ndly, Isabel, sister and heir of Hugh de Ferrers, of Oakham, in Rutlandshire, and of Lechelade and Lagebiry in Glou.ester-shire. All which lands he inherited upon the death of the said Hugh Ferrers; and by the lady he had three sons, Ralph, Robert, and Philip. He d. in 1215, and was s. by his eldest son,

Hugh de Mortimer. This feudal lord in the baronial war adhered with unshaken fidelity to King John. In the 16th of that monarch's reign he had a military summons to attend the king at Cirencester, with the other Barons Marchers. He m. Annora, dau. of William de Braose, and had 100 shillings in land with her. But having been severely wounded in a tournament, departed this life in November, 1227, leaving no issue, when he was s. by his half brother,

Ralph de Mortimer, who, in the 12th Henry III., paying £100 for his relief, had livery of all his lands, lying in the cos. of Gloucester, Southampton, Berks, Salop, and Hereford. This nobleman being of a martial disposition, erected several strong castles, by which he was enabled to extend his possessions against the Welsh; so that Prince Lewelin, seeing that he could not successfully cope with him, gave him his dau. Gladuse Luy, widow of Reginald de Braose, in marriage, and by this

lady he had issue, Roger, his successor; Peter John, a gray friar at Shrewsbury; Hugh, of Chelmersh, and a dau. Isolda, m. 1st. to Walter Balem, and 2ndly, to Hugh, Lord Audley. He d. in 1246, and was s. by his eldest son,

Roger de Mortimer, who in the 31st Henry III., paying 2000 marks to the king, had livery of all his lands, excepting those whereof Gladuse, his mother then surviving was endowed In six years afterwards he attended the king in his expedition into Gascony, and in a few years subsequently, when Lewelin, Prince of Wales, began again to make incursions upon the marches, received command to assist Humphrey de Bohun, Earl of Hereford, in the defence of the country lying between Montgomery, and the lan ls of the Earl of Gloucester. In the 42nd of the same reign he had another military summons to march with the king against the Welsh; and being in that service, had a special discharge of his scutage for th.se twenty-six knights' fees, and a sixth part which he held in right of Maud, his wife, one of the daus. and co-heirs of William de Braose, of Brecknock. In two years afterwards he was made captain-general of all the king's forces in Wales, all the barons marchers receiving command to be attendant on him with their whole strength; and he was the same year constituted governor of the castle of Hereford. But notwithstanding this extensive power, and those great resources, he was eventually worsted by Lewelin, and constrained to sue for permission to depart, which the Welsh prince, owing to his consanguinity, conceded. After this he took an active part in the contest between Henry III. and the insurrectionary barons in favour of the former. He was at the battle of Lewes, whence he fled into Wales, and afterwards successfully planned the escape of Prince Edward. The exploit is thus detailed by Dugdale: "Seeing therefore his sovereign in this great distress, and nothing but ruine and misery attending himself, and all other the king's loyal subjects, he took no rest till he had contrived some way for their deliverance; and to that end sent a swift horse to the prince, then prisoner with the king in the castle of Hereford, with intimation that he should obtain leave to ride out for recreation, into a place cal.ed Widemersh; and that upon sight of a person mounted on a white horse, at the foot ot Tulington Hill, and waving his bonnet (which was the Lord of Croft, as it was said), he should haste towards him with all possible speed. Which being accordingly done (though all the country thereabouts were thither called to prevent his escape), setting spurs to that horse he overwent them all. Moreover that being come to the park of Tulington, this Roger met him with five hundred armed men; and seeing many to pursue, chased them back to the gates of Hereford, making great slaughter amongst them." Having thus accomplished his prince's freedom, Mortimer, directing all his energies to the embodying a sufficient force to meet the enemy, soon placed Prince Edward in a situation to fight and win the great battle of Evesham (4 August, 1265), by which the king was restored to his freedom and his crown. In this celebrated conflict Mortimer commanded the third division of the royal army, and for his faithful services obtained, in the October following, a grant of the whole earldom and honour of Oxford, and all other the lands of Robert de Vere, Earl of Oxford, at that time and by that treason forfeited. The Dictum of Kenilworth followed soon after the victory of Evesham, by which the defeated barons were suffered to regain their lands upon the payment of a stipulated fine; but this arrangement is said to have caused great irritation amongst the barons marchers, (Mortimer with the rest), who had acquired grants of those estates. He was, however, subsequently entrusted, by the crown, with the castle of Hereford, which he had orders to fortify, and was appointed sheriff of Herefordshire. After the accession of Edward I. he continued to enjoy the sunshine of royal favour, and had other valuable grants from the crown. He m., as already stated, Maud, dau. and co-heir of William de Braose, of Brecknock, and had, with other issue, three sons, Edmund, William, and Geffrey; upon whom, having procured the honour of knighthood to be conferred by King Edward I., he caused a tournament to be held, at his own cost, at Kenilworth, where he sumptuously entertained an hundred knights and as many ladies, for three days, the like whereof was never before known in England; and there began the round table, so called from the place wherein they practised those feats, which was encompassed by a strong wall, in a circular form. Upon the 4th day the golden lion, in token of triumph, having been yielded to him, he carried it (with all that company) to Warwick. The fame whereof being spread into foreign countries occasioned the Queen of Navarre to send him certain wooden bottles, bound with golden bars and wax, under the pretence of wine, but in truth filled with gold, which for many ages after were preserved in the Abbey of Wigmore. Whereupon for the love of that queen, he had added a *carbuncle* to his arms. By his wife he had several sons, whereof

Ralph (Sir), *d. v p.*

Edmund (Sir), was his successor.

Roger, was Lord of Chirke, which lordship his grandson sold to Richard Fitz-Alan, Earl of Arundel. It subsequently passed to the family of Middleton (*see* Mortimer of Chirke).

William (Sir). an eminent soldier, who *m.* Hawyse, heir of Robert de Musegross, but *d. s. p.*

Geffrey (Sir), *d. s. p., v. p.*

This celebrated feudal lord *d.* in 1282, and was *s.* by his eldest surviving son,

Sir Edmund Mortimer, Lord of Wigmore, who *m.* Margaret, dau. of Sir William de Fiennes. In the 10th Edward I., he *s.* his father, and the next year doing his homage, had livery of his lands. He was afterwards constantly employed in the Welsh wars, and was summoned to parliament as a baron, from 8 June, 1294, and from 23 June, 1295, to 2 June, 1302. His lordship was mortally wounded in 1303 at the battle of Buelt, against the Welsh, and dying almost immediately, at Wigmore Castle, was buried in the abbey there. He left issue,

Roger, his successor.

John, accidentally slain in a tournament at Worcester, 12th Edward II. by John de Leyburne, being not more than eighteen years of age.

Hugh, a priest, rector of the church at Old Radnor.

Walter, a priest, rector of Kingston.

Edmund, a priest, rector of Hodnet, and treasurer of the cathedral at York.

Maud, *m.* to Theobald de Verdon.

Joan, } nuns.
Elizabeth, }

His lordship was *s.* by his eldest son,

Roger Mortimer, 2nd baron, summoned to parliament from 22 February, 1306, to 3 December, 1326 (from the accession of Edward II., with the addition of "De Wigmore"). This nobleman, so notorious in our histories as the paramour of Isabel, queen consort of the unfortunate Edward II., was in his sixteenth year at the time of his father's decease, and was placed by the king (Edward I.) in ward with Piers Gaveston, so that to redeem himself, and for permission to marry whom he pleased, he was obliged to pay Gaveston 2,500 marks, and thereupon *m.* Joane, dau. of Peter de Genevill, son of Geffrey de Genevill, Lord of Trim, in Ireland. In 34th Edward I. he received the honour of knighthood, and the same year attended the king into Scotland; where we find him again in the 3rd Edward II., and the same year he was constituted governor of the castle of Buelt, in Brecknockshire. In the 7th, 8th and 10th years he was likewise in Scotland, and was then appointed lord-lieutenant of Ireland. During the remainder of the unhappy Edward's reign he attached himself to the interests of the queen, and at length fled with her and Prince Edward into France. Returning, however, and his party triumphing, he was advanced to the dignity of Earl of March soon after the accession of King Edward III., and he held a round table the same year at Bedford. But hereupon becoming proud beyond measure (so that his own son, Geffrey, called him the King of Folly), he kept a round table of knights in Wales, in imitation of King Arthur. "Other particulars," says Dugdale, " of his haughtiness and insolence were these, viz., that with Queen Isabel, he caused a parliament to be held at Northampton, where an unworthy agreement was made with the Scots, and Ragman's Roll of Homage of Scotland was traitorously delivered as also the black cross, which King Edward I. brought into England, out of the abbey of Scone, and then accounted a precious relique. That (with the queen) he caused the young king to ride twenty-four miles in one night, towards Bedford, to destroy the Earl of Lancaster and his adherents, saying that they imagined the king's death. That he followed Queen Isabel to Nottingham, and lodged in one house with her. That he commanded the treasure of the realm, and assumed the authority, which by common consent in parliament was conferred upon Henry, Earl of Lancaster, at the king's coronation." His career was not however of long continuance, for, the king becoming sensible of his folly and vices, had him suddenly seized in the castle of Nottingham, and conveyed prisoner to London, where, been impeached before parliament, he was convicted under various charges, the first of which was privity to the murder of King Edward II. in Berkeley Castle; and receiving sentence of death was hanged in 1330, at the common gallows, called Elmes, near Smithfield, where his body was permitted to hang two days and two nights naked, before it was interred in the Grey Friers; whence in some years afterwards it was removed to Wigmore. The Earl of March left issue four sons and seven daus., viz.,

Edmund (Sir), of whom presently

Roger (Sir), who m., 1321, Lady Joane Butler.

Geffrey (Sir), Lord of Towyth.

John, slain in a tournament at Shrewsbury.

Katherine, *m.* to Thomas de Beauchamp, Earl of Warwick.

Joane, *m.* to James, Lord Audley.

Agnes, *m.* to Laurence, Earl of Pembroke.

Margaret, *m.* 1st, to Robert, 6th Earl of Oxford; and 2ndly, to Thomas (son and heir of Maurice), Lord Berkeley.

Maud, *m.* to John de Cherlton, son and heir of John, Lord Powis.

Blanch, *m.* to Peter de Grandison.

Beatrix, *m.* 1st, to Edward, son and heir of Thomas of Brotherton, Earl Marshal of England, and 2ndly, to Sir Thomas de Braose.

Upon the execution and attainder of the earl all his honours became forfeited. But his eldest son,

Sir Edmund Mortimer, although he did not succeed to the earldom, was summoned to parliament, as Lord Mortimer, 20 November, 1331. His lordship *m.* Elizabeth, one of the daus., and at length co-heirs of Bartholomew (commonly called the Rich), Lord Badlesmere, of Ledes Castle, in Kent, by whom (who m.. after his decease, William de Bohun, Earl of Northampton) he had an only surviving son, his successor in 1331,

Roger Mortimer, *b* 1328, summoned to parliament as Baron Mortimer, and Baron Mortimer, *of Wigmore*, from 20 November, 1348, to 15 March, 1354. This nobleman at the time of his father's decease, was only three years of age, and during his minority his castles in the marches of Wales were committed to the custody of William, Earl of Northampton, who had *m.* his mother. In the 20th Edward III. he accompanied the king into France, and then received the honour of knighthood. In the 26th he was in a similar expedition, and in two years afterwards, obtaining a reversal of the attainder of his grandfather, he was restored to the Earldom of March, and to his forfeited lands. His lordship the next year was constable of Dover Castle, and warden of the Cinque Ports, and for some years afterwards he was in the wars of France. He *m.* Philippa, dau. of William de Montacute, 1st Earl of Salisbury, and had issue,

Roger, who *d. v. p.*

Edmund, his successor.

Margery, *m.* to John, Lord Audley.

His lordship *d.* at Romera, in Burgundy, in 1359, being then commander of the English forces there, and a knight of the Garter. He was *s.* by his son,

Edmund Mortimer, 3rd Earl of March, *b.* 1352. This nobleman at the time of his father's death, was in minority, yet by reason of his singular knowledge and parts, he was employed at eighteen years of age, to treat with the commissioners of the King of France, touching a peace betwixt both realms In the 1st Richard II., he was sworn to the privy council, and in two years afterwards, constituted lord lieutenant of Ireland, in which government he *d.* in 1381. His lordship *m.* the Lady Philippa Plantagenet, dau. and heir of Lionel, Duke of Clarence (by Elizabeth, his wife, dau. and heir of William, son and heir of John de Burgh, Earl of Ulster), by whom he had issue,

Roger, his successor.

Edmund (Sir), *m.* the dau. of Owen Glendour, and his issue is said to have settled in Scotland.

John (Sir), who, being arraigned in parliament, *temp.* Henry VI., for treasonable speeches, was condemned and executed.

Elizabeth. *m.* 1st, to Henry Percy, the celebrated Hotspur; and 2ndly, to Thomas, Lord Camois, K.G.

Philippa, *m.* 1st, to John, Earl of Pembroke; 2ndly, to Richard, Earl of Arundel; and 3rdly, to John Poynings, Lord St. John.

His lordship *d.* in 1381, and was *s.* by his eldest son,

Roger Mortimer, 4th Earl of March, who being but seven years old, at the decease of his father, was committed in ward, by the king, to Richard, Earl of Arundel; and when he came of age, found, by the care of those who had the management of his estate, all his castles and houses in good repair, and amply stored with rich furniture, while his lands were completely stocked with cattle, and in h s treasury, no less than 40,000 marks. This Roger being a hopeful youth, and every way accomplished, was, soon after his father's death, made lieutenant of Ireland; and in parliament, held 9th Richard II., was declared, by reason of his descent from Lionel, Duke of Clarence, heir presumptive to the crown. His lordship *m.* Alianore, dau. of Thomas Holland, Earl of Kent, sister of Thomas, Duke of Surrey, and sister and co-heir of Edmund, Earl of Kent, by whom (who *m.* 2ndly, Edward, Lord Powis, and 3rdly, John, Lord Dudley), he had issue,

Edmund, his successor.

Roger, *d. s. p.*

Anne, *m.* to Richard Plantagenet, Earl of Cambridge, younger son of Edmund, Duke of York (5th son of King Edward III.), and conveyed the right to the crown to the House of York.

Allanore, *m.* to Edward, son of Edward Courtenay, Earl of Devon, but *d. s. p.*

His lordship was slain in battle, in Ireland, in 1398, and was *s.* by his son,

EDMUND MORTIMER, 5th Earl of March. This nobleman being but six years of age, at his father's death, was committed by King HENRY IV., to Henry, Prince of Wales, his son; out of whose custody he was shortly after stolen away by the Lady de Spencer; but being discovered in Chittham Woods, they kept him afterwards, under stricter guard, for he was the rightful heir to the crown of England, by his descent from Lionel, Duke of Clarence. This nobleman was frequently engaged in the wars of France, *temp.* HENRY V., and in the 1st HENRY VI. he was constituted lord lieutenant of Ireland. His lordship *m.* Anne, dau. of Edmund, Earl of Stafford, but *d. s. p.*, in 1424, when the Earldom of March became EXTINCT, but the Baronies of Mortimer, created by the writs of EDWARD I. and EDWARD III. devolved upon his lordship's nephew,

RICHARD PLANTAGENET, Duke of York, son of his sister Anne, Countess of Cambridge; and upon the accession of the son and heir of the said Duke of York to the throne, as EDWARD IV., these baronies, with his other dignities, became merged in the crown.

Thus terminated the male line of the illustrious family of Mortimer, Earls of March; and their great estates, with the right to the throne, passed to RICHARD, DUKE OF YORK, son of the last earl's sister, the LADY ANNE MORTIMER, by her husband, Richard Plantagenet, Earl of Cambridge.

Arms—Barry of six, or and az., on a chief of the 1st, two pallets between two base esquierres of the 2nd, over all an inescocheon arg.

MORTIMER—BARON MORTIMER, OF RICHARD'S CASTLE.

By Writ of Summons, dated 26 January, 1297.

Lineage.

The founder of this branch of the MORTIMERS in England, was,

ROBERT DE MORTIMER (the presumed son or brother of the the 1st Hugh de Mortimer, of Wigmore, ancestor of the Earls of March), who *m.* Margery, only dau. and heiress of Hugh de Ferrers, and grand-dau. of Hugh de Say,* Lord of Richard's Castle, co. Hereford, by which alliance he acquired that, and other considerable manors, and in the 12th HENRY II. he certified his knights' fees of this honour to be in number twenty-three. In the 17th JOHN he had a grant from the king of all those lands in Berwic, in Sussex, which had belonged to Mabel de Say, mother of Margery, his wife, and then in the possession of Robert Marmion, the younger. He *d.* about the year 1219, and was *s.* by his son,

HUGH DE MORTIMER, who, in the 43rd HENRY III., upon the death of William de Stutevill, 2nd husband of his mother, had livery of all those lands of her inheritance, upon the payment of £100 for his relief, which he the said William held as tenant by the courtesy of England during his life. In the next year, Hugh Mortimer, being one of the Barons Marchers, had command to repair personally to his house, at Richard's Castle, and there to attend the directions of Roger, Lord Mortimer, of Wigmore, whom the king had then constituted captain-general of all his forces in those parts, to oppose the hostilities of Llewelyn, Prince of Wales. In the contest between HENRY III. and the barons, this feudal lord siding with the former, was obliged to surrender Richard's Castle, after the defeat of Lewes, but he regained possession of that and all his other lands, by the triumph of Evesham, In the 1st EDWARD I., he executed

* HUGH DE SAY was feudal lord-of Richard's Castle, co Hereford. one of the possessions of his ancestor, RICHARD (surnamed Scrupe), in EDWARD THE CONFESSOR's days, whence it derives its denomination. In the 22nd HENRY II., this Hugh paid 20 marks to the king for trespassing in the royal forests, and in the 31st of the same reign, 200 marks for livery of his lands. He *m.* Lucia, dau. of Walter de Clifford, and left an only dau. and heir,

Mabel, who *m.* HUGH DE FERRERS, by whom she had an only dau. and heir,

MARGERY FERRERS, who *m.* Robert Mortimer, as in the text.

385

the office of sheriff for the cos. of Salop and Stafford, and dying in two years afterwards, was *s.* by his son,

ROBERT DE MORTIMER, who *m.* Joice, dau. and heir of William La Zouch, 2nd son of Roger, 2nd Baron Zouch, of Ashby, and had issue,

HUGH, his successor.

William, who inheriting from the Zouches the lordship of Ashby de la Zouch, assumed the surname of ZOUCHE (*see* ZOUCHE, of Mortimer).

This feudal lord *d.* in 1287, and was *s.* by his elder son,

HUGH DE MORTIMER, who was summoned to parliament as a Baron, 26 January, 1229, and from that time to 10 April, 1299, in which latter year he was in the wars of Scotland. His lordship *d.* in 1304, leaving by Maud, his wife, two daus., his co-heirs, viz.,

I. JOANE MORTIMER, *m.* 1st, to Thomas de Bikenore, by whom she had no issue, and 2ndly, to Sir Richard Talbot (a younger son of Richard, Lord Talbot, of Eccleswall, in Herefordshire), who thus founded the House of TALBOT, *of Richard's Castle*. By this, her 2nd husband, Joane Mortimer had three sons, JOHN (Sir), Thomas, and Richard, and was *s.* by the eldest,

SIR JOHN TALBOT, of Richard's Castle, who *m.* Joane, dau of Roger, Lord Grey, of Ruthyn, and was *s.* by his elder son,

JOHN TALBOT, of Richard's Castle, who left at his decease, in 1375, two sons, Richard and John, who both *d. unm.*, the former in 1382, and the latter 1388, and three daus., his eventual heirs, viz.,

ELIZABETH TALBOT, *m.* to Sir Warine Archdeckne, of Lanherne, in Cornwall.

PHILIPPA TALBOT, *m.* to Sir Matthew Gournay.

ELEANOR TALBOT. *d. unm.* 1390.

II. MARGARET MORTIMER, *m.* to Geffery Cornwall, and was mother of Sir Geoffrey Cornwall, of Burford.

Upon the decease of his lordship, the Barony of Mortimer, of Richard's Castle, fell into ABEYANCE, in which state it is supposed still to remain, amongst the descendants and representatives of his above-mentioned daus.

Arms—Similar to those of the Earls of March, with a bend gules.

MORTIMER—BARON MORTIMER OF CHIRKE.

By Writ of Summons, dated 26 August, 1307.

Lineage.

ROGER MORTIMER, 2nd son of Roger Mortimer, 5th feudal Lord of Wigmore, by Maud, dau. of William de Braose, of Brecknock, settled himself at Chirke, part of the territor es of Griffith ap Madoc, and was summoned to parliament from 6 February, 1299, to 3 November, 1306, as "Rogers de Mortuomari," an l as BARON MORTIMER, *of Chirke*, from 26 August, 1307, to 15 May, 1321. The manner in which his lordship acquired Chirke, is thus detailed by Powel, the Welsh historian:— "Griffith ap Madoc," saith he, "took part with King EDWARD III. and King EDWARD I., against the Prince of North Wales, and died. leaving his children within age; shortly after which followed the destruction of two of them; for King EDWARD gave the wardship of Madoc (the elder of them), who had for his part the lordship of Bromfield, &c., as also the castle of Dinas-Bran, to John, Earl of Warren; and of Llewelin, the younger, to whose part the lordships of Chirke, &c., fell, to Roger Mortimer, a younger son of Roger Mortimer, Lord of Wigmore; which guardians forgetting the services done by Griffith ap Madoc, their father, so guarded these, their wards, that they never returned to their possessions, and shortly after obtained these lands to themselves by charter."* Being thus

* Griffith and Llewelyn were the sons of MADOC VYCHAN, Lord of Bromfield, in Powys, living 22 December, 1270. and 3 December, 6th EDWARD I, when he was under age, son of Griffith ap Madoc, Lord of Bromfield, great-grandson and representative of Madoc ap Meredith, last Prince of Powys-Fadoc (*refer* to Cheriton of Powys). By Margaret, his wife, who was living 4 January, 9th EDWARD I., and 3 May, 12th EDWARD I., Madoc Vychan was father of the two children referre1 to; 1 GRIFFITH AP MADOC VYCHAN; 2 Llewelyn Vychan ap Madoc Vychan, whose territory EDWARD I., by charter dat.d at Salop,

ated here, he built the castle of Chirke; and during the reign of EDWARD I., was constantly employed in the wars of France, Scotland, and Wales, of which latter he was constituted the king's lieutenant, having all the castles in the principality committed to his custody; and he was subsequently made justice of all Wales. In the time of EDWARD II., his martial spirit continued and we find him ever in the field, either in Scotland or in Wales; he ended his career, however, in the Tower; for being one of the opponents of the Spencers, and amongst those lords who condemned them to exile, so soon as the king recovered his authority, his lordship and his nephew, Lord Mortimer of Wigmore, submitting themselves, were committed to the Tower of London, in which confinement this nobleman is said to have died, anno 1336. His lordship m. Lucia, dau. of Sir Robert de Wafre, Knt., and dying 1336, was s. by his son,

ROGER MORTIMER, of Chirke, never summoned to parliament, who m. Joane Turberville, and was s. by his son,

JOHN MORTIMER, who was never summoned to parliament, nor were any of his descendants. This personage sold his lordship of Chirke to Richard Fitz-Alan, Earl of Arundel.

Arms—Same as the Earls of March, with due difference.

MORTIMER—EARL OF ULSTER.

(*See* MORTIMER, Earl of March.)

MOWBRAY — EARLS OF NOTTINGHAM, DUKES OF NORFOLK, EARLS-MARSHAL, EARLS OF WARREN AND SURREY.

Earldom by Charter, anno 1377, and re-created 1383.
Dukedom, by Charter, 29 September, 1396.
Earldom of Warren and Surrey, 29 March, 1451.

Lineage.

The MOWBRAYS, DUKES OF NORFOLK, were from an ancient period a great baronial family, and made a succession of fortunate alliances. The royal match of John, Lord Mowbray, with Elizabeth Segrave, whose mother was Margaret, Countess of Norfolk, dau. and heir of Thomas, Earl of Norfolk, son of King EDWARD I., may be considered the first step from baronial rank. King RICHARD II., constituted Thomas, son of the great alliance, Earl Marshal in 1386, and created him Duke of Norfolk in 1396, when his grandmother, Margaret, was also advanced to be Duchess of Norfolk. The duke, preparing in 1398 to fight a duel with Henry, Duke of Hereford, afterwards King HENRY IV., was banished, and d. in exile next year. The family was restored and continued for four generations down to Anne, the infant dau. and heiress of John, 4th duke, whom King EDWARD IV. m. as a child, to his 2nd son, Richard, Duke of York, then a young boy, and he made a settlement of the title and estate upon him and his heirs. She d. immediately afterwards, in 1478, but the Duke of York continued in possession till he was murdered with his brother, King EDWARD V., by their uncle, RICHARD, 20 June, 1483. All EDWARD's plans for seizing the Mowbray property being thus terminated, and RICHARD III., wishing to secure vigorous allies, the succession

2 June, in the 10th year of his reign, 1282, granted to Roger Mortimer, the younger. The elder son, GRIFFITH AP MADOC VYCHAN, was living 11 January, 6th EDWARD I., 1278, and 7 October, 10th EDWARD I., at which latter date the English monarch, by charter, dated at Rhuddlan, granted to John de Warren, Earl of Surrey, " Castrum Dinas Bran qd. fuit in manu pria. in pncipio. psentes. guerre nre. Wåll et totam terram de Bromfield que Griffinus et Lewelinus filii Madoci Vaghan p. se vl. p. tutores seu custodes suos in pcipio. guerre illius tenerit (except the castle of Hope); also terram de Yal que fuent Griffini Vaghan fil Griffini de Bromfield, inimici nre " A charter dated at Rhuddlan, 12 February, 11th EDWARD I., sets forth " sciatis quod ad requisitem. . . . Johannis de Warren, Comitis Surr. concesss. Griffino Vaghan filio Madc ei qd. teneat teiram de Glyndordo de nob. voluntatem bram."

to the estates was allowed to open to the Berkeleys and Howards, the heirs of the daus. of the duke, who d. in exile in 1400, eighty-three years before, and King RICHARD, on the 3rd day of his reign, 28 June, 1483, created William, Viscount Berkeley, Earl of Nottingham, and John, Lord Howard (who had been first raised to be a baron by his brother EDWARD), at once Duke of Norfolk and Marshal of England.

The family was founded by

NIGIL DE ALBINI, brother of William de Albini, from whom the ancient Earls of Arundel descended. The Albinis, who were maternally of the house of Mowbray, came into England with the CONQUEROR, and obtained large possessions after the victory of Hastings. Nigil's grants lay in the cos. of Bucks, Bedford, Warwick, and Leicester, and comprised several extensive lordships. In the reign of RUFUS, he was bow-bearer to the king: and being girt with the sword of knighthood by King HENRY I., had the manor of Egmanton, with divers parks in the forest of Shirwood, of that monarch's gift; which lordship he transferred however, to his particular friend, Robert Davil. But when King Henry had further experience of his great valour and military skill, he augmented his royal bounty, and conferred upon him the vavassories of Camvile and Wyvile; which gracious mark of favour so attached Albini to the interests of his sovereign, that he espoused with the most devoted zeal the cause of HENRY, against his brother, Robert Curthose, and taking a conspicuous part at the battle of Tenerchebray, he there slew the horse of Curthose, and brought the prince himself to the king; for which eminent service, HENRY conferred upon him the lands of Robert, Baron of Frontebeof, namely Stutevile, in England, which Frontebeof had fortified in behalf of Curthose. After which, King Henry besieging a castle in Normandy, this gallant Sir Nigil first entered the breech, sword in hand, and delivered up the fortress to the king, which achievement was remunerated by a royal grant of the forfeited lands of his maternal uncle, Robert de Mowbray, Earl of Northumberland, both in Normandy and England; as also his castles, with the castle of Bayeux and its appurtenances; so that he had no less than 120 knights' fees in Normandy, and as many in England; thus becoming one of the most powerful persons of the period in which he lived. Sir Nigil de Albini m. 1st, Maud, dau. of Richard de Aquila, by permission of Pope PASCHALL; her husband Robert de Mowbray, Earl of Northumberland, before-mentioned, being then alive, and in prison for rebellion against WILLIAM RUFUS; from this lady he was, however, divorced, on account of consanguinity, and by her he had no issue. He m. 2ndly, in 1118, Gundred, dau. of Gerald de Gorney, by the special advice of King HENRY I., and had two sons,

ROGER, his successor, who, possessing the lands of Mowbray, assumed, by command of King HENRY, the surname of MOWBRAY.
Henry, who had the lordship and barony of Cambo, and was ancestor of the Albinis, feudal lords of that place.

This great feudal baron d. at an advanced age, and was buried with his ancestor, in the abbey of Bec, in Normandy. He was s. by his elder son,

ROGER DE MOWBRAY, who, although not yet of age, was one of the chief commanders, at the memorable battle fought, anno 1138, with the Scots, near Northallerton, known in history as the battle of the Standard; and adhering to King STEPHEN, in his contest with the empress, he was taken prisoner with that monarch at the battle of Lincoln. In 1148, he accompanied LEWIS, King of France, to the Holy Land, and there acquired great renown by vanquishing a stout and hardy Pagan in single combat. He was afterwards involved in the rebellion of Prince Henry, against King HENRY II., and lost some of his castles. His grants to the church were munificent in the extreme; and his piety was so fervent, that he again assumed the cross, and made a second journey to the Holy Land, where he was made prisoner, but redeemed by the knights Templars; he d. however, soon after in the East, and was buried at Sures. Some authorities say that he returned to England, and living fifteen years longer, was buried in the abbey of Riland. He m. Alice de Gant, and was s. by his elder son,

NIGIL DE MOWBRAY, who attended amongst the barons, in the 1st RICHARD I., at the solemn coronation of that monarch; and in the 3rd of the same reign, assuming the cross, set out for Palestine, but d. upon his journey. He m. Mabel, dau. of the Earl of Clare, and had issue, WILLIAM, Robert, Philip, 1st of Barnbougle in Scotland, and Roger ancestor of Mowbray, of Kirklington. Nigil de Mowbray d. 1191, and was s. by his eldest son,

WILLIAM DE MOWBRAY, who in the 6th RICHARD I., paying £100 for his relief, had livery of his lands. This feudal lord upon the accession of King JOHN, was tardy in pledging his allegiance, and at length only swore fealty upon condition that

Mowbray.
(D.Norfolk.)

Netterville.
(V.Netterville.)

Neville.
(E.Westmoreland.)

Noel.
(E.Gainsborough.)

O'Brien.
(E.Thomond.)

O'Dempsey.
(V.Clanmalier.)

O'Donnell.
(E.Tyrconnell.)

Parr.
(M.Northampton.)

Payne.
(B.Lavington.)

Pierrepoint
(D.Kingston.)

Pole.
(D.Suffolk.)

Poynings.
(B.Poynings.)

the king should render to every man his right. At the breaking out of the baronial war, it was no marvel then, that he should be found one of the most forward of the discontented lords, and so distinguished, that he was chosen with his brother, Roger, amongst the twenty-five celebrated barons appointed to enforce the observance of Magna Charter. In the reign of HENRY III., adhering to the same cause, he was at the battle of Lincoln, and taken prisoner there, when his lands were seized, and bestowed upon William Mareshal, the younger, but he was subsequently allowed to redeem them. After which he appears to have attached himself to the king, and was with the royal army at the siege of Bitham Castle, in Lincolnshire. He m. Agnes, dau. of the Earl of Arundel, and dying in 1222, was s. by his elder son,

NIGEL DE MOWBRAY, who, in the 8th HENRY III., paying £500 for his relief, had livery of his lands. He m. Maud, dau. and heiress of Roger de Camvil, but dying s. p. in 1228, was s. by his brother,

ROGER DE MOWBRAY, then in minority. This feudal lord had several military summonses to attend King HENRY III. into Scotland and Wales. He m. Maud, dau. of William de Beauchamp, of Bedford, and dying in 1266, was s. by his eldest son,

ROGER DE MOWBRAY, who, in the 6th EDWARD II., upon making proof of his age, had livery of his lands. He was engaged in the wars of Wales and Gascony, and was summoned to parliament as a Baron, from 23 June, 1295, to 26 August, 1296. His lordship m. Rose, great grand-dau. of Richard de Clare, Earl of Hertford, and dying in 1298, left two sons, JOHN, his heir, and Alexander, who went to Scotland. The son and heir,

JOHN DE MOWBRAY, 2nd baron, summoned to parliament from 26 August, 1307, to 5 August, 1320. This nobleman during his minority, was actively engaged in the Scottish wars of King EDWARD I., and had livery of all his lands before he attained majority, in consideration of those services. In the 6th EDWARD II., being then sheriff of Yorkshire, and governor of the city of York, he had command from the king to seize upon Henry de Perey, then a great baron in the north, in consequence of that nobleman suffering Piers de Gaveston, Earl of Cornwall, to escape from Scarborough Castle, in which he had undertaken to keep him in safety. The next year Lord Mowbray was in another expedition into Scotland, and he was then constituted one of the wardens of the marches towards that kingdom. In the 11th of the same reign he was made governor of Malton and Scarborough Castles, in Yorkshire, and the following year he was once more in Scotland, invested with authority to receive into protection all who should submit to King EDWARD. But afterwards taking part in the insurrection of Thomas, Earl of Lancaster, he was made prisoner with that nobleman and others at the battle of Boroughbridge, and immediately hanged at York, anno 1321, when his lands were seized by the crown, and Aliva, his widow, with her son, imprisoned in the Tower of London. This lady, who was dau. and co-heir of William de Braose, Lord Braose, of Gower, was compelled, in order to obtain some alleviation of her unhappy situation, to confer several manors of her own inheritance upon Hugh le Despencer, Earl of Winchester. In the next reign, however, she obtained from the crown a confirmation of Gowerland, in Wales, to herself and the heirs of her body by her deceased husband, with remainder to Humphrey de Bohun, Earl of Hereford and Essex, and his heirs. Lady Mowbray m. 2ndly, Sir R. de Peshale, Knt., and d. in the 5th EDWARD III. Her ladyship's son,

JOHN DE MOWBRAY, 3rd baron, was summoned to parliament from 10 December, 1327, to 20 November, 1360. This nobleman found much favour from King EDWARD III , who, in consideration of the eminent services of his progenitors, accepted of his homage, and gave him livery of his lands before he came of full age. He was subsequently the constant companion in arms of his martial sovereign, attending him in his glorious campaign in France, where he assisted at the siege of Nantes, and the raising that of Aguillon. He was likewise at the celebrated battle of Durham (20th EDWARD III.), and at one time was governor of Berwick-upon-Tweed. His lordship m. the Lady Joane Plantagenet, dau. of Henry, Earl of Lancaster, by whom he had issue, JOHN, his successor. Lord Mowbray, who was styled in the charters, Lord of the Isle of Axholme, and of the honour of Gower and Brember, d. in 1361, and was s. by his son,

JOHN DE MOWBRAY, 4th baron, summoned to parliament from 14 August, 1362, to 20 January, 1366, as "John de Mowbray of Axholme." This nobleman in the lifetime of his father was in the wars of France; and he eventually fell, anno 1368, in a conflict with the Turks, near Constantinople, having assumed the cross, and embarked in the holy war. His lordship m Elizabeth, dau. and heiress of John, Lord Segrave, by

Margaret, Duchess of Norfolk (dau. and eventually sole heiress, of Thomas Plantagenet, of Brotherton, Earl of Norfolk —see that dignity), whereby he acquired a great inheritance in lands, and the most splendid alliance in the kingdom. By this lady he had two sons, JOHN and THOMAS, and several daus., of whom one m. Roger, Lord De la Warr; and another m. John, Lord Welles; and a 3rd, Anne, was abbess of Barkyng His lordship was s. by his elder son,

JOHN DE MOWBRAY, 5th baron, who was created EARL OF NOTTINGHAM, upon the day of the coronation of King RICHARD II., anno 1377, with a special clause in the charter of creation, that all his lands and tenements whereof he was then possessed, should be held sub honore comitali, and as parcel of this earldom. His lordship d. two years afterwards, still under age, and unmarried, when the Earldom of Nottingham expired, but the Barony of Mowbray and his great possessions devolved upon his brother,

THOMAS DE MOWBRAY, as 6th baron, then seventeen years of age, who was created EARL OF NOTTINGHAM, as his brother had been, by charter, dated 12 February, 1383, and three years afterwards was constituted EARL MARSHAL, by reason of his descent from Thomas, of Brotherton; his lordship being the first who had the title of earl attached to the office. In the 10th RICHARD II. his lordship participated in the naval victory achieved by Richard, Earl of Arundel, over the French and Spaniards, and the subsequent conquest of the castle of Brest. In the 16th of the same reign he was made governor of Calais, and in four years afterwards obtained the king's charter of confirmation of the office of earl marshal of England to the heirs male of his body. and that they, by reason of the said office, should bear a golden truncheon, enamelled with black at each end, having at the upper end the king's arms, and at the lower, their own arms engraven thereon. Moreover, he stood in such favour, that the king, acknowledging his just and hereditary title to bear for his crest a golden leopard, with a white label, which of right belonged to the king's eldest son, did, by letters patent, grant to him and his heirs, authority to bear the golden leopard for his crest, with a coronet of silver about his neck, instead of the label ; and the same year appointed him justice of Chester and Flintshire for life. In the 18th RICHARD he attended the king into Ireland, but afterwards siding with the parasites, who controlled that weak and unfortunate prince, he not only aided in the destruction of his father-in-law, Richard, Earl of Arundel—being one of the chief persons that guarded the unhappy nobleman to the place of execution— but he is also accused of being an accomplice in the murder of Thomas, of Woodstock, Duke of Gloucester, the king's uncle. Certain it is that he was at this period in high estimation with the prevailing party, and obtained a grant of all the lands of the unfortunate Lord Arundel, with those of Thomas Beauchamp, Earl of Warwick, which had also vested in the crown, by forfeiture. These grants bore date 28 September, 1396, and the next day he was created DUKE OF NORFOLK (his grandmother, Margaret, Duchess of Norfolk, being still alive). Prosperous, however, as this nobleman's career had hitherto been, it was doomed eventually, to a disgraceful termination. Henry, Duke of Hereford (afterwards HENRY IV.), having accused his Grace of Norfolk, of speaking disrespectfully of the king, a challenge ensued, and a day was named for the combat, when the lists were accordingly set up, at Gosford Green, Coventry, and the king and court were present; but just as the combatants were about to engage, and the charge had been sounded, RICHARD interfered, and by the advice of his council, prohibited the conflict, banishing the Duke of Hereford for ten years, and the Duke of Norfolk for life—who, thereupon going abroad, d. at Venice, of the pestilence, but according to Sandford, of grief, in 1400. The duke, who, along with his other great honours, was a knight of the Garter, m. 1st, Elizabeth, dau. of John, Lord Strange, of Blackmere, but had no issue; he m. 2ndly, Lady Elizabeth Fitz-Alan, dau. of Richard, Earl of Arundel, sister and co-heir of Thomas, Earl of Arundel, and widow of William de Montacute, by whom he had issue,

I. THOMAS, who simply bore the title of Earl Marshal.
II. JOHN. of whom hereafter, as restored Duke of Norfolk.
   I. ISABEL, m. 1st, Henry, son and heir of William, 5th Lord Ferrers of Groby, and had an only child. Elizabeth, heiress of Groby, b. 1419. Isabel, m 2ndly, James, 5th LORD BERKELEY, and had a son William, whom EDWARD IV. made a viscount in 1481, RICHARD III. advanced to the Earldom of Nottingham, and HENRY VII. promoted to be Earl Marshal and Marquess of Berkeley.
II. MARGARET, m. Sir Robert Howard, Knt. This lady became eventually co-heiress of the Mowbrays. and her son,
   Sir John Howard, Knt., was created DUKE OF NORFOLK, and Earl Marshal, and became ancestor of the illustrious house of Howard, Dukes of Norfolk.
III. ELIZABETH, m. 1st, Nicholas. Lord Audley, who d. 1391;

2ndly, John, Lord Beaumont, who d. 1396; and 3rdly, Michael, 3rd Earl of Suffolk, who d. 1415. The issue of Elizabeth became extinct.

The elder son,

THOMAS DE MOWBRAY, 7th Baron Mowbray, was but fourteen years of age, at the decease of his father, and never had the title of Duke of Norfolk, but was simply styled EARL MARSHAL. He was beheaded at York, in 1405, for participating in the conspiracy of Richard Scrope, archbishop of York, against HENRY IV. His lordship m. Constance, dau. of John Holland, Duke of Exeter, but having no issue, was s. by his brother,

JOHN DE MOWBRAY, 8th Baron Mowbray, who was restored, 3rd HENRY VI., in the parliament then held at Westminster, to the dignity of DUKE OF NORFOLK, having previously used only the titles of Earl of Nottingham, and Earl Marshal. This nobleman was engaged in the French wars of King HENRY V., and was only prevented by indisposition, from sharing the glories of Agincourt. His grace, who was a knight of the Garter, m. the Lady Katherine Nevil, dau. of Ralph, Earl of Westmoreland (who subsequently m. Thomas Strangways, Esq., and after his decease, John, Viscount Beaumont, and lastly, Sir John Widvile, Knt.), and dying in 1432, was s. by his son,

JOHN DE MOWBRAY, 3rd Duke of Norfolk. This nobleman attained majority in the 14th HENRY VI., and in three years afterwards was sent ambassador into Picardy, to treat of peace, with the King of France. In the 23rd of the same reign, upon obtaining a confirmation of the Dukedom of Norfolk, he had a place assigned him in parliament, and elsewhere, next to the Duke of Exeter. His grace m. Eleanor, dau. of William, Lord Bourchier, and dying in 1461, was s. by his son,

JOHN DE MOWBRAY, Earl of Warren and Surrey (so created 29 March, 1451), as 4th Duke of Norfolk, and Earl Marshal. This nobleman, in the 14th EDWARD IV., was retained to serve the king in his wars in France, for one year, and he was made a knight of the Garter. His grace m. the Lady Elizabeth Talbot, dau. of John, Earl of Shrewsbury, by whom he had an only dau.,

Lady Anne Mowbray, contracted to Richard, son of King EDWARD IV., but d. before consummation of marriage.

The duke d. in 1475, when all his honours, except the Baronies of Mowbray and Segrave, EXPIRED; but those, on the decease of Lady Anne Mowbray above-mentioned, fell into ABEYANCE, amongst the descendants of the Ladies Isabel Berkeley and Margaret Howard (refer to issue of Thomas, 1st Duke of Norfolk), and so continued until the suspension of the Barony of Mowbray was terminated by the summoning of Henry Howard, son, and heir apparent of Thomas, Earl of Arundel, Norfolk, and Surrey, to parliament, 13 April, 1639, as BARON MOWBRAY. The eldest son of that nobleman was restored to the Dukedom of Norfolk, and the barony merged in that dignity, until the death of Edward, 11th duke, in 1777, when, with several other baronies, it again fell into ABEYANCE, between the two daus. and co-heirs of Philip Howard, Esq., younger brother of the said duke, namely,

Winifred, m. to Charles-Philip, 15th Lord Stourton,
Anne, m. to Robert-Edward, 9th Lord Petre,

And so remained until ALFRED-JOSEPH, 19th LORD STOURTON, had the abeyance of the Barony of Mowbray, as well as of the barony of Segrave terminated in his favour, 3 January, 1878.

Arms—Gu., a lion rampant, arg.

———

MULTON—BARONS MULTON, OF EGREMONT.

By Writ of Summons, dated 26 February 1297.

Lineage.

In the time of King HENRY I.,

THOMAS DE MULTON, so called from his residence at Multon, in Lincolnshire, bestowed at the funeral of his father, in the Chapter House, at Spalding (his mother, brothers, sisters, and friends, being present), the church of Weston, upon the monks of that abbey. After this Thomas, came

LAMBERT DE MULTON, who, in the 11th HENRY II., residing

then in Lincolnshire, was amerced 100 marks. In the 9th and 10th of King JOHN, flourished another

THOMAS DE MULTON, who at that period was sheriff of the co. Lincoln, and in the 15th of the same reign, attended the king in his expedition then made into Poictou. This Thomas gave 1,000 marks to the crown for the wardship of the daus. and heirs of Richard de Luci, of Egremont, co. Cumberland, and bestowed those ladies afterwards in marriage upon his two sons, Lambert and Alan. In the 17th JOHN, being in arms with the rebellious barons, and taken at Rochester Castle, he was committed to the custody of Peter de Mauley, to be safely secured, who conveyed him prisoner to the castle of Corff, but in the 1st HENRY III., making his peace, he had restitution of his liberty and his lands. The next year having m. Ada, dau. and co-heir of Hugh de Morvill, widow of Richard de Lacy, of Egremont, without the king's license, command was sent to the archbishop of York, to make seizure of all his lands in Cumberland, and to retain them in his hands until further orders. Multon giving security, however, to answer the same, whensoever the king should require him so to do, he had livery of all those lands which had been seized for that transgression, with the castle of Egremont. In three years afterwards he paid £100 fine to the king, and one palfrey for the office of forester of Cumberland, it being the inheritance of Ada, his wife. In the 17th HENRY III., he was sheriff of Cumberland, and remained in office for several succeeding years. Moreover, he was one of the justices of the king's Court of Common Pleas. from the 8th HENRY III., and a justice itinerant for divers years, from the 9th of the same reign. He m. twice, by his 1st wife he had issue,

LAMBERT, m. Annabel, dau. and co-heir of Richard de Lucie.
Alan, m. Alice, dau. and co-heir of Richard de Lucie, and had a son.

THOMAS DE MULTON, who assumed the surname of LUCIE (see LUCY, of Egremont).

Thomas de Multon m. 2ndly, Ada, dau. and co-heir of Hugh de Morville, and had, by that lady,

THOMAS (see MULTONS, of Gillesland).
Julian, m. to Robert le Vavasour.

This celebrated feudal lord, who was a liberal benefactor to the church, is thus characterized by Matthew Paris: " In his youth he was a stout soldier, afterwards very wealthy, and learned in the laws; but overmuch coveting to enlarge his possessions, which lay contiguous to those of the monks of Crowland, he did them great wrong in many respects." He d. in 1240, and was s. by his eldest son,

LAMBERT DE MULTON, who, as stated above, m. Annabel, the elder dau. and co-heir of Richard de Lucy, of Egremont, and in 1246, obtained by large gifts from the Pope, an extraordinary privilege; namely, that no one should have the power to excommunicate him, but by a special mandate from his holiness. But he, who had this liberty, saith Matthew Paris, riding with rich trappings very proudly, from a trial at law, no sooner alighted from his horse, but (meriting God's judgment) was suddenly smitten with a grievous disease, of which falling to the ground, he died before his spurs could be taken off, being then at his house at Multon, in Lincolnshire. By his 1st wife, he had a son, THOMAS, his successor. He m. 2ndly, Ida, widow of Geoffrey de Oilli, but had no issue. His death occurred in 1247, when he was s. by his son,

THOMAS DE MOULTON, designated of Egremont, who was in arms against the king, in 49th HENRY III., with the rebellious barons of that period. In the 22nd EDWARD I., he had a grant of free warren in all his demesne lands, at Egremont, and dying in 1294, was s. by his son,

THOMAS DE MULTON, who was summoned to parliament as BARON MULTON, of Egremont, from 26 January, 1297, to 15 May, 1320. During which interval, he was almost constantly engaged in the Scottish wars. His lordship d. in 1322, and was s. by his son,

JOHN DE MULTON, 2nd baron, summoned to parliament from 27 January, 1332, to 24 July, 1334. This nobleman m. Annabel, dau. and heiress of Laurence de Holbeche, but dying s. p., in 1334, his estates, including the manors of Thurstaneston, in Suffolk, and Egremont and Cockermouth, in Cumberland, were divided amongst his three sisters, thus, viz.,

JOANE, wife of Robert, Baron Fitz-Walter, had for her share the Castle of Egremont, with the third part of that manor and the third part of other manors.
ELIZABETH, wife of Walter de Bermichan. had certain lands at Gosford, parcel of the manor of Egremont, and a proportion of other manors. This Elizabeth was 1st m. to Robert, son and heir of John, 1st Lord Harington.
MARGARET, wife of Thomas de Lucy, had certain lands in Cumberland, parcel of the manor of Egremont, besides a proportion of other estates.

while the Barony of Multon, of Egremont, fell into ABEYANCE amongst those ladies, as it still continues with their descendants and representatives.

Arms—Arg., three bars, gules.

MULTON—BARON MULTON, OF GILLESLAND.

By Writ of Summons, dated 26 August, 1307.

Lineage.

THOMAS DE MULTON, Lord of Multon, in Lincolnshire, who d. 1240 (*see* MULTON *of Egremont*), m. for his 2nd wife, Ada, dau. and co-heir of Hugh de Moreville, and had, with a dau., Julian, who m. Robert de Vavasour, a son,

THOMAS DE MULTON, who inherited the office of forester of Cumberland from his mother, and in the 36th HENRY III., paid a fine of 400 marks to the crown, for trespassing in the forests there, and for the future enjoyment of all the privileges which his ancestors had possessed with the forestership. In the 42nd of the same reign, he had a military summons to march with the other northern barons into Scotland, for the purpose of rescuing the Scottish monarch, King HENRY's son-in-law, from the restraints imposed upon him by his own subjects: and again in the 55th, to take up arms against the Welsh. This feudal baron m. MAUD, only dau. and heiress of HUBERT DE VAUX,* Lord of Gillesland, and with her acquired that lordship. He d. in 1270, and was s. by his son,

THOMAS DE MULTON, who doing his homage, had livery of his lands, and the ensuing year, upon the death of Helewise de Levinton, widow of Eustace de Baliol, was found to be her heir as to a moiety of the Barony of Burgh upon the Sands (he already enjoyed the other moiety by inheritance), and divers other considerable manors. He d. in 1293 (his mother, the heiress of Gillesland, being still alive), and was s. by his son,

THOMAS DE MULTON, who doing his homage the same year, had livery of his lands, but d. in two years afterwards, being then seized of the manor of Donham, in Norfolk; of Burgh-upon-Sands; of Kirk-Oswald; and of the Barony of Gillesland, with divers other estates, all in the co. Cumberland. He was s. at his decease in 1295 (his widow, Isabel, m. Sir John de Caster) by his son,

THOMAS DE MULTON. This feudal lord having been engaged in the Scottish wars, in the 31st and 34th EDWARD I., was summoned to parliament as BARON MULTON, *of Gillesland*, upon the accession of EDWARD II. from 26 August, 1307, to 26 November, 1313. After which we find his lordship again upon the theatre of war, in Scotland, in the 3rd and 4th years of the new monarch: and he subsequently obtained some immunities from the crown, in the shape of grants for fairs and markets upon his different manors. He d. in 1313, leaving by Margaret, his wife, an only dau. and heiress,

MARGARET DE MULTON, who m. Ranulph de Dacre, Lord Dacre, of the North, and conveyed her great estates with the Barony of Multon, to the DACRE family (*see* DACRE, *of Gillesland*).

Arms—Az., three bars, gules.

---

* RANULPH DE MESCHINES, in the time of the CONQUEROR, granted the Barony of Gillesland ' to a Norman called

HUBERT, who was ever afterwards denominated either HUBERT VAULX, or "HUBERT DE VALLIBUS." He was s. by his son and heir,

ROBERT DE VAUX, who m. Ada, dau. and heir of William Engaine, and widow of Simon de Moreville, and was s. by his elder son,

ROBERT DE VAUX. This baron outliving his only son, was s. at his decease, by his brother,

RANULPH DE VAUX, who was father of

ROBERT DE VAUX, one of the barons who took up arms against King JOHN. He was s. by his son,

HUBERT DE VAUX, who left at his decease, an only dau. and heir,

MAUD DE VAUX, who m., as in the text, THOMAS DE MULTON, and conveyed to him the BARONY OF GILLESLAND.

' *Gill*, in the provincial dialect of Cumberland, signifies a *dale* or *valley*, which corresponds with the Latin word, *vallis*, whence the French derived their term, *Vaulx*.

MUNCHENSI—BARON MUNCHENSI.

By Writ of Summons, dated 24 December, 1264.

Lineage.

It was not long after the Norman Conquest, that HUBERT DE MUNCHENSI, made grants of lands to the monks of Eye and Thetford, in the cos. of Suffolk and Norfolk. "It is said that this Hubert," observes Dugdale, "had issue, WARINE DE MUNCHENSI, and he another Hubert, which is likely enough to be true; for in the 33rd HENRY II., it appears that Hubert de Munchensi was in ward to the bishop of Ely, with his land at Stratford, part of the honour of Henry de Essex. At the same time also Agnes de Munchensi (widow of Warine, as I guess) dau. of Payne Fitz-John, then sixty years of age, had three sons, viz., Ralph and William, both knights, and Hubert, a clerk; as also two daus., the one m. to Stephen de Glanvile, and the other to William Painell, her lands at Holkham, in Norfolk, being then valued at £11 per annum." His son and heir,

WARINE DE MUNCHENSI, was father of

HUGH DE MUNCHENSI, living in 1186. The next member of the family upon record is

WILLIAM DE MUNCHENSI, who d. about the 6th JOHN, and was s. by his son,

WILLIAM DE MUNCHENSI, who was s. at his death s. p. in about seven years afterwards, by his uncle,

WARINE DE MUNCHENSI, a person of military reputation, *temp.* HENRY III. He m. Joan, dau. and heir of William Marshall, Earl of Pembroke, and had issue,

WILLIAM, his successor.

Joane, m. to William Valence, the King's half brother,

Warine d. 1255, and was s. by his son,

WILLIAM DE MUNCHENSI. This feudal lord was one of the leading persons who took up arms against HENRY III., and one of the chief commanders at the battle of Lewes. After this victory he was summoned to parliament 24 December, 1264, by the baronial government, acting in the name of the king. His lordship was subsequently made prisoner at Kenilworth, and his lands being seized, were transferred to his brother-in-law, William Valence. They were soon, however, restored upon his making the necessary submission. He was eventually slain *anno* 1289, in battle, by the Welsh. He left a dau. and heiress,

DIONISIA MUNCHENSI, who m. Hugh de Vere, younger son of Robert, Earl of Oxford.

This dignity can hardly be deemed, however, an inheritable barony. A younger brother of Warine de Munchensi, William de Munchensi, m. Beatrix, dau. and co-heir of William de Beauchamp, Baron of Bedford, and d. in 1286, leaving William, his son and heir, who d. in 1302, leaving male issue, but none of this branch were ever summoned to parliament.

Arms—Or, three escutcheons, barry of six, vair and gu.

MURRAY—EARLS OF ANNANDALE.

By Letters Patent, dated 13 March, 1624-5.

Lineage.

SIR JOHN MURRAY, Knt., youngest son of Sir Charles Murray of Cockpool, by Margaret, his wife, eldest dau. of Hugh, 5th Lord Somerville, rising high in favour with JAMES VI., was appointed master of the horse, and upon his Majesty's accession to the throne of England, accompanied his royal master to London as one of the gentlemen of the privy chamber, and was created VISCOUNT ANNAND, and LORD MURRAY, *of Lochmaben*. On 13 March, 1624-5, he obtained the EARLDOM OF ANNANDALE. His lordship, who s. his brother, Sir Richard Murray, Bart., in the old family estate of Cockpool, m. Elizabeth, dau. of Sir John Schaw, Knt.; and dying, September, 1640, was s. by his son,

JAMES MURRAY, 2nd Earl of Annandale, who inherited the VISCOUNTY OF STORMONT, under the limitation in the patent, at the decease of Mungo, the 2nd viscount. His lordship joined Montrose after the battle of Kilsyth, and upon that heroic chieftain's defeat, retired to England, where he d. 28 December, 1658. He m. Lady Elizabeth Carnegie, eldest dau. of James, 2nd Earl of Southesk, but by her (who m. 2ndly, in 1659,

David, 4th Viscount Stormont) had no issue. At Lord Annandale's decease, the titles of Annandale, Annand, and Murray of Lochmaben, became EXTINCT, and those of Stormont and Scoon devolved on David, 2nd Lord Balvaird.

Arms—Az., a crescent, between three stars, all within a double tressure, flory, counterflory with fleurs-de-lis, arg.; and a dexter canton of the 2nd, charged with a thistle, vert, crowned, or, as an augmentation.

MURRAY—EARL OF TULLIBARDINE.

Lineage.

JOHN MURRAY, eldest son of John, 1st Marquess of Athole, was appointed in 1695, one of the principal secretaries of state for Scotland, and in the following year (27 July) created EARL OF TULLIBARDINE, VISCOUNT OF GLENALMOND, and LORD MURRAY, for life. In 1703, he *s.* his father as 2nd Marquess of Athole, and was raised to a dukedom shortly after. His grace *d.* 14 November, 1724, when the dignities which had been conferred on him for life, of course became EXTINCT, but his hereditary honours devolved on his son,

JAMES, 2nd Duke of Athole.

MURRAY — VISCOUNTESS BAYNING, OF FOXLEY, CO. WILTS.

By Letters Patent, dated 17 March, 1674.

Lineage.

The Hon. ANNE BAYNING, 2nd dau. of Sir Paul Bayning, Bart., 1st VISCOUNT BAYNING, *of Sudbury, co. Suffolk,* and sister of Paul, 2nd Viscount Bayning, was created for life, after the decease of the latter lord, without male issue, and the extinction of the honours of her family, VISCOUNTESS BAYNING, o *Foxley, co. Wilts,* 17 March, 1674. She had previously *m.* Henry Murray, Esq., one of the grooms of bedchamber to King CHARLES I. Her ladyship *d.* in 1698, when the dignity of course EXPIRED. Mr. Murray's eldest dau. and co-heiress, by Lady Bayning,

The Hon. Elizabeth Murray, *m.* General Randolph Egerton, and had a dau.,

  ANNE EGERTON (sole heiress of her father), who *m.* Lord William Paulet, 2nd son of Charles, 1st Duke of Bolton, by whom she had an only dau.,

    HENRIETTA PAULET (heiress of her father), who *m.* the Hon. William Townshend, 3rd son of Charles, 2nd Viscount Townshend, K.G., and left a son,

      CHARLES TOWNSHEND, who was created BARON BAYNING, *of Foxley,* 27 October, 1797, and was father of the late and present LORDS BAYNING (*see* BURKE's *Extant Peerage*).

MUSGRAVE—BARON MUSGRAVE.

By Writ of Summons, dated 25 November, 1350.

Lineage.

The MUSGRAVES are said to have come originally from Germany, and to have been MUSGRAVES, or Lords Marchers there. Banks tells the following story of their good fortune in obtaining an alliance with the imperial family:—"The emperor had two great generals, who made court to his daughter at the same time; and as he had experienced singular services from both, did not care to prefer one before the other. But to decide the matter, ordered the two heroes to run at the ring for her (an exercise then in use): it so happened that this Musgrave (one of the contending generals) had the fortune to pierce the ring with the point of his spear; by which action he gained her for a reward of his gallantry and dexterity, and had 'six annulets, or,' given him for his coat of arms; and for his crest, two arms in armour, holding an annulet. From this marriage issued that MUSGRAVE, who being a man of an enterprising genius, accompanied WILLIAM THE CONQUEROR into England, and was the founder of the Musgraves in this country."

SIR THOMAS MUSGRAVE, one of the commanders in the van of the English army that gave battle to, and totally defeated DAVID, King of Scotland, at Durham, 20th EDWARD III., was summoned to parliament as a Baron from 25 November, 1350, to 4 October, 1373. His lordship appears to have been generally employed upon the borders in resisting the incursion of the Scotch. He was made (21st EDWARD III.) governor of Berwick-upon-Tweed; and sole justiciar through all the lands in Scotland, whereof the king had then possession. He was afterwards sheriff of Yorkshire and governor of the castle of York. His lordship *m.* Isabel, widow of Robert, son of Robert, Lord Clifford, and dau. of Thomas, Lord Berkeley; but the barony did not continue in his descendants, nor have any of those been deemed barons of the realm. Descended from his lordship are the three existing houses of Musgrave, Baronets, viz.,

The MUSGRAVES of Eden Hall, in Cumberland, created Baronets 29 June, 1611.
The MUSGRAVES of Hayton, created baronets in 1638.
The MUSGRAVES of Tourin, co. Waterford, created baronets of Ireland, in 1782.

Arms—Gu., six annulets, or.

NANSLADRON—BARON NANSLADRON.

By Writ of Summons, dated 29 December, 1299.

Lineage.

In the 29th EDWARD I.,
SERLO DE NANSLADRON, or LANSLADRON, was in the expedition then made into Scotland, and had summons to parliament as a Baron, from the 28th to the 34th of the same reign, but never afterwards, and of his lordship nothing further is known.

Arms—Sa., three chevronels, arg.

NASSAU—EARLS OF ROCHFORD.

By Letters Patent, dated 10 May, 1695.

Lineage.

FREDERICK DE NASSAU, natural son of Henry-Frederick de Nassau, Prince of Orange (grandfather of King WILLIAM III.), by the dau. of the Bourgue Mestre d'Emmeric, was endowed by his father with the lordship of Zuylestein, and thereupon assumed that surname. He subsequently commanded the infantry in the service of the States-General, when his country was invaded by the French, in 1672. In that gloomy conjuncture, when the Prince of Orange was elected Stadtholder, his highness's first action was an attack on Naerden; in furtherance of which, he detached General Zuylestein to take up a position between Utrecht and the object of the prince's operations; whereupon the Duke of Luxemburgh marched to relieve the besieged, and fell, with between 8,000 and 9,000 men, on General Zuylestein, who bravely met the assault, and repulsed his assailant. The town was afterwards bombarded, and reduced to such extremity, as to be compelled to offer terms of capitulation: in which interval the Duke of Luxemburgh, having been reinforced, marched through swamps guided by peasants to Voordam, and re-attacked General Zuylestein. who, after a gallant resistance, fell, sword in hand, 12 October, 1672. The son of this brave soldier (by Mary, his wife, dau. of Sir William Killigrew, Bart., Chamberlainto Queen Catharine, consort of CHARLES II.),

WILLIAM-HENRY DE ZUYLESTEIN, confidential friend of WILLIAM III., accompanied that prince to England, and was elevated to the peerage 10 May, 1695, as *Baron of Enfield, Viscount Tunbridge,* and EARL OF ROCHFORD. His lordship *m.* Jane, dau. and heiress of Sir Henry Wroth, of Durans, co. Middlesex, by whom he had four sons and five daus. He *d.* at Zuylestein, in 1708, and was *s.* by his eldest son,

WILLIAM-HENRY DE NASSAU, 2nd earl. This nobleman was a military officer of considerable renown, and participating in the triumphs of the Duke of Marlborough, was the bearer of the despatches announcing the glorious victory of Blenheim, 2 August, 1704. His lordship fell at the battle of Almanza, in Spain, 27 July, 1710; and, as he *d. unm.,* the honours devolved upon his brother,

FREDERICK NASSAU, 3rd earl, then one of the nobles of the province of Utrecht. His lordship m. Bessey, dau. and heiress of Richard Savage, Earl of Rivers, by whom (who m. 2ndly, the Rev. Mr. Carter), he left two sons,

    I. WILLIAM-HENRY, his successor.
    II. Richard-Savage, one of the clerks of the Board of Green Cloth, and M.P.; b. in 1723; m. in December, 1751, Elizabeth, dau. and heiress of Edward Spencer, Esq , of Rendlesham, Sussex, and Dowager of James, Duke of Hamilton and Brandon, by whom (who d. 9 March, 1771,) he left at his decease, May, 178¹,
      1 WILLIAM-HENRY, last earl.
      2 George-Richard-Savage, b. 5 September, 1756; d. s. p.
      1 Lucy, d. unm.

His lordship d. 14 June, 1738. and was s. by his elder son, WILLIAM-HENRY NASSAU, 4th earl, who was installed a knight of the Garter, in 1778, having previously resided as ambassador at the courts of Madrid and Versailles, and filled the offices of groom of the stole, first lord of the bedchamber, and secretary of state. His lordship m. Lucy, dau. of Edward Young, Esq., of Durnford, co. Wilts, by whom (who d. 9 January, 1773,) he had no issue. He d. 20 September, 1781, and was s. by his nephew, WILLIAM-HENRY NASSAU, 5th earl, b. 28 July, 1754, at whose decease, unm., 3 September, 1830, all his honours became EXTINCT.

Arms—Quarterly: 1st, az., semée of billets, or, a lion rampant. of the 2nd, for NASSAU; 2nd. or, a lion rampant, gu., ducally crowned, az., for DIETZ; 3rd, gu., a fesse, arg., for VIANDEN: 4th, gu., two lions passant gardant, in pale, or, for CATZNELLOGEN; over all, in an escocheon gu., three zules, arg., in chief, a label of three points of the last, for ZUYLESTEIN.

NASSAU, OR DE AUVERQUERQUE—EARL OF GRANTHAM.

By Letters Patent, dated 24 December, 1698.

Lineage.

HENRY DE NASSAU, Lord of Auverquerque, or d'Ouwerkerck, general of Dutch infantry, and governor of Hortogenbosh, d. 28 February, 1668, leaving by his wife, Elizabeth, dau. of Count de Horn, the following issue,

    Maurice, Earl of Nassau. being so created by the Emperor LEOPOLD, Lord of La Leek, in Holland, and governor of Sluice, d. in 1683.
    William Adrian, Lord of Odyke, Zeist, &c., was created likewise a count of the empire, and was premier nobleman of Zealand.
    HENRY, of whom presently.
    Emilia, m. to the celebrated Thomas Butler, Earl of Ossory, son and heir of James, Duke of Ormond.
    Isabella, m. to Henry Bennett, Earl of Arlington.
    Mauritia, m. to Colin Lindsey, Earl of Balcarres.
    Charlotte, lady of the bedchamber, d. unm. in 1702.
    Anne-Elizabeth, m. to Heer van Baron Ruytenburgh, and was mother of Anne-Elizabeth, who m. George, 2nd Earl of Cholmondeley.

The youngest son,
HENRY DE NASSAU, Lord of Auverquerque, came into England with the Prince of Orange, in 1670, and being with his highness when he visited the University of Oxford, had the degree of Doctor of Civil Law conferred upon him. He was subsequently the companion in arms of the prince, and at the battle of St. Denuis, before Mons, in 1678, had the good fortune to save his life, by striking to the ground an officer in the act of charging his highness; for which gallant achievement, the States-general presented him with a sword, whereof the hilt was of massy gold, a pair of pistols richly inlaid with gold, and a pair of gold horse buckles. Being captain of the guard to the Prince of Orange, he attended him in that station into England, anno 1688; and upon the accession of WILLIAM and MARY to the throne, he was naturalised by act of parliament, and appointed master of the horse. His lordship was at the battle of the Boyne, and subsequently attended his royal master in all his campaigns against the French. "The gallant manner (we quote Macaulay) in which Auverquerque brought off the remains of Mackay's division (at Steinkirk) was long remembered and talked of with grateful admiration by the British camp fires." On his death-bed, King WILLIAM "strained his feeble voice to thank Auverquerque for the affectionate and loyal services of thirty years." At the monarch's decease, Auverquerque returned to Holland, and was appointed by the States, velt-marshal of the army. In the campaign of 1708, his

lordship lost his life in the field, as he had always desired. He d. in the camp at Rouselaer, in the sixty-seventh year of his age, after a procrastinated indisposition, 17 October, 1708, and was interred with great pomp at Auverquerque. His lordship m. Isabella van Aersen, dau. of Cornelius, Lord of Sommelsdyck and Plaata. by whom he had issue,

    Louis, d. 2 August, 1687. aged eighteen.
    HENRY. of whom presently.
    Cornelius, Count de Nassau, Lord of Wondenburg. lieut.-gen. in the service of the States-general, gained the battle of Wynendahl, and was killed at the battle of Denain, anno 1712.
    Maurice, Count de Nassau, lieut.-gen. in the service of the States-general, and governor of Sluice.
    Francis, Count de Nassau, colonel of dragoons, killed at the battle of Almenare, 27 July, 1710, in Spain.
    Isabella, m. in 1691, to Charles, Lord Lansdown, heir-apparent to John Granville, 1st Earl of Bath, by whom he had an only son,
      William-Henry, 3rd Earl of Bath.
    Frances, m. to Nanfant Coote, Earl of Bellamont, in the peerage of Ireland.

HENRY D'AUVERQUERQUE, the eldest surviving son, had been elevated to the peerage in the lifetime of his father, 24 December, 1698, by the titles of Baron Alford, Viscount Boston, and EARL OF GRANTHAM, with remainder, failing his male issue, to his younger brothers, Cornelius, Maurice and Francis d'Auverquerque, and the male issue of their bodies. His lordship m. Lady Henrietta Butler, dau. and eventually heiress of Thomas, Earl of Ossory, Lord Butler of Moore Park, eldest son of James, Duke of Ormonde, by whom he had issue,

    Henry, Viscount Boston, d. 19 June, 1718, unm.
    Thomas, Viscount Boston, d. 27 April, 1730, unm.
    Frances, m. in 1737, Captain Elliot; d. s. p. 1772.
    Emilia-Maria, d. at ten years of age.
    Henrietta, m. 27 June, 1732, to William, 2nd Earl Cowper, ancestor, by her, of Earl Cowper.

His lordship d. in 1754, when all his honours EXPIRED.

Arms—Quarterly: 1st, az., semée of billets, and a lion rampant. or; 2nd. or, a lion rampant guardant, gu., crowned with a ducal coronet, az.; 3rd, gu., a fesse arg.; 4th, gu. two lions passant guardant in pale, or, over all in an escutcheon, arg., a lion rampant, sa.

NEREFORD—BARON NEREFORD.

By Writ of Summons, dated 26 January, 1297.

Lineage.

In the year 1206, ROBERT DE NEREFORD, and his wife, Alice, dau. of John Pouchard, founded the abbey of Pree, co. Norfolk, as also an hospital there, for thirteen poor people. This Robert was governor of Dover Castle, in the 1st HENRY III., under Hubert de Burgh, Justiciary of England. He was s. by

WILLIAM DE NEREFORD, who had been in arms with the barons against King JOHN, and had his lands seized, but returning to his allegiance in the beginning of the next reign, they were restored to him. He m. Petronill, one of the daus. and co-heirs of John de Vaux, without license, for which offence he paid a fine of £230 to the crown. In the division of the lands of de Vaux, with William de Ros, who had m. the other co-heir, this William de Nereford had the manors of Sherston and Sholesham, in the co. of Norfolk, with other lands in the same shire, and in the cos. Suffolk and Cambridge. In the 22nd EDWARD I., he received command, with divers other great men, to attend the king, with his best advice, upon the great affairs of the realm, and was summoned to parliament as a Baron in the 22nd and the 25th of the same reign, but never afterwards. His lordship was s. by his son,

JOHN DE NEREFORD, who does not appear to have been summoned to parliament as a Baron. He d. s. p., and was s. by his brother,

THOMAS DE NEREFORD, who was father of

SIR JOHN DE NEREFORD, Knt., who was slain in the wars in France, in the 38th EDWARD III., leaving an only dau., and heiress,

MARGERY DE NEREFORD, then but five years old, who afterwards vowed chastity.

Arms—Gu., a lion rampant, ermine

NETTERVILLE — VISCOUNT NETTER-VILLE.

By Letters Patent, dated 3 April, 1622.

Lineage.

This very ancient Anglo-Norman family has been settled in Ireland since the reign of HENRY II. The heir male, temp. JAMES I.

NICHOLAS NETTERVILLE, of Dowth, co. Meath, was raised to the peerage of Ireland, 3 April, 1622, as VISCOUNT NETTERVILLE. He m. 1st, Eleanor, dau. of Sir John Bathe, of Drumcondragh, co. Dublin; and 2ndly, Mary, relict of Sir Thomas Hibbots, chancellor of the Exchequer in Ireland; by the former of whom he left issue (with five daus., Mary, m. to Sir Luke FitzGerald, of Teroghan; Margaret, m. to Pierce, son and heir of Edward, Viscount Galmoye; Alison, m. to Walter Chevers, Esq.; Ellen, m. to Thomas Fleming, Esq.; and Jane, m. to Matthias, Lord Trimleston), eight sons, viz.,

 I. JOHN, his heir.
 II. Lucas, m. Margaret, dau. of Sir Patrick Barnewall, of Turvey; but d. s. p.
 III. PATRICK, m. Mary, dau. of Peter Duffe, Gent., of Drogheda; and dying in 1676, left a son and successor, NICHOLAS, of Lecarrow, who m. 1st, Mary, dau. of Sir Redmond Burke, Bart. of Glinsk, and had by her two sons, whose issue failed. He m. 2ndly, Mary, dau. of Christopher Betagh, Esq., and dying in 1719, left by her, Christopher, d. unm., JAMES, Nicholas, Peter, and Francis. The 2nd son of the 2nd marriage, JAMES, m. Reddis, dau. of D'Arcy Hamilton, Esq., of Fahy, co. Galway, and d. in 1782, leaving four sons, NICHOLAS, Hamilton, Mark, and Robert. The eldest, NICHOLAS, m. Bridget, dau. of Bartholomew French, Esq., of Ballykenean, and d. in 1788, leaving a son, JAMES, 7th Viscount Netterville.
 IV. Robert, of Crucerath, ancestor of ARTHUR, 8th and last VISCOUNT NETTERVILLE.
 V. Richard.   VI. Christopher.
 VII. Thomas.   VIII. Nicholas.

Lord Netterville d. in 1654, and was s. by his eldest son,
 JOHN, 2nd viscount, who m. Elizabeth, dau. of Richard, Earl of Portland, K.G.; and d. 1659, the title descended regularly to
 JOHN, 6th viscount; at whose decease, unm., 15 March, 1826, the title remained dormant until adjudged by the House of Lords, 14 August, 1834, to
 JAMES, 7th viscount, co. Meath, who m. 7 April, 1834, Eliza, 3rd dau. of Joseph Kirwan, Esq., of Hillsbrook, co. Galway, and had issue, two daus., his co-heiresses,

 I. ELIZABETH - GWENDOLINE - THEODORA, m. 1876. Michael Cahill, Esq., of Ballyconra, co. Kilkenny, J.P., high sheriff, 1863, who d. Sept. 1877.
 II. MARY-REDDIS, m. 22 November, 1860, to Joshua-James MacEvoy, Esq., J.P. co. Kildare (who took, in 1865, by royal licence, the surname and arms of NETTERVILLE), second son of James MacEvoy, Esq., of Tobertynan, co. Meath, and grandson of Sir Joshua Meredyth, Bart., and has seven daus., Mary-Netterville; Theresa; Elizabeth; Rose; Barbara; Victoria; and Pauline.

Lord Netterville d. 13 February, 1854, and the title lay dormant, until adjudged by the House of Lords, in 1867, to
 ARTHUR-JAMES, 8th viscount (see ante, Robert Netterville, of Crucerath, 4th son of the 1st Viscount). He m. 27 October, 1841, Constantia Frances, dau. of Sir Edward-Joseph Smythe, 6th Bart., of Eshe Hall, by whom (who d. 21 January, 1870) he had an only dau.,
 Frances-Constantia, m. 3 December, 1860, to M. Charles Viditz.

Lord Netterville d. 7 April, 1882, when the viscounty became EXTINCT.

For full details of this family and the descent of the title, see ADDENDA.

Arms—Arg., a cross, gu., fretty, or.

NEVILL—BARONS NEVILL, OF RABY, EARLS OF WESTMORELAND.

Barony, by Writ of Summons, dated 8 June, 1294.
Earldom, by Charter, dated 29 September, 1397.

Lineage.

This noble, ancient, and illustrious family, which "was to mediæval England what the Douglas was to Scotland," was founded in England, by

GILBERT DE NEVIL, a Norman, one of the companions in arms of the CONQUEROR, and called by some of our genealogists his admiral; although there is no mention of him, or of any person of the name, in the General Survey. The grandson, it is presumed, of this Gilbert,
 GEOFFREY DE NEVILL (son and heir of Geoffrey de Neville), m. Emma, dau. and heir of Bertram de Bulmer, Lord of Brancepeth, a great baron of the north, and d. 1194, having issue,
 HENRY, who d. s. p. in 1227.
 Isabel.

By the heiress of Bulmer, Geoffrey de Nevill acquired extensive estates, which, after the death of his son, as stated above, without issue, devolved upon his dau.,
 ISABEL DE NEVILL. This great heiress m. ROBERT FITZ-MALDRED, the Saxon, Lord of Raby, in the bishopric of Durham, and had a son, GEOFFREY, who, adopting his maternal surname, and inheriting the estates, became
 GEOFFREY DE NEVILL, of Raby, and left (by Margaret, his wife,) two sons, viz.,
 ROBERT, his successor.
 Geoffrey, who, in the 54th HENRY III., was constituted governor of Scarborough Castle, and a justice itinerant. He m. Margaret, dau. and heir of Sir John Longvillers, of Hornby Castle, in Lancashire, and d. in the 13th EDWARD I., being then seized of the manor of Appleby, and other lands in Lincolnshire; the castle and manor of Hornby, co. Lancaster; and Hoton-Longvillers, and other manors in Yorkshire; the entire of which he acquired by his wife. He was ancestor of the NEVILLS of Hornby.

The elder son,
 ROBERT NEVILL, had livery in the 30th HENRY III., upon doing his fealty, of all the lands which he inherited from his grandfather, Robert Fitz-Maldred. In the 42nd of the same reign, he had a military summons to march to the relief of the King of Scotland, and he was then constituted governor of the Castles of Norham and Werke. In the next year, he was entrusted with Bamborough Castle: and two years afterwards, made warden of all the king's forests beyond Trent; which was followed by the appointment of justice-itinerant, for the pleas of those forests. In the 47th, he was one of the barons who undertook for the king's observance of the ordinances of Oxford; and in the same turbulent period, was made captain-general of all the king's forces beyond Trent, as also sheriff of Yorkshire, and governor of the castle of York; but notwithstanding these great trusts, he subsequently joined the baronial banner, yet was fortunate enough, after the discomfiture of his party, not only to obtain his pardon, but to be constituted governor of Pickering Castle, in Yorkshire. He m. Ida, relict or dau. of Robert Bertram, and had a son,
 ROBERT, who m. (54th HENRY III.,) Mary, elder dau. and co-heir of Ralph Fitz-Randolph, Lord of Middleham, by which alliance he acquired that manor, with the manor of Houton, co. Norfolk, and Snape, co. York. He d. v. p., leaving a son,
 RANULPH, who s. his grandfather.

Robert de Nevill d. in 1282, and was s. by his grandson,
 RANULPH, or RALPH DE NEVILL, who, being in minority, at the time of his grandfather's decease, obtained liberty of the king, that his friends might plough and manage his lands; and in the 13th EDWARD I., had livery of certain manors, part of his inheritance; soon after this, he had a warm contest with the prior of Durham, about the presentation of a stag, upon St. Cuthbert's Day, in September; "which, in truth" (says Dugdale), "was rather a rent than an obligation, in regard he held Raby, with the eight adjoining townships, by the yearly rent of £4 and a stag. For, contrary to the custom of his ancestors, he not only required that the prior of Durham, at the offering of that stag, ought to feast him, and all the company he should bring, but that the prior's own menial servants should, for that time, be set aside, and his peculiar servants and officers be put in their stead. Whereupon, amongst other of his guests, he invited John de Baliol, of Barnard Castle, who refused to go with him, alleging that he never knew the Nevills to have such a privilege there; Sir William de Brompton, the bishop's chief justice, likewise acknowledging that he himself was the first that began that extravagant practice; for being a young man, and delighting in hunting, he came with the Lord Nevill at the offering of the stag, and said to his companions, 'Come, let us go into the abbey and wind our horns,' and so they did. The prior father adding, that before the time of this Ranulph, none of his predecessors ever made any such claim; but when they brought the stag into the hall, they had only a breakfast, nor did the lord himself ever stay dinner, except he were invited." This Ranulph was summoned to parliament as a Baron, 8 June, 1294, and from that period, to 18 February, 1331. His lordship was in the wars of France, temp. EDWARD I., and in those of Scotland in the next reign. It is said, however, that he

little minded secular business, but devoted the principal part of his time to conversation with the canons of Merton and Coverham, upon whom he bestowed some considerable grants. He *m*. 1st, Euphemia, dau. of Robert and sister of John de Clavering, and had two sons,

ROBERT, of Middleham, called from his love and show of finery, the *Peacock of the North*, who *d. s. p.* in his father's life-time.

RALPH, his successor.

Margaret, *m*. William, Lord Ros, of Hamlake.

Anastasia, *m*. to Walter de Fauconbridge.

His lordship *m*. 2ndly, Margery, dau. of John, son of Marmaduke de Thweng, but had no issue. He *d*. in 1331, was buried on the south side of the altar at Coverham, and was *s*. by his only surviving son,

RALPH DE NEVILL, 2nd baron, summoned to parliament, from 20 November, 1331, to 20 January, 1336. This nobleman, in the time of his father was retained by indenture to serve the Lord Henry de Percy for life, in peace and war, against all men except the king, with twenty men-at-arms, whereof five to be knights receiving £100 sterling per annum. The dispute with the prior of Durham, regarding the presentation of the stag was revived, and finally set at rest, in the abandonment of his claim, by this Lord Nevill. The matter is thus detailed by Dugdale: "In this year likewise, doing his fealty to William, prior of Durham, upon Lammas day, for the manor of RABY, he told him, ' that he would offer the stag as his ancestors had done: saving that, whereas his father required that the prior's servants should be set aside at that time, and his own serve in their stead, he would be content that his should attend together with those of the prior's; and whereas, his father insisted, that his servants should only be admitted at dinner; he stood upon it that his should be there entertained the whole day and likewise the morrow at breakfast.' Whereupon the prior made answer, ' that none of his ancestors were ever so admitted, and that he would rather quit the stag, than suffer any new custom to the prejudice of their church.' But, to this Ralph replied ' that he would perform the whole service, or none, and put the trial of his right upon the country,' The prior, therefore, knowing him to be so powerful, and that the country could not displease him, declined the offer; howbeit, at length, to gain his favour, in regard he had no small interest at court, and might do him a kindness or a displeasure, was content for that one time he should perform it as he pleased, so that it might not be drawn into example afterwards: and to the purpose proposed, that indentures should be made betwixt them. Whereupon the Lord Nevill brought but few with him, and those more for the honour of the prior, than a burthen ; and so shortly after dinner took his leave, but left one of his servants to lodge there all night, and to take his breakfast there on the next day; ' protesting, that being both a son and tenant to the church, he would not be burthensome to it, in respect it would be no advantage to himself, but might much damnifie him, if he should bring with him as great a train as he would, saying, ' *what doth a breakfast signify to me ? nothing*. And likewise, that if the prior would shew that he had no right to what he so claimed, he would freely recede therefrom; and if he had a right, he would accept of a composition for it, rather than be burthensome to the convent; but if they should put him to get his right by law, then he would not abate anything thereof.' Whereupon inquiry being made amongst the eldest monks of the house, they affirmed, that being of eight years standing when his father was before repulsed, they had often seen the stag offered, and that he never staid dinner, but when the prior invited him; and some ancient men of the country testified as much : as also, that so soon as the stag was brought they carried him to the kitchen, and those who brought him were taken into the hall to breakfast, as they that bring their rents used to be.

" Moreover, when it happened any of the Lords Nevill to be desired to stay dinner with the prior, his cook was admitted into the kitchen to prepare a dish for him ; so likewise, another servant in the cellar, to choose his drink, and in like manner, some other at the gate, who knew his servants and followers, merely to let them in, and keep out others, who, under pretence of being servants might then intrude. But this was only done by the prior, as out of courtesy and respect, and not at all out of right."

In the 7th EDWARD III., Lord Nevill was one of the commissioners sent into Scotland, there to see that the covenants between EDWARD DE BALIOL, King of Scots, and his royal master, were ratified by the parliament of that kingdom; and the next year he was joined with Henry de Percy, in the wardenship of the marches of Northumberland, Cumberland, and Westmoreland. He had, subsequently other high and confidential employments, and was constantly engaged in the wars of Scotland and France. His lordship *m*. Alice, dau. of Sir Hugh

de Audley, and by her (who *m*. 2ndly, Ralph, Lord Greystock, and *d*. 1374,) had issue,

JOHN (Sir), his successor.

William (Sir), a distinguished soldier, gentleman of the bed-chamber to RICHARD II.

Thomas, *m*. Margaret, dau. of William Babington, and had a dau. and heir,

Jane, *m*. 1st, to Thomas Thurland ; and 2ndly, to Sir Gervase Clifton, Knt.

Robert (Sir), of Eldon, eminent in arms, from whom derive their descent the NEVILES, *of Grove, Notts.*, Baronets, the NEVILES, *of Wellingore, co. Lincoln*, the NEVILES, *of Thorney, Notts.*, the NEVILES, *of Badsworth*, and *Skelbrook Park, co. York,* &c.

Alexander, archbishop of York, and lord high chancellor, *d*. in 1391.

Ralph (Sir), of Candall.

Euphemia, *m*. 1st, Reginald de Lucy ; 2ndly, Lord Clifford.

Catherine, *m*. to Lord Dacre, of Gillesland.

Margaret, *m*. 1st, to William, 4th Lord Ros, of Hamlake, and 2ndly, to Henry Percy, Earl of Northumberland.

Isabel, *m*. to Hugh FitzHugh.

Eleanor, *m*. to Geoffrey Le Scrope.

He *d*. in 1367, and was buried in the church of Durham, on the south side thereof, being the first layman that had sepulture there, which favour he obtained from the prior and convent, for a vestment of red velvet, richly embroidered with gold silk, great pearls, and images of saints, standing in tabernacles, by him given to St. Cuthbert. His body being brought in a chariot drawn by seven horses to the boundary of the churchyard, and thence conveyed upon the shoulders of knights into the middle of the church, where the abbot of St. Mary's in York (by reason of the bishop's absence and impotency of the dean), performed the office of the dead, and celebrated the morrow mass, at which were offered eight horses, viz., four for the war, with four men armed, and all their harness and habiliments: and four others for peace ; as also three cloths of gold, of blue colour, interwoven with flowers. Four of those horses were redeemed, after the funeral, by Sir JOHN, his son and heir, for 100 marks. His lordship was *s*. by his eldest son,

SIR JOHN DE NEVILL, 3rd baron, summoned to parliament as LORD NEVILL, *of Raby*, from 24 February, 1368, to 28 July, 1388. This nobleman was carried by his father to witness the battle of Durham, being then scarcely five years old; and received the honour of knighthood some years afterwards when in arms before the barriers of Paris. In the 44th of the same reign he was again in the wars with France, and then constituted admiral of the king's fleet from the mouth of the Thames northwards. During the remainder of King EDWARD's reign he was constantly in active service either in France or Scotland. In the 2nd RICHARD II. he was constituted lieutenant of Aquitaine, and he was likewise seneschal of Bordeaux. It is reported of this nobleman that he was some time employed against the Turks; and that being lieutenant of Aquitaine, he reduced that province to tranquillity, and that in his service in those parts, he won, and had rendered to him, 83 walled towns, castles, and forts. His lordship was a knight of the Garter. He *m*. 1st, Maud, dau. of Henry, Lord Percy, by whom he had issue,

RALPH, his successor.

Thomas, who *m*. Joane, only dau. and heiress of William de Furnival, Lord Furnival, and was summoned to parliament in her right, as LORD FURNIVAL (*see* Furnival, Lords Furnival).

Maud, *m*. to William, Lord Scrope.

Alice, *m*. to William, Lord Deincourt.

Eleanor, *m*. to Ralph, Lord Lumley.

His lordship *m*. 2ndly, Elizabeth, dau. and heir of William, Lord Latimer, K.G., and had by her (who *m*. 2ndly, Sir Robert de Willoughby), issue,

JOHN, who, in right of his mother, was summoned to parliament as LORD LATIMER (*see* LATIMER, BARONS LATIMER, *of Danby*).

Elizabeth, *m*. to Sir Thomas Willoughby, Knt.

Margaret.

He *d*. at Newcastle, 17 October, 1388, was buried in the south side of the nave of Durham Cathedral, and was *s*. by his eldest son,

RALPH DE NEVILL, 4th baron, summoned to parliament from 6 December, 1389, to 30 November, 1396. This nobleman took a leading part in the political drama of his day, and sustained it with more than ordinary ability. In the life-time of his father (9th RICHARD II.), he was joined with Thomas Clifford, son of Lord Clifford, in the governorship of the city and castle of Carlisle, and was appointed a commissionership for the guardianship of the West Marches. In three years after this he succeeded to the title, and in two years subsequently he was one of the commissioners appointed to treat with the Kings of France and Scotland, touching a truce made by them with the King of England. In the 21st RICHARD II. he was made constable of the Tower of London, and shortly afterwards advanced

In full parliament to the dignity of EARL OF WESTMORELAND. His lordship was of the privy council to King RICHARD, and had much favour from that monarch, yet he was one of the, most active in raising HENRY, *of Lancaster*, to the throne, as HENRY IV., and was rewarded by the new king in the first year of his reign, with a grant of the county and honour of Richmond for his life, and with the great office of Earl Marshal of England. Soon after this he stoutly resisted the Earl of Northumberland in his rebellion, and forced the PERCIES, who had advanced as far as Durham, to fall back upon Prudhoe, when the battle of Shrewsbury ensued, in which the gallant Hotspur sustained so signal a defeat, and closed his impetuous career. The earl was afterwards governor of the town and castle of Carlisle, warden of the West Marshes towards Scotland, and governor of Roxborough. He was also a knight of the Garter. His lordship m. 1st, Lady Margaret Stafford, dau. of Hugh, Earl Stafford, K.G., for which marriage a dispensation was obtained from Pope URBAN V., the earl and his bride being within the third and fourth degrees of consanguinity: by this lady he had issue,

> JOHN, Lord Nevill, who, in the 12th HENRY IV., was made governor of Roxburgh Castle for ten years, and the next year constituted warden of the West Marches towards Scotland. His lordship m. Lady Elizabeth Holland, dau. of Thomas, Earl of Kent, and sister and co-heir of Edmund, Earl of Kent, by whom (dying in 1423, his father still living) he left issue,
>> RALPH, who s. as 2nd Earl of Westmoreland.
>> John, slain at Towton, in 1461, m. Lady Anne Holland, dau. of John, Duke of Exeter, and widow of his nephew, John, Lord Nevill, and left a son,
>>> RALPH, who s. as 3rd Earl of Westmoreland.
>> Thomas.
>
> Ralph, who m. Margery, dau. and co-heir of Lord Ferrers, of Wemme, and left a son,
>> John of Oversley who m. Elizabeth, dau. and heir of Robert Newmarch, and left an only dau. and heir, Joane, wife of Sir William Gascoigne.
> Maud, m. to Peter. Lord Mauley.
> Phillippa, m. to Thomas, Lord Dacre.
> Alice. m. 1st, to Sir Thomas Grey, Knt., of Heton, and 2ndly, to Sir Gilbert Lancaster, Knt.
> Margaret, m. to Richard, Lord Scrope of Bolton.
> Anne, m. to Sir Gilbert Umfravill.
> Margery, abbess of Barking.
> Elizabeth, a nun.

The earl m. 2ndly, Joane de Beaufort, dau. of John of Gaunt, by Katherine Swynford, and widow of Robert, Lord Ferrers, of Wem, by whom he had issue,

> RICHARD, who m. Lady Alice de Montacute, only dau. and heiress of Thomas, Earl of Salisbury, and was created EARL OF SALISBURY himself (*see* NEVILL, EARL OF SALISBURY).
> William (*s* e NEVILL, LORD FAUCONBERG AND EARL OF KENT).
> George (*see* NEVILL, LORD LATIMER).
> Edward (Sir), K.G., who m. Lady Elizabeth Beauchamp, only dau. and heiress of Richard Beauchamp, Lord Bergavenny, and Earl of Worcester, and was summoned to parliament, *jure uxoris* as Baron Bergavenny; a dignity enjoyed by his lordship's lineal descendant, the present EARL OF ABERGAVENNY.
> Robert, a churchman, bishop of Durham.
> Cuthbert, }
> Henry,   } *d. s. p.*
> Thomas, }
> Catherine, m. 1st, to John Mowbray, Duke of Norfolk; 2ndly, to Sir Thomas Strangwayes; 3rdly. to John, Viscount Beaumont; 4thly, to Sir John Widvile, Knt., son of Richard, Earl Rivers.
> Eleanor, m. 1st, to Richard, Lord le Despencer, and 2ndly, to Henry Percy, Ear of Northumberland.
> Anne, m. 1st, to Humphrey, Duke of Buckingham, and 2ndly, to Walter Blount, Lord Mountjoy.
> June, a nun.
> Cicely, m. to Richard Plantagenet, Duke of York.

This great earl d. in 1425, and was s. by his grandson,

RALPH NEVILL, 5th Baron Nevill, of Raby, and 2nd Earl of Westmoreland. This nobleman, after the death of Elizabeth, his mother, had £40 per annum, allowed him by the king for his maintenance, being then in minority. His lordship m. 1st, Elizabeth, dau. of Henry, Lord Percy (Hotspur), and widow of John, Lord Clifford, by whom he had issue,

> JOHN, Lord Nevill, who m. Lady Anne Holland, dau. of John, Duke of Exeter, and d. in the life-time of his father s. p. His widow re-m. her late husband's uncle, Sir John Nevill; and 3rdly, James, Earl of Douglas, K.G.

The earl m. 2ndly, Margaret, dau. of Sir Reginald Cobham, Knt., but had no issue. His lordship d. in 1485, and was s. by his nephew,

RALPH NEVILL, 6th Baron Nevill, of Raby, and 3rd Earl of Westmoreland. This nobleman m. Margaret, dau. of Roger Booth, of Sawley, by Catherine, his wife, dau. of Ralph Hutton, of Mollington, and had an only son,

RALPH. Lord Nevill, who m. Editha, or Elizabeth, dau. of Sir William Sandys, and dying in the life-time of his father, left a son and dau., viz.,

> RALPH, who s. as 4th earl.
> Anne. m. to Sir William Conyers, Knt., of Hornby.

The earl is said to have died of grief for the loss of his son at Hornby Castle, in 1523, and was s. by his grandson,

RALPH NEVILL, 7th Baron Nevill, of Raby, and 4th Earl of Westmoreland. This nobleman was made a knight of the Garter by King HENRY VIII., and was one of those who signed the celebrated letter to Pope CLEMENT regarding the divorce of Queen Katherine. His lordship m. Lady Catherine Stafford, dau. of Edward, Duke of Buckingham, and had issue,

> I. HENRY. Lord Nevill, his successor.
> II. Thomas (Sir).   III. Edward.
> IV. Christopher, attainted 1569.
> V. George.   VI. Ralph.   VII. Cuthbert.
> I. Eleanor.
> II. Dorothy, m. to John Vere, Earl of Oxford.
> III. Mary, m. to Sir Thomas Danby, Knt.
> IV. Joane.
> V. Margaret, m. to Henry Manners, 2nd Earl of Rutland.
> VI. Elizabeth, m. to Thomas, Lord Dacre, of Gillesland.
> VII. Eleanor, m. to Sir Bryan Stapleton, Knt.
> VIII. Anne. m. to Sir Fulke Greville, Knt., of Beauchamps Court, co. Warwick.   IX. Ursula.

The earl d. in 1549, and was s. by his eldest son,

HENRY NEVILL, 8th Baron Nevill, of Raby, and 5th Earl of Westmoreland, who m. 1st, Lady Anne Manners, dau. of Thomas, Earl of Rutland, and had issue,

> CHARLES, Lord Nevill.
> Eleanor, m. to Sir William Pelham, Knt.
> Katherine, m. to Sir John Constable, Knt., of Kirby Knowle, co. York.
> Adeline. d. unm.

His lordship m. 2ndly, Jane, dau. of Sir Richard Cholmondeley, Knt., and widow of Sir Henry Gascoigne, Knt., by whom he had two daus., Margaret and Elizabeth. The earl, who was a knight of the Garter, d. in 1563, and was s. by his son,

CHARLES NEVILL, 9th Baron Nevill, of Raby, and 6th Earl of Westmoreland. This nobleman, joining in the insurrection of Henry Percy, Earl of Northumberland, in the 13th ELIZABETH, was attainted, and preserved his life only by first flying into Scotland, "where he found concealment and protection for a long time at Fernyhurst Castle, in Roxburghshire. Eventually he succeeded in effecting his escape to Flanders, but his vast inheritance was confiscated, and he suffered the extremity of poverty. Brancepeth, the stronghold of the Nevills in war, and Raby, their festive hall in peace, had passed into stranger hands, and nothing remained for the exiled lord. He was living in the Low Countries in 1572, on a miserable pittance allowed him by the bounty of the King of Spain."[*] His lordship m. Jane, dau. of Henry Howard, Earl of Surrey, and sister of Thomas, Duke of Norfolk, by whom he had issue,

> KATHERINE, m. to Sir Thomas Grey, of Chillingham, and d. s. p.
> Eleanor, d. unm.
> Margaret, m. to Sir Nicholas Pudsey.
> Anne, m. David, brother of Sir William Ingleby, Knt., of Ripley, and had three daus., co-heirs, viz., Mary, m. to Sir Peter Middleton, of Stockeld; Frances, m. to Sir Robert Hodshon; and Ursula, m. to Robert Widdrington, Esq.

The earl d. in 1584; under his attainder the old Barony of Nevill, of Raby, and the Earldom of Westmoreland became both FORFEITED.

Arms—Gu., a saltier, arg.

NOTE.—In the reign of JAMES I., the Earldom of Westmoreland was claimed by Edward Nevill, and the case appears thus :—

In the time of RICHARD II., Ralph, Lord Nevill, of Raby, was created Earl of Westmoreland, to him and the heirs male of his body; and had issue by his 1st wife a son, Ralph, whose issue male. during several successions, enjoyed the title, and to him Charles, last Earl of Westmoreland, was heir male. That Ralph, the 1st earl. by his 2nd wife, had issue, George Neville, Lord Latimer. of whom the then claimant, Edward Neville, was the lineal descendant, and heir male. And that Charles, then late Earl of Westmoreland, was attainted for high treason. It was, however, adjudged that Edward Neville should not succeed to the earldom, though heir male of the first degree. The authority for which decision was grounded on the statute of 26th HENRY VIII., cap. 13, whereby, in cases of high treason, it is enacted, that the offender shall forfeit all such lands, tenements. and *hereditaments*, wherein he shall have *any estate of inheritance*.—BANKS

_____

* BURKE's *Vicissitudes of Families*.

NEVILL—EARLS OF SALISBURY, EARL OF WARWICK, BARON MONTACUTE, BARON MONTHERMER.

Earldom of Salisbury, by Letters Patent, dated 4 May, 1442.
Earldom of Warwick, by Letters Patent, dated 4 May, 1442.
Barony of Montacute, by Writ of Summons, dated 8 June, 1294.
Barony of Monthermer, by Writ of Summons, dated 4 March, 1309.

Lineage.

RICHARD NEVILL, K.G., eldest son of Ralph Nevill, 1st Earl of Westmoreland, by his 2nd wife, Joane de Beaufort, dau. of John of Gaunt, and widow of Robert, Lord Ferrers, of Wem, m. the Lady Alice Montacute, dau. and heir of Thomas, 4th Earl of Salisbury (see Montacute, Earl of Salisbury), and had that earldom revived in his person, by letters patent, dated 4 May, 1442, with remainder to the said Alice, and with £20 annual rent out of the issues of the co. of Wilts. Her ladyship inherited the old Baronies of MONTACUTE and MONTHERMER, which had been so long in her family. This nobleman obtained from King HENRY VI. numerous substantial grants, and some of the highest and most important trusts, amongst others he was appointed warden of the marches towards Scotland, and governor of Carlisle, and had large territorial gifts from the crown, with a grant of £9,083 6s. 8d. per annum, out of the customs for thirty years, yet he was one of the earliest to espouse the cause of the house of York, and one of the most determined in maintaining it. His lordship fought and won, in conjunction with the Duke of York, the first pitched battle, that of St. Albans, between the contending Roses; and he followed up his success by defeating the Lord Audley at Blore Heath in 1458, and again in 1460, at Northampton, when he was constituted by the Yorkists Lord Great Chamberlain of England. The fortune of war changing, however, in the very next rencounter, the battle of Wakefield, the Duke of York fell, the Yorkists were routed, Salisbury's son, Sir Thomas Nevill, slain, and the earl himself made prisoner, when his head was immediately cut off, and fixed upon a pole over one of the gates of the city of York. His lordship had issue by the heiress of the Montacutes (who d. 1463),

RICHARD, Earl of Warwick, his successor.
Thomas (Sir), m. Maud, widow of Lord Willoughby, and was slain at Wakefield, d. s. p.
John (Sir), created MARQUESS OF MONTAGU (see that dignity).
George, in holy orders, became Archbishop of York, and Chancellor of England.
Ralph, } d. young.
Robert, }
Joane, m. to William Fitz-Alan, Earl of Arundel.
Cicely, m. 1st, to Henry Beauchamp, Duke of Warwick, and 2ndly, to John Tiptoft, Earl of Worcester.
Alice, m. to Henry. Lord Fitz-Hugh.
Eleanor. m. to Thomas Stanley, 1st Earl of Warwick.
Katherine, m. to William, Lord Bonville.
Margaret, m. 1st, to John de Vere, Earl of Oxford; and 2ndly, to William, Lord Hastings.

The decapitation of the earl (who was a knight of the Garter) occurred in December, 1460, when his eldest son,

RICHARD NEVILL, K.G., the stout Earl of Warwick, became 2nd Earl of Salisbury, and he inherited from his mother the Baronies of Montacute and Monthermer His lordship m. Lady Anne Beauchamp, dau. of Richard, 5th Earl of Warwick, and heiress of the Beauchamps, on the decease, in 1449, of her young niece, Anne, Countess of Warwick, dau. and heiress of Henry, Duke of Warwick, and had a confirmation of the EARLDOM OF WARWICK, with all its pre-eminences to himself and his wife, the said Lady Anne Beauchamp, by letters patent, dated 23 July, in the same year. This nobleman so well known in English history as the king maker, "the greatest and last of the old Norman chivalry—kinglier in pride, in state, in possessions, and in renown than the King himself," espoused the fortunes of the house of York at the very commencement of the contest between the Roses, and was made captain-general of Calais after the first battle of St. Albans. He subsequently commanded the van of the Yorkists at Northampton, where Margaret of Anjou sustained so signal a defeat. He shared, however, in the reverses of his party in the ensuing battles of Wakefield and St. Albans, but out-generalled the heroic Margaret, in reaching London, with the young Lord of March, son of the Duke of York, before her victorious army. Here he caused his protegé to be proclaimed as EDWARD IV., and following the Queen and Lancastrians into the north, fixed the sceptre in the hand of the new

monarch by the great victory of Towton Field. After which he was constituted general warden of the east marches towards Scotland, constable of Dover Castle, lord great chamberlain of England for life, and lord high steward. He likewise obtained immense grants from the crown, so that his revenues are said to have amounted, independently of his own heritable estates, to the annual income of four score thousand crowns! It is not possible, however, in a work of this description, to enter into anything like a detail of the deeds of this, probably most potent, noble in the whole range of English story. We must, therefore, be content in briefly stating, that his lordship, becoming in a few years discontented with the order of things which he had thus established, projected the restoration of the Lancastrian monarch, HENRY VI., and having embodied an army under the sanction of his former foe, Margaret of Anjou, landed in the west of England from Normandy, proclaimed King HENRY VI., forced King EDWARD to fly the kingdom, marched upon London, and releasing the restored monarch from his captivity in the Tower, re-established him upon the throne; when he was himself constituted lord high admiral of England. This revolution was, however, but of brief endurance, for within one short year King EDWARD reappeared upon the scene of action, and soon found himself at the head of a sufficient force to contend for, and to recover his diadem. The battle was fought on Easter-day, 1471, at Barnet Field, when, notwithstanding the personal valour and great martial prowess of the Earl of Warwick and his brother, the Marquess of Montagu, victory declared for the Yorkists, but his lordship survived not the defeat—he fell in the brunt of the conflict, with a numerous train of eminent associates. The earl's remains, with those of his brother, the Marquess of Montagu, were conveyed to London, and there exposed to public view in the cathedral of St. Paul, whence they were transferred to Bitham, in Berkshire, and interred in the tomb of the Montacutes. Comines reports, that the earl was so popular at Calais, of which he was governor, that everybody wore his badge, no man esteeming himself gallant whose head was not adorned with his ragged staff; nor no door frequented that had not his white cross painted thereon. Moreover, he saith, that this earl never used to fight on foot; but his manner was, when he had led his men to the charge, then to take horse. And if the victory fell on his side, to fight among his soldiers, otherwise to depart in time. But in this last battle he was constrained by his brother, the Marquess of Montagu, to alight and to send away his horse. Of his extraordinary hospitality, it is recorded that, at his house in London, six oxen were usually eaten at breakfast, and every tavern full of his meat; "for, who that had any acquaintance in his family, should have as much sodden and roast as he might carry upon a long dagger." As admiral to King HENRY VI., his lordship was styled Great Captain of the Sea, and through the favour of the same monarch, he had a grant of precedency above all the earls of England, and to augment his grandeur, had a peculiar office at arms, for his services in martial employments, called Warwick Herald. After his lordship's death, his countess (such the mutability of human affairs), the great heiress of the Beauchamps, endured the deepest distress, be ng constrained to take sanctuary in the abbey of Beaulieu, in Hampshire, where she continued a long time in a very mean condition; thence removing privately into the north, she there too abode in most humble circumstances. all her vast inheritance being, by authority of parliament, taken from her and settled upon ISABEL and ANNE, her two daus. and heirs, as if she herself had been naturally dead. But upon the death of these ladies, without surviving issue, her inheritance was restored, 3rd HENRY VII., with power to alienate the same or any part thereof. This appears, however, to have been merely granted, in order that she might transfer it to the king; for soon after, by special deed, and a fine thereupon, she passed the Warwick estates, of no less than 114 lordships, together with the Isles of Jersey, &c., to King HENRY VII., and his issue male, with remainder to herself and her heirs for ever. When she died is not exactly known, but she was living in the 5th HENRY VII. By this lady the Earl of Warwick left two daus.,

I. ISABEL. b. 5 September, 1451, m. to George Plantagenet, Duke of Clarence, K.G., brother of King EDWARD IV., and d. 1476, having had issue.

1 EDWARD, EARL OF WARWICK and SALISBURY, beheaded 1499.

1 Margaret, restored as Countess of Salisbury, 5th HENRY VIII., beheaded, 27 May, 1541. She m. Sir Richard Pole, K.G., and had a son,

HENRY POLE, who was summoned into his mother's Barony of Montacute. He m. Jane, dau. of George, Lord Abergavenny, and had two daus., viz.,

1 Katherine, who m. Francis, Earl of Huntingdon, K.G., and d. 23 September, 1576, having had two sons,

Henry Earl of Huntingdon, K.G., *d. s. p.*

George, Earl of Huntingdon, who *d.* 1604, and was father of

Francis, Lord Hastings, who had a son, Henry, Earl of Huntingdon, who *d.* 1643, leaving a son,

Ferdinand, Earl of Huntingdon, who *d.* 1665, and was father of

Theophilus, Earl of Huntingdon, who had two sons,

George, Earl of Huntingdon, *d. s. p.*, 1705.

Theophilus, Earl of Huntingdon, father of

Elizabeth, Lady Hastings, who *m.* John, Earl of Moira, in Ireland, and was great grandmother of HENRY, MARQUESS OF HASTINGS.

2 Winifred, *m.* 1st, Sir Thomas Hastings, who *d. s. p.*; and 2ndly, Sir Thomas Barrington, who *d.* 1581. She *d.* 1601, leaving a son,

SIR FRANCIS BARRINGTON, Bart., who *m.* Joan, dau. of Sir Henry Cromwell, and was father of

SIR THOMAS BARRINGTON, Bart., who *m.* Frances, dau. and co-heir of John Gobert, Esq., and was father of

SIR JOHN BARRINGTON, Bart., whose son,

THOMAS BARRINGTON, *m.* Anne. dau. and co-heir of Robert Rich, Earl of Warwick. He *d. v p.* 1681, leaving, with other issue, a dau.,

ANNE, who *m.* Charles Shales, and *d.* 1729, having had issue,

Richard, *d. s. p.*   John, *d. s. p.*

Anne, *m.* Charles Lowndes, Esq , of Chesham, and *d.* 1759, leaving a son,

William Lowndes, Esq., who *m.* Lydia-Mary, dau. of Robert Osborne, Esq., and had a son,

William Lowndes. who *m.* 1st, Elizabeth, dau. of Robert James, Esq.; and 2ndly, in 1803, Harriet - Wilson, dau. of John Kingston, Esq., and by her had a son and heir,

WILLIAM LOWNDES, of Chesham, co. Bucks, Esq., one of the co-heirs of the Baronies of Monthermer and Montacute.

Essex, *m.* Richard Lowndes, Esq., of Winslow, and had a son,

William Lowndes, of Whaddon, who took the name of Selby, *m.* Mary, dau. of Thomas Goosetrey, Esq., and had a son,

WILLIAM SELBY LOWNDES, Esq , *m.* 1st, Maria, dau. of Sir Thomas Sheppard, Bart., and had a dau., Maria-Selby Lowndes, *d. unm.*, January, 1856; and 2ndly, Anne-Eleonora-Isabella, dau. of the Rev. Graham Hanmer, and had a son and heir,

WILLIAM SELBY LOWNDES, Esq., of Whaddon, one of the co-heirs of the Baronies of Monthermer and Montacute.

II. ANNE, *m.* 1st, to Edward, Prince of Wales, son of King HENRY VI.; and 2ndly, to Richard, Duke of Gloucester, afterwards RICHARD III. By RICHARD she had a son,

EDWARD PLANTAGENET, who was created by his uncle, King EDWARD IV., EARL OF SALISBURY, in the 1st year of his reign, and afterwards Earl of Chester, and PRINCE OF WALES. He *d.* the next year, 1484, when all his honours became EXTINCT.

An attainder immediately followed the death of the great Earl of Warwick, and the Earldoms of Warwick and Salisbury became FORFEITED.

Arms—Gu., a saltier, arg.

NEVILL—BARON NEVILL, OF MONTAGU, EARL OF NORTHUMBERLAND, MARQUESS OF MONTAGU.

Barony, by Writ of Summons, dated 30 July, 1460.
Earldom, by Letters Patent, dated 27 May, 1467.
Marquisate, by Letters Patent, dated 25 May, 1470.

Lineage.

SIR JOHN NEVILL. 3rd son of Richard Nevill, Earl of Salisbury, by the Lady Alice Montacute, dau. and heir of Thomas Montacute, Earl of Salisbury, was summoned to parliament as BARON NEVILL, *of Montague* by King HENRY VI., in 1460, and afterwards espousing, with his father and elder brother,

Richard, the celebrated Earl of Warwick, the interests of the house of York, he had similar summons upon the accession of King EDWARD IV., which latter monarch constituted him general warden of the east marches towards Scotland, and the ensuing year (27 May, 1467) advanced him to the dignity of EARL OF NORTHUMBERLAND (in consequence of the flight of Henry Percy, Earl of Northumberland, into Scotland, with HENRY VI.) His lordship in this year defeated the Lancastrians under the Duke of Somerset, at Hexham; and he was subsequently rewarded with extensive grants from the forfeited lands in the cos. of Norfolk, Leicester, Nottingham, Suffolk, and York. In the 10th EDWARD IV., the earl was induced to resign the peerage of Northumberland, in order that *the Percy* might be restored; and in lieu thereof, he was created MARQUESS OF MONTAGU. Soon after this, however, his lordship joined his brother, the Earl of Warwick, in the restoration of King HENRY VI., and eventually shared the fate of that eminent nobleman, at the battle of Barnet, 14 April, 1471; in that conflict both brothers fell, and both were afterwards attainted. The marquess *m.* Isabel, dau. and heir of Sir Edmund Ingoldsthorp, Knt., and by her (who *m.* 2ndly, Sir William Norris), had issue,

GEORGE, who was created DUKE OF BEDFORD, 5 January, 1469, by King EDWARD IV., with the intention of bestowing upon him, in marriage, his eldest dau., the Lady Elizabeth Plantagenet. After the attainder of his father, and the consequent confiscation of his heritable estates, having no means of sustaining the ducal dignity, his grace was degraded from all his dignities and honours by parliament, in 1477. He *d.* in 1483, *s. p.*, and was interred at Sheriff Hutton.

John, *d.* and was buried at Salston, in Cambridgeshire.

Anne, *m.* to Sir William Stonor. Knt., of Stonor, Oxfordshire.

Elizabeth, *m.* 1st, Thomas, Lord Scrope, of Upsall; and 2ndly Sir Henry Wentworth.

Margaret, *m.* 1st, Sir John Mortimer; and 2ndly, Charles Brandon, Duke of Suffolk, K.G.

Lucy, *m.* 1st, to Sir Thomas Fitz-William, of Aldwarke. Knt., and 2ndly, to Sir Anthony Browne, Knt., standard-bearer of England. Her ladyship's grandson,

SIR ANTHONY BROWNE, Knt., was created Viscount Montagu.

Isabel, *m.* to Sir William Huddleston, Knt., of Salston, co. Cambridge.

Under the attainder of this nobleman, the Barony of Nevill, of Montagu, and the Marquessate of Montagu, became FORFEITED.

Arms—Gu. a saltier, arg., a label gobonny arg. and az., crescent for difference.

NEVILL—DUKE OF BEDFORD.

(See Nevill, MARQUESS OF MONTAGU.)

NEVILL, AND FAUCONBERG — BARONS FAUCONBERG, EARL OF KENT.

Barony, by Writ of Summons, dated 23 July, 1295.
Earldom, by Letters Patent, dated 1462.

Lineage.

Of this ancient family, the first upon record is

PETER DE FALKEBERGE, son of Agnes de Arches, foundress of the house of nuns, Nunkelling, in Holderness, co. York. This Peter had three sons,

William.

Walter, *m.* Agnes, one of the three daus. and co-heirs of Simon Fitz-Simon, by Isabel, his wife, dau. and heir of Thomas de Cukeney, founder of Welbeck Abbey, in Nottinghamshire.

Stephen, *m.* Petronill, another of the daus. and co-heirs of Simon Fitz-Simon.

To Walter de Falkeberge (the 2nd son), succeeded

PETER DE FAUCONBERO, who was *s.* by his son,

WALTER DE FAUCONBERG, of Ryse, in Holderness, who, in the 8th HENRY III., was constituted governor of Plympton Castle, co. Devon. He *m.* Agnes. one of the sisters and co heirs of Peter de Bruss of Skelton Castle, and by her acquired that castle, with other extensive lands, in all of which he obtained charter for free warren, in the 8th En-

WARD I. In the 22nd of the same reign, he had summons to attend the king, amongst divers other persons of note, to advise concerning the important affairs of the realm, and soon after had a military summons to be at Portsmouth, in order to sail with the king into France. He was summoned to parliament as a Baron from 23 June, 1295, to 24 July, 1301, and d. in 1303 : his eldest son,

WALTER DE FAUCONBERG, 2nd baron, does not appear from the existing enrolments to have been ever summoned to parliament. His lordship m. Isabel, dau. of Robert, 1st Lord Ros, of Hamlake, by whom he had a numerous family. He was s. by his eldest surviving son,

SIR WALTER DE FAUCONBERG, 3rd baron, summoned to parliament from 12 November, 1303, to 25 August, 1318. This nobleman distinguished himself in the Scottish wars. His lordship m. Anastasia, dau. of Ralph de Nevil, and dying in 1318, was s. by his son,

JOHN DE FAUCONBERG, 4th baron, summoned to parliament from 22 January, 1336, to 10 March, 1349. This nobleman was in the wars of Scotland, 7th EDWARD III., and he was afterwards in the expedition made into Flanders. In the 15th of the same reign, he was constituted sheriff of Yorkshire, and governor of the castle of York; and the next year he was made governor of Berwick-upon-Tweed. His lordship d. in 1349, and was s. by his son,

SIR WALTER DE FAUCONBERG, 5th baron, summoned to parliament, from 25 November, 1359, to 14 August, 1362. This nobleman being a banneret, had an assignation, in the 24th EDWARD III., of £239 9d., to be paid out of the exchequer, for wages due to him, for his services and expenses in the wars beyond sea. In two years afterwards, upon an apprehended invasion by the French, his lordship was appointed, with the Lord Mowbray, and other eminent persons, to guard the sea coast of Yorkshire; and he was subsequently again in the wars of France. He m. 1st, Maud, dau. of John, Lord Pateshull, and sister and co heir of William de Pateshull, and had issue,

I. THOMAS, his heir.
II. Roger.   III. Walter.
IV. Roger (Sir), of Holme, in Spaldingmore, who m. Margaret Darcy, heir of Flixburgh, dau. of Robert, son of Sir John Darcy, who was son of Richard Darcy, Lord of Flixburgh, and by her had a son,
   Sir Walter Fauconberg, of Whittor, co. Lincoln, who by Maud, his wife, had issue,
     1 Roger, d. s. p.
     1 Margaret, m. to Sir John Constable, of Holme.
     2 Isabel. m. to Sir Edmund Perchay, of Ryton.
     3 Constance, d. unm.

His lordship m. 2ndly, Isabel, sister of John Bigot. He d. in 1362, and was s. by his son,

SIR THOMAS DE FAUCONBERG, 6th baron, who does not appear to have been summoned to parliament. This nobleman was with William de Windsore, in the expedition made into Ireland, in the 43rd EDWARD III., and in the 50th of the same reign he was in the wars of France. He m. Joane, sister of Thomas Bromflete. He d. about the year 1376, leaving an only dau. and heiress,

JOAN DE FAUCONBERG, who married

SIR WILLIAM NEVILL, Knt. (youngest son of Ralph, 1st Earl of Westmoreland, by his 2nd wife, Joane de Beaufort, dau. of John of Gaunt); he was summoned to parliament, jure uxoris, as LORD FAUCONBERG, from 3 August, 1429, to 23 May, 1461. His lordship, who was a military person of great valour, distinguished himself at the siege of Orleans, in the 9th HENRY VI., and subsequently took a leading part in the wars of France. He was governor of the castle of Roxborough, in the same reign ; but being sent ambassador into Normandy to treat of peace, he was perfidiously seized upon by the French, and detained for some time a prisoner in France. In consideration of which captivity, he had an assignation, in the 30th HENRY VI., of £4,180, then in arrear, due to him for his pay, whilst he was governor of Roxborough, to be received out of the customs of the ports of Bristol, Kingston-upon-Hull, and Ipswich. After this he was again constituted, in conjunction with Sir Ralph Grey, governor of Roxborough Castle for twelve years, and they were to receive jointly, in times of truce, £1000 per annum, and in time of war, double that income. In the 35th of the same reign, he was again in the wars of France, in the retinue of his nephew, Richard, Earl of Warwick, then governor of Calais, and lieutenant of the marches there. His lordship espousing the cause of EDWARD

IV., and fighting valiantly for that prince, at the battle of Towton, was rewarded, after the accession of the new monarch, by being raised to the dignity of EARL OF KENT, constituted lord admiral of England, and made a knight of the Garter. But those honours his lordship enjoyed a few months only, as he d. some time in the same year, 1463, leaving three daus., his co-heirs, viz.,

Joane, m. to Sir Edward Bechom, Knt., called by Drummond (History of Noble British Families) Sir Edward Bethune. She d. s. p.

Elizabeth, m. to Sir Richard Strangeways, Knt., and their grand-daus. and co-heirs were, Maria, m. Robert Ros, of Ingmanthorpe, and Joan, m. 1st, John Bygod, and 2ndly, Sir W. Mauleverer.

Alice, m. Sir John Conyers, K.G., and her eldest son,
   SIR WILLIAM CONYERS was summoned to parliament by King HENRY VIII., as LORD CONYERS. His lordship m. Lady Anne Neville, dau. of Ralph, Earl of Westmoreland, and dying in 1524, left issue,
     CHRISTOPHER, his successor.
     Katherine, m. to Sir Francis Bigod, of Settrington.
     Margaret, m. to Richard, son of Sir Roger Cholmeley, of Rockley. Knt.
   His lordship was s. by his son,
   SIR CHRISTOPHER CONYERS, 2nd baron, who m. Anne, dau. of William, Lord Dacre, of Gillesland, and had issue,
     JOHN his successor.
     Leonard.
     Elizabeth, m. to George Playce, Esq., of Halnaby.
     Jane, m to Sir Marmaduke Constable, Knt.
   His lordship was s. by his elder son,
   JOHN CONYERS, 3rd baron. This nobleman m. Maud, dau. of Henry Clifford, 1st Earl of Cumberland, and d. in 1557, leaving three daus., his heirs, viz.,
     Anne, m. to Anthony Kempe, Esq., of Slindon.
     Elizabeth, m. to Thomas D'Arcy (see D'Arcy, Barons Conyers).
     Catherine, m. to John, son and heir of John Atherton, Esq., of Atherton, in Lancashire.
   Of these daus., the descendants of Elizabeth, Lady D'Arcy alone remain, and one of those, Sackville-George Lane-Fox, s. to the BARONY OF CONYERS, on the death, in 1859, of his maternal uncle, the late Duke of Leeds, in whom that barony had vested (see BURKE'S Extant Peerage).

Upon the decease of the Earl of Kent, the Earldom of Kent became EXTINCT, while the Barony of Fauconberg fell into ABEYANCE between his three daus., as it still continues with their representatives.

Arms—Gu., a saltier, arg., a mullet, sa., for difference.

NOTE.—By an old Inquisition, it was found that Henry de Fauconberge held the manor of Cukeney, in Nottinghamshire, by serjeanty, for shoeing the king's horses when the Sovereign went to Mansfield, a place which our kings were wont frequently to retire to, for the purpose of enjoying the chase.

NEVILL—BARON LATIMER.

(See LATIMER, BARONS LATIMER, of Danby.)

NEVILL—BARONS LATIMER.

By Writ of Summons, dated 25 February, 1432.

Lineage.

Upon the decease, without issue, of John Nevill, Lord Latimer, of Danby, several of his lordship's estates passed to his elder brother of the half-blood,

RALPH NEVILL, 1st Earl of Westmoreland, who settled those lands by feoffment on Sir George Nevill, one of his sons by his 2nd wife, Joane, dau. of John of Gaunt, which

SIR GEORGE NEVILL was, thereupon, the next ensuing year, 25 February, 1432, summoned to parliament as BARON LATIMER, and from that date until 7 September, 1469. In the 13th HENRY VI. this nobleman was one of the chief commanders of the king's forces then raised in the north, for the defence of those parts against the Scots. And the same year his lordship came to an agreement with Maud, Countess of Cambridge, (widow of his half-uncle, John, Lord Latimer, of Danby), to this effect, viz. :—That if they should, by advice of their counsel, grant unto Sir John Willoughby, Knt. (for the pur-

* NICHOLAS doubts whether this writ could be deemed a regular summons to parliament, as none of the higher temporal nobility, nor any of the spiritual peers were included in the summons, nor was there any day fixed for the meeting.

397

pose of avoiding litigation), any of those lands which formerly belonged to the said John, Lord Latimer, that she should give of the said grants, two parts, and he Lord Latimer, one. And in case of any suit commenced by Sir John Willoughby against them (by reason of his being the next heir of blood of the said John, Lord Latimer, of Danby), for any of those lands, she to pay two-third parts, and he the other part of the costs incurred thereby. Lord Latimer m. Lady Elizabeth Beauchamp, 3rd dau. by his 1st wife of Richard, Earl of Warwick, by whom he had issue,

    ι. HENRY (Sir), who m. Joanna, dau. of John Bourchier, Lord Berners, and falling at the battle of Edgcot, near Banbury, in the 9th EDWARD IV., his father still living, left two sons and a dau., viz.,

        1 RICHARD (Sir), successor to his grandfather.
        2 Thomas of Mathon, co. Worcester, and Shenstone. co. Stafford.
        1 Joane, m. to Sir James Ratclyffe.

    ιι. Thomas, of Shenstone, co. Stafford.
    ι. Jane, m. to Oliver Dudley.
    ιι. Catherine.

Lord Latimer, it appears, in the latter years of his life became an idiot, and King EDWARD IV., in consequence, committed all his lands and lordships to the care of his nephew, Richard Nevill, Earl of Warwick. He d. 30 December, 1469, and was s. by his grandson,

SIR RICHARD NEVILL, 2nd baron, summoned to parliament from 12 August, 1492, to 3 November, 1529. This nobleman was one of the commanders (1st HENRY VII.) of the king's army at the battle of Stoke, wherein John de la Pole, Earl of Lincoln, and his adherents, sustained so signal a defeat. In the 6th HENRY VII. he had special livery of all the lands which descended to him, by the death of his grandfather; and the next year he was again a commander in the English army, under the Earl of Surrey, which marched to the relief of Norham Castle, then invested by the Scots; but the besiegers raised the siege and fled at the approach of the English forces. In the 5th HENRY VIII., Lord Latimer acquired high reputation at the battle of Flodden Field, where the Scottish army was totally routed, and King JAMES IV. of Scotland, slain. In the 28th of the same reign he was one of the peers who subscribed the letter to Pope CLEMENT VII., touching the king's divorce from Queen Katherine. His lordship m. Anne, dau. of Sir Humphrey Stafford, of Grafton, and had issue,

JOHN, his successor.
William, of Penwyn, m. Elizabeth, dau. of Sir Giles Greville, Knt., and his issue became extinct in 1631.
Thomas, of Pigott's Hardley, co. Essex, m. Mary, dau. and co-heir of Sir Thomas Teye, and had a son,
    Thomas.
Marmaduke, of Marks Teye. m. Elizabeth, dau. and co-heir of Sir Thomas Teye, and had issue,
    Christopher, who d. young.
    Alianore, who m. Thomas Teye, Esq , of Layer-de-la-Hay.
George.   Christopher.
Margaret. m. to Edward, son and heir of Robert, Lord Broke.
Dorothy, m. to Sir John Dawney, Knt.
Elizabeth, m. to Sir Christopher Danby.
Catherine.
Susanna, m. to Richard Norton, Esq., high sheriff of Yorkshire 13th ELIZABETH. From a younger son of this marriage, Edmund Norton, the Lords Grantley are said to derive.
Joane.

Lord Latimer* d. in 1530, and was s. by his eldest son,
SIR JOHN NEVILL, 3rd baron, summoned to parliament from 5 January, 1534, to 16 January, 1542. This nobleman, upon the insurrection in Yorkshire, temp. HENRY VIII., called the Pilgrimage of Grace, was one of those deputed by the rebels (the others were the Lords Scrope, Lumley, and Darcy,) to treat with the Duke of Norfolk, then advancing at the head of an

---

* Memorable, also, is this Richard, Lord Latimer, for the dispute he had with Robert, Lord Broke, touching the Barony of Latimer; to which, as next heir in blood to John, Lord Latimer, of Danby, who d. s. p., the 9th HENRY VI., he claimed a right. But to end the contention, the Lord Broke was informed by an herald, that Sir George Nevill, grandfather to Richard, was created Lord Latimer by a new title, which therefore lineally descended to Richard, by Henry, son and heir of the said George: and that the Lord Broke had made a wrong claim: who should have claimed his style from William Latimer, first created Lord Latimer, of Danby (the head manor of his barony), temp. EDWARD I., on this, the Lord Broke, perceiving his error, and having a title of his own, was contented to conclude a match between their children, and Richard suffered a recovery on certain manors and lordships demanded by the Lord Broke; with which adjustment both parties were well satisfied.—BANKS.

---

army against them. His lordship m. 1st, Lady Dorothy de Vere, dau. and co-heir of John, Earl of Oxford, and had issue,
JOHN, his successor.
Margaret.

He m. 2ndly, Catherine, dau. of Sir Thomas Parr, of Kendall, Knt., by whom (who became, after his decease, the last wife of King HENRY VIII.) he had no issue. His lordship d. in 1542, and was s. by his son,
SIR JOHN NEVILL, 4th baron, summoned to parliament from 14 June, 1543, to 6 January, 1581. His lordship m. Lucy, dau. of Henry, Earl of Worcester, and had issue,

ι. Katherine, m. to Henry Percy, 8th Earl of Northumberland, and their descendant and heir-general is the DUKE OF ATHOLE, senior co-heir of the Barony of Latimer.
ιι. Dorothy, m. to Thomas Cecil, 1st Earl of Exeter, and had issue,
    WILLIAM, 2nd Earl of Exeter, who d. 1640, and left three daus., viz.,
        Elizabeth, m. to Thomas, Earl of Berkshire. Their heir-general is WINCHCOMBE-HENRY-HOWARD HARTLEY, Esq., of Bucklebury, Berks, one of the co-heirs of the Barony of Latimer.
        Diana, m. 1st, to Thomas, Earl of Elgin, and 2ndly, to the Earl of Aylesbury, and d. s. p.
        Anne, m. to Henry Grey, Earl of Stamford, and their co-representatives, co-heirs of the Barony of Latimer, are, SIR RAINALD KNIGHTLEY, Bart., of Faw ley, co. Northampton: and TROTH, widow of Rev. Richard Jenkins, D.D., dean of Wells.
ιιι. Lucy, m. to Sir William Cornwallis, Knt. of Brome, and had two sons, who both d. s. p., with four daus., viz.,
    1 Frances, m. to Sir Edmund Withipool, and their representative Sir ROBERT BURDETT, Bart., of Foremark is one of the co-heirs of the Barony of Latimer.
    2 Elizabeth, m. 1st, Sir William Sandys; and 2ndly, Richard, Viscount Lumley, and d s. p. 1661.
    3 Cornelia, m. Sir Richard Fermor, of Somerton, and their co-representatives (co-heirs of the Barony of Latimer) are Sir CHARLES-ROBERT TEMPEST, Bart., CHARLES STANDISH, Esq., of Standish, co. Lancaster, and JOHN WRIGHT, Esq., of Kelvedon, co. Essex.
    4 Anne, m. to Archibald, Earl of Argyll, and d. 1634; their heir-general is John Rogerson, LORD ROLLO, one of the co-heirs of the Barony of Latimer.
ιν. Elizabeth, m. to Sir John Danvers, Knt., of Dantsey, and had issue,
    1 SIR CHARLES DANVERS, Knt., d. s. p. 1602.
    2 Sir Henry Danvers, Knt., created EARL OF DANBY. His lordship, who was a knight of the Garter, d. in 1643, unm., when his honours became extinct.
    3 Sir John Danvers, of Chelsea, one of the Judges of King CHARLES I., d. in 1655 His co-representatives (co-heirs to the Barony of Latimer) are GEORGE-WILLIAM VILLIERS, Esq., and MONTAGU, EARL OF ABINGDON.
    4 Elizabeth Danvers, m. Thomas Walmsley, Esq., of Dunkenhagh, co. Lancaster, and left a dau.,
        Anne, who m. 1st, William Middleton, Esq., of Stokeld, co. York, and 2ndly, Sir Edward Osborne, Bart., whose son,
            Sir Thomas Osborne, was created Viscount Latimer, Earl of Danby, and afterwards Marquess of Carmarthen, and DUKE OF LEEDS.

Lord Latimer d. in 1577, when the Barony of Latimer fell into ABEYANCE between his lordship's four daus. and co-heirs, as it still continues with their descendants and representatives.

Arms—Gu., a saltire, arg., an annulet for difference.

NEVILL—BARON FURNIVAL.

See FURNIVAL.

NEVILL—BARONS NEVILL OF ESSEX.

By Writ of Summons, dated 22 January, 1336.

Lineage.

In the 8th HENRY III., HUGH DE NEVILL was constituted principal warden of the king's forests throughout England, and chief justice of the same. This Hugh m. Joane, dau. and co-heir of Warine Fitz-Gerald, by Alice, his wife, dau. and heir of William de Courcy, and paid 100 marks for livery of the moiety of the manor of Stoke-Courcy, with the castle there, and moiety of the knight's fees thereunto belonging, which he had of her inheritance.

He found 'd the priory of Stoke-Courcy, co. Devon, and was s. by his son,

JOHN DE NEVILL, who, like his father, was chief warden of the forests. In the 26th HENRY III. this John had a military summons to attend the king into France; but in two years afterwards, being convicted of trespassing in the royal forests, he was fined 2000 marks and dismissed from the wardenship with disgrace; which so affected him, that he d. in the same year of a broken heart, at his manor house of Walperfield. He was s. by his son,

HUGH DE NEVILL, a minor at the time of his father's decease, then removed to Windsor Castle, there to be educated with other of the king's wards. For the custody of this Hugh, and benefit of his marriage, John de Courtenay paid to the crown, 31st HENRY III., 2500 marks. From this Hugh, Dugdale surmises, descended

HUGH DE NEVILL, who was father of

JOHN DE NEVILL, who in the 9th EDWARD III., upon doing his homage, had livery of his lands, and was summoned to parliament as JOHANNES DE NEVILL, of Essex, from 22 January, 1336, to 10 March, 1349. His lordship was in the wars of France and Flanders. He d. in 1358, seized of two parts of the manors of Great and Little Wakering, in Essex, for life only, the remainder to William de Bohun, Earl of Northampton; and also jointly with Alice, his wife, the manors of Wethers's-field, Parva, Halyngbury, Chigenhale-Zoin, Chigenhale-Tany, and Peltingdon; the reversion of all which belonged to the said William, Earl of Northampton.

Upon the decease of Lord Nevill without issue, the Barony of Nevill, of Essex, became EXTINCT.

NOTE—The connection, if any, between this family of Nevills, and the Nevills of Raby, does not appear.

NEVILL—BARON NEVILL.

By Writ of Summons, dated 25 February, 1342.

Lineage.

ROBERT DE NEVILL was summoned to parliament, as a Baron, 25 February, 1342, but never afterwards, nor is there anything further known of himself or his family. It is presumed that the barony became, at his decease, EXTINCT.

NEWBURGH—EARLS OF WARWICK.

Creation of WILLIAM THE CONQUEROR.

Lineage.

The first who bore the title of Earl of Warwick, after the Norman Conquest, was

HENRY DE NEWBURGH (so called from the castle of that name in Normandy), a younger son of Roger de Bellomont, Earl of Mellent. When this eminent person obtained the earldom is not exactly ascertained, but Sir William Dugdale presumes the period to be towards the close of the CONQUEROR'S reign, "for then," saith he, "King WILLIAM, having begirt Warwick with a mighty ditch, for the precinct of its walls, and erected the gates at his own charge, did promote this Henry to the earldom, and annexed thereto the royalty of the borough, which at that time belonged to the crown." But, though Henry de Newburgh was made Earl of Warwick by the first Norman sovereign, he was not invested with all the lands attached to the earldom until the ensuing reign, as we find WILLIAM RUFUS, soon after his accession to the throne, conferring upon him the whole inheritance of Turchil de Warwick, a Saxon, who, at the coming of Duke William, had the reputation of earl; and thenceforth the "bear and ragged staff," the device of Turchil's family, derived from the chivalrous Guy, Earl of Warwick, was assumed by the first of the Newburgh dynasty; and it has been continued ever since as a badge of the successive Earls of Warwick. The name of this Henry, Earl of Warwick, appears as a witness to the charter of King HENRY I., whereby that prince confirmed the laws of EDWARD THE CONFESSOR, and granted many other immunities to the clergy and laity. His lordship m. Margaret, dau. of Geffrey, Count de Moreton, and sister of Rotrode, Earl of Perch, and had issue, two daus., whose names are not mentioned, and five sons, viz.,

ROGER, his successor.
Henry.   Geffrey.
Rotrode, bishop of Eureux.
Robert, seneschal and justice of Normandy. This Robert was a great benefactor to the abbey of Bec, in which he was afterwards shorn a monk, and d. in 1123.

This Earl Henry commenced imparking Wedgenock, near his castle of Warwick, following the example of his sovereign, King HENRY, who made the first park that had ever been in England, at Woodstock. His lordship, who was so memorable for pious foundations as distinguished for military achievements, d. in 1123, and was s. by his eldest son,

ROGER DE NEWBURGH, 2nd Earl of Warwick. This nobleman in the contest between the Empress MAUD and King STEPHEN, espoused the cause of the former, but his lordship is much more known by his munificent grants to the church than his martial deeds. He m. Gundred, dau. of William, Earl of Warren, and had issue,

WILLIAM, } successive earls.
WALERAN, }
Henry, who had for his patrimony Gowerland, in Wales: he d. s. p.
Agnes, m. to Geffery de Clinton, the king's chamberlain, son of Geffery, founder of Kenilworth Castle.

The earl d. 12 June, 1153, and was s. by his eldest son,

WILLIAM DE NEWBURGH, 3rd Earl of Warwick, who in the 12th HENRY II., upon the assessment of aid for marrying the king's dau., certified the number of his knights' fees to be one hundred and five, and one-half, an enormous fortune at that period. His lordship m. 1st, Maud, elder dau. and co-heir of William, Lord Percy, and 2ndly, Margaret D'Eivill, but had no issue. This nobleman was distinguished by the splendour of his style of living, and was, like his father, a liberal benefactor to the church. He d. in the Holy Land, 15 November, 1184, and was s. by his brother,

WALERAN DE NEWBURGH, 4th Earl of Warwick. This nobleman, Dugdale says, "had much ado a great part of his time touching his inheritance; there starting up one who feigned himself to be his brother, Earl William, deceased in the Holy Land, which occasioned him no little trouble and vexation; so that it is thought by some, that the grant which he made to Hubert, archbishop of Canterbury, then chancellor of England, of the advowson of all the prebendaries belonging to the collegiate church, in Warwick, to hold during his life, was to purchase his favour in that weighty business." His lordship m. 1st, Margery, dau. of Humphrey de Bohun, Earl of Hereford, by whom he had issue,

HENRY, his successor.
Waleran, who had the manors of Gretham and Cotismore, co. Rutland, d. s. p.
Gundred, who took the veil at Pinley.

He m. 2ndly, Alice, dau. of John de Harcourt, and widow of John de Limesi, by whom he had an only dau.,

ALICE, m. to William Mauduit, feudal Baron of Hanslape, (great grandson of William Mauduit, chamberlain to King HENRY I., by Maud, dau. and heiress of Michael de Hanslape), and had issue,
    William Mauduit, Baron of Hanslape, who eventually s. to the Earldom of Warwick.
    Isabel, m. to William Beauchamp, Baron of Elmley, from whom the Beauchamps, Earls of Warwick, descended.

The earl d. in 1205, and was s. by his elder son,

HENRY DE NEWBURGH, 5th Earl of Warwick, a minor at his father's decease, committed to the guardianship of Thomas Basset, of Hedendon, who accordingly had livery of his lands, with the castle of Warwick. His lordship attained majority in the 15th King JOHN, and, although that monarch had, during his minority, taken away his inheritance of Gower, in Wales, and bestowed it upon William de Braose, his lordship, nevertheless, adhered to the royal cause in all the subsequent conflicts between the crown and the barons, in the reigns of King JOHN and his son HENRY III. His lordship m. 1st, Margery, elder dau. and co-heir of Henry D'Oyly, of Hocknorton, co. Oxford, by whom he had issue,

THOMAS, his successor.
Margery, m. 1st, to John Mareschal, and 2ndly, to John de Plessetis, both of whom, in her right, assumed the Earldom of Warwick.

The earl m. 2ndly, Philippa, one of the three daus. and heirs of his guardian, Thomas Basset, of Hedendon, but had no issue. This countess, outliving his lordship, paid 100 marks to King HENRY III., that she might not be compelled to marry again, but that she might select her own husband, provided he were a loyal subject. She afterwards m. Richard Siward, a turbulent person, but of a martial disposition his youth, who took an active part with the barons. From this boisterous soldier her ladyship was, however, eventually divorced. Henry, 5th Earl of Warwick, was *s.* at his decease in 1229, by his son,

THOMAS DE NEWBURGH, 6th Earl of Warwick. This nobleman *m.* Ela, dau. of William Longespee, Earl of Salisbury, but dying *s. p.*, 1242 the earldom and great inheritance devolved upon his sister,

The Lady MARGERY DE NEWBURGH, then wife of

JOHN MARESCHAL, who assumed the title of Earl of Warwick, but as he *d.* the following year, 1243, *s. p.*, the countess *m.*, by especial appointment of the king,

JOHN DE PLESSETIS, an eminent Norman, who came to England in the beginning of the reign of HENRY III., and achieved a high reputation in the Welsh wars. In the 28th of the same reign this John was made constable of the Tower of London, but not by the title of Earl of Warwick, nor does it appear that he acquired that designation for some time after his union with the heiress of Warwick. He eventually assumed it, however, under a clause in a fine levied in the 31st HENRY III., whereby William Mauduit, and Alice, his wife, did, as much as in them lay, confer the earldom upon him for life, so that, if he outlived the countess, his wife, he should not be forced to lay it aside. In the August ensuing the King, granting to him license to fell oaks in the forest of Dene, styles him EARL OF WARWICK, and thenceforward he bore the dignity. His lordship appears to have been one of the first favourites of King HENRY III., and to have enjoyed every honour and privilege that monarch could confer. At the commencement of the troubles between Henry and the barons the earl was appointed sheriff of the cos. of Warwick and Leicester, but he lived not to witness the issue of those conflicts, for, falling sick in the beginning of the month of February, 1263, he *d.* before its expiration. His lordship left issue by his 1st wife (*see* Plessetis, Baron Plessetis), but none by the Countess of Warwick. Lady Warwick survived her husband but a short time, when the Earldom of Warwick, and the great inheritance of the Newburghs, reverted to the son of her aunt, Lady Alice Mauduit (*refer to* issue of Waleran, 4th earl), her cousin,

WILLIAM MAUDUIT, who inherited the feudal Barony of Hanslape at the decease of his father in the year 1256, and upon succeeding the Countess of Warwick, assumed the title of Earl of Warwick, in which dignity he had summons to attend the king at Worcester, to march against the Welsh (47th HENRY III). During the civil war between King HENRY and the barons, his lordship was surprised by a division of the baronial army, under John Giffard, governor of Kenilworth, at his castle of Warwick, and being taken prisoner with his countess, Alice, dau. of Gilbert de Segrave, was detained at Kenilworth until freed by paying a ransom of 1,900 marks. The earl *d.* 1267, *s. p.* when his sister, Isabel, wife of William Beauchamp, of Elmley, called the Blind Baron, became his lordship's heir (*see* Beauchamp, Earls of Warwick), and thus terminated the Earls of the houses of Newburgh, Plessetis, and Mauduit.

Arms—Newburgh, Earls of Warwick—Lozengy, or and az., on a bordure, gu., eight plates. Mauduit, Earl of Warwick—Arg., two bars, gu.

NEWCOMEN—BARON AND VISCOUNT NEWCOMEN.

Barony, by Letters Patent, dated 29 July, 1800.
Viscounty, by Letters Patent, dated 25 January, 1803.

Lineage.

SIR ROBERT NEWCOMEN, of Kenagh, co. Longford, was knighted at Dublin Castle, by Sir Arthur Chichester, L.D., 9 June, 1605, and was created a Baronet of that kingdom, 30 December, 1623. He *m.* Catherine, 2nd dau. of Sir Thomas Molyneux, Knt., chancellor of the exchequer in Ireland, and sister of Daniel Molyneux, Ulster King of Arms, and dying 28 September, 1629, was *s.* by his eldest son,

SIR BEVERLEY NEWCOMEN,* 2nd bart., who *m.* Margaret,

---

* Sir Beverley Newcomen left an illegitimate son, the Right Hon. SIR THOMAS NEWCOMEN, of Sutton, co. Dublin, Knt., who *m.* 1st, Frances, dau. of Sir William Talbot, of Cartown, and 2ndly, Jane, dau. and heir of Edward Brabazon, Esq., and left issue.

3rd dau. of Sir William Usher, Knt., and had a son, ARTHUR, and a dau., Catherine, *m.* to Richard Parsons, Esq.. Sir Beverley, who commanded the "Swallow" man-of-war, was drowned at Passage, near Waterford, 28 April, 1637, together with his only son, whereupon the baronetcy devolved on his brother,

SIR THOMAS NEWCOMEN, 3rd baronet, who *m.* Elizabeth, dau. of Sir Charles Pleydell, Knt., but *d. s. p.*, April, 1642, when the title was inherited by his brother,

SIR ROBERT NEWCOMEN, 4th baronet, who *m.* 1st, Anna Bullen, styled "consanguinea ELIZABETHÆ Reginæ Angliæ," and 2ndly, 31 March, 1650, Katharine Verschoyle. By the former he had issue,

THOMAS, his heir.
Catherine, *m.* 1st, to Sir Alexander Stewart, Knt., and 2ndly, to Arthur, 1st Earl of Granard.
Anne, *m.* 1st, to William Tynte, Esq., of Carmoon, co Cork, and 2ndly, to William Digby, Esq., of Newtown, King's co.

Sir Robert *d.* in 1668, and was *s.* by his only son,

SIR THOMAS NEWCOMEN, 5th baronet, who was killed at the siege of Enniskillen, leaving by Sarah, his 2nd wife, dau. of Sir George St. George, Bart., of Carrickdrumrusk, co. Leitrim, six sons and one dau., viz.,

I. ROBERT (Sir), his heir, 6th baronet, M.P. for the co. of Longford, in 1731, *m.* Lady Mary Chichester, dau. of Arthur, 2nd Earl of Donegal, and was *s.* by his only son,

SIR ARTHUR NEWCOMEN, 7th baronet, M.P. for the co. of Longford, who *m.* 1st, Elizabeth, dau. of Thomas Moore, Esq., of Marlfield, co. Tipperary, and had by her, THOMAS, his heir, and John, who *d. s. p.* He *m.* 2ndly, Sarah, dau. of William Gore, Esq., and had by her two daus., Katherine, *d. unm.* 1793, and Sarah, *d. unm.* Sir Arthur *d.* 20 November, 1759, and was *s.* by his son,

SIR THOMAS NEWCOMEN, 8th baronet, of Mosstown, *b.* in 1740, M.P. for the co. of Longford, who *m.* in 1761, Margaret, dau. of John, 1st Earl of Mayo, but *d. s. p.* 27 April, 1789, when the baronetcy became EXTINCT.

II. George, killed at Limerick, *s. p*
III. Arthur, of Chester, barrister-at-law, *m.* Margaret Kendrick.
IV. Thomas, of Dove Hill, co. Tipperary. who *m.* Elizabeth, dau. of William, 1st Viscount Duncannon, and widow of Richard, Lord Kilworth, and had issue,

Ponsonby, collector of Clonmel, who *d.* in 1746, leaving issue.
William, collector of excise in the port of Cork.
Robert.
Sarah, *m.* 1st, to James Dawson, Esq., of Newforest, co. Tipperary, and 2ndly, to William Dawson, Esq.

V. Beverley (Col.), *d. unm.* 2 November, 1731.
VI. CHARLES, of Droming.
I. Katherine, *m.* William Gore, Esq., of Woodford, and *d.* 14 January, 1747.

The youngest son,

CHARLES NEWCOMEN, Esq., of Droming, co. Longford, whose will, dated 2 July, 1732, was proved 8 November, following, *m.* Edith, dau. of Sir Henry Caldwell, Bart., of Castle Caldwell, co. Fermanagh, and had issue,

I. THOMAS, of Droming, who *m.* and had issue.
II. James, *d. unm.*
III. CHARLES, of whom presently.
I. Frances.   II. Sarah.

The 3rd son,

CHARLES NEWCOMEN, Esq., of Carrickglass, in the co. Longford, *m.* (license dated 1 November, 1740) Charlotte, dau. of George Babe, of Dublin, merchant, and had an only dau. and heir,

CHARLOTTE NEWCOMEN, who *m.* William Gleadowe, Esq. of Killester, co. Dublin, and that gentleman assumed the surname and arms of Newcomen, and was created a baronet, 9 October, 1781. By him, her ladyship had issue,

THOMAS, her heir.
Jane, *m.* 9 March, 1818, to Charles Gordon Ashley, Esq., of Butcomb Court, co. Somerset, and *d.* 9 January, 1847.
Teresa, *m.* 1st, 2 September, 1796, to Sir Charles Turner, Bart, of Kirkleatham, co. York, who *d.* 1810; and 2ndly, 21 July, 1812, to Henry Vansittart, Esq., of Kirkleatham, who *d.* 22 April, 1848, leaving an only dau., THERESA, *m.* to Arthur Newcomen, Esq., R.H. art.
Charlotte, *d.* 26 June, 1840.
Catherine, *m.* 21 September, 1818, to Charles Newcomen, Esq. of Clonahard, co. Longford.

Lady Newcomen was raised to the peerage of Ireland, 29 July, 1800, as BARONESS NEWCOMEN, of Mosstown, and advanced to the dignity of VISCOUNTESS NEWCOMEN, 25 January, 1803. Her ladyship *d.* 16 May, 1817, and was *s.* by her son,

Sir Thomas Newcomen, Bart., Viscount Newcomen; at whose decease *unm.*, 15 January, 1825, the honours became EXTINCT.

Arms—Arg., a lion's head, erased, sa., between three crescents, gu.

NEWMARCH—BARON NEWMARCH.

By Writ of Summons, dated 24 December, 1264.

Lineage.

Amongst the companions of the CONQUEROR was

BERNARD DE NEWMARCH, who won the province of Brecknock, in Wales, and settled there. In this place he founded a priory of Benedictine monks, and, endowing it with extensive lands and revenues, gave it to the abbey of Battell, which his victorious master had founded in commemoration of the conquest. This Bernard *m.* Nesta, or Agnes, dau. of Griffyn, son of Llewelyn, Prince of Wales, and had a son, MABEL, who, by the infamous conduct of his mother, was deprived of his inheritance. She was a woman of licentious habits, and her son having enraged her by offending one of her paramours, she swore before the king that he was not the off-pring of her husband, but had been begotten in adultery. Upon which, Mabel, being excluded, the estates devolved to his sister, Sibyl, and in her right to her husband, Miles, Earl of Hereford, whose only surviving child and heiress, BERTHA, inherited eventually the co. Brecknock, and *m.* Philip de Braose.

The next person of this name mentioned, but unascertained how allied, if at all to the last, is

ADAM DE NEWMARCH; and after him comes

WILLIAM DE NEWMARCH, who, in the 10th RICHARD I., paid £100 for his relief, and £100 for livery of his father's lands. But of him nothing further is stated, than that he became a leper, and that Godfrey de St Martin had custody of his lands in Hampshire. From this William we pass to

HENRY DE NEWMARCH, who, upon the assessment of the aid for marrying the king's dau., 12th HENRY II., certified his knights' fees to be sixteen, an half, two thirds, and two fifth parts, for which he paid £11 14*s.* 2*d.* To this feudal lord, who *d. s. p., s.* his brother and heir,

JAMES DE NEWMARCH, who *d.* about the year 1232, leaving two daus., his co-heirs, viz.,

ISABEL DE NEWMARCH. *m.* to Ralph Russel, who, in the 8th HENRY III., had livery of her lands in the cos. Somerset, Wilts and Gloucester.

HAWYSE DE NEWMARCH, *m.* 1st, to John de Botreaux, who, in the 2nd HENRY III., had livery of her proportion of her father's property. She *m.* 2ndly, Nicholas de Moels.

Thus terminated this branch of the family: but there was another, of which was

ADAM DE NEWMARCH, who, joining the baronial standard, *temp.* HENRY III., was summoned to parliament as a Baron, after the battle of Lewes, by the lords who then usurped the government, but he was subsequently made prisoner, and compounded for his estates under the Dictum de Kenilworth. He *m.* a dau. of Roger de Mowbray, and had a son and successor,

HENRY DE NEWMARCH, who does not appear to have been summoned to parliament. In the 11th EDWARD II., he had free warren granted him, in certain demesne lands, in the co. York; and left a son ROGER, but nothing further is recorded of the family.

Arms—Gules, five lozenges conjoined in fesse, or.

NEWPORT — BARONS NEWPORT, VISCOUNTS NEWPORT, EARLS OF BRADFORD.

Barony, by Letters Patent, dated 14 October, 1642.
Viscounty, by Letters Patent, dated 11 March, 1675.
Earldom, by Letters Patent, dated 11 May, 1694.

Lineage.

The NEWPORTS were of great antiquity in the co. Salop, and descended from

JOHN DE NEWPORT, a person of some note, in the time of EDWARD I. From him, after several generations, sprang

THOMAS NEWPORT, Esq., who marrying Anne, dau. and co heir of John Ercall, Esq., of High Ercall, in Shropshire, settled there, and made it the designation of his family. From this marriage lineally descended,

SIR RICHARD NEWPORT, Knt., of High Ercall, who, for his eminent services to King CHARLES I., was elevated to the peerage by that monarch, 14 October, 1642, as BARON NEWPORT, *of High Ercall.* His lordship *m.* Rachel, dau. of John Leveson, Esq., of Haling, and sister and co-heir of Sir Richard Leveson, of Trentham, K.B., co. Stafford, and had issue,

I. FRANCIS, his successor.
II. Andrew, a commissioner of the customs, *d. unm.*
I. Bea*t*rix. *m.* to Sir Henry Bromley, Knt., of Shrawarden Castle. Salop.
II. Christian, *d. unm*
III. Mary, *m.* 1st, to John Steventon, Esq., of Dothill, in Shropshire, and 2ndly, to Francis Forester, Esq., of Watling-street, in the same co.
IV. Margaret, *m.* to Richard Fowler, Esq., of Harnage Green, co. Salop.
V Anne, *m.* to Edward Corbett, Esq., of Longnor, co. Salop.
VI Elizabeth, *m.*'to Henry Powle, Esq., of Williamsthorpe, co. Gloucester.

Lord Newport having suffered much during the civil wars, and being aged and infirm, retired into France and *d.* there, 8 February, 1650, when he was *s.* by his eldest son,

FRANCIS NEWPORT, 2nd Baron Newport. This nobleman, in the time of his father, fought valiantly under the royal banner until 1644, when he was taken prisoner by the parliamentarians. Upon the Restoration, he was constituted by King CHARLES II., first, comptroller, and afterwards, treasurer of the household, and was advanced to the dignity of VISCOUNT NEWPORT, *of Bradford*, by letters patent, dated 11 March, 1675. His lordship *m.* Lady Diana Russell, dau. of Francis, Earl of Bedford, and had issue,

RICHARD, his successor.
THOMAS, elevated to the peerage, 25 June, 1716, as BARON TORRINGTON, in the co. Devon, but *d. s. p.* in 1718, when the barony became EXTINCT.
Francis, *d. unm.*
Elizabeth. *m.* 1st, to Sir Henry Littleton, of Frankley, Bart., and 2ndly, to Edward Harvey, Esq., of Combe, co. Surrey.
Catherine, *m.* to Henry, Lord Herbert, of Cherbury.
Diana, *m.* 1st, to Thomas, son of Sir Robert Howard, Knt., of Ashstead, co. Surrey, and 2ndly, to William Fielding, brother of Basil, Earl of Denbigh.
Anne, *d. unm.*

His lordship, after the Revolution, was created EARL OF BRADFORD, by letters patent, dated 11 May, 1694. He *d.* in 1708, and was *s* by his eldest son,

RICHARD NEWPORT, 2nd earl. This nobleman *m.* Mary, dau. of Sir Thomas Wilbraham, Bart., of Woodhey, co. Chester, and had issue,

HENRY, 3rd earl.
Richard, *d. unm.* 3 December, 1716.
THOMAS, 4th earl.
William, *d. s. p.*
Mary, *d. unm.*
Elizabeth. *m.* to James Cocks, Esq., and *d. s. p.*
Anne, *m.* to Sir Orlando Bridgeman, Bart., and her eldest son.
SIR HENRY BRIDGEMAN, was created in 1794, BARON BRADFORD. His lordship *d.* in 1803, and was *s.* by his son,
ORLANDO BRIDGEMAN, 2nd baron, who was created VISCOUNT NEWPORT, and EARL OF BRADFORD, 30 November, 1815: he *d.* in 1825, and was *s.* by his son,
GEORGE-AUGUSTUS-FREDERICK-HENRY, 2nd EARL OF BRADFORD, of the 2nd creation.
Diana, *m.* to Algernon Coote, Earl of Mountrath, in Ireland. by whom she had an only son,
Charles-Henry, Earl of Mountrath, who *d. s. p.* in 1802.

His lordship, who was lord-lieutenant and custos-rotulorum of the co. Salop, *d.* in 1723, and was *s.* by his eldest son,

HENRY NEWPORT, 3rd earl. who *d.* without legitimate issue, in 1734, and was *s.* by his next brother,

THOMAS NEWPORT, 4th earl. This nobleman *d.* a lunatic, in 1762, when, as he had no issue, the Barony of Newport, of High Ercall, the Viscounty of Newport, and the Earldom of Bradford became EXTINCT.

Arms—Arg., a chevron, gu., between three leopards' faces, sa.

N O E

NEWPORT—BARON TORRINGTON.

Refer to NEWPORT. Earls of Bradford (Thomas, 2nd son of the 1st Earl of Bradford, was created Baron Torrington, 20 June, 1716: he *d. s. p.* 1719).

NOEL—BARONS WENTWORTH, VISCOUNTS WENTWORTH, OF WELLESBOROUGH, CO. LEICESTER.

(*Refer to* WENTWORTH, Barons Wentworth).

NOEL—BARONS NOEL, OF RIDLINGTON, VISCOUNTS CAMPDEN, BARONS NOEL, OF TITCHFIELD, EARLS OF GAINS-BOROUGH.

Barony, by Letters Patent, dated 23 March, 1617.
Viscounty, by Letters Patent. dated 5 May, 1628.
Barony, by Letters Patent, dated 3 February, 1681.
Earldom, by Letters Patent, dated 1 December, 1682.

Lineage.

It is evident, say modern genealogists, from the foundation of the priory of Raunton, in Staffordshire, that NOEL, the ancestor of this family, came into England with the CONQUEROR in 1066, and for his services obtained the manors of Ellenhall, Wiverstone, Podmore, Milnese, and other lands, by grants from the new monarch. His eldest son,

ROBERT, was Lord of Ellenhall, &c., and in the reign of HENRY I. had a grant of the greatest part of Granborough, co. Warwick, from Lawrence, the prior of Coventry, and the monks of that house. In the reign of HENRY II., he founded the priory of Raunton, or Ronton, near Ellenhall, his chief seat, for Canons Regular of St. Augustine. This Robert had two sons,

Thomas, who was Sheriff of Staffordshire for seven years, in the reign of HENRY II., and for one year upon the accession of RICHARD I., left, at his decease, two daus.,
  Alice, m. to William Harcourt, of Stanton Harcourt, and had Ellenhall and other estates as her moiety of her father's property.
  Joan, m. to William de Dunstan, and had for her share, Ronton, &c.
PHILIP.

The 2nd son,
PHILIP NOEL, had Hilcote, in Staffordshire, from his father, and was *s.* by his son,
ROBERT NOEL, Lord of Hilcote, who m. Joan, dau. of Sir John Acton, Knt., and from this Robert we pass to his lineal descendant,
JAMES NOEL, Esq., of Hilcote, who, in the 5th HENRY VIII., was nominated, by act of parliament, one of the Justices of the peace for assessing and collecting the poll tax, &c. He m. a dau. of Richard Pole, of Langley, co. Derby, by whom he had seven sons, of which ROBERT, the eldest, continued the line at Hilcote, while another branch was founded by the 3rd son,
ANDREW NOEL, Esq., who, at the dissolution of the monasteries, had a grant of the manor and site of the late preceptory of Dalby-upon-Wold, in Leicestershire, which had belonged to the knights of St. John of Jerusalem, and of the manor of Purybarre, in Staffordshire. In the 28th HENRY VIII., he was sheriff of the co. Rutland, as he was afterwards, both in the reign of EDWARD VI. and in that of MARY. In 1548 he purchased the seat and manor of Brook, in Rutlandshire, and was elected for that co. in the first parliament of Queen MARY. He m. 1st, Elizabeth, dau. and heir of John Hopton, Esq., of Hopton, in Shropshire, and widow of Sir John Perient, by whom he had ANDREW, his heir, and several other children. He m. 2ndly, Dorothy, dau. of Richard Conyers, Esq., of Wakerley, co. Northampton, and widow of Roger Flower, Esq., by whom he had one son,
JOHN, father of
WILLIAM NOEL, Esq., of Kirby Mallory, high sheriff of Leicester, in the 2nd JAMES I., whose son and successor,

VERE NOEL, Esq., of Kirby Mallory, was created a baronet in 1660, and was ancestor of
SIR EDWARD NOEL, who *s.* to the Barony of Wentworth in 1762, and was created VISCOUNT WENTWORTH.

Mr. Noel was *s.* at his decease by the eldest son of his 1st marriage,
SIR ANDREW NOEL, Knt., of Dalby, co. Leicester, who was a person of great note in the time of ELIZABETH, living in such magnificence as to vie with noblemen of the largest fortunes. Fuller, in his Worthies of England, observes, that this Andrew, "for person, parentage, gesture, valour, and many other excellent parts (amongst which skill in music), was of the first rank in the court." He was knighted by Queen ELIZABETH, and became a favourite, but the expenses in which he was involved obliged him to sell his seat and manor at Dalby. Her majesty is said to have made the following distich upon his name—

  "The word of denial, and letter of fifty,
    Is that gentleman's name, who will never be thrifty."

He was thrice sheriff of the co. Rutland, and member for that shire in several parliaments during the reign of Queen ELIZABETH. Sir Andrew m. Mabel, 6th dau. of Sir James Harrington, Knt., and sister and heir of John, Lord Harrington, of Exton, by whom he had issue,

EDWARD (Sir), his heir.
Charles, *d. unm.* in 1619.
Arthur.   Alexander, of Whitwell.
Lucy, m. to William, Lord Eure.
Theodosia, m. to Sir Edward Cecil, afterwards Lord Wimbledon.
Elizabeth, m. to George, Earl of Castlehaven, in Ireland.

He *d.* at his seat, Brook, in Rutlandshire, 9 October, 1607, and was *s.* by his eldest son,
SIR EDWARD NOEL, Knt., who was created a baronet 29 June, 1611, and elevated to the peerage, by letters patent, dated 23 March, 1616-17, as BARON NOEL, *of Ridlington, co. Rutland.* His lordship m. in 1605, Julian, eldest dau. and co-heir of Sir Baptist Hicks, Bart., which Sir Baptist was created *Baron Hicks, of Hilmington, co. Warwick,* and VISCOUNT CAMPDEN, in Gloucestershire, 5 May, 1628, with remainder to his son-in-law, Lord Noel ; and upon his decease, 18 October, in the following year, these dignities were inherited by his lordship. He had issue,

BAPTIST, his successor.
Henry, m. Mary, dau. of Hugh Perry, Esq., of London, but *d. s. p.*
Anne.
Penelope, m. to John, Viscount Chaworth.
Eleanor.
Mary, m. to Sir Erasmus de la Fountain, of Kirby Bellers, co. Leicester.

On the breaking out of the civil war, Lord Noel raised forces for the royal cause, and departed this life in his garrison at Oxford, 10 March, 1643, when he was *s.* by his elder son,
BAPTIST NOEL, 2nd Baron Noel, and 3rd Viscount Campden. This nobleman was as faithful a cavalier as his father, and raised a troop of horse and company of foot for the service of the king. For his estates he was obliged to pay to the sequestrators £9,000 composition, and an annuity of £150 settled on the Teachers of the period; and moreover, he sustained the loss of his princely seat at Campden, which had been burnt down by the royal army to prevent its becoming a garrison to the parliamentarians. His lordship lived to witness the restoration of the monarchy, and was made lord-lieutenant of the co. Rutland. He m. 1st, Lady Anne Fielding, dau. of William, Earl of Denbigh, by whom he had no surviving issue. He m. 2ndly, Anne, widow of Edward, Earl of Bath, and dau. of Sir Robert Lovet, Knt., but had only one still-born child. His lordship m. 3rdly, Hester, dau. and co-heir of Thomas, Lord Wotton, by whom he had issue,

EDWARD, his successor.
Henry, of North Luffenham, in Rutlandshire, who m. Elizabeth, dau. and heir of Sir William Wale, and left an only dau. and heir,
  JULIANA, who m. Charles Boyle, Earl of Burlington.
Mary, m. to James, Earl of Northampton.
Juliana, m. to William, Lord Alington.
Elizabeth, m. to Charles, Earl Berkeley.

The viscount m. 4thly, Lady Elizabeth Bertie, dau. of Montagu, Earl of Lindsey, and had issue,

Lindsey, *d.* young.
BAPTIST, of Luffenham, co. Rutland, M.P. for that shire, m. Susan, dau. and heir of Sir Thomas Fanshawe, of Jenkins, co. Essex, and left at his decease, one son,
  BAPTIST, who inherited, as 3rd Earl of Gainsborough.

John, m. Elizabeth, dau. of Bennet, Lord Sherrard, and had issue,

John, M.P. for Northamptonshire, who d. unm.
Thomas, m. Elizabeth, widow of Baptist, 4th Earl of Gainsborough.
Bennet, m. to ——, dau. of Adam, Esq.
Elizabeth, d unm.
Bridget, m. to David, Earl of Portmore.
Alice.
Catherine, m. to John, Earl of Rutland, afterwards Duke of Rutland.
Martha-Penelope, m. to — Dormer, Esq.

His lordship d. at Exton, 29 October, 1682, and was s. by his eldest son,

EDWARD NOEL, 3rd Baron Noel, and 4th Viscount Campden, who had been created by King CHARLES II., by letters patent, dated 3 February, 1681, BARON NOEL, of Titchfield, with remainder, in default of male issue, to the younger sons of his father, and was advanced to the dignity of EARL OF GAINS-BOROUGH, 1 December, 1682, with similar limitation. His lordship was constituted lord lieutenant of the co. Southampton, warden of the New Forest, and governor of Portsmouth. He m. 1st, Lady Elizabeth Wriothesley, dau. and co-heir of Thomas, 4th Earl of Southampton, by whom he acquired the lordship of Titchfield, and had issue,

WRIOTHESLEY-BAPTIST, his successor.
Frances, m. to Simon, Lord Digby, and d. in 1684.
Jane, m. to William, Lord Digby, brother and successor of Simon, Lord Digby.
Elizabeth, m. to Richard Norton, Esq., of the co. Southampton.
Juliana, d. unm.

The earl m. 2ndly, Mary, widow of Sir Robert Worsley, of Appuldercombe, in the Isle of Wight, and dau. of the Hon. James Herbert, of Kingsey, in Buckinghamshire. He d. in 1689, and was s. by his son,

WRIOTHESLEY-BAPTIST NOEL, 4th Baron Noel, 5th Viscount Campden, and 2nd Earl of Gainsborough, who m. Catherine, eldest dau. of Fulke Greville, 5th Lord Brooke, and had two daus., his co-heirs, viz.,

Elizabeth, m. in 1704, to Henry, 1st Duke of Portland
Rachael, m. in 1705-6, to Henry, 2nd Duke of Beaufort.

His lordship d. 21 September, 1690, when all the honours devolved upon his kinsman (refer to issue of Baptist, 3rd Viscount Campden, by his 4th marriage),

BAPTIST NOEL, Esq., of Luffenham, co. Rutland, as 3rd Earl of Gainsborough. His lordship m. Lady Dorothy Manners, dau. of John, Duke of Rutland, and had issue,

BAPTIST, Viscount Campden, his successor.
John, d. in 1718.
James, M.P. for Rutlandshire, d. unm. in 1752.
Susan, m. to Anthony, 4th Earl of Shaftesbury.
Catherine.   Mary, d. in 1718.

The earl d. in 1714, and was s. by his son,

BAPTIST NOEL, 4th Earl of Gainsborough. This nobleman m. Elizabeth, dau. of William Chapman, Esq., by whom (who m. 2ndly, Thomas Noel, Esq., grandson of the 3rd Viscount Campden,) he had issue,

BAPTIST, } 5th and 6th earls.
HENRY, }
Charles, d. young.
Elizabeth.
Jane, m. to Gerard-Anne Edwards, Esq., of Welham Grove, co. Essex, and her only son, GERARD EDWARDS, having been created a baronet, and assuming the name and arms of NOEL, upon inheriting the estates of his uncle, Henry, 6th Earl of Gainsborough, was the late

SIR GERARD-NOEL NOEL, Bart., whose eldest son and heir,

CHARLES-NOEL NOEL, Lord Barham, was created, 16 August, 1841, EARL OF GAINSBOROUGH (see BURKE's Extant Peerage.)

Juliana, m. to George Evans, Lord Carbery, and d. in 1760.
Penelope, d. young.   Anne.
Lucy, m. to Sir Horatio Mann, K.B.
Mary.   Susanna.
Sophia, m. to Christopher Nevile, Esq., grandfather by her of the late HENRY NEVILE, Esq., of Walcot, co. Northampton, and of GEORGE NEVILE, Esq., of Stubton, Notts.

His lordship d. 21 March, 1750-51, and was s. by his eldest son,

BAPTIST NOEL, 5th earl, who d. in minority. on his travels, at Geneva, in 1759, when the honours devolved upon his brother,

HENRY NOEL, 6th earl, at whose decease, unm., in 1798, the Earldom of Gainsborough, and all the other honours became EXTINCT; while the estates passed to his lordship's nephew,

403

Gerard-Noel Edwards, Esq., who, thereupon assuming the surname and arms of NOEL, and being created a baronet, became Sir Gerard-Noel Noel (refer to children of 4th earl).

Arms—Or, fretty gu., a canton erm.

NORREYS—VISCOUNT THAME, EARL OF BERKSHIRE.

By Letters Patent, dated 28 January, 1620.

Lineage.

This family was one of consideration in King EDWARD III.'s time, and then of knightly degree. In the reign of HENRY VI.,

JOHN NORREYS was first usher of the chamber, next, esquire of the body, and afterwards master of the wardrobe to that monarch. He was subsequently sheriff of the co. Devon and Berks, and in the next reign (EDWARD IV.) he was continued in the post of esquire of the body to the king. He resided at Patenden, in Berkshire, and dying in the 6th EDWARD IV., was interred at Bray, in an aisle of that church, built at his own expense. He was s. by his son and heir,

SIR WILLIAM NORREYS, of Yatenden, one of the knights of the body to King EDWARD IV. In the 2nd HENRY VII., this gentleman had a command in the royal army at the battle of Stoke; and in the 19th of the same reign he obtained a grant from the king of the custody of the manor of Langley, which manor was then in the crown by reason of the minority of EDWARD, son and heir of Isabel, late wife of George, Duke of Clarence, and he had the stewardship of several other manors in the co. of Oxford, part of the property of the said EDWARD, and situated similarly during his minority. Sir William m. 1st, Isabel, dau. and heir of Edmund Ingoldesthorpe, and widow of John Nevil, Marquess of Montacute, by whom he had three sons who all d. young, and three daus., viz.,

A dau., m. to Sir John Langford, of Bradfield.
Joane, m. to John Cheney, Esq., of Wodhey, co. Berks.
Elizabeth, m. to William Fermer, Esq., of Somerton, co Oxford.

He m. 2ndly, the Lady Jane de Vere, dau. of John, Earl of Oxford, and had a son,

SIR EDWARD NORREYS, Knt., who m. Fridiswide, dau. and co-heir of Francis, Viscount Lovel, by whom he had two sons,

JOHN, one of the esquires of the body to King HENRY VIII., m. Elizabeth, sister of Edmund, Lord Bray, but d. without legitimate issue, in the 6th ELIZABETH.
Henry.

The younger son,

HENRY NORREYS, or NORRIS, who s. eventually to the estates and representation of the family, was made usher of the black rod, upon the resignation of Sir William Compton, Knt., in the 18th HENRY VIII. He was also esquire of the body to the king, and one of the gentlemen of his privy chamber; but being afterwards involved in the fall of Anne Boleyn, he was committed to the Tower as one of her paramours. It is said, however, that the King felt some compunction in putting him to death, and offered him a pardon conditionally, that he would confess his guilt; but Norreys resolutely replied, "That in his conscience, he thought the Queen guiltless of the objected crime; but whether she were or not, he could not accuse her of anything; and that he had rather undergo a thousand deaths than betray the innocent." Upon the report of which declaration, the King cried out, "Hang him up, hang him up." He suffered death accordingly, 14 May, 1536, and was attainted in parliament the same year. He had m. Mary, dau. of Thomas, Lord Dacre of the south, and left a dau. Mary, m. 1st, to Sir George Carew, Knt., of Mohun's Ottery, and 2ndly, to Sir Arthur Champernowne, of Dartington, Devon, Knt., and a son,

HENRY NORREYS or NORRIS, Esq., who resided at Wytham, in Berks, and received, in 1566, the honour of knighthood. In the 14th ELIZABETH, Sir Henry was sent ambassador into France, and in consideration of his good services upon that occasion, as well as the sufferings of his father, he was summoned to parliament, 8 May, 1572, as BARON NORRIS, of Rycote. His lordship m. Margery, younger dau. and co-heir of John, Baron Williams, of Thame (and one of the co-heirs of the said Barony of Williams) by whom he acquired the lordship of Rycote, and had issue,

WILLIAM, Marshal of Berwick, who m. Elizabeth, dau. of Sir Richard Morrison, Knt., and dying v. p., left an only son,

FRANCIS, who s. his grandfather.

John (Sir), a very eminent and gallant soldier, temp. ELIZA-BETH, distinguished in the wars of the Low Countries, and in those of Ireland, in which latter kingdom he filled the office of president of the Council of Munster, and d. there unm.

Edward, governor of Ostend. d. s. p.

Henry, d. of a wound received in action.

Thomas (Sir), of Mallow, co. Cork, president of Munster, and some time justice of Ireland. His only dau. and heiress, ELIZABETH NORREYS, m. the Right Hon. SIR JOHN JEPH-SON, Knt., of Froyle, Hants, and their descendant, Sir Charles Denham Orlando Jephson-Norreys, of Mallow, was created a baronet, 6 August, 1838.

Maximilian, slain in Britanny.

His lordship d. in 1600, and was s. by his grandson,

FRANCIS NORREYS, 2nd Baron Norreys, of Rycote, summoned to parliament, from 17 October, 1601, to 5 April, 1614. His lordship at the creation of King JAMES's son, Prince Charles, Duke of York, was made a knight of the Bath, and some years afterwards, 28 January, 1620, advanced to the dignities of Viscount Thame, and EARL OF BERKSHIRE. His lordship m. Lady Bridget de Vere, dau. of Edward, Earl of Oxford, and had an only dau. and heiress,

ELIZABETH, who m. Edward Wray (3rd son of Sir William Wray, of Grentworth), one of the grooms of the bed-chamber to King CHARLES I., and left an only dau.,

BRIDGET WRAY, who m. Edward, son of Edward, Earl of Dorset, and became, after his decease, 2nd wife of Montagu Bertie, Earl of Lindsay. lord great chamberlain of England : by the latter she had a son,

JAMES BERTIE, who in her right, inherited the Barony of Norreys, of Rycote. He was afterwards created EARL OF ABINGDON—honours enjoyed by his descendant, the present Earl of Abingdon.

His lordship, who was a person of impetuous temperament, was at one time committed to the Fleet Prison, for a rude assault upon the Lord Scrope, in the House of Lords, while the peers were actually sitting, and the Prince present. He d. in 1623, from the effects of a wound which he had inflicted upon himself with a crossbow. The Barony of Norris, of Rycote, passed eventually, through his grand-dau., into the family of BERTIE, and has since merged in the Earldom of Abingdon, while the Viscounty of Thame and Earldom of Berkshire became EXTINCT.

Arms—Quarterly: arg. and gu., a fesse, az., in the 2nd and 3rd quarters, a fret, or.

NORTH—BARONS GREY, OF ROLLESTON, CO. STAFFORD.

By Writ of Summons, dated 17 October, 1673.

Lineage.

The HON. CHARLES NORTH, son and heir-apparent of Dudley, 4th Baron North, and brother of the Lord Keeper North, 1st Lord Guilford, having m. Katherine, widow of Sir Edward Moseley, Bart., of Rough, co. Lancaster, and dau. of William Grey, of Chillingham, 1st Lord Grey, of Werke, was summoned to parliament in the life-time of his father, 24 October, 1673, as BARON GREY, of Rolleston, co. Stafford. His lordship succeeded as 5th Baron North in 1677, and d. in 1690, when he was s. by his elder son,

WILLIAM NORTH, 6th Baron North, and 2nd Lord Grey. This nobleman being bred to arms, served under the Duke of Marlborough, in all his campaigns, and had his right hand shot off at the battle of Blenheim. He was subsequently made lieutenant-general of the forces, and governor of Portsmouth. His lordship m. Maria-Margaretta, dau. of Mons. Elmet, receiver-general to the States of Holland ; but d. in 1734, s. p., when the Barony of North devolved upon his cousin, Francis, 3rd Lord Guilford, and the Barony of Grey, of Rolleston, became EXTINCT.

Arms—Az., a lion passant, or, between three fleurs-de-lis, arg.

NORTHWODE—BARONS NORTHWODE.*

By Writ of Summons, dated 8 January, 1313.

Lineage.

In the 42nd HENRY III., upon the death of Reginald de Cobham, at that time sheriff of Kent,

SIR ROGER DE NORTHWODE, one of his executors, accounted to the exchequer for the sums he had received during his sheriffalty. This Sir Roger served in the wars under HENRY III. and EDWARD I. He m. Bona, sister and heiress to John de Wanton, of Shorne, in Kent, and d. in the 14th EDWARD I., whereupon his son and heir,

SIR JOHN DE NORTHWODE, doing his homage had livery of his lands. He was b. circa 38th HENRY III., and had summons to attend the king to advise upon the affairs of the realm in the 22nd EDWARD I. He had afterwards in the same reign a military summons; served in the wars of Flanders; accompanied EDWARD I. in his wars in Scotland, and was present at the siege of Carlaverock, in the 28th year of his reign, where he was knighted. He was sheriff of Kent in 20th, 21st, 28th, 33rd, and 34th EDWARD I. For his services on different public occasions he was summoned to parliament as a Baron, from 8 January, 1313, to 20 March, 1319. He m. 10th EDWARD I., Joane, eldest dau. of Sir Bartholomew Badlesmere, and sister and co-heiress to Giles, Lord Badlesmere. He d. 12th ED-WARD II., and was s. by (the son of his deceased son, Sir John de Northwode, by Agnes, dau. of William de Grandison) his grandson,

SIR ROGER DE NORTHWODE, 2nd baron, b. circa 1st EDWARD II., summoned to parliament, 3 April, 1360. This nobleman served in the wars of Flanders and France, in the 14th and 16th EDWARD III. His lordship m. 1st, 14th EDWARD II., when under fifteen, Julian, dau. of Sir Geoffrey de Say, which lady d. 3rd EDWARD III.; 2ndly, 4th EDWARD III., Elizabeth, dau. of Sir John de Segrave, Lord of Folkestone, which lady d. s. p. 9th EDWARD III.; 3rdly, in 13th EDWARD III., Margery, widow of Sir Nicholas de Halgton, and she d. s. p. 13th EDWARD III.; 4thly, in 15th EDWARD III., Joane, widow of Thomas de Feversham, which lady d. s. p. 30th EDWARD III.; 5thly, 30th EDWARD III., Agnes, widow of Sir John de Cobham. He d. 35th EDWARD III., and was s. by his son,

SIR JOHN NORTHWODE, 3rd baron, summoned to parliament, from 1 June, 1363, to 20 January, 1376. This nobleman was in the French wars of King EDWARD III., and shared in the glory of that martial reign. He was b. 14th EDWARD II., and m. 23rd EDWARD III.. Joane, dau. and co-heiress of Robert Hart, of Faversham, co. Kent, and dying in 1379, was s. by his son,

SIR ROGER NORTHWODE, 4th baron, who was never summoned to parliament. He was b. 30th EDWARD III., d. s. p., and was s by his brother,

WILLIAM NORTHWODE, 5th baron, never summoned to par-liament. This nobleman (if he ever assumed the dignity) did signal service at the battles of Agincourt and Verneuil. He was buried at Bredhurst, where there was once a brass plate in the church to the memory of him and four of his sons, who also lie buried there. The epitaph was: " Hic jacet Williel-mus Northwood cum quatuor suis filiis verus hæres domini de Northwood." He had issue,

JOHN, his successor.

Elizabeth, m. to Peter Cat, but of her descendants nothing is known.   Isabel.

Eleanor, m. to John Adam, whose male descendant (after five generations),

Richard Adam, although m. twice, appears to have had no issue, but his brother,

Roger Adam, had six children, viz.,

Richard.   John.   William.

Bridget, m. to Adam Shepherd.

Margery, m. to William Hawe.

Anne.

This William d. about the year 1406, and was s. by his son,

JOHN NORTHWODE, 6th baron, who d. s. p. in 1416, when the Barony of Northwode fell into ABEYANCE, and is now pre-sumed to be vested in the descendants of the above-Roger Adam.

Arms—Ermine, a cross engrailed, gu.

---

* (See BURKE's Landed Gentry, tit. NORWOOD OF KENT.)

NORWICH—BARON NORWICH.

By Writ of Summons, dated 25 February, 1342.

Lineage.

GEOFFREY DE NORWICH, the first person of this name upon record, was involved in the baronial contest with King JOHN, and committed to prison in consequence. From him descended, it is presumed,

WALTER DE NORWICH, who, in the 5th EDWARD II., was constituted one of the barons of the exchequer, and at the same time obtained a charter of free warren in all his demesne lands. In some years afterwards he was made treasurer of the exchequer, and had a grant of the manors of Dalham and Bradfield, with the advowson of the church of Dalham, co. Suffolk. To this learned judge, who d. in 2nd EDWARD III., succeeded

SIR JOHN DE NORWICH, Knt., who was in the wars of Flanders and Scotland in the reign of EDWARD III., and was summoned to parliament as a Baron, from 25 February, 1342, to 3 April, 1360. His lordship had grants from the crown for his services, and licence to make castles of his houses at Metyngham, in Suffolk, and at Blackworth, and Lyng, in Norfolk. He d. in 1362, and was s. by his grandson,

JOHN DE NORWICH, 2nd baron, who does not appear to have been summoned to parliament. This nobleman d. in 1374, s. p., when the Barony of Norwich became EXTINCT. His lordship's estates devolved upon his cousin, CATHERINE DE BREWS, dau. and heir of Thomas de Norwich, his grand-uncle, but that lady taking the veil at Dartford, William de Ufford, Earl of Suffolk, by Margery, his wife, sister of Thomas de Norwich, father of the said Catherine, inherited as her heir.

Arms—Per pale gu. and az., a lion rampant, ermine.

NOTE.—From this Baronial house is said to have sprung the eminent family seated at Brampton, co. Northampton, of which Sir Erasmus Norwich, in the time of WILLIAM III., m. Annabella, dau. of Thomas Savage, Earl Rivers. For its ultimate fall and present decadence, *see Vicissitudes of Families.*

NUGENT—BARON NUGENT, AND VISCOUNT CLARE.

Viscounty, by Letters Patent, dated 19 January, 1767.

Lineage.

SIR THOMAS NUGENT, Knt., 2nd son of Richard, 7th Baron of Delvin, was seated at Carlanstown, co. Westmeath, and became ancestor of the branch of the family seated there, whose representative,

EDMOND NUGENT, Esq., of Carlanstown, was member in King JAMES's parliament for Mullingar. He m. Clara, dau. of Robert Cusack, Esq., of Rathgare, and had issue,

ROBERT, d. s. p. in 1728.
MICHAEL, of whom presently.
Christopher.
Margaret, m. to John Chevers, Esq., of Macetown.
Anne, m. to James Reynolds, Esq., of Loughscur. co. Leitrim, and had issue, George-Nugent Reynolds, Anne Reynolds, and others.
Martha, m. Ignatius Palles, Esq., of Aughterava, co. Cavan, and had a dau., Mary, wife of John Nugent, Esq., of Killasona, and a son, Andrew, of Mount Palles, co. Cavan, grandfather of Andrew-Christopher Palles, Esq., of Little Mount Palles, co. Cavan, and of Dublin.
Frances, m. to Edward Nugent, Esq., of Dungomine, co. Cavan.
Mary-Anne, who d. unm. 1744.
Mary, m. to Edward Nugent, Esq., of Donore, ancestor by her of Sir Percy Nugent, Bart., of Donore.
Elizabeth, m. to Garrett Dardis, Esq., of Giggenstown.
Another dau. m. to Mr. Mapother, of the co. Roscommon.

The 2nd son,

MICHAEL NUGENT, Esq., who s. to Carlanstown, upon the demise of his brother, in 1728, m. Mary, 5th dau. of Robert, Lord Trimleston, and by her, who d. in 1740, had issue,

Edmond, who d. at Buda, aged twenty-one, in 1736.
ROBERT, of whom presently.
Mary, m. in 1748, to Henry, 3rd son of Geoffrey Browne, Esq., of Castlemagarret, co. Mayo.
Clare, m. in 1740, to George Byrne, Esq., of Cabintely, co. Dublin.   Margaret,

Mr. Nugent d. in 1739, and was s. by his son,

ROBERT NUGENT, Esq., of Carlanstown, elected M P. for St. Mawes, in 1747, who having filled several important offices, was advanced to the peerage of Ireland as *Baron Nugent, of Carlanstown, co. Westmeath,* and VISCOUNT CLARE, 19 January, 1767, and subsequently, 27 June, 1776, was created EARL NUGENT, with remainder, in default of male issue, to George Grenville Nugent, of Wotton, Bucks. His lordship m. 1st, in 1730, Lady Emilia Plunket, 2nd dau. of Peter, 4th Earl of Fingall, and had by her a son, Edmond, lieut.-col. 1st foot guards, who d. unm., at Bath, in 1771. He m. 2ndly, in 1736, Anna, dau. of James Craggs, Esq., postmaster-general, sister and heir of the Right Hon. James Craggs, and relict of Robert Knight, Esq., of Gosfield Hall, Essex. By this lady he had no issue. Lord Nugent m. 3rdly, in 1757, Elizabeth, Countess Dowager of Berkeley, by whom he had two daus.,

MARY-ELIZABETH, m. to George, Marquess of Buckingham, K.G., who inherited under the limitation, the EARLDOM OF NUGENT (*see* BURKE's *Peerage*).
LOUISA, m. in 1784, to Admiral Sir Eliab Harvey, G.C.B., of Rolls Park, Chigwell, Essex, and had issue,
  1 Edward, lieut. in the 3rd regiment of guards, slain at Burgos.
  2 William, d. 1823, aged twenty-one.
  1 Louisa, m. William Lloyd, Esq., of Aston, Salop.
  2 Emma, m. to General William Cornwallis Eustace, C.B., K.C.H.
  3 Maria, m. to the Rev. William Tower, of Weald Hall, Essex.
  4 Georgiana, m. 16 February, 1830, to William Drummond, Esq.
  5 Eliza, m. in 1830, to Thomas-William Bramston, Esq., of Skreens, in Essex.   6 Mary.

The earl d. 14 October, 1788, and was buried at Gosfield, co. Essex, when the barony and viscounty became EXTINCT.

Arms—Erm., two bars, gu.

NUGENT—BARON NUGENT.

By Letters Patent, dated 29 December, 1800.

Lineage.

MARY-ELIZABETH, MARCHIONESS OF BUCKINGHAM, dau. and co heir of Robert, Earl Nugent, and wife of George, 1st Marquess of Buckingham, was created a peeress of Ireland, as BARONESS NUGENT, *of Carlanstoun, co. Westmeath,* with remainder to her 2nd son, Lord George-Nugent Grenville, and the heirs male of his body, by patent, dated 29 December, 1800. The Marchioness d. 16 March, 1812, and was s. by her said 2nd son,

GEORGE-NUGENT GRENVILLE, Baron Nugent, knight grand cross of St. Michael and St. George, and of the Greek order of the Saviour; b. 31 December, 1789; who m. 6 September, 1813, Anne-Lucy, 2nd dau. of the late Hon. Major-Gen. Vere Poulett, and niece of Earl Poulett (who d. 19 May, 1848), but had no issue. His lordship sat in the House of Commons as member for Aylesbury. In 1832, he was appointed lord high-commissioner of the Ionian Isles, and held the government until 1835. He d. s. p. 26 November, 1850, when his title became EXTINCT.

NUGENT—MARQUESS OF WESTMEATH.

(See BURKE's *Extant Peerage,* WESTMEATH, E.)

O'BRIEN—EARL OF THOMOND.

By Letters Patent, dated 1 July, 1543.

Lineage.

"It has been," says O'Donoghue, in his *Historical Memoir of the O'Briens,* "the fortune of the race of O'Brien to form an exception to those instances in which families once occupying a regal station, have, after their declension, sunk into obscurity. A reader of Irish history will find the names of the O'Briens so often mentioned in the pages of its annals, that he cannot hesitate to conclude, that, whether as kings of the whole island, or later, of the southern half, or again, after the arrival of the Anglo-Normans, ruling their restricted principality of Thomond with independent authority, as asserted by Sir John Davis of them and others, the descendants of Brian Boriomhe have written their names in indelible characters in the history of their country. In no part of the kingdom can so many memorials of the energy and power of the native princes be found at this day, as in the territory of Thomond, before it was restricted to the present co. of Clare. The erection of the monasteries of Manister-nenagh, Holycross, the cathedral of Limerick, the abbey of Ennis, and many others, too numerous to mention, devoted to the promotion of learning and piety, exhibit to the modern traveller proofs of the genius and vigour of the descendants of Brien. And notwithstanding the various changes which the state of society has for so many ages undergone, and the downfall of so many of the ancient fam lies of the country, we find the descendants of Brian of the Tributes still holding their own, while we may search in vain even amongst some of the royal houses on the continent of Europe for a line of greater antiquity, or one whose descent is more clearly traced through the historic records of their country."

CONNOR O'BRIEN, who was inaugurated King and Prince of Thomond, in 1528, d. in 1540, when his son DONOUGH was set aside, and his brother,

MORROUGH O'BRIEN, was elected the O'BRIEN and Prince of Thomond, according to the Brehon law. He surrendered his royalty to King HENRY VIII., and was created in consequence by that monarch, 1st July, 1543, Earl of Thomond, with remainder to his deposed nephew, DONOUGH O'BRIEN, and BARON OF INCHIQUIN, to the heirs male of his own body. His lordship d. in 1551, when the Barony of Inchiquin devolved on his son, DERMOD, and is now enjoyed by Morrough's male representative, the present LORD INCHIQUIN (see BURKE'S Extant Peerage). The Earldom of Thomond passed, however, to Murrough's nephew,

DONOUGH O'BRIEN, who, on surrendering the patent to King EDWARD VI, obtained a new grant of the dignities to himself and the heirs male of his body, by patent, dated 7 November, 1552, and also possession of all the honours and lands which had fallen to the crown,by the death of his uncle. He m. Ellen, dau. of Pierce, Earl of Ormonde, and d. 1553, having had issue,

  I. CONNOR, 3rd earl.
  I. Margaret, m. to Dermod, Lord Inchiquin.
  II. More or Maud, m. to Teige Macnamarareagh.

The son and heir,

CONNOR O'BRIEN, 3rd Earl of Thomond, m. 1st, Joan, only dau. of Sir Thomas, 16th Lord Kerry, by whom he had one dau., who d. young. He m. 2ndly, Una or Wonafrit, dau. of Turlough O'Brien, of Arra, co. Tipperary, and had issue,

  I. DONOGH, his heir.
  II. Teige, of Dromore, who m. 1st, Slana, dau. of Teige McMurrough; and 2ndly, Joane, dau. of Sir Dermod O'Shaughnessy, and relict of Sir William Bourke, Knt. By the latter he had issue, Dermod and Mortaugh, who both d. s. p.
  III. DANIEL (Sir), VISCOUNT O'BRIEN, OF CLARE (see that title).
  IV. Hugh, whose grandson, Conor, d. s. p.
  I. Mary, m. to Terlaugh Roe MacMahon, Lord of East Corcavaskin.
  II. Margaret, m. to James Butler, Lord Baron of Dunboyne.
  III. Honora, m. to Thomas Fitzmaurice, Lord Baron of Kerry and Lixnaw.

The eldest son,

DONOGH O'BRIEN, 4th Earl of Thomond, and lord-president of Munster, called "the great earl," m. 1st, Ellen, dau., Margaret, m. to Charles McCarthy, 1st Lord Viscount Muskerry. He m. 2ndly, Elizabeth, dau. of Gerald, Earl of Kildare, and by her (who d. 12 January, 1617) had issue two sons,

  I. HENRY, 5th earl.
  II. BRYAN or BARNABY, 6th earl.

The earl d. 5 September, 1624, and was s. by his eldest son,

HENRY O'BRIEN, 5th Earl of Thomond, who was summoned to parliament, 1615, as Lord O'Brien; he m. Mary, dau. of Sir William Brereton, and had issue,

  I. Mary, m. to Edward Cockayne, Lord Viscount Cullen.
  II. Margaret, m. to Edward Somerset, Marquess of Worcester.
  III. Elizabeth, m. to Dutton, Lord Gerrard of Bromley.
  IV. Anne, m. Henry, 7th Earl of Thomond.
  V. Honora, m. 1st, to Sir Francis Inglefield, Knt., of Wotton-Bassett; and 2ndly, to Sir Robert Howard, Knt., son of the Earl of Berkshire.

The earl d. in 1639, and was s. by his brother,

SIR BRYAN or BARNABY O'BRIEN, 6th Earl of Thomond, knighted by King JAMES, 21 July, 1615. He was created MARQUESS OF BILLING, by privy seal, 1645, but the great seal not being then within the royal power, the patent never passed. He m. Mary, dau. of Sir James Fermer, Knt., and by her (whose will bears date 22 February, 1672), he had issue,

  I. HENRY, 7th earl.
  I. Penelope, wife of Henry, 2nd Earl of Peterborough.

The son and heir,

HENRY O'BRIEN, 7th Earl of Thomond, custos rotulorum co. Clare, 1663, m. 1st, 1641, Anne, dau. and co-heiress of Henry O'Brien, 5th Earl of Thomond, and by her (who d. 1645), had a son,

Henry, Lord Ibrackan, M.P. for Clare, 1661, m. 1664 Lady Catherine Stuart, sister of Charles, Duke of Richmond and Lennox, Baroness Clifton, in her own right, and by her (who m. 2ndly, Sir Joseph Williamson) ha t issue,
  Donogh, Lord Ibrackan, drowned with H.R H the Duke of York, going to Scotland. He m. Lady Sophia Osborne, dau. of Thomas, Duke of Leeds, and d. s. p.
  George, d. young.
  Mary. m. to John FitzGerald, Earl of Kildare.
  Catherine, m. to Edward Hyde, Earl of Clarendon, and d. 11 August, 1706, leaving issue,
    Edward, Baron Cornbury and Baron Clifton, d. s. p. 12 February, 1712.
    Catherine, d. unm.
    Theodosia, Baroness Clifton, eventually sole heir, m. 25 August, 1704, John Bligh, of Rathmore, co Meath. created Baron Clifton, Viscount and Earl of Darnley, in the peerage of Ireland.

Lord Ibrackan d. 1 December, 1678.

The earl m. 2ndly, in 1660, Sarah, dau of Sir Francis Russell, of Chippenham, co. Cambridge, Knt., and had issue,

  I. HENRY-HORATIO, Lord Ibrackan, m. 1686, Henrietta, 2nd dau. of Henry Somerset, Duke of Beaufort, K.G., and d. v. p., aged twenty-one, at Chester, having had issue,
    HENRY, 8th Earl of Thomond.
    Henrietta, widow of Lord Ibrackan, m. 2ndly, Henry, Earl of Suffolk.
  I. Elizabeth, d. unm. 3 June, 1688.
  II. Penelope, m. Henry Howard. Earl of Suffolk and Bindon and was mother of Charles-William, 7th Earl of Suffolk. She d. in December, 1703, and was buried at Saffron Walden.
  III. MARY, m. to Sir Matthew Dudley, Bart., of Clopton, Northamptonshire, and d. 9 November, 1735, leaving issue.

The earl d. at his seat, Billing, co. Northampton, May 1691, and was s. by his grandson,

HENRY O'BRIEN, 8th Earl of Thomond, b. 14 August, 1688, was M.P. for Arundel, in Sussex, and was created a peer of England by the title of VISCOUNT TADCASTER, co. York, 19 October, 1714. He m. 4 June, 1707, the Lady Elizabeth Seymour, eldest dau. of Charles, Duke of Somerset, but by her (who d. 2 April, 1734,) had no issue. He d. in Dublin, 20 April, 1741, and was buried with his ancestors in the cathedral church of Limerick. By his will dated 14 October, 1738, he left his estate to Murrough, Lord O'Brien, son and heir of the Earl of Inchiquin, with remainder to Percy Wyndham (see WYNDHAM O'BRIEN, Earl of THOMOND). At the earl's death. the Viscounty of Tadcaster EXPIRED. and the Earldom of Thomond became DORMANT.

Arms—Gu., three lions passant guardant, in pale, party per pale, or and arg.

O'BRIEN—VISCOUNT O'BRIEN, OF CLARE.

By Letters Patent, dated 11 July, 1662.

Lineage.

SIR DANIEL O'BRIEN, Knt., of Carrigky Chouly, or Carrigaholt, 3rd son of Connor, 3rd Earl of Thomond, having performed signal service in the wars of Ireland, was created 11 July, 1662, VISCOUNT O'BRIEN, of Clare. He m. Catherine, dau. of Gerald, 16th Earl of Desmond, and relict of Maurice, Viscount Roche of Fermoy, and had issue,

  I. Donogh, d. s. p. 6 August, 1638, buried in St. Mary's Church in Limerick, m. Elizabeth, dau. of Sir Thomas Southwell, Knt., and relict of Sir J. Dowdall, Knt.
  II. CONNOR, 2nd viscount.
  III. Murrough, m. Eleanor, dau. of Richard Wingfield, Esq., and d. s. p
  IV. Teigue, m. Honora, dau. of Gerald Fitzgerald, Esq , of Ballyglagiane, and had a son,
    Donogh, living in England, in 1694.

The 2nd son,

CONNOR O'BRIEN, 2nd viscount O'Brien, of Clare, m. Honora, dau. of Daniel O'Brien, of Duagh; and dying about 1670, left (with six daus., Margaret, m. to Hugh O'Reilly; Ellen, m. to Sir Roger O'Shaghnessy; Honora, m. John Fitzgerald, Knight of Kerry; Catherine, m. 1st. to Garret Fitzgerald, Esq., of Castleishen, and 2ndly, to John Macnamara, Esq.; Sarah, m. to

Daniel O'Sullivan Bear; and Mary, *m.* to — Power, of Dounil), a son and successor,

DANIEL O'BRIEN, 3rd Viscount O'Brien, of Clare; who attended CHARLES II. in his exile, and with unshaken zeal for the royal house of Stuart, fought for JAMES II. at the Boyne, for which he was outlawed. His lordship *d.* in 1690, leaving by Philadelphia, his wife, dau. of Francis Lennard, Lord Dacre and sister of Thomas Dacre, Earl of Sussex, two sons,

DANIEL, 4th viscount, who accompanied King JAMES to France, and there *d. s. p.*

CHARLES, 5th viscount, entered the French service and was mortally wounded at Ramilies, 11 May, 1706 He *m.* the eldest dau. of Henry Buckley, Esq., and by her (who *m.* 2ndly, to Mr. Omane had a dau., Laura, *m.* to the Comte de Breteuil, and a son,

> CHARLES, 6th viscount, *b.* in 1699: the distinguished MAR-SHAL THOMOND, of the French service. He became, on the death of Henry, Earl of Thomond, heir male of the Earls of Thomond, and would have been entitled to the dignity of Earl of Thomond, which he assumed, if his grandfather's attainder had not barred his right. He *m.* in 1755, Marie-Geneviève-Gauthier de Chiffreville, Marchioness de Chiffreville, in Normandy; and dying 9 September, 1761, aged sixty-two, left with a dau. (Antoinette-Charlotte-Marie-Septimanie, *m.* the Duc de Choiseuil-Praslin), a son and heir,
>
>> CHARLES, 7th viscount, *b.* in 1756; who *d.* young and *unm.* at Paris, 1764.

Arms—Gu., three lions passant guardant, in pale, per pale, or and arg.

O'BRIEN — EARL OF INCHIQUIN, MARQUESS OF THOMOND, IN THE PEERAGE OF IRELAND, AND BARON THOMOND AND BARON TADCASTER, IN THE PEERAGE OF THE UNITED KINGDOM.

Earldom, by Letters Patent, dated 21 October, 1654.
Marquessate, by Letters Patent, dated 30 December, 1800.
Baronies by Letters Patent, dated 2 October, 1801, and 3 July, 1826.

Lineage.

The EARLDOM OF INCHIQUIN was conferred by letters patent dated 21 October, 1654, on MURROUGH, 6th Baron Inchiquin afterwards Viceroy of Catalonia; and descended in a direct line (*refer to* BURKE's *Extant Peerage*) to

MURROUGH O'BRIEN, 5th Earl of Inchiquin in Ireland, who was created MARQUESS OF THOMOND, also in Ireland, by letters patent bearing date 30 December, 1800, with remainder to his brother Edward, and the heirs male of his body, and was made a peer of the United Kingdom by letters patent, dated 2 October, 1801, as BARON THOMOND, *of Taplow, co. Bucks.* His lordship *m.* 1st, Mary, Countess of Orkney, and had several children, of whom one dau. alone survived, namely,

MARY, who, succeeding her mother, became COUNTESS OF ORKNEY. Her ladyship *m.* the Hon. Thomas Fitz-Maurice.

The marquess *m.* 2ndly, Mary, dau. of John Palmer, Esq., of Torrington, co. Devon, and niece of Sir Joshua Reynolds, but by her had no issue. His lordship *d.* in consequence of a fall from his horse, 10 February, 1808, when the Barony of Thomond became EXTINCT, while his Irish honours devolved upon his nephew,

WILLIAM, 2nd Marquess of Thomond, K.P., who *m.* 16 September, 1799, Elizabeth, only dau. and heir of Thomas Trotter, Esq., of Duleck, and by her (who *d.* 3 March, 1852), had issue,

> I. SUSAN-MARIA, *m.* 1824, Rear-Admiral Hon. George-F. Hotham, and *d.* 1857.
> II. SARAH, *m.* 1830, Major William-Stanhope Taylor, and *d.* 1859.
> III. MARY, *m.* 1836, Richard, Earl of Bantry, and *d.* 1853.
> IV. ELIZABETH, *m.* 1835, Sir George Stucley Stucley, Bart.

The marquess was created a peer of the United Kingdom as BARON TADCASTER *of Tadcaster, co. York,* 3 July, 1826. His lordship *d.* 21 August, 1846, when this last named barony became EXTINCT, but the Irish honours devolved on his brother,

JAMES, 3rd Marquess of Thomond, G.C.H., admiral R.N., who *m.* 1st, 25 November, 1800, Eliza-Bridgeman, 2nd dau. of James Willyams, Esq., of Carnanton, Cornwall (which lady *d.* 1802); 2ndly, Jane, 3rd dau. of Thomas Ottley, Esq., of Antigua, and relict of Valentine-Horne Horsford, Esq., also of Antigua (which lady *d.* 8 September, 1843); and 3rdly,

5 January, 1847, Anne, widow of Rear-Admiral Fane, and sister of the late Sir Charles Flint. The marquess *d.* 3 July, 1855, when the Marquessate of Thomond, and the Earldom of Inchiquin became EXTINCT, but the old Barony of Inchiquin devolved on Sir LUCIUS O'BRIEN. Bart., of Dromoland, who established his right before the Committee for Privileges, as 13th Lord Inchiquin in 1862.

Arms—Gu., three lions passant guardant, in pale, per pale, or and arg.

O'BRIEN—VISCOUNT TADCASTER.

By Letters Patent, dated 19 December, 1714.

See O'BRIEN, EARL OF THOMOND.

O'CARROLL—LORD OF ELY O'CARROLL.

It is stated that a barony was granted in 1552 to TEIGE O'CARROLL, as Baron of Ely O'Carroll, but the patent or the record of the patent is nowhere to be found.

O'DEMPSEY—VISCOUNT CLANMALIER.

By Letters Patent, dated 22 December, 1631.

Lineage.

The old Irish sept of O'Dempsey, whose country was Clanmalier, incorrectly written Glenmalire, extending on both sides of the river Barrow, partly in the King's County, and partly in the Queen's County, springs from a common ancestor with the family of O'Conor Faley, and may be traced in the Irish annals from a very early period.

DERMOT O'DEMPSEY, chief of Clanmalier and for a long time Lord of Offaly, founded, *circa* 1178, on the site of an ancient church dedicated to St. Evin, the great Cistercian Abbey of Monasterevan, which he richly endowed. His charter of foundation is given in the *Monasticon Anglicanum.* Dermot *d.* in 1193.

In the 12th century the O'Dempseys contended with the English forces under Strongbow, Earl of Pembroke, who in the year 1173, together with his son-in-law Robert de Quincy, constable and standard bearer of Leinster, marched a powerful force into Kildare and Offaly: but being opposed by the Irish clans, commanded by the chiefs of Clanmalier, the English were defeated with great slaughter, and, amongst the slain was de Quincy, the standard bearer; the affair is thus mentioned by Maurice Regan in HARRIS's *Hibernica*. "From thence the earl (Strongbow) went to Kildare making many incursions into Offaley, upon O'Dempsey, lord of that country, who refused to come unto him, and to deliver hostages; the earl to subdue him made a journey in person upon him, Offaley was burned and harassed, the whole prey of the country taken and the army retired towards Kildare; in the retreat the earl with 1000 men marched in the vanguard, and the rere was commanded by Robert de Quincy; in the pass when the vanguard was passed, O'Dempsey gave upon the rere, at which charges Robert de Quincy with many others were slain and the banner of Leinster lost; and for his death, as well by the earl as the whole army, great lamentation was made."

The Four Masters further record that "Dermod, son of Conbroghda O'Diomusaigh, a long time chief of Clan Maollughra and Lord of Hy Failge, *d.* A.D. 1193;" and that "Dermod O'Dempsey, Lord of Clanmalire (in Queen's County), was slain by the English in 1383." Passing down to a more recent period, we come to

OWEN O'DEMPSEY. Lord of Clanmalier, Queen's County, son of Hugh O'Dempsey, Lord of Clanmalier, who had a grant of the town of Coolroddery, *d. s p.* before 1578, and was *s.* by his, nephew,

TERENCE O'DEMPSEY, of Ballybrittas, who *d. s. p.,* (*Inq. p. m.* 1578), and was *s.* by his brother,

HUGH O'DEMPSEY, Esq., of Loghire, Queen's Co., who had three sons,

> I. Owen Mac Hugh, *d. s p.*
> II Terence, *d. s. p.*
> III. DERMOT, of whom we treat.

The 3rd son,

DERMOT O'DEMPSEY, was father of

SIR TERENCE O'DEMPSEY, who was heir to his great uncle in the estate of Coolroddery. This Terence who was knighted at Kiltenan in Munster, 22 May, 1599, was created *Baron of Phillipstown*, and VISCOUNT CLANMALIER, 22 December, 1631, when he adopted, for "Supporters" to his Arms, two knights in armour ppr., chained one to the other, from the right leg of the one to the left leg of the other. He *m.* Fitzgerald of the House of Lakagh, and by her (who *d.* 4 January, 1614,) he had issue,

  1. OWNY, of Clonygawny, King's Co., *m.* 1st, Mary, dau. of Christopher Nugent, Lord Delvin, and by her (who *d.* 1618), had issue,

    1 Christopher, knighted 13 July, 1624, *m.* Cleopatra Cary, but by her (who *d.* 28 March, 1628) he left no issue,
    2 Lewis, of whom presently.
    3 Henry.   4 Charles, *d.* young.
    5 Stephen, *d. unm.*   6 John, beyond seas.
    7 Matthew, *d. unm.*
    1 Elizabeth, *d. unm.*
    2 Giles, *m.* to Conn MacGeoghegan, of Beallanurrighir, co. Westmeath.
    3 Mary.   4 Margaret.
    5 Eleanor, *m.* to Robert Reeves, Esq.
    6 Cicely.   7 Julia, *d. unm.*

He *m.* 2ndly, Jane, dau. of Sir John Moore of Croghan, King's Co., Knt.,, by whom he had one son and one dau , James, and Dorothy, who *d.* an infant. He *m.* 3rdly, Dame Ismae, dau. of Sir Christopher Bellew, Knt., and relict of Sir William Taaffe, Knt., but by her had no issue. His will bears date 24 February, 1637. He was buried in the chapel of Killmolahy, Queen's co.

  1. Anne, wife of Gerald Fitzgerald, Esq.

LEWIS O'DEMPSEY, 2nd Viscount Clanmalier, eldest surviving son of Owny O'Dempsey, and heir to his grandfather was attainted for the rebellion of 1641. He *m.* Martha, dau. of John Itchingham, Esq., of Dunbrody, co. Wexford, and had issue,

  I. MAXIMILIAN, of whom presently.
  II. Terence, living, 1691, *m.* Joan, dau. of Conly Mac Geoghegan. and had a dau. Alice, wife of Thomas O'Gorman, Esq., of Inchiquin, co. Clare.
  1 Mary, *m.* to John Quinn, of Quinnsborough, co. Kildare.
  II Elizabeth, *m* to Hugh O'More, of Ballynakil, Queen's co.

The eldest son,

MAXIMILIAN O'DEMPSEY, 3rd viscount, lord lieutenant of the Queen's co., *m.* Anne, dau. and co-heir of Walter Bermingham, Esq., of Dunfert, co. Kildare, but by her (who *d.* 27 June, 1708), he had no issue. He *d.* intestate, and administration was granted to his nephew Dominick Quin, 13 January, 1714.

Dr. O'Donovan (*Annals of the Four Masters*) states that the O'Dempseys have fallen altogether from their high estate and can now be only traced among the farmers and peasantry of Ireland. Dr. O'Donovan adds that Mr Dempsey, of Liverpool was, at the time he wrote, the most conspicuous person of the name of whom he was aware.

Arms.—Gu., a lion rampant, arg., between two swords, points upwards, one in bend dexter, and the other in bend sinister, all ppr,

---

O'DONNELL—EARL OF TYRCONNELL.

By Letters Patent, dated 27 September, 1603.

Lineage.

Dr. O'Donovan, in his edition of the *Four Masters*, and John Cornelius O'Cullaghan in his *History of the Irish Brigade*, have dwelt at much length on the ancestry of the illustrious House of O'DONNELL. Suffice it for our purpose to commence with MAGNUS, or MANUS O'DONNELL, "Rex Tirconnelliæ," who succeeded his father Hugh Duy O'Donnell as Chieftain, in 1537 : he was *m.* four times, and *d.* in 1563. Of his sons, we will confine ourselves to two, viz., CALVAGH O'DONNELL, and HUGH O'DONNELL, of whom in the sequel. The former, CALVAGH O'DONNELL, Prince of Tyrconnel, "Capitanus Nationis Suæ, de antiquis Regibus sive Principibus Tirconnelliæ, in rectâ lineâ oriundus," *d.* 1566, leaving one son, CON O'DONNELL, Prince of Tyrconnel, who *m.* a dau. of Sir Turlough Luineach O'Neill, and had several sons, of whom, it appears from McFirbis, three only left issue, viz , NIALL GARV, HUGH BOY, and CON OGE ; the eldest, the famous SIR NIALL GARV O'DONNELL. " Vir animo magno et audaci, et rei militaris scientiâ prœditus," was in constant hostility with his cousin, Hugh Rory O'Donnell, but incurring eventually the suspicion of the English govern-

ment, he was arrested at Raphoe, in 1608, and *d.* in 1626, after a confinement of eighteen years in the Tower of London. HUGH BOY O'DONNELL, the 2nd son, was a person of weight among the Catholic confederates in the great civil war, and *l.* in 1649 : his son, JOHN O'DONNELL, an officer in the Spanish service, *m.* Catherine O'Rorke, and was father of HUGH BALLDEARG O'DONNELL,[*] or " O'Donnell of the Red Spot." From

---

[*] This Hugh bore, with the sanction of the Spanish Crown. the title of Conde de Tyrconnell in that king-dom. He was probably the testamentary heir of Hugh-Albert O'Donnell, for though born in Ireland, he possessed property in Spain and possessed also and transmitted the family papers of Earl Rory and his son, including the original letters patent of JAMES I. for the earldom, which, with the great seal of Ireland still attached, remains among the muniments of Count Maximilian O'Donnell in Vienna. Hugh, whose memory has long been hardly dealt with by his countrymen, is commonly known in Ireland by the name of "*Ballde-rg* O'Donell, or O'Donell of the Red Spot," for many of the genuine O'Donells have a curious red blood-mark beneath the skin, usually on the side ; and the " old rhyming prophecies " spoke of an O'Donell with the red mark. who was to be a mighty champion of the Irish race. He was the son of John O'Donell, an officer in the Spanish service, and of Catherine O'Rorke, of the old princely lineage of Brefny. His grandfather was Hugh O'Donell, of Ramelton, who acted a leading part in the Catholic Confederacy, and who, from documents of the time, appears to have been looked up to as "the O'Donell" from 1642, or at least from 1646 to 1649, in which year he died. Hugh of Ramelton was son of Conn, who was the son of Calvagh, P.ince of Tyrconnell, the eldest son of Prince Manus ; the common ancestor of the principal existing branches as well as of the still more distinguished junior line, which was illustrated by the chivalry of Red Hugh, and by the calamities of Earl Rory and his children ; and here I may remark, that in all the transmissions of native dignities, the line of hereditary succession gave way to the " worthiest elder of the blood," a point that should never be lost sight of in the modern and ancient bickerings about the claims of the representation of the Celtic chieftainries.

In the Spanish service, BALLDEARG had risen to the rank of a brigadier, and comman ted an Irish regiment in the Spanish pay, when the news of the Jacobite war in Ireland sounded in his heart like the trumpet call of duty. Already he had frequently offered his services to the Stuarts. when CHARLES and JAMES were still, like himself, in exile. He now craved permission of the Spanish monarch to go and serve his lawful king in Ireland. It was refused. Listening to no voice but the cry of his patriotic conscience, he fled from Spain like a deserter ; but addressing an eloquent justification of his act to the Spanish government, and taking shipping, he reached Cork just four days after the battle of the Boyne had struck dismay into the adherents of JAMES. On the fugitive king he waited in Kinsale Harbour, on board the vessel that bore that luckless sovereign to France. By his Majesty he was recommended to Richard Talbot, Duke and Earl of Tyrconnell, and by Talbot, as viceroy, was given a commission to raise 5,000 men. " If you can collect fifteen thousand," added Talbot, " the King will be better served, and your country the more grateful." Armed with this authority, Balldearg, by the sole magic of his name, raised, in the space of six brief weeks, eight regiments of foot and two of horse. If these fresh levies were ill armed, and consequently remained during the war less efficient than they might have been, it must not be imputed to O'Donell, but to the jealousy of that knot of narrow-minded men, who renewed, in this most critical conjuncture, the internecine animosities of the old English Pale against the ancient native houses thus damaging fearfully the cause which they had not only sworn to defend, but for which they in truth made otherwise such noble sacrifices. It is told by Macaulay, in his glittering language, how O'Donell looked upon himself as no less royal than JAMES, and it is hinted that his object was to found a Celtic monarchy, of which he was to be the sovereign. Right royally proud of his regal blood, O'Donell doubtless was : but his nature seems to have been less open to narrow jealousies than those of his rivals His insular prejudices had been mitigated by a foreign education, and many years of foreign service, during which his views had become more just. It was not he that revived the jealousies of Celt and Norman then. He came to bind Celt and Norman together, for the nation's sake, in the cause of JAMES.

When fate declared against that monarch, when the fight at Aghrim was lost, and Galway had fallen, and Limerick was about to surrender, terms were generously offered by Ginkel to O'Donell. The chieftain refused as long as a ray of hope remained, but his memory has been stained in Ireland for having, in that supreme hour, while stipulating favourable and honourable terms for his faithful followers, accepted what was miscalled in his country, a "pension" from the victorious party. The simple truth is this : he had abandoned his fortune and position in Spain, he had no fortune in Ireland, having given to his brother, who was King JAMES's lord lieutenant of Donegal, whatever fortune he may have been entitled to, and even that was doubtless exhausted by the sacrifices made to serve King JAMES. He could not enter Spain, where he had forfeited his rank, and was liable to be treated as a deserter, for having gone, contrary to the king's will, to serve his native monarch. He could not, like other adherents of the fallen cause of JAMES, and like that monarch

Hugh Boy descended the O'DONNELLS of Larkfield, co. Leitrim, of which line was CONNELL, COUNT O'DONNELL, a field-marshal in the Austrian service. CON OGE O'DONNELL, the 3rd son of Con O'Donnell, Prince of Tyrconnell, was ancestor, *inter alios*, of LEOPOLD O'DONNELL, DUKE of TETUAN, in Spain, and of MAXIMILIAN,* COUNT O'DONNELL, of Austria.

We must now revert to the 2nd son of Manus O'Donnell, Prince of Tyrconnell, viz.,

Sir HUGH O'DONNELL, Prince of Tyrconnell. This Hugh *m.* Inneen Ddu (dark Ina) dau. of the House of the Macdonnells of the Isles, and had issue,

I. HUGH ROE, his heir.
II. RORY, of whom presently, as EARL of TYRCONNELL.
I. Joan, wife of Henry, Earl of Tyrone.

The elder son,

HUGH ROE O'DONNELL, was perhaps the most dangerous antagonist the English Government ever had to contend with in Ireland : he was *b.* in 1571, and, in early life, not only displayed considerable genius and independence of spirit, but made these qualities prized among his clansmen and countrymen, by the noble generosity of his manners, and the matchless symmetry of his form.

In former times, the O'Donnells of Tyrconnell, and the O'Neills of Tyrone, were often addressed by the English monarch as his equals, and did against foreign foes as more than once asked of them, as peers in royalty, by English monarchs. In 1244, HENRY III, King of England, solicited help by a letter, still on record, addressed, "Donaldo Regi de Tirconnell;" and some of the successors of the puissant HENRY of England, and the scarcely less proud King Donell of Tyrconnell, interchanged these royal courtesies as peers in degree. It was not unnatural that the high-spirited young Hugh should desire to substantiate an independence so often and so distinctly recognized. He made no secret of his intentions, which were soon the theme of conversation throughout Ireland, and which reaching the ears of the Lord Justice, alarmed in no light measure the royal council in Dublin Castle. Sir John Perrott,

then at the head of the Anglo-Irish government, instead of courting the haughty young chieftain with honours and favour, framed a plot to seize him, which, though successful at the time, conduced eventually to render implacable the proud and injured youth.

In the year 1587, a ship, laden with Spanish wines, was fitted out and dispatched to one of the harbours of Tyrconnell, and the young Hugh O'Donnell, Prince of Tyrconnell, having been lured by false appearances to trust himself on board, he was made prisoner and conveyed to Dublin Castle. There he was held captive full three years, but in 1591, he managed to elude his keepers, and found means to pass into Tyrconnell, where, his aged father resigning in his favour, he was proclaimed by the tribes chief of his name, and the white wand, the simple sceptre of his sway, was placed in his hands, with solemn and time-honoured rites, by the Coarb of Kilmacrinan.

For the sixteen years following he was the scourge and terror of the government. He kept his mountain territory of Donegal, in spite of ELIZABETH's best generals: carried his excursions to the remotest parts of Munster, and made his power dreaded, and his name a word of terror, "even in the rich plains of Meath, and to where the Shannon blends its waters with the Atlantic."

At last, the only military fault he was ever known to commit led to his total rout at Kinsale, in the early spring of 1601, by Lord Mountjoy, one of the ablest generals, and perhaps the wisest statesman ever sent by England to Ireland.

HUGH ROE, Prince of Tyrconnell, this bold and ill-fated chieftain, was the first exile of the O'Donnells.

After the defeat of the Irish, and the inefficient force of their Spanish allies at Kinsale, he sailed for Spain to crave further succours of PHILIP III. In the known religious sympathies of the Spanish king, the exile set his trust; and, as the annalists quaintly tells us, "Moreover, on account of that monarch's love for the Gaels, from their having primally come out of Spain to invade Ireland, as is manifest in the Book of Invasions."

---

himself, accept the pay of France, for France was then the foe of Spain, and to Spain O'Donnell and his family were bound by the fealty of gratitude for nearly a century of protection, as well as by the fealty of military honour, for he had sworn to her allegiance. He stipulated from William, the ally of Spain, for the pay of a brigadier, which was his Spanish rank ; and instead of going to fight for the Dutch, as he has been supposed to have done, he retired to the Spanish Low Countries, thence to Spanish Italy, and at length to Barcelona, and after serving for the space of five or six years as a volunteer with Spanish troops, he was rewarded for his constancy by being restored to his Spanish military station, and soon after, promoted to that of major-general, and sent to a command in the Low Countries. (BURKE's *Vicissitudes of Families*.)

* Count Maximilian O'Donnell was aide-de-camp to the Emperor of Austria, FRANCIS JOSEPH I., whom he saved from assassination in 1853. For this signal service, the Emperor granted him a special patent of nobility, from which we make the following extracts, illustrative of the services of the O'Donnells :—" He is descended from the exceedingly ancient and very illustrious race, the chiefs of Donegal, and dynasts of the former Tyrconnell, in Ireland History speaks of them in early ages, when Christianity was first introduced into that country ; and extols the zeal with which they founded churches and monasteries to assist in the propagation of the true faith. In later times they exercised princely power in the land of their descent, and enjoyed widely extended martial fame. Shortly before the final incorporation of Ireland with the royal crown of Great Britain, Roderick, one of this ancient princely race, was invested with the dignity of Earl of the above-named province, as we have satisfactorily ascertained by the original document of King JAMES I., with the seal of Ireland thereto attached, and dated the 10th day of February, in the first year of his reign in England, and thirty-seventh year of his reign in Scotland. Various concurrences in ecclesiastical and political affairs, unnecessary now to enumerate, compelled the above named to quit his native land and seek refuge in a Catholic foreign country, as his elder brother Hugh had previously done. The latter met with a distinguished reception at the court of PHILIP III., of Spain, and the former was welcomed with paternal kindness by the paternal head of the Church, Pope PAUL V.; since that period their descendants have devoted themselves to the service of the monarchs of the Spanish line of our most serene archducal House in the kingdom of Spain, and in latter times, in the beginning of the past century, to that of our most serene predecessors in the imperial government. During their stay in the land of Spain, as well as in that of Austria, they ever enjoyed the consideration and respect due to the rank of count, and to their original nobility. It is to us a grateful and pleasing thing to bring to mind the banished (but with honour and dignity expatriated) forefathers, and relatives of our beloved, loyal, Maximilian Charles, Count O'Donnell, here mentioned, whose virtues and deeds for the greatest welfare of our most serene House, and the highest interests of the State, shine with such peculiar and distinguished lustre. Charles (*i. e.* Connell), Count O'Donnell, general of

cavalry, and colonel proprietor of his regiment, distinguished himself at the battle of Torgau, November 3rd. 1760. when appointed successor in command to Field Marshal Count Daun, and performed the important service of repelling the advance of the enemy on Dresden ; for which achievement it was unanimously resolved by the chapter of the order of Maria Theresa, that although he was not a knight thereof, he should be invested with the grand cross of the order, which honour was conferred upon him, December 21st, 1761. John, Count O'Donnell, field-marshal, lieutenant and knight of the order of Maria Theresa, distinguished himself at the battle of Leuthen, December 5th, 1757, and at Maxen, November 20th, 1759. Henry, Count O'Donnell, commanded as major of the 49th regiment of infantry, and volunteered to lead in person the storming of the principal gate of the fortress of Schweidnitz, September 30th, 1761, by which the same was taken ; and for which achievement. by a resolution of the chapter, April 30th, 1762, the knight-cross of the order of Maria Theresa was conferred upon him. In due gradation he attained the rank of major-general. Francis-Joseph, Count O'Donnell was president of the chief council, and the ministerial bank committee, and also of the board of finance and commerce, and was decorated with the grand cross of the order of St. Stephen. John, Count O'Donnell, was one of the first to offer himself as a volunteer for the campaign of 1809, and as such headed a corps with the greatest devotion and courage. Hugh, Count O'Donnell, also a major, was killed at the storming of the bridge of Kehl; and Charles, Count O'Donnell, a major-general, was killed in the battle of Aspern. Maurice, Count O'Donnell, distinguished himself as a commander of a battalion, in the defence of the bridge of Ebersburg, in 1814, and afterwards attained the rank of field-marshal lieutenant Our well-beloved, trusty Maximilian Charles O'Donnell, son of the above-named Maurice, and grandson of Francis Joseph, Count O'Donnell, was born October 29th, 1812, and entered our service in the year 1830, and in regular gradation was promoted to his present rank. In 1848, he served in the campaign of Italy, and in 1849, in that of Hungary ; and on every occasion was distinguished for his valour. Already did WE, as a mark of our confidence in his zeal and abilities, appoint him as aide-decamp to our person. At all times he has fulfilled the high expectations we formed of him ; and most fully was this exemplified, when, at the risk of being personally sacrificed, he warded off our imperial person the murderous attack on the 18th February in the present year, whereby he rendered to ourselves, to our royal house, and to our realm. a never to be forgotten service. We rewarded him by investing him with the cross of our order of St. Leopold. But that he may enjoy an enduring and conspicuous mark of our just acknowledgment, which can be transmitted to his posterity, we grant him further all the rights, privileges, of an Austrian Count; and as a further proof of imperial and royal grace and favour, we augment henceforth his hereditary and family arms, by the insertion of our own initials and shield of our most serene ducal house of Austria : and finally, the double-headed eagle of our empire, to be and endure as a visible and imperishable memorial of his proved and devoted services."

On the 6th of January, 1602, O'Donnell, with his brave companions, took shipping at Castlehaven, near Bantry; and on the 14th of the same month, he landed at Corunna. where he was nobly received by the Conde de Caragena, then Governor of Galicia, who invited him to lodge in his house.

The *Four Masters* record faithfully the princely welcome King PHILIP gave him; but O'Donnell's course was well-nigh run. On his arrival at Simancas, two leagues from the court, which was confided at Valladolid, the exiled chieftain took his death sickness, and *d.* 10 September, 1602, in the house which the King of Spain had in that town of Simancas. This celebrated Irishman had no child and was consequently *s.* by his brother,

RORY or RODERIC O'DONNEL, the O'Donnel and Prince or Lord of Tyrconnell. who submitting to the English government, obtained a regrant of his lands from the crown, to be held *in capite*, and was created 27 September, 1603, *Baron of Donegal*, and EARL OF TYRCONNELL, and to his heirs male, with remainder to his brother Geoffry *alias* Caffrie O'Donnell, and his heirs male with the title of Baron of Donegal to his heir apparent.

He soon, however, with reason or not, suspected the government of plotting his ruin, and fled to the continent for safety, perhaps for succour.[*]

He bore with him his only son, Hugh, then aged but eleven months. With them fled the earl's brother, Caffrie, together with his only son, Hugh, aged about two years and a-half, and Caffrie's young wife, the sister of the chivalrous Sir Cahir O'Doherty, chief of Innishowen. With them too fled their sister, the Lady Nuala O'Donnell, wife of her valiant but turbulent kinsman, Sir Niall garbh O'Donell, who, after refusing from the government the title of Baron of Lifford, *d.* in the Tower of London, having lain there for a quarter of a century, a state prisoner of the government in whose service he had often risked life and honour against the cause of his tribe and his co-religionists.

Earl Rory *m.* Lady Bridget FitzGerald, dau. of Henry, Earl of Kildare, and, as we have seen, left an only and infant son, named Hugh, subsequently Hugh-Albert, or Albert-Hugh. He lived in Spain and the Low Countries, and styles himself, in existing documents, of almost regal character, Earl of Tyrconnell and Donegal, Baron of Lifford, Lord of Sligo and Lower Connaught, and knight commander of the order of Al antara. He rose to be a general in the Spanish service, *m.* the dau. of a knight of the Golden Fleece (of a now extinct house in the Low Countries, hardly second at that time to any subject family on the continent), Anna-Margaret, dau. of Maximilian de

---

[*] Macaulay affirms that Earl Rory fled to the court of Madrid, but this was not the fact. The fugitive never set foot on the soil of Spain. He landed in France. proceeded to Brussels, and thence through Germany to Rome, where he *d.* in the first year of his foreign sojourn, and was there interred, with the following inscription:

D. O. M.

RODERICO PRINCIPI O'DONALLIO
Comiti Tirconalliæ in Hibernia
Qui pro religione Catholica
Gravissimis defunctus periculis
In sago pariter et in toga
Constantissimus cultor et defensor
Apostolicæ Romanæ Fidei
Pro qua tuenda et conservanda e patria profugus
Lustratis in Italia, Gallia-Belgio
Præcipuis sanctorum monumentis
Atq. ibidem principum Christianorum
Singulari amore et honore
Sanctiss. etiam P. ac D. Pauli P. P. V.
Paterno affectu susceptus
In maximis Catholicorum votis de felici ejus reditu
Summum dolorem attulit suis
Et mœrorem omnibus in hac urbe ordinibus
Immatura morte quam obiit III. Kalendas Sextiles
Anno Salutis MDCVIII ætatis suæ XXXIII.
Quem mox secutus eodem tramite
Ut eadem cum beatitate frueretur
CALFURNIUS frater
Periculorum et exilij socius
In summa spe et expectatione bonorum
De ejus nobilitate animi
Quem virtus et optima indoles exornavit
Ut reliquit desiderium et mœstitiam coexulibus
XVIII. Kal. Oct. proxime sequentis anno ætatis XXV.
Utrunque antecessit ætate et fati ordine
Frater primogenitus
HUGO Princeps
Quem pie et Catholice pro fide et patria cogitante
Philippus III. Hispaniarum Rex
Et vivum benevole amplexus et in viridi ætate
Mortuum honorifice funerandum curavit
Vallisoleti in Hispania IIII Idus Septemb. A.S. MDCII.

410

Hennin, Count de Bossut, and a near kinswoman of the last eccentric Duke of Guise.

When Earl Rory *d.*, this only son was aged about two years and a-half. For some few years one loses sight of both him and his cousin german, Hugh, son of Caffrie, but in all probability they were confided to the charge of Caffrie's youthful widow, the Lady Rose O'Doherty, who *m.* 2ndly, Owen Roe O'Neill, the famous general of the confederate Catholics, in the war against the Parliamentarians. It may be presumed that she brought back these children from Rome to the archducal court at Brussels; for from the *Livre des Depenses de l'Archiduc Albert*, governor of the Low Countries, which is preserved in MS., and which extends over the years between 1612 and 1618, we learn that from 1615 the "Conde de Tyrconnell" and Don Hugo O'Donnell were in the receipt of a modest pension from his Imperial Highness. As both boys were called Hugh, there was added to the name of him who was chief of his house that of the archduke his protector, who was in all likelihood his godfather in confirmation; and henceforward this Hugh is equally styled Hugh-Albert or Albert-Hugh. About this time he was attached as page to the court of the Infanta Isabella, the consort of Archduke Albert.

That the two young O'Donnells were brought up at the University of Louvaine is clear, from the authority of Vernulæus, who, in his *Academia Lovaniensis*, enumerates among the men of distinction that were educated in that celebrated school, "Albert Hugh O'Donnell, Earl of Tyrconnell, Baron of Lifford Lord of Lower Connaught, of the ancient stock of the Kings of Ireland; and Hugh O'Donnell, paternal cousin german of the aforesaid Albert, died a captain during the siege of Breda."

The Irish naturally cherished a generous memory of this heir of one of their most famous chieftains. The court of Spain was fully alive to the political importance of the exile. Even at the cautious Roman Court there appears to have been some that partook in a measure of the illusions of the native Irish, that the exiled O'Donnells and O'Neills might one day be placed by circumstances in a position to renew the stern struggle for their faith and lands, in which fate had declared against their fathers. In 1641, when the Irish rose in arms to oppose the Parliamentarians, many an anxious eye was turned towards Albert Hugh, the banished heir of Tyrconnell, who was then a Spanish general of reputation. His military rank and experience, his undoubted claim to the position of chief, though not senior of his clan, the popular belief that he was alluded to in the "old rhyming prophecies," which for ages had such a strong hold upon the Celtic imagination, and even still are not forgotten—all contributed to make some of the ablest of his countrymen look anxiously for his return to his native land. He seems indeed, to have craved permission of the Spanish court to place himself at the service of his country; but owing to the war with France, in which he was employed, this permission was refused; and he *d.* or as some say was drowned in 1642, the year following that in which his country had again taken up arms.

Albert Hugh does not appear to have had any issue. The title attainted by King JAMES I., still remains under forfeiture.

Arms—Gu., issuing from the dexter side of the shield a cubit sinister arm, vested. az., cuffed or, the hand ppr., grasping a cross fitchee, of the 3rd.

ODO—EARL OF KENT.

Creation of WILLIAM THE CONQUEROR, *anno* 1067.

Lineage.

ODO, bishop of Bayeux, in Normandy, half brother of the CONQUEROR, having with "divers monks, and secular clerks," assisted at the battle of Hastings, "with their devout prayers and councils," had the whole county of Kent committed to his charge after the victory, and was joined with William Fitz-Osborne, one of the principal generals, afterwards Earl of Hereford, in the superintendency of the military forces of the kingdom, as well in field as garrison. He was likewise a count palatine, and a justiciary of England. In the Lent succeeding his coronation, King WILLIAM having visited Normandy, Odo and Fitz-Osborne were constituted *custodes Angliæ*, or *regents*, during his absence, with authority to erect castles in all fit and proper places Being thus seated in Kent, and so powerful that no man durst oppose him, he possessed himself of divers lordships belonging to the archbishopric of Canterbury; of which, when Lanfranke became archbishop, a complaint was made by that prelate to the king, who immediately ordered a convocation of the men of Kent, versed in old customs and usages, to sit upon the matter; a meeting took pl ce, accordingly, at Penenden Heath. Geffrey, bishop of Constance, presiding for the king, when judgment was given in favour of Lanfranke, viz.—"That he should enjoy the lands belonging to his church, as freely as the king himself did enjoy his own demesne lands." In 1074, Odo, and the bishop of Constance, suppressed the rebellion of the Earls of Hereford and Norfolk; and in four years afterwards, being "*next to the king*" in authority, Odo went at the head of an army to waste Northumberland, by reason that the men of those parts had risen in insurrection and murdered Walcher, bishop of Durham. The Earl of Kent is accused of exercising great cruelty upon this occasion, and of despoiling the church of Durham of some rich ornaments, amongst which was a rare crosier of sapphire; certain it is, that his lordship was not proof against the seductions of unlimited power, and that he became proud and oppressive; the more so, it was alleged, because it had been foretold by certain soothsayers of Rome, that he was destined, at no remote period, to fill the papal chair, then the first throne in Christendom, and nothing short of that could now satisfy his ambition. He purchased a magnificent palace at Rome, attached the Senators to his interest by munificent gifts, and induced Hugh, Earl of Chester, by promise of ample rewards, to accompany him with a chosen body of soldiers, into Italy. King WILLIAM becoming, however, acquainted with Odo's proceedings, hastened back to England, and casually meeting the earl at the head of this pompous retinue, in the Isle of Wight, upon his route to Normandy, assembled the nobles together, and in a passionate harangue impeached his conduct, concluding by a command that the guards should seize upon the delinquent; but no one daring to do so on account of his episcopal character, the king himself arrested him : when Odo exclaimed, "That he was a clerk and a minister of God, and that he was amenable to the papal authority, by which alone he could be sentenced." To this the king replied, "I neither sentence any clerk or bishop, but my own earl, whom I made my vicegerent in my kingdom, resolving that he shall give an account of that his trust." Odo was immediately conveyed into Normandy, and during the remainder of the CONQUEROR's reign, he was kept close prisoner in the castle of Roan. He obtained his freedom, however, upon the accession of RUFUS, and was restored to his Earldom of Kent, but not to the high office of justiciary, which had been conferred upon William, bishop of Durham. This latter circumstance, with the consequent diminution of his authority, kindling his wrath, induced him to fling off his allegiance to RUFUS, his benefactor, and to espouse the cause of Robert Curthose. He raised the standard of rebellion in Kent, and wasted with fire and sword, several towns belonging to the king, and to his great enemy. Lanfranke, archbishop of Canterbury, but he was afterwards besieged by RUFUS, in Rochester Castle, and forced, upon surrendering, to relinquish all his honours, and to abjure the kingdom for ever. Thence he repaired to Normandy, where being cordially received by Prince Robert, he had the entire government of the dukedom committed to his care. He d. at Palermo, in 1099, and was there interred. This very eminent personage is thus characterized by one of the old historians—"He was eloquent and magnanimous, courtly, and (to speak according to the world) courageous; he was a great honourer of religious men; his clergy he stoutly defended, with his tongue and sword, and furnished his church with rich ornament, as his buildings, vestments, and plate of gold and silver, which he gave thereto, do testifie."

The Earl of Kent held after the Conquest in England, by the gift of his brother, no less than 439 lordships; in Kent, 184; in Essex, 39; in Oxfordshire, 32; in Herefordshire, 23; in Buckinghamshire, 30; in Worcestershire, 2; in Bedfordshire, 8; in Northamptonshire, 12; in Nottinghamshire, 5; in Norfolk, 22; in Warwickshire, 6; and in Lincolnshire, 76.

Arms—Gu., a lion rampant, arg., debruised with a croiser's staff, gu.

OGILVY—EARL OF FINDLATER.

Barony, by Letters Patent, dated 4 October, 1616.
Earldom, by Letters Patent, dated 20 February, 1638.

Lineage.

ALEXANDER OGILVY son of Sir James Ogilvy (who d. in 510), by Agnes, natural dau. of George, 2nd Earl of Huntly, and great-grandson of Sir Walter Ogilvy, of Auchleven (by

Margaret, his wife, dau. and heir of Sir John Sinclair of Deskford and Findlater), from whose 2nd son. Sir Walter, descended the Lord Banffs (*see* that title), obtained a charter in 1511 for incorporating the lands of Deskford, Findlater, and Keithmore, into one entire barony, to be designated by the name of Ogilvy. He m. Janet, 2nd dau. of James Abernethy, 3rd Lord Saltoun, and had a son, JAMES, whom he disinherited, settling his estates upon John Gordon, 2nd son of George, 4th Earl of Huntly; but after a feud and some bloodshed between the Gordons and Ogilvys, the baronies of Deskford and Findlater were restored by an arbitration, of which Queen MARY was *overswoman*, to the rightful heir,

JAMES OGILVY, of Cardell, who m. 1st, Janet, dau. of Sir Robert Gordon, of Lochinvar; and 2ndly, Marian Livingstoun, of the family of Linlithgow, and by the latter only had issue, a son and dau., the latter predeceasing him, he was s. by his grandson,

SIR WALTER OGILVY, Knt. (son of Alexander Ogilvy, by Barbara, dau. of Walter Ogilvy, of Boyne), who was elevated to the peerage of Scotland, 4 October, 1616, by the title of BARON OGILVY, *of Deskford*. His lordship m. 1st, Agnes, dau. of Robert, 3rd Lord Elphinstone, by whom he had a dau., Christian, m. to Sir John Forbes, of Pitsligo; he m. 2ndly, Lady Mary Douglas, dau. of William, Earl of Morton, and by her had (besides two daus., Margaret, m. 1st, to James Douglas, Earl of Buchan, and 2ndly, to Andrew, 8th Lord Gray; and Mary, m. to Sir John Grant, of Grant), a son and successor,

JAMES OGILVY, 2nd baron; who was created, 20 February, 1638, *Earl of Findlater*. His lordship m. 1st, Elizabeth, dau. of Andrew, 2nd Earl of Rothes, by whom he had two daus., Elizabeth, m. to Sir Patrick Ogilvy, of Inchmarten, and Ann, m. to William, 9th Earl of Glencairn. He m. 2ndly, Marian, dau. of William Cunningham, 8th Earl of Glencairn, by whom he had no issue. The earl not having a son, procured a renewed patent, dated 18 October, 1641, conferring the titles of *Earl* and *Countess of Findlater* upon his son-in-law, Sir Patrick Ogilvy, Knt., of Inchmartin, and that gentleman's wife, Lady Elizabeth Ogilvy, his lordship's eldest dau. : and at his decease the peerage so devolved upon

SIR PATRICK OGILVY and his wife, ELIZABETH, as Earl and Countess of Findlater. His lordship d. 30 March, 1658, and was s. by his son,

JAMES OGILVY, 3rd earl; who m. 1st, Anne, dau. of Hugh, 7th Earl of Eglinton; and 2ndly, Lady Mary, 3rd dau. of William, 2nd Duke of Hamilton, but by the former only had issue, three sons, Walter, d. unm., JAMES, and Patrick, and two daus. : and dying in 1711, was s. by his eldest surviving son,

JAMES OGILVY, 4th earl; a lawyer of great eminence at the Scottish bar, who filled successively the offices of Solicitor-General and Secretary of State for Scotland, Lord Chief Baron of the Exchequer, and High Commissioner to the General Assembly of the Church. His lordship had been elevated to the peerage before the decease of his father, 28 June 1698, by the title of *Viscount Seafield*, and created, 24 June, 1701, *Viscount Reidhaven*, and EARL OF SEAFIELD, with remainder, in default of direct heirs male, to heirs-general. The earl m. Anne, dau. of Sir William Dunbar, Bart., of Durn, by whom he had three sons and two daus., Elizabeth, Countess of Lauderdale, and Janet, Countess of Fife. This nobleman made a motion in the House of Lords, 1 June, 1713, for leave to bring in a bill to dissolve the union with Scotland, which was refused by a majority of *four* only. In the same year, he was appointed keeper of the great seal in Scotland, and presided as chancellor in the court of Session. His lordship d. in 1730, and was s. by his eldest son,

JAMES OGILVY, 5th Earl of Findlater, and 2nd Earl of Seafield; who m. 1st, Lady Elizabeth Hay, dau. of Thomas, 6th Earl of Kinnoull, by whom he had issue,

JAMES, his successor.
Margaret, who m. Sir Lodovick Grant, Bart. of Grant, and had (with seven daus.) a son,
  SIR JAMES GRANT, Bart. *b.* 1738, who m. in 1763, Jean, only child of Alexander Duff, Esq., of Hatton, and left, with other issue, a son and heir,
    SIR LEWIS-ALEXANDER GRANT, who s. as 5th EARL OF SEAFIELD. (*See* BURKE's *Extant Peerage*.)

Anne, the wife of John, 2nd Earl of Hopetoun.

The earl m. 2ndly, Sophia, dau. of Charles, Earl of Hopetoun but had no issue. His lordship d. in 1764, and was s. by his only son,

JAMES OGILVY, 6th Earl of Findlater, and 3rd Earl of Seafield. This nobleman m. 9 June, 1749, Mary, dau. of John, Duke of Athole; and dying 3 November, 1770, was s. by his only child,

JAMES OGILVY, 7th Earl of Findlater, and 4th Earl of Sea-

'eld, who m. Christina-Teresa, dau. of Joseph, Count Murray, of Melgum, and d. s. p., 5 October, 1811, when the Earldom of Findlater, and the Viscounty of Seafield EXPIRED; but the other dignities reverted to his cousin, SIR LEWIS-ALEXANDER GRANT, Bart., who assumed the surname of Ogilvy in addition to that of his paternal family. and became 5th Earl of Seafield.

ALEXANDER OGILVIE (see next article OGILVY, LORD BANFF), M.D., Deputy-Inspector-General Royal Artillery, claimant to the Barony of Banff, would if that claim were established be, as a sequitur, male representative of the Earls of Findlater, and Barons of Deskford.

Arms—Or, a lion passant guardant gu., imperially crowned, ppr.

OGILVY—LORD BANFF.

By Letters Patent, dated 31 August, 1642.

Lineage.

SIR WALTER OGILVY, of Boyne, co. Banff, and of Auchleven, in the Barony of Boyne (whose elder brother, Sir James Ogilvy, was ancestor of the Earls of Findlater, see that title), m. 27 March, 1491, Margaret, 2nd dau. and co-heiress of Sir James Edmonstone, of that ilk, Thane of Boyne, and d. 1504, leaving two sons,

  GEORGE, 2nd Baron of Boyne, from whom ALEXANDER OGILVIE, M.D., present claimant to the Barony of Banff, deduces his descent (see infra).
  WALTER, of Dunlugus.

The younger son,

SIR WALTER OGILVY, of Dunlugus, m. Alison, dau. and co-heir of Sir Patrick Hume, of Fastcastle, and d. in 1538, leaving, with a dau. (Magdalen, wife of Sir Alexander Fraser, of Philorth), two sons,

  GEORGE, his heir,.
  Walter, of Carnousie.

The elder,

SIR GEORGE OGILVY, of Dunlugus, who acquired the thanedom of Boyne from the elder branch of his family, m. Beatrix, 4th dau. of George, 5th Lord Seton, and had three sons,

  WALTER, his heir.
  George, father of Sir George Ogilvy, 1st baronet of Carnousie.
  James.
  Janet, wife of William Forbes, of Tolquhoun.

The eldest son,

SIR WALTER OGILVY, of Banff and Dunlugus, s. his father in 1621, and marrying Helen, dau. of Walter Urquhart, of Cromarty, left a dau. (Beatrix, m. to Alexander Seton, of Pitmedden,) and two sons, of whom the elder,

SIR GEORGE OGILVY, of Dunlugus, created a baronet of Nova Scotia, 10 July, 1627, was distinguished in Montrose's wars, and in consideration of his eminent services in the royal cause was created a peer, 31 August, 1642, as BARON OGILVY, of *Banff*, with limitation to his heirs male for ever. His lordship m. 1st, Margaret, dau. of Sir Alexander Irvine of Drum, and had by her an only dau., Helen, m. to James, 2nd Earl of Airlie. He m. 2ndly, Mary, dau. of Alexander Sutherland, laird of Duffus, by whom he left at his decease, 11 August, 1663, with two daus., a son and successor,

GEORGE OGILVY, 2nd Lord Banff, who m. Agnes, dau. of Alexander Falconer, Lord Halkerton, and had issue,

  GEORGE, his heir.
  Alexander (Sir), of Forglen, M.P., created a baronet, 29 June, 1701, and constituted one of the senators of the college of justice, 23 July, 1705. He d. in 1727, having had by Mary, his 1st wife, eldest dau. of Sir John Allardice, of Allardice, co. Kincardine, three sons and four daus. The eldest surviving son,
    ALEXANDER, of Forglen, m. Jean Friend, of Bellenrichie, in Ireland, and by her (who m. 2ndly, Archibald Campbell, of Stonefield) dying v. p. left a son,
      ALEXANDER, who s. as 7th Lord Banff.
  Agnes, m. to Francis Gordon, of Craig.
  Mary, m. to John Forbes, of Balfluig.
  Helen, m. to Sir Robert Lauder, of Bielmouth.
  Janet, m. to John Leith, of Leithhall.

Lord Banff d. in 1668, and was s. by his son,

GEORGE OGILVY, 3rd Lord Banff, who m. Lady Jean Keith, 3rd dau. of William, 7th Earl Marischal, and dying in 1713

(he was burnt to death at Inchdruer), left. with a dau. (Mary, m. 1st, to John Joass, of Colleonard; and 2ndly, to the Rev William Hunter), a son and successor,

GEORGE OGILVY, 4th Lord Banff, b. 4 August, 1670, who m. in 1712, Helen, dau. of Sir John Lauder, Bart., of Fountainhall, and by her (who m. 2ndly, James Hay, Esq.) left at his decease, in 1718, two sons. by the elder of whom,

JOHN-GEORGE OGILVY, 5th Lord Banff, he was succeeded. His lordship was accidentally drowned, 29 July, 173, and as he left no issue by Mary, his wife, dau. of Capt. James Ogilvy, the title devolved on his brother,

ALEXANDER OGILVY, 6th Lord Banff, captain R.N.; who d. unm. at Lisbon, in 1746, and was s. by his kinsman,

SIR ALEXANDER OGILVY, Bart. as 7th Lord Banff (see supra); who m. 2 April, 1749, Jean, dau. of William Nisbet, Esq., of Dirleton, co. Haddington, and had issue,

  WILLIAM, his heir.
  Archibald, d. in 1763.
  David, captain in the army, d. unm. 10 August, 1796,
  Jane (eventually heiress), m. to Sir George Abercromby, Bart., of Birkenbog.
  Sophia.
  Janet, m. to the Rev. John Willison.
  Mary, m. to Alexander Murray, of Ayton.
  Grace, m. to William Douglas.

Lord Banff d. in 1771, and was s. by his son,

WILLIAM OGILVY, 8th Lord Banff, d. unm. 4 June, 1803, since which period the title has remained DORMANT. This Barony of Banff was, however, claimed by ALEXANDER OGILVIE, M.D., Deputy Inspector-General Royal Artillery, as "male descendant and representative of George Ogilvy, 2nd Baron of Boyne, and as heir-male of George, 1st Baron Ogilvy, of Banff." The claimant, Dr. Alexander Ogilvie, a distinguished medical officer of the Royal Artillery, was b. 9 May, 1789, and m. 20 December, 1830, Elizabeth-Frances, dau. and eventual sole heiress of — Warcup, Esq., and widow of Major J. Fogerty, 33rd regiment, and had an only child,

  ALEXANDER-WALTER-ARMSTRONG OGILVIE, capt. R.A., who, b. at Gibraltar, 20 January, 1834, m. 5 June. 1860, Gertrudis-Juana-Antonia, elder dau. (by his wife, Maria del Rosario, a lady of a noble Spanish family) of Vice-Admiral John-Alexander Duntze, R.N., grand niece of Sir John Duntze, 2nd baronet of Rockbere House, Devon (see BURKE's *Peerage*), and cousin of the Right Hon. Sir A.-J.-G. Cockburn, Bart, lord chief justice of England, and dying, 21 June, 1865, left an only child, ALEXANDER.

Arms—Arg., a lion passant guardant, gu., crowned with an imperial crown, or.

OGLE—VISCOUNT OGLE.

The Viscounty of Ogle, of Catherlough, was conferred, in 1645, on RICHARD OGLE, but EXPIRED with him in 1670.

OGLE—BARONS OGLE.

By Writ of Summons, dated 26 July, 1461.

Lineage.

This family, one of great antiquity in the co. of Northumberland, assumed its surname from the lordship of Oggil, its principal seat.

SIR ROBERT DE OOLE, son of Robert Ogle, by Margaret, his wife, dau. and heir of Sir Hugh Gubium, and grandson of Sir John de Ogle, Knt., and Annabella, his wife, dau. of Sir Walter Selby (HODGSON's *Northumberland*), obtained license 15th EDWARD III., to make a castle of his manor house there. In four years afterwards this Robert Ogle, upon the incursion of the Scots under the command of William Douglas, when they burnt Carlisle, Penrith, and other places, accompanied John de Kirkeby, then bishop of Carlisle, in a charge which he made, upon a strong party of the invaders, and encountering their chief commander, wounded him in the side with his lance, being severely wounded himself; while the bishop was unhorsed, but gallantly recovering his saddle, escaped unhurt. Sir Robert Ogle m. Joan, dau. and heir of Sir Robert Hepphale, Knt., and was father of

ROBERT OGLE, Jun.. who m. Helen, dau. and heir of Sir Robert Bertram, Knt., feudal Baron of Bothal Castle, Northumberland, by whom he acquired a considerable accession of property, and had a son,

SIR ROBERT OGLE. This feudal lord having been made prisoner by the Scots, in the 2nd HENRY IV., obtained a grant from the king, of 100 marks, towards the payment of his ransom; after which, in the 6th of the same reign, he served in the garrison of Berwick-upon-Tweed, under John Plantagenet, afterwards Duke of Bedford, then governor thereof. The next year, upon the death of David de Holgrave, the last husband of his mother, Helen, he had livery, upon doing his homage, of the castle and manor of Bothal. Whereupon being thus possessed of that manor and castle, as also of the manor of Hepphale, and the town of Lour-bottil, he entailed the same upon the heirs male of his body, upon condition that every such heir-male should bear the surname of Ogle, with the arms of Ogle and Bertram quarterly. He m. Joan, 3rd dau. and co-heir of Sir Alan de Heton, Knt., of Chillingham, and had livery of her property in the 12th of RICHARD II. He d. 31 October, 1410, and was s. by his eldest son,

ROBERT OGLE, who forcibly possessed himself of the castle and manor of Bothal, which had been settled upon John, his brother, who bore the name of BERTRAM. Whereupon complaint being made in parliament, it was ordered that a writ should be sent to the sheriff of Northumberland to require all those who then held that castle, to depart thence, and to command the said Robert to appear at Westminster by a certain day, to make answer to the king, for this misdemeanour. In the 5th HENRY V. he was constituted sheriff of Northumberland; and in the 2nd HENRY VI., he was joined with Henry, Earl of Northumberland, and other great men, in those parts, to conduct JAMES, King o' Scotland, from Durham, into his own realm; that prince, being then, upon hostages given, enlarged after an imprisonment of some years. He departed this life in the 15th HENRY VI., leaving issue,* by his wife, Maud, dau. of Sir Thomas Grey, of Heton, by Alice, his wife, dau. of Ralph, 1st Earl of Westmoreland and Werke, by Catherine Mowbray, according to Collins, eight daus., m. to persons of the first rank in the county, and three sons, viz.,

ROBERT (Sir), his successor.
John (Sir).
William (Sir), from whom one account derives the OGLES of Kirkley, co. Northumberland, and the OGLES of Worthy, in Hampshire, baronets (see BURKE's *Peerage and Baronetage*).

He was s. by his eldest son,

SIR ROBERT OGLE, who, in the 16th HENRY VI., was made sheriff of Northumberland, and in the 38th of the same reign, was in a commission to treat regarding a truce with the Scots. In the 1st EDWARD IV., he was made warden of the east marches, and in consideration of his good services had a grant of the offices of steward and constable of Alnwick, and other castles in Northumberland. Shortly after this he was summoned to parliament as a Baron (from 26 July, 1461, to 7 September, 1469), and in the same year he obtained from the crown a grant in special title of the Lordship of Redisdale, and castle of Herbotel, then vested therein by the attainder of Sir William Talboys. In the 2nd EDWARD IV., his lordship was with the king in arms against the Lancastrians, and assisting at the siege of Bamburgh Castle, was made governor of that fortress upon its surrender. He m. Isabel, dau. and heir of Alexander de Kirkeby, of Kirkeby, co. Lancaster, eldest son of Sir Richard de Kirkeby, Knt., by whom he had issue,

OWEN, his successor.
Isabel, who m. 1st, Sir John Heron, of Chipchase, Knt., and 2ndly, John Widrington.

His lordship d. 1 November, 1469, and was s. by his son,

OWEN OGLE, 2nd baron, summoned to parliament 6th HENRY VII. This nobleman was in the battle of Stoke, 2nd HENRY VII., on the part of the king against the Earl of Lincoln, and his adherents, and is the same that Polydore Virgil calls by mistake George. In two years afterwards he marched with the rest of the northern nobles, under Thomas, Earl of Surrey, to relieve Norham Castle, then besieged by the Scots. His lordship who d. 1485, m. Eleanor, dau. of Sir William Hilton, Knt., of Hilton Castle, co. Durham, and by her (who m. 2ndly, George Percy, Esq.,) had an only son,

RALPH OGLE, 3rd baron, summoned to parliament from 17 October, 1509, to 29 November, 1511. This nobleman m. Margaret, dau. of Sir William Gascoigne, Knt., and had issue,

* Dugdale enumerates his issue thus:—
ROBERT, his successor.
Margaret, m. to Sir Robert de Harbottle, Knt.
Anne, m. to Sir William Heron, Knt.
Constance, m. to Sir John Milford, Knt.
Joane, m. to — Manera.

ROBERT, his successor
William (Sir), m. Margaret, dau. of John Delaval, Esq., and had issue,
James, of Cawsey Park.
John, of Bedsyde.
John, from whom the Ogles of Kirkley, co. Northumberland, are said by some accounts to derive.
Anne, m. to Humphrey, son and heir of Sir William Lisle, Knt., and 2ndly, Sir John Delaval.
Dorothy, m. 1st, to Sir Thomas Forster, and 2ndly, to Sir Thomas Grey, of Horton, Knt.
Margery, m. to George Harbottle, Esq.

His lordship d. in 1512, and was s. by his eldest son,

ROBERT OGLE, 4th baron, summoned to parliament from 23 November, 1514, to 3 November, 1529. This nobleman was in the vanguard of the English army at the battle of Flodden, where the King of Scotland sustained so signal a defeat, but continuing in the Scottish wars, he fell eventually at Paunherhaugh, in 1529. His lordship m. Anne, dau. of Thomas, son and heir of George, Lord Lumley, by whom he had three sons, and was s. by the eldest surviving,

ROBERT OGLE, 5th baron, but never summoned to parliament. This nobleman m. 1st, Dorothy, dau. of Sir Henry Widdrington, of Widdrington, by whom he had issue, ROBERT, his successor; Margery, m. to Gregory Ogle, Esq. His lordship m. 2ndly, Jane, eldest dau. of Sir Cuthbert Ratcliffe, Knt., of Dilston, and by her (who m. 2ndly, Sir John Forster), had two sons, viz.,

CUTHBERT, successor to his brother.
Thomas, who m. Isabella, dau. of Sir Thomas Grey, of Horton, but d. without surviving issue.
Jane.
Margaret, m. to Robert Widdrington, Esq.

Lord Ogle fell at the battle of Halidon, in 1544, and was s. by his eldest son,

ROBERT OGLE, 6th baron, summoned to parliament from 14 August, 1553, to 5 November, 1558. His lordship m. Joan, dau. and heir of Sir Thomas Mauleverer, Knt., of Allerton Mauleverer, co. York, but dying s. p. in 1562, was s. by his half brother,

CUTHBERT OGLE, 7th baron, summoned to parliament from 11 January, 1563, to 17 October, 1601. This nobleman m. Catherine, dau. and co-heir of Sir Reginald Carnaby, Knt., and had issue,

Joane, m. to Edward Talbot (eventually 8th Earl of Shrewsbury), son of George, 6th Earl of Shrewsbury, but d. s. p in 1627.
Catherine, m. to Sir Charles Cavendish, Knt., of Welbeck, co. Nottingham.

His lordship d. in 1597, and the Barony of Ogle fell into ABEYANCE between his two daus., and so continued until the decease of JOANE, COUNTESS OF SHREWSBURY, the elder, without issue, in 1627, when it was called out in favour of the younger,

CATHERINE CAVENDISH, relict of Sir Charles Cavendish, who obtained especial letters patent under the great seal, from King CHARLES I., dated 4 December, 1628, declaring her ladyship to be BARONESS OGLE, and ratifying the dignity to her heirs for ever. Her ladyship d. the next year, and was s. by her only surviving son,

SIR WILLIAM CAVENDISH, K.G., who had been created Baron Ogle, and Viscount Mansfield, 3 November, 1620. (For the particulars of this nobleman, afterwards so celebrated in the civil wars, as DUKE OF NEWCASTLE, refer to Cavendish, Baron Ogle, Duke of Newcastle, &c.) His grace d. 1676, and was s. by his only son,

HENRY CAVENDISH, 2nd Duke of Newcastle, &c., and 9th Baron Ogle, K.G. This nobleman m. Frances, dau. of William, 2nd son of Robert Pierpoint, Earl of Kingston, by whom he had a son, HENRY, who d. s. p. in 1680, and five daus., viz.,

I. Elizabeth, m. 1st, to Christopher Monk, Duke of Albemarle, and 2ndly, to Ralph, Duke of Montagu, but d. s. p.
II. Frances, m. to John, 2nd Earl of Breadalbane, and d. s. p.
III. Margaret, m. to John Holles, Earl of Clare, afterwards created Duke of Newcastle, by whom she had an only dau.,
LADY HENRIETTA-CAVENDISH HOLLES, who m. Robert Harley, 2nd Earl of Oxford, and left an only dau.,
LADY MARGARET CAVENDISH HARLEY, who m. William Bentinck, 2nd Duke of Portland, K.G., and was mother of
WILLIAM-HENRY-CAVENDISH, 3rd Duke of Portland, K.G., great-grandfather of William-John-Arthur-Charles-James, DUKE OF PORTLAND.
IV. Catherine, m. to Thomas, 6th Earl of Thanet, and had five daus., to survive, viz.,
1 Catherine, m. to Edward, Viscount Sondes, heir apparent to the Earl of Rockingham.
2 Anne, m. to James, 5th Earl of Salisbury, and from this marriage descends the MARQUESS OF SALISBURY.

3 Margaret, *m.* to Thomas Coke, Earl of Leicester, but *d. s. p.*

4 Mary, *m.* 1st, Anthony Grey, Earl of Harold, who *d. s. p.*; and 2ndly, John, Earl of Gower, by whom she had issue.

5 Isabella, *m.* 1st, Lord Nassau Paulett, and 2ndly, Sir Francis Blake-Delaval, K.B.

v. Arabella, *m.* Charles, Earl of Sunderland, and left an only dau.,

Frances, who *m.* Henry, 4th Earl of Carlisle.

His grace *d.* in 1691, when all his honours became EXTINCT, except the Barony of Ogle, which fell into ABEYANCE, and still continues amongst the representatives of those of his daus. who left issue.

Arms—Arg., a fesse between three crescents, gu.

O'HARA—BARON TYRAWLY, AND BARON KILMAINE.

By Letters Patent, dated 10 January, 1706, and 8 February, 1721.

Lineage.

The O'Haras are an ancient Milesian family, settled in the west of Ireland.

SIR CHARLES O'HARA, Knt., a native of the co. of Mayo, was a distinguished military officer in Spain, and was raised to the peerage of Ireland, as BARON TYRAWLY, 10 January, 1706. In the following year, his lordship commanded the left wing of the allied army at the battle of Almanza, and remained in the Peninsula until the conclusion of the war, when he returned to Ireland, took his seat in the house of peers, and was constituted commander-in-chief of the forces in that kingdom. He *m.* Frances, dau. of Gervase Rouse, Esq., of Rouse Lench, co. Worcester, and had issue, JAMES, his heir, and Mary, whose will dated 28 February, 1759, was proved 7 April, 1759. He *d.* 8 June, 1724, aged eighty-four, and was buried 11 June following in the chancel vault of St. Mary's church, Dublin. His son, JAMES O'HARA, 2nd Baron Tyrawly, *b.* in 1690, who had been previously, 8 February, 1721, created Baron Kilmaine, of Kilmaine, co. Mayo, in recompense for his eminent military services during Queen Anne's wars, attained the rank of general in the army, filled several high diplomatic appointments, and was for a period, governor of Minorca. His lordship *m.* Mary, only surviving dau. of William, Viscount Mountjoy, but *d. s. p.* in 1774, when the titles became EXTINCT.

Arms—Vert, on a pale, radiant, or, a lion rampant, sa.

OLDCASTLE—BARON COBHAM.

By Writ of Summons, dated 8 January, 1313.

Lineage.

For an account of this nobleman, the celebrated Lollard leader, SIR JOHN OLDCASTLE, Baron Cobham, refer to *Cobham*, BARONS COBHAM.

OLIPHANT—LORD OLIPHANT.

Created before 1456.

Lineage.

Referring to CHALMERS' *Caledonia* for the more early pedigree, we need only mention that the 6th in descent from Sir William Oliphant, of Aberdalgie, the knightly warrior who so gallantly defended Stirling Castle against EDWARD I. in 1304, and whose tombstone is still extant, recording his death on 5 February, 1329, was

SIR LAURENCE OLIPHANT (eldest son and heir of Sir John Oliphant, of Aberdalgie, by Isabel, his wife, dau. of Walter Ogilvy, of Auchterhouse, and grandson of Sir William Oliphant), a minor in 1450, who was created BARON OLIPHANT before 1456, when he got a seisin of Auchterhouse, and was designed a noble and worshipful man, Laurence, Lord Oliphant and Aberdalgie. He obtained bonds of manrent from thirteen gentlemen in his neighbourhood, binding themselves to be his followers. He *d.* soon after 1495, leaving three sons, viz.,

JOHN, his heir.

William, of Berriedale, who *m.* Christian, only dau. and heir

of Alexander Sutherland, of Duffus, in Morny, Strabrok, in Linlithgow, and Berriedale, in Caithness. As the connexion with the latter county is important to the history of this family, it may be remarked that Christian, besides representing a branch of the Earls of Sutherland, and the Morays, Cheynes, and Chisholms, of Moray, was co-heir to the Earldom of Caithness, of which she inherited a fourth part. Their son, Andrew, was so harassed in that district, where he was looked on as an intruder, that at length having no son by Dame Janet Sinclair, his wife, he gave up his estates to his chief, in 1520, on condition that Lord Oliphant should provide suitable matches and tochers (fortunes) for his daus. He accordingly *m.* two of the three to cousins of his and their own, probably at a small expense, viz.,

Margaret, *m.* to William Oliphant, of Newton.

Katherine, *m.* to Andrew Oliphant, of Binzian.

Helen.

George, of Balmactorn.

The eldest son,

JOHN OLIPHANT, 2nd Lord Oliphant, was served heir in 1500. He *m.* Elizabeth, dau. of Colin, 1st Earl of Argyll, and *d.* in 1516, leaving his wife surviving. His eldest son,

COLIN OLIPHANT, Master of Oliphant, was slain *vita patris* at Flodden in 1513. He *m.* Elizabeth Keith, who survived him, and *m.* William, Lord Sinclair. The Master of Oliphant left three sons, viz.,

LAURENCE, his heir.

Peter, ancestor of the Oliphants of Langton.

William, of Newton, ancestor of the Oliphants of Gask, in Perthshire, whose representative, the late JAMES BLAIR-OLIPHANT, Esq., of Gask, *d. s. p.*, 7 December, 1847. His widow, Henrietta, dau. of James Gillespie Grahame, Esq., *s.* to the estate of Orchill, co. Perth.

The eldest son,

LAURENCE OLIPHANT, 3rd Lord Oliphant, is designed son and heir of Umquhill Colin, master of Oliphant, and grandson and heir of Umquhill John, Lord Oliphant, 18 November, 1516, when a gift of the ward of his lands passed. The 3rd lord purchased his cousin's whole estate in Caithness. He *m.* Margaret, eldest dau. of James Sandiland of Cruvie, and *d.* at Aldwick, in Caithness, 26 March, 1566, leaving an eldest son and heir,

LAURENCE OLIPHANT, 4th Lord Oliphant, who joined the association on behalf of Queen MARY at Hamilton. He *m.* Lady Margaret Hay, 2nd dau. of George, 7th Earl of Erroll; and dying in 1593, was *s.* by his grandson,

LAURENCE OLIPHANT, 5th Lord Oliphant (son and heir of Laurence, Master of Oliphant, by Christian, his wife, dau. of William, 2nd Earl of Morton). This nobleman *m.* Lilias Drummond, eldest dau. of James, 1st Lord Madherty, and had an only child, Anne, whose claim to the peerage was compromised by giving her husband the title of Mordington, while that of Oliphant was confirmed to her father's cousin german, Patrick, grandson of the 4th lord by his only younger son, John,

PATRICK OLIPHANT, who thus became 6th Lord Oliphant. By his 1st wife, Elizabeth, dau. of Sir Patrick Cheyne, of Esslemont, he had an only child, Lilias, *m.* to Sir Lawrence Oliphant, of Gask; and by his 2nd wife, Mary, dau. of James Crichton, of Frendraught, three sons, CHARLES, WILLIAM, and FRANCIS, who all inherited the title. The eldest son,

CHARLES OLIPHANT, 7th Lord Oliphant, *m.* Mary, dau. of Ogilvy of Milton, and relict of Patrick Meldrum, of Leathers, by whom he had a son,

PATRICK OLIPHANT, 8th Lord Oliphant; at whose decease without issue, in 1721, the title devolved on his uncle,

WILLIAM OLIPHANT, 9th Lord Oliphant, colonel in the army; who *d. s p.*, and was *s.* by his brother,

FRANCIS OLIPHANT, 10th Lord Oliphant; who *m.* in 1747, Mrs. Mary Lingley, of York; and *d. s. p.* at Islington, 19 April, 1748. At his lordship's decease, William Oliphant, son of Charles Oliphant, of Langton, one of the clerks of Session, assumed the title as 11th Lord Oliphant, and voted at the election of 1750. He *d. s. p.* in 1751, acknowledging Laurence Oliphant, of Gask, to be heir to his peerage.

Arms—Gu., three crescents, arg.

OLMIUS—BARON WALTHAM.

By Letters Patent, dated 22 June, 1762.

Lineage.

JOHN OLMIUS, Esq., of New Hall, co. Essex, a merchant of the city of London, descended from an ancient family settled at Arlon, in the Duchy of Luxembourg, was chosen deputy-governor of the bank of England in 1731, returned to parliament by the boroughs of Weymouth and Melcombe Regis, in 1737, and raised to the peerage of Ireland as BARON WALTHAM *of Philipstown*, King's Co., 22 June, 1762. He *m.* 8 September, 1741, Anne, dau. and heir of Sir William Billers, Knt., some time Lord Mayor of London, and had issue,

DRIGUE-BILLERS, his heir.
Elizabeth, *m.* 1766, to John Luttrell, Earl of Carhampton.

Lord Waltham *d.* in September, 1762, and was *s.* by his only son,

DRIGUE-BILLERS OLMIUS, 2nd Lord Waltham, *b.* 12 March, 1746; who *m.* 5 June, 1767, Miss Coe; but *d. s. p.* in 1787, when the title became EXTINCT.

Arms—Per fess, az. and arg., a fess, counter-embattled, or, in chief, a mullet of six points of the 2nd; in base, out of a mount, vert, an elm-tree, p; r.

O'MALLUN—BARON GLEAN-O'MALLUN.

By Letters Patent, dated 5 October, 1622.

Lineage.

SIR DERMOT O'MALLUN, or MULLANE, was created by patent, dated 5 October, 1622, Baron of Glean-O'Mallun, co. Clare, for life, with remainder to Albert O'Mallun, and the heirs male of his body. These are the words of the creation:—" R. Vto. die Octobris creavit Dermicium O'Mallun milit. in gradum et dignitatem Baronis de Glean-O'Mallun in Com. Clare, in Regno Hiberniæ duran. vita. Ac etiam creavit Albertum O'Mallun in gradum Baronis de Glean O'Mallun imediate post mortem pdict. Dermicii sibi et heredibus masculis." *(Patent Rolls,* 20th JAMES I, p. 3, N. 29.) The O'Mulluns were distinct from the Malones, and probably of the same house as the MacMullanes.

Arms–Arg., a bend, vert.

O'NEILL—EARL OF TYRONE, AND BARON DUNGANNON.

Earldom, by Letters Patent, dated 1 October, 1542.
Barony, by Letters Patent, dated 1 October, 1542.

Lineage.

The O'Neills of Ulster were for ages the most formidable of the aboriginal clans in Ireland.

HENRY MACOWEN O'NEILL, chief of his nation, in the 15th century, *m.* the dau. of MacMurrogh, and by her, who was living 1452, he had issue,

I. CON MORE, of whom presently.
II. Henry, slain at the house of Art O'Neill, of the Fews, 1498, he had a son, Felim.
III. Donald, competitor with his brother Henry, *d.* 6 August, 1509.   IV. Bryan.

The eldest son,

CON MORE O'NEILL, who founded the Franciscan Monastery of Ballinesaggart, in Tyrone, 1489, *m.* Elinor, dau. of Thomas, 7th Earl of Kildare, and was murdered by his brother Henry, 1493. He had issue,

I. CON BACCACH. of whom presently.
II. Art Oge, slain by Art O'Neill, of the Castle. He had issue, Neil Conalagh, who *m.* Rose, dau. of Manus O'Donnell, Lord of Tyronnel, and was father of

Sir Tirlogh Luineach O'Neill, Captain of all Tyrone, who assumed the title of O'Neill on the death of Shane a Diomais, was knighted 6 October, 1588, and *d.* 1595, leaving issue.

III. Cormac, alias Donnorrie, *alias* Kinard, co. Tyrone, father of Sir Henry O'Neill, of Drommorrie, and of two younger sons, John, surnamed Gealagh, from whom a family resident in France were said to have been descended, and Art O'Neill: the eldest son, SIR HENRY O'NEILL, had a son and heir,

Sir Henry Oge O'Neill, who was knighted 28 August, 1604, and slain in the king's service, leaving four sons and one dau., viz.,

1 Tirlogh, who *d. v. p.*, leaving by Catherine, his wife, two sons,

Phelim Roe (Sir), the first actor in the great war of 1641, attainted and executed in Dublin, 1652. He *m.* 1st, Lady Jane Gordon, dau. of George, Marquess of Huntly, and widow of Claud, Earl of Abercorn; and 2ndly, a dau. of General Thomas Preston, and had a son,

Gordon, brigadier-general *d.* at St. Germain-en-Laye, in France, in 1704, having had Charles, *d.* in France, and Mary-Anne, wife of Richard Bourke, commonly called Baron Castle Connell.

Tirlogh, of Ardgonnel.

2 Bryan, had custodiam of lands during minority of Phelim Roe. He had a son, Cormac, father of Colonel Con O'Neill, who had three sons, Art, Cormac, and John.

3 Cormac, father of John, father of Bryan.
4 Con, had custodiam of lands of Phelim, father of Con Oge.
1 Catherine, *m.* to Art Oge O'Neill, Esq., of Tassagh.

IV. Tirlogh, governor of Kinnard, father of Neill, father of Neill Oge.
V. Bryan, father of Con, father of Tirlogh, father of Rory, father of Art.
I. Joane, *m.* to Manus O'Donnell.

The eldest son,

CON BACCACH O'NEILL, having, according to Moryson, joined in the Geraldine Rebellion, and fearing the king's vengeance " sayled into England," and renouncing the title of O'Neill, had a regrant of his lands by patent, dated 1 October, 34th HENRY VIII., and was created 1 October, 1542, EARL OF TYRONE, for life with remainder to his son, MATTHEW, otherwise FEARDORAGH, O'NEILL, and the heirs male of his body. (The words of the patent are " ac post decessum predicti Conacii probatissimo viro subdito nostro Matheo, alias Ferdoraghe, O'Nele, filio predicti Conacii, ac heredibus masculinis de corpore predicti Mathei exeuntibus remanere." Pat. Rot. 33, 34, and 35 HENRY VIII., Mem. 2 fs.) He *m.* Alice, dau. of Gerald, 8th Earl of Kildare, and had issue,

I. Shane or John a Diomais, the Proud, who went to London in 1561 (to effect a reconciliation with Queen ELIZABETH), attended by his body guard of galloglasses with their Captain, MacSweeny, and his standard bearer, MacCaffry. Camden relates how the Londoners were astonished at the appearance in their streets of these stalwart warriors, habited in the military costume of their country. Shane a Diomais was slain by the MacDonnells in 1567; he *m.* Margery, dau. of Manus O'Donnell, Lord of Tyrconnell, and by her had issue,

1 Henry, who fled into Ulster when Hugh Roe O'Donnell effected his second and successful escape from Dublin Castle.
2 Art, died in the co. Wicklow from fatigue in his flight from confinement in Dublin.

Shane had, by Lady Jane, wife of Calvagh O'Donnell, Lord of Tyrconnell, an illegitimate son, HUGH NA GAVALLOCH, who was hanged by order of the Earl of Tyrone, and not, as Camden insinuates, by that Chieftain's own hand.

II. Phelim Caach, father of Tirlogh O'Neill Breassalagh, who had issue, 1 Hugh, 2 Cormack, 3 Con, 4 Art, 5 Phelim, 6 Edmund, 7 Tirlagh, 8 Bryan-Ceannfhionain, 9 Ever-an-locha. III. Tirlogh.
I. Mary, *m.* to Sorley Boy MacDonnell, father of the 1st Earl of Antrim.

Con Baccach O'Neill, 1st Earl of Tyrone, had also by Alison, the wife of a blacksmith at Dundalk, an illegitimate son,

MATTHEW O'NEILL, called " Feardoragh," who was created by patent, 1 October, 1542, BARON DUNGANNON. He *m.* Joanna, dau. of Constantine Maguire, son of Constantine, son of Bryan, son of Philip, son of Thomas Maguire, and by her (who was afterwards the wife of Henry O'Neill of the Fews) he had issue,

I. Bryan, murdered by McDonnell.
II. Hugh, of whom presently.
III. Cormac (Sir), knighted 23 August, 1605, by Sir Arthur Chichester. He *m.* the dau. of Sir Hugh O'Donnell, Lord of Tyrconnell, and dying in the Tower of London, about 1616, left a son, Constantine O'Neill, who *d. s. p.*
IV. Barnaby.
V. Art, who had three sons.

1 Art-Oge, father of HUGH O'NEILL, a major-general, and governor of Limerick, 1650, who assumed the title of EARL OF TYRONE, as appears by his letter, soliciting the restoration of his family to the favour of the King, dated from Madrid, 27 October, 1660, addressed to the Marquess of Ormonde, and supported by the recommendation of the English ambassador, Henry Bennet, who sets forth Hugh's lineal succession to the title *(Carte M.S.S. vol. 31, p. 33).*
2 OWEN-ROE, the famous general of the Confederates in 1642; who achieved the victory of Benburb, and was one of the greatest of Irish commanders. He *d.* 1649, in the castle of Cloughouter, co. Cavan, and was buried in the cemetery of the ancient Franciscan monastery in the town of Cavan, leaving by his wife, Rose O'Dogherty, widow of Calvagh O'Donnell, four sons,

Henry, born in Spain, executed by order of Sir Charles Coote, at Derry, 1650, having had a son Hugh, who *d. s. p.*
Bryan, father of Owen, titular Earl of Tyrone, *d. s. p.*
Con (captain) had two sons, Owen, a colonel in the French service, and Lewis, an officer in the French service.
John, a priest.

3 Con, had two sons, Daniel and Bryan Roe, father of Con, who *d.* young in Spain.

The 2nd son,

HUGH O'NEILL, Earl of Tyrone, was chiefly educated at the Court of Queen ELIZABETH, where he learnt, from the English statesmen Burghley, Leicester, and Hatton, that knowledge of political craft which marked his entire career. Eventually, throwing off his allegiance to the English Sovereign, "the Arch Rebel," as he was styled, disclaimed the title of Earl of Tyrone (which had been confirmed to him by charter, 10 May, 1587) and proclaimed himself the O'Neill. He conquered every army sent against him by ELIZABETH; until after the siege of Kinsale in 1603, he found his cause hopeless and surrendered to Lord Mountjoy, by whom he was received into protection. Subsequently, in 1607, he fled to France, and thence proceeded to Louvain, and finally to Rome, where he was maintained on a monthly allowance granted by PAUL V. and the King of Spain. He m. 1st, a dau. of Sir Brian McPhelim, from whom he was legitimately divorced; 2ndly, Judith, dau. of Manus O'Donnell, and sister of the celebrated Red Hugh O'Donnell, and by her had issue,

   I. HUGH, Baron of Dungannon, d. at Rome, 1609, unm.

   II. HENRY, a colonel of an Irish regiment, in the archduke's service, killed in Spain.

   III. JOHN, called El Condé de Tyrone, in Spain, in which kingdom he had attained the rank of lieutenant-general, killed in Catalonia.

   IV. BRYAN or BERNARD, page to the archduke, murdered at Brussels, 1617.

   V. CON, a prisoner in the Tower of London, 1617.

   I. Mary, m. to Sir Bryan McMahon, Knt. of Monaghan.

   II. ——, m. to Donnell Ballagh O'Cahan.

   III. Sarah, m. to Arthur Magennis, Viscount Iveagh.

   IV. Margaret, m. to Richard Butler, 3rd Viscount Mountgarrett.

He m. 3rdly, Mabel, sister of Sir Henry Bagenall, marshal of the Queen's forces in Ireland, to whom he was m. by Jones, bishop of Meath, 1591, she d. s. p.; and 4thly, the dau. of the Lord Iveagh, who accompanied him to Rome where she died. This lady is described by Peter Lombard, archbishop of Armagh, thus : "Ætate quidem juniorem, sed educatione, prudentiâ, piétate maturam;" de Reg. Hib. p. 383. Tyrone d. at Rome, blind and old, 20 July, 1616, and was buried with great pomp in the church of San Pietro Montorio, where the tombs of 'O'Donnell and O'Neill, Baron of Dungannon, are objects of attraction to English and Irish sojourners in the Eternal City. The tomb of the Earl of Tyrone is no longer in existence, but happily the inscription it bore is still preserved in the Book of Obits, of San Pietro's monastery, and runs thus :

D. O. M,
Hic Quiescunt Ossa
Hugonis Principis O'Neill.

It would appear that this brief epitaph was suggested by that on the tomb of Tasso in the neighbouring church of St. Onofrio. Hugh, Earl of Tyrone, was attainted in 1612.

Arms—Arg., a sinister-hand affronté and couped, gu.

O'NEILL—BARONS VISCOUNTS AND EARL O'NEILL.

Baronies, by Patent, dated 25 October, 1793.
Viscounty, by Patent, dated 3 October, 1795.
Earldom, by Patent, dated August, 1800.

Lineage.

NIALL THE GREAT, Monarch of Ireland at the close of the 4th century, having subdued the Picts and Britons, and ravaged the coasts of Gaul, was assassinated on the banks of the Loire, near Boulogne. His son, Prince Owen, was the ancestor of the house of O'Neill. Daniel O'Neill, surnamed *Ardmach*, the 46th monarch of the Hy-Niall race, d. A.D. 1004; he was s. by Malachy, a South Hy-Niall Prince, in whose reign the ancient dynasty was interrupted by Bryan Boru (O'Brien), King of Munster, who obtained the crown, but at his death at the battle of Clontarf, 1014, Malachy resumed the sceptre, and d. 1048. Thenceforward, for nearly a century and a quarter, Princes of other houses, the O'Conors of Connaught, and the O'Briens of Munster, contended for the sovereignty.

HUGH DUFF O'NEILL, King of Ulster, 6th in descent from the Monarch, Daniel Ardmach, d. 1230; he was ancestor of the house of O'NEILL, of Clanaboy, as his brother Prince Neill Roe, was of O'NEILL, of Tyrone. Aodh-Buidhe, i.e., Hugh-boy or Yellow Hugh O'Neill, King of Ulster, 1260, grandson of Hugh Duff, recovered from the English the territories in the cos. Antrim and Down, called after him Clan Hugh-boy, *Anglicé* Clanaboy, and had for his chief castle, Edenduffcarrig, now Shane's Castle. The last of this royal house who bore the title of King of Ulster, was DONALD O'NEILL, who d. 1325. In the celebrated appeal made by him, and the princes, nobles, and Irish people in general to Pope JOHN XXII., against the English, in 1315, as recorded by John Fordun, he is styled "*Donald O'Neyl, King of Ulster, and rightful successor to the throne of all Ireland.*"

SIR SHANE O'NEILL, Knt. of Edenduffcarrig, *alias* Shane's Castle, m. 1st, Rose, dau. of Sir Arthur Magennis, Viscount Iveagh, and had by her a son, HENRY. He m. 2ndly, Anne, dau. of Bryan Carrah O'Neill, lord of the barony of Loughinsholin, and d. 23 April, 1617, having had two sons,

   I. Arthur, who m. Grace, dau. of Cahal O'Hara, of Crebilly, co. Antrim, and was father of CAPT. JOHN O'NEILL, whose son, COL. CHARLES O'NEILL, successor to the estates at Lady Antrim's death.

   II. Phelim Duff, who m. Shela, 2nd dau. of Cahal O'Hara, Esq., and had a son, BRIAN, who m. Elinor, dau. of Edmund Magennis, Esq., of Kilwarlin, and was father of JOHN, known as "French John," who s. his cousin Charles.

The eldest son of Sir Shane,

SIR HENRY O'NEILL, Knt. of Edenduffcarrig, or Shane's Castle, m. Martha, dau. of Sir Francis Stafford, governor of Ulster, and d. 13 September, 1637, leaving an only child, ROSA, who m. Randall, 1st Marquess of Antrim, and d. s. p. in 1707, when the estates passed to her cousin,

COL. CHARLES O'NEILL, who m. Mary, dau. of Charles, Duke of Bolton, and d. s. p. in 1716. His kinsman and heir,

JOHN O'NEILL, Esq. of Edenduffcarrig, or Shane's Castle, known as "French John," m. Charity, dau. of Sir Richard Dixon. His will, which bears date 16 September, 1737, was proved 1 May, 1739. He had issue,

   I. HENRY (disinherited), m. Mary, widow of Captain Jo'n Bickerstaffe, of Rosegift in the Largy, and d. 1721, v. p., leaving an only child and heiress,

     MARY, who m. Rev. Arthur Chichester, grandson of John Chichester, Esq., brother of Arthur, 2nd Earl of Donegal, and had a son,

     REV. WILLIAM CHICHESTER, LL.D., rector of Broughshane, co. Antrim, and Clonmanny, co. Donegal; he m. 1st, Mary-Anne, dau. of George Harvey, Esq. of Malin Hall, and had a son,

     Arthur (Sir), of Greencastle, M.P., created a Baronet 13 September, 1821; d. unm. 25 May, 1847, when his baronetcy became extinct.

     He m. 2ndly, Mary-Anne, dau. of the Rev. Edward Hart, of Kilderry, and d. 31 October, 1816, leaving a son,

     REV. EDWARD CHICHESTER, rector of Kilmore, co. Armagh, m. 23 April, 1812, Catherine, dau. of Robert Young, Esq. of Culdaff House, co. Donegal, and d. in June, 1840, having had by this lady, who d. 15 April, 1875,

     WILLIAM, Lord O'Neill, b. 4 March, 1813; s. to the O'Neill estates under the will of the 3rd Viscount O'Neill, 1855, assumed the surname and arms of O'Neill, by royal license, and was created Baron O'Neill, of Shane's Castle, by patent, dated 18 April, 1868. He m. 1st, 3 January, 1839, Henrietta, dau. of the Hon. Robert Torrens, one of the judges of the court of common pleas in Ireland, and by her (who d. 17 January, 1857) has issue,

       EDWARD, M.P. co. Antrim, 1863 to 1880, b. 31 December, 1839 ; m. 30 June, 1873, Lady Louisa-Katharine-Emma Cochrane, eldest dau. of the Earl of Dundonald, and has issue,

         WILLIAM-THOMAS-COCHRANE, b. 16 November, 1874; d. 24 July, 1882.

         Arthur-Edward-Bruce, b. 19 September, 1876.

         Louisa-Henrietta-Valdevia, b. 8 October, 1879.

       Arthur, b. 13 September, 1843; d. 12 January, 1870.

       Robert-Torrens, M.A., b. 10 January, 1845.

       Anne.

      He m. 2ndly, 8 April, 1858, Elizabeth-Grace, dau. of the Ven. John Torrens, D.D., Archdeacon of Dublin.

      Robert, b. 6 April, 1814; in holy orders; m. 1st, 5 March, 1840, Frances-Alicia-Anne, dau. of Gen. George-Vaughan Hart, of Kilderry, which lady d. August, 1867; and 2ndly, 1869, Henrietta, dau. of the Rev. Townley Blackwood Price, rector of Bright, co. Down, and d. 2 June, 1878, leaving issue.

      Arthur, who d. young in 1830.

      George-Vaughan (Rev.), rector of Wotton, Dorking, Surrey; m. Harriett, dau. of Hugh Lyle, Esq. of Knocktarna, co. Antrim, and has issue, Edward; Henry; William (d. in infancy); Arthur; Alfred; Frances-Harriett, m. 28 October, 1873, to William-John Evelyn, Esq. of Wootton House, Surrey; Ada, m. 22 June, 1876, to Reginald, son of Isaac Braithwaite, Esq of Hookfield, Epsom, and 4, Gloucester Square, London; Helen; and Mary.

   II. CHARLES, of whom presently.

   III. Clotworthy, d. unm. His will which bears date 1 May, 1749, was proved 2 August, 1750.

   I. Catherine, m. to Richard Butler, Lord Viscount Mountgarrett.

II. Anne, *m.* to Captain William Sharman.

III. Mary, *m.* to Robert Burrowes, Esq. of Ballybrittas, co Kildare.

IV. Jane, *m.* to the Hon. Arthur Dawson, Baron of the Exchequer.

v. Rachel.   VI. Elinor.   VII. Rose.

French John O'Neill, *d.* 1739 (his will, dated 16 September, 1737, was proved 1 May, 1739), and was *s.* by his 2nd son,

CHARLES O'NEILL, Esq. of Shane's Castle, who *m.* (license dated 20 January, 1786) Catherine, dau. of the Right Hon. St. John Brodrick, of Midleton, and had issue,

    I. JOHN, of whom presently.

    II. St. John, *b.* 6 May, 1741; *m.* Frances, dau. of Robert Borrowes, Esq. of Ballybrittas, and *d.* 1790, leaving an only child, Mary, who *d. unm.*

    III. Anne, *m.* to Right Hon. Richard Jackson, and had issue, SIR GEORGE JACKSON, who was created a Baronet, 3 November, 1812, *d. s. p.*; Major Robert Jackson, *d. s. p.*; Anne Jackson, wife of Nathaniel Alexander, Bishop of Meath; Mary, *m.* to John-Hamilton O'Hara, Esq. of Crebilly, and *d. s. p.*; and Harriet, *d. unm.*

Charles O'Neill, whose will bears date 10 July, 1769, and was proved 4 November following, *d.* in August, 1769, and was *s.* by his elder son,

JOHN O'NEILL, Esq. of Shane's Castle, M.P., *b.* 18 January, 1740, was proved to the peerage of Ireland, 25 October, 1793, as *Baron O'Neill, of Shane's Castle;* and advanced to the dignity of VISCOUNT O'NEILL, 3 October, 1795. His lordship *m.* 18 October, 1777, Henrietta, only child of Charles Boyle, Lord Dungarvan, and by her (who *d.* 3 September, 1793) had issue, CHARLES-HENRY-ST. JOHN, his heir; and JOHN-BRUCE-RICHARD, last viscount. Lord O'Neill *d.* of wounds received in action with the insurgents in Ireland, 17 June, 1798, and was *s.* by his elder son,

CHARLES-HENRY-ST. JOHN, 2nd Viscount O'Neill, K.P., lord-lieutenant of the co. Antrim, and colonel of its militia; *b.* 22 January, 1779, was created Viscount Raymond and EARL O'NEILL, in August, 1800. His lordship *d. unm.* 25 March, 1841, when the higher honours became EXTINCT, and the Viscounty of O'Neill devolved on his brother,

JOHN-BRUCE-RICHARD O'NEILL, 3rd Viscount O'Neill, one of the representative lords; *b.* 20 December, 1780. His lordship, a general in the army, *d.* 12 February, 1855, when the peerage became EXTINCT, and the estates devolved on the heir general, the REV. WILLIAM CHICHESTER, who assumed by royal license, the surname and arms of O'NEILL, and was created LORD O'NEILL, of Shane's Castle.

Arms—Per fesse, wavy, the chief arg., and the base representing waves of the sea, in chief a dexter hand couped at the wrist, gu., in base, a salmon naiant in fess, ppr.

ONGLEY—BARON ONGLEY.

(*See* ADDENDA.)

ORREBY—BARON ORREBY.

(*See* ADDENDA.)

PAGET—BARONS BURTON, EARLS OF UXBRIDGE.

Barony, by Letters Patent, dated 31 December, 1711.
Earldom, by Letters Patent, dated 19 October, 1714.

Lineage.

WILLIAM PAGET was, says Dugdale, "a person endowed with excellent parts, as may seem from his ascent from so low a condition to those high preferments, whereunto, by sundry degrees, he attained: being son to Paget, one of the serjeants at mace in the city of London, who was born near Wednesbury, in Staffordshire, of mean parentage, where there were some of that generation, till of late years, remaining." In the 23rd HENRY VIII., this William Paget, through his great abilities alone, obtained the appointment of clerk of the signet; in a few years afterwards he was made clerk of the council: he next became clerk of the privy seal, and then clerk of the parliament, having the latter office conferred upon him for life. He subsequently received the honour of knighthood, was employed by King HENRY VIII., upon several diplomatic occasions of high importance, and appointed one of his Majesty's executors, and of the council to his son, for that monarch upon his death-bed. In the 2nd year of the new reign (EDWARD VI.), Sir William Paget had a grant in fee from the crown of Exeter House (formerly belonging to the Bishops of that see), with a parcel of ground lying within the garden of the Middle Temple, adjoining thereto;

which mansion he rebuilt for his own residence, and called it Paget House. But it did not retain that designation for any length of time, it being afterwards called Leicester House, and then Essex House. In the 4th EDWARD VI., Sir Edward was accredited ambassador extraordinary to the Emperor CHARLES V., and became so great a favourite with that monarch, that his imperial majesty was heard to say, "that Sir Edward Paget deserved to be a king as well as to represent one." Once, too, as the English ambassador came to court, the emperor observed, "Yonder is the man to whom I can deny nothing." At another time, his majesty remarked, that England sent three sorts of ambassadors to him; the first was Wolsey, whose great retinue promised much, but he did nothing; the second, Morisin, promised, and did much; the third, Paget, promised nothing, and did all. In the same year, Sir Edward being then a kn ght of the Garter, was constituted comptroller of the king's household: made chancellor of the Duchy of Lancaster, and summoned to the House of Lords as BARON PAGET, *of Beaudesert,* co. *Stafford,* by writ, dated 23 January, 1552; after which he was sent with the Earl of Bedford and Sir John Mason, again to treat of peace with the French. Notwithstanding, however, these eminent services, he was accused by his enemies on the fall of the Protector Somerset, of divers offences, and committed to the Tower, deprived of the insignia of the Garter, and fined £6,000, two of which were remitted, on condition that the other four were paid within a year. At the demise of King ED-WARD, his lordship, espousing the cause of MARY, rode post with the Earl of Arundel, to convey the announcement of the King's death to her Majesty, and of her proclamation by the city of London; for which loyal proceeding he was ever afterwards highly esteemed by her Majesty, and in the 3rd year of her reign, was made lord privy seal. His lordship *m.* Anne, dau. and heir of Henry Preston, Esq., of the co. Lancaster (son of Lawrence, 2nd son of Thomas Preston, Esq., of Preston Patrick and Under Levins Hall), and had issue,

HENRY (Sir), his successor.

THOMAS. who *s.* as 3rd lord.

Charles, attainted with his brother Thomas, Lord Paget. Hollingshed relates that Charles Paget was principal agent for the Roman Catholics, as it was proved on examination of the Earl of Northumberland's case, viz.: that in September, 1583, he came privately beyond sea to the Earl of Northumberland, at Petworth, where the Lord Paget met him; and that on Throgmorton's being committed to the Tower, the Earl of Northumberland prevailed on the Lord Paget to quit the realm, and provided him a ship on the coast of Sussex, wherein he embarked.

Etheldreda, *m.* to Sir Christopher Allen, Knt.

Eleanor. *m.* 1st, to Jerome Palmer, Esq., and 2ndly, to Sir Rowland Clerk, Knt.

Grisild, *m.* 1st, to Sir William Waldegrave, and 2ndly, to Sir Thomas Rivet, Knt.

Joan, *m.* to Sir Thomas Kitson, Knt.

Dorothy, *m.* to Sir Thomas Willoughby, son of Sir Henry Willoughby, of Woollaton, co. Notts.

Anne, *m.* to Sir Henry Lee, Knt.

He *d.* 1563, and was *s.* by his eldest son,

SIR HENRY PAGET, 2nd baron, summoned to parliament 30 September, 1566. His lordship *m.* Catherine, dau. of Sir Henry Knyvett, Knt., and had an only dau.,

ELIZABETH, *d.* in infancy, 29 June, 1571.

He *d.* in 1568, and was *s.* by his brother,

THOMAS PAGET. 3rd baron, summoned to parliament from 4 April, 1571, to 6 January, 1581. This nobleman, being a zealous Roman Catholic, was obliged, in the reign of ELIZABETH, to seek personal security in France, but he was attainted in parliament with his brother, Charles, as a well-wisher to the Queen of Scots, when the Barony of Paget became FORFEITED, and his lands bei g confiscated, the Earl of Leicester got a grant of Paget House. His lordship *m.* Nazaret, dau. of Sir Henry Newton, Knt., and left at his decease (*anno* 1589, at Brussels), an only son,

WILLIAM PAGET, who was with the Earl of Essex in the memorable attack upon Cadiz, 39th ELIZABETH, and being restored to the lands and honours forfeited by his father, was summoned to parliament as BARON PAGET, from 5 November, 1605, to 7 March, 1628. His lordship *m.* Lettice, dau. and co-heir of Henry Knollys, Esq., a younger son of Sir Henry Knollys, K.G., by whom he had issue,

WILLIAM, his successor.

Henry, } both *d. unm.*
Thomas, }

Mary, *m.* to Sir William Hicks, Bart., of Buckholt, Essex.

Dorothy, *d. unm.*

Catherine, *m.* to Sir Anthony Irby, Knt., of Boston, co. Lincoln, ancestor of the Lords Boston.

Anne, *m.* 1st, to Sir Simon Harcourt, Knt., of Stanton Harcourt, co. Oxford, and 2ndly, to Sir William Waller, Knt., of

Osterley Park, co. Middlesex, the celebrated parliamentary general.

He d. in 1629, and was s. by his eldest son,

WILLIAM PAGET, 5th baron, summoned to parliament from 13 April, 1639, to 8 May, 1661. His lordship was made a knight of the Bath at the coronation of King CHARLES I. He m. Lady Frances Rich, dau. of Henry, Earl of Holland, and had issue,

WILLIAM, his successor.

Henry, who settled in Ireland, m. Anne, dau. of Robert Sandford, Esq., of Sandford, co. Salop, by Anne, his wife, dau. of Peter Daniel, Esq., M.P., of Tabley, and had (with a dau., Dorothy, who m. Sir Edward Irby, Bart.) a son,

THOMAS, a brigadier-general in the army, who m. Mary, dau. and co-heir of Peter Whitcombe, Esq., of Great Braxted, in Essex, by whom he had an only dau. and heiress,

CAROLINE PAGET, who m. Sir Nicholas Bayly, Bart., and had a son,

HENRY BAYLY, who inherited as 9th Baron Paget. His lordship assumed the surname and arms of PAGET, and was created EARL OF UXBRIDGE. He was father of Henry-William, 2nd Earl of Uxbridge, created, in 1815, MARQUESS OF ANGLESEY (see BURKE's Extant Peerage).

Thomas, d. unm.

Isabel, d. unm.

Lettice, m. to Richard Hampden, Esq., of Great Hampden, Bucks.

Elizabeth, d. unm.

Frances, m. to Rowland Hunt, Esq., of Boreatton, co. Salop.

Penelope, m. to Philip Foley, Esq., of Prestwood, Staffordshire.

Diana, m. to Sir Henry Asshurst, Bart

Anne, d. unm.

His lordship d. in 1678, and was s. by his eldest son,

WILLIAM PAGET, 6th baron, summoned to parliament, 6 March, 1679. This nobleman m. 1st, Frances, dau. of Francis Pierrepont, and granddau. of Robert, Earl of Kingston, by whom he had two sons,

William, who d. unm., v. p.

HENRY, successor to the title.

His lordship m. 2ndly, Isabella, dau. of Sir Anthony Irby, Knt., of Boston, by whom he had another son, William, who d. young. This nobleman, "the reputation of whose great abilities," says Banks, "will last as long as the memory of that celebrated peace of Carlowitz, concluded in 1698, shall remain in history," d. at an advanced age, 25 February, 1713, and was s. by his son,

HENRY PAGET, BARON BURTON (a dignity to which he had been raised in the life-time of his father, by letters patent, dated 3 December, 1711), as 7th Baron Paget. His lordship was advanced to the EARLDOM OF UXBRIDGE, 19 October, 1714. He filled many high and important offices, but resigned all his employments in 11.5. His lordship m. 1st, Mary, dau. and co-heir of Thomas Catesby, Esq., of Whiston, co. Northampton, and had a son,

THOMAS-CATESBY, Lord Paget: he was colonel of a regiment of foot, who d. v. p., anno 1742, leaving by his wife Lady Elizabeth Egerton, dau. of John, Earl of Bridgewater,

HENRY, who s. as 2nd Earl of Uxbridge.

The earl m. 2ndly, Elizabeth, dau. of Sir Walter Bagot, Knt., but had no issue. He d. in 1743, and was s. by his grandson,

HENRY PAGET, 2nd Earl of Uxbridge. This nobleman d: unm. in November, 1769, when the Barony of Paget devolved upon his kinsman, Henry Bayly, Esq., as 9th baron (refer to issue of Henry, 2nd son of 5th lord), while the Barony of Burton and Earldom of Uxbridge became EXTINCT.

Arms—Sa., on a cross engrailed between four eagles displayed arg., five lions passant of the 1st.

PALMER—EARL OF CASTLEMAINE.

By Letters Patent, dated 11 December, 1661.

Lineage.

SIR THOMAS PALMER, Knt., of Wingham, in Kent, the representative of a very ancient family, was created a Baronet, 29 June, 1621 (see BURKE's Extinct Baronetage, and BURKE's Peerage and Baronetage, under PALMER, BART., of Wanlip Hall). He m. Margaret, dau. of John Pooley, Esq., of Badley, co. Suffolk, and had three sons,

417*

I. THOMAS (Sir), m. Margaret, dau. of Herbert Pelham, Esq., and dying v. p., left

THOMAS (Sir), 2nd baronet, who m. Elizabeth, dau. and co-heiress of Sir John Shirley, Knt. of Isfield, co. Sussex, and was grandfather of

Sir Thomas Palmer, whose dau. Elizabeth, m. Hon. Edward Finch (son of Daniel, 6th Earl of Winchelsea).

II. Roger (Sir), K.B., cup-bearer to Henry, Prince of Wales, and to his brother afterwards King CHARLES I., d. s. p.

III. James (Sir), of Dorney, Bucks, knight of the bedchamber to King JAMES I., and chancellor of the Order of the Garter, m. 1st, Martha, dau. of Sir William Garrard, of Dorney, Bucks, by whom he had a son, PHILIP, cup-bearer to King CHARLES II., ancestor of the PALMERS, of Dorney Court. Sir James m. 2ndly, Catherine, dau. of William Herbert, Earl of Powys, and relict of Sir Robert Vaughan, and had a son, ROGER, 1st Earl of Castlemaine. This

ROGER PALMER, Esq., was sent as ambassador to Constantinople, and afterwards to Rome, and raised to the peerage of Ireland as Baron Palmer, and EARL OF CASTLEMAINE, co. Kerry, 11 December, 1661, honours which EXPIRED 28 July, 1705. His lordship m. Barbara, only dau. and heir of William Villiers, 2nd Viscount Grandison, and had a dau., Lady Anne Palmer, m. to Thomas Lennard, Earl of Sussex. Lady Castlemaine, becoming the mistress of King CHARLES II., was created by his majesty, DUCHESS OF CLEVELAND. (See FITZROY, Duke of Cleveland.)

The portraits of the Earl and Countess of Castlemaine (by Lely), the earl's will, some private letters, and a very handsome book of vellum, dedicated to Lady Anne Palmer, containing the whole pedigree of the family, authenticated by the signature of Sir William Segar, Garter, with the different arms, quarterings, &c., are now in the possession of the Rev. HENRY PALMER, of Dorney Court, Bucks (see CORRIGENDA).

Arms—Or, two bars, gu., each charged with three trefoils, arg., in chief, a greyhound courant, sa.

PARKE—BARON WENSLEYDALE.

(See ADDENDA.)

PARKER—BARONS MORLEY, BARONS MONTEAGLE.

Barony of Morley, by Writ of Summons, dated 29 Dec. 1299.
Barony of Monteagle, by Writ of Summons, dated 23 Nov. 1514

Lineage.

ROBERT MORLEY, Baron Morley (a dignity created by writ of EDWARD I., dated as above), d. in 1442, leaving a dau. and heiress,

ALIANORE MORLEY, who m.

SIR WILLIAM LOVEL, 2nd son of William, Lord Lovel, of Tchinersh, which William was summoned to parliament in right of his wife, as Lord Morley. He d. in 1476, and was s. by his son,

HENRY LOVEL, Lord Morley, but never summoned to parliament. This nobleman, b. in 1468, d. in 1489, s. p., when his sister,

ALICE LOVEL, became his heir. Her ladyship m. 1st,

SIR WILLIAM PARKER, standard bearer, and privy councillor to King RICHARD III., and 2ndly, Sir Edward Howard, 2nd son of Thomas, Duke of Norfolk; by the latter she had no issue, but by the former she had a son,

SIR HENRY PARKER, who was summoned to parliament as BARON MORLEY from 15 April, 1523, to 28 October, 1555. This nobleman was one of the peers who signed the letter, 22nd HENRY VIII., to the Pope, regarding the king's divorce from Queen KATHERINE. His lordship m. Alice, dau. of Sir John St. John, of Bletsho, co. Bedford, and had an only son,

HENRY, who was created a knight of the Bath at the coronation of Queen ANNE BOLEYN, and d. in the 5th EDWARD VI. his father then living. He m. 1st, Grace, dau. of John Newport, Esq., of Brent Pelham, Herts, and had issue,

HENRY, successor to his grandfather.

Jane, m. to George Boleyn. Lord Rochford

Margaret, m. to Sir John Shelton, Knt.

Sir Henry Morley m. 2ndly, Elizabeth, dau. and heir of Sir Philip Calthorp, Knt., of Erwarton, co. Suffolk, and had by her a son, Sir Philip Parker, Knt. of Erwarton, ancestor of the Parkers of Erwarton, extinct baronets, whose last male descendant, Sir Philip Parker-A.-Morley-Long, Bart., the last male heir of the Lords Morley, d. without male issue, 20 June, 1740-1: his daus. and co-heirs, Martha, wife of John, Lord Chedworth, and Elizabeth, wife of James Plunket, Esq., both d. s. p., whereupon the representation of the family devolved on Sir Philip's sisters, Catherine, m. to John Perceval, 1st Earl of Egmont, and Mary, m. to Daniel Dering, Esq.

In WALPOLE's *Catalogue of Noble Authors*, Lord Morley is mentioned as a voluminous writer, and Anthony Wood says, he was living, an ancient man, highly esteemed by the nobility, in the latter end of HENRY VIII.'s reign. He *d.* in the time of PHILIP and MARY, *anno* 1555, and was *s.* by his grandson,

HENRY PARKER, Lord Morley, summoned to parliament from 20 January, 1558, to 8 May, 1572. This nobleman *m.* Lady Elizabeth Stanley, dau. of Edward, Earl of Derby, and had issue,

EDWARD, his successor.
Alice, *m.* to Sir Thomas Barrington, Knt.
Mary, *m.* to Sir Edward Leventhorpe, Knt.

His lordship was *s.* at his decease, by his son,

EDWARD PARKER, Lord Morley, summoned to parliament from 26 January, 1581, to 5 April, 1614. This nobleman was one of the peers that sat in judgment upon MARY, Queen of Scots; on Philip, Earl of Arundel, and on Robert, Earl of Essex, all in the reign of ELIZABETH; his lordship *m.* Elizabeth, only dau. and heiress of William Stanley, Baron Monteagle, and had issue,

WILLIAM, his successor.
Henry.   Charles.
Mary, *m.* to Thomas Abington, Esq., of Hinlip.
Elizabeth, *m.* to Sir Alexander Barlow, of Barlow, in Lancashire.
Frances, *m.* to Christopher Danby, Esq., of Leighton, co York.

He *d.* in 1618, and was *s.* by his eldest son,

WILLIAM PARKER, who had been summoned to parliament in the life-time of his father, in right of his mother, as BARON MONTEAGLE, and was summoned as LORD MORLEY AND MONTEAGLE from 30 January, 1621, to 4 November in the same year. This is the nobleman to whom the memorable anonymous letter was addressed, by which the Gunpowder-plot was fortunately discovered. It is said to have been written by his sister, Mary, wife of Thomas Abington (or Habington), of Hinlip, which Thomas had been cofferer to Queen ELIZABETH. Abington was concerned in many projects for the release of MARY, Queen of Scotland, and contrived various places of concealment in his old mansion at Hinlip. He was condemned to die for concealing Garnet and Oldcorn, the Jesuits, but was pardoned, at the intercession of his wife and Lord Monteagle. Lord Morley and Monteagle *m.* Elizabeth, dau. of Sir Thomas Tresham, Knt., and had issue,

HENRY, his successor.
William, *d. s. p.*   Charles, *d. s. p.*
Frances, *d.* a nun.
Katherine, *m.* to John Savage, Earl Rivers.
Elizabeth, *m.* to Edward Cranfield, Esq.

His lordship *d.* in 1622, and was *s.* by his eldest son,

SIR HENRY PARKER, K.B., summoned to parliament as BARON MORLEY AND MONTEAGLE from 12 February, 1624, to 3 November, 1639. His lordship *m.* Philippa, dau. and co-heir of Sir Philip Carrel, of Shipley, in Surrey, and dying in 1655, was *s.* by his only child,

THOMAS PARKER, summoned to parliament as BARON MORLEY AND MONTEAGLE from 8 May, 1661, to 19 May, 1685. His lordship *m.* Mary, dau. of Henry Martin, Esq., of Landsworth, in the co. of Berks, but *d. s. p.* about the year 1686, when the Baronies of Morley and Monteagle fell into ABEYANCE between the issue of his two aunts, and so con·tinue with their representatives. Those aunts were

1. KATHERINE, who *m.* John Savage, 2nd Earl of Rivers, and had issue

THOMAS, who *s.* to the Earldom of Rivers, and was *s.* by his son,

RICHARD, Earl of Rivers, who *d.* in 1712, and was *s.* by his cousin,

JOHN SAVAGE, Earl of Rivers, with whose son,

JOHN, the earldom expired.

John, *d. s. p.*
Richard, who has left no descendants.
Elizabeth, *m.* to William, Lord Petre, but had no issue.
Jane, *m.* 1st, to George, Lord Chandos; 2ndly, to Sir William Sidley, Bart.; and 3rdly, to GEORGE PITT, Esq., *of Strathfieldsaye, co. Hants.* Her ladyship's great-grandson by her last husband, GEORGE PITT, Esq., of Strathfieldsaye, was created, in 1776, BARON RIVERS, *of Strathfieldsaye,* and in 1802, BARON RIVERS, *of Sudley Castle,* with a special remainder. His lordship *d.* in 1803, and was *s.* by his son,

GEORGE PITT, 2nd baron, at whose decease, in 1828, the 1st Barony of Rivers expired, but the 2nd devolved, according to the limitation, upon his nephew,

HORACE-WILLIAM BECKFORD, Esq., as 3rd baron, he *d.* in 1831, and was *s.* by his son,

GEORGE, 4th Lord Rivers.

Catherine, *m.* to Charles, brother of Sir William Sidley.
Mary, *m.* to William Killigrew, Esq.
Frances, *d.* young.
II. Elizabeth, *m.* to Edward Cranfield, Esq.

Arms—Az., between two bars, sa., charged with three bezants, a lion passant, gu., in chief three bucks' heads caboshed of the 2nd.

PARKYNS—BARON RANCLIFFE.

By Letters Patent, dated 1 October, 1795.

Lineage.

RICHARD PARKYNS, Esq., barrister-at-law, recorder of Nottingham and Leicester, purchased the manor of Bunny, co. Nottingham, and was *s.* in 1603, by his son,

SIR GEORGE PARKYNS, Knt., who *m.* Mary, dau. and heir of Edward Isham, Esq., of Walmer Castle, co. Kent; and dying in 1626, was *s.* by his eldest son,

ISHAM PARKYNS, Esq., of Bunny. This gentleman held the rank of colonel in the royal army during the civil wars, and being governor of a garrison called The Place, in Ashby-de-la-Zouch, resisted to the last the power of Cromwell. He *m.* Katherine, dau. of Henry Cave, E.q., of Barrow, co. Leicester, and was *s.* at his decease, by his son,

THOMAS PARKYNS, Esq., of Bunny, who was created a Baronet, 18 May, 1681. Sir Thomas *m.* Anne, dau. and heir of Thomas Cressy, Esq., of Byrkin, and was *s.* at his decease, 15 July, 1684, by his eldest surviving son,

SIR THOMAS. This gentleman *m.* 1st, Elizabeth, dau. and heir of John Sampson, Esq., of Breaston, co. Derby, and granddau. and heir of John Sampson, Esq., of Hewby, co. York, an alderman of London, by whom he had two sons, who predeceased him (the elder, Sampson, leaving a son, Thomas, whose only dau., Jane, *m.* the 3rd baronet). He *m.* 2ndly, in 1727, Jane, dau. of Mr. Alderman Barnat, of the city of York, by whom he had two sons. Sir Thomas Parkyns, designated "Luctator," was distinguished by his benevolence and philanthropy as well as by his love of what he termed "the noble science of wrestling." He *d.* in March, 1740-1, and was *s.* by his eldest surviving son,

SIR THOMAS, *b.* in December, 1728; who *m.* 7 April, 1747, his grand-niece, Jane, dau. and heir of Thomas Parkyns, Esq. (son of Sampson Parkyns, Esq., eldest son, by his 1st marriage, of Sir Thomas, the 2nd baronet), by whom he had one son and two daus., THOMAS, his heir; Jane, *m.* to Clement Winstanley, Esq., of Braunston Hall; and Elizabeth, *m.* to Stephen Charlesworth, Esq. Sir Thomas *m.* 2ndly, in 1765, Sarah, dau. of Daniel Smith, Esq., by whom he had two sons, Frederic and Richard, who both *d. s. p.,* and three daus. who all *m.* and had issue; the Countess Metaxa is the dau. of one of these ladies, and the Rev. T. Parkyns Dodson of another. Sir Thomas *m.* 3rdly, Miss Jane Boultbee, and had one son, Thomas-Boultbee, who *m.* Miss Smith, of Edwalton, and left issue, Sir Thomas-George-Augustus Parkyns, who *s.* to the baronetcy at the death of Lord Rancliffe, and Mansfield Parkyns, the well-known traveller. The eldest son of Sir Thomas

THOMAS-BOOTHBY PARKYNS, Esq., *b.* 24 July, 1755, was elevated to the peerage of Ireland, 1 October, 1795, by the title of BARON RANCLIFFE. His lordship *m.* in December, 1783, Elizabeth-Anne, dau. and sole heir of Sir William James, Bart., of Eltham Park, co. Kent, by whom (who *d.* in 1797,) he had issue,

GEORGE-AUGUSTUS-HENRY-ANNE, 2nd peer.
Elizabeth-Anne, *m.* 8 December, 1810, Sir Richard Levinge, Bart., of Knockdrin Castle, co. Westmeath, and left with other issue, a son,

SIR RICHARD LEVINGE, Bart., senior co-representative of the Lords Rancliffe.

Henrietta-Elizabeth, *m.* 13 July, 1809, to Sir William Rumbold, Bart.; and *d.* 24 August, 1833.
Maria-Charlotte, *m.* 1st, in 1817, to the Marquess de Choiseul, who *d.* in 1823; and 2ndly, 3 June, 1824, to Prince Auguste Jules Armand de Polignac, the unfortunate minister of CHARLES X., King of France.

His lordship *d.* 17 November, 1800, and was *s.* by his only son,

GEORGE-AUGUSTUS-HENRY-ANNE PARKYNS, 2nd baron, *b.* 10 June, 1785, who *s.* to the baronetcy as 4th bart., at the decease of his grandfather, 17 March, 1806. He *m.* 15 October, 1807, Elizabeth-Mary, eldest dau. of George, 6th Earl of Granard, and *d. s. p.* 1 November, 1850, when the Barony became EXTINCT.

Arms—Arg., an eagle displayed, sa.; on a canton, or, several billets, ermines.

PARR—BARON PARR OF KENDAL, EARL OF ESSEX, MARQUESS OF NORTHAMPTON.

Barony, by Letters Patent, dated in 1538.
Earldom, by Letters Patent, dated 23 December, 1543.
Marquessate by Letters Patent, dated 16 February, 1546-7.
Marquessate revived, 13 January, 1559.

Lineage.

The surname of PARR is local, being derived from a manor in the parish of Prescot, co. Lancaster, of which the family of Parr were anciently lords.

SIR JOHN DE PARRE, Knt. of Parre, living about 1350, m. Matilda, dau. of Sir Richard de Leyborne, and was father of SIR WILLIAM DE PARRE, who m. 1383, Elizabeth, dau. of John de Ros, and grand-dau. and heiress of Sir Thomas de Ros, Baron of Kendal, and had livery of her inheritance.* On the accession of the Duke of Lancaster as HENRY IV., Sir William stood so high in the estimation of the new monarch, that he was deputed, with the bishop of St. Asaph, to announce the revolution to the court of Spain. He d. 4 October, 1405, being then seized of the fourth part of the manor of Kirby in K ndal, in right of the heiress of Ros, and was s. by his eldest son,†

JOHN PARRE, of Parre and Kendal, who m. Agnes, dau. and heir of Sir Thomas Crophull, and relict of Sir Walter Devereux, and dying in 1409, was s. by his son,

SIR THOMAS PARRE, of Kendal, who, taking part with Richard, Duke of York, was attainted in the parliament held at Coventry, 38th HENRY VI. He m. Alice, dau. of Sir Thomas Tunstall, of Thurland Castle, and had issue,

I. WILLIAM, his heir.
II. John (Sir), appointed sheriff of Westmoreland for life, in 1462, m. a dau. of Sir John Yonge, lord mayor of London, and had issue. From him it is stated derived a branch of the family long seated in Derbyshire, and the late Rev. SAMUEL PARR, LL.D.
III. Thomas, slain at Barnet-field, 1472.
I. Margaret. m. Sir Thomas Radclyffe, of Derwentwater.
II. Anne, m. William Harington, of Cartmell.
III. Elizabeth, m. Sir Christopher Moresby, of Moresby.
IV. Agnes, m. Sir Thomas Strickland, of Syzergh.
V. Maud, m. Humphrey, Lord Dacre, of Gillesland.
VI. Eleanor, m. Sir Henry Agard.

Sir Thomas d. 1464. His eldest son,
SIR WILLIAM PARRE, was high in favour with King EDWARD IV., and repaid it with great fidelity. He was one of the commissioners appointed to adjust with JAMES III. of Scotland some alleged violations of the truce then subsisting between the two kingdoms; and on the return of King EDWARD, again to contest his right to the crown, with Margaret of Anjou, supported by the king maker, Earl of Warwick, Sir William Parre met him at Northampton with a considerable force, and thence marched to Barnet-field, where the contest was decided in favour of his royal master. He was M.P. for Westmoreland in the 6th and 12th EDWARD IV., and served as sheriff of Cumberland in 1473. In the 22nd of the same reign he was constituted chief commissioner for exercising the office of constable of England; he was also created a knight banneret, and a knight of the Garter. Sir William m. Elizabeth, dau. of Henry, 5th Baron Fitz-Hugh, by whom (who m. 2ndly, Nicholas, Lord Vaux,) he had issue,

I. THOMAS, his successor.
II. WILLIAM, created LORD PARR, of Horton.
III. John, m. Constance, dau. and co-heir of Sir Henry Vere, of Addington, co. Northampton, d. s. p. 1504.
I. Anne, m. Sir Thomas Cheney, of Tithlingborough, whose dau. and heiress,
Elizabeth Cheney, m. Thomas, 2nd Lord Vaux.

He d. before 1512, and was s. by his eldest son,
SIR THOMAS PARR, of Parr and Kendal, who upon the decease of his first cousin, George, 7th Baron Fitz-Hugh, in 1512, was found joint heir of that nobleman's barony and lands. He m. Maud, dau. and co-heir of Sir Thomas Greene, of Greene's Norton, co. Northampton, by w..om, who d. 1532, he had issue,

WILLIAM.
KATHERINE, m. 1st, Edward Borough; 2ndly, John Neville,

Lord Latimer; 3rdly, King HENRY VIII.; and 4thly, Thomas, Lord Seymour, of Sudely. She d. 5 September, 1548.*
Anne, m. William Herbert, Earl of Pembroke, and her male descendant continues to inherit that earldom, but Philip, 8th Earl of Pembroke, leaving at his decease an only dau.,
LADY CHARLOTTE HERBERT, who m. 1st, John, Lord Jeffreys; and 2ndly, Thomas, Viscount Windsor, the co-heirship to the Barony of Fitz-Hugh, was thus severed from the Earldom of Pembroke. The representatives of her ladyship's two marriages are the Earl of Pomfret and the Marquess of Bute.

Sir Thomas, who was master of the Wards, and comptroller to HENRY VIII., served as sheriff of Northamptonshire in 1509, and of Lincolnshire in 1510. He d. in 1518, and was buried in Blackfriars Church, London.† His son,

WILLIAM PARR, was brought to Court by his sister, and rose rapidly into royal favour. He was first made one of the esquires of King HENRY VIII.'s body, and he attended his royal master in the celebrated interview with FRANCIS, king of France, where he took part in the justing and feats of arms, being amongst the challengers on the English side. In the 30th of the same reign, he was advanced to the dignity of BARON PARR, of Kendal; but upon what day or month the enrolment of his patent mentions not. He was summoned in the next year, and took his seat in parliament 28 April, 1539, to 4 June, 1543. His lordship m. 1st, Lady Anne Bourchier, only dau. and heiress of Henry Bourchier, 2nd Earl of Essex, (which marriage was dissolved by act of parliament, and the issue bastardized), and was soon after the elevation of his sister, Katherine, to the dignity of Queen Consort, created, being then a knight of the Garter, by letters patent, dated 23 December, 1543, EARL OF ESSEX, with the precedency which the late Henry Bourchier, Earl of Essex, had enjoyed. His lordship was constituted by King HENRY VIII. one of his executors, and upon the accession of his nephew, EDWARD VI, he was advanced to the MARQUESSATE OF NORTHAMPTON. by letters patent, dated 16 February, 1546-7. In four years afterwards he was made lord great chamberlain of England for life, and having about this time m for his 2nd wife, Elizabeth, dau. of George, Lord Cobham, he obtained in the 5th EDWARD VI., an especial act of parliament for annulling his marriage with the Lady Anne Bourchier, as also for ratifying his marriage with the said Elizabeth, and legitimating the children that might be born of that lady. Shortly, after this his lordship was sent ambassador extraordinary to the King of France, to present to his majesty the order of the Garter, and to treat with him touching certain private affairs, being accompanied by the bishop of Ely, and other distinguished personages. Before the close of this year he was one of the peers who sat on the trial of the protector, Somerset. Espousing the cause of Lady Jane Grey, and joining the Duke of Northumberland, in proclaiming her Queen of England, upon the demise of King EDWARD, the marquess, on the total failure of the project, was committed to the Tower, and being afterwards arraigned, had sentence of death passed upon him, and all his honours became FORFEITED. Notwithstanding which, execution was forborne, and before the close of the year he was restored in blood by parliament, but not to his honours, so that he had no other title than William Parr, Esq., late Marquess of Northampton, and stood in no higher degree until Queen ELIZABETH ascended the throne, when her Majesty was graciously pleased to create him, by letters patent, dated 13 January, 1559, MARQUESS OF NORTHAMPTON, to restore him to his lands, to make him one of her privy council, and to re-invest him with the order of the Garter. His lordship outliving his 2nd wife, m. 3rdly, Helen, dau. of Wolfangus Snavenburgh, but had no issue. The delight of this nobleman is said to have been music and poetry, and his exercise war; though his skill in the field answered not his industry, nor his success, his skill. Yet King EDWARD called him "his honest uncle," and King HENRY "his integrity." His lordship d. in 1571, and was buried in the collegiate church at Warwick, where about half-a-century before Sir William Dugdale wrote, his body being dug up, was found perfect, the skin entire, dried to the bones; and the rosemary and bag lying in the coffin, fresh and green. His children by his 1st lady were illegitimated, and, as he had none by his other wives all his honours at his decease became EXTINCT.

Arms—Arg., two bars, az., a border engrailed, sa.

PARR—BARON PARR OF HORTON.

By Letters Patent, dated 23 December, 1543.

Lineage.

Sir William Parr, younger son of Sir Thomas Parr, of Kendal, became seated at Horton, co. Northampton, in consequence of his marriage with Mary, dau. and co-heir of John Salisbury, Esq. He was constituted chamberlain to his niece, Katherine, wife of King Henry VIII., and advanced to the peerage in December, 1543, as Baron Parr, *of Horton.* He had issue, four daus., only,

Maud, *m.* Sir Ralph Lane.
Anne, *m.* Sir John Digby, of Ketilby, co. Lincoln.
Elizabeth, *m.* Sir Nicholas Woodhull.
Mary, *m.* Sir Thomas Tresham, of Rushton.

Lord Parr *d.* 10 September, 1546, and was buried at Horton, where a splendid monument to his memory, and that of his wife, is to be seen. As he left no male issue, the Barony EXPIRED.

Arms—As Parr, of Kendal.

PARSONS—EARL OF ROSSE.

By Letters Patent, dated 16 June, 1718.

Lineage.

William Parsons, who settled in Ireland about the close of Queen Elizabeth's reign, being a commissioner of plantations, obtained very considerable territorial grants from the crown. In 1602, Mr. Parsons *s.* Sir Geoffrey Fenton as surveyor-general of Ireland; in 1610, he obtained a pension of £30 a-year, English, for life; in 1613, he was joined with his brother, Lawrence, in the supervisorship of the crown lands, with a fee of £60 a-year for life; in 1620, presenting to the king, in person, surveys of escheated estates, in his capacity of surveyor-general, he received the honour of knighthood, and was created a baronet 10 November in the same year. Sir William represented the county of Wicklow in parliament in 1639, and was nominated lord deputy with Lord Dillon, in 1640; but that nobleman being soon removed, he was resworn, with Sir John Borlace, master of the ordnance. He continued in the government until 1643, when he was removed, charged with treason, and committed to prison, with Sir Adam Loftus, and others. Sir William *m.* Elizabeth, eldest dau. of Mr. Alderman John Lane, of Dublin, and dau. of Sir Geoffrey Fenton, and *d.* at Westminster, in February, 1650, having had issue,

  I. Richard, M.P., 1639, for the town of Wicklow, *m.* Lettice, eldest dau. of Sir Adam Loftus, of Rathfarnham, vice-treasurer of the Exchequer, by Jane, his wife, dau. of Walter Vaughan, Esq., of Golden Grove, and by her (who *d.* 26 October, 1633, and was buried in St. Patrick's) had issue,

    1 William, successor to his grandfather.
    1 Jane. *m.* 1657, to John Franks, Esq.
    2 Elizabeth, *m.* to Sir Thomas Worsop, of Dunshaghlin, co. Meath, Knt., by whom he had a numerous issue.

  II. John, *m.* Elizabeth, dau. of Sir Walsingham Cooke, of Tomduffe, co. Wexford, by his wife, dau. and co-heir of Sir Edward Fisher, of Fisher's Prospect, in that co., and had issue,

    1 Arthur, of Tomduffe. *m.* 1st, Eleanor, dau. of John Pennington, of St. James's-street, Dublin, but by her (who *d.* 1 December, 1667) he had no issue; he *m.* 2ndly, Lady Bridget Fielding, youngest dau. of George, 1st Earl of Desmond, which lady *d.* 20 July, 1669; he *m.* 3rdly, Mary, dau. of Moyses Hill, Esq., by whom he had issue,

      Michael, of Tomduffe, *m.* Clotilda, 2nd dau. of Christian Borr, Esq., of Drynogh, co. Wexford. and dying 1700, left

        Arthur, who *d.* in August, 1701, leaving William, his uncle and heir, who, by will dated 21 February, 1705, left his estate to Sir William Parsons, Bart., of Birr, and soon after *d. s. p.*

      William, who *s.* his nephew.
      Ellen.   Anne.
      Penelope, *m.* Christopher White, Esq., of Donoghmore, and *d.* 2 February, 1716.
      Mary.

    1 Elizabeth, *m.* to Michael Hare, Esq., of Monkstown, co. Dublin.
  III. Francis, of Garrydice, co. Leitrim *m.* Sarah, dau. of Mr. Faircloath, and dying in 1668, left issue,

---

William, his heir.
  Elizabeth, *m.* to Philip Moore.
  Mary, *m.* to Jonas Percy.   Frances.
  IV. James, *d. unm.*
  V. William, *d. unm.*
  I. Catherine, *m.* Sir James Barry, created Lord Santry.
  II. Margaret, *m.* Thomas Stockdale, Esq., of Bilton Park, co. York.
  III. Elizabeth, *m.* Sir William Ussher, of the castle of Grange, co. Wicklow, grandson of Sir William Ussher, clerk of the Council.
  IV. Jane, *m.* to Sir John Hoey, Knt. of Dunganstown, co. Wicklow.
  V. Mary, *m.* to Arthur Hill, Esq., of Hillsborough, co. Down.
  VI. Anne, *m.* to Sir Paul Davis, secretary of state in Ireland.
  VII. Judith, *m.* to Thomas Whyte, Esq., of Redhills, co. Cavan.

The grandson and heir,

Sir William Parsons, of Bellamont, co. Dublin, 2nd baronet, *m.* Catherine, eldest dau. of Arthur, Viscount Ranelagh, and dying 31 December, 1658, was *s.* by his only surviving son,

Sir Richard Parsons, 3rd baronet, who was elevated to the peerage, 2 July, 1681, as *Baron of Oxmantown,* and *Viscount Rosse,* with remainder to the male issue of his great-grandfather. His lordship *m.* 1st, Anne Walsingham; 2ndly, Catherine Brydges, dau. of George, Lord Chandos, both of whom *d. s. p.*; and 3rdly, in 1685, Elizabeth, eldest dau. of Sir George Hamilton, Count Hamilton, and niece of Sarah, Duchess of Marlborough, by whom he had two sons and three daus.,

Richard, his heir.
George, *d. unm.* 20 March. 1709.
Frances, *m.* 30 May, 1704, to John, Viscount Netterville.
Catherine, *m.* to James Hussey, Esq., of Westown, co. Dublin.
Elizabeth, *d. unm.*

He *d.* 30 January, 1702-3, and was buried in St. Patrick's Cathedral. His elder son,

Richard Parsons, 2nd viscount, was advanced to the Earldom of Rosse, 16 June, 1718. His lordship *m.* 1st, in 1715, Mary, eldest dau. of Lord William Paulet, by whom he had issue, Richard, his heir; James, *d.* 1739; and Elizabeth. Lord Rosse, *m.* 2ndly, 1719, Frances, dau. of Thomas Claxton, Esq. His lordship dying in 1741, was *s.* by his elder son,

Richard Parsons, 2nd earl, at whose decease, 27 August, 1764, *s.p.* all the honours EXPIRED, and the representation of the family devolved on Sir William Parsons, 4th baronet of Birr Castle, King's co., grandfather of William, 3rd Earl of Rosse, K.P. (*See* Burke's *Extant Peerage.*)

Arms—Gu., three leopards' faces, arg.

PASTON—VISCOUNTS YARMOUTH, EARLS OF YARMOUTH.

Viscounty, by Letters Patent, dated 19 August, 1673.
Earldom, by Letters Patent, dated 30 July, 1679.

Lineage.

This very ancient and "worshipful" family of Paston, of Paston, was settled in the co. of Norfolk, time out of mind, and formed many high alliances. Passing over the earlier ancestry, we will begin with

John Paston, Esq., of Paston (son of William Paston, a judge of the Court of King's Bench), who *m.* 1st, Margaret, dau. and heir of John Mantby, and had by her a son, John, and several other children; he *m.* 2ndly, Lady Ann Beaufort, dau. of Edmund, Duke of Somerset, and by her was father *inter alios* of Sir William Paston, one of whose daus. and co-heirs, Anna, *m.* Sir Gilbert Talbot, of Grafton. The eldest son and heir,

Sir John Paston, of Paston, *m.* Margery, dau. of Sir T. Brews, Knt., and was father of

Sir William Paston, of Paston, whose wife was Bridget, dau. of Sir Henry Heydon, of Baconsthorpe, by whom he had issue,

  I. Erasmus, his heir.   II. Henry.
  III. John, *m.* Anne, dau. of John Moulton, and left two daus., her co-heirs, viz., Bridget, *m.* to Sir Edward Coke, attorney-general to Queen Elizabeth; and Ann, *m.* to Anthony Germain, brother of Sir Robert Germain.
  IV. Thomas (Sir), *m.* Ann, dau. of Sir John Leigh, and had issue.   V. Clement, *d. s. p.*
  I. Allanore, *m.* to Thomas, Earl of Rutland.
  II. Ann, *m.* to Sir Thomas Tindall.
  III. Elizabeth, *m.* to Sir Francis Leke, of Walton.
  IV. Mary, *m.* to Sir John Chaworth.
  V. Margaret, *m.* to John Leke, of Worcop.

The son and heir,

ERASMUS PASTON, Esq., of Paston, who m. Mary, dau. of Sir Thomas Windham, Knt., of Felbrigg, and was father of

SIR WILLIAM PASTON, of Paston, who m. Frances, dau. of Sir T. Clere, of Stokesley, and d. leaving, with four daus., Alianore, m. to John Echingham, Ann, m. 1st, to George Chaworth, Viscount Armagh; 2ndly, to Sir Nicholas L'Estrange; and 3rdly, to Sir Anthony Cope; Frances, m. to Thomas Greayan, and Gertrude, m. to William Read, a son and heir,

CHRISTOPHER PASTON, of Paston, who m. Anna, dau. of Philip Audeley, Esq., and left a dau., Bridget, m. to John Heveningham, and a son,

SIR EDMUND PASTON, of Paston, who m. Katherine, dau. of Thomas Knevitt, Esq., of Ashwellthorpe, and was father of

SIR WILLIAM PASTON, of Paston, created a baronet in 1641. He m. Lady Katherine Bertie, dau. of Robert, Earl of Lindsey, and was s. by his son,

SIR ROBERT PASTON, 2nd Bart., of Paston, who having devoted his fortune and energies to the royal cause, during the civil wars, was elevated to the peerage by King CHARLES II., 19 August, 1673, as Baron Paston, of Paston, and VISCOUNT YARMOUTH, both in the co. of Norfolk His lordship m. Rebecca, dau. of Sir Jasper Clayton, Knt., of London, and had with other issue,

WILLIAM, his successor.

Robert, m. 1st, Hester Mainwaring; and 2ndly, Anne, dau. and co-heir of Philip Harbord, Esq., and had an only dau. and heir, ANN.

Jasper, m. Lady Fairborne, widow of Sir Palmes Fairborne.

Thomas, a colonel in the army, drowned in 1693, leaving by his wife, Dorothy, dau. of Edward Darcy, Esq.,

Robert, captain R.N.

Rebecca, dau. to Admiral Sir Stafford Fairborne.

Margaret, m. to Hieronimo Alberto de Conti, a German.

The viscount was advanced to the EARLDOM OF YARMOUTH, 30 July, 1679. He was esteemed a man of refined taste and learning, and dying in 1682, æt. fifty-two, was s. by his eldest son,

WILLIAM PASTON, 2nd Earl of Yarmouth. This nobleman m. 1st, Charlotte-Jemima-Maria, natural dau. of King CHARLES II., by the Viscountess Shannon, wife of Francis Boyle, Viscount Shannon, and dau. of Sir William Killigrew, and had issue,

CHARLES, Lord Paston, b. 1673, a brigadier in the army, who predeceased him.

William, captain R.N., b. 1682, d. unm. 1711.

Charlotte, m. 1st, to Thomas Herne, Esq., of Heveringland, in Norfolk, and 2ndly, Major Weldron.

Rebecca, m. to Sir John Holland, of Quidenham, Bart.

His lordship m. 2ndly, Elizabeth, dau. of Lord North, and widow of Sir Robert Wiseman, but had no issue. He d. in 1732, when leaving no male issue, and the male line of his brothers having previously ceased, the barony, viscounty, and earldom became EXTINCT.

Arms—Arg., six fleurs-de-lis, three, two, and one, and a chief indented, or.

PATESHULL—BARON PATESHULL.

By Writ of Summons, dated 25 February, 1342.

Lineage.

In the time of King HENRY III.,

SIMON DE PATESHULL, held the manor of Bletsho, co. Bedford, of the Barony of Bedford, by the service of one knight's fee. In the 17th of the same reign,

HUGH DE PATESHULL, uncle to Maud, wife of Nigel de Mowbray, gave to Hubert de Burgh, 300 marks fine on behalf of the said Maud, that she might marry whom she thought fit, and enjoy her dowry.

To either of the above Simon, or Hugh, s. another,

SIMON DE PATESHULL, who m. Isabel, dau. and heir of John de Steingreve, and was s. by

SIR JOHN DE PATESHULL, who had summons to parliament as a Baron, 25 February, 1342, but not afterwards. He d. in 1349, leaving by Mabel de Grandison, heiress of Lydiard Tregory, a son and heir,

SIR WILLIAM DE PATESHULL, who was never summoned to parliament, nor can he have been esteemed a baron, for his father had but one writ of summons, and there is no proof of sitting. The Barony of Pateshull must therefore be considered V EXTINCT, at the decease of John, Lord Pateshull.

420

William d. in 1360, when his estates devolved upon his sisters as co heirs, viz.,

  I. Alice, m. to Thomas Wake, of Blyseworth.

  II. Sybyl. m. to Roger de Beauchamp, and conveyed to him the manor of Bletsho, which manor was transferred by MARGARET, heiress of the Beauchamps, to her husband, Sir Oliver St. John.

  III. Mabel, m. to Walter de Fauconberg.

  IV. Katherine, m. to Sir Robert de Tudenham, Knt.

Arms—Arg., a fesse, sa., between three crescents, gu.

PAULET—DUKES OF BOLTON.

By Letters Patent, dated 9 April, 1689.

Lineage.

JOHN PAULET, 5th Marquess of Winchester, so celebrated in the civil wars (see BURKE's Extant Peerage), left by his 1st wife, Jane, dau. of Thomas, Viscount Savage, an only son,

CHARLES PAULET, 6th Marquess of Winchester, who, for his zeal in promoting the Revolution, was created DUKE OF BOLTON, by letters patent, dated 9 April, 1689. His grace m. 1st, Christiana, dau. of John, Lord Freshville, by whom he had one son, John, who d. in infancy. The duke m. 2ndly, Mary, one of the illegitimate daus. of Emanuel Scroop, Earl of Sunderland, by whom he acquired that considerable estate at Bolton, in Yorkshire, whence he derived the title of his dukedom: and had issue,

CHARLES, Marquess of Winchester.

William, who m. twice, and left issue by both marriages.

Jane, m. to John, Earl of Bridgewater.

Mary, d. unm.

Elizabeth, m. to Toby Jenkins, Esq., of Grimston, co. York.

His grace d. 26 February, 1698-9, and was s. by his elder son,

CHARLES PAULET, 2nd duke, K.G., appointed lord-lieutenant of Ireland in 1717. His grace m. 1st, Margaret, dau. of George, Lord Coventry, by whom he had no issue. He m. 2ndly, Frances, dau. of William Ramsden, Esq., of Byrom, co. York, and had,

CHARLES,} successively DUKES OF BOLTON.
HENRY. }

Mary, m. 1st, to Charles O'Neal, Esq. and 2ndly, to Arthur Moore, Esq., 2nd son of Henry, Earl of Drogheda.

Frances, m. to John, Lord Mordaunt.

The duke m. 3rdly, Henrietta Crofts, natural dau. of James Scott, Duke of Monmouth, by Eleanor, younger dau. of Sir Robert Needham, Knt., and had one son,

Nassau, K.B., and M.P. for co. Southampton, who m. Isabella, dau. of Thomas. Earl of Thanet. Lord Nassau Paulet d. in 1741, leaving an only dau.,

Isabella, m. to John-James, 3rd Earl of Egmont.

His grace d. 21 January, 1721-2, and was s. by his eldest son,

CHARLES PAULET, 3rd duke, K.G., constable of the Tower of London. His grace m. 1st, Anne, only dau. and heir of John, Earl of Carbery, in Ireland, by whom he had no issue. He m. 2ndly, Lavinia Fenton, well known as an actress, in the character of Polly Peachum, by whom he had no issue after marriage, but had three sons previously. He d. 26 August, 1754, when the honours devolved upon his brother,

HARRY PAULET, 4th duke, an officer in the army, and aide-de-camp to Lord Galway, in Portugal. His grace m. Catherine, dau. of Chas. Parry, Esq., of Oakfield, in Berkshire, and had issue,

CHARLES,} successively dukes.
HARRY, }

Henrietta, m. to Sir Robert Colebrook, Bart.

Catherine, m. 1st, to William Ashe, Esq., and 2ndly, to Adam Drummond, Esq.

The duke d. in 1758, and was s. by his elder son,

CHARLES PAULET, 5th duke, at whose decease, unm., 5 July, 1765, the honours devolved upon his brother,

HARRY PAULET, 6th duke. This nobleman being bred to the sea service, attained the rank of admiral of the white. His grace m. 1st, in 1752, Henrietta, dau. of — Nun, Esq. of Eltham, by whom he had a dau.,

Mary-Henrietta, m. to John, Viscount Hinchinbroke, eldest son of the 5th Earl of Sandwich.

The duke m. 2ndly, Catherine, dau. of Robert Lowther, Esq., and sister of James, Earl of Lonsdale, by whom he had two daus.,

Katherine, *m.* to William-Henry, 3rd Earl of Darlington, who was created Duke of Cleveland, and *d.* in 1842.
Amelia.

His grace *d.* 24 December, 1794, and, after a considerable time consumed in establishing his right, the Marquessate of Winchester passed to George Paulet, Esq., of Amport, while the Dukedom of Bolton became EXTINCT.

Arms—Sa., three swords in pile, points in base, arg., pommels and hilts, or.

PAYNE—BARON LAVINGTON,

By Letters Patent, dated 1 October, 1795.

Lineage.

MR. BERTRAND PAYNE, in his splendid *Armorial of Jersey*, gives a full pedigree of the ancient and distinguished family of PAYNE.

"In Jersey," says that accomplished writer, "amongst the primeval Norman settlers are found seigneurs and other high officials, whose names are written indifferently, Payen, Paien, and Payn. Hugh Payen, Valvasor and Jurat, is one of the first officers of the Royal Court of Jersey, on record, and from that period to the last century, the family has never lacked representatives in the church or state of its native island.

In the oldest record possessed of the King's tenants in Jersey, the *extente* of 1331, several entries occur of sundry names of the Payn family, proving it to have then been of consequence and wealth. In the subsequent *extentes*, also, several landowners named Payn, are recorded.

The number of fiefs held at various times by members of this house, is perhaps greater than has ever been possessed by any other family in the island of Jersey. At different periods they have been seigneurs of Oulande, la Godelibre, Samarés, le Hommet, la Fosse, Burey, Ponterrin, Gruchy, Montfort, Diblament, les Cras, le Chastelet, Grainville, Quetivel, la Malletière, Sauteur, le Niesmes, the Fief Payn in St. Helier, the Fief Jourdain Payn in St. Laurence, and the Fief Guille Payn in St. Martin, which last alone remains, of all these immense possessions, "attached to its ancient owners."

ABRAHAM PAYNE, *b.* 1616, son of Abraham Payn, constable of St. Martin, by Susan, his wife, dau. of Michael Sarre, seigneur of the fief of Guille Payn was some time constable of St. Martin, and emigrated with his son to the neighbouring coast of Devonshire, from cause, it is supposed, connected with the political troubles of the period. From him descended a family which rendered itself conspicuous by the zeal with which its members espoused the royalist side at the time of the Rebellion, and to which belonged Colonel Payne, who succoured, and was the host of CHARLES II., after the battle of Worcester. Its chief representative in the early part of the last century, emigrated to St. Christopher's, and there attaining wealth and influence, was rewarded with a baronetcy, an honour which was repeated in the person of another representative of this branch, while a third eminent member of the same family became a peer of the realm.

RALPH PAYNE, distinguished for his attachment to CHARLES I., early joined the royal standard, and was present at the battle of Worcester. He left issue,

ABRAHAM.
Charles, created a baronet, 31 October, 1737.
Nathaniel, who left an only dau., who *m.* William Woodley, Esq., governor of the Leeward Islands.

The eldest son,
ABRAHAM PAYNE, Esq., *m.* Anne, dau. of Ralph Willett, Esq. and was *s.* by his son,
RALPH PAYNE, Esq. This gentleman *m.* 1st, Alice, dau. and heir of Francis Carlisle, Esq., of Antigua, and had issue,

RALPH, created 1 October, 1795, BARON LAVINGTON.
John.
Elizabeth.

He *m.* 2ndly, Miss Margaret Gallwey, by whom he had, with other issue,

Stephen, of Tofts Hall, Norfolk, who assumed the name and arms of GALLWEY. His only dau. and heir, Charlotte, *m.* in 1797, John Moseley, Esq., of Glemham House, Suffolk, and was mother of an only dau., Charlotte, *m.* to Sir Joshua-R. Rowley, Bart., of Tendring Hall, Suffolk.
John, rear-admiral of the Red, appointed commander-in-chief

of the squadron sent to conduct her Majesty Queen Caroline to England, and *d. unm.*
WILLIAM, created a baronet, 8 December, 1812, and assumed, by sign-manual, in 1814, the surname and arms of GALLWEY, in compliance with the testamentary injunction of Tobias-Wall Gallwey, Esq., of the island of St. Christopher.
Martha.   Lucretia.

The eldest son,
SIR RALPH PAYNE, K.B., was raised to the peerage of Ireland, 1 October, 1795, as BARON LAVINGTON, *of Lavington*; but *d s. p.* in 1807, when the title became EXTINCT.

Arms—Gu., a fesse, between two lions passant, arg.

PAYNEL—BARON PAYNELL.

By Writ of Summons, dated 29 December, 1299.

Lineage.

SIR JOHN PAYNELL, of Drax, co. York, was summoned to parliament as a Baron, from 29 December, 1299, to 25 August, 1318. This nobleman is supposed to have died before 1326. No account is given of his issue, nor does Dugdale in his Baronage take any notice of him; but in his writs of summons to parliament the name of "Johannes Paynell de Drax" occurs amongst the barons summoned to parliament, the 28th and 30th EDWARD I., and the 11th and 12th EDWARD II. The same name also occurs in the 32nd, 33rd, 34th, and 35th EDWARD I., and in the 1st and 3rd EDWARD II., which is presumed, by Nicolas, to be that of the same person.

Arms—Or, two bars, az., within an orle of eight martlets, gu.

PEACHEY—BARON SELSEY.

By Letters Patent, dated 13 August, 1794.

Lineage.

HENRY PEACHEY, Esq. of New Grove (eldest son and heir of William Peachey, Esq., of Newgrove, by Mary, his wife, dau. of Henry Bulstrode, Esq.,) was created a baronet, 21 March, 1736, with remainder, in default of male issue to his brother John Peachey, Esq., of the city of London. Sir Henry *m.* Jane, dau. of William Garrett, Esq., by whom he had two sons and three dau., all of whom, however, *d. unm.*, except Jane, who became the wife of G.-H. Nash, Esq., of Petworth. Sir Henry, who represented Sussex in parliament, *d.* 14 August, 1737, and was *s.*, according to the limitation of the patent, by his brother,
SIR JOHN PEACHEY, M.P., who *m.* Henrietta, dau. of George London, Esq., of Long Ditton, and dau., Mary, wife of Michael Seers, Esq., and two sons. He *d.* 12 April, 1744, and was *s.* by his eldest son,
SIR JOHN PEACHEY, M.P. This gentleman *m.* Elizabeth, dau. of John-Maeres Fagg, Esq., of Glenley, co. Sussex, and *d.* without issue, 3 July, 1768, when the title devolved upon his brother,
SIR JAMES PEACHEY, who, having filled some elevated situations about the court, was advanced to the peerage, 13 August, 1794, as the title of BARON SELSEY, *of Selsey, co. Sussex*. His lordship *m.* in 1747, Lady Georgiana-Caroline Scott, eldest dau. of Henry, 1st Earl of Deloraine, by whom he had a son, John, and a dau., Georgiana, who *m.* in 1771, George, Earl of Warwick. His lordship *d.* 1 February, 1808, and was *s.* by his only son,
JOHN PEACHEY, 2nd baron, *b.* 16 March, 1749. This nobleman *m.* in 1784, Hester-Elizabeth, dau. of George Jennings, Esq., of Newcells, co. Herts, by whom he left issue,
HENRY-JOHN, 3rd baron.
John-William, in holy orders, *b.* 15 December, 1788; *d. unm.* 1837.
Caroline-Mary, *m.* in August, 1815, to the Rev. Leveson-Venables Vernon, son of Edward, Lord Archbishop of York.

His lordship *d.* 27 June, 1816, and was *s.* by his son,
HENRY-JOHN PEACHEY, F.R.S., 3rd baron, *b.* 4 September, 1787, who *m.* 21 October, 1817, Anna-Maria-Louisa, dau. of Frederick, 2nd Lord Boston, by whom he had no issue. Lord Selsey, who was a captain in the royal navy, *d.* 10 March, 1838, when the title became EXTINCT.

Arms—Az., a lion rampant, double queued, erm., ducally crowned, or, on a canton of the last a mullet, pierced, gu.

PECHE—BARON PECHE, OF BRUNNE.

By Writ of Summons, dated 29 December, 1299.

Lineage.

HAMON PECHE was sheriff of the co. Cambridge from 'he 2nd to the 12th year of King HENRY II. He m. Alice, one of the daus. and co-heirs of Pain Peverell, and was, in her right, Lord of Brunne, in the same shire. To this Hamon, at his decease, in 1190, s. his son and heir,

GILBERT PECHE, who, in the 6th of RICHARD I., upon the collection of the scutage, then assessed for the king's redemption, paid £29 1s. 8d. for the knights' fees of his paternal inheritance, and 2 marks and a-half for those of the honour of Brunne, which descended to him through his mother. He d. before the year 1217, and w..s s. by his son,

HAMON PECHE, who d. in 1241, in his pilgrimage to the Holy Land, and was s. by his eldest son,

GILBERT PECHE. This feudal lord d. in 1291, and was s. by his son,

GILBERT PECHE, who, having served in the wars of Gascony, 22nd EDWARD I., was summoned to parliament as a Baron, from 29 December, 1299, to 3 November, 1306, and again 14 March, 1322. His lordship m. 1st, Maude de Hastings, by whom he had a son and heir, GILBERT, who, however, was not summoned to parliament, nor is any account given of their descendants. Lord Peche m. 2ndly, Joane, dau. of Simon de Grey, and to his children by that lady, he left the greater part of his property, making King EDWARD I. heir to the rest of the barony. He d. in 1323.

Arms—Arg., a fess between two chevronels, gu.

PECHE — BARON PECHE, OF WORM-LEIGHTON.

By Writ of Summons, dated 15 May, 1321.

Lineage.

The connection of the Lords Peche of Wormleighton with the Lords Peche of Brunne has not been ascertained, nor is it at all certain that they were of the same stock: the arms would seem to indicate a different lineage. ROBERT PECHE, Bishop of Coventry *temp.* STEPHEN, belonged to the Wormleighton line.

SIR JOHN PECHE, of Wormleighton (son and heir of Richard Peche, who was Lord of Wormleighton, co. Warwick, in right of his mother, Petronile, dau. and heir of Richard Walsh), sided with King HENRY III. against the barons, and was summoned to parliament as BARON PECHE, from 13 May, 1321, to 22 January, 1336. His lordship was in the wars of Scotland, and was governor of Warwick Castle in the 16th EDWARD II.; he was afterwards governor of Dover Castle, and warden of the Cinque Ports. He d. about the year 1339, leaving his grandson,

SIR JOHN PECHE, Knt., his heir. This feudal lord was never summoned to parliament, nor esteemed a baron, for we find him serving as one of the knights for the co. Warwick, in the parliament held at Westminster, in the 28th EDWARD III., and again in the 47th of the same reign. He d. in 1376, and was s. by his son,

SIR JOHN PECHE (never summoned to parliament, nor esteemed a baron), who attended, 9th RICHARD II., John, Duke of Lancaster, then bearing the title of King of Castile and Leon, into Spain, and is supposed to have d. there in the same year, leaving two daus., viz., JOANE, who d. s. p., and MARGARET, m. to Sir William de Montfort.

Arms—Gu., a fess between six cross-crosslets, arg., with a label of three points in chief.

PELHAM-HOLLES—DUKE OF NEWCASTLE.

(*See* HOLLES-PELHAM.)

PENNANT—BARON PENRHYN.

By Letters Patent, dated 1783.

Lineage.

This family derived its descent from TUDOR TREVOR, Lord of Hereford.

THOMAS PENNANT, son of David ap Tudor Pennant, of Bychton, co. Flint, by Anne, his 2nd wife, dau. of John Done, Esq., of Utkington, co. Chester, and half-brother of Rees Pennant, of Bychton, ancestor of the PENNANTS of Downing, was abbot of Bassingwerk, Flintshire, and is celebrated by Guttyn Owain, a Welsh bard of the year 1480, who records the hospitality of the abbot, in a poem, printed in the collection of Mr. Rhys Jones. The poet is so liberal of his praise as to say, "That he gave twice the treasure of a king in wine." Guttyn Owain and Tudor Aled, another noted bard. speak not only of the abbot's works of utility; of the water and windmills he erected, of his having enlarged and beautified the abbey; but also compliment him on his prowess in battle. Thomas Pennant, quitting his profession, became in the law term, a monk *derainge*, and m. Angharad, dau. of Gwilim ap Griffith, of the great house of Penrhyn, in Carnarvonshire by whom he had, with two daus., three sons,

  I. EDWARD, of Holywell.
  II. THOMAS, vicar of Holywell.
  III. Nicholas, abbot of Bassingwerk, who m. and had a son, Edward, of Holywell, whose grandson, John Pennant, of Holywell, left a dau. and heir, Margaret, wife of David Pennant, Esq., of Bychton.

The eldest son,

EDWARD PENNANT, was seated at Holywell, in Flintshire. He m. Catharine, dau. of David ap Davydd Ithel Vychan, and had with other issue, an eldest son,

HENRY PENNANT, Esq., of Holywell and Bagillt, who, by Margaret, his wife, dau. of John ap Griffith Vychan, of Pant y Llongdy, had, with eight daus., three sons,

  I. EDWARD, of Bagillt, whose great-grandson Edward. of Bagillt, high sheriff in 1753, d. *unm.* at Marseilles. in 1778, having previously, in 1776, sold Bagillt Hall, and all his estates in Holywell township, to Thomas Pennant, Esq., of Downing.
  II. GIFFORD, of whom we treat.
  III. George.
  I. Frances, m. to Robert Owen, bishop of St. Asaph.
  II. Elizabeth, m. to Philip Longton, Esq.
  III. Anne, m. to Edward Parry, Esq.
  IV. Jane.
  V. Mary, m. to John Mostyn. Esq., of Brynford.
  VI. Winifred.   VII. Agnes.
  VIII. Mildred.

The 2nd son,

GIFFORD PENNANT, Esq., a military officer, went to Jamaica, in 1655. He m. 7 September, 1669, Elizabeth Aldwinkle, and d. in 1676, leaving with a dau. m. to — Lewis, Esq., a son,

EDWARD PENNANT, Esq., of Clarendon, in Jamaica, chief justice of the Island, b. in 1672, who m. Elizabeth, dau. of Col. John Moore, and aunt of Sir Henry Moore, Bart., lieutenant-governor of Jamaica, by whom he had issue,

  I. Edward.
  II. JOHN, of whom presently.
  III. Samuel (Sir). Knt., Lord Mayor of London in 1749, d. in the following year.
  IV. Gifford.   V. Henry.
  I. Judith, m. to John Lewis, Esq.
  II. Smart, m. to the Rev. William May, rector of Kingston, killed in the storm of 1722.
  III. Elizabeth, m. to Henry Dawkins, Esq., of Jamaica, and had, with a younger son, James Dawkins (the Oriental traveller), an elder son,
    Henry Dawkins, Esq., of Standlynch, co. Wilts, who m. the Lady Julia Colyer. dau. of the Earl of Portmore, and by her had six sons, of whom the 3rd was the late George-Hay Dawkins-Pennant, Esq. of Penrhyn Castle.
  IV. Sarah, m. to Col. Thomas Rowden.
  V. Mary, m. to John Morant, Esq.

The 2nd son,

JOHN PENNANT. Esq., m. Bonella Hodges, and had two sons, John, the elder, d. s. p., and

RICHARD PENNANT, Esq., of Winnington and Penrhyn Castle, who was created in 1783, Baron Penrhyn, of the kingdom of Ireland. His lordship m. Anne-Susannah, dau. and heir of General Hugh Warburton, but d. s. p. in 1808, when the title became EXTINCT; the estates devolving on his cousin, GEORGE-HAY DAWKINS, Esq., who then became of Penrhyn Castle, and assumed the surname and arms of PENNANT. He m. 1st, 25 June, 1807, the Hon. Sophia-Mary-Maude, dau. of Cornwallis,

1st Viscount Hawarden, which lady d. 23 January, 1812; and 2ndly, 4 May, 1814, Elizabeth, elder dau. of the late Hon. William-Henry Bouverie, uncle to the Earl of Radnor. Mr. Dawkins-Pennant d. 17 December, 1840, leaving daus. his co-heirs : the younger, Emma, m. Hon. T. C. Hanbury Tracy; the elder, Juliana-Isabella-Mary, m. Hon. Edward Gordon Douglas (brother of George Sholto, Earl of Morton), who has assumed the surname of Pennant and is now of Penrhyn Castle

Arms—Party per bend, sinister erm. and ermines, a lion rampant, or, langued and armed, gu.

PERCY—BARONS PERCY, EARLS OF NORTHUMBERLAND, BARONS POYNINGS, BARONS PERCY, OF COCKERMOUTH, EARLS OF NORTHUMBERLAND.

Barony of Percy, by Writ of Summons, dated 6 February, 1299. Earldom of Northumberland, by Charter of Creation, dated 16 July, 1377.
Restored, 11 November, 1414.
Again restored, 1470.
Barony of Poynings, by Writ of Summons, dated 23 April, 1337. Barony of Percy, of Cockermouth, &c., by Creation, dated 3 April, 1557.
Earldom of Northumberland (New Creation), dated 1 May, 1557.

Lineage.

The illustrious family of Percy derived descent from one of the Norman chieftains (William de Percy) who accompanied William the Conqueror into England in 1066; and it took its name from the village of Percy, near Villedieu. The family of Percy, of Normandy, sprang from Geoffrey (son of Mainfred, a Danish chieftain), who assisted Rollo, in 912, in subjugating that principality, and acquired considerable possessions there.

William de Percy, surnamed Algernon, being high in favour with the victorious duke, obtained, according to Madox, in his *Baronia Anglica*, a barony of thirty knights' fees from that monarch, in his new dominions, and thus became a feudal lord of the realm from the Conquest. This Lord William de Percy, who was distinguished amongst his contemporaries by the addition of Algernons (William with the whiskers), whence his posterity have cons'antly borne the name of Algernon, restored, or rather refounded, the famous abbey of St. Hilda, in Yorkshire, of which his brother, Serlo de Percy, became first prior. Accompanying, however, Duke Robert, in the first Crusade, 1096, he d. at Mountjoy, near Jerusalem, the celebrated eminence whence the pilgrims of the cross first viewed the Holy City, leaving four sons and two daus., by his wife, Emma de Port, a lady of Saxon descent, whose lands were amongst those bestowed upon him by the Conqueror, according to an ancient writer, "he wedded hyr that was very heire to them, in discharging of his conscien e." His lordship was s. in his feudal rights and possessions by his eldest son,

Alan de Percy, 2nd baron, surnamed the Great Alan, who m. Emma, dau. of Gilbert de Gaunt (which Gilbert was son of Baldwin, Earl of Flanders, and nephew of Queen Maude, wife of William the Conqueror), and was s. by his eldest son,

William de Percy, 3rd baron; at whose decease the eldest branch of the first race of Percys from Normandy became extinct in the male line, and their great inheritance devolved upon his lordship's two daus. (by Alice de Tunbridge, his wife, dau. of Richard, Earl of Clare, who was usually styled de Tunbridge, from his castle of that name), the Ladies Maude and Agnes de Percy, successively.

Maude de Percy, the senior, was 2nd wife of William de Plessetis, Earl of Warwick, by whom (who d. in the Holy Land, 1184), she had no issue. Her ladyship d. in 1204 or 1205, and then the whole possessions of the Percys descended to the family of her sister,

Agnes de Percy, who m. Josceline, of Louvain, brother of Queen Adelisa, 2nd wife of Henry I., and son of Godfrey Barbatus, Duke of Lower Loriain, and Count of Brabant, who was descended from the Emperor Charlemagne. Her ladyship, it is stated, would only consent to this great alliance, upon condition that Josceline should adopt either the surname or arms of Percy; the former of which, says the old family tradition,[*]

[*] Mr. Hylton Dyer Longstaffe in his *Old Heraldry of the Percys*, considers this tradition erroneous in all respects, and is unable to discover any traces of the *blue lion* until the reign of Edward I.

he accordingly assumed, and retained his own paternal coat, in order to perpetuate his claim to the principality of his father, should the elder line of the reigning duke at any period become extinct. The matter is thus stated in the great old pedigree at Sion House: "The ancient arms of Hainault, this Lord Joceline retained, and gave his children the surname of Percie." Of this illustrious alliance there were several children, of whom,

Henry de Percy, the eldest son, who appears to have d. before his mother, m. Isabel, dau. of Adam de Brus, Lord of Skelton, with whom he had the manor of Levington, for which he and his heirs were to repair to Skelton Castle every Christmas-day, and to lead the lady of the castle from her chamber to the chapel to mass, and thence to her chamber again, and after dining with her, to depart. This Henry left two sons,

    William, of whom presently.
    Henry, ancestor of the Percys, of Hesset, Sussex.

Richard de Percy, the youngest son of Agnes and Josceline, got possession of the entire property of his aunt, Maud, Countess of Warwick, and even of a great proportion of that of his mother, and retained the same during the principal part of his life : at length, subsequently to infinite litigation, it was settled between him and his nephew, William de Percy, to whom the inheritance belonged, after a solemn hearing before the king in person, 6 July, 1234 (18th Henry III.), that the estates should be divided into equal portions between the parties during Richard's life; and that after his death, all the ancient patrimony of the Percy family should devolve upon his nephew aforesaid; a small reservation having been made for Richard's son and heir, Henry de Percy. This Richard de Percy continued for the whole of his life at the head of the family, and enjoyed all its baronial rights. He was one of those powerful feudal lords who took up arms, in 1215, against John, and having a principal hand in extorting the great charters of English freedom, was chosen one of the twenty-five guardians to see the Magna Charta duly observed. He d. about 1244, and then his nephew,

William de Percy, came into full possession of all those rights and properties which had been usurped at the decease of his mother; but did not live long to enjoy them, for he d. in 1245, and was s. by his son (by his 2nd wife, Elena, dau. of Ingelram de Baliol, by whom he obtained in dower, Dalton, afterwards called Dalton Percy, in the bishopric of Durham),

Henry de Percy, who m. Eleanor, dau. of John Plantagenet, Earl of Warren and Surrey; and dying in 1272, was s. by his only surviving son,

Henry de Percy, 9th feudal lord, who was summoned to parliament from 6 February, 1299 (27th Edward I.) to 29 July, 1315 (8th Edward II.) This nobleman, obtained, 19 November, 1309, from Anthony Beck, bishop of Durham, by purchase, a grant of the Barony of Alnwick, co. Northumberland. His lordship was one of the great barons who subscribed, in 1301, the celebrated letter to Pope Boniface VIII., upon the attempt of his holiness to interpose in the affairs of the kingdom, intimating, "That their king was not to answer in judgment, for any rights of the crown of Engl nd, before any tribunal under heaven, &c., and that, by the help of God, they would resolutely, and with all their force, maintain against all men." He m. Eleanor, dau. of John Fitz-Alan, Earl of Arundel; d. in 1315, and was s. by his eldest son,

Henry de Percy, 2nd Lord Percy, of Alnwick. This nobleman had a grant from the crown in the 2nd Edward III., of the reversion of the barony and castle of Warkworth, &c. He had summons to parliament from 1322 to the time of his death, 26 February, 1351-2, when he was s. by his eldest son (by Idonia, dau. of Robert, Lord Clifford),

Henry de Percy, 3rd Lord Percy, of Alnwick; who, in the lifetime of his father, had participated in the glories of Cressy (26 August, 1346). His lordship m. 1st, in her ladyship's fourteenth year, Lady Mary Plantagenet, dau. of Henry, Earl of Lancaster, which Henry was son of Edmund, Earl of Lancaster, Leicester, &c., 2nd son of King Henry III., by this alliance his lordship had two sons,

    Henry, his successor.
    Thomas, created in 1397, Earl of Worcester. K.G., a very eminent warrior and statesman in the reigns of Edward III., Richard II., and Henry IV., d. s. p. 1402.

His lordship m. 2ndly, Joan, dau. and heiress of John de Oreby, of Lincolnshire, one of the barons in the reign of Edward III., by whom he left one dau.,

    Mary, who m. John, Lord Ros, of Hamlake, but d. s. p. in 1395.

He d. 17 June, 1368, and was s. by his elder son,

Henry de Percy, 4th Lord Percy, of Alnwick, a distinguished military commander in the reign of Edward III., who, assisting as marshal of England at the coronation of King Richard II., was advanced on the same day, 6 July, 1377, to the *Earldom of Northumberland*, with remainder to his heirs generally, and, like a barony in fee, transmissible, it would appear, to female as well as male heirs. He m. 1st, 1358, Margaret, dau. of Ralph, Lord Nevill, of Raby, and had issue,

HENRY (Sir), the renowned Hotspur, so celebrated in all our histories. He fought the famous battle of Otterbourn, near the Cheviot Hills, in Northumberland (Chevy Chace), where James, Earl of Douglas, was slain, and himself and his brother, Sir Ralph Percy, made prisoners. He m. Philippa, dau. of Edmund Mortimer, Earl of March, by Philippa, dau. and heir of Lionel Plantagenet, Duke of Clarence, and falling at the battle of Shrewsbury in 1403, left issue,

HENRY, who s. as 2nd Earl of Northumberland.
Elizabeth. m. 1st, to John, Lord Clifford, and 2ndly, to Ralph, Earl of Westmoreland.
Thomas (Sir), of Athole, m. Elizabeth, elder dau. and co-heir of David Strathbogie, Earl of Athol, by whom (who m. 2ndly, Sir Henry Scrope), he had issue,

Henry Percy, of Athole, governor of Alnwick, who m. Elizabeth, widow of Robert, Lord Scales, and dying in 1433, left two daus. and co-heirs, viz.,

Elizabeth, m. 1st, to Thomas, Lord Burgh, and 2ndly, to Sir William Lucy.
Margaret, m. 1st, to Henry, Lord Grey, of Codnor, and 2ndly, to Richard, Earl of Oxford.
Sir Thomas d. in Spain, in 1388.
Ralph (Sir), m. Philippa, the other dau. and co-heir of David Strathbogie, Earl of Athole, but d. s. g. in Palestine, 1399.
Alan d. young.
Margaret, d. young.
The earl m. 2ndly, Maud, sister and heir of Anthony, Lord Lucy, which Anthony settled upon his lordship and his heirs the honour and castle of Cockermouth, with other great estates, on condition that her arms should be for ever quartered with those of the Percys. In the 7th year of RICHARD II., the earl having been elected one of the knights of the Garter. the king bestowed upon him the robes of the order out of the royal wardrobe. In some years afterwards, however, being proclaimed a traitor, and his lands declared forfeited by King RICHARD, his lordship, in conjunction with his son, Sir Henry Percy, surnamed Hotspur, and Henry, Duke of Lancaster, accomplished the dethronement of that monarch, and placed the crown upon the head of Henry, Duke of Lancaster, under the title of HENRY IV. In requital, the king gave Percy the Isle of Man, by the tenure of carrying in the left hand the sword (which he wore when he landed in Holderness) at the oronation of himself and his successors. Again dissatisfied with the government, the duke is charged with concerting the rebellion, in which his son, Hotspur, and his brother, the Earl of Worcester, engaged, in 1403, for transferring the sceptre to Mortimer, Earl of March, then a boy. Of these two eminent persons, Sir Henry Percy, the renowned Hotspur, fell, performing prodigies of valour, at Battle-field, near Shrewsbury, 21 July, 1403, and Thomas Percy, Earl of Worcester, was beheaded, after the battle, at Shrewsbury. The Earl of Northumberland fell subsequently (29 February, 1407-8), in arms against the king, at Bramham Moor, near Haslewood, when his honours became forfeited under an attainder, but were restored, in 1414, to his grandson (Hotspur's only son),

HENRY DE PERCY, 2nd Earl of Northumberland, who m. Lady Eleanor Nevil, dau. of Ralph, 1st Earl of Westmoreland, and Joan de Beaufort, dau. of John of Gaunt, and aunt of King HENRY V. Of this nobleman and his countess, and their issue, the following account is given in a very curious MS. preserved in the British Museum, and there said to be extracted *Ex Registro Monasterij de Whitbye;*—"Henry Percy, the son of Sir Henry Percy, that was slayne at Shrewsbury, and of Elizabeth, the dau. of the Erle of Marche, after the death of his father and grauntsyre, was exiled into Scotland, in the time of King HENRY V.: by the labour of Johanne, the Countess of Westmoreland (whose dau., Alianor, he had wedded in coming into England), he recovered the king's grace, and the county of Northumberland, so was the 2nd Earl of Northumberland. And of this Alianor, his wife, he begat IX sonnes and III daughters, whose names be Johanne, that is buried at Whitbye; Thomas (created) Lord Egremont; Katheyne Grey, of Ruthyn (wife of Edmund, Lord Grey, afterwards Earl of Kent); Sir Raffe Percy; William Percy, a byshopp; Richard Percy; John, that dyed without issue: another John (called by Vincent, in his MS. Baronage in the Heralds' office, John Percy, senior, of Warkworth); George Percy, clerk; Henry, that dyed without issue; besides the eldest sonne and successor, Henry, 3rd Erle of Northumberland." His lordship, who was at the battle of Agincourt, was made lord high constable by King HENRY VI., and fell at St. Alban's, 23 May, 1455, fighting under the banner of that monarch, and was s. by his eldest surviving son,

HENRY PERCY, 3rd earl, who had m. Eleanor, dau. and sole heiress of Richard Poynings, who d. in the life-time of his father, Lord Poynings; by which marriage the Baronies of Poynings, Fitzpayne, and Bryan, came into the family of Percy; and Sir Henry Percy was summoned to parliament, while his father, the Earl of Northumberland, yet lived (29th HENRY VI.), as Baron Poynings. His lordship fell leading the van of the Lancastrians, sword in hand, at the battle of Towton, 29 March, 1461, and his honours became subsequently forfeited by an act of attainder, but were restored to his only son,

HENRY PERCY, 4th earl, K.G., who was confined in the Tower of London, from the death of his father until 27 October, 1469, when, being brought before EDWARD IV., at his palace of Westminster, he subscribed an oath of allegiance, and was restored to his freedom and dignity, although the reversal of his father's attainder does not appear upon the rolls of parliament. The king had previously created John, Lord Montague, Earl of Northumberland, but upon the re-establishment of the rightful earl Lord Montague was created Marquess of Montague. This Henry, 4th Earl of Northumberland, fell a victim, in 1489, to the avarice of King HENRY VII. In that year, parliament having granted the king a subsidy for carrying on the war in Bretagne, the Earl of Northumberland, as lord-lieutenant of his county, was empowered to enforce the same; but the tax causing a general commotion, his lordship wrote to inform the king of the discontent, and praying an abatement, to which HENRY peremptorily replied, "that not a penny should be abated:" which message being delivered incautiously by the earl to the populace, who had assembled to complain of their grievances, they broke into his house, Cocklodge, in Yorkshire, and murdered his lordship and some of his attendants, 28 April, 1489. The earl m. Maud, dau. of William Herbert, 1st Earl of Pembroke, and had, with three daus., four sons, HENRY-ALGERNON; William (Sir), a commander at Flodden; Alan, master of the college at Arundel; and Joscelin, of Beverley.

HENRY-ALGERNON PERCY, 5th earl, K.G., who m. Catherine, dau. and co-heiress of Sir Robert Spencer, Knt., of Spencer-Combe, Devon, by Eleanor, his wife, dau., and, at length, co-heir of Edmund Beaufort, Duke of Somerset, by whom he had
HENRY. his successor.
Thomas (Sir), executed for Ask's conspiracy, 1537, leaving, by Eleanor, his wife, dau. and co-heir of Sir Guischard Harbottle, two sons and a dau.,
THOMAS,⎫ successively Earls of Northumberland.
HENRY, ⎭
Mary, m. to Sir Francis Slingsby, Bart.
Ingelram (Sir).[*]
Margaret, m. to Henry Clifford, 1st Earl of Cumberland.
Maud, m. to William, Lord Coniers.

His lordship (we quote from Alexander Sinclair) "lived in great state and splendour, as his 'Household Book' shows, and although he was at the battles of Blackheath and Spurs, he d. in peace in 1527." He was s. by his eldest son,

HENRY PERCY, 6th earl, K.G., styled "the unthrifty," who was an attendant on Cardinal Wolsey, and a lover of Anne Boleyn. This nobleman m. Mary, dau. of George Talbot, Earl of Shrewsbury; but as he d. s. p. in 1537, and his brother, Sir Thomas Percy had been previously attainted and executed, all the honours of the family became forfeited, and the Dukedom of Northumberland was conferred, by King EDWARD VI., upon John Dudley, Earl of Warwick; but that nobleman having forfeited his life and honours, by treason against Queen MARY, in 1553, her Majesty was pleased to advance, by letters patent, dated 30 April, 1557,

THOMAS PERCY, son of the attainted Sir Thomas Percy, to the degree of a baron, by the title of *Baron Percy, of Cockermouth,* and on the day following, his lordship was created *Earl of Northumberland,* with remainder to Henry Percy, his brother, and his issue male. The earl m. Anne, 3rd dau. of Henry Somerset, 2nd Earl of Worcester, and had issue,

1. Thomas, d. young, 1560.
1. ELIZABETH, m. to Richard Woodroffe, Esq., of Wolley, co. York.
11. LUCY, m. Sir Edward Stanley, K.B., of Tong Castle, and had two daus.,

FRANCES STANLEY, who m. Sir John Fortescue, of Salden, Bart., and had a son,

Sir John Fortescue, Bart., father of Frances Fortescue, who m. Henry-Benedict Hall, Esq., of High Meadow, and had a son,

---

[*] From this Sir Ingelram Percy, JAMES PERCY, known as the trunk-maker, who so pertinaciously claimed the honours of the house of Percy, asserted that he derived descent (see BURKE's *Vicissitudes of Families*).

PER

PER

Benedict Hall, of High Meadow, who d. 1719, leaving a dau. and sole heir,

Benedicta-Maria-Theresa Hall, who m. Thomas, 1st Viscount Gage, father of

Hon. Thomas Gage, a general officer, father of Henry, 3rd viscount, who d. 1808, leaving a son,

Henry, 4th viscount Gage, b. 1791 (*See* Burke's *Extant Peerage*).

Venetia Stanley, m. Sir Kenelm Digby, and had a son, John Digby, of Gothurst, who had a dau., and at length sole heir,

Margaret-Maria, who m. Sir John Conway, Bart., of Bodryddan, and had a son, Henry Conway, who d. v. p., leaving a dau. and sole heir.

Honora Conway, who m. Sir John Glynne, Bart. of Hawarden, father, by her, of

Sir Stephen Glynne, 7th bart., who d. 1780, leaving a son,

Sir Stephen-Richard Glynne, 8th bart., b. 1780, father of

Sir Stephen-Richard Glynne, Bart., b. 1807.

III. Jane, m. Lord Henry Seymour, and d. s. p.
IV. Mary, prioress of the English nunnery at Brussells.

This nobleman having conspired against Queen Elizabeth, was beheaded at York, 22 August, 1572 (avowing t e Pope's supremacy, and affirming the realm to be in a state of schism, when his honours would have fallen under the attainder, but for the reversionary clause in favour of his brother,

Henry Percy, who s. as 8th earl. His lordship m. Katherine, eldest dau. and co-heiress of John Neville, Lord Latimer, by whom (who d. 1596) he had eight sons, and three daus. The earl having been committed to the Tower, for participating in a supposed plot in favour of Mary Queen of Scots, was found dead in his bed there, wounded by three bullets from a pistol, 21 June, 1585, when he was s. by his eldest son,

Henry Percy, 9th earl, K.G. This nobleman, after every effort to involve him in the Gunpowder Plot had proved ineffectual was "cast" (says Osborne) "into the star chamber," by which he was sentenced to a fine of £30,000, with imprisonment in the Tower during his Majesty's pleasure, and he actually suffered several years' incarceration. His lordship m. Dorothy, sister of Queen Elizabeth's favourite, the Earl of Essex., and widow of Sir Thomas Perrot, Knt., and dying 5 November, 1632, was s. by his eldest surviving son,

Algernon Percy, 10th earl, K.G., who had been summoned to parliament in the lifetime of his father, 1626, as *Baron Percy.* This nobleman took an active part during the civil wars, against King Charles I., but was entirely free of any participation in his Majesty's death. He subsequently promoted the Restoration. His lordship d. 13 October, 1668, and w s s. by his only son (by Lady Elizabeth Howard, 2nd dau. of Theophilus, 2nd Earl of Suffolk),

Joscelyn Percy, 11th earl. This nobleman m. Elizabeth, youngest dau. of Thomas Wriothesley, Earl of Southampton, lord high treasurer of England, by whom he left, at his decease, 21 May, 1670, an only dau.,

Lady Elizabeth Percy, who m. 1st, when only fourteen years of age (1679), Henry Cavendish, Earl of Ogle (son and heir of Henry, Duke of Newcastle , who assumed the name of Percy, but his lordship d.s.p. 1 November, 1680, and her ladyship m. in 1682 (3rdly, it is stated, but she appears to have been only contracted to Thomas Thynne, Esq., of Longleate, who was assassinated by Koningsmark, 12 February, 1681-2), Charles Seymour, 6th Duke of Somerset, who also assumed, by preliminary engagement, the surname and arms of Percy, but from that stipulation he was released, when her grace attained majority. By this marriage the Duchess (who d. 1722) had thirteen children, the eldest surviving whom,

Algernon Seymour, was summoned to parliament, in 1722, as *Baron Percy.* His lordship s. to the Dukedom of Somerset, in 1748, and was created *Baron Warkworth, of Warkworth Castle, co. Northumberland,* and *Earl of Northumberland,* 2 October, 1749, with remainder to

Sir Hugh Smithson, Bart., who had m. his grace's dau., the Lady Elizabeth Seymour, and who s. to those honours upon the demise of the duke, in 1750, obtaining in the same year an act of parliament to allow himself, and his countess to assume the surname and arms of Percy. His lordship was installed a knight of the Garter in 1757: and created *Earl Percy,* and *Duke of Northumberland,* 18 October, 1766. His grace's eldest son, Hugh, 2nd Duke of Northumberland, K.G., was father of two sons, Hugh, 3rd Duke. K.G., and Algernon, 4th Duke, K.G., and also of four daus., all of whom, d. s. p. or unm., except the youngest, Emily, wife of James, Lord Glenlyon, whose grandson, John-James-Hugh-Henry Murray, Duke of Athole, as heir-general of the Dukes of Northumberland, inherited the Barony of Percy. The 2nd son of the 1st Duke of Northumberland, Algernon, Earl

425

of Beverley, was father of George, 5th Duke of Northumberland.

Upon the decease of his lordship (Joscelyn, 11th earl), all the honours of the Percys, save the baronies became extinct.

Arms—Quarterly. four grand quarters; 1st and 4th, or, a lion rampant, az. (being the ancient arms of the Duke of Brabant and Lovaine); 2nd and 3rd, gu., three lucies, or pikes, haurient, arg., for Lucy; 2nd grand quarter, az . five fusils, in fesse, or, for Percy: 3rd, gu., on a saltier arg., a rose of the field, barbed and seeded ppr., for Neville; 4th quarterly, gu. and or, in the 1st quarter a mullet, arg., for Vere.

Mr. Alexander Sinclair in his *Remarks on the far descended and renowned title of Lord Percy,* gives this statement of some of the Percy estates:—

1 Spofforth and Topcliff in Yorkshire, came into the family at the Conquest.
2 Petworth, from Queen Adeliza, to her brother Josceline de Louvaine, husband of Agnes de Percy.
3 Alnwick, in 1309, from Anthony Bec, bishop of Durham.
4 Sion House, by grant from the crown to Henry, 9th Earl of Northumberland.
5 Northumberland House, formerly Northampton House, by Elizabeth Howard, 2nd wife of Algernon, 10th earl.

PERCY—BARON EGREMONT.

By Letters Patent, dated 20 December, 1449.

Lineage.

Sir Thomas Percy, Knt., 3rd son of Henry, 2nd Earl of Northumberland, was created by King Edward IV., in consideration of his good services, Baron Egremont, of Egremont Castle, in Cumberland. His lordship fell at the battle of Northampton, in 1460, when the king was taken prisoner. He d. according to Dugdale, "without issue," when the Barony of Egremont became extinct. Some other authorities state, however, that he left a son, Sir John Percy, who never assumed the title.

PERCY—BARON PRUDHOE.

By Letters Patent, dated 27 November, 1816.

Lineage.

Lord Algernon Percy, K.G., 2nd son of Hugh, 2nd Duke of Northumberland, was created Baron Prudhoe, of Prudhoe Castle, Northumberland, 27 November, 1816, and s. to the ducal honours as 4th Duke of Northumberland, at the decease of his brother, Hugh, 3rd duke. His Grace, m. 25 August, 1842, Eleanor, dau. of Richard, 2nd Marquess of Westminster, but d. s. p. 12 February, 1865, when the Barony of Prudhoe became extinct.

The Barony of Percy passed to his grand-nephew, and heir-general the Duke of Athole, and the dukedom devolved on the heir male, the Earl of Beverley.

Arms—Quarterly: 1st and 4th grand quarters, 1st and 4th, or, a lion rampant, az. (being the ancient arms of the Duke of Brabant and Lovaine): 2nd and 3rd, gu., three lucies. or pikes, haurient, arg., for Lucy; 2nd and 3rd grand quarters, az., five fusils, in fesse, or, for Percy.

PERCY—EARL OF WORCESTER.

Created 29 September, 1397.

Lineage.

Sir Thomas Percy, a younger brother of Henry, 1st Earl of Northumberland, having distinguished himself in the council and the camp, temp. Edward III. and Richard II., was created by the latter monarch Earl of Worcester. Towards the end of Edward III.'s reign, Sir Thomas was the companion in arms of the Black Prince; and had a grant of 100 marks per annum for life, out of the exchequer, for his good services, with a similar annuity for his especial services to the Prince. In the 1st Richard II., he assisted at the coronation of that king, his brother, Henry, being then marshal of England.

The next year as admiral of the north seas, he was associated with Sir Hugh Calveley, Knt., and meeting with seven ships and one man of war, laden with wine, brought them all into Bristol. He was subsequently employed with the Earl of Buckingham to suppress Jack Straw's insurrection: and in the 10th of the same reign he was made admiral of the fleet, for the great army of 20,000 men then sent into Spain, with John of Gaunt, to establish that prince's right to the throne of Castile and Leon. In three years afterwards he was constituted justice of South Wales, and subsequently vice-chamberlain to the king. In the 18th he was sent ambassador to France, being then steward of the king's household, and in a few years afterwards appointed admiral of the king's fleet for Ireland. Notwithstanding his lordship's high position in the estimation of King RICHARD, upon the deposition of that monarch, he seems to have made his ground good with the new king, for we find him d. puted with the bishop of Durham to announce to the court of France the revolution that placed the sceptre in the hand of HENRY IV., and reconstituted soon after, steward of the household. Subsequently, however, joining his brother, the Earl of Northumberland, and his nephew, Hotspur, in an effort to restore the dethroned monarch he was made prisoner at the battle of Shrewsbury, where his gallant nephew fell, and was beheaded immediately after, anno 1402. His lordship was a knight of the Garter; he d. s. p. when the Earldom of Worcester became EXTINCT.

Arms—Same as Percy, Earls of Northumberland.

PERY—VISCOUNT PERY.

By Letters Patent, dated 30 March, 1785.

Lineage.

EDMOND PERY, Esq , of Stackpole Court, co. Clare (son of Edmond Pery, Esq., by Susannah, his wife, only dau. and heir of Stephen Sexton, Esq.), a colonel in his Majesty's service, d. about the year 1721, leaving issue,

I. Sexton, of Stackpole Court, d. s p. in 1730.
II. STACKPOLE, of whom we treat.

The 2nd son,

THE REV. STACKPOLE PERY, of the co. Limerick, b. about the year 1686, m. 2 April, 1716, Jane, dau. of the Rev. Wm. Twigg, archdeacon of Limerick (by Diana, his wife, dau. of Sir Drury Wray, of Rathcannon, co. Limerick, Bt.). and by her (who d. 31 August, 1767) had issue,

I. EDMOND SEXTON, of whom presently.
II. William-Cecil, D.D., bishop of Limerick, Ardfert, and Aghadoe, b. 26 July, 1721, bapt. 3 August following, created BARON GLENTWORTH, of Mallow, 21 May, 1790. (See BURKE'S Extant Peerage—Earl of Limerick).
III. Stackpole, d. young.
IV. Wray, d. an infant.
V. Sexton, d. an infant.
I. Diana, m. 8 October, 1733, the Rev. Henry Smyth, son of Thos. Smith, D.D., bishop of Limerick.
II. Dymphna, m. in 1751, to William Monsell, Esq., of Tervoe, co. Limerick.
III. Anne, d. an infant.   IV. Frances.
V. Lucy. m. 23 December, 1751, Sir Henry Hartstonge, of Bruff, Bart.
VI. Mary.
VII. Jane, m. June. 1774, Lancelot Hill, Esq., of Limerick.

The Rev. Stackpole Pery d. 8 June, 1739, and was interred in Christ Church-yard, in the city of Cork. His eldest son,

THE RIGHT HON. EDMOND SEXTON PERY, having filled the Speaker's chair of the Commons of Ireland from 1771 to 1785, was, on his retirement, elevated to the peerage of Ireland, 30 March, in that year, as VISCOUNT PERY, of Newtown Pery, co. Limerick. His lordship m. 1st, 11 June, 1785, Patty, youngest dau. of John Martin, Esq. ; and 2ndly, 27 October, 1762 (his 1st wife d. s. p. in 1757), Elizabeth, eldest dau. of John, Lord Knapton, sister of Sir Thomas Viscount de Vesci, and widow of Robert Handcock, Esq., of Waterstown, co. Westmeath, by whom he had issue,

DIANA-JANE. m. 2 June, 1785, to Thomas, 2nd Viscount Northland, afterwards Earl of Ranfurly, and d. 24 November, 1839.
Frances, m. in January, 1789, to Nicholson Calvert, Esq., M.P., of Hunsdon House, Herts, who d. 1841.

Lord Pery d. in 1806, and with him the viscounty EXPIRED.

Arms—Quarterly : gu. and or, on a bend, arg., three lions passant, sa.

PETTY—EARL OF SHELBURNE.

By Letters Patent, dated 29 April, 1719.

Lineage.

SIR WILLIAM PETTY, M.D., the celebrated Surveyor-General of Ireland, b. at Romsey, in Hampshire, in 1623, acquired by his public appointments great estates in Ireland, and founded the noble house of Shelburne. He m. in 1667, Elizabeth, dau. of Sir Hardress Waller, Knt., of Castletown, co. Limerick, and widow of Sir Maurice Fenton, Bart., by whom (who was created, in the first year of her widowhood, 1688, BARONESS SHELBURNE, for life,) he left at his decease, 16 December, 1687, a dau., Anne, m. in 1692, to Thomas Fitzmaurice, 1st Earl of Kerry, and two sons; of whom the elder,

CHARLES PETTY, Esq., was created in 1688, Baron Shelburne, of the kingdom of Ireland. His lordship m. in June, 1690, Mary, dau. of Sir John Williams, Bart., of Minster Court, Kent, b t by her (who m. 2ndly, Maj.-Gen. Henry Conyngham, of Slane; and 3rdly, Col. Robert Dalway, and d. 1760), he left no issue at his decease in April, 1696, when the title became EXTINCT, but the estates passed to his brother,

HENRY PETTY, Esq., who was created 16 June, 1699, Baron Shelburne, co. Wexford, and advanced to the dignities of Viscount Dunkerron, co. Kerry, and EARL OF SHELBURNE, 29 April, 1719. His lordship m. in 1699, Arabella, 5th dau. of Charles Boyle, Lord Clifford, and by her (who d. in October, 1740,) had issue,

JAMES, Viscount Dunkeron; who m. 21 April, 1737, Elizabeth, sister and co-heir of Sir James Clavering, Bart., of Axwell, but predeceased his father, without surviving issue, 17 September, 1750.
Anne, m. 26 March, 1722, to Francis, son and heir of Francis Bernard Esq., one of the Judges of the Court of Common Pleas ; but d. s. p.

Lord Shelburne survived his son but a few months, and d. 17 April following, when all his honours became EXTINCT His great estates his lordship bequeathed to his neph w, the Hon. John Fitzmaurice, who was created Viscount Fitzmaurice, 7 October, 1751, and EARL OF SHELBURNE, 26 June, 1753, was father of William, 2nd Earl of Shelburne, the Prime Minister of 1782, who was created MARQUESS OF LANSDOWNE.

Arms—Erm., on a bend, az., a magnetic needle pointing to the polar star, or.

PHILIPPS—BARON MILFORD.

By Letters Patent, dated 1776.

Lineage.

SIR RICHARD PHILIPPS, 7th Baronet of Picton Castle, co. Pembroke (see BURKE'S Extant Peerage and Baronetage), was elevated to the peerage of Ireland, as BARON MILFORD, in 1776; but d. s. p. 28 November, 1823, when the title became EXTINCT.

Arms—Arg., a lion rampant, sa., ducally gorged and chained, or.

PHILIPPS—BARON MILFORD.

By Letters Patent, dated 21 September, 1847.

Lineage.

RICHARD BULKELEY-PHILIPPS PHILIPPS, Esq., of Picton Castle, co. Pembroke, b. 7 June, 1801, son of John Grant, Esq., of Nolton, by Mary-Philippa-Artemisia, his wife, only dau. and heir of James Child, Esq., of Bigelly Hou e, co. Pembroke, by Mary-Philippa-Artemisia, his wife, only dau. and heir of Bulkeley Philipps, Esq., of Abercover, 2nd son of Sir John Philipps, 4th bart., of Picton Castle, assumed by sign-manual, in 1824, in respect of the memory of his maternal cousin, Sir Richard Philipps, Baron Milford, the surname and arms of PHILIPPS, and was created a Baronet in 1828, and advanced to the peerage of the United Kingdom as BARON MILFORD, of Picton Ca tle, co. Pembroke, 21 September, 1847. He m. 1st, Eliza, only dau. of the late John Gordon, Esq., of Hanwell, co. Middlesex, which lady *d.* 24 March, 1852; and 2ndly, 8 June, 1854, Lady Anne-Jane Howard, 4th dau. of the Earl of Wicklow; but *d. s. p.* 3 January, 1857, when the title became EXTINCT. His widow *m.* 2ndly, 4 June, 1861, Thomas-J. Eyre, Esq., of Uppercourt, co. Kilkenny.

Arms—Arg., a lion rampant, sa., ducally gorged and chained, or.

PHIPPS—BARON MULGRAVE.

By Letters Patent, dated 7 July, 1790.

Lineage.

CONSTANTINE-JOHN PHIPPS, 2nd Baron Mulgrave, of New Ross, in the peerage of Ireland, an enterprising naval officer, who made an effort to discover a north-west passage, was created a peer of Great Britain by letters patent, dated 7 July, 1790, in the dignity of BARON MULGRAVE, of *Mulgrave, co. York.* His lordship *m.* in 1787, Anne-Elizabeth, youngest dau. of Nathaniel Cholmley, Esq., of Howsham, co. York, and had an only dau.,

ANNE-ELIZABETH-CHOLMLEY, who *m.* Lieut.-Gen. Sir John Murray, Bart., and *d.* 10 April, 1848.

Lord Mulgrave *d.* in 1792, and was *s.* in the Irish peerage by his brother, HENRY (father of the 1st MARQUESS OF NORMANBY), while the Barony of Mulgrave, of Mulgrave, in the peerage of Great Britain, became EXTINCT.

Arms—Quarterly: 1st and 4th, sa , a trefoil, slipped, between eight mullets arg., for PHIPPS; 2nd and 3rd, paly of six, arg. and az., over all a bend gu., for ANNESLEY.

PIERREPONT—BARON PIERREPONT, OF ARDGLASS.

(*See* PIERREPONT, Baron Pierrepont, of Hanslope, in the *Extinct Peerage of England.*)

PIERREPONT — VISCOUNTS NEWARK, EARLS OF KINGSTON-UPON-HULL, MARQUESSES OF DORCHESTER, DUKES OF KINGSTON-UPON-HULL.

Viscounty, by Letters Patent, dated 29 June, 1627.
Earldom, by Letters Patent, dated 25 July, 1628.
Marquessate, by Letters Patent, dated 25 March, 1644.
Dukedom, by Letters Patent, dated 10 August, 1715.

Lineage.

SIR HENRY DE PIERREPONT, a person of great note at the period in which he lived, and representative of the Anglo-Norman family of Pierrepont, *m.* Annora, dau. of Michael, and sister and heir of Lionel de Manvers, whereby he acquired an extensive land property in co. Nottingham, with the lordship of Holme, now called Holme-Pierrepont. Sir Henry *d.* about the 20th EDWARD I., and was *s.* by his elder son,

SIMON DE PIERREPONT, who in the 32nd EDWARD I., was one of those that by special writ, bearing date 8 June, had summons amongst the barons of the realm, to repair with all speed to the king, wheresoever he should then be in England, to treat of certain weighty affairs, relating to his and their honour; the sheriffs of every county having also command to cause two knights for each shire, as also two citizens, and two burgesses for each city and borough, to attend the king at the same time, "to advise and consent for themselves and the commonalty of their respective shires, cities, and boroughs, unto what the earls, barons, and nobles, should at that time ordain." This Simon leaving a dau. (only), Sibilla, who *m.* Edmund Ufford, was *s.* by his brother,

ROBERT DE PIERREPONT, a very eminent person in the reigns of EDWARD I. and EDWARD II., distinguished in the wars of Scotland. He *m.* Sarah, dau. and eventually heir of Sir John Heriz, Knt., and was direct ancestor of

427

SIR GEORGE PIERREPONT, who, at the dissolution of the monasteries, in the reign of HENRY VIII., purchased large manors in the co. Nottingham, part of the possessions of the abbot and convent of Welbeck, and others in Derbyshire, which had belonged to the monastery of Newsted. He *d.* in the 6th ELIZABETH, and was *s.* by his son,

SIR HENRY PIERREPONT, who *m.* Frances, elder dau. of Sir William Cavendish, of Chatsworth, and sister of William, Earl of Devonshire, and was *s.* by his son,

ROBERT PIERREPONT. who was advanced to the peerage by King CHARLES I., as BARON PIERREPONT, *of Holme Pierrepont, co. Nottingham*, and VISCOUNT NEWARK, by letters patent, dated 29 June, 1627, and the next year was created EARL OF KINGSTON-UPON-HULL At the breaking out of the civil war, his lordship was one of the first and most zealous to espouse the royal cause, and he is said to have brought no less than 4000 men immediately to the standard of the king. He was soon after constituted lieutenant-general of all his Majesty's forces, in the cos. of Lincoln, Rutland, Huntingdon, Cambridge, and Norfolk ; and was amongst the most popular of the cavalier commanders. His lordship became, therefore, an object of more than ordinary watchfulness to the parliamentarians, and was at length surprised and made prisoner by Lord Willoughby, of Parham, at Gainsborough, whence he was despatched in an open boat towards Hull. But Sir Charles Cavendish, pursuing the boat, and overtaking it, demanded the release of the earl, which being refused, his men fired, and, unhappily, killed Lord Kingston, and his servant, though they captured the boat and put the crew to the sword. This melancholy event occurred 30 July, 1643. His lordship bore so high a character for benevolence, hospitality, and liberality, that he was usually styled by the common people, "the good Earl of Kingston." He *m.* Gertrude, dau. and co-heir of Henry Talbot, 3rd son of George, Earl of Shrewsbury, and by her (who *d.* 1649, æt. sixty-one), had issue,

HENRY, Viscount Newark.
William, of Thoresby, *m.* Elizabeth, dau. and co-heir of Sir Thomas Harris, of Tong Castle, co. Salop, and had

  ROBERT, who *m.* Elizabeth, dau. and co-heir of Sir John Evelyn, and had issue,

    ROBERT, } 3rd and 4th Earls of Kingston.
    WILLIAM, }
    EVELYN, 5th earl, and 1st duke.
    Gertrude, *m.* to Charles, Viscount Newhaven.

GERVASE, created Baron Pierrepont, of Hanslope.
Frances, *m.* to Henry, Earl of Ogle.
Grace, *m.* to Gilbert, Earl of Clare.
Gertrude, *m.* to George, Marquess of Halifax.

This William was one of the leading members of the House of Commons, during the civil wars : he *d.* after the Restoration, in 1679.

Francis, *m.* Elizabeth, dau. and co-heir of Thomas Bray, Esq.' of Eyam, co. Derby, and *d.* in 1657, leaving,

  Robert, who *m.* Anne, dau. of Henry Murray, Esq., and left issue,

    Francis, } *d. s. p*
    George, }
    William, whose sons *d. s. p.*
    Jane, *m.* to Rev. Bernard Gilpin.
    Anne, *m* to Thomas Newport, Lord Torrington.
  William.   Henry.
  Frances, *m.* to William, son and heir of William, 5th Lord Paget.

Robert, *d. unm.*
Gervase, *d. unm.*, in Holland, *anno* 1679, bequeathing £10,000 to the first member of his family who should obtain the honour and title of a duke.

George, of Old Cotes, in Derbyshire, *m.* Miss Jones, sister of Sir Samuel Jones, of Corthen Hall, Notts, by whom he had two sons,

  Henry, } both *d. unm.*
  Samuel, }

Frances, *m.* Philip Rolleston, Esq.

His lordship was *s.* by his eldest son,

HENRY PIERREPONT, 2nd Earl of Kingston. This nobleman remaining, like his father, most faithfully attached to the fortunes of King CHARLES I., was sworn of the privy council to that monarch, and created 25 March, 1644, MARQUESS OF DORCHESTER. His lordship *m.* 1st, Cecilia, dau. of Paul, Viscount Bayning, and had surviving issue,

  Anne, *m.* to John, Lord Ros (afterwards Duke of Rutland), from whom she was divorced in 1668.
  Grace, *d. unm.*

The earl *m.* 2ndly, Lady Katherine Stanley, dau. of James, Earl of Derby, but had no surviving issue His lordship. who was a man of learning, particularly in law and physic, *d.* in 1680, when the Marquessate of Dorchester became EXTINCT, but his other honours devolved upon his grand nephew (*refer to descendants of William Pierrepont, of Thoresby, 2nd son of the 1st earl*),

ROBERT PIERREPONT, 3rd Earl of Kingston. This nobleman *d. unm.* while on his travels at Dieppe, in France, *anno* 1682, and was *s.* by his brother,

WILLIAM PIERREPONT, 4th earl, who *m.* Anne, dau. of Robert, Lord Brooke, but *d. s. p.*, in 1690, when the honours devolved upon his brother,

EVELYN PIERREPONT, 5th earl, who was advanced 23 December, 1706, to the MARQUESSATE OF DORCHESTER, with remainder to his uncle, Gervase, Lord Pierrepont, of Hanslope, and was created 10 August, 1715, DUKE OF KINGSTON-UPON-HULL. His grace was subsequently made a knight of the Garter, and he was constituted, four different times, one of the lords justices, during his Majesty's absence in his Hanoverian dominions. His grace *m.* 1st, Lady Mary Fielding, dau. of William, Earl of Denbigh, and had issue,

WILLIAM, Marquess of Dorchester, who *d.* in the duke's lifetime, 1713, leaving by Rachel, his wife, a son and a dau.,

EVELYN, who inherited as 2nd duke.

Frances, *m.* 1734, to Philip, son of Sir Philip Medows, Knt., and had, with other issue,

CHARLES MEDOWS, Esq., who succeeding to the estates of his uncle, Evelyn, Duke of Kingston, in 1773, assumed the surname of PIERREPONT, and was elevated to the peerage as Baron Pierrepont. He *d.* in 1816, and was *s.* by his son,

CHARLES, late Earl Manvers, who *d.* in 1860, and was *s.* by his eldest surviving son,

CHARLES, 3rd EARL MANVERS.

Mary, *m.* to Edward Wortley-Montagu, Esq., and became celebrated as Lady Mary Wortley-Montagu.

Frances, *m.* to John, Earl of Mar.

Evelyn, *m.* to John, Lord Gower.

The duke *m.* 2ndly, Lady Isabella Bentinck, dau. of William, Earl of Portland, by whom he had,

Carolina, *m.* to Thomas Brand, Esq.

Anne, *d. unm.*

His grace *d.* in 1726, and was *s.* by his grandson,

EVELYN PIERREPONT, 2nd duke. This nobleman *m.* Elizabeth, Chudleigh, one of the maids of honour to the Dowager Princess of Wales, and only dau. of Colonel Thomas Chudleigh, of Chelsea Hospital, (2nd son of Sir George Chudleigh, Bart., of Ashton, co. Devon) but this lady, so notorious as Duchess of Kingston, was afterwards convicted by her peers of bigamy. The trial took place in 1776, the Lord Chancellor Apsley officiating as high steward. His grace *d. s. p.* in 1773, when all his honours became EXTINCT, while his estates devolved upon his nephew, Charles Medows, Esq., who assumed the name of PIERREPONT, and was created EARL MANVERS.

Arms—Arg., semée of cinquefoils, gu., a lion rampant, sa.

PIERREPONT—BARON PIERREPONT, OF HANSLOPE.

By Letters Patent, dated 19 October, 1714.

Lineage.

GERVASE PIERREPONT, 2nd son of the Hon. William Pierrepont, 2nd son of Robert, 1st Earl of Kingston, was created a peer of Ireland as Baron Pierrepont, of Ardglass, 29 March, 1703, and of Great Britain (19 October, 1714), as BARON PIERREPONT, *of Hanslope, co. Bucks.* His lordship *m.* Lucy, dau. of Sir John Pelham, Bart., of Loughton, in Sussex, but *d. s. p.* 22 May, 1715, when all his honours became EXTINCT.

Arms—Same as the Earls and Dukes of Kingston, with due difference.

PIGOT—BARON PIGOT, OF PATSHUL.

By Letters Patent, dated 18 January, 1766.

Lineage.

The house of Pigott was founded in England by Pigott, Baron of Boome, in Normandy, one of the knightly companions of WILLIAM THE CONQUEROR. From GILBERT PIGOTT, Lord of Croxton, co. Chester, cotemporary with that monarch, derived the family of Pigott, of Butley, in the same co., ancestor of

RICHARD PIGOT, Esq., of Butley, who *m.* Jocosa, heiress of Chetwynd, co. Salop, elder dau. and co-heir of Richard de Pershall, of Chetwynd, living 17th HENRY IV. (brother of Nicholas de Pershall, Lord of the manor of Pershall, and Horsley, co. Stafford, and grandson of Sir Richard de Pershall, Knt., high-sheriff of Shropshire, 50th EDWARD III., 1377, by Johanna, his wife, heiress of Chetwynd, dau. and heir of Reginald, son and heir of Sir John Chetwynd, of Chetwynd). The grandson of Richard Pigot, by the heiress of Pershall, of Chetwynd,

ROBERT PIGOTT, of Chetwynd, high sheriff of Shropshire in 1517, bore, "Azure, a chevron between three mullets, or. on a chief, ermine, three fusils, sable." From the marriage of this Robert and Margaret, his wife, dau. of Sir John Blount, Knt., of Kinlet, derived 7th in descent,

ROBERT PIGOTT, Esq., of Chetwynd, high sheriff of Shropshire in 1697, who *m.* Frances, dau. of the Hon. William Ward, of Willingsworth, co. Stafford, brother of Edward, Lord Dudley and Ward, by whom he had, *inter alios*, ROBERT-PIGOTT, eldest son, and the Rev. William Pigott, rector of Edgemond and Chetwynd, ancestor of the PIGOTTS, of Doddershall Park, Bucks, represented by William-Harvey Pigott, Esq., of Doddershall Park (*refer* to that name, BURKE's *Landed Gentry.*) The eldest son,

ROBERT PIGOTT, Esq., of Chetwynd, who *d.* May, 1770, was father by Anne, his wife, dau. of — Piers, Esq., of Croggian, co. Montgomery, of two sons,

I. Robert Pigott, Esq., of Chetwynd, high sheriff of Shropshire, in 1774, who sold Chetwynd, which he had inherited through twelve generations, retired abroad, and *d.* 7 July, 1794, having had a son who predeceased him.

II. The Rev. William Pigott, of Edgmond, co. Salop, rector of Chetwynd and Edgmond, who *m.* Arabella, dau. of John Mytton, Esq., of Halston, co. Salop, father of the REV. JOHN DRYDEN PIGOTT, of Edgmond, rector of the same place, and of Habberley.

From the Pigotts of Chetwynd, claim descent two families, both of which bear "Ermine, three fusils, sable," the Pigotts, of Knapton, Queen's co., Ireland, baronets, so created 3 October, 1808, represented by the present SIR CHARLES-ROBERT PIGOTT, Bart., of Knapton, and an English branch. The immediate ancestor of the latter,

HUGH PIGOTT, of Peploe, co. Salop, who *d.* in 1697, was father, by Elizabeth Duke, his wife, of a 7th son,

RICHARD PIGOT, Esq., of Westminster, who *m.* Frances, dau. of Peter Goode, Esq., and had issue, with a dau., Margaret, who *m.* in 1755, Thomas Fisher, Esq., three sons,

I. GEORGE.

II. ROBERT, successor to his brother.

III. Hugh, vice-admiral, who *m.* 1st, Elizabeth, dau. of Peter Le Neve, Esq., and had, with a dau., Isabella, a son,

Sir Henry Pigot, G.C.M.G., a general officer, to whom Malta was surrendered by the French, *d. s. p.* 1840.

He *m.* 2ndly, Frances, dau. of Sir Richard Wrottesley, Bart., and by her, who *d.* 1811, had a son and two daus.,

1 Sir Hugh Pigot, K.C.B., admiral of the white, who *d.* 30 July, 1857, æt. eighty-two.

1 Frances.

2 Caroline, *m.* in 1800, to Lord Henry Fitzroy, prebendary of Westminster, eldest son (by his 2nd wife, Elizabeth, dau. of Sir Richard Wrottesley, Bart.), of Augustus, 3rd Duke of Grafton, and by him, who *d.* 9 June, 1828, left at her decease, 1825, with other issue, an eldest son, Hugh Fitzroy, lieut.-colonel, grenadier guards, *b.* 14 May, 1808.

Mr. Pigot, who *d.* in 1729, was *s.* by his eldest son,

GEORGE PIGOT, governor of Fort St. George, Madras, created a Baronet, 5 December, 1764, with remainder, in default of male issue, to his brother, Robert, and on failure of his issue to his brother, Hugh and his heirs male. Sir George was created a peer of Ireland 18 January, 1766, as BARON PIGOT, *of Patshul, co. Dublin,* but, at his death, *s.p.*, in illegal confinement in India, 17 April, 1777, the barony EXPIRED, while the baronetcy devolved, according to the limitation, upon his brother,

BRIGADIER-GENERAL SIR ROBERT PIGOT, an officer of high distinction during the American war, grandfather of the present SIR ROBERT PIGOT, of Patshul, 4th baronet.

Arms—Erm., three lozenges, in fesse, sa.

PINKNEY—BARON PINKNEY.

By Writ of Summons, dated 6 February, 1299.

Lineage.

In the time of King HENRY I.,

GILO DE PINCHENI gave certain lands lying at Wedon, in Northamptonshire, to the monks of St. Lucian, in France, who thereupon transplanted part of their convent to that place, and made it a cell to their monastery. To this Gilo *s.* his son,

RALPH DE PINCHENI, who was *s.* by his son,

GILBERT DE PINCHENI, who, in the 3rd, 5th, and 6th HENRY II., was sheriff of the county of Berks: and upon the assessment in aid for marrying that king's dau. in six years subsequently, certified his knights' fees at fourteen and a half. He was *s.* by his son,

HENRY DE PINCHENI, who *d.* about 1209, and was *s.* by his son,

ROBERT DE PINCHENI, one of the barons who took up arms against King John, in consequence of which his lands were seized upon by the crown, and given to Waleran Tyes. But making his peace, they were restored to him, in the 1st year of HENRY III. He was *s.* by his son,

HENRY DE PINCHENI, who *m.* Alice, sister and heir of Gerard de Lindesey, and dying in 1254, seized of the Barony of Wedon, co. Northampton, which he held of the king *in capite* by barony, besides lands in Bucks and Essex, was *s.* by his son,

HENRY DE PINCHENY. This baron had a military summons to attend the king against the Welsh, in the 42nd HENRY III. He was *s.* at his decease in 1277, by his son,

ROBERT DE PINCHENY, who, in the 10th EDWARD I., being in the king's service, in Wales, had scutage of all his tenants by military service in the cos. of Northampton, Bucks, Bedford, Essex, Herts, Warwick, Oxford, Berks, Suffolk, Norfolk, and Somerset. He was afterwards in the wars of Gascony, and dying about the year 1295, was *s.* by his brother,

HENRY DE PINKNEY, of Wedon, who was in the wars of Scotland, in the 26th EDWARD I., and was summoned to parliament as a Baron, in the 25th, 27th, and 28th of the same reign. His lordship, having no issue, made a surrender of his lands in 1301 to the king, and his heirs for ever. At his decease the Barony of Pinkney became EXTINCT.

Arms—Or, four fusils in fesse, gu.

PIPARD—BARON PIPARD.

By Writ of Summons, dated 6 February, 1299.

Lineage.

RALPH PIPARD, said to be a younger son of Ralph Fitz-Nicholas, steward of the household to King HENRY III., having distinguished himself in the Welsh and Scottish wars, *temp.* EDWARD I., was summoned to parliament as a Baron from 6 February, 1299, to 24 July, 1302. In the 30th EDWARD I. his lordship was made governor for life of Bolesover and Hareston Castles, co. Derby. Lord Pipard *d.* in 1309, leaving JOHN, his son and heir, but neither he nor any of his descendants were ever summoned to parliament, nor esteemed barons.

Arms—Arg., two bars, gu., on a canton, az., a cinquefoil, or.

PITT—BARONS AND EARL OF CHATHAM.

Barony, by Letters Patent, dated 4 December, 1761.
Earldom by Letters Patent, dated 4 August, 1766.

Lineage.

THOMAS PITT, Esq., of Blandford, co. Dorset, was appointed in the reign of Queen ANNE, Governor of Fort St. George, in the East Indies, where he purchased for 48,000 pagodas

(£20,400) the very celebrated diamond, weighing 127 carats; which he sold to the Regent of Orleans for £135,000, which is still considered as the most precious jewel in the crown of France. Mr. Pitt was subsequently governor-general of Jamaica. He sat in four parliaments for Old Sarum, and Thirsk. He *m.* Jane, dau. of James Innes, Esq., and had issue,

  I. ROBERT, of Boconnoc.
  II. THOMAS, a colonel of horse, who marrying Frances, dau. and co-heiress of Robert Ridgway, Earl of Londonderry, was himself created in 1719, Baron, and in 1726, EARL OF LONDONDERRY (*see that title*).
  III. John, M.P., and lieutenant-colonel of 1st foot guards, *m.* 5 April, 1721, Mary, eldest dau. of Thomas, Viscount Fauconberg.
  I. Lucy, *m.* 24 February, 1712-13, James, 1st Earl Stanhope, and had issue.
  II. Essex, *m.* 1714, to Charles Cholmondely, Esq., of Vale Royal, M.P. for Cheshire, and had issue, Thomas, M.P., (father of Thomas, created Baron Delamere, 17 July, 18 1.) Jane, *m.* to Richard Meyrick, Esq. of Bodorgan; and Mary, *m.* to Rev. William Wannup of Walden.

Governor Pitt *d.* 1726, and was buried in Blandford Church, where a monument was erected to his memory: his eldest son, ROBERT PITT, Esq., of Boconnoc, co. Cornwall, M.P., and one of the clerks of the green-cloth, *m.* Harriet, sister of John Villiers, Earl of Grandison, and *d.* 21 May, 1727, having had issue,

  I. Thomas, of Boconnoc, father of THOMAS, 1ST BARON CAMELFORD (*see that title*).
  II. WILLIAM, 1st EARL CHATHAM.
  I. Harriet, *m.* 21 May, 1753, to Robert Needham, Esq., M.P. for Newry.
  II. Elizabeth, *m.* 1743, to George Tomlinson, Esq.
  III. Sarah, Maid of Honour to Queen Caroline.

The 2nd son,

WILLIAM PITT, Esq., *b.* at Boconnoc, 15 November, 1708, was educated at Eton and Oxford, and commenced life as cornet in the Blues, but, on being returned to parliament for Old Sarum, in 1735, he abandoned the military profession and devoting himself to politics, soon distinguished himself as one of the most eloquent senators and ablest statesmen of the reigns of GEORGE II., and GEORGE III., becoming secretary of State in 1756, and obtaining, 4 December, 1761, a peerage for his wife, Hester Grenville, only dau. of Richard Grenville, Esq., and sister of Earl Temple, by the style of *Baroness of Chatham*. He was himself created, 4 August, 1766, *Viscount Pitt, of Burton Pynsent, co. Somerset*, and EARL OF CHATHAM. His lordship had issue,

  I. JOHN, late earl.
  II. William, *b.* 28 May, 1759, educated at Pembroke Hall, Cambridge, under Dr. Pretyman, and called to the bar at Lincoln's Inn, 1780. This great statesman, who entered parliament as member for Appleby, was Prime Minister, with but one short interruption, from 1783 to 1806, during years, the most eventful in the annals of England. He *d. unm.* 23 January, 1806, and was buried at the public expense in Westminster Abbey, where a national monument has been erected to his memory. To the immortal credit of this powerful minister, who had the almost uncontrolled management of the public purse for a long series of years, he died in circumstances so far from affluent, that parliament found it necessary to devote £40,000 to the liquidation of his debts.
  III. James-Charles, R.N., *d.* in 1780.
  I. Hester, *m.* 19 December, 1774, to Charles, 3rd Earl Stanhope, and *d.* 20 July, 1780, leaving three daus., Lady Hester-Lucy Stanhope, who *d.* in Syria, 23 June, 1849; Griselda, *m.* 29 August, 1800, John Jekell, Esq., and *d.* 13 October, 1851; and Lucy-Rachel, *m.* 26 April, 1796, Thomas Taylor, Esq., of Sevenoaks, and *d.* 1 March, 1814.
  II. Harriet, *m.* the Hon. Edward-James Eliot, eldest son and heir-apparent of Edward, Lord Eliot, St. Germans, and *d.* in 1786, leaving an only child,
    Hester-Harriet-Pitt Eliot, who *m.* Lieutenant-General Sir William-Henry Pringle, G.C.B., M.P.

The death of Lord Chatham was sudden and impressive. In an effort to speak in the House of Lords, when labouring under infirmities, he suddenly dropt down, and, although dissolution did not immediately ensue, his lordship survived but a few weeks; he was stricken, 8 April, and died at Hayes, in Kent, 11 May, 1778. His remains were honoured with public obsequies in Westminster Abbey, a splendid monument was erected to his memory at the national expense and a pension of £4,000 a year, settled upon the Earldom of Chatham. "History," to borrow the eloquent words of Macaulay, "History, while, for the warning of vehement, high and daring natures, she notes his many errors, will yet deliberately pronounce, that, among the eminent men whose bones lie near his, scarcely one has left a more stainless, and none a more splendid name." The countess *d.* 3 April, 1803. The elder son,

JOHN PITT, 2nd Earl of Chatham, *b.* 10 September, 1756 K.G., was a general officer in the army, colonel of the 4th regt ment of foot, and governor-general of Gibraltar. As lieutenant general he commanded the unlucky expedition to Walcheren in 1809. His lordship *m.* 9 July, 1783, Mary-Elizabeth, 2nd dau. of Thomas, 1st Viscount Sydney, by whom (who *d.* 20 May, 1821,) he had no issue. He was an Elder Brother of the Trinity House, governor of the Charter House, and high steward of Colchester. He *d.* 24 September, 1835, when all his honours became EXTINCT.

Arms—Sa., a fesse chequy, arg. and az., between three be-zants.

PITT—BARONS CAMELFORD.

By Letters Patent, dated 5 January, 1784.

Lineage.

THOMAS PITT, Esq., of Boconnoc, Cornwall (elder brother of William, 1st Earl of Chatham), was M.P. for Okehampton and Old Sarum, warden of the stannaries, and steward of the Duchy of Cornwall and Devon to Frederick, Prince of Wales. He *m.* Christian, dau. of Sir Thomas Lyttleton, of Hagley, and *d.* in 1761, having had a son, THOMAS, and two daus., Amelia, *m.* to William Spry, LL.D., and Christian *m.* to Thomas Saunders, governor of Fort St. George. The son,

THOMAS PITT, Esq., of Boconnoc, *b.* in 1737, was elevated to the peerage, 5 January, 1784, as BARON CAMELFORD, *of Boconnoc, co. Cornwall.* His lordship *m.* Anne, dau. and co-heiress of Pinkney Wilkinson, Esq., of Burnham, in Norfolk, and had issue,

THOMAS, his successor.
Anne, *m.* to William, Lord Grenville (uncle of the Duke of Buckingham). His lordship *d. s. p.* in 1834; his widow survived unt l 1864.

He *d.* in 1793, and was *s.* by his son,

THOMAS PITT, 2nd baron, a post captain, R.N. This nobleman fell in a duel with a gentleman of the name of Best, in 1804 (*see* BURKE'S *Romance of the Aristocracy*), and as he *d. unm.,* the BARONY OF CAMELFORD became EXTINCT, while his estates devolved upon his sister, Anne, Lady Grenville, and are now enjoyed, under her ladyship's will, by the Hon. George Matthew Fortescue, 2nd son of Hugh, 1st Earl Fortescue.

Arms—Sa., fesse chequy, arg. and az., between three be-zants.

PITT—EARL OF LONDONDERRY.

By Letters Patent, dated 9 October, 1726.

Lineage.

THOMAS PITT, Esq., colonel of horse, and M P. for Wilton (2nd son of Thomas Pitt, governor of Fort St. George, *see* EARL CHATHAM), *m.* Lady Frances Ridgeway, dau. and co-heir of Robert, Earl of Londonderry, and was created, 3 June, 1719, BARON OF LONDONDERRY, in the kingdom of Ireland, and 8 October, 1726, advanced to the dignities of Viscount Galen Ridgeway, and EARL OF LONDONDERRY. His lordship was subsequently constituted captain-general of the Leeward Isles; he *d.* at St. Kitts, 12 September, 1729, and was buried in the family vault at Blandford, co. Dorset, leaving two sons (THOMAS and RIDGEWAY), and one dau., Lucy, *m.* to Pierce Meyrick, Esq., youngest son of Owen Meyrick, Esq., of Bodorgan, in the Island of Anglesey. The elder son,

THOMAS PITT, 2nd Earl of Londonderry, *d. unm.* 25 Augu t, 1735, and was *s.* by his brother,

RIDGEWAY PITT, 3rd Earl of Londonderry, at whose decease, also *unm.* in 1764, the honours became EXTINCT.

Arms—Sa., a fesse, chequy, arg. and az , between three be-zants.

PITT-RIVERS—BARON RIVERS.

(*See* ADDENDA.)

PLANTAGENET—EARLS OF CORNWALL.

Creation, 30 May, 1226.

Lineage.

JOHN PLANTAGENET, youngest son of King HENRY II., bore the title of EARL OF CORNWALL, in the life-time of his brother,

King RICHARD I., but on succeeding that monarch, in 1199, *so* King JOHN, the EARLDOM OF CORNWALL merged in the crown ; and so remained until it was conferred upon the same monarch's younger son,

RICHARD PLANTAGENET, who was made EARL OF POITOU AND CORNWALL by his brother, King HENRY III., 30 May, 1226. This prince acquired high reputation in the council and the field, and during the reign of his brother was one of the leading characters of Europe. In 1241, he was in the Holy Land, and then entered into a truce with the Soldan of Babylon, upon condition that the French prisoners there should be released ; that J rusalem, with all the parts adjacent, should be free from all molestation, and that other immunities should be granted to the Christians. In 1252, the earl, journeying through France with a pompous retinue, viz., forty knights, all in rich liveries, five waggons, and fifty sumpter horses (his lady and his son Henry being also with him), the Pope, being then at Lyons, sent all his cardinals, except one, besides a number of clerks, to meet the earl, and conduct them thither. And receiving the prince with great respect, feast d him at his own table. In 1255, upon a full meeting of the nobles in parliament assembled at Westminster, the king especially applied himself to the Earl of Cornwall in a formal speech for a large supply of money, viz., forty thousand pounds, the Pope having also written to him letters for that purpose; but the prince appears not to have complied with the request. In about two years afterwards, certain nobles of Almaine, having arrived in England, stated to the whole baronage, then met in full parliament, that, by the unanimous consent of the princes of the empire, the Earl of Cornwall was elected King of the Romans; and those ambassadors were followed by the archbishop of Cologne, and a numerous train of nobility, who ca i e for the purpose of doing homage to the new monarch. Whereupon he gave them 500 marks towards their travelling expenses, and presented the prelate with a rich mitre, adorned with precious stones. Soon after this the earl repaired to his new dominions, and was solemnly crowned King on ascension-day. In the contest which subsequently took place between the barons and King HENRY, he adhered with great fidelity to the latter, and commanded the main body of the royal army at the unfortunate battle of Lewes, where he was made prisoner. But he lived to see the termination of those troubles, and departing this life in 2 April, 1272, at his manor of Berkhamstead, was buried in the abbey of Hales, which he had founded. The prince had married, 1st, the Lady Isabel Marshall, 3rd dau. and co-heir of William, Earl of Pembroke, by whom he had four sons and a dau., who all died young, except

HENRY, *b.* 1235, who was taken prisoner with his father at the battle of Lewes, in which he had a principal command. Subsequently, having embarked in the Crusade, and being at Viterbuin, in Italy, on his return he was barbarously murdered there in the church of St. Lawrence, at high mass, by Guy, son of Simon Montfort, Earl of Leicester, the general of the baronial army, in revenge of his father's death, who had been slain at the battle of Evesham.

The King of Almaine *m.* 2ndly, Sanchia, 3rd dau. and co-heir* of Raymond, Earl of Provence, by whom he had one surviving son,

EDMUND, his successor.

He *m.* 3rdly, Beatrix, niece of Conrad, archbishop of Cologne, but had no child by that lady. The prince was *s.* as Earl of Cornwall, by his son,

EDMUND PLANTAGENET, who accomplishing his full age, in the 55th HENRY III., received the honour of knighthood, upon St Edward's day, and was invested, soon after, with the title of EARL OF CORNWALL, by cincture, with the sword. In the 16th EDWARD I., he was made warden of England, during the king's absence in the wars of Scotland, and then marching into Wales, besieged Droselan Castle, and demolished its walls. The next year, he was constituted sheriff for the co. of Cornwall in fee. His lordship *m.* Margaret, dau. of Richard de Clare, Earl of Gloucester, but *d. s. p.,* in 1300, when his great inheritance devolved upon the king, as his next of kin and heir-at-law, while the Earldom of Cornwall became EXTINCT.

Arms—Of RICHARD, King of the Romans: Arg., a lion rampant, gu., crowned, or, a bordure, sa., bezantée.

Richard Plantagenet.
(E. Cornwall.)

Edmund Plantagenet.
(E. Lancaster.)

Thomas of Brotherton.
(E. Norfolk.)

Edmund of Woodstock.
(E. Kent.)

Lionel of Antwerp.
(D. Clarence.)

John of Gaunt.
(D. Lancaster.)

Thomas of Woodstock.
(D. Gloucester.)

Edmund of Langley.
(D. York.)

George Plantagenet.
(D. Clarence.)

Thomas Plantagenet.
(D. Clarence.)

John Plantagenet.
(D. Bedford.)

Humphrey Plantagenet
(D. Gloucester.)

PLANTAGENET— EARLS OF CHESTER, EARLS OF LEICESTER, EARL OF DERBY, EARL OF LINCOLN, DUKE OF LANCASTER.

Earldom of Chester, *anno* 1253.
Earldom of Leicester, 25 October, 1264.
Earldom of Derby, 16 March, 1337.
Earldom of Lincoln, 20 August, 1349.
Dukedom of Lancaster, 6 March, 1351.

Lineage.

EDMUND PLANTAGENET, surnamed *Crouch'back*, second son of King HENRY III., was born at London, in February, 1245, and when he had attained his eighth year, was solemnly invested by the Pope, in the kingdom of Sicily and Apulia. About this time too, he was made EARL OF CHESTER. But neither of these honours turned out eventually of much value, for the real King of Sicily, CONRAD, was then living; and the Earldom of Chester is said to have been transferred to the prince's elder brother, Edward, afterwards EDWARD I. He soon obtained, however, both possessions and dignities, for upon the forfeiture of Simon de Montfort, Earl of Leicester, the king, by letters patent, granted him the inheritance of the EARLDOM OF LEICESTER, as also the honour and stewardship of England: with the lands likewise of Nicolas de Segrave, an associate in the treason of Montfort. And the next ensuing year he had another grant from the crown of all the goods and chattels, whereof Robert de Ferrers, Earl of Derby, was possessed upon the day of the skirmish at Chesterfield. He subsequently had grants of the honour of Derby, with the castles, manors, and lands, of the said Robert de Ferrers; and the honour of Leicester, with all the lands of Simon de Montfort, late Earl of Leicester: to hold to himself and the heirs of his body. About the 54th HENRY III., the earl went into the Holy Land, and returned within two years. In the reign of EDWARD I., he was in the Scottish wars and had the grants which he had received from his father confirmed, with additional castles, manors, and lands of great extent. In the 21st of that reign, he procured licence from the crown to make a castle of his house, in the parish of St. Clement's Danes, in the co. Middlesex, called the Savoy; and founded the nunnery, called the Minoresses, without Aldgate, in the suburbs of London. He was afterwards in the Welsh wars; and then proceeded to France, being sent with the Earl of Lincoln, and twenty-six bannerets, into Gascony. He eventually invested Bordeaux, but not succeeding in its reduction, the disappointment affected him so severely, that it brought on a disease which terminated his life in the year 1295. The prince's remains were brought over to England, and honourably interred in Westminster Abbey. Upon his death-bed, he directed " that his body should not be buried 'till his debts were paid." This earl *m.* 1st, in April, 1269, Aveline (dau. of William de Fortibus, Earl of Albemarle), COUNTESS OF HOLDERNESS, heir to her father, and by her mother, Countess of Devon and the Isle of Wight, but this great heiress *d.* the following year *s. p.* The prince *m.* 2ndly, 1276, Blanche, dau. of Robert, Earl of Artois (3rd son of LEWIS VIII., King of France), and widow of HENRY, King of Navarre, by whom he had surviving issue,

THOMAS, his successor.
HENRY, of whom hereafter. as restored Earl of Lancaster.
John *d.* in France.

His highness was *s.* by his elder son,
THOMAS PLANTAGENET, Earl of Lancaster, who in the 26th EDWARD I., doing his homage, being then esteemed of full age by the king, had livery of his lands, except the dowry of Blanche, his mother; and thereupon marched into Scotland, the king himself being in the expedition. The earl, who was hereditary sheriff of Lancashire, substituted Richard de Hughton, his deputy in that office. For the remainder of this reign the Earl of Lancaster was constantly employed in the wars of Scotland. In the 4th EDWARD II., having *m.* Alice, only dau. and heiress of Henry de Lacy, Earl of Lincoln, he had livery of the castle of Denbigh, and other lands of her inheritance; his homage for them being performed the ensuing year, in the presence of divers bishops, earls, and barons, and other of the king's council, in a certain chamber within the house of the Friars Preachers, in London. The earl is said to have borne the title of EARL OF LINCOLN, in right of this lady; after his decease, she *m.* Eubold le Strange, who *d. s. p.*, and 3rdly, Hugh le Frenes; the which Eubold and Hugh, are deemed, by many writers to have been Earls of Lincoln. The said Alice styled herself Countess of Lincoln and Salisbury, and *d. s. p.* in 1348. In the 5th EDWARD II., the Earl of Lancaster joined the con-

431

federation against Piers Gaveston, and was made their general by those nobles and great personages, who had united for a redress of grievances. It is said that his father-in-law, Henry de Lacy, Earl of Lincoln, had charged him upon his death-bed, to maintain the quarrel against Gaveston, and that thereupon he joined with the Earl of Warwick, and caused the favourite to be put to death. From this period he was never fully restored to the confidence of the king, but was esteemed the great champion of the popular party, in whose cause he eventually laid down his life; for taking up arms against the Spencers, he was made prisoner in a skirmish at Boroughbridge, and being thence conveyed to Pontefract, was beheaded on a plain without the town (where a beautiful church was afterwards erected in honour of his memory), in April, 1321. Dugdale details the events that immediately preceded the earl's untimely death, thus—"That being come to Boroughbridge, he there found Sir Andrew de Harcla, Warden of Carlisle, and the Marches, and Sir Simon Ward, sheriff of Yorkshire, ready to encounter him. Where relating to Harcla his just quarrel to the Spencers, (he the earl) promised him, if he would favour his cause, to give him one of those five earldoms which he had in possession; and that Harcla refusing, he told him that he would soon repent it, and that he should die a shameful death (as it afterwards happened). Also, that Harcla, then causing his archers to shoot, the fight began, in which many of this earl's party being slain, he betook himself to chapel, refusing to yield to Harcla, and looking to the crucifix, said, ' *Good Lord, I render myself to thee, and put myself into thy mercy.*' Also, that they then took off his coat armor, and putting upon him one of his men's liveries, carried him by water to York, where they threw balls of dirt at him. Moreover, that from thence they brought him back to the king at Pontefract Castle, and there put him in a tower, towards the abbey which he had newly made. Likewise, that soon after, being brought into the hall, he had sentence of death by these justices, viz. :—Aymer, Earl of Pembroke. Edmund, Earl of Kent, John de Bretaigne, and Sir Robert Malmethorpe, who pronounced the judgment. Whereupon, saying, '*shall I die without answer?*' A certain Gascoigne took him away, and put a pill'd broken hood on his head, and set him on a lean white jade, without a bridle; and that then he added, ' *King of Heaven, have mercy on me, for the king of earth nous ad guerthi.*' And that thus he was carried, some throwing pellets of dirt at him (having a fryer-preacher for his confessor), to an hill without the town, where he kneeled down towards the east, until one Hugh de Muston caused him to turn his face towards Scotland, and then a villain of London cut off his head. After which the prior and monks obtaining his body from the king, buried it on the right hand of the high altar. The day of his death was certainly upon the Monday next preceding the *Annunciation of the Blessed Virgin.* Touching his merits," continues the same authority, "there happened afterwards very great disputes : some thinking it fit that he should be accounted a saint, because he was so charitable, and so much an honour of the religious; as also that he died in a just cause; but chiefly because his persecutors came within a short period to untimely ends. On the other side many there were who taxed him for adultery, in keeping of sundry women, notwithstanding he had a wife. Aspersing him likewise for cruelty, in putting to death some persons for small offences; and protecting some for punishment who were transgressors of the laws ; a lying also, that he was chiefly swayed by one of his secretaries ; and that he did not fight stoutly for justice, but fled and was taken unarmed. Nevertheless, many miracles were reported to have been afterwards wrought in the place where his corpse was buried; much confluence of people coming thereto, in honour thereof, till the king, through the incitation of the Spencers, set guards to restrain them. Whereupon, they flocked to the place where he suffered death; and so much the more eagerly, as endeavours had been used to restrain them, until a church was erected on the place where he suffered." All the honours of this prince became FORFEITED under his attainder : yet his brother and heir (Thomas Plantagenet having himself no issue),

HENRY PLANTAGENET, being a distinguished soldier in the Scottish wars, had livery of his lands in the 17th EDWARD II., and was restored to the dignity of EARL OF LEICESTER. This prince was subsequently one of the leaders in the great confederacy which overturned the power of the Spencers, and deposed King EDWARD II. Upon the accession of EDWARD III., the earl had the honour of girding him with the sword of knighthood, and as soon as the new monarch was crowned, he was appointed, the king being a minor, his guardian. After which, in the parliament begun at Westminster, the attainder against his brother being reversed, he was restored to all the lands of his father and brother, with the EARLDOMS OF LANCASTER AND LEICESTER, and the same year (1st EDWARD [....]) he was constituted captain-general of all the king's forces in the marches of Scotland. The earl m. Maud, dau. and heiress of Sir Patrick Chaworth, Knt., and had issue,

HENRY, Earl of Derby, his successor.
Maud, m. 1st, to William de Burgh, Earl of Ulster, by whom she had an only dau. and heiress,

ELIZABETH DE BURGH, m. to Lionel, Duke of Clarence.

The Lady Maud m. 2ndly, Ralph de Ufford, justice of Ireland, temp. EDWARD III., and brother of Robert, Earl of Suffolk, by whom she had an only dau.,

MAUD, m. to Thomas, son of John de Vere, Earl of Oxford.
Blanche, m. to Thomas, Lord Wake, of Lydell, and d. s. p.
Eleanor, m. 1st, to John, son and heir of Henry, Earl of Buchan; and 2ndly, to Richard Fitz-Alan, Earl of Arundel.
Jane, m. to John, 3rd Lord Mowbray.
Isabel, prioress of Ambresbury.
Mary, m. to Henry, Lord Percy.

His lordship d. in 1345, was buried at Leicester (where his obsequies were attended by the king and queen in person), and was s. by his son,

HENRY PLANTAGENET, called "of Gresmont," from a castle in Monmouthshire, the place of his birth, who, having distinguished himself in the lifetime of his father in the Scottish wars, was made captain-general of all the king's forces there, had considerable grants from the crown, and was created EARL OF DERBY (11th EDWARD III.) The next year he was with the king in the wars of Flanders, as he was in two years afterwards in the great naval engagement with the French off Sluges.' In the 15th EDWARD III. we find the prince again in the wars of Scotland, being then the king's lieutenant for the northern parts of England, and general of his army against the Scots: in which capacity he was authorized to treat of peace. After this, as EARL OF DERBY (his father still alive), he became one of the first and most successful captains of the age, reducing no less than fifty-six French cities and places of note to the dominion of the king of England, and taking immense treasure in gold. In the year of those great exploits his father died, so that he was prevented assisting the deceased earl's funeral. He had afterwards a chief command at the siege of Calais, bearing then the title of Earl of Lancaster, Derby, and Leicester, and Steward of England; at which time he had, of his own retinue, 800 men-at-arms, and 2,000 archers, with 30 banners, which cost him, in hospitality, a daily disbursement of £100. In the 22nd EDWARD III., after having had previously for his brilliant services, extensive grants from the crown, he was made the king's lieutenant in Flanders and France, and the next year was created by letters patent, EARL OF LINCOLN, soon after which he was constituted the king's lieutenant and captain-general of Poictou, made a knight of the Garter (one of the Founders of the Order*) and created DUKE OF LANCASTER. To the latter high dignity he was raised in full parliament, and invested with power to have a chancery in the co. Lancaster, and to enjoy all other liberties and royalties appertaining to a county palatine, in as ample a manner as the Earls of Chester did, in the county palatine of Chester. About this time, too, he was constituted admiral of the king's whole fleet westward. The same year, having obtained license to go abroad to fight against the infidels, he was surprised in his journey, and forced to pay a large ransom for his liberty: which surprisal having occurred through the Duke of Brunswick's means, the English prince expressed his resentment in language so unmeasured, that the duke sent him a challenge; which being accepted, a day was appointed for the combat; but when it arrived, the Duke of Brunswick so panic struck, that he could not wield his shield, sword, or lance; while the Duke of Lancaster, with the most undaunted firmness, in vain awaited his attack. They were, however, afterwards reconciled, by the interference of the French monarch; and thus the English prince acquired great renown for personal valour, while his adversary was covered with disgrace. The close of this heroic nobleman's martial career, was quite as splendid as its opening, and after a most brilliant course of achievements, he d. 24 March, 1360-1, deeply lamented by all classes of his countrymen, including his gallant companions in arms. He lived in one of the most glorious periods of English history, and he was himself the chief actor in that splendid era. The prince m. Isabel, dau. of Henry, Lord Beaumont, and left two daus., his co-heirs, viz.,

MAUD, who had been 1st, the betrothed wife of Ralph, son and heir of Ralph, Lord Stafford, and at the age of six years his widow; she m. 2ndly, 1352, William, Duke of Zealand and Bavaria, and d s. p.
BLANCHE, m. to John of Gaunt, Earl of Richmond, 4th son of King EDWARD III.,

---

* The Prince occupied, in St. George's Chapel, the second stall at the sovereign's side, next to that of the Royal Founder.

432

Which

JOHN (PLANTAGENET), b. 1340, styled of Gaunt, from the place of his birth, who had been created EARL OF RICHMOND, in 1342, was advanced to the DUKEDOM OF LANCASTER, by his father, King EDWARD III., in the 36th year of his reign. After the decease of his 1st wife, BLANCH, the great heiress of the Duke of Lancaster, he m. Constance, elder dau. and co-heiress of PETER, King of Castile, and in her right assumed the title of King of Castile and Leon, in which regal dignity, as well as in those of Duke of Lancaster, Earl of Richmond, Derby, Lincoln, and Leicester, he had summons to parliament; he was likewise Duke of Aquitaine, and a knight of the Garter. On the decease of EDWARD III., this prince was joined in the administration of affairs during the minority of his nephew, RICHARD II. He subsequently attempted the conquest of Spain at the head of a fine army; and landing at the Groyne, advanced to Compostella, where he was met by JOHN, King of Portugal, between whom and his eldest dau., the Lady Philippa, a marriage was concluded. Thence he marched into Castile, and there ratified a treaty of peace, by which he abandoned his claim to the throne of Castile and Leon, in consideration of a large sum of money, and the marriage of Henry, Prince of Asturias, with his only dau. by his 2nd wife, the Lady Katherine Plantagenet. In the latter part of his life he dwelt in retirement, having incurred the displeasure of King RICHARD, by a motion which he had made in parliament, that his son, Henry of Bolingbroke, should be declared heir to the crown. He d. at Ely House, Holborn, in 1399.

JOHN of Gaunt m. 1st, in 1359, as already stated, Lady Blanche Plantagenet, the eventual heiress of the Duke of Lancaster, and had by her,

HENRY, surnamed of BOLINGBROKE, who, having m. Mary, dau. and co-heir of Humphrey de Bohun, last Earl of Hereford, was created Earl of Hereford, 29 September, 1397.
Philippa, m. to JOHN, King of Portugal, from this marriage descend quartering the royal arms of England, MARY-ISABELLA, Queen of Spain; FERDINAND, King of Naples; PEDRO, Emperor of the Brazils; Henry de Bourbon, Duke of Bordeaux; FREDERICK-AUGUSTUS, King of Saxony; the Emperor of Austria; &c.
Elizabeth, m. 1st, to John Holand Earl of Huntingdon; and 2ndly, to Sir John Cornwall. This lady by her 1st husband had issue,

John Holand, Duke of Exeter, K.G., who m 1st, Anne, widow of Edward Mortimer, Earl of March, and dau. of Edmund, Earl of Stafford, and had by her a son,

Henry, 2nd Duke of Exeter, who m. Lady Anne Plantagenet, sister of King EDWARD IV., and d. 1473.

John Holand, Duke of Exeter, m. 2ndly, Lady Anne Montacute, dau. of John, Earl of Salisbury, and had by her a dau.,

Anne, eventually heiress, who m. 1st, John Lord Nevill (son and heir of Ralph, Earl of Westmoreland), who fell at Towton-field, s. p.; and 2ndly, Sir John Nevill, Knt., by whom she had a son,

Ralph Nevill, 3rd Earl of Westmoreland, who m. Margaret, dau. of Roger Booth, of Sawley, and had an only son,

Ralph, Lord Nevill, who m. Elizabeth, dau. of Sir William Sandys, and d. v. p., leaving a son and successor,

Ralph, 4th Earl of Westmoreland, whose grandson Charles, 6th Earl of Westmoreland, m. Anne, dau. of Henry Howard, Earl of Surrey, and had issue, four daus., his co-heirs, viz.,

1 Katherine, m. Sir Thomas Grey, and d. s. p.
2 Eleanor, d. unm.
3 Margaret, m. to Nicholas Pudsey, Esq.
4 Anne, m. to David Ingleby, Esq. Among the co-representatives of Lady Ann, wife of David Ingleby, Esq., we may enumerate the following,
Sir Rowland Errington, 9th bart., of Hooton, co. Chester.
Sir John-De Marie Haggerston, Bart., of Haggerston Castle, co. Northumberland.
Marmaduke-Constable Maxwell, of Everingham, Lord Herries.
William Middleton, Esq., of Middleton Lodge, and Stockeld, co. York.
Thomas Constable, Esq., of Manor House, Otley, co. York.

John of Gaunt m. 2ndly, 1372, Constance, elder dau. and co-heir of PETER, King of Castile, and by her had an only dau.,

Katherine, m. to Henry, Prince of Asturias, afterwards HENRY III., King of Castile and Leon. From this marriage descend the royal families of (Bourbon) France, Spain, Naples, Saxony, and Austria.

The duke m. 3rdly, in 1396, Catherine, dau. of Sir Payn Roet, Guyenne King of Arms, and widow of Sir Otho de Swynford, Knt., by whom, before marriage, he had issue,

JOHN DE BEAUFORT, Earl of Somerset, who m. Margaret, dau. of Thomas Holand, Earl of Kent, and had a son, JOHN, Duke of Somerset, whose only dau. and heir, MARGARET, m. Edmund Tudor, Earl of Richmond, and was mother of King HENRY VII.

HENRY DE BEAUFORT, cardinal of St. Eusebeus, and bishop of Winchester.

THOMAS DE BEAUFORT, Earl of Dorset, and Duke of Exeter, d. s. p.

JOAN DE BEAUFORT, m. 1st, to Robert, Lord Ferrers, of Wemme, and 2ndly to Ralph Neville, 1st Earl of Westmoreland.

These children were legitimated by act of parliament for all purposes, save succession to the throne, in the 20th RICHARD II., and derived their surname from the castle of Beaufort, the place of their birth. JOHN of Gaunt, who bore for arms, "France and England quarterly, a label of three points, erm," was s. by his eldest son,

HENRY PLANTAGENET, b. 1366, surnamed of Bolingbroke, Earl of Hereford, who, upon the deposition of RICHARD II., was called to the throne as King HENRY IV., when his great inheritance, with the Dukedom of Lancaster, and the Earldoms of Hereford, Derby, Lincoln, and Leicester, merged in the crown.

Arms of Edmund Crouchback—Gu., three lions passant guardant, or, a label of three points, az., each charged with as many fleur-de-lis, or.

PLANTAGENET, SURNAMED DE BROTHERTON—EARL OF NORFOLK AND EARL MARSHAL.

By Special Charter, dated 16 December, 1312

Lineage.

THOMAS PLANTAGENET, eldest son of King EDWARD I., by his 2nd wife, Margaret, dau. of PHILIP III., or the Hardy, of France, was born at Brotherton in Yorkshire, anno 1301, whence the surname, "DE BROTHERTON," and before he had attained his thirteenth year, was advanced by special charter of his half brother King EDWARD II (at the dying request of his predecessor), dated 16 December, 1312, to all the honours which Roger le Bigod, sometime Earl of Norfolk, and Marshal of England did enjoy by the name of earl, in the co. Norfolk, with all the castles, manors, and lands, which the said Roger possessed in England, Ireland, and Wales, which had become vested in the crown, by the surrender of the said Roger. But in some years afterwards, the king seized upon the marshalship in the Court of King's Bench, because the Earl of Norfolk had failed to substitute some person on his behalf, to attend the justices of that court, upon their journey into Lancashire; he had, however, restitution of the high office, upon paying a fine of £100. This prince was repeatedly in the wars of Scotland, temp. EDWARD II. and EDWARD III., in the latter of which reigns he had a confirmation of the Earldom of Norfolk, and the office of earl marshal. He m. 1st, Alice, dau of Sir Roger Halys, Knt., of Harwich, by whom he had issue,

MARGARET, of whom hereafter.

Alice, m. to Edward de Montacute, and had a dau.,

JOAN, who m. William Ufford, Earl of Suffolk, and d. without male issue.

The prince m. 2ndly, Mary, dau. of William, Lord Roos, and widow of William Braose, and had a son,

John, who became a monk at the abbey of Ely.

Thomas of Brotherton d. in 1338, when the Earldom of Norfolk became EXTINCT. But his elder dau. and co-heir, who eventually became sole heiress,

The LADY MARGARET PLANTAGENET, was created DUCHESS OF NORFOLK for life, by King RICHARD II., 29 September, 1397. Her grace, at the time styled Countess of Norfolk, claimed the office of earl marshal, at the coronation of that monarch, and prayed that she might execute the same by her deputy; but her claim was not allowed, owing to the want of sufficient time to investigate its merits, and the prior appointment, for the occasion, of Henry, Lord Percy. This illustrious lady m. 1st, John, Lord Segrave, and had issue,

Anne, abbess of Barking.

Elizabeth, m. John, Lord Mowbray (see Mowbray, Earl of Nottingham, and Duke of Norfolk). From this marriage descend the HOWARDS, and the BERKELEYS.

The duchess m. 2ndly, Sir William Manny, K.G., and had an only surviving dau.,

433

Anne, m. to John Hastings, Earl of Pembroke.

Her grace d. in 1399, when the dignity became EXTINCT.

Arms—Gu., three lions passant guardant, or, a label of three points, arg. for difference.

PLANTAGENET—DUCHESS OF NORFOLK.

(Refer to PLANTAGENET, surnamed "De Brotherton," Earl of Norfolk).

PLANTAGENET—BARONS OF WOODSTOCK, EARLS OF KENT.

Barony, by Writ of Summons, dated 5 August, 1320.
Earldom, by Charter, dated 28 July, 1321.

Lineage.

EDMUND PLANTAGENET, b. 5 August, 1301, surnamed of Woodstock, from the place of his birth, 2nd son of King EDWARD I., was summoned to parliament, by writ, directed "Edmundo de Wodestok," 5 August, 1320, about two years before he attained majority. He had previously been in the wars of Scotland, and had obtained considerable territorial grants from the crown. In the next year he was created EARL OF KENT, and had a grant of the castle of Okham, in the co. Rutland, and shrievalty of the county. About the same time he was constituted governor of the castle of Tunbridge, in Kent; and upon the breaking out of the insurrection, under Thomas Plantagenet, Earl of Lancaster, he was commissioned by the king, to pursue that rebellious prince, and to lay siege to the castle of Pontefract. The Earl of Lancaster was subsequently made prisoner at Boroughbridge, and the Earl of Kent was one of those who condemned him to death. From this period, during the remainder of the reign of his brother, Edmund, of Woodsto k, was constantly employed in the cabinet or the field. He was frequently accredited on embassies to the Court of France, and was in all the wars in Gascony and Scotland. But after the accession of his nephew, King EDWARD III., he was arrested and sentenced to death, for having conspired, with other nobles, to deliver his brother, the deposed EDWARD II., out of prison. Whereupon, by the management of Queen ISABEL and her paramour, Mortimer, he was beheaded at Winchester (1380), after he had remained upon the scaffold, from noon until five o'clock in the evening, waiting for an executioner; no one being willing to undertake the horrid office, till a malefactor from the Marshalsea was procured to perform it. The earl m. Margaret, dau. of John, Lord Wake, and sister and heiress of Thomas, Lord Wake, by whom (who d. 29 September, 1349,) he had issue,

EDMUND, } successively Earls of Kent.
JOHN,

Margaret, m. to Amaneus, eldest son of Bernard, Lord de la Brette, and d. s. p.

JOANE, from her extraordinary beauty, styled "the Fair Maid of Kent," m. 1st, William Montacute, Earl of Salisbury, from whom she was divorced;* 2ndly, Sir Thomas Holland, K.G., (who d. 26 December, 1360); and 3rdly, the renowned hero, EDWARD, Prince of Wales, K.G., the Black Prince, by whom (who d. 8 July, 1376), she was the mother of King RICHARD II.

The unfortunate earl's eldest son,

EDMUND PLANTAGENET was restored in blood and honours by parliament, the year in which his father suffered, and thus became Baron Woodstock and EARL OF KENT—but d. soon after in minority, unm., and was s. by his brother,

JOHN PLANTAGENET, 3rd Earl of Kent, who m. Elizabeth, dau. of the Duke of Juliers, but d. s. p. in 1352, when the Earldom of Kent, and Baronies of Woodstock and Wake, devolved upon his only surviving sister,

JOANE, the Fair Maid of Kent, who m. Sir Thomas Holland, Lord Holland, K G. (see Holland, Earl of Kent).

Arms of Edmund Woodstock—England, within a bordure, arg.

* Collins, in explanation of the divorce, states, that the Earl of Salisbury had intended to have married her, had she not been previously contracted to Sir Thomas Holland; yet, during the absence of Sir Thomas, the earl made a subsequent contract, and withheld the lady, until the Pope decided against him—when acquiescing, it was said, she was divorced.

PLANTAGENET--EARL OF CORNWALL.

By Patent, anno 1328.

Lineage.

JOHN PLANTAGENET, 2nd son of King EDWARD II., commonly called "John of Eltham," from the place of his birth, was created by patent, dated in 1327, EARL OF CORNWALL. This prince *d. unm.* in 1336, when the Earldom of Cornwall became EXTINCT.

Arms—Same as the other branches of the House of Plantagenet.

PLANTAGENET—DUKE OF CORNWALL.

By Patent, dated in 1337.

Lineage.

EDWARD PLANTAGENET, the gallant Black Prince, eldest son of King EDWARD III., was advanced by patent, in 1337, to the dignity of DUKE OF CORNWALL, with the following limitation:—"Habend. et tenend. eidem Duci et ipsius et heredum suorum Regum Angliæ filiis primogenitis et dicti loci ducibus in regno Angl' hereditar' succesur." He was subsequently created PRINCE OF WALES, and the dukedom merged in the principality. Since the dignity was so conferred upon Prince Edward, it has been vested in the heir apparent of the throne of England, who, at his birth, or at the decease of an elder brother, becomes Duke of Cornwall, and is always created Prince of Wales. The Black Prince *m.* his cousin, Joane, commonly called the *Fair Maid of Kent*, dau. of Edmund, Earl of Kent, and widow of Sir Thomas Holland, by whom he left, at his decease, 8 July, 1376, his father, King EDWARD still living, an only surviving son,

RICHARD, afterwards King RICHARD II.

PLANTAGENET—DUKE OF CLARENCE.

Created 15 September, 1362.

Lineage.

GILBERT DE CLARE, Earl of Hertford and Gloucester, who fell at the bat le of Bannockburn in 1313, leaving no issue, his titles became extinct, while his estates devolved upon his sisters, as co-heirs, of whom

ELIZABETH DE CLARE, the youngest sister, had *m.* JOHN DE BURGH, son of Richard, Earl of Ulster, and through this alliance the honour of Clare came into the possession of the De Burghs. The heiress of Clare left a son,

WILLIAM DE BURGH, Earl of Ulster, who *m.* Maud, sister of Henry Plantagenet, Duke of Lancaster, and left an only child and heiress,

ELIZABETH DE BURGH, who married

LIONEL PLANTAGENET, *b.* 29 November, 1339 (of Antwerp), 3rd son of King EDWARD III. who became *jure uxoris*, Earl of Ulster, and was created 15 September, 1362, DUKE OF CLARENCE.* The prince was likewise a knight of the Garter. He had an only child by the heiress of Ulster,

PHILIPPA PLANTAGENET, *b.* 16 August, 1355, who *m.* Edmond Mortimer, 3rd Earl of March, and had, with other issue,

ROGER MORTIMER, Earl of March, *b.* 1377, who, in the parliament held 9th RICHARD II., was declared next heir to the throne. This nobleman, slain at Kenlis, in Meath, 1398, had, with other issue,

EDMOND, his successor.

Anne (sister and heir of her brother, Edmond, Earl of March), who *m.* Richard Plantagenet, of Coningsburgh, Earl of Cambridge, younger son of Edmond, Duke of York, 5th son of EDWARD III., and had a son,

RICHARD, Duke of York, K.G., who fell at Wakefield, 31 December, 1460, leaving,

EDWARD, Duke of York, who ascended the throne as EDWARD IV.

George, Duke of Clarence, K.G., father of MARGARET PLANTAGENET, COUNTESS OF SALISBURY (see that title).

RICHARD, Duke of Gloucester, who ascended the throne as RICHARD III.

Lionel, Duke of Clarence, *m.* 2ndly, 15 June, 1368, Valentina, dau. of Galeazzo, or Galeas II., Duke of Milan, but by her had no issue. About four years after the death of the Duchess Elizabeth (25 April, 1368), King EDWARD concluded the terms of a new marriage for his son, the Duke of Clarence, with Violanta, or Jolantia, the dau. of Galeas, or, as he was more classically called, Galeasius, prince of Milan, and sister to John Galeas, who subsequently became 1st Duke of Milan. The bargain, for such it was in the strictest meaning of the word, was struck at Windsor, upon which occasion the wealthy and munificent Prince Galeas paid down for his daughter's dowry, the sum of 100,000 florins. This, however, was but a prelude to the unbounded magnificence with which he received his son-in-law, and his small but chosen retinue of English nobles, who in number amounted to about 200. When the duke married his affianced bride, the luxury of the various feasts that followed upon the nuptials, and the richness of the gifts presented by Galeas to the bridegroom and his followers, were such as fairly to confound the imagination. The whole scene, as described by Paulus Jovius, is only to be paralleled by the wild dreamings of some eastern story. At one banquet, when the celebrated Petrarch was present, thirty courses succeeded each other, all composed of the choicest viands that the earth or sea could supply, and between each course, as many rare gifts were brought in by Galeas himself, and presented by him to Clarence.

"But not five months after, the Duke of Clarence (having lived with this new wife after the manner of his own country, forgetting, or not regarding his change of air, and addicting himself to immoderate feasting), spent and consumed with a lingering disease, departed this world at Alba Pompeia, called also Longuevil, in the Marquisate of Montserrat, in Piedmont, on the vigil of St. Luke the Evangelist, viz., the 17th day of October, anno 1368."

The duke was first buried in the city of Pavia, but was afterwards brought over to England by Thomas Narbonne and others of the retinue, who had accompanied him in his nuptial expedition. The body was then conveyed to the church of the Augustine Friars, at Clare, in Suffolk, and finally deposited near the remains of his 1st wife, Elizabeth de Burgh. Violanta herself was afterwards *m.* to Otho, Marquis of Montserrat; but, as the chronicler quaintly observes, her 2nd marriage was not more fortunate than her first;—Otho soon perished ignobly in the mountain, being slain by a country stable-keeper.

At the death of Lionel, the Dukedom of Clarence became EXTINCT.

Arms—Gu., three lions passant guardant, or.

PLANTAGENET—EARL OF CAMBRIDGE, DUKES OF YORK, DUKE OF ALBEMARLE.

Earldom, 13 November, 1362.
Dukedom, 6 August, 1385.
Dukedom of Albemarle, 29 September, 1397

Lineage.

EDMUND PLANTAGENET, *b.* 5 June, 1341, surnamed Langley, from the place of his birth, 5th son of King EDWARD III., was created by his father, 13 November, 1362, EARL OF CAMBRIDGE, and by his nephew, King RICHARD II., 6 August, 1385, DUKE OF YORK. This prince *m.* 1st, 1372, Isabel, dau. and co-heir of PETER THE CRUEL, King of Castile and Leon, and sister of Constance, the wife of John of Gaunt, by whom (who *d.* in 1894) he had issue,

I. EDWARD his successor in the Dukedom of York.
II. RICHARD, of Coningsburgh, who *s.* to the Earldom of Cambridge. This prince was beheaded at Southampton for conspiring against HENRY V., in 1415, when the Earldom of Cambridge became forfeited. He had *m.* Anne,* sister and heir of Edmond Mortimer, Earl of March, and dau. of Roger Mortimer, Earl of March, son of Edmond, 3rd Earl of March, by Philippa, his wife, only dau. and heiress of Lionel, of Antwerp, Duke of Clarence, 2nd son of King EDWARD III.:

----

* The title of Clarence was derived from the honour of Clare.

* Through this alliance the house of York derived its right to the crown.

by Anne Mortimer, his wife, the Earl of Cambridge left an only son and a dau., viz.,

RICHARD, who *s.* his uncle as Duke of York.

Isabel, *m.* to Henry Bourchier, Earl of Essex.

1. Constance, *m.* to Thomas de Spencer, Earl of Gloucester.

Edmund, Duke of York, *m.* 2ndly, Joane, dau. of Thomas Holland, Earl of Kent, and sister and co-heir of Edmund, Earl of Kent, but had no issue. The Duke of York attained the highest reputation as a statesman and a soldier, and after vainly endeavouring to sustain his nephew, King RICHARD, upon the throne, he retired to his estate in Hertfordshire, and *ubi spiravit, ibi expiravit ;*—at Langley he was born, and at Langley he died 1 August, 1402, "having lived to see England's sceptre in three several hands, in which the royal stream never kept its immediate channel." In compliance with the terms of his will, he was buried at the Friary of Langley, under a tomb of alabaster and black marble; but upon the dissolution of the religious houses, both the monument, and the body which it had covered, were removed to the parish church of the same town, and placed in the east corner of the chancel. The prince, who was a knight of the Garter, was *s.* by his eldest son,

EDWARD PLANTAGENET, 2nd Duke of York, who had been created Duke of Albemarle, 29 September, 1397, and was restored to the Dukedom of York in 1406, which he had been previously rendered incapable of inheriting : he was also invested with the Garter. This gallant prince, who had become eminent in arms, fell at Agincourt in 1415, and his brother having been previously put to death, the Dukedom of York (the prince leaving no issue) devolved upon his nephew.

RICHARD PLANTAGENET, K.G., who was restored to the Earldom of Cambridge, and allowed to inherit as 3rd Duke of York. This prince becoming afterwards one of the most powerful subjects of the period in which he lived, laid claim to the throne as the descendant of Lionel, Duke of Clarence, 2nd son of EDWARD III., whereas the reigning monarch, HENRY VI., sprang from John of Gaunt, Duke of Lancaster, 3rd son of the same king : thus originated the devastating war of the Roses. In his pretensions, the Duke was supported by the Nevils and other great families, but his ambitious projects closed at the battle of Wakefield in 1460, where his party sustained a signal defeat, and he was himself slain. The prince had *m.* Cecily, dau. of Ralph Nevil, Earl of Westmoreland, and by her (who d. 31 May, 1495, and was buried at Fotheringhay) left issue,

EDWARD, his successor.

EDMUND, said to have borne the title of Earl of Rutland. This prince at the age of twelve was barbarously murdered by Lord Clifford, after the battle of Wakefield.

GEORGE, Duke of Clarence (*see* Plantagenet Duke of Clarence).

RICHARD, Duke of Gloucester (afterwards King RICHARD III.) Anne, *m.* 1st to Henry Holland, Duke of Exeter, from whom she was divorced; and 2ndly, to Sir Thomas St. Leger, Knt., by whom she had a dau.,

ANNE ST. LEGER, who *m.* Sir George Manners, Lord Ros, ancestor of the ducal house of RUTLAND.

Elizabeth, *m.* to John de la Pole, Duke of Suffolk.

Margaret, *m.* to Charles, Duke of Burgundy, but had no issue. This was the Duchess of Burgundy, so persevering in her hostility to HENRY VII., and her zeal in the cause of York, who set up the pretended Plantagenets, Warbeck and Symnel.

Ursula.

Richard, Duke of York, was *s.* by his son,

EDWARD PLANTAGENET, 4th Duke of York, who, after various fortunes at the head of the Yorkists, finally established himself upon the throne as EDWARD IV., when the Dukedom of York merged in the crown.

Arms—France and England. with a label of three points, arg., each charged with as many torteaux.

PLANTAGENET—EARLS OF BUCKINGHAM, DUKE OF GLOUCESTER.

Earldom, *anno* 1377.

Dukedom, 12 November, 1385.

Lineage.

THOMAS PLANTAGENET. *b.* at the royal Manor House, Woodstock co. Oxford, 7 January, 1355, and thence surnamed "THOMAS OF WOODSTOCK," youngest son of King EDWARD III., *m.* the Lady Eleanor de Bohun, eldest dau. and co-heir of Humphrey, Earl of Hereford, Essex, and Northampton; and

In consideration of that alliance was shortly afterwards made constable of England (a dignity enjoyed for nearly two centuries by the Bohuns). At the coronation of his nephew, King RICHARD II., the prince was advanced to the EARLDOM OF BUCKINGHAM, with a grant of 1,000 marks per annum, to be paid out of the exchequer, until provision of so much value should be made otherwise for him, and twenty pounds a-year out of the issues of the county, whence he derived his title. From this period, he was constantly employed as a commander in foreign wars, until the 9th of the same reign, when, for his eminent services, he was created 12 November, 1385, DUKE OF GLOUCESTER. Previously, he had been likewise sent into Essex, at the head of a large force, to suppress the insurrection of Jack Straw. The ceremony of his creation, as Duke of Gloucester, was performed at Hoselow Lodge, in Tividale, by girding with a sword, and putting a cap with a circle of gold, upon the prince's head ; the parliament being then sitting at London, and assenting thereto. The parliamentary rolls tell us the king "*ipsum ducem de prælictis titulo, nomine, et honore, per gladii cincturam, et pilei ac circuli aurei, suo capiti impositionem, maturius investivit,*"—that instalment being by girding on the sword, and adorning his head with a coronet and cap of estate. This is the more worthy of being remembered, as, at a later period, we find dukes invested, " per appositionem cappæ suo capiti, ac traditionem virgæ aureæ"—by the imposition, that is, of a cap of estate and the delivery of a golden rod. In two years afterwards, he was constituted Justice of Chester, but he subsequently forfeited the favour of the king, by his opposition to Robert de Vere, Duke of Ireland, and his coalition with the lords who assembled in arms, at Haringey Park, to put an end to the power of that celebrated minion. After the disgrace and banishment of De Vere, the Duke of Gloucester obtained some immunities from the crown, but the king never pardoned the course he had pursued in that affair, and eventually it cost the duke his life. The story of his destruction is thus told by Froissart :—" The king rode to Havering, in the county of Essex, as it were on a hunting party, and came to Plessy, where the duke then resided, about five o'clock, the duke having just newly supped, who hearing of his coming (with the duchess and his children) met him in the court. The king hereupon being brought in, a table was spread for his supper. Whereat being set, he told the duke, that he would have him ride to London with him that night ; saying, that the Londoners were to be before him on the morrow, as also his uncles of LANCASTER and YORK, with divers others of the nobles; and that he would be guided by their counsels, wishing him to command his steward to follow with his train. Hereupon the duke suspecting no hurt, so soon as the king had supp't, got on horseback, accompanied with no more than seven servants (three esquires and four yeomen), taking the way of Bondelay, to shun the common road to London : and riding fast, approached near Stratford, on the river Thames. Being got thus far, and coming near to the ambuscado* which was laid, the king rode away a great pace, and left him somewhat behind. Whereupon the earl marshal with his band, came galloping after, and overtaking him, said : *I arrest you in the king's name.* The duke therefore discerning that he was betrayed, call'd out aloud to the king, but to no purpose, for the king rode on, and took no notice of it. This was done about ten or eleven o'clock in the night ; whence he was forthwith carried into a barge, and so into a ship, which lay in the Thames, wherein they conveyed him, the next day, to Calais. Being thus brought thither, he askt the earl marshal the cause thereof, saying : *Methinks you hold me here as a prisoner ; let me go abroad, and let me see the fortress ;* but the earl marshal refused." Froissart concludes by stating : "That the duke hereupon fearing his life, desired to have a priest, who sang mass before him, that he might be confessed; and so he had. When, soon after dinner, having washed his hands, there came into the chamber four men, who suddenly casting a towel about his neck, strangled him." After this violent death, the body of the prince was laid naked in his bed, and it was rumoured that he died of a palsy; the earl marshal going into deep mourning for his lamented cousin. This account of the duke's death is, however, according to Dugdale, erroneous, "As appeareth " (saith that celebrated antiquary) " by the deposition of John Hall, a servant to the earl marshal, then present, and in some sort assisting in that most barbarous murder, viz. 'That in the month of September, 21st RICHARD II., Thomas, Earl Marshal and Nottingham, whom the deposition calls Duke of Norfolk' (by reason he was soon afterwards advanced to

* This plot to take away the life of the Duke of Gloucester, was previously concerted with Thomas Mowbray. Earl Marshal, and Earl of Nottingham, Richard's great confidant.

that honour, as a reward for this bloody fact), and one John Colfox, his esquire, came in the night-time to the chamber of the said Hall, in Calais; and that Colfox calling him out of his bed, commanded him to come forthwith to his lord. Also, that when he came, the Duke of Norfolk asked him, If he heard nothing of the Duke of Gloucester;' and that he answered, ' *He supposed him to be dead.*' Whereupon the Duke of Norfolk replied, ' *No, he is not ; but the king hath given charge that he shall be murthered ;*' and farther said, ' that he himself, with the Earl of Rutland' (afterwards made Duke of Aumarle), ' had sent certain of their esquires and yeomen, to be then there:' and likewise told him, the said Hall, ' that he should also be present, in his (Norfolk s) name;' but that Hall said, ' No;' desiring that he might rather lose all he had, and depart, rather than be present thereat: and that the duke then replied, ' He should do so, or die for it;' giving him a great knock on the pate.

" ' Moreover, that the said duke, with Colfox and Hall went to the church of Nostre Dame, in Calais, where they found William Hampsterley and — Bradeston (two esquires of the Duke of Norfolk), as also one William Serle, a yeoman of the chamber to the king; — Fraunceys, a yeoman of the chamber to the Earl of Rutland; William Rogers and William Dennys, yeomen of the said Duke of Norfolk, and another yeoman of the Earl of Rutland's, called *Cock of the Chamber*, and that there it was told to this Hall, that all the rest had made oath, that they should not discover anything of their purpose, causing him in like manner, to swear upon the sacrament, in the presence of one Sir William, a chaplain of St. George, in the church of Nostre Dame, that he should keep counsel therein. Furthermore, that after the oath thus made, they went along with the Duke of Norfolk, to a certain hostel, called Prince's Inn; and being come thither, that the said duke sent Colfox, Hampsterley, Bradeston, Serle, Faunceys, William Roger, William Dennys, Cock of the Chamber, and Hall, into a house within that inn, and then departed from them, with some unknown persons. Likewise, that so soon as they were come into that house, there entered one John Lovetoft, with divers other esquires, unknown, who brought with him the Duke of Gloucester, and delivered him to Serle and Fraunceys, in an inner room of the house, and said, ' Here are Serle and Fraunceys;' and that they, thereupon, taking the duke from Lovetoft, brought him to a chamber, and said, ' They would speak with him;' adding, ' it was the king's pleasure that he must suffer death.' Whereunto he answered, ' *If it be so, it is welcome.*' Also, that Serle and Fraunceys, forthwith appointed a priest to confess him; and that being done, made him lie down upon a bed, and laying a feather-bed upon him, held it about his mouth till he died, William Roger, William Dennys, and Cock of the Chamber, holding down the sides of it; and Colfox, Hampsterley and Bradeston, upon their knees all the while, weeping and praying for his soul, Hall himself keeping the door. Which being done, he was attainted in the parliament, held on Monday next, ensuing the feast of the Exaltation of the Holy Cross, of the same year.'" Of those assassins, Hall, in the 1st HENRY IV., had judgment in parliament, to be drawn from Tower Hill to Tyburn, and there hanged and quartered; and Serle being taken in Scotland, in the year 1404, had a similar sentence. The others, it is presumed, never returned into England. The Duke of Norfolk ended his days, and died of grief, in exile; and Edward Plantagenet, Earl-of Rutland, afterwards Duke of York, was slain at the battle of Agincourt. Thus the principal instigators a of this foul deed, all met their deserts. The fate of King RICHARD, himself, is too well known, to require particularizing here. The death of the Duke of Gloucester occurred in 1397. In due time, his friends—or rather, the enemies of his enemies —being uppermost, the empty honours of a noble interment were bestowed upon his grace. His body was conveyed to Plashy, where it was laid in a handsome sepulchre, which he had caused to be built during his lifetime in the college of Canons Regular, founded by himself, and dedicated to the Holy Trinity. At a yet later period, his reliques were again removed, and were then deposited under a marble, inlaid with brass, in the royal chapel in Westminster Abbey, upon the south side of the shrine of EDWARD THE CONFESSOR. The Duke left by the Lady Eleanor de Bohun, his wife (who *d.* a nun, 3 October, 1399), one son and three daus., viz.,

HUMPHREY PLANTAGENET.

Anne Plantagenet (eventual heiress), *m.* 1st, to Thomas, Earl of Stafford. by whom she had no issue; and 2ndly, by virtue of the king's especial license (22nd RICHARD II.), to the said Thomas's brother, Edmund, Earl of Stafford, K.G., by whom (who was slain at Shrewsbury, 22 July, 1403,) she had a son,

Humphrey, created Duke of Buckingham. (*See* STAFFORD.)

Her ladyship *m.* 3rdly, William Bourchier, Earl of Eu, in Normandy, and *d.* in 1438-9, being buried at Lanthony Abbey. She had by him a son, Henry, Earl of Ewe and Essex, from whom descend entitled to quarter the Plantagenet arms: 1, Duke of Buckingham and Chandos; 2, Marquess Townshend; 3, Marmion-Edward Ferrers, Esq., of Baddesley, and H. T. Boultbee, Esq.; 4, the Earl of Loudoun and other co-heirs of the late Marquess of Hastings; 5, Earl Ferrers; 6, Shirley, of Ettington : 7; Lord Hatherton; 8, the sisters and co-heiresses of Sir Robert Burdett, 6th Bart., of Foremark; 9, Sir Francis Burdett, 7th Bart.; 10, Viscount Hereford; 11, Sir Rainald Knightley, Bart., of Fawsley; 12, Troth, wife of the Rev. Richard Jenkyns, D.D., Master of Baliol College, Oxford; 13, Sir Henry-Bourchier Toke Wrey, Bart.; 14, John Bruton, Esq.; 15, Wrey-Chichester Bruton, Esq.; 16, George-Barnard-Knighton Drake, Esq.; 17, Baroness Berners; and 18, the families of Strangwayes Knyvett, &c., &c.

Joane, was designed to be the wife of Gilbert, Lord Talbot, but *d. unm.*

Isabel, a nun.

The duke's son,

HUMPHREY PLANTAGENET, who was styled Earl of Buckingham, after the murder of his father, was conveyed to Ireland, by King RICHARD, and imprisoned in the castle of Trim, where he remained until the accession of HENRY IV., who purposed restoring him to all the honours, but he *d. s. p.* upon his return to England, at Chester, in 1399.

Arms—Quarterly, France and England, a bordure, arg.

NOTE.—Thomas of Woodstock, Duke of Gloucester, was summoned to parliament in 1385, as Duke of Aumarle, but never afterwards by that title, nor did his above son, Humphrey, ever assume the dignity.

PLANTAGENET—EARL OF ALBEMARLE, DUKE OF CLARENCE.

Created, 9 July, 1411.

Lineage.

THOMAS PLANTAGENET, K.G.. son of King HENRY IV., was created by his father, 9 July, 1411, *Earl of Albemarle* and DUKE OF CLARENCE. This martial and valiant prince being engaged in the wars of HENRY V., fell at the battle of Baugy in 1421, and dying without legitimate issue,* his honours became EXTINCT.

PLANTAGENET—EARL OF KENDALL, DUKE OF BEDFORD.

By Letters Patent, dated 6 May, 1414.

Lineage.

JOHN PLANTAGENET, 3rd son of King HENRY IV., by his 1st consort, the Lady Mary de Bohun, dau. and co-heir of Humphrey, Earl of Hereford, was created by his brother, King HENRY V., by letters patent, dated 6 May, 1414, EARL OF KENDALL and DUKE OF BEDFORD, being designated previou ly, "John de Lancaster." The achievements of this eminent person form so prominent an era in the annals of the Plantagenets, and have been detailed so much at length by all our great historians, that it would be idle to attempt more than a mere sketch of his most conspicuous actions, in a work of this description. His first public employment in the reign of his father, was that of constable of England, and governor of the town and castle of Berwick-upon-Tweed. In the 3rd HENRY V., he was constituted lieutenant of the whole realm of England, the king himself being then in the wars of France, and the next year he was retained by indenture to serve in those wars, being appointed general of the king's whole army, both by sea and land; whereupon he set sail, and encountering the French near Southampton, achieved a great naval victory over them. In the year ensuing, the king making another expedition into France, the duke was again constituted lieutenant of the king-

---

* He had a natural son, SIR JOHN CLARENCE, called the "Bastard of Clarence," who accompanied the remains of his gallant father from Baugy to Canterbury for their interment. This Sir John Clarence had a grant of lands in Ireland from King HENRY VI., and according to Camden, he bore for arms, "Per chevron gu. and az., in chief, two lions combatant, and guardant, or, and in base, a fleur-de-lis, of the last.

dom during his absence. In the 7th HENRY V., he sailed with large reinforcements to the king in Normandy; and the next year assisted at the siege of Melon, which held out fourteen weeks and four days, before it surrendered. Upon the accession of HENRY VI., the duke was constituted chief counsellor and protector to the king, then an infant, and appointed at the same time Regent of France.

The prince, who, with his other honours, had been invested with the Garter, *m.* 1st, Anne, dau. of John, Duke of Burgundy, and 2ndly, Jacqueline, dau. of Peter, of Luxemburgh, Earl of St. Paul, but as he had no issue, the Earldom of Kendall, and Dukedom of Bedford became EXTINCT, at his decease in 1435. The duke's remains were interred in the cathedral of Notre Dame, at Roan, under a plain tomb of black marble. He was deeply lamented by the English people. He had ever borne the character of one of the first captains of his age, and the greatest generals of his time. His widow Jacqueline of Luxemburgh, *m.* 2ndly, Sir Richard Wideville, and had, with other issue, Elizabeth Wideville, who *m.* 1st, Sir John Grey, of Groby, and after his decease in the second battle of St. Albans, became Queen Consort of King EDWARD IV.

LEWIS XI. of France, says Banks, being counselled to deface the Duke of Bedford's tomb, is reported to have used these generous expressions:—

" What honour shall it be, either to us or you, to break this monument, and to rake out of the earth the bones of one, who, in his lifetime, neither my father, nor any of your progenitors with all their puissance, were ever once able to make fly one foot backwards; that by his strength or policy, kept them all out of the principal dominions of France, and out of this noble Duchy of Normandy. Wherefore I say, first, God save his soul and let his body rest in quiet: which when he was living, would have disquieted the proudest of us all; and as for his tomb, which I assure you is not so worthy as his acts deserve, I account it an honour to have him remain in my dominions."

Arms—France and England, a label per pale of five points, the first two erm., the other three az., charged with nine fleurs-de-lis, or.

PLANTAGENET—DUKE OF GLOUCESTER.

Created, 26 September, 1414.

Lineage.

HUMPHREY-PLANTAGENET, 4th son of King HENRY IV., by his 1st wife, the Lady Mary de Bohun, dau. and co-heiress of Humphrey. Earl of Hereford, Essex, and Northampton, constable of England, was made a knight of the Bath at his father's coronation, along with his brothers, THOMAS, afterwards Duke of Clarence, and JOHN, Duke of Bedford. In the 1st HENRY V., he obtained with other grants, the castle and lordship of Pembroke; shortly after which, being made DUKE OF GLOUCESTER, in the parliament held at Leicester, he had summons by that title, as well as by the title of EARL OF PEMBROKE, 26 September, 1414. In the 3rd of the same reign, the prince assisted at the siege of Harfleur, and he received soon after a dangerous wound in the celebrated battle of Agincourt. During the remainder of the reign of his martial brother, the Duke of Gloucester was almost wholly engaged in the wars of France; and upon the accession of HENRY VI., he was constituted, as he had been twice before, upon temporary absences of the king, lieutenant of the realm. In this year it was, that he was involved in a serious dispute with William, Duke of Brabant, by reason of marrying that prince's wife Jaqueline, Duchess of Hainault, who had come to England, upon some disagreement with her husband. The matter led to open hostilities, and a challenge to single combat passed between the two dukes, and was accepted; but that mode of deciding the affair was prevented by the Duke of Bedford, and the contest was finally terminated by the Duke of Gloucester's bowing to the decision of the Pope, and withdrawing from the lady. He then *m.* his concubine, Eleanor, dau. of Reginald, Lord Cobham; and in a few years afterwards a complaint was made to parliament, against him, by one "Mistress Stokes and other bold women," because he suffered Jaqueline, his wife, to be a prisoner to the Duke of Burgundy, and for living himself with an adultress. In the 14th HENRY VI., he obtained a grant for life, of the Earldom of Flanders, which was held of the king *in capite*, in right of his crown of France; and he had numerous and most valuable grants of manors and lordships in England; he had also an annuity of 2000 marks, out of the exchequer, during the king's

pleasure. The duke incurring, however, the jealousy of Margaret of Anjou, fell, at length, a victim to her machinations. Attending a parliament which had been called at St. Edmundsbury, he was arrested upon the 2nd day of the session, by the Viscount Beaumont, constable of England, accompanied by the Duke of Buckingham, and some others, and put in ward; all his servants being taken from him, and thirty-two of the chief of them sent to different prisons. The following night, the prince was found dead in his bed, supposed to have been either strangled or smothered; and his body was exhibited to the lords as though he had died of apoplexy.

The duke, who received from the people the title of *Good*, and was called " the father of his country," had with his other honours been invested with the Garter. He was a proficient in learning; wrote some tracts; laid the foundation of the Bodleian library, and built the divinity schools in the University of Oxford. The death of the prince happened in 1446, and as he left no issue, his honours became EXTINCT.

Arms—Quarterly: France and England, a border, arg.

PLANTAGENET—DUKE OF GLOUCESTER.

Created in Parliament, 1461.

Lineage.

RICHARD PLANTAGENET, brother of King EDWARD IV., was created according to Dugdale. *anno* 1461, DUKE OF GLOUCESTER, but he was not summoned to parliament until 10 August, 1469. He usurped the throne, upon the murder of his nephews EDWARD V. and the Duke of York in the Tower, under the title of RICHARD III.; he had previously governed the realm as Protector. RICHARD fell at Bosworth Field, 22 August, 1485, and his rival Henry, Earl of Richmond, *s.* him as HENRY VII. When the Duke of Gloucester assumed the reins of government as king, the dukedom merged in the crown.

Arms—France and England, on a label of three points, ermine, as many cantons, gu.

NOTE.—The body of King RICHARD was buried in the chapel of the monastery at Leicester, at the dissolution whereof, the place of his burial happened to fall into the bounds of a citizen's garden; which being afterwards purchased by Mr. Robert Kerrick (sometime Mayor of Leicester), was by him covered with a handsome stone pillar, 3 feet high, with this inscription: " Here lies the body of RICHARD III., sometime king of England." This he shewed me walking in his garden, 1612 (see PECK's *Collection of Curious Historical Pieces*, p. 85.)—BANKS.

PLANTAGENET—DUKE OF CLARENCE, EARLS OF WARWICK AND SALISBURY.

Dukedom of Clarence, by Letters Patent, *anno* 1461.
Earldom of Warwick and Salisbury, by Letters Patent, dated 25 March, 1472.

Lineage.

GEORGE PLANTAGENET, K.G., son of Richard, Duke of York, and brother of King EDWARD IV., was created DUKE OF CLARENCE, in 1461, and having *m.* the Lady Isabel Nevil, dau. and co-heir of Richard Nevill, Earl of Salisbury, and Earl of Warwick, was advanced to those dignities by letters patent, dated 25 March, 1472. This unhappy prince was attainted of high treason, and suffered death, by being drowned, it is said, in a butt of Malmsey, in the Tower, 1477, when his honours became FORFEITED. King EDWARD IV. assented, of course, to the execution, but he is said subsequently to have most deeply lamented having done so, and upon all occasions when the life of a condemned person was solicited, he used openly to exclaim, " Oh, unhappy brother, for whose life no man would make suit." The Duke of Clarence left issue,

EDWARD, who, after his father's death, was entitled EARL OF WARWICK. This unhappy prince was born the child of adversity, and spent almost the whole of his melancholy life in prison. After the decease of his uncle, King EDWARD IV., his other uncle, the Duke of Gloucester, had him removed to the castle of Sheriff-Hutton, in Yorkshire, where he remained until the defeat of the Yorkists at Bosworth placed him in the hands of HENRY VII, by whose order he was transferred to the Tower of London, and there more closely confined than before, solely because he was the last male Plantagenet living. He was not allowed, however, a protracted existence, for being arraigned for high treason and betrayed under a promise of pardon, into an acknowledgment of guilt, he was condemned, and executed upon Tower Hill, in 1499.

MARGARET. This lady upon the execution of her brother, became the last member of the royal and illustrious house of Plantagenet (*see* Plantagenet, Countess of Salisbury).

Arms—France and England quarterly; a label of three points, arg., each charged with a canton, gu.

NOTE—From the period that George Plantagenet, Duke of Clarence, lost his life in 1477, the Dukedom of Clarence lay dormant, until revived in the person of His Royal Highness PRINCE WILLIAM-HENRY (Guelph), 3rd son of His Majesty King GEORGE III., who was created DUKE OF CLARENCE AND ST. ANDREWS, in the peerage of Great Britain, and EARL OF MUNSTER, in that of Ireland. 19 May, 1789, all which honours merged in the crown upon the accession of the duke in 1830, as KING WILLIAM THE FOURTH.

PLANTAGENET — COUNTESS OF SALISBURY.

By Letters Patent, dated 14 October, 1513.

Lineage.

MARGARET PLANTAGENET, dau. of George, Duke of Clarence, and the Lady Isabel Nevil, eldest dau., and eventually sole heir, of Richard, Earl of Warwick and Salisbury, son and heir of Alice, dau. and heir of Thomas Montacute, Earl of Salisbury, became the LAST OF THE PLANTAGENETS, upon the execution of her brother, Edward Plantagenet, called Earl of Warwick, by HENRY VII. in 1499, and petitioned parliament in the 5th King HENRY VIII., to be restored to the honours of her maternal family. Whereupon she was advanced to the dignity of COUNTESS OF SALISBURY, 14 October, 1513, and obtained at the same time letters patent, establishing her in the castles, manors, and lands of Richard, late Earl of Salisbury, her grandfather, which had fallen to the crown by the attainder of her brother, Edward, called Earl of Warwick. Notwithstanding these substantial marks of royal favour, an opportunity in several years after was seized upon to destroy the only remaining branch of the Plantagenets in this illustrious lady; and at a period of life too, when, in the natural progress of events, her course was nearly closed. At the advanced age of seventy years, 31st HENRY VIII., her ladyship was condemned to death, unheard by parliament, and beheaded on Tower Hill in two years afterwards, 27 May, 1541, when her dignity as Countess of Salisbury, fell under the attainder. Her ladyship had m. Sir Richard Pole, K.G., and had issue,

HENRY, summoned to parliament as BARON MONTAGU (*see* Pole, Baron Montagu).
Geffry (5n), upon whose testimony his elder brother, Lord Montagu, was convicted of, and executed for, high treason. He received sentence of death himself, but did not suffer.
Arthur, was charged, in the reign of ELIZABETH, with projecting a scheme for the release of the Queen of Scots, and had judgment of death; but by reason of his near alliance to the crown, no execution followed
Reginald, in holy orders, was educated at Oxford, and obtained the deanery of Exeter by the gift of King HENRY VIII. He was abroad at the period that king abolished the papal authority in England, and not attending when summoned to return, he was proclaimed a traitor and divested of his deanery. He was afterwards, *unno* 1536, made a cardinal, and, as CARDINAL POLE, presided (one of three presidents) at the celebrated Council of Trent. When Queen MARY ascended the throne, his eminence returned to England as legate from Pope JULIUS III., and had his attainder reversed by special act of parliament. He was made, at the same time, archbishop of Canterbury, in which high episcopal dignity he continued until his death, which occurred 17 November, 1558, being the very day upon which Queen MARY herself died; the tidings of that event are said to have broken the cardinal's heart, being at the time much weakened by a quartan ague. Whereupon his remains were interred in the cathedral at Canterbury. Few churchmen have borne so unblemished a reputation as this eminent prelate, and few have carried themselves with so much moderation and meekness.
Ursula, m. to Henry, Lord Stafford.

Among the co-representatives of Margaret, Countess of Salisbury, may be mentioned the Marquess of Hastings; William Lowndes, Esq., of Chesham; William Selby Lowndes, Esq., of Whaddon.

PLANTAGENET—VISCOUNT L'ISLE.

By Letters Patent, dated 26 April, 1533.

Lineage.

ARTHUR PLANTAGENET (natural son of King EDWARD IV., by the Lady Elizabeth Lucy), having m. Elizabeth, dau. of Edward Grey, 1st Viscount L'Isle of that family; sole heir of her niece, Elizabeth, Countess of Devon, and widow of Edmund Dudley (*see* Grey, Viscounts L'Isle), was created Viscount L'Isle, with limitation to his heirs male, by the said Elizabeth, by letters patent, dated 26 April, 1533, upon the surrender of that dignity by Charles Brandon,* afterwards Duke of Suffolk. His lordship had issue by the heiress of Grey,

Bridget, m. to Sir William Carden, Knt.
Francis, m. 1st, to John Basset. Esq., of Umberleigh, co. Devon, and 2ndly, to Thomas Monk, of Potheridge, in the same shire, from whom the celebrated General Monk descended.
Elizabeth, m. to Sir Francis Jobson, Knt., lieutenant of the Tower, and master of the jewel office to Queen ELIZABETH.

In the 24th HENRY VIII., Lord L'Isle was constituted lieutenant of Calais, and some time after, incurring suspicion of being privy to a plot to deliver up the garrison to the French, he was recalled and committed to the Tower of London; but his innocence appearing manifest upon investigation, the king not only gave immediate orders for his release, but sent him a diamond ring, and a most gracious message; which made such an impression upon the sensitive nobleman, that he died the night following, 3 March, 1541, of excessive joy. His lordship was a knight of the most noble order of the Garter. At his decease, the Viscounty of L'Isle became EXTINCT.

Arms—The coat of his lordship's father, King EDWARD IV., quartered with Ulster and Mortimer under a baton.

PLANTAGENET—EARLS OF SURREY

(*Refer to* WARREN, Earls of Surrey.)

PLANTAGENET—EARL OF ULSTER.

(*See* PLANTAGENET, Duke of Clarence.)

PLAYZ—BARON PLAYZ.

By Writ of Summons, dated 1297.

Lineage.

In the 17th King JOHN, HUGH DE PLAYZ held seven knights' fees in co. Sussex, and was one of the barons who took up arms against that prince. He m. 1st, Beatrix de Say, widow of Hugh de Nevill, but was divorced from that lady, and m. 2ndly, Philippa, one of the daus. and co-heirs of Richard de Montfichet, by whom he had his successor,

RICHARD DE PLAYZ, who, in the 53d HENRY III., as one of the nephews and heirs of Richard de Montfichet, paid his relief for a third part of the said Richard's lands. To this Richard de Playz, s. his son,
RALPH DE PLAYZ, who d. s. p., and was s. by his brother,
RICHARD DE PLAYZ, to whom succeeded,
GILES DE PLAYZ. This feudal lord had summons to attend the king on the affairs of the realm, in the 22nd EDWARD I. He had afterwards a military summons to proceed to Gascony, and ultimately summons to parliament as a Baron, in the 25th of the same reign, but not afterwards. He d. in 1303, seized of the manor of Fulmere, co. Cambridge, and was s. by his son,

---

* Elizabeth Grey, only dau. and heiress of John, last Viscount L'Isle, of the Grey family, was contracted to Charles Brandon, who was created in consequence Viscount L'Isle, but the lady refusing, when she had attained maturity, to fulfil the engagement, the patent was cancelled. She afterwards m. Henry Courtenay, Earl of Devon

RICHARD DE PLATZ, 2nd baron, summoned to parliament, from 20 November, 1317, to 14 March, 1322. This nobleman was *s.* at his decease in 1327, by his son,

RICHARD DE PLATZ, 3rd baron, but never summoned to parliament. This nobleman was found in the 8th EDWARD III., heir to John de Lancaster, of co. Essex; he *d.* in 1359-60, and was *s.* by his son,

SIR JOHN DE PLAITZ, 4th baron, but never summoned to parliament, who *d.* in the 33rd EDWARD III., leaving an only dau. and heiress,

MARGARET, who *m.* Sir John Howard (his 1st wife), and was mother of

SIR JOHN HOWARD, whose dau. and heir,

FLIZABETH HOWARD, *m.* John de Vere, 12th Earl of Oxford, and had with an elder son, John, 13th Earl of Oxford, a younger son,

SIR GEORGE VERE, who *d.* in 1503, leaving a son and heir,

JOHN, 14th Earl of Oxford, who *d. s. p.* in 1526, when the Barony of Plaitz fell into abeyance between his three sisters and co-heirs, viz.,

Dorothy, *m.* to John Nevil, Lord Latimer: for the co-heirs of this marriage (the senior of whom is the Duke of Athole), *see* p. 393.

Elizabeth, *m.* to Sir Anthony Wingfield, K.G., and had issue: the co-heirs of this marriage are ADRIEN, MARQUIS DE COURONNELL, in France, and Vice-Admiral SIR WILLIAM-HENRY DILLON.

Ursula, *m.* 1st, to George Windsor, and 2ndly, to Sir Edward Knightley, but *d. s. p.* 1560.

The Barony of Playz, or Plaitz, is now in ABEYANCE between the co-heirs of the sisters of the 14th Earl of Oxford.

Arms—Per pale, or and gu., a lion passant, arg.

PLESSETS, OR PLESSETIS—EARL OF WAR-WICK, BARON PLESSETS.

Earldom, *jure uxoris. temp.* HENRY III.
Barony, by Writ of Summons, dated 6 February, 1299.

Lineage.

The first of this family mentioned is

JOHN DE PLESSETS, a domestic servant in the court of King HENRY III., and a Norman by birth; who having served in the Welsh wars, was constituted governor of the castle of Devizes, in Wiltshire, and warden of the forest of Chippenham, in the same shire. In the 24th King HENRY's reign he was sheriff of Oxfordshire, and in two years afterwards he had a grant of the wardship and marriage of John Bisset: and likewise of the heirs of Nicholas Malesmaines. Certain it is that he enjoyed in a high degree the favour of his royal master, for upon the death of John Mareschal, who had *m.* Margery, the sister and heir of Thomas de Newburgh, Earl of Warwick, the king sent his mandate to the archbishop of York, the bishop of Carlisle, and William de Cantilupe, requiring them that they should earnestly persuade this opulent widow to take John de Plessets for her 2nd husband. Nay, so much did he desire the union, that upon Christmas-day in the same year, being then at Bordeaux, he granted to John Plessets, by patent, the marriage of this Margery, in case he could procure her consent; and if not, that then he should have the fine, which the lady would incur by marrying without the king's license. This course of his majesty, however, prevailed, and his favourite obtained the hand of Margery de Newburgh, Countess of Warwick, and widow of John Mareschal, styled Earl of Warwick. De Plessets was subsequently constituted constable of the Tower of London, but not by the title of Earl of Warwick, nor did he assume that dignity for some time afterwards. He did, however, eventually assume it, for we find him so styled (31st HENRY III.) by the king in a license granted him, to cut down oak timber in the forest of Dene; ever after which he is called Earl of Warwick. His lordship was appointed in four years afterwards one of the justices itinerant to sit at the Tower, for hearing and determining such pleas as concerned the city of London; and at the breaking out of the contest between HENRY and the barons, he was constituted sheriff of the cos. Warwick and Leicester; but he lived not to see the issue of those troubles. His lordship *d.* in 1263; not having had issue by the Countess of Warwick, the Earldom of Warwick passed at her ladyship's decease to the heir-at-law (*see* Newburgh, Earls of Warwick). But he left, by a former wife, Christian, dau. and heir of Hugh de Sandford, a son and heir,

HUGH DE PLESSETS, who doing his homage, in the April ensuing, had livery of the manors of Oxenardton, Kedelinton, and Stuttesdon, co. Oxford, which were of his mother's inheritance; the two former being holden of the king by barony, for which manors in the 48th HENRY III., he paid £100 for his relief. This feudal lord *m.* Isabel, dau. of John de Riparius, and dying in 1291, was *s.* by his son,

HUGH DE PLESSETS, who being engaged in the Scottish wars was summoned to parliament as a Baron, 6 February, 1299, but Dugdale gives no further account of the family.

Arms—Arg., six annulets, gu., a chief chequy, or and sa.

NOTE.—Hutchins, in his *History of Dorsetshire*, says, that ROBERT DE PLECY, or PLESSETS, son of Sir Hugh, brother, or a near kinsman of John de Plessets, Earl of Warwick, in the 19th EDWARD I., held Upwinborne Placy in that co., which passed through several generations to

JOAN DE PLECY, dau. and heiress, who *m.* Sir John Hamelyn, whose dau. and eventual heiress,

EGIDIA HAMELYN, *m.* for her 2nd husband, Robert Ashley, and conveyed to him the manor of Upwinborne-Plecy. The descendant of this marriage,

SIR ANTHONY ASHLEY, Knt., of Winborne, St. Giles, left an only dau. and heiress,

ANNE ASHLEY, who *m.* Sir John Cooper, Bart., from which marriage the extant Earls of Shaftesbury descend, and through which they inherit the manor of Upwinborne-Plecy.

PLUGENET—BARONS PLUGENET.

By Writ of Summons, dated 24 June, 1295.

Lineage.

In the beginning of HENRY II.'s reign, HUGH DE PLUGENET had lands given him in the co. Oxford, and in some years afterwards was owner of Lamburne, in Berkshire. He *m.* Sibell, dau. and co-heir of Josceus de Dinant, and had two sons, Alan and Josceus. To one of whom succeeded,

SIR ALAN DE PLUGENET, Lord of Kilpec, who, after the battle of Evesham, in the 49th HENRY III., was made governor of Dunster Castle, co. Somerset, and in three years subsequently, obtained a grant from his maternal uncle, Robert Walrond, of certain manors in the cos. Wilts, Dorset, and Somerset, with the castle of Kilpeck, &c., co. Hereford, and at the death of the said Robert without issue, in the 1st EDWARD I., had livery of the same. This Sir Alan de Plugenet, distinguishing himself in the Welsh wars, and being esteemed a person of wisdom, and of military knowledge, was summoned to parliament as a Baron from 24 June, 1295, to 26 January, 1297. He *d.* in 1299, and was *s.* by his son,

SIR ALAN DE PLUGENET, 2nd baron, K.B., summoned to parliament, 19 December, 1311. This nobleman was constantly engaged in the wars of Scotland. He *d.* about 1325, leaving his sister,

JOAN DE BOHUN, heir to the Barony of Plugenet, at whose decease *s. p.* in 1327, that dignity became EXT.NCT.

Arms—Erm., a bend engrailed, gu.

POINTZ—BARONS POINTZ.

By Writ of Summons, dated 24 June, 1295.

Lineage.

This family, and that of CLIFFORD, is said to have sprung from a common ancestor, PONZ, whose grandson, WALTER, derived his surname from the place of his abode, Clifford Castle, co. Hereford, and another of whose descendants was father of

OSBERT FITZ-PONZ, from whom sprang

HUGH POINTZ, who with his father, Nicholas Pointz, taking part with the revolted barons, had his lands, in the 17th JOHN, in the cos. of Somerset, Dorset, and Gloucester, seized by the crown, and given to Godfrey de Crancumbe. He was afterwards imprisoned in the castle of Bristol, but not strictly, as his friends had permission to visit him, and to supply him with necessaries. This Hugh *m.* Helewis, dau. of William, and sister and co-heir of William Mallet, of Carry-Malet, co. Somerset, and was *s.* by his son,

NICHOLAS POINTZ, who, residing in Gloucestershire, had military summons from the crown to march against the Welsh, in the 41st and 42nd HENRY III., but afterwards joined the other barons who took up arms against the king. He *d.* in the 1st EDWARD I., seized of the manor of Carry-Malet, co. Somerset, and several other estates. He *m.* Elizabeth, dau. of William de la Zouch, and was *s.* by his son,

SIR HUGH POINTZ, who having been engaged in the wars of Wales, Gascony and Scotland, was summoned to parliament as a Baron by King EDWARD I., from 24 June, 1295, to 1 August, 1307. His lordship *m.* Margaret, dau. of Sir William Paveley, and *d.* in 1307, having had regular summonses to that year, and was *s.* by his son,

NICHOLAS POINTZ, 2nd baron, summoned to parliament from 4 March, 1309, to 16 June, 1311. This nobleman was in the Scottish wars, before and after his father's decease. He *m.* 1st, Elizabeth, dau. of Eudo de Zouche, by Milicent, dau. of William Cantilupe, Lord of Bergavenny, and co-heir of her brother George; by whom he had the manor of Batecumbe, in free marriage. He is stated to have *m.* 2ndly, Matilda, dau. and heir of Sir John Acton, of Iron Acton, co. Gloucester, by whom he left a son,

Sir John Poyntz, of Iron Acton, who *m.* Elizabeth, dau. and co-heir of Sir Philip Clanvowe, and was ancestor of the families of POYNTZ of Iron Acton, co., Gloucester, and of POYNTZ, of Midgham, co. Berks, whose last male heir was WILLIAM-STEPHEN POYNTZ, Esq., of Cowdray Park, in Sussex, and of Midgham, Berks, who *m.* Hon. Elizabeth-Mary Browne, sister and heir of Samuel, 6th Viscount Montagu, and *d.* leaving three daus. his co-heirs.

He *d.* in 1312, and was *s.* by his son,

HUGH POINTZ, 3rd baron, K.B., summoned to parliament, from 20 November, 1317, to 24 February, 1343. This nobleman was *s.* by his son,

SIR NICHOLAS POINTZ, 4th baron, but never summoned to parliament. This nobleman *m.* Alianore, dau. of Sir John Erleigh, Knt., and had two daus., viz.,

AVICIA, *m.* to John Barry, and had a son John, who *d. s. p.*
MARGARET, *m.* to John de Newburgh, and had issue.

At his lordship's death the Barony of Pointz, fell into ABEYANCE between his daus.

Arms—Barry of eight, or, and gu.

POLE — BARONS DE LA POLE, EARLS OF SUFFOLK, MARQUESS OF SUFFOLK, EARL OF PEMBROKE, DUKES OF SUF-FOLK.

Barony, by Writ of Summons, dated 20 January, 1366.
Earldom of Suffolk, by Letters Patent, dated 6 August, 1385.
Earldom of Pembroke, 21 February, 1443.
Marquess, 14 September, 1444.
Dukedom, 2 June, 1448.

Lineage.

The founder of this family, which eventually attained such an exalted station, was

WILLIAM DE LA POLE, an opulent merchant at Kingston-upon-Hull, who left two sons,

WILLIAM, of whom presently.
Richard, to whom King EDWARD III., in the 11th year of his reign, gave, "for his extraordinary merits," £1,000 sterling, out of the exchequer. This Richard left a son and heir, WILLIAM, who *m.* Margaret, sister and heiress of John Peverel, of Castle Ashby, co. Northumberland, and had a son and heir,

JOHN, who left, by Joane, his wife, sister and heiress of John, Lord Cobham, an only dau. and heiress,

JOANE, who *m.* Reginald Braybroke, and had a dau. and heiress,

JOANE BRAYBROKE, *m.* to Thomas Broke, who became in her right, Lord Cobham.

The elder son,

WILLIAM DE LA POLE, was, like his father, a merchant, at Kingston-upon-Hull, and mayor of that borough. In the 10th King EDWARD III., this William contracted to furnish the navy in Scotland, with wine, salt, and other provisions, but losing part of the cargo, in the transmission to Berwick-upon-Tweed, he had an allowance for the same in passing his accounts. In three years afterwards, being a person of great opulence, he was enabled to advance the sum of £1,000, in gold, to the king, who then lay at Antwerp: for which important service,

EDWARD being much in want at the time of supplies, he was constituted 2nd baron of the exchequer, and advanced to the degree of banneret, with a grant out of the customs at Hull, for the better support of that rank. He was afterwards known as Sir William de la Pole, senior. He *m.* Catherine, dau. of Sir Walter Norwich, and dying in the 40th EDWARD III., possessed of extensive estates in the co. of York, had issue,

MICHAEL, his heir.
Thomas.   Edmond.
Katherine.
Blanche, *m.* to Richard, Lord Scrope, of Bolton.
Margaret.

The eldest son,

MICHAEL DE LA POLE, had, in the lifetime of his father, a grant in reversion, of £70 a-year, to himself and his heirs from EDWARD III., in consideration of that opulent person's services, whom the king denominated his "Beloved Merchant;" which annuity, William, his father, and Richard, his uncle, had previously enjoyed. This Michael de la Pole, despite of Walsingham's observation, "That as a merchant himself and the son of a merchant, he was better versed in merchandize, than skilled in martial matters;" was an eminent soldier, and distinguished himself in the French wars, at the close of EDWARD III.'s reign, when ne served immediately under the Black Prince. In the 1st year of RICHARD II., he accompanied John, Duke of Lancaster, then called King of Castile, in his voyage to sea; and the same year had the chief command of all the king's fleet to the northward; in which his own retinue were 140 men-at-arms, 140 archers, one banneret, eight knights and 130 esquires. In the next year he was employed upon a mission to the court of Rome; and in four years after, constituted chancellor and keeper of the great seal—having had summons to parliament as a Baron since the 39th King EDWARD III. In the 8th RICHARD II., his lordship procured license to castellate his manor houses at Wyngfield, Skernefield, and Huntingfield, co. Suffolk, and to impark all his woods and lands in the vicinity. And in the 9th of the same monarch, being still chancellor he was created by letters patent, dated 6 August, 1385, EARL OF SUFFOLK, with a grant of 1,000 marks per annum, to be received out of the king's exchequer. In the parliament held at this period, a dispute is recorded as having taken place between his lordship and Thomas Arundel, bishop of Ely, in consequence of the king's having restored, at the earnest solicitation of that prelate, the temporalities to the bishop of Norwich. The chancellor opposing the Restoration, thus interrogated the bishop, when he moved that measure:—"What is this, my lord, that you desire? Is it a small matter to part with those temporalities which yield the king more than a thousand pounds per annum? The king hath no more need of such advisers to his loss." To which the bishop answered, "What is that you say, Michael? I desire nothing of the king which is his own; but that which belongs to another, and which he unjustly detains, by thy wicked council, or such as thou art, which will never be for his advantage; (I think) if thou beest so much concerned for the king's profit, why hast thou covetously taken from him a thousand marks per annum, since thou wast made an earl?"

After this, in the same year, we find the earl, notwithstanding his being lord chancellor, retained to serve the king, being a banneret, in his Scottish wars for forty days, and obtaining a grant in consequence, to himself and his heirs male, of £500 per annum, lands, part of the possessions of William de Ufford, late Earl of Suffolk, deceased, viz., the castle, town, manor, and honour of Eye. In this year, too, he marched troops from all quarters to London and its vicinity, in order to resist a menaced invasion of the French. But he was soon afterwards impeached by the commons for divers misdemeanours and frauds, particularly for purchasing lands, while chancellor, "in deception of the king," and being found guilty was sentenced to death and forfeiture. Upon the dissolution of parliament, however, he seems, through the protection of the king, to have set his foes for the moment at defiance, and to have relinquished the chancellorship only. But subsequently, the storm again gathering, he fled the kingdom with Robert de Vere, Duke of Ireland, and repairing to Calais, approached the castle, of which his brother, Edmund de la Pole, was captain, in the disguise of a Flemish poulterer, having shaved his head and beard; but it is said that Edmund refused him admission without the previous permission of William de Beauchamp, the governor. "Brother," said the captain of the castle, "you must know that I dare not be false to the king of England for the sake of any kindred whatsoever; nor admit you in without the privity of William de Beauchamp, governor of this town." Whether this be true or false, certain-it is that the earl never afterwards came back to England, but *d.* at Paris, an outlaw, in 1388, his dignities having previously fallen under the outlawry. His lordship, who, amongst his other honours, had the Garter, was, like all the great nobles of the period, a benefactor to the church, having founded a Carthusian monastery, without the north-gate, at Kingston-upon-Hull, and endowed it with lands of great value. He m. Katherine, dau. and heiress of Sir John Wing-field, Knt., and had issue,

MICHAEL, (Sir).
Richard, *d s. p.*
Anne, *m.* to Gerard, son of Warine, Lord L'Isle.

Wh'ch
SIR MICHAEL DE LA POLE, *b.* 1368, in the 21st RICHARD II., obtained the annulment of the judgment against his father; and upon the accession of King HENRY IV. was fully restored to the castle, manor, and honour of Eye, with the other lands of the late lord, as also to the EARLDOM OF SUFFOLK, with a reversionary proviso, that those lands and honours should, in default of his male issue, devolve upon the male heir of his deceased father. This nobleman, who spent his time chiefly in the French wars, *d.* 14 September, 1415, at the siege of Har-fleur. His lordship *m.* Lady Catherine de Stafford, dau. of Hugh, 2nd Earl of Stafford, and left three daus., Kathe-rine, abbess of Barking, Elizabeth, *m.* to John de Foix, Earl of Kendal, and Isabel, *m.* to Thomas, Lord Morley) four sons, MICHAEL, WILLIAM, Thomas, and John (Sir). The eldest
MICHAEL DE LA POLE, *s.* as 3rd Earl of Suffolk, but this gallant nobleman lost his life within a month of his accession to the title, at the battle of Agincourt, 25 October, 1415. He *m.* Lady Elizabeth Mowbray, dau. of Thomas, Earl Marshal (widow of Nicholas, Lord Audley, and John, Lord Beaumont), and had three daus., who all *d. s. p.* At the decease of his lordship the Barony of De la Pole and the Earldom of Suffolk devolved on his brother,

WILLIAM DE LA POLE, 4th Earl of Suffolk, who, in the 6th King HENRY V., making proof of his age, had livery of his in-heritance. his homage being respited. This nobleman was actively engaged in the glorious wars of that monarch, and, for his eminent services, was made a knight of the Garter. At the death of King HENRY, his lordship was left in France with the Earl of Salisbury, to defend the castles and towns which had fallen to the English arms, and in the 1st year of King HENRY VI., his two nieces, Elizabeth and Isabel, dying in minority without issue, and the other, Katherine, having taken the veil, his lordship inherited the entire property of his deceased brother, Earl Michael. About this period, the Earl, in con-junction with the Earl of Salisbury, achieved a great victory over the French at Verneuil, and continued for several years afterwards to sustain the British banner upon the same soil. In the 6th HENRY VI. his lordship, with his companion in arms, Lord Salisbury, invested Orleans, and the latter nobleman being slain, the Earl of Suffolk was appointed captain of the siege, by the celebrated general, John Plantagenet, Duke of Bedford. In this affair he appears, however, to have been un-fortunate, but he afterwards retrieved his reputation at Aumerle, which he carried with its fortress, after no less than twenty-four assaults. In the 9th of the same reign he assisted at the solemn coronation of King HENRY at Paris. In four years afterwards his lordship was deputed ambassador to Arras to treat of peace with the French, having license to take with him gold, silver, plate, and jewels, to the value of £2,000; and the next year was joined, in commission with the Duke of York, to proceed in the treaty. From this period the earl continued actively engaged as a military commander, or diplomatist, in the service of the crown, for which he was most amply compensated, by numerous and valuable grants (amongst which was the reversion of the Earldom of Pembroke, should Humphrey Plantagenet, Duke of Gloucester and Earl of Pem-broke, the king's uncle, die without issue), until the 23rd year of HENRY's reign, when he was created MARQUESS OF SUFFOLK (14 September, 1444), by cincture with a sword, and putting a coronet of gold upon his head. This dignity was accompanied by a grant of £35 yearly out of the issues of the cos. of Nor-folk and Suffolk. Being at this period lord steward of the household, the marquess was sent into Sicily, to perform the solemnity of marriage with Margaret of Anjou, dau. of Reg-nier, titular King of Sicily, and Duke of Anjou, as proxy for King HENRY VI., and to conduct the Princess into Eng-land. In the next year he was employed in negotiating peace with France, and he was soon after appointed lord chamberlain, and then lord high admiral of England. On the death of the Duke of Gloucester, in 1446, his lordship suc-ceeded to the Earldom of Pembroke, and he was created DUKE OF SUFFOLK, 2 June, 1448. Which latter dignity is said to have been conferred upon him for advising the murder of the Duke of Gloucester; but be that as it may, his grace's prosperity en-

441

dured not many years longer. For affairs becoming disastrous both at home and abroad, the popular voice became loud against him. He was charged with the loss of Anjou and Nor-mandy, of having caused the murder of the good Duke of Glou-cester, of rapacity, and of the numerous other crimes which are generally attributed to an unsuccessful minister, in a season of calamity, by a disappointed people. Parliament soon after as-sembling, he was regularly impeached by the Commons, of high crimes and misdemeanors, and committed prisoner to the Tower; but he was released within a month, and restored to the k ng's favour. This act of royal clemency exciting, however, univer-sal clamour, the king was obliged at length to banish him the realm; with the intention of recalling him, however, so soon as the storm had abated. But the unfortunate nobleman was doomed to immediate destruction, for after embarking at Ipswich for France, he was boarded by the captain of a ship of war belonging to the Duke of Exeter, then constable of the Tower of London, called the *Nicholas of the Tower*, and being brought into Dover Road, was decapitated without further trial, on the side of the cock-boat. It is recorded of this gallant personage that he served in the wars of France, full twenty-four years, seventeen of which were in uninterrupted succes-sion without once visiting his native country. He was at one time made prisoner, whilst only a knight, and paid £20,000 for his ransom. His grace was fifteen years a member of the privy council, and thirty, one of the knights of the Garter.

It is said that he first *m.* privately, the Countess of Hainault, and by her had a dau., who *m.* — Barentine, but that after-wards taking to wife, Alice, dau. and heiress of Thomas Chaucer, a grand-daughter of Geoffrey Chaucer, the poet, and widow of Sir John Philip, Knt., that daughter was proved a bastard.

All the duke's honours, including the old Barony of Dela-pole, which he inherited from his nieces, devolved on his eldest son,
JOHN DE LA POLE, who, having *m.* the Lady Elizabeth Planta-genet, sister of King EDWARD IV. and King RICHARD III., was confirmed as DUKE OF SUFFOLK, by letters patent, dated 23 March, 1463. After which, in the 11th of the same reign, he was one of the lords then assembled in parliament, who recog-nized the title of Prince Edward, eldest son of that king, and made oath of fidelity to him. Upon the accession of King HENRY VII. his grace was made constable of Wallingford. The duke had issue,

JOHN, who, by special charter, dated 13 March, 1467, was created EARL OF LINCOLN, and in the 2nd RICHARD III., was appointed lord lieutenant of Ireland. After this, he was de-clared, by his uncle, the same monarch, heir to the crown of England, in the event of the decease of his own son, Prince Edward. His lordship, in the next reign, having reared the standard of revolt, fell at the battle of Stoke, 16 June, 1487 (*see* De la Pole, Earl of Lincoln).
EDMUND, who *s.* his father.
Humphrey, a priest.
Edward, archdeacon of Richmond.
RICHARD, of whom hereafter.
Catherine, *m.* to William, Lord Stourton.
Anne, a nun at Sion.
Dorothy, *d. unm.*
Elizabeth, *m.* Henry Lovel, Lord Morley.

His grace, who was a knight of the Garter, *d.* in 1491, and was *s.* by his eldest surviving son,
EDMUND DE LA POLE, 2nd Duke of Suffolk. We find this nobleman, although one of the last persons of rank remaining of the house of York, and of a family previously devoted to that cause, engaged in the beginning of HENRY VII.'s reign, in that monarch's service; and so late as the 12th year, he was in arms with the Lords Essex and Mountjoy, against Lord Audley and the Cornish men, who suffered so memorable a defeat on Blackheath. But his grace being subjected to the ignominy of a public trial and condemnation (although immediately par-doned), for "killing an ordinary person in wrath," became so indignant that he immediately withdrew, without permission, to the court of his aunt, Margaret, Duchess of Burgundy (sister of the Kings EDWARD IV. and RICHARD III.), then the asylum for all the discontented spirits, who retained any feeling of attachment to the House of York, or had any cause of dissatis-faction with the existing order of things in England. He re-turned, however, soon after, and excusing himself to the king, assisted at the nuptials of Prince Arthur, with Katherine of Arragon. But he again departed for Flanders, accompanied by his brother, Richard. and remained in exile, until treacher-ously delivered up to the English monarch, by Philip, Duke of Burgundy, upon an express stipulation, however, that his life should not be endangered. On arriving in England, he was immediately committed to the Tower, where he remained a close prisoner until the 5th HENRY VIII., when that monarch caused the unfortunate duke, solely from being a Yorkist, to be

decapitated on Tower Hill, 30 April, 1513. His grace m. Margaret, dau. of Richard, Lord Scrope, and left an only dau.,

Anne, who became a nun, in the convent of Minoresses, without Aldgate, in the suburbs of the city of London.

Notwithstanding the attainder of this duke, and the consequent forfeiture of his honours, the title, after his decease, was assumed by his brother,

RICHARD DE LA POLE, as 3rd Duke of Suffolk, then living an exile in France. This gallant person commanded 6,000 French at the siege of Therouenne, when assaulted by King HENRY VIII., and he fell at the battle of Pavia, in 1524, where his heroic conduct extorted the praise even of his foes; and the Duke of Bourbon honouring his remains with splendid obsequies, assisted in person, as one of the chief mourners. Thus terminated the male line of this gallant and highly gifted race; and the Dukedom of Suffolk passed by a new creation to King HENRY VIII.'s brother-in-law, the celebrated Charles Brandon.

Arms—Azure, a fesse between three leopards' heads, or.

POLE—EARL OF LINCOLN.

By Special Charter, dated 13 March, 1467.

Lineage..

JOHN DE LA POLE, eldest son of John de la Pole, Duke of Suffolk, by the Lady Elizabeth Plantagenet, sister of Kings EDWARD IV. and RICHARD III., was created, in the 7th year of the former monarch, his father being then living, EARL OF LINCOLN. Upon the accession of his uncle, RICHARD, his lordship obtained several important grants of land from the crown, and was soon afterwards appointed lord-lieutenant of Ireland. Firmly attached to the house of York, the earl could ill brook the triumph of King HENRY VII., and accordingly, upon the accession of that prince, removed to the court of his aunt, Margaret, Duchess of Burgundy, where he entered zealously into the affair of Lambert Simnel; in promotion of whose pretensions to the crown his lordship returned at the head of four thousand German soldiers, under the immediate command of Martin Swart, and having first landed in Ireland, and proclaimed the Pretender there, made a descent upon Lancashire, whence marching towards Newark-upon-Trent, co. Nottingham, he encountered the royal army at Stoke, 16 June, 1487, where he sustained a signal defeat, and fell himself in the conflict. His lordship *d. s. p.*, when his honours became EXTINCT.

POLE —BARON MONTAGU.

By Writ of Summons, dated 5 January, 1553.

Lineage.

The first of this family of whom anything memorable occurs is

SIR RICHARD POLE, Knt. (son of Sir Jeffrey Pole, Knt., of Buckinghamshire, by Edith, dau. of Sir Oliver St. John, and aunt of HENRY VII.), who, being a valiant and expert commander, was first retained to serve King HENRY VII. in the wars of Scotland, and being a person highly accomplished, was made chief gentleman of the bed-chamber to Prince Arthur, and a knight of the Garter. He m. the LADY MARGARET PLANTAGENET (afterwards COUNTESS OF SALISBURY—(see Plantagenet, Countess of Salisbury), and had, with junior issue,[*] a son and heir,

HENRY POLE, who, in the 5th HENRY VIII., had special livery of the lands of his inheritance, and in eight years afterwards was restored to the king's favour by the title of LORD MONTACUTE. But as to any creation, by patent or otherwise, nothing appears until the 24th of the same reign, when his lordship had summons to parliament as "Henrico Pole de Montacute." He attended King HENRY in the celebrated interview with FRANCIS, King of France, and was made a knight of the Bath at the coronation of Anne Boleyn. But in a few years afterwards being charged, along with the Marquess of Exeter, by his own brother, Sir Jeffrey Pole, with a design to elevate his

[*] For the particulars of the younger sons, amongst whom was the celebrated CARDINAL POLE, refer to Plantagenet, Countess of Salisbury.

442

youngest brother, Reginald, dean of Exeter, to the throne, he was convicted of high treason before the Lord Audley (lord chancellor), acting as high steward of England, at Westminster, and was beheaded on Tower Hill, 9 January, 1539, when the Barony of Montagu became FORFEITED. His lordship left by his wife, Jane, dau. of George Nevill, Lord Abergavenny, two daus., his co-heirs, namely,

Katherine, m. to Francis, 2nd Earl of Huntingdon, K.G., lately represented by the MARQUESS OF HASTINGS, one of the co-heirs of the Barony of Montacute.

Winifred, m. 1st, to Sir Thomas Hastings (a younger brother of the Earl of Huntingdon), who *d. s. p.*; and 2ndly, to Sir Thomas Barrington, of Barrington Hall, in Essex, of which latter marriage, WILLIAM LOWNDES, Esq., of Chesham, Bucks, and WILLIAM SELBY LOWNDES, Esq., of Whaddon, in the same co., were the representatives, being as such co-heirs of the BARONY OF MONTACUTE.

In the 1st year of PHILIP and MARY, these ladies being restored in blood and honours, the Barony of Montagu was then placed in ABEYANCE, as it so continues.

Arms—Per pale, or and sa., a saltier engrailed, counterchanged.

PONSONBY—VISCOUNT PONSONBY.

(*See* ADDENDA.)

POPE—EARL OF DOWNE.

By Letters Patent, dated 16 October, 1628.

Lineage.

WILLIAM POPE, Gent., of Dedington, co. Oxford, d. in 1523, having had by Margaret, his wife, two sons,

1. Thomas (Sir), b. at Dedington, about the year 1508, the celebrated Founder of Trinity College, Oxford. He filled, during the reigns of HENRY VIII. and Queen MARY, several high official appointments, and from EDWARD VI received a grant of the manor of Tittenhanger, Herts. He m. three times: his last wife being Elizabeth, eldest dau. of Walter Blount, Esq, and *d. s. p.* in 1559.

II. JOHN, of whom presently.

1. Alice, m. to Edward Love, Esq., of Eynore, co. Oxford, and was mother of

Frances Love, who m. William Blount, Esq., of Osberston, and had a son,

SIR THOMAS POPE BLOUNT, Knt., who eventually *s.* to the manor of Tittenhanger: his descendant, CATHERINE, dau. and heiress of SIR THOMAS POPE BLOUNT, 2nd Baronet of Tittenhanger, m. 1731, the Rev. William Freeman, D.D., and left an only child, CATHERINE, wife of the Right Hon. Charles Yorke, and mother of Philip, 3rd Earl of Hardwicke.

The 2nd son,

JOHN POPE, Esq., of Wroxton, who d. in 1583, m. 1st, Anne Stavely, of Bygnell, and had by her a dau., m. in 1573, to Edward Blount, Esq., of Burton-on-Trent. He m. 2ndly, a dau. of Sir John Brocket, Knt., of Brocket Hall, Herts, by whom he had, with six daus., a son, WILLIAM (Sir), his heir; and 3rdly, a dau. of Sir Edmund Wyndham, by whom he had no issue. His only son,

SIR WILLIAM POPE, K.B., of Wroxton, was created a Baronet of England, 29 June, 1611, and 16 October, 1628, raised to the peerage of Ireland, as Baron of Belturbet, and EARL OF DOWNE. His lordship m. in 1595, Anne, dau. of Sir Owen Hopton, lieutenant of the Tower of London, and relict of Henry, Lord Wentworth, by whom he had two sons, namely,

I. WILLIAM (Sir, Knt.), b. in 1596, who *d. v. p.* in 1624, leaving three sons, viz.,

    THOMAS, successor to his grandfather.
    John, b. in 1623. } *
    William, b. in 1624.

II. THOMAS, who *s.* his nephew as 3rd earl.

The Earl of Downe d. 2 July, 1631, was buried at Wroxton, and was *s.* by his grandson,

SIR THOMAS POPE, Bart., 2nd Earl of Downe, b. at Cogges, in 1622, an active royalist during the civil war; who m. Lucy, dau. of John Dutton, Esq., of Sherborne, and had an only dau. and heir, Elizabeth, m. 1st, to Sir Francis-Henry Lee, Bart.; and 2ndly, to Robert, Earl of Lindsay. Lord Downe d. at Oxford, 28 December, 1660, and was *s.* by his uncle.

SIR THOMAS POPE, Bart., 3rd Earl of Downe, b. at Wroxton, in 1598, who m. in 1636. Beata, dau. of Sir Henry Poole, of Saperton, in Gloucestershire, and had issue,

[*] Mr. Warton inadvertently puts the supposition that one of these was grandfather of Alexander Pope, the poet. From the circumstance that their brother, Thomas, 2nd Earl of Downe, was *s* in the title by his uncle, it is clear that these two gentlemen must have d. without legitimate male issue.

THOMAS, his heir.

Anne, m. to Sir Bryan Boughton, Bart., and d. s. p.

Beata, m. in 1668, to Sir William Soames, Bart., and d. s. p.

Frances, m. to Sir Francis North, the celebrated Lord Keeper, afterwards Lord Guilford, and d. in 1678. leaving issue. The heir-general of this marriage is BARONESS NORTH, present possessor of Wroxton.

Finetta, m. to Robert Hyde, Esq , son of Dr. Hyde, bishop of Salisbury.

The earl d. 11 January, 1667, and was s. by his son,

SIR THOMAS POPE, 4th earl, who d. unm. 18 May, 1668, when all his honours became EXTINCT.

Arms—Per pale, or and az., on a chevron. between three griffins' heads, erased, four fleurs-de-lis, all counterchanged.

POWER—EARL OF TYRONE.

By Letters Patent, dated 9 October, 1673.

Lineage.

SIR ROGER DE LA POER, Knt., who accompanied Strongbow into Ireland, obtained for his services there very considerable territorial grants. Of Sir Roger, Cambrensis writes, " It might be said without offence, that there was not a man who did more valiant acts than Roger le Poer, who, although he were young and beardless, yet he shewed himself a lusty, valiant, and courageous gentleman, and who grew into such good credit, that he had the government of the country about Leighlin, as also in Ossory, where he was traitorously killed; on whose slaughter a conspiracy was formed among the Irish to destroy the English, and many castles were destroyed." Sir Roger m. a niece of Sir Amory St. Laurence (ancestor of the noble house of Howth), and left a son,

JOHN LE POER, from whom descended

NICHOLAS LE POER, who had summons to parliament as BARON LE POER, 23 November, 1375, and thrice afterwards. in 1378, 1381, and 1383, being the most ancient writs to be found in the Rolls' office of Ireland. This nobleman was s. by his son,

RICHARD LE POER, 2nd baron, who was created *Lord Le Poer, Baron of Curraghmore*, by King HENRY VI., in 1452. His lordship m. Catherine, dau. of Sir Richard Butler, Earl of Ormonde, and was s. by his son,

PETER, 3rd Baron Le Poer and 2nd Baron of Curraghmore, who m. the dau. of Lord Decies, and left a son,

RICHARD LE POER, who was re-created 13 September, 1535, *Lord Le Poer, Baron of Curraghmore.* This nobleman m. Catherine, dau. of Pierce, 8th Earl of Ormonde, and was father of

JOHN, Lord Le Poer (More), b. in 1527. Of this nobleman, Sir Henry Sidney, in his account of the province of Munster to the lords of the council, thus writes: " 27 Feb. 15:5. The day I departed from Waterford, I lodged that night at Corragmore, the house that the Lord Power is baron of, where I was so used, and with such plenty and good order entertained (as adding to it the quiet of all the country adjoining, by the people called *Power Country*, for *that* surname has been since the beginning of Englishman's planting inhabitants there), it may be well compared with the best ordered country in the *English Pale.* And the lord of the country, though he be of scope of ground a far less territory than his neighbour is, yet he lives in shew far more honourably and plentifully than he or any other, whatsoever he be, of his calling that lives in this province." His lordship m. Ellen, dau. of James, 15th Earl of Desmond, and left, with a dau. m. to Hon. Peter Butler, a son and heir,

RICHARD LE POER, Lord Le Poer, who m. Catherine, dau. and heiress of John, Viscount Buttevant, and d. 2 August, 1607, having had issue,

I. JOHN (Oge), his heir, who d. v. p.

II. Pierce, of Monalargy. co. Waterford, who m. Catherine, 4th dau. of Walter, Earl of Ormonde.

i. Julia, m. in 1615, Thomas, Lord Kerry.

II Ellen. m. to David Condon, chief of his sept.

III. Elizabeth, m. 1st, to David, Viscount Buttevant; and 2ndly, Patrick, son of Sir John Sherlock, Knt., of Ballina Clarahan, co. Tipperary.

Lord Le Poer was s. by his grandson,

JOHN LE POER, Lord Le Poer (son of John Oge, the late lord's eldest son, who was killed in his father's lifetime, by Edmund Fitzgerald, the *White Knight*), by Helen, dau. of David, Viscount Buttevant). His lordship m. Ruth, dau. and heiress of Robert Pyphoe, Esq. of St. Mary's Abbey, Dublin, and had issue,

I. RICHARD, his successor.

II. Pierce. of Killowen, co. Waterford, who m. Honora, dau. of John, 2nd Lord Brittas. and had a son Richard, who d. in February. 1635, leaving by Ellen, his wife. dau. of William Butler. of Ballboe, co. Tipperary, Gent., John, who m Ellen, dau. of Daniel Magragh, of Mountain Castle, co. Waterford; Pierce ; James; Ellen; and Anne.

III. Robert.

IV. John, d. unm. in Dublin.

V. David, who d. 17 August, 1661, and was buried at St. Michan's.

I. Ellen, m. to Thomas Walsh, Esq., of Piltown.

II. Catherine, m. to John Fitzgerald, Esq., of Dromana. whose only dau., Catharine, was mother of John, Earl of Grandison.

III. Margaret.   IV. Mary.

The eldest son,

RICHARD POWER, Lord Le Poer and Curraghmore. This nobleman was advanced. 9 October, 1673, to the *Viscounty of Decies* and *Earldom of Tyrone.* His lordship m. 1st, in 1654, Dorothy, dau. of Arthur, Earl of Anglesey ; and 2ndly, 20 May, 1673, Catherine, dau. and heir of John Fitzgerald, Esq.. of Dromana and the Decies, which lady m. 2ndly, Edward Fitzgerald-Villiers, Esq. By his 1st wife, his lordship had issue, and dying 14 October, 1690, was s. by his eldest surviving son,

JOHN POWER, 2nd earl; at whose decease, unm., 14 October. 1693, in the twenty-ninth year of his age, the honours devolved upon his brother,

JAMES POWER, 3rd earl, who m. 13 December, 1692, Anne, elder dau. and co-heiress of Andrew Rickards, Esq., of Dangan Spidoge, co. Kilkenny, by whom (who d. 26 September, 1729), he left at his decease, 19 August, 1704, aged thirty-seven, an only dau. and heiress,

LADY CATHARINE, who m. 16 July, 1717, Sir Marcus Beresford, Bart., M.P., created 4 November, 1720, Baron Beresford, and Viscount of Tyrone, and advanced, 18 July, 1746, to the EARLDOM OF TYRONE. (*See* Burke's *Extant Peerage.*)

Upon the decease of James, 3rd earl, the Earldom of Tyrone, and all his other honours, except the original barony by writ, EXPIRED, but that devolved upon his dau., as BARONESS LE POER.

Arms—Arg., a chief indented, sa..

POWER—VISCOUNT VALENTIA.

By Letters Patent, dated 1 March, 1620.

Lineage.

SIR HENRY POWER, Knt., of Bersham, in Denbighshire, constable of the castle of Maryborough, knight mareschal of Ireland, governor of Leix, and a privy councillor, was raised to the Irish peerage, as VISCOUNT VALENTIA, co. Kerry, 1 March, 1620. His lordship m. Grizel, dau. of Sir Richard Bulkeley, Knt. of Beaumaris and Cheadle, but d. s. p. 25 May, 1642, when his peerage became EXTINCT.

POWLETT—BARON BAYNING.

(See TOWNSHEND.)

BOYNINGS—BARONS POYNINGS.

By Writ of Summons, dated 23 April, 1337.

Lineage.

In the time of King HENRY II.,

ADAM DE POYNINGS, of Poynings, co. Sussex, was a benefactor to the monks of Lewes. This Adam left three sons, Adam, William, and John ; the eldest of whom was father of MICHAEL, the father of THOMAS, whose son.

SIR LUKE DE POYNINGS, Lord of Crawley, was father by Isabel, his wife, dau. and co-heir of Robert d'Aguillon, of a son and heir,

SIR MICHAEL DE POYNINGS, who, in the 17th JOHN, adhered to the rebellious barons, and was s. by his son,

THOMAS DE POYNINGS, who held ten knights' fees in Poynings, and had issue, two sons, Michael and Lucas. The elder of whom,

SIR MICHAEL DE POYNINGS, received summons 8 June, 1294 (22nd EDWARD I.), to attend the king, with other great men of the time, in order to advise touching the most important affairs of the realm ; and he had military summons immediately after, to proceed in the expedition against France, which had been the result of that council. He was likewise actively engaged

In the Scottish wars both in the reign of EDWARD I. and in that of EDWARD II. He was *s.* by his son,

THOMAS DE POYNINGS, who was summoned to parliament as a Baron, 23 April, 1337. His lordship *m.* Agnes de Rokesle, one of the co-heirs of John, son of Bartholomew de Cryol, and was slain in the great sea-fight with the French at Sluse, in 1339. He was *s.* by his elder son,

MICHAEL DE POYNINGS, 2nd baron, summoned to parliament from 25 February, 1342, to 24 February, 1368. Upon the decease of the last lord, the king, by his letters patent, dated the 14th of the same month, acknowledging his great valour and eminent merits, and reciting that he was slain in his service, received the homage of the present baron though then under age; and in recompense of those his father's sufferings, not only granted him livery of his lands, but the full benefit of his marriage, taking security for the payment of his relief. This Michael, Lord Poynings, participated in the glories of the reign of EDWARD III., and was amongst the heroes of Cressy. His lordship *m.* Joane, dau. of Sir Richard Rokesley, and widow of Sir John de Molyns, Knt., and *d.* in 1369; he was *s.* by his son,

THOMAS DE POYNINGS, 3rd baron, *b.* 19 April, 1349, who does not appear to have been summoned to parliament. This nobleman *m.* Blanche de Mowbray (who *m.* 2ndly, Sir John de Worthe, Knt., but dying *s. p.* in 1375, was *s.* by his brother,

RICHARD POYNINGS, 4th baron, summoned to parliament from 7 January, 1383, to 3 September, 1385. This no' 'eman *m.* Isabel, dau. and heir of Robert Grey, of Charlton-Grey, co. Somerset, who assumed the surname of FITZ-PAYNE (*see* Fitz-Payne, Barons Fitz-Payne), by his wife, Elizabeth, dau. and co-heir of Sir Guy de Bryan; which Isabel inherited eventually the estates of her maternal grandfather, as well as those of her father. Lord Poynings accompanied John of Gaunt into Spain, and dying there in 1387, was *s.* by his son,

ROBERT DE POYNINGS, 5th baron, summoned to parliament from 25 August, 1404, to 13 January, 1415. This nobleman who was in the French wars of HENRY IV., HENRY V., and HENRY VI., fell at the siege of Orleans in 1446. His lordship *m.* Elizabeth or Eleanor, dau. of Reginald, Lord Grey de Ruthyn, and had two sons, viz.,

RICHARD, who *m.* Alianore, dau. of Sir John Berkeley, of Beverstone, Knt., and dying before his father, 1430, left an only dau. and heir,

Alianore, who *m.* Sir Henry Percy, son and heir of Henry, 2nd Earl of Northumberland, and *d.* 10 February, 1482.

ROBERT, of Est Hall, Faukham-Aske, and Chellesfield (for whom and his descendants, *see* POYNINGS, Baron Poynings, by letters patent).

Upon the decease of Robert, Lord Poynings, his grand-dau., Alianore, became heir to his estates and barony, and her husband,

SIR HENRY PERCY, was summoned to parliament as BARON POYNINGS, from 14 December, 1446, to 26 May, 1455, in which latter year his lordship succeeded to the EARLDOM OF NORTHUMBERLAND; and the BARONY OF POYNINGS, thenceforward shared the fortunes of the superior dignity. With the earldom it was forfeited in 1408—restored in 1414—forfeited in 1461—restored 1471. On the death of Henry, 6th Earl of Northumberland, *s.p.* in 1537, the Barony of Poynings, with the earldom, became EXTINCT, in consequence of the attainder of the earl's brother, Sir Thomas Percy. On the 30 April, 1557, Thomas Percy, son and heir of the attainted Sir Thomas Percy, was created by patent, Baron Percy, of Cockermouth and Petworth, with remainder, failing issue male, to his brother, Henry Percy, and his issue male; and he was shortly afterwards advanced to the dignity of Earl of Northumberland, with the same reversionary grant. This Henry Percy, the person in remainder, inherited the honours, and they remained vested in his descendants, until the demise of JOCELINE, 11th Earl of Northumberland, without male issue, in 1670, when all the honours conferred by the patent to Thomas Percy, became EXTINCT.

Arms—Barry of six, or, and vert, a bend, gu.

POYNINGS—BARON ST. JOHN, OF BASING.

By Writ of Summons, dated 29 December, 1299.

Lineage.

LUCAS DE POYNINGS, younger son of Thomas 1st Lord Poynings, under the writ of EDWARD III., having *m.* in the 23rd EDWARD III., Isabel, widow of Henry de Burghersh, dau. of

444

Hugh de St. John, Lord St. John, of Basing (a barony created by writ in the 28th EDWARD I., *see* St. John), and sister and co-heir of Edmund, Lord St. John, had an assignation of all the lands of her inheritance, and in some years afterwards, on the death of Margaret, the said Isabel's mother, he had a further assignation of the manors of Basing and Shireborne. This Lucas was in the wars of France, and had summons to parliament in his wife's barony (it is supposed) of St. John of Basing, from 24 February, 1368, to 20 January, 1376. His lordship *d.* about the year 1385, and was *s.* by his son,

HUGH DE ST. JOHN, Knt., who obtained license in the 2nd HENRY IV., by the title of LORD ST. JOHN, to go on a pilgrimage to Jerusalem, but was never summoned to parliament. His lordship *m.* four times, and by his first wife, Joan, dau. of Roger, Lord Strange, had an only son,

HUGH, who *m.* 1st, Elizabeth, dau. and heir of Martin Ferrers, of Bere Ferrers; and 2ndly, Eleanor, dau. of John, Lord Welles; he *d. v. p.* in 1426, leaving

JOANE (by first wife), *m.* to Thomas Bonville, and had a son, John.

CONSTANCE (by second wife), who *m.* 1st, John Paulet, and was grandmother of

SIR WILLIAM PAULET, 1st Marquess of Winchester. (*See* BURKE's *Extant Peerage*.)

Constance *m.* 2ndly. Henry Greene, of Drayton, and had a dau., Constance, wife of John Stafford, Earl of Wiltshire.

Alice, *m.* 1st, to John Orrell; and 2ndly, to Sir Thomas Kingeston.

Lord St. John *d.* about the 7th HENRY VI., when his grandchildren above-mentioned became his heirs, and the Barony of St. John, of Basing, fell into ABEYANCE amongst them, as it still continues with their descendants.

POYNINGS—BARON POYNINGS.

By Letters Patent, dated 30 January, 1545.

Lineage.

ROBERT DE POYNINGS, 2nd son of Robert, 5th and last Lord Poynings, of the family, under the writ of EDWARD III. (*see* Poynings, Baron Poynings, by summons), was seized of the manors of East Hall, Faukam-Ayske, and Chellesfield, and was *s.* at his decease, 9th EDWARD IV., by his son,

SIR EDWARD POYNINGS, who, taking an active part in the revolution which placed HENRY VII. upon the throne, was sworn of the privy council to that monarch, and during the whole of the reign enjoyed the king's full confidence. He was one of the chief commanders sent in the 5th HENRY VII., to the assistance of the Emperor MAXIMILIAN, against the French; and he was subsequently despatched at the head of a large force, to put down the supporters of Perkyn Warbeck, in Ireland; of which realm, Sir Edward (10th EDWARD VII.), was made deputy in the absence of Prince Henry, the king's younger son, then lieutenant thereof. In ten years afterwards he was constituted constable of Dover Castle, and was in the same office at HENRY's decease. Sir Edward was the third of eighteen councillors, bequeathed by the king to his successor; a privy council, in which it is said, there was not one lawyer but a complete body of active and experienced men in their own orb. In the 1st HENRY VIII., being then a knight of the Garter, and comptroller of the king's household, he was again made constable of Dover Castle, and warden of the Cinque Ports. In the 5th of the same reign, he was with the king at the siege of Therouenne, at the head of 600 chosen men in the body of the army, and upon the surrender of that place, he was left its governor with a strong garrison. Sir Edward Poynings *m.* Elizabeth, dau. of Sir John Scott, but had no surviving issue. He had, however, by four concubines, three sons and four daus., viz.,

THOMAS (Sir), of whom presently.

Adrian (Sir), Governor of Portsmouth, in 1561. Sir Adrian *d.* in the 13th ELIZABETH, leaving by his wife, Mary, dau. and heir of Sir Owen West, three daus., viz.,

Elizabeth, *m.* to Andrew Rogers, Esq.

Mary, *m.* to Edward More, Esq., of Odiham.

Anne, *m.* to George More, Esq., of Loseley.

Edward, slain at Boloin, in the 38th HENRY VIII.

Jane, *m.* to Thomas Clinton, Lord Clinton.

Margaret, *m.* to Edmund Barry, of Sunnington, co. Kent.

Maria, *m.* to Sir Thomas Wilford, Knt.

Rose, *m.* to Robert Leukenore, of Leigh.

Sir Edward *d.* 14th HENRY VIII. The eldest of the above illegitimate sons,

SIR THOMAS POYNINGS, Knt., was with Charles Brandon, Duke of Suffolk, at the siege of Burcs, in the 36th HENRY VIII., and was despatched with an account of the progress of the siege to the king, who was then before Boloin, at the head of a powerful army. Sir Thomas was graciously received, and, for his gallant services, elevated to the peerage by letters patent, dated 30 January, 1545, as BARON POYNINGS, being at the same time appointed general of the king's whole army at Boloin; after which nothing further is recorded. His lordship *m.* Katherine, dau. and co-heir of John, Lord Marney, and widow of George Ratcliffe, Esq., but had no issue. By this lady he acquired considerable property in the county of Dorset, two parts of which he entailed upon his brothers successively, and after them upon the children of his sisters. He *d.* in 1545, when the Barony of Poynings became EXTINCT.

Arms—Same as the Barons Poynings, by writ.

PRESTON—VISCOUNTS TARA.
By Letters Patent, dated 2 July, 1650.
Lineage.

THE HON. THOMAS PRESTON (2nd son of Christopher, 4th Viscount Gormanston), was appointed a General in the army of the Confederate Catholics of Ireland in 1642, and was created VISCOUNT TARA, *co. Meath*, in the peerage of Ireland, by a patent dated at Ennis, 2 July, 1650. His son and successor,

ANTHONY PRESTON, 2nd Viscount Tara, *m.* Margaret, dau. of Anthony Warren, Esq., of the King's co., and was father of several daus. and a son (with whom the title EXPIRED),

THOMAS PRESTON, 3rd Viscount Tara, who was killed 6 July, 1674, by Sir Francis Blundell, Knt., of the King's co., and his brothers, William and Winwood Blundell. These gentlemen being all, however, acquitted of murder, received his Majesty's pardon in the December of the same year.

In the Carte MSS., Bodleian Library, Oxford, Vol. 42, p. 191, occurs the following Royal Letter with reference to Thomas, last Viscount Tara:—

Whitehall, August 14, 1662.

My Lo. Orrery,—When I came first to Bruges in Flanders, and was far from being in a good condition, I found my Lord of Taragh there, who invited me to his hous where I lodged neer a month till I could provide another place for myself; and during the whole time of my abood in those parts he gave me frequent evidences of his good affection and dutye to me, which I resolved to have requited if he had lived. And therefore since hee and his wife are dead, I must particularly recommend his children to you, and likewise their aunt, Miss Warren, who was there likewise at Bruges, to your care, that they may be out of hand put into the possession of ye severall [   ] which belonging to them, of which you are to advertise the other Lords Justices to the end that you may *all* give effectual orders to the Commissioners to that purpose, and let them know I expect a good account of this business.

Your very affectionate friend,
CHARLES R.

(Endorsed)
"This Ltre. all written with ye King's own hande."

Arms—Or, on a chief, sa., three crescents, gold, a crescent for difference.

PRESTON—BARON TARA.
By Letters Patent, dated 31 July, 1800.
Lineage.

HUGH PRESTON, of Bolton, in the co. of Lancaster, gent. (no described in his son's Funeral Entry, Ulster's Office, vol. 13, p. 137), was father of

JOHN PRESTON, alderman of Dublin and mayor of the city 1653, who in 1665 applied to Richard St. George, Ulster, for a grant of armorial bearings, and requested Ulster, as set forth in the patent, dated 12 September, 17 CHARLES II., "to assign to him such armes and creast as he may lawfully bear without prejudice to any other of that name beinge descended of a family of that surname in ye county of Lancaster." He had a grant under the Act of Settlement, dated 10 July, 1666, of 12,677 acres in Ardsallagh, and other lands in co. Meath and of Emo, and other lands in the Queen's Co., and had a patent for holding fairs at Ballyroan, 29 June and 7 November, every year dated 30 April, 1675. Alderman Preston was M.P. for Navan from 1661 to his death; he *m.* 1st, Mary, dau. of John Morris, of Bolton, co. Lancaster, gent., by whom he had ten children, five sons and two daus. of whom died in his lifetime. The survivors were,

I. PHINEAS, of Ardsallagh, entered Trinity College, Dublin, 21 May, 1666, *m.* Letitia, dau. of Robert Hamond, Esq., of Chertsey, and had an only son,

JOHN, of Ardsallagh, *b.* 1672, entered Trinity College, Dublin, 6 October, 1687, aged 15, whose will, dated 17 April, 1702, was proved 28 April, 1703. He had by Mary, his wife,

PHINEAS, of Ardsallagh, *d. s. p.*
Mary, heiress to her brother, *m.* by licence 31 May, 1710, Peter Ludlow, Esq., M.P. co. Meath, and was mother of PETER LUDLOW, 1st *Earl of Ludlow.*

II. Samuel, of Emo, *m.* Mary, dau. of Theophilus Sandford, Esq., of Moyglare, co. Meath, and *d.* 1692, having had two daus., Anne and Mary, the elder of whom,

ANNE, heiress of Emo, *m.* Ephraim Dawson, Esq., of Dawson's Grove, and was mother of WILLIAM HENRY, 1st *Viscount Carlow*, whose son, JOHN, 2nd viscount, was created, 1785, *Earl of Portarlington.*

III. Mary, *m.* 1st, Rev. Edward Baynes, of Dublin; and 2ndly, Nehemiah Donellan, Esq., councellor-at-law, son of Sir James Donellan, lord chief justice of common pleas. She *d.* 26 September, 1684, and was buried at Christ Church Cathedral, Dublin.

He *m.* 2ndly, Katherine, dau. of John Ashburnham, Esq., and widow of Sir John Sherlock, Knt., by whom he had no issue; and 3rdly, Anne, dau. of Alderman Richard Tighe, of Dublin, and widow of Theophilus Sandford, Esq., of Moyglare, by whom he had,

IV. JOHN, of whom hereafter.

V. Nathaniel, who had a son, Nathaniel.

Mr. Preston *d.* at Ardsallagh, 13 July, 1686, and was buried at Christ Church Cathedral. His eldest son by his third wife, JOHN PRESTON, Esq., of Balsoon, *b.* 23 April, 1677, M.P. co. Meath, *m.* by licence 10 February, 1698, Lydia, dau. of Joseph Pratt, Esq., of Cabra, co. Cavan, by whom (who *d.* 5 February, 1714) he had,

I. JOHN, his heir.

II. Joseph, major in Gen. Bligh's regiment of horse, *m.* 5 December, 1747, Frances, dau. of Henry Sandford, Esq., of Castlerea, co. Roscommon, and widow of Michael Cuffe, Esq., M.P., co. Mayo, *d. s. p.*; his will, dated 23 October, 1753, was proved 9 May, 1754.

III. Nathaniel, of Swainstown, M.P. for Navan, ancestor of PRESTON, *of Swainstown* (*see* BURKE'S *Landed Gentry*).

Mr. Preston *m.* 2ndly, by licence of 11 October, 1720, Henrietta, dau. of Sir Thomas Taylor, 1st Bart. of Kells, by whom (who *d.* 15 January, 1729) he had three daus.,

I. Henrietta.

II. Sophia.

III. Sarah.

Mr. Preston *d.* 23 September, 1732, and was *s.* by his eldest son, JOHN PRESTON, Esq., of Bellinter, *b.* 25 January, 1700, M.P. for Navan; *m.* by licence 21 January, 1731, Alice, dau. of Peter Ludlow, Esq., of Ardsallagh, M.P, co. Meath, and sister of Peter, 1st Earl of Ludlow, and by her (who *d.* 7 January, 1778) had issue,

I. JOHN, his heir.

II. Joseph, of Dublin, M.P. for Navan 1761 to 1769.

Mr. Preston *d.* 27 December, 1753, and was *s.* by his eldest son, JOHN PRESTON, Esq., of Bellinter, M.P. for Navan, *m.* 25 April, 1758, Mary, dau. of James Smyth, Esq., of Tinny Park, co. Wicklow, M.P., sister of Right Hon. Sir Edward Skeffington Smyth, Bart., and granddau. of Right Rev. Edward Smyth, Bishop of Down and Connor, by whom he had issue,

I. JOHN, his heir, created *Lord Tara.*

II. James, *d. s. p.*

III. JOSEPH (Rev.), *s.* to Bellinter on the death of his brother, Lord Tara; *m.* Mary, dau. of Godfrey Massy, Esq., of Ballywire, co. Tipperary; and *d.* 1839, having had issue,

 1 JOHN JOSEPH, of Bellinter, *b.* 1815: *m.* 1842, Sarah, dau. of Denis O'Meagher, Esq., of Kilmoyler, by whom he had one dau.,

  Helen Maria Agnes, *m.* 6 June, 1865, John Joseph Roche Kelly, Esq., of Rockstown Castle, co. Limerick; and *d.* 28 July, 1873.

 2 Francis, *d.* 1834.

 3 Joseph, *d.* 1841, lost on board the "Thames" steamer.

 4 Skeffington (Rev.), rector of Drumconda.

 5 James, *d.* 1841, lost on board the "Thames" steamer.

 6 Mary-Jane, *m.* 1835, Rev. John Dixon Manghan.

IV. Skeffington (Rev.), *d.* 1842.

V. Francis, *d.* 1841.

I. Mary, *m.* 1801, James Falls, Esq.

II. Elizabeth, *m.* 29 December, 1794, Hon. Henry Forbes, 2nd son of the 5th Earl of Granard.

III. Emma.

Mr. Preston *d.* 19 January, 1781, and was *s.* by his eldest son, JOHN PRESTON, Esq., of Bellinter, *b.* 1764; M.P. for Navan, who was created a peer of Ireland, as BARON TARA of Bellinter, co. Meath, by letters patent, dated 31 July, 1800. Lord Tara *m.* 1801, Harriet, dau. of Thomas Jelf Powys, Esq., of Berwick House, co. Salop, and *d. s. p.* 1821, when the title became extinct, and his estates passed to his brother, Rev. Joseph Preston.

Arms—Ermines on a chief, arg., three crescents gu.

PULTENEY—EARL OF BATH.

By Letters Patent, dated 14 July, 1742.

Lineage.

Sir William Pulteney, Knt., of Misterton, co. Leicester (of very ancient descent), one of the leading members of the House of Commons, *temp.* Charles II., *m.* Grace, dau. of Sir John Corbett, Bart., of Stoke, and had issue, 1 William, his heir; 2 John (father, by Lucy, his wife, of Daniel); 1 Catherine, *m.* to Sir Charles Heron, Bart.; and 2 Anne, *m.* to Charles, Duke of Cleveland. The eldest son,

William Pulteney, Esq., *m.* 1st, Mary Floyd, and 2ndly, Arabella, dau. of George, Earl of Berkeley: by the latter he left two daus., Arabella and Elizabeth, and by the former four sons, William, Henry, Corbet, and Thomas, who all *d. s. p.* The eldest son,

William Pulteney, Esq., was the popular statesman of the reigns of the two first sovereigns of the House of Brunswick. In 1714, Mr. Pulteney was appointed Secretary of State, an office which he resigned in 1717. In 1723 he was made cofferer of the household, and sworn of the privy council; but he re-signed again in 1725. In the reign of George II., he was leader of the opposition to the administration of Sir Robert Walpole, and so keenly was his eloquence felt by the court, that his name was erased in 1731 from the list of privy councillors. That proceeding having no other effect, however, than ren dering Pulteney more popular, Sir Robert, at length, discovered that the only manner in which he could hope to triumph over so gifted a rival, was to cajole him into the acceptance of a peerage; and for that purpose the following letter was written to his royal master:—

"Most Sacred,

"The violence of the fit of the stone, which has tormented me for some days, is now so far abated, that although it will not permit me to have the honour to wait on your majesty, yet is kind enough to enable me so far to obey your orders, as to write my sentiments concerning that troublesome man, Mr. Pulteney; and to point out (what I conceive to be) the most effectual method to make him perfectly quiet. Your majesty well knows, how, by the dint of his eloquence, he has so captivated the mob, and attained an unbounded popularity, that the most manifest wrong, appears to be right, when adopted and urged by him. Hence it is, that he has become not only trouble-some but dangerous. The inconsiderate multitude think he has not one object but the public good in view; although, if they would reflect a little, they would soon perceive, that spleen against those your majesty has honoured with your confidence, has greater weight with him than patriotism. Since, let any measure be proposed, however salutary, if he thinks it comes from me, it is sufficient for him to oppose it. Thus, Sir, you see the affairs of the most momentous concern are subject to the caprice of that popular man; and he has nothing to do, but to call it a ministerial project, and bellow out the word *favourite,* to half an hundred pens drawn against it, and a thou-s-nd mouths open to contradict it. Under these circumstances he bears up against the ministry (and, let me add, against your majesty itself); and every useful scheme must be either abandoned, or if it is carried in either house, the public are made to believe it is done by a corrupted majority. Since then things are thus circumstanced, it is become necessary for the public tranquillity, that he should be made quiet; and the only method to do that effectually, is to destroy his popularity, and ruin the good belief the people have it, him.

"In order to do this, he must be invited to court; your majesty must condescend to speak to him in the most favour-able and distinguished manner; you must make him believe that he is the only person upon whose opinion you can rely, and to whom your people look up for useful measures. As he has already several times refused to take the lead in the adminis-tration, unless it was totally modelled to his fancy, your majesty should close in with his advice, and give him leave to arrange the administration as he pleases, and put whom he chooses into office (there c n be no danger in that, as you can dismiss him when you think fit); and when he has got thus far (to which his extreme self-love, and the high opinion he entertains of his own import nce, will easily conduce), it will be necessary that your majesty should seem to have a great regard for his health; signifying to him, that your affairs will be ruined if he should die; and that you want to have him constantly near you, to have his sage advice; and that, therefore, as he is much disordered in body, and something infirm, it will be necessary for his preservation, for him to quit the House of Commons, where malevolent tempers will be continually fretting him; and where indeed, his presence will be needless,

as no step will be taken but according to his advice; and that he will let you give him a distinguished mark of your approba-tion, by creating him a peer. This he may be brought to; for if I know anything of mankind, he has a love of honour and money; and notwithstanding his great haughtiness and seeming contempt for honour, he may be won, if it be done with dexterity. For as the poet Fenton says,

'Flattery is an oil that softens the thoughtless fool.'

"If your majesty can once bring him to accept of a coronet, all will be over with him; the changing multitude will cease to have any confidence in him; and when you see that, your majesty may turn your back to him, dismiss him from his post, turn out his meddling partizans, and restore things to quiet; for then if he complains, it will be of no avail; the bee will have lost his sting, and become an idle drone, whose buzzing nobody heeds.

"Your majesty will pardon me for the freedom with which I have given my sentiments and advice; which I should not have done, had not your majesty commanded it, and had I not been certain that your peace is much disturbed by the con-trivance of that turbulent man. I shall only add, that I will dispose several whom I know to wish him well, to solicit for his establishment in power, that you may seem to yield to their entreaties, and the finesse be less liable to be discovered.

"I hope to have the honour to attend your majesty in a few days: which I will do privately, that my public presence may give him no umbrage.

(Signed)   "Robert Walpole."

"24th January, 1741."

In this scheme the king acquiesced, and William Pulteney having been restored to the privy council. was created by letters patent, dated 14 July, 1742, *Baron of Heydon, co. York, Viscount Pulteney, of Wrington, in Somersetshire,* and Earl of Bath. His lordship *m.* Anna-Maria, dau. of John Gumley, Esq., of Isleworth, co. Middlesex, by whom he had a son, William, Viscount Pulteney, who *d. unm., v. p., anno* 1763; he had likewise a dau., who *d.* in 1741, at the age of fourteen. The earl *d.* in 1764. when failing male issue, all his honours became extinct. His lordship's great estates devolved on his brother, General Henry Pulteney, who *d.* in 1765, and was *s.* in the Pulteney property by his cousin Frances, dau. of Daniel Pulteney, Esq., son of John Pulteney, Esq., uncle of the Earl of Bath. This lady, Frances Pulteney, was wife of William Johnstone, Esq., who took the name of Pulteney, and *s.* his brother as 5th baronet of Westerhall: their only dau. and co-heiress, Henrietta-Laura Johnstone, who assumed the name of Pulteney, was created Baroness of Bath with limitation to the barony to her male issue, 26 July, 1792, and Countess of Bath, with similar limitation 26 October, 1806. Her ladyship *m.* Sir James Murray, Bart., and *d. s. p.* 14 August, 1808, when her titles also became extinct.

Arms—Arg., a fesse indented, gu., in chief, three leopards' heads, sa.

PULTENEY—BARONESS BATH, COUNTESS OF BATH.

Barony, by Letters Patent, dated 23 July. 1792.
Earldom, by Letters Patent, dated 26 October, 1803.

Lineage.

Sir William Johnstone, Bart., of Westerhall, co. Dum-fries, *m.* Frances, dau. and heir of Daniel Pulteney, Esq., first cousin of William, Earl of Bath (which lady was eventually heiress to his lordship's estates), and had an only dau.,

Henrietta-Laura Johnstone, who, succeeding to the great Pulteney fortune, assumed the surname and arms of Pul-teney, and was elevated to the peerage, 26 July, 1792, as Baroness Bath, with limitation to the dignity of Baron Bath to her issue male. Her ladyship was created Countess of Bath, with a similar reversion of the Earldom of Bath, by letters patent, dated 26 October, 1803. She *m.* General Sir James Murray, Bart., who adopted likewise the name of Pul-teney, but had no issue. The Countess *d.* in 1808, when the Barony and Earldom of Bath both became extinct.

Arms—Arg., a fesse indented, gu., in chief, three leopards' heads, sa.

Radcliffe.
(E.Derwentwater.)

Rich.
(E.Warwick.)

Roche.
(V.Fermoy.)

Savage.
(E.Rivers.)

Saville.
(M.Halifax.)

Scales.
(B.Scales.)

Scrope.
(E.Sunderland.)

Segrave.
(B.Segrave.)

Seton.
(E.Winton.)

Stafford.
(D.Buckingham.)

Strange.
(B.Strange.)

Sutton.
(B.Dudley.)

QUEROUAILLE — DUCHESS OF PORTS-MOUTH.

By Letters Patent, dated 19 August, 1673.

Lineage.

In the retinue of Henrietta, Duchess of Orleans, sister of King CHARLES II., came to the court of St. James's, a young French lady,

LOUISE RENÉE DE PERRENCOURT DE QUEROUAILLE, who, captivating the English monarch. CHARLES II., was mother, by his Majesty, of a son, CHARLES LENNOX, DUKE OF RICHMOND, founder of the present noble house of Richmond, and was created FOR LIFE, by letters patent, dated 19 August, 1673, *Baroness Petersfield, Countess of Fareham*, and DUCHESS OF PORTSMOUTH, all in Hampshire. Her grace being of a noble family in Britanny, LOUIS XIV., in 1684, conferred upon her the DUCHY OF AUBIGNY. a dignity still held by the Dukes of Richmond. The duchess, to whom CHARLES II. was strongly attached during the whole course of his life, proved a great means of supporting that monarch's connection with her native country of France. "A life of frivolity and vice," says Macaulay, "had not extinguished in the Duchess of Portsmouth all sentiments of religion, or all that kindness, which is the glory of her sex." At the death-bed of King CHARLES, she stood in an agony of grief, and it was by her intercession and entreaty alone that the dying monarch received the last consolation of religion. She d. at an advanced age at Paris, in the year 1734.

Arms—Az., three bars, arg.

QUINCY—EARLS OF WINCHESTER.

By Creation of King JOHN, about the year 1210.

Lineage.

In the reign of King HENRY II.,

SAIER DE QUINCY had a grant from the crown, of the manor of Bushby, co. Northampton, formerly the property of Anselme de Conchis. He *m.* Maud de St. Liz, and had two sons,

Robert, a soldier of the cross, and one of the companions in arms of RICHARD CŒUR DE LION.

And

SAIER DE QUINCY, who was created EARL OF WINCHESTER, by King JOHN. This nobleman was one of the lords present at Lincoln, when WILLIAM, King of Scotland, did homage to the English monarch, and he subsequently obtained large grants and immunities from King JOHN; when, however, the baronial war broke out, his lordship's pennant waived on the side of freedom, and he became so eminent amongst those sturdy chiefs, that he was chosen one of the celebrated twenty-five barons, appointed to enforce the observance of Magna Charta. Adhering to that same party, after the accession of HENRY III., the Earl of Winchester had a principal command at the battle of Lincoln, and there being defeated, he was taken prisoner by the royalists. But submitting in the following October, he had restitution of all his lands; and proceeded soon after, in company with the Earls of Chester and Arundel, and others of the nobility, to the Holy Land, where he assisted at the siege of Damietta, *anno* 1219, and *d.* in the same year, in his progress towards Jerusalem. His lordship *m.* Margaret, younger sister and co-heir of Robert Fitz-Parnell, Earl of Leicester, by which alliance he acquired a very considerable inheritance, and had issue,

Robert, who *d.* in the Holy Land. leaving issue by his wife, Hawyse, dau. of Hugh Keveliok, Earl of Chester, an only dau..

Margaret. who *m.* 1st, John de Lacie, Earl of Lincoln ; and 2ndly, Walter, Earl of Pembroke.

Mabel, *m.* to Hugh Audley.

ROGER, successor to the earldom.
Robert, *m.* the Princess Helen, widow of John Scot, Earl of Huntingdon, and 8th Earl Palatine of Chester, who *d. s. p.*, June, 1244 (brother of WILLIAM THE LION, King of Scotland). By this princess, who was eldest dau. of Llewelyn the Great, Prince of North Wales, by his 3rd consort, Joan, illegitimate dau. of JOHN King of England, Robert de Quincy, who *d.* 41st HENRY III.. 1257, in the tournament at Blie, had three daus and co-heirs,

447

1 Anne a nun.
2 Joane, *m.* to Humphrey de Bohun, the younger.
3 Margaret, *m.* to Baldwin Wake, a powerful feudal lord, and by him, who *d.* in 1282, was mother of John Wake, summoned to parliament as a Baron, 1 October, 1295.

At the decease of the earl, his 2nd son,

ROGER DE QUINCY (his elder brother being still in the Holy Land,) had livery of his father's estates, and he subsequently *s.* to the Earldom of Winchester. This nobleman marrying Helen, eldest dau. and co-heir of Alan, Lord of Galloway, became, in her right, constable of Scotland. By this lady he had issue,

Margaret, *m.* to William de Ferrers, Earl of Derby, and brought to her husband the Manor and Barony of Groby.
Elizabeth, *m.* to Alexander Comyn, Earl of Buchan. in Scotland.
Ela, *m.* to Alan, Lord Zouch, of Ashby.

His lordship *m.* 2ndly, Maud, dau. of Humprey de Bohun, Earl of Hereford (widow of Anselme Mareschall, Earl of Pembroke), and 3rdly, Alianore, dau. of William de Ferrers, Earl of Derby, and widow of William de Vaux (this lady survived the earl, and *m.* after his decease, Roger de Leybourne). Dugdale says, that the earl had another dau., but by which wife he could not discover, namely,

Isabell. with whom a contract of marriage was made, by John, son of Hugh de Nevil, for his son, Hugh.

His lordship *d.* in 1264, when the Earldom of Winchester became EXTINCT, and his great landed possessions devolved upon his daus., as co-heiresses.

Arms—Robert de Quincy—or, a fesse, gu, a label of twelve points, az. Roger de Quincy—gu., seven mascles, or, three, three, and one. The arms of Quincy, Earl of Winchester. are mentioned by Habingdon, as in the church of Ribbesford, Worcestershire.

RADCLIFFE — EARLS OF DERWENTWATER.

By Letters Patent, dated 7 March, 1688.

Lineage.

The Radcliffes, of Derwentwater, were one of the oldest families in Cumberland. In that county, beyond Hay Castle, the river Derwent, runs along the mountains, called Derwent-Fells. and " spreads itself into a spacious lake wherein are three islands : one the seat of the family of Radcliffe, Knt., *temp.* HENRY V., who *m.* Margaret, dau. and heir of Sir John de Derwentwater, Knt.; another inhabited by miners; and the third supposed to be that wherein Bede mentions St. Herbert to have led a hermit's life." From the time of the CONQUEST, up to the reign of HENRY III., the castle of Dilston was possessed by the family bearing the local name, and, after having passed through many hands, the Tynedales, the Crafters, and the Claxtons, at length devolved on the Radcliffes, in the person of Sir Nicholas Radcliffe, who *m.* the heiress of the Derwentwaters.

SIR FRANCIS RADCLYFFE, Baron of Dilston, co. Northumberland, was elevated to the peerage by King JAMES II., as *Baron Tyndale, Viscount Radcliffe and Langley*, and EARL OF DERWENTWATER. His lordship *m.* Catherine, dau. and heir of Sir William Fenwick, of Meldon, co. Northumberland, and had issue,

I. FRANCIS, Viscount Radcliffe, his successor.
II. Edward, *d. unm.*
III. Thomas, a military officer.
IV. William.   V. Arthur.
I. Anne, *m.* to Sir Philip Constable, Knt., of Flamborough, in Yorkshire.
II. Catherine.   III. Elizabeth.   IV. Mary.

His lordship *d.* in 1696, and was *s.* by his eldest son,

FRANCIS RADCLIFFE, 2nd earl, who had *m.* in his father's life-time. Mary Tudor, natural dau. of King CHARLES II., by Mrs. Mary Davis, and had issue,

JAMES, Viscount Radcliffe, his successor.
Francis, *d. s. p.*
CHARLES. of whom hereafter.
Mary-Tudor.

His lordship *d.* in April, 1705, and was *s.* by his eldest son,

JAMES RADCLIFFE, 3rd earl. This ill-fated nobleman who became the victim of his steadfast, though misguided loyalty, embarked with his brother Charles in the attempt to place the CHEVALIER ST. GEORGE upon the throne. He was a perfect cavalier, and a fine specimen of an English nobleman; amiable, brave, open, generous, hospitable, and humane, "of so universal a benefic-ence that he seemed to live for others." He gave bread to multitudes of people whom he employed upon his estate; the poor, the widow, the orphan, rejoiced in his bounty. Having been taken prisoner, he was sent to the Tower of London, and, having been soon afterwards found guilty of high treason, was, when only twenty-eight years of age, beheaded on Tower Hill, 24 February, 1715-16, when all his honours became FORFEITED. The best authenticated account affirms that the earl was buried in the church of St. Giles-in-the-Fields, but there is also a tradition extant of his having found his last resting place at Dilstone: but let Derwentwater's bones be where they may, his memory is still cherished by the people, and lives in many a rude ballad: the exquisitely touching lament, *Farewell to Lochaber*, is said to have been written by the earl, and addressed to his wife, on the eve of his departure for the miserable venture wherein he forfeited life, lands, and nobility. His lordship left a young and beautiful widow, Anna-Maria, the dau. of Sir John Webb, Bart., and two infant children to deplore his untimely fate, and suffer by his attainder. Those children were,

JOHN, Viscount Radcliffe, *d.* in 1731.
Mary, *m.* 1732, Robert-James, 8th Lord Petre.

His lordship's brother,
CHARLES RADCLIFFE, one of the most unbending adherents of the house of Stuart, took a prominent part in those stirring times. He was made prisoner at Preston, 14 November, 1715, and being transferred to London, was condemned for high treason. After his conviction, in 1716, he received several reprieves from time to time, and probably on account of his youth, and the government wishing to shed no more of the blood of his house, he would have been pardoned, but he and thirteen others made their escape from Newgate 11 December, 1716, and thus placed themselves beyond the benefit even of the general act of grace which was passed about that time. Radcliffe, on reaching the continent, went to Rome, and obtained a small pension from the Chevalier; he then settled in Paris, and there became, in 1724, the 2nd husband of Charlotte-Maria, Countess of Newburgh, in her own right. By her he had two sons: I. James-Bartholomew Radcliffe, Earl of Newburgh (father of an only son, Anthony-James, Earl of Newburgh who *d. s. p.* 29 November, 1814); II. James-Clement, *d. s. p.*; and four daus., the youngest of whom, Lady Mary, *m.* Francis Eyre, Esq., of Hassop (*refer to* BURKE'S *Peerage*). In 1731, on the death of his nephew, John, Viscount Radcliffe, called Earl of Derwentwater, Charles Radcliffe assumed the title of EARL OF DERWENTWATER, though attainted. Twice, during his exile, he came to London, and, though his presence was known to government, his visits passed unmolested. The rising of 1745 brought him again into action. Still adhering to the fortunes of the Stuarts, he embarked from Calais, in the November of that year, on board the "Espérance," a French man-of-war, or privateer, with his son, and with some other officers, and a quantity of ammunition of war, to join CHARLES-EDWARD. The vessel, no doubt bound for Scotland in aid of the insurgents (though there was no legal proof given of the fact) was seized in open sea by the "Sheerness" man-of-war, and brought to Deal. Radcliffe and his son were immediately committed to the Tower. The son being deemed a foreigner, was exchanged on the first cartel; but Radcliffe himself was confined till the rebellion was over, when, in Michaelmas term, 1746, he was brought to the bar of the court of King's Bench, to have execution awarded against him under his former sentence. He pleaded that he was not the same person as the party convicted, and prayed time to bring witnesses; but as he would not deny, in his affidavit relative to the absence of witnesses, that he was the attainted Charles Radcliffe, the court proceeded, and decided against his plea. He then wished to plead the general pardon of 1716, but the court (one judge, Sir Michael Foster, dissenting) would hear no further plea, and the prisoner was ordered for execution. Though then, legally, no nobleman, regard was so far paid to the rank and station of his family that he did not undergo the, in those days, ordinary and horrible punishment for treason, but, like his brother, the Earl of Derwentwater, he was decapitated on Tower Hill, 8 December, 1746. He behaved at his execution with dignified calmness and courage. This ill-starred Charles Radcliffe was the mainspring of the support his house gave to the Chevalier; he and his brother, the earl, besides their lives, lost in the cause £300,000 in real value. A book, entitled, *Impartial Memoirs of the Life and Character of Charles Radcliffe, Secretary to the Young Pretender*, with a portrait, was published in London, 1746.

448

The EARLDOM OF DERWENTWATER fell under the attainder of JAMES, the 3rd earl; if it had been, however, restored to the male heir of Charles Radcliffe, JAMES-BARTHOLOMEW, 3rd Earl of Newburgh, it would have became EXTINCT upon the decease of that nobleman's son and successor, ANTHONY-JAMES, 4th Earl of Newburgh, without male issue, in 1814, unless there remain some male descendants of Thomas, William, and Arthur, the younger sons of FRANCIS, the 1st earl.

Arms—Ar., a bend engrailed, sa.

RAMSAY—LORD OF BOTHWELL.

Lineage.

SIR JOHN RAMSAY, Lord of Bothwell, was son of John Ramsay, of Corstoun, descended from the house of Carnock, in Fife, by Janet Napier, his wife, who afterwards *m.* John Wilson, burgess of Edinburgh. His genius and accomplishments recommended him to the notice of King JAMES III., and he was the only one of the favourites of that monarch that escaped execution at Lauder, July, 1482, owing his safety to his clasping the person of JAMES, and jumping behind him on horseback. His Majesty bestowed on him the lands, barony, and lordship of Bothwell, in Lanarkshire, together with 40 marks of land of the Barony of Monipennie, which fell into the king's hand by recognition, and he sat in parliament as a peer, by the title of LORD BOTHWELL. His lordship was ambassador from JAMES III. to England, 1486; and in 1487 was employed in arranging a treaty of peace between the two kingdoms. His attachment to King JAMES III. occasioned his proscription; he was FORFEITED in the parliament held at Edinburgh by King JAMES IV., 8 October, 1488; and the lordship of Bothwell was conferred on Patrick, Lord Hales, created Earl of Bothwell, 17 October, 1488. The forfeited lord fled to England, and entered into a nefarious scheme with HENRY VII. to deliver into his hands the King of Scots and his brothers. Eventually, however, in 1498, he received a royal pardon under the simple recognition of John Ramsay, and obtained, at the same time, some lands including the Barony of Balmain, co. Kincardine, which gave designation to his descendants, the RAMSAYS of Balmain, Baronets of Nova Scotia.

Arms—Arg., an eagle displayed, sa., beaked and membered, gu., charged on the breast with a rose of the field.

RAMSAY — VISCOUNT HADDINGTON AND EARL OF HOLDERNESS.

Viscounty, by Letters Patent, dated 11 June, 1606.
Earldom, by Letters Patent, dated 22 January, 1621.

Lineage.

SIR JOHN RAMSAY, of an ancient Scottish family (brother of George, 1st Lord Ramsay, of Dalhousie, *see* BURKE'S *Peerage*: DALHOUSIE), was one of the pages of honour of King JAMES (VI.) I., and had the good fortune to be one of the chief agents in the preservation of King JAMES VI from the attempt of the Earl of Gowrie and his brother, Alexander Ruthven, at Perth, in August, 1600. His Majesty had been induced by Alexander Ruthven to accompany him to the Earl of Gowrie's house at Perth, and soon after his arrival had been murderously attacked by Ruthven. At the moment young Ramsay, the page, happened to be hurrying to the stable for his horse, and heard the King crying, from the window of Gowrie's house, "Treason! murder!" The royal attendants, who had rushed up the principal staircase to his assistance, found the doors locked, but Ramsay fortunately entered the room by a back stair, and perceiving Alexander Ruthven struggling with the king, drew his dagger, plunged it twice into Alexander's body, and then threw him down stairs, where he was met by Sir Thomas Erskine and Hugh Harris, the king's physician, who dispatched him, and went up to the king. Just then the Earl of Gowrie rushed into the apartment, with a sword in each hand, followed by six of his attendants completely armed, but was met by Ramsay, Erskine, and Harris, and after a mortal struggle, was slain. For these acceptable services, Ramsay, rewarded with knighthood, had the Barony of Eastbarns, co. Haddington, conferred on him, and had a charter of the same, 15 November, 1600. He was also created VISCOUNT OF HADDINGTON, and LORD RAMSAY, of Barns, 11

June, 1606; and had an augmentation of honour to his arms, viz.: an arm holding a naked sword with a crown on the middle thereof, and a heart at the point, with the motto, "*Hæc dextra vindex Principis et patriæ.*" Upon the accession of King James to the throne of England, his lordship accompanied his royal master to London, and in some years afterwards, 22 January, 1621, was made a peer of the king's new dominions, by the titles of *Baron Kingston upon Thames*, and Earl of Holderness, with this especial addition to the honour, that annually, on 5 August (the thanksgiving day for the king's deliverance from the Earl of Gowrie and his brother), he and his heirs male should bear the sword of state before the king, in the solemnization of that day's service. His lordship *m.* 1st, 9 February, 1608, Lady Elizabeth Ratcliffe, dau. of Robert, Earl of Sussex, by whom he had no surviving issue. He *m.* 2ndly, Martha, 3rd dau. of Alderman (Sir William) Cockayne, of the city of London, and of Rushton, co. Northampton, but by her (who *m.* 2ndly, Montagu, Earl of Lindsay) had no issue. As he died without leaving issue in February, 1625, his titles became EXTINCT.

Arms—Two coats, per pale; 1st, arg., an eagle, displayed, sa., beaked and membered, gu., on his breast a crescent of the field; 2nd, azure, issuing out of the sinister part of the escutcheon, or, an arm holding in a dexter hand a sword erected, arg., hilted and pommelled, or; piercing a man's heart, gu., the point supporting an imperial crown, ppr. This coat was granted in honour of his service to King James VI.

RANDOLPH—EARL OF MORAY.

Created about 1312.

Lineage.

The 1st Earl of Moray was the renowned
Sir Thomas Randolph, the warrior, statesman, and patriot of a very memorable period of Scottish history. He was nephew of Robert Bruce, being the son of Lady Isabel Bruce, that monarch's sister by her husband, Thomas Randolph, Lord of Strathnith. Our confined space permits but a passing reference to Randolph's capture by assault of the castle of Edinburgh, in 1313, and to his glorious participation in the victory of Bannockburn in 1314. On that famous field, he commanded a division of the Scottish army, and mainly contributed to the successful issue of the day. Subsequently, he accompanied Edward Bruce to Ireland, in principal command of the Scotch troops, and displayed his usual military ability in that campaign. He returned to Scotland before the disastrous battle of Dundalk, in which Edward Bruce was slain; and not long after was sent at the head of a large army, across the Border, with the object ot compelling Edward to raise the siege of Berwick. This object was effectually performed by the defeat at Mitton, in Yorkshire, of the troops collected by the archbishop of York. At the death of his uncle, Robert Bruce, Randolph became Regent of Scotland, and guardian of the young King David, and applied himself with great vigour to the internal settlement of the kingdom. At length, in 1332, while leading the Scottish army to provide against the threatened descent of Baliol, he *d.* at Musselburgh, 20 July in that year. The Earl of Moray *m.* Isabel, only dau. of Sir John Stewart, of Bonkyl, and had issue,

Thomas,⎫
John, ⎬ successively earls.
Agnes, of whom hereafter.

The elder son,
Thomas Randolph, 2nd Earl of Moray, adopting, like his illustrious father, the profession of arms, fell in action at Duplin, 12 August, 1332, just twenty-three days after the late earl's decease: dying *unm.*, he was *s.* by his brother,
John Randolph, 3rd Earl of Moray, also a great warrior of his time, who commanded the first body of the Scottish army at Halidon Hill, 19 July, 1333, and, escaping from the carnage of that dreadful day, fled to France. Returning to Scotland the next year, he resumed his military career, and in 1342, invaded England, King David II., serving as a volunteer under him, and in 1346 (17 October) fell in command of the right wing of the Scots at the battle of Durham. He *m.* Isabel, dau. of Sir Alexander Stewart, of Bonkyl, but *d. s. p.*, whereupon the Earldom of Moray was assumed by his lordship's sister,
Agnes, wife of Patrick Dunbar, 10th Earl of Dunbar and March, who took in her right, the title of Earl of Moray. This great heiress is memorable for her successful defence at the castle of Dunbar against the English. She *d. circa* 1369,

leaving two sons, George, Earl of Dunbar and March, and John, Earl of Moray. The 2nd son,
John Dunbar, obtained, 9 March, 1371-2, from Robert II., a charter confirmatory of the whole Earldom of Moray. He fought at Otterburn, and was killed in a tournament in 1394. He *m.* Marjory, dau. of King Robert II., and left with a dau., Mabella, Countess of Sutherland, two sons, Thomas and Alexander, of Frendraught. The elder son,
Thomas Dunbar, Earl of Moray, was at the battle of Homildon Hill, and was there taken prisoner by the English in 1402: his son,
Thomas Dunbar, Earl of Moray, was one of the hostages for King James I., 31 May, 1421 and 13 December, 1423. He was *s.* by his cousin,
James Dunbar, Earl of Moray (son of Alexander, of Frendraught), who *m.* Lady Janet Gordon, and had two daus., Janet, styled "Countess of Moray," *m.* to James, 2nd Lord Crichton, and Mary. The Earl of Moray *d.* without male issue, in 1430, when the husband of the dau. of Earl Thomas, Lady Elizabeth Dunbar,
Archibald Douglas, (3rd son of the 7th Earl of Douglas) obtained the Earldom of Moray. This nobleman joining his brother, the Earl of Douglas, in arms against James II., fell at Arkinholm, 1 May, 1455, and was afterwards attainted, when the Earldom of Moray became vested in the crown of Scotland.

Arms—Or, three cushions within a double tressure flory, counterflory, gu.

RATCLIFFE—BARONS AND VISCOUNT FITZ-WALTER, EARLS OF SUSSEX.

Barony, orignally, by Writ of Summons dated 23 June, 1295.
Barony, to the Ratcliffes, by Writ of Summons, dated 15 September, 1485.
Viscounty, by Letters Patent, dated 18 June, 1525.
Earldom, by Letters Patent, dated 28 December, 1529.

Lineage.

The family of Ratcliffe or Radcliffe took its name from the village of Radcliffe, near Bury, in Lancashire, one of decidedly Saxon origin.
Richard de Radclyffe, of Radclyffe Tower, co. Lancaster, seneschal and minister of the forests of Blackburnshire, accompanied King Edward I. in his wars in Scotland, and received from that prince, in the 32nd year of his reign, a grant of a charter of free warren and free chase, in all his demesne lands of Radclyffe, &c. He *m.* a dau. of Boteler, of Bewsey, Baron of Warrington, and had issue: I. Robert, of Radclyffe Tower, ancestor of the Radclyffes of Smithills; II. William, of Colceth and Edgworth, and afterwards of Radclyffe Tower, usually styled the "Great William," ancestor of the Radclyffes of Radclyffe Tower, and of the Radclyffes, Barons Fitz-Walter and Earls of Sussex; III. John (Sir), of Ordshall, co. Lancaster, ancestor of the Radclyffes of Ordshall, Foxdenton, &c., co. Lancaster, the Radcliffes of Hitchin Priory, Herts, &c., &c. A descendant of the 2nd son, William of Colceth,
Sir John Ratcliffe, Knt., governor of Trounsak, in Aquitaine, had 1,000 marks per annum allowed to him for the guard thereof, 7th King Henry V., and in the 1st Henry VI., being retained to serve the king, as seneschal of that duchy, had an assignation of 4s. per day for his own salary, and 20 marks a piece per annum for 200 archers. In the 4th year of the same monarch, Sir John had a grant of the wardship of Ralph, Earl of Westmoreland, in consideration of 2,000 marks, then due to him by the king, for wages in his military capacity; and in seven years afterwards, he had an assignation of all the revenues of the crown, issuing out of the counties of Caernarvon and Merioneth, as also out of the lordships of Chirk, and Chirkland, to liquidate another arrear of service money, to the amount of £7,029 13s. 1d. This eminent soldier, who was a knight banneret, and a knight of the Garter, *m.* Elizabeth Fitz-Walter, only dau. and heiress of Walter Fitz-Walter, last Baron Fitz-Walter of that family (*revert* to Fitz-Walter, Baron Fitz-Walter), and was *s.* at his decease by his son,
Sir John Ratcliffe, who, in the 39th Henry VI., obtained a pardon of intrusion, for entering upon the lands of his inheritance without livery; and in the 1st Henry VII., 15 September, 1485, was summoned to parliament in right of his mother, as Baron Fitz-Walter. In which year, being at that time steward of the king's household, he was joined in commission with Sir Reginald Bray, Knt., for exercising the office of chief justice of all the forests beyond Trent. And at the coronation of King

Henry's consort, Queen Elizabeth, his lordship was associated with Jasper Tudor, Duke of Bedford, for performing the duties of High Steward of England. But afterwards implicated in the conspiracy in favour of Perkyn Warbeck, he was attainted of high treason, and being carried prisoner to Calais, whence he endeavoured to make his escape, by corrupting his keepers, he was there beheaded in the year 1495, when the Barony of Fitz-Walter became forfeited. Nevertheless his son and heir, Robert Ratcliffe, K.G., found much favour from Henry VII., and was restored in blood and honours by act of parliament in the 1st Henry VIII., when he became 2nd Lord Fitz-Walter of the Ratcliffe family. In the 4th of the same reign, his lordship attended the king in the great expedition then made to Therouenne and Tournay; and in ten years afterwards, he commanded the van of the army sent into France, under the Earl of Surrey; for which eminent services he was created, by letters patent, dated 18 June, 1525, Viscount Fitz-Walter. His lordship was one of those peers, who, in four years afterwards, subscribed the articles against Cardinal Wolsey. He was subsequently made a knight of the Garter, and elevated to the Earldom of Sussex, 8 December, 1529. The next year he subscribed the remonstrance of the peers to Pope Clement VII., regarding the king's divorce from Queen Katherine, and he was one of the nobles who attended Henry into France, in 1532; after which he obtained a special patent to himself, and his heirs male of the office of Sewer, at the time of dinner, upon the coronation day of all the future kings and queens of England, with a fee of £20 per annum out of the exchequer; and was constituted Lord High Chamberlain of England for life, upon the attainder of Thomas Cromwell, Earl of Essex. Besides all those honours, his lordship in the spoliation of the church, was a considerable participator, having obtained from his royal master grants of the site of the abbey of Cleve, in Somersetshire, with its revenues; and of the college and chantry of Attleburgh, in Norfolk. The earl m. 1st, Elizabeth, dau. of Henry, Duke of Buckingham, and had issue,

Henry, his successor.
George.
Humphrey (Sir). of Elnestow, co. Bedford, left issue,
Edward, who inherited as 6th and last Earl of Sussex.
Frances, m. to Henry Cheeke, Esq.

His lordship m. 2ndly, Lady Margaret Stanley, dau. of Thomas, Earl of Derby, and had,

Anne, m. to Thomas, Lord Wharton.
Jane, m. to Anthony, Viscount Montague.

He m. 3rdly, Mary, dau. of Sir John Arundel, of Lanherne. In Cornwall, and had an only son,

John (Sir), who d. s. p.

His lordship d. in 1542, and was s. by his eldest son, Sir Henry Ratcliffe, K.G., as 3rd Lord Fitz-Walter, and 2nd Earl of Sussex, who, in the 1st Edward VI., upon the expedition then made into Scotland, had the command of 1,600 demi-lances; in which service, being unhorsed, he escaped very narrowly with his life. At the demise of King Edward, the Earl of Sussex was amongst the first that declared for Queen Mary, and was in consequence constituted by that sovereign, soon after her accession, warden and chief justice itinerant of all the forests south of Trent. He was also made a knight of the Garter. His lordship m. 1st, Lady Elizabeth Howard, dau. of Thomas, Duke of Norfolk, and had issue,

Thomas, } successive Earls of Sussex.
Henry, }
Francis.

He m. 2ndly, Anne, dau. of Sir Philip Calthorpe, Knt., by whom he had a son and dau., viz.,

Egremont, who, being a principal actor in the northern rebellion, was attainted and forced to fly the kingdom. He was afterwards put to death at Namurs, by Don John of Austria, for purposing to murder that prince.
Frances, m. to Sir Thomas Mildmay, Knt., of Mulsh, co. Essex, and had issue,

   Sir Thomas Mildmay, Bart., who d. s. p. 13 February, 1625-6.
   Sir Henry Mildmay, Knt., who, in 1610, claimed, by petition to the Long Parliament, in right of his mother, the Barony of Fitz-Walter, but owing to the civil wars, nothing was done at that time therein. Sir Henry m. Elizabeth, dau. of John Darcy, Esq., of Toleshunt Darcy, co. Essex, and dying in 1654, left three sons, viz.,

      1 Robert, m. Mary, dau. and co-heir of Sir Thomas Edmonds, Knt., and had issue,

         Henry, d. s. p.
         Benjamin, who was allowed the Barony of Fitz-Walter in 1669 (see Mildmay, Barons Fitz-Walter).
         Mary, m. to Henry Mildmay, Esq., of Graces, and had issue,

450

Mary, m. to Charles Goodwin, Esq., of Rovant, co. Sussex, and d. s. p.
Lucy, m. to Thomas Gardiner, Esq., of Tollesbury, Essex, and had, with other issue, who d. s. p., two daus., Lucy, who m. in 1728, Sir Richard Bacon, Bart., but their issue is extinct; and Jemima, who is stated to have m. John Joseph, surgeon, and to have had an only dau., Jemima, wife of Robert Duke, woollen draper, of Colchester, who, it is asserted, settled in America.
Elizabeth, m. to Edmund Waterson, Esq., and d. s. p.
Frances, m. to Christopher Fowler, Esq., and d. in 1705, leaving a son, Edmund Fowler, of Graces, who m. Elizabeth Pateshall, and d. in 1751, leaving a dau. and heir, Fanny, wife of Sir Brook Bridges, Bart., and mother of Sir Brook-William Bridges, Bart., whose son and heir, Sir Brook-William Bridges, Bart., was one of the co-heirs, if not sole heir, of the Barony of Fitz-Walter, and was created Baron Fitz-Walter, by Patent, 1868, but d. s. p. 1875.
Katherine, m. to Colonel Thomas Townshend, and had issue, but since extinct.

2 Henry, d. s. p.
3 Charles, m. to Martha, dau. and heir of Sir Cranmer Harris, Knt., and left an only dau.,

   Mary, m. to Sir Charles Tyrrell, Bart., of Thornton.

The earl, being divorced from his 2nd countess, obtained a special act of parliament in the 2nd and 3rd Philip and Mary, to debar her from jointure and dower. He d. 17 February, 1556, and was s. by his eldest son,

Sir Thomas Ratcliffe, K.G., 4th Lord Fitz-Walter, and 3rd Earl of Sussex, b. in 1526. In the life-time of his father, he was deputed ambassador by Queen Mary to the Emperor Charles V. to treat of a marriage between herself and Prince Philip, the emperor's eldest son; and he proceeded afterwards to the court of Spain to the prince himself to obtain a ratification of the treaty. In the 2nd and 3rd Philip and Mary, Sir Thomas Ratcliffe was constituted lord deputy of Ireland, and soon after his father's decease, his lordship was made chief justice of all the forests south of Trent. In the 4th and 5th of the same reign, the earl being then a knight of the Garter, and captain of the pensioners, had his commission as deputy of Ireland renewed: which high office was confirmed to him upon the accession of Queen Elizabeth, with instructions to reduce the revenues of Ireland to the standard of England. In the 3rd Elizabeth he was constituted lord-lieutenant of the same kingdom, and in six years afterwards he had the honour of bearing the order of the Garter to the Emperor Maximilian. He was afterwards engaged in negotiating a matrimonial alliance between his royal mistress, and the Archduke Charles of Austria. In the 12th Elizabeth he was lord president of the north, and the next year, upon an incursion of the Scots, his lordship invaded Scotland and laid several of their towns and castles in ashes; amongst which were the castles of Annand and Caerlaveroc. He sat subsequently upon the trial of the Duke of Norfolk; and he was one of the commissioners (24th Elizabeth), to treat regarding a marriage between her Majesty and the Duke of Anjou. His lordship m. 1st, Lady Elizabeth Wriothesley, dau. of Thomas, Earl of Southampton, by whom he had two sons, Henry and Robert, who both d. young. He m. 2ndly, Frances, dau. of Sir William Sidney, Knt., sister of Sir Henry Sidney, Knt., but by her (who was foundress of Sydney-Sussex College, Cambridge, and d. 19 March, 1589, aged fifty-eight) Lord Sussex had no issue.

This Thomas, Earl of Sussex, Sir Robert Naunton, in his Fragmenta Regalia, describes " as a goodly gentleman; of a brave noble nature, and constant to his friends and servants:" and goes on to state, " that there was such an antipathy in his nature to that of the Earl of Leicester's, that being together at court, and both in high employments, they grew to direct forwardness, and were in continual opposition; the one setting the watch and the other the sentinel, each on the other's actions and motions: for this Earl of Sussex was of great spirit, which backed with the Queen's special favour, and supported by a great and antient inheritance, could not brook the other's empire: in so much as the queen, upon sundry occasions, had somewhat to do to appease and attain them, until death parted the competition, and left the place to Leicester." Upon his death-bed his lordship is said, by the same authority, thus to have addressed his friends: "I am now passing into another world, and I must leave you to your fortunes, and the queen's grace and goodness; but beware of the gipsey (meaning Leicester), for he will be too hard for you all; you know not the beast so well as I do."—He d. in June, 1583, at his house of Bermondsey, in Southwark, and was buried at Boreham, in Sussex; but leaving no issue surviving, was s. by his brother,

Sir Henry Ratcliffe, 5th Lord Fitz-Walter, and 4th Earl of Sussex, captain and chief governor of Portsmouth, and knight of the Garter. He had a grant from Queen Elizabeth of sundry rectories and lands in Ireland by patent, in 1577. His lordship *m.* Honora, dau. of Anthony Pound, Esq., of Hampshire, and dying 10 April, 1593, was *s.* by his only child,

ROBERT RATCLIFFE, K.G., 6th Lord Fitz-Walter, and 5th Earl of Sussex. This nobleman was with the Earl of Essex in the attack and sacking of the city of Cadiz in the 39th ELIZABETH, and was installed a knight of the Garter, 19th of the ensuing reign (1621). His lordship *m.* 1st, Bridget, dau. of Sir Charles Morrison, Knt., of Cashiobury, co. Hertford, and had issue,

Henry, who *m.* Jane, dau. of Sir Michael Stanhope, Knt.
Thomas.
Elizabeth, *m.* 9 February, 1608, to Sir John Ramsey. Viscount Haddington, afterwards Earl of Holderness (*see that name*).
Honora.

All of these, however, *d. s. p.* before himself. The earl *m.* 2ndly, Frances, dau. of Hercules Meutas, Esq., of Hame, in Essex, but had no issue by her. His lordship *d.* in 1629, when the Barony of Fitz-Walter devolved upon the descendants of his aunt, of the half blood, Lady Frances Mildmay (*refer to* issue of Henry, 2nd Earl of Sussex, by his 2nd marriage; and *see* MILDMAY, Lord Fitz-Walter), and the other honours devolved upon his cousin,

SIR EDWARD RATCLIFFE, as 6th Earl of Sussex, *d.* in 1641 *s. p.*, when his honours became EXTINCT.

Arms—Arg., a bend engrailed, sa,

RAWDON—EARL OF MOIRA, AND RAWDON - HASTINGS, MARQUESS OF HASTINGS AND EARL OF RAWDON.

(*See* ADDENDA.)

RAWSON—VISCOUNT CLONTARFE.

Created for life, 5 November, 1541.

Lineage.

SIR JOHN RAWSON, Knight of Rhodes, and Prior of Kilmainham, co. Dublin, a man in whom the English Government placed the highest confidence, and one of the lords of the privy council, surrendered, with the consent of the convent, to King HENRY VIII. the hospital of St. John of Jerusalem at Kilmainham, 22 November, 1541, and was in accordance with a king's letter, dated at Windsor, 5 November, in that year, confirmed in his pension of 500 marks, and created VISCOUNT CLONTARFE (with an annuity of £10) for life. Several grants by him are enrolled in the Chancery Records of Ireland. He *d.* in 1560, when the title of course became EXTINCT.

The following representation preceded, and appears to have influenced the marks of royal favour he received :—

"May it further please your Majesty," writes the Lord Deputy St. Leger, in 1540, to King HENRY VIII, "according to your high commandment, I, at my repair to these parts, moved the Lord Kilmainham, Lord of St. John's here, concerning the surrender of his name and lands, and how good and gracious your Majesty is to him, assigning unto him for term of his life five hundred marks by the year. The said Lord Kilmainham is not only glad and willing to obey your said commandment and pleasure, but also desired me to render unto your excellent Majesty his most humble thanks for your said goodness towards him. And also he, perceiving your said pleasure, hath not only given to me, your poor servant, certain implements very necessary for the house there, with corn, hay, and other things whereof I had great need, but also hath caused the principal house there to be well and substantially repaired in all places needful, which assuredly is a good house, and great pity that it should decay. And forasmuch, as by the report of the most part of the counsel here, the said Lord Kilmainham hath, for the long time of his abode here, been the person which, next your Majesty's Deputy, hath always kept the best house, and English sort, and at all times, when strangers of other countries hath repaired thither, feasted and entertained them to your Highness's honour; and also for that it is thought by those of your English counsellors here, that it shall be a great lack to miss him out of council, and also out of the parliament (when any shall be), as well for his honesty as for his long experience, they have all desired me to write unto your most excellent Majesty in favour of the said Lord Kilmainham, that for as much as your Majesty hath assigned him so honourable pension, and that he intended here to remain for term of his life, that your Majesty would be so good and gracious as to give him the name of honour of Viscount of Clontarf, which is a place where he intendeth with your Majesty's favour, to make his abode, and to be a Lord of the Parliament and of your Council, assigning to him such

annuity with the said name of honour, as shall stand with your Highnesse's pleasure. Wherefore in accomplishment of their said requests, I most humbly beseech your Majesty to be good unto him in this their humble suits and mine. The man is very aged, and not like to charge your Majesty very long."[*]

This request was further urged by a memorial from the Privy Council to the king, signed by the Master of the Rolls (John Alen), the Archbishop of Dublin, the Bishop of Meath, Dean Basnet, Lord Gormanston, Justices Aylmer and Luttrell, Thomas Eustace, afterwards created Lord Baltinglass, and three others. (For further particulars *see* ADDENDA.)

RAYMOND — BARONS RAYMOND, OF ABBOT'S LANGLEY, CO. HERTFORD.

By Letters Patent, dated 15 Januray, 1731.

Lineage.

In the reign of King CHARLES II.,

SIR THOMAS RAYMOND. Knt., was one of the judges of the King's Bench, and his name is handed down to posterity by his *Law Reports*. He was father of

ROBERT RAYMOND, another eminent lawyer, who became chief justice of the Court of King's Bench, and was elevated to the peerage by letters patent, dated 15 January, 1731, in the dignity of LORD RAYMOND, BARON OF ABBOT'S LANGLEY, *co.* Hertford. His lordship *m.* Anne, dau. of Sir Edward Northey, Knt., of Epsom, co Surrey, attorney-general, *temp.* Queen ANNE, and King GEORGE I., and dying in 1732, was *s.* by his only son,

ROBERT RAYMOND, 2nd baron. This nobleman *m.* Chetwynd, dau. and co-heir of Montagu, Viscount Blundell, in Ireland, but *d.* in 1753 *s. p.*, when the barony became EXTINCT.

Arms—Sa., a chevron between three eagles displayed, arg.; on a chiet, or, a rose between two fleurs-de-lis, gu.

RICH—BARONS RICH, EARLS OF WARWICK, BARONS KENSINGTON, EARLS OF HOLLAND.

Barony of Rich, by Letters Patent, dated 16 February, 1547.
Earldom of Warwick, by Letters Patent, dated 6 August, 1618.
Barony of Kensington, by Letters Patent, dated 8 March, 1622.
Earldom of Holland, by Letters Patent, dated 24 September, 1624.

Lineage.

The founder of this family, RICHARD RICH, was an opulent mercer of London, who served the office of sheriff for that city, in 1441. He *d.* in 1469, leaving a son,

JOHN RICH, whose grandson,

RICHARD RICH, having studied law in the Middle Temple, was appointed, in the 21st HENRY VIII., autumnal reader to that society. Shortly after which, he advanced through several eminent employments, to great wealth and high honours. In the 24th year of the same king, he was constituted attorney-general for Wales, and in the next year, appointed the king's solicitor-general. In the 27th, he had a grant of the office of chirographer to the Common Pleas; and about that time, visiting Sir Thomas More, ex-lord chancellor, then a prisoner in the Tower, used his utmost exertions to persuade that great and eminent person to acknowledge the king's supremacy in spiritual affairs. In this year, too, he was appointed chancellor of the Court of Augmentations, a court formed to take cognizance of the revenues of the monasteries, which had considerably augmented the funds of the crown; and he had a grant of the site of the priory of Leeze, with the manor thereunto appertaining, in the county of Essex. Upon the accession of King EDWARD VI., being then a knight, he was elevated to the peerage, by letters patent, dated 16 February, 1547 (the fourth day before the coronation), as BARON RICH, *of Leeze*, and constituted 30 November following, lord chancellor of England. But within five years, observing the dangers of the times, by the Duke of Somerset's fall, and other circumstances equally ominous, and having amassed a very large fortune, "like a discreet pilot," says Dugdale, "who seeing a storm at hand, gets his ship into harbour, he made suit to the king, by reason of some bodily infirmities, that he might be discharged of his office, which being granted, the great seal was delivered to Thomas Goodrick, bishop of Ely; after which, he (Lord Rich) lived many years, and at his own charge built the tower steeple at Rochford, in Essex." The cause of his lordship's resignation of the chancellorship is thus, however, more feasibly accounted for: "The Lord Rich being a fast friend to the great Duke of Somerset, then in the Tower, was endeavouring to serve him with the king; and for that purpose had written him notice of something designed against him by the council; and being in haste, directed the letter only 'to the duke,' bidding his servant carry it to the Tower, without giving him any particular directions 'to the Duke of Somerset.' The servant not knowing that his master was intimate with Somerset, but knowing that he was so with the Duke of Norfolk (then also in the Tower), gave the latter nobleman the letter by mistake. When the chancellor found out his error at night, fearful that Norfolk would discover him, he immediately repaired to the king, and desired to be discharged his office, feigning illness, which was merely to raise pity for himself, and prevent the malice of his enemies." The reputation of Lord Rich suffered deeply in the opinion of all honourable men, by the baseness of his conduct to Sir Thomas More. Upon the trial of the ex-chancellor, Rich was a witness against him, as to a pretended conversation in the Tower: and when he gave his evidence, Sir Thomas made answer: "If I were a man, my lord, that had no regard to my oath, I had no occasion to be here a criminal; and if this oath, Mr. Rich, you have taken, be true, then I pray I may never see God's face; which, were it otherwise, is an imprecation I would not be guilty of to gain the world." Sir Thomas then proceeded to charge him with being "light of tongue, a great gamester, and a person of no good, in the parish where they had lived together, or in the Temple, where he was educated." After which, he went on to show how unlikely it was, that he should "impart the secrets of his conscience to a man, of whom he always had so mean an opinion."

His lordship m. Elizabeth, sister of William Jenks, of London, grocer, and had issue, ROBERT, his successor, with three other sons, all of whom d. s. p., and nine daus., viz.,

Margery, m. to Henry Pigot, Esq., of Abingdon.
Agnes, m. to Edmund Mordaunt, Esq.
Mary, m. to Sir Thomas Wrothe, Knt.
Dorothy, m. to Francis Barley, Esq.
Elizabeth, m. to Robert Peyton, Esq.
Winifride, m. 1st, to Sir Henry Dudley, Knt.; and 2ndly, to Roger, Lord North.
Etheldreda, m. to Robert Drury, Esq.
Anne, m. to Thomas Pigot, Esq.
Frances, m. to John, Lord Darcy, of Chiche.

Lord Rich d. in 1568, and was s. by his eldest son,

ROBERT RICH, 2nd baron. This nobleman was one of the peers upon the trial of the Duke of Norfolk, in the reign of ELIZABETH, and was afterwards employed by her Majesty upon a diplomatic mission to France, as well as on some complicated affairs in Ireland. His lordship m. Elizabeth, dau. and heir of George Baldry, Esq., son and heir of Sir Thomas Baldry, Knt., of London, and had issue,

Richard, m. to Katherine, dau. and co-heir of Sir Henry Knevitt, Knt., and d. s. p. v. p.
ROBERT, his successor.
Edwin (Sir), of Mulbarton, in Norfolk, m. Honora, dau. of Charles Worlick, Esq., and had issue,
  Robert, who d. s. p.
  Edwin (Sir), of Lincoln's Inn, d. s. p. in 1675.
  Richard, d. s. p.
  Charles, created a Baronet by King CHARLES II., a dignity which expired with Lieut.-General Sir Robert Rich, Bart., whose only dau. and heiress,
    MARY-FRANCES RICH, m. 4 January, 1784, the Rev. Charles Bostock, LL.D., of Shirley House, Hants, who assumed the surname and arms of RICH, and was created a Baronet, 11 June, 1791 (see Baronetage).
  Frances, m. to Nathaniel Acton, Esq.
  Margaret.   Honora.
Frances, m. to Thomas Camock, Esq.
Elizabeth, m. to — Castleton, Esq.

His lordship d. in 1581, and was s. by his eldest son,

ROBERT RICH, 3rd baron. This nobleman, in the 40th ELIZABETH, was at the sacking of Cadiz, under the Earl of Essex, and was advanced by King JAMES I., 6 August, 1618, to the EARLDOM OF WARWICK. His lordship m. 1st, Lady Penelope Devereux, dau. of Walter, Earl of Essex, and had issue,

I. ROBERT, Lord Rich, his successor.
II. HENRY (Sir), K.B., captain of the king's guard, "incomparably the most accomplished English courtier of his time, who, under a veil of universal complaisance and condescension concealed the purest selfishness." He was elevated to the peerage, by letters patent, dated 8 March, 1622, as BARON KENSINGTON. His lordship was subsequently employed to negotiate a marriage between Prince Charles (afterwards CHARLES I.), and the Spanish Infanta; and when that treaty proved abortive, he was sent into France to sound the French Court, regarding a consort for the English prince. He was advanced, 24 September, 1624, to the dignity of EARL OF HOLLAND, co. Lincoln, and installed shortly after a knight of the Garter. His lordship m. Isabel, dau. and heir of Sir Walter Cope, of Kensington, co. Middlesex, Knt., by whom he acquired the manor and mansion of Kensington,* and had (with four daus., Frances, m. to Sir James Thynne; Susannah, m to James, Earl of Suffolk; Mary, m. to John, Earl of Breadalbane; and Diana) three sons,

ROBERT, 2nd Earl of Holland, and 5th Earl of Warwick.
Charles.   Henry,
Cope, m., and had a son,
  COPE, whose son,
    EDWARD eventually was the last Earl of Warwick and of Holland.

Henry, the 1st Earl of Holland, after King CHARLES I., became a prisoner in the Isle of Wight, took up arms, with other loyal persons, to effect his restoration, but miscarrying at Kingston-upon-Thames, 7 July, 1648, he was pursued, made prisoner, and committed to the Tower, where he remained until after the execution of the king, when, being brought to trial with the Duke of Hamilton, the Earl of Norwich, Sir John Owen, &c., he was condemned to death, and executed by decapitation before the gates of Westminster Hall, 9 March, 1649.
III. Charles (Sir), slain at the Isle of Rhee, in the expedition under the Duke of Buckingham.
I. Lettice, m. 1st, to Sir George Cary, Knt., of Cockington, co. Devon, and 2ndly, to Sir Arthur Lake, Knt.
II. Penelope, m. to Sir Gervase Clifton, Bart., of Clifton, co Nottingham.
III. Essex, m. to Sir Thomas Cheeke, Knt., of Pirgo, in Essex.
IV. Isabel, m. to Sir John Smythe, Knt.

Lord Rich being divorced from his 1st countess (who re-m. Charles Blount, Earl of Devon), m. 2ndly, Frances, widow of Sir George Paul, and dau. of Sir Christopher Wray, Knt., lord chief justice of the court of King's Bench, but had no other issue. His lordship d. in the same year in which he was advanced to the earldom (anno 1618), and was s. by his eldest son,

ROBERT RICH, 2nd Earl of Warwick. This nobleman was a very distinguished personage in the time of the civil war. He was admiral for the long parliament, and during the usurpation, enjoyed the full confidence of Cromwell. Lord Clarendon says, "That he was a man of a pleasant and companionable wit and conversation; of an universal jollity; and such a license in his words, and in his actions, that a man of less virtue could not be found out. But with all these faults he had great authority and credit with the people; for by opening his doors, and spending a good part of his estate, of which he was very prodigal, upon them, and by being present with them at his devotions, and making himself merry with them, and at them, which they dispensed with, he became the head of that party, and got the style of a godly man." His lordship m. 1st, Frances, dau. of Sir William Hatton, alias Newport, Knt. (by Elizabeth, his wife, dau. and heir of Sir Francis Gawdi, Knt., lord chief justice of the court of Common Pleas), by whom he had issue,

ROBERT, Lord Rich, his successor.
CHARLES, who inherited as 4th earl.
Henry, } both d. unm.
Hatton, }
Anne, 2nd wife to Edward Montagu, 2nd Earl of Manchester, the celebrated parliamentary general, distinguished by his victory over Prince Rupert, at Marston Moor.
Lucy, m. to John Roberts, Baron Roberts, of Truro, afterwards Earl of Radnor.
Frances, m. to Nicholas Leke, Earl of Scarsdale.

The earl m. 2ndly, Eleanor, dau. of Sir Edward Wortley, Knt., but had no other issue. He d. in 1658, and was s. by his eldest son,

ROBERT RICH, 3rd Earl of Warwick, who was made a knight of the Bath at the coronation of King CHARLES II. His lord-

* This ancient and venerable pile has from that period borne the name of Holland House. It has since been in the possession of the family of Fox, Lords Holland; having been purchased by Henry Fox (who from it assumed the title of HOLLAND), from William Edwardes, 1st Lord Kensington of the 2nd creation.

ship m. 1st, Lady Anne Cavendish, dau. of William, Earl of Devonshire, and had issue,

  ROBERT, who m. in the life-time of his grandfather, Frances, youngest dau. of the Protector Cromwell, and d. in about two months after, 16 February, 1657-8.

He m. 2ndly, Anne, widow of Richard Rogers, Esq., and dau. of Sir Thomas Cheeke, of Pirgo, and had three daus., viz.,

  Anne, m. to Sir John Barrington, Bart., of Barrington Hall, co. Essex.
  Mary, m. to Sir Henry St. John.
  Essex, m. to Daniel Finch, 6th Earl of Winchilsea.

The earl d. 29 May, 1659, leaving no male issue, when the honours devolved upon his brother,

  CHARLES RICH, 4th Earl of Warwick, who m. Lady Mary Boyle, dau. of Richard, 1st Earl of Cork, and had a son, CHARLES, Lord Rich, who m. Lady Anne Cavendish, dau. of William, 3rd Earl of Devonshire, but d. s. p. v. p.　The earl d. 24 August, 1673, when his estates, except Warwick House, in Holborn, passed to his co-heirs, and his honours devolved upon his kinsman (refer to Henry, 1st Earl of Holland, 2nd son of Robert, 1st Earl of Warwick),

  ROBERT RICH, Lord of Holland, as 5th Earl of Warwick. This nobleman m. 1st, Elizabeth, dau. of Sir Arthur Ingram, Knt., by whom he had one surviving son,

    HENRY, Lord Kensington, who m. Christiana, dau. of Andrew Riccard, Esq., and d. s. p. v. p.　His widow m. John, Lord Berkeley, of Stratton.

The earl m. 2ndly, Lady Anne Montagu, dau. of Edward, Earl of Manchester, and had issue,

  EDWARD, his successor.
  Elizabeth, m. to Francis Edwardes, Esq., of Haverfordwest, 2nd son of Owen Edwardes, Esq., of Trefgarne, co. Pembroke, and had an only surviving son,
    WILLIAM EDWARDES Esq., who inherited the estates of his cousin, EDWARD-HENRY RICH, 4th EARL OF HOLLAND, and 7th EARL OF WARWICK, and was created a peer of Ireland in 1776, as BARON KENSINGTON. (See BURKE's Peerage.)

His lordship d. in 1675, and was s. by his son,
EDWARD RICH, 3rd Earl of Holland, and 6th Earl of Warwick. His lordship m. Charlotte, dau. of Sir Thomas Middleton, by whom (who m. 2ndly, the Right Hon. Joseph Addison) he had an only son, his successor, at his decease in 1701,
EDWARD-HENRY RICH, 4th Earl of Holland, and 7th Earl of Warwick, at whose decease unm. in 1721, his fortune passed to his cousin, WILLIAM EDWARDES, Esq., created LORD KENSINGTON, as above mentioned, while the honours reverted to his kinsman (refer to Cope, youngest son of HENRY, 1st EARL OF HOLLAND, 2nd son of ROBERT, 1st Earl of Warwick),
EDWARD RICH, Esq., 5th Earl of Holland, and 8th Earl of Warwick. This nobleman m. Miss Stanton, dau. of Samuel Stanton, Esq., of Lyme Regis, and had an only dau., Catherine. His lordship d. in 1759, when all the titles became EXTINCT.

Arms—Gu., a chevron between three crosses-botonny, or.

RICHARDSON—LORD CRAMOND.

By Letters Patent, dated 1628.

Lineage.

SIR THOMAS RICHARDSON, Knt., b. at Hardwick, in Suffolk, 3 July, 1569, the son of Dr. Thomas Richardson, adopting the legal profession, became eminent as a lawyer, was made king's serjeant, elected Speaker of the House of Commons, and at length constituted lord chief justice of the court of King's Bench. Sir Thomas the well-known opponent of Laud, m. 1st, Ursula, dau. of John Southwell, Esq., of Barham Hall, in Suffolk, and had by her one son and four daus. viz.,

  THOMAS (Sir), who d. 1642, aged forty-five. He m. 1st, Elizabeth, dau. of Sir William Hewett, Knt., and by her had with other children, who d. young,
    THOMAS, Lord Cramond.
    William, serjeant-at-law; whose will is dated 8 March, 1681.
    Charles, who m. Miss Wiseman, and had Charles, Ursula, Anne, and Margaret.
    Elizabeth, m. to Richard Mansel, of West Leek, Derbyshire.
  Sir Thomas, jun., m. 2ndly, Mary, relict of Sir Miles Sandys, Knt., and had by her a son,
    Edward.

453

Ursula, m. to Sir William Yelverton, Bart. of Rougham.
Mary, m. to John Webb, Esq. of Beccles.
Elizabeth, m. to Robert Wood, Esq. of Bracon Ash.
Susan, d. unm.

Sir Thomas m. 2ndly, ELIZABETH, dau. of SIR THOMAS BEAUMONT, Knt. of Stoughton Grange, co. Leicester, and relict of Sir John Ashburnham, Knt. of Ashburnham, but by her had no issue. This lady was raised to the peerage of Scotland, as BARONESS CRAMOND, in 1628, the dignity being conferred on her for her life, with remainder to the son by a former wife of her 2nd husband, Sir Thomas Richardson, and his heirs male; which failing, to the heirs male of the body of his father. Lady Cramond survived her 2nd husband (who d. in 1634) and was s. at her decease 16 April, 1651, by the grandson of that gentleman,

THOMAS RICHARDSON, Lord Cramond, M.P. for the co. Norfolk, who m. Anne, dau. of Sir Thomas Richardson, lord mayor of London; and dying 16 May, 1674, was s. by his eldest son,

HENRY RICHARDSON, Lord Cramond, b. in 1650; who m. Frances, dau. of Sir John Napier, Bart. of Luton Hoo, and relict of Sir Edward Barkham, of Southacre, in Norfolk; but dying s. p., 5 January, 1701, was s. by his brother,

WILLIAM RICHARDSON, Lord Cramond, b. 2 August, 1654; who m. 1st, Elizabeth, dau. and heir of Edward Barkham, Esq. of Southacre; and 2ndly, Elizabeth, dau. and heir of James Daniel, of Norwich, goldsmith. The former had no issue; but by the latter his lordship left one son and one dau., viz.,

  WILLIAM, his heir.
  ELIZABETH, heiress to her brother; m. in 1735, to William Jermy, Esq., only son of John Jermy, Esq., of Bayfield, in Norfolk. They sold Southacre Hall, the last remaining portion of the great Cramond property in Norfolk, to Sir Andrew Fountaine, Knt. of Salle, Norfolk, warden of the Mint.

Lord Cramond d. 7 March, 1719, and was s. by his son,
WILLIAM RICHARDSON, Lord Cramond, b. in 1714; at whose decease unm. 28 July, 1735, the peerage is supposed to have become EXTINCT.

Of this family the Richardsons of Aber Hirnant, co. Merioneth, claim to be a branch.

Arms—Or, on a chief, as., three lions' heads erased, of the field; to which CHARLES I. added "a canton, az., charged with a St. Andrew's cross, arg."

RIDGEWAY—BARONS RIDGEWAY AND EARLS OF LONDONDERRY.

Barony, by Letters Patent, dated 25 May, 1616.
Earldom, by Letters Patent, dated 23 August, 1622.

Lineage.

SIR THOMAS RIDGEWAY, Knt., son of Thomas Ridgeway, Esq. of Tor, co. Devon, was employed in Ireland in a military capacity, temp. ELIZABETH. In 1612 he was made a Baronet of England; created a peer of Ireland, 25 May, 1616, as BARON OF GALLEN RIDGEWAY; and advanced to the EARLDOM OF LONDONDERRY, 23 August, 1622. He m. Cicely, sister and co-heir of Henry Mackwilliam, and was s. by his son,

SIR ROBERT RIDGEWAY, 2nd Earl of Londonderry; who m. Elizabeth, dau., and heir of Sir Simon Weston, Knt. of Lichfield, and was father of

SIR WESTON RIDGEWAY, 3rd Earl of Londonderry; who m. Martha, dau. of Sir Richard Temple, Bart., and left with several daus., two sons, ROBERT and Thomas. The elder,
SIR ROBERT RIDGEWAY, 4th Earl of Londonderry, m. Lucy, dau. of Sir William Jopson, Bart., and had two daus. his co-heirs,

  LUCY, m. to Arthur, 4th Earl of Donegall, and d. s. p. 10 July, 1736.
  FRANCES, m. the Right Hon. Thomas Pitt, M.P., who was created Earl of Londonderry.

His lordship d. 7 March, 1713-14, when all his honours became EXTINCT.

Arms—Sa., a pair of wings, conjoined and elevated, arg.

RIPARIIS, OR DE RIVERS—BARON RIPARIIS.

By Writ of Summons, dated 6 February, 1299.

Lineage.

JOHN DE RIPARIIS was summoned to parliament, as a Baron, from 6 February, 1299, to 26 August, 1307. His lordship signed the celebrated letter to the Pope, 29th EDWARD I., as "Johannes de Ripariis, Dominus de Angre." He d. in 1311, and was s. by his son,

JOHN DE RIPARIIS, 2nd baron, summoned to parliament from 8 June, 1313, to 16 October, 1315. This John de Ripariis was, according to Courthope (Historic Peerage), living in 1339, and left at his decease a dau. Christiana, wife of J. Bulkeley, and a son and heir, Edmund de Rivers, whose only child, Katherine, was wife, 1st of William Lekhull, and 2ndly, of John Hall. Eventually, by the failure of the issue of Katherine, the Barony of Ripariis became vested in the Bulkeleys of Eaton.

RIVERS—BARON RIVERS.

(See PITT-RIVERS, ADDENDA.)

ROBERTS OR ROBARTES—BARONS ROBERTS OF TRURO, EARLS OF RADNOR.

Barony, by Letters Patent, dated 16 January, 1625.
Earldom, by Letters Patent, dated 23 July, 1679.

Lineage.

RICHARD ROBERTS, Esq., of Truro, in Cornwall, had the honour of knighthood conferred upon him by King JAMES I., at Whitehall, in 1616, and was created a baronet in 1621. In four years afterwards he was advanced, through the influence of the favourite Buckingham, to the peerage, in the dignity of BARON ROBERTS, of Truro. For this, Sir Richard is said to have paid £10,000; and one of the charges brought against the Duke of Buckingham in parliament, anno 1626, was, "that, knowing Roberts to be rich, he forced him to take that title of honour; and that, in consideration thereof, he paid ten thousand pounds to the duke's use." Lord Roberts m. Frances, dau. and co-heir of John Hender, Esq., of Botreaux Castle, in Cornwall, and had issue,

JOHN, his successor, of whom presently.
Mary, m. to William Rous, Esq., of Halton, in Cornwall.
Jane, m. to Charles, Lord Lambart, created in 1647, Earl of Cavan.

His lordship d. in 1634, and was s. by his son,

JOHN ROBERTS, 2nd baron. Although this nobleman fought under the parliamentary banner, he was favourably received by King CHARLES II., after the Restoration; sworn of the privy council, appointed lord privy seal, and afterwards lord lieutenant of Ireland. In 1679, his lordship was advanced to the dignities of Viscount Bodmin and EARL OF RADNOR (he was first created Earl of Falmouth, but the title was altered at the desire of the king). His lordship m. 1st, Lady Lucy Rich, dau. of Robert, Earl of Warwick (see that name), and had issue,

I. ROBERT, Viscount Bodmin, a person of eminent talents, who d. about the year 1681, in his embassy at the court of Denmark. His lordship m. Sarah, dau. and heir of John Bodvile, Esq., of Bodvile Castle, in Carnarvonshire, and left issue,

CHARLES-BODVILE, successor to the honours.
Russel, one of the tellers of the Exchequer, m. Lady Mary Booth, dau of Henry, Earl of Warrington, and had issue,

HENRY, who s. as 3rd Earl of Radnor.
Mary, who m. Thomas Hunt, Esq. of Mollington, co. Chester, and had issue, the younger son,

GEORGE HUNT, Esq., s. to the estates of the EARLS OF RADNOR, and became of Lanhydrock in Cornwall, but dying s. p., was s. by his niece ANNA-MARIA, dau. of his elder brother, Thomas Hunt, Esq., of Mollington, by Mary, his wife, dau. of Peter Bold, Esq., of Bold. This lady, m. 15 November, 1804, the Hon. CHARLES-BAGENAL AGAR, and was mother of THOMAS-JAMES AGAR-ROBARTES, Esq., of Lanhydrock, co. Cornwall, who assumed the additional surname of Robartes, as representative of the EARLS OF RADNOR.

Isabella, m. to Colonel Legh, of Adlington, co. Chester.
Sarah, d. unm.
Lucy, m. to the Hon. George Booth, 2nd son of George, 1st Lord Delamere.
Essex, d. unm.

II. Hender, M.P. for Bodmin, temp. CHARLES II. and JAMES II., d. unm.
III. John, d. young

The earl m. 2ndly, Isabella, dau. of Sir John Smith, Knt., of Kent, and had four other sons and five daus., viz.,

I. Francis, M.P. in the reigns of CHARLES II., JAMES II., WILLIAM III., and Queen ANNE. Mr. Robartes was a person of great learning, and vice-president of the Royal Society. He m. Anne, relict of Hugh Boscawen, Esq., of Tregothnan, and dau. of Wentworth, 17th Earl of Kildare, by whom he had,

JOHN, who s. as 4th EARL OF RADNOR.
Francis, m. to Mary, dau. of William Wallis, Esq., of Groveby, in Wiltshire, and d. in 1734, leaving one son, John.

Mr. Robartes d. at Chelsea, in February, 1717-18.
II. Henry, m Miss Frances Coryton, and d. s. p.
III. Warwick.
IV. Charles, d. unm.
I. Letitia-Isabella, m. 1st, in 1669, to Charles, 2nd Earl of Drogheda, and 2ndly to the celebrated William Wycherley, Esq., of Shropshire.
II. Diana, d. unm.
III. Aramintha, m. to Ezekiel Hopkins, bishop of Derry.
IV. Olimpia.
V. Essex, m. to John Speccot, Esq., of Penhaile, in Cornwall.

The Earl of Radnor, was "a stanch presbyterian; sour and cynical; just in his administration, but vicious under the semblance of virtue; learned above any of his quality; but stiff, obstinate, proud, and jealous, and every way intractable." He d. in 1685, and was s. by his grandson,

CHARLES BODVILE ROBARTES, 2nd Earl of Radnor, who m. Elizabeth, dau. and heir of Sir John Cutler, Knt., of the city of London, but d. s. p. in 1723, when his honours devolved upon his nephew,

HENRY ROBARTES, 3rd earl, at whose decease, unm., at Paris, in 1741, the estates passed to his nephew George Hunt, Esq., and the honours passed to his cousin (refer to Francis, eldest son of the 1st earl, by his 2nd wife),

JOHN ROBARTES, as 4th earl, d. in 1764, unm., when the Earldom of Radnor became EXTINCT.

Arms—Az., three estoiles of six points, and a chief, wavy, or.

ROBERTSON—BARON MAJORIBANKS.

(See BURKE's Extant Peerage, MAJORIBANKS, BART.)

ROBSART—BARON ROBSART.

(Refer to BOURCHIER, Barons Bourchier, and Earls of Essex.)

ELIZABETH BOURCHIER, Baroness Bourchier, m. for her 2nd husband, Sir Lewis Robsart, K.G., who assumed the title, jure uxoris, of LORD BOURCHIER, but was summoned to parliament in the name of ROBSART, from 1425 to 1429: he d. s. p. 1 July, 1433.

ROCHE—VISCOUNT ROCHE OF FERMOY.

Lineage.

The family of Roche was established in Ireland by ADAM DE RUPE, of Roch Castle, co. Pembroke, who accompanied Robert FitzStephen to that country in 1196.

DAVID ROCHE, Lord Roche, surnamed "the Great," sat in parliament as VISCOUNT ROCHE, of Fermoy, in the reigns of EDWARD IV., and HENRY VII. He m. Joanna, dau. of Walter de Burgo, called MacWilliam, and had issue,

MAURICE, his heir.
Redmond, of Ballymagly.
Ulick, of Cragh.
Theobald, of Ballyhindon and Clash.
William, of Ballyhowly.
Philip, of Scrall and Rahan.
Gerald, of Ballyhonan.
Edmund, of Ballenime.
Jacob.
Ellena, m. to James, 13th Lord Kingsale.

The eldest son,

MAURICE ROCHE, Viscount Roche, of Fermoy, was present in the parliament of 6th HENRY VII, anno 1490, being styled "Dominus de Fermoy," and was placed next after William, Lord Buttevant. In 1487, he m. Joan, dau. of James, 9th Earl of Desmond, and by her had David, his heir; and Ellen, m. to Maurice, 10th Earl of Desmond. He m. 2ndly, More, dau. of — O'Brien, and by her had Edmund, in the army, who also m. an O'Brien. The son and heir,

DAVID ROCHE, Lord Roche of Fermoy, m. Catharine, dau. of Teige MacCarthy More, and had a son and heir,

MAURICE ROCHE, Viscount Fermoy, generally called the Mad,

liv'ng in 1541, 33rd HENRY VIII., who, by Grany, dau. of Cormac MacTeige MacCarthy, chief of Muskerry, had three sons and three daus., viz.,

i. DAVID, his heir.
ii. William, of Carrickdownan, who *m.* Ellen, dau. of John Tobin, of Compshinagh, co. Tipperary, Esq., and had issue, John, James, and Edward: John, the eldest son, was father of William, father of Ulick, of Carrigdownan, co. Cork, Gent., to whom a special livery of his estate was granted 29 May, 1629, for the fine of £6 Irish.
iii. John, who *d. unm.*
i. Ellen, *m.* to John, Lord Barry.
ii. Margery, *m.* to James Barrett, of Ballincolly.
iii. Catharine, *m.* to Conogher or Connor O'Callaghan, of Clonmeen, co. Cork, chief of his name.

The eldest son,
DAVID ROCHE, Viscount Roche and Fermoy, who succeeded, *m.* Ellen, dau. of James, Lord Dunboyne, by whom he had seven sons and two daus., viz.,

i. MAURICE, his heir.
ii. William, of Ballingaugin, who *m.* a dau. of James Tobin, of Killakin, co. Tipperary, Esq.
iii. Richard, *d. unm.*
iv. Theobald, who *m.* Grany, dau. of Murrough O'Brien Ara, and was killed by the Seneschal of Imokilly, in the Queen's wars.
v. John.   vi. Redmond.
vii. A son, killed by the rebels in the Queen's wars.
i. Joan, *m.* to Patrick, 17th Lord of Kerry.
ii. Helen. *m.* David, Viscount Buttevant, father to David, 1st Earl of Barrymore.

The son and heir,
MAURICE ROCHE, Viscount Roche and Fermoy, sat in the parliament, held by Thomas, Earl of Sussex, 12 January, 1559, and 17 May, 1580, was joined in commission of martial law with Sir Cormac MacTeige MacCarthy, of Muskerry, and had power to give provision for fifteen days to any other than the principal rebels. By letters from Greenwich, 19 July, 1581, his lordship had a grant in fee farm of the lands of Dounemughell, and others in the county of Cork. "But his lordship and his wife being suspected in their loyalty, were sent for by the government to Cork, and the next day were brought thither by Capt. Walter Raleigh, from the castle of Ballinharsh; when his lordship being examined did so well answer for himself, that he was acquitted and taken for a true and good subject, and which in time was known by experience, for not he himself, but all his sons and followers did attend to and perform all such services as were laid upon them, and in which three of his sons were killed in her Majesty's service by the enemy. On the 18 October, 1577, he had a grant from Queen ELIZABETH for 30 years, of all the lands in Ballindrehed alias Ballindre, in Roche, and county; on the 26 October, 1588, the Queen granted to him and other of his body, a castle and lands in Johnstowne and Downe; and 24 October, 1600, he *d.* at his seat of Glanogher (as by inquisition), seized of the manor of Castletown and county." He *m.* 1st, Ellener, dau. of Sir Maurice Fitz-John, 3rd son of John, 14th Earl of Desmond, and 2ndly, Catharine, 3rd dau. of Gerald, 16th Earl of Desmond; by the latter, who survived him, he had no issue, yet by another inquisition he is said to have had his children by her; they were three sons and two daus., viz.,

i. DAVID, his heir.
ii. Theobald, who *m.* Grany, dau. of Sir Owen MacCarthy, on whom he settled divers lands, 25 January, 1602, and making his will, 21 January, 1620, *d.* 27th of that month, seized in fee of the castles, towns, and lands of Croagh-Mac-piers, containing five plough-lands, and several other lands and premires in co. Cork, held of the king *in capite* by knight's service, of which he made a settlement by indenture, dated 1 April, 1620, having issue by his said wife, who survived him, David, his heir, then aged sixteen years.
iii. John.
i. Ellen, or rather Joan, *m.* to Donogh, 3rd Earl of Thomond.
ii. Amy. *m.* to Dermot MacCarthy, of Duhallow, *alias* Mac-Donogh.

The son and heir,
DAVID ROCHE, Viscount Fermoy, "was never touched with the least disloyalty against Queen ELIZABETH, yea, such loyal *constanceis* did he always impress and practice, that in the universal inundation of treasons, when all Munster in general, and his father in particular, did combine against their anointed sovereign, at that time, and ever since did he continue himself within the *lists* of an obedient subject; 13 April, 1603, attended with about 800 soldiers and others, he proclaimed King JAMES I. in the north suburbs of the city of Cork, near Shandon bridge, the mayor of Cork refusing to do it; 22 February, 1604, he had a special livery of his estate; was present in the parliament of 1613, 1614, and 8 July, 1615, was rated £200 to the subsidy then granted; 16 December, 1611, upon his surrender, made 9th of

that month, the king granted and confirmed to his lordship in fee (in consideration of his faithful services to his Majesty and Queen ELIZABETH, and also at his humble suit) the manor of Dounegroe, *alias* Castletown, and all other his estates in co. Cork, with the usual privileges belonging to manors; and to hold three weekly markets and three yearly fairs upon the premises Also by letters from Westminster, 8 July, 1614, his Majesty, for the foregoing reasons, and in respect that he had been always true and loyal to the crown, and as a mark of his princely favour and royal bounty towards him, was pleased to direct a grant to be made to him and his heirs, of so many manors, lands, and other hereditaments, either abstracted or unjustly detained from the crown, as should be of the clear yearly value of £50 sterling, or thereabouts, as the same should be valued by the surveyor-general, and likewise such and so many other lands, being then in charge, as should amount to other £50 English per annum; which said lands, by deed dated 18 February following, his lordship assigned to Sir Gerald Aylmer, of Munctown, co. Dublin." He *m.* Joan, dau. of James, Viscount Buttevant, and dying at Castletown, 22 March, 1635, was buried 12 April in the abbey of Bridgetown, "with a solemne funerall according to his degree," having had issue five sons and four daus., viz.,

i. MAURICE, his heir and successor.
ii. John, deaf and dumb, who *d. unm.* after 1642.
iii. Theobald (Sir), who *m.* Julia, dau. of Dominick, 1st Viscount Kilmallock, and left no issue by his said wife, who re-married with Philip Barry-Oge, of Rincorran, co. Cork, Esq.
iv. Ulick, who *m.* Gyles (Cecilia), dau. of John O'Conor Kerry, of Carrigfoyll, co. Kerry, Esq., and had Theobald, of Ballymagoulan, who took to wife, Anne, dau. of John Boyle, and had Francis; David. who *m.* Miss Lundy; Joan, who *m.* Sir Tyrlogh MacMahon, Bart.; and Catharine, the wife of Charles MacCarthy, of Carrignevar, Esq.
v. Redmond, who, 4 December, 1641, accompanied Sir William St. Leger, president of Munster, to quell the rebellion in co. Waterford. He *m.* 1st, Joan, dau. and co-heir to Sir John Dowdall, of Kilfinny, co. Limerick, Knt.; and 2ndly, Alice, dau. of Sir Richard Smyth, of Ballynatray, co. Waterford, Knt., but had no issue.
i. Ellen, *m.* 1st, to Donell MacCarthy Reagh, of Kilbritain, co. Cork, Esq.; 2ndly, to Charles, Viscount Muskerry; and 3rdly, to Thomas Fitzmaurice, 4th son of Thomas, 18th Lord Kerry.
ii. Ellinor.   iii. Joan.
iv. Amy or Catherine, who *m.* John Everard, of Fethard, cc. Tipperary, Esq.

The son and heir,
MAURICE ROCHE, Viscount Fermoy, took his seat in the House of Peers, 26 October, 1640, by proxy, when it was ordered by the lords, that the placing of him before the Lord Viscount Mountgarret, should be with a salvo jure to that lord who claimed precedence of him. After the commencement of the troubles in 1641, it appears, from sundry depositions, that his lordship was deeply engaged therein; he was a colonel in the Munster army, under their general, Garret Barry, and was at the siege of the garrison of Limerick, and the reduction of other places in that province, for which he was outlawed in the co. Cork, 23 October, 1643; and his estate, then forfeited, was divided by Cromwell amongst his followers, Viscount Roche, of Fermoy being excepted, by act of parliament, 12 August, 1652, from pardon for life or estate.[*] He *m.* Ellen, dau. of

---

[*] The following interesting document, transcribed from the Records of the Auditor-General's Office, Custom House, Dublin (Vol. 17, folio 112), furnishes some information respecting the Viscount:—

"March, 1660-1—To the Right Honourable ye L. L. Justices of Ireland.

"*The humble peticon, of* Maurice, LORD VISCOUNT ROCHE, *of Fermoy.*

"Most humbly sheweth that your Peticoner. hath been seaven yeares agoe dispossessed of his whole estate havinge the chardge of Foure young daughters, unpreferred, to whose misery was added the losse of their mother your Peticoner's wife by an unjust illegal proceeding, as is knowne and may be attested by ye best Protestant Nobility and Gentry of the County of Corke who have heard and seene it. And whose charitable compassion it moved:

"That your Peticoner. and his said children ever since have lived in a most disconsolate condition, destituted of all kinde of subsistence (except what Almes some good Christians did in charity afford them) by occasion whereof one of your Peticoner's. daughters falling sick about three yeares agoe died for want of requisite accomodacon either for her cure or diett:

"That your Peticoner. had often supplicated those in authority in ye late Government for Releefe who after ten months' attendance in Dublin gave him noe other succour but an order to ye Commissioners in Connaught to set out some lands for him *De Bene Esse* there or in ye County of Clare:

"That your Peticoner. being necessitated to goe from Dublin

John, eldest son of Richard Power, Lord of Power and Curragh-more, and had issue,

    I. DAVID, his heir,
    II. John, m. Catharine Condon, and had issue,
      1 ULICK, of whom presently.
      2 David.   3 Theobald, *d. s. p.*
      1 Elinor, living 1703.
    1. Ellen, m. to William, Lord Castle Connell.

The elder son,

DAVID ROCHE, Viscount Fermoy, a naval officer, was drowned near Plymouth, in the great storm of 1703, and dying *unm.*, was *s.* by his nephew,

ULICK ROCHE, called Viscount Fermoy, who m. Miss Anne Carr, of the co. Northumberland, and *d.* 1733 (his will dated 6 November, 1729, was proved 16 June, 1733), leaving an only dau., ANNA-MARIA, who *d.* 1763; the title was subsequently assumed by

DAVID ROCHE, of Ballydangan, a general in the King of Sardinia's service, who greatly distinguished himself in the war between Maria-Theresa and France, particularly at the siege of Gerona, in 1746.

Since his death, the title has not been assumed. The Roches of Trabolgan, co. Cork, descend from Philip Roche, merchant, of Cork, who by deed, dated April, 1554, purchased from Gerald, Lord Kingsale, the estates now enjoyed partly by Thomas Cuthbert-Kearney, Esq., of Garretstown, co. Cork, and by the Right Hon. EDMUND-BURKE ROCHE, LORD FERMOY, who was elevated to the peerage of Ireland as BARON FERMOY, 10 September, 1856 (*see Peerage*).

Arms—Gu., three roaches, naiant, in pale, arg.

ROCHFORT—BARONS AND VISCOUNTS BELLFIELD, EARLS OF BELVEDERE.

Baron, by Letters Patent, dated 16 March, 1787.
Viscount, by Letters Patent, dated 5 October, 1751.
Earl, by Letters Patent, dated 29 November, 1756.

Lineage.

ROBERT ROCHFORT, Esq., *b.* 9 December, 1652 (the descendant of a very ancient family, and son of Prime Iron Rochfort, Esq., lieutenant-colonel in Cromwell's army, who was executed, under the sentence of a court-martial, for killing Major Turner), having adopted the legal profession, became attorney-general, 6 June, 1695, was chosen Speaker of the Irish House of Commons 27th of the following August, and made chief baron of the Exchequer, 30 June, 1707. He m. Hannah, eldest dau. of William

---

a foote to attende on them in Athlone and Loughreagh for six monethe more (in which prosecution and attendaunce he ran himself One Hundred Pounds in debt) yet at last had but 2,500 acres, part in ye Owles in Oonnaughte, and part in ye remotest parts of Thomond, all waste and unprofitable at that time assigned him. Both which before and after were by ye said Commissioners disposed of by Final Settlements to others who evicted your Peticoner, before he could receive any maner of profitt soe as that colour of succor and releefe proved rather an increase and addition of misery to your said Peticoner, who is now in that very low condition, that he cannot in person attende on your Londships, much less make a jorney to His Sacred Majesty to set forth his sufferings and to implore releefe.

"The premises tenderly considered and for that it hath beene unheard of in all former ages That a Peere of this Realme, of English extraction though never so criminous should be reduced to such extremitie of misery, his cause not heard, and without conviction or attainder by his Peers or otherwise contrary to the knowne laws of the land. And ye rights and privilege of the Nobility and Peerage. And for that your Peticoner, is in that forlorne condition that he cannot any longer hould out unlesse speedily relcoved, your Ldpps. may be pleased to aford your Peticoner. some present succor and releefe and to enable him to discharge the said £100 debt. And hee will ever pray, &c."

The Viscount was father of

DAVID ROCHE, Viscount Fermoy. In an intercepted letter of the titular archbishop of Cashel, addressed to " Monsr. Tirell, Docteur en Théologie, Superieur des Hibernois à l'Abbaye d'Arras," and dated from " Limerick, 31st January, 1650 (*nostro compoto*)," read in parliament, on Tuesday, 22 April, 1651, is the following passage :—

"My Lord Castlehaven is Lord General in Munster, and in the field with a very considerable party of horse and foot. My Lord of Muskerry and Mr. DAVID ROCH (son and heir unto Lord Roch) have a good party in the west of Ireland."—*Several Proceedings in Parliament, &c.,* No. 81, p. 1256.

Handcock, Esq., of Twyford, co. Westmeath (ancestor of Lord Castlemaine). Mr. Rochfort's will, dated 30 May, 1726, was proved at Dublin, 13 January, 1727. His widow *d.* 2 July, 1732, and her will was proved in that month. They had two sons,

    I. GEORGE, of whom presently.
    II. John, of Clogrenane, co. Carlow, and of New Park, co. Dublin, M.P. for Ballyshannon, and for Mullingar. *b.* in 1690; *m.* in, 1709, Deborah, only dau. of Thomas Staunton, Esq., M.P., and was father of

John Rochfort, Esq. in 1710, who *m.* in 1733, Emilia, dau of John Eyre, Esq. of Eyrecourt, co. Galway, and (with two daus., Mary, *m.* in 1767, to Thomas Maunsell, Esq., and Deborah, *m.* to George Bishop, Esq. of Bishop's Hall, co. Kildare) had one son,

JOHN, baptized 25 July, 1735; *m.* in 1759, Dorothea, dau. of Thomas Burgh, Esq., of Bert, and had issue. The grandson of this marriage is the present

HORACE-WILLIAM-NOEL ROCHFORT, Esq., of Clogrenane, co. Carlow.

The elder son,

THE RIGHT HON. GEORGE ROCHFORT, of Gaulstown, chief chamberlain of the court of Exchequer, and M.P. for the co. Westmeath, *m.* 24 January, 1704, Lady Elizabeth Moore, younger dau. of Henry, 3rd Earl of Drogheda, and had issue,

    I. ROBERT, his heir.
    II. Arthur, LL.D., M.P. for Westmeath; *b.* 7 November, 1711, *m.* Sarah, dau. of the Rev. Rowland Singleton, of Drogheda, and had issue, with two daus., Elizabeth, *m.* to Richard Wilson, Esq.; and Patience, *m.* to John Dutton, Esq , five sons, viz.,

      GEORGE, general of artillery, whose dau. and heir, Eliza, *m.* George Clarke, Esq., of Hyde Hall, co. Chester.
      Singleton, an officer in the army.
      Philip.
      Rowland, an officer in the army.
      Henry an officer in the 28th regiment, assistant-commissary-general on the Irish establishment, *m.* Henrietta, dau. of John Hill, Esq. of Barnhill, co. Carlow, and dying 4 October, 1816, left issue,

        JOHN, formerly major 18th regiment.
        GUSTAVUS-ROBERT, commander R.N., *b.* in 1789, a distinguished naval officer, *m.* 12 September, 1814, Maria, dau. of George Leonard, Esq. of Dover Castle, in Sussex Vale, New Brunswick, North America, and had issue, two daus., HENRIETTA-CAROLINE, and SARAH-NAPIER, *d. unm.* 25 September, 1839.
        Catherine, *m.* to John Rae, Esq., captain 72nd regiment.
        Elizabeth, *d. unm.* 10 February, 1830.

    III. George, of Rochfort, co. Westmeath. *b.* in 1713; *m.* in 1746, Alice, dau. of Sir Gustavus Hume, Bart., of Castle Hume, co. Fermanagh, and had an only son,

      GUSTAVUS-HUME ROCHFORT, Esq., M.P. for Westmeath, who sold Rochfort. He *m.* in 1779, Frances, 3rd dau. of John Bloomfield, Esq. of Redwood, and had issue,

        GUSTAVUS, M.P., colonel in the army, *m.* 1806, his cousin Dora Nixon, and dying 1848, left a son, GUSTAVUS ROCHFORT, Esq., captain 4th dragoon-guards, *d. unm.* 1855.
        Richard. late comptroller of the customs of Cork, *m.* 1833, his cousin, Augusta, dau. of Col. Nixon, and *d.* 1842, leaving issue, George, captain 49th regiment, killed at the Redan.
        Henry, in holy orders, *m.* 1829, his cousin, Sarah Rochfort, and *d.* 1854, leaving a dau.
        William, captain R N., *m.* 1833, Arabella, dau. of John Calcraft, Esq., M.P., and *d.* 1847, leaving issue, three daus.
        Charles, of Rochfort Lodge, co. Sligo, late captain rifle brigade, with which he served at Waterloo, *m.* 1832, Hannah, eldest dau. of Colonel Pratt, of Cabra Castle, and *d.* 1844, leaving issue, a son, CHARLES-GUSTAVUS, captain H.M. 20th regiment, *b.* 1837: and a dau., Emily.
        Jane, *m.* to Mervyn Archdale, Esq., of Castle Archdale, general in the army.
        Alice.
        Elizabeth, *m.* to Thomas-Fane Uniacke, Esq.
        Frances-Jocelyn, *m.* to William-Dutton Pollard, Esq., of Castle Pollard, and *d.* 1812.
        Dora, *m.* to Thomas Wade, Esq., of Fairfield House, co. Galway, a descendant of the elder brother of the celebrated Field-Marshal Wade.

    IV. John, *d.* young.
    V. William, of Clontarf, in the army; *b.* in 1719; *m.* in 1743, Henrietta, elder dau. of Colonel John Ramsay. His will dated 23 October, 1772, was proved in Dublin, 10 December, 1772; and his widow's, dated 1 May, 1783, was proved in 1784. They had issue,

      George, called " eldest son " by his father, but not mentioned in his mother's will.
      John. called " eldest son " in his mother's will.
      William.   Henry.
      Ann. *m.* Mr. Weeks.
      Diana, *m.* Mr. Doyly.

Henrietta, m. Mr. Kilpatrick.

Mary, m. Mr. Grange.   Judith.

i. Mary, m. to Sir Henry Tuite, Bart., of Sonnagh, co. Westmeath.

ii. Hannah, d. young.

iii. Elizabeth, d. young.

iv. Alice, m. in 1734, to Thomas Loftus, Esq., of Killyon, M.P.

v. Thomazine, m. to Gustavus Lambert, Esq., of Beau Parc, co. Meath, M.P. for Kilbeggan.

vi. A ne, m. to Henry Lyons, Esq., of River Lyons, King's co.

Mr. Rochfort's will, dated 5 April, 1730, was proved in Dublin, 7 September, following. His eldest son,

Robert Rochfort, Esq., M.P. for the co. Westmeath, b. 26 March, 1708, was elevated to the peerage of Ireland 16 March, 1737, as Baron of Bellfield, advanced to the Viscounty of Bellfield, 5 October, 1751, and created Earl of Belvedere, 29 November, 1756. His lordship m. 1st, Elizabeth, elder dau. of Richard Tenison, Esq., of Thomastown, co. Louth, by whom he had no issue; and 2ndly, 7 August, 1736, Mary, eldest dau. of Richard, Viscount Molesworth, by whom he had issue,

i. George, his heir.

ii. Richard, lieutenant-colonel 39th foot, who m. the dau. and heir of James Mervyn, Esq., but d. s. p.

iii. Robert, M.P., who m. Fanny, eldest dau. of John Nugent, Esq., of Clonlost, co. Westmeath, but d. s. p.

i. Jane, m. 26 January, 1754, to Brinsley, 2nd Earl of Lanesborough, and had issue. The 2nd dau. Lady Catherine Butler m. George Marlay, Esq., of Twickenham, co. Middlesex, and had a son and heir George Marlay, Esq., lieutenant colonel, C.B., who m. Catherine-Louisa-Augusta, dau. of James Tisdall, Esq., of Bawn and d. 1830, leaving a dau. Catherine-Louisa-Georgina, widow of Lord John Manners and two sons, James Marley, who d. in 1843, and Charles-Brinsley Marlay, Esq., of Belvedere, co. Westmeath.

The Earl of Belvedere d. in April, 1772, and was s. by his son, George Rochfort, 2nd Earl of Belvedere, b. 12 October, 1738; who m. 1st, 20 August, 1775, Dorothea, dau. of John Bloomfield, Esq., of Redwood; and 2ndly, Jane, dau. of the Rev. James Mackay, but d. s. p. in 1814, when the title became extinct. His lordship's widow m. 2ndly, 1815, Abraham Boyd, Esq., King's counsel, and had by him an only son, the present George-Augustus Boyd, Esq., of Middleton Park, co. Westmeath, who has inherited from his mother a great portion of the Belvedere estates. Another very considerable portion has devolved on Charles Brinsley Marlay, Esq.

Arms—Az., a lion rampant, arg., armed and langued, gu.

ROLFE—BARON CRANWORTH.

(*See* Addenda.)

ROLLE—BARON ROLLE.

By Letters Patent, dated 8 January, 1748; and 20 June, 1796.

Lineage.

This family was originally of the co. Dorset, and the first of its members that removed into Devon, was

George Rolle, a merchant of great opulence and high reputation in the city of London, who became an extensive purchaser of abbey lands. Besides which he bought *temp.* Henry VIII., the seat, manor, and large demesnes of Stevenstone, in Devonshire, from the Moyles, who had acquired the property by marriage with the heiress of the Stevenstones, the former lords. This George Rolle married thrice, and had no less than twenty children. By his 2nd wife, Eleanor, 2nd dau. of Henry Dacres, Esq., of London, merchant, he had (with two daus.) six sons, viz.,

John, his successor, whose male line became extinct.

George, of whom presently.

Christopher, d. unm.

Henry, who m. Mary, dau. and heir of Robert Yeo, Esq., of Heanton, and was grandfather of two brothers, Sir Samuel Rolle, ancestor (in the female line) of Lord Clinton; and Henry Rolle, an eminent lawyer, who became lord chief justice, and one of the council of state, during the first years of the Commonwealth, from 1648 to 1655.

Robert.   Maurice.

The 2nd son,

George Rolle, Esq., m. Margaret, dau. and heiress of Edmund Marrais, Esq., of Marrais, in Cornwall, and was s. by his son,

Andrew Rolle, Esq., of Marrais, whose son,

Sir John Rolle, K.B., inherited Stevenstone, and became chief of the family upon the failure of the male line of John Rolle, Esq., his great uncle in 1647. This gentleman, who was zealously attached to King Charles II., accompanied that monarch from Holland upon his Restoration, and was made a knight of the Bath, at the ensuing coronation. Sir John Rolle afterwards represented Devon in parliament, and was a leading member

of the House of Commons. He m. Florence, dau. and co-heir of Dennis Rolle, Esq., and dying at an advanced age, in 1706 (accounted the wealthiest commoner in England), was s. by his grandson,

Robert Rolle, Esq., M.P. (son of John Rolle and the Lady Christian Bruce, his wife), he d. s. p. in 1710, and was s. by his brother,

John Rolle, Esq., M.P. for the co. Devon. This gentleman is said to have been offered an earldom by Queen Anne's last ministry, and to have declined it. He m. Isabella, dau. of Sir William Walter, Bart., of Sarsden, in Oxfordshire, and granddau. (maternally) of Robert, Earl of Ailesbury, by whom he had issue,

i. Henry, his successor.

ii. John, M.P., co. Devon, who assumed the surname of Walter, d. in 1779.

iii. William, d. s. p.

iv. Dennis. of Tuderly, Hants, and of Shapwick, co. Somerset, father of John, last Lord Rolle.

i. Christian, m. to Henry Stevens, Esq., of Winscot, co. Devon.

ii. Isabella, m. to Robert Duke, Esq , of Otterton.

iii. Letitia.   iv. Lucilla.

Mr. Rolle d. 6 May, 1730, and was s. by his eldest son,

Henry Rolle, Esq., M.P., co. Devon, D.C.L., b. 7 November, 1708, who was elevated to the peerage, 8 January, 1747-8, by the title of Baron Rolle, of *Stevenstone, co. Devon.* His lordship d. unm. in 1759, when the dignity became extinct, but the estates devolved on his brother,

Dennis Rolle, Esq., who then became of Stevenstone. He m., 1748, Ann, dau. of Arthur Chichester, Esq., of Stowford and Hall, co. Devon, and was s. at his decease, 25 July, 1797, by his son,

John Rolle, Esq., of Stevenstone, and Bicton, b. 16 October, 1756, who was elevated to the peerage, 20 June, 1796, as Baron Rolle, *of Stevenstone, co. Devon:* he m. 1st, 22 February, 1778, Judith Maria, dau. and heir of Henry Walrond, Esq., of Bovey, co. Devon, which lady d. 1 October, 1820; and 2ndly, 24 September, 1822, the Hon. Louisa Trefusis, 2nd dau. of Robert-George-William, 16th Lord Clinton. His lordship d. s. p. 1842, when the barony expired.

Arms—Or, on a bar dancettè, between three billets, az., charged with as many lions rampant of the 1st, three bezants.

ROMARE—EARL OF LINCOLN.

Created *circa* 1142.

Lineage.

The first of this name upon record,

Robert de Romare, feudal Lord of Bolingbroke, co. Lincoln, m. Lucia, dau. and co-heir of Ivo de Tailboys; by whom (who m. after his decease, Ranulph de Meschines, Earl of Chester), he had a son and successor,

William de Romare, Lord of Bolingbroke, who, in 1118, being governor of the garrison of Newmarch, in Normandy, stoutly resisted Hugh de Gournay, then in rebellion there; and remaining firm in his allegiance to King Henry I., was with that monarch at the battle of Brennevill, where a glorious victory was achieved over Lewis, King of France. Long after this, however, having laid claim, unsuccessfully, to those lands in England, of his mother's inheritance, which Ranulph, Earl of Chester, her last husband, had delivered up to the king, in exchange for the earldom, he returned to Normandy in great indignation, and rearing the standard of rebellion in favour of William, son of Robert Curthose, continued in open hostility for two years, but the king at length made him compensation and restored him to the greater part of his right. Whereupon being honourably reconciled, Henry gave him in marriage a noble lady, viz., Maud, dau. of Richard de Redvers, Earl of Devon. Upon the decease of Henry I., and the accession of Stephen, this eminent person espoused the cause of the new monarch, who appointed him one of his principal delegates to administer justice in Normandy: but he soon after went over to the Empress Maud, and joined his half-brother, Ranulph, Earl of Chester, in the surprisal of the castle of Lincoln (anno 1141). He had subsequently a command at the battle of Lincoln, so disastrous to the fortunes of Stephen, and the next year (1142) bore the title of Earl of Lincoln, in the grant by which he founded the Cistercian monastery at Revesby, in that co. His lordship had issue,

William, who d. v. p. (1152), leaving by Hawise, dau. of Stephen, Earl of Albemarle, a son,

William.

Hawyse, m. to Gilbert de Gant (*see* Gant, Earls of Lincoln)

The earl was *s.* at his decease, by his grandson,

WILLIAM DE ROMARE, Lord of Bolingbroke, who never assumed the title of Earl of Lincoln. In the 12th HENRY II., on the assessment of aid for marriage of the king's dau., he certified his knights' fees *de veteri feoffamento*, to be thirty-two, and those *de novo*, twenty-five, a fourth and a third part. This feudal lord *d.* without issue, when the male line of the family ceased, and the earldom passed through the dau. of Earl William, to the house of Gant (*See* GANT, Earls of Lincoln).

Arms—Gu., seven mascles and semée of crosslets, or.

ROPER—VISCOUNT BALTINGLASS.

By Letters Patent, dated 27 June, 1627.

Lineage.

THE RIGHT HON. SIR THOMAS ROPER, Knight, a member of the Irish privy council, "a very valiant comaunder in this said realme of Ireland, in the reigne of Queen ELIZABETH, of most famous memory," *m.* Dame Ann, dau. of Sir Henry Harrington, some time of Baltinglass, Knt., brother to Sir John Harrington, Knt., Lord Harrington in England, and had issue six sons and three daus., viz., I. THOMAS; II. Christopher, who *m.* Anne, dau. of Rolland Wilcokes, of Coventry, Esq., and widow of Sherrington Talbot, Esq., and had two daus., Ruth, *m.* to Thomas Langley, Esq., and Dorothea; III. Henry; IV. John, slain at Marston Moor; V. CARY; VI. Robert; I. Ruth, *m.* to Sir Edward Denny, of Tralee, co. Kerry, Knight; II. Mary, 2nd wife of Rev. Thomas Fuller, D.D., author of "The Worthies;" III. Elizabeth, *m.* to Thomas Humphrey, Esq., of Swepston.

Sir Thomas had an assignment of the site of the dissolved monastery and lordship of Baltinglass, and other lands confirmed to him by royal patent of CHARLES I., 10 November, 1626, "in regard of the many acceptable services done unto our father and the late Queen ELIZABETH," and "having performed many worthy services in the last war, and gained an extraordinary reputation in the eminent employments of command and government,"—(*King's Letter*, dated at Westminster, 18 May, 3rd of King CHARLES I.), he was by letters patent, bearing date 27 June of that year, 1627, created a Baronet of Ireland, and raised to the Irish peerage as *Baron of Bantry, co. Cork*, and VISCOUNT BALTINGLASS, *co. Wicklow*, with remainder to the heirs male of his body. By a king's letter of 26 February, 1629, the viscount had a respite of £2,000 arrears due upon his farm of the licensing of ale houses, and £1,000 received from the clergy, and a pension of six shillings a-day assigned by the viscount to one of his sons, as well as his pay as captain of a company of fifty to be secured to him. The viscount *d.* 15 February, 1637, and was buried in St John's church, Dublin, 20th same month. His eldest son and successor,

THOMAS ROPER, 2nd Viscount Baltinglass, *m.* Anne, dau. of Sir Peter Temple, Bart., of Stowe, Bucks, but *d. s. p.* in 1665, and was *s.* by his brother,

CARY ROPER, 3rd Viscount Baltinglass, who *d* and was buried at Castle Lyons in 1676.

Arms—Erm., two chevrons, paly, or and gu.

ROS, OR ROOS—BARONS ROS.

By Writ of Summons, dated 24 December, 1264.

Lineage.

"That Peter, the ancestor of this great and noble family," says Dugdale, "did originally assume his surname in the time of HENRY I., from that lordship in Holderness, called Ros, where he then had his residence, needeth not to be doubted." This

PETER DE ROS, or Roos, a feudal baron, *m.* Adeline, one of the sisters and co-heirs of the famous Walter Espec, Lord of the manor of Helmesley, called sometimes Helmeslac but oftener Hamlake, in the north riding of Yorkshire, and was *s.* at his decease, by his son,

ROBERT DE ROS, who, in the 3rd HENRY II., paid 1,000 marks of silver to the king for livery of the lands inherited by his mother from her brother, Walter Espec. This Robert was a munificent benefactor to the Knights Templars. He *m.* Sybell de Valoines (who, after his decease, *m.* Ralph de Albini,) and dying sometime about the middle of the 12th century, was *s.* by his son,

EVERARD DE ROS, a minor, and in ward to Ranulph de Glanvil. In the 12th HENRY II., this feudal lord held of the crown eight knights' fees, and in two years afterwards, upon collection of the aid for marrying the king's dau., answered 112*s.* for those which were *de veteri feoffamento*, and 31*s.* 1*d.* for what he had *de novo*. He *m.* Roysia, dau. of William Trusbut, of Wartre, in Holderness, and at the decease of her brothers, *s. p.*, co-heir to her father's estate, which estate was eventually inherited by her descendants, Lords Ros, her sisters and co-heirs having no posterity. They had two sons. This Everard de Ros must have been a very considerable personage at the period in which he lived, for we find him in the year 1176, paying the *then* very large sum of £526 as a fine for his lands, and in four years subsequently, £100 more to have possession of those which the Earl of Albemarle held. He *d.* about 1186, and was *s.* by his elder son,

ROBERT DE ROS, surnamed *Furfan*, who, in the 1st RICHARD I., paid 1,000 marks fine to the crown for livery of his lands. In the 8th of the same reign, being with the king in Normandy, he was committed to the custody of Hugh de Chaumont, for what offence appears not; with especial charge to the said Hugh, that he should keep him as safe as his own life; but Chaumont trusting William de Spiney with his prisoner, that person being corrupted, allowed him to escape out of the castle of Bonville. De Ros eventually gained nothing, however, by this escape, for RICHARD caused him nevertheless to pay 1,200 marks for his freedom, while he had the false traitor Spiney, hanged for his breach of faith. In the next reign, however, Robert de Ros found more favour, for upon the accession of King JOHN, that monarch gave him the whole barony of his great-grandmother's father, Walter Espee, to enjoy in as large and ample a manner as he, the said Walter, ever held it. Soon after which he was deputed, with the bishop of Durham, and other great men, to escort WILLIAM, King of Scotland into England, which monarch coming to Lincoln, swore fealty there to King JOHN, upon the cross of Hubert, archbishop of Canterbury, in the presence of all the people. About the 14th of King JOHN's reign, Robert de Ros assumed the habit of a monk, whereupon the custody of all his lands, viz., Werke Castle, in the co. Northumberland, with his whole barony, was committed to Philip de Ulcote, but he did not continue long a recluse, for we find him the very next year executing the office of sheriff for the county of Cumberland. At the commencement of the struggle between the barons and JOHN, this feudal lord took part with the king, and obtained, in consequence, some grants from the crown; but he subsequently espoused the baronial cause, and was one of the celebrated twenty-five appointed to enforce the observance of Magna Charter. In the reign of King HENRY III. he seems, however, to have returned to his allegiance, and to have been in favour with that prince, for the year after the king's accession, a precept was issued by the crown to the sheriff of Cumberland, ordering the restoration of certain manors granted by King JOHN to De Ros. This feudal lord was the founder of the castle of Helmesley, otherwise Hamlake, in Yorkshire, and of the castle of Werke, in Northumberland—the former of which he bequeathed to his elder son—the latter to the younger, with a barony in Scotland, to be held of the elder by military service. In his latter days he became a Knight Templar, to which order himself and his predecessors had ever been munificently liberal, and dying in that habit, *anno* 1227, was buried in the Temple Church. Robert de Ros *m.* Isabel, natural dau. of WILLIAM THE LION, King of Scotland, and widow of Robert de Brus, and had issue two sons,

WILLIAM, his successor.

ROBERT, *Baron Ros, of Werke*, concerning whom *see* next article.

He was *s.* by his elder son,

WILLIAM DE ROS, of Hamlake, who, upon giving security for the payment of £100 for his relief, had livery of his lands. This feudal lord, in the lifetime of his father, was an active supporter of the baronial cause, and was made prisoner at the battle of Lincoln (1st HENRY III.;) by the royalists, but soon after released and delivered up to his father upon bail. He was subsequently engaged in the wars of Gascony, and he had two military summonses in the 42nd HENRY III., march against the Scots and Welsh. By the deaths of his two great aunts, the sisters of his grandmother, Rose Trusbut, *s. p.*, he became sole heir of the baronial estate of Trusbut and Watre. He *m.* Lucia, dau. of Reginald Fitz-Piers, of Blewleveny, in Wales, and *d.* in 1258. He was *s.* by his son,

ROBERT DE ROS, who had *m.* in the lifetime of his father, Isabel, dau. and heiress of William de Albini, feudal lord of Belvoir, in Leicestershire, by whom he acquired Belvoir Castle, co. Lincoln (*see* Daubeney, Barons Daubeney, and Earl of Bridgewater), and other extensive landed possessions. This great heiress was in ward to the king, and a mandate upon her marriage, bearing date at Windsor, 17 May, 1244, was directed to Bernard de Savoy and Hugh Giffard, to deliver her to her husband, the said Robert: "but not," says Dugdale, "without a round composition, for it appears that both he and his wife, in the 32nd HENRY III., were debtors to the king in no less than the sum of £3,285 13s. 4d., and a palfrey; of which sum the king was then pleased to accept by 200 marks a year until it should be all paid." In the 42nd of the same reign he had two military summonses with his father, to march against the Scotch and Welsh—but afterwards rearing, with the other barons, the standard of revolt, he had a chief command at the battle of Lewes, so disastrous to the royalists; and to his custody in the castle of Hereford, was especially committed the person of Prince Edward. He was at the same time summoned 24 December, 1264, as *Baron de Ros*, to the parliament then called in the king's name by the victorious lords. But the fortune of war changing at the subsequent battle of Evesham, his lands were all seized by the crown, and held until redeemed by his lordship under the Dictum of Kenilworth. In two years after this he must, however, have regained somewhat of royal favour, for he had then permission to raise a new embattled wall around the castle of Belvoir. He *d.* 16 June, 1285, leaving issue by the heiress of Belvoir,

WILLIAM, his successor.
Robert (Sir), knighted 1296.
Isabel, *m.* to Walter de Fauconberge.

His lordship was *s.* by his elder son,

WILLIAM DE ROS, 2nd baron, *b.* 1255; summoned to parliament as *Baron Ros, of Hamlake*, from 23 June, 1295, to 6 October, 1315. This nobleman was one of the competitors for the crown of Scotland, in the 19th EDWARD I., 1296, through his grandmother, Isabel, natural dau. of WILLIAM THE LION, King of Scotland. He was subsequently engaged in the wars of Gascony and Scotland, and discovering the intention of his kinsman, Robert de Ros, then Lord of Werke, to deliver up that castle to the Scots, he lost no time in apprising the king, who thereupon despatched him with 1000 men to defend that place, but the Scots attacking this force upon its march, cut it to pieces; when EDWARD himself advancing from Newcastle-upon-Tyne, soon obtained possession of the fort, and appointed Lord Ros its governor—allowing him, during his absence in Gascony, to nominate his brother, Robert, lieutenant. In a short time after, he had a grant of this castle, with its appurtenances, forfeited by the treason of his before-mentioned kinsman; and for several subsequent years, his lordship was actively engaged in Scotland. In the 1st EDWARD II., he was constituted the king's lieutenant, between Berwick and the river Forth, and in six years afterwards, he was appointed warden of the west marches of Scotland. He *m.* Maud, or Matilda, one of the daus. and co-heirs of John de Vaux, who brought him the manor of Feston, and lands in Boston, co. Lincoln, and had issue,

I. WILLIAM, his successor.
II. JOHN, a very eminent person, *temp.* EDWARD II. and EDWARD III. In the former reign, he took an active part against the Spencers, and, upon the accession of the latter king he was appointed steward of the household, and entrusted with a command in Scotland. He was likewise constituted one of the governors of the young monarch. In the 10th of the same reign, he was made admiral of the seas, from the river Thames, northwards; and the next year, he was with the king in Gascony, as he was again in two years afterwards. He was summoned to parliament as BARON DE ROS, from 27 January, 1332, to 15 June, 1338, but *d. s. p.* in the latter year, when the barony became EXTINCT, while his property devolved upon his brother, William, Lord Ros, of Hamlake.
III. Thomas.
I. Margaret.
II. Anne, *m.* to Paine, son of Robert de Tibetot.
III. Mary, *m.* 1st, to William Braose, and 2ndly, to Thomas de Brotherton, Duke of Norfolk.

His lordship *d.* in 1316, and was *s.* by his elder son,

WILLIAM DE ROS, 3rd baron, summoned to parliament, from 20 November, 1317, to 12 September, 1342. This nobleman, in the 5th EDWARD II., was one of the commissioners appointed to negotiate peace with ROBERT BRUCE, King of Scotland, about which time he came to an agreement with the king, regarding the castle of Werke, which he then exchanged with the crown for other lands. He was subsequently much engaged in the wars of Gascony and Scotland. His lordship *m.* Margery, elder sister and co-heir of Giles de Badlesmere, of Ledes Castle, in Kent, a great feudal baron, by whom he had issue,

WILLIAM, his heir.
THOMAS, who *s.* his brother.
Margaret.   Maud, *m.* to John, Lord Welles.
Alice, *m.* Nicholas, Lord Meinell.
Milicent, *m.* to William, Lord d'Eyncourt.

He *d.* 16 February, 1342-3, and was *s.* by his elder son,

WILLIAM DE ROS, 4th baron, *b.* 1326, summoned to parliament, from 25 November, 1350, to 20 November, 1351. This nobleman was one of the eminent martial characters of the glorious reign of EDWARD III. He was at the memorable battle of Cressy, a leader in the 2nd brigade of the English army; he had a command at Newcastle-upon-Tyne, in the conflict, where DAVID BRUCE, King of Scotland, and many of his nobles, after sustaining a defeat, fell into the hands of the English; and he was subsequently (21st EDWARD III.) at the siege of Calais with the Black Prince. His lordship *m.* Margaret, dau. of Ralph, Lord Nevill (who *m.* after his decease, Henry, Lord Percy), but dying in the Holy Land, in 1352, *s p.*, he was *s.* by his brother,

THOMAS DE ROS, 5th baron, summoned to parliament, from 24 August, 1362, to 3 March, 1384. This nobleman was also engaged in the French wars, and is supposed to have shared the glory of Poictiers. His lordship *m.* Beatrix, dau. of Ralph, 1st Earl of Stafford, and widow of Maurice, Fitz-Maurice, 2nd Earl of Desmond, by whom he had issue, JOHN, William, Thomas, Robert, Elizabeth, *m.* 1st to Lord Zouche, of Haryngworth, and 2ndly, to Thomas, son and heir of Roger, Lord Clifford; and Margaret. He *d.* in 1384, and was *s.* by his eldest son,

JOHN DE ROS, 6th baron, summoned to parliament, from 8 August, 1386, to 13 November, 1393. This nobleman was in the naval expedition in the 11th RICHARD II., under Richard, Earl of Arundel, and the next year he was joined with Henry, Earl of Northumberland, and Ralph, Lord Nevill, in the government of Carlisle, and wardenship of the west marches of Scotland. His lordship, who was not less distinguished for piety than valour, *d.* upon his pilgrimage to Jerusalem, at Paphos, in the Isle of Cyprus, *anno* 1393-4. He *m.* Mary, dau. of Henry de Percy, but having no issue, was *s.* by his brother,

WILLIAM DE ROS, 7th baron, summoned to parliament, from 20 November, 1394, to 24 December, 1413. This nobleman was appointed lord treasurer of England, in the 4th HENRY IV., and in the 6th he obtained, in consideration of his services, a grant from the crown of 100 marks per annum for his life, to be paid out of the exchequer. In the 16th of the same reign, being then one of the king's council, and in such esteem that his residence near the court was deemed indispensable, he had the town of Chyngilford, in Essex, assigned him, for the abode of his servants and horses. It was about this period that his lordship preferred a complaint in parliament against Robert Tirwhit, one of the justices of the King's Bench, for withholding from him, and his tenants, of the manor of Melton Roos, co. Lincoln, certain commonage of pasture and turbay, and with lying in wait for him, with 500 men. To which charges, Mr. Justice Tirwhit pleading guilty in the presence of the king, and craving pardon, the case was referred to the chief justice, Sir William Gascoine, who determined that Tirwhit, attended by all his party, should meet Lord Ros, at the common in dispute, and bring with him two tuns of Gascony wine, with two fat oxen, and twelve fat sheep, as provision for a dinner, to be then eaten by the assembled friends and adherents of the disputants, and that Tirwhit, in the presence of all, should make Lord Ros, a most submissive apology, tendering him, at the same time, 500 hundred marks, as a compensation. To which, it was also settled by the arbitrator, that the baron should reply; "At reverence of the king, who hath shewed himself to be a good and righteous lord; I will take nothing but the oxen and sheep, for the dinner of these here collected." A free and open act of forgiveness was to follow this speech to Tirwhit and his partisans, and thus the matter terminated. His lordship *m.* Margaret, dau. of Sir John Arundel, son of John Fitzalan, Lord Maltravers, 2nd son of Richard, 9th Earl of Arundel. Lord De Ros *d.* at Belvoir, 1 September, 1414, having had issue,

I. JOHN, of whom presently.
II. Thomas.
III. Robert (Sir), whose dau , Elizabeth, *m.* 1st, Robert Lovel, 2ndly, Thomas Proude, and 3rdly, Sir Richard Haut.
IV. William.
V. Richard, who had a dau., Mary, *m.* to Sir Giles Capel.
I. Beatrice, a nun.   II. Alice.
III. Margaret, *m.* 1st, Reginald, Lord Grey de Ruthyn, and 2ndly, to James, Lord Audley.
IV. Elizabeth, *m.* to Robert, 6th Lord Morley.

The eldest son,

JOHN DE ROS, 8th baron, but never summoned to parliament. His lordship was retained in the 4th HENRY V., to serve the king in France, being then scarcely eighteen years of age. In two years afterwards he was with the Dukes of Exeter and Clarence at the siege of Roan, where he so gallantly distinguished himself, that he had a grant of the castle of Basqueville, in Normandy, to himself and his heirs male for ever. Continuing in those wars, he was slain within two years, *anno* 1421, at Beaugé, in which disastrous battle his brother, William de Ros, as well as the Duke of Clarence (under whom he served), and a great many of the flower of the English nobility fell. His lordship m. Margaret, dau. and heir of Sir Philip Despenser, but having had no issue (his widow m. 2ndly, Sir Roger Wentworth), was s. by his next brother,

SIR THOMAS DE ROS, 9th baron, summoned to parliament 12 July, and 3 August, 1429. This nobleman m. Alianor, dau. of Richard Beauchamp, Earl of Warwick, and was s. at his decease, 18 August, 1431, by his eldest son,

THOMAS DE ROS, 10th baron, b. 9 September, 1427. During the minority of this nobleman, his great uncle, Sir Robert Ros, Knt., was deputed by the king to perform the office of chamberlain to the archbishop. of Canterbury upon the day of his installation, which office belonged to the Lord Ros, in right of the tenure of a certain manor. His lordship, who was in ward to the crown, had, by especial favour, the livery of his lands in the 24th HENRY VI. In the memorable contests commenced in that monarch's reign between the houses of Lancaster and York, Lord Ros entered zealously into the cause of the former, and participated in its disasters, particularly at the battle of Towton-field. Being with the king at York, when tidings of the defeat reached the unfortunate monarch, he fled with his royal master to Berwick, and was attainted in the 1st EDWARD IV., when his lands were confiscated, and Belvoir Castle granted to the Lord Hastings, who eventually dismantled the splendid structure, which remained from that period little better than a heap of ruins until the reigns of HENRY VIII. and ELIZABETH, when its renovation was commenced, and completed by Thomas and Henry Manners, 1st and 2nd Earls of Rutland. His lordship m. Philippa, dau. of John, Lord Tiptoft, and sister and co-heir of John, Earl of Worcester, and by her (who m. 2ndly, Sir Thomas Wingfield, and 3rdly, Edward Grimston) had issue,

EDMUND.   John, d. s. p
ELEANOR, m. to SIR ROBERT MANNERS, M.P., ancestor of the Earls and Dukes of Rutland and of the present LORD DE ROS.
ISABEL, m. 1st, to Sir Thomas Everingham, 2ndly, to Thomas Grey, youngest son of Sir Ralph Grey, of Werke, and 3rdly, to Sir Thomas Lovel, K.G.: she d. s. p. 1524.
MARGARET, d. unm.

Lord Ros was summoned to parliament from 2 January, 1449, to 30 July, 1460. He was attainted 4 November, 1461, and his honours thereupon became forfeited. He d. in the same year. The Barony of Ros lay under the attainder until the complete triumph of the Lancastrians, by the accession of King HENRY VII., when the elder son,

EDMUND DE ROS, obtained (1st HENRY VII.) an act of parliament, annulling and making entirely void the act by which his father was attainted, and restoring to him all the estates and honours of the family. He was never, however, summoned to parliament. His lordship d. 13 October, 1508, unm., when the Barony of Ros fell into ABEYANCE between his three sisters and co-heirs, but the two younger sisters having d. s p., the abeyance terminated in favour of SIR GEORGE MANNERS, the son and heir of Sir Robert and Lady Eleanor Manners. His eldest son was created EARL OF RUTLAND, and the title of Ros descended for some generations in that family. (For particulars refer to BURKE's Peerage).

Thus terminated the male line of the family of DE ROS, BARONS ROS, of Hamlake, but the barony has long survived its original possessors, and after having remained in ABEYANCE from the year 1687, was after the lapse of nearly a century and a quarter, called out of abeyance in 1806 in favour of Lady Henry Fitzgerald, who assumed the additional surname of DE ROS, and was mother of the late and present LORDS DE ROS. For particulars of more recent lineage, refer to the Extant Peerage.

Arms—Gu., three water-bougets, arg.

ROS—BARON ROS, OF WERKE.

By Writ of Summons, dated 24 June, 1295.

Lineage.

ROBERT DE ROS, feudal Lord of Hamlake (refer to that family), conferred the castle and Barony of Werke, co. Northumberland, which he held of the crown by the service of two knights' fees, upon his younger son,

ROBERT DE ROS, who, in the 21st HENRY III., was constituted chief justice of the forest in the counties of Nottingham, Derby, York, Lancaster, Northumberland, and

Cumberland, which office he held for several years afterwards. In the 39th of the same reign he made a temporary surrender of his castle of Werke to the king, who was then advancing with an army upon Scotland, and deemed it impolitic to permit so strong a fort to remain in private hands. About this time charges were preferred against Robert de Ros, to whose care and guidance, with John de Baliol, the kingdom of Scotland, as well as its King, ALEXANDER III., and the Queen MARGARET (dau. of the English monarch), were committed, for arbitrary conduct in the discharge of his duty; for which he was, eventually, fined no less than 100,000 marks, but his innocence appearing afterwards manifest, the penalty was entirely remitted. In the 22nd EDWARD I , he had summons with other of the barons to repair to the king, to advise upon the affairs of the realm; and the next year he was summoned to parliament, 24 June, 1 October, and 2 November, by writ addressed "Roberto de Roos de Werke," but never afterwards. In a short time, subsequently, however, falling in love with a Scottish lady, he deserted to the Scots, having previously endeavoured to seduce from his allegiance, his kinsman, Lord Ros, of Hamlake. But that nobleman repairing to King EDWARD divulged the treason, and was forthwith despatched at the head of 1,000 men to take possession of Werke, whither he was proceeding, when Robert de Ros, with a great body of Scots, surprised him at the village of Prestfen, and cut the whole English force to pieces. King EDWARD very shortly, however, most amply avenged himself, at the battle of Dunbar, where no less than 10,053 Scotsmen fell: and Werke coming into the possession of the crown, was conferred upon Lord Ros, of Hamlake.

Robert, Lord Ros, of Werke, m. Margaret, one of the four sisters and co-heirs of Peter de Brus of Skelton, but regarding his heirs the records differ, but the more reliable state that he had a son, WILLIAM, to whom his mother gave the castle of Kendal; and from whom descended his eventual heir ELIZABETH de Ros, m. Sir William Parr, Knight, from whom sprang the Parrs of Kendal, ennobled by that title, which see. The barony of Ros of Werke EXPIRED under the treason of the baron.

Arms—Gu., three water-bougets, arg.

ROS, OR ROOS—BARON ROS.

By Writ of Summons, dated 27 January, 1332.

Lineage.

(See ROS, LORD ROS, of Hamlake.)

John de Ros, 2nd son of William de Ros, 2nd Baron Ros, of Hamlake.

ROSS—LORD ROSS.

Lineage.

SIR JOHN ROSS, of Halkhead, in Renfrewshire, son and heir of Sir John Ross, of Halkhead, was one of the conservators of a treaty with the English, 20 September, 1484, under the designation of John Rosse de Halkhede, miles. Ross Dominus de Halkhed occurs among the barons in the parliament, 3 February, 1489-90; and Ross de Halkhed is inserted among the Domini barones in the parliament, 11 March, 1503-4. His son and heir,

JOHN ROSS, 2nd Lord Ross, of Halkhead, fell at the battle of Flodden, 9 September, 1513. By Christian, his wife, dau. of Archibald Edmonston, of Duntreath, he had a son,

NINIAN ROSS, 3rd Lord Ross, of Halkhead, one of the Scottish nobles who, in 1515, despatched ambassadors to France, to endeavour to include Scotland in the pacification with England. He m. 1st, Lady Janet Stewart, 3rd dau. of John, Earl of Lennox, by whom he had a son, ROBERT, Master of Ross, killed at Pinkie in 1547, leaving a dau., Elizabeth, wife of John, Lord Fleming. Lord Ross m. 2ndly, Elizabeth, dau. of William, 1st Lord Ruthven, and relict of William, 5th Earl of Erroll, by whom he had a son,

JAMES ROSS, 4th Lord Ross: who d. in April, 1581, leaving by Jean, his wife, dau. of Robert, 3rd Lord Semphill, two sons,

ROBERT, his heir.
William (Sir), of Muiriston.
Elizabeth, *m.* to Alan Lockhart, jun., of Cleghorn.
Jean, *m.* to Sir James Sandilands, of Calder.

The son and heir,

ROBERT ROSS, 5th Lord Ross, *m.* Jean, dau. of Gavin Hamilton, of Raploch, by whom he had a dau. (Grizel, *m.* to Sir Archibald Stirling, of Keir and Cawder,) and a son,

JAMES ROSS, 6th Lord Ross; who *m.* Margaret, eldest dau. of Walter, 1st Lord Scott, of Buccleuch, and by her (who *m.* 2ndly, Alexander, 6th Earl of Eglinton, and *d.* in October, 1651) he had issue,

JAMES, 7th Lord Ross.
WILLIAM, 8th Lord Ross.
ROBERT, 9th Lord Ross.
Margaret, *b.* 19 December, 1615; *m.* to Sir George Stirling, of Keir and Cawder; and *d.* 10 March, 1633, aged eighteen, leaving one dau., Margaret, who *d.* 11 May, 1633.
Mary, *m.* to John Hepburn, of Waughton.
Jean, *m.* to Sir Robert Innes, Bart. of Innes.

JAMES ROSS, 7th Lord Ross, the eldest son, was served heir of his father in the lordship and Barony of Melville, &c., 18 September, 1634, and had charters of Halkhead, Melville, Craig, and Balgone, 25 January, 1636; also of Easter Stanley, in Renfrewshire. He *d. unm.* 17 March, 1636, and was *s.* by his brother,

WILLIAM, 8th Lord Ross; who also *d. unm.* in August, 1640, and was *s.* by his brother,

ROBERT ROSS, 9th Lord Ross; who *d. unm.* in August, 1648, when his estates and titles devolved on the heir male (the son of Sir William Ross, of Muiriston, 2nd son of James, 4th Lord Ross),

SIR WILLIAM ROSS, of Muiriston, as 10th Lord Ross. His lordship was colonel of foot in the cos. of Ayr and Renfrew, in 1648, and one of the committee of estates in 1649. He *d.* in 1656, leaving by Helen, his wife, eldest dau. of George, 1st Lord Forrester, of Corstorphine, a son and heir,

GEORGE ROSS, 11th Lord Ross; who, on the restoration of CHARLES II., was sworn a privy councillor, and appointed lieutenant-colonel of the royal regiment of guards. He *m.* 1st, Lady Grizel Cochrane, only dau. of William, 1st Earl of Dundonald, and had issue,

WILLIAM, 12th Lord Ross.
Grizel, *m.* to Sir Alexander Gilmour, Bart., of Craigmiller, co. Edinburgh.

His lordship *m.* 2ndly, Lady Jean Ramsay, eldest dau. of George, 2nd Earl of Dalhousie, and by her (who took to her 2nd husband, Robert, Viscount of Oxford) had issue,

Charles, of Balnagowan, colonel of the 5th, or royal Irish regiment of dragoons, from 1695 to 1716, and again from 1726 to 1732; who ranked as general in the army from 1 April, 1712. He *d. unm.* at Bath, 5 August, 1732, and was buried at Fearn, in Ross-shire.
Jean, *m.* to William, 6th Earl of Dalhousie, and had issue.

The eldest son,

WILLIAM ROSS, 12th Lord Ross, *b.* 1656, *s.* his father, 1682. He entered zealously into the revolution, 1689; was a privy councillor to King WILLIAM and Queen ANNE, high commissioner to the church of Scotland, 1704; one of the lords of the treasury, and a commissioner for the Union, of which treaty he was a stanch supporter. He was chosen one of the sixteen representatives of the Scottish peerage at the general election, 1715; appointed lieutenant of the co. of Renfrew, the same year; and *d.* at Halkhead, 15 March, 1738, in the eighty-second year of his age. His lordship *m.* 1st, 7 February, 1679, Agnes, dau. and heiress of Sir John Wilkie, of Foulden, co. Berwick, and by her had issue,

GEORGE, 13th Lord Ross.
Eupheme, *m.* to William, 3rd Earl of Kilmarnock, and had issue.
Mary, *m.* in 1710, to John, 1st Duke of Athole, and had issue.
Grizel, *m.* to Sir James Lockhart, Bart., of Carstairs, co. Lanark, who *d.* 31 July, 1755: the great grandson and heir male of this marriage is the present SIR CHARLES-WILLIAM-AUGUSTUS ROSS, Bart., of Balnagowan.

Lord Ross *m.* 2ndly, a dau. of Philip, Lord Wharton, but she *d. s. p.*; and 3rdly, Lady Anne Hay, eldest dau. of John, 2nd Marquess of Tweeddale, by whom he had one dau.,

Anne, who *d. unm.*

He lordship *m.* 4thly (contract dated 16 June, 1731), Henrietta, dau. of Sir Francis Scott, of Thirlestane, but by her, who *d.* at Edinburgh, 16 January, 1750, had no issue. His only son,

GEORGE ROSS, 13th Lord Ross, was appointed one of the commissioners of excise in Scotland, 24 November, 1726, and one of the commissioners of customs, 21 September, 1730. He *s.* his

father in 1738; made a settlement of his estates 17 June, 1751, on his son, and the heirs of his body; which failing, on his daus., Jane, Elizabeth, and Mary, respectively, and the heirs male of their bodies, remainder to his nearest heirs and assigns; and dying 17 June, 1754, in the 73rd year of his age, was buried at Renfrew. He *m.* Lady Elizabeth Kerr, 3rd dau. of William, 2nd Marquess of Lothian, and by her, who *d.* at Halkhead, 22 May, 1768, had issue,

WILLIAM, 14th Lord Ross.
Charles, M.P. for Renfrewshire, who, in 1732, *s.* to the estate of Balnagowan, in virtue of an entail executed by his uncle, 1727. He held a commission in the army, and fell at the battle of Fontenoy, 30 April, 1745, *unm.;* the estate of Balnagowan devolving on his father.
George, *d. s. p.*
Jane, *m.* 28 July, 1755, to John Mackye of Polgowan, M.P., who took the name of Ross, but *d. s. p.*, at Clifton, 19 August, 1777.
Elizabeth (eventually heiress), *m.* 11 June, 1755, to John Boyle, 3rd Earl of Glasgow, and had issue: the son and heir, GEORGE, 4th Earl of Glasgow, G.C.H., was created a peer of the United Kingdom, 11 August, 1815, and took the title of BARON ROSS, *of Halkhead, co. Renfrew.*
Mary, *d. unm.* at London, 22 October, 1762, aged thirty-two.

The only surviving son,

WILLIAM ROSS, 14th Lord Ross, was an officer in the royal army commanded by Lord Loudoun, and in the march to surprise the Chevalier at Moy, in February, 1746, was thrown down by the cavalry, and much hurt. He *s.* his father in June, 1754, but enjoyed the title only two months, dying at Mount Teviot, the seat of his uncle, the Marquess of Lothian, of gout in his head, 19 August, 1754, aged thirty-four, *unm.* The title became EXTINCT; the estate of Balnagowan went to his cousin, Sir James Ross Lockhart, after an ineffectual opposition from Sir Alexander Gilmour; and his other property devolved on his sisters, and is now possessed by the Earl of Glasgow.

Arms—Quarterly: 1st and 4th, arg., a chev., chequy, of the field and sa., between three water bougets, of the last, for Ross; 2nd and 3rd, gu., three crescents, within a bordure, arg., the latter charged with eight roses of the field, barbed and seeded, ppr., for MELVILLE.

ROWLEY—VISCOUNT LANGFORD.

(*See* BARON LANGFORD in BURKE's *Extant Peerage.*)

RUPERT—DUKE OF CUMBERLAND.

By Letters Patent, dated 24 June, 1644.

Lineage.

The Princess ELIZABETH, of England, *b.* 19 August, 1569, only dau. of King JAMES I., *m.* 14 February, 1612-13, FREDERICK V., Duke of Bavaria, Elector Palatine of the Rhine, and King of Bohemia, and had issue,

I. CHARLES-LEWIS, successor to the Dukedom of Bavaria, whose dau. and heir, CHARLOTTE, *m.* Philippe, Duke of Orleans.
II. RUPERT, Count Palatine of the Rhine, of whom presently.
III. Maurice, the companion in arms during the civil wars of his gallant brother, Prince RUPERT, known in English history as "Prince Maurice," *d. unm.* (shipwrecked), in 1654.
IV. Edward, Duke of Bavaria, Count Palatine of the Rhine, K.G., *m.* Anne de Gonzaga of Mantua, and *d.* 10 March, 1663, leaving three daus., viz.,

  1 ANNE, *m.* to Henry-Julius Prince of Condé.
  2 BENEDICTA, *m.* to John-Frederick, Duke of Brunswick-Lunenburgh.
  3 LOUISA-MARIA, *m.* to Charles-Theodore, Prince of Salms.

V. Philip, killed in battle, *unm.* in 1650.
I. Elizabeth, Abbess of Hervorden, *d.* 1680.
II. Louisa, Abbess of Maubisson.
III. Henrietta, *m.* to Sigismund, Prince of Transylvania, and *d. s. p* 1651.
IV. SOPHIA, *b.* 13 October, 1630; *m.* in 1658, to Ernest-Augustus, Duke of Brunswick-Lunenburgh, Elector of Hanover, and was mother of GEORGE-LEWIS, who ascended the British throne, as King GEORGE I.

The 2nd son,

PRINCE RUPERT, coming into England in 1642, was elected knight of the Garter, and created by his uncle, King CHARLES I., 24 June, 1644, *Baron of Kendal, co. Westmoreland, Earl of*

Holderness, and DUKE OF CUMBERLAND. His highness, with his gallant brother, Prince MAURICE, was ever found amongst the most intrepid, enterprizing, and indefatigable of the cavalier commanders; RUPERT, as general of the royal horse, and MAURICE, in command of some forces in the west. Indeed Rupert's fiery disposition appears frequently to have outrun his better judgment, and he has acquired the reputation of a bold and high-spirited officer, rather than of a cool and able commander. To his unbridled zeal the loss of Marston Moor has been attributed, and upon that the fate of King CHARLES I. mainly depended. In glancing at the chapter of English history, which records the great Civil War, we find much to console us, and much to retrieve the character of the country, in the gallant bearing assumed by the gentlemen of England, and the thorough devotedness of her high-minded nobility. The foes of royalty may decry, with as much malignity as they please, the cause in which the cavaliers so nobly fought and bled; but they must concede to those chivalrous men, the meed of loyalty, the most enthusiastic; fidelity, the most disinterested; and valour, the most heroic. Prince RUPERT retired into France when the royal cause became hopeless, but returned at the Restoration, and subsequently filled some high official situations. In the different naval engagements with the Dutch, his highness was particularly signalized by his able conduct and his characteristic bravery. He d. *unm.* 19 November, 1682, in the sixty-third year of his age, when the Dukedom of Cumberland (of this creation) and the minor honours became EXTINCT.

Arms—Quarterly: 1st and 4th, sa., a lion rampant, or; 2nd and 3rd paly bendy, arg., and az.

NOTE.—Prince RUPERT had by FRANCES, dau. and co-heir of Henry Bard, Viscount Bellamont, in Ireland, an illegitimate son, DUDLEY RUPERT, who was slain at the siege of Buda, a volunteer in the imperial army. His highness had likewise, by Mrs. Margaret Hughes, a dau., RUPERTA, *m.* to Emanuel-Scroope Howe, brother of Scroope, Viscount Howe.

RUSSELL—EARL OF ORFORD.

By Letters Patent, dated 7 May, 1697.

Lineage.

EDWARD RUSSELL, 2nd son (by Penelope, his wife, dau. of Sir Moyses Hill, of Hillsborough), of the Hon. Edward Russell, 4th son of Francis, 4th Earl Bedford (*refer to Extant Peerage*), had been, says Burnet "bred at sea, and was bedchamber-man to the King (JAMES II.). when Duke of York; but upon Lord Russell's death, retired from the court. He was a man of much honour and great courage. He had good principles and was firm to them." Strenuously supporting the Revolution, he obtained high naval commands from the new King (WILLIAM III.); attained to the rank of admiral; and distinguished himself as one of the most eminent naval heroes of the period particularly by the splendid victory which, while commander of the fleet, he achieved in 1692 over the French under Count de Tourville, off La Hogue, for which, and his other gallant services, he was created 7 May, 1697, BARON OF SHINGAY, co. Cambridge (with remainder to the issue male of LETITIA, his elder sister), *Viscount of Barfleur, in the Duchy of Normandy*, and EARL OF ORFORD, co. Suffolk. His lordship *m.* his cousin, Lady Margaret Russell, dau. of William, 1st Duke of Bedford, but d. *s. p.* in 1727, when (his sister LETITIA having deceased previously without male issue), all his honours became EXTINCT.

Arms—Arg., a lion rampant, gu., on a chief, sa., three escallops of the field: a crescent for difference.

RUTHERFORD—EARL OF TEVIOT, AND BARON RUTHERFORD.

Barony, by Letters Patent, dated 19 January, 1661.
Earldom, by Letters Patent, dated 2 February, 1663

Lineage.

ANDREW RUTHERFORD, only son of William Rutherford, of Quarryholes, a cadet of Rutherford, of Hunthill, by Isabel, dau. of James Stuart of Traquair, was by King CHARLES II., created

a peer of Scotland, by the title of LORD RUTHERFORD, by diploma or patent of dignity, dated 19 January, 1661, to him and the heirs male of his body, "quibus deficientibus, quamcunque aliam personam seu personas quas sibi quoad vixerit, quinetiam in articulo mortis, ad ei succedendum, ac fore ejus hæredes talliæ et conscribendam in eadem dignitate, nominare et designare placuerit, secundum nominationem et designationem manu ejus subscribendam, subque provisionibus restrictionibus et conditionibus a dicto Andreā, pro ejus arbitrio, in dictā designatione exprimendis. "Being chosen governor of Tangier," says Mr. Alexander Sinclair, in his learned *Dissertation on Heirs Male*, "his lordship. before departing, executed a settlement, which is probably the most curious patent of honor extant, as his title, lands, legacies, debts, and execulry, are all intermingled in his appointment of heirs, who were SIR THOMAS RUTHERFORD, of Hunthill, then to the eldest son of Sir Thomas, and failing thereof, to the nearest heir male of the said Sir Thomas, and then to Sir Thomas's eldest daughter. This deed in connection with the patent was quite sufficient, on his being slain by the Moors next year, to convey the peerage to his nominee and distant cousin, who thus became 2nd Lord Rutherford." His lordship, in two years after (2 February, 1663), was advanced to the EARLDOM OF TEVIOT, with limitation to the heirs male of his body. He d. *s. p.* (being killed at Tangier), 4 May, 1664, when the earldom became EXTINCT; but the barony under the settlement made by the earl, in accordance with the special provisions of the patent above quoted, devolved on his kinsman,

SIR THOMAS RUTHERFORD, of Hunthill, as 2nd Lord Rutherford. This nobleman *m.* Christian, dau. of Sir Alexander Urquhart, of Cromarty, but by her (who *m.* 2ndly, James, 2nd Viscount Frendraught; and 3rdly, Alexander Monson, of Bognie) had no issue. He d. in 1668, leaving no issue, and was *s.* by his youngest brother,

ARCHIBALD RUTHERFORD, 3rd Lord Rutherford, who *d.* without male issue, in 1685, when the title devolved on the youngest brother,

ROBERT RUTHERFORD, 4th Lord Rutherford, who *d. s. p.* in 1724.

After his lordship's decease, George Durie, Esq., of Grange, Fifeshire, grandson of Christian Rutherford (sister of the Earl of Teviot) by her husband, Robert Durie, of Grange, voted without objection, as Lord Rutherford, at the election of a representative peer, in 1733. In 1734, he again entered his vote, but under protest from the procurator of Captain John Rutherford, and in 1739, both George Durie and John Rutherford voted, which they continued to do at several elections. "Claimants" observes Mr. Alexander Sinclair, "have repeatedly come forward as heirs male to the last lord, and others as heirs general of the first lord, so that from 1734, for two generations, the rival parties continued voting at elections, each protesting that the other had no right, the alleged heir male stating that the peerage was granted first to heirs male, and that no provision whatever had been made for the succession of the 1st lord's female relations, and the undoubted heir-general asserting that the other could not prove any male connexion with his pretended cousins, either the first or the last peer. There was no settlement of these conflicting claims when they dropped in 1782; but in 1786, the House of Lords resolved that the vote of the heir-general should have been rejected, and assuredly he could have no right whatever. The original destination to Sir Thomas and his heirs male having been admitted to include collaterals in general, the succession could not open to heirs-general while any male branch of the Hunthill family existed; and if they did fail, the ultimate clause in favour of females was to the 2nd lord's daughter, and not to the 1st lord's sister, whom her brothers had cut off probably from her inferior status. The 4th lord appointed Thomas Rutherford one of the family of Edgerston to succeed him; but this could not affect the settlement of the peerage. This is a case of the admission of collateral succession under a settlement on heirs-male, simply; as the proviso, regarding the name and arms, refers to the case of Sir Thomas's daughter becoming the heir, and her husband and issue not being Rutherfords by birth."

MARGARET RUTHERFORD, only sister of the last Lord Rutherford, named in the limitation, *m.* Charles, 2nd son of Sir John Scott, Bart., of Ancrum, and left one son, JOHN SCOTT, of Belford, who *m.* Marion Bailie, of Ashestiel: this gentleman was engaged in the rising of 1745, and did not set up a claim to the peerage: his representatives are his great-grandsons, SIR ALEXANDER COCKBURN CAMPBELL, Bart., and JOHN HOOD, Esq., of Stoneridge, co. Berwick (by double descent), and his great great-grandson, Sir Stafford H. Northcote, Bart.

Arms—Arg., an orle, gu., and in chief, three martlets, sa.

RUTHVEN — BARONS RUTHVEN AND EARLS OF GOWRIE.

Barony, created 29 January, 1487-8.
Earldom, by Letters Patent, dated 23 August, 1581.

Lineage.

Sir WILLIAM DE RUTHVEN was created a lord of parliament, 29 January, 1487-8. He *m.* 1st, Isabel, dau. of Livington, of Saltcoats, co. Haddington, and relict of Walter Lindsay, of Beaufort, by whom he had two sons, born before marriage, and a dau., viz.,

   I. WILLIAM, slain at Flodden, who had a legitimation under the great seal, 2 July, 1480. He *m.* Catherine Buttergask, and had a son,
     WILLIAM, heir to his grandfather.

   II. John, who obtained a legitimation under the great seal, 2 July, 1480, with his brother William, wherein they were styled natural sons of William de Ruthven, of Ruthven.
   I. Margaret, *m.* 1st, to Alexander, 2nd Earl of Buchan.

William, Lord Ruthven, *m.* 2ndly, Christian, dau. of John, Lord Forbes, and by her had a son, and a dau.,

   WILLIAM, of Ballindean, ancestor of the EARL OF FORTH.
   Elizabeth, *m.* 1st, to William, 4th Earl of Erroll, and 2ndly, to Ninian, 2nd Lord Ross, and had issue to both.

Lord Ruthven was *s.* by his grandson,

WILLIAM RUTHVEN, 2nd Lord Ruthven, who *s.* in 1528. He was appointed an extraordinary lord of session, 16 February, 1539, and keeper of the privy seal in 1547. He *d.* before 16 December, 1552. He *m.* Janet, eldest dau. and co-heir of Patrick, Lord Halyburton, of Dirleton, with whom he got that barony, and a considerable accession to his estate, and had issue by her,

   I. PATRICK, 3rd Lord Ruthven.
   II. JAMES, of Forteviot. There is a charter to William, Lord Ruthven, Janet Haliburton, his wife, and James, their son, of half of the lands of Forteviot, 24 January, 1535-6, and another to James, 2nd son of William, Lord Ruthven, of the Barony of Segge, in Kinross-shire, 5 February, 1550-1. He *d. s. p.*, as Patrick, Lord Ruthven, was served heir to James Ruthven, of Forteviot, his brother, 9 January, 1553.
   III. ALEXANDER, of Freeland, ancestor of the LORDS RUTHVEN, of Freeland.
   I. Lilias, *m.* to David, 2nd Lord Drummond.
   II. Catharine, *m.* to Sir Colin Campbell, of Glenurchy.
   III. Cecilia, *m.* to Sir David Wemyss, of Wemyss.
   IV. Barbara, *m.* to Patrick, 6th Lord Gray.
   V. Ganet, *m.* to John Crichton, of Strathurd.
   VI. Margaret, *m.* to John Johnston, of Elphinston.
   VII. Christian, *m.* to William Lundin, of Lundin.

The eldest son,

PATRICK RUTHVEN, 3rd Lord Ruthven and Dirleton, *b.* about 1520, acted a prominent part in the political and religious controversies of his time, but is most known as the principal actor in the murder of David Rizzio, 9 March, 1566. He *m.* 1st, Janet Douglas, natural dau. of Archibald, Earl of Angus, and 2ndly, Janet, Lady Methven, dau. of the 2nd Earl of Athole, and by the former had issue,

   I. PATRICK, master of Ruthven, *m.* Margaret, eldest dau. of Patrick, 5th Lord Gray, and *d. s. p. v. p.*
   II. WILLIAM, 4th Lord Ruthven.
   III. Alexander.
   I. Jean, *m.* 1st, to Henry, 2nd Lord Methven, and 2ndly, to Andrew, 5th Earl of Rothes.
   II. Isabel, *m.* to James, 1st Lord Colvill, of Culross, and had issue.

Lord Ruthven, after the murder of Darnley, fled to England, and *d.* in that country three months after, 13 June, 1566-7. His eldest surviving son,

WILLIAM RUTHVEN, 4th Lord Ruthven and Dirleton, took part with his father in the murder of David Rizzio, 9 March, 1566, and fled into England; but eventually making his peace with the Scottish court, he obtained, by means of the Earl of Morton, the Queen's pardon, was appointed treasurer for Scotland for life, by patent, dated 24 June, 1571, and one of the extraordinary lords of Session, 25 November, 1578, and created EARL OF GOWRIE, by patent, dated 23 August, 1581. Subsequently joining in the treasonable conspiracy for seizing on the king (JAMES VI.), known in history as the "Raid of Ruthven," he was tried and found guilty of high treason, at Stirling, 28 May, 1584, and executed between eight and nine in the evening of the same day. He *m.* Dorothea, 2nd dau. of Henry, Lord Methven (by his 2nd wife, Lady Janet Stewart, afterwards *m.* to his father, Lord Ruthven), and had issue by her,

JAMES, 2nd Earl of Gowrie.
JOHN, 3rd Earl of Gowrie.
Alexander, engaged in "the Gowrie conspiracy" at Perth, 5 August, 1600, in which he was killed.
William, who went abroad, and became famous for his knowledge in chemistry.
Patrick, an eminent physician, who was confined for many years in the Tower of London, from which he was released in 1619. His dau. Mary *m.* Sir Anthony Vandyke, the famous painter, and left a dau. and sole heiress,
   JUSTINA, *m.* to SIR JOHN STEPNEY. Bart.
Margaret, *m.* to James, 4th Earl of Montrose, and was mother of the gallant Marquess of Montrose.
Mary, *m.* 1st, to John, 5th Earl of Athole, and 2ndly, to John, Lord Innermeath, created Earl of Athole.
Sophia, *m.* to Ludovick, 2nd Duke of Lennox, but *d. s. p.*
Jean, *m.* to James, Lord Ogilvy, of Airly, and was mother of the 1st Earl of Airly.
Beatrix, *m.* to Sir John Home, of Coldingknows, and had issue.
Isabel, *m.* 1st, to Sir Robert Gordon, of Lochinvar, and had issue. She was divorced from him, and *m.* 2ndly, George, 1st Lord Loudoun, and had issue.
Dorothea, *m.* to James Wemyss, of Pittencrieff, co. Fife.

The eldest son,

JAMES RUTHVEN, 2nd Earl of Gowrie, Provost of Perth, was restored to his estate and honours in 1586, and *d.* in the fourteenth year of his age, 1588, when his brother,

JOHN RUTHVEN, *s.* as 3rd Earl of Gowrie, Provost of Perth. He was killed at Perth, 5 August, 1600, with his brother Alexander, in the mysterious attempt on the person of King JAMES VI., known as the "Gowrie Conspiracy." A life of him, by the Rev. James Scott, of Perth, was printed at Edinburgh, in 1818, and all the evidence respecting the conspiracy is ably investigated in *Pitcairn's Criminal Trials of Scotland.* (*See* RAMSAY, EARL OF HOLDERNESSE.) The dead bodies of the Ruthvens were afterwards arraigned and convicted of treason at Edinburgh, and the honours and the whole of the estates of the deceased declared FORFEITED by parliament.

Arms—1st and 4th, paly of six, arg. and gu., for Ruthven; 2nd, or, three bars, gu., for Cameron; 3rd, or, on a bend. az., three mascles of the 1st, for Haliburton; all within a border, or, flory and counterflory, gu.

RUTHVEN—LORD RUTHVEN OF ETTRICK, EARL OF FORTH AND EARL OF BRENTFORD.

By Letters Patent, dated in 1639; 27 March, 1642; and 27 May, 1644.

Lineage.

PATRICK RUTHVEN (son of William Ruthven of Ballindean, and grandson of William Ruthven, only son of the 1st Lord Ruthven) served with great distinction in the wars of Sweden, Denmark, Russia, Poland, Prussia, and also in the German wars under Gustavus-Adolphus, attained the rank of lieutenant-general, and upon the surrender of Ulm, in 1632, was appointed governor of that important place, which he gallantly defended. Returning home, General Ruthven was created a peer of Scotland, as Lord Ruthven of Ettrick, in 1639; made governor of the castle of Edinburgh, and advanced to the EARLDOM OF FORTH, in the peerage of Scotland, 27 March, 1642. Subsequently, having drawn his sword in the cause of King CHARLES I., and taken a leading part as a cavalier commander, he distinguished himself at Edghill, where, on the death of Lord Lindsey, he had the chief command, was made general of the king's army, and created a peer of England by letters patent, dated 27 May, 1644, as EARL OF BRENTFORD, deriving his title f om the town of Brentford, where he had defeated the parliamentary forces in 1642. Clarendon, although strongly prejudiced in his estimate of this gallant officer, is constrained to admit that " in the field he well knew what was to be done." His lordship *m.* Miss Clara Barnard, and had issue,

PATRICIA, *m.* to the Hon. Sir Thomas Ogilvy, son of James, 1st Earl of Airlie, and had issue. (*See Peerage.*)
JEAN or JANE, who alone survived her father, *m.* James, 2nd Lord Forrester, and had issue.
ELSPETH or ELIZABETH. *m.* Major George Pringle. (*See* PRINGLE, *of Yair*, in BURKE'S *landed Gentry.*)

The earl *d.* at Dundee, very old, in 1651, without male issue, and with him all his honours EXPIRED.

Arms—Paly of six, arg and gu.; a crescent for difference.

RUVIGNY—EARL OF GALWAY.

(See Massue.)

RYTHRE—BARON RYTHRE.

By Writ of Summons, dated 29 December, 1299.

Lineage.

In the 25th Edward I.

Sir William de Rythre, having taken a part in the Scottish and French wars, was summoned to parliament, as a Baron, by King Edward I., 29 December, 1299, and he had writs from that period to 26 August, 1807. His lordship was *s.* by his son,

John de Rythre, 2nd baron, who was never summoned to parliament. In the 11th Edward II. he was governor of Skypton Castle, and in the 17th of the same reign, had a charter for free warren in all his demesne lands at Haselwode, &c., and Adington, in Yorkshire. Neither this lord, nor any of his descendants, having had summons to parliament, Dugdale gives no further account of the family, although modern genealogists (borne out by a Visitation entry signed by James Rythre, of Harewood), have endeavoured to connect with this old baronial house the existing one of Ryder.

Arms—Az., three crescents, or.

SACKVILLE—BARONS BUCKHURST AND EARLS AND DUKES OF DORSET.

Barony, by Letters Patent, dated 8 June, 1567.
Earldom, by Letters Patent, dated 13 March, 1603.
Dukedom, by Letters Patent, dated 13 June, 1720.

Lineage.

The Sackvilles or Saukevilles, as the name was originally written, were persons of considerable power, wealth, and influence from the Conquest, and the house of Dorset traced its foundation to

Sir Robert de Saukeville, Knt., 3rd son of Herbrand de Sakavilla, one of the chieftains in the army of the Conqueror. From this Robert descended

Sir Richard Sackville, Knt., member of the privy council in the reigns of Mary and Elizabeth; chancellor of the court of Augmentation in the former and under treasurer of the Exchequer in the latter; M.P. for the co. Kent, and subsequently for the co. Surrey. Sir Richard m. Winefred, dau. of Sir John Bruges, lord mayor of the city of London, and dying .n 1556, left by her (who m. 2ndly, John, Marquess of Winchester, and d. 1586,) a dau. Anne, wife of Gregory, Lord Dacre, and a son and successor,

Thomas Sackville, Esq., who was knighted in the presence of Queen Elizabeth, by the Duke of Norfolk, 8 June, 1567, and on the same day created a peer of the realm, as Baron Buckhurst, of Buckhurst, co. Sussex. In 1594, his lordship was appointed lord high treasurer of England, and 13 March, 1603-4, he was elevated to an earldom as Earl Dorset. Of this nobleman Warton says, "At both universities (he had been a student at Oxford and Cambridge) he became celebrated as a Latin and English poet; and he carried his love of poetry, which he seems to have almost solely cultivated, to the Inner Temple. It was now fashionable for every young man of fortune before he began his travels or was admitted into Parliament, to be initiated in the study of the law. But instead of pursuing a science which could not be his profession, and which was unaccommodated to the bias of his genius, he betrayed his predilection to a more pleasing species of literature, by composing the tragedy of *Gorboduc*; which tragedy was exhibited in the great hall of the Inner Temple, by the students of that society, as part of the entertainments of a grand Christmas festival, and afterwards before Queen Elizabeth, at Whitehall, 18 January, 1561." His lordship m. Cecily, dau. of Sir John Baker, Knt., and d. suddenly at the council table at Whitehall, 19 April, 1608, having had issue,

i. Robert, his heir.
ii. Henry.
iii. William (Sir), who was knighted in France by King Henry IV, in October, 1589, at the age of nineteen years, and lost his life in the wars in that country in 1591.

iv. Thomas, who distinguished himself against the Turks, in 1595.
i. Anne, *m.* to Sir Henry Glemham, of Glemham, co. Suffolk.
ii. Jane, *m.* in February, 1591, to Anthony, Viscount Montague.
iii. Mary, *m.* to Sir Henry Neville, son and successor to Edward, Lord Abergavenny, whom he *s.* in that title.

The eldest son,

Robert Sackville, 2nd earl, who enjoyed the family honours but a few months, and *d.* 25 February, 1608-9. m. 1st, Margaret, dau. of Thomas, Duke of Norfolk, which lady dying 4 September, 1591, he m. 2ndly, Anne, dau. of Sir John Spencer, of Althorp. co. Northampton, and widow of Henry, Lord Compton. He had issue by his 1st wife,

i. Richard, his successor.
ii. Edward, successor to his brother Richard.
i. Cecily, *m.* to Sir Henry Compton, K.B., 3rd son of Henry, Lord Compton.
ii. Anne, *m.* 1st, to Edward Seymour, Lord Beauchamp, grandson to Edward, Earl of Hertford, and afterwards to Sir Edward Lewes, Knt.

The elder son,

Richard Sackville, 3rd earl, *b.* 28 March, 1589, *m.* Anne, dau. and sole heiress of George (Clifford), Earl of Cumberland, by whom he had two daus.,

Margaret, *m.* to John, Earl of Thanet.
Isabella, *m.* to James, Earl of Northampton.

He *d.* in 1624, when the honours devolved upon his brother,

Edward Sackville, 4th earl, K.G., who *m.* Mary, dau. and heiress of Sir George Curzon, of Croxhall, co. Derby, by whom he had issue, two sons. His lordship, before he attained the title, was concerned in a fatal duel, which is thus mentioned by Lord Clarendon:—"He entered into a fatal quarrel upon a subject very unwarrantable, with a young nobleman of Scotland, the Lord Bruce; upon which they both transported themselves in Flanders, and attended by only two chirurgeons placed at a distance, and under an obligation not to stir but at the fall of one of them, they fought under the walls of Antwerp, when the Lord Bruce fell dead upon the place; and Sir Edward Sackville (for so he was then called) being likewise hurt, retired into the next monastery which was near at hand." His lordship *d.* in 1652, having had two sons,

i. Richard, his successor.
ii. Edward, who *m.* Bridget, Baroness Norreys, dau. and sole heir to Edward Wray, 3rd son of Sir William Wray, of Glentworth. co. Lincoln, Bart., by his wife Elizabeth, dau. and heir of Francis, Lord Norreys, Earl of Berkshire.

The eldest son,

Richard Sackville, 5th earl, *m.* Frances Cranfield, eldest dau. of Lionel, Earl of Middlesex, by whom he had several children, viz.,

i. Charles, his successor.
ii. Edward, *b.* 2 April, 1641, *d. unm.* 1678.
iii. Lionel, *b.* 25 June, 1645.
iv. Richard, *b* 30 April, 1646, and *d.* 1712.
v. Lionel. *b.* 25 October, 1656, *d.* young.
vi. Cranfield, *b.* 18 December, 1660.
vii. Thomas, *b.* 3 February, 1662, *d.* 14 August, 1675.
i. Elizabeth, *d.* young. ii. Anne, *d.* young.
iii. Catherine, *d.* young.
iv. Mary, *b.* 4 February, 1646, *m.* Roger Boyle, Lord Broghill, son and heir of Roger, 1st Earl of Orrery.
v. Anne, *b.* 7 June, 1650, *m.* Alexander, 4th Earl of Hume, in Scotland.
vi. Frances, *b.* 6 February, 1655, *m.* 11 December, 1683, Sir George Lane, of Tulske, co. Roscommon, Bart., afterwards created Lord Lanesborough.

His lordship *d.* 1667, and was *s.* by his elder son,

Charles Sackville, K.G., 6th earl, *b.* 24 January, 1637, who succeeding also in right of his mother to the estates of the Earl of Middlesex, had been created 4 April, 1675, *Earl of Middlesex and Baron Cranfield, of Cranfield, co. Bedford.* His lordship's 2nd wife was Mary, dau. of James Compton, Earl of Northampton, by whom, besides a dau., he had his successor,

Lionel-Cranfield Sackville, K.G., 7th earl, *b.* 18 January, 1688, created Duke of Dorset, 13 June, 1720. His grace m. in June, 1708-9, Elizabeth, dau. of Lieut.-General Walter Philip Colyear, and niece of David, Earl of Portmore, by whom he had issue,

i. Charles, his successor.
ii. John-Philip, *b.* 22 June, 1713, *m.* in 1744, Frances, dau. of John, Earl of Gower, and dying 1765, left

John-Frederick, who *s.* as 3rd duke.
Mary, *m.* 30 August, 1767, to Sackville, 8th Earl of Thanet.
iii. George, the well known Lord George Sackville, *b.* 26 January, 1715-16, assumed by act of parliament, 16 February, 1770, the surname of Germain, pursuant to the will of Sir John and Lady Elizabeth Germain of Drayton, co. Northampton. This nobleman was distinguished as a soldier

and statesman. In the former he was less fortunate than in the latter, having incurred the displeasure of the commander-in-chief, Ferdinand, Prince of Brunswick, at the battle of Minden, and being censured by a court-martial held at his own request on returning to England. His lordship was endowed with very considerable talents, and filled subsequently some of the highest offices in the administration. He was elevated to the peerage, 11 February, 1782, as BARON BOLEBROKE and VISCOUNT SACKVILLE. of *Drayton*. He *m*. 3 September, 1754, Diana, 2nd dau. and co-heiress of John Sambrooke, Esq., by whom (who *d*. 15 January, 1778) he had issue,

1 CHARLES, 2nd Viscount Sackville, and 5th and last Duke of Dorset.

2 George, *b*. 7 December, 1770 ; *m*. December, 1814, Miss Harriet Pearce, and by her (who *d*. 18 April, 1835), left at his decease, 31 May, 1836, an only child,

CAROLINE-HARRIET, *m*. 2 June, 1837. to William Bruce Stopford, Esq., now of Drayton, co. Northampton.

1 Diana, *m*. to John, 2nd Earl o' Glandore, and *d*. 1814.
2 Elizabeth, *m*. to Henry Arthur Herbert, Esq., of Muckruss, co. Kerry.
3 Caroline, *d. unm.* 1789.

He *d.* 26 August, 1785.
I. Lady Anne, *d.* 23 March, 1720-1, aged eleven years.
II. Lady Elizabeth, *m* 6 December, 1726, Thomas, Viscount Weymouth, and *d.* 9 June, 1729.
IV. Lady Caroline, *m.* 27 July, 1742, to Joseph Damer, Lord Milton, and *d.* 24 March, 1775.

His grace *d.* 10 October, 1765, and was *s.* by his eldest son,

CHARLES, 2nd duke, *b.* 6 February, 1710-11, who *d. s. p.* 6 January, 1769, when the honours devolved upon his nephew, JOHN-FREDERICK SACKVILLE, 3rd duke. His grace was lord-lieutenant and custos rotulorum of the co. Kent, and of the city of Canterbury, vice-admiral of the coasts of that county, and, in 1783, ambassador to the court of France. He *m.* 4 January, 1790, Arabella-Diana, dau. and co-heiress of Sir Charles Cope, Bart., of Brewerne, and dying in 1799, left issue,

I. GEORGE-JOHN-FREDERICK, his heir.
I. MARY, *m.* 1st, Other-Archer, 6th Earl of Plymouth ; and 2ndly, William Pitt, Earl Amherst. This lady *d. s. p.* 20 July, 1864.
II. ELIZABETH. *m.* 21 June, 1813, George-John, Earl Delawarr, who assumed by royal license, 6 November, 1843, the additional surname and arms of SACKVILLE. The Countess Delawarr was created in 1864. BARONESS BUCKHURST. of Buckhurst, co. Sussex, with limitation to her 2nd son, REGINALD WINDSOR SACKVILLE, present EARL DE LA WARR (*see Extant Peerage*).

His grace was *s.* by his only son,

GEORGE-JOHN-FREDERICK SACKVILLE, 4th duke, *b.* 15 November, 1793, killed by a fall from his horse while hunting near Dublin, 14 February, 1815, being on a visit at the time to his mother, who had *m.* Charles, Lord Whitworth, then lord-lieutenant of Ireland. As he *d. unm.*, the family honours devolved upon his cousin,

CHARLES SACKVILLE-GERMAIN. 2nd Viscount Sackville, who became 5th Duke of Dorset, K.G., P.C., *b.* 27 August, 1767, and *d. unm.*, 29 July, 1843, when all his honours became EXTINCT.

Arms—Quarterly : or and gu , over all a bend, vair.

ST. AMAND—BARONS ST. AMAND.

By Writ of Summons, dated 29 December, 1299, and 22 March, 1313.

Lineage.

In the 6th year of HENRY III.,

ALMARIC DE ST. AMAND obtained a grant of two parts of the manor of Liskaret, in Cornwall, for his support in the king's service, and in nine years afterwards, being in the expedition then made into Wales, deported himself so gallantly, that the king remitted to him a debt, due by Walter de Verdon, his uncle (whose heir he was), which otherwise he should have paid to the exchequer by 10 marks annually. The next year he had a grant of the manor of Bloxham, in Oxfordshire, and soon afterwards we find him governor of St. Briavels Castle, in Gloucestershire, and warden of the forest of Dene, as also sheriff of Herefordshire, and governor of Hereford Castle. In the 21st of the same reign, he was again entrusted with the same important fortresses ; and standing high in favour at court, he was one of the sponsors at the font when Prince Edward (son of HENRY III.) was baptized, by Otto, the Pope's legate. He was *s.* by his son,

RALPH DE ST. AMAND, who *m* Asceline, dau. and co-heir of Robert de Albini, son of Robert de Albini, Baron of Caynho.

co. Bedford, and paid in the 25th HENRY III., £25 for his relief of one moiety of the lands of Joane de Beauch .mp, another of the daus. and co-heirs of the said Robert de Albini. This Ralph *d.* in five years afterwards, and was *s.* by his son,

ALMARIC DE ST. AMAND, for whose wardship, and the benefit of his marriage, Paulyne Peyvre, a great personage at that period, gave 1000 marks. In the 40th HENRY III., Almaric, however, made proof of his age, and had then livery of his lands: and the next year had a military summons to march against the Welsh. He *d.* in the 14th EDWARD I. (1285-6). He was *s.* by his eldest son,

GUY DE ST. AMAND, who *d. s. p.* soon after, and was *s.* by his brother,

ALMARIC DE ST. AMAND. This feudal lord distinguished in the wars of France and Scotland, was summoned to parliament as a Baron, from 29 December, 1299, to 16 June, 1311. His lordship was at one time governor of Bordeaux. He *d. s. p.* in 1312, when the Barony of St. Amand became EXTINCT, but his lands devolved upon his brother,

JOHN DE ST. AMAND, a professor of the canon law, and at that time called *Magister Johannes de Sancto Amand*, who, doing his fealty, had livery of the deceased lord's lands, and was summoned to parliament as a Baron from 22 March, 1313, to 10 October, 1325. His lordship *d.* in 1330, leaving by his wife, Joane, dau. of Hugh le Despencer, Earl of Winchester, a son,

ALMARIC DE ST. AMAND, 2nd baron, summoned to parliament from 8 January, 1371, to 22 August, 1381. This nobleman was in the Scottish and French wars, *temp.* EDWARD II. and EDWARD III. In the 31st of the latter king (1357-8) he was made justice of Ireland, and had forty men at arms. with 100 archers on horseback, assigned to attend him there, over and above the usual number of men at arms which appertained to his high office. In the 47th EDWARD III., he was made steward of the forest of Rockingham, and governor of the castle. He *d.* in 1381, and was *s.* by his son,

ALMARIC DE ST. AMAND, 3rd baron, summoned to parliament from 9 August, 1382, to 2 December, 1401. This nobleman, by indenture in the 8th RICHARD II. (1384-5). was retained to serve the king in his wars of Scotland, and in the 1st of HENRY IV. (1399-1400,) was made a knight of the Bath, at the coronation of that monarch. By Ida, his 1st wife, he had issue,

ALIANORE, who *m.* Sir Gerard de Braybroke, Knt., and was mother of

GERARD DE BRAYBROKE, who left issue,

ELIZABETH, who *m.* 1st Sir WILLIAM DE BEAUCHAMP, afterwards summoned to parliament as LORD ST. AMAND. and 2ndly. Sir Roger Tocotes.
Maud, *m.* to John Babington, and *d. s. p.* 5th HENRY VI.
Alianore, *d. unm.* 7th HENRY VI.

His lordship *m.* 2ndly, Alianore, heiress of the St. Elen family, and left a dau.,

IDA, *m.* to Sir Thomas West, Knt., and *d. s p.* 1416.

Lord St. Amand *d.* in 1403, leaving his younger dau.. IDA, and his grandson, GERARD DE BRAYBROKE (son of his deceased elder dau., Alianore), his heirs; between whom the Barony of St. Amand fell into ABEYANCE, and so continued until the year 1449, when it was called out in favour of Sir William de Beauchamp. husband of the deceased lord's great granddau., ELIZABETH DE BRAYBROKE (*refer to* BEAUCHAMP, BARONS ST. AMAND).

Arms—Or, fretté, sa.. on a chief of the 2nd, three bezants.

ST. GEORGE—BARONS ST. GEORGE OF HATLEY ST. GEORGE, COS. ROSCOMMON AND LEITRIM.

1st Barony by Letters Patent, dated 16 April, 1715.
2nd Barony, by Letters Patent. dated 24 May, 1763.

Lineage.

This family deduces its pedigree from

BALDWIN ST. GEORGE, one of the companions in arms of the CONQUEROR, whose descendants flourished in England for several centuries, and frequently represented the co. Cambridge in Parliament. A full pedigree of the family and all its branches is registered in Ulster's Office, from which it appears that

BALDWIN DE ST. GEORGE, living anno 13 HENRY I., was father of,

WILLIAM DE ST. GEORGE, living temp. HENRY II., whose son,

BALDWIN DE ST. GEORGE, lived in the reigns of RICHARD I. and KING JOHN. He had four sons,

I. BALDWIN, his heir.
II. Robert, of Haliverton, anno 7 HENRY III., m. Anne, dau. and heir of William de Alneto, and widow of Hugh de Ardres, and had issue,

  1 Baldwin.
  2 William (Sir).
  3 Felicia, living anno 29 HENRY III.
  4 Cecilia, living anno 29 HENRY III.
  5 Agnes, m. William Graffan.
  6 Albrede, m. — Windleberg.

III. Henry, living anno 7 HENRY III.
IV. William, living anno 7 HENRY III.

The eldest son,

BALDWIN DE ST. GEORGE, living anno 12 HENRY III., had two sons, WILLIAM, his heir; Baldwin: and a dau., Amicia, m. Sir Philip Abbington, Knt. The eldest son,

SIR WILLIAM DE ST. GEORGE, Knt., living anno 26 HENRY III., was s. by his son,

SIR BALDWIN DE ST. GEORGE, Knt., living anno 40 HENRY, m. Roesia de Upwood, and d. anno 1 EDWARD I., leaving a son,

SIR WILLIAM DE ST. GEORGE, living anno 29 EDWARD I., m. Margaret, dau. and co-heir of Egbaud de Turnbard, of Upton, co. Nottingham, who brought her husband certain manors in the cos. of Cambridge and York, by her he had a dau., Margaret, m. Robert Haringale, of co. York, and a son,

BALDWIN DE ST. GEORGE, who d. vitâ patris, leaving by Johanna, his wife (who was living anno 13 EDWARD III.), a dau., Basilca and a son,

SIR WILLIAM DE ST. GEORGE, Knt. of Hatley St. George, co. Cambridge, who s. his grandfather, was living anno 21 EDWARD III., and was s. by his son,

SIR BALDWIN DE ST. GEORGE, Knt., of Hatley St. George, living anno 31 EDWARD III., who m. Elizabeth, dau. and co-heir of Sir John Argentine, Knt., of Wimondesley, co. Hertford, and other manors, in cos. Cambridge and Norfolk, by Margaret, his wife, dau. and heir of Robert Darcy, of Strettin, and had, John, Giles, Thomas, Elizabeth (all living anno 4 RICHARD II.), and his successor,

SIR BALDWIN DE ST GEORGE, Knt., of Hatley St. George, m. anno 4 RICHARD II., Johanna, dau. and co-heir of Sir John Engaine, by Margaret, his wife, dau. of William Delahay, and granddau. and heir of Sir John Delahay, Knt., of Shepereth, co. Cambridge, and had issue,

I. John, m. Matilda, dau. and co-heir of Sir William Cogshall, and d. vitâ patris, leaving a son,

WILLIAM (Sir), heir to his grandfather.

II. Baldwin, living anno 4 EDWARD IV.
III. William.

Sir Baldwin d. 18 February, 1485, and was s. by his grandson,

SIR WILLIAM ST. GEORGE, Knt., of Hatley St. George, who was knighted before St. Ormes, in France, by Humphry, Duke of Gloucester. He m. 1st, Alianore, dau. and co-heir of Sir William Arundel, by whom he had one son,

I. Thomas, who d. s. p. in his mother's lifetime.

Sir William m. 2ndly, Katherine, dau. of Sir John Maningham, and widow of Peter Beauchamp, of Lydiard Tregoze, and had by her,

II. RICHARD (Sir), his heir.

Sir William m. 3rdly, Margaret, widow of Richard Cotton, but had no further issue; he was s. by his only surviving son,

SIR RICHARD ST. GEORGE, Knt., of Hatley St. George, who was aged 26 anno 11 EDWARD IV., and claimed the villenage of Robert Aumfriese, as holding the manor of Papworth Everard. He m. Anne, dau. of Thomas Burgoine, Esq., of Impington, co. Cambridge, and d. 1st HENRY VII., leaving a son,

466*

THOMAS ST. GEORGE, Esq., of Hatley St. George, m. 1st, Alice, dau. of Sir John Rotheram, by whom he had a son, George, d. s. p.; 2ndly, Etheldreda, dau. of Clement Higham, Esq., of Giffords, co. Suffolk; and d. 32 HENRY VIII, leaving, with a dau., Anne, m. John Dockwra, a son, his eventual heir,

FRANCIS ST. GEORGE, Esq., of Hatley St. George, co. Cambridge, of full age 1 EDWARD VI., m. Rohesia, dau. of Thomas Hatton, of Drayton, co. Cambridge, and had two sons,

I. John, of Hatley St. George, living 1628, had two sons,

Baldwin, d. s. p., and
John, of Hatley St. George, who had three sons,

  1 JOHN.
  2 Thomas.
  3 Richard.

II. RICHARD.

The 2nd son,

SIR RICHARD ST. GEORGE, Clarenceux King-of-Arms, appointed Norroy, King of Arms, 1603, and Clarenceux, September. 1623, knighted 28 September, 1616, m. 1575, Elizabeth, dau. of Nicholas St. John, Esq. of Lydiard Tregoze, Wilts, by whom he had issue,

I. William }
II. John } both slain in Ireland; d. unm.

III. Henry (Sir), Garter King-of-Arms, appointed Rouge Rose pursuivant, May, 1610; Blue Mantle, December, 1611; Richmond Herald, March, 1615; Norroy, King of Arms, July, 1635; and Garter, April, 1644: m. 1614, Mary, dau. of Sir Thomas Dayrell. Knt. of Lillingston Dayrell; and d. 5 November, 1644, leaving issue,

Sir Thomas St. George, Garter King-of-Arms, 9 March, 1686; m. Clara, dau. of Rev. John Pymlow, rector of Cliff, co. Northampton, and d. 6 March. 1703.
William, St. George (Col.), a Cavalier, killed at the storming of Leicester.
Sir Henry St. George, Clarenceux King-of-Arms, and appointed Garter, temp. GEORGE I.; d. 1715, aged 91.
Richard St. George, Ulster King-of-Arms, appointed August, 1660; resigned, 1683. He m. Mary, dau. of Sir Henry Hastings, Knt., of Bramston, co. Lincoln, and d. s. p.
Elizabeth, m. Col. Richard Bourke.
Mary, m. Ferdinand Hastings, Esq.; Frances, m. George Tucker, Esq.
Rebecca, m. George Cook, Esq.

IV. GEORGE (Sir), of whom presently.
V. Richard, capt., went to Ireland, in the 17th century. in the royal army, and was appointed governor of the town and castle of Athlone. m. 20 February, 1625, Ann, dau. of Michael Pinnock, Esq., of Turrock, co. Roscommon, and left (with two daus., Mary, wife, 1st. of Thomas Ashe, Esq., of St. Johns, co. Meath, and 2ndly, of Strafford Lightburne, Esq., of Adamstown, and Ann, wife of Major Wood, an only surviving son,

HENRY ST. GEORGE, Esq., of Athlone, an officer in the Irish army of CHARLES II.; he obtained a grant of the estate of Woodsgift, co. Kilkenny, in 1666; he was b. 15 October, 1638; m. 3 June, 1669, Anne, dau. of Ridgeley Hatfield, alderman of the city of Dublin, by whom he had four sons,

1 RICHARD, of Kilrush, a lieut.-gen. in the army, m. 1696, Elizabeth, dau. of Lord Coote, of Co oony, and d. in Dublin in 1755, without legitimate issue.
2 Henry, d. unm. 1723.
3 ARTHUR, D.D., Dean of Ross, d. 24 September, 1772, aged 91. leaving, by his 2nd wife, June, dau. of Sir Thomas Molyneux, Bart.,

  Richard, of Kilrush, co. Kilkenny, m. 1763, Sarah, eldest dau. of the Very Rev. Richard Handcock, Dean of Achonry, and had a son, Richard, of Kilrush, b. 1766; d. unm. June, 1840.
  THOMAS, M.P. for Clogher, a commissioner of the Barrack Board, b. October, 1738; m. 15 August, 1776, Hon. Lucinda Acheson, 4th dau. of Archibald Acheson, Lord Gosford, and d. 1 April, 1785, leaving by her (who m. 2ndly, Jeremiah French, Esq., capt. 8th regt.) issue, ancestor of ST. GEORGE, of Woodpark see BURKE's Landed Gentry).
  Camel, d. in the West Indies.
  Arthur, d. in the West Indies.
  Howard (Rev.), D.D., who purchased Kilrush, m. Mary, the eldest dau. of Edward Lucas, Esq., of Cas leshane, and had issue; ancestor of St. GEORGE, of Kilrush.
  Henry (Rev.), m. 1st, Mary, dau. of Philip Percival, Esq., of Temple House, co. Sligo, and by her had a son, Arthur, b. 1776; d. unm. 1845. He m. 2ndly, Jane, dau. and co-heir of William Walsh, Esq., co. Limerick, and by her had four sons and four daus.
  Catherine, m. to Clement Wolseley, Esq., of Wolseley Bridge, son of Sir Richard Wolseley, 1st bart. of Mount Wolseley, and had issue.

4 GEORGE, of Woodsgift, M.P., m. Elizabeth, dau. of Thomas Bligh, Esq., of Rathmore, co. Meath, by whom he had three sons and a dau.,

Henry, M.P., d. unm. in 1763.
RICHARD, of Woodsgift, who was created a BARONET OF IRELAND, 12 March, 1706. ancestor of St. GEORGE, Bart., of Woodsgift (see BURKE's Peerage and Baronetage).
George, capt. in the army, m. Miss Bathurst, and had issue.
Elizabeth.

Sir Richard d. 17 May, 1635, and was buried in the chancel of St. Andrew's Church, Holborn, London. His 4th son,

SIR GEORGE ST. GEORGE, Knt., of Carrickdrumrusk, co. Leitrim, Deputy Admiral of Connaught 1620, m. Katherine, dau. of Richard Gifford, Esq., of Castle Jordan, co. Meath, and had issue,

I. OLIVER (Sir), his heir.
II. George (Sir), Knt. of Dunmore, co. Galway, m. Elizabeth, dau. of bir Robert Hannay, a Scotch knight, and had issue,

1 Richard, captain in the army, m. Anne, dau. of John Eyre, Esq., of Eyre Court, co. Galway, and d. s. p. 1726.
2 George, d. s. p.
1 Jane, m. St. George Ashe, D.D., Bishop of Clogher, and d. 5 August, 1741.
2 Katherine, m. Charles Crow, D.D., Bishop of Clogher.
3 Lettice.
4 Elizabeth, m. Sir William Parsons, 2nd Bart. of Birr Castle, and d. 6 February, 1739.
5 Emilia, m. Very Rev. Robert Carleton, Dean of Cork.

III. John, d. s. p.
IV. Henry, d. s. p.
V. Richard, d. s. p.
I. Lettice, m. Arthur Dillon, Esq., of Lismullen, co. Meath.
II. Mary, m. Richard, 1st Lord Colooney, and was mother of Richard, 1st Earl of Bellamont.
III. Elizabeth, d. unm.
IV. Anne, m. Sir Henry Brooke, Knt. of Brookesborough, co. Fermanagh.
V. Eleanor, m. Sir Arthur Gore, 1st Bart. of Newtown Gore, co. Mayo.
VI. Sarah, m. Sir Thomas Newcomen, 5th Bart. of Kenagh, co. Longford.

Sir George, whose will, dated 29 March, 1659, was proved 3 June, 1662, was s. by his eldest son,

SIR OLIVER ST. GEORGE, 1st Bart. of Carrickdrumrusk, so created 5 September, 1666, being the first baronet created after the Restoration, was appointed a Commissioner for settling the affairs of Ireland; m. Olivia, dau. of Michael Beresford, Esq. of Coleraine, co. Londonderry, and widow of George Thornhill, Esq., and had issue,

I. GEORGE (Sir), 1st baron.
II. Oliver, a privy councillor, captain of a troop of dragoons 1685, m. 1701, Mary, dau. of Thomas Knox. Esq. of Dungannon; and d. s. p. 1729.
III. Thomas, d. s. p. Buried at St. Andrew's, Dublin, 2 April, 1662.
IV. John, d. s. p. Buried at St. Andrew's, Dublin, 19 March, 1678.
I. Katherine, m. Sir Edward Crofton, 2nd bart., of Mote, co. Roscommon.
II. Olivia, m. 1st, Sir Robert Colville, Knt., of Newtown, co. Down; 2ndly, Pierce, 4th Viscount Ikerrin; 3rdly, — Worth, Esq., of Epsom, co. Surrey; and d. 1722.
III. Mary, d. unm. Buried at St. Andrew's, Dublin, 16 December, 1661.

Sir Oliver d. October, 1695, and was s. by his eldest son,

SIR GEORGE ST. GEORGE, 2nd bart., of Carrickdrumrusk, b. 1651, M.P. for Carrick-on-Shannon 1703, and for co. Roscommon 1713. Created by Patent, 16 April, 1715, BARON ST. GEORGE, of Hatley St. George, co. Roscommon and co. Leitrim, in the Peerage of Ireland, with remainder to the heirs male of his body, and in default of such heirs, remainder to the heirs male of the body of his deceased father, Sir Oliver St. George, Bart., and was appointed Vice-Admiral of Connaught, 25 October, 1727. He m. 29 November, 1681, Hon. Margaret Skeffington, dau. of John, 2nd Viscount Massereene, and by her (who d. 1711) had an only dau.,

MARY, heiress to her father.

Lord St. George d. 4 August, 1735, when his title became extinct and his estates devolved on his only dau.,

HON. MARY ST. GEORGE, b. 10 May, 1693; who m. 20 December, 1714, John Usher, Esq., M.P. for Carrick-on-Shannon from 1715 to 1741, Governor co. Galway, and Vice-

Admiral of Connaught, 3rd son of Beverley Usher, Esq., of K'lmeadon, co. Waterford, who was 5th son of Arthur Usher, Esq., of Donnybrook, co. Dublin (see BURKE's Landed Gentry, USHER, of Eastwell), and had by him (who d. 1741),

ST. GEORGE, who, 25 May, 1734, assumed the surname of ST. GEORGE, and s. to the estates, of whom hereafter.

Olivia, m. 23 January, 1736, Arthur French, Esq., of Tyrone House, co Galway, and had by him (who d. 8 May, 1779) three daus.. Olivia, m. Anthony Nugent, Esq., of Pallas (Lord Riverstown), and was grandmother of the 9th Earl of Westmeath; Julia. m. Christopher French, Esq., of Brook Lodge; and Nichola; one son,

CHRISTOPHER FRENCH ST. GEORGE, Esq., of Tyrone. b 13 April, 1754, who adopted, in 1774, the surname of ST. GEORGE, in compliance with the settlement of his great-grandfather, Lord St. George, who m. 1778, Anne, dau. of Henry Bingham, Esq., of Newbrook, co. Mayo. and left, with two daus.. Letitia, m. to James Kelly, Esq., and Olivia, m. to William-Robert Wills, Esq., of Willsgrove, a son and heir,

ARTHUR FRENCH ST. GEORGE, Esq., of Tyrone, b. 8 August, 1780, who assumed by royal licence, dated 30 April, 1811, the surname and arms of ST. GEORGE; m. 22 January, 1801, lady Harriet St. Lawrence, eldest dau. of William, 2nd Earl of Howth, and co-heir of her mother, Lady Mary Bermingham, dau. and co-heir of Thomas, 22nd Lord Athenry, and Earl of Louth; and d. 1 January, 1844, leaving issue,

CHRISTOPHER, of Tyrone, J.P. and D.L., b. 15 March, 1810, M.P. for Galway 1847 to 1852; d. s. p. 12 November, 1877.
ARTHUR-ST. GEORGE, of Tyrone, J.P., b. 6 May, 1813. Mary, m. to Francis Cuff, Esq., of Creagh, co. Mayo. Matilda, m. to Lieut. Col. Charles Pepper.
Louisa, m. to Capt. H. Bingham.
Anne.
Harriet.

Mr. St. George was s. by his son, the present CHRISTOPHER ST. GEORGE, Esq.

Judith, m. George Lowther, Esq., of Kilrue, co. Meath, and had issue (see BURKE's Landed Gentry).

Hon. Mary St. George Usher, heiress of St. George, d. May, 1741, and was s. by her only son,

ST. GEORGE USHER ST. GEORGE, Esq., of Headford, co. Galway, M.P. for Carrick-on-Shannon from 1741 to 1763, who was created BARON ST. GEORGE, of Hatley St. G orge, cos. Roscommon and Leitrim, in the peerage of Ireland, by patent dated 24 May, 1763; m. 18 July, 1752, Elizabeth, dau. and heir of Christopher Dominick, Esq., Dublin, and had by her (who d. 26 February, 1813, aged 81) one son, b. January, 1761 (who d. 17 December, 1765) and an only dau. and heir,

OLIVIA EMILY, m. 4 November, 1775, WILLIAM ROBERT, 2nd Duke of Leinster, K.P. (see EXTANT Peerage).

His lordship d. January, 1775, when the barony became EXTINCT.

Arms—ST. GEORGE, ar., a chief az. over all, a lion rampant gu. ducally crowned or.; USHER, az. a chev. erm. between three billets ar.

ST. JOHN—BARONS ST. JOHN, OF STANTON ST. JOHN, CO. OXFORD.

By Writ of Summons, dated 24 December, 1264.

Lineage.

THOMAS DE ST. JOHN, of Stanton St. John, 2nd son of JOHN DE ST. JOHN, of Stanton St. John, co. Oxford, and younger brother of Roger de St. John, ancestor of the St. Johns, of Basing, was father of

ROGER DE ST. JOHN, who, in the 22nd HENRY II., was amerced £133 6s. 8d., for trespassing in the king's forests, in the co. Oxford. This Roger, who d. before 1215, was s. by his son,

JOHN DE ST. JOHN, living 1229, who was s. by his son,

ROGER DE ST. JOHN. This feudal lord having taken up arms with the barons against King HENRY III., was summoned to parliament after the victory of those lords at Lewes, 24 December, 1264, and appointed governor of the castle of Oxford. He was slain, however, the following year at Evesham, where his party sustained so signal a defeat. His lordship *m.* a sister of Richard de Luci, by whom he acquired a moiety of the lordship of Wolnestede, co. Surrey, and had an only son,

JOHN, who was never summoned to parliament, nor were his descendants. He *d. s. p.*

The Barony of St. John, of Stanton, EXPIRED therefore with the 1st lord.

Arms—Arg., on a chief, gu., two mul'ets, or.

ST. JOHN—BARONS ST. JOHN, OF LAGEHAM.

By Writ of Summons, dated 21 September, 1299

Lineage.

In the 46th HENRY III.,
ROGER DE ST. JOHN, younger son of the 1st baron, obtained license to fortify his house at Lageham, co. Surrey, and so to hold the same, whilst himself and his heirs should continue loyal to the king; but within two years he joined the baronial standard, and, after the battle of Lewes, was one of the nine barons chosen to form the council of state. To this turbulent feudal lord succeeded
JOHN DE ST. JOHN, who had summons to parliament as a Baron, from 21 September, 1299, to 6 October, 1315, after the 6th EDWARD II., with the addition of " de Lageham." This nobleman was actively engaged in the Scottish wars, *temp.* EDWARD I. and EDWARD II. His lordship *d.* in 1316, and was *s.* by his son,
JOHN DE ST. JOHN, 2nd baron, summoned to parliament, from 20 November, 1317, to 18 September, 1322. His lordship was in the expedition made into Scotland, 11th EDWARD II., and dying in 1322, was *s.* by his son,
JOHN DE ST. JOHN, 3rd baron, summoned to parliament, from 1 August, 1327, to 18 February, 1331, being the last summons received by a member of this house. This nobleman *m.* Katharine, dau. of Geffrey de Say, and dying in 1349, was *s.* by his son,
ROGER DE ST. JOHN, 4th baron, who in the 25th EDWARD III., released to Sir Nicholas de Lovoyane, Knt., and Margaret, his wife, all his right in the manor of Lageham, and *d.* shortly after (in 1353), *s. p.*, leaving PETER DE ST. JOHN, his kinsman (son of his brother William), his next heir. He *d. s. p.*, whereupon the representation vested in the heir of Nicolas St. John, of Glimpton, co. Oxford, younger son of John, 1st Baron of Lageham, whose descendants continued for several generations, but none of the family were subsequently summoned to parliament.

Arms—Ermine, on a chief, gu., two mullets, or.

ST. JOHN — BARONS ST. JOHN, OF BASING.

By Writ of Summons, dated 29 December, 1299.

Lineage.

At the time of the General Survey,
HUGH DE PORT held fifty-five lordships of the crown, in Hampshire, whereof Basing was one, and the head of the barony. He had also lands in the cos. Dorset and Cambridge. In the reign of RUFUS, he took the cowl at Winchester, and was *s.* by his son,
HENRY DE PORT, Lord of Basing, who was *s.* by his son,
JOHN DE PORT, who, in the 12th HENRY II. (1165-6), contributed for his knights' fees (seven in number) to the assessment for marrying the king's dau., 57 marks. He was *s.* by his son,
ADAM DE PORT, Lord of Basing. This feudal baron was governor of the castle of Southampton, in the 15th (1213-14) King JOHN; and in the 22nd HENRY II., was fined 300 marks for trespassing in the king's forests. In the 26th of the same reign, he gave 1000 marks to the king for livery of his wife's

inheritance in Normandy; and that he might be restored to the king's favour, and do his homage. He *m.* Mabel, dau. of Reginald de Aurevalle, and grandchild and heir through her mother, Muriell, of Roger de St. John, and Cecily, his wife, dau. and heir of Robert de Haya, Lord of Halnac, co. Sussex; and his posterity ever afterwards bore the surname of ST. JOHN. By this lady he had two sons, WILLIAM and Robert. The elder,
WILLIAM DE ST. JOHN, assuming that surname, wrote himself *Willielmus de Sancto Johanne filius et hæres Adæ de Port*, and in the 15th JOHN, gave 500 marks to the king for livery of all the lands of ADAM DE PORT, his father. The two following years he executed the sheriff's office for the co. Southampton; but was subsequently in arms with the other barons against the crown, and did not return to his allegiance until some time after the accession of HENRY III. He made his peace, however, effectually, for we find him in the 11th of that king, appointed governor of the islands of Guernsey and Jersey. He *m.* Godchild, dau. of N. Paganell, and was *s.* by his son,
ROBERT DE ST. JOHN, who had a military summons in the 42nd HENRY III., to oppose the incursions of the Welsh, and in three years afterwards, obtained a license to fix a pale upon the bank of his moat at Basing; as also to continue it so fortified, during the king's pleasure.[*] In the 50th of the same reign he was constituted governor of Porchester Castle, and dying soon after, 1266, left (by his wife, Agnes, dau. of William de Cantilupe,)
JOHN, his heir.
William, of Faumont, co. Glamorgan, ancestor of the ST. JOHNS, Barons of Bletshoe, and of the Viscounts Bolingbroke.

The elder son,
JOHN DE ST. JOHN, Lord of Basing, succeeded likewise to the governorship of Porchester Castle. This baron acquired high military reputation in the wars of EDWARD I.; and, in his capacity of lieutenant of Aquitaine, achieved some important conquests. In 1296, he took the city of Bayonne by assault, and its castle surrendered after a siege of eight days. Thence marching to Bellegard, at the time invested by the Earl of Arras, he was made prisoner, and conveyed to Paris; being, however, redeemed (it was said by ALFONSUS, King of Castile), he was again in the wars of Gascony, as well as in those of Scotland; and was afterwards deputed ambassador to France, with John, Earl of Warren, and other persons of rank. He *d.* in 1301, having *m.* Alice, dau. of Reginald Fitz-Piers, and had issue,

JOHN, his successor.
William.

The elder son,
JOHN DE ST. JOHN, had been summoned to parliament as a Baron, in the life-time of his father, from 29 December, 1299, to 12 November, 1303, under the designation of "John de St. John, *Junior*," but afterwards, viz., from 14 March, 1322, to 10 October, 1325, as "St. John of Basing." This nobleman was eminent in the wars of Scotland, *temp.* EDWARD I. and EDWARD II. His lordship *m.* Isabel, dau. of Hugh de Courtenay, and *d.* in 1329, was *s.* by his son,
HUGH DE ST. JOHN, 2nd Baron St. John, of Basing, who *d.* in 1337, without being summoned to parliament, leaving him surviving, besides his wife, Mirabelle,[†] dau. of Thomas Wake,
EDMUND, his successor, aged then four years
Margaret, *m.* to John de St. Philibert, and had a son, John, who *d.* infancy. She *d.* 35th EDWARD III. (1361-2).

---

[*] Basing House, supposed to have occupied the site of the old castle of the St. Johns, was built by Sir William Paulet, Baron St. John, and Marquess of Winchester. It is famous for the siege which it underwent during the parliamentary wars, when, under Lord Winchester's command, it held out nearly two years for the king. Cromwell finally carried it by storm, massacred nearly the whole of its valiant garrison, and burned it to the ground. He is reported to have said that Basing was a fitter abode for a sovereign than a subject. In the chivalric spirit of the time Winchester named his house *aimez loyauté*—ever since the family motto, and so rich were its stores of plate, jewels, furniture, &c., that each soldier of the besiegers had £300 worth of plunder. The gate-house, built of brick in the style of the 15th century, and portions of the ballium yet remain.
[†] BANKS, quoting *Berry's Sussex Genealogies*," says there was a 3rd dau. of Hugh de St. John, named Alice, who *m.* John Kingstone, and had a son, Thomas Kingstone. Banks also surmises that Roger de St. John, summoned, with his wife, to the coronation of EDWARD II., was an elder brother of Edmund, last Lord St. John, but that he predeceased his father, and *d. s. p.*

ISABEL, m. 1st, to Henry de Burghersh, who d. s. p., and 2ndly, to Lucas de Poynings, who was summoned to parliament, it is presumed, *jure uxoris*, 24 February, 1369, and on to 1372.

His lordship was s. by his elder son,

EDMUND ST. JOHN, 3rd Baron St. John, of Basing, b. 1333, who dying in minority, 21st EDWARD III. (1347-8), then a ward of the king, his sisters, MARGARET and ISABEL, became his heirs. The elder sister, Margaret, did not long survive, and her only issue, John de St. Philibert, dying an infant, the whole of the inheritance centered in the younger sister, Isabel, then m. to her 2nd husband, LUCAS DE POYNINGS, who in her right was summoned to parliament, and the Barony of St. John, of Basing, was thus conveyed to the family of Poynings (see Poynings, Barons St. John).

ST. JOHN—EARLS OF BOLINGBROKE.

By Letters Patent, dated 28 December, 1624.

Lineage.

SIR OLIVER ST. JOHN, of Penmark, co. Glamorgan, (of the family of St. John of Stanton St. John), m. Margaret,[*] dau. of Sir John de Beauchamp, and sister and heir of John, Lord Beauchamp, of Bletshoe, and had two sons, viz., JOHN, his heir, and Oliver, ancestor of the present VISCOUNT BOLINGBROKE. The elder son,

SIR JOHN ST. JOHN, K.B., of Bletshoe, m. Alice, dau. of Sir Thomas Bradshaigh, of Haigh, co. Lancaster, and was s. by his son,

SIR JOHN ST. JOHN, K.B. of Bletshoe, who m. Sibyl, dau. of Morgan ap Jenkyns ap Philip, and had besides several daus., three sons, JOHN, (Sir) his heir; Oliver (Sir), of Sharnbrook, co. Bedford, and Alexander, of Thorley, co. Herts, whose great grandson, Oliver, was lord chief justice of the Common Pleas, and was grandfather of Sir Francis St. John, created a baronet in 1715. SIR JOHN was s. by his eldest son,

SIR JOHN ST. JOHN, who m. Margaret, dau. of Sir William Waldegrave, of Smallbridge, co. Suffolk, K.B., and his son and successor,

OLIVER ST. JOHN, was elevated to the peerage 13 January, 1559, as BARON ST. JOHN, of Bletshoe, and d. in 1582; his elder son and heir,

JOHN ST. JOHN, 2nd Lord St. John of Bletshoe, d. in 1596, leaving an only dau. and heiress, Anne, m. to William, Lord Howard, (son and heir-apparent of Charles, Earl of Nottingham) in whose descendants the Barony of Bletshoe became vested. He was s. by his brother,

OLIVER ST. JOHN, 3rd Baron St. John, of Bletshoe, who d. in 1618, leaving with other issue,

  I. OLIVER, his successor.
  II. Rowland (Sir), K.B., whose son Oliver was created a baronet, and was father of Sir Andrew St. John, 2nd baronet whose youngest son, JOHN, eventually s. to the Barony of St John, and was ancestor of the present Baron St. John. (See BURKE's *Extant Peerage*).

The elder son,

OLIVER ST. JOHN, 4th Lord St. John, of Bletshoe, was advanced, by letters patent, dated 28 December, 1624, to the dignity of EARL OF BOLINGBROKE. His lordship m. Elizabeth, dau. and heir of William Paulet, grandson of St. George Paulet, a younger brother of William, 1st Marquess of Winchester, and had issue,

OLIVER, Lord St. John, summoned to parliament by writ in his father's lifetime, in the Barony of St. John, and took his seat 14 May, 1641; made knight of the Bath at the coronation of King CHARLES I. This nobleman fell fighting under the royal banner at Edgehill, 23 October, 1624. He had m. Lady Arabella Egerton, dau. of John, 1st Earl of Bridgewater, and left four daus., viz.,

  Frances, m. Sir William Beecher, Knt., of Howberry, co. Bedford.
  Elizabeth, m. to George Bennett, Esq., of Cotsback, in Leicestershire.
  Arabella, m. to Sir Edward Wyse, K.B., of Sydenham, Devon.
  Dorothy, m. to Francis Charlton, Esq., of Apley Castle, Salop.

---

[*] This lady m. 2ndly, John Beaufort, Duke of Somerset, K.G., by whom she was mother of Lady MARGARET BEAUFORT, who m. Edward Tudor, Earl of Richmond, and had a son, HENRY, EARL OF RICHMOND, who ascended the throne as HENRY VII. The Duchess of Somerset m. 3rdly, John, VISCOUNT WELLES, K.G.

467

PAULET (Sir), made knight of the Bath, at the coronation of King CHARLES I.; m. Elizabeth, dau. and heir of Sir Rowland Vaughan, of the Spital, near Shoreditch, in the suburbs of London, and dying before his father, left,

OLIVER, } successively Earls of Bolingbroke.
PAULET, }

Francis, d. unm.
Anthony, m. a dau of — Kensham, Esq., of Tameford.
Dorothy, m. to John Carey, Lord Rochford, eldest son of Henry, Earl of Dover.

His lordship d. in 1646, and was s. by his grandson,

OLIVER ST. JOHN, 2nd Earl of Bolingbroke, and 5th Lord St. John of Bletshoe. His lordship m. Lady Frances Cavendish, dau. of William, Duke of Newcastle, but dying s. p., 18 March, 1687-8, was s. by his brother,

PAULET ST. JOHN, 3rd Earl of Bolingbroke, and 6th Lord St. John, of Bletshoe. This nobleman d. unm. 17 October, 1711, when the Barony of St. John, of Bletshoe, passed t · the heir-at-law, Sir Andrew St. John, of Woodford, co. Northampton (see BURKE's *Extant Peerage and Baronetage*), and the Earldom of Bolingbroke became EXTINCT.

Arms—Arg., on a chief, gu., two mullets pierced, or.

ST. JOHN—BARON TREGOZE OF HIGH-WORTH.

By Letters Patent, dated 21 May, 1626.

Lineage.

SIR OLIVER ST. JOHN, of Lydiard Tregoze, an eminent soldier, obtained great renown in the Irish wars of ELIZABETH and JAMES, was created Viscount Grandison, in the peerage of Ireland, *temp.* JAMES I., with limitation to the male issue of his nephew Sir Edward Villiers. He was first president of Munster, and was afterwards constituted lord deputy of that kingdom. His lordship returned, in the 20th of the same monarch, and by his majesty's successor. was made a peer of England, 21 May, 1626, in the dignity of BARON TREGOZE, of *Highworth*, co. *Wilts*. His lordship m. Joan, dau. and heir of Henry Roydon, Esq., of Battersea, and widow of Sir William Holcroft, but had no issue. He d. in 1629, when the Barony of Tregoze became EXTINCT; the Viscounty of Grandison passed in accordance with the limitation to the family of Villiers, and the manors of Battersea and Wandsworth devolved on his lordship's nephew, Sir John St. John, Bart., ancestor of the VISCOUNTS BOLINGBROKE.

ST. LEGER—VISCOUNT DONERAILE.

(See BURKE's *Extant Peerage*.)

ST. LIZ—EARLS OF HUNTINGDON.

Creation of WILLIAM THE CONQUEROR.

Lineage.

The county which gave designation to this earldom was, according to Dr. Heylin, a thickly wooded forest, until the reign of the 2nd HENRY, when the timber was first cleared away; the chief town, from the celebrity of the forest as a chase, was called Huntingtown, which soon became abbreviated into Huntington, or Huntingdon. The Earldom of Huntingdon was conferred, by WILLIAM THE CONQUEROR, upon

WALTHEOF (son of Syward, the Saxon Earl of Northumberland), who had m. the dau. of that monarch's sister, by the moth 'r's side, JUDITH. He was also Earl of Northampton, and of Northumberland: but conspiring against the Normans, he was beheaded, in 1073, at Winchester, leaving issue,

Maud, m. 1st, to Simon de St. Liz; and 2ndly, to David, brother of ALEXANDER, King of Scotland.
Judith, m. 1st, to Ralph de Toney, and afterwards to Robert, 5th son of Richard de Tonbridge, ancestor of the Lords Fitz-Walter.

After the execution of Waltheof, King WILLIAM offered Judith, his niece. the deceased earl's widow, in marriage to Simon St. Liz, a noble Norman, but the lady peremptorily rejected the alliance, owing, Dugdale says, to St. Liz's *halting in one leg;* which refusal so displeased the CONQUEROR, that he immediately seized upon the castle and honour of Huntingdon, which the Countess held in dower, exposing herself and her dau. to a state of privation and obscurity in the Isle of Ely, and other places; while he bestowed upon the said Simon St. Liz the town of Northampton, and the whole hundred of Falkeley, then valued at £40 per annum, to *provide shoes for his horses.* St. Liz thus disappointed in obtaining the hand of the Countess of Huntingdon, made his addresses, with greater success, to her elder dau., the Lady Maud, who became his wife, when William conferred upon the said

SIMON DE ST. LIZ, the Earldoms of Huntingdon and Northampton. This nobleman built the castle of Northampton, as also the priory of St. Andrews here, about the 18th year of the CONQUEROR's reign, and was a liberal benefactor to the church. His lordship was a witness to King HENRY I.'s laws in 1100, after which he made a voyage to the Holy Land, and d. on his return (1115), at the abbey of Charity, in France, leaving issue,

    SIMON, who *s.* to the Earldom of Northampton, but was excluded from that of Huntingdon. He was, subsequently, however, restored.
    Waltheof, Abbot of Melrus, in Scotland.
    Maud, *m.* 1st, to Robert, son of Richard de Tonbridge; and 2ndly, to William de Albini, according to Dugdale; but Hornby, in his remarks upon Dugdale's errors, proves that such alliances, if not impossible, were very improbable. A Maud de St. Lis is mentioned as wife of Saier de Quincy, being father and mother of Saier, 1st Earl of Winchester.

Upon the death of Simon. Earl of Huntingdon and Northampton, his elder son, Simon, should have succeeded to both dignities, but it appears he only inherited the former. The Earldom of Huntingdon being assumed by

DAVID, son of MALCOLM III., King of Scotland, who had *m.* the deceased earl's widow, the Countess Maud, under the especial sanction of King HENRY I. This nobleman succeeded to the Scottish throne, on the decease of Alexander, his elder brother, in 1124; and invading England, was met upon the border by King STEPHEN, when their differences were amicably adjusted; and

HENRY, son of the said DAVID, King of Scotland, on condition of swearing allegiance to STEPHEN, had the Earldom and honour of Huntingdon, with the borough of Doncaster and Carlisle as an augmentation thereto. Nay, he was in such high estimation with King STEPHEN, that upon that monarch's solemn celebration of the feast of Easter, he placed the Earl of Huntingdon on his right hand; which gave such displeasure to the nobility then present, that William Corbois, or Corbel, Archbishop of Canterbury, Ranulph, Earl of Chester, and several others, withdrew from court, He *m* Ada, sister of William, Earl of Warrenne and Surrey, and had issue,

    MALCOLM,|
    WILLIAM, | successively Kings of Scotland.
    David.
    Ada, *m* to Floris, Earl of Holland.
    Margaret, *m.* to Conan le Petit, Earl of Britanny.

The earl *d.* in 1153, a little before his father, and upon his decease,

SIMON DE ST. LIZ, Earl of Northampton, was restored to the Earldom of Huntingdon. This nobleman was a zealous supporter of King STEPHEN, against the Empress MAUD, and continued ever opposed to any amicable adjustment of the contest. He *m.* Isabel, dau. of Robert, Earl of Leicester, and had issue,

    SIMON, who succeeded to the Earldom of Northampton, but not to *that* of Huntingdon. He was, however, restored. *temp.* HENRY II.
    Amice.   Hawyse.

His lordship* *d.* about the year 1154, and after his decease, King HENRY II., in the 1st year of his reign, conferred, in exchange for the cos. of Northumberland, Cumberland, and Westmoreland (which the Scots had subjugated , upon

MALCOLM, King of Scotland, son of Henry, Earl of Huntingdon, the Earldom of Huntingdon. This monarch *d.s.p.,* in 1165, and was *s.* by his brother,

WILLIAM, King of Scotland, as Earl of Huntingdon. This monarch taking up arms in favour of Prince Henry, so exaspe

rated King HENRY II., that he immediately sent an army against him, and promised that the castle and earldom should be restored to the family of St. Liz, the rightful heirs; whereupon Simon St. Liz, Earl of Northampton, son and heir of Simon, last Earl of Huntingdon, of that family, levied troops, and appeared before the castle, when WILLIAM, of SCOTLAND, finding it untenable, made a surrender to St. Liz of that fortress, which the King of England ordered to be demolished, but, nevertheless,

SIMON DE ST. LIZ was restored to the Earldom of Huntingdon, circa 1174, which he enjoyed for the remainder of his life. He *d. s. p.,* in 1184, whereupon King HENRY II. restored the Earldom to King WILLIAM, of Scotland, and that monarch transferred it to his younger brother, who thus became

DAVID, Earl of Huntingdon. This prince accompanied King RICHARD I. to the Holy Land, with 500 men in his train; but upon his return, his fleet being scattered, his lordship was made prisoner by the Egyptians, and eventually redeemed by the Venetians. He *m.* Maud, dau. of Hugh Kyvelioc, and sister and co-heir of Ralph, Earl of Chester, and had surviving issue,

    JOHN, surnamed Le Scot.
    Margaret, *m.* to Alan, of Galloway and had two daus.,
        Christian, *m.* to William, Earl of Albemarle, and *d. s. p.*; and
        DEVORGILDA, *m.* to JOHN BALIOL (*see* BALIOL).
    Isabel, *m.* to Robert Bruce, of Annandale.
    Ada, *m.* to Henry de Hastings, Lord Hastings.
    Maud, *d. unm.*

His lordship *d.* in 1219, and was *s.* by his son,

JOHN LE SCOT, as Earl of Huntingdon, who, in right of his mother, became likewise Earl of Chester (*see* Scot, Earl of Chester). This nobleman *d.* in 1237, *s. p.,* when the Earldom of Huntingdon became EXTINCT, but his great possessions devolved upon his sisters as co-heirs.

Arms—Per pale, indented, arg. and az.

ST. MAUR—BARONS ST. MAUR.

By Writ of Summons, dated 29 July, 1314.

Lineage.

The first of this family upon record (though the name DE ST. MAURO entered England contemporaneously with the CONQUEROR),

MILO DE ST. MAUR, was involved in the baronial war against King JOHN. He was father of Peter, Lord of Weston, in Gordano and Kingston Seymour, co. Somerset, *temp.* HENRY III., father of Maud, who *m.* Simon de Ludgate, and their son assumed the name of St. Maur, but had, as in the preceding generation, an heiress only, named Milicent, *m.* to Sir John de Perceval. Returning to the male line, though the connection between them does not appear, the next is

GEFFREY DE ST. MAUR, who *m.* the dau. and heir of William de Rughdon : and after him

LAURENCE DE ST. MAUR, who in the 11th EDWARD I., obtained a grant for a weekly market at his manor of Rode, co. Somerset, and *d.* in the 24th of the same reign. He *m.* Isabella, dau. and co-heiress of Hugh de Morewick, widow of Sir Roger Lumley, and was *s.* by his son,

NICHOLAS DE ST. MAUR. This feudal lord having been engaged in all the expeditions made into Scotland from the 27th to the 34th EDWARD I., was summoned to parliament as a Baron in the 8th of the ensuing reign. His lordship *m.,* 1st, Eva de Meysy; and 2ndly, Elena, eldest dau. and co heir of Alan le Zouche, Lord Zouche, of Ashby, co. Leicester, and dying in 1316, was *s.* by his elder son, by his 1st marriage,

THOMAS DE ST. MAUR, 2nd baron, but never summoned to parliament. This nobleman *d. s. p.* in 1358 (leaving his nephew, John Worthy, his heir of the whole blood), and was *s.* by his half-brother,

SIR NICHOLAS DE ST. MAUR, 3rd baron, summoned to parliament from 15 November, 1351, to 20 November, 1360. This nobleman was in the wars of France, *temp.* EDWARD III., first in the retinue of Maurice de Holand. His lordship *m.* Muriel, dau. and heir of Thomas de Holand His lordship *m.* Muriel, dau. and heir of James Lovel, only son of Sir Richard Lovel, Lord Lovel, of Kari, by whom he acquired the estates of Winfred-Eagle, co. Dorset, and of Castle Kary, in Somersetshire, with the Barony of Lovel. He *d.* in 1361, and was *s.* by his elder son.

NICHOLAS DE ST. MAUR, 4th baron, *b.* 1353, who also *d.* in 1361, under age, and was *s.* by his brother,

RICHARD DE ST. MAUR, 5th baron, summoned to parliament, under the name of SEYMOUR, from 26 August, 1380, to 3 October, 1400. This nobleman was in the wars of France, in

* This earl is stated to have had a brother also called Simon de St. Liz. whose descendants settling at Seton, co. Rutland, assumed the surname of SETON. The heir female of this family *m.,* in the reign of HENRY VI., Sir William Fielding, ancestor of the Fieldings. Earls of Denbigh.

the 10th RICHARD II., in the retinue of Richard, Earl of Arundel, admiral of England. His lordship *m.* Ela, dau. and co-heir of Sir John St. Lo, Knt., and by her (who made her will in 14t9) had issue,

RICHARD, his successor.

John (Sir), *m.* Margaret, dau. and heir of Sir John Erlegh, son of Sir John Erlegh, by Margaret, his wife, sister and eventually co-heir of Sir Gui de Bryan, and was *s.* by his son,

> JOHN, who *m.* Elizabeth, dau. of Thomas, Lord Cobham, and left a son,
>
>> THOMAS (Sir), who got a share of the Bryan inheritance, in 1488. and *d.* in the beginning of HENRY VII.'s reign. He *m.* Philippa, dau. of Sir Edward Hungerford, and had a son,
>>
>>> JOHN, of Rode, in the co. of Somerset, who *d. v. p.*, leaving
>>>
>>>> WILLIAM, whose only dau. and heiress,
>>>>
>>>>> JOANE, *m.* Sir Robert Drury, and *d. s. p.*
>>>>>
>>>>> Anne, *m.* to Robert Stawell, Esq., ancestor of the Lord Stawell.
>>>>>
>>>>> Margaret, *m.* to William Bampfylde, and had a son,
>>>>>
>>>>>> SIR EDWARD BAMPFYLDE, who *m.* Elizabeth, dau. of Sir Michael Wadham, and had a dau.,
>>>>>>
>>>>>>> ELIZABETH, who *m.* George Perceval, Esq., Lord of Tykenham, co. Somerset, ancestor of the Earls of Egmont.

Nicholas.

The baron *d.* in 1401, and was *s.* by his eldest son,

RICHARD DE ST. MAUR, 6th baron, summoned to parliament from 21 June, 1402, to 26 August, 1408, by writ addressed "Ricardo Seymour." This nobleman went into Ireland with Thomas, Duke of Surrey, in the 22nd of RICHARD II., then lieutenant of that kingdom; and in the 4th HENRY III., he was in the wars of France. His lordship *m.* Mary, dau. and heir of Thomas Peyver, by Margaret, his wife, dau. and co-heir of Sir Nigel Loring, and *d.* 1409, leaving his wife, then *enciente*, who was afterwards delivered of a dau.,

ALICE ST. MAUR, *b.* in the house of Thomas Cressy, citizen and mercer of London, in the parish of St. Lawrence, Cripplegate, in that city. This lady *m.* WILLIAM ZOUCHE, 5th Baron Zouche, of Haryngworth, and the BARONY OF ST. MAUR continued vested in the Lords Zouche until the decease of

EDWARD, 11th Baron Zouche, in 1625, when the Baronies of Zouche of Haryngworth, of St. Maur, and of Lovel of Kary, fell into ABEYANCE between his lordship's two daus. and co-heirs, viz.,

> ELIZABETH, *m.* 1597, to Sir William Tate, M.P., of De la Pre, Northamptonshire, and *d.* 1617: their descendant in the 4th generation,
>
>> CATHERINE TATE, dau. and co-heir (with her sisters, Mary, wife of Samuel Long, Esq., and Susannah, who *d. unm.*) of Bartholomew Tate, Esq., of De la Pré Abbey, *m.* 1720, Charles Hedges, Esq., of Finchley, and was grandmother of SIR CECIL BISSHOPP, Bart.
>
> Mary, *m.* 1st, to Thomas Leighton, Esq., and 2ndly, to William Connard, Esq.

The BARONY OF ZOUCHE was, however, called out in favour of SIR CECIL BISSHOPP, 27 August, 1815, to whom succeeded his dau., HARRIET-ANNE, BARONESS ZOUCHE.

The Baronies of St. Maur, and of Lovel of Kary, fell into ABEYANCE, as stated above, upon the decease of Edward, 11th Baron Zouche, of Haryngworth, in 1625, between his daus., ELIZABETH, wife of Sir William Tate, of De la Pre, co. Northampton, and MARY, wife of Thomas Leighton, Esq., as they still continue amongst the descendants of those ladies.

Arms—Az., two chevrons, gu., in chief a label of three points, as.

ST. MAUR—BARON ST. MAUR.

By Writ of Summons, dated 20 November, 1317.

Lineage.

WILLIAM ST. MAUR, supposed to have been of the old baronial family of St. Maur, was summoned to parliament as a Baron, under the name de Sancto Mauro, from 20 November, 1317, to 14 March, 1322, but there is nothing further known of his lordship or his descendants.

469

BANKS conjectures (with a strong appearance of probability) that this William St. Maur was elder brother of Thomas de St. Maur, 2nd baron, under the creation set forth in the preceding article (*which see*).

ST. PHILIBERT—BARONS ST. PHILIBERT.

By Writ of Summons, dated 6 February, 1299.

Lineage.

NICHOLAS DE ST. PHILIBERT, in the 15th JOHN, was in the expedition then made in Poictou; and in the same reign,

HUGH DE ST. PHILIBERT was in arms with the other barons against the crown, and did not return to his allegiance before the 1st HENRY III., when he had restitution of his lands. In the 10th of the latter king he was made governor of the island of Jersey. After this Hugh, came

ROGER DE ST. PHILIBERT, one of the rebellious barons made prisoner in 47th HENRY III., at the battle of Northampton. And about the same time,

WILLIAM DE ST. PHILIBERT was also in the baronial ranks, and assisted in the defence of Dover Castle. But after the battle of Evesham, making his peace, and returning to his allegiance, he had restitution of his lands which had been seized, in the co. Northampton. The next of the family we find, is

HUGH DE ST. PHILIBERT, who, having been engaged in the French and Scottish wars, was summoned to parliament by King EDWARD I., as a Baron, 6 February, 1299, but never afterwards. His lordship was *s.* by his son,

JOHN DE ST. PHILIBERT, who had livery of his lands 7th EDWARD II., and like his predecessor, was in the French and Scottish wars; and in the 5th EDWARD III., was constituted mayor of Bordeaux. He *d.* in two years afterwards, leaving Ada, his wife, him surviving, and was *s.* by his son,

JOHN DE ST. PHILIBERT, who, in the 21st EDWARD III., making proof of his age, and doing his homage, had livery of his lands, and was summoned to parliament, 20 November, 1348, and 1 January, and 10 March, 1349. His lordship was in the wars of France, temp. EDWARD III., and *d.* in 1359. He *m.* Margaret, dau. of Hugh de St. John, and one of the co-heirs of her brother, Edmund de St. John, by whom he left a son,

JOHN DE ST. PHILIBERT, who *d.* in infancy, when the Barony of St. Philibert became EXTINCT.

Arms—Bendy of six, arg. and az.

ST. QUINTIN—BARON ST. QUINTIN.

By Writ of Summons, dated 8 June, 1294.

Lineage.

This family is said to have adopted its surname from the town of St. Quintin, the capital of Lower Picardy.

SIR HERBERT DE ST. QUINTIN came into England with the CONQUEROR, and was father of OLIVER, father of

SIR ROBERT DE ST. QUINTIN, who, in the time of RUFUS, was one of the twelve knights who divided, with Robert Fitz-Hamon, certain lands in Wales, which they had won by conquest, and there he erected the castle of St. Quintin. The brother of this Sir Robert,

SIR HERBERT ST. QUINTIN, was father of

AMATELLUS ST. QUINTIN, who, in the reign of RICHARD I., was entitled BARON ST. QUINTIN, and was *s.* by his son,

HERBERT ST. QUINTIN, also styled Baron St. Quintin, who *m.* Agnes, or Anne, sister and co-heir of Anselm de Stutevill, and had five sons, of whom the three elder, Herbert, John, and Amatellus, *d. s. p.* WILLIAM, the 4th, carried on the line of the family, and Alexander is said to be ancestor of the baronets of the name, viz., the ST. QUINTINS of Harpham, co. York. He had also two daus., viz., Margery, *m.* to Sir William Rochfort, Knt., and Agnes, *m.* to Sir Fulke Constable, Knt. The 4th son,

WILLIAM ST. QUINTIN, had, by Beatrix, his wife, a son, HERBERT, Baron of St. Quintin, who by his wife, Margery, dau. of Walter de Fauconberg, of Skelton, had issue, HERBERT, who *d. v. p.*, leaving by his wife, Anastasia, dau. of John, Lord Maltravers, HERBERT, Baron of St. Quintin, husband of Lora, dau. of William, Lord Fauconberg, of Skelton (on occasion of which marriage a dispensation was obtained owing to the near relationship of the parties) and had a son and heir,

HERBERT ST. QUINTIN, who was summoned to parliament as BARON ST. QUINTIN, by King EDWARD I., 8 June, 1294.* This nobleman *m.* Margery, sister of Gerard de Lisle, and dau. and co-heir of Warine de Lisle, and left two daus., viz.,

ELIZABETH, who is called, by one account, wife of John. Lord Grey, of Rotherfield, *d. s. p.*, but she is stated by Banks, on the authority of an ancient record in the Tower of London, to have *m.* John Marmion.

LORA, *m.* Robert de Grey, of Rotherfield, who took the name of Marmion ; in the record Robert, brother to John Marmion, had an only dau. and heir,

    ELIZABETH GREY, who *m.* Henry, Lord Fitz-Hugh, and her grandson,

      HENRY, Lord Fitz-Hugh (*see* Fitz-Hugh), left, with other issue,

        ELIZABETH FITZ-HUGH, 2nd dau., who *m* Sir William Parr, Knt., and had (with an elder son,) William, created Lord Parr),

          SIR THOMAS PARR, who left,

          WILLIAM PARR, Marquess of Northampton.

          ANNE PARR, *m.* to William Herbert, Earl of Pembroke. from which period the titles of ST. QUINTIN and MARMION have been numbered amongst the honours of the house of Pembroke.

          KATHARINE PARR, wife of HENRY VIII.

Arms—Or, three chevrons, gu., a chief barry of two, vairy.

SANDFORD—BARON MOUNT SANDFORD.

By Letters Patent, dated 31 July, 1800.

Lineage.

CAPTAIN THEOPHILUS SANDFORD, of Moyglare, co. Meath, *d.* February, 1668, leaving by Anne, his wife, dau. of Richard Tighe, Esq., a son and heir,

HENRY SANDFORD, of Castlerea, M.P., co. Roscommon, *m.* 1692, Elizabeth, sister of Robert FitzGerald, Earl of Kildare, and *d.* 9 September, 1733, leaving a dau., Frances, wife of Michael Cuffe, Esq., and a son and heir,

ROBERT SANDFORD, Esq., of Castlerea, M.P. co. Roscommon, *m.* 1717, Henrietta, dau. of William O'Brien, Earl of Inchiquin, and had issue,

  I. HENRY, his heir.

  II. Robert. general in the army, *d.* 1793.

  I. Rachael. *m.* to Thomas Crofton, Esq.

  II. Mary, *m.* to Robert Cooke, Esq.

  III. Anne, *m.* to John Bourne, Esq.

  IV. Henrietta, *m.* to Edward Nicholson, Esq.

The son and heir,

HENRY SANDFORD, Esq., of Castlerea, *m.* 21 September, 1750, Sarah, dau. of Stephen Moore, Viscount Mountcashell, and by her (who *d.* 1764), had issue,

  HENRY-MOORE, created Baron Mount Sandford.

  William, in holy orders, *b.* 1752, *d.* 17 August, 1809, having *m.* 1789. Jane, 2nd dau. of the Right Hon. Silver Oliver, of Castle Oliver, co. Limerick, and had issue,

    HENRY, 2nd baron.

  Mary, *b.* 1791. *m.* William Robert Wills, Esq., of Willsgrove, co. Roscommon, and was mother of Thomas-George Wills-Sandford, Esq., of Castlerea and Willsgrove.

  Eliza, *b.* 1796, *m.* Hon. and Very Rev. Henry Pakenham,

---

dean of St. Patrick's, son of Thomas, 2nd Earl of Longford.

  Louisa, *b.* 1759 ; *m.* 1783, William-Worth Newenham, of Coolmore, co. Cork, Esq.

Mr. Henry Sandford *d.* 12 February, 1797.

HENRY-MOORE SANDFORD, Esq., of Castlerea, *b.* 28 July, 1751, was, by letters patent, dated 31 July, 1800, created BARON MOUNT SANDFORD, *of Castlerea*, with limitation to his brother, and the male heirs of his body. He *m.* Katherine, eldest dau. of the Right Hon. Silver Oliver, of Castle Oliver, but by her, who *d.* 1818, had no surviving issue. He *d.* 14 June, 1814, and was *s.* by his nephew,

HENRY SANDFORD, 2nd Baron Mount Sandford, *b.* 1805. who was killed at a riot at Windsor. He *d. unm.* 14 June, 1828, and was *s.* by his uncle,

GEORGE SANDFORD, 3rd Baron Mount Sandford, who *d. unm.* 25 September, 1846, when the title became EXTINCT.

Arms—Per chevron, or and ermine, in chief, two boars' heads, erased, sa.

SANDILANDS—LORD ABERCROMBIE.

By Letters Patent, dated 12 December, 1647.

Lineage.

JAMES SANDILANDS, the first of this branch of the noble house of Torphichen, was son of Sir James Sandilands, of Calder, by his 2nd wife, Margaret, dau. of Andrew Ker. He *m.* Catherine, dau. of Sir William Scott, of Balwearie, and had, with a son, three daus.,

  JAMES, his heir.

  Margaret, *m.* to Lawrence, 3rd Lord Oliphant.

  Mary, *m.* to David Forrester, of Carden.

  Helen, *m.* to George Towers, of Innerleath.

The son and heir,

JAMES SANDILANDS, of Cruvy and St. Monance, *m.* Elizabeth, Meldrum (said to have been a dau. of Alexander Meldrum, of Segie), and had three sons and a dau., viz.,

  I. JAMES. *d. v. p.* leaving by Elizabeth, his wife, dau. of Robert Bethune, of Creich, a son,

    WILLIAM (Sir), successor to his grandfather.

  II. David.

  III. Andrew, tutor to James, Lord Torphichen, in 1586.

  I. Elizabeth, *m.* to Sir John Boswell, of Balmuto.

James Sandilands *d.* in November, 1586, and was *s.* by his grandson,

SIR WILLIAM SANDILANDS, of St. Monance, who *m.* Jean Bothwell, and had with two daus., Margaret, *m.* to Sir James Learmonth, of Balerny, a lord of session, and Christian, *m.* to Adam Bothwell, of Pitcally, a son,

  James, who predeceased him, leaving a son,

    JAMES (Sir), successor to his grandfather.

Sir William *d.* in October, 1644, æt. seventy-two, and was *s.* by his grandson,

SIR JAMES SANDILANDS, of St. Monance, who was served heir to his grandfather, Sir William Sandilands, 5 and 16 July, 1645, in considerable possessions in the co. Fife, including the Barony of Petlair, lordship of St. Monance, with the tower and portalice thereof, called the Newark, and was raised to the peerage by King CHARLES I., as LORD ABERCROMBIE, by letters patent, dated at Carisbrooke Castle, 12 December, 1647, to himself and the heirs male of his body. "Being a riotous youth," says Sir William Douglas, "he wasted his whole estate in five years after his succession to his grandfather; and, in 1649, disposed of his property in Fife, including St. Monance and the castle of Newark, to Lieut.-Gen. David Lesly, who took the title of Lord Newark from thence." His lordship *m.* Lady Agnes Carnegie, 2nd dau. of David, 1st Earl of Southesk, and by her had a son and successor,

JAMES, 2nd lord, who *d. s. p.* in 1681, when the barony became EXTINCT.

⁂ The Lords of Session, in their return to the House of Peers, 1740, observe, that "it does not appear that either the patentee, or any successor of his in that right, ever sat or voted in parliament, nor has any one offered to vote in right of that peerage at any election, general or particular, since the Union."

Arms—Quarterly : 1st and 4th, arg., a bend, az., for SANDILANDS ; 2nd and 3rd, arg., a man's heart, ensigned with an imperial crown, ppr. ; on a chief, az., three mullets of the 1st, for DOUGLAS.

---

* Nicolas does not consider this writ a regular summons to parliament, nor the person summoned under it a baron of the realm. Because "none of the higher temporal nobility, nor any of the spiritual peers, were included in it ; nor was there any day fixed for the meeting." "It is also to be observed," continues the same authority, "that the writ in question is the earliest on record, excepting that of 49th HENRY III., that the majority of the persons summoned in the 22nd EDWARD I. were never again summoned, excepting in the 25th of the same king ; that several of the persons were not considered barons by tenure ; and that of those who were barons by tenure, and summoned on those occasions, many were never included in any subsequent summons to parliament. The writ of the 22nd EDWARD I. has, however, on one occasion (in the case of the Barony of Ros), been admitted as a writ of summons to parliament at the bar of the House of Lords : but the last 'General Report of the Lords Committee, appointed to search for Matters touching the dignity of a Peer of the Realm,' appears to confirm the objections here expressed." Yet under this, at least, doubtful writ, the *extant* EARLS OF PEMBROKE assume the dignity of BARONS OF ST. QUINTIN.

470

SANDYS—BARON SANDYS, OF THE VINE.

By Writ of Summons, dated 3 November, 1529.

Lineage.

SIR WILLIAM SANDYS (son of Sir William Sandys of the Vine by Elizabeth, his wife, dau. of Sir John Cheney, of Shurland) was an eminent soldier in the reigns of HENRY VII. and HENRY VIII. In the 7th of the former king he was in the expedition sent into Flanders, under the Earls of Derby, Shrewsbury, and other English noblemen, to aid the Emperor MAXIMILIAN against the French; and in five years afterwards he shared in the victory over the Cornishmen at Blackheath. In the 4th HENRY VIII. he was sent, with other gallant persons from England, to assist Ferdinand of Arragon, against the French; and he was subsequently, being at the time a knight of the Garter, one of the commissioners deputed to make a palace before the castle gate at Guisnes, preparatory to the celebrated interview between HENRY VIII. and FRANCIS I. Upon the attainder of the Duke of Buckingham, Sir William Sandys obtained a grant of the manors of Willesford and Stratton, co. Wilts, and in the 14th HENRY VIII. he was treasurer of Calais: in which latter he led, in conjunction with Sir Richard Wingfield, the rear of the army sent under the command of the Earl of Surrey into France; and for his good services was summoned to parliament by warrant directed *Willielmo Sandys (de Vine) chivalier*, from 3 November, 1529, to 16 January, 1542. (Dugdale states from Stow, that six years previously viz., 27 April, 1523, he had been advanced to the degree of a baron of the realm by the title of LORD SANDS at the king's royal palace of Bridewell, but that no patent of the creation is upon record). He certainly bore the title of Lord Sandys long before the first of these summonses, and so designated, led the van of the army sent, under the Duke of Suffolk into France, in the 15th HENRY VIII., and in two years afterwards, as Lord Sandys, had a reversionary grant of the office of lord chamberlain, after the death of Charles, Earl of Worcester. His lordship was in the train of Wolsey, when the cardinal was deputed to complain to the King of France, of the sacking of Rome by the Duke of Bourbon. He subsequently subscribed the articles of impeachment against that celebrated prelate, and he signed the letter to Pope CLEMENT regarding HENRY's divorce from Queen Katharine

The principal seat of the Sandys family, anciently at the Vine near Basingstoke in Hampshire, had been alienated by an heiress to the family of Brocas, but was recovered by this Lord Sandys, who rebuilt the manor house there. His lordship m. Margery, only dau. and heir of John Bray, Esq. (brother and heir of Reginald Bray) by whom he eventually acquired a considerable property. He d. in 1542, having had issue,

  I. Thomas, who s. as 2nd baron.
  II. Reginald, a priest, d. unm.
  III. John, a priest, d. unm.
  I. Mary, wife 1st, of Sir William Pelham, and 2ndly of John Palmer, of Augmering.
  II. Alice, 2nd wife of Walter, Lord Hungerford, of Heytesbury.
  III. Elizabeth, wife of Sir Humphrey Forster, of Aldermaston, Berks.
  IV. Margaret, m. to Sir Thomas Essex.

The eldest son,
THOMAS SANDYS, 2nd baron, summoned to parliament from 14 June, 1543. to 5 November, 1558. This nobleman m. Elizabeth, dau. of George Manners, Lord Ros, and had issue,

  HENRY, who m. Elizabeth, dau. of William Windsor, 2nd Baron Windsor, and dying v. p., left issue,
    WILLIAM, successor to the title.
    Thomas.
    Margery, m. to Henry Carey, Esq., of Hamworthy, co. Dorset.
  Walter (Sir).

His lordship (who is stated by Leland to have had four sons and six daus., a junior of the former being, says THYNNE's *Chronicle*, executed at St. Thomas Waterings, 18 June, 1556, for a robbery of £3,000,) was s. at his decease by his grandson, WILLIAM SANDYS, 3rd baron, summoned to parliament from 8 May, 1572, to 14 November, 1621. This nobleman was one of the peers who sat upon the trial of the Duke of Norfolk, and upon that of MARY, Queen of Scotland. Afterwards taking part, 43rd ELIZABETH, with the Earl of Essex, in that nobleman's insurrection, he suffered imprisonment. His lordship m. 1st, Christian, dau. of Bryan Annesley, Esq., of Lewisham, in Kent, and had a son, WILLIAM, his successor. He m. 2ndly, Catherine, called "the Fair Brydges," dau. of Edmund, Lord Chandos by whom he had an only dau.,

471

ELIZABETH, who m. Sir Edwin Sandys, Knt., son of Miles Sandys, of Latimers, and had issue,
HENRY SANDYS, a colonel in the royal army during the civil wars—of whom hereafter—as successor to the 4th baron.

His lordship d. in 1623, and was s. by his son,
WILLIAM SANDYS, 4th baron, but never summoned to parliament. His lordship m. Alathea, eldest dau. and co-heir of John Panton, Esq., of Brinneskid, co. Denbigh, but d. s. p. in 1629, when the barony devolved upon his nephew of the half blood,
COLONEL HENRY SANDYS, 5th baron, but owing to the civil wars never summoned to parliament. This nobleman, who was a brave and active cavalier officer, received a mortal wound in the fight at Bramdene, near Alresford, in Hants, 29 March, 1644, and d. 6 April ensuing. His lordship m. Jane, dau. of Sir William Sandys, Knt., of Missenden, co. Gloucester, and had issue,

WILLIAM,
HENRY, } 6th and 7th barons.
Miles, d. s. p.
EDWIN, 8th baron.
Hester, m. to Colonel Humphrey Noye, of Carnanton, son of Sir William Noye, attorney-general to King CHARLES I., and his dau. and heiress,
  CATHERINE NOYE, marrying William Davies, Esq., of St. Erith, they had issue,
    JOHN, whose dau. and heiress,
      Catherine, was wife of the Rev. Edward Giddy, A.M., whose son,
        DAVIES O DDY, Esq., on marrying the heiress of Gilbert took that name, and was father of
          JOHN DAVIES GILBERT, Esq., who m. the Hon. Anne Carew, and had issue,
            CAREW DAVIES GILBERT, Esq , of Trelissick, co. Cornwall, now senior co-heir to the Barony of SANDYS.
Alathea, m. to Francis Goston, Esq., of Alderidge, co. Hants.
Mary, m. to Dr. Henry Savage, principal of Balliol College, Oxford.
Jane, m. to John Harris, Esq., of Old Woodstock, co. Oxford.
Margaret, m. to Sir John Mill, Bart., ancestor of the late Sir John Barker Mill, Bart.
Margery, m. to Sir Edmund Fortescue, Bart., of Fallapit, co. Devon. and had (with two daus, Jane, m. to William Coleman, Esq., and Sarah, who d. unm. 1685), a son and heir SIR SANDYS FORTESCUE, Bart. of Fallapit, who had an only child Elizabeth.

Lord Sandys d. in 1644, and was s. by his eldest son,
WILLIAM SANDYS, 6th baron summoned to parliament, 8 May, 1661. This nobleman m. Lady Mary Cecil, dau. of William, 2nd Earl of Salisbury, but d. s. p. in 1668. During the time of this lord in the year 1653, the ancient family mansion of the Vine, erected by the 1st baron, in the reign of HENRY VIII., was sold to Challoner Chute, Esq., M.P. for Middlesex, in 1656, afterwards Speaker of Richard Cromwell's House of Commons. Lord Sandys was s. by his brother,
HENRY SANDYS, 7th baron, summoned to parliament from 6 March, 1679, to 21 March, 1680 ; at whose decease s. p. in 1680, the title devolved upon his brother,
EDWYN SANDYS, 8th baron, who was never summoned to parliament. This nobleman d. s. p. about the year 1700, when his estates devolved upon his sisters, as co-heirs (*refer* to issue of the 5th lord), and the Barony of Sandys, of the Vine, fell into ABEYANCE amongst those ladies, as it still continues with their representatives, of which the senior as before said is Mr. Davies-Gilbert of Trelissick.

Arms—Arg., a cross raguly, sa.

SANDYS—BARONS SANDYS, OF OMBERSLEY.

By Letters Patent, dated 20 December, 1743.

Lineage.

This family of Sandys was originally seated at St. Bees, in Cumberland.
GEORGE SANDYS, Esq. (son of William Sandys, by Margaret, his wife, dau. and heir of William Rawson), m. Margaret, dau. of John Dixon, of London, and had six sons,

  I. George, slain fighting against the Scotch, 1547.
  II. William, of Conishead, who left an only son,
    Francis, who d. s p. in ward to Queen ELIZABETH.
  III Edwin, D.D., archbishop of York.

iv. Christopher of Graythwaite ancestor in the female line of Sandys of Graythwaite and Tytup

v. Myles, ancestor of Sir Edwin-Bayntun Sandys, Bart., of Missenden Castle, co. Gloucester.

vi. Anthony, ancestor in the male line of SANDYS *of Graythwaite.*

The 3rd son,

THE REV. EDWIN SANDYS, D.D., archbishop of York, *d.* 1588, leaving behind him a deservedly high reputation for learning and virtue. His place *m.* Cecilia, dau. of Thomas Wilford, of Cranbrook, co. Kent, and had issue,

I. SAMUEL (Sir), ancestor of the Lo.ds SANDYS of Ombersley.

II. EDWIN (Sir, a distinguished politician of the time of JAMES I., dying 16.9, as buried in the church of Northbourne, in Kent, where he had a seat and fair estate. His direct male descendant, REV. EDWIN SANDYS, assumed in 1 30, in right of his wife, the surname and arms of LUMSDAINE.

III. Myles (Sir), afterwards created a baronet, 161.; but the baronetcy expired in his eldest son, Sir Myles-Sandys Sandys, Bart., who *d. s. p.*

IV. George, celebrated as a traveller and poet, *d.* in 1643.

SAMUEL SANDYS, Esq., his grace's eldest son, inherited the manor of Ombersley, in Worcestershire, and served the office of sheriff for that co., *temp.* JAMES I. He *m.* Mercy, only dau. of Martin Colpeper, and had four sons, EDWIN, Martin, John, and William, and seven daus., Cecilia, *m.* to John Brace, Esq.; Margaret, *m.* to Sir Francis Wyat; Anne, *m.* to Sir Francis Wenman; Mary, *m.* to Richard Humfrys, Esq.; Mercy, *m.* to — Ewbank: Joyce, *m.* to John Dyneley, Esq.; and Elizabeth, *m.* 1st, to Edward Pytts, Esq., and 2ndly, to George Walsh, Esq. The eldest son

SIR EDWIN SANDYS of Ombersley, *s.* his father, 18 August, 1623, and *d.* 6 September following. By Penelope, his wife, dau. of Sir Richard Bulkeley, he had issue, SAMUEL, his heir; Richard, killed at Edgehill, 1642; Edwin; Martin; Catharine, *m.* to Stephen Anderson, Esq.; and Mercy, *d.* young. The eldest son,

SAMUEL SANDYS, Esq., of Ombersley, a gallant cavalier commander, governor of Evesham, M.P. for Worcestershire, *m.* 1st, Mary, only dau. of Dr. Hugh Barker, dean of the Arches, and 2ndly, Elizabeth, widow of Col. Washington, and dau. of Sir John Pakington, Bart., and dying in 1685, was *s.* by his eldest son,

SAMUEL SANDYS, Esq. of Ombersley, M.P., who *m.* Elizabeth, only dau. of Sir John Pettus, Knt., and had issue,

I. EDWIN, M.P. co. Worcester, *m.* Alice, dau. of Sir James Rushout, Bart., and *d. v. p.* 1699, leaving a son, SAMUEL, heir to his grandfather.

II. Henry, *d.* young.

III. Martin, fellow of New College, and barrister-at-law, *m.* Elizabeth Burton, and left issue.

I. Elizabeth, *d.* young.

II. Penelope, *m.* to Henry Townsend, Esq.

III. Mary, *m.* to Price, Viscount Hereford.

IV. Frances, *m.* to Samuel Pytts, Esq., of Kyre, co. Worcester.

Mr. Sandys *d.* 4 August, 1701, and was *s.* by his grandson,

SAMUEL SANDYS, Esq., M.P., who was elevated to the peerage by King GEORGE II., 20 December, 1743, as BARON SANDYS, *of Ombersley,* having previously filled the office of chancellor of the Exchequer, and held other high and important situations. His lordship, after his elevation to the peerage, was made speaker of the House of Lords. He *m.* Letitia, dau. of Sir Thomas Tipping, Bart., of Wheatfield. co. Oxford (by Anne, his wife, dau. and eventually heir of Thomas Cheeke, Esq., of Pyrgo, in Essex, by Letitia, dau. and heir of the Hon. Edward Russell, brother to William, 1st Duke of Bedford), and had issue,

I. EDWIN, his successor.

II. Cheek, } both *d.* young.

III. Thomas, }

IV. Martin, a colonel in the army, *m.* Mary, dau. of William Trumbull, Esq., of East Hampstead Park, Berks, son of Sir William Trumbull, secretary of state, *temp.* WILLIAM III., by Mary, one of the daus. and co-heirs of Montagu, Viscount Blundell, in Ireland. Col. Sandys had issue,

  1 William, *d.* young.

  2 Edward, *d.* young.

  1 MARY, who *m.* in 1786, Arthur Hill, Marquess of Downshire, in Ireland, and was created in 1802 BARONESS SANDYS, *of Ombersley,* with remainder to her 2nd and younger sons by the marquess, and their heirs male in succession, in default whereof to the eldest son and his heirs male. She *d.* 1 August, 1836.

Colonel Sandys *d.* 26 December, 1768.

V. William, *d.* in 1749.

VI. John. *d.* in 1758.

VII. Henry, *d.* in 1737,

I. Letitia.

II. Anne, *m.* to Christopher Bethell, Esq.

III. Catherine, *d* young.

His lordship *d.* in 1770, and was *s.* by his eldest son,

EDWIN SANDYS, 2nd baron, who *m.* in 1769, Anna-Maria, dau. of James Colebrooke, Esq., and widow of Paine King, Esq., of Finchampstead Abbey, Northamptonshire, but *d. s. p.* in 1797, when his estates devolved upon his sister, Mary, Marchioness of Downshire, and the Barony of Sandys, of Ombersley, became EXTINCT.

Arms—Or, a fesse dancetté, between three cross-crosslets fitchée, gules.

SARSFIELD—EARL OF LUCAN.

Lineage.

SIR THOMAS and STEPHEN DE SARSFIELD were summoned among the magnates of Ireland to the Scottish war, in 1302. ROGER SARSFIELD, Esq., of Sarsfieldstown, co. Meath, had a 2nd son,

JOHN SARSFIELD, mayor of Dublin in 1531, who had issue,

Patrick, "a worshipful gentleman," mayor of that city in 1554, whose hospitality is mentioned by Holinshed; and

SIR WILLIAM SARSFIELD, Knt., of Lucan, co. Dublin, who, being mayor of Dublin in 1566, was knighted 16 November of that year, by Sir Henry Sidney, lord deputy of Ireland, for having rescued Lady Sidney from the Irish, and for his services against Shane O'Neill. He *d.* 27 November, 1616, leaving, by Margaret, his wife, dau. of Andrew Tyrrell, Esq. of Athboy,

JOHN, his heir.

Patrick, who left several children.

Katherine, *m.* Sir Robert Dillon, Knt.; and 2ndly, Sir Christopher Bellew, Knt.

Mary, *m.* Christopher Bathe, Esq.

Jennet, *m.* to Sir John Plunket, Knt., of Dunsoghly.

The eldest son,

JOHN SARSFIELD, Esq. of Lucan, *m.* Margaret, dau. of Sir Luke Dillon, Knt., and had with other issue (of which a dau., Jane, *m.* Robert Alen, Esq., of St. Wolstans), an eldest son,

WILLIAM SARSFIELD, Esq. of Lucan, *b.* 1582; who *m.* Anne, dau. of Sir Patrick Barnewall, Knt., of Gracedieu, and had a son,

PATRICK SARSFIELD, Esq., whose estates were sequestrated by Cromwell, but who recovered them at the Restoration by the interference of the Queen-mother. He had issue,

WILLIAM, his successor, of Lucan, *m.* Mary, natural dau. of CHARLES II., and sister of James, Duke of Monmouth, by whom (who *m.* 2ndly, William Fanshawe, Esq,) he had an only child,

CHARLOTTE, *m.* to Agmondisham Vesey, Esq., and had two daus., co-heirs, viz., Anne, *m.* to Sir John Bingham, Bart., and Henrietta, *m.* to Cæsar Colclough, Esq., of Duffrey Hall.

PATRICK.

Anne, *m.* to Edward Cheevers, Viscount Mount Leinster.

Mary, *m.* to Thomas Rositer, Esq. The great great-great grandson of this marriage was the late Sir William-Sarsfield Rositer Cockburn, Bart.

The 2nd son,

PATRICK SARSFIELD, was created by JAMES II., EARL OF LUCAN, in 1689. This celebrated general, whose skill and address compelled King WILLIAM to sign the articles of Limerick, was slain at the battle of Landen, 29 July, 1693. He *m.* Lady Honora Burke, 2nd dau. of William, 7th Earl of Clanricarde, which lady *m.* 2ndly, James, Duke of Berwick. The earl's issue was a son, who *d. unm.* in Flanders.

Arms—Az., an eagle, or, crowned, az.

SARSFIELD—VISCOUNT SARSFIELD.

Lineage.

SIR DOMINICK SARSFIELD, Knt., chief justice of the Court of Common Pleas in Ireland, was created the 1st baronet in Ireland, 30 September, 1619, and raised to the peerage of Ireland by Privy Seal, 13 February, 1624, as Baron of Barrett's county, and Viscount Kingsale, both in the co. Cork; which privy seal having no effect by reason of the death of King James, the title was conferred by King Charles; but a dispute arising between him and the Lord Courcy, of Kingsale, it was referred to commissioners appointed for that purpose, who decreed that he, Sarsfield, should relinquish the title of Kingsale, and take the title of Viscount of Roscarbrie or any other place in Ireland at his election, whereupon he chose the title of Viscount Sarsfield, of Kilmallock, co. Limerick, which was conferred without loss of precedence or place, as if he had continued his former honour of Kingsale. Soon after, Sir Dominick was made Viscount Sarsfield, of Kilmallock, with precedence of the former patent. He had two sons,

  I. WILLIAM, his heir.
  II. Dominick, whose will is dated 1642, was father of Edmund, mentioned in his father's and uncle William's will. He had besides two younger sons who d. unm., two sons,

Dominick, Viscount of Kilmallock, after his kinsman David's death, s. p. He was colonel of a regiment of cavalry in the Irish army, went to France, and was afterwards first lieutenant of the body-guards, of which the Count Lusan was captain, and subsequently colonel of the king's regiment.
David, Viscount of Kilmallock, after his brother Dominick, was colonel of dragoons in the Spanish service, governor and commandant at Badajoz. He had, with younger issue, Dominick, his heir, Viscount of Kilmallock, who d. unm.; and Edward, who s. his brother as Viscount Kilmallock. He was b. at Perpignan, 11 June, 1693, and had (with a younger son Patrick, who went to Spain, in the navy, and d. s. p. at Carthagena,) an elder son and heir, Edward Sarsfield, Viscount of Kilmallock, who m. in 1784, and had issue.

The elder son,
WILLIAM SARSFIELD, 2nd Viscount Kilmallock, was father of DAVID SARSFIELD, 3rd Viscount Kilmallock; who suffered attainder in 1691, and under that forfeiture the title fell.

SAUNDERSON—BARON SAUNDERSON, OF SAXBY, VISCOUNT CASTLETON, EARL OF CASTLETON.

Viscounty of Ireland, by Letters Patent, dated 16 July, 1627.
Barony, by Letters Patent, dated 19 October, 1714.
Viscounty, by Letters Patent, dated 7 July, 1716.
Earldom, by Letters Patent, dated 18 June, 1720.

Lineage.

A full and elaborate pedigree of this family is given in BURKE's Extinct Baronetage.
SIR NICHOLAS SAUNDERSON, Bart., of Saxby, sheriff of Lincolnshire, in the 34th ELIZABETH, was created VISCOUNT CASTLETON, in the peerage of Ireland, 16 July, 1627. He m. Winifred, dau. and heir of John Elltoft, Esq., of Boston, co. Lincoln, and had issue,

  I. NICHOLAS.   II. PEREGRINE.   III. GEORGE.
  IV. Rutland.   V. Francis.   VI. Charles.
  I. Mildred, m. to Thomas, Viscount Fauconberg.
  II. Grace, d. unm.

His lordship was s. by his eldest son,
SIR NICHOLAS SAUNDERSON, Bart., 2nd Viscount Castleton, whose will was proved 1 January, 1641. He m. Frances, dau. of Sir George Manners, of Haddon, and was s. by his eldest son,
SIR NICHOLAS SAUNDERSON, Bart., 3rd Viscount Castleton, who d. s. p., and was s. by his brother,
SIR PEREGRINE SAUNDERSON, Bart., 4th Viscount Castleton, whose will bears date 4 November, 1649, his brother and heir,
SIR GEORGE SAUNDERSON, Bart., 5th Viscount Castleton, m. 1st, Grace, dau. of Henry Bellasis, son and heir of Thomas, Lord Fauconberg; and 2ndly, Sarah, relict of Sir John Wray, and of Thomas, Viscount Fanshawe, and dau. of Sir John Evelyn. By the former he had with other issue, who d. s. p., two sons, NICHOLAS, his heir apparent (who m. Elizabeth, dau. and heir of Sir John Wray, of Glentworth, and left an only child Wray, who d. s. p. in the lifetime of his grandfather), and JAMES. Lord Castleton d. at Sandbeck, 27 May, 1714: his son,
SIR JAMES SAUNDERSON, 6th Viscount Castleton, was created a peer of England, 19 October, 1714, as BARON SAUNDERSON, of Saxby, co. Lincoln, made VISCOUNT CASTLETON, of Sandbeck, co. York, 7 July, 1716, and raised to the EARLDOM OF CASTLETON, 18 June, 1720. He d. s. p. 22 May, 1723, when all his honours became EXTINCT. His great estates he bequeathed to his cousin on the mother's side, Thomas Lumley,

473

3rd Earl of Scarborough, who assumed, in consequence, by act of parliament, the additional surname of SAUNDERSON.
The family of Saunderson, of Castle Saunderson, co. Cavan, claims descent from this noble house.

Arms—Paly of six, arg. and az., a bend, sa.

SAVAGE—VISCOUNTS SAVAGE, VISCOUNTS COLCHESTER, EARL RIVERS.

Viscounty of Savage, by Letters Patent, dated 6 November, 1626.
Viscounty of Colchester, by Letters Patent, dated 5 July, 1621.
Earldom, by Letters Patent, dated 4 November, 1626.

Lineage.

Of this family, whose chief seat, for many generations, had been at the Castle of Frodsham, in Cheshire, and partly at another house, more recently erected, at Clifton, on the opposite side of the river, called Rock Savage, was
JOHN SAVAGE, Esq. (descended of the Savages of Steinesbre, co. Derby), who m. about 49th EDWARD III., Margaret, widow of John Radcliffe and dau. and heir of Sir Thomas Daniers (commonly called Daniels), of Bradley, in Appleton, and in right of this marriage became of Clifton. By this lady (who m. 3rdly, Piers Legh, of Maxfield, by whom she had two sons, Piers, ancestor of the Leghs of Lyme, and John, ancestor of the Leghs, of Ridge), John Savage was father of
SIR JOHN SAVAGE, of Clifton, Knt., who m. Maud, dau. and heir of Sir Robert Swinnerton, and had issue, JOHN, his heir; William; Arnold; George; Roger; Margaret, m. to John, 2nd son and eventual heir of Sir Piers Dutton, of Dutton, and Maude, m. to Sir Thomas Booth, of Barton, co. Lancaster. Sir John Savage d. 1 August, 1450, and was s. by his eldest son,
JOHN SAVAGE, Esq., of Clifton, who had besides two daus. Margery m. 1st, to Edmund Leigh, Esq., of Baggeley, co. Chester, and 2ndly, to Thomas Leycester, Esq., of Nether Tabley and Margaret m. 1st, to John Maxfield; and 2ndly, to Randle, 3rd son of Randle Mainwaring, Esq., of Over-Pever, a son and heir,
SIR JOHN SAVAGE, of Clifton, Knt., who m. Catherine, dau. of Sir Thomas Stanley, afterwards Lord Stanley, and sister of Thomas Stanley, Earl of Derby, and had with other issue,

John (Sir), his heir.
Thomas, archbishop of York, 1501, d. 1508.
Homfrey (Sir).
Edmund (Sir), knighted by the Earl Hertford, at Leith, 11 May, 1544, m. Mary, dau. and heir of William Sparke, of Surrey, and widow of Roger Legh, of Ridge, High Maxfield.
William-George.
Richard.
Ellen, m. to Peter Legh, Esq., of Lyme, co. Chester.
Katherine, m. Thomas Legh, Esq., of Adlington, co. Chester.
Margaret. m. to Edmund Trafford, of Trafford, co. Lancaster.
Alice, m. to Roger Pilkington.
Elizabeth, m. to John, son of William Leeke, of Longford, co Derby.

Sir John d. 22 November, 1495, aged seventy-three. The eldest son,
SIR JOHN SAVAGE, one of the adherents of Henry, Earl of Richmond, who, by the victory of Bosworth, placed the crown on that nobleman's head, as HENRY VII. Sir John Savage was afterwards in the wars of France, and fell at the siege of Boloine, in the life-time of his father, leaving a son,
SIR JOHN SAVAGE, of Clifton, knighted about 13th HENRY VII., who was sheriff of Worcestershire twenty-four years together from the death of his father. He m. Anne, dau. and heir of Raufe Bostock, Esq., of Bostock, and d. 2 March, 1527, when he was s. by his eldest son,
SIR JOHN SAVAGE, Knt., who m. Elizabeth, dau. of Charles Somerset, the 1st Earl of Worcester, and by her, who m 2ndly, William Brereton, of the bedchamber to HENRY VIII., had issue, JOHN, his heir, Henry, Margaret, m. Sir Richard Buckley, of Beaumaris, and Mary, m. to John Hampden, of Hampden. Sir John d. 27 July, 1528, and was s. by his elder son,
SIR JOHN SAVAGE, Knt., of Clifton, who m. Lady Elizabeth Manners, dau. of Thomas, 1st Earl of Rutland, and had issue to survive infancy,

John, his successor.
Edward.
Margaret, m. to Sir William Brereton, afterwards Baron Leighlin, in Ireland.

Elizabeth, m. to Thomas Langton, Baron of Newton, in Lancashire.

Elenora, m. 1st, to Sir Henry Bagnall, son and heir of Sir Nicholas Bagnall, Knt.; and 2ndly, to Sir Sackville Trevor.

Mary, m to Sir Richard Milles, of Hampshire.

Frances, m. to Thomas Wilkes, Esq., of Surrey.

Sir John m. 2ndly, Elenora, widow of Sir Richard Pexhull, of Beaurepair, co. Hants, and dau. of John Cotgreve, and dying 5 December, 1597, was s. by his eldest surviving son,

Sir John Savage, of Rock Savage, who was created a baronet 9th James, 1611, being the 19th advanced to the rank of baronet, upon the institution of that order. He m. Mary, dau. and co-heir of Richard Allington, and had issue,

John, d. young.
Thomas, his successor.
John.   Richard.
William.
Elizabeth, m. 1st, to Thomas Mainwaring; and 2ndly, to Sir Raufe Done, of Duddon, co. Chester.
Grace, m. to Sir Richard Wilbraham, Bart., of Woodhey.

Sir John Savage, who was mayor of Chester in 1607, and sheriff of Chester the same year, d. in July (buried the 14th), 1615, and was s. by his eldest surviving son,

Sir Thomas Savage, Knt. He m. Elizabeth, eldest dau. and eventually co-heir of Thomas, Lord D'Arcy, of Chiche; which Lord D'Arcy (who d. 1639), was created, 5 July, 1621, Viscount Colchester, and elevated, 4 November, 1626, to the dignity of Earl Rivers, both honours to revert, in default of male issue, to his son-in-law, Sir Thomas Savage, and his heirs male, who was himself created, in two days afterwards, Viscount Savage, of Rock Savage, co. Chester. Lord Savage had issue by the Lady Elizabeth D'Arcy, (who was created Countess Rivers for life, 21 April, 1641, and d. in 1650), seven sons and six daus., viz.,

John, his successor.
Thomas, m. Elizabeth, dau. and co-heir of William Whitmore, Esq., of Leighton, in Cheshire (by Margaret, his wife, sister and co-heir of Sir George Beeston, of Beeston, co. Chester), and widow of Sir Edward Somerset, 5th son of Edward Somerset, Earl of Worcester, and had issue,

D'Arcy, who s. at Leighton, and left a dau.,
Bridget Savage, who m. Sir Thomas Mostyn, Bart. of Mostyn.
Elizabeth, m. to Marmaduke, Lord Langdale.

Francis.
William, }
James,   } all d. s. p.
Richard, }
Charles, left a dau.,
Mary Savage, who m. Jeremy Thoresby, of Leeds, and left two daus.,
Elizabeth.   Mary.

Jane, m. to John, Marquess of Winchester.
Dorothy, m. to Charles, Viscount Andover.
Elizabeth, m. to Sir John Thimbleby, Knt., of Irnham, in Lincolnshire.
Anne, m. to Robert, son and heir of Thomas, Lord Brudenell, afterwards Earl of Cardigan.
Catherine, a nun at Dunkirk.
Henrietta-Maria, m. to Ralph Sheldon, Esq., of Beoley.

His lordship d. in 1635, and was s. by his eldest son,

John Savage, 2nd Viscount Savage, who s. his maternal grandfather in 1639, as Viscount Colchester and Earl Rivers. His lordship m. 1st, Catherine, dau. of William Parker, Lord Morley and Monteagle, and had issue,

Thomas, his successor.
John, d. s. p.
Richard, who m. Alice, dau. and heir of Thomas Trafford, of Bridge-Trafford, co. Chester, and widow of John Barnston, of Churton, and left a son,
John, who inherited as 5th and last Earl.

Elizabeth, m. to William, Lord Petre.
Jane, m. 1st, to George, Lord Chandos; 2ndly, to Sir William Sidley, Bart.; and 3rdly, to George Pitt, Esq., of Strathfieldsaye, in Hampshire. By her last husband, her ladyship left a son,
George Pitt, Esq., of Strathfieldsaye, M.P. for the co. of Hants, whose grandson,
George Pitt, Esq, was created, in 1776, Baron Rivers, of Strathfieldsaye (see Burke's Extant Peerage).

Catherine, m. to Charles Sidley, Esq., brother of Sir William.
Mary, m. to Henry Killegrew, Esq., groom of the bed-chamber to James, Duke of York.
Frances, d. young.

The earl m. 2ndly, Mary Ogle, and by her had one son, Peter. His lordship d. 10 October, 1654, and was s. by his eldest son,

Thomas Savage, 3rd Earl Rivers, who became, in 1686, in

right of his mother, heir of one moiety of the Baronies of Morley, Mounteagle, and Marshal. His lordship m. 1st, Elizabeth, natural dau. of Emanuel Scrope, Earl of Sunderland (which lady, with her sisters, Mary, Marchioness of Winchester, and Arabella, wife of John Grubham Howe, Esq., eventually s. to the ancient inheritance of the Scropes), by whom he had issue,

Thomas, Lord Colchester, who m. Lady Charlotte Stanley, dau. of Charles, Earl of Derby, and dying before his father, left an only dau.,
Charlotte, who d. unm.
Richard, his successor.
Elizabeth.
Annabella, m. to Sir Erasmus Norwich, of Brampton, in the co. of Northampton, and d. s. p.

The earl m. 2ndly, Lady Arabella Lindsey, dau. of Robert Bertie, Earl of Lindsey, but had no issue. He d. 14 September, 1694, and was s. by his only surviving son,

Richard Savage, 4th Earl Rivers. This nobleman m. Penelope, dau. and heir of Roger Downes, Esq., of Wardley, in Lancashire, by whom he had surviving issue,

Elizabeth, m. to James, Earl of Barrymore, in Ireland, and left an only dau.,
Penelope, who m. Major-General James Cholmondeley, 2nd surviving son of George, Earl of Cholmondeley, and d. s. p.

His lordship,* who was an eminent soldier and statesman in the reigns of William III. and Queen Anne, d. in 1712, when his honours passed to his kinsman (revert to Richard, 3rd son of John, 2nd Viscount Savage),

John Savage, Esq., a Roman Catholic priest, as 5th Earl Rivers, at whose decease, unm. in 1728, the Viscounty of Savage, the Viscounty of Colchester, and the Earldom of Rivers, became extinct.

Arms—Arg., six lions rampant (three, two and one), sa

SAVAGE—COUNTESS OF RIVERS.

By Letters Patent, dated 21 April, 1641.

Lineage.

Lady Elizabeth Savage, dau. of Thomas D'Arcy, Lord D'Arcy, of Chiche, and Earl Rivers, and widow of Thomas Savage, 1st Viscount Savage, of Rock Savage, was created 21 April, 1641, Countess Rivers, for life. Her ladyship d 9 March, 1650, when the title became of course extinct.

SAVILE — BARONS SAVILE, EARLS OF SUSSEX.

Barony, by Letters Patent, dated 21 July, 1628.
Earldom, by Letters Patent, dated 25 May, 1644.

Lineage.

The family of Savile is of great antiquity in the north of England. In the reign of Edward III., Sir John Savile, Knt., of Eland, in Yorkshire, was constituted escheator for the cos. Northumberland, Cumberland, and Westmoreland, and in the next reign was sheriff of Yorkshire, and governor of the castle of York. In the 2nd Henry V. (1414-15),

Thomas Savile, of Thornhill, co. York, being at that time one of the Esquires to Edward, Duke of York, was, in consideration of his good services, made forester of that Prince's chase and park at Aryngden, in the same shire. From this Thomas descended

Sir Henry Savile, of Thornhill, K.B., temp. King Henry VIII., who by his wife, a dau. and co-heir of Thomas Southill, Esq., of Southill, had a son and heir, Edward, who d. s. p., and a dau., Dorothy, m. to John Kay, Esq., of Woodsome, co York. He had also, by a concubine, named Barkston, another son,

Sir Robert Savile, alias Barkston, Knt., who, in the 15th Elizabeth, served the office of high sheriff for the co.

---

* The 4th Earl Rivers had two illegitimate children, a dau. Bessy, wife of Frederick, Earl of Rochford, and a son, the ill-fated Richard Savage, the poet.

Lincoln. He *m.* a sister of John, Lord Hussey, and widow of Sir Richard Thimelby, and was *s.* by his son,

SIR JOHN SAVILE, Knt., of Howley, in Yorkshire, high sheriff for Lincolnshire, in the 32nd ELIZABETH, and member of parliament for the co. York, *temp.* King JAMES I. and King CHARLES I. He was likewise high steward for the honour of Pontefract, and was elevated to the peerage, by letters patent, dated 21 July. 1628, as BARON SAVILE, *of Pontefract.* His lordship was subsequently sworn of the privy council, and appointed comptroller of the household. Lord Savile *m.* 1st, Catherine, dau. of Lord Willoughby, of Parham, but had no issue. He *m.* 2ndly, Elizabeth, dau. of Sir Edward Carey, Knt., and had issue,

Henry, who *m.* Helen, dau. and co-heir of William Oglethorpe, Esq., and *d. v. p.,* leaving a son,
    JOHN, who *d.* also before Lord Savile.
Edward, *m.* Anne, dau. and heir of Richard Tolson, Esq., of Cumberland, but *d. s. p.*
THOMAS (Sir), who *s.* to the peerage.
Robert, } *d. unm.*
Edmund, }
Catherine, *m.* 1st, to Sir Thomas Bland, of Kippax Park, in Yorkshire, and 2ndly, to Walter Welsh, Esq.
Anne, *m.* to Piers Leigh, son and heir of Sir Piers Leigh, of Lyme.
Elizabeth, *m.* 1st, to Alveray Cooper, Esq., of Batley, in Yorkshire. and 2ndly, to Richard Banks, Esq.
Frances, *m.* to the Rev. Thomas Bradley, D.D., rector of Castelford, co. York.

His lordship *d.* in 1630, and was *s.* by his eldest surviving son,

SIR THOMAS SAVILE, Knt., 2nd Baron Savile. This nobleman was created 11 June, 1628, Viscount Savile, of Castlebar, in the peerage of Ireland. His lordship was comptroller of the household, and attending King CHARLES I. at Oxford, was advanced. by letters patent, dated 25 May, 1644, to the dignity of EARL OF SUSSEX. During the whole of the civil wars he remained faithfully attached to the fortunes of his royal master, and his services merited fully the honours he received. His lordship *m.* 1st, Frances, dau. of Sir Michael Sondes, Knt., of Throwley, in Kent, and widow of Sir John Leveson, but had no issue. He *m.* 2ndly, Lady Anne Villiers, dau. of Christopher, Earl of Anglesey, and eventually sole heir of her brother, Charles, last Earl of Anglesey, of the family of Villiers. By this lady he had issue,

JAMES, Lord Savile, his successor.
Frances, *m.* to Francis, Lord Brudenel, son and heir of Robert, Earl of Cardigan, by whom she had issue,
    GEORGE, 3rd Earl of Cardigan.
    James.
Mary, *m.* to Richard, Viscount Molineux.
Anne, *m.* 1st, to Henry, Lord Belasyse, of Worlaby, and 2ndly, to Charles Lenox, Duke of Richmond.
Frances, *m.* 1st, to Charles Levingston, 2nd Earl of Newburgh, and 2ndly, to Richard, Lord Bellew.

His lordship *d.* in 1646, and was *s.* by his son,

JAMES SAVILE, 2nd Earl of Sussex. This nobleman *m.* Anne, dau. of Robert Wake a merchant at Antwerp, but *d. s. p.,* in 1671, when the Earldom of Sussex, and the minor honours became EXTINCT, while his lordship's estates devolved upon his only sister, FRANCES, LADY BRUDENEL (*see Extant Peerage*).

*Arms—*Arg., on a bend, sa, three owls of the 1st, properly differenced.

SAVILE — VISCOUNT SAVILE, IN THE PEERAGE OF IRELAND.

(*See* SAVILE, Earl of Sussex.)

SAVILE—VISCOUNTS HALIFAX, EARLS OF HALIFAX, MARQUESSES OF HALIFAX.

Viscounty, by Letters Patent, dated 13 January, 1668.
Earldom, by Letters Patent, dated 16 July, 1679.
Marquessate, by Letters Patent, dated 22 August, 1682.

Lineage.

The principal legitimate branch of the SAVILE family was represented by

SIR GEORGE SAVILE, Bart., of Thornhill, co. York (*see* PURKE's *Extinct Baronetage*), who *m.* Lady Mary Talbot, dau. of George, 6th Earl of Shrewsbury. and was grandfather of

SIR WILLIAM SAVILE. Bart., who *m.* Anne, dau. of Thomas, Lord Coventry, and was *s.* by his son,

SIR WILLIAM SAVILE, Bart., of Thornhill, who, in consideration of his own and his father's eminent services during the civil wars, was elevated to the peerage by King CHARLES II., 13 January, 1668, as *Baron Saville, of Eland, co. York,* and VISCOUNT HALIFAX On 16 July, 1679, his lordship was created EARL OF HALIFAX, and MARQUESS OF HALIFAX, 22 August, 1682. He *m.* 1st, Lady Dorothy Spencer, dau. of Henry, Earl of Sunderland, and had issue,

HENRY, who *m.* Esther, dau. and co-heir of Charles de la Tour, Marquess of Gouvernet, in France, and *d. s. p., v. p.*
WILLIAM, his successor.
George, fell at the siege of Buda, in 1688, and *d. unm.*
Anne, *m.* to John, Lord Vaughan.

His lordship *m.* 2ndly, Gertrude, dau. of William Pierrepont, of Thoresby, 2nd son of Robert, 1st Earl of Kingston, by whom he had an only dau.,

ELIZABETH, who *m.* Philip, eldest son of Philip Stanhope, 2nd Earl of Chesterfield.

The Marquess of Halifax was lord privy seal, and some time president of the council, *temp.* CHARLES II. He was esteemed a statesman of the first grade. Burnet characterizes him "as a man of great and ready wit, full of life, and very pleasant, but much turned to satire; his imagination was too hard for his judgment; and a severe jest took more with him than all arguments whatever. He let his wit run much on matters of religion, which got him the reputation of a confirmed atheist; but he denied the charge. Friendship and morality were great topics with him; and punctuality and justice more remarkable in his private dealings. In relation to the public, he went backwards and forwards, and changed sides so often, that, in the conclusion, no side would trust him." Macaulay bears more flattering testimony to the merit of this eminent politician :— "The memory of Halifax," says that brilliant writer, "is entitled in an especial manner to the protection of history. For what distinguishes him from all other statesmen is this, that, through a long public life, and through frequent and violent revolutions of public feeling, he almost invariably took that view of the great questions of his time which history has finally adopted. He was called inconstant, because the relative position in which he stood to the contending factions was perpetually varying. As well might the pole star be called inconstant because it is sometimes to the east and sometimes to the west of the pointers. To have defended the ancient and legal constitution of the realm against a seditious populace at one conjuncture, and against a tyrannical government at another; to have been the foremost champion of order in the turbulent parliament of 1680, and the foremost champion of liberty in the servile parliament of 1685; to have been just and merciful to Roman Catholics in the days of the Popish Plot, and to Exclusionists in the days of the Rye House Plot; to have done all in his power to save both the head of Stafford and the head of Russell; this was a course which contemporaries, heated by passion and deluded by names and badges, might not unnaturally call fickle, but which deserves a very different name from the late justice of posterity."

His lordship *d.* in 1695, and was *s.* by his eldest surviving son,

WILLIAM SAVILE, 2nd marquess. This nobleman *m.* 1st, Elizabeth, dau. of Sir Samuel Grimston. Bart., of Gorhambury, co. Herts, and sister and heir of Sir Harbottle Grimston, by whom he had to survive, an only dau.,

ANNE, *m.* to Charles, 4th Earl of Elgin, and 3rd Earl of Ailesbury, and was mother of a dau. and eventual heiress, LADY MARY BRUCE, who *m.* 1728. Henry Brydges, 2nd Duke of Chandos, and had one son James, 3rd Duke of Chandos (whose dau. and heiress. Anne-Eliza, *m.* 1796, Richard, Earl Temple, afterwards Duke of Buckingham and Chandos), and one dau. Caroline, wife of John Leigh, Esq., of Adlestrop.

His lordship *m.* 2ndly, Lady Mary Finch, dau. of Daniel, Earl of Nottingham, by Lady Essex Rich, dau. and co-heir of Richard, Earl of Warwick and Holland, and had, with two sons, who both *d.* young, three daus., viz.,

Essex, *d.* young.
Dorothy, *m.* to Richard Boyle, Earl of Burlington.
Mary, *m.* to Sackville Tufton, Earl of Thanet.

The marquess *d.* 31 August, 1700, when his estates devolved upon his daus., as co-heirs, and all his honours became EXTINCT.

*Arms—*Arg., on a bend, sa., three owls of the 1st.

SAYE, OR SAY—BARONS SAYE.

By Writ of Summons, dated 22nd EDWARD I.

Lineage.

The first member of the family of SAY mentioned by Sir William Dugdale, is

PICOT DE SAY, who, in the time of the CONQUEROR, and living in 1083, was one of the principal persons in the co. Salop, under Roger de Montgomery, Earl of Shrewsbury. The next is

INGELRAM DE SAY, one of the stanchest adherents of King STEPHEN in his contest with the Empress MAUD, and made prisoner with that monarch at the battle of Lincoln. After this gallant and faithful soldier, we come to

WILLIAM DE SAY, son of WILLIAM DE SAY, and grandson of WILLIAM DE SAY, who came into England with the CONQUEROR. He m. Beatrix, the divorced wife of Hugh Talbot, and dau. of Geoffrey de Mandeville, Earl of Essex, sister of Geoffrey, and aunt, and eventually heiress of William de Mandeville, Earls of Essex, by whom he had issue,

> William, who d. v. p.. leaving two daus., viz.,
>
> Beatrix, who m. Geoffrey Fitz-Piers, and from whom descended the Fitz-Piers's, who subsequently s. to the Earldom of Essex.
> Maud, m. to William de Bocland.
> GEOFFREY.

The 2nd son, and eventual heir male,

GEOFFREY DE SAY, was one of the barons chosen to proceed with William de Longchamp, bishop of Ely, chancellor of England, with the covenanted ransom of 70,000 marks of silver for the release of RICHARD I. He m. Lettice, sister, and at length heir, of Walkeline Maminot, and dying in 1214, was s. by his son,

GEOFFREY DE SAYE, who, in the 16th JOHN, paid 400 marks to the king for livery of the lands of his inheritance both by father and mother. In the next year this Geoffrey was in arms with the other barons against the king, and was one of the twenty-five appointed to enforce the observance of Magna Charta. His lands in the cos. of Northampton, Cambridge, Essex, Herts, Norfolk, Suffolk, and Lincoln, were in consequence seized, and given to Peter de Crohim; but returning to his allegiance in the next reign he had full restitution, and on levying the scutage of Montgomery, 8th HENRY III., answered for 42 knights' fees. He m. Alice, dau. and co-heir of John de Cheyney, and dying in 1230, was s. by his son,

WILLIAM DE SAY, or SAYE, who, in the 44th HENRY III., was constituted governor of the castle at Rochester, but being afterwards at the battle of Lewes, on the side of the king, he fled from the field on the defeat of the royalists. He d. 56th HENRY III., 1272, and was s. by his son,

WILLIAM DE SAY. This feudal lord had summons (by a writ, the regularity of which as a summons to parliament, is doubtful, and which, though on one occasion admitted in the general report of the Lords' Committee, has been finally rejected), with other great men, in the 22nd EDWARD II., to advise with the king upon the most important affairs of the realm; and he had subsequently a military summons to march into Gascony. He d. in 1295, and was s. by his son,

GEOFFREY DE SAY, then only fourteen years of age, whose wardship was given to William de Leyburne, in order that he might marry Idonea, dau. of the said William. In the 34th EDWARD III., he had livery of his lands upon doing his homage; and was in the expedition made at that period into Scotland. In the 7th EDWARD II. (26 July, 1313), he was summoned to parliament as a Baron, and thenceforward to the 14th of the same reign. His lordship m. Idonea de Leyburne, d. in 1322, and was s. by his son,

GEOFFREY DE SAY, 2nd baron, who, making proof of his age, 19th EDWARD II., had livery of his lands, and was summoned to parliament, from 25 February, 1342, to 15 July, 1353 (27th EDWARD III.) In the 8th EDWARD III., he obtained the king's charter for free warren in all his demesne lands within his lordships of Greenwich, Deptford, &c., and in two years afterwards he was constituted admiral of the king's fleet, from the mouth of the Thames westwards, in which service, besides himself then a banneret, he had of his retinue, four knights, twenty men at arms, and three archers. From this period Lord Say was constantly employed in the wars of France and Flanders, and deported himself with great gallantry. His lordship m. Maud, dau. of Guy de Beauchamp, Earl of Warwick, and had issue (besides, it appears, two sons, Thomas and John, who d. unm. and young),

476

WILLIAM, his successor.
Idonea, who m. Sir John Clinton, Knt., of Maxtock, m. Warwick. 3rd BARON CLINTON, the 8th in descent, from whom THOMAS CLYNTON (DE SAY), primog nitus Comitis Lincoln, was summoned to parliament, 18 February, 1604, v. p., as Lord Clinton. To this Idonea, Charles Rudolph, present LORD CLINTON, is elder co-heir.
Elizabeth, m. to Thomas, or John, de Aldone, and d. s. p.
Joane, m. 1st. to Sir William Fiennes, and her grandson, Sir JAMES FIENNES, or FYNES, Knt., was summoned to parliament in 1447, by King HENRY VI., as BARON SAYE AND SELE, a dignity still extant, and now enjoyed by FREDERICK, 13th LORD SAYE and SELE, who is 20th in descent from Geoffrey, Lord Saye, the Baron of Magna Charta. Joane Say m. 2ndly, Stephen de Valoines.

Lord Say d. in 1359, and was s. by his son,

WILLIAM DE SAY, 3rd baron, summoned to parliament, from 14 August, 1362, to 4 October, 1373. This nobleman m. Beatrice, dau. of Thomas de Braose, and had issue,

> JOHN.   Elizabeth.

He d. 1375, and was s. by his son,

JOHN DE SAY, 4th baron, who d. in minority, a ward to the king, in 1382, leaving his sister,

ELIZABETH DE SAY, his heir. This lady m. 1st, Sir John de Fallesle, or Falvesley, who was summoned to parliament as a Baron (see Falvesley), and 2ndly, Sir William Heron (d.1404), also summoned to parliament as a Baron (see Heron), but d. s. p. in 1399, leaving the descendants of her aunts, IDONEA, Lady Clinton, and JOANE, Lady Fiennes (refer to issue of 2nd baron), her heirs, amongst whose representatives the Barony of Say has continued from that period to the present in ABEYANCE.

Arms—Quarterly : or and gu.

SCALES—BARONS SCALES.

By Writ of Summons, dated 6 February, 1299.

Lineage.

ROBERT DE SCALES, Lord of Newselles, co. Herts, who, in the 26th HENRY III., paid a fine of £10 to the king, to be exempted from serving in the wars of Gascony, at that time, d. in 1265, leaving, by Muriel, his wife, two sons,

William, who became a canon at Blackburgh, co. Norfolk.

And his heir,

SIR ROBERT DE SCALES. This feudal lord having distinguished himself in arms both in Scotland and France, in the reign of EDWARD I., was summoned to parliament as BARON SCALES, by that monarch, from 6 February, 1299, to 22 January, 1305, and dying in the latter year, left, by Alice, his wife, a son,

ROBERT DE SCALES, 2nd baron, summoned to parliament from 3 November, 1306, to 14 March, 1322. This nobleman being made a knight of the Bath, with Prince Edward and several others, attended him in the expedition made, at that time, into Scotland. He was also summoned as a peer to the coronation of EDWARD II. His lordship m. Evelina, dau. of Hugh de Courtenay, and sister of Hugh, Earl of Devon, and dying in 1322, was s. by his son,

ROBERT DE SCALES, 3rd baron, then in minority, for whose guardianship, his mother paid a fine of 200 marks to the king. His lordship attained his majority in the 7th EDWARD III., and in two years afterwards, we find him in the expedtion made into Scotland, in the retinue of William de Ufford. He was again in Scotland the ensuing year, and in the 12th of the same reign he attended the king into Flanders. From this period, until the 30th EDWARD, he was almost unremittingly engaged in France. His lordship m. Katherine, dau. of Robert de Ufford, sister and co-heir of William de Ufford, Earls of Suffolk, and had issue,

1. ROGER, his successor.
1. Margaret, m. Sir Robert Howard, and by him (who d. in 1389,) left a son and heir,

> Sir John Howard, M.P. co. Cambridge, m. 1st, Margaret, dau. and heir of Sir John de Playtz; and 2ndly, Alice, dau. and heir of Sir William Tendring; by the latter he had a son, ROBERT, ancestor of the DUKES OF NORFOLK; and by the former he had a son,
>
> > Sir John Howard, who dying v. p., left an only dau. and heiress,
> >
> > > ELIZABETH, heiress of her grandfather; this lady m. John de Vere, 12th Earl of Oxford. Of this marriage, the co-representatives (all being co-heirs of the Barony of Scales), are 1 the DUKE OF ATHOLE; 2 WINCH-

COMBE-HENRY-HOWARD HARTLEY, Esq., of Bucklebury; 5 SIR RAINALD KNIGHTLEY, Bart.; 4 MRS. TROTH JENKINS; 5 SIR ROBERT BURDETT, Bart., of Foremark; 6 SIR CHARLES-ROBERT TEMPEST, Bart., of Broughton; 7 CHARLES STANDISH, Esq., of Standish; 8 JOHN WRIGHT, Esq., of Kelvedon, co. Essex; 9 JOHN-ROGERSON, LORD ROLLO; 10 GEORGE-WILLIAM VILLIERS, Esq.; and 11 MONTAGU, EARL OF ABINGDON.

III. Elizabeth, m. to Sir Roger de Felbrigg, and had issue,

Sir Simon de Felbrigg. who m. Margaret, dau. and heiress of the Duke of Silesia, and left an only dau. and heiress,

ALENA, m. Sir William Tyndall, of Dene, co. Northampton, father of Sir Thomas, the father of Sir William Tyndall, K.B., temp. HENRY VII., who was found, by the inquisition taken after the death of Anthony, Earl of Rivers and 8th Lord de Scales, to be one of the two co-heirs of Elizabeth, Lady de Scales; a direct descendant of Sir William Tyndall—possibly his representative—JOHN TYNDALL (son of Deane Tyndall) d. aged ninety, in 1706, leaving an only dau., Elizabeth, who m. 8 January, 1700-1, Jasper Blythman. Esq., of New Lathes, co. York, and by him had an only dau., LUCY, who m. Charles King, Esq., and was mother of two daus., her co-heirs, viz., Elizabeth, wife of REV. WM. CAMPBELL, and Lucy, wife of REV. RICHARD BULLOCK. Mrs. Campbell d. 1779, s. p.; Mrs. Bullock, in 1784. leaving two sons, William and Edward; the elder of these (William Bullock) d. in 1832, leaving three daus., Lucy, Marianne. wife of Sir James Douglas, K.C.B., and Emily, wife of John Cay, Esq.

Lord Scales, who had summons to parliament, from 25 February, 1342, to 6 April, 1369, d. in the latter year, and was s. by his son,

ROGER DE SCALES, 4th baron, summoned to parliament from 28 December, 1375, to 3 September, 1385. This nobleman was in the expedition made into France, in the 46th EDWARD III.; and upon the breaking out of the insurrection under Jack Straw, temp. RICHARD II., his lordship was one of those eminent persons whom the insurgents seized, and compelled to march along with them. In the 5th of the same reign, Lord Scales, by an inquisition, was found to be one of the co-heirs to William de Ufford, Earl of Suffolk. His lordship m. Joan, dau. and heiress of Sir John de Northwode, and dying in 1386, was s. by his son.

ROBERT DE SCALES, 5th baron, summoned to parliament from 30 November, 1396, to 3 October, 1400. His lordship, at his accession to the dignity, was in his fourteenth year. In the 1st HENRY IV., Lord Scales was one of the lords in parliament, that voted for the safe custody of the late King RICHARD II., and he embarked soon afterwards in the expedition made into Aquitaine. His lordship m. Elizabeth, dau. of William, Lord Bardolf, by whom (who m., after his decease, Sir Henry Percy, of Athol,) he had issue,

ROBERT, } successive lords.
THOMAS, }

He d. in 1402, and was s. by his elder son,

ROBERT DE SCALES, 6th baron. but never summoned to parliament. This nobleman dying unm., in 1418, was s. by his brother,

THOMAS DE SCALES, 7th baron, summoned to parliament from 13 January, 1445, to 9 October, 1459. This nobleman attained high military renown in the reign of HENRY V. and HENRY VI. In 1436, upon the death of John Plantagenet, Duke of Bedford, the Normans rebelling, this Lord Scales was sent out with others, against them; when, after he had destroyed many of the rebels. and some of the towns and villages, the country was reduced to obedience. For this especial service, he obtained from the crown a grant of £100 per annum. for life. In the 21st HENRY VI., his lordship was constituted one of the ambassadors then deputed to France, for the purpose of negotiating a peace. In the 28th of the same reign, we find Lord Scales in arms against Jack Cade; and in the subsequent conflicts between the Houses of York and Lancaster, he remained ever faithful to King HENRY VI. His lordship m. Emma, dau. of John Walesborough, and had issue,

THOMAS, who d. v. p.
Elizabeth, m. 1st, to Henry Bourchier, 2nd son of Henry, Earl of Essex. but he d. s. p.; and 2ndly, to Anthony, son and heir of Richard Widvile, Earl of Rivers, who was summoned to parliament in her right, as Lord Scales, but afterwards s. to the Earldom of Rivers, and was beheaded in 1483. Lady Scales d. previously s. p.

Lord Scales, is said by Story to have been murdered 25 July, 1460, but Dugdale merely says, that he departed this life. After his lordship's decease, the 2nd husband of his only dau. and heiress, Elizabeth, Anthony Widvile, was summoned to parliament, jure uxoris as Lord Scales, and upon the death of the said Elizabeth, s. p., the Barony of Scales fell into ABEYANCE, between the descendants of Margaret, Lady Howard and

Elizabeth, Lady Felbrigg (refer to issue of Robert, 3rd baron), as it still continues with their representatives.

The noble family of Scales resided for many generations, in great splendour and power, at the castle of Middleton, near Lynn, co. Norfolk.

Arms—Gu., six escallop shells arg., three, two, one.

SCHOMBERG—DUKES OF SCHOMBERG.

By Letters Patent, dated 9 March, 1689.

Lineage.

JOHN MEINHARDT SCHONBERG, or SCHOMBERG, a German, of an ancient and noble family in the Palatinate, m. Anne, dau. of Edward Sutton, Lord Dudley, and was father of

FREDERIC SCHOMBERG, a military officer of high reputation. This eminent person commenced his gallant career in the service of the States General; he was afterwards in Portugal, where he commanded the Portuguese army against the Spaniards, and in 1668, achieved by arms, the full recognition of the right of the House of Braganza to the crown of Portugal. We next find him in the service of LOUIS XIV., by whom he was raised to the rank of a Marshal of France. In 1688, he accompanied the Prince of Orange into England, and when His Highness obtained the sceptre as WILLIAM III., was elevated to the peerage, by letters patent, dated 9 March, 1689, as BARON TEYES, and EARL OF BRENTFORD, co. Middlesex, MARQUESS OF HARWICH, and DUKE OF SCHOMBERG, all in remainder to his 2nd surviving son, Charles, and his issue male; failure of which, to his eldest surviving son, Meinhardt, and his male descendants His grace m. 1st, Johanna-Elizabetha, the dau. of his paternal uncle, and had issue,

Frederick, who resided in Germany.
MEINHARDT, who was created in the peerage of Ireland, in 1690-1, Baron of Tarragh, Earl of Bangor, and DUKE OF LEINSTER.
Otto, who fell at the siege of Valenciennes.
Henry, d. at Brussels.
CHARLES, successor to the honours, under the patent.

The duke m. 2ndly, Susanna, dau. of Count Anmale de Harcourt, in France, but had no issue. His grace, besides his other honours, had been made a knight of the Garter and Master of the Ordnance, and had been granted by parliament £100,000. At length, after a long and glorious military career, Schomberg fell at the Boyne, in 1690, aged eighty-four, and was buried at St. Patrick's, Dublin, with the following inscription—

"Underneath lies the body of Frederick, Duke of Schomberg. slain at the battle of the Boyne, in the year 1690. The dean and chapter of this church, again and again, besought the heirs of the duke, to cause some monument to be here erected to his memory. But when, after many entreaties by letters and friends, they found they could not obtain their request, they themselves placed this stone: only that the indignant reader may know where the ashes of Schomberg are deposited.

"Thus did the fame only of his virtue obtain more for him from strangers, than nearness of blood from his own family."

His grace was s. according to the limitation, by his son,

CHARLES SCHIOMBERG, 2nd duke. who dying unm. of a wound, received at the battle of Marsaglia, in Piedmont, anno 1693, was s. by his elder brother,

MEINHARDT SCHIOMBERG, Duke of Leinster, in Ireland, as 3rd Duke of Schomberg. This nobleman m. Charlotte, dau. of Charles-Lewis, Elector Palatine, and had issue,

Charles, Marquess of Harwich, colonel of horse, who d. v. p., anno 1713, s. p.
Mary, m. to Count Dagenfieldt.
Caroline, d. unm.
Frederica, m. 1st, to Robert D'Arcy, Earl of Holderness; and 2ndly, to Benjamin Mildmay, Earl Fitz-Walter, and d. in 1751.

His grace, who, like his father, was a military man of high reputation, d. in 1719. when, for want of an heir male, all his honours became EXTINCT.

Arms—Arg., an inescutcheon, ss. surmounted by an escarbuncle of eight rays, or.

SCHOMBERG—DUKE OF LEINSTER.

(See SCHOMBERG, Duke of Schomberg.)

SCHULENBERG—DUCHESS OF MUNSTER. AND DUCHESS OF KENDAL.

Dukedom of Ireland. by Letters Patent, dated 16 July, 1716.
Dukedom of Great Britain. by Letters Patent, dated 19 March, 1719.

Lineage.

ERENGARF MELOSINE SCHULENBERG, Princess of Eberstein, in Germany, mistress to King GEORGE I.. was created, 16 July, 1716. a peeress of Ireland. as Baroness of Dundalk, Countess and Marchioness of Dungannon, and Duchess of Munster, for life. On 19 March. 1719, her ladyship was enrolled among the nobility of Great Britain. in the dignities of Baroness Glastonbury, co. Somerset, Countess of Feversham, and DUCHESS OF KENDAL, also for life. She was. likewise advanced to the rank of Princess of Eberstein. in the Germanic empire.

Her grace d. in May, 1743, when all her honours became EXTINCT.

Arms—Quarterly: 1st and 4th, or, a lamb passant in fesse quartered gu. and arg. ensigned on its head with three standards of the 2nd; 2nd and 3rd, arg.. three eagles' legs couped at the thigh, gu. And as a princess of the empire. in a shield surtout az., a lion rampant, arg., imperially crowned ppr.

SCHULENBERG—COUNTESS OF WALSINGHAM.

By Letters Patent, dated 7 April, 1722.

Lineage.

MELESINA DE SCHULENBERG, natural dau. of King GEORGE I., was elevated to the peerage of England, by letters patent, dated 7 April, 1722, as BARONESS OF ALDBOROUGH, co. Suffolk, and COUNTESS OF WALSINGHAM, co. Norfolk, both dignities for life only. Her ladyship m. Philip Stanhope, the celebrated EARL OF CHESTERFIELD, but d. in 1778, s. p., when her honours became EXTINCT.

Arms—In a lozenge two coats quarterly: 1st and 4th, or, a lamb passant in fesse, quartered, gules and arg., ensigned on the head with three standards of the 2nd; 2nd and 3rd arg., three eagles' legs couped at the thigh, gules.

SCOT—EARL OF CHESTER.

By Inheritance, anno 1231.

Lineage.

THE LADY MAUD DE MESCHINES, eldest dau. of Hugh (surnamed Kevelick), 3rd Earl of Chester, m. David, Earl of Huntingdon, brother of WILLIAM THE LION, King of Scotland, and had with four daus. (see MESCHINES, Earls of Chester), an only son,

JOHN LE SCOT, who, upon the demise in 1231, of his uncle (his mother being d. previously), RANULPH DE MESCHINES (surnamed Blundevil), 4th EARL OF CHESTER, without issue, succeeded to the whole Palatine of Chester, and became, in consequence, Earl of that county. This nobleman carried the sword, called Curtana, at the marriage of King HENRY III., anno 1236; and Selden, in his titles of honour, says, that his lordship then bore the express designation of "Earl Palatine;" observing, that until the time of the 2nd HENRY he had never found "Palatine" so applied. In the same year his lordship assumed the cross, but it is doubtful whether he ever set out for the Holy Land or not. He d. in 1244, by poison, suspected to have been administered by his wife, Helen, dau. of Llewellin, Prince of North Wales; and as he left no issue, the Earldom of Chester was annexed to the crown for ever (in 1246); " He

478

tam præclara dominatio inter colos fœminarum dividi contingeret;"—" Lest so fair a dominion should be divided amongst women:" the king bestowing upon the deceased lord's sisters other lands instead

Arms—Or, three piles, gu.

SCOTLAND, KINGS OF—EARLS OF HUNTINGDON.

(See ST LIZ, Earls of Huntingdon).

SCOTT (FITZ-ROY) — DUKE OF MONMOUTH.

By Letters Patent, dated 14 February, 1663.

Lineage.

JAMES, natural son of King CHARLES II., by Mrs. Lucy Walters, dau. of Richard Walters, of Haverford West, co. Pembroke, was elevated to the peerage, 14 February, 1663, in the dignities of Baron Tynedale. co. Northumberland, Viscount Doncaster, and DUKE OF MONMOUTH, and afterwards invested with the Garter. His grace b. at Rotterdam, 9 April, 1649, and bore for several years the name of Crofts, but on his marriage 20 April, 1663, with the celebrated heiress, LADY ANNE SCOTT, Countess of Buccleuch, dau. and sole heir of Francis, 2nd Earl of Buccleuch, he assumed her name of SCOTT, and was created Duke of Buccleuch. By this lady he left two sons, and one dau., viz.,

JAMES, Earl of Dalkeith, from whom the present Duke of Buccleuch lineally descends.
Henry, created Earl of Deloraine, a title that became extinct in 1807.
Anne, who d. of grief a few days after her father, in her eleventh year.

The fate of the Duke of Monmouth, is an historical event, so well known, that it would be idle to enlarge upon it here—suffice it to state, that his grace, soon after the accession of King JAMES II., took up arms to depose that monarch, and to establish his own right to the throne, as the legitimate son of King CHARLES II. (under the allegation, that the king had married his mother)—that he came to a pitched battle with the royal army at Sedgemore, 6 July, 1685, and sustained a decisive overthrow—that he was soon afterwards made prisoner, and brought to the block, on the 15th of the same month, when the Dukedom of Monmouth, and the minor honours became EXTINCT, under the attainder. Burnet characterizes his grace, "as possessed of many good qualities, and of some that were bad; that he was soft and gentle, even to excess; and too easy to those who had credit with him; sincere and good-natured, and understood war well; but too much given to pleasure and to favourites." The duke had separated from his duchess, and lived with Henrietta, Lady Wentworth. Immediately prior to his execution, Rapin states, that Dr. Jennison and Dr. Hooper, the divines in attendance upon him, "tried, but in vain, to obtain satisfaction, regarding his connexion with this lady, though he had a duchess of his own, and his pretending to be lawfully married to her before God; alleging that his first marriage was null, as being too young when he gave his consent. All the pains taken by the two doctors to convince him of the falsehood of this opinion were fruitless, nay, he chose rather to deprive himself of the communion, than own his engagements with that lady to be unlawful."

Macaulay gives a painful description of Monmouth's execution: "At length, after many blows of the axe, life was extinguished, and the head and body were placed in a coffin covered with black velvet, and were laid privately under the communion table of St. Peter's Chapel, in the Tower."

Henrietta. Baroness Wentworth, had a sad and sorrowful history: her romantic and devoted attachment to the Duke of Monmouth she sacrificed her maiden honour and the hope of a splendid alliance: she abandoned all for him, and was his one loved companion in exile and in misfortune up to the very hour of his death: that event she survived but a few brief months, and then sank broken-hearted to the grave. "Near the quiet village of Toddington, in Bedfordshire," remarks Macaulay, "stood an ancient and stately Hall, the seat of the Wentworths. The transept of the parish church had long been their burial place. To that burial place, in the spring which followed the death of Monmouth, was borne the coffin of the young Baroness Wentworth, of Nettlestede. Her family reared a sumptuous mausoleum* over her remains; but a less costly memorial of her was long contemplated, with far deeper interest. Her name, carved by the hand of him whom she loved too well, was, a few years ago, still discernible on a tree in the adjoining park."

Arms—The royal arms of King CHARLES II., viz.: quarterly, 1st and 4th, *France and E gland*, quarterly; 2nd *Scotland;* 3rd *Ireland* debruised, with a baton sinister, arg.

SCOTT—EARL OF DELORAINE.

By Letters Patent, dated 29 March, 1706.

Lineage.

LORD HENRY SCOTT, *b.* in 1676 (3rd, but 2nd surviving, son of James, Duke of Monmouth, and his wife, Anne, Duchess of Buccleuch), was, by Queen ANNE, created EARL OF DELORAINE, Viscount Hermitage, and Baron Scott, of Goldielands, by patent dated 29 March, 1706. His lordship, who attained the rank of major-general, and was one of the Scottish representative peers, *d.* 25 December, 1730, in his fifty-fifth year, and was buried at Leadwell, in Oxfordshire. He *m.* 1st, Anne, dau. and heir of William Duncombe, of Battlesden, co. Bedford, one of the lords justices of Ireland, 1693, and comptroller of army accounts in the reign of Queen ANNE, and by her (who *d.* 22 October, 1720) had issue,

Francis, 2nd Earl of Deloraine.
Henry, 3rd Earl of Deloraine.
Anne, *d.* an infant.

He *m.* 2ndly, Mary, dau. of Philip Howard, a younger son of Thomas, 1st Earl of Berkshire, and by her (who *m.* 2ndly, William Wyndham, Esq., and *d.* at London, 12 November, 1744) had two daus.,

Georgiana-Caroline, *b.* February, 1727, *m.* 19 August, 1747, to Sir James Peachey, Bart., of Westdean, in Sussex, master of the robes to the king, created Lord Selsey, 1794. He *d.* in 1808; she *d.* in Berkeley-square, London, 15 October, 1809, in her eighty-third year, leaving issue.
Henrietta, *b.* 1728; *m.* to Nicholas Boyce, Esq.

The elder son,
Francis Scott, 2nd Earl of Deloraine, *b.* 5 October, 1710, *d. s. p.* at Bath, 11 April, 1739, in his twenty-ninth year. He *m.* 1st, Mary, dau. of Matthew Lister, Esq., of Burwell, co. Lincoln, which lady *d.* 1737, aged twenty-two, and was buried in the cathedral of Lincoln. He *m.* 2ndly, in July, 1737, Mary, dau. of Gervase Scrope, Esq., of Cockerington, co. Lincoln. She *d.* at Lincoln, 11 March, 1767, having *m.* a 2nd husband, Thomas Vivian, Esq , by whom she had a dau., Mary, *m.* to Joshua Scrope, Esq., and *d.* 3 February, 1795. The earl's brother and successor,
Henry Scott, 3rd Earl of Deloraine, capt. R.N., *b.* 11 February, 1712, *m.* Elizabeth, dau. of John Fenwick, Esq., and by her (who, surviving her husband more than fifty-four years, *d.* in Upper Brook-street, London, 5 June, 1794), had two sons,

Henry, his heir.
John, *b.* 6 October, 1738, commissioner of bankrupts, *d.* in Gray's Inn, London, 31 December, 1788, in his fifty-first year. He *m.* in 1757, Miss Isabella Young, and by her (who *d.* 17 August, 1791), had a son, John, who *d.* in America, 1799.

The elder son,
Henry Scott, 4th Earl of Deloraine, *b.* 8 February, 1737, *s.* his father, 1740. In early life, his lordship was one of the leaders of fashion, and dissipated a fine estate. At length, when his whole fortune was well nigh spent, he changed his course, secured from the wreck of his property an annuity of £1000 per annum, and passed in privacy the rest of his life. His lordship *m.* at London, 16 November, 1763, Frances, dau. of Thomas Heath, Esq., and widow of the Hon. Henry Knight, eldest son and heir apparent of Robert, Lord Luxborough, afterwards Earl of Catherlough, but had no issue by her (who *d.* in a convent in France, in 1782, after several

---

years separation from her husband). The Earl of Deloraine *d.* in London, in September, 1807, in the seventy-first year of his age, when his honours became EXTINCT.

Arms—Or, on a bend, az., a star, between two crescents of the field, with a crescent for difference.

SCOTT—EARL OF TARRAS.

By Letters Patent, dated 4 September, 1660.

Lineage.

WALTER SCOTT, of High Chester, eldest son of Sir Gideon Scott, of High Chester, 2nd son of Sir William Scott, of Harden, was *m.* at Wemyss Castle, 9 February, 1659, to Mary, Countess of Buccleuch, the greatest heiress then in Scotland; her ladyship had not completed her eleventh, nor Mr. Scott his fourteenth year. In consequence of this alliance, he was created EARL OF TARRAS, Lord Alemoor and Camp Castell, for his life only, by patent, dated 4 September, 1660. Mary, Countess of Buccleuch, *d.* at Wemyss, 12 March, 1661, in her thirteenth year *s. p.*, when her title and estates devolved on her sister, Anne, afterwards Duchess of Buccleuch, wife of the Duke of Monmouth. The Earl of Tarras, who was implicated in the treasonable designs of the Duke of Monmouth, his brother-in-law, was brought to trial, 5 January, 1685, and found guilty, whereupon his titles and estates were forfeited, and his arms ordered to be torn. He obtained, however, a remission, 5 February following, and his liberty out of the castle the same day. The Earl of Tarras was one of the first who engaged in the Revolution of 1688, and *d.* in 1693, aged about forty-eight, when his title became EXTINCT. His lordship *m.* 2ndly, 31 December, 1677, Helen, eldest dau. of Thomas Hepburn, of Humbie, co. Haddington, by whom he had, with three daus., three sons,

GIDEON, of High Chester, father of two sons, Walter, of Harden, and John, also of Harden, who both *d. s. p.*
WALTER, who *s.* to Harden at the death, in 1734, of his nephew, John; he was ancestor of Lord Polwarth.
Thomas, *d. unm.*

Arms—Or, two mullets in chief, and a crescent in base, arg.

SCOTT—BARON STOWELL.

By Letters Patent, dated 17 July, 1821.

Lineage.

WILLIAM SCOTT, Esq., a merchant of Newcastle-upon-Tyne, *m.* Jane, dau. of Henry Atkinson, Esq., and granddau. of John Lawson, Esq., of Longhirst, Northumberland, by whom (who *d.* in 1800, at the advanced age of ninety-two) he left at his decease, in 1776, three sons and two daus., viz.,

I. WILLIAM, of whom presently.
II. Henry, who *s.* to his father's business, and *d.* in 1779, leaving by Mary, dau. of John Cook, Esq., of Togston, an only dau., Mary, *m.* to Joseph Forster, Esq., of Seaton Burn.
III. JOHN, created EARL OF ELDON, 7 July, 1821
I. Barbara, *d. unm.* in 1828.
II. Jane, *m.* to Sir Thomas Burdon, Knt., and *d.* in 1822.

The eldest son,
WILLIAM SCOTT, D.C.L., *b.* 1745, a very eminent civilian, was appointed in 1791, judge of the court of Admiralty, and created in 1821, BARON STOWELL, *of Stowell Park, co. Gloucester*. He *m.* 1st, in 1782, Anna-Maria, eldest dau. and co-heir of John Bagnall, Esq., of Earley Court, Berkshire, and 2ndly, in 1813, Louisa-Catherine, Marchioness Dowager of Sligo. By the former he had issue,

I. WILLIAM, *b.* in 1794; *d. unm.* in 1835.
I. MARIANNE, *m.* 1st, 16 March, 1809, to Thomas, eldest son of Gore Townsend, Esq., of Honington Hall, co. Warwick, and 2ndly, 29 July, 1823, to Henry, Viscount Sidmouth, and *d. s. p.* 26 April, 1842.

Lord Stowell *d.* 28 January, 1836, when the title became EXTINCT.

Arms—Arg., three lions' heads erased, gu., two and one, between the upper ones an anchor, sa., on a chief, wavy, az., a portcullis with chains, or

---

SCRIMGEOUR — VISCOUNTS DUDHOPE, AND EARL OF DUNDEE.

Viscounty, by Letters Patent, dated 15 November. 1641.
Earldom, by Letters Patent, dated 8 September, 1660.

Lineage.

SIR JOHN SCRIMGEOUR, of Dudhope, hereditary King's Standard Bearer for Scotland, representative of the Scrimgeours, Constables of Dundee, was raised to the peerage, by patent, dated at Holyrood House, 15 November, 1641, as VISCOUNT OF DUDHOPE, and LORD SCRIMGEOUR, with the eventual limitation to his heirs male whatsoever. He d. 7 March, 1643, leaving by his wife, Margaret Seton, of the family of Parbroath, co. Fife, two daus., Jean, m. to Sir Thomas Thomson, Bart.; and Mary, m. to Sir James Haliburton, a son and successor,

JAMES SCRIMGEOUR, 2nd Viscount of Dudhope, who m. Lady Isabel Ker, 3rd dau. of Robert, 1st Earl of Roxburgh, and by her had (with two daus., Mary and Margaret, wife of John Graham, of Fintry) two sons. His lordship d. from the effects of a wound he received at Marston Moor, 22 July, 1644, and was s. by his son,

JOHN SCRIMGEOUR, 3rd Viscount of Dudhope, colonel of horse in the engagement to attempt the rescue of King CHARLES I., under the Duke of Hamilton, in 1648. His lordship accompanied CHARLES II. to the battle of Worcester, and escaping thence, and joining General Middleton in the highlands of Scotland, was taken with a party of Middleton's forces in the braes of Angus, by the English, in November, 1654. At the Restoration, he was, in consideration of his services and sufferings in the royal cause, sworn a privy councillor, and created EARL OF DUNDEE, Viscount of Dudhope, Lord Scrimgeour and Inverkeithing, 8 September, 1660; the limitations are not known, the patent not being on record. He m. in 1644, Lady Anne Ramsay, 2nd dau. of William, 1st Earl of Dalhousie, by whom (who took to her 2nd husband, Sir Henry Bruce, of Clackmannan) he left no issue at his decease, 23 June, 1668.

The representative of the distinguished family of Scrimgeour devolved, at the decease of the Earl of Dundee, on the Scrimgeours, of Kirkton, whose male heir, FREDERICK-LEWIS SCRIMGEOUR WEDDERBURN, Esq., of Wedderburn, s. as heritable royal standard-bearer for Scotland.

Arms—Gu., a lion rampant, or, armed and langued, az., holding in his dexter paw a crooked sword or scimitar, arg.

SCROPE—BARONS SCROPE, OF BOLTON, EARL OF SUNDERLAND.

Barony, by Writ of Summons, dated 8 January, 1371.
Earldom, by Letters Patent, dated 19 June, 1627.

Lineage.

The great baronial house of Scrope had an unbroken male descent from the Conquest, if not from the time of EDWARD THE CONFESSOR.

SIR WILLIAM LE SCROPE, Knt. (son of William le Scrope, and grandson of Henry le Scrope, who were both buried with their ancestors at Wensley) possessed lands in Bolton, co. York, 1296. Several deponents in the Scrope and Grosvenor Controversy, report him to have been celebrated for his conduct in the field, and "the best knight of the whole country at jousts and tournaments." He left issue,

I. HENRY LE SCROPE, his heir.
II. Geoffry le Scrope, of Masham, knight-banneret, and chief justice to both EDWARD II. and EDWARD III.; with the latter of whom he also served in a military capacity throughout his French and Scotch wars. He was likewise celebrated for his achievements in the lists and tournaments, and many interesting anecdotes are given concerning him, by the deponents in the Scrope and Grosvenor Controversy. He was the progenitor of the line of the LORDS SCROPE OF MASHAM.

SIR HENRY LE SCROPE, eldest son of Sir William le Scrope, became a judge of the Court of King's Bench, 2nd EDWARD II. He was a trier of petitions in the parliament which met at Lincoln, 9th EDWARD II., 1316, and in the following year was made Chief Justice of his court, which judicial office he filled for seven years. He was in high favour throughout the greater part of the reign of EDWARD II., and was employed in various situations of high trust. On the accession of EDWARD III., he was re-appointed Chief Justice of the King's Bench, and subsequently made Chief Baron of the Exchequer. He obtained charters of free warren for his manors of Bolton,

and others in Yorkshire; and for his large benefactions was considered the founder of the wealthy abbey of St. Agatha, of Richmond. He d. in 1336, and left issue by his wife, Margaret, dau. of Lord Ross,
I. WILLIAM LE SCROPE.
II. Stephen le Scrope, who d. s. p.
III. RICHARD LE SCROPE, who became heir to his brother William.

The eldest son,

SIR WILLIAM LE SCROPE accompanied King EDWARD III., in several of his French and Scotch expeditions. He was at the battle of Vironfoss, in Picardy, in 1339; at the siege of Tournay, in 1340; and at that of Vannes, in 1342. He d. of a wound received at the siege of Morlaix, in 1344, and was buried in the abbey of St. Agatha. He was s. by his brother,

SIR RICHARD SCROPE, 1st BARON SCROPE OF BOLTON, b. in 1327. This gallant soldier was knighted by EDWARD III. at the battle of Durham, where the Scotch were defeated in 1346, and was present at the siege of Calais in the same year. Without attempting to follow this nobleman through all his martial exploits, which, however, stand recorded by their eye-witnesses, the several royal, noble, and knightly deponents in the celebrated controversy sustained by him with Sir Richard Grosvenor, for the right of bearing his family coat of arms, it is enough to say, that between 1346 and 1385, a period of forty years, there was scarcely a battle of note in England, France, Spain, or Scotland, where the English forces were engaged, in which Scrope did not gain honour. But as a statesman he was still more distinguished. He was lord high treasurer to EDWARD III., and twice lord chancellor of England in the reign of RICHARD II., by both which sovereigns he was entrusted with many other employments of honour and confidence. Walsingham states him to have been remarkable for his extraordinary wisdom and integrity, and records his firmness in refusing to put the great seal as chancellor to the profuse grants made by RICHARD II. to his favourites. When RICHARD, incensed at this, sent messenger after messenger to Scrope, "desiring him forthwith to return the great seal, he refused to deliver it to any other person than to the king himself." Lord Scrope was summoned to parliament continuously during the reigns of EDWARD III. and RICHARD II., and was a trier of petitions on many occasions. In 1385, he challenged the right of Sir Robert Grosvenor to bear the arms, "Azure, a bend. or." and the memorable suit, instituted for the decision of this heraldic controversy, lasted upwards of four years, and was at length decided in his favour, Scrope having established, by the evidence of a vast number of deponents, consisting of the most distinguished men of the day, from John of Gaunt, the King's uncle, to Chaucer, the poet, who was then a squire at arms, that "his ancestors had continually borne the contested coat from the Conquest." Lord Scrope built the stately castle of Bolton, in Richmondshire, and d. full of honours, at the age of seventy-three, 4th HENRY IV., 1403. His name is among those of the peers who assented to the deposition of RICHARD II.: but his heir apparent, the Earl of Wilts, sacrificed his life in the service of that unfortunate sovereign; and his younger son, Sir Stephen Scrope, adhered to the dethroned monarch with admirable fidelity. Lord Scrope m. Blanche, dau. of Sir William de la Pole, by whom (who d. before 1378) he had issue,

I. SIR WILLIAM SCROPE, K.G., created EARL OF WILTES, and appointed treasurer of England, in the reign of RICHARD II., by which sovereign he was greatly esteemed, and employed in numerous important services. (See SCROPE, EARL OF WILTS.)
II. ROGER, 2nd LORD SCROPE OF BOLTON, who s. his father in the title and estates, and was the continuator of the family of SCROPES, BARONS OF BOLTON.
III. STEPHEN (Sir), Knt., of Bentley and Castle Combe, ancestor of the SCROPES of Castle Combe, Wilts. (See BURKE's Landed Gentry).
IV. Richard. archbishop of York, beheaded for conspiring against HENRY IV.

Lord Scrope, who was a noble benefactor to the church, d. in 1403, and was s. by his eldest surviving son,

SIR ROGER LE SCROPE, 2nd Baron Scrope, of Bolton, summoned to parliament, 2 October, and 23 November, 1403. His lordship m. Margaret, eldest dau. and co-heir of Robert, Lord Tiptoft, or Tibetot, with whom he acquired the manor of Langor, Notts, and dying 3 December, 1403, was s. by his son,

SIR RICHARD LE SCROPE, 3rd baron. but never summoned to parliament. This nobleman, in the 7th HENRY V., attended the king in the expedition then made into France, but d. soon after, anno 1420. His lordship m. Lady Margaret Nevil, dau. of Ralph, Earl of Westmoreland, and by her (who m. 2ndly, William Cressener, Esq.), had two sons,

HENRY (Sir), his heir.
Richard, b. 1419, bishop of Carlisle, d. 22 May, 1468.

His lordship d. 29 August, 1420, and was s. by his son,

SIR HENRY LE SCROPE, 4th baron, b. 4 June, 1418, summoned t∴ parliament from 3 December, 1441, to 26 May, 1455, as LORD SCROPE, of Bolton. This nobleman, during his minority, accompanied John, Lord Scrope, of Upsal, in his embassy to the Grand Master of the Order of St. John of Jerusalem; and in the 18th HENRY VI., making proof of his age, had livery of his lands. His lordship m. Elizabeth, dau. of John, Lord Scrope, of Masham and Upsal, by whom he had issue,

  I. JOHN (Sir), his successor.
  II. Richard (Sir), Knt., m. Eleanor, dau. of Norman Washbourne, Esq., of co. Worcester, and by her (who m. 2ndly, Sir John Wyndham, of Felbrigg, co. Norfolk), had a son, Stephen, who d. s. p., and eight daus. and co-heirs, viz.,

    Elizabeth, m. 1st, to William, 2nd Viscount Beaumont; and 2ndly, to John de Vere, 13th Earl of Oxford, K.G.
    Eleanor, m. to Sir Thomas Wyndham, of Felbrigg.
    Mary, m. 1st, to Sir Edward Jerningham, of Somerleyton, co. Suffolk; and 2ndly, to Sir Wiliam Kingston, K.G.
    Katherine, m. to Richard Audley, Esq., of Swaffham.
    Jane, m. to Thomas Brewes, of Wenham, co. Suffolk.
    Anne.   Frances.
    Dorothy, d. unm.

  III. Ralph, archdeacon of Northumberland, d. 11 March, 1513.
  IV. Robert, by Katherine Zouche, his wife, had four daus. and co-heirs, Elizabeth, m. to Sir John Percehay; Anne, m. to Thomas Redman, of Bassall; Margaret, a nun; and Agnes.
  I. Agnes, m. 1st. to Sir Christopher Boynton, Knt., of Sadbury, and 2ndly, to Sir Richard Radclyffe, K.G., who was slain at Bosworth
  II. Elizabeth, m. 1st, to Sir John Bigot; 2ndly to Henry Rochfort, Esq., of Stoke Rochfort, co. Lincoln; and 3rdly, to Oliver St. John, Esq.
  III. Margaret, m. 1st, to Plessington; 2ndly, to Hugh Stafford; and 3rdly, to John Bernard, of Abingdon.

He was s. at his decease, 14 January, 1459, by the eldest son,

SIR JOHN LE SCROPE, 5th baron, summoned to parliament from 30 July, 1460, to 16 January, 1497. This nobleman espoused the cause of York, and during the reign of EDWARD IV. was a person of great influence and power. His lordship was a knight of the Garter, and fought against the Lancastrians, as well as the Scots, particularly at Norham Castle, when that fortress was relieved by the Earl of Surrey, and the besiegers driven beyond the Scottish border. He m. 1st, Joane, dau. of William, Lord Fitz-Hugh; and 2ndly, Elizabeth, dau. of Sir Oliver St. John, and relict of Lord Zouche; and 3rdly, Anne, dau. and heir of Sir Robert Harling, of East Harling, co. Norfolk, and widow, 1st, of Sir William Chamberlain, K.G., and 2ndly, of Sir Robert Wingfield. By his 2nd wife, his lordship had a dau., Mary, m. to Sir William Conyers, and was s. at his death, 17 August, 1498, by his son (by his 1st wife),

SIR HENRY LE SCROPE, 6th baron. This nobleman m. Elizabeth, dau. of Henry, Earl of Northumberland, by whom he had issue,

  I. HENRY, his successor.
  II. John, of Spennithorne, co. York, and Hambleton, Bucks, who m. Phillis, dau. of Ralph Rokeby, Esq., of Mortham, co. York, and was ancestor of the SCROPES, of Danby, co. York, and the SCROPES, of Cockerington, co. Lincoln. SIMON THOMAS SCROPE, Esq., of Danby, is now HEIR MALE of the illustrious house of SCROPE, and, as such, claims the EARLDOM OF WILTES. (See p. 483.)
  I. Elizabeth.   II. Katherine.
  III. Agnes.   IV. Jane.

Dying in 1506, he was s. by his elder son,

HENRY LE SCROPE, 7th baron, summoned to parliament from 23 November, 1514, to 9 August, 1529. This nobleman was at the battle of Flodden in the 5th HENRY VIII., and he was one of the peers, who, in the same reign, signed the celebrated letter to the Pope regarding the divorce of Queen Katherine. His lordship m. 1st, Alice, dau. and heir of Thomas, 6th Lord Scrope of Masham, and by her had two daus., Alice and Elizabeth, both d. young. He m. 2ndly, Margaret, dau. of Thomas, Lord Dacre, and had issue,

  JOHN, his successor.
  Anne, m. to John Vavasour, Esq., of Haslewood, co. York.
  Joane, m. to John, Lord Lumley.
  Elizabeth, m. to Sir Bryan Stapleton, Knt., of Carlton, co. York.
  Anne, m. to Thomas Rither, Esq., of Harewood, in Yorkshire.

He d. about the year, 1532, and was s. by his elder son,

JOHN LE SCROPE, 8th baron, summoned to parliament from 5 January, 1533, to 5 January, 1553. His lordship had livery of his lands in the 25th HENRY VIII., but in three years afterwards was involved in the conspiracy occasioned by the dissolution of the monasteries, called the Pilgrimage of Grace. He m. Catherine, eldest dau. of Henry, Earl of Cumberland, and by her (who m. 2ndly, Sir Richard Cholmley, of Roxby, co. York,) had issue,

John, d. s. p., v. p.
HENRY, his successor.
George,
Edward, } d. s. p.
Thomas,
Margaret, m. to Sir John Constable, Knt., of Burton Constable, co. York, and was grandmother of Henry Constable, Viscount Dunbar.
Elizabeth, m. to Thomas Pudsey, Esq., of Bolton, in Craven, and was great-grandmother of Ambrose Pudsey, Esq.
Alianore, m. to Sir Richard Tempest, of Bracewell, d. s. p.
Catherine, d. unm.

His lordship d. 3rd EDWARD VI., and was s. by his eldest son,

HENRY LE SCROPE, 9th baron, summoned to parliament from 21 October, 1555, to 4 February, 1589. This nobleman, in the 5th ELIZABETH, was constituted governor of the castle of Carlisle, and warden of the west marches towards Scotland. He was subsequently in arms against the insurgents under the Earls of Northumberland and Westmoreland, and was made a knight of the Garter. His lordship m. 1st, Alianore, dau. of Edward, Lord North, and had by her an only dau.,

  MARY, who m. SIR WILLIAM BOWES, of Bradley Hall, co. Durham (eldest son of Sir George Bowes, Knt., of Streatlam Castle in the same county) and left an only dau. and heir,

    MARY BOWES, who m. Sir William Eure, and was mother of

    WILLIAM EURE, of Elvet, who m. Mary, dau. of Peter Forcer, Esq., and had a dau.,

    MARY EURE, eventually sole heiress, who m. Michael Johnson, Esq., of Twyzell Hall, co. Durham; their eldest dau. and eventual heiress,

    MARY JOHNSON, m. 1st, John Brockholes, Esq., of Claughton, co. Lancaster (by whom she had a dau., Catherine, Duchess of Norfolk, whose issue is extinct), and 2ndly, 2 January, 1723-4, Richard Jones Esq., of Caton, co. Lancaster, by whom she had a son,

    MICHAEL JONES, of Caton, b. 23 November, 1729, m. 23 October, 1773, Mary, dau. of Mathew Smith, Esq., and widow of Edward Coyney, Esq., of Weston Coyney, in Staffordshire, and d. at Lancaster, 24 July, 1801, leaving issue,

      1 CHARLES JONES, captain 1st regiment of dragoon guards, d. 1840; his son and heir,

        HENRY-JAMES JONES, Esq., is heir-general of the BARONY OF SCROPE of Bolton.

      2 Michael Jones, barrister-at-law, F.S.A., d. s. p.
      3 Edward Jones, captain (half-pay) 29th regiment of foot.
      4 James Jones, lieutenant-colonel in the army, knight of the Guelphic order of Hanover, and of the order of CHARLES III. of Spain.
      1 Mary Jones, m. in April, 1818, to Monsieur Pierre de Sandelin, Chevalier de St. Lewis, Seigneur de Halines, &c., near St. Omer.
      2 Constantia Jones.
      3 Katherine, d. unm.

The 9th Lord Scrope m. 2ndly, Lady Margaret Howard, sister of Thomas, Duke of Norfolk and left by her at his decease in 1591, a son and heir,

THOMAS LE SCROPE, 10th baron, K.G., summoned to parliament from 19 February, 1593, to 6 October, 1610, who m. Philadelphia, dau. of Henry Carey, Lord Hunsdon, and dying 2 September, 1609, was s. by his only child,

EMANUEL LE SCROPE, 11th baron, summoned to parliament from 5 April, 1614, to 17 May, 1625. This nobleman, in the reign of JAMES I., was president of the king's council in the north, and was created by King CHARLES I., 19 June, 1627, EARL OF SUNDERLAND. His lordship m. Lady Elizabeth Manners, dau. of John, Earl of Rutland, but by her had no child. He d. without legitimate issue* 30 May, 1630 (being buried at Langar), when the Earldom of Sunderland became EXTINCT; and "the Barony of Scrope of Bolton devolved (says Nicolas) on the representative of MARY, only dau. of HENRY, 9th Lord, CHARLES JONES, Esq., captain 1st dragoons, he being heir-general of the body of Henry, 9th baron, although he never urged his claim to the dignity." Captain Jones was likewise

---

* Emanuel, Earl of Sunderland, last Lord Scrope, of Bolton, left three natural daus., by Martha Jeanes, his servant, besides a son, John, Fellow Com., Trin. Coll., Oxon, who d. unm., who were afterwards legitimated and given precedence as such, and among them the estates of the Scropes were divided, viz.,

  I. MARY, m. 1st, to the Hon. Henry Carey, 2nd son of Henry, Earl of Monmouth; and 2ndly, to Charles, Marquess of Winchester; which nobleman acquired the estate at Bolton, co. York, and was afterwards created Duke of Bolton.
  II. Elizabeth, m. to Thomas Savage, Earl Rivers.
  III. Annabella, m. to John Grubham Howe, Esq., ancestor of the Earls and Viscounts Howe. Mr Howe obtained the manor of Langar, in Nottinghamshire, which came to the Scropes with the heiress of the Tiptofts.

e'dest co-heir of the Barony of Tiptoft, created by writ of EDWARD II., dated 10 March, 1308; and co-heir of one moiety of the Barony of Badlesmere. He d. February, 1840, leaving a son, HENRY-JAMES JONES, Esq., now heir-general of the LORDS SCROPE, of Bolton.

Arms—Az., a bend, or.

SCROPE—BARONS SCROPE, OF MASHAM AND UPSAL.

By Writ of Summons, dated 25 February, 1342.

Lineage.

GEFFREY LE SCROPE (younger brother of Sir Henry le Scrope, the Chief Justice, father of Richard, Lord Scrope, of Bolton, *see* p. 480), a great landed proprietor in the reign of King EDWARD II., obtained from that monarch license to make a castle of his house at Clifton-upon-Yore, co. York, and had, at the same time, free warren in all his demesne lands at Clifton, and Parnewick, in Yorkshire, and at Whalton, in Northumberland. In the 17th of the same monarch, he was constituted Chief Justice of the court of King's Bench, as he was again in the 4th and 6th of EDWARD III., but being the next year sent abroad upon the king's affairs, he resigned his judicial office. He was afterwards in the wars of Flanders, and attained the rank of banneret. He *m.* Ivetta, or Rametta, dau. of William Ros, of Ingmanthorpe, and widow of Sir John Ufflete, and had issue,

HENRY, his successor.
John
William (Sir), served in the wars in France, Spain and Scotland, *m.* Maud, dau. of John Neville, of Raby, K.G., and *d. s. p.*
Thomas, (Sir), *d. v. p.*
Stephen (Sir), held lands in the town of Leyburn, in Thornton, and other places in Yorkshire. By Isabella, his wife, he left an only dau. and heir,
  Joan, *m.* 1st, to William de Pert, of the co. York ; and 2ndly, Sir Roger Swyllington, Knt., and had issue by both. She *d.* 20 September, 1427.

Beatrix, *m.* to Sir Andrew Luttrell.
Constance, *m.* to Sir Geoffrey Luttrell, brother of Sir Andrew.
Ivetta, *m.* to John de Hotham.

This learned and gallant person *d.* about 1340, and was *s.* by his elder son,

HENRY LE SCROPE, who in the 5th EDWARD III., was in the wars of Scotland, and was summoned to parliament the next year as a Baron, and from that period to 15th RICHARD II., 1391. In the 19th EDWARD III., his lordship was in the wars of France, and the next year he fought at the battle of Durham, where DAVID, King of Scotland, sustained so signal a defeat. He was afterwards one of the commissioners for arraying the co. York upon a menaced invasion by the French, and during the remainder of EDWARD III.'s reign, he was either actively engaged in the wars, or as a diplomatist. In the 2nd RICHARD II., being then a banneret, his lordship was sent ambassador, with others, to treat with CHARLES, King of Navarre, regarding a league between that prince and the King of England. By Joan, his wife he had issue,

  I. Geoffrey, *b.* 1340, served at the siege of Rennes, 1357, and before Paris, 1360 when he was knighted. Slain in Lithuania, 1362, *v. p. s. p.*
  II. STEPHEN, his successor.
  III. Richard, archbishop of York, 1398: beheaded 8 June, 1405.
  IV. Henry, an esquire in the army before Paris, 1360.
  V. John (Sir), *b.* about 1345; *m.* before 1402, Elizabeth, dau. and co-heir of David Strabolgi, Earl of Athol, and widow of Sir Thomas Percy, knt., and by her, who *m.* after his decease Robert de Thorley, Esq., had two daus., and co-heirs, Elizabeth, *m.* to Sir Richard Hastings; and Margaret, *m.* to Thomas Clavel, of Aldwark, co. York.
  I. Joan, *m.* to Henry, Lord Fitzhugh.
  II. Isabel, *m.* to Sir Robert Plumpton, Knt.

His lordship *d.* 31 July, 1291, and was *s.* by his eldest son,

SIR STEPHEN LE SCROPE, 2nd baron, then aged forty, summoned to parliament from 23 November, 1392, to 1 January, 1406. This nobleman received the honour of knighthood for his martial services in the lifetime of his father, and distinguished himself both by sea and land. His lordship *m.* Margery, dau. of John, Lord Welles, and widow of John, son of Sir William de Huntingfield, Knt., and had issue,

482

I. HENRY, his successor.
II. JOHN, of whom *presently.*
III. Stephen, archdeacon of Richmond, *t.* about the 2nd HENRY VI.
IV. William, *d.* 1463.

He *d.* 26 January, 1406, possessed of large estates in the cos. Essex, Notts, Stafford, Lincoln, and York, and was *s.* by his eldest son,

SIR HENRY LE SCROPE, 3rd baron, summoned to parliament from 26 August, 1408, to 26 September, 1414, as LORD SCROPE, *of Masham*. His lordship, in the 7th HENRY IV., was employed in the embassy to Isabel, Queen of Denmark, and ERIC, King of Denmark, to treat concerning the dowry of Philippa, the dau. of King HENRY, then consort of the King of Denmark; and for a league between the two crowns. In four years after he was made treasurer of the king's exchequer, and the next year the king considering his great abilities, as also the necessity of his presence in parliament and council, assigned him, during his stay at Westminster, or London, the towns of Hamstede and Hendon, co. Middlesex, for lodging and entertainment of his servants and horses. In the reign of HENRY V. Lord Scrope was appointed ambassador to treat of peace with the French. "But this great trust," says Dugdale, "he shamefully abused; for being a person in whom the king had so great a confidence, that nothing of private or public concernment was done without him; his gravity of countenance, modesty in his deportment and religious discourse, being always such, that whatsoever he advised was held as an oracle; upon this his solemn embassy into France, (which none was thought so fit to manage himself,) he treated privily with the king's enemies, (being in his heart totally theirs), and conspired the king's destruction, upon promise of reward from the French; his confederates in this design being Richard, Earl of Cambridge (brother of the Duke of York) and Sir Thomas Grey, a northern knight. But before this mischievous plot could be effected (which was to have killed the king and all his brethren ere he went to sea; five ships being ready at Southampton to waft the king over into France), it was discovered. Whereupon he had a speedy trial before Thomas, Duke of Clarence, and other peers, at Southampton, and being found guilty there lost his head, in August, 1415." His lordship had *m.* 1st, Philippa, dau. of Sir Guy de Brien, and 2ndly, Joane, Duchess of York, sister and co-heir of Edmund Holand, Earl of Kent, but had no issue. Upon his lordship's attainder, the Barony of Scrope, of Masham, became FORFEITED, and his lands were seized, part of which, including Masham, the king conferred upon Henry, Lord Fitz-Hugh, for life. He was *s.* by his brother,

SIR JOHN LE SCROPE, who, upon the death of his brother, Stephen, archdeacon of Richmond, 2nd HENRY VI., on doing his homage, had livery of his lands; and immediately, thereupon, by the consent of the lords in parliament, obtained a grant from the king, of the farms and rents of all those lordships which came to the crown by the attainder of Henry, Lord Scrope, his brother, to hold for four years. This Sir John Scrope wrote himself of Masham and Upsal, and was summoned to parliament as LORD SCROPE, *of Masham and Upsal*, from 7 January, 1426, to 26 May, 1455, having previously, according to Nicolas, (in 1421), obtained a restoration of his brother's honours and inheritance. His lordship was afterwards in high favour at court, and constituted treasurer of the king's exchequer. He *m.* Elizabeth, dau. of Sir Thomas Chaworth, of Wiverton, co. Notts, and heiress of her mother, Nicola, dau. and heir of Sir Gerard Braybrooke, Knt., and had issue,

Henry, who *d.* young.
John, who *d. s. p.*
THOMAS, his successor.
Alianore, *m.* 1st Richard, son and heir of Sir John Darcy, ancestor of the Barons Darcy and Conyers, and 2ndly, William Claxton, Esq., of Briggeford, Notts.
Elizabeth, *m.* to Henry, Lord Scrope, of Bolton.

His lordship *d.* 15 November, 1455, and was *s.* by his eldest surviving son,

SIR THOMAS LE SCROPE, 5th baron, summoned to parliament from 9 October, 1459, to 19 August, 1472. This nobleman *m.* Elizabeth, dau. of Ralph, Lord Greystoke, and by her who *m.* 2ndly, Sir Gilbert Talbot, Knt., of Grafton, had issue,

THOMAS, his successor.
HENRY, }
RALPH, } successively barons.
GEFFRY, }
Alice, *m.* to Sir James Strangways: and their daus. and eventual co-heiresses were, 1 MARIA, who *m.* Robert Ros, of Ingmanthorpe, and their heir-general, Elizabeth Ros, was wife of William Thomas, Esq., of Essex, and 2 JOAN, *m.* 1st, to John Bygod, and 2ndly, to Sir William Mauleverer.
Margaret, who *m.* Sir Christopher Danby, of Farnley, co. York, and had a son, SIR CHRISTOPHER DANBY, who *m.*

Elizabeth, daughter of Richard Neville, Lord Latimer, and was ancestor of the DANBYS, of Swinton, co. York, in whose representative vests a co-heirship to the Barony of Scrope, of Masham: HARRIETT, only child of Charles-Burrell Massingberd, Esq., of Ormsby, co. Lincoln, and widow of Charles-Godfrey Mundy, Esq., of Burton, appears to be such heir-general, entitled to a co heirship of the Barony of Scrope, through heiresses of Dobson, Tancred, Armytage, and Danby.

Elizabeth, m. to Sir Ralph Fitz-Randolph, Knt., of Spennithorne, co. York, and had, with a son, John, who d. s. p., five daus., Elizabeth Fitz-Randolph, wife of Sir Nicholas Strelley, of co. Nottingham; Alice Fitz-Randolph, m. Charles Dromfield, Esq (and had Ralph, d. s. p., and four daus., one of them Isabel, wife of John Swale, of Swinton; Elizabeth, m.— Warcop, of Sandall; Anne, m. Frances Percy, of Scotton, Dorothy Fitz-Randolph, m. John Forster, of Leyburn); Mary Fitz-Randolph, m. Ralph Batty, d. s. p.; Dorothy Fitz-Randolph, m. Lancelot Ashe, and had issue; and Agnes Fitz-Randolph, 5th dau, m. Marmaduke Wyvill, of Little Burton, Esq., and had Christopher, who, by his wife. Margaret, had Sir Marmaduke, a baronet, who m. Magdalen, dau. of Sir Christopher Danby, of Thorpe Park, co. York, and had six sons and two daus.

His lordship d. in 1475, and was s. by his eldest son,

SIR THOMAS LE SCROPE, 6th baron, summoned to parliament from 15 November, 1482, to 12 August, 1492. His lordship m. 1st Alice, dau. of Sir Walter Wrottesley, Knt.; and 2ndly, Elizabeth, dau. and co-heir of John Nevil, Marquess of Montacute, by whom (who m. 2ndly, Sir Henry Wentworth) he had an only dau., Alice, who became the wife of Henry, Lord Scrope, of Bo'ton, by whom she had two daus., Alice and Elizabeth, who both d. young and s. p. His lordship d. in 1494, and the barony appears then to have devolved upon his dau., ALICE, wife of Lord Scrope, of Bolton, but at her decease, s. p., in 1501, it reverted, to her ladyship's uncle,

SIR HENRY LE SCROPE, 7th baron, who was summoned to parliament, 28 November, 1511, "as Henricus Scrope de Scrope et Upsall ch'l'r," and dying s. p. about 1512, was s. by his brother,

RALPH LE SCROPE, 8th baron, never summoned to parliament. This nobleman d. s. p. in 1515, of which year his will bears date, and in which he mentions his wife, Johanna, and Geffery Scruope, Clerk, his brother, upon whom the barony devolved. This

GEFFERY LE SCROPE, 9th baron, was never summoned to parliament. His lordship dying s. p. in 1517, the Barony of Scrope of Masham and Upsal fell into ABEYANCE between his three sisters (refer to daus. of Thomas, 5th baron), as it still continues with their numerous representatives.

Arms—Az., a bend, or, in chief, a label of three points, ar y.

SCROPE—EARL OF WILTES.

By Charter, dated 29 September, 1397.

Lineage.

SIR WILLIAM LE SCROPE, K.G., eldest son of Richard, 1st Baron Scrope, of Bolton (see p. 480), was made seneschal of Aquitaine, 6th RICHARD II., and afterwards constituted custos of the castle of Queensboro'. In the 16th of the same reign he was appointed vice-chamberlain of the household, and he purchased, about that time from William de Montacute, Earl of Salisbury, the Isle of Man, with the crown thereof; it being then a right belonging to the lord of that island, to be crowned with a regal crown, and to bear the title of king. He was subsequently constituted lord chamberlain of the household, and was one of the ambassadors deputed to France to contract a marriage for King RICHARD with Isabel, eldest dau. of CHARLES VI., King of France. After this, having large grants of confiscated lands from the crown, he was created, by charter, dated 29 September, 21st RICHARD II., EARL OF WILTES, "to have to him and his heirs male for ever." He was constituted justice of Chester, North Wales, and Flint, with a grant of the office of surveyor of all the forests within the principality of Chester. He was also made a knight of the Garter. He purchased the sovereignty of the Isle of Man from the Earl of Salisbury, and in 1394, when the truce was confirmed with France, "Guilliam le Scrop" is recorded to have assented to it "pour la seigneurie du Man." as one of the "allies" of the King of England. He is the person of whom Shakespeare makes the Lord Roos to say:—

"The Earl of Wiltshire hath the realm in farm."
RICHARD II., Act 2, sc. I.

On the invasion of th kingdom by Henry, Duke of Lancaster,

the Earl of Wilts defended the castle of Bristol for the king, but was taken by the usurper's troops and beheaded, 29 July, 1399, v. p.

Since this earl's death, the title has remained dormant, but it has been claimed unsuccessfully by SIMON-THOMAS SCROPE, Esq., of Danby, co. York, the heir male of the family of SCROPE.

Arms—Az., a bend, or.

SCUDAMORE—VISCOUNT SCUDAMORE.

By Letters Patent, dated 2 July, 1628.

Lineage.

The Scudamores, one of the most eminent families in the West of England, have been established in Herefordshire for many centuries. At an early period they became divided into two distinct families, the Scudamores of Holme Lacy, and the Scudamores of Kentchurch, but the exact period when the branches separated, has not been accurately ascertained.

SIR JOHN SCUDAMORE (son of William Scudamore, and grandson of John Scudamore, Esq., of Holme Lacy, by Sybell, his wife, dau. of Watkyn Vaughan, of Hergest), was gentleman usher to Queen ELIZABETH, received the honour of knighthood, and was elected by the co. of Hereford in five successive parliaments during that reign. He m. 1st, Eleanor, dau. of Sir James Croft, and had issue,

JAMES (Sir), who was knighted for his valour at the siege of Calais, and in the 1st JAMES I., served in parliament for Herefordshire. Sir James m. Anne, dau. of Sir Thomas Throckmorton and dying v. p., left issue,

JOHN, successor to his grandfather.

Mary, m. to Sir Giles Brydges, of Wilton Castle.

Alice.

Ursula, wife of Alexander Walwyn, Esq., of Oldcourt.

Sir John Scudamore, the Sir Scudamore of Spencers' "Fairie Queen," was s. by his grandson,

JOHN SCUDAMORE, Esq., of Holme Lacy, who, at a very early age m. Elizabeth, only dau. and heir of Sir Arthur Porter, Knt., and was created a baronet, 1620, in which year he served in parliament for the co. Hereford, as also in 21st JAMES I., and was created Baron of Dromore, and VISCOUNT SCUDAMORE, of Sligo, by letters patent, 2 July, 1628. In 1634, he was sent ambassador to the court of France, in which employment he acquitted himself with singular prudence and honour. In the beginning of the civil wars, he was surprised in Hereford by Sir John Waller, and was sent prisoner to London, some of his houses were besieged, plundered, and burnt by the rebels, and his whole estate sequestered for several years, after which he compounded for his liberty and property as other royalists had done. The remarkably studious, pious, and hospitable life he led, made him respected and esteemed by all good men, especially by Bishop Laud, who generally visited him in going to and from his diocese of St. David's, and found his entertainment as kind and full of respect as ever he did from any friend. Lord Scudamore d. universally lamented in the seventy-first year of his age, 8 June, 1671, and was buried in the south aisle of the chancel in the parish church of Holme Lacy. Of six sons of this truly great and noble lord, only James lived to man's estate, and dying v. p., his son,

SIR JOHN SCUDAMORE, 2nd Viscount Scudamore, succeeded to the title and estates of his grandfather. He m. Frances, dau. of John, Earl of Exeter, and d. 22 July, 1697, having had three sons and three daus. He was s. by his 2nd son,

SIR JAMES SCUDAMORE, 3rd Viscount Scudamore; who m. Frances, only dau. of Simon, Lord Digby, and d. 2 December, 1716, aged thirty-two (when all his honours became EXTINCT), leaving an only dau. and heir,

FRANCES, b. in 1711, who m. 1st, Henry Somerset, Duke of Beaufort, from whom she was divorced; and 2ndly, Charles Fitzroy, Esq., who assumed the name and arms of SCUDAMORE; by him she had an only dau. and heiress, FRANCES, m. in 1762, to the Hon. Charles Howard, afterwards Earl of Surrey and Duke of Norfolk, who d. 15 December, 1815. The duchess did not very long survive him. She d. 22 October, 1820, when there being no issue by that marriage, the estates of Holme Lacy devolved upon SIR EDWYN-FRANCIS STANHOPE, Bart., as lineal descendant of Mary, wife of Sir Giles Brydges, of Wilton Castle, co. Hereford, dau. of Sir James Scudamore, Knt., and sister of John, 1st Viscount Scudamore. Sir Edwyn Stanhope assumed the additional surname and arms of Scudamore, by royal sign manual, on coming into possession of the Holme Lacey estates.

Another portion of the Scudamore property devolved on Daniel Higford Davall Burr, Esq., M.P., also a descendant of the Scudamores.

Arms—Gu., three stirrups, leathered and buckled, or.

SEEZ—EARL OF DORSET.

Creation of WILLIAM THE CONQUEROR.

Lineage.

OSMUND DE SEEZ, a noble Norman, was made bishop of Salisbury, by his kinsman, King WILLIAM THE CONQUEROR, and afterwards created EARL of the co. of Dorset. This eminent prelate, who filled the high office of Lord Chancellor of England, *d.* in 1099, and was buried at Old Sarum. In nearly three centuries and a half (1457) subsequently, he was canonized by Pope CALIXTUS, for the purity of his life, and the great services he had rendered to religion.

SEGRAVE—BARONS SEGRAVE OF BARTON SEGRAVE.

By Writ of Summons, dated 24 June, 1295.

Lineage.

In the 12th year of HENRY II.,

GILBERT DE SEGRAVE, Lord of Segrave, co. Leicester (whence he assumed his surname) held the fourth part of one knight's fee of William de Newburgh, Earl of Warwick, and in the 4th RICHARD I., he was joint sheriff with Reginald Basset, for the cos. Warwick and Leicester, under Hugh de Novant, bishop of Coventry, in which office he continued two whole years. He subsequently, 10th RICHARD I., gave 400 marks to the king towards the support of his wars. This Gilbert was *s.* by his son,

STEPHEN DE SEGRAVE, who, in the 5th King JOHN, was constable of the Tower of London, and remaining faithful to that monarch in his conflicts with the barons, obtained a grant (17th JOHN) of the lands of Stephen de Gant, lying in the cos. Lincoln and Leicester, with the manor of Kintone, co. Warwick. In the 4th HENRY III., he was made governor of Saubey Castle, Leicestershire, and the next year constituted sheriff of the cos. Essex and Hertford, and afterwards of Leicestershire. In the 8th of the same reign, he was governor of the castle at Hertford, and in two years after, one of the justices itinerant in the cos. Nottingham and Derby. About this period we find this successful person, whom Matthew Paris says, in his young days " from a *clerk* was made a *knight*," acquiring large landed property by purchase. In the 13th HENRY III., he bought the manor of Cotes, in the co. Derby, from the daus. and heirs of Stephen de Beauchamp, and he afterwards purchased from Ranulph, Earl of Chester and Lincoln, all the lands which that nobleman possessed at Mount Sorrell, co. Leicester, without the castle; as also two carucates and a half lying at Segrave, which himself and his ancestors had previously held at the rent of 14*s.* per annum. In the 16th HENRY III., he obtained a grant of the custody of the castle and county of Northampton, as also of the cos. Bedford, Buckingham, Warwick, and Leicester, for the term of his life ; taking the whole profit of all those shires for his support in that service; excepting the ancient farms, which had usually been paid into the exchequer. And, having been of the king's council for several years, as also chief justice of the Common Pleas, he succeeded in the 16th HENRY III., Hubert de Burgh in the great office of justiciary of England, being at the same time constituted governor of Dover, Canterbury, Rochester, &c., and constable of the Tower of London. After this we find him, however, opposed by the bishops and barons, and his manor house at Segrave burnt to the ground by the populace, as well as another mansion in the co. Huntingdon. The king, too, in this perilous crisis, deserted him, and cited him, along with Peter de Rupibus, bishop of Winchester, and others who had been in power, to appear forthwith at court in order to answer any charge regarding the wasting of the public treasure, which might be preferred against them. Some of those persons, conscious of guilt, fled to sanctuary, and Stephen de Segrave sought an asylum in the abbey of Leicester, where he openly declared that he was and had been a priest, and that he resolved to shave his crown

again to be a canon of that house. Nevertheless upon second thoughts, he braved the storm, and appeared at court, under the archbishop's protection; where the king called him a *wicked traitor*, and told him that it was under his advice that he had displaced Hubert de Burgh from the office of justiciary, and cast that eminent person into prison; nay, that had he gone the full length of his council, Hubert would have been hanged, and divers of the nobility banished. In twelve months subsequently, however, Stephen de Segrave made his peace by paying 1000 marks to the king, and he afterwards grew again into such favour, that in the 21st HENRY III., he was the means of reconciling the king with some of his most hostile barons. Subsequently, he was made justice of Chester, and the king's chief councillor, and " being now," says Dugdale, " advanced in years, deported himself by experience of former times, with much mo.e temper and moderation than heretofore." This eminent person *m.* twice— 1st, Robese, dau. of Thomas le Despencer, and 2ndly, Ida, sister of Henry de Hastings, with whom he had in frank-marriage, the manor of Bruneswaver, co. Warwick. Of Stephen de Segrave, so distinguished in the reign of HENRY III., Matthew Paris, thus speaks—" This Stephen, though come of no high parentage, was in his youth, of a clerk made a knight; and in his latter days, through his prudence and valour, so exalted, that he had the reputation of one of the chief men of the realm, managing the greatest affairs as he pleased. In doing whereof, he more minded his own profit than the common good ; yet for some good deeds, and making a discreet testament, he *d.* with much honour." He departed this life in 1241, and was *s.* by his son,

GILBERT DE SEGRAVE. This feudal lord having *m.* Annabil, dau. and co-heir of Robert de Chaucumbe, obtained a grant, in the 15th HENRY III., from Simon de Montfort, lord of Leicester, of the whole town of Kegworth, co. Leicester, and in two years after, had a grant from the crown, of the manor of Newcastle-under-Lyme, co. Stafford ; being the same year constituted governor of Bolsover Castle. In the 26th HENRY III., he was made justice of all the royal forests, south of Trent, and governor of Kenilworth Castle. In the 35th of the same reign, he was constituted one of the justices of *Oyer and Terminer*, in the city of London, to hear and determine all such causes as had usually been tried before the justice itinerant, at the Tower of London. But in three years afterwards, being deputed, with Roger Bigod, Earl Marshal, on an embassy, was treacherously seized (along with John de Plasets, Earl of Warwick, and divers others of the English nobility,) by the French, as he was returning, and *d.* within a short period, of the severe treatment he had received in prison. His decease occurred somewhat about the year 1254, when he was *s.* by his son,

NICHOLAS DE SEGRAVE, who, in the 43rd HENRY III., attended that monarch into France, but soon after espoused the cause of the barons, and became one of their most active leaders. In the 47th of HENRY's reign, he was amongst those who appeared openly in arms, and fortified Northampton, for which proceeding, his lands were seized by the crown. Upon the subsequent fall of Northampton to the royalists, Nicholas de Segrave fled to London, where the citizens having raised a large army for the barons, made him their general. At the head of this force, he marched with Gilbert de Clare, and Henry de Hastings, to the siege of Rochester, and thence to Lewes, at which place, the celebrated battle, so disastrous to the king, commenced, by a charge made by Segrave, at the head of the Londoners; in this, however, he was worsted by Prince Edward, who, flushed with success, pursued his advantage too far, and thus mainly contributed to the defeat which the royal arms sustained. The issue of this battle is well known. The king, Prince Edward, and the chief of their adherents became prisoners to the rebels, who followed up their triumph, by immediately summoning a parliament in the king's name, to which Nicholas de Segrave was summoned as BARON SEGRAVE, 24 December, 1264. But the tide soon ebbing, he was among the defeated at Evesham, where he was wounded and made prisoner. He was, however, admitted to the benefit of the Dictum de Kenilworth, and obtained a full pardon, with restoration of his lands, which had been seized. In four years afterwards, he attended Prince Edward to the Holy Land, and when that prince ascended the throne, he appears to have enjoyed a large share of royal favour. In the 4th year of EDWARD's reign, he was with the king in a campaign against the Welsh, and was subsequently employed in Scotland and Ireland, having had a second summons to parliament, 24 June, 1295. His lordship *m.* Maud de Lucy, by whom he had issue,

    I. JOHN, 2nd baron.
    II. NICHOLAS, of Barton Segrave, of whom hereafter.
    III. Geoffrey, sheriff co. Leicester 1 Edward II.

iv Peter.
v. Gilbert, Bishop of London, 1313-1316.
vi. Annabel, m. John de Plessetis, son of Sir Hugh de Plessetis, Knt.

Lord Segrave, d. 1295, and was s. by his eldest son,

JOHN DE SEGRAVE, 2nd baron, b. 1256, summoned to parliament, from 26 August, 1296, to 6 May, 1325. This nobleman, in the lifetime of his father, having been taken prisoner in the wars of Scotland (9th EDWARD I.), obtained from the king, in consideration of his services there, the grant of £100 towards the liquidation of his ransom. He was subsequently much engaged in the Scottish wars, and in the 24th of the same reign was constable of the English army in that country. The next year he was by indenture retained to serve Roger le Bigod, Earl of Norfolk, with six knights, himself accounted, as well in time of peace as in war, for the term of his whole life, in England, Wales, and Scotland: viz., in time of peace with six horses, so long as the earl should think fit, taking Bouche of Court for himself and his knights, and for his esquires, hay and oats; as also livery for six more horses, and wages for six grooms and their horses; likewise for himself two robes yearly, as well in time of peace as war, as for a banneret; and for his five knights, as for his other bachelors, viz., two yearly. Moreover, in time of war he was bound to bring with him his five knights with twenty horses; and in consideration thereof, to receive for himself and his company, with all those horses, 40s. per day, but if he should bring no more than six horses, then 32s.; it being likewise agreed that the horses should be valued to the end that a fair allowance might be made for any which should be lost in the service For the performance of this covenant he had a grant of the manor of Lodene, co. Norfolk.

In the 26th EDWARD I., his lordship was again in Scotland, and had a principal command at the battle of Falkirk. In three years after, he obtained license to make a castle at his manor house, of Bretteby, co Derby, and he was next constituted governor of Berwick-upon-Tweed, as also warden of Scotland. Subsequently we find him with King EDWARD at the celebrated siege of Caerlaverock. After the accession of EDWARD II., he was again made warden of Scotland, and within a short time, attending the king into that usual theatre of war, was amongst the worsted in the great defeat sustained by the English arms at Bannockburn, and was made prisoner by the Scots, who detained him for a year, until he was exchanged for Thomas de Moram, and other prisoners of that realm, who were incarcerated in London. His lordship eventually lost his life in Gascony, whither he was sent by the king, who had conceived some displeasure against him, for the escape of Roger Mortimer out of the Tower of London, under pretence of defending those parts, with Edmund, Earl of Kent, and others, where, being a great mortality, he d. anno 1325. His lordship m. in the lifetime of his father, in 1270, Christian, dau. of Sir Hugh de Plessetis, Knt., by whom he had issue,

i. STEPHEN, the companion in arms of his gallant father in the Scottish wars, but in the 12th EDWARD II., one of the partisans of Thomas, Earl of Lancaster. Submitting himself, however, he obtained his pardon, and 16th EDWARD II., was made constable of the Tower of London. In the 18th EDWARD, he attended his father into Gascony, and d. there v. p. He m. Alice de Arundel, and left issue,

JOHN DE SEGRAVE, 3rd baron, summoned to parliament, from 29 November, 1336, to 15 November, 1351. This nobleman appears, like his predecessors, a distinguished personage in the field, during his comparatively short career; for he did not live beyond the age of thirty-eight. In the wars of France and Scotland temp. EDWARD III., he took an active part, and was more than once retained to serve the king by indenture. His lordship made an illustrious alliance in marrying the Lady Margaret Plantagenet, dau., and eventually sole heiress of Thomas de Brotherton, Earl of Norfolk, Marshal of England, younger son of King EDWARD I.; by this lady he left, at his decease, in 1353, an only dau. and heiress,

ELIZABETH, who m. John de Mowbray, 4th Baron Mowbray (slain near Constantinople on his way to the Holy Land in 1368), and had issue,

JOHN, 5th Lord Mowbray, who was four years old at the time of his father's death. He was created Earl of Nottingham at the Coronation of RICHARD II. in 1377, and he and William de Latimer made claim to exercise on that day the office of Almoner, which had belonged to their ancestor, William de Beauchamp, of Bedford. He d. under age and unmarried, in 1382, and was s. in his family dignities by his brother,

THOMAS, 6th Lord Mowbray, created after the decease of his brother, Earl of Nottingham, and Duke of Norfolk, Earl Marshal, and K.G. His grace, for his military services, was authorised to bear for his crest a golden leopard, with a coronet of silver. In 1398 he

was accused by Henry Bolingbroke, Earl of Hereford, of having spoken slanderously of the king, whom he charged with a design of destroying the principal members of the nobility. Norfolk denied the accusation, and desired Hereford to prove its truth in single combat. The lists were set at Coventry in the presence of the king and the peers of the disputants, but on the eve of the contest the king interposed, and forbade the combat. Both Norfolk and Hereford were banished, the former for life, and the other for ten years. Norfolk d. of the plague at Venice in 1399. By his first wife, Elizabeth, dau. and heir of John, Lord Strange, of Blackmere, he had no issue. By his second wife, Elizabeth, dau. and co-heir of Richard Fitz Alan, Earl of Arundel and Surrey, he left two sons and two daus., viz.,

1 THOMAS, who never bore the title of Duke of Norfolk, but was denominated simply, Earl Marshal; beheaded, 6th HENRY IV., and d. s. p. 1399.

2 JOHN, restored to the Dukedom of Norfolk, s. in 1432 by his son,

JOHN, 3rd Duke of Norfolk, d. in 1461, and was s. by his son,

JOHN, 4th Duke of Norfolk, left, at his decease in 1475, an only dau.,

ANNE, LADY MOWBRAY AND SEGRAVE, then six years of age. She is styled in her father's inquisition "Domina de Mowbray." In January, 1476, she was affianced to Richard, Duke of York, second son of EDWARD IV. He was created Duke of Norfolk and Earl Warren; and was murdered in 1483. The Duchess had previously died under age and without issue. By this event the inheritance of the Mowbrays reverted to the heirs of Margaret and Isabel, daughters of Thomas de Mowbray, first Duke of Norfolk, and wives respectively of Sir Robert Howard and James, Lord Berkeley, and the Barony of Mowbray, as well as those of Segrave and Braose, fell into abeyance between the sons of Sir Robert Howard and Lord Berkeley.

1 MARGARET, m. to SIR ROBERT HOWARD, from whom the HOWARDS, DUKES OF NORFOLK derive, as well as the LORD MOWBRAY, SEGRAVE, AND STOURTON.

2 ISABEL, m. 1st, to Sir Henry Ferrers, Knt. by whom she had an only child, Elizabeth, m. to Edward Grey, 2nd son of Reginald, Lord Grey, of Ruthyn. Her ladyship m. 2ndly, James, 5th Lord Berkeley, from whom the extant Earl of Berkeley and the Baroness Berkeley derive.

Upon the decease, s. p., of Lady Anne Mowbray, only dau. and heiress of John Mowbray, 4th and last Duke of Norfolk, of that family, the Barony of Segrave reverted to the descendants of the two daus. of Thomas Mowbray, 1st Duke of Norfolk, namely, Lady Margaret Howard and Lady Isabel Berkeley, and fell into ABEYANCE amongst them, and so continued until terminated in favour of one of the co-heirs of Lady Margaret Howard, Alfred Joseph, 19th Lord Stourton, who was summoned as Baron Segrave, 3 January, 1878.

Having carried down the line of the eldest son, John, 2nd Baron, we revert to that of his brother,

NICHOLAS DE SEGRAVE, of Barton Segrave, co. Northampton, being in the king's service in Gascony, was summoned to parliament as a baron, 24 June, 1295. His lordship was soon after in the wars of Scotland, and shared in the victory of Falkirk. In the 33rd EDWARD I. Lord Segrave, whom Matthew Paris calls "one of the most worthy knights in this realm," being accused of treason by Sir John de Cromwell, Knt., challenged, in defence of his innocence, his accuser to single combat, according to the custom of the period, but the king not giving his consent to the duel, his lordship crossed the sea, for the purpose of meeting his antagonist without the realm. Having done so, however, unlicensed, he was taken into custody upon his return, and immediately brought to trial. The affair puzzled the judges, who were at a loss to come to a decision; however, after three days' consultation they declared that his lordship deserved death, and that all his goods should be confiscated; yet added, that in regard he departed not from England in an affront to the king, but to avenge his own quarrel, the king would do well to pardon him. EDWARD was much displeased at the boldness of the judges who seemed to set bounds to his prerogative, and gave them a severe reprimand. But he, nevertheless, pardoned Segrave, and restored him to his possessions; several of the nobility having interceded for him, and entered into security for his future good conduct.

In the 1st EDWARD II., his lordship was constituted governor of the castle at Northampton, and marshal of England, and in four years after he obtained license to make a castle of his manor house at Barton Segrave.

Upon the grant of the marshalship to Lord Segrave, much

animosity arose between him and William le Mareschall; which was allayed, however, by the king's interference. His lordship *d.* in 1322, leaving an only dau. and heiress,

MAUD SEGRAVE, who *m.* Edmund de Bohun, and in the representatives of this marriage (if any exist) the Barony of Segrave, of Barton Segrave, is now vested.

Arms—Sa., a lion rampant, arg., crowned, or.

SETON—BARONS SETON AND EARLS OF WINTOUN.

Earldom, by Charter, dated 16 November, 1600.

Lineage.

GEORGE SETON, of Seton, only son of Sir William Seton, slain at Verneuil, 1424, was soon after, 23 April, 1448, created a peer of parliament. He *d.* in the place of the Blackfriars at Edinburgh, after 15 July, 1478 (the date of a charter granted by him), and was buried in the choir of the same, having given to the community 20 merks of annual rents out of his lands. He *m.* 1st, Lady Margaret Stewart, only dau. and heiress of the gallant John, Earl of Buchan, constable of France, killed at Verneuil, and had a son,

JOHN, who *d. v. p.*, leaving, by Christian, his wife, dau. of John, 1st Lord Lindsay of Byres (which lady *m.* 2ndly, Robert, Lord Kilmaurs, properly 2nd Earl of Glencairn,) a son, George, successor to his grandfather.

He *m.* 2ndly, Christian Murray, of the house of Tullybardine, by whom he had a dau.,

Christian, *m.* to Hugh Douglas, of Corehead.

GEORGE SETON, 2nd Lord Seton, who *s.* his grandfather, and was one of the commissioners for settling differences on the marches appointed by the treaty of Nottingham, 22 September, 1484, founded the collegiate church of Seton, 20 June, 1493, and endowed it for the support of a provost, six prebendaries, and two singing boys. George, Lord Seton, was one of the conservators of treaties with the English, 30 September, 1497, and 12 July, 1499, and witnessed the assignation of the dower of Margaret, Queen of Scotland, 24 May, 1503. He *m.* Lady Margaret Campbell, eldest dau. of Colin, 1st Earl of Argyll, and by her had issue,

GEORGE, 3rd Lord Seton.
John, who *m.* the heiress of Sinclair of Northrig, and was ancestor of the Setons of Northrig.
Martha, *m.* to Sir William Maitland, of Leighthington.

The elder son,

GEORGE Seton, 3rd Lord Seton, fell at the battle of Flodden, 9 September, 1513. He *m.* Lady Janet Hepburn, eldest dau. of Patrick, 1st Earl of Bothwell, and had (with a dau. Mariot, *m.* 1st, to William, Master of Borthwick; and 2ndly, to Hugh, 2nd Earl of Eglinton,) a son,

GEORGE SETON, 4th Lord Seton, who *m.* 1st, Elizabeth, dau. of John, Lord Hay, of Yester, by whom he had issue,

GEORGE, 5th Lord Seton.
John, who, during the absence of his elder brother abroad, assumed the title of Lord Seton, and sat in parliament as a peer. On his brother's return, however, he surrendered estate and dignity: he *m.* Isabel Balfour, of Cariston, co. Fife, and was ancestor of the SETONS of Cariston, now represented by GEORGE SETON, Esq., M.A.
James.
Marian, *m.* to John, 4th Earl of Menteth; and 2ndly, to John, 11th Earl of Sutherland.
Margaret, *m.* to Sir Robert Logan, of Restalrig.
Eleanor, *m.* to Hugh, 7th Lord Somerville.
Beatrix, *m.* to Sir George Ogilivie, of Dunlugus.

Lord Seton *m.* 2ndly, Mary Pyerres or Peris, a French lady, who accompanied Mary of Lorraine to Scotland; and by whom he had a son, Robert. The eldest son,

GEORGE SETON, 5th Lord Seton, was one of the commissioners appointed by the parliament of Scotland, 17 December, 1557, to be present at the marriage of Queen MARY with the Dauphin of France. His lordship adhered to the party of the queen-dowager against the lords of the congregation, in 1559; and on Queen MARY's return from France, was sworn a privy councillor, and appointed master of the household for her Majesty. After the murder of Lord Darnley, the Queen and Bothwell went to Seton, where they passed some days, and where the contract of marriage between them was signed. Lord Seton was one of those who waited for the Queen on the banks of Lo.hlevin, in May, 1568, when she effected her escape, con-

ducted her by his castle of Niddry to Hamilton, and joined the association in her behalf. After the battle of Langside, Lord Seton retired to Flanders, where he remained in exile two years, and drove a waggon with four horses, for his livelihood. His picture in that employment was painted on the north end of the long gallery of Seton. Lord Seton was in Scotland in April, 1570, actively employed in the cause of Queen MARY; and in the same year he was sent to the Low Countries to solicit the Duke of Alva to assist the friends of her Majesty in Scotland. In 1583, he went as ambassador to France, but *d.* 8 January following, aged about fifty-five, and was buried at Seton, where a monument remains to his memory. His lordship *m.* Isabel, dau. of Sir William Hamilton, of Sanquhar, high treasurer of Scotland, and by her (who *d.* 12 November, 1606, aged about seventy-five,) had issue,

George, Master of Seton, *d.* in March, 1562. His brother Robert was served heir of him, 3 February, 1603.
ROBERT, 6th Lord Seton.
John (Sir), of Barns, knight of the order of St. Jago, master of the household, and one of the gentlemen of the bedchamber to King PHILIP II. of Spain. Being recalled into Scotland by King JAMES VI., he was appointed one of the extraordinary lords of session, in room of his brother Alexander (constituted an ordinary lord,) 17 February, 1587; and he *d.* before 11 June, 1594, when a successor was appointed in his place. He *m.* Anne, youngest dau. of William, 7th Lord Forbes, and was ancestor of the Setons, of Barns. Sir John Seton, of Barns, was served heir of his father, Sir John Seton, of Barns, 3 October, 1615.
ALEXANDER, high chancellor of Scotland, created 4 March, 1605-6, EARL OF DUNFERMLINE. His lordship *d.* in 1622, and was *s.* by his son,
  Charles Seton, 2nd earl of Dunfermline, who had, with a dau. (Henriet, *m.* 1st, to William, 5th Earl of Wigton; and 2ndly, to William, 15th Earl of Crawford), two sons; the elder,
    ALEXANDER, 3rd Earl of Dumfermline, *d. s. p.*, and was. *s.* by his brother,
    JAMES, 4th Earl of Dunfermline, who was outlawed and forfeited in 1690, for his participation in the battle of Killicranky. His lordship *d. s. p.* at St. Germains, in 1694.
William (Sir), of Killismore.
Margaret, wife of Lord Claud Hamilton, commendator of Paisley, and mother of the 1st Earl of Abercorn; she *d.* in March, 1616.

The eldest surviving son,

ROBERT SETON, 6th Lord Seton, who stood high in the favour of JAMES VI., was created EARL OF WINTOUN, Lord Seton and Tranent, by charter, dated 16 November, 1600, erecting the lordship of Seton into the Earldom of Wintoun, to him and his heirs male. He *d.* in 1603, and was buried 5 April, in that year, being the day King JAMES VI. commenced his royal journey to England. He *m.* (contract dated 10 April, 1582,) Lady Margaret Montgomery, eldest dau. of Hugh, 3rd Earl of Eglinton, heiress of her nephew, the 5th earl, and by her (who *d.* 9 April, 1624) had issue,

ROBERT, 2nd Earl of Winton.
GEORGE, 3rd Earl of Winton.
ALEXANDER, 6th Earl of Eglinton.
Thomas (Sir), ancestor of the Setons, of Olivestob.
John (Sir), whose only dau. *m.* Alexander Menzies, of Couterallers.
Isabel, *b.* 30 November, 1593; *m.* 1st, to James, 1st Earl of Perth; and 2ndly, to Francis Stewart, eldest son of Francis, Earl of Bothwell.

The eldest son,

ROBERT SETON, 2nd Earl of Winton, *m.* Anne, dau. of John, Lord Thirlestane, high chancellor of Scotland, sister of John, 1st Earl of Lauderdale, but by her (who *d.* 6 July, 1609, aged twenty) had no issue. His brother,

GEORGE SETON, 3rd Earl of Winton, was *b.* in December, 1584. He twice entertained King CHARLES I. at Seton, and rebuilt Winton House in 1619. His lordship *d.* 17 December, 1650, aged sixty-five, and was buried at Seton. He *m.* 1st, Lady Anne Hay, eldest dau. of Francis, 8th Earl of Erroll, and had issue,

I: GEORGE, Lord Seton, *b.* 1645, fought with Montrose and was made prisoner at Philiphaugh. He *d.* 4 June, 1648 leaving by Lady Henriet Gordon, his wife, 2nd dau. of George, 2nd Marquess of Huntley (who *m.* 2ndly, John, 2nd Earl of Traquair), a son,
  GEORGE, successor to his grandfather.
II. Christopher, *b.* 2 March, 1617; *d.* 30 June, 1618.
III. ALEXANDER, Viscount of Kingston. (*See that title.*)
IV. Francis, *b.* 1 May, 1623; *d.* young.
I. Margaret, *b.* 28 March, 1615; *d. unm.* in 1637.
II. Elizabeth, *m.* in 1637, to William, 7th Earl Marischal, and had issue; and *d.* in 1650, aged twenty-eight.

The Earl of Winton *m.* 2ndly, Elizabeth, dau. of John, Lord Herries, and by her had issue,

ɪ. Christopher, b 28 June, 1631, a youth of learning and promise, who, going on his travels with his brother William, was
lost on the coast of Holland, in July, 1648.

ɪɪ. William, b. 8 January, 1633, who perished with his brother,
1648.

ɪɪɪ. John (Sir), of Gairmiltoun (now Garletoun), ancestor of
the Setons, of Garletoun.

ɪv. Robert (Sir), of Windygoul, created a baronet in 1671,
d. s. p.

ɪ. Isabel, m. to Francis, Lord Sempill.

ɪɪ. Sophia, d. young.

ɪɪɪ. Anne, m. April, 1654, to John, 2nd Earl of Traquair.

ɪv. Jean, d. unm.

v. Mary, m. to James, 4th Earl of Carnwath.

The earl d. in 1650, and was s. by his grandson,

GEORGE SETON, 4th Earl of Winton, who commanded the
East Lothian regiment at the defeat of the Covenanters at
Pentland, in 1666, and at the battle of Bothwell Bridge, in
1679. He m. in 1662, Lady Mary Montgomery, eldest dau. of
Hugh, 7th Earl of Eglinton, by whom he had no surviving
issue: and 2ndly, Christian, dau. of John Hepburn, of Alder-
s on, by whom (who d. in 1704) he left at his decease, 6 March,
1704, two sons,

GEORGE, 5th earl.
Christopher, who d. unm. 1704.

The elder son,

GEORGE SETON, 5th Earl of Winton, joining the rising
of 1715, was taken at Preston, 14 November, in that year,
att iinted, and left for execution. His lordship found means,
however, to escape from the Tower of London in 1716, and fled
to France and eventually to Rome, where he d. unm. 19 December, 1749.

Thus fell one of the noblest and most ancient houses in Scotland, after an honourable existence of full 600 years. In 1840,
the Earl of Eglinton, as the lineal representative of Sir Alexander Seton, 3rd son of the 1st Earl of Winton, was served
" nearest and lawful heir male general, and also nearest and
lawful heir male of provision to George, 4th Earl of Winton."

Arms—Or, three crescents, within a double tressure, flory
counterflory, gu.

SETON—EARL OF DUNFERMLINE.

(See SETON, Earl of Winton.)

SETON—VISCOUNT OF KINGSTON.

By Letters Patent, dated 6 February, 1650.

Lineage.

THE HON. ALEXANDER SETON, b. 1621, 2nd son of George,
2nd Earl of Winton was employed in several negotiations of
importance by CHARLES II., and discharging his trust to his
Majesty's satisfaction, was created VISCOUNT OF KINGSTON, with
limitation to the heirs-male of his body, 6 February, 1650. His
lordship m. 1st, Jean, dau. of Sir George Fletcher, Knt., by
whom he had one dau.,

Jean, m. to James, 3rd Lord Mordington.

The viscount m. 2ndly, Elizabeth, dau. of Sir Archibald Douglas,
of Whittinghame, co. Haddington, and had issue,

ɪ. Charles, Master of Kingston, who d. v. p. unm.

ɪɪ. George, for some years a captain in Douglas's regiment in
France; d. young.

ɪɪɪ. Alexander, a great scholar, who d. young.

ɪv. ARCHIBALD, 2nd Viscount of Kingston.

v. John, d. aged nine years.

vɪ. JAMES, 3rd Viscount of Kingston.

ɪ. Isabel, d. aged eight years.

ɪɪ. Barbara, d. aged sixteen years.

ɪɪɪ. Elizabeth, m. to Hon. William Hay, of Drumelzier; their
grandson, Robert Hay, of Drumelzier and Whittinghame, d.
1807, leaving WILLIAM HAY, Esq., of Dunse Castle, co. Berwick, and other issue.

The viscount m. 3rdly, the Hon. Elizabeth Hamilton, 3rd dau.
of John, 1st Lord Belhaven; and 4thly, 3 August, 1686, Lady
Margaret Douglas, dau. of Archibald, Earl of Angus, sister of
James, 2nd Marquess of Douglas, but had no other issue. His
eldest surviving son,

ARCHIBALD SETON, 2nd Viscount of Kingston, was, under the
style of Master of Kingston, served heir of Charles, Master of

Kingston, his brother, 9 October, 1683, and of Elizabeth Douglas, his mother, 8 September, 1684. He d. unm. 1713. His
brother,

JAMES SETON, 3rd Viscount of Kingston, engaging in the
rebellion, 1715, was attainted by act of parliament, and his
estates and honours forfeited to the crown. He m. Lady Anne
Lindsay, eldest dau. of Colin, 3rd Earl of Balcarres, and relict of
Alexander, 5th Earl of Kellie, but by her, who d. at Edinburgh,
4 February, 1743, had no issue. His lordship d. about 1726,
and in him terminated the male line of the body of Alexander,
1st Viscount of Kingston.

Arms—Quarterly: 1st and 4th, or, three crescents, within a
double tressure, flory, counterflory, gu.; 2nd and 3rd, arg., a
dragon, vert.

SEYMOUR—VISCOUNTS BEAUCHAMP, OF HACHE, EARLS OF HERTFORD, DUKES OF SOMERSET, MARQUESSES OF HERTFORD, BARONS SEYMOUR, OF TROWBRIDGE.

Viscounty, by Letters Patent, dated 5 June, 1536.
Earldom, by Letters Patent, dated 18 October, 1537.
Dukedom, by Letters Patent, dated 16 February. 1547.
Marquessate, by Letters Patent, dated 3 June, 1640.
Barony, by Letters Patent, dated 19 February, 1641.

Lineage.

Of this family which derived its descent from Sir Roger
Seymour, of Evenswinden, co. Wilts, Knt., who m. Cecilia, one
of the sisters and co-heirs of John, Lord Beauchamp, of Hache,
was

SIR JOHN SEYMOUR, of Wolf Hall, Wilts, who, in the 9th
HENRY VIII., being then one of the knights of the body to the
king, obtained a grant of the constablewick of Bristol Castle,
to himself, and Edward, his son, in as ample manner as Giles,
Lord D'Aubeney, held the same. Sir John m. Margery, dau.
of Sir Henry Wentworth, K.B., of Nettlested, co. Suffolk, and
had issue,

EDWARD, of whom presently.

Henry (Sir), K.B., whose line is supposed to be extinct.

THOMAS, created Baron Seymour, of Sudeley.

JANE, who became Queen Consort of King HENRY VIII., and
was mother of EDWARD VI.

Elizabeth, m. 1st, to Sir Anthony Oughtred, Knt.; and 2ndly,
to Gregory, Lord Cromwell.

Dorothy, m. 1st, to Sir Clement Smith, Knt., and 2ndly, to
Thomas Laventhorpe, Esq.

The eldest son,

SIR EDWARD SEYMOUR, was one of the esquires of the body
to King HENRY VIII., and when his sister, Jane (who had been
maid of honour to Queen Anne Boleyn) became the wife of
his royal master, his advancement to rank and influence was
rapid and unrestricted. At the nuptials (28th HENRY VIII.)
he was elevated to the peerage by the title of VISCOUNT BEAU-
CHAMP, of Hache, and appointed in two days afterwards
captain of the Isle of Jersey. His father, Sir John Seymour,
d. the next year, when his lordship had livery of his lands;
and he was created, by letters patent, dated 18 October,
1537, EARL OF HERTFORD, with remainder to his issue male,
thereafter to be begotten. He was next constituted lord
great chamberlain of England for life, and the same year he
accompanied the Duke of Norfolk, lieutenant-general of the
English army, consisting of 20,000 men, into Scotland. His
lordship, during the remainder of the reign of his brother-in-
law, was constantly engaged in the wars of France; and upon
the decease of that monarch was chosen unanimously by the
council, Protector to the young king, his nephew, EDWARD VI.,
and within a month constituted lord treasurer of England.
As he was not previously a baron of the realm, that dignity,
under the title of BARON SEYMOUR, was conferred upon him 16
February, 1547, and he was created the next day DUKE OF
SOMERSET, both honours in remainder to the heirs male of his
body, by Anne, his 2nd wife; failing which to " Sir Edward
Seymour, son of the Earl of Hertford, by Katherine, his 1st
wife, and the heirs male of Sir Edward Seymour the son."[*] His

---

* This singular limitation is copied from the statement in page
49 of the Third General Report of the Lords Committee to
search for documents relative to the dignity of a peer of the
realm, to which is added the following remark on the effect of
the attainder of the said duke on the descendants of Sir Edward

grace was immediately after constituted earl marshal of England for life; and in the ensuing March he obtained a patent for the great office of Protector, and governor of the king and realms. On 3 November following, his grace had a special grant that he should sit alone, and be placed at all times (as well in the king's presence in parliament, as in his absence) upon the middle of the bench or stool, standing next on the right hand of the king's seat royal, in his parliament chamber. In the 1st year of the duke's administration he concluded a peace with France, directing then all his attention to bringing about a marriage between Mary, only dau. and heir of James V., of Scotland, and his nephew, the English king. But the negotiation proving abortive, he subsequently invaded Scotland with a large army, and fought and won the celebrated battle of Musselburgh, chiefly by his own courage and conduct. Thus having traced the rise of this eminent person, it now remains for us briefly to narrate his fall. Exciting by his extraordinary prosperity the envy of his contemporaries, and incurring by his barbarous treatment of his brother, Lord Seymour, of Sudeley, the hostility of the people, it required no great effort to hurl him from his giddy pre-eminence; and when he did fall, the recollection of his having signed the death warrant of his own brother, deprived him of much public sympathy. The moment he affixed his signature to that deed of fratricide his own doom was signed; and it was generally observed, that with his left hand he had cut off his right. Persons of his own rank designated him a blood-sucker and murderer, and declared aloud, that it was unfit that the king should remain under the protection of so ravenous a wolf. "Besides," (Sir William Dugdale writes) "many well disposed minds conceived a very hard opinion of him, for causing a church near Strand bridge, and two bishops' houses, to be pulled down, to make a site for his new building, called Somerset House, in digging the foundation whereof the bones of many, who had been there buried, were cast up, and carried into the fields. And because the stones of that church and those houses were not sufficient for that work, the steeple, and most part of the church of St. John of Hierusalem, near Smithfield, were mined and overthrown with powder, and the stones carried thereto. So likewise the cloister on the north side of St. Paul's Cathedral, and the charnel house on the south side thereof, with the chapel, the tombes and monuments therein being all beaten down, the bones of the dead carried into Finsbury fields, and the stones converted to this building; and it was confidently affirmed, that for the same purpose he intended to have pulled down St. Margaret's Church, at West minster, but that the standing thereof was preserved by his fall." The duke's great rival and most bitter foe was John Dudley, Viscount L'Isle, afterwards Earl of Warwick and Duke of Northumberland. This nobleman, observing the gathering storm around the Protector, availed himself of it, and retired from court, accompanied by eighteen other influential members of the privy council. A course of proceedings ensued which compelled Somerset to remove the King from Hampton Court to Windsor, and finally terminated in placing the protector himself at the mercy of his enemies. His grace was brought from Windsor, a prisoner, to London, and conducted on horseback through Holborn, between the Earls of Southampton and Huntingdon, followed by lords and gentlemen to the number of three hundred, all on horseback to the Tower; where he was afterwards waited upon by certain lords of the council, who laid before him a list of twenty-eight articles of impeachment, to which they required his immediate answer. To these Somerset was induced to subscribe with his own hand an acknowledgment of guilt, and to offer at the same time to sue, upon his knees, to the king for pardon. This humble bearing saved his life; but he was stripped of his offices of protector, treasurer, and marshal, lost all his goods, and nearly

£2,000 in lands. Subsequently working by the most abject submission upon the feelings of the king, he was released from his imprisonment, his fines remitted, and his lands, save those which had been given away, restored. Within a short interval too, he was feasted by the king, with a great show of favour, and resworn of the privy council. A reconciliation was likewise effected between him and Dudley, who had become Earl of Warwick, and his grace's daughter was married to the earl's son and heir, Lord L'Isle. But this alliance was found to be no cement to the new-born friendship, nor was it sufficiently strong to preserve even the semblance of good feeling between the rival noblemen. Somerset was soon after accused of meditating the assassination of Warwick, who was then Duke of Northumberland, and being committed, with his duchess to the Tower, was arraigned at Westminster Hall, 1 December, 1551, before the Marquess of Winchester, then lord treasurer, as high steward for the occasion, and twenty-seven other peers, on five distinct charges, viz.,

1. Of raising men in the northern parts of the realm.
2. Of assembling men to kill the Duke of Northumberland.
3. Of resisting his attachment.
4. Of killing the gens d'armes, and raising London.
5. Of assaulting the lords, and devising their deaths.

To which he pleaded not guilty, and was eventually acquitted of high treason, but convicted of felony, whereupon he had judgment to be hanged: a sentence which most of our historians say, he might have avoided by praying the benefit of his clergy, but upon a closer inquiry it will be found, that he was thus condemned under a specific statute then in force, which made the conspiring the death of a privy councillor felony, without the benefit of clergy. After conviction he was detained nearly two months in prison, when he was at length brought to the scaffold, on Tower Hill, 22 January, 1552, and being attainted, his honours were supposed to have become forfeited. The duke's character differed entirely from that of his brother, Thomas, Lord Seymour, of Sudeley. Dugdale says, "that Thomas was a person of great courage, courtly in fashion, in personage stately, in voice magnificent, but, somewhat empty in matter. The duke greatest in favour with the people; Sudeley most respected by the nobility; both highly esteemed by the king; both fortunate alike in their advancements; both ruined alike by their own vanity and folly. Both so well affected to the king, that the one might well be termed his sword, the other his target." His grace m. 1st, Katherine, dau. and co-heir of Sir William Fillol, of Fillols Hall, co. Essex, and had issue,

EDWARD (Sir), of Berry Pomeroy, from whom descended Sir Edward Seymour Bart., who s. as 8th Duke of Somerset, and Francis Seymour, created Lord Conway, ancestor of the extant Marquesses of Hertford. (see BURKE's Peerage and Baronetage).
John (Sir).

The duke m. 2ndly, Anne, dau. and heir of Sir Edward Stanhope, Knt., of Shelford, co. Notts (by Elizabeth, his wife, great-grand-dau. of William Bourchier, Earl of Ewe, in Normandy, by Anne, his wife, dau., and at length sole heir, of Thomas of Woodstock, Duke of Gloucester, youngest son of EDWARD III.) By this lady, he had

EDWARD, created Baron Beauchamp, of Hache, and Earl of Hertford.
Anne, m. 1st, to John Dudley, commonly called Earl of Warwick, eldest son of John, Duke of Northumberland, and 2ndly, to Sir Edward Umpton, K.B.
Margaret,} d. unm.
Jane, }
Mary, m. 1st, to Andrew Rogers, Esq., eldest son of Sir Richard Rogers, Knt., of Brianston, co. Dorset, and 2ndly to Sir Henry Payton, Knt.
Katherine, d. unm.
Elizabeth, m. to Sir Richard Knightley, Knt,

The only son of the attainted duke, by his 2nd wife,
SIR EDWARD SEYMOUR, upon whom the chief honours of his father were especially entailed, was created, by Queen ELIZABETH, by letters patent, dated 13 January, 1559, Baron Beauchamp, of Hache, and EARL OF HERTFORD. This nobleman incurred subsequently the displeasure of the Queen, by marrying without her consent the Lady Catherine Grey, dau. of Henry, Duke of Suffolk, and great grand-dau. of King HENRY VII., for which offence he had to pay a fine of £5,000, and to endure nine years incarceration: while the unhappy lady, being also committed to the Tower, was only released by death. The validity of this marriage was finally established at common law, by the verdict of a jury, of which John Digby, Esq., of Coleshill, was foreman. By this lady his lordship had three sons and one dau., viz.,

I. EDWARD, Lord Beauchamp, who, in the 6th of JAMES I., obtained letters patent, that himself and the heirs male of his

Seymour his son:—"The attainder of the Duke of Somerset, his father, and forfeiture of his dignities, by act of parliament, of the 5th and 6th EDWARD VI., did not affect the dignity of the Duke of Somerset granted to Sir Edward Seymour, and the heirs male of his body. By the terms of the grant, that dignity had vested immediately after the patent passed the great seal, in Sir Edward Seymour, with limitation to the heirs male of his body, though the actual enjoyment of it by Sir Edward, and the heirs male of his body, was made to depend on the failure of heirs male of the body of his father by his 2nd wife; and it is confidently affirmed, that, on the extinction of the heirs male of the Duke of Somerset, by his 2nd wife, that dukedom would have de volved on the heirs male of Sir Edward Seymour, above-mentioned, even had not the act of restoration, in 1660, taken place, 'because so far as the said limitation was in question, it wanted no such act for its preservation.' As the Barony of Seymour was granted with the same limitation, the preceding observations prove that it would have descended in a similar manner to the Dukedom of Somerset."
488

body, after the decease of his father, should be barons of parliament, and have place and voice therein ; and also letters patent, for the enjoyment of the Earldom of Hertford after his said father's decease. His lordship died however before that nobleman. He m. Honora, dau. of Sir Richard Rogers, of Bryanston, co. Dorset, and had issue,

Edward (Sir), K.B., who m. Anne, dau. of Richard, Earl of Dorset, and d. before his grandfather, 1618.

WILLIAM (Sir), successor to his grandfather.

FRANCIS (Sir), created 19 February, 1641, BARON SEYMOUR, of Trowbridge, co. Wilts. His lordship m. 1st, Frances, dau. and heir of Sir Gilbert Prinne, of Allington, Wilts, and had issue,

    CHARLES, his successor.
    Frances, m. to Sir William Ducie.

Lord Seymour of Trowbridge m. 2ndly, Catherine, dau. of Sir Robert Lee, but had no issue. He d. in 1664, and was s. by his son,

CHARLES, 2nd Lord Seymour, of Trowbridge, who m. 1st, Mary, dau. and sole heir of Thomas Smith, Esq., of Foley, by whom he had surviving issue,

    Catherine, d. unm.
    Frances, m. to Sir George Hungerford, Bart

His lordship m. 2ndly, Elizabeth, dau. of William, Lord Alington, and by her (who m. 2ndly, Sir John Ernle, of Whelham), had issue,

    1 FRANCIS.
    2 CHARLES, 6th Duke of Somerset.
    1 Honora, m. to Sir Charles Gerard.

He d. in 1665, and was s. by his elder son,

FRANCIS, 3rd Lord Trowbridge, who inherited as 5th DUKE OF SOMERSET.

II. Thomas, m. to Isabel, dau. of Edward Onley, Esq., of Catesby, co. Northampton, and d. s. p.

III. Edward.

I. Catherine, who d. young.

The earl m. 2ndly, Frances, sister to Charles, Earl of Nottingham, and 3rdly, Frances, dau. of Thomas, Viscount Howard of Bindon, but had issue, by neither. He d. at an advanced age in 1621, and was s. by his grandson,

SIR WILLIAM SEYMOUR, 2nd Earl of Hertford, who was created 3 June, 1640, MARQUESS OF HERTFORD. He had previously incurred the displeasure of King JAMES I., by marrying without his Majesty's consent, Arabella Stewart, for which himself and his wife were committed to the Tower; whence his lordship found means to escape, and passed beyond the seas. But the Lady Arabella, remained a prisoner until her decease (see STUART). The marquess during the civil wars, continued faithfully attached to the royal cause, and, upon the restoration of the monarchy was made a knight of the Garter, and restored in 1660, by special act of parliament, to the DUKEDOM OF SOMERSET, with all the privileges as fully and amply as though the attainder of the Protector Somerset had never occurred. The duke m. 2ndly, Lady Frances Devereux, dau. of Robert, 2nd Earl of Essex, and had issue,

William, } who both d. unm.
Robert, }

Henry, who m. Mary, dau. of Arthur, Lord Capel, and dying in his father's lifetime, 1656, left issue,

    WILLIAM, successor to his grandfather.
    Elizabeth, who had a warrant from King CHARLES II., conferring upon her the rank and precedency of a duke's dau. Her ladyship m. Thomas, Lord Bruce, afterwards Earl of Ailesbury, to whom, as heir of her brother, the Duke of Somerset, she brought a considerable estate.

John, who s. his nephew as Duke of Somerset.

Arabella, d. unm.

Frances, m. 1st, to Richard, Viscount Molyneux ; 2ndly, to Thomas, Earl of Southampton, lord treasurer ; and 3rdly, to Conyers D'Arcy, son and heir of Conyers, Lord D'Arcy.

Mary, m. to Heneage, Earl of Winchilsea.

Jane, m. to Charles, Lord Clifford, of Lanesborough, son of Richard, Earl of Burlington.

His grace d. in 1660, and was s. by his grandson,

WILLIAM SEYMOUR, 3rd Duke of Somerset. This nobleman d. in minority, unm., in 1671, when his estates devolved upon his sister, Lady Elizabeth Seymour, who m. Thomas, 2nd Earl of Ailesbury, and his honours reverted to his uncle,

JOHN SEYMOUR, as 4th Duke of Somerset. His grace m. Sarah, dau. of Sir Edward Alston, Knt., and widow of George Grimston, Esq., but d. s. p. 20 April, 1675, when the Marquessate of Hertford became EXTINCT, but the other honours devolved upon his cousin (refer to Francis, 3rd son of Edward, Lord Beauchamp, eldest son of Sir Edward Seymour, son and successor of the Protector),

FRANCIS SEYMOUR, 3rd Lord Seymour, of Trowbridge, as 5th Duke of Somerset. This nobleman did not, however, long enjoy his elevation. In his travels in Italy, visiting the church of the Augustinians, at Lerice, near Genoa, with some French gentlemen, his grace or one of his party was said to have in-

sulted in the church some ladies of the family of Botti, for which supposed affront he was shot dead by Horatio Botti, the husband of one of them, at his inn door (April, 1678), when, dying unm., his honours devolved upon his brother,

CHARLES SEYMOUR, 6th Duke of Somerset, known as "the proud Duke of Somerset, a man in whom the pride of birth and rank amounted almost to a disease." This nobleman was made a knight of the Garter by King CHARLES II., and was of the privy council and a lord of the bedchamber to King JAMES II. He was subsequently, however, a promoter of the Revolution, and in the reign of WILLIAM, was constituted president of the council. His grace was one of the commissioners for the union with Scotland, temp. Queen ANNE, and upon the accession of King GEORGE I., he was sworn of the privy council, and appointed master of the horse. He m. 1st, Lady Elizabeth Percy, only dau. of Joscelyn, 11th Earl of Northumberland, K.G., and heiress of the illustrious house of Percy, by whom he had issue,

ALGERNON, his successor.

Percy, M.P., d. unm. 1721.

Charles, d. unm. 1710.

Elizabeth, m. to Henry O'Brien, Earl of Thomond, and d. s. p. 1734.

Katherine, w. to Sir William Wyndham, baronet, of Orchard Wyndham, and had issue : 1, Sir Charles Wyndham, who succeeded his uncle, the Duke of Somerset, as Earl of Egremont; 2, Percy Wyndham created EARL OF THOMOND (see that title) ; and Elizabeth, m. to Right Hon. George Grenville.

Frances, d. unm.

Anne, m. to Peregrine Osborne, Marquess of Carmarthen, afterwards Duke of Leeds.

The duke m. 2ndly, Charlotte, dau. of Daniel, Earl of Winchilsea, and had two daus.,

Frances, m. to John Manners, the celebrated Marquess of Granby, and was mother of Charles, 4th Duke of Rutland.

Charlotte, m. to Heneage Finch, Earl of Aylesford.

His grace d. in 1748, and was s. by his eldest son,

ALGERNON SEYMOUR, 7th Duke of Somerset. This nobleman m. Frances, dau. of Henry, son of Thomas Thynne, Viscount Weymouth, by whom he had a son, GEORGE, who d. in 1744, in the life-time of his grandfather and father, and a dau.,

ELIZABETH, who m. Sir Hugh Smithson, Baronet, afterwards Duke of Northumberland.

Upon the decease of his mother, in 1722, his grace was summoned to parliament, as BARON PERCY; and was created, 2 October, 1749, Baron Warkworth, of Warkworth Castle, and Earl of Northumberland, with remainder, failing his own male issue, to his son-in-law, Sir Hugh Smithson, Baronet, and his male heirs, by the Lady Elizabeth, his wife; in default of which, the dignities of Baroness Warkworth and Countess of Northumberland, to the said Lady Elizabeth and her heirs male. He was further created the next day, Baron Cockermouth, and Earl of Egremont, both in Cumberland, with remainder, failing his issue male, to his nephew, Sir Charles Wyndham, Baronet, by Katherine, his sister, and his issue male; failure of which, to Percy Wyndham (who assumed the name of O'Brien, and was created Earl of Thomond, in Ireland), brother of the said Sir William Wyndham, and his issue male.

The duke d. in 1750, when the Dukedom of Somerset devolved on Sir Edward Seymour, Baronet (the descendant of Sir Edward Seymour, of Berry Pomeroy, elder son of the Protector Somerset, by his 1st wife), as 8th Duke of Somerset. The Earldoms of Northumberland and Egremont passed according to the patents, while the Earldom of Hereford, Viscounty of Beauchamp, and Barony of Seymour, of Trowbridge, became EXTINCT.

Arms—Quarterly : 1st and 4th, or, on a pile gules between six fleurs-de-lis. az., three lions of England (being the coat of augmentation, granted by HENRY VIII., on his marriage with Jane Seymour); 2nd and 3rd, gu., two wings conjoined in lure, tips downwards, or.

SEYMOUR—BARONS SEYMOUR, OF TROWBRIDGE.

By Letters Patent, dated 19 February, 1641.

(Refer to SEYMOUR, Viscounts Beauchamp of Hache, Dukes of Somerset, &c.)

SEYMOUR — BARON SEYMOUR, OF SUDELEY.

By Letters Patent, dated 16 February, 1547.

Lineage.

SIR THOMAS SEYMOUR, brother of the celebrated Protector Somerset, and of Jane Seymour, Queen Consort of HENRY VIII., was elevated to the peerage by King EDWARD VI., 16 February, 1547, as BARON SEYMOUR, of *Sudeley, co. Gloucester.* His lordship was lord high admiral of England, and a privy councillor. He *m.* the Queen Dowager, Katherine (Parr), who *d.* in childbed, 2nd EDWARD VI. His lordship, in the reign of his brother-in-law, had distinguished himself in arms, and was esteemed a person of lofty bearing, but turbulent, fierce, and ambitious. Conspiring against the power of his brother, the Protector, and paying court to the Lady Elizabeth, dau. of King HENRY VIII., with whom he was on the point of contracting a private marriage, he was committed to the Tower by parliament, and condemned without any form of trial. The parliament was soon after dissolved, and his lordship was beheaded on the 6th day succeeding, under the warrant of his brother, the Duke of Somerset. Lord Seymour dying *s. p.,* the Barony of Seymour, of Sudeley, would have become EXTINCT, had it not fallen under the ATTAINDER.

On 14 October, 1786, at which time Sudeley Castle was possessed by Lord Rivers, the Rev. Dr. Nash, in company with the Honourable John Somers Cocks, and Mr. John Skipp, of Ledbury, made an examination of the grave of Queen KATHERINE, and its contents. "Upon opening the ground," says Dr. Nash,[*] "and heaving up the lead, we found the face totally decayed, the bones only remaining; the teeth, which were sound, had fallen out of their sockets. The body, I believe, is perfect, as it has never been opened; we thought it indelicate and indecent to uncover it, but observing the left hand to lie at a small instance from the body, we took off the cere-cloth, and found the hands and nails perfect, but of a brownish colour; the cere-cloth consisted of many folds of coarse linen, dipped in wax, tar, and perhaps some gums; over this was wrapt a sheet of lead fitted exactly close to the body. I could not perceive any remains of a wooden coffin. On that part of the lead which covered the breast was this inscription:—

> ' K. P.
> Here Lycthe quene
> Katerine wife to Kyng
> Henry the VIII. and
> Last the wife of Thomas
> Lord of Sudeley highe
> Admyrall of England.
> And vncle to Kyng
> Edward the VI.,
> dyed
> 5 September
> MCCCCC.
> xlviii.'"[†]

The letters K. P. above the inscription was the signature she commonly used, though sometimes she signs herself, "Keteryn, the Quene." It seems at first extraordinary that she should be buried so near the surface of the ground; but we should consider that a pavement, and perhaps some earth had been taken away since she was first interred; and as she was buried within the communion rails, probably that ground might be formerly two or three steps higher than the rest of the chapel.

Arms—Same as Seymour, Viscounts Beauchamp, of Hache, &c.

SHAUNDE — EARL OF BATH.

By Letters Patent, dated 6 January, 1485.

Lineage.

PHILIBERT DE SHAUNDE, a native of Britanny, having promoted the cause of the Earl of Richmond, was raised to the peerage of England by HENRY VII., in the dignity of EARL OF

BATH, by letters patent, dated 6 January, 1485, wherein he is styled by the king, "consanguineus noster," but of his lordship or family nothing further is known.

Arms—Arg., on a cross, sa., a leo, ard's head, or.

SHEFFIELD — BARONS SHEFFIELD, OF BUTTERWICKE, CO. LINCOLN, EARLS OF MULGRAVE, MARQUESSES OF NOR-MANBY, DUKES OF NORMANBY, DUKES OF BUCKINGHAM.

Barony, by Letters Patent, dated 16 February, 1547.
Earldom, by Letters Patent, dated 7 February, 1626.
Marquessate, by Letters Patent, date 10 May, 1694.
Dukedom of Normanby, by Letters Patent, dated 9 March, 1703
Dukedom of Buckingham, by Letters Patent, dated 23 March, 1703.

Lineage.

The family of Sheffield attained importance so early as the reign of HENRY III., when

SIR ROBERT SHEFFIELD, Knt., flourished. He was *s.* by his son,

ROBERT SHEFFIELD, who *m.* Anne, dau. and co-heiress of Sir Simon Goure, and was *s.* by his son,

SIR ROBERT SHEFFIELD, who *m.* Genette, eldest dau. and co-heir of Alexander Lownde, of Butterwicke, co. Lincoln, and thus became possessed of that lordship. From this Sir Robert descended

SIR ROBERT SHEFFIELD, who, in the 2nd HENRY VII., was one of the commanders in the royal army, against John, Earl of Lincoln, and his adherents, at the battle of Stoke. Sir Robert was afterwards Speaker of the House of Commons, and recorder of London. He *m.* Helen, dau. and heiress of Sir John Delves, Knt., and was *s.* by his son,

SIR ROBERT SHEFFIELD, of Butterwicke, who *m.* Margaret, dau. of Sir John Zouche, of Codnor, and left a son,

EDMUND SHEFFIELD, who was advanced to the peerage. 16 February, 1547 (two days before the coronation of King EDWARD VI.), in the dignity of BARON SHEFFIELD, *of Butterwicke, co. Lincoln.* The next year, his lordship having accompanied the Marquess of Northampton, to suppress the rebellion of Ket, in Norfolk, lost his life in the conflict. He had *m.* the Lady Anne Vere, dau. of John, Earl of Oxford, and left issue,

JOHN, his successor.
Frances, *m.* to — Metham, Esq.
Eleanor, *m.* to Denzil Holles, Esq., 2nd son of Sir William Holles, Knt., of Houghton, Notts.
Elizabeth.

His lordship was *s.* by his son,

JOHN SHEFFIELD. 2nd Baron Sheffield. This nobleman *m.* Douglas, dau. of William, Lord Howard of Effingham, by whom (who *m.* 2ndly, Dudley, Earl of Leicester,) he had issue,

EDMUND, his successor.
Elizabeth, *m.* to Thomas, Earl of Ormonde.

His lordship *d.* in 1569, and was *s.* by his son,

EDMUND SHEFFIELD, 3rd baron. This nobleman distinguished himself in arms, in the reign of Queen ELIZABETH, particularly in the celebrated defeat of the formidable Armada. He was subsequently made governor of the Brill, and in the same reign, a knight of the Garter. By King JAMES I., his lordship was constituted president of the council for the northern parts of the realm; and created by the succeeding monarch, 7 February, 1626, EARL OF MULGRAVE. He *m.* 1st, Ursula, dau of Sir Robert Tirwhit, of Ketilby, co. Lincoln, and had no less than fifteen children, of whom, Charles *d. unm., v. p.*

JOHN (Sir), *m.* Griseld, dau. of Sir Edmund Anderson, chief justice of the Court of Common Pleas, and dying *v. p.,* left a son,

EDMUND, who *s.* his grandfather.

Margaret, *m.* to Walter Walsh, Esq., of Castle Hoel, in Ireland, and her 2nd dau. and co-heiress,

URSULA WALSH, *m.* John Bryan, Esq., of Bawnmore, co. Kilkenny (his 2nd wife). The only surviving child and heiress of this marriage,

ELIZABETH BRYAN, marrying Oliver Grace, Esq., M.P., of Shanganagh, in the Queen's co., a portion of the Shef-

---

[*] In his communication to the Archæological Society—Archæologia, Vol. IX., pp. 1-15.

[†] The inscription is here given as it now appears on the coffin. When Dr. Nash made his examination, it was in all probability too much encrusted to be distinctly legible. On the last inspection it was first carefully cleaned.

field property came, eventually, into the Grace family, and is at present enjoyed by
Sir William Grace, Baronet.

Elizabeth, m. 1st, to Sir Edward Swift, Knt.; and 2ndly, to Sir John Bourchier.
Mary, m. to Sir Ferdinand Fairfax.
Frances, m. to Sir Philip Fairfax.
Triphena, m. to George Verney, Esq.

His lordship m. 2ndly, Mariana, dau. of Sir William Urwyn, Knt., by whom he had James, d. 1664; Thomas; Robert; Margaret m. Symon Thelwall, Esq., of Plâs-y-Ward, co. Denbigh; and Sarah. He d. at eighty years of age, in 1646, and was s. by his grandson,

EDMUND SHEFFIELD, 2nd Earl of Mulgrave, who m. Lady Elizabeth Cranfield, dau. of Lionel, Earl of Middlesex, and dying in 1658, was s. by his only son,

JOHN SHEFFIELD, 3rd Earl of Mulgrave. This nobleman, who became one of the most eminent personages of the period in which he lived, first attained distinction in arms; being in the great sea fight at Solhay, and afterwards captain of the Royal Catherine. In 1674, he was installed a knight of the Garter, and soon after made gentleman of the bed-chamber to King CHARLES II. He was at the same time appointed colonel of the old Holland regiment, governor of Hull, and entrusted with the command of the forces sent to Tangier. In the 1st JAMES II., his lordship was sworn of the privy council, and constituted lord chamberlain of the household. After the Revolution, he was sworn of the new privy council, and created by King WILLIAM, 10 May, 1694, MARQUESS OF NORMANBY, co. Lincoln. His lordship was further advanced, 2nd Queen ANNE, 9 March, 1703, to the DUKEDOM OF NORMANBY, and created in a fortnight afterwards, DUKE OF THE COUNTY OF BUCKINGHAM. The duke aspired to the fame of a man of letters, as well as a soldier and a statesman; and his literary productions have attained some popularity, but his abilities as a writer have been, of course, differently estimated.

Dryden says: "His thoughts are always just, his numbers harmonious, his words chosen, his expressions strong and manly, his verse flowing, and his turns so happy as they are easy." Walpole on the contrary, thus characterizes his lordship:—

"The life of this peer takes up fourteen pages and a half, in folio, in the 'General Dictionary,' where it has little pretensions to occupy a couple. But his pious relict was always purchasing places for him, herself, and their son, in every suburb of the temple of fame: a tenure, against which, above all others, quo warranto's are sure to take place. The author of the article in the 'Dictionary,' calls the duke one of the most beautiful prose writers, and greatest poets of this age; which is also, he says, proved by the finest writers his contemporaries; ce tificates that have little weight. where the merit is not proved by the author's own works. It is certain, that his grace's compositions in prose have nothing extraordinary in them; his poetry is most indifferent; and the greatest part of both is already fallen into total neglect. It is said, that he wrote, in hopes of being confounded with his predecessor in the title; but he would more easily have been mistaken with the other Buckingham, if he had never written at all. He had a great deal of bravery, and understood a court. Queen ANNE, who undoubtedly had no turn to gallantry, yet so far resembled her predecessor, ELIZABETH, as not to dislike a little homage to her person. This duke was immediately rewarded, on her accession, for having made love to her before her marriage. Though attached to the house of Stewart and their principles, he maintained a dignity of honour in some points, independent of all connections; for he ridiculed King JAMES's religion, though he attended him to his chapel; and warmly took the part of the Catalans against the Tory ministry, whom he had helped to introduce to the queen."

His grace m. 1st, Ursula, dau. of Colonel Stawel, and widow of the Earl of Conway, by whom he had no issue; 2ndly, Catherine, dau. of Fulke Grevile, Lord Brooke, and widow of Baptist, Earl of Gainsborough, who also d. s. p. in 1703-4; and 3rdly, Catherine, natural dau. of King JAMES II. (by Catherine, dau. of Sir Charles Sidley, Baronet, and widow of James, Earl of Anglesey, by whom he had three sons and a dau., one of whom, EDMUND, alone survived infancy. His grace* d. in 1721, and was s. by his son,

---

* His grace left an illegitimate son, by a Mrs. Lambert, called
CHARLES HERBERT, who, at the decease of Edmund, the last Duke, succeeded to a great part of the estates, including Normanby, co. Lincoln, and assumed by the will of his father, the surname of SHEFFIELD; he was created a baronet in 1755, and the present Sir Robert Sheffield is his great-grandson and successor.

EDMUND SHEFFIELD, 2nd Duke of Buckingham. This young nobleman served in 1734, as a volunteer, under the command of his uncle, the Duke of Berwick, in Germany, and was an ai 'e-de-camp at the siege of Fort Kiel and Philipsburgh, where that eminent general lost his life. His grace d., however, the following year at Rome, of a rapid consumption, not having attained majority, and with him, the honours and male line of the ducal house of Sheffield, EXPIRED.

Arms—Arg., a chevron between three garbs, gu.

SHERARD—BARONS AND EARLS OF HARBOROUGH.

Barony, by Letters Patent, dated 19 October, 1714.
Earldom, by Letters Patent, dated 8 May, 1719.

Lineage.

The house of Harborough claimed descent from a family of Shirard, which it is stated was powerful and opulent at the Conquest, in the counties of Chester and Lancaster. Its representative, temp. HENRY VI.,

GEOFFREY SHERARD, high-sheriff of Rutlandshire in 1468, 1480. and 1484, m. Joyce, dau. of Thomas Ashby, Esq., of Lowsby, in Leicestershire, and had two sons; the younger, Robert, of Lobethorpe, was ancestor of the SHERARDS, Baronets of Lobethorpe (see BURKE's Extinct Baronetage); and from the elder, THOMAS, descended the immediate founder of the dignities of the ennobled line,

WILLIAM SHERARD, Esq., of Stapleford, co. Leicester (sprung, through a long line of eminent ancestors, from Robert Sherard, Lord of Bromhall, in Cheshire, temp. King STEPHEN), who received the honour of knighthood from JAMES I., at Oatlands, 3 July, 1622, and was elevated to the peerage of Ireland by the succeeding monarch, 10 July, 1627, as *Baron Sherard, of Leitrim*. He m. Abigail, eldest dau. and co-heir of Cecil Cave, Esq., by Anne, his wife, dau. and sole heir of Anthony Bennet, Esq. of Greenwich, by whom he had seven sons and four daus.; of whom, BENNET s. to the honours; PHILIP (the 2nd son), seated at Whissendine, was father of BENNET, whose son, PHILIP, s. as 2nd EARL OF HARBOROUGH; and George (the 3rd son), was ancestor of PHILIP-CASTELL SHERARD, Esq. of Glatton, Hunts, who s. as 9th BARON SHERARD, 28 July, 1859. (See Extant Peerage). William, 1st Lord Sherard, d. 16 April, 1640, and was s. by his eldest son,

BENNET, 2nd baron, who m. Elizabeth, dau. and co-heir of Sir Robert Christopher, Knt., of Alford, co. Lincoln, and dying in 1700, was s. by his only surviving son,

BENNET, 3rd baron, who was enrolled amongst the peers of Great Britain, as *Baron Harborough, of Harborough, co. Leicester*, 19 October, 1714, with remainder, in default of male issue, to Philip Sherard, Esq. of Whissendine. co. Rutland (refer to Philip, 2nd son of the 1st lord). His lordship was advanced to a viscounty, 31 October, 1718, by the title of *Viscount Sherard, of Stapleford*; and created 8 May, 1719, EARL OF HARBOROUGH, with the like reversionary clause in the patent of creation (of the earldom) as had already been granted in that of the barony. His lordship m. Mary, dau. and sole heir of Sir Henry Calverley, Knt., of Ayerholme, in the bishopric of Durham; and d. s. p. 16 October, 1732, when the viscounty became extinct; but the earldom devolved upon his cousin,

PHILIP SHERARD, Esq. of Whissendine, as 2nd earl, who inherited also, as direct heir, the Irish dignity. This nobleman m. Anne, only dau. and heir of Nicholas Pedley, Esq., eldest son of Sir Nicholas Pedley, Knt., of Huntingdon, serjeant-at-law, by whom he had issue,

I. BENNET, his successor.
II. John, d. unm. in 1746.
III. ROBERT, 4th earl.
IV. Daniel, R.N., d. unm. 1744.
V. Philip, a lieut.-gen. in the army; d. unm. 14 September, 1790.

The family of Phipps, which now possesses the titles of Mulgrave and Normanby, was connected with the Sheffields, by William Phipps, Esq., father of the Earl Mulgrave, marrying Lady Catherine Annesley. only dau. and heiress of James, 1st Earl of Anglesey, by Catherine, natural dau. of King JAMES II., which Catherine m, 2ndly, JOHN SHEFFIELD, Duke of Buckingham and Normanby, and by him was mother of EDMUND, the last Duke of Buckingham. which Edmund was thus half-brother to the said Lady Catherine Annesley, wife of William Phipps.

1. Dorothy. _m._ to the Rev. James Torkington. of Great Stukeley, co. Huntingdon.
II. Lucy, _d._ 1731.   III. Susan, _d._ 1765.
IV. Ursula, _d._ 1745.

He _d._ 20 July, 1758, and was _s._ by his son,

BENNET SHERARD, 3rd earl. This nobleman _m._ four times: 1st, 27 June, 1748, Elizabeth, eldest dau. of Ralph, Earl of Verney, by whom he had several children, who all _d._ in infancy; 2ndly, 3 July, 1757, Frances, dau. of the Hon. William Noel, one of the judges of the Court of Common Pleas, by whom he had a dau., Frances, _m._ 18 April, 1776, to Major-Gen. George Morgan; 3rdly, 21 March, 1761, Margaret, dau. of Thomas Hill, Esq. of Tern, in Shropshire, M.P., by whom he had no surviving issue; and 4thly, in 1767, Elizabeth, eldest dau. of Sir Thomas Cave, Bart., LL.D., of Stanford Hall, co. Leicester, which lady _d. s. p._ His lordship _d._ 23 February, 1770, when the honours devolved upon his brother,

THE REV. ROBERT SHERARD, prebendary and canon-residentiary of Salisbury, as 4th earl, _b._ 21 October, 1712. His lordship _m._ 1st, in 1762, Catherine, eldest dau. and co-heir of Edward Hearst, Esq. of Salisbury, by whom he had no child; 2ndly, 1767, Jane, dau. of William Reeve, Esq., by whom he had a dau. (Lucy, who was _m._ 1st, to Sir Thomas Cave, Bart., M.P., and 2ndly, to the Hon. Philip Pusey, and _d._ the widow of the latter, 28 March, 1858) and a son, PHILIP, his successor; and 3rdly, 1772, Dorothy, dau. of William Roberts, Esq. of Glaiston, co. Rutland, by whom he had Dorothea-Sophia. He _d._ 21 April, 1799, and was _s._ by his son,

PHILIP SHERARD, 5th earl, _b._ 10 October, 1767; who _m._ 4 July, 1791, Eleanor, dau. of the Hon. John Monckton, of Fineshade, co Northampton, by whom (who _d._ 9 October, 1809) he had issue,

I. ROBERT, his heir.
I. Lucy-Eleanor, _m._ 19 May, 1817, to Col. the Hon Henry-C. Lowther, 2nd son of William, Earl of Lonsdale, K.G., and _d._ 8 June, 1848, leaving Henry Lowther, Esq., M.P., and other issue.
II. Anna-Maria, _m._ 7 March, 1816, to William Cuffe, Esq. of St. Albans. co. Kilkenny, and _d._ 22 November, 1848.
III. Sophia, _m._ 1st, 9 April, 1818, to Sir Thomas Whichcote, Bart; and 2ndly, 23 April, 1840, to William-Charles-Evans Freke, Esq., 4th son of the Hon. Percy Evans-Freke, nephew to Lord Carbery.
IV. Jane, _d._ 18 December, 1856.
V. Charlotte. _d unm._ 1856.
VI. Susan. _m._ 11 July, 1 21, to Lieut.-Gen. John Reeve, of the grenadier guards, and had. with other issue, a son, Col. John Reeve, of Leadenham House, co. Lincoln, late grenadier guards, _b._ 1 June, 1822, _m._ 18 August. 1857, Frances-Wilhelmina, eldest dau. of Sir G. Erle Welby, Bart.

His lordship _d._ 10 December, 1807, and was _s._ by his son,

ROBERT SHERARD, 6th earl, _b._ 26 August, 1797, who _m._ 27 November, 1843, Mary-Eliza, dau. of Edward Temple, Esq. (only son of the late Rev. Thomas-William Temple, D.D.), by Caroline, his wife, dau. of Sir John Honywood, Bart., of Evington, and the Lady Frances Courtenay, his wife, sister of the late Earl of Devon. The earl _d._ 28 July, 1859, when the Earldom and Barony of Harborough became EXTINCT, and the Irish Barony of Sherard devolved upon PHILIP-CASTELL SHERARD, Esq., as 9th BARON SHERARD.

Arms—Arg., a chevron, gu., between three torteaux.

SHERARD—VISCOUNT SHERARD.

(_See_ SHERARD, EARL OF HARBOROUGH.)

SHULDHAM—BARON SHULDHAM.

By Letters Patent, dated 31 July, 1776.

Lineage.

This is a branch of the very ancient family of Shuldham, seated for full 500 years at Shuldham's Manor, co. Norfolk.

EDMOND SHULDHAM, Esq. of Dublin, crown solicitor, 1713, _m._ Mary, dau. and heir of M'Carthy Spanuagh, of Dunmanway, and had with other issue, a son,

THE REV. LEMUEL SHULDHAM, of Dublin, who _m._ Elizabeth, dau. of Daniel Molyneux. Esq. of Ballymulvey, by Catherine, his wife, dau. of Thomas Pooley, Esq. of the city of Dublin, and granddau.. by Mary, his wife, dau. and co heiress of

492

William Dowdall, Esq., of Mount-town, co. Meath, of Col. Adam Molyneux of Ballymulvey, M.P for co. Longford in 1661, who was son of Daniel Molyneux, Esq. of Newlands, co. Dublin, Ulster King of Arms, M.P. for Strabane in 1613, and grandson of Thomas Molyneux, chancellor of the exchequer in Ireland, _temp._ ELIZABETH, who _d._ 3 January, 1596. By Elizabeth Molyneux, who was sole heir of her brother, Pooley Molyneux, Esq. of Ballymulvey, who _d. s. p._ in 1772, the Rev. Lemuel Shuldham had issue,

LEMUEL, ancestor of the SHULDHAMS of Ballymulvey and Molg House, co. Longford (_see_ BURKE'S _Landed Gentry_.)
MOLYNEUX, of whom presently.
Rebecca, _d._ in 1785, _unm._

The 2nd son,

MOLYNEUX SHULDHAM, vice-admiral R.N., and M.P. for Fowey, was elevated to the peerage of Ireland, as BARON SHULDHAM, 31 July, 1776. His lordship _m._ 4 October, 1790, Margaret-Irene, dau. of John Sarney, Esq. of Somerset House, London, and widow of John Harcourt, Esq. of Ankerwycke, Bucks, but by her (who _m._ 3rdly, 13 July, 1805, Richard, 2nd Earl of Clanwilliam) had no issue. He _d._ October, 1798, and with him the title EXPIRED. His lordship had two uncles, one of whom, Edmond, was ancestor of the SHULDHAMS, of Dunmanway, co. Cork.

Arms—Az., an eagle, displayed, or.

SIDLEY—COUNTESS OF DORCHESTER.

By Letters Patent, dated 20 January, 1685-6.

Lineage.

CATHERINE SIDLEY (only dau. of Sir Charles Sidley, Bart., of Southfield, co. Kent), mistress to King JAMES II., was created by that monarch, 20 January, 1685-6, _Baroness of Darlington_, co. _Durham_, and COUNTESS OF DORCHESTER, _for life._ By his Majesty, her ladyship had an only surviving dau.,

LADY CATHERINE DARNLEY, who _m._ 1st, James Annesley, 3rd Earl of Anglesey, by whom she had an only dau.,
LADY CATHERINE ANNESLEY, who _m._ William Phipps. Esq., son of Sir Constantine Phipps, Knt., Lord Chancellor of Ireland, and had a son,
CONSTANTINE PHIPPS, who was created BARON MULGRAVE, in the peerage of Ireland; a dignity inherited by the present Marques of Normanby.

Her ladyship being divorced from Lord Anglesey, for cruelty and causeless ill-treatment on her husband's part. _m._ 2ndly, John Sheffield, Duke of Buckingham, by whom she was mother of Edmund, 2nd Duke of Buckingham and Normanby

The countess, after the dissolution of her connection with the King, _m._ Sir David Colyear. subsequently Earl of Portmore, by whom she left one only surviving son, Charles, 2nd Earl of Portmore. The conduct of this lady made so strong an impression upon the honourable mind of her father, Sir Charles Sidley, that he conceived ever after a rooted hatred to her royal paramour, and was a zealous promoter of the Revolution. Being asked one day, why he appeared so warm against the king, who had created his dau. a countess, he replied, " it was from gratitude; for as his Majesty had made his daughter a _countess_, it was but fit he should do all he could to make his daughter _a qu en._"

Her ladyship _d._ in 1692, when all her honours became, as a matter of course, EXTINCT.

SINCLAIR—EARL OF ORKNEY.

Lineage.

The Scandinavian Earls of Orkney trace their descent from the noblest and most heroic of the ruling dynasties of the north. IVAR, Prince of the Uplands in Norway, who claimed a descent from the deified hero THOR, was the father of EYSTEIN, who had issue ROGENWALD and MALAHULE. The latter was ancestor of the great Norman race of De Toeny, who were the hereditary Standard bearers of Normandy, and from whom the house of Lindsay is descended. ROGENWALD, was a supporter of King HAROLD HARFAGR, and assisted him in obtaining the mastery over the other independent Norwegian chiefs, and in establishing himself as King of all Norway. He was Earl of

More and Raumdahl in Norway, and in 888, he obtained from King Harold a grant of the Orkney and Shetland islands. One of his sons, Rollo, conquered Neustria, founded the line of sovereign Dukes of Normandy, and was ancestor to William the Conqueror. Another of the sons of Earl Rogenwald was Eynar, to whom his father assigned the Orkney and Shetland Isles, and whom King Harold created earl. He was the ancestor of the line of great Scandinavian earls who reigned over the Orkney and Shetland Islands during five centuries. The alliances of these insular magnates with royalty were frequent. Besides more remote intermarriages between them and the family of Harold Harfagr, four deserve especial notice.

Sigurd, 2nd Earl of Orkney, who was slain at the battle of Clontarf in 1014, m. one of the daus. and co-heirs of Malcolm II., King of Scotland; and his descendants and representatives share the honour of being heirs general of the ancient Scoto-Pictish kings, with the reigning family of Great Britain.

Paul, Earl of Orkney, who, in 1066, accompanied King Harold Hardrada in his ill-omened expedition against England, m. the dau. of Earl Haco and Princess Ragenhilda, dau. of Magnus, the good King of Norway, who d. in 1048; and the descendants of this marriage became heirs-general of a branch of the royal family of Norway. The grand-dau. and eventual heir of this marriage, Margaret, Countess of Orkney, m. about the middle of the 12th century, Madoch, Earl of Athole, son of Earl Melmare, younger son of King Duncan I., and brother of King Malcolm Canmore. Her descendant, John, Earl of Orkney, who d. in 1305, m. a Norwegian Princess, dau. of Magnus, King of Norway, by Ingeborga, dau. of Eric, King of Denmark. The son of this marriage,

Magnus, 5th Earl of Orkney, was admitted by his uncle, Haco, King of Norway, in 1308, to be a prince of the blood royal, and to take his place along with the immediate sons of the Norwegian kings; he m. Catherine, Countess of Caithness, in her own right, and in 1320, he joined the other Magnates Scotiæ, in signing the famous letter to the Pope, in which the independence of Scotland was asserted. This great earl was the last of the Scandinavian sovereigns of the Orkneys. He was s. by his dau., the Countess Isabella, who carried the Earldoms of Orkney, and Caithness, together with the right of representation of her illustrious blood, into a great Scottish family, by marrying Malise, 6th Earl Palatine of Stratherne. The son of this marriage was

Malise, 7th Earl Palatine of Stratherne, and Earl of Orkney and Caithness, one of the most illustrious and powerful of the magnates of Scotland. He had no male issue. His dau. Isabella outlived all her sisters, and their descendants, and carried her extensive possessions and magnificent claims into the great Norman house of Sinclair, or De Sancto Claro. Isabella of Stratherne, m. William St. Clair or Sinclair, Lord of Rosslyn, and transmitted her right to the Earldom of Orkney to Henry her son. The remote ancestor of William St. Clair was a noble Norman baron, descended from Waleran, Count of St. Clair in Normandy, by a dau. of Richard, the Norman duke, who settled in Scotland in the reign of King David I., and obtained from that monarch, before the middle of the 12th century, the Lordship of Rosslyn, in the shire of Midlothian. His descendant William St. Clair, Lord of Rosslyn, the companion in arms of King Robert Bruce, perished along with James, Lord of Douglas, in battle against the Moors in Spain, in 1330, while carrying that monarch's heart to the Holy Sepulchre, in Jerusalem. The son of this hero,

William St. Clair, Lord of Rosslyn, m. Isabella, of Stratherne, dau. and eventual sole heir of Malise, 7th Earl Palatine of Stratherne, Earl of Orkney and Caithness, by whom he had issue,

I. Henry, who became Earl of Orkney.
II David, who had from his brother in 1391, the confirmation of Newburgh, and of some lands in Orkney and Shetland.
I. Margaret, wife 1st, in 1353, of Thomas, Earl of Angus and 2ndly, of Sir William St. Clair, of Hermandston. This is the first connexion that can be traced between the two distinct branches of the Norman race of De Sancto Claro.

Henry St. Clair, the eldest son, s. his father as Lord of Rosslyn, and in right of his mother he successfully prosecuted his claim to the Earldom of Orkney, which, being a female fief, was granted to him by Haco, 6th King of Norway, as heir of the old Scandinavian earls, in 1379 ; and he was immediately thereupon recognized as Earl of Orkney, by his native sovereign, Robert, 2nd King of Scotland. Earl Henry is said to have m. 1st, Florentia, a lady descended from the royal family of Denmark, by whom he had no issue. He m. 2ndly, Jean, dau. of Sir John Haliburton, Lord of Dirleton, by whom he had issue,

I. Henry, his successor.
II. John, who, in 1418, did homage to Eric, King of Norway, for Shetland.

III. William.
I. Elizabeth, wife of Sir John Drummond, of Stobhall, brother to Annabella, Queen of Robert III. of Scotland.
II. Mary, wife of Thomas Somerville, of Carnwath, ancestor to Lord Somerville.
III. Jean, wife of Sir John Forester, ancestor to Lord Forester.
IV. Marjory, wife of Sir David Menzies of Weem.
V. Beatrix, wife of James, 7th Earl of Douglas; in some genealogies this lady is stated to have been dau. to the 2nd earl.

Henry, Earl of Orkney, d. in 1400, having been survived by his mother Isabella, through whom he had claimed, and obtained the earldom. He was s. by his eldest son,

Henry St. Clair, 2nd Earl of Orkney, and Lord Sinclair. There is no doubt that this earl held the Barony of Sinclair as a subordinate title to his great earldom. He m. Egidia, dau. and heir of William Douglas, Lord of Nithsdale, by the Princess Egidia, dau. of Robert II., King of Scotland, who brought great possessions to her husband, and who survived him for many years, being alive in 1438. The earl d. in 1422, and was s. by his son,

William St. Clair, 3rd Earl of Orkney, and Lord Sinclair. In 1456 the Earl resigned to the crown his Lordship of Nithsdale, and received in compensation the Earldom of Caithness, which was granted to him, and his heirs female as well as male. King James III. having on his marriage with the Princess Margaret of Denmark, acquired from his father-in-law, King of Denmark and Norway, the over lordship of the Orkney Islands, compelled the earl to resign it as a royal fief to the crown in 1470, and gave him as a most inadequate compensation, the lands of Dysart and Ravensheugh, and the castle of Ravenscraig, co. Fife. He m. 1st, the Lady Elizabeth Douglas, dau. of Archibald, 4th Earl of Douglas, and Duke of Touraine, by the Princess Margaret, dau. of Robert III., King of Scotland. This lady had been previously twice m., 1st to John Stewart, Earl of Buchan, Constable of France, son of Robert, Duke of Albany, Regent of Scotland; and 2ndly, to Thomas Stewart, styled Earl of Garioch. By her the Earl of Orkney had issue, a son, William, ancestor to the Lords Sinclair, and a dau., Catherine, wife of Alexander, Duke of Albany, 2nd son of James II., King of Scotland. He m. 2ndly, Marjory, dau. of Alexander Sutherland, of Dunbeath, by Mariotta, dau of Donald, Lord of the Isles and Earl of Ross, by whom he had issue,

I. Oliver, founder of the cadet branch of St. Clair of Rosslyn, now extinct in the male line.
II. William, founder of the family of Sinclair, Earl of Caithness.
III. David.
IV. John, bishop of Caithness.
I. Eleanor, wife of John Stewart, Earl of Athol, half-brother of King James II.
II. Marian, wife of Sir John Houston of Houston.
III. Margaret, wife of David Boswell, of Balmuto.
IV. Marjory, wife of Andrew Leslie, Master of Rothes.

The earl being resolved to disinherit his eldest son William, resigned the Earldom of Caithness to the crown in 1476, and got a new grant of it with remainder to his 3rd son, William, and his heirs male and female. He d. in 1480, and at the time of his death was Earl of Caithness and Lord Sinclair. He left nothing to his eldest son, William, Master of Orkney and Caithness, to whom, during his life, he had given the Barony of Newburgh, in Aberdeenshire. He left his great estates of Rosslyn, Herbertshire. &c., to Sir Oliver, the eldest son of his 2nd marriage, and the Earldom of Caithness, with the estates thereto belonging to William, the 2nd son of his 2nd marriage. As he had not resigned the lordship of Sinclair, it went to his eldest son,

William, the disinherited Master of Orkney and Caithness, who thus became Lord Sinclair. His life was spent in a struggle with his more favoured brothers for a share of the paternal inheritance, and he compelled Sir Oliver to resign to him the estates of Dysart and Ravensheugh, and the castle of Ravenscraig, co. Fife; and he was solemnly recognized by Sir Oliver, and William, Earl of Caithness, as their chief and head of their house. Immediately after bringing this family arrangement to a conclusion, William the Master of Orkney and Caithness, d. in 1487, leaving by his wife, Lady Christian Leslie, dau. of George, 1st Earl of Rothes, a son and heir,

Henry Sinclair, who immediately upon his father's death was in 1488, recognized as a peer of parliament, by the king and parliament as Lord Sinclair. He was not then so created, but recognized as Lord Sinclair, his father, grandfather, and great-grandfather before him having held that title. As he was the first of the family who held that title alone, he is generally styled 1st Lord Sinclair, but he was in fact the 4th lord, dating the origin of the title from the 2nd Earl of O.kney. The Barony of Sinclair was a female title. It has been ruled in law in the case of the old lordship of Lindsay, which was attached to the Earldom of Crawford, that a lordship for which there was no patent, and which was held as an inferior title along with a great earldom, followed the course of succession of that superior title. It accordingly follows that the lordship of Sinclair was determined as to its succession by the great Earldoms of Orkney and Caithness, to which it was attached as an inferior title, and as they were not limited to male succession, but were descendible to heirs general, the lordship of Sinclair consequently was a peerage which descended to heirs-general. HENRY SINCLAIR, who thus in 1488 became 1st, or more properly, 4th Lord Sinclair, m. Margaret, dau. of Adam Hepburn, Lord Hailes, and sister of the 1st Earl of Bothwell, by whom he had issue, a son, and four daus.,

  I. WILLIAM, his heir.
  I. Catherine, wife of Sir David Wemyss, of Wemyss, ancestor to the Earls of Wemyss.
  II. Helen, wife of James, 4th Lord Ogilvie, of Airlie.
  III. Jean, wife of Alexander Lindsay, Master of Crawford, son of the 8th earl.
  IV. Agnes, wife of Patrick Hepburn, 3rd Earl of Bothwell; her son, James, 4th Earl of Bothwell, and Duke of Orkney, was 3rd husband of Mary Queen of Scots.

Henry, Lord Sinclair, was slain at Flodden in 1513, and was s. by his s n,
WILLIAM SINCLAIR, 2nd or more properly 5th Lord Sinclair. m. 1st, in 1515, Lady Elizabeth Keith, dau. of William, 3rd Earl Marischal, and descended from JAMES I., King of Scotland (widow of Colin, Master of Oliphant), by whom he had issue,

  I. HENRY.   II. Magnus.
  I. Margaret.

He m. 2ndly, Agnes Bruce. He d. in 1570, and was s. by his son, HENRY SINCLAIR, 3rd or more properly 6th Lord Sinclair. He m. 1st, Janet, dau. of Patrick, 6th Lord Lindsay, of the Byres, by whom he had issue,

  I. JAMES, Master of Sinclair.
  II. Patrick, of Balgreggie. He m. Catherine, dau. of James Boswell, of Balmuto, by whom he was ancestor of a line of Sinclairs of Balgreggie, which did not fail in the male line until 1710, in the person of John Sinclair of Balgreggie, who as he survived the last Lord Sinclair in the male line for thirty-four years, was during that long period head of the house of Sinclair, and if the title had been limited to heirs male, would have had an undoubted right to it. His family is now represented in the female line by Aytoun, of Inchdarnie.
  III. Andrew.   IV. Magnus.
  I. Helen, wife of Andrew Kinninmont, of Kinninmont.

Lord Sinclair m. 2ndly, Elizabeth, dau. of William, 7th Lord Forbes, by whom he had issue,

  I. Laurence.   II. William.
  I. Elizabeth, wife of Sir Duncan Campbell, of Glenorchy, ancestor to the Earls of Breadalbane.
  II. Jane.

Henry, Lord Sinclair, d. in 1601. His eldest son, James, Master of Sinclair, d. before his father in 1592. He m. Lady Isabella Leslie, dau. of Andrew, 4th Earl of Rothes, by whom he had issue, 1 HENRY; 2 James; 3 Patrick, all successively Lords Sinclair; 1 Catherine; 2 Margaret, wife of William, Lord Ber.iedale, eldest son of the 5th Earl of Caithness; her grandson was George, 6th Earl of Caithness. The 3rd lord was s. by his grandson,
HENRY SINCLAIR, 4th or more properly 7th Lord Sinclair, d. in 1602, and was s. by his brother,
JAMES SINCLAIR, 5th, or more properly 8th Lord Sinclair, who d. in 1607, and was s. by his brother,
PATRICK SINCLAIR, 6th, or more properly 9th Lord Sinclair. He m. Margaret, dau. of Sir John Cockburn, of Ormiston, Lord Justice Clerk of Scotland by whom he had issue,

  I. JOHN, his heir.
  II. Henry. d. unm. 1670.

And dying in 1615, was s. by his eldest son,
JOHN SINCLAIR, 7th or more properly, 10th Lord Sinclair. This nobleman took an active part in the political troubles of the times, and was a zealous royalist. He was taken prisoner at the battle of Worcester in 1651, and was detained in prison until 1660. He was the last lord of the male line of the family, and on his death in 1676, at the age of sixty-six, the honour of being male representative of the great house of Rosslyn and Orkney devolved on John Sinclair, of Balgreggie, until his death without male issue in 1710; while the ancient Sinclair peerage and the family estates were transmitted through the 7th lord's dau., Catherine, Mistress of Sinclair, to her son as heir general. The original constitution of the Sinclair peerage proves it to have been a female title; and this is confirmed by a long series

494

of charters from the crown to successive Lords Sinclair and their heirs-general. John, 7th lord, m., in 1631, Lady Mary Wemyss, eldest dau. of John, 1st Earl of Wemyss, by Jane, eldest dau. of Patrick, 7th Lord Gray, by whom he had an only dau. and heir, CATHERINE SINCLAIR, Mistress of Sinclair, who, 15 April, 1659, m. John St. Clair, eldest son of Sir John St. Clair, of Hermandston, by Elizabeth, dau. of Sir John Sinclair, Baronet of Stevenson, by whom she had issue, 1 HENRY, heir to his grandfather, b. 1660; 2 John. b. 1663. d. unm.; 1 Mary, b. 1666, d. unm. The Mistress of Sinclair d. in 1666, and was followed to the grave by her husband, while their son was in his minority. John, 7th Lord Sinclair, d. in 1676, and was s. in his title and estates by his daughter's son,
HENRY ST. CLAIR, who was thus heir male of Hermandston, and heir-general of Rosslyn and Orkney, uniting in his person the two great unconnected Norman lines De Sancto Claro. As the 7th lord had never surrendered or resigned his peerage to the crown, Henry St. Clair inherited it, along with the estates of Dysart and Ravenscraig, in right of his mother Catherine, the Mistress of Sinclair. During his minority he was under the guardianship of his paternal grandfather, Sir John St. Clair, of Hermandston, and in the year 1677, a new patent of the Sinclair peerage was obtained from King CHARLES II., purporting to be founded on a designation made by John, 7th lord, in Henry's favour; and introducing an entirely new series of heirs, excluding all the heirs male and female of the ancient Lords Sinclair, and substituting in place of them, the cadet branches of the entirely alien family of Hermandston. By this patent the peerage was granted, in default of the male heirs of Henry, Lord Sinclair's own body, in remainder to the heirs male of his father, the cadet branches of the family of Hermandston, who were of a totally different race, and in no way descended from the Lords Sinclair. But previous to the granting of this new patent there was no resignation to the crown of the original peerage of Sinclair. That peerage therefore continued to exist, and was, in no way affected by the limitations of the patent of 1677, which must be held to convey a different peerage, while the old peerage stands exactly on the footing on which it stood anterior to the new patent, and the right to which is vested in the undoubted representative and heir-general of Henry, 8th or 11th Lord Sinclair, viz., John Anstruther Thomson, of Charleton, who is thus, de jure, Lord Sinclair, of the original creation. Henry St. Clair. 8th or more properly 11th Lord Sinclair, m. in 1680, Grizzel, dau. of Sir James Cockburn, Bart., of Cockburn, by whom he had issue,

  I. JOHN, of whom hereafter.
  II. JAMES, of whom hereafter.
  III. William, a major in the army, d. s. p. in 1762.
  IV. David, d. young.
  V. Henry, d. unm. in 1756.
  VI. Matthew, d. unm. in 1747.
  I. Grizzel, of whom hereafter as carrying on the line of the family as heir-general.
  II. Catherine, b. 1685, wife of Sir John Erskine. Bart., of Alva. Her son, Sir Henry Erskine, Bart., m. Janet Wedderburn, sister to the Lord Chancellor, Lord Loughborough, created Earl of Rosslyn, with remainder to her son, Sir James Erskine, Bart, who s. his maternal uncle as 2nd Earl of Rosslyn, and s. by special destination to the estates of Dysart and Rosslyn, on the death of his father's cousin, Colonel Paterson St. Clair, in 1789, on which he assumed the additional name of St. Clair. His son is James Alexander, 3rd and present Earl of Rosslyn.
  III. Margaret, wife of Sir David Baird, Bart., of Newbythe. Her son d. s. p.
  IV. Elizabeth, wife of David, 3rd Earl of Wemyss, by whom she had issue, two daus. 1 Elizabeth, wife of William, 16th Earl of Sutherland; 2 Margaret, wife of James, 7th Earl of Moray.

By descent from these three daus. of the 8th Lord Sinclair, Grizzel, Catherine, and Elizabeth, John Anstruther Thomson, is heir-general of the Earls of Orkney and the Lords Sinclair, through the eldest, while the Earl of Rosslyn is representative of the 2nd, and the Duke of Sutherland, is representative of the 3rd. Henry, 8th Lord Sinclair, d. in 1723, and was s. in the family estates by his eldest son,
JOHN ST. CLAIR, Master of Sinclair, born 1683, who having been engaged in the rebellion in 1715, was attainted and never assumed the title of Lord Sinclair. In 1735, he had the satisfaction of purchasing the ancient ancestral castle of Rosslyn from the last male heir of that cadet branch, and he added it to the family estates. He m. 1st, in 1733, Lady Margaret Stewart, dau. of James, 5th Earl of Galloway and widow of James, 5th Earl of Southesk, by whom he had no issue. He m. 2ndly, in 1750, Amelia, dau. of Lord George Murray, and sister of the 3rd Duke of Athol (she m. 2ndly, 1754, James Farquharson, of Invercauld) by whom he had no issue, and dying in 1750, he was s. by his brother,
JAMES ST. CLAIR, a general in the army, and de jure 9th

Lord Sinclair, although he never assumed the title; he was a distinguished diplomatist, as well as a military commander, and was ambassador at the courts of Turin and Vienna. During forty years until the time of his death he was a member of the British parliament. He m. Janet, dau. of Sir David Dalrymple, Bart., of Hailes, and widow of Sir John Baird, Baronet, by whom he had no issue, and dying in 1762, he was s. by his nephew Colonel James Paterson, son of his eldest sister,

The Hon. Grizzel St. Clair, eldest dau. of Henry, 8th Lord Sinclair. She m. John Paterson, of Preston Hall, eldest son of the Most Rev. John Paterson, last archbishop of Glasgow, and elder brother of Sir William Paterson, 1st baronet of Eccles. She d. in 1737, and had issue a son, James, and a dau., Margaret, of whom hereafter. Her son,

James Paterson, a colonel in the army, on succeeding to the Dysart and Rosslyn estates, on the death of his uncle General St. Clair, assumed the name of St. Clair, as heir general of the family. He was moreover entitled to the original Sinclair peerage which has continued dormant since the death of the 8th lord. Whilst the peerage confirmed by the patent of 1677, by King Charles II., was claimed in 1780, by Charles St. Clair, of Hermandston, descended from a younger son of Sir John St. Clair of Hermandston, but in no way either descended from, or connected with the original Lords Sinclair. He, being included in the remainder of the patent of 1677, had his claim allowed by the House of Lords, and in 1782, became Lord Sinclair, being the first of his race that has borne the title. Colonel Paterson St. Clair, d. unm. in 1789. He was s. in the Dysart and Rosslyn estates by his cousin, Sir James Erskine, Baronet, afterwards 2nd Earl of Rosslyn, according to a special destination; whilst he was s. as heir-general of the house of Sinclair, by John Anstruther, his grandnephew, grandson of his sister,

Margaret Paterson, who in 1744, m. John Thomson, of Charleton, son of John Thomson, of Charleton, by Rachel, dau. of — Brymer, of Edrom, and by him she had issue, i. Rachel, wife of Colonel Macdonald, of Lochgarry, and d. in early life, s. p.; ii. Grizzel Maria, heiress of Charleton.

Grizzel-Maria Thomson, sole heiress of Charleton, m. Col. John Anstruther, 2nd son of Sir Philip Anstruther, 2nd baronet of Balcaskie, by Catharine Hay, dau. of Lord Alexander Hay of Spott, son of John Hay, 1st Marquess of Tweeddale, by Lady Jean Scott, dau. of Frances, Earl of Buccleugh. Colonel John Anstruther was 18th in direct paternal descent from William de Candela, Lord of Anstruther, in 1100, the founder of the house of Anstruther, in Scotland. By John Anstruther, she had issue, a son, John, her heir, and two daus., one of whom d. unm., and the other was wife of her cousin, General James Durham of Largo.

John Anstruther, on succeeding to his mother's estate of Charleton, assumed the name of Thomson, and became John Anstruther Thomson of Charleton. On the death of his grand-uncle, Colonel James Paterson St. Clair, of Dysart and Rosslyn, he became heir-general of the Earls of Orkney and Lords Sinclair, and inherited the claim to the original Sinclair peerage. He was also heir-general of the St. Clairs of Hermandston, Lord Sinclair of that family being descended from a younger son. He m. Clementina, only dau. of the Right Hon. William Adam, M.P., of Blair Adam, baron of Exchequer, lord chief commissioner of the Jury Court, lord-lieutenant of the co. Kinross, by the Hon. Eleanor Elphinstone, dau. of Charles, 10th Lord Elphinstone, by Lady Clementina Fleming, dau. and heir of John Fleming, 6th Earl of Wigton, and heir-general of the Earls of Wigton, and Marischal and Perth. By Clementina Adam, John Anstruther Thomson had issue,

i. John, his heir.
ii. William, a colonel in the army. commander of the body guard of the governor-general of India, m. Isabella, dau. of Col. Steele, by whom he has issue a son and a dau. He d. 1865.
1 Eleanor, wife of James Montgomery eldest son of Archibald Montgomery of Whim, son of Sir James Montgomery, Bart., of Stanhope, lord chief baron of exchequer.
ii. Louisa.   iii. Clementina.
iv. Mary, wife of the Rev. A. Ramsay Campbell, rector of Aston, son of Sir Archibald Campbell, Bart., of Garscube, a lord of session in Scotland.
v. Jean St. Clair.

John Anstruther Thomson was s. by his eldest son,

John Anstruther Thomson, now of Charleton, heir-general of the Earls of Orkney and Lords Sinclair, and 20th in descent from William de Candela, Lord of Anstruther, b. 1819, an officer in the 9th lancers and 13th light dragoons. He m. in August, 1852, Caroline-Maria-Agnes-Robina, only child of the Rev. John Hamilton Gray of Carntyne, by Elizabeth-Caroline, eldest dau. of James Raymond Johnstone of Alva. John Hamilton Gray is only son of Robert Gray of Carntyne, representative of Gray of Dalmarnock, and Hamilton of Newton, cadet of Hamilton, Bart., of Silverton Hill, by Mary-Anne, dau. of G. Hamilton, of Westburn, by Agnes Dundas, heiress of Duddingston, and co-heir-general of the Earls of Crawford and Lindsay and Viscounts Garnock. James Raymond Johnstone of Alva, was grandson of Sir James Johnstone, 3rd Bart., of Westerhall. He m. Elizabeth-Mary Cholmeley, dau. of Montague Cholmeley of Easton, and sister of Sir Montague Cholmeley, Bart. The issue of this marriage is

i. John St. Clair, b. June, 1853.
ii. Charles-Frederick St. Clair, b. May, 1855.
iii. William, b. 1859.
i. Clementina-Caroline.
ii. Rosia-Mary.

Original Barony of Sinclair.

The title of Lord Sinclair was held by Henry Sinclair, 2nd Earl of Orkney, as a subordinate title, along with his earldom. In a confirmation by the Duke of Albany, Regent of Scotland, in 1407, of the charter of the Barony of Herbertshi e, from Archibald, Earl of Douglas, to Henry, Earl of Orkney, he is styled Lord Sinclair. In the grant by King James II., in 1455, of the Earldom of Caithness to William, 3rd Earl of Orkney, son of Earl Henry, he is styled Lord Sinclair: and again, in a charter by King James III. to the same nobleman, in 1471.

In the settlement between William Sinclair, Master of Orkney and Caithness, eldest son of Earl William, and his brother Oliver, in 1481, the former is styled Lord Sinclair; and in a charter of confirmation to this nobleman in 1487, he is styled Lord Sinclair.

On 26 January, 1488-9, Henry Sinclair, the son and heir of William, Master of Orkney, was recognized by the king and parliament of Scotland as Lord Sinclair, "his grandsire and his father having been Lords Sinclair." He was not then created Lord Sinclair. He was then recognized as actually holding a title which he had derived from his ancestors. He was the 4th lord, although he is generally reckoned as the 1st, he being the first of the family who did not hold that title in conjunction with another of superior dignity. Thus, the antiquity of the Sinclair peerage, dating prior to 1407, leads to the presumption that it was one which descended to heirs general.

The Earldom of Orkney, and also the Earldom of Caithness (as originally constituted) were titles that descended to heirs general. And as the peerage of Sinclair was attached to them as an inferior title, it must be presumed to have followed the course of succession of those superior titles. This sequence of an inferior title without a patent to the greater titles to which it was attached, has been ruled in law in the case of the ancient Barony of Lindsay.

All the grants and fiefs given to the Sinclair family as Earls of Orkney, Earls of Caithness (as originally constituted), and Lords Sinclair were invariably given to heirs general.

These grants and arguments tell in favour of the peerage of Sinclair having been a title which descended to heirs ge eral, provided that there was no subsequent resignation of the original peerage to the crown, of which there is no trace whatever.

Henry, 4th, or as he is generally reckoned, 1st Lord Sinclair, fell at Flodden in 1513. And the title was transmitted in regular succession to his descendant John, 10th, or as he is generally reckoned, 7th lord, who as his father in 1615. He was devoted to the cause of Charles I., and suffered severely for his principles both in his person and in his fortune. He had an only dau. and sole heir, Catherine, Mistress of Sinclair, who, in 1659, m. John St. Clair, eldest son of Sir John St. Clair of Hermandston, the head of a very ancient and distinguished family of the same name, but in no way descended from the Lords Sinclair, or even from the house of Rosslyn and Orkney. She pre-deceased her father in 1666, and her husband did not long survive her. She left, with two other children that had no succession, a son, Henry St. Clair, heir to his grandfather, John, 7th Lord Sinclair. This nobleman d. in 1676, leaving his grandson, Henry, as his heir general, and his 2nd cousin, John Sinclair of Balgreggie as his heir male, who survived him until 1710, when he also d. without male issue. John, Lord Sinclair was s. in his title and estates by his grandson, Henry, at that time a minor, having been b. in 1660, and under the guardianship of his paternal grandfather, Sir John St. Clair of Hermandston.

John, 7th Lord Sinclair, had made a settlement of his honours and estates in favour of his grandson and heir-general, Henry. As the title was one descendible to heirs-general, no opposition was offered to his succession by the heir male, John Sinclair of Balgreggie, who would have been clearly entitled to it, if it had been restricted to heirs male.

immediately upon the death of John, 7th Lord Sinclair, a patent was procured in 1677, from King CHARLES II., which conferred the title of Lord Sinclair upon the minor HENRY; at the same time that it altogether changed the line of succession to the peerage, and introduced a new and alien set of heirs. This patent states that it proceeds upon a designation by John, 7th Lord Sinclair, of his honours and estates in favour of his grandson, Henry. It is the royal confirmation of the designation or nomination of the deceased lord, which was unaccompanied by any resignation or surrender to the crown. It conveyed a Barony of Sinclair, with the precedence of the original barony, to a totally new line of heirs, limiting it, in the first instance, to the male line of Henry, the patentee, failing which, to the collateral younger branches of his father's family of Hermandston, who were total aliens to the house of Sinclair, to the exclusion of his own heirs general, and of all the heirs of the original lords. It seems clear that this confirmation or new creation in 1677, could not exclude the right of the previous heirs, owing to the want of a resignation, by which alone they could be barred. The patent does not found upon a resignation; but upon something quite different, viz., a "designation" or nomination, by John, Lord Sinclair. Therefore we may conclude that there was no resignation; otherwise it would have been stated in the patent. No new grant of the sovereign could have the slightest effect in altering the destination of the original dignity, so long as that dignity had not been actually resigned by the holders. There is not the slightest pretence for holding that such a resignation took place on the part of John. 7th Lord Sinclair, and therefore the title was actually vested in his grandson, Henry, at the time when the new patent was passed, and the dignity which he so inherited, must duly descend to his posterity according to the original course of succession, which was to heirs general. No resignation can be proved, and no constructive resignation can be presumed. There is not the smallest ground for supposing that John, Lord Sinclair's "designation" extended to the younger branches of his son-in-law's family of Hermandston, who were absolute aliens. It is indeed clear that it did not do so from the terms of the patent itself. The preamble of the patent only states the "designation" of the 7th lord as having been in favour of his grandson, and not a word is said of the family of Hermandston. The introduction of the cadet branches of that family into the body of the new patent, while they are excluded from its preamble makes the patent inconsistent with itself. In the preamble the king limits his reason for granting the patent to his favour for John, 7th Lord Sinclair, and his desire to reward his services in the person of his descendants. And yet in the body of the patent there is an alien race introduced, who have nothing to do with John, Lord Sinclair, to the exclusion of his descendants.

The new patent of 1677 granted to Henry, the heir of the deceased lord, then a minor and under the guardianship of his paternal grandfather, seems to have been procured through that gentleman's influence, in order to divert the peerage into his own family. And it must, in fact, be regarded as conveying a separate peerage, and in no way interfering with, or controlling, the succession to the ancient original Sinclair peerage which existed prior to 1407, and which was solemnly recognized in 1488. There is no mention of a resignation and nothing is more certain than that without that mention in the most specific terms, no resignation can exist. The original Sinclair peerage, therefore, must be held to exist although dormant, and its undoubted heir is the heir-general of the original lords, viz., John Anstruther Thomson of Charleton.

HENRY ST. CLAIR, the 8th Lord Sinclair, who inherited the original peerage as heir-general of his grandfather, and on whom a peerage was conferred by patent, by King CHARLES II. in 1677, during his minority, had numerous issue. Besides several sons who predeceased their elder brothers and left no succession, he had,

1. JOHN, Master of Sinclair, his heir.
II. JAMES, who s. his brother.
1. Grizzel, who carried on the line of heirs-general.
II. Catherine wife of Sir John Erskine, Bart., of Alva. Her grandson, Sir James Erskine, Bart., s. to the Sinclair estates by special entail on the death of Colonel James Paterson St. Clair, in 1789. He became Earl of Rosslyn, and his son is James-Alexander, present Earl of Rosslyn.
III. MARY, wife of Sir William Baird, Bart., of Newbythe. Her line failed.
IV. Elizabeth, wife of David, 3rd Earl of Wemyss. Her heir is the Duke of Sutherland.

Henry, 8th Lord Sinclair, d. in 1723, and was s. by his son,
JOHN, Master of Sinclair, who, having been attainted during his brother's lifetime, for his share in the rebellion in 1715, never assumed the title. Dying s. p. in 1750, he was s. by his brother,

496

THE HON. JAMES ST. CLAIR, a general in the army, and a distinguished ambassador, and during the greater part of his life a leading member of the House of Commons. He was de jure 9th Lord Sinclair, but he never assumed the title, and he d. s. p. in 1762. On his death, the male issue of Henry, 8th Lord Sinclair became extinct; and according to the limitations in the patent of 1677, the claim to the peerage which that patent conferred, opened to the cadet branches of the St Clairs of Hermandston, and was brought forward in 1780, by Charles St. Clair, who in 1782 became Lord Sinclair in virtue of the patent of 1677. While the right to the original unresigned peerage of Sinclair was vested in the heir-general of the ancient lords, Colonel James Paterson, only son of the
HON. GRIZZEL ST. CLAIR, eldest dau. of Henry, 8th lord, wife of John Paterson of Prestonhall, eldest son of the Most Reverend John Paterson, last archbishop of Glasgow, and elder brother of Sir William Paterson, 1st Baronet of Eccles. She d. in 1737, leaving issue, a son, JAMES, and a dau., Margaret, wife of John Thomson of Charleton.
JAMES PATERSON was a colonel in the army, and on the death of his uncle, the Hon. General James St. Clair, he s. to the Sinclair estate, became heir-general of the ancient Lords Sinclair, and took the name of St. Clair. Dying in 1789, he was s. in the representation of the Lords Sinclair, and in the claim to their ancient peerage, by his grand-nephew,
JOHN ANSTRUTHER THOMSON of Charleton, grandson and heir of his sister,
MARGARET PATERSON, wife of John Thomson, of Charleton, by whom she had a dau. and heir,
GRIZZEL MARIA THOMSON, heiress of Charleton, wife of Col. John Anstruther, 2nd son of Sir Philip Anstruther, Bart., of Balcaskie, by Catherine, dau. of Lord Alexander Hay, son of John, 1st Marquess of Tweeddale, by Lady Jean Scott, dau. of the Earl of Buccleugh. By him she had a son,
JOHN ANSTRUTHER, who, on inheriting his mother's estates of Charleton, took the name of Thomson, and on the death of his grand-uncle, Col. Paterson St. Clair, became heir-general and representative of the Lords Sinclair.

SKEFFINGTON—EARL OF MASSEREENE.

By Letters Patent, dated 16 July, 1756.

Lineage.

SIR WILLIAM SKEFFINGTON, Knt, of Fiskerwick, co. Stafford, who was appointed by HENRY VIII., in 1529, his Majesty's commissioner to Ireland, arrived there in the August of that year, empowered to restrain the exactions of the soldiers, to call a parliament, and to provide that the possessions of the clergy might be subject to bear their part of the public expense. Sir William was subsequently a very distinguished political personage in Ireland; and d. in the government of that kingdom, as lord deputy, in December, 1535. His great-grandson,
JOHN SKEFFINGTON, Esq., of Fisherwick, co. Stafford, m. Alice, 7th dau. of Sir Thomas Cave, of Stanford, and was father of
SIR WILLIAM SKEFFINGTON, Knt., of Fisherwick, who was created a Baronet by CHARLES I. He m. Elizabeth, dau. of Richard Dering, Esq., and had issue,

JOHN, 2nd baronet, whose son,
WILLIAM, 3rd baronet, d. s. p.
RICHARD, 4th baronet.
Elizabeth, m. to Michael Biddulph, Esq.
Cicely, m. to Edward Mytton, Esq.
Mary, m. to Richard Pyott, Esq.
Heather, m. to Sir W. Bowyer, Bart.
Lettice, m. to John Bayly, Esq.
Alice, m. to Alexander Walthall, Esq.

The 2nd son,
SIR RICHARD SKEFFINGTON, Bart., was father of
SIR JOHN SKEFFINGTON, 5th Bart.; who m. Mary, only dau. and heir of
SIR JOHN CLOTWORTHY, Knt., of Antrim, who, for his activity and zeal in promoting the Restoration of CHARLES II., was elevated to the peerage of Ireland, 21 November, 1660, as Baron of Loughneagh, and VISCOUNT MASSEREENE, with remainder, in default of male issue, to his son-in-law, the said Sir John Skeffington, Bart., and his issue male by MARY, his said wife; in default of which, to the heirs-general of the said Sir John Clotworthy. The viscount d. in 1665, and the honours devolved, according to the reversionary proviso, upon the said
SIR JOHN SKEFFINGTON, Bart., as 2nd viscount; who d. in 1695, leaving with two daus., Mary, m. to Sir Charles Hoghton, and Margaret, m. to Sir George St. George, Bart., an only son,

CLOTWORTHY SKEFFINGTON, 3rd viscount. This nobleman m-'n March, 1684, Rachael, dau. of Sir Edward Hungerford, K.B., of Farley Castle, co. Somerset, and had issue,

t. CLOTWORTHY, his successor.
II. John, d. unm., 1741.
I. Mary, m. to the Right Rev. Edward Smyth, D.D., bishop of Down and Connor.
II. Frances-Diana.
III. Rachael, m. 1st, to Randal, 4th Earl of Antrim; and 2ndly, to Robert-Hawkins Magill, Esq.; and d. 13 April, 1739.
IV. Jane, m. to Sir Hans Hamilton, Bart.

His lordship d. 14 March, 1713, and was s. by his son,
CLOTWORTHY SKEFFINGTON, 4th viscount; who m. 9 September, 1713, Lady Catherine Chichester, eldest dau. of Arthur, 4th Earl of Donegal, and by her ladyship (who d. 1 July, 1749) had issue,

CLOTWORTHY, his heir.
Arthur. M.P. for the co. Antrim; d. s. p. 8 April, 1747, buried at St. Mary's, Dublin.
John, in holy orders; m. a dau. of Henry Thornton, Esq., of Muff; and d. 25 December, 1753, leaving a son, John.
Hungerford, M.P., d. in 1768.
Hugh, d. 1768.
Catherine, m. 3 January, 1739, to Arthur, Viscount Done-raile; and d. 3 April, 1751.
Rachel, d. unm.

The viscount d. 11 February, 1738, and was s. by his eldest son,
CLOTWORTHY SKEFFINGTON, 5th viscount; who was created, 16 July, 1756, EARL OF MASSEREENE. His lordship m. 1st, 16 March, 1741, Anne, eldest dau. of Richard Daniel, dean of Down, but by that lady (who d. 27 March, 1740,) had no issue; he m. 2ndly, 25 November, 1741, Anne, only dau. of Henry Eyre, Esq., of Rowter, co. Derby, by whom he had,

CLOTWORTHY, his successor.
HENRY, successor to his brother.
William-John, constable of the castle of Dublin; d. unm. 10 January, 1814.
CHICHESTER, who inherited as 4th earl.
Alexander, d. s. p.
Elizabeth, m. to Robert. 1st Earl of Leitrim.
Catherine, m. 7 June, 1784, to Francis, 1st Earl of Llandaff; and d. 9 February, 1796.

The earl d. 14 September, 1757, and was s. by his eldest son,
CLOTWORTHY SKEFFINGTON, 2nd earl, b. 28 January, 1742. This nobleman m. 1st, in August, 1789, Mademoiselle Mary-Anne Barcier; and 2ndly, Elizabeth Lane, but had no issue. He d. 28 February, 1805 (his widow m. 2ndly, George Doran, Esq.; and 3rdly, the Hon. George Massy), and was s. by his brother,
HENRY SKEFFINGTON, 3rd earl; who d. unm. 12 June, 1811, when the peerage devolved on his next surviving brother,
CHICHESTER SKEFFINGTON, 4th earl. This nobleman m. in 1780, Lady Harriet Jocelyn, eldest dau. of Robert, 1st Earl of Roden, by whom he had an only dau., Harriet. The earl d. in 1816, when the earldom and baronetcy EXPIRED, while the Viscounty of Massereene and the Barony of Loughneagh devolved upon his only dau., HARRIET, as VISCOUNTESS MASSEREENE. Her ladyship m. 29 November, 1810, Thomas-Henry Foster, Viscount Ferrard (who assumed the name of Skeffington), and had issue (see BURKE's Extant Peerage).

Arms—Quarterly: 1st and 4th, arg., three bulls' heads, erased, sa., armed, or, for SKEFFINGTON; 2nd and 3rd, az., a chev., erm., between three chaplets, or, for CLOTWORTHY.

SMITH, OR SMYTH—BARONS AND VIS-COUNTS CARRINGTON.

Barony, by Letters Patent, dated 31 October, 1643.
Irish Viscounty, by Letters Patent, dated 4 November, 1643.

Lineage.

From SIR MICHAEL CARINGTON, Knt., standard bearer to King RICHARD I. in the Holy Land, descended
JOHN CARINGTON, who, in the beginning of HENRY IV.'s reign, having stoutly adhered to the deposed monarch, RICHARD II., was obliged to expatriate himself, and after residing some time abroad, is stated to have assumed for security the very general surname of SMITH. From this gentleman claimed descent
JOHN SMITH, Esq., who being the lord treasurer's remembrancer in the exchequer, was constituted, in the 38th HENRY VIII., 2nd baron of that court. This learned person m. Anne, dau. and heir of John Harewell, Esq., of Wotton Waven, co. Warwick, and from that union sprang
FRANCIS SMITH, Esq., of Ashby Folville, co. Leicester, and of

Wootton Waven, co. Warwick, who m. Maria, dau. and heir of John Morton, Esq., of Ashby Folville, and d. 3 September, 1606, leaving a son,
GEORGE SMITH, Esq., of Ashby Folville, who m. Anne, dau. of Sir Thomas Giffard, of Chillington, co. Stafford, Knt., and d. 31 July, 1607, leaving with other issue, a son,
SIR FRANCIS SMITH, of Wootton Waven and Ashby Folville, Knt., who m. Anne, dau. of Thomas Markham, of Allerton, co. Notts., Esq., and d. 6 May, 1629, æt. fifty-nine, and was buried at Ashby Folville. He had, besides daus., four sons,

I. CHARLES (Sir), of whom presently.
II. Thomas (Sir), of Broxton, Knt.   III. Francis.
IV. John (Sir), slain ex parte Regis, at the battle near Alresford, Hants, 30 March, and was buried 1 April, 1644, at Christ Church, Oxford.

Sir Francis Smith's will, which bears date 28 February, 1628, was proved 8 October, 1629. His eldest son,
SIR CHARLES SMITH, Knt., was, in consideration of his fidelity to King CHARLES I., elevated to the peerage 31 October, 1643, as LORD CARRINGTON, BARON OF WOOTTON WAVEN, co. Warwick, and was advanced 4 November following, to the dignity of VISCOUNT CARRINGTON, of Barrefore or Burford, in Connaught, in the peerage of Ireland. His lordship m. Elizabeth, dau. of Sir John Caryll, Knt., of South Harting, in Sussex, and had issue,

FRANCIS, his successor.   CARYLL, d. s. p., m.
CHARLES, successor to his brother.
Mary, m. to Sir George Wintour, Knt., of Huddington.
Lucy, } d. unm.
Anne, }
Margaret, m. to Sir Francis Hungate, Bart. of Huddleston, in Yorkshire.
Mary, d. unm.

Lord Carrington having occasion to visit France, and lodging at Pontoise, was there barbarously murdered by one of his own servants, 21 February, 1664, for the sake of his money and jewels; and his remains were interred in the church at that place, under a marble tomb erected to his memory. His lordship was s. by his eldest son,
FRANCIS SMITH, 2nd viscount, and Baron Carrington. This nobleman m. 1st, Juliana, dau. of Sir Thomas Walmesley, of Dunkenhalgh, in Lancashire, by whom he had an only son,

CHARLES, who d. in infancy.

His lordship m. 2ndly, Lady Anne Herbert, dau. of William, Marquess of Powis, but had no issue. His will, dated 18 January, 1700, was proved 30 April, 1701. He was s. by his brother,
CHARLES SMITH, 3rd Viscount and Baron Carrington, who m. Frances, 2nd dau. and co-heir of Sir John Pate, Bart. of Sysonby, co. Leicester, d. s. p. May 1706, and was buried at Ashby Folville. With him the peerage honours became EXTINCT.

Arms—Arg., a cross, gu., between four peacocks, az.

SMYTHE—VISCOUNT STRANGFORD.
(See ADDENDA.)

SOMERIE—BARON DUDLEY.

By Writ of Summons, dated 10 March, 1308.

Lineage.

SIR JOHN DE SOMERIE (lineally descended from the marriage of John de Somerie, with Hawyse, sister and heir of Gervase Pagnell, Lord of Dudley, co. Stafford), was for his services in the Scottish wars, temp. EDWARD I. and EDWARD II., summoned to parliament as a Baron,* from 10 March, 1308, to 14 March, 1322. His lordship d. in the latter year s. p., when his barony became EXTINCT, and his castles and lands devolved upon his sisters, as co-heirs, thus,

---

* Although this barony is uniformly considered to be that of "DUDLEY," it appears very questionable if such is the proper designation. That antecedent to the latter part of the reign of EDWARD I., the tenure of the castle of Dudley constituted the family of SOMERIE, barons by tenure, can scarcely be doubted; but that such tenure did not establish a right in the possessor of the castle to demand a writ of summons to parliament, may be inferred from this fact, that John de Somerie, who was first summoned in 1308 (1st EDWARD II.) and who continued to be regularly summoned to 1322 (15th EDWARD II.) is never once designated as "DE DUDLEY," but is merely described as "Johanni de Somery."—NICOLAS.

MARGARET, *m.* to John de Sutton. had the Castle of Dudley, with the manor of Seggesley, chase of Pensnet, and manor of New Synford Regis, co. Stafford; as also the town of Dudley (*see* Sutton, Barons Dudley).

JOANE, *m.* to Thomas Botetourt, eldest son and heir of John, Lord Botetourt, had the manors of Bradfield, Solcham, and Rastenden, co. Berks: with Rowley-Somery, and other lands in Staffordshire (*see* Botetourt, Barons Botetourt).

Arms—Or, two lioncels passant, az.

SOMERS—BARON SOMERS.

By Letters Patent, dated 2 December, 1697.

Lineage.

JOHN SOMERS, or SOMMERS, Gent., of Clifton on Severn, an attorney in the city of Worcester, *m.* in 1648, Catherine, youngest dau. of John Severne, Esq., of Powyck, co. Worcester (ancestor of the Severnes, of Wallop Hall, co. Salop), and by her (who *d.* in 1709) left at his decease, January, 1680-1, one son and two daus., viz.,

  I. JOHN, LORD SOMERS.
    I. Mary, *m.* Charles Cocks, Esq., M.P., and had issue.
    II. Elizabeth, *m.* Sir Joseph Jekyll, master of the rolls; and *d. s. p.* 1745.

The son and heir,

JOHN SOMERS, *b.* at Worcester, in 1652, having been brought up to the higher grade in the legal profession, acquired such reputation as an advocate, that he was engaged in the important case of the Seven Bishops, *temp.* JAMES II., and his speech upon that occasion will ever be regarded as one of the boldest, most impressive, and constitutional, delivered at the bar. After the Revolution, Mr. Somers was appointed successively (1689) solicitor, and (1692) attorney-general, and received the usual honour of knighthood. In 1695, he became Lord Keeper, and in 1697 was constituted Lord Chancellor of England, and elevated to the peerage as LORD SOMERS, BARON OF EVESHAM, *co. Worcester.* Of this great and learned personage, Walpole, in his *Catalogue of Noble Authors*, observes, "That Lord Somers was one of those divine men, who, like a Chapel in a Palace, remain unprofaned, while all the rest is tyranny, corruption and folly: and that all the traditional accounts of him, the historians of the last age, and its best authors, *represent him* as the most uncorrupt lawyer, and the honestest statesman; a master orator; a genius of the finest taste; and as a patriot of the noblest and most extensive views; as a man who dispensed blessings by his life, and planned them for posterity: at once the model of Addison, and the touchstone of Swift." Macaulay considers him in some respects the greatest man of the age in which he lived: "He was," says that brilliant historian, "equally eminent as a jurist and as a politician, as an orator, and as a writer. His speeches have perished: but his State Papers remain and are models of terse, luminous and dignified eloquence. In truth, he united all the qualities of a great judge, an intellect comprehensive, quick and acute, diligence, integrity, patience, suavity. In council, the calm wisdom which he possessed in a measure rarely found among men of parts so quick, and of opinions so decided as his, acquired for him the authority of an oracle." Macaulay winds up his panegyric in these words: "He was at once a munificent and a severely judicious patron of genius and learning. Locke owed opulence to Somers. By Somers, Addison was drawn forth from a cell in a college. In distant countries, the name of Somers was mentioned with respect and gratitude by great scholars and poets who had never seen his face."

Lord Somers survived, however, his great mental powers, and *d.* in dotage, *unm.*, April 1716, when the Barony of Somers became EXTINCT, and his estates devolved upon his sisters as co-heirs, the elder of whom,

MARY SOMERS, *m.* Charles Cocks, Esq., M.P., in 1692, for the city of Worcester, and had issue,

  1 JAMES COCKS, M.P., of Bruckmans, Herts, whose only son, James, was killed at St. Cas, on the coast of France, 11 September, 1758.
  2 JOHN COCKS, of Castleditch, co. Hereford, whose eldest son and successor,
    CHARLES COCKS, Esq., of Castleditch, M.P., was created a baronet in 1772, and elevated to the peerage as LORD SOMERS, *Baron of Evesham,* in 1784. (See BURKE'S *Extant Peerage.*)
  1 Katherine Cocks, *m.* to James Harris, Esq., of Salisbury.
  2 Margaret Cocks, *m.* to Philip Yorke, 1st Earl of Hardwicke, lord chancellor.

Arms—Vert, a fosse dancetté, orm.

SOMERSET—VISCOUNT SOMERSET.

By Letters Patent, dated 8 December, 1626.

Lineage.

THE HON. SIR THOMAS SOMERSET, K.B., 3rd son of Edward, 4th Earl of Worcester, was raised to the peerage of Ireland, as VISCOUNT SOMERSET, *of Cashel, co. Tipperary,* 8 December, 1626. His lordship *m.* Eleanor, dau. of David, Viscount Buttevant, and had an only dau., Elizabeth, who *d. unm.* Lord Somerset *d.* in 1651, and with him the title became EXTINCT.

Arms—Quarterly: France and England, within a bordure, compony, arg. and az.

SOMERVILLE—BARONS SOMERVILLE.

(*See* ADDENDA.)

SONDES—EARL OF FEVERSHAM.

By Letters Patent, dated 8 April, 1676.

Lineage.

SIR GEORGE SONDES, Bart., of Lees Court, co. Kent, was elevated to the peerage, in consideration of the services he had rendered to King CHARLES I., by letters patent, dated 8 April, 1676, in the dignities of *Baron Throwley, Viscount Sondes, of Lees Court,* and EARL OF FEVERSHAM, with remainder, failing his own male issue, to Lewis, Lord Duras, the husband of his elder dau. His lordship *m.* 1st, Jane, dau. and heir of Sir Ralph Freeman, Knt., by whom he had three sons,

  I. Freeman, who *d.* young.
  II. George, inhumanly murdered in his bed by his younger brother,
  III. Freeman, who suffered death for the atrocious deed of fratricide.

The earl *m.* 2ndly, Mary, dau. of Sir William Villiers, of Brokesby, co. Leicester, Bart., and had two daus.,

Mary, *m.* to Lewis, Lord Duras, K.G. (*see* that dignity), and *d. s. p.* in 1709.
Catherine, *m.* to Lewis Watson, Lord Rockingham. This lady succeeded, on the decease of her sister, *s. p.*, to the entire fortune of her father.

His lordship *d.* in 1677, when his honours devolved, according to the limitation, upon his son-in-law, Lord Duras.

Arms—Arg. three blackamoors' heads, couped, ppr., between two chevronels, sa.

SPENCER—VISCOUNT OF TEVIOT.

By Letters Patent, dated 20 October, 1685.

Lineage.

THE HON. ROBERT SPENCER, brother of Henry, 1st Earl of Sunderland, and 2nd son of William, 2nd Lord Spencer, of Wormleighton, by Lady Penelope Wriothesley, his wife, eldest dau. of Henry, Earl of Southampton, was created a Peer of Scotland, as VISCOUNT OF TEVIOT, 20 October, 1685. He *m.* Jane, eldest dau. and co-heiress of Sir Thomas Spencer, Bart., of Yarnton, co. Oxford, but *d. s. p.*, when the title became EXTINCT.

Arms—Quarterly: arg. and gu., in the 2nd and 3rd quarters, a fret, or, over all, on a bend, sa., three escallops of the 1st.

STAFFORD—BARONS STAFFORD, EARLS OF STAFFORD, DUKES OF BUCKINGHAM, BARONS STAFFORD.

Barony, by Writ of Summons, dated 6 February, 1299
Earldom, dated 5 March, 1351
Dukedom, dated 14 September, 1444.
Barony, dated 1547.

Lineage.

The first that assumed this surname,

ROBERT DE STAFFORD, possessed, at the time of the General Survey, lordships in Suffolk, Gloucestershire, Lincolnshire, Warwickshire, and Staffordshire, in all 131, and Dugdale surmises, that the assumption of the surname of Stafford arose from his being governor of Stafford Castle, which had been erected by the CONQUEROR; for his name originally was De Toenei, and he is said to have been a younger son of Roger de Toenei, standard bearer of Normandy. Of this Robert de Stafford, who lived till HENRY I.'s time, nothing further is known than his founding an Augustine priory, at Stone, in Staffordshire, upon the spot where Enysan de Waltone, one of the companions of the CONQUEROR, had killed two nuns and a priest. 1.s m. Avice de Clare, and was s. by his son,

NICHOLAS DE STAFFORD, who was sheriff of Staffordshire, *temp.* King HENRY I. This feudal lord was s. by his son,

ROBERT DE STAFFORD, who was sheriff of Staffordshire from the 2nd to the end of the 6th year, inclusive, of King HENRY II.'s reign, and in six years afterwards paid towards the marriage portion of the king's dau. 60 marks for 60 knights' fees. This Robert performed a pilgrimage to Jerusalem, and *d.* about the year 1176, and was s. by his son,

ROBERT DE STAFFORD, at whose decease, about 1139, s. p., the feudal barony and lordships devolved upon his only sister and heiress,

MILICENT DE STAFFORD, who m. in the 5th RICHARD I. a Staffordshire gentleman of ancient family, named Hervey Bagot. This Hervey paying a fine of 300 marks to the crown, had livery of his wife's inheritance, but in order to raise that sum he was obliged to sell the lordship of Drayton to the canons of St. Thomas, near Stafford. The son and heir of this Hervey and Milicent, assuming his maternal surname, inherited the estates as

HERVEY DE STAFFORD. This feudal lord was with King HENRY III. at the siege of Bitham Castle, in Lincolnshire, in the 5th of that monarch's reign. He m. Petronill, sister of William de Ferrers, Earl of Derby, and dying in 1237, was s. by his son,

HERVEY DE STAFFORD, who d. s. p. in 1241, and was s. by his brother,

ROBERT DE STAFFORD, who, in the 25th HENRY III., upon doing homage, and paying £100 for his relief, had livery of his lands. This feudal lord was in the wars of Gascony, 38th HENRY III., and in four years afterwards he had a military summons to march against the Welsh. He m. Alice, one of the daus. and co-heirs of Thomas Corbet, of Caus, co. Salop, and dying in 1282, was s. by his son,

NICHOLAS DE STAFFORD. This feudal lord, who was actively engaged against the Welsh, in the reign of King EDWARD I., was killed before Droselan Castle, about 1293, and was s. by his son,

EDMUND DE STAFFORD, who, having distinguished himself in the Scottish wars, was summoned to parliament as a Baron, by King EDWARD I., from 6 February, 1299, to 26 August, 1308, the year of his decease. He m. Margaret, dau., and at length heir of Ralph, Lord Basset, of Drayton, and had issue,

RALPH, his successor.
Richard, m. Maud, dau. and heir of Richard de Camville, of Clifton, and was styled " Sir Richard Stafford, of Clifton, Knt." (*see* STAFFORDS, of Clifton).

His lordship d. in 1308, and was s. by his elder son,

RALPH DE STAFFORD, 2nd baron, summoned to parliament, from 14 January, 1337, to 25 November, 1350. This nobleman attaining majority in the 17th EDWARD II., and then doing his homage, had livery of his father's lands, and the next ensuing year, being made a knight by bathing, and other sacred ceremonies, had robes, &c., as a banneret, allowed him out of the king's wardrobe for the solemnity; after which he soon became a personage of celebrity in the wars of King EDWARD III. His lordship was first engaged in Scotland for some years, and he then embarked for Britanny, where he was made prisoner at the siege of Nantes. In the 19th EDWARD III., he was sent into Gascony, with Henry of Lancaster, Earl of Derby, and while that nobleman assaulted Bergerath by land, Lord Stafford commanded the force which attacked it by sea. The next year he was constituted seneschal of Aquitaine, when John, son and heir of PHILIP, King of France, coming to besiege Aguillon, where his lordship then resided, he stoutly defended that place against the whole power of the French, until King EDWARD came to his relief, and forced the enemy to raise the siege. After this, joining his troops with the army of King EDWARD, he had a principal command in the van of the English at the glorious battle of Cressy. On the termination of this great conflict, his lordship being sent with Sir Reginald Cobham, and three heralds, to view the slain, reported the number to be 11 great princes, 80 bannerets, 1,200 knights, and more than 30,000 common soldiers. He was afterwards, when Calais surrendered, appointed, together with Sir Walter Manny, and the Earl of Warwick, to take possession of that place for the king; and subsequently his lordship was one of the ambassadors deputed to the cardinals of Naples and Claremont, to treat of peace between King EDWARD and Philip de Valois, then assuming the title of King of France. The next year he had license to make castles of his manor houses at Stafford and Nadeley; as also a grant from the king of £573, for his expenses in foreign service.

About this time his lordship was elected a knight of the Garter, being one of the original members of that noble order. In the 24th EDWARD III., he was in commission with the bishop of Durham, and the Lords Percy and Nevill, to treat with the nobles of Scotland, at York, for a firm and final peace between the two realms; for all which eminent services, he was created, 5 March, 1351, EARL OF STAFFORD, and constituted lieutenant and captain-general of the Duchy of Aquitaine. His lordship m. Margaret, only dau. and heiress of Hugh de Audley, Baron Audley, and in right of his wife, EARL OF GLOUCESTER, by which alliance he acquired a considerable inheritance, and the BARONY OF AUDLEY is presumed to have merged in that of STAFFORD. He had issue,

Ralph, who m. Maud, dau. of Henry, Earl of Derby, Duke of Lancaster, but d. v. p., s. p.
HUGH, his successor.
Beatrice, m. 1st, Maurice, son and heir of Maurice Earl of Desmond; 2ndly, Thomas, Lord Ros, of Hamlake; and 3rdly, Sir Richard Burley, Knt.
Joane, m. to John, son and heir of John Cheriton, Lord Powis.
Elizabeth, m. to Fulke le Strange.
Margaret, m. to Sir John Stafford, Knt.

His lordship d. 31 August, 1372; was buried at Tunbridge, and was s. by his only surviving son,

HUGH DE STAFFORD, 3rd baron, and 2nd Earl of Stafford, who, following the steps of his noble father in those martial times, came very early into action, for at the age of seventeen he was in the wars of France, and again when he attained majority, being then in the retinue of the Black Prince. At the period he succeeded to the honours of his family, he was twenty-eight years of age, and he was subsequently distinguished in all the wars of EDWARD III., and in those at the beginning of King RICHARD II.'s time. In the 9th of the latter monarch, his lordship having obtained license to travel, undertook a pilgrimage to the Holy Sepulchre, and on his return d. at Rhodes, October 1386, having had issue by his wife, the Lady Philippa Beauchamp, dau. of Thomas, Earl of Warwick,

Ralph, who was murdered in 1385 by Sir John Holand, half-brother to King RICHARD II. (*Froissart*).
THOMAS,   } successors, alternately, to the honours of the
WILLIAM,   } family.
EDMUND,   }
Hugh (Sir), K.G., m. Elizabeth Bourchier, only dau. and heiress of Bartholomew, Lord Bourchier, and was summoned to parliament as Baron Bourchier. His lordship d. s. p. in 1420 (*see* p. 502.)
Margaret, m. to Ralph, 1st Earl of Westmoreland.
Katherine, m. to Michael, son of Michael de la Pole, 2nd Earl of Suffolk.
Joane, m. to Thomas Holland, Earl of Kent.

The earl, who was a knight of the Garter, was s. by his eldest surviving son,

THOMAS DE STAFFORD, 4th baron, and 3rd Earl of Stafford, who, in the 14th RICHARD II., making proof of his age, and doing his homage, had livery of his lands, and about the same time, upon the decease of Ralph, the last Lord Basset, of Drayton, was found to be one of his co-heirs.[*] His lordship was in the wars of France, in the 15th RICHARD II., under the conduct of Thomas of Woodstock, Duke of Gloucester, whose dau., the Lady Anne Plantagenet, he had married, but d. s. p. in 1392. when he was s. by his brother,

WILLIAM DE STAFFORD, 5th baron, and 4th Earl of Stafford, b. 1378. This nobleman was but fourteen years of age when he came to the title, and in ward to the Duke of Gloucester. He d. in three years after, and the honours devolved upon his next brother,

EDMUND DE STAFFORD, 6th baron, and 5th Earl of Stafford, who, in the 22nd RICHARD II., by virtue of the king's special license, m. Anne, sister and heir of Humphrey Plantagenet, Earl of Buckingham, and widow of Thomas, 3rd earl of Stafford, his eldest brother (which marriage of the said Thomas and Anne had never been con umated, owing to the tender years of the earl). At the coronation of King HENRY IV., this Edmund, Earl of Stafford, was made a knight of the Bath, as was also Hugh, his younger brother. He was subsequently made a knight of the Garter, but he was killed soon after, at the battle of Shrewsbury, fighting on the part of the king, 22 July, 1403. By Anne, his wife, who d. 1438-9, his lordship (who was buried at the Augustine Friars, Stafford,) left issue,

HUMPHREY, his successor.
Philippa, d. young.
Anne, m. 1st, to Edmund Mortimer, Earl of March, and 2ndly, to John Holland, Earl of Huntingdon.

_____

[*] Thus, Margaret Basset, great aunt of the above-mentioned Ralph, Lord Basset, was the wife of Edmund, 1st Lord Stafford, the earl's great grandfather. For this inheritance he had a contest with the Shirleys.

The earl was *s.* by his son,

HUMPHREY DE STAFFORD, 7th baron, and 6th Earl of Stafford, who, in the 2nd HENRY VI., making proof of his age, had livery of his lands; as also of those which had descended to him by the death, *s. p.*, of his uncle, Sir Hugh Stafford, Lord Bourchier. In the 6th of the same reign, his lordship obtained license from the king to be absent from the realm of Ireland for ten years, but nevertheless to receive the revenue of all his castles, lordships, and lands there. From this period he served for several years in France, and was constituted, 19th HENRY VI., captain of the town of Calais, and tower of Risbanke; as also of the marches of Calais: in consequence of which services, and his near alliance in blood to the royal family, he was created, 14 September, 1444, DUKE OF BUCKINGHAM, with precedence before all dukes whatsoever, next to those of the blood royal; but a great dispute regarding this matter immediately arose between his grace and Henry Beauchamp, Duke of Warwick, which required a special act of parliament to adjust, giving to the rival dukes precedency alternately, year about; the question was, however, finally set at rest by the death of the Duke of Warwick, *s. p.*, in about two years after. In the 28th of HENRY VI., the Duke of Buckingham was made constable of Dover Castle, and warden of the Cinque Ports; and in the 34th of the same reign, after the fatal battle of St Albans, where the Duke of York being victorious, Humphrey, Earl of Stafford, his eldest son, lost his life; seeing what specious pretences were made by the Yorkists, to obtain the favour of the people, his grace, with the Duke of Somerset, made his way privately to Queen Margaret, and apprised her of the danger that impended Continuing faithfully attached to the Lancastrian interest, the duke fell gallantly fighting under that banner at the battle of Northampton, 27 July, 1460. His grace, along with his other honours, was a knight of the Garter. His wife was the Lady Anne Nevill, dau. of Ralph, 1st Earl of Westmoreland, by whom (who *m.* 2ndly, Walter Blount, Lord Mountjoy,) he had issue,

I. HUMPHREY, Earl of Stafford, slain in the battle of St. Albans, 22 May, 1455, leaving by Margaret, dau. and co-heir of Edmund, Duke of Somerset,

'HENRY, who *s.* his grandfather.

II. Henry (Sir), *m.* Margaret, Countess of Richmond, mother of King HENRY VII.

III. Edward.

IV. George, and V. William, twins.

VI. JOHN, created EARL OF WILTSHIRE (*see* STAFFORD, Earls of Wilts.)

I Anne, *m.* 1st, to Aubrey de Vere, son and heir-apparent of John, 12th Earl of Oxford, and 2ndly, to Sir Thomas Cobham, son of Reginald, Lord Cobham, of Sterborough.

II. Joane, *m.* 1st, to William, Viscount Beaumont, and 2ndly, to Sir William Knyvet, of Buckenham, co. Norfolk.

III. Catherine, *m.* to John Talbot, Earl of Shrewsbury.

IThe duke was *s.* by his grandson,

HENRY DE STAFFORD, 2nd Duke of Buckingham, who, being in ward to King EDWARD IV., was committed with Humphrey, his brother, to the tuition of Anne, Duchess of Exeter, the king's sister, with an assignation of 500 marks per annum, for their maintenance. This nobleman was little heard of during the remainder of the reign of EDWARD IV., but being a main instrument in elevating RICHARD III. to the throne, he was made a knight of the Garter, and constable of England by that monarch; besides being promised the possession of the great inheritance of the Bohuns, Earls of Hereford, to which he pretended a right. But whether through disappointment at this promise not being fulfilled, or from a conscientious feeling, certain it is that he soon afterwards entered into a conspiracy to place the Earl of Richmond upon the throne, and actually took up arms for the purpose; but the Courtenays and his other associates, not being able to second his movements, he found himself deserted, and was forced to seek an asylum at the house of an old servant, Humphrey Banaster, near Shrewsbury; by this servant he was, however, betrayed and delivered up to his enemies, but the king refused to reward the betrayer, observing, "that he who could be untrue to so good a master, would be false to all other." The duke was beheaded soon after, in the market-place at Salisbury, 2 November, 1483, without any arraignment, or legal proceeding. His grace had *m.* Katherine, dau. of Richard Widville, Earl of Rivers, and by her (who *m.* 2ndly, Jasper, Duke of Bedford; and 3rdly, Sir Richard Wingfield, K.G.,) left issue,

EDWARD, his successor.
Henry, created Earl of Wiltshire.
Elizabeth, *m.* to Robert Ratcliffe, Lord Fitz-Walter.
Anne, *m.* 1st, to Sir Walter Herbert, Knt., and 2ndly, to George, Earl of Huntingdon.

The earl was *s* by his elder son,

EDWARD DE STAFFORD, who was restored by King HENRY VII. to the Dukedom of Buckingham, Earldom and Barony of Stafford, and all the other honours of his father. This nobleman was in arms against the Cornish men, who rebelled in favour of Perkin Warbeck, and in the 24th HENRY VII., obtained several considerable grants. He was likewise made a knight of the Garter, and lord high constable of England. In the 2nd HENRY VIII., he had license to impark 1000 acres of land at his lordship of Thornbury, in Gloucestershire, and was then in high favour with the king. But in some years afterwards, exciting the enmity of Wolsey, that ambitious prelate planned, and finally succeeded, in accomplishing his grace's ruin. It is stated that the offence given by the duke to the cardinal arose thus:—His grace upon some occasion holding a bason to the king, so soon as his majesty had washed, Wolsey dipped his hands in the water, which appeared so derogatory to the rank of nobility, that he flung the contents of the ewer into the churchman's shoes; who, being highly incensed, menaced that he would stick upon the duke's skirts; a threat which his grace met by coming to court soon after richly dressed, but without any skirts—and the king demanding the cause of so strange a fashion, the duke replied, that it was intended to *prevent the cardinal's design.* The duke, like his father, was doomed, however, to fall by domestic treason, for having discharged one Knevet, a steward, for oppressing his tenantry, that individual became a fit instrument in the hands of Wolsey to effect the object he had so much at heart. Knevet declared that the duke had contemplated the assassination of the king, in order that he might ascend the throne himself as next heir, if his majesty died without issue, and upon this frivolous information, one of the most illustrious noblemen in England was arraigned at Westminster, before Thomas, Duke of Norfolk, then sitting as lord high steward of England for the occasion.

The duke pleaded his own cause, and sustained the character of an able and accomplished advocate, but to no purpose; he was found guilty, and sentenced to death. Upon which he addressed the high steward thus:—"My Lord of Norfolk, you have said as a traitor should be said to; but I was never any. I nothing malign you, for what you have done to me; but the eternal God forgive you my death. I shall never sue to the king for life, though he be a gracious prince; and more grace may come from him than I desire; and so I desire you and all my fellows to pray for me." The duke was executed by decapitation in pursuance of the judgment passed upon him, on Tower Hill, 17 May, 1521. When the emperor CHARLES V. heard of the event, he is said to have exclaimed, "A butcher's dog has killed the finest buck in England." His grace had *m.* the Lady Alianore Percy, dau. of Henry, Earl of Northumberland, and left issue,

HENRY, of whom presently.
Elizabeth, *m.* to Thomas Howard, Duke of Norfolk.
Katherine, *m.* to Ralph Nevill, Earl of Westmoreland.
Mary, *m.* to George Nevill, Lord Bergavenny.

A bill of attainder followed the judgment and execution of the duke, and all his honours became FORFEITED. The fate of this illustrious house was marked by a more than ordinary degree of misfortune:

Edmund, Earl of Stafford, and his son,	all fell in the war of the Roses.
Humphrey, Duke of Buckingham, and his son,	
Humphrey, Earl of Stafford,	
Henry, 2nd Duke of Buckingham, and his son,	were both beheaded and sacrificed to the feuds of party, and to private malignity.
Edward, 3rd and last Duke of Buckingham,	

With the last Duke sunk for ever the splendour, princely honours, and great wealth of the ancient and renowned family of Stafford. Upon passing the bill of attainder against the duke, the parliament enacted also a bill to restore in blood, but not in honours and lands, his grace's only son,

HENRY STAFFORD, to whom, however, the king made immediate grants of manors in the co. Stafford and elsewhere, which had belonged to his father, and he obtained from the crown, in some years after, the castle and manor of Stafford, with other of the estates of the deceased duke; but altogether producing only a comparatively small annual income. He was summoned to parliament, from 24 November, 1548, to 5 November, 1558. In the 1st EDWARD VI., *anno* 1547, an act of parliament passed,* again restoring him in blood, and declar-

* Dugdale states, that he was restored in blood in 1522: but on a reference to the authorized collection of the statutes it appears, that, in the 14th and 15th HENRY VIII., the act in

ing, "that the said Henry, Lord Stafford, and the heirs male of his body coming, may be taken, and reputed as Lord Stafford, with a seat and voice in parliament as a baron; and further that the said Henry be restored in blood as son and heir of Edward, late Duke of Buckingham, &c." His lordship *m.* Ursula, dau. of Sir Richard Pole, K.G., and Margaret Plantagenet, Countess of Salisbury, dau. and heir of George, Duke of Clarence, and niece of Kings EDWARD IV. and RICHARD III., by whom he had issue,

HENRY, his heir.
EDWARD, successor to his brother.
Richard, *m.* Mary, dau. of John Corbet, of Lee, co. Salop, Esq. and had issue,
    ROGER, who claimed the barony upon the decease of Henry, 4th lord, in 1637, but was denied it on account of his poverty. He *d. unm.* in 1640.
    Jane, who *m.* a joiner, and had a son a cobbler, living at Newport, in Shropshire. in 1637 : thus the great-great-grandson of Margaret Plantagenet, dau. and heiress of George, Duke of Clarence, sunk to the grade of a mender of old shoes.
Walter.
Dorothy, *m.* to William Stafford, of Grafton, and from this lady, Mr. Richard Stafford Cooke, who claimed the ancient Barony of Stafford, derived descent. "But admitting this descent," says Nicolas, "it is difficult to find any real claim which it affords to the Barony of Stafford. The ancient barony undoubtedly became forfeited on the attainder of Edward, Duke of Buckingham, in 1521, and which attainder has never been reversed. Henry Stafford, his son and heir, was created Baron Stafford, *de novo*, with an express limitation, to *the heirs male of his body coming*, by act of parliament, 1st EDWARD VI., 1547, and which dignity became *extinct* on the termination of the male descendants of the said Henry, about the year 1640."
Elizabeth, *m.* to Sir William Nevil, Knt., of Chebsey.

This nobleman, who was esteemed for his learning and piety, *d.* in 1562, and was *s.* by his son,
HENRY STAFFORD, 2nd Baron Stafford, who *d. s. p.* 8 April, 1566, and was *s.* by his brother,
EDWARD STAFFORD, 3rd Baron Stafford, of the new creation, summoned to parliament in the 23rd ELIZABETH. His lordship *m.* Mary, dau. of Edward, Earl of Derby, and had issue,

EDWARD, his successor.
Ursula, *m.* to Walter Erdeswick, Esq.
Dorothy, *m.* to Gerveis of Chadsden.

He *d.* 18 October, 1603, and was *s.* by his son,
EDWARD STAFFORD, 4th baron. This nobleman *m.* Isabel, dau. of Thomas Forster, of Tonge, in Shropshire, whom Banks surmises to have been a chambermaid, from a paragraph in a letter of Rowland White, to Sir Robert Sydney, dated 22 November, 1595 (Sidney Papers): "My Lorde Stafford's sonne is basely married to his mother's chambermaid." His lordship had issue,

EDWARD, *b.* in 1600, *m.* Anne, dau. of James Wilford, Esq., of Newnham Hall, co. Essex, and *d.* 1621, *v. p.*, leaving issue,
    HENRY, who *s.* his grandfather.
Mary, *m.* to Sir William Howard, K.B., younger son of Thomas, Earl of Arundel (*see* HOWARD, Baron and Viscount Stafford).

The baron *d.* 25 September, 1625, and was *s.* by his grandson,
HENRY STAFFORD, 5th baron, who *d. unm.* in 1637, when the barony devolved upon his kinsman (*revert to* children of Henry Stafford, the restored baron in 1547).
ROGER STAFFORD, *b.* at Malpas, in Cheshire, about the year 1572. "This unfortunate man (says Banks) in his youth went by the name of Fludd, or Floyde : for what reason, has not yet been explained : perhaps with the indignant pride, that the very name of Stafford should not be associated with the obscurity of such a lot! However, one Floyde, a servant of Mr. George Corbett, of Cowlesmore, near Lee, in Shropshire, his mother's brother, is recorded in a manuscript which was once part of the collections of the Stafford family: and it is not improbable, that this was some faithful servant, under whose roof he might have been reared, or found a shelter from misfortunes, when all his great alliances, with a cowardly and detestable selfishness might have forsaken him; and that he might have preferred the generous, though humble name of Floyde, to one that had brought him nothing but a keener memorial of his misfortunes. At the age of sixty-five he became, by the early death of Henry, Lord Stafford (the great grandson of his father's elder brother,) in 1637, heir male of the family ;" and petitioned parliament accordingly, but eventually submitted his claim to the decision of King CHARLES, who decided *that the said Roger Stafford, having no part of the inheritance of the said Lord*

Stafford, nor *any other lands or means whatsoever*, should make a resignation of all claims and title to the said Barony of Stafford, for his Majesty to dispose of as he should see fit. In obedience, and performance of which said order, the said Roger Stafford, who was never married, did by his deed enrolled, dated 7 December, 1639, grant and surrender unto his Majesty the said Barony of Stafford, and the honour, name, and dignity of Lord Stafford. After which surrender, the king, by patent dated 12 September, 1640, created Sir William Howard, and Mary Stafford, his wife, Baron and Baroness Stafford, with remainder to the heirs *male of their* bodies, failure of which, to the heirs of their bodies, with such place or precedence, as Henry, Lord Stafford, brother of the said Mary, ought to have had as Baron Stafford.

With this unfortunate ROGER STAFFORD, who *d. circa* 1640, the male line of the Staffords became EXTINCT, as did the Barony of Stafford, created in 1547. (*See* BURKE's *Vicissitudes of Families.*)

Arms—Or, a chevron, gules.

STAFFORD—BARON STAFFORD, OF CLIFTON.

By Writ of Summons, dated 8 January, 1371.

Lineage.

SIR RICHARD DE STAFFORD, younger son of Edmund, 1st Lord Stafford (*see* Stafford, Barons and Earls Stafford), having *m.* Maud, dau. and heiress of Richard de Camvile, of Clifton, co. Stafford, acquired that lordship, and was thence designated. Sir Richard Stafford distinguished himself in the French wars of King EDWARD III., and was seneschal of Gascony in that monarch's reign. He was *s.* at his decease by his son,
RICHARD DE STAFFORD, who, having been engaged in the French wars, was summoned to parliament, by King EDWARD III., as BARON STAFFORD, *of Clifton*, 8 January, 1371, and he had regular summons from that period to 20 October, 1379 ; he *d.* in 1381, leaving his son and heir,
EDMUND DE STAFFORD, in holy orders, who was afterwards bishop of Exeter, and lord keeper of the great seal, who *d.* in 1419
And another son,
SIR THOMAS STAFFORD, who came to possess the estate, and was *s.* by his son,
THOMAS STAFFORD, who *d. s. p.*, leaving an only sister and heiress,
KATHERINE STAFFORD, who *m.* Sir John Arderne, of Elford, co. Stafford, Knt., and left an only child,
MAUD ARDERNE.[*] This lady *m.* Sir Thomas Stanley, 2nd son of Sir John Stanley, K.G., and although none of the Staffords were summoned but Richard, the 1st lord, yet the barony still existed, and was conveyed to the family of her husband by this Maud, and continues vested in the representatives of that lady.

Arms—Same as Stafford, Earls Stafford, a crescent for difference.

STAFFORD—BARON STAFFORD, OF SUTH-WYK, EARL OF DEVON.

Barony, first by Writ of Summons, dated 26 July, 1461, and afterwards by Patent, dated 24 April, 1464. Earldom, created 17 May, 1469.

Lineage.

This branch of the ancient house of Stafford sprang from SIR JOHN STAFFORD, son of William Stafford, of Bromshull, co. Stafford, and a descendant of Hervey Bagot and Milicent Stafford (*see* Stafford, Lords Stafford, Dukes of Buckingham, &c.); which Sir John *m.* Margaret, youngest dau. of Ralph Stafford, 1st Earl of Stafford, and left issue,

I. HUMPHREY (Sir), his heir.
II. Ralph, who *m.* Maud, dau. and co-heir of Sir John Hastang, and was ancestor of the Staffords of Grafton, co. Worcester, and of the Staffords of Blatherwycke, co. Northampton.

The elder son,
SIR HUMPHREY STAFFORD, a distinguished soldier in the martial reign of King EDWARD III., and one of the retinue of the Black Prince. He *m.* the dau. and heir of — Gre'nvil, and was *s.* by his son,

---

question was passed, and which merely enabled the said Henry, and Ursula, his wife, and their heirs, to hold and enjoy certain estates, granted them by letters patent, dated 20 December, 1522.—NICOLAS.

* Some accounts make Maud the dau. of Sir John Arderne, *junior*, and *granddau.* of Sir John Arderne, by Katherine Stafford, his wife.

SIR HUMPHREY STAFFORD. called "Humphrey with the silver hand," who m. 1st, Elizabeth, dau. and heir of Sir William Aumerle, and widow of Sir John Maltravers, of Hooke, co. Dorset, by whom he had no issue. He m. 2ndly, Elizabeth Cheyney, and had two sons,

HUMPHREY, his successor,
John, bishop of Bath and Wells, and afterwards archbishop of Canterbury, d. about the 30th HENRY VI.

This Sir Humphrey was sheriff of the cos. Somerset and Dorset, in the reign of HENRY IV., and dying in 1413, was s. by his elder son,

SIR HUMPHREY STAFFORD, who m. Elizabeth, dau. and eventually sole heiress, of Sir John Maltravers, Knt., of Hooke, and had livery of the lands of her inheritance in the 8th HENRY IV. By this lady he had issue,

    I. John (Sir), m. Anne, dau. of William, Lord Botreaux, and dying v. p., left a son, HUMPHREY, who s. his grandfather.
    II. William, m. to Katherine, dau. of Sir John Chidiock, and by her (who m. 2ndly, Sir John Arundel), had a son, HUMPHREY, of whom hereafter, as Lord Stafford, and Earl of Devon.
    I. Alice, m. 1st, to Sir Edmund Cheney, of Brooke, co. Wilts, and had issue,
        Elizabeth Cheney, m. to Sir John Coleshill, Knt., and d. s. p., 1st RICHARD III.
        Anne Cheney, m. Sir John Willoughby, and had issue,
        Sir Robert Willoughby, summoned to parliament as Lord Willoughby de Broke.
    Alice, Lady Cheney, m. 2ndly, Walter Talboys, by whom she had an only dau.,
        Eleanor, who m. Thomas Strangwayes, Esq., of Melbury, co Dorset.

Sir Humphrey Stafford was s. at his decease by his grandson,
SIR HUMPHREY STAFFORD, who was slain 30th HENRY VI., in rencontre with the rebels under Jack Cade, at Sevenoaks, co. Kent, and was s. by his son,

HUMPHREY STAFFORD, appointed steward of the Duchy of Cornwall, in the 1st HENRY IV., but d. the same year s. p., when the estates devolved upon his cousin (refer to issue of William, son of Sir Humphrey Stafford, and Elizabeth, heiress of Maltravers),

HUMPHREY STAFFORD, of Suthwyk, who was summoned to parliament as a Baron by writ addressed "Humfrido Stafford de Suthwyk," from 26 July, 1461, to 28 February, 1463. His lordship was created, by patent, dated 24 April, 1464, LORD STAFFORD, of Suthwyck, and advanced to the EARLDOM OF DEVON, 17 May, 1469; after the execution and attainder of Thomas Courtenay, Earl of Devon, who had been made prisoner at Towton Field. But this latter dignity he enjoyed only a few months: for being sent with 800 archers to assist the Earl of Pembroke in suppressing the northern rebellion under Sir John Conyers, he deserted the earl's banner owing to some personal slight, and caused the total defeat of that nobleman and his army; which conduct so irritated King EDWARD IV., that he immediately dispatched letters to the sheriffs of Somerset and Devon, commanding them to seize Stafford wheresoever they should find him, and to put him to immediate death. His lordship was, in consequence, taken at a village called Brentmarsh, and thence conveyed to Bridgewater, where his head was cut off 17 August, 1469. He had m. Elizabeth, dau. of Sir John Barre, Knt., and had two daus., Elizabeth and Anne, who both d. unm. All his honours fell, however, under the attainder; but "his estates, comprising divers manors in the co. of Dorset, by a feoffment made to John Stafford, archbishop of Canterbury, Sir William Bonvill, and others, by Sir Humphrey Stafford with the silver hand (which feoffers passed them to Katherine, late wife of William Stafford, Esq., to hold for life, with remainder to Sir Humphrey, son of the said William, and his lawful heirs; and in default of such issue, to the right heirs of Sir Humphrey with the silver hand), descended to Elizabeth, wife of Sir John Coleshill, in the co. of Devon: Sir Robert Willoughby, son and heir of Anne Cheney, otherwise Willoughby, and Eleanor Strangwayes, as heirs of Sir Humphrey Stafford with the silver hand" (revert to issue of Alice, only dau. of Sir Humphrey Stafford, and Elizabeth, heiress of Sir John Maltravers)

Sir John Coleshill dying s. p., 1st RICHARD I., the estates were then divided between the Willoughbys and Strangwayes. From the Willoughbys, their dividend passed to the Paulets and the Blounts, and at length centred entirely in the former, who thereby became possessors of the manor of Hooke, co. Dorset.

Arms—Or, a chevron gu., within a bordure engrailed, sa.

STAFFORD—EARLS OF WILTSHIRE.

Created 5 January, 1470, and 1509.

Lineage.

LORD JOHN STAFFORD, youngest son of Humphrey, 1st Duke of Buckingham. was elevated to the peerage by King EDWARD IV., as EARL OF WILTSHIRE, and in three years afterwards was joined in commission with the Earl of Northumberland, and others, to treat with the ambassadors of JAMES III., King of Scotland, for the adjustment of grievances complained of by both realms. His lordship m. Constance, dau. and heiress of Sir Henry Greene, of Drayton, co. Northampton. The earl, who was remarkable for little more than his devotion to the house of York, by which he acquired the peerage and the Garter, d. in 1473, and was s. by his only child,

EDWARD STAFFORD, 2nd Earl of Wiltshire. This nobleman m. Margaret, one of the daus. and co-heirs of John Grey, 2nd Viscount L'Isle, but d. s. p. 24 March, 1499, when the earldom became EXTINCT. In some years afterwards the deceased lord's 1st cousin,

LORD HENRY STAFFORD, younger son of Henry, 2nd Duke of Buckingham, was created by King HENRY VIII. (in the first year of his reign 1509), EARL OF WILTSHIRE. His lordship m. 1st, Margaret, Countess of Wilts, widow of the deceased lord, and 2ndly, Cecily, dau. and heiress of William Bonvile, Lord Harington, and widow of Thomas Grey, Marquess of Dorset, but d. s. p. in 1523, when the Earldom of Wiltshire became again EXTINCT.

Arms—See Stafford, Duke of Buckingham.

STAFFORD — BARON STAFFORD, OR BOURCHIER.

(See p. 499, and also BOURCHIER, Barons Bourchier and Earls of Essex.)

SIR HUGH STAFFORD, K.G., m. Elizabeth Bourchier, Baroness Bourchier, and in her right was summoned to parliament as a Baron, from 21 September, 1411, to 22 March, 1413. He d. however s. p. in 1420; his widow m. Sir Lewis Robsert, K.G., and d. s. p. 1 July, 1433, when the barony devolved on Henry Bourchier, Earl of Ewe, in Normandy.

STANHOPE — BARONS STANHOPE, OF HARRINGTON.

By Letters Patent, dated 4 May, 1605.

Lineage.

The family of STANHOPE was of great antiquity in the co. Nottingham, although it did not attain the dignity of the peerage, until comparatively modern times. In the 48th EDWARD III.,

JOHN STANHOPE, of Rampton, served the office of escheator for Nottinghamshire, and the co. Derby, a public station at that time little inferior to that of sheriff. From him descended another,

JOHN STANHOPE, who m. Elizabeth, dau. and heir of Steven Maulovel (cousin and heir of Sir John Longvilliers, grandson to Thomas Longvilliers, Baron Longvilliers, temp. EDWARD III.), and was s. by his son,

SIR RICHARD STANHOPE, Knt., who, in the 6th HENRY IV., was sheriff of the cos. Nottingham and Derby. From this Sir Richard descended,

SIR EDWARD STANHOPE, Knt., constable of Sandale Castle, temp. HENRY VII., whose 2nd son,

SIR MICHAEL STANHOPE, Knt., obtained a grant, temp. HENRY VIII., of the manor of Shelford, co. Nottingham, with its members, parcel of the possessions of the then dissolved monastery there, as also grants of lands in the cos. Lincoln and Derby. Sir Michael had a numerous family, of which the eldest son,

SIR THOMAS STANHOPE. inherited Shelford, and was grandfather of Philip, 1st Earl of Chesterfield.

And the 3rd son,

SIR JOHN STANHOPE, Knt., of Harrington, co. Northampton,

M P. for that shire, having enjoyed high favour at the courts of ELIZABETH and JAMES I., was elevated to the peerage by the latter monarch, to whom he was vice-chamberlain, as BARON STANHOPE, *of Harrington*, 4 May, 1605. His lordship m 1st, Joan, dau. and heir of William Knolls, by whom he had no issue; and 2ndly, Margaret, dau. and co-heir of Henry M'Williams, Esq., of Stanborne, in Essex, by whom he had issue,

CHARLES, his successor.
Elizabeth, *m.* to Sir Lionel Tollemache, Bart., of Helmingham, ancestor of the Earls of Dysart.
Catherine, *m.* to Robert, Viscount Cholmondeley, of Kells, in Ireland, afterwards Earl of Leinster.

Lord Stanhope *d.* 9 March 1620, and was *s.* by his son,
CHARLES STANHOPE, 2nd baron. This nobleman lived abroad during the civil wars, *temp.* CHARLES I. He *m.* Dorothy, sister of Edward, Lord Barret, of Newburgh, but *d. s. p.* in 1675, aged eighty-two, when the Barony of Stanhope, of Harrington, became EXTINCT.

Arms—Quarterly : erm. and gu.

STANLEY—BARONS STANLEY.

By Writ of Summons, tested 15 January, 1456.

Lineage.

This family, according to Dugdale, is "a branch of that, whose chief seat hath been for many ages at Hooton, in Cheshire;" and it originally assumed its surname from the lordship of Standleigh, Stondleigh, or Stanley, in Staffordshire, which lordship was so called from the nature of the soil, it being rough and stony, with divers craggy rocks around it. Stondleigh was formerly possessed by the Lords Aldithley, or Audley, and was exchanged by Adam, the son of Lydulph de Aldithley, with his cousin, William, son of his uncle, Adam de Aldithley, which William became in consequence,

WILLIAM DE STANLEIGH: from him descended,
SIR JOHN STANLEY, K.G., who *m.* Isabel, dau. and heiress of Sir Thomas Lathom, and acquired thereby the estates of Lathom and Knowesley, co. Lancaster.. Sir John was, subsequently, one of the most powerful personages in the kingdom. In the reign of HENRY IV., he obtained, being then steward of the household, license to fortify a house near Liverpool, which he had newly built, with embattled walls. He was afterwards lord deputy of Ireland. In 1399, he was lord justice and lord lieutenant of the same kingdom. In the 1st year of HENRY V., being then constable of Windsor Castle, he was installed a knight of the Garter, and was a second time constituted lord-lieutenant of Ireland, for six years, in which government he *d.* 6 January, 1414. By the heiress of Lathom he left two sons,

JOHN, his successor.
Thomas (Sir), who *m.* Maud, dau. and heir of Sir John Arderne, of Elford, co. Stafford, and so long as his male line continued, Elford was their chief seat. From this marriage descended the STANLEYS of Elford, Pipe, &c.

The elder son,
JOHN STANLEY, Esq., was made governor of Carnarvon Castle, and marrying Isabel, sister of Sir William Harrington, Knt., of Hornby, had a son,
SIR THOMAS STANLEY, Knt., who, in the 9th HENRY VI., was constituted lord-lieutenant of Ireland, as his grandfather had been for six years, and he was subsequently made lord chamberlain to the king. With King HENRY, Sir Thomas was in high favour, and having been commissioned by that monarch upon several occasions to negotiate peace with his enemies, he was made a knight of the Garter, and had summons to parliament as BARON STANLEY, by special writ, tested 15 January, 1456, but never afterwards *m.* Joan, dau. and heir of Sir Robert Goushill, Knt., by Elizabeth, his wife, widow of Thomas Mowbray, Duke of Norfolk, and had issue,

I. THOMAS, his successor.
II. William (Sir), of Holt.
III. John (Sir), ancestor of the STANLEYS of ALDERLEY, co. Chester.
IV. James, archdeacon of Carlisle.
I. Margaret, *m.* to Sir William Troubeck, Knt.
II. Elizabeth, *m.* to Sir Richard Molyneux, Knt.

His lordship *d.* in 1458-9, and was *s.* by his eldest son,
THOMAS STANLEY, 2nd baron, summoned to parliament, from 30 July, 1460, to 9 December, 1483. This nobleman, who was steward of the household to King EDWARD IV., stood faithful to the interests of his son, EDWARD V., and incurred, in con-

503

sequence, the jealousy of the Protector Gloucester, from the moment that daring personage contemplated seizing upon the government. Lord Stanley was at the council, when Lord Hastings was arrested by order of the Protector, and then very narrowly escaped with his life, having received a violent blow on the head from a halbert. He was afterwards committed to prison, when the Protector threw off the mask, and usurped the crown as RICHARD III., but was released, lest his son, George, Lord Strange, should stir up the people to revolt. To ensure his support, the new monarch loaded his lordship with honours; constituting him lord steward of the household, constable of England for life, investing him with the Garter, &c.; but his having married for his 2nd wife, Margaret Tudor, Countess of Richmond, and mother of RICHARD's rival, HENRY, Earl of Richmond, made him still an object of distrust to Richard. So soon, therefore, as RICHARD was apprised of the Earl of Richmond's arrival in Britanny, and his projects regarding the English sceptre, Lord Stanley was commanded to discharge all his servants, and strictly prohibited holding any communication with his stepson. Subsequently he obtained permission to retire into the country, but was obliged to leave his son and heir, GEORGE, Lord Strange, as hostage. This young nobleman, RICHARD afterwards threatened to put to death, should his father appear in arms on the part of Richmond, but the menace failed in keeping Lord Stanley from the field, who distinguished himself as one of the most active commanders at Bosworth, and when victory at length declared for Lancaster, had the high honour of crowning upon the field of battle, his son-in-law and chief, and proclaiming him King of England, under the title of HENRY VII. His lordship was soon afterwards created EARL OF DERBY, and sworn of the privy council. He *m.* 1st, Lady Eleanor Neville, dau. of Richard, Earl of Salisbury, and had issue,

I. GEORGE (Sir), K.B. and K.G., who *m.* Joane, dau. and heir of John, Lord Strange, of Knokyn, and in her right was summoned to parliament, as Lord Strange. He *d. v. p.* 5 December, 1497, leaving,
     1 THOMAS, who *s.* as 2nd Earl of Derby,
     2 John, *d.* young.
     8 James (Sir), of Crosshall, ancestor of the present EARL OF DERBY.
II. EDWARD, afterwards Lord Monteagle.
III. James, bishop of Ely.
I. Margaret, *m.* to Sir John Osbaldeston.

His lordship *m.* 2ndly, as already stated, Margaret, Countess of Richmond, mother of King HENRY VII., but by her had no issue. He *d.* in 1504, and from that period the Barony of Stanley merged in the Earldom of Derby, until the decease of FERDINANDO STANLEY, 5th Earl of Derby, and 6th Baron Stanley, 16 April, 1594, when it fell into ABEYANCE, together with the Barony of Strange, of Knokyn, amongst that nobleman's three daus. and co-heirs, viz.,

ANNE, *m.* 1st, to Grey Bruges, Lord Chandos, and 2ndly, to Mervin, Earl of Castlehaven.
FRANCES, *m.* to Sir John Egerton, afterwards Earl of Bridgewater. Of this marriage the co-heirs are the EARL OF JERSEY and the DUKE OF SUTHERLAND.
ELIZABETH, *m.* to Henry, Earl of Huntingdon: the co-heirs of whom are the Earl of Loudoun, and his aunts, the daus. of the 2nd Marquess of Hastings.

Arms—Arg., on a bend, az., three bucks' heads, caboshed, or.

STANLEY—BARONS MONTEAGLE.

By Writ of Summons, dated 23 November, 1514.

Lineage.

SIR EDWARD STANLEY, 2nd son of Thomas, 1st Earl of Derby, having commanded in the 5th HENRY VIII., the rear guard of the English army, at the battle of Flodden Field, and contributed by extraordinary valour, at the head of a body of archers, to the total overthrow of the Scottish army, was the next year proclaimed LORD MONTEAGLE, by King HENRY, then holding his court at Eltham, in consideration of his gallant conduct, and in commemoration of having won an elevated position from the Scots: in which dignity he was summoned to parliament from 23 November, 1514, to 12 November, 1515. He was also made a knight of the Garter.

"This nobleman's birth," says Banks, "his active childhood and martial spirit had brought him early to HENRY's notice and company, and his aspiring manhood to his service. The camp was his school, and his learning was a pike and sword. Whenever his Majesty met him, his greeting was, 'Ho, my soldier.' Twice did he and Sir John Wallop land, with only

600 men, in the heart of France; and four times did he and
Sir Thomas Lovel save Calais; the first time by intelligence,
the second by stratagem, the third by valour and resolution,
the fourth by hardship, patience, and industry." His lordship
m. Anne,[*] dau. and co-heir of Sir John Harrington, Knt., and
had issue,

　THOMAS, his successor.
　Elizabeth, *m.* to Sir Thomas Langton, Knt., of Newton, in
　Lancashire.

He *d.* in 1523, and was *s.* by his son,
　THOMAS STANLEY, 2nd baron, summoned to parliament from
3 November, 1529 to 23 January, 1559. This nobleman was
made a knight of the Bath at the coronation of ANNE BOLEYN.
His lordship *m.* Lady Mary Brandon, dau. of Charles, Duke of
Suffolk, by whom he had issue,

　WILLIAM (Sir), his successor.
　Francis,⎱ both *d.* young and *s. p.*
　Charles, ⎰
　Elizabeth, *m.* to Richard Zouche, of Staffordel, co. Somerset.
　Margaret, *m.* 1st, to William Sutton, and 2ndly, to John
　Tallard.
　Anne, *m.* to Sir John Clifton, Knt., of Barrington, in Somer-
　setshire.

Lord Monteagle *m.* 2ndly, Helen, dau. of Thomas Preston, Esq.,
of Levens, in Westmoreland, but had no issue. He *d.* in 1560,
and was *s.* by his son,
　SIR WILLIAM STANLEY, 3rd baron, summoned to parliament
from 11 January, 1563, to 6 January, 1581. His lordship *m.*
1st, Anne, dau. of Thomas Preston, and widow of Sir James
Leybourne, Knt., by whom he had an only child,

　ELIZABETH, who *m.* Edward Parker, LORD MORLEY, and her
　son,
　　William Parker, was summoned to parliament as LORD
　　MORLEY and MONTEAGLE (*see* Parker, Barons Morley and
　　Monteagle).

He *m.* 2ndly, Anne, dau. of Sir John Spencer, of Althorp, co.
Northampton, by whom (who *m.* after his lordship's decease
Henry, Lord Compton, and afterwards Robert, Lord Buckhurst,)
he had no issue. His lordship *d.* in 1581, when the Barony of
Monteagle devolved upon his only dau. and heiress, ELIZABETH
STANLEY, who conveyed it to the family of her husband, Edward
Parker, LORD MORLEY.

Arms—Arg., on a bend, az., three bucks' heads caboshed, or;
a crescent for difference.

STANLEY—BARONS STRANGE, OF KNOKYN.

Refer to STRANGE, Barons Strange, of Knokyn.

STAPLETON—BARONS STAPLETON.

By Writ of Summons, dated 8 January, 1313.

Lineage.

The surname of this ancient family is derived from Stapleton-
on-Tees, a little village on that river, between Richmond and
Darlington.
The representative of the elder or Carlton branch is the
present Lord Beaumont.
HERTON or HERMAN, Lord of Stapleton-on-Tees, became
seised of that manor in 1052. His descendant was
SIR MILES STAPLETON, Knt., who, having distinguished himself, *temp.* EDWARD I. and II., in the wars of Gascony and
Scotland, in the retinue of Edward, Prince of Wales, was summoned to parliament as a Baron 8 January, 23 May, and 26
July, 1313. He *d.* in 1314, and was *s.* by his son,
SIR NICHOLAS STAPLETON, 2nd baron, summoned to parliament, 25 February, 1342. This nobleman in the time of
EDWARD II. was involved in the insurrection of Thomas, Earl
of Lancaster, and was fined 2,000 marks to save his life, but
the fine was remitted in the 1st EDWARD III. He *m.* Sibill,
dau. and heir of Sir John de Bella-aqua (Beaulieu or Bellew),
the last baron of that name, by his wife Laderina, sister and

co heir of Peter Bruce, the 6th and last Baron of Skelton Castle.
In her right he became Lord of Carlton, which is still the property of the elder branch of the family; and he was also Lord
of Wighill at his death in 1343. He had issue,

　I. MILES.
　II. Gilbert, a priest of St. Leonard's Hospital at York.

The elder son,
　SIR MILES STAPLETON, Knt., 3rd baron, summoned to parliament in 1358, was one of the first knights of the Garter, at
the foundation of the order by EDWARD III. This nobleman
was a person of great note at the period in which he lived. He
participated in many of the French campaigns of EDWARD III.,
and when Philip, brother of the King of Navarre, came to
England to obtain help, he was chosen as "an expert soldier,"
and marched with his banner to within nine leagues of Paris,
when the French were obliged to enter into a truce. He was
high sheriff of Yorkshire in 1353, and again in 1355, for five
years consecutively. He *d.* in 1373, leaving issue,

　I. SIR NICHOLAS, whose son, THOMAS, was 4th baron, but was
　　never summoned to parliament, having *d.* the same year he
　　inherited. Having left no issue, his sister ELIZABETH, wife of
　　SIR THOMAS METHAM, became. his heir, and the barony has
　　since been vested in her descendants. Her son and heir, Sir
　　Alexander Metham, Knt., was the ancestor of Sir Thomas
　　Metham, Knt., who fell at Marston Moor, *ex parte Regis*.
　　He *m.* Barbara, dau. of Philip Constable, Esq., and left, with
　　an only son, Thomas, who *d. unm.*, two daus., Catherine,
　　who *m.* Edward Smyth, Esq., of Eshe, and Barbara, *m.* to
　　THOMAS DOLMAN, Esq., of Badsworth and Pocklington, co.
　　York; JOHN THOMAS DOLMAN, Esq., now of Souldern House,
　　co. Oxford, petitioned the Crown, some years since, as heir-
　　general of this marriage, for a confirmation of his right to
　　the Barony of Stapleton. The petition was referred to H. M.'s
　　attorney-general, but no further proceedings were taken.
　II. GILBERT, *m.* Agnes, eldest dau. and one of the heirs of Sir
　　Bryan Fitzalan, Lord of Bedale, the last baron of that name,
　　Sir Bryan left two daus. only, the elder *m.* Sir Gilbert Stapyl-
　　ton, and Catherine, *m.* to Sir John. Lord Grey of Rotherfield,
　　K.G., whose heirs merged in the families of Lovel and
　　Beaumont. Sir Gilbert had issue,
　　1 Sir Miles Stapleton of Bedale and Ingham, *m.* Joan, widow
　　　of Roger, Lord Strange of Knockyn, and dau. and co-heir
　　　of Sir Oliver Ingham of Ingham, co. Norfolk, in whose
　　　right he became possessed of Ingham. This line terminated
　　　after several generations, in two daus., Elizabeth, *m.* 1st,
　　　Sir Philip Calthorp; 2ndly, Sir John Fortescue, chief
　　　justice of England; and 3rdly, Sir Edward Howard, lord
　　　high admiral of England; and Joan, *m.* 1st, to Christopher
　　　Harcourt, Esq. of Stanton Harcourt; 2ndly, to Sir John
　　　Hudleston.
　　2 SIR BRYAN STAPLETON, K.G., ancestor of the Stapyltons
　　　of Carlton, whose representative is now LORD BEAUMONT, and
　　　the STAPYLTONS of Wighill, co. York, now represented by
　　　HENRY-EDWARD CHETWIND-STAPYLTON, Esq.

Arms—Az., a lion rampant, sa.

STAWEL—BARONS STAWEL, OF SOMERTON.

By Letters Patent, dated 15 January, 1683.

Lineage.

This family is said to have been of antiquity, but it arrived
at no distinction until a period of comparatively modern date.
　SIR JOHN STAWEL, K.B., *m.* Elizabeth, dau. of George Touchet,
Lord Audley, and left a son,
　SIR JOHN STAWEL, of Somerton, co. Somerset, who distinguished himself by his zeal in the royal cause during the civil
wars. He was *s.* by his son,
　RALPH STAWEL, Esq., who, in consideration of the sufferings
of his father, and his own eminent services in the same cause,
was elevated to the peerage by King CHARLES II., 15 January,
1683, as BARON STAWEL, of *Somerton, co. Somerset*. His lord-
ship *m.* 1st, Anne, dau. of John Ryves, Esq., of Ranston, co.
Dorset, and had an only son, JOHN, his successor. He *m.* 2ndly,
Abigail, dau. of William Pitt, Esq., of Hartley Wespal, co
Stafford, by whom he had issue,

　WILLIAM,⎱ who *s.* successively to the title.
　EDWARD, ⎰
　Elizabeth, *m.* to William Bromley, Esq., of Bagenton.
　Catherine, *m.* to the Rev. William Higden, D.D.
　Lucy.　　　　　Diana.

His lordship *d.* in 1689, and was *s.* by his eldest son,
　JOHN STAWEL, 2nd Baron Stawel of Somerton. This nobleman *m.* Lady Margaret Cecil, dau. of James, Earl of Salisbury,

---

[*] Edmondson says he had a former wife, Elizabeth, dau. and
heir of Thomas Vaughan, Esq., but had no issue.

504

by whom he left an only dau., who *m.* 1st, James D'Arcy, grandson of Conyers, Earl of Holdernesse; and 2ndly, John Barber, Esq., of Sunning Hill. His lordship *d.* at the early age of twenty-four, in 1692, and was *s.* by his half brother,

WILLIAM STAWEL, 3rd baron, who *m.* Elizabeth, widow of William Foster, Esq , of Bamborough Castle, and dau. of William Pert, Esq. (by Elizabeth, his wife, dau. of William Forster, Esq., and sister of Sir Humphrey Forster, Bart.) By this alliance his lordship acquired the mansion and estate of Aldermaston, in Berkshire (which had come to the Forsters by the heiress of Delamere, and to the Delameres through the heiress of Achard, which latter family obtained it by grant of HENRY I.) Lord Stawel had issue,

William, who *d. unm.* in the life-time of his father, in February, 1739-40.
Charlotte, *m.* 1st, to Major Ruishe Hasell, and 2ndly, to Ralph Congreve. Esq., M.P. Mr. Congreve survived his wife, and *d. s. p.,* having devised the estate of Aldermaston, co. Berks (which had been settled on the survivor) to the eldest branch of the Congreves, settled at Congreve, co. Stafford.

His lordship *d.* in 1742, and was *s.* by his brother,

EDWARD STAWEL, 4th baron. This nobleman *m.* Mary, dau. and co-heir of Sir Hugh Stewkley, of Hinton Ampner, co. Hants, by whom he had issue,

Stewkley, who *d.* at Westminster School ·in the life time of his father.
MARY, *m.* to Henry Bilson Legge, Esq This lady having inherited the estates of her family, as sole heiress of her father, was created in 1760, BARONESS STAWEL, *of Somerton,* with remainder to her heirs male by Mr. Legge, (*see* Legge, Baroness Stawel). Her ladyship *m.* 2ndly, Wills, Earl of Hillsborough.

His lordship *d.* in 1755, when the Barony of Stawel, of Somerton, became EXTINCT.

Arms—Gu., a cross of lozenges, arg.

STEWART—EARL OF BLESINTON, BARON STEWART, VISCOUNT MOUNTJOY.

Barony and Viscounts, by Letters Patent, dated 19 March, 1682.
Earldom, by Letters Patent, dated 7 December, 1745.

Lineage.

SIR WILLIAM STEWART, Knt., being in great favour with King JAMES I., became an undertaker for the plantation of escheated lands in the province of Ulster, and was created a Baronet of Ireland, 10 April, 1623. Sir William was a privy councillor in the reigns of King JAMES I. and King CHARLES I., and having served as a military officer in the troubles of Ireland, received in satisfaction for arrears of pay due prior to 5 June, 1649, one debenture of 4,000 and odd pounds; while his son, Sir Alexander Stewart, was allotted for his services a debenture for £2,599. Sir William *m.* Frances, 2nd dau. of Sir Robert Newcomen, Bart. of Mosstown, co. Longford, and had issue,

I. ALEXANDER (Sir), of whom presently.
II. William, *d. unm.*   III. John, *d. unm.*
IV. Robert, *d. unm.*
V Thomas, a captain in the army, *m.* a dau. of John Montgomery, and was ancestor of SIR ANNESLEY STEWART, of Fort Stewart, co. Donegal, who *s.* as 6th bart. at the death of William, Earl of Blesinton.
I. Catherine, *m.* in 1630, to Sir James Montgomery, of Rosemount, co. Down.
II. Anne, *m.* to Sir William St. Paul, otherwise Semple, of Letterkenny, co. Longford, Knt.

The eldest son,

SIR ALEXANDER STEWART, was killed at the battle of Dunbar, 3 September, 1653. He *m.* Catharine, dau. of ·Sir Robert Newcomen, Bart. (3rd son of the said Robert), by Anna Boleyne, his wife, of kin, it is alleged, to Queen ELIZABETH, and by her (who *m.* 2ndly, Sir Arthur Forbes, created Earl of Granard,) he had an only son,

SIR WILLIAM STEWART, who *s.* his grandfather, Sir William Stewart, as 2nd baronet, and was advanced to the peerage of Ireland, 19 March, 1682, by the titles of *Baron Stewart of Ramalton and Viscount Mountjoy;* his lordship being constituted at the same time master-general of the ordnance for life and colonel of a regiment of foot. The viscount served in Hungary, at the siege of Buda, in 1686, and upon his return to Ireland was raised to the rank of brigadier-general, with the pay of £497 10s. a-year. His lordship undertaking, with the Lord Chief Baron, Sir Stephen Rice, in 1688,

a mission from the Lord Deputy Tyrconnel to King JAMES II. then at Paris, was immediately upon his arrival in that city thrown into the Bastile, and there confined until the year 1692, when, being released, he waited upon King WILLIAM in Flanders and lost his life 24 August, in the same year, at the battle of Steinkirk. Lord Mountjoy *m.* Mary, eldest dau. of Richard, Lo d Colooney, by whom he had with two daus. (Mary, *m.* 1st, to Phineas Preston, Esq., of Ardsallah, and 2ndly, to George, Earl of Granard; and Catherine, *m.* to Arthur Davis, Esq. of Carrickfergus,) six sons,

I. WILLIAM, his successor.
II. Alexander, who was a captain of foot, *m.* Mary, eldest dau. of William Tighe, Esq. of Dublin; and dying in 1701, left an only dau. and heiress, Anne, who *m.* the Right Hon. Luke Gardiner, treasurer of Ireland; from which marriage, Gardiner, Earl of Blesinton, descended.
III Richard, who in 1704 and 1713 was elected to parliament for Castlebar and the co. Tyrone, in 1715 for Strabane, and in 1727 for said co.; he *d. unm.* 4 August, 1728.
IV. Arthur, a captain in the army, buried by his brother Alexander, 1 August, 1723
V. Charles, M.P. co. Tyrone, vice-admiral of the White, *d.* 5 February, 1740.
VI. James, *b.* in October, 1687, *s.* his brother Richard in parliament for the co. Tyrone. *m.* 15 February, 1731, Rebecca, elder dau. and co-heir of Robert Stewart, Esq., of Castle· rothery, co. Wicklow, and *d.* 9 March, 1747.

His lordship was *s.* by his eldest son,

SIR WILLIAM STEWART, 2nd Viscount Mountjoy, a lieutenant-general in the army, and master-general of the ordnance; who *m.* 23 November, 1696, Anne Boyle, younger dau. and eventually heiress of Murrough Boyle, Viscount Blesinton; and dying in London, 10 January, 1727, had issue by her (who *re-m.* with John Farquharson, Esq., and *d.* 27 October, 1741), five sons and four daus., who all *d.* infants, except Mary, the wife of James, Lord Tyrawley, and

SIR WILLIAM STEWART, 3rd Viscount Mountjoy, *b.* 7 April, 1709, who was created EARL OF BLESINTON, 7 December, 1745. His lordship *m.* 10 January, 1733, Eleanor, dau. and heiress of Robert Fitzgerald, Esq. of Castle Dod, co. Cork, by whom he had two sons, William, *b.* 14 March, 1734, *d. v. p.,* Lionel-Robert, *b.* 12 April, 1736, buried 23rd of that month ·in the chancel of St Michans Church. The earl *d.* 14 August, 1769, when the peerage EXPIRED, but the baronetcy devolved on his heir-at-law, Sir Annesley Stewart, M.P., of Fort Stewart, co. Donegal, and is now enjoyed by Sir Augustus Stewart, Bart.

Arms—Gu., a fesse chequy, arg. and az., between three lions rampant, or.

STEWART—DUKE OF ALBANY.

Lineage.

ROBERT STEWART, 3rd, but 2nd surviving son of King ROBERT II., by Elizabeth Mure, his wife, *b.* in 1339, obtained the great Earldom of Menteith by his marriage with Margaret, Countess of Menteith, dau. and heir of Alan, Earl of Menteith, and became subsequently EARL OF FIFE and MENTEITH, and was created ·DUKE OF ALBANY, according to Fordun, in 1398. In 1383, he was appointed great chamberlain of Scotland, which office he held till 1408, when he resigned it in favour of his son, John, Earl of Buchan; and in 1389, was recognized as governor of the kingdom. By Margaret, Countess of Menteith, who was his 1st wife, he had issue,

MURDOCH, 2nd Duke of Albany.
Isabel, *m.* 1st, to Alexander, Earl of Ross, and 2ndly, to Walter, Lord Haliburton, of Dirleton.
Marjory, *m.* to Sir Duncan Campbell, of Lochow, created Lord Campbell, 1445.
Elizabeth, *m.* to Sir Malcolm Fleming, of Cumbernauld.
Margaret, *m.* to Robert, Lord Lorn and Innermeath.
Beatrix, *m.* to James, 7th Earl of Douglas, Duke of Tourraine.
A dau., *m.* to Sir George Abernethy, of Salton.

The regent *m.* 2ndly, Muriella, eldest dau. of Sir William Keith, Great Marischal of Scotland, and had by her,

JOHN, Earl of Buchan.
Andrew, *d. s. p.*
Robert, killed with his brother, the Earl of Buchan, at the battle of Verneuil, 1424, *s. p.*

This powerful nobleman governed Scotland under ROBERT II. and ROBERT III., and as regent for JAMES I., for fifty years, and *d.* at the age of eighty and upwards. "The Duke of Albany," says Scott, "as a statesman, was an unprincipled politician; and as a soldier, a man of suspected courage." Winton and Bower, however, speak of him in high terms of praise, and even Pinkerton cannot deny him some kind of commendation. The eldest son,

MURDOCH STEWART, 2nd Duke of Albany, *m.* in 1391, Isabel, dau. of Duncan, Earl of Lennox, and had the EARLDOM OF LENNOX settled on him, his wife, and their issue, after the death of his father-in-law, Duncan, without heirs male of his body. In 1419, Murdoch *s.* his father as Duke of Albany, and in his office of regent of Scotland, but with far inferior talents for government.

By this great heiress, Albany had four sons, who, as is said by a contemporary writer (Cupar MSS. of the Scotichronicon,) were men of "princely stature and lovely person, eloquent, wise, agreeable, and beloved." Robert, the eldest, *d. s. p., v. p.,* in 1421. Walter and Alexander were beheaded along with their father, and James survived to transmit the blood of his race, through many lines, to our own day.

King JAMES I., on his restoration to power was not slow in commencing the work of vengeance on the race by whom he had been long supplanted. The first victim was Walter, the regent's eldest surviving son, who was called Walter of the Lennox, as heir to the earldom of his maternal grandfather. He was carried off before t 1e king's coronation, and confined in the Rock of the B ss. Soon after, the aged grandfather, Duncan, Earl of Lennox, was seized with Sir Robert Graham, and confined in the castle of Edinburgh. In March, 1425, JAMES felt himself sufficiently secure on his throne to order the arrest of the late regent himself, along with twenty-six of the most illustrious men in Scotland, many of whom, however, were immediately released, and were, in fact, compelled to sit in judgment on the distinguished and foredoomed victims. When the regent was arrested, the Duchess Isabella was also seized, at their castle of Doune, and dragged to the fortress of Tantallon. James, the youngest son, alone escaped, and being a daring youth, he made one desperate effort to succour or avenge his family. With a body of armed followers he sacked Dumbarton, and put to death its commander, John Stewart, of Dundonald, natural son of King ROBERT II.; but his struggle was unavailing, and he fled to Ireland, where he became father of many families which have been great in the h'story of their country.

In a parliament, where the king presided, in May, 1425, Walter Stewart of the Lennox was tried by his peers, convicted, and instantly beheaded. On the next day his brother, Alexander, had his head struck off; and he was followed to the scaffold, a few hours later, by Duke Murdoch, his father; and the Earl of Lennox also perished, at the age of eighty. They were all put to death on the castle hill of Stirling, from which high position the unhappy ex-regent was enabled to cast a last look on his rich and romantic territory of Menteith, and the hills of Lennox, to which his duchess was heir; and he could even descry the stately castle of Doune, which had been his own vice-regal palace. The companion of these most unhappy princes, Sir Robert Graham, was released, and he lived to consummate his long-planned vengeance on the king, in 1437. He it was who, when James cried for mercy, in his extremity, replied, "Thou cruel tyrant, thou never hadst any mercy on lords born of thy blood, therefore no mercy shalt thou have here!"

This ruin seems to have smitten the house of Albany most unexpectedly. On May, 1424, Duke Murdoch, as Earl of Fife, seated his royal cousin on the throne, to receive the unction and the crown. His son, Alexander, was then made a belted knight by the king's hands, and the duchess appeared as the first lady at the court; but in the commencement of the following year she had to mourn the violent deaths of her husband, her father, and her two sons.

The widowhood of the Duchess of Albany was long and dreary, though rich and great. She inherited the vast estates of her father, which were not confiscated, and his earldom, which was not forfeited. She retired within her princely domains to her feudal castle of Inchmurran, in an island of Loch Lomond, where she bore, with punctilious ceremony, the lofty names of Albany and Lennox, and possessed all the broad and fair domains around that beautiful lake. Yet, widowed and childless, she was haunted by the recollection that her race was extingu shed by the hand of the executioner, and that her fair and handsome sons would never return at her call—

"To renew the wild pomp of the chase and the ball."

The widowed duchess outlived the destroyer of her family for twenty-three years; and, if she harboured feelings of revenge against him, they were amply gratified by his murder, in 1437, which was attended by every circumstance of horror,

There are many charters of the Duchess of Albany, which prove her to have lived at her castle in Loch Lomond, and in

possession of the power and wealth of her family until the year 1460. A very interesting one, conveying lands for the pious purpose of offering prayers for the souls of her murdered husband, father, and sons, and dated 18 May, 1451, is attested by Murdoch, Arthur, and Robert Stewart of Albany, who all seem at that time to have been domesticated with her at Inchmurran Castle.

Who were these three Stewarts of Albany? They were three of the seven illegitimate children of James Stewart, the duke's youngest son, who fled to Ireland, and who there formed a connection with a lady of the house of the Lord of the Isles, v hich produced a flourishing progeny. These youths seem to have been adopted, after their father's death, by their grandmother, to bear her company in the melancholy, deserted halls of her feudal castle. These seven sons are all well-known to history. Many of them were legitimated, which, however, did not entitle them to succeed to the possessions of their family, though some of them and their descendants reached the highest rank and offices in the state, and founded great families. When the Duchess Isabella died, in 1460, her title of Lennox seems to have become dormant. She had no legitimate descendants, and those of her two sisters had each some claim to the succession. Her 2nd sister, Margaret, was wife of Sir Robert Menteith of Ruskey, and her daus. carried her claims into the families of Napier and Haldane. Her 3rd sister, Elizabeth, was wife of Sir John Stewart of Darnley, and her grandson, John, created a lord of parliament, as Lord Darnley, assumed the title of Earl of Lennox, in 1478, and was the direct paternal ancestor of JAMES I., King of Great Britain.

A rapid review of the varied fortunes of the seven sons of James Stewart[*] of Albany, the youngest of the fair and noble princes of the house of Albany, and heir of the line of Lennox will not inappropriately conclude this memoir.

I. Andrew, was invited from Ireland by King JAMES II., raised to high honours, created Lord Avondale in 1459, was appointed in 1160, lord high chancellor of Scotland (which office he held for twenty-five years), and had a grant for life of the landed estates belonging to the Earldom of Lennox. He *d. s. p.* in 1488.

VI. Walter, was grandfather of Andrew Stewart, who was Lord Avondale in 1501; and he was the father of three distinguished sons,

  1 Andrew, 3rd Lord Avondale, who exchanged his title for that of Ochiltree. His direct representative, Andrew, 3rd Lord Ochiltree, resigned his Scottish title, settled in Ireland, and was created a peer as Lord Castlestewart, in 1619. His descendant is the present Earl of Castlestewart, who is the representative of the House of Albany. A younger son of the 2nd Lord Ochiltree, Captain James Stewart, achieved a bad notoriety under King JAMES VI., when for a few years he was all-powerful as Earl of Arran and Lord High Chancellor; but his fall was as sudden as his rise had been.

  2 Henry Stewart was created Lord Methven in 1528, and *m.* in 1620, Princess Margaret of England, widow of King JAMES IV. He had no issue by the Queen, and his issue by a 2nd wife failed.

  3 James Stewart of Beath, was father of James, created Lord Doun in 1581. His grandson, James, Lord Doun, *m.* the dau. and heir of the Regent Earl of Moray, natural son of King JAMES V., and the descendant of this marriage is the present Earl of Moray.

The four intermediate sons between Andrew and Walter were less distinguished, and do not appear to have left issue. They were MURDOCH, ARTHUR, ROBERT, and ALEXANDER; and three of them seem to have been the companions of their widowed grandmother.

VII. JAMES STEWART, the youngest, was ancestor to the still existing families of Stewart of Ardvohrlich, and Stewart of Glenbuckey.

The Dukedom of Albany continued forfeited to the crown till it was conferred on

ALEXANDER STEWART, 2nd son of King JAMES II.; King JAMES III., having imbibed an unhappy prejudice against his two brothers, the Duke of Albany and the Earl of Marr, they were arrested by his orders, 1479, and Marr put to death. Albany was committed prisoner to the castle of Edinburgh, whence he made his escape by the aid of two casks of malmsey wine, with which he intoxicated his guards, and, according to Pitscottie, killed them. "One of the casks," says Douglas, "contained a coil of rope, which was let down from a retired part of the wall (the king was then in the castle); Albany's servant

---

[*] The Hon. and Rev. Andrew Godfrey Stuart, M.A., in his *Sketch of the House of Castle Stuart*, maintains, and with strong evidence to support his assertion, that Andrew, 1st Lord Avondale, was son of Walter, Duke Murdoch's eldest son.

first descended, but from the shortness of the rope, fell and broke his thigh. The duke guarded against the same fate by lengthening the cord with the torn sheets of his bed, and descended safely, first carrying his faithful domestic upon his back to a place of security, whence proceeding to Newhaven, he was received on board a French ship lying off that place, which immediately sailed for France. He was forfeited 4 October, 1479, and troops were sent to besiege his castle of Dunbar, which soon yielded, the garrison escaping in boats to England. He met with an honourable reception at Paris, where his expenses were defrayed by Louis XI., and he remained there till 1482, when he proceeded to England, where he entered into an agreement with King Edward IV., disgraceful to himself, and treasonable to his country. By that agreement, Edward obliged himself to assist in reducing Scotland, and maintaining his royalty against James." Albany assumed the title of Alexander, King of Scotland, by gift of the English king; and consented to pay homage to Edward, and to give up to him some counties and places in the south of Scotland, particularly Berwick. He afterwards joined the English army, which advanced against Berwick, and after taking that town, marched to Edinburgh. His grace nevertheless found means to make his peace with his brother, King James III., who engaged to restore his estates and offices, and to grant an amnesty to his followers, and having delivered the king from the power of the Earl of Atholl, his uncle, who kept him a prisoner in Edinburgh Castle, he acquired great favour. However, in 1483, Albany renewed his former treasonable agreement with King Edward IV., and having previously placed his castle of Dunbar in the hands of the English, he and the Earl of Douglas invaded Scotland with 500 cavalry and some infantry. They suffered a defeat at Lochmaben, 22 July, 1484, when Douglas was taken prisoner, and Albany, escaping by the swiftness of his horse, retired into France. By act of the parliament of Scotland, 1 October, 1487, the lands forfeited by Alexander, Duke of Albany, Earl of March, Marr, and Garioch, Lord of Annandale and Man, were annexed to the crown. These lands were the Lordship and Earldom of March, the Baronies of Dunbar and Colbrandspath, with the castle of Dunbar, and tower and fortalice of Colbrandspath, and the lordship of Annandale, with the castle of Lochmaben. Alexander, Duke of Albany, was accidentally killed at Paris in 1485, by the splinter of a lance at a tournament between the Duke of Orleans and another knight, and was buried in the Celestines in that city. He m. 1st, Lady Catherine Sinclair, eldest dau. of William, Earl of Orkney and Caithness, but sentence of divorce was pronounced between the parties by the official of Lothian, 2 March, 1477-8, on account of propinquity of blood. By her he had one son, Alexander, who was declared illegitimate by act of parliament, 13 November, 1516. He had first, the priory of Whithorn, in Galloway; afterwards, the abbey of Inchaffray; then that of Scone; was consecrated bishop of Murray, 1527, and dying in 1534, was buried at Scone. Alexander, Duke of Albany, m. 2ndly, 16 February, 1480, Anne de la Tour, 3rd dau. of Bertrand, Comte d'Auvergne and de Bouillon, and by her (who m. 2ndly, 15 February, 1487, Louis, Comte de la Chambre, father of Cardinal Phillipe de la Chambre, and dying 13 October, 1512, was buried in the Carmelite monastery de la Rochette, in Savoy) had one son,

John Stewart, Duke of Albany, "who, in 1514," says Douglas, "was invited to assume the regency of Scotland, during the minority of King James V., arrived at Dumbarton, 18 May, 1515, with eight ships laden with ammunition, warlike stores, and the gold and luxuries of France; the peers and chiefs crowded to his presence; his exotic elegance of manners, his condescension, affability, and courtly demeanour, won all hearts. As soon as the forms would admit, a parliament was assembled at Edinburgh, where the first care, after the restitution of his honours and estates, was to inaugurate Albany in the regency, a ceremony performed with great splendour. A sword was delivered, a crown was placed upon his head, and the peers paid solemn obeisance, while Albany was with martial music proclaimed protector and governor of Scotland, till the period of the king's attaining the age of eighteen years." This, the celebrated Regent Albany of the reign of James V., after governing the kingdom with great incapacity and extreme unpopularity for eight years, made his final retreat to France in 1523, loaded with the curses and reproaches of the nation. John, Duke of Albany, m. 8 July, 1505, his cousin-german, Anne de la Tour, Comtesse D'Auvergne and de Lauragais, with whom he got the county of Lauragais, and the seigneuries of Douzenac, Courreze, and Boussac. She was eldest dau. of John de la Tour, Comte D'Auvergne, by Jane de Bourbon, his wife, eldest dau. of John, Comte de Vendôme, and must have been very young at her nuptials, as her father and mother's contract of marriage is

dated 11 January, 1495. She d. s. p. at St. Saturnin. Her sister, Madeline de la Tour, m. 13 June, 1518, Lorenzo de Medici, Duke of Urbino, nephew of Pope Leo X., and d. in the following year, leaving one child, Catherine de Medici, Countess of Auvergne and Lauragais, Queen of Henry II. of France.

The next possessor of the title of Albany was
Henry Stewart, Lord Darnley, Earl of Ross, eldest son of Matthew, 4th Earl of Lennox, who was created Duke of Albany, to him and the heirs male of his body legitimately to be procreated, 20 July, 1565, nine days before his nuptials with Mary, Queen of Scots. The next on the list was
Charles Stewart, 2nd son of King James VI., who was, at his baptism, 23 December, 1600, created Duke of Albany, Marquess of Ormond, Earl of Ross, and Lord Ardmanoch, and ascended the throne as Charles I. The last time the dukedom of Albany was conferred on a Royal Stewart, was 31 December, 1660, when the title was given to
James Stewart, Duke of York, 2nd son of King Charles I., and at His Royal Highness's accession to the throne, 1685, the dukedom vested in the crown.

The direct line of the Royal Stuarts terminated with the late Cardinal York, in 1807. He was the 2nd son of the old "Pretender," James-Francis-Edward, only son of King James II., by Mary-Clementina, his wife, dau. of Prince James Sobieski (see p. 518), and was born at Rome, 26 March, 1725, where he was baptized by the name of Henry Benedict Maria Clemens. In 1745, he went to France to head an army of 15,000 men assembled at Dunkirk for the invasion of England, but the news of Culloden's fatal contest counteracted the proposed plan. Henry Benedict returned to Rome, and exchanging the sword for the priest's stole, was made a cardinal by Pope Benedict XIV.

Eventually, after the expulsion of Pius VI. by the French, Cardinal York fled from his splendid residences at Rome and Frascati to Venice, infirm in health, distressed in circumstances, and borne down by the weight of seventy-five years. For a while he subsisted on the produce of some silver plate which he had rescued from the ruin of his property, but soon privation and poverty pressed upon him, and his situation became so deplorable, that Sir John Cox Hippisley deemed it right to have it made known to the King of England. George III. immediately gave orders that a present of £2,000 should be remitted to the last of the Stuarts, with an intimation that he might draw for a similar amount in the following July, and that an annuity of £4,000 would be at his service so long as his circumstances might require it. This liberality was accepted, and acknowledged by the Cardinal in terms of gratitude, and made a deep impression on the Papal Court. The pension, Cardinal York continued to receive till his decease in June, 1807, at the age of eighty-two. From the time he entered into holy orders, his eminence took no part in politics, and seems to have laid aside all worldly views. The only exception to this line of conduct was his having medals struck at his brother's death, in 1788, bearing on the face a representation of his head, with this inscription—"Henricus Nonus Magnæ Britanniæ Rex; non voluntate hominum, sed Dei Gratiâ."* Those who have visited Rome will not fail to recollect Canova's monument in St. Peter's to the last of the Stewarts.

With Cardinal York, expired all the descendants of King James II.; and the representation of the royal houses of Plantagenet, Tudor, and Stuart thereupon vested by inheritance in Charles Emmanuel IV., King of Sardinia, who was eldest son of Victor-Amadeus III., the grandson of Victor-Amadeus, King of Sardinia, by Anna-Maria, his wife, dau. of Henrietta, Duchess of Orleans, dau. of King Charles I. of England. Charles Emmanuel IV. d. s. p. in 1819, and was succeeded by his brother, Victor-Emmanuel I., King of Sardinia, whose co-representatives are Maria-Theresa, of Modena, Archduchess of Austria, wife of Louis, Prince of Bavaria, niece and heiress of Francis Ferdinand V., ex-Duke of Modena; Mary-Theresa, Duchess of Parma; Anne, Empress of Austria, and Francis II., ex-King of Naples.

Arms—Of Robert Stewart, Duke of Albany—Quarterly: 1st and 4th, or, a lion rampant, and in chief, a label of three points, az., for the title of Albany, 2nd and 3rd, or, a fesse chequy, az. and arg., a label of three points in chief.

STEWART—EARL OF ARRAN.

By Charter, dated 22 April, 1581.

Lineage.

Captain James Stewart, of Bothwellmuir (2nd son of Andrew, Lord Ochiltree, whose mother, Lady Margaret Hamilton, was

* Burke's Vicissitudes of Families.

507

only child of James, 1st Earl of Arran by his 1st wife, Beatrix Drummond) served for some years in the army of the States of Holland, against the Spaniards. Returning to Scotland in 1579, he found means to obtain the favour of JAMES VI., who, in a few days after his appearance at court, appointed him a gentleman of his bedchamber, a privy councillor, captain of his guard, and tutor to the Earl of Arran, who had been declared an idiot. "Captain Stewart immediately commenced an opposition to the Earl of Morton, regent of Scotland; and 30 December, 1580, preferred an accusation against that nobleman before the king in council, at Holyrood House, of being accessory to the death of Lord Darnley; and Morton was, on that accusation, tried, convicted, and executed. Captain Stewart's proceedings in this affair were approved of in council as good service to his Majesty. Captain Stewart had a charter of the Earldom of Arran, the Baronies of Hamilton and Kinniel, and the other estates of the Hamilton family in the cos. of Bute, Lanark, Kirkcudbright, Berwick, and Linlithgow, 22 April, 1581; and he obtained a letter of confirmation under the great seal, 28 October, 1581, of new ratifying the old creation of the Earldom of Arran, and creating him and his heirs male Earl of Arran, Lord of Avane and Hamilton." So far we quote from WOOD's *Douglas*. Robertson thus delineates Stewart, Earl of Arran:—"Stewart, Earl of Arran, was remarkable for all the vices which render a man formidable to his country, and a pernicious counsellor to his prince, nor did he possess one virtue to counterbalance these vices, unless dexterity in conducting his own designs, and an enterprising courage superior to the sense of danger, may pass by that name. Unrestrained by religion, regardless of decency, and undismayed by opposition, he aimed at objects seemingly unattainable; but under a prince void of experience, and blind to the defects of those who had gained his favour, his audacity was successful, and honours, wealth, and power were the reward of his crimes." In 1584, Arran succeeded the Earl of Argyll as high chancellor of Scotland, and subsequently procured the appointment of lieutenant of the kingdom, in which character he had a private and confidential conference on the borders with Lord Hunsdon, the relative and envoy of ELIZABETH. For nearly two years after, Arran exercised almost regal authority, and acted with venality and arrogance, until at length the lords whom he had banished, taking up arms, surprised Stirling, 2 November, 1585. Arran, finding that resistance was hopeless, fled to the north, and was deprived of his honours, and declared an enemy to his country by public proclamation. The title of Arran was restored to the Hamilton family, and is still enjoyed by the Duke of Hamilton, and the chancellor's place was given to Sir John Maitland, of Thirlestane. After this, Captain Stewart, as he was now styled, lived privately at Newtown, an estate he possessed in Ayrshire, till 1595, when he was again brought to the king, who held out some hopes of a renewal of royal favour: but the general alarm and disgust were so great, at the reappearance of this ill-omened and wicked man, that he was counselled to withdraw himself in all haste from court, and return to Ayrshire, where he had been permitted to remain unnoticed and in obscurity. As he rode back through Simonstown, near Douglas, in Lanarkshire, accompanied only by a servant or two, he was attacked and slain by Sir James Douglas, of Torthorald, nephew of the Regent, Morton; his head was cut off and carried on the point of a lance in a kind of triumph through the country. The body of this once proud and all-powerful man is said to have been neglected on the waste road, until it was mangled by swine. Captain Stewart *m.* 6 July, 1581, Lady Elizabeth Stewart, eldest dau. of John, 4th Earl of Athole, and widow 1st, of Hugh, 6th Lord Lovat, and 2ndly, of Robert, Earl of Lennox and March, grand-uncle of King JAMES VI.; by her he had issue,

    I. JAMES (Sir) of Killeith, Lord Ochiltree. (*See that title.*)
    II. Henry, grantee from King CHARLES I., of the manor of Corrigan, in Killyman, Ireland, father of a son, William (whose only child, Harry, *d. s. p.*), and of two daus., Catherine, *m.* to Henry, Lord Methven; and Barbara, *m.* to Col. Stuart, who eventually *s.* to the manor of Corrigan.
    III. Frederick, who appears to have *d. s. p.*

STEWART—EARL OF ATHOLL.

By Charter, dated 6 March, 1595-6.

Lineage.

SIR ROBERT STEWART, son of Sir James, 4th son of Sir John Stewart, of Bonkyll, was designed of Innermeath, in a donation to the abbey of Culross, 1362, and in the parliament of King ROBERT II., at Scone, in 1373. He *d.* 1386, leaving issue a dau., Catherine, wife of John Bethune, of Balfour, and two sons, I. JOHN, ancestor of the Stewarts of Innermeath and Lorn, and II. ROBERT, of Durisdeer, who *m.* Janet de Ergadia, dau. and heir of Ewen de Ergadia, Lord of Lorn, by Joanna de Izac, granddau. maternally of King ROBERT BRUCE. Robert, of Durisdeer, transferred his wife's lordship of Lorn to his elder brother John, of Innermeath; he was killed at the battle of Shrewsbury, in 1403, and was ancestor of the Stewarts of Rossyth, co. Fife, and of Craigie Hall and Newhalls, co. Linlithgow.

SIR JOHN STEWART, of Innermeath, the elder son, who acquired from his brother the lordship of Lorn, and is designed of Innermeath, Lord of Lorn, in 1407 and 1412, had issue,

    ROBERT, his heir.
    Archibald, living in 1452.
    JAMES (Sir), the BLACK KNIGHT OF LORN.
    Alexander, ancestor of the STEWARTS of Grandtully
    William.
    Christian, *m.* to James Dundas, of Dundas.
    Isabel, *m.* 1st, to Sir William Oliphant, of Aberdalgy; and 2ndly, to Sir David Murray, of Tullibardine.

The eldest son,

ROBERT STEWART, of Lorn, was created a lord of parliament, and is a witness, under the title of "Robertus, Dominus Lorn," to a charter, dated 5 September, 1439. He *m.* Margaret, dau. of Robert, Duke of Albany, governor of Scotland, and left, with two daus., *m.* respectively to Robert, Lord Erskine, and to John, 1st Lord Lindsay, of the Byres, a son and successor,

JOHN STEWART, 2nd Lord Lorn; who had, on his own resignation, a charter of the Lordship of Lorn, Barony of Innermeath, and lands of Redcastle, 20 June, 1452, to himself and the heirs male of his body; which failing, to Walter, Alan, David, and Robert, his brothers; Archibald Stewart, his uncle; Sir James Stewart, Knt., and Thomas Stewart, his cousins; and the heirs male of their bodies respectively. His lordship left three daus., his co-heirs, viz.,

    ISABEL, *m.* to COLIN, 1st EARL OF ARGYLL.
    MARGARET, *m.* to Sir Colin Campbell, of Glenurchy.
    MARION, *m.* to Arthur Campbell, of Otter.

WALTER STEWART, on the demise of his brother, John, Lord Lorn, without legitimate male issue, *s.* to the Lordship of Lorn; but having exchanged that barony with the Earl of Argyll for that of Innermeath in 1470, he was thenceforward styled Lord Innermeath. He *m.* Margaret, dau. of John, Lord Lindsay, of Byres, and was *s.* by his son,

THOMAS STEWART, 2nd Lord Innermeath, slain at Flodden in 1513. His lordship *m.* Lady Janet Keith, and left (with a dau., Marion, wife of Patrick Ogilvy, of Inchmartin,) a son and successor,

RICHARD STEWART, 3rd Lord Innermeath; who *m.* Margaret, dau. of John, Lord Lindsay, of Byres, and by her (who *m.* 2ndly, Sir James Stewart) left at his decease, in 1529, a son and successor,

JOHN STEWART, 4th Lord Innermeath, who *m.* Elizabeth, dau. of Sir John Bethune, of Creich, and had three sons, JAMES, John and Alexander. The eldest,

JAMES STEWART, 4th Lord Innermeath, *m.* Helen, dau. of James, 4th Lord Ogilvy, of Airly, and had (with three daus., Margaret, *m.* to Sir William Ruthven, of Bandean; Janet, *m.* to Alexander Cuming, of Culter; and Grizel, *m.* to Thomas Gordon, of Cluny,) a son and successor,

JOHN STEWART, 6th Lord Innermeath, to whom King JAMES granted a charter of the EARLDOM OF ATHOLL, 6 March, 1595-6. He *m.* 1st, Margaret, 2nd dau. of Sir David Lindsay, of Edzell, Earl of Crawford; and 2nd'y, Lady Mary Ruthven, Dowager of John, 5th Earl of Atholl. By the latter he had no issue; but by the former he left at his decease, in 1605 (with a dau., Margaret, *m.* 1st, to Sir James Stewart, of Ballechin; and 2ndly, to Sir Robert Crichton, of Cluny), a son and heir,

JAMES STEWART, 2nd Earl of Atholl, who *m.* Lady Mary Stuart, 2nd dau. of John, 5th Earl of Atholl; but *d. s. p.* in 1625, when the earldom, under the terms of the charter, reverted to the crown.

Arms—Quarterly: 1st and 4th, or, a fesse chequy, az. and arg., in chief a garb (another, a fleur-de-lis, and in Balfour's blazon, a buckle) of the 2nd; 2nd and 3rd, arg., a galley with flames of fire issuing out of the fore and hinder parts, and out of the top of the mast, for the Lordship of Lorn.

STEWART—EARL OF ATHOL.

Lineage.

Sir James Stewart, the Black Knight of Lorn, 3r.l son of Sir John Stewart, of Innermeath and Lorn, m., 1438, Lady Joanna Beaufort, Dowager of King James I. of Scotland, and by her had three sons,

John, his heir.
James, Earl of Buchan.
Andrew, bishop-of-Moray.

The eldest,

Sir John Stewart, of Balveny, created Earl of Athol, in 1457, acted a conspicuous part in the political transactions of his time, and was mainly instrumental in suppressing the rebellion of the Earl of Ross, upon which occasion he assumed the motto, still borne by his descendants, "Furth fortune and fill the fetters." He m. 1st, Lady Margaret Douglas, relict of William, 8th Earl of Douglas, and only dau. of Archibald, 5th Earl of Douglas, and had by her two daus., Janet, m. to Alexander, 3rd Earl of Huntly; and Elizabeth, wife of Andrew, Lord Gray. The earl m. 2ndly, Lady Eleanor Sinclair, dau. of William, Earl of Orkney and Caithness, and by her had issue.

I. John, 2nd Earl of Athol.
II. Andrew, prebend of Craig, postulate of Dunkeld, 1515, consecrated bishop of Caithness, 1518, d. 1542.
I. Jean, m. to Sir Robert Gordon, of Pitlurg.
II. Catherine, m. to John, Lord Forbes.
III. Elspeth, m. about 1510, to Robert Innes, of Innermarky.
IV. Marjory, m. to Sir Colin Campbell, of Glenurchy.
V. Margaret, m. to William Murray, of Tullibardine.
VI. Isabel, m to Alexander Robertson, of Strowan.
VII. Anne, m. to John, 3rd Earl of Lennox.

He d. 19 September, 1512, and was s. by his son,

John Stewart, 2nd Earl of Athol, who fell at Flodden the year after his succession. He m. Lady Mary Campbell, dau. of Archibald, Earl of Argyll, and left issue,

I. John, his successor.
I. Isabel, m. to Kenneth Mackenzie, of Kintail.
II. Elizabeth, m. to William Sutherland, of Duffus.
III. Helen, m. to John, 6th Lord Lindsay, of Byres.
IV. Janet, m. 1st, Alexander, Master of Sutherland; 2ndly, Sir Hugh Kennedy, of Girvan Mains; 3rdly, Henry, 1st Lord Methven; and 4thly, Patrick, Lord Ruthven.
V. Isabel, m. to James Herring, of Lethendy and Glasclune.
VI. Jean, m. to James Arbuthnot, of Arbuthnot.

The son and heir,

John Stewart, 3rd Earl of Athol, a nobleman of princely hospitality and magnificence, who d. in 1542, leaving issue by Grizel, his 1st wife, dau. of Sir John Rattray, of that ilk,

John, his heir.
James (Sir), of Balveny.
Helen, m. to John Grant, of Grant.
Helen, m. to Walter Wood, of Balbegno.
Elizabeth, m. to Thomas Stewart, of Grandtully.

He m. 2ndly, Jean, youngest dau. of John, 6th Lord Forbes, and by her, who m. 2ndly, Alexander Hay, of Dalgety, and 3rdly, William Leslie, of Balquhain, had two daus.,

Barbara, m. to James Menzies, of Weem.
Jean, m. 1st, to John Otterburn, of Redhall, and 2ndly to George Crawford, of Leifnerris.

The son and heir,

John Stewart, 4th Earl of Athol, high chancellor of Scotland, was a distinguished actor in the troubled times in which he lived. His lordship m. 1st, Lady Elizabeth Gordon, 3rd dau. of George, 4th Earl of Huntly, and had by her two daus., Elizabeth, m. 1st, to Hugh, 6th Lord Lovat; 2ndly, to Robert, Earl of Lennox; and 3rdly, James Stewart, Earl of Arran; and Margaret, wife of George, 7th Lord Saltoun. The earl m. 2ndly, Margaret, 3rd dau. of Malcolm, 3rd Lord Fleming, by whom he had,

John, his heir.
Grizel, m. to David, 10th Earl of Crawford.
Jean, m. to Sir Duncan Campbell, of Glenurchy.
Anne, m. to Francis, 9th Earl of Erroll.

The Chancellor Athol d. in 1579, and was interred with great solemnity in the south aisle of the cathedral church of St. Giles, Edinburgh; he was s. by his son,

John Stewart, 5th Earl of Athol, who m. Lady Mary Ruthven, 2nd dau of William, 1st Earl of Gowrie, and by her (who m. 2ndly, John, Lord Innermeath, created Earl of Athol, in 1596) had issue,

Dorothea, m. 1604, to William Murray, 2nd Earl of Tullibar-

dine, and was mother of John Murray, created Earl of Athol.
Mary, m. to James Stewart, Earl of Athol, d. s. p.
Jean, m. 1st, to Henry, Lord St. Colme, and 2ndly, to Nicol Bellenden.
Anne, m. to Andrew, Master of Ochiltree.

The earl d in 1595, when the earldom reverted to the Crown.

STEWART—LORD AVONDALE.

Lineage.

Robert Stewart, 3rd son of Robert II., acquired the Earldom of Menteith by his marriage with Margaret, Countess of Menteith, and afterwards succeeding to the Earldom of Fife, became Earl of Fife and Menteith. This nobleman, subsequently regent of Scotland, was one of the first persons honoured with a dukedom in the Scottish peerage. In 1398, the heir apparent to the throne having been created Duke of Rothsay, the Regent Fife was at the same time raised to the Dukedom of Albany. His grace, who fills a conspicuous place in Scottish history, d. in 1419, and was s. by the only son of his 1st marriage,

Murdoch Stewart, 2nd Duke of Albany, who m. Isabel, eldest dau. and co-heir of Duncan, Earl of Lennox Previously to the decease of his father, this nobleman was a captive for thirteen years in England, having been made prisoner at the battle of Homildon, in 1402. He s. the late duke in the regency as well as the dukedom, but with talents for such a station of a very inferior order. Within a few short years, he was brought to the block, with his two elder surviving sons, and his father-in-law, the Earl of Lennox (anno 1425), when the Dukedom of Albany reverted to the crown. His grace's next son,

Sir James Stewart, called James the Gross, upon being apprised of the imprisonment of his father by James I., flew to arms, and with the aid of the bishop of Argyll, raising a band of highland freebooters, assaulted and burnt the town of Dumbarton, and put Sir James Stewart, of Dundonald, natural son of Robert II., governor of the castle, to the sword, 3 May, 1424. For these acts of violence he was proclaimed a felon, and forced to seek an asylum in Ireland, whence he never afterwards returned, but d. there in 1451. He had issue,

I. Andrew, Lord Avondale.
II. Alexander, d s. p.
III. Murdoch, (Sir), knighted by King James III., 1465.
IV. Arthur, d. s. p.
V. Walter, of Morphie, m. Elizabeth, dau. of Arnot, of Arnot, and had issue,
    1 Alexander, who d. before 1490, leaving a son,
      Andrew, 2nd Lord Avondale.
    2 John.
    3 George, of Johnston, ancestor of Stuart of Inchbreck and Laithers.
    1 Margaret, m. to Alexander Cunningham, of Drumquharth.
VI. James.
I. Matilda, m. to Sir William Edmondstone, of Duntreath, Bart.

The statement that Andrew Stewart and his brothers were the children of James More, the younger brother of Walter, and the younger son of Murdoch, Duke of Albany, rests originally on the authority of the learned genealogist, Crawford, whom subsequent writers have adopted as their guide; but Buchanan, Drummond of Hawthornden, and several MSS. in the Harleian Collection, one signed apparently by Segar, Garter, make them children of Walter, Duke Murdoch's eldest son. This latter view is that taken by the Hon. and Rev. A.-G. Stuart in his memoirs of the Stuarts of Castlestuart. Be the fact, however, what it may, certain it is that

Andrew Stewart, 1st Lord Avondale, was grandson of Murdoch, Duke of Albany. This Andrew was brought over from Ireland by James II., and created, in 1459, Lord Avondale; he was afterwards chancellor of Scotland, and dying s. p. 1488, was s. by his grand-nephew,

Andrew Stewart, 2nd Lord Avondale, who was son of Alexander, and grandson of Walter of Morphie: he m. Margaret, dau. of Sir John Kennedy, of Blairquhan, in Ayrshire, and had issue.

I. Andrew, 3rd Lord Avondale.
II. Henry, Lord Methven.
III. James (Sir), of Beath, ancestor of the Earl of Moray.
I. Agnes, m. to John Boswell, of Auchinleck.
II. Anne, m. to Bartholomew Crawford, of Carse.
III. Barbara, m. 1st, to Sinclair of Santry, and 2ndly, to Macleod of Lewes.

The eldest son,

ANDREW STEWART, 3rd Lord Avondale. who, having ex changed his barony with Sir James Hamilton for that of Ochiltrie, was ordained to be called LORD STEWART, *of Ochiltrie,* in time to come, by act of parliament, 15 March. 1542-3. His lordship m. Margaret Hamilton, only child of James, 1st Earl of Arran, by his 1st wife, Beatrix, dau. of John, Lord Drummond, and had a son,

ANDREW STEWART. 2nd Lord Stewart, of Ochiltrie, commonly called the *good Lord Ochiltrie.* who m. 1st, Agnes, dau. of John Cunningham, of Caprington, and 2ndly, a dau. of the Earl of Glencairn, and had issue,

  I. ANDREW, Master of Ochiltrie, who m. Margaret, dau. of Henry, Lord Methven, and had issue,
    1 ANDREW, 3rd Lord Ochiltrie.
    2 Josias, of Bonnyton.
    1 Anne, *m.* to Andrew, 1st Lord Jedburgh.
    2 Margaret, m. to Sir John Stewart, of Traquair.
    3 Marjory, m. to Sir Roger Ashton.
    4 Martha, m. to Rutherford, of Hundeley.
    5 Mary, m. to Sir George Crawford, of Lifnorris.
    6 Janet, m. to Gilbert Kennedy, of Bargany.
  II. JAMES, Earl of Arran.
  III. William (Sir), of Monkton.
  IV. Henry (Sir).
  V. Robert (Sir), of Wester Braco.
  1. Isabel, m. to Thomas Kennedy, of Bargany.
  II. Margaret, 2nd wife of JOHN KNOX.

The good Lord Ochiltrie was *s.* at his decease, in 1592, by his grandson,

ANDREW STEWART, 3rd Lord Ochiltrie; a lord of the bedchamber to JAMES I. of England. who having sold, through pecuniary embarrassment, the Barony of Ochiltrie to his cousin, Sir James Stewart, of Killeith, and relinquished his title to that gentleman, was created, 7 November, 1619, LORD STUART, BARON OF CASTLE-STUART, co. *Tyrone,* in the peerage of Ireland. His descendant is the present EARL OF CASTLE-STUART.

Arms—Quarterly: 1st, or, a lion rampant, gu., within a double tressure, flory-counterflory, of the last, for SCOTLAND; 2nd, or, a fesse, chequy, arg. and az., in chief a label of three points, gu., for STUART; 3rd, arg., a saltier between four roses, gu, for LENNOX; 4th, or, a lion rampant, gu., the whole within a bordure, compony, of the 2nd and 1st.

STEWART—EARL OF BOTHWELL.

Lineage.

JOHN STEWART, prior of Coldinghame, natural son of JAMES V., by Elizabeth, dau. of Sir John Carmichael, m. 4 January, 1561-2, Lady Jean Hepburn, on'y dau. of Patrick, 3rd Earl of Bothwell, and by her (who m. 2udly, John, Master of Caithness) was father of

FRANCIS STEWART, created by JAMES VI., in consideration of his descent from the Hepburns, EARL OF BOTHWELL, in 1587. This nobleman, perhaps the most turbulent, the most versatile, and most treacherous of the age, was at length, after several unsuccessful conspiracies against his royal master, finally driven from Scotland, and compelled to seek a refuge in France. Even this retreat he forfeited by his turbulent temper, and banished thence, went successively to Spain and Naples, dying at the latter place in poverty and infamy. His titles fell under the attainder which was passed against him, and his principal possessions were bestowed upon Scott of Buccleuch, and Ker of Cessford. The earl m. Lady Margaret Douglas, eldest dau. of David, 7th Earl of Angus, and relict of Sir Walter Scott, of Buccleuch, and had issue,

  FRANCIS. who m Lady Isabel Seton, only dau. of Robert, 1st Earl of Wintoun, and dowager of James, 1st Earl of Perth, an l had issue, a dau., Margaret, and a son. Charles Stewart, *b.* in 1618, who is stated by Scott, of Scottstarvet, to have been a trooper in the civil wars.
  John. commendator of Coldinghame, father of Francis, who is mentioned in *Creighton's Memoirs* as a private gentleman in the horse-guards of CHARLES II., by whom he was made captain of dragoons. He commanded the cavalry on the left in the action against the Covenanters at Bothwell Bridge. John Stewart had also a dau., Margaret, who m. Sir John Home, of Renton, and was ancestor of SIR CHARLES E. F. STIRLIN , Bart., of Glorat, who is heir-general of Hepburn and Stewart, Earls of Bothwell.
  Henry.
  Elizabeth, m. to the Hon. James Cranstoun.
  Margaret, m. to Alan, 5th Lord Cathcart.
  Helen, m. to John Macfarlane, of Macfarlane.

Lineage.

The Earldom of Buchan can be traced to the time of WILLIAM THE LION, when

FERGUS, Earl of Buchan, made a grant of a mark of silver annually to the Abbacy of Aberbrothwick, founded by that monarch The only dau. and heiress of this feudal chieftain,

MARJORY, Countess of Buchan, *m.* circa 1210,

WILLIAM COMYN, justiciary of Scotland, who then became in her right Earl of Buchan: their son, ALEXANDER COMYN, 2nd Earl of Buchan (of the Comyns), was also justiciary of Scotland, and one of the six guardians of Scotland in 1286. He m. Elizabeth, dau. of Roger de Quinci, Earl of Winchester, and dying 1289, was *s.* by his son,

JOHN COMYN, 3rd Earl of Buchan, in 1308. This nobleman m. Isabel, dau. of Duncan, Earl of Fife, a lady celebrated for her patriotism and high spirit in placing the crown on the head of ROBERT BRUCE at his coronation at Scone, 29 March, 1306, her brother, Duncan, Earl of Fife, to whom, as the successor of Macduff, that privilege belonged, being then in the English interest. On this account she is denominated by the English writers the most impious of all traitoresses. Falling the same year into the hands of EDWARD I., that monarch avenged himself in a manner which sufficiently indicated the importance of the service her ladyship had rendered to BRUCE. He issued immediate orders that the chamberlain of Scotland do, in one of the turrets of the castle of Berwick-upon-Tweed, caused to be constructed a cage, strongly latticed with wood, cross-barred, and secured with iron, in which he shall put the Countess of Buchan, and that he do cause her to be so strictly guarded that she may not speak with any one of the Scottish nation, nor with any one else, saving with the woman who shall be appointed to attend her, or with the guard who shall have the custody of her person; and that the cage be constructed so that the countess may have therein the convenience of a decent chamber, &c. In this terrible state of incarceration her ladyship remained until released by EDWARD II., in 1313.

The Earldom of Buchan was next granted (having reverted to the crown by the forfeiture of the COMYNS)) by ROBERT II. to his 3rd son, by his wife Elizabeth, dau. of Sir Adam Mure, of Rowallan,

SIR ALEXANDER STEWART, who had also a proportion of the lands of the Comyns. On the demise of this nobleman without legitimate issue, in 1394, the Earldom of Buchan passed to (the eldest son of his brother, Robert, Duke of Albany, by his 2nd wife, Murielia, dau. of Sir William Keith, Grand Marischal of Scotland) his nephew,

JOHN STEWART, EARL OF BUCHAN, *b.* in 1380. This nobleman, a renowned warrior of his time, was sent to France by the Duke of Albany, in command of 7,000 Scotch troops to aid CHARLES VII. against the English, and gained great glory by his victory over the Duke of Clarence, at Beaugé, in Anjou, 22 March, 1421. In this engagement the Duke of Clarence was slain, having been stunned and unhorsed by Buchan himself with a blow of his mace. For this exploit, CHARLES VII. conferred upon him the sword of constable of France. The earl fell gloriously at the battle of Verneuil, 17 August, 1424, and was thus spared the pain of witnessing the utter ruin of his family, which took place the following year. By his wife, Lady Elizabeth Douglas, dau. of Archibald. 4th Earl of Douglas, Duke of Tourraine, he left an only child, MARGARET, who m. George, 2nd Lord Seton. Margaret, Lady Seton, was progenetrix of the great families of SETON, EARL OF WINTON and MONTGOMERIE, EARL OF EGLINTON. The Earl of Eglinton is now her heir male, and it would seem that her heir general is William Hay, Esq., of Dunse Castle. At the death of the Constable Buchan, his earldom devolved, according to the limitation, upon Murdoch, Duke of Albany, and reverted to the crown by the forfeiture of that nobleman the following year.

Arms—Quarterly: 1st and 4th, or, a fesse chequy, az. and arg.; 2nd and 3rd, az., three garbs, or, for the EARLDOM OF BUCHAN.

STEWART—EARL OF CAITHNESS.

Lineage.

DAVID STEWART, Earl Palatine of Strathern, eldest son of King ROBERT II., by his 2nd wife, Euphame Ross, was, by his father created EARL OF CAITHNESS, early in his reign, and is styled Earl Palatine of Strathern, and Earl of Caithness, in several charters. His dau.,

EUPHAME STEWART, Countess Palatine of Strathern, resigned the Earldom of Caithness in favour of her uncle,

WALTER STEWART, Lord Brechin, 2nd son of King ROBERT II., by Euphame Ross, who accordingly obtained from King ROBERT III. a charter of the EARLDOM OF CAITHNESS and regality thereof, by resignation of the Countess Palatine, called Euphame Stewart, Countess Palatine of Strathern, blench, for a reid haulk. He was afterwards created Earl of Athol,* and resigned the Earldom of Caithness in favour of his 2nd son,

ALAN STEWART. Earl of Caithness, who obtained from King JAMES I. a grant dated at Perth, 15 May, 1430, of all and whole the Earldom of Caithness, to himself and the legitimate heirs male of his body; which failing, to Walter, his father, and his heirs, but he did not long enjoy that title. Donald Balloch, a relation of Alexander, Lord of the Isles, landing in Lochaber with a considerable force the next year, 1431, and finding Alexander, Earl of Marr, and Alan, Earl of Caithness, stationed at Inverlochy, co. Inverness, to defend the western coast, he attacked and utterly defeated them. In this conflict the Earl of Caithness was killed, as well as many barons and knights, and several of the earl's personal attendants. Lord Caithness had no child, and his earldom, in terms of the charter, reverted to his father, and on his attainder for the murder of his nephew, and benefactor, JAMES I., in 1437, was forfeited, and annexed to the crown.

STEWART—EARL OF CARRICK.

Lineage.

JOHN STEWART, Lord of Kyle, great-grandson of King ROBERT BRUCE, eldest son of Robert, steward of Scotland, Earl of Strathern, had the EARLDOM OF CARRICK conferred on him by his granduncle, King DAVID II , by a charter in the parliament of Scone, 22 June, 1363. After the accession of his father to the throne, he resigned the Earldom of Carrick into his Majesty's hands, and obtained a new charter thereof to him and Annabella, his wife, in life rent, and to the heirs procreated, or to be procreated betwixt them, in fee, 1 June, 1374. On his succession to the crown of Scotland, by the style of ROBERT III., he conferred the Earldom of Carrick on his eldest son, DAVID, who is designed Duke of Rothesay, Earl of Carrick and of Athayle, in a charter of 14 November, 1398. After the death of the Duke of Rothesay, ROBERT III. granted 10 December, 1404. in free regality to his son and heir, James, steward of Scotland (afterwards King JAMES I.), the whole lands of the stewartry of Scotland, including the EARLDOM OF CARRICK. That earldom has ever since composed part of the inheritance of the princes and steward of Scotland, and is now one of the titles of the Prince of Wales

---

STEWART—EARL OF CARRICK (IN ORKNEY).

Lineage.

JOHN STEWART, 2nd son of Robert, Earl of Orkney, a natural son of JAMES V., was created a peer of Scotland, by the title of Lord Kinclevin, 10 August, 1607, and EARL OF CARRICK, in Orkney, in 1630. His lordship m. at Chelsea, 26 October, 1604, Lady Elizabeth Howard, dau. of Charles, Earl of Nottingham, relict of Sir Robert Southwell, of Woodrising, in Hertfordshire, and by her, who was buried at Greenwich, 31 January, 1646, had a dau.,

Margaret, m. to Sir John Mennes, Knt., by whom she had one dau., Margaret, who was twice m. Her 2nd husband was Sir John Heath, of Brastede, in Kent. She was buried at

---

* As Earl of Athol, Walter Stewart was involved in the murder of his nephew, JAMES I., and beheaded at Edinburgh, in April, 1437. He m. Margaret, only dau. and heir of Sir David de Barclay, Lord of Brechin, and had two sons,

DAVID, one of the hostages for the ransom of JAMES I., d. in England, leaving a son,

ROBERT (Sir), private chamberlain to JAMES I., who engaging in Sir Robert Graham's conspiracy against his royal benefactor, was apprehended soon after the monarch's assassination, and put to death at Edinburgh.

ALAN, Earl of Caithness.

511

Brastede, 1676, leaving an only dau., Margaret Heath, who carried the estate of Brastede to her husband, George Verney, Lord Willoughby de Broke; and d. 18 October, 1729, leaving issue.

The earl d. without male issue, in 1652, when his honours appear to have become EXTINCT.

STEWART OR STUART—BARONS DARNLEY, EARLS AND DUKES OF LENNOX, IN SCOTLAND, EARLS OF MARCH, EARLS AND DUKES OF RICHMOND, AND EARL OF LITCHFIELD, IN ENGLAND.

Barony of Darnley, created circa 1460.
Duke of Lennox, created 5 August, 1581.
Earl of Richmond, created 6 October, 1613.
Duke of Richmond, created 17 May, 1623.
Earl of March, created 7 June, 1619.
Earl of Litchfield, created 10 December, 1645.

Lineage.

ALEXANDER, 5th Lord-High-Steward of Scotland, living in the reigns of ALEXANDER II. and ALEXANDER III , m. Jean, dau. and heiress of Angus Macrory, Lord Bute, and had, with one dau. two sons,

JAMES, 7th lord high-steward; from whom the royal family of STUART derived, in a direct male line, down to JAMES V., whose dau. and heiress was MARY Queen of Scots.

And

SIR JOHN STEWART, of Bonkill, who fell at the battle of Falkirk in 1298, leaving by his wife, Margaret, dau. and heiress of Sir Alexander de Bonkill,

Alexander, of Bonkyll, ancestor of the Stewarts, Earls of Angus.
ALAN, from whom the Stewarts, Earls of Lennox, descended.
Walter, ancestor, through an heiress, of the Earls of Galloway.
James, progenitor of the EARLS OF ATHOLE, the STEWARTS of Durisdeir, and the Grandtully family.
John.

The 2nd son,

SIR ALAN STEWART, of Dreghorn, had a charter, 4 June, 1330, from his cousin Robert, the Steward of Scotland, of liberty to purchase heritably the lands of Cruckisfle, co. Renfrew. He fell at Halidon Hill in 1333, leaving three sons, John (Sir) of Derneley, who d. s. p. ; Walter, d. s. p.; and ALEXANDER. The 3rd son,

SIR ALEXANDER STEWART, of Derneley, had a charter from DAVID II., 26 December, 1347. He was father of

SIR ALEXANDER STEWART, of Derneley, who m. Janet, dau. and heir of Sir William Keith, of Galstoun, and had issue,

I. JOHN, his heir.
II. William (Sir), killed at the siege of Orleans, 12 February, 1428-9.
III. Alexander, of Torbane and Galliston.
IV. Robert.   V. James.
I. Janet, m. 1391, to Thomas de Somerville.

The eldest son,

SIR JOHN STEWART, of Derneley, s. his father before 5 May, 1404. In 1420 he was sent to France with the Scots auxiliaries, and was so highly distinguished at the battle of Beaugé, that Charles, the Dauphin, conferred on him the lands of Aubigny and Concressault. Continuing his gallant services in the French wars, he was slain in an engagement near Orleans, 12 February. 1428-9. He m. 1392, Elizabeth, dau. of Duncan, Earl of Lennox, and had three sons, viz.,

I. ALAN, his heir.
II. Alexander, d. s. p., m
III. John, Lord of Aubigny and Concressault, in France, knight of the order of St. Michael, and captain of 100 men-at-arms, d. 1482, leaving by his wife, Beatrix d'Apecher, an only son, the renowned

BERNARD STUART, Chevalier d'Aubigny, so gloriously distinguished by his martial achievements in the service of France, during the campaigns in Italy against Gonsalvo de Cordova: and at various times viceroy of Naples, constable of Sicily and Jerusalem, Duke of Terra Nova, Marquis de Giruce and Squillazzo, Comte de Beaumont, D'Arcy and Venassac, Lord of Aubigny, and governor of Melun. He d. in 1508, leaving by Anne de Naumont, his wife, an only dau., Anne, wife of Robert Stuart, of Aubigny, Marshal of France.

The eldest son,

SIR ALAN STEWART or STUART, of Derneley, was treacherously slain by Boyd, of Kilmarnock, in 1439, leaving by Catherine, his wife, eldest dau. of Sir William Seton, of Seton (which lady m. 2ndly, Herbert, Lord Maxwell), two sons, JOHN, his heir, and ALEXANDER of Galstoun. The elder son,

SIR JOHN STEWART, of Derneley, who s. his father in 1439, was created a lord of parliament, by the title of LORD DERNELEY, most probably at the coronation of King JAMES III., who ascended the throne, 3 August, 1460. Stewart was served heir of Duncan, Earl of Lennox, his great-grandfather, 23 July, 1473, and assumed the title of EARL OF LENNOX. His lordship m. 1438, Margaret, eldest dau. of Alexander, 1st Lord Montgomery, and had issue,

MATTHEW, 2nd Earl of Lennox.
Robert, of Aubigny, in France, a highly distinguished military commander in the service of that kingdom was created a Marshal of France by FRANCIS I. He m. 1st, his cousin, Anne, only dau. of Bernard Stuart, of Aubigny; and 2ndly, Jacqueline de Longueville, but d. s. p. 1543.
William, chevalier, Seigneur d'Oyzon et de Grey, counsellor and chamberlain of the king, captain of a hundred lances, mentioned as such in 1499.
John, of Henriestoun, rector of Kirkinner, and also of the University of Glasgow. He m. Marion, dau. of Thomas Semple, of Eliotstoun, and had one child, Margaret, m. to John Fraser, of Kuoik, in Ayrshire.
Alexander, described as brother of Matthew, Earl of Lennox, in a charter, 1495, an archer de la garde Ecossaise in France, 1538.
Alan, of Cardonald, 1496, father of John, who had a son, James, who had two sons, James, of Cardonald, and Alan, made abbot of Crossregal, in 1564, both of whom d. s. p., and the estate of Cardonald went to the son of their sister Margaret, Walter, 1st Lord Blantyre.
Elizabeth m. to Archibald, 2nd Earl of Argyll.
Marion, a. to Robert, 1st Lord Crichton, of Sanquhar.
Janet, va. to Ninian, 2nd Lord Ross, of Halkhead.
Margaret, m. to Sir John Colquhoun, of Luss.

The eldest son,

MATTHEW STUART, 2nd Earl of Lennox, s. his father, 1494. He and the Earl of Argyll commanded the right wing of the Scottish army, at Flodden Field, 9 September, 1513, and both fell in that disastrous conflict. His lordship m. Elizabeth Hamilton, dau. of James, Lord Hamilton, and niece of JAMES III, and by her had issue,

I. WILLIAM, Master of Lennox, m. Lady Margaret Graham, eldest dau. of William. 1st Earl of Montrose, but had no issue by her, who m. 2ndly, John Somerville, of Cambusnethan.
II. JOHN, 3rd earl.
    1. Margaret, m. 1st, to John, 2nd Lord Fleming ; 2ndly, to Alexander Douglas, of Mains.
    II. Elizabeth, m. to Sir Hugh Campbell, of Loudoun.
    III. Agnes, m. to William Edmonstone, of Dundreath.

The 2nd son,

JOHN STEWART, 3rd Earl of Lennox, one of the most estimable characters of the age in which he lived, who was taken prisoner by the Laird of Pardovan, and murdered in cold blood by Sir James Hamilton, of Finnart, natural son of Arran. His lordship m. Lady Anne Stewart, 8th dau. of John, Earl of Atholl, uterine brother of King JAMES II., and had issue,

MATTHEW, 4th Earl of Lennox.
ROBERT, 6th Earl of Lennox.
JOHN, Lord of Aubigny, in right of his wife, the dau. of De la Verrey, Lord of Aubigny. He appears to have lived constantly in France, where he was captain in the Scots gens d'armes and governor of Avignon, and d. in 1567, leaving a son, ESME, Lord of Aubigny, who in 1579, was created DUKE OF LENNOX, by King JAMES VI.
Helen, m. 1st, to William, 6th Earl of Erroll ; and 2ndly, to John, 10th Earl of Sutherland.

The eldest son,

MATTHEW STUART, 4th Earl of Lennox, s. his father, 1526. The early part of his life was passed in the service of the crown of France in the wars in Italy, where he served with gallantry and distinction. He returned home at the death of JAMES V.; and after acting a leading part in the political transactions of the time, was constituted, in 1570, Regent of Scotland. This high office he held for little more than a year, being slain 4 September, 1571. His lordship m. Lady Margaret Douglas, dau. of Archibald, Earl of Angus, by Margaret, Queen Dowager of Scotland, sister of HENRY VIII., and by her (who d. at Hackney, 9 March, 1577, in her sixty-second year, and was buried in Westminster Abbey), had four sons and four daus., all of whom d. young, except two sons,

I. HENRY, Lord Darnley, b. at Temple Newsom, co. York, 1545; created DUKE OF ALBANY, Earl of Ross and Lord Ardmannock, in 1565; m. 29 July, 1565, MARY Queen of Scotland, and was murdered 9 February, 1566 7, leaving one son, King JAMES VI. His last male descendant was CARDINAL YORK (see p. 507).
II. CHARLES, 5th Earl of Lennox.

The Regent Lennox was s. by his only surviving son,

CHARLES STUART, 5th Earl of Lennox, who had four charters dated 18 April, 1572, for the purpose of conveying to him and to his heirs male the Earldom of Lennox and various other lands belonging to the Darnley family, which had devolved on King JAMES VI. in right of blood, and he became accordingly 5th Earl of Lennox. Dying at London in 1576, aged twenty-one, he was buried in HENRY VII.'s chapel, in Westminster Abbey, as appears from the inscription on his mother's monument there. He m. in 1574, Elizabeth, dau. of Sir William Cavendish, and sister of William, 1st Earl of Devonshire, by whom he had an only dau.,

LADY ARABELLA STUART, the ill-fated victim of the jealous timidity and state policy of JAMES I. "Her double connexion with the blood royal was equally obnoxious to the jealousy of ELIZABETH and the timidity of JAMES; and they secretly dreaded the supposed danger of her having a legitimate offspring Yet we find the Scottish monarch, at one time not unwilling to wed his fair cousin to Esme Stuart, whom he had created DUKE OF LENNOX. The banns, however, were forbidden by the English Queen, and the luckless maiden consigned to prison. The hand of the lady remained not long unsought: a curious project of the Pope, favoured, it is said, by HENRY IV., of France, was to marry her to a brother of the Duke of Parma; to set aside JAMES from the succession, and to place the Lady Arabella on the throne Another aspirant was a son of the illustrious house of Percy, and a fourth, no less a personage than the King of Poland. But JAMES I., from political motives, invariably rejected all matrimonial offers made to his kinswoman; the Lady Arabella submitting with ill grace to this species of tyranny. Every noble youth who sighed for distinction ambitioned her notice; and she was frequently contriving a marriage herself. At length, undeterred by a censure passed on her a short time previously, for listening to a clandestine proposal, she ventured to receive similar overtures from William Seymour, 2nd son of Lord Beauchamp and grandson of the Earl of Hertford ; on discovery of which, both parties were summoned before the privy council and reprimanded. Their love, formed in childhood, had been renewed in after years, and appears to have survived all their sorrow and sufferings. To the king's prohibition Seymour submitted. 'But love' (says D'Israeli), 'laughs at privy councils, and the grave promises made by two frightened lovers.' The parties were secretly married in 1610, and the contract came to the knowledge of the king in the July of the following year. They were then separately confined ; Arabella at the house of Sir Thomas Parry, at Lambeth, and the bridegroom in the Tower, for 'his contempt in marrying a lady of the royal family without the king's leave.' Their imprisonment does not, however, seem to have been very close or rigorous. The lovers soon effected their escape; Seymour got safe to Flanders, but the Lady Arabella was recaptured and brought back to the Tower, where, 'her bright intellect overthrown and the temple of reason desolate and forsaken,' she lingered in hopeless misery four lonely years, dying 27 September, 1615. Seymour was afterwards permitted to return, and made a figure, as a cavalry commander in the subsequent reign. He was then Marquess of Hertford, and had eventually the Dukedom of Somerset restored to him. His character has been finely described by Clarendon. He loved his studies and his repose; but when the civil wars broke out, he closed his volumes and drew his sword, and was both an active and a skilful general. To his life's latest hour he cherished his romantic passion for the object of his early love; and, though he married again, he christened the daughter of his 2nd wife by the fondly remembered name of Arabella Stuart."[*]

ROBERT STEWART, 2nd son of John, 3rd Earl of Lennox, was created EARL OF LENNOX, by royal charter, dated 15 June, 1578, by which the Earldom of Lennox, the Barony of Torboltoun, the lands of Cruckisfee, Derneley, and others, in the shires of Renfrew, Ayr, Dumbarton, and Stirling, we e granted to him and the heirs male of his body. "He was bred," says Douglas, "to the church; the first promotion he had was that of provost of the collegiate church of Dumbarton, and after that he was preferred to the episcopal see of Caithness, in 1542; but while he was only elect, taking part with his brother, the Earl of Lennox, against the Earl of Arran, he was deprived of his bishopric, and lived in exile till 1563, when he was again restored, at least to the profits of the see; and complying with the Reformation, he had for his share of the riches of the church, the priory of St. Andrew's given him by the crown. He became 6th Earl of Lennox in virtue of the charter, 1578, but afterwards agreed to accept of the Earldom of March, and Lordship of Dunbar in lieu of the Earldom of Lennox, so that the king might be at liberty to bestow the lands and honours of Lennox upon Esme, Lord of Aubigny. In confirmation of this arrangement, a charter was granted, 15 October, 1582, of the Earldom of March and Lordship of Dunbar, in favour of

Robert Stuart, containing a new erection of these lands into an earldom, and creating him Earl of March. After this he li red privately at St. Andrew's, in a studious and retired manner, happily free from any faction till his death, 29 August, 1586, in the seventieth year of his age." He *m.* Lady Elizabeth Stewart, eldest dau. of John, 4th Earl of Athol, and relict of Hugh, 6th Lord Lovat (who *d.* in January, 1576-7,) but had no issue by her, who obtained a divorce from him, and *m.* 6 July, 1581, James Stewart, Earl of Arran. The next in succession was

Esme Stewart, Lord of Aubigny, son of John, Lord of Aubigny, 3rd son of the 3rd Earl of Lennox. He was educated in France, and being sent for by King James VI., landed at Leith, 8 September, 1579, and was graciously received. On 5 March, 1579-80, he was created Earl of Lennox, and 5 August, 1581, Duke of Lennox, Earl of Derneley, Lord of Aubigny, Torbolton, and Dalkeith. His grace took a prominent part in the affairs of Scotland, especially those affecting episcopacy, and attained such power and influence, that the Earl of Gowrie remarked, that "the realm could not suffer two kings." The duke, after the "raid of Ruthven," had to quit Scotland. He retired to France and *d.* at Paris, 28 May, 1583. He *m.* 1572, Catherine de Balsac, youngest dau. of William de Balsac, Seigneur d'Entragues et de Marcoussis, governor of Havre de Grace, mortally wounded at the battle of Rentz, in 1555, and by her had issue,

Ludovic, 2nd Duke of Lennox.
Esme, 3rd Duke of Lennox.
Henriet, *m.* 21 July, 1588, to George, 1st Marquess of Huntly; dying in France, 2 September, 1642, she was buried at Lyons.
Mary, the 2nd wife of John, Earl of Marr.
Gabriella, contracted, in April, 1598, to Hugh, 5th Earl of Eglinton, but the marriage did not take effect. Sir Robert Gordon says she was a nun at Glatteny, in Berry, in France.

The eldest son,
Ludovic Stuart, 2nd Duke of Lennox, in Scotland, *b.* 29 September, 1574, held the high office of great chamberlain of Scotland, as well as high admiral, and went as ambassador from James VI. to Henry IV. of France. He attended his sovereign to England on his accession to the English throne, and was created, by letters patent dated 6 October, 1613, *Baron Setrington, of Setrington, co. York*, and Earl of Richmond. He was constituted master of the household, and first gentleman of the bedchamber, invested with the Garter, appointed commissioner to the parliament in 1607, and advanced in 1623, to the dignities of *Earl of Newcastle*, and Duke of Richmond. His grace *m.* 1st, Sophia, dau. of William, Earl of Gowrie, in Scotland; 2ndly, Jean, dau. of Sir Matthew Campbell, of Loudon; and 3rdly, Frances, dau. of Thomas Howard, Viscount Bindon, and widow of Edward, Earl of Hertford, but *d.* without legitimate issue, 16 February, 1624, when his English honours became extinct, while those of Scotland devolved upon his brother,

Esme Stuart, Lord D'Aubigny, as 3rd Duke of Lennox, K.G. This nobleman had been created by King James I., 7 June, 1619, *Baron Stuart, of Leighton Bromswold*, and Earl of March. His lordship *m.* Katherine, only dau. and heir of Sir Gervase Clifton, Lord Clifton, of Leighton Bromswold, by writ of summons, dated 9 July, 1608, and had surviving issue,

  1. James, his successor.
  ii. George, Lord D'Aubigny, who fell in the king's service at the battle of Edgehill, 23 October, 1642. He *m.* Catherine, dau. of Theophilus, Earl of Suffolk, and by her (who *m.* 2ndly, James, Earl of Newburgh,) had issue,

    1 Charles, created Earl of Litchfield, who *s.* as 6th Duke of Lennox, and 3rd Duke of Richmond.
    2 Katherine, who *m.* 1st, Henry O'Brien, Lord Ibrackan, son and heir apparent of Henry, 7th Earl of Thomond, and by him (who *d.* 1678) had an only dau.,

      Katherine O'Brien, Baroness Clifton, who *m.* Edward Hyde, 3rd Earl of Clarendon, and dying in the lifetime of her mother, left

        Edward, Viscount Cornbury, *d. unm.* 1712.
        Theodosia, who *m.* John Bligh, Esq., M.P., afterwards created Earl of Darnley. Her ladyship eventually inherited the Barony of Clifton, which had been conferred, by writ, upon her ancestor, Sir Gervase Clifton, and that dignity is now enjoyed by her descendant, the Earl of Darnley.

    Catherine, Lady Ibrackan, *m.* 2ndly, Sir Joseph Williamson.

  iii. Lodovick, Seigneur d'Aubigny, canon of the cathedral of Notre Dame, Paris, named cardinal in 1665. He *d.* in Paris in November of that year, just after the arrival of the courier who brought him the announcement from Rome. He was buried in the church of the Chartreux, where the inscription on his monument runs thus :—"Qui cum in cardinalium

collegio mox cooptandus est, immaturâ morte peremptus est anno ætatis 46, r. l., 1665, 3tio id. Novembris."
  iv. Bernard, commander of the king's troop of guards, in the civil wars, killed at Rowton Heath near Chester, in 1645.
  v. John, general of horse on the royal side, fell at the battle of Bramdene, in 1644.
  i. Elizabeth, *m.* to Henry-Frederick Howard, Earl of Arundel.
  ii. Anne, *m.* to Archibald Douglas, Earl of Angus, son and heir of William, 1st Marquess of Douglas.
  iii. Frances, *m.* to Jerome Weston, Earl of Portland.

His grace *d.* 30 July, 1624, and was buried in Westminster Abbey. His widow, Katherine, *m.* 2ndly, James, Earl of Abercorn, and was granted by King Charles I. a royal letter declaring that, notwithstanding her second marriage, she should retain the title and rank of Duchess of Lennox. The Duke's eldest son,

James Stuart, 4th Duke of Lennox, in Scotland, 2nd Earl of March, in England, was advanced, by letters patent, dated 8 August, 1641, to the Dukedom of Richmond, with remainder in default of heirs male of his own body, to his brothers and their heirs male primogenitively. His grace was lord great chamberlain, and admiral of Scotland, lord steward of the household, warden of the Cinque Ports, gentleman of the bedchamber, and a knight of the Garter. He *m.* Lady Mary Villiers, only dau. of George, Duke of Buckingham, and relict of Charles, Lord Herbert, and had issue,

Esme, his successor.
Mary, *m.* Richard Butler, Earl of Arran, and *d. s. p.*, 1667.

The Duke of Richmond and Lennox adhered with unshaken fidelity to the king during the civil wars, and when money was raised upon loans to support the royal cause, he subscribed £40,000, "although there was not a man in England," says Duncan Stewart, "that offered more than £10,000, except Strafford, lord-lieutenant of Ireland, who offered £20,000; and yet at the same time, the duke had not the most considerable or profitable posts about the king, nor was his estate the greatest either; and when he was taken notice of by Sir Philip Warwick for his offer, he smilingly replied, 'I will serve the king in his person, though I carry but his cloak, as well and as cheerfully, as any in the greatest trust'; reflecting upon Hamilton. He paid his last duty to his master, King Charles, by putting him in his grave at Windsor." His grace *d.* 30 March, 1655, and was *s.* by his son,

Esme Stuart, 5th Duke of Lennox, in Scotland, 3rd Earl of March, and 2nd Duke of Richmond. This nobleman *d.* in his minority *unm.*, 14 August, 1660, and was buried in Westminster Abbey. His cousin and heir was

Charles Stuart, 6th Duke of Lennox, in Scotland, 4th Earl of March, and 3rd Duke of Richmond, K.G. This nobleman, in consideration of his father, George, Lord D'Aubigny's, and his uncle, Bernard Stuart's gallant services in the royal cause, had been created, by King Charles I., by letters patent, dated 10 December, 1645, *Baron Stuart, of Newberry, co. Berks*, and Earl of Litchfield. His grace *m.* 1st, Elizabeth, relict of Charles, Viscount Mansfield, and dau. of Richard Rogers, Esq., of Bryanston, co. Dorset; 2ndly, Margaret, widow of William Lewis, Esq., of the Van, and dau. of Lawrence, son and heir of Sir Robert Banaster, Bart. of Papenham, Bucks; and 3rdly, Frances-Theresa, dau. of Walter Stuart, 3rd son of Walter, Lord Blantyre, but *d. s. p.* December, 1672, at Elsenure, where he resided as ambassador-extraordinary from King Charles II., to the court of Denmark. At his lordship's decease, the Barony of Clifton (that created by writ) devolved upon his only sister, Catherine, Lady Ibracken, whose grand-dau., and eventual representative, Lady Theodosia Hyde, *m.* John Bligh, Esq., M.P., afterwards Earl of Darnley, and conveyed the barony to the Bligh family. All his grace's other honours appear to have become extinct, those of England certainly, but there is a question as to the extinction of the Dukedom of Lennox,* and the matter remains as yet undecided.

Frances, Duchess of Lennox, his grace's widow, survived until 15 October, 1702. By her will, she bequeathed a con-

---

* In 1829, John Bligh, Earl of Darnley, presented a petition to the king, claiming the Dukedom of Lennox, in the peerage of Scotland, as heir of line of Charles, 6th Duke of Lennox, and 4th Duke of Richmond, at whose death, in 1672, King Charles II. was served his grace's heir. As his Majesty's (legitimate) issue became extinct in 1807 with the Cardinal York, and as that personage was the last heir male of the Stuarts, the Earl of Darnley put forward his claim as heir-general, being descended from Catherine, sister of the duke mentioned above. The petition was referred to the House of Lords, and their lordships have not hitherto decided upon it.

siderable portion of her fortune to Lord Blantyre, who bought with it, the estate of Lethington, near Haddington, which, in grateful remembrance of his benefactress, he named Lennox Love.

Arms—Or, a fesse chequy, az. and arg., surmounted of a bend, sa., charged with three buckles, or ; subsequently a bordure, gu., charged with buckles, or, was used.

STEWART—EARL OF MAR.

Lineage.

Isabel, Countess of Mar, grandniece and eventual heir of Thomas, 13th Earl of Mar, m. 1st, Sir Malcolm Drummond, of Drummond, who d. s. p. ; and 2ndly, Alexander Stewart, "the Wolf of Badenoch," natural son of Alexander, Earl of Buchan, 4th son of Robert II. The first appearance of this person in life was at the head of a formidable band of robbers in the highlands of Scotland, when storming the Countess of Mar's castle of Kildrummie, he obtained her ladyship in marriage, either by violence or persuasion. The countess subsequently made a free grant of all her honours and inheritance to her said husband; and d. s. p. 1419, when

Alexander Stewart, designed, in right of the deceased countess, Earl of Mar and Lord of Garioch, resigned those honours to the crown, whereupon they were regranted to him, 28 May, 1426, in remainder to his natural son, Sir Thomas Stewart, to revert, in case of failure of male issue of the latter to the crown. His lordship was ambassador to England in 1406, and again in 1407, when he engaged in a tournament with the Earl of Kent. The following year he went to France and Flanders with a noble company, and eminently distinguished himself in the service of the Duke of Burgundy, who employed him to assist in quelling a rebellion of the people of Liege against their bishop, John of Bavaria. The earl commanded the royal army at the battle of Harlaw, against the Lord of the Isles, in 1411; and was appointed ambassador-extraordinary to England in 1416; and soon afterwards warden of the marches. He d. in 1435, and his natural son mentioned above, having predeceased him, the Earldom of Mar, according to the charter, reverted to the crown, when it was claimed, in 1435, by Sir Robert Erskine, of Erskine, as lineal descendant of Lady Elyne Mar, but though the descent was indisputably established, the earldom was not conferred upon the Erskines until it had been enjoyed by four earls of different families, the last of whom was the celebrated Regent Moray, a period of 130 years having elapsed, when at last it was restored, in 1565, by Queen Mary, to John, 5th Lord Erskine.

STEWART—EARL OF MAR.

Lineage.

The Earldom of Mar was conferred in 1457, on John Stewart, 3rd son of King James II., but became extinct in 1479, when the unfortunate prince, accused by the king's favourite of plotting by spells and machinations against the sovereign, was bled to death in Craigmillar Castle by order of his brother James III.

STEWART—EARL OF MAR AND GARIOCH.

Lineage.

Alexander Stewart, 3rd son of King James III., was created Earl of Mar and Garioch, in 1486, but d. s. p., whereupon the title became extinct.

STEWART—LORD METHVEN.

By Letters Patent, dated 1528.

Lineage.

Henry Stewart, 2nd son of Andrew, Lord Avondale, appearing at court in 1524, made a deep impression on Queen Margaret of England, dowager of King James IV., and wife

of Archibald, Earl of Angus. So great indeed was his influence that the Queen Dowager gave him the offices of high chancellor and treasurer, and, having obtained a divorce from Angus, m. him, in March, 1526. James V., incensed at Stewart's presumption, refused for some time his sanction to the match, but at length withdrew his opposition, and Stewart was created a peer of Scotland, as Lord Methven, in 1528 ; the title being derived from the lands of Methven, in Perthshire, which were part of the dower lands of the Queen Dowager. By his royal consort, Lord Methven had an only dau. who d. an infant; but by Lady Janet Stewart, his 2nd wife (eldest dau. of John, 2nd Earl of Athol, and widow of Alexander, Master of Sutherland and of Sir Hugh Kennedy, of Girvanmains), had issue,

Henry, 2nd Lord Methven.
Joanna, m. to Colin, 6th Earl of Argyll.
Dorothea, m. to William, 1st Earl of Gowrie.
Margaret, m. 1st, to Andrew, Master of Ochiltree; 2ndly, to Uchtred Macdowall, of Garthland.

The only son,

Henry Stewart, 2nd Lord Methven, s. his father, and was killed at the siege of the castle of Edinburgh by a cannon shot from that garrison, 3 March, 1571-2. Walpole, in his *Royal and Noble Authors*, notices Lord Methven's *Tragedie*, 1572, written by Lord Sempill. He m. Jean, eldest dau. of Patrick, 3rd Lord Ruthven, and by her (who m. 2ndly, Andrew, 5th Earl of Rothes) had a son,

Henry Stewart, 3rd Lord Methven; who m. Catherine, dau. of Henry Stewart, son of James, Earl of Arran, but d. s. p. when the title became extinct. After Lord Methven's death in 1584, the Lordship of Methven was granted to Ludovic, Duke of Lennox, and became eventually (by purchase, in 1664, from the Lennox family,) the property of the Smythes, of Braco.

STEWART—LORD OCHILTREE.

Lineage.

Sir James Stewart, of Killeith, eldest son of Captain Stewart, the well-known Earl of Arran, purchased from Andrew, 3rd Lord Ochiltree, that lordship, and obtained a regrant of the title by charter, dated 7 June, 1615, to himself "Domino Jacobo Stewart of Killieth, milit. et hæredibus suis masculis." He m. and had an only son,

William, 2nd Lord Ochiltree, who d. under age in 1675. With this William, 2nd Lord Ochiltree, this branch of the family, which had borne the title of Ochiltree for about sixty years, became extinct.

STEWART—LORD OCHILTREE.

(*See* Stewart, Lord Avondale.)

STEWART—EARL OF ORKNEY.

Lineage.

Robert Stewart, abbot of Holyrood House, natural son of James V., conformed to the Protestant faith in 1559, had a grant of the crown lands of Orkney and Zetland in 1565, and was created Earl of Orkney, 28 October, 1581. He m. Lady Janet Kennedy, eldest dau. of Gilbert, 3rd Earl of Cassilis, and had, with four daus., three sons,

Patrick, his successor.
John, Earl of Carrick ; who d. s. p., when that title became extinct.
James (Sir), of Tullas, on whom the Earldom of Orkney was also entailed. He left issue,
   Captain Robert Stewart, of Eday, who m. the Lady Jane Gordon, dau. of the Earl of Sutherland, and left a son, Captain Robert Stewart, of Eday, who m. Miss Isabella Graem, of Graemshall, and left a dau., Jane, m. to Robert Richan, Esq., of Linklater, head of an ancient and distinguished Danish family which settled in the Orkneys in the 9th century. He left a son, the late Captain William Richan, of Rapness, who left a son, and several daus.
Colonel John Stewart, of Newark, who d. s. p.

He was s. by his eldest surviving son,

Patrick Stewart, 2nd earl ; who was condemned for high treason, and beheaded at the market-cross of Edinburgh, 6

February, 1614. He *m.* Margaret, dau. of William, 6th Lord Livingstone, and *d. s. p.*: his estates and honours were FOR-FEITED to the crown; the former of which King JAMES VI. granted to Bishop Law.

STEWART—LORD PITTENWEEM.

Lineage.

The lands and baronies belonging to the priory of Pitten-weem were erected into a temporal lordship, by act of parliament, in 1606, with limitation to the grantee's heirs and assigns, in favour of

FREDERICK STEWART, son of JAMES VI.'s unworthy favourite, William Stewart or Stuart, commendator of Pittenweem, by Isabel, his wife, dau. of Sir Patrick Hepburn, of Waughton, and grandson of Thomas Stewart, of Galstoun, who was great-great-great-grandson of Alan Stewart, of Derneley. His lordship *d. s. p.*, and the title has not, since his decease, been claimed by an heir-general or an assignee.

STEWART—DUKE OF ROSS.

Lineage.

JAMES STEWART, 2nd son of King JAMES III., was named at his baptism, 1476, MARQUESS OF ORMONDE, in 1481, made EARL OF ROSS, Lord of Brechin, Navar, and Ardmanach; and by royal charter, dated 29 January, 1487-8, created DUKE OF ROSS, Marquess of Ormonde, and Earl of Edirdale. This prince, immortalized by Ariosto, in the Orlando Furioso, obtained the archiepiscopal see of St. Andrew's in 1498, and was constituted high chancellor of the kingdom in 1502. His grace *d.* in 1504, and was buried in the chancel of St. Andrew's Cathedral.

STEWART—LORD ST. COLME.

Lineage.

HENRY STEWART, of St. Colme Abbey, co. Fife, 2nd son of James, Lord Doune, and brother of James, Earl of Moray, was created a peer of Scotland, as LORD ST. COLME, 7 March, 1611. He *m.* Lady Jean Stewart, dau. of John, 5th Earl of Atholl, and dying 12 July, 1612, left a son and successor.

JAMES STEWART, 2nd Lord St. Colme, a colonel in the service of GUSTAVUS ADOLPHUS, King of Sweden, who *d. s. p.* 1642, and his title became EXTINCT. His estates in the cos. of Edinburgh, Fife, Haddington, Perth, &c., which formerly belonged to the abbacy of St. Colme, devolved on the Earl of Moray.

STRABOLGI—EARL OF ATHOL.

(*See* STRATHBOLGIE.)

STRANGE — BARONS STRANGE, OF KNOKYN.

By Writ of Summons, dated 29 December, 1299.

Lineage.

It is stated, that at Justs, held in the Peke of Derbyshire, at Castle Peverell, where, amongst other persons of note, were present Owen, Prince of Wales, and a son of the King of Scots, there were also two sons of the Duke of Bretaigne; the younger of them being named Guy, was called

GUY LE STRANGE, and from him that the several families of Strange subsequently descended. This statement may or may not be true: but it is certain that, in the time of HENRY II. there were three brothers named le Strange, who possessed lands in Shropshire. Those brothers were,

I. GUY LE STRANGE, who had a grant from King HENRY II., to hold by the service of one knight's fee of the manors of Weston and Alvithele, co. Salop, and was sheriff of that shire

from the 6th to the 11th of the same reign, and from the 17th to the 25th. He *d.* before the accession of King JOHN, leaving,

     RALPH LE STRANGE, his successor, who *d. s. p.*, when his lands devolved upon his sisters as co-heirs.

     Margaret le Strange, *m.* to Thomas Noell.

     Joane le Strange, *m* to R chard de Wapenburl.

     Matilda, *m. circa* 1196 Griffin ap Iorwerth, Lord of Sutton and *d.* 4 May, 1242. From this marriage the family of KYNASTON derives descent.

II. HAMON LE STRANGE, Lord of Wrockwardine, of whom nothing more can be said then that he gave his whole part of the common woods at Wombrugge, Salop, to the canons of that house, and *d. s. p.*

III. JOHN LE STRANGE, who, in the 11th King JOHN, possessed the lordships of Nesse and Cheswardine, co. Salop, which he held by grant of HENRY II. In the 18th JOHN he was sheriff of the cos. Salop and Stafford, and in the 3rd HENRY III., he obtained the king's precept to the sheriff of Shropshire, for aid to rebuild part of his castle at Knokyn, and to repair the rest of it. And, having been a liberal benefactor to the canons of Wombrugge, departed this life shortly after, when he was *s.* by his son—

JOHN LE STRANGE, a person of great note in his time. In the 16th JOHN, his father then living, he was in the wars of Poictou; and in the 15th HENRY III., he obtained a grant of the inheritance of the manor of Wrockwurdine, for the yearly rent of £8, to be paid to the king, and his heirs and successors. In the 21st of the same reign he was appointed sheriff of the cos. Salop and Stafford, and constituted governor of the castle of Salop and Bruges. He was afterwards one of the barons marchers, and had command as such to reside in the marches, in order to resist the incursions of the Welsh. In the contest between HENRY III. and the barons, his lordship adhered with great fidelity to the king, and obtained for his loyalty a grant of the lands of Walter de Mucegros, which had been forfeited in that rebellion. By Amicia, his wife, he had issue,

JOHN, his successor.

Hamon, of Ellesmere, from whom descended the Stranges, of Blackmere (*see* STRANGE, Barons Strange, of Blackmere).

He *d.* in 1269, and was *s.* by his eldest son,

JOHN LE STRANGE, Lord of Knokyn. This feudal baron, in the time of his father, was deputy governor of Winchester Castle; and in the 48th HENRY III., he was constituted governor of the castle of Montgomery. He subsequently espoused the baronial cause, and after the triumph of the barons at Lewes, was reinstated in the governorship of Montgomery Castle. In the 3rd EDWARD I., he surrendered to his brother, Robert, his entire right in the manor of Wrockwardine. His lordship *m.* Joane, one of the daus. and heirs of Roger de Someri, Baron of Dudley, by his 1st wife, Lady Nichola de Albini, sister and co-heir of Hugh, 4th Earl of Arundel, and *d.* in 1276, when all his lands were seized upon by the crown, but in two years afterwards they were restored to his son and heir,

JOHN LE STRANGE, who, upon paying his relief, had livery thereof. This feudal lord, in the 14th EDWARD I., answered for 300 marks to the king; which sums John, his grandfather, had borrowed from the Cheshire men, to maintain the wars of Wales. He was, subsequently, engaged in the wars of Gascony and Scotland, and, for his good services, was summoned to parliament as BARON STRANGE, *of Knokyn*, from 29 December, 1299, to 12 December, 1309, and likewise made a knight of the Bath. His lordship *m.* Maud, dau. and heir of Ebulo de Montibus, Lord of Ketton, and by her (who *m.* 2ndly, Thomas de Hastang) had issue,

JOHN, his successor.

EBULO, who *m.* Alice de Laci, dau. and sole heir of Henry de Laci, Earl of Lincoln, and widow of Thomas Plantagenet, Earl of Lancaster. In right of this lady, Ebulo le Strange bore the title of EARL OF LINCOLN, but he *d. s. p.*, and Alice, his countess, surviving, *m* 3rdly. Hugo de Frenes, who was also styled Earl of Lincoln, but he likewise *d. s. p.* This great heiress *d.* n the 22nd EDWARD III., and was buried at Berling Abbey, with her 2nd husband, Ebulo le Strange.

Hamon, ancestor of the L'ESTRANGES of Hunstanton, co. Norfolk. SIR NICHOLAS L'ESTRANGE, 3rd Bart. of Hunstanton, *d.* 1724, leaving by Anne, his wife, dau. of Sir Thomas Wodehouse, of Kimberley, two sons, Thomas and Henry, successive barts., both of whom *d. s. p.*, and two daus., ARMINE, wife of NICHOLAS STYLEMAN, Esq., of Snettisham, and LUCY, wife of SIR JACOB ASTLEY, KNT. Of these co-heiresses, Lucy, Lady Astley, the younger, was ancestor of LORD HASTINGS, and Armine the elder was great-grandmother of Henry L'Estrange Styleman, Esq., of Hunstanton, who assumed in 1839, the ancient surname of his ancestors, LA STRANGE (*see* BURKE's *Landed Gentry*). A younger son of the L'Estranges, of Hunstanton, Richard L'Estrange, settled in Ireland, and was ancestor of the L'ESTRANGES of Moystown, King's co., and of the L'ESTRANGES of the co. of West meath.

His lordship *d.* in 1310, and was *s.* by his eldest son,

JOHN LE STRANGE, 2nd baron, summoned to parliament, 13 June, 1311. This nobleman before and after his accession to the title, was in the Scottish wars. He *m.* Isolda, dau. and heir of John de Walton, of Walton D'Eiville, *d.* the year after his father, and was *s.* by his elder son,

JOHN LE STRANGE, 3rd baron, summoned to parliament, 8 January, and 26 July, 1313. His lordship *d.* in 1324, *s. p.,* and was *s.* by his brother,

ROGER LE STRANGE, 4th baron, summoned to parliament, from 25 February, 1342, to 10 March, 1349. This nobleman was made a knight of the Bath, in the 20th EDWARD II., and in the reign of EDWARD III. was in the wars of Scotland and France. His lordship *m.* 1st, Joane, dau. and co-heir of Oliver, Lord Ingham, and 2ndly, a lady, named Maud, in whose right he held the manor of Middleton, in Cambridgeshire. His lordship *d.* in 1349, and was *s.* by his son,

ROGER LE STRANGE, 5th baron, summoned to parliament, from 20 September, 1355, to 9 August, 1382, *b.* 1327. This nobleman was constantly engaged in the wars of Gascony and Britanny, *temp.* EDWARD III. and RICHARD II. His lordship *m.* Lady Aliva Fitz-Alan, dau. of Edmund, Earl of Arundel, and dying in 1382, was *s.* by his son,

JOHN LE STRANGE, 6th baron, summoned to parliament, from 20 August, 1383, to 18 July, 1397, *b.* 1362. This nobleman, in the 10th RICHARD II., was in the garrison of Berwick-upon-Tweed, and the next year in the Scottish wars. He *m.* Maud, dau. and eventually co-heir of Sir John de Mohun, of Dunster, and dying about the year 1398, was *s.* by his son,

RICHARD LE STRANGE, 7th baron, summoned to parliament, from 25 August, 1404, to 2 January, 1449. This nobleman making proof of his age in the 6th HENRY IV., had livery of all his lands, Maud, his mother, being then dead. He was likewise, maternally, nephew and heir of Philippa, Duchess of York. By his 1st wife, Constance, he had no issue, but by his 2nd, Elizabeth, dau. of Reginald, Lord Cobham, he left at his decease, in 1449, an only son,

JOHN LE STRANGE, 8th baron, summoned to parliament, from 28 February, 1466, to 19 August, 1472. This nobleman *m.* Jaquetta, dau. of Richard Widville, Earl Rivers, and sister-in-law of King EDWARD IV., by whom he left at his decease, 15 October, 1477, an only dau. and heiress,

JOHANNA LE STRANGE, who *m.*

SIR GEORGE STANLEY, K.B. and K.G., eldest son of Sir Thomas Stanley, 1st Earl of Derby, and conveyed the Barony of Strange, of Knokyn, to the family of her husband, Sir George being summoned to parliament in that dignity, *jure uxoris,* from 15 November, 1482, to 16 January, 1497. This nobleman was sworn of the privy council, upon the accession of HENRY VII., and the next year he was one of the principal commanders who defeated John, Earl of Lincoln, and his adherents at Stoke. His lordship *d.* in 1497, his father, the Earl of Derby, then living, leaving issue,

THOMAS, his successor.
James.
Jane, *m.* to Robert Sheffield, Esq.
Elizabeth.

Lord Strange was *s.* by his eldest son,

THOMAS STANLEY, as 10th Baron Strange, who *s.* his grandfather as 2nd Earl of Derby, in 1504; and the Barony of Strange, of Knokyn, merged in the superior dignity, until the decease of

FERDINANDO STANLEY, 5th Earl of Derby, and 13th Baron Strange, in 1594. This nobleman *m.* Alice, dau. of Sir John Spencer, of Althorp, co. Northampton, and left three daus., viz.,

ANNE, *m.* 1st, to Grey Bruges, 5th Lord Chandos, and 2ndly, to Mervyn, Earl of Castlehaven.
FRANCES, *m.* to Sir John Egerton, Knt., afterwards Earl of Bridgewater.
ELIZABETH, *m.* to Henry Hastings, afterwards Earl of Huntingdon.

Amongst these ladies the Barony of Strange, of Knokyn, with that of Stanley, fell into ABEYANCE. as both still continue with their representatives.

Arms—Gu., two lions passant, arg

STRANGE—BARON STRANGE, OF ELLES-MERE.

By Writ of Summons, dated 24 June, 1295.

Lineage.

HAMON LE STRANGE, eldest son of Hamon of Ellesmere, 2nd son of John le Strange, of Knokyn, by Amicia, his w.fe, having stood firmly by King HENRY III., in his contest with Montfort, Earl of Leicester, was rewarded by a grant from the crown of the manors of Ellesmere and Stretton. He went to the Holy Land, and *d.* there *s. p.,* having previously given Ellesmere to his brother,

SIR ROGER LE STRANGE, who thus became of Ellesmere, and served the office of sheriff for the co. York, in the 53rd HENRY III., and again in the 56th of the same monarch. In the 4th EDWARD I., he obtained a confirmation of the grant made to him by his brother Hamon, of the castle and hundred of Ellesmere; and in some years afterwards he was made justice of all the forests south of Trent. In the 22nd of the same reign, he had a military summons to march against the French, and he was summoned to parliament as a Baron from 24 June, 1295, to 26 August, 1296. His lordship *m.* Maud, widow of Roger de Mowbray, and one of the daus. and co-heirs of William Beauchamp, of Bedford. Dugdale states that he was living in 1303, but "that further he cannot say of him." It is presumed that he *d. s. p.,* when the barony became EXTINCT.

Arms—Same as Strange, of Knokyn.

STRANGE—BARONS STRANGE, OF BLACK-MERE.

By Writ of Summons, dated 13 January, 1308.

Lineage.

This branch of the STRANGES sprang from

ROBERT LE STRANGE, Lord of Chauton, Hants, 3rd son of Hamon le Strange of Ellesmere, who was younger son of John Le Strange of Knokyn, by Amicia his wife. He obtained from his brother all that feudal lord's right in the manor of Wrockwordine, and marrying Alianore, sister and co-heir of William de Blancminster, *alias* Whitechurch, acquired the manor of Whitechurch, in Shropshire. He *d.* in the 4th EDWARD I., and was *s.* by his elder son,

JOHN LE STRANGE, designated of Blackmere, by reason that his manor house of Whitechurch was situated close to a mere, so called from the dark colour of its waters. This John *d. unm.* soon after attaining majority, and was *s.* by his brother,

FULK LE STRANGE, who, having been engaged in the wars of Scotland and France, *temp.* EDWARD I. and EDWARD II., was summoned to parliament as BARON STRANGE, from 13 January, 1308, to 13 September, 1324. In the 12th EDWARD II., his lordship obtained pardon for adhering to Thomas, Earl of Lancaster, and in four years afterwards he was constituted seneschal of the Duchy of Aquitaine. He *m.* Alianore, dau. and co-heir of John Giffard, of Brimsfield, and in her right acquired one-third part of the manor of Thornhagh, in Nottinghamshire. His lordship *d.* in 1324, and was *s.* by his son,

JOHN LE STRANGE, 2nd baron, summoned to parliament as BARON STRANGE, *of Blackmere,* from 6 September, 1330, to 26 April, 1343. This nobleman in the 4th EDWARD III., was made governor of Conway Castle; he was afterwards in the wars of Scotland and France, and attained the high military rank of Banneret. His lordship *m.* Ankaret, dau. of William le Boteler, of Wemme, and sister and co-heir of Edmund le Boteler, Clerk, and dying in 1349, had (with a dau. Eleanor, *m.* Reginald, Lord Grey de Ruthven,) an elder son,

FULK LE STRANGE, 3rd baron, who dying in minority, and *s. p.,* 23rd EDWARD III., was *s.* by his brother,

JOHN LE STRANGE, 4th baron, summoned to parliament 3 April, 1360. His lordship *m.* Lady Mary Fitz-Alan, sister of Richard, Earl of Arundel, and had issue,

JOHN, his successor.
ANKARET, *m.* to Sir Richard Talbot.

He *d.* in 1361, and was *s.* by his son,

JOHN LE STRANGE, 5th baron. This nobleman *m.* Lady Isabel Beauchamp, dau. of Thomas, Earl of Warwick, and widow of William de la Pole, 2nd Earl of Suffolk, and by her (who *m.* 3rdly, Robert de Ufford), he left at his decease *infra œtatem*, 3 August, 1375, an only dau. and heiress,

ELIZABETH LE STRANGE, who *m.* Thomas Mowbray, Earl of Nottingham, but *d. s. p.* 23 August, 1383.

At the decease of her ladyship, the estates and Barony of Strange, of Blackmere, reverted to her aunt, ANKARET, LADY TALBOT, whose husband, Sir Richard Talbot, was summoned to parliament as LORD TALBOT, *of Blackmere*, and on the death of his father, became 4th Baron Talbot. (*See* TALBOT, Barons Talbot).

Arms—Same as Strange, of Knockyn.

STRATFORD—EARL OF ALDBOROUGH.

(*See* ADDENDA.)

STRATHBOGIE—EARLS OF ATHOL AND BARONS STRATHBOGIE.

Earldom, created *temp.* ALEXANDER I.
Barony, by Writ of Summons, dated 14 March, 1322.

Lineage.

This Earldom of Athol was as ancient as the time of King ALEXANDER I, to whose foundation charter of the Monastery of Scone A.D. 1115, Madach, 1st Earl of Athol, son of King DONAL BANE, was a witness. This Madach, is styled by Torfæus, the Danish Historian, as "Omnium Scotiæ principum facile nobilissimus." From Madach, the Earldom of Athol passed by descent through heiresses to ADA, COUNTESS OF ATHOL, dau. and heiress of Ferelith, Countess of Athol, by her husband, David de Hastings. Ada *m.* JOHN DE STRATHBOGIE, and in 1253, she and her husband confirmed the grant made by Ferelith, to the Monastery of Cupar, for the soul of Sir David de Hastings. The son and heir of Ada, and John de Strathbogie, was,

DAVID DE STRATHBOGIE, Earl of Athol, in Scotland, who, by Isabel de Chilham, one of the co-heirs of Richard de Chilham, of Chilham Castle, in Kent, and Roese de Dover, his wife, had issue,

JOHN DE STRATHBOGIE, Earl of Athol, who in the 32nd EDWARD I., upon the death of Joane, widow of Richard de Dover, had livery of the manor of Lesnes, in Kent, which descended to him through his mother. "It is reported" says Dugdale, "that, in 1306, King EDWARD I., being victorious in Scotland, taking much to heart the slaughter of John Comin, and the crowning of ROBERT DE BRUS, king of that realm, exercised a sharp revenge upon all whom he could discover to have had a hand therein; and that thereupon this John de Asceles (for so he is called) fled the country; but being driven back from sea by contrary winds, was taken, carried to London, and sentenced to death in Westminster Hall. In respect, however, of his descent from royal blood, he was not drawn as traitors usually are, but set on horseback, and hanged upon a gibbet fifty feet high, his head fixed on London Bridge, and his body burnt to ashes." Being thus executed for treason, all his lands in Scotland were conferred by the crown upon Ralph Monthermer, Earl of Gloucester; but those lands were soon after recovered by purchase, and the recovery received the confirmation of the king, by the deceased nobleman's son and heir,

DAVID DE STRATHBOGIE, who, pursuing a different course to that of his father, and taking an active part in favour of the English interests, against BRUCE, had a grant, from the crown, of the manor and honour of Chilham, in Kent, and was summoned to parliament, as a Baron, by King EDWARD II., in the same year, 1322, and from that period to 3 December, 1326. "David, 11th Earl of Athol" (we quote Alexander Sinclair), "was restored by EDWARD I., yet was made high constable by King ROBERT BRUCE in 1311, but joining Baliol's party, he was forfeited and expelled in 1315. By King EDWARD II., he was summoned to parliament as Earl of Athol, 1322. By his grandmother he had Chilham in Kent, and by his wife, Joan Cumyn, he became co-heir to her brother John, Lord of Badenoch, another banished Scotch grandee, and also shared in a still greater succession in this way: Aymer de Valence, Earl of Pembroke, the Jew, half-nephew of King HENRY III., and governor of Scotland just before Bannockburn, was murdered attending EDWARD II.'s Queen Isabel in France, in 1323, leaving no children, but having estates in twenty-five counties in England, out of forty, besides Wales and Ireland. John Cumyn was nephew, and one of the nearest heirs of these vast properties, and he *d.* two years after, in 1325-6, also without issue, leaving only two sisters, his heirs, Elizabeth, the eldest, being wife of David, 11th Earl of Athol." By his said wife Joan, dau.

of John Comyn, Lord of Badenoch, eldest sister and co-heir of John Comyn, of Badenoch, and one of the co-heirs of Aymer de Valence, Earl of Pembroke, the earl left a son and heir,

DAVID DE STRATHBOGIE, 12th Earl of Athol, 2nd baron, summoned to parliament from 25 January, 1330, to 24 July, 1334. This nobleman, at the decease of his father was but nineteen years of age, when Henry de Beaumont paid 1000 marks for his wardship and marriage; notwithstanding which, he stood in such fair esteem with the king, that in the 1st EDWARD III., although he had not then attained majority, he was allowed to do homage, and had livery of his lands. He subsequently inherited estates from his uncle, John Comyn; and lands also as one of the co-heirs of Aymer, Earl of Pembroke. His lordship, in the Scottish wars, was at one time engaged against the English monarch, and at another in his favour; he eventually, however, fell fighting under King EDWARD's (III.) banner, "Thus perished" (says Wood's Douglas) "in the twenty-eighth year of his age, David de Strathbogie, of royal descent, nobly allied, and possessing estates above the rank of a subject. He died seized of the manors of Gainsborough, in Lincolnshire, Bulindon in Buckinghamshire, Posewyke, West Lexham, Styvely, and Rockham in Norfolk; Mitford Castle, and other lands, in Northumberland." He *m.* Katherine Beaumont, dau. of Henry, styled Earl of Buchan, and was *s.* 3 November, 1335, by his only son,

DAVID DE STRATHBOGIE, 3rd Baron Strathbogie, and 13th Earl of Athol, aged three at his father's death; summoned to the parliament of England from 20 January, 1366, to 6 April, 1369 He was afterwards in the wars of France under the Black Prince. His lordship *m.* Elizabeth, dau. of Henry, Lord Ferrers, of Groby, and had issue,

> ELIZABETH, *b.* 1361, *m.* 1st, to Sir Thomas Percy (*jure uxoris*) of Athol, Knt., 2nd son of Henry, Earl of Northumberland, by whom (who *d.* in Spain, in 1388) she had issue,
> > Sir Henry Percy, of Athol, governor of Alnwick for his grandfather, the earl; he escaped the ruin of his family and *d.* in 1433; he *m.* Elizabeth, dau. of Sir William Brewse, of Gower, and widow of Robert, Lord Scales, and left two daus., his heirs, viz.,
> > > Elizabeth, *m.* 1st, to Thomas, Lord Burgh, and 2ndly, to Sir William Lucy. The co-heirs general of Elizabeth, Lady Burgh, are Archdeacon Thomas Thorp, Henry-William Lord Berners, and Hubert de Burgh, Esq., of West Drayton.
> > > Margaret, *m.* 1st, to Henry, Lord Grey, of Codnor, and 2ndly to Sir Richard Vere, Knt.
>
> Her ladyship *m.* 2ndly, Sir John Scrope, Knt.
> PHILIPPA, *m.* 1st, to Sir Ralph Percy, who *d. s. p.*, younger brother of Sir Thomas, and 3rd son of Henry, Earl of Northumberland, and 2ndly, to Sir John Halsham.

His lordship *d.* 10 October, 1375, when the Barony of Strathbogie fell into ABEYANCE between his daus., as it still continues with their representatives.

Arms—Paly of six, or and sa.

STRYVELIN—BARON STRYVELIN.

By Writ of Summons, dated 25 February, 1342.

Lineage.

In the 9th EDWARD III.,

SIR JOHN DE STRYVELIN was in the garrison of Edinburgh Castle, and in the 16th of the same monarch he was constituted one of the commissioners, with the bishop of Durham, Ralph, Lord Nevill, and others, to treat of peace with the Scots He was summoned to parliament as a Baron, from 25 February, 1342, to 8 January, 1371; and he was in the famous expedition made into France in the 20th EDWARD III. Lord Stryvelin *d. s. p.* 15 August, 1378, whereupon the barony became EXTINCT. On this failure of issue to Sir John Stryvelyn, Baron Stryvelyn, certain lands, that he died possessed of, descended to Sir John Middleton and CHRISTIAN DE STRYVELIN, his wife, but the relationship of Christian to Sir John is not shown. Certain it is that she was not his daughter and consequently she could not succeed to the barony.

Arms—Arg., on a chief, gu., three round buckles in fess, or.

STUART—DUKE OF YORK.

By Letters Patent, dated 6 January, 1605.

Lineage.

JAMES I., King of England, Scotland, France, and Ireland, Defender of the Faith, &c., b. at Edinburgh, 19 June, 1566; crowned King of England, 25 July, 1603; m. 20 August, 1590, Anne, dau. of FREDERICK II., King of Denmark, and by her (who d. 2 March, 1619) had,

1. HENRY-FREDERICK, K.G., Prince of Wales, b. 19 February, 1594, d. unm. v. p. 6 November, 1612, in his nineteenth year.
11. CHARLES, Prince of Wales, successor to the crown.
1. Elizabeth, b. 19 August, 1596; m. 14 February, 1612-13, FREDERICK V., Duke of Bavaria, Elector Palatine of the Rhine, and King of Bohemia, and had issue,
 Henry-Frederick, accidentally drowned in 1629.
 CHARLES-LEWIS, Elector Palatine, who m. Charlotte, of Hesse Cassel, and had a dau and heir, Elizabeth-Charlotte, b. 1652, m. Philip, Duke of Orleans, and was direct ancestor of LOUIS-PHILIP, late King of the French.
 Rupert, so gallantly distinguished during the civil wars as Prince Rupert, d. unm. 19 November, 1682.
 Maurice (known in English history as Prince Maurice), d. unm. (shipwrecked) in 1654.
 Edward, Duke of Bavaria, Count Palatine of the Rhine, K.G., m. Anne de Gonzaga, of Mantua, and d. in March, 1663, leaving three daus.,
  LOUISA-MARIA, m. to the Prince of Salms, and had issue, Louis-Otto, Prince of Salms, Louisa, and Eleanora.
  ANNE, m. to Henry-Julius, Prince of Condé, and had issue.
  BENEDICTA, m. to John-Frederick, Duke of Brunswick-Lunenburgh, and had issue.
 Philip, slain in battle, d. unm. in 1650.
 Elizabeth. Abbess of Hervorden, d. in 1680.
 Louisa, Abbess of Maubisson, d. in 1709.
 Henrietta, m. to Sigismund, Prince of Transylvania, d. s. p. in 1651.
 SOPHIA, b. 13 October, 1630; m. 1658. to Ernest-Augustus, Duke of Brunswick-Lunenburgh, Elector of Hanover, by whom she had GEORGE-LEWIS. who ascended the British Throne, under the Act of Settlement, by the title of King GEORGE I.; five other sons, who d. unm.: and one dau., Sophia-Charlotte, m. to FREDERICK-WILLIAM, King of Prussia.

The King's 2nd son,

PRINCE CHARLES STUART, Duke of Albany, in Scotland, was created by letters patent, dated 6 January. 1605, DUKE OF YORK. At the decease of his elder brother, HENRY-FREDERICK, Prince of Wales, in 1612, his royal highness inherited the Dukedom of Cornwall, and, in 1616, was created PRINCE OF WALES. He s. his father 27 March, 1625, as King CHARLES I., when the Dukedom of York merged in the crown.

Arms—Royal arms of England.

STUART—DUKE OF YORK AND EARL OF ULSTER.

Dukedom, by Letters Patent, dated 27 January, 1643.
Earldom of Ireland, by Letters Patent, dated 10 May, 1659.

Lineage.

JAMES STUART, 2nd son of King CHARLES I., was declared DUKE OF YORK at his birth, so created by letters patent, dated 27 January, 1643, and made Earl of Ulster, in Ireland, 10 May, 1659. His royal highness m, 1st, 3 September, 1660 (having been previously, 24 November, 1659, contracted to her), LADY ANNE HYDE, eldest dau. of Edward, Earl of Clarendon, lord high chancellor of England, and had issue,

Charles, b. 22 October, 1660,
James, } Dukes of
Charles, Duke of Kendal. Cambridge. { all of whom d. in infancy or childhood.
Edgar, Duke of Cambridge,
MARY, m. WILLIAM-HENRY, Prince of Orange, and ascended the British throne with her husband, at the Revolution Her Majesty d. s. p. in 1694.
ANNE, m. Prince GEORGE, of Denmark, and ascended the throne as Queen ANNE; d. in 1714, without surviving issue.

The Duchess of York d. in 1671, and the Duke m. 2ndly, 21 November, 1673, MARY-BEATRICE-ELEANOR D'ESTE, dau. of ALPHONSO III., Duke of Modena. She was sister of Francis, Duke of Modena, and of Isabella, Princess of Parma and Placentca. Her mother was Laura Martinozzi, niece to Cardinal Mazarin, being dau. of COUNT JEROME MARTINOZZI, by that celebrated statesman's eldest sister, Margaret Mazarin. By

---

this illustrious lady (who d. 8 May, 1718), his royal highness had issue to survive, a dau., Louisa, who d. unm. 1712, and two sons,

Charles Duke of Cambridge, who d. an infant, 1677.
JAMES-FRANCIS-EDWARD, b. 10 June, 1688: his father being then King, he was declared PRINCE OF WALES, and was bapt. 15 October in the same year. The Pope's nuncio held the prince at the baptismal font, in his holiness's name, who was godfather, and the queen-dowager, godmother. This prince upon the decease of his father, in 1701, was proclaimed, by LOUIS XIV., at Paris, King of Great Britain, &c., and he endeavoured, in 1715, to establish his right by arms He was attainted by the Act 13 and 14 WILLIAM III. He m. in 1719, Clementina Sobieski, dau. of Prince JAMES SOBIESKI, son of John Sobieski, King of Poland, by whom he had two sons,
 CHARLES-EDWARD, Duke of Albany, b. 31 December, 1720, called "the young Pretender," who made so bold an attempt, in 1745, to regain the crown. He m. in 1773, Ludovica, Princess of Stolberg, but d. s. p. 30 January, 1788.
 HENRY-BENEDICT, b. at Rome, 25 March, 1725. This prince became a churchman, and having obtained a cardinal's hat, bore the designation of CARDINAL YORK. His eminence d. in July, 1807, and with him expired the male line of the ROYAL HOUSE OF STUART. (See p. 507).

The prince ascended the throne, as King JAMES II., 6 February, 1685, when the Dukedom of York merged in the crown.

Arms—Royal arms of England

STUART—EARL OF CAMBRIDGE, DUKE OF GLOUCESTER.

By Letters Patent, dated 13 May, 1659.

Lineage.

CHARLES I., b. at Dumfermline, 19 November, 1600, crowned 2 February, 1625; m. 1 May following, HENRIETTA-MARIA, dau. of HENRY IV., of France, and by her (who d. 10 September, 1669, aged sixty,) had issue,

CHARLES, Prince of Wales.
JAMES, Duke of York, who s. his brother as King JAMES II.
HENRY, Duke of Gloucester. b. in July, 1640; d. in 1660. unm.
Mary, m. 2 May, 1648, to WILLIAM II., Prince of Orange, by whom she had an only son,
 WILLIAM-HENRY, Prince of Orange, who ascended the British throne, as WILLIAM III.
Elizabeth, d. of grief, 8 September, 1650, aged fifteen.
Henrietta-Maria, b. 10 June, 1644; m. 31 March, 1661, Philip, Duke of Orleans, and d. 30 June, 1670, leaving issue,
 Philip-Charles, Duc de Valois, d. in 1666, aged two.
 Maria Aloisia, b. in 1662; m. in 1679, to CHARLES II., King of Spain, but d. s. p. in 1689.
 Anna-Maria, b. 31 August, 1669; m. in 1684, to VICTOR AMADEUS II., Duke of Savoy and King of Sardinia; of this marriage,
  FRANCIS V., Duke of Modena, b. 1 June, 1819, is senior heir of line.

The 3rd son,

PRINCE HENRY STUART, b. at Oatlands, 8 July, 1640, and thence denominated "HENRY, of Oatlands," was created, by letters patent, dated 13 May, 1659, EARL OF CAMBRIDGE AND DUKE OF GLOUCESTER. He was also elected a knight of the Garter. His royal highness was in exile with his brother, CHARLES, during the usurpation, and returned to England when that prince was restored to the crown, but d. in 1660 unm., when all his honours became EXTINCT.

Arms—Royal arms of England, duly differenced.

STUART—DUKES OF CAMBRIDGE.

By Letters Patent, dated in 1661, 1664, 1667, 1677.

Lineage.

The following children of James, Duke of York, afterwards King JAMES II., were created DUKES OF CAMBRIDGE, viz.,

CHARLES STUART, created in 1661, d. the same year, an infant, when the Dukedom EXPIRED.
JAMES STUART, created in 1664, d. in 1667, an infant, when the Dukedom became EXTINCT.
EDGAR STUART, created in 1667, d. in 1671, an infant, when the dignity EXPIRED.
CHARLES STUART, created in 1677, d. the same year, an infant, when the honour became EXTINCT.

Arms—Royal arms of England, duly differenced.

STUART—DUKE OF KENDAL.

By Letters Patent, dated 1666.

Lineage.

CHARLES STUART, 3rd son of James, Duke of York (afterwards JAMES II.), was created DUKE OF KENDAL, in 1666. He d. the next year, an infant, when the dignity became EXTINCT.

Arms—Royal arms of England, duly differenced.

STUART—BARON STUART DE ROTHESAY.

By Letters Patent, dated 22 January, 1828.

Lineage.

LIEUT.-GEN. THE HON. SIR CHARLES STUART, K.B. (4th son of John, 3rd Earl of Bute, by Mary, his wife, only dau. of Edward Wortley-Montagu, Esq., M.P.), was governor of the island of Minorca, which, amongst his other military services, he had reduced in 1798. He m. 19 April, 1778, Louisa, 2nd dau. and co-heiress (with her sister, Albinia, Countess of Buckinghamshire,) of Lord Vere Bertie, 3rd son of Robert, 1st Duke of Ancaster, and had issue,

> CHARLES, created LORD STUART DE ROTHESAY.
> John, capt. R.N.; *b.* in 1782; *m.* 26 September, 1807, Albinia, eldest dau. of the Right Hon. John Sullivan, and left at his decease, in 1811, an only son, Charles, an officer in the army. *b.* 16 March, 1810; *m.* 4 September, 1839, Hon. Georgiana. dau. of the late Vice-Admiral Sir John Gore, K.C.H. Mrs. Stuart *m.* 2ndly, the Rev. Marmaduke Thompson, and d. in 1827.

Sir Charles d. 25 May, 1801, and was s. by his son,

SIR CHARLES STUART, G C.B., an eminent diplomatist, *b.* 1779, who was at one time ambassador extraordinary to the court of Paris, and obtained his peerage by patent of creation, dated 22 January, 1828. He m. 6 February, 1816, Elizabeth-Margaret, 3rd dau. of Philip, 3rd Earl of Hardwicke, and had issue,

> Charlotte, *m.* 5 September, 1835, to Charles-John, Viscount Canning, and d. 18 November, 1861
> Louisa, *m.* 8 June, 1842, to Henry, 3rd Marquess of Waterford, K.P.

His lordship d. 6 November, 1845, when the title became EXTINCT.

Arms—Or, a fesse, chequy, az. and arg., within a double tressure, flory, counterflory, gu., a mullet for difference.

STUART—BARON STUART DE DECIES.

(*See* BURKE's *Extant Peerage*, BUTE, M.)

STUART—DUKES OF LENNOX AND RICHMOND.

(*See* STEWART.)

STUART—BARONS STUART AND EARLS OF TRAQUAIR.

Barony, by Letters Patent, dated 19 April, 1638.
Earldom, by Letters Patent, dated 22 June, 1683.

Lineage.

JAMES STUART, 2nd son of Sir James Stuart, Black Knight of Lorn, by Jean, Queen-dowager of King JAMES I., who was created Earl of Buchan in 1469, left a son by a lady of the family of Murray, of Philliphaugh,

JAMES STUART, who obtained a charter of legitimacy, 20 February, 1488-9, and received, by deed of gift, the Barony of Traquair, which was confirmed by royal charter, dated 18 May, 1492. He m. Katharine, dau. and sole heiress of Richard Rutherford, of that ilk, with whom he acquired the baronies of Rutherford and Wells, co. Roxburgh. He fell at Flodden, in 1513, and was s. by his son,

WILLIAM STUART, of Traquair, who m. Christian Hay, 2nd dau. of John, 2nd Lord Yester, by whom he had four sons,

519

1. ROBERT, his heir.
11. John (Sir), successor to his brother.
111 William (Sir), one of the gentlemen of the bedchamber to King JAMES VI., and governor of Dumbarton Castle, *d. unm* 20 May. 1605.
IV. JAMES.

The eldest son,

ROBERT STUART, of Traquair, *d. s. p.* 9 September, 1548, and was *s.* by his brother,

SIR JOHN STUART, of Traquair, captain of the guards to Queen MARY of Scotland. He also *d. s. p.* His last surviving brother,

JAMES STUART was lieutenant in the guards under his brother, Sir John. He was served heir of his brother, Sir William, 7 August, 1605, and *d.* 9 May, 1606. He had issue,

1. JOHN, *m.* Margaret, dau. of Andrew Stewart, Master of Ochiltree, and dying *v. p.*, left a son, JOHN, heir to his grand father.
11. Robert (Sir), of Schelynlaw, tutor to his nephew, John.

The grandson and heir,

SIR JOHN STUART, was elevated to the peerage of Scotland, 19 April, 1638, by the title of BARON STUART, *of Traquair*, to him and his heirs male bearing the name and arms of Stuart, and was created, by patent, dated at Holyrood House, 22 June, 1683, BARON LINTON AND CABARSTON, and EARL OF TRAQUAIR to him and his heirs male for ever, bearing the name and arms of Stuart. This nobleman was constituted lord-treasurer-deputy of Scotland by King CHARLES I.; and, when that unfortunate prince was subsequently confined in the Isle of Wight, his lordship raised a regiment of horse for his majesty's service, and marching at its head to the battle of Preston, himself and his son, Lord Linton, fell into the hands of the rebels, and were committed to the castle of Warwick, where the earl remained four years; being at last, however, released, he returned home, and suffered extreme poverty. His lordship *m.* Katharine, dau. of David, 1st Earl of Southesk, by whom he had one son and four daus.,

1. JOHN, 2nd earl.
1. Margaret, *m.* to James, 2nd Earl of Queensberry, and was mother of the 1st Duke.
11. Elizabeth, *m.* to Patrick, 2nd Lord Elibank, and had issue.
111. Anne, *m.* Sir John Hamilton, of Redhouse, and had issue.
IV. Catherine, *m.* to John Stewart, Esq., and had two sons and a dau.

His lordship *d.* in 1659, and was *s.* by his son,

JOHN STUART, 2nd earl; who *m.* 1st, in 1649, Harriet, 2nd dau. of George, Marquess of Huntly, by whom he had no issue; and 2ndly, Anne, dau. of George. 2nd Earl of Wintoun; and dying in 1666, was *s.* by his eldest son,

WILLIAM STUART, 3rd earl. This nobleman dying *unm.*, the honours devolved upon his only surviving brother,

CHARLES STUART, 4th earl. His lordship *m.* Lady Mary Maxwell, dau. of Robert, 4th Earl of Nithsdale, by whom he had two sons and six daus., viz., Lucy; Anne; Mary, wife of John Drummond, styled Duke of Perth; Catherine, wife of William, Earl of Nithsdale; Barbara; and Margaret. The elder son,

CHARLES STUART, 5th earl. *m.* Theresa, dau. of Sir Baldwin Conyers, Bart., of Great Stoughton, co. Huntingdon: but *d. s. p.* in 1764, when the honours devolved upon his brother,

JOHN STUART, 6th earl. This nobleman *m.* Christiana, dau. of Sir Philip Anstruther, of Anstrutherfield, co. Fife, and widow of Sir William Weir, Bart., of Blackwood, and left issue,

1. CHARLES, his successor.
1. Christina, *m.* to Cyrus Griffin, Esq.
11. Mary.   111. Lucy.

The earl dying 22 March, 1779, was *s.* by his only son,

CHARLES STUART, 7th earl, *b.* in 1746; who *m.* 19 August, 1773, Mary, dau. and co-heiress of George Ravenscroft, Esq., of Wickham, co. Lincoln, and by her (who *d.* 11 July, 1796), had issue,

1. CHARLES, his heir.
1. Louisa of Traquair Castle, co. Peebles, *b.* 20 March, 1776; who *d.* 1875, whereupon her cousin, Hon. Henry Maxwell (brother of Lord Herries) became of Traquair, and assumed the surname of STUART.

His lordship *d.* 14 October, 1827, and was *s.* by his son,

CHARLES STUART, 8th earl, *b.* 31 January, 1781, who *d. unm.* 2 August, 1861. Since that time, the Earldom of Traquair has remained DORMANT.

Arms—Quarterly: 1st, or, a fesse, chequy, az., and arg., for STUART; 2nd, az., three garbs, or, for BUCHAN, 3rd, arg., an orle, gu., in chief three martlets, sa., for RUTHERFORD; 4th, sa., a mullet, arg., for TRAQUAIR.

SUDELEY—BARONS SUDELEY.

By Writ of Summons, dated 29 December, 1299.
By Letters Patent, dated 10 September, 1441.

Lineage.

HAROLD, according to Dugdale, the son of Ralph, Earl of Hereford, but, by other authorities, an illegitimate son of King HAROLD, possessed, at the time of the General Survey, numerous lordships in England, amongst which was Sudeley, in Gloucestershire, the chief place of his residence. He had two sons,

JOHN, his heir.
Robert, who had the castle of Ewyas, and assumed therefrom the surname of EWYAS. His dau., Sybilla de Ewyas, m. 1st, Robert de Tregoz, of Lydiard, Wilts, sheriff 5th RICHARD I.; and 2ndly, Roger de Clifford, ancestor by her of the Earls of Cumberland.

The elder son, assuming his surname from Sudeley, the chief seat which he inherited, became
JOHN DE SUDELEY, Lord of Sudeley and Toddington, in 1140. He m. Grace, dau. and heir of Henry de Traci, feudal Lord of Barnstaple, and had issue,
RALPH DE SUDELEY, founder of the priory of Erdburie.
WILLIAM, who adopted his mother's name of DE TRACI, and was ancestor of the TRACYS of Toddington and Stanway, co. Gloucester, the late Viscounts Tracys, of Rathcoole, and of the present LORD SUDELEY, of Toddington.

He was s. by his elder son,
RALPH DE SUDELEY, who, in the 12th HENRY II., certified his knights' fees in number, four. He m. Emme, dau. of William de Beauchamp, of Elmley, and was s. by his son,
OTWELL DE SUDELEY. This feudal baron d. s. p., about the year 1195, and was s. by his brother,
RALPH DE SUDELEY, who, in the 10th RICHARD I., gave 300 marks to the king for livery of his lands; in which sum 60 marks were included, which had been imposed upon his deceased brother, as a fine for the defect of a soldier, whom he ought to have maintained in Normandy. This Ralph was s. by his son, another
RALPH DE SUDELEY, who m. Isabel, dau. of Roger Corbet, of Chadesley, and was s. by his son,
BARTHOLOMEW DE SUDELEY. This feudal lord was sheriff of Herefordshire, and governor of the castle of Hereford, in the latter end of the reign of HENRY III. He m. Joane, dau. of William de Beauchamp, of Elmley, and sister of William, 1st Earl of Warwick, and dying in 1274, was s. by his son,
JOHN DE SUDELEY, an eminent soldier in the reign of EDWARD I., and lord chamberlain to that king. He was in the French and Scottish wars, and had summons to parliament as a Baron, from 29 December, 1299, to 15 May, 1321. He m. a dau. of William, Lord Saye and dying 1336, left
JOHN DE SUDELEY, his grandson (son of Bartholomew de Sudeley, by his wife, Maud Montfort, of Beaudesert,) his next heir. This John m. Eleanor, dau. of Robert, Lord Scales, and dying in the 14th EDWARD III., left issue,
JOHN, who d. unm. 1367.
Joane, m. to William Boteler, of Wemme, and had a son, THOMAS, who obtained Sudeley Castle.
Margery, m. Sir Robert Massy, Knt., and d. s. p.

Eventually the barony vested in
SIR RALPH BOTELER, K.G., of Sudeley Castle, brother of John Boteler, who d. s. p., and son of Thomas Boteler, whose mother was JOANE DE SUDELEY as above. This Ralph Boteler becoming a person of eminence, temp. HENRY VI., was created, by letters patent, 10 September, 1441, BARON SUDELEY. This nobleman, being a strenuous Lancastrian, excused himself from coming to parliament after the accession of EDWARD IV., by the reason of his advanced age, and had so much favour shown him, that he obtained letters patent of exemption from the duty during life. He was afterwards, however, attached and brought prisoner to London; when it is stated, that as he was departing from his seat, he cast a lingering look upon Sudeley Castle, and exclaimed, "Sudeley Castle, thou art the traytor, not I." This castle he is said to have built out of the spoils he had obtained in the wars of France. Leland tells us, "The Lord Sudeley that builded the castle was a famous man of war in King HENRY's the fifth and sixth dayes, and was an admiral (as I have heard) on sea; whereupon it was supposed and spoken that it was partly builded ex spoliis Gallorum; and some speake of a towre in it called Portmare's Towre, that it should be made of a ransom of his." From its present remains, it would seem that Fuller does not exaggerate when in his quaint phraseology he declares, "It was of subjects' castles the most hand-

some habitation, and of subjects' habitations the strongest castle." These relics, however, would rather indicate its having been a superb castellated mansion than a baronial fortress.* He m. Alice, dau. and heir of Sir William Deincourt, but, as he left no issue, at his decease in 1473, the Barony became EXTINCT, but the barony by writ fell into abeyance between his sisters as co-heirs, namely,

ELIZABETH, m. to Sir John Norbury.
JOANE, m. to Hamond Belknap, Esq.

Arms—SUDELEY, or, two bendlets, gu.; BOTELER, gu., a fesse chequy, arg. and sa., between six cross crosslets, or.

SUTTON—BARONS DUDLEY.

By Writ of Summons, dated 25 February, 1342.

Lineage.

Sir William Dugdale commences his account of the SUTTON family by the following observations: "In the time of Queen ELIZABETH, when Ambrose Dudley, Earl of Warwick, and Robert, his brother, Earl of Leicester (sons to John Dudley, some time Viscount L'Isle, Earl of Warwick, and lastly, Duke of Northumberland), powerful men in their days, did flourish, the most learned and expert genealogists of that age, spared not their endeavours to magnifie this family, whence those great men did, by a younger son, derive their descent; some deducing it from Sutton, of Sutton, in Holdernesse; some from the Suttons, of Sutton Madoc, in Shropshire; but others from Sutton, of Sutton-upon-Trent, near Newark; whence the Suttons, of Aram (near at hand), are descended. Of which opinion was the right learned and judicious Robert Glover, then Somerset Herald; and Henry Ferrers, of Badsley Clinton, co. Warwick, Esq. (a person likewise much versed in those studies), all of them giving probable reasons for those their various conjectures. But, that these Suttons, of Dudley, did spring from Hugh de Sutton, most of them do agree."

HERVEY DE SUTTON, Lord of Sutton-upon-Trent, near Tuxford, co. Notts, gave the church of Sutton to the canons of Radford, near Worksop, Notts. He had issue,

I. ROBERT, heir apparent, d. abroad, s. p.
II. Richard, who had issue; Agnes, m. Gilbert de Muschamp, and had issue; Margery, m. Stephen de Coverham, and had issue; Alice; Mary, m. Guichard de Charrons, and had issue; Elizabeth, mother of William de Caunton.
III. ROWLAND, of whom we treat.

The 3rd son,
ROWLAND DE SUTTON, m. Alice, dau. of Richard de Lexington, and sister and co-heir of Robert, Baron Lexington, and Henry, bishop of Lincoln, and had two sons,

I. WILLIAM, of whom presently.
II. Robert, ancestor of ROBERT SUTTON, created BARON LEXINGTON, of Aram, 21 November, 21st CHARLES I.

The elder son,
WILLIAM DE SUTTON, d. 52nd HENRY III., seized of the manor of Worksop, co. Notts, leaving to Matilda, his wife, a son and heir,
ROBERT DE SUTTON, Lord of Worksop, who m. Johanna, who had lands at Ekering and Allerton, in dower, 2nd EDWARD I. He d. 1st EDWARD I., seised of the manor of Theydon ad Montem, Essex, and the manors of Aston and Byfeld, co. Northampton, leaving a son and heir,
RICHARD DE SUTTON, m. Isabel, dau. and heir of Roderic, the son of Griffin, Lord of the Castle of Shokelach, in Cheshire, by Beatrix, his wife, dau. and co-heir of David de Malpas, and was father of
SIR JOHN DE SUTTON, Knt., who m. Margaret, dau. of Roger de Somerie, and elder sister and co-heir of John de Somerie, Lord Dudley, by whom the Sutton family acquired the castle of Dudley, and other considerable estates (refer to Somerie, Baron Dudley). This Sir John Sutton passed away by deed, bearing date at Westminster, 19 October, in the 19th EDWARD II., all his right and title to the castle and manor of Dudley, with other lands, to Hugh le Despenser, son of Hugh, Earl of

---

* Sudeley Castle, afterwards the residence of Lord Seymour, of Sudeley, and his wife Queen Katharine Parr, was granted by Queen MARY, to Sir John Brydges, of Coberley, who also took title from it as LORD CHANDOS, of Sudeley. From the family of Brydges, Sudeley passed to that of Pitt, and was eventually purchased by Messrs. John and William Dent, of Worcester.

Winchester. But the grant thus made being extorted from him while in prison, and in fear of being put to death, it was cancelled upon the accession of EDWARD III., and the property restored. Sir John was *s.* by his son,

JOHN DE SUTTON, who was summoned to parliament as BARON SUTTON, *of Dudley*, 25 February, 1342. His lordship *m.* Isabel, dau. of John de Cherlton, Lord of Powis, and dying in 1359, was *s.* by his only son,

JOHN DE SUTTON, 2nd baron. The wardship of this nobleman, he being in minority at his father's decease, was granted to Richard, Earl of Arundel, and sold by him to Sir Philip le Despenser, in the 5th RICHARD II., for 350 marks. He *m.* twice; by his 1st wife, Margaret, dau. of Roger de Mortimer, Baron of Wigmore, he had no issue, but by his 2nd wife, Johanna, he had two sons,

   I. JOHN, of whom presently.
   II. Thomas.

The 2nd Lord Dudley *d.* 1376, and was *s.* by his son,

JOHN DE SUTTON, 3rd baron, *m.* 1st, Alice, dau. of Philip le Despenser; and 2ndly, Constance, dau. of Sir Walter le Blount, Knt., of Barton, co. Derby, and Belton, co. Rutland, and by her had,

   I. JOHN, of whom presently.
   II. Thomas, father of Thomas, who *m.* Elizabeth, dau. and co-heir of Robert Goddard, and had a dau., Elizabeth, *m.* Sir A. Billesley, Knt.

He *d.* in 1407. His elder son,

JOHN DE SUTTON, 4th baron, K.G., carried the standard at the solemn obsequies of HENRY V.; and, being also a knight in the 2nd HENRY VI., bore the title of BARON OF DUDLEY, at which time he was in the garrison of the castle of Ghisnes, under its governor, Humphrey, Duke of Gloucester, and continued there for some time. In the 6th of the same reign he was constituted lieutenant of Ireland for the term of two years; and for his good services was summoned to the parliament, then held at Reading, 15 February, 1440: in which year he was likewise appointed one of the commissioners to negotiate a truce with the Duke of Burgundy, or his ambassadors; and in the 27th of the same reign, being then one of the lords of the king's council, he was employed as ambassador to the same prince, to treat with him, and certain commissioners from the Flemings, touching *a freedom of trade* between England and the Low Countries. His lordship being a stanch Lancastrian, was made prisoner in two years after at Gloucester, by Richard, Duke of York, and sent to the castle of Ludlow. He was, subsequently, wounded at Bloreheath, and obtained from King HENRY VI., to whom he was treasurer, various grants of divers lordships, as also of the stewardship of Montgomery, Chirbury, &c., for life, to be executed either personally or by deputy. But, notwithstanding his fidelity to his royal master, he so far acquiesced in the rule of EDWARD IV., that he had a discharge from that prince of all the debts he owed the crown, and he afterwards obtained other immunities from the same king. Towards the latter end of HENRY VI.'s reign, he was invested with the Garter, and he had summons to parliament regularly from 18th of that king to the 3rd HENRY VII. His lordship *m.* Elizabeth, dau. of Sir John Berkeley, of Beverstone, and widow of Sir Edward Cherlton, Knt., Lord Powis, by whom he had issue,

   I. EDMUND (Sir), who *m.* 1st, Joice, dau. of John Lord Tiptoft, and aunt and, in her issue, co-heir of Edward, Earl of Worcester, and had issue,

     EDWARD, who *s.* his grandfather.
     Joyce, *m.* to Sir E. Bensted.

   He *m.* 2ndly, Matilda, dau. of Thomas, Lord Clifford, by whom he had,

     Thomas, who *m.* Grace, dau. and co-heir of Lancelot Threlkeld, of Yeawith, Esq., and had issue, 1 Richard Sutton, alias Dudley, of Yeawith, *m.* Dorothy, dau. of Edward Sandford, of Askam, and had Edmund, Robert, Elizabeth, Anne, Johanna, Jane, and Grace. 2 John Dudley, of Newington, *m.* the dau. of — Gardener, and had a dau. and heir ; 3 Thomas ; 1 Elizabeth, *m.* to Alan Thacksted ; 2 Winifred, *m.* to Anthony Blencowe, Esq., of Blencowe, and 3 Lucy, *m.* to Albany Fetherston, Esq.
     Richard, in holy orders.
     Oliver.   Robert, *s. p.*
     George, in holy orders.
     Joice, *m.* to William Middleton, Esq., of Stockeld, co. York.
     Margaret.
     Alice, *m.* to Sir John Ratcliffe, of Ordsal, Lancashire.
     Dorothy, *m.* 1st, to Sir John Musgrave, Knt.; and 2ndly, to Richard Wrottesley, Esq., of Wrottesley.

   Sir Edmund Sutton *d. v. p.*

   II. John, who assumed the surname of DUDLEY, and became ancestor of the Dudleys, Earls of Warwick. He *m.* Elizabeth, one of the daus. and co-heirs of John Bramshot, Esq., of Bramshot, and was father of

521

EDMUND DUDLEY, the notorious minister of HENRY VII (*'ce* Dudley, Earls of Warwick.)

   III. William, bishop of Durham.
   I. Margaret. *m.* to Sir John Longueville, of Little Billing, co. Northampton, Knt.
   II. Jane, *m.* to Thomas Maynwaring, of Ightfield.
   III. Eleanor, *m.* to Henry Beaumont, of Woodsop, Knt.

His lordship *d.* in 1487, and was *s.* by his grandson,

EDWARD SUTTON, 6th baron, K.G., summoned to parliament from 12 August, 1492, to 3 November, 1529. This nobleman was elected a knight of the Garter in the beginning of HENRY VIII.'s reign. He *m.* Cecilie, dau. of Sir William Willoughby, Knt., and had issue,

   I. JOHN, his successor.
   II. Geoffrey, *m.* Eleanor Talbot, and had a son,
     Thomas, of Russels.
   III. Thomas.   IV. Arthur.
   I. Elizabeth.   II. Alice.
   III Eleanor, *m.* to Charles Somerset, Earl of Worcester, ancestor of the present Duke of Beaufort.
   IV. Joyce, *m.* to Sir John Leighton, Knt. of Wattlesborough.
   V. Johanna, *m.* to Sir Thomas Fiennes, Knt., son and heir apparent of Thomas, Baron Dacre.
   VI. Margaret, *m.* to John Grey, Baron Powys.
   VII. Catherine, *m.* to Sir George Gresley, of Drakelow, co. Derby, Knt.

His lordship *d.* in 1531, and was *s.* by his son,

JOHN SUTTON, 7th baron, but never summoned to parliament. "It is reported," writes Dugdale, "by credible tradition, of this John, Lord Dudley, that, being a weak man of understanding, whereby he had exposed himself to some wants, and so became entangled in the usurer's bonds, John Dudley, then Viscount L'Isle, and Earl of Warwick (afterwards Duke of Northumberland), thirsting after Dudley Castle (the chief seat of the family), made those money merchants his instruments to work him out of it; which, by some mortgage, being at length effected, this poor lord became exposed to the charity of his friends for subsistence; and spending the remainder of his life in visits amongst them, was commonly called *Lord Quondam*." His lordship *m.* Lady Cicely Grey, dau. of Thomas, Marquess of Dorset, and had issue,

   EDWARD, his successor.
   George.   Henry.
   Dorothy.   Elizabeth.

He *d.* 1553, and was *s.* by his eldest son,

SIR EDWARD SUTTON, 8th baron, summoned to parliament from 12 November, 1554, to 15 October, 1586. This nobleman, when Sir Edward Sutton, was in the expedition made into Scotland in the 1st EDWARD VI., and was appointed governor of Hume Castle upon the surrender of that fortress to the English. His lordship afterwards enjoyed so much favour from Queen MARY, that her Majesty restored to him, by letters patent, Dudley Castle, and other lands of great value, which had vested in the crown, by the attainder of John Dudley, Duke of Northumberland. Her Majesty constituted him likewise lieutenant of the castle of Hampnes, in Picardy, for life. Lord Dudley *m.* 1st, Catherine, dau. of John Brydges, Lord Chandos, of Sudley, by whom he had an only dau.,

   Agnes, *m.* 1st, Francis Throckmorton, Esq., and 2ndly, Thomas Wylmer, Esq, barrister-at-law.

He *m.* 2ndly, Lady Jane Stanley, dau. of Edward, Earl of Derby, by whom he had two sons,

   EDWARD, his successor.
   John, who *m.* Elizabeth, dau. of Thomas Whorwood, of Compton, and had a son and heir,
     Whorwood.

His lordship *m.* 3rdly, Mary, dau. of William, Lord Howard of Effingham, but by her (who *m.* 2ndly, Richard Mompesson) had no issue. He *d.* in 1586, and was *s.* by his son,

EDWARD SUTTON, 9th baron, summoned to parliament, from 19 February, 1593, to 3 November, 1639. This nobleman *m.* Theodosia, dau. of Sir James Harrington, Knt., of Exton, by Lucy Sydney, his wife, and had issue,

   FERDINANDO (Sir), who was made a knight of the Bath at the creation of Henry, Prince of Wales, in 1610. He *m.* Honora, dau. of Edward, Lord Beauchamp, eldest son of Edward, Earl of Hertford. Of this marriage, Mr. Porry writes, in a letter to Sir Ralph Winwood, dated London, 17 July, 1610, "Sir Ferdinando Dudley, heir to the Lord Dudley, was yesterday married to my Lord Beauchamp's only daughter, who hath £5000 in present to her marriage, and shall have £5000." Sir Ferdinando *d. v. p.*, leaving an only dau. and heir,

     FRANCES, who *s.* her grandfather.

   Mary, *m.* to Alexander, Earl Hume, in Scotland.
   Anne, *m.* to Meinhardt, Count Schomberg, and was mother of

the celebrated General Frederick, Duke of Schomberg, K.G., who fell in the Boyne, in 1690.

Margaret, m. to Sir Miles Hobart, K.B.

Theodosia.

Lord Dudley having lavished a great portion of his property on a concubine, and his children by her, and having thus involved himself and the estates of the family very much in debt, was obliged, according to Dugdale, in order to extricate them, to bestow the hand of his grand-dau., and heiress, FRANCES SUTTON, upon Humble Ward, the only son of William Ward, an opulent goldsmith in London, and jeweller to the queen. His lordship d. 1643, and was s. by his grand-dau.,

FRANCES WARD (wife of the above-mentioned Sir Humble Ward, Knt., who was created by King CHARLES I., 23 March, 1644, Lord Ward, of Birmingham), as Baroness Dudley. This lady had issue,

   I. EDWARD, who s. his father as Lord Ward, in 1670.

   II. William, who m. Anne. dau. and sole heir of Thomas Parkes. Esq., of Willngsworth, co. Stafford, by whom he acquired that and other estates, and had issue,

      WILLIAM, his successor.

      Frances, m. to Robert Pigot, Esq., of Chetwynd, Salop.

      Jane, m. to Daniel Jevon, Esq.

      Rebecca, d. unm.

   Mr. Ward was s. by his son,

      WILLIAM WARD, Esq., of Willingsworth, M.P. for co. Stafford, temp. Queen ANNE and King GEORGE I. He m. Mary, dau. of the Hon. John Grey, of Enville Hall, and had issue,

         1 JOHN, of Sedgley Park, co. Stafford, who inherited the Barony of Ward, at the decease of William. 5th baron, in 1740, and was grandfather of John-William Ward, late Earl of Dudley.

         2 William, rector of Himley, ancestor of the present EARL OF DUDLEY.

   III. Humble, d. young.

   I. Honora, m. to William Dilke, Esq., of Maxtocke Castle, co. Warwick.

   II. Frances. m. to Sir William Noel, Bart., of Kirkby Mallory, co. Leicester.

   III. Theodosia, m. 1st, to Sir Thomas Brereton, and 2ndly, to Charles Brereton.

Her ladyship d. in 1697, and was s. by her eldest son,

EDWARD WARD, 2nd Lord Ward, of Birmingham, as (11th successor to the Barony of Dudley, and) 10th Baron Dudley. His lordship m. Frances, dau. of Sir William Brereton, Bart., of Handford, in Cheshire, and sister and sole heir of Sir Thomas Brereton, by whom he had issue,

   I. John, who d. young, in 1675.

   II. WILLIAM, m. Frances. dau. of Thomas Dilke, Esq., of Maxtocke Castle, co Warwick, and had issue,

      1 EDWARD, who s. his grandfather.

      2 WILLIAM, successor to his nephew.

      1 FRANCES, m. 1706, to William Lea, Esq., of Hales-Owen-Grange, co. Salop, and had issue,

         FERDINANDO-DUDLEY LEA, of whom hereafter, as 14th Baron Dudley, upon the decease of William, 13th baron, in 1740.

         William Lea, d. unm.

         ANNE, m. to William Smith, Esq., of Ridgeacre, co. Salop.

         Frances, m. to Walter Woodcock, Esq.

         Mary, m. to Dr. Hervey, a physician, of Stourbridge.

         Catherine, m. to Thomas Jordan, of Birmingham.

         Elizabeth, m. to the Rev. Benjamin Briscoe.

   III. Ferdinando, d. unm. 1717.

   I. Catherine, m. to the Hon. John Grey, of Enville Hall, and was mother of

      Harry Grey, 3rd Earl of Stamford.

   II. Lettice, d. young.

   III. Humbletta, m. to Thomas Porter, Esq.

His lordship d. in 1701, and was s. by his grandson,

EDWARD WARD, 11th Baron Dudley, and 3rd Lord Ward. This nobleman m. Diana, dau. of Thomas Howard, Esq., of Ashted, co. Surrey, and dying 28 March, 1704, was s. by his posthumous son,

EDWARD WARD, 12th Baron Dudley, and 4th Lord Ward, at whose decease, unm., 6 September, 1731, the honours reverted to his uncle,

WILLIAM WARD, 13th Baron Dudley, and 5th Lord Ward. This nobleman d. also unm., 21 May, 1740, when the Barony of Ward, of Birmingham, passed to his kinsman, JOHN WARD, Esq., of Sedgeley Park (refer to WILLIAM, 2nd son of Frances Ward, Baroness Dudley), and the Barony of Dudley devolved upon his nephew (revert to FRANCES, dau. of William Ward, eldest surviving son of Edward, 2nd Lord Ward, and 10th Baron Dudley),

FERDINANDO-DUDLEY LEA, Esq., as 14th Baron Dudley (15th in succession, one of the inheritors being a baroness). This nobleman d. unm. in 1757, and his brother having pre-deceased him, also unm., the Barony of Dudley fell into ABEYANCE amongst his lordship's sisters, as it still continues with their descendants. Of those ladies, the eldest, ANNE, wife of William Smith, Esq., of Ridgeacre, was great grandmother of FERDINANDO-DUDLEY-LEA SMITH, Esq., of Halesowen Grange, co. Salop, senior co-heir of the Barony of Dudley; the second, FRANCES, wife of Walter Woodcock, Esq., had, with two sons, who d. s. p., six daus., and eventually co-heirs, viz., MARY, m. Benjamin Smart; FRANCES, m. Joseph Green, and d. s p.; ELIZABETH, m. John Green, and had issue; ANNE, m. William Wilmot; SARAH, m. to the Rev. Thomas Hughes, and had issue; and Katherine, d. s. p.

The youngest sister and co-heir of Ferdinando-Dudley Lea, 14th Lord Dudley, was ELIZABETH, wife of the Rev. Benjamin Briscoe, rector of Stanton, co. Worcester, by whom she had a son, the Rev. WILLIAM-LEA BRISCOE, LL.D., J.P. for the co. Wilts.

The following extract from the author's work, the *Vicissitudes of Families*, may not be deemed irrelevant here:—

"The Barony of Dudley, at the death, in 1757, of Ferdinando-Dudley Lea, 14th baron, fell into abeyance amongst his lordship's sisters. One of these sisters, Frances, became the wife of Walter Woodcock, Esq., 'Justice Woodcock,' as he was called, to whose descendants Dame Fortune has been most chary in the distribution of her favours. Their dau. Anne, became the wife of William Wilmot, and another dau., Mary, was married to Benjamin Smart. Some seventeen or eighteen years ago, the traveller on the Dudley road, on reaching the toll-gate of Cooper's Bank, and depositing the usual fees of the pike in the hands of that inflexible personage, the toll-bar keeper, little dreamt that the poor man following this lowly occupation was next brother of one of the co-heirs of the Barony of Dudley! But so it was: George Wilmot, the toll-bar keeper of Cooper's Bank, was a descendant of the very Lords Dudley, whose proud castle towered in the distance; and when he died on Christmas day, 1846, his remains were borne from the turnpike-gate to Dudley, and deposited by the ashes of his kindred. One nephew, Daniel-Sinclair Wilmot, filled the office of second clerk of the customs at Bristol, and another, John K. Wilmot (son of his eldest brother, Pynson), at this moment one of the co-heirs of the Barony of Dudley, is residing in an humble station, at No. 1, Cleveland Grove, Mile End.

"At Oatenfield Farm, Halesowen, in Worcestershire, another and a senior co-heir of the barony resides, Joseph Smart, a worthy farmer; and at the town of Halesowen, his only brother, Robert Smart, carries on the business and trade of grazier and butcher.

"Mr. Joseph Smart has in his possession an ancient and curious family record, tracing his descent from the old Lords Dudley, and setting forth his royal line through the Suttons, the Seymours, the Greys, and the Brandons from HENRY VII., and Elizabeth of York. After which comes the following curious inventory:—' An account of jewels and gold rings in the possession of Walter Woodcock, Esq., in an oak chest, at Dovehouse Fields, in the parish of Salop: 1. a mourning ring, with inscription engraved within it, 'Edward, Lord Dudley Ward, obt. 6 Sept. 1731, aged 27;' also three gold ear-rings, apparently diamonds, supposed to have been his said lordship's mother's Lady Dudley Ward, of Dudley Castle, and by her given to her daughter, Frances Ward, who married with William Lea, of the Grange, Halesowen, by whom she had issue;' and then follows the genealogy of her descendants to the present day.

"Where can we find a more striking contrast than this mournful tale of the Barony of Dudley? The history of that famous title speaks in its first chapter of chivalry, warlike achievement, and magnificent hospitality in the ancient castle from which the barony took its name. The last chapter tells the story of the Halesowen farmer, the custom-house clerk, and the toll-bar keeper, all resident within range of that very castle."

Arms—Of the SUTTONS: Or, a lion rampant, vert, queue fourché. Of the WARDS: chequy, or and az., a bend, erm.

SUTTON — BARONS LEXINTON, OF ARAM.

By Letters Patent, dated 21 November, 1645.

Lineage.

ROBERT SUTTON, Esq., of Aram, co. Nottingham, descended from a common ancestor, with the family of Sutton, Barons Dudley, was, in consideration of the eminent services he had rendered to the royal cause, during the civil war, elevated to the peerage, by letters patent, dated 21 November, 1645, as BARON LEXINTON,* of *Aram.* His lordship m. 1st, Elizabeth, dau. of Sir George Manners, of Haddon, co. Derby; 2ndly, Anne, dau. of Sir Guy Palmes, of Lindley, co. York, and widow of Sir Thomas Browne, and 3rdly, Mary, dau. of Sir Anthony St. Leger, Knt.: by the last wife, only, he had issue, viz.,

ROBERT, his successor.
Bridget, m. to John, eldest son of Conyers Darcy, son and heir-apparent of Conyers, Lord Darcy.

His lordship d. in 1668, and was s. by his son,
ROBERT SUTTON, 2nd baron, who m. Margaret, dau. and heir of Sir Giles Hungerford, of Colston, co. Wilts, by whom he had issue,

WILLIAM-GEORGE, who d. unm., v. p., anno 1713.
Eleonora-Margaretta, d. unm.
Bridget, m. 1717, to John Manners, 3rd Duke of Rutland, K.G., and had issue,

JOHN, Marquess of Granby, ancestor of the Dukes of Rutland.
Robert, who assumed the surname of SUTTON, on succeeding to the Lexinton estates. His lordship d. s. p. in 1772, when those estates devolved upon his next brother,
GEORGE, who then assumed the additional surname of SUTTON. Lord George Manners-Sutton m. 1st, in 1749, Diana, dau. of Thomas Chaplin, Esq., of Blankney, co. Lincoln, and had issue,

1 JOHN, who d. in 1826: his grandson is the present JOHN-HENRY MANNERS-SUTTON, Esq., of Kelham, Notts.
2 CHARLES, archbishop of Canterbury, m. Mary, dau. of Thomas Thoroton, Esq., and left at his decease, in 1828, with other issue,

SIR CHARLES MANNERS-SUTTON, G.C.B., Speaker of the House of Commons, created VISCOUNT CANTERBURY, 10 March, 1835 (see BURKE's Extant Peerage).

3 Thomas, appointed lord chancellor of Ireland, and created BARON MANNERS, of Foston, in 1807.
1 Diana, m. 21 April, 1778, to Francis Dickins, Esq., of Wollaston, co. Northampton, and Branches Park, co. Suffolk, who d. 1834, aged eighty-five.
2 Louisa-Bridget, m. 1790, to Edward Lockwood Percival, Esq.
3 Charlotte, m. 1789, to Thomas Lockwood, Esq.

Lord George m. 2ndly, Mary, dau. of Joshua Peart, Esq., and had a dau.,

Mary, m. 1799, to the Rev. Richard Lockwood, prebendary of Peterborough, who d. 1830.

Lord Lexinton, who had been envoy-extraordinary to the Court of Vienna, and was appointed ambassador-extraordinary to that of Spain, and for the treaty of Ryswick, d. in 1723, when the Barony of Lexinton, of Aram, became EXTINCT, and the Sutton estates passed eventually to his grandson, LORD GEORGE MANNERS.

Arms—Arg., a canton, sa.

---

* LEXINTON.
This name is taken from Lexington, now called Laxton, co. Nottingham, which lordship
RICHARD LEXINTON held, in the reign of King JOHN, and was s. by
ROBERT LEXINTON, a learned judge, temp. HENRY III., and justice itinerant for several northern counties. He was s. by his brother,
JOHN LEXINTON, who, in the reign of HENRY III., was chief justice of all the forests north of Trent, and dying s. p., in the 41st of the same reign, was s. by another brother,
HENRY LEXINTON, bishop of Lincoln, who d. the next year, leaving Richard Markham, and WILLIAM DE SUTTON, from whom the Lord Lexinton, of Aram, derived, his heirs.

SUTTON—BARON SUTTON.

By Writ, 20 July, 1332.

Lineage.

JOHN SUTTON, of Sutton, in Holderness, co. York, was summoned to parliament, from 20 July, 1332, to 15 November 1338, in which latter year he died. His son and heir,
JOHN DE SUTTON, 2nd baron, held the manor of Sutton "de Dominâ Isabellâ filiâ Domini Regis," and was summoned to parliament, from 25 August, 1339, to 20 April, 1344, and again 3 April, 1360. He d. in 1362, his brother, Sir Thomas Sutton, Knt., being his heir. This Sir Thomas left three daus. co-heiresses, viz., Margery, m. Peter, 6th Lord Mauley; Agnes, m. 1st, to Edmond Hastings, and 2ndly, to Ralph de Bulmer; and Constance, m. to John Godard.

SWIFT—VISCOUNT CARLINGFORD.

By Letters Patent, dated 26 March, 1627.

Lineage.

The family of Swyft, or Swift, was of long consideration in Yorkshire, and from one of its branches DEAN SWIFT is reputed to have descended.
ROBERT SWYFT, Esq.,* "the rich mercer of Rotheram" (son of Robert Swyft, by Agnes, his wife, dau. of Martin Anne, of Frickley), m. Anne, dau. of William Taylor, of Sheffield, and had with two daus. (the elder, Anne, wife of Lionel Reresby, Esq. of Thribergh; and the younger, Margaret, of Richard, son and heir apparent of Sir Thomas Waterton, Knt., of Walton,) two sons, viz.,

ROBERT, of Rotheram, who m. Ellinor, dau. and sole heir of Nicholas Wickersley, co. York, and d. v. p. 1558, leaving three daus., his co-heirs, viz.,
ANNE, m. to Richard Jessop, Esq., and had issue. (For full details of the Jessops of Broom Hall, and their representatives, the Wilkinsons and Lawsons, see BURKE's Commoners.)
MARY, m. to Francis Wortley, Esq. of Wortley.
FRANCES, m. to Sir Francis Leke, Knt. of Sutton, co. Derby.
WILLIAM.

The 2nd son,
WILLIAM SWYFT, Esq. of Rotheram, m. Margaret, dau. of Hugh Worral, Esq. of Lovershall, and widow of Thomas Ricard, of Hatfield, and left issue,

I. ROBERT, of whom presently.
I. Anne, m. to Ralph Beeston, Esq. of Beeston, co. York.
II. Barbara, m. to — Gemby.
III. June.

The son,
SIR ROBERT SWYFT, Knt. of Rotheram and Doncaster, high-sheriff of Yorkshire, 42nd ELIZABETH and 16th JAMES I., and bow-bearer of the royal chase of Hatfield, was bapt. at Sheffield, 5 December, 1568. He m. 1st, Bridget, youngest of the three daus. and co-heirs of Sir Francis Hastings, of Fenwick, co. York, and by her had issue,

I. Edward (Sir), of Rotheram, knighted 23 April, 1603, m. 1st, Elizabeth, dau. of Edmund, Earl of Mulgrave, Lord Sheffield, lord-president of the north: but by her (who m. 2ndly, Sir John Bouchier,) he had no issue.
I. Mary, sole heir of the whole blood of her brother, m. Robert Ryther, Esq. of Harewood Castle; her will was proved 22 September, 1632.

He m. 2ndly, Ursula, dau. of Stephen Barnham of Lewes, co Sussex, and co-heir to her brother, Martin Barnham, Esq., and by her (who d. at Doncaster, 28 May, 1632,) had issue,

I. BARNHAM, created Viscount Carlingford.
II. Darcy, d. unm., administration granted 31 December, 1629.
I. Anne, under age in 1626.
II. Penelope, m. to William, 2nd Earl of Dumfries.
III. Rosamond, b. after 1612.

Sir Robert d. at Doncaster, 14 March, 1625. His son, was
BARNHAM SWIFT, Esq., who was created a peer of Ireland, 26 March, 1627, as VISCOUNT CARLINGFORD, co. Louth, with limitation to the heirs male of his body. His lordship m. Lady Mary Crichton, dau. of William, 1st Earl of Dumfries,

---

* To Robert Swyft and his wife there is a splendid monument in Rotheram Church, erected in 1561.

and d. 28 January, 1634, leaving an only dau., MARY, who was so unfortunate as to marry the thoughtless and profligate Honourble Robert Fielding, of the court of CHARLES II., who squandered the Swyft property. The title became EXTINCT at his lordship's death.

Arms—Or, a chev., barry nebulée, arg and az., between three roebucks courant, ppr.

SWILLINGTON—BARON SWILLINGTON.

By Writ of Summons, dated 3 December, 1326.

Lineage.

Of this family, which assumed its surname from a lordship in the west riding of Yorkshire, was

ADAM DE SWILLINGTON, who, in the times of EDWARD I. and EDWARD II., was in the Scottish wars, and in the latter reign obtained charter for free warren, in all his demesne lands at Swillington, Thorpe-Pyron, and Thorpe o' the Hill, co. York, and was summoned to parliament as a Baron, 3 December, 1326, but afterwards siding with the Earl of Lancaster against the Spencers, he was fined 1,000 marks. On the accession of EDWARD I., however, matters being changed, that judgment was reversed by parliament, and his lordship marched again into Scotland. Moreover, the next year he had another charter for free warren in his demesne lands, and had summons to parliament, to 5 March, 1328, but nothing further is known of his lordship or his descendants.

Arms—Arg., a chevron, az.

SWYNNERTON—BARON SWYNNERTON.

By Writ of Summons, dated 23 April, 1337.

Lineage.

This family (one of great antiquity in the co. Stafford,) derived its surname from the lordship of Swynnerton, co. Stafford.

SIR THOMAS SWINNERTON, Knt., of Swinnerton, m. Matilda, dau. of Sir Robert de Holland, and had two sons, viz.,

I. ROGER (Sir), his heir.
II. John (Sir), who d. 14th EDWARD III., leaving by Anne, dau. of Philip de Montgomery, his wife, two sons, viz.,

  1 JOHN seneschal of Cannock, whose lineal descendant,

  HUMPHREY SWINNERTON, of Swinnerton, m. Cassandra, dau. of Sir John Giffard, Knt., and dying in 1562 left two daus., his co-heirs, viz.,

    MARGARET, m. to Henry Vernon, Esq., of Sudbury, co. Derby, and conveyed to her husband, the estate of Hilton, co. Stafford.

    Elizabeth, m. 1st, in 1552, to William, 4th son of Sir Anthony Fitz-Herbert, of Norbury, the celebrated judge of the Court of Common Pleas, *temp.* HENRY VIII., and conveyed the manor of Swinnerton to her husband. Elizabeth, m. 2ndly, Francis Gatacre. Esq., of Gatacre.

  2 Thomas, of Butterton, co. Stafford, ancestor of the SWINNERTONS of that place, whose last male descendant, THOMAS SWINNERTON, Esq., of Butterton, m. 1793, Mary, dau. and heir of Charles Milhorne, Esq. of Wonaston, by the Lady Martha Harley, his wife, and left three daus., his co-heirs, viz., Martha, m. to Wm. Bagot, Esq.; Mary, m. to Sir William Pilkington, Bart., of Chevet; and Elizabeth, m. to Charles-John Kemeys-Tynte, Esq., M.P.

The eldest son of Sir Thomas,

SIR ROGER DE SWYNNERTON, had, in the 34th EDWARD I., a charter for free warren in all his demesne lands, at his manor of Swynnerton, and for holding a market there on Wednesday every week, and a fair yearly upon the festival of our Lady's Assumption; and in the 4th EDWARD II. was in the wars of Scotland. In the 11th EDWARD II., he was governor of the town of Stafford, and in three years after of the stronghold of Hardelagh, in Wales. In the 15th of the same reign, he had the custody of Eccleshall Castle (during the vacancy of the bishoprick of Lichfield whereunto it belonged), and was some years after constituted constable of the Tower of London. In the 2nd EDWARD III., being then a banneret, he had an assignation out of the exchequer of £145 13s. 8d., as well for his wages of war in that expedition made into Scotland, as for his services in attending Queen ISABEL. In the 9th EDWARD III., he was again in the Scottish wars, and in two years subsequently,

524

23 April, 1337, had summons to parliament among the barons of the realm. He m. Johanna, dau. of Sir Robert de Hastange, and dying 1338, left two sons, ROGER his heir, and Robert, aged fifteen at the death of his father. The elder son,

SIR ROGER DE SWINNERTON, Knt., of Swinnerton, left, by Matilda, his wife, a son and successor,

SIR THOMAS SWYNNERTON, Knt., who m. Matilda, dau. of Sir Robert Holland, and was s. by his son,

SIR ROBERT SWYNNERTON, Knt., who m. Elizabeth, dau. and heir of Sir Nicholas Beke, Knt., by whom he left an only dau. and heir,

MAUD SWYNNERTON, who m 1st, William Ipstone, by whom she had issue,

  William, who *d. s. p.*
  Christiana, aged six, } *d.* in 1399.
  Alicia, aged three,

She m. 2ndly, Humphrey Peshall; and 3rdly, Sir John Savage, of Clifton.

Arms—Az., a cross florée, sa.

NOTE—Of this family was Sir Thomas Swinnerton, Lord Mayor of London, whose 3rd son,

THOMAS SWINNERTON, Esq., of Stanway Hall, Essex, left an only dau. and heiress,

THOMASINE SWINNERTON, m. William Dyer, Esq., who was created a Baronet in 1678, and was great-great-grandfather, of

SIR THOMAS-RICHARD-SWINNERTON DYER, Bart.

SYDNEY—BARONS SYDNEY, OF PENSHURST, VISCOUNTS L'ISLE, EARLS LEICESTER.

Barony, by Letters Patent, dated 13 May, 1603.
Viscounty, by Letters Patent, dated 4 May, 1605.
Earldom, by Letters Patent, dated 2 August, 1618.

Lineage.

This family, anciently seated at Cranleigh, in Surrey, and at Kyngesham, in Sussex, derived its descent from

SIR WILLIAM SYDNEY, chamberlain to King HENRY II. with which monarch he came into England from Anjou. From this Sir William lineally sprang,

NICHOLAS SYDNEY (son of William Sydney, of Stoke D'Abernon), who m. Ann, dau. and co-heir of Sir William Brandon, Knt., cousin of Charles, Duke of Brandon, and was father of

SIR WILLIAM SYDNEY, who in the 3rd HENRY VIII., being then one of the esquires of the king's house, accompanied Thomas, Lord D'Arcy into Spain, for the assistance of the Spaniards against the Moors; and when other persons of rank received the dignity of knighthood at the hands of King FERDINAND, excused himself from partaking thereof. The next year he was captain of one of the ships of war employed against the French, and came into action off the coast of Brest. In the 5th of the same reign, Sir William (then a knight) was a chief commander at the battle of Flodden Field; and the next ensuing year he accompanied the Duke of Suffolk, the Marquess of Dorset, and other persons of distinction to Paris, there to make proof of their skill in arms against the Dauphin of France, and nine other select persons, whom he had chosen for his assistants at those solemn justs, there held in the month of November for all comers, being gentlemen of name and arms. The English noblemen and gentlemen landed at Calais, arrayed in green coats and hoods, that they might not be known. Sir William was subsequently one in the second band of the English at the justs held before the courts of HENRY VIII. and FRANCIS I., on the field of the Cloth of Gold. He was also chamberlain and steward to King HENRY, and in the 18th of that monarch, accompanying the Duke of Suffolk into France, he shared in the glory then acquired by the English arms. After this, on the attainder of Sir Philip Vane, he had a grant of the honour of Penshurst, and manor of Enfield, with the park of Penshurst, and other manors and lands in Kent. Sir William m. Anne, dau. of Hugh Pagenham, Esq., and by her (who d. 22 October, 1544,) had issue,

HENRY (Sir), his successor.
Frances, m. to Thomas Ratcliffe, Earl of Sussex, whom she survived, and founded Sydney-Sussex College, at Cambridge.
Agnes, m. to Sir William Fitz-Williams, Knt.
Mary, m. to Sir William Dormer, Knt., of Ascot.
Lucy, m. to Sir James Harrington, Knt.

Sydney
(E. Leicester)

Talboys
(B. Talboys)

Thomson
(B. Sydenham)

Tudor
(E. Richmond)

Tufton
(E. Thanet)

Ufford
(E. Suffolk)

Umfravill
(E. Angus)

Valence
(E. Pembroke)

Verdon
(B. Verdon)

Vere
(E. Oxford)

Villiers
(D. Buckingham)

Warren
(E. Surrey)

He d. in the 7th EDWARD VI., and was s. by his son,

SIR HENRY SYDNEY, K.G., who had been ambassador to France four years before, and the next year was constituted cupbearer to the king for life. In the 2nd and 3rd PHILIP and MARY, he was made vice-treasurer, and general governor of all the revenues of the crown in Ireland, and he was soon afterwards invested with the temporary government of that kingdom as lord justice during the absence of the lord-deputy, the Earl of Sussex. In the 2nd ELIZABETH he was appointed lord-president of Wales, and in the 5th, sent upon a confidential mission into France. In 1564 (6th ELIZABETH), he was made a knight of the Garter, and in some years afterwards, was thrice constituted lord deputy of Ireland. He d. 1586. This eminent person m. Lady Mary Dudley, dau. of John, Earl of Northumberland, and sister of Robert, Earl of Leicester, by whom he had issue,

PHILIP, the accomplished SIR PHILIP SYDNEY, whom Camden describes as "the great glory of his family, the great hope of mankind, the most lively pattern of virtue, and the glory of mankind." He was a soldier and a scholar, illustrious in letters and in arms, but more illustrious still by his deeds of benevolence and humanity. He was mortally wounded in September. 1586, at the battle of Zutphen, in Guelderland. and d. 16 October following. Sir Philip Sydney m. Frances, dau. and heir of Sir Francis Walsingham. and by her (who m. 2ndly, Robert, Earl of Essex; and 3rdly, Richard, Earl of Clanricade,) he left an only dau.,

     Elizabeth, m. Roger, 5th Earl of Rutland, and d. s. p.

ROBERT (Sir), of whom presently.

Thomas (Sir), d. s. p.

Mary, m. Henry, Earl of Pembroke. K G., and d. 25 September, 1621. To this lady Sir Philip Sydney dedicated his "Arcadia;" and Ben Jonson wrote her epitaph.

The 2nd son,

SIR ROBERT SYDNEY, s. as next heir male upon the death of his elder brother, Sir Philip. This gallant person, like his predecessors, acquired renown in arms, first under his uncle, Robert Dudley, Earl of Leicester, in the Netherlands, and afterwards with Sir Francis Vere, when he shared in the victory achieved at Turnholt, in Brabant, anno 1597. For these services, he was, on the accession of King JAMES I., elevated to the peerage as BARON SYDNEY, of Penshurst, co. Kent, by letters patent, dated 13 May, 1603, and on 24 July, in the same year (it being the day of the King and Queen's coronation), he was appointed lord chamberlain to the queen. The next year he was created VISCOUNT L'ISLE. In 1616 he was installed a knight of the Garter, and raised 2 August. 1618, to the EARLDOM OF LEICESTER, the ceremony of creation being performed in the hall of the bishop's palace at Salisbury. His lordship m. 1st, Barbara, dau. and heir of John Gamage, Esq., of Coyty, Glamorganshire, and had issue,

William (Sir), who d. unm., v.p.

ROBERT (Sir), made knight of the Bath at the creation of Henry, Prince of Wales. s. his father.

Mary, m. to Sir Robert Wroth, Knt.

Elizabeth-Catherine, m. to Sir Lewis Mansel, Bart., of Margam.

Philippa, m. to Sir John Hobart, Knt., eldest son of Sir Henry Hobart, Knt , lord chief justice of the Common Pleas, from whom the Earls of Buckinghamshire descend.

Barbara, m. 1st, to Sir Thomas Smythe, afterwards Viscount Strangford; and 2ndly, to Sir Thomas Colepepper.

His lordship m. 2ndly, Lady Smith, widow of Sir Thomas Smith, Knt.; he d. in 1626, and was s. by his eldest surviving son,

SIR ROBERT SYDNEY, K.B., 2nd Earl of Leicester. This nobleman, who lived to the age of eighty years and eleven months, was esteemed of great learning, observation, and veracity. He m. Lady Dorothy Percy, dau. of Henry, 9th Earl of Northumberland, and had issue,

PHILIP, Viscount L'Isle. his successor.

ALGERNON, the celebrated patriot, who suffered death by decapitation on Tower Hill, 7 December, 1683, as a participator in the Rye House Plot. Of this eminent person Burnet writes, "he was too rough and boisterous in his temper to bear contradiction; he seemed to be a Christian, but in a particular form of his own : for Christianity he thought was to be like a divine philosophy of the mind, without all public worship, or any sign of a visible church. Stiff he was in all republican principles, and such an enemy to every thing that looked like monarchy, that he opposed Cromwell after he was made PROTECTOR : but he had studied the history of government in all its branches; had a knowledge of mankind, and of their tempers; and could insinuate himself into people that would hearken to his notions with a wonderful dexterity."

Robert d. in 1674.

HENRY, created Earl of Romney.

Dorothy (Waller's "Sacharissa,") m. 1st, to Henry, Earl of Sunderland, and 2ndly, to Robert Smythe, Esq., of Bounde.

Lucy, m. to Sir John Pelham, Bart.

Anne, m. to the Rev. Joseph Cart.

Isabella, m. to Philip, Viscount Strangford.

His lordship d. in 1677, and was s. by his eldest son,

PHILIP SYDNEY, 3rd Earl of Leicester. This nobleman was, in the life-time of his father, a zealous republican, and during the Commonwealth one of the Protector's council, with a salary of £1000 a-year. He had been from his youth trained up a diplomatist, attending on his father to the States-General, and the courts of Denmark and France. His lordship m. Lady Catherine Cecil, dau. of William, Earl of Salisbury, and had issue,

ROBERT, Viscount L'Isle. summoned to parliament in his father's life-time, by writ addressed "ROBERTO SYDNEY, de Penshurst, Chev.," 11 July, 1689.

Dorothy, m. to Thomas Cheeke, Esq.

The earl d. in March, 1697-8, and was s. by his son,

ROBERT SYDNEY, 4th Earl of Leicester. His lordship m. Lady Elizabeth Egerton, dau. of John, Earl of Bridgewater, and had issue,

PHILIP, Viscount L'Isle, his heir.

JOHN, who s. as 6th earl.

JOSCELYN, 7th earl.

Thomas, who m. Mary, dau. of Sir Robert Reeve, Bart., and left two daus., co-heirs, viz.,

     MARY, m. to Sir Brownlow Sherard. Bart. and d. s. p.

     ELIZABETH, m. to William Perry, Esq., of Wormington, co. Gloucester. This lady succeeded eventually as sole heiress to Penshurst, and the other estates of the Sydneys She claimed, in 1782, the Barony of Sydney, of Penshurst, under the presumption that Robert, Earl of Leicester, her grandfather, having been summoned in 1689, in the lifetime of his father, in that nobleman's barony, a barony in fee had been created, but the claim was dismissed by the House of Lords. Mrs. Perry left an only dau. and heiress,

         ELIZABETH-JANE SYDNEY, who became the 2nd wife of Sir Bysshe Shelley, Bart., of Castle Goring, and had, with junior issue,

            JOHN SHELLEY, who assumed, in 1793, the additional surname of SYDNEY, and having inherited the Sydney estates, was created a baronet, as SIR JOHN SHELLEY SYDNEY, of Penshurst Place, Kent: he m. 1799, Henrietta, dau. of Sir Henry Hunloke, Bart.. and dying in 1849, was s. by his son, Sir Philip-Charles Sidney, G.C.H., who had been created a peer as Lord de L'Isle and Dudley, 13 January, 1835. (See BURKE's Extant Peerage.)

Elizabeth. m. to Sir Harcourt Masters.

Catherine, m. to William Barker, Esq.   Frances

His lordship d. in 1702, and was s. by his eldest son,

PHILIP SYDNEY, 5th earl, who m. Anne, dau. and co-heir of Sir Robert Reeve, of Thwaite, in Suffolk, but d. without surviving issue, in 1705, when the honours devolved on his brother,

JOHN SYDNEY, 6th earl. This nobleman was constituted in 1717, warden of the Cinque Ports and governor of Dover Castle ; and on the revival of the order of the Bath, he was elected one of the knights. His lordship d. unm. in 1737, and was s. by his only surviving brother,

JOSCELYNE SYDNEY, 7th earl. This nobleman m. Elizabeth, dau. and heiress of Lewis Thomas, Esq., of Glamorganshire, with which lady his lordship had long pending disputes regarding her misconduct, but he never obtained a divorce. He d. 7 July, 1743, when the estates devolved upon (the dau. of his brother, Colonel Thomas Sydney) his niece, ELIZABETH, who had m. Robert Perry, Esq., and all the estates were conveyed by her dau. and heiress, ELIZABETH-JANE-SYDNEY PERRY to the Shelleys : while all the honours of the house of Sydney became EXTINCT ; his lordship having d. s. p.[*]

Arms—Or, a pheon, az.

_____

[*] By a trial at bar on a writ of right, at Westminster, 11 February, 1782, for Penshurst Place, park, and premises, in the co. Kent, it appeared that this Jocelyne, Earl of Leicester, never was divorced from his wife, the said Elizabeth Thomas; and that she had a child, a son, John Sydney, the demandant at the trial aforesaid ; which John, therefore, in the eye of the law, was to be considered as a legitimate person, and as such, well entitled to the inheritance of the honours of the family. But with respect to the inheritance of the estates demanded by him, he failed to establish a better right than the tenant in possession. This (according to the statement at the trial) arose from his averment, that his father, Earl Joscelyne, was possessed thereof in fee, and not as tenant for life, which was the fact, as opened by the tenant; and further contended, that even had he been possessed thereof in fee, then by this will the earl had given them away to a third party. The event of this trial going to admit the legitimacy of the demandant, embraces an important question, as to the absolute extinction of the honours.—BANKS. The John Sydney, referred to by Banks, as "the demandant at the trial," m. Elizabeth, dau. of the Rev. John Apsley, D.D., and d. 1812, leaving, 1 PAUL ALGERNON; 2 John-Apsley; 3 Richard-Chase; 4 Philip, d. s. p.; 5 William-Robert (Sir), Knt., of Bournebridge Lodge, Berkshire ; 6 James-Waller, and several daughters.

_____

SYDNEY—VISCOUNT SYDNEY, EARL OF ROMNEY.

Viscounty, by Letters Patent, dated 9 April, 1689.
Earldom, by Letters Patent, dated 14 May, 1694.

Lineage.

HENRY SYDNEY, youngest son of Robert, 2nd Earl of Leicester, having contributed zealously to effect the Revolution, was created, in the 1st WILLIAM and MARY, by letters patent, dated 9 April, 1689, BARON SYDNEY, *of Milton*, and VISCOUNT SYDNEY, *of Sheppey, both in the co. Kent*, and advanced 14 May, 1694, to the EARLDOM OF ROMNEY. His lordship held many lucrative employments under the crown. He *d. unm.* in 1704, when all his honours became EXTINCT.

Arms—Or, a pheon, az., a crescent for difference.

TAAFFE—EARLS OF CARLINGFORD.

By Letters Patent, dated 26 June, 1662.

Lineage.

SIR JOHN TAAFFE, Knt., son of Sir William Taaffe, Knt., of Harleston, was advanced to the peerage of Ireland, 1 August, 1628, in the dignities of BARON *of Ballymote*, and VISCOUNT TAAFFE, *of Corren, both in the co Sligo*. His lordship *m.* Anne, dau. of Theobald, 1st Viscount Dillon, by whom he had (with other issue),

THEOBALD (Sir), who *s.* to the honours.
Lucas, a major-general in the army, appointed governor of Ross, in 1649, to defend that place against Cromwell. He was subsequently obliged to expatriate himself, and served as a colonel in Italy and Spain. He returned, however, and *d.* in Ireland.
Francis, a colonel in the rebellion of 1641; *m.* an Italian lady, and left a son, CHARLES.
Edward, *d. unm.*
Peter, a canon of the order of St. Augustine, killed at Drogheda, 1649.
Jasper, slain in battle, and *d. s. p.*
WILLIAM, *m.* Margaret, dau of Connor O'Kennedy Roe, by whom he had, with three daus,

  FRANCIS, who *m.* Anne, dau. of John Crean, Esq., of Olrean's Castle, in Sligo, and had issue,
    NICHOLAS, who inherited as 6th Viscount Taaffe.
  Anne. *m.* to John Brett, Esq., of Rathdoony, co. Sligo.
  Mary, *m.* to Theodore Verdon, Esq., of Clunigashell; and *d. s. p.*

His lordship *d.* 1642, and was *s.* by his eldest son,

THEOBALD TAAFFE, 2nd viscount; who was advanced to the EARLDOM OF CARLINGFORD, 26 June, 1662. This nobleman espoused zealously the royal cause during the civil wars, and had his estate sequestered by Cromwell. After the Restoration, he obtained, however, a pension of £800 a-year; and upon being advanced in the peerage, received a grant of £4000 a-year, of the rents payable to the crown out of the retrenched lands of adventurers and soldiers during such time as the same remained in the common stock of reprisals, and out of forfeited jointures, mortgages, &c. The earl was *s.* at his decease, 1677, by his eldest surviving son by his 1st wife, Mary, dau. of Sir Nicholas Whyte, of Leixlip,

NICHOLAS TAAFFE, 2nd earl and 3rd viscount, who fell at the battle of the Boyne, in the command of a regiment of foot under King JAMES, and as he left no issue the honours devolved upon his brother,

FRANCIS TAAFFE, 3rd earl, the celebrated Count Taaffe of the Germanic empire. This nobleman, who was sent in his youth to the city of Olmutz to prosecute his studies, became first, one of the pages of honour to the Emperor FERDINAND, and soon after obtained a captain's commission from Charles, 5th Duke of Lorraine, in his own regiment. He was subsequently chamberlain to the Emperor, a marshal of the empire, and councillor of the state and cabinet. His lordship was so highly esteemed by most of the crowned heads of Europe, that when he succeeded to his hereditary honours, he was exempted from forfeiture by a special clause in the English act of parliament, 1st WILLIAM and MARY; and in the acts passed in Ireland, 9th of the same reign, to hinder the reversion of divers outlawries and attainders, it was provided, that nothing therein contained should extend to attaint or convict of high treason, Nicholas,

526

Earl of Carlingford, or his brother, &c., &c. The earl *d. s. p.* in August, 1704, when the honours devolved upon his nephew,

THEOBALD TAAFFE, 4th earl (son of the Hon. Major John Taaffe, who fell before Londonderry, in the service of King JAMES, by Lady Rose Lambart, dau. of Charles, 1st Earl of Cavan). This nobleman *m.* Amelia, youngest dau. of Luke, 3rd Earl of Fingall; but *d. s. p.* in 1738, when the Earldom of Carlingford EXPIRED, while the viscounty and barony passed to his lordship's next heir male, NICHOLAS, Count Taaffe of the Germanic empire, as 6th Viscount Taaffe. (*See* BURKE'S *Extant Peerage*.)

Arms—Gu., a cross, arg., fretty, az.

TALBOT—BARONS TALBOT.

By Writ of Summons, dated 5 June, 1331.

Lineage.

RICHARD DE TALBOT, mentioned in Domesday Book, *m.* the dau. of Gerard de Gournay, Baron of Yarmouth, and had two sons, GEOFFREY, ancestor of the TALBOTS of Bashall, co. York, and HUGH, ancestor of the house of Shrewsbury. The 2nd son,

HUGH TALBOT, governor of Plessey Castle, in Essex, who, in the decline of life, assumed the cowl in the monastery of Beaubeck, in Normandy, to which he had been a liberal benefactor, was *s.* upon his retirement by his eldest son,

RICHARD TALBOT, who, in the beginning of HENRY II.'s reign, obtained from the crown a grant of the lordship of Eccleswall and Linton, co. Hereford, which RICHARD I. afterwards confirmed for 200 marks. This Richard Talbot was *s.* by his son,

GILBERT TALBOT, who was present at the coronation of King RICHARD I.; his son,

RICHARD TALBOT, *m.* Aliva, dau. of Alan Basset, of Wicombe, co. Buckingham, sister of Philip Basset, justi e of Englan t, and widow of Dru Montacute. He was *s.* by his son,

GILBERT TALBOT, who, in the 45th HENRY III., was constituted one of the justices itinerant for the co. Hereford, and in two years afterwards, upon the disturbance made by the Welsh, was ordered by the king to fortify Monmouth Castle, and other castles, of which he was then governor. He *m.* Gwendaline, dau, and at length heiress of Rhys ap Griffith ap Rhys ap Griffith ap Rhys ap Tewdwr Mawr, King of South Wales. In consequence of this alliance, the TALBOTS, instead of their own arms, " *Bendy of ten, arg. and gu.,*" adopted those of the Princes of South Wales, viz., " *gu., a lion rampant, or.*" He *d.* in 1274, seized of the manors of Longhope and Redley, co. Gloucester, and the manors of Eccleswall and Linton, in Herefordshire ; and was *s.* by his son,

RICHARD TALBOT, who, in 10th EDWARD I., was in the expedition made into Wales, and in the 24th and 25th of the same reign, he was in the wars of Gascony ; in which latter year, he was constituted governor of the castle of Cardiff. He had afterwards a military summons to prevent an invasion of the Scots, and he was a member of the great council or parliament held at Lincoln, in the 29th EDWARD I., when, with the other barons, he subscribed the letter to the Pope, in which was asserted the King of England's right to the realm of Scotland. He *m.* the Lady Sarah Beauchamp, dau. of William, Earl of Warwick, and had issue,

  GILBERT, his successor.
  Richard, who *m.* Joane, dau. and co-heir of Hugh de Mortimer. of Richard's Castle, co. Hertford, and obtaining that seat, this branch of the Talbots was afterwards designated of " Richard's Castle." He was *s.* by his son.
    SIR JOHN TALBOT, of Richard's Castle, who was *s.* by his son,
      JOHN TALBOT, of Richard's Castle, who *d.* in the 12th RICHARD II., *s. p.*, leaving his sisters, amongst whom the estates were divided. his heirs, viz.,
        ELIZABETH, *m.* to Sir Warine Archdekne, Knt.
        PHILIPPA, *m.* to Sir Matthew Gournay, Knt.
        ELEANOR, *unm.*

Lord Talbot *d.* in 1306, and was *s.* by his elder son,

GILBERT TALBOT, who was in the expedition made into Scotland in the 26th EDWARD I.; and having been implicated in the murder of Piers Gaveston, obtained a pardon, in the 7th EDWARD II. In the 16th of the same reign, he was constituted governor of the town and castle of Gloucester, but being afterwards engaged in the insurrection of Thomas, Earl of Lancaster, against the power of the Spencers, he was compelled, in order to save his life and preserve his estates, to enter into a recognisance to pay £200, and also £2,000 more, with one tun of wine. Upon the accession of EDWARD III., however, that obligation was cancelled. Moreover, being then a banneret, he became so active for the king in all his military affairs, that there was due to him £116 3s. 8d. for the service of himself and his men-at-arms. In the 4th EDWARD III, he was constituted justice of South Wales, and he was summoned to parliament as a Baron, in the same year, and from that period to the 17th (1343). His lordship m. Anne, dau of William Boteler, of Wemme, and dying in 1346, was s. by his son,

RICHARD TALBOT, 2nd baron, summoned to parliament from 5 June, 1331, to 22 October, 1355, by writ directed to "Ricardo Talbot de Castro Goderici," co. Hereford. This nobleman m. Elizabeth, dau. and co-heir of John Comyn, of Badenoch, by Joan,, his wife, sister and co-heir of Aymer de Valence, Earl of Pembroke ; and in her right, claiming (anno 1331) certain lands in Scotland, and adhering to Edward Baliol, who then preferred pretensions to the crown, would have entered that kingdom by land, but was prevented by King EDWARD III., whose sister, Joane, had been married to David Bruce, the son of ROBERT, King of Scotland. He invaded it, however, by sea, at the head of 300 armed men, and soon after achieved a great victory over the Scots at Gleddesmore; but he was subsequently made prison r, and had to pay 2,000 marks for his redemption. In the 11th EDWARD III., his lordship was appointed governor of Berwick-upon-Tweed, as also justice there, and of all other the king's lands in Scotland. The same year being a banneret, he had an assignation of £200 of the tenth, then given in parliament, out of the city of Bristol, for his better support in the governorship of Berwick. In four years afterwards he was again in the wars of Scotland, and subsequently (20th EDWARD III.) in the expedition made into France; at which latter period (he laid the foundation of the priory of Flanesford, within his lordship of Goderich Castle ; and at this time too, he obtained from the king a grant for a prison at Goderich Castle, for punishing malefactors. His lordship d. in 1356, and was s. by his elder son,

GILBERT TALBOT, 3rd baron, summoned to parliament, from 14 August, 1362, to 8 August, 1386. This nobleman served under the Black Prince, in the wars of France; and in the 1st RICHARD II., he was in the king's fleet at sea, with Michael de la Pole, admiral for the north. His lordship m. 1st, Petronille, dau. of James, Earl of Ormonde, by whom he had,

    RICHARD, who having m. Ankaret, sister and eventually sole heir of John, Baron Strange, of Blackmere, was summoned to parliament in the life-time of his father, from 3 March, 1384, to 17 December, 1387, by writ directed to "Ricardo Talbot de Blackmere."

Elizabeth, m. to Henry, Lord Grey de Wilton.

Lord Talbot m. 2ndly, Joane, dau. of Ralph, Earl of Stafford. He d. in 1387, and was s. by his son,

SIR RICHARD TALBOT, Lord Talbot, of Blackmere, as 4th Baron Talbot, summoned to parliament, in 1387 (the same writ in which he was also designated of "Blackmere"), as TALBOT, of Goderich Castle, and from that period to 1393. His lordship was in the wars of Scotland, and attained the rank of banneret. In the 15th RICHARD II., he succeeded to the lands of the family of Hastings, Earls of Pembroke, derived through his great grandmother, Joane de Valence, sister and co-heir of Aymer, Earl of Pembroke, and wife of John Comyn, of Badenoch. By Ankaret le Strange, the heiress of Blackmere, he had four sons,

    GILBERT, his successor.
    JOHN, of whom hereafter, as successor to the barony.
    Richard, archbishop of Dublin.
    Thomas, of Wrockwardine, co. Salop.

His lordship d. in 1396, and was s. by his elder son,

SIR GILBERT TALBOT, 5th baron, summoned to parliament, from 25 August, 1404, to October, 1417. This nobleman, as heir to the Earls of Pembroke, claimed to carry the great spurs at the coronation of HENRY V.; soon after which he was constituted justice of Chester, and he was subsequently engaged in the French wars. In the 4th of the same reign his lordship was appointed guardian and captain-general of the Marches of Normandy, and he was likewise a knight of the Garter. He m. 1st, Joan, dau. of Thomas, of Woodstock, Duke of Gloucester, by whom he had no issue. His lordship m. 2ndly, Beatrix, a Portuguese lady, widow of Thomas, Earl of Arundel, and illegitimate dau., it is stated, of JOHN I., King of Portugal, by whom he had a dau., ANKARET. He d. in 1419, and was s. in the Baronies of Talbot and Strange, of Blackmere, by his dau.,

ANKARET TALBOT, at whose decease, in minority, anno 1431, those honours reverted to her uncle,

SIR JOHN TALBOT, as 6th Baron Talbot, who having m. Maud de Nevill, eldest dau. and co-heir of Thomas, 5th Lord Furnival, had been summoned to parliament as LORD TALBOT, of

Furnival, from 26 October, 1409, to 26 November, 1421. This is the renowned SIR JOHN TALBOT, one of the most illustrious characters in the whole range of English history. In 1412 he was appointed chief justice of Ireland, and in two years after wards constituted lord lieutenant of the same kingdom. He subsequently distinguished himself in the wars of HENRY V., but his splendid reputation was acquired under the Regent (John Plantagenet, Duke of) Bedford, temp. HENRY VI., when his name alone became terrible to the soldiers of France, owing to the numerous victories he had achieved. His lordship was attacked, however, by the Maid of Orleans, hear Patay, in 1429, when, his army being entirely routed, he was taken prisoner. This defeat of Lord Talbot was followed by the loss of divers places of importance to the English. His lordship was detained in captivity for no less than four years, but obtained at length his freedom by the payment of a large sum of money, and in exchange for Ambrose de Lore, an eminent captain of the French. Again taking the field, and again becoming renowned for his triumphs, he was granted, in consideration of those eminent services, 20 May, 1442, the EARLDOM OF SHREWSBURY, "nomen et honorem comitis Salop." After this, we find him reconstituted lord lieutenant of Ireland, and made a peer of that kingdom (anno 1446), as Earl of Waterford, having at the same time the city of Waterford, with the castles, honour, land, and Barony of Dungarvan granted to him, and the heirs male of his body, as well as the great office of Lord High Steward or Great Seneschal of Ireland. A few weeks afterwards, his son, Sir John Talbot, was appointed lord chancellor of that k ngdom. His lordship was now far advanced in life, but the English interests declining in France, he was once more induced to place himself at the head of the army there, and his courage and conduct restored for some time, at least, its glory. He was appointed lieutenant of the Duchy of Acquitaine, having under him as captains of his men-at-arms and archers, his son, John Talbot, Viscount L'Isle, Sir John Hungerford, Lord Molines, Sir Roger Camoys, Sir John L'Isle, and John Beaufort, the bastard of Somerset. Marching immediately to the place of his government he took the city of Bordeaux, and placed a garrison in it; and thence proceeded to the relief of Chastillon, where an engagement with the French army ensued, which terminated in the total defeat of the English, and the death of their gallant general, who was killed by a cannon ball. Thus fell sword in hand, John Talbot, Earl of Shrewsbury, at the great age of eighty, 20 July, 1453 (Inq. p. m.), after having won no less than forty pitched battles, or important rencounters. His remains were conveyed to England, and interred at Whitchurch, co. Salop, where a noble monument was erected in the south wall of the chancel, with this epitaph :

    " Orate pro animâ prænobilis domini, domini
    " Johannis Talbot, quondam Comitis Salopiæ, domini
    " Furnivall, domini Verdon, domini Strange de
    " Blackmere, et Marescalli Franciæ, qui obiit in
    " Bello apud Burdeuus, vis Julii, MCCCCLIII."

By the heiress of Furnival, his lordship had issue,

    Thomas, who d. in France, v. p.
    JOHN, his successor, 2nd Earl of Shrewsbury, K.G.
    Christopher (Sir).

The earl m. 2ndly, the Lady Margaret Beauchamp, dau. and co-heir of Richard, Earl of Warwick, and had,

    JOHN, created Baron and Viscount L'Isle (see that dignity).
    Humphrey (Sir), Marshal of Calais, d. s. p. in 1492.
    Lewis (Sir), of Penyard, Herts.
    Joane, m. to James, 1st Lord Berkeley.
    Elizabeth, m. to John Mowbray, Duke of Norfolk.

At the period of his lordship's advancement to the Earldom of Shrewsbury, the Barony of Talbot, with those of Strange, of Blackmere, and Furnivall merged in that dignity, and so continued until the decease of

GILBERT TALBOT, 7th Earl of Shrewsbury, and 12th Baron Talbot, in 1626, when all three fell into ABEYANCE amongst his daus. and co-heirs, viz.,

    Mary, m. to William, 3rd Earl of Pembroke, and d. s. p.
    Elizabeth, m. to Henry Grey, 8th Earl of Kent, and d. s. p.
    ALATHEA, m. to Thomas Howard, who had been restored in 1603 to the Earldoms of Arundel and Surrey, and created Earl Marshal in 1621.

At the decease of Mary and Elizabeth, the two elder co-heirs, as stated above, without issue, the ABEYANCE of the Baronies of Talbot, Strange, and Furnivall terminated, and those dignities then vested in the 3rd co-heir, ALATHEA, widow of Thomas Howard, Earl of Arundel, and thenceforward they merged in the Earldom of Arundel, and Dukedom of Norfolk, until the decease of

EDWARD HOWARD, 9th Duke of Norfolk, in 1777, s. p., when

the Baronies of Talbot, Strange, of Blackmere, and Furnivall, fell again into ABEYANCE between his grace's nieces, the two daus. and co-heirs of his brother, Philip Howard, Esq., namely,

WINIFREDE HOWARD, who m. William, Lord Stourton.
ANNE HOWARD, who m. Robert-Edward, Lord Petre.

And so the said baronies remain between the present Lords Stourton and Petre.

Arms—Gu., a lion rampant, or, within a bordure engrailed of the 2nd.

TALBOT—BARON L'ISLE, OF KINGSTON L'ISLE, CO. BERKS, VISCOUNT L'ISLE.

Barony, by Letters Patent, dated 26 July, 1443.
Viscounty, by Letters Patent, dated 30 October, 1452.

Lineage.

The Hon. JOHN TALBOT, eldest son of John Talbot, the 1st and great Earl of Shrewsbury, by his 2nd wife, the Lady Margaret Beauchamp, dau. and co-heir of Richard, 12th Earl of Warwick, and great grand-dau. of Warine, 2nd Baron L'Isle (*see* L'Isle, Barons L'Isle), was created BARON L'ISLE, of Kingston L'Isle, co. Berks, by patent,* dated 26 July, 1443, limiting the dignity to the said John and his heirs and assigns for ever, being tenants of the manor of Kingston L'Isle, and was advanced to the dignity of VISCOUNT L'ISLE, 30 October, 1452. This nobleman, who served under his gallant father in France, was slain with that heroic personage at Chastillon, *anno* 1453. His lordship m. Joan, dau. and co-heir of Sir John or Sir Thomas Chedder, of Chedder, co. Somerset, and widow of Richard Stafford, Esq., and had issue,

THOMAS, his successor.
Elizabeth, m. to Sir Edward Grey (2nd son of Edward, Lord Ferrers, of Groby), who was created Viscount L'Isle (*see* Grey, Viscount L'Isle).
Margaret, m. to Sir George Vere, Knt., and d. s. p.

The viscount was s. by his son,

THOMAS TALBOT, 2nd Baron and Viscount L'Isle. This nobleman having a great contest with William, Lord Berkeley, of Berkeley Castle, concerning certain lands which he claimed in right of his grandmother, Margaret Beauchamp, Countess of Shrewsbury, lost his life by an arrow shot through the mouth, in a skirmish between the parties, at Wotton-under-Edge, in Gloucestershire, 20 March, 1469. His lordship m. Lady Margaret Herbert, dau. of William, Earl of Pembroke, but as he left no issue, his sisters became his co-heirs. The Viscounty of L'Isle EXPIRED at his lordship's decease. "But," says Nicolas, "it is a very doubtful point into what state the barony then fell. In the third report of the lords' committee on the dignity of a peer of the realm, the case is most ably stated, and to it he (Nicolas) refers in support of the following conclusions: first, that the patent to John Talbot, in 1443, did not (though evidently intended so to do) affect the barony created by the writ to Gerard L'Isle, in 31st EDWARD III., and which, consequently, still remained in abeyance, but created a *new* barony, descendible according to the provisions of the patent: and secondly, with respect to the extremely difficult question, 'in

*This patent, NICOLAS, in his Synopsis, terms one of the most extraordinary on record—and he proceeds. "The patent recites as a fact, that 'Warine de L'Isle, and his ancestors, by reason of the lordship and manor of Kingston L'Isle, had, from time whereof the memory of man was not to the contrary, the name and dignity of Baron and Lord L'Isle, and by that name had seat in parliament, &c., as other barons of the realm had;' an assertion satisfactorily proved by the lords' committee on the dignity of a peer of the realm, in their third report, to have been entirely without foundation; for not only had the said manor never been held in capite by the crown, but a period of above sixty years had elapsed, viz., from 23 EDWARD I. to 31st EDWARD III., after writs of summons were generally issued, before the family of L'Isle, tenants of the manor of L'Isle, were ever summoned to parliament. Many arguments might be adduced to support the conclusion stated in the text relative to this dignity, but they are rendered useless, by the statement of the case in the report of the Lords' committee just cited, page 191, *et seq.*, and by the opinions of the great legal authorities, Coke and Blackstone. It is therefore sufficient to remark, that this singular creation probably arose from the powerful influence possessed by the Earl of Shrewsbury, in a reign when more anomalies connected with dignities are to be found than under any preceding or subsequent monarch."

whom is *that* barony now vested?' it is to be observed that, according to the high authority of Lord Chief Justice Coke and of Justice Blackstone, John Talbot, and his heirs, under the patent, had only a base or qualified fee in that dignity, and ' that the instant he or his heirs quitted the seigniory of this manor the dignity was at an end.' On the death of Thomas, 2nd viscount (continues Nicolas), in 1469, without issue, his two sisters became his heirs, viz., Margaret, the wife of Sir George Vere, Knt., and Elizabeth, Lady Grey, when it is presumed the Barony of L'Isle became suspended, for although the said Elizabeth was possessed of the manor, she was not *sole* heir of John Talbot, her father, and consequently had not the two constituent qualifications necessary to entitle her to the dignity. On the death of her sister, Lady Vere, however, s. p., she appears to have become legally seized of the barony, as is recited in the patent granted to her husband."

Arms—Gu., a lion rampant, within a bordure engrailed, or.

TALBOT—BARONS FURNIVAL.

(*See* FURNIVAL, and TALBOT, Barons Talbot.)

TALBOT—EARL TALBOT.

By Letters Patent, dated 10 March, 1761.

(*See* BURKE's *Extant Peerage*, SHREWSBURY, E.)

TALBOT—DUKE OF SHREWSBURY.

By Letters Patent, dated 30 April, 1694.

Lineage.

CHARLES TALBOT, Lord Talbot, b. 24 July, 1660, s. his father as 12th Earl of Shrewsbury, 16 March, 1667, and, in 1681, was constituted lord lieutenant and custos rotulorum of the co. Stafford, but was dismissed from both offices by King JAMES II. At the coronation of that monarch, the earl bore the Curtance or pointless sword; and, the same year, was appointed colonel of the 6th regiment of horse; but disgusted with the proceedings of the court he resigned soon after his military rank, and went over to the Prince of Orange, whom he tendered his purse and sword: Burnet states that Lord Shrewsbury was one of the nobles in whom the Prince placed the utmost confidence, and by whose advice he was upon all occasions principally guided. Thus promoting the Revolution, when that measure was accomplished by the elevation of WILLIAM and MARY to the throne, his lordship was immediately sworn of the privy council, and made principal secretary of state. In March, 1694, he was elected a knight of the Garter, and the next month created *Marquess of Alton*, and DUKE OF SHREWSBURY. In 1695 and 1697 his grace was one of the lords justices during the temporary absences of the king; and in 1699 he resigned the seals as secretary of state, but was constituted soon after lord chamberlain of the household—an office which he subsequently held in the reign of Queen ANNE; and was also (*anno* 1713) appointed by her Majesty lord lieutenant of Ireland. On the accession of King GEORGE I. the duke was made groom of the stole and privy purse, and sworn a member of the new privy council. He was subsequently declared lord chamberlain of his Majesty's household, while his duchess was appointed one of the ladies of the bedchamber to Caroline, Princess of Wales. His grace m. Adelhida, dau. of the Marquess of Paliotti, in Italy, descended maternally from Sir Robert Dudley, son of Robert Dudley, Earl of Leicester, the celebrated favourite of Queen ELIZABETH, but d. s. p. 1 February, 1717-18, when the honours he had inherited passed to the heir-at-law, and the Marquessate of Alton and Dukedom of Shrewsbury became EXTINCT.

This, the great Duke of Shrewsbury, is thus described by Macaulay. "His person was pleasing, his temper singularly sweet, his parts such as, if he had been born in a humble rank, might well have raised him to civil greatness. All these advantages he had so improved that, before he was of age, he was allowed to be one of the finest gentlemen and finest scholars of his time."

Arms—Gu., a lion rampant, within a border engrailed, or

TALBOT—EARL AND DUKE OF TYR-CONNELL.

Lineage.

WILLIAM TALBOT, Esq., who acquired the estate of Cartown, co. Kildare, and was created a baronet of Ireland, 4 February, 1622, was son of Robert of Carton, 3rd son of Sir Thomas Talbot of Malahide, co. Dublin. He m. Alison, dau. of John Netterville, Esq., of Castleton, co. Meath, d. 16 March, 1633, and was buried 1 April following, leaving issue,

I. ROBERT (Sir), of Cartown, Bart., who m. Grace, dau. of George Calvert, Lord Baltimore, and had a dau.,

    FRANCES, m. Richard Talbot, Esq., of Malahide, and d. in 1718. Their descendant, LORD TALBOT DE MALAHIDE is now representative of the Talbots of Cartown, as well as of the Duke of Tyrconnel.

II. JOHN.

III. Garret, m. Margaret, dau. of Henry Gaidon, Esq. of the co. Louth, and had a son William, Condé de Tyrconnel.

IV. James.   v. Thomas.

VI. Peter, Roman Catholic archbishop of Dublin, a very celebrated Catholic divine, who was arrested in 1678 at Luttrellstown, on suspicion of being concerned in what was termed "the Popish Plot," and d. in prison in 1680.

VII. Gilbert.

VIII. RICHARD, Earl of Tyrconnel.

I. Mary, m. to Sir John Dongan, Bart.

II. Bridget, m. to John Gaidon, Esq., of Irishtown.

III. Margaret, m. to Henry Talbot, Esq., of Templeogue.

IV. Frances, m. 1st. to James Cusack, Esq., of Cushenstown, and 2ndly, to Right Hon. Sir Thomas Newcomen, Knt.

V. Elizabeth.   VI. Jane.

VII. Catherine.

VIII. Eleanor, m. to Sir Henry O'Neill, Bart.

COLONEL RICHARD TALBOT (the youngest son), was by patent, dated 20 June, 1685, created Baron of Talbot's-town, Viscount of Baltinglass, and EARL TYRCONNELL, with remainder in tail mule to his nephews; and subsequently, 20 March, 1689, advanced to the dignity of MARQUESS and DUKE OF TYRCONNELL, by JAMES II., in whose service as chief governor of Ireland he died, and for his attachment to whom, his honours were attainted in 1691. "Of Richard Talbot, Duke of Tyrconnell (says an eloquent writer), much ill has been written, and more believed; but his history, like that of his unfortunate country, has only been written by the pen of party, steeped in gall, and copied servilely from the pages of prejudice by the lame historians of modern times. more anxious for authority than authenticity. Two qualities he possessed in an eminent degree—wit and valour; and if to gifts so brilliant and so Irish be joined devotion to his country, and fidelity to the unfortunate and fated family with whose exile he began life, and with whose ruin he finished it, it cannot be denied that in his character the elements of evil were mixed with much great and striking good. Under happier circumstances, the good might have predominated, and he whose deeds are held even by his own family in such right estimation, might have shed a lustre on his race by those talents and heroism which gave force to his passions and celebrity to his errors." His grace m. 1st, Katherine Boynton; and 2ndly, Frances (the "Belle Jenyns" of the court of CHARLES II.) eldest dau. and co-heir of Richard Jenyns, Esq., of Sandridge, in Hertfordshire, widow of George, Count Hamilton, and sister to Sarah, Duchess of Marlborough. Her ladyship, after the duke's death, was permitted to erect a house, still standing, in King-street, Dublin, as a nunnery for poor Clares, and in this obscure retirement, burying all the attractions and graces which once so adorned the court of England, she d. at the age of ninety-two, and was interred in St. Patrick's Cathedral, 9 March, 1730. By Tyrconnell she had two daus., of whom Charlotte, was m. to the Prince de Vintimiglia, and had issue two daus., the Countess de Verac, and the Princess Belmonte; but both dying s.p., Richard-Wogan Talbot, Baron Talbot de Malahide, became heir-general to the Duke of Tyrconnell, as descendant and sole heir of FRANCES, the duke's niece.

Arms—Arg., a lion rampant, gu., armed and langued, az.

TALBOYS—BARON TALBOYS.

By Writ of Summons, dated in 1529.

Lineage.

WILLIAM DE KYME, Baron Kyme, son of Philip, Baron de Kyme, d. in 1338, s.p., when his estates, including the lordship of Kyme, in Lincolnshire, devolved upon his sister,

LUCY DE KYME, who had m. Robert de Umfravill, Earl of Angus, and had issue,

GILBERT, Earl of Angus, who d. 1381, leaving an only son,

    ROBERT, d. s. p., v. p.

Elizabeth, who m. Gilbert Burdon or Baradon, and had a dau. and heir,

    ELEANOR or ELIZABETH BARADON.

This

ELEANOR or ELIZABETH BARADON, b. 1341, inherited Kyme and the other lands through her mother, and married HENRY TALBOYS (æt. thirty, A.D. 1365): from them lineally descended, SIR GEORGE TALBOYS (æt. twenty-eight, A.D. 1495), who, by Elizabeth, his wife, dau. of Sir William Gascoigne, had issue,

    GILBERT, of whom presently.
    William, a priest, 33rd HENRY VIII.
    Elizabeth, m. to Sir Christopher Willoughby, Knt.
    Cecilia, m. 1st, to William Ingleby, Esq., of Ripley, co. York, and 2ndly, to John Torney, Esq., of Kainely.
    Anne, m. 1st, to Sir Edward Dymoke, Knt., and 2ndly, to Sir Robert Carr, Knt.

Sir George d. 21 September, 1538, and was s. by his son,

GILBERT TALBOYS, of Kyme, who was summoned to parliament as BARON TALBOYS, *of Kyme*, by King HENRY VIII., in 1536. His lordship m. Elizabeth,* dau. of Sir John Blount, by whom (who m. 2ndly, Edward Clinton, 1st Earl of Lincoln) he had two sons, George and Robert, who both d. s. p., v. p., and an only dau.,

    ELIZABETH TALBOYS, who m. 1st, Thomas Wimbish, Esq. and 2ndly, Ambrose Dudley, Earl of Warwick, but ha1 no issue.

At the decease of his lordship in 1539, the barony devolved upon his dau.,

ELIZABETH WIMBISH, and her husband, Mr. Wimbish, claimed the dignity *jure uxoris*, when it was solemnly decided, in the presence of King HENRY VIII., "That no man, husband of a baroness, should use the title of her dignity, until he had a child by her, whereby he should become tenant by the courtesie of her barony." Her ladyship, as stated above, m. 2ndly, the Earl of Warwick, but d. s. p., when the Barony of Talboys became EXTINCT; while the estates passed to the heirs general, and in the division the manor of Kyme fell to the Dymokes, of Scrivelsby, co. Lincoln, from whom, after a considerable time, it was sold to strangers.

Arms—Arg., a saltier, gu., on a chief of the 2nd, three escallops of the 1st.

TATTESHALL—BARONS TATTESHALL.

By Writ of Summons, dated 24 June, 1295.

Lineage.

Amongst the companions in arms of the CONQUEROR, were two stanch friends, and as Dugdale calls them, sworn brothers in war, but not otherwise allied.

EUDO and PINSON, on whom, in requital of their gallant services, WILLIAM THE CONQUEROR conferred large grants of land, whereof Tatteshall, with the hamlet of Thorpe, and town of Kirkeby, co. Lincoln, were a part; Eudo to hold his proportion of the king, and Pinson his of St. Cuthbert, of Durham. The former,

EUDO, seated himself at Tatteshall, and from him lineally descended,

ROBERT DE TATTESHALL, who, in the 10th HENRY III., had custody of Bolsover Castle, and the next year was governor of that of Lincoln. In four years afterwards he had license to build a castle at his manor of Tatteshall. This feudal lord m. 1st, Amabill, dau. and eventual co-heir of William de Albini, Earl of Arundel and Sussex, with whom he acquired the castle and manor of Buckenham, in Norfolk. He m. 2ndly, a dau. of John de Grey, and had with her the manor of Scondebury, Berks, held of the king by serjeanty, viz., the service of falconry. He d. in 1249, and was s. by his son,

ROBERT DE TATTESHALL, who, in the 38th HENRY III., on levying the aid for making the king's eldest son knight, paid £50 for the twenty five knights' fees, which he held, and in the 42nd of the same reign, received command to attend the king

---

* This lady, after the death of her 1st husband, had an illegitimate child by King HENRY VIII., HENRY FITZROY, created DUKE OF RICHMOND.

at Chester, well fitted with horse and arms, to oppose the incursions of the Welsh. In the baronial wars, Robert de Tatteshall, sided at first with the king, and was in the royal army at the battle of Lewes, but afterwards joining the opposite party, he fought at the battle of Evesham. In the reign of EDWARD I., he became, however, eminently distinguished in the Welsh, Scotch, and French wars, and was summoned to parliament as BARON TATTESHALL, from 24 June, 1295, to 26 August, 1296. His lordship *m.* Joan, dau. and co-heir of Ralph Fitz-Ralph, feudal Lord of Middleham, co. York, by whom he acquired a considerable accession of property, and had issue,

    ROBERT, his successor.

    Emma, *m.* to Sir Osbert de Cayly, and had issue,

        Sir Thomas Cayly, Lord of Buckenham, in right of his mother.

    Joan, *m.* to Sir Robert Driby, and left a dau. and heiress,

        Alice, *m.* to Sir William Bernake, whose dau., and the eventual heiress of her brother,

        Maud Bernake, *m.* Sir Ralph de Cromwell.

    Isabel, *m.* to Sir John Orreby.

The baron *d.* in 1272, and was *s.* by his son,

ROBERT DE TATTESHALL, 2nd baron, summoned to parliament from 6 February, 1299, to 13 September, 1302. This nobleman is supposed, on strong presumptive evidence, to have had a younger brother John de Tatteshall, ancestor of the Tatteshalls of Wanstede and Little Waltham, Essex, and of Finchampsted, Berks. The 2nd Lord Tatteshall served in the Scotch and French wars, and dying in 1303, was *s.* by his son,

ROBERT DE TATTESHALL, 3rd baron, at whose decease in minority, the barony fell into ABEYANCE, between

    Sir Thomas Cayly, son of Emma Tatteshall, by Sir Osbert de Cailly.

    Joan de Tatteshall, *m.* to Sir Robert Driby.

    Isabel de Tatteshall, *m.* to Sir John Orreby.

As it still continues with their descendants, while the estates passed thus:

    To Sir Thomas Cayly, the castle of Buckenham, with a fourth part of that manor, and half the parks thereunto belonging, and other lands in co. Norfolk; from this Sir Thomas Cayly's uncle, Sir Hugo de Cayly of Owby, the existing Baronets Cayly, of Brompton, co. York, deduce their descent.

    To Lady Driby, the castle and manor of Tatteshall, and other estates in co. Lincoln.

    To Lady Orreby, the manor of Tybenham, and a part of the manor of Buckenham, with other lands in co. Norfolk.

Arms—Chequy, or and gu., a chief, ermine.

TEMPLE—VISCOUNT PALMERSTON.

By Letters Patent, dated 12 March, 1722.

Lineage.

SIR WILLIAM TEMPLE, Knt., a learned and eminent person in the reign of ELIZABETH, removed into Ireland, and was appointed provost of Trinity College, Dublin, which university he represented in parliament in 1613. He received the honour of knighthood, 4 May, 1622, from the Lord Deputy St. John, and was appointed one of the Masters in Chancery. Sir William *m.* Martha, dau. of Mr. Robert Harrison, of the co. Derby, by whom he had two sons, John and Thomas, in holy orders, minister of Battersea (ancestor, it is presumed, of the TEMPLES of the co. of Westmeath), and two daus., Katherine, *m.* 1st, John Archdall, of Archdall, co. Fermanagh; and 2ndly, Sir John Veel, Knt.; and Mary, *m.* to Job Ward, Esq. Sir William *d.* 15 January, 1626-7, and was *s.* by his son,

SIR JOHN TEMPLE, Knt., *b.* in 1600, who was constituted Master of the Rolls in Ireland, and sworn of the privy council there. He filled, for a series of years, high and confidential places in the government of Ireland; and was appointed, in 1648, joint commissioner of the great seal with Sir William Parsons. He joined, however, the standard of Cromwell, but was nevertheless retained as Master of the Rolls after the Restoration, when he was constituted vice-treasurer of Ireland. He *m.* Mary, dau. of John Hammond, M.D., of Chertsey, in Surrey, and had two surviving sons and two daus., viz.,

    I. WILLIAM (Sir), created a baronet 1665, and sworn of the privy council. Sir William's "Memoirs" and "Letters" display much acquaintance with men and books, and are important also, in an historical point of view. The great Sir William Temple *d.* January, 1698, and was buried in Westminster Abbey : by direction of his will, his heart, in a silver box, was placed under the sun-dial in his garden,

530

at Moor Park, opposite to the window from which he used to contemplate the works of nature. He *m.* Dorothy, 2nd dau. of Sir Peter Osborne, of Chicksands, co. Bedford, and had (with other issue, who *d.* young), a son,

    JOHN, of Moor Park, whose melancholy death by suicide in 1689, is so graphically narrated by Macaulay : he left by his wife, a French lady, Mary, dau. of Monsieur Du Plessis Rambouillet, two daus.,

        ELIZABETH, *m.* to John Temple, Esq.

        DOROTHY, *m.* to Nicholas Bacon, Esq., of Shrubland Hall, Suffolk.

    II. JOHN.

    I. Martha, *m.* Sir Thomas Gifford, of Castle Jordan, co. Kildare, Bart.

    II. Mary, *m.* 1st, to Abraham Yarner, Esq.; and 2ndly, to Hugh Eccles, Esq.

Sir John *d.* 14 November, 1677. His younger son,

SIR JOHN TEMPLE, Knt., who was solicitor and attorney-general, and Speaker of the House of Commons in Ireland, had several grants of land in Ireland, including one adjoining the Phœnix Park, Dublin, near Chapel Izod, which was called "Palmerston." He *m.* 4 August, 1663, Jane, dau. of Sir Abraham Yarner, Knt., of Dublin, and had issue,

    HENRY, his successor.

    John, who *m.* Elizabeth, elder dau. of John Temple, Esq., of Moor Park, in Surrey, and grand-dau. of Sir William Temple, Bart., by whom he acquired that estate, and had a numerous family. His male issue soon became extinct.

    Catherine, *m.* 1st, to Charles Ward, Esq., of Killough; and 2ndly, to Charles King, Esq., of Dublin.

    Dorothy, *m.* 1st, to Francis Colvill, Esq.; and 2ndly, to Sir Basil Dixwell, Bart., and *d. s. p.*

    Elizabeth, *d. unm.*

    Mary, *m.* 1683, to Thomas Flower, Esq., of Durrow.

    Lucy-Jane, *m.* 1st, John, Lord Berkeley, of Stratton; and 2ndly, William Bentinck, Earl of Portland.

    Frances, *m.* William, Lord Berkeley, of Stratton, and had with other issue, who *d. s. p.*, a son, Charles, whose only surviving child, SOPHIA, *m.* JOHN, 1st LORD WODEHOUSE, great-grandfather by her of John, Earl of Kimberley.

Sir John *d.* in 1704, and was *s.* by his eldest son,

HENRY TEMPLE, Esq., Chief Remembrancer of the Court of Exchequer, in Ireland, who was created a peer of that kingdom, as *Baron Temple, of Mount Temple*, co. Sligo, and VISCOUNT PALMERSTON, of *Palmerston*, co. Dublin, by letters patent, bearing date 12 March, 1722, and describing Henry Temple the grantee, "præclaris ortum majoribus." His lordship *m.* 1st, Anne, dau. of Abraham Houblon, Esq., of London, and by that lady (who *d.* 8 December, 1735), had issue,

    HENRY, who *m.* 1st, 18 June, 1753, Elizabeth, eldest dau. of Col. and Lady Elizabeth Lee, and sister of Caroline, wife of Gen. William Haviland, of Penn, Bucks, but had no issue. He *m.*, 2ndly, in 1738, Jane, dau. of Sir John Bernard, Bart., lord mayor of London, and left at his decease, 18 August, 1740, an only son,

        HENRY, successor to his grandfather

    Richard, M.P., *m.* Henrietta, dau. of Thomas Pelham, Esq., of Stanmer, in Sussex; and *d.* 8 August, 1749. His widow *m.* George Neville, 1st Earl of Abergavenny, and *d.* 1768.

The viscount *m.* 2ndly, 11 May, 1738, Isabella, dau. of Sir Francis Gerard, Bart., and relict of Sir John Fryer, Bart., but by her (who *d.* 10 August, 1762), had no other issue. His lordship *d.* 10 June, 1757, and was *s.* by his grandson,

HENRY TEMPLE, 2nd viscount, *b.* 4 December, 1739; who *m.* 1st, 6 October, 1767, Frances, only dau. of Sir Francis Poole, Bart., of Poole Hall, co. Chester, but by her (who *d.* 2 June, 1769), had no issue. His lordship *m.* 2ndly, at Bath, 5 January, 1783, Mary, dau. of Benjamin Mee, Esq., and sister of Benjamin Mee, Esq., Director of the Bank, by whom (who *d.* 8 February, 1805) he left,

    HENRY-JOHN, his heir.

    William (Sir), K.C.B., minister plenipotentiary to the Court of Naples; *b.* 19 January, 1788; *d. unm.* 24 August, 1856.

    Frances, *m.* 9 August, 1820, to Captain (afterwards vice-admiral) William Bowles, R.N., and *d.* in 1838.

    Elizabeth, *m.* in 1811, Right Hon. Laurence Sulivan, of Ponsbourne Park, Herts, some time deputy secretary at-war, and a commissioner of the royal military asylum; and *d.* 1837, leaving with an elder son (who *d.* at Lima in 1856),

        REV. HENRY WILLIAM SULIVAN, M.A., rector of Yoxall, co. Stafford.

    ELIZABETH, *m.* 8 May, 1851, Henry Hippisley, Esq., of Lamborne Place and Sparsholt House, Berks.

    MARY, *m.* 6 July, 1865, Rev. R. G. Baker, vicar of Fulham, and prebendary of St. Paul's.

The viscount, who sat in the English House of Commons for East Looe and Borobridge, *d.* 17 April, 1802, and was *s.* by his son,

HENRY-JOHN TEMPLE, 3rd viscount, K.G., G.C.B., P.C., D.C.L.; Lord Warden of the Cinque' Ports, b. at Broadlands, near Romsey, Hants, 20 October, 1784, and educated at Harrow, Edinburgh, and Cambridge. In 1806, he contested, unsuccessfully with Lord Henry Petty, the representation of the University of Cambridge, and again in 1807, with a similar result, but in 1811, he was more fortunate, being then returned for that constituency, which he continued to represent up to 1831. He had meanwhile entered the House of Commons as M.P. for Helston, and held office as a Lord of the Admiralty in 1807. From 1809 to 1828 he was secretary at war; and Foreign Secretary from 1830 to 1834, from 1835 to 1841, and from 1846 to 1851. In December, 1852, he was constituted Secretary of State for the Home Department; and 8 February, 1855, FIRST LORD OF THE TREASURY, which office he resigned 26 February, 1858, but resumed it 24 June, 1859, and held it up to the period of his decease. His lordship, after his retirement from the representation of the University of Cambridge, sat for Bletchingley, 1831, for South Hants from 1832 to 1834, and for Tiverton from 1835 to 1865. He m. 16 December, 1839, Emily-Mary, dau. and (by the deaths of her brothers, Viscount Melbourne, the Prime Minister, and Lord Beauvale), sole heiress of Peniston Lamb, 1st Viscount Melbourne, and widow of Peter-Leopold, 5th Earl Cowper, but had no issue. His lordship, a most distinguished, able, and popular statesman, d. 18 October, 1865, deeply lamented by the nation at large, irrespectively of politics or party, and was buried in Westminster Abbey, in a grave closely adjoining those of Pitt and Canning. At his death the honours of his family became EXTINCT.

Arms—Quarterly: 1st and 4th, or, an eagle displayed, sa., 2nd and 3rd, arg., two bars sa., each charged with three martlets, or.

THOMPSON—BARON HAVERSHAM.

By Letters Patent, dated 4 May, 1696.

Lineage.

SIR JOHN THOMPSON, Bart., a leading member of the House of Commons, and a zealous promoter of the Revolution, was elevated to the peerage 4 May, 1696, as BARON HAVERSHAM, of Haversham, co. Bucks. His lordship m. 1st, Lady Frances Wyndham, widow of Francis Wyndham, Esq., and dau. of Arthur Annesley, 1st Earl of Anglesey, by whom he had issue,

MAURICE, his successor.
George, who d. s. p.
Helen, m. to the Rev. Thomas Gregory, rector of Toddington, co. Bedford. Their son, John Wentworth Nanzianzen Gregory, Esq., had an only dau. and heiress, Frances-Annesley, m. 1772, to Robert Austen, Esq., of Shalford, co. Surrey.
Elizabeth, m to Joseph Grange, Esq
Mary, m. to Arthur Annesley, 5th Earl of Anglesey.
Frances, m. to Thomas Armstrong, Esq.
Martha, m. to Sir John Every, Bart.
Catherine, m. to Mr. White.
Dorothy, m. to Capt. Beckford, of the East India service.
Althamia, m. to Mr. Francis of Bristol.

Lord Haversham m. 2ndly, Martha, widow of Mr. Grahme, but had no other issue. He d. in 1709, and was s. by his elder son,
MAURICE THOMPSON, 2nd baron. This nobleman, in the lifetime of his father, served in the French war, and obtained distinction at the siege of Namur, where he was dangerously wounded. He was subsequently a colonel in the guards, and before his accession to the title, a member of the House of Commons. His lordship m. 1st, Elizabeth, dau. of John Smith, Esq., of Hertfordshire, by whom he had two daus.,

ELIZABETH, m. 1724, John Carter, Esq., of Weston Colville, co. Cambridge, and had a dau. and eventual heiress, ELIZABETH, m. to Gen. Hall, of Wratten Park, co. Cambridge, and had one son, JOHN HALL, Esq., of Weston Colville, and one dau., Elizabeth-Anne Hall, wife of John Morse, Esq., of Sprowston Hall, co. Norfolk.
Anne, m. to Richard Reynolds, Esq., son of Richard, bishop of London, and d. s. p. in 1737.

His lordship m. 2ndly, Elizabeth, widow of William Green, Esq., and sister of Richard, Earl of Anglesey, but by her had no issue. He d. in 1745, when the Barony of Haversham became EXTINCT.

Arms—Or, on a fesse dancetté az., three stars, arg., a canton of the 2nd, charged with the sun in glory ppr.

THOMSON—BARON SYDENHAM.

By Letters Patent, dated 19 August, 1840.

Lineage.

JOHN THOMSON, Esq., of Crichton, a banker at Edinburgh, m. Elizabeth, dau. of Andrew Ronaldson, Esq., and left at his decease (he was buried at Edinburgh, in the Grey Friars, in 1746), with other children who d. s. p., a dau., Agnes, m. to Andrew Bonar, Esq., 2nd son of John Bonar, Esq., of Kilgraston, co. Perth, and a son,
ANDREW THOMSON, Esq., of Roehampton, co. Surrey, who m. Harriet Wright (widow), 3rd dau., and at length sole heiress of Colonel John Buncombe, of Gothurst, co. Somerset, and representative of her great-grandfather, Edward Poulett, Esq., of Gothurst, and by her (who d. in 1787, and was buried at Putney,) had issue,

I. JOHN, his heir.
I. Elizabeth, m. to John Hankey, Esq., of London.
II. Maria, m. to Sir Joshua Van Neck, Lord Huntingfield.
III. Anne, m. 1779, to Thomson Bonar, Esq., of Roehampton, co. Surrey.
IV. Agnes, m. to Samuel Ibbetson, Esq.

Mr. Thomson d. in 1795, and was buried at Putney. His only son and heir,
JOHN THOMSON, Esq., of Roehampton and Waverley Abbey, co. Surrey, assumed, by royal license, the surnames and arms of BUNCOMBE and POULETT. He m. 1781, Charlotte, dau. of John Jacob, M.D., of Salisbury, by Margaret, his wife, dau. and co-heir of the Very Rev. John Clarke, dean of Salisbury, and had issue,

I. ANDREW-HENRY, of the city of London, b. August, 1786, at Lee, in Kent; m. January, 1813, Sophia, dau. of George Holme Sumner, Esq., of Hatchlands, M.P. for Surrey, and left two sons, deceased, and a dau., CHARLOTTE, m. in 1837, to Thomas-Mathias Weguelin, Esq., M.P., and had issue.
II. GEORGE-POULETT, of Castle Combe, Wilts, J.P. and D.L., late M.P. for Stroud, b. 1797, who m. 1821, Emma-Phipps, dau. and heir of the late William Scrope, Esq., of Castle Combe, Wilts, and Cockerington, co. Lincoln; and assumed, by royal license, 22 March, 1821, the name and arms of SCROPE only.
III. CHARLES, created LORD SYDENHAM.
I. Harriet, m. to Rev. George Locke, rector of Lee, Kent.
II. Charlotte, m. to Sir Charles-Wm. Taylor, Bart.
III. Emily, m. to Charles Hammersley, Esq., of Great Cumberland Place, London.
IV. Frances, m. 1st, to Wm. Baring, Esq., of Portswood, Hants, son of Sir Francis Baring, Bart.; and 2ndly, to Arthur Eden, Esq.
V. Julia, m. to Baron Maltzalin.
VI. Sophia, m. to Baron Biel.

The 3rd son,
CHARLES POULETT-THOMSON, Esq., b. September, 1799, M.P., having taken a prominent part in political life was appointed governor-general of Canada, and created by letters patent, bearing date 19 August, 1840, BARON SYDENHAM, of Sydenham, co. Kent, and Toronto, Canada. His lordship did not survive to take his seat in the House of Lords, but d. unm. in Canada, 19 September, 1841, when the title became EXTINCT.

Arms—Arg., a buck's head cabossed, gu., attired, or: on a chief, az., a cross-crosslet fitchée of the third, between two mullets of the field: quartering POULETT, sa., three swords in pile, their points in base, arg., pomels and hilts, or., a crescent for difference.

THORPE—BARON THORPE.

Lineage.

JOHN DE THORPE was summoned to parliament as a Baron from 11 June, 1309, to 10 October, 1325. Dugdale does not mention this Baron, but Banks endeavours to identify him with John de Thorpe, Lord of Creke, co. Norfolk, who left issue.

THORPE—BARON THORPE.

Lineage.

WILLIAM DE THORPE was summoned to parliament as a Baron, from 16 July, 1381, to 12 September, 1390. Nothing further, with any degree of accuracy, is known of this nobleman, or his descendants. He is not mentioned at all by Dugdale.

THWENG—BARONS THWENG.

By Writ of Summons, dated 22 February, 1307.

Lineage.

Of this family, anciently Lords of Kilton Castle, in York-shire, was

SIR ROBERT DE THWENG, who, in the 22nd HENRY III., was deputed by the other barons to repair to Rome, and to lay at the foot of the pontifical throne, a complaint of the nobles of England, regarding some encroachment upon their ecclesiastical rights, by the holy see. He was *s.* by his son,

MARMADUKE DE THWENG. This feudal lord had a military summons to march into Scotland, 42nd HENRY III., when the Scots had risen in rebellion against their king, the son-in-law of the English monarch. He *m.* Emma, sister and heir of Duncan Darell, and left a son,

ROBERT DE THWENG, who *m.* the widow of Sir John de Oketon, and was *s.* by his eldest son,

MARMADUKE DE THWENG, Lord of Kilton, who *m.* Lucia, one of the sisters and co-heirs of Peter de Brus, of Skelton (*see* Bruce, of Annandale), and acquired thereby considerable estates in the co. York. In the 22nd EDWARD I., this Marmaduke had summons amongst the other great men of that time, to repair with all speed to the king, and to afford him his advice touching the most important affairs of the realm. He had subsequently a military summons to march against the French. He had three sons, viz.,

I. ROBERT, his heir.
II. MARMADUKE, successor to his brother.
III. Edward, who *m.* Alice, dau. and heir of Walter Helmesley, of Over Helmesley, co. York, and became ancestor of the THWENGS of Upper Helmesley, whose male representative, MARMADUKE THWENGE, Esq., of Upper Helmesley, *b.* in 1560, left a dau. and heiress, MARGERY, *m.* 1st, to George Wilmer, Esq., of Stratford-le-Bow; and 2ndly, to the Hon. Henry Fairfax.

The eldest son,

ROBERT DE THWENG, Lord of Kilton, left an only dau.,

LUCY, who *m.* 1st, William le Latimer, (un., Baron Latimer (*see that title*), but being divorced from him, as there mentioned, *m.* 2ndly, Bartholomew de Fancourt; and 3rdly, Robert de Everingham.

He was *s.* at his decease by his brother, as next heir male,

MARMADUKE DE THWENG, one of the most eminent soldiers of the period in which he lived, who, being highly distinguished in the wars of Scotland, was summoned to parliament as a Baron from 22 February, 1307, to 18 September, 1322. His lordship *m.* Isabel, dau. of William de Ros, of Igmanthorpe, co. York, and had issue,

I. WILLIAM, his successor.
II. ROBERT, } both priests, successively barons.
III. THOMAS, }
I. LUCIA, *m.* to Sir Robert de Lumley, and her son,

SIR MARMADUKE DE LUMLEY, assumed the arms of Thweng. His son,

SIR RALPH DE LUMLEY, was summoned to parliament as BARON LUMLEY, in 1384, but, on his attainter, his honours expired. The attainder was, however, repealed in the reign of EDWARD IV. (*see* LUMLEY).

II. MARGARET, *m.* to Sir Robert de Hilton, Knt.
III. KATHERINE, *m.* to Sir Ralph D'Aubenie.

His lordship *d.* in 1323, and was *s.* by his eldest son,

WILLIAM DE THWENG, 2nd baron, summoned to parliament 30 December, 1324. He *m.* Katherine, dau. of Thomas, Lord Furnival, of Hallamshire, and dying *s. p.* in 1341, was *s.* by his brother,

ROBERT DE THWENG, who, doing homage in the same year, had livery of his lands. This baron was in holy orders, and *d.* of course *unm.* in 1344, when he was *s.* by his brother,

THOMAS DE THWENG, also a clergyman. This baron being rector of the church at Lytham, founded a chantry of twelve priests and four clerks, in the parochial church there, to pray for the good estate of himself, and Henri, Lord Percy, and for the souls of their ancestors; likewise for the souls of Robert de Thweng, and Maud, his wife; Marmaduke de Thweng, and Lucy, his wife, &c., &c. His lordship *d.* in 1374, when his estates devolved upon the heirs of his sisters, and the Barony of Thweng fell into ABEYANCE amongst them, as it still continues with their representatives.

Arms—Or, a fesse, gules.

THYNNE—BARON CARTERET.

By Letters Patent, dated 29 January, 1784.

Lineage.

The HON. HENRY-FREDERICK THYNNE, 2nd son of Thomas, 2nd Viscount Weymouth, by the Lady Louisa Carteret, his wife, dau. of John, 2nd Earl Granville, having succeeded, by will, to the estates of his maternal grandfather, assumed, by sign-manual, the surname of "Carteret," and was created, 29 January, 1784, BARON CARTERET, *of Hawnes, co. Bedford*, with remainder, in default of male issue, to each of the sons in succession (except the eldest) of his brother, Thomas, 1st Marquess of Bath, and the heirs male of their bodies. His lordship *d. unm.* 17 June, 1826, aged ninety-one, when the barony devolved, according to the limitation, upon his nephew (the 2nd son of Thomas, 1st Marquess of Bath),

LORD GEORGE THYNNE, as 2nd Lord Carteret, *b.* 23 January, 1770, *m.* May, 1797, Harriet, 5th dau. of William, 2nd Viscount Courtenay, but *d. s. p.* 19 February, 1838, when the barony devolved on his only surviving younger brother,

LORD JOHN THYNNE, as 3rd Lord Carteret, *b.* 23 December, 1772, *m.* in 1801, Mary-Anne, dau. of Thomas Master, Esq., of the Abbey, co. Gloucester, and *d.* 1 March, 1849, when the title became EXTINCT His widow *d.* 22 February, 1863.

Arms—Quarterly: 1st and 4th, barry of ten, or and sa ; 2nd and 3rd, arg , a lion rampant, gu.

TIBETOT—BARONS TIBETOT.

By Writ of Summons, dated 10 March, 1308.

Lineage.

In the 1st year of HENRY III.,

HENRY DE TIBETOT, being in arms for the king, had a grant in conjunction with Thomas Botterel, of the possessions lying in the cos. York and Lincoln, of Adam Painel, who fought on the other side, and dying in the 34th of the same reign, was *s.* by his son,

ROBERT DE TIBETOT, who, in the 50th HENRY III., was made governor of the castle of Porchester, and having attended Prince Edward to the Holy Land, was high in favour, after he had ascended the throne, as EDWARD I., being then constituted governor of Nottingham Castle, justice of South Wales, and governor of the castles of Carmarthen and Cardigan. In the 13th of the same reign, he had a grant from John, the son of Gerard de Rodes, to himself, his wife, and his son, in fee, of the manors of Langar and Berneston, in Nottinghamshire. In the 20th, being then the king's lieutenant for Wales, he fought and defeated Rees ap Meredeth, in a great battle, wherein 4,000 Welshmen were slain, and Rees himself having been made prisoner, was conveyed to York, and there executed. Robert de Tibetot was subsequently in the wars of Gascony and Scotland. He *m.* Eve, dau. (or granddau.) of Pain de Chaworth, and had issue,

PAIN, his successor.
Hawyse, *m.* to John Clavering, son of Robert Fitz-Roger.
Eve, *m.* to Robert, son of Robert de Tatshall.

He *d.* in the 26th EDWARD I., and was *s.* by his son,

PAIN DE TIBETOT, who, serving in the Scottish wars, during the latter part of the reign of EDWARD I., was summoned to parliament as a Baron, upon the accession of EDWARD II., from 10 March, 1308, to 26 November, 1313. He was subsequently Justice of the forests beyond Trent, and governor of the castle of Northampton. His lordship, who had made several campaigns into Scotland, fell eventually at the battle of Strivelin, *anno* 1314. He *m.* Agnes, dau. of William de Ros, of Hamlake, and was *s.* by his son,

SIR JOHN DE TIBETOT, 2nd baron, summoned to parliament, from 1 April, 1335, to 20 January, 1366. This nobleman was in the wars of France and Scotland, and was constituted governor of Berwick-upon-Tweed in the 20th EDWARD III. His lordship *m.* 1st, Margaret, dau. of Bartholomew, Lord Badlesmere, and co-heir of her brother, Giles, Lord Badlesmere, by whom he acquired a great accession of landed property (including Castlecombe, Wilts) and had issue,

I. ROBERT, his successor.
II. John, *d. s. p.*

The 2nd Lord Tibetot *m.* 2ndly, Elizabeth, dau. of Sir Robert Aspall, and widow of Sir Thomas Wauton, and had by her a son,

Pain (Sir), from whom the EARLS OF WORCESTER of this family descended.

He *d.* in 1367, and was *s.* by his elder son,

ROBERT DE TIBETOT, 3rd baron, summoned to parliament, from 24 February, 1368, to 8 January, 1371. His lordship *m.* Margaret, dau. of William Deincourt, Lord Deincourt, and by her (who *m.* 2ndly, John Cheyne) had issue,

> MARGARET (who inherited Langar, Notts), *m.* to Roger, 2nd Lord Scrope, of Bolton: the heir-general of this Margaret is HENRY-JAMES JONES, ESQ.
> MILICENT (who inherited the manors of Castlecombe, Wilts, and Oxenden, Gloucestershire), *m.* to Stephen le Scrope, brother of the above Roger: the heir-general of this co-heiress is EMMA PHIPPS, wife of GEORGE-POULETT SCROPE, Esq., of Castlecombe, Wilts, and only child of the late William Scrope, Esq., of Castlecombe.
> ELIZABETH (who inherited Nettlested, co. Suffolk), *m.* to Philip le Despencer, the younger: the heir-general of this co-heiress, Elizabeth, is LORD WENTWORTH.

Lord Tibbetot *d.* in 1372, when his lands devolved upon his daus. as co-heirs, and in the division thereof, Langar fell to the eldest (and was conveyed by her to the SCROPES, whence it passed through an illegitimate dau. of Emanuel Scrope, Earl of Sunderland, to the family of HOWE), Castlecombe devolved on the second, and the manor of Nettlested fell to the Despencers, from whom it passed by marriage to the Wentworths, afterwards summoned to parliament under the title of "Wentworth of Nettlested." The Barony of Tibetot, or Tiptoft, fell into ABEYANCE amongst these three co-heiresses of Robert, 3rd Lord Tibetot, as it still continues with their representatives.

Arms—Arg., a saltier engrailed, gu.

TIBETOT, OR TIPTOFT—BARONS TIBETOT, OR TIPTOFT, EARLS OF WORCESTER.

Barony, by Writ of Summons, dated 7 January, 1426.
Earldom, by Letters Patent, dated 16 July, 1449.

Lineage.

SIR PAIN DE TIBETOT, youngest son of John, 2nd Lord Tibetot, *m.* Agnes, sister of Sir John Wrothe, Knt., of Enfield, Middlesex, and was *s.* by his son,

SIR JOHN DE TIPTOFT, who, in the 1st HENRY IV., being retained in the service of that king, during his life, had, in consideration thereof, a grant of 100 marks per annum, payable out of the issues of the co. Cambridge; and in six years afterwards, upon the attainder of Thomas Mowbray, Earl Marshal and Nottingham, had, in conjunction with Ralph de Rochfort, a grant from the king, of all the apparel pertaining to the body of that earl, and all his harness, for peace and war, as well for great horses called coursers, as saddles for tilts and tournaments. In the 8th of the same reign, upon the rebellion and forfeiture of Owen Glendower, he obtained all the lands of Rhys ap Griffith (an adherent to Owen), lying within the principality of South Wales, and the same year he was constituted chief butler of England. He was, subsequently, made treasurer of the household, and in the reign of HENRY V., he was seneschal of Aquitaine, president of the king's exchequer in Normandy, and treasurer of that duchy. In the 3rd HENRY VI., he was appointed chief steward of the king's castles and lordships throughout Wales and the Marches, and the next year he had summons to parliament as a Baron. (Dugdale says he bore the title of Lord Tiptoft and Powys, but he was never summoned by any other writ than that addressed "Johanni Tiptoft, Chl'r,") His lordship *m.* 1st, Philippa, dau. of Sir John Talbot, and sister and co-heir of Sir John Talbot, of Richard's Castle, co. Hereford, Knt., and widow of Sir Matthew de Gournay, Knt., but by her had no issue. He *m.* 2ndly, Joyce, 2nd dau. and co-heir of Edward Cherlton, Lord Powys, by whom he acquired a considerable estate, and had issue,

JOHN, his successor.
Philippa, *m.* to Thomas, Lord Ros; one of the heirs-general of this Philippa, is the present LORD DE ROS.
Joane, *m.* to Sir Edmund Ingoldsthorpe (*refer to* Neville, Marquess of Montacute, for the co-heirs of this Joane).

Joyce, *m.* to Edmund Sutton, son and heir-apparent of John, Lord Dudley (*see* SUTTON).

Lord Tiptoft *d.* in 1443, and was *s.* by his son,

JOHN DE TIPTOFT, 2nd baron, who was created just as he had attained majority, 16 July, 1449, EARL OF WORCESTER. In 1457 his lordship was lord deputy of Ireland, and in the 1st EDWARD IV. he was constituted justice of North Wales for life. He was soon after made constable of the Tower of London, and the next year, being then treasurer of the exchequer, he assisted the king at the siege of Bamburgh Castle, held at the time by the Duke of Somerset, and other Lancastrians. His next great appointment was that of chancellor of Ireland, and in the 7th of the same reign being deputy of that kingdom to George, Duke of Clarence, he resided there for the protection of the realm. In three years afterwards he was constituted lieutenant of Ireland; as also constable of England, and again treasurer of the exchequer. At this time on his coming to Southampton, the king caused him to sit in judgment upon several of the Lancastrian party, who had then been made prisoners at sea, and the execution of twenty of those persons followed. Besides all this, it is further memorable of this nobleman, that having been bred a student at Baliol College, Oxford, and attained to an eminent degree in learning, he went to Jerusalem, and sojourned there for some time, whence he travelled into other countries, and returning through Italy, proceeded to Rome, for the express purpose of visiting the library at the Vatican. Here he made, it is said, so eloquent an oration to Pope PIUS II., that it drew tears from the eyes of his holiness. His lordship translated into English *Publius Cornelius* and *Caius Flaminius*; and wrote several learned Tracts, of which Bale makes mention. In Walpole's *Royal and Noble Authors*, he is also noticed with high commendation. Being a stanch Yorkist, the earl, upon the temporary restoration of HENRY VI., was placed in danger, and forced to conceal himself from his enemies, but being at length found in the upper branches of a high tree, he was conveyed to London, and being adjudged to suffer death, was beheaded on Tower Hill, *anno* 1470, when all his honours became FORFEITED. His lordship *m.* 1st, Cecily, dau. of Richard, Earl of Salisbury, and widow of Henry Beauchamp, Duke of Warwick, but had no issue. He *m.* 2ndly, Elizabeth, dau. of Robert Greyndour, by whom he had a son, John, who *d.* in infancy. He *m.* 3rdly, Elizabeth, dau. of Thomas Hopton, Esq., and widow of Sir Roger Corbet, Knt., of Moreton Corbet, co. Salop, by whom he had an only son,

EDWARD DE TIPTOFT, at whose decease *unm.*, in 1485, the Earldom of Worcester became EXTINCT, while the Barony of Tiptoft fell into ABEYANCE amongst his aunts (*see* children of the 1st lord), as it still continues with their representatives.

Arms—Az., a saltier engrailed, gu.

TICHBORNE—BARON FERRARD.

By Letters Patent, dated 26 September, 1715.

Lineage.

SIR HENRY TICHBORNE (4th son of Sir Benjamin Tichborne, 1st Baronet, of Tichborne, Hants), *b.* 1581, governor of the castle of Lifford, was knighted by King JAMES I. at Tichborne, 29 August, 1623; and being appointed, at the outbreak of the rebellion of 1641, to a command in Ireland, he gained great renown by his successful defence of the town of Drogheda. In consideration of these services, he was sworn of the privy council, and 12 May, 1642, made one of the lords justices of Ireland, in the place of Sir William Parsons. Lord Clarendon refers to the appointment in these words:—"Sir Harry Tichborne being a man of so excellent a fame, that though the parliament was heartily angry at the removal of the other, and knew this would never be brought to serve their turn, yet they had nothing to object against him." By King CHARLES II., Sir Henry was constituted field-marshal of his forces in Ireland, which post he held till his death, 1667, at the age of eighty-five. He was buried at Drogheda. He *m.* Jane, dau. of Sir Robert Newcomen, Bart., and by her (who *d.* about 1664) he had five sons and three daus., viz.,

I. BENJAMIN, a captain of horse in the service of CHARLES I, killed by the rebels at Belruddery, co. Dublin, in the twenty-first year of his age.
II. WILLIAM, his successor.
III. Richard, major of the horse-guards in Ireland, *d. unm.*
IV. Henry, *d. unm.*
V. Samuel, *d.* young.

i. Dorcas, *m.* to William Toxteth, Esq., of Drogheda, a native of Lancashire.

ii. Amphilis, *m.* to Richard Broughton, Esq., major of foot-guards in Ireland, younger brother of Sir Edward Broughton.

iii. Elizabeth, *m.* to Roger West, Esq., of the Rock, co. Wicklow.

The eldest surviving son,

SIR WILLIAM TICHBORNE, of Beaulieu, co. Louth, knighted by King CHARLES II., *m.* Judith, dau. and co-heir of John Ilyase, Esq., lord chief baron of the exchequer in Ireland, and *d.* 12 March, 1693, having had issue,

i. HENRY, of whom presently.

ii. Benjamin, killed in the thirty-ninth year of his age, at the battle of Blenheim, 1704. By Elizabeth, his wife, dau. of Major Edward Gibbs, of the city of Gloucester, he had three daus., of whom Judith, *m.* 1st, Charles, Earl of Sunderland, and 2ndly, Sir Robert Sutton, K.B.

iii. William, a captain in the sea service.

iv. John, colonel of his Majesty's forces, and governor of Athlone.

v. Richard, M.A., T.C.D., 1692.

vi. Bysse, captain, lost his life in defence of Gibraltar, 1704.

i. Margaret, *m.* Stephen Stanley, Esq., of Grange Gormon, co. Dublin, father of Sir John Stanley, Bart.

The eldest,

SIR HENRY TICHBORNE, of Beaulieu, co. Louth. *b.* 1663, was knighted by King WILLIAM III , in 1694, created a Baronet of England, 12 July, 1697 ; and 26 September, 1715, advanced to the peerage of Ireland, as BARON FERRARD, *of Beaulieu.* He *m.* 1683, Arabella, dau. of Sir Robert Cotton, of Combermere, co. Chester, and had issue,

i. Henry, *b.* 20 April, 1684, *m.* Mary, dau. and sole heir of John Fowke, of Atherdee, Esq. On his passage to England in 1709, he was unfortunately cast away in the bay of Liverpool

ii. William, *m.* Charlotte-Amelia, 2nd dau. of Robert, late Lord Viscount Molesworth, of the kingdom of Ireland, by whom he left no issue

iii. Cotton, *d.* young.

i. Salisbury, *m.* William Aston, Esq., of co. Louth, and had issue, of which SOPHIA ASTON, heiress of her brother, Tichborne Aston, Esq., *m.* February, 1741-2, Thomas Tipping, Esq. (son of Thomas Tipping, Esq., of Castletown, co. Louth, by Mabella, his wife, dau. of William Stannus, Esq., of Carlingford), and left three daus. and co-heirs, viz.,

1 ELIZABETH TIPPING, *m.* to Cadwallader, Lord Blayney.

2 SOPHIA-MABELLA, *m.* Rev. Robert Montgomery, rector of Monaghan, and had *inter alios,* a son, the Rev. Alexander Johnston-Montgomery, of Beaulieu, father of the present Richard-Thomas Montgomery, Esq., of Beaulieu.

3 SALISBURY WILHELMINA.

On his lordship's death, in 1731, the honours became EXTINCT,

Arms—Vair, a chief, or.

TONI—BARON TONI.

By Writ of Summons, dated 10 April, 1299

Lineage.

ROBERT DE TONI (the lineal descendant of Ralph de Toni, Lord of Toni in Normandy, standard bearer of that duchy, and one of the soldiers of Hastings) having distinguished himself *temp.* EDWARD I., in the wars of Scotland and Gascony, had summons to parliament as BARON TONI, from 10 April, 1299, to 16 June, 1311. His lordship *d. s. p.* about the latter year, when the Barony became EXTINCT. His estates devolved upon his sister, Alice de Toni, who *m.* 1st,Thomas Leybourne ; 2ndly, Guy de Beauchamp, Earl of Warwick, and 3rdly, William de la Zouche, of Ashby, co. Leicester

Arms—Arg., a maunch, gu.

TONSON—BARON RIVERSDALE.

By Letters Patent, dated 13 October, 1783

Lineage.

The first member of the Tonson family who settled in Ireland was

MAJOR RICHARD TONSON, who obtained a grant of land in the co. Cork from CHARLES II., for his distinguished exertions in favour of royalty during the civil wars, and purchased the castle and lands of Spanish Island, in the same county. He *m.*

Elizabeth, sister of Thomas Becher, Esq , of Skerkin, co. Cork, and had issue,

HENRY, his successor.

Elizabeth, *m.* to Colonel Daniel O'Donovan. of Banlaghan, M.P. in 1689.

Major Tonson *d.* in 1693, and was *s.* by his son,

HENRY TONSON, Esq., of Spanish Island, who *m.* in May. 1692, Elizabeth, 2nd dau. of Sir Richard Hull, one of the judges of the Court of Common Pleas, in Ireland (great-grandniece of Richard Boyle, 1st Earl of Cork), and had surviving issue,

RICHARD, his successor.

Elizabeth, *m.* 1st, in 1713, to John Reading, Esq., of St. Off. co. York ; and 2ndly, to the Rev. Percy Meade, and by the latter, had an only dau. and heir, Elizabeth-Peniel, *m.* 6 September, 1759, to John Rye, Esq., of Ryecourt. co. Cork. Mabella, *m.* in 1722, to Thomas Addison, Esq., and *d. s. p.*

Mr. Tonson *d.* in 1703, and was *s.* by his son,

RICHARD TONSON, Esq., of Spanish Island and Dunkettle, *b.* 6 January, 1695, who was returned to parliament by the borough of Baltimore in 1727, and represented the same place for forty-six years afterwards. This gentleman acquired a considerable accession of property from Major Anthony Butler, who, having no issue, settled his estate upon him in 1718, through friendship for his grandfather, Major Tonson, with whom Major Butler had served in the civil wars. Mr. Tonson *m.* 1st, Elizabeth, dau. of Henry Tynte, Esq., by whom he had an only dau. ELIZABETH, who *d. unm.* He *m.* 2ndly, Peniel, dau. of Colonel Gates, and relict of Michael Becher, Esq., of Affadown, co. Cork; and *d.* 24 June, 1773. He devised his estates to Col. William Hull, on condition that he took the surname and arms of Tonson, which he consequently did, and became

COL. WILLIAM TONSON. This gentleman, *b.* 3 May, 1724 ; was a military officer of rank, lieutenant-governor of Cork, and a member of the Irish parliament, who was elevated to the peerage 13 October, 1783, as BARON RIVERSDALE, *of Rathcormac* (of which borough he was patron). His lordship *m.* 13 November, 1773, Rose, eldest dau. of James Bernard, Esq., of Castle Bernard, M.P. for the co. Cork, and sister of Francis, 1st Earl of Bandon, by whom (who *m.* 2ndly, Captain Millerd of the 55th foot, and *d.* in 1810) he had issue,

WILLIAM, his heir.

James-Bernard, *d. unm.* 11 February, 1803.

Richard, lieutenant of the 55th foot ; *d.* 17 September, 1794.

Francis, midshipman R.N. ; *d.* 1 November, 1793.

Charles-Ludlow, *b.* 9 July, 1781 ; *d. unm.* 20 August, 1837.

Henry, lieutenant 34th foot; *d.* in 1805.

LUDLOW, last peer.

Esther-Charlotte, *m.* 27 February, 1802, to Major General Joseph Baird (who *d.* 4 April, 1816), brother of the late General Sir David Baird, Bart., G.C.B., and had William and other issue. She *d.* 27 June, 1850.

Charlotte, *d. unm.* in 1830.

His lordship *d.* 4 December, 1787, and was *s.* by his son,

WILLIAM, 2nd lord, *b.* 8 December, 1775; who *m.* 21 October, 1799, Charlotte-Theodosia, dau. of St. Leger Aldworth, 1st Viscount Doneraile, but had no issue. His lordship. who was colonel of the South Cork militia, *d.* 3 April, 1848. Lady Riversdale *d.* 12 May, 1853. His lordship was *s.* by his brother,

LUDLOW TONSON, D.D., 3rd lord, bishop of Killaloe, *b.* 6 March, 1784, who *d. unm.* 13 December, 1861, when the title became EXTINCT. By his will, his lordship devised his estates to William-Thomas-Jonas Stawell, 2nd son of Col. Alcock-Stawell, of Kilbrittain Castle, co. Cork, and directed that he, William T. J. Stawell, should take the name of RIVERSDALE.

Arms—Gu., on a fesse, arg., two pellets; in chief, a right-hand gauntlet, erect, between two castles, arg.

TOUCHET—BARON TOUCHET.

By Writ of Summons, dated 29 December, 1299.

Lineage.

WILLIAM TOUCHET, supposed to have been a kinsman of the Lords Audley (although the arms he bore were different), having distinguished himself in the wars in Gascony and Scotland, was summoned to parliament, as a Baron, from 29 December, 1299, to 3 November, 1306, but of his lordship nothing further is recorded.

TOUCHET—EARLS OF CASTLEHAVEN.

By Letters Patent, dated 6 September, 1616.

Lineage.

JAMES, THE 4th LORD AUDELEY, was twice married, 1st to Joan, dau. of Roger Mortimer, Earl of March; and 2ndly, to Isabella, dau. of William Malbank. By his 1st wife he had a son, Nicholas Audeley, who *s.* him as Lord Audeley, and two daus., Joan and Margaret. Margaret, *m.* Sir Roger Hillary, and survived her brother; and Joan, *m.* Sir John Touchet, and *d.* in the lifetime of her brother, leaving her grandson, John Touchet, her heir. James, Lord Audeley, had issue by Isabella, his 2nd wife, a son, Thomas Audeley, who *d. s. p.* 24 January, 1385, and an only dau., Margaret, who *m.* Fulk, Lord Fitz Warine. Lady FitzWarine *d.* in the lifetime of her brother, Nicholas, leaving her grandson, Fulk, Lord FitzWarine, her heir. James, the 4th Lord Audeley, *d.* in April, in the 9th RICHARD II., 1386, and was *s.* by his only son, Nicholas, the 5th Lord Audeley. Nicholas, the 5th Lord Audeley *d. s. p.* in July, in the 15th RICHARD II., 1392. His surviving sister, Dame Margaret Hillary, and his grandnephew John Touchet, were his heirs of the whole blood, and the said Dame Margaret Hillary and John Touchet together with Fulk, Lord Fitz-Warine were the heirs of line, and the heirs of James, Lord Audeley, and his ancestors Lords Audeley, and the Barony of Audeley fell into ABEYANCE between the said Dame Margaret Hillary, John Touchet, and Fulk, Lord FitzWarine. The manor of Heleigh and other estates had been entailed upon Nicholas, the 3rd Lord Audeley, the father of James, the 4th Lord Audeley, and the heirs of his body, and upon the decease of Nicholas, the 5th Lord Audeley they descended in purparty upon Dame Margaret Hillary, John Touchet, and Fulk, Lord FitzWarine. John Touchet was twenty years of age. and Fulk, Lord FitzWarine three years of age at the time of the death of Nicholas, the 4th Lord Audeley.

John Touchet came of age in the 16th of RICHARD II., 1393. The abeyance of the Barony of Audeley was determined in his favour in or prior to the 6th HENRY IV., 1403, and he was summoned to parliament 20 October in that year. Dame Margaret Hillary, the eldest dau. of James, Lord Audeley, and the senior co-heir of Nicholas, Lord Audeley, was then living, and 12 June, 1404, 5th HENRY IV. (the 5th year of his reign having commenced 30 September, 1403), she obtained the king's release in respect of certain demands made against her as the executrix of her late husband Sir Roger Hillary. (Memoranda Roll, 5th HENRY IV., ro. 7). Fulk, Lord Fitz-Warine, the other co-heir of the Lords Audeley, *d.* in the 9th HENRY IV., and from him there are many descendants now in existence. John Touchet, in whose favour the abeyance of the Barony of Audeley was determined in the 5th HENRY IV., *d.* in the 10th HENRY IV. His widow survived until the 24th HENRY VI., and in the king's writ, directing an inquisition to be taken after her decease, she is described as Elizabeth Audeley, who was the wife of John Touchet, late Lord Audeley, and in the inquisition she is described in the same manner, and her son is spoken of as James Touchet, knight, Lord Audeley; and in a proceeding in parliament in the 9th HENRY V., John, Lord Audeley is styled "John Touchet, Chevalier, Jadiz 'Seigneur de Audeley,'" and his son as "James, Seigneur de Audeley." (Inquisition, 25th HENRY VI., No. 33, Rolls of Parliament, v. 4, p. 164). The Lords Audeley of the family of Touchet at all times after the determination of the abeyance held the place and precedence of the original Lords Audeley. These remarks on her descent of the Barony of Audeley, we derive from a very learned House of Lords' paper, "The additional case on behalf of Sir Charles Robert Tempest, of Broughton, co. York, Bart."

SIR GEORGE TOUCHET, Knt., the 18th Baron Audley, of Heley, was created 6 September, 1616 (old style), *Baron Orier*, and EARL OF CASTLEHAVEN, in the peerage of Ireland. His lordship *m.* Lucy, dau. of Sir James Mervyn, Knt., of Fonthill, Wilts; *d.* 20 February, 1616 (old style), and had issue,

  I. MERVYN, of whom presently.
  II. Ferdinando, K.B., *m.* the widow of Sir John Rodney, of Pilton, co. Somerset.
  I. Anne, *m.* to Edward Blount, Esq., of Harleston, co. Derby.
  II. Elizabeth, *m.* 1st, Sir John Stawel, of Stawel, co. Somerset, K.B., and 2ndly, Sir Thomas Griffin, of Dingley, co. Northampton, Knt.
  III. Mary, *m.* to Sir Thomas Thynne, of Longleate, co. Wilts.
  IV. Christian, *m.* to Sir Henry Mervyn, of Petersfield, co. Southampton, Knt., admiral of the fleet.
  V. Eleanor, *m.* 1st, to Sir John Davis, Knt., the king's attorney in Ireland; and 2ndly, Sir Archibald Douglas, Knt.

The son,

MERVYN TOUCHET, 2nd Earl of Castlehaven, and also Lord Audley. This nobleman being accused of certain high crimes, and by virtue of a commission of oyer and terminer, thereupon arraigned, had sentence of death passed upon him, and was executed accordingly on Tower hill, 14 May, 1631. His lordship *m.* 1st, Elizabeth, dau. and co-heir of Benedict Barnham, alderman of London; and 2ndly, Anne, dau. of Ferdinando, Earl of Derby, and widow of Grey Bridges, Lord Chandos. By his 1st wife, he had issue,

  I. JAMES, his heir.
  II. George, a Benedictine monk at Douay.
  III. MERVYN, successor to his brother.
  I. Lucy, *m.* 1st. John Anketell, of Compton, in Wiltshire, and of Newmarket, co. Cork; and 2ndly, to Gerald FitzMaurice, brother of Lord Kerry.
  II. Dorothy, *m.* to Edmund Butler, Viscount Mountgarret.
  III. Frances, *m.* to Richard Butler, brother of James, Duke of Ormonde.

The eldest son,

JAMES TOUCHET, obtained a new patent, 3 June, 1634, creating him *Lord Audeley*, and EARL OF CASTLEHAVEN. His lordship during the civil wars of Ireland, commanded under the Duke of Ormonde; and in 1649, being chosen general of the Irish forces, acted against Cromwell and the parliamentarians. On the subjugation of the kingdom by Cromwell, his lordship withdrew into France, whence he returned to England at the Restoration, and obtained a special act of parliament, in 1678, restoring to him the honour, dignity, place and precedence, as Lord Audley, enjoyed by his ancestors, but forfeited by his father, with remainder, in default of issue of his own body, to his brother, Mervyn Touchet, 3rd son of the late lord (passing over George, a Benedictine monk, his next brother), and the heirs of his body, and in default of issue of the said Mervyn, to the daus. (his sisters) of the deceased lord. The earl *m.* Elizabeth, dau. of Grey Bridges, Lord Chandos; but *d. s. p.*, 11 October, 1684, when his lordship's honours devolved upon his brother,

MERVYN TOUCHET, 4th Earl of Castlehaven. His lordship *m.* Mary, 3rd dau. of John, 10th Earl of Shrewsbury, and relict of Charles Arundel, Esq., and *d.* in 1686, having had issue,

  I. JAMES, 3rd earl.
  II. John. *m.* Elizabeth, 2nd dau. of Thomas Saville, Earl of Sussex. by whom he had a dau. Mary, who *m.* Cadwallader, Lord Blaney.
  I. Eleanor, *m.* to Sir Henry Wingfield, Bart., of Easton, Suffolk.
  II. Mary, *d. unm.*
  III. Anne, *d. unm.*

The elder son,

JAMES TOUCHET, 5th Earl of Castlehaven, *m.* Elizabeth Bard, a co-heiress, and was *s.* at his decease, 12 August, 1700, by his only child,

JAMES TOUCHET, 6th Earl of Castlehaven; who *m.* Elizabeth, dau. of Henry, Lord Arundell, of Wardour, and had issue,

JAMES, his heir.
JOHN TALBOT, successor to his brother.
Mary, *m.* in November, 1749, to Captain Philip Thicknesse, lieutenant-governor of Landguard Fort (younger brother of Ralph Thicknesse, Esq., of Barterley, co. Stafford), by whom she had GEORGE, who *s.* as Baron Audley, and other children.

His lordship *d.* in November, 1740, and was *s.* by his son,

JAMES TOUCHET, 7th Earl of Castlehaven, also Lord Audley, who *d. unm.* 8 May, 1769, and was *s.* by his brother,

JOHN TALBOT TOUCHET, 8th Earl of Castlehaven and also Lord Audley; who *d. s. p.* 22 April, 1777, when the earldom EXPIRED. The Barony of Audley, however, having been (although twice FORFEITED, in 1397 and in 1631.) fully restored by act of parliament. Being a barony in fee it descended to the son of the earl's deceased sister,

GEORGE THICKNESSE, who then became BARON AUDLEY. *See* ADDENDA.

Arms—Erm., a chev., gu.

TOUCHETT—BARONS AUDLEY.

(*See* ADDENDA.)

TOWNSHEND—BARONESS OF GREENWICH.

By Letters Patent, dated 28 August, 1767.

Lineage.

JOHN CAMPBELL, 2nd Duke of Argyll, *b.* 10 October, 1680, having, as lord high commissioner, given the royal assent, in the parliament of Scotland, to the introduction of the act of union with England, 21 September, 1705, was created by Queen ANNE, 26 November following, *Baron Chatham*, and EARL OF GREENWICH, in the peerage of England. In the next year, his grace made the campaign under the Duke of Marlborough, and distinguished himself at Ramillies, at the siege of Ostend, and in the attack of Menin; but his highest military reputation was acquired in 1708, at the battle of Oudenarde, where he commanded a division of the army, comprising 20 battalions, which was the first brought into action, and which maintained its ground, against a great disparity of numbers. On his return to England he was sworn of the privy council, and subsequently commanded in chief, as lieutenant-general, the English forces under General Schulemberg, at the attack of the city and citadel of Tournay. In 1710, the duke was installed a knight of the Garter. In 1712 he was constituted commander-in-chief of all the land forces in Scotland, and captain of the company of foot, in Edinburgh Castle. At the death of Queen ANNE, his grace was one of the seven lords justices, in whom the government was vested, under the act of parliament, until the arrival of King GEORGE I. from Hanover. After which he was again appointed general and commander-in-chief of the forces in Scotland, and in that capacity, suppressed the rebellion of 1715, by his victory of Dumblain, and his subsequent proceedings. For all these eminent services, he was advanced to a British dukedom, 30 April, 1718, as DUKE OF ARGYLL, and declared lord steward of the household. He was subsequently master-general of the ordnance, and in 1735-6, was constituted field-marshal of all his Majesty's forces.

His grace m. 1st, Mary, dau. of John Brown, Esq., and niece of Sir John Duncombe, Knt. (lord mayor of London, in 1708), but had no issue. He m. 2ndly, Jane, dau. of Thomas Warburton, Esq., of Winnington, in Cheshire, and had five daus., viz.,

    I. CAROLINE, of whom presently.
    II. Anne, m. to William Wentworth, Earl of Strafford, but d. s. p.
    III. Jane, d. young, January, 1735.
    IV. Elizabeth, m. to the Right Hon. James Stewart Mackenzie, brother of John, Earl of Bute.
    V. Mary, m. to Edward, Viscount Coke, heir-apparent of Thomas, Earl of Leicester, but d. s p.

This illustrious nobleman, commonly called "The great Duke of Argyll," who was as conspicuous for patriotism and eloquence in parliament, as he had been for valour and conduct in the field, d. 4 October, 1743, when his Scottish honours devolved upon his brother, and those of England became EXTINCT. The duke has been immortalized by Pope. There is a fine monument to his memory by Roubiliac, on which is chiselled, the personification of History, employed in writing the following lines:—

    Britons, behold! if patriot worth be dear,
    A shrine that claims thy tributary tear,
    Silent that tongue—admiring senates heard;
    Nerveless that arm—opposing legions fear'd.
    Nor less, O Campbell, thine the power to please,
    And give to grandeur all the grace of ease,
    Long from thy life, let kindred heroes trace
    Arts, which ennoble still the noblest race.
    Others may owe their future fame to me,
    I borrow immortality from thee.

His eldest dau.,

LADY CAROLINE (Countess of Dalkeith), who had m. 1st, Francis, Earl of Dalkeith, eldest son of Francis, Duke of Buccleugh, and was then the wife of the Right Hon. John Townshend, first lord of the treasury, and chancellor of the exchequer, was created 28 August, 1767, a peeress in her own right, as BARONESS GREENWICH, with the degree of Baron in remainder to the heirs male of her body, by the said John Townshend. Her ladyship, by her 1st husband, Lord Dalkeith, had no issue, but by the 2nd had two sons and a dau., viz.,

    Thomas-Charles, } both predeceased their mother, s. p.
    William-John, }
    Anne, m. 1st, in 1779, to Richard Wilson, Esq., of Tyrone, in Ireland, and left a son, and 2ndly, John Tempest, Esq., of Lincolnshire.

The countess d. in 1794, when the Barony of Greenwich became EXTINCT.

Arms—TOWNSHEND: az. a chev. erm. between three escallops arg.; CAMPBELL: quarterly: 1st and 4th, girony of eight pieces, or and sa ; 2nd and 3rd, arg., a galley with her sails furled close, flag and pendants flying, and oars in action, all sa.

TOWNSHEND—EARL OF LEICESTER.

(*See* BURKE's *Extant Peerage*, MARQUIS OF TOWNSHEND.)

TOWNSHEND—BARON BAYNING OF FOXLEY.

By Letters Patent, dated 20 October, 1797.

Lineage.

HON. WILLIAM TOWNSHEND, son of Charles, 2nd Viscount Townshend (*see* Extant Peerage, TOWNSHEND, M. OF), m. 29 May, 1725, Henrietta, only dau. and heir of Lord William Powlett, and had issue,

    I. CHARLES, his heir.
    I. Caroline, wife of Most Rev. Frederick Cornwallis, D.D., Archbishop of Canterbury.
    II. Anne, m. to Charles Hedges, Esq.
    III. Dorothy, m. to Miles-Buller Allen, Esq.

The Hon. William Townshend d. in 1738, and was s. by his son,

CHARLES TOWNSHEND, Esq., who, having filled some public offices of importance, was created, 20 October, 1797, BARON BAYNING, of Foxley, co. Berks, in the Peerage of Great Britain. He m. in 1777, Annabella - Powlett, dau. of Rev. Richard Smyth, and granddau. and heir of William Powlett, Esq., by whom (who d. 3 January, 1825) he had issue (with four daus., who d. unm.) two sons,

    I. CHARLES-FREDERICK-POWLETT, 2nd baron.
    II. Henry, 3rd baron.

His lordship d. 16 May, 1810, and was s. by his elder son,

CHARLES-FREDERICK-POWLETT, 2nd Baron Bayning, b. in 1785, at whose decease, unm., 2 August, 1823, the dignity devolved upon his brother,

HENRY, 3rd Baron Bayning, who was b. 8 June, 1797, and assumed by sign manual, in 1823 (in lieu of his patronymic, Townshend) the names of his maternal great-grandfather, William Powlett. He m. 9 August, 1842, Emma, only dau. of William-H. Fellowes, Esq., of Ramsey Abbey, co. Huntingdon, and had a son,

Charles-William, b. 9 October, 1844, d. 9 June, 1864.

Lord Bayning, who was Vicar of Honingham, Norfolk, d. 5 August, 1866, and, as he left no issue, the title became extinct.

Arms—Az., a chev., erm. between three escallops, ar., a mullet for diff.

TRACY—VISCOUNT TRACY OF RATHCOOLE.

By Letters Patent, dated 12 January, 1642.

Lineage.

SIR JOHN TRACY, of Toddington, who received knighthood from King JAMES I., in 1609. was advanced, by letters patent, dated 12 January, 1642, to the peerage of Ireland, as VISCOUNT TRACY, of Rathcoole. He m. Anne, dau. of Sir Thomas Shirley, Knt., of Isfield, co. Sussex, and was s. at his decease by his son,

ROBERT TRACY, 2nd Viscount Tracy, was knighted by King CHARLES I., and sat in parliament as member for Gloucestershire. His lordship m. 1st, Bridget, dau. of John Lyttelton, Esq., of Frankley Court, co. Worcester, by Meriel, his wife, dau. of Sir Thomas Bromley, lord chancellor, and had by her,

    I. JOHN, his heir.
    II. Robert, d. s. p.
    III. Thomas, d. s. p.
    IV. William, d. s. p.
    I. Anne, who m. William Somerville, Esq., of Edston, co. Warwick, and was grandmother of the author of *The Chase*, and other poems.
    II. Meriel, m. to Sir William Poole, of Saperton.
    III. Frances, m. to Dr. Hinckley.
    IV. Mary, d. unm.

His lordship m. 2ndly, Dorothy, dau. of Thomas Cocks, Esq., of Castleditch, co. Hereford, and had by her,

    I. Robert, of Coscomb, one of the Judges of the Court of King's Bench, and a commissioner of the Great Seal, m. Anne, dau. of William Dowdeswell, Esq., of Pull Court, co. Worcester, and d. 11 September, 1735, aged eighty, having had issue,

        1 RICHARD, of Coscomb, who m. Margaret, dau. of Owen Salusbury, Esq., of Rûg, co. Merioneth, and left at his decease, in 1734, an only child, ROBERT, of Coscomb, who d s. p. in 1756.

2 Robert, of the Middle Temple, d. 1732.
1 Dorothy, m. to John Pratt, Esq.
2 Anne, m. 1st, to Charles Dowdeswell, Esq., of Forth-ampton Court, co. Gloucester, and 2ndly, to Charles Wild, Esq.
II. Benjamin.
1. Dorothy, m. to William Higford, Esq., of Dixton, co. Gloucester.

The 2nd viscount d. in 1662, and was s. by his eldest son,

JOHN TRACY, 3rd viscount, who m. Elizabeth, eldest surviving dau. of Thomas, 1st Lord Leigh, of Stoneleigh, and by her (who d. in 1688) had, with a dau., the wife of Sir John Every, three sons, viz.,

I. WILLIAM, his heir.
II. Charles, d. unm. 3 May, 1676.
III. Ferdinando, b. in 1659, who became possessed of Stanway, by the will of Sir John Tracy, last baronet of that branch. He m. in 1680, Katherine, dau. of Sir Anthony Keck, and d. in 1682, leaving an only child,

JOHN, of Stanway, who m. Anne, only dau. of Sir Robert Atkyns, of Saperton, chief baron of the exchequer, and d. in 1735, leaving issue,

1 Robert, M.P.
2 Anthony, who assumed the surname of KECK; he m. Lady Susan Hamilton, dau. of James, 4th Duke of Hamilton, and dying 30 May, 1769, left two daus., Henrietta-Charlotte, m. to Edward, Viscount Hereford; and Susan, m. to Francis, Lord Elcho.
3 Thomas, of Sandywell, M.P.
4 John, who assumed the surname of ATKYNS, and was Curaitor Baron of the Exchequer,
1 Anne, m. to John Travell, Esq.
2 Frances, m. to Gustavus-Guy Dickens, Esq., colonel of the 3rd regiment of guards.

His lordship was s. by his eldest son,

WILLIAM TRACY, 4th viscount, who m. 1st, Frances, dau. of Leicester Devereux, Viscount Hereford, by whom he had an only dau., Elizabeth, m. 1st, to Robert Burdet, Esq.; 2ndly, to Ralph Holden, Esq., of Aston, co. Derby. His lordship m. 2ndly, Jane, 3rd dau. of the Hon. Sir Thomas Leigh, son of Thomas, 2nd Lord Leigh, and d. in 1712, leaving by her r dau., Anne, m. to Sir William Keyt, Bart., and a son and heir,

THOMAS-CHARLES TRACY, 5th viscount, who m. 1st, Elizabeth, eldest dau. of William Keyt, Esq., son of Sir William Keyt, Bart., of Ebrington, and by her (who d. in 1719) had issue,

William, d. vitâ patris
THOMAS-CHARLES, heir to the title.
Jane, who m. 7 October, 1743, Capel Hanbury, Esq., of Pontypool Park, M.P. for Monmouthshire, and d. 7 March, 1787, leaving issue.

Lord Tracy m. 2ndly, Frances, eldest dau. of Sir John Pakington, Bart., of Westwood, co. Worcester, and by her (who d. 23 April, 1751) had issue,

JOHN, successor to his half brother as 7th viscount.
Robert Pakington, d. s. p. at Bombay, 1748.
HENRY, 8th viscount.
Frances, bedchamber woman to Queen Charlotte, d. unm.
Anne, m. to John Smith, Esq., of Combhay, co. Somerset.
Dorothy, d. young.
Elizabeth, d. young.

The 5th viscount d. 4 June, 1756, and was s. by his son,

THOMAS-CHARLES TRACY, 6th viscount, b. in July, 1719, who m. Harriet, dau. of Peter Bathurst, Esq., of Clarendon Park, Wilts, by the Lady Selina Shirley, his wife, dau. of Robert, Earl Ferrers, but d. s. p. in 1792, and was s. by his half-brother,

JOHN TRACY, 7th viscount, warden of All Souls' College, Oxford, at whose decease unm. in 1793, aged seventy-one, the honours and estates passed to his brother,

HENRY TRACY, 8th viscount, b. 25 January, 1732, who m. Susannah, dau. of Anthony Weaver, Esq., of Morvil. co. Salop, and left at his decease, 27 April, 1797, an only surviving child and heiress,

The HON. HENRIETTA-SUSANNA TRACY, b. 30 November, 1776, who m. 29 December, 1798, her cousin, CHARLES HANBURY, Esq., who had assumed, by royal license, 10 December, previously, the additional surname and arms of TRACY, and who having been raised to the peerage in 1838, was the 1st BARON SUDELEY, of Toddington.

Since his lordship's decease, the peerage has been DORMANT. It was at one time claimed by James Tracy, who asserted that he was descended from the Hon. Robert Tracy, the judge, and who submitted his case to the House of Lords, by whom it was dismissed. At present another claimant, Benjamin-Wheatley Tracy, Esq., lieut. R.N., asserts a right to the title.

Arms—Or, two bends, gu., in the chief point an escallop, sa.

TREGOZ—BARON TREGOZ.

By Writ of Summons, dated 6 February, 1299.

Lineage.

ROBERT DE TREGOZ, a feudal lord, was sheriff of Wiltshire, in the 3rd RICHARD I., and in three years afterwards was in an expedition then made into Normandy. He m. Sibel, dau. of Robert de Ewyas, and in the 7th JOHN, upon collecting the scutage of that king's reign, answered 38 marks for nineteen knights' fees, belonging to the honour of the said Robert de Ewyas. He was s. by his son,

ROBERT DE TREGOZ, who had a military summons to march against the Welsh, in the 42nd HENRY III., but joining the baronial banner in the same reign, he fell at the battle of Evesham, leaving by Julia, his wife, dau. of William, Lord Cantelupe, two sons, viz.,

JOHN, his heir.
Henry, of Goring, summoned to parliament.

The elder son,

JOHN TREGOZ, doing his homage in the 52nd HENRY III., had livery of his lands; and had such favor from the king, notwithstanding his father's treason, that he was acquitted of 50 marks of the £100 then due for his relief. After which, 10th EDWARD I., he attended the king in an expedition then made into Wales, and in the 22nd of the same reign, being in the campaign of Gascony, he had permission for his wife and family to reside in the castle of Devizes, and to have fuel for their fires there. He was subsequently in the Scottish wars, and was summoned to parliament as a Baron 6 February and 10 April, 1299. His lordship m. Mabel, dau. of Fulk, Lord Fitzwarren, and had issue,

CLARICE, m. to Roger de la Warre, and left a son,
JOHN DE LA WARRE.
SYBIL, m. to Sir William de Grandison, Knt.

He d. in 1300, seised of the castle of Ewyas-Harold, with its members in the marches of Wales, which he held by barony: the manor of Eton-Tregoz, in the co. Hereford, and estates in the cos. Wilts, Salop, and Northampton. At his lordship's decease the Barony of Tregoz fell into ABEYANCE between his grandson, John de la Warre, and his 2nd dau., Sybil de Grandison, as it still continues with their representatives.

Arms—Gu., two bars gemels, and in a chief a lion passant guardant, or.

TREGOZ—BARON TREGOZ.

By Writ of Summons, dated 22 January, 1305.

Lineage.

HENRY DE TREGOZ, of Goring, co. Sussex, a distinguished soldier in the Scottish wars, temp. EDWARD I. and EDWARD II., was summoned to parliament as a Baron, from 22 January, 1305 to 14 March, 1322. He m. Margaret, dau. and heir of John Goring, and was father of

SIR THOMAS DE TREGOZ, who was summoned to parliament as a Baron, 4 January, 1316, and from 20 October, 1332, to 1 April, 1335. He m. Joan, dau. of Lord Poynings, and left a son, Henry, whose line failed, and a dau., Margaret, who m. Sir John D'Oyly, and their dau. and heir, Joan D'Oyly, wife of Thomas Lewknor, was ancestor of Sir Roger Lewknor, Knt, who d. in 1543, leaving four daus., his co-heirs, among whose representatives this Barony of Tregoz is in ABEYANCE.

TREVOR—BARONS TREVOR, AND VISCOUNTS HAMPDEN.

Barony, by Letters Patent, dated 31 December, 1711.
Viscounty, by Letters Patent, dated 14 June, 1776.

Lineage.

This very ancient family derived from one of the most distinguished stocks in Cambrian genealogy, deducing descent from Tudor Trevor, Lord of Hereford, Bromfield, Chirk, both the Maelors, and Oswestry. Eigh'h in descent from this chief was

OWAIN AP BLETHIN, who m. Efa, widow of Iorwerth, son of Owain Brogyntyn, Lord of Edeirnion, Dinmael, and Abertanat, and dau. and co-heiress of Madoc, Lord of Mawddwy, in Merionethshire, younger son of Gwenwynwyn, Prince of Powys-Wenwynwyn. By her he had issue,

I. IORWERTH GAM AP OWAIN, of whose line we have to treat.
II. Thomas ap Owain, progenitor of the PENNANTS OF DOWNING.
III. Owain Vychan ap Owain, from whom derive the DYMOCKS of Penley Hall.

The eldest son,
IORWERTH GAM AP OWAIN, m. Angharad, dau. and co-heir of Griffith ap Meilir ap Elidir, of the Tribe of the Lord of Hereford, and was ancestor of,
EDWARD AP DAVID AP EDNYFED GAM AP IORWERTH VOEL, who m. Angharad, dau. (by Lowrie, sister of OWEN-GLENDOWER, and dau. of Griffith Vychan, Lord of Glyndwrdwy, co. Merioneth,) of Robert Puleston, of Emrall, co. Flint, Esq., and dying in 1448, had issue, I. JOHN; II. Richard-Trevor, progenitor of the TREVORS OF OSWESTRY co. SALOP. The elder son,
JOHN AP DAVID, who assumed the name of TREVOR, acquired the estate of Brynkynallt, co. Denbigh. He m. Agnes, dau. and heir of Peter Cambre, of Poole, and had issue,

I. ROBERT, of Brynkynallt, who m. Catherine, dau. and heir of Llewelyn ap Ithel, of Mold and Plasteg, co. Flint, and from this marriage derived the TREVORS OF BRYNKYNALLT, whose eventual representative, Sir John Trevor, Knt. of Brynkynallt, Speaker of the House of Commons, and First Lord Commissioner of the Great Seal, left an only dau. and heiress, ANNE, who m. Michael Hill, Esq. of Hillsborough, co. Down, and had two sons, TREVOR, created Viscount Hillsborough; and ARTHUR, who inherited the estates of his maternal grandfather, Sir John Trevor, in 1762, upon which he assumed the surname of TREVOR, and was created 27 April, 1765, Baron Hill and Viscount Dungannon.
II. Edward, who m. Anne, dau. of Geoffrey Kyffin, and was presumed ancestor of Col. Mark Trevor, who distinguishing himself by his devotion to the cause of CHARLES I. was raised to the peerage of Ireland as Viscount Dungannon, in 1661. His lordship m. Anne, dau. and heir of John Lewis, Esq., and widow of John Owen, Esq., son and heir of Sir Hugh Owen, of Orielton, co. Pembroke, Bart., but d. s. p. in 1670, when the title became EXTINCT.
III. Richard, of whose line we have to treat.
IV. Roger, who m. and had issue.
V. Thomas, m. Margaret, dau. of John Hanmer, Esq., of Lightwond, and left issue.

The 3rd son,
RICHARD TREVOR, m. Matilda, dau. and heir of Jenkyn ap David ap Griffith, of Allington, co. Denbigh, by whom he had
JOHN TREVOR, of Allington, who m. Margaret, dau. and heir of David ap Rhys ap Kendrick, of Cwm, and was father of
JOHN TREVOR, of Allington, who m. Anne, dau. of Randal Broughton, of Broughton, Esq., and had with other issue, an eldest son and a dau., viz.,

I. JOHN.
II. MARGARET, who m. Roger Jones, of Llwynon, co. Denbigh, Esq.

The eldest son,
JOHN TREVOR, was seated at Trevallyn, in Denbighshire. He m. Mary, dau. of Sir George Bruges, Knt., of London, and had issue,

I. Richard (Sir), of Allington, who m. Catherine, dau. (by Anne, dau. of Richard Grosvenor, of Eaton, co. Chester, Esq.) of Roger Puleston, of Emrall, co. Flint, Esq., and left four daus., his co-heirs, viz.,
Magdalen, m. 1st, Arthur Bagnall, Esq. of Staffordshire; and 2ndly, to — Tyringham, Esq. of Tyringham, co. Bucks.
Mary, m. Evan Lloyd, of Bodidris in-Yale, co. Denbigh, Esq., son of Sir John Lloyd, Knt., Banneret, of Bodidris, and was mother, with other issue, of two sons,
1 John, of Bodidris, father, by Margaret, his wife, dau. of Sir Bevis Thelwall, Knt., of Sir Evan Lloyd, of Bodidris, Bart., so created in 1646.
2 Trevor, ancestor of the LLOYDS OF GLOSTER, King's county.

538

Dorothy, m. Sir John Hanmer, Bart., of Hanmer, co. Flint
Margaret, m. John Griffith, Esq., of Lynn, co. Carnarvon.
II JOHN (Sir), of whom presently.
III. Randulph, d. unm. 21 July, 1590.
IV. Sackville (Sir), a naval officer of high reputation, temp. JAMES I.
V. Thomas (Sir), chief baron of the exchequer, temp. CHARLES I., b. 6 July, 1586, m. Prudence, dau. of Henry Botiler, Esq., and dying 21 December, 1656, was s by his only son and heir, Sir Thomas Trevor, of Enfield, co. Middlesex, Bart., so created 11 August, 1641, m. Anne, dau and heir of Robert Jenner, of London, but d. s. p., when the baronetcy became EXTINCT.
I Winifred, m. Edward Puleston, Esq., of Allington, co. Denbigh.

Mr. Trevor d. 15 July, 1589, and was s. by his 2nd son,
SIR JOHN TREVOR, of Trevallyn, knighted 7 June, 1618, who m. Margaret, dau. of Hugh Trevannion, Esq., of Cornwall, and had issue,

I. John (Sir), who pre-deceased his father, and was one of the principal secretaries of state, and member of the privy council in the reign of CHARLES II. He m. Ruth, dau. of John Hampden, Esq., of Great Hampden, co. Bucks, and left at his decease, 28 May, 1672, with two younger sons, Richard and Edward, two elder sons,
1 JOHN, of Trevallyn, who m. Elizabeth (Clark), widow of William, eldest son of Colonel Herbert Morley, of Glynde, M.P. for Lewes, and by her (who m. 3rdly, the Lord Viscount Cutts,) had issue,
1 JOHN-MORLEY, his heir.
2 Thomas, b. in 1684, d. in 1707.
3 William.
1 Elizabeth, m. to David Polhill, Esq., of Otford, co. Kent.
2 Arabella, m. 1st, to Robert Heath, Esq., of Lewes; and 2ndly, to Col. Edward Montague, only brother of George, Earl of Halifax.
The eldest son,
JOHN-MORLEY TREVOR, Esq., of Trevallyn, Plasteg, and Glynde, b. in 1681, m. Lucy, dau. of Edward Montague, Esq., of Horton, co. Northampton, and dying 12 April, 1719, left issue,
1 John-Morley, d. in 1706, aged two years.
2 Thomas, d. in 1807, aged three months.
3 JOHN-TREVOR, of Trevallyn, Plasteg, and Glynde, commissioner of the Admiralty in 1742, d. s. p in 1745, having m. Elizabeth, dau. of Sir Thomas Frankland, of Thirkleby, co. York, who pre-deceased him in 1742.
1 Lucy, b. in 1706, m. Edward Rice, Esq., of Newtown, M.P. for Carmarthen, and was mother of George Rice, Esq., of Newtown, M.P. for Carmarthenshire, who m. 16 August, 1756, Cecil, Baroness Dynevor, only dau. of William Talbot, 2nd Baron, and 1st Earl Talbot, created Baron Dynevor, of Dynevor (see BURKE's Extant Peerage).
2 Grace, d. unm.
3 Mary, b. in 1708, d. unm.
4 ANN, m. 17 July, 1743, the Hon. George Boscawen, a general in the army, and by him who d. 3 May, 1775, had issue,
George, of Trevallyn and Plasteg, b. 4 September, 1745, m. Annabella, 2nd dau. of the Rev. Sir William Bunbury, Bart., and d. s. p. 14 October, 1833.
WILLIAM, b. in 1752, m. in 1786, Charlotte, 2nd dau. of the Rev. James Ibbetson, D.D., archdeacon of St. Albans, and d. in 1811, leaving issue,
Grace-Trevor-Charlotte, m. 1st, in 1828, William Fleming Esq., and 2ndly, in 1838, the Rev. James-Sydney Darvell.
Anne-Arabella, m. the Rev. Christopher Parkins, of Gresford.
Catherine-Emily, m. 1st, in 1823, Henry Rowlands, Esq., and 2ndly, to the Rev. Fletcher Fleming, of Rayrigg, Westmoreland.
ELIZABETH-MARY, m. to Thos. Griffith, Esq., after wards seated at Trevallyn.
Julia, d. unm. in 1832.
Anne, maid of honour to Queen CHARLOTTE, d. in 1831
Charlotte, d. in 1829, aged eighty-two.
5 Margaret, b. in 1710, d. unm.
6 Ruth, b. in 1712, d. unm. in 1764.
7 Gertrude, m. to the Hon. Charles Roper, 3rd son of Henry, 8th Baron Teynham, and had issue,
1 Charles-Trevor Roper, 18th Lord Dacre.
2 Henry, lieut.-col. in the army, killed in a duel, m. 1 Gertrude, who s. her brother in the Barony of Dacre.
(See BURKE's Extant Peerage.)
8 Arabella, b. in 1714, d. unm.
9 Lucy, d. an infant.
2 THOMAS, of whom we treat
3 Richard.
II. William.   III. Richard, M.D.
I. Anne, m. to Robert Weldon, Esq., of London.
II. Jane, m. to the Hon Sir Francis Compton, 5th son of Spencer, Earl of Northampton.
III. Elizabeth, m. to William Masham, Esq., eldest son of Sir William Masham, Bart.

Sir John Trevor *d.* in 1673, and his eldest grandson, John Trevor Esq., inherited Trevallin, while the next,

THOMAS TREVOR, was brought up to the profession of the law, and having attained reputation at the bar, was made solicitor-general in 1692, when he received the honour of knighthood. In 1695, he became attorney-general, and on the accession of Queen ANNE, was constituted lord chief justice of the Court of Common Pleas, when he was elevated to the peerage, 31 December, 1711, as BARON TREVOR, *of Bromham, co. Bedford.* In 1726, he was appointed lord privy seal, and the next year he was declared one of the lords justices. On the accession of GEORGE II. he was again sworn lord privy seal, and in three years afterwards constituted president of the council. His lordship *m.* 1st, Elizabeth, dau. and co-heir of John Searle, Esq., of Finchley, co. Middlesex, by whom he had issue,

  I. THOMAS, } successively Lords Trevor.
  II. JOHN, }
  I. Anne.
  II. Lætitia, *m.* to Peter Cock, Esq., of Camberwell.
  III. Elizabeth.

Lord Trevor *m* 2ndly, Anne, dau. of Robert Weldon, Esq., and widow of Sir Robert Bernard, Bart., of Brampton, co. Huntingdon, and by her had issue,

  III. ROBERT, who *s.* as 4th lord.
  IV. Richard, in holy orders, consecrated bishop of St. David's in 1744, translated to the see of Durham in 1752, and *d. unm.* 9 June, 1771.
  V. Edward, *d.* young.

His lordship *d.* 19 June, 1730, and was *s.* by his eldest son,

THOMAS TREVOR, 2nd baron. This nobleman *m.* Elizabeth, dau. of Timothy Burrell, Esq., of Cuckfield, co. Sussex, barrister at law, by whom he had an only dau.,

ELIZABETH, *m.* to Charles, 2nd Duke of Marlborough.

He *d.* 22 March, 1753, and was *s.* by his brother,

JOHN TREVOR, 3rd baron, who had previously served in parliament for Woodstock, was a king's counsel, and one of the Welsh judges. His lordship *m.* Elizabeth, dau. of the celebrated SIR RICHARD STEELE, and left an only dau., Diana, *b.* 10 June, 1744. He *d.* 27 September, 1764, and was *s.* by his half brother,

ROBERT TREVOR, 4th baron, *b.* in 1701. This nobleman, in compliance with the testamentary injunction of John Hampden, Esq., of Great Hampden, assumed the surname and arms of Hampden. His lordship was several years envoy-extraordinary to the States-General, and was constituted in 1746 one of the commissioners of the revenue in Ireland. In 1759 he was made joint postmaster-general with the Earl of Bessborough, which office he held until the year 1765, and was created 14 June, 1776, VISCOUNT HAMPDEN, of Hampden, co. Bucks. His lordship *m.* in 1743, Constantia, dau. of Peter Anthony de Huybert, Lord of Van Kruningen, of Holland, and had issue,

  I. THOMAS, his successor.
  II. John, who was appointed, 8 April, 1780, minister-plenipotentiary to the diet at Raleston, and 22 February, 1783, to the court of Sardinia. He *s.* to the honours as 3rd viscount.
  I. Maria-Constantia, *m.* 25 May, 1764, to Henry Howard, 12th Earl of Suffolk, and 5th Earl of Berkshire, by whom she had no surviving issue. Her ladyship *d.* in 1767.
  II. Anne, *d. unm.* in 1760.

His lordship, who was distinguished by his classical taste, *d.* 22 August, 1783, and was *s.* by his elder son,

THOMAS TREVOR-HAMPDEN, 2nd viscount. This nobleman *m.* in 1768, Catherine, dau. of General David Græme, but *d. s. p.* in 1824, when the honours devolved upon his brother,

JOHN TREVOR-HAMPDEN, as 3rd viscount, *b.* 24 February, 1748-9. His lordship *m.* in 1773, Harriet, only dau. of the Rev. Daniel Burton, D.D., canon of Christ-church, but had no issue. His lordship, at one time envoy to the court of Sardinia, *d.* in 1824, when all his honours became EXTINCT.

Arms—Per bend, sinister, ermine and erminois, a lion rampant, or.

TREVOR—VISCOUNT DUNGANNON.

By Letters Patent, dated 28 August, 1662.

Lineage.

COLONEL MARK or MARCUS TREVOR (presumed to have descended from Edward, younger brother of Robert Trevor, Esq., of Brynkinallt, co. Denbigh), having distinguished himself by his devotion to the cause of CHARLES I., and for his signal gallantry in wounding Oliver Cromwell at Marston

539

Moor, was created Baron Trevor, of Rose Trevor, co. Down, and VISCOUNT DUNGANNON, 28 August, 1662. He *m.* 1st, Frances, dau. and co-heir of Sir Marmaduke Whitechurch, of Loughbrickland; and 2ndly, Anne, dau. and heir of John Lewis, Esq., and relict of John Owen, Esq., of Oriclton. His eldest dau. (by his 1st wife) Mary, became the 2nd wife of William Hill, Esq., of Hillsborough, co. Down, and was mother of MARCUS HILL, Esq., of Holt Forest, Hants, who *d. unm.*, 6 April, 1751, having bequeathed his property to Lord Hillsborough. The title became EXTINCT, 8 November, 1706.

Arms—Per bend, sinister, erm. and erminois, a lion rampant, or.

TREVOR—VISCOUNTS DUNGANNON.

By Letters Patent, dated 27 April, 1765.

Lineage.

MICHAEL HILL, Esq., of Hillsborough, co. Down, who *m.* Anne, only dau. of Sir John Trevor, Knt., of Brynkinallt, co. Denbigh, Speaker of the English House of Commons, and subsequently first lord-commissioner of the great seal (chief of a branch of the "Tribe of the Marches," established by Tudor Trevor, Lord of Hereford), had by her two sons, TREVOR, created *Viscount Hillsborough,* founder of the noble house of Downshire; and ARTHUR HILL, Esq., M.P. for the co. Down in 1727, who *s.* to the estates of his maternal grandfather, Sir John Trevor, in 1762, upon which occasion he assumed the additional surname of TREVOR, and was created 27 April, 1765, VISCOUNT DUNGANNON, *of Dungannon, co. Tyrone, and Baron Hill, of Olderfleet, co. Antrim,* in the peerage of Ireland. His lordship *m.* 1st, Anne, 3rd dau. and co-heir of the Right Hon. Joseph Deane, chief baron of the court of Exchequer in Ireland, but had no issue. He *m.* 2ndly, 12 January, 1737, Anne, dau. and heir of Edmund-Francis Stafford, Esq., of Mount Stafford, co Antrim, by whom he had,

  Arthur, M.P., *b.* 24 December, 1738, *m.* 27 February, 1762, Letitia, eldest dau. of Hervey, 1st Viscount Mountmorres, and by her (who *m.* 2ndly, Randal-William, 1st Marquess of Antrim, and *d.* 7 December, 1801) left at his decease, 19 June, 1770, an only son, ARTHUR, 2nd viscount.
  Anne, *b.* 23 June, 1742, *m.* to Garret, 1st Earl of Mornington; her ladyship, who was mother of the great Duke of Wellington, *d.* 10 December, 1831.
  Prudence, *b.* 17 March, 1745, *m.* 22 May, 1765, to Charles-Powell Leslie, Esq., who *d.* in 1800

The viscount *d.* 30 January, 1771, and was *s.* by his grandson,

ARTHUR HILL-TREVOR, 2nd viscount, *b.* 2 October, 1763, *m.* 30 July, 1795, Charlotte, dau. of Charles, 1st Lord Southampton, and by her ladyship (who *d.* 22 November, 1828,) had two sons,

  ARTHUR, 3rd and last viscount.
  Charles-Henry, *b.* 21 September, 1801, *d. unm.* 18 September, 1823.

His lordship *d.* 14 December, 1837, and was *s.* by his only surviving son,

ARTHUR HILL-TREVOR, 3rd viscount, M.A., F.A.S., M.R.I.A., and M.R.S.L., a representative peer, *b.* 9 November, 1798, *m.* 10 September, 1821, Sophia, 4th dau. of Colonel Gorges-Marcus D'Arcy-Irvine, of Castle Irvine, co. Fermanagh, and *d. s. p.* 11 August, 1862, when his honours became EXTINCT. Brynkinallt and his other estates devolved on his kinsman, Lord Arthur Edwin Hill (only surviving brother of the Marquess of Downshire), who has assumed, by royal license, the additional surname and arms of TREVOR.

Arms—Quarterly: 1st and 4th, party per bend sinister, erm. and ermines, a lion rampant, or, for TREVOR; 2nd and 3rd, sa., on a fesse, arg., between three leopards passant-guardant, or, spotted of the field, three escallops, gu., for HILL

TRUSSEL—BARON TRUSSEL.

By Writ of Summons, dated 25 February, 1342.

Lineage.

Of this very ancient Warwickshire family, was

RICHARD TRUSSEL, who fell at the battle of Evesham, 4th HENRY III., as also,

WILLIAM TRUSSEL, of Cublesdon, co. Stafford (which manor the Trussels acquired by Roese, dau. and heir of William Pandolf, who had married into the family). This William was father of another

WILLIAM TRUSSEL, who *m.* Maud, dau. and heir of Warine Mainwaring, and from him descended

SIR WILLIAM TRUSSEL, who *m.* Bridget, dau. of William Kene (by Elizabeth, dau. of William Chicele, and niece of Henry Chicele, archbishop of Canterbury, *temp.* HENRY VI.), and was father of

SIR EDWARD TRUSSEL, K.B., *m.* Margaret, dau. of Sir John Dun, and had,

John, *d. s. p.* 1499.
ELIZABETH TRUSSEL, *m.* in the time of HENRY VIII., John Vere, Earl of Oxford.

But the principal branch of the family remaining, according to Dugdale, was that some time resident at Cublesdon, of whi h was

WILLIAM TRUSSEL, who, in the 22nd EDWARD I., A.D. 1294, received command to repair to the king, to consult upon the important affairs of the realm; and had subsequently a military summons to march into Gascony. He was *s.* by (his supposed nephew) another

WILLIAM TRUSSEL, who, in the 15th EDWARD II., A.D 1322, being one of the adherents of Thomas, Earl of Lancaster, was exiled in consequence, but returned in five years afterwards with Queen Isabel and Prince Edward, at the head of a considerable force, against the power of the Spencers, one of whom being brought afterwards to trial, had judgment passed upon him by this William, who was at that time in such estimation with the commons in convention assembled, as to be chosen their organ to pronounce the deposition of the unfortunate EDWARD II., which duty he executed in the following words;—" Ego Will. Trussell, *vice omnium de Terrâ Angliæ et totius parliamenti procurator, tibi Edwardo reddo homagium prius tibi factum et extunc diffido te, et privo omne potestate regiâ et dignitate.*" On the accession of EDWARD III , 1327, he was constituted escheator-general on the south of Trent, but soon after, being opposed as strongly to the influence of Mortimer as he had previously been to that of the Spencers, he was again obliged to fly the kingdom, and to remain in exile until the favourite's fall; when, returning, he was reinvested with the escheatorship. In the 13th EDWARD III., he was admiral of the royal navy, from the mouth of the Thames westward; and in two years afterwards, being then a knight, he was in the expedition made into Flanders, and the same year in the Scottish campaign. In the 16th, A.D. 1342, being in the great expedition made into France, he was summoned to parliament as a Baron, and constituted admiral of all the fleet, from the mouth of the Thames to Berwick-upon-Tweed, his lordship's residence being then at Cublesdon. For the two following years he continued employed in the French campaigns, and two years afterwards he sat in judgment with Sir William Thorpe, chief justice of the Court of King's Bench, at the Tower of London, upon the Earls of Fife and Monteith, when the latter nobleman was hanged, drawn, and quartered, but the former spared. His lordship appears to have had but one summons to parliament, and the barony at his decease, became EXTINCT.

Arms—Arg. frettée, gu., on each joint a bezant.

NOTE.—Besides the above, there was another
WILLIAM TRUSSEL, who, in the 37th EDWARD III , 1363, was at the battle of Poictiers, in the immediate retinue of the Black Prince, and for his services, obtained from that gallant personage, a grant of £40 per annum for life, to be paid out of the exchequer at Chester. This William *m.* Idonea, sister of Edward de Boteler, and left an only dau., MARGARET TRUSSEL, who *m.* Fulk de Pembruge, and *d. s. p*

TUDOR—EARLS OF RICHMOND.

By Letters Patent, dated 23 November, 1452.

Lineage.

EDNYFED VYCHAN AP KENDRIG, Lord of Brynffenigl, in Denbighland, and Krigeth in Efinoydd, chief counsellor, chief Justice, and general of LLEWELYN AP IORWERTH, King of North Wales, was one of the most prominent historical characters of the period. Commanding in the wars between Llewelyn, Prince of North Wales, and JOHN, King of England, he attacked the army of Ranulph, Earl of Chester, and achieving a signal victory, killed three chief captains and commanders of the enemy, whose heads he laid at the feet of his sovereign. For this exploit he had conferred on him new armorial ensigns emblematic of the occasion, which continue to be borne by the LLOYDS *of Plymog,* and other families derived from him.

He *m.* twice, 1st, Tangwystyl, dau. of Llowarch ap Bran, Lord of Menai, in Anglesey, cotemporary with Owen Gwynedd, Prince of North Wales, and by her had issue,

I. Tudor (Sir), ap Ednyfed Vychan, of Nant and Llangynhafal, one of the commissioners for the conclusion of peace between EDWARD I., King of England, and LLEWELYN AP IORWERTH, King of North Wales. He *m.* Adlais, dau. of Richard, son of Cadwallader, 2nd son of GRIFFITH AP CYNAN, King of North Wales, and was ancestor of I. Morgans of Golden Grove; II. Williamses of Cochwillan; III. Williamses of Meillionydd and Ystymcollwyn; IV. Williams-Bulkeleys of Penrhyn, Barts.; v. Williamses of Vaenol, Barts.; VI. Owens of Penmynydh; VII. Griffiths, Lords of Penrhyn; VIII. Hughes of Prestatyn and Feador; IX. Lloyds of Nant.
II. Llewellyn ap Ednyfed Vychan, who had a moiety of Creuthyn in Yale
III. KENDRIG AP EDNYFED VYCHAN, ancestor of the Lloyds of Plymog, co. Denbigh.
IV Rhys ap Ednyfed Vychan, of Garth Garmon.
v. Howel ap Ednyfed Vychan, consecrated bishop of St. Asaph, 25th HENRY III.
VI. Rhys ap Ednyfed Vychan, of Garth Garmon, ancestor of the LLOYDS of Gydros.
VII. Iorwerth ap Ednyfed Vychan, Lord of Abermarlais, in Glandowi, co. Carmarthen.
I. Angharad, *m.* Einion Vychan ap Einion, of Plas-yn-nant, in Llanganhafel, co. Anglesey.
II. Gwenllian, *m.* Llewellyn the Great, Prince of North Wales.

Ednyfed Vychan *m.* 2ndly, Gwenllian, dau. of Rhys ap Griffith, Lord of South Wales, representative of the sovereign princes of South Wales, by whom he had issue,

I. GRONO AP EDNYFED VYCHAN, Lord of Tref-Gastel.
II. Griffith ap Ednyfed Vychan, of Henglawdd, father of Sir Rhys Griffith, Knt., whose son, SIR GRIFFITH LLWYD, received from EDWARD I. the honour of knighthood on bringing him intelligence of the birth of his son, Edward of Carnarvon.

The eldest son of Ednyfed Vychan, by Gwenllian, his 2nd wife,

GRONO AP EDNYFED VYCHAN, Lord of Tref-Gastel, in Anglesey, chief counsellor of Llewelyn ap Griffith, Prince of North Wales, *m.* Morfydd, dau. of Meuric ap Ithel, Lord of Gwent, and had, with junior issue,

TUDOR AP GRONO, of Penmynedd, who built the priory of Bangor, and did homage for his lands to EDWARD I. at Chester. By Angharad, his wife, dau. of Ithel Vychan, of Englefield, in Flint, he left at his decease in 1311, an only son,
GRONO AP TUDOR, captain of twenty archers in Aquitaine, 43rd EDWARD III. He *m.* Gwervyl, dau. of Madoc ap David, Baron of Hendwr, co. Merioneth, and *d.* in 1331. The eldest son of this marriage,
SIR TUDOR AP GRONO, Knt., of Penmynedd, who *d.* in 1367, *m.* Margaret, dau. and co-heir (with her elder sister, Eleanor, wife of Griffith Vychan, Lord of Glyndwrdwy, and mother of OWEN GLENDOWER) of Thomas ap Llewelyn Lord of South Wales, representative of the sovereign princes of South Wales, by Eleanor Goch, his wife, dau. and heir of Philip, Lord of Iscoed in Cardigan, by Princess Catherine, dau and heir of Llewelyn, last Prince of North Wales. Of this alliance there was, with other issue, a son,
MEREDITH AP TUDOR, who *m.* Margaret, dau. of David Vychan ap David Llwyd, of Anglesey, and was father of
SIR OWEN TUDOR, who *m.* Queen Katherine of Valois, widow of King HENRY V. of England, and dau. of CHARLES VI. of France, by whom he had issue,

I. EDMUND, of whose line we now treat.
II. JASPER, created Earl of Pembroke. (*See* next article.)
I. Tacina, *m.* to Sir Reginald Grey, Lord Grey, of Wilton.

Sir Owen Tudor, who was taken prisoner at the battle of Mortimer's Cross, fighting for the Red Rose, was beheaded in 1461. His elder son,
EDMUND TUDOR, surnamed of Hadham, having been *b.* at that place in co. Bedford, was created by his half-brother, King HENRY VI., 23 November, 1452, EARL OF RICHMOND, with precedency of all other earls; and the same year he had a grant from the king, in fee, of the mansion-house of Baynard's Castle, in the city of London. He *m.* the Lady Margaret Beaufort, dau. and heiress of John, Duke of Somerset, and great-granddau. of John of Gaunt, by his last wife Catherine Swineford. It has been discovered, that in the original patent of legitimacy to the BEAUFORTS, the children of John of Gaunt, born before wedlock, of his last wife, Catherine Swineford (which, as it was ratified by parliament, parliament alone could alter), the exception of inheritance to the crown does not occur; the words "excepta dignitate regali," being inserted only by the caution of HENRY IV., in his confirmation ten years after. The Earl of Richmond *d.* in 1456, and his remains were interred in the cathedral of St. David's in Wales, with the following epitaph:—
" Under this marble stone here inclosed, resteth the bones of the noble Lord, Edmund, Earl of Richmond, father and

brother to kings; the which departed out of this world in the year of our Lord, 1456, the 3rd of the month of November; on whose soul, almighty Jesus have mercy, Amen."

The Countess of Richmond having outlived her husband, m. 2ndly, Henry, a younger son of Humphrey Stafford, Duke of Buckingham, and 3rdly. Thomas, Lord Stanley, afterwards Earl of Derby; but had issue by neither. Her ladyship provided in her last will, dated 6 January, 1508, for two perpetual readerships in divinity, the Margaret Professorships of Divinity, one at each of the universities; and she founded the school at Cambridge, called Christ's Church; she also left provision for "a perpetual preacher of the word of God," in the same university. This exemplary lady d. 29 June, 1509.

At the death of the Earl of Richmond in 1456, he was s. by his son,

HENRY TUDOR, 2nd Earl of Richmond, then but fifteen weeks old. This noble infant being removed by his uncle, Jasper, Earl of Pembroke, into Brittany, remained there during the whole of EDWARD IV.'s reign, under the protection of Francis, Duke of Provence, notwithstanding various efforts made by the English monarch to obtain possession of his person. At one time, Polydore Virgil relates, the duke, confiding in the pledge of EDWARD, to marry the young earl to his dau., Elizabeth, and thus unite for ever the red and white roses, had actually delivered him up to the English ambassadors, and that they had conveyed him to St. Malo, on his way to England, but were detained by the earl's falling ill of a dangerous fever. In the interim, one John Chenlet, who had great influence in the ducal court, flew to the presence of the duke, and feelingly depicted the perils in which he had placed this last scion of Lancaster. To which his highness replied, "Hold thy peace, John, there is no such danger at all; for King EDWARD resolves to make him his son-in-law." But to this Chenlet instantly returned: "Believe me, most illustrious duke, he is already very near death; and if you permit him to be carried one step out of your dominions, no mortal man can preserve him from it." At which the duke, being not a little troubled, immediately despatched Peter Landose, his third treasurer, to St. Malo, with orders to bring the earl back. Peter, on hastening thither, is said to have detained the ambassadors 'rith a long speech, while his servants conveyed the object of his care to a sanctuary in the city, whence he was soon after conducted in safety to his former residence. The subsequent contest between the Earl of Richmond and RICHARD III., our historians and poets have so minutely detailed, that it would be idle to pursue the subject here, further than to record the simple fa t, that the victory of Bosworth placed the crown of England on the head of Richmond, and terminated the wars of the ROSES. Upon the earl ascending the throne as HENRY VII., the Earldom of Richmond merged in the crown.

Arms—Quarterly: France and England, a border. az., charged with eight martlets, or.

TUDOR—EARL OF PEMBROKE, DUKE OF BEDFORD.

Earldom, 6 March, 1453.
Dukedom, 27 October, 1485.

Lineage.

JASPER TUDOR, surnamed of Hatfield, the place of his birth, 2nd son of Sir Owen Tudor, by KATHERINE, Queen Dowager of King HENRY V. (*see preceding article*), was advanced by his half-brother, HENRY VI., in the parliament held at Reading, *anno* 1453, to the EARLDOM OF PEMBROKE, at the same time that his brother, EDMUND, of Hadham, was made Earl of Richmond. This nobleman being afterwards one of the main pillars of the cause of Lancaster, was attainted and forced to fly when EDWARD IV. obtained the crown, and the Earldom of Pembroke was then conferred upon William Herbert, Lord Herbert, of Chepstow. Joining, subsequently, with the Earl of Warwick, he had a principal part in the temporary restoration of HENRY VI., and at that period he had the good fortune to find his nephew, Henry, Earl of Richmond, in the custody of William Herbert's (Earl of Pembroke) widow, and presenting the boy to King HENRY, that monarch is said prophetically to have exclaimed—"This is he who shall quietly possess, what we and our adversaries do now contend for." The total overthrow of the Lancastrians at Barnet Field, and the re-establishment of EDWARD upon the throne again, however, broke down the

fortunes of Jasper Tudor, and forced him, after some hair-breadth escapes, to seek an asylum for himself and his nephew, at the court of Brittany. Here, during the remainder of the reign of EDWARD IV., protection was afforded them, and here, in the reign of RICHARD III., they planned the enterprize which led to the triumph of Bosworth. Upon the accession of his nephew, as HENRY VII., Jasper Tudor was created DUKE OF BEDFORD at the Tower of London, 27 October, 1485. He was next sworn amongst the chief of the privy council, and constituted one of the commissioners to execute the duties of high steward of England at the king's coronation. His grace was afterwards appointed justice of South Wales, and lord-lieutenant of Ireland for two years; he likewise obtained considerable grants from the crown, and was invested with the Garter. Upon the insurrection of the Earl of Lincoln in behalf of the Pretender Simnell, the Duke of Bedford was nominated joint commander with the Earl of Oxford, of the forces sent to oppose the Simnellites, and he ever enjoyed the entire confidence of the king. He m. Catherine, 6th and youngest dau. of Richard Wydeville, Earl Rivers, and widow of Henry, Duke of Buckingham, by whom (who m. after his decease Sir Richard Wingfield, K.G.,) he had no issue. He left, however, an illegitimate dau., Helen, who m. William Gardiner, citizen of London, and was mother of Stephen Gardiner, bishop of Winchester. He d. 21 December, 1495, when the Earldom of Pembroke and the Dukedom of Bedford became EXTINCT.

Arms—Quarterly: France and England, a border, az., charged with eight martlets, or.

TUDOR—DUKE OF YORK.

By Letters Patent, dated 31 October, 1494.

Lineage.

HENRY TUDOR, 2nd son of King HENRY VII., was created 31 October, 1494, DUKE OF YORK, but at the death of his elder brother, Arthur, he s. to the Dukedom of Cornwall, and was created Prince of Wales. His royal highness subsequently ascended the throne as HENRY VIII., when all his honours merged in the crown.

TUDOR—DUKE OF SOMERSET.

By Letters Patent, *anno* 1499.

Lineage.

EDMUND TUDOR, 3rd son of King HENRY VII., was created, in 1499, DUKE OF SOMERSET. He d. however, under five years of age, in 1499, when the dukedom became EXTINCT.

TUFTON—BARONS TUFTON AND EARLS OF THANET.

Barony, by Letters Patent, dated 1 November, 1626.
Earldom, by Letters Patent, dated 5 August, 1628.

Lineage.

The surname of this family, TOKETON, as originally written, was derived from a place of that name in Kent, of which its remote ancestors were feudal lords.

NICHOLAS TUFTON, of Northyam, co. Sussex, m. Margaret, dau. and heiress of John Heaver, of Cranbrook, in Kent, and dying 31 December, 1538, was s. by his son,

JOHN TUFTON, Esq., of Hothfield, co. Kent, sheriff of that shire, 4th Queen ELIZABETH, who m. Mary, eldest dau. of Sir John Baker, of Sisinghurst, chancellor and under-treasurer of the exchequer, and left at his decease, 10 October, 1567, a dau., Cecily, m. to Sir Thomas Sondes, and an only son,

SIR JOHN TUFTON, Knt., of Hothfield, high sheriff of Kent, 18th Queen ELIZABETH, who was created a Baronet, 19 June, 1611. Sir John m. 1st, Olympia, dau. and heiress of Christopher Blower, Esq., of Sileham, in Kent, and had three daus. viz., Anne, m. to Francis Tresham, Esq., of Rushton; Elizabeth, d. young; and Margaret, m. to Sir Thomas Carill, Knt., of Benton and Shipley, co. Sussex. He *m.* 2n.lly, Christian, dau. and co-heiress of Sir Humphrey Brown, Knt., one of the justices of the Court of Common Pleas, by whom he had six sons and four daus. He *d.* 2 April, 1624, and was *s.* by his eldest son,

Sir Nicholas Tufton, Knt. This gentleman, being amongst those who met King James I. at Newcastle-upon-Tyne, on his coming into England, received the honour of knighthood from that monarch, 13 April, 1603, and was elevated to the peerage, 1 November, 1626, in the dignity of *Baron Tufton, of Tufton, co. Sussex,* and created Earl of Thanet, 5 August, 1628. His lordship *m.* Lady Frances Cecil, dau. of Thomas, 1st Earl of Exeter, and had issue to survive,

John, his successor.
Cecil, father of Sir Charles Tufton, Knt., of Twickenham.
Elizabeth, *m.* to Sir Edward Dering, Bart.
Dorothy, *m.* to Sir Ralph Assheton, Bart.
Mary, *m.* to Sir Edward Bisshopp, Bart.
Diana, *m.* to Sir Robert Curzon, of Water Pery, co. Oxon, Knt.
Christian, *m.* to William Milward, of Chilcote, co. Derby, son and heir of Sir Thomas Milward, of Eaton, co. Derby, Knt.

He *d.* 1 July, 1632, and was *s.* by his eldest surviving son,
John Tufton, 2nd earl, who *m.* 21 April, 1629, Lady Margaret Sackville, eldest dau. and co-heiress of Richard, 3rd Earl of Dorset, by Anne, Baroness Clifford, only dau. and heiress of George, Earl of Cumberland, and had issue, Nicholas, John, Richard, Thomas, successively Earls of Thanet; Sackville; and George, buried at Raynham, 1670; Anne, *d.* young; Margaret, *m.* to George, Lord Coventry; Frances, *m.* to Henry Drax, Esq., of Boston, co. Lincoln; Cecilie, *m.* to Christopher, Lord Hatton; Mary, *m.* to William, son and heir of Sir William Walter, of Saresden, co. Oxon, Bart.; Anne, *m.* to Samuel Grimston, son and heir of Sir Harbottle Grimston, Bart., master of the Rolls. This nobleman was obliged to compound for his estate with the sequestrators of the rebel parliament at no less a sum than £9000, which, it is observable, is the largest compromise in the list of 1654. His lordship *d.* 6 May, 1664. His eldest son,
Nicholas Tufton, 3rd earl, *b.* 7 August, 1631, *m.* 11 April, 1664, Elizabeth, 2nd dau. of Richard Boyle, Earl of Burlington, by whom (who *d.* in 1725) he had no issue. In 1655, the earl was committed by Cromwell to the Tower, but soon afterwards released. He was, however, re-committed, in 1656, and detained for nearly two years. In 1678 he inherited the Barony of Clifford at the decease of his mother, but *d. s. p.* 24 November, 1679, when all his honours devolved upon his brother,
John Tufton, 4th earl, *b.* 7 August, 1638, who had previously *s.* his mother, one of the co-heiresses of the Earl of Dorset, in the estates of Clifford, Westmoreland, and Vesey; and his cousin, Lady Alathea Hungerford, wife of Edward Hungerford, Esq., and only dau. and heiress of James, Earl of Northampton, by Isabella, youngest dau. and co-heiress of his grandfather, Richard, Earl of Dorset, whereby he became possessed of the whole inheritance of his grandmother Anne, only dau. and heiress of George, Earl of Cumberland, who *m.* 1st, Richard, Earl of Dorset, and after his decease, Philip, Earl of Montgomery and Pembroke. The Earl of Thanet dying *unm.* 27 April, 1680, all his honours and estates passed to his brother,
Richard Tufton, 5th earl, who *d. unm.* 8 March, 1683-4, when the honours devolved upon his brother,
Thomas Tufton, 6th earl. This nobleman *m.* in 1684, Lady Catherine Cavendish, dau. and co-heiress of Henry, Duke of Newcastle, by whom he had three sons, who *d.* in infancy, and five daus., his co-heirs, viz.,

Catherine, *m.* to Edward Watson, Viscount Sondes, heir-apparent of Lewis, Earl of Rockingham, and had issue, Lewis, 2nd Earl of Rockingham; Thomas, 3rd Earl of Rockingham; Edward, *d. unm.*; Catherine, *m.* to Edward Southwell, Esq., of King's Weston, and her son. Edward Southwell, inherited, in 1776, the Barony of De Clifford.
Anne, *m.* to James, 5th Earl of Salisbury.
Margaret, *m.* to Thomas Coke, Earl of Leicester, and was declared, in 1734, Baroness Clifford.
Mary, *m.* 1st, to Anthony Grey, Earl of Harold, and 2ndly, to John, 1st Earl Gower.
Isabella, *m.* 1st, to Lord Nassau Paulett, and 2ndly, to Sir F. Blake-Delaval, K.B.

His lordship claimed the Baronies of Clifford and Vesey, in right of inheritance from his grandmother, and that of Clifford was confirmed to him by the House of Lords, 12 December, 1691, when he assumed the additional title of *Baron Clifford,* which barony at his decease, in 1729, fell into abeyance between his daus. and co-heirs, and so continued until the crown, in 1734, interposed in favour of Margaret, Countess of Leicester, his lordship's 3rd dau.; but at her lady-

542

ship's decease without issue, in 1775, it relapsed into abeyance between her sisters, which abeyance the crown again terminated, in 1776, in favour of Edward Southwell, as stated above. The Earl of Thanet's other honours reverted to his nephew,
Sackville Tufton, Esq., as 7th earl (eldest surviving son of the Hon. Col. Sackville Tufton, of the guards, by Elizabeth, his wife, dau. and sole heir of Ralph Wilbraham, Esq., of Newbottle, co. Northampton, 2nd son of Sir Thomas Wilbraham, Bart). This nobleman *m.* in 1722, Lady Mary Savile, youngest dau. and co-heiress of William, Marquess of Halifax, by whom he had surviving issue,

Sackville, his successor.
Mary, *m.* to Sir William Duncan, Bart., one of the royal physicians, and *d.* in 1806.
Charlotte, *d.* in 1803.

His lordship *d.* 4 December, 1753, and was *s.* by his son,
Sackville Tufton, 8th earl, *b.* 1733; *m.* 30 August, 1767, Mary, dau. of Lord John Sackville, and granddau. of Lionel, 1st Duke of Dorset, and sister of John-Frederick, the 3rd duke, by whom he had,

Sackville, his successor.
Charles, who *s.* his brother.
Henry, last earl.
Elizabeth, *m.* 16 September, 1819.
Caroline, *m.* 26 July, 1792, to Joseph-Foster Barham, Esq., M.P., who *d.* 28 September, 1832. Lady Caroline Barham *d.* 3 November in the same year, leaving with other issue, the late John-Foster Barham, Esq., of Treewn, co. Pembroke, M.P., and the late Rev. Charles-Henry Barham, of Treewn.

His lordship *d.* 10 April, 1786, and was *s.* by his eldest son,
Sackville Tufton, 9th earl, *b.* 30 June, 1769; *m.* 28 February, 1811, Anne-Charlotte de Bojunovitz, a noble lady of Hungary, who *d. s. p.* in 1819. His lordship *d.* in January, 1825, when the honours of the family devolved upon his next brother,
Charles Tufton, 10th earl, *b.* 10 September, 1770, who dying *unm.*, in April, 1832, was *s.* by his only surviving brother,
Henry Tufton, 11th Earl, *b.* 2 January, 1775. His lordship, who was lord lieutenant of Kent, and hereditary sheriff of the co. Westmoreland, *d. unm.*, 12 June, 1849, when the title became extinct. His nephew and representative is the Rev. Charles Henry Barham, of Treewn.

Arms—Sa., an eagle, displayed, erm., within a bordure, arg.

TYES—BARON TYES.

By Writ of Summons, dated 6 February, 1299.

Lineage.

In the time of King Henry III.,
Henry de Tyes held Shireburne, in Oxfordshire, by the grant of Richard, Earl of Cornwall, and was summoned to parliament as a Baron, from 6 February, 1299, to 26 August, 1307. In the 28th Edward I., his lordship had free warren in all his demesne lands at Shireburne and Allerton, both in the co. Oxford. He *d.* in 1308, and was *s.* by his son,
Henry de Tyes, 2nd baron, summoned to parliament from 8 January, 1313, to 15 May, 1321. This nobleman who in the wars of Scotland, and for several years adhered faithfully to King Edward II., but afterwards joining in the insurrection of Thomas, Earl of Lancaster, he was taken prisoner at Boroughbridge, and being conveyed to London, was there beheaded for high treason, in 1321. His lordship *d. s. p.*, leaving his sister,

Alice de Tyes, who *m.* Warine de L'Isle, his heir, in whose descendants this Barony of Tyes is now vested.

Arms—Arg., a chevron, gu.

TYES—BARON TYES.

By Writ of Summons, dated 6 February, 1299.

Lineage.

In the 25th Edward I., A.D. 1297,
Walter de Tyes, in conjunction with Isabel, his wife, obtained numerous grants from the crown, lands in the cos Bedford, York, Essex, and Bucks, and having served in the Scottish wars, had summons to parliament as a Baron from 6 February, 1299, to 26 August, 1307. In the 11th Edward II.,

his lordship was joint governor of the city of York, with Robert de Hasting. He *m.* Isabel, dau. of John de Steyngreve, and widow of Simon Patshull, but *d. s. p.* in 1324, leaving MARGARET DE TYES, dau. of his brother, Roger, his heir, when this Barony of Tyes became EXTINCT.

Arms—Arg., a chevron, gu.

UFFORD—BARONS UFFORD, EARLS OF SUFFOLK.

Barony, by Writ of Summons, dated 13 January, 1308.
Earldom, by Creation in Parliament, dated 16 March, 1337.

Lineage.

Of this family, says Sir William Dugdale, which afterwards arrived to great honour, I have not seen anything memorable, until the 53rd HENRY III., when Robert, a younger son of John de Peyton, of Peyton, co. Suffolk, [assuming his surname from the lordship of Ufford, in that shire, became

ROBERT DE UFFORD. This Robert was justice of Ireland in the reign of HENRY III., and again in the reign of EDWARD I. He *m.* Mary, widow of William de Say, and dying in the 26th of the latter king, was *s.* by his son,

SIR ROBERT DE UFFORD, Knt., who was summoned to parliament as a Baron from 13 January, 1308, to 19 December, 1311. His lordship was in the expedition made into Scotland, in the 34th EDWARD I. He *m.* Cecily, one of the daus. and co heirs of Sir Robert de Valoines, Knt., Lord of Walsham, and had issue,

ROBERT, his successor.
John, archbishop of Canterbury, *d.* 1318.
Ralph, justice of Ireland in the reign of EDWARD III. *(see* Ufford, Baron Ufford).
Edmund.

He *d.* in 1316, and was *s.* by his eldest son,

ROBERT DE UFFORD, 2nd baron, K G., summoned to parliament from 27 January, 1332, to 14 January, 1337. This nobleman was in the wars of Gascony in the reign of EDWARD II., and he obtained, in the beginning of EDWARD III.'s reign, in requital of his eminent services, a grant for life of the town and castle of Orford, co. Suffolk, and soon after, further considerable territorial possessions, also by grant from the crown, in consideration of the personal danger he had incurred in arresting, by the king's command, MORTIMER, and some of his adherents, in the castle of Nottingham. His lordship was solemnly advanced in the parliament to the dignity of EARL OF SUFFOLK, 16 March, 1336, "habendum sibi et hæredibus suis." Whereupon he was associated with William de Bohun, Earl of Northampton, and John Darcy, steward of the king's household, to treat with David Brus, of Scotland, touching a league of peace and amity. And the same year, going beyond sea on the king's service had an assignation of £300 out of the exchequer, towards his expenses in that employment, which was in the wars of France; for it appears that he then accompanied the Earl of Derby, being with him at the battle of Cagant. After which time he was seldom out of some distinguished action. In the 12th EDWARD III., being in the expedition made into Flanders, he was the next year one of the marshals when King EDWARD besieged Cambray; and his lordship within a few years subsequently was actively engaged in the wars of Brittany. In the 17th of this reign the Earl of Suffolk was deputed to the court of Rome, there to treat in the presence of his holiness, touching an amicable peace and accord between the English monarch and Philip de Valois, and he marched the same year with Henry of Lancaster, Earl of Derby, to the relief of Loughmaben Castle, then besieged by the Scots. Soon after this he was made admiral of the king's whole fleet northward. For several years subsequently his lordship was with King EDWARD in France, and he was one of the persons presented by that monarch with harness and other accoutrements for the tournament at Canterbury, in the 22nd year of his reign. In seven years afterwards we find the earl again in France, with the Black Prince; and at the celebrated battle of Poictiers, fought, and so gloriously won in the following year, his lordship achieved the highest military renown by his skill as a leader, and his personal courage at the head of his troops. He was subsequently elected a knight of the Garter. His lordship *m* Margaret, sister of Sir John Norwich, and widow of S r Thomas Cailly, and had issue,

ROBERT, summoned to parliament 25 February, 1342, by writ directed " Roberto de Ufford le Fitz;" he *m.* Elizabeth, dau. of Richard, son of Richard, Earl of Arundel, and *d. v. p., s. p.*

543

WILLIAM, his successor.
Cecilie, *m.* to John, 3rd Lord Willoughby de Eresby; whose co-heirs-general are Lord Willoughby de Eresby and the Marquess of Cholmondeley.
Catherine, *m.* to Robert, Lord Scales *(see* SCALES).
Margaret, *m.* to William, Lord Ferrers, of Groby *(see* FERRERS).

The earl's last testament bears date in 1368, and he *d.* in the following year. Amongst other bequests, he leaves to his son, William, " the sword, wherewith the king girt him, when he created him earl; as also his bed, with the eagle entire; and his summer vestment, powdered with leopards." His lordship was *s.* by his only surviving son,

WILLIAM DE UFFORD, 2nd Earl of Suffolk, K.G., who had been summoned to parliament, as a Baron, in the lifetime of his father, 4 December, 1364, and 20 January, 1366. This nobleman was in the French wars at the close of EDWARD III.'s reign, and in the beginning of that of RICHARD II. In the 50th EDWARD he was constituted admiral of the king's whole fleet northward. At the breaking out of Jack Straw's insurrection, 4th RICHARD II., his lordship understanding that the common people contemplated forcing him into their ranks, and thus to represent him as one of their leaders, hastily arose from supper, and pursuing an unfrequented route, reached the king at St. Albans, with a wallet over his shoulder, under the assumed character of servant to Sir Roger de Bois; but afterwards, being chosen by the Commons in parliament assembled, to represent to the lords certain matters of importance to the public welfare, the earl while ascending the steps to their lordships' house, suddenly fell down dead, to the amazement and sorrow of all persons, rich and poor, 15 February, 1381. His lordship *m.* 1st. Joane, dau. of Edward de Montacute, and grand-dau. maternally, of Thomas, of Brotherton, Earl of Norfolk. and 2ndly, Isabel, dau. of Thomas de Beauchamp, Earl of Warwick, and widow of John le Strange, of Blackmere, but as he left no issue, the Earldom of Suffolk and the Barony of Ufford fell into ABEYANCE, between his sisters and heirs, (refer to children of Robert, 1st earl), as it still continues amongst their representatives.

Arms—Sa., a cross engrailed, or.

UFFORD—BARON UFFORD.

By Writ of Summons, dated 3 April, 1360.

Lineage.

SIR RALPH DE UFFORD, brother (according to Dugdale and Nicolas) of Robert, 1st Earl of Suffolk, having served in the wars of France and Flanders, in the martial reign of EDWARD III., obtained large grants of land from that monarch, in the co. Berks and Dorset. Subsequently (20th EDWARD III.,) being justice of Ireland, we are told " he landed in that realm, with a great number of men-at-arms and archers." This distinguished person *m.* 1st, Maud, widow of William de Burgo, Earl of Ulster, and dau. of Henry Plantagenet, Earl of Lancaster, by whom he had an only dau.,

MAUD, buried before 21st EDWARD III.

He *m.* 2ndly (says Dugdale), Eve, dau. and heiress of John de Clavering, and widow of Thomas de Audeley, by whom he had issue,

JOHN, of whom presently.
Edmund (Sir), who inherited the estates of the family at the decease of his brother. Sir Edmund *m.* Sybil, dau. of Robert or Simon Pierpont, and had issue,
    Robert (Sir), who *m.* Eleanor, dau. of Sir Thomas Felton, Knt., and left issue three daus., his co-heirs, viz.,
        Ella, *m.* to Richard Bowet, Esq.
        Sybil, a nun at Barking.
        Joan, *m.* to William Bowet, Esq., brother of Richard, and left one dau. and heiress,
            Elizabeth, *m.* to Thomas, son of Thomas, 7th Lord Dacre.

Ralph de Ufford *d.* in 1346, and was *s.* by his eldest son,

JOHN DE UFFORD, who was summoned to parliament as BARON UFFORD, 3 April, 1360, but *d. s. p.* the following year, when the dignity became EXTINCT, while his estates passed to his brother, Sir Edmund Ufford, Knt.

Dugdale, followed by Nicolas, is the authority for this pedigree; but Vincent maintains that John de Ufford, summoned to parliament in 1360, was son of Thomas, a younger son of Robert de Ufford, by Mary de Say, his wife, and that Eve de Clavering was the wife of the said Thomas, and not of Ralph (See ADDENDA.)

Arms—Sa., a cross engrailed, or.

UGHTRED—BARON UGHTRED.

By Writ of Summons, dated 30 April, 1343.

Lineage.

Of this family, which was of great antiquity in the co. York, was

ROBERT UGHTRED, Lord of Scarborough, who, in the 28th EDWARD I., obtained a charter for free warren, in all his demesne lands in that shire. He d. 3rd EDWARD II., and was s. by his son,

SIR THOMAS UGHTRED, K.G., who became a person of great note in his time, and was celebrated in the Scottish wars temp. EDWARD II. and EDWARD III. In the 10th of the latter reign, he was made admiral of the king's whole fleet to the northward, and for some years afterwards he was again in the Scottish wars, when he attained the rank of banneret, and was constituted governor of Perth. He was subsequently in the wars of Flanders, and had summons to parliament as a Baron, from 20 April, 1343, to 4 December, 1364. His lordship d. in 1365, leaving by Margaret, his wife, a son and heir,

SIR THOMAS UGHTRED, who does not appear from the existing enrolments to have been summoned to parliament as a Baron. Sir Thomas, like his father, was a military man, and became eminent likewise in the wars of Scotland. In the 50th EDWARD III. he was made constable and chamberlain of Lochmaben Castle, and he was afterwards engaged in the wars of France. He d. 3rd HENRY IV., and was s. by his grandson,

THOMAS UGHTRED (son of William), who had m. Margaret, dau. and co-heir of Sir John Goddard, Knt., by Constance, his wife, dau. and co-heir of Sir Thomas Sutton, of Holderness; and had issue, according to Banks, two sons, ROBERT and THOMAS (Sir), of whom the elder was ancestor of the UGHTREDS, of Kexby, co. York.

Arms—Gu., on a cross moline, or, five mullets of the field.

UMFRAVILL—BARONS UMFRAVILL, EARLS OF ANGUS.

Barony, by Writ of Summons, dated 24 June, 1295.
Earldom, by Writ of Summons, dated 26 January, 1297.

Lineage.

In the 10th year of his reign, WILLIAM THE CONQUEROR granted the forest, valley, and lordship of Riddesdale, in Northumberland, to his kinsman,

SIR ROBERT DE UMFRAVILL, Knt.,* otherwise *Robert with the beard*, Lord of Tours and Vian, to hold, by the service of defending that part of the country for ever, from enemies and wolves with the sword which King WILLIAM had by his side when he entered Northumberland. By this grant he had likewise authority for holding, governing, exercising, hearing, and judging, in all the pleas of the crown, as well as others occurring within the precincts of Riddesdale. The next of this family we will mention is

RICHARD DE UMFRAVILL, a feudal lord who appears, in the 7th RICHARD I., to have pledged his lands of Turney, to Aaron, a Jew, for a debt of £22 6s. In the 5th King JOHN he obtained the right of preventing all persons from grazing, hunting, or cutting down timber in the forest of Riddesdale; and in nine years afterwards, the times being then turbulent, he delivered up his four sons in hostage, with his castle of Prudhoe, as guarantee for his loyalty, upon the condition, that if he transgressed, the said castle became forfeited, and that he should himself be dealt with as a traitor: notwithstanding which, no sooner did the barons take up arms, than he appeared amongst them, when his lands were seized and granted to Hugh de Baliol. In the reign of King HENRY III., however, he made his peace, and had restitution of the castle of Prudhoe, &c., but he was nevertheless far from enjoying the confidence of that monarch, as we find the king soon after issuing a precept to the sheriff of Northumberland, directing a jury of twelve knights to be empanelled, to inspect certain buildings at the castle of Herbotil, which this Richard de Umfravill was then erecting, and to demolish all that bore the appearance of fortifications. His son,

GILBERT DE UMFRAVILL, Lord of Prudhoe, Redesdale, and Harbottle, Northumberland, according to Matthew Paris, "a

---

* This Robert de Umfravill, had a grandson, Robert, father of Gilbert, which last two adhered to DAVID I., King of Scotland, who gave Gilbert, Kinnaird and Dunipace, in Stirlingshire.

famous baron, guardian and chief flower of the north," m. in 1243, Maud, Countess of Angus, and d. in 1245, leaving his son and heir "of tender years," which son and heir,

GILBERT DE UMFRAVILL, was committed to the guardianship of Simon de Montfort, Earl of Leicester, in consideration of 10,000 marks paid by that nobleman to the king. This Gilbert attained majority in the 43rd HENRY III., and in six years subsequently we find him in arms with the barons, but he made his peace prior to the battle of Evesham, and obtained then some immunities from the crown. In the 20th EDWARD I. he was governor of the castle of Forfar, and the whole territory of Angus, in Scotland, and appears to have borne the title of Earl of Angus, in right of his mother. He was summoned to parliament, however, in three years afterwards, as BARON UMFRAVILL only, but in the 25th of the same reign, and from that period to the 1st EDWARD II., his writ of summons was addressed "Gilberto de Umfravill, Comiti de Anggos." But this dignity the English lawyers refused to acknowledge (Angus not being within the kingdom of England,) until he had openly produced the king's writ in public court, by which he was called to parliament, under the title of EARL OF ANGUS. In the 27th EDWARD I., his lordship was constituted one of the king's commissioners for manning and fortifying the castles within the realm of Scotland, and to appoint wardens of the Marches. The next year he founded a chantry for two priests, to celebrate divine service daily in the chapel of our lady, within the castle of Prudhoe. The earl m. Lady Agnes Comyn, dau. of Alexander, Earl of Buchan, d. in 1308, and was s. by his eldest surviving son,

ROBERT DE UMFRAVILL, summoned to parliament as Earl of Angus, from 4 March, 1309, to 30 December, 1324. This nobleman distinguished himself in the lifetime of his father in the Scottish wars, and soon after his accession to the title he was joined in commission with William, Lord Ros, of Hamlake, and Henry, Lord Beaumont, in the lieutenancy of Scotland. In the 11th EDWARD II., his lordship was appointed one of the commissioners to treat with Robert de Brus and his partisans for a truce between both realms. The earl m. 1st, Lucy, dau. of Philip, and eventually heiress of her brother, William de Kyme, by whom he had issue,

GILBERT, his successor.

Elizabeth, m. Gilbert Burdon, or Baradon, and had an only dau. and heiress,

ELIZABETH, or ALIANORE, heiress to her uncle, Earl Gilbert, m. to Henry Talboys, from which marriage the Lord Talboys descended.

His lordship's 2nd wife, was named Alianore, but of what family is not mentioned; by this lady (who m. 2ndly, Roger Mauduit,) he had issue,

Robert (Sir), who d. s p.

Thomas (Sir), of Harbottle Castle, m. Joane de Roddam, d. 1386, and left issue,

1 Thomas (Sir), b. 1364, d. 1391, who, by Agnes, his wife, left issue,

Gilbert (styled "Earl of Kyme," probably from the tenure of the castle of Kyme,) d. s. p., being s'ain at Beaugé, 1421.

Elizabeth, m. Sir William Elmedon, and left four co-heiresses; one of whom, Isabella, m. Sir Rowland Tempest, Knt., and was ancester of the Tempests, extinct Barts. of Stella, and through them, the Chaytors of Croft, Swinburnes of Capheaton, &c.

Joane, m. to Sir Wm. Lambert.

Margaret, m. 1st, to William Lodington, and 2ndly, to John Constable of Halsham.

Agnes, m. to Thomas Hagerston.

2 Robert, K.G., lord high admiral temp. HENRY IV., d. s. p. 27 December, 1436.

Annora, m. to Stephen Waleys, son and heir of Sir Richard Waleys.

The earl d. in 1325, and was s. by his eldest son,

GILBERT DE UMFRAVILL, summoned to parliament, as 3rd Earl of Angus, from 27 January, 1332, to 26 August, 1380. This nobleman acquired great reputation in the Scottish wars, and was a chief commander at the battle of Durham, 20th EDWARD III., where DAVID BRUS, the Scottish monarch was totally defeated and made prisoner by the English. In the 25th EDWARD III., his lordship had permission, upon petition to the king and parliament, to transfer the prisoners, made within the liberty of Redesdale, whom he had the privilege of detaining, from his prison of Herbotil Castle (then in a state of dilapidation), to Prudhoe Castle, for the ensuing ten years. His lordship m. Maud, sister of Anthony de Lucy, and next heir of Joane, dau. and heir of the said Anthony, by whom he had an only son,

ROBERT (Sir), who m. Margaret, dau. of Henry Lord Percy, and d. v. p., s p.

The earl d. 7 January, 1381, leaving Alianore, his niece, wife of Henry Talboys, his heir of the whole blood, and Thomas Umfravill, his brother of the half blood, his next male heir, but none of the family were ever subsequently summoned to parliament. The Barony of Umfravill, created by writ of 23rd EDWARD I., is, however, vested in the descendants and representatives of the said Thomas de Umfravill—(see children of Robert, 2nd Earl of Angus, by his 2nd wife).

Arms—Gu., a cinquefoil within an orle of cross crosslets, or.

UMFRAVILLE—EARL OF ANGUS.

(See UMFRAVILLE, Baron Umfraville.)

UNDERWOOD—DUCHESS OF INVERNESS.

By Letters Patent, dated 10 April, 1840.

Lineage.

LADY CECILIA-LETITIA GORE, eldest dau. of Arthur Saunders, 2nd Earl of Arran, K.P. (by his 3rd Countess, Elizabeth, dau. of Richard Underwood, Esq.), m. 14 May, 1815, Sir George Buggin, who d. 12 April, 1825. She assumed by royal licence, dated 2 May, 1831, the surname of her mother's family, UNDERWOOD, and was created, by patent, dated 10 April, 1840, DUCHESS OF INVERNESS in the peerage of the united kingdom. Her Grace d. s. p. 1 August, 1873, when her peerage became EXTINCT.

Arms—Quarterly: 1st and 4th, az., on a fess, erm., between three annulets, or., a lion passant, of the first, for UNDERWOOD; 2nd and 3rd, gu., a fess, between three crosses-crosslet, fitchée, or., for GORE.

UVEDALE—BARON UVEDALE.

By Writ of Summons, dated 27 January, 1332.

Lineage.

PETER DE UVEDALE was summoned to parliament as a Baron, from 27 January, 1332, to 22 January, 1336. He appears to have d. s. p., when the Barony of Uvedale became EXTINCT. From Thomas, his brother, derived descent, according to Banks, the UVEDALES, of Wickham, Hants, and the UVEDALES, of More Crichill, co. Dorset.

VALENCE—EARLS OF PEMBROKE.

Lineage.

WILLIAM DE LUZIGNAN, otherwise DE VALENCE, son of Hugh le Brun, Comte de la Marche, in Poictou, by Isabel, his wife, dau. of Aymer, Comte d'Angouleme, and widow of King JOHN, derived his surname from the place of his birth, as the rest of his brothers did from theirs, and being so nearly allied to King HENRY III. (half brother, by the mother) was brought into England, in 1247, with Guy de Luzignan, his elder brother, and Alice, his sister, in consequence of being oppressed by the King of France. Not many months after his arrival he was made governor of Goderich Castle, and through the influence of the king, obtained the hand of Joane, dau. and eventually heir of Warine de Monchensy, by Joane, his wife, 2nd sister and co-heir of Anselme Marshal, Earl of Pembroke.

William de Valence had, subsequently, a grant from the crown of the castle and honour of Hertford, as also another grant to himself and his lady, and to their issue, of all those debts which William de Lancaster did then owe to the Jews throughout the whole realm. " About this time," writes Dugdale, " this William de Valence, residing at Hertford Castle, rode to the Park at Hatfield, belonging to the bishop of Ely,

545

and there hunting without any leave, went to the bishop's manor house, and readily finding nothing to drink but ordinary beer, broke open the buttery doors, and swearing and cursing the drink, and those who made it; after all his company had drunk their fills, pulled the spigots out of the vessels, and let out the rest on the floor; and that a servant of the house hearing the noise, and coming to see what the matter was, they laughed him to scorn, and so departed."

In the 34th HENRY III., William de Valence was in the Holy Land, and in the 42nd had a military summons to march against the Welsh, but he was soon afterwards obliged to fly the kingdom, when the barons took up arms against the influence of himself and other foreigners; he came back, however, after an exile of only two years, under the protection of the king, but was not suffered to land by the barons, until he had sworn to observe the ordinances of Oxford. Nevertheless, the contest again breaking out, he had a chief command in the royal army, and with the prince, assaulted successfully the town of Northampton, when the whole baronial force was put to the rout, but soon rallying, owing to the junction of the Londoners, the battle of Lewes ensued, and victory deserted the regal banner. In this action, the king and his son became prisoners; but Valence, who then bore the title of EARL OF PEMBROKE, with the Earl of Warren, and others, escaped by flight, first to Pevensey, and thence into France. His lands were, however, seized by the triumphant barons, and his wife, who was residing at Windsor Castle, ordered to retire immediately into some religious house. The battle of Evesham again, however, changing the fortune of war, and the power of the king being re-established, the Earl of Pembroke, with the other stanch adherents of royalty, were restored to their possessions; and his lordship had, subsequently, large grants from the crown. In the 18th EDWARD I., the earl, with Joane, his wife, presented a petition to parliament, setting forth, " tha', whereas, upon the death of William de Monchensi (brother to her, the said Joane), they had obtained a bull from the Pope directed to the archbishop of Canterbury, touching the inheritance of the lands of the said William de Monchensi, thereby desiring that the king would please to commit the tuition of Dionysia, the daughter of the said William, unto some person who might appear before the said archbishop, and such other judges as were named in the bull." But it was answered, that the admission of that bull would tend to the diminution of the king's authority and power, by reason that such cases of hereditary succession ought not to be determined but in his own courts. Wherefore, inasmuch, as it did appear, that the object of the earl was to invalidate the sentence of the bishop of Worcester, which had declared the said Dionysia to be legitimate, and his design to make her a bastard, in order that he might enjoy her estate, his lordship and his lady were prohibited to prosecute their appeal any further. His lordship was afterwards engaged in the wars of France, and was slain there in 1296, when his remains were conveyed to England, and interred in Westminster Abbey, under a splendid monument. The earl had issue by the heiress of Monchensi three sons and four daus., viz.,

I. John, who d. young.
II. William, killed by the Welsh, v. p.
III. AYMER, his successor.
I. Anne, m. 1st, to Maurice Fitz-Gerald; 2ndly, to Hugh de Baliol, and 3rdly, to John de Avennes, but had no issue.
II. Isabel, m. to John de Hastings.
III. Joan, m. to John Comyn, feudal lord of Badenoch (son of John Comyn, by Mary, his wife, dau. of John Baliol), Lord of Barnard Castle, and sister of King John Baliol, and had issue,

John Comyn, slain at Striveling in 1314, s. p.
William Comyn, made prisoner in the same action, d. s. p.
Joan Comyn, b. 1296, m. to David de Strathbogie, Earl of Atholl.
Elizabeth Comyn, b. 1300, m. to Richard, 2nd Lord Talbot, ancestor, by her, of the Earls of Shrewsbury.
IV. Margaret.

His lordship was s. by his only surviving son,

AYMER DE VALENCE, 2nd Earl of Pembroke. This nobleman was in the wars of Scotland, temp. EDWARD I., and obtained considerable grants from the crown, in that kingdom. His lordship being with King EDWARD at Burgh upon the Sands, immediately before the monarch's death, was one of those to whom the king recommended his son, and enjoined him not to suffer Piers de Gaveston to come into England again. For which he was ever after much hated by Piers, "being called by him-*Joseph the Jew*, in regard he was tall and pale of countenance." His lordship subsequently joined the coalition against the power of Gaveston, and assisted at the siege of Scarborough Castle, in which, upon its surrender, the favourite was made prisoner, and was soon afterwards beheaded, by orders of the Earl of Warwick, at Blackton Hill, near Warwick.

In the 8th EDWARD II., his lordship was constituted general of all the king's forces, from the river Trent, northwards, to Roxborough, and he obtained license to make a castle of his house at Bampton, in Oxfordshire. Two years later he was again in the Scottish wars, but being made prisoner in his journey towards the court of Rome, by John Molley, a Burgundian, and sent to the emperor, he was constrained to give twenty thousand pounds of silver for his ransom; by reason, Molley alleged, that he himself having served the King of England, had not been paid his wages. After obtaining his liberty, his lordship returned to the wars of Scotland, and for several subsequent years was engaged in that kingdom. In the 15th EDWARD II. he was one of the lords who sat in judgment upon Thomas Plantagenet, Earl of Lancaster, and condemned that prince to death: "but this mercenary and time serving act of infamy," it is said, was speedily atoned for by his own death, which occurred in two years after in France, where, attending Queen Isabel, he was murdered, 27 June, 1323. His lordship m. 1st, Beatrix, dau. of Ralph de Clermont, Seigneur de Nele, constable of France; 2ndly, a dau. of the Comte de Barre, and 3rdly, Mary,* dau. of Guy de Chastillon, Comte de St. Paul, but had no issue. His remains were conveyed to England, and buried in Westminster Abbey. On his lordship's decease, his estates passed to his sisters as co-heirs, and the Earldom of Pembroke became EXTINCT.

Arms—Barry, arg. and az., an orle of martlets, gu.

VANE—BARON AND VISCOUNT VANE.

By Letters Patent, dated 13 September, 1720.

Lineage.

The Hon. WILLIAM VANE, of Fairlawn, Kent, M.P. for co. Durham, and afterwards for Steyning, 2nd son of Christopher, Lord Barnard, was created a peer of Ireland, 13 September, 1720, as Baron Vane, of Dungannon, and VISCOUNT VANE. His lordship m. Lucy, dau. and co-heir of William Jolliffe, Esq., of Caveswell, co. Stafford, and by her (who d. 27 March, 1742) had three sons, Christopher, John, and WILLIAM. The two elder d. under age, unm., the 3rd,

WILLIAM VANE, 2nd Viscount Vane, s. his father, 20 May, 1734, and dissipated in reckless extravagance, the large fortune he then inherited. His lordship m. 19 May, 1735, Anne, dau. and heir of Francis Hawes, Esq., of Purley Hall, Berks, and widow of Lord William Hamilton, but d. s. p. in 1789, when the honours became EXTINCT.

Arms—Az., three sinister gauntlets, or, on a canton, erm., a pile, sa., charged with a mullet of five points, arg.

VANSITTART—BARON BEXLEY.

By Letters Patent, dated 1 March, 1823.

Lineage.

The Vansittarts are of German origin, and have been established in England nearly two centuries.

PETER VANSITTART, the 1st settler in England, was son of William-J. Van Sittart, of Dantzic, and became an eminent Russian merchant. He m. Susannah, dau. of Robert Saunderson, of London; and d. in 1705, leaving, inter alios, a 5th son,

ARTHUR VANSITTART, Esq., of Shottesbrook, verdurer of Windsor Forest, who m. in 1723, Martha, eldest dau. of Sir John Stonhouse, Bart. of Radley; and dying in 1760, left issue,

  I. ARTHUR, of Shottesbrook, Berks, M.P. for that co., m. Anne, sister of Lord Coleraine, and left, at his decease, in 1804, three sons,

    1 ARTHUR, of Shottesbrook, who m. the Hon. Caroline Eden, and d. in 1829, leaving by her (who d. 3 March, 1851,) four daus., Caroline, m. in 1828, George, Lord Vaux;

---

* This lady, who was great-grand-dau., maternally, of King HENRY III., founded by grant from her cousin EDWARD III., the college of Mary de Valence, in Cambridge, now called Pembroke Hall.

Charlotte-Eleanor, m. in 1842, the Rev. Edward-Serocold Pearce-Serocold; Louisa, m. in 1841, William Chapman, Esq. of Southill, co. Westmeath; and Sophia, m. in 1840, to Thomas-A. Anstruther, Esq. several sons, of whom the eldest, Arthur Vansittart, Esq., of Shottesbrook, m. Diana, dau. of General Sir John Crosbie. of Watergate, Sussex, and d. 1859, leaving issue. (See BURKE'S Landed Gentry).
2 Robert, d. 26 December, 1838.
3 William, D.D., prebendary of Carlisle, m. Charlotte, dau. of General Warde, and left issue.
  II. Robert, d. unm. in 1789, professor of civil law at Oxford.
  III. HENRY, of whom presently.
  IV. George, of Bisham Abbey, M.P. for Berks, b. 15 September, 1745; m. Sarah, dau. of Sir James Stonhouse, Bart., by Anne, his wife, eldest dau. of John Neale, Esq., of Allesley, co. Warwick, and d. in 1825. leaving issue.

    1 George-Henry, a general officer, m. in 1818, Anna-Maria, only surviving child of Thomas Copson, Esq., and d. in 1824, leaving two sons, GEORGE-HENRY, of Bisham Abbey, co. Berks, b. in 1823; and Augustus-Arthur, b. in 1824. (See BURKE'S Landed Gentry.)
    2 Edward, rector of Taplow, Bucks, assumed by sign manual, the surname of NEALE in 1805. He m. twice, and had issue. (See BURKE'S Landed Gentry).
    3 Henry, rear-admiral of the red, d. in March, 1843.
    4 Caroline-Anne, m. to Augustus-Henry East, Esq., who d. in 1928.
    5 Laura, m. Fulwar Craven, then of Chilton House, Esq., and d. in 1844.
    6 Henrietta.
  V. Susannah.
  VI. Anne, m. to Sir Robert Palk, Bart.

The 3rd son,
HENRY VANSITTART, Esq., governor of Bengal, b. in 1732, m. Amelia, dau. of Nicholas Morse, Esq., governor of Madras by whom (who d. in 1819) he had issue,

  I. Henry, m. Catherine-Maria Powney, and by her (who m. 2ndly, George-Nesbitt Thomson, Esq., of Penton Lodge, near Andover) left at his decease, 12 October, 1787, a son,
    Henry, of Kirkleatham, co. York, high sheriff, in 1820. b. 10 July, 1784; m. in 1812, Hon. Theresa-Gleadowe Newcomen, 2nd dau. of Charlotte, Viscountess Newcomen, and Sir William-Gleadowe Newcomen, Bart., and widow of Sir Charles Turner, Bart., and d. 22 April, 1848, leaving a dau.,
      THERESA, m. 11 May, 1841, to ARTHUR NEWCOMEN, Esq., of the royal horse artillery.
  II. NICHOLAS, of whom presently.
  1. Sophia, deceased.
  II. Emilia, m. to Edward Perry, Esq., and is deceased.

Governor Vansittart was one of the committee of three, appointed by the directors of the East India Company, supervisors of their affairs in the east, who were lost, in 1770, on board the "Aurora" frigate. The 2nd son,
The RIGHT HON. NICHOLAS VANSITTART, F.R.S. and S.A., of Bexley, co. Kent; b. 29 April, 1766, was for many years a member of administration, and filled the office of chancellor of the exchequer from 1812 to the beginning of 1823. In the latter year (1 March), on retiring, he was created BARON BEXLEY, of Bexley, co. Kent. Lord Bexley was a commissioner of the land-tax and of the Royal Military College, a director of Greenwich Hospital, and a privy councillor for Great Britain and Ireland. He m. 22 July, 1806, Catherine-Isabella, 2nd dau. of William, 1st Lord Auckland; became a widower 10 August, 1810; and d. s. p. 8 February, 1851, when the title became EXTINCT.

Arms—Erm., an eagle displayed, sa., on a chief, gu., a ducal crown, or, between two crosses-patée, arg.

VAUGHAN — BARONS VAUGHAN AND EARLS OF CARBERY, AND BARONS VAUGHAN, OF EMLYN.

Barony of Ireland, by Letters Patent, dated 29 July, 1621.
Earldom of Ireland, by Letters Patent, dated 5 August, 1628.
Barony in the Peerage of England, dated 25 October, 1643.

Lineage.

The Vaughans of Golden Grove, derived their descent from Hugh Vaughan, Esq., of Kidwelly, gentleman usher to King HENRY VII. During the great tournament held by that monarch at Richmond in Surrey, in May, 1492, this Hugh Vaughan fought a duel with one Sir James Parker, Knt., concerning the arms which Mr. Garter had given to the said Hugh, and which the king permitted him to use, when Parker was slain accidentally as it would seem in the first encounter. From the following entry in a book of the first household expenses of King HENRY VII., it appears that Hugh Vaughan was living, and in his service in 1497. "It. to Hugh Vaughan for ij harpers, xiiis. 10d., 2 Jan., 1497." He m. Jane, dau. of Morris ap Owen, and had one son,

JOHN VAUGHAN, Esq., of Golden Grove, who having m. Katherine, dau. of Henry Morgan, Esq., of Moddlescombe, was father of one son,

WALTER VAUGHAN, of Golden Grove, living in 1590, who m. Katherine, dau. of Griffith ap Rhys of Newton, co. Carmarthen, and grand-dau. of Rhys ap Griffith, by Katherine, his wife, who was dau. of Thomas Howard, first Duke of Norfolk, Earl Marshal of England, K.G., &c., by his 1st wife, Agnes, sister and co-heir of Sir Philip Tilney of Boston, co. Lincoln, and consequently a relation in blood to Queen ELIZABETH, who was great grand-dau. of the said Thomas Howard, Duke of Norfolk, by his 2nd wife, Elizabeth, dau. and heir of Sir Frederic Tilney, Knt. By the said Katherine, his wife, Walter Vaughan had issue,

I. JOHN (Sir), of whom presently.
II. William (Sir), Knt., of Terracoyd. co. Carmarthen. Who had also lands in Newfoundland and America, was living in England in 1630. He m. Anne, dau. and heir of John Christmas, of Colchester, co. Essex, and had with other issue a son,

   SIR EDWARD VAUGHAN, of Terracoyd, who m. Jemima, dau. of Nicholas Bacon, Esq., of Shrubland, co. Suffolk, and had, with other issue, an eldest son,

      RICHARD VAUGHAN, Esq., of Terracoyd, and afterwards of Shenfield, co. Essex, who m. 1st, Jemima, dau. of John Vaughan, Esq., of Llanelly, and had issue. He m. 2ndly, Elizabeth, dau. and co-heir of Sir William Appleton, Bart., of Shenfield, and had with other issue, a son,

      JOHN VAUGHAN, of Shenfield, who succeeded to the estate of Golden Grove, by will of Anne, Duchess of Bolton. He m. 1st, Ellen, dau. and heir or co-heir of Nicholas Partridge, Esq., of Doddinghurst, co. Essex; and 2ndly, Elizabeth, dau. and co-heir of John Vaughan, Esq., of Court Derllys, and widow of Thomas Lloyd, Esq., of Danyrallt, who d. 20 January, 1754. He d. 27 January, and was buried at Shenfield, 5 February, 1765, having had issue, by his 1st wife, one son,

         RICHARD VAUGHAN, Esq., of Shenfield, and of Golden Grove, who m. 1st, Elizabeth-Philippa, dau. of Charles Phillips, Esq., of Llanelly, and had by her, two sons, John, of Shenfield and Golden Grove, and Charles-Richard, who both d. s. p. He m. 2ndly, 12 September, 1767, Susannah, dau. of John Warner, Esq., of Swansea, and 'd. at Shenfield, in 1781, having by her (who d. March, 1810) had an only dau.,

         SUSANNA ELEANORA VAUGHAN, b. 21 December, 1768, who m. at Marylebone, 22 January, 1795, the Rev. Thomas Watkins, M.A., F.R.S., F.S.A., &c., of Pennoyre, co. Brecon, rector of Llandefailog, and Landefalley, and left, with other issue,

           JOHN-LLOYD-VAUGHAN WATKINS, Esq., late of Pennoyre and Rhosferig, co. Brecon, and Broadway, co. Carmarthen. (See BURKE'S *Landed Gentry*.)

The elder son,
SIR JOHN VAUGHAN, Knt., of Golden Grove, co. Carmarthen, was created a peer of Ireland, as LORD VAUGHAN, of *Mullingar*, co. *Westmeath*, 29 July, 1621, and 5 August, 1628, advanced to the dignity of EARL OF CARBERY, also in Ireland. His lordship m. 1st, Margaret, dau. of Sir Gilly Meyrick, Knt., by whom he had one surviving son, RICHARD, his successor; and a dau., Mary, m. to Sir Francis Lloyd. He m. 2ndly, Jane, dau. of Sir Thomas Palmer, Knt., but had no issue. His lordship was s. at his decease, by his son,

RICHARD VAUGHAN, 2nd Earl of Carbery, who was made a knight of the Bath, at the coronation of King CHARLES I., and was afterwards distinguished in the civil wars as a cavalier leader, being lieutenant-general for the cos. of Carmarthen, Pembroke, and Cardigan; in which command, acting with great zeal and gallantry, he was rewarded with a peerage of England, 25 October, 1643, as BARON VAUGHAN, of *Emlyn*, co. *Carmarthen*; and he was constituted after the Restoration, lord president of the principality of Wales. His lordship, m. 1st, Bridget, dau. and heir of Thomas Lloyd, Esq., of Llanleer, co. Cardigan, by whom he had no surviving issue. He m. 2ndly, Frances, dau. and co-heir of Sir John Altham, Knt., of Oxby, in Hertfordshire, by whom he had issue,

Francis, who m. Lady Rachel Wriothesley, dau. of Thomas, Earl of Southampton, and d. s. p., v. p.
JOHN, his successor.
Altham.
Frances.   Althamia.

He m. 3rdly, Lady Alice Egerton, dau. of John, Earl of Bridgewater, but had no issue. His lordship d. in 1687, and was s. by his elder surviving son,

JOHN VAUGHAN, 3rd Earl of Carbery, and 2nd Lord Vaughan, of Emlyn. This nobleman was for some time governor of Jamaica. His lordship m. Mary, dau. of George Brown, Esq., of Green Castle, co. Carmarthen, but had no issue. He m. 2ndly, Lady Anne Montagu, dau. of George, Marquess of Halifax, and by her had an only dau. and heir,

LADY ANNE VAUGHAN, who m. Charles Paulet, Marquess of Winchester, afterwards Duke of Bolton.

The earl d. 16 January, 1712, when the Barony of Vaughan, of Emlyn and his Irish honours became EXTINCT.

Arms—Or, a lion rampant, gu.

VAVASOUR—BARON VAVASOUR.

By Writ of Summons, dated 6 February, 1299.

Lineage.

Of this family, which derived its surname from the high office of "King's Valvasor" (a dignity little inferior to the baronial), and flourished for many ages in Yorkshire, was,

SIR ROBERT LE VAVASOUR, who in the 9th King JOHN, paid a fine of 1,200 marks and two palfreys, that Maud, his dau., widow of Theobald Walter, might be married to Fulke Fitz-Warine, an eminent baron in those days. In the 31st HENRY III., he was sheriff of the cos. Nottingham and Derby, and so continued until the 39th of the same reign, having in the interim had the custody of the honour of Peverell committed to his charge. He m. Juliana, dau. of Gilbert de Ros, of Steeton, in Yorkshire, and was s. by his son,

SIR JOHN LE VAVASOUR, who m. Alice, dau. of Sir Robert Cockfield, Knt., and had two sons, WILLIAM, his heir; and MALGER, ancestor of the VAVASOURS of Denton, and of Weston Hall, co. York, who preserved a male succession until recent times.

SIR WILLIAM LE VAVASOUR (the elder son) had, 18th EDWARD I., license to make a castle of his manor house at Haslewood, co. York, and in three years afterwards was in an expedition made into Gascony. He was subsequently in the wars of Scotland, and had summons to parliament as a Baron from 6 February, 1299, to 7 January, 1313. His lordship m. Nicola, dau. of Sir Stephen Wallis, and had three sons, WALTER, ROBERT (Sir), and HENRY, and was s. at his decease by the eldest,

WALTER LE VAVASOUR, 2nd baron, summoned to parliament 26 July, 1313, who d. s. p. Accounts vary as to his heir: Mr. Courthope (*Historic Peerage*) states that his niece, Elizabeth, only child of Sir Robert le Vavasour, was his heir, and that she m. Sir Robert Strelly, Knt., of Nottinghamshire: but two inquisitions taken on Sir Robert le Vavasour's death, find that Henry le Vavasour, his brother, was his heir. This HENRY LE VAVASOUR, was the direct ancestor of Thomas Vavasour, Esq., of Hazlewood, who was created a baronet in 1628.

Arms—Or, a fesse dancettée, sa.

NOTE.—Of this family it was remarked that in twenty-one descents from Sir Mauger le Vavasour, temp. WILLIAM THE CONQUEROR, not one of them had ever married an heir, or ever buried his wife.—BANKS.

VERDON—BARONS VERDON.

By Writ of Summons, dated 24 June, 1295.

Lineage.

At the General Survey,
BERTRAM DE VERDUN (stated to have been son of Godfreye, Comte de Verdun, surnamed "le Caplif,") possessed Farnham Royal, in Buckinghamshire, holding the same by grand serjeanty: viz., by the service of providing a glove on the day of the king's coronation for his right hand; and of supporting the monarch's right arm during the same ceremony, so long as he bore the royal sceptre. Bertram had three sons,

I. NORMAN, his heir.
II. Milo, d. in Ireland.

III. William, of Brisingham, co. Norfolk, witness to a charter, A.D. 1100, ancestor of the VERDONS of Norfolk, Suffolk, and Northampton.

The eldest son,

NORMAN DE VERDON, living 1140. *m.* Lasceline, dau. of Geoffrey de Clinton, lord-chamberlain and treasurer to King HENRY I., and had issue,

I. BERTRAM, his heir.
II. Nicholas, abbot of Burton.
III. Robert, *m.* Joan, dau. and co-heir of Henry de Bourton, of Warwickshire, and was ancestor of the VERDONS of Draycot, co. Warwick, and of Ibstock, co. Leicester.
IV. Simon.
I. Alicia, *m.* to Ivo de Pantulf, of Wem, co. Salop.

BERTRAM DE VERDON, the eldest son, was sheriff of Leicestershire, from the 16th to the 30th of King HENRY II.'s reign, inclusive. He subsequently attended RICHARD I. to the Holy Land, and was at the siege of Acon, which place, upon its surrender, was committed to his custody. This Bertram founded the abbey of Croxden, co. Stafford, anno 1176, and was otherwise a liberal benefactor to the church. He *m.* 1st, Maud, dau. of Robert de Ferrers, Earl of Derby, by whom he had no issue; and 2ndly, Roesia, but of what family is unknown. He *d.* at Joppa, in 1192, having had issue,

I. William, *d. s. p.* 1199.
II. THOMAS, of whom presently.   III. Bertram.
IV. Robert.   V. NICHOLAS, successor to his brother.
VI. Walter, constable of Bruges Castle, in Valois, and had a son, Ralf de Verdon.
I. Leceline, *m.* to Hugh de Lacy.

The 2nd son and heir,

THOMAS DE VERDON, *m.* Eustachia, dau. of Gilbert Bassett, and by her (who *m.* 2ndly, Richard Camville,) he had no issue. He *d.* in Ireland, anno 1199, *s. p.*, when he was *s.* by his brother,

NICHOLAS DE VERDON, who, in the 6th JOHN, paid to the king £100, as also a courser and palfrey, for livery of those lands in Ireland whereof his father died possessed. But in twelve years afterwards, he took part with the rebellious barons, whereupon all his lands were seized by special precepts from the crown to the sheriffs of Warwick, Leicester, Stafford, Lincoln, Bucks, and Oxford, and placed in the custody of William de Cantilupe, during the king's pleasure. On his submission, however, to King HENRY III., those lands were restored to him in the first year of that monarch, and he appears afterwards to have enjoyed the favour of the king. He died in 1231, leaving (by Joan, his wife,) an only dau. and heiress,

ROESIA DE VERDON, who *m.* THEOBALD LE BOTILLER, of the noble family of Butler, of Ireland, but being so great an heiress, retained her maiden name after marriage, which her husband adopted. At the time of her father's decease, she appears to have been a widow. This lady, who founded the abbey of Grace Dieu, for Cisterian Monks, at Beldon, in Leicestershire, *d.* in 1248, leaving issue,

JOHN, her heir.
Humphrey, rector of Alveton, *d.* at Paris, 1285.
Nicholas, who had the manor of Clonmore, in Ireland, *d. s. p.*
THEOBALD DE VERDON, ancestor of the VERDONS, Lords of Darlaston and Biddulph, co. Stafford.
Maud, *m.* to John Fitz-Alan, Earl of Arundel.

Roesia was *s.* by her eldest son,

JOHN DE VERDON (alias Le Botiller). This great feudal lord, being one of the barons marchers, had orders, in the 44th HENRY III., on the incursions of the Welsh, to keep his residence upon the borders. After which he was one of the barons who adhered to the king, in the conflict between the crown and the nobles; and upon the triumph of the royal cause at Evesham, he was commissioned to raise forces in Worcestershire, for the purpose of attacking the only remaining hold of the barons, at Kenilworth. But these troubles being at length ended, John de Verdon was signed with the cross, and accompanied Prince Edward to the Holy Land. John de Verdon *m.* 1st, Margerie, dau. of Gilbert de Lacie, and co-heir to her grandfather, Walter de Lacie, Lord Palatine of Meath, in Ireland, by which alliance the castle of Weobley, co. Hereford, came into the Verdon family; and 2ndly, Alianore, whose surname is unknown. At his death, being slain in Ireland, 1278, he left issue,

I. NICHOLAS (Sir), of Ewyas Lacie, *d. v. p.* and *s. p.* 1271.
II. John, Lord of Weobley, *d. s. p.*, circa 1295.
III. THEOBALD, of whom presently.
IV. Thomas, of Staffordshire; returned as a man-at-arms, 17th EDWARD II.; ancestor, it is believed, of Sir Thomas de Verdon, Knt., of Denston, co. Stafford, and of his brother, Sir John de Verdon, sheriff of Staffordshire, 34th EDWARD III., who *d. s. p.*, leaving his sister, JOAN, wife of JOHN DE WHITMORE, Lord of Whitmore, his heir. This Joan left two daus. and co-heirs, viz.: Joan, *m.* to Henry Clerk, of Ruyton,

548

co. Salop; and Elizabeth, *m.* to James de Boghay, Lord of Whitmore. (*See* BURKE's *Landed Gentry*, "Mainwaring of Whitmore.")
I. Agnes, *d.* 1305.

The 3rd son,

THEOBALD DE VERDON, lord of the moiety of Meath, in Ireland, had, in the 3rd EDWARD I., on doing homage, livery of his lands, paying £100 for his relief. At this period, he held the office of constable of Ireland. For some years subsequently, this eminent person seems to have enjoyed the favour of the crown, and to have received several immunities; but in the 19th of EDWARD's reign, we find him arraigned for treason, and divers other misdemeanors, before the king and council, at Bergavenny, and condemned to imprisonment and confiscation; the king, however, taking into consideration the good servi- es of his ancestors, and his own submission, freed him for a fine of 500 marks; and he was soon after summoned to parliament as BARON VERDON. In the 29th of the same reign (EDWARD I.), his lordship was one of the barons in the parliament of Lincoln, who, by a public instrument, under their seals, sent to Pope BONIFACE VIII., asserted the right of King EDWARD, as superior lord of the whole realm of Scotland. Lord Verdon having had summons to parliament to 3 November, 1306, *d.* in 1309. By Margery, or Elenor, his wife, he had issue,

I. John (Sir), *d. v. p.* and *s. p.* 1297.
II. THEOBALD, of whom presently.

The elder son,

SIR THEOBALD DE VERDON, 2nd baron, had summons to parliament in the life-time of his father, as "Theobald de Verdon, junior," from 29 December, 1299, to 22 February, 1307, and afterwards, without the word "Junior," from 4 March, 1309, to 24 October, 1314. This nobleman, in the 6th EDWARD II., was constituted justice of Ireland, having likewise the lieutenancy of that realm, and the fee of £500 per annum, then granted to him. His lordship *m.* 1st, Maud, dau. of Edmund, Lord Mortimer, of Wigmore, by whom, who *d.* at Alveton Castle, 1315, he had issue,

I. John, *d. s. p.*   II. William. *d. s. p.*
I. JOAN, *m.* 1st. William de Montagu; and 2ndly. Thomas de Furnival, 2nd Lord Furnival, and *d.* in 1334. Joan had the castle of Alveton as co-heiress of her father.
II. ELIZABETH, *m.* to Bartholomew, Lord de Burghersh. Elizabeth had the castle of Ewyas Lacie as her share.
III. MARGARET, *m.* 1st. Marcus Hussee; 2ndly, William le Blount; and 3rdly, Sir John Crophull. Margaret had the castle of Weobley, as 3rd co-heiress. By Sir John Crophull, she had a son,

Thomas Crophull, whose dau. and heiress,
Agnes, *m.* Sir Walter Devereux, Knt.

He *m.* 2ndly, Elizabeth, widow of John de Burgh, Earl of Ulster, and dau. and eventually co-heir of Gilbert de Clare, Earl of Gloucester, by Jane Plantagenet, dau. of King EDWARD I., by whom (who *m.* 3rdly, Sir Roger d'Amorie) he had an only dau.,

IV. ISABEL, who had the Castle of Ludlow, as 4th co-heiress, *m.* to Henry Ferrers, Lord Ferrers, of Groby, which Henry *d.* 17th EDWARD III., leaving by the said Isabel,

William, Lord Ferrers.
Philippa, *m.* to Guy de Beauchamp.
Elizabeth, *m.* to — de Assells.

Theobald, Lord Verdon, *d.* at Alveton Castle, and was buried at Croxden, aged circa thirty-four, in 1316, when the Barony of Verdon fell into ABEYANCE amongst his daus., and so continues with their representatives.

Arms—Or, a fret, gu.

VERDON—BARON VERDON.

By Writ of Summons, dated 27 January, 1332.

Lineage.

WILLIAM DE VERDON, of Brisingham, co. Norfolk, 3rd son of Bertram de Verdun the Norman (*see* preceding memoir), was ancestor of the Verdons of Brisingham, whose representative,

JOHN DE VERDUN, a minor at his father's decease, *m.* Margaret, dau. and heir of Simon Fitz de Lisle, of Brixworth, co. Northampton, and *d.* circa 1300, having had issue,

I. JOHN, *d.* circa 1302.
II. THOMAS, of whom presently.
I. Susan, wife of Sir Nicholas Seyton.

The 2nd son,

THOMAS DE VERDUN, Lord of Brisingham, Brixworth, &c., d. 9th EDWARD II., leaving a son,

SIR JOHN DE VERDUN, Knt., of Marthesham, co. Suffolk (having removed from Brisingham) who, dying 1346, left by Maud, his wife, three sons,

I. Thomas (Sir). on whom Brixworth was settled in 1329; he d. v. p., leaving by his wife, Alice, an only son, Thomas, who d. s. p. before 25th EDWARD III.

II. JOHN, of whom presently.

III. Christopher (Sir).

The 2nd son,

SIR JOHN DE VERDON, was summoned to parliament as a Baron, from 27 January, 1332, to 22 January, 1336, and again 25 February, 1342. He m. twice: by Maud, his 1st wife, he had a son, Edmund, d. s. p., v. p., and a dau., MARGARET, m. 1st, to Hugh or Henry Bradshaw; and 2ndly, to Sir John Pilkington; and by Isabel, his 2nd wife, dau. of Sir John Vise de Lore, he had a dau., Isabel. m. to Sir Imbert Noon, Knt., among whose heirs-general this Barony of Verdon is now in ABEYANCE.

VERE—EARLS OF OXFORD, MARQUESS OF DUBLIN, DUKE OF IRELAND.

Earldom, Creation of the Empress MAUD, and confirmed by HENRY II., anno 1135.
Marquessate, Creation of RICHARD II., 1385,
Dukedom, Creation of RICHARD II., 1386.

Lineage.

"The noblest subject in England, and indeed, as Englishmen loved to say, the noblest subject in Europe, was Aubrey de Vere, twentieth and last of the old Earls of Oxford. He derived his title through an uninterrupted male descent, from a time when the families of Howard and Seymour were still obscure, when the Nevills and Percys enjoyed only a provincial celebrity, and when even the great name of Plantagenet had not yet been heard in England. One chief of the house of De Vere had held high command at Hastings; another had marched, with Godfrey and Tancred, over heaps of slaughtere d Moslems, to the sepulchre of Christ. The first Earl of Oxford had been minister of Henry Beauclerc. The third earl had been conspicuous among the lords who extorted the great charter from JOHN. The seventh earl had fought bravely at Cressy and Poictiers. The thirteenth earl had, through many vicissitudes of fortune, been the chief of the party of the Red Rose, and had led the van on the decisive day of Bosworth. The seventeenth earl had shone at the court of ELIZABETH, and had won for himself an honourable place among the early masters of English poetry. The nineteenth earl had fallen in arms for the Protestant religion, and for the liberties of Europe, under the walls of Maestricht. His son, Aubrey, in whom closed the longest and most illustrious line of nobles that England has seen, a man of loose morals, but of inoffensive temper, and of courtly manners, was lord-lieutenant of Essex and colonel of the Blues." To these remarks, the author of this work, in his Vicissitudes of Families, ventured thus to refer:—

"Such is Macaulay's glowing and eloquent eulogium on the De Veres—so eloquent, indeed, that one regrets that the panegyric is somewhat exaggerated, and scarcely consistent with recorded fact. The line of the Earls of Oxford was certainly the longest, but as certainly, not the most illustrious that England has seen. In personal achievement and historical importance the De Veres can bear no comparison within the Talbots, the Howards, the Nevills, the Percys, or the Scropes; in antiquity of descent, the Courtenays, the De Bohuns, and the Beauchamps were in all respects their equals, and in splendour of alliances, many a less distinguished family far surpassed them. There was scarcely one of our grand old houses of the times of the HENRYS and the EDWARDS that had not more of royal blood. Nevertheless, I must freely admit, although I cannot subscribe to the pre-eminence Macaulay assigns, that this famous house, if inferior to any, was only so to the very first, to the most historic and to the most illustrious of our ancient nobility."

The first mention of the De Veres is in the General Survey of England, made by WILLIAM THE CONQUEROR, wherein ALBERIC DE VER possessed numerous lordships in different shires, of which Chenisiton (now Kensington), co. Middlesex, was one, and Hedingham, co. Essex, where his castle was situated, and where he chiefly resided, another This Alberic

m. Beatrix, Countess of Ghisnes in her own right, by whom he had five sons, Alberic, Geoffrey, Roger, Robert, and William. Alberic de Vere, in the latter end of his days assumed the cowl, and d. a monk in 1088; he was buried in the church of Colne Priory, which he founded, and was s. by his son,

ALBERIC LE VERE, who being in high favour with King HENRY I., was constituted by that monarch Great Chamberlain of England, to hold the same in fee, to himself and his heirs, with all dignities and liberties thereunto appertaining, as fully and honourably as Robert Malet, lord of the honour of Eye, in Suffolk, who had then been banished and disinherited, had holden the said office. His lordship m. Adeliza, dau. of Gilbert de Clare (or, according to Collins, Adeline, dau. of Roger de Yvery), and had issue,

Alberic, or Aubrey, his successor.
——, canon of St. Osyth's, in Essex.
Robert, Lord of Twiwell, co. Northampton,
Geffery.
William, chancellor of England.
Adeliza, m. to Henry de Essex.
Juliana, m. to Hugh Bigod, Earl of Norfolk.
Bohesia, m. 1st, to Geoffrey Mandeville, Earl of Oxford, and 2ndly, Payne Beauchamp, of Bedford.

In the 6th year of King STEPHEN, when joint sheriff (with Richard Basset, then justice of England,) of Surrey, Cambridge, Essex, and several other counties, his lordship was slain in a popular tumult at London, and was s. by his eldest son,

AUBREY DE VERE, who, for his fidel'ty to the Empress MAUD, was confirmed by that princess in the office of Great Lord Chamberlain, and all his father's territorial possessions. He had likewise other important grants with the Earldom of Cambridge, provided that dignity was not vested in the King of Scots, but if it were, then his lordship was to have his choice of the Earldoms of Oxford, Berkshire, Wiltshire, or Dorsetshire, all which grants being ratified by King HENRY II., his lordship was created EARL OF OXFORD, with the usual grant to earls, of the third penny of the pleas of the county. In the 12th King HENRY II., on the levy of the aid for portioning the king's daughter, the Earl of Oxford certified his knights' fees to be in number twenty-eight, for which he paid £20, and in the 2nd year of King RICHARD I., he paid a fine of 500 marks to the king, "for the sister of Walter de Bolebec, to make a wife for his son." In four years afterwards his lordship contributed £30 2s. 6d. for the knights' fees he then held, towards the sum at that time raised for the ransom of the king. The earl m. 1st, Euphamia, dau. of Sir William de Cantilupe, by whom he had no issue, and 2ndly, Lucia, dau. and heiress of William de Abrincis, by whom he had

AUBREY, } successively Earls of Oxford.
ROBERT, }
William, bishop of Hereford, anno 1186, d. in 1199.
Henry.
Adeliza.   Sarah.

His lordship d. in 1194 (being styled in his monumental inscription Earl of Ghisnes and 1st Earl of Oxford), and was s. by his elder son,

AUBREY DE VERE, 2nd Earl of Oxford and Great Chamberlain. This nobleman was sheriff of Essex and Herefordshire from the 10th to the 15th King JOHN, inclusive, and was reputed one of the evil councillors of that monarch. His lordship d. in 1214, and having no issue, was s. by his brother,

ROBERT DE VERE, 3rd Earl of Oxford and Great Chamberlain, who, pursuing a different course from that of his deceased brother, was one of the celebrated twenty-five barons appointed to enforce the observance of Magna Charta. In the beginning of the reign of HENRY III., having made his peace, his lordship appears, from a fine levied before him and others, to have been one of the judges in the Court of King's Bench. He m. Isabel, dau. of Hugh, and sister and heir of Walter de Bolebec, by whom he had issue,

I. HUGH, his successor.

II. Henry (Sir), of Great Addington, co. Northampton, whose son, SIR ROBERT, was father of

Richard de Vere, who m. Isabel, dau. of John Greene, Esq., of Drayton, and heiress of her brother, whereby the manor of Drayton, co. Northampton, came into this branch of the Vere family, the male line of which terminated with

Sir Henry Vere, of Great Addington, Drayton, &c., who left by his wife, Isabel, dau. of Sir Thomas Tresham, four daus., his co-heirs, viz.,

Elizabeth, m. to John, Lord Mordaunt.
Anne, m. to Sir Humphrey Brown, chief justice of the Common Pleas, 34th HENRY VIII.
Constance, m. to John Parr, Esq., younger son of Sir William Parr, K.G.
Etheldred, m. to John Brown, Esq.

The earl *d.* in 1221, and was *s.* by his elder son,

Hugh de Vere, 4th Earl of Oxford and 5th Great Chamberlain. In the 17th King Henry III. he was knighted at Gloucester, the King at that time solemnizing the feast of Pentecost there. In 1245 his lordship's mother died, and he then, upon giving security for payment of his relief, namely, the sum of £100, and doing homage, had livery of the lands of her inheritance. In the 30th Henry III. he was one of the subscribing barons to the letter transmitted to the Pope, complaining of the exactions of his holiness upon this realm, and he sat in the parliament, 32nd Henry III., wherein the king was upbraided with his prodigal expenditure, and informed that neither his treasurer nor chancellor had the confidence of their lordships. The earl *m.* Hawise, dau. of Sayer de Quincy, Earl of Winchester, and *d.* in 1263, having had issue, i. Robert, his heir; ii. Aubrey; iii. Richard: i. Margaret, *m.* to Hugh de Cressi; ii. Maud; iii. Isabel, *m.* to John de Courtenay. The eldest son,

Robert de Vere, 5th Earl of Oxford and 6th Great Chamberlain, having arrayed himself under the banner of Montfort, Earl of Leicester, was amongst those who were surprised with young Hugh de Montfort, at Kenilworth, a few days before the battle of Evesham, and taken prisoner, but he made his peace soon after, under the "Dictum de Kenilworth," and we find him employed by King Edward I. against the Welsh, in the 14th of that monarch's reign. His lordship *m.* Alice, dau. and heiress of Gilbert de Saundford,* chamberlain in fee to Eleanor, Queen of Henry III., and had, with other issue,

Robert, his successor.

Alphonsus, *m.* Jane, dau. of Sir Richard Foliot, Knt., and had a son,

John, who *s.* as 7th Earl of Oxford.

Hugh, Baron Vere (*see that title*),

Joane, *m.* to William de Warren.

Lora, *m.* to Reginald de Argentein.

The earl *d.* in 1296, and was *s.* by his eldest son,

Robert de Vere, 6th Earl of Oxford and 7th Great Chamberlain, who took part in the wars of Scotland, 24th and 27th Edward I. His lordship *m.* Margaret, dau. of Roger Mortimer, Earl of March, but *d. s. p.* in 1331, when his honours devolved upon his nephew,

John de Vere, as 7th Earl of Oxford and 8th Great Chamberlain. This nobleman, who was a military personage of great renown, shared in all the glories of King Edward III.'s martial reign. When he *s.* to the earldom, he had but just attained his eighteenth year, and very soon afterwards we find him with the army in Scotland, where he appears to have been engaged for some years. In the 14th Edward III., he attended the king into Flanders. The next year he assisted "at the great feast and justing in London, which King Edward III. caused to be made, as it was said, for the love of the Countess of Salisbury." In the 16th year he was again in the wars of France, to which service he brought forty men-at arms (himself included), one banneret, nine knights, twenty-nine esquires, and thirty archers on horseback, and had an allowance of fifty-six sacks of wool for the wages of himself and his retinue. The next year he accompanied Henry de Lancaster, Earl of Derby, and divers other great personages, into Scotland, for raising the siege of Lochmaban Castle. And in the 18th, he was in Gascony, at the surrender of Bergerath, after which, proceeding to assault the castle of Pellegrue, he was taken prisoner in his tent, but soon after exchanged for the Viscount de Bonquentyne, when he marched with the Earl of Derby to Attveroche, then besieged by the French, and relieved it. "But about the feast of the Blessed Virgin," writes Dugdale, "returning out of Brittany, he was by tempest cast upon the coast of Connaught, in Ireland, where he and all his company suffered much misery from those barbarous people there, who pillaged them of all they had."

His lordship returned to France soon after this event, and continued with little interruption during the remainder of his life actively and gallantly engaged in the wars in that country.

---

* This Gilbert inherited the manor of Hormade Magna, co. Herts, and held it by serjeanty of service, in the queen's chamber, which manor was conveyed by his heiress, Alice, to her husband, the Earl of Oxford, and sold by his successor, Edward, Earl of Oxford, *temp.* Elizabeth, to Anthony Cage, citizen of London, whose representative, Daniel Cage, at the coronation of King James I., claimed the office of chamberlain to the queen; but the court for determining claims came to no decision upon the case, because the Earl of Oxford held three manors by this office, and there was no proof that Ginges, one of the three, was yet severed from the earldom.

He was one of the heroes of Cressy, and he had a command upon the glorious field of Poictiers. He eventually lost his life from fatigue, in the English army, encamped before the walls of Rheims, 24 January, 1360. The earl *m.* Maud, sister and heiress of Giles, Lord Badlesmere, and widow of Robert Fitz-Payn, by whom he had issue,

Thomas, his successor.

Aubrey, who, upon the reversal of the attainder of his nephew, Robert, Duke of Ireland, *s.* as 10th Earl of Oxford (of this nobleman presently).

John, *d. s. p.*

Margaret, *m.* 1st, to Sir Nicholas Lovain; 2ndly, to Henry, Lord Beaumont, and 3rdly, to Sir John Devereux, Knt.

His lordship, who left vast landed possessions in the cos. Hereford, Bedford, Leicester, Essex, Buckingham, Hertford, Dorset, Wilts, Suffolk, and Cambridge, was *s.* by his eldest son,

Sir Thomas de Vere, Knt., 8th Earl of Oxford and 9th Great Chamberlain. Of this nobleman little more is mentioned than his being engaged in foreign warfare like his father, but not with the same renown. His lordship *m.* in the life-time of the late earl, Maud, dau. of Sir Ralph de Ufford, brother of Robert, Earl of Suffolk, and was *s.* at his decease, 18 September, 1371, by his only son,

Robert de Vere, 9th Earl of Oxford and 10th Lord Chamberlain, K.G., who doing homage, and making proof of his age, in the 6th King Richard II., had livery of his lands. His lordship becoming subsequently the favourite of that weak and unfortunate prince, obtained large territorial grants from the crown, amongst which was the castle of Okeham, in Rutland, and was advanced to a new dignity in the peerage, by the title of Marquess of Dublin, for life, in which he had summons to parliament, 8 August, 1386. On his elevation to the marquessate his lordship obtained a grant of the lordship and domain of Ireland, with all profits, revenues, and regalities, as amply as the king himself ought to enjoy the same, to hold by homage and allegiance. With the lordship and domain thereof, as aforesaid, "*quoad vixerit*," he was created Duke of Ireland on 8 August, 1386, on his surrender of the Marquessate. These high honours and immunities exciting the jealousy of the nobles, and the favourite bearing his fortune imperiously, several of the great lords assembled at Haringhay House, near Highgate, co. Middlesex, and evinced open hostility to the royal minion. Thence, at the desire of the king, who became alarmed, they transferred their deliberations to Westminster, and in reply to an interrogatory put to them by the bishop of Ely, then lord chancellor, they demanded that the king should dismiss the traitors that surrounded him, amongst whom they particularized Robert de Vere, Duke of Ireland. For the moment, however, Richard allayed this tumult by fair promises, but De Vere not considering himself safe, soon after effected his escape, in disguise, to the continent, accompanied by Michael de la Pole, Earl of Suffolk. He subsequently returned to England, at the head of 4000 or 5000 men, and marching into Oxfordshire, was met at Radcote Bridge, on the river Isis, by the Earl of Derby and Duke of Gloucester, where his troops being surrounded, he could secure personal safety only by abandoning his two gauntlets and armour, and thus swimming down the stream. In the pursuit, his grace's chariot having fallen into the hands of his foes, it is said that they discovered there letters from the king, calling on him to hasten to London, and the Monarch would be ready to live or die for him. In a parliament soon after convened, through the influence of the nobles, the duke, not appearing to a citation, was sentenced to banishment, and at the same time outlawed and attainted. He again, however, effected his escape to the continent, where, being wounded by a wild boar, while hunting, he died of the hurt at Lovaine, *anno* 1392, in great distress and poverty; his English property being all confiscated, and his honours extinguished by the attainder. When the news of the duke's death reached England, King Richard caused his body to be brought over, had the coffin opened, that he might once again see the features of the friend he had loved so well, and attended the corpse himself, in grand procession, to its interment at Earl's Colne, in Essex.

His grace *m.* 1st, Lady Philippa De Coucy, dau. and co-heiress of Ingelram, Earl of Bedford, by his wife, the Princess Isabel, dau. of King Edward III., which noble lady, in the zenith of his prosperity, he repudiated, and *m.* 2ndly, a Portuguese girl, named Lancerona, stated by some accounts to have been a joiner's daughter, but by others, styled "the Landgravine," who came out of Bohemia, with Anne, Queen consort of King Richard. This lady was the companion of De Vere's banishment and adversity; and there may yet be seen at Earl's Colne, among the De Vere memorials, the tomb and effigy of Lancerona, Duchess of Ireland, conspicuous from the quaint head-dress of "piked horns," introduced by Anne of

Bohemia. The duke had no issue, and at his decease the representation of the family reverted to his uncle,

AUBREY DE VERE, who, in the 16th RICHARD II., was, by consent of parliament, restored to all those lands which had been, by fine, entailed previously to the attainder of the deceased duke; having the Earldom of Oxford likewise restored to himself and the heirs male of his body. His lordship, in consequence, took his seat in the House of Peers, as 10th earl; but the office of Great Chamberlain, so long in the Vere family, was bestowed by the king, owing to the restored lord being infirm, upon John Holland, Earl of Huntingdon, for life. The infirmities of his lordship continuing, he had especial license to absent himself from the parliament held at Shrewsbury,.in the 21st RICHARD II., in which the judgment passed ten years previously against his nephew, the Duke of Ireland, was revoked and annulled. The earl m. Alice, dau. of John, Lord Fitz-Walter, and had issue,

RICHARD, his successor.
John, d. |s. p. 9th HENRY V.
Alice, m. 1st, Gui d'Albon; 2ndly, to Sir John Fitz-Lewes, Knt., and 3rdly, Nicholas Thorley.

His lordship d. in 1400, and was s. by his elder son,

RICHARD DE VERE, 11th Earl of Oxford, K.G. This nobleman was fourteen years of age at the decease of his father, and had a grant of £100 a year out of his own lands for his maintenance during his minority. His lordship inherited very extensive estates in the cos. Essex, Kent, Cambridge, &c., and in the 8th HENRY IV., being then of full age, having assented. that Philippa, Duchess of Ireland, first wife of the attainted duke, should enjoy her dower out of the entailed lands, the king, in compliance with an act of parliament, granted to his lordship and his heirs, all those lands and tenements, which, by the forfeiture of Duke Robert, came to the crown; excepting such as had been disposed of by himself or King RICHARD II.

"About this time," says Dugdale, "or not long before, Maud, Countess of Oxford, widow of Earl Thomas, and mother of Robert, Duke of Ireland, still surviving, caused it to be divulged that King RICHARD II. was alive; and that he would forthwith lay claim to his ancient honour; and procured Harts to be made of silver and gilt (which were badges that king gave to his friends, souldiers, and servants) to be in the king's name distributed in the countrey, whereby the people might be the sooner allured to rise on his behalf; giving it farther out, that he was privately kept in Scotland till he could have a fit opportunity to come in with an army of French and Scots. Whereupon she was committed to prison, and her goods confiscated." This lady d. in 1422, leaving her cousin, Robert de Willoughby, her next heir. The Earl of Oxford m. Alice, dau. of Sir Richard Serjeaulx, Knt., of Cornwall, by Lady Philippa-FitzAlan, his wife, and had issue,

JOHN, his successor.
Robert, m. Joane, widow of Sir Nicholas Carew, and dau. of Sir Hugh Courtenay, and had issue,
    JOHN DE VERE, who m. Alice, widow of Sir Walter Courtenay, and dau. of Walter Kilrington, and left a son,
        JOHN, who s. as 15th Earl of Oxford.

His lordship, who had been in the French wars, and was honoured with the Garter, d. in 1417, and was s by his elder son,

JOHN DE VERE, 12th Earl of Oxford, then in his 9th year. In the 4th HENRY VI. his lordship had the honour of knighthood conferred upon him by that monarch, at Leicester, when the king himself received a similar honour at the hands of his uncle, the Duke of Bedford. In the 7th of the same reign, being still in ward, the earl had to pay a fine of £2000 for marrying Elizabeth, dau. of Sir John Howard, Knt., the younger, without license; but before the close of that year, having attained majority, and done homage, he had livery of his lands. In the 13th, his lordship obtained license to travel towards the Holy Land, with twelve persons of his company; and to take with him £100 in money, and to receive 600 marks more by way of exchange. In the next year he went into Picardy for the relief of Calais, and the same year performing his homage had livery of all those lands, which, by the death of Margaret, the wife of Sir John Howard, Knight, descended to her dau. Elizabeth, Countess of Oxford, his lordship's consort. After this we find the earl joined in commission with John, Duke of Norfolk, and others, to treat with Charles de Valoys, or his ambassadors, touching a peace with France; and during the whole reign of HENRY VI., being a stanch Lancastrian, always enjoying the confidence of the crown; but upon the accession of EDWARD IV., sharing the fate of his party, he was attainted in the 1st parliament of that monarch, with his eldest son, Aubrey, and beheaded on Tower Hill, anno 1461.

His lordship m. as already stated, Elizabeth, only dau. and

heiress of Sir John Howard (uncle by the half-blood of John Howard, 1st Duke of Norfolk) and heiress, through her grandmother, Margaret, dau. of Sir John de Platz, to the Barony of Platz, and co-heiress, through her great-grandmother, Margaret, to the Barony of Scales (see p. 476). By Elizabeth, his wife, the earl had issue,

I. Aubrey, who m. Anne, dau. of Henry, 1st Duke of Buckingham, but had no issue. He was beheaded with his father, 1st EDWARD IV.
II. JOHN, restored as 13th earl.
III. George (Sir), m. Margaret, dau. and heiress of Sir William Stafford, Knt., of Frome, and d. 1503, having had issue,
  1 George, who d. in his father's lifetime, 1498.
  2 JOHN, who inherited as 14th Earl of Oxford.
  1 DOROTHEA, m. to John Nevill, Lord Latimer, and had issue; for the co-heirs of this marriage, the senior of whom is the DUKE OF ATHOLE (refer to p. 398).
  2 Elizabeth, m. to Sir Anthony Wingfield, K.G., the co-heirship of the marriage centered in Adrien, MARQUESS DE COURONNELL, of France, and VICE-ADMIRAL SIR WILLIAM-HENRY DILLON.
  3 Ursula, m. 1st, to George Windsor. Esq., and 2ndly, to Sir Edmund Knightly. She d. s. p. in 1500.
IV Richard (Sir), m. Margaret Percy.
V. Thomas (Sir), d. s. p. in 1489.
I. Mary, a nun at Barking
II. Joane, m. to Sir William Norris, Knt., of Yatenden.
III. Elizabeth, m. to William Bourchier, son and heir of Henry, Earl of Essex.

On the attainder and execution of John, 12th Earl of Oxford, all the honours of the family EXPIRED, but his lordship's 2nd and eldest surviving son,

JOHN DE VERE, was restored as 13th Earl of Oxford, K.G., during the temporary triumph of the House of Lancaster in the 10th EDWARD IV., when he sat as lord high steward at the trial of John Tiptoft, Earl of Worcester, who was condemned and beheaded on Tower Hill. But his lordship, with Richard Nevill, the stout Earl of Warwick, being soon after totally routed by the Yorkists, at Barnet, and King EDWARD re-established upon the throne, himself and his two brothers, Sir George and Sir Thomas Vere, were attainted, but pardoned as to their lives. Subsequently escaping from prison, and ardently embarking in the cause of Henry, Earl of Richmond, Oxford commanded the archers of the vanguard, at Bosworth Field, and there mainly contributed, by his valour and skill, to the victory which terminated the bloody and procrastinated contest between the Houses of York and Lancaster. On the accession of his chief to the crown of England as HENRY VII., his lordship was immediately restored to all his possessions, and sworn of the privy council; and at the coronation of the king he was constituted one of the commissioners for executing the office of lord high steward of England. The earl had besides large grants of confiscated property, and was made constable of the Tower of London, and lord high admiral of England, Ireland, and the Duchy of Aquitaine. At the coronation of the Queen consort, 3rd HENRY VII., his lordship was again one of the commissioners for executing the office of lord high steward, and he had subsequently a chief command in suppressing the rebellion of Lambert Simnell and his partizans; as he had a few years afterwards in opposing Lord Audley and the Cornish men at Blackheath. Upon the accession of King HENRY VIII., the Earl of Oxford was restored to the office of Great Chamberlain of England, originally granted to his ancestor, Aubrey de Vere, by King HENRY I., in which year he had the constableship of the castle of Clare, co. Suffolk, confirmed to him for life; as also a grant and confirmation of the castle of Colchester, which MAUD, the Empress conferred upon his family. Of this distinguished personage (who was celebrated for his splendid hospitality, and was esteemed a gallant, learned, and religious man,) and King HENRY VII., the following story is told:

The monarch visiting the earl's castle of Hedingham, was there sumptuously entertained by the princely noble; and at his departure his lordship's livery servants ranged on both sides, made an avenue for the king; which attracting his highness's attention, he called out to the earl and said, "My lord, I have heard much of your hospitality, but I see it is greater than the speech. These handsome gentlemen and yeomen, which I see on both sides of me, are surely your menial servants?" The earl smiled, and said, "It may please your grace they were not for mine ease; they are most of them my retainers, that are come to do me service at such a time as this; and chiefly to see your grace." The king started a little, and rejoined, "By my faith, my lord, I thank you for my good cheer, but I may not endure to have my laws broken in my sight; my attorney must speak with you." It is added that this affair cost his lordship eventually no less than 15,000 marks in the shape of compromise.

The earl m. 1st, Lady Margaret Nevill, dau. of Richard, Earl of Salisbury, by whom he had a son, John, who d. young in the Tower of London during his father's exile. His lordship m. 2ndly, Elizabeth, dau. of Sir Richard Scrope, Knt., and widow of William, Viscount Beaumont, but had no issue. The earl who with his other honours was a knight of the Garter, d. in 1513, and was s by (the eldest surviving son of his deceased brother, Sir George Vere) his nephew,

JOHN DE VERE, as 14th Earl of Oxford, commonly called, "Little John of Campes," from his diminutive stature, and residence at Castle Campes, in Cambridgeshire. His lordship m. Lady Anne Howard, dau. of Thomas, Duke of Norfolk, but had no issue. He d. in 1526, when his sisters (refer to children of Sir George Vere, son of John, 12th earl,) became heirs to the ancient baronies * of the family, and those fell into ABEYANCE between them, as they still continue with their descendants, while the Earldom of Oxford passed to his cousin and heir-at-law (refer to descendants of the Hon. Robert Vere, 2nd son of Richard, 11th earl),

JOHN DE VERE, as 15th Earl of Oxford and Great Chamberlain, K.G. This nobleman was a privy councillor in the reign of HENRY VI'I., and supported the measures of the court. He signed the articles exhibited by the King against Cardinal Wolsey, and his name was to the letter addressed to the Pope (CLEMENT VII.) by several of the nobility and divers churchmen, declaring that unless his holiness sanctioned the king's divorce from Queen Katharine. the supremacy of the holy see within this realm would terminate.

The earl m. Elizabeth, dau. and heiress of Sir Edward Trussel, Knt., of Cubleadon, co. Stafford, by whom he had issue,

JOHN, his successor,

Aubrey, m. Margaret, dau. of John Spring, Esq., of Lavenham, co. Suffolk, and had, with other. issue,

HUGH, m. Eleanor, dau. of — Walsh, Esq., and left a son,

ROBERT, who s. as 19th Earl of Oxford.

Geffery, who m. Elizabeth, dau. of Sir John Hardkyn of Colchester, and had, with other issue,

Francis (Sir), some time governor of Brill, in the Netherlands.

HORATIO, the celebrated Lord Vere, of Tilbury. (See that dignity.)

Frances, m. to Sir Robert Harcourt, Knt., ancestor of the extinct Earls of Harcourt.

Elizabeth, m. to Thomas, Lord Darcy. of Chiche.
Anne. m. to Edmund Sheffield, Lord Sheffield.
Frances, m. to Henry, Earl of Surrey.

His lordship, who was a knight of the Garter, d. in 1539, and was s. by his eldest son,

JOHN DE VERE, 16th Earl of Oxford and Great Chamberlain, who, in the 32nd HENRY VIII , had livery of those lands which descended to him from Elizabeth, his mother, sister and heir of John Trussel, Esq.: and in the 36th of the same monarch was in the expedition into France, when Bulloigne was besieged and taken. His lordship m. 1st, Lady Dorothy Nevill, dau. of Ralph, Earl of Westmoreland, by whom he had an only dau.,

Katherine, m. to Edward, Lord Windsor.

The earl m. 2ndly, Margery, dau. of John Golding, Esq., of Halstead, co. Essex, auditor of the exchequer, and sister of Sir Thomas Golding, Knt., of Notts, by whom (who m. 2ndly, Christopher Tyrrell, and d. 2 December, 1568,) he had issue,

EDWARD, his successor.

Mary, m. to Peregrine Bertie, 10th Lord Willoughby de Eresby, by whom she had,

ROBERT, 11th Lord Willoughby de Eresby, who claimed the Earldom of Oxford and the office of Great Chamberlain, in right of his mother; but s. in the latter only. He was, however, created EARL OF LINDSAY. In this earldom and the subsequent Dukedom of Ancaster, the Barony of Willoughby and the chamberlainship continued, until the extinction in 1809, of those dignities, when the Great chamberlainship devolved jointly upon the last Duke of Ancaster's sisters and heirs, Priscilla, Lady Gwydyr, and Georgiana-Charlotte, Marchioness of Cholmondeley, and it is now vested in Lord Willoughby de Eresby and the Marquess of Cholmondeley.

The earl d. in 1562, and was s. by his elder son,

EDWARD DE VERE, 17th Earl of Oxford and Great Chamberlain, who was one of the peers appointed, 29th ELIZABETH, to sit in judgment upon the unhappy MARY Queen of Scotland, and had a command in the fleet equipped to oppose the Armada, in 1588. His lordship was one of the wits of the period

in which he lived, and distinguished alike by his patriotism and chivalrous spirit. In the tournaments of ELIZABETH's reign he was pre-eminently conspicuous, and on two occasions was honoured with a prize from her Majesty's own hand, being conducted, armed by two ladies, into the presence chamber for the purpose of receiving the high reward. Walpole says that he obtained reputation as a poet, and was esteemed the first writer of comedy in his time. His lordship m. 1st, Anne, dau. of William Cecil, the celebrated, Lord (Treasurer) Burghley, and had issue,

Elizabeth, m. to William, Earl of Derby ; the heir-general of this marriage is the DUKE OF ATHOLE.

Bridget, m. to Francis, Lord Norris, of Rycote ; the heir-general of this marriage is the EARL OF ABINGDON.

Susan, m. to Philip Herbert, Earl of Montgomery ; the heir-general of this marriage is the MARQUESS OF BUTE.

The earl m. 2ndly, Elizabeth, dau. of Thomas Trentham, Esq., of Rowcester, co. Stafford, by whom he had an only child,

HENRY, his successor.

This Lord Oxford was the first person who introduced perfumes and embroidered gloves into England, and on his presentation of a pair of the latter to Queen ELIZABETH, her Majesty was so pleased.with them, that she had her picture painted with those gloves on. His lordship, who seems to have dissipated the noble inheritance of his family, lived to an advanced age, and dying in 1604, was s. by his son,

HENRY DE VERE, 18th Earl of Oxford, and Great Chamberlain, who m. Lady Diana Cecil. 2nd dau. of William, Earl of Exeter, one of the greatest fortunes and most celebrated beauties of the period, but had no issue. His lordship d. at the siege of Breda, in the Netherlands, where he had the command of a regiment in 1625, when his honours devolved upon his cousin (refer to descendants of Aubrey, 2nd son of John, 15th earl),

ROBERT DE VERE, as 19th Earl of Oxford. In the 2nd CHARLES I , there was great controversy between this Robert and Robert Bertie, then Lord Willoughby de Eresby, in consequence of the latter claiming in right of his mother, Mary, dau. of John, 16th Earl of Oxford, and sister and heiress of Edward, 17th earl, the Earldom of Oxford, with the baronies in fee belonging to the family, and.the Great Chamberlainship of England. The judges, gave their opinion, however, in parliament, "that the earldom was well descended upon the heir male ; but that the baronies having devolved upon heirs female, the three sisters of John, 14th earl (refer to children of Sir George Vere, 3rd son of the 12th earl,) were then in ABEYANCE." As to the office of Great Chamberlain, it was also referred to the judges, then attending in parliament, to report, whether "that Robert, Earl of Oxford, who made the entail thereof, temp. RICHARD II., on the heir male, was at that time seized thereof or not, and admitting that he was, then whether such an office might be conveyed by way of limiting of uses." On this reference three of the judges, Dodridge, Yelverton, and Trevor, decided for Lord, Willoughby,* and two, Chief Justice Crew, and Chief Baron Walter, for the heir male ; five of their lordships only attending. Whereupon the Lord Willoughby was admitted 13 April, 13th CHARLES I., into the house with his staff of office; and took his place above all the barons, according to the statute of 31st HENRY VIII., and the next day, Robert de Vere took his seat as Earl of Oxford, next to the Earl of Arundel. His lordship m. a Dutch lady, Beatrix Van Hemmend, by whom he left, at his decease in 1632 (falling at the siege of Maestrich, where he commanded a regiment,) an only surviving child, his successor,

AUBREY DE VERE, 20th Earl of Oxford, K.G. This nobleman, at the decease of his father, was but six years of age, and in ward to King CHARLES I. In 1648 he had command of a regiment of English infantry in the service of the States General. During the civil wars he espoused the royal cause, and suffered much in consequence, but after the Restoration he was sworn of the privy council, made a knight of the Garter, and appointed lord-lieutenant of the co. Essex. His lordship m. 1st, Anne, dau. and co-heir of Paul, Viscount Bayning, by whom he had no issue. He m. 2ndly, Diana, dau. of George Kirke, Esq., one of the grooms of the bedchamber to King CHARLES I., by whom he had,

Charles,
Charlotte, } both d. young.

Diana, m. to Charles Beauclerk (illegitimate son of CHARLES

---

* This decision appears strangely at variance with our present notions; Lord Willoughby was not the heir-general of the De Veres, but was simply the nearest relation by the full blood to the last holder of the title. (See Vicissitudes of Families, vol 2, p. 431.)

II.,) DUKE OF ST. ALBANS. This lady became. eventually, sole heiress of her father, and representative of Aubrey de Vere, last Earl of Oxford.

Mary,
Henrietta, } both *d. unm.*

The earl *d.* "at a miserable cottage" 12 March, 1702 (having acquiesced in the expulsion of the royal house, which he had previously so zealously upheld,) and with him the very ancient Earldom of Oxford, which had passed through twenty generations, is supposed to have become EXTINCT. How can this brief epitome of the history of the De Veres be more appropriately concluded, than by the following quotation from the summing up of Chief Justice Crew, at the great controversy of the time of CHARLES I.—"This great and weighty cause" (these are the chief justice's words,) "incomparable to any other that hath happened at any time, requires great deliberation, and solid and mature judgment to determine it; and I wish that all the judges of England had heard it (it being a fit case for all), to the end we all together might have given our humble advice to your lordships herein. Here is represented to your lordships *certamen honoris*, and, as I may well say, *illustris honoris*, illustrious honour. I heard a great peer of this realm, and a learned, say, when he lived there was no King in Christendom had such a subject as Oxford. He came in with the CONQUEROR, Earl of Guynes; shortly after the Conquest, made Great Chamberlain of England, above 500 years ago, by HENRY I., the CONQUEROR'S son, brother to RUFUS; by MAUD, the empress, Earl of Oxford; confirmed and approved by HENRY II., Alberico comiti, so earl before. This great honour, this high and noble dignity hath continued ever since in the remarkable surname of De Vere, by so many ages, descents and generations, as no other kingdom can produce such a peer in one and the self same name and title. I find in all this length of time, but two attainders of this noble family, and those in stormy and tempestuous times, when the government was unsettled, and the kingdom in competition. I have laboured to make a covenant with myself, that affection may not press upon judgment, for I suppose there is not many that hath any apprehension of gentry or nobleness, but his affection stands to the continuance of so noble a name and house, and would take hold of a twig or a twine thread to uphold it. And yet, time hath its revolutions; there must be a period and an end to all things temporal—*finis rerum*—an end of names and dignities and whatever is terrene, and why not of De Vere? For where is Bohun? Where is Mowbray? Where is Mortimer? Nay, which is more and most of all, where is Plantagenet? They are entombed in the urns and sepulchres of mortality! And yet let the name and dignity of De Vere stand so long as it pleaseth God."

A family of VERE seated at Carlton, Notts, which traces back its ancestry to William Vere, of Hints, co. Stafford, temp. JAMES I., has long asserted a claim to the Earldom of Oxford.

Arms—Quarterly: gu. and or; in the first quarter a mullet, arg.

VERE—BARON VERE.

By Writ of Summons, dated 27 September, 1299.

Lineage.

HUGH DE VERE, one of the younger sons of Robert, 5th Earl of Oxford, a military personage of high reputation, was summoned to parliament as a Baron from 27 September, 1299, to 3 March, 1318. In the 25th EDWARD I., he was joined in an embassy to France with the bishop of Gloucester, for negotiating peace between the two crowns; and the next year he was deputed to the court of Rome on a mission of great importance. He was, subsequently, employed upon other diplomatic occasions, and was actively engaged in the Scottish wars. His lordship *m.* Dyonisia, dau. and heiress of William, son of Warine de Monchensy, which lady *d. s. p.* in 1313, when Adomare de Valence, son of the Lady Joane de Valence, was found to be her next heir. Lord Vere does not appear to have *m.* a second time, and the barony became therefore, at his decease, EXTINCT.

Arms—Same as De Vere, Earl of Oxford, with proper difference.

VERE—BARON VERE, OF TILBURY, CO. ESSEX.

By Letters Patent, dated 24 July, 1625.

Lineage.

GEOFFREY DE VERE, 3rd son of John, 15th Earl of Oxford, and brother of John, 16th earl, *m.* Elizabeth, dau. of Sir John Hardkyn, Knt., of Colchester, and had issue,

John, of Kisby Hall, co. Essex, *m.* Thomasine, dau. of — Porter, Esq., and had two sons,

John,
Robert, } who both *d. s. p.*

Francis (Sir). Of the exploits of this gallant person an account appeared in 1657, under the title of *The Commentaries of Sir Francis Vere, being divers pieces of service, wherein he had command, written by himself,* published by William Dellingham, D.D. Sir Francis *m.* Elizabeth Dent, dau. and co-heir of a citizen of London, by whom he had several children, all of whom, however, predeceased himself *unm.* He *d.* in 1608. and was interred in Westminster Abbey, under a splendid monument.

Geoffrey, *d. unm.*

HORATIO, of whom presently.

Frances, *m.* to Sir Robert Harcourt, ancestor of the Earls of Harcourt.

The youngest son,

SIR HORATIO VERE, Knt., becoming one of the most eminent persons of the period in which he lived, was elevated to the peerage for his distinguished services, by King CHARLES I., in the dignity of BARON VERE, *of Tilbury,* co. Essex, 24 July, 1625. The exploits of this gallant personage form a brilliant page in British History, and it would be in vain to attempt even to epitomize them here. He was so great a military officer that the first generals were proud of having served under him; and Clarendon in mentioning Edward, Lord Conway, says, "he was bred up a soldier, in several commands under the particular care of Lord Vere." He also observes, that "Monk, Duke of Albemarle, had the reputation of a good foot officer, when he was in the Lord Vere's regiment in Holland." Fuller in his *Worthies* thus characterizes his lordship: "Horace, Lord Vere, had more meekness and as much valour as his brother; of an excellent temper: it being true of him what is said of the Caspian Sea, that it doth never ebb, nor flow, observing a constant tenor, neither elated or depressed with success. Both lived in war much honoured, and died in peace much lamented." Lord Vere *m.* Mary, dau. of Sir William Tracy, Knt., of Toddington, co. Gloucester, and relict of William Hoby, Esq., and had five daus., his co-heirs, viz.,

Elizabeth, *m.* to John Holles, 2nd Earl of Clare, and had issue,

GILBERT, 3rd Earl of Clare, whose son,

JOHN, 4th Earl of Clare. was created DUKE OF NEWCASTLE, K.G., and *d.* in 1711, leaving an only dau. and heiress,

Lady Henrietta Cavendish Holles. who *m.* Edward Harley, 2nd Earl of Oxford, and had an only dau. and heiress.

Lady Margaret Cavendish Harley, *m.* to William, 2nd Duke of Portland.

On the demise of John Holles, Duke of Newcastle, the honours of the Holles family expired, but they were revived in his grace's nephew. Thomas, Lord Pelham, from whom the extant Dukes of Newcastle derive.

Mary, *m.* to Sir Roger Townshend, Bart., of Raynham, co. Norfolk, from which marriage the extant Marquesses Townshend derive. Her ladyship *m.,* after the decease of Sir Roger, Mildmay Fane, 2nd Earl of Westmoreland, and had issue, Vere, who *s.* his half-brother, Charles, as 4th Earl of Westmoreland.

Catherine, *m.* 1st, Oliver, son and heir of Sir John St. John, of Lydiard Tregoze, and 2ndly, John, Lord Paulet.

Anne, *m.* to the celebrated parliamentary general, Sir Thomas Fairfax, Lord Fairfax. By whom she had an only dau. and heiress, Mary, *m.* to George Villiers, 2nd Duke of Buckingham.

Dorothy, *m.* to John Wolstenholme, Esq., eldest son of Sir John Wolstenholme, Bart. of Nostel, co. York. by whom she had no issue. Mr. Wolstenholme predeceased his father and was buried at Stanmore under a stately monument of white marble.

His lordship *d.* 2 May, 1635, when the Barony of Vere, of Tilbury, became EXTINCT. Horatio, Lord Vere, was interred near his brother, Sir Francis, in Westminster Abbey.

Arms—See those of Vere, Earls of Oxford, duly differenced.

VERE—MARQUESS OF DUBLIN AND DUKE OF IRELAND.

(*See* VERE, Earls of Oxford.)

VERNEY—VISCOUNTS FERMANAGH AND EARLS VERNEY.

Viscounty, by Letters Patent, dated 16 June, 1703.
Earldom, by Letters Patent, dated 22 March, 1742.

Lineage.

JOHN VERNEY, Esq., son of SIR RALPH VERNEY, m. Margaret, dau. and heir of Sir Robert Whittingham, of Penley, co. Hertford, sheriff of London, 1419, and had a son,

RALPH VERNEY, Esq., lord mayor of London, who received the honour of knighthood. He m. Margaret, dau. and heir of Francis Iwardby, Esq., of Quinton, Bucks, by whom he had two sons and three daus., viz.,

    I. RALPH (Sir), his heir.
    II. John (Sir), of Penley, who was sheriff of Bedford and Bucks, 21st EDWARD IV., and of Essex and Hertford, 14th HENRY VII.
    I. Eleanor, m. to Sir Edward Greville.
    II. Catherine, m. to Sir John Conway, of Arrow, co. Warwick, knight banneret.
    III. Margaret, m. to Sir Edward Raleigh, of Farnborough, Knt.

The elder son,

SIR RALPH VERNEY, of Penley, Herts, and Middle Claydon, Bucks, m. Elizabeth, 2nd dau. of Edmund, Lord Braye, and sister and co-heir of John, last Lord Braye, and had issue,

    EDWARD, his heir.
    John, d. s. p.,
    EDMUND, succeeded his brother.
    Francis.   Ralph.
    Urian.
    Richard (Sir), sheriff of Warwick and Leicester.
    Anne, m. to Sir Nicholas Poyntz.
    Jane, m. to Sir Francis Hinde.

The eldest son,

EDWARD VERNEY, Esq., m. Dorothy, dau. of Sir Edward Peckham, but d. s. p., 1558, when the estate devolved on his brother,

SIR EDMUND VERNEY, who received the honour of knighthood. He was sheriff of the co. Bucks and Hertford. He m. 1st, Frances, dau. of John Hastings, Esq., of Yelford, co. Oxford, by whom he had no issue; and 2ndly, Audrey, widow of Sir Peter Carew, and dau. of William Gardiner, Esq., of Fulmer, and by her had,

    Francis (Sir), who m Ursula, dau. of William St. Barbe, Esq., and d. s. p.

He m. 3rdly, Mary, dau. of John Blankey, Esq., of Sparrowham, and widow of G. Turvile, Esq., and had issue, by her.

SIR EDMUND VERNEY, of Middle Claydon, b. in London, 7 April, 1596, knight mareschal of the household. He m. Margaret, eldest dau. of Sir Thomas Denton, Knt., of Hillesden, in Bucks, by whom he had issue,

    I. RALPH (Sir), his heir.   II. Thomas.
    III. Edmund (Sir), who commanded a regiment of horse, and being deputy-governor of Drogheda, was killed 11 September, 1649, at the taking of that town by Cromwell.
    IV. Henry, a colonel, also in the king's service.
    V John.
    VI. Richard.

The eldest son,

SIR RALPH VERNEY, M.P., a member of the parliament which, in 1660, restored King CHARLES II., was by patent dated 16 March, 1661, created a baronet. He m. Mary, dau. and heir of John Blackwell, of Wasing and Abingdon, co. Berks, and had issue,

    I. Edmund, m. and had a dau., Mary, and two sons, Ralph and Edmund, who both d. young.
    II. JOHN, his successor.
    III. Ralph.

The 2nd son,

SIR JOHN VERNEY, 2nd baronet of Middle Claydon, co. Bucks, M.P. for that shire, was raised to the peerage of Ireland, 16 June, 1703, as Baron Verney, of Belturbet, and VISCOUNT OF FERMANAGH. His lordship m. 1st, Elizabeth, dau. of Daniel Baker, of London, Esq.; 2ndly, Mary, dau. of Sir Francis Lawley, of Spoonhill, in Shropshire, Bart.; and 3rdly, Elizabeth, dau. of Ralph Palmer, Esq., of Little Chelsea,

554

in Middlesex, and by her (who d. 12 December, 1736, and was buried at Hertford), he had issue,

    RALPH, his heir.
    Elizabeth, d. unm.
    Mary, m. to Col. John Lovett, of Soulbury, Bucks; all her issue d. unm.
    MARGARET, m. to Sir Thomas Cave, Bart., of Stanford Hall, co. Leicester. Her great-granddau. and representative,
        SARAH OTWAY CAVE, widow of Henry Otway, Esq., of Castle Otway, co. Tipperary, claimed to be one of the co-heirs of the Barony of Braye, as the descendant of Elizabeth Braye, by her husband, Sir Ralph Verney, of Middle Claydon; and having established her claim, had the ABEYANCE of the barony terminated in her favour, 3 October, 1839.

Lord Fermanagh d. 23 June, 1717, and was s. by his son,

RALPH VERNEY, 2nd Viscount Fermanagh, who was created 22 March, 1742, EARL VERNEY. He m. Catherine, eldest dau. and co-heir of Henry Paschall, Esq., of Baddow Hall, Essex, and by her (who d. 28 November, 1748) had issue,

    John, who m. in 1736, Mary,* dau. of Jonas Nicholson, Esq.; but d. v. p., 3 June, 1737, leaving his wife enceinte. She was afterwards delivered of a dau.,
        MARY, created in 1792, BARONESS FERMANAGH. Her ladyship d. unm. 15 November, 1810 (when her title EXPIRED), having bequeathed her estates to her half-sister, Mrs. Wright.
    RALPH, his father's heir.
    Elizabeth, m. to Bennet, Earl of Harborough, and had several children, who d. in infancy.
    Catherine, d. unm. in 1750.

The earl d. 4 October, 1752, and was s. by his son,

RALPH VERNEY, 2nd Earl Verney, F.R.S., who m. 11 September, 1740, Mary, dau. and co-heiress of Henry Herring, Esq., of Egham, in Surrey, a merchant of London and director of the Bank; but d. s. p. 31 March, 1791, when all his honours became EXTINCT.

Arms—Az., on a cross, arg., five mullets, pierced, gu.

VERNON — BARON ORWELL, OF NEWRY, AND EARL OF SHIPBROOK.

Barony, by Letters Patent, dated 17 April, 1762
Earldom, by Letters Patent, dated 28 January, 1777.

Lineage.

The Vernons were a family of noble Norman origin, and their ancestors were seigneurs of Vernon, in Normandy. William de Vernon founded and richly endowed the collegiate church of St. Mary there, in 1052, where he is interred. His eldest son, Richard, accompanied WILLIAM THE CONQUEROR to England, and was one of the barons created by Hugh Lupus, to whom King WILLIAM, in the 20th year of his reign, granted the county palatine of Chester. His great-grandson, Warine de Vernon, 4th Baron of Shipbrook, was father of William, who married the heiress of Avenel, of Haddon, co. Derby.

WARINE DE VERNON had an elder son, Richard, who carried on the line of the elder branch, the Barons of Shipbrook, of whom one of the descendants,

RALPH VERNON (2nd son of Ralph Vernon, of Haslington, Esq., by Isabella, his wife, dau. of Thomas Leversege, of Willock, co. Chester), m. Elizabeth, sister of Thomas Moreton, and had issue; his 2nd son,

FRANCIS VERNON, of London, merchant, m. a Dutch lady, and had issue; his eldest son,

FRANCIS VERNON, of London, m. Anne, dau. of Mr. Alderman Smithies, of London, and had with other issue, a son,

THE RIGHT HONOURABLE JAMES VERNON, one of the principal Secretaries of State, temp. WILLIAM III. (A.D. 1697), m. Mary, dau. of Sir John Buck, of Hamby Grange, Lincolnshire, Bart., and had issue,

    I. JAMES, of whom presently.
    II. Francis.
    III. EDWARD, of Nacton, in Suffolk, b. 1684, in Westminster, a very distinguished naval officer, who attained the rank of admiral of the white, and was employed in many important services; in 1739, he captured Portobello, in the West Indies; and in 1741, commanded at the attack on Carthagena. He m. Sarah, dau. of Thomas Best, Esq., of Chatham, in Kent, and d. 29 October, 1757, having had three sons, James,

---

* She m. 2ndly, Richard Calvert, Esq., and was mother of Catherine (wife of the Rev. Robert Wright), who eventually inherited the estates of Mary, Lady Fermanagh, and assumed the surname of VERNEY. She d. s. p. in 1827, and was s. in her estates by her cousin, SIR HARRY CALVERT, Bart., who has also taken the name of VERNEY.

Thomas, and Edward, who *d. s. p.* Admiral Vernon was at one time a prominent member of the House of Commons.

I. Mary, *m.* to — Harrison, Esq., son of Sir Edward Harrison, of Armagh.

II. Theodosia.

Mr. Secretary Vernon (whose will bears date 1 May, 1726, and was proved 20 October, 1730), was *s.* by his elder son,

JAMES VERNON, Esq., ambassador to the court of Denmark. commissioner of excise, who *m.* Arethusa, dau. of Charles Clifford, son of Richard, Earl of Burlington, and *d.* 17 April, 1756, leaving issue,

I. Henry, who *m.* Elizabeth, dau. of Thomas Payne, of Hough, in Lincolnshire, Esq., and had an only dau. and heir,

Arethusa, who *m.* Sir Robert Harland, Bart., of Sproughton Hall, Suffolk, and *d. s. p.*

II. FRANCIS, Lord Orwell, and EARL OF SHIPBROOKE.

III. Charles.   IV. James, *d. unm.*

V. Richard, *d. unm.*

I. Arethusa.

The 2nd son,

FRANCIS VERNON, Esq., of Nacton, co. Suffolk, M.P. for Ipswich, was created, 7 April, 1762, a peer of Ireland as Baron Orwell, of Newry, co. Down, and 28 January, 1777, made EARL OF SHIPBROOK. His lordship *m.* Alice, dau. and co-heir of Samuel Ibbetson, Esq., of Denton Park, co. York; but *d. s. p.* in 1783, when the honours became EXTINCT. Orwell Park was eventually sold by Lord Shipbrook's heir, Sir Robert Harland, Bart., to the Tomline family.

Arms—Or, on a fess, az., three garbs of the field.

VESCI—BARONS VESCI.

By Writ of Summons, dated 24 December, 1264.

Lineage.

Amongst the most valiant of the Norman nobility in the train of the CONQUEROR were

ROBERT DE VESCI, who possessed at the General Survey the lordship of Badebrock, in Northamptonshire, with divers other estates in the cos. Warwick, Lincoln, and Leicester: and

YVO DE VESCI, on whom King WILLIAM bestowed in marriage, Alda, only dau. and heiress of William Tyson, Lord of Alnwick, in Northumberland, and Malton, in Yorkshire (which William's father, Gilbert Tyson, fell at Hastings, fighting under the Anglo-Saxon banner). By this great heiress Yvo had an only dau. and heir,

BEATRICE DE VESCI, who *m.* EUSTACE FITZ-JOHN,[*] Lord of Knaresborough, in Yorkshire, and had two sons,

WILLIAM, of whom presently

Geoffrey.

The elder son of Beatrice, having inherited the great possessions of his mother's family, assumed its surname, and became

WILLIAM DE VESCI. This feudal lord was sheriff of Northumberland, from the 3rd to the 15th HENRY II. inclusive, and he was subsequently sheriff of Lancashire. In the 12th of the same reign, upon levying the aid for marrying the king's dau., he certified his knights' fees, *de veteri feoffamento*, to be in number twenty, for which he paid £17 13*s.*, and for his knights' fees, *de novo feoffamento*, £1 8*s.* 6*d.* In 1174, he joined

---

[*] EUSTACE FITZ-JOHN, nephew and heir of Serlo de Burgh (of the great family of Burgh), the founder of Knaresborough Castle, in Yorkshire, and son of JOHN, called Monoculus, from having but one eye, is said by an historian of the period in which he lived, to have been "one of the chiefest peers of England," and of intimate familiarity with King HENRY I., as also a person of great wisdom and singular judgment in councils. He had immense grants from the crown, and was constituted governor of the castle of Bamburgh, in Northumberland, *temp.* HENRY I., of which governorship, however, he was deprived by King STEPHEN; but he subsequently enjoyed the favour of that monarch. He fell in ensuing reign, *anno* 1157, in an engagement with the Welsh, "a great and aged man, and of the chiefest English peers, most eminent for his wealth and wisdom." By his 1st wife, the heiress of Vesci, he had two sons, as in the text, and by Agnes, his 2nd wife, dau. of William Fitz-Nigel, Baron of Halton, and constable of Chester, he left another son, called

RICHARD, FITZ-EUSTACE, Baron of Halton, and constable of Chester, who *m.* Albreda Lisours, half-sister of Robert de Lacy, and had issue,

JOHN, who becoming heir to his uncle, the said Robert de Lacy, assumed the surname of LACY, and was ancestor of the Earls of Lincoln, of that family (*see* Lacy, Earls of Lincoln).

ROGER, surnamed Fitz-Richard, progenitor of the great families of Clavering (*see* Clavering).

Ranulph de Glanvil, Bernard Baliol, and Robert de Stutevil in repelling an invasion of the Scots, and fought and won the great battle of Alnwick, wherein the King of Scotland himself was made prisoner, after his whole army had been routed. This William de Vesci *m.* Burga, sister of Robert de Estoteville, or Stuteville, Lord of Knaresborough, by whom he acquired the town of Langton, and had two sons,

EUSTACE, his successor.

Warine, Lord of Knapton, whose only dau. and heiress,

MARGERIE DE VESCI, *m.* Gilbert de Aton, and his great-grandson,

GILBERT DE ATON, inherited eventually all the lands of the De Vescis (*see* ATON, Barons Aton).

He was *s.* at his decease in 1184, by the elder,

EUSTACE DE VESCI, who attaining majority in the 2nd RICHARD I., gave 2,300 marks for livery of his lands, with liberty to marry whom he pleased. In the 14th King JOHN, when the first commotion arose amongst the barons, the king hastening to London, summoned all the suspected lords thither, and forced each to give hostages for his peaceable demeanour. But this Eustace, one of the most suspected, refused to attend the summons, and fled into Scotland, when all his possessions in England were seized upon by the crown, and a special command issued to demolish his castle at Alnwick. But a reconciliation between the king and his turbulent nobles soon afterwards taking place through the influence of the legate Pandulph, Eustace had restitution of his estates. But this was a deceitful calm—the winds were only stilled, to rage with greater violence—the baronial conflict ere long burst forth more furiously, and was only allayed by those concessions on the part of the crown, which have immortalized the plains of Runnymede. The cause of this celebrated quarrel, in which, by the way the people had little or no *immediate* interest, was doubtless, of long standing, and was based on the encroachment of the Sovereign on the privileges of the nobility, but the spark that ignited the flame was personal injury; an affront inflicted by King JOHN on this Eustace de Vesci. "Hearing," writes Sir William Dugdale, "that Eustace de Vesci had a very beautiful wife, but far distant from court and studying how to accomplish his licentious desires towards her, sitting at table with her husband, and seeing a ring on his finger he laid hold on it, and told him that he had such another stone, which he resolved to set in gold, in that very form. And having thus got the ring, presently sent it to her, in her husband's name; by that token conjuring her, if ever she expected to see him alive, to come speedily to him. She, therefore, upon sight of the ring, gave credit to the messenger, and came with all expedition. But so it happened, that her husband casually riding out, met her on the road, and I marvelling much to see her there, asked what the matter was? and when he understood how they were both deluded, resolved to find a common woman, and put her in apparel to personate his lady." The king afterwards boasting of the favours he had received to the injured husband himself, Eustace had the pleasure of undeceiving him, "whereat the king grew so enraged, that he threatened to kill him; Eustace, therefore, apprehending danger, hastened into the north, and in his passage, wasted some of the king's houses; divers of the nobles whose wives the king had vitiated, accompanying him. And being grown strong by the confluence of their friends, and others, seized his castles, the Londoners adhering to them." When JOHN was, subsequently, brought to submission, EUSTACE DE VESCI was one of the twenty-five Barons appointed to enforce the observance of Magna Charta, but he was slain soon after, about 1216, by an arrow from the ramparts of Barnard Castle (belonging to Hugh de Baliol), which he had commenced besieging, or was about to attack. He had *m.* Margaret, natural dau. of WILLIAM, King of Scotland, and was *s.* by his son,

WILLIAM DE VESCI, who, being in minority, was placed under the guardianship of William de Longespée, Earl of Salisbury. In the 10th HENRY III. he obtained livery of all his lands, as well as of the castle of Alnwick (but the castle of Knaresborough had been alienated previously to the Stutevil's Dugdale surmises, in the time of JOHN). After this we find no more of him until the 29th of the same reign, when he had a grant of five bucks and ten does, to be taken out of the king's forests at Northumberland, to stock his park at Alnwick, and he then paid to the king, upon collection of the aid for marrying his dau., £12, for his twelve knights' fees in Northumberland. He *m.* 1st, Isabel, dau. of William Longespée, Earl of Salisbury, but had no issue. He *m.* 2ndly, Agnes, dau. of William Ferrers, Earl of Derby, by whom he had two sons, JOHN and William, and dying in 1253, was *s.* by the elder,

JOHN DE VESCI, then in minority, and in ward, with Alnwick Castle to Peter de Savoy. This feudal lord was one of King HENRY III.'s chief commanders in the wars of Gascony, but afterwards joining with Montfort, Earl of Leicester, and the other barons, who had taken up arms to compel the king to observe the ordinances of Oxford, he was summoned to parliament, as a Baron by those lords, 24 December, 1264, when their power became dominant after the battle of Lewes, but he was afterwards made prisoner at Evesham, and forced to avail himself of the protection of the *Dictum de Kenilworth.* His lordship subsequently assumed the cross, and made a pilgrimage to the Holy Land. On his return, in the 2nd EDWARD I., he was constituted governor of Scarborough Castle, and in the 10th of the same reign was in the wars of Wales. This was the Sir John Vesci, who returning from the King of Arragon, brought over a great number of Gascoignes to King EDWARD to serve him in his Welsh wars. His lordship *m.* Mary, sister of Hugh de Lezinian, Earl of March and Angolesme; and 2ndly, Isabel de Beaumont, sister of Henry Lord Beaumont, styled Earl of Bucban, and kinswoman of Queen Eleanor but *d.* in 1289, *s. p.,* when the great possessions of the family devolved upon his brother (then forty years of age),

WILLIAM DE VESCI, who was a person in great esteem with EDWARD I., and constituted by that monarch, in the 13th year of his reign, justice of the royal forests beyond Trent, and the next year one of the justices itinerant touching the pleas of the forests. After succeeding his brother he was made governor of Scarborough Castle, and the year ensuing, doing his homage, had livery of all those lands in Ireland which were of the inheritance of Agnes, his mother, and he was made at the same time justice of that kingdom. But during his sojourn there, he was accused in open court, in the city of Dublin, in the presence of Gilbert de Clare, Earl of Gloucester, and others, of felony, and challenged to the combat by John Fitz-Thomas; for which he subsequently instituted a suit before the chief justice of Dublin against the said Fitz-Thomas on a charge of defamation, in saying, that he the said William de Vesci, had solicited him to a confederacy against the king; which charge being denied by Fitz-Thomas, and a schedule by him delivered into court, containing the words which he acknowledged, he was, thereupon, challenged to the combat by this William, and he accepted the challenge. But the king being apprised of the proceedings, prohibited the battle, and ordered the combatants to appear before him at Westminster; to which place William de Vesci came accordingly, mounted upon his great horse covered, as also completely armed with lance, dagger, coat of mail, and other military equipments, and proffered himself to the fight; but Fitz-Thomas, although called, appeared not. The affair was afterwards brought before parliament, but dismissed owing to some informality. It was finally submitted to the award of the king, but the ulterior proceedings are not recorded. In the 23rd EDWARD I. William de Vesci was again in the wars of Gascony, and he was summoned to parliament as a Baron 24 June, 1 October, and 2 November, 1295. His lordship was one of the competitors for the crown of Scotland, through his grandmother, Margaret.* He *m.* Isabel dau. of Adam de Periton, and widow of Robert de Welles, by whom he had an only son,

> JOHN, who was justice of the forests south of Trent, and was in the wars of Gascony. He *m.* Clementina, a kinswoman of Queen Eleanor, but *d. s. p., v. p.*

On the decease of his son, his lordship enfeoffed Anthony Beke, bishop of Durham, in the castle of Alnwick, and divers other lands, in trust for William, his bastard son, who became possessed of all his other estates. This trust the prelate is said to have basely betrayed, and to have alienated the property by disposing of it for ready money to William Percy; since which time the castle of Alnwick, and those lands, have been held by the Percys and their representatives. His lordship *d.* in 1297, when all his great inheritance passed to his bastard son, WILLIAM DE KILDARE, save the estates above-mentioned, in Northumberland; and the Barony of Vesci, became EXTINCT.

VISCOUNT DE VESCI, of Ireland, claims descent from this old Baronial family.

Arms—Gu., a cross, arg.

---

* The illegitimacy of this lady and her sisters, daus. of WILLIAM THE LION, is obviously established by the fact of their claim being at once dismissed. Whereas had they been legitimately born, their pretensions were prior to those of either Baliol or Bruce, who had sprung from David, Earl of Huntingdon, brother of King WILLIAM.

VESCI—BARON VESCI.

By Writ of Summons, dated 8 January 1313.

Lineage.

WILLIAM DE VESCI, of Kildare, presumed to have been a natural son of WILLIAM, LORD DE VESCI, who *d.* in 1297, having become possessed, by gift of his father, of all the Vesci estates, except the castle of Alnwick and the lands in Northumberland, of which he is said to have been defrauded by the celebrated prelate, Anthony Beke, was summoned to parliament as a Baron from 8 January, 1313, to 29 July, 1314. His lordship *d. s. p.* in the following year, when his estates reverted to the heirs general of his father, the said William, Lord De Vesci, the family of ATON (*see* Aton, Barons de Aton) and the Barony of Vesci became EXTINCT.

Arms—Gu., a cross, arg., with the mark of illegitimacy.

VILLIERS — BARONS WHADDON, VISCOUNTS VILLIERS, EARLS OF BUCKINGHAM, MARQUESSES OF BUCKINGHAM, DUKES OF BUCKINGHAM.

Viscounty, by Letters Patent, dated 27 August, 1616.
Earldom, by Letters Patent, dated 5 January, 1617.
Marquessate, by Letters Patent, dated 1 January, 1618.
Dukedom, by Letters Patent, dated 18 May, 1623.

Lineage.

This family, which is still extant, in the noble houses of Jersey and Clarendon, claimed descent from the Villiers, Seigneurs of L'Isle Adam, in Normandy, through one of that house, who came into England with the CONQUEROR.

SIR GEORGE VILLIERS, Knt., of Brokesby, co. Leicester, a person of eminent note, *m.* 1st, Audrey, dau. of William Sanders, Esq. of Harrington, co. Northampton, and had issue,

> WILLIAM, created a baronet in 1619, a dignity which expired with his grandson, Sir William Villiers, in 1711.
> EDWARD, from whom the present EARLS OF JERSEY and CLARENDON descend. (*See* BURKE'S *Extant Peerage and Baronetage.*)
> Elizabeth, *m.* to John, Lord Butler, of Bramfield.
> Anne, *m.* to Sir William Washington, Knt., of Pakington, co. Lincoln.
> Frances.

Sir George Villiers *m.* 2ndly, Mary, dau. of Anthony Beaumont, Esq., of Glenfield, co. Leicester, which lady survived her husband, and was created Countess of Buckingham for life: by her he had issue,

> JOHN (Sir), created VISCOUNT PURBECK (*see* Villiers, Viscounts Purbeck).
> GEORGE, of whom presently.
> CHRISTOPHER, created Earl of Anglesey (*see* Villiers, Earls of Anglesey).
> Susan, *m.* to William Fielding, Earl of Denbigh.

Sir George, who was sheriff of the co. Leicester, in 1591, *d.* 4 January, 1605. His 2nd son by his last wife,

GEORGE VILLIERS, *b.* at Brokesby, 28 August, 1592, received the first rudiments of his education at Billesden school, in Leicestershire, whence being removed at the age of thirteen, by his mother, he was sent to France, and there soon attained perfection in all polite accomplishments. On his return home, he came first to London as a suitor to the dau. of Sir Roger Ashton, one of the gentlemen of the bedchamber, and master of the robes to King JAMES I., but was dissuaded from the connection by another courtier, Sir John Graham, another of the gentlemen of the privy chamber, who encouraged him to "*woo fortune in the court.*" Soon after this he attracted the attention of King JAMES, and succeeded the favourite Carr, Earl of Somerset, as cup-bearer to his Majesty (being, says Dugdale, of stature tall and comely, his comportment graceful and of a most sweet disposition). From this period he rose rapidly in royal estimation, and the queen through the influence of Abbot, archbishop of Canterbury, an enemy of Somerset's, being induced also to protect him, his fortune was at once established. The first honour he received was that of knighthood, which was conferred in her Majesty's bedchamber, with the prince's rapier; he was then sworn a gentleman of the bedchamber (23 April, 1615) with an annual pension of £1,000 payable out of the Court of Wards. The ensuing January he succeeded the Earl of Worcester as master of the horse, and in a few months after was installed a knight of the Garter. Before the close of the year (27 August, 1616) he was advanced to the peerage, by the title of BARON WHADDON, co. *Bucks,* the ceremony of creation being performed at Woodstock, the Lords Compton and Norris introducing the new peer, and Lord Carew carrying his robe: and he was very soon after created VISCOUNT VILLIERS. On 5 January, 1616-7, his lordship was created EARL OF BUCKINGHAM, with a special remainder, in default of male issue, to his brothers John and Christopher, and their male issue; and on the 1st of the same month, in the ensuing year, MARQUESS OF BUCKINGHAM. This last dignity was succeeded by his appointment to the great office of lord high admiral, and his being sworn of the privy council; and about this time his lordship was constituted chief justice in Eyre; master of the King's Bench office; high steward of Westminster; constable of Windsor Castle; and chancellor of the university of Cambridge.

In 1623 the marquess was sent into Spain with Prince Charles, to accelerate the marriage then in contemplation between his royal highness and a Spanish princess. The journey, a very singular one, commenced 18 February, when the Prince and Marquess, putting on false beards, assumed the names of Thomas and John Smith, their sole attendant being Sir Richard Graham, master of the horse. Riding post to Canterbury, where they took fresh horses, they were stopped by the mayor as suspicious persons, whereupon the marquess was constrained to take off his beard, and to satisfy Mr. Mayor, by stating that he was going in that private manner to survey the fleet, as lord high admiral. At Dover, they found the prince's private secretary, Sir Francis Cottington, and Mr. Endymion Porter, who had provided a vessel for their use, on which they embarked, and landing at Boulogne, proceeded to Paris, and thence travelled through France to Madrid. During their sojourn in Paris, the marquess is said to have fallen in love with the Queen of France (Anne, of Austria, consort of Louis XIII.) Certain it is, that, on his return, Richelieu refused him permission to land in a French port. At Madrid, Buckingham was involved in a dispute wi h the Comte d'Olivares, and received some affronts for his haughty bearing, *French part,* and great familiarity with the prince. His royal master continuing however to lavish favours upon him, sent out letters patent, dated 18 May, 1623, creating him DUKE OF BUCKINGHAM and EARL OF COVENTRY. The prince and duke, failing in the object of their journey, departed from Madrid 12 September, and arrived at Portsmouth in October, when his grace was made lord warden of the Cinque Ports, and steward of the manor of Hampton Court. The death of King JAMES followed in about a year and a half, but the influence of Buckingham experienced no diminution. His grace officiated as lord high steward at the coronation of the new king; and was soon after sent upon an embassy into Holland, where he purchased a rare collection of Arabic manuscripts, procured in remote countries by the industry and diligence of Erpinius, a famous linguist. Those valuable papers were presented to the university of Cambridge, for which he intended them, after the duke's death. His grace continued to bask in the same sunshine of royal favour under King CHARLES that he had so beneficially enjoyed in the last reign, but with the people he had become an object of great detestation. His influence was paramount, and to that influence were attributed all the grievances of the nation. The failure, too, of an expedition to the Isle of Rhee, for the relief of the Rochellers, completed his unpopularity. To recover the ground he had lost by this untoward enterprize, his grace projected another expedition, and had repaired to Portsmouth in order to forward its sailing. Here, while passing through a lobby, after breakfasting with Sir Thomas Fryer, and other persons of distinction, he was stabbed to the heart with a penknife by one John Felton, a lieutenant in Sir John Ramsey's regiment, and died instantaneously. The assassination of the duke* took place 23 August, 1628, when he had just com-

pleted his thirty-sixth year. His duchess was in the house in an upper room, hardly out of bed, and the King and Court at Sir Daniel Norton's, at Southwick, not much more than six miles off.

His Grace had *m.* 1620, Lady Katherine Manners, only dau. and heiress of Francis, 6th Earl of Rutland and Baron de Ros (which latter dignity she inherited at the decease of her father in 1632,) and by her (who *m.* 2nd.y, Randal Macdonell, Marquess of Antrim,) had issue,

GEORGE, his successor.

Francis (posthumous), called by Aubrey "the beautiful Francis Villiers," killed in a skirmish with the parliamentarians after a most gallant resistance, in 1648, and *d. unm.*

MARY, who, by letters patent, dated 31 August, 1628, had the title of Duchess of Buckingham limited to her in case of the failure of the male issue of her father; *m.* 1st, in 1634, Sir Charles Herbert, K.B., Lord Herbert, son of Philip, 4th Earl of Pembroke, who *d.* in a few weeks afterwards of the small pox, without cohabiting with his bride. Her ladyship *m.* 2ndly, James Stuart, Duke of Richmond and Lennox, K.G., and had an only son, Esme Stuart, Duke of Richmond and Lennox, who *d. unm.* 14 August, 1660; and a dau., Mary, *m.* to Richard, Earl of Arran. Her grace *m.* 3rdly, Thomas Howard, brother of Charles, Earl of Carlisle, but had no issue. She *d.* in 1685.

The duke was *s.* by his eldest son,

GEORGE VILLIERS, 2nd Duke of Buckingham, and in right of his mother, Baron de Ros; he was *b.* at Wallingford House, St. Martin's-in-the-Fields, 30 January, 1627-8. This nobleman was very young at the time of his father's murder, and spent some years abroad after that event, travelling. He returned to England during the civil war, and had a command in the royal army at the battle of Worcester, 3 September, 165`, from which unfortunate field, making his escape with difficulty, he reached London, and was thence enabled to make good his retreat to Holland. At the restoration of the monarchy his grace, with General Monk, rode uncovered before the king on his public entry into London, and he was soon after made a knight of the Garter. The Duke of Buckingham formed one of the unpopular administration of King CHARLES II., which was designated the *Cabal,* from the initial letters of the ministers' names. "But towards the latter end of that monarch's reign," says, B nks, " by his strange conduct and unsteady temper, he sunk very low in the opinion of most people. He first seduced the wife of Francis Talbot, Earl of Shrewsbury, and then killed the earl in a duel."

Walpole, in his Catalogue of Noble Authors observes, "when this extraordinary man, with the figure and genius of Alcibiades, could equally charm the presbyterian Fairfax, and the dissolute CHARLES; when he alike ridiculed the witty king, and his solemn chancellor; when he plotted the ruin of his country with a cabal of bad ministers, or equally unprincipled, supported its cause with bad patriots, one laments that such parts should be devoid of every virtue. But when Alcibiades turns chemist, when he is a real bubble, and a visionary miser, when ambition is but a frolic, when the worst designs are for the foolishest ends, contempt extinguishes all reflections on his character."

This nobleman, profligate as he was, held an elevated place amongst the *beaux esprits* of his day, and was a wit was equalled but by few of his contemporaries.

The *Rehearsal,* a well-known comedy, and other plays, were among his literary productions.

"He began life (says Banks), with all the advantages of fortune and person which a nobleman could covet; and afterwards, by favour of the King, had great opportunities of making himself as considerable as his father had been. But he miserably wasted his estate, forfeited his honour, damned his reputation, and, at the time of his death, is said to have wanted even the necessaries of life, and not to have had one friend in the world."

Dryden, with admirable truth, thus portrays the second Buckingham:—

---

* It is said, on the relation of Bishop Burnet, that the apparition of Sir George Villiers, his father, appeared to a man who had been formerly an old servant of the family, entreating him to go to the duke, and warn him that some sad fatality would certainly happen to him, unless he did something to please the people, and remove their grievances. The old man, surprised at such a vision, was terrified: but on the same appearing a second and a third time, he at last resolved to see the duke; and having obtained an interview, acquainted him with what had passed, and by a communication of certain events, touching a peculiar circumstance in the duke's life, convinced his grace so perfectly of what he had seen, that the duke exclaimed, "*It must be*

true," for excepting to himself and one person more (who was not likely to disclose it,) the same was not known to any one living. It is also related, that, the day after the duke's death, John Buckridge, Bishop of Ely, was pitched upon as the properest person to make known to the Countess of Denbigh, the melancholy tidings of her brother's death, whom she tenderly loved; that hearing, when he came to wait upon her, she was at rest, he attended till she should wake of herself, which she did with the affrightment of a dream; her brother seeming to pass through a field with her in her couch, where hearing a sudden shout of the people, and asking the reason of it, was answered, "that it was for joy the Duke of Buckingham was dead." This dream she had scarce told her gentlewoman, when the bishop entered the room to acquaint her with the mournful news.— BANKS.

"A man so various that he seem'd to be
Not one, but all mankind's epitome;
Stiff in opinion— always in the wrong—
Was everything by starts, but nothing long;
Who, in the course of one revolving moon
Was chemist, fiddler, statesman, and buffoon;
Then, all for women, painting, rhyming, drinking;
Besides a thousand freaks that died in thinking."

Pope's description of the Duke in his "Moral Essays" is greatly exaggerated. It was not in "the worst inn's worst room," but at a tenant's house at Kirby Moorside that he died, after a few days' fever, produced by a chill, consequent on a fox chase. The following are Pope's lines:—

"Behold what blessings, wealth to life can lend,
And see what comfort it affords our end!
In the worst inn's worst room, with mat half hung,
The floor of plaster and the walls of dung;
On once a flock-bed, but repaired with straw;
With tape-tyed curtains never meant to draw;
The George and Garter dangling from that bed,
Where tawdry yellow strove with dirty red,
Great Villiers lies: alas! how changed from him,
That life of pleasure and that soul of whim!
Gallant and gay, in Cliveden's proud alcove,
The bow'r of wanton Shrewsbury and love;
Or just as gay at council, in a ring
Of mimic statesmen, and their merry king.
No wit to flatter left of all his store;
No fool to laugh at, which he valued more!
There, victor of his health, of fortune, friends,
And fame, this lord of useless thousands ends."

His grace m. Mary, only dau. and heiress of Thomas, Lord Fairfax, the parliamentary general, and granddau. maternally of Horatio, Lord Vere, of Tilbury, but had no issue. He d. 16 April, 1687, and the event is thus recorded in the parish register of Kirby Moorside:—" George Vilaus, Lord dooke of bookingham." His sister MARY, to whom the Dukedom of Buckingham was in remainder, provided she had outlived the male descendants of her father, having predeceased him, all the honours* which he had inherited from his father became EXTINCT, while the Barony of Ros, derived from his mother, fell into ABEYANCE between the heirs general of the sisters and heirs of George Manners, 7th Earl of Rutland.

Arms—Arg., on a cross gu., five escallops, or, a martlet for difference.

VILLIERS—COUNTESS OF BUCKINGHAM.

By Letters Patent, dated 1 July, 1618.

Lineage.

MARY VILLIERS, dau. of Anthony Beaumont, Esq., of Glenfield, co. Leicester, widow of Sir George Villiers, of Brokesby, and mother of George Villiers, Duke of Buckingham, was created COUNTESS OF BUCKINGHAM, for life, by letters patent, dated 1 July, 1618. Her ladyship m. 2ndly, Sir William Rayner, and 3rdly, Sir Thomas Compton, Knt., brother of William, 1st Earl of Northampton, and d. 19 April, 1632, in her sixty-third year, being buried in St. Edmund's Chapel, Westminster Abbey. At the countess's death the dignity of course EXPIRED.

VILLIERS—BARON VILLIERS, OF STOKE, CO. BUCKS, VISCOUNT PURBECK.

By Letters Patent, dated 19 July, 1619.

Lineage.

SIR JOHN VILLIERS, Knt., elder brother of King JAMES's celebrated favourite, George, Duke of Buckingham (see VILLIERS, Dukes of Buckingham), was elevated to the peerage, 19 July, 1619, as Baron Villiers, of Stoke, co. Bucks, and VISCOUNT OF PURBECK, co. Dorset. His lordship m. 1st, Frances, dau. of the eminent Chief Justice (Sir Edward) Coke, a lady who eloped from him, in 1621, with Sir Robert Howard, and after her misconduct assumed the name of Wright, and gave birth, privately, to a son, who also bore that surname. She d. in the king's garrison, at Oxford, in 1645, and was buried in St. Mary's Church. His lordship m. 2ndly, Elizabeth, dau. of Sir

* The Earldom of Buckingham was subsequently, but fruitlessly claimed, by the alleged descendant of his grace's uncle, Sir John Villiers (see Villiers, Viscount Purbeck).

William Slingsby, of Kippax, co. York, but had no issue. The viscount d. in 1657, when the Barony of Villiers, of Stoke, and the Viscounty of Purbeck became EXTINCT.

Arms—Arg., on a cross, gu., five escallops, or, a mullet for difference.

THE following narrative gives a succinct account of the celebrated Purbeck case, and of the line of the Villiers family which claimed to be entitled to the VISCOUNTY OF PURBECK:—
The father of George Villiers, the favourite raised by King JAMES to the Dukedom of Buckingham, was twice married. The descendants of the first marriage ascended slowly to the honours of the peerage, and are now represented in the male line by the Earls of Jersey and of Clarendon. The sons of the second marriage, brothers of the whole blood to the favourite, were ennobled with a rapidity proportioned to that of his own elevation. John Villiers, the eldest son of this second family, had, in the dawn of the fortunes of his honour, aspired to the hand of Frances, the daughter of Sir Edward Coke, but his advances had been repulsed. To the girl herself the proposals were most distasteful; and the friends of the daughter of the successful lawyer and courtier, "a lady of transcending beauty," and sole heiress of the great wealth and high blood of her mother,* might well expect for her a more advantageous alliance than any member of the Villiers family then afforded. Soon, however, Fortune reversed her wheel, and Coke, pursued by the united hostility of George Villiers and Francis Bacon, was, in the year 1617, deprived of the chief justiceship, expelled the privy council, and threatened with the terrors of the Star-chamber for some portion of the legal reports which he had published. In this crisis of his fate, the father bethought himself that, by the sacrifice of his daughter, he might appease the angry elements, which, gathering round his political horizon, seemed ready to overwhelm him: and the venerable sage of the law immediately volunteered to confer the disconsolate fair one, together with a large portion, on the late rejected brother of George Villiers—the price of the favour of the young ex-cupbearer. The ambition of Sir Edward Coke surmounted the extraordinary difficulties which were opposed to his plan; but the subsequent disgrace of his daughter, and the deferred hopes and evaded claims of her male descendants, present a fearful warning to such success as his.
Bacon, then lord keeper, determined to spare no effort to hinder the accomplishment of a plan, which tended to transfer to his rival all the court influence of Buckingham: with him, therefore, in a letter written in the summer of 1617, he thus remonstrated on the subject:—
"The mother's consent is not had, nor the young gentlewoman's, who expecteth a great fortune from her mother, which, without her consent, is endangered. This match, out of my faith and freedom towards your Lordship, I hold very inconvenient both for your brother and yourself. First, he shall marry into a disgraced house, which in reason of state is never held good. Next he shall marry into a troubled house of man and wife, which in religion and Christian discretion is disliked. Thirdly, your Lordship will go near to lose all such your friends as are adverse to Sir Edward Coke, myself only except, who, out of a pure love and thankfulness, shall ever be firm to you. And lastly, and chiefly, it will greatly weaken and distract the king's service." He, therefore, earnestly recommends that that match should be broken off, "or not proceeded in without the consent of both parents, required by religion and the law of God."
Having given to Buckingham this recommendation:

"The brightest, wisest, meanest, of mankind,"

did all in his power to prevent the possibility of the mother consenting; though, as he himself had been a rejected suitor of Lady Hatton, he would have been deterred—could any feelings of delicacy have deterred him—from interfering in the family affairs of his successful rival. There had, however, been a connection between the family of Bacon and that of

* The second wife of Lord Chief Justice Coke was Elizabeth Cecil, dau. of the 1st Earl of Exeter, by Dorothy Neville, the co-heiress of the last Lord Latimer. For her first husband she had married Sir William Newport, who, having succeeded to the property of his maternal uncle, Sir Christopher Hatton, the lord chancellor, took the name of Hatton. By this marriage, says Lord Campbell, in his Lives of the Chancellors, Coke "got possession of Chancellor Hatton's estate, along with a companion who kept him in trouble the rest of his days."

Lady Hatton* (as in spite of her second marriage she continued to be called), which might have afforded him facilities for tendering his advice. And, with Bacon's concurrence, Lady Hatton carried off her daughter from her father's house, and concealed her in the residence of Sir Edmund Withipole, near Oatlands. The ex-chief justice traced the flight of the young lady, and then demanded a warrant from the lord keeper to recover her. The warrant being refused, the father, accompanied by the sons of his first marriage, and at the head of a band of armed men, proceeded to the retreat of Miss Frances Coke, and forcibly resumed possession of her.

"For this alleged outrage he was summoned, and several times examined before the Council; and, by the Lord Keeper's direction, Yelverton, the Attorney General, filed an information against him in the Star-chamber.

"Intelligence of these events being brought to Edinboro' (where James was then staying), the King and Buckingham put an end to the sullen silence they had for some time observed towards the Lord Keeper, and wrote him letters filled with bitter complaints, invectives and threats. Bacon suddenly awoke from a trance, and all at once saw his imprudence and his danger. In an agony of terror, he ordered the Attorney General to discontinue the prosecution in the Star-chamber; he sent for Lady Hatton, and tried to reconcile her to the match, and he made the most abject submission to Buckingham's mother who had complained of being insulted by him."

In the end Bacon was allowed to retain the great seal; Coke was restored to the privy council; and Frances Coke, having first been tied to the bed-post and whipped† into consent, became, 29 September, 1617, the struggling and reluctant bride of Sir John Villiers.

Enriched by this alliance, Sir John Villiers was, 19 July, 1619, created Baron Villiers, of Stoke Poges,‡ and Viscount Purbeck; and he and his heirs male were placed next in remainder for the titles of Baron Whaddon, Viscount Villiers, and Earl of Buckingham, in the event of the failure of the issue male of his brother, the duke.

About two years after his elevation to the peerage, it has been stated that Lord Purbeck was afflicted with insanity; and that his wife, parting from him, cohabited with Sir Robert Howard,§ 5th son of the Earl of Suffolk, lord high chamberlain. And, however little confirmation there may be for the former allegation there is unfortunately abundant for the latter. A son having been born (who will presently be treated of), Lady Purbeck and the reputed father, Sir Robert Howard, were both prosecuted for adultery in the Court of High Commission; and were convicted and sentenced to do penance. Lady Purbeck escaped the humiliating ceremony by concealing herself, but her paramour had probably to undergo it, for in 1640, when the Court of High Commission was abolished, a fine of £500 was, at the suit of Sir Robert Howard, imposed on Archbishop Laud, who had passed the sentence. No attempts to obtain a divorce or legal separation were made by Lord Purbeck; but henceforward Lady Purbeck, together with her son, are stated to have been taken care of by her mother, Lady Hatton. Lady Purbeck d. in 1645, and was buried at St. Mary's Church, Oxford. Lord Purbeck m. 2ndly, Elizabeth, dau. of Sir William Slingsby, of Kippax, in Yorkshire; but had no issue by her. He d. in 1657, and was buried at Charlton, near Greenwich.

The child, to whom it has been mentioned that Lady Purbeck had given birth, was, bapt. clandestinely, 20 October, 1624, at St. Giles's, Cripplegate, London, under the name of "Robert Wright," and, though reputed to be the son of Sir Robert Howard, he afterwards bore the name of Villiers, and joined with Lord Purbeck, as his son, in the conveyance of some lands. Finally, having m. 23 November, 1648, Elizabeth, dau. and co-heiress, of Sir John Danvers, of Chelsea, M.P., one of the judges who condemned CHARLES I., he availed himself of the circumstance to obtain a patent from Cromwell to relinquish the surname of Villiers and assume that of Danvers, professing to

hate the former name on account of the many disservices which, as he alleged, the family bearing it had done to the commonwealth. He disclaimed the peerage, and sat in the House of Commons, in the Convention Parliament of 1659, as M.P. for Westbury; when, being accused in the House of Lords of treasonable expressions, namely, that "he hated the Stuarts, and that, if no person could be found to cut off the King's head, he would do it himself," and in consequence summoned to attend there in his place as a peer, to answer to the charge, he refused to attend, on the ground that he was a member of the lower House. This plea, however, did not avail him, and he was compelled to kneel and ask pardon for it at the bar of the Lords. Still anxious to divest himself of his peerage, he, under legal advice, and with the consent of CHARLES II., levied a fine of his titles in possession and remainder. Latterly he retired to his estate called Siluria, in the parish of Houghton, in Radnorshire, but d. in Calais, in 1675. In the administration of his goods, granted at Doctors' Commons in 1676, he is described as "Robert Danvers, alias Villiers, Esquire." His wife survived him; and, considering, as she states in a letter to her steward, that the possession of a title would assist her son to an advantageous alliance, now again called herself Viscountess Purbeck. She m. 2ndly, but at a period of life too advanced for issue, John Duval, Esq., a colonel in the army. Her will in which she styles herself "Elizabeth Viscountess Purbeck, of Hatton Garden, widow," was dated 14 July, 1709, and proved at Doctors' Commons, in the autumn of the same year. In it she mentions her two grandsons, "John Villiers, Earl of Bucks," and "George Villiers," and her three daus., "Dame Frances Deerham," "Mrs. Elizabeth Maurice," and "Dame Mary Wogan, widow of Sir William Wogan, Knt., and Sergeant-at-Law." Lady Purbeck was buried at Chelsea, 22 August, 1709.

To Robert and Elizabeth Villiers, or Danvers, were born two sons, Robert and Edward, who, each resuming the name of Villiers, were the respective fathers of the two grandsons mentioned in the will. The elder of these sons, Robert, claimed after his father's death, the title of which his father had laboured to divest himself. He petitioned CHARLES II. on the subject, and was referred to the House of Lords. His claim was there opposed on two grounds: that the fine levied by his father barred his right to the honours, and that his father was not, in fact, the son of John Villiers, the 1st Viscount Purbeck.

In 1678 the Lords came to the important resolution—one involving a great constitutional principle—that "no fine now levied nor at any time hereafter to be levied to the King, can bar a title of honour or the right of any person claiming such title under him that levied or shall levy such fine." The House further resolved, that the king should be petitioned to give leave that a bill may be brought in to disable the petitioner from claiming the title of Viscount Purbeck. To this latter resolution a protest was made signed by seven peers, stating that "the said claimant's right (the bar of the fine of his ancestors being removed) did, both at the hearing at the bar and debate in the House, appear to them clear in fact and law, and above all objection." The king, on a petition in conformity with the resolution of the House of Lords being presented to him, answered that he "would take it into consideration;" and, as the bill contemplated was never brought in, the family continued to claim its old titles, together with those which subsequently devolved on it, on the death of the last Duke of Buckingham of the Villiers name, although no writ was issued summoning its representatives to the House of Lords. The 3rd Viscount Purbeck was killed at the age of twenty-eight, in a duel fought at Liege with Colonel Luttrell, in 1684; in the June of which year he is described, in the administration taken out to his goods at Doctors' Commons, as "Robert Lord Viscount Purbeck, alias Villiers, alias Danvers, Esquire." He had m. Margaret,* relict of Charles, Viscount Muskerry and only child of Ulick de Burgh, 1st Marquess of Clanricarde, in Ireland, and 2nd Earl of St. Albans in England, and by her had issue, an only surviving child, John Villiers, who was seven years old at his father's death.

This John Villiers, after 16 April, 1697, when the 2nd Duke of Buckingham, "in the worst inn's worst room," had breathed his last, assumed the title of Earl of Buckingham, by which henceforward he was known, instead of that of Viscount Purbeck. Having lived a life of debauchery, and squandered his

---

* The second wife of Lord Keeper Nicolas Bacon, and mother of the celebrated Francis Bacon, lord keeper, and alderman chancellor, was sister of the second wife of the 1st Lord Burghley, stepmother to the Earl of Exeter, Lady Hatton's father.

† Cole's MSS., vol. xxxiii., p. 17.

‡ Stoke Poges, in Buckinghamshire, was settled by Sir Edward Coke upon his daughter and her husband, to come to them after the deaths of himself and his wife. Lyson's Mag. Brit., vol. i., p. 636. Aylsham Burgh manor in Norfolk, formed a part of the portion which Lady Purbeck received from her father, and was retained by her descendants till the latter end of the last century. (See Blomefield's History of Norfolk, vol. iii., p. 655.)

§ Cole's MSS., vol. xxxiii., p. 17.

---

* From her father she inherited the estate of Sommerhill, near Tunbridge; a portion of which her extravagance compelled her to part with—Hasted's History of Kent, vol. 2, p. 341 Lord Purbeck was her 2nd husband. The 1st husband was Lord Muskerry, and her 3rd was Colonel Robert Fielding, known in his day under the soubriquet of "Beau Fielding." She died at Sommerhill (according to Cole's MSS., vol. 33, p. 5), 14 August, 1698.

fortune, he m. Frances, the dau. of the Rev. Mr. Moyser, and widow of George Heneage, Esq., of Lincolnshire, a woman of dissolute character, whose only recommendation was her large jointure. He d. 10 August, 1723, at Dancer's Hill, in the parish of South Mimms, in Middlesex; and the parish register there, for the year 1723, contains the following entry :—"Lord Buckingham, buried August ye 18th." He had no sons, and his claims, therefore to the Villiers peerages passed to a younger branch of the family, which will presently be treated of. His wife is described as having been the mother of two daus., who d. unm. Of one of these the burial register of Merton, in Surrey, for 18 May, 1703, thus disposes — "Lady Mary Villiers, daughter of the Right Honourable Earl of Buckingham and Lord Viscount Purbeck, of this parish." The other dau., Lady Elizabeth Villiers, is stated in an imperfect modern pedigree, in the Heralds' College, to have been born in 1701. In the 56th vol. of the Gentleman's Magazine, p. 620, is a long obituary and genealogical notice of her, stating that she had died in Tavistock Court, Tavistock Street, London, 4 July, 1786.

Returning to the children of Robert Villiers and Elizabeth Danvers, his wife, we shall recollect that there was a younger son, Edward Villiers. He was born at Knighton, in Radnorshire, 28 March, 1661, became a captain in the army, and d. at Canterbury, in 1691. He had m. Joan, dau. of Mr. William Heming, a brewer, at Worcester. The marriage took place in the private chapel of the bishop of Worcester, in consequence of the bride being related to Dr. Thomas, who then possessed this see.

The issue of this marriage was George Villiers, who was born at Worcester, 11 April, 1690, and educated at Westminster school. He matriculated at Christ Church, Oxford, 28 June, 1709, and was thus described on this occasion in the books of the University : "George Villiers Edvardi de Civitat. Worcester gen. fil." He took his degree of M.A., 20 April, 1716; and, entering holy orders, became vicar of Chalgrove, in Oxfordshire. On the death of his first cousin, John Villiers, in 1723, without male issue, he claimed the title of Earl of Buckingham, but appears to have abstained from using it. He d. at Chalgrove in 1748. By his will, dated 30 March, 1748, and proved at Doctors' Commons, 10 May following—after reciting that he had settled his real property by a deed dated 20 May, 1731, and that he had given her fortune to his dau., Catherine, on her marriage to the Rev. Mr. Lewis—he directs that Mary, his other daughter, shall receive a like fortune, bequeaths to Mr. Lewis his wife's portrait, in water colours, and appoints his own wife sole executrix. He had married, according to a pedigree at p. 5 of a MS. vol. in the Heralds' College, lettered B.P., the dau. of T. Stephens, Esq.; and his will is proved by Catherine, his widow.

The Rev. George Villiers and Catherine, his wife, had the following issue : George, Edward, Catherine (by whom alone the family was continued), and Mary.

George,[*] the eldest son, was entered at Christ Church, Oxford, 2 July, 1742, and having taken holy orders, was instituted vicar of Frodsham, in Cheshire, in 1772, and d. 24 June, 1774, aged fifty. His will, in which he styles himself of St. George, the parish of the Martyr, in Southwark, Surrey, Clerk, is dated 30 June, 1770, and proved 16 December, 1774. In it he devises to his wife, Mary, for life, and, in default of issue, to his right heir, his manor and rectory of Aylsham Burgh,— a property which had been settled by Sir Edward Coke on his dau. He d. s. p.

His brother, Edward, d. a bachelor; and, with these two brothers, expired the male line of this family.[†] Their sister, Mary, d. unm.

It has already been stated that the husband of Catherine Villiers was named Lewis. He, the Rev. John Lewis, was instituted dean of Ossory, in Ireland, 24 May, 1755. His wife, dying 13 April, 1756, he m. a second time, and had a second family, and d. 28 June, 1783.

The children of the marriage of Catherine Villiers and John

Lewis, were John Joseph Lewis, who d. unm. in early manhood, and is believed to have been drowned at sea, Villiers William Lewis, of whom presently, Elizabeth-Catherine Lewis, who was m. to William Surtees, Esq., of Seaton-burn, near Newcastle-on-Tyne, and had issue, and Cassandra Lewis, presumed to have d. unm.

Villiers William Lewis, inheriting Aylsham Burgh Manor, as the right heir to his uncle, the Rev. George Villiers, of Frodsham, took the surname of Villiers, and marrying Matilda, dau. of the 11th Lord St. John of Bletsoe, had an only son, George-William Villiers, who was accidentally killed at Tours, in 1841. The eldest son of this gentleman, GEORGE-WILLIAM VILLIERS-VILLIERS, Esq., of Bath, became, through his great-grandmother, Catherine Villiers, the representative of this unfortunate, but historic line, and also one of the co-heirs of the Baronies of Scales, Playtz, &c.

VILLIERS—EARLS OF ANGLESEY.

By Letters Patent, dated 18 April, 1623.

Lineage.

CHRISTOPHER VILLIERS, youngest brother of George, 1st Duke of Buckingham (see Villiers, Dukes of Buckingham,) was elevated to the peerage, 18 April, 1623, as Baron Villiers of Daventry, co. Northampton, and EARL OF ANGLESEY. His lordship m. Elizabeth, dau. of Thomas Sheldon, Esq. of Houby, co. Leicester, and by her (who m. 2ndly, Hon. Benjamin Weston,) had issue,

CHARLES, his successor.

Anne, m. 1st, to Thomas, Viscount Savile, afterwards Earl of Sussex, and had

JAMES, 2nd Earl of Sussex, who d. s. p. in 1761, when his honours EXPIRED.

Frances, m. Francis, Lord Brudenel, son and heir of Robert, Earl of Cardigan.

Her ladyship m. 2ndly, — Barde, Esq., of Weston.

The earl, who was gentleman of the horse to King JAMES I., d. in 1630, and was s. by his son,

CHARLES VILLIERS, 2nd Earl of Anglesey, who m. Mary, dau. of Paul, Viscount Bayning, and widow of William, Viscount Grandison, but d. s. p. in 1659, when all his honours became EXTINCT; while his sister Anne, Countess of Sussex, s. to the estates of the family.

Arms.—Arg., on a cross, gu., five escallops, or, a mullet for difference.

VILLIERS—DUCHESS OF CLEVELAND.

(See FITZ-ROY, Duke of Cleveland and Southampton.)

VILLIERS—EARL OF GRANDISON.

By Letters Patent, dated 11 September, 1721, and 19 February, 1767.

Lineage.

WILLIAM VILLIERS, Esq., of Brookesby, eldest son of Sir George Villiers, Knt. (by his 1st marriage with Audrey, dau. and heiress of William Sanders, Esq. of Harrington, co. Northampton,) was created a Baronet, 19 July, 1619, but the title ceased in 1711. at the demise of the grandson of the first possessor, s. p. The eldest son, by his 2nd marriage, of Sir George Villiers, and the half-brother of Sir William, the 1st baronet, was George, DUKE OF BUCKINGHAM, the celebrated favourite of JAMES I. and CHARLES I., who fell by the hand of the assassin Felton, 23 August, 1628. The 2nd son of the above Sir George Villiers, Knt., by his 1st wife, and consequently brother of Sir William Villiers aforesaid, was

SIR EDWARD VILLIERS, who received the honour of knighthood, 7 September, 1616, having been employed, in 1620, as ambassador to Bohemia, and was, in 1622, through the interest of his half-brother, the Duke of Buckingham, nominated President of the province of Munster, in Ireland, at the decease of the Earl of Thomond. Sir Edward m. Barbara, eldest dau. of Sir John St. John, of Lidiard Tregoze, co. Wilts, and niece of Sir Oliver St. John, who was created 3 January, 1620,

* During the youth of this gentleman, some efforts are said to have been made by the family to obtain a summons to the House of Lords, which his devotion to the Jacobite cause is supposed to have rendered hopeless. Mr. Murray, afterwards Lord Mansfield, was consulted on the subject of the claim; and exchanged with this family assurances of devotion to the exiled Stuarts, which, when he received office, he was imagined to have betrayed, to the disadvantage of his former clients. Republicans during the reign of the Stuarts—Jacobites during the reign of the Guelphs—this unfortunate family seems always to have "had hold of the wrong end of the stick."

† It is to be observed that, in consequence of the claims of this family, the title of Buckingham was not again conferred till after its extinction in the male line; and that the Sheffields, though commonly called Dukes of Buckingham, were in fact created Dukes of Buckinghamshire.

560

Viscount Grandison, in the peerage of Ireland, with remainder to the issue male of his sister, Lady Villiers. By this marriage Sir Edward had four sons and three daus.,

  i. WILLIAM, his heir.
  ii. JOHN, successor to his brother.
  iii. GEORGE, successor to his brother John.
  iv. EDWARD (Sir), ancestor of the EARLS OF JERSEY.
  1. Anne, m. 1st, Richard, only son and heir of Lord Wenman; and 2ndly, to James Howard, 3rd Earl of Suffolk.
  ii. Ellen.

Sir Edward d. 7 September, 1626, lamented more deeply than any governor who had previously ruled the province, and was interred in the Earl of Cork's chapel at Youghal, where the following lines were engraven upon his tomb:—

> "Munster may curse the time that Villiers came
> To make us worse by leaving such a name
> Of noble parts as none can imitate
> But those whose hearts are married to the state;
> But if they press to imitate his fame,
> Munster may bless the time that Villiers came."

The eldest son,

WILLIAM VILLIERS, Esq., s. to the estates of his father, and, on the demise of his uncle in 1630, became 2nd Viscount Grandison. Actively espousing the cause of CHARLES I., his lordship received a wound at the siege of Bristol, 26 July, 1643, of which he d. in the following month at Oxford, leaving, by Mary, his wife, dau. of Paul, Viscount Bayning, an only dau., Barbara (wife of Roger Palmer, Earl of Castlemaine, in Ireland,) afterwards Duchess of Cleveland, and mistress of CHARLES II. His brother and heir,

JOHN VILLIERS, 3rd Viscount Grandison, d. s. p., when the honours devolved upon his brother,

GEORGE VILLIERS, 4th viscount, who m. Lady Mary Legh, 2nd dau. [and co-heiress of Sir Francis Legh, Bart., created *Lord Dunsmore* in 1628, and *Earl of Chichester* in 1644, and had two sons and two daus.,

  i. Edward, a brigadier-general in the army, and lieut.-col. of the Queen's regiment of horse; m. in 1677, Catherine, dau. and heir of John Fitzgerald, Esq., of Dromana, co. Waterford, by whom he obtained a considerable landed property in that county. He d. in 1693, leaving

    1 JOHN, who s. to the viscounty.
    2 William.
    1 Mary, m. to Brigadier-Gen. Stuart.
    2 Harriet, m. to Robert Pitt, Esq., by whom she was mother of WILLIAM PITT, 1st EARL OF CHATHAM.

Mrs. Villiers obtained a patent from King WILLIAM in 1699, granting her the privilege to enjoy the same title and precedence as if her husband had survived his father, and had actually been possessed of the honour of VISCOUNT GRANDISON. She m. 2ndly, Lieut.-Gen. William Steuart, M.P., P.C., appointed, in 1711, commander-in-chief of the army during the Duke of Ormonde's absence.

  ii. William, d. 7 September, 1723, having m. Catherine, 2nd dau. of Sir Edward Villiers, his father's younger brother, and widow of Lewis-Jame Le Vassen, Marquess de Puissars, in France.
  1. Audrey, m. to Richard Harrison, Esq., of Balls, near Hertford.
  ii. A dau. m. to Skinner Byde, Esq.

Lord Grandison d. in 1699, and was s. by his grandson,

JOHN VILLIERS, 5th Viscount Grandison, who was created EARL GRANDISON, *of Limerick*, 11 September, 1721. His lordship m. Lady Frances Cary, dau. of Anthony, Viscount Falkland, by whom he had issue: 1 JAMES, Lord Villiers, M.P., who m. Jane, dau. and heir of Richard Butler, Esq., and had three children, who d. in infancy: he d. 12 December, 1732: his widow m. 2ndly, Lucius-Charles, Viscount Falkland; 2 WILLIAM, Lord Villiers, d. unm., 1739; and 3 ELIZABETH, eventual heiress. The earl d. 14 May, 1766, when the earldom EXPIRED, the viscounty descended to his kinsman, William, 3rd Earl of Jersey, and his estates passed to his dau.,

LADY ELIZABETH VILLIERS, who had been elevated to the peerage of Ireland, 10 April, 1746, as VISCOUNTESS GRANDISON, *of Dromana, co. Waterford*, and was, after her father's death, advanced to be COUNTESS GRANDISON, 19 February, 1767. Her ladyship m. 1st, 12 June, 1739, Aland John Mason, Esq., M.P.; and 2ndly, Gen. Charles Montague Halifax; by the former of whom she left at her decease, 29 May, 1782, an only surviving child,

GEORGE MASON-VILLIERS, 2nd Earl of Grandison, b. 23 July, 1751; who m. 10 February, 1774, Lady Gertrude Conway, 3rd dau. of Francis, Earl of Hertford, and had an only dau. and heir,

GERTRUDE-AMELIA, who m. 7 June, 1777, Lord Henry Stuart, son of John, 1st Marquess of Bute, and left, with other issue, a son and heir,

HENRY VILLIERS-STUART, Lord Stuart de Decies.

The Earl of Grandison d. in July, 1800, and with him the honours became EXTINCT.

Arms—Arg., on a cross, gu., five escallops, or.

FAMILY OF FITZGERALD OF THE DECIES

GERALD FITZ-GERALD, 2nd son of James, Earl of Desmond, was the first of the family of the Decies (see FITZ-GERALD, EARL OF DESMOND): he m. Margaret, dau. of MacRichard Burke, and had issue by her,

  i. JOHN, of whom presently
  ii. Gerald.
  iii. Maurice, m. Anne, dau. of James Fitz-Gerald, 3rd son of Thomas, 7th Earl of Kildare, and had daus.
  iv. Thomas.

The eldest son,

JOHN FITZ-GERALD, Lord of the Decies, co. Waterford, m. Ellen, dau. of Fitzgibbon, the White Knight, and d. 17 April, 1533, being buried at Youghal, 24 April following. He left issue, one son,

GERALD FITZ-GERALD, Lord of the Decies, seised of the Barony of Comragh, co. Waterford: he m. Ellice, dau. of Pierce, Earl of Ormonde, and d. 1553, leaving issue,

  i. SIR MAURICE FITZ-GERALD, Lord of the Decies, m. Ellen, dau. of John, Earl of Desmond, and d. 28 December, 1572, s. p.
  ii. SIR JAMES FITZ-GERALD, of Dromana, Lord of the Decies, co. Waterford, æt. thirty, 1572, m. Ellen Carty, dau. of Mac-Carty Reagh, and d. 16 December, 1581, leaving an only son, GERALD, of Dromana, who m. Honora, dau. of David Barry, Lord Barry, and d. s. p.; his will, dated 1616, was proved in Dublin; he was buried in the abbey of St. Francis, at Youghal.
  iii. GERALD, of whom hereafter.
  i. Mary, wife of Sir Oliver Grace, Knt., of Leagan Castle, and of Ballylinch, co. Kilkenny.

GERALD FITZ-GERALD, 3rd son, of Ballihenni, co. Waterford, Esq., m. Ellinor, dau. of John Butler, of Derryloskan, co. Tipperary, Esq., and d. 1 May, 1509, leaving issue an only son.

SIR JOHN FITZ-GERALD, of Dromana, Knt., who had a grant of a fair at Dromana, on St. Bartholomew's Day, and on vigil of St. James, at the rock near White Mount, 1 December, 1607. He m. Ellen Fitzgibbon, dau. of Maurice, the White Knight, and by her, whose will was dated 30 May, 1630, he left at his decease, before 26 May, 1608,

  i. JOHN, of whom presently.
  i. Catharine, wife of James Prendergast, Esq., of Newcastle, co. Tipperary, J.P.
  ii. Ellinor, wife of James Butler of Nodstown.
  iii. Anne, wife of Tibbot Butler.
  iv. Mary, wife of Patrick Courcy, grandfather of Gerald, Lord Kinsale.
  v. Ellen, wife of Gerald de Courcy, Lord of Kinsale.
  vi. Ellice, wife 1st, of Thomas, Lord Cahir; and 2ndly, of Sir Thomas Esmonde, Bart.

The only son,

SIR JOHN OGE FITZGERALD, of Dromana, knighted by the Lord Deputy St. John, m. Elinor, dau. of James, Lord Dunboyne, by Dame Margaret, his wife, and d. 1 March, 1626 (administration dated 25 November, 1626) leaving issue,

  i. SIR GERALD, of whom presently.
  ii. John.   iii. Maurice.
  i. Ellen.   ii. Margaret, wife of — Roche.
  iii. Giles, wife of John Power, of Kilmeadon, Esq.
  v. Mary.

The eldest son,

SIR GERALD FITZ-GERALD, of Dromana, Knt., m. Mabel, dau. of Sir Robert Digby, and dying 6 August, 1643, left issue by her, viz.,

  i. JOHN, of whom presently.
  i. Lettice, wife of Richard Franklyn of Coolbagh, co. Wexford, Esq.
  ii. A dau., wife of Thomas Walsh of Piltown, co. Waterford.

The son and heir,

SIR JOHN FITZ-GERALD, of Dromana, Knt., M.P. for Dungarvan, m. 1st, Catharine, dau. of John, Lord Poer, she d. 22 August, 1660, and 2ndly, Helen, dau. of Donogh MacCarthy, Earl of Clancartay; he d. 1 March, 1664, leaving issue by his 1st wife, an only dau.,

CATHARINE, m. in 1677, to EDWARD VILLIERS, eldest son of George, Viscount Grandison, *ut supra*.

WAHULL—BARONS DE WAHULL.

By Writ of Summons, dated 26 January, 1297.

Lineage.

WALTER DE FLANDERS came into England with the CONQUEROR, and held, as a feudal lord, at the time of the General Survey, considerable estates in the cos. Bedford and Northampton, of which WAHULL (now Wodhull or Odhull,) in the former shire, was the head of his barony. To this Walter succeeded

WALTER DE WAHULL, whose son,

SIMON DE WAHULL, in the time of King HENRY I. or STEPHEN, with Sibyll, his wife, gave the church of Langford to the Knights Templars. His son and successor,

WALTER DE WAHULL, certified, 12th HENRY II., on the assessment of the aid for marrying the king's dau., his knights' fees, *de veteri feoffamento*, to be twenty-seven, and those *de novo*, three. He was subsequently concerned in the insurrection of Robert, Earl of Leicester, and was made prisoner in a battle near St. Edmundsbury. By his 1st wife, Albreda, widow of Guy de St. Valery, he had no issue, but by Roesia, his 2nd, he had two daus. and two sons, SIMON and John, and was *s.* by the elder,

SIMON DE WAHULL, who was fined in the 22nd HENRY II., 10 marks for trespassing in the king's forests; and in the 2nd RICHARD I., upon levying the scutage of Wales, paid £13 10s. for his knights' fees: in the 6th of the same reign, he paid £27 towards the sum levied for the king's redemption. This Simon gave to the nuns at Godstone, into which convent his daus., Mary and Cicely had entered, a moiety of the church of Pateshill, in Northamptonshire. He *d.* in two years afterwards, when Henry, archbishop of Canterbury, paid £333 6s. 8d., for the wardship of his heir, and benefit of his marriage, which heir was

JOHN DE WAHULL. This feudal lord *d.* 1216, leaving his sisters his heirs, viz., ROESIA, *m.* to Robert L'Isle; and Agnes, *m.* 1st, to Robert de Bassingham, and 2ndly, to William Fitz-Warine; but neither sister appears to have had any surviving issue. At John de Wahull's death, the honour of Wahull devolved upon the heir male of the family, son of his uncle,

SAIHER DE WAHULL, who *d.* in 1250, and was *s.* by his son,

WALTER DE WAHULL, who, upon doing his homage, and giving security to pay £100 for his relief, had livery of the honour of Wahull, and the other lands of his inheritance. He *m.* Helewyse, dau. of Hugh de Vivon, and dying in 1269, was *s.* by his son,

JOHN DE WAHULL, who, attaining majority in the next year, and doing his homage, had livery of his lands. In the 22nd EDWARD I., he had a military summons to march into Gascony, and had, subsequently, a similar summons to proceed against the Welsh, but *d.* in two years afterwards, seized of the manor of Wahull or Wodhull, which he held by the service of two knights' fees. He *m.* Agnes, dau. of Sir Henry Pinkeney, of Wedon Pinkeney, and dying 1295, was *s.* by his son,

THOMAS DE WAHULL. This feudal lord was summoned to parliament as a Baron,* 26 January, 1297, 25th EDWARD I. He *d.* in 1304, seized of the Barony of Wahull, as also of the manor of Wahull, co. Bedford, and Pateshill, in Northamptonshire, leaving, by his wife Hawise, dau. of Henry Praers, an infant son and heir,

JOHN DE WAHULL, who, although possessing the honour of Wahull, had no similar summons to parliament, nor had any of his descendants. He *d.* in the 10th EDWARD III., leaving by Isabella, his wife, two sons,

  I. JOHN (Sir), whose line terminated in heiresses, his granddaus.,

    Elizabeth, } who both *d. s. p*
    Eleanor. }

  II. NICOLAS.

---

* NICOLAS doubts if this writ constituted a parliamentary Baron because it was only directed to the temporality. "The writ,' he observes, "commands the persons to whom it is addressed, to attend at Salisbury, on Sunday, the feast of S. Matthew the Apostle next ensuing. viz., 21st September, 'nobiscum super dictis negotiis colloquium et tractatum specialiter habituri, vestrumque consilium impensuri; et hoc, sicut nos et honorem nostrum ac salvationem regni, nostri ac incolarum diligitis, nullatenus omittatis;' and it was directed to six earls and seventy-five barons, and to the judges: but not one of the bishops or abbots were included." He admits, however, that two subsequent writs in the same year supplied this omission, and he states, that the validity of the writ had never before been questioned, and that in a special case brought before parliament (that of Fresheville,) the slightest objection was not made.

The 2nd son (or his son), upon the termination of the line of the elder Sir John de Wahull, *s.* to the estates, and became NICHOLAS DE WAHULL, of Wahull. He *m.* Margaret, dau. and heir of John Foxcote, Esq., and had issue,

  THOMAS, his successor.
  Richard.
  Edith, *m.* to — Emesworth.
  Margaret, *m.* to Simon Brown.

He *d.* in the 12th HENRY IV., and was *s.* by his elder son,

THOMAS DE WAHULL, who *m.* Elizabeth, sister and heir of Sir Thomas Chetwode, Knt., and had two sons, THOMAS and William. He *d.* 9th HENRY V., and was *s.* by the elder,

THOMAS DE WAHULL, who *m.* Isabel, eldest dau. of Sir William Trussell, of Elmesthorpe, and had issue,

  JOHN.   Thomas.
  Isabel, *m.* to — Bowden.

He was *s.* by his elder son,

JOHN DE WAHULL, or WOODHULL. This gentleman *m.* Jean, dau. of Henry Etwell, of London, and had four sons, FULK, Thomas, William, and John; and three daus., Elizabeth, Anne, and Mary. He was *s.* by his eldest son,

FULK WOODHULL, who *m.* Anne, dau. and heir of William Newman, of Thenford (by Margaret, his wife, one of the daus. and co-heirs of Thomas Lamport,) and had issue,

  NICHOLAS, his successor.
  Thomas.
  Lawrence, of Molington, co. Warwick.
  Mary, *m.* to Edward Cope, Esq., of Towes, co. Lincoln.
  Jane, *m.* to William Bellingham, Esq.
  Isabel, *m.* to Richard Tresham, Esq., of Newton, Northamptonshire.

Mr. Woodhull *d.* 24th HENRY VII., and was *s.* by his eldest son,

SIR NICHOLAS WOODHULL, Knt. This gentleman *m.* 1st, Mary, dau. of Richard Raleigh, Esq., of Farnborough, co. Warwick, and had issue, ANTHONY; Barbara, *m.* to Edmund Medwinter, Esq.; and Joice. He *m.* 2ndly, Elizabeth, dau. and co-heir of Sir William Parr, Lord Parr, of Horton, and had,

  Fulk, who *m.* Alice, dau. of William Coles, of Leigh, and was ancestor of the Wodhulls of Thenford.
  Anne, *m.* to David Seamer, Esq.
  Mary, *m.* to Richard Burnaby, Esq., of Watford, Northamptonshire.

Sir Nicholas *d.* 23rd HENRY VIII., and was *s.* by his eldest son,

ANTHONY WODEHULL, who, coming of age in the 31st HENRY VIII., had livery of his lands; but dying in two years after, left by Anne, his wife, dau. of Sir John Smith, an only dau. and heiress,

AGNES WODEHULL, who *m.* 1st, Richard Chetwode, Esq. (3rd son of Roger Chetwode, Esq. of Oakley, by Ellen Masterson, his wife,) and had a son and heir,

RICHARD CHETWODE, of whom presently.

She *m.* 2ndly, Sir George Calverley, Knt., and had two sons, who both predeceased her. Lady Calverley was *s.* at her decease, 18th ELIZABETH, by her only son,

SIR RICHARD CHETWODE. This gentleman, in the time of JAMES I., preferred a claim to the BARONY OF WAHULL, or WODHULL, as possessor of the manor and castle of Odell (Wahull) and his petition being referred to the Duke of Lennox, the Lord Howard, and the Earl of Nottingham, these noblemen returned the following certificate :—

"According to your majesty's direction, we have met and considered the petition of Sir Richard Chetwode, and find that the petition is true: and that before any usual calling of barons by writs, his ancestors were barons in their own right, and were summoned to serve the kings in their wars, with other barons; and were also summoned to parliament. And we conceive the discontinuance to have arisen from the lords of the honour dying at one year of age, and the troubles of the time ensuing : but still the title of baron was allowed in all the reigns by conveyances of their estates, and by pardon of alienation from the crown by the king's own officers, and £9 per annum, being the ancient fee for the castle guard of Rockingham, was constantly paid, and is paid to this day : so that, though there has been a disuse, yet the right so fully appearing, which cannot die, we have not seen or heard of any one so much to be regarded in grace, and in consideration of so many knights' fees, held from the very time of the Conquest, and by him held at this day; and a pedigree both on the father and mother's side, proved by authentic records from the time of the CONQUEROR (which in such cases are very rare), we hold him worthy the honour of a baron, if your majesty thinks meet

        Signed,   Lennox.
                  Howard.
                  Nottingham."

It appears, however, that notwithstanding so favourable a report, the king did not think fit to summon the petitioner in the ancient barony, but he offered to make him BARON OF WODHULL, by patent. This Sir Richard thought derogatory, and declined. Sir Richard Chetwode m. twice, but had issue only by his 1st wife, Jane, dau. and co-heir of Sir William Drury, Knt., viz.,

William, who d. v. p.

RICHARD, also d. v. p., leaving issue by his wife Anne, dau. and heiress of Sir Valentine Knightley, a son,

VALENTINE CHETWOOD, who m. Mary, dau. and co-heir of Francis Shute, Esq., of Upton, co. Leicester, and had two sons,

Knightley Chetwood, dean of Gloucester, whose son and dau. both d. unm.

JOHN CHETWOOD, in holy orders, D.D., whose son,

KNIGHTLEY CHETWOOD, of Woodbrook, Queen's co., m. Hester, dau. and heir of Richard Brooking, Esq., of Totness, co. Devon, and had issue,

   1 VALENTINE-KNIGHTLEY CHETWOOD, who m Henrietta-Maria, dau. of Sir Jonathan Cope, of Oxfordshire, and left the late

     JONATHAN CHETWOOD, Esq., of Woodbrooke, Queen's co., who m. Margaret, dau. and co-heir of Laurence Clutterbuck, Esq., of Derrylusken, co. Tipperary, and d. s. p.

   2 CREWE, of Woodbrooke, who m. Anna-Maria, dau. of Allan Holford, co. Chester, and relict of Ralph Sneyd, Esq., of Keele, co. Stafford, and had, with two daus., one son,

     John, in holy orders, of Glanmire, co. Cork, who m. Elizabeth, dau. of William Hamilton, Esq., and had a son, John, captain in the 33rd regiment (who m. Eliza, dau. of G. Patton, Esq., governor of St. Helena, and d. leaving an only dau., ELIZA - CONSTANCE, heir-general of the BARONY OF WAHULL, m. to PETER AIKEN, Esq., of Clifton), and several daus., the eldest of whom, Elizabeth-Hester, m 23 September, 1798, Robert-Rogers Wilmot, elder son and heir of Edward Wilmot, Esq., by Martha, his dau. and co-heir of Charles Moore, Esq., of Lisapooka, and grandson of Robert Wilmot, elder brother of Dr. Ryder Wilmot, archbishop of Tuam, and had issue, Edward Wilmot-Chetwode, Esq., of Woodbrooke, and Emily-Margaret, m. William Brooke, Esq., master in chancery, in Ireland.

Arms—Or, three crescents, gu.

WAKE—BARONS WAKE.

By Writ of Summons, dated 1 October, 1295.

Lineage.

In the time of HENRY I.,

HUGH LE WAKE, m. Emma, dau. and eventually heiress of Baldwin Fitz-Gilbert, by Adelidis, his wife, dau. of Richard de Rullos, which Baldwin was uncle of Gilbert de Gant, 1st Earl of Lincoln of that family. This Hugh le Wake gave the lordship of Wilesford, co. Lincoln, to the monks of Bec, in Normandy, when it became a cell to that great abbey. He d. in 1172, and was s. by his son,

BALDWIN WAKE, who, in the 12th HENRY II., on the assessment in aid of marrying the king's dau., certified his knights' fees to be in number ten, and that they were bestowed upon his ancestor by King HENRY I. This Baldwin was one of the barons who assisted at the coronation of King RICHARD I., on the accession of that monarch. He d. in 1201, and was s. by his son,

BALDWIN WAKE, who m. Agnes, dau. of William de Humet, constable of Normandy, by whom he acquired the manor of Wichéndon. He was s. by his son,

BALDWIN WAKE. This feudal lord m. Isabel, dau. of William de Briwere, and dying about the year 1213, was s. by his son,

HUGH WAKE, who m. Joane, dau. and eventual heiress of Nicholas de Stuteville, Lord of Liddell, and at the death of his uncle, William de Briwere, s. p., in 17th HENRY III., s. to his property. This Hugh d. at Jerusalem in 1246 (his widow m. 2ndly, Hugh Bigod), and was s. by his son,

BALDWIN WAKE. This feudal lord, who took up arms with the barons in the reign of HENRY III., was made prisoner at the storming of the castle of Northampton, in the 48th of that monarch's reign; but afterwards participated in the success of his party at Lewes. He was again, however, taken prisoner

with young Simon de Montfort, at Kenilworth, but by some means or other effected his escape, and made head once more after the defeat of Evesham, with Robert Ferrers, Earl of Derby, under whom he fought at the battle of Chesterfield, but had the good fortune to escape with his life. He subsequently submitted to the king, and received a pardon, with restitution of his lands. He m., according to Dugdale, Hawise, dau. and co-heir of Robert de Quinci, and was s. by his son,

JOHN WAKE, who was summoned to parliament as a Baron, 1 October, 1295, and from that period to 29 December, 1299. This nobleman was engaged in the French and Scottish wars of King EDWARD I., and in the 27th of that monarch, his lordship was one of the commissioners assigned (with the archbishop of York and others) to see to the fortification of the castles of Scotland, and guarding the marches. He d. in 1304, and was s. by his son,

THOMAS WAKE, 2nd baron, summoned to parliament from 20 November, 1317, to 20 November, 1348. This nobleman taking part with Queen ISABEL against EDWARD II., was appointed by that princess, acting in the name of the king, justice of all the forests south of Trent, and constable of the Tower of London. On the accession of EDWARD III., his lordship was constituted governor of the castle of Hertford, and obtained license to make a castle of his manor-house of Cotingham, co. York. He was subsequently a leading personage for seventeen years of the reign of King EDWARD, during which period he was constantly in the wars of Scotland, and once in those of France. He was also governor of Jersey and Guernsey, and constable of the Tower of London. His lordship m. Blanche, dau. of Henry Plantagenet, Earl of Lancaster, but d. s. p. in 1349, leaving his sister Margaret, Countess of Kent, widow of Edmund of Woodstock, Earl of Kent, his heir, who carried the Barony of Wake into the family of Plantagenet, whence it was conveyed by

JOANE PLANTAGENET, the Fair Maid of Kent, the countess's eventual heiress into the family of her 1st husband, Sir Thomas Holland, Lord Holland, K.G. (See Plantagenet, Barons of Woodstock, and Earls of Kent. See likewise, Holland, Barons Holland, Earls of Kent, and Duke of Surrey).

Arms—Or, two bars, gu., in chief three torteaux.

NOTE.—From this old baronial family, the Wakes, Baronets of Clevedon, co. Somerset, claim descent.

WALCHER — EARL OF NORTHUMBERLAND, BISHOP OF DURHAM.

Lineage.

On the execution and attainder of Waltheof, Earl of Northumberland, in 1075 (he was beheaded at Winchester, and the first so put to death after the Norman Conquest),

WALCHER DE LORRAINE, bishop of Durham, was entrusted with the government or earldom of the co. Northumberland. This prelate, a native of Lorraine, was a person of excellent endowments, greatly esteemed for his piety, integrity, and benevolence, but of so gentle a disposition, that he was unable to repress the arbitrary proceedings of his servants and soldiers; whereupon loud murmurs arose amongst the people, and a day was at length appointed for an amicable adjustment, when oppressors and oppressed assembled at a place called Gateshead, near Newcastle-upon-Tyne. But instead of a peaceable result, a violent turmoil commenced, in which the church, where the bishop sought safety, was set on fire, and the venerable prelate barbarously murdered, *anno* 1080.

Arms—Az., a cross between four lions rampant, or: these are still the arms of the bishops of Durham.

WALEYS—BARON WALEYS.

By Writ of Summons, dated 15 May, 1321.

Lineage.

RICHARD WALEYS, had summons to parliament as a Baron, 15 May, 1321, but never afterwards. Of this nobleman, Dugdale gives no account, nor are there any particulars recorded of him.

He, however, left (Courthope's *Historic Peerage*) a son, Stephen, living in 1348, whose only dau. and heiress, Elizabeth, *m.* Sir John Depedene, Knt. On his death it is presumed that the Barony of Waleys became EXTINCT.

WALLACE—BARON WALLACE.

By Letters Patent, dated 2 February, 1828.

Lineage.

It appears from Hutchinson's *History of Cumberland*, published 1794, that this family claims descent from a cadet of Craigie-Wallace, in Ayrshire; and a pedigree of that house states that many of the posterity of Alexander, 2nd son of John Wallace, of Craigie, who s. about the year 1500, settled upon the eastern border of England; and there is also a stone in the east wall of St. Mary's porch, in the church of St. Nicholas, at Newcastle-upon-Tyne, with the arms of the Scottish Wallaces, quartering those of "Lindsay of Craigie." In 1550, Henry Wallace is described in a MS. in the British Museum, as one of the gentlemen inhabiting the middle marches in Northumberland; in 1552, he was one of the commissioners of enclosures there; in 1553, he is rated as owner of property in Lambley in Tyndale Ward; and the same year (6th EDWARD VI.) he, and Albany Featherstonhaugh, are appointed by the lord warden, overseers of the watches, 1st at Bellistar and Milner Peth: 2nd at Cowenwoodburn and Lambley: 3rd at Purkenford and Shawbenfoot; and 4th, the rest of the lordship of Knaresdale.

THOMAS WALLACE, of Lambley, living in the reigns of JAMES I. and CHARLES I., purchased lands in Asholme, co. of Northumberland, 13 December, 1637. He is said to have been slain in the battle of Worcester, on the side of the royalists, 3 September, 1651; by his wife, an heiress of the Blenkinsop family, he had three sons, of whom,

THOMAS WALLACE, of Asholme, s. his father, and added to the property the manor or lordship of East and West Coanwood, contiguous to Asholme, 8 March, 1657. By Alice, his wife, a dau. of Sir Thomas Carleton, Knt., he had two sons, of whom, the elder,

ALBANY WALLACE, of Asholme, succeeded. His will, dated 17 November, 1677, was proved at Durham, 1678, in which will he devises "all his lands, farms, and farmholds, with woods and all privileges thereupon to his eldest son, Thomas, as his right, being his only heir." By Isabella, his wife, a dau. of the family of Graham, of Breckonhill Castle, co. Cumberland, he had two sons; I. Thomas, his heir; and II. John. The elder,

THOMAS WALLACE, of Asholme, is styled in the *Haltwhistle Registers* "Lord of the Asholme, &c., &c." By Grace, his 1st wife (who *d.* 1695), he had no issue; and he *m.* 2ndly, 17 May, 1696, Margaret, dau. of Hugh Ridley, of Plenmeller (Chief Ridley), and by her had two sons, and two daus. This gentleman was buried at Haltwhistle, 4 July, 1721, having greatly reduced his estate by prodigal living, and s. by his eldest son,

THOMAS WALLACE, of Asholme, attorney-at-law, b. 1697, who purchased an estate at Brampton, co. Cumberland, where he resided. He *m.* 2 January, 1728, Dulcibella, 7th dau. of John Sowerbye, of Brampton-Gillesland and Botcherby, 2nd son of Daniel Sowerbye, of Sleetbeck and Sowerbyca, by whom he had issue, two sons and one dau.,

I. JAMES, his heir.
II. JOHN, of Sedcop House and Golden Square (of whom hereafter).
1. Margaret, baptised 4 July, 1735, *m.* 30 September, 1762, Edward Atkinson, lieut. R.N., and *d.* (leaving issue) in April, 1812.

Mr. Wallace, dying 11 December, 1737, his widow *m.* 2ndly, the Rev. William Plaskett, vicar of Ganton, co. York, and Brampton, co. Cumberland, by whom she had a dau., Anne, *b.* 4 August, 1741, who *m.* 1st, 22 October, 1761, John, son and heir of the Rev. John Tomlinson, lord of the manors of Blencogo and Allonby, in Cumberland, and 2ndly, 17 January, 1782, John Law, D.D., lord bishop of Elphin, brother to Edward, 1st Lord Ellenborough. Mr. Wallace's elder son,

JAMES WALLACE, Esq., of Asholme, baptised 12 March, 1729, added to his paternal estates the manors of Knaresdale and Thornhope, and Featherstone Castle, all near Asholme. He was called to the bar in 1757; appointed solicitor-general in 1777, and attorney-general in 1780; and sat in parliament for Horsham, co. Sussex, from 1770 till his death. He *m.* 8 January, 1767, Elizabeth, only dau. and sole heir of Thomas

Simpson, Esq., of Carleton Hall, co. Cumberland (by Elizabeth, his wife, dau. and co-heir of John Pattinson, Esq., of Carleton Hall, a'near relative of Thomas Pattinson, Esq., of Melmerby, high sheriff for the county in 1793), by whom (who *d.* 18 April, 1811) he had one son and one dau.,

I. THOMAS, his heir.
I. Elizabeth, baptised 2 April, 1770, *d. unm.* 12 May, 1792.

Mr. Wallace *d.* in the office of attorney-general, and was buried in Exeter Cathedral, 16 November, 1783. His only son,

THOMAS WALLACE, Esq., of Asholme, Knaresdale, and Featherstone Castle, *b.* in 1768, was sworn of the privy council, 21 May, 1801, and created BARON WALLACE, *of Knaresdale*, 2 February, 1828, having previously, as a member of the administration, filled several public offices, and sat in parliament at different elections for many places, and lastly, for Weymouth. He *m.* 16 February, 1814, Lady Jane Hope, dau. of John, 2nd Earl of Hopetoun, and relict of Henry, 1st Viscount Melville, by whom (who *d.* 6 June, 1829) he had no issue. His lordship *d.* 23 February, 1844, when the title became EXTINCT. The estates devolved on John-George-Frederick-Hope Wallace, Esq., and the representation of the family devolved upon the issue of his uncle. That gentleman,

JOHN WALLACE, Esq., long resident at Sedcop House, Kent, and in Golden Square, baptised 26 March, 1733 (2nd son of Thomas Wallace, of Asholme and Brampton, and only brother to the Attorney-General), was an eminent contractor in London, in the commission of the peace for the ca. Middlesex, and treasurer to the New Westminster Lying-in Hospital. He *m.* 6 March, 1764, Elizabeth, only child of Robert French (son and heir of David French, of Frenchland, M.P. for the borough of New Galloway, in the Scotch parliament of 1702, and lineal representer of the Frenches, of Frenchland and Thornidkes, in Annandale and the Merse), by Elizabeth, dau. of Christopher Hull, of Brampton, and sister to Christopher Hull, of Sedcop House, by whom he had six sons and five daus.,

1 James, A.B., in holy orders, and formerly a fellow commoner of Christ's College, Cambridge, *b.* 4 February, 1766, *m.* Miss Mercey Coombes, and *d.* 14 January, 1829.
2 JOHN, *b.* 13 December, 1770, late commercial-resident at Irgeram, in the Madras Presidency, who succeeded to the representation of the family on the death of his cousin-german, Lord Wallace, which, on his demise, 4 August, 1846, fell (as already mentioned) to his next brother, Albany.
3 Thomas-Hull, in the H.E.I.C.'s service at Madras, *b.* 15 June, 1774, *d.* in India, in 1800, *s. p.*
4 William, a captain in the 90th regiment of foot, *b.* 8 September, 1785; *d.* in the year 1804, of the yellow fever, on his passage homewards from the West Indies, *s. p.*
5 ALBANY, late of Queen Anne Street, Cavendish Square, and of Worthing, Sussex, *b.* 27 June, 1788.
6 Robert-Clerke, a colonel in the army, late major in the king's dragoon-guards, and K.H., *b.* 1 November, 1789; *m.* 22 February, 1814, Henrietta, dau. of Major Ellis, of Abbeyfeal, co. Cork (and sister to the late Thomas Ellis, Esq., one of the four masters in chancery in Ireland, and M.P. for Dublin), by whom he had eight sons and two daus.,

John, *b.* 3 April, 1815, a lieut. in the 94th and 41st regts., *d.* at Callao, in Peru, South America, 27 June, 1845, *s. p.*
Robert, *b.* 31 August, 1816, a capt. in the H.E.I.C.'s service, and late major in the Essex rifle militia, *m.* 30 July, 1840, Corbetta, dau. to Edward Lord, Esq., of Van Diemen's Land (brother to Sir John Owen, Bart., M.P. of Orielton, co. Pembroke), by whom he had three sons, Robert-Edward, ensign, 91th regt.; Albany-John, who *d.* in infancy; and Charles-Mansel, who *d.* young; and three daus., Mary-Eliza-Owen; Henrietta-Ellis, who *d.* in childhood; and Corry-Janetta.
Richard-Ellis, *d.* an infant.
Thomas-French, *b.* 12 February, 1819, *m.* 20 April, 1839, Eliza, dau. of the Rev James Wallace, and had issue, six sons, Robert-French-Algernon; James-Charles-Stuart; John-Henry; Albany-French; Thomas-Alexander, who *d.* an infant; and Charles-Malcolm, who also *d.* in infancy; and six daus., Mercy-Louisa Elizabeth; Henrietta-Adeliza; Elizabeth-Mary-Emily; Mary-Blanch-Annie; Louiza-Eliza; and Alice-Fanny-Maude.
William, *d.* an infant.
Albany-French, *b.* 11 April, 1821, a capt. in the 7th royal fusiliers, who *d.* at Varna, in Turkey, in consequence of a fall from his horse, in June, 1854; this meritorious officer had served in China and India, and had a medal with several clasps.
Charles-James-Stewart, *b.* 16 May, 1823, major in the 25th regt., *m.* 27 October, 1857, Florence, only dau. of Capt. T. Macnamara, R.N., of the family of Doolan, co. Clare, and has issue, Charles-Albany-Ellis, *b.* 6 February, 1863; Florence-Dora-Anna; and Mabel-Henrietta.
Henry, *d.* young.

Mary-Anne-French, m. 15 June, 1853, John, 3rd son of Ferson Manners, Esq., of Kemton Park, Middlesex, and has issue.

Henrietta-Elizabeth.

Col. R.-C. Wallace d. 25 March, 1863.

1 Elizabeth, b. 17 May, 1767; d. unm. 11 May, 1810.
2 Anne, b. 16 May, 1777; m. 3 December, 1810, Roger, 2nd son of James Partridge, of Nymet-Rowland Barton, co. Devon (who d. 27 May, 1851), and d. (leaving issue) 18 May, 1821.
3 Louisa, d. unm. 4 December, 1792.
4 Emma, b. 12 November, 1781; m. 18 June, 1808, Richard Taylor, Esq., late of the War Office (who d. in 1831), and d. 9 May, 1855, leaving issue.
5 Mary, d. at Sedcop, in infancy, 29 November, 1785.

Arms – Gu., a lion rampant, in chief, two crosses patonce, arg., all within a bordure invected, componé, erm. and az.

WALMODEN—COUNTESS OF YARMOUTH.

By Letters Patent, dated 4 April, 1740.

Lineage.

AMELIA SOPHIA DE WALMODEN, the presumed mistress of King GEORGE II. (a young married lady of the first fashion at Hanover, and niece of Erangard Melosine de Schulemberg, Duchess of Kendal), was elevated to the peerage, by letters patent, dated 4 April, 1740, conferring the dignity for life, under the titles of BARONESS AND COUNTESS OF YARMOUTH.

The Countess d. at Hanover, 20 October, 1765, when her honours EXPIRED. She left by her husband two sons, one chamberlain at the Court of Hanover, the other a major-general in the Hanoverian Guards.

Field-marshal Count Walmoden (of Hanover) was generally deemed her ladyship's representative.

Arms – Or, three morions per pale, arg. and az., banded, gu.

WALPOLE—EARLS OF ORFORD.

By Letters Patent, dated 6 February, 1742.

Lineage.

This family is said to have been established in England before the Norman Conquest, and to have derived their surname from WALPOLE, in Norfolk, where they were enfeoffed of lands belonging to the see of Ely. Camden states " that the owner of Walpole gave both that and Wisbich in the Isle of Ely to the monastery of Ely, at the same time that he made his younger son, Alwin, a monk there." We will commence, however, with

HENRY DE WALPOL, who, in the baronial war, in the time of JOHN, taking part against the crown, was made prisoner, and forced to pay £100 for his deliverance. In the last year of HENRY III.'s reign that monarch commands the sheriff of Lincoln to restore to him all those lands in the county, whereof he had been possessed when he fell from his allegiance to King JOHN. This letter was dated at Oxford, 29 June, 1217, and sealed with the seal of William, Earl Marshal, styled the king's justice, because (as the record says) the king had yet no seal. He was s. by

SIR JOHN DE WALPOL, who had been also involved in the baronial contest, and likewise returned to his allegiance in the reign of HENRY III. He had by Isabel, his wife, several sons, of whom

HENRY, was his successor.

RALPH was in holy orders, and became bishop of Norwich, and subsequently of Ely; he obtained the archdeaconry of the latter place in 1271, and was elected bishop of Norwich, 11 November, 1288: on his confirmation, John Peckham, archbishop of Canterbury, addressed him in these memorable words:—" My lord elect, there has an evil custom prevailed in the diocese of Norwich of receiving the first fruits of the livings in your diocese, which proceeds from a spirit of covetousness, and is displeasing both to God and man. Let me therefore persuade you, if you have any concern for your soul's health, to lay aside this evil custom, which will thus tend to the public advantage:" to which he made reply, " I shall freely consent to what you have desired of me, and promise to do all that is in my power to prevent it." This took place at South-Malling, in Kent, after his return to

England from waiting upon the king on the frontiers of Arragon, where he obtained the royal assent; and by patent, dated 7 February, the king recites, *that the church of Norwich, having elected this discreet man, Mr. Rolph de Walpol, archdeacon of Ely, to the bishopric of Norwich,* he confirms the said election, and commands John Peckham, archbishop of Canterbury, William de Redham, and Peter de Leycester. to deliver to him the temporalities, &c. Whereupon he was consecrated in the church of Canterbury, 20 March ensuing. He sat in this see about ten years, and then, upon the death of William de Luda, bishop of Ely, was translated by the Pope to that bishopric. The convent of Ely had obtained the king's leave to proceed to an election, but could not agree amongst themselves; one part (the majority) made choice of John Salmon, their prior; the other selected John de Langton (then king's chancellor), afterwards bishop of Chichester; and the election being thus in dispute, the merits were submitted to Robert Winchelsea, archbishop of Canterbury, who, keeping the cause depending, an appeal was made to the Pope. and both parties repaired to Rome, when his Holiness unwilling to set aside Salmon, sent the monks to a new election; but that proving equally unsatisfactory, the Pope, then to terminate the contest, translated Walpol to Ely, by a bull, bearing date 15 July, 1299, and made Salmon bishop of Norwich. His lordship d. 20 March, 1301-2.

Sir John Walpol was s. by his eldest son,

SIR HENRY DE WALPOLE, in the manors of Walpole and Houghton, who, in the 5th Edward I., is mentioned in a certain deed made by the prior and chapter of Ely as having a mansion house in Ely. In the same reign he had military summonses to march into Flanders and into Scotland. He m. Isabel, dau., of Sir Peter Fitz-Osbert, and heir to her brother, Sir Roger Fitz-Osbert (which lady, after his decease, m. Sir Walter Jernegan, of Stoneham Jernegan, ancestor of the Jerninghams, Lord Stafford, and brought the lordship of Somerleyton, and other lands, into that family). Sir Henry Walpole was s. by his son,

SIR HENRY DE WALPOLE, who, with Robert Baynard, was chosen knight of the shire for the co. of Norfolk, in the parliament that met at Lincoln in the 9th EDWARD II., wherein it was ordered that none should depart without the king's especial license. In the 17th of the same reign he was returned into chancery amongst the knights, who (with other persons of note) were certified to *bear ancient arms from their ancestors.* This Sir Henry Walpole purchased divers lands in Walpole and Houghton, and dying soon after the 9th EDWARD III., was s. by his son,

HENRY DE WALPOLE, of Houghton, who was returned one of the knights of the shire for the co. Norfolk, to the parliament summoned to meet at York, in the 7th EDWARD III., and was s. at his decease by his son,

HENRY WALPOLE, Esq., a person of great note in the co. Norfolk, temp. HENRY VI. He m. Margaret, dau. of Sir Oliver le Grosse, Knt., of Costwick, co. Norfolk, and was s. by his eldest son,

HENRY WALPOLE, Esq., of Walpole and Houghton, who m. Margery, dau. of Sir John Harsick, of Southacre, in Norfolk, and was s. by his son,

JOHN WALPOLE, Esq., of Houghton. This gentleman m. Elizabeth, dau. of Robert Shawe, Esq., of Derby, and was s. by his son,

THOMAS WALPOLE, Esq., who had a grant from William Fawkes, and others, of lands in Houghton, in the 1st HENRY VII., and he had subsequently further grants of lands in the same reign. He m. twice: by his 2nd wife, Alice, he had no issue; but by his 1st, Joane, dau., of William Cobbe, Esq., of Sandringham, he had three sons and a dau., viz.,

John, who d. v. p., leaving a widow, Anne Walpole, but no child.

EDWARD, successor to his father.

Henry, who m. Margaret, dau. and co-heir of Holtofte, of Whaplode, in Lincolnshire, and had issue,

THOMAS, of Whaplode, ancestor of the Walpoles, of Lincolnshire.

JOHN, an eminent lawyer, temp. EDWARD VI., M.P. for Lynn in 1553; and called to the degree of serjeant-at-law, with seven others, in the following year: the feast upon which occasion was kept with the greatest splendour in the Inner Temple Hall, 16 October, 1554, several officers being appointed for the management thereof; and each serjeant presented to the king and queen rings of the finest gold, of the value. besides the fashion, of £3 6s. 8d. Serjeant Walpole m. Katherine, dau. of Edmund Knivett, Esq., of Ashwellthorpe (by his wife, Jane, dau., and eventually sole heir of Sir John Bourchier, Lord Berners), by whom he left at his decease, in 1557,

WILLIAM, who d. s. p.

Mary,
Jane,
Katherine,
Anne,
} co-heirs to their brother.

Francis.
Christopher, of Docking, co. Norfolk.
Agnes, *m.* to William Russel.

Mr. Walpole *d.* 14 January, 1513-14, and was *s.* by his eldest surviving son,

EDWARD WALPOLE, Esq., who *m.* Lucy, dau. of Sir Terry Robsart, and heiress of her grandfather, the celebrated Sir John Robsart. K.B. and K.G. (in consequence of the decease of her brother, Sir John Robsart, and his dau., Amie Robsart, wife of Sir Robert Dudley, afterwards Earl of Leicester, without issue), by whom he had issue,

JOHN, his successor.
Richard, of Brakenash, co. Norfolk, who, by his will, dated 26 March, 1568, left his whole estate to his younger brother, Terry, who *d.* in 1582, leaving issue by two wives.
Elizabeth, *m.* to Martin Cobb, Esq., of Snetisham, in Norfolk.

Mr. Walpole *d.* in 1558-9, and was *s.* by his eldest son,

JOHN WALPOLE, Esq., who inherited the manor of Sidestern, co. Norfolk, and other lands, as heir of Amie Dudley (Robsart), the 1st wife of Robert Dudley, Earl of Leicester. Mr. Walpole *m.* Catherine, dau. and co-heir of William Calybut, Esq., of Coxforth, co. Norfolk, and had issue,

Edward, who *d.* upon his travels in 1559.
CALIBUT, successor to his father.
Thomas.
Catherine, *m.* to Philip Russell, Esq., of Burnhamthorp, co. Norfolk.
Bona. *m.* to John Amyas, Esq., of Delpham. co. Norfolk.
Elizabeth, *m.* to Richard Bunting, Esq., of Southcreeke, co. Norfolk.
Bridget, *m.* to Henry Paynell, Esq., of Bellaugh, co. Norfolk.

Mr. Walpole *d.* in 1588, and was *s.* by his son,

CALIBUT WALPOLE, Esq., of Houghton, who *m.* Elizabeth, dau. of Edmund Bacon, Esq., of Hesset, Suffolk, and had issue,

I. ROBERT, his successor.
II. John, of Southcreeke, *m.* Abigail, dau. and sole heir of Froximer Crocket, Esq.. of Bromesthorpe, Norfolk, and acquired thereby that estate. He left three daus., co-heirs, viz.,

Elizabeth, *m.* to Edward Pepys, Esq., barrister-at-law, and conveyed to him a portion of Bromesthorpe.
Bridget, *m.* to Francis Thoresby, Esq., of Gaywood, Norfolk.
Susan, *m.* to John Hare, Esq., of Snitterton, and conveyed to him a portion of Bromesthorpe.
III. Calibut, }
IV. Bacon, } both *d. unm.*
I. Elizabeth, *m.* in 1612, to Thomas Clifton, Esq., of Toftrees, Norfolk.
II. Anne, *m.* 1st in 1614, to Thomas Pettus, Esq., son and heir of Sir Augustus Pettus, Knt., and brother of Sir Thomas Pettus. Bart., of Rackheath; and 2ndly, in 1619, to Sir Henry Hungate, Knt., of Bradenham, in Norfolk.

Mr. Walpole *d.* 4 May, 1646, and was *s.* by his eldest son,

ROBERT WALPOLE, Esq., who *m.* Susan, dau of Sir Edward Barkham, Knt., of Southacre, lord mayor of London, 19th JAMES I., and had issue,

EDWARD, his successor.
Jane.
Elizabeth.

He *d.* in 1663, and was *s.* by his son,

SIR EDWARD WALPOLE, K.B., of Houghton an eloquent and leading member of the parliament which voted the restoration of King CHARLES II., and also of the long parliament, in both representing the borough of King's Lynn. Sir Edward *m.* in 1649, Susan, 2nd dau. and co-heir of Sir Robert Crane, Bart., of Chilton, co. Suffolk, and had surviving issue,

ROBERT, his successor.
Horatio, who *m.* Lady Anne Osborne, dau. of Thomas. Duke of Leeds, and widow of Robert Coke, Esq., of Holkham, in Norfolk, but *d. s. p.* 17 October, 1717.
Edward, Fellow of Trinity College, Cambridge. *d.* in 1688, *unm.*
Anne, *m.* to Montfort Spelman, Esq , of Narborough. Norfolk, and *d. s. p.* in 1691.
Dorothy, *d. unm.* in 1694.
Mary. *m.* to John Wilson, Esq., of Leicestershire, and *d. s. p.*
Elizabeth, *m.* in 1665, to James Hoste, Esq., of Sandringham. Norfolk.

He *d.* in 1667, and was *s.* by his eldest son,

ROBERT WALPOLE, Esq., M.P. for Castle Rising, co. York, from 1st WILLIAM and MARY until his decease; deputy-lieutenant of co. Norfolk, and colonel of its militia. He *m.* Mary, only dau. and heir of Sir Jeffrey Burwell, Knt., of Rougham, co. Suffolk, and had surviving issue,

I. ROBERT, his successor.
II. HORATIO, *b.* in 1678. This gentleman, who was a diplomatist of the first grade during the administration of his brother, was elevated to the peerage 4 June, 1756, as BARON

WALPOLE, *of Wolterton, co. Norfolk.* His lordship *m.* in 1720, Mary Magdalen, dau. and co-heir of Peter Lombard, Esq., and dying in 1757, left

1 HORATIO, 2nd Baron Walpole, of Wolterton, who *s.* his cousin, the celebrated HORACE WALPOLE, 4th Earl of Orford. in the Barony of Walpole, of Walpole, and was created Earl of Orford. 10 April, 1806, from him descends the pr.sent Earl of Orford.
2 Thomas, whose elder son was the late Thomas Walpole, Esq., of Stagbury Park, co. Surrey (*see* BURKE's *Extant Peerage*).
3 Richard, M.P. for Yarmouth, *m.* 22 November, 1757. Margaret, dau. of Sir Joshua Van Neck, Bart., and sister of Joshua, 1st Lord Huntingfield. and dying 18 August, 1795, left issue by her (who *d.* in 1818),

Richard, *d. s. p.* 15 August, 1811.
Robert. *d. unm.* 18 May, 1834.
Edward, *d. unm.* 1 October, 1844.
Mary-Rachel, *m.* January, 1798, Rev. Ashton Vade, and *d.* his widow, 16 September, 1827, leaving a son, Richard-Henry Vade-Walpole, Esq., of Freethorpe, Norfolk.
Caroline. *m.* 1787, Hon. G.-H. Nevill, and *d.* 1841.

III. Galfridus. a naval officer, and M.P., *temp.* GEORGE I. This gentleman was treasurer of Greenwich Hospital, and afterwards (1711) joint postmaster-general. He *m.* Cornelia. dau. of Mr. Hays, of London, but *d. s. p.* in 1726. His widow *m.* — Kyrwood, Esq., of Herefordshire.
I. Mary, *m.* to Sir Charles Turner, of Warham, Norfolk.
II. Dorothy, *m.* to Charles, Viscount Townshend (his lordship's 2nd wife).
III. Susan, *m.* to Anthony Hamond, Esq., of Wootton, Norfolk. (See BURKE's *Landed Gentry* "HAMOND of Westacre.")

Colonel Walpole *d.* in 1700, and was *s.* by his eldest son,

SIR ROBERT WALPOLE, K.G., *b.* 26 August, 1676, educated at Eton and Cambridge. This gentleman, who attained so much celebrity as Prime Minister, *temp.* King GEORGE I. and King GEORGE II., was first returned to parliament by the borough of King's Lynn, in 1700, and so long as he remained a commoner he sat for the same place, excepting one session: that in which he was a prisoner in the Tower, from 4 January, 1711-12, to the prorogation of the parliament 21 June following.

In June, 1705, Mr. Walpole was commissioned as one of the council in the affairs of the admiralty to the lord high admiral, Prince George of Denmark; and he was appointed secretary of war in two years afterwards. In January, 1709-10, he was made treasurer of the navy. but on the change of ministry soon after he was removed from all his employments. At the accession of King GEORGE I., his eminent abilities were again enlisted on the side of the government. In 1714, five days after the new king's landing, he was made paymaster of the guards and garrisons at home, and of the forces abroad; and in the same year he was sworn of the privy council. In 1715 he was constituted First Lord Commissioner of the Treasury, and chancellor of the Exchequer; and in the same year was chosen chairman of the committee of secrecy, appointed by the House of Commons, to inquire into the conduct of those evil ministers "that brought a reproach on the nation, by the unsuitable conclusion of a war which was carried on at so vast an expense, and was attended with such unparalleled successes." The result of this impeachment of the Tory ministers of ANNE was the flight of Ormonde and Bolingbroke, and the condemnation of Harley, Earl of Oxford, Prior, and some others, but the whole in the end escaped with impunity. In 1717 Mr. Walpole again withdrew with his friends from office, but in 1721 he returned, and was appointed paymaster-general. The next year he was placed in his former situation of First Lord of the Treasury, and chancellor of the Exchequer: was constituted one of the lords justices in 1723, and sworn sole secretary of state during the king's absence in Hanover, attended by the Lords Townshend and Carteret. In 1725 his Majesty conferred upon him the order of the Bath, and he was in the same year again named one of the lords justices during another visit of the king to Hanover. In 1726 he was made a knight of the Garter, and on the accession of King GEORGE II., he was re-sworn of the privy council, and continued in his official employments of First Lord of the Treasury, and chancellor of the Exchequer. At the coronation of the new monarch Sir Robert assisted as a privy councillor, and as a knight of the Garter, in the full habit and collar of the order. In 1740 he was again one of the lords justices, and on retiring from office, he was elevated to the peerage by letters patent, dated 6 February, 1742, as *Baron of Houghton, Viscount Walpole, in Norfolk,* and EARL OF ORFORD, *co. Suffolk.* Thus have we simply enumerated the high offices and the high honours of this celebrated statesman. His lordship rebuilt the ancient family seat at Houghton, and adorned it with a noble collection of pictures and statues. He

Wandesford
(E. Wandesford)

Wenman
(V. Wenman)

Wentworth
(E. Strafford)

Weston
(E. Portland)

Wharton
(D. Wharton)

Willington
(B. Willington)

Willoughby
(B. Willoughby)

Wilmot
(E. Rochester)

Wriothesley
(E. Southampton)

Wyndham
(E. Egremont)

Yelverton
(E. Sussex)

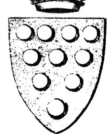

Zouche
(B. Zouche)

m. 1st, Catherine, dau. of Sir John Shorter, of Bybrook, in Kent. Lord Mayor of London, and by her (who *d.* 20 August, 1737) had issue,

ROBERT, his successor, who was created 10 June, 1723, LORD WALPOLE, *of Walpole, co. Norfolk*, with remainder to Edward and Horatio, his brothers, and in default of their heirs male to his father. Sir Robert Walpole, and after him to the heirs male of Robert Walpole, Esq., Sir Robert's father.

Edward (Sir), installed a knight of the Bath in 1753, M.P. for Lostwithiel, and afterwards for Great Yarmouth. On the appointment of the Duke of Devonshire to the lord lieutenancy of Ireland, Sir Edward Walpole was made chief secretary, and sworn of the privy council of that kingdom. He was afterwards joint secretary of the treasury and clerk of the pells. He *d. unm.*[*]

HORACE, who inherited as 4th Earl of Orford.

Katherine, *d. unm.*

MARY, *m.* 14 September, 1723, to GEORGE, 3rd EARL OF CHOLMONDELEY, K.B.

His lordship *m.* 2ndly, Maria, dau. and sole heir of Thomas Skerret, Esq., but by her had no issue. He *d.* 18 March, 1745, and was *s.* by his eldest son,

ROBERT WALPOLE, Lord Walpole, 2nd Earl of Orford. This nobleman *m.* 1724, Margaret, dau. and sole heir of Samuel Rolle, Esq., of Heanton, co. Devon (which lady *m.* 2ndly, the Hon. Sewallis Shirley, and *s.* to the Barony of Clinton), and dying in 1751, was *s.* by his only son,

GEORGE WALPOLE, 3rd Earl of Orford. This nobleman sold to the Empress of Russia, the splendid collection of pictures made by his grandfather, Sir Robert Walpole. His lordship *d. unm.* in 1791, when the honours reverted to his uncle, the celebrated

HORACE WALPOLE, as 4th Earl of Orford, *b.* in 1717, and educated at Eton and Cambridge. For this his youngest child, the Minister Walpole procured the places of usher of the receipt of the exchequer, comptroller of the great roll, and keeper of the foreign receipts. His lordship had for several years a seat in the House of Commons, but he was distinguished more in the literary than the political arena. Soon after returning from his travels he purchased a villa at Twickenham, which he changed into a Gothic mansion, and there (the renowned "Strawberry Hill,") he continued ever afterwards principally to reside. At that favourite retirement he established a private press, where he not only printed his own works, but many other curious compositions. From this press first issued, *The Catalogue of Royal and Noble Authors*, 1758, 2 vols., 12mo.; *Anecdotes of Painting*, 1762; *Historic Doubts*, 1768; *Mysterious Mother*, 1768; *Miscellaneous Antiquities*, 1772, 4to. His lordship *d. unm.* 2 March, 1797, when the Barony of Walpole, of Walpole, passed, according to the limitation to his cousin, HORATIO, 2nd Baron Walpole, of Wolterton (*refer* to 2nd son of Robert Walpole, Esq., father of the 1st earl), and the Earldom of Orford, with the minor dignities, became EXTINCT.

Arms—Or, on a fesse between two chevrons, sa., three crosscrosslets of the 1st.

WANDESFORD — VISCOUNTS CASTLE-COMER AND EARL WANDESFORD.

Barony by Letters Patent, dated 15 March, 1706.
Earldom, by Letters Patent, dated 15 August, 1758.

Lineage.

THOMAS WANDESFORD, Esq. of Kirklington, descended from John de Wandesford, of Westwick, co. York, by Elizabeth,

[*] Sir Edward Walpole left three illegitimate daus., viz.,

Laura, *m.* to the Hon. and Rev. Frederick Keppel, son of William-Anne, 2nd Earl of Albemarle.

Maria, *m.* 1st, James, 2nd Earl Waldegrave, by whom she had issue,

Elizabeth-Laura, *m.* to her cousin, George, 4th Earl of Waldegrave.

Charlotte-Maria, *m.* to George, Duke of Grafton.

Anna-Horatio, *m.* to Lord Hugh Seymour.

The countess *m.* 2ndly, H.R.H. WILLIAM-HENRY, Duke of Gloucester, and was mother of their royal highnesses,

WILLIAM-FREDERICK, 2nd Duke of Gloucester, K.G., G.C.B., *d. s. p.* 30 November, 1834.

PRINCESS SOPHIA-MATILDA, of Gloucester, *d.* 29 November, 1844.

Charlotte, *m.* to Lionel, 4th Earl of Dysart.

his wife, dau. and heir of Sir Henry de Musters, of Kirklington, and widow of Alexander Mowbray, *m.* Margaret, dau. of Sir Henry Pudsey, and had four sons and two daus., viz.,

I. CHRISTOPHER, his heir.

II. William, of Woodel, co. Bedford.

III. Michael, whose grandson,

Sir Rowland Wandesford, Knt. of Pickhay, co. York, was attorney at the court of wards and liveries in 1637. His dau.,

Elizabeth, *m.* Philip, 4th Lord Wharton, and their only dau.,

ELIZABETH WHARTON, *m.* Robert Bertie, 3rd Earl of Lindsey.

IV. John, rector of Kirklington.

I. Ellen, *m.* to Ambrose Lancaster, Esq., of Westmoreland.

II. Elizabeth, *m.* to Ralph Claxton, Esq., of the co. Durham.

The eldest son,

CHRISTOPHER WANDESFORD, Esq., of Kirklington, living *temp.* EDWARD IV. and HENRY VII., *m.* Anne, dau. of John Norton, Esq., of Norton, and had

I. FRANCIS, his heir.

II. Christopher, who *m.* twice, and had issue.

The elder son,

FRANCIS WANDESFORD, Esq., of Kirklington, who *m.* Jane, 2nd dau. and co-heir of John Foulthorpe, Esq., of Hipswell, and had by her,

I. CHRISTOPHER (Sir).   II. John, *d. s. p.*
I. Jane.

He was *s.* in 1559, by his elder son,

SIR CHRISTOPHER WANDESFORD, of Kirklington, who was knighted and served as sheriff of Yorkshire in 1578. He *m.* Elizabeth, dau. of Sir George Bowes, of Streatlam, and was *s.* 11 July, 1591, by his eldest son,

SIR GEORGE WANDESFORD, of Kirklington, *b.* 20 May, 1573, and knighted by King James I. He *m.* 1st, Catharine, dau. and co-heir of Ralph Hansby, Esq., of Beverley, and had issue,

I. CHRISTOPHER, his successor.

II. John, M.P. in 1639.

III. Nicholas, M.P. for Thomastown, in the parliament of Ireland.

IV. Michael, in holy orders, successively dean of Limerick and Derry.

I. Anne, *m.* to Manger Norton, Esq., of St. Nicholas, near Richmond, Yorkshire.

II. Mary.

Sir George *m.* 2ndly, Mary, dau. of Robert Pamplin, and by her had ad au., Margaret, wife of James Blanchard, and one son,

WILLIAM, citizen and merchant tailor of London, to whom and his heirs his eldest brother, 30 June, 1637, gave £20 per annum, issuing out of the manor of Castlecomer, and payable upon Strongbow's tomb in Christ Church, Dublin. In 1639 he was member in the Irish parliament for Ballynakill, in the Queen's co.

Sir George *d.* 4 September, 1612. His eldest son,

CHRISTOPHER WANDESFORD, Esq., of Kirklington, being upon close habits of intimacy and friendship with Sir Thomas Wentworth, Earl of Strafford, accompanied that eminent and ill-fated nobleman into Ireland when he was constituted chief governor of that kingdom, and was appointed in 1633, Master of the Rolls, at the same time being sworn of the privy council; of this office he had soon after a grant by patent for life. He was one of the lords justices in 1636 and 1639, and was appointed 1 April, 1640, lord deputy; but the fate of his friend Lord Strafford had so deep an effect upon him that he *d.* 3 December, in that year. He *m.* 1st, the dau. of William and sister of Sir John Ramsden, Knt., of Byrom, in Yorkshire, but by that lady had no issue. He *m.* 2ndly, Alice, dau. of Sir Hewet Osborne, of Kiveton, in the same co., and had issue,

I. GEORGE, his heir.

II. CHRISTOPHER, successor to his brother.

III. John, *d. unm.*

I. Alice, *m.* to William Thornton, Esq., of Newton, co. York.

II. Catherine, *m.* to Sir Thomas Danby, Knt., of Farnley, near Leeds, and *d.* in childbed of her fifteenth child, aged thirty.

He was *s.* by his eldest son,

GEORGE WANDESFORD, Esq., of Kirklington, M.P. for Clogher, in 1639, *d. s. p.*, and was *s.* by his brother,

CHRISTOPHER WANDESFORD, Esq., of Kirklington, co. York, *b.* 19 August, 1626, who was created a Baronet, 5 August, 1662. He *m.* Eleanor, dau. of Sir John Lowther, Bart., of Lowther Hall, co. Westmoreland, and had issue,

I. CHRISTOPHER, his heir.

II George, who *m.* Elizabeth, widow of Garett Foulke, Esq.

III Charles, *d. s. p.*

I. Mary, d. unm.
II. Eleanor, m to Amias Bushe, Esq., of Kilfane, in the co. of Kilkenny.
III. Catherine, m. to Sir Richard Pyne, chief justice of the King's Bench, and d. in 1731, aged sixty-four.
IV. Frances, m. to Robert Maude, Esq. of Ripon, in Yorkshire, and Kilkenny; d. 5 January, 1690.
V. Alice, d. unm.
VI. Christiana, m. to Richard Lowther, Esq., of Leeds, 2nd son of Sir William Lowther, Knt., of Swillington.

Sir Christopher, who was M.P. for Ripon, d. in February, 1686, and was s. by his eldest son,

SIR CHRISTOPHER WANDESFORD, who was attainted by King JAMES's parliament in 1689, and had his estate sequestered; but on the Revolution he was sworn of the privy council by King WILLIAM, and again in 1702, by Queen ANNE, who advanced him to the peerage of Ireland 1706, as BARON WANDESFORD and VISCOUNT CASTLECOMER. He m. Elizabeth, dau. of George Montagu, Esq., of Horton, co. Northampton, and by that lady (who d. 13 November, 1731,) had issue,

I. CHRISTOPHER, his successor.
II. GEORGE, of whom hereafter, as heir to his nephew.
III. John, in holy orders, rector of Kirklington and Catterick. d. s. p. March, 1747-8.
IV. Richard, d. unm. 1719.
I. Henrietta, m. to William Maynard, Esq., of Curryglass, in the co. of Cork, M.P., and d. 19 April, 1736.

His lordship d. in London, 13 September, 1707, and was s. by his eldest son,

CHRISTOPHER WANDESFORD, 2nd Viscount Castlecomer, member in the British parliament in 1710, for Morpeth, and in 1714 for Ripon. In the latter year he was sworn of the privy council to King GEORGE I., and the next year appointed governor of the co. Kilkenny. In 1717 he was constituted secretary-at-war, and d. 23 June, 1719, leaving by his wife, Frances, 2nd dau. of Thomas, Lord Pelham, and sister to Thomas, Duke of Newcastle, an only child,

CHRISTOPHER WANDESFORD, 3rd Viscount Castlecomer, b. in 1717; who d. in London, of the small-pox, unm., 8 May, 1736, and was s. by his uncle,

GEORGE WANDESFORD, 4th Viscount Castlecomer, who m. Susannah, dau. of the Rev. John Griffith, archdeacon of Killaloe, and by her (who d. 10 September, 1757) he had several children, of whom but three survived, viz.,

JOHN, his heir, b. 1726.
Susannah, m. to Thomas Newenham, Esq., of Coolmore, in the co. of Cork.
Elizabeth, d. unm. 17 March, 1764.

He d. 25 June, 1751, and was s. by his son,

JOHN WANDESFORD, 5th Viscount Castlecomer, who took his seat in the Irish House of Lords in 1751, and was created in 1758 EARL OF WANDESFORD, co. Kilkenny. He m. 11 August, 1750, Agnes-Elizabeth, dau. and heir of John Southwell, Esq., of Enniscouch, co. Limerick, and had issue,

I. JOHN, Viscount Castlecomer, b. 23 April, 1753; d. young before the earl.
I. ANNE, m. 13 February, 1769, to John Butler, Esq., of Garryricken, to whom the EARLDOM OF ORMONDE was restored by the House of Lords in Ireland in 1791. There were four sons and two daus., issue of this marriage: the 3rd son, JAMES, became by the death of his eldest brother, 19th EARL OF ORMONDE; and the 4th son succeeding to the estates of the Wandesfords, assumed the surname and arms of WANDESFORD, and was the late Hon. Charles-H. Butler-Clarke-Southwell-Wandesford, of Castlecomer and Kirklington.

His lordship d. 12 January, 1784, and his son having predeceased him, all his honours, including the baronetcy, became EXTINCT.

Arms—Or, a lion rampant, double queud, az.

WARD—EARL OF DUDLEY.

(See WARD, Earl of Dudley, in BURKE's Extant Peerage.)

WARD—BARONS DUDLEY.

(Refer to SUTTON, Barons Dudley.)

SIR HUMBLE WARD, m. FRANCES SUTTON, Baroness Dudley and the Wards thus acquired that barony.

WARDE—BARONS DE LA WARDE.

By Writ of Summons, dated 29 December, 1299.

Lineage.

In the 31st year of King EDWARD I.,
ROBERT DE LA WARDE was in the wars of Scotland, and again in the 34th, at which time he was steward of the king's household. He had been previously summoned to parliament as a Baron, from 29 December, 1299, to 3 November, 1306. His lordship d. 1307, and was s. by his son,

SIMON DE LA WARDE, 2nd baron, summoned to parliament from 30 December, 1324, to 24 July, 1334. This nobleman, who was governor of York, upon the insurrection of Thomas, Earl of Lancaster, in the 15th EDWARD II., brought considerable forces to Boroughbridge in aid of the royal cause, where the earl received so signal a defeat, and, being taken prisoner, was conveyed to Pontefract, and there beheaded. Lord de la Warde was subsequently constituted governor of Pontefract Castle, but of his lordship, or his posterity, nothing further is known.

Arms—Vairé, arg. and sa.

WARREN—EARLS OF SURREY.

Creation of WILLIAM RUFUS

Lineage.

WILLIAM DE WARRENNE, Earl of Warrenne, in Normandy, a near kinsman of WILLIAM THE CONQUEROR, came into England with that prince, and having distinguished himself at the battle of Hastings, obtained an immense portion of the public spoliation. He had large grants of lands in several counties amongst which were the Barony of Lewes, in Sussex, and the manors of Carletune and Beningtun, in Lincolnshire. So extensive indeed were those grants that his possessions resembled more the dominions of a sovereign prince than the estates of a subject He enjoyed, too, in the highest degree, the confidence of the king, and was appointed joint justice-general, with Richard de Benefactis, for administering justice throughout the whole realm. While in that office, some great disturbers of the public peace having refused to appear before him and his colleague, in obedience to citation, the Earl took up arms, and defeated the rebels in a battle at Fagadune, when he is said, for the purpose of striking terror, to have cut off the right foot of each of his prisoners. Of those rebels, Ralph Wahir or Guader, Earl of Norfolk, and Roger, Earl of Hereford, were the ringleaders. His lordship was likewise highly esteemed by King WILLIAM RUFUS, and was created by that monarch EARL OF SURREY. He m. Gundred, dau. of the CONQUEROR, and had issue,

WILLIAM, his successor.
Reginald or Raynald, one of the adherents of Robert Curthose. Watson (History of the House of Warren) makes this Reginald the husband of Alice Wirmgay, and the grandfather of the two co-heiresses.
Gundred-Edith, m. 1st, to Girard de Gornay; and 2ndly, to Drew de Monceux.
A dau., m. to Ernise de Culungis.

This potent noble built the castle of Holt, and founded the priory of Lewes, in Sussex. He resided principally at the castle of Lewes, and had besides Castle-Acre, in Norfolk, and noble castles in Coningsburg and Sandal. He d. 24 June, 1088, and Dugdale gives the following curious account of his parting hour. "It is reported that this Earl William did violently detain certain lands from the monks of Ely; for which, being often admonished by the abbot, and not making restitution, he died miserably. And, though his death happened very far off the Isle of Ely, the same night he died, the abbot lying quietly in his bed, and meditating on heavenly things, heard the soul of this earl, in its carriage away by the devil, cry out loudly, and with a known and distinct voice, Lord have mercy on me : Lord have mercy on me. And, moreover, that the next day after, the abbot acquainted all the monks in chapter therewith, And likewise that about four days after, there came a messenger to them from the wife of this earl, with 100 shillings for the good of his soul, who told them that he died the very hour that the abbot had heard the outcry. But that neither the abbot nor any of the monks would receive it; not thinking it safe for them to take the money of a damned person." "If this part of the story," adds Dugdale, "as to the abbot's hearing the noise, be no truer than the last, viz., that his lady sent them 100 shillings, I shall deem it to be a mere fiction, in regard the lady was certainly dead about three years before." The earl was *s.* by his elder son,

WILLIAM DE WARRENNE (Earl of Warrenne), 2nd Earl of Surrey, This nobleman joined Robert de Belesmé, Earl of Arundel and Shrewsbury, in favour of Robert Curthose, against HENRY I., and in consequence forfeited his English earldom and estates: but those were subsequently restored to him, and he was ever afterwards a good and faithful subject to King HENRY. His lordship *m.* Isabel, dau. of Hugh the Great, Earl of Vermandois, and widow of Robert, Earl of Mellent, by whom he had issue,

WILLIAM, his successor.

Reginald, who marrying Alice, dau. and heir of William de Wirmgay, became Lord of Wirmgay, in Norfolk. He founded the priory of Wirmgay, and left a dau., Alice, wife of Reginald de Dunstavil, and a son, William, who *m.* twice, having issue only by his 1st wife, Beatrix, dau. of Hugh de Perepont. a son, Reginald, who *d. s. p.*, and two daus., viz.,

   1 BEATRIX DE WARREN, who *m.* 1st, Dodo Bardolf, Baron of Shelford, and left a son,

      WILLIAM BARDOLF (see Bardolf.)
   She *m.* 2ndly, Hubert de Burgh. Earl of Kent.

   2 Isabel, who is stated by Watson to have *m.* Geoffrey de Merlay.

Watson, in his *History of the House of Warren*, corroborated by Camden and Ormerod, makes this Reginald to have *m.* Aldelia de Mowbray, and to have had a son, William, from whom he deduces the family of Warren, of Poynton, co. Chester.

Ralph, *d. s. p.*

Gundred, *m.* 1st, to Roger de Newburgh, Earl of Warwick; and 2ndly, to William de Lancaster, Baron of Kendal.

Adeline, *m.* to Henry, son of DAVID, King of Scotland.

The earl *d.* 11 May, 1138, and was *s.* by his eldest son,

WILLIAM DE WARRENNE (Earl of Warrenne) 3rd Earl of Surrey, who zealously espoused the cause of King STEPHEN, and had a chief command in the army of that monarch, in the battle fought at Lincoln, between him and the adherents of t.ie Empress MAUD. His lordship *m.* Adela, dau. of William Talvace, son of Robert de Belesme, Earl of Shrewsbury, and by her (who *m.* 2ndly, Patrick de Eureux, Earl of Salisbury,) had an only dau. and heir,

ISABEL, who *m.* 1st, WILLIAM DE BLOIS, natural son of King STEPHEN; and 2ndly, HAMELINE PLANTAGENET, natural son of Geoffrey, Earl of Anjou, father of King HENRY II.

In 1147, the Earl of Warrenne and Surrey assumed the cross, and accompanied LEWIS, King of France, to the Holy Land, against the Saracens. From this unfortunate enterprise the earl never returned, but whether he fell in battle, or died in captivity, has not been ascertained. His only dau., as stated above,

ISABEL DE WARREN, *m.* 1st,

WILLIAM DE BLOIS, Earl of Moreton, in Normandy, natural son of King STEPHEN, and this nobleman became, in consequence, EARL OF SURREY, having, by the grant of Henry, Duke of Normandy, upon the accord made between him and King STEPHEN, all those lands which STEPHEN held before he was King of England, as well in Normandy as in England, or elsewhere. Amongst these where the castle and town of Norwich, with the whole county of Norfolk, excepting what belonged to the churches, religious houses, and other earls, and, especially, excepting the *Tertium Denarium*, by reason whereof Hugh Bigot was Earl of Norfolk. He had also all the honour of Pevensey. This nobleman, who was of an unambitious disposition, and enjoyed the favour of HENRY II., accompanied that monarch to the siege of Thoulouse, and *d.* there *s. p.* in 1160. His widow, Isabel, heiress of the Warrens, *m.* subsequently, in 1163,

HAMELINE PLANTAGENET, natural brother to King HENRY II., who likewise obtained, *jure uxoris*, the EARLDOM OF SURREY, and assumed the surname and arms of DE WARREN. This nobleman bore one of the three swords at the second coronation of RICHARD I., and in the 6th of the same reign, he was with that king in his army in Normandy. He *d.* 7 May, 1202, four years after the countess, having had issue,

  I WILLIAM, his heir.
  I. Adela, *m.* to Sir William Fitzwilliam.
  II. Maud.
  III ——, *m.* to Gilbert de Aquila.
  IV. Isabel, *m.* to Roger, Earl of Norfolk.
  v. Margaret, *m.* to Baldwin, Earl of Devon.

The son and heir,

WILLIAM DE WARREN (Plantagenet), Earl of Warren and Surrey, sided at the commencement of the contest between King JOHN and the barons, and for a long time after, with his royal kinsman, but eventually joined the banner of LEWIS of France. On the death of King JOHN, how-

ever, he returned to his allegiance, and swore fealty to King HENRY III.; at the solemn nuptials of which monarch he had the honour of serving the king, at the banquet, with his royal cup in the Earl of Arundel's stead, who, being in minority, could not perform that office, as he had not been girt with the sword of knighthood. His lordship *m.* 1st, Lady Maud de Albini, dau. of the Earl of Arundel, but by her ladyship had no issue. He *m.* 2ndly, Maud, dau. of William Marshal, Earl of Pembroke, and widow of Hugh Bigot, Earl of Norfolk, by whom he had,

JOHN, his successor
Isabel, *m.* to Hugh de Albini, Earl of Arundel.

He *d.* in 1240, and was *s.* by his son,

JOHN DE WARREN (Plantagenet), Earl of Warren and Surrey. This nobleman was but five years of age at the time of his father's decease, and was placed in ward with Peter de Savoy, the Queen's brother. When he attained majority, he attached himself zealously to HENRY III. in his conflicts with the barons, and maintained the cause of the king with his sword at the battle of Lewes. His lordship was a person of violent and imperious temper, and was often betrayed into acts of great intemperance; as in the instance of assaulting Sir Alan Zouch, and Roger, his son, in Westminster Hall, when he almost killed the one and wounded the other. And again, when EDWARD I. issued the first writs of Quo Warranto, his lordship being questioned as to the title of his possessions, exhibited to the justices an old sword, and unsheathing it, said, " Behold, my lords, here is my warranty, my ancestors coming into this land with WILLIAM *the Bastard*, did obtain their lands by the sword, and I am resolved with the sword to defend them, against whomsoever shall endeavour to dispossess me ; for that king did not himself conquer the land, and subdue it, but our progenitors were sharers and assistants therein." The earl was constituted, by King EDWARD, general of all his forces on the north of Trent, for the better restraining the insolence of the Scots; whereupon he marched into Scotland, and so terrified the inhabitants that they immediately sued for peace, and gave hostages for their future good conduct. But the war soon after breaking out afresh, his lordship sustained a signal defeat at Strivelin, when his troops fled first to Berwick, and thence into England. The earl *m.* 1st, 1247, Alice, dau. of Hugh le Brun, Count de la March, and half sister by the mother of King HENRY III., and 2ndly, Joan, dau. of William, Lord Mowbray, and by the former only had issue,

WILLIAM, who was killed in a tournament at Croydon in his father's life-time, 12 December, 1285. He *m.* Joane, dau. of Robert de Vere, Earl of Oxford. and left a posthumous son,

  JOHN, who *s.* his grandfather, and a dau.,

  ALICE, *m.* to Edmund Fitz-Alan, Earl of Arundel This lady, upon the decease of her brother, *s. p.*, inherited the great estates of the Warrens, and conveyed them to the Fitz-Alans, and her son, RICHARD, Earl of Arundel, succeeded to their honours.

Alianore, *m.* to Henry, Lord Percy.
Isabel, *m.* to John de Baliol, afterwards King of Scotland.

His lordship *d.* in 1304, and was *s.* by his grandson,

JOHN DE WARREN (Plantagenet). Earl of Warren and Surrey. This nobleman had the honour of knighthood conferred upon him, with 200 other persons of distinction, in the 34th EDWARD I., when Prince Edward was also knighted with great solemnity. In the last year of King EDWARD, his lordship was in the expedition made into Scotland, wherein that victorious prince died. In the 4th of the next reign he was again in Scotland, and so much in favour with the king, that he obtained a free grant of the castle and honour of Peke, in Derbyshire, with the whole forest of High Peke, to hold during his life, in as full and ample manner as William Peverel anciently enjoyed the same, before it came to the kings of England by escheat. In the ensuing year we find his lordship, along with the Earl of Pembroke, besieging Piers Gaveston, in Scarborough Castle, and forcing him to surrender. He was, some years afterwards, one of those who invested the castle of Pontefract, at that time held by Thomas, Earl of Lancaster, and his adherents; and he subsequently sat in judgment upon, and condemned to death that eminent personage. In the reign of EDWARD III. the earl appears constantly engaged in the wars of Scotland. His lordship *m.* 1st, Joane, dau. of the Count de Barre, by whom he had no issue. In the life-time of this lady he cohabited publicly with Maud de Nereford,[*] a person of good family in

---

[*] By Maud de Nereford he had three sons and three daus.,
  1 JOHN DE WARREN.
  2 WILLIAM DE WARREN.   3 Thomas de Warren.
  1 Joan, of Basing.
  2 Catherine, wife of Robert Heveningham.
  3 Isabel.

Norfolk, but was at length obliged, by the archbishop of Canterbury, to break off the connection. He obtained a divorce, however, from his countess, on the ground of a precontract with this Maud. He m. subsequently, Johanna, eldest dau. and heir of Malise, 7th Earl of Strathern, in Scotland. and had a grant of that earldom from Edward Baliol. His wife was forfeited by ROBERT BRUCE for marrying the Earl of Surrey. He d. 30 June, 1347, aged sixty-one, when as he left no legitimate issue, his sister, Alice, wife of Edmund Fitz-Alan, 8th Earl of Arundel, became his heir, and conveyed the great estates of the Warrens (Plantagenets), into the Fitz-Alan family. Her ladyship's son, Richard Fitz-Alan, 9th Earl of Arundel, is considered to have succeeded to the EARLDOM OF SURREY, and so styled himself, but it is doubtful if he were ever formally invested with the dignity. He d. in 1375, and was s. by his son and heir, RICHARD FITZ-ALAN, Earl of Arundel and Surrey, who was beheaded in 1397, when all his honours became FORFEITED (see Fitz-Alan, Earls of Arundel).

Arms—OF THE WARRENNES—Chequy, or and az. OF BLOIS—Gu.. three pallets, vairé, on a chief, or, an eagle displayed, gu., membered, az. OF PLANTAGENET—Semée of France, and a border of England. This coat was abandoned for that of Warrenne.

WATSON—BARONS ROCKINGHAM, EARLS OF ROCKINGHAM, BARONS OF MALTON, EARLS OF MALTON, MARQUESSES OF ROCKINGHAM.

Barony, by Letters Patent, dated 29 January, 1645.
Earldom, 19 October, 1714.
Barony of Malton, 28 May, 1728.
Earldom of Malton, 19 November, 1734.
Irish Earldom of Malton, 17 September, 1750.
Marquessate, 19 April, 1746.

Lineage.

Of the ancient family of WATSON, which flourished for several ages in the cos. Rutland, Northampton, and Cambridge, was

EDWARD WATSON, of Lydington, co. Rutland, who lived in 1460, and had fifteen children : the eldest of whom, his son and heir,

EDWARD WATSON, d. in 1530, leaving by his wife, Emma, dau. and co-heir of Anthony Smith, Esq., an only son,

EDWARD WATSON, Esq., of Rockingham Castle, co. Northampton, who m. Dorothy, eldest dau. of Sir Edward Montague, Knt., lord chief justice of the King's Bench, and was s. by his son,

SIR EDWARD WATSON, who served the office of high sheriff for Northamptonshire, 34th ELIZABETH, and was knighted at the Charter House, in London, in May, 1603. He m. Anne, dau. of Kenelm Digby, Esq., of Stoke, co. Rutland, by whom he had issue,

LEWIS, his successor.
Edward, d. in 1658.
Anne, m. to Sir Charles Norwich, of Brampton, co. Northampton.
Emma, m. to John Grant, Esq.
Mary, m. to Sir Anthony Mayney, Knt., of Linton, in Kent.
Elizabeth, m. 1st, to Sir John Needham, of Litchborough, co. Northampton, and 2ndly, to Sir Edward Tyrell, Bart., of Thornton, co. Bucks.

Sir Edward d. in 1616, and was s. by his elder son,

SIR LEWIS WATSON, Knt., who was created a Baronet, 23 June, 1621. He was high sheriff of Northamptonshire 9th CHARLES I., and, in consideration of his loyalty to that prince, for whom he garrisoned the castle of Rockingham, was advanced 29 January, 1645, to the dignity of BARON ROCKINGHAM, *of Rockingham, co. Northampton.* His lordship m. 1st, Catharine, dau. of Peregrine Bertie, Lord Willoughby, of Eresby, but by that lady had no surviving issue. He m. 2ndly, Eleanor, dau. of Sir George Manners, of Haddon, co. Derby, Knt., and sister of John, Earl of Rutland, by whom he had one son and three daus., viz.,

EDWARD, his successor.
Grace, m. to Sir Edward Barkham, Bart., of Southouse, in Norfolk.
Frances, m. to Edward Dingley, Esq., of Charlton, in Worcestershire.
Eleanor, m. to Sir Charles Dymoke, Knt., of Scrivelsby, co. Lincoln, hereditary champion of England.

His lordship d. in 1652, and was s. by his son,

EDWARD WATSON, 2nd Baron Rockingham, who m. Lady Anne Wentworth, dau. of Thomas, 1st Earl of Strafford, by whom he had surviving issue,

I. LEWIS, his successor.
II. Edward, d. unm.
III. Thomas, who succeeded, at the death of his uncle, William Wentworth, Earl of Strafford, in 1695, to the great bulk of that nobleman's estates, and assumed the additional surname of WENTWORTH. He was M.P. for Higham Ferrers, and afterwards for Malton, in the reign of Queen ANNE. He m. Alice. only dau. of Sir Thomas Proby, Bart., of Elton, co. Huntingdon, and dying in 1723, left an only child,

    THOMAS WATSON-WENTWORTH, who was created 28 May, 1728, BARON OF MALTON, and advanced 19 November, 1734, to the dignites of *Baron of Wath and Harrowden, Viscount Higham, of Higham Ferrers, and EARL OF MALTON.* His lordship inherited the Barony of Rockingham at the decease of his cousin, in 1746.

IV George.
I. Eleanor, m. to Thomas, Lord Leigh, of Stoneleigh, and d in 1705.
II. Arabella, m. to Sir James Oxenden, Bart., of Dene, in Kent.
III. Anne, } both d. unm.
IV. Margaret, }

His lordship d. in 1691, and was s. by his eldest son,

LEWIS WATSON, 3rd baron. This nobleman, in his father's life-time, sat for Higham Ferrers, in the convention parliament, and was lord-lieutenant and custos rotulorum for the co. Kent, *temp.* Queen ANNE and GEORGE I. His lordship m. Catherine, younger dau. and co-heir of Sir George Sondes, of Lees Court, co. Kent, K.B. (afterwards created Earl of Feversham), and eventually heiress to her elder sister, Mary, wife of Lewis, Lord Duras. In consequence of this alliance Lord Rockingham, on being advanced in the peerage by letters patent, dated 19 October, 1714, assumed two of the titles borne by his deceased father-in-law, namely, *Baron Throwley, and Viscount Sondes, of Lees Court,* both in the co. Kent. He was also created by the same patent, EARL OF ROCKINGHAM. His lordship had issue,

I. EDWARD, Viscount Sondes, M.P. for New Romney, m. in 1709 Lady Catherine Tufton, eldest dau. and co-heir of Thomas, 6th Earl of Thanet, and dying 21 March. 1721-2, left issue.

    LEWIS, who succeeded his grandfather as Earl of Rockingham.
    THOMAS, who inherited the honours on the decease of his brother, s. p.
    Edward, d. unm.
    Catherine, m. to Edward Southwell, Esq., of King's Weston, co. Gloucester, and had a son,

        EDWARD SOUTHWELL, who succeeded, in 1776, to the Barony of De Clifford.

II. George, d. in 1735.
I. Mary, m. to Wray Saunderson, Esq., of Glentworth, co Lincoln.
II. Anne, d. young
III. Arabella, m. to Henry Furnese, Esq., son and heir of Sir Robert Furnese, Bart., of Waldershare, in Kent.
IV. Margaret, m. 1725, to Sir John Monson, Bart., K.B., of Burton, co. Lincoln, who was created in 1728, BARON MONSON, and had,

    1 JOHN, who s. to the Barony of Monson, and was great-grandfather of

        FREDERICK-JOHN, 5th Lord Monson, who was s. by his cousin,

        WILLIAM-JOHN, 6th Lord Monson (See BURKE'S *Extant Peerage*).

    2 LEWIS, who assumed the surname of WATSON, and was created 20 May, 1760, BARON SONDES, of Lees Court (see BURKE's *Extant Peerage*).
    3 George. a brigadier-general, d. in 1777, s. p.

The earl d. in 1724, and was s. by his grandson,

LEWIS WATSON, 2nd Earl of Rockingham. who m. Anne, dau. of Sir Henry Furnese, Bart. of Waldershare, but d. s. p. in December, 1745, when the honours devolved on his only surviving brother,

THOMAS WATSON, 3rd Earl of Rockingham, who d. in a few months afterwards, anno 1746, unm., and devised his estates to his cousin, the Hon. Lewis Monson (refer to children of his aunt, Margaret), upon condition that he assumed the surname and arms of WATSON. At the decease, thus, of this nobleman, all his honours became EXTINCT, except the Barony of Rockingham, which passed to his kinsman and next heir male (refer to Thomas, 2nd son of Edward, 2nd Baron Rockingham),

THOMAS WATSON-WENTWORTH, Earl of Malton, K.B., as 5th Baron Rockingham. His lordship was created 19 April, 1746, MARQUESS OF ROCKINGHAM. He m. Lady Mary Finch, 4th dau. of Daniel, Earl of Winchilsea and Nottingham, and had surviving issue,

WAY

WED

L. Charles, who was created, *vitâ patris*, 17 September, 1750, Earl of Malton, in the peerage of Ireland.
I. Anne, m. in 1744, to William, 3rd Earl Fitz-William, and was mother of

William, 4th Earl FitzWilliam, who was grandfather of William-Thomas Spencer Wentworth FitzWilliam, present Earl FitzWilliam.

II. Mary, m. in 1764, to John Milbanke, Esq., 4th son of Sir Ralph Milbanke. Bart., of Halnaby Hall, and had an only child, Mary, m. to John Gage, of Rogate, Hants, brother of Henry, 3rd Viscount Gage.
III. Henrietta-Alicia, m. October, 1764, Mr. William Sturgeon, and had issue,

1 Thomas-William Sturgeon, a naval officer, m. Elizabeth-Wells, only dau. of Edmund Wells-Fortescue, Esq., of Fallapit. co. Devon, and *d. s. p.*
2 Charles-Alexander Sturgeon, of London, m. Ann, dau. of George Smirthwaite, Esq., of West Hall, near Wakefield, and had, with two daus., Charlotte, m. to Lieut. Forbes, R.N., and Harriet-Alicia, m. to Lieut. Roberts, a son, Charles Sturgeon, Esq., of the Inner Temple, barrister-at-law, who m. 1st, Eleanor, dau. of Rev. Peter Geary, by whom he had no issue; and 2ndly, Jane-Sydney-Louisa, dau. of Col. George Pinckney, by whom he had a son Charles-Wentworth-Dillon Sturgeon, m. 1st, Caroline-Seymour, dau. of Jonathan Sadler, Esq., of the co. Tipperary, by Anne-Alicia-Seymour Lynn, his wife, dau. of Charles-Seymour Lynn, Esq., R.N., Groom of the Wardrobe to King George III., by whom he had no issue; he m. 2ndly, Lucy-May, dau. of the late Joseph Lillie, Esq., of Ardwick and Moss Side, Manchester.
3 Henry - Robert Sturgeon, roy. eng., col. in the South Guides on the Duke of Wellington's Staff in the Peninsular war; m. 1805, Sarah, youngest dau. of Right Hon. John-Philpot Curran, Master of the Rolls in Ireland, but by her (who *d.* 5 May, 1808, aged 26) he had no issue. This lady, the betrothed of Robert Emmet, was the subject of one of Moore's most touching melodies, and of Washington Irving's sketch of "The Broken Heart."
1 Charlotte, m. 1789, to James, 2nd son of James Edwards, Esq., of Old Court, co. Wicklow.
2 Agnes, m. to Pierre Jacques La Chesnay, of Rouen.

This nobleman, who rebuilt the ancient family seat, Wentworth House, in a very splendid manner, *d.* 1750, and was s. by his son, Charles Watson-Wentworth, Earl of Malton, K.G., as 2nd Marquess of Rockingham. This nobleman, at the coronation of King George III., presented to his Majesty, as deputy to the Duke of Norfolk, in his grace's capacity of lord of the manor of Worksop, a right hand glove, before the king received the sceptre with the cross from the Archbishop of Canterbury, and after the king was enthroned, and whilst he received the homage of the peers spiritual and temporal, his lordship held the said sceptre, with the cross. He was elected knight of the Garter in February, 1760, and installed in the May following. In 1765 he was appointed First Lord of the Treasury in the room of the Hon. George Grenville, and sworn of the privy council; but he held the Premiership then only a single year, and from that period was leader of a strong party opposed to the measures of administration, until restored to office in 1782, in his former post of First Lord of the Treasury, and chief of a government, which has since borne in history the title of "the Rockingham Administration," and of which Charles James Fox and Edmund Burke formed a part. Under his lordship's auspices, a pacific negotiation with the revolted states of America commenced, but he did not live to complete his project. He died the same year that he had returned to power. The marquess was esteemed for his purity, his principle, and his patriotism, but he was not considered a man of more than ordinary abilities. He m. Mary, dau. and heir of Thomas Bright, Esq., of Badsworth, co. York, but, as he had no issue, all his honours, at his decease, became extinct. His remains were interred in the Earl of Strafford's vault, in York Minster, 20 July, 1782, and the principal part of the Wentworth estates, including Wentworth House and Malton, co. York, devolved on his lordship's nephew, William, Earl Fitz-William, who assumed the additional surname of "Wentworth."

Arms—Arg., on a chevron ingrailed, az., between three martlets, sa., as many crescents, or, for Watson.

WAYER, OR GUADER — EARL OF NORFOLK AND SUFFOLK.

Creation of William the Conqueror.

Lineage.

Ralph de Wayer, Guader, or De Waet, was constituted by William the Conqueror, Earl of Norfolk and Suffolk.

571

Some of our historians affirm that this nobleman was an Englishman by birth, born in Norfolk; but others, that he was a native of Brittany, which is the more probable, as he was owner of the castle of Guader, in that province. Of this earl there is nothing memorable beyond his conspiracy against his royal master, whom he sought to destroy or expel; and to that end drew into his plans, Roger Earl of Hereford, Waltheof, the great Earl of Northumberland, and other persons of distinction. He m. Emma, sister of the Earl of Hereford, and he took the opportunity of his wedding day to disclose to the conspirators, when they were elated with wine, the whole of his projects. As soon, however, as they had recovered the effect of inebriation, the greater number refused to participate, and the Earl of Hereford alone joined him in openly resorting to arms. The rebellion was quickly, however, suppressed by those stout and warlike prelates, Odo, bishop of Bayeux, and Geffery, bishop of Worcester. The Earl of Norfolk fled into Brittany, leaving his followers to their fate in their encampment at Cambridge: of those, many were put to the sword, and more taken prisoners. The castle of Norwich was subsequently besieged, and his countess obliged to surrender, but she was suffered to go beyond sea. In the end this turbulent person assumed the cross, and joined an expedition under Robert Curthose, to Jerusalem, against the Turks; where he afterwards became a pilgrim, and died a great penitent. He left issue, two sons and a dau., viz.,

Ralph.   Alan.
Amicia, m. to Robert, Earl of Leicester, son of Robert, Earl of Mellent, and brought to him most part of the lands, which William Fitz-Osborne, her grandfather, held in Normandy.

By the treason of Ra'ph de Wayer his earldom became forfeited.

Arms—Per pale, or and sa., a bend vairé.

WEDDERBURN — BARON LOUGHBOROUGH, OF LOUGHBOROUGH, CO. LEICESTER.

By Letters Patent, dated 14 June, 1780.

Lineage.

Alexander Wedderburn, eldest son of Peter Wedderburn, of Chest. rhall, North Britain, (a lord of session, under the titulary designation of Lord Chesterhall,[*]) having been brought up to the English bar, and having attained high reputation as a lawyer, was appointed solicitor general in 1771, attorney-general in 1778, and lord chief justice of the court of Common Pleas in 1780, when he was elevated to the peerage as Baron Loughborough, *of Loughborough, co. Leicester*. In 1783 his lordship was constituted first commissioner for keeping the great seal; and, 27 January, 1793, lord high chancellor of Great Britain. In 1795, Lord Loughborough, having no issue of his own, obtained a new patent, creating him Baron Loughborough, of Loughborough, co. Surrey, with remainder to his sister Janet's sons, by her husband, Sir James Erskine, Bart.,) his nephews, Sir James St. Clair Erskine, Bart., and John Erskine, Esq.; and he was advanced, in 1801, to the Earldom of Rosslyn with a similar remaindership. His lordship m. 1st, Betty-Anne, dau. and heir of John Dawson, Esq., of Morley, in Yorkshire, and 2ndly, Charlotte, dau. of William, Viscount Courtenay, but had no issue. He *d.* 3 January, 1805, when the honours created by the patents of 1795 and 1801, devolved, according to the limitation, upon his nephew, Sir James St. Clair Erskine, Bart., who was father of the 3rd Earl of Rosslyn (*see* Burke's *Extant Peerage*); and the Barony of Loughborough, co. Leicester, became extinct.

Arms—Arg., on a chevron between three roses, gules, barbed and seeded, ppr., a fleur-de-lis, arg.

[*] In Scotland the judges assume, on being raised to the bench, the designation of nobility, but they are merely *titular* lords. In England a practice somewhat similar anciently prevailed, the judges being usually summoned to parliament amongst the barons, *to give their advice*; but they were not regarded as peers of the realm, nor did the writ of summons constitute an hereditary peerage in the family of the person summoned.

WELLES—BARONS WELLES.

By Writ of Summons, dated 6 February, 1299.

Lineage.

The first of this family mentioned by Sir William Dugdale is ADAM DE WELLES, who, in the 6th of RICHARD I.,* paid 10 marks for adhering to John, Earl of Moreton, who at that time assumed more authority, during his brother's captivity, than he was afterwards able to justify. After this Adam came

WILLIAM DE WELLES, who, in the 9th of JOHN, gave 50 marks for one knight's fee in Grimsby, co. Lincoln, and was *s.* by another

WILLIAM DE WELLES, who, in the 11th EDWARD I., obtained license for a weekly market and a yearly fair at his manor of Alford, in Lincolnshire. H: m. Isabel de Vesci, and had two sons, William, a minor, 49th HENRY III., and

ADAM DE WELLES, who in the 22nd EDWARD I. was in the wars of Gascony, and was summoned to parliament, as a Baron, 6 February, 1299, in which year he was made constable of Rockingham Castle, and warden of the forest. The next year he was in the wars of Scotland, and again in 1301 and 1302; and had regular summonses to parliament to the year of his decease, 1311. He m. Joane, dau. and heir of John d'Engayne, and had a son,

ROBERT DE WELLES, baron, never summoned to parliament. This nobleman d. in two years after he had attained majority, *anno* 1320, and leaving no issue by his wife, Maud de Clare, widow of Roger de Clifford, he was *s.* by his brother,

ADAM DE WELLES, 3rd baron, summoned to parliament from 20 July, 1332, to 20 April, 1343. This nobleman, at the period of his brother's death, was only sixteen years of age: he attained his majority in the 20th EDWARD II., and doing his homage had livery of his lands. In the 7th EDWARD III his lordship was in the wars of Scotland, and again in two years afterwards, at which latter period he was a knight. In the 16th of the same reign he was charged with ten men-at-arms and ten archers for the king's service in France, and the like number in the next year. He m. Margaret, dau. of John, Lord Bardolf, and dying 1345, left with a dau., Margaret, who m. William, son of William, Lord Deincourt, a son,

JOHN DE WELLES, 4th baron, summoned to parliament 15 December, 1357, and 20 November, 1360. The wardship of this nobleman, who was a minor at his father's decease, was granted to Margaret, widow of William, Lord Ros, of Hamlake. In the 22nd EDWARD III., although still in minority, he caused his father's executors to purchase a rent of ten pounds per annum, from the monks of Bardney, for the behoof of the abbess and nuns of Grenefield, which monastery was founded by his ancestors; in consideration whereof they obliged themselves, and their successors, to find two fitting priests, to celebrate *masses, matins, placebo, dirge,* and *commendation,* every day in the chapel of our lady, within that their monastery of Grenefield, for the health of the souls of his lordship's predecessors. Lord Welles had livery of his lands in the 29th EDWARD III., and in four years afterwards he was in the wars of Gascony. He m. Maud, dau. of the aforesaid Margaret, Lady Ros, *d.* in 1361, and was *s.* by his son,

JOHN DE WELLES, 5th baron, summoned to parliament from 20 January, 1376, to 26 February, 1421. This nobleman served in the expedition made into Flanders, in the retinue of John, Duke of Lancaster, in the 27th EDWARD III., and in the 1st RICHARD II. was in the wars of France. The next year he was in the garrison of Berwick, under Henry Percy, Earl of Northumberland, its governor. His lordship subsequently obtained license to travel beyond sea, and returning in the 8th RICHARD II., had leave to go abroad again for the vindication of his honour, having received some affront from a knight in France. He seems to have come home solely to procure letters testimonial vouching for his credit and reputation. After this we find him in the Scottish wars; and in the 19th of the same reign, he was ambassador to Scotland, where during h.s sojourn, being at a banquet, where deeds of arms becoming the subject of conversation, his lordship exclaimed, "*Let words have no place; if ye know not the chivalry and valiant deeds of Englishmen, appoint me a day and place when ye list, and ye shall have experience.*" This challenge was immediately accepted by David, Earl of Crawford, and London Bridge ap-

pointed as the place of combat. The battle was fought on St. George's Day, and the Scottish earl was declared victor. Indeed he displayed such an extraordinary degree of prowess, that notwithstanding the spear was broken upon his helmet and visage, he remained so immovably fixed in his saddle, that the spectators cried out that in defiance of the laws of arms, he was bound thereto. Whereupon he dismounted, and got up again, and ran a second course; but in the third, Lord Welles was unhorsed and flung to the ground; on which Crawford dismounting, embraced him, that the people might understand that he had no animosity, and the earl subsequently visited *his lordship with great courtesy until his recovery. Of this* Lord Welles nothing further is known than the period of his decease, *anno* 1421; although for eight years afterwards, summonses appear to have been regularly issued to his lordship. But there are other instances upon record, of summonses having been directed to barons after their deaths, probably from ignorance that the decease occurred. The case of Maurice, the 4th Lord Berkeley, is a remarkable instance; he *d.* in 1368, and summonses were addressed to him until 1380. Lord Welles m. Margaret, or Eleanor, dau. of John, Lord Mowbray, and had two daus., Margaret, m. 1st, John de Huntingfield; 2ndly, Stephen, 2nd Lord Scrope, of Masham; and Anne m. to James, 3rd Earl of Ormonde. He was *s.* by (the son of his deceased eldest son, Eudo, by his wife, Màude, dau. of Ralph, Lord Greystock) his grandson,

SIR LEO, or LIONEL DE WELLES, as 6th baron, summoned to parliament from 25 February, 1432, to 30 July, 1460. This nobleman received the honour of knighthood, in the 4th HENRY VI., from the Duke of Bedford at Leicester, with the young king himself, and divers other persons of rank. His lordship for several years after served with great honour in France, and was made lieutenant of Ireland for seven years, in the 16th of the same reign. When the fatal feud between the houses of York and Lancaster broke out, Lord Welles arrayed himself under the banner of the latter, and adhering to his colours with unbending fidelity, fell at the battle of Towton Field, on Palm Sunday, 1461. His remains were deposited in Waterton Chapel, at Methley, co. York. His lordship m. 1st, Joan, or by some accounts, Cecilia, only dau. of Sir Robert Waterton, of Waterton and Methley, co. York, and sister and heir of Sir Robert Waterton, also of Waterton, Knt., and had issue,

RICHARD (Sir), who m. Joane. dau. and heir of Robert, Lord Willoughby de Eresby, and was summoned to parliament in her right, as LORD WILLOUGHBY, from 26 May, 1455, to 28 February, 1466.

I. ALIANORE. *m.* 1st, Thomas, Lord Hoo and Hastings; BETHELL WALROND, Esq., of Dulford House, co. Devon is, by descent from this marriage, one of the co-heirs of the Barony of Welles; Alianore, *m.* 2ndly, James Lawrence.

II. CECILY, *m.* Sir Robert Willoughby, and had issue; the representatives of Cecily are the MARQUESS OF CHOLMONDELEY, and LORD WILLOUGHBY DE ERESBY, both co-heirs of the Barony of Welles.

III. MARGARET, *m.* to Sir Thomas Dymoke, of Scrivelsby, co. Lincoln, and had issue.

IV. CATHERINE, *m.* 1st, Sir Thomas de la Launde, Knt., and had issue, two daus., his co-heirs, viz.,

JOAN, *m.* to William Denton, Esq., and had a son, JOHN DENTON.

Margaret, *m.* to Thomas Berkeley, Esq., and had two sons, William and Maurice.

She m. 2ndly, Robert Tempest, and had two sons, John and Thomas, who *d. s. p.*

Lord Welles m. 2ndly, Margaret, sister and heir of Sir John Beauchamp, of Bletshoe, and widow of John Beaufort, Earl of Somerset (by whom she was mother of Margaret, Countess of Richmond, mother of King HENRY VII.), and had another son,

JOHN, created VISCOUNT WELLES *(see that dignity)*.

An attainder followed his lordship's decease, under which the BARONY OF WELLES became forfeited; but his son,

SIR RICHARD WELLES, Lord Willoughby, had a grant in the 4th EDWARD IV., through the king's especial favour, of all the goods, chattels, and moveables, whereof his father died possessed; and the next ensuing year had restitution of the manors of Welles, and other estates in the co. of Lincoln, with lands in Northumberland. In three years afterwards (1468,) his lordship obtained a full restitution in blood and honours. But this good fortune had a brief endurance, for the next year, Richard Nevill, the stout Earl of Warwick, taking up arms for the restoration of HENRY VI., made Sir Robert Welles, son and heir of Lord Willoughby and Welles, a brave and able commander, general of the Lancastrian forces. Whereupon Sir Robert drove Sir Thomas Burgh, a knight of the king's house, out of Lincolnshire, pulled down his dwelling, seized upon all his goods and chattels, and at the head of 30,000 of the people, raised the standard of Lancaster, and cried King HENRY. Of

---

* In *Camden*, RICHARD DE WELLES is stated to have held the manor of Welles ever since the Conquest, by the service of being baker to the king.

this insurrection so soon as King EDWARD had intelligence, he summoned the Lord Willoughby and Welles to his presence, but that nobleman on arriving in London, with his brother-in-law, Sir John Dymoke, and learning that the king was highly incensed, fled to sanctuary at Westminster, and there determined to remain until his wrath was assuaged. The king hoping, however, to terminate the disturbance in Lincolnshire, without being obliged to take the field, sent for his lordship, and induced him to leave his asylum, on a solemn promise of safety. He then required of Lord Welles to command his son to lay down his arms, and in the interim marched at the head of what forces he could collect into Lincolnshire, taking Lord Welles and Sir John Dymoke with him. But when he arrived within two days' journey of Stamford, where his adversaries were stationed, he learned that Sir Robert Welles had refused to obey the injunctions of his father, which had been conveyed to him by letter, and becoming enraged at the refusal, he caused, in violation of his royal promise, the heads of Lord Welles and Sir John Dymoke to be forthwith cut off. In revenge of this act of treachery, Sir Robert Welles, without awaiting the coming up of Warwick, attacked the royal army, although superior in number to that which he commanded, but after a most gallant and obstinate struggle, he sustained a defeat, and being made prisoner, was immediately beheaded. The death of the father and his heroic son took place almost at the same time in 1469, and they were both attainted after the restoration of EDWARD IV., in 1474. Lord Willoughby and Welles had issue, by the heiress of Willoughby,

ROBERT (Sir), the gallant soldier whose fate we have just recorded. He d. s. p., leaving a widow, Elizabeth, dau. of John Bourchier, Lord Berners. Her ladyship survived her husband but one year, when she bequeathed her body to be interred with his, in the church of the friars, at Doncaster.

JOANE, m. 1st, Richard Pigot; and 2ndly, Richard Hastings, Esq., brother of William, Lord Hastings, chamberlain to King EDWARD IV.

To Sir Robert Welles, succeeded his only sister, the above mentioned

JOANE HASTINGS, whose husband,

SIR RICHARD HASTINGS, had so much favour from King EDWARD, that he obtained a special livery of all the castles, manors, lordships, and lands, whereof Richard, Lord Welles and Willoughby, and his son, Sir Robert Welles, died possessed,* and was summoned to parliament, as "*Richardo Hastinges de Welles, Ch'r,*" 15 November, 1482, and 9 December, 1483. His lordship had an only son, Anthony, who predeceased him. He d. himself in 1503, when, if his summons to parliament be deemed a continuation of the old Barony of Welles (but it must be recollected that the attainder was never reversed), that barony fell into ABEYANCE, amongst the descendants of the daus. of LEO, the 6th Lord Welles; but if the summons be considered a new creation, the barony at his lordship's decease became then EXTINCT.

Arms—Or, a lion rampant, double queued, sa.

WELLES—VISCOUNT WELLES.

By Letters Patent, *temp.* HENRY VII.

Lineage.

JOHN WELLES, only child of Leo, 6th Lord Welles, by his 2nd wife, Margaret, Countess Dowager of Somerset, having taken up arms in behalf of his kinsman, HENRY, of Richmond,† was made constable of the castle of Rockingham, and steward of Rockingham Forest, after the accession of that personage to the throne as HENRY VII. He was also elevated to the peerage by letters patent (but the date is not known), as VISCOUNT WELLES, and was summoned to parliament in that dignity, 1 September, 1487. He was afterwards made a knight of the Garter. His lordship m. the Lady Cecily Plantagenet, dau. of King EDWARD IV., and sister-in-law to King HENRY VII., and is stated to have had an only dau.,

ANNE, who d. an infant.

---

* In the act of attainder special provision is made that Richard Hastings should enjoy certain manors that belonged to the said barons, in consideration of his having married Joane, sister and heir of Robert de Welles, and also of his loyalty and services.

† He was uncle by the half blood to Henry, Earl of Richmond, afterwards HENRY VII.

573

He d. in 1498, when the Viscounty of Welles became EXTINCT. His lordship's widow m. Sir John Kyme, of Lincolnshire.

Arms—Or, a lion rampant, double queued, sa., armed and langued, gu.

WELLESLEY—BARON AND MARQUESS WELLESLEY.

Barony, by Letters Patent, dated 20 October, 1797.
Marquessate, by Letters Patent, dated 2 December, 1799.

Lineage.

RICHARD COLLEY WELLESLEY, 2nd Earl of Mornington, K.G., K.P. (eldest brother of Arthur, 1st Duke of Wellington, K.G.), b. 20 June, 1760, was created BARON WELLESLEY, *of Wellesley, co. Somerset*, in the peerage of Great Britain, 20 October, 1797, and MARQUESS WELLESLEY, of *Norrah*, in the peerage of Ireland, 2 December, 1799; the latter conferred in consideration of his eminent services as governor-general of India, when he triumphed over the Sultan TIPPOO, and destroyed the empire of Mysore. His lordship m. 1st, in 1794, Hyacinthe-Gabrielle, only dau. of Mons. Pierre Roland, but by that lady (who d. 5 November, 1816) had no legitimate issue. He m. 2ndly, 29 February, 1825 (being then Viceroy of Ireland), Marianne, dau. of Richard Caton, Esq., of the United States of America, granddau. of Charles O'Carroll, of Carrollstown, in Maryland, and widow of Robert Paterson, Esq., whose sister, Elizabeth, was the 1st wife of Jerome Bonaparte, King of Westphalia, and Marshal of France. The Marchioness Wellesley d. 17 December, 1853. The marquess, who was at one time Ambassador to Spain, and subsequently Secretary of State for Foreign Affairs, and twice Lord-Lieutenant of Ireland, d. 26 September, 1842, and was s. in the Earldom of Mornington and minor honours by his brother,

WILLIAM-WELLESLEY-POLE, Lord Maryborough, b. 20 May, 1763, as 3rd Earl of Mornington; his lordship had obtained the Barony of Maryborough by patent of creation, dated 17 July, 1821. He m. 17 May, 1784, Katharine-Elizabeth, eldest dau. of Admiral the Hon. John Forbes, 2nd son of George, Earl of Granard, and by her (who d. 23 October, 1851, aged ninety-one) had issue,

WILLIAM, Viscount Wellesley, 4th Earl of Mornington.
Mary-Charlotte-Anne, m. 24 July, 1806, to the Right Hon. Sir Charles Bagot, G.C.B. (who d. in 1843), and d. his widow, 2 February, 1845.
Emily-Harriet, m. 13 March, 1814, to Field-Marshal FitzRoy, 1st Lord Raglan, G.C.B.
Priscilla-Anne, m. 26 June, 1811, to John, 11th Earl of Westmoreland.

The earl, who was constable of Maryborough Castle, custos-rotulorum of the Queen's County, and captain of Deal Castle, d. 22 February, 1845, and was s. by his son,

WILLIAM POLE-TYLNEY-LONG-WELLESLEY, 4th Earl of Mornington, b. 22 June, 1788; m. 1st, 14 March, 1812, Catharine, eldest dau. and eventual heir of Sir James Tylney-Long, Bart., of Draycot, Wilts, by Catharine, his wife, dau. of Other Windsor, 4th Earl of Plymouth; on his marriage he assumed the additional surnames of TYLNEY and LONG. By this lady (who d. 12 September, 1825) his lordship had issue,

WILLIAM-RICHARD-ARTHUR, 5th earl.
James-FitzRoy-Henry-William, 12th lancers, b. 11 August, 1815: d. 30 October, 1851.
Victoria-Catharine-Mary.

He m. 2ndly, in 1828, Helena, 3rd dau. of Colonel Thomas Paterson (by Anne, his wife, dau. and co-heir of Boyd Porterfield, Esq., of Porterfield, co. Renfrew), and widow of Thomas Bligh, Esq., captain Coldstream-guards, eldest son of Thomas-C. Bligh, Esq., of Brittas, co. Meath. The earl d. 1 July, 1857, and was s. by his elder and only surviving son,

WILLIAM-RICHARD-ARTHUR, 5th earl, who was b. 7 October, 1813, and who d. unm. at Paris, 25 July, 1863, when the Barony of Maryborough became EXTINCT, and the Earldom and Barony of Mornington, and Viscounty of Wellesley, Irish honours, devolved on his lordship's cousin, ARTHUR-RICHARD, 2nd DUKE OF WELLINGTON.

Arms—Quarterly: 1st and 4th, gu., a cross, arg., between five plates, saltierwise, in each quarter; 2nd and 3rd, or, a lion rampant, gu., ducally gorged, or: an honourable augmentation, viz.. "an inescocheon purpure, charged with as estoile radiated wavy between eight spots of the Royal Tiger in pairs saltierwise, ppr.," representing the Standard of the Sultan of Mysore, taken at Seringapatam, was granted 18 December, 1799, to Richard, Marquess Wellesley.

WELLESLEY—BARON MARYBOROUGH.

By Letters Patent, dated 17 July, 1821.

(*See* WELLESLEY, Marquess Wellesley.)

WEMYSS - LORD BURNTISLAND.

By Letters Patent, dated 15 April, 1672.

Lineage.

SIR JAMES WEMYSS, of Caskieberry, husband of Margaret, Countess of Wemyss in her own right, was created a peer of parliament, for life, by the title of Lord Burntisland, 15 April, 1672. This peerage of course became EXTINCT on his death, 1685, and did not devolve on his son, David, who *s.* his mother, as Earl of Wemyss in 1705.

WENLOCK—BARON WENLOCK.

Created in 1461.

Lineage.

In the 17th HENRY VI.,

JOHN WENLOK, or WENLOCK, was constituted escheator for the counties of Buckingham and Bedford; shortly after which coming to court, he was made usher of the chamber to Queen MARGARET, when he had the title of esquire. He was next knighted, and appointed governor of Bamburgh Castle, in Northumberland. In the 28th of the same reign he was constituted chamberlain to the queen, and he fought on the side of Lancaster at the first battle of St. Albans, when he was severely wounded. After this, we find him advancing a sum of money, as a loan, to King HENRY VI., and subsequently chosen a knight of the Garter. Notwithstanding these high honours, Sir John Wenlock joined, soon after, the standard of York, and fought under that banner at the battle of Towton Field, for which desertion he was rewarded, by King EDWARD IV., with the grant of the offices of chief butler of England, and steward of the castle and lordship of Berkhampsted, in Hertfordshire. He was also raised to the degree of a baron, as LORD WENLOCK, *of Wenlock, co. Salop,* and sworn of the privy council. In the first period of King EDWARD's reign his lordship was employed upon confidential embassies to the courts of Burgundy and France, and he was constituted lieutenant-governor of Calais, and the marches adjacent. But afterwards joining the Earl of Warwick, in the attempt to restore HENRY VI., he had a command at the battle of Tewkesbury, where he is said to have been slain by the Duke of Somerset, who furiously cleft his head with his battle-axe, for neglecting to come up in time, whereby the battle was lost, and the fate of the King HENRY VI. decided for ever. His lordship *m.* Elizabeth, dau. and co-heir of Sir John Drayton, but had no issue. He d. in 1471, when the Barony of Wenlock became EXTINCT. His lordship's estates devolved on THOMAS LAWLEY, who appears to have been his heir-general, and from whom descended SIR ROBERT LAWLEY, Bart., who was elevated to the peerage as BARON WENLOCK, *of Wenlock,* in 1831, but who d. *s. p.* 10 April, 1832. His property and the baronetcy passed eventually to his brother, Paul Beilby Lawley-Thompson, who had been created in 1839, BARON WENLOCK, *of Wenlock* (*see* BURKE's *Extant Peerage*).

Arms—Arg., a chevron between three blackamoors' heads, erased, sa.

WENMAN—VISCOUNT WENMAN.

By Letters Patent, dated 30 July, 1628.

Lineage.

HENRY WAINMAN or WENMAN, of Blewbury, co. Berks, living 1452, *m.* Emmota, dau. of Simkin Hervey, co. Hertford, and by her (who *m.* 2ndly, Thomas Fermor, *alias* Richards, of Witney, co. Oxford) had a son,

RICHARD WAINMAN, of Witney, who *m.* Anne Humphrey; and d. 1500, leaving a son,

RICHARD WAINMAN, of Witney, merchant of the staple of Calais, *m.* Anne, dau. of John Bushe, of Northleach, co. Gloucester; and d. 1533, leaving a son,

SIR THOMAS WAINMAN or WENMAN, Knt. of Witney and Caswell, co. Oxford, merchant of the staple of Calais, "suffered in his goods by the loss of Calais, under Lord Wentworth," knighted by Queen ELIZABETH; *m.* Ursula, dau. and heiress of Thomas Gifford, Esq. of Twyford, co. Buckingham (by Mary, his wife dau. and heiress of William Staveley, Esq. of Bignell, co. Oxford), and by her, who d. 7 December, 1558, had a son,

RICHARD WENMAN, Esq. of Thame Park, co. Oxford, and of Caswell, Sheriff co. Oxford, 1562 and 1570, *m.* Isabella, dau. and co-heiress of John, Lord Williams, of Thame, and by her (who *m.* 2ndly, Richard Huddlestone, Esq. of Little Haseley, and *d.* 1587) had, with three daus., Elizabeth, Margaret, and Frances, as many sons,

I. THOMAS, his heir.

II. Henry, *d. s. p.*

III. Francis, of Caswell, living 1572, *m.* Frances, dau. of Sir Henry Goodier, Knt. of Bagginton, co. Warwick; and d. in Ireland, leaving by his wife (who *m.* 2ndly, Sir Charles Manners) a son,

Francis, of Caswell, M.P. co. Oxford, 1640; *m.* Anne, dau. of Sir Samuel Sandys, Knt. of Omberslade, co. Worcester, and had a dau., Anne, *m.* Sir John Fettiplace, 1st Bart. of Chilbury; and a son,

Francis (Sir), of Caswell, created a Baronet 29 November, 1662, *m.* 1st, Hon. Mary Wenman, dau. and co-heir of Thomas, 2nd Viscount Wenman, by whom he had,

Francis, *b. cir.* 1652; *d.* 5 September, 1663.

RICHARD, 4th viscount, of whom hereafter.

Sir Francis *m.* 2ndly, Mary, dau. of Edward Fettiplace, Esq. of Swinbrook, co. Oxford, by whom he had a dau., Dozelina, *m.* Richard Smith, Esq., of Padbury, Bucks.

Mr. Wenman d. 1572, and was *s.* by his eldest son,

SIR THOMAS WENMAN, Knt. of Thame Park, M.P. for Oxford, 1555, *m.* 9 June, 1572, Hon. Jane West, dau. of William, 8th Lord De la Warr, by whom (who *m.* 2ndly, James Cressie, Esq.; 3rdly, Sir Thomas Tasburgh; and 4thly, Ralph Sheldon, Esq. of Beoly) he had three sons and a dau.,

I. RICHARD (Sir), 1st viscount.

II. Ferdinand, *m.* Frances Ryley, of Chetwoode, Bucks.

III. Thomas (Sir), M.P. for Oxford, 1626.

I. Elizabeth, *m.* to Sir Thomas Tredway, Knt. of Beaconsfield, co. Buckingham.

Sir Thomas d. 22 July, 1577, and was *s.* by his eldest son,

RICHARD, 1st Viscount Wenman, *b.* 1573, M.P. for Oxford, 1620 and 1625; high sheriff, 1627; created, by patent, dated 30 July, 1628, Baron Wenman, of Kilmainham, and Viscount Wenman, of Tuam, in the peerage of Ireland. He *m.* 1st, Agnes, dau. of Sir George Fermor, Knt. of Easton Neston, co. Northampton, by whom, who was buried at Twyford, 4 July, 1617, he had issue,

I. THOMAS, 2nd viscount.

II. Edward, *d. s. p.*   III. Charles, *d. s. p.*

IV. PHILIP, 3rd viscount.

I. Penelope, *m.* to Sir John Dynham, Knt. of Boarstall.

II. Jane, *m.* to John Goodwin, Esq. of Winchendon.

III. Mary, *m.* to Sir Martin Lister, Knt. of Thorpe Arnold, co. Leicester.

Lord Wenman *m.* twice afterwards but had no further issue. He d. 3 April, 1640, and was *s.* by his son,

THOMAS, 2nd Viscount Wenman, *b.* 1596, one of the adventurers in Ireland when that kingdom was reduced by the English parliament, one of the commissioners to carry the propositions for peace to the King at Oxford, in 1644; again named commissioner for the treaty at Uxbridge, in the same year; and for the treaty at Newport, in 1648. He *m.* Margaret, dau. and heir of Edmund Hampden, Esq., of Hartwell, Bucks, and had,

I. Richard, *m.* Barbara, dau. of Sir Edward Villiers, Knt., of Brokesby, by whom (who *m.* 2ndly, James, 3rd Earl of Suffolk) he had no issue. He d. *vitâ patris,*

I. Frances, *m.* Richard Samwell, Esq., of Upton.

II. Penelope, *m.* Sir Thomas Cave, 1st Bart., of Stanford.

III. Elizabeth, *m.* Sir Greville Verney, Knt., of Compton Verney, co. Warwick.

IV. Mary, *m.* Sir Francis Wenman, 1st Bart., of Caswell.

Lord Wenman d. 25 Jan. 1664, and was *s.* by his brother,

PHILIP, 3rd Viscount Wenman, who had been elected M.P. for Oxford, 1660; his only dau.,

Mary, *m.* William Croft, Esq., of Croft Castle, co. Hereford.

Lord Wenman d. 20 April, 1696, and was *s.* by virtue of a new entail (*see* ADDENDA) procured from CHARLES II., 30 January, 1683, extending the succession to his next heir male, Sir Richard Wenman, Bart., of Caswell, with the same precedence as the original creation, viz. :—

RICHARD, 4th Viscount Wenman; who *m.* Catherine, elder dau. and co-heir of Sir Thomas Chamberlayne, Bart., of Wickham, and Northbrooke, co. Oxford, and by her (who *m.* 2ndly, James, 1st Earl of Abingdon; and 3rdly, Francis Wroughton, Esq., of Heskett, Wilts) had (with two daus., of whom the elder, Catharine, *m.* 1st, the Hon. Robert Bertie, and 2ndly, Sir William Osbaldeston, Bart., of Chadlington; and the younger, John Wicksted, Esq.) a son, RICHARD, 5th Viscount. Lord Wenman d. about 1691, and was *s.* by his only son.

RICHARD, 5th Viscount Wenman, who m. Susanna, dau. of Seymour Wroughton, Esq., of Heskett, and had two sons, PHILIP, 6th Viscount; and Richard, m. 1773, Jemima, relict of Col. Caulfeild. Lord Wenman d. 28 November, 1729, and was s. by his elder son,

PHILIP, 6th Viscount Wenman, D.C.L., b. 23 November, 1719, M.P. for Oxford, who m. 13 July, 1741, Sophia, eldest dau. and co-heir of James Herbert, Esq., of Tythrop, co. Oxford, and by her (who d. 19 July, 1787) had issue,

  I. PHILIP, 7th Viscount.
  II. Thomas-Francis, D.C.L., b. 18 November, 1745.
  III. Richard, b. 13 November, 1746; d. young.
  IV. Henry-Herbert, b. 18 July, 1749; d. young.
  I. SOPHIA, m. 30 December, 1768, William-Humphrey Wykeham, Esq., of Swalcliffe, co. Oxford, and had issue,
    1 Richard-Wykeham, of Swalcliffe, father of SOPHIA-ELIZABETH WYKEHAM, created BARONESS WENMAN, 3 June, 1834 (see that title).
    2 Philip-Thomas Wykeham, of Tythrop, father (by Hester-Louisa, his 1st wife, dau. of Fiennes Trotman, Esq., of Lyston Court, co. Gloucester) of two sons,
      PHILIP-THOMAS-HERBERT WYKEHAM, of Tythrop House, co. Oxford, and Thame Park; d. 21 May, 1879, when Thame Park and Swalcliffe devolved on his brother Aubrey.
      Aubrey-Wenman Wykeham, of Thame Park and Swalcliffe, m. 1836, Georgiana, dau. of Sir James Musgrave, Bart.; and d. 21 October, 1879, leaving with other issue, a son and successor, WENMAN-AUBREY WYKEHAM-MUSGRAVE, of Thame Park, Swalcliffe Park and Barnsley Park (see BURKE's Landed Gentry).
    1 Sophia-Anne, d. unm.
    2 Harriet-Mary, m. to Rev. Willoughby Bertie; and 2ndly, to Sir Edward Johnston, K.C.S.
  II Susanna, d. young.
  III. Mary, d. 1757.

Lord Wenman d. 16 August, 1760, and was s. by his son, PHILIP, 7th Viscount Wenman, b. 18 April, 1742; who m. 7 July, 1766, Lady Anne-Eleanora Bertie, dau. of Willoughby, 3rd Earl of Abingdon, but d. s. p. 26 March, 1800, when all his honours became EXTINCT.

Arms—Per pale, gu. and az., a cross patonce, or.

WENTWORTH — BARONS WENTWORTH, OF WENTWORTH-WOODHOUSE, VISCOUNT WENTWORTH, BARONS RABY, EARLS OF STRAFFORD.

Barony, by Letters Patent, dated 22 July, 1628.
Viscounty, by Letters Patent, dated 10 December, 1628.
Earldom and Barony of Raby, by Letters Patent, dated 12 January, 1640.
Earldom, by Letters Patent, 4 September, 1711.

Lineage.

The ancient stock of Wentworth-Woodhouse, co. York, has been rooted in that shire from the earliest period to which the geneaologist can usually ascend in his investigations. Of the orthography of the lands, whence originated the name, Domesday Book, and all the old charters have it *Winteworth*, and such is still the pronunciation of the common people, who do not easily fall into new modes of speech. As to its derivation, Mr. Hunter, in his *History of Doncaster*, makes the following remarks: "The latter half of the name (*worth*) is one of the most frequent local terminals, and appears to denote some degree of cultivation. The former half affords room for conjecture. It has been suggested that it may be the word *givint*, preserved in the Breton language, which is a dialect of the Celtic, where it denotes *elevation*. This sense would undoubtedly apply well to Wentworth, which stands high, as does also another place of the same name, in the Isle of Ely, relatively to the fens around it. Celtic etymologies are, however, to be admitted with great caution in investigating the names of places cultivated or populated; and perhaps the scribe of Domesday, who, in one of the five instances in which the word occurs, has written it thus, *Wintrerworde*, may have presented us with an ancient and expiring orthography, from whence we may conclude that the name of Wentworth is to be classed with Winterton, Winterburn, Winteredge, and other places, which have obtained those names from their high, exposed, or cold situations." While the lands of Wentworth-Woodhouse continued to be the seat of the chiefs, and descended from sire to son, in an unbroken series, till the succession of male heirs failed with William, the 2nd Earl of Strafford, the junior scions of the family founded, in several instances, houses of rank and

influence, the Wentworths of Woolley, of North and South Elmsal,* of Bretton, of Nettlested, &c.

WILLIAM DE WYNTWORD, of Wyntword, m. in the time of HENRY III., Emma, dau. and heir of William Wodehous, of Wodehous, by whom he acquired that estate, and taking up his abode there, the family were subsequenty designated the "Wentworths of Wentworth-Woodhouse." He was s. by his son,

WILLIAM DE WENTWORTH, of Wentworth-Woodhouse, who m. Beatrix, dau. of Gilbert Thakel, and had two sons,

WILLIAM, his successor.
Richard, bishop of London, and chancellor of England in 1338.

The elder son,

WILLIAM DE WENTWORTH, m. 1st, Dyonisia, dau. of Peter de Rotherfield, and 2ndly, Lucy, dau. of Sir Adam Newmarch, and by the former had two sons,

WILLIAM, his successor.
John, m. the dau. and heir of Elmsall, of Elmsall, in York shire, by whom he acquired that estate, and dying s. p., left it to his nephew, JOHN.

The elder son,

WILLIAM DE WENTWORTH, s. his father in 1295, and m. Isabel, dau. and co-heir of William Pollington, of Pollington, co. York, and had issue,

WILLIAM (Sir), his heir.
John, who inherited Emsall from his uncle, and marrying Joan, dau. of Richard le Tyas, of Burgh-Walleys, co. York, was ancestor of the WENTWORTHS of Elmsall, of the WENTWORTHS of Bretton, of the WENTWORTHS, Barons and Viscounts Wentworth; and of divers other branches.

William de Wentworth was s. by his elder son, SIR WILLIAM WENTWORTH, who m. Isabel, dau. and co-heir of Walter, son and heir of Henry de Tynsley, of Tynsley, also in Yorkshire, and was s. by his son,

WILLIAM WENTWORTH, who m. Joan, dau. of Sir William Fleming, Knt., of Walth, and was father of

WILLIAM DE WENTWORTH, who m. Lucy, dau. of Isabel, wife of William Sheffield, of Bolderstoun, and left a son,

WILLIAM DE WENTWORTH, who m. 1st, Isabella, dau. of Thomas Durrant; and 2ndly, Isabel, dau. of Sir Thomas Beresby, of Thryberg, co. York, and was father of

SIR THOMAS WENTWORTH, who fought valiantly on the side of King HENRY VI., at the battle of Hexham, 3 April, 1463, when he was made prisoner with the Duke of Somerset and others. He m. Joan, dau. of Sir Richard Redman, Knt., of Harwood Tower, and was s. by his elder son,

WILLIAM WENTWORTH, Esq., of Wentworth-Woodhouse, who m. in the 39th HENRY VI., Isabel, dau. of Sir Richard Fitz-William, of Aldwark, York, by whom he had four sons, THOMAS, his successor, Ralph, George, William, and a dau., Elizabeth, who m. 1st, Thomas Lea, Esq, of Middleton, and 2ndly, Henry, Arthington, Esq. Mr. Wentworth d. in 1477, and was s. by his eldest son,

SIR THOMAS WENTWORTH, of Wentworth Woodhouse, who received the honour of knighthood for his bravery in the battle of Spurs. This gentleman, being a person of great opulence, went by the name of Golden Thomas. He paid a fine to be excused from being created a knight of the Bath; and in 1528, he obtained a license from HENRY VIII. to wear his bonnet and be covered in the royal presence, because he was infirm. He m. Beatrix, dau. of Sir Richard Woodruffe, of

---

* The Wentworths of North Elmsal acquired that estate *temp.* EDWARD III., in marriage with Alice, dau. and heiress of John Bissett, and continued there for several centuries, until the year 1741, when their male line expired with Sir Butler-Cavendish Wentworth, Bart., the estates devolving on that gentleman's half-sister, CATHERINE WENTWORTH, who m. Hugh Cholmley, Esq., of Whitby, co. York, M.P. for Hedon, and high sheriff of that shire in 1724. The Wentworths of South Elmsal, sprung from a younger son of Thomas Wentworth, of North Elmsal, are also now extinct.
The Wentworths of Bretton, deriving from Richard Wentworth, of Everton, in the co. Nottingham, 3rd son of John Wentworth, of Elmsal, by Agnes, his wife, sister and co-heir of Sir William Dronsfield of Bretton, became extinct in the male line upon the demise of Sir Thomas Wentworth Blackett, Bart., 9 July, 1792. The estates of Bretton, &c., are now enjoyed by the Beaumont family.
The Wentworths of Wentworth Castle were founded by Sir William Wentworth, of Ashby, in Lincolnshire, slain at Marston Moor, who was a younger son of Sir William Wentworth, Bart., of Wentworth-Woodhouse, and brother to Thomas, 1st Earl of Strafford. They became extinct in the male line in 1799. The estates are now possessed by Frederick-William-Thomas Vernon-Wentworth, Esq., of Wentworth Castle.
The Wentworths of Nettlested became Earls of Cleveland, and Barons Wentworth. (See p st.)

Woolley, Knt., and widow of John Drax, Esq., of Woodhall, and had issue,

WILLIAM, his successor.
Gervase.
Michael, of Mendham Priory, co. Suffolk, cofferer to King HENRY VIII., and comptroller to the queen, m. Isabel, dau. and heir of Percival Whitley, Esq., of Whitley, co. York, and was father of Thomas Wentworth, Esq., of Mendham Priory, co. Suffolk, and of Whitley, co. York, who m. Susan, dau. of Christopher Hopton, Esq., of Armley Hall, co. York, and had a son and successor, MICHAEL WENTWORTH, Esq., who purchased, from Francis Woodruffe, Esq., Wooley, and other lands in Yorkshire, and was ancestor of the WENTWORTHS of Woolley (see BURKE's Landed Gentry).
Thomas, of Scorby, m. Grace, dau. of John Gascoigne, Esq., of Lasingcroft, co. York, and had issue.
Bryan.
Elizabeth, m. to Ralph Denham, Esq.
Isabel, m. to Nicholas Wombwell, Esq., of Thunnercliffe, co. York.
Beatrice, m. to Thomas Worrall, Esq., of Loversall, co. York.

Sir Thomas d. 5 December, 1548, and was s. by his eldest son,
WILLIAM WENTWORTH, Esq., of Wentworth-Woodhouse, who m. Catherine, dau. of Ralph Beeston, Esq., of Beeston, and dying 4 July, 1549, was s. by his eldest son,
THOMAS WENTWORTH, Esq., of Wentworth-Woodhouse, high sheriff of co. York in the 25th ELIZABETH; m. Margaret, dau. and heir of Sir William Gascoigne, Knt., of Gawthorpe, by which alliance he acquired the manor and seat of Gawthorpe, Cusworth, &c., and his descendants became co-heirs to the Baronies of Ferrers of Wemme, and Boteler, of Wemme, then (and still) in ABEYANCE. By her he had issue,

WILLIAM (Sir), his successor.
Elizabeth, m. to Thomas Danby, Esq., of Farnley.
Barbara, d. unm.
Margaret, m. 1st. to Michael, son and heir of John, Lord Darcy; and 2ndly, to Jasper Blythman, Esq., of New Lathes.
Catherine, m. to Thomas Gargrave, Esq., of Nostel Priory, in Yorkshire.

Mr. Wentworth d. 14 February, 1586-7, possessed of a great landed estate in co. York, and was s. by his son,
SIR WILLIAM WENTWORTH, of Wentworth-Woodhouse. Gawthorpe, &c. This gentleman was high sheriff of Yorkshire in the last year of Queen ELIZABETH, and was created a Baronet, 29 June, 1611. He m. Anne, dau. and heir of Robert Atkinson, Esq., of Stowell, co. Gloucester, by whom he had three surviving sons and three daus., viz.,

I. THOMAS, his successor.
II. William (Sir), of Ashby-Puerorum, co. Lincoln, who was knighted by King CHARLES I., and fell at Marston-Moor, ex parte regis. He m. Elizabeth, dau. and co-heir of Thomas Savile, of Hasselrion Hall, co. York, and had with a dau. Anne, who m. Edward Skinner, Esq., of Thornton College, Lincoln, one surviving son,
  WILLIAM (Sir), high sheriff of Yorkshire, 24th CHARLES II.; m. Isabella, dau. of Sir Allen Apsley, Knt., treasurer of the household to James, Duke of York, and had issue,
    William, a military officer, d. unm. in 1693, while serving as captain of horse in Flanders.
    THOMAS, who s. his cousin, the Earl of Strafford, in the Barony of Raby.
    Peter, of Henbury, co. Dorset, m. Juliana, only dau. of Thomas Horde, Esq., of Cote, co. Oxford, and had surviving issue,
      1 WILLIAM, his successor, who m. Susanna, dau. of John-Chamberlayne Slaughter, Esq., of Upper Slaughter Hall, co. Gloucester, and had two sons and three daus.,
        FREDERICK-THOMAS, who s. to the Earldom of Strafford, at the death of his cousin, Thomas, 2nd Earl of the second creation.
        George, d. unm.
        Caroline, d. unm.
        Augusta Anne, m. 30 May, 1772, to John-Hatfield Kaye, Esq., of Hatfield Hall, Yorkshire; she s. to Wentworth Castle, on the death of her brother Frederick-Thomas, 3rd Earl of Strafford, and d. s. p. in 1802, leaving that estate to her kinsman, FREDERICK-WILLIAM-THOMAS VERNON, Esq., of Hilton who therefore assumed the additional surname of WENTWORTH (see BURKE's Landed Gentry).
      1 Harriet, m. to Thomas, son and heir of Francis Arundel, Esq., of Stoke-Bruers Park, co. Northampton.
    Paul, fell at the siege of Namur, in 1695, unm.
    Allan, killed in storming the citadel at Liege, in 1702, and d. unm.
    Frances-Arabella, m. to Walter, Lord Bellew, of Ireland.
    Anne, m. to James Donelan, Esq., of Ireland.
    Isabella, m. to Francis Arundel, Esq., of Stoke-Bruers Park.
    Elizabeth, m. to John, Lord Arundel, of Trerise.

III. George (Sir), M.P for Pontefract, in 1640, but disabled from sitting on account of his loyalty to King CHARLES I., received the honour of knighthood, made general of the forces in Ireland, and sworn of the privy council of that kingdom. Sir George m. Frances, dau. and co-heir of Sir Francis Ruishe, Knt., of Sarre, in the Isle of Thanet, and left a son,
  RUISHE WENTWORTH, of Sarre, who m. Susanna, sister of James Adye, Esq., of Barham, in Kent, and dying in 1686, left an only child and heir,
    MARY, m. to Thomas, Lord Howard of Effingham.
I. Mary, m. to Sir Richard Hooton, Knt., of Goldesburgh, in Yorkshire.
II. Anne, m. to Sir Gervase Savile, Bart., of Thornhill, co York.
III. Elizabeth, m. to James, 3rd Earl of Roscommon, and was mother of the celebrated poet.

Sir William Wentworth d. in 1614, and was s. by his eldest surviving son,
SIR THOMAS WENTWORTH, 2nd baronet, b. 13 April, 1593, who became afterwards so conspicuous in the troubled times of the first CHARLES. In the reign of JAMES I., Sir Thomas was member of parliament for the co. of York, and also in the beginning of that of his successor; but the latter monarch, soon after his accession, elevated Sir Thomas Wentworth to the peerage, by letters patent, dated 22 July, 1628, as BARON WENTWORTH, of Wentworth-Woodhouse, and further advanced him, 10th of the ensuing December, to the degree of VISCOUNT WENTWORTH. The next year his lordship was sworn of the privy council, made lord lieutenant of the co. of York, and president of the north. In February, 1632-3, he was nominated lord deputy of Ireland; from which government he was recalled to command as lieutenant-general in the army then raised against the Scots. In 1640 he was created BARON RABY, of Raby Castle, in the bishopric of Durham (with remainder, default his own male issue, to his younger brothers, and their issue male), and EARL OF STRAFFORD. Soon after he was made a knight of the Garter, and constituted lord lieutenant of Ireland. About this period the republican and puritanical parties prevailing in parliament, Strafford became an object of their greatest distrust, and the destruction of his lordship was deemed indispensable to the accomplishment of their ulterior projects. An impeachment against him was therefore immediately voted by the Commons, and Pym deputed to carry it up to the House of Lords. The earl was just entering to take his seat, when he was apprised of the prosecution, and ordered into custody. He was subsequently brought to trial 22 March, 1640-1, but his prosecutors were unable to establish their charges, according to the laws of the land, and were therefore, after an investigation which lasted eighteen days, in which Strafford deported himself with a degree of firmness, moderation, and wisdom that extorted admiration from his bitterest foes, obliged to resort to the very unusual and unconstitutional mode of proceeding by bill of attainder. So determined, however, were the Commons to condemn him, that the bill was brought in, and passed on the same day. It was read twice in the morning, and the third time in the afternoon; and carried by 204 voices against 59. But in the Lords its progress was not so triumphant; and when it finally passed 45 peers only were present, of whom 26 voted in the affirmative. In the end Strafford was sacrificed to the clamour of the mob, and his own magnanimous consideration for the precarious position of his royal master. The populace goaded to frenzy, flocked around Whitehall, where the King resided, calling aloud for justice, and accompanying their vociferations with open and furious menaces. The Queen and council were appalled; they advised CHARLES to sign the doom of the most faithful of his servants. Juxon, bishop of London, alone had the fortitude to counsel the king not to act contrary to his conscience. But the earl hearing of his Majesty's irresolution and anxiety, immediately addressed him, and with a devotion almost unparalleled, besought him for the sake of public peace, to put an end to his unfortunate, however blameless, life, and to quiet the tumultuous populace, by conceding the request for which they were so importunate.[*] The king gave at last a most reluc-

---

[*] Last letter from Thomas, Earl of Strafford, to King CHARLES I.

"May it please your Sacred Majestye,
"It hath bin my greatest griefe in all these troubles to be taken as a person which should endeavour to represent and set things amisse between your majesty and your people; and to give counsells tending to the disquiet of the three kingdomes.
"Most true it is, that this miine owne private condition considered, it hath beene a great madnesse, since through your gracious favour I was so provided, as not to expect in any kind

tant arsent; and Thomas Earl of Strafford, the firmest prop of the monarchy, was thus, in the forty-ninth year of his age, consigned to the scaffold. He suffered death with his characteristic firmness upon Tower Hill, 12 May, 1641. His lordship is allowed to have possessed many amiable qualities—to have been endowed with great natural parts—to have had a cultivated understanding,—a brave and noble bearing; but he is accused of pride, arrogance, and ambition—and the epitaph, which Plutarch says that Sylla wrote for himself, is quoted as most appropriate to his tomb, "That no man did ever exceed him in doing good to his friends, or in doing mischief to his enemies; for his acts of both kinds were most notorious." His government of Ireland has been characterized as tyrannical and rapacious. Amongst his bitterest foes was Sir Harry Vane, and he is said to have incurred the enmity of that celebrated person by taking the title of Raby, from Raby Castle, then in Vane's possession. The earl m. 1st, Lady Margaret Clifford, dau. of Francis, Earl of Cumberland, which lady d s p. He m. 2ndly, Lady Arabella Holles, dau. of John, Earl of Clare, by whom he had issue,

WILLIAM, his successor.

Anne, m. to Edward Watson, Earl of Rockingham, and had issue,

    LEWIS WATSON, 3rd Earl of Rockingham
    THOMAS WATSON, who assumed the name of WENTWORTH on succeeding to the estates of his maternal uncle (refer to WATSON.)

Arabella, m. to Justin McCarthy, created Viscount Mountcashell by JAMES II. 1689, son of the Earl of Clancarty.

to mend my fortune, or please my mind, more, then by resting where your bounteous hands had placed me.

"Nay, it is most mightily mistaken, for unto your majesty it is well knowne, my poore and humble advises concluded still in this, that your majesty and your people could never bee happy, till there were a right understanding betwixt you and them; no other means to effect and settle this happinesse, but by the councell, and assent of parliament; or to prevent the growing evils upon this state, but by entirely putting your selfe in the last resort, upon the loyalty and good affections of your English subjects.

"Yet, such is my misfortune, this truth findeth little credit, the contrary seemeth generally to be believed, and myselfe reputed, as something of seperation between you and your people; under a heavyer censure then which I am persuaded no gentleman can suffer.

"Now, I understand the minds of men are more incensed against me, notwithstanding your majesty has declared, that in your princely opinion, I am not guilty of treason, nor are you satisfyed in your conscience to passe the bill.

"This bringeth me into a very great streight, there is before me the ruine of my children and family hitherto untouched, in all the branches of it with any foule crimes. Here is before me the many ills, which may befall your sacred person, and the whole kingdome, should yourselfe and parliament part lesse satisfied one with the other, then is necessary for the preservation both of king and people. Here are before me the things most valued, most feared, by mortal man, life or death.

"To say, Sir, that there hath not beene a strife in me, were to make me lesse man, then God knoweth my infirmities give me. And to call a destruction upon myselfe and young children (where the intentions of my heart, at least have beene innocent of this great offence), may be believed, will find no easie consent from flesh and bloud.

"But with much sadnesse, I am come to a resolution, of that which I take to be most becoming in me, to looke upon that which is most principall in itself; which doubtlesse is the prosperity of your sacred person and the common-wealth, infinitely before any private man's interest.

"And therefore, in few words, as I put myselfe wholly upon the honour and justice of my peers, so clearly as to beseech your majesty might have spared that declaration of yours on Saturday last, and entirely to have left me to their lordships; so now to set your majesty's conscience at liberty, I doe most humbly beseech your majesty, in prevention of mistakes which may happen by your refusall to passe this bill; and by this meanes remove (praysed be God), I cannot say, this accursed (but I confesse) this unfortunate thing forth of the way, towards that blessed agreement, which God, I trust shall ever establish betweene you and your subjects.

"Sir, my consent shall more acquit you herein to God, then all the world can doe besides. To a willing man there is no injury done. And as by God's grace I forgive all the world with a calmnesse and meeknesse of infinite contentment to my dislodging soule, so, Sir, to you can I give the life of this world with all the cheerfulnesse imaginable; in the just acknowledgment of your exceeding favours. And only begge that in your goodnesse, you would vouchsafe to cast your gracious regard upon my poore sonne, and his three sisters, lesse or more, and no otherwise, then as their (in present) unfortunate father, may hereafter appear more or lesse guilty of this death.

"God long preserve your Majestye,
"Your Majesties most faithful and
"humble Subject and Servant,
"STRAFFORD.

* _Tower, 4th May, 1641._"

The earl m. 3rdly, Elizabeth, dau. of Sir Godfrey Rodes, Knt., of Great Houghton, co. York, by whom he had a son, Thomas, and a dau., Margaret, both of whom d. unm. His elder son,

WILLIAM WENTWORTH, was restored by patent 1 December 1641, and by Act of Parliament, 19 May, 1662, to all his father's honours. He was also installed a knight of the Garter. His lordship m. 1st, Lady Henrietta-Maria Stanley, dau. of James, Earl of Derby, and 2ndly, Henrietta, dau. of Frederick Charles de Roy de la Rochefoucauld, generalissimo of the forces of the King of Denmark, but d. s. p. in October, 1695, when the greater part of his estates devolved upon his nephew, the Hon. Thomas Watson, son of Edward, Earl of Rockingham, and all his honours became EXTINCT, save the Barony of Raby, which passed, according to the special limitation in the patent, to his kinsman (revert to issue of Sir William Wentworth, of Ashby Puerorum, 2nd son of the 1st baronet),

THOMAS WENTWORTH, as 3rd Baron Raby. This nobleman had in early life adopted the profession of arms, and served under WILLIAM III. in Flanders, where he acquired high reputation, particularly at the battles of Steinkirk and Landen. In the reign of Queen ANNE he shared in several of the glorious campaigns of Marlborough, and was repeatedly ambassador to the courts of Berlin, Vienna, and the States General. His lordship was advanced in consideration of his eminent services, by letters patent, dated 4 September, 1711, to the dignities of _Viscount Wentworth, of Wentworth-Woodhouse, and of Stainborough,_ and _Earl of Strafford,_ with special remainder to his brother, Peter. His lordship m. Anne, dau. and heir of Sir Henry Johnson, Knt., of Bradenham, co. Bucks, by whom he had issue,

I. WILLIAM, his successor.
  1. ANNE, m. to the Right Hon. William Conolly, one of his Majesty's privy council in Ireland, and had issue,
    1 RIGHT HON. THOMAS CONOLLY, of Castletown, co. Kildare. P.C., d. s. p., 27 April, 1803.
    1 Catherine, m. 1754, Ralph Gore, Earl of Ross, and d. s. p., 1771.
    2 ANNE CONOLLY, m. George Byng, Esq., M.P. of Wrotham Park, Middlesex, and was mother, inter alios, of Field-Marshal Sir John Byng, G.C.B., who was created BARON STRAFFORD in 1835, and EARL OF STRAFFORD in 1847 (see BURKE'S Peerage).
    3 HARRIET CONOLLY, m. the Right Hon. John Staples, and had two daus., of whom the younger, HENRIETTA-MARGARET STAPLES, m. Richard, 2nd Earl of Clancarty, G.C.B; and the elder, LOUISA-ANNE STAPLES, was wife of Admiral the Hon. SIR THOMAS PAKENHAM, G.C.B., and mother of EDWARD-MICHAEL PAKENHAM, who s. to the estate of Castletown, and assumed the name and arms of CONOLLY.
    4 Frances Conolly, m. Viscount Howe, K.B. and d. s. p.
    5 Caroline Conolly, m. John, Earl of Buckinghamshire, and left a dau., Emily, Marchioness of Londonderry.
  II. LUCY, m. 1747, to Field-Marshal Sir George Howard, K.B., M.P., and dying 1771, left an only child to survive her, viz.,
    ANNE, who m. 1780, General Richard Vyse, and d. 1784, leaving a son and heir,
      Richard-William-Howard Howard-Vyse, Esq., of Stoke Place, Bucks. (See BURKE's Landed Gentry.)
  III. HENRIETTA, m. 1743, Henry Vernon, of Hilton Park, co. Stafford, and had, with other issue, a son and successor,
    Henry Vernon, Esq., of Hilton, who m. 1st, Penelope, dau. and co-heir of Arthur Graham, Esq., by whom he had a son, HENRY-CHARLES-EDWARD VERNON, Esq., of Hilton; and 2ndly, Margaret, dau. of Thomas Fisher, Esq., by whom he had a son,
      FREDERICK-WILLIAM-THOMAS VERNON, who s. to the estate of Wentworth Castle, under the will of his maternal relation, Mrs. Hatfield Kaye, and assumed the additional surname of WENTWORTH (see BURKE's Landed Gentry).

His lordship, who was a knight of the most noble order of the Garter, d. 15 November, 1739, and was s. by his son,

WILLIAM WENTWORTH, 2nd Earl of Strafford, of the new creation, who m. 28 April, 1741, Lady Anne Campbell, dau. and co-heir of John, Duke of Argyle, but d s. p. in 1791, when the honours passed, according to the limitation, to his cousin (revert to issue of Sir William Wentworth, 2nd son of Sir William, the 1st baronet),

FREDERICK-THOMAS WENTWORTH, as 3rd Earl of Strafford, b. 1732. This nobleman m. 17 February, 1772, Elizabeth, 3rd dau. of Thomas Gould, Esq., of Milborne St. Andrews, and Frome Bellet, co. Dorset, by Mary, his wife, dau. of William Freke, Esq., but by her (who m. 2ndly, W. Churchill, Esq., and d. 1 May, 1811) had no issue. The earl d. at his seat, Honbury, in Dorsetshire, 7 August, 1799, when the Barony of Raby, the Viscounty of Wentworth, and Earldom of Strafford became EXTINCT.

Arms—Sa., a chevron between three leopards' heads, or.

WENTWORTH — MARQUESSES OF ROCKINGHAM.

(Refer to WATSON, Barons Rockingham, &c.)

The Hon. THOMAS WATSON, 2nd son of Edward Watson, 2nd Lord Rockingham, by Lady Anne Wentworth, succeeded to the Wentworth estates on the demise of his uncle, William, Earl of Strafford, in 1695, and assumed the additional surname of WENTWORTH; from this gentleman descended the Marquesses of Rockingham.

WENTWORTH — EARL OF CLEVELAND, VISCOUNT WENTWORTH, OF WELLESBOROUGH.

Earldom, by Letters Patent, dated 7 February, 1625.
Viscounty, by Letters Patent, dated 4 May, 1762.

Lineage.

This family, although of great antiquity in the co. York, did not attain the honour of the peerage until the time of HENRY VIII., when

THOMAS WENTWORTH, Esq., son of Sir Richard Wentworth, Knt., of Nettlested, co. Suffolk, was summoned to parliament by writ, as BARON WENTWORTH. His lordship m. Margaret, dau. of Sir Adrian Fortescue, Knt., by Anne, his wife, dau. and heir of Sir William Stonor, Knt. (by Anne, dau. and co-heir of John Nevil, Marquess of Montacute), and had issue,

THOMAS, his successor.
Henry (Sir), m. Elizabeth, dau. of Sir Christopher Glenham.
Richard, m. to Margaret Roydon.
Philip, m. the dau. of Sir Richard Corbet, Knt.
John.   Edward.
James.   Roger.
Anne, m. to Sir John Poley, of Bradley, co. Suffolk, Knt.
Cicily, m. to Sir Robert Wingfield, Knt.
Mary, m. to William Cavendish.
Margaret, m. 1st, to John, Lord Williams: 2ndly, to Sir William Drury, and 3rdly, to Sir John Crofts.
Joan, m. to Henry, Lord Cheney.
Dorothy, m. to Paul Withypoole, Esq.
Elizabeth.   Catherine.
Margery.

His lordship, who was lord chamberlain of the household, d. in 1551, and was s. by his eldest son,

THOMAS WENTWORTH, 2nd baron, summoned to parliament, from 23 January, 1552, to 4 February, 1589. This nobleman, on the demise of EDWARD VI., was one of the first who appeared for Queen MARY, and upon her Majesty's accession his lordship was sworn of the privy council, and constituted deputy of Calais, and the marches thereof, in which high trust he continued until the surrender of that place, January, 1558, to the overwhelming force of the Duke of Guise, after being held by the English for upwards of two centuries. Lord Wentworth was subsequently tried by his peers on suspicion of cowardice or treachery, but honourably acquitted. In the reign of ELIZABETH, his lordship was one of the noblemen who sat in judgment upon the Duke of Norfolk, and upon MARY, Queen of Scotland. He m. Anne, dau. of Sir John Wentworth, Knt., of Gosfield, co. Essex, and had issue,

Thomas, who m. Elizabeth, dau. of William Cecil, Lord Burghley, but d. s. p., v. p.
HENRY, his successor.
Elizabeth, m. to William Hynde, Esq., son and heir of Sir Francis Hynde, Knt.

His lordship d. in 1590, and was s. by his son,

HENRY WENTWORTH, 3rd baron, summoned to parliament, 19 February, 1593. His lordship m. Anne, dau. of Sir Owen Hopton, Knt., and widow of Sir William Pope, Knt., by whom he had issue,

THOMAS, his successor.
Henry, major-general in the service of King CHARLES I., d. in 1641.
Jane, m. to Sir John Finet, Knt., of West Keele, co. Lincoln.

His lordship d. in 1594, and was s. by his elder son,

THOMAS WENTWORTH, 4th baron, who was created 7 February, 1625, Baron Wentworth, of Nettlested, and EARL OF CLEVELAND. This nobleman was one of the most zealous supporters of the royal cause during the unhappy times of CHARLES I., and suffered much, including imprisonment in the Tower of London. He had the satisfaction, however, of witnessing the restoration of the monarchy, and headed a body of 300 noblemen and gentlemen in the triumphal procession of

CHARLES II. into London. His lordship m. 1st, Anne, dau. of Sir John Crofts, of Saxham, co. Suffolk, Knt., and had surviving issue,

THOMAS, who was summoned to parliament as Lord Wentworth, of Nettlested, 16th CHARLES I. His lordship m. Philadelphia, dau. of Sir Ferdinando Carey, Knt., and dying v. p. (in 1664), left an only dau.,
  HENRIETTA WENTWORTH, who s. her grandfather in the Barony of Wentworth.
ANNE, who m. John, Lord Lovelace, and s. her niece in the Barony of Wentworth

The earl m. 2ndly, Catherine, dau. of Sir John Wentworth, Knt., of Gosfield Hall, co. Essex, and had an only child,

Catherine, who m. William Spencer, Esq., of Cople, co. Bedford, and d. s. p.

His lordship d. in 1667, when the Earldom of Cleveland became EXTINCT, and the old Barony of Wentworth devolved upon the grand-dau.,

HENRIETTA WENTWORTH, as Baroness Wentworth. This lady resided at Toddington, co. Bedford, with James, Duke of Monmouth, whose attachment to her ladyship continued until his decease. Lady Wentworth survived his grace's execution but a few months, and her remains were interred under a costly monument at Toddington (refer to SCOTT, Duke of Monmouth). Her ladyship d. in 1686, when the barony reverted to her aunt (refer to issue of the Earl of Cleveland),

LADY ANNE WENTWORTH, as Baroness Wentworth. This lady (as stated above) m. John, Lord Lovelace, and had issue,

JOHN, who s. to the Barony of Lovelace on the death of his father, and dying in the life-time of his mother, left, by his wife, Martha, dau. and co-heir of Sir Edmund Pye, Bart., of Bradenham, co. Bucks, an only surviving child,
  MARTHA LOVELACE, who s. her grandmother in the Barony of Wentworth.
Anne, d. unm.
Margaret, m. to Sir William Noel, Bart., of Kirkby-Malory, co. Leicester, and had issue,
  SIR THOMAS NOEL, Bart., who d. in 1688, s. p., and was s. by his brother,
  SIR JOHN NOEL, Bart., who m. Mary, dau. and co-heir of Sir John Cloberry, of Winchester, Knt., and had two sons and a dau., viz.,
    1 SIR CLOBERRY NOEL, Bart., who m. Elizabeth, dau. of Thomas Rowney, Esq., of Oxford, and had a son,
      SIR EDWARD NOEL, who inherited the Barony of Wentworth on the decease of Martha Lovelace, Lady Wentworth, in 1745.
    2 William Noel, one of the judges of the court of Common Pleas, m. Susanna, dau. of Sir Thomas Trollope, Bart., of Casewick, co. Lincoln, and had four daus., his co-heirs, viz.,
      Susanna-Maria, m. to Thomas Hill, Esq., and was mother of
        NOEL HILL, created in 1784, BARON HILL.
      Anne, d. unm.
      Frances, m. to Bennet, 3rd Earl of Harborough.
      Elizabeth.
    3 Anne Noel, who m. 1713, Francis Mundy, Esq., of Osbaston and Markeaton, co. Derby, M.P. for Leicestershire, and had, with younger children, a son and heir,
      WRIGHTSON MUNDY, Esq., of Markeaton, M.P. for Leicestershire, m. Anne, sister of Sir Robert Burdett, Bart., of Foremark, and was s. at his decease, 18 June, 1762, by his son,
      FRANCIS-NOEL-CLARKE MUNDY, Esq., of Markeaton. This gentleman was the author of the descriptive Poems, Needwood Forest, and the Fall of Needwood. He left at his decease, 23 October, 1815, by Elizabeth, his wife, dau. of Sir Robert Burdett, Bart., two sons, the younger, Charles-Godfrey, of Burton Hall (see p. 483), and the elder,
        FRANCIS MUNDY, Esq., of Markeaton, M.P. for co. Derby, who m. 16 December, 1800, Sarah, dau. of John Leaper Newton, Esq., of Mickleover, co. Derby, and was father of
          WILLIAM MUNDY, Esq., of Markeaton, co. Derby, M.P., m. 1830, Harriet-Georgiana, eldest dau. of James Frampton, Esq., of Moreton, by Lady Harriet-Strangways, his wife, and dying 1877, left a son, FRANCIS-NOEL, of Markeaton.

Anne, Lady Wentworth, d. in 1697, and was s. by her grand-dau. (the barony being adjudged to her in parliament by descent, and confirmed in 1702),

MARTHA LOVELACE, as Baroness Wentworth. This lady assisted at the coronation of Queen ANNE, and walked in the procession, in her place, as a peeress. She m. Sir Henry Johnson, Knt., but d. s. p. in 1745, when the Barony of Wentworth passed to the family of Noel, and her ladyship's cousin (*refer* to issue of Margaret, dau. of Lady Anne Wentworth, Baroness Wentworth),

SIR EDWARD NOEL, Bart., of Kirkby Malory, became BARON WENTWORTH. His lordship *m.* Judith, dau. and heir of William Lamb, Esq., of Farndish, and had issue,

THOMAS, his successor.

JUDITH, *m.* to Sir Ralph Milbanke, Bart. This lady and her husband assumed the additional surname of NOEL at the decease of her brother, Thomas, Viscount Wentworth. She *d.* in 1822, leaving an only dau. and heiress (Sir Ralph *d.* in 1825),

ANNE-ISABELLA, *b.* 17 May, 1792, who *m.* 2 January, 1815, the celebrated poet, GEORGE GORDON, LORD BYRON, and had an only child,

AUGUSTA-ADA BYRON, *b.* 10 December, 1815, *m.* 8 July, 1835, William, Lord King, afterwards Earl of Lovelace, and *d.* 27 November, 1852, leaving with a dau., two sons, the younger and only survivor of whom, RALPH-GORDON-NOEL, *Viscount Ockham*, is now BARON WENTWORTH.

Lady Byron became, at the death of her cousin, Lord Scarsdale, by the termination of the abeyance, BARONESS WENTWORTH. Her ladyship *d.* 16 May, 1860.

Elizabeth, *m.* in 1777, to James-Bland Burgess, Esq. (afterwards Sir James Lamb, Bart.), but *d. s. p.* in 1779.

Sophia-Susanna, *m.* 18 August, 1777, to Nathaniel, Lord Scarsdale, and dying 1782, left issue,

NATHANIEL CURZON, 3rd Baron Scarsdale, who *d. unm.* 12 November, 1856.

William Curzon, killed at Waterloo.

Sophia-Caroline Curzon, *m.* in 1800, to Robert, Viscount Tamworth, who *d.* in 1824. She *d. s. p.* 1849.

His lordship was advanced, by letters patent, dated 4 May, 1762, to the dignity of VISCOUNT WENTWORTH, *of Wellesborough, co. Leicester*, and dying in 1774, was *s.* by his son,

THOMAS NOEL, 2nd Viscount Wentworth, and 9th successor to the Barony of Wentworth. His lordship *d. s. p.* 17 April, 1815, when the Viscounty became EXTINCT, but the Barony of Wentworth fell into ABEYANCE between his lordship's sister, JUDITH, LADY MILBANKE, and his nephew, the HON. NATHANIEL CURZON, afterwards 3rd Lord Scarsdale. Judith, Lady Milbanke, *d.* 22 January, 1822, and Nathaniel, 3rd Lord Scarsdale, *d. unm.* 12 November, 1856. On the occurrence of the latter event, Lady Milbanke's only child, Anne-Isabella, Lady Byron, became Baroness Wentworth.

Arms.—Of the WENTWORTHS—Sa., a chevron between three leopards' heads, or, a crescent for difference.

WENTWORTH—EARL OF MALTON.

(*See* WATSON WENTWORTH, Marquess of Rockingham.)

WESTERN—BARON WESTERN.

By Letters Patent, dated 28 January, 1833.

Lineage.

The family of Western was established in London, *temp.* HENRY VII. RICHARD WESTERN, of London, was father of WILLIAM, also of London, who *m.* Frances, dau of Martin Trott, Esq., and *d.* in July, 1640, æt. sixty-four, leaving issue,

I. Henry Western, *m.* 1st, Sarah, dau. of — Lavender, Esq.; 2ndly, Jane, dau. of — Child, Esq.; and *d.* in 1660, æt. sixty.

II. William. *m.* the dau. of — Alsworth, Esq., and *d.* in 1660, æt. fifty-five.

III. Richard, *m.* and had issue.

IV. THOMAS

The 4th son,

THOMAS WESTERN, of Rivenhall Place, Esq. (which estate he purchased in 1693), fined for alderman of London, and *d.* 11 January, 1707, æt. eighty-three, having *m.* 30 September, 1651, Martha, dau. of Samuel Gott, M.P. for Winchelsea, and by her left issue,

I. Samuel Western, Esq., thrice M.P. for Winchelsea, *m.* Anna-Maria, only dau of William Finch, Esq., and *d. v. p.* 20 August, 1699, having had issue,

1 Samuel, *d.* 5 February, 1697.

2 WILLIAM WESTERN, of Rivenhall Place, Esq. (to which estate he *s.* on the death of his grandfather, 1707), *m.* Anne, dau. of Sir James Bateman, Knight, lord mayor of London,

and sister of William, 1st Viscount Bateman, who *m-m* in February, 1735, George Dolliffe, Esq., of London. He *d.* 22 September, 1729, æt. thirty-six, having had issue,

James, who *d.* 19 March, 1730, æt. fourteen.

Sarah, sister and co-heir, *m.* 10 February, 1735, William Hanbury, Esq., of Kelmarsh, co. Northampton, and was grandmother of William Bateman-Hanbury, Lord Bateman.

Wilhelmina-Anne, sister and co-heir, *m.* Richard Stephens, Esq

II. THOMAS, of whom presently.

III. MAXIMILIAN, of Great Abington, co. Cambridge, Esq., *m.* Anne, dau. of — Mathews, Esq., and had, with other issue,

1 THOMAS, his successor.

2 Maximilian, of Cokethorpe, co. Oxford, and of Lincoln's Inn-fields, co. Middlesex, a director of the East India Company, *m.* Anne, dau. of — Tahourden, Esq., and *d.* leaving issue,

Maximilian, who *m.* a dau. of — Fowkes, Esq., of Norfolk, and had issue,

Maximilian, who *m.* Miss Loder, but *d. s. p.*

Elizabeth, *m.* 1st, Francis-Sackville Lloyd-Wheate, Esq. of Glympton Park, co. Oxford; and 2ndly, Rev. William Way, rector of Denham.

Frances, *m.* Walter Strickland, Esq., of Flamborough, co. York. 3rd son of Sir George Strickland, Bart.

Frances, *m.* 14 August, 1773, John Larpent, Esq , of East Sheen, co. Surrey (secretary to the Marquess of Hertford, lord lieutenant of Ireland), the father of the late Sir George-Gerard de Hochepied Larpent, Bart., M.P., for Nottingham.

Dorothy, *m.* 12 May, 1796, Sir Edmund Head, Bart., of the Hermitage, co. Kent, who *d.* 21 November, 1796; she *d. s. p.* in 1807.

Olive.

1 Olive, *m.* Thomas White, Esq., of Tattingstone Place, co. Suffolk, and had issue.

The eldest son of Maximilian, of Great Abington,

THOMAS WESTERN, Esq., *b.* June, 1691; *m.* 19 December, 1726, Catherine, younger of the two daus. and co-heirs of Charles-Harman Le Gros, Esq., of Crostwight, co. Norfolk (grandson of Sir Charles Le Gros, Knight, by Muriel, his wife, eldest dau. of Sir Thomas Knyvett, Knight., great-grandson of Edmund Knyvett, Esq., Serjeant Porter to King HENRY VIII., by Jane, his wife, dau. and co-heir, and eventually sole heir of Sir John Bourchier, Lord Berners, K.G., *temp.* EDWARD IV., who was great grandson, of * Sir William Bourchier, who was created by patent, 10 June, 1419, Earl of Ewe, in Normandy, who *m.* the Lady Anne Plantagenet, dau. of Thomas (of Woodstock), Duke of Gloucester, K.G., 6th and youngest son of King EDWARD III.) ; by this marriage Mr. Thomas Western was father of (besides two daus., Anne, *m.* Richard Townley, Esq., of Belfield, co. Lancaster; and Frances, *b.* in February, 1733 ; *m.* 22 November, 1767, Elisha Biscoe, Esq., of London), an only son.

THOMAS WESTERN, of Great Abington, Esq., *b.* 22 July, 1735 ; *m.* 7 May, 1759, Jane, dau. of Felix Calvert, Esq., of Albury Hall, co. Herts, M.P. for Wendover, and *d.* 30 June, 1781, leaving issue,

I. CHARLES, M.A., of Great Abington, rector of Kingham, co. Oxford, *b.* 22 March, 1760 ; *m.* 7 July, 1784, Mary-Peniston (who *d.* 15 January, 1849), dau. of William Goostrey, captain R.N., and *d.* 1 October, 1835, having had issue, an only dau., Hannah-Maria, who *d. unm.* 5 August, 1851, and a son,

CHARLES-MAXIMILIAN-THOMAS WESTERN, Esq., lieut.-colonel in the army, and knight-commander of the Portugese order of the Tower and Sword, *b.* 4 June, 1790 ; *m.* 4 November, 1813, Harriet, dau. of Christopher Clark, of Twickenham, King's co., in Ireland, captain in the army ; she *d.* in June. 1846 ; he *d.* 14 May, 1824, leaving with two surviving daus., Mary Harriet, *m.* 18 August, 1840, to Edward Lees, Esq., of Dublin, and Jane-Harriet, *m.* November, 1842, to Patrick Byrne, Esq., of Coltique, co. Wexford, a son and heir,

CHARLES-MAXIMILIAN-THOMAS, present representative of the Western family, *b.* 14 February, 1824; *m.* 3 October, 1850, Harriet, dau. of William Balfour, Esq., of Trenaby, in Orkney, and has issue,

1 Charles-Maximilian-Thomas, *b.* 2 September, 1855.

2 Edward-Lees, *b.* 15 July, 1857.

3 William-George-Balfour, *b.* 2 May, 1861.

1 Mary-Harriet.

II THOMAS, of Tattingstone Place, co. Suffolk, and of Aldham. co. Essex, a rear-admiral and knight commander of the Royal Portuguese Military Order of the Tower and Sword, *b.* 16 May, 1761 ; *m.* 4 October, 1794, Mary, dau. of Thomas Burch, Esq., of Bermuda, in the West Indies; and *d.* 26 December, 1814, leaving with other issue,

1 THOMAS-BURCH, created a baronet, 20 August, 1864 (*see* BURKE's *Peerage and Baronetage*).

---

* Sir William Bourchier held the manor of Bourchier's Hall, in Rivenhall, now in the possession of Sir Thomas-Burch Western, Bart.

III. George, one of the surveyors of the General Post Office, *b.* 1 August, 1762; *d. u.m.* April, 1821.
IV. John, lieutenant R.N., *b.* 22 June, 1770; killed in the expedition to Holland, 21 March, 1793.
V. James, of Bath, co. Somerset, *b.* 6 February, 1774; *m.* 7 December, 1805, Charlotte, eldest dau. of Rev. Robert Hallifax, vicar of Standish, co. Gloucester, and *d.* 15 November, 1864, having by her (who *d.* 4 June, 1864) with other issue,

Edward, *b.* 22 August, 1808; *m.* 23 April, 1835, Frances, eldest dau. of John-Adolphus Young, Esq., of Hare Hatch, co. Berks, and *d.* 10 April, 1862, leaving Edward-Young, *b.* 3 March, 1837; George-Adolphus, *m.* 4 October, 1865, Emily, dau. of Guy Atkinson, Esq., of Cangort; and other issue.

VI. Roger-Peter, of the East India Company's service, *b.* 26 April, 1775; *m.* 1st, in 1798, Helen, widow of Major Thomas Hook, of Bombay; 2ndly, Anna-Maria Wiggett, who *d.* 20 August, 1853; he *d. s. p.* 28 November, 1834.
VII. William-Brydges, an officer in the East India Company's service, at Bengal *b.* 12 November, 1779; *d. unm.* 18 October, 1818.
I. Jane, *d. unm.* 5 March, 1852.
II. Anne, *m.* 1st, Rev. Chaloner-Byng Baldock, vicar of Milton Abbey, co. Dorset: 2ndly, in December, 1800, Rev Edward Valpy, rector of Stanford, co. Berks, and had issue by both husbands.
III. Mary, *d. young.*
IV. Charlotte, *d. unm.* 1 August, 1859.
V. Caroline, *m.* 21 June, 1794, Edward Knipe, Esq., of Epsom, co. Surrey, and *d. s. p.* 17 November, 1837.
VI. Mary, *d. unm.* 30 August, 1853.

IV. William Western, of Rivenhall, co. Essex, Esq., *d. unm.* in 1706.
V. Robert, of the parish of St. Peter's, Cornhill, *m.* 26 December, 1698, Anne, eldest sister and co-heir of the said Sir Richard Shirley, Bart., of Preston, co. Sussex, and *d.* in June, 1728, leaving issue, an only son, Thomas, who *d. s. p.*, and three daus., his co-heirs, viz:—

1 Judith, *m.* John Morris, Esq., and had issue.
2 Sarah, *m.* Sir Thomas Mostyn, Bart., of Mostyn. co. Flint, and *d.* 28 March, 1740, leaving issue.
3 Anne, *m.* Hugh-Hume-Campbell, Viscount Polwarth, afterwards Earl of Marchmont, and *d.* 9 May, 1747.

I. Elizabeth, *d.* an infant.
II. Martha, *m.* Peter Gott, Esq., of Fairchurch in Wadhurst, co. Sussex.
III. Elizabeth, *d.* an infant.
IV. Mary. *m.* Francis Tyssen, of Hackney, co. Middlesex, who *d.* in 1710, leaving issue.
V. Sarah, *m.* Hon. Francis Brydges, receiver-general of the salt duty, 3rd son of James, 8th Lord Chandos, and brother of James, 1st Duke of Chandos; he *d. s. p.* 25 September, 1714.
VI. Frances, *m.* Heneage Featherstone, Esq., of Terling. co. Essex (*jure uxoris*), who *d.* 19 June, 1711; she *d.* 24 June, 1746.

The 2nd son of Thomas Western, of Rivenhall, and Martha Gott, his wife,
THOMAS WESTERN, Esq., *m.* Ann, dau. of Captain Fisher, and dying 1 April, 1733, left an only child,
THOMAS WESTERN, Esq., who *s.* to Rivenhall at the decease of his cousin James in 1730, and was M.P. for Sudbury: he *m.* Mary, sister and co-heir of Richard Shirley, Esq., of Preston, in Sussex, and was *s.* by his only son,
THOMAS WESTERN, Esq., of Rivenhall, who *m.* Ann, dau. of Robert Callis, Esq., and sister of Admiral Smith Callis, and by that lady (who *d.* January, 1776,) left at his decease, 1765, aged fifty-six (with three daus., Anna, *m.* in 1768, to Sir Thomas Shirley, Bart.; Frances; and Judith, the wife of Robert Houlton, Esq.), two sons to survive him, viz., CHARLES, his heir, and Thomas-Walsingham, LL.D., rector of Rivenhall, *d. s. p.*, 2 September, 1824. The son and heir,
CHARLES WESTERN, Esq., of Rivenhall, *b.* 27 September, 1747, *m.* 24 October, 1766, Frances-Shirley, only child of William Bollan, Esq., of London (by Frances, his wife, sister of Sir Thomas Shirley, Bart., of Oathall), and left at his decease, 24 July, 1771 (with a younger son, Shirley, in holy orders, rector of Rivenhall, who *d. unm.*, 30 April, 1824), an elder son and heir,
CHARLES-CALLIS WESTERN, of Rivenhall Place and Felix Hall, Essex, *b.* 9 August 1767, M.P. for Essex for twenty years, and for Maldon for twenty-two years, who was created BARON WESTERN, *of Rivenhall, co. Essex,* 28 January, 1833, but *d. unm.* 4 November, 1844, when the title became EXTINCT.

Arms—Sa., a chevron, between two crescents and a trefoil, slipped in base, or.

WESTON—BARONS WESTON, OF NEYLAND, EARLS OF PORTLAND.

Barony, by Letters Patent, dated 13 April, 1628.
Earldom, by Letters Patent, dated 17 February, 1633.

Lineage.

This family derived its origin from Hamon de Weston, Lord of Weston-under-Lyzard, co. Stafford, *temp.* HENRY II. The first of the family to settle in Essex, about 14th EDWARD I., was
MICHAEL WESTON, younger son of Sir William de Weston, Knt., of Boston. He left two sons, Thomas (Sir), whose only dau. and heir, Margaret, *m.* John de Loveyn, Lord of Little Estayne, and whose dau. and heir. *m.* Sir William Bourchier, Knt., from whom the Earl of Essex, of that name derived; and
HUMFREY DE WESTON, who settled at Prested Hall, in Fering, co. Essex, where he was living in 1360, and where his descendants continued for several generations. Of these
WILLIAM WESTON, was of Prested Hall, and of London, in 1512; by Margaret, his wife, he had, with other issue,
Richard, his eldest son and heir, whose grandson, Robert, of Prested Hall. *d.* 6 June, 1601, leaving two daus. and co-heirs.
JOHN, 4th son, of whose line we treat.

The latter,
JOHN WESTON, left (besides a dau., Mary, wife of John Ball, of Suffolk) a son.
RICHARD WESTON, who, being bred to the law, laid the foundation of the greatness of the family. He was appointed one of the judges of the Common Pleas in 1559. He *m.* 1st, Wiburga, dau. of Michael Catesby, of Seaton, co. Northampton, and relict of Richard Jenour, of Great Dunmow; 2ndly, Miss Burnaby; and 3rdly, Elizabeth, dau. of Thomas Lovett, of Astwell, co. Northampton, and widow 1st of Anthony Cave, Esq., of Chicheley, and 2ndly of John Newdegate, Esq., M.P., and had issue by the first only, a son, JEROME, and two daus., Amphalis, *m.* to Sir Benjamin Tichborne, and Margaret, *m.* 1st, to John Loveday, and 2ndly, to Andrew Glascock. He *d.* 6 July, 1572, and was *s.* by his son,
SIR HIEROME WESTON, Knt., of Roxwell, in Essex, high sheriff of the county 41st ELIZABETH, who *m.* 1st, Mary, dau. and co-heir of Anthony Cave, Esq., of Chicheley, Bucks, and 2ndly, Margery, dau. of George Pert, of London, and relict of — Thwayts, and by the former had issue,
RICHARD, his heir.
William.
Anne, *m.* to John Williams, of Brentwood, executed for treason.
——, wife of — Gardner, of Sussex.
Winifrida, *m.* to Nicolas Cotton, Esq., of Romford.
Dorothy, *m.* to Sir Edward Pinchon, Knt., of Writtle: their son, John Pinchon, Esq., of Writtle, left daus., his co-heirs, one of whom, Anne, *m.* John Woolfe, Esq., and was mother of a dau. and co-heir, Bridget, wife of John Webbe, Esq., ancestor by her of the family of Webbe-Weston, of Sutton Place, co. Surrey.
Margaret, *m.* to Edward Leventhorp.

He *d.* 31 December, 1603; his elder son and heir,
SIR RICHARD WESTON, Knt., *b.* 1577, was employed in the reign of JAMES I., as ambassador to Bohemia and subsequently to Brussels, to treat with the ambassadors of the emperor and king of Spain, regarding the restitution of the palatine. Soon after which he was constituted chancellor of the Exchequer, and elevated to the peerage, 13 April, 1628, as BARON WESTON, *of Neyland, co. Essex.* His lordship was subsequently made lord treasurer of England, invested with the Garter, and created, 17 February, 1633, EARL OF PORTLAND. He *m.* 1st, Elizabeth, dau. of William Pinchon, Esq., of Writtle, co. Essex, by whom he had issue,
Richard, *d. unm.* in the earl's lifetime.
Elizabeth, *m.* to Sir John Netterville, Knt., son and heir of Viscount Netterville.
Mary, *m.* to Sir Walter Aston, Knt., son and heir of Walter, Lord Aston.
The earl *m.* 2ndly, Frances, dau. and co-heir of Nicholas Walgrave, Esq., of Boreley, in Essex, and had four sons and four daus., viz.,
JEROME, his successor.
THOMAS, who *s.* his nephew as Earl of Portland.
Nicholas, *d. s. p.*
Benjamin, of Walton-on-Thames, who *m.* Elizabeth, dau. of Thomas Sheldon, Esq., of Houby, in Leicestershire, and widow of Charles Villiers, Earl of Anglesey, and had two daus., Elizabeth, *m.* to Sir Charles Shelley, Bart., and Anne, *d.* an infant.

Anne, m. to Basil Fielding, son and heir of William, Earl of Denbigh.

Mary-Frances, m. to Philip Draycote, Esq. of Paynsly, co. Stafford.

Catherine, m. to Richard White, Esq., of Hutton, in Essex.

His lordship d. 13 March, 1634, and was s. by his eldest son,

JEROME WESTON, 2nd Earl of Portland, who m. Lady Frances Stuart, dau. of Esme, Duke of Lennox, and had CHARLES, his heir, with four daus., Henrietta-Mary, Frances, Katharine, and Elizabeth, all of whom entered into religious orders. His lordship d. 16 May, 1662, and was s. by his son,

CHARLES WESTON, 3rd Earl of Portland. This nobleman, falling in the great naval engagement with the Dutch, 3 June, 1665, and dying s. p., was s. by his uncle,

THOMAS WESTON, 4th Earl of Portland, who m. Anne, d. u. of John, Lord Butler, of Bramfield, and widow of Mountjoy Blount, Earl of Newport, but d. s. p. about the year 1688, when his estates passed to his nieces (the children of the 2nd earl), as co-heirs, while the honours became EXTINCT.

Arms—Or, an eagle regardant and displayed, sa.

WHARTON—BARONS WHARTON, EARLS WHARTON, MARQUESSES OF MALMESBURY, AND OF WHARTON, DUKE OF WHARTON.

Barony, by Writ of Summons, dated 30 January, 1545.
Earldom, by Letters Patent, dated 24 December, 1706.
Marquessate by Letters Patent, dated 1 January, 1715.
Dukedom, by Letters Patent, dated 20 January, 1718.

Lineage.

Of this family, which derived its surname from "a fair lordship" situated upon the river Eden, and was of great antiquity in the co. Westmoreland, was

HENRY WHARTON, of Wharton, co. Westmoreland, living 10th HENRY V., who m. Elizabeth, dau. of Sir James Musgrave. Knt., of Harcla Castle, and had issue,

 I. THOMAS, of whom we treat.

 II. Gilbert, who m. Joan, dau. and heir of Kirkby, of Kirkby Thore, and was ancestor of the WHARTONS, of Kirkby Thore, co. Westmoreland; the WHARTONS, of Old Park, co. Durham; the WHARTONS, of Dryburn, also in Durham; the WHARTONS, of Gillingwood and Skelton Castle, co. York, &c.

The elder son,

THOMAS WHARTON, Esq., of Wharton and Croglin, m. a dau. of Lowther, of Lowther, and was father of HENRY WHARTON, who m. Alice, dau. of Sir John Conyers, of Hornby, and had a son and heir, THOMAS WHARTON, who m. Agnes, dau. of Reginald Warcop, Esq., and was father of

SIR THOMAS WHARTON, Knt., governor of the town and castle of Carlisle, who in the 34th HENRY VIII., assisted by Sir William Musgrave, at the head of only 300 men, gallantly resisted an incursion of the Scots, put them to the rout, and made prisoners of the Earls of Cassillis and Gleucairn, with several other personages of note. In two years after he marched into Scotland with the Lord Dacre, and was at the taking of Dumfries; for which and other eminent services, he was summoned to parliament as BARON WHARTON, from 30 January, 1545, to 30 September, 1566. In the 1st PHILIP and MARY, his lordship was constituted warden of the middle marches, and the next year he was made general warden of all the marches towards Scotland, and governor of Berwick. His lordship m 1st, Eleanor, dau. of Sir Bryan Stapleton, of Wighill, co. York, and had issue,

THOMAS, his successor.

Henry (Sir), m. Jane, dau. and heir of Sir Thomas Mauleverer.

Joane, m. to William Penington, Esq., of Muncaster, co. Cumberland.

Anne, m. to Sir Richard Musgrave, Knt., of Harcla Castle, in Westmoreland.

He m. 2ndly, Lady Anne Talbot, dau. of George, Earl of Shrewsbury, but had no other children. He d. in 1568, and was s. by his elder son,

THOMAS WHARTON, 2nd baron, summoned to parliament from 2 April, 1571, to 8 May, in the next year. His lordship m. Lady Anne Devereux, dau. of Robert, Earl of Sussex, and had issue,

PHILIP, his successor.

Mary, m. to Roger Gower, Esq., of Henham, in Yorkshire

Anne, m. to William Woolrich, Esq.

His lordship d. in 1572, and was s. by his son, then seventeen years of age,

PHILIP WHARTON, 3rd baron, summoned to parliament, from 6 January, 1581, to 17 May, 1625. This nobleman m. Lady Frances Clifford, dau. of Henry, Earl of Cumberland, and had issue,

George (Sir), who m. Lady Anne Manners, dau. of John, Earl of Rutland. Sir George Wharton fell in a duel with his friend, Sir James Stuart, son of Lord Blantyre. In this unfortunate conflict both combatants were slain, and both interred in one grave at Islington, by the king's command, 10 November, 1609. Sir George d. s. p.

THOMAS (Sir), m. Lady Philadelphia Carey, dau. of Robert, Earl of Monmouth, and dying v. p. in 1622, left two sons,

 PHILIP, successor to his grandfather.

 Thomas (Sir), K.B., of Edlington, co York, m. Mary, dau. of Henry Carey, Earl of Dover, and had a son, PHILIP, Warder of the Mint, who m. the dau. and heir of Richard Hutton, Esq., and left at his decease, 23 February, 1684–5, a dau. and heir, MARY, m. 1st, to James Campbell, brother of Archibald, 1st Duke of Argyle; and 2ndly (the former marriage having been dissolved by parliament), to Robert Bierley, Esq., M.P.

Margaret, m. to Edward Wotton, Baron Wotton.

Eleanor, m. to William Thwaytes, Esq., of Long Marston.

Frances, m. to Sir Richard Musgrave, Bart., K.B., of Edenhall, in Cumberland.

His lordship d. in 1625, and was s. by his grandson,

PHILIP WHARTON, 4th baron, b. 1613, summoned to parliament from 3 November, 1639, to 19 May, 1685. This nobleman who attained majority in 1634, m. 1st, Elizabeth, dau. of Sir Rowland Wandesford, Knt., of Pickhay, co. York, and had an only dau.,

Elizabeth, who m. Robert Bertle, then Lord Willoughby de Eresby, afterwards 3rd Earl of Lindsey, and is now represented by LORD WILLOUGHBY DE ERESBY and the MARQUESS OF CHOLMONDELEY.

His lordship m. 2ndly, 7 Sept. 1637, Jane, dau. and heir of Arthur Goodwyn, Esq., of Upper Winchendon, co. Bucks, and had two sons and four daus., viz.,

 I. THOMAS, his successor.

 II. Goodwin, M.P., d. 1704.

 I. Anne, m. to William, only son of William Carr, groom of the bedchamber to King JAMES I.

 II. Margaret, m. 1st, to Major Dunch, of Pusey, in Berkshire, and 2ndly, to Sir Thomas Sulyarde, and 3rdly, to William Ross, Esq. By her 1st husband she had issue,

  Wharton Dunch, d. unm. 1705.

  Jane Dunch, m. to Francis Keck, Esq. of Great Tew, co. Oxford, and d. s. p.

  Margaret Dunch, d. unm. 1690.

 III. Mary, m. 1st, to William, son and heir of Edmund Thomas, Esq., of Wenvoe, co. Glamorgan; and 2ndly, to Sir Charles Kemeys, Bart., of Kevanmably, in the same shire, M.P. for the county. Her ladyship's children by her 1st husband, d. s. p.; her dau. and heiress by her 2nd husband,

  JANE KEMEYS, m. Sir John Tynte, 2nd bart., of Halsewell, M.P. for Bridgwater, and was mother of

   1 SIR HALSEWELL TYNTE, 3rd baronet, who d. s. p. in 1730.

   2 SIR JOHN TYNTE, 4th baronet, in holy orders, d. unm. in 1740.

   3 SIR CHARLES KEMEYS-TYNTE, 5th baronet, who, on the decease of his uncle, Sir Charles Kemeys, Bart., s. p., became representative of that ancient family, and inherited its great estates. Sir Charles Tynte represented the co. of Somerset in parliament. He d. s. p. 1785, when the baronetcy EXP.RED, and his estates devolved upon his only sister's dau.

   4 JANE TYNTE, m. to Major Hassell, of the royal horse guards (blue), son of John Hassell, Esq., by Anne, his wife, dau. and heir of Thomas St. Quintin, Esq., and left a dau.,

    JANE HASSEL, who inherited the estates of the Kemeys and Tynte families upon the death of her uncle, Sir Charles Kemeys-Tynte. She m. Colonel Johnstone, of the foot guards, groom of the bedchamber to George, Prince of Wales, afterwards GEORGE IV., who assumed, by sign manual, the surnames of KEMEYS-TYNTE. He d. in 1807, and was s. by his only son,

     CHARLES-KEMEYS KEMEYS-TYNTE, Esq., M.P. for Bridgwater, colonel of the Somerset cavalry, who m. Anne, dau. of the Rev. T. Leyson, relict of Thomas Lewis, Esq., of St. Pierre, co Monmouth, and had issue,

      1 CHARLES-JOHN KEMEYS-TYNTE, Esq., of Halsewell House, co. Somerset, and of Kevanmably, co. Glamorgan, one of the co-heirs of the Barony of Wharton (*see* BURKE'S *Landed Gentry*).

      1 Anne, m. to Sir William-Henry Cooper, Bart., of Gogar, who d. 1836.

2 Jane, *d. unm.* 1834.
3 Louisa, *m.* to Simon-Fraser Campbell, Esq.
4 Henrietta-Anne, *m.* to T.-A. Kemmis, Esq.

IV. Philadelphia, *m.* 1st, to Sir George Lockhart, Knt., of Carnwath, and 2ndly, to Captain John Ramsay. The co-representation of the marriage of Hon. Philadelphia and Sir George Lockhart, vested in ALEXANDER-DUNDAS-ROSS, Lord Lamington, of Lamington, co. Lanark, and in GEORGE-ANTHONY AUFRERE, Esq., of Foulsham, Norfolk, both co-heirs of the Barony of Wharton.

Lord Wharton *m.* 3rdly, Anne, dau. of William Carr, already mentioned as groom of the bedchamber to King JAMES I., and widow of Edward Popham, Esq., by whom he had a son, William, killed in a duel December, 1689. His lordship who was a violent Puritan, and an active parliamentary partisan, *temp.* CHARLES I , *d.* 5 February, 1695, and was *s.* by his eldest son,

THOMAS WHARTON, 5th baron. This nobleman, who was esteemed a profound and eloquent statesman, having devoted himself zealously to accomplish the Revolution, was created by Queen ANNE, by letters patent, dated 24 December, 1706, VISCOUNT WINCHENDEN, *co. Bucks*, and EARL WHARTON, *in Westmoreland.* His lordship was advanced, 15 February, 1715, to the dignities of MARQUESS OF MALMESBURY, *in Wiltshire*, and MARQUESS OF WHARTON; and, 12 April, following, he was made a peer of Ireland, as Baron Trim, Earl of Rathfarnham, and Marquess of Catherlough. His lordship *m.* 1st, 1654, Anne, one of the two daus. and co-heirs of Sir Henry Lee, of Ditchley, co. Oxford, but by that lady had no issue. He *m.* 2ndly, Lucy, dau. of Adam Loftus, Lord Lisburn, in Ireland, by Lucy, his wife, dau. of George Brydges, Lord Chandos, and by her (who *d.* 1716) had issue,

PHILIP, his successor.
Jane, } both *d. s. p.* Lady Jane *m.* 1st, John Holt, Esq.,
Lucy, } and 2ndly, Robert Coke, Esq., of Hillingdon; and Lady Lucy *m.* (and was divorced from) Sir William Morice. Lady Jane Coke, the survivor of the two sisters, bequeathed her estate by will, proved 19 January, 1761, to Miss Anna-Maria Drayton, of Clarges Street, London, afterwards the wife of George, 2nd Earl of Pomfret.

The marquess filled. with great éclat, the high appointment of Lord Lieutenant of Ireland, and took with him Addison as his Secretary. His lordship *d.* in London, 12 April, 1715, and was *s.* by his only son,

PHILIP WHARTON, 6th baron, and 2nd marquess, who was created DUKE OF WHARTON, 20 January, 1718. Of this, the profligate, eccentric, witty, and gifted Lord Wharton, Walpole thus speaks: "With attachment to no party, though with talents to govern any, this lively man changed the free air of Westminster for the gloom of the Escurial; the prospect of King GEORGE'S garter for the Pretender's; and with indifference to all religion, the frolic lord, who had written the ballad on the archbishop of Canterbury, died in the habit of a Capuchin." After he had received a dukedom from GEORGE I. he became a strenuous opponent of the king's government, eventually espoused the tenets of the ancient church, and adopted the cause of the banished dynasty. In parliament his grace attained the reputation of an able and eloquent speaker; and his speeches against the ministers were delivered with much effect: in the instance of the South Sea affair Lord Stanhope was so excited by one of those tirades, that, in replying with extreme warmth, he burst a blood-vessel and died. On the bill of Pains and Penalties against Bishop Atterbury, his grace is accused of having deceived the minister by pretending to take part against the bishop, and having thus extorted from him, immediately prior to the third reading of the bill, the whole of his argument, came down to the House of Lords the next day, after a night of debauch without going to bed, and made one of the most masterly speeches in favour of the prelate, anticipating and answering all the arguments which could be adduced against him. His grace subsequently, retired into Spain, openly adopting the colours of the "Pretender" (by whom he was given the title of "Duke of Northumberland"), was a volunteer in the Spanish army before Gibraltar in 1727, and was attainted by parliament in the following year. The duke *m.* 1st, Martha, dau. of Major-General Holmes, by whom he had an only child, Thomas, who *d.* an infant; and 2ndly, Maria-Theresa-O'Neill O'Beirne, maid of honour to the Queen of Spain, and dau. of Colonel Henry O'Beirne, an Irish officer, in the Spanish service, by Henrietta, his wife, dau. of Henry O'Neill, by whom (who survived until 1777) he had no issue. The duke retired at last into the Spanish monastery of St. Bernard, near Tarragona, and *d.* there 31 May, 1731, age thirty-two, when all his honours, save the Barony of Wharton, independently of the attainder, became EXTINCT; but were that act repealed the barony would be in abeyance between the Marquess Cholmondeley, Lord Wil-

loughby de Eresby, Charles-J.-K. Kemeys-Tynte, Esq., M.P., of Halsewell House, in Somersetshire, Alexander-Dundas-Ross-Wishart-Baillie-Cochrane, Esq., and George-Anthony Aufrere, Esq.

Arms—Sa., a manch, arg., within a border, or, an orle of lions' gambs, erased in saltier, gu. The border, &c., being an augmentation granted by EDWARD VI.

WHARTON—MARQUESS OF CATHER-LOUGH.

(*See* WHARTON, Duke of Wharton.)

WHITWORTH—BARON WHITWORTH.

By Letters Patent, dated 9 January, 1720.

Lineage.

The Whitworths were an ancient and respectable Staffordshire family. The eldest of the six sons of RICHARD WHITWORTH, Esq. of Adbaston, in that co., by Anne, his wife, dau. of the Rev. Francis Mosley, rector of Winslow, co. Chester, uncle of Sir Oswald Mosley, 1st Bart., of Rolleston and Ancoats, was CHARLES WHITWORTH, Esq., a distinguished diplomatist, celebrated for the number and importance of his embassies, who was raised to the peerage of Ireland, 9 January, 1720, as BARON WHITWORTH, *of Galway ;* but *d. s. p.* 20 October, 1725, when the title EXPIRED. His lordship's youngest brother, FRANCIS, who represented Minehead, was grandfather of CHARLES, EARL WHITWORTH, in the peerage of England. (*See that title.*)

Arms—Same as Earl Whitworth.

WHITWORTH — BARON WHITWORTH, VISCOUNT WHITWORTH, EARL WHITWORTH.

Irish Barony, by Letters Patent, dated 4 April, 1800.
Viscounty by Letters Patent, dated 14 June, 1813.
Earldom, by Letters Patent, dated 25 November, 1815.

Lineage.

The Whitworths, an ancient Staffordshire family, produced a nobleman of the kingdom of Ireland, in the beginning of the last century, CHARLES WHITWORTH, *Baron Whitworth, of Galway*, between whom and his namesake, the eminent person of whom we are about to treat, there are many points of singular similarity. Like his noble kinsman (our English lord,) he was celebrated for the number and importance of his embassies, like him created Baron Whitworth, of Galway, and, as if to complete the resemblance, *d.* in the year 1725 (the last lord, it will be seen, *d.* in 1825,) leaving no heir to his title. The brother of this Lord Whitworth, of Galway,

FRANCIS WHITWORTH, Esq. (youngest son of Richard Whitworth, Esq. of Adbaston, co. Stafford, by Anne, his wife, dau. of Rev. Francis Mosley, rector of Winslow), was M.P. for Minehead, surveyor-general of woods and forests, and secretary of Barbadoes, settled at Leybourne, in Kent. He *d.* in 1743, and was *s.* by his son,

SIR CHARLES WHITWORTH, Knt., of Leybourne, co. Kent, and of Millington, co. Chester, M.P. for Saltash, lieutenant-governor of Tilbury Fort, governor of Gravesend, and treasurer of the Foundling Hospital, who *m.* in 1749, Martha, eldest dau. of Richard Shelley, Esq., commissioner of the Stamp Office, brother of Sir John Shelley, Bart., and had three sons and four daus.,

I. CHARLES, his heir.
II. Francis (Sir), lieut.-col., *d.* 1805.
  I. Priscilla, *m.* 1st, to Sir Bellingham Graham, Bart.; and 2ndly, to Francis-Gerard, 2nd Viscount Lake.
III. Richard, capt. R N., lost at sea.
II. Catherine, *m.* 1st, 1774, to Henry, 4th Lord Aylmer; and 2ndly, to Howel Price, Esq. She *d.* 1805.
III. Mary, *m.* to Thomas Lloyd, Esq.
IV. Anna-Barbara, *m.* 1782, Sir Henry Russell, Bart., chief justice of Bengal, and *d.* 1814.

Sir Charles d. at Bath, 22 August, 1778, and was s. by his son,

CHARLES WHITWORTH, Esq., baptised at Leybourne, 29 May, 1752, and educated at Tunbridge School, under the poet Cawthorne. Soon after he had completed his studies, Mr. Whitworth obtained a commission in the guards. In 1776 he removed with his father to Stanmore, having joined that gentleman in obtaining an act of parliament to authorize the sale of Leybourne to James Hawley, Esq., M.D. and F.R.S., which seat is now the residence of Dr. Hawley's descendant, Sir Joseph-Henry Hawley, Bart.

Mr. Whitworth's first diplomatic employment was at the court of Poland in 1786. Warsaw was then the centre of intrigues. A new partition of Poland happened to be in contemplation, and the generous effort for national independence, sealed then, as recently, the doom of this valiant and noble people. Mr. Whitworth was recalled from Poland in 1788, and accredited envoy extraordinary and plenipotentiary to the court of Russia. In 1793, when the English cabinet had embarked in the confederacy against France, it was deemed proper to invest the ambassador at St. Petersburgh with the order of the Bath, to add to the dignity of his mission; and Sir Charles Whitworth from that moment assumed a conspicuous position in the field of European politics. On his return from this embassy he was created, 4 April, 1800, a peer of Ireland, by the title of BARON WHITWORTH, of Newport Pratt, co. Galway; and his lordship repaired soon after, as plenipotentiary extraordinary, to Copenhagen. His next mission, his lordship having been previously sworn of the privy council, was in 1802, to the consular court of France, where his sojourn was but of brief duration. After numerous preliminary conferences with Talleyrand on the subject of the retention of Malta by the British government, Napoleon sent at length for the English ambassador, and a long and important interview ensued, unsatisfactory to both parties. A subsequent conference took place, when the First Consul instead of healing, appears to have widened the breach, and Lord Whitworth's prompt and dignified repression of Napoleon's intemperate address, before a full court, and all the foreign ambassadors, has been celebrated throughout Europe. He soon afterwards left Paris, and for the succeeding ten years remained in retirement. On 2 March, 1813, Lord Whitworth was made a lord of the bedchamber, and created 14 June following, a peer of the United Kingdom, as VISCOUNT WHITWORTH, of Adbaston, co. Stafford, within two months after he succeeded the Duke of Richmond as Viceroy of Ireland, and he was advanced, 25 November, 1815, to the dignities of BARON ADBASTON and EARL WHITWORTH. He continued in the government of Ireland until 1817. His lordship m. 7 April, 1801, Arabella-Diana, eldest dau. and co-heir of Sir Charles Cope, Bart., of Brewern, in Oxfordshire, and widow of John-Frederick, 3rd Duke of Dorset, but had no issue. He d. 12 May, 1825, when all his honours became EXTINCT, and his estates devolved upon his widow, the Duchess of Dorset, at whose decease in the August following, they passed to her two daus. and co-heirs,

MARY, Countess of Plymouth, and
ELIZABETH, Countess of Delawarr.

Arms—Arg., a bend, sa., in the sinister chief point a garb, gu.

WIDDRINGTON—BARONS WIDDRINGTON.

By Letters Patent, dated 10 November, 1643.

Lineage.

Sir WILLIAM WIDDRINGTON, Bart., of Widdrington, co. Northumberland, M.P., b. in 1611, descended from a very ancient Northumbrian family, having raised a considerable force for the royal cause, and participated in the victories of the Duke of Newcastle, under whom he fought, was elevated to the peerage by King CHARLES I., by letters patent, dated 10 November, 1643, as BARON WIDDRINGTON, of Blankney, co. Lincoln. His lordship eventually fell in the fight at Wigan Lane, when the Earl of Derby was defeated by Colonel Lilburne, in August, 1651. Of this nobleman, Lord Clarendon observes, that "he was one of the most goodly persons of that age, being near the head higher than most tall men, of a very fair fortune, and one of the four of which King CHARLES made choice to be about the person of the prince, his son, as gentleman of the privy chamber. He was a man of great courage, but of some passion; by which he incurred the ill-will of many, who imputed it to an insolence of nature, which no one was further from in reality." His lordship m. Mary, dau. and sole heir of Sir Anthony Thorold, Knt., of Blankney, co. Lincoln, and had surviving issue,

I. WILLIAM, his successor.
II. Edward. captain of dragoons, who fell at the battle of the Boyne. He m. Dorothy, elder dau. and co-heir of Sir John Horsley, Knt., of Horsley, Northumberland, and left an only son,

  EDWARD. of Felton, b. 1658, who m. Elizabeth, dau. of Caryl, 3rd Viscount Molyneux, and left at his decease, 1705,

    Edward-Horsley, of Felton, who m. Elizabeth, dau of Humphrey Weld, Esq., of Lulworth, co. Dorset, and had an only dau. and heiress,

      ELIZABETH, m. to THOMAS RIDDELL, Esq, of Swinburne Castle, co. Northumberland, jure uxoris, of Felton. From this marriage descend the RIDDELLS, of Felton Park and Swinburne Castle.

    Theresa, m. to Sir William Wheler, Bart., and was ancestor of Sir Trevor Wheler, Bart., of Leamington Hastang, co. Warwick.
    Bridget.

III. Ralph, was engaged in the Dutch war, and lost his sight therein.
IV. Anthony, d. unm.
V. Roger, fell at the siege of Maestricht.
I. Mary, m. to Francis Crane, Esq., of Woodrising, in Norfolk.
II. Jane, m. to Sir Charles Stanley, K.B., grandson (through one of his younger sons) of William, Earl of Derby.

His lordship was s. by his eldest son,

WILLIAM WIDDRINGTON, 2nd baron. This nobleman m. Elizabeth, dau. and heir of Sir Peregrine Bertie, Knt., of Evedon, co. Lincoln, and grand-dau. of Robert, Earl of Lindsey, by whom he had four sons, and six daus., viz.,

I. WILLIAM, his successor.
II. Roger, of Blankney, d. 1715.
III. Henry, whose will bears date 1729.
IV. Edward.
I. Mary, m. to Richard Forster.
II. Elizabeth, } these ladies were both nuns.
III. Dorothy, }
IV. Anne, m. in 1659, to John Clavering, Esq., of Callaly, co. Northumberland (a descendant of the Barons Clavering, see CLAVERING), and of this marriage, Edward-John Clavering, Esq., of Callaly, is the representative.
V. Jane.
VI. Catherine, m. Edward Southcote, Esq., of Blitheborough, and d. 1758.

His lordship d. in 1676, and was s. by his eldest son,

WILLIAM WIDDRINGTON, 3rd baron, who m. Alathea, dau. and heir of Charles, Viscount Fairfax, and had issue,

I. WILLIAM, his successor.
II. Charles, supposed to have d. at St. Omers, in 1756.
III. Peregrine, m. Mary, Duchess of Norfolk, dau. and heir of Sir Nicholas Sherburne, of Stonyhurst, Bart., but d. s. p.
I. Mary, m. Richard Towneley, Esq., of Towneley Hall, co. Lancaster, and d. July, 1731.
II. Elizabeth, m. Marmaduke, 4th Lord Langdale.

His lordship d. in 1695, and was s. by his eldest son,

WILLIAM WIDDRINGTON, 4th baron. This nobleman, with his brothers, engaging in the rebellion of 1715, for the restoration of the Stuarts, they were all three made prisoners at Preston, and subsequently tri. d and convicted of high treason, 7 July, 1716. But in the next year, his lordship, with the Messrs. Widdrington, and several more, received a royal pardon, while his honours became forfeited under the attainder. He m. 1st, Jane, dau. and heir of Sir Thomas Tempest, of Stella, in the bishopric of Durham. and 2ndly, Mrs. Catherine Graham. He d. at Bath, in 1743, leaving by his 1st wife (who d. 1714), Henry-Francis Widdrington, Esq., who m. Anne Gattonby, and d. s. p. 1774; William Tempest, who m. Anne Philips, but d. s. p. about 1753; and two daus., Alathea, who became a nun, and Mary, b. 1713, m. to Rowland Eyre, Esq., of Hassop, co. Derby.

Arms—Quarterly: arg. and gu, a bend, sa.

WIDVILE OR WYDEVILE — BARONS RIVERS, EARLS RIVERS.

Barony, by Letters Patent, dated 29 May, 1448.
Earldom, by Letters Patent, dated 24 May, 1466.

Lineage.

The family of Wideville, Widvile, Woodvile, or Wydeville may be traced to the 12th century.

RICHARD DE WYDVILL, of Grafton (great-great-great-grandson of William de Wydvil, of Grafton,) was constituted sheriff of Northamptonshire, 35th EDWARD III., and governor of the castle there, and again in two years after. In the 43rd of the same reign, he was made escheator for the cos. of Northampton and Rutland, and the year ensuing he was once more sheriff of Northamptonshire, and governor of Northampton Castle. He m. Elizabeth, dau. and heir of Sir John Lyons, of Warkworth, and widow of Sir Nicholas Chetwode, of Chetwode, and dying *circa* 1378, left issue, JOHN, his heir; Thomas, who m. twice, and had issue; Elizabeth, m. to John Pashley, of Kent; and Margaret, m. to William Hawe. The son and heir,

JOHN DE WYDEVILE, of Grafton, was sheriff of Northamptonshire 4th, 9th, and 14th RICHARD II. He was s. by his son,

THOMAS DE WYDEVILE, of Grafton, who d. s. p., and was s. by his brother,

RICHARD DE WYDEVILE, of Grafton, esquire of the body to HENRY V., and Constable of the Tower, who m. Elizabeth, dau. of John Bedelgate, by Mary, his wife, dau. of William Beauchamp, of Wellington, and had issue,

  I. RICHARD, his heir.
  II. Edward (Sir), commonly called "Lord Wideville," slain at St. Albin, in Brittany, 1488.
  1. Joan, m. 1429, William Haute.

The son and heir,

SIR RICHARD DE WYDEVILE, of Grafton, was in the 3rd HENRY VI., governor of the Tower of London, and the next year he received the honour of knighthood from the king at Leicester. Soon after this, we find him lieutenant of Calais, under the Duke of Bedford, and residing there. From that period for several succeeding years, Sir Richard Wydevile was constantly engaged in the wars of France. In the interval, he married, without license, Jacqueline or Jacquetta of Luxembourgh, dau. of Peter I., Comte de St. Pol, and Brienne, Chevalier de la Toison d'Or, and widow of his late commander, the king's uncle, John, Duke of Bedford; for which transgression, and for the livery of the castles, manors, and lands, constituting her grace's dower, he paid a fine of £1000. He served afterwards under Richard, Duke of York, and was elevated to the peerage, by letters patent, dated 9 May, 1448, as BARON RIVERS. His lordship was further rewarded by grants from the crown, amongst which was the manor of Westhall, co. Essex. He was made likewise a knight of the Garter, and appointed seneschal of Aquitaine. In the contest between the houses of York and Lancaster, Lord Rivers was a stanch supporter of the latter, until his daughter became Queen consort of EDWARD IV., and then of course he veered to the new order of affairs. His Lancastrian predilections were forgotten by his royal son in-law, and he was raised to high honours, and entrusted with high offices. His lordship was first made treasurer of the exchequer, and afterwards Lord High Constable of England, for life, with remainder to his son, Anthony, Lord Scales, also for life. He was likewise advanced in the peerage to the dignity of EARL RIVERS, by letters patent, dated 24 May, 1466; but the next year he was taken out of his manor-house of Grafton, by Robin of Ridsdale, at the head of the revolted Lancastrians, and carried to Northampton, where his head was cut off. Stow gives a different version of the manner of his lordship's death. He states that being defeated in a battle by Robin of Ridsdale, near Banbury, the earl flying from the field, was made prisoner in the forest of Dene (or rather Whittlebury), and conveyed to Northampton, where he was beheaded by order of the Duke of Clarence, and the Earl of Warwick, then 'n hostility to King EDWARD. By Jacqueline of Luxembourg (who d. 1472), his lordship had issue,

  I. ANTHONY, his successor, who m. Elizabeth, widow of Henry Bourchier, and only dau. and heiress of Th mas, Lord Scales, in whose right he was summoned to parliament as BARON SCALES, from 22 December, 1462, to the 23rd of the ensuing February.
  II. John (Sir), put to death with his father.
  III. Lionel, bishop of Salisbury, d. 1485.
  IV. Edward, d. s. p.
  V. RICHARD, who s. his eldest brother in the honours of the family.
  1. ELIZABETH, m. 1st, Sir John Grey, Lord Grey of Groby, by whom she had issue,

    SIR THOMAS GREY, created MARQUESS OF DORSET.
    Sir Richard Grey, beheaded in the 1st year of RICHARD III.

  Lord Grey fell in the second battle of St. Albans, fighting under the Lancastrian banner, and her ladyship m. 2ndly, King EDWARD IV., by whom she was mother of

    EDWARD V., King of England. } Supposed to have been murdered in the Tower, by the command of RICHARD III.
    RICHARD, Duke of York. }

    Elizabeth, m. to King HENRY VII.
    Cecily, m. 1st, to John, Viscount Welles, and 2ndly, to Sir John Kyme, d. s. p.
    Anne, m. to Thomas Howard, Duke of Norfolk. d. s. p.
    Katherine, m. to William Courtenay, Earl of Devon.

  II. Margaret, m. 1464 to Thomas Fitz-Alan, Earl of Arundel.
  III. Anne, m. 1st, to William, Lord Bourchier, eldest son of Henry, Earl of Essex: 2ndly, to George Grey, Earl of Kent, and 3rdly, to Sir Anthony Wingfield, Knt.
  IV. Jacquetta, m. to John, Lord Strange, of Knokyn.
  V. Mary, m. 1466, to William Herbert, Earl of Huntingdon.
  VI. Katherine, m. 1st, to Henry Stafford, Duke of Buckingham; 2ndly, to Jasper Tudor, Duke of Bedford; and 3rdly, to Sir Richard Wingfield, K.G.
  VII. Another dau., stated by Dugdale to have been m. to Sir John Bromley, Knt., who is called son of the renowned Sir John Bromley, who recovered the standard of Guyen, in the memorable battle of Le Corby, against the French.

The melancholy death of the gallant and accomplished Lord Rivers occurred in 1469, and he was s. by his eldest son,

ANTHONY WIDVILE, Lord Scales, as 2nd Earl Rivers, K.G. This nobleman, when Lord Scales, in the beginning of the reign of EDWARD IV., marched with the king into the north against the Lancastrians, and was one of the principal commanders at the siege of Alnwick Castle. He was soon afterwards made a knight of the Garter, and he obtained a grant in tail of the Isle of Wight; his lordship about this period acquired great fame in a tournament at London, wherein he contested successfully with Anthony, the Bastard of Burgundy, brother of Charles, Duke of Burgundy. Dugdale thus details the combat: "Upon Thursday next after *Corpus Christi*-day, the king being present, they ran together with sharp spears: and parted with equal honour. Likewise, the next day on horseback; at which time this Lord Scales's horse having a long sharp pike of steel on his chaffron, upon their coping together, it ran into the nose of the bastard's horse. Which making him to mount, he fell on his side, with his rider. Whereupon the Lord Scales rode about him, with his sword drawn, till the king commanded the marshal to help him up: no more being done that day. But the next day coming into the lists on foot, with pole axes, they fought valiantly, till the point of this lord's weapon entered the sight of the bastard's helm. Which being discerned by the king, he cast down his warder, to the end the marshal should sever them. Hereupon the bastard requiring that he might go on in the performance of his enterprise, and consultation being had with the Duke of Clarence, then constable, and the Duke of Norfolk, marshal, whether it might be allowed or not, they determined that if so, then by the law of arms, the bastard ought to be delivered to his adversary, in the same condition as he stood, when the king caused them to be severed, which, when the bastard understood, he relinquished his further challenge." During the temporary restoration of HENRY VI., Lord Scales fled with his brother-in-law, King EDWARD, into Holland, and returned with him before the close of the year, bearing the title of EARL RIVERS, his father and brother having been put to death in the interval. After the re-establishment of the power of EDWARD, his lordship was constituted governor of the town and castle of Calais, of the tower of Rysebank, as also of the castle of Guysnes, and the marches adjacent for seven years. He was likewise appointed captain-general of the king's army, and of all his forces, both by sea and land. In the 13th EDWARD IV., upon the creation of Prince Edward to be Prince of Wales, and Earl of Chester, Lord Rivers, being made governor to him, obtained the office of chief butler of England, and shortly after visited the shrine of St. James in Galicia, and from Spain passed into Italy where he journeyed to Rome and made many pilgrimages. The fate of this accomplished and gallant nobleman, after the decease of EDWARD IV., marks the commencement of an era in our history. He was one of the first victims to the ambition of RICHARD III.; an ambition which not long after closed the dynasty of the Plantagenets. His lordship, with his nephew, Sir Richard Grey, was treacherously seized by the Duke of Gloucester and his partisans, at Northampton, and some time afterwards beheaded in front of Pontefract Castle, where he had been confined, by order of the governor, Sir Richard Ratcliffe, without any form of trial, or being allowed to speak one word in his own vindication. Walpole assigns Lord Rivers a place in his Noble Authors, and observes, "that though Caxton knew '*none like to the Erle of Worcester*,' and thought that all learning in the nobility perished with Tiptoft, yet there flourished about the same period, a noble person (Anthony, Earl Rivers,) by no means inferior to him in learning and politeness; in birth his equal, by alliance his superior, greater in feats of arms, and in pilgrimages more abundant." After the decease of his 1st wife, the heiress of Scales, his lordship m. Mary, dau. and heir of Henry Fitz-Lewis, but by her had no issue.[*] His unhappy decease took place in 1483, when

---

[*] The earl had an illegitimate daughter, Margaret, m. to Sir Robert Poynes, Knt.

he was s. in all his honours, but the Barony of Scales, by his only surviving brother,

RICHARD WIDVILE, 3rd Earl Rivers. This nobleman, a Knight Hospitaller of St. John of Jerusalem, d. unm. in 1491. By his testament, bearing date, 20 February, 1490, his lordship directed his body to be buried in the Abbey of St. James's, near Northampton. He bequeathed to the parish church of Grafton all such cattle as he then had at Grafton, viz., two oxen. five kine, and two bullocks, to the intent that they should yearly keep an obit for his soul, and he appointed his nephew, Thomas, Marquess of Dorset, his heir, to whom he devised all his lands whatsoever; desiring that there might be as much underwood sold, in the woods of Grafton, as would purchase a bell, to be a tenor to the bells already there, for a remembrance of the last of his blood. At the decease of his lordship, the Barony and Earldom of Rivers became EXTINCT.

Arms—Arg., a fesse, and canton. gu.

WILLIAMS—BARON WILLIAMS OF THAME.

By Writ of Summons, dated 2 April, 1554.

Lineage.

This nobleman descended, it is stated, from a common progenitor with the Sir Robert Williams, Knt., who assumed the name of CROMWELL, and was ancestor of the Protector. The first person of this branch of the family,

JOHN WILLIAMS, 2nd son of Sir John Williams, of Burfield, in Berkshire (by his wife, Elizabeth, dau. and co-heir of Richard More, Esq., of Burfield), was a servant to King HENRY VIII., and had in the 18th of that monarch £10 per annum, granted to him by patent, for the keeping of a greyhound. In some years afterwards he was clerk of the king's jewel office; and had interest enough to procure a patent for the office of master or treasurer of the same office. This, however, he was obliged to surrender, and to accept of a new patent jointly with Thomas Cromwell, then secretary of state. Having by these lucrative employments amassed considerable wealth, he purchased, in the 30th HENRY VIII., from Giles Heron, Esq., of Shakewell, co. Middlesex, the manors of Great and Little Ricott, in Oxfordshire. In the next year, being then a knight, he had a grant from the crown of the chief stewardship of the manors of Grafton and Hertwell, co. Northampton, with the keepership of the parks there: as also of the manors of Wytham, Weston-on-the-Green, and Botley. And he was soon after constituted chief supervisor of all the swans within the river Thames, and all other waters in England excepting those of the Duchy of Lancaster. Moreover, about this time he had a special patent for retaining ten persons, gentlemen and yeomen, in his household, and to give livery badges to them; and he had another grant of the office of treasurer of the court of augmentation. Upon the demise of EDWARD VI., Sir John Williams was one of the first who appeared in behalf of Queen MARY, and upon the accession of her Majesty to the crown, was solemnly created LORD WILLIAMS, *of Thame*, at the palace of St. James's. He was summoned the next year (2 April, 1554) in that dignity to parliament, but no patent of creation was ever enrolled. After which, upon surrendering his office of treasurer of the court of augmentation, he had in lieu thereof a grant of £320 per annum from the crown; and was constituted, on the marriage of the queen, lord chamberlain of the household to King PHILIP. Nor did his lordship enjoy less favour from Queen ELIZABETH, being, in the first year of her Majesty's reign, appointed lord president of Wales. He subsequently resided as lord president in the Castle of Ludlow. His lordship m., 1st, Elizabeth, widow of Andrew Edmundes, of Gressing Temple, in Essex, and dau. and co-heir of Thomas Bledlow, Esq. (son and heir of Thomas Bledlow, sheriff of the city of London, in 1472), by whom he had issue,

Henry, who m. Anne, dau. of Henry, Lord Stafford, and d. s. p., v. p.
Francis, also d. s. p., v. p.
Isabel, m. Richard Wenman, sheriff of Oxfordshire, 1562, and had a son, Sir Richard Wenman, Knt. of Thame, co. Oxford, who m. Jane, dau. of William, Lord De la Warr, and had with junior issue, an eldest son and successor,
  Richard, 1st Viscount Wenman, whose only son, Thomas, 2nd Viscount Wenman, left two daus., his co-heirs, viz., Frances, m. to Richard Samwell, Esq., of Upton Hall, co. Northampton, and Penelope, m. to Sir Thomas Cave, Bart., of Stanford Hall, co. Leicester; in the heirs-general of these marriages a co-heirship of the Barony of Williams is vested.

585

Margery, m. to Sir Henry Norreys, Knt., to whom she conveyed the manor of Ricott, or Rycote, in Oxfordshire, and Sir Henry was summoned to parliament from 8 May, 1572, to 24 October, 1597, as BARON NORREYS, *of Rycote;* their grandson,

FRANCIS NORREYS, Lord Norreys, of Rycote, was created in 1620, Viscount Thame, and Earl of Berkshire, his lordship's heir-general is the EARL OF ABINGDON, one of the co-heirs of the Barony of Williams.

He m. 2ndly, Margery, dau. of Thomas, Lord Wentworth, but had no issue. His lordship d. in 1559, when his estates devolved upon his daus., as co-heirs, and the Barony of Williams, of Thame, fell into ABEYANCE between the same ladies, as it still continues with their representatives. Of Margery, the younger sister, the Earl of Abingdon is now heir-general.

Arms—Az. an organ pipe in bend sinister saltierwise. surmounted of another dexter, between two crosses patee, arg.

WILLINGTON—BARONS WILLINGTON.

By Writ of Summons, dated 14 June, 1329.

Lineage.

JOHN DE WILLINGTON, of Willington, co. Derby, lived at, or immediately after, the time of WILLIAM THE CONQUEROR, since we find that his son,

NICHOLAS DE WILLINGTON, of Willington, was contemporaneous with Robert, Abbot of Burton in the reign of King STEPHEN. He was s. by his son,

NICHOLAS DE WILLINGTON, of Willington. A dau. and heiress of this Nicholas m. Hugo de Finderne, from which marriage descends Sir J. Harpur-Crewe, Bart., of Calke Abbey, In Dugdale's *Monasticon*, it appears that both this Nicholas and his father were liberal benefactors to the convent of Repton, and according to Lysons, the manor and church of Willington were given to the convent by these Willingtons. His brother,

RALPH DE WILLINGTON, settled at Sandhurst, in Gloucestershire, *temp.* King JOHN, whence the manor-house obtained the name of Willington Court. In the 8th HENRY III., he was governor of Bristol Castle, and had a grant of the wardenship of the forest, with that of the chase of Rainsham, in the 17th of the same reign. He was governor of Devizes Castle, in Wiltshire. He founded St. Mary's Chapel, in the abbey of St. Peter's, at Gloucester, now called "the Ladye Chapel." He m. Olympias, dau. and heir of Sir Humphrey Franc, Knt. He d. about 21st HENRY III., and was father of

SIR RALPH DE WILLINGTON, living 37th HENRY III., who m. Joan, dau. and heir of Sir William Champernowne, of Umberleigh, co. Devon. After this marriage, their descendants, as is recorded by Sir William Pole, in his *History of Devon*, left their own arms, and took those of Champernowne, omitting the billets, viz., gules, a saltier, vairé. Their son,

SIR RALPH DE WILLINGTON, of Willington Court, co. Gloucester, and of Umberleigh, co. Devon, styled by Risdon, "a worthy warrior," was governor of the castle at Exeter, 38th HENRY III., and sheriff of Devon. He m. Juliana (supposed by Sir William Pole to be), the dau. and heir of Sir Richard de Lomen, as the lands of Lomen came to their descendants. They had issue,

JOHN WILLINGTON, who, in the reign of EDWARD I., had several grants from the crown, but in that of EDWARD II., being involved in the Earl of Lancaster's insurrection, all his lands were seized, but his life was spared. He and his younger brother, Sir Henry de Willington, were taken prisoners at the battle of Boroughbridge, when the sentence against Sir Henry was that he should be drawn for his treason, and hanged for his homicides, which being carried into effect in 1322 (*see* Parliamentary Writs, vol. 2, div. 2, part. 2, pp. 261, 262), miracles were afterwards said to be worked by his body in 1323, then hanging in chains, at Bristol, on account of which a commission issued for the trial of Reginald de Montfort, and others who were alleged to have feigned the same. This Sir Henry Willington m. Margaret, dau. of Sir Alexander Frevill and Joan, his wife, a co-heiress of the Marmions of Tamworth. John de Willington was restored to favour by King EDWARD III., and by that monarch was summoned to parliament as a Baron, from 14 June, 1329, to 15 November, 1338. He d. the following year, and was s. by his son,

RALPH DE WILLINGTON, 2nd baron, who was summoned to parliament, 25 February, 1342. He was in the wars of Scotland and France. He m. Elynor, dau. of John, 1st Lord Mohun, of

Dunster, but *d. s p.* in 1348, when his uncle, Reginald de Willington, became his heir. Reginald *d. s. p.*, 29th EDWARD III., leaving John, the son of Henry, and grandson of Henry, who had been executed at Bristol, his heir. This line became EXTINCT in the male descent, 20th RICHARD II., when John Willington, brother of Ralph, and son of the John who was the heir of Reginald, *d.* leaving two sisters, his co-heirs, who m. into the families of Worth and Beaumont, whence, through heiresses, descend the Bassets, present owners of Umberleigh; as also the Baronet family of Chichester, and the Marquess of Donegal. A younger branch of the Willingtons, after remaining in Gloucestershire for two or three descents, settled in Warwickshire, *temp.* King HENRY VII. In which county William Willington was seated at Barcheston, and having m. Anne, dau. of Richard Littleton, of Pillaton, *d.* leaving seven daus., co-heiresses, for whose marriages *see* BURKE's *Landed Gentry.*

THOMAS WILLINGTON, a younger brother of William Willington, of Barcheston, settled at Hurley, co. Warwick, where his descendants were resident for several centuries, becoming EXTINCT in the male line in 1815; from him descended the Willingtons, of Whateley and Tamworth.

Arms—Gu., a saltier, vairée, arg. and az.

WILLOUGHBY — BARONS WILLOUGHBY, OF PARHAM.

By Letters Patent, dated 16 February, 1547.

Lineage.

The family of Willoughby, by a pedigree drawn up in the time of ELIZABETH, appears to be descended from SIR JOHN DE WILLOUGHBY, a Norman knight, who had the lordship of Willoughby, in Lincolnshire, by gift of the CONQUEROR. From this successful soldier we pass to
SIR WILLIAM DE WILLOUGHBY (son of Robert Willoughby, and Margaret, his wife, dau. and heiress of John de Orreby), who, in the 54th HENRY III., was signed with the cross, and accompanied Prince Edward into the Holy Land. He. m. Alice, dau. of John, Lord Beke, of Eresby, and eldest co-heir of her brother Walter, Lord of Eresby, and had issue,

ROBERT (Sir), his successor.
Thomas. m. Margaret, sister and co-heir of Alun de Munby and had a son, who, assuming the surname of his mother, became
    William Munby. He *d. s. p.*, and his estates were divided amongst his sisters.
Margaret, m. to Walter, son of Sir Walter Hamby, Knt.

Sir William was *s.* by his elder son,
SIR ROBERT DE WILLOUGHBY, who inherited in the 4th EDWARD II., as next heir, the estates of Anthony Bec, bishop of Durham, and was summoned to parliament in three years afterwards as BARON WILLOUGHBY DE ERESBY. He m. Margaret, dau. of Edmund, Lord Deincourt. From this nobleman we pass to his lineal descendant,
WILLIAM WILLOUGHBY. 5th Baron Willoughby de Eresby, who m. 1st, Lucy, dau. of Roger, Lord Strange, of Knokyn, and had issue,

ROBERT, his successor, and 6th Baron Willoughby de Eresby.
Thomas (Sir), of whose descendants we are about to treat.

His lordship m. 2ndly, Joane, widow of Edward Plantagenet, Duke of York, and dau of Thomas Holland, 2nd Earl of Kent. He *d.* in 1409, and was *s.* in his title by his elder son, ROBERT; but we proceed with the younger,
SIR THOMAS WILLOUGHBY, of Parham, co. Suffolk; a gallant soldier, and one of the heroes of Agincourt. He m. Joane, dau. and heir of Sir Richard Fitz-Alan, Knt. (son of John Fitz-Alan, Lord Maltravers, 2nd son of Sir Richard Fitz-Alan, 3rd Earl of Arundel), and was *s.* by his son,
SIR ROBERT WILLOUGHBY, who m. Cecilia, dau. of Leo, Lord Welles, and had two sons,

ROBERT. } both knights.
Christopher,

Sir Robert *d.* 30 May, 1465, and was *s.* by his elder son,
SIR ROBERT WILLOUGHBY, who *d.* in minority, and was *s.* by his brother,
SIR CHRISTOPHER WILLOUGHBY, who was made a knight of the Bath, 6 July, 1483, at the coronation of RICHARD III. In the next reign he raised forces to assist the king against the Earl of Lincoln, Lambert Simnel, and their adherents, and was afterwards at the battle of Stoke. He m. Margaret,

586

dau. of Sir William Jenny, of Knotshall, in Suffolk, and had issue,

WILLIAM, who inherited the Barony of Willoughby de Eresby at the decease of JOANE WELLES in 1506, after the dignity had been out of the Willoughby family for half a century. His lordship became possessed also of the manors of Grimsby and Grimesthorp, with the greater part of the estates of the Lord Welles.
CHRISTOPHER, of whom presently.
George.
THOMAS, from whom the extant Willoughbys, Lords Middleton derive.
John.
Dorothy.
Catherine, m. to Sir John Heydon, Knt., of Baconsthorp, co. Norfolk.
Elizabeth, m. to William, Lord Eure.

The 2nd son,
SIR CHRISTOPHER WILLOUGHBY, received the honour of knighthood for his valiant conduct at the siege of Tournay, *temp.* HENRY VIII. He m. Elizabeth, dau. of Sir George Talboys, and sister of Gilbert, Lord Talboys, of Kyme, by whom he had issue,

WILLIAM, his successor.
Dorothy, m. to Ralph Hopton, Esq., of Wytham, co. Somerset.
Elizabeth, m. to Sir John Breuse, of Wenham, co. Suffolk.
Anne, m. to Robert Hall, Esq., of Gretford, co Lincoln.

Sir Christopher was *s.* by his eldest son,
SIR WILLIAM WILLOUGHBY, Knt., who was elevated to the peerage, by letters patent, dated 20 February, 1547, in the dignity of LORD WILLOUGHBY, *of Parham.* His lordship having distinguished himself in the wars of HENRY VIII., was made lieutenant of Calais, and the adjacent marches, in the 4th EDWARD VI., and he resided there during the remainder of that king's reign. He m. 1st, Elizabeth, dau. and heir of Sir Thomas Heneage, Knt., of Hainton and Knaith, co. Lincoln, by whom he acquired considerable estates, and had issue,

CHARLES, his successor.
Mary, m. to William Metham, Esq., of Bolington, co. Lincoln.

He m. 2ndly, Margaret, dau. of Robert Garnish, Esq., of Kenton, in Suffolk, and widow of Walter, 1st Viscount Hereford. His lordship *d.* in 1574, and was *s.* by his son,
CHARLES WILLOUGHBY, 2nd Baron Willoughby, of Parham, who m. Lady Margaret Clinton, dau. of Edward, 1st Earl of Lincoln, and had issue,

I. WILLIAM, who m. Elizabeth, dau. and heir of Sir Christopher Hildyard, Knt., of Winstead, in Yorkshire, and dying *v. p.*, left with other issue,
    WILLIAM, successor to his grandfather.
    Elizabeth, m. to Sir William Hickman, of Gainsborough, co. Lincoln.
    Catherine. m. to Joseph Godfrey, Esq., of Thorock, in the same shire.
    Mary, m. to Sir William Booth, of Killingholm, also in Lincolnshire.
II. Ambrose (Sir), of Matson. co. Gloucester, m. Susan, dau. of Richard Brookes. Esq., and sole heir of her maternal grandfather, R chard Pate, Esq., of Matson, and by her (who m. 2ndly, Sir Robert Lovett, of Lipscombe,) he left an only son,
    EDWARD, who m. Rebecca, dau. of Henry Draper, Esq., and had surviving issue,
        HENRY, who emigrated to Virginia, and *d.* there in 1685, leaving by Mary, his wife, a son,
        HENRY, who m. Elizabeth, dau. of William Pidgeon, Esq., of Stepney, co. Middlesex, and had issue,
        1 HENRY, declared 15th baron in 1767.
        2 William, who m. ——, dau. of — Knochton and left a son,
            William, who *d. s. p.*
        3 Edward, } *d. s. p.*
        4 Joseph.
        5 FORTUNE, who m. Hannah, dau. of Thomas Barrow, and widow of Cook Tollet, Esq., of Swanscomb, in Kent, and dying 1720, left a son,
            GEORGE, who *s.* as 16th baron.
        Richard, whose line ceased with his sons.
        Sarah, m. to — Birt.
        Rebecca, m. to Richard Hull.
III. Edward, m. Elizabeth, dau. of Francis Manby, Esq., of Elsham, and widow of John Prescot, and had a son,
    Edward, who *d.* young.
IV. Charles. *d. s. p.*
V. Thomas (Sir), m. Mary, dau. of — Thorney, Esq., and had issue,
    THOMAS, who *s.* as 11th lord, under the supposition that the line of Sir Ambrose was extinct.
    William, in holy orders, in the church of Rome.
    Mary, m. 1st, to Augustine Wingfield, and 2ndly, to —
    Beal.

vi. Catherine, *m.* to Sir John Savile, of Howley, co. York.

vii. Margaret, *m.* to — Erle, Esq. of Corpsey.

viii. Anne, *m.* to Si: William Pelham, Knt., of Brokelsby in Lincolnshire.

Charles, 2nd Lord Willoughby, *d.* in 1603, and was *s.* by his grandson,

WILLIAM WILLOUGHBY, 3rd Lord Willoughby, of Parham. This nobleman, *m.* Lady Frances Manners, dau. of John, 4th Earl of Rutland, and had issue,

HENRY, }
FRANCIS, } successively Lords Willoughby.
WILLIAM, }

Frances, *m.* to Sir Bulstrode Whitlock, Knt., of Chilton, co. Wilts.

Elizabeth, *d. unm.*

His lordship *d.* in 1617, and was *s.* by his eldest son.

HENRY WILLOUGHBY, 4th lord, at whose decease, in infancy, the title devolved upon his brother,

FRANCIS WILLOUGHBY, 5th lord, who *m.* Elizabeth, 2nd dau. and co-heir of Edward Cecil, Viscount Wimbledon, and had surviving issue,

Diana, *m.* to Heneage, 2nd Earl of Winchilsea.

Frances, *m.* to William, Lord Brereton, of the kingdom of Ireland.

Elizabeth, *m.* to Richard Jones, 1st Earl Ranelagh.

This nobleman was drowned at Barbadoes, in 1666, and was *s.* by his brother,

WILLIAM WILLOUGHBY, 6th Baron Willoughby, of Parham. His lordship was governor of the Caribbee Islands, and *d.* at Barbadoes, 10 April, 1673. He *m.* Anne, dau. of Sir Philip Carey, Knt., of Stanwell, co. Middlesex, and had, with other issue,

GEORGE, his successor.

JOHN, }
CHARLES, } who became successively Lords Willoughby.

William, living July, 1668.

Henry, Governor of Antigua.

Frances, *m.* 1st, to Sir John Harpur, Knt., of Swarkeston; 2ndly, to Charles-Henry Kirkhoven, Earl of Bellomont; and 3rdly, to Henry Heveningham, Esq., of Heveningham.

Anne, *m.* to Sir John Harpur, Bart., of Calke, co. Derby.

Catharine, *m.* to Charles Cockayne, 3rd Viscount Cullen.

Lord Willoughby *d.* in 1673, and was *s.* by his eldest son,

GEORGE WILLOUGHBY, 7th baron, who *m.* Elizabeth, dau. and co-heir of Henry Fiennes, otherwise Clinton, Esq., by whom he had issue,

JOHN, his successor.

Anne, *d.* young.

Elizabeth, *m.* to the Hon. James Bertie, 2nd son of James, 1st Earl of Abingdon, and was mother of Willoughby, 3rd Earl of Abingdon.

His lordship *d.* at Knaith, in 1674, and was *s.* by his son,

JOHN WILLOUGHBY, 8th baron, who *d.* in 1678, *unm.*, when the barony reverted to his uncle,

JOHN WILLOUGHBY, 9th baron. This nobleman *m.* Anne Bolterton, and dying *s. p.* in 1678, was *s.* by his brother,

CHARLES WILLOUGHBY, 10th baron, who *m.* Mary, dau. of Sir Beaumont Dixie, Bart., of Bosworth, co. Leicester, but *d. s. p.* in 1679, devising his estate to his niece, Elizabeth, wife of the Hon. James Bertie. At the decease of his lordship, the barony, *by right*, should have devolved upon the descendant of Sir Ambrose Willoughby, 2nd son of Charles, the 2nd lord; but that gentleman's grandson, Henry Willoughby, having emigrated to America, the second branch remained in ignorance of the failure of the elder, and as the senior line put in no claim to the title, it was presumed to have become likewise EXTINCT; the Barony of Willoughby, of Parham, under these circumstances, was adjudged *erroneously* to the son and heir of Sir Thomas Willoughby, youngest son of the 2nd lord (*refer* to issue of Charles, 2nd baron.) and he was summoned to parliament accordingly, 19 May, 1685, by writ, addressed "Thomæ Willoughby de Parham, Chl'r." This

THOMAS WILLOUGHBY, Baron Willoughby, of Parham, *m.* Eleanor, dau. of Hugh Whittle, Esq., of Horwath, Lancashire, and had, with other issue,

HUGH, his successor.

Francis, *m.* to Eleanor, dau. of Thomas Rothwell, of Haigh, co. Lancaster, and had issue,

Thomas, *d. unm.* 1703.

EDWARD who *s.* his uncle as Lord Willoughby.

CHARLES who *s.* his brother.

His lordship *d.* in 1692, and was *s.* by his eldest son,

HUGH WILLOUGHBY, Baron Willoughby of Parham. This nobleman *m.* 1st, Anne, dau. of Lawrence Halliwell, Esq., of Tockholes, in Lancashire, and had a son,

Thomas, who *d.* young.

His lordship *m.* 2ndly, in 1692, Honora, widow of Sir William Egerton, and dau. of Sir Thomas Leigh, son and heir of Thomas, 1st Lord Leigh, but *d. s. p.* in August, 1712, when he was *s.* by his nephew,

EDWARD WILLOUGHBY, Baron Willoughby, of Parham, who, when the honour devolved upon him, was abroad as a *private soldier* in the confederate army, under John, Duke of Marlborough. His lordship did not, however, enjoy the peerage long, for he *d.* in 1713, and was *s.* by his brother,

CHARLES WILLOUGHBY, 14th baron, *b.* 25 December, 1681, who *m.* Hester, dau. of Henry Davenport, Esq., of Darcy Lever, by whom he had, HUGH, his successor. Helena, *m.* to Baxter Roscoe, of Anglezark, Bolton; and Elizabeth *m.* to John Shaw. He *d.* 12 July, 1715, and was *s.* by his son,

HUGH WILLOUGHBY, Baron Willoughby, of Parham. This nobleman was elected vice-president of the Royal Society in 1752, and president of the Society of Antiquaries in two years afterwards. His lordship was esteemed a man of abilities, but according to Cole's MSS. in the British Museum, he was a presbyterian of the most rigid class. "I have heard" (says Cole) "Mr. Coventry, of Magdalen College, Cambridge, declare that his conscience was so nice, that he could not bring himself to receive the sacrament in the church of England on his knees, without scruple, and thought it idolatry. He had a very small estate, and when he came to it, with the title, was in a very humble capacity in the army.' He *d. unm.* 21 January, 1765, when the barony was claimed by

HENRY WILLOUGHBY, representative of the elder branch (*refer* to Sir Ambrose Willoughby, 2nd son of the 2nd lord,) and the House of Lords adjudged, in 1767, "That he had a right to the title, dignity, and peerage of Willoughby, of Parham; which was enjoyed from the year 1680 to 1765 by the male line (now EXTINCT,) of Sir Thomas Willoughby, youngest son of Charles, Lord Willoughby, of Parham, who were successively summoned to parliament by descent, in virtue of letters patent, bearing date 16 February, 1st EDWARD VI., and sat as heirs male of the body of Sir William, created Lord Willoughby of Parham, by the said letters patent, contrary to the right and truth of the case; it now appearing that Sir Ambrose Willoughby, the 2nd son of the said Charles (and elder brother of the said Thomas,) who was averred to have died without issue, left a son; and that Henry Willoughby, Esq., the claimant, is great-grandson and heir male of the body of such son, and consequently heir male of the said Sir William, who was created Lord Willoughby, of Parham, the male line of the elder son, Charles, Lord Willoughby, of Parham, having failed in or before the year 1680." Mr. Willoughby became, therefore, 16th BARON WILLOUGHBY, *of Parham*, and took his seat in the House of Peers, 25 April, 1767. His lordship *m.* Susannah, dau. of Robert Gresswell, Esq., of co. Middlesex, by whom he had one surviving dau., Elizabeth, who *m.* 1st, John Halsey, Esq., of Tower Hill, and 2ndly, Edward Angles, Esq. He *d.* 29 January, 1775, and was *s.* by his nephew,

GEORGE WILLOUGHBY, 17th baron, who *d. s. p.*, 29 October, 1779, since which period the Barony, created by patent, 20 February, 1547, has remained DORMANT.

A short extract from the *Vicissitudes of Families* will appropriately conclude this memoir of the Willoughbys of Parham:

"The Barony of WILLOUGHBY OF PARHAM was conferred by letters patent, in 1547, on Sir William Willoughby, Knt., and the heirs male of his body, and devolved at his death, on his son and heir, Charles, 2nd lord, who had with other children, three sons, who all left issue. In the descendants of the eldest son, the barony continued vested until the decease, without issue, of the 10th lord, in 1679. At his lordship's decease, the title ought, by right, to have gone to the heir of Sir Ambrose, the second son of the second lord; but as his branch had emigrated to America, it was presumed to have become extinct, and the Barony of Willoughby of Parham, was adjudged erroneously to the son of the second lord's youngest son, and that personage and his descendants continued to sit in parliament as Lords Willoughby of Parham. Meanwhile, the descendant of Sir Ambrose came back from America, proved his pedigree, and thus created a remarkable state of things. He, the true lord, was excluded from his rights as a peer, while his cousin, the false lord, sat and voted. In course of time, however, right prevailed. '*Dormit aliquando jus, moritur nunquam.*' The male line of the false lord expired, and Henry Willoughby, Sir Ambrose's representative, claimed his peerage, and had it adjudged to him by a memorable decision of the House of Lords, which admitted that the intermediate lords had 'sat contrary to the right and truth of the case.'

"The decision, one should have supposed, would have ended all perplexity connected with the title of Willoughby of Parham. But it was not so. As the first false lord was summoned to parliament under the erroneous presumption that he was a peer, and took his seat accordingly under the writ, an Independent barony in fee was thereby created, descendible to his heirs general.

"For instance, when the eldest son of an earl is summoned up in the name of a barony not vested in his father and it afterwards turns out that the earl had no such barony, then a substantive barony by writ is created; whereas, on the contrary, had the earl pcssessed a barony, the effect of the writ to his heir-apparent, would only be to accelerate the descent of the dignity, and to make it still descendible according to the original limitation.

"There still being an heir-general of the false Lord Willoughby, is not such heir-general, in this view of the case, entitled to a barony in fee?"

Arms—1st and 4th, or, fretté, az., 2nd and 3rd, sa., a cross engrailed, or.

WILMOT—VISCOUNTS WILMOT IN IRELAND, BARONS WILMOT AND EARLS OF ROCHESTER, IN ENGLAND.

Irish Viscounty, by Letters Patent. dated 4 January, 1620.
English Barony, by Letters Patent, dated 29 June. 1643.
Earldom, by Letters Patent, dated 13 December, 1652.

Lineage.

SIR CHARLES WILMOT, or WILLMOTT, lord president of Connaught, and privy-councillor to JAMES I. and CHARLES I., was raised to the peerage of Ireland, as VISCOUNT WILMOT, *of Athlone*, 4 January, 1620: taking the locality his title from the seat of his government (Athlone) as lord president of Connaught. His lordship received very considerable grants of land in Ireland. "In regard of the long and faithful services done to Queen ELIZABETH and the crown by Sir Charles Willmott, and the better to encourage and enable him to persevere therein, the King was pleased, at his humble suit, to direct by privy seal, dated at Westminster, 15 June, 1614, and at Windsor, 4 September, the Lord Deputy Chichester, to accept of him (Sir Charles Willmott) by grant or surrender, an estate in fee simple of lands in Ireland of the clear yearly value of £200 English and his surrender (within twelve months), of two pensions of £250 a-year granted to him for life, and 10s. a-day Irish harpes, granted to him in respect of his government of Kerry, during pleasure, in consideration whereof he was to receive a grant to him and his heirs, or such as he should nominate, in fee simple so many crown lands as should amount to £200 a-year English, according to the rents rateably for each parcel remaining of record. And Sir Charles having by petition, declared yea many difficulties and great expence of time he must suffer in acquiring lands fit for his majesty to accept, all which time his grant was to stay, the king was pleased, by letters from Windsor, 4 September, 1614. to enlarge his warrant, and to direct the lord deputy, without delay, to pass patent to him of £100 lands of the said £200 a-year before he should surrender. and lands to the king and to take caution of him to make the said surrenders, within one year." Accordingly, were granted by this patent the abbey and monastery of Carrickfergus, co. Antrim, with lands in the co. of Waterford and various other counties. Sir Charles had subsequently other extensive estates assigned to him throughout Ireland, including the monastery and lordship of Baltinglass, co. Wicklow. Lord Willmott m. twice; by his 2nd wife, Mary, widow of Garret, 1st Viscount Moore, and dau. of Sir Henry Colley, of Castle Carbery, co. Kildare, which lady was buried "at Drogheda in the Lord Moore's tomb, 3 July, 1654," he does not appear to have had issue; but by his 1st wife, was father of ARTHUR, who m. a dau. of Sir Moyses Hill, but d. s. p. 31 October, 1632; and of CHARLES, his successor. This latter, Lord Willmott's only surviving son,

HENRY WILMOT, 2nd Viscount Wilmot, of Athlone, had been previously, to the death of his father, created a baron of England, by letters patent, of King CHARLES I., dated 29 June, 1643, as LORD WILMOT, *of Adderbury, co. Oxford*. He was at that time lieutenant of the horse, in his majesty's armies throughout England and Wales, and attained high reputation, particularly at the battle of Roundway Down. His lordship afterwards remained faithfully attached to King CHARLES II., during his exile, and was mainly instrumental in enabling his Majesty to effect his escape after the fatal battle of Worcester. In consideration of these eminent services he was advanced by letters patent, dated at Paris, 13 December, 1652, to the EARLDOM OF ROCHESTER. His lordship m. Anne, widow of Sir

Henry Lee, of Dichley, co. Oxford, and dau. of Sir John St-John, Bart., of Lyddiard Tregoz. co. Wilts, and of Batterscaand Wandsworth, so created 22 May, 1611, and grandaunt of the celebrated statesman and author, Viscount Bolinbroke. The earl d. at Dunkirk, in 1659, and was s. by his only surviving son,

JOHN WILMOT, 2nd Earl of Rochester. This is the nobleman who became so celebrated in the reign of CHARLES II., at the gifted, witty, but licentious companion of the merry monarch. His lordship, Walpole characterises as a poet, whom the muses inspired, but were ashamed to own, and who practised without the least reserve, the secret which can make verses more read for their defects than for their merits. Lord Rochester's poems are truly described by the same author, as having more obscenity than wit, more wit than poetry, and more poetry than politeness. His lordship m. Elizabeth, dau. and heir of John Mallet, Esq., of Enmore, co. Somerset, "*la triste héritière*," named by Grammont, and of whom mention is made by Burnet. By her he had issue,

I. CHARLES, his successor.
I. ANNE, of whom presently, as eldest sister and co-heir of her brother.
II. Elizabeth, m. Edward Montague, 3rd Earl of Sandwich, and was by him (who d. 20 October, 1729) mother of

Edward-Richard, Viscount Hinchinbroke, who d. 1727, father of John, 4th Earl of Sandwich, the diplomatist and statesman, from whom derives the present Earl of Sandwich.

III. Malet, m. John Vaughan, Viscount Lisburne, so created 26 June, 1695, and by him (who d. in 17.0) was mother o Wilmot, 3rd Viscount Lisburne, ancestor of the present Earl of Lisburne.

The earl d. in 1680, and was s. by his son,

CHARLES WILMOT, 3rd Earl of Rochester, who d. unm. and in minority the year after his father, when all his honours became EXTINCT, and his co-representation devolved on his eldest sister,

LADY ANNE WILMOT, who m. twice: her 2nd husband was the Hon. Francis Greville, ancestor by her of the Grevilles, Earls of Warwick; her 1st husband was Henry Bayntun, Esq., of Bromham, Wilts, M.P. for Chippenham in 1685, eldest son and heir of Sir Edward Bayntun, of Bromham, M.P. for Calne, in 1658, high sheriff for Wilts, 1656, CHARLES I., 1661; commissioner of parliament in the Scots army, and created at the Restoration a knight of the Bath, derived 8th in descent, through a succession of knightly ancestors and distinguished alliances, from Sir John Bayntun, Knt.,[*] of Falston, 25th HENRY IV., and Joan, his wife, dau., by Sir Richard Dudley, Knt., of Elizabeth, in her issue, heiress of her nephew, Richard de Beauchamp, 2nd Baron St. Amand, who d. 1505, and dau. of Sir Walter de Beauchamp and Elizabeth, his wife, heiress of Bromham, dau. and co-heir of Sir John Roche, Knt., of Bromham. By this gentleman, who was baptised 17 November, 1664, and d. in 1691, Lady Anne was mother of one son and one dau. The former of whom,

JOHN BAYNTUN, Esq., m. Catherine Brounker, and dying s. p. 1716-17, was s. by his sister and heir,

ANNE, heiress of Bromham. This lady m. twice: 1st, Edward Rolt, Esq., of Saccomb Park, co. Hertford, M.P. for Chippenham, son of Sir Thomas Rolt, Knt., of Saccomb Park. President of the East India Company at Surat, knighted at Whitehall, 1 October, 1682, and high sheriff of Hertfordshire 1696. She m. 2ndly, in 1724, James Somerville, 13th Baron Somerville, and the eldest surviving grandson of this marriage,

Kenelm, 17th Baron Somerville, was father of HUGH, 18th BARON SOMERVILLE.

By her 1st marriage the heiress of Bromham had issue,

I. THOMAS, in whose line the representation of the line continued.
II EDWARD, of whom presently.
III. John Rolt, Rector of Bromham and Yatesbury, who had issue and d. 25 October, 1793.
IV. Henry Rolt, colonel, horse guards, 1737.
V. Wilmot Rolt, d. unm.
VI. James Rolt, Gentleman Usher to the Princess Amelia, d. 5 March, 1795, æt. seventy-four.

---

[*] GUIDO DE TABLIER, Lord of Falston, was father of a dau. and heir, EDITH, heiress of Falston, who by her husband, Richard de Grimsted, was mother of a dau. and co-heir, MARGARET, heiress of Falston, who m. Thomas de Bayntun, and was mother of NICHOLAS DE BAYNTUN, Lord of Falston, b. 1335, living 45th EDWARD III., who m. Joan, dau of Gilbert de Berwick. Their son, NICHOLAS DE BAYNTUN, Lord of Falston, was father of NICHOLAS DE BAYNTUN. b. 1382, living 6th HENRY IV., who m. JANE, dau. and co-heir (with her sister, Elizabeth, wife of Sir Walter de Beauchamp), of Sir John Roche, Knt., of Bromham, Wilts, and was father by her of Sir John Bayntun, Knt., of Falston, father, as above stated (by JOAN. in her issue, heiress of Richard Beauchamp, 2nd Baron St. Amand), of Sir John Bayntun, Knt., of Falston.

1. Elizabeth, *m.* John Prideaux, Esq., brigadier-general, 2nd son of Sir John Prideaux, Bart., and was by him mother of SIR EDMUND-SAUNDERSON PRIDEAUX, 9th baronet.
II. Anna-Maria Rolt, *d. unm.* 27 November, 1723.

The 2nd son of the heiress of Bromham and Mr. Rolt, viz.,
EDWARD ROLT, Esq., of Spye Park, Bromham, assumed the additional surname of BAYNTUN. and was created a baronet 9 July, 1762. Sir Edward Bayntun-Rolt, who was M.P. for Chippenham, and groom of the bedchamber to the Prince of Wales, *m.* Mary Poynter, of Herryard, co. Southampton, and had issue, one son and two daus.,

SIR ANDREW BAYNTUN-ROLT, of whom presently.
Elizabeth, who *m.* Andrew Stone, Esq., and *d.* 5 June, 1782. Her son, Bayntun Stone, lieut.-col. 58th foot, by Anne, his wife, only dau. and heir of John Stone, Esq., of Badbury, Wilts, was father of an eldest son, Henry Stone, Esq., of Badbury, sometime an officer in the 6th Inniskilling dragoons. This gentleman *b.* in 1824, *m.* 17 January, 1850, Catherine-Charlotte-Mary, sister of Anthony-John Wright-Biddulph, Esq., of Burton Park, co. Sussex. and elder dau. of Anthony-George Wright, Esq., who assumed the additional surname of Biddulph after that of Wright, on succeeding to Burton Park, and had issue.
Constantia, *m.* Richard Foster, Esq., of Thames Bank, co. Buckingham, and had issue, five sons and two daus.,
   I. Augustus Foster, Esq., of Warmwell House, Dorset, lord of the manor of Warmwell, high sheriff for Dorset in 1852, deputy lieutenant and justice of the peace for that county, and late captain 40th light dragoons, *b.* 1787; who *m* in 1813, Judith-Letitia, only dau. and heir of Thomas Billet, Esq., of Warmwell House, and had issue,
     1 Augustus-Billet Foster, Esq., Warmwell, co. Dorset, J.P. and D.L., *b.* August, 1824.
     2 Richard-Bayntun Foster, capt. R.N.
     3 Frederic-Wilmot Foster, captain 78th highlanders.
     1 Anna-Maria-Letitia-Constantia.
     2 Matilda, *m.* Thomas Pryor, Esq., of High Elms, co. Hertford.
   II. Edmund Foster, Esq., B.A. 1851, of Clewer Manor, Berks, deputy-lieutenant and justice of the peace for that county, *m.* Maria, only child and heir of John Benson, Esq., of Millington and New Cross, Uxbridge, and left at his decease,
     Edmund-Benson Foster, Esq., B.A., of Clewer Manor, deputy-lieutenant for Berkshire, *b.* 8 April, 1824.
     Eliza-Constantia Foster, *d. unm.* June, 1862.
   III. Bayntun Foster, R.N., drowned.
   IV. Richard Foster, an officer East India Company's service, drowned in embarking from India to England.
   V. Frederick Foster, R.N., drowned.
   I. Constantia, who *m.* Hill D'Arley, Esq., and *d. s. p.*
   II. Caroline-Anne, *m.* 30 May, 1816, James Elmslie, Esq., of Gray's Inn, and Serge Island, Jamaica, and of Brighton, 2nd but eldest surviving son of John Elmslie. Esq., of those places, and left at her decease in August, 1862,
     1 John-Foster Elmslie, Esq., of Gray's Inn and Serge Island, and of Westow Hill, Upper Norwood, Surrey, *m.* 9 April, 1842, his cousin, Helen. dau. of John Elmslie, Esq., of Island Head Estate, Jamaica, and has had issue,
       John-Elmslie Elmslie, *b.* 29 May, 1843.
       Graham Elmslie, *b.* 5 March, 1845.
       Francis-Logan Elmslie, *b.* 15 June, 1846.
       Alfred Elmslie, *b.* 24 September, 1847.
       Bayntun Elmslie, *b.* 2 December, 1848.
       William Elmslie, *b.* 4 March, 1852.
       Richard-Foster Elmslie, *b.* 3 March, 1855.
       Wilmot-Edward Elmslie, *b.* 29 December, 1860.
       Helen Eliza.   Constance-Edith, *d.* young.
       Maud-Margaret.
     2 James Elmslie, Esq., of Norfolk Square, Hyde Park Gardens, who *m.* Mary-Johanna, eldest dau. of Major-General John-Gregory Baumgardt, C.B.
     3 Edmund-Wallace Elmslie, Esq., of Great Malvern, *m.* Theodora-Honora Price.
     4 Augustus-Frederick Elmslie, Esq., of Kingston, Surrey, *m.* Louisa, youngest dau. of Major-General John-Gregory Baumgardt. C.B.
     1 Constantia-Anne, *m.* 22 June, 1829, Henry Richardson, Esq., of Ryde, Isle of Wight, who assumed by royal sign manual the name and arms of Cornfoot.
     2 Louisa-Beacher Elmslie.

Sir Edward Bayntun-Rolt, who *d.* 1800, æt. ninety, was *s.* by his only son,
SIR ANDREW BAYNTUN-ROLT, 2nd baronet of Spye Park, high sheriff for Wilts in 1802. He *m.* 1st. 1777. Lady Maria-Alicia, 2nd dau. of George, 6th Earl of Coventry, from whom he was divorced in 1783, by Act of Parliament, and 2ndly, Anna-Maria Maude, and *d.* 12 August, 1816. By his 1st wife who *d.* 1784, he had an only dau. whose
ANNA BARBARA, heiress of Spye Park, who *m.* in 1797, the Rev. John Starky, D.D., rector of Charlynch, co. Somerset, and by him, who *d.* 1 April, 1834, was mother, with other issue, of an eldest son,

JOHN-EDWARD-ANDREW STARKY, Esq., of Spye Park, Bromham, who *m.* Charlotte, dau. of William Wyndham, Esq., of Dinton, Wilts, and was *s.* by his son and heir,
JOHN-BAYNTUN STARKY, Esq., of Spye Park, who *m.* 14 July, 1857, Frances-Anne, dau. of the Rev. James-Hunt Grubb, of Potterne, and has, with other issue, an eldest son, George-Bayntun Starky.
The heiress of Bromham *d.* in 1734, and her eldest son, by her 1st husband, Mr. Rolt, viz.,
THOMAS ROLT, Esq., of Saccomb Park, who was buried 20 February, 1754, *m.* Anne, dau. of Felix Calvert, Esq., of Nine Ashes in Hunsdon, co. Hertford. By this lady, who was buried 3 October, 1756, he had issue,
   I. THOMAS.
   II. CECILIA-ETHELREDA.
   III. MARY-CONSTANTIA.

The son,
THOMAS ROLT, Esq., of Saccomb Park, captain 1st regiment of guards, was killed near the Bay of St. Cass, Brittany, France, 11 September, 1758, æt. twenty-five, and was *s.* by his sister,
CECILIA-ETHELREDA ROLT, of Saccomb Park, who *d. unm.* 6 January, 1761. æt. twenty-three, and was *s.* by her sister,
MARY-CONSTANTIA, of Saccomb Park, who *m.* 28 January, 1762, Timothy Caswall, Esq., LL.D., *jure uxoris,* of Saccomb Park. an officer in the guards, who served in the expedition of St. Cass, a commissioner of excise, M.P. for Hertford, and subsequently in 1771 for Brackley, brother of John Caswall, Esq., great-grandfather of the late Alfred Caswall, Esq., of Elmgrove, Binfield, Berks, and of the Inner Temple, barrister, and younger son of Sir George Caswall, Knt., M.P. for Leominster. By Dr. Caswall, who *d.* 24 August, 1802, the heiress of Bromham, left at her decease, 7 July, 1767, a son,
GEORGE CASWALL, Esq., of Saccomb Park, nominated high sheriff for Herts 1807. He *m.* at Gretna Green, 1786, Anne Newman, and had issue (with a 1st and 2nd dau., who *d.*, and a 3rd. Eliza Caswall, who *d. unm.* 22 October, 1815, in the lifetime of her parents), an only surviving son,
GEORGE-NEWMAN CASWALL, Esq., senior heir-general of CHARLES WILMOT, 3rd and last EARL OF ROCHESTER.

Arms—Arg., or. a fesse. gu., between three eagles' heads erased, sa., as many escallops, or.

WINDSORE —BARON WINDSORE.

By Writ of Summons, dated 22 August, 1381.

Lineage.

At the time of the General Survey,
WALTER FITZ-OTHER possessed three lordships in Surrey, two in Hampshire, three in Bucks, and four in Middlesex; of which Stanwell, in the latter county, was the chief place of abode of himself and his descendants for several succeeding ages. Those lordships, manors, and lands, moreover, were held by his father, Sir Other, in the reign of EDWARD THE CONFESSOR. Walter Fitz-Other was warden of all the forests in Berkshire, and castellan of Windsore in the time of WILLIAM THE CONQUEROR. The name and family of his wife are in doubt, as likewise the seniority of his three sons,[a]

WILLIAM, his successor.
Robert, Lord of Eston, afterwards called Estains, in Essex, in which he was *s.* by his son,
   William, who left a dau., his heir,
     Delicia, *m.* to Robert de Hastings, and had a dau., Delicia, who *m.* Henry de Cornhill, whose only dau. and heir, Jane, being *m.* to Sir Godfrey de Lovaine, was mother of Sir Matthew de Lovaine, who held the said manor of Estaine by barony.

---

[a] GERALD, is called, in the Duke of Leinster's pedigree, the *eldest,* although placed *youngest* on the pedigree of the Earls of Kerry, and the latter disposition is supported by Segar, Dugdale, and Anstis, all eminent members of the Heralds' College. These Heralds maintain, that the appellation of *Fitz-Walter* was given to Gerald because he was the youngest son. LODGE, however, protests against such a conclusion, and says, "It deserves an inquiry, how the consequences of his being a younger son can be drawn from his having the appellation of Fitz-Walter! The custom of that age," he continues, "warrants the affirmation of the contrary; and that the eldest son, especially, assumed for his surname the christian name of his father, with the addition of *Fitz,* &c. And this continued in use until surnames came to be fixed about the time of EDWARD I., and among many families until long after that time, younger sons being not so frequently known, or called by their fathers' christian name, as by that of his office or employment. For which reason the two brothers of Gerald are not called Fitz-Walter, but Windsore."

Gerald, who bore the surname of FITZ-WALTER, and being successfully employed by King HENRY II., against the Welsh, was constituted governor of Pembroke Castle, and afterwards made president of the co. Pembroke. He m. Nesta, dau. of Rhese, Prince of Wales, and from their union sprang the Fitz-Geralds, Earls of Kildare, Dukes of Leinster, and other eminent families.

The eldest son,

WILLIAM bore the surname of WINDSORE, and s. his father in his offices of warden of the forests of Berkshire, and Castellan of Windsore. The Empress MAUD confirmed to him, at Oxford, all the grants made to his ancestors of the custody of Windsor Castle, and of all lands, in as full a manner as they had enjoyed them in the time of her father, HENRY I. He assumed the designation of Windsore from his office, and left two sons,

WILLIAM, his successor.

Hugh de Windsore, lord of the manor of West Horsley, co. Surrey, which, by heirs female, devolved upon the Barons de Berners.

The elder son and heir,

SIR WILLIAM DE WINDSORE, was also a powerful baron in the reign of HENRY II., and in 1165, upon the assessment for a marriage portion for that monarch's daughter, he certified that he held sixteen knights' fees and a half *de veteri feoffamento*, and three and a half *de novo*, for which he afterwards paid £12 2s. 6d. In 1194, he attended the king in his expedition into Normandy, when he raised the siege of Vernuel, and beat the French in several skirmishes. Sir William de Windsore, it is supposed, eventually fell in that campaign. He left two sons, WALTER and William, and was s. by the elder,

WALTER DE WINDSORE, who had accompanied his father in the expedition into France. This baron having no male issue, divided, by virtue of a fine levied in the 9th RICHARD I., the whole barony of his father, with his brother, William de Windsore. He d. about the year 1205, leaving two daus, his co-heirs, viz.,

Christian, m. to Duncan de Lascelles.
Gunnora, m. to Ralph de Hodeng.

In the division of the estates, as mentioned above, the deceased lord's brother, and the male representative of the family,

WILLIAM DE WINDSORE, had the lordships of Stanwell and Hakeburn, with other lands, &c., of considerable value; and in 1212, he paid into the exchequer, £100 for livery of some part of the estates which was possessed by his nieces. He was s. by his son and heir,

WILLIAM DE WINDSORE, who d. about the year 1275, and was s. by his elder son,

WILLIAM DE WINDSORE, of Stanwell, who m. Margaret, dau. of John Drokensford, and sister of Sir John Drokensford, Knt, and had issue, RICHARD, his successor, Walter, and a dau., Margaret, who took the veil, and was a nun at Ankerwyke Monastery, near Staines. He was s. by his elder son,

SIR RICHARD DE WINDSORE, who, attaining majority in the 13th EDWARD I., had livery of the manor of Stanwell, in Middlesex, and of West Hakeburn, in Berkshire. In the 23rd and 25th of the same reign he was returned one of the knights for the co. Berks. In 1297, he had a military summons to march under Edmund, Earl of Lancaster, into Gascony, and he subsequently sat in parliament as one of the knights for the co. Middlesex. In the 17th EDWARD II., upon an inquisition in every county, returned into chancery, of such as inherited arms from their ancestors, Sir Richard de Windsore was named amongst those of the cos. Middlesex and Berks. He d. in two years afterwards, seized of the manors of Stanwell, in Middlesex, and West Hakeburn, in Berkshire; as also the ward of the castle of Windsore. He left issue by his wife, Julian, dau. of Sir Nicholas Stapleton, of Hachilsay, co. York, William, rector of the church of Stanwell, and an elder son, his successor,

RICHARD DE WINDSORE, who served in parliament, *temp.* EDWARD III., for the cos. Middlesex and Berks. He m. twice: by his 1st wife, Joane, he had one child, a daughter. He m. 2ndly, Julian, dau. and co-heir of James Molyns, of the co. Southampton, and had two sons,

JAMES (Sir), his successor, ancestor of the Lords Mountjoy, Earls of Plymouth, &c.

WILLIAM (Sir), of whom presently

Richard de Windsore m. 3rdly, Claricia, dau. of John Drokensford, and widow of John Yorke. He d. in 1367, and was s. in his estates by his elder son, but we pass to the younger,

SIR WILLIAM DE WINDSORE, an eminent warrior and states-

590

man, in the reigns of EDWARD III. and RICHARD II.; by the former monarch he was constituted Lieutenant of Ireland, and by the latter summoned to parliament as a Baron, from 22 August, 1381, to 3 March, 1384. His lordship m. about the year 1378, the famous and beautiful ALICE PIERS or PERRERS,[*] but appears to have d. s. p. in 1384, as by the post-mortem inquisition taken before Nicholas Brembre, mayor of London, after enumerating his estates, it is stated, "that he died September 15th, 8th RICHARD II., leaving his three sisters his heirs, viz.,

"Isabel, thirty-eight years of age, *unm.*
"Christian, thirty-four years of age, *m.* to Sir William Moraux, Knt.
"Margery, aged thirty-two, *m.* to John Duket."

At his lordship's decease the Barony of Windsore became EXTINCT. Sir William Dugdale says, that Lord Windsore left daughters, but Collins considers those the issue of his wife, Alice, by another husband, and he quotes, in corroboration, a passage from her will; wherein styling herself widow of Sir William Windsore, she bequeaths to Joan, her youngest dau., her manor of Gaynes. This Joane m. Robert Skerne, of Kingston upon-Thames.

Arms—Gu. a saltier, arg., between twelve crosslets, or, with proper difference.

WINDSOR—EARL OF PLYMOUTH.

By Letters Patent, dated 6 December, 1682.

Lineage.

This baronial family descended from

WALTER FITZ-OTHER, warden of all the forests in Berkshire, and castellan of Windsor in the reign of WILLIAM THE CONQUEROR, and in which offices he was s. by his son and heir,

WILLIAM FITZ-WALTER, who assumed the surname of WINDSOR, from his office. His eldest son and heir,

---

[*] Of this celebrated woman, BARNES, in his *History of the Reign of King Edward III.*, states, "That being a person of extraordinary beauty, she was (48th EDWARD III.) made Lady of the Sun, and rode from the Tower of London through Cheapside, accompanied with many lords, knights, and ladies; every lady leading a lord or knight, by his horse's bridle, till they came into West Smithfield; where presently began solemn justs, which held for seven days together. That she had been constantly misrepresented by most of our writers (one taking it from another), as being King EDWARD's concubine, but that it was improbable, from the reputation she had of being taken in marriage by so considerable a person as the Lord William Windsore; and that King EDWARD, who never else is said to have gone astray, even in the flower of his age, should, within five years of the queen's death, when he was very infirm, burn in flames. That the records wherein she is mentioned are not severe on her reputation, as appears from the charge against her, brought into parliament in the 1st RICHARD II., in these words:—

"Dame Alice Perrers was introduced before the lords, and by Sir Richard le Scrope, Knt., steward of the king's household, charged for pursuing of matters, contrary to orders taken two years before; namely, that no woman should, for any advantage, present any cause in the King's Court, on pain of losing all they had, and being banished the realm for ever. That, particularly she had procured Sir Nicholas Dagworth to be called from Ireland, whether he was sent; and that she also procured, from the king, restitution of lands and goods, to Richard Lyon, merchant of London, whereas the same lands, having been forfeited by him, had been given to the king's own sons. To all which the said Dame Alice replied, that she had not pursued any such thing for any advantage of her own. Whereupon divers officers, counsellors, and servants to King EDWARD III., being examined, proved that she made such pursuit; and that, in their conceits, for her own private gain. Then judgment was given by the lords against the said dame, that according to the order aforesaid, she should be banished, and forfeit all her goods and lands whatsoever."

Sir Robert Cotton, in his *Abridgment of Records*, makes this remark on the above judgment: "To say truth of the devil is counted commendable, and therefore surely the record against the said lady, being very long, proves no such heinous matter against her; only it sheweth, that the same dame was in such credit with EDWARD III., as she sat at his bed's head, when all of the council, and the privy chamber, stood waiting without doors; and that she moved those suits that they dared not; and these two suits, whereof she was condemned, seemed very honest; her mishap was, that she was friendly to many, but all were not so to her."

The effect of this conviction was, however, subsequently removed.

WILLIAM DE WINDSOR was a powerful baron in the reign of HENRY II., which monarch he attended in his expedition into Normandy, where he *d.*, leaving two sons, Walter, who left only two daus., and

WILLIAM DE WINDSOR, who became male heir, and was *s.* by his son,

WILLIAM DE WINDSOR, surnamed the "Great Seal," who *d.* about 1275, leaving, by Agnes, his wife, two sons, WILLIAM and Hugh, who left an only dau., Joan, *m.* to Sir Richard de Dray, Knt. The former,

WILLIAM DE WINDSOR, was seated at Stanwell. He *m.* Margaret, sister of Sir John Drokensford, Knt., and dying 7th EDWARD I., was *s.* by his eldest son,

SIR RICHARD DE WINDSOR, who served in several parliaments for Berkshire and Middlesex. He was summoned with other great men to attend the king at Berwick-upon-Tweed, well appointed with horse and arms, to march against the Scots. He *m.* 1st, Julian, dau. of Sir Nicholas Stapleton, Knt., of Hachilsay, co. York, and by her had two sons, RICHARD, his heir, and William, in holy orders, rector of Stanwell. Sir Richard had no issue by his 2nd wife, Joan, and dying 19th EDWARD II., was *s.* by his eldest son,

RICHARD DE WINDSOR, M.P. for Berks and Middlesex, who *m.* thrice, having male issue only by his 2nd wife, Julian (dau. and co-heir of James Molyns, of co. Hants, by Margaret, his wife, dau. and co-heir of William de Bintworth), two sons,

JAMES, his heir.

William (Sir). a great military commander, who distinguished himself in the wars in Ireland (of which country he was appointed lieutenant, 43rd EDWARD III.), Scotland, and France, and was summoned as a baron of the realm, 24 March, 4th RICHARD II., to the parliament holden at Northampton. His lordship *d.* without male issue, 15 September, 8th RICHARD II., leaving his three sisters, heirs to his estates, Isabel ; Christian, wife of Sir William Morleux, Knt. ; and Margery, wife of John Duket.

Sir Richard *d.* 1367, and was *s.* by his eldest son,

SIR JAMES DE WINDSOR, of Stanwell, knighted by EDWARD III., who *m.* Elizabeth, dau. and co-heir of Sir John Streehie, Knt., of Wombro, Wilts, and *d.* 2 October, 44th EDWARD III., leaving an only son and heir,

SIR MILES WINDSOR, Knt., who was a Witness at the Scrope and Grosvernor Controversy. He *m.* Alice, dau. of Adam de Wymondham, of Wymondham, co. Norfolk, and was *s.* by his son,

BRIAN DE WINDSOR, who, by Alice, his wife, dau. of Thomas Drewe, Esq., of Segrave, co. Leicester, had two sons : Miles, the heir, *d. unm.*, and was *s.* by his brother,

RICHARD DE WINDSOR, who *m.* Christian, dau. of Richard Falconer, and had an only son and heir,

MILES DE WINDSOR, went on a pilgrimage to the Holy Land, and *d.* on the way, 30 September, 1451, leaving, by Joan, his wife, dau. of Walter Green, Esq., of Bridgenorth, a son and heir,

THOMAS WINDSOR, Esq., of Stanwell, who *m.* Elizabeth, elder of the two daus. and co-heirs of John Andrews, Esq. of Baylham, co. Suffolk, by Elizabeth, his wife, dau. and co-heir of John Stratton, Esq., and Elizabeth, dau. and heir of Sir Hugh Luttrell, and by her (who *m.* 2ndly, Sir Robert Litton, Knt.), had issue. He *d.* 1st HENRY VII., and was *s.* by his eldest surviving son,

SIR ANDREWS WINDSOR, K.B., of Stanwell, who, in June, 1513, embarked with the king in his expedition to France, and having distinguished himself at the siege of Terrouenne and subsequent battle, was created a knight banneret. In the following year he was one of the knights banneret who attended the Princess Mary, sister to HENRY VIII., on her marriage with LEWIS XII. of France. In 1529 Sir Andrews was summoned to parliament by writ addressed " Andreæ de Windsore," and 1 December in that year, took his seat. His lordship *m.* Elizabeth, dau. of William Blount, and sister and co-heir of Edward Blount, Lord Montjoy, and had issue,

George, who *m.* Ursula, dau. of Sir George Vere, Knt., and sister and co-heir of John Vere, 14th Earl of Oxford, but *d. s. p., v. p.* His widow *m.* Sir Edmund Knightley.

WILLIAM, successor to his father.

Edmund (Sir). of Stoke Poges, co. Bucks, who had issue, Robert, Andrew, Miles, Ursula, and Agnes.

Thomas, of Bentley, who *m.* Mary, dau. and heir of Thomas Bokenham, of Burscott, Berks, and by her had issue, seven sons and three daus.

Elizabeth, *m.* to Sir Peter Vavasour, of Spaldington, co. York.

Anne, *m.* to Roger Corbet, of Moreton, co. Salop

Ed th, *m.* to George Ludlow, Esq., of Hill Deverell, co. Wilts.

Eleanor, *m.* 1st, to Ralph, Lord Scrope, of Upsall ; and 2ndly, to Sir Edward Neville, son of George, Lord Abergavenny, and by the latter was mother of Edward, Lord Abergavenny, ancestor of the present earl, and Sir Henry Nevill, Knt., of Billingbeare, ancestor of Lord Braybrook.

His lordship (probate to whose will bears date 31 July, 1543,) was *s.* by his 2nd but eldest surviving son,

WILLIAM WINDSOR, 2nd Lord Windsor, K.B., who built the Manor House of Bradenham. He *m.* 1st, Margaret, dau. and heir of William Sambourne, Esq., of Southcote, co. Berks, and by her had numerous issue. Of his daus., the youngest, Anne, *m.* Henry Grey, of Pergo, Essex, who was lineal male heir of Henry, Duke of Suffolk and created by JAMES I., BARON GREY, *of Groby*, and was ancestor of the present Earl of Stamford. Lord Windsor *m.* 2ndly, Elizabeth, 2nd dau. and co-heir of Peter Cowdrey, of Heriott, or Herriard, co. Hants, and widow of Richard Powlet, Esq., and by her had a son and dau., who survived him, but *d. s. p.* His lordship *d.* 20 August, 1558, and was buried with great pomp at Bradenham: his eldest surviving son,

SIR EDWARD WINDSOR, 3rd Lord Windsor, distinguished at the siege of St. Quintin, entertained Queen ELIZABETH at Bradenham, in 1566, when Miles Windsor, a kinsman of his lordship, spoke a Latin oration to Her Majesty's infinite satisfaction. Lord Windsor *m.* Catherine, dau of John Vere, Earl of Oxford, by Dorothy, his wife, dau. of Ralph, Earl of Westmoreland, and dying 24 January, 1574, was *s.* by his eldest son,

FREDERICK WINDSOR, 4th Lord Windsor, who dying *unm.* 24 December, 1585, was *s.* by his brother,

HENRY WINDSOR, 5th Lord Windsor, who *d.* 6 April, 1605, leaving by Anne, his wife, dau. and co-heir of Thomas Rivet, Esq., of Chippenham, a son and two daus., viz.,

I. THOMAS.

I. Elizabeth, sen., *m.* to Dixie Hickman, Esq., of Kew, Surrey, eldest son, by Elizabeth, his wife, dau. of Nicholas Staines, of Essex, of Walter Hickman, Esq., 3rd son of Anthony Hickman, Esq., of London, by Rose, his wife, dau. of Sir William Leake, and heir to her mother, Catherine, sister and co-heir of Sir Thomas Cooke, Knt., of Wiltshire, and had issue, a son and two daus.,

THOMAS WINDSOR, who *s.* his maternal uncle as 7th Lord Windsor, and was created Earl of Plymouth, as hereafter.

Mariana. *m.* to Sir Henry Hunlocke, of Winzerworth, Bart.

Catherine, *m.* to John Columbine, Esq.

II. Elizabeth, the younger, *m.* 1st, to Andrew Windsor; and 2ndly, to Sir James Ware.

The son and heir,

THOMAS WINDSOR, 6th Lord Windsor, was one of the noblemen chosen to be knights of the Bath, in 1610, at the creation of Henry, Prince of Wales. He was subsequently rear-admiral of the fleet sent by King JAMES to bring Prince Charles out of Spain, and, on that occasion, entertained on board-ship the Grandees of the Court of Spain, with princely magnificence. His lordship *m.* Catherine. dau. of Edward, Earl of Worcester, but *d. s. p.* 6 December, 1642, when he was *s.* in all his possessions, and at length in his peerage, by his nephew (son of his elder sister, Elizabeth,)

THOMAS WINDSOR-HICKMAN, who became 7th Lord Windsor, and by letters patent dated 6 December, 1682, was advanced to the dignity and degree of EARL OF PLYMOUTH. He *m.* 1st, Anne, dau. of Sir William Savile, Bart., of Thornhill, co. York, and sister to George, Marquess of Halifax, and by her had a son and dau., OTHER, his heir, and Mary, *m.* to Sir Thomas Cookes, Bart., of Bentley. His lordship *m.* 2ndly, Ursula, youngest dau. and co-heir of Sir Thomas Widdrington, Knt. of Sherburne Grange, co. Northumberland, and by her had issue to survive, viz.,

THOMAS, created Viscount Windsor, in Ireland, 19 June, 1699, and Baron Montjoy, in the Isle of Wight, 31 December, 1711, both of which titles are now EXTINCT. (*See* WINDSOR, Baron Montjoy.)

Dixey, *b.* 1672, Fellow of Trinity College. Cambridge, and M.P. for the university in six succeeding parliaments. He *m.* Dorothy, youngest dau. of Sir Richard Stote, Knt., and co-heir of her brother, but *d. s. p.,* 20 October, 1743.

Andrews, brigadier-gen. in the army, M.P.

Ursula, *m.* in 1703, to Thomas Johnson, Esq., of Walthamstowe, Essex.

Elizabeth, *m.* to Sir Francis Dashwood, Bart.

The Earl of Plymouth *d.* 3 November, 1687, and was *s.* by his grandson, son of his eldest son Other (who *d. v. p.,* 11 November, 1684), by Elizabeth, his wife, dau. and eventually sole heir of Thomas Turvey, Esq., of Walcote, co. Worcester,

OTHER, 2nd Earl of Plymouth, *b.* 27 August, 1679, who *m.* Elizabeth, dau. and heir of Thomas Whitley, Esq., of Peel, co. Chester, and *d.* 28 December, 1727, when he was *s.* by his elder son and heir,

OTHER, 3rd Earl of Plymouth, *b.* 30 June, 1707, who *m.* Elizabeth, only dau. and heir of Thomas Lewis, Esq. of Soberton, co. Hants, and dying 23 November, 1732, was *s.* by his only son and heir,

OTHER-LEWIS, 4th Earl of Plymouth, *b.* in 1731, who *m.* in 1750, Katherine, dau. of Thomas, Lord Archer, and had

i. OTHER-HICKMAN, his heir.
ii. ANDREWS 7th earl.
iii. HENRY, 8th earl.
iv. Thomas, R.N., b. in 1752; d. in 1832.
i. Katharine-Sidney, m. to Sir James Tilney Long, Bart.
ii. Elizabeth, m. to Gore Townsend, Esq. of Honington.
iii. Anne, m. in 1787, to Sir Thomas Broughton, Bart.
iv. Sarah, m. to Sir William Champion de Crespigny, Bart.

The earl d. 20 April, 1771, and was s. by his son,
OTHER-HICKMAN, 5th Earl of Plymouth, b. in 1751, who m. in 1778, Sarah, dau. and co-heir of Andrew, Lord Archer, and by her (who m. 2ndly, William Pitt, Earl Amherst), had,

    OTHER-ARCHER 6th earl.
Maria, m. 25 October, 1811, to Arthur, 3rd Marquess of Downshire, and d. his widow, 7 April, 1855.
Harriet (BARONESS WINDSOR), m. in 1819, to Hon. Robert-Henry Clive, who d. 20 January, 1854.

The earl d. 12 June, 1799, and was s. by his son,
OTHER-ARCHER, 6th Earl of Plymouth, b. in 1789; who m. in 1811, Mary, eldest dau. of John-Frederick Sackville, 3rd Duke of Dorset, but by her (who m. 2ndly, William Pitt, Earl Amherst,) had no issue. He d. 10 July, 1833, when the Barony of Windsor fell into ABEYANCE between his two sisters, and remained so until terminated in 1855, in favour of Lady Harriet Clive, now Baroness Windsor. The earldom devolved on his uncle,
ANDREWS, 7th Earl of Plymouth, b. in 1789, who d. unm. 19 January, 1837, and was s. by his brother,
HENRY, 8th Earl of Plymouth, b. 1 February, 1768, who m. 12 July, 1798, Ann, dau. of Thomas Copson, Esq., and d. s. p. 8 December, 1843, when the earldom of Plymouth became EXTINCT. His lordship's widow d. 30 January, 1850.

Arms—Gu., a saltier, arg., between twelve cross-crosslets, or.

WINDSOR — VISCOUNTS WINDSOR AND BARONS MONTJOY.

Barony by Letters Patent, dated 31 December, 1711.
Viscounty of Ireland by Letters Patent, dated 19 June, 1699.

Lineage.

WALTER BLOUNT, 1st Lord Montjoy of Thurveston, co. Derby, and lord treasurer of England, m. 1st, Helen, dau. of Sir John Byron, of Clayton; and 2ndly, Anne, relict of Humphrey, Duke of Buckingham, and had by the former three sons, viz.,

i. WILLIAM BLOUNT, who m. Margaret Echingham, and dying v. p. left issue,
  1 EDWARD BLOUNT, 2nd Lord Montjoy, who d. aged eight, in 1475.
  2 Elizabeth, m. to Sir Andrews Windsor, K.B., of the old baronial family of Windsor, who was summoned to parliament, as BARON WINDSOR, in 1529.
  3 Anne, m. 1st, Thomas Oxenbridge, and 2ndly, Sir David Owen, of Midhurst. By the former she had three daus co-heirs, viz., Margaret, m. to John St. Paul: Katherine, m. to Sir Thomas Thimelby, of Irnham; and Elizabeth, m. to William Munson, of Saulton.
ii. JOHN BLOUNT, 3rd Lord Montjoy (see p. 55.)
iii. James Blount, knight banneret.

From the above Elizabeth Blount, and her husband, Andrews, Lord Windsor, lineally descended (see WINDSOR, EARL OF PLYMOUTH),
THOMAS WINDSOR, 6th Baron Windsor, K.B., who d. s. p. in 1642, when the Barony of Windsor fell into ABEYANCE between his two sisters, viz.,

Elizabeth, sen., m. to Dixie Hickman, Esq., and had issue,
  THOMAS HICKMAN, who inherited his uncle's estates.
Elizabeth, jun., m. 1st, Andrews Windsor, and 2ndly, Sir James Ware.

And it so remained until called out by the crown, 16 June, 1660, in favour of the above-named
THOMAS HICKMAN, as 7th Baron Windsor, who thereupon assumed the additional surname of WINDSOR, and was created 6 December, 1682, Earl of Plymouth. His lordship m. 1st, Anne, dau. of Sir William Savile, Bart., of Thornhill, co. York, by whom he had a son, OTHER, who d. v. p., leaving a son, OTHER, who inherited the Earldom of Plymouth, &c. The earl m. 2ndly, Ursula, dau. and co-heir of Sir Thomas Widdrington, of Sherburn Grange, co. Northumberland, and had, with other issue, a son,
THOMAS WINDSOR, who, having distinguished himself in the wars of Flanders, was created, by King WILLIAM III. a peer of Ireland in the dignity of *Viscount Windsor*, and made a baron

---

of the realm by Queen ANNE, 31 December, 1711, as Lord MONTJOY, *of the Isle of Wight.* His lordship m. Charlotte, widow of John Jeffries, 2nd Baron Jeffries, of Wem, and only dau. and heir of Philip Herbert, Earl of Pembroke, by whom he had surviving issue,

HERBERT, his successor.
Ursula, m. to John Wadman. Esq., of Imber, co. Wilts.
Charlotte, m. to John Kent, Esq., of Salisbury
Catherine, m. in Holland.   Elizabeth.

He d. in 1738, and was s. by his son,
HERBERT WINDSOR, 2nd Baron Montjoy, and 2nd Viscount Windsor. This nobleman m. Alice, sister and co-heir of Sir James Clavering, Bart., and left two daus., his co-heirs, viz.,

CHARLOTTE-JANE, m. 12 November, 1766, John, 1st Marquess of Bute, and d. 28 January, 1800, leaving issue (see BURKE's *Extant Peerage*).
ALICE-ELIZABETH, m. 1768, Francis, Viscount Beauchamp, eldest son of Francis, Earl of Hertford, and died without surviving issue, in 1772.

His lordship d. in 1758, when all his honours in default of male issue, became EXTINCT.

Arms—Gu., a saltire, arg., between twelve cross-crosslets, or, a crescent for difference.

WINGFIELD—VISCOUNT POWERSCOURT.

(See BURKE's *Extant Peerage*, article "POWERSCOURT.")

WOLFE — BARONS AND VISCOUNTS KILWARDEN.

Baronies, by Letters Patent, dated 30 September, 1795, and 3 July, 1798.
Viscounty by Letters Patent, dated 29 December, 1800.

Lineage.

RICHARD WOLFE, Esq., of Forenaghts, co. Kildare, son of John Wolfe, Esq., and his wife, Mary Cowper, m. Lydia Page, and had with other issue,

i. JOHN, of whom presently.
ii. THOMAS, of Blackhall, co. Kildare, who m. 1733, Margaret Lombard, and was father of
THEOBALD WOLFE, Esq., of Blackhall, who m. Frances, dau. of Rev. Peter Lombard, and had issue; Peter; James; Edward; Richard; Charles; Mary; and Margaret; the youngest son, the Rev. Charles Wolfe, b. in Dublin, 14 December, 1791, was author of the exquisite elegy on the death of Sir John Moore; another of the sons was MAJOR JAMES WOLFE, who m. Elizabeth Walker, and d. 9 July, 1840, leaving, with four daus., three sons, GEORGE, of Bishop Land, J.P. co. Kildare; John-Charles, rector of Ematris; and Charles, late British chaplain at Havre (see BURKE's *Landed Gentry*).

The elder son,
JOHN WOLFE, Esq., of Forenaghts, m. Mary, dau. of William Philpott, by his wife, a dau. of James Butler of Rathlin, and had with other issue,

i. PHILPOTT, of Forenaghts, m. Mary, dau. of Thomas Burgh, Esq., of Drumkeen, and had a son and successor, the late COLONEL JOHN WOLFE, of Forenaghts.
ii. ARTHUR, of whom we treat.

The 2nd son,
ARTHUR WOLFE, Esq., b. 30 January, 1739, having attained considerable eminence at the Irish bar, was nominated solicitor-general of Ireland in 1787, promoted to the attorney-generalship in 1789, and appointed lord chief justice of the court of King's Bench in 1798, when he was elevated to the peerage, 3 July, 1798, as BARON KILWARDEN, *of Newlands*, and advanced to the VISCOUNTY OF KILWARDEN, 29 December, 1800. His lordship m. in 1769, Anne, dau. of William Ruxton, Esq., of Ardee, co. Louth, M.P. (which lady was created BARONESS KILWARDEN, *of Kilteel*, 30 September, 1795, and d. 23 August, 1804), by whom he had issue,

JOHN, his heir.
Arthur, colonel in the army; d. unm., 29 June, 1805.
Marianna, m. to Hardwicke Shute, Esq., M.D., of Gloucester, and d. 1814.
Elizabeth, b. 31 August, 1778; d. 24 May, 1806.

Lord Kilwarden, one of the brightest ornaments of the Irish

bench, was murdered, while on his way to the castle of Dublin for the purpose of assisting in council, 23 July, 1803, during the riot incited by Emmet; his lordship, falling accidentally into the hands of a body of insurgents, was barbarously assassinated, along with his nephew and companion, the Rev. Mr. Wolfe. His son and successor,

JOHN WOLFE, 2nd Viscount Kilwarden, b. 11 November, 1769, registrar of deeds in Ireland, s. to the Barony of Kilwarden of Kilteel at the death of his mother. He d. s. p., 16 May, 1830, and with him the honours became EXTINCT.

Arms—Arg., three wolves' heads, erased, sa., ducally gorged, or; a crescent for difference.

WOOD—BARON HATHERLEY.

(*See* BURKE's *Extant Peerage*, WOOD, Bart.)

WOTTON—BARONS WOTTON.

By Letters Patent, dated 13 May, 1603.

Lineage.

SIR NICHOLAS WOTTON, son of William Wotton, Esq., by his wife, Mary Wyverton, and grandson of John Wotton, was an alderman of London, of which he served as sheriff, 8th HENRY IV., and was twice lord mayor. He m. Joane, only dau. and heir of Robert Corbye, Esq., of Boughton Malherbe, by Alice, his wife, dau. and co-heir of Sir John Gousal, Knt., and acquired with this lady the manor of Boughton Malherbe. He d. 14 September, 1448, æt. seventy-six, and was s. by his son and heir,

NICHOLAS WOTTON, Esq., of Boughton Place, who m. Elizabeth, dau. and heir of John Bamburgh, Esq., of Paddlesworth, and dying 9 April, 1499, was s. by his son,

SIR ROBERT WOTTON, of Bocton Malherbe, who had been knighted by King EDWARD IV., who made him lieutenant of Guisnes, and knight porter and comptroller of Calais, where he died. He m. Anne, dau. of Sir Henry Belknap, and sister and co-heir of Sir Edward Belknap, Knt., and by her had issue, viz.,

I. EDWARD (Sir).
II. Nicholas, doctor of laws, who was of the privy council, and one of the executors to the will of King HENRY VIII., and was frequently accredited on diplomatic missions to the courts of France, Spain, and Germany. In the reign of EDWARD VI. he was one of the principal secretaries of state, as he was afterwards in the reigns of MARY and ELIZABETH. He was a person of great learning, being versed in the Latin, French, Italian, and German languages. He d. unm. 26 January, 1586, aged seventy, and was buried in the cathedral church at Canterbury, where a splendid monument was erected to his memory by his nephew, Thomas Wotton, Esq.
I. Idonea, m. to Thomas Norton.
II. Margaret, m. 1st to William Medley; and 2ndly, to Thomas Grey, Marquess of Dorset.
III. Mary, m. 1st, to Sir Henry Guldeford; and 2ndly, to Sir Gawen Carew.

The elder son,

SIR EDWARD WOTTON, b. 1489, was a member of the privy council, temp. HENRY VIII., and treasurer of the town and marches of Calais. He was likewise one of the executors to King HENRY, and named by that prince of the council to his son, Prince Edward: "being," says Dugdale, "of such great abilities, that he might have been lord chancellor of England, but that he modestly declined it." Sir Edward m. 1st, Dorothy, 4th dau. and co-heir of Sir Robert Read, Knt., justice of the common pleas, and 2ndly, Ursula, dau. of Sir Robert Dymoke, Knt., and widow of Sir John Rudston, Knt., lord mayor of London, but left issue only by the former, three sons, and one dau., of whom, THOMAS, the eldest, s. him; William, the 3rd son, m. Mary, dau. of John Dannet, and d. s. p., and the dau. Anne, m. 1st, James Cromer, Esq., and 2ndly, Robert Rudston, Esq. Sir Edward d. 8 November, 1550, and was s. by his son,

THOMAS WOTTON, Esq., b. 1521, who served as high sheriff both during the reigns of MARY and ELIZABETH, and had the honour of entertaining the latter sovereign with her whole court, in July, 1573, in her Majesty's progress through Kent. He m. 1st, Elizabeth, dau. of Sir John Rudstone, of Bocton Monchensy, and had issue,

EDWARD, his successor.
Robert, d. s. p., v. p.
James, who received the honour of knighthood for his gallantry in the expedition to Cadiz, temp. ELIZABETH, d. 20 October, 1628.
John, knighted by Queen ELIZABETH, m. Lucy, sister of Henry Percy, Earl of Northumberland, but d. s. p.
Henry (Sir), knighted by JAMES I., d. v. p.
Elizabeth, m. John Dering, of Egerton, co. Kent.

He m. 2ndly, Eleanor, dau. of Sir William Finch, of Eastwell, in Kent, and widow of Robert Morton, and had another son,

Henry, who was knighted by King JAMES I., and sent thrice ambassador to Venice; once to the States General, twice to the court of Savoy, and upon several other equally important diplomatic missions. Sir Henry was subsequently appointed provost of Eton College, and d. in December, 1639.

Mr. Wotton d. 11 January, 1587, and was s. by his eldest son,

SIR EDWARD WOTTON, Knt., b. 1548. This gentleman, having been accredited as ambassador to the court of Portugal, was elevated to the peerage by King JAMES I., by letters patent, dated 13 May, 1603, as BARON WOTTON, of Maherly, or Marley, co. Kent. His lordship, like the other members of his family, was distinguished by great mental powers and superior attainments. He m. 1st. Hesther, dau. and co-heir of Sir William Puckering, Knt., of Oswald Kirk, co. York, and 2ndly, Margaret, dau. of Philip, Lord Wharton, and by the former only had issue to survive him, viz., a son, THOMAS, his successor, and a dau., Philippa, who m. Sir Edmund Bacon, Bart. He was s. at his decease, about 1604, by his son,

THOMAS WOTTON, 2nd baron. This nobleman m. Mary, dau. and co-heir of Sir Arthur Throckmorton, of Paulers Perry, in Northamptonshire, and had issue,

I. Katherine, who m. 1st, Henry, Lord Stanhope, by whom who predeceased his father, she was mother of
  Philip, 2nd Earl of Chesterfield.
  Mary, d. unm.
  Katherine, m. to William, Lord Alington.
Her ladyship m. 2ndly, John Poliander Kirckhoven, Lord of Heenvliett, in Holland, and had a son,
  CHARLES-HENRY KIRCKHOVEN, who was created BARON WOTTON, of Wotton, 31 August, 1650, EARL OF BELLAMONT, in Ireland, 11 February, 1680. He m. Frances, dau. of William, Lord Willoughby, of Parham, and widow of Sir John Harpur, Bart., of Calke, co. Derby, but d. s. p. 5 January, 1682, when these dignities became EXTINCT.
She m. 3rdly, Colonel Daniel O'Neile, one of the grooms of the bed-chamber to CHARLES II. Her ladyship was governess to the Princess of Orange, dau. of King CHARLES I., and attending her highness into Holland, sent over money, arms, and ammunition to his Majesty's aid, for which service she was created, by CHARLES II., COUNTESS OF CHESTERFIELD, for life.
II. Hesther, m. to Baptist, Viscount Campden: the heir-general of this co-heiress of Lord Wotton, was the late D ke of Devonshire, K.G.
III. Margaret, m. to Sir John Tufton. Knt.
IV. Anne, m. to Sir Edward Hales, Knt., of Tunstall, Kent.

His lordship d. at Bocton, 2 April, 1630, aged forty-two, when the Barony of Wotton, in default of male issue, became EXTINCT.

Arms—Arg., a cross-patée fitchée, sa.

WOTTON—COUNTESS OF CHESTERFIELD.

By Letters Patent, dated 29 May, 1660.

Lineage.

KATHERINE WOTTON, eldest dau. and co-heir of Thomas Wotton, 2nd Lord Wotton, of Marley, and widow of Henry, Lord Stanhope, was created, by King CHARLES II., COUNTESS OF CHESTERFIELD for life, 29 May, 1660. She m. 2ndly, John Kirckhoven, alias Poliander, Lord of Heenvliett, in Holland, and 3rdly, Colonel Daniel O'Neile. Her ladyship d. in 1667, when the title became EXTINCT (see WOTTON, Barons Wotton).

WRIOTHESLEY—BARONS WRIOTHESLEY, EARLS OF SOUTHAMPTON, EARLS OF CHICHESTER.

Barony, by Letters Patent, dated 1 January, 1544.
Earldom, by Letters Patent, dated 16 February, 1547.
Earldom of Chichester, by Letters Patent, dated 3 June, 1644

Lineage.

Of this family the first mentioned,

JOHN WRIOTHESLEY (commonly called *Wrythe*), was Faucon Herald in the reign of EDWARD IV., and had letters patent for the office of Garter King of Arms, in the 1st RICHARD III. He had two sons,

THOMAS, who was first a Herald, by thet itle of *Wallingford*, and in the 20th HENRY VII. was constituted Garter King of Arms.

William, was also a member of the College of Arms as York Herald.

The younger son,

WILLIAM WRIOTHESLEY, York Herald, left a son,

THOMAS WRIOTHESLEY, who, in the 27th HENRY VIII., was made coroner and attorney in the court of common pleas; and in three years afterwards, being then one of the principal secretaries of state, was sent ambassador to treat of a marriage between his royal master and Christiana, 2nd dau. of the King of Denmark. In the 32nd of the same reign, subsequently to his having had the honour of knighthood, he was made constable of the castle of Southampton. He was soon afterwards accredited one of the commissioners to treat with the Emperor CHARLES V., and he was elevated to the peerage, by letters patent, dated 1 January, 1544, in the dignity of BARON WRIOTHESLEY, of *Titchfield, co. Hants;* which *Titchfield* was one of the dissolved monasteries he had obtained by grant from the crown. Soon after this, upon the decease of Lord Audley, his lordship was constituted Lord Chancellor of England, and the same year he was made a knight of the Garter. He was subsequently appointed, by King HENRY, one of his executors, and named of the council to his son EDWARD VI.; three days before whose coronation he was created, by letters patent, dated 16 February, 1547, EARL OF SOUTHAMPTON. His lordship did not long, however, maintain his influence in this reign. Prior to the accession of the king he was opposed to the Duke of Somerset, and he had little chance, under the new order of affairs of sustaining himself against so powerful a rival. The earl, in order that he might have the greater leisure to attend to public business, had, of his own authority, put the great seal into commission, and had empowered four lawyers, two of whom were canonists, to execute, in his absence, the duties of his high office. Complaints were made of this irregularity to the council, which, influenced by the Protector, readily seized the opportunity to depress his lordship. The Judges were consulted upon the occasion, and gave it as their opinion, that the commission was illegal, and that the chancellor, by his presumption in granting it, had justly forfeited the great seal, and had even subjected himself to punishment. His lordship was immediately cited before the council, and, notwithstanding a most able defence, it was declared that he had forfeited the chancellorship, that a fine should be imposed upon him, and that he be confined to his own house during the king's pleasure. This eminent person was esteemed a man of learning, a good lawyer, and a most excellent chancellor. He was accustomed to observe, that "*Force awed, but justice governed the world;*" and that "he loved a bishop to satisfy his conscience, a lawyer to guide his judgment, a good family to keep up his interest, and an university to preserve his name." He *m.* Jane, dau. and heir of William Cheney, Esq., and had issue,

HENRY, his successor.

Mary, *m.* 1st. to William Shelley, Esq., of Michelgrove, Sussex, and 2ndly, to the son and heir of Sir Michael Lyster, Knt.

Elizabeth, *m.* to Thomas Ratcliffe, Earl of Sussex.

Katherine, *m.* to Thomas Cornwallis, Esq.

Mabel, *m.* to Sir Walter Sands, Knt.

Anne, *m.* to Sir Oliver Lawrence, Knt.

His lordship *d.* in 1550, and was *s.* by his son,

HENRY WRIOTHESLEY, 2nd Earl of Southampton. This nobleman was a friend of Thomas, Duke of Norfolk, and involved himself in trouble by promoting the contemplated marriage of that nobleman with MARY Queen of Scots, "to whom and her religion (says Dugdale) he stood not a little affected." He *m.* Mary, dau. of Anthony Browne, Viscount Montagu, and had issue,

HENRY, Lord Wriothesley.

Mary, *m.* to Thomas, Lord Arundell, of Wardour.

His lordship *d.* in 1581, and was *s.* by his son,

HENRY WRIOTHESLEY, 3rd Earl of Southampton. This nobleman was the companion in arms of the Earl of Essex, and a participator in the treason by which that unhappy nobleman forfeited his life in the reign of ELIZABETH. Lord Southampton was also tried, condemned, and attainted, but his life was spared; and upon the accession of King JAMES I., he was released from prison, restored in blood by act of parliament, and created by a new patent, dated 21 July, 1603, EARL OF SOUTHAMPTON, with the same rights, precedency, and privileges that he had formerly enjoyed. He was also made a knight of the Garter, and constituted captain of the Isle of Wight, and castle of Carisbroke. His lordship *m.* Elizabeth, dau. of John Vernon, Esq., of Hodnet, co. Derby, by Elizabeth, sister of Walter Devereux, 1st Earl of Essex, and dying in 1624, left issue,

THOMAS, Lord Wriothesley.

Penelope, *m.* to William, Lord Spencer, of Wormleighton.

Anne, *m.* to Robert Wallop, Esq., M.P., of Farley Wallop, co. Southampton.

Elizabeth, *m.* to Sir Thomas Estcourt, Knt., one of the Masters in Chancery.

The earl was *s.* by his son,

THOMAS WRIOTHESLEY, 4th Earl of Southampton, who was a staunch supporter of King CHARLES I., was installed a knight of the Garter at the Restoration, and was constituted lord treasurer of England. His lordship *m.* 1st, Rachel, dau. of Daniel de Massu, Baron de Ruvigny, in France, by whom he had two sons, who both *d.* young, and three daus., viz.,

Elizabeth, *m.* to Edward Noel, eldest son of Baptist, Viscount Campden.

Rachael, *m.* 1st, to Francis, son and heir of Richard, Earl of Carbery, in Ireland, and 2ndly, to the celebrated patriot, William, Lord Russell, beheaded in 1683, son of William, 5th Earl of Bedford.

Magdalen, who *d.* young.

He *m.* 2ndly, Frances, dau. of Francis Leigh, Baron Dunsmore, which nobleman, was created, 3 June, 1644, EARL OF CHICHESTER, with remainder, failing his own male issue, to his son-in-law, the Earl of Southampton and the heirs male of his body by his lordship's dau., the said Frances Leigh. He *d.* in 1653, and the honours of Lord Southampton, were then augmented by the Earldom of Chichester. By this lady, his lordship had four daus.,

Audrey, who *d. unm.*

Penelope, *d.* young.

Elizabeth, *m.* 1st, Josceline, Earl of Northumberland, and 2ndly, to Ralph, Duke of Montagu, of Boughton.

Penelope, *d.* in infancy.

The earl *m.* 3rdly, Frances, dau. of William, Duke of Somerset, and widow of Richard, Viscount Molineux, but had no issue. He *d.* at Southampton House, "near Holburne, in the suburbs of London," 16 May, 1667, when all his honours, including the Earldom of Chichester, became EXTINCT.

Arms—Az., a cross, or, between four falcons close, arg.

WYKEHAM—BARONESS WENMAN.

(*See* ADDENDA.)

WYNDHAM—EARL OF EGREMONT.

By Letters Patent, dated 3 October, 1749.

Lineage.

This noble family claimed descent from Ailwardus, an eminent Saxon of the co. Norfolk, who, being possessed of an estate there, in Wymondham (subsequently called Wyndham), is stated to have assumed, soon after the Norman Conquest, the surname of WYNDHAM.

WILLIAM, son of RALPH DE WIMONDHAM, was possessed 10th EDWARD II., of the manors of Crownthorpe and Wicklewode, co. Norfolk, and in which he was *s.* by his son,

SIR JOHN DE WIMONDHAM, who *m.* Catherine, dau. of Sir John de Redisham. Knt., and was father of

THOMAS DE WIMONDHAM, who *m.* Margaret, dau. of Sir Robert Walcot, Knt., and had a son, JOHN, whose son, another JOHN WIMONDHAM, *m.* Margaret, dau. of Sir John Segrave, Knt., and was father of

JOHN WYNDHAM, Esq., of Crownthorpe, and of Felbrigg, which latter he purchased of the trustees of Sir John Felbrigg, K.G. This John Wyndham, in the 38th HENRY VI., being one of the knights for the co. Norfolk in the parliament held at Coventry, wherein the Earl of Warwick, and other accomplices of the Duke of York, were attainted of high treason. He *m.* Margery, dau. of Sir Robert Clifton, of Bokenham Castle, co. Norfolk, and relict of Sir John Hastings, and was *s.* by his son,

SIR JOHN WYNDHAM, who was in the battle of Stoke, *anno* 1487, against the Earl of Lincoln, Lambert Simnel, and their adherents, and was knighted immediately after the victory; but being afterwards engaged in the interests of the house of York, he was condemned for high treason, and beheaded, with Sir James Tyrrell, lieutenant of Guisnes Castle, 17th HENRY VII. Sir John Wyndham *m.* 1st, Margaret, dau. of John Howard, Duke of Norfolk, by whom he had THOMAS, his successor, and other children. He *m.* 2ndly, Eleanor, dau. of Norman Washbourne, Esq., of Washbourne, co. Worcester, and widow of Sir Richard Scrope. Sir John was *s.* by his eldest son,

SIR THOMAS WYNDHAM, of Felbrigg, who was a distinguished naval commander, and attended King HENRY VIII., as one of the knights of his body at the siege of Therounne and Tournay, &c. He *m.* 1st, Eleanor, dau and co-heir of Sir Richard Scrope, Knt., of Upsal, co. York, by whom he had issue,

I. EDMUND (Sir), of Felbrigg. This gentleman obtained from HENRY VIII., with whom he was a favourite, large grants out of the confiscated church lands. He *m.* Susan, dau. of Sir Roger Townshend, of Raynham, Norfolk, and was *s.* by his son,

   FRANCIS (Sir), barrister-at-law, who was made one of the judges of the Court of Common Pleas, 21st ELIZABETH. His lordship and his two brothers dying *s. p.*, Felbrigg and other estates devolved upon the heirs of their uncle, JOHN, of whom presently.

II. JOHN (Sir), of Orchard Wyndham.
  I Margaret, *m.* to Sir Andrew Luttrell, Knt., of Dunster Castle, co. Somerset
  II. Mary, *m.* to Sir Erasmus Paston, Knt., ancestor of the Earls of Yarmouth.
  III. Elizabeth, *d. s. p.*

Sir Thomas *m.* 2ndly, Elizabeth, dau. of Sir Henry Wentworth, K.B., of Nettlested, and relict of Sir Roger D'Arcy, by whom he had one son, Sir Thomas Wyndham, an eminent naval officer. The line of the eldest son of Sir Thomas failing as above, we proceed with the 2nd son,

SIR JOHN WYNDHAM, who was knighted at the coronation of EDWARD VI., he *m.* Elizabeth, dau. and co-heir of John Sydenham, Esq., of Orchard, co. Somerset, and thus acquired that estate which now retains the name of Orchard-Wyndham. Sir John had (with four daus., Margaret, *m.* to John Fraunceis; Eleanor, *m.* to Thomas Carne; Catherine, *m.* to Christopher Wood; and Elizabeth, *m.* to — Welch,) four sons,

I. JOHN, who *m.* Florence, dau. of John, and sister and co-heir of Nicholas Wadham, Esq., of Merrifield, co. Somerset (founder of Wadham College, Oxford,) by whom he left at his decease, 25 August, 1572, *s. p.*, an only son,
  JOHN (Sir), heir to his grandfather.

II. Edmund, of Kentsford, *m.* Mary, dau. and co-heir of Richard Chamberlaine, Esq., alderman of London, and had with other issue,
  Thomas (Sir), of Kentsford, *m.* Elizabeth, dau. of Richard Coningsby, Esq., of Hampton Court, and by her had several children; of the sons most of them were engaged in the service of CHARLES I. The 4th son,
    Colonel Francis Wyndham, is memorable for having conducted King CHARLES II., to his seat at Trent, after the battle of Worcester. Colonel Wyndham, for his devotion to the royal cause during the civil wars, was created a baronet. He *m.* Anne, dau. and co-heir of Thomas Gerard, Esq., of Trent, with whom he acquired that estate, and *d.* in 1676, leaving three sons,
    1 THOMAS (Sir), 2nd baronet, of Trent, whose only dau. and heir,
      ANNE, *m.* William James, Esq., of Ightham Court, in Kent, and was great-grandmother of DEMETRIUS-GREVIS JAMES, Esq., of Ightham Court. (*See* BURKE'S *Landed Gentry.*)
    2 Gerard, *d. unm.*
    3 FRANCIS (Sir), 3rd baronet; whose son. Thomas, *d. v. p.*, leaving a son, FRANCIS, 4th baronet, who *d.* young; and a dau., FRANCES. *m.* to Henry Bromley, Esq., afterwards Lord Montford.
    Hugh (Sir), 4th son, created a Baronet 4 August, 1641, but by Mary, his wife, dau. of Christopher Alanson, Esq., of London, leaving only daus. and co-heirs, his title became EXTINCT.

III. Humphrey, of Wiveliscombe, in Somersetshire, whose only dau. and heir, Elizabeth, *m.* John Colles, Esq., of Barton.
IV. Charles, ancestor of the WINDHAMS *of Sandhill.*

Sir John Wyndham was *s.* by his grandson,
SIR JOHN WYNDHAM, Knt., of Orchard-Wyndham, who *m.* Joan, dau. of Henry Portman, Esq., of Orchard, and had issue,

I. JOHN, his heir.
II. Henry, *d. unm.* 1613.
III. Thomas, of Felbrigg, ancestor of the distinguished statesman, the Right Hon. WILLIAM WINDHAM, of Felbrigg, who *d.* in 1810.
IV. Humphrey, ancestor of the WYNDHAMS, of Dunraven Castle, co. Glamorgan; his son, HUMPHREY WYNDHAM, Esq., of Dunraven Castle, *m.* Joan, dau. of Sir John Carne, of Ewenny Abbey, and was father of JOHN WYNDHAM, Serjeant-at-law, who *m.* Jane, dau. of William Strode, Esq., and had a son, JOHN WYNDHAM, Esq., whose dau. JANE, heiress of Dunraven, *m.* Thomas Wyndham, of Clearwell.
V. Hugh (Sir), of Silton, baron of the exchequer, and afterwards one of the justices of the common pleas, *d.* 1684, aged eighty-two. Sir Hugh *m.* thrice. 1st, June, dau. of Sir Thomas Wodehouse, Bart., of Kimberly; 2ndly, Elizabeth, dau. of Sir William Minn of Woodcote, co. Surrey, and relict of Sir Henry Berkeley, Bart.; and 3rdly, Catherine, dau. of Sir Thomas Fleming of Stoneham, and relict of Sir Edward Hooper, Knt., but had issue only by his 1st wife, two sons,

John and Hugh, both *d.* young. and three daus. Blanche, *m.* to Sir Nathanie' Napier, Bart. ; Joan, *d.* young; and Rachel, *m.* to John, Earl of Bristol.
VI. Wadham (Sir), one of the judges of the court of King's Bench, ancestor of Baron Wyndham, of Finglass (*see* that title); and of the WYNDHAMS, of Dinton, Salisbury, &c. (*See* BURKE'S *Landed Gentry.*)
VII. George, of Uffords, near Cromer. Norfo'k, *m.* twice, but had issue only by his 2nd wife, Frances, dau. and co-heir of James Davy, Esq., of Suffield, a son and successor,
  FRANCIS WYNDHAM, Esq., Lord of Uffords, *m.* Sarah, dau. of Sir Thomas Dayrell, of Shudy Camps, co. Cambridge, and dying 1694, left issue,
    FRANCIS, of Ufford's Manor, whose son, JOHN, of Cromer, *m.* Elizabeth, only child of Richard Dalton, Esq., and was ancestor of the WYNDHAMS, of Cromer Hall, co. Norfolk, extinct in the male line.
    Thomas, who *m.* 1st, Jane, dau. of John Wyndham, Esq., of Dunraven, and 2ndly, Anne, dau. and eventually heiress of Samuel Edwin, Esq., of Llanmihange, co. Glamorgan; he *d.* 1751, leaving by his 2nd wife, a son, CHARLES WYNDHAM, Esq., of Clearwell, who took the name of Edwin, and *d.* 1801, he *m.* Eleanor, dau. of George Rooke, Esq., of Bigswear, and was father of THOMAS WYNDHAM, Esq., of Dunraven Castle, who *m.* Anna-Maria-Charlotte, dau. of Thomas Ashby, Esq., and by her (who *m.* 2ndly, John-Wick Bennet, Esq., of Laleston) he left at his decease in 1814, an only dau. and heiress,
      CAROLINE WYNDHAM, wife of Windham-Henry, 2nd EARL OF DUNRAVEN.

I. Joan, *m.* to John Giffard, Esq. of Brightley.
II. Margaret, *m.* to John Courtenay, Esq. of Molland.
III. Florence, *m.* to John Harris, Esq. of Hayne.
IV. Rachel, *m.* to Thomas Moore, Esq of Heytesbury.
V. Margery, *m.* to Thomas Carew, Esq. of Crowcombe.
VI. Anne, *m.* to Sir John Strode, Knt.

Sir John *d.* 1645, aged eighty-seven, and was *s.* by his eldest son,
JOHN WYNDHAM, Esq., of Orchard Wyndham, *m.* Catherine, dau. and co-heir of Robert Hopton, Esq., of Witham, co. Somerset, and sister and co-heir of her brother Ralph, Lord Hopton, and dying 1649, left (with four daus., Florence, *m.* to Sir John Malet; Mary, *m.* to W. Okeden; Anne, *m.* to Anthony Bullen; and Catharine, *m.* 1st, to John Specot; and 2ndly, to John Tanner, a very eloquent Member of the House of Commons,) an eldest son,
WILLIAM WYNDHAM, Esq., of Orchard-Wyndham, who was created a Baronet, 9 September, 1661. This gentleman *m.* Frances, dau. of Anthony Hungerford, Esq., of Farley Castle, and had issue,

  EDWARD, his heir.
  Rachel, *m.* 1st, to Sir George Speke, Bart., of Haselbury; and 2ndly, to Richard Musgrave, Esq.
  Elizabeth, *m.* to General Thomas Erle, of Charborough, co. Dorset.
  Frances, *m.* to Nathaniel Palmer, Esq. of Fairfield.
  John, *m.* to William Cary, Esq., of Clovelly, co. Devon.

Sir William Wyndham dying in 1683, was *s.* by his son,
SIR EDWARD WYNDHAM, Bart., who *m.* Catherine, dau. of Sir William Leveson-Gower, Bart., and sister of John, Lord Gower, by whom he had a son WILLIAM, and a dau., Jane, *m.* to Sir Richard Grosvenor, Bart., of Eaton, and was *s.* by the former,
SIR WILLIAM WYNDHAM, Bart., of Orchard-Wyndham, *b.* 1687. This gentleman filled, in the reign of Queen ANNE, the high offices of master of the buckhounds, secretary-at-war, and chancellor of the exchequer, and was sworn of her Majesty's privy council. He *m.* 1st, Lady Catharine Seymour, 2nd dau. of Charles, 6th Duke of Somerset, K.G., by Lady Elizabeth Percy, his wife, and had two sons and two daus. His 2nd son, PERCY, succeeding to the estate of his uncle, Henry, Earl of Thomond, bore the surname and arms of O'BRIEN, and was created *Earl of Thomond, in Ireland.* Of Sir William's 2nd marriage with Maria-Catharina, dau. of Mr. Peter D'Jong, of the province of Utrecht, in Holland, and relict of William, Marquess of Blandford, there was no issue. He *d.* 17 June, 1740, after a few days' illness, and was *s.* by his eldest son,
SIR CHARLES WYNDHAM, Bart., who also succeeded, on the demise of his uncle, Algernon, Duke of Somerset, without male issue, 7 February, 1750, to the *barony of Cockermouth* and *earldom of Egremont,* his grace having obtained those dignities by patent, dated 3 October, 1749, with remainder to the sons of his sister, Lady Catherine Wyndham His lordship *m.* 12 March, 1750-1, Alicia-Maria, dau. of George, 2nd Lord Carpenter, by whom (who *m.* 2ndly, Count Bruhl, of Saxony, and *d.* 1 June, 1794,) he had issue,

I. GEORGE-O'BRIEN, 3rd earl.
II. Percy-Charles, *b.* 3 September, 1757; secretary and clerk of the courts and prothonotory of the Common Pleas in Barbadoes; *d. unm.* 5 August, 1833.

m. Charles-William, *b.* 8 October, 1760; *m.* in 1801, Lady Anne-Barbara-Frances Lambton, 2nd dau. of George-Bussey. 4th Earl of Jersey, widow of William-Henry Lambton, Esq., and mother of the 1st Earl of Durham. Her ladyship *d.* 21 April, 1832. Mr. Wyndham *d.* 8 July, 1828.

IV. William-Frederick, *b.* 6 April, 1763; *m.* 1st, 21 July, 1784, Frances-Mary Harford, natural dau. of Frederick Calvert, Lord Baltimore, by whom he had issue,

  1 GEORGE, 4th earl.
  1 Frances, *m.* 1st, in 1809, to William Miller, Esq., of Ozle-worth Park, Gloucestershire; and 2ndly, 11 March, 1847, to Augustin-Denis-Pinon Duclos, Vicomte de Valmer, capt. in the lancers of the Garde Royale of CHARLES X.
  2 Laura, *m.* in 1812, to the Rev. Charles Boultbee, by whom (who *d.* in 1833,) she left, at her decease, an only child, Julia-Frances-Laura, *m.* 1835, to the Hon. Francis Scott.
  3 Julia, *d. unm.* in 1811.

Mr. Wyndham *m.* 2ndly, Julia de Smorzewska, Countess de Spyterki ; and *d.* in 1829.

I. Elizabeth, *m.* to Henry, 1st Earl of Carnarvon; and *d.* in 1826.

II. Frances, *m.* to Charles, 1st Earl Romney; and *d.* in 1795.

His lordship, who was secretary-of-state, 1761, *d.* 21 August, 1763, and was *s.* by his eldest son,

GEORGE-O'BRIEN WYNDHAM, 3rd earl, F.R.S. and F.S.A.; *b.* 18 December, 1751. His lordship, who was lord-lieutenant, custos rotulorum, and vice-admiral of the co. of Sussex, *d. unm.* 11 November, 1837, and was *s.* by his nephew,

GEORGE-FRANCIS WYNDHAM, 4th earl, *b.* in 1786; who *m.* in 1820, Jane, 3rd dau. of the Rev. William Roberts, Vice Provost of Eton, but *d. s. p,* 2 April, 1845, when the peerage honours became EXTINCT.

Arms—Az., a chevron between three lions' heads, erased, or.

WYNDHAM—BARON WYNDHAM.

By Letters Patent, dated 17 September, 1731.

Lineage.

SIR WADHAM WYNDHAM, Knt., of Norrington, co. Wilts, youngest son of Sir John Wyndham, Knt., of Felbrigg, co. Norfolk, by Joan, his wife, dau. of Sir Henry Portman, Knt., of Orchard Portman, in Somersetshire, adopted the legal profession, and was constituted in 1660, one of the judges of the court of king's bench. He *m.* Barbara, dau. of Sir George Clarke, Knt., of Walford, Northamptonshire, and had, with other issue,

I. JOHN, his heir.
II. William, ancestor of the WYNDHAMS of Dinton, Wilts, now represented by WILLIAM WYNDHAM, Esq., of Dinton, the present heir male of the family of WYNDHAM. (*See* BURKE'S *Landed Gentry*).
III. Wadham, of St. Edmund's College, Salisbury, *m.* Sarah, Hearst, of Sarum, and by her (who *d.* in 1768), left at his decease in 1736, a son,

  HENRY WYNDHAM, of Sarum, who *m.* Arundel, dau. of Thomas Penruddocke, Esq., of Compton, Wilts, and left, with a dau. (Letitia, Lady A'Court,) several sons; of whom the eldest,

    HENRY-PENRUDDOCKE WYNDHAM, Esq., of the College, Sarum, M.P. for Wilts, *m.* in 1768, Caroline, dau. and heir of Edward Hearst, of the College, Sarum, and *d.* in 1819, leaving (with other sons who *d. s. p.,*)

      WADHAM WYNDHAM, Esq., of the College, Sarum, M.P. *m.* Ann-Eliza, dau. of Lieut.-Gen. Slade, and *d. s. p.* 1843.

      CAROLINE-FRANCES, *m.* John Campbell, Esq., of Dunoon, co. Argyll. and of Blunham, co. Bedford, and *d.* 3 December, 1845, leaving with two daus. (Julia-Anne-Frances, wife of S.-E. Thornton, Esq.; and Ellen-Christian, wife of R. King, Esq.) a son and heir, JOHN-HENRY-CAMPBELL WYNDHAM, Esq., of the College, Sarum, and Corhampton House. Hants, who assumed the surname and arms of WYNDHAM.

The eldest son,
JOHN WYNDHAM, Esq., of Norrington, *m.* Alice, dau. of Thomas Fownes, Esq., and left three sons, namely,

  JOHN, of Ashcombe, whose only dau. and heir (by Anne Barber, his wife), ANNE, *m.* in 1751. the Hon. James-Everard Arundell, and was mother of James-Everard, 9th Lord Arundell, of Wardour.
  Wadham, *d. s. p.*
  THOMAS.
  Alicia, *m.* Sir Edward Knatchbull, Bart.

The 3rd son,
THOMAS WYNDHAM, Esq., a distinguished lawyer, was made

596

---

lord chancellor of Ireland, 21 December, 1727, and raised to the peerage of that kingdom, as BARON WYNDHAM, *of Finglass, co. Dublin*, 17 September, 1731. His lordship *d. s. p.* 24 November 1745, and with him the title became EXTINCT.

Arms—Az., a chev., between three lions' heads, erased,

WYNDHAM-O'BRIEN—BARON IBRACKAN AND EARL OF THOMOND.

By Letters Patent, dated 11 December, 1756.

Lineage.

SIR WILLIAM WYNDHAM, Bart., P.C., chancellor of the exchequer, *m.* 1st, 21 July, 1708, Lady Catherine Seymour, 2nd dau. of Charles, Duke of Somerset, K.G., by whom he had two sons and two daus.,

I. CHARLES WYNDHAM, Earl of Egremont.
II. PERCY O'BRIEN, of whom we treat.
I. Catherine, who *d. unm.* in April, 1734.
II. Elizabeth (who *d.* at Wootton, in Buckinghamshire, 5 December, 1769). *m.* 1749, to the Hon. George Grenville, 2nd son of Hester, Countess Temple, and had issue, three sons, George, Marquess of Buckingham, the Right Hon. Thomas Grenville, William-Wyndham, Lord Grenville, and four daus.

He *m.* 2ndly, Lady Maria-Catharina, dau. of M. Peter D'Jong, of the province of Utrecht, in Holland, and relict of William. Marquess of Blandford, but by her had no issue. He *d.* 17 July, 1740. The 2nd son,

PERCY WYNDHAM, Esq., of Shortgrove, in Essex, *s.* to the estate of his uncle Henry O'Brien, 8th Earl of Thomond, assumed in consequence the surname and arms of O'BRIEN, and was advanced to the dignity of BARON IBRACKAN and EARL OF THOMOND, in the kingdom of Ireland. 11 December, 1756, but *d. unm.* 21 July, 1774, when the titles became EXTINCT.

Arms—Quarterly: 1st and 4th grand quarters, 1st and 4th, gu., three lions passant guardant, in pale, per pale, or and arg., for O'BRIEN; 2nd, arg., three piles meeting in point issuing from the chief, gu.; 3rd, or, a pheon, az. 2nd and 3rd grand quarters, az . a chevron between three lions' heads erased, or, for WYNDHAM.

YELVERTON—VISCOUNTS LONGUEVILLE, EARLS OF SUSSEX AND BARONS GREY DE RUTHYN,

Viscounty, by Letters Patent, dated 21 April, 1690.
Earldom, by Letters Patent, dated 26 September, 1717.

Lineage.

Of this family, one of great antiquity in the co. of Norfolk, was

ANDREW YELVERTON, living in the reign of EDWARD II., who was father of

ROBERT YELVERTON, who was seated, *temp.* EDWARD III., at Rackheath, in the vicinity of Norwich, and marrying Cecilia, dau. of Sir Thomas Bardolfe, left a son and heir,

JOHN YELVERTON, of Rackheath, who had, by his 1st wife, a son and successor,

ROBERT, who *d.* about the year 1420, leaving a son,

  THOMAS, of Rackheath, who *d. s. p.*

John Yelverton *m.* 2ndly, Elizabeth, dau. of John Read, of Rougham, co. Norfolk, and had a son,

SIR WILLIAM YELVERTON, a lawyer of great eminence, who was constituted one of the judges of the court of king's bench in the 22nd HENRY VI. This learned person appears to have stood equally well with the monarchs of both the Roses, as we find him not only continued in his judicial office by King EDWARD IV., but made a knight of the Bath, in order to grace that prince's coronation; and upon the temporary restoration of King HENRY, appointed by patent, dated 9 October, 1470, one of the judges of the court of common pleas. He *m.* Agnes, dau. of Sir Oliver le Gross, of Crostwick, co. Norfolk, Knt., and was *s.* by his son,

JOHN YELVERTON, Esq., of Rackheath, who *m.* Margery, dau. of William Morley, Esq., and had issue,

WILLIAM (Sir), his successor,
Anne, *m.* to Thomas Farmey, Esq., of Helmingham.

He was *s.* by his son,

Sir WILLIAM YELVERTON, Knt., who was retained by indenture, *anno* 1474, to serve the king (EDWARD IV.) in person in his wars in France, with two men at arms, and four archers. He *m.* 1st, Anne, dau. of John Paston, Esq., of Paston Hall, co. Norfolk, by whom he had issue,

WILLIAM, who *d. v. p., s. p.*
Anne. *m.* to Thomas Jermy, Esq., son of Sir John Jermy, Knt.
Margaret, *m.* to John Palgrave, Esq., of Norwood Barningham. co. Norfolk.
Eleanor, *m.* to John Conyers, Esq., scn and heir of Sir Robert Conyers.

Sir William *m.* 2ndly, Eleanor, dau. of Sir Thomas Brewse, Knt., and had a son, his successor,

WILLIAM YELVERTON, Esq., of Rougham and Rackheath. This gentleman *m.* Catherine, dau. of John Randes, Esq., of the co. Essex, and had five sons, viz., WILLIAM, his successor, John, Nicholas. Edward, and Adam, and a dau., Anne, *m.* to Matthew Canne, Esq., of Wessenham, in Norfolk. He was *s.* at his decease by his eldest son,

WILLIAM YELVERTON, Esq., of Rougham, who, by Margaret, his wife, (and executrix of his Will, proved 17 August, 1541,) he had two sons, WILLIAM and John, and three daus., viz.,

Mary, *m.* 1st, to William Baker, Esq., and 2ndly, to Henry Wayte, Esq.
Susan. *m.* 1st, to Edward Eston, Esq., of Rainham, in Norfolk, and 2ndly, to Edward Harvey, Esq.
Eleanor. *m.* to Richard Draper, Esq., of Marham, Norfolk.

William Yelverton *d.* in the year 1541, and was *s.* by his elder son,

WILLIAM YELVERTON, Esq., of Rougham. This gentleman *m.* 1st, Anne, dau. and heir of Sir Henry Fermor, Knt., of East Barsham, in Norfolk, by whom he acquired a great increase to his landed possessions, and had issue,

HENRY, who inherited Rougham, and the other estates of his father, as son and heir. He *m.* Bridget, dau. of Sir William Drury, of Hawsted, in Suffolk, Knt., and had issue,

WILLIAM, his successor, created a baronet in 1620. He *m.* Dionesse, dau. of Richard Stubbs, Esq., of Sedgeford, in Norfolk, and left

WILLIAM (Sir), 2nd baronet, who *m.* Ursula, dau. of Sir Thomas Richardson, Knt., speaker of the House of Commons, and afterwards lord chief justice of the King's Bench, by whom he had, WILLIAM, and two daus., Elizabeth and Ursula. He *d.* in 1648, and was *s.* by his son,

WILLIAM (Sir), 3rd baronet, who *d. s. p.*, 15 November, 1649, when the baronetcy expired.

Henry (Sir), *m.* Alice, dau. and co-heir of the Right Rev. William Barlow, bishop of Lincoln.
Margaret, *m.* to Thomas Tyrrell, Esq., of Gippinge, co. Suffolk.

William, *m.* Grace Newport.
CHRISTOPHER, of whom presently
Humphrey.   Launcelot.
Winifred, *m.* to Owen Duckett, Esq., of Worthing, in Norfolk.
Anne, *m.* 1st, to Thomas Reade, Esq., of Wishbyche, and 2ndly, to John Hawkins, Esq., of Essex.
Martha, *m.* 1st, to Thomas Fyncham, Esq., of Fyncham, co. Norfolk, and 2ndly, to John Higham, Esq., of Gifford, in Sussex.

Mr. Yelverton *m.* 2ndly, Jane, dau. of Edward Cocket, Esq., of Ampton, in Suffolk, by whom he had,

Edward.   Charles.
Jane, *m.* 1st, to Edmund Lummer, Esq., of Mannington, in Norfolk, and 2ndly, to John Dodge, Esq., of Wrothani, in Kent.
Chrysold, *m.* 1st, to the son and heir of Sir Nicholas L'Estrange, of Hunstanton, and 2ndly, to Sir Philip Wodehouse, Bart., of Kimberley, M.P.

The 3rd son of William Yelverton, by his 1st wife, Anne Fermor,

CHRISTOPHER YELVERTON, being bred to the bar, and called to the degree of serjeant-at-law, was constituted queen's serjeant in the 31st ELIZABETH. Some years afterwards he was chosen speaker of the House of Commons, and in the 44th of the same reign he was constituted one of the judges of the court of King's Bench. On the accession of King JAMES, his patent, as a judge, was renewed, and he was then made a knight. Sir Christopher *m.* Mary, dau. of Thomas Catesby, Esq., of Whiston, co. Northampton, and had issue,

HENRY, his successor.
Christopher (Sir).
Isabel, *m.* to Sir Edward Cope, of Canon's Ashby, co. Northampton.

597

Anne, *m.* 1st, to Thomas Sherland, Esq., of co. Suffolk, and 2ndly, to Sir Edward Cocket, Knt., of Ampton, in the same shire.
Mary, *m.* to Sir William Gardiner, of Lagham, in Surrey.
Judith, *m.* to Edmund Abdy, Esq., of Lincoln's Inn.

His lordship *d.* in 1607, at Easton-Mauduit, a seat which he had purchased in Northamptonshire, and was *s.* by his elder son,

HENRY YELVERTON, Esq., of Easton-Mauduit. This gentleman having, like his father, adopted the profession of the law, was appointed solicitor-general in 1613, and knighted about the same period. In 1617, Sir Henry Yelverton was made attorney general; previously, however, he is said to have displeased the king by refusing to appear against the Earl of Somerset, at his trial for the murder of Sir Thomas Overbury, and in the October of the year in which he was advanced to the attorney-generalship we find him writing a letter to his royal master, complaining "of his unhappiness to fall under his Majesty's displeasure, who had made him almost the wonder of his favour; that he conceived it to arise from some accident, befel in the late business of the marriage of Sir John Villiers; as also from a report, as if he had uttered some speeches to the dishonour of the Earl of Buckingham." He pleaded his cause so successfully, however, that he very soon recovered any ground which he might have lost in JAMES'S opinion, but he was not so fortunate with the Duke of Buckingham, who seems, for a long time afterwards, to have regarded him with an evil eye. In 1620, principally through the machinations of that favoured nobleman, he was involved, with the lord mayor of London, and others, in a star-chamber prosecution, regarding the passing of certain clauses in a charter to the city of London, not authorized by the king's warrant; for this offence, although he made every submission, and that the charter was given up, he was adjudged to pay a fine of £4000, to be deprived of the office of attorney-general, and to be committed to the Tower. He was subsequently prosecuted before parliament upon another account, and the House of Lords, 16 May, 1621, proceeded to sentence, and declare, "That the said Sir Henry Yelverton for his speeches, uttered here in court, which do touch the king's majesty's honour, shall be fined to the king in ten thousand marks, be imprisoned during pleasure, and make submission to the king: and for those which touched the Marquess of Buckingham, he should be fined five thousand marks, &c." Upon which Buckingham stood up, and did freely remit his portion of the fine; and the prince and the House agreed to move his Majesty to mitigate the other part of the judgment. What proportion of the fine was ultimately forgiven is nowhere mentioned, but his misfortunes very soon afterwards terminated. The Duke of Buckingham visited him *incognito* in the Tower, and Sir Henry making a sufficient apology to his grace, he was presently set at liberty, and became again a practising barrister, until April, 1625, when a gentleman from the duke brought him a warrant from the king, appointing him one of the judges of the court of Common Pleas. In this situation he remained until his decease, 24 January, 1629-30, when his remains were interred in the parish church of Easton-Mauduit. Of this eminent person the following character is given by one of his own profession:

"Memorandum, That upon Sunday morning, being the 24th of January, 1629-30, died Sir Henry Yelverton, puisne judge of the Common Pleas, who before had been attorney-general to King JAMES, and afterwards incurring his displeasure, was displeased and censured in the star-chamber. He then became a practiser again at the bar, from which he was advanced, by King CHARLES, to be a judge. He was a man of profound knowledge in the common laws, and ingenious and eloquent in expression; and for his life, of great integrity and piety, and his death universally bewailed." His lordship *m.* Margaret, dau. of Robert Beale, Esq., clerk of the council to Queen ELIZABETH, and was *s.* by his eldest son,

SIR CHRISTOPHER YELVERTON, Knt., of Easton-Mauduit, who was created a baronet 30 June, 1641. He *m.* in 1630, Anne, youngest dau. of Sir William Twisden, Bart., of Roydon Hall, Kent, by whom he had issue,

HENRY, his successor.
Anne. *m.* 1st, to Robert, Earl of Manchester, and 2ndly, to Charles, Earl of Halifax.

Sir Christopher *d.* 4 December, 1654, and was *s.* by his son,

SIR HENRY YELVERTON, 2nd baronet, member for Northamptonshire, in the parliament that voted the restoration of King CHARLES II. He *m.* Susan, Baroness Grey de Ruthyn, dau. and heiress of Charles Longueville, Lord Grey de Ruthyn, and great grand-dau. of Charles Grey, Earl of Kent (*see* Grey, Earl of Kent), by whom he had issue,

CHARLES, his successor.
HENRY, heir to his brother.
Christopher.
Frances, m. to Christopher, Viscount Hatton.

Sir Henry d. 28 January, 1676, and was s. by his eldest son,
SIR CHARLES YELVERTON, 2nd baronet, who, on the decease of his mother, 28 January, 1676, became BARON GREY DE RUTHYN. His lordship d. unm., of the small-pox, 17 May, 1679, and was s. by his brother,
SIR HENRY YELVERTON, as 3rd baronet, and as Lord Grey de Ruthyn. This nobleman claimed, by inheritance from the Hastings. Earls of Pembroke, the right of carrying the golden spurs at the coronation of King JAMES II., and his claim being admitted, he bore them accordingly. His lordship m. Barbara, dau. of John Talbot, Esq., of Lacock, co. Wilts, and had, with other issue,

TALBOT, his successor.
Henry, m. a dau. of Major Carle, and had an only dau., Barbara, who d. young. He d. 1765.
Barbara, m. to Reynolds Calthorpe, Esq., of Elvetham, Hants.

His lordship was advanced to the dignity of VISCOUNT LONGUEVILLE, 21 April, 1690. He d. in 1704, and was s. by his elder son,
TALBOT YELVERTON, 2nd Viscount Longueville, who was created 26 September, 1717, EARL OF SUSSEX, with remainder, in default of his own male issue, to his brother, the Hon. Henry Yelverton, and the heirs male of his body. His lordship was appointed deputy earl-marshal of England in 1725, and he officiated as such at the coronation of King GEORGE II. He was made a knight of the Bath upon the revival of that order, and subsequently sworn of the privy council. His lordship m. Lucy, dau. of Henry Pelham, Esq., of Lewes, in Sussex, clerk of the pells, and uncle of Thomas, Duke of Newcastle, by whom (who d. 1730) he had two sons,

GEORGE-AUGUSTUS, } successively inheritors of the honours.
HENRY,

The earl, who carried the golden spurs at the coronation of GEORGE I., d. 27 October, 1731, and was s. by his elder son,
GEORGE-AUGUSTUS YELVERTON, 2nd Earl of Sussex. This nobleman was one of the lords of the bedchamber to Frederick, Prince of Wales, and afterwards to his Majesty, King GEORGE III. He d. unm. 8 January, 1758, and was s. by his brother,
HENRY YELVERTON, 3rd Earl of Sussex. b. 1729. This nobleman m. 1st, Hester, dau. of John Hall, Esq., of Mansfield Woodhouse, Notts, and by her (who d. in 1777), had an only surviving dau.,

LADY BARBARA YELVERTON, who m. Edward-Thoroton Gould, Esq., of Woodham Mansfield, co. Notts, and dying v. p., 9 April, 1781, left issue,
HENRY-EDWARD-GOULD, s. his grandfather as 19th Lord Grey de Ruthyn.
Barbara-Gould, d. unm.
Mary-Gould, m. to the Hon and Rev. Frederick Powys, son of Lord Lilford, and d. 19 January, 1837.

The earl m. 2ndly, Mary, dau. of John Vaughan, Esq. of Bristol, but had no issue. He d. in 1799, when the Viscounty of Longueville, with the Earldom of Sussex, became EXTINCT, but the Barony of Grey de Ruthyn devolved upon his grandson,
HENRY-EDWARD GOULD, 19th Lord Grey de Ruthyn, who thereupon assumed the surname of YELVERTON. He m. in 1809, Anna-Maria, dau. of Mr. William Kelham, and by her (who m. 2ndly. Hon. and Rev. William Eden), he left at his decease an only dau. and heiress,
BARBARA YELVERTON, Baroness Grey de Ruthyn, Marchioness of Hastings, who m. 1st, 18 August, 1831, George-Augustus-Francis, Marquess of Hastings, and had issue,
PAULYN-REGINALD-SERLO, s. his father, 13 January, 1844, as 3rd Marquess of Hastings, b. 2 June, 1832; d. unm. in the lif. time of his mother, 17 January, 1851.
HENRY-WEYSFORD-CHARLES-PLANTAGENET, 4th Marquess of Hastings, who s. his mother as 21st Lord Grey de Ruthyn.
EDITH-MAUD, COUNTESS of LOUDOUN, wife of C.-F. Abney-Hastings, Esq., created 4 May, 1880, Lord Donington, and had issue. The eldest son is the present Earl of Loudoun.
Bertha-Lelgarde, m. 11 December, 1855, to Capt. Augustus-Wykeham Clifton, son of Thomas Clifton, Esq. of Lytham Hall, co. Lancaster, and has issue, two sons and two daus.
Victoria-Maria-Louisa, m. 31 October, 1859, to J.-F -Stratford Ki wan, Esq. of Moyne, co. Galway, and has issue two sons and three daus.
Frances-Augusta-Constance, m. 30 July, 1863, to Charles, 4th Earl of Romney, and has issue.

Lady Grey de Ruthyn, Marchioness of Hastings, m. 2ndly, 9 April, 1845, Captain Reginald-Hastings-Henry, R.N. (grandson maternally of William-Robert, 2nd Duke of Leinster, K.P.), who thereupon assumed the surname and arms of Yelverton,

and was afterwards Admiral Sir Reginald-Hastings Yelverton, G.C.B., and d. 23 July, 1878, leaving by the Marchioness an only dau.,
Barbara, m. 23 September, 1872, John, 1st Lord Churston, and has issue.

Lady Grey de Ruthyn, Marchioness of Hastings, d. 18 November, 1858, and was s. by her only surviving son,
HENRY-WEYSFORD-CHARLES-PLANTAGENET, 4th Marquess of Hastings, as 21st Baron Grey de Ruthyn, b. 22 July, 1842. His lordship m. 16 July, 1864, Lady Florence-Cecilia Paget, youngest dau. of Henry, 2nd Marquess of Anglesey, but by her (who m. 2ndly, 1870, Sir George Chetwynd, Bart.), had no issue. He d. 10 November, 1868, when the Marquessate of Hastings and his Irish honours became EXTINCT; the Scotch honours passed to his eldest sister, and the Barony of Grey de Ruthyn fell into abeyance between his sisters, the Countess of Loudoun, Lady Bertha Clifton, Lady Victoria Kirwan, the Countess of Romney, and his half-sister, Lady Churston.

Arms—Ar., three lions ramp., gu., a chief of the last.

YORKE—BARON DOVER.

By Letters Patent, dated 18 September, 1788.

(See BURKE's Extant Peerage, HARDWICKE, E.)

ZOUCHE—BARON ZOUCHE, OF ASHBY, CO. LEICESTER.

By Writ of Summons, dated 25 January, 1297.

Lineage.

That the Zouches branched from the Earls of Brittany, is admitted by all genealogists, but they do not coincide in the exact line of descent.

WILLIAM LA ZUSCHE, in confirming to the monks of Swavesey, in Cambridgeshire, the grants made by his ancestors to the abbey St. Segius and Bacchus, in Anjou (to which the priory of Swavesey was a cell), calls Roger la Zusche, his father, and Alan la Zusche, his grandfather. This William d. in the 1st JOHN, and was s. by his brother,
ROGER LA ZUSCHE who, for his fidelity to King JOHN, had a grant from that monarch of the manors of Petersfield and Maple Durham, co. Southampton, part of the lands of Geffrey de Mandeville, one of the rebellious barons then in arms. In the next reign he was sheriff of Devonshire, and had further grants from the crown. By Margaret, his wife, he had issue,
ALAN, his successor.
William, who left an only dau.
Joice, who m. Robert Mortimer, of Richard's Castle, and had issue,
HUGH MORTIMER, summoned to parliament as Lord Mortimer, of Richard's Castle.
WILLIAM MORTIMER, who assumed the surname of ZOUCHE, and was summoned to parliament as LORD ZOUCHE, of Mortimer.

He was s. by his elder son,
SIR ALAN LA ZOUCHE, who, in the 26th HENRY III., had a military summons to attend the king into France, and in ten years afterwards had the whole county of Chester, and all North Wales placed under his government. In the 45th of the same reign he obtained a charter for a weekly market at Ashby-la-Zouche, in Leicestershire, and for two fairs in the year at Swavesey. About the same time he was constituted warden of all the king's forests south of Trent, as also sheriff of Northamptonshire. In the 46th he was made justice itinerant for the cos. Southampton, Buckingham, and Northampton; and upon the arbitration made by LEWIS, King of France, between HENRY III. and the barons, he was one of the sureties on behalf of the king. In three years afterwards he was constituted constable of the Tower of London, and governor of the castle at Northampton. Sir Alan Zouche was violently assaulted in Westminster Hall, in 1268, by John, Earl of Warren and Surrey, upon occasion of a dispute between them regarding some landed property, and with his son, Roger, who happened to be with him, severely wounded. He m. Elena, dau. and heir of Roger de Quinci, Earl of Winchester, and by her (who d. 1296) had issue,
ROGER, his successor.
Eudo, from whom the Zouches, Barons Zouche, of Harynworth (extant) derive.

Alan le Zouche d. in 1269, and was s. by his elder son,
ROGER LA ZOUCHE, who m. Ela, dau. and co-heir of Stephen de Longespée, 2nd son of William, Earl of Salisbury, and dying in 1285, was s. by his son,
ALAN LA ZOUCHE. This feudal lord, b. 1267, having died

tinguished himself in the wars of Gascony, and Scotland, *temp.* EDWARD I., was summoned to parliament by that monarch as a Baron, 26 January, 1297, and he had regular summonses from that period until 7th EDWARD II., 26 November, 1313. In the 5th EDWARD II. his lordship was constituted governor of Rockingham Castle, in Northamptonshire, and steward of Rockingham Forest. He *d.* in 1314, leaving by Eleanor, his wife, dau. of Nicholas de Segrave, three daus., his co-heirs, viz.,

  I ELLEN, *m.* 1st, Nicholas St. Maur, and 2ndly, Alan de Charlton : the eventual heiress-general of Ellen le Zouche, was (*see* p. 469).

    ALICE ST. MAUR, who *m.* William, 5th Lord Zouche of Haryngworth, and was ancestress of EDWARD, 11th Lord Zouche, of Haryngworth, who *d.* 1625, leaving two daus., his co-heirs, viz.,

      1 ELIZABETH ZOUCHE, who *m.* Sir William Tate, of Delapré, and was great-grandmother of BARTHOLOMEW TATE, Esq., of Delapré, who *d* 1704, leaving one son, whose issue failed, and two daus.; 1 CATHARINE *m.* 1720, to Charles Hedges, Esq., ancestor by her of HARRIET-ANNE, BARONESS DE LA ZOUCHE, and of KATHERINE-ANNABELLA, wife of Sir George-Richard Pechell, Bart., and 2 MARY. *m.* 1723. to Samuel Long, Esq., and had, besides daus., three sons, of whom the eldest, ROBERT LONG, Esq., left three daus. and co-heirs. viz., JANE, wife of John Oliver. Esq.; MARY-CHARLOTTE, wife of Samuel Scudamore Heming. Esq., and LUCY-ANN, wife of Thomas-Bayley Howell, Esq., of Prinknash Park, co. Gloucester.

      2 MARY ZOUCHE, *m.* 1st, Thomas Leighton, Esq., and had issue; and 2ndly, William Connard, Esq., by whom she had no issue.

  II MAUD, *m.* Robert, Lord Holland : their great-grand-dau. and heir-general, MAUD HOLLAND, *m.* 1373, JOHN LOVEL, LORD LOVEL, of Tichmersh, and the descendants and co-heirs-general of this marriage are HENRY, LORD BEAU-MONT and MONTAGU, EARL OF ABINGDON (*see* p. 333).

  III. ELIZABETH, a nun at Brewood, co. Stafford.

Amongst these three daus. and co-heirs of Alan le Zouche, a partition was made in the 8th EDWARD II., of their father's lands, excepting the manor of Ashby-de-la-Zouche, which the deceased lord gave to his kinsman, WILLIAM DE MORTIMER, who thereupon assumed the surname of ZOUCHE. At the decease of Lord Zouche, the Barony of Zouche, of Ashby, fell into ABEYANCE between his daus., as it still continues with their representatives.

Arms—Gu., ten bezants, or.

ZOUCHE—BARON ZOUCHE, OF MORTI-MER.

By Writ of Summons, dated 26 December, 1323.

Lineage.

WILLIAM DE MORTIMER, younger son of Robert Lord Mortimer, of Richard's Castle, by Joice, dau. and heir of William la Zouche, having obtained the lordship of Ashby-de-la-Zouche, from his kinsman Alan, Lord Zouche, of Ashby, assumed the surname of ZOUCHE; and was summoned to parliament as BARON ZOUCHE *of Mortimer*, from 26 December, 1323, to 14 January, 1337, In the reign of EDWARD III., his lordship was made justice of all the forests, south of Trent, and constable of the Tower of London. He *m.* 1st, Alice de Tony, widow of Guy de Beauchamp, Earl of Warwick, and had a son, ALAN, his successor. He *m.* 2ndly, Alianore, dau. and heir of Gilbert de Clare, Earl of Gloucester, by whom also he had a son. His lordship *d.* and was *s.* by his son,

ALAN LA ZOUCH, one of the eminent warriors of the reign of EDWARD III. He was constantly engaged in the French and Scottish wars, and was in the celebrated battle of Cressy, shortly after which he died and was *s.* by his son,

HUGH LA ZOUCHE, who, says Courthope (*Historic Peerage*), "*d.* 1368, *s. p.,* when ROBERT LA ZOUCHE, his uncle, was found to be his heir and then æt. fifty; but Robert, the uncle, also dying *s. p.,* by a second inquisition, 1st HENRY IV., 1399, JOYCE, wife of Hugh, 2nd Baron Burnell, and granddau. of John, Baron Botetourt, son of Joyce, sister of Alan, his father, and Robert, his uncle, was found to be his cousin and next heir, and then æt. thirty ; she *d. s. p.,* 1406." The manor of Ashby-de-la-Zouche came afterwards into the possession of the Earls of Ormonde, and on the attainder of John Butler, 5th Earl of Ormonde and Earl of Wiltshire, fell to the crown. It was subsequently granted to William de Hastings, ancestor of the family of Hastings, Earls of Huntingdon and Marquesses of Hastings.

Arms—Gu., ten bezants, or.

ADDENDA.

ABERCROMBY—BARONS DUNFERMLINE.

By Letters Patent, dated 7 June, 1839.

Lineage.

THE RIGHT HON. JAMES ABERCROMBY, b. 7 Nov. 1776, 3rd son of the famous SIR RALPH ABERCROMBY and BARONESS ABERCROMBY (see Extant Peerage, ABERCROMBY, B.), was called to the Bar in 1800, and after being a commissioner of bankruptcy, was appointed judge-advocate-general in 1827, chief baron of Scotland in 1830, and master of the Mint and a member of the Cabinet in 1834. He was chosen Speaker of the House of Commons in 1835. In 1839, he resigned the Speakership, and was raised to the peerage of the United Kingdom as LORD DUNFERMLINE, of Dunfermline, co. Fife, the 7th June of that year. He m. 14 June, 1802, Mary-Anne, dau. of Egerton Leigh, Esq., of the West Hall, High Leigh, co. Chester; and dying 17 April, 1858, was s. by his only child,

SIR RALPH ABERCROMBY, 2nd Lord Dunfermline, K.C.B. b. 6 April, 1803; m. 18 September, 1838, Lady Mary Elizabeth Elliot, eldest dau. of Gilbert, 2nd Earl of Minto, and had a dau.,

Mary-Catherine-Elizabeth, m. 27 October, 1876, Capt. John Mowbray Trotter, 4th son of Archibald Trotter, Esq., of Dreghorn, co. Midlothian, and has issue.

His lordship has filled several very high diplomatic appointments, was sent as British Minister to the Hague, 30 May, 1840, and resigned in 1858; he was made a K.C.B., 1 March, 1851; and d. 2 July, 1868, when, as he left no male issue, his title became EXTINCT.

Arms—Arg., a fesse, embattled, gu., between, in base, the ancient family arms of ABERCROMBY, being a chevron, indented, gu., between three boars' heads, erased, az.; and in chief, issuing out of the battlements of the fesse, a dexter arm, embowed, in armour, ppr., garnished, or, the cubit part of the arm encircled by a wreath of laurel, and the hand grasping a French republican military flag, in bend sinister.

AIREY—BARON AIREY.

By Letters Patent, dated 29 November. 1876.

Lineage.

LIEUT.-GEN. SIR GEORGE AIREY, K.C.H., col. 39th regt., m. Hon. Katherine Talbot, 3rd dau. of Baroness Talbot of Malahide, and by her (who d. 13 May, 1852), left at his decease (18 February, 1833), six sons and three daus. Of the former, the eldest,

SIR RICHARD AIREY, G.C.B., a general in the army, col. 71st foot, Knight Commander of the Legion of Honor, and Commander of the 1st Class of the Military Order of Savoy, and of the Medjidie, b. April, 1803; m. January, 1838, Hon. Harriett-Mary-Everard Talbot, dau. of James, 3rd Lord Talbot de Malahide, by whom (who d. 28 July, 1881) he had issue,

I. George-Aylmer, b. 27 August, 1839; d. May, 1853.
II. Richard-John, lieut. 73rd regt., b. March, 1844; d. 3 September, 1865.
III. Dy-Frederic, b. 6 June, 1848; d. August, 1857.
I. Louisa-Anne, b. 1841; d. January, 1849.
II. Katherine-Margaret, b. 6 January, 1843; m. 14 September, 1865, to Sir Geers-Henry Cotterell, 3rd bart.
III. Juliet-Fanny, b. May, 1846; d. July, 1863.

This distinguished officer entered the army in 1821, and attained the rank of general 1871. He was in the command of ✝ brigade as acting quartermaster-general in the Crimea, and

took part in the battles of the Alma, Balaklava, and Inkermann, and was at the siege and fall of Sebastopol. In 1855, he was appointed quartermaster-general, was military secretary to the Commander-in-Chief from 1862 to 1864, was Governor and Commander-in-Chief at Gibraltar from 1865 to 1870. and from 1870 to 1875 adjutant-general of the forces. He was made a K.C.B. in 1855, G.C.B. in 1867, and a peer of the United Kingdom by the title of BARON AIREY, of Killingworth, co. Northumberland, by Letters Patent, 29 November, 1876. Lord Airey d. without surviving male issue, 14 September, 1881, when the barony became EXTINCT.

Arms—Az., on a chev. arg. between, in chief three mullets of the last and in base a mural crown or, as many cinquefoils of the field.

Page 15.

ATON—BARONS ATON.

WILLIAM DE ATON, who was summoned to parliament, 8 January, 1371, had by Isabel, his wife, dau. of Henry, Lord Percy, a son, WILLIAM (who d. v. p.), and three daus., who became his co-heirs. Of these Anastacia, m. Edward de St. John; Catherine, m. Sir Ralph de Eure; and Elizabeth, m. 1st, William Playz; 2ndly, John Coniers; the representatives of which co-heirs are EDWARD SOUTHWELL, Lord de Clifford; ROBERT ARTHUR TALBOT, Marquess of Salisbury; and JOHN LEVESON GOWER, Esq., of Bill Hill, co. Berks, descended (through the TUFTONS, Earls of Thanet), from Anastacia de Aton, eldest dau. and co-heir of William, Lord Aton, and wife of Edward St. John; SIR CHARLES WILLIAM STRICKLAND, 8th Bart. of Boynton, the heir-general of Catherine de Aton, the second co-heir; and FRANCIS ROBERT, Lord Camoys, the descendant of Elizabeth de Aton, the third co-heir.

BLAYNEY—BARONS BLAYNEY.

By Letters Patent, dated 29 July, 1621.

Lineage.

The Blayneys, of Gregynog, in the parish of Tregynnon, co. Montgomery, were of the tribe of Brochwel Ysgythrog.

SIR EDWARD BLAYNEY, Knt. (a soldier from his youth, in the service of ELIZABETH), is stated in the Funeral Entry of Jane, Lady Blayney, to have been son of John Blayney, of Tregonog, co. Montgomery. He accompanied the Earl of Essex to Ireland in 1598, being then a colonel in the army. In the next reign he was granted, 21 February, 1607, the lands of the Ballybetaghs, of Ballinlurgan, alias Ballinfort, and Ballynockaluske, co. Monaghan, to be "forfeited if he does not build a strong castle surrounded with a stone trench, called a bawne, within the next four years." Immediately on the passing of his patent, Sir Edward commenced the building of Castle Blayney above the beautiful lake of Mucknoe, not far from the present house; and in 1610 became governor or seneschal of the County of Monaghan, being greatly trusted by the English Interest in Ireland. Acquiring fame and fortune in the subsequent wars, he was elevated to the peerage of Ireland, 29 July, 1621, as LORD BLAYNEY, Baron of Monaghan, co. Monaghan. His lordship m. Anne, 2nd dau. of Adam Loftus, D.D., Archbishop of Dublin, and chancellor of Ireland, by whom he had,

I. HENRY, 2nd baron.
II. Arthur (Sir), of Shien Castle, co. Monaghan, m. Joyce, dau. and heir of John Blayney, Esq., of Gregynnoge, co. Montgomery, and had, with a dau., Elizabeth, four sons,

1 John, d. unm.
2 Edward, m. Elizabeth, dau. of John Scrimshire, Esq., of Norbury, and d. s. p.
3 Henry, m. Elizabeth, dau. of Rev. Dr. Seddon, co. Lancaster, and had, with six daus. (1 Mary ; 2 Alice ; 3 Joyce ; 4 Elizabeth ; 5 Bridget ; 6 Margaret), one son,
John.
4 Arthur, m. 1st, Margaret Forbes, by whom he had two daus. (Jane and Elizabeth) and three sons,
Edward.
Richard.
Henry.
He m. 2ndly, Jane Smothergil, by whom he had six children.
i. Anne, m. James, 1st Lord Balfour, of Glenawley.
ii. Jane, m. 1st, Sir James Moore, Knt., of Ardee ; and 2ndly, Sir Robert Stirling, Knt.
iii. Mary, d. unm.
iv. Elizabeth, d. unm.
v. Martha, m. Walter Cope, Esq., of Drummilly.
vi. Lettice, m. John O'Neill, Esq.

Lord Blayney dying 11 February, 1629, was buried in the church of Monaghan (his Funeral Entry is recorded in Ulster's Office), and was s. by his elder son,

HENRY, 2nd baron, who had been knighted in his father's lifetime. It was this Lord Blayney who, at the surprisal of his house at Castle Blayney by the Irish, 23 October, 1641, brought the news of the outbreak to Dublin. He m. January, 1623, Hon. Jane Moore, dau. of Garrett, 1st Viscount Drogheda, by whom (who d. 22 October, 1686) he had issue,

i. EDWARD, 3rd baron.   ii. Charles, d. young.
iii. RICHARD, 4th baron.   iv. Arthur, d. young.
v Garrett, d. unm.   vi. John, d. unm.
i. Thomasine, m. 1st, Sir Henry Piers, Bart., of Shercock ; and 2ndly, Joseph Fox, Esq., of Graige.
ii. Alice, m. 1st, Thomas Sandford, Esq., of Sandford Court ; and 2ndly, John Langrishe, Esq , of Knocktopher.
iii. Mary, m. 1st, Captain Henry Moreton, of Newtown, co. Meath: and 2ndly, Charles Meredith, Esq. She d. January, 1675.
iv. Penelope, d. young.
v. Sarah, m. Very Rev. Thomas Bladen, D.D., Dean of Ardfert, who d. July, 1695.
vi. Jane, m. John Gorges, Esq., of Somerset, co. Derby.

Lord Blayney, who was a military man, fell at the battle of Benburb, co. Tyrone, 5 June, 1646, and was s. by his elder son,

EDWARD, 3rd baron, who dying unm. in 1669, was s. by his brother,

RICHARD, 4th baron. This nobleman was high in favour with OLIVER CROMWELL, and was appointed by him, in 1656, custos rotulorum of the co. Monaghan and escheator of the co. Tyrone. He m. 9 March, 1653, Elizabeth, eldest dau. of Thomas Vincent, alderman of Dublin, M.P., by whom he had issue,

i. Vincent, b 17 March, 1654, buried at Camberwell, co. Surrey, 29 March, 1655.
ii HENRY VINCENT, 5th baron.
iii. Edward, d. unm.   iv. Thomas, d. unm.
v. WILLIAM, 6th baron.
i. Jane, m. Blayney Owen, Esq., of Newgrove, co. Monaghan.
ii. Sarah, m. Maurice Annesley, Esq., of Little Rath.
iii. Elizabeth, m. Henry Owen, Esq. of Ballydrumny, and d. s. p. 1725.
iv. Joanna-Maria, d. unm.

Lord Blayney m. 2ndly, Jane, dau. of John Mallock, Esq., but had no further issue. He d. 5 November, 1670 (his widow m. 2ndly, Hugh Montgomery, Esq.), and was s. by his eldest surviving son,

HENRY-VINCENT, 5th baron. This nobleman m. Margaret Moore, eldest sister of John, 1st Lord Tullamoore, by whom (who m. 2ndly, 1 October, 1691, Charles Dering, Esq., auditor of the Exchequer, and d. 1 May, 1725) he had two daus.,

i. Elizabeth, b. 1687 ; d. 1692.
ii. Elinor, b. 14 May, 1689 ; m. 14 February, 1709, Nicholas Mahon, barrister-at-law ; and d. 10 June, 1743, leaving issue.

Lord Blayney d. August, 1689, and was s. by his brother,

WILLIAM, 6th baron. His lordship m. in 1686. Hon. Mary-Caulfeild, eldest dau. of William, 1st Viscount Charlemont, widow of Arthur Dillon, Esq , of Lismullen, co. Meath, and had by her (who d. 3 January, 1705),

i. Henry, d. young.
ii. CADWALLADER, 7th baron.
i. Jane, b. 1688 ; m. January, 1720, John Clark, Esq., of Portadown, and d. August, 1745, leaving issue.
ii. Alice, b. 1694 ; m. February, 1720, Thomas, eldest son of Edward Lucas, Esq., of Castle Shane, M.P., and had issue.
iii. Elizabeth, b. 1696 ; m. 1718, Capt. Joshua Johnston, of Armagh, and had issue.
iv. Anne, d unm.

Lord Blayney d. 3 January, 1705, and was s. by his only surviving son,

CADWALLADER, 7th baron, who m. 22 April, 1714, Mary, dau. of Hon. John Touche (second son of Mervyn, 4th Earl of Castlehaven), and niece of Charles, Duke of Shrewsbury, then lord-lieut. of Ireland, by whom (who d. September, 1741) he had,

i. CHARLES TALBOT, 8th baron.
ii. CADWALLADER, 9th baron.
iii William, d. unm.
i. Mary, b. 16 March, 1716 ; m 1st, in December, 1736, Nicholas Mahon, Esq.; and 2ndly, 1743, John Campbell, Esq., Dublin. of the House of Argyle.
ii. Martha, d. unm.

Lord Blayney m. 2ndly, 1724, Mary, dau. and heir of Sir Alexander Cairnes, Bart., of Monaghan, by whom, who m. 2ndly, Col. John Murray, he had no issue ; he d. 19 March, 1732, and was s. by his eldest son,

CHARLES TALBOT, 9th baron, Dean of Killaloe. b. 27 January, 1714 ; m. November, 1734, his cousin Elizabeth, dau. of Nicholas Mahon, Esq., barrister-at-law, by whom he had a son,

Henry-Vincent, b. 28 December, 1737 ; d. vitâ patris, 30 March, 1754.

Lord Blayney d. 15 September, 1761, and was s. by his brother,

CADWALLADER, 9th baron, b. 2 May, 1720 ; m. 1767, Sophia, dau. of Thomas Tipping, Esq., of Beaulieu, co. Louth, and had issue,

CADWALLADER-DAVIS, 10th baron.
ANDREW-THOMAS, 11th baron.
Sophia, m. 1788, to John Armstrong, Esq.
Mary, m. 1794, to Edmund Tipping, Esq., of Bellurgan Park, co. Louth, and d. in 1800, leaving issue, Catherine, m. 1815, to the Rev. Richard Hamilton, rector of Culdaff and Cloncha, co. Donegal (see BURKE's Landed Gentry, HAMILTON, of Abbotstown), who d. 1842, leaving issue, 1 Edward-James, in holy orders, m. 1844, Georgina-Susan, dau. of Gen. George-Vaughan Hart, of Kilderry, late M.P., and has issue ; 2 Richard-Tipping, poor law inspector, m. Anna, dau. of Latham Blacker, Esq., and has issue ; 3 Alicia, m. 1835, to Evory Kennedy, Esq., of Belgarde Castle, co. Dublin ; 4 Harriette-Catherine, m. to Sir John Laird-Mair Lawrence, Bart., afterwards BARON LAWRENCE.

Lord Blayney, who was a lieut.-gen. in the army and col. 38th regt., d. 13 November, 1775, and was s. by his elder son,

CADWALLADER-DAVIS, 10th baron, b. in 1769 ; at whose decease, unm. 2 April, 1784, the title devolved upon his brother,

ANDREW-THOMAS, 11th baron, a lieut.-gen. in the army; b. 30 November, 1770 ; m. 5 July, 1796, Lady Mabella Alexander, eldest dau. of James, 1st Earl of Caledon, and by her (who d. 4 March, 1854) had,

i. CADWALLADER-DAVIS, 12th baron.
i. Anne, m. 20 November, 1818, Admiral Charles Gordon, R.N., C.B., brother of the Right Hon. Sir J. Willoughby Gordon, Bart., and d. 11 December, 1882, leaving an only dau.,

Jane, m. 1st, 1840, Rev. James Henry Scudamore Burr; 2ndly, 1853, Rev. Francis Lewis, of St. Pierre, co. Monmouth ; and 3rdly, Captain Rolland.

ii. Elizabeth-Harriet, d. May, 1818.
iii. Charlotte-Sophia, m. in 1833, to Frederic Angerstein, Esq., and d. s. p. 5 August, 1863.

Lord Blayney d. 8 April, 1834, and was s. by his only son,

CADWALLADER-DAVIS, 12th baron, one of the representative peers; he was b. 19 December, 1802, and d. unm. 13 January, 1874, when the barony became EXTINCT. The Castle Blayney estate was purchased from the last Lord Blayney in 1853, by Henry Thomas Hope, Esq., of Deepdene, Surrey.

Arms—Sa. three nags' heads erased arg.

BLOOMFIELD—BARONS BLOOMFIELD.

Barony Irish Peerage, by Letters Patent, dated 14 May, 1825.
Barony United Kingdom, by Letters Patent, dated 7 August, 1871.

Lineage.

BENJAMIN BLOOMFIELD, or BLUMFIELD, of Eyre Court, co. Galway, made his will 17 July, 1737, which was proved 13 January following. By Dorthy, his wife, he left four sons and two daus.,

i. John, of Redwood, co. Tipperary, high sheriff 1753, ancestor of BLOOMFIELD, of Redwood (see BURKE's Landed Gentry).
ii. Joseph, entered Trin. Coll., Dublin, 14 October, 1726, aged 14 B.A. 1731.

III. Benjamin, of whom hereafter.
IV. Richard
I. Dorothy.
II. Anne.

The 3rd son,

Benjamin Bloomfield, Esq., of Meelick, co. Galway, was father of

John Bloomfield, Esq., of Newport, co. Tipperary, m. Charlotte, dau. of Samuel Waller, Esq., barrister-at-law (by Anne, his wife, dau. of Thomas Jocelyn, Esq.), and sister of Sir Robert Waller, 1st Bart., of Newport, by whom he had issue,

I. Benjamin, created Lord Bloomfield.
I. Anne, m. Thomas-Ryder Pepper, Esq., of Loughton, co. Tipperary.
II. Charlotte, m. Very Rev. Thomas Bunbury Gough, Dean of Derry.

The only son,

Sir Benjamin Bloomfield, 1st Lord Bloomfield, a lieut.-general in the army, col. commandant of the royal regiment of artillery, G.C.B. and G.C.H., b. 13 April, 1762, was 1808 appointed gentleman-attendant upon His Royal Highness the Prince of Wales, and, during the subsequent regency, filled the offices of marshal and chief equerry to the Regent. In 1815, he received the honour of knighthood; and in 1817, on the resignation of Sir John MacMahon, succeeded that gentleman as receiver-general of the duchy of Cornwall, and private secretary and keeper of the privy purse to the Prince. In September, 1824, he was appointed minister-plenipotentiary and envoy-extraordinary to the Court of Sweden, and was elevated to the peerage of Ireland as Baron Bloomfield, of Redwood and Oakhampton, co. Tipperary, by patent, dated 14 May, 1825. Lord Bloomfield m. 7 September, 1797, Harriott, dau. of John Douglas, Esq., of Grantham, co. Lincoln, and had by her (who d. 13 September, 1868),

John-Arthur Douglas, 2nd baron.
Harriett-Mary-Anne, m. 5 June, 1833, Col. Thomas-Henry Kingscote, of Kingscote, co. Gloucester, and by him (who d. 19 December, 1861) had Fitzhardinge, Henry-Bloomfield, and other issue.
Georgiana-Mary-Emilia, m. 22 October, 1836, to Henry, 2nd son of William Trench, Esq., of Cangort Park, King's County, and had Henry-Bloomfield Trench, and other issue.

Lord Bloomfield, d. 15 August, 1846, and was s. by his son,

Sir John-Arthur-Douglas, 2nd Lord Bloomfield, G.C.B., P.C., b. 12 November, 1802; m. 4 September, 1845, the Hon. Georgiana Liddell, youngest dau. of Thomas-Henry, 1st Lord Ravensworth. In 1844 he was appointed Ambassador to Russia, in 1851 to Prussia, in 1860 to Austria, and in 1871, created a peer of the United Kingdom, as Baron Bloomfield of Ciamhaltha, co. Tipperary. Lord Bloomfield d. s. p. 17 August, 1879, when his titles became extinct, and his estate devolved on his sister the Hon. Harriett-Mary-Anne Kingscote.

Arms—Arg., three lozenges, conjoined, in fesse, gu., between as many cinquefoils, az.: on a canton of the last, a plume of three ostrich feathers of the field, issuing through the rim of a royal coronet, or.

BURY—EARLS OF CHARLEVILLE, VISCOUNTS CHARLEVILLE, AND BARONS TULLAMOORE.

Barony, by Letters Patent, dated 7 November, 1797.
Viscounty, by Letters Patent, dated 29 December, 1800.
Earldom, by Letters Patent, dated 16 February, 1806.

Lineage.

Phineas Bury, Esq., had a grant of lands in co. Limerick, 14 November, 1666, and in the Barony of Barrymore, co. Cork, 10 June, 1668, and was High Sheriff of the latter co., 1673. His 2nd son,

John Bury, Esq., of Shannon Grove, co. Limerick, took out administration to his elder brother, Richard, 11 January, 1691. He m. Jane, only dau. of William Palliser, Archbishop of Cashel, and had issue,

I. William, his heir.
II. John, assumed the name and arms of Palliser. His will, dated 12 July, 1766, was proved 28 February, 1769. He was ancestor of Palliser, of Derryluskan, co. Tipperary, and Comragh, co. Waterford, represented by John Palliser, Esq., of Derryluskan and Comragh, C.M.G., b. 29 January, 1817. (See Burke's Landed Gentry.)
III. Richard, of Mount Pleasant, co. Clare, m. Anne, dau. of Mountiford Westropp, of Attyflin, co. Limerick, which lady m. 2ndly, Wm. Spaight, Esq.
IV. Thomas, of Curraghbridge, co. Limerick. Will dated 11 September, 1767; proved 19 April, 1774; d. s. p.
V. Phineas, of Little Island, co. Cork, m. 1734, Hester, dau.

of Thos. Moland, Esq., and was ancestor of Bury, of Little Island and Curraghbridge, co. Cork, represented by Phineas Bury, Esq., of Little Island and Curraghbridge, b. 7 March, 1841. (See Burke's Landed Gentry.)
I. Elizabeth, m. to Mountiford Westropp, Esq., of Attyflin.

John Bury, of Shannon Grove, d. 1722, and was s. by his eldest son,

William Bury, Esq., of Shannon Grove, m. 27 January, 1723, Hon. Jane Moore, only dau. of John, 1st Lord Tullamoore, and sister and eventual heiress of Charles, 2nd Lord Tullamoore and Earl of Charleville (see Moore, Earl of Charleville, page 379) and had issue,

I. John, his successor.
II. Charles.
III. William.
IV. Richard.
V. Thomas.
I. Jane.
II. Georgiana, m. Richard, 4th Viscount Boyne.
III. Mary.
IV. Elizabeth.

The eldest son,

John Bury, Esq., of Shannon Grove, s. to Charleville Forest, in the King's Co., on the death s. p. of his uncle, Charles, Earl of Charleville, 17 February, 1764. He m. Catherine, 2nd dau. and co-heir of Francis Sadleir. Esq., of Sopwell Hall, co. Tipperary, and by her (who m. 2ndly, 2 June, 1766, Henry Prittie, afterwards Lord Dunalley) left at his decease, 4 August, 1764, an only son,

Charles-William Bury, Esq., of Shannon Grove, b. 30 June, 1764; who was raised to the peerage of Ireland, as Baron Tullamoore, 26 November, 1797; created Viscount Charleville, 29 December, 1800, and Earl of Charleville, 16 February, 1806. He m. 4 June, 1798, Catherine-Maria, widow of James Tisdall, Esq., of Bawn, co. Louth, and dau. and sole heir of Thomas-Townley Dawson, Esq., of Kinsealy, co. Dublin, by whom he left at his decease, in October, 1835, an only son,

Charles-William, 2nd earl, b. 29 April, 1801; m. 26 February, 1821, Harriet-Charlotte-Beaujolois, 3rd dau. of Col. John Campbell, of Shawfield, and niece of the Duke of Argyll, and by her (who d. 1 February, 1848) had issue,

Charles-William-George, 3rd earl
John-James, capt. R.E., b. 22 October, 1827; m. 24 June, 1852, Charlotte-Theresa, only dau. of Thomas Austin, Esq., and d. 20 January, 1861, having had issue, Beaujolois-Arabella-Charlotte, d. 1 November, 1865; Georgiana-Florence, m. 24 June, 1879, Edward-Guy-Selby Smyth, Esq.; Louisa-Emily-Austin, d. 1881; and Ada-Tighe.
Alfred, 5th earl.
Katherine-Eleanora-Beaujolois, m. 30 June, 1853, to Hastings Dent, Esq. (who d. 7 June, 1864), son of John Dent, Esq., M.P.

The earl d. 14 July, 1851, and was s. by his eldest son,

Charles-William-George, 3rd earl; b. 8 March, 1822; lieut. 43rd foot; m. 7 March, 1850, Arabella-Louisa, youngest dau. of Henry Case, Esq., of Shenston Moss, co. Stafford, and by her (who d. 8 July, 1857) had,

Charles-William-Francis, 4th earl.
John-William, b. 31 August, 1854; d. 20 August, 1872.
Katherine-Beaujolois-Arabella, m. 5 June, 1873, to Lieut.-Col. Edmund-Bacon Hutton, royal dragoons.
Harriet-Hugh-Adelaide, accidentally killed by a fall, 3 April, 1861.
Emily-Alfreda-Julia, s. to the Charleville estates; m. 20 September, 1881, Kenneth Howard (son of Hon. James-Kenneth Howard, and grandson of Thomas, Earl of Suffolk and Berkshire), who assumed, by royal licence, dated 14 December, 1881, the additional surname and arms of Bury.

The earl d. 19 January, 1859, and was s. by his elder son,

Charles-William-Francis, 4th earl; he was b. 16 May, 1852; and d. unm. 3 November, 1874, when he was s. by his uncle,

Alfred, 5th earl, b. 19 February, 1829; m. 20 June, 1854, Emily-Frances, 3rd dau. of Gen. Sir William Wood, K.C.B., K.H., col. 14th foot. He d. s. p. 28 June, 1875, when the titles became extinct.

Arms—Quarterly: 1st and 4th, vert, a cross-crosslet, or, for Bury; 2nd and 3rd, az., on a chief, indented, or, three mullets, pierced, gu., a crescent for difference, for Moore.

CAMPBELL—BARON CLYDE.

By Letters Patent, dated 16 August, 1858.

Lineage.

Sir Colin Campbell, G.C.B., K.S.I., D.C.L., a general in the army, colonel of the coldstream guards, was created a Peer of the United Kingdom, 16 August, 1858, as Baron Clyde, of Clydesdale, in Scotland. This eminent military commander was b. near Glasgow, 20 October, 1792; the son of

Mr. John M'Liver, a native of Mull, resident in Glasgow; he descended, through his mother, from a family of CAMPBELLS, who settled in Islay near two centuries ago, along with their chief, the ancestor of the Earls of Cawdor. His maternal kinsmen often served in the army; one uncle, after whom he was called, was killed a subaltern in the war of the American Revolution, and another, under whose directions he was educated, was Colonel John Campbell. Young Colin M'Liver entered the British army 26 May, 1808, being gazetted an ensign in the 9th foot, under the name of Campbell, which he bore ever afterwards. He proceeded at once on foreign service, served at Vimiera and at Corunna, and was in the Walcheren expedition, after which, returning to Spain, he shared in all the remainder of the Peninsular War, until 1814, being at the battles of Barossa and Vittoria, and being severely wounded twice in the forlorn hope at the siege of San Sebastian, and again at the passage of the Bidassoa. When the Peninsular War was over, Campbell, then a captain, was drafted into the 60th rifles, and served in America during 1814 and 1815. He became a lieut.-col. in 1832, and a colonel and aide-de-camp to the Queen in 1842, and in that year he commanded the 98th at the siege and capture of Chinkeanfoo, during the Chinese war. In 1848, he went to India as commander of the 3rd division of the Punjaub, in the second Sikh war. Here he mainly contributed to the British being masters of the field in the terrible battle of the Chillianwallah, and he again did good work at the victory of Goojerat. For these services he was created a K.C.B. and received the thanks of Parliament and of the East India Company. Sir Colin Campbell was at the head of the highland brigade and high land division during the Crimean war, and to him, in a great measure, belonged the credit of the victory of the Alma. He received the thanks of parliament for his services in that campaign. He was made a major-general 20 June, 1854, and colonel of the 67th foot, 24 October same year; and received the local rank of general, in Turkey, 1855, and that of lieut.-general in the army 4 June, 1856; he became a general 14 May, 1858. He was appointed commander-in-chief of the forces in India in 1857, with the local rank of general; and his success there in crushing the Sepoy rebellion proved most effective, his principal achievements being the storming of Lucknow, in November, 1857, when he relieved Sir Henry Havelock and Sir James Outram; and his final capture of the same place, in March, 1858. He concluded by completely restoring order and re-establishing British supremacy. Sir Colin Campbell was raised to the peerage 16 August, 1858, as LORD CLYDE, of Clydesdale. He received again the thanks of parliament, in 1859, for his services in India, and he was appointed colonel of the coldstream guards. He was made a knight of the Star of India in 1861.

This great and gallant soldier, who rose from a lowly station to the highest position in the British army, achieved his success "by the mere force of sterling ability, complete knowledge of his profession, sound sense, high honour, and an honest, industrious, and laborious performance of duty. Perhaps he owed as much to the qualities of his heart as to those of his head and his will. The positions he won are hardly open to equal abilities, if marred by an impracticable or ungenerous nature. But his nature was so retiring, and his modesty so complete that he excited no personal envy or jealousy. His rise was felt to be simply the natural recognition of talents which the country could not spare: and at the same time his entire generosity prevented his retaining any grudge at past disappointments, and made him always ready to serve others, whenever and wherever he was wanted." Lord Clyde d. at the Government House, Chatham, 14 August, 1863, and on the 22nd of that month his remains were buried near the grave of Outram in Westminster Abbey, but, agreeably to his own wish, with little of the ceremony that commonly attends interment there.

As his lordship d. unm. the title became EXTINCT.

Arms—Or, on a fesse, gu., a mural crown of the field.

CANNING—VISCOUNT AND EARL CANNING.

Viscounty, by Letters Patent, dated 22 January, 1828.
Earldom, by Letters Patent, dated 21 May, 1859.

Lineage.

GEORGE CANNING, Esq., of the Middle Temple, eldest son of Stratford Canning, Esq., of Garvagh, co. Londonderry, and uncle of George, 1st Lord Garvagh (see BURKE's Peerage), m. May, 1768, Miss Mary-Anne Costello, of Wigmore Street,

London, and d. 8 April, 1771, having incurred the displeasure of his father and the penalty of disinheritance by this improvident marriage, leaving an only child.

THE RIGHT HON. GEORGE CANNING. This celebrated orator and statesman, b. in London, 11 April, 1770, was educated at Eton and Oxford, entered Parliament in 1793, and, in 1796, became under secretary of state. In 1807, he was appointed secretary of state for Foreign Affairs, but resigned in consequence of a duel with Lord Castlereagh. In 1812, he was elected M.P. for Liverpool, in 1814 went as Ambassador to Portugal, and in 1816 became President of the Board of Control. In 1822, he was selected as the Marquess of Hastings' successor in the government of India, but, while he was preparing for his departure, Lord Londonderry's death occurred, and Mr. Canning was constituted secretary for foreign affairs, in his stead. Finally, 17 February, 1827, he attained to the highest position under the Crown, and was nominated First Lord of the Treasury and Chancellor of the Exchequer, but his tenure of power was very brief. After the stormy session of 1827, broken in health and spirit, he sought repose and change of air at the Duke of Devonshire's villa at Chiswick, but hopelessly. On the 8th of August following, he breathed his last, in the very room in which Fox died; and his remains were laid in Westminster Abbey, close to the resting place of William Pitt. Mr. Canning m. 8 July, 1800, JOAN, youngest dau. and co-heir of Major-General John Scott, of Balcomie, co. Fife, by Margaret, his wife, youngest dau. of Robert Dundas, of Arniston, lord president of the Court of Session, by Henrietta Baillie, the heiress of Lamintoun. A few months after Mr. Canning's decease, his widow, JOAN, was elevated to the peerage of the United Kingdom, as VISCOUNTESS CANNING, of Kilbrahan, co. Kilkenny, 22 January, 1828. Her ladyship d. 15 March, 1837: the issue of her marriage consisted of three sons and one dau., viz.,

I. George-Charles, b. 25 April, 1801; d. 31 March, 1820.
II. William-Pitt, captain R.N., drowned while bathing at Madeira, 25 September, 1828.
III. CHARLES-JOHN, of whom presently.
I. Harriet, m. 4 April, 1825, to Ulick-John, 1st Marquess of Clanricarde, K.P., and her son,

HUBERT-GEORGE, 2nd Marquess of Clanricarde, assumed the surname and arms of CANNING (see BURKE's Peerage).

The 3rd and last surviving son,

SIR CHARLES-JOHN CANNING, K.G., G.C.B., P.C., Viscount Canning, b. at Brompton, Middlesex, 14 December, 1812, was educated at Eton and Oxford, graduating as a First Class in "literis humanioribus." In 1841, he became under secretary of state for foreign affairs, and in 1846, chief commissioner of woods and forests. In 1852, he joined Lord Aberdeen's ministry as postmaster-general, and in 1855, was given the high appointment of governor-general of India, during his tenure of which the great Indian Mutiny broke out, and was suppressed. His lordship was raised to the EARLDOM OF CANNING, 21 May, 1859, and made K.G. 21 May, 1862. He m. 5 September, 1835, the Hon. Charlotte Stuart, eldest dau. and co-heir of Lord Stuart de Rothesay, which lady d. s. p. at Calcutta, 18 November, 1861. Lord Canning d. 17 June, 1862, when his honours became EXTINCT.

Arms—Quarterly: 1st and 4th, arg., three Moors' heads, couped in profile, ppr., wreathed round the temples, arg. and az.; 2nd, gu., three spear-heads, palewise, in fesse, arg.; 3rd, gu., a goat, salient, or.

CANNING—VISCOUNT STRATFORD DE REDCLIFFE.

By Letters Patent, dated 24 April, 1852.

Lineage.

STRATFORD CANNING, a merchant of London, 3rd son of STRATFORD CANNING, Esq., of Garvagh, descended from the ancient family of Canning, of Foxcote, co. Warwick (see BURKE's Peerage, Garvagh, B.), m. Mehetabel, dau. of Robert Patrick, Esq., of Somerville, co. Dublin, and had issue,

I. Henry, consul-general at Hamburgh, m. and had issue.
II. William (Rev.), canon of Windsor, d. s. p. 24 February, 1860.
III. Charles, aide-de-camp to the Duke of Wellington, killed at Waterloo.
IV. STRATFORD, of whom hereafter.
I. Elizabeth, m. to George-Henry Barnett, Esq., of Glympton Park, co. Oxford.

Mr. Stratford Canning d. May, 1787. His 4th son,

RIGHT HON. SIR STRATFORD CANNING, Viscount Stratford de Redcliffe, K.G., G.C.B., P.C., Hon. D.C.L. Oxford, and Hon.

LL.D. Cambridge, was b. 6 January, 1788, and was one of the most eminent diplomatists of his time. For more than half a century he was actively engaged as ambassador or minister in various important congresses and missions at different periods and in different countries. He was secretary to the embassy to Turkey 1809-10, and minister plenipotentiary 1810-12; was at the congress of Vienna 1814-15; ambassador to Switzerland, 1814; to the United States, 1820; went on a special mission to Russia, 1824; ambassador at Constantinople, 1825-27-29; at Madrid, 1832, and at St. Petersburgh same year. His last embassy, and one in which he has achieved historic reputation, was to Constantinople, in 1841; he resigned it in May, 1858, but went on a special mission to take leave of the Sultan in September of that year. He sat in the House of Commons for Old Sarum, 1828-31, for Stockbridge, 1831-32, and for King's Lynn, 1835-42, and was raised to the peerage of the United Kingdom by letters patent 24 April, 1852, as VISCOUNT STRATFORD DE REDCLIFFE, Somerset, chosing the designation of REDCLIFFE in remembrance of his collateral ancestor "William Cannynge," the pious founder of St. Marye Redcliffe at Bristol. His lordship m. 1st, 3 August, 1816, Harriet, dau. of Thomas Raikes, Esq., by whom (who d. 17 February following) he had no issue. He m. 2ndly, 3 September, 1825, Elizabeth-Charlotte, dau. of James Alexander, Esq., of Somerhill, by whom he had issue,

   I. GEORGE, b. 15 May, 1832; d. unm. vitâ patris, 14 February, 1878.
   I. Louisa.
   II. Katherine.
   III. Mary.

Arms—Quarterly: 1st and 4th, arg., three Moors' heads, uped, in profile, ppr., wreathed round the temples, arg. and az.; 2nd, gu., three spear heads, palewise, in fesse, arg.; 3rd, gu., a goat, salient, or.

Page 126.

COKAYNE—VISCOUNT CULLEN.

The original patent of this peerage has been lost, and was never enrolled; but in the Partition Book, vol. iv., p. 37, at the College of Arms, London, is the following entry:—"Particon made at the Office of Armes the 2d day of March, 1642, of the fees of CHARLES COKAYNE, of Rushton in Com. Northon, Esq., created BARON and VISCOUNT CULLEN in the countie of Typarary, in Ireland. Intayling the same upon his heires males of his body for ever and for want of such issue, the same Honors are intayled upon Peregrine Bertie, Richard Bertie, Vere Bertie, and Charles Bertie, 4 yonger sons of the Lo. Willoughby of Erisby and the heires males of their bodies successively. Teste xj. Augusti, 1642."

Page 126.

CRADOCK—BARONS HOWDEN OF GRIMSTON AND SPADLINGTON AND OF CRADOCKSTOWN, CO. KILDARE, BARONS HOWDEN OF HOWDEN AND GRIMSTON, CO. YORK.

Barony (Irish Peerage), by Letters Patent dated 19 October, 1819.
Barony (United Kingdom), by Letters Patent, dated 7 September, 1831.

Lineage.

JOHN CRADOCK, D.D., born at Wolverhampton, was a Fellow of St. John's Coll., Cambridge, and rector of St. Paul's, Covent Garden. Subsequently he accompanied as chaplain the Duke of Bedford, Lord Lieutenant, to Ireland, and was consecrated Bishop of Kilmore 1757, and translated to the archiepiscopal see of Dublin in 1772. He m. 28 August, 1758, Mary, dau. of William Blaydwin, Esq., of Boston, co. Lincoln, and widow of Richard St. George, Esq., of Kilrush, co. Kilkenny, and d. 11 December, 1778, leaving an only son,

GEN. SIR JOHN-FRANCIS CRADOCK, b. 12 August, 1762, created BARON HOWDEN of Grimston and Spadlington and of Cradockstown, co. Kildare, in the peerage of Ireland, 19 October, 1819, and BARON HOWDEN of Howden and Grimston, co. York, in that of the United Kingdom, 7 September, 1831. He assumed the surname of CARADOC by royal licence, dated 19 December same year. His lordship was a general officer in the army, colonel of the 43rd regiment of foot, a Knight Grand Cross of the Bath, and Knight Grand Cross of the Imperial Ottoman order of the Crescent; which orders were bestowed upon his lordship for his distinguished services in Egypt. He m. 17 November, 1798, Lady Theodosia-Sarah-Frances Meade, dau. of John, 1st Earl of Clanwilliam (by

Theodosia his wife, dau. of Robert Hawkins Magill, Esq., of Gill Hall, and the Lady Anne Bligh, his wife, who was dau. of John, 1st Earl of Darnley, by Theodosia, baroness Clifton, his wife, dau. and heiress of Edward, 3rd Earl of Clarendon), by whom he left at his decease, July, 1839, an only son,

JOHN HOBART, 2nd Baron, b. 16 October, 1799; lieut.-general in the army, equerry to H.R.H. the Duchess of Kent, steward of the Halmot Court of Howdenshire, deputy-lieut. of the co. York; G.C.B. of the Civil order, and knight of the Guelphic order of Hanover, Legion of Honour of France, St. Anne of Prussia, Leopold of Belgium, Redeemer of Greece, and Charles III. of Spain; m. 11 January, 1830, Catharine, Princess Bagration, dau. of his Excellency Paul, Count Skavronsky, and great-niece of Prince Potemkin, which lady d. 2 June, 1857. He was envoy-extraordinary to the Queen of Spain, and d. s. p. 9 October, 1873, when his titles became EXTINCT.

Arms—Arg., on a chevron, az., between a griffin, passant, gu., wings erminois, in chief, and in base a boar's head, erased, ppr., three garbs, or.

Page 126.

DE COURCY, OR DE CURCI—EARL OF ULSTER.

Lineage.

Shortly after the death of Strongbow in 1176, HENRY II. granted "Ulidia," the present counties of Down and Antrim, and afterwards called among the Anglo-Irish "Ulster," to John de Curci, one his most successful and valiant soldiers, who erected a castle at Downpatrick, but was in 1178 obliged to fly wounded to Dublin, from a battle in which he was utterly defeated by the Chief of Firli. In the latter end of 1185 he was appointed deputy to Prince John, Lord of Ireland, and continued in office as viceroy till 1189.

He m. Affreca, dau. of Godred Crovan, King of Man and the Isles, and by Scandinavian and Irish help managed to maintain his possessions of Ulidia against all the power of the Viceroy Hugh de Lacy, whom he defeated in a battle at Down in 1204; however, in May, 1205, King JOHN bestowed the Earldom on de Lacy.

In 1204 de Curci had a safe conduct to go to the King, and in 1210 proceeded to Ireland in his service, being then in receipt of a pension of £100 per annum.

He appears to have died about 1219, as in that year Affreca is described as his widow. By her (who d. in Grey Abbey, co. Down, endowed by her for Cistercians in 1193), his contemporary, Cambrensis, alleges he had no children, which appears the more probable, as neither he nor his brother-in-law, Reginald, King of Man, in their numerous endowments to monasteries ever makes mention of them among the relations whose souls are to be prayed for.

Moreover, the connexion between John de Curci, Earl of Ulster, and the English Barons of Stoke-Courcy becomes very problematical when we learn from a fine roll of 1218, quoted in Gilbert's erudite Viceroys of Ireland (from which we have drawn much of the information in this article), that he had relinquished to HENRY III. rights in Ireland, claimed as of his father Roger de Chester.

Page 162.

DE DREUX—EARLS OF RICHMOND.

I have found it impossible to reconcile the conflicting accounts of the earlier generations of the ancestry of the Earls of Richmond. Dugdale's statement differs materially from the descent given in the third general report of the Lords' Committee on the dignity of a peer, a descent followed by Nicolas and Courthope. Whereas the pedigree in the Art de Vérifier les Dates is again quite dissimilar. My esteemed and accomplished friend, the present Lord Gort, has afforded me the advantage of his researches on the subject of the De Dreux pedigree, and I have rested my narrative on what appeared to me to be the most reliable sources of information.

DE FOIX—EARL OF KENDAL.

Lineage.

SIR JOHN DE FOIX, K.G., Comte de Longueville and de Benanges, Captal de Buch, son of Gaston de Foix, Captal de Buch, Comte de Longueville, in Normandy, by Margaret D'Albret, his wife, and grandson of Archambaud de Grailly,

Captal de Buch, by Isabelle de Foix, his wife, Comtesse de Foix, and Vicomtesse de Castelbon, is stated to have been created a Peer of England, as EARL OF KENDAL, by patent, 22 August, 1446; "but," says Nicolas, "it may be doubted if this John de Foix was ever regularly created Earl of Kendal in England, for, though Dugdale cites the Rolls of Parliament, 28th HENRY VI., n. 31, as his authority, it does not appear that positive proof of the fact is afforded therein." John de Foix eventually surrendered the Garter, and became the liege subject of the King of France; he m. Margaret, dau. of Michael de la Pole, Earl of Suffolk, and d. in 1485, leaving two sons, GASTON, Comte de Candale (Kendal), and JOHN, Vicomte de Meilles, Comte de Gurson and de Fleix, ancestor of the Ducs DE RENDAN, who styled themselves afterwards COMTES DE CANDALE (Kendal). The elder son, GASTON, 2nd Comte de Candale, m. Catherine, sister of Gaston, Prince de Viane, and was father of GASTON, 3rd Comte de Candale, who m. Martha, dau. and heir of John, 3rd Comte d'Astarac, and had a son, FREDERIC, Comte de Candale, who m. 1540, Frances, dau. of Francis, 2nd Comte de la Rochefoucauld, and was father of HENRY DE FOIX, Comte de Candale, who m. 1567, Mary, a dau. of Ann, Duc de Montmorency, and d. 1573, leaving a dau. and heiress, MARGUERITE, Comtesse de Candale, m. 1587, to John-Louis Nogaret de la Vallette, Duc d'Espernon, and had issue.

Arms—Quarterly: 1st and 4th, arg., two cows passant, gu., armed and unguled, with bells about their necks, or, 2nd and 3rd, or, three pallets, gu., over all a label of three points, sa., charged with fifteen escallops, arg.

DE LACY—EARLS OF ULSTER.

See under DE LACY, EARLS OF LINCOLN.

DUNBAR—EARLS OF DUNBAR AND MARCH.

Lineage.

MALDRED, son of Crinan, m. Algitha, dau. of Uchtred, Earl of Northumberland, by Elgiva, his wife, dau. of King ETHELRED, and was father of

COSPATRIC, made Earl of Northumberland by WILLIAM THE CONQUEROR. Soon after, he was deprived of that Earldom, and fled to Scotland, where King MALCOLM CANMORE gave him Dunbar and the lands adjoining. The monks of Durham celebrated 15 December, 1069, the death of this Cospatricius, Earl and Monk; and, in 1821, a stone coffin inscribed on its lid, " + Cospatricius, Comes," was found in the monks' burial ground at Durham. His son, COSPATRIC, a great benefactor to the abbey of Kelso, is described in many of his charters to that community "Cospatricius, Comes." He d. 1139, and was s. by his son, COSPATRIC, styled in the Register of Kelso, "Cospatricius Comes, filius Cospatricii Comitis." He left issue; of which the eldest son,

EARL COSPATRIC, founded the Cistercian Convents of Coldstream and Eccles, co. Berwick, and was a liberal benefactor to the abbey of Melrose; he d. 1166, leaving two sons, WALDEVE, his heir, and PATRICK, witness to a charter, A.D. 1123, as "filius Comitis Cospatric ac frater Comitis Waldevi, Dominus de Greenlaw;" ancestor of the HOMES, EARLS OF HOME. The elder son,

WALDEVE, 5th Earl, was the first who had the territorial designation of Dunbar, about 1174. He was one of the hostages for the due performance of the treaty for the liberation of King WILLIAM I. He d. 1182, leaving by Aelina, his wife, two sons, PATRICK and Constantine, and a dau., Alicia, m. to Philip de Seton. The elder son,

PATRICK DUNBAR, 6th Earl of Dunbar, was Justiciary of Lothian and Keeper of Berwick. In 1218, he founded the House of the Red Friars, at Dunbar, and eventually, when far advanced in years, retired to a monastery, where he d. in 1232. He m. 1st, Ada, illegitimate dau. of King WILLIAM THE LYON; and 2ndly, a lady, whose Christian name was Christina; by the former he had issue,

  I. PATRICK, his heir.
  II. William, designed " Willielmus, filius Comitis Patricii," in a charter to the monastery of Kelso, m. Christianna, dau. and heir of Walter de Corbet, of Mackerston, and d. 1253, leaving issue.
  III. Adam.   IV. Robert.
  I. Ada, m. 1st, to — Courtenay; and 2ndly, to William Dunbar, ancestor by her of the EARLS OF HOME.

The eldest son,

PATRICK DUNBAR, 7th Earl, a potent noble of Scotland, joined the Crusade under LOUIS IX., commanded the Scots, and d. at the siege of Damietta, 1248. He m. Eupheme, dau. of Walter, Lord High Stewart, and had a son,

PATRICK DUNBAR, 8th Earl, who took an active part in Scotch politics, and was one of the leaders of the English party. His surprisal of the castle of Edinburgh delivered ALEXANDER III. and his Queen from the Comyns. He was, after the death of that monarch, one of the Regents of Scotland, and one of the SEVEN EARLS OF SCOTLAND—a distinct body separate from the rest of the estates of the Kingdom. The Earl of Dunbar d. in 1289, aged seventy-six, leaving by Christiana, his wife (who founded "ane house of religione in ye toune of Dunbar,") dau. of Robert Bruce, Lord of Annandale,

PATRICK DUNBAR, 9th Earl, surnamed "Black Beard," and styled also Earl of March, who swore fealty to EDWARD I. of England, and was a steadfast adherent of the English interest, but his wife, Marjory Comyn,[*] dau. of Alexander Comyn, Earl of Buchan, sided with the opposite party, and held the castle of Dunbar for Baliol, until forced to surrender it to EDWARD, in 1296. In 1298, the Earl of March was appointed the King's Lieutenant in Scotland, and in 1300 was at the siege of Carlaverock. By Marjory, his wife, he had issue, PATRICK, his heir; and GEORGE, ancestor of the family of DUNBAR, of Mochrum, the direct line of which ended in the three daus. an t co-heirs of Patrick Dunbar, of Mochrum, who all married Dunbars. Their uncle, the heir-male, was Cuthbert Dunbar, of Blantyre. The eldest son,

PATRICK DUNBAR, 10th earl, was with his father at Carlaverock; and, after the battle of Bannockburn, gave refuge to EDWARD II. in his castle of Dunbar, and secured the king's escape in a fishing boat to England. Making peace, however, with Robert Bruce, he signed the letter to the Pope in 1320, was appointed Governor of Berwick Castle, and held that fortress against EDWARD III., until the defeat of the Scots at Halidon Hill necessitated its surrender. Not long after, his Countess, known in history as "Black Agnes," dau. of the renowned Regent of Scotland, Thomas Randolph, Earl of Moray, and grandniece of Bruce, defended in the absence of her husband, in January, 1337-8, the castle of Dunbar against the English, under the Earl of Salisbury, during a fierce and determined siege of nineteen weeks, and at length forced the Earl to abandon the attempt. This gallant resistance of the Countess of Dunbar is memorable in Scottish annals, and has given subject to many a minstrel's song. "Black Agnes" became eventually heiress of her brother, John Randolph, 3rd Earl of Moray, and her husband added the Earldom of Moray to his other dignities. They left issue,

  I. GEORGE, 11th Earl of Dunbar and March.
  II. JOHN, Earl o' Moray (*see* p. 449).
  I Agnes, m. to Sir James Douglas, Lord Dalkeith, and from her came the 1st, 2nd, and 3rd Earls of Morton.
  II. Elizabeth, m. to John Maitland, of Lethington, ancestrix of the Duke of Lauderdale, who took as his second title the Marquessate of March.

The 10th Earl of Dunbar and March commanded the left wing of the Scottish army at the battle of Durham. At the age of eighty-four he denuded himself of his title, and d. plain Sir Patrick de Dunbar, Knt., in 1369. His eldest son and heir,

GEORGE DUNBAR, 11th earl, Warden of the Marches, a great and powerful noble, accompanied Douglas in his foray in England, in 1388, and, after the battle of Otterburn, took command of the Scots, and conducted them safely home. But subsequently he became the rival of the Douglases, and, in consequence of the daughter of Archibald, the Grim Earl of Douglas, having been preferred to his own as bride for the Duke of Rothsay, the king's son, Dunbar renounced his allegiance, fled to England, and offered his services to HENRY IV., who gladly received him into his protection. The earl fought on the English side at Homildon Hill, as well as at the battle of Shrewsbury, against Owen Glendower and the Percys. At last, reconciled to the Douglases, he returned to Scotland after the death of ROBERT III., in 1409, and d. there in 1420, aged eighty-two. He m. Christine, sister of Sir William Seton, and had issue,

  I. GEORGE, his heir.
  II. Gawin (Sir), of Cumnock.
  III. Patrick (Sir), of Beil.
  IV. John.   V. David.
  VI. Columba, Bishop of Moray, d. 1435.
  I. Elizabeth, who should have been Duchess of Rothsay, d. unm.
  II. Janet, m. 1st, to John, Lord Seton, and 2ndly, Sir Adam Johnstone, of Johnstone, by whom she had a son, Matthew, ancestor of the Baronets of Westerhall.
  III. Margery, m. to Sir John Swinton.

---

[*] The marriage of Patrick, 9th Earl of March, with Marjory Comyn is proved by a letter written by George, 11th Earl of March to King HENRY IV., in which the earl claims cousinship with the King, but misstates the royal connexion. It was Marjory's niece and not sister of whom HENRY IV. was grandson.

The son and heir,

GEORGE DUNBAR, 12th earl, knighted at the coronation of JAMES I., seemed to all appearance to enjoy the confidence of the new monarch, and was on many occasions employed on State affairs, but, in 1434, without any previous warning, the king seized on the castle of Dunbar, and the parliament of Perth having declared the forfeiture of the earl, confiscated his estate, and annexed it to the Crown. There had long been an effort on the part of the Scottish monarch to diminish the power of these ambitious and turbulent Earls of Dunbar, whose possession of the great fortress of Dunbar gave rise to the saying that they held the key of Scotland in their girdles; and JAMES I. seized this as a proper moment to carry his plan into effect. To make some amends for the spoliation, the Earldom of Buchan was bestowed on the forfeited Earl, but Dunbar disdained to accept the title, and retired with his son Patrick to England. Thus passed away, mainly through the jealousy of the Scottish sovereigns, and the hostility of their great rivals, the Douglasses, the famous and historic Earls of Dunbar and March, who had, for nearly four centuries, stood so foremost amongst the Scottish nobles, and acted so prominent a part in the national annals. The estate of Kilconquhar in Fife, being held under the bishop of St. Andrews, was saved from forfeiture, but the rest of the great Dunbar estate was all swept away.

King HENRY IV. gave the fugitive earl a grant of part of the estate of Thomas, Lord Bardolph, who had been involved in the forfeiture of the Earl of Northumberland. In the charter he is called Sir George de Dunbar, Knt. His only son,

PATRICK DUNBAR, styled of Kilconquhar, who m. Janet, youngest of the three co-heirs of Patrick Dunbar of Mochrum, and got, as his share, Mochrum Loch. Their grandson, ANDREW DUNBAR, d. s. p., and his eldest sister MARGARET is now represented through the Macdowalls of Freuch, and her descendant Patrick, 5th Earl of Dumfries, by the MARQUESS OF BUTE, 7th Earl of Dumfries, and heir of COSPATRICK, Earl of Northumberland, temp. Conquestoris. The families of Dunbar now existing are derived from Sir ALEX DUNBAR, of Westfield, Sheriff of Moray, which estate he got from his sister, the heir to her father James Dunbar, 5th Earl of Moray, grandson of JOHN I., Earl thereof. The two eldest of Sir Alexander's six sons m. Anne-Eupheme and Margaret, the two eldest daus. and co-heirs of Patrick Dunbar, of Mochrum, and founded the long lines of Westfield and Mochrum, many other Dunbars trace to the other sons of the founder, Sir Alexander of Westfield.

Arms—Gu., a lion rampant, arg., within a bordure of the last, charged with eight roses of the 1st; Nisbet says that the bordure of roses was the badge of the comital office of Patrick, who was first designed "Earl of March." The earlier seals exhibit simply the lion rampant.

DUNGAN, OR DONGAN—VISCOUNTS DUNGAN AND EARLS OF LIMERICK.

Viscounty, by Letters Patent, dated 14 February, 1661.
Earldom, by Letters Patent, dated 2 January, 1685.

Lineage.

JOHN DUNGAN, or DONGAN, Esq., of Dublin, d. 8 August, 1592, leaving by Margaret Foster, his wife, four sons; I. WALTER, his heir; II. William, recorder of Dublin, m. Slanny-Bryan, dau. of Morough, Baron of Inchiquin, and dying 11 December, 1622, left an only son, John, who d.s p. 28 February, 1635; III. Edward, of Kiltaghan, whose will bears date 2 March, 1639; and IV. Thomas, of Griffenrath. The eldest son,

SIR WALTER DUNGAN, of Castletown, co. Kildare, created a Baronet 23 October, 1623, m. Jane, dau. of Robert Rochfort, Esq., of Kilbride, and by her had issue,

  I. JOHN, his successor.
  II. Thomas.   III. Christopher, d. s. p.
  IV. Mark, d. s. p.   v. William.
  VI. Oliver.   VII. Luke.
  I. Margaret, m. to Thomas Barnewall, Esq , of Robertstown, co. Meath.
  II. Mary.   III. Frances, d. s. p.
  IV. Jane.

Sir Walter, whose will was proved 11 February, 1627, was s. by his eldest son,

SIR JOHN DUNGAN, 2nd bart., of Castletown, who m. Mary, dau. of Sir William Talbot, Bart., of Cartown, and had issue, Walter (Sir), Bart., one of the Confederate Catholics of Kilkenny, d. s. p.; WILLIAM (Sir), of whom presently; Edward; Robert; Michael; Jerome; THOMAS (Sir), 2nd Earl of Limerick; James;

Bridget, m. to Francis Nugent, Esq., of Dardistown; Margaret, m. Robert, Lord Trimleston, and d. 5 December, 1678; Alice, m. to Robert Nugent, Esq., of Donore. Sir John's will, dated 26 July, 1642, was proved 27 January, 1663. His 2nd son,

SIR WILLIAM DUNGAN, Knt., was created VISCOUNT DUNGAN, *of Clane, co. Kildare*, by patent, dated 14 February, 1661, with remainder to his brothers Robert, Michael, and Thomas, and their respective issue male, and was created EARL OF LIMERICK by patent, dated 2 January, 1685, with remainder to his brother, Colonel Thomas Dungan, and his heirs male; and then to John Dungan, his cousin-german, and his heirs male. The earl m., while abroad, a foreign lady, whose christian name was Euphemia, and by her had issue, WALTER, Lord Dungan, member for Naas in King JAMES's parliament of 1689, slain at the battle of the Boyne; Maria-Euphemia, and Ursula, m. to Lucas, 6th Viscount Dillon. After the defeat of his party at the Boyne, the Earl went to Limerick, and proceeded eventually, after the capitulation of that city, to France, thereby forfeiting his great estates. The attainders of 1691 include the names of Euphemia Dungan, *alias* Countess of Limerick; and William, Earl of Limerick; and under those attainders the Dungan possessions were granted to General de Ginkell. The earl d. in 1698 (O'Callaghan's *Irish Brigades*), and was s. by his brother,

THOMAS DUNGAN, 2nd Earl of Limerick, at one time colonel of an Irish regiment in the service of LOUIS XIV., and subsequently, under CHARLES II., lieut.-governor of Tangier, and governor of New York: he d. 14 December, 1715, and was buried in St. Pancras church-yard, London.

Arms—Quarterly: 1st and 4th, gu., three lions passant, or, each holding in the dexter paw, a close helmet, arg., garnished of the second; 2nd and 3rd, az., six plates, three, two, and one, on a chief or, a demi-lion rampant, gu.

FERMOR—EARLS OF POMFRET, BARONS LEOMINSTER OF LEOMINSTER.

Barony, by Letters Patent, dated 12 April, 1692.
Earldom, by Letters Patent, dated 27 December, 1721.

Lineage.

RICHARD FERMOUR, Esq., having amassed considerable wealth as a merchant at Calais, settled himself at Easton Neston, co. Northampton; but exciting the hostility of HENRY VIII., by a zealous adherence to the Church of Rome, and inciting the cupidity of Thomas Cromwell, Earl of Essex, his majesty's vicar-general, by the extent of his possessions, he was deprived of the whole of his large fortune, which was confiscated, under a præmunire, because of his having relieved Nicholas Thayne, his quondam confessor, while a prisoner in the goal at Buckingham. It was, however, partly restored by EDWARD VI.; and Mr. Fermour regained his mansion house of Easton Neston. He m. Anne, dau. of Sir William Browne, lord-mayor of London, and d. 17 November, 1552, when he was s. by his eldest son,

JOHN FERMOR, Esq., of Easton Neston, who was made one of the Knights of the Carpet at Westminster, 2 October, 1553, the day after the coronation of MARY I., in her majesty's presence, under the cloth of state, by the Earl of Arundel, commissioner for the occasion. Sir John Fermor represented the co. of Northampton in two parliaments, and was sheriff of that co. in the 4th and 5th of PHILIP and MARY. He m. Maud, dau. of Sir Nicholas Vaux, Knt., Lord Vaux of Harrowden, and was s. at his decease, 12 December, 1571, by his eldest son,

GEORGE FERMOR, Esq., of Easton Neston, who received knighthood in 1586. Sir George had the honour of entertaining JAMES I. and his Queen at Easton, in June, 1603, when his majesty was pleased to knight Sir George's eldest son. He m. Mary, dau. and heir of Thomas Curzon, Esq., of Waterperry, co. Oxford, and had,

  I. Edward, d. unm.
  II. HATTON (Sir), his heir.
  III. Robert, slain in Ireland, 1616.
  IV. George.   v. Richard.
  VI. Devereux.   VII. William; and eight daus.

He d. 1 December, 1612, and was s. by his eldest son,

SIR HATTON FERMOR, Knt., of Easton Neston, sheriff co. Northampton, 15th JAMES I. He m. 1st, Elizabeth, dau. of Sir Edmund Anderson, lord-chief-justice of the Common Pleas, but by her had no issue; and 2ndly, Anna, dau. of Sir William Cokayne, lord-mayor of London, by whom he had five sons,

  I. WILLIAM (Sir), his heir.
  II. Hatton, major of horse, fell on the side of CHARLES I., 11 January, 1645.
  III. Charles.   IV. George.   v. Richard; and six daus.

Sir Hatton *d.* 28 October, 1640, and was *s.* by his eldest son,

SIR WILLIAM FERMOR, of Easton Neston, was created a Baronet, 6 September. 1641. This gentleman, who distinguished himself during the civil wars in the royal cause, and suffered severely, had the satisfaction of living to see the monarchy restored. Sir William *m.* Mary, dau. of Hugh Perry, Esq., of London, and relict of Henry Noel, 2nd son of Edward, Viscount Campden; and *dying of the small-pox*, in 1671, was *s.* by his eldest son,

SIR WILLIAM, 2nd bart., *elevated to the peerage,* 12 April, 1692, by the title of *Baron Leominster, of Leominster, co. Hereford.* His lordship *m.* 1st, Jane, dau. of Andrew Barker, Esq., of Fairford, co. Gloucester, by whom he had a dau.,

  I. Elizabeth, *d. unm.* March, 1705.

He *m.* 2ndly, Hon. Katherine Poulett, dau. of John, 1st Lord Poulett, by whom he had a dau.,

  II. Mary, *m.* Sir John Wodehouse, 4th Bart. of Kimberley.

He *m.* 3rdly, Lady Sophia Osborne, dau. of Thomas, 1st Duke of Leeds, and widow of Donogh, Lord Ibrackan, grandson and heir of Henry, 7th Earl of Thomond, by whom he had, with three other daus., who *d. unm.,*

  I. WILLIAM, 1st earl.
  III. Matilda, *m.* Edward Conyers, Esq., of Copthall, co. Essex, and *d.* 1741.

Lord Leominster *d.* 7 December, 1711, and was *s.* by his only son,

THOMAS, 2nd baron, K.B.; who was advanced to an earldom, 27 December, 1721, by the title of EARL OF POMFRET, *or Pontefract, co. York; m.* in 1720, Henrietta-Louisa, dau. and heir of John, Lord Jeffreys, by whom he had issue,

GEORGE, 2nd earl.
William, capt. R.N.; *d. unm.* in 1744.
John, *d.* in 1729.   Thomas, *d.* young.
Henrietta, *m.* in 1747, to John Conyers, Esq., of Copt Hall, co. Essex.
Sophia, *m.* to John Carteret, Earl Granville.
Charlotte, *m.* to Right Hon. William Finch, and *d.* in 1813.
Juliana, *m.* 1751, to Thomas Penn, Esq., of Stoke Park, co Bucks.
Louisa, *m.* to Sir Thomas Clayton, Bart.
Anne, *m.* 1754, to Thomas, 1st Viscount Cremorne.

The earl *d.* 8 July, 1753, and was *s.* by his eldest son,

GEORGE, 2nd earl, one of the lords of the bedchamber, and ranger of the Little Park at Windsor, *b.* in 1722, who *m.* in 1764, Miss Anna-Maria Drayton, of Sudbury, co. Middlesex (to whom Lady Jane Coke, relict of Robert Coke, Esq., bequeathed a considerable fortune), and had issue,

GEORGE, 3rd earl.
THOMAS-WILLIAM, 4th earl.
Charlotte, *m.* 1 August, 1787, to Peter Denys, Esq., of Hans Place, Chelsea, and of Fremington, Yorkshire; and *d.* in November, 1835.

The earl *d.* 9 June, 1785, and was *s.* by his elder son,

GEORGE, 3rd earl, *b.* 6 January, 1768, who *m.* in 1793, Mary, dau. and heir of Thomas Trollope Browne, Esq., of Gretford, co. Lincoln, and Besthorpe, Norfolk; by her (who *d.* 17 September, 1839) he had no issue. The earl *d.* 1830, and was *s.* by his brother,

THOMAS-WILLIAM, 4th earl, *b.* 22 November, 1770, a lieut.-general in the army, *m.* 13 January, 1823, Amabel-Elizabeth, eldest dau. of Sir Richard Borough, 1st Bart. of Basildon, by whom (who *m.* 2ndly, Mary, 1834, Rev. William Thorpe, D.D., of Belgrave Chapel, Pimlico) he had issue,

GEORGE-WILLIAM-RICHARD, 5th earl.
Thomas-Hatton-George, an officer 2nd life-guards; *b.* 1832; *d.* 4 March, 1864.
Anna-Maria-Annabella, *m.* 10 March, 1846, to Sir Thomas Hesketh, 5th Bart., of Rufford, and *d.* 25 February, 1870, leaving, with other issue, SIR THOMAS - GEORGE - FERMOR HESKETH, 7th Bart. of Rufford.
Henrietta - Louisa, *m.* 7 August, 1856, Col. Thomas-Wedderburn Ogilvy, of Ruthven, co. Forfar.

The earl *d.* 29 June. 1833, and was *s.* by his eldest son,

GEORGE-WILLIAM-RICHARD, 5th earl, co-heir of the barony of Fitzhugh (*see* that title); *b.* 31 December, 1824; *d.* 8 June, 1867, *unm.*, when the earldom, barony, and baronetcy became EXTINCT, and the co-heirship of the baron of Fitzhugh devolved on his sisters.

NOTE.—*Of the descendants of one of the younger sons of* Sir George Fermor, Knt. of Easton Neston. 1586, the first-mentioned with certainty as settled in Ireland, as

JASPER FERMOR: he is described in a letter, dated 4 December, 1746, and from other sources, as a grandson of Sir George Fermor of Easton Neston; this Jasper was a major in the army, and was deprived of his estates in the rebellion of 1641, and was forced to seek an asylum in England, where he resided

principally at Exeter. He *m.* the eldest dau. of Anthony Gamble, Esq. of co. Cork; and *d.* in 1683, leaving several children, of whom six were sons. The eldest,

RICHARD FERMOR, or FARMAR, of Arderrack, co. Cork, *m.* in 1675, Elizabeth, eldest dau. of Robert Phaire, col. in Cromwell's army, and governor of Cork in 1650. Their direct descendant and representative,

HUGH HOVELL FARMAR, Esq. of Dunsinane, co. Wexford, *b.* 15 January, 1782; *m.* 12 January, 1815, Meliora, only dau. of Peter Rickards Mynors, Esq. of Treago, co. Hereford, and by her (who *d.* 11 November, 1854) left at his decease, 1828,

HUGH HOVELL BASKERVILLE (Rev.), present representative of the family.
William Roberts, a col. in the army, assistant-commandant Royal Victoria Hospital, Netley, *o.* 14 March, 1825; served in 50th regt., and was severely wounded at the battle of Aliwal; served throughout the Indian Mutiny, of 1857-8 in the 82nd regt.; *m.* 1st, 20 May, 1851, Alicia Mary, only child of Edward Stone Cotgrave, Esq., capt. R.N., and by her (who *d.* 10 April, 1861) had issue,
  Richard D. Malpas Cotgrave, *b.* 2 December, 1853.
  Alicia-Mildred Cotgrave, *d.* 14 November, 1864.
  Meliora-Alianor Cotgrave.
  Grace-Ursula Cotgrave.
Col. Farmar *m.,* 2ndly, 11 June 1863, Ellinor-Louisa, eldest dau. of Rev. William Lewis Girardot, of Hinton Charterhouse, and has issue by her,
  Hugh-Henry-Foxcroft, *b.* 21 August, 1870.
  George-Jasper, *b.* 20 July, 1872.
  Beatrice-Emily.
  Cecily-Eleanor, *d.* 17 May, 1871.
  Juliet-Mary.
  Rose-Dorothea.
  Ella-Katherine.
  Violet-Eleanor.
Meliora Mynors, *m.* 1861, Edward A. Blundell, Esq., Governor of Singapore.
Anna-Catharina Rickards, *m.* 12 June, 1855, Rev. William Hirzel Le Marchant, Vicar of Harlsfield.
Jane-Philippa-Baskerville, *m.* 9 December, 1852, John Whitehead, Esq., barrister-at-law.

Arms—Arg., a fesse, sa., between three lions' heads, erased, gu.

FITZHERBERT—BARON ST. HELENS.

Barony of Ireland, by Letters Patent, dated 26 January, 1791. Barony of the United Kingdom, by Letters Patent, dated 31 July, 1801.

Lineage.

WILLIAM FITZHERBERT, Esq., of Tissington, co. Derby, recorder of Derby (an estate acquired by his progenitor, Nicholas Fitzherbert, of Upton, with his wife, Cicely, dau. and co-heir of Robert Francis, Esq., of Foremark), succeeded his uncle in 1696. He *m.* Rachel, dau. and at length heir of Thomas Bagshaw, Esq., of Bakewell and Ridge, co. Derby, and was *s.* by his eldest son,

WILLIAM FITZHERBERT, Esq., of Tissington, M.P., who *m.* Mary, eldest dau. of Littleton-Poyntz Meynell, Esq., of Bradley, co. Derby, and had issue,

WILLIAM, of Tissington, created a Baronet, 10 December, 1783 (*see* BURKE'S *Extant Peerage and Baronetage*).
John, *d.* young in the East Indies, in 1776.
Thomas, a lieut. in the army; *d. unm.* in 1767.
ALLEYNE, created *Lord St. Helens* in 1791.
Selina, *m.* to Henry-Gally Knight, Esq., barrister-at-law, of Langold, co. Notts; and *d.* 2 January, 1823, leaving a son, the late Henry-Gally Knight, Esq. of Firbeck and Langold, M.P. for Notts.
Catherine, *m.* in 1755, to Richard Bateman, Esq. of Hartington Hall, in Derbyshire, and had a son, Sir Hugh Bateman, Bart.

The 4th son,

SIR ALLEYNE FITZHERBERT, G.C.B., M.A., *b.* 1 March, 1753, and educated at Eton and Cambridge, commenced his diplomatic career at Brussels in 1777. After negotiating as sole plenipotentiary, a peace between France, Spain, and the States-General, in 1783, he had a leading share in that concluded with America at the same period. In 1783, he was appointed envoy extraordinary to the court of St. Petersburgh, and in 1787, sworn of the Privy Council, and made Chief Secretary for Ireland. In April, 1789, he went as ambassador extraordinary to the Hague, and in the following November, in the same capacity to Madrid, where he negotiated the convention between the crowns of Great Britain and Spain, which was signed at the Escurial 28 October, 1790; but the climate disagreeing, he went ambassador to the Hague in 1794, till the government was overthrown by the invasion of the French in the following winter. His last foreign mission was to St. Petersburgh, March, 1801, to congratulate the Emperor ALEXANDER on his accession, whose coronation he attended at Moscow the following September, and having accommodated the differences between Great Britain and the three Baltic powers, he finally closed his diplomatic labours. This eminent diplomatist was created a peer of Ireland as BARON ST. HELENS, 26 January, 1791, and a peer of the United Kingdom, as BARON ST. HELENS, *of the Isle of Wight*, 31 July, 1801. His lordship *d. unm.* in 1839, when his honours became EXTINCT.

Arms—Gu., three lions rampant, or.

Page 208.

FITZ-JAMES—DUKE OF BERWICK.

The Duke of Alba (brother-in-law of the Empress Eugenie), by descent, DUKE OF BERWICK, succeeded also to four Spanish dukedoms, ALBA and LIRIA (conferred on his great ancestor, Marshal Berwick), MONTORO and OLIVAREZ.

Page 218.

FLEMING—EARLS OF WIGTON.

The following is the earlier lineage of this noble family:—

SIR MALCOLM FLEMING (elder son of SIR ROBERT FLEMING, of Cumbernauld, the adherent of ROBERT BRUCE, and brother of Sir Patrick Fleming, of Biggar, *jure uxoris*, a dau. and co-heir of Sir Simon Fraser,) fought in the second body of the Scots army, at Halidonhill, 19 July, 1333, and was one of the few who were not slain. His subsequent participation in the conveyance of King DAVID II., to France, and his many gallant services were requited on the king's return, in 1341, by a grant of a charta, dated 9 November, 1341, conferring on him the title of EARL OF WIGTON. The earl was taken prisoner at the battle of Durham, 17 October, 1346, and with his royal master, endured a long and dreary captivity in the Tower of London, but eventually he sat in the parliament of Scotland, at Edinburgh, 26 September, 1357. He is said to have had two daus., one *m.* to Sir John Danielston, and Marjory, *m.* to William de Fawsyd; he had also a son,

JOHN FLEMING, one of the hostages for the ransom of King DAVID II., under the style of "Johan Flemyng, heir au Counte de Wygeton." It is, however, probable that he was dead before 1351, and that Johan is a mistake for Thomas. His son,

THOMAS FLEMING, 2nd Earl of Wigton, was, under the style of Thomas Fleming, grandson of the Earl of Wigton, one of the hostages for DAVID II., when he was permitted to visit his dominions, 4 September, 1351. By deed of sale, dated at Edinburgh, 8 February, 1371-2, this Thomas sold "pro unâ certâ et notabili summâ pecuniæ" the Earldom of Wigton to Archibald Douglas, and the sale was confirmed by the king. Henceforward, he was styled "Thomas Flemyng, *dudum* Comes de Wigton." He was *s.* by his cousin,

SIR MALCOLM FLEMING, of Biggar (son of Sir Patrick Fleming, of Biggar, by his wife, a co-heiress of Sir Simon Fraser, of Oliver Castle,) who had charters from King DAVID II., of the lands of Leigne, forfeited by John Kennedy. He had two sons,

I. DAVID, of whom presently.
II. Patrick, ancestor of the Flemings of Bord.

The elder son,

SIR DAVID FLEMING, of Biggar and Cumbernauld, distinguished himself at the battle of Otterburn, in 1388, and had several charters from King ROBERT III. He *m.* 1st, Jean, only dau. of Sir David Barclay, of Brechin, and by her had one dau.,

MARION, *m.* to William Maule, of Panmure, who in his right, claimed the Barony of Brechin.

He *m.* 2ndly, Isabel, heiress of Monycabon, by whom he had two sons,

I. MALCOLM (Sir).
II. David, whose son, Malcolm Fleming, of Boghull, and Elizabeth de Horeston, his wife, had a charter of the lands of Boghull and Haddoliston, in the shire of Renfrew, 15 June, 1452.

The elder son,

SIR MALCOLM FLEMING, of Biggar and Cumbernauld, was knighted by King ROBERT III. He *m.* Lady Elizabeth Stewart, 3rd dau. of Robert, Duke of Albany, Regent of Scotland, and by her had issue,

I. MALCOLM, who appears to have *d. v. p.*, and *s. p.*
II. ROBERT, of whom presently.
I. Margaret, *m.* to Patrick, Master of Gray.

Sir Malcolm was arrested with the Duke of Albany, in 1425, but was soon after released. Eventually, accompanying William, Earl of Douglas, to Edinburgh Castle, he was, after a hurried trial, there beheaded, 1440. His 2nd son,

SIR ROBERT FLEMING, of Biggar and Cumbernauld, was created a peer of parliament as LORD FLEMING, but the date of his creation is not known. He *m.* 1st, Lady Janet Douglas, 3rd dau. of James, 7th Earl of Douglas, and by her had issue,

I. MALCOLM, his heir.
II. Robert, mentioned in the records of parliament, 12 June, 1478.
I. Elizabeth, *m.* to John, Lord Livingston.
II. Beatrix, *m.* to Sir William Stirling, of Kier.

He *m.* 2ndly, Margaret, dau. of John Lindsay, of Covingtoun, but by her had no issue. The elder son,

MALCOLM FLEMING, of Monycabon (who *d. v. p.*), *m.* Eupheme, dau. of James, Lord Livingston, and had issue,

I. David (Sir), *d.* in the life-time of his grandfather.
II. JOHN, 2nd Lord Fleming.
I. Elizabeth, *m.* to George Fleming, son and heir apparent of William Fleming, of the Bord.
II. Isabel.

The 2nd son,

JOHN FLEMING, 2nd Lord Fleming, succeeded his grandfather, 1494, went as ambassador to France, and became Chamberlain of Scotland. He *m.* Eupheme, 5th dau. of David, Lord Drummond, and by her (who was poisoned with two of her sisters, in 1501), had issue,

I. MALCOLM, 3rd Lord Fleming.
I. Elizabeth, *m.* to William, Lord Crichton, of Sanquhar.
II. Margaret, *m.* to John Cunningham, of Glengarnock.
III. Johanna, *m.* 1st, to John Sandilands, of Calder; and 2ndly, to David Crawford, of Kerse.

He *m.* 2ndly, Lady Margaret Stewart, eldest dau. of Matthew, 2nd Earl of Lennox, which lady *m.* 2ndly, Alexander Douglas, of Mains. Lord Fleming *m.* 3rdly, Agnes Somerville, relict of the deceased John, Lord Fleming. The 2nd Lord Fleming was assassinated 1 November, 1524. His son and heir,

MALCOLM FLEMING, 3rd Lord Fleming, *s.* his father as Great Chamberlain of Scotland; he *m.* Johanna or Janet Stewart, natural dau. of King JAMES IV., by Isabel Stewart, dau. of James, Earl of Buchan, and had issue,

I. JAMES, 4th Lord Fleming.
II. JOHN, 5th Lord Fleming.
I. Janet, *m.* 1st, John Livingston, eldest son of Alexander, 5th Lord Livingston.
II. Agnes, *m.* to William, 6th Lord Livingston.
III. Margaret, *m.* 1st, to Robert, Master of Montrose; 2ndly, to Thomas, Master of Marr; and 3rdly, John, 4th Earl of Atholl, high chancellor of Scotland.
IV. Mary, *m.* 6 January, 1567, to William Maitland, of Leightington.

The 3rd Lord Fleming founded the Collegiate Church of Biggar. He was slain at Pinkie, 1547, and *s.* by his son,

JAMES FLEMING, 4th Lord Fleming, Great Chamberlain of Scotland, *m.* Lady Barbara Hamilton, eldest dau. of James, Duke of Chatelherault, governor of Scotland, and by her had a dau., Jane, *m.* 1st, to John, Lord Thirlestane, high chancellor of Scotland. The 4th Lord Fleming, one of the eight commissioners chosen by parliament to represent the Scottish nation at the nuptial of MARY, Queen of Scots, with the Dauphin of France, *d.* at Paris, 15 December, 1558. He was *s.* by his brother,

JOHN FLEMING, 5th Lord Fleming, Great Chamberlain of Scotland, who *m.* Elizabeth, only child of Robert, Master of Ross, and by her had a son,

I. JOHN, 6th Lord Fleming.
I. Mary, *m.* to James Douglas, of Drumlanrig.
II. Jane, *m.* to William Bruce, of Airth.
III. Margaret, *m.* to Sir James Forrester, of Carden.

The 5th Lord Fleming, a devoted adherent of Queen MARY was accidentally wounded at Edinburgh, and *d.* shortly after, 6 September, 1572. The son and heir,

JOHN FLEMING, 6th Lord Fleming, was created EARL OF WIGTON, Lord Fleming and Cumbernauld by patent, dated at Whitehall, 19 March, 1606.

(The continuation is at page 218.)

Page 228.

GENEVILL—BARON GENEVILL.

SIR SIMON DE GEYNVILLE or JOINVILLE, who *m.* Joan, dau. and heir of Richard FitzLeon, succeeded in her right' to Culmolyn. His son, Nicholas, dying *v. p.* without issue, his, Sir Simon's heirs, were the son of his dau. Joan, who *m.* John Cusack, the son of his dau. Elizabeth, who *m.* William de Loundres, and Simon, Lord Slane, the son of his dau., Matilda who *m.* Baldwin, Lord Slane. Matilda appears to have been the eldest dau., and, in her right, her son succeeded to Culmolyn, which remained in the Fleming family until the forfeiture in 1691.

GREY—EARLS OF WARRINGTON AND BARONS DELAMER, OF DUNHAM MASSEY.

By Letters Patent, dated 22 April, 1796.

Lineage.

GEORGE HARRY GREY, 5th Earl of Stamford, son and heir of Harry, 4th Earl, by LADY MARY BOOTH, his wife, only dau. and heiress of George, 2nd and last EARL OF WARRINGTON, of that family (*see that title*), b. 1 October, 1737; was created 22 May, 1796, *Baron Delamer*, of Dunham Massey, co. Chester, and EARL OF WARRINGTON, in the peerage of Great Britain, the honours enjoyed by his maternal grandfather. He m. in 1763, Lady Henrietta Cavendish Bentinck, dau. of William, 2nd Duke of Portland, and by her (who d. 4 June, 1827) left issue,

GEORGE-HARRY, 6th earl.
> William-Booth, b. 10 September, 1773; m. 1st, 7 April, 1802, Frances-Anne, eldest dau. of Thomas Pryce, Esq., of Duffryn, co. Glamorgan (which lady d. in 1837); and 2ndly, 28 August, 1838, the Hon. Frances Somerville, who d. in 1849), sister of the 16th Lord Somerville. He d. s. p. 11 March, 1852.
> Anchitel, b. 16 December, 1774; d. unm. 20 December, 1833.
> Henrietta, m. 26 October, 1785, to Sir John Chetwode, 4th Bart., of Chetwode, and d. 12 July, 1826.
> Maria, m. to John Cotes, Esq., of Woodcote, co. Salop; and d. in 1838.
> Louisa, d. unm. in February, 1830.
> Sophia, m. 21 October, 1809, to Booth Grey, Esq., of Aston Hayes, co. Chester, and d. 7 January, 1849.
> Amelia, m. 18 October, 1800, Sir John Lister Kaye, 1st bart., of Grange, and d. 29 October, 1849.

The earl d. 1819, and was s. by his eldest son,

GEORGE-HARRY, 2nd Earl of Warrington, lord-lieutenant and custos-rotulorum of the co. Chester, b. 31 October, 1765; m. 23 December, 1797, Lady Henrietta - Charlotte - Elizabeth Charteris, eldest dau. of Francis, Lord Elcho (eldest son of Francis, 6th Earl of Wemyss, who predeceased his father), by whom (who d. 30 January, 1839), he had issue,

> I. GEORGE-HARRY, *Lord Grey, of Groby*, b. 5 April, 1802; summoned to the House of Lords in his father's barony Grey, of Groby in 1832; m. 20 December, 1824, Lady Katherine Charteris Wemyss, 4th dau. of Francis, 7th Earl of Wemyss and March, and d. 24 October, 1835, leaving by her (who d. 4 January, 1844) issue,
>> GEORGE-HARRY, 3rd earl.
>> Margaret-Henrietta-Maria, m. 6 October, 1846, Henry-John Milbank (who d. 4 June, 1872), son of Mark and Lady Augusta Milbank, of Thorp Perrow, and d. 7 March, 1852, leaving issue,
>>> 1 Katherine-Henrietta-Maria, m. 12 June, 1869, to Arthur-Duncombe, Esq., barrister-at-law (son of Adm. the Hon. Arthur Duncombe), and had issue,
>>>> Alice-Louisa, b. 1874.
>>>> Cicely, b. 1877.
>>>> Muriel-Katherine, b. 16 March, 1880.
>>> 2 Louisa, b. 28 January, 1849; m. 2 January, 1868, to Francis Arkwright, Esq.
> II. Henry-Booth, b. 29 January, 1807; an officer in the army; d. March, 1857.
>> I. Henrietta-Charlotte, m. 16 December, 1820, to the Rev. James-Thomas Law, chancellor of dio., Lichfield, son of the Hon. and Rt Rev. George-Henry Law, Bishop of Bath and Wells, and d. March, 1866.
>> II. Jane, m. 8 November, 1825, to John-Benn, 1st Lord Ormathwaite, and d. 22 June, 1877.

His lordship d. 26 April, 1845, and was s. by his grandson,

GEORGE-HARRY, 3rd Earl of Warrington and 7th Earl of Stamford, b. 7 January, 1827: m. 1st, 23 December, 1848, Elizabeth (who d. 22 October, 1854), dau. of John Billige, of Wincanton, co. Somerset; and 2ndly, 29 August, 1855, Katherine, 2nd dau. of Henry Cocks, Esq. The earl d. s. p. 2 January, 1883, when the earldom of Warrington and barony of Delamer, of Dunham Massey, became extinct.

Arms—Barry of six, ar. and az.

HOBHOUSE—BARON BROUGHTON.

Created 1851.

(*See* BURKE's *Extant Peerage and Baronetage*, HOBHOUSE, Bart.)

Page 327.

LIVINGSTONE—BARONS LIVINGSTONE AND EARLS OF LINLITHGOW.

In the United States of America may be found descendants of some of the ancient nobility of England, Scotland, and Ireland. The family of Livingstone, of New York, (unquestionably descended in the direct male line from the old Lords

Livingstone) is a memorable case in point: its immediate ancestor was the celebrated divine, John Livingstone, b. in 1603, who, from religious persecution, went or was exiled to Holland. He was a man of talent and influence, and was sent to the Hague to solicit King CHARLES II. to resume the throne. He m. a Flemish lady, and d. in 1672, leaving issue. His diary, on parchment, as well as his portrait (by Rembrandt), is still preserved. The diary has been printed. To his son, ROBERT LIVINGSTONE, Queen ANNE, granted a very considerable tract of land, in the State of New York, which became the manor of Livingstone, and continues to be the seat of the family.

The original grant was of vast extent, and its proprietors, the Livingstones, were all called lords of the manor, until the War of Independence destroyed titles and entails. At the death of the 3rd and last lord of the manor, the manor was divided into four portions, HENRY-WALTER LIVINGSTONE, of Teviotdale, inheriting two of those portions. Beside the possession of their landed estates, the Livingstones of America have gained distinction by their conspicuous abilities and great public services.

ROBERT-R. LIVINGSTONE, b. at New York, 27 November, 1746, was one of the family who drew up the declaration of Independence. In 1780, he was appointed Secretary of Foreign Affairs, and, on the adoption of the constitution of New York was constituted chancellor of that state. In 1801, he went, as minister plenipotentiary to the court of France, and gained the especial favour of Napoleon, who gave Livingstone, his portrait, by Isabey, surrounded by valuable diamonds. During his diplomatic residence at Paris, Livingstone accomplished, with the aid of Mr. Munro, the transfer of Louisiana to the United States. His memoirs have been published as well as the life of his brother Edward Livingstone, a famous American legislator. Robert Livingstone formed the acquaintance, while in Paris, of Robert Fulton, and was associated with that eminent engineer (who married his niece, Harriet Livingstone) in great steam navigation enterprises. Chancellor Livingstone, who was founder and first president of the New York Academy of the Fine Arts, d. 26 March, 1813, honoured as an able statesman, an upright and useful citizen, and "highly distinguished public servant."

Another eminent member of the family was Governor Livingstone (governor of the State for life) whose dau. m. the celebrated John Jay. Some years ago, several members of the American family visited Admiral Sir Thomas Livingstone, in Scotland (then keeper of the Royal Palace of Linlithgow), who received them with great kindness, and afterwards corresponded with them until his death.

McNEILL—BARON COLONSAY.

By Letters Patent, dated 26 February, 1867.

Lineage.

This family of McNeills is descended from a common ancestor with the McNeills of Taynish, of Gigha, and of Gallachallie.

TORQUILLE McNEILL, of Taynish, Keeper of Castle Sween, *ante* 1449, had two sons, NEILL and HECTOR.

NEILL McNEILL, who s. his father, d. s. p., and was s. by his brother,

HECTOR McNEILL, who d. about 1473, leaving a son, NEILL McNEILL, who s. his father, and was s. by his son,

NEILL McNEILL, who had two sons, NEILL, ancestor of the McNEILLS *of Taynish and of Gigha*; and JOHN OIG, ancestor of the McNEILLS *of Gallachallie, of Couctronon,* and *of Crear, &c.,* afterwards *of Colonsay.* The 2nd son,

JOHN OIG McNEILL, had two sons,

> DONALD, ancestor of the McNEILLS *of Gallachallie.*
> MALCOLM BEG, ancestor of the McNEILLS *of Arichonan,* and McNEILLS *of Crear, &c.,* afterwards *of Colonsay.*

The 2nd son,

MALCOLM BEG McNEILL, had a son, NEILL OIG McNEILL, who had three sons, 1 Malcolm, of Arichonan: 2 John, afterwards of Arichonan; 3 DONALD, of Crear, &c. The 3rd son,

DONALD McNEILL, of Crear, &c., m. Mary, dau. of Lachlan McNeill, of Tirfeargus, and 1700, acquired from Archibald, Duke of Argyll, the Islands of Colonsay and Oronsay in exchange for his lands of Crear, Drimdrishaig, and others. He was s. by his son,

MALCOLM McNEILL, of Colonsay and Oronsay, m. Barbara, dau. of Campbell, of Dunstaffnage, and had two sons,

> I. DONALD, his heir.
> II. Alexander, of Oronsay, m. Mary, dau. of Alex. McDougall, of McDougall, Chief of that clan, and had six sons,

1 John. of Oronsay, who acquired the estates of Colonsay and Ardlussa, from his cousin, Archibald, of whom hereafter.
2 Malcolm, of the H.E.I.Co.'s naval service.
3 James, M.D. and inspector of hospitals.
4 Donald, lieut.-col. in the army.
5 Alexander, d. early.   6 Archibald, lieut. R.N.

The eldest son,
DUNCAN McNEILL, of Colonsay and Oronsay, acquired also the estate of Ardlussa, in the island of Jura; m. Miss McNeill, of Belfast, and had a son, Archibald, who succeeded him in the estates of Colonsay and Ardlussa, m. 1796, Lady Georgiana-Anne Forbes, dau. of George, 5th Earl of Granard, and sold the estates of Colonsay and Ardlussa to his cousin, John McNeill, Esq. This cousin,
JOHN McNEILL, Esq., of Colonsay, Oronsay, and Ardlussa, b. 1767; m. Hester, dau. of Duncan McNeill, Esq., of Dunmore, by whom (who d. June, 1843) he had, with daus., six sons,

I. ALEXANDER, of Colonsay, Oronsay, and Ardlussa, b. 17 January, 1791, acquired the estates of Gigha, and sold the Islands of Colonsay and Oronsay to his next brother, Duncan. He m. 24 June, 1830, Anne-Elizabeth, dau. and co-heiress of John Carstairs, Esq., of Stratford Green, co. Essex, and Worboys, co. Huntingdon, and d. June, 1851, leaving issue,

SIR JOHN-CARSTAIRS McNEILL, K.C.M.G., C.B., V.C., of Colonsay, major-general in the army, Equerry to the Queen, b. 29 March, 1831.
Alexander, late Bengal engineers, b. 24 February, 1834; m. 1859, Mary, dau. of Col. Leighton, and has issue.
Duncan, late capt. royal Scots greys, chief constable of the West Riding co. York, b. 10 July, 1836; m. June, 1861, Fanny-Charlotte-Emma, dau. of Admiral Sir Charles Talbot, K.C.B., of the noble house of Shrewsbury, and has issue.
Malcolm, of North Manor Place, Edinburgh, late 78th highlanders, inspector under the Poor Law Board of Scotland, b. 15 November, 1839; m. 1st, 1 January, 1863, Clara-Elizabeth, dau. of Robert Buchanan, Esq., of Ardoch, by whom he had issue,

1 Duncan, b. 19 August, 1864.
2 Donald-Buchanan, b. November, 1869; d. August, 1872.
1 Hester-Mary, b. October, 1865: d. October, 1870.
2 Helen-Eva-Forbes, b. 1 November, 1867.

He m. 2ndly, 18 April, 1871, Susan-Carruthers, dau. of Archibald M'Neill, Principal Clerk of Session of Edinburgh, by whom he had further issue,

3 Neill-Archibald, b. 19 February, 1873.
3 Ina-Erskine, b. 4 September, 1874.

Cecil Anne. d. unm.
Helen, m. 1861, Alexander-E.-C. Streatfeild, Esq., of Charts Edge, Kent.
Hester-Mary, d. young.

II. DUNCAN, acquired in 1848, by purchase from his brother, Alexander, the ancestral estates of Colonsay and Oronsay, and was created BARON COLONSAY, as hereafter.
III. John (Sir), G.C.B., D.C.L., b. 1795, formerly envoy and minister plenipotentiary to the Court of Persia, K.L.S. of Persia of the first class; m. 1st, 1814, Innes, 4th dau. of George Robinson, Esq., of Clormiston, Midlothian, who d. 1816; 2ndly, 1823, Elizabeth, 4th dau. of John Wilson, Esq, which lady d. 1868; and 3rdly, 26 August, 1870, Lady Emma-Augusta Campbell, dau. of John, 7th Duke of Argyll.
IV. Malcolm, lieut.-col. and brigadier H.E.I.Co.'s cavalry, governor of Vellor, military commandant of Arcot, fell leading the attack on Frome, 1852.
V. Archibald, b. 1803, writer to the signet, one of the principal clerks of session, formerly director of chancery.
VI. Forbes, of the H.E.I.Co.'s naval service, afterwards merchant in London; d. 1843.

John McNeill d. February, 1846. His second son,
THE RIGHT HON. DUNCAN McNEILL, b. 1793, P.C., LL.D., was admitted to the Scottish bar, 1816, and was sheriff co. Perth, from 1824 to 1834. He was solicitor-general for Scotland from November, 1834, to April, 1835, and from September, 1841, to October, 1842, from which time till July, 1846, he was lord advocate. In 1843 he was chosen dean of the faculty of advocates, and continued to hold that appointment til' he was made a lord of session and justiciary in May, 1851. He was M.P. co. Argyll, from 1843 to 1851, and was appointed lord-justice-general, May, 1852, and was made a privy councillor, 1853. He was raised to the peerage of the united kingdom as BARON COLONSAY, of Colonsay and Oronsay, in the co. of Argyll, by letters patent, dated 26 February, 1867, and resigned the office of lord-justice-general the same year. He d. unm. 1874, when the title became EXTINCT.

Arms—Quarterly: 1st and 4th, az., a lion rampant arg.; 2nd, arg., a sinister hand couped tessways in chief gu., in base wavy az., a salmon naiant of the first; 3rd, or., a galley sa., her oars in saltire gu, on a chief of the second three mullets of the first; the whole within a bordure erm.

Page 348.

MAGENNIS—VISCOUNT MAGENNIS, OF IVEAGH.

The following curious documents describe the condition of the Lords Iveagh after the Restoration—
The state of the Claime of the Lord of Iveaghe is as followeth:—
The Lord of Iveaghe had two Mannor Houses in the county of Doune before the warres, vizt., Rathfrilan and Narrow-water, both of them are now demolished.
At Rathfrilan, one Mr. Hawkins, an Adventurer, hath built a house, which, as he alleadgeth cost him £300 or thereabouts.
The lande about that Mannor for 2 miles every way is not worth six pence per Acre as they stand now in Lease from the said Adventurer, and the most parte of the land contiguous thereto being in Mortgage with Colonell Hill for £1000; soe as all the said inconveniences and encumbrances being in that place hath hindered the Lord of Iveaghe to make his Election there.
The Mannor of Narrow-water is, 1500 acres contiguous about it, leased by one Mr. Barker Deane, an Adventurer, to Mr. Charles Bolton for £40 per annum for severall years to come, which lease is also given over by Mr. Bolton to the Lord of Dungannon, so as the Lord of Iveaghe could not fix on 2000 acres in that place.
Wherefore his hath made his election on a place called Keilmore. On this Keilmore the late Lord of Iveaghe built a house before the warres, and was dwelling therein the summer before his death, and his Lady. It was proved by two witnesses in the Court of Claimes that the said late Lord dwelled there, and that Sir William Brownlow and Mr. Burly the then High Sheriffe of the county of Doune did dine with His Lordship at Keilmore. Wherefore the now Lord of Iveaghe made his election and claime of 2000 acres contiguous, at Keilmore, although the house built thereon be demolished as the other houses are, which election he humbly conceiveth is suitable to His Matie's intencons and Royall favours declared in the Act of Explanacon intended for him as one of the Nominees therein mencioned.
Notwithstanding it was objected by the Councell and the persons in possession of the premises that it was not due election, none of the said Mannor Houses being fixed upon, and it is further alledged that the most parte of the said 2000 acres was in the Dowager Lady Iveaghe's possession in Anno 1641, as parte of her joynture, given her upon a writt of Dower sued out of the Cumon place after the late Lord of Iveaghe's death, in the minority and wardshippe of the now Lord of Iveaghe.
In answer to these objections, the said Lord offers that his father having built and lived at Keilmore as aforesaid that it is grounds sufficient enough for him to make his election there. And as to the other parte of the objection he saith that it appeareth by a Deede of feoffment inserted in an office taken after the death of Arthure Lord Viscount of Iveaghe, the now Lord of Iveaghe's grandfather, that upon the intermarriage between the late Lord of Iveaghe and the Lady Dowager now living that other lands were made over to the said Lady in liewe of her joynture, which lands were in particular nominated in the said Deede of which lands the 2000 acres of Keilmore aforesaid claimed by the now lord is noe parte: that a writt of Dower could not give her any other joynture but what was made over to her as aforesaid, that she taking then advantage of the now Lord of Iveaghe's minority, tooke out the said writt of Dower unknowne to the Master of the Wardes, and to his guardian the Lord Marquis of Antrim.
That for all the reasons aforesaid hee humbly prayeth his said election may stand, and that the said 2000 acres may forthwith be assigned out, in regard he hathe not a foote of land in Conaught or elsewhere to subsist by or live uppon as the other Nominees have; and that the rather as the said Lady Dowager now living hath not a foote of land as a Dower or joynture nor provided of any wayes either by the Acte of Settlement or Explanacon.
Carte MSS., Bodlein Library, Oxford,
Vol. 35, p. 139.

Patrick Ma Ginn to His Grace the Duke of Ormonde.
Whitehall, this 9th April, 1666.

My Lord,—At this very instant I received a letter from poore my Lord Iveaghe's agent acquainting me how he is hindered in order to getting his 2000 akers by the power and creditt of his adversaryes. The poore man hath no body to support him there, nor I noe friend to rely upon but your Grace. Therefore I humbly begg of your Grace to shew your selfe in this conjuincture his friend, specially seeing his right is so cleere as the Commissioners themselves tould me there, it being a generall rule that any nominee could chuse out of their estates any 2000 ackers. You know my Lord how troublesome I have been heretofore both to the King and to your Grace for this poore man, and how often your Grace gave me all the hopes I could expect to favour him: Now is the time: My Lord, one word in his behalfe to the Commissioners will do his businesse, which I dare promise myselfe your Grace will doe as well for his sake as for the justness of his cause. I will trouble you noe more upon this subject but wish your Grace all happinesse and long health, for which shall ever pray,

My Lord,

Your most humble and addicted servant,

PATRICK MA GINN.

Carte MSS., Vol. 35, p. 140.

Magennis, styling himself Viscount Iveagh, was colonel of the Irish brigade in Spain, at or shortly before the breaking out of the great French Revolution. Documents signed by him, as "Viscount Iveagh," are in existence.

Page 359.

MARTIN—BARON MARTIN.

NICHOLAS MARTIN (the only son of Nicholas, the baron by tenure), who d. before his father, had a son, WILLIAM, and a dau., MARIA, who m. RICHARD FLEMING, BARON OF SLANE.

WILLIAM MARTIN, the son of William, was summoned to parliament after his succession, 19th EDWARD II., and d. in the next year.

ELEANOR, his sister, who m. William de Columbers, d. s. p., and the barony devolved upon James, Lord Audeley, who had livery of all the Martin estates. On the death of Nicholas, Lord Audeley, the son of James, the Barony of Martin fell into abeyance between his three sisters.

Page 360.

MASSUE DE RUVIGNY—EARL OF GALWAY.

DANIEL DE MASSUE, Baron de Ruvigny (son of Nicholas de Massue, by Helen D'Ally, his wife), was father of a dau., Rachel, wife of Thomas Wriothesley, Earl of Southampton (and mother of Rachel, Lady Russell), and a son, HENRY, MARQUIS DE RUVIGNY, who emigrated from France, and left, by Marie Tallemand, his wife, two sons; the elder was HENRY MASSUE DE RUVIGNY, EARL OF GALWAY; and the younger, named CAILLEMOT, the famous Williamite officer, slain at the battle of the Boyne.

"THE MARQUESS OF RUVIGNY," says Macaulay, "had been during many years an eminently faithful and useful servant of the French government. So highly was his merit appreciated at Versailles, that he had been solicited to accept indulgencies which scarcely any other heretic could by any sollicitation obtain. Had he chosen to remain in his native country, he and his household would have been permitted to worship God privately according to their own forms. But Ruvigny rejected all offers, cast in his lot with his brethren, and, at upwards of eighty years of age, quitted Versailles, where he might still have been a favourite, for a modest dwelling at Greenwich. That dwelling was, during the last months of his life, the resort of all that was most distinguished among his fellow exiles. His abilities, his experience, and his munificent kindness, made him the undisputed chief of the refugees. He was at the same time half an Englishman: for his sister had been Countess of Southampton, and he was uncle of Lady Russell. He was long past the time of action. But his two sons, both men of eminent courage, devoted their swords to the service of WILLIAM. The younger son, who bore the name of CAILLEMOT, was appointed colonel of one of the Huguenot regiments of foot. The two other regiments of foot were commanded by La Melloniere and Cambon, officers of high reputation. The regiment of horse was raised by Schomberg himself, and bore his name. Ruvigny lived just long enough to see these arrangements complete."

MAYNARD — BARON AND VISCOUNT MAYNARD.

Irish Barony, by Letters Patent, dated 30 May, 1620.
English Barony, by Letters Patent, dated 14 March, 1628.
Viscounty, by Letters Patent, dated 18 October, 1766.

Lineage.

SIR HENRY MAYNARD, Knt. (grandson of John Maynard, Esq., M.P. for St. Albans), secretary to the Lord-Treasurer Bur-

leigh, purchased the estate of Estains, in Essex, and was designated therefrom. He represented the co. in parliament, and was sheriff in the last year of ELIZABETH. He m. Susan, dau. and co-heir of Thomas Pearson, Esq., and had, with other issue,

I. WILLIAM, his successor.
II. John (Sir), of Tooting, Surrey, K.B. and M.P. for Lostwithiel in 1640. Sir John expressing a strong dislike to the army, and exerting himself that it might be disbanded in 1647, was impeached of high-treason, expelled the House of Commons, and committed prisoner to the Tower. He d. in 1658, and his male line failed with him, Sir John Maynard, K.B., in 1665, whose only dau. and heir, Mary, m. 1st, William Adams, Esq.; 2ndly, Sir Bushout Cullen, Bart.; and 3rdly, Francis Buller, Esq. of Shillingham, in Cornwall.
III. Charles, auditor of the Exchequer, temp. CHARLES II., baptized 4 September, 1599, m. Mary, dau. of Zeger Corsellis, of London, merchant; and dying November, 1665, left a son,
WILLIAM MAYNARD, Esq. of Walthamstow, who was created a baronet, 1 February, 1681, and was s. by his son,
1 SIR WILLIAM, 2nd baronet, who d. unm. and was s. by his brother,
2 SIR HENRY, 3rd baronet, who was s. by his son,
SIR WILLIAM, 4th baronet, b. 19 April, 1721; to whom the remainder of the dignities of Viscount and Baron Maynard was granted in 1766. He m. in 1751, Charlotte, 2nd dau. of Sir Cecil Bishopp; and dying 18 January, 1772, left issue by that lady (who d. 16 May, 1762),
SIR CHARLES, 5th bart., of whom hereafter, as 2nd Viscount Maynard.
Henry (Rev.), Rector of Radwinter, and vicar of Thaxted in Essex; b. 30 October, 1758; d. May, 1806, leaving by Susan his wife, dau. of Rev. F. Barnard, Rector of Caxton, one son and three daus., viz.,
HENRY, who s. his uncle, as 3rd Viscount Maynard,
Harriet, d. in 1851.
Susan, d. in 1850.
Mary-Anne.
Sir William d. in 1772.

Sir Henry d. in 1616, and was s. by his eldest son,
WILLIAM MAYNARD, who with the greater part of the estates of the family, inherited the seat at Easton, received the honour of knighthood 7 March, 1608; was created a baronet 29 June, 1611; elevated to the peerage of Ireland 30 May, 1620, as Lord Maynard of Wicklow; and made a peer of England, as Baron Maynard, of Estaines, co. Essex, 14 March, 1628. His lordship d. 18 December, 1639. He m. 1st, Lady Margaret Cavendish, only dau. of William, 1st. Earl of Devonshire, which lady d. 1 September, 1613, leaving one dau. Anne, who d. young. He m. 2ndly, Anne, only dau. and heir of Sir Anthony Everard, Knt., of Langleys, in Essex, and by her (who d. 5 August, 1647,) he had issue,

I. WILLIAM, 2nd baron.
I. Susan, d. unm.
II. Jane, m. to Edward Eyre, Esq. co. Galway, whose dau. and co-heir, Margaret, m. Francis Annesley, Esq., eldest son of John, brother of Arthur, 1st Earl of Anglesey.
III. Anne, wife of Sir Henry Wrothe, Knt., of Durance, co. Middlesex.
IV. Elizabeth, m. to John Wrothe, Esq., of Loughton, in Essex.
V. Mary, m. to Sir Ralph Bovey, Knt., of Caxton and Longstone, co. Cambridge.

The son,
WILLIAM MAYNARD, 2nd baron, was appointed, after the Restoration, comptroller of the Household, and sworn of the Privy Council, which office he also filled in the reign of JAMES II. His lordship m. 1st, Dorothy, dau. and sole heir of Sir Robert Banaster, Knt. of Passenham, co. Northampton, by whom (who d. 30 October, 1649,) he had two surviving sons,

BANASTER, his successor.
William, who m. 1st, Jane, dau. and co-heir of Sir John Prescot, Knt., and widow of Sir Thomas Fisher, Bart., which lady d. s. p. 1 March, 1675. He m. 2ndly, Susan, only dau. and heir of Thomas Egans, Esq. of Bow, Middlesex, and had two sons and a dau., Thomas and Prescot, both of whom d. unm., and Anne.

He m. 2ndly, Lady Margaret Murray, dau. of James, Earl of Dysart, by whom he had another son Henry, and a dau., Elizabeth, m. to Sir Thomas Brograve, Bart., of Hamels, co. Hertford. He d. 3 February, 1698, and was s. by his eldest son,
BANASTER MAYNARD, 3rd baron. His lordship m. Lady Elizabeth Grey, only dau. of Henry, 10th Earl of Kent, by whom, who d. 24 September, 1714, he had eight sons and three daus,

I. William, d. v. p. 8 March, 1716-17, and was buried at Little Easton.
II. Banaster, d. young.
III. HENRY, 4th Lord Maynard.
IV. Banaster, d. young.

v. Anthony, *d.* young.
vi. Robert, *d.* young.
vii. GREY, 5th Lord Maynard.
viii. CHARLES, 6th Lord Maynard.
1. Annabella, *m.* William Lowther, Esq., of Swillington, co. York (afterwards created a Bart.), and *d.* 8 August, 1734.
ii. Dorothy, *m.* to Sir Robert Hesilrige, Bart., of Noseley, co. Leicester, and *d.* 11 September, 1748, and was buried at Noselev.
iii. Elizabeth, *d. unm.* 1720.

He *d.* 4 March, 1717-18, and was *s.* by his 3rd but eldest surviving son,

HENRY MAYNARD, 4th baron; who *d. unm.* 7 December, 1742, and was *s.* by his brother,

GREY MAYNARD, 5th baron; who also *d. unm.* 27 April, 1745, and was *s.* by his brother,

CHARLES MAYNARD, 6th baron. This nobleman was created 18 October, 1766, *Baron Maynard, of Much Easton,* and VISCOUNT MAYNARD, *of Easton Lodge, both in the co. Essex,* with remainder, in default of male issue, to the descendants male of his kinsman, Sir William Maynard, Bart., of Waltons, in the same co. His lordship *d. unm.,* at the age of eighty-five, 30 June, 1775, when the baronetcy and the original Irish and English baronies expired; but the viscounty and last barony devolved, according to the reversionary clause in the patent, upon

SIR CHARLES MAYNARD, 2nd viscount, who was the 5th baronet, of Waltons, co. Essex (*refer* to descendants of Charles, 3rd son of Sir Henry Maynard, Knt., Lord Burleigh's secretary). This nobleman *b.* 9 August, 1751; *m.* in 1776, Mrs. Anne Horton; but *d. s. p.* 10 March, 1824, and was *s.* by his nephew,

HENRY MAYNARD, 3rd viscount; lord-lieutenant and vice-admiral of Essex; *b.* 3 March, 1786; who *m.* 28 December, 1810, Mary, dau. of Reginald Rabett, Esq., of Bramfield Hall, Suffolk, and by her (who *d.* 22 October, 1857) had issue,

1. Charles-Henry, an officer in the guards, and col. West Essex militia; *b.* in 1814; *m.* 1st, 16 January, 1840, Lady Frances-Julia Murray, sister of George, 6th Duke of Athole, by whom (who *d.* 4 November, 1858) he had no issue. He *m.* 2ndly, 13 October, 1860, Blanche-Adeliza, 2nd dau. of Henry Fitz-Roy, Esq., of Salcey Lawn, co. Northampton, and by her (who *m.* 2ndly, 8 November, 1866, Robert-Francis, 4th Earl of Rosslyn) had two daus.,

  FRANCES-EVELYN, *b.* 10 December, 1861; *m.* 30 April, 1881, Francis, Lord Brooke, eldest son of the 4th Earl of Warwick.
  BLANCHE, *b.* 14 February, 1864.

He *d.* 2 January, 1865.
i. Charlotte-Mary, *m.* 22 December, 1834, to the Hon. Adolphus-Frederick-Charles-Molyneux Capell, brother of the 6th Earl of Essex, and *d.* 27 June, 1871, having had issue.
ii. Emma, *m.* in 1836, to J.-Robert Ives, Esq. of Bentworth Hall, Hants (who *d.* 1865) and has, Gordon-Maynard, lieut.-col. late Coldstream guards; and Cecil-Robert-St. John, lately colonel commanding royal horse guards, and silver stick-in-waiting on Her Majesty, *m.* 7 April, 1864, Hon. Susan-Anne Talbot, eldest dau of the 4th Lord Talbot de Malahide, and has Violet Maud-Cecil; Marion; Kathleen-Emma; and Frances-Edith.
iii. Catherine-Harriet, *d. unm.* February, 1865.
iv. Augusta-Julia, *d. unm.* 20 July, 1868.

His lordship *s.* his uncle as 3rd viscount, 10 March, 1824, and *d.* 19 May, 1865, when his honours became EXTINCT.

Arms—Arg., a chevron, az., between three sinister hands couped at the wrist, gu

---

METCALFE—BARON METCALFE.

(*See* BURKE'S *Extant Peerage and Baronetage*).

MONCK—EARL OF RATHDOWNE.

By Letters Patent, dated 12 January, 1822.

Lineage.

HENRY-STANLEY MONCK, 2nd Viscount Monck, in the Peerage of Ireland, *b.* 26 July, 1785, was created EARL OF RATHDOWNE, 12 January, 1822. His lordship *m.* 28 July, 1806, Lady Frances Le Poer Trench, dau. of William, 1st Earl of Clancarty, by whom (who *d.* 22 November, 1843) he had three sons, who *d.* in infancy, and ten daus., viz.,

1. Anne-Florinda, *b.* 18 September, 1807; *d.* 30 October, 1876.
ii. Frances-Isabella, *b.* 20 July, 1809; *m.* 1834, to Owen-Blayney Cole, Esq., of Brandrum, deputy-lieut. of the co. Monaghan, high sheriff of that co. in 1835. She *d.* 9 June, 1871.
iii. Elizabeth-Louise-Mary, *b.* 1 March, 1814; *m.* 23 July, 1844, to Charles Stanley, 4th Viscount Monck.
iv. Emily, *b.* 5 April, 1818; *m.* 7 February, 1837, William-Barlow Smythe, Esq., of Barbavilla House, co. Westmeath; and *d.* 22 November following.

---

v. Louisa-Dorothea, *b.* 3 March, 1820; *d.* 16 May, 1870.
vi. Georgina-Ellen, *b.* 30 June, 1821; *m.* 17 May, 1841, to Edward Croker, Esq., of Ballynagarde, co. Limerick.
vii. Caroline-Letitia, *b.* 20 April, 1823.
viii. Henrietta-Margaret, *b.* 26 March, 1825.
ix. Mary, *b* 17 September, 1828; *d.* 3 June, 1880.
x. Selina-Gertrude, *d.* in infancy.

His lordship *d.* 20 September, 1848, when the Earldom of Rathdowne became EXTINCT and the Viscountcy of Monck devolved on his brother, CHARLES-JOSEPH-KELLY, as 3rd Viscount Monck. (*See* BURKE'S *Extant Peerage.*)

Arms—Gu., a chev. between three lions' heads, erased, arg.

NETTERVILLE—VISCOUNTS NETTERVILLE.

By Letters Patent, dated 3 April, 1622.

Lineage.

The Nettervilles settled at Dowth, co. Meath, *temp.* HENRY II.

SIR LUKE NETTERVILLE, of Dowth, a justice of the Queen's Bench, 15 October, 1559; *m.* Margaret, dau. of Sir Thomas Luttrell, of Luttrellstown, and had issue,

1. JOHN, of whom presently.
ii. Richard, of Corballis, co. Meath, who acquired considerable estates in Meath and Tipperary, *m.* Alison, dau. of Sir John Plunket, of Dunsoghly, chief justice of the Queen's Bench, and *d. s. p.* 5 September, 1607.

The elder son,

JOHN NETTERVILLE, *s.* his father at Dowth, and was M.P. for co. Meath, in 1585. He *m.* Eleanor, dau. of Sir James Gernon, of Kilmacoole, co. Louth, and dying 20 September, 1601, left by her (who *d.* 29 January, 1626) an only son,

NICHOLAS NETTERVILLE, of Dowth, co. Meath, who was raised to the peerage of Ireland, 3 April, 1622, as VISCOUNT NETTERVILLE. He *m.* 1st, Eleanor, dau. of Sir John Bathe, of Athcarne and Drumconrath, co. Meath, which lady *d.* 27 October, 1634; and 2ndly, Mary, dau. of Alderman Brice, of Drogheda, widow. 1st, of John Hoey, Esq., serjeant-at-arms; and 2ndly, of Sir Thomas Hibbots, chancellor of the exchequer in Ireland, which lady *d. s. p.* By his 1st wife, Lord Netterville left issue,

1 JOHN, his heir.
ii. Lucas, who, under the will of his great uncle, Richard Netterville, *s.* to the estate of Corballi-; he *m.* Mabel, dau. of Sir Patrick Barnewall, Bart., and *d.* before 1652, having had by her (with another son, Richard, who *d.* an infant) a son, Francis, who *m.* Mary, dau. of Gen. Thomas Preston, and *d.* before 1660, having had issue, Thomas and Mary.
iii. PATRICK, of Lecarrow, co. Galway, *m.* Mary, dau. of Peter Duffe, Esq., of Drogheda; and dying in 1676, left (with three younger sons, Luke, who *m.* and *d. s. p.*; Richard, who *m.* Honestas, dau. of Christopher Netterville, Esq., of Fethard, and *d. s. p.*; and John, who *d. s. p.*), a son,

NICHOLAS, of Lecarrow, who *m.* 1st, Cicily, dau. of Sir Edmund Burke, Bart., of Glinsk, and had by her two sons,

1 Patrick Netterville, of Longford, co. Galway, who *m.* Margaret, sister of James Ferrall, Esq., of Kilmore, co. Roscommon, and dying in 1736, left (with three daus., Cisley, *m.* to Sir Henry Burke, Bart.; Margaret, *m.* to John Fallon, Esq., of Runnemead, co. Roscommon; and Bridget, *m.* to Dr. James Tully, of Dublin) an only son, Edmund Netterville, Esq , of Longford, co. Galway, and Glasnevin, co. Dublin, who settled his estates by will dated 15 November, 1765; he *m.* Margery, dau. of Frederick Trench, Esq., M.P., and dying in 1777, left (with a dau., Margery, *m.* to Walter Lawrence, Esq., of Woodfield, co. Galway) an only son, Frederick Netterville, Esq., of Longford and Glasnevin, who *m.* Mary dau. of Mr. Keogh, and *d.* in 1785, leaving (with two younger sons, who *d. unm.,* and three daus., of whom the two youngest *d. unm.,* and the eldest, Marcella, *m.* John Gerrard, Esq., of Gibbstown, co. Meath, and *d. s. p.* 1865; by the death intestate of Mrs. Gerrard, representative of the NETTERVILLES, *of Lecarrow,* her extensive estates in the co. of Galway devolved on her next heirs, the 9th Viscount Netterville, John Fallon, Esq., of Netterville Lodge, co. Galway, and Sir John Bradstreet, Bart., the heirs general of Patrick Netterville, of Lecarrow) a son, Edmund Netterville, Esq., of Longford and Glasnevin, who *d. unm.* in 1814.
2 Edward Netterville, of Sligo, who *m.* Dorothea Douglas, and *d.* in 1744, leaving an only son, Patrick, who *d. s. p.,* and a dau , Cisley, wife of George Abbott, Esq., of Castlegar, co. Galway.

Nicholas Netterville, of Lecarrow, *m.* 2ndly, Mary, dau. of Christopher Betagh, Esq., and dying in 1719, left by her, Christopher, *d. s. p.*, James, Nicholas, Peter, and Francis, which last three *d. s. p.* The 2nd son of the second marriage, JAMES, *m.* Reddis, dau. of D'Arcy Hamilton, Esq., of Fahy, co. Galway, and *d.* in 1782, leaving four sons, NICHOLAS, Hamilton, Mark, and Robert. The three younger *d. s. p.*, and the eldest, NICHOLAS, *m.* Bridget, dau. of Bartholomew French, Esq., of Ballykenean, and *d.* in 1788, leaving a son, JAMES, 7th Viscount Netterville.

IV. ROBERT, of Cruicerath, co. Meath, who eventually inherited the Tipperary estates of his great uncle, Richard Netterville; and who *m.* Jane, dau. of Sir William Rigdon, and had a son, NICHOLAS, of Cruicerath, who *m.* Catherine, dau. of William, Viscount Fitzwilliam, and *d.* 1716, leaving a son, WILLIAM, of Cruicerath, who *m.* Mary, dau. of Robert Preston, Esq., of Charlestown, co. Dublin, and *d.* in 1757, leaving issue,

  1 Robert, of Cruicerath, who *m.* Margaret, dau. of Sir Andrew Aylmer, and widow of H. Luttrell, Esq., and *d. s. p.* 1791.
  2 WILLIAM, of whom we treat.
  3 Thomas, in holy orders of the church of Rome.

The 2nd son,
WILLIAM, inherited Cruicerath at the death *s. p.* of his eldest brother, and *m.* Margaret, dau. of James Madan, Esq., and *d.* 1801, having had a son, William, who *m.* Susanna, dau. of Sir Ulick Burke, Bart, and *d. v. p.* 1788, leaving a son, ROBERT-WILLIAM, of Cruicerath, his grandfather's successor, who *m.* Mary, dau. of John Bernard, Esq., of Ballynegar, co. Kerry, and *d.* 1834, having had issue,

ARTHUR-JAMES, 8th and last viscount.
Robert, formerly capt. of hussars in Austrian service, *b.* 1804; *m.* 1838, Annette, 2nd dau. of Hatton-Ronayne Conron, Esq., of Grange House, co. Cork, which lady *d. s. p.* 1849. He *d.* 10 August, 1880.
John, *b.* 1812; *d.* 8 September, 1880.
Thomas, in the Austrian service, *b.* 1814; *m.* 1853, Eleanor-Maria-Theresa, dau. of Edmund Balfe, Esq., of Rockfield, and *d.* 7 March, 1855, leaving a dau., Mary-Thomasina.
PIERCE, *b.* 1816; *m.* 1846, Julia, dau. of Henry Robinson, Esq., of Hyde Park House, London.
  Maria.   Susan.

V. Richard, *d. s. p.*
VI. Christopher, in holy orders of the church of Rome.
VII. Thomas.
VIII. Nicholas, in holy orders of the church of Rome.

Lord Netterville *d.* in 1654, and was *s.* by his eldest son,
JOHN, 2nd viscount; who *m.* in 1623, Elizabeth, elder dau. of Richard, Earl of Portland, K.G., and had issue,

I. NICHOLAS, 3rd viscount.
II. Richard, *d.* in Italy.
III. Hierome, in holy orders of the church of Rome.
IV. James, lieut. in the army, *m.* Eleanor, dau. of Sir William Talbot, 1st bart. of Cartown.
V. Lucas, *d. s. p.*   VI. Patrick, *d. s. p.*
VII. Robert, *d. s. p.*
I. Margaret, *m.* 1661, Henry, 2nd Viscount Kingsland.
II. Frances.
III. Margaret, *m.* William Archbold, Esq., of Timolin.
IV. Eleanor, *d.* young.

The viscount *d.* in 1659, and was *s.* by his son,
NICHOLAS, 3rd viscount; who *m.* Margaret, dau. of Thady O'Hara, Esq., of Crebilly, co. Antrim, and had three sons,

JOHN, 4th viscount.
Nicholas, *d. s. p.* in 1698.
Luke, of Staleen, co. Meath, who *m.* Anne, dau. of Mr. Stanley, of Drogheda, and whose only dau. and eventually heiress, Margaret, *m.* Oliver, Lord Louth.

The viscount *d.* 1689, and was *s.* by his eldest son,
JOHN, 4th viscount, *s.* his father in 1689. He *m.* Frances, dau. of Richard, Viscount Rosse, and was *s.* at his decease, at Liege, in Flanders, 12 December, 1727, by his only son,
NICHOLAS, 5th viscount; who *m.* Catherine, dau. of Samuel Burton, Esq., of Burton Hall, co. Carlow, and had issue,

I. JOHN, 6th viscount.
I. Frances, *m.* to Dominick Blake, Esq., of Castle Grove, co. Galway, and *d.* in 1764, leaving issue.
II. Anne, *d. unm.* in 1756.

The viscount *d.* 19 March, 1750, and was *s.* by his son,
JOHN, 6th viscount, *b.* 1744; at whose decease, *unm.*, 15 March, 1826, the title remained dormant until adjudged by the House of Lords, 14 August, 1834, to
JAMES, 7th viscount (*see ante*, issue of Patrick Netterville, of Lecarrow): his lordship *m.* 7 April, 1834, Eliza, 3rd dau. of Joseph Kirwan, Esq., of Hillsbrook, co. Galway, and had issue two daus., his co-heiresses,

I. ELIZABETH-GWENDOLINE-THEODORA, *m.* 1876, Michael-Cahill, Esq., of Ballyconra, co. Kilkenny, J.P., high sheriff 1863, who *d.* September, 1877.
II. MARY-REDDIS, *m.* 22 November, 1860, to JOSHUA-JAMES MACEVOY, Esq., J.P. co. Kildare (who took, in 1865, by royal licence, the surname and arms of NETTERVILLE), second son of James MacEvoy, Esq., of Tobertynan, co. Meath, and Theresa, his wife, dau. and co-heir of Sir Joshua-Colles Meredyth, 8th bart. of Greenhills, and has seven daus..

614

Mary-Netterville.   Theresa.   Elizabeth.
Rose.   Barbara.   Victoria.   Pauline.

Lord Netterville *d.* 13 February, 1854, and the title lay dormant, until adjudged by the House of Lords, in 1867, to
ARTHUR-JAMES, 8th Viscount NETTERVILLE (*see ante*, issue of Robert Netterville, of Cruicerath), *m.* 27 October, 1841, Constantia-Frances, 2nd dau. of Sir Edward-Joseph Smythe, 6th bart. of Eshe Hall, co. Durham, by whom (who *d.* at Paris, 21 January, 1870) he had an only child,

Frances-Constantia, *m.* 3 December, 1860, to M. Charles Viditz.

Lord Netterville *d.* without male issue, 7 April, 1882, when his Viscounty became EXTINCT.

Arms—Arg., a cross, gu., fretty, or.

Page 394.

NEVILL—EARL OF WESTMORLAND.

RALPH, LORD NEVILL, of Raby, only son of Ralph, 3rd Earl of Westmorland, *m.* Editha, dau. of Sir William Sandys; and *d. v. p.*, leaving one surviving son, RALPH, Lord Nevill, of Raby, who succeeded his grandfather as 4th Earl of Westmorland; and one dau., CICELY, who was married to John Weston, Esq., of Lichfield, 4th son of John Weston, of Hagley, near Rugeley, descended from the Westons of Weston-under-Lyzard, co. Stafford.

Lady Conyers was daughter, not granddau. of the 3rd Earl of Westmorland.

ONGLEY—BARONS ONGLEY OF OLD WARDEN.

By Letters Patent, dated 20 July, 1776.

Lineage.

ROBERT HENLEY, Esq., M.P. for the co. of Bedford, assumed the surname and arms of ONGLEY, upon succeeding to the estates of his great-uncle, Sir Samuel Ongley, Knt., and was elevated to the peerage of Ireland, 20 July, 1776, as BARON ONGLEY, *of Old Warden*. He *m.* in 1763, Frances, dau. and co-heir of Richard Gosfright, Esq., of Langton Hall, co. Essex, by whom he had issue,

ROBERT, 2nd baron.
Samuel-Henry, *b.* 16 June, 1774; *m.* 3 October, 1809, Frances, dau. and co-heir of Sir Philip Monoux, Bart., and *d.* 1822.
Frances.
Catherine, *m.* 27 March, 1790, to Col. J.-E. Fremantle, C.B., aide-de-camp to the Queen. He *d. s. p.*
Sarah, *m.* 27 June, 1791, to William-Robert Phillimore, Esq., of Kendall's Hall, co. Hertford, and *d.* 1850, leaving issue.

Lord Ongley *d.* 23 October, 1785, and was *s.* by his eldest son,
ROBERT, 2nd baron, who *m.* 11 July, 1801, Frances, only dau. of Lieut.-Gen. Sir John Burgoyne, 7th Bart., of Sutton, by whom (who *d.* in December, 1841) he left issue,

ROBERT, 3rd baron.
Samuel, capt. grenadier-guards, *d.* 1826. aged 20.
Montagu, *b.* 22 February, 1808, capt. Coldstream guards; *d. s. p.* 13 February, 1856.
George, *b.* 11 April, 1809, capt. Coldstream guards, *d. s. p.* 22 May, 1871.
Frederick, lieut. royal horse guards, *b.* 8 November, 1810; *d. s. p.* 26 August, 1846.
Frances-Elizabeth, *m.* 10 May, 1848, to Barff Tucker, Esq.
Charlotte, *m.* 26 July, 1837, to Capt. Charles Magra, 75th regt., and *d.* 1854, leaving issue.

Lord Ongley *d.* 20 August, 1814, and was *s.* by his eldest son,
ROBERT, 3rd baron, *b.* 9 May, 1803; who *d. unm.* 21 January, 1877, when his title became EXTINCT.

Arms—Quarterly: 1st and 4th, arg., a fesse, gu.; 2nd and 3rd, arg., in chief three piles, gu.; in base, a mount, vert; on a canton, az., a sun, or.

ORREBY—BARON ORREBY.

By Writ of Summons, dated 4 March, 1309.

Lineage.

In the 22nd HENRY II.
HERBERT DE ORREBY (son of Alard de Orreby) with Agnes, his wife, founded the priory of Hagneby, co. Lincoln. He had three sons, viz.,

I. JOHN, whose only dau. and heiress *m.* Robert Willoughby, of Eresby.
II. PHILIP, of Alvaniey.
III. Herbert, grantee of Gawsworth, co. Chester, from Richard de Aldford.

The 2nd son,

PHILIP DE ORREBY, of Alvanley, Justiciary of Cheshire, 1209 to 1228, m. Alice de Bamville, and had two sons, viz.,

I. PHILIP, of Alvanley, m. Lucy, dau. and heir of Roger de Montalt, and had an only dau. and heiress, Agnes, wife of Walkelynde Arderne.

II. FULKE.

The 2nd son,

FULKE DE ORREBY, justice of Chester in the 44th HENRY III., to whom the custody of the castles of Chester, Beeston, Vaenor, Shotwick, and Dyserth, was then committed He m. (ORMEROD's *Cheshire*) the dau. and heir of Strange, Lord of Dalby, and had a dau., Alicia, m. to Peter Corbet, of Leighton, and a son,

SIR JOHN DE ORREBY, of Dalby and Fulke Stapleford, co. Chester, who was summoned to parliament from 4 March, 2nd EDWARD II., 1309, to 16 June, 4th EDWARD II., 1311. He m. 1st, Isabella, youngest sister and co-heiress of Robert, Lord de Tatteshall; and 2ndly, Jane, by whom (who remarried Henry Fitz-Henry) he left (according to ORMEROD's *Cheshire*) a son and heir,

PHILIP DE ORREBY, who was never summoned to parliament, neither was his son,

JOHN or PHILIP DE ORREBY, who left a dau. and heir,

JOAN, the 2nd wife of Henry, 3rd Lord Percy, by whom she had an only child, Mary, who m. John, Lord Ros of Hamlake, and d. s. p. Inq. p. m., 5th HENRY IV.

Arms—Ermine, five chevronels, gu., on a canton of the 2nd, a lion passant, or.

PARKE — BARON WENSLEYDALE, CO. YORK, AND BARON WENSLEYDALE, OF WALTON, CO. LANCASTER.

Barony of Wensleydale, co. York, by Letters Patent, dated 16 Jan. 1856.
Barony of Walton, co. Lancaster, by Letters Patent, dated 23 July, 1856.

Lineage.

THOMAS PARKE, Esq., of Highfield, near Liverpool, m. Anne Preston, and had issue,

I. Thomas, d. s. p.
II. John, d. s. p.
III. Ralph, d. s. p.
IV. Preston-Fryer, d. s. p.
V. JAMES (SIR), created Baron Wensleydale.
I. Hannah, d. unm.
II. Alice, m. Sir Sitwell Sitwell, 1st Bart. of Renishaw, and d. May, 1797.
III. Anne, m. John Groome Smythe, Esq., of Hilton, co. Salop; and d. 4 November, 1852.

The youngest son,

RIGHT HON. SIR JAMES PARKE, one of the most distinguished lawyers and judges of his time, b. 22 March, 1782, was called to the Bar from the Lower Temple, 1813, and made a judge of the Court of Queen's Bench, a privy councillor, and knighted 1828, and afterwards appointed a Baron of the Court of Exchequer. He was raised to the peerage of the United Kingdom as Baron Wensleydale, of Wensleydale, in the North Riding of the co. York, for the term of his natural life, by letters patent, dated 16 Jan. 1856, and by a subsequent patent, dated 23 July, 1856, made BARON WENSLEYDALE, of Walton, in the co. palatine of Lancaster, with limitation of the title to the heirs male of his body. Lord Wensleydale m. 8 April, 1817, Cecilia-Arabella-Frances, dau. of Samuel-Francis Barlow, Esq. of Middlethorpe, co. York, and had, with three sons, Thomas; Thomas-James; and James, who all d. in infancy, three daus., viz.,

I. Cecilia-Anne, m. 21 September, 1841, to Sir Mathew White Ridley, 4th Bart., of Heaton Hall, and d. 20 April, 1845, leaving SIR MATHEW RIDLEY, 5th bart , and other issue.
II. Mary-Priscilla-Harriett, m. 8 August, 1842, to the Hon. Charles-W.-G. Howard, M.P., 5th son of George, 6th Earl of Carlisle, K.G., and d. 26 August, 1843, leaving a son, GEORGE-JAMES-HOWARD, Esq. of Naworth Castle (see BURKE's *Extant Peerage*, CARLISLE, E. OF).
III. Charlotte - Alice, m. 17 December, 1853, to William Lowther, Esq., 2nd surviving son of Col. Hon. William Lowther, M.P., brother of Henry, 3rd Earl of Lonsdale, and has issue (see *Extant Peerage*, LONSDALE, E. OF).

Lord Wensleydale d. 25 Feb. 1868, when his titles became EXTINCT.

A. m —Gu., on a pale, engrailed, plain cottised, arg., three stags' heads, caboshed, of the field attired, or.

PEMBERTON-LEIGH—BARON KINGS-DOWN.

By Letters Patent dated 28 Aug. 1858.

Lineage.

ALEXANDER LEIGH, Esq. of Bretherton, co. Lancaster, m. as his 2nd wife, Dorothy, dau. of Robert Holt, Esq. of Sherrington, and had, with other issue,

I. HOLT, his heir.
II. Edward, of Bispham Hall, co. Lancaster, whose eldest dau. and co-heir,

Margaret, m. 24 July, 1788, Robert Pemberton, Esq., of the Inner Temple, barrister-at-law (son of Edward Pemberton, M.D., of Warrington, by Ellen, his wife, dau. of John Lyon, Esq., of Appleton), and had issue,

THOMAS PEMBERTON, of whom hereafter.
Edward-Leigh Pemberton, of Wrinsted Court, Sittingbourne, co. Kent, b. 18 February, 1795; m. 23 December, 1820, Charlotte, dau. of Samuel Compton Cox, Esq., master in Chancery, and had issue,

1 EDWARD-LEIGH PEMBERTON, of Torry Hill and Wrinsted, co. Kent, and of Lincoln's-inn, barrister-at-law, J.P., M.P. for East Kent, b. 14 May, 1823; m. August, 1849, Matilda-Catherine-Emma, dau. of the Hon. and Rev. Francis-James Noel, and has, with three daus., two sons,

ROBERT-LEIGH PEMBERTON, late grenadier guards, b. 25 December, 1852.
Wilfred-Leigh Pemberton, b. 19 June, 1854.

2 Robert-Leigh Pemberton, d. 18 April, 1850.
3 Charles-Leigh Pemberton (Rev.), Rector of Curry-Mallet, co. Somerset, m. Sarah-Elizabeth, dau. of John Woodcock, Esq., of the Elms, near Wigan, and by her (who d. 27 December, 1862) has had issue.
4 Loftus-Leigh Pemberton.
5 Wykeham-Leigh Pemberton, C.B., col. in the army, late 60th rifles.
6 Henry-Leigh Pemberton.
1 Emily-Leigh, m. Capt. Leach, royal engineers.
2 Margaret-Leigh, m. to Lieut.-Col. Muller, royal regt., and d. 2 January, 1856.
3 Charlotte-Leigh, m. to Gerard-Coke Meynell, Esq.

Frances-Ellen Pemberton, m. Rev. Edward-Collins Wright, Rector of Pitsford, co. Northampton, and d. 28 October, 1867.

The eldest son,

HOLT LEIGH, Esq., of Whitley, m. 1785, Mary, dau. and co-heir of Thomas Owen, Esq., of Up Holland Abbey, and had issue,

I. ROBERT-HOLT, his successor.
II. Alexander, of Leeds.
III. Roger-Holt, d. 1831.
I. Johannah.

The eldest son,

SIR ROBERT HOLT LEIGH, Bart., of Whitley, b. 25 Dec. 1762, s. his father, and was created a bart. 22 May, 1815, with remainder, in default of male issue of his body, to the male issue of his father. He d. s. p. Jan. 1843, when his estates devolved on his cousin,

THOMAS PEMBERTON-LEIGH, Esq., of Kingsdown, in the co. of Kent, Q.C., P.C., b. 11 Feb. 1793; an eminent equity lawyer, called to the bar in 1816, and made a king's counsel in 1829. He was appointed attorney-general to the Prince of Wales in 1841, and his chancellor in 1843. He sat in Parliament for the boroughs of Rye and Ripon, and was raised to the peerage of the United Kingdom 28 Aug. 1858, by the title of BARON KINGSDOWN, of Kingsdown, co. Kent. Upon succeeding, Jan. 1843, to the estates of his mother's cousin, Sir Robert-Holt Leigh, Bart., he assumed, in compliance with that gentleman's will, the additional surname and arms of LEIGH, by royal licence, dated 7 March, 1843. Lord Kingsdown d. unm, 7 Oct. 1867, when his title became EXTINCT, and his estate devolved on his brother, EDWARD LEIGH-PEMBERTON, Esq., of Wrinsted and Torry.

Arms—Quarterly: 1st and 4th, gu., a cross, engr., arg., between four lozenges, erm., for LEIGH; 2nd and 3rd, erm., an estoile or, between three buckets, sa., hoops and handles gold, for PEMBERTON.

PITT-RIVERS—BARON RIVERS OF STRATHFIELDSAYE AND BARONS RIVERS OF SUDELEY CASTLE.

Barony of Strathfieldsaye, by Letters Patent, dated 20 May, 1776.

Barony of Sudeley Castle, by Letters Patent, dated 1 April, 1802.

Lineage.

This family, the branches of which extended through the cos. of Dorset, Somerset, Southampton, &c., descended from NICHOLAS PITT, who lived in the reign of HENRY VI., and whose grandson,

JOHN PITT, clerk of the Exchequer in the reign of Queen ELIZABETH, m. Joan, dau. of John Swayne, and had, with two daus., three sons,

WILLIAM, of whom presently.

John, who settled in Ireland.

Thomas, of Blandford, co. Dorset, ancestor of the extinct Earls of Londonderry, the Earls of Chatham, and the Lords Camelford (see those titles).

The eldest son,

SIR WILLIAM PITT, Knt., comptroller of the household, and a principal officer in the Exchequer in the reign of JAMES I., m. Edith, youngest dau. and co-heir of Nicholas Cadbury, Esq. of Arne, co. Dorset, and was s. in 1636, by his eldest son,

EDWARD PITT, Esq. of Strathfieldsaye, co. Hants, who m. in 1620, Rachel, dau. of Sir George Morton, Bart. of Milbourne St. Andrew, co. Dorset, and was s. in 1643, by his eldest surviving son,

GEORGE PITT, Esq. of Strathfieldsaye, an officer in the royal army during the civil wars, m. in 1657, Jane, eldest dau. of John Savage, 2nd Earl of Rivers (a dignity which expired with John, 5th earl, in 1728—see that title), and widow of George, 6th Lord Chandos, by whom he had four sons and four daus., and was s. by his eldest son,

GEORGE PITT, Esq. of Strathfieldsaye, M.P. for the co. Hants, who m. 1st, Lucy, dau. of Thomas Pile, Esq. of Beeverstock, co. Wilts, and widow of Laurence Lowe, Esq., by whom (who d. November, 1697) he had issue,

I. GEORGE, his heir.
II. Thomas, d. s. p.
I. Lucy, d. unm. 24 February, 1768.

He m. 2ndly, Lora, only dau. and heir of Audley Grey, Esq. of Kingston, co. Dorset, by whom (who d. June, 1750) he had issue,

III. William, m. Elizabeth Wyndham, and d. s. p. 1774.
IV. John, of Encombe, M.P., who d. in 1787, leaving by Marcia, his wife, dau. of Marcus Morgan, Esq., a dau., Marcia, wife of George-James Cholmondeley, Esq., and a son,

WILLIAM-MORTON PITT, Esq., M.P., of Kingston House, co. Dorset, whose dau.,

SOPHIA, m. Charles, Earl of Romney.

V. Thomas, d. s. p.
II. Elizabeth, m. 22 April, 1738, William Burton, Esq., M.P. co. Rutland.
III. Lora, m. Francis George, Esq. of Ford Abbey, co. Dorset.
IV. Anne.   V. Mary.

Mr. Pitt d. 22 Feb. 1734, and was s. by his eldest son,

GEORGE PITT, Esq. of Strathfieldsaye, who m. Louisa, dau. of John Bernier, Esq., by whom he had issue,

I. GEORGE, 1st Lord Rivers.
II. James, d. s. p.   III. Thomas, d. s. p.
IV. William-Augustus (Sir), K.B., of Heckfield, co. Southampton, gen. in the army; m. Hon. Mary Howe, dau. of Emanuel Scrope, 2nd Viscount Howe, and d. s. p. December, 1809.
I. Lucy, m. James Ker, Esq. of Morriston and Kessfield, co. Berwick.
II. Mary, d. August, 1744.

Mr. Pitt d. in December, 1745, and was s. by his eldest son,

GEORGE PITT, Esq. of Strathfieldsaye, M.P. for the co. Dorset, and a diplomatist of the first grade, who was elevated to the peerage of Great Britain, 20 May, 1776, by the title of Baron Rivers, of Strathfieldsaye. His lordship obtained a second patent, 1 April, 1802, creating him BARON RIVERS of Sudeley Castle, co. Gloucester, with remainder, in default of male issue, to his brother, Sir William-Augustus Pitt, K.B., and after him to the male issue of his dau., Louisa, Mrs. Beckford. The limitation did not, however, include the children of his dau., Marcia-Lucy, wife of James Fox-Lane, Esq. His lordship m. 5 January, 1745-6, Penelope, dau. of Sir Henry Atkins, 4th bart. of Clapham, co. Surrey, and had issue,

616

I. GEORGE, 2nd baron.
I. Penelope. m. 1st, to Edward, Earl Ligonier; and 2ndly, in 1784, to Capt. Smith.
II. Louisa, m. 22 March, 1773, to Peter Beckford, Esq. of Stapleton, co. Dorset, M.P. for Morpeth, and d. in 1791, leaving issue,
1 HORACE-WILLIAM, 3rd baron.
1 Harriet, m. in 1807, to Henry Seymer, Esq. of Hanford, co. Dorset, who d. in 1834 (see BURKE's Landed Gentry).
III. Marcia-Lucy, m. 23 July, 1789, to James Fox-Lane, Esq. of Bramham Park, Yorkshire, M.P. for Horsham, and d. 5 Aug. 1822, leaving by him (who d. 7 April, 1821),
1 George Lane-Fox, Esq. of Bramham Park, b. 4 May, 1793; m. 20 September, 1814, Georgiana-Henrietta, dau. of Edward Pery Buckley, Esq. of Minestead; and d. 15 November, 1848, leaving,
GEORGE LANE-FOX, Esq. of Bramham Park, b. 13 November, 1816, and other issue (see BURKE's Landed Gentry).
2 William-Lane Fox, grenadier guards, m. 31 December, 1817, Lady Caroline Douglas, dau. of Hon. John Douglas, and sister of George Sholto, 18th Earl of Morton, and d. 11 February, 1832, leaving,
William-Edward Lane-Fox, Esq., b. 1818; d. unm. 1852.
AUGUSTUS-HENRY-LANE FOX-PITT-RIVERS, F.R.S., of Rushmore, Salisbury, lieut.-gen. in the army, b. 14 April, 1827, assumed by royal licence, dated 25 May, 1880, the additional surname and arms of PITT RIVERS, under the will of his grand-uncle, the 2nd Lord Rivers. By the same warrant his children took the name of PITT only after Fox. He m. 3 February, 1853, Hon. Alice-Margaret Stanley, dau. of Edward-John, 2nd Lord Stanley of Alderley, and has,
Alexander-Edward-Lane, b. 2 November, 1855.
St. George-William-Lane, b. 14 September, 1856.
William-Augustus-Lane, b. 9 January, 1858.
Lionel-Charles-Lane, b. 5 November, 1860.
Douglas-Henry-Lane, b. 17 December, 1864.
Arthur-Algernon-Lane, b. 11 April, 1866.
Ursula-Katherine-Lane, m. 14 January, 1880, to William Scott, Esq., only son of Gen. W.-H. Scott.
Alice-Augusta-Laurentia-Lane.
Agnes-Geraldine-Lane.
3 Sackville-Walter Lane Fox, m. 22 May, 1826, Lady Charlotte-Mary-Anne-Georgiana Osborne, only dau. of George-William-Frederick, 6th Duke of Leeds, and 10th Baron Conyers, and d. 18 August, 1874, having had by her (who d. 17 January, 1836),
SACKVILLE-GEORGE LANE FOX, 12th Baron Conyers, and other issue (see BURKE's Extant Peerage).

His lordship d. 7 May, 1803, and was s. by his son,
GEORGE, 2nd baron, b. 19 September, 1751, one of the lords of the bedchamber. His lordship's estate of Strathfieldsaye was purchased in 1814 for the Duke of Wellington. Lord Rivers d. 20 July, 1828, unm., when the barony of RIVERS of Strathfieldsaye expired, while that of RIVERS of Sudeley Castle devolved, according to the limitation, upon his nephew,
HORACE-WILLIAM, 3rd baron, b. 2 December, 1777, who m. 9 February, 1808, Francis, only dau. of Col. Francis-Hale Rigby, of Mistley Hall, co. Essex, by Frances, his wife, dau. of Sir Thomas Rumbold, Bart., governor of Madras, and by her (who d. 6 September, 1860) had,
I. GEORGE, 4th baron.
II. HORACE, 6th baron.
I. Fanny, m. 24 July, 1834, to Frederick-William Cox, Esq., and d. 1 Feb. 1836.
II. Harriet-Elizabeth, maid of honour to the Queen, m. in September, 1841, to Charles-Dashwood Bruce, Esq., grandson of the 5th Earl of Elgin and Kincardine.

Lord Rivers relinquished entirely his surname of BECKFORD, and took, by royal licence, 26 November, 1828, that of PITT-RIVERS. He d. 23 January, 1831, and was s. by his elder son,
GEORGE, 4th baron, who was b. 16 July, 1810. and m. 2 February, 1833, Lady Susan-Georgiana Leveson-Gower, dau. of Granville, 1st Earl Granville, and by her (who d. 30 April, 1866) had issue,
I. George-Horace, b. 20 March, 1834; d. 20 December, 1850.
II. Granville-Beckford, b. 26 July, 1838; d. 20 August, 1855.
III. William-Frederick, b. 21 October, 1845; d. 8 July, 1859.
IV. HENRY-PETER, 5th baron.
I. Susan-Harriet, m. 30 July, 1872, to Edmund Oldfield, Esq., Fellow of Worcester College, Oxford.
II. Fanny-Georgiana, m. 16 January, 1861, to George Godolphin, 9th Duke of Leeds.
III. Blanche-Caroline.
IV. Alice-Charlotte, m. 26 April, 1865, to Col. William Arbuthnot, 14th hussars, nephew of Sir Robert-Keith Arbuthnot, 2nd bart., and was accidentally killed, 21 June, 1865, by a stroke of lightning, while ascending Schelthorne, one of the Bernese Alps.
V. Mary-Emma, maid of honour in ordinary to the Queen.
VI. Margaret-Grace.
VII. Gertrude-Emily.
VIII. Constance-Elizabeth, d. 2 June, 1875.

Lord Rivers *d.* 28 April, 1866, and was *s.* by his son,

HENRY-PETER, 5th baron, who was *b.* 7 April, 1849, and *d.* 15 March, 1867, when he was *s.* by his uncle,

HORACE, 6th baron, lieut.-col. royal horse guards, *b.* 12 April, 1814; *m.* 1st, 10 April, 1845, Miss Eleanor Suter, who *d.* September, 1872; and *m.* 2ndly, 26 June, 1873, Emmeline, dau. of Capt. John-Pownall Bastard. Lord Rivers *d. s. p.* 31 March, 1880, when the barony of RIVERS *of Sudeley Castle* became EXTINCT.

Arms—Quarterly, 1st and 4th, sa. a fesse chequy arg. and az., between three bezants, for PITT; 2nd and 3rd, per pale gu. and az. on a chevron arg., between three martlets or, an eagle displayed sa., for BECKFORD.

PONSONBY — BARONS PONSONBY, OF IMOKILLY, VISCOUNT PONSONBY.

Barony, by Letters Patent, dated 13 March, 1806.
Viscounty, by Letters Patent, dated 12 April, 1839.

Lineage.

THE RIGHT HON. JOHN PONSONBY (2nd son of Brabazon, 1st EARL OF BESSBOROUGH, *see that title,* BURKE'S *Peerage*), speaker of the House of Commons in Ireland, and six times one of the lords-justices of that kingdom; *b.* 29 March, 1713; *m.* 22 September, 1743, Lady Elizabeth-Cavendish, dau. of William, 3rd Duke of Devonshire, by whom he had, with other issue,

I. WILLIAM-BRABAZON, 1st lord.
II. John, *b.* 24 December, 1748; *d.* 9 August, 1761.
III. George, *b.* 4 March, 1755, M.P. Inistioge, 1784; an eminent lawyer and statesman, constituted lord-high chancellor of Ireland in 1806; *m.* in 1781, Lady Mary Butler, dau. of Brinsley, 2nd Earl of Lanesborough; and *d.* in 1817, leaving an only dau.,

Elizabeth, who *m.* in 1803, the Hon. Francis-Aldborough Prittie; and *d.* 11 January, 1849.

IV. Richard, *b.* 17 July, 1758; *d.* young.
V. Frederick, *b.* 18 March, 1763; *d.* 28 July, 1769.
I. Catherine, *m.* 15 December, 1763, Richard, 2nd Earl of Shannon; *d.* in 1827.
II. Frances, *m.* 13 December, 1774, Cornelius, 1st Lord Lismore; *d.* in 1827.
III. Charlotte, *m.* 10 July, 1780, to the Right Hon. Denis-Bowes Daly, of Dalystown, co. Galway; and *d* 26 August, 1781.
IV. Henrietta, *b.* 12 March, 1765.

Mr. Speaker Ponsonby *d.* 12 December, 1789, and was *s.* by his eldest son,

WILLIAM-BRABAZON, 1st baron, *b.* 15 September, 1744; M.P. co. Kilkenny, and joint postmaster-general for Ireland, 1784; *m.* 26 December, 1769, Hon. Louisa Molesworth, dau. of Richard, 3rd Viscount Molesworth, by whom he had issue,

I. JOHN, 2nd baron.
II. William (Sir), K.C.B., a major-general in the army; *m.* 26 January, 1807, Hon. Georgiana, FitzRoy, 6th dau. of Charles, 1st Lord Southampton, by whom (who *d.* 6 February, 1835) he left,

1 WILLIAM, 3rd baron.
1 Anne-Louisa, *m.* 27 September, 1832, to William-Tighe Hamilton, Esq., and *d.* at Nice, 24 January, 1863. This lady and her surviving sister had a patent of precedence as daus. of a baron, 4 September, 1855.
2 Charlotte-Georgina, *m.* 1st, 8 July, 1834, to Lieut.-Col. John-Horace-Thomas Stapleton; and 2ndly, 11 December, 1838, to Rear-Admiral Sir Charles Talbot, K.C.B. (*see* SHREWSBURY, WATERFORD, and TALBOT, E. BURKE's *Peerage*), and had by him (who *d.* 8 August, 1876) the following issue,

CHARLES-WILLIAM TALBOT-PONSONBY, of Inchiquin, Youghal, J.P., lieut. R.N., *b.* 29 May, 1843, assumed, by royal licence, 1866, the additional surname and arms of PONSONBY, on succeeding to the estate of Imokilly, *m.* 15 January, 1868, Constance-Louisa, youngest dau. of F.-P. Delmé Radcliffe, Esq., of Hitchin Priory, Herts, and has had issue, William-Charles-Francis, *b.* 14 October, 1868, *d.* 1870: John-Seymour-William, *b.* 1 May, 1870; Edward-Frederick, *b.* 21 October, 1872; Charles-George, *b.* 1 May, 1874; Evelyn-Mary-Georgiana, *b.* 22 February, 1876.
Francis-Arthur-Bouverie-Talbot, lieutenant and adjutant 43rd foot, *b.* 27 September, 1851; *m.* 16 November, 1878, Alice-M. Beatrice, 2nd dau. of Col. E. Melville Lawford, comt. 4th Madras cavalry, and has issue,

Francis-Eustace-George, *b.* 6 October, 1849.
Edward-Charles, *b.* 9 April, 1881.

George-Ponsonby Talbot, *b.* 29 April, 1853
Georgy-Melosina-Mary-Elizabeth, *m.* 14 April, 1874, to Francis Delmé-Radcliffe, Esq., R.N., 2nd surviving son of F.-P. Delmé-Radcliffe, Esq., of Hitchin Priory, Herts.

Fanny-Charlotte-Emma, *m.* 6 June, 1861, to Capt. Duncan McNeill, Scots greys, 3rd son of the late Capt. Alexander McNeill, of Colonsay.
Edith, *m.* 2 March, 1878, to Lieut. Charles Davis Sherston, of the rifle brigade.
Rose (twin with Edith).

3 Mary-Elizabeth, *m.* 1 August, 1835, to the Rev. Henry-George Talbot: and *d.* 14 September, 1838.
4 Frances-Isabella, *m.* 22 January, 1840, to the Rev. Windham Beadon, vicar of Cricklade, co. Wilts; and *d.* in 1845.

Sir William fell at Waterloo, in 1815.
III. Richard (Right Rev.), D.D., Bishop of Derry; *m.* in 1804, Frances, 2nd dau. of the Right Hon. John Staples; and *d.* 27 October, 1853, having had issue,

1 WILLIAM-BRABAZON, 4th baron.
1 Harriet-Catherine, *m.* 1 December, 1835, to the Rev. Thomas Lindsay; and *d.* in 1858.
2 Louisa-Elizabeth-Eleanor, *m.* 11 August, 1836, to Simon-George Purdon, Esq., of Tinerana, co. Clare. This lady and her surviving sister had a patent of precedence as daus. of a baron. 1862.
3 Frances-Charlotte.
4 Emily-Augusta-Grace, *m.* 1852, the Rev. Charlton Maxwell, rector of Lockpatrick, and *d.* 11 August, 1856.

IV. George, of Woodbeding, near Midhurst, co. Sussex; *m.* 1st, 7 April, 1807, the eldest dau. of John Jacob Gladstanes, Esq., by whom (who *d.* 18 July, 1808) he had a son,

William-Gladstanes, barrister-at-law, *b.* in 1808: and *d.* in 1841.

He *m.* 2ndly, 1812, Diana-Juliana-Margaretta, dau. of Hon. Edward Bouverie, and *d.* 5 June, 1863, having by her had issue,

1 Robert-Wentworth, *b.* in 1814; *d.* 28 September, 1840.
1 Diana, *m.* 16 August, 1842, Edward-Granville-George, Lord Lanerton, who *d. s. p.* 8 October, 1880, 4th son of George, 6th Earl of Carlisle.

V. Frederick, *d. unm.* in 1849.
I. Mary-Elizabeth, *m.* 18 November, 1794, to Charles, 2nd Earl Grey, and *d.* 26 November, 1861.

Mr. Ponsonby was elevated to the peerage of the united kingdom, as BARON PONSONBY *of Imokilly*, 13 March, 1806. He *d.* 5 November, 1806, and was *s.* by his son,

JOHN, 2nd baron, G.C B., a distinguished diplomatist, H.M. ambassador at Constantinople from 1832 to 1837, and at Vienna from 1846 to 1851, created VISCOUNT PONSONBY, 12 April, 1839. He *m.* 13 January, 1803, Lady Frances Villiers (who *d.* 14 April, 1866), dau. of George, 4th Earl of Jersey; but *d. s. p.* 21 February, 1855, when the viscounty became EXTINCT, but the barony devolved on his lordship's nephew,

WILLIAM, 3rd baron, who was *b.* 6 February, 1816; *m.* 12 April, 1851, Mademoiselle Maria-Theresa Duerbeck, of Munich, and *d. s. p.* at Rottach-Tegernsee, Bavaria, 2 October, 1861, and was *s.* by his cousin,

WILLIAM-BRABAZON, 4th baron, capt. in the 7th fusiliers, *b.* 18 August, 1807; he *d.* 10 September, 1866, on board his yacht, the Lufra, off Plymouth. He was never married, and with him the title became EXTINCT, and the estates devolved on his cousin, CHARLES-WILLIAM-TALBOT, who then assumed the surname of PONSONBY.

Arms—Gu., a chevron, between three combs, arg.

RAWDON — EARLS OF MOIRA, BARONS RAWDON, OF RAWDON, CO. DOWN, MARQUESSES OF HASTINGS, EARLS OF RAWDON, VISCOUNTS LOUDOUN, AND BARONS RAWDON, OF RAWDON, CO. YORK.

Barony of Rawdon, co. Down, by Letters Patent, dated 9 April, 1750.
Earldom of Moira, by Letters Patent, dated 15 December, 1761.
Barony of Rawdon, co. York, by Letters Patent, dated 5 March, 1783.
Marquessate of Hastings, &c., by Letters Patent, dated 7 December, 1816.

Lineage.

JOHN DE RAWDON, of Rawdon, co. York, with whom the regular pedigree in Glover's Visitation commences, *m.* the dau. of Thomas Bradford, and was *s.* by his son,

MICHAEL RAWDON, of Rawdon, who *m.* Elizabeth, dau. of Richard Thorneton, of Tyreshall, and had a son,

GEORGE RAWDON, of Rawdon, *m.* Anne, dau. of John Beckwith, of Scough, and was father of

Francis Rawdon, of Rawdon, living, at Glover's Visitation, in 1612. He m. Dorothy, dau. of William Aldborough, of Aldborough, and had issue,

George, 1st bart.
Anne, m. John Stanhope, Esq., of Horsforth.
Elizabeth, m. Rev. Philip Tandy, vicar of Glanavy.
Mary, m. John Dunbar, gent.
Mercy, d. unm..   Priscilla, d. unm.

The only son,

Sir George Rawdon, 1st bart. of Moira, settled in Ireland, and took an active part, as military commander, during the rebellion in 1641, in that kingdom; and subsequently, until his decease in 1684, in the general affairs of Ireland, and was created a Baronet of England 20 May, 1665, being denominated of Moira, co. Down. Sir George m. 1st, Ursula, dau. of Sir Francis Stafford, Knt., of Bradney, co. Salop, and widow of Francis Hill, Esq., of Hill Hall, by whom he had an only son,

1. Francis, d. young.

He m. 2ndly, September, 1654, Hon. Dorothy Conway, dau. of Edward, 2nd Viscount Conway and Killultagh, by whom (who d. 1676) he had issue,

1. Edward, b. 1655; killed in France, 1676.
11. John, b. 1656; killed in France, 1677.
111. Arthur, 2nd bart.
1. Mary, b. 1661; m. October, 1678, Arthur, 2nd Earl of Granard.
11. Dorothy, b. 1667; d. unm. 12 April, 1737; buried at St. George's, Dublin.
111. Brileana, b. 1668; d. unm. 11 October, 1712; buried at St. Mary's, Dublin.

Sir George d. August, 1684, and was s. by his only surviving son,

Sir Arthur Rawdon, 2nd bart. of Moira, b. 17 October, 1662; who m. Helen, dau. and heir of Sir James Graham, and granddau. of William, 7th Earl of Monteith, and had by her (who d. 17 March, 1709, aged 47),

1. Edward, d. young.
11. John, 3rd bart.
1. Dorothy, d. unm.
11. Isabella, m. March, 1719, Sir Richard Levinge, 2nd bart., of Parwich, and d. 2 November, 1731.

Sir Arthur d. 17 October, 1695, and was s. by his only surviving son,

Sir John Rawdon, 3rd bart. of Moira, M.P. co. Down, b. 1690; who m. 3 March, 1717, Dorothy, 2nd dau. of Sir Richard Levinge, 1st Bart. of Parwich, Speaker of the House of Commons in Ireland, and had by her (who m. 2ndly, Most Rev. Charles Cobbe, D.D., Archbishop of Dublin) issue,

1. George, bapt. 13 February, 1718; buried at St. Mary's, Dublin, 27 June, 1719.
11. John, 1st Earl of Moira.
111. Richard, b. 6 October, 1721; buried at St. Mary's, Dublin, 9 March, 1723.
1v. Arthur, of Rathmolyan, b. 1723, sheriff co. Meath, 1746; m. Arabella Cheshire, heiress of Hallwood, co. Chester; and d. s. p. 6 June, 1766.

Sir John d. 1 February, 1723, and was s. by his eldest surviving son,

Sir John, 1st Earl of Moira, who was elevated to the peerage of Ireland, 9 April, 1750, as Baron Rawdon, of Rawdon, co. Down, and created Earl of Moira, 15 December, 1761. He m. 1st, 10 November, 1741, Lady Helena Perceval, dau. of John, 1st Earl of Egmont, by whom he had two daus.,

Catherine, m. 30 April, 1764, Joseph Henry, Esq., of Straffan, co. Kildare.
Helena, m. 3 June, 1769, Stephen, 1st Earl Mountcashell.

The earl m. 2ndly, 23 December, 1746, Hon. Anne Hill, dau. of Trevor, 1st Viscount Hillsborough, by whom he had no issue; and 3rdly, 26 November, 1752, Lady Elizabeth Hastings, eldest dau. of Theophilus, 9th Earl of Huntingdon (by his countess, Selina, 2nd dau. and co-heir of Washington, Earl Ferrers), who inherited the Baronies of Hastings, &c., in the peerage of England (created by summons, in the 14th and 15th centuries), upon the demise of her brother, Francis, 10th Earl of Huntingdon, without issue, 1789. By this last union his lordship had issue,

1. Francis, 2nd earl.
11. John-Theophilus, b. 19 November, 1756, m. Frances, dau. of Joseph-William Hall Stephenson, Esq., and granddau. of John Hall (afterwards Stevenson) Esq., of Skelton Castle, co. York, who d. in 1785 (the Eugenius, of Sterne); and dying in 1808, left an only dau., Elizabeth-Anne, who m. Lord George-William Russell, and d. 10 August, 1874.
111. George, b. 9 January, 1761, major 16th regt.
1. Anne-Elizabeth, m. 15 February, 1788, Thomas, 1st Earl of Ailesbury ; and d. in 1813.
11. Selina-Frances, m. 10 May, 1779, George, 6th Earl of Granard, and d. in 1827.
111. Charlotte-Adelaide-Constantia, m. in 1814, Hamilton Fitzgerald, Esq., and d. in 1834.

The earl d. 20 June, 1793, and was s. by his eldest son,

Sir Francis, 2nd Earl of Moira, and 1st Marquess of Hastings, &c., b. 9 Dec. 1754, K.G., G.C.B., F.R.S., F.S.A., and M.R.I.A., a gallant soldier, an eloquent senator, and a popular statesman. His lordship inherited, at the decease of his mother, in 1808, the ancient Baronies of Botreaux, Hungerford, De Molyns, and Hastings, and was created, 7 Dec. 1816, a peer of the United Kingdom, by the titles of Viscount Loudoun, Earl of Rawdon, and Marquess of Hastings. He had been previously created a peer of Great Britain, 5 March, 1783, by the title of Baron Rawdon, of Rawdon, co. York. The marquess m. 12 July, 1804, Flora - Muir (Campbell), Countess of Loudoun in her own right, in the peerage of Scotland, by whom (who d. 8 Jan. 1840) he had issue,

1. George-Augustus-Francis, 3rd earl and 2nd marquess.
1. Flora-Elizabeth, lady of the bedchamber to the Duchess of Kent; d. unm. 5 July. 1839.
11. Sophia-Frederica-Christina, b. 1 February, 1809; m. 10 April, 1845, John, 2nd Marquess of Bute; she d. 28 December, 1859.
111. Selina-Constance, m. 25 June, 1838, Charles-John Henry, Esq., son of John-Joseph Henry, Esq., of Straffan, co. Kildare, and d. 8 November, 1867.
1v. Adelaide-Augusta-Lavinia, m. 8 July, 1854, to Sir William-Keith Murray, 7th bart., of Ochtertyre, and d. 6 December, 1860.

His lordship, at one time Governor-General of India, was, at his decease, governor and commander-in-chief of the Island of Malta and its dependencies, constable and chief-governor of the Tower of London, lord-lieut. and custos rotulorum of the Tower division, a general officer in the army, and col. of the 27th regt., a governor of the Charterhouse, and council of the king in Cornwall and North Britain. The marquess assumed the surname of Hastings, in addition to that of Rawdon. He d. 28 Nov. 1826, and was s. by his son,

Sir George-Augustus-Francis, 3rd Earl of Moira, 2nd Marquess of Hastings, b. 4 Feb. 1808, who m. 1 Aug. 1831, Barbara, Baroness Grey de Ruthyn in her own right, and by her had issue,

Paulyn-Reginald-Serlo, 4th earl and 3rd marquess.
Henry-Weysford-Charles-Plantagenet, 5th earl and 4th marquess.
Edith-Maud Abney-Hastings, of Willersley Hall, heiress, at the death of her brother, to the earldom of Loudoun, and to the co-heirship of the English baronies, the abeyance of which was terminated in her favour in 1871. Her ladyship m. 1853, Charles - Frederick Clifton, afterwards Abney-Hastings, created Lord Donington in 1880; and d. 23 January, 1874, leaving with other issue,

Charles-Edward-Hastings, Earl of Loudoun, &c. (see Burke's Extant Peerage, Loudoun, E. of).

Bertha-Lelgarde, m. 11 December, 1855, to Capt. Augustus-Wykeham Clifton, son of Thomas Clifton, Esq., of Lytham Hall, Lancashire, and has issue.
Victoria-Maria-Louisa, m. 31 October, 1859, John-Forbes-Stratford Kirwan, Esq., of Moyne House, co. Galway.
Frances-Augusta-Constance, m. 30 July, 1863, Charles, 4th Earl of Romney.

His lordship d. 13 Jan. 1844. (The marchioness m. 2ndly, 19 April, 1845, Admiral Sir Hastings-Reginald Henry, afterwards Yelverton, G.C.B., R.N., and d. 18 Nov. 1858). His eldest son,

Sir Paulyn-Reginald Serlo, 4th Earl of Moira, and 3rd Marquess of Hastings, an officer in the army, b. 2 June, 1832; d. unm. 17 Jan. 1851, and was s. by his uncle,

Sir Henry Weysford-Charles-Plantagenet, 5th Earl of Moira, and 4th Marquess of Hastings, b. 22 July, 1842. He inherited the Barony of Grey de Ruthyn, 18 Nov. 1858, at the decease of his mother; m. 16 July, 1864, Lady Florence-Cecilia Paget, dau. of Henry, 2nd Marquess of Anglesey, and d. s. p. 12 Nov. 1868, when the Earldom of Moira, and Barony of Rawdon (peerage of Ireland), Barony of Rawdon (peerage of Great Britain), Marquessate of Hastings, Earldom of Rawdon, and Viscounty of Loudoun (peerage of the United Kingdom), with the baronetcy, became extinct. The Earldom of Loudoun, and other titles in the peerage of Scotland, descended to his eldest sister, then Lady Edith Abney-Hastings ; the baronies of Hastings, Hungerford, Botreaux, and De Molyns (peerage of England), fell into abeyance between his four sisters of the whole blood, and was terminated, 21 April, 1871, in favour of the eldest, Edith, Countess of Loudoun, and the barony of Grey de Ruthyn fell into abeyance between his said four sisters of the whole blood, and his sister of the half-blood, Hon. Barbara Yelverton, afterwards Lady Churston, and so continues.

Arms -Rawdon, Earl of Moira, Ar. a fesse between three pheons, sa; Rawdon - Hastings, Marquess of Hastings, Quarterly, 1st and 4th, Ar. a maunch sa., for Hastings; 2nd and 3rd, Ar. a fess between three pheons, sa., for Rawdon.

Page 451.

RAWSON—VISCOUNT CLONTARFF.

The Rawsons of Fryston, in Yorkshire, from whom the Prior of Kilmainham is presumed to have descended, are recorded in the Visitations of 1563, 1584, 1585, and 1612.

Richard Rawson, probably a brother of James Rawson of Fryston, was elected alderman of the Ward of Farringdon Without in 1475, was sheriff of London in 1476, and senior warden of the Mercer's Company in 1478 and 1483. He d. in the latter year and was buried at St. Mary Magdalen's, Old Fish Street. By Isabella Craford, his wife (who d. in 1497) he had issue,

I. John, Prior of Kilmainham.
II. Avery, of Alvethley, Essex, father of Nicholas Rawson, whose dau. and co-heiress, Anne, m. Sir Michael Stanhope.
III. Christopher, of London, merchant of the Staple of Calais; d. 1518.
IV. Richard, D.D., rector of St. Olaves, Hart Street, London
v. Nicholas, master of the Free Chapel, of Grysenhale, Norfolk.

The eldest son,
John Rawson, admitted to the freedom of the Mercers' Company in 1492, joined the Order of Knights of St. John, and is mentioned in his mother's will, dated 1 September, 1497, as "a knight of Rhodes." In 1511 he was appointed Prior of Kilmainham, near Dublin, and sworn of the privy council of Ireland. In 1517, he was lord treasurer of that kingdom, and sat, as Prior of Kilmainham, in the Irish House of Peers. When the Sultan Solyman attacked Rhodes with a mighty host, and the Grand Master summoned to his aid all the knights in every country, we find Sir John Rawson's name at the head of the list of knights of St. John reviewed by the Grand Master, Villiers l'Isle Adam, for the defence of the island. In 1525, Sir John Rawson was Turcopilier, and subsequently returned to Ireland, taking an active part in the council as Prior of Kilmainham. In 1540, he surrendered the priory of Kilmainham, receiving in recompense a grant of 500 marks per annum for life out of the estates of the hospital, and in 1541 was created Viscount Clontarff for life, with a pension of £10. He survived until 1560, when his life peerage expired with him.

Arms—Quarterly, 1st and 4th: Rawson, per fess undée, sa. and az., a castle with four towers, arg.; 2nd and 3rd, Craford, or, on a chev, vert., three ravens heads, erased, arg., with the cross of the order of St. John, in chief. This coat armour,'thus marshalled, was borne by Sir John Rawson, Viscount Clontarff, Knight of St. John of Jerusalem.

ROLFE—BARON CRANWORTH, OF CRANWORTH, CO. NORFOLK.

By Letters Patent dated 20 Dec. 1850.

Lineage.

The Rev. Waters Rolfe, A.B. of Caius College, Rector of North Pickenham and Houghton, b. in 1688, m. 27 Sept. 1720, Allen, dau. of Robert Shuldham, Esq. of Kettlestone, and d. 11 June, 1748, leaving a son,
The Rev. Robert Rolfe, A.M., some time fellow of Caius College, Rector of Hilborough, who s. to the estates of his uncle, Francis Shuldham, Esq. of Kettlestone. He m. Alice, 2nd dau. of the Rev. Edmund Nelson, Rector of Hilburgh, aunt to Horatio, Viscount Nelson, and by her (who d. 24 July, 1823, aged 93) had issue,

I. Edmund, of whom presently.
II. Robert (Rev.), A.B. of Caius College; s. his brother as rector of Cockley Clay, domestic chaplain to Viscount Nelson, b. 4 May, 1767; m. 1st, Frances, youngest dau. of the Rev. Robert Crever, A.M, vicar of Wymondham, and relict of Thomas-Vertue Mott, Esq., of Great Barningham, M.A., of Caius College, and by this lady (who d. 14 August, 1803) had an only child,
Frances-Alice, m. Joseph Everett, Esq., of Heytesbury, co. Wilts, F.S.A., J.P. and D.L. for that county.
Mr. Robert Rolfe m. 2ndly, 6 December, 1808, Elizabeth, only surviving dau. of John Rose, Esq., of Eye, and by her had, besides several other children,
Edmund-Nelson (Rev.), A.M. of Caius College, rector of Morningthorpe, Norfolk, and domestic chaplain to Thomas, second Earl Nelson, b. 28 November, 1810.
III. Randyll, d. young, in 1775
I. Ellen, m. to the Rev. William Taylor, A.M.

Mr. Rolfe d. 7 May, 1785, aged 64. His eldest son,
The Rev. Edmund Rolfe, A.B., of Cranworth, Norfolk, Rector of Cockley Clay, m. Jemima, 4th dau. of William

Alexander, Esq., and granddau. of the celebrated Dr. Monsey, physician to Chelsea College, and by her (who d. 25 June, 1827, aged 64) had,
Robert-Monsey (Sir), created Baron Cranworth. William, lieut. R.N., d. unm. in 1825.

Mr. Rolfe d. 24 July, 1795, aged 32. His eldest son,
Right Hon. Sir Robert-Monsey Rolfe, b. 18 Dec. 1790. A distinguished lawyer who was called to the bar in 1816, made king's counsel in 1832, solicitor-general in 1834, and a Baron of the Exchequer in 1839. He had been from 1832 to 1839 M.P. for Penryn. He was knighted in 1835. In 1850 he became Vice-Chancellor of England, and on the 20 Dec. of the same year was created Baron Cranworth, of Cranworth, co. Norfolk, in the peerage of the United Kingdom. He was subsequently a Judge of the Court of Appeal in Chancery, and was constituted Lord High Chancellor in Dec. 1852, which high office he resigned in 1858, was reappointed to it in 1865, and again resigned in 1866. Lord Cranworth m. 9 Oct. 1845, Laura, dau. of T. W. Carr, Esq. of Frognal and Eshott, co. Northumberland, but by her (who d. 15 Feb. 1868) he had no issue. He d. 26 July, 1868, when his title became extinct.

Arms—Gyronny of eight, arg. and gu., an eagle, displayed, sa., charged on the breast with a sun in splendour, or.

SOMERVILLE—BARONS SOMERVILLE.

Created before 15 December, 1430.

Lineage.

The remotest ancestor of this family upon record is,
Sir Gualter de Somerville, one of the companions of the Norman Conqueror, who became Lord of Whichnour, co. Stafford, and his descendants possessed considerable property, about the close of the 12th century, in the co. Lanark, and in other parts of Scotland. He had three sons, ancestors of Somerville of Whichnour, co. Stafford, Somerville of Linton, co. Roxburgh, and Somerville of Aston, co. Gloucester, the last descendant of which house, William Somerville, author of "The Chase," d. 19 July, 1742, having settled his estate on James, 13th Lord Somerville. The second son of Sir Gualter de Somerville,
William de Somerville attached himself to David I., King of Scots, and settled in Scotland He was witness to the Foundation Charter of Melrose, and d. 1142, leaving two sons.
Walter, the younger, was witness to a charter of Malcolm IV. 1154 60. The elder,
William de Somerville was witness to a charter of David I. to the Abbey of Kelso, 1144, and to several charters of Malcolm IV. He d. before 1161, leaving a son,
William de Somerville, who is stated to have obtained the lands of Linton, co. Roxburgh, from King William the Lion, for killing a serpent that infested that quarter, and to have been father of
William de Somerville, of Linton and Carnwarth, who was one of the barons appointed at the marriage of Alexander II. (whose reign commenced in 1214) to exercise in a tournament at the castle of Roxburgh. He m. Margaret, dau. of Walter de Newbigging, of Dunsire, and had a dau., Margaret, m. Sir Archibald Campbell, of Lochow, and a son,
Sir William de Somerville, of Linton and Carnwarth, gave, with consent of his father, the church of Carnwarth to the see of Glasgow; d. 1282, leaving a son,
Thomas de Somerville, of Linton and Carnwarth. Swore fealty to Edward I., 15 May, 1296; joined Sir William Wallace, 1297; d. 1300, leaving (with a younger son, John (Sir), an adherent to Robert I., King of Scots, and taken prisoner by the English, 1306. An elder son,
Sir Walter de Somerville, of Linton and Carnwarth, m. Giles, dau. and heiress of Sir John Herring, with whom he got the lands of Gilmerton, Drum. and Gooltrees. He d. about 1330, when his eldest surviving son,
Sir Thomas de Somerville, of Lincoln and Carnwarth, who m. Elizabeth, dau. of Sir James Douglas, of London, and was s. by his eldest son,
Sir William de Somerville, of Linton and Carnwarth, one of the hostages for the ransom of King David II., in 1357; who d. in 1403, and was s. by his elder son,
Thomas de Somerville, of Linton and Carnwarth (one of the ambassadors deputed, in 1423, to the court of London, to treat for the ransom of King James I.) who was created, 15 December, 1430, Lord Somerville, in the peerage of Scotland. His lordship m. Janet, dau. of Sir Alexander Stewart, of Dernley, with whom he acquired the barony of Cambusnethan; and had issue,

I. WILLIAM, 2nd baron.
I. Mary, said to have m. Sir William Hay, of Yester.
II. Giles, m. Sir Robert Logan, of Restalrig.
III. Margaret, said to have m. 1st, Roger Kirkpatrick, of Closeburn; and 2ndly, Sir Thomas Kerr, of Fernihirst.

The baron d. 1445, and was s. by his only son,
WILLIAM, 2nd baron, who m. Janet, dau. of Sir John Mowat, of Stanhouse, and had issue,

I. JOHN, 3rd baron.
II. Thomas, of Plane, had a charter of those lands and Crannok and Glorat co. Stirling, and Fordale, co. Fife, 26 February, 1450. He was ancestor of SOMERVILLE of Plane.
I. Janet, m. Ralph Weir, of Blackwood.
II. Mary, m. William Cleland, of Cleland.

The baron d. 1456, and was s. by his eldest son,
JOHN, 3rd lord, m. 1st, Helen Stepburn, sister of Patrick, 1st Earl of Bothwell, and had issue,

I. WILLIAM, Master of Somerville, m. 1st Marjory Montgomery, sister of Hugh, 1st Earl of Eglingtoun; and 2ndly, Janet, dau. of William Douglas, of Drumanrig, and d. vitâ patris, leaving by his 1st wife, two sons,
  1 JOHN, 4th baron.
  2 HUGH, 5th baron.
I. Elizabeth, m. Archibald Campbell, eldest surviving son of Duncan, 1st Lord Campbell, of Lochow, and was mother of Colin, 1st Earl of Argull.
II. Helen, m. Sir John Jardine, of Applegirth.

Lord Somerville m. 2ndly, Mariot, dau. of Sir William Baillie, of Lamington, by whom he had further issue,

II. John (Sir), of Cambusnethan, fell at Flodden, 9 September, 1513, and was ancestor of SOMERVILLE of Cambusnethan.
III. Mary, m. Sir Stephen Lockhart, of Cleghorn.

The baron d. in 1491-2, and was s. by his grandson,
JOHN, 4th lord, at whose decease s. p. the dignity devolved upon his brother,
HUGH, 5th lord, who m. Janet, dau. of William Maitland, of Leithington, and had issue,

I. JAMES, 6th baron.
II. John, d. s p.
III. Hugh, ancestor of SOMERVILLE of Spittel.
I. Margaret, m. Charles Murray, of Cockpool.
II. Marjory, m. James Tweedie, of Drumelzier.
III. Elizabeth, m. Sir John Carmichael, of Carmichael.

The baron d. 1549, and was s. by his eldest son,
JAMES, 6th lord. This nobleman was a strenuous opposer of the Reformation, saying, with the Earl of Atholl and Lord Bothwick, "that he would believe as his fathers had done before him." His lordship joined Queen MARY, at Hamilton, May, 1568, with three hundred horse, at whose head he fought at the battle of Langside, and was severely wounded. He m. Agnes, dau. of Sir James Hamilton, of Finnart, and had issue,

I. Hugh, 7th baron.
II. Another son, who got part of Carnwarth from his father, and whose posterity were existing in 1813.
I. Margaret, d. s. p.
II. Agnes, m. Somerville, of Plane, co. Stirling.

The baron d. 1569, and was s. by his elder son,
HUGH, 7th lord, who m. Eleanor, dau. of George, Lord Seton, and had, with four daus., four surviving sons,

I. William, d. s. p. vitâ patris.
II. Robert, accidentally killed by his eldest brother 1597.
III. GILBERT, 8th baron.
IV. HUGH, 9th baron.

The baron d. 1597, and was s. by his son,
GILBERT, 8th lord. This nobleman entertained King JAMES VI. most sumptuously at his castle of Cowthaly, which the monarch jocularly called Cow-daily, from seeing a cow and ten sheep killed daily. His lordship, by a course of similar extravagance, ran entirely through his estates. He m. Margaret, dau. of John Somerville, of Cambusnethan, and had three surviving daus.,

Mary, m. 1st, to James, Lord Torphichen, and 2ndly, to Sir William Douglas, of Pumpherstoun.
Margaret, m. to Sir Humphrey Colquhoun, of Balvie.
A dau., m. to Stewart, of Minto.

His lordship d. in 1618, and as he left no male issue, the title devolved upon his brother,
HUGH, 9th lord, but he never assumed the honour. He m. Margaret, dau. of Gavin Hamilton, of Raploch, and had issue,

I. JAMES, 10th baron.   II. Gavin.
I. Jean, m. Thomas Tenant, of Cairns.
II. Margaret, d. s. p.

The baron d. 1640, and was s. by his elder son,
JAMES, 10th lord (but he likewise declined assuming the dignity), m. Lilias, dau. of Sir James Bannatyne, of Newhall, a lord of Session; and d. 3 January, 1677, when he was s. by his only son.

620

JAMES, 11th lord (but unassumed), m. 1st, Martha, dau. of Bauntyne, of Corhouse; and 2ndly, 15 March, 1685, and had issue by the former only, viz., three sons,

I. JAMES, m. 1671, Elizabeth, dau. of George Graham, of Edinburgh, merchant, and d. of wounds received in a drunken quarrel, 8 July, 1682, leaving a son,

JAMES, 12th baron.

II. John, lieut.-col. in Gen. Ramsay's regt.
III. George, adjutant-gen. to the foot guards.

The baron d. in 1690, and was s. by his grandson,
JAMES 12th lord (still unassumed), who m. Margaret, dau. of Murray, of Deuchar, and had issue,

I. JAMES, 13th baron.
II. George, of Dinder, co. Somerset, d. 6 July, 1776, leaving with two daus., two sons,
  1 George (Rev.), of Bilney, co. Gloucester, m. Miss Seaman, and d. s p.
  2 William, lieut. R.N., d. s. p. 10 September 1758.
III. John, d. s. p.   IV. William, d. s. p.
I. Euphemia, b. 26 June, 1696; d. unm.
II. Elizabeth, d. unm.

The baron d. in 1700, and was s. by his eldest son,
JAMES, the 13th lord; whose claim being disputed, was confirmed by parliament, 27 May, 1723, and he was chosen one of the representative lords in 1741. His lordship m. 1st, in 1724, Anne, only dau. of Henry Bayntum, Esq. of Spye Park, co. Wilts, and relict of Edward Rolt, Esq., of Sacombe Park, co. Herts, by whom he had issue,

I. JAMES, 14th baron.
II. Hugh, lieut.-colonel, b. in 1729; m. 1st, 23 November, 1763, Elizabeth, dau. and heir of Christopher Lethbridge, Esq. of Westaway, co. Devon, by whom (who d. 11 October, 1765) he had an only son,
  1 JOHN, who s. as 15th lord.

Colonel Somerville m. 2ndly, 26 October, 1778, Mary, eldest dau. of the Hon. Wriothesley Digby, of Meriden, co. Warwick, by whom (who d. 8 Sept. 1794) he left at his decease, 7 May, 1795,

1 MARK, 16th lord.
2 Hugh, in E.I C.'s civil service, m 1807, Amicia, dau. of George Heming, Esq., of Weddington, co. Warwick (who d. 22 Jan. 1859), and d. at Bengal, s. p. 1808.
3 KENELM, 17th lord.
4 William (Rev.), Rector of Harford, co. Warwick, b. 14 October, 1789; m. 5 May, 1830, Charlotte, dau. of the late Rev. Walter Bagot, of Blithfield, co. Stafford, and d 6 July, 1857, having by her (who d. 24 October. 1865) had issue,

Walter-Digby, b. 17 December, 1831; d. at Paris, 17 May, 1865.
Everard-William, b. 3 July, 1833.
Reginald-Hugh, b. 16 December, 1835, lieut. R.W. fusiliers, killed in the assault before Sebastop l, 8 September, 1855.
AUBREY-JOHN, 19th baron.
Augustus, b. 8 August, 1839; d. 7 April, 1869.

1 Mary, m. to the Rev. Charles Digby; d. 28 April, 1834.
2 Frances, m. in 1838, to the Hon. W.-Booth Grey.
3 Harriet, m. to William, 15th Earl of Erroll, and d. his widow, 28 January, 1864.
4 Julia-Valenza, m. 20 May, 1816, to Sir Francis-Bond Head. Bart., K.H.

I. Anne-Whichnour, m. in December, 1748, to George Burgess, Esq. of Greslee, co. Berks.
II. Frances-Anne, m. to James-Roper Head, Esq. of The Hermitage, co. Kent.
III. Mary-Anne, d. unm.

The baron m. 2ndly, in 1736, Frances, dau. and co-heiress of John Rotherham, Esq., of Muchwaltham, co. Essex, and had another dau.,

IV. Elizabeth, b. 16 December. 1737; d. at Holyrood-House, 1740.

Lord Somerville augmented his fortune considerably by an arrangement with his kinsman, William Somerville, Esq., of Eadstone, co. Warwick, and of Somerville-Ashton, co. Gloucester, the celebrated poet, and author of The Chase, representative of the English and elder branch of his lordship's family; by which, in consideration of certain sums applied to the relief of burdens, the poet who was unmarried, settled the reversions of his estate upon Lord Somerville; and d. in 1742, when the baron inherited accordingly. His lordship was s. by his eldest son,

JAMES, 14th lord; who d. unm. in 1796, when the dignity reverted to his nephew,
JOHN, as 15th lord, b. 21 Sept. 1765 (refer to Hugh, 2nd son of James, 13th lord). This nobleman has transmitted his name to posterity by the introduction of the breed of Merino sheep from Lisbon into Great Britain. He d. unm. in 1819, and was s. by his half-brother,

MARK, as 16th lord, b. 26 October, 1784, and dying *unm.* 3 June, 1842, was *s.* by his brother,

KENELM, 17th lord, admiral R.N., who was b. 14 November, 1787, and *m.* 3 September, 1833, Frances-Louisa, only dau. of John Hayman, Esq., and had issue,

   I. HUGH, 18th baron.
   II. Frederick-Noel, lieut. rifle brigade, b. 8 October, 1840; *d. s. p.* 8 January, 1866.
   I. Louisa-Harriet, *m.* 21 October, 1871, Col. Charles-Stewart Henry, C.B., royal horse artillery.
   II. Emily-Charlotte, *m.* 29 April, 1869, Rev. Thomas-Bond-Bird Robinson, rector of Milton, diocese of Winchester.
   III. Mary-Agnes, *m.* 18 June, 1872, Sir Theophilus-William Biddulph, 4th bart. of Westcombe.
   IV. Selina-Constance, *m.* 6 August, 1861, to Ralph Smyth, Esq. of Gaybrook, co. Westmeath.
   V. Julia-Frances, *m.* 23 November, 1871, Col. Edward-William Blackett, A.D.C. to the Queen, eldest son of Sir Edward Blackett, 6th bart. of Matfen.

Lord Somerville *d.* 19 October, 1864, and was *s.* by his elder son,

HUGH, 18th lord, b. 11 October, 1839; *d. unm.*, killed while out hunting 17 November, 1868, when he was *s.* by his cousin, AUBREY-JOHN, 19th lord, b. 1 February, 1838; *d. s. p.* 28 Aug. 1870, since which time the title has been DORMANT or EXTINCT.

Arms—Az., three mullets, two and one, between seven crosses crosslet, fitchée, three, one, two, and one, or.

SMYTHE—VISCOUNTS STRANGFORD AND BARONS PENSHURST OF PENSHURST.

Viscounty by Letters Patent, dated 17 July, 1628.
Barony by Letters Patent, dated 26 January, 1825.

Lineage.

JOHN SMYTHE, Esq., of Corsham, co. Wilts, living *temp.* HENRY VIII., *m.* Joan, dau. of Robert Brouncker, Esq. of Melksham, and *d.* in 1538, leaving issue,

   I. John, whose descendants where living in 1620.
   II. THOMAS, of whom presently.
   III. Henry, whose son Henry, of Baydon, Wilts, entered his pedigree at the Visitation of 1620.
   IV. Robert, living in 1592.
   V. Richard.
   I. Ann.   II. Jane.
   III. Elizabeth, *m.* to Simon Horsepool, of London.

The 2nd son,

THOMAS SMYTHE, Esq., b. about 1522, removed from Corsham, and seated himself at Osterhanger, co. Kent. This gentleman was Farmer of the Customs in the reign of ELIZABETH, and amassed considerable wealth. He *m.* Alice, dau. and heiress of Sir Andrew Judde, Knt., of Ashford, by whom he acquired the manor of Ashford, and had with other issue,

   I. John, his heir.
   II. Thomas (Sir, Knt.), ambassador to Russia in 1604; *m.* Sarah, dau. and heir of William Blount, Esq., and had by her (who *m.* 2ndly, Robert Sydney, 1st Earl of Leicester) two sons: of whom the elder,

      JOHN (Sir, Knt.), of Bidborough, Kent, *m.* Lady Isabella Rich, dau. of Robert, 1st Earl of Warwick, and left a son, Robert, of Sutton-at-Hone and Bounds, Kent, who *m.* 8 July, 1652, Lady Dorothy Sydney (the poet Waller's "Sacharissa"), dau. of Robert, 2nd Earl of Leicester (widow of Henry, 1st Earl of Sunderland, and by that Earl, mother of Robert, 2nd Earl, lineal ancestor of the Dukes of Marlborough and Earls Spencer), and had issue,

         Robert Smythe, Esq., governor of Dover Castle, who *m.* Catherine, dau. of William Stafford, Esq., of Blatherwick, co. Northampton, and had,

           Henry, his heir, father of Sir Sydney-Stafford Smythe, of Bounds, chief baron of the Exchequer in 1772, who *m.* Sarah, elder dau. of Sir Charles Farnaby, 3rd bart., of Kippington, and *d. s. p.* 1777, when this branch of the family terminated.

   II. Richard (Sir), Knt., of Leeds Castle, co. Kent.

Mr. Smythe *d.* 1591. Through his marriage with Alice Judde, his descendants, the Lords Strangford became representatives of Sir Andrew Judde, the founder of Tonbridge free-school, and eldest co-heir of Sir Robert Chicheley, lord-mayor of London, eldest brother of Henry Chicheley, Archbishop of Canterbury, founder of All Souls, Oxford. The eldest son,

SIR JOHN SMYTHE, Knt. of Osterhanger and Ashford, b. 1556; *m.* 1578, Elizabeth, dau. and heiress of John Fineux, Esq., of Hawhouse, co. Kent (son of Chief-Justice Sir John Fineux), and had issue,

THOMAS, 1st viscount.
Katherine, *m.* Sir Henry Baker, 1st bart., of Sisinghurst.
Elizabeth, *m.* Sir Henry Neville, Knt., of Billingbear.

Sir John *d.* 1609, and was *s.* by his son,

SIR THOMAS SMYTHE, K.B., who was created a peer of Ireland, 17 July, 1628, as VISCOUNT STRANGFORD. His lordship *m.* Lady Barbara Sydney, 7th dau. of Robert, 1st Earl of Leicester, K.G., and niece of the ever-memorable Sir Philip Sydney, and by her (who *m.* 2ndly, Sir Thomas Colepepper) had issue,

   I. PHILIP, 2nd viscount.
   I. Barbara, *m.* Peter Rycaut, Esq. of Eastwell, co. Kent.
   II. Elizabeth.   III. Philippa.   IV. Dorothy.

The Viscount *d.* 1635, and was *s.* by his only son,

PHILIP, 2nd viscount, b. 1634; who *m.* 1650, his cousin, Lady Isabella Sydney, dau. of Robert, 2nd Earl of Leicester, by whom (who *d.* in 1663) he had,

Diana, b. 1660; *m.* John Aelst, and *d. s. p.*

Lord Strangford *m.* 2ndly, Mary, dau. of George Porter, Esq., eldest son of Endymion Porter, Esq., groom of the bedchamber to CHARLES I., and by her (who *d.* 13 November, 1730) had

ENDYMION, 3rd viscount.
Elizabeth, *m.* Henry Audley, Esq. of Berechurch, co. Essex.
Olivia, *m.* John Darell, Esq. of Calehill, co. Kent.
Katherine-Clare, *m.* Henry, 8th Lord Teynham.

The viscount *d.* 1708, and was *s.* by his son,

ENDYMION, 3rd viscount, *m.* Elizabeth, dau. and heiress of Jean Larget de Bresville, of Chalons; and dying 9 September, 1724 (his widow *m.* Gen. Vander Horst and *d.* in Holland, in June, 1764), was *s.* by his only son,

PHILIP, 4th viscount, LL.D., Dean of Derry; b. 14 March, 1715; who *m.* in 1741, Mary, dau. of Anthony Jephson, Esq., of Mallow Castle, co. Cork, M.P., and dying 29 April, 1787, left, with two daus., Mary and Anne, an only son,

LIONEL, 5th viscount, b. 19 May, 1753. This nobleman entered early in life into the army, and distinguished himself in North America; he subsequently took holy orders, and became a clergyman of the established church. His lordship *m.* 5 September, 1779, Maria-Eliza, eldest dau. of Frederick Philipse, Esq., of Philipseburg, New York, by whom (who *d.* in April, 1838) he had issue,

PERCY-CLINTON-SYDNEY, 6th viscount.
Lionel, b. 28 March, 1783.
Eliza-Maria-Sydney, b. 5 September, 1781; *m.* 1824, to James Sullivan, M.D.
Louisa-Sarah-Sydney, b. 2 March, 1785; *m.* 17 November, 1807, to John Eld, Esq., of Seighford, co. Stafford.

The viscount *d.* 1801, and was *s.* by his son,

PERCY-CLINTON-SYDNEY, 6th viscount; b. 31 August, 1780; who was created Baron Penshurst of Penshurst, Kent, in the peerage of the United Kingdom, 26 January, 1825; he *m.* 17 June, 1817, Ellen, youngest dau. of Sir Thomas Burke, 1st Bart. of Marble Hill, and relict of Nicholas Browne, Esq., of Mount Hazel, co. Galway, by whom (who *d.* 26 May, 1826) he had issue,

   I. GEORGE - AUGUSTUS - FREDERICK - PERCY - SYDNEY, 7th viscount.
   II. Lionel-Philip-Thomas-Henry, b. 5 August, 1821; *d.* 18 July, 1844.
   III. PERCY-ELLEN-FREDERICK-WILLIAM, 8th and last viscount.
   I. Philippa-Eliza-Sydney, *m.* 29 December, 1840, to the Right Hon. Henry-James Baillie, of Redcastle, co. Ross, M.P. co. Inverness, and *d.* 3 June, 1854.
   II. Louisa-Ellen-Frances-Augusta, *m.* 3 May, 1847, George-John, 3rd Marquess of Sligo, and *d.* 23 November, 1852.

Lord Strangford was appointed ambassador to the court of Lisbon in 1806, to Sweden in 1817, to the Sublime Porte in 1820, and to Russia in 1825. His lordship acquired literary reputation by his English version of the smaller poems of Camoëns, the Portuguese poet. He *d.* 29 May, 1855, and was *s.* by his eldest son,

GEORGE-AUGUSTUS-FREDERICK-PERCY-SYDNEY, 7th viscount, b. 13 April, 1818; *m.* 9 November, 1857, Margaret, eldest dau. of John Lennox Kincaid Lennox, Esq., of Castle Lennox, N.B. (which lady was *m.* 2ndly, 17 October, 1861, to Charles Spencer, second son of William Hanbury, 1st Lord Bateman, and she and her husband assumed, by royal licence, in 1862, the surnames of Kincaid-Lennox, in addition to, and after those of Bateman-Hanbury). The viscount dying 23 November, 1857, was *s.* by his next surviving brother,

PERCY-ELLEN-FREDERICK-WILLIAM, 8th and last viscount, a Grandee of Portugal, D.L. for Canterbury; b. 26 November, 1825; *m.* 6 February, 1862, Emily-Anne, youngest dau. of Admiral Sir F. Beaufort, K.C.B., and *d. s. p.* 9 January, 1869, when all his honours became EXTINCT.

Arms—Az., a chevron, engrailed, between three lions passant-guardant, or.

STRATFORD—EARLS OF ALDBOROUGH, VISCOUNTS ALDBOROUGH AND AMIENS, AND BARONS OF BALTINGLASS.

Barony, by Letters Patent, dated 21 May, 1763.
Viscounty of Aldborough, by Letters Patent, dated 23 July, 1776.
Earldom and Viscounty of Amiens, by Letters Patent, dated 9 July, 1777.

Lineage.

In the year 1660,

ROBERT STRATFORD settled in Ireland, and was one of the original burgesses in the charter constituting Baltinglass a borough town. He represented the co. Wicklow in parliament, and m. (marriage licence, 11 February, 1662) Mary, dau. of Oliver Walsh, Esq., of Ballykilcaven, Queen's Co., by whom he had issue,

1. EDWARD, his successor.
11. Francis, b. 1667, consul at Bordeaux, d. s. p.
1. Grace, b. 2 May, 1666; m. (marriage licence, 22 May, 1686) Benjamin Burton, Esq., M P. for Dublin, 1703-23.
11. Mary, b. 1 April, 1668; m. (marriage licence, 27 June, 1688) Henry Persse, Esq., of Roxborough.
111. Elizabeth, b. 27 September, 1672; m. Thomas Hickman, Esq., of Barntic.
1v. Abigail, b. 1673; m. (marriage licence, 19 April, 1697) 1st, to George Canning, Esq., of Garvagh; and 2ndly, to Major Cudmore.
v. Jane, b. 5 June, 1674; m. John Carleton, Esq., of Darlinghill, co. Tipperary, who d. 1730.
v1. Anne, m. Colonel Samuel Eyre, M.P. for Galway.
v11. Catherine, b. 3 May, 1676; m. to John Spencer, Esq., co. Dublin, M.P.

Mr. Stratford, whose will dated 8 November, 1698, was proved 29 January, 1699, was s. by his elder son,

EDWARD STRATFORD, who purchased Great Belan, and other lands in the co. of Kildare, from Lord Fitzhardinge. This gentleman was a staunch promoter of the Revolution, and entertained King WILLIAM at Belan. He m. (marriage licence, 28 January, 1683) Elizabeth, dau. of Euseby Baisley, Esq., of Ricketstown, co. Carlow, and had issue.

1. ROBERT, of Corbally, in the Queen's Co., m. Mrs. Sisson, widow, and had five daus,

  1 Grace, m. Samuel Richardson, Esq., Dublin.
  2 Anne, m. Rev. Chaworth Chambre.
  3 Jane, m. James Wemys, Esq., of Danesfort, M.P.
  4 Mary, m. Henry O'Neill, Esq., of Ballybollan.
  5 Penelope.

11. Euseby, of Corbally, whose will, dated 9 September, 1745, was proved 23 July, 1753, m. the dau. of Edward Warren, Esq., of Lowhill, co. Kilkenny, and had issue,

  1 BENJAMIN, of Corbally, entered Trin. Coll., Dublin, 18 June, 1733, aged 17 years, made his will, 27 September, 1771, which was proved 21 October same year, m. (marriage licence, 29 June, 1768) Jane, dau of Patrick Wemys, Esq., of Danesfort, M.P., and had one son,

    EUSEBY.

  2 Euseby, of Dublin, m. (marriage licence, 15 April, 1755) Jane, dau. of Rev. James Robinson, D.D., prebendary of St. John's, Christ's Church, Dublin, and d. intestate (adm. 5 May, 1778), leaving two sons,

    Euseby.
    James.

  3 Francis (Rev.) rector of Baltinglass, m. Jane Slack.
  1 Elizabeth, m. Stephen FitzGerald, Esq., of Ballythomas, in the Queen's Co.
  2 Mary, m. Richard FitzGerald, Esq., of Dorinson; in the Queen's Co.

111. JOHN, 1st Earl of Aldborough, of whom hereafter.
1. Elizabeth, m. (marriage licence, 3 March, 1713) Charles Plunkett, Esq., of Dunleer, co. Louth, and d. 1729.

Mr. Stratford m. 2ndly, Mrs. Penelope Echlin, widow, but had no further issue. He d. 23 February, 1740, having settled his estates in cos. Wicklow, Carlow, and Kildare, on his youngest son,

JOHN STRATFORD, Esq., of Belan, M.P., for Baltinglass in the reigns of the first three GEORGES, who was advanced to the peerage of Ireland, on 21 May, 1763, as *Baron of Baltinglass, co. Wicklow;* 23 July, 1776, he was created *Viscount Aldborough of Belan, co. Kildare;* and 9 July, 1777, *Viscount Amiens* and EARL OF ALDBOROUGH, *of the palatinate of Upper Ormonde.* He m. Martha, dau. and co-heiress of the Ven. Benjamin Neale, Archdeacon of Leighlin, by Hannah his wife, dau. and co-heir of Col. Joshua Paul, and had by her,

1. EDWARD, 2nd earl.
11. JOHN, 3rd earl.
111. Francis-Paul (Rev.), of Mount Neale, d. s. p.
1v. BENJAMIN NEALE, 4th earl.
v. Robert, capt. R.N., d. unm. 1778.

v1. William, d. unm.
1. Hannah.
11. Elizabeth, m. Robert Tynte, Esq., of Dunlavin, co. Wicklow.
111. Martha, m. Morley Pendred, alias Saunders, Esq., of Saunders Grove, co. Wicklow.
1v. Anne, m. George Powell, Esq., of Newgarden, co. Limerick.
v. Grace.
v1. Amelia, m. Richard, 3rd Viscount Powerscourt, and had, with other issue,
  Richard, 4th Viscount Powerscourt.
  John-Wingfield, b. 2 August, 1772, who assumed in 1802 the additional surname of STRATFORD (see BURKE's *Peerage,* POWERSCOURT, V.).
v11. Henrietta, m. Robert Hartpole, Esq., of Shrule Castle, in the Queen's Co.
v111. Frances, m. (marr. lic. 26 April, 1781) William Holt, of Dublin, and d. May, 1792.
1x. Letitia.

The Earl d. 29 June, 1777, and was s. by his eldest son,

EDWARD, 2nd earl. His lordship m. 1st, Barbara, dau. and sole heiress of the Hon. Nicholas Herbert, of Great Glenham, co. Suffolk, and granddau. of Thomas, 8th Earl of Pembroke and Montgomery; and 2ndly, Anne-Elizabeth, only dau. of Sir John Henniker, 2nd Bart., of Newton Hill, co. Essex, and 1st Lord Henniker, by whom (who m. 2ndly, George Powell, of Newgarden, and d. 14 July, 1802) he had no issue. He d. s. p. 2 January, 1801, and was s. by his brother,

JOHN, 3rd earl, m. (Mar. Lic. 14 March, 1777) Elizabeth, dau. of Rev. Frederick Hamilton, Vicar of Wellingborough, granddau. of Lord Archibald Hamilton, and great-granddau. of William, 3rd Duke of Hamilton, by whom (who d. 29 January, 1845) he had three daus.,

1. LOUISA-MARTHA, m. 19 October, 1799, Admiral Hon. John Rodney, 3rd son of John, 1st Lord Rodney, and d. 2 December, 1814, leaving to him (who d. 21 May, 1792),

  1 JOHN-STRATFORD RODNEY, b. 14 May, 1802; m. 1st, 22 March, 1824, Miss Boyce, of Bombay, who d. 3 February, 1825; and 2ndly, in 1826, Eleanor, 3rd dau. of Joseph Hume, Esq., and d. 1854, leaving an only son, Tollemache-Montagu-Brydges, who d. s. p. 1858, and one dau.,

    KATHERINE-DORA RODNEY, m. 8 May, 1860, Henry-Craven St. John, Esq., of Stokefield, co. Gloucester, capt. R.N. (see BURKE's *Peerage,* BOLINGBROOKE and ST. JOHN, V.), and has issue.

  2 Maitland-Thomas Rodney, capt. R.N.; b. 14 October, 1804; m. 10 January, 1849, Elizabeth-Frances, 5th dau. of Col. Dickson, and great granddau. of Col. Gardiner (who fell at Preston Pans) by the Lady Frances Erskine, his wife, and d. 18 July, 1842.
  1 Louisa-Frederica, m. 29 June, 1818. Lord John-George Lennox, and d. 12 January, 1865.
  2 Angela, m. 8 January, 1825, Col. Alexander Browne, R.E.
  3 Eliza, m. 1832, James-Sedgewick Wetenhall, Esq.
  4 Emily-Georgiana, m. in 1835, William-Marsden Wetenhall, Esq., lieut.-col. 10th regt.; and d. in 1842.
  5 Henrietta.
  6 Caroline-Stuart, m. 3 April, 1830, Campbell-Drummond Riddell, Esq.

11. ELIZABETH, m. 28 February, 1797, Admiral John Richard Delap Tollemache, Vice-Admiral of the Red, by whom (who d. 16 July, 1837) she had issue,

  1 JOHN. 1st Lord Tollemache, so created 17 January, 1876, b. 5 December, 1805; m. 1st, 2 August, 1826, Georgina-Louisa, dau. of Thomas Best, Esq., by Lady Emily Stratford his wife, and by her (who d. 18 July, 1846) has issue,

    WILBRAHAM-FREDERIC TOLLEMACHE, b. 4 July, 1832; m. 1st, 2 December, 1858. Lady Emma-Georgiana Stewart, 2nd dau. of the 9th Earl of Galloway, and by her (who d. 24 January, 1869) has issue, 1 Lyonel-Plantagenet, b. 28 October, 1860; m. 13 April, 1882, Lady Blanche-Sybil King, only dau. and heir of Robert Edward, 7th Earl of Kingston; 2 Wilbraham, b. 5 February, 1865; 3 Randolph-Stewart, b. 5 April, 1866; 4 Arthur-Wilbraham, b. 9 September, 1867; 1 Blanche; 2 Grace. He m. 2ndly, 2 October, 1878, Mary-Stuart, dau. of the Right Hon. Lord Claud Hamilton, M.P. (see BURKE's *Peerage,* ABERCORN, D.)

    Lyonel-Arthur Tollemache, b. 28 May, 1838; m. 25 January, 1870, Hon. Beatrice-Lucia-Catherine, youngest dau of Lord Egerton of Tatton.

  Lord Tollemache m. 2ndly, 17 January, 1850, Minnie, dau. of James Duff, Esq., and step dau. of Lord Rendlesham, and has issue,

    John-Richard-Delap Tollemache, b. 22 October, 1850; m. 26 December, 1872, Eleanor, fourth dau. of Hon. Henry Starnes, President of Council for the Province of Quebec, Canada.
    Hamilton-James Tollemache, b. 22 January, 1852; m. 21 October, 1879, Mabel, second dau. of Robert-Culling Hanbury, Esq., M.P., of Bedwell Park, co. Hertford.
    Murray Tollemache, b. 21 May, 1853.
    Stanhope Tollemache, b. 28 August, 1855.
    Duff Tollemache, b. 5 January, 1859.

Douglas Tollemache, *b.* 27 June, 1862.
Stratford Tollemache, *b.* 25 June, 1864.
Ranulph Tollemache, *b.* 1 January, 1866.
Mortimer Tollemache, *b.* 12 April, 1872.
Rhona-Cecilia-Emily, *b.* 25 September, 1857.

2 Wilbraham-Spencer Tollemache, of Dorfold Hall, co. Chester, Coldstream guards, *b.* 3 October, 1807; *m.* 1844, Anne, eldest dau. and heiress of Rev. James Tomkinson, of Dorfold Hall, and has issue, 1 Henry-James, J.P., *b.* 1846; 2 Algernon-Edward (Rev.), vicar of Weston, near Crewe, *b.* 1851, *m.* 14 September, 1875, Agnes-Mary, dau. of Metcalfe Larken, Esq.; 1 Julia-Elizabeth-Anne, *m.* 10 May, 1873, Charles-Saville Roundell; 2 Alice-Georgiana.
3 William-Augustus Tollemache, 2nd life guards, *b.* 23 November, 1817; *m.* Marguerite, dau. of John Home-Purves, Esq., and step-dau. of the 1st Vicount Canterbury.
1 Elizabeth-Jane-Henrietta, *m.* 19 June, 1826, to James Thomas, 7th Earl of Cardigan. K.C.B., and *d.* 15 July, 1858.
2 Emily, *m.* 1819, Charles Tyrwhitt Jones, Esq., and *d.* 1821.
3 Jane, *m.* 1819, to George Finch, Esq., of Burley-on-the-Hill, co. Rutland, and *d.* 1821.
4 Louisa, *d.* 1821.
5 Marcia, *m.* to Admiral Frederick-Edward Vernon-Harcourt, R.N., and *d.* 27 December, 1855.
6 Marianne, widow of Hubert de Burgh, Esq., of West Drayton.
7 Selina, *d.* 1832; *m.* Capt. William Locke, 1st life guards.
8 Charlotte, *m.* 1833, to Capt. G. Hope, R.N., and *d.* 1837.
9 Georgina, *m.* 1848, Right Hon. William Cowper-Temple, created 1880, LORD MOUNT TEMPLE (*see that title*).

III. EMILY, *m.* Thomas Best, Esq., who *d.* 1829. She *d.* 22 May, 1863, and her dau., Georgina-Lucy, *m.* her cousin, John, 1st, Lord Tollemache.

The earl *d.* March, 1823, and was *s.* by his brother,
BENJAMIN NEALE, 4th earl, who *m.* Martha, only child and heiress of John Burton, Esq., and niece and heiress of Mason Gerard, Esq., and by her (who *d.* 24 August, 1816) had issue,

MASON-GERARD, 5th earl.
Eliza, *d. unm.* 1848.
Sophia, *d. unm.* 1864.

The earl *d.* 11 July, 1863, and was *s.* by his only son,
MASON GERARD, 5th earl, who *m.* 2 August, 1804, Cornelia-Jane, eldest dau. of Charles-Henry Tandy, Esq., and had issue,

BENJAMIN O'NEALE, 6th earl.
Charles-Henry, an officer in the army, *b.* 11 July, 1809, *d. unm.* at Suez, 23 October, 1842.
Martha-Eliza, *d. unm.* in 1831.   Eliza, *d.* young in 1824.

The earl *d.* 15 October, 1849, and was *s.* by his eldest son,
BENJAMIN O'NEALE, 6th earl, capt. 1st dragoon guards, *b.* 10 June, 1809, J.P. and D.L. co. Wicklow, who *d. s. p.* 1875, when his titles became EXTINCT.

Arms—Barry of ten, arg. and az., a lion ramp., gu.

TOUCHET—BARONS AUDLEY.

By Writ of Summons, dated 21 December, 1403.

Lineage.

The family of Touchet came into England with the Conqueror, and is recorded in the Battle Abbey Roll, and in the Chronicles of Normandy.
WILLIAM TOUCHET, distinguished himself in the wars of Gascony and Scotland, *temp.* EDWARD I. and had summons to parliament as a BARON, from 29 December, 1209, to 3 November, 1306; but of his lordship Dugdale gives no further account. Contemporary with this Lord Touchet was
SIR ROBERT TOUCHET, Knt., of Tattenhale, co. Chester, who was *s.* by his son,
SIR THOMAS TOUCHET, who *d.* in the 23rd of EDWARD III., leaving a son,
SIR JOHN TOUCHET, Knt., a gallant and distinguished soldier in the martial times of EDWARD III., fell in a sanguinary conflict with the Spaniards of Rochelle, in the 44th of the same king. He *m.* Joane, eldest dau. of James Aldethley or Audley, Lord Audley, of Heleigh (a dignity created by writ of summons, 8 January, 1313), and sole heiress in 1392, of her brother, Nicholas, last Baron Audley, of that family. Sir John was *s.* by his son,
JOHN TOUCHET, who was summoned to parliament as *Lord Audley*, 21 Decembr, 1405, in the peerage of England, and was ancestor of the TOUCHETS, *Lords Audley* and *Earls of Castlehaven* (*see that title at page* 535).
JOHN, 17th Lord Audley and 5th and last Earl of Castlehaven, *d.* without issue, 22 April, 1777, when the earldom ceased; but the barony of Audley, being a barony in fee,

descended to his nephew (the son of his deceased sister, Mary, and her husband, Capt. Philip Thicknesse, lieut.-governor of the fort at Languard Point*),
GEORGE, 18th Baron Audley, *b.* 4 February, 1758. In 1783, his lordship, by royal permission, assumed the surname of TOUCHET, and the arms of Touchet and Audley. Lord Audley *m.* 1st, 21 May, 1781, Elizabeth, dau. and co-heir of John Hussey, 2nd Lord Delaval, by whom he had issue,

GEORGE-JOHN, 18th baron.
John, killed at Copenhagen, 2 April, 1801.
Elizabeth-Susannah, *m.* in November, 1805, to John Cossins, Esq.

Lady Audley, dying 11 July, 1785, his lordship *m.* 2ndly, Augusta, widow of Col. Moorhouse, and younger dau. of the Rev. Andre Boisdaune, by Elizabeth Strode, sister of Col. Strode, of South Hill, co. Somerset, but had no other issue. He *d.* August, 1818, and was *s.* by his son,
GEORGE-JOHN, 19th baron, *b.* 23 January, 1783; *m.* 18 April, 1816, Anne-Jane, eldest dau. of Vice-Admiral Sir Ross Donelly, K.C.B., and by her (who *d.* 18 August, 1855) he had,

I. GEORGE-EDWARD, 20th baron.
II. John, *b.* 8 November, 1819; *m.* 6 September, 1842, Elizabeth, 3rd dau. of the late John-Henry Blennerhasset, Esq., and *d.* 21 July, 1861, having had, George-John, *b.* 27 April, 1847, *d.* 11 November, 1866; Elizabeth; Maria-Anne, *d.* 15 February, 1867; Charlotte-Anne, *m.* 16 June, 1875, to Thomas Jesson, eldest son of Thomas Jesson, Esq., of Clarendon Terrace, Brighton; and Dorothea-Susan, *m.* 24 January, 1878, to the Hon. and Rev. Charles-Samuel Twisleton (*see* SAYE and SELE, B.).
III. William-Ross, *b.* 23 November, 1821.
IV. James, *b.* in 1825; *d.* an infant.
I. Jane-Elizabeth.   II. Susan, *d.* 14 July, 1872.

He *d.* 14 January, 1837, and was *s.* by his eldest son,
GEORGE-EDWARD, 20th baron, *b.* 26 January, 1817; *m.* 16 April, 1857, Emily, 2nd dau. of Col. Sir Thomas-Livingstone Mitchell, D.C.L., the eminent geographer, and granddau. of Gen. Blunt, and by her (who *d.* 1 April, 1860) had two daus.,

MARY, *b.* 13 August, 1858.
EMILY, *b.* 29 November, 1859.

Lord Audley *m.* 2ndly, 15 February, 1868, Margaret-Anne, widow of James-William Smith, Esq., of 15, Gloucester Square, Hyde Park, and sister of the Rev. Thomas-Dawson Hudson, of Frogmore Hall, co. Hertford. He *d.* 18 April, 1872, when the barony fell into abeyance between his daus.

Arms—Quarterly: 1st and 4th, erm., a chev. gu., TOUCHET; 2nd and 3rd, gu., a fret, or., for AUDLEY.

Page 543.

UFFORD—BARON UFFORD.

Gilbert, in his *History of the Viceroys of Ireland*, speaking of Sir Ralph de Ufford, Viceroy *temp.* EDWARD III., relates that " the colonial chroniclers of the time, reflecting to some extent the feelings of the settlers, declared that de Ufford's death was hailed with joy by clergy and laity, who, in consequence, celebrated their Easter with merry hearts, the tempests and floods, which had continually prevailed from the day of his arrival, suddenly 'ceasing when he died. They denounced him as an unjust man, greedy of gain, doing everything by violence, equitable to none, a robber and oppressor of both rich and poor, adding, that he revoked and cancelled grants which he had made under the king's seal, and extorted money by indicting and imprisoning ecclesiastics as well as laymen. Much of his severity was ascribed to the counsels of his wife, of whom the colonial writers recorded, with malignant satisfaction, that she, who had for a time maintained the state of a queen, subsequently, with her people, bearing de Ufford's remains in a leaden coffin, in which her treasure was secreted, passed privately from Dublin Castle, evading her clamorous creditors, and returned ingloriously to England, in horrible grief of heart, sad and mournful, with the doleful badges of death, sorrow, and heaviness. The Viceroy was interred by his widow in the nunnery of St. Clare, at Cumpsey, or Camesey, near the town of Ufford, co. Suffolk, the burial place of her first husband, William de Burgh, Earl of Ulster, and, through the influence of her brother, Henry, Earl of Lancaster,

* In this Captain Thicknesse's will, proved 24 January, 1793, occurs the following singular bequest, " I leave my right hand, to be cut off after death, to my son, Lord Audley, and I desire it may be sent him, in hopes that such a sight may remind him of his duty to God, after having so long abandoned the duty he owed to a father who once affectionately loved him."

she obtained licence from EDWARD III. to found there a charity of five priests, to offer up prayers perpetually for the repose of their souls."

The fact, stated by Gilbert, that Ufford's remains were interred by his widow in the nunnery of St. Clare, at Campsey, near the town of Ufford, the burial place of her first husband, William de Burgh, Earl of Ulster, clearly proves that the second marriage of de Ufford, mentioned by Dugdale, could not have taken place, and that Vincent's account of the Ufford pedigree is the more accurate.

Page 574.

WENMAN—VISCOUNT WENMAN.

The following is the extension of the limitation of the dignity of VISCOUNT WENMAN to SIR RICHARD WENMAN, 2nd Bart. of Caswell, in the event of failure of issue male of his kinsman, PHILIP, 3rd Viscount Wenman:—

PATENT ROLL, 35 CHARLES II., PART 4, No. 10.

King CHARLES II. by his Letters Patent, dated at Westminster the 30th June, in the 35th year of his reign (A.D. 1683), reciting the creation by patent dated 30th July, 5 CHARLES I. (A.D. 1629), of Sir Richard Wenman, Kt., as Baron Wenman, of Kilmaynham, county Dublin, and Viscount Wenman, of Tuam, county Galway, both in the kingdom of Ireland, to him and the heirs male of his body, lawfully begotten, and reciting that Philip, now Viscount and Baron Wenman, has no surviving issue in whom the honours may be carried on, and that Sir Richard Wenman, of Caswall, in the county of Oxford, Baronet, is nearest of kin to the said Philip, Viscount and Baron Wenman, the King therefore grants to the said Sir Richard Wenman, Baronet, that if Philip, now Viscount and Baron Wenman, die without heir male of his body, that then and thenceforth the aforesaid Sir Richard Wenman, Baronet, and the heirs male of his body, lawfully begotten, and to be begotten, shall have, hold, and bear and enjoy, and every of them successively and respectively shall have, hold, bear, and enjoy the estates, ranks, dignities, titles, and honours of Baron Wenman, of Kilmaynham, county Dublin, and Viscount Wenman, of Tuam, county Galway, both in the kingdom of Ireland, and that they and every of them successively and respectively shall be held in all things, and shall be treated and reputed as Barons and Viscounts Wenman. And that they shall have hold and possess a seat, place, and voice in the parliaments and public assemblies and councils of the king, his heirs and successors, within the realm of Ireland, among the other barons as barons, and among the other viscounts as viscounts (and in this capacity) before all barons, and that they and every of them shall enjoy and use, by the names of Baron and Viscount Wenman, respectively, all and singular, such rights, privileges, pre-eminences, and immunities to the estates of Baron and Viscount respectively, rightfully, and lawfully in all things pertaining, as the other barons and viscounts of the realm of Ireland have heretofore and now respectively enjoy and use, and that the said Sir Richard Wenman, Baronet, may be the better able to support the charges incumbent upon the aforesaid estate of Viscount Wenman, of Tuam, therefore the king grants further to the said Sir Richard Wenman, Baronet, and his heirs male aforesaid, the fee or rent of £13 6s. 8d. yearly. To have and perceive yearly the said fee to the same Sir Richard Wenman, Baronet. and his heirs male aforesaid, from the issues of the great and small customs and subsidies granted to the king, his heirs and successors, arising within the port of the city of Dublin, at the feasts of Easter and Michaelmas by equal portions. The first payment thereof to begin at such of the aforesaid feasts as shall happen next after the death of the aforesaid Philip, now Viscount Wenman, without heirs male of his body, lawfully begotten. Provided always, that these Letters Patent be enrolled in the Court of Chancery in Ireland within the year next after the date of these presents.—By Writ of Privy Seal.

WYKEHAM—BARONESS WENMAN.

By Letters Patent dated 3 June, 1834.

Lineage.

The family of Wykeham has been settled at Swalcliffe from a very remote period; we find mention made of a SIR RALPH WYKEHAM, living in the time of King JOHN, and of a SIR ROBERT WYKEHAM, contemporary with HENRY III.; but of these knights little more is recorded. The great luminary of the family was the celebrated Bishop of Winchester,

WILLIAM OF WYKEHAM, the Founder of Winchester College, and of New College, Oxford. It is still, however, a contested point, whether this eminent churchman was or was not a lineal descendant of the Wykehams of Swalcliffe. They have from time immemorial claimed him as one of their race; and in later times an intermarriage has taken place between Richard Wykeham, of Swalcliffe, and the sister of Richard Fiennes, last Viscount Saye and Sele, who was the lineal descendant of Agnes Champneis, sister of WILLIAM OF WYKEHAM. From the time of the above Sir Robert Wykeham, there is a chasm until about the commencement of the fourteenth century, when

ROBERT WYKEHAM, Lord of Swalcliffe, m. Maud, dau. and heiress of Reginald Waterville. He was s. by

SIR ROBERT WYKEHAM, Knt., Lord of Swalcliffe and Wykeham, who m. Elizabeth, dau. and heiress of Sir John Le Sore, and was s. by his son,

JOHN WYKEHAM, who m. Alys Lyggrade, and had a son and successor,

THOMAS WYKEHAM, whose son and heir, by his wife, Joyce Hanbury,

SIR EDWARD WYKEHAM, m. Isabella, dau. of Gyles Powlton, and was s. by his son,

HUMPHREY WYKEHAM, Esq., living in 1569, who m. Mary, dau. of Edward Underhill, of Ettington, co. Warwick, and left a son and successor,

RICHARD WYKEHAM, Esq., who m. Anne Houldbrook, and was s. by his son,

HUMPHREY WYKEHAM, Esq. of Swalcliffe. This gentleman m. Martha, dau. of Rowley Warde, Esq., serjeant-at-law, and had issue, Humphrey, b in 1668: Richard; Joyce; Anne; and Martha. He was s. by his eldest son,

HUMPHREY WYKEHAM, Esq., of Swalcliffe, who m. in 1693, Susanna, dau. of Richard Orlebar, Esq., of Hinwick House, and dying in 1703, was s. by his only surviving child,

RICHARD WYKEHAM, Esq., of Swalcliffe, who m. Vere-Alicia, dau. of the Rev. Richard Fiennes, and sister and co-heir of Richard, 6th and last Viscount Saye and Sele, by whom (who d. in 1768) he had issue,

WILLIAM-HUMPHRY, his heir.

Richard (Rev.), Vicar of Sulgrave and Chacombe, ancestor of WYKEHAM MARTIN, of Leeds Castle, co. Kent. (See BURKE'S Landed Gentry.)

George, R.N., m. Mary Waddington, and had issue.

Vere, m. Rev. Richard Nicoll, D.D., of Boddicot House; chaplain to GEORGE III.; and had a son, Rev. Thomas-Vere-Richard Nicoll, rector of Cherington, co. Warwick, J.P., whose dau. Mary-Anne, m. William Lucy, Esq., of Birmingham, J.P.

Susanna, m. to Benjamin Holloway, Esq., of Lee Place, and left issue.

Mr. Wykeham d. in 1751, and was s. by his eldest son,

WILLIAM-HUMPHRY WYKEHAM, Esq., of Swalcliffe, b. 1734; who m. 1768, the Hon. Sophia Wenman, eventually sole heiress of her brother Philip, Viscount Wenman, and had issue,

I. WILLIAM-RICHARD, his heir.

II. PHILIP THOMAS WYKEHAM, of Tythrop, m. 1st September, 1806, Hester Louisa. dau. of Fiennes Trotman, Esq., of Syston Court, co. Gloucester, and by her (who d. 26 October, 1823) had two sons,

1 PHILIP - THOMAS - HERBERT WYKEHAM, of Thame Park, and Tythrop House, co. Oxford, J.P. for Bucks and Oxon, b. 9 September, 1807, high sheriff co. Oxford 1837, and capt. comm. 8th Oxford volunteer rifle corps, served for some years in the 7th hussars, and afterwards for a quarter of a century as a capt. in the Oxford yeomanry cavalry. Mr. Wykeham s. to the Tythrop, Emmington, and Kingsey estates at the death of his father, 5 September, 1832, and to the Thame Park estates at the death of his cousin, Baroness Wenman, 9 August, 1870. He d. unm. 21 May, 1879, when Thame Park and Swalcliffe were inherited by his brother Aubrey.

2 Aubrey Wenman, of Chinnor, and afterwards of Thame Park and Swalcliffe, co. Oxford, b. 15 April, 1809; m. 22 June, 1836, Georgiana, dau. and eventually heiress of Sir James Musgrave, 8th bart. of Barnsley Park, co. Gloucester, and assumed, in 1875, by Royal Licence, the additional surname of MUSGRAVE; he d. 21 October, 1879, leaving issue,

WENMAN-AUBREY WYKEHAM-MUSGRAVE, of Thame Park, Swalcliffe, and Barnsley Park, m. 1870, Jane, 3rd dau. of Admiral Hon. George Grey, and has with other issue, Herbert Wenman, b. 26 March, 1871 (see BURKE'S Landed Gentry).

Philip-James-Digby, of Tythrop House, co. Oxford, m. 1871, Georgina-Caroline, 2nd dau. of J. J. Henley, Esq., and has issue.

He m. 2ndly, 24 January, 1825, Elizabeth, eldest dau. of Fiennes Wykeham-Martin, Esq. of Leeds Castle, Kent, but by her had no issue. He d. 5 September, 1832.

I. Sophia-Anne, d. unm.

II. Harriet-Mary, m. 1st, Rev. Willoughby Bertie; and 2ndly, Sir Edward Johnson, K.C.S.I.

Mr. Wykeham d. in 1783, and was s. by his son,

WILLIAM-RICHARD WYKEHAM, Esq., of Swalcliffe, b. 24 October, 1769; who m. 1st, Elizabeth, dau. of W. Marsh, Esq. (who d. in July, 1791); and 2ndly, Miss Hughes (who m. 2ndly, Joseph Pain, Esq.). By the 1st he left at his decease, in 1800,

SOPHIA-ELIZABETH (BARONESS WENMAN), of Thame Park, co. Oxford; so created in the peerage of the United Kingdom, 3 June, 1834; d. unm. 9 Aug. 1870, when her title became EXTINCT.

Arms—Arg., two chevronels between three roses, gu.

YOUNG—BARON LISGAR OF LISGAR.

By Letters Patent, dated 2 November, 1870.

Lineage.

SIR WILLIAM YOUNG, 1st bart., of Baillieborough Castle (*see* BURKE's *Peerage and Baronetage*), an East India director, was created a Baronet, 28 August, 1821. He m. 20 September, 1806, Lucy, dau. of Lieut.-Col. Charles Frederick, eldest son of Sir Charles Frederick, K.B., brother of Sir John Frederick, 4th bart., of Burwood Park, co. Surrey, and by her (who d. 8 August, 1856) had,

JOHN, 2nd bart., created BARON LISGAR.

Thomas, Bengal civil service, b. January, 1810; m. 24 June, 1844, Mary-J. Duncan, dau. of William-Pitt Muston, Esq., and d. 1846, leaving a dau., Lucy, and a son,

WILLIAM-NEED-MUSTON, 3rd baronet.

Charles, b. 1811; d. at Calcutta, 18 March, 1838.

William, a Bengal cavalry officer, b. June, 1817; d. 1850.

Helenus-Edward, a Bengal cavalry officer, b. June, 1822; m. 4 December, 1844, Frances, eldest dau. of Capt. Frederick Nepean-Skinner, and d. 1851. His widow m. 1853, Col. Charles Needham:

Anna, m. 14 June, 1860, to Adolphe-Christophe Edouard, Baron Von Barnekow; d. at Lauban, Prussia, 21 May, 1862. Lucy.

Augusta-Maria, m. 3 April, 1841, to George Rolleston, Esq., of Pan Manor, Isle of Wight, and has, William-Vilette, Augustus Carr-Vilette, Arthur-Hampden-Vilette, and five daus., viz., Elizabeth-Harriet, wife of Rev. G.-A. Clarkson; Laura, wife of Capt. E.-F. Thompson; Georgina, wife of Capt. F.-O. Passy, R.N ; Blanche - Albinia, wife of Capt. W.-L. Martin, R.N; and Lucy-Vilette, m. 23 December, 1879, John-St. Patrick Teather, Esq., of Alstonby, co. Cumberland.

Sir William d. 10 March, 1848, and was s. by his eldest son, RIGHT HON. SIR JOHN YOUNG, 2nd Bart., P.C., G.C.B , G.C.M.G., who was created a peer of the United Kingdom, as BARON LISGAR, of Lisgar and Baillieborough, co. Cavan, 2 November, 1870. His lordship was M.P. for co. Cavan, 1831 to 1855; successively joint secretary of the treasury from 1841 to 1844; chief secretary for Ireland from 1852 to 1855; lord high commissioner of the Ionian Isles from 1855 to 1859; governor of New South Wales from 1860 to 1867 ; and governor-general of Canada, and governor and commander-in-chief of the Island of Prince Edward from 1868 to 1872. He was b. 31 August, 1807; m. 8 April, 1835, Adelaide-Annabella, dau. of Edward-Tuite Dalton, Esq., by his wife, Olivia, afterwards Marchioness of Headfort, and d. s. p. 6 October, 1876, when the Barony of Lisgar became EXTINCT, but the baronetcy devolved on his nephew, SIR WILLIAM-NEED-MUSTON YOUNG, as 3rd bart. Lord Lisgard's widow m. 2ndly, 3 August, 1878, Sir Francis-Charles-Fortescue Turville, K.C.M.G., of Bosworth Hall, co. Leicester.

Arms—Arg., three piles, ss., each charged with a trefoil, slipped, or; on a chief, of the 2nd, three annulets, of the 3rd.

BARONAGE OF IRELAND.

In addition to the PEERAGES of IRELAND by Creation, included in the body of this work, a MS., entitled *Baronage of Ireland* (Ulster's Office), gives the following lists of Barons of Ireland by Tenure, and by Writ of Summons. It would appear, however, that these Writs of Summons did not, as in England, create hereditary peerages descendible to heirs-general. The subject is very ably discussed in LYNCH'S *Feudal Dignities,* from which we make the following extracts:—

"It seems to be now admitted that from the reign of WILLIAM THE CONQUEROR to the middle of the thirteenth century at least, the dignity of Baron in England was annexed to territorial possessions derived from the crown, for which the grantee was bound to render homage, fealty, and military or honorary services. To these possessions there was annexed a right of holding courts, or the civil and criminal jurisdiction as it has been called, which right sometimes passed with the seigniory as an incident without being expressly named: but more generally was specially granted by the words, 'justitiam,' 'curiam,' or 'socha' and 'sacha, infangthef and outfangthef,' &c. In such courts justice was administered by the Baron to his tenants and vassals, or those under him. Besides attending the king in his wars with the number of knights reserved by his tenure to the crown, the baron, as its vassal, was bound to attend the king's court, or '*Curia Regis.*' This court, at first held at stated periods in each year, was afterwards extended to the *Magnum Concilium,* or *Commune Concilium,* to which the king summoned his barons, for their *advice* and *consent,* at such times and on such occasions as his exigencies required. When *extra-feudal* services were agreed on by the barons in this court, the consent of their tenants or vassals was also sought by the lords of such seigniories in the respective Courts Baron; and in the possession of one of those seigniories as a *Feodum Nobile,* with its incident service of attending the *Curia Regis* or *Commune Concilium,* originated the dignity of the Feudal Peerage.

"For so far the origin of those dignities in England and Ireland seems perfectly similar; but in or about the forty-ninth year of HENRY the Third, an alteration was effected in the rights of the English Baronage, by which it was established that no person should attend Parliament, or the *Commune Concilium,* without express writs from the king, and such writ, with a sitting in consequence, has since been held to have vested in the person so summoned, and his heirs lineally, an hereditary barony. This alteration however was not extended to Ireland.

"The effects of a writ of Summons were so well known in Ireland at the end of the seventeenth century, that at a period when the state of public affairs would not admit of the necessary time for preparing patents in due form, King JAMES the Second, wishing to confer peerages on Thomas Nugent, second son of the Earl of Westmeath, John Bourke, second son of the Earl of Clanrickarde, and Sir Alexander Fitton, addressed his special summons to them, and commanded their presence at the Parliament to be held in Dublin on the 7th May following, with others his Prelates, Magnates, and Proceres of that kingdom; but knowing that mere summons to Parliament could not in Ireland effect an hereditary peerage, and that even in England at that time the law could scarcely be considered as settled on the point, King JAMES added a clause of creation for that purpose in the following words:—'Volumeus etiam vos et heredes vestros masculos de corpore vestro legitime exeuntes Barones Nugent de Riverston in comitatu Westmidie existere.' There is but one other instance of a similar creation, namely, that of Henry Bromfiet, who was created Baron de Vessy in England by a clause inserted in the summons which HENRY the Sixth directed to him. It must be added that those three letters of summons being known to operate as creations, they were duly entered on the Chancery Rolls, while none of the other instruments of summons for that Parliament appear to have been made matter of record.

"In fact, an usuage has prevailed in Ireland in this respect as in many others; and though it may now be considered as an *usage peculiar* to that country, yet it is really but the observance of that law or custom in favour of heirs-male which long prevailed in England, and which was introduced into Ireland with all the other feudal institutions by King HENRY the Second."

With these few introductory remarks of a very learned Peerage Lawyer, we will proceed with the MS. entitled "Baronage of Ireland," in Ulster's office:

BARONS ARE OF THREE KINDS, NAMELY,—

(1) By Tenure (who, in regard thereof, ought to be summoned to Parliament).
(2) By Writ of Summons.
(3) By Creation, or Letters Patent.

Barons by Tenure were of old the king's principal tenants, or freeholders, who holding any honour, castle, or manor of the king *in capite* by barony (*per integram Baroniam*) were called his barons majores, having their titles usually from their principal seats, or heads of their baronies, and continued to be the only barons summoned to parliament until the 49th year of King HENRY III. (1265), when that king, having overcome the rebellious barons in the battle of Evesham, called a parliament, in order to have such of them as were slain, taken prisoners, or escaped, attainted and disinherited; but the number of his faithful barons being small, he supplied their number with other persons of known worth, wisdom, and repute, who, by means thereof were thenceforth barons by Writ, although they had no possessions that were honorary baronies (Salden, p. 715), for they were only the tenants *in capite,* which were no real barons, yet were often called to great councils, as barons, peers (Brady agst. Petyt, pp. 68, 32, &c.), and this continued to be the practice until King RICHARD II., in the 11th year of his reign (1388), introduced the creation of barons by Letters Patent.

A perfect list of barons by Tenure and Writ is not to be expected; the loss of the ancient records and summons to parliament renders such a list impossible to be compiled at this day. The following must suffice. The order of time cannot be observed, the barons being differently placed in different parliaments, but where the year is mentioned they appear possessed of their baronies:—

RICHARD DE CLARE (surnamed Strongbow), EARL OF PEMBROKE,
} **LORD OF LEINSTER, AND CONSTABLE OF IRELAND, 1172,**

By marriage with Eva, the only dau. of McMurgh, King of Leinster, whose inheritance King HENRY II., granted to him consisting of the province of Leinster, in which were contained Wexford, Kildare, Kilkenny, Ossory, and Catherlogh. He d. in May, 1177, and left an only dau. and heir, Isabel, who being married to

WILLIAM MARESCHAL, now Marshall (Mareschal to the King), he became EARL OF PEMBROKE,
} **LORD OF LEINSTER, AND LORD MARSHAL OF IRELAND, 1207,**

Having then a grant of the whole province of Leinster. He d. 16 March, 1219, having issue, five sons and five daus. His sons, William, Richard, Gilbert, Walter, and Anselme, all succeeded to the Earldom of Pembroke and Lordship of Leinster, the last of whom dying s. p. 21 December, 1245 (30th HENRY III.), the title of Pembroke became EXTINCT, and the Lordship of Leinster was divided amongst the five daus., viz., (1) Maud, who being m. to Hugh le Bigod, Earl of Norfolk, had issue,

ROGER LE BIGOD, EARL OF NORFOLK,
} **LORD OF CATHERLOGH AND MARSHAL OF IRELAND, 1245,**

In right of his mother upon his uncle's death. He was s. by his nephew, Roger, Earl of Norfolk and Lord of Catherlogh, who dying s. p. in 1306 (35th EDWARD I.), that king gave the earldom, marshalship, and all his lands to his own eldest son by his 2nd wife,

THOMAS PLANTAGENET DE BROTHERTON, EARL OF SUFFOLK,
} **LORD OF CATHERLOGH, 1306,**

He d. in 1337 (12th EDWARD III.), leaving his eldest dau. and co-heir,

MARGARET DE BROTHERTON,
} **LADY OF CATHERLOGH, 29 SEPTEMBER, 1397,**

She was then advanced to the dignities of Duchess of Norfolk, &c., and d. 24 March, 1399, and having m. John, Lord Segrave, their dau. and heir, Elizabeth,, was m. to John, Baron Moubray, by whom she had,

THOMAS, LORD MOWBRAY, DUKE OF NORFOLK, &c.,
} **LORD OF CATHERLOGH, 1399,**

He d. at Venice the next year (1400), and his great great grand-dau., Anne, dau. of his great grandson, John, Duke of Norfolk, who d. in 1475 (15th EDWARD IV.), was m. 15 January, 1477, to Richard, Duke of York, surnamed of Shrewsbury, 2nd son of King EDWARD IV., who being murdered with his brother, King EDWARD V., by their uncle, Richard, Duke of Gloucester, in 1483, issue the inheritance through heirs female descended to the families of Howard and Berkeley, who forfeited the same by reason of their absence from Ireland, by virtue of the statute of Absentees.

(2) Joan, dau. and co-heir to William Mareschal, Earl of Pembroke, and Lord of Leinster, being married to

WARINUS DE MONTECANISIO (Montchensy), an English Baron, he thereby became
} **LORD OF WEXFORD, 1245,**

Their only dau., Joan, heir to her brother William, was married to

WILLIAM DE VALENCE, EARL OF PEMBROKE, half brother to King HENRY III.,
} **LORD OF WEXFORD,**

He d. in 1294 (23rd EDWARD I.), and his son, Audomar, Earl of Pembroke, and Lord of Wexford, dying s. p. in 1322, his two daus. became heirs, and were: (1) Isabel, m. to John, Lord Hastings and Abergavenny, whose son, John, had Lawrence, created Earl of Pembroke, 13 October, 1345 (19th EDWARD III.), and Elizabeth, m. to Roger, Lord Grey of Ruthyn.

LAWRENCE, LORD HASTINGS (afterwards EARL OF PEMBROKE,)
} **LORD OF WEXFORD, 1340,**

Upon the death of his grandson, John, Earl of Pembroke, and Lord of Wexford, 13 December, 1390, the inheritance and honour of Wexford descended to

REGINALD, LORD GREY OF RUTHYN (grandson and heir of the said Roger, Lord Grey, and Elizabeth, sister to Lawrence, Earl of Pembroke),
} **LORD OF WEXFORD, 1390,**

Edmund, Lord Hastings, Weishford and Ruthyn (grandson of the said Reginald), was created Earl of Kent, by King EDWARD IV., and he and his descendants used, among their other titles, this of Lord of Weishford.

(3) Dau. and co-heir, Isabel, of William Mareschal, Earl of Pembroke, and Lord of Leinster, was m. to Gilbert de Clare, Earl of Gloucester, and their son in her right,

RICHARD DE CLARE, EARL OF GLOUCESTER AND HERTFORD, was
} **LORD OF KILKENNY, 1245,**

He d. in 1262, leaving Gilbert, his successor, surnamed the Red, who, 2 May, 1290, m. to his 2nd wife, Joan of Acres, 2nd dau. of King EDWARD I., and dying in December, 1295, left issue, one son, Gilbert, and three daus., co-heirs to their brother. Their mother re-married in 1296, with a servant of her 1st husband, named

RALPH DE MONTHERMER, EARL OF GLOUCESTER AND HERTFORD, and
} **LORD OF KILKENNY, 1296,**

Who enjoyed these honours and estate until Gilbert de Clare, son of the last earl (but five years old at his father's death), succeeded upon his mother's decease, 10 May, 1305, and the said Ralph's formal surrender thereof in 1307 (1st EDWARD II.), but being killed in the battle of Bannockburn, near Stryvelin, 24 June, 1314, the inheritance was divided between his said three sisters in 1316 (10th EDWARD II.), who were

(1) Eleanor, m. to Hugh Le Despencer, the younger son of Hugh, Earl of Gloucester.

(2) Margaret, m. 1st, to Piers Gaveston, Earl of Cornwall, and 2ndly, to Hugh de Audley, created Earl of Gloucester after her brother's death.

(3) Elizabeth, m. 1st, to John de Burgh, who d. before his father, Richard, Earl of Ulster; 2ndly, to Theobald, Lord Verdon, and 3rdly, to Roger D'Amory, Baron of Armoy.

(4) Sybil, 4th dau. and co-heir of William Mareschal, Earl of Pembroke, and Lord of Leinster, married

WILLIAM DE FERRERS, EARL OF FERRERS, NOTTINGHAM, and DERBY,
} **LORD OF KILDARE, 1245,**

In her right. He d. 23 March, 1254, leaving by her, his 1st wife, seven daus., of whom Agnes, the eldest, carried this lordship to her husband,

WILLIAM, LORD VESEY, of Alnwick	LORD OF KILDARE, 1254, He was Lord Justice of Ireland, and forfeited his estate here to John, Lord O'Haley, in 1291, who was created Earl of Kildare. (5) Eva. youngest dau. and co-heir to William Mareschal, Earl of Pembroke, and Lord of Leinster, was *m.* to
WILLIAM BRUCE, or DE BRAWSE, Lord of Brecknock	LORD OF LEIX, or OSSORY, otherwise DOWMAS, or DUMAS IN OSSORY, 1245, In her right. His dau. and heir was *m.* to Lord Mortimer.
HUGH DE LACI (a Baron of England),	LORD OF MEATH, 1172, Extinct by the death of his son Walter, without issue. His lands became divided between his grand-daus., children of Gilbert, his son, who *d.* in his life-time, and he was succeeded in England by his brother, Hugh de Laci, Earl of Ulster.
ROBERT FITZ-STEPHEN,	LORD OF THE MOIETY OF THE KINGDOM OF CORKE, patent dated at Oxford, 1177.
MILES DE COGAN,	LORD OF THE MOIETY OF THE KINGDOM OF CORKE, patent dated at Oxford, 1177. This kingdom of Corke was held by the service of 60 knights' fees, and became by heirs-general the inheritance of Robert de Carren (Carew) and Patrick de Courcy, in 1236, and so continued until the Irish, taking advantage of a division among the English, expelled them, and recovered the country to themselves in the beginning of EDWARD III.'s reign.
SIR JOHN DE COURCY,	LORD OF CONAUGHT, AND EARL OF ULSTER.
RICHARD DE BURGO,	LORD OF CONAUGHT AND TRIM, 17 September, 1215. For the succession, *see* Earls of Ulster.
PHILIP DE BROASE,	LORD OF LIMERICK, 1179, But he could not be prevailed upon to settle there. This honour was confirmed to his nephew, William, &c.
SIR THOMAS DE CLARE,	LORD OF THOMOND, 1179. He obtained a grant of Thomond about the year 1179, and Thomas de Clare was Lord of Thomond in 1290.
OTHO DE GRANDISON,	LORD OF TIPPERARY, 1179.
ROBERT LE POER,	LORD OF WATERFORD, 1179,
JOHN DE MARREIS, or DE MARISCO.	LORD OF Extinct in 1491.
THEOBALD LE BOTILLER,	LORD OF CARRICK, 1177-1247.
JOHN DE COURCY (natural son of John, Earl of Ulster),	LORD OF RATHENNY AND KILBARROCK. CO. DUBLIN, He was murdered by Walter Lacy, Lord of Meath, and Hugh Lacy, Earl of Ulster in 1203.
SIR GEOFFREY FITZ-ROBERT,	LORD OF He was dead in 1211.
RICHARD DE ST. MICHAEL,	LORD OF RHEBAN, CO. KILDARE. His dau., Rose, was married to Thomas, Lord Offaley.
MAURICE FITZ-GERALD,	LORD OF OFFALEY, CO. KILDARE, 1205, 1270.
PETER DE BERMINGHAM,	LORD OF ATHNERY, now ATHENRY, CO GALWAY.
PETER DE BERMINGHAM,	LORD OF THETMOY.
MILES DE COURCY (son of John, Earl of Ulster),	LORD COURCY, OF KINSALE AND RINGRONE, CO. CORK, 1223. Confirmed by patent in 1397.
THOMAS FITZ-MAURICE,	LORD OF KERRY AND LIXNAWE, In 1199 (1st JOHN) he had a grant of ten knights' fees. Patrick, Lord of Kerry and Lixnawe, was placed next below Gerald, Lord of Courcy, of Kinsale, and next above William Fleminge, Lord of Slane, by the Commissioners for executing the office of Earl Marshal of England, by a warrant from them, dated 1 January, 1615.
ARCHIBALD FLEMINGE,	LORD OF SLANE, CO. MEATH. Attainted 16 April, 1691.
SIR WILLIAM NUGENT, Knt.,	LORD OF DELVIN, CO. WESTMEATH. Peter Misset is said to be Lord and Baron of Delvin in 1212 (14th King JOHN). But the Barony of Delvin was given by Hugh de Laci, Lord of Meath, to Gilbert de Nugent, who conveyed the same to his brother, Richard, whose dau. and heir being *m.* to
JOHN FITZ-JOHN,	LORD OF DELVIN, 1357, He possessed the Barony of Delvin in her right, which continued in his family until it was again carried by his heir-general to the said Sir William Nugent, Baron of Delvin, in 1407 (8th HENRY I.)
GEOFFRY CUSACK,	LORD OF KILLEEN, 12 , His heir-general, Genet, dau. and heir of Sir Lucas Cusack, Lord of Killeen, carried this barony to
SIR CHRISTOPHER PLUNKET, Knt.,	LORD OF KILLEEN, CO. MEATH, in or before 1432.

SIR ALMERICUS ST. LAU-
RENCE,
	LORD OF HOWTH, CO. DUBLIN, 1181,
	
	    The lands of Howth were confirmed by patent, dated 4 March, 1489.
	
	        (N.B.—The Barons of Athenry, Courcy of Kingsale, Kerry, Slane, Delvin, Killeen, and
	        Howth were marshalled in this order in the parliament of 1613.)

JOHN MARESCHAL (Mar- shal), nephew to WIL- LIAM, EARL OF PEM- BROKE,	LORD MARSHAL OF IRELAND, 1207, He obtained a grant in fee of the office of Marshal of Ireland, with lands there, to hold by knights' service from King John, and had livery of the said office, and what appertained to it, with the privilege to depute a knight to execute it. He d. in 1235 (19th HENRY III.), and his heir- general, Hawise, carried this honour to her husband,
ROBERT DE MORLEY,	LORD MARSHAL OF IRELAND, 1317, Whose family continued Lord Marshal, or Mareschal of Ireland to the death of Robert, Lord Morley, who left an only dau., Eleanor, m. to William, 2nd son of William, Lord Lovell, who thereby became Lord Morley, and having issue by her, Henry, Lord Morley, who d. s. p. in 1489 (4th HENRY VII.), and Alice, m. to Sir William Parker, Knt., her son, Henry, was summoned to parliament 21st HENRY VIII., by the title of Lord Morley.
WILLIAM FITZ - PHILIP BARRY,	LORD OF OLETHAN, &c., patent dated at Woodstock, 8 November, 1208.
ALMARIC GRAS,	BARON OF GRAS, 1385.
DAVID DE BARRY,	LORD OF BUTTEVANT, CO. CORKE, before 1273,
ADAM LE PETIT,	LORD OF DUNBOYNE, CO. MEATH, The dau. and heir of Adam, Lord of Dunboyne, carried the honour to her husband.
SIR THOMAS BUTLER, Knt.,	LORD OF DUNBOYNE, 1274.
WILLIAM FITZ-MAURICE,	LORD OF NAAS, CO. KILDARE, His dau. and heir, Emma, was m. to David Laundres, de Londres, or London.
DAVID DE LONDRES,	LORD OF NAAS, In her right, and his heir-general being m. to
SIR CHRISTOPHER PRESTON, Knt.,	LORD OF NAAS, Carried the barony into that family In 1460 (38th HENRY VI.), for placing Gormanston in the place of his father and grandfather, as Lord of Kells, he shall have place in parliament next to the place of David Fleming, and his heirs, 2nd EDWARD IV.
WALTER DE RIDLEFORD,	LORD OF BRAY, CO. DUBLIN, 12 , His only dau and heir, Emelina, was m. 1st, to Hugh de Laci, the younger Earl of Ulster, who d. in 1243; and 2ndly, to Stephen de Longue Espée, who d. lord justice of Ireland, in 1260, whose dau., Emelina, was m. to Gerald, Lord Offaley.
THEOBALD DE VERDON (a Baron of England),	LORD OF ERGAL, 1234, By marriage with Margaret, dau. and co-heir to Walter de Laci, Lord of Meath. The barony ended in his son, Theobald, who d. s. p. in 1309.
JOHN DE VERDON,	LORD OF LOUGHSEWDY, 1308.
GEOFFRY DE GENEVILE,	LORD OF TRIM, 1234, By marriage with Matilda, dau. and co-heir to Walter de Laci, Lord of Meath. Jane, dau. and heir of Sir Peter de Geneville, Lord of Mede, Vanclour, and Trim, was m. to Roger Mortimer, Earl of March, Lord of Trim, in her right.
SIR ROBERT DE LACY,	LORD OF IVECOLYEN,
ROGER ROCHFORT,	LORD OF KELLADOWN, He d. 9 April, 1489.
MATTHEW CANTON, or CON- DON,	LORD CONDON,
ROBERT DE PERCIVAL,	LORD OF , 1285, Extinct in 1322.
SIR ROGER DAMORY, Knt.,	LORD OF ARMOY, CO. ANTRIM, 13 His wife was Elizabeth, sister and co-heir to Gilbert de Clare, Earl of Gloucester; and dying in rebellion his lands were seized, but restored to his wife for life, remainder to his only dau., Elizabeth, wife of William, Lord Bardolf.

(Uncertain. — bracketing KELLADOWN and CONDON)

        SIR RICHARD COX, in his *History of Ireland*, page 86, gives the following list of a PARLIA-
MENT held by JOHN WOGAN, LORD JUSTICE in 1295 (23rd EDWARD I.)

RICHARD DE BURGO,	EARL OF ULSTER,	
GEOFREY DE GENEVIL,		NOTE.—Dr Brady, in his answer to Mr. Petit's book, in-
JOHN FITZ-THOMAS,	Afterwards EARL OF KILDARE,	tituled *The Rights of the Commons asserted, p. 32, &c.*,
THOMAS FITZ - MAURICE (Nappagh),		says that, "Barons by Writt were not actually Barons, but were called to sit among the Lords sometimes,
THEOBALD LE BUTLER,		and sometimes again omitted in several kings'
THEOBALD DE VERDUN,		reigns."
PETER DE BERMINGHAM OF	ATHENRY.	
PETER DE BERMINGHAM OF	THETMOY.	

EUSTACE DE POER,
JOHN DE POER,
HUGH DE PURCEL,
JOHN DE COGAN,
JOHN DE BARRY,
WILLIAM DE BARRY,
WALTER DE LACY,
RICHARD DE EXCESTER,
JOHN PIPARD,
WALTER L'ENFANT,
JORDAN DE EXON,
ADAM DE STANTON,
SYMON DE PRIPO,
WILLIAM CADEL,
JOHN DE VAL,
MORRIS DE CAREW,   Nicholas de Carrew was Baron of Idrone in the reign of EDWARD I., and so was John de Carren, 1349.

GEORGE DE LA ROCH (or RUPE), } COSLEA, co. WATERFORD, and 1318 (12th EDWARD II.).

MAURICE DE ROCHFORT,

MAURICE FITZ-THOMAS, of Kerry, } KERRY.

King EDWARD I. directed his Writ, dated at Morpeth, 23rd February, 1302 (30th EDWARD I.), to Geoffry de Geynvill, requiring him and John Wogan, Lord Justice of Ireland, to convene and treat with Richard, Earl of Ulster, the nobility (magnates), and others of his land of Ireland to assist him in his intended expedition against the Scots at the end of the truce, in case peace did not ensue. For which end Writts of the same date were directed to the said Richard, Earl of Ulster, and the following persons, which I have transcribed from Rymer's *Fœdera*, tome ii. p. 896, to shew the state of the Baronage, and of the Tenures *in capite*, by knights' service, and consequently the state of the kingdom at that time:—

John Fitz-Thomas.
Maurice Fitz-Thomas.
Reginald de Dene.
John de Barry.
Peter Fitz-James de Burmyngham.
Maurice de Rocheford.
Peter Fitz-Meiler (de Burmyngham.)
John de Cogan.
Jordan de Exon (Excestre).
Walter de Lacy.
Maurice de Cauneeton.
William de Barry.
Edmund Le Butiller.
Maurice de Carreu.
John Mautravers.
John Le Botiller.
Eustace Le Poer.
George de Rupe.
John Le Poer.
Hugh Purcel.
Odo de Barry.
Thomas de Cantewell.
Herbert Damareys.
Richard Talire.
Mathew de Caunceton.
William de Burgo.
Richard de London.
Henry de Vernoill.
Thomas de Maundevill.
Peter Le Petit.
Reginald de Kynet.
Reymund de Burgo.
John Drull.
John Fitz-Robert.
Philip Christophre.
David de Rocheford.
Robert Haket.
John Fitz John.
Henry de Castell.
Maurice de Lees.
Hugh de Lees.
John Harald.
John de Dandon.
Henry Russel.
William Le Waleys.
Thomas Engleys.
Thomas Fitz-Idis.
Philip Le Mareschall.
Almaric de Beause.
Robert Bagot.
Nicholas Deveneys.
Philip Olf.
Robert de Bonevill.
Thomas Maunsell.
Robert de Lees.
Thomas del Ille.

Maurice de London.
Geoffry Fitz-Richard.
John Fitz-Pointz.
John Bretmanth.
Richard Le Botiller.
William Le Botiller.
John Le Botiller.
John Christophre.
John Fitz-Rob. le Poer.
Richard de Whitfeld.
Miles Le Bret.
Geoffry Le Bret.
Geoffry de Cogan.
Richard de Val.
Walter de Val.
David Fitz-Adam de Sto. Albins (St. Albans).
Geoffry de Norragh.
Stephen Le Poer.
Miles de Rochfort.
Henry Fitz-Henry de Rochfort.
Henry Fitz-Simon de Rochfort.
David Masmer.
John de Bonevill.
Robert de Persevall.
Walram de Wylesleye.
John Comyn.
Henry Fitz-Ririth.
Gerald Tyrel.
John de Hothmo.
Oliver Fitz-Eynon.
Fulke de la Treignee.
William Le Graunt.
William de St. Leger.
Anselm de Gras.
David de Gras.
John Le Ercedekne.
Silvester Le Ercedekne.
William Le Ercedekne.
David de Barry de Rathetomok (Rath-cormack).
Mathew de Milburn.
Robert Fitz-David.
Henry de Bermyngham.
William Le Poer.
Walter Le Poer.
Miles, Baron de Overk.
Robert de Sorthales (Shortall).
Edmund de Gras.
John Fitz-Hugh de Rochfort.
Laurence de Rochfort.
Philip Purcel.
Maurice Purcel.
Adam Purcel.
John Talum.
Muler Candal.

William Trahern.
John de Lyvet.
Gilbert de Sutton.
Adam de Rupe (Baron of Poolcastle, co. Corke, in the reign of EDWARD II.).
John Fitz-Henry.
Richard Wytteye.
Hamon de Gras.
Simon Fitz-Richer.
Geoffry Harold.
John Fitz-Ririth.
Walter de Kenleye.
James de Ketyng.
John Assyk (John Assick was Baron of Duleeke, co. Meath, in 1426, 19th EDWARD II.).
Nicholas Crok.
William Fitz-William.
Reymund de Carreu.
David Burdun.
Aubert de Kenleyne.
Theobald de Verdun.
Hugh de Lacy.
Edmund de Lacy.
Richard Tyrel.
Thomas de Ledwich.
John Tuyt.
Richard Manneyfin.
Richard Fitz-John.
Thomas Fitz-Alfred.
Philip de Barry de Rencorran.
David de la Roche.
John Fitz-John Le Poer.
Thomas Fitz-Philip.
Gilbert Le Waleys.
William de Cantelon.
William de Caunceton.
Maurice Le Ercedekne.
Reymund Keneseg.
Baldewin Fitz-Philip.
Gerard Fitz-Maurice.
John Crok.
Nigil Le Brun.
John Le White, of Rathregois.
Donald (Roth) Macarthi.
Thetheric Ebryan.
John Haket.
Walter Appelgard.
Thomas de Saresfeld.
Stephen de Saresfeld.
David Fitz-John de Cogan.
Bernard de Mithe.
William de Staunton.
Miles Fitz-Thomas.
Robert Baret.

Robert de Caunceton.
Philip Le Bret.
John de la Pille.
Richard de la Pille.
William Fitz-Philip Barry.
William Fitz-William Barry.
Robert Arundel.
Robert Fitz-Pierse.
Edmund de Courcy (Miles de Courcy

was a Baron by Tenure as appears by Inquisition taken after his death in 1372 (46th EDWARD III), when it was found that he died without issue male).
John Fitz-Robert de Obathun.
David de Caunceton.
Jordan de Caunceton.
William Fitz-Philip de la Roche.

Philip de Mithe.
John de Mithe.
Henry de Cogan.
James de la Chapele.
Richard Clement.
Gioto Kokerel.
Odo O'Tonethor.
Donald O'Nel.

ALMARICE DE ST. AMAND
(a Baron of England),   }   LORD OF GORMANSTON, CO. MEATH, 1358.

RALPH, EARL OF EU,   LORD OF LOUTH, 1364.

BY SUMMONS TO PARLIAMENT, 25 March, 1374 (48th EDWARD III.):—

William Le Londres, Knt.
Patrick de la Freigne, Knt.
Simon de Cusake, Knt.
Robert de Preston, Knt. (He was only summoned as one of the King's council.)
Nicholas de Castro-Martyn, Knt.
Walter de Cusak, Knt.
James Delahyde, Knt.
Thomas Tuyt, Knt.
Thomas Bruyn, Knt.
Robert Calf (Calvus), Baron of Norracht.
John Husee, Baron of Galtrim.
John Belleau (or Bedelewe, now Bellew).

Richard Plunkett.
John Tyrrell.
Oliver Fitz-Eustace.
William Wellysley. (John and William de Wellesley were summoned to parliament as Barons in 1339, 13th EDWARD III., Gerald, or Garrett Wesley, was styled Lord of Dengyn, and was succeeded by his son and heir, William, styled Lord of Dengyn, in a special livery of his estate, granted 10 March, 1538, 30th HENRY VIII., and was maternal ancestor to Garrett, Earl of Mornington)

William L'Enfaunt.
Adam de Lyt.
John Cruce.
William Dolthin.
John Creef.
Roger Gernon.
John Haddeshore, now Hadsor.
Geffry White, of Dundalk.
Richard Taaf.
John Balf.
Thomas Talbot, Knt.
Nicholas Houth.
Geffry Tryvers, Knt.
Mathew Darcy.

BY SUMMONS TO PARLIAMENT, 22 November, 1374:—

Thomas Fitz-John, Knt.
Patrick de la Freigne. Knt.
Robert de la Freigne, Knt.
Richard de Burgo. Knt.
John Fitz-Nicholas, Knt.
Thomas Clifford, Knt.
Robert Swetman, Knt.
Walter L'Enfaunt, Knt. (He set forth by petition to the lord justice and council that, whereas he, tanquam Tenens per Baroniam, was summoned to the late parliament, holden in Dublin, and for not attending was grievously fined; whereas he never was Tenens per Baroniam, as was found by an Inquisition taken at his suit, upon the premises before the said lord justice, and therefore prayed that the said fine might be remitted; and the same being recorded and

testified by the said lord justice, and that it had not hitherto been the law or custom in Ireland, that any person who did not hold per Baroniam were summoned to parliament, or fined for non-attendance, the king remitted the said fine by writt directed to the treasurer and barons of the exchequer, bearing date at Cork, 12 June, 1377.)
David de Barry, Knt.
Nicholas Houthe.
Patrick Verdon.
William de London, Knt.
Robert Calf, Knt.
Simon Cusak, Knt.
Nicholas Castelmartyn, Knt.
Thomas Tuyt, Knt.
Thomas Brune, Knt.
Thomas Vernaill, Knt.

Walter Cusak, Knt.
Thomas Talbot, Knt.
Hugh Byset, Knt
Henry Savage, Knt.
Roger Gernon.
Richard Taaf.
John Balf.
Richard Plunket.
John Husee, Baron Galtrym.
John Bedelewe.
Maurice Fitz-Richard.
Thomas Oge Botiller.
Nicholas Poer.
Philip Fitz-William Barry.
Geffry de la Laund.
Matthew Fitz-Henry.
Richard Wyttey.
William Wellesley.
Oliver Fitz-Eustace.
Geffry Vale.

BY SUMMONS TO PARLIAMENT, 22 January, 1377:—

David de Barry, Knt.
Richard de Burgo, Knt.
Thomas Fitz-John, Knt.
Patrick de la Freigne, Knt.
Robert de la Freigne, Knt.

Simon de Cusake, Knt.
William de Londres, Knt.
Walter de Cusake, Knt.
Hugh Byset, Knt.
Henry Savage, Knt.

Thomas Tuyt, Knt.
Thomas Vernayll, Knt.
Robert Calf, Knt
Thomas Clifford, Knt

NOTE.—The King's Council, or those de Consilio Domini Regis are placed here between those that were Knights, and those that were not.

John Husee, Baron Galtrym.
Maurice Fitz-Richard.
Richard Oge de Burgo.
John Roche de Fermoy.

Thomas Oge Botiller.
Walter Bermyngham de Athnery.
Nicholas Le Poer.
Philip Fitz-William de Barry.

Geffrey de Laund.
Matthew Fitz-Henry.
Maurice Dexcestre.
Richard Whittey.

BY SUMMONS TO PARLIAMENT, 11 September, 1380:—

William de Loundres, Knt.
Thomas Fitz-John, Knt.
Patrick de la Freigne. Knt.
Robert de la Freigne, Knt.
Simon Cusak, Knt.

Hugh Byset, Knt.
Walter de Cusak, Knt.
Henry Savage, Knt.
Thomas Tuyt, Knt.

Thomas Vernayll, Knt.
Edmund Husee.
David de Barry, Knt.
Richard de Burgo, Knt.

NOTE.—The King's Council, or those de Consilio Domini Regis are placed here between those that were Knights, and those that were not.

Maurice Fitz-Richard.
John Roche de Fermoy,

Walter Bermyngham de Athnery.
Philip Fitz-William de Barry.

Nicholas Le Poer.

BY SUMMONS TO PARLIAMENT, 29 April, 1382:—

William de Loundres, Knt.
Thomas Fitz-John. Knt.
Patrick de la Freigne, Knt.
Robert de la Freigne, Knt.

Simon Cusak, Knt.
Walter de Cusak, Knt.
Thomas de Vernayll, Knt.
David de Barry, Knt.

Hugh Byset, Knt.
Henry Savage, Knt.
Edmund Husee.
Richard de Burgo, Knt.

NOTE.—The King's Council, or those de Consilio Domini Regis are placed here between those that were Knights, and those that were not.

Maurice Fitz-Richard.
John Roche de Fermoy.

Nicholas Le Poer.
Walter Bermyngham de Athnery.

Philip Fitz-William de Barry.

INDEX.

ARRANGED BY TITLES, WITH YEAR OF CREATION, AND FAMILY NAMES.

D. *Duke.* M. *Marquess.* E. *Earl.* V. *Viscount.* B. *Baron.* S. *Scotland.* I. *Ireland.*

INDEX.

INDEX.

CPSIA information can be obtained at www.ICGtesting.com
Printed in the USA
LVOW101105100613

337816LV00008B/53/P